Fundamentals of Mathematics

Algebra I

Second Edition

Sanjay Mishra

B.Tech.
Indian Institute of Technology, Varanasi

Title : Fundamentals of Mathematics Algebra I

Language : English

Author : Sanjay Mishra

Typeset & Published by :

Career Launcher Infrastructure (P) Ltd.

A-45, Mohan Cooperative Industrial Area, Near Mohan Estate Metro Station, New Delhi - 110044

Marketed by :

G.K. Publications (P) Ltd.

Plot No. 63, Sector-27A, Near Sector - 28 Metro Station, Faridabad, Haryana-121003

ISBN : **978-81-93975-86-2**

Printer's Details : Printed in India, New Delhi.

Preface

Human mind has immense potential, much beyond any stretch of imagination. We can utilize this potential not only for thinking and venturing into endless imaginations, but also for analysing the situations and memorizing the useful results. By looking at the past history of development of human beings as a race, we find that humans have improved themselves to this stage more by application of their mind (i.e., the ability to reason) than by memorizing the observations. We have applied the analytical ability of mind to develop a number system for counting, a language for communication, different arts to amuse ourselves and so many other useful skills. Altogether, we have developed *Mathematics*, a wonderful tool to provide foundations and a medium for development of all other branches of science. Mathematics, in itself, remained an art (skill). One of the most eminent scientists, Albert Einstein, very aptly defined Mathematics as "the language in which God has written the universe."

In my yesteryears, during my high school days, as an IIT-JEE aspirant, and later as a tutor of Mathematics for last fifteen years, I always felt the need of a comprehensive text book for this subject. I always therefore had an insatiable desire to write one. This book has been written with the objective of providing a text book as well as an exercise book, focusing on problem solving. I feel this will not only fulfil the need of a beginner, pre-college student (i.e., students of standard XI and XII), but also meet the requirements of advanced level students who are preparing for various entrance examinations like the IIT-JEE, AIEEE, BITSAT and other state engineering entrance examinations. This book *Fundamentals of Mathematics—Algebra I*, gives deep insights into topics like Foundation Mathematics, Logarithm, Sequence and Progression, Theory of Equations, Inequalities, Combinatorics, Binomial Theorem and Infinite Series. These are the eight most scary but highly scoring topics of Mathematics. The Foundation Mathematics and Logarithm consist of all essential tools necessary to deal with the problem solving, pertaining to every topic of Mathematics, as well as topics of other subjects like Physics and Chemistry. These two topics are an attempt to equip the readers with those essential mathematical tools which are like oxygen for their life in Mathematics. Understanding these concepts has great importance in the light of the fact that these mathematical tools provide a way to express and understand the various branches of Mathematics.

The well-arranged content list will help students as well as teachers to access conveniently the chapters and sub-topics of their interest. Each chapter is divided into several topics. Each topic contains theory and sometimes subtopics with sufficient number of worked out illustrative problems. Students can develop applicative ability of the concepts learned. This is followed by a textual exercise of both objective and subjective problems, as per the requirements. At the end of the theory of each chapter, a large set of solved examples of both objective and subjective type is given. This will involve application of all the concepts learnt in the chapter so that students can develop mastery over the chapter. The tutorial exercise given at the end contains a large number of multiple choice problems of single and multiple correct answers, comprehension passages, column matching problems, numerical integer type questions to facilitate the students to do the thorough revision of the entire chapter and to enhance their level of understanding of the topics. For teachers, this text book will be quite helpful as it will provide a set of well graded problems and well arranged topics that can be used to give home assignments to their students.

All suggestions for improvement are welcome and shall be gratefully acknowledged.

Sanjay Mishra

Acknowledgements

I am really grateful to GK Publications, for showing faith in me and for providing me with an opportunity to transform my yearning, my vast experience of years of teaching and my knowledge into the present comprehensive text book, *Fundamentals of Mathematics—Algebra I*. I would like to thank all my friends and teachers for their valuable criticism, support and advice that was really helpful to carve out this work. I am pleased to award special acknowledgement to all my pupils. During my interactions with my students, I have got much of the inspiration of writing this text book. I feel that by interacting with them, I have learnt much more than I could have ever taught them. I wish to thank my parents and all my family members, for their patience and support in bringing out this book and donating their valuable share of time for such cause. I extend my special thanks to my team, including my assisting teachers, managers and computer operators, for their hard work and dedication in completing this task.

Sanjay Mishra

Contents

CHAPTER 1

Foundation Mathematics

INTRODUCTION

Mathematics is a pure application of brain. It is a game in which we play with the unknown situation under limited information and each of its problems are the challenges, especially those asked in exams like Olympiad, JEE and AIEEE. So to crack them successfully, an analytical approach is needed. Unfortunately, till 10th, most of you ignore the analytical part of the study resulting in the weak analytical skills of the brain.

This chapter contains the concepts and basic mathematical tools that are necessary to solve the problems of mathematics belonging to any topic, e.g., Set, Number system, Algebra, Trigonometry, Geometry, Calculus, etc.

Some of the concepts contained in this topic belong to the 9th and 10th class syllabus, only difference is that here we study them with analytical approach rather than through conventional learning (cramming) approach.

After completion of this chapter, you will feel that you have developed the aptitude of attacking and attempting questions by applying the basic principles of Mathematics.

MATHEMATICAL SYMBOLS AND THEIR MEANINGS

Symbols are used to express the meaning of words in brief and they find very important place in the language of mathematics. Some very popular symbols are mentioned below along with their meaning.

Mathematical symbols

Symbol	Meaning	Symbol	Meaning	Symbol	Meaning
$\therefore$	Therefore	$\int$	Single Integration	Δ	Triangle
$\because$	Because, Since	$\int\int$	Double Integration	$\Rightarrow$	Implies
:	Such that	Σ	Sigma	N	The set of natural numbers
::	So as	α	Proportionate to	$\Leftrightarrow$	Implies and is implied by
:	Ratio	f	Function	Z or I	The set of integers
::	Proportion	∞	Infinity	Q	The set of rational numbers
=	Equal to	$\_$	Line bracket	$\mathbb{R}$	The set of real numbers
$\neq$	Not equal to	()	Small bracket	$\|x\|$	Absolute Value of x
>	Greater than	{}	Mid bracket	i.e.	idest (that is)
<	Less than	[]	Large bracket	e.g.	example gratia (for example)
$\geq$	Greater than or equal to	$\in$	Belongs to	Q.E.D.	Quod Erat Demonstrandum

Symbol	Meaning	Symbol	Meaning	Symbol	Meaning
$\leq$	Less than or equal to	$\notin$	Does not belong to	$\not\subset$	Is not a subset of
$\nless$	Not less than	$\subset$	Is a subset of	$\cup$	Universal set
$\sqrt[n]{\ }$	nth root	$\cup$	union of sets	$\sim$	Similar to
$\sqrt[3]{\ }$	Cube root	$\cap$	Intersection of sets	iff	If and only if
$\angle$	Angle	$A \times B$	Cartesian Product of A and B	$\parallel$	Parallel
$\perp$	Perpendicular	$A - B$	Difference of two sets A and B	ϕ	Null Set(phi)
$\cong$	Congruent to	$\forall$	for all	$\frown$	Arc
$\exists$	There Exists				

Greek words (Symbols)

Symbol	Meaning	Symbol	Meaning	Symbol	Meaning
α	Alpha	β	Beta	γ	Gamma
δ, Δ	Delta	$\in, \varepsilon$	Epsilon	ξ	Zeta
η	Eta	θ	Theta	i	Iota
κ	Kappa	λ	Lambda	μ	Mu
ν	Nu	ξ	Xi	o	Omicron
π	Pi	ρ	Rho	σ, Σ	Sigma
τ	Tau	υ	Upsilon	ϕ	Phi
χ	Chi	ψ	Psi	ω	Omega

■ MATHEMATICAL REASONING

It is a well known fact that human race has evolved from lower species over the period of time and the process of evolution is still going on. Our ability to reason makes us superior to the other species. In mathematics, there are two kinds of reasoning.

(i) **Inductive reasoning**, e.g., principle of mathematical induction.

(ii) **Deductive reasoning**. Here we shall discuss some elements of deductive reasoning and the need, process and procedure of reasoning as well as proofs in mathematics.

What is reasoning and why reasoning? Reasoning is a process of logical steps that enables us to arrive at a conclusion. The need for reasoning arises out of the decision making process i.e., to decide what is right and what is wrong in case of a mathematical statement.

Statements and mathematical statements

Statement: Statement is a sentence which is complete in itself and explains its meaning. e.g., Lion is a wild animal.

Mathematical statement A given sentence will qualify as a mathematical statement if either it is true or it is false but not both. e.g.,

s_1: The sum of two odd integers is an odd integer.
s_2: Tomorrow is Wednesday.
s_3: The sum of six and seven is greater than 12.
s_4: Men are more intelligent than women.

Where statements s_1 and s_3 are mathematical statements because s_1 is always false and s_3 is always true but statements s_2 and s_4 are not because it will be true only if it is made on Tuesday and for s_4 every one will not agree to it.

Classification of mathematical statements

Mathematical Statements are classified in three types:

(i) Definition
(ii) Axiom
(iii) Theorem

Definition A mathematical statement which is used to explain the meaning of certain words used in the subject. For example: "*The numbers which are divisible by two are called even numbers*".

Axiom A mathematical statement which is accepted as true without any formal proof given for it. e.g., "*One is a natural number and every natural number has an unique successor*".

Theorem A mathematical statement which is accepted as true only when a formal proof is given for it. e.g., "*If two straight lines cut one another, the vertically opposite angles are equal*".

Conjecture A conjecture is a proposition that is unproven but it *appears* correct. e.g., "*Every integer greater than 2*".

Remarks

1. *Algorithm: A series of mathematical statements providing systematic steps to completely perform a process (i.e., to solve a mathematical problem)*
2. *Exclamatory, imperative* and *interrogative sentences are not mathematical statements.*
3. *Sentences involving today, tomorrow, yesterday and pronouns (here, there, she, he...) without referring to a particular person are not mathematical statements.*

TEXTUAL EXERCISE–1 (SUBJECTIVE)

1. Which of the following can be classified as mathematical statements? Give proper reason to support your answer.
   (i) Sum of two natural number is always positive.
   (ii) For given two integers x and y, $x - y$ is less than zero.
   (iii) $2n + 1$ is a prime number for every natural values of n.
   (iv) Tomorrow is Friday.
   (v) Bombay is far from here.
   (vi) The nearest star is Alpha Centauri

2. Which of the following cannot be classified as mathematical statements? Give proper reason to support your answer?
   (i) Sun is not a Star.
   (ii) The square of a number is an even number.
   (iii) The sides of a quadrilateral have equal length.
   (iv) The sum of all interior angles of a triangle is 180°.
   (v) Mathematics is a challenging subject.
   (vi) Is mathematics a science?

3. Test whether following statements are mathematical statements or not.
   (i) S: Since barber shaves them who do not shave themselves then barber shaves himself.
   (ii) S: S_1, S_2 and S_3 where S_1 = God is almighty
   S_2 = The world has problems of evil.
   S_3 = God does not want evil in the world.

4. State which of the following is a definition, an axiom or a theorem.
   (a) Sum of interior angles of a triangle is 180°.
   (b) Every natural number has successor.
   (c) Total angle around a point is 360°.
   (d) Ratio of sides of two similar triangles be n/m then the ratio of their area is $(n/m)^2$.
   (e) If two triangles have their sides in similar proportion, then both triangles are similar.
   (f) Angle between two lines is a physical quantity which describes the amount of rotation by which one has to be rotated to coincide with other.
   (g) An equation is unaltered if both members are multiplied by the same number.
   (h) The modulus of any number is non-negative.
   (i) $a^{1/3} = \sqrt[3]{a}$
   (j) The graph of the function $y = -3x$ passes through the origin of coordinate system.

Answer Keys

1. i **2.** ii, iii, v, vi **3.** None of these

4. (a) Theorem (b) Axiom (c) Theorem (d) Theorem (e) Axiom
(f) Definition (g) Theorem (h) Theorem (i) Definition (j) Theorem

TEXTUAL EXERCISE–1 (OBJECTIVE)

1. 'Sum of interior angles of a triangle is 180°' is
   (a) definition (b) theorem
   (c) axiom (d) None of these

2. 'Sum of interior opposite angles of a cyclic quadrilateral is 180°' is
   (a) definition (b) theorem
   (c) axiom (d) None of these

3. 'The numbers 0, 1, 2, 3, 4... are whole numbers' is
   (a) definition (b) theorem
   (c) axiom (d) None of these

4. 'A circle is the locus of a point moving on a plane so that its distance from a fixed point is always constant' is
   (a) definition (b) theorem
   (c) axiom (d) None of these

5. 'Vertically opposite angles between two intersecting lines are equal' is
   (a) definition (b) theorem
   (c) axiom (d) None of these

6. Which of the following statement(s) are mathematical?
   (a) Sum of two rational numbers is always a rational number
   (b) Sum of two odd integers is an odd integer.
   (c) Every prime greater than 2 is odd.
   (d) The roots of quadratic equation $x^2 - 5x + k = 0$ are always real $\forall k \in \mathbb{R}$

Answer Keys

1. (b) 2. (b) 3. (a) 4. (a) 5. (c, b) 6. (a, b, c)

GENERATION OF NEW STATEMENTS FROM OLD

An English Mathematician, George Bool, invented logical methods of generating a new statement from a given statement and published in a book *Laws of Thought* which involves two techniques: (i) Negation of a statement (ii) Compounding of a statement.

Negation of a statement

Denial of a statement is called negation. e.g., negation of "Chennai is a city" will be "Chennai is not a city".

REMARK

While doing negation of a statement, phrases like," It is not the case" or "It is false that" are also used.

Compounding of statements

By combining two or more component statements using the connecting words like "And", "Or" etc., we can form a compound statement.

(i) Compounding by using "Or" Given p and q are two statements.

p: x is a prime number
q: x is an even natural number

The compounded statement will be x is a prime or an even natural number. In order to understand the statements with OR, we must note that it is used in two ways (i) exclusive "Or" (ii) inclusive "Or"

Example using exclusive "Or" "You will get coffee or cold drink with your meal in this hotel". It is clearly meant that only one item (any one) will be provided but not both.

Example using inclusive "Or" "Students of biology or mathematics can take pharmacy course." It means that the students with either of the mentioned subjects are eligible for pharmacy course. Students having both mathematics and biology are not ineligible. They are also eligible.

(ii) Compounding by using "And" Given p and q are two statements.

Component statements

p: 11 is a prime number

q: 11 is an odd number

Compounded statement is 11 is a prime and odd number.

■ IMPLICATION

By using the conditional words "if-then" certain other types of statements are possible to be formed. $p \Rightarrow q$ means if the statement p is true then the statement q will be true E.g., x is prime and $x > 2 \Rightarrow x$ is odd.

Converse of an implication: The converse of "If p then q" is "If q then p" e.g., converse of the statement "If a number n is odd, then n^2 is odd", will be "If n^2 is odd then n is odd". If the statement $p \Rightarrow q$ and its converse i.e., $q \Rightarrow p$ both hold good then it is denoted by both way implication $p \Leftrightarrow q$ and read as "p if and only if q" or "p iff q".

"If a number is multiple of 4 then it is a multiple of 2".

Component statements:

p: a number is a multiple of 4
q: a number is a multiple of 2

Here "If p then q" means $p \Rightarrow q$ i.e., if p is true then q will hold. If a number is a multiple of 4 then it is a multiple of 2. But in case p is not true then q may or may not be true.

Similarly, "p only if q" would mean that "a number will be a multiple of 4 only if it is a multiple of 2".

The statement "p if and only if q" means "a number will be a multiple of 4 if and only if it is a multiple of 2.

■ CONTRA-POSITIVE OF AN IMPLICATION

Suppose truth of a statement p implies truth of a statement q then negation of statement q implies negation of statement p. Contra positive of the implication $p \Rightarrow q$ is $\sim q \Rightarrow \sim p$.

E.g., The contra-positive of the statement "If all sides of a triangle are equal, then it is an equilateral triangle", is given as "if a triangle is not equilateral, then its all sides are not equal".

Also, the contra-positive of the statement "If a number is divisible by 4 then it is divisible by 2", will be "If a number is not divisible by 2, then it is not divisible by 4".

REMARKS

If an implication $p \Rightarrow q$ is true then its contra positive $\sim q \Rightarrow \sim p$ is always true, but converse of a statement is not always true.

E.g., "If a number is divisible by 21, then it is divisible by 7" is a true statement but "If a number is divisible by 7, then it is divisible by 21" is a false statement as 14 is divisible by 7 but it is not divisible by 21.

Special words and phrases

Quantifiers These are phrases like "There exists ∃", "for all ∀", Examples:

(a) There exists a triangle having all sides equal.
(b) For all prime numbers, the only two divisors are 1 and the number itself.
(c) For every $x > 0$, if $y > x$, then $y > 0$
(alternatively, for every $x > 0$, there exists a positive number $y > 0$ such that $y < x$.)

Validation of statements

Analysing the statements to understand its meaning and to decide the condition and its validity (i.e., truth/falsifiability) is called validation of statements. And to complete this task, the analysis of the special words and phrases (like or, and, if, iff) and quantifiers ∀, ∃ etc., used in the statements is to be done very carefully. Depending upon the stated conditions, certain rules do apply for the statements to be true.

For statement with "And"

"p and q" validation requires the following steps:

Step I: To show that first statement (p) is true.

Step II: To show that second statement (q) is true.

For statement with "Or"

"p or q" validation requires following cases:

Case I: Even if p is not true, show that q is (still) true.

Case II: Even if q is false, show that p is (still) true.

For statement with "if-then"

"If p then q" validation would require following cases:

Case I: When p is true, prove that q is also true.
Case II: When q is not true, prove that p is also not true.

This is direct contra-positive method.

For statement with "if and only if"

"p if and only if q" validation will require the following cases:

Case I: To show that if p is true then q is true.
Case II: To show that if q is true then p is true.

ILLUSTRATION 1: Check the validity of statement: If $x, y \in I$ and x, y are odd then xy is odd.

SOLUTION: *Method (I)*: Let p be the statement $x, y \in I$ and x, y are odd and q be a statement xy is odd. Using rule 3, we take $x = 2p + 1$ and $y = 2k + 1: p, k \in I$

$\Rightarrow \quad xy = \{4pk + 2(p + k)\} + 1 = 2\{2pk + (p + k)\} + 1 = \text{odd}$

Method (II): We will consider the negation of statement i.e., let xy (product) be even when x, y are both odd.

But xy = even is possible if any one or both of x and y are even.

So the consideration that product xy being even is not valid.

TEXTUAL EXERCISE–2 (SUBJECTIVE)

1. Make a compound statement by combining two given statements
   (a) p: The player in blue dress is from Indian team.
   q: The player in blue dress is from Australian team. **(use 'or')**
   (b) p: Malerkotla is in Punjab.
   q: Malerkotla is in Haryana. **(use 'or')**
   (c) p: The dish was sweet in taste.
   q: The dish was salty in taste. **(use 'and')**
   (d) p: Every prime number greater than two is odd.
   q: Every prime number has exactly two positive divisors. **(use 'and')**

2. For each of the following compound statements, first identify the connecting words and then break it into components.
   (a) All rational numbers are real and all real numbers are not complex.
   (b) The sand heats up quickly in the Sun and does not cool down fast at night.
   (c) $x = 2$ and $x = 3$ are the roots of equation $x^2 - 5x + 6 = 0$
   (d) Both the roots of a quadratic equation are either real or imaginary.
   (e) Golden temple is in Amritsar or Jalandhar.

3. Classify inclusive and exclusive 'or'.
   (a) x is even or odd.
   (b) Delhi is the capital of India or Nepal.
   (c) x is an integer or rational number.
   (d) He would be going to Bombay by train or by air.

4. Which type of "Or" is being used in the following statement?
   (a) To get a driving license, you should have residence proof (like ration card) or identity proof (like passport).
   (b) $\sqrt{2}$ is a rational number or an irrational number.
   (c) A rectangle is a quadrilateral or six sided polygon.
   (d) Sun rises or moon sets.
   (e) All integers are positive or negative.

5. Write down the negative of given statements.
   (a) $\sqrt{2}$ is an irrational number.
   (b) Delhi is capital of India.
   (c) Every prime number is odd.
   (d) 42 is divisible by 7

6. Write the converse of following statements.
   (i) If two integers a and b are such that $ab < 0$ then a and b are of opposite sign.
   (ii) If two integers m and n are such that $mn \neq 0$, then both m and n are non-zero.
   (iii) If number n is even then n^2 is even.

7. Write the contra-positive of following statements.
   (i) If a quadrilateral has equal sides, then it is a rhombus.

(ii) If a triangle has equal sides, then it is isosceles.
(iii) If a number is divisible by 9 then it is divisible by 3.

8. Check whether the following pair of statements are negation of each other. Give reasons for your answer.
(i) $x + y = y + x$ is true for every real numbers x and y.
(ii) There exist real numbers x and y for which $x + y \neq y + x$.

Answer Keys

1. (a) The player in blue dress is from Indian team or from Australian team.
(b) Malerkotla is in Punjab or Haryana.
(c) The dish was sweet and salty in taste.
(d) Every prime number greater than two is odd and has exactly two positive divisors.
2. (a) and (b) and (c) and (d) OR (e) OR
3. (a) exclusive (b) exclusive (c) inclusive (d) exclusive
4. (a) inclusive (b) exclusive (c) exclusive (d) inclusive (e) exclusive
5. (a) $\sqrt{2}$ is not irrational (b) Delhi is not the capital of India.
(c) At least one prime number is even. (d) 7 does not divide 42.
6. (i) If a and b are of opposite sign then $ab < 0$. (ii) If m and n are non-zero then mn is not equal to zero.
(iii) If n^2 is even then n must be even.
7. (i) If a quadrilateral is not a rhombus, then its sides are not equal.
(ii) If a triangle is not isosceles, it does not have equal sides.
(iii) If a number is not divisible by 3, then it is not divisible by 9.
8. Yes

TEXTUAL EXERCISE–2 (OBJECTIVE)

1. Negation of the statement "$\sqrt{2}$ is not a complex number" is
(a) $\sqrt{2}$ is a natural number
(b) $\sqrt{2}$ is an integer
(c) $\sqrt{2}$ is a complex number
(d) None of these

2. Negation of "Chandigarh is the capital of Punjab" is
(a) Chandigarh is the capital of U.P.
(b) It is false that Chandigarh is the capital of Punjab.
(c) Punjab is the capital of Chandigarh.
(d) None of these

3. Which type of "Or" is being used in the statement: "2 is an irrational number or it is a natural number"?
(a) Inclusive (b) Exclusive
(c) Both (a) and (b) (d) None of these

4. Contra-positive of statement 'If a number is divisible by 4 then it is also divisible by 2' is
(a) If a number is not divisible by 2, then it is divisible by 4.
(b) If a number is not divisible by 2, then it is not divisible by 4.
(c) If a number is divisible by 2, then it is divisible by 4.
(d) None of these

5. The converse of statement
If two lines are parallel, then the distance between them is constant.
(a) If the distance between two lines is not constant then they are non-parallel.
(b) If the distance between two lines is not constant then they are intersecting.
(c) If the distance between two lines is constant then they are parallel.
(d) None of these

6. Let P: 10 is divisible by 2
q: 10 is divisible by 5
then the compound statement formed by using connecting word 'and' is
(a) 10 is divisible by 2 and 10 is divisible by 5
(b) 10 is divisible by 2 and 5
(c) 2 divides 10 and 5 divides 10
(d) None of these

Answer Keys

1. (c) **2.** (b) **3.** (b) **4.** (b) **5.** (c) **6.** (b)

PROOFS IN MATHEMATICS

The proofs in mathematics consist of a set of statements given in a logical (systematic and meaningful) arrangement. And each of these statements should be justified by previously established definitions, axioms, arguments and preposition etc.

Thus proof is a process of "drawing inferences" by providing a chain of inductive/deductive arguments in which step by step way, we continue drawing conclusions and finally reach the completion. Proving can be approached in two ways:

Direct proofs In this method, directly start with the given information and conclude the result by providing inductive/deductive arguments.

Straight forward method It is a chain of arguments which leads directly from what is given or assumed, with the help of axioms, definitions or already proved theorems, to what is to be proved using rules of logic.

ILLUSTRATION 2: Prove that if $x^2 - 3x - 4 = 0$, then either $x = 4$ or $x = -1$.

SOLUTION: Given $x^2 - 3x - 4 = 0$

$\Rightarrow$ $x^2 - 4x + x - 4 = 0$ (replacing by an equivalent expression)

$\Rightarrow$ $x(x - 4) + (x - 4) = 0$

$\Rightarrow$ $(x + 1)(x - 4) = 0$ (factorizing the expression)

$\Rightarrow$ $x + 1 = 0$ or $(x - 4) = 0$ (by theorem $a.b = 0 \Rightarrow$ either $a = 0$ or $b = 0$)

$\Rightarrow$ $x + 1 - 1 = 0 - 1$ or $x - 4 + 4 = 0 + 4$ (Adding equal quantities to both side does not alter the nature of equation.)

$\Rightarrow$ $x = -1$ or $x = 4$

Note that or is not inclusive here.

Method of mathematical induction In this method, we prove the result for $n = 1$ and assume that the result is true for a natural number 'm' and show that the result is true for $(m + 1)$.

Therefore by induction, the result is true for every positive integer n.

(We shall discuss P.M.I in detail before Textual Exercise 9)

ILLUSTRATION 3: Prove that the sum of first n odd natural numbers is n^2.

PROOF: Let us take $n = 1$

$\therefore$ Sum of first odd natural no. $= 1 = (1)^2$

$\therefore$ The result is true for $n = 1$

Let us assume that the result is true for a natural number (m)

i.e., $1 + 3 + 5 + ... + (2m - 1) = m^2$ (i)

We prove the result for $n = m$

Now consider

$1 + 3 + 5...... + (2m - 1) + (2m + 1) = m^2 + (2m + 1)$ ...[by (i)] $= (m + 1)^2$

Thus the result is also true for $n = m + 1$, whenever it is true for $n = m$

$\therefore$ By the principle of mathematical induction, the result is true for all natural numbers n

Method of exhaustion (All possible case method) This method consists of examining every possible case of the hypothesis. It is practically convenient only when the number of possible cases are few.

ILLUSTRATION 4: Prove that $n^3 - n$ is divisible by $6 \forall n \in N$

SOLUTION: Since any integer when divided by 3 leaves remainder 0 or 1 or 2 so an integer n can always be taken as $3k$, $3k + 1$, $3k + 2$ where $k \in \mathbb{Z}$

Case 1: Let $n = 3k$ then

$n^3 - n = (3k)^3 - 3k = 3k(9k^2 - 1)$ clearly divisible by 3

Case 2: if $n = 3k + 1$

$n^3 - n = (3k + 1)^3 - (3k + 1)$

$= 27k^3 + 1 + 9k(3k + 1) - (3k + 1) = 27k^3 + 27k^2 + 6k$

$= 3k(9k^2 + 9k + 2)$ again divisible by 3

Case 3: $n = 3k + 2$

$n^3 - n = (3k + 2)3 - (3k + 2) = 27k^3 + 8 + 54k^2 + 36k - 3k - 2$

$= 27k^3 + 54k^2 + 33k + 6 = 3[9k^3 + 18k^2 + 11k + 2]$

Also if n is even $\Rightarrow n^3 - n$ is even and if n is odd $\Rightarrow n^3 - n$ is even

$\therefore$ $n^3 - n$ is an even integer

Hence $n^3 - n$ is divisible by LCM of 3 and 2, i.e., 6.

ILLUSTRATION 5: Show that in any ΔABC, $\dfrac{a}{\sin A} = \dfrac{b}{\sin B} = \dfrac{c}{\sin C}$ where a, b, c are lengths of sides of triangle and A, B, C are corresponding opposite angles. (This expression leads to sine rule of the triangle).

SOLUTION: Consider an acute angled, a right angled and an obtuse angled triangle ABC.

Case 1: For an acute angled triangle

Drop perpendicular AD from A on BC (may be on extended BC)

Now in acute angled Δ ABC

$AD = AB \sin B \Rightarrow AD = c \sin B$ (i)

also $AD = AC \sin C \Rightarrow AD = b \sin C$ (ii)

From (I) and (II) $\dfrac{b}{\sin B} = \dfrac{c}{\text{Sin} C}$ By dropping perpendicular from other points the other cases will lead us to conclude

$$\frac{a}{\sin A} = \frac{b}{\sin B} = \frac{c}{\sin C}$$

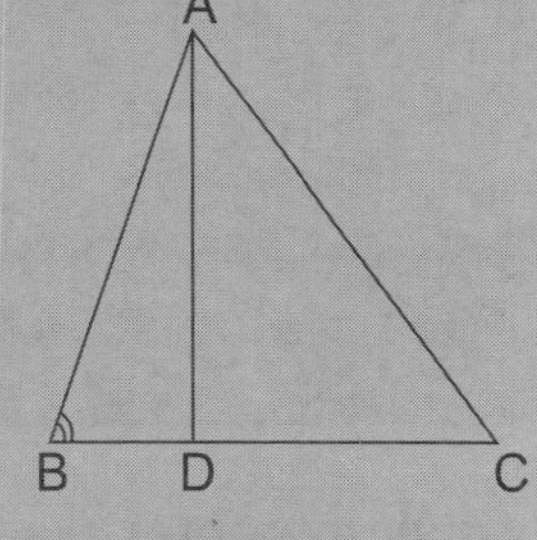

FIGURE 1.1

Case 2: In right angled ΔABC

$AD = AB \sin B = c \sin B$

as $AD = AC$ or $AD = AC \sin 90° = b \sin C$

$\therefore$ $\dfrac{b}{\sin B} = \dfrac{c}{\sin C}$

Finally proceeding for other points, we will be able to conclude $\dfrac{a}{\sin A} = \dfrac{b}{\sin B} = \dfrac{c}{\sin C}$

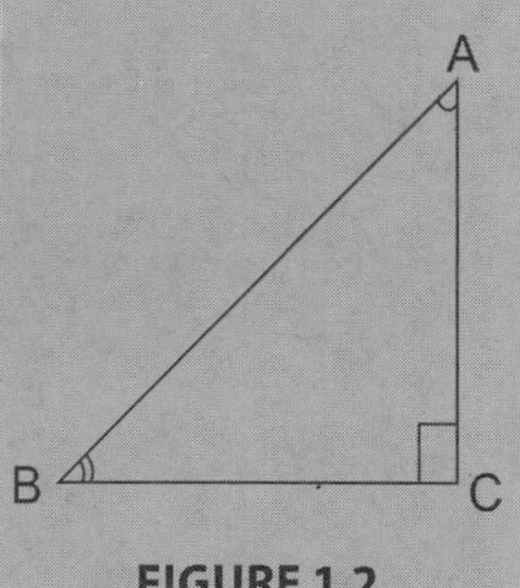

FIGURE 1.2

Case 3: In obtuse angled ΔABC

$AD = AB \sin B$ or $AD = c \sin B$

also $AD = AC \sin(180° - C) = b \sin C$

$\therefore \quad \frac{b}{\sin B} = \frac{c}{\sin C}$; On the same line, we will get $\frac{a}{\sin A} = \frac{b}{\sin B} = \frac{c}{\sin C}$

So irrespective of the type of triangle, we get the same result i.e.,

$\frac{a}{\sin A} = \frac{b}{\sin B} = \frac{c}{\sin C}$

A
180°
B C D

FIGURE 1.3

Indirect proof

In these methods, we establish the proof of given proposition by proving another proposition which is equivalent to the given proposition. It involves following three methods:

Proof by contradiction: Here, the statement is assumed to be false and with logical approach, the assumption is to be contradicted and we will infer that the assumption is wrong.

Method of contradiction: In this approach, negation of the statement under consideration is worked out. i.e., to check the truth of statement *p,* we assume that *p* is not true i.e., $\sim p$ is true and by this assumption, we arrive at a result which contradicts our basic assumption and therefore we conclude the results.

ILLUSTRATION 6: Using Contradiction Method, Check the validity of statement "$\sqrt{13}$ is an irrational number".

SOLUTION: Let us assume $\sqrt{13}$ as rational number i.e., $\sqrt{13} = \frac{a}{b}$ (*a*, *b* are in the lowest terms)

$\Rightarrow \quad \frac{a^2}{b^2} = 13 \Rightarrow a^2 = 13b^2 \Rightarrow 13$ divides a (i)

(because *b* does not divide *a*)

So we can safely consider $a = 13p$

$\Rightarrow \quad a^2 = 169\,p^2$ and $a^2 = 13b^2$

$\therefore \quad b^2 = 13p^2 \Rightarrow 13$ divides *b* (ii)

From (i) and (ii), 13 is the HCF of *a* and *b*. But this contradicts our assumption that *a* and *b* are integers in the lowest terms. So our assumption that $\sqrt{13}$ is rational is not true.

By giving counter example

This is a method to falsify a given statement and it involves an example of a situation where the statement becomes invalid and it is called as ***counter example.***

ILLUSTRATION 7: Using a counter example, falsify the statement "Every odd integer is *a* prime number"

SOLUTION: We know that $2n + 1$ is an odd integer $\forall n \in \mathbb{Z}$ but when $n = 4, 7$ ...etc., Statement fails to be true, because 9, 15, ... are not primes. Hence falsified.

ILLUSTRATION 8: Prove that the set of all prime numbers is infinite.

SOLUTION: We proceed by taking the set of all prime numbers to be finite.

So our set may be having *m* elements listed as p_1, p_2, p_3 ...., p_m

Now we can take a number $N = (p_1, p_2, p_3 \text{ ....}, p_m) + 1$ (i)

N will be larger than any of $p_1, p_2 \text{.............} p_m$. If *N* is taken as prime then the list $p_1, p_2, p_3, \text{............} p_m$ is not complete.

If N is taken as composite, then there should be some prime divisor (s) of N. But we observe that any prime number from the list will leave 1 as remainder. So N cannot be composite.

In these two approaches, we end up with contradiction. So our assumption is wrong, which means the set of primes is infinite.

Proof by using contra positive statement: In this method, instead of proving $p \Rightarrow q$. We try to prove $\sim q \Rightarrow \sim p$. The contra-positive of a condition can be formed by interchanging the conclusion and the hypothesis and negating both.

ILLUSTRATION 9: Prove that if $x^2 - 3x = 0$ then x is either 0 or 3.

SOLUTION: To prove above statements, let us consider a statement p: $x^2 - 3x = 0$ and another statement q: x is either 0 or 3. Therefore $\sim p$: $x^2 - 3x \neq 0$ and $\sim q$: x is neither 0 nor 3.
Let $x^2 - 3x \neq 0 \quad \Rightarrow \quad x \neq 0$ and $x - 3 \neq 0, \quad \Rightarrow \quad x \neq 0$ and 3

ILLUSTRATION 10: Prove by contra-positive method that $f: R \to R$, given by $f(x) = \frac{1}{3}x + 4$ is one – one by contra-positive method we begin with $x_1 \neq x_2 \Rightarrow \frac{1}{3}x_1 \neq \frac{1}{3}x_2$

SOLUTION: By adding 4 to both sides $\frac{1}{3}x_1 + 4 \neq \frac{1}{3}x_2 + 4$
$\Rightarrow \quad f(x_1) \neq f(x_2)$
since "$\sim q \Rightarrow \sim p$" which is equivalent to "$p \Rightarrow q$"
which completes the proof.

Proof by counter example: Sometimes it is difficult to prove a statement then we search for an example to dis-approve.

ILLUSTRATION 11: Verify the truth of statement " $4n - 1$ is a prime number for $n \in \mathbb{N}$ ".

SOLUTION: "$4n - 1$ is prime number for $n \in \mathbb{N}$ " We check by putting $n = 1, 2, 3, \ldots \ldots$ and observe that for $n = 4$, $4n - 1 = 15 = 3 \times 5$, which is composite number. So our statement is false.

ILLUSTRATION 12: Verify the truth of statement " Every continuous function is differentiable."

SOLUTION: Consider examples $F(x) = |\sin x|$ or $G(x) = |x|$
The graph of function is as shown in the figure.
The derivative at $x = 0$ does not exist for both these functions.
So the statement that "every continuous function is differentiable" is false.

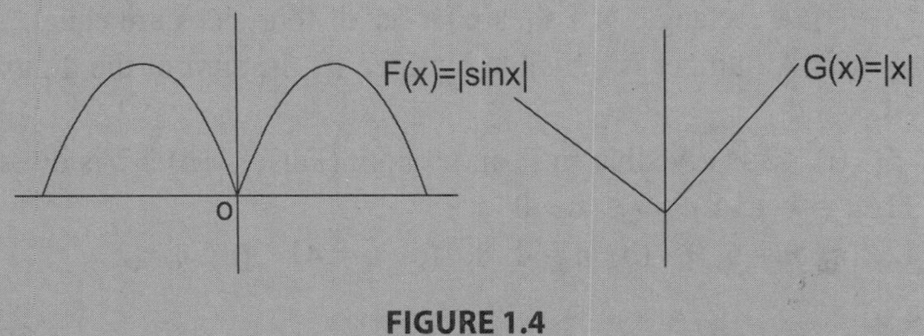

FIGURE 1.4

TEXTUAL EXERCISE–3 (SUBJECTIVE)

1. Identify the quantifier in the following statements and write the negation of the statements.
   - (i) There exists a number which is equal to its square.
   - (ii) For every real number x, x is less than $x + 1$.
   - (iii) There exists a capital for every state in India.
   - (iv) There exists a successor for every real number x.
   - (v) Square of every real number is non-negative.

2. Form the compound statements by using the implications given in braces
   - (i) p: x is a whole number **(use 'if-then')**
     q: x is an integer
   - (ii) p: x^2 is non-negative quantity, **(use 'if-then')**
     q: x is a real number
   - (iii) p: Δ_1 and Δ_2 are similar triangles **(use 'only if')**
     q: Δ_1 and Δ_2 are congruent triangles

(iv) **p:** x is a real number **(use 'only if')**

q: x is a natural number

(v) **p:** Δ_1 and Δ_2 are similar triangles **(use 'if and only if')**

q: corresponding angles of Δ_1 and Δ_2 are equal.

(vi) **p:** x^2 is non positive quantity. **(use 'if and only if')**

q: x is purely imaginary

3. Given below are two pairs of statements. Combine these two statements using 'if and only if'.

(i) **p:** If a rectangle is a square, then all its four sides are equal.

q: If all the four sides of a rectangle are equal, then the rectangle is a square.

(ii) **p:** If the sum of digits of a number is divisible by 3, then the number is divisible by 3.

q: If a number is divisible by 3, then the sum of its digits is divisible by 3.

4. Check the validity of the statement: If $x, y \in I$ and x, y are odd then xy is odd.

5. Form a compound statement using the following statements with connecting words.

(i) "And" (ii) "Or".

p: 42 is divisible by 7;

q: 42 is divisible by 9. Also check the validity of the statements formed

6. If $\frac{(2a+7)(a+b+c)}{abc}, \frac{(2b+7)(a+b+c)}{abc}, \frac{(2c+7)(a+b+c)}{abc}$ are not in *A.P.* then by using contradiction method, prove that a, b, c are not in *A.P.*

7. By using contradiction method, prove that the expression $x^4 + 9x^2 + 14$ does not vanish for any real value of x.

8. By using direct method, prove that the truth of following statement "If x is a real number such that $2x^3 + 9x = 0$, then $x = 0$".

9. Prove that the statement "$2x^2 - 5 = 0$ cannot have roots lying between 0 and 2" is false.

10. Prove that $n^2 \geq 6n - 9$ for all $n \in N$.

11. "For any real number x and y, $x^2 - y^2 = 0, \Rightarrow x = y$" falsify the above statement by giving counter example.

12. Providing counter examples, falsify the following statements:

(a) $6n - 1$ is a prime number for all natural numbers n.

(b) $6n + 1$ is a prime number for all natural numbers n.

(c) $n^2 + n + 41$ is a prime number for all natural numbers n.

(d) $4n + 1$ is never a perfect square for any natural number n.

Answer Keys

1. (i) there exist (∃) (ii) For all (∀) (iii) there exist (∃) (iv) there exist (∃) (v) For all (∀)

3. (i) A rectangle is a square iff its all four sides are equal.

(ii) A number is divisible by three iff the sum of the digits is divisible by three.

4. valid

5. (i) 42 is divisible by 7 and 9 both (False) (ii) 42 is divisible by 7 or 9. (True)

11. $x = k$ and $y = -k$, $k \neq 0$

12. (a) $n = 6, 9$ (b) $n = 4, 8$ (c) $n = 41$ (d) $n = 2$.

■ SET THEORY

Definition of set

A collection of well defined objects which are distinct and distinguishable is called a set. E.g., collection of even natural numbers, collection of vowels of English alphabet.

A collection is said to be well defined if each and every element of the collection has same definition.

Notation of sets

Sets are denoted by capital letters like A, B, C or { } and the entries within the braces are known as ***elements*** of set. denoted by small letters $a, b, \ldots\ldots\ldots x, y$ etc.

Cardinal number of a set

Cardinal number of a set X is the number of elements of set X and it is denoted by $n(X)$.

E.g. for $X = \{x_1, x_2, x_3\}$, the cardinal number of $X = n(X) = 3$. For example:

If A = Set of all small English alphabets = $\{a, b, c, \ldots\ldots\ldots x, y, z\}$; $n(A) = 26$

If B = Set of all positive integers less than or equal to 10 = {1, 2, 3, 4, 5, 6, 7, 8, 9, 10}; $n(B) = 10$

If $\mathbb{R}$ = Set of real numbers = $\{x : -\infty < x < \infty\}$; $n(\mathbb{R})$ is infinite.

The elements of a set can be discrete (e.g., set of all English alphabets) or continuous (e.g., set of real numbers).

Description of sets

Sets are described by using two methods known as Roster method and Set builder method.

Set listing method (Roster method) In this method, a set is described by listing all the elements, separated by commas, within braces { }.

Set builder method (Set rule method) In this method, a set is described by *a* characterizing property $P(x)$ of its elements x. In such case, the set is described by $\{x: P(x)$ holds$\}$ or $\{x \mid P(x)$ holds$\}$, which is read as the set of all x such that $P(x)$ holds. The symbol '|' or ':' is read as such that. The set may contain finite or infinite number of elements. *A* set may contain no elements and such *a* set is called Void set or Null set or empty set and is denote by ϕ (phi). The number of elements of a set A is denoted by $n(A)$ and hence $n(\phi) = 0$ as it contains no element.

Types of sets

Finite set A set X is called a finite set if its elements can be listed by counting or labelling with the help of natural numbers and the process terminates at a certain natural number n.

e.g.,

(a) A set of English Alphabets

(b) Set of soldiers in Indian Army

(c) Set of all persons living on the earth etc.

Infinite set A set whose elements cannot be listed or if listing is possible then the process never terminates, is called an infinite set.

E.g.,

(a) A set of all points in *a* plane

(b) $X = \{x: x \in R \quad 0 < x < 0.0001\}$

(c) $X = \{x: x \in Q \quad 0 \le x \le 0.0001\}$

Singleton set A set consisting of *a* single element is called *a* singleton set. i.e., $n(x) = 1$, *e.g.*, $\{x: x \in \mathbb{N}, 1 < x < 3\}$, $\{\{\ \}\}$:Set containing an element as null set, $\{\phi\}$ is a set containing alphabet ϕ.

Null set A set is said to be empty, void or null set if it has no element in it, and it is denoted by ϕ. i.e., X is a null set if $n(X) = 0$. E.g., $\{x{:}x \in R$ and $x^2 + 2 = 0\}$, $\{x{:}x > 1$ but $x < 1/2\}$, $\{x{:}x \in R, x^2 < 0\}$

Countable and uncountable sets *A* set X is called *a countable* set if its element can be listed by counting or labelling with the help of natural numbers i.e., *a* set is called countable if it has one to one correspondence with set of natural numbers e.g., Set of odd natural numbers, set of even natural numbers etc. Otherwise the set is called *uncountable*. *e.g.*, set of irrational numbers, set of real numbers etc.

Classification of Sets

Finite Set A set X is called finite if it has limited number of elements in it. i.e., if its all elements are labelled with the help of natural numbers the process terminates at certain finite natural number. E.g., set of living people on earth.

Null Set A set X is called null/void/empty if it has no element in it. It is denoted by ϕ or {} e.g.,
A = {x: x ∈ & $x^2 + 2 = 0$}
B = {x:x ∈ & $x^2 < 0$}

Singletion Set A set X is called singleton set if it has only one element in it e.g.,
A = {x: x ∈ & $x^2 - 4 = 0$}
B = {x:x ∈ & $x^2 \le 0$}

Infinite Set A set X is called infnite if it has unlimited number of elements in it. e.g., set of rational numbers or set of points in a plane.

Countable Set
A set X is called countable if its elements can be labeled with the help of natural numbers. i.e., its elements are function of natural numbers e.g. A set of odd natural numbers.

Uncountable Set
A set X is called uncountable if its elements can not be labeled with the help of Natural numbers. i.e., its elements can not be written as function of natural numbers. e.g., set of real numbers, set of irrational numbers.

FIGURE 1.5

SOME IMPORTANT REMARKS

- ❑ *Every finite set is countable but every countable set is not necessarily finite*
- ❑ *Infinite sets may or may not be countable*

- ❑ *Uncountable sets are always infinite*
- ❑ *Every subset of a countable set is countable*
- ❑ *Every superset of an uncountable set is also uncountable*
- ❑ *Intersection of countable sets is always countable*
- ❑ *Countable union of countable sets is always countable*

Relative classification of sets

Equivalent set

Two finite sets A and B are equivalent if their cardinal numbers are same i.e., $n(A) = n(B)$. Example, set of positive integers or set of negative integers.

Equal set

Two sets A and B are said to be equal if every element of A is a member of B and every element of B is a member of A. i.e., $A = B$ if A and B are equal and $A \neq B$ if they are not equal.

Subset

A set A is said to be a subset of B if all the elements of A are also present in B and is denoted by

$A \subset B$ (read as A is subset of B) and symbolically written as:

$x \in A \Rightarrow x \in B \Leftrightarrow A \subset B$

$A \subset B \Rightarrow A$ is a proper subset of B

Properties

1. $A \subset B \Rightarrow B \supset A$ where $\supset$ is known as superset.
2. $A \subset B$ and $B \subset C \Rightarrow A \subset C$
3. Every set is subset of universal set.
4. Null set is subset of all sets

Super set

If a set A is a subset of B, then B is called superset of A and it is denoted as $B \supset$ A(read as B superset of A)

Number of subsets

Consider a set X containing n elements as $\{x_1, x_2, ..., x_n\}$, then the total number of subsets of $X = 2^n$

Power set

The collection of all subsets of set A is called the power set of A and is denoted by $P(A)$. i.e., $P(A) = \{x: x$ is a subset of $A\}$. If $X = \{x_1, x_2, x_3, ...x_n\}$ then $n(P(X)) = 2^n$; $n(P(P(x)) = 2^{2n}$

Disjoint set

Sets A and B are said to be disjoint iff A and B have no common element or $A \cap B = \phi$. If $A \cap B \neq \phi$ then A and B are said to be intersecting or overlapping sets.

Example

(i) If $A = \{1, 2, 3\}$, $B = \{4, 5, 6\}$ and $C = \{4, 7, 9\}$ then A and B are disjoint set where B and C are intersecting sets.

(ii) Set of even natural numbers and odd natural numbers are disjoint sets.

Universal set

It is a set which includes all the sets under considerations., it is a super set of each of the given set. Thus, a set that contains all sets in a given context is called the universal set. It is denoted by U or S. e.g., if

$A = \{1, 2, 3\}$, $B = \{2, 4, 5, 6\}$ and $C = \{1, 3, 5, 7\}$, then

$U = \{1, 2, 3, 4, 5, 6, 7\}$ can be taken as the universal set.

Complementary set

Complementary set of a set A is a set containing all those elements of universal set which are not in A. It is denoted by $\overline{A}$, A^c A'. So $A^c = \{x: x \in U$ but $x \notin A\}$.

E.g., If set $A = \{1, 2, 3, 4, 5\}$ and universal set $U = \{1, 2, 3, 4, ...50\}$ then $\overline{A} = \{6, 7, ...50\}$

ILLUSTRATION 13: Classify the following sets as Finite sets, Infinite sets, Countable sets, Uncountable sets, Singleton sets and, Null sets.

(a) $A = \{2, 3, 5\}$

(b) $B = \{2, 4, 6, 8, ...\}$

(c) $C = \{x : x$ is neither prime nor composite$\}$

(d) $D = \{x : x$ is a bird which can swim as well as fly$\}$

(e) $E = \{l : l$ is a straight line parallel to a given line segment $AB\}$

(f) $F = \{x : x$ is a real number which is integer as well as irrational$\}$

(g) $G = \{x : x$ is real number which is irrational$\}$

(h) $H = \{x : x$ is a real number lying between two different real numbers a and $b\}$

SOLUTION: (a) $A = \{2, 3, 5\}$

It is finite and hence countable set ($\because$ Every finite set is countable)

(b) $B = \{2, 4, 6, 8, ...\}$

It is an infinite set but its elements can be listed without leaving any element and hence is countable.

(c) $C = \{1\}$ as 1 is the number which is prime as well as composite. Thus C is singleton, finite and countable.

(d) $D = \{x : x$ is a bird which can fly as well as swim$\}$

Duck, penguin are some birds which can fly as well as swim, so the set is not singleton but being a subset of birds (which is finite) is also finite and countable.

(e) $E = \{l : l$ is a straight line parallel to a given line segment $AB\}$

We can draw uncountably many lines parallel to a given line segment AB, hence the set E is infinite and uncountable.

A

B

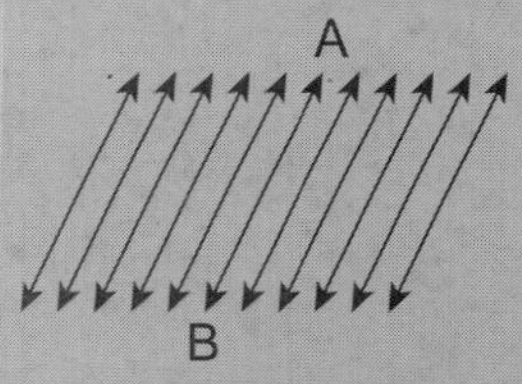

FIGURE 1.6

(f) $F = \{x : x$ is a real number which is integer as well as irrational$\}$

$F = \{\}$, as no real number is both integer as well as irrational as every integer is rational.

So F is a null set, finite set and countable set

(g) G = set of irrational numbers,

$\Rightarrow$ G is infinite and uncountable.

(h) $H = (a, b)$ = set of all real numbers lying between 'a' and 'b' which are infinitely many and can't be listed and hence uncountable.

ILLUSTRATION 14: Classify the pairs of equivalent and equal sets.

(a) $A = \{o, e, i, a, u\}$

(b) $B = \{1, 2, 3, 4, 5\}$

(c) $C = \{x : x$ is a vowel english alphabets$\}$

(d) $D = \{x : x$ is an even natural number$\}$

(e) $E = \{x : x$ is an odd natural number$\}$

(f) $F = \{x : x \leq 20; x \in N$ and x is divisible by $2\}$

(g) $G = \{x : x \leq 20; x \in N$ and x is not divisible by $2\}$

(h) $H = \{x : x$ is a real root of equation $x^3 - 4x^2 + x + 6 = 0\}$

(i) $I = \{a, b, c, d\}$;

(j) $J = \{a, b, c\}$

SOLUTION: All the sets in Roster form are:

(a) $A = \{o, e, i, a, u\}$

(b) $B = \{1, 2, 3, 4, 5\}$

(c) $C = \{a, e, i, o, u\}$

(d) $D = \{2, 4, 6, 8, ...\}$

(e) $E = \{1, 3, 5, 7, ...\}$

(f) $F = \{2, 4, 6, 8, ..., 20\}$;
$n(F) = 10$

(g) $G = \{1, 3, 5, ..., 19\}$;
$n(G) = 10$

(h) $H = \{x : x \in R \text{ and } x^3 - 4x^2 + x + 6 = 0\}$
$= \{x : x \in R \text{ and } (x + 1)(x - 2)(x - 3) = 0\} = \{-1, 2, 3\}$

(i) $I = \{a, b, c, d\}$;

(j) $J = \{a, b, c\}$

Clearly equal sets: (A, C)

Equivalent sets: (A, B) ; (B, C) ; (A, C) ; (F, G); (H, J)

Since D and E are infinite sets, but they are comparable to natural numbers, so they are equivalent sets. Also, every pair of equal sets is equivalent.

ILLUSTRATION 15: Let $A = \{5, 6, 7\}$; $B = \{8, 9, 10\}$; $C = \{1, 2, 3, 4, 5, 6, 7, 8, 9, 10\}$ then find

(i) number of subsets of C which are supersets of B.

(ii) number of subsets of C having number of element of A and B.

(iii) number of subsets of C having exactly one element from each of A and B.

SOLUTION: (i) If X is a superset of B and subset of C, then X has at least 3 elements i.e., 8, 9 and 10

Now each of the remaining elements of C except for 8, 9, 10 i.e., 1, 2, 3, 4, 5, 6, 7 has two choices either they would belong to X or does not belong to X.

Thus total number of X's = (2) (2) (2) … × (2) [7 times] = $(2)^7 = 128$

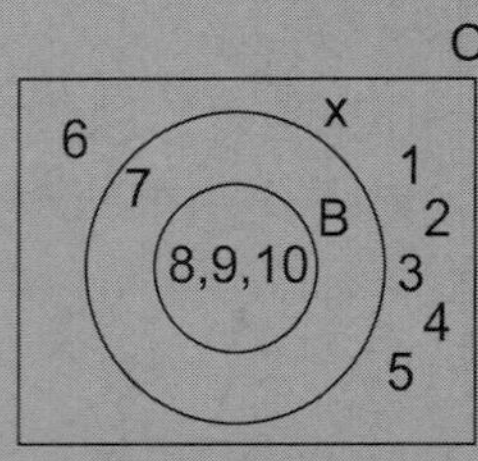

FIGURE 1.7

(ii) Let X be any subset of C, disjoint from A and B

$\therefore$ X must be formed from the elements of set of $\{1, 2, 3, 4\}$

i.e., X will be a subset of set $\{1, 2, 3, 4\} = (2)^4 = 16$

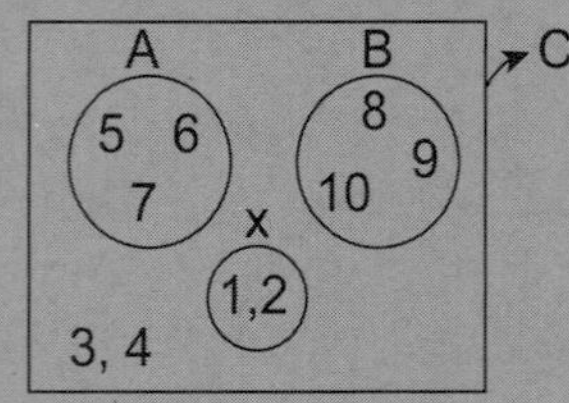

FIGURE 1.8

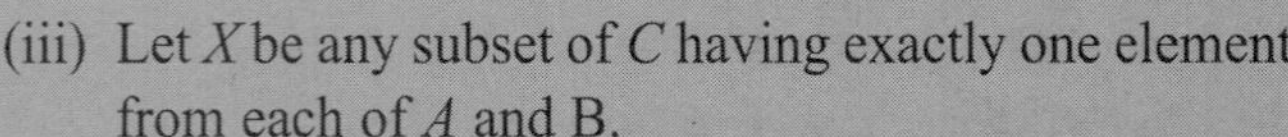

(iii) Let X be any subset of C having exactly one element from each of A and B.

Now, X has a pair of elements (a, b) ; $a \in A$ and $b \in B$

Now a has 3 choices i.e., 5, 6, 7 and b has 3 choices i.e., 8, 9, 10

$\therefore$ Total pairs $(a, b) = 3 \times 3 = 9$

Now, corresponding to each pair (a, b) contained by X, X can have or can't have the remaining elements 1, 2 or 3.

Therefore total possibilities of X are $9 \times 2 \times 2 \times 2 \times 2 = 144$.

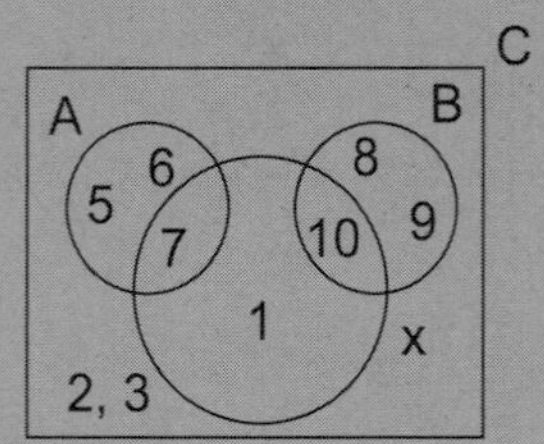

FIGURE 1.9

TEXTUAL EXERCISE–4 (SUBJECTIVE)

1. (a) Which of the following collections can be called as set?
   (i) collection of antique coins
   (ii) collection of antique coins of mughal period.
   (iii) collection of genius people on earth
   (iv) {Book, Dog, Donkey, Lion, Pen, Mango}
   (v) $\{a, b, b, c, 1, 2, 2, 3\}$
   (vi) Collection of the best Hindi novels.

   (b) Which of the following is true if $A = \{a, b, \{a\}, \{b\}\}$?
   (i) 'a' is an element of A
   (ii) $\{a, b\}$ is an element of A
   (iii) $\{b\}$ is not an element of A
   (iv) $\{\{a\}, a, b\}$ is element of A

2. Given the following sets in builder form, find their nature and their cardinal number.
   (a) $A = \{x: x$ is integer and $x^2 - 4x + 3 = 0\}$
   (b) $A = \{x: x$ is natural number and $x^2 - 3x - 4 = 0\}$
   (c) $A = \{x: x$ is positive integer divisible by 4 and $x < 50\}$
   (d) $A = \{x: x$ is a non-negative integer which leaves remainder 1 when divided by 4 and $x \le 100\}$
   (e) $A = \{x: x$ is even prime number, but $x \ne 2\}$
   (f) $A = \{x: x$ is odd natural number divisible by 5 and $x \le 50\}$
   (g) $A = \{x: x$ is natural number divisible by both 2 and 3 and $x < 100\}$
   (h) $A = \{x: x$ is natural number divisible by both 4 and 6 and $x \le 100\}$
   (i) $A = \{x: x$ is natural number divisible by either 2 or 3$\}$
   (j) $A = \{x: x$ is natural number divisible by 4 and 6$\}$
   (k) $A = \{x: m$ is non-negative integer and $x = 4m + 1$ and $x < 10\}$

3. Which of the following pairs of sets are disjoint?
   (i) $\{1, 2, 3, 4\}$ and $\{x: x$ is a natural number and $4 < x < 6\}$
   (ii) $\{a, e, i, o, u\}$ and $\{c, d, e, f\}$
   (iii) $\{x: x$ is an even integer$\}$ and $\{x: x$ is an odd integer$\}$

4. State whether each of the following statement is true or false. Justify your answer.
   (i) $\{2, 3, 4, 5\}$ and $\{3, 6\}$ are disjoint sets.
   (ii) $\{a, e, i, o, u\}$ and $\{a, b, c, d\}$ are disjoint sets.
   (iii) $\{2, 6, 10, 14\}$ and $\{3, 7, 11, 15\}$ are disjoint sets.
   (iv) $\{2, 6, 10\}$ and $\{3, 7\ 11\}$ are disjoint sets.

5. If $U = \{a, b, c, d, e, f, g, h\}$, find the complements of the following sets.
   (i) $A = \{a, b, c\}$ (ii) $B = \{d, e, f, g\}$
   (iii) $C = \{a, c, e, g\}$ (iv) $D = \{f, g, h, a\}$

6. Let $A = \{a, b, c, d\}$, $B = \{a, b, c\}$ and $C = \{b, d\}$. Find all sets X satisfying the conditions.
   (a) $X \subset B, X \subset C$
   (b) $X \subset A, X \not\subset B$

7. Let $A = \{2, 4, 6, 8\}$, $B = \{3, 4, 5\}$ and $C = \{3, 5\}$. Find a set R satisfying the conditions.
   (a) $R \subset B$ and $R \subset A$
   (b) $R \subset C, R \not\subset A$
   (c) $R \subset B, R \subset C$
   (d) R and C are disjoint, $R \subset A$

8. Let B be a subset of A and let $P(A: B) = \{X \in P(A): X \supset B\}$ then
   (a) Show that $P(A: \phi) = P(A)$
   (b) If $A = \{a, b, c, d\}$, $B = \{a, b\}$. List all members of the set $P(A: B)$.

9. Two finite sets have m, n elements. The total number of subsets of the first set is 56 more than the total number of subsets of the second set. Find the values of m, n.

10. Let $A = \{a, b, c, d\}$ then find
    (i) Number of disjoint pairs of subset of A.
    (ii) Number of pairs of subsets of A having exactly 2 elements common.
    (iii) Number of pairs of subsets of A having exactly 3 element common.

    (what if in each of above cases each pair must have different subsets)

11. Let $A = \{1, 2, 3, 4\}$ and $B = \{2, 3\}$ find the number of subsets of A which are supersets of B.

12. Let $A = \{1, 2, 3, 4, 5, 6\}$; $B = \{3, 4, 5\}$, then find the number of subsets of A.
    (i) disjoint from B (i.e., no element common with B)
    (ii) having exactly one element of B
    (iii) having exactly two elements of B
    (iv) Subsets of A and supersets of B.}

13. Let $A = \{1, 2, 3\}$; $B = \{4, 5, 6\}$; $C = \{7, 8, 9\}$. Find the number of subsets of set $D = \{1, 2, 3, 4, 5, ..., 10\}$ having exactly one element from each of sets A, B and C.

14. Let $A_1 = \{1\}$; $A_2 = \{1, 2\}$; $A_3 = \{1, 2, 3,\}$; .... $A_r = \{1, 2, 3, ..., r\}$ and so on and let $S = \{1, 2, 3, 4, 5, 6\}$. Define $P(i)$ = Number of subsets of S having exactly one element of A_i, then evaluate $\sum_{i=1}^{6} P(i)$

15. Let A = {1, 2, 3} ; $B = \{7, 8, 9\}$; $C = \{1, 2, 3, 4, ..., 9, 10\}$; then find the number of subsets of C disjoint from both A and B (i.e., no element common with A and B).

16. $A = \{x : x \in N$ and $x \le 100$ and x is divisible by $2\}$
$B = \{x : x \in N$ and $x \le 100$ and x is divisible by $3\}$
$C = \{x : x \in N$ and $x \le 100$ and x is divisible by $5\}$
$D = \{x : x \in N$ and $x \le 100$ and x is divisible by $7\}$
$E = \{x : x \in N$ and $x \le 100$ and x is divisible by $11\}$
then find the set $G = \{x : x \in N$ and $x \le 100\}$ and G is disjoint from each of the sets A, B, C, D and E. Also find cardinality of set G.

Answer Keys

1. (a) (iv) (b) (i) T (ii) F (iii) F (iv) F
2. (a) finite, countable, 2 (b) singleton (c) finite, countable, 12 (d) finite, countable, 25 (e) null set, 0 (f) finite, countable, 5 (g) finite, countable, 16 (h) finite, countable, 8 (i) infinite, countable (j) infinite, countable (k) finite, countable, 3
3. i and iii
4. (i) F (ii) F (iii) T (iv) T
5.(i) $A' = \{d, e, f, g, h\}$ (ii) $B' = \{a, b, c, h\}$ (iii) $C' = \{b, d, f, h\}$ (iv) $D' = \{b, c, d, e\}$
6.(a) $\phi; \{b\}$ (b) {d}; {a,d}, {b,d}, {c,d}, {a,b,d}, {a,c,d}, {b,c,d}, {a,b,c,d}
7.(a) $R = \{4\}$, $R = \phi$ (b) $R = \{3\}, \{5\}, \{3,5\}$ (c) $R = \phi, \{3\}, \{5\}, \{3,5\}$ (d) $R = \{2\}, \{4\}, \{6,8\}$
8. (b) {a,b}, {a,b,c}, {a,b,d}, {a,b,c,d}
9. $m = 6$, $n = 3$
10. (i) 41 (ii) 30 (iii) 4
11. 4
12. (i) 8 (ii) 24 (iii) 24 (iv) 8
13. 54
14. 120
15. 16
16. G = {1,13,17,19,23,29,31,37,41,43,47,53,59,61,67,71,73,79,83,89,97}; $n(G) = 21$

■ VENN (EULER) DIAGRAM

- ❑ The diagrammatic representation of sets for their relative study is called 'Venn diagram' or 'Euler – Venn diagram'.
- ❑ Here we represent the universal S as set of all points within rectangle and the subset A of the set S is represented by the interior of *a* circle contained in the rectangle.

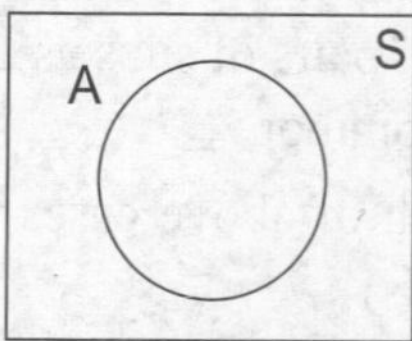

FIGURE 1.10

- ❑ If A and B are not equal but they have some common elements, then we represent A and B by two intersecting circles.

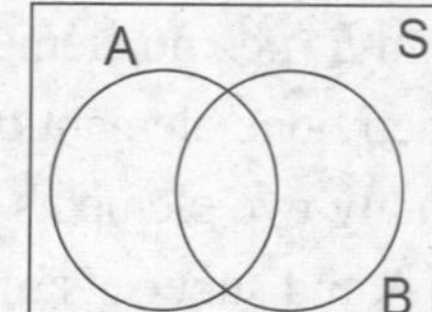

FIGURE 1.11

- ❑ If a set A is a subset of a set B, then the circle representing A is drawn inside the circle representing B.

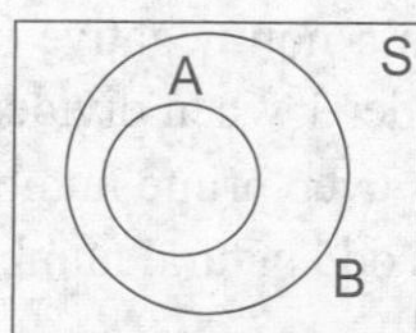

FIGURE 1.12

- ❑ Two circles having no common element are represented by two non-overlapping circles.

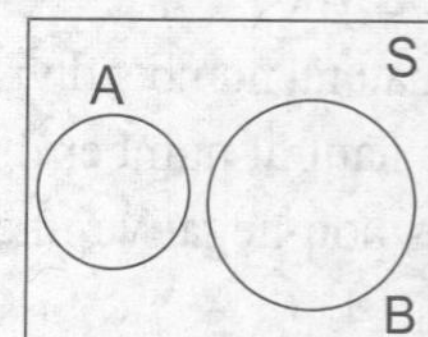

FIGURE 1.13

- ❑ The complementary set of the set A is represented by the shaded region in the figure by region lying outside the circle of set A and inside the universal set.

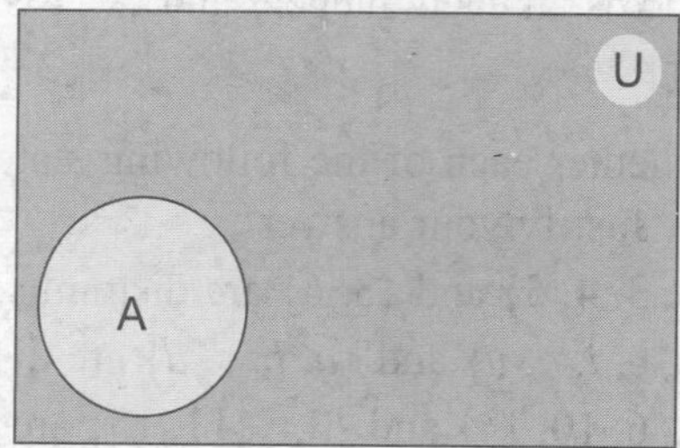

FIGURE 1.14

■ OPERATIONS ON SETS

Union of sets

Union of two or more sets is the set of all elements that belong to any of these sets. The symbol used for union of sets is '$\cup$'.

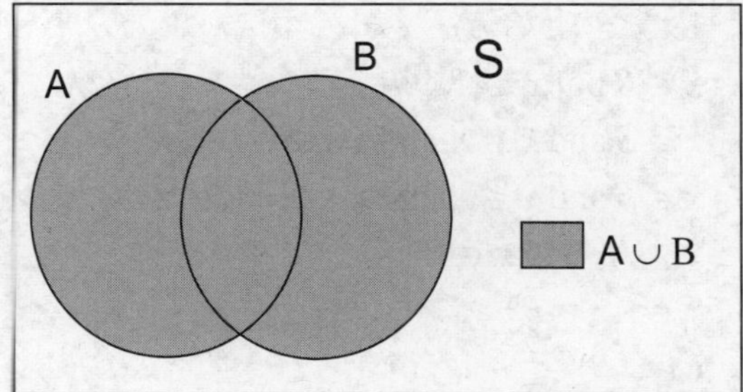

FIGURE 1.15

i.e., $A \cup B$ = Union of set A and set B $\{x: x \in A$ or $x \in B$ (both)$\}$

E.g., If $A = \{1, 2, 3, 4\}$ and $B = \{2, 4, 5, 6\}$ and $C\ \{1, 2, 6, 8\}$, then $A \cup B \cup C = \{1, 2, 3, 4, 5, 6, 8, 9\}$.

Intersection of sets

It is the set of all the elements, which are common to all the sets. The symbol used for intersection of sets is '$\cap$' i.e., $A \cap B = \{x: x \in A$ and $X \in B\}$ e.g., If $A = \{1, 2, 3, 4\}$ and $B = \{2, 4, 5, 6\}$ and $C = \{1, 2, 6, 8\}$, then $A \cap B \cap C\ \{2\}$.

Remember that $n(A \cup B) = n(A) + n(B) - n(A \cap B)$

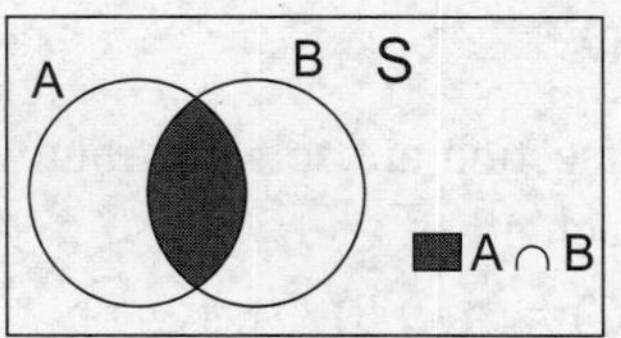

FIGURE 1.16

Difference of two sets

The difference of set A to B denoted as $A - B$ is the set of those elements that are in the set A but not in the set B.

i.e., $A - B = \{x: x \in A$ and $x \notin B\}$

Similarly, $B - A = \{x: x \in B$ and $x \notin A\}$. In general $A - B \neq B - A$.

e.g., If $A = \{a, b, c, d\}$ and $B = \{b, c, e, f\}$, then $A - B = \{a, d\}$ and $B - A = \{e, f\}$

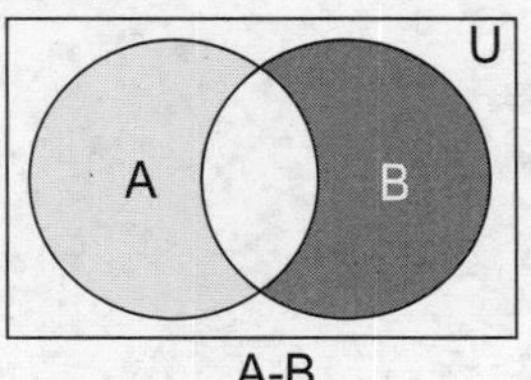

FIGURE 1.17

Symmetric difference If A and B are two sets, then symmetric difference of sets A and B is denoted by $A \Delta B$ and is given by $A\Delta B = (A - B) \cup (B - A)$

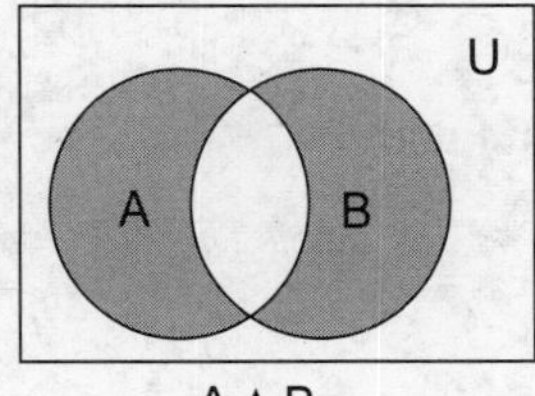

FIGURE 1.18

ILLUSTRATION 16: If $A = \{a, b, c\}$ and $B = \{b, c, d\}$ then evaluate $A \cup B$, $A \cap B$, $A - B$, $B - A$ and $A \Delta B$.

SOLUTION: $A \cup B = \{x : x \in A$ or $x \in B\} = \{a, b, c, d\}$; $A \cap B = \{x : x \in A$ and $x \in B\} = \{b, c\}$
$A - B = \{x : x \in A$ and $x \notin B\} = \{a\}$; $B - A = \{x : x \in B$ and $x \notin A\} = \{d\}$ $A \Delta B = \{a, d\}$

Algebraic structure of sets Four operations $\cup, \cap, \sim, \Delta$

Closure law Let S be set of all sets then S is closed for operation $\cup, \cap, \sim, \Delta$ .i.e., if $A, B \in S$

$\Rightarrow \quad A \cup B \in S, A \cap B \in S$ and $A \sim B \in S$

Commutative law Union and intersection of sets is commutative $A \cup B = B \cup A$ and $A \cap B = B \cap A$.

Associative law Union and intersection of sets is associative. i.e.,

For given three sets A, B and C

$(A \cap B) \cap C = A \cap (B \cap C)$

$A \cup (B \cup C) = (A \cup B) \cup C$

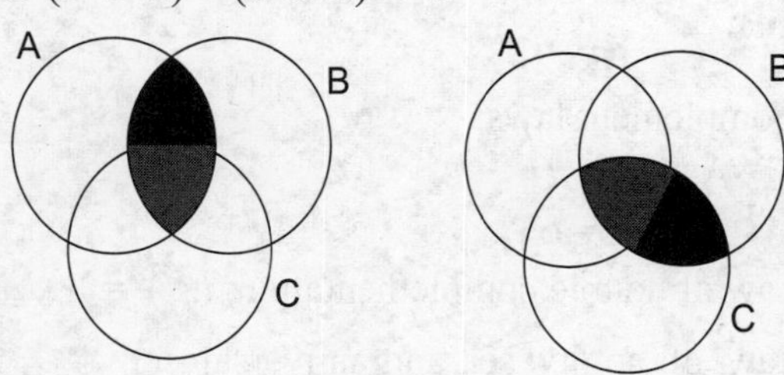

FIGURE 1.19

Distributive law

Union and Intersection are self distributive as well as distributive over each other.

$A \cup (B \cup C) = (A \cup B) \cup (A \cup C)$

$A \cap (B \cap C) = (A \cap B) \cap (A \cap C)$

$A \cup (B \cap C) = (A \cup B) \cap (A \cup C)$

$A \cap (B \cup C) = (A \cap B) \cup (A \cap C)$

Law of identity element

Null set (ϕ) is the identity element for $\cup$ because $A \cup \phi = A = \phi \cup A$

Universal set (S) is identity element for intersection because $A \cap S = A = S \cap A$.

Idempotent laws

$A \cup A = A$

$A \cap A = A$

Intersection distributes on difference:

$A \cap (B - C) = (A \cap B) - (A \cap C)$

However, $A \cup (B - C) \neq (A \cup B) - (A \cup C)$ i.e., union does not distribute over difference.

De morgan laws

For given two sets A and B

$(A \cup B)^C = A^C \cap B^C$ and $(A \cap B)^C = A^C \cup B^C$

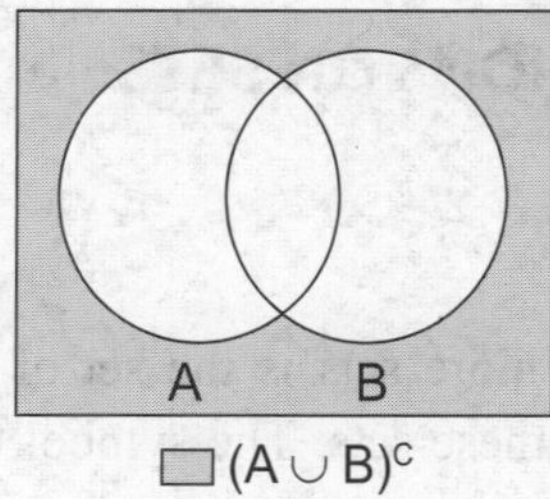

FIGURE 1.20

Proof: let $x \in (A \cup B)^C$

$\Rightarrow x \in S$ but $x \notin A \cup B$

$\Rightarrow x \in S$ and $x \notin A$ and $x \notin B$

$\Rightarrow x \in S$ and $x \notin A$ and $x \in S$ and $x \notin B$

$\Rightarrow x \in A^C$ and $x \in B^C$

$\Rightarrow x \in A^C \cap B^C$

$\Rightarrow (A \cup B)^C \subseteq A^C \cap B^C$ (i)

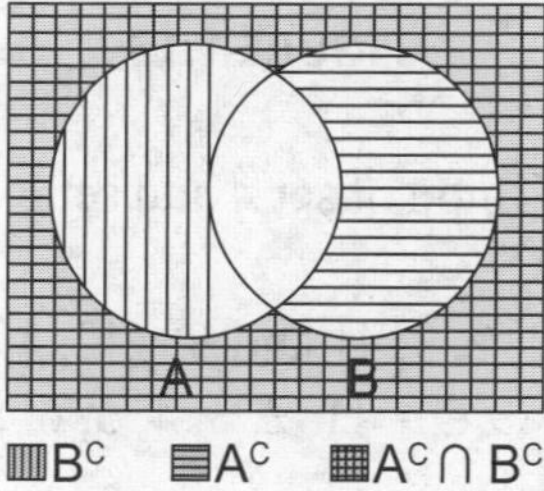

FIGURE 1.21

Similarly, we can prove $A^c \cap B^c \subseteq (A \cup B)^c$ (ii)

$\therefore$ From (i) and (ii) we have $(A \cup B)^c = A^c \cap B^c$

Similarly, we can prove the second part.

ILLUSTRATION 17: Let $(U) = 100$; $n(A) = 30$

$n(B) = 40$

$n(A \cap B) = 10$

then find $n(A^C \cap B^C)$.

SOLUTION: By Demorgan's principal, we have, $n[A^c \cap B^c]$

$= n(A \cup B)^c = n(U) - n(A \cup B)$

$= n(U) - [n(A) + n(B) - n(A \cap B)] = 100 - [30 + 40 - 10] = 100 - [60] = 40.$

The following laws can be easily verified using Venn diagrams.

(i) Complement laws:

(i) $A \cup A' = U$

(ii) $A \cap A' = \phi$

(iii) Law of double complementation: $(A')' = A$

(iv) Law of empty set and universal set: $\phi' = U$ and $U' = \phi$

■ MATHEMATICAL LOGIC AND REASONING THROUGH VENN DIAGRAM

Statement and its negation

Let P be any mathematical statement (i.e., either true or false but not both simultaneously).

Let S be the set containing all mathematical statements and Let P be a subset of S representing the mathematical statement. Thus we can express it by using Venn Diagram as shown below:

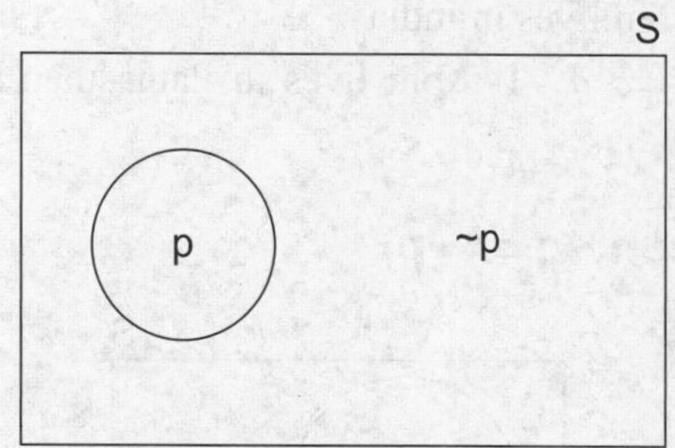

FIGURE 1.22

The complement of P represents negation of P i.e., $\sim P$. **e.g.,**

(i) P = Every whole number is a natural number.
$\sim P$ = There exists a whole number which is not natural.

(ii) P = If x^2 is even then x is even
$\sim P = x$ can be even without x^2 being even.

(iii) P = If x is a natural number dividing 2 then x is either 1 or 2.
$\sim P$ = If x is a natural number dividing 2, then it is not necessary that it is 1 or 2.
cr There exists a natural number dividing 2 other than 1 and 2.

Or statements

Let P and Q be two mathematical statements represented by two subsets of U as shown below

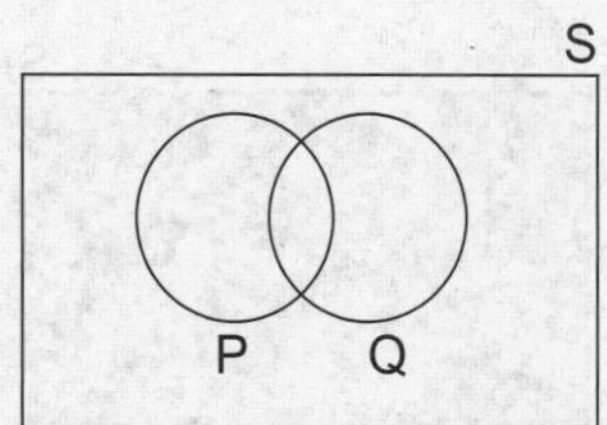

FIGURE 1.23

P* or *Q $= P \cup Q$

$\therefore$ Or statement is true if any one of p or q (or both) are true. e.g.,

(i) p = 10 is divisible by 2
q = 10 is divisible by 3
$p \cup q$ = 10 is divisible by 2 or 3.
Here p or q is true as P is true.

(ii) p = If y is father of x and z is father of y, then x is grandson of z.
q = If y is father of x and z is father of y, then x is grand daughter of z.
p or $q = p \cup q$ = If y is father of x and z is father of y then x is either grandson or grand daughter of z.

(iii) p = Every square is a rectangle
q = every square is a rhombus
$\therefore$ p or $q = p \cup q$ = Every square is either a rectangle or rhombus.

And statements

p and $q = p \cap q$ is true when both p and q are true. **e.g.**

(i) p =2 is a divisor of 10
q = 5 is a divisor of 10
p and $q = p \cap q$ = 2 and 5 are divisors of 10.

(ii) p = 2 is a divisor of 4
q = 2 is a divisor of 10
p and $q = p \cap q$ = 2 is a divisor of both 4 and 10.

(iv) p = If x is an integer, then x is rational.
q = If x is an integer, then x is real.
p and $q = p \cap q$ = If x is an integer, then x is rational and real.

~ *P* and ~*Q*: = (~*p*) ∩ (~*q*) = ~(*p* ∪ *q*) = ~(*p* or *q*) [De morgan's law]

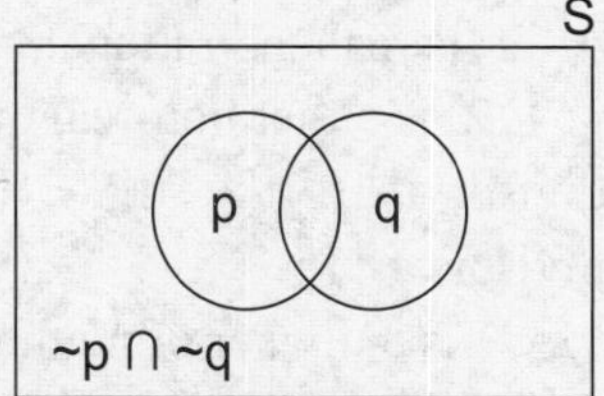

FIGURE 1.24

e.g.,

(i) p = 2 is a divisor of 3.
q = 2 is a divisor of 5.
$\sim p$ and $\sim q$ = 2 is a divisor of neither 3 nor 5.
Also $p \cup q$ = 2 is a divisor of 3 or 5.
$\sim(p \cup q)$ = 2 is a divisor of neither 3 nor 5.
$\therefore\ (\sim p) \cup (\sim q) = \sim(p \cup q)$

(ii) p = Taj Mahal is in Delhi.
q = Gateway of India is in Delhi.
$\sim p$ and $\sim q$ = Neither Taj Mahal nor Gateway of India is in Delhi.
= None of the Taj Mahal and Gateway of India is in Delhi.
$p \cup q$ = Taj Mahal or Gateway of India is in Delhi

$\sim(p \cup q)$ = Neither Taj Mahal nor Gateway of India is in Delhi.

(iii) p = L.C.M. of 2 and 4 is 8

q = L.C.M. of 2 and √3 is 2√3.

$\sim p$ and $\sim q$ = Neither L.C.M. of 2 and 4 is 8 nor L.C.M. of 2 and √3 is 2√3.

p or $q = p \cup q$ = L.C.M. of 2 and 4 is 8 and L.C.M. of 2 and √3 is 2√3. and

$\sim(p \cup q)$ = Neither L.C.M. of 2 and 4 is 8 nor L.C.M. of 2 and √3 is 2√3.

(~p) or (~q) = ~(p and q) = ~(p ∩ q) [De morgan's law]

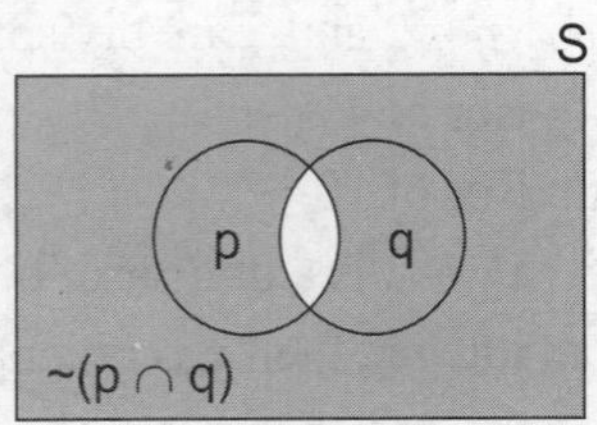

FIGURE 1.25

e.g.,

(i) p = $\sqrt{-2}$ is a real number

q = $\sqrt{-2}$ is a rational number.

(~p) or (~q) = $\sqrt{-2}$ is non-real or irrational

(p ∩ q) = $\sqrt{-2}$ is real and rational

$\sim(p \cap q)$ = $\sqrt{-2}$ is either non-real or irrational.

(ii) p = 3 is a divisor of 10

q = 3 is a divisor of 11

$(\sim p)$ or $(\sim q)$ = 3 is a divisor of neither 10 nor 11

$(p \cap q)$ = 3 is a divisor of 10 and 11

$\sim(p \cap q)$ = either 3 is not a divisor of 10 or not a divisor of 11.

p ⇒ q

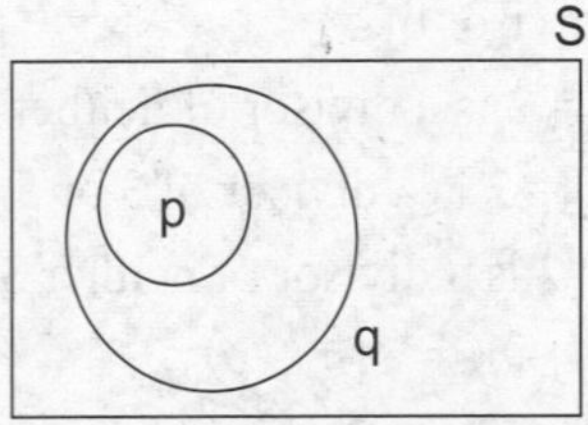

FIGURE 1.26

e.g.,

(i) p = At least two sides of given triangle are equal

q = Given triangle is an isosceles triangle.

$p \Rightarrow q$: If at least two sides of a given triangle are equal then it is an isosceles triangle.

(ii) p : x is a rational number

q : x is a real number

$p \Rightarrow q$: If x is rational, then it is real.

(iii) p : Abhi lives in Patna

q : Abhi lives in India

$\therefore$ $P \Rightarrow q$: If Abhi lives in Patna then he lives in India.

p ⇒ q then ~q ⇒ ~p

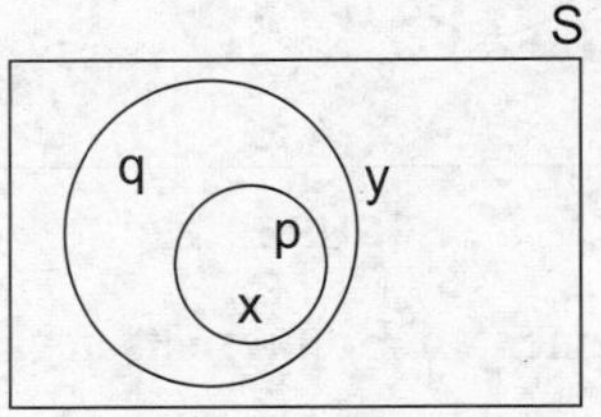

FIGURE 1.27

If x is in p, then x is in q i.e., $p \Rightarrow q$

If y is not in q then y is not in p. i.e., $\sim q \Rightarrow \sim p$ e.g.,

(i) p : x is a divisor of 8

q : x is a divisor of 16

$\sim p$ = x is not a divisor of 8

~q = x is not a divisor of 16

~q ⇒ $\sim p$: If x is not a divisor of 16, then x is not a divisor of 8.

(ii) $p : x + y$ = even ; $x, y \in \mathbb{Z}$

q : either x and y both are odd or x and y both are even (i.e., of same parity).

$p \Rightarrow q$: If for $x, y \in \mathbb{Z}$ x and y are of opposite parity then $x + y$ is not an even number i.e., odd.

Implies and is implied by: p ⇔ q

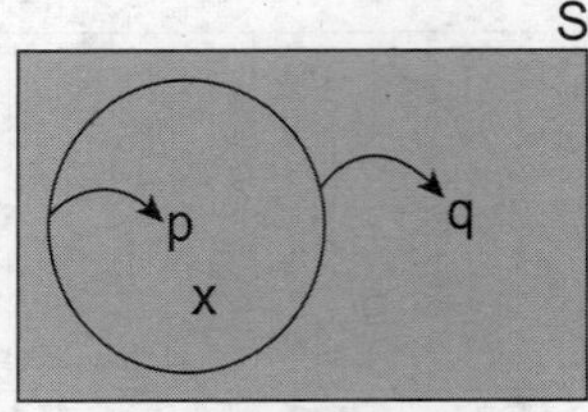

FIGURE 1.28

It is true when either both p and q are true or both p and q are false. e.g.,

(i) p : x is rational

q : x is a real

$p \Rightarrow q$: If x is rational then x is real

$q \Rightarrow p$: If x is real, then x is rational

$\therefore$ $p \Leftrightarrow q$: If x is rational, then x is real and if x is real, then x is rational or $p \Leftrightarrow q$: x is rational if and only if x is real. the above statement is false as q does not imply p as if x is real it is not necessary that x is rational as it can be irrational.

Check this yourself:

(i) Does ~p = ~q?

Try to support with relevant example.

TEXTUAL EXERCISE–5 (SUBJECTIVE)

1. Find the union of each of the following pairs of sets:

(i) $X = \{1, 3, 5\}$ $Y = \{1, 2, 3\}$

(ii) $A = \{a, e, i, o, u\}$ $B = \{a, b, c\}$

(iii) $A = \{x$: x is a natural number and multiple of 3}

$B = \{x$: x is a natural number less than 6}

(iv) $A = \{x$: x is a natural number and $1 < x \leq 6\}$

$B = \{x$: x is a natural number and $6 < x \leq 10\}$

(v) $A = \{1, 2, 3\}$, $B = \phi$

2. If $A = \{1, 2, 3, 4\}$, $B = \{3, 4, 5, 6\}$, $C = \{5, 6, 7, 8\}$ and $D = \{7, 8, 9, 10\}$; find

(i) $A \cup B$ (ii) $A \cup C$

(iii) $B \cup C$ (iv) $B \cup D$

(v) $A \cup B \cup C$ (vi) $A \cup B \cup D$

(vii) $B \cup C \cup D$

3. If $A = \{3, 6, 9, 12, 15, 18, 21\}$, $B = \{4, 8, 12, 16, 20\}$, $C = \{2, 4, 6, 8, 10, 12, 16\}$, $D = \{5, 10, 15, 20\}$; find

(i) $A - B$ (ii) $A - C$

(iii) $A - D$ (iv) $B - A$

(v) $C - A$ (vi) $D - A$

(vii) $B - C$ (viii) $B - D$

(ix) $C - B$ (x) $D - B$

(xi) $C - D$ (xii) $D - C$

4. If $a \in N$ where $aN = \{ax : x \in N\}$. Describe the set $3N \cap 7N$.

5. If A, B and C are three sets, then prove that

(a) $(A \cap B) \cap C = A \cap (B \cap C)$

(b) $A \cap (B \cup C) = (A \cap B) \cup (A \cap C)$

6. Prove the following:

(a) If $A \subset B$ and $B \subset C$, then $A \subset C$

(b) If A and B are two sets, then $A \cap B \subset A \subset A \cup B$ and $A \cap B \subset B \subset A \cup B$.

(c) Let A, B be sets, if $A \cap X = B \cap X = \phi$ and $A \cup X = B \cup X$ for some set X, then $n(A) = n(B)$.

7. Prove the following:

(a) $(A')' = A$

(b) $A \cup A' = U$

(c) $(A - B) \cap A = A \cap B'$

(d) $A \cap (B \Delta C) = (A \cap B) \Delta (A \cap C)$

(e) $C - B \subset C - A$, if $A \subset B$

8. Defined two sets A, B, such that $A = \{a$: $a \in \mathbb{N}$ and $a^2 - 7a + 12 = 0\}$ and $B = \{2, 3, 4, 5, 6\}$. Answer the following problems:

(a) Find whether $A \subset B$ or $B \subset A$ or neither.

(b) Find the set X defined as $B - A$.

(c) Express $A \cup B$ or $B \cap A$ and $A - B$ on Venn diagram.

(d) Find all the subsets of X and also find the number of elements in power set of X.

9. Defined three sets A, B and C such that $A = \{2, 3, 5, 7, 11, 13, 17, 19\}$ and $B = \{2, 5, 8, 11, 14, 17, 20\}$ $C = \{3, 5, 7, 9, 11, 13, 15\}$ and given that universal set $X = \{1, 2, 3, 5, 7, 8, 9, 11, 13, 14, 15, 17, 19, 20\}$.

Answer the following problems and express them on Venn euler diagram.

(a) Find $A \cup B$.

(b) Find the set $A - B$.

(c) Express $\overline{A \cup B}$.

(d) Find $\overline{B} \cup \overline{C}$.

(e) Find $A \cap B \cap C, A \cap B \cap \overline{C}$.

10. Write down the sets representing unshaded region in the following Venn diagrams.

(a)

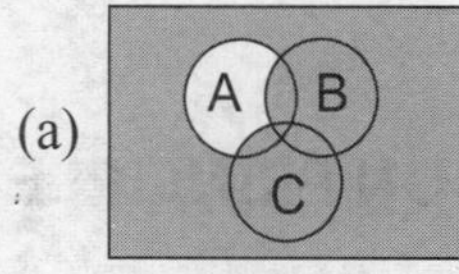

(b)

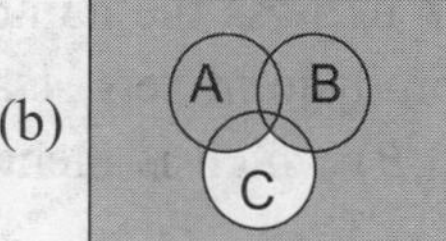

Answer Keys

1. (i) {1, 2, 3, 5}(ii) {*a*, *e*, *i*, *o*, *u*, *b*, *c*, } (iii) {1,2,3,4,5,6,9,12,15,16...}(iv) {2,3, 4, 5, 6, 7, 8, 9, 10}(v) {1, 2, 3}

2. (i) {1, 2, 3, 4, 5, 6} (ii) {1, 2, 3, 4, 5, 6, 7, 8} (iii) {3, 4, 5, 6, 7, 8} (iv) {3, 4, 5, 6, 7, 8, 9, 10} (v) {1, 2, 3, 4, 5, 6, 7, 8} (vi) {1, 2, 3, 4, 5, 6, 7, 8, 9, 10} (vii) {3, 4, 5, 6, 7, 8, 9, 10}

3. (i) {3,6,9,15,18,21} (ii) {3,9,15,18,21} (iii) {3,6,9,12,18,21} (iv) {4,8,16,20} (v) {2,4,8,10,16} (vi) {5,10,20} (vii) {20} (viii) {4,8,12,16} (ix) {2,6,10} (x) {5,10,15} (xi) {2,4,6,8,12,16} (xii) {5,15,20}

4. 21*N*

8. (a) $A \subset B$ (b) {2, 5, 6} (c) $A \cup B = \{2, 3, 4, 5, 6\}$, $B \cap A = \{3, 4\}$, $A - B = \{\} = \phi$ (d)

9. (a) $A \cup B = \{2,3,5,7,8,11,13,14,17,19,20\}$ (b) $A \sim B = \{3,7,13,19\}$ (c) $\overline{A \cup B} = \{1,9,15\}$

(d) $\overline{B \cap C} = \{1,2,3,7,8,9,13,14,15,17,19,20\}$ (e) $A \cap B \cap C = \{5,11\}$; $A \cap B \cap \bar{C} = \{2,17\}$

10. (a) $A \cap (B \cup C)^C$ (b) $A \cup (B \cap C)$

TEXTUAL EXERCISE–3 (OBJECTIVE)

1. Given the sets $A = \{1, 2, 3\}$, $B = \{3, 4\}$, $C = \{4, 5, 6\}$, then $A \cup (B \cap C)$ is
(a) {3} (b) {1, 2, 3, 4}
(c) {1, 2, 4, 5} (d) {1, 2, 3, 4, 5, 6}

2. If $N_a = [a.n : n \in N\}$, then $N_6 \cap N_8 =$
(a) N_6 (b) N_8
(c) N_{24} (d) N_{44}

3. If *A* and *B* are disjoint, then $n(A \cup B)$ is
(a) $n(A)$
(b) $n(B)$
(c) $n(A) + n(B)$
(d) $n(A).\ n(B)$

4. Given the following sets: $A = \{1, 2, 3, 4, 6\}$; $B = \{2, 3\}$; $C = \{0\}$, then *A* and *C* sets are :
(a) equal (b) equivalent
(c) disjoint (d) None of these

5. Consider the sets
A: The set of all intelligent girls in class 10th
B: Set of natural numbers
Which of the following is correct?
(a) $A \cup B$
(b) A and B are equal
(c) A and B are disjoint
(d) A is not a set

6. If $A \subset B$ ανδ $B \subset C$, then
(a) A = B (b) $A \subset C$
(c) $n(A) = n(B)$ (d) cannot predict

7. Which of the following is not a set ?
(a) A: set of primes
(b) Set of even number
(c) C: set of beautiful places of india
(d) set of squares of all odd numbers

Answer Keys

1. (b) **2.** (c) **3.** (c) **4.** (c) **5.** (d) **6.** (b) **7.** (c)

■ INCLUSION-EXCLUSION PRINCIPLE

Rule of the sum can be applied to express the number of elements in the union of two non-disjoint sets *A* and *B* in terms of $n(A)$, $n(B)$ and $n(A \cap B)$ which is mentioned below:

Since we can write *A* as the union of pair-wise disjoint sets

$$A \cap B \text{ and } A \cap B'$$

therefore $n(A) = n(A \cap B) + n(A \cap B')$ (i)

Again, since we can write *B* as the union of pair-wise disjoint set

$A \cap B$ and $A' \cap B$,

therefore $n(B) = n(A \cap B) + n(A' \cap B)$ (ii)

Also since the set $A \cup B$ can be expressed as the union of pair-wise disjoint sets $A \cap B$, $A \cap B'$ and $A' \cap B$, therefore

$n(A \cup B) = n(A \cap B) + n(A \cap B') + n(A' \cap B)$ (iii)

Adding corresponding sides of (i) and (ii) and using (iii), we have

$n(A) + n(B) = n(A \cup B) + n(A \cap B) \Rightarrow n(A \cup B) = n(A) + n(B) - n(A \cap B)$

Properties

1. $n(A \cup B) = n(A) + n(B) - n(A \cap B)$ (*inclusion-exclusion principle*)
2. $n(A \cup B)_{max} = n(A) + n(B)$ when A and B are disjoint.
3. $n(A \cup B)_{min} = \max\{n(A), n(B)\} = n(A)$ if $B \subset A$ and $n(B)$ if $A \subset B$

Proof: $n(A \cup B)_{min} = n(A) + n(B) - n(A \cap B)_{max}$

$= n(A) + n(B) - \min\{n(A), n(B)\}$

$= \max\{n(A), n(B)\}$

$$= \begin{cases} n(A) & \text{if } B \subset A \\ n(B) & \text{if } A \subset B \end{cases}$$

4. $n(A \cap B)_{max} = \min\{n(A), n(B)\} = n(B)$ if $B \subset A$ and $n(A)$ if $A \subset B$

Proof: $n(A \cap B)_{max} = \min\{n(A), n(B)\}$

$$n(A \cap B)_{max} = \begin{cases} n(A) & \text{if } A \subset B \\ n(B) & \text{if } A \supset B \end{cases}$$

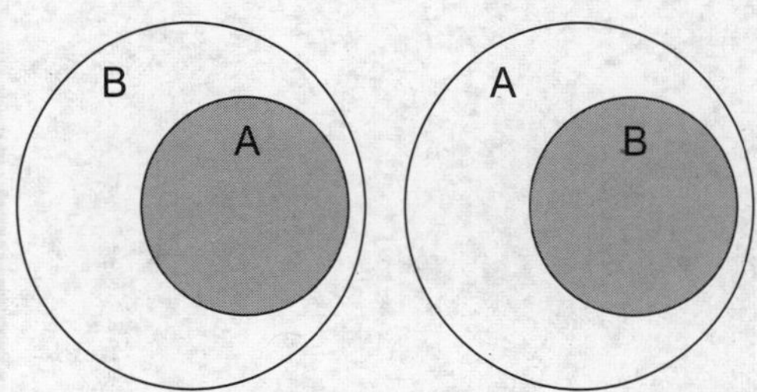

FIGURE 1.29

5. $n(A \cap B)_{min} = n\{\phi\} = 0$ when A and B are disjoint.
6. $n(A \cap B)_{min} = \max\{n(A) + n(B) - n(S), 0\}$

Proof: $n(A \cup B) = n(A) + n(B) - n(A \cap B) \le n(S)$

$\Rightarrow n(A \cap B) \ge n(A) + n(B) - n(S)$

$\Rightarrow n(A \cap B)_{min}$

$$= \begin{cases} n(A) + n(B) - n(S) & \text{if } n(A) + n(B) \ge n(S) \\ 0 & \text{if } n(A) + n(B) < n(S) \end{cases}$$

7. $n(A \cup B)_{max} = \min\{n(A) + n(B), n(S)\}$

Proof: $n(A \cup B)_{max} = n(A) + n(B) - n(A \cap B)_{min}$

$= n(A) + n(B)$

$$-\begin{cases} n(A) + n(B) - n(S) & \text{if } n(A) + n(B) \ge n(S) \\ 0 & \text{if } n(A) + n(B) < n(S) \end{cases}$$

$$= \begin{cases} n(S) & n(A) + n(B) \ge n(S) \\ n(A) + n(B) & n(A) + n(B) < n(S) \end{cases}$$

Some basic results on cardinal numbers

If A, B and C are finite sets and U be the finite universal set, then

1. $n(A') = n(\cup') - n(A)$
2. $n(A \cup B) = n(A) + n(B) - n(A \cap B)$
3. $n(A \cup B) = n(A) + n(B)$ where A and B are disjoint non-empty sets
4. $n(A \cup B') = n(A) - n(A \cap B)$
5. $n(A' \cap B') = n(A \cup B)' = n(\cup) - n(A \cup B)$
6. $n(A' \cup B') = n(A \cap B)' = n(\cup) - n(A \cap B)$
7. $n(A-B) = n(A) - n(A \cap B)$
8. $n(A \cap B) = n(A \cup B) - n(A \cap B') - n(A' \cap B)$
9. $n(A \cup B \cup C) = n(A) + n(B) + n(C) - n(A \cap B)$ $-n(B \cap C) - n(C \cap A) + n(A \cap B \cap C)$
10. If $A_1, A_2, A_3, \ldots A_n$ are disjoint sets, then $n(A_1 \cup A_2 \cup A_3 \cup \ldots \cup A_n = n(A_1) + n(A_2) + n(A_3) + \ldots n(A_n)$
11. $n(A \,\Delta\, B)$ = number of elements which belong to exactly one of A or B.

ILLUSTRATION 18: In a survey on 20,000 families of a city, it was found that 40% families read newspaper P, 20% families read newspaper Q, 10 % families read newspaper R, 4% buy P and Q, 3% buy Q and R and 5% buy P and R. If 2 % families buy all the three newspapers, then find

(a) Number of families buying newspaper P only, Q only and R only
(b) Number of families buying exactly one of the 3 newspapers

(c) Number of families buying exactly two newspapers
(d) Number of families buying at least one newspaper
(e) Number families buying no newspaper
(f) Number of families buying at most two newspapers

SOLUTION: Let here $n(U) = 20000$

A = set of families buying newspaper P
B = set of families buying newspaper Q
C = set of families buying newspaper R

$\therefore\ n(A) = 40\%$ of $20,000 = \dfrac{40}{100} \times 20,000 = 8000$

$n(B) = 20\ \%$ of $20,000 = \dfrac{20}{100} \times 20,000 = 4000$

$n(C) = 10\%$ of $20,000 = \dfrac{10}{100} \times 20,000 = 2000$

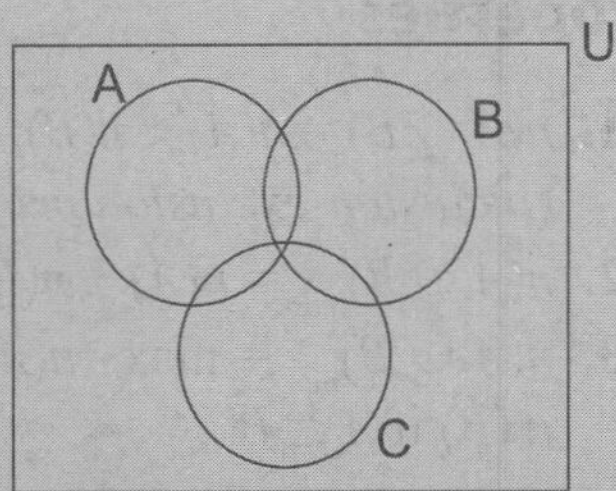

FIGURE 1.30

$n(A \cap B)$ = number of families buying newspaper P as well as $Q = 4\%$ of $20,000 = 800$
similarly $n(B \cap C) = 3\ \%$ of $20,000 = 600$
$n(A \cap C) = 5\ \%$ of $20,000 = 1000$
$n(A \cap B \cap C) = 2\ \%$ of $20,000 = 400$

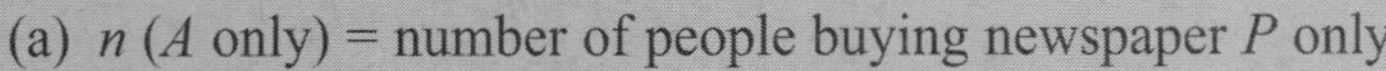

(a) n (A only) = number of people buying newspaper P only
$= n(A) - n(A \cap B) - n(A \cap C) + n(A \cap B \cap C)$
$= 8000 - 800 - 1000 + 400$
$= 6600$
Similarly, n (B only) $= n(B) - n(B \cap A) - n(B \cap C) + n(A \cap B \cap C)$
$= 4000 - 800 - 600 + 400 = 3000$
and n (C only) $= n(C) - n(C \cap A) - n(C \cap B) + n(A \cap B \cap C)$
$= 2000 - 1000 - 600 + 400 = 800$

(b) Number of families buying exactly one of the three news papers
$= n$ (A only) $+ n$ (B only) $+ n$ (C only)
$= 6600 + 3000 + 800 = 10,400$

(c) Number of families buying exactly two newspapers
$= [n(A \cap B) - n(A \cap B \cap C)] + [n(A \cap C) - n(A \cap B \cap C)]$
$+ [n(B \cap C) - n(A \cap B \cap C)]$
$= [800 - 400] + [600 - 400] + [1000 - 400] = 400 + 200 + 600 = 1200$

(d) Number of families buying at least one newspapers
$= (A \cup B \cup C) = n(A) + n(B) + n(C) - n(A \cap B) - n(B \cap C) - n(C \cap A) + n(A \cap B \cap C)$
$= 8000 + 4000 + 2000 - 800 - 600 - 1000 + 400 = 12000$

(e) Number of families buying no newspaper $= n(U) - n(A \cup B \cup C) = 20000 - 12000 = 8000$

(f) Number of families buying at most two newspaper
$= n(U) - n(A \cap B \cap C) = 20,000 - 400 = 19,600$

ILLUSTRATION 19: At a certain conference of 100 people, there are 52 Indians, which consist of 29 women and 23 men. Of these Indians, 4 are doctors and 24 are either men or doctors. There are no foreign doctors. How many foreigners and women doctors are attending the conference?

(a) 48, 1 (b) 34, 3
(c) 46, 4 (d) 42, 2

SOLUTION: $n(U)$ = Total number of persons = 100

n (I) = Total number of Indians = n (Men) + n (Women) = 23 + 29 = 52

$\therefore$ n (F) = Number of foreigners = $n(\cup) - n$ (I) = 100 – 52 = 48

n (D) = Number of Indian doctors = 4

Now, n $(M \cup D)$ = number of people which are either men or doctors

$= n$ (M) + $n(D) - n$ $(M \cap D)$

$\Rightarrow$ $24 = 23 + 4 - n(M \cap D) \Rightarrow n(M \cap D) = 3$

Now, $n(D) = n$ (Men doctor) n (Women doctor)

$\Rightarrow$ n (women doctor) = n (D) – n (Men doctor)

$\Rightarrow$ 4 – 3 = 1.

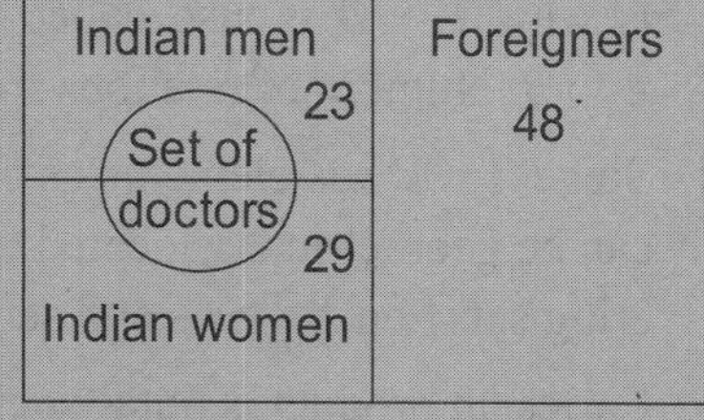

FIGURE 1.31

ILLUSTRATION 20: Let A and B be two sets containing 23 and 60 elements respectively. Find the maximum and minimum number of elements in $A \cup B$.

SOLUTION: Given $n(A) = 23$ and $n(B) = 60$

$\therefore$ by inclusion and exclusion principle

$n(A \cup B) = n(A) + n(B) - n(A \cap B)$

$\Rightarrow$ $n(A \cup B) = 23 + 60 - n(A \cap B)$

$= 83 - n(A \cap B)$

Now $n(A \cup B)$ will be maximum for min value of $n(A \cap B)$ which is zero, when A and B become disjoint sets $(A \cap B = \phi)$

$\Rightarrow$ $n(A \cup B)_{max} = 83$

Similarly, $n(A \cap B)$ is minimum when $n(A \cap B)$ is maximum (when $A \subset B$)

$\Rightarrow$ $n(A \cup B)_{min} = 83 - (n(A \cap B))_{max}$

$= 83 - 23 = 60$

■ CARTESIAN PRODUCT OF TWO SETS

Ordered Pair:

The phrase 'ordered Pair' is used frequently in mathematics. An ordered pair (a, b) is a pair of mathematical objects. The order in which the objects appear is significant. Hence the ordered pair (a, b) is different from ordered pair (b, a).

In contrary

unordered pair $\{a, b\}$ is same as $\{b, a\}$.

Let (a_1, b_1) and (a_2, b_2) be ordered pairs, then $(a_1, b_1) = (a_2, b_2)$ iff $a_1 = a_2$ and $b_1 = b_2$.

Cartesian product of A and B if denoted as $A \times B$ is a set containing the elements in the form of ordered pair (a, b) such that $a \in A$ and $b \in B$. If set $A = \{a_1, a_2, a_3\}$ and $B = \{b_1, b_2\}$ then $A \times B$ and $B \times A$ can be written as: $A \times B = \{(a, b)$: $a \in A$ and $b \in B\} = \{(a_1, b_1), (a_1, b_2), (a_2, b_1)(a_2, b_2)\ (a_3, b_1)\ (a_3, b_2)\}$ or $B \times A = \{(b, a)$: $b \in B$ and $a \in A\}$. $B \times A = \{(b_1\ a_1), (b_1\ a_2), (b_2\ a_1), (b_2\ a_2)(b_1\ a_3), (b_2\ a_3)\}$ Clearly, $A \times B \neq B \times A$ until A and B are equal.

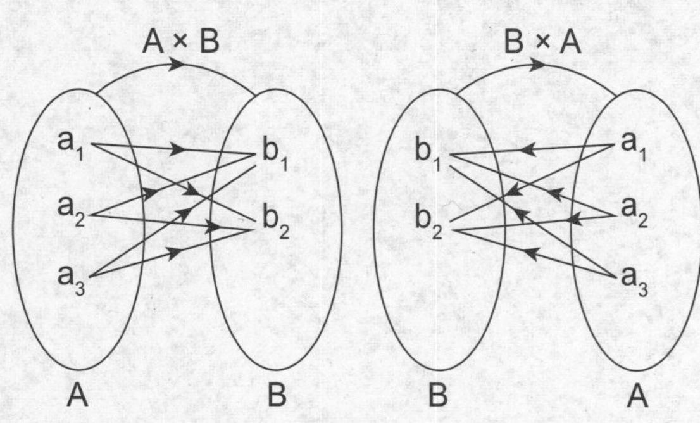

FIGURE 1.32

Some basic results on cartesian product

1. Cartesian product is not commutative, i.e., $A \times B \neq B \times A$ unless $A = B$

2. n(A x B) = n{(a, b) : a ∈ A & b ∈ B} = n(A).n(B)
   $\Rightarrow n(A \times B) = n(B \times A) = n(A).n(B) = m \times n$
3. Since $A \times B$ contains all possible ordered pairs as its elements that can be formed by pairing the elements of set A to the element of set B. Therefore every relation defined from set A to set B is subset of $A \times B$. That is why $A \times B$ is also called universal relation from A to B. Number of relations from A to $B = 2^{n(A).n(B)}$.
4. Since $A \times B$ has elements as ordered pairs therefore it can be geometrically located in $X - Y$ plane by considering set A on $X - axis$ and set B on Y-axis.
5. Cartesian product is not associative.
6. **Distributive law**
   Cartesian product distributes over union, difference intersection $A \times (B \cup C) = (A \times B) \cup (A \times C)$
   Proof: $(x, y) \in A \times (B \cup C)$
   $\Rightarrow x \in A$ and $y \in (B \cup C)$
   $\Rightarrow x \in A$ and $y \in B$ or $y \in C$
   $\Rightarrow x \in A$ and $y \in B$ or $x \in A$ and $y \in C$
   $\Rightarrow (x, y) \in (A \times B) \cup (A \times C)$
7. $A \times (B \cap C) = (A \times B) \cap (A \times C)$
8. $A \times (B - C) = (A \times B) - (A \times C)$
9. $(A \times B) \cap (S \times T) = (A \cap S) \times (B \cap T)$ where S and T are two sets
10. If $A \subseteq B$ then $(A \times C) \subseteq (B \times C)$
11. If $A \subseteq B$ and $C \subseteq D$ then $(A \times C) \subseteq (B \times D)$
12. If $A \subseteq B$ then $(A \times A) \subseteq (A \times B) \cap (B \times A)$
13. $(A \times B) = (B \times A)$ if and only if $A = B$
14. $A \times (B' \cup C')' = (A \times B) \cap (A \times C)$
15. $A \times (B' \cap C')' = (A \times B) \cup (A \times C)$
16. *If* $n(A \cap B) = k \Rightarrow n((A \times B) \cap (B \times A))$
    $n(A \cap B) \times (A \cap B) = k.k = k^2$

ILLUSTRATION 21: If $A \times B = \{(1, 1), (1, 2), (1, 3)\ (2, 1), (2, 2), (2, 3)\}$, then A is equal to

(a) {1, 2} (b) {1, 2, 3}
(c) {2, 3} (d) None of these

SOLUTION: $A X B = \{(1, 1)\ (1, 2), (1, 3), (2, 1), (2, 2)\ (2, 3)\}$
Let $(a, b) \in A \times B$, then $a \in A, b \in B$ *so*, $a = 1, 2$
$\therefore A = \{1, 2\}$

ILLUSTRATION 22: If $A = \{5, 6, 7\}$ and $B = \{1, 2, 3, 4\}$, then number of elements in set $A \times B \times B$ is equal to

(a) 36 (b) 48
(c) 16 (d) None of these

SOLUTION: There are 3 elements in A, 4 elements in B, therefore set $A X B$ has 12 elements, now $A \times B \times B$ has $12 \times 4 = 48$ elements.

ILLUSTRATION 23: If two sets A and B are having 99 elements in common, then the number of elements common to each of the sets $A \times B$ and $B \times A$ are

(a) 2^{99} (b) 99^2
(c) 100 (d) 18

SOLUTION: Given that $n\ (A \cap B) = 99$
$\therefore n\ ((A \times B) \cap (B \times A)) = n\ ((A \cap B) \times (B \cap A))$
$= n\ (A \cap B) \times n\ (B \cap A)$
$= n\ (A \cap B) \times n\ (A \cap B)$ (intersection is commutative)
$= (99)\ (99) = 99^2$

ILLUSTRATION 24: Let $A = \{x: x$ is a root of equation $x^3 + 2x^2 - x - 2 = 0\}$
$B = \{x: x$ is a prime divisor of $720\}$, then find $A \times B$ and hence verify that $n\ (A \times B)$.
$= n\ (A) \times n\ (B)$

SOLUTION: $x^3 + 2x^2 - x - 2 = 0$

By factorization

$(x^2 - 1)(x + 2) = 0$

$\Rightarrow x = \pm 1, -2$

$\therefore A = \{1, -1, -2\}$

and Prime divisors of 720 are 2, 3 and 5.

$\therefore B = \{2, 3, 5\}$

$\therefore A \times B = \{(1, 2), (1, 3), (1, 5) (-1, 2), (-1, 3), (-1, 5), (-2, 2), (-2, 3), (-2, 5)\}$

It contains 9 elements.

$\Rightarrow n(A \times B) = 9$

Also $n(A) = n(B) = 3$

$\therefore n(A) \times n(B) = n(A \times B) = 9$

Hence verified.

FIGURE 1.33

ILLUSTRATION 25: Given two sets A and B defined as $A = \{a : a \in \mathbb{N} \text{ and} -2 \le a \le 5\}$ and $B = \{b : b \in \mathbb{Z} \text{ and } 0 \le b \le 3\}$. Find $A \times B$ and $B \times$A. Represent them geometrically and also find number of elements common in $A \times B$ and $B \times A$.

SOLUTION: $A = \{a : a \in \mathbb{N} \text{ and } -2 \le a \le 5\} = \{1,2,3,4,5\}$

$B = \{b : b \in \mathbb{Z} \text{ and } 0 \le b \le 3\} = \{0,1,2,3\}$

$A \times B = \{(1,0), (1,1), (1,2), (1,3), (2,0), (2,1), (2,2), (2,3), (3,0), (3,1), (3,2), (3,3), (4,0), (4,1), (4,2), (4,3), (5,0), (5,1), (5,2), (5,3)\}$

$B \times A = \{(0,1), (0,2), (0,3), (0,4), (0,5), (1,1), (1,2), (1,3), (1,4), (1,5), (2,1), (2,2), (2,3), (2,4), (2,5), (3,1), (3,2), (3,3), (3,4), (3,5)\}$

Number of elements common in $(A \times B)$ and $(B \times A) = [n(A \cap B)]^2 = (3)^2 = 9$

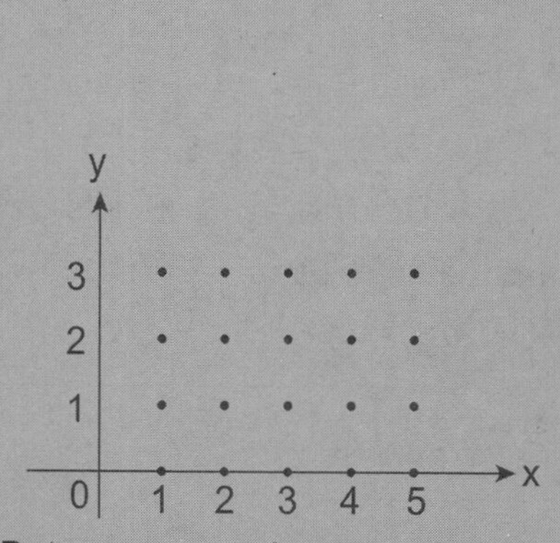

Dots represent elements of set A×B

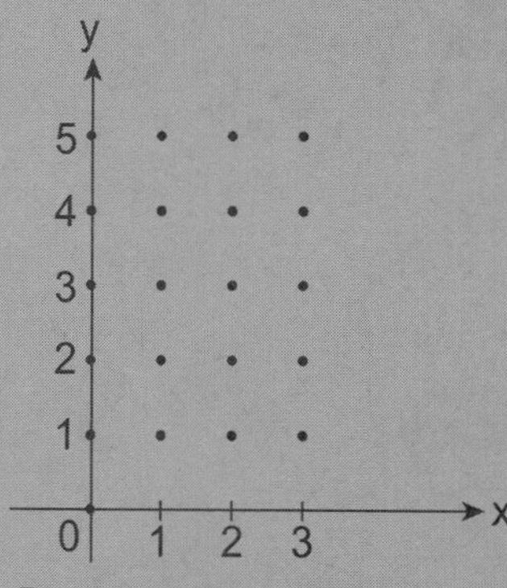

Dots represents elements of set B×A

FIGURE 1.34

ILLUSTRATION 26: Given two sets A and B defined as $A = \{a : a \in \mathbb{R} \text{ and } -2 \le a \le 3\}$ and $B = \{b : b \in \mathbb{Z} \text{ and } 0 \le b \le 4\}$. Find $A \times B$ and $B \times A$. Represent them geometrically and also find number of elements common in $A \times B$ and $B \times A$, and find the answer if $b \in \mathbb{R}$.

SOLUTION: $A = \{a : a \in \mathbb{R} \text{ and } -2 \le a \le 3\} = [-2, 3]$

$B = \{b : b \in \mathbb{Z} \text{ and } 0 \le b \le 4\} = \{0, 1, 2, 3, 4\}$

$\therefore\ A \times B = \{(x, y) : x \in [-2, 3] \text{ and } y \in \{0, 1, 2, 3\}\}$

= set of four horizontal line segments $y = 0$, $y = 1$, $y = 2$, $y = 3$ and having their left end point at $x = -2$ and right end point at $x = 3$ as shown below:

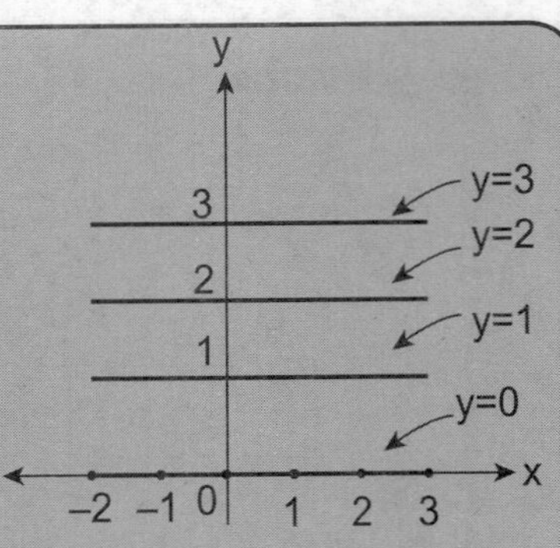

Collection of horizontal line segments representing A×B

FIGURE 1.35

Also, $B \times A = \{(x, y) : x \in \{0,1,2,3,4\} \text{ and } y \in [-2, 3]\}$

= set of fine vertical line segments $x = 0$, $x = 1$, $x = 2$, $x = 3$, $x = 4$ and having their bottom end point at $y = -2$ and top end point at $y = 3$ as shown below.

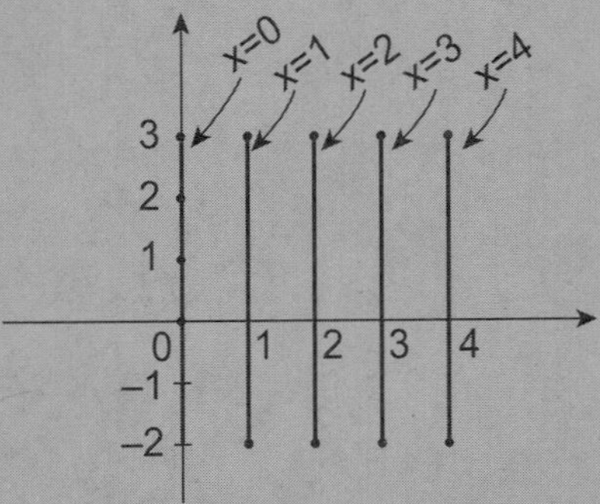

Collection of five line segments representing B×A

FIGURE 1.36

Clearly, $A \cap B = \{0,1,2,3\} \Rightarrow n[(A \times B) \cap (B \times A)]$
$= [n(A \cap B)]^2 = (4)^2 = 16$

Also if we draw the graphs of $A \times B$ and $B \times A$ on a single diagram, then their points of intersection would give us the number of elements common in $A \times B$ and $B \times A$ as shown below:

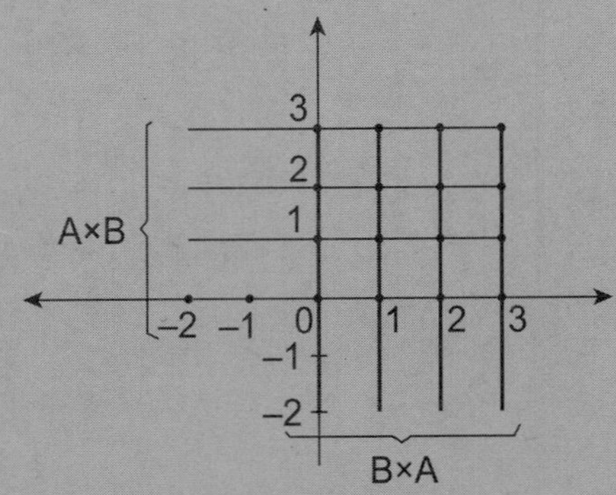

Points common in A×B and B×A

FIGURE 1.37

Next part, If $b \in \mathbb{R}$, then

$A = [-2, 3]$ and $B = [0, 4]$

then $A \times B = \{(x, y) : x \in [-2, 3] \text{ and } y \in [0, 4]\}$

= Rectangular region bounded by lines having equations $x = -2$, $x = 3$, $y = 0$ and $y = 4$ as shown below:

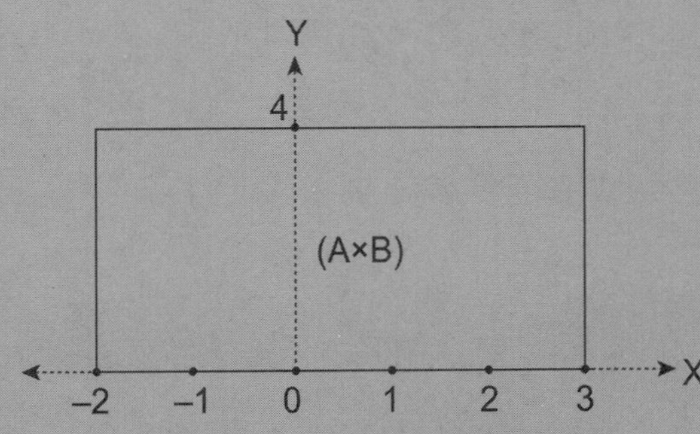

Rectangular region representing A×B

FIGURE 1.38

Similarly, $B \times A$ represents rectangular region bounded by lines having equations $x = 0, x = 4, y = -2$, and $y = 3$

and $(A \times B) \cap (B \times A)$ represents a square bounded by lines having equations $x = 0, x = 3, y = 0, y = 3$ and has infinitely many elements.

ILLUSTRATION 27: Given two sets A and B defined as and $A = \{a : a \in \mathbb{R} \text{ and } 1 \le a \le 4\}$. and $B = \{b : b \in \mathbb{Z} \text{ and } 0 \le b \le 4\}$. Find $A \times B$ and $B \times A$. Represent them geometrically and also find the area of the region common in $A \times B$ and $B \times A$. if $b \in \mathbb{R}$.

SOLUTION: $A = \{a : a \in \mathbb{R} \text{ and } 1 \le a \le 4\} = [1, 4]$

$B = \{b : b \in \mathbb{Z} \text{ and } 0 \le b \le 4\} = \{0, 1, 2, 3, 4\}$

$A \times B = \{(a, b) : 1 \le a \le 4 \text{ and } b \in \{0,1,2,3,4\}\}$

= collection of five horizontal line segments having equation $y = 0, y = 1, y = 2, y = 3, y = 4$ having their left end point at $x = 1$ and right end point at $x = 4$ as shown below.

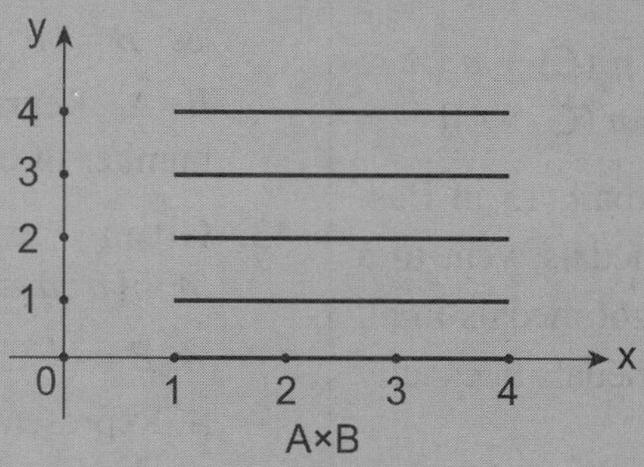

FIGURE 1.39

Similarly, graph given below represent $B \times A$

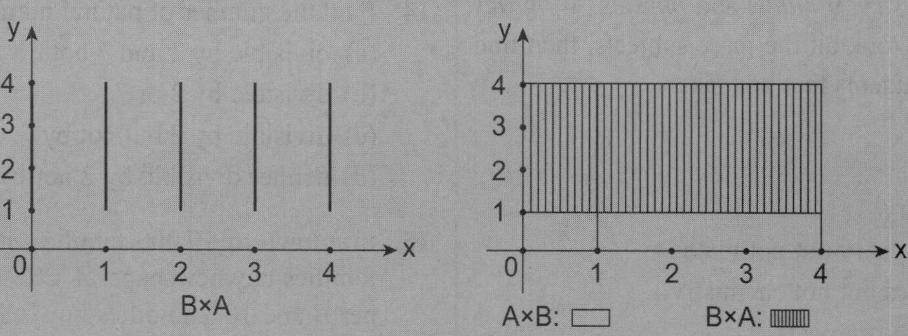

FIGURE 1.40

If $b \in \mathbb{R}$; then $A = [1, 4]$ and $B = [0, 4]$, then $(B \times A) \cap (A \times B)$ = square region bonded by lines $x = 1, x = 4, y = 1, y = 4$ and hence area of region common in $(A \times B)$ and $(B \times A) = (3)^2 = 9$ sq units.

TEXTUAL EXERCISE–6 (SUBJECTIVE)

1. If X and y are two sets of n (X) = 17, $n(Y) = 23$ and $n(X \cup Y) = 38$. Find $n(X \cap Y)$.

2. If X and y are two sets such that $X \cup y$ has 18 elements, X has 8 elements and y has 15 elements: how many elements does $X \cap y$ have?

3. In a class of 100 students, 55 students have passed in Mathematics and 67 students have passed in Physics. Then find the number of students who have passed in Physics only. Assuming that no student fails in both the subjects.

4. Evaluate the unknowns in each of the following cases:
   (a) $n(A \cup B)$, $n(A \cap B)$, if $A \subset B$, $n(A) = 30$, $n(B) = 36$
   (b) $n(B)$, if $n(A) = 30$, $n(A \cup B) = 50$, $n(A \cap B) = 10$
   (c) $n(A \cup B)$, if $n(A) = 20$, $n(A' \cap B) = 8$
   (d) $n(A \cap B)$, if $n(A - B) = 30$, $n(B - A) = 16$, $n(A \cup B) = 60$
   (e) $n(A \cup B)$, if $n(A) = 58$, $n(B) = 102$, $n(A - B) = 38$
   (f) $n(A \cup B)$, if $n(S) = 70$, $n(A) = 40$, $n(B) = 50$, $n(A \cap \bar{B}) = 27$
5. A survey of 2000 consumers reported that 1500 consumers liked product *P*, 1800 liked product *Q*. What is the least number that must have liked both the products?
6. For any three sets *A*, *B*, *C* prove that: $n(A \cup B \cup C) = [n(A) + n(B) + n(C) + n(A \cap B \cap C)] - [n(A \cap B) + n(B \cap C) + n(C \cap A)]$
7. A college awarded 38 medals in football, 15 in Basketball and 20 to Cricket. If these medals went to a total of 58 men and only three men got medals in all the three sports, how many received medals in exactly two of the three sports?
8. In a survey of 25 students, it was found that 15 had taken maths, 12 had taken physics, 11 chemistry, 5 *maths* and *chemistry*, 9 *maths* and *physics*, 4 *physics* and *chemistry*, 3 took all the three subjects, then find the number of students that had taken
   (a) only maths
   (b) only physics
   (c) only chemistry
   (d) physics, chemistry but not maths
   (e) maths, physics but not chemistry
   (f) only one of the subjects
   (g) at least one of three subjects
   (h) none of the subjects
9. Find the number of natural numbers ≤ 500 which are
   (a) divisible by 4 and 6 both
   (b) divisible by either 4 or 6
   (c) divisible by 4 but not by 6
   (d) divisible by 6 but not by 4
   (e) neither divisible by 4 nor by 6
10. Find the number of natural numbers which are divisible either by 2 or 3 or 5 but which is smaller than or equal to 300.
11. Find the cardinality of set of those positive integers ≤ 1200 which are divisible by
   (i) either of the integers 3, 4, 6
   (ii) either of the integers 2, 4, 6.
   (iii) neither of integer 2, 3, 5.
12. Given two sets *A* and *B* defined as $A = \{a : a \in \mathbb{N}\ \&\ 1 \leq a \leq 6\}$ & $B = \{b : b \in \mathbb{Z}\ \&\ -2 \leq b \leq 4\}$. Find $A \times B$ and $B \times A$. Represent them geometrically and also find number of elements common in $A \times B$ and $B \times A$.
13. Given two sets *A* and *B* defined as $A = \{a : a \in \mathbb{R}\ \&\ -1 \leq a \leq 5\}$ & $B = \{b : b \in \mathbb{Z}\ \&\ 0 \leq b \leq 6\}$. Find $A \times B$ and $B \times A$. Represent them geometrically and also find number of elements common in $A \times B$ and $B \times A$. and find the answer if $b \in \mathbb{R}$.
14. Find the number of natural numbers ≤ 300 which are
   (a) divisible by 2 and 7 both
   (b) divisible by 2 or 7
   (c) divisible by 2 but not by 7
   (d) neither divisible by 2 nor by 7
15. In a town of 10,000 families, it was found that 40% families buy newspaper *A*, 20% families buy newspaper *B* and 10% families buy newspaper *C*, 5% families buy *A* and *B*,3% buy *B* and *C* and 4% buy *A* and *C*. If 2% families buy all the three newspapers, find the number of families which buy:
   (i) *A* only
   (ii) *B* only
   (iii) None of *A*, *B* and *C*.

Answer Keys

1. 2 **2.** 5 **3.** 45
4. (a) $n(A \cup B) = 36$; $n(A \cup B) = 30$ (b) 30 (c) 28 (d) 14 (e) 140 (f) data is incorrect
5. 1300 **7.** 9 **8.** (a) 4 (b) 2 (c) 5 (d) 1 (e) 6 (f) 11 (g) 23 (h) 2
9. (a) 41 (b) 167 (c) 84 (d) 42 (e) 333 **10.** 220 **11.** (i) 600 (ii) 600 (iii) 320
12. 42, 42{(1, 1), (1, 2), (1, 3),(1, 4),(2, 1),(2, 2),(2, 3),(2, 4),(3, 1),(3, 2)(3, 3),(3, 4),(4, 1),(4, 2),(4, 3),(4, 4)}
14. (a) 21 (b) 171 (c) 129 (d) 129 **15.** (i) 3300 (ii) 1400 (iii) 4000.

TEXTUAL EXERCISE–4 (OBJECTIVE)

1. Which of the following is a null set?
(a) $\{x : |x| < 1, x \in \mathbb{N}\}$
(b) $\{x : |x| < 5, x \in \mathbb{N}\}$
(c) $\{x : x^2=1, \text{ or } |x|<1, x \in \mathbb{Z}\}$
(d) $\{x : x^2+2x+1=0, x \in \mathbb{R}\}$

2. Which of the following is a singleton set?
(a) $\{x : |x| < 1, x \in \mathbb{Z}\}$
(b) $\{x : |x| < 5, x \in \mathbb{Z}\}$
(c) $\{x : x^2 = 1, x \in \mathbb{Z}\}$
(d) $\{x : x^2 + x + 1 = 0, x \in \mathbb{R}\}$

3. A set is defined as A = { x : x is irrational and $0.1 < x < 0.101$} then
(a) A is null set (b) A is finite set
(c) A is infinite set (d) None of these

4. Which of the following has only one subset ?
(a) {} (b) {4}
(c) {4,5} (d) {0}

5. A set S contains 3 elements, the number of subsets of which of following sets is 256.
(a) S (b) $P(S)$
(c) $P(P(S))$ (d) None of these

6. If A = { ϕ, {ϕ}}, then the power set of A is
(a) A (b) {ϕ, {ϕ}, A}
(c) {ϕ, {ϕ}, {{ϕ}},A} (d) None of these

7. $(A \cap B)^C \cap A$ is equal to :
(a) B (b) $A \cap B^C$
(c) $A \cup B$ (d) $A - B$

8. $A-(B \cup C)$ is equal to
(a) $(A - B) \cap (A - C)$ (b) $(A - B) \cup (A - C)$
(c) $(A \cap B) - C$ (d) None of these

9. If A = {1,2,3} and B = {3,4},then $(A \cup B) \times (A \cap B)$ is:
(a) {3,3}
(b) {(1,3),(2,3),(3,3),(1,4),(2,4),(3,4)}
(c) {(1,3),(2,3),(3,3)}
(d) {(1,3),(2,3),(3,3),(4,3)}

10. If sets A and B are defined as
$A = \{(x,y): y = 1/x, x \in R \sim \{0\}\}$
$B = \{(x,y): y = -x, x \in R\}$ then
(a) $A \cap B = A$ (b) $A \cap B = B$
(c) $A \cap B = \phi$ (d) None of these

11. Let $n(U) = 700$, $n(A) = 200$, $n(B) = 300$ and $n(A \cap B) = 100$, then $n(A^c \cap B^c)$ is
(a) 400 (b) 600
(c) 300 (d) 200

12. Sets A and B have 3 and 6 elements respectively. What can be the minimum number of elements in $A \cup B$?
(a) 3 (b) 6
(c) 9 (d) 18

13. In a college of 300 students, every student reads 5 newspaper and every newspaper is read by 60 students. The number of newspaper is
(a) at least 30 (b) at most 20
(c) exactly 25 (d) none of these

14. Let F_1 be the set of all parallelogram, F_2 the set of rectangles, F_3 the set of rhombuses, F_4 the set of squares and F_5 the set of trapeziums in a plane then F_1 is equal to
(a) $F_2 \cap F_3$ (b) $F_2 \cup F_3 \cup F_4 \cup F_1$
(c) $F_3 \cap F_4$ (d) none of these

15. In a committee 50 people speak French, 20 speak Spanish and 10 speak both Spanish and French. The number of persons speaking at least one of these two languages.
(a) 60 (b) 40
(c) 38 (d) none of these

16. In a group of 1000 people, there are 750 people who can speak Hindi and 400 who can speak English. Then number of persons who can speak Hindi only is equal to
(a) 300 (b) 400
(c) 600 (d) none of these

17. If $A = \{x \in \mathbb{C} : x^2 = 1\}$ and $B = \{x \in \mathbb{C} : x^4 = 1\}$, then $A \Delta B$ is equal to :
(a) {–1,1} (b) {–1,1,i,–i}
(c) {–i, i} (d) none of these

18. If $A \subseteq B$, then $B'-A'$ is equal to :
(a) A' (b) B'
(c) $A - B$ (d) ϕ

19. If a set A has n distinct elements, the number of all relations on A is
(a) 2^{n^2} (b) n^2
(c) 2^n (d) None of these

20. If $A = \{x : x^2 - 3x + 2 = 0\}$, and R is a universal relation on A, then R is ;

(a) $\{(1,1),(2,2)\}$ (b) $\{1,1)\}'$
(c) $\{\phi\}$ (d) $\{(1,1),(1,2),(2,1),(2,2)\}$

21. If $A = \{5, 6, 7\}$ and $B = \{1, 2, 3, 4\}$, then number of elements in set $(A \times B) \times B$ is equal to:

(a) 36 (b) 48
(c) 16 (d) None of these

22. Let $A = \{a, b, c, d\}$, $B = \{b, c, d, e\}$. Then $n[(A \times B) \cap (B \times A)]$ is equal to

(a) 3 (b) 6
(c) 9 (d) None of these

23. If $A = \{1,2,4\}$, $B = \{2,4,5\}$, $C=\{2,5\}$ then $(A–C) \times' (B - C)$ is equal to

(a) $\{(1,4)\}$ (b) $\{(1,4),(4,4)\}'$
(c) $\{(4,1),(4,4)\}$ (d) None of these

24. Let A and B be two sets, $(A \cup B)' \cup (A' \cap B)$ is equal to:

(a) A' (b) A
(c) B' (d) None of these

25. Let U be the universal set and $A \cup B \cup C = U$ Then $\{(A–B) \cup (B - C) \cup (C - A)\}'$ is equal to:

(a) $A \cup B \cup C$ (b) $A \cup (B \cap C)$
(c) $A \cap B \cap C$ (d) $A \cap (B \cup C)$

26. If A, B, C be three sets such that $A \cup B = A \cup C$ and $A \cap B = A \cap C$, then which of the following is always true:

(a) $A = B$ (b) $B = C$
(c) $A = C$ (d) $A = B = C$

27. Out of 800 boys in a school 224 played cricket, 240 played hockey and 336 played basketball. Of the total, 64 played both basketball and hockey; 80 played cricket and basketball and 40 played cricket and hockey ; 24 played all the three games. The number of boys who did not play any game is

(a) 128 (b) 216
(c) 240 (d) 160

28. A survey shows that 63% of Indians like cheese whereas 76% like apples. If x% of the Indians like both cheese and apples, then x can be

(a) $x = 40$ (b) $x = 65$
(c) $x = 39$ (d) None of these

29. If $A = \{x : x$ is a multiple of 4$\}$ and $B = \{x : x$ is a multiple of 6$\}$, then $A \cap B$ consists of all multiple of

(a) 16 (b) 12
(c) 8 (d) 4

Answer Keys

1. (a)	**2.** (a)	**3.** (c)	**4.** (a)	**5.** (c)	**6.** (c)	**7.** (d)	**8.** (a)	**9.** (d)	**10.** (c)
11. (c)	**12.** (b)	**13.** (c)	**14.** (b)	**15.** (a)	**16.** (c)	**17.** (c)	**18.** (d)	**19.** (a)	**20.** (d)
21. (b)	**22.** (c)	**23.** (b)	**24.** (a)	**25.** (c)	**26.** (b)	**27.** (d)	**28.** (c)	**29.** (b)	

■ NUMBER SYSTEM

A number is actually a way of thinking, an idea that enables us to compare different sets of objects. It can also be called as an idea behind the act of counting to facilitate Bartar System of Trade.

Unit denotes the single things *e.g.*, one apple, one man, one Pen, etc.

Numeral is a symbol used to represent a number

Digits are alphabets of the numbers e.g., 0, 1, 2, ...9. Our present number system is known as Indo-Arabic number system. Here we are going to take up the various number systems and their algebraic structure in the order of their chronological development.

Natural numbers (ℕ) and whole numbers (W)

The numbers which are used for counting are known as natural number (*also known as set of positive integers/counting numbers*) i.e., {1, 2, 3, 4, 5, 6, ...}. If ‘0’ is included in the set of natural numbers then we obtain the set of **Whole Numbers (W).** i.e., $W = \{0, 1, 2, 3, 4, ...\} = \mathbb{N} \cup \{0\}$

Algebraic properties of natural numbers

Addition and Multiplication of natural numbers possess following properties

(a) They are Associative and Commutative, i.e., for all $a, b, c \in N$
Associative Law: $a + (b + c) = (a + b) + c$; $a(bc) = (ab)c$
Commutative Law: $a + b = b + a$; $ab = ba$

(b) Cancellation law holds for natural numbers i.e., for all $a, b, c \in N$
$a + c = b + c \Rightarrow a = b$ and $ac = bc \Rightarrow a = b$

(c) Distribution of multiplication over addition, i.e., for all $a, b, c \in N$
$a(b + c) = ab + ac$

(d) **Order properties:**

(i) **Law of trichomy:** Given any two natural numbers a and b, exactly one of the following holds.
$a > b$ or $a < b$ or $a = b$

(ii) **Transitivity:** For each triplet of natural numbers a, b and c; $a > b$ and $b > c \Rightarrow a > c$.

(iii) **Monotone property for addition and multiplication:** For each triplet of natural numbers a, b and c. $a > b \Rightarrow a + c > b + c$ and $a > b \Rightarrow ac > bc$

(e) **Existence of additive and multiplicative identity:** zero is an additive identity element and one is multiplicative identity element because addition of zero and multiplication by one to any element does not produce any change in it.

(f) **Existence of additive and multiplicative inverse:** For every integer x, there always exist its negative integer $-x$ (additive inverse of x) which, when added to x makes additive identity. multiplicative inverse of x is an element which, when multiplied to x makes multiplicative identity 1 Additive and multiplicative inverse does not exist in set of whole numbers.

Robert Peano's axioms

While the natural numbers have been known to us since the dawn of civilization, an axiomatic approach to the natural numbers was put forth only at the end of eighteenth century (1899) by Italian mathematician Peano, who gave the following axioms valid for natural numbers, commonly known as **Robert Peano's Axioms**.

$P1$: There exists natural number 1.

$P2$: Every natural number has unique successor. The successor of natural number n is denoted by $n^+ : n^+ = n + 1$.

$P3$: 1 is not the successor of any natural number.

$P4$: If a mathematical statement $P(n)$ is true for a natural number and its successor then it will be true for all natural numbers greater than or equal to n. **(Induction Axiom).**

(a) $1 \in k$

(b) $m \in k \Rightarrow m^+ \in k$ when $k = N$

This axiom is known as *induction axiom* or *postulate of induction*. Based on this axiom only the principle of Mathematical Induction has been given which is widely used in many branches of algebra, geometry and arithmetic to prove the truth of mathematical statements given for natural numbers.

Integers (Z or I)

When negative of natural numbers are included in the set of whole numbers then the set of integers are formed. That is, {....., –3, –2, –1, 0, 1, 2, 3, ...}.

Properties of integers

(a) **Closure law:** Set of integer is closed under addition, subtraction, and multiplication operations. i.e., sum difference and product of any two integer is also an integer.

(b) **Commutative and associative law:** Addition and multiplication (not subtraction/division) of integers are Associative and Commutative. i.e., for all $a, b, c \in N$
Associative Law: $a + (b + c) = (a + b) + c$; $a(bc) = (ab)c$
Commutative law: $a + b = b + a$; $ab = ba$

(c) **Cancellation law:** holds for natural numbers, i.e., for all $a, b, c \in N$
$a + c = b + c \Rightarrow a = b$ and $ac = bc \Rightarrow a = b$

(d) **Distributive law:** Distribution of multiplication over addition i.e., for all $a, b, c \in N$, $a(b + c) = ab + ac$

(e) **Order properties:**

(i) **Law of Trichomy:** Given any two natural numbers a and b, exactly one of the following holds.
$a > b$ or $a < b$ or $a = b$

(ii) **Transitivity:** For each triplet of natural numbers a, b and c; $a > b$ and $b > c \Rightarrow a > c$.

(iii) **Monotone property for addition** and **Multiplication:** For each triplet of natural numbers a, b and c.
$a > b \Rightarrow a + c > b + c$ and $a > b \Rightarrow ac > bc$

(f) **Existence of additive and multiplicative identity:** Zero is an additive identity element and one is multiplicative identity element because addition of zero and multiplication by one to any element does not produce any change in it.

(g) **Existence of additive and multiplicative inverse:** For every integer x, there always exist its negative integer $-x$ which, when added to x makes additive identity. Multiplicative inverse of x is an element which, when multiplied to x makes multiplicative identity. Multiplicative inverse does not exist in set of integers.

Division algorithm Given two integers a and m ($m \neq 0$) then $\exists$ an unique integer q and r such that $a = mq + r$ where $0 \leq r \leq | m |$, q is quotient and r is known as remainder. If $r = 0$ then m is said to be divisor of a.

Corollaries of Division algorithm:

(a) An even number a can be written in the form $a = 2q$, where q is an integer.

(b) An odd number a can be written in the form $a = 2q_1 + 1$, where q_1 is an integer

(c) An integer a which is exactly divisible by three can be written in the form $a = 3q$, where q is an integer.

(d) An integer a which is not exactly divisible by three can be written in one of the following forms: $a = 3m + 1$ or $a = 3n + 2$, where m and n are integers.

(e) An integer a which is exactly divisible by a natural number k can be written in the form $a = kq$, where q is an integer.

(f) An integer a which is not exactly divisible by a natural number k can be written in the form $a = kq + r$, where r is one of the numbers 1, 2, ...$(k-1)$ and q is an integer.

TEXTUAL EXERCISE–7 (SUBJECTIVE)

1. State whether the following statements are **True (T)** or **False (F).**
   (a) Every natural number has unique successor.
   (b) Set of natural number is closed under the operation of addition and multiplication but not under subtraction and division.
   (c) Set of integers is closed under addition, subtraction, multiplication and division.
   (d) Zero is an additive identity and one is multiplicative identity for the set of integers.
   (e) Every integer has an unique multiplicative and additive inverse.
   (f) Commutative and associative law well holds for multiplication and addition of integers.
   (g) Subtraction of integers is commutative.
   (h) Multiplication is distributive over both the operations: addition and subtraction.
2. Prove that each integer of the type $6k + 5$ can always be written as $3m + 2$ but the converse is not true.
3. Show that any positive odd integer is of the form $4q + 1$ or $4q + 3$, where q is some integer.
4. Show that any positive odd integer is of the form $6q + 1$, or $6q + 3$, or $6q + 5$, where q is some integer.
5. Show that the square of any positive integer is either of the form $3m$ or $3m + 1$ for some integer m.
6. Show that the cube of any positive integer is of the form $9m$, $9m + 1$ or $9m + 8$.
7. If x is an integer and $x+\frac{1}{x}$ is an integer, prove that $x^n+\frac{1}{x^n}$ is also an integer for all $n \in \mathbb{N}$.
8. If x and y are positive integers, and if $x - y$ is even, show that $x^2 - y^2$ is divisible by 4.
9. Prove that square of an odd integer is always an odd integer.
10. Show that the difference between any number and its square is even.

Answer Keys

1. (a) T (b) T (c) F (d) T (e) F (f) T (g) F (h) T

Prime numbers and their properties

If an integer (other than one) is not divisible by any other integer except one and itself, then it is called a prime number. i.e., 2, 3, 5, 7, 11, 13,.... etc.

Properties of prime numbers

1. For any prime p the only divisors are ± 1 and $\pm p$
2. If difference of two prime numbers is 2 then they are known as **twin primes**. e.g., {5, 7}, {11, 13} etc.
3. $\frac{p^2-1}{24} \in I \Rightarrow$ p is a prime number $[p > 3]$.
4. Prime numbers are written either as $6k - 1$ or $6k + 1$ i.e., (twins) but the converse is not true.
5. $2^{2^n} + 1$ is a number known as **Fermat's number**.

NOTE

1. *Above number was proposed to be prime number* by *Fermat, but Cauchy proved it wrong for* $n \geq 4$.

6. Composite numbers: An integer $p > 1$ is said to be *a* composite number if it has at least one divisor other than ± 1 and $\pm p$. *e.g.*, 6, 27 and 143 are composite numbers whereas -1, 1, 2, 7, 13 are not composite numbers. **Note that: 1 is neither prime nor composite**

Co-prime numbers

Two integers are said to be relatively prime or co-prime if they have no common factor i.e., their $G.C.D = 1$, e.g., 4 and 15, 3 and 16 etc.

Perfect number

If sum of all the divisors of a number n is equal to $2n$ then the number n is called perfect number. e.g., 6 is a perfect number because sum of all divisors $= 1 + 2 + 3 + 6 = 12 = 2(6)$

Factorial notation

Factorial of r is defined as product of first r natural numbers. And is denoted as $r!$.

i.e., $r! = 1 . 2 . 3.4. . . .(r - 1). r$

e.g., $1! = 1$ $2! = 2$ $3! = 6$ $4! = 24$
$5! = 120$ $6! = 720$ $7! = 5040$ $8! = 40320$.

ILLUSTRATION 28: Simplify the following.

(a) $\dfrac{8!}{5!}$ (b) $\dfrac{10!}{2!\,8!}$

(c) $\dfrac{8!}{3!\,5!}$ (d) $\dfrac{15!}{12!}$

SOLUTION: (a) Given $\dfrac{8!}{5!} = \dfrac{8\times7\times6\times(5!)}{(5!)} = 8 \times 7\times 6 = 336$

(b) Consider $\dfrac{10!}{2!8!} = \dfrac{10\times9\times(8!)}{2!(8!)} = \dfrac{90}{2} = 45$

(c) Given $\dfrac{8!}{3!5!} = \dfrac{8\times7\times6\times5!}{(3\times2\times1)\times5!} = 56$

(d) Given $\dfrac{15!}{12!} = \dfrac{15\times14\times13\times(12!)}{12!} = 15\times14\times13 = 2730$

ILLUSTRATION 29: Prove the following $\forall\, n \in \mathbb{N}$ here $n > r$ and $r \in \mathbb{N}$.

(a) $\dfrac{(n+1)!}{(n)!} = (n+1)$ i.e., $(n+1)(n!) = (n+1)!$

(b) $\dfrac{(n+2)!}{(n)!} = (n+2)(n+1)$

(c) $(n^3 - n)\left((n-2)!\right) = (n+1)!$; here $n \geq 3$

(d) $\dfrac{(n)!}{(n-r)!} = n(n-1)(n-2)(n-3)(n-4)....(n-r+1)$

SOLUTION: (a) Consider the L.H.S. of the expression

$$\frac{(n+1)!}{n!} = \frac{(n+1)n(n-1)(n-2)....3.2.1}{n!} = \frac{(n+1)(n!)}{n!} = n+1 = \text{R.H.S.}$$

(b) L.H.S. $= \dfrac{(n+2)!}{n!} = \dfrac{(n+2)(n+1)(n!)}{n!} = (n+2)(n+1)$

consider the left hand side of the identity

(c) L.H.S. $(n^2 - n)((n-2)!) = n(n-1)((n-2)!) = n((n-1)!) = n!$

$\because$ product of 1st $(n-2)$ natural numbers of multiplied to $(n-1)$ becomes product of 1st $(n-1)$ natural numbers, i.e., $(n-1)!$

Applying the definition of factorial we get

(d) $\text{L.H.S.} = \dfrac{n!}{(n-r)!} = \dfrac{n(n-1)(n-2)....(n-rH)(n-r)(n-r-1)....3.2.1}{(n-r)!}$

$= \dfrac{(n(n-1)(n-2)....(n-rH))(n-r)!}{(n-r)!} = n(n-1)(n-2)(n-3) ..... (n-r+1)$

An important result for divisibility

Product of k consecutive integer is always divisible by k!. e.g., $(n+1)(n+2)(n+3)(n+4)$ is divisible by 4!

Let P_n denote the product of k consecutive integers, the smallest of which is n. Then

$P_n = n(n+1)(n+2)...(n+k-1)$

$\therefore\ P_{n+1} = (n+1)(n+2) .... (n+k)$

$\therefore\ nP_{n+1} = (n+k)P_n = nP_n + kP_n$

i.e., $n(P_{n+1} - P_n) = kP_n$ so that

$P_{n+1} - P_n = k(P_n/n)$ (i)

Now $P_n/n = (n+1)(n+2)...(n+k-1)$

which is the product of $(k-1)$ consecutive integer beginning with $n+1$. From (i), we find that, $P_{n+1} - P_n = k \times$ product of $(k-1)$ consecutive integers.

Therefore if the product of $(k-1)$ consecutive integers is divisible by $(k-1)!$ then $P_{n+1} - P_n = M(k!)$ But $P_1 = k!$ so that P_1 is divisible by $k!$. Consequently, $P_2 P_3 ..., P_n$ are all divisible by $k!$.

Since the product of every pair of consecutive integers is divisible by 2!, it follows by the principle of finite induction that P_n is divisible by $k!$ for all positive integers n.

ILLUSTRATION 30: Prove that for any natural number n, the number $N = n^2 + 1$ is not divisible by 3.

SOLUTION: The only possible remainders upon the division of *a* natural number by 3 are 0, 1, 1, 2. In solving this problem, we therefore find it convenient to partition all the natural numbers into three classes; $3k$, Where k is a natural number ; $3k+1$, where k is *a* whole number; $3k+2$, where k is *a* whole number. If $n = 3k$, we haven $n^2 + 1 = 9k^2 + 1$. Since the first term in the right member is divisible by 3 and the second one is not, the number N is not divisible by 3 for these values of n.

If $n = 3k+1$, then $n^2 + 1 = 9k^2 + 6k + 2$. It is obvious in this case that when N is divided by there is *a* remainder of 2.

The case of $n = 3k+2$ is considered in a similar manner.

ILLUSTRATION 31: Prove that $n(n^2 + 20)$ is divisible by 48 if n is even

SOLUTION: $n(n^2 + 20) = n[n^2 - 4 + 24] = n(n^2 - 4) + n(24)$

$= n(n-2)(n+2) + 24n = 2k(2k-2)(2k+2) + 48k$ (where $2k = n$)

$= 8k(k-1)(k+1) + 48k = 8(k+1)k(k-1) + 48k$

$= 8(3!)m + 48k = 48m + 48k$ **which is divisible by 48**

Aliter: Let $n = 2k$, where k is an integer therefore $N = 8k(k^2 + 5)$

If we show that for any integer k the number $k(k^2 + 5)$ is divisible by 6, it will be clear that N is divisible by 48. Now, $k(k^2 + 5) = k(k^2 - 1 + 6) = (k-1)k(k+1) + 6k$, we see that $6k$ is divisible by 6. Here $(k-1)k(k+1)$ is a product of three successive integers and for this reason one of them is definitely divisible by 3. Out of the two successive integers, one must definitely be even. Since 2 and 3 are relatively prime, it follows that $k\ (k^2 + 5)$ is indeed divisible by 6 for any integer k.

ILLUSTRATION 32: Sum of cubes of three consecutive integers is always divisible by 9.

SOLUTION: $n^3 + (n + 1)^3 + (n + 2)^3 = 3n^3 + 1 + 3n\ (n + 1) + 8 + 6n\ (n + 2)$

$\Rightarrow\ 3n\ (n^2 + 3n + 5) + 9 = 3n\ [(n + 1)(n + 2) + 3] + 9$

$\Rightarrow\ 3n\ (n + 1)\ (n + 2) + 9(n + 1) = 3.3!\ k_1 + 9k_2 = (9k)$

ILLUSTRATION 33: If $4x - y$ is a multiple of 3, show that $4x^2 + 7xy - 2y^2$ is divisible by 9.

SOLUTION: Given $4x - y = 3k \quad \Rightarrow\ y = 4x - 3k$

Now $4x^2 + 7xy - 2y^2 = 4x^2 + 7x(4x - 3k) - 2(4x - 3k)^2 = 4x^2 + 28x^2 - 21kx - 32x^2 + 48kx - 18k^2$

$= 27kx - 18k^2 = 9k(3x - 2k)$

So $9 \mid 4x^2 + 7xy - 2y^2$

ILLUSTRATION 34: If n is greater than 2, show that $n^5 - 5n^3 + 4n$ is divisible by 120. Given n is an integer.

SOLUTION: $n^5 - 5n^3 + 4n\ ;\ n > 2 = n(n^4 - 5n^2 + 4) = n(n^2 - 1)\ (n^2 - 4) = n(n - 1)\ (n + 1)\ (n - 2)\ (n + 2)$

Being product of 5 consecutive int, divisible by 5!.

ILLUSTRATION 35: Show that $a^n - b^n$ is divisible by $a - b$ if n is any positive integer odd or even.

SOLUTION: Let $a^n - b^n = f(a)$

By remainder theorem, $f(b) - b^n = 0$ (replacing a by b)

$\therefore\ a - b$ is a factor of $a^n - b^n$

ILLUSTRATION 36: Show that $a^n - b^n$ is divisble by $(a + b)$ when n is an even positive integer, but not if n is odd.

SOLUTION: Let a $n - b^n = f(a)$

Now $f(-b) = (-b)^n - b^n = 0$ if n is even, and hence $a + b$ is a factor of $a^n - b^n$

If n is odd, $f(-b) = -b^n - b^n = -2b^n \neq 0$

ILLUSTRATION 37: If y is a prime number and x is any integer satisfying $x^2 - 2y^2 = 1$, then find all possible solutions.

SOLUTION: $x^2 - 2y^2 = 1$

$\Rightarrow\ x^2 = 2y^2 + 1$ (1)

$\Rightarrow\ x^2$ is an odd integer

Let $x = (2n + 1)$

$\Rightarrow\ (2n + 1)^2 = 2y^2 + 1 \Rightarrow\ 4n^2 + 4n + 1 = 2y^2 + 1$

$\Rightarrow\ y^2 = 2n^2 + 2n \Rightarrow\ y^2 = 2n(n + 1) = 4k\ ;\ a \in \mathbb{Z}$

$\Rightarrow\ y^2$ is even integer

$\Rightarrow\ y$ is also an even integer. But y is prime

$\Rightarrow\ y = 2$ (2)

$\therefore$ from (1) and (2) $x^2 = 2(2)^2 + 1 = 9$

$\Rightarrow\ x = \pm 3$

$\therefore$ The possible solutions are $x = 3$, $y = 2$ and $x = -3$, $y = 2$.

ILLUSTRATION 38: Find all possible natural numbers 'n' for which $\frac{5n^2-7n+84}{n}$ is divisible by 5.

SOLUTION: $\frac{5n^2-7n+84}{n}=\frac{5n^2-5n-2n+84}{n}=(5n-5)+\frac{84-2n}{n}$

$$=5(n-1)+\frac{84}{n}-2 \quad (1)$$

It will be divisible by 5

If $\frac{84}{n}-2=5k$ for some $k\in\mathbb{Z}$

$\Rightarrow \frac{84}{n}=5k+2$

$\Rightarrow n=\frac{84}{5k+2}$; $k\in\mathbb{Z}$ and $n\in\mathbb{N}$; $5k+2>0$

$\Rightarrow k>-\frac{2}{5}$ also $5k+2\le 84 \Rightarrow k\le 1604$

but $k\in\mathbb{Z} \Rightarrow k\ge 0$ and $k\le 16$

for $k=0$, $n=42$
for $k=1$, $n=12$
for $k=2$, $n=7$
for $k=8$, $n=2$
Further, we will not get any value of k for which $n\in\mathbb{N}$
$\therefore$ possible values of n are 2, 7, 12, 42.

TEXTUAL EXERCISE–8 (SUBJECTIVE)

1. Prove the following facts:
   (a) product of two consecutive integers is divisible by 2 and three consecutive integers is divisible by 6.
   (b) product of four consecutive integers is divisible by 24 = 4!.
   (c) product of two consecutive even integers is always divisible by 8
   (d) Square of any odd integers is always of the type $8k+1$ where k is some integer
2. Prove that $n(n+1)(n+5)$ is a multiple of 6
3. Show that $n(n^2-1)(3n+2)$ is divisible by 24
4. Prove that the sum of the squares of two successive integers when divided by 4 has a remainder 1.
5. Prove that the number $n(n^2+5)$ is divisible by 6 for any natural n
6. Prove that the product of three successive natural numbers, the middle number being the square of a natural number, is divisible by 60.
7. Prove that the difference between the cube of an odd number and the number itself is divisible by 24
8. Prove that if a is an integer, then a^3-a is divisible by 6. Also deduce that $5a^3+13a-30$ is divisible by 6.
9. Prove that there is no prime number p for which the numbers $p+2$ and $p+5$ are both prime.
10. Show that every number and its cube when divided by 6 leave the same remainder.
11. Show that m^n+m and m^n-m are always even, whatever m and n may be.

$n^5 - n = n(n^{5-1} - 1)$ is divisible by 5.

Also $n^5 - n = n(n-1)(n+1)(n^2+1)$

But $n(n-1)(n+1)$ is divisible by 3!. Therefore, $n^5 - n$ is divisible by both 5 and 6 i.e., 30

Hence correct answer is (a).

ILLUSTRATION 43: $7^{10} - 5^{10}$ is divisible by which of the following is/are true.

(a) 8 (b) 3
(c) 11 (d) 264

SOLUTION: Let $x = 7^{10} - 5^{10} = (7^{11-1} - 5^{11-1}) = (7^{11-1} - 1) - (5^{11-1} - 1)$.

Here 11 is a prime number, therefore by Fermat's theorem, $(7^{11-1} - 1)$ and $(5^{11-1} - 1)$ both are divisible by 11. Hence the given number $7^{10} - 5^{10}$ is divisible by 11.

Also $7^{10} - 5^{10} = (49)^5 - (25)^5$ which is divisible by 24

$\Rightarrow$ 24/x and 11/x $\Rightarrow$ 264/x

hence all options are correct.

ILLUSTRATION 44: If n is a prime greater than 3, show that $n^2 - 1$ is a multiple of 24.

SOLUTION: n is prime > 3

$n^2 - 1 = n^{3-1} - 1$ so divisible by 3 (Fermatis theorem)

Also, $n^2 - 1 = (n-1)(n+1)$; product of two consecutive odd integers so divisible by 8.

$\Rightarrow$ $24/n^2 - 1$ if $n > 3$ and n is prime

Aliter: Exhaustive method $n = 6k \pm 1$

ILLUSTRATION 45: Show that the difference of the squares of any two prime numbers greater than 6 is divisible by 24.

SOLUTION: Let p and q be prime greater than $n = 6$

$p^2 - q^2 = (p^2 - 1) - (q^2 - 1) = (24k_1 - 24k_2) = 24(k_1 - k_2)$

each factor is divisible by 3 and 8 refer to previous question.

ILLUSTRATION 46: Show that no square number is of the form $3n - 1$.

SOLUTION: $3n - 1$ cant be perfect square

Let $3n - 1 = N^2$

$N^2 + 1 = 3n$

$(N^2 - 1) + 2 = 3n$

If N is prime to 3 ; $N^2 - 1 = N^{3-1} - 1 = 3k$ (*Fermat's theorem*)

$\Rightarrow$ LHS $= 3k + 2$ hence contradiction

If N^2 is not prime to 3

$\Rightarrow N^2 = 3\lambda$

$\Rightarrow N^2 + 1 = 3\lambda + 1 \neq 3n$ again contradiction

ILLUSTRATION 47: Show that if a cube number is divided by 7, the remainder is 0, 1 or 6.

SOLUTION: Cube of any integer leaves remainder 0, 1 or 6

When divided by 7.

Method 1: Let $p = 7q + r$

$p^3 = (7q)^3 + 3(7qr)(7q + r) + r^3 = 7m + r^3$.

Method 2: If p is co-prime to 7

$\Rightarrow 7 \mid p^6 - 1$ $(\because$ Fermat $\rightarrow 7 \mid p^{7-1} - 1))$

$\Rightarrow 7 \mid (p^3 - 1)(p^3 + 1) = p^3 = 7n + 1$ or $7n - 1$

If p is not co-prime to 7 then

$\Rightarrow p^3 = 7n$ or $7n + 1$ or $7n + 13$

TEXTUAL EXERCISE–9 (SUBJECTIVE)

1. State whether the following statements are *True* (*T*) or *False* (*F*).
   (a) $x^{16} - y^{16}$ is divisible by $x - y$, $x + y$, $x^2 + y^2$.
   (b) $x^{2m+1} + y^{2m+1}$ is divisible by $x + y$.
   (c) $n^p - n$ is divisible by p, where p is prime.
   (d) $1 + (14)!$ is divisible by 13.
2. Prove that the 8th power of any natural number is of the form $17n$ or $17n \pm 1$.
3. Prove that the 12th power of any number is of the form $13n$ or $13n + 1$.
4. Prove that
   (i) $8^{10} - 1$ is divisible by 7 as well as 77, 693
   (ii) $13^{10} - 5^{10}$ is divisible by 11 as well as 88.
5. Prove that $3n^5 + 5n^3 + 7n$ is divisible by 15.
6. Prove that $2.7^n + 3.5^n - 5$ is divisible by 12.
7. If n is prime number greater than 5, show that $n^4 - 1$ is divisible by 240.
8. Prove that $11^{n+2} + 12^{2n+1}$ is divided by 133.
9. Prove that for every positive integer n, $1^n + 8^n - 3^n - 6^n$ is divisible by 10.
10. Prove that product of four consecutive positive integers increased by 1 is a perfect square.
11. Three consecutive positive integers raised to the first, second and third powers respectively, when added make a perfect square, the square root of which is equal to the sum of the three consecutive integers, find these integers.
12. Show that 13 divides $2^{70} + 3^{70}$.
13. Show that $2^{2n} - 1$ and $2^{2n-1} + 1$ are both divisible by 3 for all positive integral values of n.
14. Show that $10^n + 3.4^{n+2} + 5$ is divisible by 9.
15. If n is any prime number greater than 3, except 7, show that $n^6 - 1$ is divisible by 168.

Answer Keys

1. (a) T (b) T (c) T (d) F **11.** 3,4,5

DIVISORS/MULTIPLES OF NUMBERS

Unique factorization theorem

Let n be any integer such that $|n| > 1$. Then n is expressible as a product of unity and finitely many prime numbers. Moreover, such an expression is unique except as to the order in which the various factors occur. Any natural number N can be written as $N = p^a\, q^b\, r^c\, s^d$ ..... where p, q, r, s are prime numbers and a, b, c, d are non-negative integers. e.g., $225 = 3^2 \times 5^2$; $345 = 3 \times 5 \times 23$

Divisors/multiples and their properties

From division algorithm $a = mq + r$. When the remainder r becomes zero then $a = mq$. Here m and q are called divisors of a and a is known as multiple of m and q.

Given a natural number $N = p^a.q^b.r^c$ and a number $x = p^\alpha q^\beta r^\gamma$ is called divisor of N. If N is completely divisible by x i.e., $N = x.m$ where $m \in I$. In other words, that will be divisor of N iff all the prime factors of x are present in N. This condition can be mathematically expressed as $0 \le \alpha \le a$; $0 \le \beta \le b$; $0 \le \gamma \le c$ where α, β, γ are integers.

Number of divisor: Number of divisors of N = number of ways the integers α, β, γ can take values applying the above restrictions = $(a + 1).(b + 1).(c + 1)$

Proper and improper divisors: As unity (1) is a divisor of every natural number (N) and every natural number N is divisor of itself. These two numbers are called the improper divisor of (N) and remaining divisors are known as proper divisors.

$\therefore$ Number of proper divisors of $(N) = (a + 1)(b + 1)(c + 1) - 2$.

Sum of divisors: Divisors of the number (N) are given by the terms of the following expansion as it clear that each term of the product.

$$(1+p+p^2+...+p^a).(1+q+q^2+...+q^b).(1+r+r^2+...+r^c)$$

is a divisor of 'N' including 'N' and unity and no other number is divisor of N.

$\because$ $(1+p+p^2+...+p^a).(1+q+q^2+...+q^b).(1+r+r^2+...+r^c) = 1+p+q+r+pq+pr+qr+p^2+q^2+r^2+pqr+p^3+q^3+r^3+....+p^a.\,q^b.\,r^c$

$\therefore$ sum of all divisors of (N) is given by

$$S = (1+p+p^2+...+p^a).(1+q+q^2+...+q^b).(1+r+r^2+...+r^c)$$

$$= \left(\frac{p^{a+1}-1}{p-1}\right)\left(\frac{q^{b+1}-1}{q-1}\right)\left(\frac{r^{c+1}-1}{r-1}\right)$$

ILLUSTRATION 48: Given a natural number $n = p^2q$ where p and q are primes. Find all of its possible divisors and also find the sum of all divisors.

SOLUTION: Number of divisors = (2 + 1). (1 + 1) = 6 and they are given as $1, p, q, p^2$, pq and p^2q sum of all divisors = $(1 + p + p^2).(1 + q)$

ILLUSTRATION 49: Find the number of divisors of the number 1800, also find the summation of all divisors.

SOLUTION: Consider prime factorization of $n = 1800$

$n = 2^3 . 3^2 . 5^2$

a natural number, $x = 2^{\alpha}.3^{\beta}.5^{\gamma}$ divides n

$\Rightarrow 0 \le \alpha \le 3, \quad 0 \le \beta \le 2, \quad 0 \le \gamma \le 2$

Set of all such divisors is given as $X = \begin{cases} x : x = 2^{\alpha}\ 3^{\beta}\ 3^{\gamma} & where\ \alpha, \beta, \gamma \in W \\ \& \ 0 \le \alpha \le 3\ ;\ 0 \le \beta \le 2\ \&\ 0 \le \gamma \le 2 \end{cases}$

$\Rightarrow$ number of divisors = $n(X)$ = number of ordered triplet (α, β, γ) satisfying the above conditions = (number of possible values of α) × (number of possible values of β) × (number of possible values of γ)

= (3 + 1) (2 + 1) (2 + 1) = 36

Sum of divisors $= \left(2^0 + 2^1 + 2^2 + 2^3\right)\left(3^0 + 3^1 + 3^2\right)\left(5^0 + 5^1 + 5^2\right)$

$$= \left(\frac{2^4 - 1}{2 - 1}\right)\left(\frac{3^3 - 1}{3 - 1}\right)\left(\frac{5^3 - 1}{5 - 1}\right) = 15 \times 13 \times 31 = 6045$$

Number and sum of divisors of N divisible by a natural number $y = p^{a_1}.q^{b_1}.r^{c_1}$

Let $x = p^{\alpha} . q^{\beta} . r^{\gamma}$ be such divisors

$\because y \,|\, x \Rightarrow p^{a_1}.q^{b_1}.r^{c_1} \,|\, p^{\alpha}.q^{\beta}.r^{\gamma}$

$\Rightarrow a_1 \le \alpha \le a \ \ \&\ b_1 \le \beta \le b$ and $c_1 \le \gamma \le c$

$\Rightarrow$ number of such divisors = $(a - a_1 + 1)(b - b_1 + 1)(c - c_1 + 1)$

Sum of such divisors $S_y = \left(p^{a_1} + p^{a_1+1} + ... + p^{a}\right) . \left(q^{b_1} + q^{b_1+1} + ... + q^{b}\right) . \left(r^{c_1} + r^{c_1+1} + ... + r^{c}\right)$

$= y\left(1 + p + p^2 + ... + p^{a-a_1}\right)\left(1 + q + q^2 + ... + q^{b-b_1}\right)\left(1 + r + ... + r^{c-c_1}\right)$

$$= y\left(\frac{p^{a-a_1+1} - 1}{p - 1}\right)\left(\frac{q^{b-b_1+1} - 1}{q - 1}\right)\left(\frac{r^{c-c_1+1} - 1}{r - 1}\right)$$

ILLUSTRATION 50: Find the number of:

(a) even proper divisors and sum of even proper divisors of 180.

(b) odd proper divisors and sum of odd proper divisors of 2700

SOLUTION: (a) $180 = 2^2 \times 3^2 \times 5$

$\Rightarrow$ number of divisors = (2 + 1) (2 + 1) (2 + 1) = 18

Since even divisors are of the type $2^{a+1} . 3^b . 5^c$ where a, b, c are non negative integers.

$\Rightarrow$ number of even divisors = 2 × 3 × 2 = 12

sum of even divisors = $(2^1 + 2^2)(3^0 + 3^1 + 3^2)(5^0 + 5^1) = 6 \times 13 \times 6 = 468$

$\Rightarrow$ number of even proper divisors = 12 – 1 = 11 (*excluding the number* 180)

sum of even proper divisors = 468 – 180 = 388

(b) $2700 = 2^2 \times 3^3 \times 5^2$

Since odd divisors of above number are of the type $3^b . 5^c$

where a, b, c are non negative integers, where $0 \le b \le 3$ and $0 \le c \le 2$

$\Rightarrow$ number of odd divisors $= 4 \times 3 = 12$

sum of odd divisors $= (3^0 + 3^1 + 3^2 + 3^3)(5^0 + 5^1 + 5^2) = 1240$

$\Rightarrow$ number of odd proper divisors $= 12 - 1 = 11$ *(excluding unity)*

sum of odd proper divisors $= 1240 - 1 = 1239$.

ILLUSTRATION 51: Find the number and sum of all divisors of 3600 that are divisible by 48

SOLUTION: $3600 = 2^4.3^2.5^2$. Any required divisor of 3600 is of the form $48.(2^a\, 3^b.5^c)$.

i.e. $2^{a+4} . 3^{b+1} . 5^c$ where a, b, c are non negative integers.

$\Rightarrow$ number of such divisors = (no. of values of a) × (no. of values of b) × (no. of values of c)

$= 1 \times 2 \times 3 = 6$ since $0 \le a + 4 \le 4;$ $0 \le b + 1 \le 2$ $0 \le c \le 2$

Sum of there divisors $= 48\,(2^0)\,(3^1 + 3^2) + (5^0 + 5^1 + 5^2)$

$= 48 \times 12 \times 31 = 17856$

To find the number of ways in which a composite number can be resolved into two factors

Consider the natural number $n = p^a q^b r^c$ .... as the number of divisors of n is $(a + 1)(b + 1)(c + 1)$. Among these divisors we can always find a pair of two divisors x, y such that their product $x.y = n$.

Therefore number of ordered pairs (x, y) satisfying above equation $x.y = n$ is equal to number of divisors.

Every un-ordered pair of such divisors represents one way of resolving n into two factors. Therefore, the number of ways of resolving n into two factors is half the total number of divisors. Number of such pair of factors $= \frac{1}{2}(a+1)(b+1)(c+1)...$ But, this is true only if n is not a perfect square (*i.e. atleast one of the quantities a, b, c, ... is an odd natural number*).

In case n being a perfect square, one of the possible resolution into factors is $x = \sqrt{n}$ and $y = \sqrt{n}$, and corresponding to this there will be only one unordered pair ($(x_1;y_1) = (x_2, y_2)$ does not imply $x_1 = x_2$ and $y_1 = y_2$) of solution. While counting number of (x, y) as $(a + 1)(b + 1)(c + 1)$ the above $\left(\sqrt{n}, \sqrt{n}\right)$ has been counted only once. So to find number of unordered pair of solutions it should be counted twice and then the total must be factored by two.

Hence, number of ways of resolution is $\frac{1}{2}\{(a+1)(b+1)(c+1)+1\}$

ILLUSTRATION 52: Find the number of ordered pairs of integer x and y satisfying the equation : $x.y = 1260v$

SOLUTION: $\because$ $x/1260$ and $y/1260$

$\Rightarrow$ x, y are divisors of 1260

$\Rightarrow$ number of ordered pairs of natural number (x, y)

= number of positive divisors of $\{1260 = 2^2 \times 3^2 \times 5 \times 7\}$

$= (2 + 1)(2 + 1)(1 + 1)(1 + 1) = 36$

But if $x.y = 1260$, then $(-x)(-y) = 1260$

So for each ordered pair (x, y) satisfying the above equation the ordered pair $(-x, -y)$ also satisfies the equation.

$\Rightarrow$ Total number of integral ordered pairs $= 2 \times 36 = 72$

ILLUSTRATION 53: In how many ways 129600 can be resolved into product of two positive integers.

SOLUTION: $129600 = 2^6 \times 3^4 \times 5^2$. Here 129600 is a perfect square as every power is even

$\therefore$ Number of ways $= \frac{1}{2}\{(6+1)(4+1)(2+1)+1\} = 53$

ILLUSTRATION 54: In how many ways the number 36000 can be resolved as a product of two positive integers?

SOLUTION: Let $n = 54000 = 2^4 \times 3^3 \times 5^3$. Here n is not a perfect square.

($\because$ power of 3 and 5 are odds)

Hence the number of ways $= \frac{1}{2}\{(4+1)(3+1)(3+1)\} = 40$

NOTES

1. The number of ways of resolving ***n*** into two factors is $\frac{1}{2}(a+1)(b+1)(c+1)...,$ when *n* is not a perfect square and $\frac{1}{2}\{(a+1)(b+1)(c+1)+1\}$, when *n* is a perfect square.
2. Every number n has two improper divisors 1 and n itself and the remaining divisors are called proper divisors. E.g., number of proper divisors of 108 is 10.

Least common multiple (LCM) and greatest common divisor (GCD)

Least common multiple (LCM) LCM of set of numbers is the smallest number (integer/rational) which is completely divisible by each of them. i.e. x is said to be LCM of y and z iff y divides x, z also divides x and x is least positive of all such numbers.

e.g., To find LCM of 6, 4, 9. Let us define N_k be set of multiples of k, therefore

$N_4 = \{4x : x \in N\} = \{4, 8, 12, ..., 36, ...\}$

$N_6 = \{6x : x \in N\} = \{6, 12, 18, ..., 36, ...\}$

$N_9 = \{9x : x \in N\} = \{9, 18, 27, 36, ...\}$

$\Rightarrow$ Set of common multiples $N_4 \cap N_6 \cap N_9 = \{36, 72, 108, ...\}$

Hence least common multiple is 36.

Let x and y be two given integers $x = p^{\alpha}.q^{\beta}.r^{\gamma}.s^{\delta}$ and $y = p^{\alpha_1}.q^{\beta_1}.r^{\gamma_1}.s^{\delta_1}$ where p, q, r, are primes.

If z is LCM of x and y then

$\Rightarrow z = p^{\max(\alpha,\alpha_1)}.q^{\max(\beta,\beta_1)}.r^{\max(\gamma,\gamma_1)}.s^{\max(\delta,\delta_1)}$

Properties

(a) If x and y are co-prime then LCM (x and y) = $x.y$

(b) LCM (x and y) = LCM (y and x) {commutative}

(c) LCM of a rational and an irrational number does not exists.

(d) LCM of $\frac{a}{b}$ and $\frac{c}{d} = \frac{LCM\ (a \text{ and } c)}{HCF\ (b \text{ and } d)}$

Proof: Let the common multiple of $\frac{a}{b}$ & $\frac{c}{d}$ be $\frac{e}{f}$ where each of the above fractions are in lowest form

$\Rightarrow \frac{a}{b}\Big/\frac{e}{f}$ and $\frac{c}{d}\Big/\frac{e}{f} \Rightarrow \frac{e}{f}\times\frac{b}{a} \in \mathbb{Z}$ and $\frac{e}{f}\times\frac{d}{c} \in \mathbb{Z}$

$\Rightarrow$ e is L.C.M. of a and c where as f is H.C.F. of b and d.

$\Rightarrow LCM\left(\frac{a}{b}, \frac{c}{d}\right) = \frac{e}{f} = \frac{LCM\ (a \text{ and } c)}{HCF\ (b \text{ and } d)}$

$\Rightarrow LCM\left(\frac{a}{b}, \frac{c}{d}\right) = \frac{e_{\min}}{f_{\max}} = \frac{LCM\ (a \text{ and } c)}{HCF\ (b \text{ and } d)}$

ILLUSTRATION 55: Find the LCM of

(a) (2, 4, 6, 12, 5) (b) ($\pi/2$, $\pi/3$, π, 2π) (c) (2, π, $\pi/3$).

SOLUTION: (a) $2 = 2 \times 1$, $4 = 2 \times 2$, $6 = 2 \times 3$, $12 = 2^2 \times 3$, $5 = 1 \times 5$

hence common multiple is $2^2 \times 3 \times 5 = 60$

(b) Writing down multiples of $\pi/2$, $\pi/3$, π and 2π, we can easily see that the common multiples are 2π, 4π, 6π, ... etc., so the least common multiple is 2π

(c) Writing down multiples of 2, π and $\pi/3$ we can observe

$N_2 = \{2, 4, 6, 8, ...\}$; $N_{\pi/3} = \{\pi/3, 2\pi/3, \pi.....\}$; $N_\pi = \{\pi, 2\pi, 3\pi...\}$

there is no common multiple, So LCM does not exist.

ILLUSTRATION 56: Find the LCM of following set of numbers

(a) 1800, 1008, 1080 (b) 30/28, 35/21 (c) $3\sqrt{2}$, 4

SOLUTION: (a) consider the set of numbers in prime factorized form

$1800 = 2^3 \times 3^2 \times 5^2$;

$1008 = 2^3 \times 3^2 \times 7$;

$1080 = 2^3 \times 3^2 \times 5$

Clearly the LCM of 1800, 1008, 1080 is $2^3 \times 3^2 \times 5 \times 7$.

i.e. 2520.

(b) Considering the fractions in lowest form, $\frac{30}{28} = \frac{15}{14}$ and $\frac{35}{21} = \frac{5}{3}$

therefore LCM $= \frac{LCM\ (15\ \&\ 5)}{HCF\ (14\ \&\ 3)} = 15$

(c) Multiples of $3\sqrt{2}$ are irrationals where as all multiples of 4 are integers therefore common multiples do not exists and hence no LCM.

Greatest common divisor (GCD)/Highest common factor (HCF): HCF of a given set of numbers is the largest number which divides each of the given numbers HCF of y and z is also denoted as (y, z). therefore x is said to be GCD of y and z if x divides both y and z and x is largest of such numbers. So clearly every common divisor of y and z also divides x and $x \neq 0$.

e.g. HCF of 12 and 64 is 4. GCD of 6 and 35 is 1 (co-prime)

Method to find HCF: For two given integers x and y.

Method 1: Consider their prime factors

$x = p^{\alpha_1}.q^{\beta_1}.r^{\gamma_1}...$ and $y = p^{\alpha_2}.q^{\beta_2}.r^{\gamma_2}....$

If z is HCF of x and y $\Rightarrow$ z/x and z/y

$\therefore$ z contains the least power for each corresponding prime factor.

$\Rightarrow z = (x, y) = p^{\min\{\alpha_1,\alpha_2\}}.q^{\min\{\beta_1,\beta_2\}}.r^{\min\{\gamma_1,\gamma_2\}}...$

Method 2: To find HCF of a and b (*using division Algorithm*)

$\Rightarrow$ $a = bq_1 + r_1$ *Now dividing b by r_1*

$\Rightarrow$ $b = r_1q_2 + r_2$ *Now dividing r_1 by r_2*

$\Rightarrow$ $r_1 = r_2q_3 + r_3$ *Now dividing r_2 by r_3*

proceeding similarly till the remainder becomes zero we get

$r_{n-1} = r_nq_{n+1} + r_{n+1}$ *such that* $r_{n+1} = 0$

$\Rightarrow$ r_n is GCD of a and b.

ILLUSTRATION 57: Find the HCF of 96 and 424.

SOLUTION: $424 = 96(4) + 40$

$\Rightarrow 96 = 40(2) + 16$ $\Rightarrow 40 = 16(2) + 8$ $\Rightarrow 16 = 8(2)$

$\Rightarrow$ HCF of 96 and 424 = 8.

Properties: For all integers a, b and c

(a) $(a, b) = (b, a)$ (Commutative)

(b) $(a, (b, c)) = ((a, b), c)$ (Associative)

(c) $(ac, bc) = |c|(a, b)$ (Distributive)

(d) $(a, 0) = (0, a) = |a| \Rightarrow (a, 1) = (1, a) = 1$

(e) If a/b then $(a, b) = a$

(f) If $(b, c) = g$ and d is a common divisor of b and c, then d is a divisor of g

(g) For any $m > 0$, $(mb, mc) = m(b, c)$

(h) If d/b and d/c and $d > 0$ then $\left(\dfrac{b}{d}, \dfrac{c}{d}\right) = \left(\dfrac{1}{d}\right).(b, c)$

(i) If $(b, c) = g$, then $\left(\dfrac{b}{g}, \dfrac{c}{g}\right) = 1$

(j) If $(b, c) = g$, then there exists two integers x and y such that $g = xb + yc$

(k) If $(a, b) = 1$ and $(a, c) = 1$, then $(a, bc) = 1$

(l) Two consecutive natural numbers are co-prime to each other i.e., $(n, n + 1) = 1$

(m) If $a/bc = 1$ and $(a, b) = 1$, then $a/c = 1$

(n) $HCF\left(\dfrac{a}{b} \,\&\, \dfrac{c}{d}\right) = \dfrac{HCF\ (a \,\&\, c)}{LCM\ (b \,\&\, d)}$

Proof: Let HCF of (a/b and c/d) = e/f where each of the above fractions are in lowest form

$\Rightarrow \dfrac{e}{f}\Big/\dfrac{a}{b}$ and $\dfrac{e}{f}\Big/\dfrac{c}{d} \Rightarrow \dfrac{af}{be} \in \mathbb{Z}$ and $\dfrac{cf}{ed} \in \mathbb{Z}$

$\Rightarrow$ e/c and a and b and d/f

$\Rightarrow$ e is HCF of c and a

f is LCM of b and d

$$\Rightarrow HCF\left(\frac{a}{b}, \frac{c}{d}\right) = \frac{e_{max}}{f_{min}} = \frac{HCF(\,c \,\&\, a)}{LCM\ (b \,\&\, d)}$$

Theorem If d is the greatest common divisor of a and b, then there exist integers x and y such that $d = xa + yb$ and d is the least positive value of $xa + yb$

ILLUSTRATION 58: Find the $G.C.D$ of 6 and 24.

SOLUTION: The $G.C.D$ of 6 and 24 is 6, because 6|6 and 6|24 and every common divisor of 6 and 24 also divides 6. Thus (6, 24) = 6

ILLUSTRATION 59: If $(a, b) = d$, then, prove that $\left(\dfrac{a}{b}, \dfrac{b}{d}\right) = 1$.

SOLUTION: $\because (a, b) = d \therefore d\,|a$ and $d\,|b$ [By definition of gcd].

$\therefore$ There exist integer a_1 and b_1

such that $a = da_1$ (1)

$b = db_1$ (2)

Again $\because$ $(a, b) = d$

There exists integer x and y such that

$ax + by = d$ [By Theorem]

Putting values of a and b from (1) and (2)

$da_1x + db_1y = d$

$(a_1, b_1) = 1$ [by corollary theorem 1]

or $\left(\dfrac{a}{b}, \dfrac{b}{d}\right) = 1$

$\left[\because \text{from (1), } a_1 = \dfrac{a}{d}, \text{ from (2), } b_1 = \dfrac{b}{d}\right]$

Remark: *$(a, b) = d$ and $a = a_1d$, $b = b_1d$, then a_1 and b_1 are coprime i.e., $(a_1, b_1) = 1$.*

ILLUSTRATION 60: If $a \mid bc$ and $(a, b) = 1$, then, prove that $a \mid c$

SOLUTION: $a \mid bc$

There exists an integer d such that $bc = ad$ (1)

$\because$ $(a, b) = 1$

∴ There exist integers m and n such that $am + bn = 1$ (2)

Multiplying both sides of (2) by c, $acm + bcn = c$

putting bc = ad from (1), $acm + adn = c \Rightarrow a(cm + dn) = c \Rightarrow a \mid c$

Note: *$a \mid bc$ and $(a, b) = 1$, then $a \mid c$*

ILLUSTRATION 61: Prove that two consecutive integers are always co-prime.

SOLUTION: Let n and $n + 1$ be two consecutive integers.

Let $(n, n + 1) = d$

∴ $d \mid n + d \mid n + 1$

∴ $d \mid (n + 1) - n$ or $d \mid 1$

∴ $d = 1$

∴ $(n, n + 1) = 1$

i.e., n and $(n + 1)$ are relatively prime.

ILLUSTRATION 62: Show that gcd of $a + b$ and $a - b$ is either 1 or 2 if $(a, b) = 1$.

SOLUTION: Let $(a + b, a - b) = d$

∴ d/$(a + b)$ and d/$(a - b)$

∴ $d/(a + b + a - b)$ and $d/(a + b) - (a - b)$ or $d/2a$ and $d/2b$.

i.e., d is a common divisor of $2a$ and $2b$.

∴ $d/(2a, 2b)$ *[By definition of gcd]*

i.e., $d/2(a, b)$ [∵ $(ma, mb) = m(a, b)$]

But $a, b = 1$

∴ $d/2$

∴ $d = 1$ or $d = 2$.

TEXTUAL EXERCISE–10 (SUBJECTIVE)

1. Find the prime factorization of following numbers and mention the number of their divisors.

(a) 420 (b) 360

(c) 1008 (d) 1800

2. Find the number of divisors and sum of divisors of following numbers.

(a) $q^2.p$ (b) $q^3.p^2$

(c) 180 (d) 216

3. Find the number of even proper divisors and sum of even proper divisors of the following numbers.

(a) 216 (b) 1080

4. Find the least integral multipliers of following numbers, which makes the product a perfect square.

(a) 180 (b) 420

(c) 10500

5. Given $x = 8064$ find

(a) total number of positive integer divisors of x

(b) total number of even natural divisors of x and their sum

(c) total number of divisors of x of the form $4m + 2$.

(d) number and summation of divisors of x, that are divisible by 48.

6. State whether following statements are true/false.

(a) HCF = Product of the smallest power of each common prime factor in the numbers.

(b) LCM = Product of the greatest power of each prime factor, involved in the numbers.

(c) For any two positive integers a and b, HCF (a, b) × LCM $(a, b) = a \times b$.

(d) Product of any number of integers is equal to product of their LCM and their HCF.

7. Find the HCF of 96 and 424 by the prime factorization method. Hence, or otherwise find their LCM.

8. Find the HCF and LCM of 24, 72 and 120, using the prime factorization method.

9. Given that HCF (306, 657) = 9, find LCM (306, 657).

10. Find the LCM of following pairs of fractions:

(a) $\frac{15}{6}$ and $\frac{25}{4}$ (b) $\frac{3}{4}$ and $\frac{5}{6}$

(c) $\frac{3\pi}{4}$ and $\frac{5\pi}{2}$

11. Find the LCM of following pair of numbers:

(a) $2, \sqrt{2}$ (b) $3, \pi$

12. Use Euclid's division algorithm to find the HCF of

(i) 135 and 225 (ii) 198 and 3886

(iii) 196 and 38220 (iv) 867 and 255

13. An army contingent of 504 members is to march behind an army band of 60 members in a parade. The two groups are to march in same number of columns. What is the maximum number of columns in which they can march?

14. State whether following statements are true/false.

(a) If $p|N$ and $q|N$ and GCD$(p, q) = 1$ i.e., they are relatively prime then $pq|N$.

(b) If $q|pN$ and GCD$(p, q) = 1$ then $q|N$.

(c) If $a|N$ and $b|N$ then LCM $(a, b)|N$

(d) For some integers $n \in \mathbb{Z}$ 4^n ends with the digit zero.

15. Prove that if $2^n - 1$ is prime then n should be prime given n is the natural number larger than one but the converse is not necessarily true.

16. Find the number of integer solutions of the equation $mn = 2^3 . 3^2 . 5^4 (m + n)$

17. For every natural number n greater than one prove that $n^4 + 4$ is a composite number.

18. For every pair of natural numbers x and y such that $x^2 - y^2$ is prime prove that $x^2 - y^2 = x + y$.

Answer Keys

1. (a) $2^2.3.5.7;24$ (b) $2^3.3^2.5;24$ (c) $2^4.3^2.7;30$ (d) $2^3.3^2.5^2;36$

2. (a) 6, $(1 + p)(1 + q + q^2)$ (b) 12, $\left(\frac{1-p^3}{1-p}\right)\left(\frac{1-q^4}{1-q}\right)$ (c) 18, 546 (d) 16, 600

3. (a) 11, 344 (b)23, 2040 4. (a) 5 (b) 105 (c) 105

5. (a) 48 (b) 42; 26416 (c) 12 (d) 16; 23040 6. (a) T (b) T (c) T (d) F

7. 8, 5088 8. 24, 360 9. 22338 10. (a) 25/2 (b) 15/2 (c) 15π/2

11. (a) no LCM (b) no LCM 12. (i) 45 (ii) 2 (iii) 196 (iv) 51

13. 12 columns. 14. (a) T (b) T (c) T (d) F 16. 315

■ MATHEMATICAL INDUCTION

Mathematical induction is a tool by which we can prove correctness of any mathematical statement or proposition easily. As the name suggests, it works on the principle of induction i.e., result for higher integer gets induced from the result for lower integers. It is widely used in proving identities, inequalities, divisibility of an expression by another number or by another expression, theorems etc. It involves three steps—**Verification, Induction and Generalization**.

Let $P(n)$ be a statement involving the natural number n. To prove that $P(n)$ is true for all natural numbers n, we prove as follows.

Step I: Prove that $P(m)$ is true for some initial condition i.e., for $m = 1$ or $m = 2$ or for some other natural number.

Step II: Assuming that $P(m)$ is true and show that $P(m + 1)$ is also true. It is important that usually the 2nd step is the most difficult to prove and various mathematical tools may have to be applied for doing this according to the nature of a given question.

Step III: The statement is generalized i.e., $P(n)$ is true for all values of n.

ILLUSTRATION 63: Prove using principle of mathematical induction that $1 + 2 + 3 + ... + n = \frac{n(n+1)}{2}$, $n \in \mathbb{N}$.

SOLUTION: Let $P(n)$ be the statement $P(n)$: $1 = 2 + 3 + 4 + ... + n = \frac{n(n+1)}{2}$

Step I: Consider $P(1)$

LHS = 1 and RHS = $\frac{1(1+1)}{2} = 1$

$P(1)$ is true. (i)

Step II: Assuming $P(k)$ to be true

$P(k)$: $1 + 2 + 3 + ... + k = \frac{k(k+1)}{2}$ (ii)

Consider $p(k + 1) = 1 + 2 + 3 + ... + k + (k + 1)$

$= \frac{k(k \quad 1)}{} + (k + 1)$ *By* $P(k)$ $= (k + 1)\,(k/2 + 1) = \frac{(k+1)(k+2)}{}$

$\therefore$ $P(k + 1)$ is true

Thus we have proved that $P(n)$ is true for $n = k + 1$, if it is true for $n = k$. This can be mathematically written as

$P(k)$ is true $\Rightarrow$ $P(k + 1)$ is true

Put $k = 1 : P(1) \Rightarrow P(2)$

$k = 2 : P(2) \Rightarrow P(3)$

$k = 2 : P(3) \Rightarrow P(4)$

$\vdots$

$k = n - 1 : P(n - 1) \Rightarrow P(n)$

$\vdots$

Thus we observe that $P(n)$ is true $\forall$ $n \in N$

Now, we will see why so called "*proof by generalization*" is not a complete proof. Consider the following table, which can be easily verified.

No. of elements in a set S	No. of subsets of S
1	$2 = 2^1$
2	$4 = 2^2$
3	$8 = 2^3$
4	$16 = 2^4$

Observing the pattern we may reach a conclusion: "If a set contains n elements then it has 2^n subsets". We consider the statement proved. In this case, even though conclusion is true, the "proof" is not a proof at all. It is just generalization. It is possible that even if we verify the statement till n = one million, it may fail at the very next step.

Generalization can be useful only to the extent that it allows us to make a guess about the pattern but it cannot be considered as a proof by itself.

Let us consider the statement "$n^2 + n + 41$ is a prime number." $\forall$ $n \in \mathbb{N}$.

This statement can be verified to be true for n = 1, 2, 3 .... upto 40. If we generalize and say that $n^2 + n + 41$ is always prime, we have made a wrong conclusion, because $41^2 + 41 + 41$ is not prime.

First principle of mathematical induction

The set of statements $\{P(n): n \in N\}$ is true for each natural number $n \geq m$ is provided that:

(a) $P(m)$ is true

(b) $P(k)$ is true for $n = k$, (where $k \geq m$)
$\Rightarrow$ $P(n)$ is true for $n = k + 1$

Working Rule: Let there be a proposition or a mathematical statement namely $P(n)$, involving a natural number n. In order to prove that $P(n)$ is true for all natural numbers $n \geq m$, we proceed as follows.

(a) Verify that $P(m)$ is true

(b) Assume that $P(k)$ is true (where $k \geq m$)

(c) Prove that $P(k + 1)$ is true

Once step – (c) is completed after (a) and (b), we are through. That is $P(n)$ is true for all natural numbers $n \geq m$

ILLUSTRATION 64: Prove using first principle of mathematical induction that $1.3 + 2.4 + 3.5 + ... + n(n + 2) = \frac{1}{6} n (n + 1) (2n + 7) \forall n \in N$

SOLUTION: $P(1) = 1.3 = \frac{1}{6} (1) (1 + 1) (2 + 7) = \frac{1}{6}(1)(2) (9) = 3$

hence true for $n = 1$. Let statement be true for $n = k$

i.e., $1.3 + 2.4 + 3.5 + ... + k (k + 2) = \frac{1}{6} k (k + 1) (2k + 7) \forall k \in N$

Therefore $P(k)$ is true

$P(k + 1) = 1.3 + 2.4 + ... + k (k + 2) + (k + 1)(k + 1 + 2)$

$= P(k) + (k + 1) (k + 3) = \frac{1}{6} k(k + 1) (2k + 7) + (k + 1)(k + 3)$

$= \frac{k+1}{6} \{2k^2 + 7k + 6k + 8\} = \frac{k+1}{6} \{2k^2 + 13k + 8\}$

$= \frac{k+1}{6} \{(k + 2) (2k + 9)\}$ .Hence $P(k + 1)$ is true.

$p(k) \Rightarrow p(k + 1) \Rightarrow$ The assumption is true.

ILLUSTRATION 65: Prove using mathematical induction that you can paste a ticket of price Rs 8 or more using the tickets of Rs 3 and Rs 5 only.

SOLUTION: Let $P(n)$ represents that tickets of Rs n can be pasted using Rs 3 and Rs 5

$P(8)$: Rs 3 + Rs 5 = Rs 8 (a)

$P(9)$: Rs 3 + Rs 3 + Rs 3 = Rs 9 (b)

$P(10)$: Rs 5 + Rs 5 (c)

From (a), (b) and (c) ; $P(8)$, $P(9)$, $P(10)$ are true (d)

Assuming $p(n)$ is true for $n = k - 2$, $k - 1$ and k (e)

Consider $P(k + 1) = \text{Rs } k + 1 = \text{Rs } (k - 2) + Rs\ 3 = P(k - 2) + Rs\ 3$

$\Rightarrow P(k + 1)$ is true

$\therefore$ $P(k - 2)$, $P(k - 1)$

$P(k)$ is true

$\Rightarrow P(k + 1)$ is true (f)

$\therefore$ From (d) and (f) and by principle of Mathematical Induction

$P(n)$ is true $n \geq 8$, $n \in N$.

Second principle of mathematical induction

The set of statements $\{P(n): n \in N\}$ is true for each natural number $n \geq m$ provided that:

(a) $P(m)$ and $P(m + 1)$ are true

(b) $P(n)$ is true for $n \leq k$, (where $k \geq m$)

$\Rightarrow P(n)$ is true for $n = k + 1$

This is also called extended principle of mathematical Induction.

Working rule

(a) Verify that $P(n)$ is true for $n = m$, $n = m + 1$.

(b) Assume that $P(n)$ is true for $n \leq k$ (where $k \geq m$)

(c) Prove that $P(n)$ is true for $n = k + 1$

Once rule (c) is completed after (a) and (b), we are through. That is $P(n)$ is true for all natural numbers $n \geq m$.

This method is to be used when $P(n)$ can be expressed as a combination of $P(n - 1)$ and $P(n - 2)$. In case $P(n)$ turns out to be a combination of $P(n - 1)$, $P(n - 2)$ and $P(n - 3)$, we can verify for $n = m + 2$ also in Rule(a).

ILLUSTRATION 66: Using the mathematical induction prove that, if $x + 1/x$ is an integer, then $x^n + 1/x^n$ is also an integer $\forall\ n \in \mathbb{N}$

SOLUTION: Let $P(n)$ be the statement. $P(n)$: $x^n + 1/x^n$ is an integer for all $n \in \mathbb{N}$

Consider $P(1)$: $x + 1/x$ is an integer which is true, as it is given

$\Rightarrow P(1)$ is true (i)

Assuming $P(n)$ is true $\forall\ 1 \le n \le k$ (ii)

Consider $p(k+1)$: $x^{k+1} + \dfrac{1}{x^{k+1}} = \left(x^k + \dfrac{1}{x^k}\right)\left(x + \dfrac{1}{x}\right) - \left(x^{k-1} + \dfrac{1}{x^{k-1}}\right)$

= (integer by $p(k)$) (integer – given)-integer by $P(k-1)$ = integer

$\Rightarrow P(k+1)$ is true $\therefore P(k)$ is true $\Rightarrow P(k+1)$ is true (iii)

From equation (i) and equation (iii) and by principle of mathematical induction $P(n)$ is true $\forall\ n \in \mathbb{N}$.

ILLUSTRATION 67: Let a, b, q and r are four real numbers such that $a + b = q + r$ and $a^2 + b^2 = q^2 + r^2$. Then prove using principle of mathematical induction that $a^n + b^n = q^n + r^n\ \forall\ n \in \mathbb{N}$.

SOLUTION: $P(n)$: $a^n + b^n = q^n + r^n\ \forall\ n \in \mathbb{N}$

$P(1)$ and $P(2)$ are true (i)

$(a+b)^2 = (q+r)^2$ (*given*) (ii)

$\Rightarrow ab = qr$ ($\because a^2 + b^2 = a^2 + r^2$)

Assuming $P(n)$ is true in the region $3 \le n \le k$ (iii)

Consider $a^{k+1} + b^{k+1} = (a^k + b^k)(a+b) - ab\,(a^{k-1} + b^{k-1})$

$= (q^k + r^k)(q+r) - qr\,(q^{k-1} + r^{k-1})$ (*using result*)

$= q^{k+1} + r^{k+1}$

$\therefore P(k+1)$ is true $\therefore P(k)$ is true $\Rightarrow P(k+1)$ is true (iv)

From (i) and (iv) by principle of Mathematical Induction $P(n)$ is true $\forall\ n \in \mathbb{N}$

ILLUSTRATION 68: Prove using principle of Mathematical Induction that $3^n + 8^n$ is not divisible by 5 $\forall$ n $\in \mathbb{N}$

SOLUTION: Let $P(n)$: $3^n + 8^n$ is not divisible by 5

Consider $n = 1$: $3^1 + 8^1 = 11$ is not divisible by 5

$\therefore P(1)$ is true; Let $3^{k-1} + 8^{k-1}$ is not divisible by 5 (1)

Consider: $3^k + 8^k = 3.3^{k-1} + 8.8^{k-1} = 3\,(3^{k-1} + 8^{k-1}) + 5.8^{k-1}$

which is not divisible by 5

($\because$ of (1) $3^{k-1} + 8^{k-1}$ is not divisible by 5, whereas $5.(8)^{k-1}$ is divisible by 5)

$\Rightarrow 3^{k-1} + 8^{k-1}$ is not divisible by 5

$\Rightarrow 3^k + 8^k$ is not divisible by 5 $\therefore P(k-1)$ is true $\Rightarrow P(k)$ is true (2)

Thus from (1) and (2) and by principle of mathematical induction

$P(n)$ is true $\forall\ n \in \mathbb{N}$

ILLUSTRATION 69: Prove that there can be at the most $n(n-1)$ points of intersections of n straight lines drawn in the plane.

SOLUTION: Check for $n = 1$

Number of points of intersection $= 0$

Check for $n = 2$

Number of points of intersection $= \dfrac{2(2-1)}{2} = 1$

Let number of points of intersection of k lines is at most $P(k) = \dfrac{k(k-1)}{2}$

when $(k + 1)^{th}$ line is drawn, it will add at most k number of new points of intersections by as it may intersect all pre-existing k straight lines.

$$\Rightarrow \; P(k+1) = P(k) + k = \frac{k(k-1)}{2} + k = \frac{k^2 - k + 2k}{2} = \frac{k(k+1)}{2} = \frac{(k^2+1)(k+1-1)^2}{2}$$

Hence $P(k) \Rightarrow P(k + 1)$

ILLUSTRATION 70: Using PMI prove that $\left(\dfrac{a+b}{2}\right)^n \le \dfrac{a^n + b^n}{2} \quad a, b \in \mathbb{R}^+ \;\&\; n \in \mathbb{N}$.

SOLUTION: $P(1) = \dfrac{a+b}{2} \le \dfrac{a+b}{2}$ is clearly true

Let $P(k)$: $\left(\dfrac{a+b}{2}\right)^k \le \dfrac{a^k + b^k}{2}$ is true

For $P(k + 1)$: we have to prove that $\left(\dfrac{a+b}{2}\right)^{k+1} \le \dfrac{a^{k+1} + b^{k+1}}{2}$ is true

From assumption step we know that $\left(\dfrac{a+b}{2}\right)^k \le \left(\dfrac{a^k + b^k}{2}\right)$

$$\Rightarrow \left(\frac{a+b}{2}\right)^{k+1} \le \left(\frac{a^k + b^k}{2}\right)\left(\frac{a+b}{2}\right)$$

$$\Rightarrow \left(\frac{a+b}{2}\right)^{k+1} \le \frac{a^{k+1} + b^{k+1} + a^k b + ab^k}{4} \qquad \text{(i)}$$

$\because \; x \le y \;\&\; y \le z \Rightarrow x \le z$

So to obtain the desired result by applying above property.

Let us consider $\dfrac{a^{k+1} + b^{k+1} + a^k.b + ab^k}{4} \le \dfrac{a^{k+1} + b^{k+1}}{2}$

$$\Rightarrow \; a^{k+1} + b^{k+1} + a^k.b + b^k a \le 2\left(a^{k+1} + b^{k+1}\right)$$

$$\Rightarrow \; a^{k+1} - ab^k + b^{k+1} - ba^k \ge 0$$

$$\Rightarrow \; a\left(a^k - b^k\right) - b\left(a^k - b^k\right) \ge 0$$

$\Rightarrow \; \left(a^k - b^k\right)(a - b) \ge 0$; which is true $\forall \; a, b$.

Because $\forall \; a, b \in \mathbb{R}$; $a > b$ or $a = b$ or $a < b$

If $a \ge b$ *then* $a^k \ge b^k$ & *If* $a \le b$ *then* $a^k \le b^k$

Hence either $(a^k - b^k)$ and $(a - b)$ have same sign, or both zero. In both cases our assumption is true i.e., $\dfrac{a^{k-1} + b^{k+1} + a^k.b + a.b^k}{4} \le \dfrac{a^{k+1} + b^{k+1}}{2}$

$\Rightarrow p(k + 1)$ is true

$\therefore$ From (i) $\left(\dfrac{a+b}{2}\right)^{k+1} \le \dfrac{a^{k+1} + b^{k+1}}{2}$ Hence $p(k) \Rightarrow p\,(k + 1)$

ILLUSTRATION 71: Using PMI Prove that $n^n > (n+1)^{n-1}$ for all $n \geq 2$

SOLUTION: Let the statement $P(n)$ be $P(n)$: $\dfrac{n^n}{(n+1)^{n-1}} > 1 \ \forall n \geq 2$

$\because$ $P(2)$: $\dfrac{2^2}{(2+1)^0} > 1$ is true

let the statement $P(n)$ be true

Now consider $P(n+1)$: $\dfrac{(n+1)^{n+1}}{(n+2)^n} > 1$,

To prove this let us first try to prove: $\dfrac{(n+1)^{n+1}}{(n+2)^n} > \dfrac{n^n}{(n+1)^{n-1}}$

i.e., to prove $\dfrac{(n+1)^n(n+1)}{(n+2)^n} > \dfrac{n^n(n+1)}{(n+1)^n}$

$\Rightarrow \left(\dfrac{n+1}{n+2}\right)^n > \left(\dfrac{n}{n+1}\right)^n$

Since both sides of inequality are positive therefore taking n^{th} root of both side

i.e., to prove $\dfrac{n+1}{n+2} > \dfrac{n}{n+1}$

i.e., to prove $(n+1)^2 > n^2 + 2n$

which is always true hence assumption is true.

$\therefore$ $P(n) \Rightarrow P(n+1)$

ILLUSTRATION 72: Apply PMI to prove that $5^{2^n} - 1$ is divisible by 2^{n+2}

SOLUTION: $P(1)$ is clearly true as $8|24$.

Let $P(n)$ be true i.e. $5^{2^n} - 1 = \lambda(2^{n+2})$

Now $P(n+1) = 5^{2^{n+1}} - 1 = \left(5^{2^n}\right)^2 - 1$.

$= \left(5^{2^n} - 1\right)\left(5^{2^n} + 1\right) = 2^{n+2}(\lambda)\left(5^{2^n} + 1\right)$

Which is clearly divisible by 2^{n+2}.

TEXTUAL EXERCISE–11 (SUBJECTIVE)

1. Using PMI (*Principle of mathematical induction*) prove the following mathematical statements.

(i) $n^3 + (n+1)^3 + (n+2)^3$ is divisible by 9

(ii) $n^3 + 5n$ is divisible by 6.

(iii) Prove by induction that for all $n \in N$, whenever 3^{2n} is divided by 8 the remainder is always 1.

2. Prove by P.M.I, $1.2 + 2.5 + \ldots + n(3n-1) = n^2(n+1)$;

3. Prove by P.M.I, $1.2^2 + 2.3^2 + \ldots + (n-1)n^2 = \dfrac{n(n^2-1)(3n+2)}{12}$ for $n > 1$

4. Prove by P.M.I $\dfrac{1}{1.5} + \dfrac{1}{5.9} + \ldots + \dfrac{1}{(4n-3)(4n+1)} = \dfrac{n}{4n+1}$;

5. Prove by P.M.I $3 + 33 + \ldots + 33....3 = \dfrac{10^{n+1} - 9n - 10}{27}$.

$n \in \mathbb{N}$, *(the left hand side contains n summands)*\

Prove by induction the validity of the following inequalities for all natural $n > 1$:

6. $\dfrac{1}{2} \cdot \dfrac{3}{4} \cdot \dfrac{5}{6} \ldots \dfrac{2n-1}{2n} < \dfrac{1}{\sqrt{3n+1}}$;

7. $\frac{1}{n+1}+\frac{1}{n+2}+...+\frac{1}{2n}>\frac{13}{24}$;

8. $\sqrt{n}<1+\frac{1}{\sqrt{2}}+...\frac{1}{\sqrt{n}}<2\sqrt{n}$

9. Using P.M.I prove that number of persons who have ever lived on earth and have made odd number of hand shakes is always even.

10. Using the principle of mathematical induction, prove that
 (i) $41^n - 14^n$ is a multiple of 27
 (ii) $7^n - 3^n$ is divisible by 4.

11. Prove by the principle of mathematical induction that $n < 2^n\ \forall n \in \mathbb{N}$.

12. Prove by induction of inequality $(1 + x)^n \geq 1 + nx$ whenever x is positive and n is a positive integer.

13. Prove that $1^2 + 2^2 + 3^2 + ... + n^2 > \frac{n^3}{3}\ \forall n \in \mathbb{N}$

14. Prove that $1 + 2 + 3 +... + n < \frac{(2n+1)^2}{8}\ \forall n \in \mathbb{N}$.

15. Prove that $\forall n \in \mathbb{N}$, $10^n + 3.4^{n+2} + 5$ is divisible by 9.

16. Prove by induction that the sum of cubes of three consecutive natural numbers is divisible by 9

17. Using principle of mathematical induction prove that $4^n + 15n - 1$ is divisible by 9 for all natural numbers n.

18. Prove that

 (i) $\left(1+\frac{1}{1}\right).\left(1+\frac{1}{2}\right)...\left(1+\frac{1}{n}\right)=(n+1)\ \forall n \in \mathbb{N}$.

 (ii) $\left(1+\frac{3}{1}\right).\left(1+\frac{5}{4}\right)...\left(1+\frac{2n+1}{n^2}\right)=(n+1)^2\ \forall n \in \mathbb{N}$

Decimal representation of a number

Given a natural number $N=\overline{a_n a_{n-1} a_{n-2}...a_2 a_1 a_0}$ where a_i's are digits from 0 to 9, occupying unit, ten's, hundredth, thousandth, ... places.

So the numerical value of N is defined as,"sum of products of digits multiplied by their corresponding place values".

$$N = a_n \times \underbrace{10^n}_{\substack{\text{place value}\\ n+1^{th}\text{ place}}} ....+a_3 \underbrace{10^3}_{\substack{\text{thousand}^{th}\\ \text{place value}}} + a_2 \times \underbrace{10^2}_{\substack{\text{hundred}^{th}\\ \text{place value}}} + a_1 \times \underbrace{10^1}_{\substack{\text{ten's place}\\ \text{value}}} + a_0 \times \underbrace{10}_{\substack{\text{unit p}\\ \text{value}}}$$

ILLUSTRATION 73: The sum of the digits in a two-digit number is 6. If we add 18 to that number, we get a number consisting of the same digits written in the reverse order. Find the number.

SOLUTION: Consider two digit number $x=\overline{ab}=10a+b$

given a + b = 6 (1)

and $x + 18 = \overline{ba}$

$\Rightarrow 10a + b + 18 = 10b + a$ $\Rightarrow 9(b - a) = 18$

$\Rightarrow b - a = 2$ (2)

solving equations (1) and (2) we get b = 4 and a = 2

so the required number is 24.

Theorem: If an integer x is divided by 10 the remainder is digit at unit place of x.

Proof: $x=\overline{abcde} = a(10^4) + b(10^3) + c(10^2) + d(10) + e$
$= 10m + e \Rightarrow$ Remainder is e

Theorem: The remainder, if an integer x is divided by 5, is $\begin{cases} e & 0 \leq e \leq 4 \\ e-5 & 5 \leq e \leq 9 \end{cases}$

Where e is unit place digit of the number.

Proof: $x=\overline{abcde}$

$= a(10^4) + b(10^3) + c(10^2) + d(10) + e$

$= a(10^4) + b(10^3) + c(10^2) + d(10) + e = 5m + e; 0 \leq e \leq 9$

$= \begin{cases} 5m+e & 0 \leq e \leq 4 \\ 5m+5+e-5 & 5 \leq e \leq 9 \end{cases}$

$= \begin{cases} 5m+e & 0 \leq e \leq 4 \\ 5m_0+(e-5) & 5 \leq e \leq 9 \end{cases}$

Periodic properties of a number

As we know that the unit digit of sum of n integers say x_1, x_2, ... x_n is unit digit of sum of their digits at unit places and also the unit digit of product of these n integers is equal to unit digit of product of their digits at unit places. Application of the above two simple concepts lead to following periodic properties of integers.

1. If a number x having zero/one at its unit place then x^n ends with zero/one at its unit place, where n is any natural number.
2. If a number x having two at its unit place then x^n ends with 2, 4, 8, 6 at its unit place, for $n = 4k + 1, 4k + 2, 4k + 3, 4k$ respectively where k is any whole number.
3. If a number x having three at its unit place then x^n ends with 3, 9, 7, 1 at its unit place, for $n = 4k + 1, 4k + 2, 4k + 3, 4k$ respectively where k is any whole number.
4. If a number x having four at its unit place then x^n ends with 4, 6 at its unit place, for $n = 2k + 1, 2k + 2$ respectively where k is any whole number.
5. If a number x having five at its unit place then x^n ends with 5 at its unit place, $\forall\ n \in \mathbb{N}$ number.
6. If a number x having six at its unit place then x^n ends with 6 at its unit place, for all $n \in \mathbb{N}$ number.
7. If a number x having seven at its unit place then x^n ends with 7, 9, 3, 1 at its unit place, for $n = 4k + 1, 4k + 2, 4k + 3, 4k$ respectively where k is any whole number.
8. If a number x having eight at its unit place then x^n ends with 8, 4, 2, 6 at its unit place, for $n = 4k + 1, 4k + 2, 4k + 3, 4k$ respectively where k is any whole number.
9. If a number x having nine at its unit place then x^n ends with 9, 1 at its unit place, for $n = 2k + 1, 2k + 2$ respectively where k is any whole number.

NOTE

1. *Square of any integer can never have* 2, 3, 7, 8, *at its unit place.*
2. *Fourth power of any integer can have only* 0, 1, 5 *and* 6 *at its unit place.*

ILLUSTRATION 74: Find the digit at units place of following numbers:

(a) 1999^{1996} (b) 1999^{1997}

(c) 1947^{1947} (d) 1947^{1948}

(e) 1947^{1949} (f) 2^{2003}

(g) $(2^4)^{2^6}$

SOLUTION: (a) unit place of the base is 9 and $1996 = 2k + 2$ $\quad\therefore$ digit at unit place = 1

(b) unit place of the base is 9 and $1997 = 2k + 1$ $\quad\therefore$ digit at unit place = 9

(c) unit place of the base is 7 and $1947 = 4k + 3$ $\quad\therefore$ digit at unit place = 3

(d) unit place of the base is 7 and $1948 = 4k + 4$ $\quad\therefore$ digit at unit place = 1

(e) unit place of the base is 7 and $1949 = 4k + 1$ $\quad\therefore$ digit at unit place = 7

(f) unit place of the base is 2 and $2003 = 4k + 3$ $\quad\therefore$ digit at unit place = 8

(g) unit place of the base is 6 and $256 = 4k + 4$ $\quad\therefore$ digit at unit place = 6

ILLUSTRATION 75: Find the remainder when following numbers are divided by 2, 5, 10.

(a) $17^{19} + 19^{17}$ (b) $19^9 + 9^{19}$

(c) $13^7 + 17^3$ (d) $99^{22} + 77^{22} + 33^{31} + 88^{31}$

SOLUTION: (a) Since 17^{19} ends with 3 at unit place and 19^{17} ends with 9 at unit place, therefore the summation will end with 2 at its unit place. So, the remainder will be 0, 2, 2 when it is divided by 2, 5, 10 respectively.

(b) Since 19^9 ends with 9 at unit place and 9^{19} ends with 9 at unit place, therefore the summation will end with 8 at its unit place. So, the remainder will be 0, 3, 8 when it is divided by 2, 5, 10 respectively

(c) Since 13^7 ends with 7 at unit place and 17^3 ends with 3 at unit place, therefore the summation will end with 0 at its unit place. *So*, the remainder will be 0, 0, 0 when it is divided by 2, 5, 10 respectively.

(d) Since 99^{22} ends with 1 at unit place, 77^{22} ends with 9 at unit place, 33^{31} ends with 7 at unit place and 88^{31} ends with 2 at unit place, therefore the summation will end with 9 at its unit place. *So*, the remainder will be 1, 4, 9 when it is divided by 2, 5, 10 respectively.

ILLUSTRATION 76: Find the last digit of the number $9^{(9^9)^n}$ and of the number $2^{(3^4)}$

SOLUTION: Every even power of 9 can be represented in the form $9^{2n} = 81^n = \underbrace{81.81....81}_{n\,times}$ and, consequently, its last digit is 1. Every odd power of 9 can be written in the form $9^{2n+1} = 9.81^n$, and therefore its last digit is 9 (because such a power is the product of a number whose last digit is 1 by the number 9). In particular, $9^{(9^9)}$ is an odd power of 9, and consequently the last digit of $9^{(9^9)}$ is equal to 9. Now we note that any integral power of 6 ends with the digit 6; indeed, we have $6^1 = 6$, and 6^n ends with 6 then the last digit of $6^{n+1} = 6^n.6$ is also equal to 6. Further, the last digit of 16^n and 6^n coincide, and consequently any integral power of 2 with an exponent multiple of 4 ends with 6 (because $2^{4n} = 16^n$). But $3^4 - 1$ is divisible by $3 + 1 = 4$ and consequently, $2^{(3^4-1)}$ ends with the digit 6 while the last digit of $2^{3^4} = 2.\ 2^{(3^4-1)}$ is 2 (because this expression is the product of a number whose last digit is 6 by 2).

ILLUSTRATION 77: The product of 90 integers is equal to 1. Show that their sum cannot be zero

SOLUTION: Let $x_1, x_2, ..., x_{90}$ be such integer such that $x_1 . x_2 . x_3 .... x_{90} = 1$

Since product of two integers is one then they can be either both 1 or both –1

for instance if $x.y = 1$ then $y = 1/x$ and it is very true that only 1 and –1 have their multiplicative inverse as integer. Hence, $x_1 . x_2 . x_3 .... x_{90} = 1$

$x_k \in \{-1, 1\}$ and even number of these integers can be –1.

so as the product gets positive value.

Now $x_1 + x_2 + ... + x_{90} = 0$ is possible if 45 integers out of x_i's are 1 and rest 45 are –1 which contradicts the initial hypothesis i.e., product of all 90 integers is 1.

ILLUSTRATION 78: Find the integers x and y satisfying the equation $x^2 + y^2 + 2xy = 24973$.

SOLUTION: Given $x^2 + y^2 + 2xy = 24973$.

$\Rightarrow$ $(x + y)^2 = 24973$. where x and y are integers

which is not possible because square of any integer can never have 2, 3, 8, 7 at their unit place.

ILLUSTRATION 79: Find the number of integer solutions of equation $1! + 2! + 3! + ... + 15! = x^2$.

SOLUTION: $\because$ $k!$ is divisible by 10 $\forall\ k \geq 5$ therefore $5! + 6! + ... + 15! = 10\lambda$

$\Rightarrow$ $1! + 2! + 3! + 4! + 5! + ... + 15! = 10\lambda + 33 = 10(\lambda + 3) + 3$

which has 3 at unit place so can't be perfect square

Hence no integer solution for x.

Divisibility and concepts of divisibility

Decimal representation Decimal representation of a number x where $N = \overline{a_n a_{n-1} a_{n-2} \ldots a_2 a_1 a_0}$ (here a_i's are digits from 0 to 9) is defined as

$N = a_n(10^n) + a_{n-1}(10^{n-1}) + a_{n-2}(10^{n-2}) + \ldots + a_2(10^2) + a_1(10^1) + a_0(10^0)$

Also we know that, an integer x is said to divide an integer y if there exists an integer z such that $xz = y$. If x divides y, we can also say that x is a divisor (or factor) of y or that, y is a multiple of x. Each of these facts is often written as $x \mid y$. If x is not *a* divisor of y, we write x/y.

Above mentioned facts can be used to derive the condition of divisibility of a number $N (= a_n a_{n-1} a_{n-2} \ldots a_3 a_2 a_1$; where a_i's are digits of the number N.) by 2, 3, 4, 5, ... etc., as well as to solve other problems involving digits of a number.

Tests of divisibility

1. **Divisibility by 2:** A number N is divisible by 2 if and only if its last digit is divisible by 2. (i.e., even)

   Proof: Writing $N = a_n 10^n + a_{n-1} 10^{n-1} + .. + a_0$ as $(a_n 10^n + a_{n-1} 10^{n-1} + \ldots + 10a_1) + a_0$ we immediately get the result.

2. **Divisibility by 3:** A number N is divisible by 3 if and only if the sum of all digits are divisible by 3.

   Proof: Writing $N = \{a_n(10^n - 1) + a_{n-1}(10^{n-1} - 1) + .. + a_1(10 - 1)\} + (a_n + a_{n-1} + a_{n-2} + \ldots + a_0)$. Since $10^n - 1, 10^{n-1} - 1, \ldots$ are all divisible by 3, therefore N is divisible by 3 if and only if $a_n + a_{n-1} + .. + a_0$ is divisible by 3.

3. **Divisibility by 4:** A number N is divisible by 4 if its units digit plus twice its ten's digit is divisible by 4.

   Proof: Writing $N = a_n 10^n + a_{n-1} 10^{n-1} + .. + a_2.100) + (a_1.10 + a_0)$

   $= 4.k + 8a_1 + 2a_1 + a_0$. So n is divisible by 4 iff $2a_1 + a_0$ is divisible by 4

4. **Divisibility by 5:** A number N is divisible by 5 if and only if its last digit is divisible by 5 (i.e., if it ends in 0 or 5)

   Proof: Writing $N = (a_n 10^n + a_{n-1} 10^{n-1} + . + a_1.10) + a_0 = 10k + a_0$.

5. **Divisibility by 6:** A number N is divisible by 6 if and only if its units's digit is even and the sum of its digits is divisible by 3

   Proof: N is divisible by 6 if it is divisible by 2 and 3 both.

6. **Divisibility by 7:** A number N is divisible by 7 if and only if 3 × unit's digit + 2 × ten's digit – 1 × hundred's digit – 3 × thousand's digit –2 × ten thousand's digit + 1 × hundred thousand's digit is divisible by 7.

   i.e., $3(a_0) + 2(a_1) - 1(a_2) - 3(a_3) - 2(a_4) + 1(a_5) + 3(a_6) + \ldots$ is divisible by 7.

   i.e., If there are more digits present in the sequence of multipliers 3, 2, – 1, – 3, – 2, 1 is repeated as often necessary.

7. **Divisibility by 8:** A number N is divisible by 8 if and only if its units's digit + 2 × ten's digit + 4 × hundred's digit is divisible by 8

   Proof: Writing $N = a_n 10^n + a_{n-1} 10^{n-1} + .. + a_3.1000) + (a_2.100 + a_1.10 + a_0)$

   $= 8k + 96a_2 + 4a_2 + 8a_1 + 2a_1 + a_0 = 8k_0 + 4a_2 + 2a_1 + a_0$

8. **Divisibility by 9:** A number N is divisible by 9 if and only if the sum of its digits are divisible by 9

   Proof: Writing $N = \{a_n(10^n - 1) + a_{n-1}(10^{n-1} - 1) + .. + a_1(10 - 1)\} + (a_n + a_{n-1} + a_{n-2} + \ldots + a_1 + a_0)$

9. **Divisibility by 10:** A number N is divisible by 10 if and only if the last digit is 0

10. **Divisibility by 11:** N is divisible by 11 if and only if the difference between the sum of the digits in the odd places (starting from the right) and the sum of the digits in the even places (starting from the right) is a multiple of 11 e.g., 1221, 123321, 2783 etc.

    Proof: As we know that $10 \equiv -1$ (mod. 11),

    $10^2 \equiv 1$ (mod 11), $10^3 \equiv -1$(mod.11),

    $\Rightarrow 10^n \equiv (-1)^n$ (mod.11)

    so that $a_n 10^n + a_{n-1} 10^{n-1} + a_{n-2} 10^{n-2} + \ldots a_1. 10 + a_0$

    $\equiv a_n(-1)^n + a_{n-1}(-1)^{n-1} + a_{n-2}(-1)^{n-2} + \ldots + (-1)a_1 + a_0$ (mod.11)

    $\equiv [(a_0 + a_2 + a_4 + ..) - (a_1 + a_3 + a_5 + \ldots)]$ (mod.11)

    i.e., N is divisible by 11 if and only if $(a_0 + a_2 + a_4 + ..) - (a_1 + a_3 + a_5 + \ldots)$ is a multiple of 11.

12. **Divisibility by 13:** *A* number N is divisible by 13 if and only if 10 × units's digit – 4 × ten's digit – 1 × hundred's digit + 3 × thousand's digit + 4 × ten thousand's digit + 1 × hundred thousand's digit is divisible by 13. (*If there are more digits present, the sequence of multipli*ers 10, – 4, – 1, 3, 4, 1 *is repeated as often as necessary*)

Properties of divisibility Let a, b, c, p, q be arbitrary integers. Divisibility has the following properties:

(a) $a \mid a$ provided $a \neq 0$ *(reflexive property)*
(b) If $a \mid b$ and $b \mid c$, then $a \mid c$ *(transitive property)*
(c) If $a \mid b$, then $ca \mid cb$. $c \neq 0$ *(multiplication property)*
(d) $1 \mid a$ *(property of 1)*
(e) $a \mid 0$ *(divisibility property of zero)*
(f) If $a \mid b$ and $a \neq 0$, then (b/a).
(g) $a \mid b$ and $b \neq 0 \Rightarrow |a| \leq |b|$.
(h) $a \mid b$ and $b \mid a \Rightarrow |a| = |b|$
(i) If $a \mid b$ and $a \mid c$, then $a \mid (pb + qc)$ *(linearity property)*
(j) If $ca \mid cb$, and $c \neq 0$, then $a \mid b$. *(cancellation law)*

ILLUSTRATION 80: Test whether the integer 3201828 is divisible by 7 or not.

SOLUTION: Clearly $(3 \times 8) + (2 \times 2) + (-1 \times 8) + (-3 \times 1) + (-2 \times 0) + (1 \times 2) + (3 \times 3) = 24 + 4 - 8 + (-3) + 0 + (2) + 9 = 28$
since 28 is divisible by 7 so the given no. is divisible by 7.

ILLUSTRATION 81: Derive the condition that a three digit number $N = \overline{abc}$ is divisible by 7 if $-a + 2b + 3c$, is divisible by 7.

SOLUTION: Let N be a three digit number with digits a, b and c, then $N = 100a + 10b + c$
From the sum required by the test call it $S = -a + 2b + 3c$
Then $2S = -2a + 4b + 6c$. And $N + 2S = 98a + 14b + 7c = 7(14a + 2b + c)$
The sum $N + 2S$ is, therefore a multiple of 7, say $7M$. Now if N is multiple of 7, say $7P$,
then $2S = 7M - 7P = 7(M - P)$, and it follows from here that S must also be divisible by 7.
If conversely, S is multiple of 7, say $7Q$, then
$N = 7M - 14Q = 7(M - 2Q)$. It show that N must be a multiple of 7

ILLUSTRATION 82: Prove that the number $10^{30} + 10^{27} + 10^{24} + 10^{21} + 23$ is divisible by 3 as well as 9.

SOLUTION: $10^{30} + 10^{27} + 10^{24} + 10^{21} + 23 = (10^{30} - 1) + (10^{27} - 1) + (10^{24} - 1) + (10^{21} - 1) + 23 + 4$
$= 9k_1 + 9k_2 + 9k_3 + 9k_4 + 27$

$$\left\{\begin{array}{l}\because\ 10^n - 1 = (10)^n - (1)^n \text{ is divisible by } 10 - 1 = 9 \\ \text{or } 10^n - 1 = 999 - 9\ (n \text{ times})\end{array}\right\}$$

$= 9(k_1 + k_2 + k_3 + k_4 + 3)$
which is divisible by 3 as well as by 9.

ILLUSTRATION 83: If the number $\overline{2567X092513Y6}$ is divisible by 99, then find all possible pairs of digits (X, Y).

SOLUTION: Sum of even place digits $= S_E = y + 15$
Sum of odd place digits $= S_O = X + 31$
Sum of all digits $= S_O + S_E = X + y + 46$
As the number is divisible by 99, $S_E = S_O$ must be divisible by 11
i.e., $S_E - S_O = 11k;\ k \in \mathbb{Z}$
$X - y + 16 = 11k\ ;\ k \in \mathbb{Z}$
Now, $X, y \in [0, 9]$ and $X, Y \in \mathbb{Z}$
$\Rightarrow X - y \in [-9, 9]$ and $X - Y \in \mathbb{Z}$
$\Rightarrow X - y + 16 \in [8, 25]$ and $X - y + 16 = 11k;\ k \in \mathbb{Z}$
$\Rightarrow X - y + 16 = 11$ or 22 $\quad \Rightarrow X - y = -5$ or 6

Aliter: $S_O + S_E = X + y + 46$ must be divisible by 9

But $X + y \in [0, 18]$

$\Rightarrow X + y + 46 \in [46, 64]$ and divisible by 9

$\Rightarrow X + y + 46 = 54$ or 63 $\Rightarrow X + y = 8$ or 17

$\therefore X - y = -5$ or 6 and $X + y = 8$ or 17 $\Rightarrow X = 7, y = 1$

$\therefore$ (7, 1) is the only possible ordered pair.

ILLUSTRATION 84: Find the number of natural numbers of the type $\overline{2x35y}$ that are divisible by

(a) 3 (b) 6 (c) 4 (d) 8

when repetition of digit is allowed $x, y \in \{0, 1, 2, ..., 9\}$

SOLUTION: (a) If $3|\overline{2x35y} \Rightarrow 3|2 + x + 3 + y + 5 \Rightarrow 3|x + y + 1$

$\Rightarrow$ If $x = 0, 3, 6, 9$ then $3|y + 1$ so $y = 2, 5, 8$

and if $x = 1, 4, 7$ then $3|y + 2$ so $y = 1, 4, 7$

and if $x = 2, 5, 8$ then $3|y$ so $y = 0, 3, 6$

$\Rightarrow$ number of natural numbers $= 3(4 + 3 + 3) = 30$

(b) If $6|\overline{2x35y} \Rightarrow 2|\overline{2x35y}$ and $3|\overline{2x35y}$

$\Rightarrow$ out of 30 numbers divisible by 3 ; those divisible by 2

(i.e. $y = 2$) must also be divisible by 6.

$\Rightarrow$ Number of such number $= 4(2) + 3(1) + 3(2) = 17$

(c) $4|\overline{2x35y} \Rightarrow 4|\overline{5y} \Rightarrow 4|50 + y \Rightarrow 4|2 + y$

$\Rightarrow$ y = 2, 6 and for each of these values of y, x can take 10 possible values from {0, 1, ..., 9}

number of required numbers = 20

(d) $8|\overline{2x35y} \Rightarrow 8|\overline{35y}$

$\Rightarrow 8|350 + y \Rightarrow 8|344 + 6 + y$

$\Rightarrow 8|y + 6$

$\Rightarrow$ y = 2, only for $y = 2$; x can have 10 possible values

$\Rightarrow$ number of desired numbers = 10

TEXTUAL EXERCISE–12 (SUBJECTIVE)

1. Find the digit at unit place in the following:
   (a) $(332)^{4024}$ (b) $(123)^{216}$
   (c) $(5244)^{122}$ (d) $(4127)^{85}$
   (e) $(3285)^{885}$ (f) $(1579)^{2019}$
   (g) $(1989)^{2009}$ (h) 2^{2010}
   (i) 7777^{777}
2. Find the last digit of the number $33^{1131} + 33^{1141} + 33^{1151} + 33^{1161}$.
3. Find the remainder of 2^{1000} when divided by 5, 10.
4. Find the remainder when the following numbers are divided by 2, 5, 10.
   (a) 763^{1995} (b) $2222^{5555} + 5555^{2222}$
   (c) $777^{997} + 999^{776}$ (d) $777^{117} + 117^{777}$
   (e) $319^{1999} + 1111^{1999}$ (f) $(3233)^{120} + (5284)^{889}$
5. What digit should be placed instead of c in the number $\overline{280c}$ to obtain a number multiple of
   (a) 2 (b) 3
   (c) 4 (d) 5
   (e) 6 (f) 9
   (g) 10
6. Find the number of natural numbers of type $\overline{123AB}$, which are divisible by :-

(a) 2 (b) 3
(c) 4 (d) 5
(e) 6

7. (i) If we multiply a certain two-digit number by the sum of its digits, we get 405. If we multiply the number consisting of the same digits written in the reverse order by the sum of its digits, we get 486. Find the number.
   (ii) Find three numbers, the second of which is as much greater than the first as the third is greater than the second, if the product of the two smaller numbers is 85 and the product of the two larger numbers is 115.

8. Prove that $\overline{abcd}+\overline{bcda}+\overline{cdab}+\overline{dabc}$ is divisible by $\overline{1111}$.

9. State which of the following is true:
   (a) $\overline{222222}$ is divisible by 3 and 6 both.
   (b) Any five digit number which is made of the digits 1, 2, 3, 4, 5 without repletion is always divisible by 3.
   (c) $\overline{222222222}$ is divisible by 3, 6 and 9.
   (d) If a prime number p divides a^2 then p also divides a (where a is natural number.)
   (e) The sum/product of any two natural number has the same remainder when divided by 3 as the sum product of their remainders.

10. Find the number of the numbers of the following type (1st digit is non-zero).
   (a) $\overline{523ab}$ which are even.
   (b) $\overline{x2ab}$ which are even.
   (c) $\overline{432x}$ which are odd.
   (d) $\overline{432x}$ which are divisible by 3.
   (e) $\overline{x432}$ which are divisible by 3.
   (f) $\overline{5x012}$ and divisible by 3.

   when repetition of digits is allowed.

11. Prove that the sum $10^{13} + 5$ is divisible by 3.

12. Show that $2^{2^n} - 3$ where $n \geq 2$ always ends with 3 at unit place.

13. Find all numbers of the form $\overline{34A5B}$ which are divisible by
   (a) 24 (b) 36.

14. Consider a number $X = \overline{21A42B4}$. Find the number of ordered pairs (A, B) so that the number 'N is divisible by 22.

Answer Keys

1. (a) 6 (b) 1 (c) 6 (d) 7 (e) 5 (f) 9 (g) 9 (h) 4 (i) 7
2. 0
3. 1, 6 4. (a) 1, 2, 7 (b) 1, 3, 3 **(c)** 0, 3, 8 (d) 0, 4, 4 (e) 0, 0, 0 (f) 1, 0, 5
5. (a) 0, 2, 4, 6, 8 (b) 2, 5, 8 (c) 0, 4, 8 (d) 0, 5 (e) 2, 8 (f) 8 (g) 0
6. (a) 50 (b) 34 (c) 25 (d) 20 (e) 17 7. (i) 45 (ii) 17/2, 10, 23/2
9. (a) T (b) T (c) T (d) T (e) T 10. (a) 50 (b) 450 (c) 5 (d) 4 (e) 3 (f) 3
13. (a) 34056, 34152, 34656, 34752 (b) 34452, 34056, 34956
14. 9

■ RATIO AND PROPORTION

Ratio is a rational quantity between two quantities, that tells us what multiple/part, one quantity is of the other. Therefore if x and y are two quantities of the same kind, then their ratio is x:y which may be denoted by x/y (*This may be an integer or fraction*)

1. *A* ratio may be represented in a number of ways e.g., $\frac{x}{y}=\frac{mx}{my}=\frac{nx}{ny}=.....$ where m, n.....are non-zero numbers.
2. To compare two or more ratios, always reduce them to a common denominator.
3. Ratio of two fractions may be represented as the ratio of two integers.

   E.g, $\frac{x}{y}:\frac{z}{u}:\frac{x/y}{z/u}=\frac{xu}{yz}$ or xu:yz
4. Ratios are compounded by taking their product i.e., $\frac{x}{y}.\frac{z}{u}.\frac{v}{w}$ .... $=\frac{x.z.v}{y.u.w}$.
5. **Duplicate/Triplicate ratio:** If x:y is any ratio then its duplicate ratio is x^2: y^2; triplicate ratio is x^3: y^3 ....etc.

   If x:y is any ratio, then its sub-duplicate ratio is $x^{1/2}$: $y^{1/2}$; sub triplicate ratio is $x^{1/3}$: $y^{1/3}$ etc.

PROPORTION

When two ratios a/b and c/d are equal, then the four quantities composing them are said to be proportional.
If a,b,c,d are proportional then $a/b = c/d$, and it is written as $a:b = c:d$ or $a:b :: c: d$.

1. 'a' and 'd' are known as extremes whereas 'b and c' are called as means.
2. Product of extremes = product of means

Some important applications of proportion

If four a,b,c,d are proportional then many other useful proportions can be derived using various laws of fraction which are extremely useful in mathematical calculations and simplifications.

Invertando If $a:b = c:d$, then $b:a = d:c$

Alternando If $a:b = c:d$ then $a:c = b:d$

Componendo If $a:b = c:d$, then $\frac{a+b}{b} = \frac{c+d}{d}$

$\because \frac{a}{b} = \frac{c}{d}$ adding one to both side $\frac{a}{b}+1 = \frac{c}{d}+1$

$\Rightarrow \frac{a+b}{b} = \frac{c+d}{d}$

Dividendo If $a:b = c:d$, then $\frac{a-b}{b} = \frac{c-d}{d}$

$\because \frac{a}{b} = \frac{c}{d}$ subtracting one to both side $\frac{a}{b}-1 = \frac{c}{d}-1$

$\Rightarrow \frac{a-b}{b} = \frac{c-d}{d}$

Componendo and dividendo: If $a:b = c:d$, then applying both componendo and dividendo operations together, we get, $\frac{a+b}{a-b} = \frac{c+d}{c-d}$.

If $\frac{a}{b} = \frac{c}{d} = \frac{e}{f} = \ldots$ (say $= \lambda$) then

$$\lambda = \frac{a+c+e+\ldots}{b+d+f+\ldots.} = \frac{\text{Sum of the numerators}}{\text{Sum of the denominators}}$$

If $\frac{a}{b} = \frac{c}{d} = \frac{e}{f}$ (say $= \lambda$) then $\frac{xa+yc+ze+\ldots.}{xb+yd+zf+\ldots.}$

If, $\frac{a}{b} = \frac{c}{d} = \frac{e}{f}$ (say $= \lambda$) then $\left(\frac{xa^n+yc^n+ze^n}{xb^n+yd^n+zf^n}\right)^{1/n}$

ILLUSTRATION 85: If $\frac{x+y}{3} = \frac{y+z}{5} = \frac{z+x}{4}$ then find the ratio $x : y : z$.

Hence find the value of expression $\frac{17(x^3+y^3+z^3)}{2x^2y-y^2z+3z^2x}$

SOLUTION: Let $\frac{x+y}{3} = \frac{y+z}{5} = \frac{z+x}{4} = \lambda = \frac{\text{sum of the numerators}}{\text{Sum of the denominators}} = \frac{2(x+y+z)}{12} = \frac{x+y+z}{6}$

$$\Rightarrow \lambda = \frac{(x+y+z)-(x+y)}{6-3} = \frac{z}{3} = \frac{(x+y+z)-(y+z)}{6-5} = \frac{x}{1} = \frac{(x+y+z)-(x+z)}{6-4} = \frac{y}{2}$$

$$\Rightarrow \frac{x}{1} = \frac{y}{2} = \frac{z}{3} \Rightarrow x:y:z = 1:2:3$$

$$\Rightarrow x = \lambda, y = 2\lambda, z = 3\lambda$$

$$\therefore \frac{17(x^3+y^3+z^3)}{2x^2y-y^2z+3z^2x} = \frac{17(1+8+27)\lambda^3}{\lambda^3(2-12+27)} = 36.$$

ILLUSTRATION 86: Given a, b, c, d, e, f in continued proportion i.e., $\frac{a}{b} = \frac{c}{d} = \frac{e}{f}$, then prove that

$$\frac{a^3b+2c^2e-3ae^2f}{b^4+2d^2f-3bf^3} = \frac{ace}{bdf}.$$

SOLUTION: Consider $\frac{a}{b}=\frac{c}{d}=\frac{e}{f}=\lambda$ then $a = b\lambda$, $c = d\lambda$, $e = f\lambda$;

Now $\frac{a^3b+2c^2e-3ae^2f}{b^4+2d^2f-3bf^3}=\frac{b^4\lambda^3+2d^2f\lambda^3-3bf^3\lambda^3}{b^4+2d^2f-3bf^3}=\lambda^3=\frac{a}{b}\times\frac{c}{d}\times\frac{e}{f}=\frac{ace}{bdf}$.

ILLUSTRATION 87: If $x(b+c)=y(c+a)=z(a+b)$, then show that

(a) $\frac{x-y}{a^2-b^2}=\frac{y-z}{b^2-c^2}=\frac{z-x}{c^2-a^2}$

(b) $\frac{(b-c)(y-z)}{b+c}=\frac{(c-a)(z-x)}{c+a}=\frac{(a-b)(x-y)}{a+b}$

SOLUTION: Given proportion can also be expressed as $\frac{b+c}{1/x}=\frac{c+a}{1/y}=\frac{a+b}{1/z}=k$ (1)

$$\Rightarrow k=\frac{(c+a)-(b+c)}{\frac{1}{y}-\frac{1}{x}}=\frac{(a+b)-(a+c)}{\frac{1}{z}-\frac{1}{y}}=\frac{(b+c)-(a+b)}{\frac{1}{x}-\frac{1}{z}}$$

$$=\frac{a-b}{\frac{x-y}{xy}}=\frac{b-c}{\frac{y-z}{yz}}=\frac{c-a}{\frac{z-x}{zx}}=k \quad (2)$$

Compounding the ratios from (1) and (2), we get $\frac{a^2-b^2}{\frac{x-y}{xyz}}=\frac{b^2-c^2}{\frac{y-z}{xyz}}=\frac{c^2-a^2}{\frac{z-x}{xyz}}$

$\Rightarrow \frac{a^2-b^2}{x-y}=\frac{b^2-c^2}{y-z}=\frac{c^2-a^2}{z-x}$. $\Rightarrow \frac{x-y}{a^2-b^2}=\frac{y-z}{b^2-c^2}=\frac{z-x}{c^2-a^2}$

Applying Intervened for ratios in equation (2)

$$\frac{\left(\frac{x-y}{xy}\right)}{a-b}=\frac{\left(\frac{y-z}{yz}\right)}{b-c}=\frac{\left(\frac{z-x}{zx}\right)}{c-a}=\frac{1}{k} \quad (3)$$

Dividing the ratios from (1) and (3), we get

$\frac{b-c}{b+c}=\frac{xyz}{y-z},\frac{c-a}{c+a}=\frac{xyz}{z-x}$ and $\frac{a-b}{a+b}=\frac{xyz}{x-y}$

$$\Rightarrow \frac{(b-c)(y-z)}{b+c}=\frac{(c-a)(z-x)}{c+a}=\frac{(a-b)(x-y)}{a+b}$$

ILLUSTRATION 88: If $\frac{x}{1}=\frac{y}{2}=\frac{z}{3}$; prove that $\frac{x^2+1}{x+1}+\frac{y^2+4}{y+2}+\frac{z^2+9}{z+9}=\frac{(x+y+z)^2+36}{x+y+z+6}$.

SOLUTION: Let $\frac{x}{1}=\frac{y}{2}=\frac{z}{3}=\lambda$, so that $x = \lambda$, $y = 2\lambda$, $z = 3\lambda$;

then $\frac{x^2+1}{x+1}=\frac{\lambda^2+1}{\lambda+1}$

$$\because \frac{x^2+1}{x+1}+\frac{y^2+4}{y+2}+\frac{z^2+9}{z+3}=\frac{(\lambda^2+1)}{\lambda+1}+\frac{(\lambda^2+1)2}{\lambda+1}+\frac{(\lambda^2+1)3}{\lambda+1}$$

$$=\frac{6(\lambda^2+1)}{\lambda+1}=\frac{36\lambda^2+36}{6\lambda+6}=\frac{(\lambda+2\lambda+3\lambda)^2+36}{\lambda+2\lambda+3\lambda+6}=\frac{(x+y+z)^2+36}{x+y+z+6}.$$

ILLUSTRATION 89: Solve: $\frac{\sqrt{1+x^2}+\sqrt{1-x^2}}{\sqrt{1+x^2}-\sqrt{1-x^2}}=3$

SOLUTION: Given $\frac{\sqrt{1+x^2}+\sqrt{1-x^2}}{\sqrt{1+x^2}-\sqrt{1-x^2}}=3$ using componendo and dividendo,

$$\frac{\left(\sqrt{1+x^2}+\sqrt{1-x^2}\right)+\left(\sqrt{1+x^2}-\sqrt{1-x^2}\right)}{\left(\sqrt{1+x^2}+\sqrt{1-x^2}\right)-\left(\sqrt{1+x^2}-\sqrt{1-x^2}\right)}=\frac{3+1}{3-1}$$

(i.e.), $\frac{\sqrt{1+x^2}}{\sqrt{1-x^2}}=\frac{4}{2}$

Squaring, $\frac{1+x^2}{1-x^2}=\frac{4}{1}$ and again applying componendo and dividendo

$$x^2=\frac{3}{5}\Rightarrow\sqrt{x^2}=\sqrt{\frac{3}{5}}\Rightarrow|x|=\sqrt{\frac{3}{5}}\Rightarrow x=\pm\sqrt{\frac{3}{5}}$$

LINEAR EQUATIONS

An expression $y = ax + b$ where a and $b \in \mathbb{R}$ is called as linear polynomial function of x, y and set of points (x, y) satisfying the above relations if plotted on x-y plane, the graph obtained is a straight line e.g., $y = 2x + 3$ has solutions (0,3), (–1, 1) (–3/2, 0), (1, 5), the graph of equation is shown in the figure.

An equation of the type $ax + by + c = 0$ is termed as linear equation in x and y.

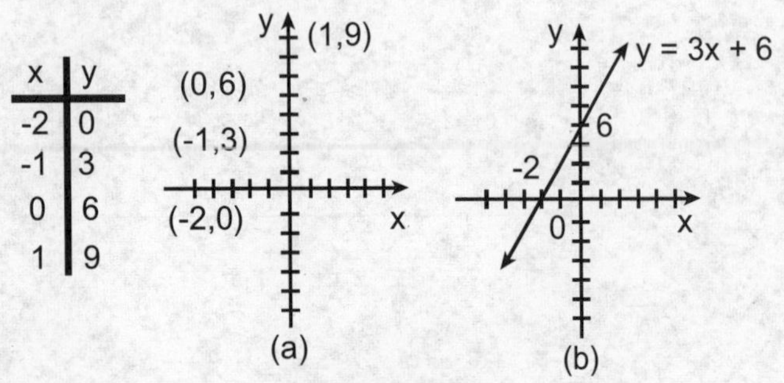

FIGURE 1.41

Solving simultaneous linear equations in two unknowns

To solve a pair of linear equation

$$a_1x + b_1y = c_1 \qquad \text{(i)}$$

$$a_2x + b_2y = c_2 \qquad \text{(ii)}$$

following three approaches are possible

Method of comparison

From both equations find the value of any one variable say y in terms of other i.e., x.

$$y=\frac{c_1-a_1x}{b_1}=\frac{c_2-a_2x}{b_2}\Rightarrow\frac{c_1}{b_1}-\frac{c_2}{b_2}=\left(\frac{a_1}{b_1}-\frac{a_2}{b_2}\right)x$$

$$\Rightarrow \frac{b_2c_1-b_1c_2}{a_1b_2-a_2b_1}$$ and similarly, we get

$$y=\frac{a_2c_1-a_1c_2}{b_1a_2-a_1b_2}$$

ILLUSTRATION 90: Find the point of intersection of two straight lines $2x - y + 3 = 0$ and $x + y + 6 = 0$.

SOLUTION: $y = 2x + 3$ and $y = -x - 6$ comparing we get

$2x + 3 = -x - 6$

$\Rightarrow 3x = -9 \Rightarrow x = -3$ and therefore $y = 3 - 6 = -3$

so the lines intersect at $(-3, -3)$

Method of substitution

To solve equation (i) and (ii) substitute the value of y from equation (i) to (ii) get x and y then can also be obtained.

$$a_2x + b_2\left(\frac{c_1 - a_1x}{b_1}\right) = c_2$$

$$a_2b_1x + b_2c_1 - b_2a_1x = b_1c_2$$

$$\Rightarrow (a_2b_1 - a_1b_2)x = b_1c_2 - b_2c_1$$

$$\Rightarrow x = \left(\frac{b_1c_2 - b_2c_1}{a_2b_1 - a_1b_2}\right)$$ and so we get

$$y = \frac{a_1c_2 - a_2c_1}{a_1b_2 - a_2b_1}$$

ILLUSTRATION 91: Solve the equation $2x + 3y = 7$ and $2x - y = 3$ (i)

SOLUTION: Substituting $y = 2x - 3$ in equation (i)

$2x + 3(2x - 3) = 7$

$\Rightarrow 8x = 16$ $\Rightarrow x = 2$ and hence $y = 1$.

$\Rightarrow$ Solution is (2, 1)

Method of elimination

$a_1x + b_1y = c_1$ (i)

$a_2x + b_2y = c_2$ (ii)

Multiplying equation (i) by a_2 and (ii) by a_1 and subtracting, x gets eliminated

$a_1a_2x + b_1a_2y = a_2c_1$ (iii)

$a_1a_2x + a_1b_2y = a_1c_2$ (iv)

subtracting (iii) and (iv)

$$y = \left(\frac{a_2c_1 - a_1c_2}{a_2b_1 - a_1b_2}\right)$$ and thus $$x = \frac{b_1c_2 - b_2c_1}{a_2b_1 - a_1b_2}$$

ILLUSTRATION 92: Solve the pair of linear equations $2x - y = 8$ and (i)

$3x + 4y = 23$ (ii)

SOLUTION: Multiplying equation (i) by 4 and adding to equation (ii) y gets eliminated $8x + 3x = 32 + 23$

$\Rightarrow 11x = 55$

$\Rightarrow x = 5$ and so $y = 2$

$\Rightarrow$ (5,2) is the obtained solutions

METHOD OF CROSS-MULTIPLICATION

It is very useful method for solving pair of linear equations in two or three variables.

Given two equations
$$a_1x+b_1y+c_1 \quad \text{(i)}$$
$$a_2x+b_2y+c_2z \quad \text{(ii)}$$

Dividing both equation by z and replacing

$\frac{x}{z}=x_0$ and $\frac{y}{z}=y_0$ *we get*

$$a_1x_0+b_1y_0+c_1 \quad \text{(iii)}$$
$$a_2x_0+b_2y_0+c_2z \quad \text{(iv)}$$

Solving by any of the above mentioned three elementary methods, we get $x_0=\frac{b_2c_1-b_1c_2}{a_2b_1-a_1b_2}=\frac{x}{z}$; $y_0=\frac{a_2c_1-a_1c_2}{a_2b_1-a_1b_2}=\frac{y}{z}$ that can be symmetrically expressed as

$$\Rightarrow \quad \frac{x}{b_1c_2-b_2c_1}=\frac{y}{c_1a_2-c_2a_1}=\frac{z}{a_1b_2-a_2b_1}$$

Thus we can conclude that the set of solution of above pair of equation can always be expressed by the ratio $x:y:$ z in terms of coefficients of the equations;

Step (1): Express the coefficients of x, y, z beginning with y in cyclic order as shown in figure and take the product of the coefficients indicated by arrows

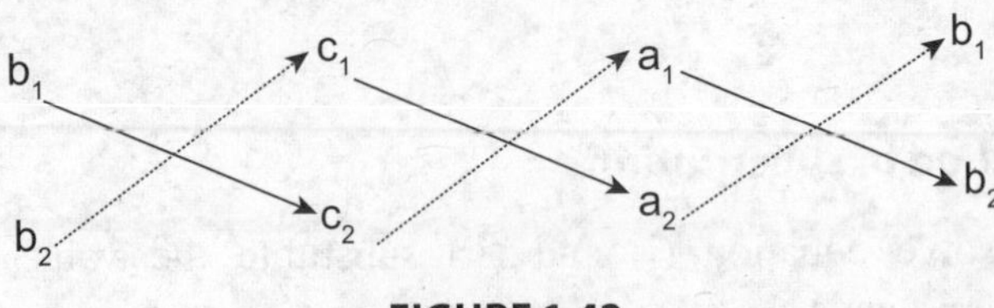

FIGURE 1.42

Step (2): The product formed by descending arrows is considered positive and those by ascending arrows is taken negative.

Step (3): So we get $x:y:z::(b_1c_2-b_2c_1):(c_1a_2-c_2a_1):(a_1b_2-a_2b_1)$

ILLUSTRATION 93: Solve the following set of three equations for unknown variables x, y and z.

$$\left.\begin{aligned} x-2y+3z=0 \quad &...(i)\\ x-y-z=0 \quad &...(ii)\\ 2x-3y+2z=0 \quad &...(iii)\end{aligned}\right\}$$

SOLUTION: Solving the equations (i) and (ii) by cross-multiplication method. We get $\frac{x}{5}=\frac{y}{4}=\frac{z}{1}$

$\Rightarrow$ x = 5λ, y = 4 λ and z = λ

Substituting in the equation (iii) we can get value of λ and hence obtaining value of x, y and z.

$\Rightarrow$ 10λ + 12λ + 2λ = 0 $\Rightarrow$ 0 = 0; which is always true.

e.g. $(x, y, z) = (5, 4, 1)$

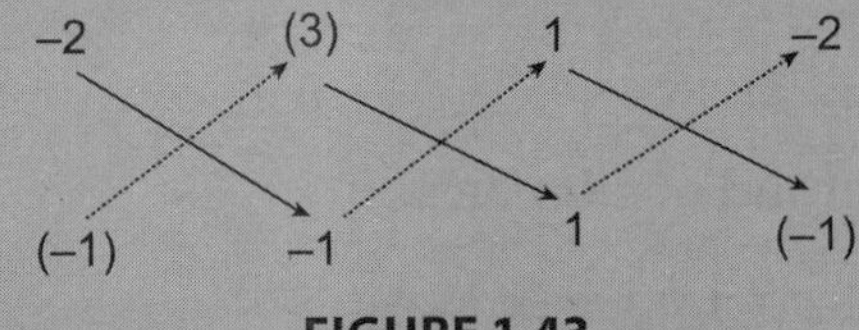

FIGURE 1.43

NOTE

In the above equations, if we put z = 1, we have $\frac{x}{b_1c_2-b_2c_1}=\frac{y}{c_1a_2-c_2a_1}=\frac{z}{a_1b_2-a_2b_1}$ *which gives solution of the equation* $a_1x+b_1y+c_1=0$, $a_2x+b_2y+c_2=0$

ILLUSTRATION 94: Solve the pair of equation $\left.\begin{aligned}2x+y-5=0\\ x-3y+1=0\end{aligned}\right\}$ using cross-multiplication method.

SOLUTION: Arranging the coefficient of both equations as described

$$\frac{x}{1-15}=\frac{y}{-5-2}=\frac{1}{-6-1} \text{ i.e., } \frac{x}{-14}=\frac{y}{-7}=\frac{1}{-7} \Rightarrow x=2 \text{ and } y=1.$$

ILLUSTRATION 95: Find the relation between $a_1, b_1, c_1; a_2, b_2, c_2; a_3, b_3, c_3$, by eliminating the unknowns x and y from the three equations $a_1x + b_1y + c_1 = 0$, $a_2x + b_2y + c_2 = 0$ and $a_3x + b_3y + c_3 = 0$.

SOLUTION: Solving the first two equations using cross-multiplication method, we get

$$\frac{x}{b_1c_2 - b_2c_1} = \frac{y}{c_1a_2 - c_2a_1} = \frac{1}{a_1b_2 - a_2b_1}$$

$$\therefore\ x = \frac{b_1c_2 - b_2c_1}{a_1b_2 - a_2b_1} \text{ and } y = \frac{c_1a_2 - c_2a_1}{a_1b_2 - a_2b_1}$$

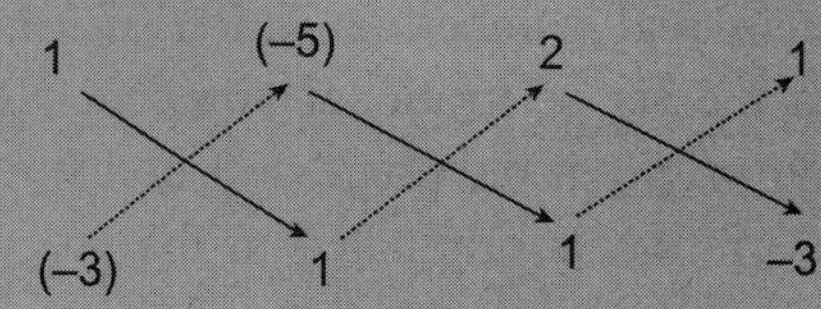

FIGURE 1.44

Substituting the values of x and y in the third equation, we get the relation between coefficients as described below

$$a_3\left(\frac{b_1c_2 - b_2c_1}{a_1b_2 - a_2b_1}\right) + b_3\left(\frac{c_1a_2 - c_2a_1}{a_1b_2 - a_2b_1}\right) + c_3 = 0$$

or $a_3(b_1c_2 - b_2c_1) + b_3(c_1a_2 - c_2a_1) + c_3(a_1b_2 - a_2b_1) = 0$

TEXTUAL EXERCISE–13 (SUBJECTIVE)

1. Find the possible ratio's $x : y$; given $2(7y^2 - x^2) = 3xy$.
2. Express x in terms of y using the equation $y = \dfrac{x^2 - 4}{x^2 + 4}$
3. If $\dfrac{a}{y+z-x} = \dfrac{b}{z+x-y} = \dfrac{c}{x+y-z}$ then prove that $\dfrac{a+b+c}{x+y+z} = \dfrac{a(b^2+c^2)+b(c^2+a^2)+c(a^2+b^2)}{2(a^2x+b^2y+c^2z)}$
4. Given a continued proportion $\dfrac{x}{a+b-c} = \dfrac{y}{b+c-a} = \dfrac{z}{c+a-b}$; prove that $(a - b)x + (b - c)y + (c - a)z = 0$
5. Given $(b+c)x = a$, $(c+a)y = b$ and $(a + b)z = c$ then show that $xy + yz + zx + 2xyz = 1$
6. Find the number of integer solutions of the equations $7x - 4y - 8z = 0$ and $12x + 11y - 3z = 0$.
7. Find a cubic polynomial $f(x) = x^3 + ax^2 + bx + c$ that vanishes at $x = 3$ and $x = -1$ and generates the values -60 and 4 at $x = -3$ and $x = 1$ respectively.
8. Solve the following set of equation for a, b, c; $a(b + c) = 44$; $b(c + a) = 50$; $c(a + b) = 54$.
9. Solve the system of equation $x + y + z = 3$; $x + y + v = 1$; $x + z + v = 4$; $y + z + v = 2$.
10. Solve the system of equation $ay + bx = c$; $cx + az = b$ and $bz + cy = a$
11. Solve the equations $\dfrac{\sqrt{x^2+1}+\sqrt{x^2-1}}{\sqrt{x^2+1}-\sqrt{x^2-1}} = \dfrac{2x^2-1}{2}$
12. Solve the following equations for x.
    (a) $\dfrac{x^3-2x^2+x+1}{x^3-2x^2-x-1} = \dfrac{2x^3+x^2+3x-2}{2x^3+x^2-3x+2}$
    (b) $\dfrac{(a+b)x-(m-n)}{(a-b)x-(m+n)} = \dfrac{(a+b)x+m+p}{(a-b)x+m-p}$

Answer Keys

1. 2 : 1 or –7 : 2 **2.** $x = \pm\sqrt{\dfrac{1+y}{1-y}}$ **6.** 4; $(4k, -3k, 5k)$ where $k \in \{-1, 0, 1, 2\}$

7. $f(x) = x^3 - 4x^2 + x + 6$ **8.** $a = \pm 4$, $b = \pm 5$, $c = \pm 6$ **9.** $x = \dfrac{4}{3}, y = -\dfrac{2}{3}, z = \dfrac{7}{3}, v = \dfrac{1}{3}$

10. $x = \dfrac{b^2+c^2-a^2}{2bc}, y = \dfrac{a^2+c^2-b^2}{2ac}, z = \dfrac{a^2+b^2-c^2}{2ab}$ **11.** $x = \pm\sqrt[4]{\dfrac{5}{4}}$ **12.** (a) $x = 0, \dfrac{11 \pm \sqrt{109}}{2}$

(b) $x = \dfrac{m(n+p)}{a(p-n)-2mb}$

RATIONAL AND IRRATIONAL NUMBERS

Set of real numbers is union of set of rational numbers and the set of irrational numbers. Rational numbers find their origin in the process of division of integers where as the irrationals originated in the process of solving higher degree algebraic equations in the search of generalization of the laws of indices.

Rational numbers (Q) and irrational numbers ($\mathbb{Q}'$)

The numbers which are in the form of p/q, where $p, q \in Z$ and $q \neq 0$ are called as rational number e.g., 2/3, 3, 1/3, 0.76, $1.23\overline{2}$ etc.

The numbers which are not rational (*not in form of p/q.*) i.e., which cannot be expressed in *p*/*q* form or whose decimal part is non-terminating non-repeating but which may represent magnitude of physical quantities are called as irrational numbers. e.g., $\sqrt{2}$, $5^{1/3}$, π, *e* ... etc.

Pie (π): π is ratio of circumference of any circle to the diameter of the same circle. It is an irrational number approximately equal to rational numbers 22/7 or 3.14.

Eular number (e): $e = 1 + \frac{1}{1!} + \frac{1}{2!} + \frac{1}{3!} + ...\infty$

$\Rightarrow 2.7 < e < 2.8$

Properties of rational numbers and irrational numbers

1. If a number *x* in decimal form is written as $x = \overline{cde}.\overline{pqr}$ then $x = c \times \underbrace{10^2}_{\text{hundred}^{th}\ \text{place-value}} + d \times \underbrace{10^1}_{\text{ten's place value}} + e \times \underbrace{10^0}_{\text{unit place value}}$ $+ p \times \underbrace{10^{-1}}_{\text{first decimal place-value}} + q \times \underbrace{10^{-2}}_{\text{Second decimal place-value}} + r \times \underbrace{10^{-3}}_{\text{third decimal place-value}}$
2. All terminating decimals are rational.
   e.g., $a.bcde = \frac{\overline{abcde}}{10^4}$; $x = a.x_1x_2x_3 ... x_n = \frac{\overline{ax_1x_2......x_n}}{10^n}$
3. If a rational *p*/*q* (*in lowest term*) is terminating decimal then $q = 2^m.5^n$. i.e., *q* must not contain any prime factor other than 2 or 5.
4. Non-terminating but repeating decimals are also rationals. e.g., $y = x.ababab... \Rightarrow y = x.\overline{ab}$ (i)
   If number of repeating digits be *n* then multiply both side by 10^n i.e., $10^2 y = xab.\overline{ab}$ (ii)
   Subtracting (i) from (ii) we get
   $y = \frac{xab - x}{99}$ (which is a rational number)
5. Non-terminating and non-repeating decimals are irrationals. 2.71354921275718 ..... (*no periodic re-occurrence up to* ∞)
6. Non-terminating, non-recurring decimals are irrational.
7. The sum of a rational and an irrational number is an irrational number.
8. Set of rational numbers ($\mathbb{Q}$) is countable set.
9. Where as set of irrationals ($\mathbb{Q}^C$) is uncountable.

ILLUSTRATION 96: Show that $5.2\overline{35}$ is a rational number.

SOLUTION: Let $5.2\overline{35}$ (1)

$\Rightarrow 10x = 52.\overline{35}$ (2)

multiplying by 10^2 we get

$10^3x = 5235.\overline{35}$ (3)

subtracting (2) from (3) $990x = 5183$

$\Rightarrow x = \frac{5183}{990}$ which is clearly a rational number.

ILLUSTRATION 97: Prove that $2 - \sqrt{3}$ is an irrational number.

SOLUTION: Let $2 - \sqrt{3} = \frac{p}{q}$ (rational number)

$\Rightarrow 2 - \frac{p}{q} = \sqrt{3}$ (1)

$$\Rightarrow \sqrt{3} = \frac{m}{n} \text{ such that } (m, n) = 1 \text{ ; where } \frac{2q-p}{q} = \frac{m}{n}$$

$$\Rightarrow 3n^2 = m^2 \qquad (2)$$

$\Rightarrow 3/m$ i.e., $m = 3k$

substituting in equation (2) we get

$\Rightarrow 3n^2 = 9k^2$ i.e., $n^2 = 3k^2$

$\Rightarrow 3/n^2$ so $3/n$

m and n are non-coprime which is contrary to our assumption therefore by method of contradiction $2 - \sqrt{3}$ is an irrational number.

n^{th} root of a number: A real number y is called n^{th} root of real number x, where n is a natural number ($n \geq 2$).

If $y^n = x$. When $n = 2$, then it is called as square root and for $n = 3$, known as cube root.

All the numbers other than zero have more than one nth roots. e.g., both 2 and –2 are square root of 4.

Principal n^{th} root: The principal n^{th} root of a real number x (*having at-least one n-th root*) is that n^{th} root which has its sign same as that of x. It is denoted by a radical symbol $\sqrt[n]{x}$

The positive integer n is known as the index of the radical symbol. Usually, we omit the index from the radical sign if index $n = 2$, and write as $\sqrt{x}$.

e.g., $\sqrt{36} = 6$, $\sqrt{\frac{27}{8}} = \frac{3}{2}$ and $\sqrt[5]{-243} = (-3)$

$\sqrt[4]{16} = 2$ where as $\sqrt[4]{-16}$ is a non-real number since fourth power of no real number can be –16 which is negative.

Properties of nth root

(i) Every positive real number x has exactly two real n^{th} roots when n is a positive even natural number ($n = 2m$) denoted by $\sqrt[2m]{x}$ and $-\sqrt[2m]{x}$.
E.g., $\sqrt[4]{256} = 4$; $-\sqrt[4]{256} = -4$ are two real fourth roots of 256.

(ii) Every real number x has only one real n^{th} roots when n is a positive odd natural number ($n = 2m + 1$) denoted by $\sqrt[2m+1]{x}$ e.g., $\sqrt[3]{125} = 5$; $\sqrt[3]{125} = -5$

(iii) nth root of a negative real number x is non-real when n is an even integer.
e.g., $\sqrt{-24}$, $\sqrt[4]{-16}$ has no real values. $\sqrt{-1}$ is a non real number symbolized as i (iota).

(iv) Zero is only real number which has only one nth root and $\sqrt[n]{0} = 0$

(v) Integers such as 1, 4, 9, 16, 25 and 49 are called perfect squares because they have integer square roots.

(vi) Integers such as 1, 8, 27, 64 are called perfect cubes as they have integer cube roots.

Square roots: If b is square root of a where a is the non-negative real number then b when squared must become equal to a.

$\Rightarrow b^2 = a \Rightarrow b^2 - a = 0$

$\Rightarrow (b - \sqrt{a})(b + \sqrt{a}) = 0$

$\Rightarrow b - \sqrt{a} = 0$ or $b + \sqrt{a} = 0$

$\Rightarrow b = \sqrt{a}$ (positive) or $b = -\sqrt{a}$ (negative)

Properties of square roots

(i) Zero has only one square root i.e., zero.

(ii) Every positive real number a (except zero) has two square roots one of them is positive (called as principle square root denoted as $\sqrt{a}$) and other is negative denoted as ($-\sqrt{a}$).

(iii) Magnitude of real number x, denoted as $|x|$ and defined as the quantity of x is

$$|x| = \sqrt{x^2} = \begin{cases} x & \text{if } x > 0 \\ 0 & \text{if } x = 0 \\ -x & \text{if } x < 0 \end{cases}$$

ILLUSTRATION 98: Find the arithmetic root of the following:

(a) $\sqrt{(-3)^2}$ (b) $\sqrt{\left(1-\sqrt{3}\right)^2}$ (c) $\sqrt{\left(\sqrt{5}-2\right)^2}$

SOLUTION: (a) $\sqrt{(-3)^2} = |-3| = -(-3) = 3$

(b) $\sqrt{\left(1-\sqrt{3}\right)^2} = \left|1-\sqrt{3}\right|$ $\because$ $1 - \sqrt{3}$ is negative real number

$= -\left(1-\sqrt{3}\right) = \sqrt{3}-1$

(c) $\sqrt{\left(\sqrt{5}-2\right)^2} = \left|\sqrt{5}-2\right|$ $\because$ $\sqrt{5} - 2$ is positive real number

$= \left(\sqrt{5}-2\right) = \sqrt{5}-2$

ALGEBRA OF RATIONAL AND IRRATIONAL NUMBERS

(i) Closure law: Set of rationals is closed under addition, subtraction, and multiplication operations. Whereas set of irrational numbers is not closed under addition, multiplication, subtraction and division.

e.g., $(3 + \sqrt{5}) + (3 - \sqrt{5}) = 6$; $(1 + \sqrt{5})(1 - \sqrt{5}) = -4$; $(1 + \sqrt{2}) - (3 + \sqrt{2}) = -2$; $(7\sqrt{5}/\sqrt{5}) = 7$ are not irrational numbers.

(a) Their sum and product are commutative and associative i.e., for all $a, b, c \in Q$ or $\mathbb{Q}'$

(ii) Commutative Law: $a + b = b + a$; $ab = ba$

(iii) Associative Law: $a + (b + c) = (a + b) + c$; $a(bc) = (ab)c$

(a) Cancellation law holds for rational/irrational numbers i.e., for all $a, b, c \in Q$ or $\mathbb{Q}'$
$a + c = b + c \Rightarrow a = b$ and $ac = bc \Rightarrow a = b$

(b) Distribution of multiplication over addition i.e., for all $a, b, c \in Q$ or $\mathbb{Q}'$; $a(b + c) = ab + ac$

(iv) Order Properties:

(a) **Law of Trichomy:** Given any two numbers a and $b \in Q$ or $\mathbb{Q}'$, exactly one of the following holds. $a > b$ or $a < b$ or $a = b$

(b) **Transitivity:** For each triplet of numbers a, b and $c \in Q$ or $\mathbb{Q}'$ if $a > b$ and $b > c \Rightarrow a > c$.

(c) **Monotone property for addition and multiplication:** For each triplet of numbers a, b and $c \in Q$ or $\mathbb{Q}'$. $a > b \Rightarrow a + c > b + c$ and $a > b \Rightarrow ac > bc$

(v) Existence of additive and multiplicative identity: Zero is an additive identity element and one is multiplicative identity element because addition of zero and multiplication by one to any element does not produce any change in it.

Note: Additive and multiplicative identity do not exist in the set of irrational numbers

(vi) Existence of additive and multiplicative inverse: For every Rational/Irrational x, there always exist its negative $-x$ which, when added to x makes additive identity. Multiplicative inverse of x is an element which, when multiplied to x makes multiplicative identity.

SURDS AND THEIR CONJUGATES

If x is not a perfect n[th] power, then $\sqrt[n]{x}$ is called a surd of the nth order. Two surds of the same order are said to be *like surds* otherwise termed as *unlike surds*.

If a Surd is of the type $a + \sqrt{b}$ where a is a rational number and b is not a perfect square of rational then a is called its rational part and $\sqrt{b}$ is known irrational part of surd. Surd $a - \sqrt{b}$ is called conjugate of the surd $a + \sqrt{b}$. If $x + \sqrt{y} = a + \sqrt{b}$ where x, y, a, b are rationals and y and b are not perfect squares then $x = a$ and $y = b$

Rationalization of denominator of an irrational number

In an expression of the form $\dfrac{x}{\sqrt{y}+\sqrt{z}}$, the denominator can be rationalized by multiplying numerator and the denominator by $\sqrt{y}-\sqrt{z}$.

e.g., to rationalize the number $\dfrac{a+\sqrt{b}}{(a-\sqrt{b})}$

Multiplying the numerator and denominator both by $a + \sqrt{b}$ we get,

$$\frac{a+\sqrt{b}}{(a-\sqrt{b})} = \frac{(a+\sqrt{b})(a+\sqrt{b})}{(a-\sqrt{b})(a+\sqrt{b})} = \frac{a^2+b}{a^2-b} + \frac{2a}{a^2-b}\sqrt{b}$$

ILLUSTRATION 99: Rationalize the denominator of the number $\dfrac{x^2 - y^2}{x^{1/3} + y^{1/3}}$.

SOLUTION: Let $x^{1/3}$ = a and $y^{1/3}$ = b now since a and b are surds of 3rd order therefore to rationalize them apply. $a^3 + b^3 = (a + b)(a^2 - ab + b^2)$

$$\Rightarrow a+b=\frac{a^3+b^3}{a^2-ab+b^2}$$

$$\Rightarrow x^{1/3}+y^{1/3}=\frac{x+y}{a^{2/3}-(xy)^{1/3}+y^{2/3}}$$

Substituting in the expression

$$\frac{x^2-y^2}{x^{1/3}+y^{1/3}}=\frac{x^2-y^2}{(x+y)\left(x^{2/3}-(xy)^{1/3}+y^{2/3}\right)^{-1}}=(x-y)(x^{2/3}-x^{1/3}y^{1/3}+y^{2/3})$$

NOTE

Similarly, to rationalize expressions containing n^{th} order surds use the identities.

$x^n - y^n = (x - y)(x^{n-1} + x^{n-2}y + y^2x^{n-3} + \ldots + y^{n-1})$ $(x^n + y^n) = (x + y)(x^{n-1} - x^{n-2}y + x^{n-3}y^2 - x^{n-4}y^3 + \ldots +(-1)^{n-1} y^{n-1})$

ILLUSTRATION 100: Rationalize the denominator of following fractions and express as equivalent fraction.

(a) $\dfrac{\sqrt{5}}{1+\sqrt{2}+\sqrt{3}}$ (b) $\dfrac{2\sqrt{a+1}}{\sqrt{a-1}-\sqrt{2a}+\sqrt{a+1}}$

SOLUTION: (a) Consider $\dfrac{\sqrt{5}}{1+\sqrt{2}+\sqrt{3}}=\dfrac{\sqrt{5}\left(1+\sqrt{2}-\sqrt{3}\right)}{\left(1+\sqrt{2}\right)^2-\left(\sqrt{3}\right)^2}=\dfrac{\sqrt{5}+\sqrt{10}-\sqrt{15}}{2\sqrt{2}}=\dfrac{\sqrt{10}+\sqrt{20}-\sqrt{30}}{4}$

(b) $\dfrac{2\sqrt{a+1}}{\sqrt{a-1}-\sqrt{2a}+\sqrt{a+1}}=\dfrac{2\sqrt{a+1}\left(\sqrt{a-1}+\sqrt{a+1}+\sqrt{2a}\right)}{\left(\sqrt{a-1}+\sqrt{a+1}\right)^2-\left(\sqrt{2a}\right)^2}$ (to rationalize denominator)

$=\dfrac{2\sqrt{a^2-1}+2(a+1)+2\sqrt{2a}\sqrt{a+1}}{\left(\sqrt{a-1}+\sqrt{a+1}\right)^2-\left(\sqrt{2a}\right)^2}$ (multiplying the numerator and rationalize denominator)

$$=\frac{\left(\sqrt{a^2-1}+a+1+\sqrt{2a^2+2a}\right)\sqrt{a^2-1}}{a^2-1}$$

ILLUSTRATION 101: Find the factor that will rationalize the following expressions:

(a) $a \quad \sqrt{b}$ (b) $\sqrt{5}-\sqrt[3]{3}$

SOLUTION: (a) Let x = a and $y = b^{1/3}$

Raising the power by LCM of indices of denominator i.e., 3

$x^3 = a^3$ and $y^3 = b$ and applying $x^3 + y^3 = (x + y)(x^2 - xy + y^2)$

so the factor that rationalize $a + b^{1/3}$ i.e., $x + y$ is $= x^2 - xy + y^2 = (a^2 - ab^{1/3} + b^{2/3})$

(b) Consider $x = \sqrt{5} = 5^{1/2}$; $y = \sqrt[3]{3} = (3)^{1/3}$

$\because$ LCM of denominators of indices = 6

Clearly $x^6 = 5^3$

$y^6 = 9$ are both rationals

$\because$ $x^6 - y^6 = (x - y)(x^5 + x^4y + x^3y^2 + x^2y^3 + xy^4 + y^5)$

So the factor that makes $x - y$ rational is

$x^5 + x^4y + x^3y^2 + x^2y^3 + xy^4 + y^5$

$= (5)^{5/2} + 25(3)^{1/3} + 5^{3/2}.3^{2/3} + 5(3) + 5^{1/2}(3)^{4/3} + (3)^{5/3}$

ILLUSTRATION 101: Find the square root of following:

(a) $8+\sqrt{60}$ (b) $2-\sqrt{3}+\sqrt{7-4\sqrt{3}}$

SOLUTION: (a) Let $\sqrt{8+\sqrt{60}} = \sqrt{a}+\sqrt{b}$ Squaring both sides

$8+2\sqrt{15} = a+b+2\sqrt{a}\sqrt{b}$

Hence a + b = 8 and $\sqrt{ab} = \sqrt{15}$

$\Rightarrow$ $a + b = 8$ and $ab = 15$

$\Rightarrow$ $a = 5$ and $b = 3$

$\Rightarrow$ $\sqrt{8+\sqrt{60}} = \sqrt{5}+\sqrt{3}$

(b) Let $\sqrt{7-4\sqrt{3}} = \sqrt{x}-\sqrt{y}$ squaring both side

$\Rightarrow 7-4\sqrt{3} = x+y-2\sqrt{xy}$

The relation $x + y = 7$ and $xy = 12$ give $x = 4$ and $y = 3$

$\Rightarrow \sqrt{2-\sqrt{3}+\sqrt{7-4\sqrt{3}}} = \sqrt{2-\sqrt{3}+2-\sqrt{3}} = \sqrt{4-2\sqrt{3}} = \sqrt{3+1-2\sqrt{3}}$

$= \sqrt{(\sqrt{3}-1)^2} = \left|\sqrt{3}-1\right| = \sqrt{3}-1$

TEXTUAL EXERCISE–14 (SUBJECTIVE)

1. Prove that the following numbers are irrational.

(a) $\sqrt{2}$ (b) $\sqrt{3} - \sqrt{2}$

(c) $3\sqrt{2}$ (d) $5-\sqrt{3}$

2. State which of the following is true.

(a) Let x be a rational number whose decimal expansion terminates. Then we can express x in the form p/q, where p and q are coprime, and such numbers are called rational number in its lowest term.

(b) Let $x = p/q$, be a rational number whose decimal expansion terminates, where p and q are coprime, then the prime factorization of q is of the form 2^n5^m where n, m are non-negative integers.

(c) Let $x = p/q$ be a rational number, such that the prime factorization of q is not of the form 2^n5^m, where n, m are non-negative integers. Then x has a decimal expansion which is non-terminating repeating (recurring).

(d) Every terminating decimal can be converted in to a decimal fraction and every non-terminating decimal can be converted in to a vulgar fraction.

3. Without actual division, find which of the following numbers are terminating decimals.

(a) 375/50 (b) 76/300

(c) 54/280

4. Show that the following numbers are rational and convert them in p/q form.

(a) 12.475 (b) $3.\overline{25}$

(c) $6.4\overline{25}$

5. State which of the following is true.

(a) Every integer is a rational number.

(b) 1/0 is not a rational number since the division by zero is not allowed.

(c) Two rational numbers a/b and c/d are called equal, written as $a/b = c/d$ if and only if $ad = bc$.

(d) The set of rational numbers excluding zero is closed under all the four fundamental operations of arithmetic.

(e) There are infinitely many rational numbers between any two rational numbers.

6. State which of the following are true.

(a) The number π is irrational, its approximate value is 22/7.

(b) The negative of an irrational number is irrational.

(c) The sum of a rational and an irrational number is irrational.

(d) The product of a non-zero rational number and an irrational number is an irrational number.

(e) The sum of two irrational numbers may not be irrational.

7. Rationalize the denominator.

(i) $\dfrac{2}{3-\sqrt{5}}$ (ii) $\dfrac{1}{2\sqrt{3}+\sqrt{7}}$

(iii) $\dfrac{2}{\sqrt{5}+\sqrt{3}+2}$ (iv) $\dfrac{12}{3+\sqrt{5}-2\sqrt{2}}$

(v) $\dfrac{x+y}{\sqrt{x}+\sqrt{y}+\sqrt{x+y}}$ (vi) $\dfrac{\left(\sqrt{3}+\sqrt{5}\right)\left(\sqrt{5}+\sqrt{2}\right)}{\sqrt{2}+\sqrt{3}+\sqrt{5}}$

8. Obtain the factor that will rationalize the following expression.

(i) $\sqrt[3]{3}+\sqrt{2}$ (ii) $\sqrt[6]{5}+\sqrt[3]{2}$ (iii) $2+\sqrt[4]{7}$

9. If x, y are rational numbers and $\dfrac{5+\sqrt{11}}{3-2\sqrt{11}} = x+y\sqrt{11}$, find the values of x and y.

10. If $\dfrac{\sqrt{5}-1}{\sqrt{5}+1}+\dfrac{\sqrt{5}+1}{\sqrt{5}-1} = a+b\sqrt{5}$, find the values of a and b.

11. Find the square root of following expressions.

(i) $16-2\sqrt{20}-2\sqrt{28}+2\sqrt{35}$

(ii) $6+\sqrt{12}-\sqrt{24}-\sqrt{8}$

(iii) $b+z+\sqrt{2bz+z^2}$

(iv) $2x-\sqrt{3x^2-2xy-y^2}$

(v) $1 + x^2 + (1 + x^2 + x^4)^{1/2}$

(vi) $21 - 4\sqrt{\ } + 8\sqrt{3} - 4\sqrt{15}$.

12. The difference $\sqrt{40\sqrt{2}+57}-\sqrt{\left|40\sqrt{2}-57\right|}$ is an integer. Find that integer.

13. Find the value of $\sqrt{2+\sqrt{3}+\sqrt{7+4\sqrt{3}}}$.

14. Express $(5^{1/2} + 9^{1/8}) \div (5^{1/2} - 9^{1/8})$ as an equivalent fraction with a rational denominator.

15. Find the number equal to $3.1\overline{45}$ when expressed as a rational number in lowest terms.

Answer Keys

2. (a) T (b) T (c) T (d) T **3.** a is terminating, b and c are non-terminating

4. (i) 499/4 (ii) 322/99 (iii) 6361/990 **5.** (a) T (b) T (c) T (d) T (e) T

6. (a) T (b) T (c) T (d) T (e) T

7. (i) $\dfrac{3+\sqrt{5}}{2}$ (ii) $\dfrac{2\sqrt{3}-\sqrt{7}}{5}$ (iii) $\dfrac{4+\sqrt{5}+3\sqrt{3}-2\sqrt{15}}{11}$ (iv) $1+\sqrt{5}+\sqrt{10}-\sqrt{2}$

(v) $\left(\dfrac{x+y(\sqrt{x}+\sqrt{y}-\sqrt{x+y})\sqrt{xy}}{2xy}\right)$ (vi) $\dfrac{(\sqrt{3}+\sqrt{5})(\sqrt{5}+\sqrt{2})\times(\sqrt{2}+\sqrt{3}-\sqrt{5})\times\sqrt{2}\times\sqrt{3}}{2\times2\times3}$

9. $x = -37/35$, $y = -13/35$ **10.** $a = 3$, $b = 0$

11. (i) $\pm(2-\sqrt{5}-\sqrt{7})$ (ii) $\pm\sqrt{3}-\sqrt{2}+1$ (iii) $\left(\sqrt{b+\dfrac{z}{2}}+\sqrt{\dfrac{z}{2}}\right)$ (iv) $\pm\left[\sqrt{\dfrac{3x+y}{2}}+\sqrt{\dfrac{x-y}{2}}\right]$

(v) $\pm\left[\sqrt{\dfrac{1+x^2+x}{2}}+\sqrt{\dfrac{1+x^2-x}{2}}\right]$ (vi) $\pm(\sqrt{5}-2-2\sqrt{3})$

12. 10 **13.** $1+\sqrt{3}$ **14.** $\dfrac{14+5^{3/2}.3^{1/4}+5.3^{1/2}+5^{1/2}.3^{3/4}}{11}$ **15.** $\dfrac{157}{495}$

■ REAL NUMBER SYSTEM ($\mathbb{R}$)

Union of set of Rationals ($\mathbb{Q}$) and set of Irrationals ($\overline{\mathbb{Q}}$) is called set of Real numbers $\mathbb{R} = \mathbb{Q} \cup \overline{\mathbb{Q}}$. It has following properties.

Properties of real numbers

(i) Square of real numbers is always non-negative. *If* $x \in \mathbb{R} \Rightarrow x^2 \geq 0$

(ii) Between any two real numbers there are infinitely many real number.

(iii) Magnitude of real number x, denoted as $|x|$ and defined as the quantity of x i.e.

$$|x| = \sqrt{x^2} = \begin{cases} x & if\ x > 0 \\ 0 & if\ x = 0 \\ -x & if\ x < 0 \end{cases}$$

(iv) They are represented on a straight line called as real number line in order of their magnitude. Such that distance of the number of x from zero is equal to magnitude of x ($|x|$).

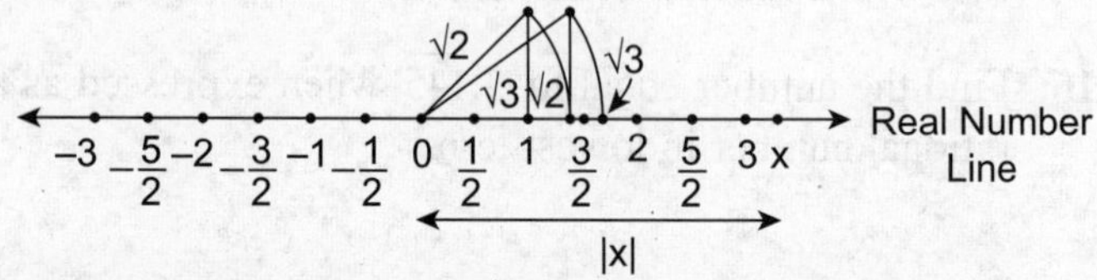

FIGURE 1.45

(v) Real number line is infinitely dense and continuous line. i.e., between any two numbers (how so ever closed they are) there lie infinitely many real numbers.

(vi) From the above figure one can observe that every real number corresponds to unique point on real number line and each point on the real number line uniquely corresponds to a real number that is why we say that there exist a one to one correspondence between set of points on real number line and set of real numbers ($\mathbb{R}$).

Concept of interval: As the set of all real numbers lying between two unequal real numbers a and b can never be expressed in roster form therefore these are expressed in set builder form using the concept of intervals.

For instance, any real number 'a' divides the the real number line in two infinite subsets geometrically represented by two rays.

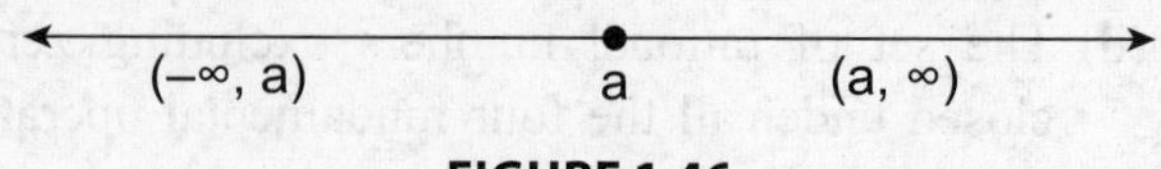

FIGURE 1.46

To represent the set $\{x : x \geq a, x \in \mathbb{R}\}$ that is read as "set of all real numbers greater than or equal to a" we use notation $x \in [a, \infty)$ and to represent set $\{x : x \leq a, x \in \mathbb{R}\}$ describing "set of all real numbers less than a" we use the interval notation $(-\infty, a)$.

Notice the fact that the square bracket (also known as *closed bracket*) at a in the interval $[a, \infty)$ indicates that the real number a is included in the set, whereas small bracket (also called as *open bracket* or parenthesise) in the interval $(-\infty, a)$ shows that a and $-\infty$ are not induced in the set.

Since infinity is not a number, it is merely a concept, so it is not included in any set of number therefore $-\infty$ and ∞ is always associated with open bracket while representing in the interval notation.

Similarly, the set of all numbers between a and b can be represented in following ways and geometrically described by a line segment obtained by truncating the real number line and classified as below.

Open interval: Denoted as (a, b) $x \in (a, b) = \{x : a < x < b, x \in \mathbb{R}\}$ i.e., end points are not included.

FIGURE 1.47

Closed interval [a, b]: $x \in [a, b] = \{x : a \leq x \leq b, x \in \mathbb{R}\}$ the end points are included.

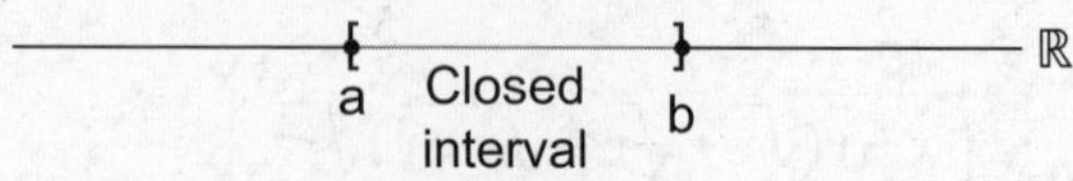

FIGURE 1.48

Semi-open interval: $x \in (a, b] \Rightarrow a < x \leq b$ and $x \in [a, b) \Rightarrow a < x \leq b$

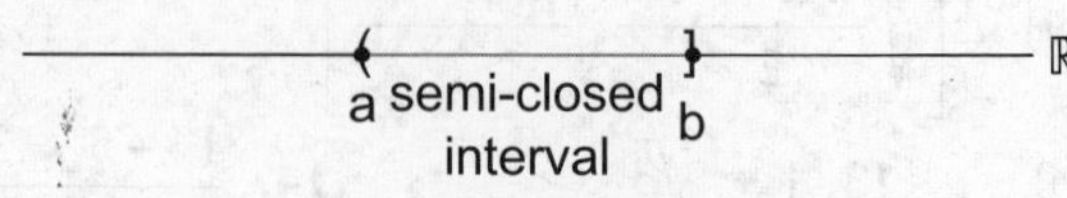

FIGURE 1.49

ILLUSTRATION 102: Express the following intervals in terms of inequality and graphically represent them on real number line.

(i) $(-2, 3)$ (ii) $[3,\infty)$

(iii) $(-\infty, -\sqrt{2})$ (iv) $[-5, 1]$

(v) $[-6, 2)$ (vi) $(-3, 4]$

SOLUTION: (i) $(-2, 3) = \{x : -2 < x < 3, x \in \mathbb{R}\}$

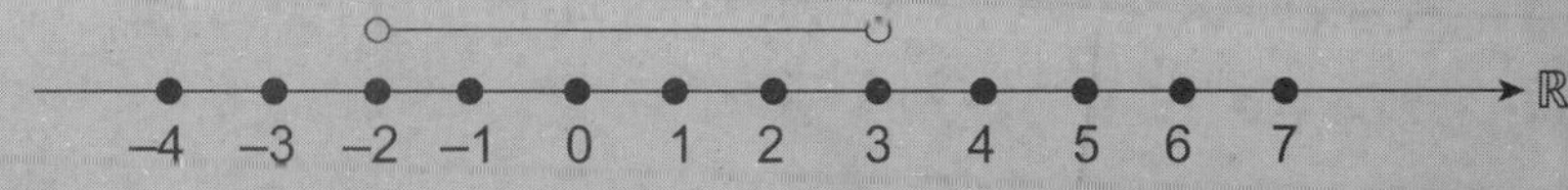

FIGURE 1.50

(ii) $[3,\infty) = \{x : 3 \le x < \infty, x \in \mathbb{R}\}$

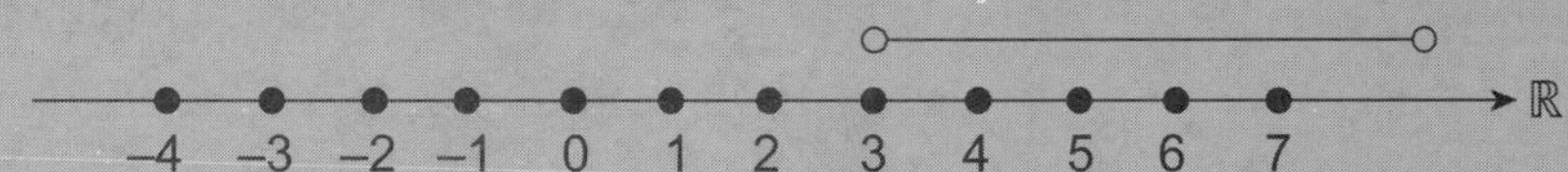

FIGURE 1.51

(iii) $(-\infty, -\sqrt{2}) = \{x : -\infty < x < \sqrt{2}, x \in \mathbb{R}\}$

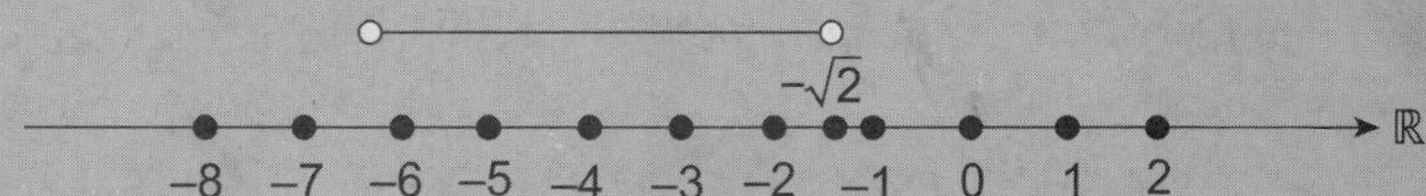

FIGURE 1.52

(iv) $[-5, 1] = \{x : -5 \le x \le 1, x \in \mathbb{R}\}$

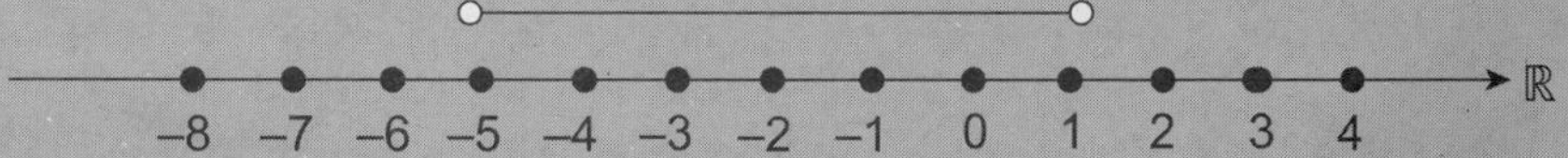

FIGURE 1.53

(vi) $[-6, 2) = \{x : -6 \le x < 2, x \in \mathbb{R}\}$

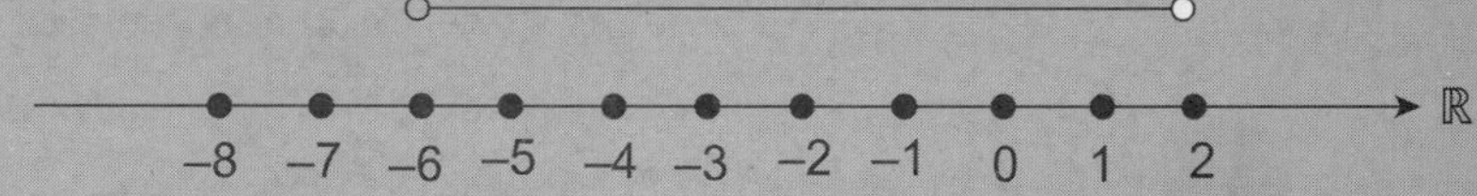

FIGURE 1.54

(vii) $(-3, 4] = \{x : -3 < x \le 4, x \in \mathbb{R}\}$

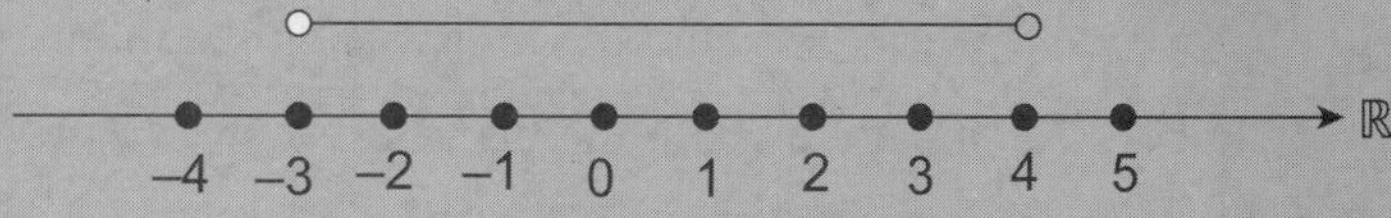

FIGURE 1.55

Intersection and union of two or more intervals: To find the union/intersection of two or more intervals, locate each interval over the same real number line and for intersection take the interval, which is common to both. For union of intervals, locate the interval which includes all the members of all the intervals considered.

If intersection of two or more intervals has no element then resulting set is written as ϕ.

If intersection of two or more interval contains finite number of element e.g., 1, 3, 5 (say) then result is written as $\{1, 3, 5\}$.

ILLUSTRATION 103: Express each set in interval notation:

(i) $(-\infty,3)\cap[-2,\infty)$ (ii) $(-4,1]\cap(-3,4)$ (iii) $(0,5]\cap(1,\infty)$

(iv) $[0,3)\cup[2,6)$ (v) $[2,\infty)\cup(4,\infty)$ (vi) $[-1,1)\cup[2,5]$

SOLUTION: (i) To find $(-\infty,3)\cap[-2,\infty)$, we plot both the interval on the number line as shown in the figure and then consider the interval on the number line which is common to both.

The resulting interval is begins at –2 and extends up to 3 but not including 3.

Therefore $(-\infty,3)\cap[-2,\infty)=[-2,3)$ which is shown as shaded portion.

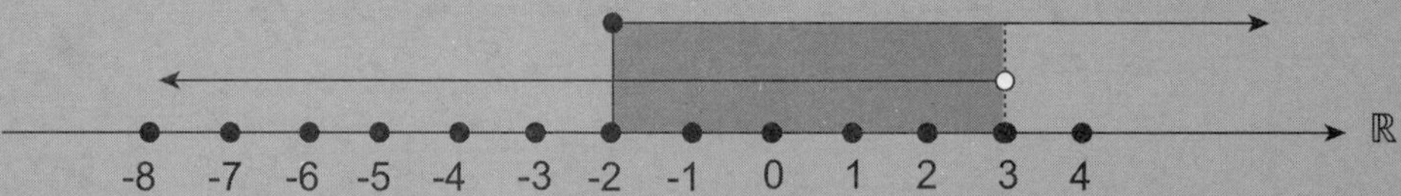

FIGURE 1.56

(ii) To find $(-4,1]\cap(-3,4)$, we plot both the intervals on the number line as shown in the figure and then consider the interval on the number line which is common to both.

The resulting interval begins at –3 and at 1 including 1 and excluding –3.

Therefore $(-4,1]\cap(-3,4)=(-3,1]$ shown as shaded portion.

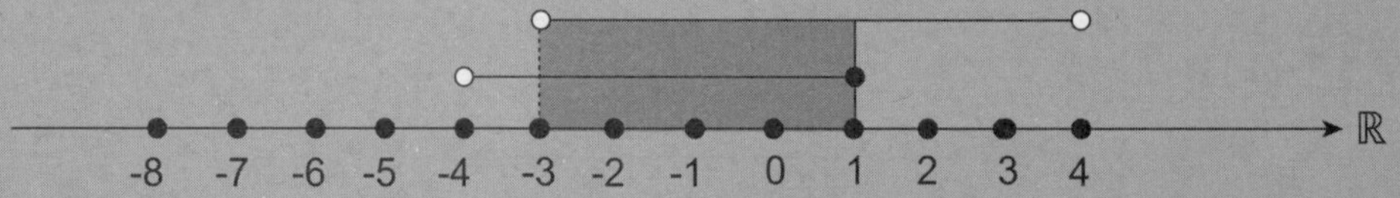

FIGURE 1.57

(iii) To find $(0,5]\cap(1,\infty)$, we plot both the intervals on the number line as shown in the figure and then consider the interval on the number line which is common to both.

The resulting interval begins at 1 and ends at 5 excluding 1 but including 5.

Therefore $(0,5]\cap(1,\infty)=(1,5]$ which is shown as shaded portion.

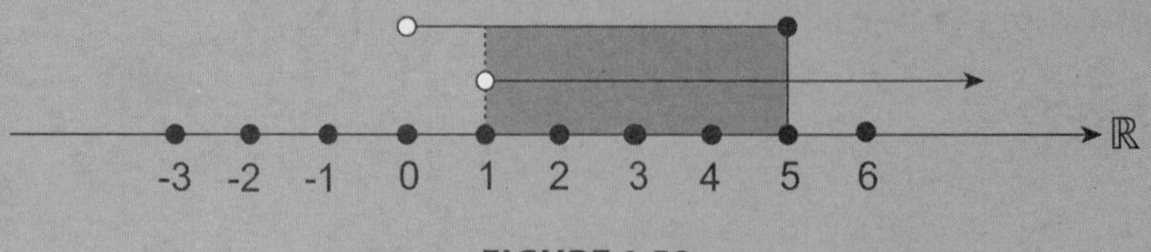

FIGURE 1.58

(iv) To find $[0,3)\cup[2,6)$, we plot both the intervals on the number line and mark the interval on the number line that unites both the intervals as shown in the figure.

The numbers belonging to either or both the intervals are given as the real numbers from 0 to 6 including 0 and excluding 6.

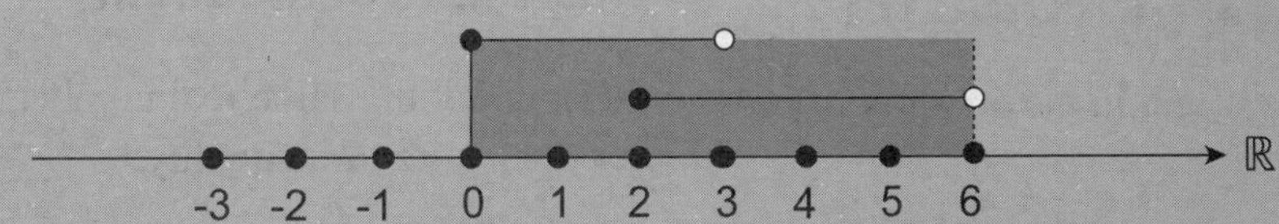

FIGURE 1.59

(v) To find $[2,\infty)\cup(4,\infty)$, locating both the intervals on the number line as shown in the figure. Clearly, the interval uniting both consists of all the real numbers larger than or equal to 2 extending upto infinity.

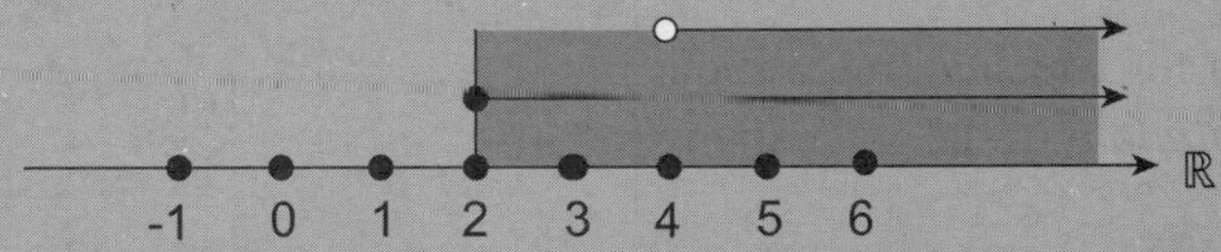

FIGURE 1.60

(vi) To find $[-1,1)\cup[2,5]$, locating both the intervals on the number line we find that the union of these can not be expressed as a single interval as the both sets are disjoint as shown in the figure so the result is written as $[-1,1)\cup[2,5]$.

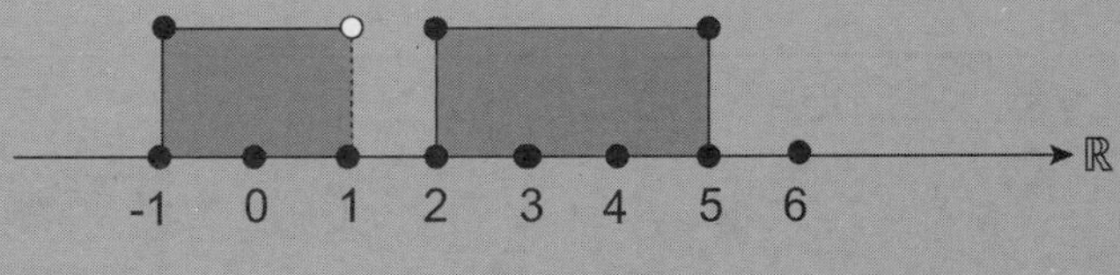

FIGURE 1.61

TEXTUAL EXERCISE–15 (SUBJECTIVE)

1. Write the intervals of real values of x which satisfies following:

(a) $x > 4$ (b) $x < -2$
(c) $-2 < x < 5$ (d) $x \geq 3$
(e) $x \geq -5$ (f) $-7 \leq x < 2$
(g) $-3 < x \leq 6$ (h) $-1 \leq x \leq 4$

2. Express each interval in terms of an inequality and graph the interval on a number line:

(i) $(-3, 3]$ (ii) $[6, 12)$
(iii) $[0, 5]$ (iv) $\left(\frac{1}{2}, \infty\right)$
(v) $[-1, \infty)$
(vi) $(-\infty, 4]$

3. Express each English phrase in both set-builder and interval notations (in all cases x is real):

(i) x is greater than 3.
(ii) x is less than or equal to 0
(iii) x lies between –2 and 5, excluding both
(iv) x lie between 3 and 7, excluding 3 and including 7.
(v) x is at least 4 and at most 9.
(vi) x is at most 7.

Answer Keys

1. (a) $(4, \infty)$ (b) $(-\infty, -2)$ (c) $(-2, 5)$ (d) $[3, \infty)$ (e) $[-5, \infty)$ (f) $[-7, 2)$ (g) $(-3, 6]$ (h) $[-1, 4]$

2. (i) $-3 < x \leq 3$ (ii) $6 \leq x < 12$ (iii) $0 \leq x \leq 5$ (iv) $1/2 < x < \infty$ (v) $-1 \leq x < \infty$ (vi) $-\infty < x \leq 4$

3. (i) $\{x : x \in \mathbb{R} \text{ and } x > 3\}$; $(3, \infty)$ (ii) $\{x : x \in \mathbb{R} \text{ and } x \leq 0\}$; $(-\infty, 0]$ (iii) $\{x : x \in \mathbb{R} \text{ and } -2 < x < 5\}$; $(-2, 5)$ (iv) $\{x : x \in \mathbb{R}; 3 < x \leq 7\}$; $(3, 7]$ (v) $\{x : x \in \mathbb{R}\ 4 \leq x \leq 9\}$; $[4, 9]$ (vi) $\{x : x \in \mathbb{R}; x \leq 7\}$; $(-\infty, 7]$

■ FUNDAMENTALS OF INEQUALITY

Concept of inequality find its origin in the property of order of real numbers.

(i) An inequation is a statement involving a sign of inequality. The signs of inequality are given as: $<, >, \leq, \geq, \nless, \ngtr, \neq$. If two algebraic expressions are connected by any one of these symbols, then the statement represents an inequation.

(ii) An inequation can have one or more variables e.g., $ax + b \geq 0$, $ax + by + c \geq 0$.

(iii) The values of the unknown for which an inequation holds good are called the *solutions* of the inequation.

Classification of inequalities

Inequalities are of four types:

If $a - b > 0 \Rightarrow a > b$ (read a greater than b)

If $a - b \geq 0 \Rightarrow a \geq b$ (read a greater than or equal to b)

If $a - b < 0 \Rightarrow a < b$ (read a is less than b)

If $a - b \leq 0 \Rightarrow a \leq b$ (read a less than or equal to b)

Basic laws of inequality

R(1): Adding same real number to both sides does not alter the nature of inequality.

$$a > b \Rightarrow a + x > b + x \quad \forall\, x \in \mathbb{R}$$
$$a < b \Rightarrow a + x < b + x \quad \forall\, x \in \mathbb{R}$$

R(2) : Transitive property: $a > b$ and $b > c \Rightarrow a > c$

R(3): Multiplying by a real number k to both sides of inequality has the following effect on the nature of inequality.

$$a > b \Rightarrow \begin{cases} ak > bk & \text{if } k > 0 \\ ak = bk & \text{if } k = 0 \\ ak < bk & \text{if } k < 0 \end{cases}$$

- If $x < y < 0 \Rightarrow |x| > |y|$ (Larger the number, smaller the magnitude)
- If $x > y > 0 \Rightarrow |x| > |y|$ (Larger the number, larger the magnitude)

ILLUSTRATION 104: Find the range of variation of y for the corresponding range given for variable x.

(i) $y = 2x + 3$; given $x \in [2, 6]$ (ii) $y = 3x - 5$; if $x \in (-3, -1]$

(iii) $y = 4 - 3x$; if $x \in [3, 5]$ (iv) $y = \frac{2}{3}x - 4$; $x \in [-2, 3)$

SOLUTION: (i) given $2 \leq x \leq 6$ (*multiplying by* 2)

$\Rightarrow 4 \leq 2x \leq 12$ (*adding* 3 *to all*)

$\Rightarrow 7 \leq 2x + 3 \leq 15$

$\Rightarrow 2x + 3 = y \in [7, 15]$

(ii) Given $x \in (-3, -1]$

$\Rightarrow -3 < x \leq -1$ (*multiplying by* 3)

$\Rightarrow -9 < 3x \leq -3$ (*subtracting* 5 *to all*)

$\Rightarrow -14 < 3x - 5 \leq -8$

$\Rightarrow 3x - 5 = y \in (-14, -8]$

(iii) Since $x \in [3, 5]$

$\Rightarrow 3 \leq x \leq 5$ (*multiplying by* –3 *inequality gets reversed*)

$\Rightarrow -9 \geq -3x \geq -15$ (*adding* 4 *to all*)

$\Rightarrow -5 \geq 4 - 3x \geq -11$

$\Rightarrow 4 - 3x = y \in [-11, -5]$

(iv) Given $x \in [-2, 3)$

$\Rightarrow -2 \leq x < 3$ (*multiplying by* 2/3)

$\Rightarrow -4/3 \leq 2x/3 < 2$ (*subtracting* 4 *to all*)

$$\Rightarrow -\frac{16}{3} \leq \frac{2}{3}x - 4 < -2 \Rightarrow \frac{2}{3}x - 4 = y \in \left[-\frac{16}{3}, -2\right).$$

ILLUSTRATION 105: If given two inequality $x + 1 > 3 > 5 - 2x$ and $x + 1 > 5 - 2x$. Solve them separately for x and mention what conclusion you can draw regarding transition property of inequality.

SOLUTION: Considering first two inequality

$x + 1 > 3$ and $3 > 5 - 2x$

$\Rightarrow x > 2$ and $x > 1$

$\Rightarrow x \in (1, \infty) \cap (2, \infty)$

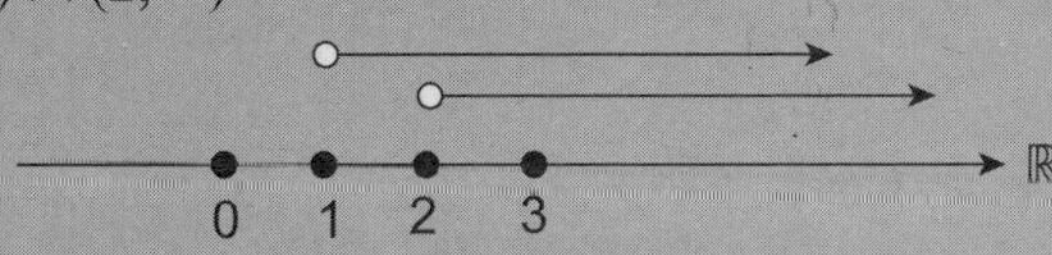

FIGURE 1.62

$\Rightarrow x \in (2, \infty)$

Now solving the third, we observe that

$x + 1 > 5 - 2x \quad \Rightarrow 3x > 4$

$\Rightarrow x > \frac{4}{3} \quad$ i.e. $x \in \left(\frac{4}{3}, \infty\right)$

Clearly, $x \in (2, \infty) \quad \Rightarrow x \in \left(\frac{4}{3}, \infty\right)$

but $x \in \left(\frac{4}{3}, \infty\right) \quad \not\Rightarrow x \in (2, \infty)$

Therefore we conclude that if $a > b$ and $b > c \Rightarrow a > c$

But the converse is not true.

R(4): Law of addition: For any set of real numbers a_k, b_k such that $k \in \{1, 2, 3, ..., n\}$.

If $a_1 > b_1$ and $a_2 > b_2$ ... and $a_n > b_n$

$\Rightarrow (a_1 + a_2 + a_3 + ... + a_n) > (b_1 + b_2 + b_3 + ... + b_n)$

R(5): Law of multiplication: For any set of positive real numbers a_k, b_k such that $k \in \{1, 2, 3, ..., n\}$.

If $a_1 > b_1 > 0$ and $a_2 > b_2 > 0$ ...... and $a_n > b_n > 0$

$\Rightarrow (a_1 . a_2 . a_3 . ... a_n) > (b_1 . b_2 . b_3 . ..... b_n)$

ILLUSTRATION 106: If $x - 3 > 2 + 6x$; $y + 6 > 5 - 12x$. Then prove that $2x + y > 9$.

SOLUTION: Considering both the inequalities

$x - 3 > 2 + 6x$ (i)

$y + 6 > 5 - 12x$ (ii)

multiplying inequality (i) by 2 and adding to (ii) we get $2(x - 3) + y + 6 > 2(2 + 6x) + 5 - 12x$

$\Rightarrow 2x + y > 9$

ILLUSTRATION 107: If given that $x_k \geq 2k - 1 \ \forall k \in \mathbb{N}$ then show that

(a) $x_1 + x_2 + x_3 + ... + x_n \geq n^2$ (b) $x_1 . x_2 . x_3 .... x_n \geq \frac{(2n!)}{2^n (n!)}$

SOLUTION: (a) Since $x_k \geq 2k - 1 \ \forall k \in \mathbb{N}$

so we get n numbers of inequalities E.g., $x_1 \geq 1, x_2 \geq 3, x_3 \geq 5,$ .... ; $x_n \geq 2n - 1,$

adding all these like inequalities by law of addition we get

$x_1 + x_2 + x_3 + ... + x_n \geq 1 + 3 + 5 + 7 + ... (2n - 1)$ (*applying Gaussian pairing method*)

$\Rightarrow x_1 + x_2 + x_3 + ... + x_n \geq \frac{n}{2}(1 + 2n - 1)$

$\Rightarrow x_1 + x_2 + x_3 + ... + x_n \geq n^2$

(b) Multiplying the above n inequalities we get

$x_1 . x_2 . x_3 .... x_n \geq 1 . 3 . 5 . 7 . ..... (2n - 3)(2n - 1)$

Now consider RHS of inequality $1 . 3 . 5 . 7 . 9 ..... (2n - 1)$

and multiplying and dividing by product of first n even natural numbers we get

$$\Rightarrow 1 . 3 . 5 . 7 . 9 ..... (2n - 1) = \frac{1.2.3.4.5......(2n-1)(2n)}{2.4.6.........(2n-2)(2n)} = \frac{(2n)!}{2^n(n!)}$$

R(6): Law of square: If a and b are two real numbers, the inequality between them and their squares is given by:

$$a > b \Rightarrow \begin{cases} a^2 > b^2 \text{ iff } |a| > |b| \\ a^2 = b^2 \text{ iff } |a| = |b| \\ a^2 < b^2 \text{ iff } |a| < |b| \end{cases}$$

which can be explained in a more specific way as below:

$$\Rightarrow \begin{cases} a^2 > b^2 & \text{if both } a \text{ and } b \text{ are non-negative} \\ a^2 = b^2 & \text{If } |a| = |b| \\ a^2 < b^2 & \text{If } a \text{ and } b \text{ are both non-positive} \end{cases}$$

and if a and b have opposite sign and $a > b$

i.e., $a > 0$ and $b < 0$ then the original rule shall be applied.

Note: The law can be extended to any even natural power ($2n$).

R(7) Law of square root: If a and b both are non-negative and $a > b \Rightarrow \sqrt{a} > \sqrt{b}$ this can be generalized for any even root i.e., $a > b \Rightarrow \sqrt[2n]{a} > \sqrt[2n]{b}$

Conclusion: If x is a variable such that $a \leq x \leq b$ then to find range of variation of x^2 we observe the following cases.

Case I: If a and b non-negative, since $a \leq x \leq b$

$\Rightarrow a^2 \leq x^2 \leq b^2 \quad \Rightarrow x^2 \in [a^2, b^2]$

Case II: If a and b non-positive, since $a \leq x \leq b$, by squaring, inquality will get reversed $\Rightarrow a^2 \geq x^2 \geq b^2$

$\Rightarrow b^2 \leq x^2 \leq a^2 \quad \Rightarrow x \in [b^2, a^2]$

Case III: If $a < 0$ and $b > 0$, as law of inequality is different for negative and positive values of x. Hence separating there intervals, we get:

$\because \; a \leq x \leq b \Rightarrow a \leq x \leq 0 \text{ or } 0 \leq x \leq b$

$\Rightarrow a^2 \geq x^2 \geq 0 \text{ or } 0 \leq x^2 \leq b^2$

$\Rightarrow x^2 \in [0, a^2] \cup [0, b^2]$

$$\Rightarrow \begin{cases} x^2 \in [0, a^2] & \text{if } |a| > |b| \\ x^2 \in [0, b^2] & \text{if } |b| > |a| \end{cases}$$

$\Rightarrow x^2 \in [0, \max(a^2, b^2)]$

R(8): Law of cube/cube root:

$\Rightarrow a^3 > b^3$ and $a^{1/3} > b^{1/3} \; \forall \; a, b \in \mathbb{R}$

This law can be extended for any odd natural power ($2n + 1$) and odd root. i.e.,

$a > b \Leftrightarrow a^{2n+1} > b^{2n+1}$ and $a^{1/2n+1} > b^{1/2n+1} \; \forall \; a, b \in \mathbb{R}$

ILLUSTRATION 108: Find the range of variation of x^2, if x is a variable described as below.

(i) $x \in [2, 6]$ (ii) $x \in (-3, -1)$.

(iii) $x \in (-3, 4]$ (iv) $x \in [-5, 2)$.

SOLUTION: (i) given $2 \leq x \leq 6$ (squaring both side)

$\Rightarrow 4 \leq x^2 \leq 36 \quad \Rightarrow x^2 \in [4, 36]$

(ii) given $x \in (-3, -1)$.

$\Rightarrow -3 < x < -1$ (by squaring both side inequality will get reversed)

$\Rightarrow 9 > x^2 > 1$

$\Rightarrow 1 < x^2 < 9$ $\Rightarrow x^2 \in (1, 9)$

(iii) given $x \in (-3, 4]$

$\Rightarrow -3 < x \leq 4$ (breaking the interval at $x = 0$, thus forming two inequalities)

$\Rightarrow -3 < x \leq 0$ or $0 \leq x \leq 4$

$\Rightarrow 9 > x^2 \geq 0$ or $0 \leq x^2 \leq 16$

$\Rightarrow x^2 \in [0, 9) \cup [0, 16]$

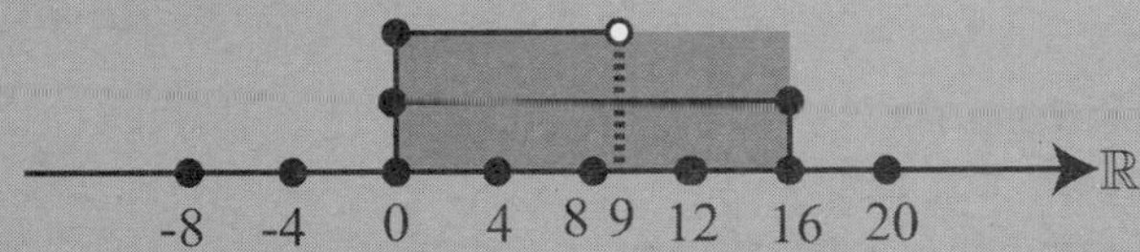

FIGURE 1.63

$\Rightarrow x^2 \in [0, 16]$

(iv) given $x \in [-5, 2)$

$\Rightarrow -5 \leq x < 2$ (breaking the interval at $x = 0$, thus forming two inequalities)

$\Rightarrow -5 \leq x \leq 0$ or $0 \leq x < 2$

$\Rightarrow 25 \geq x^2 \geq 0$ or $0 \leq x^2 < 4$

$\Rightarrow x^2 \in [0, 25] \cup [0, 4)$ $\Rightarrow x^2 \in [0, 25]$.

ILLUSTRATION 109: Given $x \in (-2, 2]$ find the range of the expression $y = \sqrt[3]{7x^3 + 8}$.

SOLUTION: $x \in (-2, 2]$

$\Rightarrow -2 < x \leq 2$ $\Rightarrow -8 > x^3 \geq 8$

$\Rightarrow -56 > 7x^3 \geq 56$ (adding 8 to all)

$\Rightarrow -48 > 7x^3 + 8 \geq 64$ (taking cube root)

$\Rightarrow \sqrt[3]{-48} < \sqrt[3]{7x^3 + 8} \leq \sqrt[3]{64}$

$\Rightarrow -2\sqrt[3]{6} < \sqrt[3]{7x^3 + 8} \leq 4$

$\Rightarrow y \in \left(-2\sqrt[3]{6}, 4\right]$

ILLUSTRATION 110: Given $x \in (-2, 5]$ find the range of the expression $y = \sqrt{8 - \frac{x^2}{4}}$.

SOLUTION: $\because \quad y = \sqrt{8 - \frac{x^2}{4}}$

$y = \frac{1}{2}\sqrt{32 - x^2}$

Now, since $x \in [-2, 5]$.

$\Rightarrow -2 \leq x \leq 5$

$x^2 \in \left[0, \max\ \{4, 25\}\right]$

$\Rightarrow 0 \leq x^2 \leq 25$ (multiplying by -1)

$\Rightarrow 0 \geq -x^2 \geq -25$ (adding 32 and taking square root)

$\Rightarrow 32 \geq 32 - x^2 \geq 7$ $\Rightarrow \sqrt{7} \leq \sqrt{32 - x^2} \leq 4\sqrt{2}$

$\Rightarrow y \in \left[\frac{\sqrt{7}}{2}, 2\sqrt{2}\right]$

R(9) Law of reciprocal: Analysing the properties of numbers and their reciprocal, one can conclude easily that as the numbers get larger their reciprocal becomes smaller for instance, $4 > 3$ therefore $\frac{1}{4} > \frac{1}{3}$ or $-2 > -3 \Rightarrow \frac{1}{2} < \frac{1}{3}$ but such conclusion leads to wrong answer if numbers have opposite sign. E.g., $-3 < -2$ but $-\frac{1}{3} < -\frac{1}{2}$.

Given two real number a and b such that $a > b$

$$\Rightarrow \begin{cases} \frac{1}{a} < \frac{1}{b} \text{ iff } a \text{ and } b \text{ have same sign} \\ \frac{1}{a} > \frac{1}{b} \text{ iff } a \text{ and } b \text{ of opposite sign} \end{cases}$$

Also it is noticeable that as a number x gets closer to zero but remains less than zero (called as $x \to 0$ from left hand side) the reciprocal of x tends to becomes very large in magnitude but negative in sign so we denote it by $\frac{1}{x} \to -\infty$ but when a number x gets closer to zero but remains greater than zero (called as $x \to 0$ from right hand side) the reciprocal of x tends to becomes very large in magnitude and remains positive in sign so we denote it by $\frac{1}{x} \to \infty$

Keeping the above facts in mind, the following laws can be concluded:

Conclusion:

Case I: Given $x \in [a, b]$: a and b of same sign

$$\Rightarrow \frac{1}{x} \in \left[\frac{1}{b}, \frac{1}{a}\right]$$

Proof: $\because a \le x \le b \Rightarrow \frac{1}{a} \ge \frac{1}{x} \ge \frac{1}{b} \Rightarrow \frac{1}{b} \le \frac{1}{x} \le \frac{1}{a}$

Case II: If $x \in [a, b]$ where $a < 0$ and $b > 0$ then, $\frac{1}{x} \in \left(-\infty, \frac{1}{a}\right] \cup \left[\frac{1}{b}, \infty\right)$

Proof: Breaking the interval at $x = 0$, because reciprocal of zero is not defined, we get; $x \in [a, 0) \cup (0, b]$

$\Rightarrow a \le x < 0 \quad or \quad 0 < x \le b$

$\Rightarrow \frac{1}{a} \ge \frac{1}{x} > -\infty \quad or \quad \infty > x \ge \frac{1}{b}$

$\Rightarrow -\infty < \frac{1}{x} \le \frac{1}{a} \quad or \quad \frac{1}{b} \le x < \infty$

$\Rightarrow \frac{1}{x} \in \left(-\infty, \frac{1}{a}\right] \cup \left[\frac{1}{b}, \infty\right)$

ILLUSTRATION 111: If x is a variable described as below then find the range of variation of $1/x$.

(i) $x \in [1/10, 2/3]$ (ii) $x \in (-5, -1/4)$.

(iii) $x \in (-1/3, 2]$ (ii) $x \in [-2, 3)$.

SOLUTION: (i) given $x \in [1/10, 2/3]$

$\Rightarrow 1/10 \le x \le 2/3$ *(taking reciprocal)*

$\Rightarrow 10 \ge 1/x \ge 3/2$ $\Rightarrow 3/2 \le 1/x \le 10$

$\Rightarrow 1/x \in [3/2, 10]$

(ii) given $x \in (-5, -1/4)$.

$\Rightarrow -5 < x < -1/4$ *(taking reciprocal)*

$\Rightarrow -1/5 > 1/x > -4$ $\Rightarrow -4 < 1/x < -1/5$

$\Rightarrow 1/x \in (-4, -1/5)$

(iii) given $x \in (-1/3, 2]$ *(breaking interval at zero)*

$\Rightarrow -1/3 < x < 0$ or $0 < x \le 2$ *(Now taking reciprocal)*

$\Rightarrow -3 > 1/x > -\infty$ or $\infty > \frac{1}{x} \ge \frac{1}{2}$

$\Rightarrow -\infty < 1/x < -3$ or $\frac{1}{2} \le \frac{1}{x} < \infty$

$\Rightarrow \frac{1}{x} \in (-\infty, -3) \cup \left[\frac{1}{2}, \infty\right)$

(iv) given $x \in [-2, 3)$ *(breaking interval at zero)*

$\Rightarrow -2 \le x < 0$ or $0 < x < 3$ *(Now taking reciprocal)*

$\Rightarrow -1/2 \ge 1/x > -\infty$ or $\infty > \frac{1}{x} > \frac{1}{3}$

$\Rightarrow -\infty < 1/x \le -1/2$ or $\frac{1}{3} < \frac{1}{x} < \infty$

$\Rightarrow \frac{1}{x} \in \left(-\infty, -\frac{1}{2}\right] \cup \left(\frac{1}{3}, \infty\right)$

ILLUSTRATION 112: Find the range of variation of y for given range of variation of variable x.

(a) $y = \frac{2x^2 - 4}{x^2 + 1}$ where $x \in [-3, 3]$

(b) $y = \frac{x^2 + 2}{x^2 - 1}$ where $x \in [-4, 5]$

SOLUTION: (a) Consider $y = \frac{2x^2 - 4}{x^2 + 1}$ where $x \in [-3, 3]$

rearranging the expression on right hand side

$y = \frac{2x^2 + 2 - 6}{x^2 + 1}$ $\Rightarrow y = 2 - \frac{6}{x^2 + 1}$

$\because -3 \le x \le 3$ $\Rightarrow 0 \le x^2 \le 9$

$\Rightarrow 1 \le x^2 + 1 \le 10$ $\Rightarrow \frac{1}{10} \le \frac{1}{x^2 + 1} \le 1$

$\Rightarrow \frac{-6}{10} \ge \frac{-6}{x^2 + 1} \ge -6$ $\Rightarrow -6 \le \frac{-6}{x^2 + 1} \le -\frac{3}{5}$

$\Rightarrow -4 \le 2 - \frac{6}{x^2 + 1} \le \frac{7}{5}$ $\Rightarrow y \in \left[-4, \frac{7}{5}\right]$

(b) Consider $y = \frac{x^2 + 2}{x^2 - 1}$ where $x \in [-4, 5]$

rearranging the expression on right hand side

$y = \frac{x^2 - 1 + 3}{x^2 - 1}$ $\Rightarrow y = 1 + \frac{3}{x^2 - 1}$

$\because -4 \le x \le 5$ $\Rightarrow 0 \le x^2 \le 25$

$\Rightarrow -1 \le x^2 - 1 \le 24$ *(breaking interval at zero)*

$\Rightarrow -1 \le x^2 - 1 \le 0$ or $0 < x^2 - 1 \le 24$

$\Rightarrow -1 \ge \frac{1}{x^2 - 1} > -\infty$ or $\infty > \frac{1}{x^2 - 1} \ge \frac{1}{24}$ *(Multiplying by 3)*

$\Rightarrow -\infty < \frac{3}{x^2 - 1} \le -3$ or $\frac{1}{8} \le \frac{3}{x^2 - 1} < \infty$ *(Adding 1 to all)*

$\Rightarrow y \in (-\infty, -2] \cup \left[\frac{9}{8}, \infty\right)$

NOTES

1. *If $0 < a < 1$ and $r \in R^+$ (set of positive real numbers), then $0 < a^r \le a^{-r}$.*
2. *Again if a and b are any two positive numbers and $a > b$ then $a^r > b^r$ if $r > 0$ and $a^r < b^r$ if $r < 0$*

TEXTUAL EXERCISE–16 (SUBJECTIVE)

1. (a) Solve $30x < 200$ when
   (i) x is a natural number
   (ii) x is an integer.
(b) Solve $5x - 3 < 3x + 1$ when
   (i) x is an integer.
   (ii) x is a real number.

2. Solve the following linear inequations and express the result in the form of intervals.
(a) $3x - 7 > x + 1$ (b) $-(x - 3) + 4 < 5 - 2x$
(c) $3x - 8 < x + 4$ (d) $2x + 7 \ge 5 - 2x$
(e) $\frac{5-2x}{3} \le \frac{x}{6} - 5$ (f) $\frac{x}{5} < \frac{3x-2}{4} - \frac{5x-3}{5}$

3. Find the limits in which y lies if …
(a) $1 < x < 9, y = -x$
(b) $-9 < x < 5, y = -x$
(c) $-9 < x < -6, y = -x/3$
(d) $-9 < x < 5, y = -3x$.

4. Find the range of x^2 for the following cases:
(i) $2 \le x \le 5$ (ii) $\frac{1}{2} < x \le \frac{5}{3}$
(iii) $\frac{1}{2} < \ < \frac{3}{2}$ (iv) $-2 < x < 3$
(v) $-3 < x < 2$ (vi) $4 \le x \le 4$

5. Find the range of values of the reciprocal of x when;
(a) $x \in [1, 5]$ (b) $x \in [2, 7]$
(c) $x \in [0, \infty]$ (d) $x \in [0, 3]$
(e) $x \in [-5, -1]$ (f) $x \in [2, 4]$
(g) $x \in [-3, 5]$

6. (a) Solve the following basic rational inequality:
   (i) $-8x + 3(x - 2) > -x + 2$
   (ii) $3x + 2 < x - 4$
   (iii) $2x + 5 > 3 - 2x$
   (iv) $2x + 5 > x + 4 > x - 1$
   (v) $3x > 6x + 9$
   (vi) $-3x + 6 < 12x - 9$
(b) Find the limit in which y lies and express the result in interval form.
   (i) $y = -x; 1 < x < 6$
   (ii) $y = -x; -1 \le x \le 5$
   (iii) $y = -x; -5 \le x \le -2$
   (iv) $y = x^2; -2 \le x < 5$
   (v) $y = x^2; -5 < x \le -1$
   (vi) $y = \frac{1}{x}; \quad -2 \le x < 1$
   (vii) $y = \frac{1}{x}; \quad -6 \le x \le -1$
   (viii) $y = x^3; 2 < x < 3$
   (ix) $y = x^3; \quad -3 \le x \le -5$
   (x) $y = \frac{1}{x^2}; \frac{1}{2} \le x \le 3$
   (xi) $y = \frac{1}{x^2}; -\frac{1}{5} \le x \le \frac{1}{5}$
   (xii) $y = \frac{1}{x^2+2}; \quad -1 \le x \le 1$

7. Solve the following polynomials for x.
(a) $x^2 - 3x + 2 < 0$ (b) $x^2 - 5x + 4 \ge 0$
(c) $x(x - 3) \le 0$ (d) $x(x - 1)(x - 2) > 0$
(e) $\frac{x}{x-5} > \frac{1}{2}$ (f) $\frac{1}{x} \le 1$
(g) $\frac{x-5}{x-9} \le 0$ (h) $\frac{5x}{3x-1} \le 0$
(i) $x \le 3 - \frac{1}{x-1}$

8. Solve the system of inequalities:

(a) $\begin{cases} 2x+3 < 3x-4 \\ 3x-2 > x+2 \\ x+8 > 3x+1 \\ 5x-1 < 4x+6 \end{cases}$

(b) $x - 1 < 11 - 3x$ and $x^2 - 4x < 0$

9. Find the greatest negative integral value of x which satisfy the system of equation $\frac{x}{8}-\frac{x}{4}+\frac{x}{2}>x+5$ and $\frac{x-2}{8}<-\frac{(x-2)}{7}$.

10. Solve the following inequalities for x.
(a) $x^3-6x\le 0$
(b) $x^4+x^3-x-1>0$
(c) $(x^2-5x+6)(x^2-3x+4)<0$

11. Find the largest integer satisfying. $(x+3)(x-3)^2(x-5)(x-4)^4(x-6)<0$

12. Find the limits in which y lies if …
(a) $-9<x<-5, y=x^2$
(b) $3<x<5, y=x^2$
(c) $-9<x<5, y=x^2$
(d) $4<x^2<9, y=x$
(e) $-9<x<5, y=\sqrt{x}$.
(f) $9<x^2<25, y=x$

13. Find the limits in which y lies if …
(a) $-9\le x\le 5, y=x^3$
(b) $27<x^3<125, y=x$
(c) $32<x^5<243, y=x$

14. Find the limits in which y lies if
(a) $2<x<5, y=1/x$
(b) $-6<x<6, y=1/x^2$
(c) $-2<x<-1, y=1/x$
(d) $-2<x<2, y=1/x^3$

15. Find the range of variation y for the following cases.
(a) $y=\frac{1}{3x-2}$ *if* $-2<x<4$
(b) $y=\frac{x-1}{x+2}$ *if* $-1<x<3$
(c) $y=\frac{1}{x^2+4}$ *if* $2\le x\le 3$.
(d) $y=\frac{x^2-1}{x^2+1}$ *if* $-1<x<3$

16. Find all pairs of consecutive odd positive integers both of which are smaller than 10 such that their sum is more than 11.

17. Find all pairs of consecutive even positive integers, both of which are larger than 5 such that their sum less than 23.

18. The longest side of a triangle is 3 times the shortest side and the third side is 2 cm shorter than the longest side, If the perimeter of the triangle is at least 61 cm, find the minimum length of the shortest side.

Answer Keys

1. (a) (i) 6 solution (ii) infinitely many solution (b) (i) $x\in[-\infty, ... 1,0,1]$ (ii) $x\in(-\infty, 2)$

2. (a) $x\in(4,\infty)$ (b) $x\in(-\infty,-2)$ (c) $x\in(-\infty,6)$ (d) $x\in\left[-\frac{1}{2},\infty\right)$ (e) $x\in[8,\infty)$ (f) $x\in\left(-\infty,\frac{2}{9}\right)$

3. (a) $y\in(-9,1)$ (b) $y\in(-5,9)$ (c) $y\in(2,3)$ (d) $y\in(-15,27)$

4. (i) [4, 25] (ii) (1/4, 25/9] (iii) (0, 9/4) (iv) (0, 9) (v) (0, 9) (vi) [0, 16]

5. (a) [1/5, 1] (b) [1/7, 1/2) (c) $(0,\infty)$ (d) $[1/3,\infty)$ (e) [–1, –1/5] (f) $\left[\frac{1}{4},\frac{1}{2}\right]$
(g) $(-\infty,-1/3]\cup[1/5,\infty)$

6. (a) (i) $x\in(-\infty,-2)$ (ii) $x\in(-\infty,-3)$ (iii) $x\in\left[-\frac{1}{2},\infty\right)$ (iv) $x\in(-1,\infty)$ (v) $x\in(-\infty,-3)$ (vi) $x\in(1,\infty)$

(b) (i) $y\in(-6,-1)$ (ii) $y\in[-5,1]$ (iii) $y\in[2,5]$ (iv) $y\in[0,25)$ (v) $y\in[1,25)$

(vi) $y\in\left(-\infty,\frac{-1}{2}\right)\cup(1,\infty)$ (vii) $y\in\left[-1,\frac{-1}{6}\right)$ (viii) $y\in(8,27)$ (ix) $y\in[-125,-27]$ (x) $y\in\left[\frac{1}{9},4\right]$

(xi) $y\in[25,\infty)$ (xii) $y\in\left[\frac{1}{3},\frac{1}{2}\right]$

7. (a) $x\in(1,2)$ (b) $x\in(-\infty,1]\cup[4,\infty)$ (c) $x\in[0,3]$ (d) $x\in(0,1)\cup(2,\infty)$ (e) $(-\infty,-5)\cup(5,\infty)$

(f) $x\in(-\infty,0)\cup[1,\infty)$ (g) $x\in[5,9)$ (h) $x\in\left[0,\frac{1}{3}\right)$ (i) $x\in(-\infty,1)\cup\{2\}$

8. (a) ϕ (b) (0, 3) **9.** –9 **10.** (a) $(-\infty,-\sqrt{6}]\cup[0,\sqrt{6}]$ (b) $(-\infty,-1)\cup(1,\infty)$ (c) (2, 3) **11.** {– 4}

12. (a) $y\in(25, 81)$ (b) $y\in(9, 25)$ (c) $y\in[0, 81)$ (d) $x\in(-3, -2)\cup(2, 3)$ (e) $\sqrt{x}\in[0,5)$

(f) $x\in(-5, -3)\cup(3, 5)$

13. (a) $y\in[-729, 125]$ (b) $y\in(3, 5)$ (c) $y\in(2, 3)$

14. (a) $x\in\left(\frac{1}{5},\frac{1}{2}\right)$ (b) $\frac{1}{x^2}\in\left(\frac{1}{36},\infty\right)$ (c) $\frac{1}{x}\in\left(-1,-\frac{1}{2}\right)$ (d) $\frac{1}{x^3}\in\left(-\infty,-\frac{1}{8}\right)\cup\left(\frac{1}{8},\infty\right)$

15. (a) $\left(-\infty,-\frac{1}{8}\right)\cup\left(\frac{1}{10},\infty\right)$ (b) $\left(-2,\frac{2}{5}\right)$ (c) $\left[\frac{1}{13},\frac{1}{8}\right]$ (d) $\left(-1,\frac{4}{5}\right)$

16. (5, 7) and (7, 9) **17.** (6, 8), (8, 10), (10, 12)

18. 9 cm

■ POLYNOMIALS

An algebraic expression involving one or more variable that contains two mathematical operations, multiplication and raising to a natural exponent (*power*) with respect to the variable//variables involved is called mononomial. e.g., ax, bx^2, $3xy$, $\frac{2}{5}x^2yz$ etc. An expression is termed as multinomial if it involves many such mononomials seperated by + sign. And each such mononomial is called a 'term' of the multinomial

E.g., $ax^3 + bx^2yz + cxy^2z^3 + dy^3 + z^3$, $ax^2 + bxy + cy^2$ etc. are polynomial with respect to variable *x, y, z*.

And if a multinomial contains only one variable (say *x*) then it is called a polynomial in that variable *x* and it is denoted by $P(x)$.

An algebraic expression of type $P(x) = a_0 + a_1x + a_2x^2 + a_3x^3 + \ldots + a_nx^n$ is called ordered polynomial in variable *x* provided powers of *x* are whole numbers.

- $x^2 - 4x + 6$; $x^2 - x + 1$ are quadratic polynomial.
- $ax^3 + ax^2 + cx + d$ is cubic polynomial
- $x^4 + x^3 + x^2 + x + 1$ is bi-quadratic polynomial.
- $2x^3 + 3x^2 - \sqrt{x} + 1$ is not a polynomial.

Coefficient

The numerical values multiplied to variable in each term are called coefficient e.g. $a_0, a_1, a_2, a_3, \ldots. a_n$, are coefficients of polynomial.

Value of polynomial expressions

In the polynomial expression $y = f(x)$, *x* is independent variable (input) *y* is called dependent variable (output).

Corresponding to each input for variable *x* the equation generates exactly one output as variable y.

E.g., Given $f(x) = x^2 - 4x + 3$

Input (x)	Output (y)	Sign of polynomial
$x = 0$	3	+ve
$x = -1$	8	+ve
$x = 2$	– 1	–ve
$x = 3$	0	---
$x = 1$	0	---
$x = 4$	3	+ve

Root of polynomial

Roots are the value of the variable *x* for which the polynomial expression vanishes. e.g., $x = 1$ and $x = 3$ are roots of quadratic polynomial $x^2 - 4x + 3$.

Study of polynomial means study of roots, sign, maximum/minmum value and graph of polynomial.

Leading term and leading coefficient

The term containing highest power of variable *x* is called leading term and its coefficient is called leading coefficient.

(because it governs the value of $f(x)$ when the input *x* is very very large (i.e., $x \to \infty$)

e.g. in the polynomial $f(x) = a_0 + a_1x + a_2x^2 + a_3x^3 + \ldots a_nx^n$ a_nx^n is leading term and a_n is the leading coefficient.

$$f(x) = x^n\left(\frac{a_0}{x^n} + \frac{a_1}{x^{n-1}} + \frac{a_2}{x^{n-2}} + \ldots + \frac{a_{n-1}}{x} + a_n\right)$$

$$\approx a_nx^n = \begin{cases} \to \infty & a_n > 0 \\ \to -\infty & a_n < 0 \end{cases}$$

We clearly observe that sign of polynomial expression at $x \to \infty$ is same as that of its leading coefficient.

Degree of polynomial

Highest power of x in the polynomial expression is called degree of polynomial i.e., (power of x in leading term).

f(x)	Degree	Leading coefficient
$x^4 - 3x^5 + 2x + 1$	5 (pentic)	–3
$x^2 - x + 1$	2 (quadratic)	1
$3x^3 + 4x^2 + 1$	3 (cubic)	3
$2x + 1$	1 (linear)	2
$6x^0$	0 (Constant)	6

Two polynomials, which are integral with respect to x, are **identical** if and only if their degrees are equal and the coefficients in like powers of x are also equal.

If a polynomial is equated with the product of other polynomials of lower degrees then equation obtained is called identity transformation of a polynomial. It is also known as **factorization** of a polynomial.

E.g., A quadratic polynomial $x^2 - 7x + 12$

$= x^2 - 4x - 3x + 12$

$= x(x - 4) - 3(x - 4)$

$= (x - 4)(x - 3)$

$= x^2 - 7x + 12 = (x - 4)(x - 3)$ is called factorization or identity transformation of polynomial.

Multivariate Polynomials:

A polynomial in more than one variable is called multivariate polynomial. e.g., $p(x, y) = x3y2 + 7x2y3 - 3x5$. p is a bivariate polynomial of degree 5. Similarly a trivariate polynomial is a polynomial in three variables.

ILLUSTRATION 113: Factorize the following polynomial consisting of vanishes x, y, z. $f(x, y, z) = x^3y + x^2y^2 + x^3z + x^2yz - y^3x - xzy^2 - y^4 - zy^3$.

SOLUTION: Rearranging the expression and grouping we get

$x^3y + zx^3 + x^2y^2 + x^2yz - y^3x - y^2xz - y^4 - y^3z = x^3(y + z) + x^2y(y + z) - y^2x(y + z) - y^3(y + z)$

$= (y + z)(x^3 + x^2y - xy^2 - y^3) = (y + z)(x^3 - xy^2 + x^2y - y^3) = (y + z)(x(x^2 - y^2) + y(x^2 - y^2))$

$= (y + z)(x^2 - y^2)(x + y)$

■ POLYNOMIAL EQUATION

- When a polynomial expression is equated to zero then it generates corresponding equation. Roots of polynomial expression are the solutions of its corresponding equation.
- Study of equation is study of the roots of polynomial. e.g. $x^2 - 6x + 8 = 0$ is a quadratic equation.
- A polynomial equation of nth degree has exactly n roots not necessarily all real. (Because it can be factorized in to exactly n linear factors)
- $a_0 + a_1x + a_2x_2 + \ldots + a_nx^n = (p_1x + q_1)(p_2x + q_2) \ldots (p_nx + q_n)$
- $x^2 + 3x + 2 = (x + 1)(x + 2)$
- $x^2 + 9 = x^2 - (-9) = (x - 3\sqrt{-1})(x + 3\sqrt{-1}) = (x - 3i)(x - 3i)$
- To solve an equation/inequality means to find set of all values of variable for which the said equation/inequality holds good for instance; $x = 3, 2$ are roots of equation $x^2 - 5x + 6 = 0$ since $x = 2$ and 3 both satisfy the above equation;
  $\because$ $(2)^2 - 5(2) + 6 = 0$ and $3^2 - 5(3) + 6 = 0$.
- While solving an equation many a times it is transformed to another equation (which has roots same as of original equation) called as equivalent equation
  e.g., $\dfrac{f(x)}{g(x)} = 0 \Rightarrow f(x) = 0$ and $g(x) \neq 0$
- Two equations or inequalities are said to be equivalent iff they possess same set of solutions for instance, $x^2 - 1 = 0$ and $(x - 1)(x + 1) = 0$ are equivalent equations.
- Solution of an equation/inequality depends upon the set of numbers over which it is considered/given. Let

us consider an example, $x^2 - x - 4 = 0$ has no root in the set of rational numbers ($\mathbb{Q}$) where as over the set of real number the same equation has two real roots given as $x = \sqrt{5}+1$ and $\sqrt{5}-1$.

■ POLYNOMIAL IDENTITY

If an equation is true for all values of variable for which it is defined then it is called identity. e.g.

$$(x+2)^2 - x^2 - 4x - 4 = 0 \quad \forall x \in \mathbb{R}$$

$$\underbrace{\frac{x^2-3x+2}{x+1} = \frac{(x-1)(x-2)}{x+1}}_{\textit{Rational identity}}$$

Conclusion:

- $ax^3 + bx^2 + cx + d = 0$ is identity
  $\Rightarrow a = b = c = d = 0$
- It has more number of roots than its degree.

Theorem: When sum of coefficients of polynomial vanishes then unity becomes a root of polynomial.

$$f(x) = a_n x^n + a_{n-1}x^{n-1} + a_{n-2}x^{n-2} + \ldots \ldots + a^2x^2 + a_1x + a_0$$
$$\text{if } a_n + a_{n-1} + a_{n-2} + \ldots\ldots + a_2 + a_1 + a_0 = 0$$
$$\Leftrightarrow f(1) = 0$$
$$\Leftrightarrow a = 1 \text{ is root of the polynomial } f(a) = 0$$

Theorem: If the difference of sum of coefficients of even power of x to that of odd power terms of x vanishes then $x = -1$ turns out to be a root of polynomial.

$$(a_0 + a_2 + a_4 + \ldots\ldots) - (a_1 + a_3 + a_5 + \ldots\ldots) = 0$$
$$\Leftrightarrow a_0 - a_1 + a_2 - a_3 + a_4 - a_5 + a_6 - \ldots\ldots = 0$$
$$\Leftrightarrow a_0(-1)^0 + a_1(-1)^1 + a_2(-1)^2 + a_3(-1)^3 + a_4(-1)^4 + \ldots a_n(-1)^n = 0$$
$$\Leftrightarrow f(-1) = 0$$
$$\Leftrightarrow x = -1 \text{ is a root of polynomial}$$

ILLUSTRATION 114: Find the roots of $x^3 - 6x^2 + 11x - 6$.

SOLUTION: Let $f(x) = x^3 - 6x^2 + 11x - 6$

$\because$ sum of coefficient $= 1 - 6 + 11 - 6 = 0$

$\Rightarrow f(1) = 0$

therefore $x = 1$ is one of its roots. To obtain other roots we will rearrange the expression so that $x - 1$ factor is extracted out as below.

$f(x) = x^3 - x^2 - 5x^2 + 5x + 6x - 6 = x^2(x-1) - 5x(x-1) + 6(x-1) = (x-1)(x^2 - 5x + 6)$

$= (x-1)(x^2 - 2x - 3x + 6) = (x-1)(x-2)(x-3)$

so roots are $x = 1, 2$ and 3

ILLUSTRATION 115: Factorise the polynomial $f(x) = x^3 - 6x^2 + 5x + 12$ and get its roots.

SOLUTION: Since sum of coefficients of even power terms - sum of coefficients of odd power terms

$= (-6 + 12) - (1 + 5) = 0$

$\Rightarrow x = -1$ is a root $\qquad \Rightarrow x + 1$ is a factor

$\Rightarrow x^3 - 6x^2 + 5x + 12 = x^3 + x^2 - 7x^2 - 7x + 12x + 12$

$= x^2(x+1) - 7x(x+1) + 12(x+1) = (x+1)(x^2 - 7x + 12)$

$= (x+1)(x^2 - 4x - 3x + 12) = (x+1)(x(x-4) - 3(x-4)) = (x+1)(x-4)(x-3)$

Hence the roots of the polynomial are $-1, 4, 3$

ILLUSTRATION 116: Solve the following equations for x. $\forall\, a \in \mathbb{R}$

(a) $a(a+2)x - 2a = 4$ $\qquad$ (b) $(a^2 - 3a)x^2 - (a^2 - 4a + 3)x + a - 3 = 0$

SOLUTION: (a) Comparing leading coefficient to zero, we get,

$a(a+2) = 0$ $\qquad$ i.e., $a = 0, -2$

Now transposing and rearranging the terms, we get,

$a(a+2)x = 2(a+2)$

Case (i) Clearly, if $a = 0$ the equation turns out to be $4 = 0$ which is an impossible case for any finite value of x therefore no solution exists in the region.

Case (ii) If $a + 2 = 0$ i.e., $a = -2$ then equation reduces to an identity $0 . x = 0$ which is true for $\forall\ x \in \mathbb{R}$ leading to infinitely many solutions

Case (iii) If $a \in \mathbb{R} \sim \{0, -2\}$ then dividing the equation by $a^2 + 2a$ we get

$x = \frac{2}{a}$ as a single finite real root. Only one root exists in this region.

(b) Consider the equation $(a^2 - 3a)x^2 \quad (a^2 + 2a - 3)x + a - 3 = 0$

Comparing leading coefficient to zero we get

$a(a - 3) = 0$ i.e., $a - 0, 3$

Now factorizing the coefficient of each term we get,

$a(a - 3)x^2 - (a + 1)(a - 3)x + a - 3 = 0$

Case (i) Clearly, if $a = 3$ then equation reduces to an identity $0 . x^2 + 0 . x + 0 = 0$ which is true for $\forall\ x \in \mathbb{R}$

Case (ii) If $a = 0$ the equation turns out to be linear equation

$3x - 3 = 0$ i.e. $x = 1$ is the only one solution

Case (iii) If $a \in \mathbb{R} \sim \{0, 3\}$ then it is a quadratic equation by

$ax^2 - (a + 1)x + 1 = 0$ and has two roots given by

$$x = \frac{(a+1) \pm \sqrt{(a+1)^2 - 4a}}{2a} = \frac{(a+1) \pm \sqrt{a^2 - 2a + 1}}{2a}$$

$$x = \frac{(a+1) \pm |a-1|}{2a}$$ i.e. 1 and $\frac{1}{a}$ are roots.

RATIONAL FUNCTION AND RATIONAL EQUATION

An expression of the form $\frac{f(x)}{g(x)}$ where $f(x)$ and $g(x)$ are two polynomials in x is known as *rational function* of x and when equated to zero. i.e., $\frac{f(x)}{g(x)} = 0$ generate a *rational equation, where* $g(x) \neq 0$.

e.g. $\frac{x^2 - 4}{x^2 + 3x + 2} = 0, \ \frac{2x - 1}{x^2 + 4} = 0$

The solution of $\frac{f(x)}{g(x)} = 0$ are the roots of the equation $f(x) = 0$ for which $g(x) \neq 0$ therefore the equation $\frac{f(x)}{g(x)} = 0 \Rightarrow f(x) = 0$ but $g(x) \neq 0$.

ILLUSTRATION 117: Solve the following rational equations for x.

(a) $\frac{x^3 - 4x}{x^2 + 3x + 2} = 0$ (b) $\frac{2x^3 + 3x^2 + 5x + 4}{x^5 - 1} = 0$

SOLUTION: (a) Consider the equation

$$\frac{x^3 - 4x}{x^2 + 3x + 2} = 0 \quad \Rightarrow \frac{x(x-2)(x+2)}{(x+1)(x+2)} = 0$$

$\Rightarrow$ $x(x-2)(x+2) = 0$ but $x \neq -1, -2$, since denominator cannot be zero.

$\Rightarrow$ $x = 0$; 2 are two real solutions

Remember that $\dfrac{x^3 - 4x}{x^2 + 3x + 2} = 0$ and $x^3 - 4x = 0$ are not equivalent equations.

(b) Given equation $\dfrac{2x^3 + 3x^2 + 5x + 4}{x^5 - 1} = 0$

$2x^3 + 3x^2 + 5x + 4 = 0$ but $x^5 \neq 1$

$\because$ $x = -1$ is root of above cubic polynomial. So rearranging and grouping to get $x + 1$ factored out

$\Rightarrow$ $2x^3 + 2x^2 + x^2 + x + 4x + 4 = 0$

$\Rightarrow$ $2x^2(x + 1) + x(x + 1) + 4(x + 1) = 0$

$\Rightarrow$ $(x + 1)(2x^2 + x + 4) = 0$

$\Rightarrow$ $x = -1$ is the only root as $2x^2 + x + 4 = 0$ has no real roots but at $x = -1$; $x^4 = 1$

so denominator of rational expression vanishes hence above rational equation has no real root.

ILLUSTRATION 118: Find the integer roots of the equation

(a) $x^3 + x^2 + x - 84 = 0$ (b) $(x - a)(x - 4) = 5$ where a is an integer.

SOLUTION: (a) Consider the equation $x^3 + x^2 + x - 84 = 0$

$x^3 + x^2 + x + 1 = 85$

$\Rightarrow$ $x^2 + 1$ is positive so $x + 1$ must be positive odd integer

and $x^2 + 1$ shall be larger than $x + 1$.

$\Rightarrow$ possible factors are $x + 1 = 1$ and $x^2 + 1 = 85$ which is not possible

or $x + 1 = 5$ and $x^2 + 1 = 17$ that gives $x = 4$ as root

$\Rightarrow$ $x = 4$ is only solution.

(b) Since $x \in \mathbb{Z}$ and a is also integer

$\Rightarrow$ $(x - a)$ and $(x - 4)$ both are integers so possible factors are

$\Rightarrow$ $x - a = 1$ and $x - 4 = 5$

or $x - a = -1$ and $x - 4 = -5$ or $x - a = 5$ and $x - 4 = 1$

or $x - a = -5$ and $x - 4 = -1$

$$\Rightarrow \begin{cases} x = 9 \text{ and } 9 - a = 1 \quad \text{i.e. } a = 8 \\ x = -1 \text{ and } -1 - a = -1 \quad \text{i.e. } a = 0 \\ x = 5 \text{ and } 5 - a = 5 \quad \text{i.e. } a = 0 \\ x = 3 \text{ and } 3 - a = -5 \quad \text{i.e. } a = 8 \end{cases}$$

therefore $a = 0$, $x = -1$ and 5 are roots and for $a = 8$, $x = 9$ and 3 are roots.

ILLUSTRATION 119: If the polynomial $f(x) = x^3 + px^2 + qx + r$ has $x = -1, 2$ as its roots, then find the possible values of p, q, r given that $p = 1 + q$.

SOLUTION: Given $x = -1, 2$ are roots of the given polynomial $f(x) = x^3 + px^2 + qx + r$

Therefore, $f(-1) = 0$ and $f(2) = 0$ so we get, $p - q + r = 1$ (1)

Since given that $p - q = 1$

therefore $r = 0$; Now from $f(2) = 0$ we get $8 + 4p + 2q = 0$

$\Rightarrow$ $2p + q = -4$ and solving with $p - q = 1$

we get $p = -1$ and $q = -2$.

TEXTUAL EXERCISE–17 (SUBJECTIVE)

1. Solve the following equations for all *a*.

(a) $(a-4)x+5=a+1$

(b) $2a(a-5)x=a-5$

(c) $ax+2x-6=2a-x$

(d) $ax+2x+3=5-x$

2. Solve the following rational equations for x.

(a) $\frac{1}{x+1}+\frac{2}{x-2}=1$

(b) $\frac{x^2-4}{x^2+3x+2}=0$

(c) $\frac{x^2+3x+2}{x^2+4x+3}=0$

3. Solve the following rational equations for x.

(a) $\frac{x^2+5x+6}{x^3+3x^2+2x}=0$

(b) $\frac{x}{x+3}+\frac{4}{x+1}=2$

(c) $\frac{2x-3}{x-1}+1=\frac{6x-x^2-6}{x-1}$

4. Find all natural number solutions of the equations. (Also find integral solution)

(a) $x^2-y^2=7$

(b) $x^2-y^2=21$

5. Let a quadratic polynomial $P(x)=px^2+qx+r$, where $p, q, r \in \mathbb{R}$. It is given that $P(5)=-3P(2)$ and that 3 is a root of polynomial $P(x)$, then find the other root of $P(x)=0$.

Answer Keys

1. (a) for $a=4$; $x\in\mathbb{R}$; for $a\neq 4$; $x=1$ (b) for $a=5$; $x\in\mathbb{R}$; for $a\neq 0, 5$ $x=\frac{1}{2a}$; for $a=0$, No solution.

(c) $x\in\mathbb{R}$ for $a=-3$; $x=2$ for $a\neq -3$ (d) No solution for $a-3$; $x=\frac{2}{a+3}$ for $a\neq -3$

2. (a) $(2\pm\sqrt{6})$ (b) 2 (c) –2 **3.** (a) –3 (b) $\frac{-3\pm\sqrt{33}}{2}$ (c) 2

4. (a) $x=\pm 4$, $y=\pm 3$ (b) $x=\pm 5$, $y=\pm 2$; $x=\pm 11$, $y=\pm 10$

5. if $p\neq 0$ then $x=3, -4$ are roots and if $p=0$ then equation and identity and has infinitely many roots.

■ RATIONAL ALGEBRAIC INEQUALITIES

Consider the following types of rational algebraic inequalities. $\frac{P(x)}{Q(x)}>0, \frac{P(x)}{Q(x)}<0, \frac{P(x)}{Q(x)}\geq 0, \frac{P(x)}{Q(x)}\leq 0$ where $P(x)$ and $Q(x)$ are polynomials in *x*.

These inequalities can be solved by the method of intervals also known as sign method.

To solve these inequalities, proceed according to following steps:

(a) Factorize $P(x)$ and $Q(x)$ into linear factors.

(b) Make coefficient of *x* positive in all factors.

(c) Equate all the factors to zero and find corresponding values of *x*.

These values are known as *Critical points.*

(d) Plot the critical points on number line. *n* critical points will divide the number line in $(n+1)$ regions.

(e) If right most region the expression bears positive sign, then and in other regions the expression bears negative and positive signs alternatively.

If $P(x)$ and $Q(x)$ can be resolved in linear factors then use wavy curve method otherwise use the following statements for solving inequalities of this kind:

(i) $\frac{P(x)}{Q(x)}>0 \Rightarrow P(x).Q(x)>0$

$\Rightarrow P(x)>0, Q(x)>0$

$or\ P(x)<0, Q(x)<0$

(ii) $\frac{P(x)}{Q(x)}<0 \Rightarrow P(x).Q(x)<0$

$\Rightarrow P(x)>0,\ Q(x)<0$ or $P(x)<0, Q(x)>0$

(iii) $\frac{P(x)}{Q(x)}\geq 0 \Rightarrow \begin{cases} P(x)Q(x)\geq 0 \\ Q(x)\neq 0 \end{cases}$

$\Rightarrow P(x)\geq 0, Q(x)>0$ or $P(x)\leq 0, Q(x)<0$

(iv) $\dfrac{P(x)}{Q(x)} \le 0 \Rightarrow \begin{cases} P(x)Q(x) \le 0 \\ Q(x) \ne 0 \end{cases}$

$\Rightarrow P(x) \ge 0,\ Q(x) < 0$ or $P(x) \le 0,\ Q(x) > 0$

■ SOLVING RATIONAL INEQUALITY

While solving rational inequality, following four facts must always be kept in mind.

$\dfrac{f(x)}{g(x)} > 0 \quad \Rightarrow$ $f(x)$ and $g(x)$ have same sign.

$\Rightarrow f(x).g(x) > 0$

$\dfrac{f(x)}{g(x)} < 0 \quad \Rightarrow$ $f(x)$ and $g(x)$ of opposite sign

$\Rightarrow f(x).g(x) < 0$

$\dfrac{f(x)}{g(x)} \ge 0 \Rightarrow$ $f(x)$ and $g(x)$ have same sign or $f(x) = 0$

$$\Rightarrow \begin{cases} f(x).g(x) > 0 \\ or \\ f(x) = 0\ \&\ g(x) \ne 0 \end{cases}$$

$\dfrac{f(x)}{g(x)} \le 0 \Rightarrow$ $f(x)$ and $g(x)$ of opposite sign or $f(x) = 0$

$$\Rightarrow \begin{cases} f(x).g(x) < 0 \\ or \\ f(x) = 0\ \&\ g(x) \ne 0 \end{cases}$$

ILLUSTRATION 120: Find the set of all real values of 'x' for which the following inequality holds true $x^2 - 3x + 2 < 0$.

SOLUTION: Given $x^2 - 3x + 2 < 0$.

$\Rightarrow (x - 1)(x - 2) < 0$ (both factors have opposite sign)

$\Rightarrow x - 1 > 0$ and $x - 2 < 0$ or $x - 1 < 0$ and $x - 2 > 0$

$\Rightarrow x > 1$ and $x < 2$ or $x < 1$ and $x > 2 \Rightarrow x \in (1, \infty) \cap (-\infty, 2)$ or $x \in (-\infty, 1) \cap (2, \infty)$

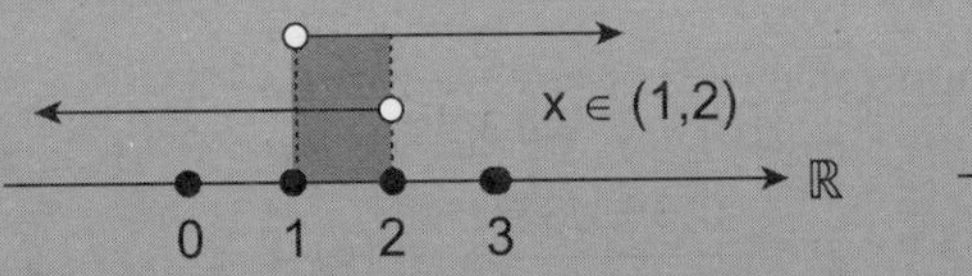

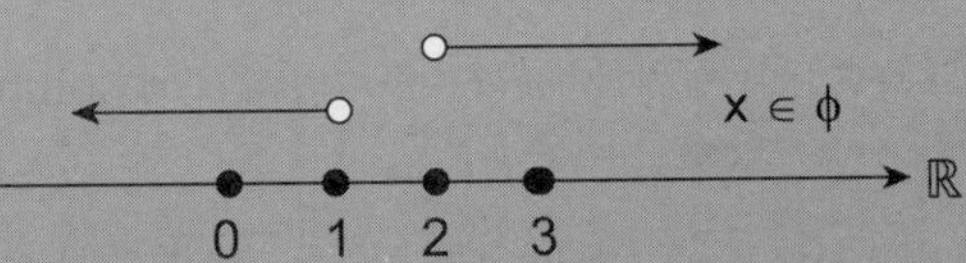

FIGURE 1.64

$\Rightarrow x \in (1, 2)$ or $x \in \phi \qquad \Rightarrow x \in (1, 2)$

ILLUSTRATION 121: Find the set of all real values of 'x' for which the inequality $(x - 1)(x + 2) \le 0$ holds good.

SOLUTION: Given $(x - 1)(x + 2) \le 0$. The following two cases arise:-

Case (i): $x - 1 \ge 0$ and $x + 2 \le 0$

$\Rightarrow x \in (1, \infty)$ and $x \in (-\infty, -2)$

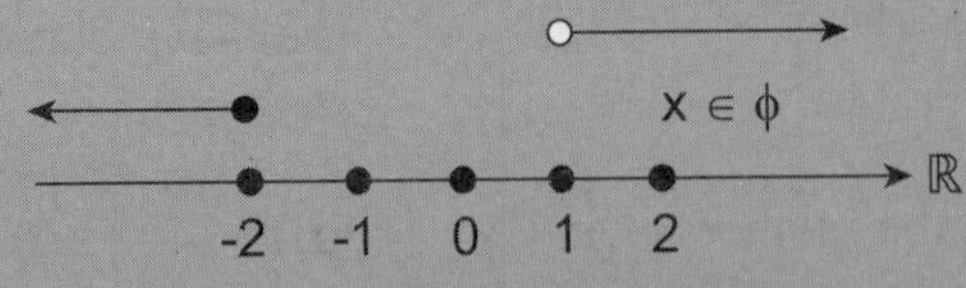

FIGURE 1.65

Case (ii): $x - 1 \le 0$ and $x + 2 \ge 0$

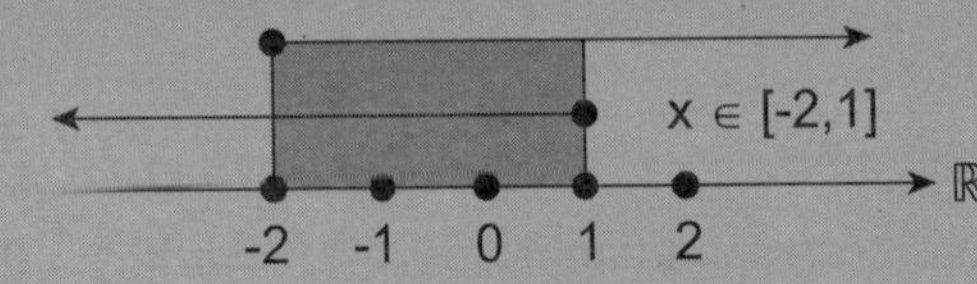

FIGURE 1.66

$\Rightarrow x \le 1$ and $x \ge -2 \qquad \Rightarrow x \in (-\infty, 1] \cap [-2, \infty) \qquad \Rightarrow x \in [-2, 1]$

We can see that the above mentioned exhaustive approach becomes very inconvenient and lengthy if the polynomial expression has more than two linear factors. Therefore to solve such rational inequalities the following algorithm is proposed, popularly known as *wavy curve method.*

WAVY CURVE METHOD/METHOD OF INTERVALS

As we know that any polynomial expression can change the sign of its expression only at its roots (the inputs at which polynomial expression vanishes). The sign of polynomial expression remains uniform (throughout positive or throughout negative) between any two consecutive roots. Above said facts lead to the conclusion that if roots of a polynomial are arranged on a number line, they divide the real number line into intervals in which the polynomial retains uniform sign. These roots are called critical points and the intervals obtained are test intervals.

To determine the test intervals and thus to find the sign of polynomial expression $f(x)$ in these intervals, following algorithm is suggested.

Step 1. Factorize the polynomial and find all the roots e.g., $f(x) = (x - \alpha)^3 (x - \beta)^2 (x - \delta) (x - \gamma)^5$ say $\alpha < \beta < \gamma < \delta$.

Step 2. Locate the roots (with their multiplicity) on real number line. *Multiplicity of root is nothing but the number of times the root is repeated in the expression.*

Step 3. Keep the sign expression in the right-most interval same as that of leading coefficient.

(+)

α 3 β 2 γ 5 δ 1 sign of leading coefficient $\mathbb{R}$

FIGURE 1.67

Step 4. Moving towards left change the sign of expression across the root with multiplicity odd. And retain the same sign across the root with multiplicity even.

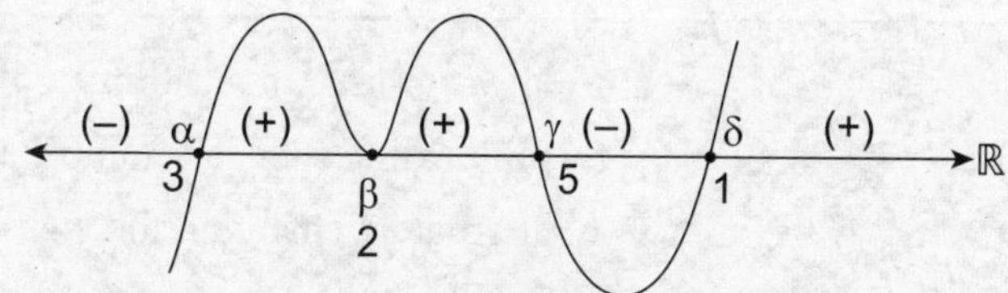

FIGURE 1.68

when $x > \delta$ all the linear factors are positive therefore the sign of expression remains positive for all $x \in (\delta, \infty)$ so we mark interval (δ, ∞) with positive sign. Now moving towards left across the point $x = \delta$ the only linear factor $x - \delta$ changes its sign (*rest of the factors retain their same sign*) therefore if the multiplicity of root δ be odd then expression contains odd power of factor $x - \delta$, consequently changing the sign of expression from positive to negative across $x = \delta$. And thus $f(x)$ becomes negative in the interval (γ, δ) and similarly, the sign of $f(x)$ changes from negative to positive across the critical point $x = \gamma$ as the factor $(x - \gamma)$ has odd power and changes its sign across $x = \gamma$. Therefore $f(x)$ remains positive in the interval (β, γ).

Now at $x = \beta$, although the sign of linear factor $(x - \beta)$ changes but as the power of $(x - \beta)$ is even, that change produces no change in the sign of expression of the polynomial $f(x)$. And hence $f(x)$ remains positive in the interval (α, β). Similarly, the sign of $f(x)$ changes from positive to negative across $x = \alpha$ since α is a root with odd multiplicity.

Conclusion from above discussion

$$f(x) > 0 \quad \Rightarrow (\alpha,\beta)\cup(\beta,\gamma)\cup(\delta,\infty)$$

Also $f(x) \geq 0$

$$\Rightarrow (\alpha,\beta)\cup(\beta,\gamma)\cup(\delta,\infty)\cup\{\alpha,\beta,\gamma,\delta\}$$

$$\Rightarrow \quad \in[\alpha,\gamma]\cup[\delta,\infty)$$

Similarly $f(x) < 0 \Rightarrow (-\infty,\alpha)\cup(\gamma,\delta)$ & $f(x) \leq 0$

$$\Rightarrow (-\infty,\alpha)\cup(\gamma,\delta)\cup\{\alpha,\beta,\gamma,\delta\} \;\; f(x) \leq 0$$

$$\Rightarrow (-\infty,\alpha]\cup[\gamma,\delta]\cup\{\beta\}$$

Aliter for Step 4. Choose a suitable value of x in each test interval and obtain the sign of the value of polynomial expression for that x, the same sign shall prevail for each value of x in that test interval. Similarly, determine the sign of expression in each interval.

ILLUSTRATION 122: Find the test intervals as well as sign of following quadratic expression

(a) $f(x) = x^2 + 2x - 8$ (b) $f(x) = x^2 + 3x - 4$ (c) $f(x) = x^2 - 3x + 4$

SOLUTION: (a) Factorising the expression and obtaining root $x^2 + 4x - 2x - 8$ $= x(x + 4) - 2(x + 4) = (x + 4)(x - 2)$

Locating the roots 2 and –4 on real number line we get the test intervals as $(-\infty, -4)$ $(-4, 2)$ and $(2, \infty)$ respectively.

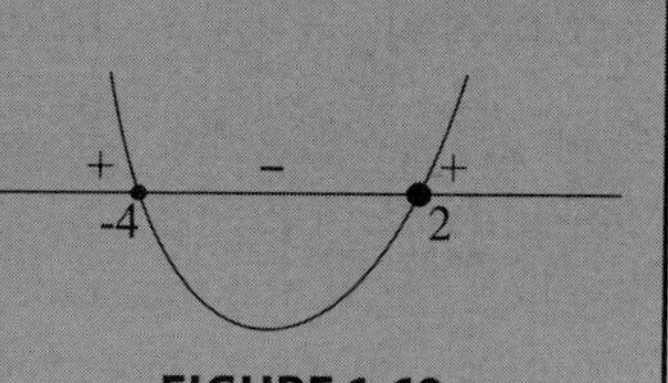

FIGURE 1.69

Now observe the leading coefficient i.e. 1 which is positive and each root is single. So locating roots on number line and keeping the sign in right most interval positive alternately changing the sign across each root we get $f(x) > 0\ \forall\ x \in (-\infty, -4) \cup (2, \infty)$

$f(x) < 0\ \forall\ x \in (-4, 2)$

(b) Factorising the polynomial equation $f(x) = x^2 + 3x - 4 = x^2 + 4x - x - 4$
$= x(x + 4) - (x + 4) = (x + 4)(x - 1)$
Test intervals are $(-\infty, 4)$, $[-4, 1]$, $(1, \infty)$
The sign of $f(x)$ is in $(-\infty, 4]$: positive; $(4, 1)$: negative; $[1, \infty)$: positive

(c) Factorising $f(x)$ is not possible. $f(x)$ can be graphed as a parabola opening upward. Hence for all real values of x, $f(x) > 0$. Since $f(x)$ will never change sign, there are no test intervals in the interval $(-\infty, \infty)$, $f(x)$ is always positive.

ILLUSTRATION 123: Find all values of a for which the set of all solutions of the system $\begin{cases} \dfrac{x^2 + ax - 2}{x^2 - x + 1} < 2 \\ \dfrac{x^2 + ax - 2}{x^2 - x + 1} > -3 \end{cases}$ is the entire number line.

SOLUTION: The system is equivalent to $\begin{cases} \dfrac{x^2 - (a+2)x + 4}{x^2 - x + 1} > 0 \\ \dfrac{4x^2 + (a-3)x + 1}{x^2 - x + 1} > 0 \end{cases}$

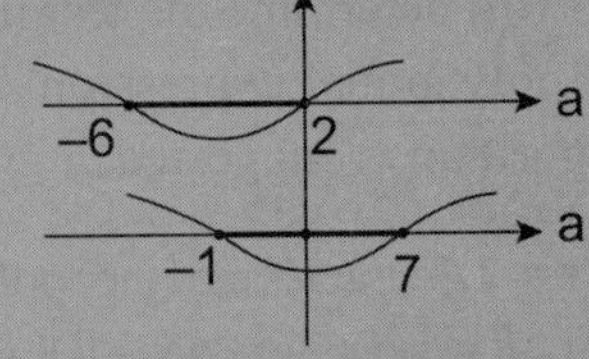

FIGURE 1.70

Since $x^2 - x + 1 = (x - 1/2)^2 + 3/4 > 0$ for any x, this system is equivalent to $\begin{cases} x^2 - (a+2)x + 4 > 0 \\ 4x^2 + (a-3)x + 1 > 0 \end{cases}$

Hence the discriminants of the both equations of this system are negative.

i.e., $\begin{cases} (a+2)^2 - 16 < 0 \\ (a-3)^2 - 16 < 0 \end{cases} \Rightarrow \begin{cases} (a+6)(a-2) < 0 \\ (a+1)(a-7) < 0 \end{cases}$

From wavy curve method: $\therefore\ a \in (-1, 2)$

■ PROCEDURE FOR SOLVING RATIONAL INEQUALITIES

To obtain the sign of rational expression $f(x)/g(x)$ i.e. to solve $\dfrac{f(x)}{g(x)} > 0$ *or* < 0 follow the steps given below.

Step 1: Write the inequality so that one side is 0. If necessary, combine terms on the other side into a single quotient.

Step 2: Locate the critical points on the real number line and obtain the *test intervals*, the critical points are the numbers for which the fraction either becomes zero or turn out to be undefined. (i.e., the roots of numerator as well as the roots of denominator)

Step 3: Choose the suitable value of the variable (say x) for each test interval and thus obtain the sign of expression in each test interval.

Step 4: The solution set for $\dfrac{f(x)}{g(x)} > 0$ is union of those intervals in which the obtained sign is positive whereas the solution set for $\dfrac{f(x)}{g(x)} < 0$ is union of those intervals in which the obtained sign is negative.

Step 5: To solve $\dfrac{f(x)}{g(x)} \le 0$ *or* $\dfrac{f(x)}{g(x)} \ge 0$ resolve the inequalities into a strict inequality and an equation and solve them separately and then take the union of both solutions.

ILLUSTRATION 124: Find the number of integer values of variable x satisfying the following pair of inequalities.

$$\frac{(x-1)(x+4)}{x-3} < 0 \ \& \ x^2+6x-27 \le 0$$

SOLUTION: Consider both inequality $\frac{(x-1)(x+4)}{x-3} < 0 \ \& \ x^2+6x-27 \le 0$

both are equivalent to polynomial inequality

$\Rightarrow (x-1)(x+4)(x-3) < 0$ and $(x+9)(x-3) \le 0$

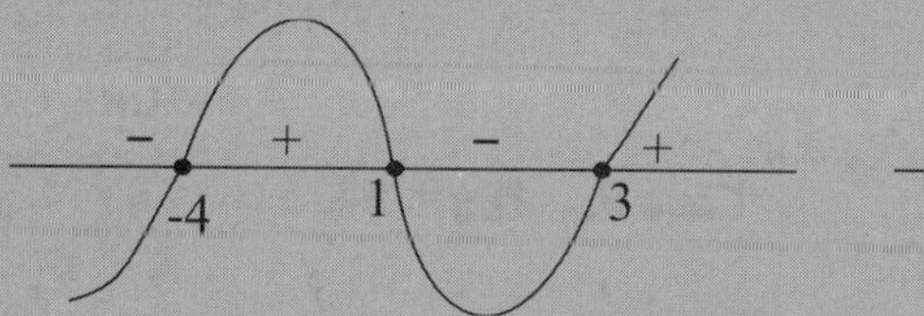

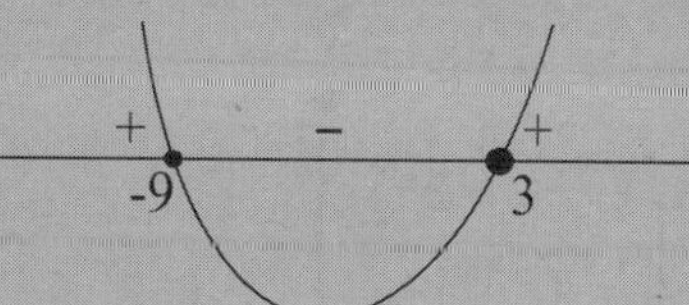

FIGURE 1.71

i.e. $x \in (-\infty,-4) \cup (1,3)$ and $x \in [-9,3]$

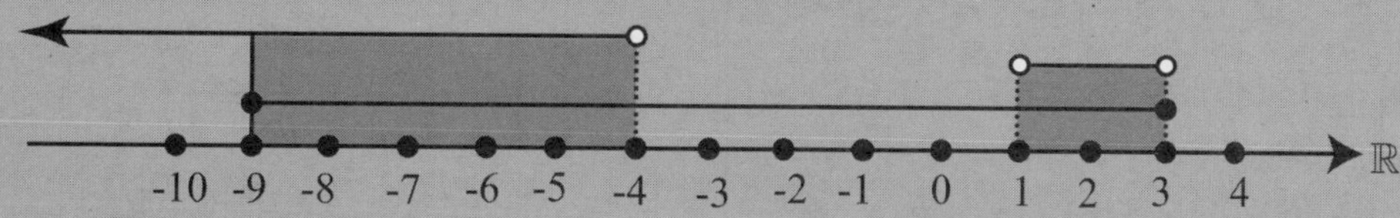

FIGURE 1.72

Taking intersection of both we get the resulting set of solution as overlapping interval on the diagram

$\Rightarrow x \in [-9,-4) \cup (1,3)$ but since x is integer $\therefore \quad x \in \{-9,-8,-7,-6,-5,2\}$

$\Rightarrow$ number of integer solutions = 6.

ILLUSTRATION 125: Solve the following inequality for x.

(a) $x^3 + 4x^2 + 5x + 2 \le 0$ (b) $x^4 - x^3 + x^2 - x + 1 \ge 0$

SOLUTION: (a) Sum of coefficients of even power terms is same as sum of coefficients of odd power terms So $x = -1$ is one root. Now rearranging and grouping to get $x + 1$ factor

$x^3 + x^2 + 3x^2 + 3x + 2x + 2 < 0$

$\Rightarrow x^2(x+1) + (3x)(x+1) + 2(x+1) < 0$

$\Rightarrow (x+1)(x^2+3x+2) < 0$ $\qquad \Rightarrow (x+1)(x+1)(x+2) < 0$

$\Rightarrow (x+1)^2(x+2) < 0$ $\qquad \because (x+1)^2 \ge 0$

$\Rightarrow x + 2 < 0$ $\qquad \Rightarrow x < -2$ $\qquad \Rightarrow x \in (-\infty,-2)$

but $x^3 + 4x^2 + 5x + 2 = 0$ $\qquad \Rightarrow (x+1)^2(x+2) = 0$

$\Rightarrow x = -1, -2$ thus $x \in (-\infty, 2] \cup \{-1\}$ is the solution.

(b) $x^3(x-1) + x(x-1) + 1 \ge 0$

$\Rightarrow (x-1)x + (x^2+1) + 1 \ge 0$

Clearly of $x(x-1) \ge 0$ i.e., $x \in (-\infty,0] \cup [1,\infty)$ then inequality holds evidently as expression remains larger than 1 but if $n \in (0, 1)$

$x^4 < x^3 < x^2 < x < 1$ and $1 - x > 0$ therefore again regrouping the terms as below:

$x^4 + (x^2 - x^3) + 1 - x = x^4 + x^2(1-x) + 1 - x = x^4 + (1-x)(x^2+1) > 0$

Hence inequality holds good $\forall x \in \mathbb{R}$.

■ MAXIMUM/MINIMUM VALUE AND SIGN OF QUADRATIC EXPRESSION

Consider a quadratic expression $y = ax^2 + bx + c \ \forall\ x \in \mathbb{R}$ completing the square and isolating the perfect square expression from above, we get

$$y = ax^2 + bx + c = a\left(x^2 + \frac{b}{a}x + \frac{c}{a}\right) = a\left(x^2 + 2\left(\frac{b}{2a}\right)x + \frac{c}{a}\right)$$

completing the square

$$= a\left(\underbrace{x^2 + 2\left(\frac{b}{2a}\right)x + \left(\frac{b}{2a}\right)^2}_{\text{complete the square}} + \frac{c}{a} - \left(\frac{b}{2a}\right)^2\right)$$

$$= a\left(\left(x + \frac{b}{2a}\right)^2 - \frac{(b^2 - 4ac)}{4a^2}\right) \Rightarrow y = a\left(x + \frac{b}{2a}\right)^2 - \frac{D}{4a}.$$

Since $y = a\left(x + \frac{b}{2a}\right)^2 - \frac{D}{4a}$.

Clearly, when $x + \frac{b}{2a} = \pm t$ i.e. at $x = -\frac{b}{2a} \pm t$ the value of expression remains equal, that is why the graph of quadratic is symmetric about the line $x = -\frac{b}{2a}$.

Case I: **If a > 0**

Since $a\left(x + \frac{b}{2a}\right)^2 \geq 0 \Rightarrow a\left(x + \frac{b}{2a}\right)^2 + a\left(\frac{-D}{4a}\right) \geq \frac{-D}{4a}$

$$\Rightarrow y \geq \frac{-D}{4a} \Rightarrow y \in \left[\frac{-D}{4a}, \infty\right)$$

$$\Rightarrow \begin{cases} y_{max} \to \infty & \text{when } x \to \pm\infty \\ y_{min} = \frac{-D}{4a} & \text{when } x = -\frac{b}{2a} \end{cases}$$

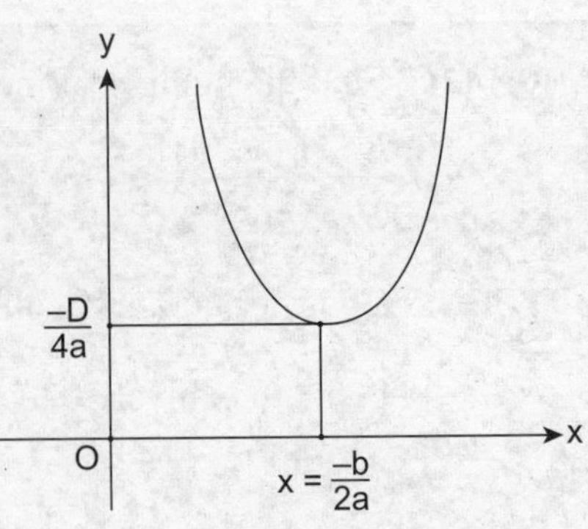

FIGURE 1.73

Case II: **If a < 0**

Since $\left(x + \frac{b}{2a}\right)^2 \geq 0 \Rightarrow a\left(x + \frac{b}{2a}\right)^2 \leq 0$

adding $\frac{-D}{4a}$ both side

$$\Rightarrow a\left(x + \frac{b}{2a}\right)^2 - \frac{D}{4a} \leq \frac{-D}{4a}$$

$$\Rightarrow y \leq \frac{-D}{4a} \Rightarrow y \in \left(-\infty, \frac{-D}{4a}\right]$$

$$\Rightarrow \begin{cases} y_{max} = \frac{-D}{4a} & \text{when } x = -\frac{b}{2a} \\ y_{min} \to -\infty & \text{when } x \to \pm\infty \end{cases}$$

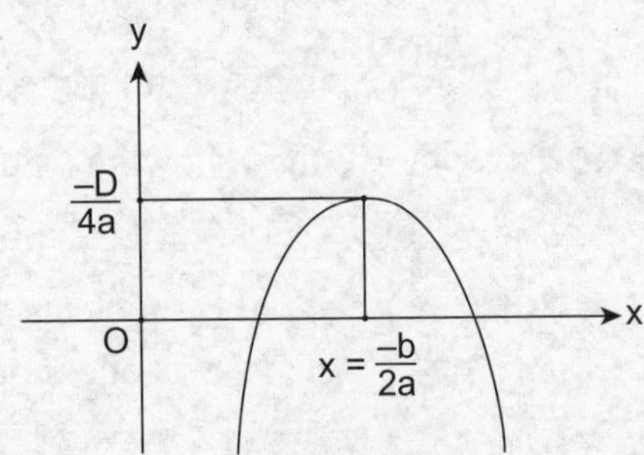

FIGURE 1.74

ILLUSTRATION 126: Find the maximum and minimum values of following quadratic expression and hence or otherwise draw their graph

(a) $y = x^2 - 4x + 3$ (b) $y = x^2 + x + 1$

(c) $y = -x^2 + 3x - 4$

SOLUTION: (a) Since leading coefficient $a = 1$ which is positive therefore the graph shall be a parabola opening upward, also $b = -4$; $c = 3$

$\Rightarrow D = b^2 - 4ac = 16 - 12 = 4$

Therefore vertex of parabola lies at $\left(\frac{-b}{2a}, \frac{-D}{4a}\right) \equiv (2, -1)$

parabola cuts y axis at (0, 3) because $y = 3$ at $x = 0$.

Completing and isolating the square, we get,

$\Rightarrow\; y = x^2 - 4x + 3 = x^2 - 4x + 4 - 1 = (x-2)^2 - 1.$

Since $(x-2)^2 \geq 0 \;\forall\; x \in \mathbb{R}$ adding –1 to both sides, we get,

$(x-2)^2 - 1 \geq -1.$ $\qquad \Rightarrow\; y \geq -1$

$\Rightarrow\; y \in [-1, \infty)$

$$\Rightarrow \begin{cases} y_{\max} \to \infty & \text{when } x \to \pm\infty \\ y_{\min} = \dfrac{-D}{4a} = -1 & \text{when } x = -\dfrac{b}{2a} = 2 \end{cases}$$

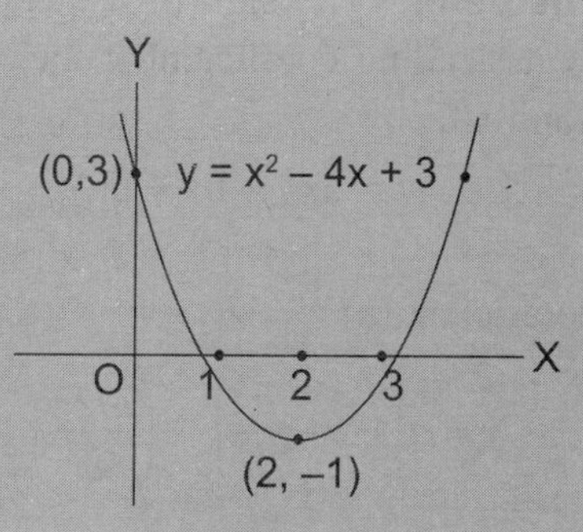

FIGURE 1.75

The graph of above parabola is shown in the figure.

(b) Since leading coefficient $a = 1$ which is positive therefore the graph shall be a parabola opening upwards also $b = 1$; $c = 1$

$\Rightarrow\; D = b^2 - 4ac = 1 - 4 = -3$

therefore vertex of parabola lies at $\left(\dfrac{-b}{2a}, \dfrac{-D}{4a}\right) \equiv \left(-\dfrac{1}{2}, \dfrac{3}{4}\right)$

Parabola cuts y axis at (0, 1) because when x becomes zero then $y = 1$

Completing and isolating the square, we get,

$\Rightarrow\; y = x^2 + x + 1 = x^2 + 2(x/2) + (1/4) + (3/4) = (x + 1/2)^2 + (3/4).$

Since $(x + 1/2)^2 \geq 0 \;\forall\; x \in \mathbb{R}$ adding (3/4) to both sides we get

$(x + 1/2)^2 + (3/4) \geq (3/4).$ $\qquad \Rightarrow\; y \geq (3/4)$

$\Rightarrow\; y \in \left[\dfrac{3}{4}, \infty\right)$

$$\Rightarrow \begin{cases} y_{\max} \to \infty & \text{when } x \to \pm\infty \\ y_{\min} = \dfrac{-D}{4a} = \dfrac{3}{4} & \text{when } x = -\dfrac{b}{2a} = -\dfrac{1}{2} \end{cases}$$

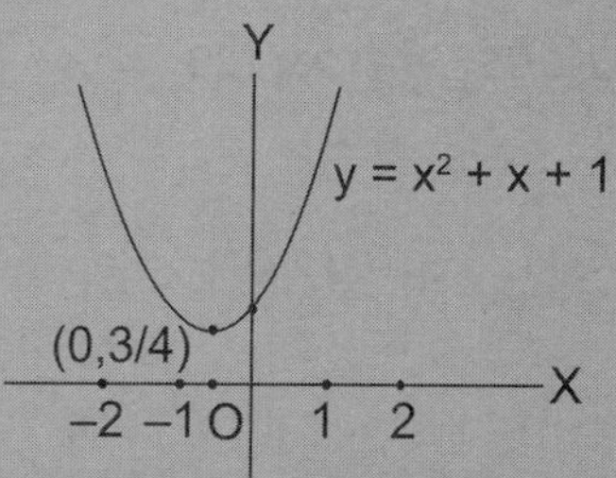

FIGURE 1.76

The graph of above parabola is shown in the figure.

(c) Since leading coefficient $a = -1$ which is negative therefore the graph shall be a parabola

opening downward also $b = 3$; $c = -4$

$\Rightarrow\; D = b^2 - 4ac = 9 - 16 = -7$

therefore vertex of parabola lies at $\left(\dfrac{-b}{2a}, \dfrac{-D}{4a}\right) \equiv \left(\dfrac{3}{2}, -\dfrac{7}{4}\right)$

parabola cuts y axis at (0, –4) because when x becomes zero then $y = -4$

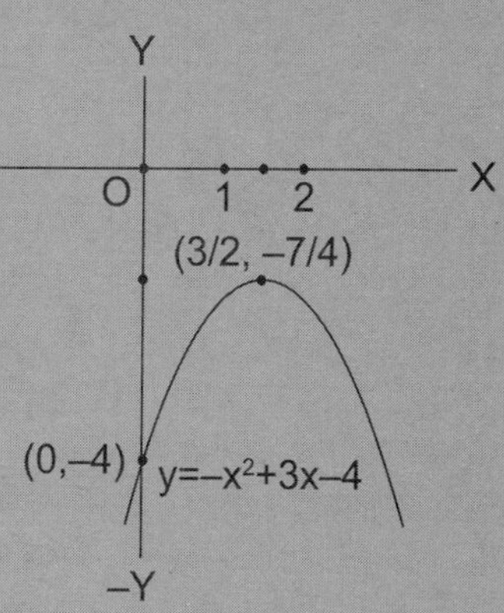

FIGURE 1.77

Completing and isolating the square, we get,

$\Rightarrow\; y = -x^2 + 3x - 4 = -[x^2 - 2(3/2)x + (9/4)] + (9/4) - 4$

$= -(x - 3/2)^2 + (-7/4).$

Since $-(x - 3/2)^2 \leq 0 \;\forall\; x \in \mathbb{R}$ adding (–7/4) to both sides, we get

$(-7/4) - (x - 3/2)^2 \leq (-7/4)$ $\qquad \Rightarrow\; y \leq (-7/4)$

$y \in \left(-\infty, -\dfrac{7}{4}\right]$

$$\Rightarrow \begin{cases} y_{\min} \to -\infty & \text{when } x \to \pm\infty \\ y_{\max} = \dfrac{-D}{4a} = -\dfrac{7}{4} & \text{when } x = -\dfrac{b}{2a} = \dfrac{3}{2} \end{cases}$$

The graph of above parabola is shown the figure.

Theorem: The sign of a quadratic expression is similar to its leading coefficient if the roots of quadratic are both non real.

i.e., $y = \underbrace{ax^2 + bx + c}_{f(x)}$ has same sign as its leading coefficient (a)

$$y = a\left(\left(x+\frac{b}{2a}\right)^2 - \left(\frac{D}{4a^2}\right)\right) = a\left[\left(x+\frac{b}{2a}\right)^2 + \left(\frac{-D}{4a^2}\right)\right]$$

$$\Rightarrow y \text{ is } \begin{cases} +ve & if\ a>0 \\ -ve & if\ a<0 \end{cases} \quad as\ D<0$$

$$\Rightarrow af(x) > 0 \quad \forall x \in \mathbb{R} \quad if \quad D<0$$

Conclusion: Sign of quadratic expression is same as of its leading coefficient when $D < 0$.

ILLUSTRATION 127: Solve the inequality $(x^2 - 5x + 6)(x^2 + 3x + 4) < 0$.

SOLUTION: Consider $(x^2 - 5x + 6)(x^2 + 3x + 4) < 0$.

$\Rightarrow (x - 3)(x - 2)(x^2 + 3x + 4) < 0$

consequently the inequality reduces to $(x - 3)(x - 2) < 0$

$\Rightarrow x \in (2, 3)$

$\because x^2 + 3x + 4 > 0 \quad \forall\ x \in \mathbb{R}$

because its leading coefficient a = 1 > 0 and discriminant $D = 9 - 16 = -7 < 0$

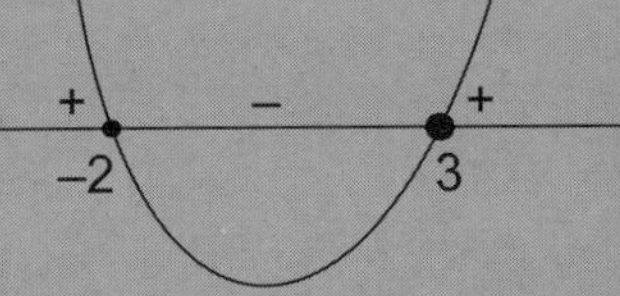

FIGURE 1.78

ILLUSTRATION 128: Solve the inequality $\dfrac{(x+1)^4(x-2)(x-3)^3(x-4)^2}{x^3-36x} \geq 0$

SOLUTION: Separating the inequality $\dfrac{(x+1^4)(x-2)(x-3)^3(x-4)^2}{x(x^2-36)} > 0$

or $(x + 1)^4 (x - 2)(x - 3)^3 (x - 4)^2 = 0$ but $(x \neq 0, -6, 6)$ transforming in to polynomial inequality

$\Rightarrow x(x + 1)^4 (x - 2)(x - 3)^3 (x + 6)(x - 6)(x - 4)^2 > 0$

or $x \in \{-1, 2, 3, 4\}$

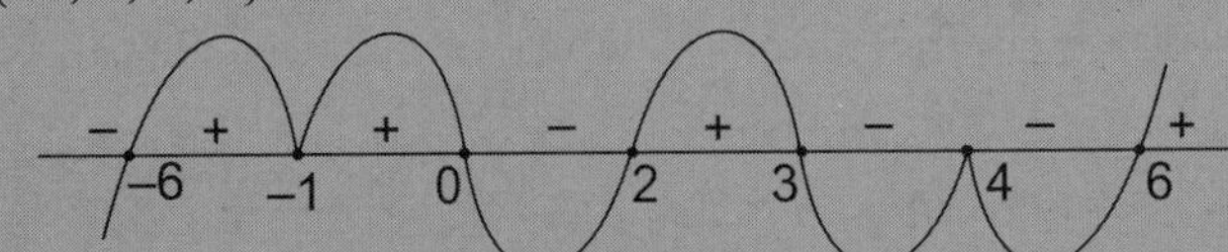

FIGURE 1.79

$x \in (-6, -1] \cup [-1,0] \cup [2,3] \cup (6, \infty)$ or $x \in \{-1, 2, 3, 4\}$

Taking union of the two sets, we get,

$\Rightarrow x \in (-6, -1] \cup [-1,0] \cup [2,3] \cup (6, \infty) \cup \{4\}$

$\Rightarrow x \in (-6, 0] \cup [2,3] \cup (6, \infty) \cup \{4\}$

ILLUSTRATION 129: Solve the inequality $\dfrac{x^3 - 4x^2 - 12x}{x+3} \geq 0$

SOLUTION : Consider $\dfrac{x^3 - 4x^2 - 12x}{x+3} \geq 0$

$\Rightarrow \dfrac{x(x^2 - 4x - 12)}{x+3} > 0$

or $x(x^2 - 4x - 12) = 0$

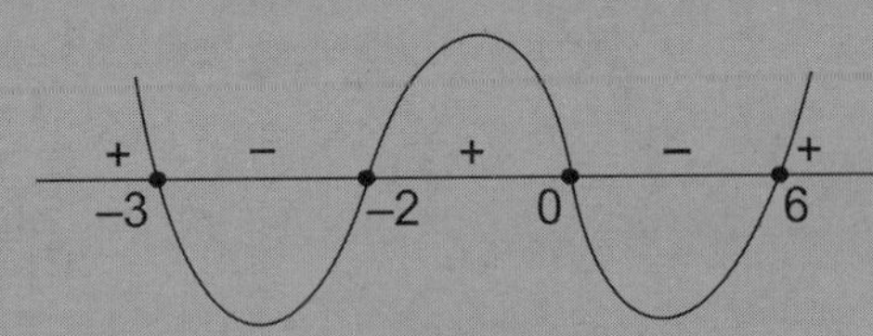

FIGURE 1.80

The equivalent polynomial inequality is

$\Rightarrow x(x-6)(x+2)(x+3) > 0$ or $x(x-6)(x+2) = 0$

$\Rightarrow x \in (-\infty, -3) \cup (-2, 0) \cup (6, \infty) \cup \{-2, 0, 6\} \Rightarrow x \in (-\infty, -3] \cup [-2, 0] \cup (6, \infty)$

The largest negative integer satisfying the inequality is –1 and smallest positive integer is 6.

ILLUSTRATION 130: Find the range of x, so that following expressions are defined

(a) $(x-1)(x-2)(x-3)^2(x-4)^5(x-5) > 0$ (b) $\dfrac{(x-1)(x-2)}{(x-3)} \geq 0$

SOLUTION: (a)

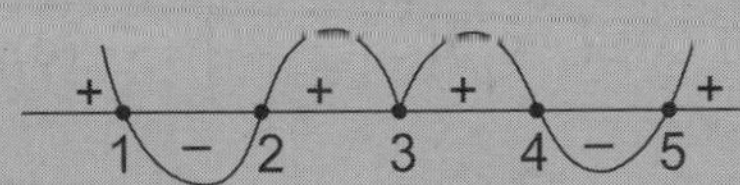

FIGURE 1.81

$\Rightarrow x \in (-\infty, 1) \cup (2, 3) \cup (3, 4) \cup (5, \infty)$

(b)

FIGURE 1.82

$\Rightarrow x \in [1, 2] \cup (3, \infty)$

ILLUSTRATION 131: If $f(x) = \dfrac{(x-3)(x+2)(x+5)}{(x+1)(x-7)}$ then find x such that

(i) $f(x) > 0$ (ii) $f(x) < 0$

SOLUTION: Given $f(x) = \dfrac{(x-3)(x+2)(x+5)}{(x+1)(x-7)}$

(i) $f(x) > 0 \Rightarrow x \in (-5, -2) \cup (-1, 3) \cup (7, \infty)$

(ii) $f(x) < 0 \Rightarrow x \in (-\infty, -5) \cup (-2, -1) \cup (3, 7)$

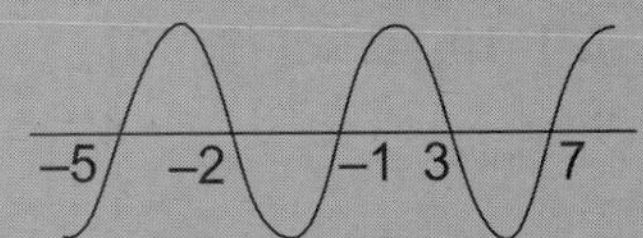

FIGURE 1.83

TEXTUAL EXERCISE–18(SUBJECTIVE)

1. Solve the following rational inequality for x.

(a) $\dfrac{x}{x-5} > \dfrac{1}{3}$ and $\dfrac{3}{x} \leq 2$ (b) $\dfrac{x+2}{x-6} \leq 0$

(c) $\dfrac{3x}{5x-4} \geq 0$ (d) $x + \dfrac{1}{x-1} \leq 3$

2. Solve the following inequality for x.

(a) $x^4 - 16 > 0$

(b) $x^3 - 4x < 0$

(c) $x^6 - x^5 + x^4 - x^3 + x^2 - x + 1 < 0$.

3. Solve the inequality for x.

$(x^2 - 16)(x^2 + 5x + 4)(x^2 - 9)(x^2 - 7x + 12) \leq 0$.

4. Solve the following inequalities and express the result in the form of intervals.

(a) $\dfrac{(x+1)^5(x-1)(x+4)^2(x-3)^4}{(x+8)(2x-3)(x-6)^2} < 0$

(b) $\dfrac{(x+1)(x-8)(x-6)^2(x-5)^4}{(x-3)^2(x-1)} < 0$

5. Solve the following inequalities and express the result in the form of intervals.

(a) $\dfrac{(x-1)^2(x+1)^3}{x^4(x-2)} \leq 0$

(b) $x^2 + 3x + 2 > 0$ and $\dfrac{x}{x+1} \leq 0$

6. Find the largest negative integer and smallest positive integer which satisfy

(a) $x^2 - 4x - 12 \geq 0$ (b) $3x^2 + 5x + 2 \leq 0$

(c) $\dfrac{x^2 - 5x + 4}{x^2 - 1} \leq 1$

7. Solve the inequality $x^2 - x - 6 \geq 0$ such that $|x| \leq 10$.

8. Solve the inequality

(a) $x^4 + 5x^3 + 5x^2 + 5x + 4 \geq 0$

(b) $x^4 - 2x^3 - x + 2 > 0$

9. Find the maximum and minimum values of quadratic expression $y = (x-2)(6-x)$ and hence or otherwise draw its graph.

10. Find the minimum and maximum value of the following expression.

(a) $4-\dfrac{3}{x^2-4x+6}$ (b) $3+\dfrac{2}{(x-2)(x-3)}$

11. If $f(x) = ax^2 + bx + c$ and a, b, c are real number such that $b^2 - 4ac < 0$, then which of the following true?

(a) $a+b+c>0$ if $a>0$
(b) $a-b+c<0$ if $a<0$
(c) $a f(x)>0$ if $a>0$
(d) $a f(x)<0$ if $a<0$

12. Show that $f(x) = x^2 + x + 1$ and $g(x) = x^2 - x + 1$ can never take negative values for any real value of x.

Answer Keys

1. (a) $x\in\left(-\infty,-\dfrac{5}{2}\right)\cup(5,\infty)$ (b) $x\in(-2,6)$ (c) $x\in(-\infty,0]\cup\left(\dfrac{4}{5},\infty\right)$ (d) $x\in(-\infty,1)\cup\{2\}$

2. (a) $x\in(-\infty,-2)\cup(2,\infty)$ (b) $x\in(-\infty,-2)\cup(0,2)$ (c) $x\in\mathbb{R}$ **3.** $x\in[-3,-1]\cup\{-4,3,4\}$

4. (a) $(-8,-4)\cup(-4,-1)\cup\left(1,\dfrac{3}{2}\right)$

(b) $(-\infty,-1)\cup(1,8)\sim\{3,5,6\}$ **5.** (a) $[-1,0)\cup(0,2)$ (b) $(-1,0]$

6. (a) –2, 6 (b) –1, no positive integer is possible (c) no negative integer, 2

7. $[-10, -2] \cup [3, 10]$ **8.** (a) $(-\infty, -4] \cup [-1, \infty)$ (b) $(-\infty, 1) \cup (2, \infty)$

9. $y_{min} \to -\infty$, $y_{max} = 4$

10. (a) $[5/2, 4)$ (b) $(-\infty, -5] \cup (3, \infty)$ **11.** (a) T (b) T (c) T, (d) F

■ IRRATIONAL INEQUALITIES

These inequalities contain the unknown under the radical sign. There are some standard forms to solve these irrational inequalities.

Type 1: The equation of the type $\sqrt[2n]{f(x)}<\sqrt[2n]{g(x)},\ n\in N$ is equivalent to the system $\begin{cases} f(x)\ge 0\\ g(x)>f(x)\end{cases}$ and inequation of the type $\sqrt[2n+1]{f(x)}<\sqrt[2n+1]{g(x)},\ n\in N$ is equivalent to the $f(x)<g(x)$.

Type 2: An inequation of the type $\sqrt[2n]{f(x)}<g(x),\ n\in N$ is equivalent to the system $\begin{cases} f(x)\ge 0\\ g(x)>0\\ f(x)<g^{2n}(x)\end{cases}$

and inequation of the type $\sqrt[2n+1]{f(x)}<g(x),\ n\in N$ is equivalent to the equation $f(x) < g^{2n+1}(x)$.

ILLUSTRATION 132: Solve the inequation $\sqrt{(x+14)}<(x+2)$.

SOLUTION: We have $\sqrt{(x+14)}<(x+2)$, this inequation is equivalent to the system $\begin{cases} x+14\ge 0\\ x+2>0\\ x+14<(x+2)^2\end{cases}$

$$\Rightarrow \begin{cases} x\ge -14\\ x>-2\\ x^2+3x-10>0\end{cases} \Rightarrow \begin{cases} x\ge -14\\ x>-2\\ (x+5)(x-2)>0\end{cases} \Rightarrow \begin{cases} x\ge -14\\ x>-2\\ x<-5 \text{ and } x>2\end{cases}$$

combining all three inequation of the system we get, $x > 2$ i.e., $x \in (2, \infty)$

Type 3: An inequation of the form $\sqrt[2n]{f(x)} > g(x), n \in N$ is equivalent to the collection of two systems of inequations

i.e., $\begin{cases} g(x) \geq 0 \\ f(x) > g^{2n}(x) \end{cases}$ or $\begin{cases} g(x) < 0 \\ f(x) \geq 0 \end{cases}$

and inequation of the form $\sqrt[2n+1]{f(x)} > g(x), n \in N$ is equivalent to the inequation $f(x) > g^{2n+1}(x)$.

ILLUSTRATION 133: Solve the inequation $\sqrt{(-x^2+4x-3)} > 6-2x$.

SOLUTION: We have, $\sqrt{(-x^2+4x-3)} > 6-2x$

This inequation is equivalent to the collection of two systems of inequations

i.e., $\begin{cases} 6-2x \geq 0 \\ -x^2+4x-3 > (6-2x)^2 \end{cases}$ or $\begin{cases} 6-2x < 0 \\ -x^2+4x-3 \geq 0 \end{cases}$

$\Rightarrow \begin{cases} x \leq 3 \\ (x-3)(5x-13) < 0 \end{cases}$ or $\begin{cases} x > 3 \\ (x-1)(x-3) \leq 0 \end{cases}$

$\Rightarrow \begin{cases} x \leq 3 \\ 13/5 < x < 3 \end{cases}$ or $\begin{cases} x > 3 \\ 1 \leq x < 3 \end{cases}$

The second system has no solution and the first system has solution in the interval $13/5 < x < 3$. Hence $x \in (13/5, 3)$ is the set of solutions of the original inequation.

ILLUSTRATION 134: Determine all real number x satisfying the inequality $\sqrt{3-x} - \sqrt{x+1} > 1/2$.

SOLUTION: Domain is $-1 \leq x \leq 3$.

Now $\sqrt{3-x} > \sqrt{x+1}$ if $3-x > x+1$ $\Rightarrow 2 > 2x \Rightarrow x < 1$

Hence for $-1 \leq x < 1$ both sides of the inequality are positive.

Squaring $-2\sqrt{3-x}\sqrt{x+1} > -\dfrac{15}{4}$

again squaring and simplifying $3 + 2x - x^2 < \dfrac{225}{8}$.

Now proceed and get answer $-1 \leq x < \dfrac{8-\sqrt{31}}{8}$

■ MODULUS OF A NUMBER

Modulus of a real number x represents the quantity of x. Also known as magnitude/absolute value of x. Geometrically, it is represented as distance of the number from zero on the real number line. Since the distance is always positive hence the modulus of a real number x is defined as

$$|x| = \begin{cases} x & \text{if } x > 0 \\ 0 & \text{if } x = 0 \\ -x & \text{if } x < 0 \end{cases} = \sqrt{x^2} = \max\{-x, x\}$$

e.g. $|3| = 3$ and $|-6| = -(-6) = 6$.

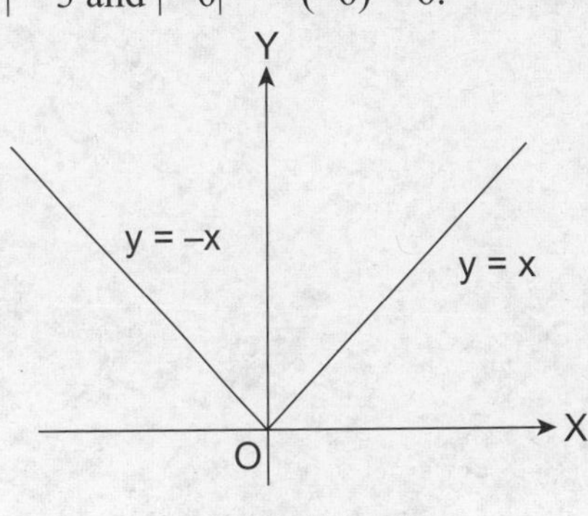

FIGURE 1.84

Properties of modulus of a real number

1. $|x.y| = |x|.|y|$
2. $|-x| = |x|$
3. $\left|\frac{x}{y}\right| = \frac{|x|}{|y|}$
4. $|-x| = |x|$
5. $|x-a| = \begin{cases} x-a & \text{when } x \geq a \\ -(x-a) & \text{when } x < a \end{cases}$
6. $|x_1.x_2.x_3...x_n| = |x_1||x_2||x_3|...|x_n| \Rightarrow |x^n| = |x|^n$
7. $|x|^{2n} = |x^{2n}| = x^{2n} \Rightarrow \forall x \in \mathbb{R}$ & $n \in \mathbb{N}$
8. $|x| = -x \Rightarrow x \in (-\infty, 0]$
9. $|x| = x \Rightarrow x \in [0, \infty)$
10. $|x| > x \Rightarrow x \in (-\infty, 0)$
11. $|x| > -x \Rightarrow x \in (0, \infty)$
12. $|x| < x \Rightarrow x \in \phi$ & $|x| < -x \Rightarrow x \in \phi$

ILLUSTRATION 135: Solve the equation $x^2 - 5|x| + 6 = 0$.

SOLUTION: The given equation is equivalent to

$$\Rightarrow \begin{cases} x^2 - 5x + 6 = 0 & \text{if } x \geq 0 \\ x^2 + 5x + 6 = 0 & \text{if } x < 0 \end{cases} \qquad \Rightarrow \begin{cases} (x-2)(x-3) = 0 & \text{if } x \geq 0 \\ (x+2)(x+3) = 0 & \text{if } x < 0 \end{cases}$$

Hence the solution of the given equation are $x_1 = 2, x_2 = 3, x_3 = -2, x_4 = -3$

ILLUSTRATION 136: Solve the following inequality for x.

(a) $|x - 6| > -5$ (b) $|2x - 5| + 2 = 0$ (c) $|x^2 - 1| < 2$

SOLUTION: (a) True for all $x \in \mathbb{R}$ as LHS is modulus of a number which will always be positive where as RHS is a negative number and positive numbers are always larger than negative numbers.

(b) $|2x - 5| + 2 = 0 \Rightarrow |2x - 5| = -2$

this can never be true since non negative number can't be equal to negative number.

(c) $|x^2 - 1| < -2$ this can never be true since a non negative number can't be less than negative number.

ILLUSTRATION 137: Evaluate the following $\forall\, x \in \mathbb{R}$

(a) $x-3+\sqrt{x^2-6x+9}$ (b) $x-3-\sqrt{x^2-6x+9}$ (c) $\frac{|x-2|}{x-2}$

SOLUTION: (a) Let $y = x-3+\sqrt{x^2-6x+9} = x-3+\sqrt{(x-3)^2}$

$$= x - 3 + |x - 3| = \begin{cases} 2(x-3) & \text{if } x \geq 3 \\ x-3+3-x & \text{if } x < 3 \end{cases} = \begin{cases} 2x-6 & \text{if } x \geq 3 \\ 0 & \text{if } x < 3 \end{cases}$$

(b) Let $y = x-3-\sqrt{x^2-6x+9} = x-3-\sqrt{(x-3)^2} = x - 3 - |x - 3|$

$$= \begin{cases} (x-3)-(x-3) & \text{if } x \geq 3 \\ (x-3)-(3-x) & \text{if } x < 3 \end{cases} = \begin{cases} 0 & \text{if } x \geq 3 \\ 2x-6 & \text{if } x < 3 \end{cases}$$

(c) Let $y = \frac{|x-2|}{x-2} = \begin{cases} \frac{x-2}{x-2} & \text{if } x > 2 \\ \frac{2-x}{x-2} & \text{if } x < 2 \\ \text{not defined} & x = 2 \end{cases} = \begin{cases} 1 & \text{if } x > 2 \\ -1 & \text{if } x < 2 \\ \text{not defined} & x = 2 \end{cases}$$

TEXTUAL EXERCISE–19 (SUBJECTIVE)

1. Solve the following equations for x:
(a) $|x| = 3$ (b) $|x| = -5.$

2. Solve the following equations for x:
(a) $x - |x| = 0$ (b) $x - |x| = 2x.$
(c) $x + |x| = 0$ (d) $x + |x| = 2x$

3. Solve the following equations for x:
(a) $\frac{|x|}{x} = 1$ (b) $\frac{x}{|x|} \geq 1$
(c) $\frac{x}{|x|} = -1$ (d) $\frac{x}{|x|} \leq 1$

4. Solve the following equations for x:
(a) $x|x| + x^2 = 0$ (b) $|x| > -x$
(c) $x^2 + |x| = 0$ (d) $x|x| - x^2 = 0$
(e) $|x| < -x$ (f) $3x\sqrt{2}$ $\sqrt{18x}$

5. Solve the equation
(a) $x^2 - 3|x| - 4 = 0$ (b) $x^2 + 3|x| + 4 = 0$
(c) $x^2 - 3|x| + 2 = 0$ (d) $|x| + x^2 + 1 = 0$

6. For what set of values of x, the following equation hold?
(a) $|x - 1| = 3$ (b) $|x + 2| = 5$
(c) $|7 + x| = 2$ (d) $|x - 3| = 3$
(e) $|2x - 5| = 3$ (f) $|3x - 5| = 3$
(g) $|2x + 5| = 3$ (h) $|2 - x| = 5$
(i) $|x| = 2x - 1$ (j) $|x| = x^2 - 1$
(k) $|x^2 - 1| = 2x - 4$ (l) $|2x + 3| - 7 = 0$
(m) $|5 - 3x| - 4 = 0$

7. Prove that

$$\sqrt{x^2 - 2x + 1} - \sqrt{x^2 + 2x + 1} = \begin{cases} 2 \text{ if } x \leq -1 \\ -2x \text{ if } x \in (-1,1) \\ -2 \text{ if } x \geq 1 \end{cases}$$

8. Simplify the following expressions:
(a) $\frac{1}{2}ab\sqrt{8a^3b} + \frac{1}{3}ab\sqrt{18ab^3} - a^2\sqrt{\frac{2b}{a}} - b^2\sqrt{\frac{2a}{b}}$
a > 0 and b > 0
(b) $x + y + \sqrt{(x-y)^2}$
(c) $(2-a)\sqrt{\frac{1}{a^2 - 4a + 4}}$ if a < 2 and what if a > 2 or a = 2
(d) $x - y - \sqrt{(x-y)^2}$

9. Simplify the expression $\sqrt{9 - 6a + a^2} + \sqrt{9 + 6a + a^2}$ if $a < -3$

Answer Keys

1. (a) $x = \pm 3$ (b) $x \in \phi$
2. (a) $x \in [0, \infty)$ (b) $x \in (-\infty, 0]$ (c) $x \in (-\infty, 0]$ (d) $x \in [0, \infty)$
3. (a) $x \in (0, \infty)$ (b) $x \in (0, \infty)$ (c) $x \in (-\infty, 0)$ (d) $\mathbb{R} \sim \{0\}$
4. (a) $x \in (-\infty, 0]$ (b) $x \in (0, \infty)$ (c) $x \in \{0\}$ (d) $x \in [0, \infty)$ (e) ϕ (f) $[0, \infty)$
5. (a) $x \in \{-4, 4\}$ (b) $x \in \phi$ (c) $x \in \{-1, 1, -2, 2\}$ (d) $\{\}$
6. (a) $\{-2, 4\}$ (b) $\{-7, 3\}$ (c) $\{-9, -5\}$ (d) $\{0, 6\}$ (e) $\{1, 4\}$ (f) $\{2/3, 8/3\}$ (g) $\{-4, -1\}$
(h) $\{-3, 7\}$ (i) $\{1\}$ (j) $\left\{\pm\left(\frac{\sqrt{5}+1}{2}\right)\right\}$ (k) $\{\phi\}$ (l) $x \in \{-5, 2\}$ (m) $\left\{\frac{1}{3}, 3\right\}$
8. (a) $\sqrt{2ab}(ab-1)(a+b)$ (b) $2x$ if $x \geq y$, $2y$ if $x < y$ (c) 1 if $a < 2$, –1 if $a > 2$, undefined if $a = 2$
(d) 0 if $x \geq y$ and $2x - 2y$ if $x < y$.
9. $-2a$

GEOMETRIC INTERPRETATION OF MODULUS

Theorem: Difference of two real numbers x and a is denoted as $|x - a|$ and represents the distance between x and a on real number line.

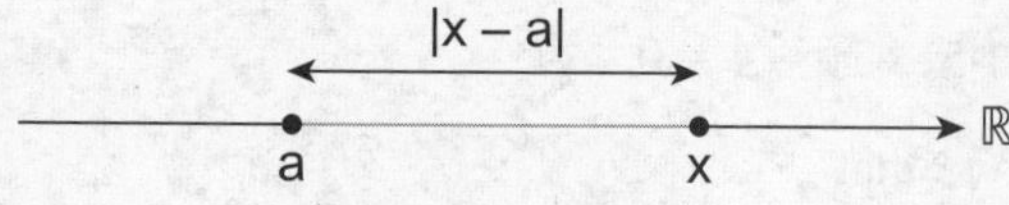

FIGURE 1.85

⇒ $|x - a|$ = distance of real number x from a.
(*considering* $a = 0$)
⇒ $|x|$ = distance of x from zero.

Conclusion: $|x| = \delta$
⇒ Distance of x from zero is δ unit
⇒ $x = -\delta$ or δ

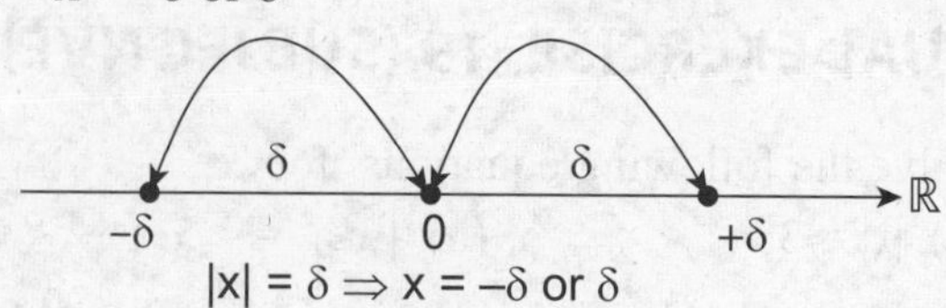

FIGURE 1.86

- $|x - a| = \delta$

⇒ Distance of x from a is δ unit
⇒ $x = a - \delta$ or $a + \delta$

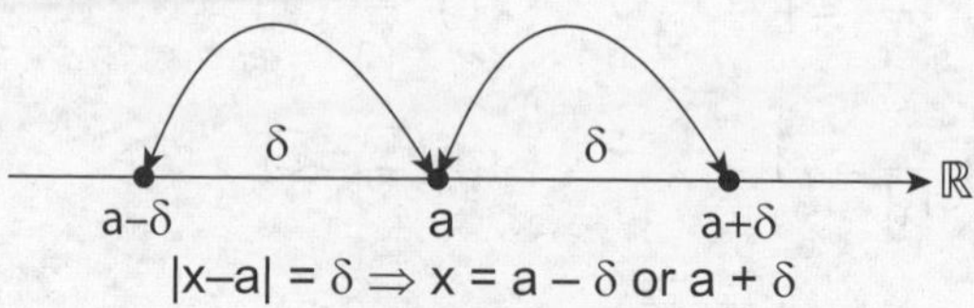

FIGURE 1.87

ILLUSTRATION 138: Solve the following equation for x.

(a) $|2x - 9| - 5 = 0$ (b) $|2x - 5| + 2 = 0$
(c) $|x + 5| - 2 = 0$

SOLUTION: (a) The given equation reduces to $|2x - 9| = 5$
⇒ distance of $2x$ from 9 is 5 units
⇒ $2x = 4$ or 14 ⇒ $x = 2$ or 7

Aliter: ∵ $|2x - 9| = 5$
Squaring both side $(2x - 9)^2 - 5^2 = 0$
⇒ $(2x - 14)(2x - 4) = 0$
⇒ $(x - 7)(x - 2) = 0$
⇒ $x = 2$ or 7.

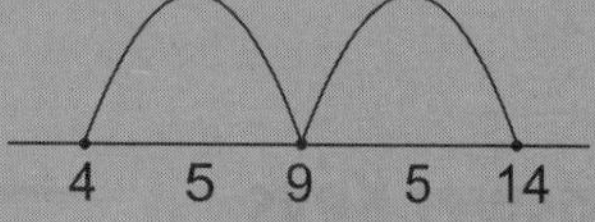

FIGURE 1.88

(b) Consider the equation $|2x - 5| + 2 = 0$
⇒ $|2x - 5| = -2$ which is never true for any value of x ⇒ $x = \phi$
(c) The given equation reduces to $|x + 5| = 2$
⇒ distance of x from -5 is 2 units
⇒ $x = -5 - 2$ or $-5 + 2$ ⇒ $x = -7$ or -3

PROPERTIES OF MODULUS INVOLVING INEQUALITY

- $|x| \le \delta$ (*where* δ *is not negative*)

⇒ Distance of x from zero is $\le \delta$ unit
⇒ $x \in [-\delta, \delta]$

Aliter: $|x| \le \delta$ ⇒ $x^2 \le \delta^2$ ⇒ $x^2 - \delta^2 \le 0$
⇒ $(x - \delta)(x + \delta) \le 0$
⇒ $x \in [-\delta, \delta]$ (*using wavy curve method*)

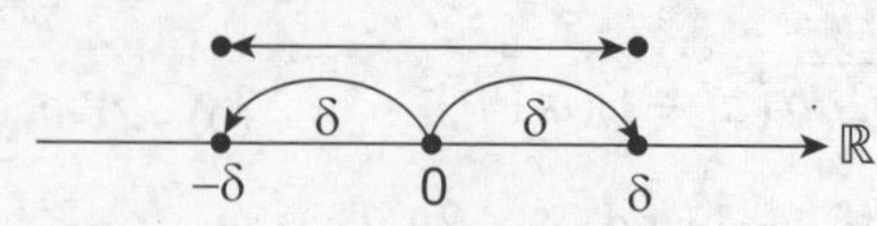

FIGURE 1.89

- $|x-a| \le \delta$ *(where δ is not negative)*

  $\Rightarrow$ Distance of x from a is $\le \delta$ unit

  $\Rightarrow x \in [a-\delta\ ,\ a+\delta]$

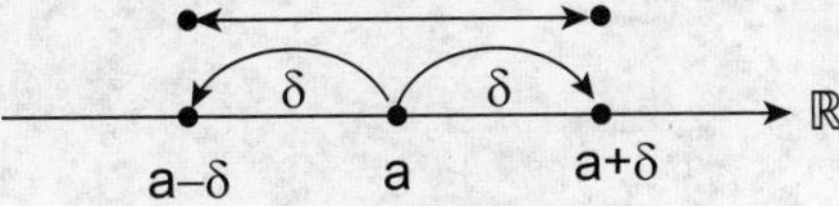

FIGURE 1.90

Aliter: $|x-a| \le \delta \Rightarrow (x-a)^2 \le \delta^2$

$\Rightarrow (x-a)^2 - \delta^2 \le 0$

$\Rightarrow (x-a-\delta)(x+a+\delta) \le 0$

$\Rightarrow x \in [a-\delta\ ,\ a+\delta]$ *(using wavy curve method)*

- $|x-a| \ge \delta$ *(where δ is not negative)*

  $\Rightarrow$ Distance of x from a is $\ge \delta$ unit

  $\Rightarrow x \in (-\infty, a-\delta] \cup [a+\delta, \infty)$

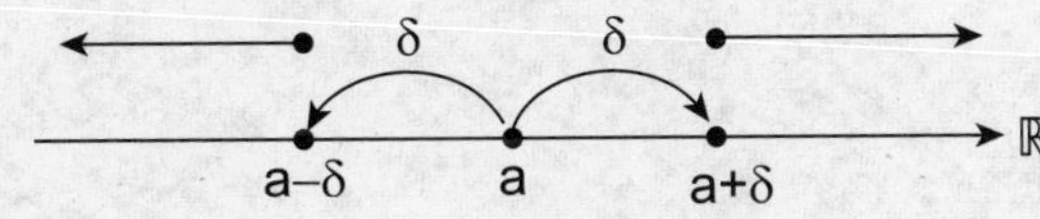

FIGURE 1.91

Aliter: $|x-a| \ge \delta \quad \Rightarrow (x-a)^2 \ge \delta^2$

$\Rightarrow (x-a)^2 - \delta^2 \ge 0 \Rightarrow (x-a-\delta)(x+a+\delta) \ge 0$

$\Rightarrow x \in (-\infty, a-\delta] \cup [a+\delta, \infty)$

(using wavy curve method)

Method of solving the equation/inequality involving |f(x)|

To solve an equation/inequality of the type

$|f(x)| = k$ (i)

or $|f(x)| < k$ (ii)

or $|f(x)| > k$ (iii)

Step I: Observe the sign of k;

if $k < 0 \Rightarrow |f(x)| = k$ and $f(x) < k$ have no solution

For Inequality : $|f(x)| > k$ holds good $\forall\ x \in \mathbb{R}$ for which $f(x)$ is defined.

Step II: If $k > 0$; consider two cases.

Case I: $f(x) \ge 0$ (iv)

$\Rightarrow |f(x)| = f(x)$

Then relation (i), (ii), (iii) respectively convert to

$f(x) = k$ (v)

$f(x) < k$ (vi)

$f(x) > k$ (vii)

Solving (v) we get the solution of equation (i) and solving (iv) and (vi) together i.e., $0 \le f(x) < k$ we get the solution of inequality (ii) and solving (vii) we get the solution of inequality (iii).

Case II: $f(x) < 0$ (viii)

$\Rightarrow |f(x)| = -f(x)$

Then relation (i), (ii), (iii) respectively convert to

$f(x) = -k$ (ix)

$f(x) > -k$ (x)

$f(x) < -k$ (xi)

Solving (ix) we get the solution of equation (i) and solving (viii) and (x) together i.e., $-k < f(x) < 0$ we get the solution of inequality (ii) and solving (xi) we get the solution of inequality (iii).

Step III: Then take union of solution of case (i) and case (ii) to get final set of solution of equation/inequality.

Method 2: If $k > 0$ given $|f(x)| = k$ (i)

Squaring both side $(f(x))^2 = k^2$ (ii)

$\Rightarrow (f(x)-k)(f(x)+k) = 0$

$\Rightarrow f(x) = k \quad or \quad f(x) = -k$

Solve both equation and take union of solution.

Similarly we can solve inequality (ii) and (iii) as well

Method 3: Use geometric definition i.e., $|f(x)| = k$

$\Rightarrow$ distance of $f(x)$ from zero or real number line is k unit

$\Rightarrow f(x) = k \ \ or \ \ -k.$

Similarly, we can solve inequality (ii) and (iii) as well

Forms of the inequality containing modulus functions

Modular Inequality	Test condition - 1	Test condition - 2
$f(\|x\|) < g(x)$	$f(x) < g(x)$ if $x \ge 0$	$f(-x) < g(x)$ if $x < 0$
$\|f(x)\| < g(x)$	$f(x) < g(x)$ if $f(x) \ge 0$	$-f(x) < g(x)$ if $x < 0$
$\|f(x)\| > g(x)$	$f(x) > g(x)$ if $f(x) \ge 0$	$-f(x) > g(x)$ if $x < 0$
$\|f(\|x\|)\| > g(x)$ or $\|f(\|x\|)\| < g(x)$	$\|f(x)\| > g(x)$ if $x \ge 0$	$\|-f(x)\| > g(x)$ if $x < 0$

ILLUSTRATION 139: Solve the inequality $\left|1-\dfrac{|x|}{1+|x|}\right| \geq \dfrac{1}{2}$.

SOLUTION: The given inequality is equivalent to the collection of system

$$\left[\begin{array}{ll}\left|1-\dfrac{x}{1+x}\right| \geq \dfrac{1}{2}, & \text{if } x \geq 0 \\ \left|\left(1+\dfrac{-x}{1-x}\right)\right| \geq \dfrac{1}{2}, & \text{if } x<0\end{array}\right. \Rightarrow \left\{\begin{array}{ll}\dfrac{1}{|1+x|} \geq \dfrac{1}{2}, & \text{if } x \geq 0 \\ \dfrac{1}{|1-x|} \geq \dfrac{1}{2}, & \text{if } x<0\end{array}\right.$$

$$\Rightarrow \left\{\begin{array}{ll}\dfrac{1}{1+x} \geq \dfrac{1}{2}, & \text{if } x \geq 0 \\ \dfrac{1}{1-x} \geq \dfrac{1}{2}, & \text{if } x<0\end{array}\right. \Rightarrow \left\{\begin{array}{ll}\dfrac{1-x}{1+x} \geq 0, & \text{if } x \geq 0 \\ \dfrac{1+x}{1-x} \geq 0, & \text{if } x<0\end{array}\right.$$

$$\Rightarrow \left\{\begin{array}{ll}\dfrac{x-1}{x+1} \leq 0, & \text{if } x \geq 0 \\ \dfrac{x+1}{x-1} \leq 0, & \text{if } x<0\end{array}\right.$$

for $\dfrac{x-1}{x+1} \leq 0$, if $x \geq 0$ (using Wavy Curve Method) $\Rightarrow 0 \leq x \leq 1$ (i)

for $\dfrac{x+1}{x-1} \leq 0$, if $x<0$ (using Wavy Curve Method)

$\Rightarrow -1 \leq x<0$ (ii)

From (i) and (ii), the solution of the given equation is $x \in[-1,1]$

Aliter: $\left|1-\left(\dfrac{|x|}{1+|x|}\right)\right|=\left|\dfrac{1}{1+|x|}\right|=\dfrac{1}{1+|x|}$ $(\because 1+|x|>0)$

$$\Rightarrow \frac{1}{1+|x|} \geq \frac{1}{2} \Rightarrow \frac{1-|x|}{1+|x|} \geq 0 \Rightarrow 1-|x| \geq 0 \Rightarrow x \in[-1,1]$$

ILLUSTRATION 140: Solve the following inequality for x.

(a) $|x-6|>5$ (b) $|2x-3|>-2$

(c) $|x+4|<-2$ (d) $|x-4| \leq 4$

SOLUTION: (a) $|x-6| \geq 5$

$\Rightarrow$ Distance of x from 6 is ≥ 5 unit

$\Rightarrow x \in(-\infty, 6-5] \cup[6+5, \infty)$

$\Rightarrow x \in(-\infty, 1] \cup[11, \infty)$

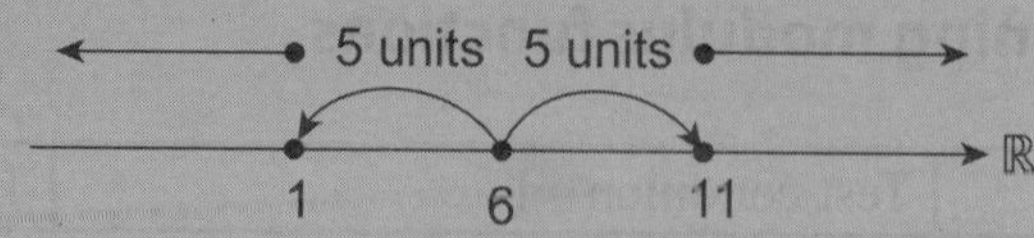

FIGURE 1.92

(b) $|2x-3|>-2$ is true $\forall x \in \mathbb{R}$ because left hand side expression being modulus of number is always positive.

(c) $|x + 4| < -2$ is not true any real x because left hand side expression being modulus of number is always positive, and thus cannot be less than negative number.

(d) $|x-4| \le 4$

$\Rightarrow$ Distance of x from 4 is $\le$ 4 unit

$\Rightarrow$ $x \in [0, 8]$

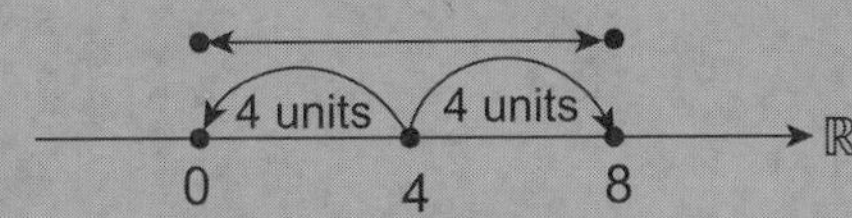

FIGURE 1.93

ILLUSTRATION 141: Solve the following inequality for x.

(a) $|x^2-2x| = -3$ (b) $|x^2-2x| > -3$

(c) $|x^2-2x| < -3$ (d) $|x^2-2x| = 3$

(e) $|x^2-2x| > 3$ (f) $|x^2-2x| < 3$

SOLUTION: (a) $|x^2-2x| = -3$ is not true any real x because left hand side expression being modulus of number is always positive, and thus can't be equal to negative number. Thus $x \in \phi$.

(b) $|x^2-2x| > -3$ is true $\forall\ x \in \mathbb{R}$ because left hand side expression being modulus of number is always positive. x is the set of all real numbers.

(c) $|x^2-2x| < -3$ is not true any real x because left hand side expression being modulus of number is always positive, and thus can't be less than negative number. Thus $x \in \phi$.

(d) ***Case I:*** $|x^2-2x| = 3$ if $x^2 - 2x \ge 0$

i.e. $x \in (-\infty, 0] \cup [2, \infty)$

$\Rightarrow |x^2 - 2x| = x^2 - 2x$ $\Rightarrow x^2 - 2x - 3 = 0$

$\Rightarrow (x - 3)(x + 1) = 0$ $\Rightarrow x = -1$ or 3

Case II: Let $x^2 - 2x < 0$

$\Rightarrow x \in (0, 2)$ $\Rightarrow |x^2 - 2x| = 2x - x^2$

Now equation becomes $2x - x^2 = 3$

$\Rightarrow x^2 - 2x + 3 = 0$; $D < 0$ $\Rightarrow x \in \phi$

$\Rightarrow x \in \{-1, 3\}$

(e) $|x^2-2x| > 3$ (i)

Case I: Let $x^2 - 2x \ge 0$ i.e. $x \in (-\infty, 0] \cup [2, \infty)$

$\Rightarrow |x^2 - 2x| = x^2 - 2x$ $\Rightarrow x^2 - 2x - 3 > 0$

$\Rightarrow (x - 3)(x + 1) > 0$

$\Rightarrow$ $x \in (-\infty, -1) \cup (3, \infty)$ taking intersection with case condition, we get,

$x \in (-\infty, -1) \cup (3, \infty)$

Case II: $x^2 - 2x < 0$

$\Rightarrow x \in (0, 2)$ $\Rightarrow |x^2 - 2x| = 2x - x$

$\Rightarrow 2x - x^2 > 3$

$\Rightarrow x^2 - 2x + 3 < 0$ which is not true for any real x because $x^2 - 2x + 3$ is > 0 always

Now taking the union of both cases we get the solution set as $x \in (-\infty, -1) \cup (3, \infty)$.

(f) Since law of trichomy of real numbers states that any real number x is either > 0, $= 0$ or $<$ 0 so solution of third inequality is complementary set of the union of the set of solution of the equation (i) and inequality (ii). therefore solution set of $|x^2-2x| < 3$ is $x \in (-1, 3)$

ILLUSTRATION 142: Solve the following inequality for x.

(a) $|2x-1|^2-3|2x-1|+2=0$

(b) $|2x-1|^2-3|2x-1|+2<0$

(c) $|2x-1|^2-3|2x-1|+2>0$

SOLUTION: (a) Let $|2x-1| = y$, substituting

$\Rightarrow y^2 - 3y + 2 = 0$

$\Rightarrow (y-1)(y-2) = 0$

$\Rightarrow y = 1$ or 2

$\Rightarrow |2x-1| = 1$

or $|2x-1| = 2$

$\Rightarrow 2x = 0, 2$

$2x = 1-2$ or $1+2$

$\Rightarrow x = 0, 1$

$x = -1/2$ or $-3/2$

(b) $y^2 - 3y + 2 < 0$

$\Rightarrow (y-1)(y-2) < 0$

applying method of intervals we get

$1 < y < 2$

Since $y = |2x-1|$

$\Rightarrow |2x-1| > 1$

and $|2x-1| < 2$

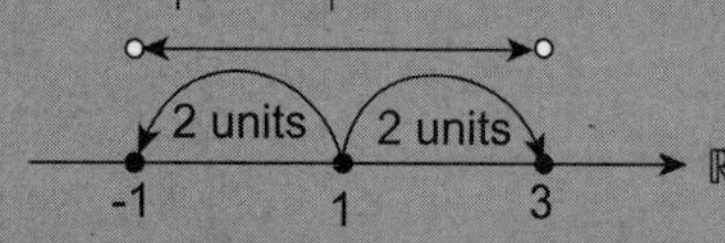

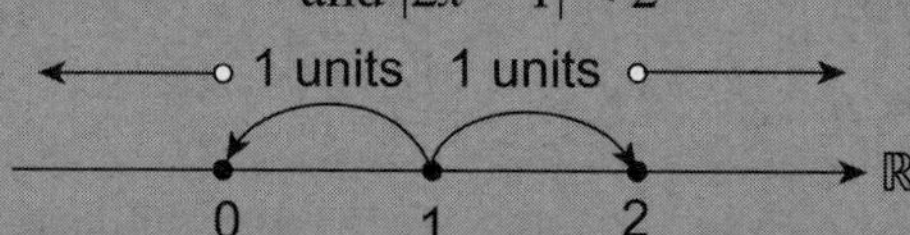

FIGURE 1.94

$\because 2x \in (-\infty,0)\cup(2,\infty)$ and $2x \in (-1,3)$

$\Rightarrow x \in (-\infty,0)\cup(1,\infty)$ and $x \in \left(-\frac{1}{2},\frac{3}{2}\right)$

taking intersection of both the sets, we get,

$x \in \left(-\frac{1}{2},0\right)\cup\left(1,\frac{3}{2}\right)$

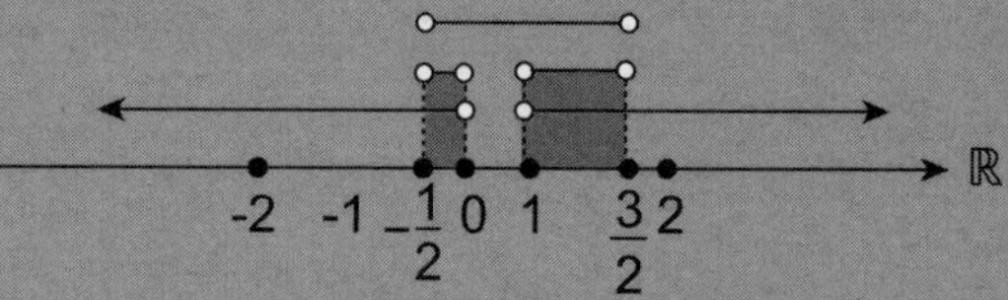

FIGURE 1.95

(c) Since law of trichomy of real numbers states that any real number x is either > 0, $= 0$ or < 0 so solution of third inequality is complementary set of the union of the set of solution of the equation (i) and inequality (ii).

Exhaustive method of solving equation/ inequality containing two or more terms involving modulus

To solve an inequality involving modulus, equate quantities inside modulus to zero and locate their roots on real number line. These points divide the real number line into test intervals, now considering each interval as a separate case, solve the equation/inequality for every case and take the intersection of solution set with case conditions as described below:

For instance, to solve an equation

$|x-1| + |x-4| = 3$ (i)

Clearly, $x = 1$ and 4 are critical points, so we will analyse the equation in following three cases.

Case I: If $-\infty < x < 1$ both $x-1$ and $x-4$ are negative numbers therefore $|x-1| = 1-x$; $|x-4| = 4-x$

Substituting in the equation (i) we get $1-x+4-x=3$

$\Rightarrow 2x = 2 \Rightarrow x = 1$

but the solution does not satisfy the case condition therefore rejected.

Case II: If $1 \le x < 4$ then $x-1$ is non-negative but $x-4$ is negative number therefore $|x-1| = x-1$; $|x-4| = 4-x$

Substituting in the equation (i) we get $x-1+4-x=3$ which is true $\forall\ x \in [1,4)$

Case III: If $x \ge 4$ then both $x-1$ and x - 4 are non-negative

$\Rightarrow |x-1| = x-1$; $|x-4| = x-4$

Substituting in the equation (i) we get

$x-1+x-4=3$

$\Rightarrow 2x = 8 \Rightarrow x = 4$

taking intersection with the case condition we get the solution $x = 4$.

Now at last taking the union of solution of the three cases, the final set of solution obtained is $x \in [1,4]$

ILLUSTRATION 143: Solve the inequality $x + |4 - 2x| > |x + 1| - 1$.

SOLUTION: Consider the roots of expression enclosed within the modulus sign in the given inequality $x + |4 - 2x| > |x + 1| - 1$ and locate them on the real number line.

Since at $x = -1$ and $x = 2$ the expressions standing inside the modulus sign vanishes.

And these points divide the number line into three intervals; $x \in (-\infty, -1)$ and $x \in [-1, 2)$ and $x \in [2, \infty)$

Considering x exhaustively on each of these intervals, we transform the original inequality is equivalent to the following three set of inequalities.

Case I: $\begin{cases} x < -1 \\ x - 2(x-2) > -(x+1) - 1 \end{cases} \Rightarrow \begin{cases} x < -1 \\ 4 - x > -x - 2 \end{cases}$

which is true $\forall\ x \in (-\infty, -1)$

Case II: $\begin{cases} -1 \le x < 2 \\ x - 2(x-2) > x + 1 - 1 \end{cases} \Rightarrow \begin{cases} -1 \le x < 2 \\ 2x < 4 \end{cases} \Rightarrow x \in [-1, 2)$ set of solution

Case III: $\begin{cases} x \ge 2, \\ x + 2(x-2) > x + 1 - 1 \end{cases} \Rightarrow \begin{cases} x \ge 2, \\ 2x - 4 > 0 \end{cases} \Rightarrow x \in (2, \infty)$ set of solution.

taking the union of solution sets of all three cases we get $x \in \mathbb{R} \sim \{2\}$ is set of solution.

TRIANGLE INEQUALITY AND ITS APPLICATIONS

When we add two real numbers x and y (*having same sign*) the resulting number $x + y$ has same magnitude as that of summation of magnitudes of x and y. (let us call it *constructive addition*). On the other hand, if we add two real numbers x and y of opposite sign the addition results into reduction of magnitude because the number with smaller magnitude gets neutralised by its additive inverse isolated from the other number and therefore the resulting number $x + y$ has its magnitude less than the summation of individual magnitudes of x and y. Consequently, we can extract the following conclusion known as triangle inequality. The name triangle inequality can be better justified when we will study these inequalities in the set of complex numbers.

- $|x + y| \le |x| + |y|$ (Triangle inequality)

  Equality holds iff x and y of same sign or at least one of them is zero.

  $\Rightarrow\ x.y \ge 0$
- $|x + y| = |x| + |y| \quad \Rightarrow x.y \ge 0$
- $|x + y| < |x| + |y| \quad \Rightarrow x.y < 0$
- $|x - y| \le |x| + |y|$ (Triangle inequality)

  Equality holds iff x and y of opposite sign or at least one of them is zero

  $\Rightarrow\ x.y \le 0$

  $|x - y| = |x| + |y| \quad \Rightarrow x.y \le 0$

  $|x - y| < |x| + |y| \quad \Rightarrow x.y > 0$

  $|x| - |y| \le |x \pm y| \le |x| + |y|$ (Triangle inequality)

ILLUSTRATION 144: Solve the following inequality for x: $|x| + |x - 3| \ge 5$.

SOLUTION: Breaking the inequality in the following test intervals

Case (i) $x < 0 < 3\ ;\ x \in (-\infty, 0)$

$|x| = -x$ and $|x - 3| = 3 - x$ the inequality reduces to form

$\Rightarrow -x + 3 - x \ge 5 \qquad \Rightarrow -2 \ge 2x$

$\Rightarrow x \le -1 \qquad \Rightarrow x \in (-\infty, -1]$

Case (ii) $0 \le x < 3$

$\Rightarrow$ $|x| = x$ and $|x-3| = 3-x$ the inequality reduces to form

$\Rightarrow$ $x + 3 - x \ge 5$ $\Rightarrow$ $3 \ge 5$ not possible

Case (iii) $x \ge 3$

$\Rightarrow$ $|x| = x$ and $|x-3| = x-3$ inequality becomes $x + x - 3 \ge 5$

$\Rightarrow$ $2x \ge 8$ $\Rightarrow x \ge 4$ $\Rightarrow$ $x \in [4, \infty)$

Now taking union of solutions of each case we get $x \in (-\infty, -1] \cup [4, \infty)$

ILLUSTRATION 145: Solve the equation for x.

(a) $|x-2| + |x+4| = 6$ (b) $|x-2| + |x+4| > 6$

(c) $|x-2| + |x+4| < 6$

SOLUTION: (a) Consider $x - 2 = a$, $x + 4 = b$

$\Rightarrow$ $6 = |6| = |(x+4) - (x-2)| = |b - a|$

$\Rightarrow$ $|a| + |b| = |b - a|$ which is true only if a and b of opposite sign or at least one of a and b vanishes

$\Rightarrow$ $a \,.\, b \le 0$ $\Rightarrow (x-2) \,.\, (x+4) \le 0$

$\Rightarrow$ $x \in [-4, 2]$

(b) Similarly, the inequality $|x-2| + |x+4| > 6$ reduces to the form $|a| + |b| > |b - a|$

$\Rightarrow$ a and b have same sign

$\Rightarrow$ $a \,.\, b \ge 0$ $\Rightarrow (x-2) \,.\, (x+4) \ge 0$

$\Rightarrow$ $x \in (-\infty, -4) \cup (2, \infty)$

(c) The inequality $|x-2| + |x+4| < 6$ is of the form $|a| + |b| < |b - a|$ which is never possible So has no solution. $x \in \phi$.

ILLUSTRATION 146: Solve the equation $\left|\dfrac{x^2 - 8x + 12}{x^2 - 10x + 21}\right| = -\left(\dfrac{x^2 - 8x + 12}{x^2 - 10x + 21}\right)$

SOLUTION: By using concept of modulus, the equation is equivalent to $\left\{\begin{matrix} |f(x)| = f(x) & \text{if } f(x) \ge 0 \\ |f(x)| = -f(x) & \text{if } f(x) < 0 \end{matrix}\right.$

The first system is equivalent to $f(x) = 0$ and the second system is equivalent to $f(x) < 0$. Then combining both systems, we get $f(x) \le 0$

$$\Rightarrow \frac{x^2 - 8x + 12}{x^2 - 10x + 21} \quad \Rightarrow \frac{(x-2)(x-6)}{(x-3)(x-7)} \le 0$$

By solving it gives $x \in [2, 3) \cup [6, 7)$

ILLUSTRATION 147: Solve $|x^2 - 4| + |x^2 - 9| = 5$

SOLUTION: There are three cases:

Case I: When $x^2 < 4$ i.e., $-2 < x < 2$

In this case, $|x^2 - 4| = -(x^2 - 4)$ and $|x^2 - 9| = -(x^2 - 9)$

So the given equation becomes $-(x^2 - 4) - (x^2 - 9) = 5$

$\Rightarrow$ $x^2 = 4 \Rightarrow x = \pm 2$ which is rejected since it does not belong to set $[-2, 2]$

Case II: When $4 \le x^2 < 9$ i.e., $-3 < x \le -2$ or $2 \le x < 3$

In this case $|x^2 - 4| = (x^2 - 4)$ and $|x^2 - 9| = -(x^2 - 9)$

So the given equation becomes $x^2 - 4 - (x^2 - 9) = 5 \Rightarrow 5 = 5$

Thus the give equation becomes an identity in this case i.e., all values of x such that $-3 < x \le -2$ or $2 \le x < 3$ satisfy the given equation.

Case III: When $x^2 \geq 9$ i.e., $x \leq -3$ or $x \geq 3$

In this case, $|x^2 - 4| = (x^2 - 4)$ and $|x^2 - 9| = (x^2 - 9)$

So the given equation becomes $(x^2 - 4) + (x^2 - 9) = 5 \Rightarrow x^2 = 9$

$\Rightarrow x = \pm 3$, Clearly, both of these values satisfy $x \leq -3$ or $x \geq 3$

$\therefore$ Solution set $= x \in [-3, -2] \cup [2, 3]$

Aliter: $x^2 - 4 = a$ and $x^2 - 9 = b$

Then $5 = |5| = |(x^2 - 4) - (x^2 - 9)| = |a - b|$

so the equation takes up the form $|a| + |b| = |a - b|$

Consequently, a and b of opposite sign or at least one of a and b becomes zero

$\Rightarrow x\,.\,b \leq 0 \Rightarrow (x^2 - 4)(x^2 - 9) \leq 0$

$\Rightarrow (x + 2)(x + 3)(x - 2)(x - 3) \leq 0$

Now applying wavy curve method.

the solution set $x \in [-3, -2] \cup [2, 3]$.

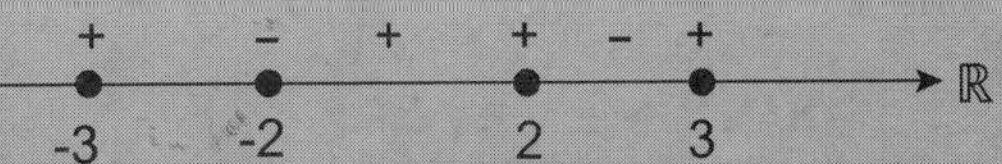

FIGURE 1.96

ILLUSTRATION 148: Find the value(*s*) of real x satisfying $|x^2 - 5x + 6| = |x^2 - 2x| + |3x - 6|$.

SOLUTION: Since $(x^2 - 2x) - (3x - 6) = x^2 - 5x + 6$

and we know that $|f(x) - g(x)| = |f(x)| + |g(x)| \Rightarrow f(x).\,g(x) \leq 0$

therefore $|x^2 - 5x + 6| = |x^2 - 2x| + |3x - 6|$

$\Rightarrow (x^2 - 2x)(3x - 6) \leq 0 \Rightarrow 3x(x - 2)(x - 2) \leq 0$

$\Rightarrow 3x(x - 2)^2 \leq 0 \Rightarrow x \leq 0$ or $x = 2 \Rightarrow x \in (-\infty, 0] \cup \{2\}$

ILLUSTRATION 149: Find the solution region of the variable in the inequality $|x2 - 2x| + |x - 4| > |x2 - 3x + 4|$

SOLUTION: $|x^2 - 2x| + |x - 4| > |x^2 - 3x + 4| \Rightarrow$ $x^2 - 2x - (x - 4) = x^2 - 3x + 4$

Hence the question reduces to $|f(x)| + |g(x)| > |f(x) - g(x)|$

$\Rightarrow f(x).g(x) > 0$

$\Rightarrow (x^2 - 2x)(x - 4) < 0$ $\Rightarrow x(x - 2)(x - 4) < 0$

$\Rightarrow x \in (0, 2) \cup (4, \infty)$

ILLUSTRATION 150: Solve for x: $|x + 2| + |x^2 - 5x + 1| \leq |x^2 - 4x + 3|$

SOLUTION: $|x + 2| + |x^2 - 5x + 1| \leq |x^2 - 4x + 3|$

Taking, $x + 2 = f(x)$; $x^2 - 5x + 1 = g(x)$

The equation reduces to $|f(x)| + |g(x)| \leq |f(x) + g(x)|$ but $|f(x)| + |g(x) < |f(x) + g(x)|$ is never possible.

Hence, the equation reduces to $|f(x)| + |g(x) = |f(x) + |g(x)|$

$\Rightarrow f(x).g(x) \geq 0$

According to for new assumption $(x + 2)(x^2 - 5x + 1) \geq 0$

Hence $x \in \left[-2, \frac{5 - \sqrt{21}}{2}\right] \cup \left[\frac{5 + \sqrt{21}}{2}, \infty\right)$

ILLUSTRATION 151: Solve for x : $|x + 3| + |x - 3| < 2x$

SOLUTION: $|x + 3| + |x - 3| < 2x$,

Case I: $x < -3$

Equation reduces to $-x - 3 + 3 - x < 2x$

$\Rightarrow -2x < 2x$ $\Rightarrow 4x > 0$ $\Rightarrow x > 0$

Hence no solution in this region

Case II: $-3 \le x < 3$

Equation reduces to $x + 3 + 3 - x < 2x \Rightarrow 6 < 2x \Rightarrow x > 3$

Hence no solution is this region

Case III: $x \ge 0$

Equation reduces to $x + 3 + x - 3 < 2x \Rightarrow 2x < 2x$, which is not possible

Hence no solution

ILLUSTRATION 152: Solve for x: $|x + 1| + |x - 1| = 2x$

SOLUTION: ***Case I:*** $x < -1$

Equation reduces to $-x - 1 - x + 1 = 2x \Rightarrow -2x = 2x \Rightarrow x = 0$

which shows no solution in this region.

Case II: $-1 \le x < 1$

Equation reduces to $x + 1 - x + 1 = 2x \Rightarrow 2 = 2x \Rightarrow x = 1$

which shows that there is no solution in the region.

Case III: $x \ge 1$

Equation reduces to $x + 1 + x - 1 = 2x \Rightarrow 2x = 2x$

Which is true, hence $x \in [1, \infty)$

ILLUSTRATION 153: Solve for x: $|x + 1| + |x - 1| > 2x$

SOLUTION: $|x + 1| + |x - 1| > 2x$

Case I: $x < -1$

Equation reduces to $-x - 1 - x + 1 > 2x$

$\Rightarrow -2x > 2x \Rightarrow 4x < 0 \Rightarrow x < 0$

Hence $x \in (-\infty, -1)$

Case II: $-1 \le x < 1$

Equation reduces to $x + 1 + 1 - x > 2 \Rightarrow 2 > 2x \Rightarrow x < 1$

In this region $x \in [-1, 1)$

Case III: $x \ge 1$

Equation reduces to $x + 1 + x - 1 > 2x$

$\Rightarrow 2x > 2x$, which is not possible

$\Rightarrow x \in (-\infty, 1)$

TEXTUAL EXERCISE–20 (SUBJECTIVE)

1. Solve the following inequality for x.

(a) $|x| > 2$ (b) $|x - 1| > 3$
(c) $|x - 2| < 1$ (d) $|x + 1| \ge 2$
(e) $|x - 1| \le 5$ (f) $|2x - 3| > 7$
(g) $|3x + 5| < 2$ (h) $|4x + 6| > 5$
(i) $|2x - 3| > -2$ (j) $|4x - 9| \le 7$
(k) $|3x + 5| \ge 2$ (l) $|2x + 3| \ge 0$
(m) $|4 - 3x| < -2$ (n) $|5 - 3x| \le 0$
(o) $\left|\frac{x-3}{x-5}\right| > 1$ (p) $\left|\frac{x+4}{x+2}\right| \le 1$
(q) $|x^2 - 4x| < 5$ (r) $|x - 3| > -1$
(s) $|3x - 2.5| \ge 2$ (t) $|x - 2| \le |x + 4|$

2. Solve the following equation for x.

(a) $|5x^2 - 3| = 2$ (b) $\left|\frac{x+4}{x+2}\right| = 3$
(c) $|x^2 - 4x| = 5$ (d) $|x + 1| + 2 = 2$

(e) $|3x - 4| = 1/2$ (f) $|x + 2| = 2(3 - x)$
(g) $|x| = -3x - 5$ (h) $x^2 + |x - 1| = 1$
(i) $|x + 1| - |2x - 3| = x - 4$

3. Solve the following equations and inequalities:
(a) $|x - 1| + |x - 3| = 2$
(b) $|x| + |x + 5| = 5$
(c) $|x - 1| + |x - 4| = 2$
(d) $|x^2 - 2x| + |x - 4| = |x^2 - 3x + 4|$
(e) $|x^2 - 2x| + |x - 4| < |x^2 - 3x + 4|$
(f) $|x^2 - 9| + |16 - x^2| = 7$

4. Solve the for x and y:
(a) $\begin{cases} |x| + y = 4 \\ x + 3|y| = 6 \end{cases}$ (b) $\begin{cases} \sqrt{(x+y)^2} = 5 \\ \sqrt{(x-y)^2} = 1 \end{cases}$

5. Solve for x: $(4a - 15)x^2 + 2a|x| + 4 = 0$

6. Solve $|x^2 + 2x + 2) + (3x + 7)| < |x^2 + 2x + 2| + |3x + 7|$

7. Solve the following equations for x:
(a) $|x + 3| + |x - 3| = 2x$
(b) $|x + 3| + |x - 3| > 2x$

8. Solve the following equations for x:
$|x + 1| + |x - 1| = |2x|$.

9. Solve the following equations for x:
$|x + 1| + |x - 1| > |2x|$.

10. Solve the following equations for x:
$|x - 1| + |x - 3| = x - 3$

11. Solve the following equations for x:
$|x - 1| + |x - 2| < x - 3$

Answer Keys

1. (a) $(-\infty, -2) \cup (2, \infty)$ (b) $(-\infty,-2)\cup(4,\infty)$ (c) $x\in(1,3)$ (d) $x\in(-\infty,-3]\cup[1,\infty)$ (e) $x\in(-4,6)$
(f) $(-\infty, -2) \cup (5, \infty)$ (g) $(-7/3, -1)$ (h) $x\in\left(-\infty,\frac{-11}{4}\right)\cup\left(-\frac{1}{4},\infty\right)$ (i) $x\in(-\infty,\infty)$ (j) $x\in\left[\frac{1}{2},4\right]$
(k) $x\in\left(-\infty,\frac{-7}{3}\right]\cup[-1,\infty)$ (l) $x\in\mathbb{R}$ (m) $x\in\phi$ (n) $x\in\left\{\frac{5}{3}\right\}$ (o) $(4, \infty) - \{5\}$ (p) $(-\infty, -3]$
(q) $(-1, 5)$ (r) $x \in (-\infty, \infty)$ (s) $x\in(-\infty,1/6]\cup[3/2,\infty)$ (t) $x\in[-1,\infty)$

2. (a) $\left\{-\frac{1}{\sqrt{5}},\frac{1}{\sqrt{5}},\pm1\right\}$ (b) $\{-1, -5/2\}$ (c) $\{-1, 5\}$ (d) $x = -1$ (e) $x = 7/6, 3/2$
(f) $x = 4/3$ (g) $x = -5/2$ (h) $x = 0, 1$ (i) $x\in(-\infty,-1]\cup\{4\}$

3. (a) $[1, 3]$ (b) $[-5, 0]$ (c) $\{\}$ (d) $x\in(-\infty,0]\cup[2,4]$ (e) $x\in\{\}$ (f) $x\in[-4,-3]\cup[3,4]$

4. (a) $(3, 1)$; $(-3/2, 5/2)$; $(-9, -5)$; $(9/2, -1/2)$ (b) $(-3, -2)$; $(-2, -3)$; $(3, 2)$; $(2, 3)$

5. $\pm\frac{a-\sqrt{a^2-16a+60}}{15-4a}$ for $a<\frac{15}{4}$; ϕ for $a\geq\frac{15}{4}$ **6.** $x < -7/3$

7. (a) $x\in[3, \infty)$ (b) $x\in(-\infty, 3)$ **8.** $x \in (-\infty, -1] \cup [1, \infty)$

9. $x \in (-1, 1)$ **10.** $x = \phi$ **11.** $x \in \phi$

■ GREATEST INTEGER FUNCTION

Any real number x can be expressed as summation of an integer (I) and a fraction (f: $0 \le f < 1$), I is called integer part of x where as f is known as fractional part of x. Integer part of x is denoted as $[x]$, and read as the greatest integer less than or equal to x. It can be defined as below.

e.g., $f(x) = [x] = -1$ *for* $-1 \le x < -2$
$[x] = 0$ *for* $0 \le x < 1$
$[x] = 1$ *for* $1 \le x < 2$
$[x] = 2$ *for* $2 \le x < 3$

The domain of the function is: $(-\infty, \infty)$ and the range is: set of *all integers*.

Properties

(a) $[x] = x \ \forall \ x \in \mathbb{Z}$
(b) $[\{x\}] = 0 = \{[x]\}$
(c) $[x + m] = [x] + m$ if m is an integer
(d) $[x] \le x \le [x] + 1$
(e) $[x] + [y] \le [x + y] \le [x] + [y] + 1$
(f) $[x] + [-x] = 0$ if $x \in \mathbb{Z}$ and equals -1 otherwise

(g) $\left[\frac{[x]}{n}\right] = \left[\frac{x}{n}\right]$ if $n \in \mathbb{Z}$

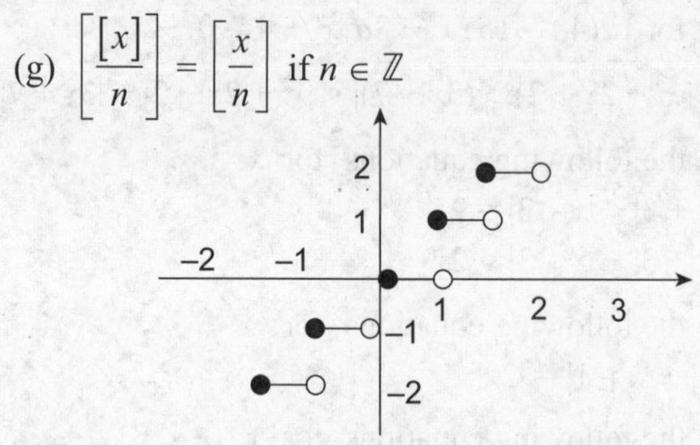

FIGURE 1.97

(h) $[x] \geq n \Rightarrow x \geq n,\ n \in \mathbb{Z}$

(i) $[x] \leq n \Rightarrow x < n + 1,\ n \in \mathbb{Z}$

(j) $[x] > n \Rightarrow x \geq n + 1,\ n \in \mathbb{Z}$

(k) $[x] < n \Rightarrow x < n,\ n \in \mathbb{Z}$

(l) $[x] - [-x] = 2n$ if $x < 2n,\ n \in \mathbb{Z}$

(m) $[x] - [-x] = 2n + 1$ if $x = n + \{x\},\ n \in \mathbb{Z}$

ILLUSTRATION 154: Find the values of $\left[\frac{3}{4}\right] + \left[\frac{3}{4} + \frac{1}{100}\right] + \left[\frac{3}{4} + \frac{2}{100}\right] + \ldots + \left[\frac{3}{4} + \frac{99}{100}\right]$.

SOLUTION: $\left[\frac{3}{4}\right] + \left[\frac{3}{4} + \frac{1}{100}\right] + \ldots. + \left[\frac{3}{4} + \frac{24}{100}\right] + \left[\frac{3}{4} + \frac{25}{100}\right] + \ldots + \left[\frac{3}{4} + \frac{99}{100}\right] \Rightarrow \left[100 \times \frac{3}{4}\right] = 75.$

■ FRACTIONAL-PART FUNCTION

Since we know that $x \geq [x]$. The difference between the number x and its integral value $[x]$ is called the fractional part of x and is symbolically denoted as $\{x\}$. Thus $\{x\} = x - [x]$

e.g., $\{2.5\} = 0.5$, $\{-1.9\} = 0.1 = -1.9 - [-1.9] = -1.9 + 2 = 0.1 = 1 - (0.9) = 1 - \{1.9\}$

Since $f(x) = \{x\}$,

$$\begin{aligned} &\{x\} = x && \text{for} && 0 \leq x < 1 \\ &\{x\} = x - 1 && \text{for} && 1 \leq x < 2 \\ \Rightarrow\ &\{x\} = x - 2 && \text{for} && 2 \leq x < 3 \\ &\{x\} = x + 1 && \text{for} && -1 \leq x < 0 \\ &\{x\} = x + 2 && \text{for} && -2 \leq x < -1 \end{aligned}$$

can be expressed graphically as shown in figure:

Properties

(a) $\{-x\} = 1 - \{x\}$ if $x > 0$

(b) $\{\{x\}\} = \{x\}$

(c) $[\{x\}] = \{[x]\} = 0$

(d) $0 \leq \{x\} \leq 1$

(e) The domain of the function is: $(-\infty, +\infty)$ and the range is: $[0, 1)$

FIGURE 1.98

(f) $\{x\} + \{-x\} = \begin{cases} 0, & x \in \text{integer} \\ 1, & x \notin \text{integer} \end{cases}$, this property is the direct consequence of above property. As we know that

$x = [x] + \{x\}$, for all $x \in R$ (i)

$\Rightarrow -x = [-x] + \{-x\}$ (ii)

From (i) and (ii), we get $[x] + [-x] + \{x\} + \{-x\} = 0$

(g) $[x + y] = \begin{cases} [x] + [y], & \text{if } \{x\} + \{y\} < 1 \\ [x] + [y] + 1, & \text{if } \{x\} + \{y\} \geq 1 \end{cases}$.

Hence $[x + y] \leq [x] + [y] + 1$

Explanation: Let $x = I_x + f_x$, $y = I_y + f_y$ where I_x and I_y represent the integral part of x and y respectively and f_x and f_y represent the fractional part of x and y respectively. It is obvious that $[x] = I_x$ and $[y] = I_y$ and

$0 \leq f_x < 1,\ 0 \leq f_y < 1$

$\Rightarrow\ 0 \leq f_x + f_y < 2 \qquad \Rightarrow [f_x + f_y] = 0$ or 1

Now $x + y = I_x + I_y + f_x + f_y$

$\Rightarrow\ [x + y] = I_x + I_y + [f_x + f_y] =$

$$\begin{cases} I_x + I_y & \text{if } 0 \leq f_x + f_y < 1 \\ I_x + I_y + 1 & \text{if } 1 \leq f_x + f_y < 2 \end{cases}$$

$\Rightarrow\ [x + y] \leq [x] + [y] + 1$

ILLUSTRATION 155: Solve $4\{x\} = x + [x]$

SOLUTION: We know $x = [x] + \{x\}$ $\therefore$ $4\{x\} = [x] + \{x\} + [x]$

$\{x\} = \dfrac{2[x]}{3}$ (i) but $0 \le \{x\} \le 1$

So $0 \le \dfrac{2[x]}{3} \le 1 \Rightarrow 0 \le [x] \le 3/2$ hence $[x] = 0$ or 1

if $[x] = 1$, then $\{x\} = 2/3$ from (i) thus $x = 5/3$ if $[x] = 0$, $\{x\} = 0$ so $x = 0$

Thus, the required solution is $x \in (0, 5/3]$

ILLUSTRATION 156: Find the range for $y = \dfrac{x-[x]}{1-[x]+x}$.

SOLUTION: Here $y = \dfrac{x-[x]}{1-[x]+x} = \dfrac{\{x\}}{1+\{x\}}$ Thus, domain $\in$ real number

Thus, from $y = \dfrac{\{x\}}{1+\{x\}}$ we have, $y + y\{x\} = \{x\} \Rightarrow \{x\} = \dfrac{y}{1-y}$

Here $0 \le \{x\} \le 1$; so, $0 \le \dfrac{y}{1-y} < 1 \Rightarrow 0 \le y < 1/2$. Hence range: $[0, 1/2)$

TEXTUAL EXERCISE–21 (SUBJECTIVE)

1. Solve for x:

(i) $[x] = 3.9$ (ii) $[x] < 3.9$

(iii) $[x] > 3.9$ (iv) $[x] > 5$

(v) $2.1 < [x] < 5$ (vi) $[x] \le 5$

(vii) $-9 \le [x] < -5.3$ (viii) $[x] \ge -5.3$

(ix) $[x] \le -5.3$ (x) $\{x\} = 0$

2. Solve for x:

(a) $[\sqrt{x}] = 3$ (b) $[x^2] = 5$

(c) $[x] + [-x] = 0$ (d) $x - [x] = 1/2$

(e) $[x]^2 - 3[x] + 2 = 0$ (f) $[x]^2 - 5[x] + 6 > 0$

(g) $[x]^2 - 3[x] + 2 < 0$ (h) $[3x] = -1$

(i) $[3x] - [-3x] = 0$ (j) $[x]^2 > 9$

(k) $[|x|] = 3$ (l) $|[x]| = 2$

(m) $4[x] - x = \{x\}$ (n) $[x] \ge n (n \in I)$

(o) $[x] < n\ (n \in I)$ (p) $-2.3 < [x] \le 3$

(q) $-2 < [x] < 5.3$

3. If $[x]^2 = [x + 2]$, where $[x]$ = the greatest integer less than or equal to x, then x must be such that

(a) $x = 2, -1$ (b) $x \in [2, 3)$

(c) $x \in [-1, 0)$ (d) None of these

4. Let $y = 2[x] + 3 = 3[x - 2] + 5$ then $[x + y]$ equals

(a) 10 (b) 15

(c) 12 (d) None of these

5. Find the complete set of values of x satisfying:

(i) $\dfrac{5[x]+4}{11[x]+7} \ge 3$ (ii) $[x]^2 - 3[x] + 2 \le 0$

6. If $[x]$ denotes the integral part of x for real x, then the value of

$$\left[\frac{1}{4}\right]+\left[\frac{1}{4}+\frac{1}{200}\right]+\left[\frac{1}{4}+\frac{2}{100}\right]+\left[\frac{1}{4}+\frac{3}{200}\right]+\text{.........}+\left[\frac{1}{4}+\frac{199}{200}\right]$$ is

(a) 44 (b) 46

(c) [50.9] (d) 50

7. Solution set of $5\{x\} = x + [x]$ and $[x] - \{x\} = \dfrac{1}{2}$ will contain

(a) no value (b) 1 value

(c) 2 value (d) None of these

8. If $0 < x < 1000$ and $\left[\dfrac{x}{2}\right]+\left[\dfrac{x}{3}\right]+\left[\dfrac{x}{5}\right]=\dfrac{31}{30}x$, where $[x]$ is the greatest integer less then or equal to x, the number of possible values of x is

(a) 34 (b) 32

(c) 33 (d) None of these

9. $[x + [x + [x]]] \le 3$ then value of x lie in the interval

(a) $(-\infty, 0)$ (b) $(-\infty, 1)$

(c) $(-\infty, 2)$ (d) None of these

10. Solve $\dfrac{[x]+3}{[x]-2} \ge \dfrac{[x]+1}{[x]-3} - 1$ (where [ ] denotes integral part)

Answer Keys

1. (i) no solution (ii) $(-\infty, 4)$ (iii) $x > 4$ (iv) $[6, \infty)$ (v) $[3, 5)$
(vi) $(-\infty, 6)$ (vii) $[-9, 5)$ (viii) $[-5, \infty)$ (ix) $(-\infty, -5)$ (x) z or I

2. (a) $[9, 16)$ (b) $(-\sqrt{6}-\sqrt{5}]\cup[\sqrt{5},\sqrt{6})$ (c) I or Z (d) $P+\frac{1}{2}, P\in I$ (e) $[1, 3)$

(f) $(-\infty,2)\cup[4,\infty)$ (g) ϕ (h) $[\frac{-1}{3},0)$ (i) $x=\frac{P}{3}, P\in I$ (j) $(-\infty-3)\cup[4,\infty)$

(k) $(-4, -3]\cup[3, 4)$ (l) $(-2, -1]\cup[2, 3)$ (m) $\{0\}$ (n) $[n, \infty)$ (o) $(-\infty, n)$ (p) $[-2, 4)$
(q) $[-1, 6)$

3. a, b, c **4.** (b) **5.** (i) no solution (ii) $[1, 3)$ **6.** (d)

7. (b) **8.** (c) **9.** (c) **10.** $(-\infty, O)\cup[5, \infty)$

■ ORIGIN OF COMPLEX NUMBERS

While solving algebraic equation many times we come across a situation where square of an unknown x is negative. e.g., $x^2 = -1$; it is very true that here x can be real but x can be written $\sqrt{-1}$ and termed as *imaginary number.* A great mathematician L.Euler coined the name: iota (symbolised as i for $\sqrt{-1}$) and thus the number system was extended to include *imaginary numbers* and termed the set obtained as set of *complex number.*

Imaginary/non-real numbers

A number whose square is not positive is termed as an imaginary number e.g., $\sqrt{-2}$ or $(1+\sqrt{-2})$ Therefore it can be said that the square root of a non positive real number is an imaginary number, for instance if $x^2 + 1 = 0$

$\Rightarrow x^2 = -1 \Rightarrow x$ is non-real no. i.e., imaginary number.

Euler introduced the symbol i for the number $\sqrt{-1}$ and is known as iota (a Greek word for 'imaginary')

Remark: Imaginary numbers do not follow the property of order i.e., for z_1 and z_2 imaginary numbers we can't say which one is greater. Since i is neither positive nor negative nor zero (*think why*?).

Purely imaginary numbers (*I*)

The number z whose square is non-positive real number (negative or zero) is termed as purely imaginary number. For example, $z^2 + a^2 = 0$ where $a \in \mathbb{R} \sim \{0\}$.

$\Rightarrow z^2 = -a^2$ Clearly, $z \notin \mathbb{R}$ as $z^2 < 0$.

$\Rightarrow z = \pm\sqrt{-a^2} \Rightarrow z = \pm a\sqrt{-1}$

$\Rightarrow z = \pm ai$ and $= \sqrt{-1}$

Note that $z = 0$ is also taken as purely imaginary number as well as real number. Thus the set of imaginary number (I) is given by $\boldsymbol{I = \{z : z = ai}$**, where** $\boldsymbol{a} \in \mathbb{R}$ **and** $\boldsymbol{i} = \sqrt{-1}\}$

Geometrical representation of purely imaginary numbers

Since $x(i^2) = x(i \times i) = -x\ (\forall x \in \mathbb{R})$, hence $-x$ can also be obtained by rotating x geometrically in anti-clockwise direction through 180° Hence twice multiplication by i is equivalent to geometrical rotation of the number by π radians in anti-clockwise direction and therefore single multiplication by i is equivalent to geometrical rotation of number by $\pi/2$ radians anti-clockwise. That is the reason why angle between real axis and imaginary axis is $\pi/2$ radians.

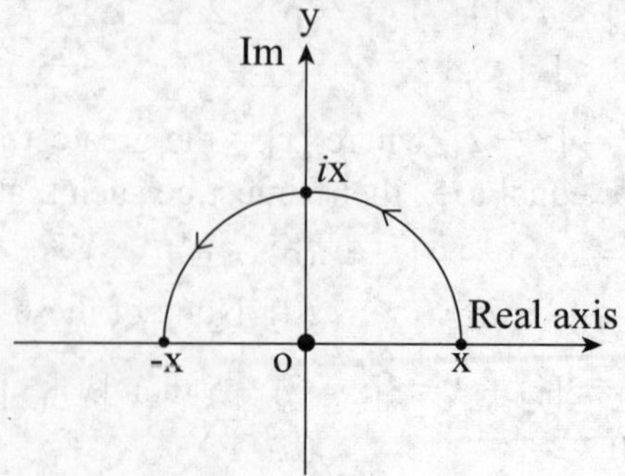

FIGURE 1.99

Therefore purely imaginary numbers are represented as points lying on y axis of argand plane. For example: $z = ai$ is represented by point $(0, a)$ on y axis as shown ahead:

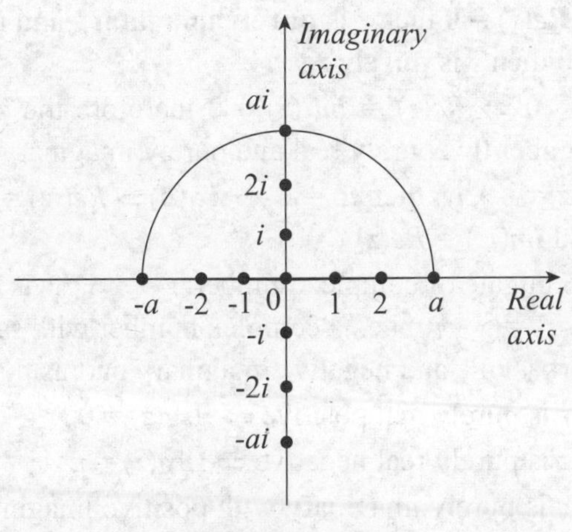

FIGURE 1.100

Properties of iota

1. $i^0 = 1, i^2 = -1, i^3 = -i, i^4 = 1$
2. Periodic properties of i
   $i^{4n} = 1, i^{4n+1} = i, i^{4n+2} = -1, i^{4n+3} = -i \ \forall\ n \in \mathbb{Z}$
3. $i^{-1} = -i$
4. Sum of four consecutive power terms of i is zero.
   i.e., $i^n + i^{n+1} + i^{n+2} + i^{n+3} = 0 \ \forall\ n \in \mathbb{Z}$
5. For any two real numbers a and b $\sqrt{a} \times \sqrt{b} = \sqrt{ab}$ is true only when atleast one of a and b is either 0 or + ve.

ILLUSTRATION 157: Prove that (i) $1 + i^{10} + i^{100} - i^{1000} = 0$

(ii) $(1 + i^{14} + i^{18} + i^{22})$ is a real number.

SOLUTION: (i) $1 + i^{10} + i^{100} - i^{1000} = 1(i^4)^2 \times i^2 + (i^4)^{25} - (i^4)^{250} = 1(i)^2 \times (-1) - (1)^{25} - (1)^{250}$

$[\because i^4 = 1]$

(ii) $1 + i^{14} + i^{18} + i^{22} = 1 + (i^4)^3 \times i^2 + (i^4)^4 \times i^2 + (i^4)^5 ' i^2$

$= 1 + (1)^3 \times (-1) + (1)^4 \times (-1) + (1)^5 \times (-1) = 1 - 1 - 1 - 1 = -2$, which is a real number.

■ COMPLEX NUMBERS

A number z resulting as a sum of a purely real number x and a purely imaginary number iy is called a complex number i.e., a number of the form $z = x + iy$ where $x, y \in \mathbb{R}$ and $i = \sqrt{-1}$ is called a complex number. Here x is called real part and y is called imaginary part of complex number and they are expressed as $Re(z) = x$, $Im(z) = y$. Here if $x = 0$ the complex number is purely imaginary and if $y = 0$ the complex number is purely real. A complex number may also be defined as an ordered pair of real numbers and may be denoted by the symbol (a, b). If we write $z = (a, b)$, then a is called the real part and b the imaginary part of the complex number z.

The set of complex numbers is denoted by $\mathbb{C}$ and is given by $\mathbb{C} = \{z : z = x + iy;$ where $x, y \in \mathbb{R}$ and $i = \sqrt{-1}\}$

Argand plane

Any complex number $z = a + ib$ can be written as an ordered pair (a, b) which can be represented on a plane by the point $P(a, b)$ (known as affix of point P) as shown below in the figure. This plane is called Argand plane, complex plane or the Gaussian plane. The Argand plane is generated by real and imaginary axis. Conversely, every point in this plane represents a complex number.

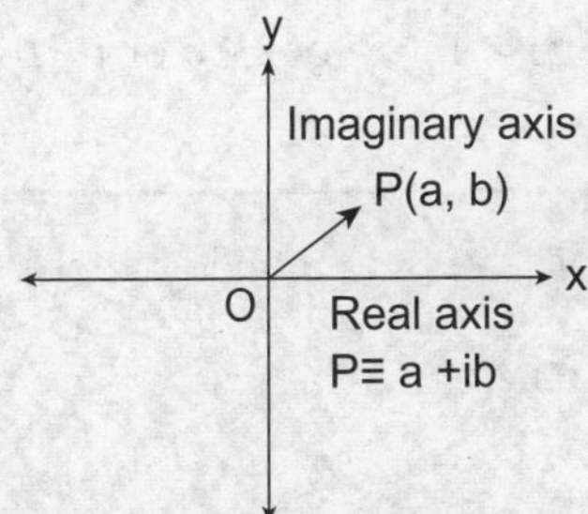

FIGURE 1.101

Representation of complex numbers

Complex numbers can be represented by following forms:

1. **Cartesian form (rectangular form):** A complex number $z = x + iy$ can be represented by the point P having coordinates (x, y).
2. **Vector form (Algebraic form):** Every complex number z is regarded as a position vector $(\overrightarrow{OP})$ which is sum of two position vectors: Purely real vector $x(\overrightarrow{OA})$ and purely imaginary vector iy $(\overrightarrow{OB})$
   $\because \overrightarrow{OP} = \overrightarrow{OA} + \overrightarrow{AP} = \overrightarrow{OA} + \overrightarrow{OB} \Rightarrow z = x + iy$

Modulus of z: Distance of point P from the origin is called modulus of complex number z and is denoted by $|z|$. It is length of vector $(\overrightarrow{OP})$. It is distance of $P(z)$ from origin.

$\therefore |z| = |\overrightarrow{OP}| = \sqrt{x^2 + y^2} = \sqrt{(R(z))^2 + (Im(z))^2}$

Argument of z: Argument of z is the angle made by $\overrightarrow{OP}$ with the positive direction of real axis. Also known as amplitude z and is denoted by $amp(z)$.

Arg(z) = θ; where $\tan\theta = \frac{y}{x}$, θ lies in the quadrant in which complex number z lies.

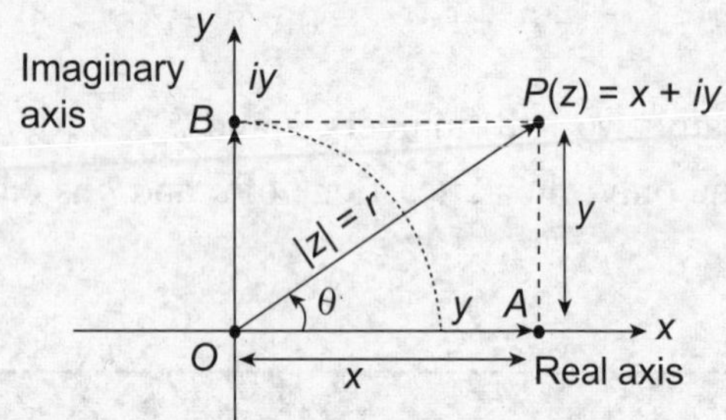

FIGURE 1.102

Properties of complex numbers

(i) Equality: Two complex numbers z_1 and z_2 are equal only when their real and imaginary parts are respectively equal. i.e., $Re(z_1) = Re(z_2)$ and $I(z_1) = I(z_2)$ or $|z_1| = |z_2|$ and $\arg(z_1) = \arg(z_2)$

(ii) Inequality: Inequality in complex number are not defined because 'i' is neither positive, zero nor negative so $4 + 3i > 1 + 2i$ or $i < 0$ or $i > 0$ is meaningless.

(iii) If $Re(z) = 0$ then z is **purely imaginary** and if $Im(z) = 0$ then z is **purely real**.

(iv) $z = 0 \Rightarrow Re(z) = Im(z) = 0$ therefore the complex number 0 is purely real and purely imaginary both.

(v) If $z = x + iy$, then $iz = -y + ix$ (a)$\Rightarrow Re(iz) = -Im(z)$ and $Im(iz) = Re(z)$

(vi) Conjugate of complex number: $z = x + iy$ is denoted as $\bar{z} = (x - iy)$ i.e., a complex number with same real part as of z and negative imaginary part as that of z.

(vii) If z is purely real positive $\Rightarrow Arg(z) = 0$

(viii) If z is purely real negative $\Rightarrow Arg(z) = \pi$

(ix) If z is purely imaginary with positive imaginary part $\Rightarrow Arg(z) = \pi/2$

(x) If z is purely imaginary with negative imaginary part $\Rightarrow Arg(z) = -\pi/2$

(xi) $Arg(0)$ is not defined

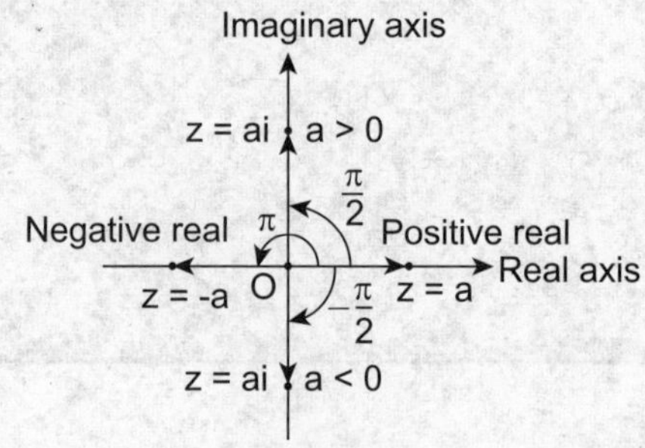

FIGURE 1.103

ILLUSTRATION 158: Find x and y when : $(2y + 7) + (4 - 3x)i = 0$

SOLUTION: We have: $(2y + 7) + (4 - 3x)i = 0$

$\Rightarrow 2y + 7 = 0$ and $4 - 3x = 0$. $[\because x + iy = 0 \Leftrightarrow x = 0, y = 0]$

$\Rightarrow 2y = -7$ and $4 = 3x$ $\Rightarrow y = -\frac{7}{2}$ and $x = \frac{4}{3}$. Hence $x = \frac{4}{3}$ and $y = -\frac{7}{2}$

Operations on set of complex numbers

(i) Addition/Subtraction of two complex numbers

Let $z_1 = x_1 + iy_1$ and $z_2 = x_2 + iy_2$

$\Rightarrow z_1 + z_2 = (x_1 + iy_1) + (x_2 + iy_2) = (x_1 + x_2) + i(y_1 + y_2)$

i.e., $z_1 + z_2 = [R(z_1) + R(z_2)] + i[I(z_1) + I(z_2)] \in C$

and $z_1 - z_2 = (x_1 + iy_1) - (x_2 + iy_2) = (x_1 - x_2) + i(y_1 - y_2)$

i.e., $z_1 - z_2 = [R(z_1) - R(z_2)] + i[I(z_1) - I(z_2)] \in C$

Geometric representation: Consider two complex numbers $z_1 = (x_1 + iy_1)$ and $z_2 = (x_2 + iy_2)$ represented by vector $z_1 = \overrightarrow{OA}$; $z_2 = \overrightarrow{OB}$ as shown in figure.

Then by parallelogram law of vector addition

$z_1 + z_2 = \overrightarrow{OA} + \overrightarrow{OB} = \overrightarrow{OC}$

Hence C represents the affix of $z_1 + z_2$

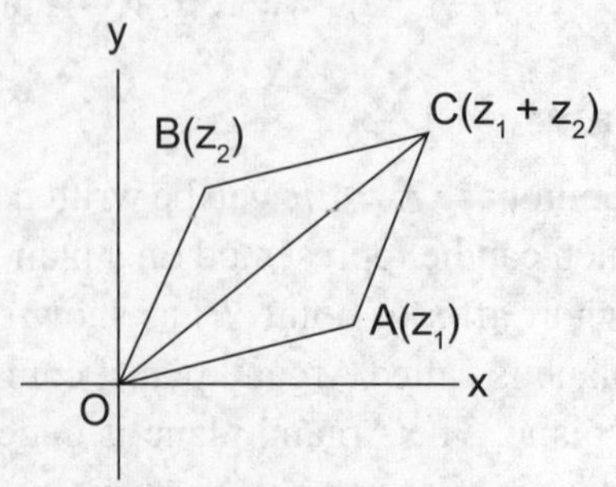

FIGURE 1.104

NOTES

1. *In ΔOAC, [Since sum of two sides of a Δ is always greater than the third side]* ∵ $OA + AC \geq OC \Rightarrow |\overrightarrow{OA}| + |\overrightarrow{OB}| \geq |\overrightarrow{OC}|$
   $\Rightarrow |z_1| + |z_2| \geq |z_1 + z_2|$ *This is called triangle inequality. Also considering ΔOAB; OA + OB ≥ AB*
   $\Rightarrow |\overrightarrow{OA}| + |\overrightarrow{OB}| \geq |\overrightarrow{BA}| \Rightarrow |z_1| + |z_2| \geq |z_1 - z_2|$
2. *In a triangle, the difference of two sides is always less than the third side*
   $\Rightarrow \left||\overrightarrow{OB}| - |\overrightarrow{OA}|\right| \leq |\overrightarrow{AB}| \Rightarrow ||z_2| - |z_1|| \leq |z_2 + z_1|$
3. *Triangle Inequality:* $||z_1| - |z_2|| \leq |z_1 \pm z_2| \leq |z_1| + |z_2|$

(ii) Multiplication of two complex numbers

Let $z_1 = x_1 + iy_1$ and $z_2 = x_2 + iy_2$

then $z_1.z_2 = (x_1 + iy_1).(x_2 + iy_2)$

$= (x_1.x_2) + ix_1y_2 + ix_2y_1 + i^2y_1y_2$

$= (x_1.x_2 - y_1y_2) + i(x_2y_1 + x_1y_2)$

$= [R(z_1).R(z_2) - I(z_1).I(z_2)] +$
$i[R(z_2).I(z_1) + R(z_1).I(z_2)] \in C$

(iii) Division of two complex numbers

Let $z_1 = x_1 + iy_1$ and $z_2 = x_2 + iy_2$

$\Rightarrow z_1/z_2 = (x_1 + iy_1)/(x_2 + iy_2)$

$= (x_1 + iy_1).(x_2 - iy_2)/(x_2 + iy_2).(x_2 - iy_2)$

$$= \frac{(x_1.x_2 + y_1.y_2) + i(x_2.y_1 - x_1.y_2)}{(x_2^2 + y_2^2)}$$

$$= \frac{(x_1.x_2 + y_1.y_2)}{(x_2^2 + y_2^2)} + \frac{i(x_2.y_1 - x_1.y_2)}{(x_2^2 + y_2^2)} \in C$$

ILLUSTRATION 159: Perform the indicated operations and write the result in the form x + iy:

(i) $(-3 - 2i) + (-6 + 3i)$ (ii) $\left(\frac{1}{2} + \frac{7}{2}i\right) - \left(4 + \frac{5}{2}i\right)$

(iii) $(1 - 2i) - i + (4 - 7i) - 2i + (5i + 3)$

SOLUTION: (i) $(-3 - 2i) + (-6 + 3i) = (-3 - 6) + (-2 + 3)i = -9 + i$

(ii) $\left(\frac{1}{2} + \frac{7}{2}i\right) - \left(4 + \frac{5}{2}i\right) = \left(\frac{1}{2} - 4\right) + \left(\frac{7}{2} - \frac{5}{2}\right)i = -\frac{7}{2} + i$

(iii) $(1 - 2i) - i + (4 - 7i) - 2i + (5i + 3) = [(1 - 2i) - i + (4 - 7i) - 2i + (5i + 3)$

$= [1 + (-2 - 1)i] + [\{(4 - 7i) - 2i\} + (5i + 3)]$

$= (1 - 3i) + [4 - 9i + 5i + 3] = (1 - 3i) + (7 - 4i) = (1 + 7) - (3 + 4)i = 8 - 7i$

ILLUSTRATION 160: Find real and imaginary parts of $\frac{1-i}{1+i}$.

SOLUTION: $\frac{1-i}{1+i} = \frac{1-i}{1+i} \times \frac{1-i}{1-i} = \frac{(1-i)^2}{1+i^2} = \frac{1-i^2-2i}{1-i^2} = \frac{1-1-2i}{1-(-1)} = \frac{-2i}{2} = -i = 0 - i$

Hence real part = 0 and imaginary part = –1

ILLUSTRATION 161: Perform the indicated operation and give your answer in the form x + iy, where x and y are real numbers and i= $\sqrt{-i}$

(i) $\left(\frac{1}{2} + \frac{1}{4}i\right)\left(-\frac{2}{3} - \frac{1}{4}i\right)$ (ii) $\frac{5+2i}{-1+\sqrt{3}i}$

(iii) $\left(\sqrt{5} - 7i\right)\left(\sqrt{5} - 7i\right)^2 + (-2 + 7i)^2$

SOLUTION: (i) $\left(\frac{1}{2}+\frac{1}{4}i\right)\left(-\frac{2}{3}-\frac{1}{4}i\right) = -\frac{1}{3}-\frac{1}{8}i-\frac{1}{6}i-\frac{1}{16}i^2$

$= \left(\frac{1}{3}+\frac{1}{16}\right)-\left(\frac{1}{8}+\frac{1}{6}\right)i = \frac{13}{48}-\frac{7}{24}i,$

which is of the form $x + iy$

Here $x = -\frac{13}{48}$ and $y = -\frac{7}{24}$

(ii) $\frac{5+2i}{-1+\sqrt{3}i} = \frac{5+2i}{-1+\sqrt{3}i} \times \frac{-1-\sqrt{3}i}{-1-\sqrt{3}i} = \frac{-5-5\sqrt{3}i-2i-2\sqrt{3}i^2}{(-1)^2-(-3i)^2}$

$= \frac{-5-5\sqrt{3}i-2i-2\sqrt{3}(-1)}{1-3(-1)} = \frac{(-5+2\sqrt{3})+(-5\sqrt{3}-2)i}{1+3} = \frac{-5+2\sqrt{3}}{4}+\frac{-5\sqrt{3}-2}{4}i,$

which is of the form $x + iy$

Here $x = \frac{-5+2\sqrt{3}}{4}$ *and* $y = \frac{-5\sqrt{3}-2}{4}$

(iii) $\left(\sqrt{5}-7i\right)\left(\sqrt{5}-7i\right)^2+\left(-2+7i\right)^2$

$\left(\sqrt{5}-7i\right)^3+\left(-2+7i\right)^2$

$= \left[5\sqrt{5}-3\left(\sqrt{5}\right)^2(7i)+3\left(\sqrt{5}\right)(7i)^2-(7i)^3\right]+\left(4-28i+49i^2\right)$

$= \left(5\sqrt{5}-105+147\sqrt{5}i^2-343i^3\right)+\left(4-28i-49\right)$

$= \left(5\sqrt{5}-105i+147\sqrt{5}-343i\right)+\left(-45-28i\right) = \left(5\sqrt{5}-147\sqrt{5}-45\right)+\left(-105i-343i-28i\right)$

$= -\left(142\sqrt{5}+45\right)+210i,$

Here $x = -\left(142\sqrt{5}+45\right)$ and $y = 210$

■ SQUARE ROOT OF A COMPLEX NUMBER

If $z = a + ib$

Let the square root of z be a complex number x + iy therefore. $z^{1/2} = x + iy = (a + ib)^{1/2}$

Squaring both sides, we get $x^2 - y^2 + 2xyi = a + i\,b$

Equating Real and Imaginary parts, we get,

$x^2 - y^2 = a$ (i)

$2xy = b$ (ii)

We have $(x^2 + y^2)^2 = (x^2 - y^2)^2 + 4x^2y^2 = a^2 + b^2$

$\Rightarrow x^2 + y^2 = \sqrt{a^2+b^2}$ [–*ve root is rejected since* $x^2 + y^2 \geq 0$]

$\therefore\ x^2 + y^2 = |z|$ (iii)

solving (i) and (iii) $x^2 = \frac{|z|+a}{2}, y^2 = \frac{|z|-a}{2}$

$\Rightarrow x = \pm\sqrt{\frac{|z|+a}{2}}, y = \sqrt{\frac{|z|-a}{2}}$

Where x, y have same sign, $b > 0$

$\Rightarrow z^{1/2} = \pm\left[\sqrt{\frac{|z|+a}{2}}+i\sqrt{\frac{|z|-a}{2}}\right]$

When x, y have different signs, $b < 0$

$\Rightarrow z^{1/2} = \pm\left[\sqrt{\frac{|z|+a}{2}}-i\sqrt{\frac{|z|-a}{2}}\right]$

Hence square roots of $z = a + ib$ are given by

$\pm\left[\sqrt{\frac{|z|+a}{2}}+i\sqrt{\frac{|z|-a}{2}}\right]$ $b > 0$ and

$\pm\left[\sqrt{\frac{|z|+a}{2}}-i\sqrt{\frac{|z|-a}{2}}\right]$ $b < 0$

ILLUSTRATION 162: Find the square root of 8 – 15*i*.

SOLUTION: Let $\sqrt{8-5i} = x+iy$

$\Rightarrow$ 8 – 15*i* = $x^2 - y^2 + i\,(2xy)$

Equating real and imaginary parts

we get, $x^2 - y^2 = 8$ (1)

and $2xy = -15$ (2)

Now, $(x^2+y^2)^2 = (x^2-y^2)^2 + 4x^2y^2 = (8)^2 + (15)^2 = 64 + 225 = 289$

$\Rightarrow x^2 + y^2 = 17$ (3)

(1) + 3 gives $2x^2 = 25$

$x^2 = 25/2 \Rightarrow x = \dfrac{\pm 5}{\sqrt{2}}$

(3) – (1) gives, $2y^2 = 9$

$y^2 = 9/2$

$y = \dfrac{\pm 3}{\sqrt{2}}$

$\because\ 2xy = -15 < 0$

$\Rightarrow$ *x* and *y* are of opposite sign

$\therefore\ \sqrt{8-5i} = \dfrac{5}{\sqrt{2}} - \dfrac{3}{\sqrt{2}}i$ or $\dfrac{-5}{\sqrt{2}} + \dfrac{3}{\sqrt{2}}i$

$\therefore\ \sqrt{8-5i} = \pm\left(\dfrac{5}{\sqrt{2}} - \dfrac{3}{\sqrt{2}}i\right) = \pm\dfrac{1}{2}(5-3i)$

■ CUBE ROOT OF UNITY

Let $\sqrt[3]{1}$ = cube root of unity

$\Rightarrow x^3 = 1$

$\Rightarrow (x-1)(x^2+x+1) = 0$

$\Rightarrow x = 1$ or $x = \dfrac{-1\pm\sqrt{1-4}}{2} = \dfrac{-1\pm\sqrt{3}i}{2} = \omega, \omega^2$

where $\omega = \dfrac{-1+\sqrt{3}i}{2}$ and $\omega^2 = \dfrac{-1-\sqrt{3}i}{2}$

$\therefore$ Cube roots of unity are 1, ω, ω^2 and ω, ω^2 are called the imaginary cube roots of unity

Properties of cube roots of unity

P(1): $|\omega| = |\omega^2| = 1$

Proof: $\left|\dfrac{-1}{2} \pm \dfrac{\sqrt{3}i}{2}\right| = \sqrt{\left(\dfrac{-1}{2}\right)^2 + \left(\dfrac{\pm\sqrt{3}}{2}\right)^2} = \sqrt{\dfrac{1}{4}+\dfrac{3}{4}} = 1$

P(2): $\bar{\omega} = \omega^2$

Proof: $\omega = \dfrac{-1}{2} + \dfrac{\sqrt{3}}{2}i \Rightarrow \bar{\omega} = \dfrac{-1}{2} - \dfrac{\sqrt{3}}{2}i = \omega^2$

P(3): $\omega^3 = 1$

Proof: $\omega^3 = \omega.\omega^2$

$= \left[\dfrac{-1+\sqrt{3}i}{2}\right]\left[\dfrac{-1-\sqrt{3}i}{2}\right]$

$= \left(\dfrac{-1}{2}\right)^2 - \left(\dfrac{\sqrt{3}}{2}i\right)^2 = \dfrac{1}{4} + \dfrac{3}{4} = 1$

P(4): $\omega^{3n} = 1$; $\omega^{3n+1} = \omega$ and $\omega^{3n+2} = \omega^2\ \forall n \in \mathbb{Z}$

Proof: $(\omega^{3n}) = (\omega^3)^n$

$= (1)^n = 1$

$\omega^{3n+1} = \omega^{3n}.\omega = 1.\omega = \omega$

$\omega^{3n+2} = \omega^{3n}.\omega^2 = 1.\omega^2 = \omega^2\ \forall n \in \mathbb{Z}$

P(5): Sum of cube roots of unity is 0 i.e., $1 + \omega + \omega^2 = 0$

Proof: $1+\omega+\omega^2$

$$= 1 + \left(\frac{-1}{2}+\frac{\sqrt{3}}{2}i\right) + \left(\frac{-1}{2}-\frac{\sqrt{3}}{2}i\right) = 0$$

Remark 1

$\because \quad \bar{\omega} = \omega^2 \quad \because \quad 1+\omega+\bar{\omega} = 0$

Remark 2

$\because \quad \bar{\omega} = \omega^2$ and $\omega = \omega.1 = \omega.\omega^3 = \omega^4 = (\omega^2)^2 = (\bar{\omega})^2$

$\because \quad 1+\omega+\omega^2 = 1 + (\bar{\omega})^2 + \bar{\omega}$

$\because \quad 1+\bar{\omega}+(\bar{\omega})^2 = 0$

P(6): $1+\omega^n+\omega^{2n} = \begin{cases} 3; \text{when } n \text{ is multiple of } 3 \\ 0; \text{when } n \text{ is not a multiple of } 3 \end{cases}$

Proof:

Case (i) When $n = 3k$; $k \in \mathbb{Z}$ then $1+\omega^n+\omega^{2n} = 1+\omega^{3k}+\omega^{6k} = 1+(\omega^3)^k+(\omega^3)^{2k} = 1+1+1 = 3$

Case (ii) When $n = 3k+1$; $k \in \mathbb{Z}$ then $1+\omega^n+\omega^{2n} = 1+\omega^{3k+1}+\omega^{6k+2} = 1+\omega+\omega^2 = 0$ $\quad [\because \omega^{3k} = \omega^{6k} = 1]$

Case (iii) When $n = 3k+2$; $k \in \mathbb{Z}$ then $1+\omega^n+\omega^{2n} = 1+\omega^{3k+2}+\omega^{6k+4} = 1+\omega^2+\omega^4 = 1+\omega^2+\omega = 0$

ILLUSTRATION 163: Prove that $a^3+b^3 = (a+b)(a+2b)(a+\omega^2 b)$.

SOLUTION: Consider RHS $= (a+b)(a+\omega b)(a+b\omega^2)$

$= (a+b)(a^2+ab\omega^2+ab\omega+b^2\omega^3)$

$= (a+b)(a^2+ab(\omega+\omega^2)+b^2) \qquad \because \omega^3 = 1$

$= (a+b)(a^2-ab+b^2) \qquad \because \omega+\omega^3 = -1$

$= a^3+b^3$.

ILLUSTRATION 164: Show that $(1+\omega-\omega^2)^5+(1-\omega+\omega^2)^5$.

SOLUTION: Consider RHS $= (1-\omega+\omega^2)^5+(1-\omega+\omega^2)^5$

$= (-2\omega^2)^5+(-2\omega)^5 = -2^5\omega^{10}-2^5\omega^5 = -2^5(\omega+\omega^2) = -2^5(-1) = 32.$

TEXTUAL EXERCISE–22 (SUBJECTIVE)

1. Prove that
   (i) $(1-i)^2 = -2i$ (ii) $(1+i)^4 \times \left(1+\frac{1}{i}\right)^4 = 16$
2. Simplify: $\sqrt{\frac{-x}{16}}+\sqrt{\frac{-x}{25}}-\sqrt{\frac{-x}{36}}$ where x is a positive real number.
3. Find real numbers x and y such that $3x+2iy-ix+5y = 7+5i$
4. Find x and y, if $(3y-2)+i(7-2x) = 0$
5. Find the sum of : $\frac{2}{3}+\frac{5}{3}i, -\frac{2}{3}i$ and $\frac{-5}{4}-i$.
6. Prove that $\left[\frac{\sqrt{7}+i\sqrt{3}}{\sqrt{7}-i\sqrt{3}}+\frac{\sqrt{7}-i\sqrt{3}}{\sqrt{7}+i\sqrt{3}}\right]$ is real.
7. Prove that
   (i) the sum of a complex number and its conjugate is real.
   (ii) The product of a complex number and its conjugate is real
8. If $1+4\sqrt{3}i = (a+ib)^2$, prove that $a^2-b^2=1$ and $ab = 2\sqrt{39}$.
9. Find the multiplicative inverse of the product of complex numbers: $3+4i$, $5-12i$.
10. Find the value of $\sqrt{3-4i}$.
11. Find the square roots of the following:
    (i) $-8-6i$ (ii) $5-12i$
    (iii) $-2+2\sqrt{3}i$
12. If 1, ω, ω^2 are the three cube roots of unity, prove that
    (i) $(1+\omega^2)^4 = \omega$
    (ii) $(1-\omega+\omega^2)(1+\omega-\omega^2) = 4$
    (iii) $(1-\omega)(1-\omega^2)(1-\omega^4)(1-\omega^5) = 9$
13. If $x = a+b$, $y = a\omega+b\omega^2$, $z = a\omega^2+b\omega$, show that
    (i) $xyz = a^3+b^3$ (ii) $x^2+y^2+z^2 = 6ab$

Answer Keys

2. $\frac{17}{60}i\sqrt{x}$ **3.** x = –1, y = 2 **4.** $x=\frac{7}{2}, y=\frac{2}{3}$ **5.** $\frac{-7}{12}$ **9.** $\frac{63}{4225}+\frac{16}{4225}i$

10. $\pm(2-i)$ **11.** (i) $\pm(1-3i)$ (ii) $\pm(3-2i)$ (iii) $\pm(1+\sqrt{3}i)$

CONCEPTS OF CONTINUED SUMS AND PRODUCTS

Continued Sum (Σ) Sigma (Σ) stands for sum of indexed terms. e.g., $\sum_{k=1}^{n} a_k = a_1 + a_2 + a_3 + \ldots + a_n$. In the above symbol, a_k is called general term and k is known as index.

Properties

1. $\sum_{k=1}^{n} a = a + a + a + \ldots + a\,(n \text{ terms}) = na$
2. Sigma distributes on addition and subtraction
$$\sum_{k=1}^{n}(a_k \pm b_k) = (a_1 \pm b_1) + (a_2 \pm b_2) + \ldots + (a_n \pm b_n)$$
3. Sigma does not distribute on product and ratio of terms i.e.,
$$\sum_{k=1}^{n}(a_k \times b_k) = (a_1 \times b_1) + (a_2 \times b_2) + \ldots + (a_n \times b_n) \neq \left(\sum_{k=1}^{n} a_k\right)\left(\sum_{k=1}^{n} b_k\right) \text{ and}$$
$$\sum_{k=1}^{n}(a_k/b_k) = (a_1/b_1) + (a_2/b_2) + \ldots + (a_n/b_n) \neq \left(\frac{\sum_{k=1}^{n} a_k}{\sum_{k=1}^{n} b_k}\right)$$
4. A constant factor can be taken out of sigma notation.
i.e., $\sum_{k=1}^{n} m.a_k = m\sum_{k=1}^{n} a_k = m\,(a_1 + a_2 + a_3 + \ldots + a_n)$

Cyclic and symmetric expressions

An expression is called symmetric in variable x and y iff interchanging x and y does not changes the expression $x^2+y^2, x^2+y^2-xy; x^3+y^3+x^2y+y^2x$. x^3-y^3 is not symmetric.

An expression is called cyclic in x, y, z iff cyclic replacement of variables does not change the expression. e.g. $x + y + z$, $xy + yz + zx$ etc. Such expression can be abbreviated by cyclic sigma notation as below:

$\Sigma x^2 = x^2 + y^2 + z^2, \Sigma xy = xy + yz + zx$

$\Sigma(x-y) = 0 \Rightarrow x + y + z + x^2 + y^2 + z^2 = \Sigma x + \Sigma x^2$

5. If sigma is defined for three variables say a, b, c occuring cyclicly, then it is evaluated as below $\sum a = a + b + c$, $\sum a.b = ab + bc + ca$, $\sum a^2 = a^2 + b^2 + c^2$

Continued products (π) Continued product of indexed terms $\prod_{k=1}^{n} a_k$ is defined as product of n number of indexed terms as $\prod_{k=1}^{n} a_k = a_1.a_2.a_3.......a_n$

Properties

1. $\prod_{k=1}^{n} a = a.a.a.......a\ (n \text{ times}) = a^n$
2. $\prod_{k=1}^{n} \lambda a_n = (\lambda a_1)(\lambda a_2)......(\lambda a_n)$
$$= \lambda^n (a_1.a_2...a_n) = \lambda \prod_{k=1}^{n} a_k$$
3. π distributes over product and ratio of indexed terms but not over sum and difference of terms. i.e.,
$$\prod_{k=1}^{n} a_k.b_k = \prod_{k=1}^{n} a_k \prod_{k=1}^{n} b_k = (a_1a_2......a_n)(b_1b_2......b_n)$$
$$\prod_{k=1}^{n}\left(\frac{a_k}{b_k}\right) = \frac{\prod_{k=1}^{n} a_k}{\prod_{k=1}^{n} b_k} = \left(\frac{a_1.a_2.a_3.....a_n}{b_1.b_2.b_3....b_n}\right)\text{s}$$
$$\prod_{k=1}^{n}(a_k \pm b_k) \neq \prod_{k=1}^{n} a_k \pm \prod_{k=1}^{n} b_k$$

NOTE

Continued product of Ist n natural numbers is called as factorial n and symbolised as n! or $\lfloor n$. i.e., $n! = \prod_{k=1}^{n} k = 1.2.3.4.....n$ clearly.

1! = 1
2! = 1. 2 = 2
3! = 1. 2. 3 = 6
4! = 1. 2. 3. 4 = 24 *etc.*

(i) $(n + 1)! = (n + 1).(n!)$ (ii) $0! = 1$ (by definition of ^nC_r) (iii) $n(n!) = (n + 1)! - n!$ etc.

TEXTUAL EXERCISE–23 (SUBJECTIVE)

1. Find the sum of following series:

(a) $\sum_{n=1}^{100}(-1)^n$ (b) $\sum_{k=1}^{n}(-1)^{2k}$

(c) $\sum_{k=0}^{80} i^{2k}$ (d) $\sum_{k=1}^{4n+3} i^k$

2. If $\prod_{k=1}^{n} k$ represents product of first n natural numbers (also denoted as n!). Then evaluate the following.

(a) 5! (b) 7!

(c) 8! (d) $\frac{8!}{6!}$

(e) $\frac{5!}{2!}$ (f) 8! + 7!

(g) $\prod_{k=1}^{n} a$ (h) $\prod_{k=1}^{5}(2k-1)$

(i) $\prod_{k=1}^{5} ak$ (j) $\prod_{k=1}^{20} 2^k$

(k) $\prod_{k=1}^{10} 2k$ (l) $\prod_{k=1}^{5}\left(\frac{2^k}{a}\right)$

3. (a) Show that $\prod_{k=1}^{n+1} k = (n+1)\prod_{k=1}^{n} k$ hence show that $(n + 1)! = (n + 1)\, n!$

(b) Evaluate 100!/98! and $n!/(n-2)!$

(c) Prove that $(p - 1)!$ is not divisible by p of p is a prime number.

(d) Prove that $(n-r+1).\frac{n!}{(n-r+1)!} = \frac{n!}{(n-r)!}$

(e) Prove that $n(n-1)(n-2)...(n-r+1) = \frac{n!}{(n-r)!}$

4. (a) Prove that

(i) $\sum_{k=1}^{n}(2k-1) = n^2$

(ii) $\sum_{k=1}^{n} k = \frac{n(n+1)}{2}$

(iii) $\sum_{k=1}^{100} k = 5050$

(iv) $\sum_{k=1}^{10} k\lambda = 55\lambda$

(v) $\sum_{j=1}^{n} jk^2 = \frac{n(n+1)}{2}k^2$

(b) Evaluate the following:

(i) $\sum_{k=1}^{n} k$

(ii) $\sum_{k=1}^{n} 2k$

(iii) $\sum_{k=1}^{n}(k^2+k)$. If it is given that

$$\sum_{k=1}^{n} k^2 = \frac{n(n+1)(2n+1)}{6}$$

(c) If Σ is defined for three variables a, b, c occuring cyclicly in the expression, then evaluate the following:

(i) Σa^2 (ii) $\Sigma(a^2 + b^2)$

(iii) $\Sigma(a - b)$ (iv) $\Sigma a(b - c)$

(v) $\Sigma a(b + c)$ (vi) Σb^2

(vii) $\Sigma a^2(b^2 - c^2)$ (viii) $\Sigma(a^2 - bc)$

Answer Keys

1. (a) 0 (b) n (c) 1 (d) –1 **2.** (i) (a) 120 (b) 5040 (c) 40320
(d) 56 (e) 60 (f) 45360 (g) a^n (h) 945 (i) $120a^5$ (j) 2^{210} (k) $10!(2^{10})$ (l) $2^{15}/a^5$

3. (b) 9900 ; $n^2 - n$

4. (b) (i) $\frac{n(n+1)}{2}$ (ii) $n^2 + n$ (iii) $\frac{n(n+1)(n+2)}{3}$ (c) (i) $a^2 + b^2 + c^2$

(ii) $2(a^2 + b^2 + c^2)$ (iii) 0 (iv) 0 (v) $2(ab + bc + ca)$ (vi) $a^2 + b^2 + c^2$ (vii) 0

(viii) $\frac{1}{2}\Sigma\left((a-b)^2\right)$

PARTIAL FRACTIONS

Types of fractions

Linear and non-repeating

When denominator $D(x)$ is expressible as the product non-repeating linear factors. Let $D(x) = (x - a_1)(x - a_2)(x - a_3)$...........Then,

$$\frac{N(x)}{D(x)} = Q(x) + \frac{A_1}{x-a_1} + \frac{A_2}{x-a_2} + \frac{A_3}{x-a_3} + \ldots\ldots \frac{A_n}{x-a_n}$$

ILLUSTRATION 164: Break the fraction $\frac{x^2}{(x-1)(2x+3)}$ into partial fractions.

SOLUTION: $\frac{x^2}{(x-1)(2x+3)} = \frac{x^2}{2x^2+x-3} = \frac{1}{2}\left[1 - \frac{x-3}{2x^2+x-3}\right]$

$\frac{1}{2}\left[1-\left(\frac{A}{x-1}+\frac{B}{2x+3}\right)\right] = \frac{1}{2}\left[1-\frac{(2x+3)A+(x-1)B}{(x-1)(2x+3)}\right] \Rightarrow x-3 = A(2x+3)+B(x-1)$

Method 1: Comparing coefficients of like terms i.e., $x - 3 = x(2A + B) + (3A - B)$

$\Rightarrow 2A + B = 1$ and $3A - B = -3 \Rightarrow A = \frac{-2}{5}$ and $B = \frac{9}{5}$

Method 2: Substituting the appropriate values of x; putting $x = 1$, we get $-2 = 5A$ $\Rightarrow A = -2/5$ Putting $x = -3/2$, we get $-9/2 = -5/2\,B \Rightarrow B = 9/5$

Linear and repeated roots

When denominator $D(x)$ is expressible as the product of linear factors such that some of them are repeating Let $D(x) = (x - a)^K (x - a_1)(x - a_2) \ldots\ldots (x - a_n)$

Then, $\frac{N(x)}{D(x)} = Q(x) + \frac{A_1}{x-a} + \frac{A_2}{(x-a)^2} + \ldots\ldots \frac{A_k}{(x-a)^k} + \frac{B_1}{x-a_1} + \frac{B_2}{x-a_2} + \ldots\ldots \frac{Bn}{x-a_n}$

ILLUSTRATION 165: Break the expression $\frac{x+1}{(x-1)^2(x-3)}$ into partial fraction.

SOLUTION: $\frac{x}{(x-1)^2(x-3)} = \frac{A}{x-1} + \frac{B}{(x-1)^2} + \frac{C}{x-3} \Rightarrow x + 1 = A(x-1)(x-3) + B(x-3) + C(x-1)^2$

Putting $x = 1$, $2 = -2B \Rightarrow B = -1$; Putting $x = 3$, $4 = 4C \Rightarrow C = 1$

Putting $x = 0$, $1 = 3A - 3B + C \Rightarrow A = -1$

$$\Rightarrow \frac{x+1}{(x-1)^2(x-3)} = \left(\frac{-1}{x-1} - \frac{1}{(x-1)^2} + \frac{1}{x-3}\right)$$

Quadratic and non-repeated roots

When some of the factors of denominator $D(x)$ are quadratic (which cannot be factorised further) but not repeating. Let $D(x) = (x^2 + ax + b)(x - a_1)(x - a_2) \ldots\ldots (x - a_n)$, then

$$\frac{N(x)}{D(x)} = Q(x) + \frac{A_1x + A_2}{(x_2 + ax + b)} + \frac{B_1}{x-a_1} + \frac{B_2}{x-a_2} + \ldots\ldots + \frac{B_n}{x-a_n}$$

ILLUSTRATION 166: Evaluate the following:

(i) $\frac{1}{x^3+1}$ (ii) $\frac{x}{(x^2+1)(x-1)}$

SOLUTION: (i) $\frac{1}{x^3+1} = \frac{1}{(x+1)(x^2-x+1)} = \frac{Ax+B}{x^2-x+1} + \frac{C}{x+1}$

$\Rightarrow 1 = (Ax + B)(x + 1) + C(x^2 - x + 1)$

Putting $x = -1$, $1 = 3C$

$\Rightarrow C = 1/3$ Comparing coeff of x, $1 = B + C$ $\Rightarrow B = 2/3$ Comparing coeff of x^2, $0 = A + C$

$\Rightarrow A = -1/3$

(ii) Decompose the fraction into partial fractions

$$\frac{x}{(x^2+1)(x-1)} = \frac{Ax+B}{x^2+1} + \frac{C}{x-1}$$

Consequently, $x = (Ax + B)(x - 1) + C(x^2 + 1)$

Setting $x = 1$ we get $1 = 2C$, $C = 1/2$; setting $x = 0$,

we get $0 = -B + C$, $B = 1/2$

Equating the coefficients of x^2, we get $0 = A + C$,

$\Rightarrow A = -1/2$.

Quadratic and repeated

When some of the factors of denominator $D(x)$ are quadratic (*which cannot be factorised further*) and are repeating.

Let $D(x) = (x^2 + a_1x + b_1)(x^2 + a_2x + b_2)\ldots\ldots\ldots (x^2 + a_nx + b_n)$

Type V: When both $N(x)$ and $D(x)$ contain only the even powers of x. To follow the steps given below: simplify the expressions

Step 1. Put $x^2 = t$ in both $N(x)$ and $D(x)$

Step 2. Make partial fractions of $N(t)/D(t)$

Step 3. Put back $t = x^2$

ILLUSTRATION 167: Evaluate $\frac{x^2}{x^4-1}$

SOLUTION: Putting $x^2 = t$, $\frac{x^2}{x^4-1} = \frac{t}{t^2-1} = \frac{1}{2}\left(\frac{1}{t-1} + \frac{1}{t+1}\right)$

Now putting back $t = x^2$, we get $= \frac{1}{2}\left(\frac{1}{x^2-1} + \frac{1}{x^2+1}\right)$

TEXTUAL EXERCISE–24 (SUBJECTIVE)

1. Evaluate the following:

(a) $\frac{x}{(x-1)(x-2)}$ (b) $\frac{(x^3-1)}{x^3+x}$

(c) $\frac{x^2-x+2}{(x+1)(x-1)}$ (d) $\frac{\cos^2\theta}{\cos^2\theta+4\sin^2\theta}$

(e) $\frac{x^3+3x+2}{(x^2+1)^2(x+1)}$ (f) $\frac{1}{(x^2+a^2)(x^2+b^2)}$

2. Resolve the following in partial functions:

(a) $\frac{1-3x^2}{(x+3)^2(x-2)}$ (b) $\frac{(2x-1)}{(x+1)(x^2+2)}$

(c) $\frac{(3x+4)}{(x^2+2x-7)(5x-2)}$ (d) $\frac{x^2+3x+6}{x^3-27}$

(e) $\frac{2x-3}{(x-1)(x^2+4)^2}$ (f) $\frac{x^2+x+1}{(x-1)^4}$

3. Express the following in partial fraction:-

(a) $\dfrac{5x-23}{(x-3)(x-7)}$ (b) $\dfrac{3x^3-x^2+19x-9}{x^4+18x^2+81}$

(c) $\dfrac{x+1}{x(x+3)(x-2)}$ (d) $\dfrac{9x}{2(2+3x)(1-3x)}$

(e) $\dfrac{2x+7}{5x^2+12x-32}$ (f) $\dfrac{2x^2}{(x-2)(x+1)^2}$

Answer Keys

1. (a) $\dfrac{-1}{x-1}+\dfrac{2}{x-2}$ (b) $1-\dfrac{1}{x}+\dfrac{(x-1)}{x^2+1}$ (c) $1-\dfrac{2}{x+1}+\dfrac{1}{x-1}$ (d) $-\dfrac{1}{3}-\dfrac{4}{9\cos^2\theta-12}$ or $\dfrac{4}{3+9\sin^2\theta}-\dfrac{1}{3}$

(e) $\dfrac{-1}{2(x+1)}+\dfrac{(x+1)}{2(x^2+1)}+\dfrac{2}{(x^2+1)^2}$ (f) $\dfrac{1}{(a^2-b^2)}\left(\dfrac{1}{x^2+b^2}-\dfrac{1}{x^2+a^2}\right)$

2. (a) $\dfrac{-11}{25(x-2)}-\dfrac{64}{25(x+3)}+\dfrac{26}{5(x+3)^2}$ (b) $\dfrac{-1}{x+1}+\dfrac{x+1}{x^2+2}$ (c) $\dfrac{-130}{151(5x-2)}+\dfrac{26x+133}{151(x^2+2x+7)}$

(d) $\dfrac{8}{9(x-3)}+\dfrac{x+6}{9(x^2+3x+9)}$ (e) $-\dfrac{1}{25(x-1)}+\dfrac{(x+1)}{25(x^2+4)}+\dfrac{(x+11)}{5(x^2+4)^2}$ (f) $\dfrac{1}{(x-1)^2}+\dfrac{3}{(x-1)^3}+\dfrac{3}{(x-1)^4}$

3. (a) $\dfrac{2}{x-3}+\dfrac{3}{x-7}$ (b) $\dfrac{3x-1}{x^2+9}+\dfrac{(-8x)}{(x^2+9)^2}$ (c) $\dfrac{1}{6x}-\dfrac{2}{15(x+3)}+\dfrac{3}{10(x-2)}$ (d) $\dfrac{2}{(3x+2)}+\dfrac{1}{(3x-1)}$

(e) $\dfrac{1}{28(x+4)}+\dfrac{51}{28(5x-8)}$ (f) $\dfrac{8}{9(x-2)}+\dfrac{10}{9(x+1)}+\left(\dfrac{-2}{3(x+1)^2}\right)$

■ REVIEW OF ELEMENTARY CONCEPTS

In this sub-topic, we are going to take a quick revision of the concepts of Geometry, Algebra,Trigonometry which you have already done in previous classes.

Geometry: Euclidian Postulates:

1. A straight line segment can be drawn joining any two points.
2. Any straight line segment can be extended indefinitely in a straight line.
3. Given any straight line segment, a circle can be drawn having the segment as radius and one end point as centre.
4. All right angles are congruent.
5. If two lines are drawn which intersect a third in such a way that the sum of the inner angles on one side is less than 90°, then the two lines must intersect on that side, if extended for enough.

Theorems related to lines and angles

Axiom I: Sum of two adjacent angles that a straight line makes with another on one side of it is always equal to two right angles.

Axiom II: If sum of two angles having a leg common is equal to two right angles then the other two legs of these two are always in straight line.

Theorems related to triangles

Theorem 1: If two triangles have two sides of the one equal to two sides of the other, each to each, and the angles included by those sides are equal, then the triangles are equal in all respects.

Theorem 2: If two angles of a triangle are equal to one another, then the sides which are opposite to the equal angles are equal to one another.

Theorem 3: If two triangles have the three sides of the one equal to three sides of another, they are equal in all respects.

Theorem 4: If one side of a triangle is greater than other then the angle opposite to the greater side is greater then the angle opposite to the smaller side.

Theorem 5: If one angle of a triangle is a greater than another then the side opposite to greater angle is greater than the side opposite to lesser angle.

Theorem 6: Any two sides of a triangle are together greater than third side.

Theorem 7: Of all straight lines drawn from a given point to a given point to a given straight line the perpendicular is the shortest.

Theorem 8: If a straight line cuts two straight lines as to make

(i) the alternate angles equal, or
(ii) and exterior angles equal to the interior opposite angles on the same side of the cutting line, or
(iii) the interior angles on the same side together equal to two right angles; then in each case the two straight lines are parallel.

Theorem 9: If a straight line cuts two parallel lines, it makes

(i) the alternate angles equal to one another
(ii) the exterior angle equal to the interior opposite angle on the same side of the cutting line
(iii) the two interior angles on the same side together equal to two right angles.

Theorem 10: If two triangles have two angles of one equal to two angles of the other, each to each, and any side of the first equal to the corresponding side of the other, the triangles are equal in all respects called congruent. (ASA congruency).

Theorem 11: Two right angled triangles which have their hypotenuses equal, and one side of one equal to one side of the other, are equal in all respects. (RHS congruency)

Theorem 12: If two triangles have two sides of the one equal to two sides of the other, each to each, but the angles included by the two sides of one greater than the angle included by the corresponding sides of the other, then the base of that which has the greater angle is greater than the base of the other.

Theorems related to parallelograms

Theorem 13: The straight lines which join the extremities of two equal and parallel line segments towards the same part are themselves equal and parallel.

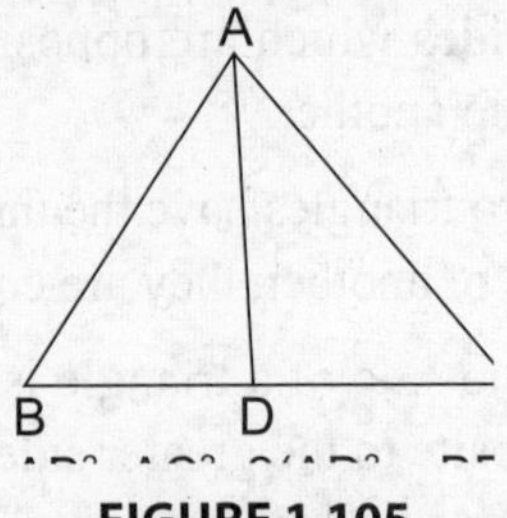

FIGURE 1.105

Theorem 14: The opposite sides and angles of a parallelogram are equal to one another, and each diagonal bisects the parallelogram.

Theorem 15: If there are three or more parallel straight lines, and the intercept made be them on any transversal are equal, then the corresponding intercept on any other transversal are also equal.

Theorem 16: Parallelograms on the same base and between the same parallels are equal in area.

Theorems related to intersection of loci

The concurrence of straight lines in a triangle.

(i) The perpendiculars drawn from the vertex to the opposite side are concurrent.
(ii) The bisectors of the angles of a triangles are concurrent.
(iii) The medians of a triangle are concurrent.

Theorem 17: Triangles on the same base and between the same parallel line are equal in area.

Theorem 18: If two triangles are equal in area, and stand on the same base and on the same side of it, they are between the same parallel lines.

Theorem 19: Pythagoras's Theorem. In a right-angled triangle, the square described on the hypotenuse is equal to the sum of the squares described on the other two sides and vice versa.

Circles

Theorem 20: If a straight line drawn from the centre of a circle bisects a chord, which does not pass through the centre, it cuts the chord at right angles. Conversely, if it cuts the chords at right angles. It bisects the chord.

Theorem 21: One circle, and only one, can pass through any three non-collinear points.

Theorem 22: If from a point within a circle more than two equal straight lines can be drawn to the circumference, that point is the centre of the circle.

Theorem 23: Equal chords of a circle are equidistant from the centre. Conversely, chords which are equidistant from the centre than the equal .

Theorem 24: Of any two chords of a circle, that which is nearer to the centre is greater than one more remote. Conversely, the greater of two chords is nearer to the centre than the less.

Theorem 25: If from any external point straight lines are drawn to the circumference of a circle, the greatest is that which passes through the centre, and the least is that which when produced passes through the centre. And of any other two such lines, the greater is that which subtends the greater angle at the centre.

Theorem 26: The angle at the centre of a circle is double of an angle at the circumference standing on the same arc.

Theorem 27: Angles in the same segment of a circle are equal. Coverse of this theorem states "equal angles standing on the same base, and on the same side of it, have their vertices on an arc of a circle, of which the given base is the chord."

Theorem 28: The opposite angles of quadrilateral inscribed in a circle are together equal to two right angles coverse of this theorem is also true

Theorem 29: The angle in a semi-circle is a right angle.

Theorem 30: In equal circular arcs arcs, which subtend cqual angles, either at the centres or at the circumferences, are equal.

Theorem 31: In equal circles, arcs which are cut off by equal chords are equal, the major arc equal, the major arc equal to the corresponding major arc, and the minor to the corresponding minor.

Theorem 32: In two equal circles, chords which cut off equal arcs are equal .

Tangents

Theorem 33: The tangent at any point of a circle is perpendicular to the radius drawn to the point of contact.

Theorem 34: Two tangent can be drawn to a circle from an external point and these two tangents are equal.

Theorem 35: If two circles touch one another, the centres and the point of contact are in one straight line.

Theorem 36: The angles made by a tangent to a circle with a chord drawn from the point of contact are respectively equal to the angles in the alternate segments of the circle.

■ SOME MISCELLANEOUS THEOREMS

Theorem 37: If two of straight lines, one is divided into any number of parts, the rectangle contained between the two lines is equal to the sum of the rectangles contained by the undivided line and the several parts of the divided line.

Theorem 38: If a straight line is divided internally at any point, the square on the given line is equal to the sum of the squares on the squares on the two segments together with twice the rectangle contained by the segments.

Theorem 39: If a straight line is divided externally at any point, the square on the given line is equal to the sum of the squares on the two segments diminished by twice the rectangle contained by the segments.

Theorem 40: In an obtuse-angled triangle, the square on the side subtending the obtuse angle is equal to the sum of the squares on the sides containing the obtuse angle together with twice the rectangle contained by one of those sides and the projection of the other side upon it.

Theorem 41: In every triangle, the square on the side subtending an acute angle is equal to the sum of the squares on the sides containing that angle diminished by twice the rectangle contained by one of these sides and the projection of the other side upon it.

Theorem 42: Steward's theorem: If D is any point on the side BC of a, then $AB^2 .DC + AC^2. BD = AC. (AD^2 + BD . DC)$

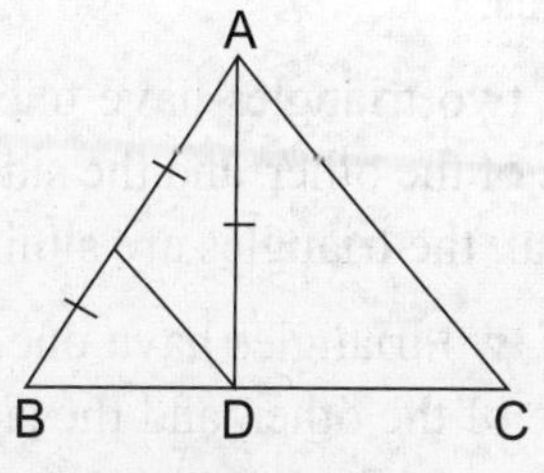

FIGURE 1.106

Theorem 43: In any triangle, the sum of the squares on two sides is equal to twice the square on half the third side together with twice the square on the median which bisects the third side.(Appolonius theorem, which is a special case of Steward's theorem).

Rectangles in connection with circles

Theorem 44: If two chords of a circle cut a point within it, the rectangle contained by their segments are equal.

Theorem 45: If two chords of a circle, when produced, cut at a point outside it, the rectangles contained by their segments are equal. And each rectangle is equal to the square on the tangent from the point of intersection.

Theorem 46: If from a point outside a circle, two straight lines are drawn, one of which cuts the circle, and the other meets it; and if the rectangle contained by the whole line which cuts the circle and the part of it outside the circle is equal to the square on the line which meets the circle, then the line which meets the circle is a tangent to it.

Proportional division of straight Lines

Theorem 47: A straight-line drawn parallel to one side of a triangle cuts the other two sides, or those sides produced proportionally.

Theorem 48: If the vertical angle of a triangle is bisected, the bisector divides the opposite side internally into segments which have the same ratio as the other sides of the triangle. Conversely, if the base is divided internally or externally into segments proportional to the other sides of the triangle, the line joining the point of section to the vertex bisects the vertical angle internally or externally.

Equiangular triangles

Theorem 49: If two triangles are equiangular to one another, their corresponding sides are proportional.

Theorem 50: If two triangles have their sides proportional when taken in order, the triangles are equiangular to one another, and those angles are equal which are opposite to corresponding sides.

Theorem 51: If two triangles have one angle of the one equal to one angle of the other, and the sides about the equal angles proportional, the triangles are similar.

Theorem 52: If two triangles have one angles of the one equal to one angle of the other, and the sides about another angle in proportional to the corresponding sides of the other, then the third angles are either equal or supplementary; and in the former case the triangles are similar.

Theorem 53: In a right-angled triangled, if a perpendicular is drawn from the right angle to the hypotenuse, the triangles on each side of it are similar to the whole triangles and to one another.

Similar figures

Theorem 54: Similar polygons can be divided into the same number of similar triangles; and the lines joining corresponding vertices in each figure are proportional.

Theorem 55: Any two similar rectilinear figures may be so placed that the lines joining corresponding vertices are concurrent.

Theorem 56: In equal circles, angles, whether at the centres or circumferences, have the same ratio as the arcs on which they stand.

Proportion applied to area

Theorem 57: The areas of similar triangles are proportional to the squares on corresponding sides.

Theorem 58: The area of similar polygons are proportional to the squares on corresponding sides.

■ MENSURATION FORMULAS

r = radius; d = diameter;
V = Volume; $S.A.$ = surface Area

1. *Circle*

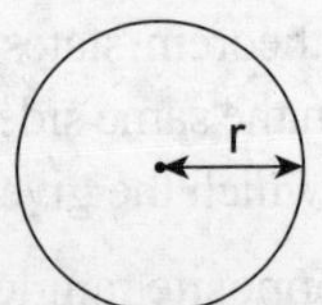

FIGURE 1.107

Perimeter: $2\pi r = \pi d$ Area : $\pi r^2 = 1/4\ \pi d^2$

2. *Sphere*

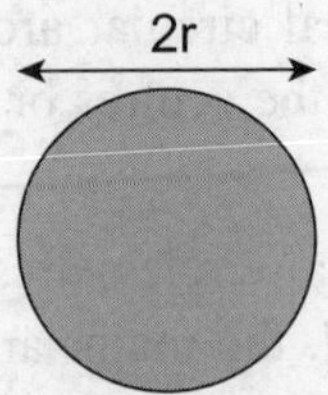

FIGURE 1.108

Surface area $= 4\pi r^2 = \pi d^2$

Volume $= 4/3\pi r^3 = 1/6\ \pi d^3$

3. *Spherical Shell (Hollow sphere)*

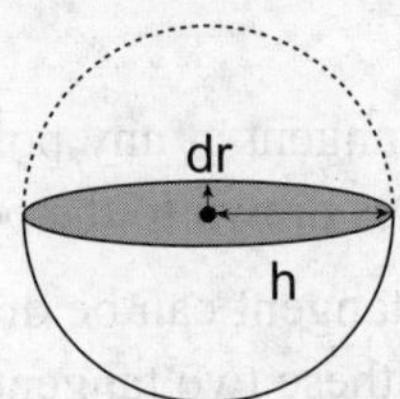

FIGURE 1.109

Surface area $= 4\pi r^2 = \pi d^2$

Volume of material used $= (4\pi r^2)(d_r)$ where d_r is thickness

4. *Cylinder*

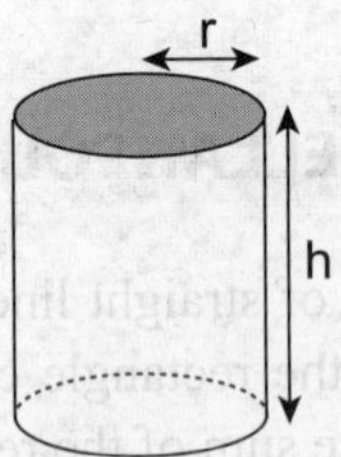

FIGURE 1.110

Lateral area $= 2\pi rh$ $V = \pi r^2 h$

Total area $= 2\pi rh + 2\pi r^2 = 2\pi r(h + r)$

5. *Cone*

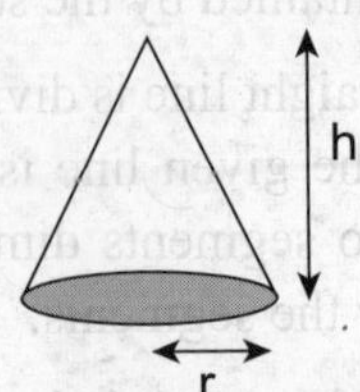

FIGURE 1.111

Lateral area = $\pi r\sqrt{r^2+h^2}$ h = height

Total area = $\pi r\left(\sqrt{r^2+h^2}+r\right)$; volume = $1/3\pi r^2 h$

6. *Ellipse*

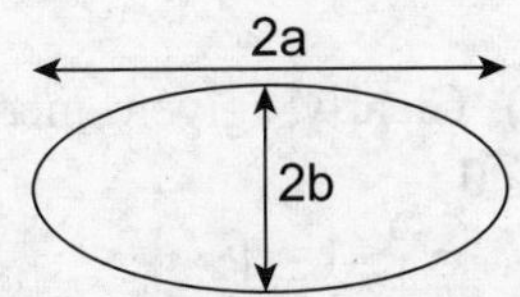

FIGURE 1.112

Circumference = $2\pi\sqrt{\dfrac{a^2+b^2}{2}}$ a = 1/2 of length of major axis; area = πab; b = 1/2 of length of minor axis

7. *Parallelogram*

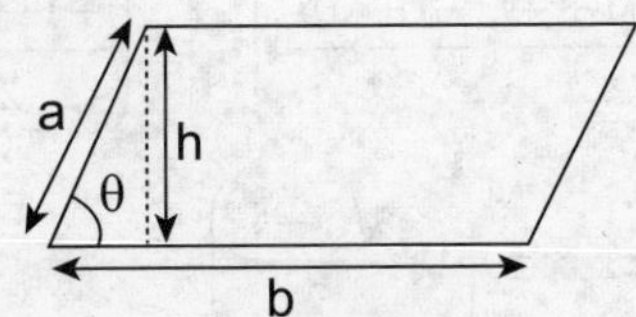

FIGURE 1.113

$A = bh$ or $= ab \sin\theta$; a = side; h = height

b = base θ = angle between sides a and b

8. *Trapeziod*

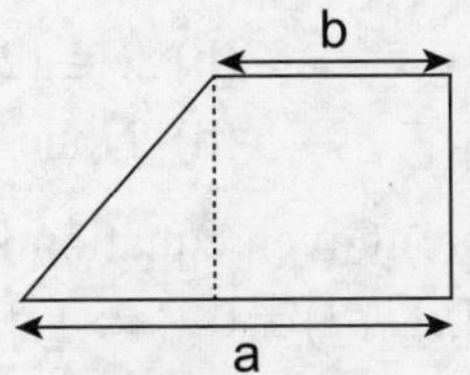

FIGURE 1.114

Area = $\dfrac{h}{2}(a+b)$

9. *Triangle*

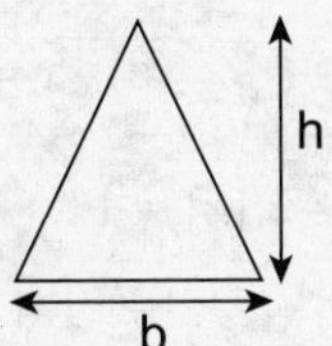

FIGURE 1.115

Area of $\Delta ABC = bh/2$ (where b = base and h = height) $= (ab/2)\sin C = (bc/2)\sin A = (ac/2)\sin B$

$= \sqrt{s(s-a)(s-b)(s-c)}$ {where $s = (a+b+c)/2$}

10. *Rectangle container*

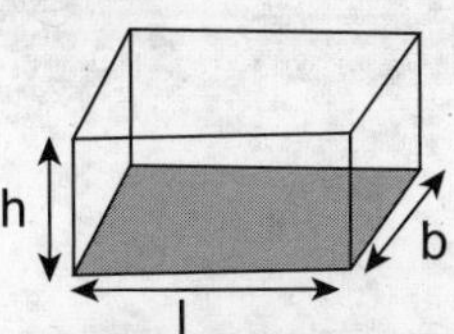

FIGURE 1.116

lateral area = $2(lb + bh + hl)$; V = lbh

Some Important Formulae

1. $(a+b)^2 = a^2+2ab+b^2 = (a-b)^2+4ab$
2. $(a-b)^2 = a^2-2ab+b^2 = (a+b)^2-4ab$
3. $a^2-b^2 = (a+b)(a-b)$
4. $(a+b)^3 = a^3+b^3+3ab(a+b)$
5. $(a-b)^3 = a^3+b^3-3ab(a-b)$
6. $a^3+b^3 = (a+b)^3-3ab(a+b) = (a+b)(a^2+b^2-ab)$
7. $a^3-b^3 = (a-b)^3+3ab(a-b) = (a-b)(a^2+b^2+ab)$
8. $(a+b+c)^2 = a^2+b^2+c^2+2ab+2bc+2ca$
   $= a^2+b^2+c^2+2abc\left(\dfrac{1}{a}+\dfrac{1}{b}+\dfrac{1}{c}\right)$
9. $a^3+b^3+c^3-ab-bc-ca$
   $=\dfrac{1}{2}\left[(a-b)^2+(b-c)^2+(c-a)^2\right]$
10. $a^3+b^3+c^2-3abc$
    $=(a+b+c)\left(a^2+b^2+c^2-ab-bc-ca\right)$
    $=\dfrac{1}{2}(a+b+c)\left[\left((a-b)^2+(b-c)^2+(c-a)^2\right)\right]$
11. $a^4-b^4 = (a+b)(a-b)\left(a^2-b^2\right)$
12. $a^4+a^2+1 = \left(a^2+1\right)^2-a^2 = \left(1+a+a^2\right)\left(1-a+a^2\right)$
13. ab = $\left(\dfrac{a+b}{2}\right)^2-\left(\dfrac{a-b}{2}\right)^2$
14. $a^2+b^2+c^2-ab-bc-ca=\left\{\left(a-b^2\right)+(b-c)^2+(c-a)^2\right\}$
15. $(x+a)(x+b) = x^2+(a+b)x+ab$
16. $(a+b+c)^3 = a^3+b^3+c^3+3(a+b)(b+c)(c+a)$
17. $a^3+b^3+c^3-3abc=(a+b+c)(a^2+b^2+c^2-ab-bc-ca)$
18. $(a+b)^4=(a+b)^2(a+b)^2=a^4+b^4+4a^3b+6a^2b^2+4ab^3$
19. $(a-b)^4=(a-b)^2(a-b)^2=a^4+b^4-4a^3b+6a^2b^2-4ab^3$
20. $(a+b)^5 = (a+b)^3(a+b)^2 = a^5+5a^4b+10a^3b^2+10a^2b^3+5ab^4+b^5$

MULTIPLE-CHOICE QUESTIONS

SECTION–I

OBJECTIVE-TYPE SOLVED EXAMPLES

1. The values of p so that the equation $3x - p + 1 = 2x - 1$ has positive solutions are

(a) $p \geq 2/3$ (b) $p < -2$

(c) $p > 2$ (d) $p > 1$

Solution: (c) $3x - 2x = p - 2 \Rightarrow x = p - 2$

for + ve solutions $x > 0$

$\Rightarrow p - 2 > 0 \qquad \Rightarrow p > 2$

2. If $x = 3 - \sqrt{8}$, then $x^3 + \dfrac{1}{x^3}$ is equal to

(a) 6 (b) 198

(c) $6\sqrt{2}$ (d) 102

Solution: (b) $x^3 + \dfrac{1}{x^3} = \left(x + \dfrac{1}{x}\right)\left(x^2 + \dfrac{1}{x^2} - 1\right)$

$= \left(3 - \sqrt{8} + 3 + \sqrt{8}\right)\left(2(9+8) - 1\right) = (6)\ [33] = 198$

3. The inequality $\dfrac{|x|^2 - |x| - 2}{2|x| - |x|^2 - 2} > 0$ holds iff

(a) $-1 < x < -2/3$ or $2/3 < x < 1$

(b) $-2 < x < 2$

(c) $2/3 < x < 1$

(d) None of these

Solution: (b) Let $|x| = y$ $= \dfrac{y^2 - y - 2}{2y - y^2 - 2} > 0$

$\Rightarrow (y^2 - y - 2)\ (2y - 2y^2 - 2) > 0$

$\Rightarrow (y^2 - y - 2)\ (y^2 - 2y + 2) < 0$

$\Rightarrow (y - 2)\ (y + 1)\ [\ (y - 1)^2 + 1] < 0$

$\Rightarrow (y - 2)\ (y + 1) < 0 \ \left[\because (y-1)^2 + 1 > 0\right]$

$\Rightarrow y \in (-1, 2)$ [By using wavy curve method)

$\Rightarrow |x| \in (-1, 2)$. But $|x| \geq 0$

$\Rightarrow |x| \in [0, 2) \qquad \Rightarrow -2 < x < 2$

4. The solution set of $x - \sqrt{1 - |x|} < 0$ is

(a) $\left[-1, \dfrac{-1+\sqrt{5}}{2}\right)$ (b) $[-1, 1]$

(c) $\left[-1, \dfrac{-1+\sqrt{5}}{2}\right]$ (d) $\left(-1, \dfrac{-1+\sqrt{5}}{2}\right)$

Solution: (a) Clearly, given inequality is valued when $1 - |x| \geq 0$

$\Rightarrow |x| \leq 1 \Rightarrow x \in [-1, 1]$ (1)

Also $x < \sqrt{1 - |x|}$ (2)

If $x \leq 0$ then (2) holds always

$\Rightarrow x \in [-1, 0]$ (3)

If $x > 0$ then squaring, we get $x^2 < 1 - |x|$

$\Rightarrow |x|^2 + |x| - 1 < 0$

or $x^2 + x - 1 < 0$ [$\because x > 0 \Rightarrow |x| = x$]

$x \in \left(\dfrac{-1-\sqrt{1+4}}{2}, \dfrac{-1+\sqrt{5}}{2}\right); x \in \left(\dfrac{-1-\sqrt{5}}{2}\ \dfrac{-1+\sqrt{5}}{2}\right)$

But $x > 0 \Rightarrow x \in \left(0, \dfrac{\sqrt{5}-1}{2}\right)$ (4)

Final solution will be the union of (3) and (4)

i.e., $x \in \left[-1, \dfrac{\sqrt{5}-1}{2}\right)$

5. If $[x]^2 - 5[x] + 6 = 0$; where [.] denotes the greatest integer function, then

(a) $x \in [3, 4)$ (b) $x \in [2, 3]$

(c) $x \in \{2, 3\}$ (d) None of these

Solution: (a,b,c) Given equation is $[x]^2 - 5[x] + 6 = 0$

$\Rightarrow ([x] - 2)\ ([x] - 3) = 0 \quad \Rightarrow [x] = 2$ or $[x] = 3$

$\Rightarrow x \in [2, 3)$ or $x \in [3, 4)$ $\therefore x \in [2, 4)$

6. The solutions of the equation $2x - 2[x] = 1$, $[x]$ is gint function, are

(a) $x = n + \dfrac{1}{2}, n \in \mathbb{N}$ (b) $x = n - \dfrac{1}{2}, n \in \mathbb{N}$

(c) $x = n + \dfrac{1}{2}, n \in I$ (d) $x = n - \dfrac{1}{2}, n \in I$

Solution: (c) $2x - 2[x] = 1$

$\Rightarrow 2x - 1 = 2[x] \qquad \Rightarrow [x] = \dfrac{2x-1}{2}$

$\Rightarrow \dfrac{2x-1}{2} \in I$ (set of integers)

$\Rightarrow 2x - 1 = 2n$ for some $n \in I$

$\Rightarrow 2x = 2n + 1 \qquad \Rightarrow x = n + \dfrac{1}{2}; n \in I$

7. The positive values of x satisfying the equations $[x]\left[x+\frac{1}{2}\right]=1$
(a) [1/2, 1) (b) [1, 2]
(c) [1, 3/2) (d) None of these

Solution: (c) ***Case I:*** $[x]=\left[x+\frac{1}{2}\right]=1$

$\Rightarrow x \in [1, 2)$ and $x + 1/2 \in [1, 2)$

$\Rightarrow x \in [1, 2)$ and $x \in \left[\frac{1}{2},\frac{3}{2}\right)$ $\therefore x \in \left[1,\frac{3}{2}\right)$

Case II: $[x]=\left[x+\frac{1}{2}\right]=-1$

$\Rightarrow x \in [-1, 0)$ and $x+\frac{1}{2} \in [-1, 0)$

But we are interested only for +ve values of x

$\therefore$ Only case (i) is possible $\therefore x \in [1, 3/2)$

8. Number of all five-digit numbers of them $34 \times 5y$ (x and y are digits) divisible by 36 are
(a) 2 (b) 3
(c) 4 (d) 5

Solution: (b) $\overline{34x5y}$ is divisible by 36. Iff it is divisible by 4 and 9

$\Rightarrow \overline{5y}$ must be divisible by 4 and $3 + 4 + x + 5 + y$ must be divisible by 9

$\Rightarrow y \in \{2, 6\}$ and $12 + x + y$ must be divisible by 9 when $y = 2$

$\Rightarrow 14 + x$ is divisible 9

$\Rightarrow x \in \{4\}$ when $y = 6$; $18 + x$ is divisible by 9

$\Rightarrow x \in \{0, 9\}$

$\therefore$ Possible numbers must be 34452, 34956, 34056 which are 3 in counting.

9. The greatest integer x satisfying the inequality $\frac{2x+1}{3}-\frac{3x-1}{2}>1$ is
(a) –1 (b) 1
(c) –2 (d) 2

Solution: (a) $2(2x + 1) - 3(3x - 1) > 6$

$\Rightarrow 4x + 2 - 9x + 3 - 6 > 0$

$\Rightarrow -5x - 1 > 0 \Rightarrow 5x + 1 < 0$

$\Rightarrow 5x < -1 \Rightarrow x < -1/5 \quad \Rightarrow x \in (-\infty, -1/5)$

$\therefore$ The greatest integer is – 1.

10. The solution of the inequality $(x^2 - 3x + 2)(x^3 - 3x^2)(4 - x^2) \geq 0$ is
(a) $(-\infty, -2) \cup (2, 3)$
(b) $(-\infty, -2)$
(c) $(-\infty, -2] \cup \{0\} \cup [1, 3]$
(d) None of these

Solution: (c) $(x^2 - 3x + 2)(x^3 - 3x^2)(4 - x^2) \geq 0$

$\Rightarrow (x - 1)(x - 2)x^2(x - 3)(2 + x)(2 - x) \geq 0$

$\Rightarrow x^2(x - 1)(x - 2)^2(x - 3)(x + 2) \leq 0$

$\Rightarrow (x - 1)(x - 3)(x + 2) \leq 0$ and $x = 0$, or 2

$\Rightarrow (x + 2)(x - 1)(x - 3) \leq 0$ and $x \in \{0, 2\}$

$\therefore$ By wavy curve method

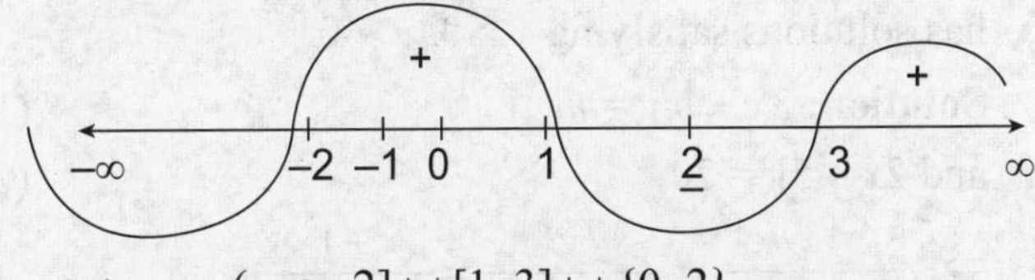

$\Rightarrow x \in (-\infty, -2] \cup [1, 3] \cup \{0, 2\}$

$\Rightarrow x \in (-\infty, -2] \cup \{0\} \cup [1, 3]$

SECTION–II

SUBJECTIVE-TYPE SOLVED EXAMPLES

1. Find the interval in which x can lie in order to satisfy following inequalities.
(a) $|x - 3| < 5$
(b) $|x + 1/2| \geq 3/2$
(c) $|3 - x| \leq 5/2$
(d) $|x^2 - 4x + 5| = |x^2 - 3x| + |5 - x|$

Solution: (a) $|x - 3| < 5 \Rightarrow -5 < x - 3 < 5$

$\Rightarrow -2 < x < 8$

(b) $|x + 1/2| > 3/2$

$\Rightarrow x + 1/2 > 3/2$

or $x + 1/2 < -3/2$

$x > 1$ or $x < -2$

(c) $|3 - x| \leq 5/2 \Rightarrow -5/2 \leq 3 - x \leq 5/2$

$\Rightarrow -5/2 \leq x - 3 \leq 5/2$

$\Rightarrow 3 - 5/2 \leq x \leq 5/2 + 3 \Rightarrow 1/2 \leq x \leq 11/2$

(d) $(x^2 - 3x)(5 - x) \geq 0$

$\Rightarrow x(x - 5)(x - 3) \leq 0 \Rightarrow x \in (-\infty, 0] \cup [3, 5]$

2. Solve the inequality $|x^2 + 3x| + x^2 - 2 \geq 0$,

Solution: By using definition of modulus we consider two cases when

(a) $x^2 + 3x \geq 0$ (b) $x^2 + 3x < 0$

In case (a) we get the inequality $2x^2 + 3x - 2 \geq 0$ the solutions of which are $x \leq -2$ and $x \geq 1/2$ condition (b) is satisfied by $x \leq -3$ and for $x \geq 0$ now the solution of case (b) as $x \leq -3$ and $x \geq 1/2$

Similarly, on solving the case (b) we get $-3 < x \leq -2/3$ as solution

$\therefore$ Combining the solution obtained in both cases, we get $x \leq -2/3$ and $x \geq 1/2$

3. Find the number of ordered pairs of integer x and y satisfying the equation: $x.y = 1260$

Solution: $\because$ $x/1260$ and $y/1260$

$\Rightarrow$ x, y are divisors of 1260

$\Rightarrow$ number of ordered pairs of natural number (x, y) = number of positive divisors of $1260 = 2^2 \times 3.5.7$ $= (2 +)(1 + 1)(1 + 1)(1 + 1) = 24$

But of $x.y = 1260$ then $(-x) = 1260$ then $(-x)(-y) = 1260$

So for each ordered pair (x, y) satisfying the above equation the ordered pair $(-x, -y)$ also satisfies the equation.

$\Rightarrow$ Total number of integer ordered pairs $= 2 \times 24$ $= 48$

4. Find the least +ve integral value of 'm', for which the system of equations $3x + my = m$; $2x - 5y = 20$ has solutions satisfying $x > 0$, $y > 0$.

Solution: $3x + my = m$ (1)

and $2x - 5y = 20$ (2)

$$\Rightarrow \frac{x}{20m+5m} = \frac{y}{-60+2m} = \frac{-1}{-15-2m}$$

$$\Rightarrow x = \frac{25m}{2m+15}; y = \frac{-60+2m}{2m+15}$$

$\because$ $x > 0 ; y > 0$

$$\Rightarrow \frac{25m}{2m+15} > 0 \text{ and } \frac{2m-60}{2m+15} > 0$$

$\Rightarrow$ $m(2m + 15) > 0$ and $(m - 30)(2m + 15) > 0$

$\Rightarrow$ $m \in (-\infty, -15/2) \cup (0, \infty)$ and $m \in (-\infty, -15/2) \cup (30, \infty)$

$\Rightarrow$ $m \in (-\infty, -15/2) \cup (30, \infty)$

$\therefore$ The smallest +ve integral value of m is 31.

5. Find the smallest value of y for which $2|y| - |2y - 1 - 1| = 2y - 1 + 1$ holds.

Solution: ***Case (i)*** when $y < 0$; $|y| = -y$

$\Rightarrow$ $2^{-y} - |2^{y-1} - 1| = 2^{y-1} + 1$ (1)

$\because$ $y < 0 \Rightarrow 2^y < 1$

Also $2^{y-1} < 2^y < 1$ [$\because$ a^x is S.I function for $a > 0$]

$\Rightarrow$ $2^{y-1} - 1 < 0 \Rightarrow |2^{y-1} - 1| = 2^{y-1} + 1$

$\therefore$ From (1) $2^{-y} + 2^{y-1} - 1 + 1 = 2^{y-1} + 1$

$\Rightarrow$ $2^{-y} = 2 \Rightarrow y = -1$ which is < 0

Case (ii) When $y \in [0, 1]$; $y - 1 \in [-1, 0]$

$\Rightarrow$ $2^{y-1} \leq 1 \Rightarrow 2^{y-1} - 1 \leq 0$ $\Rightarrow$ $|2^{y-1} - 1| = -2^{y-1} + 1$

$\therefore$ Given equation becomes $2^y + 2^{y-1} - 1 = 2^{y-1} + 1$

$\Rightarrow$ $2^y = 2$ $\Rightarrow$ $y = 1 \in [0, 1]$

Case (iii) when $y > 1$

$\Rightarrow$ $y - 1 > 0$ $\Rightarrow$ $2^{y-1} > 2^0 = 1 = 2^{y-1} - 1 > 0$

$\Rightarrow$ $|2^{y-1} - 1| = 2^{y-1} - 1$

$\therefore$ The given equation becomes $2^y - 2^{y-1} + 1 = 2^{y-1} + 1$

$\Rightarrow$ $2^y = 2 . 2^{y-1}$

$\Rightarrow$ $2^y = 2^y$ which is true $\forall$ $y > 1$

$\therefore$ Solution set is $y \in \{-1\} \cup [1, \infty)$

$\therefore$ The smallest value of y is -1

6. Find the smallest 3-digit natural number which when divides 1496 and 948 leaves the same remainder.

Solution: Let x be the required number and r be the common remainder, then $1496 = k_1x + r$; $k_1, k_2 \in Z$ (Set of integers) $948 = k_2x + r$

$\Rightarrow$ $548 = (k_1 - k_2)x$ $\Rightarrow$ $548 = (k_1 - k_2)x$

$\Rightarrow$ x is a three-digited divisor of 548.

Now $548 = 2 \times 2 \times 137 = (2)^2 \times (137)^1$

$\Rightarrow$ x can be 137 or 274 or 548

$\therefore$ Smallest value of $x = 137$

7. Define a set

$$A = \left\{x : \frac{x-1}{5} = [k] \text{ for some } k \in \mathbb{R}; 0 \leq x \leq 22\right\}$$

$$B = \left\{y : \frac{y-1}{4} = [k] \text{ for some } k \in \mathbb{R}; 0 \leq y \leq 22\right\}$$

then find

(i) $n(A-B)$ (ii) $n(B-A)$

(iii) $n(A \Delta B)$ (iv) $n(AxB)$

(v) $n[(AxB) \cap (B x A)]$

Solution: $\frac{x-1}{5} = [k]$ for some $k \in \mathbb{R}$

$\Rightarrow$ $\frac{x-1}{5}$ is an integer $\Rightarrow$ $\frac{x-1}{5} = m \in \mathbb{Z}$

$\Rightarrow$ $x = 5m + 1$; $m \in \mathbb{Z}$ But $x \geq 0, x \leq 22$

$\Rightarrow$ $x \in \{1, 6, 11, 16, 21\} = A$;

Similarly, $y = 4n + 1$; $n \in \mathbb{Z}$

But $y \geq 0$ and $y \leq 22$

$\Rightarrow$ $y \in \{1, 5, 9, 13, 17, 21\} = B$

$\therefore$ $A - B = \{6, 11, 16\}$; $B - A = \{5, 9, 13, 17\}$

$\therefore$ (i) $n(A-B) = 3$

(ii) $n(B-A) = 4$

(iii) $n(A \Delta B) = n[A - B) \cup (B - A)]$
$= n[(A \cup B)] - n[(A \cap B)] = 9 - 2 = 7$

(iv) $n(A \times B) = n(A) \times n(B) = 5 \times 6 = 30$

(v) We know that if 'n' elements are common in two sets A and B, then n^2 elements are common in $(A \times B)$ and $(B \times A)$.

$\Rightarrow n[(A \times B) \cap (B \times A)] = (2)^2 = 4$

8. For any three consecutive odd natural number, the least of which is larger than seven then the sum of the square of the two smallest is always larger than the square of the largest.

Solution: Given three consecutive odd naturals as $2x - 1, 2x + 1, 2x + 3$ s. t. $2x - 1 > 7$ i.e., $x > 4$

Now consider the difference

$\left[(2x-1)^2 + (2x+1)^2\right] - (2x+3)^2$

$= 8x^2 + 2 - (4x^2 + 12x + 9)$

$= 4x^2 - 12x - 7 = 4x^2 - 12x + 9 - 16$

$= (2x - 3)^2 - (4)^2 = (2x + 1)(2x - 7) > 0$; as $2x > 8$.

9. Find the integer solution of equation $x^2y - 72y + x^2 = 0$.

Solution: $x^2(y + 1) = 72y$

$\Rightarrow x^2 = \dfrac{72y}{y+1} \quad \Rightarrow x^2 = \dfrac{72(y+1-1)}{y+1} = 72 - \dfrac{72}{y+1}$

For integer values of x and y; $72 - \dfrac{72}{y+1} \geq 0$ and

$y + 1$ must be an integer divisor of 72.

$\Rightarrow \dfrac{72}{y+1} \leq 72 \quad \Rightarrow \dfrac{1}{y+1} \leq 1$

$\Rightarrow 1 - \dfrac{1}{y+1} \geq 0 \Rightarrow \dfrac{y}{y+1} \geq 0$

$\Rightarrow y(y+1) \geq 0$; $y \neq -1$

$\Rightarrow y \in (-\infty, 0) \cup [0, \infty)$

$\Rightarrow y + 1 \in (-\infty, 0) \cup [1, \infty)$

But $y + 1$ is an integer

$\Rightarrow y + 1$ can be any integer divisor of 72.

$\Rightarrow y + 1 = \pm1, \pm2, \pm3, \pm4, \pm6, \pm8, \pm9, \pm12, \pm18, \pm24, \pm36, \pm72$.

$\Rightarrow x^2 = (72 \pm 72), (72 \pm 36), 72 \pm 24, 72 \pm 18, 72 \pm 12, (72 \pm 9), 72 \pm 6, 72 \pm 4, \pm 3, 72 \pm 2, 72 \pm 1$

$\Rightarrow x^2 = 0, 144, 36, 81$, for $y + 1 = 1, -1, 2, -8$,

$\Rightarrow x^2 = 0, 144, 36, 81$, for $y + 1 = 1, -1, 2, -8$

$\Rightarrow x^2 = 0, 144, 36, 81$, for $y = 0, -2, 1, -9$

$\Rightarrow x^2 = 0, \pm12, \pm6, \pm9$, for $y = 0, -2, 1, -9$

$\therefore$ All possible integer solutions are (0, 0); (12, –2); (–12, –2); (6, 1); (–6, 1) ; (9, –9) ; (–9, –9).

10. If x is a prime number and y is any integer satisfying the equation $2x^2 + y^2 = 274$, then find all possible solution:

Solution: $2x^2 + y^2 = 274$, (i)

$\Rightarrow y^2 = 274 - 2x^2$

$\Rightarrow y^2$ must be an even integer

$\Rightarrow$ y must be an even integer $[\because$ *y is an integer*$]$

Let $y = 2k$

from (i) $2x^2 + 4k^2 = 274$

$\Rightarrow 4k^2 = 274 - 2x^2$

$\Rightarrow 2k^2 = 137 - x^2$ (ii)

$\Rightarrow x^2$ must be an odd integer

$\Rightarrow$ x must be an odd integer.

Also from (ii) $2k^2 = 137 - x^2$

$\Rightarrow x^2 \leq 137 \quad \Rightarrow x \leq \sqrt{137} < 12$

$\Rightarrow x$ must be and odd prime less than 12

$\Rightarrow x \in \{3, 5, 7, 11\}$

Again from (i) $y^2 = 274 - 2x^2$

For $x = 3$, $y^2 = 274 - 18 = 256 \Rightarrow y = \pm16$

For $x = 5$, $y^2 = 274 - 50 = 224$

$\Rightarrow y = \pm\sqrt{224} \notin \mathbb{Z}$

For $x = 7$, $y^2 = 274 - 98 = 176$

$\Rightarrow y = \pm\sqrt{176} \notin \mathbb{Z}$

For $x = 11$, $y^2 = 274 - 242 = 32$

$\Rightarrow y = \pm\sqrt{32} \notin \mathbb{Z}$

$\therefore x = 3$ and $y = \pm16$ are the only possible solutions

11. Show that no triangular number can be of the form $3n - 1$.

Solution: Let x be a Δ^{ar} number $x = 1 + 2 + 3 + ... + n$

$x = \dfrac{n(n+1)}{2}$; for x to be multiple of 3

$\Rightarrow 3 \mid n$ or $3 \mid n + 1$ If $m + n + 1$ not divisible by 3

$\Rightarrow n \geq 3k,\ 3k - 1 \quad \Rightarrow m = 3k + 1$

$\Rightarrow x = \dfrac{n(n+1)}{2}$

$\Rightarrow x = \dfrac{(3k+1)(3k+1)+1)}{2} = \dfrac{3k(3k+1)+(3k+1)}{2}$

$= \dfrac{3k(3k+3-2)}{2} + 3k + 1 = \dfrac{9k(k+1)}{2} + 3k + 3k + 1$

if $n = 3k$ then $3/x$

$= \dfrac{9k(k+1)+1}{2}$ if $n = 3k - 1$ then,

$3/x$ is $3m + 1$ type

$\Rightarrow$ x count be $3n + 1$ type.

12. If $2n + 1$ is a prime number, show that $1^2, 2^2, 3^2, .., n^2$ when divided by $2n + 1$ leave different remainders.

Solution: Method for contradiction:

Let $p, q \in \{1, 2, 3, \ldots, n\}$

$p = (2n + 1)k + r$

$q = (2n + 1)k1 + r$

$\Rightarrow p^2 - q^2 = (2n + 1)k0$ i.e., $2n + 1/p^2 - q^2$

But $p^2 - q^2 = (p + q)(p - q)$ each factor being less than $2n$

$\Rightarrow 2n + 1/(p - q)(p + q)$; As $2n + 1$ is prime

$\Rightarrow 2n + 1/p - q$ or $2n + 1/p + q$ both of which is wrong.

$\Rightarrow 2n + 1/(p^2 - q^2)$

$\Rightarrow$ Assertion that p, q leaves same remainder w.r.t division by $2n + 1$ is false

$\Rightarrow$ Contrary to our assumption p^2 and q^2 shall leave different remainders when divided by $2n + 1$.

13. Show that $n^{36} - 1$ is divisible by 33744 if n is coprime to 2, 3, 19 and 37.

Solution: $37 \mid n^{37-1} - 1$ as $(n, 37) = 1$

$\Rightarrow 37 \mid n^{36} - 1$

$\Rightarrow 19 \mid n^{18} - 1$ as $(n, 18) = 1$

$\Rightarrow 19 \mid (n^{18} - 1)(n^{18} + 1) \quad \Rightarrow 19 \mid n^{36} - 1$

$\Rightarrow 3 \mid n^2 - 1$ as $(n, 3) \quad \Rightarrow 3 \mid n^{36} - 1$

$\because$ N is odd as $(n, 2) = 1$

$\because 2/n^{36} - 1$

Also $n^{36} - 1 = (n^9 - 1)(n + 1)(n^8 + 1)$

$= (n^3 - 1)(n^3 + 1)(n^9 + 1)(n^{18} + 1)$

Each of there factor is even

$\Rightarrow 16/n^{36} - 1 \qquad \Rightarrow 3 \times 16 \times 19 \times 37/n^{36} - 1$

$\Rightarrow 33744/n^{36} - 1$.

14. Prove that $4^n + 15n - 1$ is always divisible by 9.

Solution: $4^n + 15n - 1 = (4n - 1) + 15n$

$= (4 - 1)(4^{n-1} + 4^{n-2} + 4^{n-3} + \ldots\ 4 + 1) + 15\text{ n}$

$= 3[4^{n-1} + 4^{n-2} + 4^{n-3} + \ldots.\ 4 + 1 - \text{n} + \text{n} + 5n]$

$$= 3\left[\left(4^{n-1}-1\right)+\left(4^{n-2}-1\right)+\left(4^{n-3}-1\right)+\ldots+(4-1)+6n\right]$$

$$= 3\left[6k_1 + 3k_2 + 3k_3 + \ldots.. + 3(1) + 3(2n)\right]$$

$$= 9\left[k_1 + k_2 + \ldots.. + 1 + n\right] = 9\lambda.$$

15. If m is a prime number, and a, b two numbers less than m, $a^{m-2} + a^{m-3}b + a^{m-4}b^2 + \ldots. + b^{m-2}$ is a multiple of m.

Solution: $a - b/a^{m-1} - b^{m-1}$ and $m/a^{m-1} - b^{m-1}$

as $m/\left(a^{m-1}-1\right)-\left(b^{m-1}-1\right)$

$\because m/(a-b)-\left(a^{m-2}+a^{m-3}.b+a^{m-4}.b^2+\ldots+a.b^{m-2}\right)$

but $m/(a-b)$ becomes both a and b < m

Hence a – b < m

$\Rightarrow m/a^{m-2}+a^{m-3}.b+a^{m-4}.b^2+\ldots+a.b^{m-2}$

16. Prove that $36 \mid 7^n - 1 - 6n$

Solution: $\because\ 7 - 1 \mid 7^n - 1$

$\Rightarrow 7n - 1 - 6n = 6(7^{n-1} + 7^{n-2} + 7^{n-3} + \ldots.. + 7 + 1 - \text{n})$

$= 6(7^{n-1} - 1) + (7^{n-2} - 1) + \ldots.. + (7^2 - 1) + (7 - 1) + (1 - 1) = 6(6k_1 + 6k_2 + 6k_3 + \ldots. + 6(8) + 6)$

$$= 36\underbrace{\left(k_1 + k_2 + k_3 + \ldots.. + 8 + 1\right)}_{\text{integer}} = 36/7^n - 1 - 6n$$

17. Solve the following irrational equation for real values of variable x.

$$\sqrt{x+2-4\sqrt{x-2}}+\sqrt{x+7+6\sqrt{x-2}}\le 8\cdot$$

Solution: Given inequality is

$$\sqrt{(x+2)-2.2\sqrt{x-2}}+\sqrt{(x+7)+2(3)\sqrt{x-2}}\le 8$$

Clearly it is defined for $x \in [2, \infty)$ only

Now rearranging the term within radical sign.

$$\sqrt{(x+2)+4-2(2)\sqrt{x-2}}+\sqrt{(x-7)+9+2(3)\sqrt{x-2}}\le 8$$

$$\sqrt{\left(\sqrt{(x-2)}\right)^2}+\sqrt{\left(\sqrt{(x-2)}+3\right)^2}\le 8$$

$$\left|\sqrt{(x-2)}-2\right|+\left|\sqrt{(x-2)}+3\right|\le 8$$

the given inequality is equivalent to following set of inequality.

$$\begin{cases} x \geq 4 \text{ and} \\ \sqrt{x-2}-2+\sqrt{x-2}+3\le 8 \end{cases} \text{ or}$$

$$\begin{cases} 2\le x<4 \text{ and} \\ 2-\sqrt{x-2}+\sqrt{x-2}+3\le 8 \end{cases}$$

which is always true

$$x\in\left[4,\frac{57}{4}\right]\cup[2,4)$$

$$\Rightarrow x\in\left[2,\frac{57}{4}\right) \text{ is set of solution.}$$

Comprehension Passage

A: Given $A = \{x\!: x - 5m,\ m \in N$ and $x \le 30\}$, $B = \{y\!: y = 4k,\ k \subset W$ and $k \le 8\}$ and $C = \{x\!: x$ is prime number and $x \le 16\}$, $U=\{x: x\le 35x\in\mathbb{N}\}$. Where W is the set of whole numbers and N is the set of natural numbers. Based on this information, now answer the following questions:

18. Number of elements in $(A \cup B)$ will be
(a) 14 (b) 9
(c) 10 (d) None of these

19. Number of elements in $(A \cup B \cup C)$ will be
(a) 18 (b) 19
(c) 20 (d) None of these

20. Number of elements in $(A - C)$ $(C - B)$ is equal to
(a) 11 (b) 9
(c) 12 (d) 10

21. Number of elements in $A \Delta B$ (The symmetric difference of A and B)
(a) 10 (b) 13
(c) 9 (d) None of these

22. Number of elements in $(A \cup B)'$ will be
(a) 21 (b) 20
(c) 24 (d) None of these

23. Number of elements in $(A' \cap (B \cup C)$ will be
(a) 10 (b) 11
(c) 12 (d) 13

Solution: $A = \{x: x=5m, m \in N \text{ and } x \leq 30\}$
$= \{5, 10, 15, 20, 25, 30\}$ and
$B = \{y: y = 4k, k \in W \text{ and } k \leq 8\}$
$= \{0, 4, 8, 12, 16, 20, 24, 28, 32\}$
$C = \{x: x \text{ is a prime no and } x \leq 16\}$
$= \{2, 3, 5, 7, 11, 13\}$ and
$U = \{x: x \leq 35 ; x \in N\} = \{1, 2, 3, 4, ...35\}$

18. Number of elements in $(A \cup B)$
$= n(A \cup B) = n(A) + n(B) - n(A \cap B)$
$= 6 + 9 - 1 \left[\because A \cap B = \{20\}\right]$
$\therefore$ **Ans (a)**

19. No of elements in $(A \cup B \cup C) = n(A) + n(B) + n(C) - n(A \cap B) - n(B \cap C) - n(A \cap C) + n(A \cap B \cap C) = 6 + 9 + 6 - 1 - 0 - 1 + 0 = 19$
$\therefore$ **Ans (b)**

20. No of elements in $(A - C) \cup (C - B)$
$= n[\{10, 15, 20, 25, 30\} \cup \{2, 3, 5, 7, 11, 13\}]$
$= n\{2, 3, 5, 7, 10, 11, 13, 15, 20, 25, 30\} = 11$
$\therefore$ **Ans (a)**

21. $n(A \Delta B) = n[(A - B)] \cup (B - A)] = n(A \cup B) - n(A \cap B) = 14 - 1 = 13$
$\therefore$ **Ans (b)**

22. $n(A \cup B)' = n(\cup) - n(A \cup B) = 35 - 14 = 21$
$\therefore$ **Ans (a)**

23. $n[A' \cap (B \cup C)] = n[(B \cup C) - A \cap (B \cup C)] = n[\{2, 3, 5, 7, 11, 13, 0, 4, 8, 12, 16, 20, 24, 28, 32\} - \{5, 20\}] = 13$
$\therefore$ **Ans (d)**

B: Let two numbers x and y be given by $x = p^a . q^b$ and $y = p^\alpha . q^\beta$ (Where p, q are prime numbers).
The number of divisors of x will be $= (a + 1)(b + 1)$. The number of proper divisors will exclude two divisors namely 1 and the number itself.
The sum of all divisors of x.
$= \left(1 + p + p^2 + ... + p^a\right)\left(1 + q + q^2 + ... + q^b\right)$
$= \dfrac{p^{a+1} - 1}{p - 1} . \dfrac{q^{b+1} - 1}{q - 1}$

On the same line, the number of divisors which are common to both x and y = Number of divisors of $p^l . q^m$. where l = minimum of (a and α) and m = minimum of (b and β).
Using this information and guideline, now answer the following questions:

24. When $x = 2^5 . 3^4$ and $y = 2^3 . 3^8$. The number of common but proper divisors of both x and y are
(a) 18 (b) 19
(c) 21 (d) None of these

25. When $x = 385$, the sum of all the divisors will be
(a) 576 (b) 538
(c) 575 (d) None of these

26. Sum of common but proper divisors of $x = 2^3 . 3^4$ and $y = 2^4 . 3^3$ will be
(a) 597 (b) 599
(c) 598 (d) 615

27. If sum of all the divisors of a number x (say) becomes $2x$, then it is called a perfect number. Find which of the following is a perfect number.
(a) 15 (b) 20
(c) 25 (d) 6

Solution: 24. $x = 2^5 . 3^4$; $y = 2^3 . 3^8$, number of common divisors of x and y
$=$ no of divisors of $2^3 . 3^4 = (3 + 1)(4 + 1)$
$= (4)(5) = 20$
But it includes 1 which is improper common divisor of x and y
$\therefore$ Number of proper common divisor of x and y $= 20 - 1 = 19$
$\therefore$ **Ans (b)**

25. $x = 385 = 5 \times 7 \times 11$

$\therefore$ Sum of divisors $= (1 + 5)\ (1 + 7)\ (1 + 11)$
$= 6 \times 8 \times 12 = 576$

$\therefore$ **Ans (a)**

26. $x = 2^3 . 3^4 ;\ y = 2^4 . 3^3$

Common divisors of x and y = divisors of $2^3.3^3$

$\therefore$ Sum of common divisors
$= (1 + 2 + 2^2 + 2^3)\ (1 + 3 + 3^2 + 3^3)$ and

Sum of proper common divisors
$= (1 + 2 + 2^2 + 2^3)(1 + 3 + 3^2 + 3^3) - 1$

$= 1.\dfrac{(2^4-1)}{(2-1)}.\dfrac{(3^4-1)}{(3-1)} - 1 = (15)\ (40) - 1$

$= 600 - 1 - 599$

$\therefore$ **Ans (b)**

27. If $x = 15 = 3^1 \times 5^1$; Sum of divisors
$= (1 + 3)\ (1 + 5) = (4)\ (6) = 24 \neq 2x$

If $x = 20 = 2^2 \times 5^1$; sum of divisors
$= (1 + 2 + 2^2)\ (1+5) = 42 \neq 2x$

If $x = 25 = (5)^2$; Sum of divisors
$= (1 + 5 + 5^2) = 31 \neq 2x$

If $x = 6$, then $x = 2^1 \times (3)^1$

$\therefore$ Sum of divisors $= (1 + 2)\ (1 + 3) = (3)\ (4)$
$= 12 = 2x$

$\therefore$ $X = 6$ is a perfect number

$\therefore$ **Ans (d)**

Matrix Match Type

28. Column I

(i) Set $\left\{\dfrac{1}{1.2}, \dfrac{1}{1.2} + \dfrac{1}{2.3}, \dfrac{1}{1.2} + \dfrac{1}{2.3} + \dfrac{1}{3.4}, \ldots\ldots\right\}$ is equivalent to:

(ii) If x, y, z are three consecutive prime numbers, such that $n(A \cup B \cup C) = 33$ and then the set $\{x, y, z\}$ is

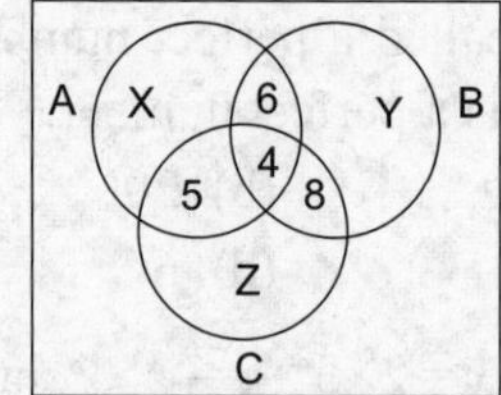

(iii) $\{x$: x is the positive integer greater than 1 which leaves remainder equal to the lowest common positive divisor of 24 and 10 when divided by the greatest common divisors of 125 and 185$\}$ is

(iv) If $A = \{1, 0, -1, -2, -4, -5\}$ and $B = \{1, 2, 3, 4, 5, 6\}$ then range of subset R of cartesian product $A \times B$ defined by, $R = \{(x, y)\ x \in A$ and $y \in B$ and $x + 2y = 5\}$ is

Column II

(a) set $\{1, 1+3, 1+3+5, 1+3+5+7, \ldots, \}$

(b) Solution set of linear equations, $2x - y + z = 6$, $x + 2y - z = 3$, $2x + 3y - z = 8$

(c) Set $\{6, 11, 16, 21, 26, 31, \ldots\ldots\ldots\ldots, \}$

Ans. (i) a, b, d, (ii) c, (iii) b, d (iv) c

Solution:

(i) Set $= \left\{\dfrac{1}{1.2}, \dfrac{1}{1.2} + \dfrac{1}{2.3}, \dfrac{1}{1.2} + \dfrac{1}{2.3} + \dfrac{1}{3.4}, \ldots.\right\}$

$= \left\{\dfrac{2-1}{1.2}, \dfrac{2-1}{1.2} + \dfrac{3-1}{2.3}, \dfrac{2-1}{1.2} + \dfrac{3-2}{2.3} + \dfrac{4-3}{3.4}, \ldots\ldots\right\}$

$= \left\{1 - \dfrac{1}{2}, 1 - \dfrac{1}{3}, , 1 - \dfrac{1}{4}, \ldots\ldots\right\} = \left\{1 - \dfrac{1}{n+1}; n \in \mathbb{N}\right\}$

$= \left\{\dfrac{n}{n+1}; n \in \mathbb{N}\right\}$

(ii)

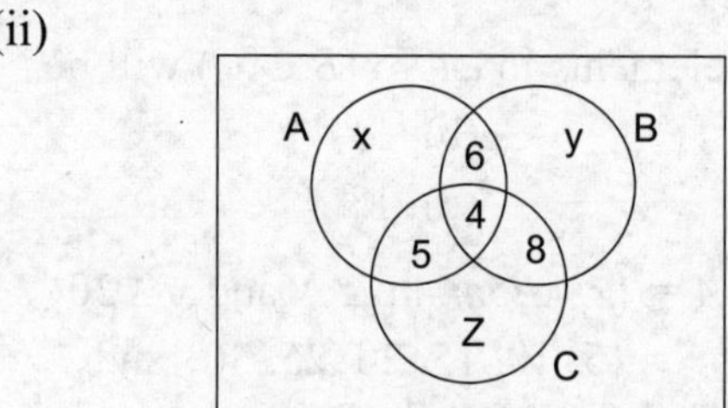

$n\,(A \cup B \cup C) = \mathbf{33}$

$\Rightarrow$ $x - y + z + 6 + 4 + 5 + 8 = 33$

$\Rightarrow$ x, y, z are three consecutive Prime numbers and their sum is 10.

$\Rightarrow$ $x, y, z \in \{2, 3, 5, 7\}$ $\Rightarrow$ Also $2 + 3 + 5 = 10$

$\Rightarrow$ $\{x, y, z\} = \{2, 3, 5\}$

(iii) $\{x$: x is the +ve integer which leaves remainder equal to the lowest common (+ve) divisor of 24 and 10 when divided by the greatest common divisor of 125 and 185$\}$

Now, lowest (+ve) common divisor of 24 and $10 = 1$, g.c.d of 125 and 185 is 5

$\therefore$ $x = 5k + 1$; $k \in \mathbb{Z}$ But x is a +ve integer

$\Rightarrow$ The set is $\{1, 6, 11, 16, 21, 26, 31\ldots..\}$ But x is greater than 1

$\therefore$ The set becomes $\{6, 11, 16, 21, 26, 31\ldots..\}$
$= \{5k + 1;\ k \in \mathbb{N}\}$

(iv) If $A = \{1, 0, -1, -2, -4, -5\}$ and $B = \{1, 2, 3, 4, 5, 6\}$ then we are to find the range of subset of Cartesian product $= \{(x, y);\ x \in A$ and $y \in B$ and $x + 2y = 5\}$
$= \{(1, 2), (-1, 3), (-5, 5)\}$

$\therefore$ Range $= \{2, 3, 5\}$

Column-II

(a) Set {1, 1+3, 1+3+5, 1+3+5+7, ...}

T_n = Sn of A.P 1, 3, 5, 7.... = $\frac{n}{2}$ [2 + 2n – 2] = n^2

∴ Set = {n^2; $n \in \mathbb{N}$}

(b) x is that natural number such that when it is divided by 5 leaves remainder 1 and greater than 5.

⇒ $x = 5k + 1$; $k \in \mathbb{N}$

∴ The set is {x: $x = 5k + 1$; $k \in \mathbb{N}$}

$2x – y + z = 6$; $x + 2y – z = 3$ and

$2x + 3y – z = 8$

Clearly $x = 2$, $y = 3$ and $z = 5$

∴ Solution set is given by = {2, 3, 5}

(c) Set = {6, 11, 16, 21, 26, 31, ...}

= {$5k + 1$; $k \in \mathbb{N}$}

Two sets are said to be equivalent if they have same number of elements

Any two sets which are enumerable (i.e.,] a one-one and onto function f $\mathbb{N} \rightarrow$ set) are considered to be equivalent.

SECTION–III

OBJECTIVE-TYPE (ONLY ONE CORRECT ANSWER)

1. If $X \cup \{1, 2\} = \{1, 2, 3, 5, 9\}$, then
(a) The smallest set X is {3, 5, 9}
(b) The smallest set X is {2, 3, 5, 9}
(c) The largest set X is {1, 2, 3, 4, 9}
(d) The largest set X is {2, 3, 4, 9}

2. Given n (U) = 20, n (A) =12, n (B) = 9, $n(A \cap B) = 4$, where U is the universal set, A and B are subsets of U, then then n $(A \cup B)^C)$ is equal to
(a) 17 (b) 9
(c) 11 (d) 3

3. The common value of x satisfying $\frac{x-1}{x+2} \geq 0$ and $\frac{2x-5}{x-2} \leq 1$ is
(a) $(2, \infty]$ (b) (2, 3]
(c) $(-\infty, 3]$ (d) None of these

4. The set of values of x satisfying the inequality $2x – 7 < 4x – 2$ and $–5 \leq 2x + 6 < 4$ is given as
(a) $\left[\frac{-11}{2}, \frac{-5}{2}\right]$ (b) $\left[\frac{-11}{2}, -5/2\right)$
(c) (–5/2, –1) (d) None of these

5. The set of values of x satisfying the inequality $x^2 – x < 6$ and $3x^2 – x –2 > 0$ is given as
(a) $(-\infty, -2/3) \cup (3, \infty)$ (b) $(-2, -2/3) \cup (1, 3)$
(c) (–2, 3) (d) None of these

6. Which of the following statements are not true?
(a) Difference of two irrational numbers is irrational.
(b) Any number of the form p/q such that $p, q \in I$ $q \neq 0$*is* always rational.
(c) The inequality $x \leq y$, $y \leq z$ and $z \leq x \Rightarrow x = y = z$
(d) The operation of exponentiation is commutative in nature i.e., $(a^m)^n = (a^n)^n$.

7. The equation $|x^2 – x| + |x + 1| = 5$ has
(a) two rational solution
(b) two irrational roots
(c) one rational and one irrational roots
(d) no real solution

8. The smallest integer k satisfying the inequality $\frac{x-5}{x^2+5x-14} > 0$ is
(a) –7 (b) –6
(c) 6 (d) None of these

9. Number of integer values of x satisfying the inequality $\frac{x^2+6x-7}{|x+4|} < 0$ is
(a) 6 (b) 7
(c) 8 (d) None of these

10. Set of real values of x satisfying $|x + 4| = 3x – 2$ is given as
(a) $\left\{-\frac{1}{2}, 3\right\}$ (b) $\left\{-\frac{1}{2}\right\}$
(c) {3} (d) None of these

11. The complete set of solution of $2|x + 1| + |x – 3| = 4$ is given by
(a) $\left\{\frac{5}{3}\right\}$ (b) {–1}
(c) $\left\{-1, \frac{5}{3}\right\}$ (d) None of these

12. LCM of integer solutions satisfying the inequality $\frac{x^2+2x-3}{x^2+1} \leq 0$ is
(a) 0 (b) 2
(c) Not defined (d) None of these

13. The inequality $\frac{|x-3|}{x^2-5x+6} \geq 2$ is given as

(a) $\left[\frac{3}{2}, 2\right] \cup \left[2, \frac{5}{2}\right]$ (b) $\left[\frac{3}{2}, 2\right]$

(c) $\left[\frac{3}{2}, \frac{5}{2}\right]$ (d) $\left[\frac{3}{2}, 2\right)$

14. Number of integral solutions of $|3x - 1| = 2x$

(a) 0 (b) 1

(c) 2 (d) 3

15. Number of real solutions of equation $|x^2+x| = 5$ are

(a) 2 (b) 4

(c) 0 (d) None of these

16. Number of negative integers which satisfies $2|x + 1|^2 - |x + 1| = 3$ are

(a) 1 (b) 2

(c) 0 (d) None of these

17. Complete set of real values of x which satisfies $\frac{(x-1)(x-2)}{x+5} > 1$ is

(a) $(-5, 2-\sqrt{7})$

(b) $(2+\sqrt{7}, \infty)$

(c) $(-5, 2-\sqrt{7}) \cup (2+\sqrt{7}, \infty)$

(d) None of these

18. If $x = \sqrt{3+2\sqrt{2}}$ then value of $x^2 + \frac{1}{x^2}$ is equal to

(a) $2\sqrt{2}$ (b) 8

(c) 6 (d) 1

19. The value of function $y = |2x + 1| + 2|x - 2|$ in the interval $-\frac{1}{2} \leq x < 2$ is

(a) $4x - 3$ (b) $3x - 1$

(c) 5 (d) 1

20. The solution set of equation $|2x + 3| - |x - 1| = 6$, is

(a) $x \in (-10, 2)$ (b) $x \in [-10, 2)$

(c) $x \in [-10, 2]$ (d) $x \in \{-10, 2\}$

21. The product of all the solutions of the equation $(x - 2)^2 - 3|x - 2| + 2 = 0$ is

(a) 2 (b) –4

(c) 0 (d) None of these

22. A 3-digit number has, from left to right, the digits a, b and c with $a > c$, when the number with the digits reversed is subtracted from the original number, the unit's digit in the difference is 4. The next two digits from right to left are

(a) 5 and 9 (b) 9 and 5

(c) 5 and 4 (d) 4 and 5

23. Which of these four numbers $\sqrt{\pi^2}$, $\sqrt[3]{0.27}$, $\sqrt[4]{0.00256}$, $\sqrt[3]{-8}$, $\sqrt{(0.04)^{-1}}$, is (are) rational?

(a) only the fourth (b) only the first

(c) the first and fourth (d) none

24. The number $x = 3.1\overline{45}$ when expressed as a rational number in lowest form, then $55x$ is equal to

(a) 172 (b) 173

(c) 174 (d) none of these

25. If $x = 3 - \sqrt{8}$, then the value of the expression $x^3 + \frac{1}{x^3}$ is equal to

(a) 6 (b) 198

(c) $6\sqrt{2}$ (d) 102

26. If $\frac{3+2\sqrt{2}}{3-\sqrt{2}} = a + b\sqrt{2}$ then a and b $(a, b \in \mathbb{Q})$ are respectively equal to

(a) $\frac{9}{7}, \frac{13}{7}$ (b) $\frac{13}{7}, \frac{9}{7}$

(c) $\frac{7}{9}, \frac{7}{13}$ (d) $\frac{13}{7}, \frac{7}{9}$

27. A set of 'n' numbers has the sum 's'. Each number of the set of increased by 20, then multiplied by 5 and then decreased by 20. The sum of the numbers in the new set thus obtained is,

(a) s + 20n (b) 5 s + 80n

(c) s (d) 5s + 4n

28. If $x = \sqrt[3]{7+5\sqrt{2}} - \frac{1}{\sqrt[3]{7+5\sqrt{2}}}$ then the value of $x^3 + 3x - 14$ is equal to

(a) 1 (b) 0

(c) 2 (d) 4

29. The value of x satisfying the equation $\frac{6x+2a+3b+c}{6x+2a-3b-c} = \frac{2x+6a+b+3c}{2x+6a-b-3c}$ is

(a) ab/c (b) 2ab/c

(c) ab/3c (d) ab/2c

30. If a number $\overline{774958A96B}$ is to be divisible by 8 and 9, the possible non-zero values of A and B, respectively, will be

(a) 7, 8 (b) 9, 8

(c) 5, 8 (d) none of these

31. The number of positive integral solutions of, $\frac{x^2(3x-4)^3(x-2)^4}{(x-5)^5.(2x-7)^6} < 0$ is

(a) 1 (b) 2
(c) 3 (d) 4

32. Values of x satisfying the inequality $|x-1|+|x-2|+|x-3|\geq 6$
(a) $(-\infty, 0] \cup (4, \infty)$ (b) $(-\infty, 1] \cup (4, \infty)$
(c) $(-\infty, 2] \cup [4, \infty)$ (d) $(-\infty, 0] \cup [4, \infty)$

33. Values of x satisfying the equality $|x^2+8x+7| = |x^2+4x+4| + |4x+3|$ for $x \in R$ are
(a) $(-2, \infty)$ (b) $\left(\frac{3}{4}, \infty\right)$
(c) $\{2\} \cup \left[-\frac{3}{4}, \infty\right)$ (d) $\left[-\frac{1}{3}, \infty\right)$

34. The set of values of x satisfying the equality $\left|\frac{x+1}{x}\right| + |x+1| = \frac{(x+1)^2}{|x|}$ are
(a) $(0, \infty)$ (b) $\{-1\}$
(c) $(-1, \infty)$ (d) $\{-1\} \cup (0, \infty)$

35. If $x^2+x+|x|+1 \leq 0$, then x belong to the set
(a) $(0, \infty)$ (b) $(-\infty, 0)$
(c) $\mathbb{R}$ (d) ϕ

36. The number of solutions to the equation $|2x^2-5x+3| + (x-1) = 0$ is
(a) 1 (b) 2
(c) 0 (d) infinite

37. The number of real roots of $|x^2+4|x|+3| = 11-2x$.
(a) 1 (b) 2
(c) 3 (d) None of these

38. The quadratic expression $21 + 12x - 4x^2$ takes:
(a) the least value 5
(b) the highest value 30
(c) the highest value 21
(d) none of these

39. The complete set of positive reals which satisfies $\frac{4}{1+x} + \frac{2}{1-x} < 1$ is
(a) $(1, \infty)$ (b) $[1, \infty)$
(c) $(-\infty, -1) \cup (1, \infty)$ (d) None of these

40. The solution set of the inequality $||x-1|+2| \leq 2$ is
(a) a singleton set (b) a null set
(c) an infinite set (d) None of these

41. Number of integers satisfying $(x-1)\sqrt{x^2-x-2} \geq 0$ are
(a) 6 (b) 10
(c) 12 (d) Infinite

42. The combined solution of $x^3-5x^2+4x \leq 0$ and $(x+1)(x-1)^2(x-3) \leq 0$ is
(a) $[-1, 3]$ (b) $[-1, 1) \cup (1, 3]$
(c) $[-1, 0] \cup [1, 3]$ (d) None of these

43. The values of x which simultaneously satisfies $(3x-4)(x-7) \leq 0$ and $|3x-5| \geq 1$ is
(a) $[2, 7] \cup \{4/3\}$ (b) $[2, 9) - \left\{\frac{4}{3}\right\}$
(c) $\left[\frac{4}{3}, 2\right] \cup [2, 7]$ (d) None of these

44. The set of integer solutions of equation $|2^x-1| + |2^x+1| = 2$
(a) A subset of $(-\infty, -1]$
(b) Contains infinitely many integer
(c) Contains finitely many integer
(d) none of the above

45. The complete set of real values of x which satisfies $|x| + 2|x-1| - 3|x-2| = 4$ is
(a) $\{2\}$ (b) $(2, \infty)$
(c) $[2, \infty)$ (d) $(-\infty, \infty)$

46. The largest positive integer which satisfies $\frac{8x^2+16x-51}{(2x-3)(x+4)} < 3$ is
(a) 1 (b) 3
(c) 4 (d) None of these

47. The solution set of the inequality $\left|\frac{y-3}{y+1}\right| < 2$ is given by
(a) $(-\infty, -5) \cup (3, \infty)$
(b) $(-\infty, -5) \cup (\frac{1}{3}, \infty)$
(c) $(-\infty, -1) \cup (\frac{1}{3}, \infty)$
(d) None of these

48. The complete set of values of x which satisfies $\frac{x^2+x+1}{(x-1)(x+1)} \geq 0$ and $|x| \leq 2$ is
(a) $[-2, -1) \cup (1, 2]$ (b) $[-2, -1] \cup (1, 2]$
(c) $(-2, -1) \cup (1, 2)$ (d) $[-2, 2]$

49. The common value of x satisfying $\frac{x-1}{x+2} \geq 0$ and $\frac{2x-5}{x-2}$ and $\frac{2x-5}{x-2} \leq 1$ is

(a) $(2, \infty]$ (b) $(2, 3]$
(c) $(-\infty, 3]$ (d) None of these

50. The combined solution of $x^3 - \sqrt{x^2} + 4x \le 0$ and $(x + 1)(x - 1)^2(x - 3) \le 0$ is
(a) $[-1, 3]$
(b) $[-1, 1) \cup (1, 3]$
(c) $[-1, 0] \cup [1, 3]$
(d) None of these

51. The value of x which simultaneously satisfies $(3x - 4)(x - 7) \le 0$ and $|3x - 5| \ge 1$ is
(a) $[2, 7] \cup \{4/3\}$ (b) $[2,9)-\left\{\frac{4}{3}\right\}$
(c) $[-1, 0] \cup [2, 7]$ (d) None of these

52. The set of value of x satisfying the inequality $2x - 7 < 4x - 2$ and $-5 \le 2x + 6 < 4$ is given as
(a) $\left[\frac{-11}{2}, \frac{-5}{2}\right]$ (b) $\left[\frac{-11}{2}, -5/2\right)$
(c) $(-5/2, -1]$ (d) None of these

53. If $|x - 4| = \max\{(x - 4), -(x - 4)\} + \min\{(x - 4), -(x - 4)\}$ then x is equal to
(a) –4 (b) 0
(c) 4 (d) 8

54. If $\left|5^{|x|}\right|^{|x|} = 125$, then value/values of x are
(a) 3, –3 (b) $\sqrt{3}, -\sqrt{3}$
(c) $\pm 1/\sqrt{3}$ (d) $\sqrt{3}$, 3

55. A point y is vibrating along y–axis with point (0, 10) as mean position and with amplitude of vibration equal to 4, then which one is true?
(a) $|y - 10| \ge 4$ (b) $|y - 10| \le 8$
(c) $|y - 10| \le 4$ (d) $|y - 10| \ge 8$

56. How many positive integers are there which when divide 1245 and 920 leaves the same remainder?
(a) 3 (b) 4
(c) 5 (d) 6

57. The locus of a point $x \in \mathbb{R}$ such that $|x + 2| + |x - 3| = 5$ is
(a) Straight line segment joining the points (–2, 0) and (3, 0)
(b) *A* straight line segment joining the points (2, 0) and (–3, 0)
(c) *A* straight line segment joining the points (–2, 0) and (5, 0)
(d) None of these

58. A point (x, y) is moving along a straight line in between the points (2, 3) and (4, 6) then.
(a) $|x - 3| + |x - 4| = 2$ and $|y - 3| + |y - 6| = 3$
(b) $|x - 2| + |x - 4| < 2$ and $|y - 3| + |y - 6| < 3$
(c) $|x - 2| + |x - 4| = 2$ and $|y - 3| + |y - 6| = 3$
(d) None of these

59. A (2, 1) ; B(6, 1); C(6, 4) and D(2, 4) are the vertices of a rectangle $ABCD$. Let (x, y) be any point in the region of rectangle then
(a) $|x - 2| + |x - 6| = 4$ and $|y - 1| + |y - 4| = 3$
(b) $|x - 2| + |x - 6| > 4$ and $|y - 1| + |y - 4| > 3$
(c) $|x - 1| + |x - 4| = 3$ and $|y - 2| + |y - 6| = 4$
(d) None of these

60. The least number (+ve integer) which when divided by 2 leaves remainder 1, when divided by 3 leaves remainder 2, when divided by 4 leaves remainder 3, and so on ...... when divided by 10 leaves remainder 9 is
(a) 2529 (b) 2539
(c) 2549 (d) 2519

61. The set of odd integer values of x from the set of integers $A = \{x: x \in z \text{ and } |x - 6| \le 8\}$ satisfying $\frac{(2x-1)(x-1)^2(x-2)^3}{(x-4)^4} > 0$ is given as
(a) {–1, 1, 3, 5, 7, 9, 11, 13}
(b) {–1, 1, 3, 5, 7, 9}
(c) {–1, 3, 5, 7, 9, 11, 13}
(d) None of these

62. Number of ordered pairs (x, y) satisfying the equation $\sqrt{x^2 + 12y} + \sqrt{y^2 + 12x} = 33$ and $x + y = 23$ is given as
(a) one (b) two
(c) three (d) None of these

63. Find the number of integer satisfying the inequality $\frac{(x-5)^2(x+2)^3(x-4)}{(x-3)^4} \le 0.$
(a) 4 (b) 8
(c) 7 (d) none of these

64. Find the number of natural numbers satisfying the inequality $\frac{(x-2)(x+2)^2(x-4)^2}{x(x+1)(x-3)} \le 0$
(a) 4 (b) 2
(c) 3 (d) none of these

SECTION–IV

OBJECTIVE-TYPE (MORE THAN ONE CORRECT ANSWER)

1. Which of the following is true about following inequality $||x-1|+2| \le 4$?
   (a) It contains 5 integer solutions
   (b) It contains only 3 integer solutions
   (c) Its set of solution is $[-1, 3]$
   (d) None of these

2. The solution set of $\left|\dfrac{x^2-1}{x^2+x+1}\right| < 1$ consists of
   (a) All positive reals (b) All negative reals
   (c) $\left(-2,-\dfrac{1}{2}\right)\cup(0,\infty)$ (d) None of these

3. The set of all real 'a' such that $5a^2 - 3a - 2$, $a^2 + a - 2$ and $2a^2 + a - 1$ are the lengths of sides of a triangle,
   (a) $\left[\dfrac{3+\sqrt{57}}{8}, \dfrac{5-\sqrt{17}}{8}\right]$
   (b) $\left[\dfrac{3-\sqrt{57}}{8}, \dfrac{5+\sqrt{17}}{4}\right]$
   (c) $\left(\dfrac{3+\sqrt{57}}{8}, \dfrac{5+\sqrt{17}}{4}\right)$
   (d) $\dfrac{3+\sqrt{57}}{8} < a < \dfrac{5+\sqrt{17}}{4}$

4. Which of the following is/are true?
   (a) $\sqrt{x^2} = |x| \ \forall\, x \in \mathbb{R}$
   (b) $|x^n| \ne |x|^n$; $x \in \mathbb{R}$
   (c) If $(x-a)(x-b) > 0$ where $a, b, \in \mathbb{R}$ and $a < b$, then either $x < a$ or $x > b$
   (d) The magnitude of all irrational numbers cannot be expressed numerically, but it can be expressed geometrically for some irrational numbers.

5. If X and y are two sets and their cartesian product is $X \times y = \{(x, y)\ ; x \in X$ and $y \in Y\}$ then $n(P(A \times B))$ where. $A = \{a, e, i, o, u\}$ and $B = \{c, d, \}$ is equal to
   (a) 5102
   (b) 1024
   (c) $1 + (1+2^1 + 2^2 + 2^3 + \ldots\ldots + 2^9)$
   (d) 256.

6. If 'a' and 'b' are two +ve real numbers, and their arithmetic mean and geometric mean are given by A.M. $= \dfrac{a+b}{2}$, and G.M. $= \sqrt{ab}$, then which of the following is/are true?
   (a) A.M. ≤ G.M.
   (b) A.M. ≥ G.M.
   (c) A.M. = G.M. if a = b
   (d) $a \le$ A.M. ≤ G.M. ≤ b

7. Two circular rings of radius r and R are moving in side a rectangle as shown below, then the area Ar of set $(B - A)$ has range

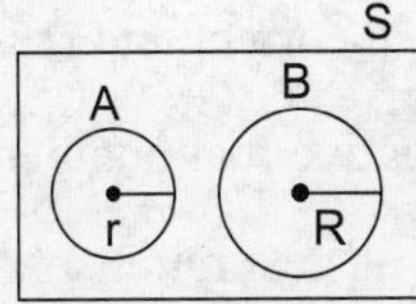

   (a) $Ar \in [5\pi, 9\pi]$ for $r = 2$ and $R = 3$ units
   (b) $Ar \in [0, 4\pi]$ for $r = R = 2$ units
   (c) Ar is not defined
   (d) $Ar \in [0, \infty)$ for $r \le R$

8. The equation $\dfrac{2x^3-3x^2+x+1}{2x^3-3x^2-x-1} = \dfrac{3x^3-x^2+5x-13}{3x^3-x^2-5x+13}$ has
   (a) at least one real solution
   (b) exactly three real solution
   (c) exactly one irrational solution
   (d) complex roots.

9. The value of 'k' for which the curve, $y = x^2 + kx + 4$ touches the x-axis is equal to
   (a) 4 (b) 2
   (c) –4 (d) –2

10. Which of the statements are true?
   (a) If $\dfrac{1}{|a|} > \dfrac{1}{b}$, then $|a| < b$, where a, b are non-zero real number
   (b) If $\dfrac{1}{a} > \dfrac{1}{|b|}$, then $a < |b|$ where a and b are non-zero real number.
   (c) If x, y, z are all different real numbers, then $\dfrac{1}{(x-y)^2} + \dfrac{1}{(y-z)^2} + \dfrac{1}{(z-x)^2} = \left(\dfrac{1}{x-y} + \dfrac{1}{y-z} + \dfrac{1}{z-x}\right)^2$
   (d) None of these

SECTION–V

ASSERTION AND REASON TYPE

The questions given below consist of an assertion (A) and the reason (R). Use the following key to choose the appropriate answer.

(a) If both assertion and reason are correct and reason is the correct explanation of the assertion.

(b) If both assertion and reason are correct but reason is not correct explanation of the assertion.

(c) If assertion is correct, but reason is incorrect

(d) If assertion is incorrect, but reason is correct

1. A: If x is negative real number then $\sqrt{x^2} = -x$

R: Since for all real number x ; $\sqrt{x^2} = |x|$

2. A: The distance between $(a + b, a)$ and $(a - b, a)$ is $2\,|b|$

R: For any real number x ; $\sqrt{x^2} = |x|$ and $|xy| = |x|.\,|y|$

4. A: LCM of $\sqrt{2}$ and 3 is $3\sqrt{2}$.

R: If x and y are two coprime numbers, then their LCM is $x.\,y$.

5. A: If $2 \le x \le 8$ then $\frac{1}{x} \in \left[\frac{1}{8}, \frac{1}{2}\right]$

R: If $a \le x \le b \;\forall$ a, b, $\in$ IR then $\frac{1}{x} \in \left[\frac{1}{b}, \frac{1}{a}\right]$

6. A: The expression $\frac{(x-3)(x+4)}{(x+5)}$ can change sign only at $x = 3, -4$ and -5.

R: The zeros of an expression decide the sign scheme of the expression.

7. A: If $0 < a < b$ then $\sqrt{a} < \sqrt{b}$ also holds true always.

R: $|x| < |y| \Leftrightarrow x^2 < y^2$

8. A: $x < x^2$ then $x < 0$ or $x > 1$.

R: Square of a real number is never negative.

9. A: If $|x| < \delta$ for every positive number 6, then $x = 0$.

R: $|x| < \delta \Rightarrow -\delta < x < \delta$ and $\delta \to 0, -\delta \to 0$.

10. A: $|x - 1| + |3 - x| = 2$ then $x \in [1, 3]$.

R: $|x| + |y| \ge |x + y|$ and equality holds if x and y have same sign or atleast one of them is zero.

11. A: $|x - 3| + |4 - x| > 1$ then $x \subset (-\infty, 3) \cup (4, \infty)$.

R: $|x + y| < |x| + |y|$ and inequality holds iff x and y have opposite sign.

12. A: If A set $x = \{a, b, c\}$ then number of subsets of its power set is 256.

R: Power set of a set A is a set containing all sub-sets of A and If $n\ (A) = m$ number of subsets of $A = 2^m$.

13. A: Set of prime numbers is countable set.

R: Every subset of countable set is also a countable set.

14. A: $A = \{\sqrt{2p+1} : p \in$ set of prime number$\}$, A is a uncountable set

R: Set of irrational numbers is uncountable.

SECTION–VI

LINKED COMPREHENSION TYPE

B: A number is represented as product of powers of different prime numbers e.g., $x = p^a.q^b.r^c$ (let $p = 2$)

To get even divisors we will rewrite $x = 2^1\ \{p^{a\ 1}.q^b.\ r^c\}$.Now number of even divisors of x = number of all the divisors of $p^a\!-\!1.q^b.r^c = a\,(b + 1)(c + 1)$. Similarly to get odd divisors we rewrite $x = p^a(q^b.r^c)$ (where $p = 2$). We will get number of odd divisors $= (b + 1)\,(c + 1)$. The two divisors *viz.*, 1 and the number itself are called improper divisors.

Based on this information, answer the following questions:

1. For $x = 2^3.3^4.5^2$ the number of even divisors will be

(a) 44 (b) 40
(c) 45 (d) None of these

2. When $x = 2^8.3^4.5^5$, the number of odd proper divisors will be

(a) 30 (b) 28
(c) 27 (d) None of these

3. For $x = 2^5.3^4.6^3$, the number of proper even divisors will be

(a) 64 (b) 63
(c) 62 (d) None of these

4. For $x = 2^3.3^5.5^3$, the number of proper odd divisors will be
(a) 22 (b) 24
(c) 23 (d) None of these

C: Let $f(x) = x$ and $g(x) = |x|$ be two real valued functions, $\phi(x)$ be a function satisfying the condition; $[\phi(x) - f(x)]^2 + [\phi(x) - g(x)]^2 = 0, x \geq 0$ then,

5. The function $\phi(x)$ is
(a) $x + |x|$ (b) $|x|$
(c) $-x$ (d) None of these

6. The solution set of inequality $\phi(x - 2) \leq 2$ is
(a) [0, 4] (b) [2, 4]
(c) [–2, 2] (d) None of these

7. Solution set of inequality $\phi(x - 2) + \phi(x + 2) \leq 4$
(a) [0, 4] (b) [–2, 2]
(c) [0, 2] (d) None of these

D: Modulus of real number x is defined as $|x| = x$ if $x \geq 0$; $|x| = -x$ if $x < 0$. Also inequations of the type $|x| < a \Rightarrow -a < x < a$ and $|x| > a \Rightarrow x > a$ or $x < -a$. The solution of simultaneous system of inequations is obtained by taking intersection of solution of each inequation. Also inequations of the type $|x - a| < |x - b|$ can be solved by squaring both sides.

8. Solution of $|x + 2| < 4$ is
(a) (– 6, 2) (b) (– 6, 0)
(c) (2, 6) (d) (0, 2)

9. Solution of $|x - 1| \geq |x - 3|$ is
(a) $x \leq 2$ (b) $x \geq 2$
(c) [1, 3] (d) None of these

10. If $x^2 - 1 \leq 0$ and $x^2 - x - 2 \geq 0$, then x lies in the interval
(a) (– 1, 2) (b) (–1, 1)
(c) (1, 2) (d) None of these

E: An inequation of the form $\sqrt{f(x)} < g(x)$ is solved by taking intersection of solution of system of inequations $f(x) \geq 0$, $g(x) \geq 0$ and $f(x) < [g(x)]^2$. Inequations of the form $\sqrt{f(x)} < g(x)$ is equivalent to system of inequation $f(x) \geq 0$, $g(x) > 0$ and $f(x) < g(x)$. $\sqrt{f(x)} > g(x)$ is equivalent to the system of inequations $g(x) \geq 0$, $f(x) \geq 0$ and $f(x) > [g(x)]^2$. Using these conceptions and taking care of general cautions for solving equations and inequalities, answer the following questions.

11. Solution of inequation $\sqrt{x+14} < x + 2$ are
(a) (– 2, ∞) (b) (2, ∞)
(c) (– 5, – 2) (d) None of these

12. $\sqrt{x+7} < \sqrt{2x+3}$ has solution set
(a) (– 7, ∞) (b) (4, ∞)
(c) (– 3/2, 4) (d) None of these

13. Solution of inequation $\sqrt{-x^2+4x-3} > 6 - 2x$ is
(a) $\left(\frac{13}{5}, 3\right)$ (b) $(-\infty, 3)$
(c) $(3, \infty)$ (d) $\left(-3, \frac{13}{5}\right)$

F: Consider the number $N = \overline{7\,7\,4\,9\,5\,8\,P\,9\,6\,Q}$ answer the following questions.

14. If $P = 2$ and the number N is divisible by 3, then number of possible values of Q is/are
(a) 0 (b) 2
(c) 3 (d) 4

15. If N is divisible by 4, then
(a) P can be any integer and $Q = 0, 2, 4, 6, 8$
(b) P can be any rational number and $Q = 0, 4, 8$
(c) P can be any single digit whole number and $Q = 0, 4, 8$
(d) P can be any real number and $Q = 0,4, 8$

16. If N is divisible by 8 and 9 both, then number of possible ordered pair (P, Q) is/are
(a) 3 (b) 2
(c) 1 (d) 0

G: If $f(x)$ and $g(x)$ are two polynomials then $\frac{f(x)}{g(x)}$ defines a rational function of x. The resolution of $\frac{f(x)}{g(x)}$ into partial fractions depends upon the nature of the factors of $g(x)$.

Case – I: When $g(x)$ is expressible as the product of non repeating linear factors

i.e., $g(x) = (x - a_1)(x - a_2) \ldots\ldots (x - a_n)$. Then

$$\frac{f(x)}{g(x)} = \frac{A_1}{x-a_1} + \frac{A_2}{x-a_2} + \ldots + \frac{A_n}{x-a_n}$$

Where $A_1, A_2, \ldots, A_n$ are constants and can be determined by equating the numerator on RHS to the numerator on LHS and then substituting $x = a_1, a_2, \ldots, a_n$.

Case – II: When $g(x)$ is expressible as the product of the linear factors, such that some of them are repeating.

Let $g(x) = (x-a)^k (x-a_1)(x-a_2) \ldots (x-a_n)$. Then

$$\frac{f(x)}{g(x)} = \frac{A_1}{x-a} + \frac{A_2}{(x-a)^2} + \ldots + \frac{A_k}{(x-a)^k}$$

$$+ \frac{B_1}{(x-a_1)} + \frac{B_2}{(x-a_2)} + \ldots + \frac{B_r}{(x-a_r)}$$

Solving this as in case–I, constants can be determined.

17. If $\frac{3x+4}{(x+1)^2(x-1)} = \frac{A}{x-1} + \frac{B}{(x+1)} + \frac{C}{(x+1)^2}$, then A is equal to

(a) –1/2 (b) 15/8
(c) 7/4 (d) –1/4

18. If $\frac{3x+7}{x^2-3x+2} = \frac{13}{x-2} + \frac{B}{x-1}$ then B has value

(a) –10
(b) 10
(c) 13
(d) –13

19. If $\frac{3x}{(x-6)(x+a)} = \frac{2}{x-6} + \frac{1}{x+a}$, then a the value of unknown 'a' is

(a) 1 (b) 2
(c) 3 (d) 4

SECTION–VII

MATRIX–MATCH TYPE

This section contains 5 questions. Each question contains statements given in two columns which have to be matched. Statements (i, ii, iii, iv) in **column** A have to be matched with statements (*a, b, c, d*) in **column** B. The answers to these questions have to be appropriately bubbled as illustrated in the following example. If the correct matches are i-a, d, ii-b, c, iii-a, b, iv-d, then the correctly bubbled 4 *x* 4 matrix should be as follows:

	a	b	c	d
i	(a)	(b)	(c)	(d)
ii	(a)	(b)	(c)	(d)
iii	(a)	(b)	(c)	(d)
iv	(a)	(b)	(c)	(d)

1. Column A

(i) {*x*: *x* is prime number and $x \leq 40$}
(ii) {*x*: $x = 4n - 1$ $n \in$ IN and $x \leq 71$}
(iii) {*x*: $x \in$ I+ $x \leq 260$ and divisible by 3 and 7}
(iv) {*x*: *x* is natural number divisible by 4 and 6 both and $x < 225$}

Column B

(a) the cardinal number of set is 12
(b) it is a finite set
(c) the cardinal number of set is 18
(d) it is an infinite set

2. (Given: *p*, *q* are two different natural prime numbers)

Column A

(i) Number of proper divisors of *pq*
(ii) Number of divisors of p^2q^2
(iii) Number of even proper divisors of 108
(iv) Number of odd divisors of 180

Column B

(a) HCF of (91, 119)
(b) the lowest prime number
(c) lowest composite divisor of $n(n+1)(n+2)$
(d) square of a prime number

3. Column I

(i) Number of integers for which $\frac{|x+2|-x}{a} < 2$
(ii) Number of values of *x* satisfying $\sqrt{x+1} - \sqrt{x-1} = \sqrt{4x-1}$
(iii) Number of positive values of *x* satisfying $x^2 - 5|x| + 6 = 0$ are
(iv) Number of integers satisfying $\sqrt{x-5} - \sqrt{9-x} > 1$ are

Column II

(a) one
(b) infinitely many
(c) no solution
(d) two

4. Column A

(i) $\frac{(x+3)^2(2x+1)^4}{(2x-1)^3(3-x)} \geq 0$ for *x* belongs to
(ii) Find values of *x* for which $\frac{(x-5)(x^3-4x^2-4x-5)}{(2x^2+2x+1)} \leq 0$

(iii) The Number of integers which satisfies x2 – $2x \geq 0$ and $x^2 - 6x + 5 \leq 0$

(iv) $\dfrac{(2x-1)}{(2x^3+3x^2+x)}$ is positive in the interval

Column B

(a) $\left(-\infty, -\dfrac{3}{2}\right)$

(b) 4

(c) 5

(d) $\left(\dfrac{1}{2}, 3\right)$

5. Match the following:

Column – I

(i) Even number

(ii) Rational number

(iii) Irrational number

(iv) Real number

Column – II

(a) 22/7

(b) π

(c) 0

(d) $\sqrt{2}$

SECTION–VIII

INTEGER-TYPE QUESTIONS

1. Find the solution of equation $\sqrt{x^2+x-5}+\sqrt{x^2+8x-4}$ = 5.

2. Solve the equation $(\sqrt{3}+1)^{2x}+(\sqrt{3}-1)^{2x}=2^{3x}$.

3. Find the number of pairs of natural numbers, the difference of whose squares is 45.

4. If the number 497A is divisible by 3 and the number 562 B is divisible by 4, then find the number of possible ordered pairs (A, B). (where A and B are digits)

5. If $4x^4-(a-1)x^3+ax^2-6x+1$ is divisible by $(2x-1)$, then find the value of a.

6. Find the number of real solution (s) of the equation $|x-3|^{3x^2-10x+3}=1$.

7. Find the number of integral solutions (x, y) of the equation $|2x-y|+|x-y|=1$.

8. If $g(x)=[x^2]-[x]^2$ where [.] denotes the greatest integer function, and $x \in [0, 2]$ then find the sum of all possible values of $g(x)$.

9. Let a function f satisfy $x - f(x) = 8\left[\dfrac{x}{8}\right]-5\left[\dfrac{f(x)}{5}\right]$ for all x, where $11 < f(10) < 14$, then find the value of $f(10)$.

10. If the sum of magnitudes of all possible roots of the equation $\left(a+\sqrt{b}\right)^{x^2-15}+\left(a-\sqrt{b}\right)^{x^2-15}=2a$ (where $a^2 - b = 1$) is given by $p+2\sqrt{q}$; then find the value of q.

11. The positive integers p, q and r are all primes if $p^2 - q^2 = r$, then the sum of all possible value of r is

12. Given $x + y = 1$ and $x^3 + y^3 = 19$, then the value of $x^2 + y^2$ is equal to

13. If A, B, C are digits for which the equation $\overline{7A2}-\overline{48B}=\overline{C73}$ holds good then find value of $A + B + C$.

14. Find the number of ordered pair (m, n) satisfying the relation $m^2 = n^2 + 2002$ where m and n are natural number.

15. If $a+b+c=0$ and $a^2+b^2+c^2=1$, then find the value of $16(a^4+b^4+c^4)$ is

Answer Keys

SECTION–III

1. (a)	**2.** (d)	**3.** (b)	**4.** (c)	**5.** (b)	**6.** (a)	**7.** (c)	**8.** (b)	**9.** (a)	**10.** (c)
11. (b)	**12.** (c)	**13.** (d)	**14.** (b)	**15.** (a)	**16.** (c)	**17.** (c)	**18.** (c)	**19.** (c)	**20.** (d)
21. (c)	**22.** (b)	**23.** (a)	**24.** (b)	**25.** (b)	**26.** (b)	**27.** (b)	**28.** (b)	**29.** (a)	**30.** (b)
31. (c)	**32.** (d)	**33.** (c)	**34.** (d)	**35.** (d)	**36.** (a)	**37.** (b)	**38.** (b)	**39.** (c)	**40.** (a)
41. (d)	**42.** (c)	**43.** (a)	**44.** (b)	**45.** (c)	**46.** (d)	**47.** (b)	**48.** (a)	**49.** (b)	**50.** (d)
51. (a)	**52.** (c)	**53.** (c)	**54.** (b)	**55.** (c)	**56.** (d)	**57.** (a)	**58.** (c)	**59.** (a)	**60.** (d)
61. (c)	**62.** (b)	**63.** (c)	**64.** (b)						

SECTION–IV

1. (a, c)	**2.** (a, c)	**3.** (c, d)	**4.** (a, c, d)	**5.** (b, c)	**6.** (b, c)	**7.** (a, b, d)	**8.** (a, b)
9. (a, c)	**10.** (b, c)						

SECTION–V

1. (a)	**2.** (a)	**3.** (d)	**4.** (c)	**5.** (a)	**6.** (a)	**7.** (b)	**8.** (a)	**9.** (a)	**10.** (a)
11. (a)	**12.** (a)	**13.** (a)							

SECTION–VI

1. (c)	**2.** (d)	**3.** (b)	**4.** (c)	**5.** (b)	**6.** (a)	**7.** (c)	**8.** (a)	**9.** (b)	**10.** (d)
11. (b)	**12.** (b)	**13.** (a)	**14.** (d)	**15.** (c)	**16.** (b)	**17.** (c)	**18.** (a)	**19.** (c)	

SECTION–VII

1. (i) → (a, b)	(ii) → (b, c)	(iii) → (a, b)	(iv) → (b, c)
2. (i) → (b)	(ii) → (d)	(iii) → (a)	(iv) → (c)
3. (i) → (c)	(ii) → (a)	(iii) → (d)	(iv) → (a)
4. (i) → (d)	(ii) → (c)	(iii) (b, c)	(iv) → (a, d)
5. (i) → (c)	(ii) → (a, c)	(iii) → (b, d)	(iv) → (a, b, c, d)

SECTION–VIII

1. 2	**2.** 1	**3.** 3	**4.** 9	**5.** 13	**6.** 3	**7.** 4	**8.** 3	**9.** 12	**10.** 14
11. 5	**12.** 13	**13.** 17	**14.** 0	**15.** 8					

HINTS AND SOLUTIONS

TEXTUAL EXERCISE–1: (SUBJECTIVE)

1. **(i)** It is true statement, hence is a mathematical statement.
(ii) Given two integers $x - y < 0$
$\Rightarrow$ $x < y$ But for $x > y$
$\Rightarrow$ $x - y > 0$, hence this may be true or false thus, it does not quality as a mathematical statement.
(iii) $n = 4$ it is not true; $n = 1$ it is true. Hence, it is not a mathematical statement.
(iv) This is true on Thursday but not Saturday, thus it is not a mathematical statement.
(v) This also may or may not be true depending on the place referred to by the word 'here'.
(vi) Alpha centuari is nearest with respect to our scalar system but not to other galaxy. Hence it is not a mathematical statement.

2. **(i)** It is always true. Hence it can be classified as mathematical statements.
(ii) It is true only if the number itself is even otherwise false. Hence it cannot be classified as mathematical statements.
(iii) It is true for a square but false for a rectangle, thus cannot be classified as a mathematical statement.
(iv) It is always true; hence it is a mathematical statement.
(v) This may be true for some statement not for the other. Hence does not qualify as a mathematical statement.
(vi) An interrogative statement cannot be a mathematical statement.

3. **(i)** Neither true nor false, hence not a mathematical statement.
(ii) Ambiguous statements which can't be proved true or false to be classified as a mathematical statement.

4. **(a)** Theorem – it can be proved using linear pair axiom and properties of parallel lines.
(b) Axiom – it cannot be proved.
(c) Theorem – it can be proved using linear pair axiom.
(d) Theorem – It can be proved using properties of similarity of triangles.
(e) Axiom – it cannot be proved.
(f) Definition – that is how an angle has been defined.
(g) Theorem – it can be proved $ax + by = a_2x + b_2y$ multiplying both sides by m.
$m(a_1x + b_1y)$, $m(a_2x + b_2y)$
Let us suppose, they are not equal $m\,(a_1x + b_1y) = m(a_2x + b_2y) + k$
$\Rightarrow$ $m[(a_1x + b_1y) - ({}^{a}{}_{2}x + b_2y)] = k$
$\Rightarrow$ $k = 0$; Hence they are equal, hence proved.
(h) Definition – as $|x| = \begin{cases} = x \text{ if } x \geq 0 \\ = -x \text{ if } x < 0 \end{cases}$
(i) Definition – that is how cubic root of a number is defined.
(j) Theorem – it can be proved using graph.

TEXTUAL EXERCISE–1: (OBJECTIVE)

1. **(b)** Theorem

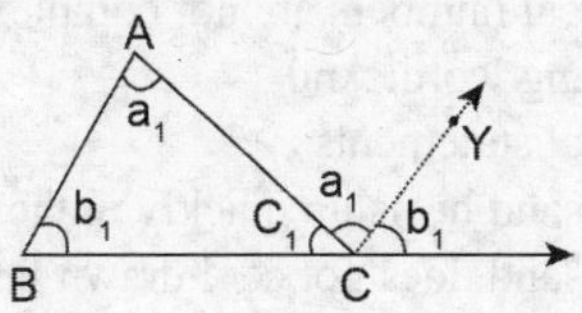

$CY \parallel AB$
Thus $A + C$; $a_1 + b_1 + c_1 = 180°$ by linear pair axiom.

2. **(b)** Theorem

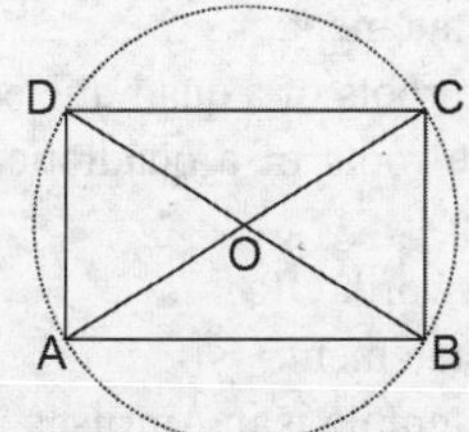

Let $ABCD$ be a cyclic quadrilateral, O be the centre.
By a property of circles:
$\angle DCB = 1/2 < (DOBA)$ (i)
$\angle DAB = 1/2 < BODC$ (ii)
Adding (i) and (ii), we get $\angle DCB + \angle DAB = 1/2\,(\angle(DOBA) + \angle BODC) = 1/2\,(360°) = 180°$

3. **(a)** Definition of whole numbers

4. **(a)** This statement is the definition of circle

5. **(b), (c)** If linear pair is assumed to be an axiom

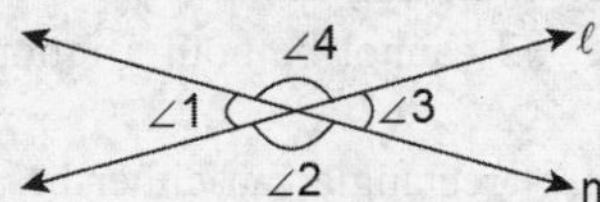

Let two lines ℓ and m intersect. By linear pair axiom
$\angle 4 + \angle 3 = 180°$ (i)
$\angle 2 + \angle 3 = 180°$ (ii)
By (i) and (ii), we have $\angle 4 + \angle 3 = \angle 2 + \angle 3$
$\Rightarrow$ $\angle 4 = \angle 2$
Similarly $\angle 1 = \angle 3$.
Let if linear pair is considered as a theorem, vertically opposite angles are equal as an axiom.

6. **(a)** True statement
(b) False statement
(c) True statement
(d) May or may not be real depending upon the value of k.
$k = 6$; $x = 3, 2$ are roots which are real
$k = 7$; roots are non-real. Hence it is not a mathematical statement.

TEXTUAL EXERCISE-2: (SUBJECTIVE)

1. Answers already given in the Answer Keys
2. **(a)** Connecting word: And
   Individual statement:
   (i) All rational numbers are real.
   (ii) All real numbers are not complex.
   (b) Connecting word: And
   Individual statements
   (i) The sand heats up quickly in the sun
   (ii) The sand does not cool drawn fast at night.
   (c) Connecting word: And
   Individual statement:
   (i) $x = 2$ is a root of the equation $x^2 - 5x + 6 = 0$
   (ii) $x = 3$ is a root of the equation $x^2 - 5x + 6 = 0$
   (d) Connecting word: OR
   Individual statement:
   (i) Both the roots of a quadratic equation are real.
   (ii) Both the roots of a quadratic equation are imaginary.
   (e) Connecting word: OR
   Individual statement:
   (i) Golden temple is in Amritsar.
   (ii) Golden temple is in Jalandhar.
3. **(a)** x can be either even or odd but not both. Thus OR is exclusive.
   (b) Delhi can be the capital of either India or Nepal but not both. Thus OR is exclusive.
   (c) a number can quality as both integer and a rational number. Thus OR is Inclusive.
   (d) a Person can go either by train or by air but not by both. Thus OR is exclusive.
4. **(a)** Inclusive, one can have both residence and identity proof to get a driving license
   (b) Exclusive, $\sqrt{2}$ cannot be both a rational and irrational number.
   (c) Exclusive, *A* rectangle can either be a quadrilateral or six-sided polygon but not both
   (d) Inclusive, Both sun rise and moon set actions can take place together.
   (e) Exclusive, An integer cannot be both positive or negative.
5. Answers already given in Answer Keys
6. Answers already given in Answer Keys
7. **(i)** If a quadrilateral is not a rhombus, then its sides are not equal.
   (ii) If a triangle is not isosceles, it does not have equal sides.
   (iii) If a number is not divisible by 3, then it is not divisible by 9.
8. Yes, negation of statement $x + y = y + x$ real x and y is there exist x and y for which $x + y \neq y + x$ which is statement.

TEXTUAL EXERCISE-2: (OBJECTIVE)

1. **(c)** Negation $\sqrt{2}$ is a complex number.
2. **(b)** Negation: It is false that Chandigarh is the capital of U.P.
3. **(b)** OR is used exclusively used as a number (base 2) cannot be both irrational as well as a natural number.
4. **(b)** Contra positive of $p \Rightarrow q$ *is* $-q \Rightarrow \neg p$
   Thus for the given statement, if a number is not divisible by 2, then it is not divisible by 4.
5. **(c)** The converse of the given statement is:
   If the distance between two lines is constant, then the lines are parallel.
6. **(b)** Compound of these two statements is given by: 10 is divisible by 2 and 5.

TEXTUAL EXERCISE-3: (SUBJECTIVE)

1. Selection already given is Answer Keys
2. **(i)** If x is a whole number, then it is an integer.
   (ii) If x^2 is non-negative quantity, then it is a real number.
   (iii) Δ_1 and Δ_2 are congruent triangle only if Δ_1 and Δ_2 are similar triangles.
   (iv) x is a real number only if x is a natural number.
   (v) Δ_1 and Δ_2 are similar triangles if and only if the corresponding angles of Δ_1 and Δ_2 are equal.
   (vi) x^2 is non-positive quantity if and only if x is purely imaginary.
3. **(i)** A rectangle is a square if and only if all its four sides are equal.
   (ii) A number is divisible by 3 if and only if the sum of the digits is divisible by 3.
4. Let us verify by taking $x = 3, y = 5; xy = 15$ is also odd, (very simply if 2 does not divide x and y, then it cannot divide xy also). Hence the statement holds.
5. **(i)** Using AND
   42 is divisible by 7 and 9.
   42 is divisible by both 7 and 9. The statement is true.
   $7 \mid 42$ are well as $9 \mid 42$.
   (ii) 42 is divisible by 7 or 9.
   $7|42$, thus the statement is true.
   Notice that OR has been used inclusively as 9 can also divide 42 (which is true infact).
6. To prove this statement by contradiction. Let us assume the negation to be true.
   If $\frac{(2a+7)(a+b+c)}{abc}, \frac{(2b+7)(a+b+c)}{abc}, \frac{(2c+7)(a+b+c)}{abc}$
   are not in *A.P.*, then *a, b, c* are in *A.P.*
   For $a = 1, b = 2, c = 4$, they are not in *AP* which
   $\frac{(2a+7)(a+b+c)}{abc} = \frac{63}{8}, \frac{(2b+7)(a+b+c)}{abc} = \frac{77}{8},$

$\frac{(2c+7)(a+b+c)}{abc} = \frac{135}{8}$ are not in *A.P.* Which is a contradiction to the assumed statement.

7. Let us assume that the negation of the statement is true, $x^4 + 9x^2 + 14$ vanishes for at least one real value of x. $x^4 + 9x^2 + 14 = (x^2 + 7)(x^2 + 2)$ roots are $x^2 = -7$, $x^2 = -2$. Thus there are no real statements for x. Thus the expression does not vanish for any real value of x which is a contradiction to the assumed statement. Hence, $x^4 + 9x^2 + 14$ does not vanish for any real value of x.

8. $2x^3 + 9x = x(2x^2 + 9) = 0; x \in \mathbb{R}$
$x = 0$ or $x^2 = -9/2$
Thus $x = 0$ is the only real solution of the equation, hence if $x \in \mathbb{R}$ and $2x^3 + 9x = 0$, then $x = 0$.

9. $2x^2 - 5 = 0 \quad \Rightarrow \quad x^2 = \sqrt{\frac{5}{2}} - \sqrt{2.5} \simeq 1.581$
$\Rightarrow x^2 = 1.581 \quad \Rightarrow \quad x = \pm 1.257$
Which certainly lies between 0 and 2. Hence the statement is false.

10. We know that $(n - 3)^2 \geq 0 \ \forall \ n \in \mathbb{N}$ (square of a number is always positive)
$\Rightarrow n^2 - 6n + 9 \geq 0$
$\Rightarrow n^2 \geq 6n - 9 \ \forall \ n \in \mathbb{N}$; which is the required statement. Hence proved

11. Let $x = 2, y = -2; x^2 - y^2 = 4 - 4 = 0$, but $x = 2 \neq y = -2$; hence the statement is false.

12. **(a)** Let us check for $n = 6$; $6n - 1 = 35$, which is not a prime number
Hence the statement is false, similarly for $n = 9$.
(b) Check for $n = 4$; $6n + 1 = 25$ which is not a prime number, hence the statement is false, similarly for $n = 8$.
(c) Check for $n = 41$; $(41)^2 + 41 + 41$ which is divisible by 41. Hence it is not prime. The statement is false.

TEXTUAL EXERCISE–4: (SUBJECTIVE)

1. **(a)** **(i)** No, antique is qualitative
(ii) No, antique is qualitative
(iii) No, genius is qualitative
(iv) Yes, it is a set
(v) No, best is qualitative
(b) **(i)** True
(ii) False, the set $\{a, b\}$ is not an element of A
(iii) False, $\{b\}$ is an element of A.
(iv) False, A does not contains $\{\{a\}, a, b\}$

2. **(a)** $A = \{-3, -1\}$ is roster form
Clearly, it is finite, countable $n(A) = 2$
(b) $A = \{a\}$ is roster form; It is a singleton set.
(c) $A = \{4, 8, 12, 16, 20, 24, 28, 32, 36, 40, 44, 48\}$ is roster form
It is finite, countable set, cardinal number of $A = 12$
(d) $A = \{1, 5, 9, 13, 17, 21, 25, 29, 33, 37, 41, 45, 49, 53, 57, 61, 65, 69, 73, 77, 81, 85, 89, 93, 97\}$ is roster form.
It is a finite, countable set $n(A) = 25$
(e) $\therefore$ 2 is the only even prime number. A is a null set. Cardinal number of $A = 0$
(f) $A = \{5, 15, 25, 35, 45\}$ it is a finite, countable set $n(A) = 5$
(g) $A = \{6, 12, 18, 24, 30, 36, 42, 48, 54, 60, 66, 72, 78, 84, 90, 96\}$
A is finite and countable. Cardinal number of $A = 16$
(h) $A = \{12, 24, 36, 48, 60, 72, 84, 96\}$
A is finite and countable, cardinal number = 8.
(i) $A = \{2, 3, 4, 6, 8 \ldots\}$ is roster form, a is infinite and countable.
(j) $A = \{12, 24, 36, \ldots.\}$; A is infinite and countable.
(k) $A = \{1, 5, 9\}$ is roster form, it is finite and countable, $n(A) = 3$

3. **(i)** $\{1, 2, 3, 4\}$ and $\{5\}$ there two sets have nothing is common. Thus they are disjoint.
(ii) e is common to both sets. They are not disjoint.
(iii) We do not have an integer which is both odd and even. Thus they are disjoint.

4. **(i)** False, 3 is common to both sets.
(ii) False, a is common to both sets.
(iii) True no element is common.
(iv) True no element is common.

5. **(i)** $A' = \{d, e, f, g, h\}$
(ii) $B' = \{a, b, c, h\}$
(iii) $C' = \{b, d, f, h\}$
(iv) $D' = \{b, c, d, e\}$

6. **(a)** $X \subset B, X \subset C$
$X = \{b\}; \phi$
(b) $X \subset A, X \not\subset B$
$X = \{a, b, d\}; \{d\}; \{a, d\}; \{b, d\}; \{c, d\}; \{a, c, d\}; \{b, c, d\}; \{a, b, c, d\}$

7. **(a)** $\{4\}, \phi$
(b) $\{3\}, \{5\}, \{3, 5\}$
(c) $\{3\}, \{5\}, \{3, 5\}, \phi$
(d) $\{2\}; \{4\}; \{6\}; \{8\}; \{2, 4\}; \{6, 8\}; \{2, 4, 6\}; \{4, 6, 8\}; \{6, 8, 2\}; \{2, 4, 8\}$

8. **(a)** By the question $P(A : \phi) = \{x \in P(A) : \phi \subset X\}$, but ϕ is a subset of every set, so $P(A : \phi\} = P(A)$
(b) $P(A : B) = \{\{a, b\}, \{a, b, c\}, \{a, b, d\}, \{a, b, c, d\}$.

9. Number of subsets of the set having m element = $2m$
Number of subsets of the set having n element = $2n$
By the question $2^m = 2^n + 56$
$\Rightarrow 2^m - 2^n = 56 = 2^6 - 2^3 \quad \Rightarrow m = 6, n = 3$
Thus, the first set has 6 elements and the set has 3 elements.

10. **(i)** $A = \{a, b, c, d\}$
Let P and Q be two disjoint subsets of A. Now every elements of A has 3 choices i.e., P, Q or $\overline{P \cup Q}$.
Thus there are $3 \times 3 \times 3 \times 3 = (3)^4 = 81$ possible ordered pairs of disjoint subsets. One of these is (ϕ, ϕ) excluding this pair from 81; we are left with 80 such

ordered pairs. Therefore total number of ordered pairs $=\frac{1}{2}(80)+1=41$; (1 pair (ϕ, ϕ) is added)

(ii) Out of 4 elements a, b, c, d, two can be chosen in ${}^4C_2 =$ 6 ways.
Consider a, b be the common elements, then following 5 required types of pairs are possible.
(i) $\{a, b\}, (a, b)$ (ii) $\{a, b\}, \{a, b, c\}$
(iii) $\{a, b\}; \{a, b, d\}$ (iv) $\{a, b, c\}, \{a, b, d\}$
(v) $\{a, b\}, \{a, b, c, d\}$
∴ Total possible pairs $= 6 \times 5 = 30$

(iii) 3 elements in common, each pair must have at least 3 elements.
$\{a, b, c\}$ can be paired with $\{a, b, c, d\}$
$\{a, c, d\}$ can be paired with $\{a, b, c, d\}$
$\{b, c, d\}$ can be paired with $\{a, b, c, d\}$
$\{b, d, a\}$ can be paired with $\{a, b, c, d\}$
Thus 4 pairs in total

11. $A = \{1, 2, 3, 4\}; B = \{2, 3\}$
The set A has 24 = 16 subsets. The subsets of A that are superset to B must include $B = \{2, 3\}$
$= 2^4 -$ those subsets which do not include $\{2, 3\}$
$= 2^4 - \{$subsets of $\{1, 4\}$ + subsets of $\{1, 3\}$ + subsets of $\{1, 2, 3\}$
$= 2^4 - 3.2^2 = 16 - 3.4 = 4$

12. (i) Subsets disjoint from B; $A = \{1, 2, 3, 4, 5, 6\}$
Number of subsets of $A = 2^6$; Sets disjoint from $B = \{3, 4, 5\}$ = Subsets of $\{1, 2, 6\} = 2^3 = 8$

(ii) Having exactly one element of B. B has three elements. It 3 is common
Number of such sets = Number of subsets of $\{1, 2, 6, 3\}$ is which 3 is included
= Number of subset of $\{1, 2, 6, 3\}$ – Number of subsets of $\{1, 2, 6\}$
$= 2^4 - 2^3 = 16 - 8 = 8$
Similarly if 4, 5 are common there 8 possibilities for each.
Total = 24 subsets.

(iii) Having exactly two elements of B:
Again there are three possibilities. The common elements can be (3, 4), (4, 5), (3, 5).
Number of such subsets = Number of subsets of $\{1, 2, 3, 4, 6\}$ in which (3, 4) is always included.
= Number of subsets of $\{1, 2, 3, 4, 6\}$ – Number of subsets of $\{1, 2, 6, 3\}$
– Number of subsets of $\{1, 2, 6, 4\}$ + Number of subsets of $\{1, 2, 6\}$
$= 2^5 - 2^4 - 2^4 + 2^3 = 2^3 = 8$
Similarly for (4, 5) and (3, 5) there are 8 possibilities each.
Thus a total of 24 possibilities.

(iv) Subsets of A and supersets of B:
= Subsets of A having $\{3, 4, 5\}$ (all elements)
= Number of subsets of A – Number of subsets of A disjoint from B
– Number of subsets of A having exactly one element in common
– Number of subsets of A having exactly two elements in common
$= 2^6 - 8 - 24 - 24 = 56 - 48 = 8$
Thus, there are 8 such subsets of A which are supersets of B.

13. It is given that the subset must have exactly one element from A, B and C.
Say $\{1, 4, 7\}$ is one such subset. It cannot include any number from $\{2, 3, 5, 6, 8, 9\}$ only number left is 10.
So there are two possible combinations $\{1, 4, 7\}$ and $\{1, 4, 7, 10\}$
Similarly we can have $3 \times 3 \times 3 = 27$ such combination from A, B and C. For each there are two possibilities thus $27 \times 2 = 54$ is the total number of subsets.

14. $i = 1$, P_1 = Number of subsets of 5 which have 1 in then = Total subsets of 5 – subsets which do not have $= 2^6 - 2^5$.
$i = 2$, P_2 = subsets which have out of $\{1, 2\}$.
Say 1 is there and 2 not there = subsets of $\{1, 3, 4, 5, 6\}$ in which 1 is there. $= 2^5 - 2^4$
For the other case if 2 is there and 1 not there $= 2^6 - 2^5$.
Total $= 2(2^5 - 2^4)$
$i = 3$; P_3 = Subsets which have either 1 or 2 or 3.
Say 1 is there then 2 and 3 must be excluded.
= 4 subsets of $\{1, 4, 5, 6\}$ in which 1 is there
Similarly for other two cases total $= 3(2^4 - 2^3)$
$i = 4$; P_4 = Subsets which have one of $\{1, 2, 3, 4\}$ say 1 is there 2, 3, 4 are not there
= Subsets of $\{1, 5, 6\}$ in which one is there $= 2^3 - 2^2$
Total $= 4(2^3 - 2^2)$
$i = 5$; P_5 = subsets which have one of $\{1, 2, 3, 4, 5\}$ say 1 is there 2, 3, 4, 5 are not there
= Subsets of $\{1, 6\}$ in which 1 is there $= 2^2 - 2$
Total $= 5(2^2 - 2)$
$i = 6$; P_6 = Subsets which have one of $\{1, 2, 3, 4, 5, 6\}$ = 6
Total $= 2^6 - 2^5 + 2(2^5 - 2^4) + 3(2^4 - 2^3) + 4(2^3 - 2^2) + 5(2^2 - 2) + 6$
$= 2^5 + 2(32 - 16) + 3(16 - 8) + 4(8 - 4) + 5 \times 2 + 6 =$ $32 + 32 + 24 + 16 + 10 + 6 = 120$

15. Number of subsets of C disjoint from both A and B.
= Subsets of C which have none out of $\{1, 2, 3, 7, 8, 9\}$
= Subsets of $\{4, 5, 6, 10\}$
$= 2^4 = 16$. Thus, there are 16 subsets of C which are disjoint from both A and B.

16. $A = \{2, 4, 6, 8 \ldots 100\}$; $n(A) = 50$
$B = \{3, 6, 9, 12, \ldots, 99\}$; $n(B) = 33$
$C = \{5, 10, 15, 20, \ldots, 100\}$; $n(C) = 19$
$D = \{7, 14, 21, \ldots, 98\}$; $n(D) = 14$
$E = \{11, 22, 33, \ldots, 99\}$; $n(E) = 9$
G is the set that has none of the elements of A, B, C, D, E
Clearly $G = \{1, 13, 17, 19, 23, 29, 31, 37, 41, 43, 47, 53, 59, 61, 67, 71, 73, 79, 83, 89, 97\}$
$n(G) = 21$

TEXTUAL EXERCISE–5: (SUBJECTIVE)

1. **(i)** $X \cup Y = \{1, 2, 3, 5\}$

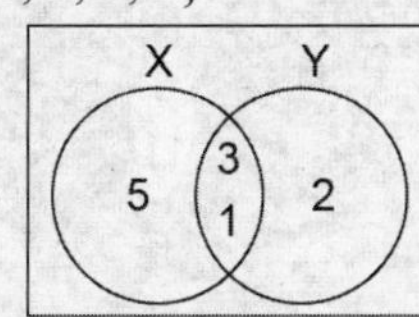

From Venn Diagram $(X \cup Y) = \{1, 2, 3, 5\}$
Similarly produced for other parts

(ii) $A \cup B = \{a, b, c, e, i, o, u\}$

(iii) $A = \{3, 6, 9, 12, ...\}$
$B = \{1, 2, 3, 4, 5, 6\}$
$A \cup B = \{1, 2, 3, 6, 9, 12, 15, ...\}$

(iv) $A = \{2, 3, 4, 5, 6\}$
$B = \{7, 8, 9, 10\}$
$A \cup B = \{2, 3, 4, 5, 6, 7, 8, 9, 10\}$

(v) $A = \{1, 2, 3\}$
$B = \phi$
$A \cup B = \{1, 2, 3\}$

2. **(i)** $A \cup B = \{1, 2, 3, 4, 5, 6\}$
(ii) $A \cup C = \{1, 2, 3, 4, 5, 6, 7, 8\}$
(iii) $B \cup C = \{3, 4, 5, 6, 7, 8\}$
(iv) $B \cup D = \{3, 4, 5, 6, 7, 8, 9, 10\}$
(v) $\{1, 2, 3, 4, 5, 6, 7, 8\}$
(vi) $\{1, 2, 3, 4, 5, 6, 7, 8, 9, 10\}$
(vii) $\{3, 4, 5, 6, 7, 8, 9, 10\}$

3. **(i)** $A - B = \{3, 6, 9, 15, 18, 21\}$
(ii) $A - C = \{3, 9, 15, 18, 21\}$
(iii) $A - D = \{3, 6, 9, 12, 18, 21\}$
(iv) $B - A = \{4, 8, 16, 20\}$
(v) $C - A = \{2, 4, 8, 10, 16\}$
(vi) $D - A = \{5, 10, 20\}$
(vii) $B - C = \{20\}$
(viii) $B - D = \{4, 8, 12, 16\}$
(ix) $C - B = \{2, 6, 10\}$
(x) $D - B = \{5, 10, 15\}$
(xi) $C - D = \{2, 4, 6, 8, 12, 16\}$
(xii) $D - C = \{5, 15, 20\}$

4. By the question; $3N = \{3x : x \in \mathbb{N}\}$
$3N = \{3, 6, 9, 12, \ldots\}$
Similarly $7N = \{7, 14, 21, \ldots\}$
$3N \cap 7N = \{21, 42, 63, ...\} = 21N$

5. By Venn - Diagram

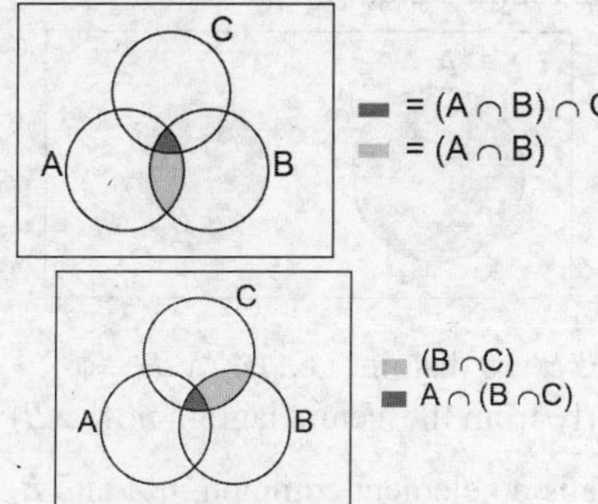

By both the Venn-diagrams $A \cap (B \cap C) = (A \cap B) \cap C$

6. **(a)** By Venn-diagram

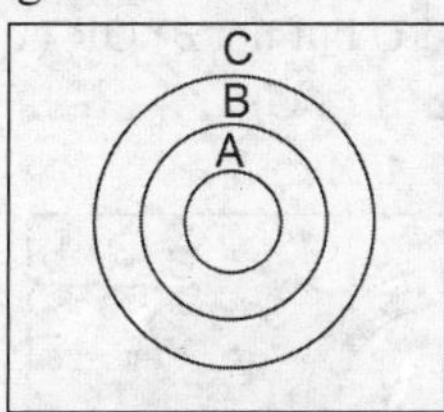

$A \subset B;\ B \subset C$, then $(A \subset C)$

(b) Proceed as done in above question by Venn-diagram
Let $A = \{1, 2, 3, 4, 5\};\ B = \{2, 3, 6\}$
$A \cap B = \{2, 3\} \subset A$
$(A \cup B) = \{1, 2, 3, 4, 5, 6\}$
$A = \{1, 2, 3, 4, 5\}$
Clearly $A \subset (A \cup B)$
Thus, $A \cap B \subset B \subset A \cup B$
Similarly $A \cap B \subset B \subset A \cup B$

(c) $A \cap X = B \cap X = \phi$
$\Rightarrow$ A and X are disjoint
$\Rightarrow$ B and X are disjoint
Also $A \cup X = B \cup X$
$\Rightarrow$ $n(A) + n(X) - n(A \cap X) = n(B) + n(X) - n(B \cap X)$
$\Rightarrow$ $n(A) = n(B)$
$\Rightarrow$ Numbers of elements in A and B are equal.

7. **(a)** $(A')'$; let U be the universal set $(A')' = U - A'$

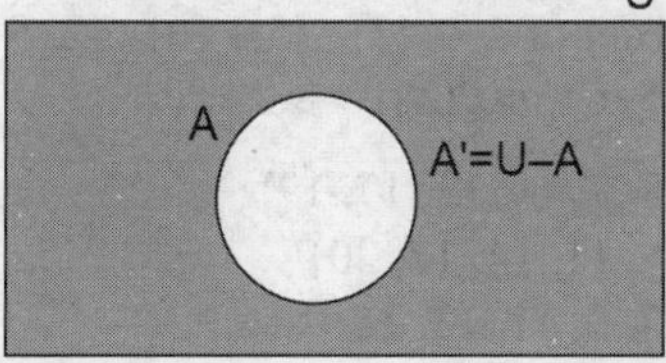

$= U - (U - A) = A$
Thus $(A')' = A$

(b) $A \cup A' = A \cup (U - A)$ {U is the universal set}
By the Venn diagram given in the previous question)
$A \cup A' = x \in A$ or $x \in U - A = x \in U$
$A \cup A' = U$

(c) $(A - B) \cap A$

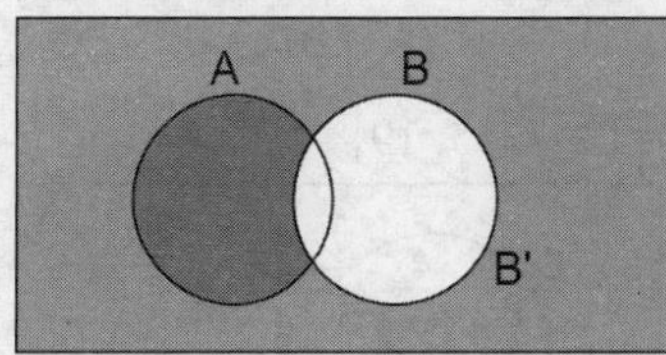

By Venn-diagram $(A - B) \cap A = A - B$
$(A \cap B') = x$ such that $x \in A$ and x does not belong to B
$= A - B$
Hence $(A - B) \cap A = A \cap B'$

(d) $A \cap (B \Delta C)$

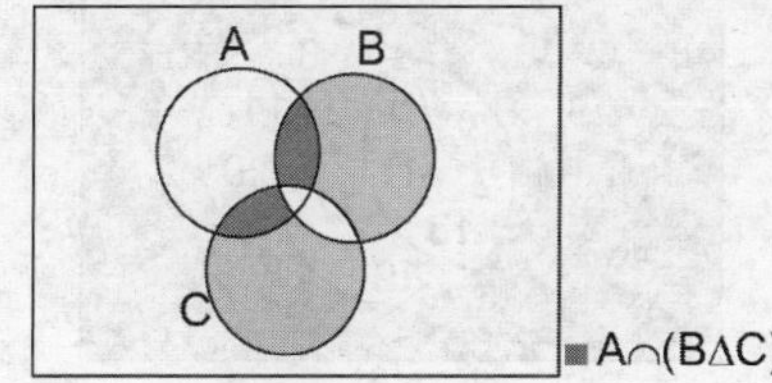

$A \cap (B \,\Delta\, C)$ contains x such that

$= (x \in A$ and C but not $B)$ OR $(x \in A$ and B but not $C)$

$= (A \cap B) \,\Delta\, (A \cap C)$

(e) $C - B \subset C - A,\ A \subset B$

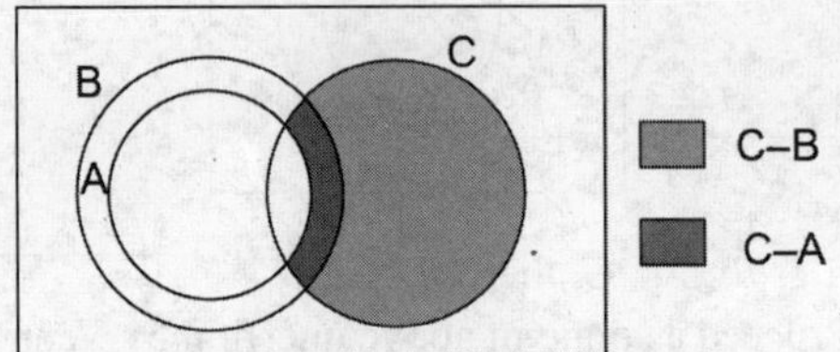

By the Venn - diagram if $x \in C - B$ then $x \in C - A$

$\Rightarrow\ C - B \subset C - A$ if $A \subset B$

8. $A = \{4, 3\}$; $B = \{2, 3, 4, 5, 6\}$

(a) $A \subset B$

(b) $B - A = \{2, 5, 6\}$

(c) $A \cup B = \{2, 3, 4, 5, 6\} = B$

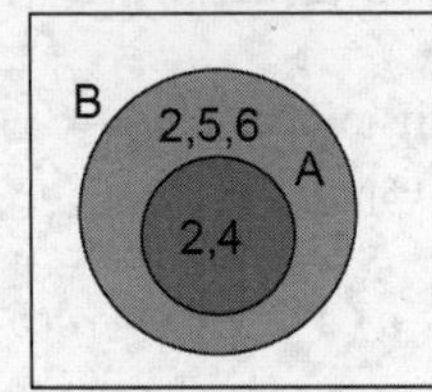

$A - B = \phi$

$A \cap B = \{3, 4) = A$

(d) $X = B - A = \{2, 5, 6\}$

All subset of $X = \{2\}, \{5\}, \{6\}, \{2, 5\}, \{2, 6\}, \{5, 6\}$, ϕ, $\{2, 5, 6\}$, $n(P(X)) = 8$

9. $A = \{2, 3, 5, 7, 11, 13, 17, 19\}$

$B = \{2, 5, 8, 11, 14, 17, 20\}$

$C = \{3, 5, 7, 9, 11, 13, 15\}$

(a) $\{2, 3, 5, 7, 11, 13, 17, 19, 8, 14, 20\}$

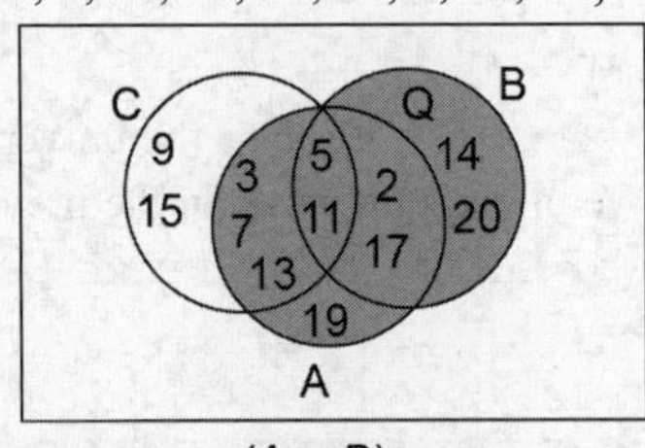

(A ∪ B)

(b) $A - B = \{3, 7, 13, 19\}$

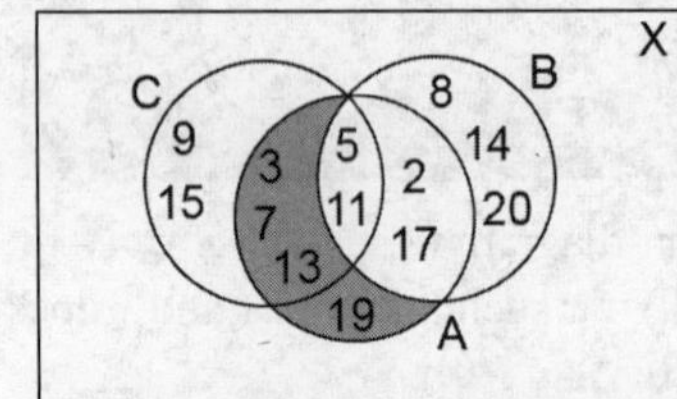

(c) $\overline{A \cup B} = \{1,9,15\}$

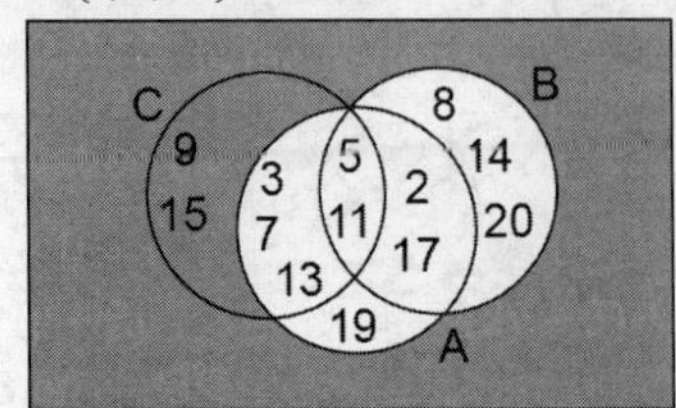

(d) $\bar{B} \cup \bar{C}$

$\bar{B} = \{1,3,7,9,13,15,19\}$

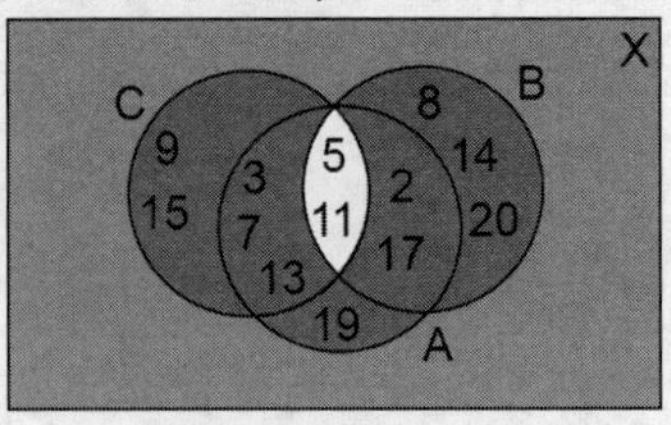

$\bar{B} \cup \bar{C}$

$\bar{B} \cup \bar{C} = \{1, 2, 3, 7, 8, 9, 13, 14, 15, 17, 19, 20\}$

(e) $(A \cap B \cap C) = \{5, 11\}$

$(A \cap B \cap \bar{C}) = \{2,17\}$

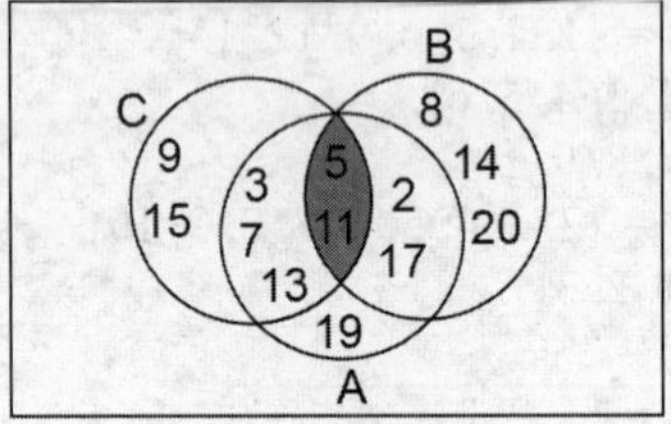

(A ∩ B ∩ C)

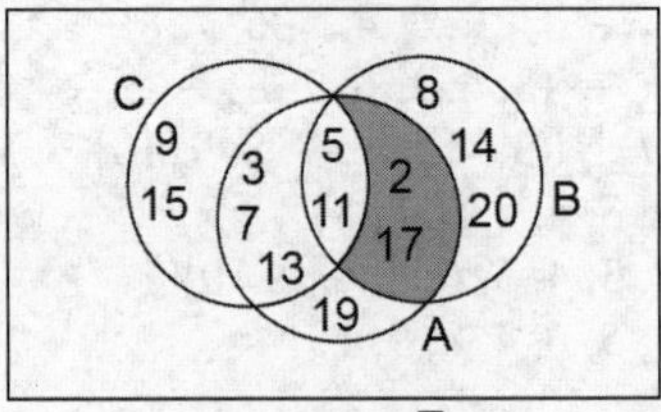

(A ∩ B ∩ $\bar{C}$)

10. **(a)** Clearly, unshaded region contains those elements which are in A but neither in B nor in C i.e., $A \cap (B \cup C)^C$

(b) Clearly, unshaded region contains those elements which are in A or both in B and C as well i.e., $A \cup (B \cap C)$

TEXTUAL EXERCISE–3: (OBJECTIVE)

1. **(b)** $A = \{1, 2, 3\}$; $B = \{3, 4\}$; $C = \{4, 5, 6\}$; $(B \cap C) = \{4\}$; $A \cup (B \cap C) = \{1, 2, 3, 4\}$

2. **(c)** $N_a = \{a_n : n \in \mathbb{N}\}$

$N_6 = \{6, 12, 18, 24, \ldots..\}$

$N_8 = \{8, 16, 24, \ldots.\}$

$N_6 \cap N_8 = \{24, 48, \ldots.\} = N_{24}$

3. **(c)** In the Venn diagram given below

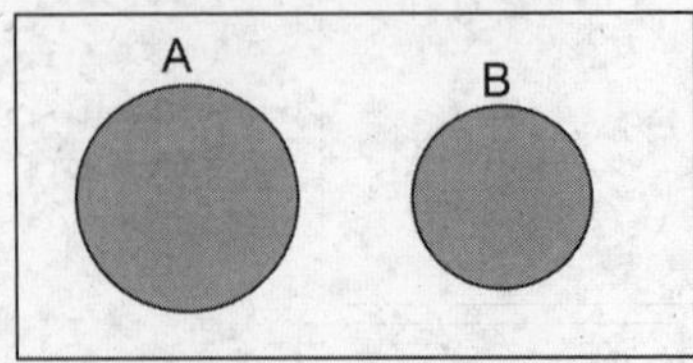

A and B are disjoint i.e., $(A \cap B) = \phi$

Clearly from the Venn diagram $n(A \cup B) = n(A) + n(B)$

4. **(d)** There is no element common in A and B

$\Rightarrow\ (A \cap B) = \phi$

5. **(d)** A: is the set defined by qualitative behaviors. Hence it is not a set.

6. **(b)** According to transitive a R b, b R c
$\Rightarrow a R c \quad \Rightarrow A \subset C$

7. **(c)** The set C is defined qualitatively. Hence it is not a well defined collection $\Rightarrow C$ is not a set

TEXTUAL EXERCISE–6: (SUBJECTIVE)

1. $n(X \cup Y) = n(X) + n(Y) - n(X \cap Y)$ (By Inclusion-Exclusion Principle)
$\Rightarrow n(X \cap Y) = n(X) + n(Y) - n(X \cup Y)$
$\Rightarrow 17 + 23 - 38 = 40 - 38 = 2$

2. $n(X \cup Y) = 18$; $n(X) = 8$; $n(Y) = 15$
Similarly by inclusion-exclusion principle $n(X \cap Y) = n(X) + n(Y) - n(X \cup Y) = 8 + 15 - 18 = 5$

3. **P:** Set of students passed in Physics
M: Set of statements passed in Mathematics
$n(P) = 67$; $n(M) = 55$
S: set of total student $n(S) = 100$
Assuming no student fails in both the subjects $n(S) = n(P \cup M)$
By inclusion-exclusion principle; $n(P \cup M) = n(P) + n(M) - n(P \cap M)$
$\Rightarrow n(P \cap M) = 67 + 55 - 100 = 22$
Number of students passed in physics only $= n(P) - n(P \cap M) = 67 - 22 = 45$

4. **(a)** $n(A) = 30$; $n(B) = 36$
$A \subset B$
$(A \cup B) = B$
$n(A \cup B) = n(B) = 36$
$A \cap B = A$
$n(A \cap B) = n(A) = 30$
(b) $n(A) = 30$, $n(A \cup B) = 50$, $n(A \cap B) = 10$
$n(A \cup B) = n(A) + n(B) - n(A \cap B)$ by inclusion – exclusion principle
$n(B) = n(A \cup B) + n(A \cap B) - n(A) = 50 + 10 - 30 = 30.$
(c) $n(A) = 20$; $n(A' \cap B) = 8$

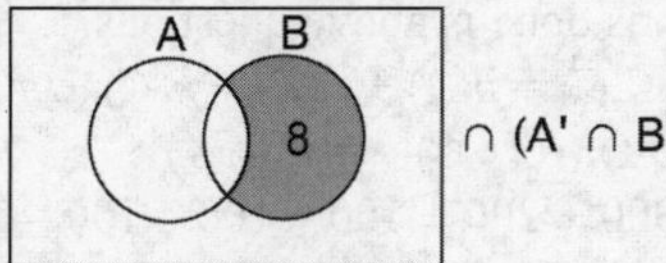

By Venn-diagram $n(A \cup B) = n(A) + n(A' \cap B) = 20 + 8 = 28$
(d) $n(A - B) = 30$; $n(B - A) = 16$; $n(A \cup B) = 60$

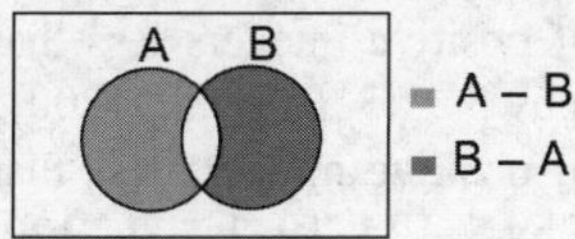

Clearly from Venn-Diagram $n(A \cup B) = n(A - B) + (B - A) + n(A \cap B)$
$\Rightarrow n(A \cap B) = n(A \cup B) - n(A - B) - n(B - A) = 60 - 30 - 16 = 14$

(e) $n(A) = 58$; $n(B) = 102$; $n(A - B) = 38$
$n(A \cap B) = n(A) - n(A - B) = 58 - 38 = 20$
By inclusion exclusion principle $n(A \cup B) = n(A) + n(B) - n(A \cap B)$
$= 58 + 120 - 20 = 102 + 38 = 140$
(f) $n(A \cap \bar{B}) = 27$; $n(A) = 40$; $n(B) = 50$
By Venn-diagram, $n(A \cap \bar{B}) + n(B) = n(A \cup B) = 27 + 50$

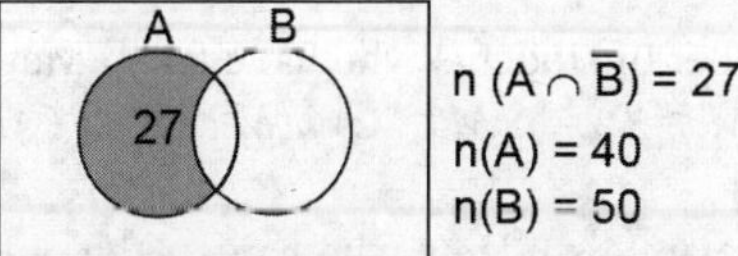

$n(A \cup B) = 77$, but $n(S) = 70$
This is not possible, hence information is incorrect.

5. **P:** set of consumers who liked product P.
Q: set of consumers who liked product Q.
$n(P \cup Q) = 2000$ {for minimum value of $n(P \cap Q)$}
$n(P) = 1500$; $n(Q) = 1800$
$n(P \cap Q) = n(P) + n(Q) - n(P \cup Q) = 1500 + 1800 - 2000 = 1300$

6. By inclusion-exclusion principle
$n((A \cup B) \cup C) = - n(A \cup B) + n(C) - n((A \cup B) \cap C)$
$= n(A) + n(B) - n(A \cap B) + n(C) - n((A \cup B) \cap C) = n((A \cup B) \cap C) = n(A \cap C) \cup n(B \cap C)$
$= n(A) + n(B) + n(C) - n(A \cap B) - n(B \cap C) - n(C \cap A) + n(A \cap B \cap C)$
$= [n(A) + n(B) + n(C) + n(A \cap B \cap C)] - [n(A \cap B) + n(B \cap C) + n(C \cap A)]$

7. **f:** Set of medals awarded in Football; B: Set of medals awarded in Basketball; C: Set of medals awarded to Cricket
$n(f) = 38$; $n(B) = 15$; $n(C) = 20$
By the question, $n(f \cup B \cup C) = 58$; $n(f \cap B \cap C) = 3$

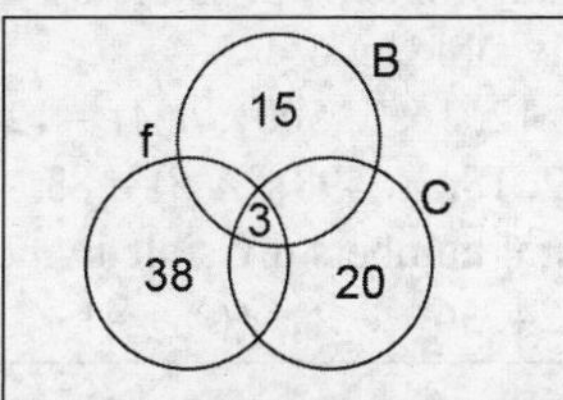

By previous question, $n(A \cup B \cup C) = n(A) + n(B) + n(C) + n(A \cap B \cap C) - n(A \cap B) - n(B \cap C) - n(C - A)$
Similarly $n(f \cap B) + n(f \cap C) + n(B \cap C) = n(f) + n(B) + n(C) + n(f \cap B \cap C) - n(f \cap B \cup C) = 38 + 15 + 20 + 3 - 58 = 76 - 58 = 18$
But this included those men also whose get medals in are the three sports.
Minimum who received medals in only two of the three sports $= 18 - (3 \times 3) = 9$

8. **M:** Set of students who have taken Maths; **C:** Set of students who have taken Chemistry;
P: Set of students who have taken Physics
By the question, $n(M) = 15$; $n(P) = 12$; $n(C) = 11$; $n(M \cap C) = 5$; $n(M \cap P) = 9$; $n(P \cap C) = 4$; $n(M \cap P \cap C) = 3$

(a) By Venn diagram

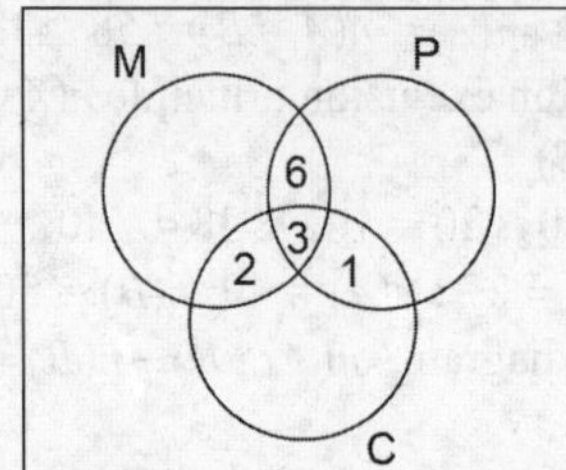

Number of students who have taken Maths only = $n(M) - n(M \cap P) - n(M \cap C)\ n(M \cap P \cap C) = 15 - 9 - 5 + 3 = 4$

There are 4 students who have taken only Maths

(b) Number of students who have taken only Physics = $n(P) - n(P \cap M) - n(P \cap C) + n(M \cap P \cap C) = 12 - 9 - 4 + 3 = 2$

2 students have taken only Physics.

(c) Number of students who have taken only chemistry = $n(C) - n(P \cap C) - n(M \cap C) - n(P \cap C \cap M) = 11 - 4 - 5 + 3 = 5$

There are five students who took my chemistry

(d) Number of students who took physics, chemistry but not Maths = $n(P \cap C) - n(M \cap P \cap C) = 4 - 3 = 1$

(e) Number of students who took Maths, physics but not chemistry = $n(M \cap P) - n(M \cap P \cap C) = 9 - 3 = 6$

(f) Only one subject = Number of students with only Maths + only chemistry + only physics = 5 + 2 + 4 = 11

(g) At least one of the three subjects = $n(M \cup C \cup P) = n(M) + n(C) + n(P) + n(M \cap P \cap C) - n((P \cap C) - n(C \cap M) - n(P \cap M)$

= 15 + 12 + 11 – 5 – 9 – 4 + 3 = 23

(h) None of the subjects = 25 – 23 = 2

There are two students who took none of the three subjects

9. **A:** Set of natural numbers divisible by 4; *B:* Set of natural numbers divisible by 6.

$A = \{4, 8, 12, 16, ...,500\}$; $n(A) = 125$

$B = \{6, 12, 18, ... 498\}$; $n(B) = 83$

C: Set of natural numbers divisible by both 4, 6

$C = \{12, 24, 36, ...\}$; $n(C) = 41$

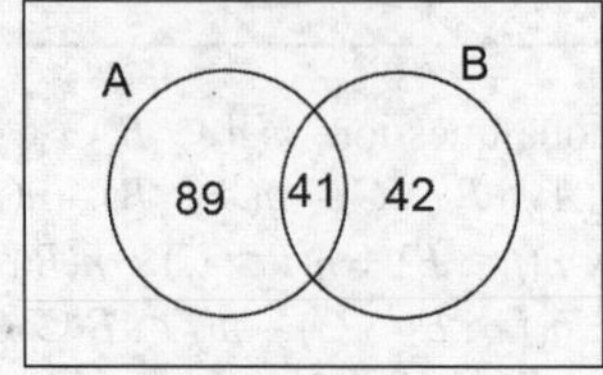

(a) Numbers divisible by 4 and 6 both $n(A \cap B) = 41$

(b) Either 4 or 6

$n(A \cup B) = n(A) + n(B) - n(A \cap B) = 125 + 83 - 41 = 167$

(c) Divisible by 5 but not by 6; $n(A - B) = 84$

(d) Divisible by 6 but not by 4; $n(B - A) = 42$

(e) Numbers divisible by neither 4 nor by 6

$500 - n(A \cup B) = 500 - 167 = 333$

10. **A:** Set of numbers divisible by 2; **B:** Set of numbers divisible by 3; **C:** Set of numbers divisible by 5

$A = \{2, 4, 6, ...,300\}$; $n(A) = 150$; $B = \{3, 6, 9, 12, ...,300\}$; $n(B) = 100$; $C = \{5, 10, 15, ... 300\}$; $n(C) = 60$

Number of natural numbers less than or equal 300 which are divisible by 2 and 3 = {6, 12, ... 300) = 50

Number of natural numbers less than or equal to 300 which are divisible by 2 and 5 = {10, 20, ... 300} = 30

Number of natural numbers less than or equal to 300 which are divisible by 3 and 5 = {5, 30, 45, 300} = 20

Number of natural numbers less than or equal to 300 which are divisible by 2, 3 and 5

= {30, 60, 90, 120, 150, 180, 210, 240, 270, 300} = 10

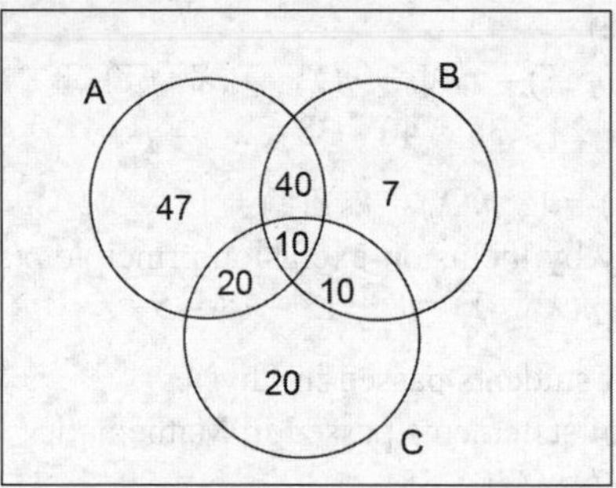

Numbers divisible either by 2 or 3 or 5 = $n(A \cup B \cup C) = n(A) + n(B) + n(C) + n(A \cap B \cap C) + n(A \cap B \cap C) - n(A \cap B) - n(B \cap C) - n(A \cap C)$

= 150 + 100 + 60 + 10 – 30 – 20 – 50 = 220

Thus there are 220 numbers less than or equal to 300 which are divisible by either 2, 3, or 5.

11. $S = \{1, 2, 3, ..., 1200\}$

(i) Either of 3, 4, 6

A = divisible by 3 = {3, 6, 9, 12, ..., 1200}; B = divisible by 4 = {4, 8, 12, ..., 1200}; C = divisible by 6 = {6, 12, 18, ..., 1200}

$n(A) = 400$; $n(B) = 300$; $n(C) = 200$

Divisible by 3 and 4 = {12, 24, 36, ..., 1200} = 100 numbers

Divisible by 3 and 6 = {6, 12, 18, ..., 1200} = 200 numbers.

Divisible by 6 and 4 = {12, 24, ..., 1200} = 100 numbers.

Divisible by 3, 4 and 6 = {12, 24, ..., 1200} = 100 numbers.

Similarly as done is above questions.

$n(A \cup B \cup C) = n(A) + n(B) + n(C) + n(A \cap B \cap C) - n(A \cap B) - n(B \cap C) - n(C \cap A)$

= 400 + 300 + 200 + 100 – 100 – 100 – 200 = 600

(ii) Produces done in above questions

(iii) Neither of 2, 3, 5.

A: Set of positive integers less than or equal to 1200 divisible by 2 = {2, 4, 6, 8, ..., 1200}; $n(A) = 600$

B: Set of positive integers less than or equal to 1200 divisible by 3 = {3, 6, 9, ..., 1200}; $n(B) = 400$

C: Set of positive integers less than or equal to 1200 divisible by 5 = {5, 10, 15, ..., 1200}; $n(C) = 240$

Numbers less than or equal to 1200 divisible by 2 and 3 = 200

Numbers less than or equal to 1200 divisible by 3 and 5 = 80

Numbers less than or equal to 1200 divisible by 5 and 2 = 120

Numbers less than or equal to 1200 divisible by 30 = 40

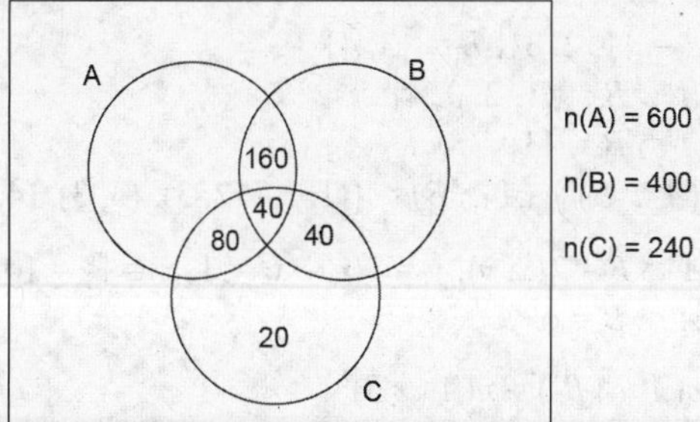

$n(A \cup B \cup C) = n(A) + n(B) + n(C) + n(A \cap B \cap C) - n(A \cap B) - n(B \cap C) - n(A \cap C)$

$= 600 + 400 + 240 + 40 - 200 - 80 - 120 = 880$

Neither of 2, 3, 5 = $1200 - n(A \cup B \cup C) = 1200 - 880 = 320$

12. $A = \{1, 2, 3, 4, 5, 6\}$; $B = \{-2, -1, 0, 1, 2, 3\ 4\}$

$A \times B = \{(1, -2), (1, -1), (1, 0), (1, 1), (1, 2), (1, 3), (1, 4), (2, -2), (2, -1), (2, 0), (2, 1), (2, 3), (2, 4), (3, -2), (3, -1), (3, 0), (3, 1), (3, 2), (3, 3), (3, 4), (4, -2), (4, -1), (4, 0), (4, 1), (4, 2), (4, 3), (4, 4), (5, -2), (5, -1), (5, 0), (5, 1), (5, 2), (5, 3), (5, 4), (6, -2), (6, -1), (6, 0), (6, 1), (6, 2), (6, 3), (6, 4)\}$

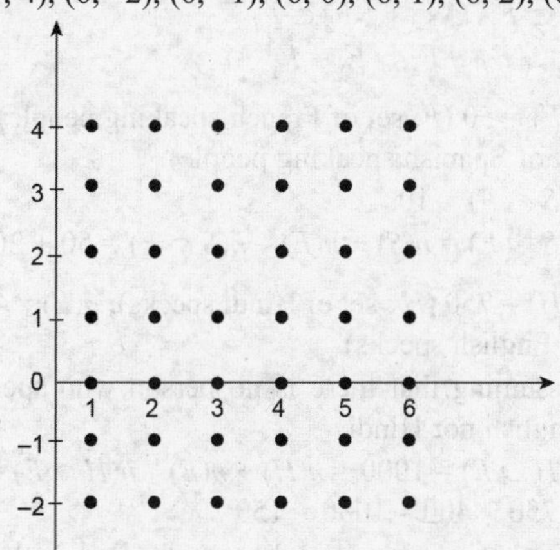

Graphical representation of A × B

Similarly $B \times A = \{(-2, 1), (-2, 2), \ldots\ldots, (-2, 6)$
$(-1, 1), (-1, 2), \ldots\ldots, (-1, 6)$
: : : : : :
: : : : : :
$(4, 1), (4, 2) \ldots\ldots(4, 6)$

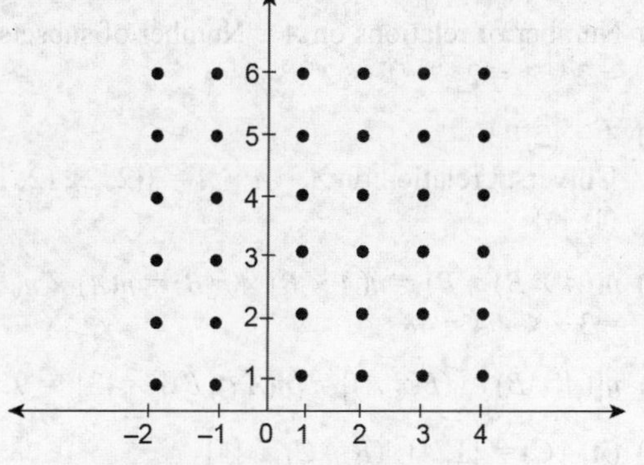

graphical representation of B × A

Number of elements common in $(A \times B)$ and $(B \times A) = (n(A \cap B))^2 = (4)^2 = 16$

13. $A = [-1, 5]$; $B = \{0, 1, 2, 3, 4, 5, 6\}$

$A \times B = \{\{(x, y): x \in [-1, 5] \text{ and } y \in \{0, 1, 2, 3, 4, 5, 6\}\}$

= Set of 7 horizontal line segments $y = 0, y = 1, y = 2, \ldots, y = 6$ with left end at $x = -1$ right end at $x = 5$

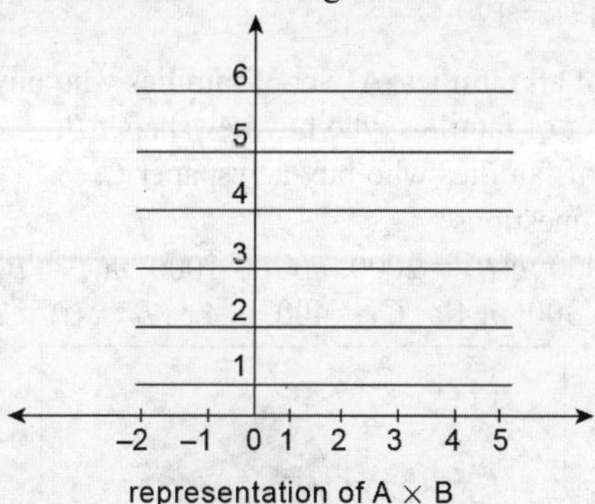

representation of A × B

$B \times A = \{x, y) : x \in \{0, 1, 2, 3, 4, 5, 6\}$ and $y \in [-1, 5]\}$

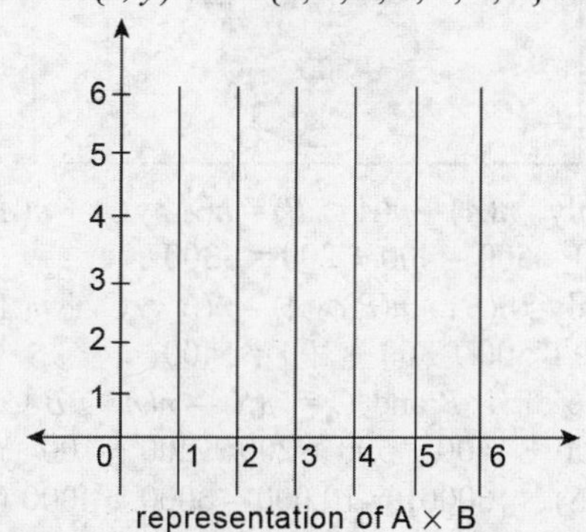

representation of A × B

Number of elements common to $(B \times A)$ and $(A \times B) = [n(A \cap B)]^2 = (7)^2 = 49$

Now if $b \in \mathbb{R}$; $B = [0, 6]$

$A \times B = \{(x, y): x \in [-1, 5] \text{ and } y \in [0, 6]\}$

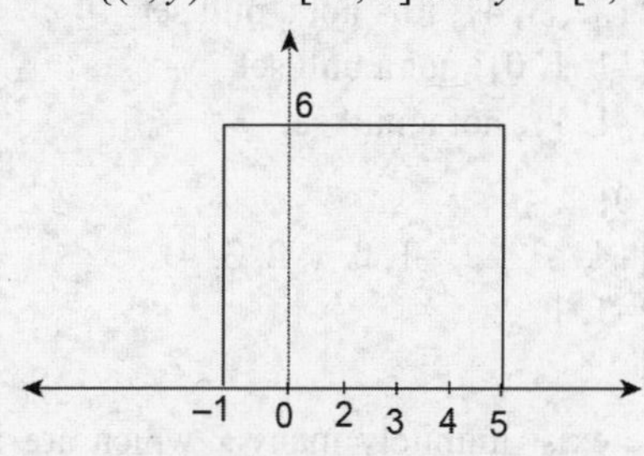

representation of B × A

Similarly proceed for $B \times A$

14. **A:** The set of natural numbers less than 300 divisible by 2

B: The set of natural numbers less than 300 divisible by 7

C: The set of natural numbers less than 300 divisible by both 2 and 7

$n(A) = 150; n(B) = 42; n(C) = 21$

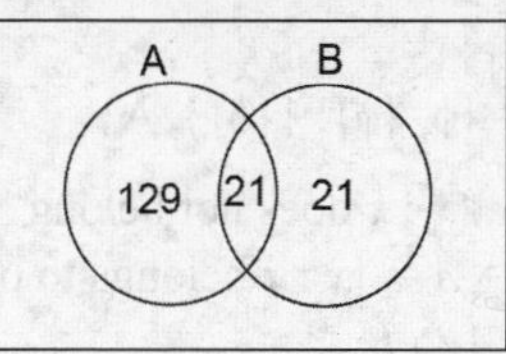

(a) Divisible by 2 and 7 both: 21

(b) Divisible by 2 or 7: $n(A \cup B) = n(A) + n(B) - n(A \cap B)$ $= 150 + 42 - 21 = 171$

(c) Divisible by 2 but not 7: $n(A - B) = 129$ (by Venn-diagram)

(d) Neither divisible by 2 nor by 7 : $300 - n(A \cup B) = 300 - 171 = 129$

15. S: Set of all families; A: Set of families who buy newspaper A; B: Set of families who buy newspaper B;
C: Set of families who buy newspaper C.
By the questions
$n(A)$ 4000; $n(B) = 2000$; $n(C) = 1000$; $n(A \cap B) = 500$; $n(B \cap C) = 300$; $n(A \cap C) = 400$; $n(A \cap B \cap C) = 200$

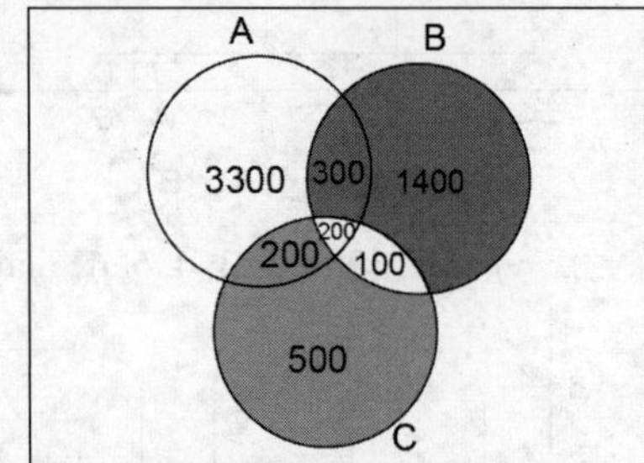

(i) A only : $n(A) - n(A \cap B) - n(A \cap C) + n(A \cap B \cap C) =$ $4000 - 500 - 400 + 200 = 3300$

(ii) B only : $n(B) - n(B \cap A) - n(B \cap C) + n(A \cap B \cap C) =$ $2000 - 500 - 300 + 200 = 1400$

(iii) None of A, B and $C = n(S) - n(A \cup B \cup C) = n(S) -$ $\{3300 + 1400 + 500 + 200 + 200 + 100 + 300\}$ $= n(S) - \{6000\} = 10{,}000 - 6000 = 4000$ families.

TEXTUAL EXERCISE–4: (OBJECTIVE)

1. (a) **(a)** ϕ; it is a null set
(b) $\{1, 2, 3, 4\}$; it is not a null set
(c) $\{-1, 1, 0\}$; not a null set
(d) $\{-1, 1\}$; not a null set

2. (a) **(a)** $\{0\}$
(b) $\{-4, -3, -2, -1, 0, 1, 2, 3, 4\}$
(c) $\{-1, 1\}$
(d) ϕ

3. (c) There exist infinitely many x which are irrational and $0.1 < x < 0.101$

4. (a) **(a)** $2^0 = 1$ has only one subset
(b) $2^1 = 2$; has two subjects
(c) $2^2 = 4$; has 4 subjects
(d) $2^1 = 2$ has 2 subjects.

5. (c) $n(P(S)) = 2^3 = 8$ elements.
$n(P(P(S)) = 2^8 = 256$ elements.

6. (c) $A = \{\phi, \{\phi\}\}$
Subjects = $\{\phi, \{\phi\}, \{\{\phi\}\}, A\}$

7. (d) $(A \cap B)^C = \{x : x$ does not belong A and B both$)$
$(A \cap B)^C \cap A = \{x : x$ belongs to only A but not $B)$
$= A - B = A \cap B^C$.

8. (a) $A - (B \cup C)$: {x: x belongs to A but not to B or C} : {x: x belongs to A not B and x belongs to A not C} $= (A - B) \cap (A - C)$

9. (d) $A = \{1, 2, 3\}$; $B = \{3, 4\}$
$A \cup B = \{1, 2, 3, 4\}$
$A \cap B = \{3\}$
$(A \cup B) \times (A \cap B) = \{(1, 3), (2, 3), (3, 3), (4, 3)\}$

10. (c) $A \cap B = \{(x, y): y = 1/x, -x^2 = 1, x \in \mathbb{R} - \{0\}] = \phi$
$\Rightarrow A \cap B = \phi$

11. (c) $n(A' \cap B') = n(A \cup B)'$
$n(A \cup B) = n(A) + n(B) - n(A \cap B)$
$= 200 + 300 - 100 = 400$
$n(A \cup B)' = n(U) - n(A \cup B)$
$= 700 + 400 = 300$

12. (b) $n(A) = 3$; $n(B) = 6$
$n(A \cup B)_{\min} = \max\ \{n(A), n(B)\}$
$= \max\ \{3, 6\} = 6$

13. (c) Let there be N newspapers
$\Rightarrow \dfrac{60 \times N}{5} = 300 \qquad \Rightarrow \quad N = \dfrac{1500}{60} = 25$

14. (b) $F_2 \subset F_1,\ F_3 \subset F_1,\ F_4 \subset F_1$
$\Rightarrow F_2 \cup F_3 \cup F_4 \cup F_1 = F_1$

15. (a) $n(F) = 50$ (F: set of French speaking people); $n(S) = 20$ (S : set of Spanish speaking people)
$n(S \cap F) = 10$
$n(S \cup F) = n(S) + n(F) - n(S \cap F) = 50 + 20 - 10 = 60$

16. (c) $n(H) = 750$ (H : set of Hindi specks); $n(E) = 400$ (E : Set of English specks)
Assuming that there is no person who speaks neither English nor Hindi
$\Rightarrow n(H \cup E) = 1000 = n(H) + n(E) - n(H \cap E) = h(H \cap E)$
$= 750 + 400 - 1000 = 150$
Number of persons who speak Hindi only = $\{750 - 150\} = 600$

17. (c) $A \Delta B = (A - B) \cup (B - A)$
$A = \{i, -i, 1, -1\}$; $\quad B = \{-1, 1\}$
$A \Delta B = \{-i, i\} \cup \phi = \{-i, i\}$

18. (d) $B' - A' = \{x : x$ does not belong to B but to $A\} = A - B$
But $A \subseteq B \qquad \Rightarrow \ A - B = \phi$

19. (a) Number of relations on A = Number of subsets $A \times A$
$= 2^{n(A \times A)} = 2^{n(A)\,.\,n(A)} = 2^{n^2}$

20. (d) $A = \{2, 1\}$
Universal relation on $A = A \times A = \{(2, 2), (2, 1), (1, 2), (1, 1)\}$

21. (b) $n((A \times B) \times B) = n(A \times B) \times n(B) = n(A) \times n(B) \times n(B)$
$= 3 \times 4 \times 4 = 48$

22. (c) $n[(A \times B) \cap (B \times A)] = [n(A \cap B)]^2 = [3]^2 = 9$

23. (b) $(A - C) = \{1, 4\}$; $(B - C) = \{4\}$
$(A - C) \times (B - C) = \{(1, 4), (4, 4)\}$

24. (a) $(A \cup B)' \cup (A' \cap B)$
$\Rightarrow$ $A' \cap B' \cup (A' \cap B)$
$\Rightarrow$ $[U - n(A \cup B)] \cup (B - A) = A'$

25. (c) $\{(A - B) \cup (B - C) \cup (C - A)\}' = (A - B)' \cap (B - C)' \cap (C - A)\}' = [(U - (A - B)) \cap (U - (B - C)) \cap (U - (C - A))]$

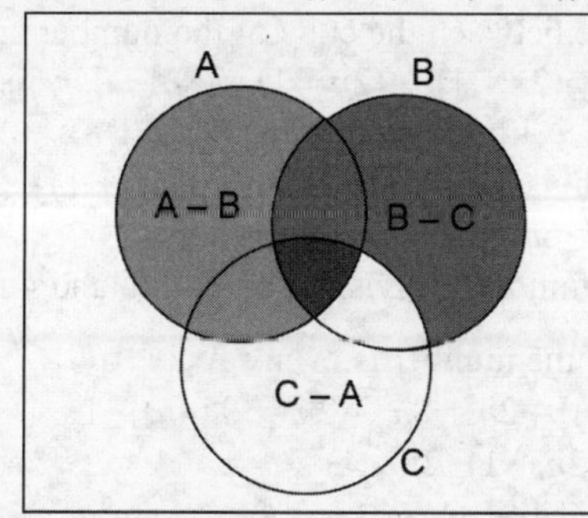

By Venn – diagram = $(A \cap B \cap C)$

26. (b) $(A \cap B) = (A \cap C)$
$\Rightarrow$ $A' \cup B' = A' \cup C'$
Also $A \cup B = A \cup C \Rightarrow B = C$

27. (d) $n(c) = 224$ (c is the set of Cricket players)
$n(h) = 240$ (h is the set of Hockey players)
$n(b) = 336$ (b is the set of Basket ball players)
$n(b \cap h) = 64$; $n(c \cap b) = 80$;
$n(c \cap h) = 40$; $n(c \cap b \cap h) = 24$
$n(c \cup b \cup h) = n(h) + n(c) + n(b) - n(b \cap h) - n(c \cap b) - n(c \cap h) + n(c \cap b \cap h)$
$= 224 + 240 + 336 - 64 - 80 - 40 + 24 = 640$
Boys who played none of the games = $n(c \cup b \cup h)$ = $800 - 640 = 160$

28. (c) Let us consider 100 Indians (who line either apple or cheese)
$n(ch) = 63$ (ch: set of Indians who like cheese); $n(ap) = 76$ (ap: set of Indians who like apple)
$n(ch \cap ap) = n(ch) + n(ap) - n(ch \cup ap) = 63 + 76 - 100 = 139 - 100 = 39$

29. (b) $A = \{4, 8, 12, 16, \ldots\}$; $B = \{5, 12, 18, \ldots\}$
$A \cap B = \{12, 24, 36, \ldots\}$
$\Rightarrow$ $A \cap B = \{x : x \text{ is a multiple of } 12\}$

TEXTUAL EXERCISE–7 (SUBJECTIVE)

1. (a) True; (already proved in Textual Exercise –1)
(b) True; $\{2 - 3 = -1$ does not belong to $\mathbb{N}$, 2/3 does not belong to $\mathbb{N}\}$
(c) False; 2/3 is not an integer
(d) True; $0 + I = I = I + 0$; I is any integer
$1 \times I = I = I \times 1$; I is any integer
(e) False; Multiplicative inverse does not exist in case of integers e.g. M.I. of $5 = \frac{1}{5}$ but $\frac{1}{5} \notin \mathbb{Z}$
(f) True; as given in properties of integers.
(g) False; $2 - 3 \neq 3 - 2$
(h) True; as given in properties of integers.

2. Given, $6k + 5$ is an integer
If $6k + 5$ is divided by 3, then by division algorithm $6k + 5 = 3(2k + 1) + 2 = 3m + 2$ $\{m = 2k + 1\}$
Since, there is a m for every k (both integers) but there may exist m say $m = 4$ for which there is no k (in integers).

3. q is any integer, by division algorithm
$a = 49 + 1$ or $49 + 2$ or $49 + 3$ or 49 (when an integer a is divided by 4)
if $a = 49$; q is even
$= 49 + 2 = 2(29 + 1)$; a is even
$= 49 + 3$; a is odd
$= 49 + 1$; a is odd
Thus, if a is odd, it can be expressed as $49 + 1$, $49 + 3$.

4. Proceed as in question number 4
$a = 69 + 1$ or $69 + 2$ or $69 + 3$ or $69 + 4$ or $69 + 5$ or 69.

5. Let a be any integer if a is divided by 3, then by division algorithm $a = 3b + 1$ or $3b + 2$ or $3b$
Square of a would be $a^2 = ab^2 + 6b + 1 = 3(3b^2 + 6b) + 1 = 3m + 1$; $\{m = 3b^2 + 6b\}$
or $= 9b^2 + 6b + 1 = 3(3b^2 + 6b) + 1 = 3m + 1$ $[m = 3b^2 + 4b + 1]$
or $= 9b^2 = 3m$ $[m = 3b^2]$

6. Let a be any integer, if a is divided by 3, then by division algorithm $a = 3b + 1$ or $3b + 2$ or $3b$
Cube of a can be $a^3 = 27b^3 + 1 + 27b^2 + 9b = 9(3b^3 + b + 3b^2) + 1 = 9m + 1$ $\{m = 3b^2 + b + 3b^2\}$
or $a^3 = 27b^3 + 8 + 54b^2 + 36b = 9(3b^3 + 6b^2 + 4b) + 8 = 9m + 8$ $\{m = 3b^3 + 6b^2 + 4b\}$ or $a^3 = 27b^3 = 9(3b^3) = 9b$ $(m = 3b^3)$
Hence cube a any positive integer is either of the form $9m$ or $9m + 1$ or $9m + 8$.

7. Given x is an integer $x + \frac{1}{x}$ is an integer.
$\Rightarrow$ $\left(x + \frac{1}{x}\right) - x = \frac{1}{x}$ is an integer. {Set of integers is closed over subtraction}
If x is integer $\Rightarrow$ x^n is an integer
$1/x$ is an integer $\Rightarrow$ $\left(\frac{1}{x}\right)^n$ is an integer
$\Rightarrow$ $x^n + \left(\frac{1}{x}\right)^n$ is an integer. {Sum of two integers is an integer}

8. Since x-y is even, there are two possibilities
(i) x, y are both even, say $2p$ and $2q$ respectively
(ii) x, y are both odd, say $2p + 1$ and $2q + 1$ respectively
Case I: $x = 2p$; $y = 2q$
$x - y = 2(p - q)$
$x + y = 2(p + q)$
$\Rightarrow$ $x^2 - y^2 = 4(p^2 - q^2)$; which is divisible by 4
Case II: $x = 2p + 1$; $y = 2q + 1$
$x - y = 2(p - q)$
$x + y = 2(p + q + 1)$
$\Rightarrow$ $x^2 - y^2 = 4(p - q)(p - q + 1)$; which is divisible by 4

9. By division algorithm, an odd number a can be written in the form $a = 2q_1 + 1$ where q_1 is an integer

Now $a^2 = 4a_1 + 1 + 4q_1 = 2(2q_1^2 + 2q) + 1 = 2q_2 + 1$; where $\{q_2 = 2q_1^2 + 2q_1\}$
Hence, square of an odd integer is an odd integer.

10. **Case I:** Integer is odd say $2q + 1$; q is an integer
Square of this number $= 4q^2 + 4q + 1$
Difference between the number and square $= 4q^2 + 4q + 1 - 2q - 1 = 4q^2 + 2q = 2(2q^2 + q)$ which is even.
Case II: Integer is even say $2q$; q is an integer
Square of this number $= 4q^2$
Difference between and square $= 4a^2 - 2q = 2(2a^2 - q)$; which is even
Hence in both the cases the difference between the square of a number and the number is even.

TEXTUAL EXERCISE–8 (SUBJECTIVE)

1. **(a)** We have proved that product of k consecutive integer is always divisible by $k!$
$\Rightarrow$ Product of 2 consecutive integers is divisible by $2! = 2$
$\Rightarrow$ Product of 3 consecutive integers is divisible by $3! = 6$
(b) Produced in part 1
(c) Let one integer be $2q$, the other consecutive even integer would be $2q + 2$
Product $= 2q\,(2q + 2) = 2.2q\,(q + 1) = 2.2.2m = 8$; which is divisible by 8.
(d) Any odd integer shall be of the form $(2q + 1)$
Its square is given by $(2q + 1)^2 = 4q^2 + 1 + 4q = 4q(q + 1) + 1 = 4.2m + 1 = 8m + 1$

2. $n(n + 1)\,(n + 5) = n(n + 1)\,(n + 2 + 3) = n(n + 1)\,(n + 2) + 3n(n + 1)$
$\therefore$ Product of k consecutive integers is divisible by $k!$
$= 6m + 3.2k = 6(m + k)$ which is divisible by 6.

3. $n(n^2 - 1)\,(3n + 2) = n(n + 1)\,(n - 1)\,(4n - (n - 2))$
$= n(n + 1)\,(n - 1).4n - n(n + 1)\,(n - 1)\,(n - 2)$
$= 4n.6m - 24k = 24\,mn - 24k = 24(mn - k)$; which is divisible by 24.

4. Let an integer be n. Successive integer $= n + 1$
Sum of the squares $= n^2 + n^2 + 1 + 2n = 2n^2 + 2n + 1 = 2n(n + 1) + 1 = 4m + 1$
Thus sum of the squares when divided by 4 leaves the remainder 1.

5. $n(n^2 + 5) = n(n^2 + 6 - 1) = n(n^2 - 1) + 6n = n(n - 1)\,(n + 1) + 6n = 6m + 6n = 6(m + n)$; which is divisible by 6

6. Let the middle number be m^2
$\Rightarrow$ $(m^2 - 1)\,m^2\,(m^2 + 1)$ is the required product in the question.
$\Rightarrow$ $(m + 1)(m - 1)m\,.\,m\,(m^2 + 1) = p$
If m is odd
$\Rightarrow (m + 1)$ and $(m - 1)$ both are even $\Rightarrow 4 \mid p$
Similarly if m is even $4 \mid p$ $\quad \Rightarrow 4 \mid p$
$\Rightarrow$ $(m - 1)\,m\,(m + 1)$ is the product of 3 consecutive numbers
$\Rightarrow$ $3 | p$
There are two possibilities
If $5 \mid m \Rightarrow 5 \mid p$
If 5 does not divide m
$P = (m^4 - 1)\,m^2 = (m^{5-1} - 1)\,m^2$; which is divisible by 5
$\Rightarrow p$ is divisible by $5 \times 3 \times 4 = 60$

7. An odd number will be of the form $(2n + 1)$.
Difference between the cube of the number and the number is given by $(2n + 1)^3 - (2n + 1) = (8n^3 + 1 + 6n(2n + 1)) - (2n + 1) = 8n^3 + 12n^2 + 4n = 4(2n^3 + 3n^2 + n)$
$\Rightarrow$ It is divisible by $4 = 4n(2n + 1)\,(n + 1) = 2n(2n + 1)\,(2n + 2) = 6m$ which is divisible by 6
$\therefore$ The number is divisible by both 6 and 4 thus 24.

8. **Case I:** if the number is even say $2n$
$= (2n)^3 - 2n = 8n^3 - 2n = 2n(4n^2 - 1)$
$= 2n(2n + 1)\,(2n - 1)$
Hence divisible by 6
Case II: Already proved in (7) that difference in the cube of a number and the number is divisible by 6, if it is odd.

9. Let us assume that there is such *a* prime number p.
Case I: $p = 6k - 1$, then $p + 2 = 6k + 1$, which may be *a* prime.
But $p + 5 = 6k + 4 = 2(3k + 2)$, which is not a prime.
Case II: $p = 6k + 1$; $p + 2 = 6k + 3 = 3(2k + 1)$, which is not a prime.
$P + 5 = 6k + 6 = 6(k + 1)$, which is not a prime
Hence such a prime number does not exist.

10. Let a leave remainder k, when divided by 6.
$a = 6m + k$; $k \in \{0, 1, 2, 3, 4, 5\}$
By question 8: $a^3 - a = 6p$
$a^3 = 6p + a = 6p + 6m + k = 6(p + m) + k$
Thus both leave the same remainder on division by 6.

11. **Case I:** m is even: $m^n + m = m(m^{n-1} + 1)$. Since m is even, it is also even. $m^n - m = m(m^{n-1} - 1)$ which is even
Case II: m is odd: $m^n + m = m(m^{n-1} + 1)$. Since m is odd m^{n-1} is odd
$\Rightarrow$ $m^{n-1} + 1$ is even.
Hence $m(m^{n-1} + 1)$ is even $m^n - m = m(m^{n-1} - 1)$
Since m is odd m^{n-1} is odd $\Rightarrow m^{n-1} - 1$ is even
Hence, $m(m^{n-1} - 1)$ is even

TEXTUAL EXERCISE–9: (SUBJECTIVE)

1. **(a)** True: $x^{16} - y^{16}$ is divisible by $x - y$
Also $x^{16} - y^{16}$ is divisible by $x + y$
$(x^2)^8 - (4^2)^8$ is divisible by $x^2 + y^2$
(b) True: $x^{2m+1} + y^{2m+1}$ is divisible by $(x + 4)$ as $2m + 1$ is odd.
(c) True: as given by Fermat's theorem
(d) False: 13 is a prime number
$\Rightarrow$ $13|14!$
For 13 to divide $1 + 14!$
$\Rightarrow$ 13 must divide 1, which is not possible.

2. $17 \mid N^{17-1} - 1$ by formats theorem
$17 \mid N^{16} - 1$ $\quad\Rightarrow\ N^{16} = 17n + 1$

Also $17 \mid (N^8 - 1)(N^8 + 1)$
$\Rightarrow$ Either $N^8 - 1 = 17n$ or $N^8 + 1 = 17n$
$\Rightarrow$ $N^8 = 17n \pm 1$
If $(N, 17) \neq 1$ $\Rightarrow N = 17k$
$\Rightarrow$ $N^8 = (17k)^8 = 17n$
$\Rightarrow$ N^8 is either $17n - 1$, $17n$ or $17n + 1$

3. k^{12} if is a factor of 13, then clearly $k^{12} = 13n$
if not, then by Fermet's theorem $k^{12} - 1 = k^{13-1} - 1 = 13n = k^{12} - 13n + 1$
Hence k^{12} is either of the form $12n$ or $12n + 1$.

4. (i) $8^{10} - 1$ is equal to $8^{10} - 1^{10}$ which is divisible by $8 - 1 = 7$
Also $8^{11} - 1$ by Fermert's theorem is divisible by 11.
$8^{10} - 1^{10}$ is divisible by $8 + 1 = 9$ {10 is even}
Hence $8^{10} - 1$ is divisible by 7, $7 \times 11 \times 7 = 693$
(ii) $13^{10} - 5^{10}$ is divisible by $13 - 5 = 8$
Also $P = 13^{11-1} - 1 = 11m$ (Fermat's theorem)
$Q = 5^{11-1} = 11n$ (Fermat's theorem)
$P - Q = 13^{10} - 5^{10} = 11(m - n)$ which is divisible by 11
Hence divisible by $11 \times 8 = 88$

5. $3n^5 + 5n^3 + 7n = 3n^5 + n(5n^2 + 7)$ $\{n^2 - 1 = 3p\}$ $= 3n^5 + n(5(3p + 1) + 7) = 3n^5 + n(15p + 12) = 15np + 3n(n^4 + 4)$
$= 15np + 3n(5q + 5)$ $\{n^4 - 1 = 5q\}$
$= 15np + 15nq + 15$ which is divisible by 15

6. $2\times 7^n + 3 \times 5^n - 5 = 2 \times 7^n - 2 + 3 \times 5^n - 3$
$2(7^n - 1) + 3(5^n - 1) = 2\times 6m + 3\times 4q = 12m + 12q = 12(m + q)$ which is divisible by 12.

7. If n is a prime number greater than 5.
$n^2 - 1$ is divisible by 24
$\Rightarrow$ $n^2 - 1 = 24k$
$n^4 - 1 = (n^2 + 1)(n^2 - 1) = 24k(n^2 + 1)$ it is divisible by 24
$n^2 + 1$; where n is a prime
$n = 6k \pm 1$ thus, $n^2 + 1$ is divisible by 2.
Also $n^4 - 1 = n^{5-1} - 1$ is divisible by 5. (Fermat's theorem)
$\Rightarrow$ $n^4 - 1 = (n^2 + 1)(n^2 - 1)$ is divisible by $2 \times 5 \times 24 = 240$.

8. Let as write it as $11^{n+2} + 12n^{n+1} = 11.11^{n+1} + 144.12^{2n-1} = 11(11^{n+1} + 12^{2n-1}) + 133.12^{2n-1}$
$\Rightarrow$ 133.12^{2n-1} is divisible by 133
$\Rightarrow$ $11(11^{n+1} + 12^{2n-1})$ is divisible by 133

9. $1^n + 8^n - 3^n - 6^n = 1^n - 6^n + 8^n - 3^n = 8^n - 3^n - (6^n - 1^n) = 5m - 5p = 5(m - p)$
$\therefore$ Thus it is divisible by 5.
Also $1^n + 8^n - 3^n - 6^n = (8^n - 6^n) - (3^n - 1^n) = 2k - 2q = 2(k - q)$
$\therefore$ Thus it is divisible by 2
Since the number is divisible by both 2 and 5, hence 10.

10. Let the first integer be m; $m(m + 1)(m + 2)(m + 3) + 1 = n^2$
$\Rightarrow$ $(m^2 + 3m)(m^2 + 3m + 2)$
$\Rightarrow$ $p(p + 2)$ (where $p = m^2 + 3m$)
$\Rightarrow$ $p^2 + 2p$
$\Rightarrow$ $(p + 1)^2 - 1$ (which is a perfect square an addition of 1)

11. By the question m, $(m + 1)^2$, $(m + 2)^3$
$\Rightarrow$ $m + (m + 1)^2 + (m + 2)^3$
The square root is $m + m + 1 + m + 2$
$\Rightarrow$ $(m + m + 1 + m + 2)^2 = m + (m + 1)^2 + (m + 2)^3$
$\Rightarrow$ $(3m + 3)^2 = m^2 + m^2 + 1 + 2m + m^3 + 8 + 6m^2 + 12m$
$\Rightarrow$ $9m^2 + 18m + 9 = 8m^2 + m^3 + 14m + 9$
$\Rightarrow$ $m^3 - m^2 - 4m = 0$
Solution are $m = 0$, $m = 3$, $m = -1$
$\Rightarrow$ Integers are 3, 4, 5

12. $13 | 2^{70} + 3^{70}$
$\Rightarrow$ $2^{70} + 3^{70} = (2^{12})^5.2^{10} + (3^{12})^5.3^{10}$
$\Rightarrow$ $2^{12} - 1$ is divisible by 13
$\Rightarrow$ $3^{12} - 1$ is divisible by 13
$\Rightarrow$ $13 = 2^2 + 3^2$ divides $2^{70} + 3^{70}$

13. $2^{2n} - 1 = 4^n - 1^n$ which is divisible by $4 - 1 = 3$.
$\therefore$ if $2^{2n} - 1$ is divisible by 3
$\Rightarrow$ $2^{2n} - 1 + 3 = 2^{2n} + 2$ is divisible by 3.
$\Rightarrow$ $2(2^{2n-1} + 1)$ is divisible by 3
$\Rightarrow$ $2^{2n-1} + 1$ is divisible by 3
Hence both $2^{2n} - 1$ and $2^{2n-1} + 1$ are divisible by 3, hence proved.

14. Which can be written as $10^n - 1 + 3.4^{n+2} + 6 = 10^n - 1 + 6(2^{2n+3} + 1)$
Using standard rule of divisibility as $2n + 3$ is odd
$= 9k + 6.3k' = 9k + 9.2k' = 9(k + 2k')$; which is always divisible by 9.

15. By Fermat's theorem $n^6 - 1$ is divisible by 7, also $n^2 - 1$ is divisible by 3
$\Rightarrow$ $n^6 - 1$ is also divisible by 3
$\Rightarrow$ $n^6 - 1$ is divisible by 21 and n is a prime number, $(n > 3 \neq 7)$
$\Rightarrow$ $n^2 - 1$ is divisible by 8
$\Rightarrow$ $n^6 - 1$ is divisible by 168.

TEXTUAL EXERCISE–10: (SUBJECTIVE)

1. (a) $420 = 2 \times 2 \times 3 \times 5 \times 7 = 2^2 \times 3 \times 5 \times 7$
Number of divisors: $(2 + 1)(2)(2)(2) = 12(2) = 24$ divisors
(b) $360 = 2^3 \times 5 \times 3^2$
Number of divisors $= (3 + 1)(2 + 1)(2) = 4.3.2 = 24$ divisors
(c) $1008 = 2^4 \times 3^2 \times 7$
Number of divisors $= (4 + 1)(2 + 1)(2) = 5.3.2 = 30$ divisors
(d) $1200 = 2^3 \times 3^2 \times 5^2$
Number of divisors $= (3 + 1)(2 + 1)(2 + 1) = 36$ divisors.

2. (a) $q^2.p$
Number of divisors $= (2 + 1)(2) = 6$ divisors
Sum of divisors $= (p^0 + p^1)(q^0 + q^1 + q^2) = (1 + p)(1 + q + q^2)$
(b) $q^3.p^2$
Number of divisors $= (3 + 1)(2 + 1) = 4 \times 3 = 12$ divisors
Sum of divisors $= (p^0 + p^1 + p^2)(q^0 + q^1 + q^2 + q^3) = \left[\frac{1 - p^3}{1 - p}\right]\left[\frac{1 - q^4}{1 - q}\right]$

(c) $180 = 2^2 \times 3^2 \times 5$
Number of divisors = (3).(3) (2) = 18 divisors.
Sum of divisors = $(1 + 2 + 2^2)(1 + 3 + 3^2)(1 + 5) = (7)(13)(6) = 546$.

(d) $216 = 2^3 \times 3^3$
Number of divisors = (3 + 1) (3 + 1) = 16 divisors
Sum of divisors = $(1 + 2 + 2^2 + 2^3)(1 + 3 + 3^2 + 3^3)$
$= (1 + 2 + 4 + 8)(1 + 3 + 9 + 27) = (15)(40) = 600$

3. (a) $216 = 2^3 \times 3^3$
Number of even proper divisors
Even divisors are of type $2^{a+1}.3^b$; *a, b, c* are non-negative non - negative integers
$3 \times 4 = 12$
Even proper divisors = 12 – 1 = 11 (excluding itself)
Sum of even divisors = $(2^1 + 2^2 + 2^3)(3^0 + 3^1 + 3^2 + 3^3)$
$= (2 + 4 + 8)(1 + 3 + 9 + 27) = (14)(40) = 560$
Sum of even proper divisors = 560 – 216 = 344.

(b) $1080 = 2^3 \times 3^3 \times 5$
Even divisors are of type $2^{a+1}.3^b.5^c$; where *a, b, c* are non-negative integers.
Number of even divisors = 3 × 4 ×2 = 24
Number of even proper divisors = 24 – 1 = 23
Number of even divisors = $(2^1 + 2^2 + 2^3)(3^0 + 3^1 + 3^2 + 3^3)(5^0 + 5^1) = 560 \times 6 = 3360$
Sum of even proper divisors = 3360 – 1080 = 2280

4. (a) $180 = 2^2 \times 3^2 \times 5$
5 is the least integer which can be multiplied by the number to make to a perfect square
Such that $2^2 \times 3^2 \times 5^2$ = a perfect square.

(b) $420 = 2^2 \times 3 \times 5 \times 7$
Least integer multiplier to make it a perfect square = 3 × 5 × 7 = 105
Such that $420 \times 3 \times 5 \times 7 = (2)^2 \times (3)^2 \times (5)^2 \times (7)^2$ which is a perfect square.

(c) $10500 = 2 \times 2 \times 3 \times 5 \times 5 \times 5 \times 7$
Least integer multiplier to make it a perfect square 3 × 5 × 7 = 105
Such that $10500 \times 3 \times 5 \times 7 = (2)^2 \times (3)^2 \times (5)^2 \times (7)^2$

5. (a) $x = 8064 = 2^7 \times 3^2 \times 7$
Number of positive integer divisors = (7 + 1) (2 + 1) (1 + 1) = 8 × 3 × 2 = 48 divisors.

(b) Even natural divisors are of the form $2^{a+1}.3^b.7^c$
Number of even natural divisors = (7 × 3 × 2) = 42 divisors
Sum of even natural divisors = $(2 + 2^2 + 2^3 + 2^4 + \ldots + 2^7)(3^0 + 3^1 + 3^2)(7^0 + 7^1) = 2\left(\frac{2^7-1}{2}\right)(13)(8) = 26416$

(c) Divisors of the form $(4m + 2) = 2(2m + 1) = 2$ (all odd divisors)
Odd divisors are of type = $3^b.7^c$; $0 \le b \le 2$; $0 \le c \le 1$
Number of odd divisors = 3 × 2 = 6
Divisors of form $2(2m + 1) = 12$

(d) Divisors of *x* that is divisible by 48
$x = 2^7 \times 3^2 \times 7$
Any such divisors will be of the form = $48(2^a.3^b.7^c) = (2^{a+4}.3^{b+1}.7^c)$; $0 \le a + 4 \le 7; 0 \le b + 1 \le 2; 0 \le c \le 1$
Number of such divisors = 4 × 2 × 2 = 16
Sum of such divisors = $48(2^0 + 2^1 + 2^2 + 2^3)(3^1 + 3^2)(7^0 + 7^1)$
$= 48(15)(4)(8) = 23040$

6. (a) True (refer to the definition of HCF)
(b) True (refer to the definition of LCM)
(c) True (evident from above statements (a) and (b))
(d) False (true only pair-wise)
In fact,
$$abc = \frac{LCM(a,b,c)) \times HCF(a,b) \times HCF = (b,c) \times HCF(c,a)}{HCF(a,b,c)}$$

7. $96 = 2^5 \times 3$; $424 = 2^3 \times 5^3$;
HCF of these numbers = $2^3 = 8$
LCM of these numbers = $2^5 \times 3 \times 53 = 5088$

8. $24 = 2^3 \times 3$; $72 = 2^3 \times 3^2$; $120 = 2^3 \times 3 \times 5$
HCF of these number = $2^3 \times 3 = 24$
LCM of these numbers = $2^3 \times 3^2 \times 5 = 8 \times 9 \times 5 = 360$

9. We already know for two positive integers *a* and *b*.
$a \times b$ = HCF (*a, b*) × LCM (*a, b*)
$$\text{LCM}(306,657) = \frac{306 \times 657}{HCF(306,657)} = \frac{306 \times 657}{9} = 22338$$

10. (a) $LCM\left(\frac{15}{6}, \frac{25}{4}\right) = \frac{LCM(15,25)}{HCF(6,4)} = \frac{25}{2}$

(b) $LCM = \left(\frac{3}{4}, \frac{5}{6}\right) = \frac{LCM(3,5)}{HCF(4,6)} = \frac{15}{2}$

(c) $LCM\left(\frac{3\pi}{4}, \frac{5\pi}{2}\right) = \frac{LCM(3\pi,4\pi)}{HCF(4,2)} = \frac{15\pi}{2}$

11. (a) 2, $\sqrt{2}$
Multiples of $\sqrt{2}$ are irrational while multiples of 2 are not. Hence common multiples will not exist.
(b) 3, π LCM does not exist for similar reason as in part (a).

12. (i) 135, 225
$\Rightarrow 225 = 135(1) + 90$
$\Rightarrow 135 = 90 \times (1) + 45$
$\Rightarrow 90 = 45 \times (2) + 0$
Thus, HCF = 45

(ii) 198, 3886
$\Rightarrow 3886 = (198)(19) + 124$
$\Rightarrow 198 = (124) \times 1 + 74$
$\Rightarrow 124 = (74) \times 1 + 50$
$\Rightarrow 74 = (50) \times 1 + 24$
$\Rightarrow 50 = (24 \times 2) + 2$
$\Rightarrow 24 = (2 \times 12) + 0$
Hence, HCF = 2

(iii) 196 and 38220
$\Rightarrow 38220 = (196)(195) + 0$
Hence LCM = 196

(iv) 867 and 255
$\Rightarrow 867 = (255)(3) + 102$

$\Rightarrow$ $255 = (102)(2) + 51$

$\Rightarrow$ $(102) = (51) \times 2 + 0$

Hence HCF = 51

13. Maximum number of columns = HCF (504, 60)

$\Rightarrow$ $504 = 2^3 \times 3^2 \times 7$

$\Rightarrow$ $60 = 2^2 \times 3 \times 5$

HCF (504, 60) = $2^2 \times 3 = 12$

Hence in maximum 12 columns they can march.

14. **(a)** True; let $p = 2, q = 3$

GCD (2, 3) = 1

$P|12$ and $q|12$

Hence $pq \mid 12$

(b) $q|pN$ and GCD $(p, q) = 1$

Let $p = 2; q = 3$ $\Rightarrow$ GCD (2, 3) = 1

$q|p \times 6$ $(N = 6)$, then $q|6$; which is true

(c) $a|N$ and $b|N$, then LCM $(a, b) \mid N$

Let $a = 2, b = 3$

$a|12$; $b|$ 12, then LCM $(a, b) = 6|12$, which is true

(d) If 4^n ends with a zero.

$\Rightarrow$ 4^n has 5 has one of its divisors which is not possible. Hence false

15. Let r and p be some positive integer such that $n = rp$, then $x^{rp} - 1 = (x^p - 1)(x^{rp-1} + x^{rp-2} + \ldots + x^1 + 1)$

If n is composite, then $2^n - 1$ is also composite (because it is divisible by $2^p - 1$) $\Rightarrow$ n must be prime.

16. $mn = 2^3.3^2.5^4\,(m + n)$

$mn = 2^3.3^2.m + 2^3.3^2.5^4 n$ (i)

Consider the product $(2^3.3^2.5^4 - m)(2^3.3^2.5^4 - n) = 2^6.3^4.5^8 - 2^3.3^2.5^4 n - 2^3.3^2.5^4 m + mn$

By (i) = $2^6.3^4.5^8$

$\Rightarrow$ $(2^3.3^2.5^4 - m)(2^3.3^2.5^4 - n) = 2^6.3^4.5^8$

$\therefore$ $2^6.5^4.5^8$ has $(6 + 1)(4 + 1)(8 + 1) = 315$

Thus there are possible 315 values for (m, n)

17. $n^4 + 4$

$n^4 + 4n^2 + 4 - 4n^2 = (n^4 + 4n^2 + 4) - 4n^2$

$= (n^2 + 2 + 2n)(n^2 + 2 - 2)$

Since $n > 1$, both factors are larger than one. Hence $n^4 + 4$ is composite.

18. $x^2 - y^2$ is a prime

$\Rightarrow$ $x^2 - y^2 = (x + y)(x - y)$

For x; $y \in \mathbb{N}$ and $x - y \in \mathbb{N}$

Hence for $x^2 - y^2$ to be prime $x + y = 1$ or $x - y = 1$

But $x + y = 1$ has no solution thus $x - y = 1$ for $x^2 - y^2$ to be prime.

TEXTUAL EXERCISE–11 (SUBJECTIVE)

1. **(i)** $P(n) : n^3 + (n + 1)^3 + (n + 2)^3 = 9m$

$P(1) = 1 + 2^3 + 3^3 = 36 = 9 \times 4$ which is true

$P(k) = k^3 + (k + 1)^3 + (k + 2)^3 = 9m$

Let as assume $P(k)$ is true.

$P(k + 1) = (k + 1)^3 + (k + 2)^3 + (k + 3)^3$

$= 9m - k^3 + k^3 + 27 + 9k^2 + 27k = 9m + 9(k^2 + 3k + 3)$

Which is divisible by 9.

$P(k) \Rightarrow P(k + 1)$, hence the assumption is true.

(ii) $n^3 + 5n$

$P(n) : n^3 + 5n = 6m$

$P(1) = 6$ which is divisible by 6.

$P(k) = k^3 + 5k = 6m$

Let us assume $P(k)$ to be true.

$P(k + 1) = (k + 1)^3 + 5(k + 1) = k^3 + 1 + 3k^2 + 3k + 5k + 5$

$= k^3 + 3k^2 + 8k + 6 = k^3 + 5k + 3k^2 + 3k + 6$

$= k^3 + 5k + 3k(k + 1) + 6 = k^3 + 5k + 3.2p + 6$ $\{k(k + 1)$ is always divisible by 2$\}$

$= 6m + 6p + 6 = 6(m + p + 1)$ which is divisible by 6.

$P(k) \Rightarrow P(k + 1)$ the assumption is true.

(iii) $P(n) : 3^{2n} = 8m + 1$

$P(1)$: LHS = 9; RHS = 9

$P(1)$ holds true

$P(k) = 3^{2k} = 8m + 1$, let us assume $P(k)$ is true

$P(k + 1) : 3^{2(k+1)} = 3^{2k}3^2 = (8m + 1)9 = 9.8m + 8 + 1 = 8(9m + 1) + 1$, which is holds true

Thus $P(k) \Rightarrow P(k + 1)$ the assumption is true.

2. $1.2 + 2.5 + \ldots. + n(3n - 1) = n^2(n + 1)$

$P(n) : 1.2 + 2.5 + \ldots + n(3n - 1) = n^2(n + 1)$

$P(1)$ = LHS = 1(2) = 2; RHS = 1(2) = 2, hence $P(1)$ holds true.

$P(k) : 1.2 + 2.5 + \ldots + k(3k - 1) = k^2(k + 1)$

Let us assume $P(k)$ to be true.

$P(k + 1) : 1.2 + 2.5 + \ldots.. + k(3k - 1) + (k + 1)(3k + 2)$

By $P(k)$ we can write $1.2 + 2.5 + \ldots. + k(3k - 1) + (k + 1)(3k + 2)$.

Can be written as $k^2(k + 1) + (k + 1)(3k + 2)$

$(k + 1)(k^2 + 3k + 2)$

$(k + 1)^2 (k + 2)$ witch holds

Thus $P(k) \Rightarrow P(k + 1)$, hence are assumption is true.

3. $P(n)$: $1.2^2 + 2.3^2 + \ldots. + (n - 1)(n^2) = \dfrac{n(n^2-1)(3n+2)}{12}$

$P(2)$: L.H.S. $= 1.2^2 = 4$

R.H.S. $= \dfrac{2(3)(8)}{12} = 4$, hence $P(2)$ is true

$P(k)$: $1.2^2 + 2.3^2 + \ldots. + (k - 1)(k^2) = \dfrac{k(k^2-1)(3k+2)}{12}$

Let us assume $P(k)$ to be true

$P(k + 1)$: $1.2^2 + 2.3^2 + \ldots\ldots + (k - 1)(k^2) + k(k + 1)^2$

By $P(k)$: We can write $\dfrac{k(k^2-1)(3k+2)}{12} + k(k+2)^2$

$= \dfrac{k(k^2-1)(3k+2)+12k(k+1)^2}{12}$

$= \dfrac{(k+1)(k(k-1)(3k+2)+12k(k+1))}{12}$

$= \dfrac{k(k+1)(3k^2+2k-3k-2+12k)}{12} = \dfrac{k(k+1)(3k^2+11k-2)}{12}$

$= \dfrac{k(k+1)(k-1)(3k+2)+12(k+1))}{12}$

$= \dfrac{k(k+1)(3k^2+2k-3k-2+12k+12)}{12}$

$$= \frac{k(k+1)(3k^2+11k+10)}{12} = \frac{k(k+1)(3k^2+6k+5k+10)}{12}$$

$$= \frac{k(k+1)(3k(k+2)+5(k+2))}{12}$$

$$= \frac{k(k+1)(3k+5)(k+2)}{12} = \frac{(k+1)((k+1)^2-1)(3k+5)}{12}$$

$$= \frac{(k+1)((k+1)^2-1)(3(k+1)+2)}{12} \text{ which is true}$$

$P(k) \Rightarrow P(k+1)$, hence, the assumption holds true.

4. $P(n): \frac{1}{1.5}+\frac{1}{5.9}+...+\frac{1}{(4n-3)(4n+1)} = \frac{n}{4n+1}$

$P(1): \frac{1}{1.5} = \frac{1}{5}(\text{L.H.S.})$; R.H.S. $= \frac{1}{4(1)+1} = \frac{1}{5}$

$P(k): \frac{1}{1.5}+\frac{1}{5.9}+....+\frac{1}{(4k-3)(4k+1)} = \frac{k}{4k+1}$

Let us assume $P(k)$ to be true

$P(k+1): \frac{1}{1.5}+\frac{1}{5.9}+....+\frac{1}{(4k-3)(4k+1)}+\frac{1}{(4k+1)(4k+5)}$

By $P(k+1)$: $\frac{k}{4k+1}+\frac{1}{(4k+1)(4k+5)}+\frac{(4k+5)k+1}{(4k+1)(4k+5)}$

$$= \frac{4k^2+5k+1}{(4k+1)(4k+5)} = \frac{4k^2+4k+k+1}{(4k+1)(4k+5)}$$

$$= \frac{4k(k+1)+k+1}{(4k+1)(4k+5)} = \frac{(k+1)(4k+1)}{(4k+1)(4k+3)} = \frac{(k+1)}{4k+3}$$

$$= \frac{(k+1)}{4(k+1)+1}$$

Thus, $P(k) \Rightarrow P(k+1)$

Hence the assumption is correct.

5. $P(n)$: 3 + 3.3 + 3.3.3 + ……. $= \frac{10^{n+1}-9n-10}{27}$

$P(1)$ = LHS = 3; RHS $= \frac{10^2-9-10}{27} = \frac{81}{27} = 3$

$P(k) = 3+3.3+3.3.3+....+\underbrace{3.3.3....}_{k \text{ times}} = \frac{10^{k+1}-9k-10}{27}$

Let us assume $P(k)$ is true;

$P(k+1)$: $3+3.3+3.3.3+....+\underbrace{3.3.3.3}_{k \text{ times}}+......+\underbrace{3.3.3.3.3}_{(k+1) \text{ times}}$

By assumption $\frac{10^{k+1}-9^k-10}{27}+3(10^k+10^{k-1}+.....+1)$

$$= \frac{10^{k+1}-9^k-10}{27}+3\frac{(10^{k+1}-1)}{9} = \frac{10^{k+2}-9(k+1)-10}{27}$$

Hence $P(k) \Rightarrow P(k+1)$

$\Rightarrow$ Assumption is true.

6. $P(n): \frac{1}{2}.\frac{3}{4}.\frac{5}{6}.....\frac{2n-1}{2n} < \frac{1}{\sqrt{3n+1}}$

$P(2)$: L.H.S. $= \frac{1}{2}.\frac{3}{4} = \frac{3}{6}$

R.H.S. $= \frac{1}{\sqrt{7}}$; L.H.S. < R.H.S., hence $P(2)$ holds.

Let us assume that $P(n)$ holds.

Given n is a natural number.

Clearly, $P(n+1) = P(n).\frac{2n+1}{2n+2}$

$P(n+1) < \frac{2n+1}{2n+2}.\frac{1}{\sqrt{3n+1}}$

Squaring R.H.S. $= \left[\frac{2n+1}{2n+2}.\frac{1}{\sqrt{3n+1}}\right]^2 = \frac{(2n+1)^2}{(2n+2)^2}\frac{1}{(3n+1)}$

$$= \frac{(2n+1)^2}{(4n^2+4+8n)3n+1} = \frac{(2n+1)^2}{(4n^2+4+8n)(3n+1)}$$

$$= \frac{(2n+1)}{[(2n+1)^2.(3n+4)+n]} < \frac{(2n+1)}{[(2n+1)^2.(3n+4)]} = \frac{1}{3n+4}$$

$\Rightarrow P(n+1) < \frac{1}{\sqrt{3n+4}}$, hence $P(n+1)$ holds

$\therefore$ $P(n) \Rightarrow P(n+1)$, the assumption is correct.

7. $P(n): \frac{1}{n+1}+\frac{1}{n+2}+....+\frac{1}{2n} > \frac{13}{24}$

$P(2): \frac{1}{3}+\frac{1}{4} = \frac{7}{12} = \frac{14}{24} > \frac{13}{24}$

Hence $P(2)$ holds

Let us assume $P(n)$ to be true. Now, without any loss of generality

$$P(n) - \frac{1}{n+1}+\frac{1}{2n+1}+\frac{1}{2n+2} > P(n)$$

$$\Rightarrow P(n+1) > P(n) > \frac{13}{24} \Rightarrow P(n+1) > \frac{13}{24}$$

Hence $P(n) \Rightarrow P(n+1)$, the assumption is correct.

8. $\sqrt{n} < 1+\frac{1}{\sqrt{2}}+....+\frac{1}{\sqrt{n}}$

$P(n): \sqrt{n} < 1+\frac{1}{\sqrt{2}}+\frac{1}{\sqrt{3}}+....+\frac{1}{\sqrt{n}}$

$P(2)$: R.H.S.: $1+\frac{1}{\sqrt{2}}$; LHS = $\sqrt{2}$

L.H.S. < R.H.S. which holds

Let us assume $P(n)$ is true.

Add $\frac{1}{\sqrt{n+1}}$ to both sides of $P(n)$, we get

$$\sqrt{n}+\frac{1}{\sqrt{n+1}} < 1+\frac{1}{\sqrt{2}}+....+\frac{1}{\sqrt{n}}+\frac{1}{\sqrt{n+1}}$$

$\therefore$ $n^2 < n^2 + n$ (as given)

$$\Rightarrow n < \sqrt{n(n+1)} \qquad \Rightarrow 1+n < \sqrt{n(n+1)}+1$$

$$\Rightarrow \sqrt{1+n}\frac{\sqrt{n(n+1)}+1}{\sqrt{n+1}} \qquad \Rightarrow \sqrt{1+n} < \sqrt{n}+\frac{1}{\sqrt{n+1}}$$

$$\Rightarrow \sqrt{1+n} < 1+\frac{1}{\sqrt{2}}+....+\frac{1}{\sqrt{n+1}}$$

$P(n) \Rightarrow P(n+1)$

Hence, this part of the inequality is proved.
Now let us consider the other part

$P(n): 1+\frac{1}{\sqrt{2}}+....+\frac{1}{\sqrt{n}}<2\sqrt{n}$

$P(2): 1+\frac{1}{\sqrt{n}}$(L.H.S.)

R.H.S. = $2\sqrt{2}$
L.H.S. < R.H.S., which holds true
Hence, $P(2)$ holds. Let as assume $P(n)$ is true.
Without loss of generality we can write $4n^2 + 4n + 1 > 4n^2 + 4n$

$\Rightarrow\ 4n^2 + 4n + 1 > 4(n^2 + n)$

$\Rightarrow\ (2n+1)>2\sqrt{n^2+n}$

$\Rightarrow\ 2(n+1)-1>2\sqrt{n}\sqrt{n+1}$

$\Rightarrow\ 2\sqrt{n}<\frac{2(n+1)-1}{\sqrt{n+1}}$

$\Rightarrow\ 2\sqrt{n}+\frac{1}{\sqrt{n+1}}<2\sqrt{n+1}$ (1)

Adding $\frac{1}{\sqrt{n+1}}$ to both sides of $P(n)$, we get

$1+\frac{1}{\sqrt{2}}+....+\frac{1}{\sqrt{n}}+\frac{1}{\sqrt{n+1}}<2\sqrt{n}+\frac{1}{\sqrt{n+1}}$

From (i) ,

$1+\frac{1}{\sqrt{2}}+....+\frac{1}{\sqrt{n}}+\frac{1}{\sqrt{n+1}}<2\sqrt{n}+\frac{1}{\sqrt{n+1}}<2\sqrt{n+1}$

$\Rightarrow\ 1+\frac{1}{\sqrt{2}}+....+\frac{1}{\sqrt{n+1}}<2\sqrt{n+1}$

$P(n) \Rightarrow P(n + 1)$, hence proved.

9. Let m be those people who have shaken hands an even number of times and let n be those people whose have shaken hands an odd number of times. Before a handshake even took place the number of elements $n = 0$, hence even.

We assume the statement is true for k handshakes and hence prove it for $(k + 1)$ handshakes.
There arise three cases for $(k + 1)^{\text{th}}$ handshake.

- Two people from m shake hands.
- Two people from n shake hands.
- One from m and one from n shake hands.

In each of the case the parity of the set consisting of n remains same (which we assumed to be even)
Simply $P(n) \Rightarrow P(n + 1)$, hence the assumption is true.

10. **(i)** $41^n - 14^n$.
$P(n) = 41^n - 14^n = 27m$
$P(1) : 41 - 14 = 27$, which is divisible by 27
Let as assume it to be true for $P(n)$
$= P(n + 1) : 41^{n+1} - 14^{n+1} = 41.41^n - 14^{n+1} = 41(27m + 14^n) - 14^{n+1} = 41.27m + 41.14^n - 14^{n+1}$
$= 41.27m + 14^n (41 - 14) = 41.27m + 14^n27$, which is divisible by 27.
$P(n) \Rightarrow P(n + 1)$, hence proved.

(ii) $P(n) = 7^n - 3^n = 4m$
$P(1) = 7 - 3 = 4$, which is divisible by 4.
Let as assume the statement is true for n.
$P(n + 1) : 7^{n+1} - 3^{n+1} = 7.7^n - 3^{n+1} = 7(4m + 3^n) - 3^{n+1} = 28m + 7.3^n - 3^{n+1} = 28m + 3^n (7 - 3)$
$= 28m + 4.3^n$, which is clearly divisible by 4
$P(n) \Rightarrow P(n + 1)$, the assumption is correct.

11. $P(n) : n < 2^n ; n \in \mathbb{N}$
$P(n)$: L.H.S. = 2; R.H.S. = $2^2 = 4$
Hence $P(2)$ is true
$P(n + 1)$: L.H.S. = $n + 1$, R.H.S. = $2^n.2$
Let as assume that $P(n)$ is true i.e., $n < 2^n$ (i)
$\therefore\ 1 < 2^n$ (ii) (n is a natural number)
Adding both the equation (i) and (ii), we get $n + 1 < 2^n + 2^n$
$\Rightarrow\ n + 1 < 2 . 2^n = 2^{n+1}$
Hence $P(n) \Rightarrow P(n + 1)$. The assumption is true.

12. $P(n) : (1 + x)^n \geq 1 + nx$; which n is a positive integer and x is positive
$P(1)$: L.H.S. = $(1 + x)$; R.H.S. = $1 + x$
Thus $P(1)$ holds
$P(n + 1) : (1 + x)^{n+1} \geq 1 + (n + 1)^x = (1 + x)^{n+1} \geq 1 + nx + x$
Let us assume $P(n)$ is true
$\Rightarrow\ (1 + x)^n \geq 1 + nx$ (i)
$\therefore\ (1 + x)^n \geq 1$ (given n is a positive integer)
$\Rightarrow\ x(1 + x)^n > x$ (given x is positive) (ii)
Adding equation (i) and equation (ii), we get $(1 + x)^n + x(1 + x)^n \geq 1 + nx + x$
$\Rightarrow\ (1 + x)^n (1 + x) \geq 1+ (n + 1)x$
$\Rightarrow\ (1 + x)^{n+1} \geq (1+ (n + 1)x)$
$P(n) \Rightarrow P(n + 1)$, hence, the assumption is correct.

13. $P(n) : 1^2 + 2^2 + 3^2 + ... + n^2 > \frac{n^3}{3}\ \forall\ n \in \mathbb{N}$
$P(2)$: L.H.S. = $1^2 + 2^2 = 5$; R.H.S. = 8/3
L.H.S. > R.H.S.
Hence $P(2)$ holds

$P(n + 1) : 1^2 + 2^2 + ... + (n + 1)^2 > \frac{(n+1)^3}{3}$

Let us assume $P(n)$ to be true $1^2 + 2^2 + 3^2 + ... + n^2 > \frac{n^3}{3}$

Now, $1^2 + 2^2 + 3^2 + ... + (n + 1)^2 > \frac{(n+1)^3}{3}$

By $P(n)$ it is true if $(n+1)^2>\frac{1+3n+3n^2}{3}$

Which is true if $3n^2 + 3 + 6n > 1 + 3n + 3n^2 = 3(1 + 3n) > 1 + 3n$, which is true (as n is a natural number)
Hence $P(n) \Rightarrow P(n + 1)$
Hence the assumption is true.

14. $P(n) : 1 + 2 + 3 + ... + n < \frac{(2n+1)^2}{8}; \forall\ n \in \mathbb{N}$

$P(1)$: L.H.S. = 1; R.H.S. = $\frac{(3)^2}{8}=\frac{9}{8}$

L.H.S. < R.H.S, hence $P(1)$ holds

$P(n + 1) : 1 + 2 + ... + n + 1 < \frac{(2n+3)^2}{8}$

Let us assume $P(n)$ is true

By $P(n): 1 + 2 + 3 + ... + n < \frac{4n^2+1+4n}{8}$

Adding $(n + 1)$ to both sides, we get $1 + 2 + 3 + ... + (n+1) < \frac{4n^2+1+4n+8n+8}{8}$

$\Rightarrow\ 1+2+....+(n+1) < \frac{4n^2+12+9}{8}$

$\Rightarrow\ 1+2+....+(n+1) < \frac{(2n+3)^2}{8}$

$\Rightarrow\ 1+2+....+(n+1) < \frac{(2(n+1)+1)^2}{8}$

Hence $P((n) \Rightarrow P(n + 1)$, the assumption is correct.

15. $P(n): 10^n + 3.4^{n+2} + 5 = 9m$

$P(1)$: L.H.S. = $10 + 3.4^2 + 5 = 10 + 48 + 5 = 63 = 9 \times 7$, which is divisible by 9, hence $P(1)$ holds

$P(n + 1) : 10^{n+1} + 3.4^{n+3} + 5 = 9k$

Let us assume $P(n)$ is true $= 10.10^n + 3.4^3 . 4^n + 5$, which can be written as $10.10^n + 3.4^3.4^n + 9m - 10^n - 3.4^{n+2}$

$= 10^n.9 + 4^{n+2}(9) + 9m = 9(10^n + 4^{n+2} + m)$, which is divisible by 9

$P(n) \Rightarrow P(n + 1)$, hence the assumption is correct.

16. $P(n) : n^3 + (n + 1)^3 + (n + 2)^3$ is divisible by 9

$P(1) : 1 + 2^3 + 3^3 = 36$ which is divisible by 9.

Hence $P(1)$ holds

$P(n + 1) : (n + 1)^3 + (n + 2)^3 + (n + 3)^3$ is divisible by 9

Let us assume $P(n)$ is true, then $(n + 1)^3 + (n + 2)^3 + (n + 3)^3$ can be written as $9m - n^3 + (n + 3)^3$

$= 9m - n^3 + n^3 + 9 + 9n^2 + 27n = 9(m + n^2 + 1 + 3n)$

Which is also divisible by 9; where $P(n) \Rightarrow P(n + 1)$

Hence the assumption is correct.

17. $P(n) : 4^n + 15n - 1$ is divisible by 9

$P(1) = 4^1 + 15 - 1 = 18$; which is divisible by 9.

Hence $P(1)$ holds

Let as assume it is true for same k. ($k \in \mathbb{N}$)

$\Rightarrow\ 4^k + 15k - 1 = 9m$

Let us test this for $(k + 1)$

$4^{k+1} + 15(k + 1) - 1 = 4.4^k + 15k + 15 - 1 = 3.4^k + 4^k + 15k + 15 - 1$

$= 3.4^k + 15 + \underbrace{(4^k + 15k - 1)}_{\text{is assumed to be divisible by 9}}$

Also $= 3(4^k - 1) + 18 + (4^k + 15k - 1)$

Both 18 and $4^k + 15k - 1$ are divisible by 9.

We are left with $3(4^k - 1)$ to prove that $3(4^k - 1)$ is divisible by 9, it is sufficient to prove $4^k - 1$ is divisible by 3.

$\therefore\ 4^k - 1^k$ is divisible by $(4 - 1 = 3)\ \forall\ k \in \mathbb{N}$. Hence $3(4^k - 1)$ is divisible by 9

Hence, $3(4^k - 1) + 18 + (4^k + 15k - 1)$ is divisible by 9.

Hence $P(n) \Rightarrow P(n + 1)$, hence the assumption is true.

18. (i) $P(n) = \left(1+\frac{1}{1}\right).\left(1+\frac{1}{2}\right)....\left(1+\frac{1}{n}\right)$

$P(2)$: L.H.S. $= (2).\left(\frac{3}{2}\right) = 3$; R.H.S. $= 2 + 1 = 3$

Let as assume $P(n)$ is true

$P(n+1) = P(n).\left(1+\frac{1}{n+1}\right)$

By the assumption $(n+1)\left(1+\frac{1}{n+1}\right) = (n+1)+1 = n+2$

Hence $P(n) \Rightarrow P(n + 1)$, hence the assumption is correct.

(ii) $P(n) = \left(1+\frac{3}{1}\right)\left(1+\frac{5}{4}\right)....\left(1+\frac{2n+1}{n^2}\right) = (n+1)^2$

$P(2) = 4.\left(1+\frac{5}{4}\right) = 4.\frac{9}{4} = 9$(L.H.S.)

R.H.S. $= (2 + 1)^2 = 9$, hence $P(2)$ holds

$P(n+1): \left(1+\frac{3}{1}\right)\left(1+\frac{5}{4}\right).....\left(1+\frac{2n+1}{n^2}\right)\left(1+\frac{2n+3}{(n+1)^2}\right)$

Let us assume $P(n)$ to be true, then we can write $(n+1)^2\left(1+\frac{2n+3}{(n+1)^2}\right) = ((n + 1)^2 + (2n + 3)) = (n^2 + 1 + 2n + 2n + 3)$

$= (n^2 + 4n + 4) = (n + 2)^2$

Hence $P(n) \Rightarrow P(n + 1)$. Hence are assumption is correct.

TEXTUAL EXERCISE–12: (SUBJECTIVE)

1. (a) $(332)^{4024}$; units place of the base is 2 and $4024 = 4k$. Hence it ends with 6.

(b) $(123)^{216}$; unit place of the base is 3 and $216 = 4k$. Hence it ends with 1.

(c) $(5244)^{122}$; unit place of the base is 4 and $122 = 2k$. Hence it ends with 6.

(d) $(4127)^{85}$; unit place of the base is 7 and $85 = 4k + 1$. Hence it ends with 7.

(e) $(3285)^{885}$; unit place of the base is 5. Hence it ends with 5.

(f) $(1579)^{2019}$; unit place of the base is 9 and $2019 = 2k + 1$. Hence it ends with 9.

(g) $(1989)^{2009}$; units place of base = 9 and $2009 = 2k + 1$. Hence the number ends with 9.

(h) 2^{2010}; units place of the base is 2 and $2010 = 4k + 2$. Hence the number ends with 4.

(i) $(7777)^{777}$; units place of base is 7 and $777 = 4k + 1$. Hence it ends with 7.

2. Last digits of $33^{1131} + 33^{1141} + 33^{1151} + 33^{1161}$.

Last digits of 33^{1131} : 7; Last digits of 33^{1141} : 3; Last digits of 33^{1151} : 7; Last digits of 33^{1161} : 3

Their summation would end with 0.

3. Clearly 2^{1000} end with 6. Hence it leaves remainder 1 on divisible by 5 and 6 on division by 10.

4. (a) 763^{1995}; unit digit of base 3.

$1995 = 4k + 3$, hence it ends with 7 on division by 2 it leaves remainder 1, on division by 5 is leaves 2 and 7 on division by 10.

(b) $2222^{5555} + 5555^{2222}$
2222^{5555} end with 8; 5555^{2222} ends with 5
Their summation ends with 3.
On division by 1 it gives 1; On division by 5 it gives 3; On division by 10 it gives 3.

(c) $777^{997} + 999^{776}$ $\Rightarrow$ 777^{997} ends with 7
$\Rightarrow$ 999^{776} ends with 1
Their sum would end with 6.
On division by 2 = 0; on division by 5 = 3; on division by 10 = 8

(d) $777^{117} + 117^{777}$ $\Rightarrow$ 777^{117} ends with 7
$\Rightarrow$ 117^{777} ends with 7
Their sum would end with 4.
On division by 2 = 0; On division by 5 = 4; On division by 10 = 4

(e) $319^{9999} + 1111^{1999}$ $\Rightarrow$ 319^{9999} ends with = 9
$\Rightarrow$ $(1111)^{1999}$ ends with = 1
Hence their sum would end with 0
On division by 2 $\to$ 0; On division by 5 $\to$ 0; On division by 10 $\to$ 0

(f) $3233^{120} + (5284)^{889}$ $\Rightarrow$ $(3233)^{120}$ ends with 1
$\Rightarrow$ $(5284)^{889}$ ends with 4
Their sum would end with 5.
On division by 2 $\to$ 1; On division by 5 $\to$ 0; On division by 10 $\to$ 5

5. (a) A number is divisible by 2, if its units place is even
$\Rightarrow$ $c \in [0, 2, 4, 6, 8]$

(b) A number is divisible by 3, if sum of the digits is divisible by 3.
$\Rightarrow$ $3|2 + 8 + 0 + c$ $\Rightarrow$ $3|10 + c$
$\Rightarrow$ $c \in [2, 5, 8]$

(c) A number is divisible by 4
$\Rightarrow$ $4|2 \times 0 + c$ $\Rightarrow$ $4|c$
$\Rightarrow$ $c \in [8, 0, 4]$

(d) Clearly $c \in [5, 0]$

(e) A number is divisible by 6 if sum of the digits is divisible by 3 and unit digit is even.
$3 \mid 2 + 8 + 0 + c$
$\Rightarrow$ $3|0 + c$ and c is even, hence $c \in [2, 8]$

(f) N is divisible by 9 if $9|\ 2 + 8 + 0 + c$
$9 \mid 10 + c$ $\Rightarrow$ $c \in [8]$

(g) Clearly, N is divisible by 0 if there is a zero at its unit place $c \in [0]$.

6. (a) $B \in [0, 2, 4, 6, 8]$; $A \in [0, 9]$
Total number = 10 × 5 = 50

(b) $3|1 + 2 + 3 + A + B$ $\Rightarrow$ $3A + B$
$A \in (0, 9)$; $B \in (0, 9)$
If $A = 0$; $B = 0, 3, 6, 9$ (4)
$A = 1$; $B = 8, 2, 5$ (3)
$A = 2$; $B = 1, 4, 7$ (3)
$A = 3$; $B = 0, 3, 6, 9$ (4)
$A = 4$; $B = 2, 5, 8$ (3)
$A = 5$; $B = 1, 4, 7$ (3)
$A = 6$; $B = 0, 3, 6, 9$ (4)
$A = 7$; $B = 2, 5, 8$ (3)
$A = 8$; $B = 1, 4, 7$ (3)
$A = 9$; $B = 0, 3, 6, 9$ (4)
Total = 34 possibilities

(c) N is divisible by 4 if $4|2A + B$
$B = 0$; $A = 0, 2, 4, 6, 8$
$B = 1$; $A = A$ has no possibilities
$B = 2$; $A = 1, 3, 5, 7, 9$
$B = 3$; $A = A$ has no possibilities
$B = 4$; $A = [0, 2, 4, 6, 8]$
$B = 5$; $A = A$ has no possibilities
$B = 6$; $A = [1, 3, 5, 7, 9]$
$B = 7$; $A = A$ has no possibilities
$B = 8$; $A = [0, 2, 4, 6, 8]$
$B = 9$; $A = A$ has no possibilities
Hence 5 × 5 = 25 possibilities

(d) N is divisible by 5 iff its last digits is 0 or 5.
$B = 0, 5$
$A = 0, 1, 2, 3,\ldots..,9$
$\Rightarrow$ Number of natural number = 20

(e) N is divisible by 6 if and only if units place digit is even and sum of digits is divisible by 3.
$B = 0, 2, 4, 6, 8$ (units digits is even) and $3|1 + 2 + 3 + A + B$
$\Rightarrow$ $3|\ A + B$
$B = 0$; $A = 0, 3, 6, 9$
$B = 2$; $A = 1, 4, 7$
$B = 4$; $A = 2, 5, 8$
$B = 6$; $A = 0, 3, 6, 9$
$B = 8$; $A = 1, 4, 7$
Total number of natural number = 17.

7. (i) Let as consider the number $N = \overline{AB} = (10 \times A + B)$
Sum of digits = $(A + B)$
By the question, $(10 \times A + B)(A + B) = 10A^2 + 10AB + BA + B^2$
$= 10A^2 + B^2 + 11AB = 405$ (i)
Similarly $(10 \times B + A)(A + B) = 486$
$= 10BA + 10B^2 + A^2 + AB = 486$
$= 11AB + A^2 + 10B^2 = 486$ (ii)
Subtracting (i) from (ii), we get $9B^2 - 9A^2 = 81$
$B^2 - A^2 = 9$
$B = 3, A = 0$ or $B = 5, A = 4$
$B = 3, A = 0$ it not valid
Hence $B = 5, A = 4$ thus, the number is 45.

(ii) Let the number by N_1, N_2, N_3 say $N_3 > N_2 > N_1$
By the question $N_2 - N_1 = N_3 - N_2$ (i)
And $N_1 N_2 = 85$ (ii)
$N_2 N_3 = 115$ (iii)
By $N_2 - N_1 = N_3 - N_2$
$\Rightarrow$ $2N_2 = N_1 + N_3$
Adding (ii) and (iii), we get $N_2(N_1 + N_3) = 200$
$\Rightarrow$ $2N_2^2 = 200$ $\Rightarrow$ $N_2 = 10$
$\Rightarrow$ $N_1 = \dfrac{85}{N_2} = \dfrac{17}{2}$ $\Rightarrow$ $N_3 = \dfrac{115}{N_2} = \dfrac{23}{2}$

Hence the three number are $10, \dfrac{17}{2}, \dfrac{23}{2}$

8. $N = \overline{abcd} + \overline{bcda} + \overline{cdab} + \overline{dabc}$
N can be written in expanded form as
$= 1000(a+b+c+d) + 100(a+b+c+d) + 10(a+b+c+d) + 1(a+b+c+d)$
Which can further be written as $= (a + b + c + d)$ (1111); which is clearly divisible by 11

9. **(a)** True; It is divisible by 2 as the number is even. It is divisible by 3 as $3|2+2+2+2+2+2$ or $3|12$.
Hence it divided $2 \times 3 = 6$
(b) True; For whatever permutation of 1, 2, 3, 4, 5; $1 + 2 + 3 + 4 + 5 = 15$ is divisible by 3.
Hence the number is also divisible by 3.
(c) True; It is divisible by 2 (even)
$3|2+2+2+2+2+2+2+2+2$ $(3|18)$ hence divisible by 3.
$\Rightarrow$ $9|18$ hence divisible by 9
(d) True; $p \mid q^2$ $\Rightarrow P|a \times a$
Since p is a prime number $\Rightarrow p \mid a$
(e) True; Let us consider two numbers a and b ($\in \mathbb{N}$)
$a = 3k_1 + R_2$; $R_2 \in \{0, 1, 2\}$
$b = 3k_3 + R_4$; $R_4 \in \{0, 1, 2\}$
Where R_2, R_4 are remainders
Sum of there natural numbers is given by $a + b = 3(k_1 + k_3) + R_2 + R_4$
Product of these natural numbers $a.b = 9k_1k_3 + 3k_1R_4 + 3.R_2k_3 + R_2R_4 = 3(3k_1k_3 + k_1R_4 + R_2k_3) + R_2R_4$.

10. **(a)** For even number, $b \in \{0, 2, 4, 6, 8\}$, $a \in \{0, 1, 2, 3, \ldots\ldots, 9\}$
$\Rightarrow$ 50 numbers
(b) For even number, $b \in \{0, 2, 4, 6, 8\}$, $a \in \{0, 1, 2, 3, \ldots\ldots, 9\}$, $x \in \{0, 1, 2, 3, \ldots\ldots, 9\}$
$\Rightarrow$ 450 possibilities
(c) For odd number, $b \in \{1, 3, 5, 7, 9\}$
$\Rightarrow$ hence there are 5 such numbers.
(d) For divisibility by 3, $3|4 + 3 + 2 + x$
$\Rightarrow$ $3|x$ $\Rightarrow$ $x \in \{0, 3, 6, 9\}$
$\Rightarrow$ 4 numbers.
(e) For divisibility by 3, $3|x + 4 + 3 + 2$
$\Rightarrow$ $3|x$
$\Rightarrow$ $x \in \{3, 6, 9\}$ as 1st digit is non zero.
$\Rightarrow$ 3 such number
(f) For divisibility by 3, $3|5 + x + 0 + 1 + 2$; $3|x + 2$
$\Rightarrow$ $x \in \{1, 4, 7\}$ $\Rightarrow$ 3 such numbers

11. Clearly $10^{13} = 1$ followed by 13 zeroes
Sum of the digits $= 1 + \underbrace{0 + 0 + \ldots + 0}_{13\text{ zeros}} + 5 = 6$ which is divisible by 3.
Hence $10^{13} + 5$ is divisible by 3.

12. $\because$ $2^2 = 4$, $2^3 = 8$, $2^4 = 16, \ldots\ldots$
$\Rightarrow$ 2^n is of type $4k_n$ for $n \geq 2$; k_n is a positive integer corresponding to n.
$\therefore$ $(2)^{2^n} - 3 = (2)^{4k_n} - 3$ for $n \geq 2 =$ (number ending at 6) $- 3 =$ number ending at 3
$\Rightarrow$ $(2)^{2^n} - 3$ always has unit place 3 digit 3 $\forall\, n \geq 2$ and $n \in \mathbb{N}$

13. **(a)** $N = \overline{34A5B}$
N is divisible by 24 iff N is divisible by 8 and 3.
$= 8|B + 2 \times 5 + 4 \times A = 8|B + 4A + 10$
$\Rightarrow$ $8|4A + B + 2$ and $3|A + B$; from there two conditions $A = \{0, 1, 6, 7\}$; $B = \{2, 6\}$
Thus possible numbers are 34056, 34152, 34656, 34752.
(b) N is divisible by 36 if divisible by 9 and 4.
$9|3 + 4 + A + 5 + B$ $\Rightarrow$ $9|3 + A + B$
$4|10 + B$ $\Rightarrow$ $4|B + 2$; $B \in [2, 6]$
$\Rightarrow$ $A \in [4, 0, 9]$
Hence the possible numbers are 34452, 34056 and 34956.

14. If x is divisible by 22, then x is divisible by 11 and 2.
x is already divisible by 2 for divisible by 11
$11|\,[(4 + 2 + A + 2) - (B + 4 + 1)]$
$11|8 + A - B - 5$ $\Rightarrow$ $11|3 + A - B$
Ordered pairs possible are (0, 3); (1, 4); (2, 5); (3, 6); (8, 0); (9, 1); (4, 7); (5, 8); (6, 9)
Thus in total 9 pairs.

TEXTUAL EXERCISE-13: (SUBJECTIVE)

1. $2(7y^2 - x^2) = 3xy$, dividing throughout by xy, we get $\frac{14y}{x} - \frac{2x}{y} = 3$. Let $\frac{x}{y} = a$
Substituting $\frac{x}{y} = a$ $\Rightarrow$ $\frac{14}{a} - 2a = 3$
$= -2a^2 - 3a + 14 = 0 = 2a^2 + 3a - 14 = 0$
$= 2a^2 + 7a - 4a - 14 = 0 = a(2a + 7) - 2(2a + 7) = 0$
$= (a - 2)(2a + 7) = 0 \Rightarrow$ $a = 2$
$x : y$ is $2 : 1$ *or* $-7 : 2$.

2. $y = \frac{x^2 - 4}{x^2 + 4}$ $\Rightarrow$ $x^2y + 4y = x^2 - 4$
$\Rightarrow$ $x^2y - x^2 = -4 - 4y$
$\Rightarrow$ $x^2 = \frac{-4(1+y)}{y-1} = \frac{4(1+y)}{(1-y)} \Rightarrow x = \pm 2\sqrt{\frac{1+y}{1-y}}$

3. $\frac{a}{y+z-x} = \frac{b}{z+x-y} = \frac{c}{x+y-z} = (say = k)$
$\Rightarrow$ $k = \frac{a+b+c}{x+y+z}$
Multiplying the denominator and numerator by $(b^2 + c^2)$, $(a^2 + c^2)$, $(a^2 + b^2)$ respectively, we get
$$= \frac{a(b^2+c^2)}{(b^2+c^2)(y+z-x)} = \frac{b(a^2+c^2)}{(a^2+c^2)(z+x-y)} = \frac{c(a^2+b^2)}{(a^2+b^2)(x+y-z)}$$
$$= \frac{a(b^2+c^2) + b(a^2+c^2) + c(a^2+b^2)}{2(a^2x + b^2y + c^2z)}$$

4. $\frac{x}{a+b-c} = \frac{y}{b+c-a} = \frac{z}{c+a-b} = \frac{x+y+z}{a+b+c}$
$\Rightarrow$ $\frac{x-y}{2a-2c} = \frac{y-z}{2b-2a} = \frac{x-z}{2b-2c} =$ say λ
$\therefore$ $(a-b)x + (b-c)y + c(c-a)z = ax - bx + by - cy + cz - az$

$= a(x - z) + b(y - x) + c(z - y) = a(2b\lambda - 2c\lambda) + b(2c\lambda - 2a\lambda) + c(2a\lambda - 2b\lambda)$
$= 2ab\lambda - 2ac\lambda + 2bc\lambda - 2ab\lambda + 2ac\lambda - 2bc\lambda = 0$

5. $(b + c)x = a$, $(c + a)y = b$ and $(a + b)z = c$

$\Rightarrow\ x = \dfrac{a}{b+c};\ y = \dfrac{b}{c+a};\ z = \dfrac{c}{a+b}$

$\Rightarrow\ xy = \dfrac{ab}{(b+c)(c+a)};\ yz = \dfrac{bc}{(a+c)(a+b)};$

$xz = \dfrac{ac}{(b+c)(a+b)};\ xyz = \dfrac{abc}{(a+b)(b+c)(c+a)}$

$\Rightarrow\ xy + yz + xz + 2xyz$

$= \dfrac{ab}{(b+c)(c+a)} + \dfrac{bc}{(a+c)(a+b)}$

$+ \dfrac{ac}{(b+c)(a+b)} + \dfrac{2abc}{(a+b)(b+c)(c+a)}$

$= \dfrac{(a+b)ab + (b+c)bc + (a+c)ac + 2abc}{(a+b)(b+c)(a+c)}$

$= \dfrac{a^2b + ab^2 + b^2c + bc^2 + a^2c + ac^2 + 2abc}{(a+b)(b+c)(c+a)}$

$= \dfrac{b(a^2 + c^2 + 2ac) + ab^2 + b^2c + a^2c + ac^2}{(a+b)(b+c)(c+a)}$

$= \dfrac{b(a+c)^2 + b^2(a+c) + ac(a+c)}{(a+b)(b+c)(c+a)}$

$= \dfrac{(a+c)(ba + bc + b^2 + ac)}{(a+b)(b+c)(c+a)} = \dfrac{(a+b)(b+c)(c+a)}{(a+b)(b+c)(c+a)} = 1$

6. $7x - 4y - 8z = 0$
$12x + 11y - 3z = 0$
Coefficients may be written as

4	–8	7	–4
–11	–3	12	11

$\Rightarrow\ \dfrac{x}{100} = \dfrac{y}{-75} = \dfrac{z}{125}\quad \Rightarrow\ \dfrac{x}{4} = \dfrac{y}{-3} = \dfrac{z}{5} = \text{say } k$

$(x, y, z) = (4k, -3k, 5k) = 4$ if $k \in (-1, 0, 1, 2)$

7. $f(x) = x^3 + ax^2 + bx + c$
$f(3) = 27 + 9a + 3b + c = 0$ (by the question) (i)
$f(-1) = -1 + a - b + c = 0$ (by the question) (ii)
$f(-3) = -27 + 9a - 3b + c = -60$ (by the question) (iii)
$f(1) = 1 + a + b + c = 4$ (by the question) (iv)
Adding (i) and (ii) $= 2(9a + c) = -60$
Adding (ii) and (iv) $= 2a + 2c = 4$
$\Rightarrow\ 9a + c = -30 \qquad \Rightarrow\ a + c = 2$
$\Rightarrow\ 9(2 - c) + c = -30 \qquad \Rightarrow\ 18 - 8c = -30$
$\Rightarrow\ c = \dfrac{48}{8} = 6 \qquad \Rightarrow\ a = 2 - c = -4$ and $b = 1$

Hence, the polynomial comes out to be $x^3 - 4x^2 + x + 6$.

8. $a(b + c) = 44$ (i) $ab + bc = 44$
$b(c + a) = 50$ (ii) $bc + ab = 50$
$c(a + b) = 54$ (iii) $ca + cb = 54$
(i) – (iii) $\Rightarrow\ a(b - c) = -4$
Adding this to (i), we get $2ab = 40$
$\Rightarrow\ ab = 20$ (a)
(i) – (ii) $\Rightarrow c(a - b) = -6$
Adding it to (iii), we get $2ca = 48$
$\Rightarrow\ ca = 24$ (b)
Similarly $bc = 30$ (c)

$\dfrac{(a)}{(b)} = \dfrac{b}{c} = \dfrac{5}{6} \qquad \Rightarrow\ b = \dfrac{5c}{6}$

By (c) $bc = 36 \qquad \Rightarrow\ \dfrac{5c^2}{6} = 30$

$\Rightarrow\ c = \pm 6$
Similarly $a = \pm 4$, $b \pm 5$, $c = \pm 6$

9. $x + y + z = 3$ (i)
$x + y + v = 1$ (ii)
$x + z + v = 4$ (iii)
$y + z + v = 2$ (iv)
Adding (iii) and (iv), we get $x + y + z + z + 2v = 6$
$\Rightarrow\ 3 + z + 2v = 6 \qquad \Rightarrow\ z + 2v = 3$ (a)
By (ii), $x + v = 1 - y \Rightarrow\ 1 - y + z = 4$
$\Rightarrow\ z - y = 3$ (b)
$\Rightarrow\ y + 3 + y + v = 2 \qquad \Rightarrow\ 2y + v = -1$ (c)
$\therefore$ (a) – (b), we get $2v + y = 0$
$\Rightarrow\ y = -2v$
Putting $y = -2v$ in (c), we get
$2(-2v) + v = -1 \qquad \Rightarrow\ -4v + v = -1$
$\Rightarrow\ v = 1/3$
$\Rightarrow\ y = -2v; \qquad \Rightarrow\ y = -2/3$
$\Rightarrow\ z = y + 3 = 7/3 \qquad \Rightarrow\ x = 3 - y - z = 3 + 2/3 - 7/3$
Hence, $x = 4/3$; $y = -2/3$; $z = 7/3$; $v = 1/3$ is the correct set of solution.

10. $ay + bx = c$ (i)
$cx + az = b$ (ii)
$bz = cy = a$ (iii)

By (i), we get $x = \dfrac{c - ay}{b}$

Putting this value of x in (ii), we get $\dfrac{c(c - ay)}{b} = az + b$

$\Rightarrow\ z = \dfrac{\left[b - \dfrac{c(c-ay)}{b}\right]}{a}$

Putting this value in (iii), we get $\dfrac{b^2 - c(c - ay)}{a} + cy = a$

$\Rightarrow\ acy - c^2 + acy + b^2 = a^2$
$\Rightarrow\ 2acy = a^2 - b^2 + c^2$

$\Rightarrow\ y = \dfrac{a^2 + c^2 - b^2}{2ac} \qquad \Rightarrow\ x = \dfrac{c - \dfrac{(a^2 + c^2 - b^2)}{2c}}{b}$

$\Rightarrow\ x = \dfrac{c^2 + b^2 - a^2}{2bc}$

Similarly, $z = \dfrac{b - \left(c^2 - \left(\dfrac{a^2 + c^2 - b^2}{b}\right)\right)}{b}$

$= \dfrac{b^2 - \left(\dfrac{c^2 - a^2 + b^2}{2a}\right)}{b} \Rightarrow z = \dfrac{a^2 + b^2 - c^2}{2ab}$

11. $\frac{\sqrt{x^2+1}+\sqrt{x^2-1}}{\sqrt{x^2+1}-\sqrt{x^2-1}}=\frac{2x^2-1}{2}$

Applying componendo and dividendo, we get

$\frac{2\sqrt{x^2+1}}{2\sqrt{x^2-1}}=\frac{2x^2+1}{2x^2-3}$

$\Rightarrow \frac{\sqrt{x^2+1}}{\sqrt{x^2-1}}=\frac{2x^2+1}{2x^2-3}$

Squaring both sides, we get $\frac{x^2+1}{x^2-1}=\frac{4x^4+1+4x^2}{4x^4+9-12x^2}$

Again applying componendo and dividendo, we get

$\frac{2x^2}{2}=\frac{8x^4+10-8x^2}{16x^2-8}$

$\Rightarrow 16x^4-8x^2=8x^4-8x^2+10$

$\Rightarrow 8x^4-10=0$

$\Rightarrow x^4=5/4 \quad \Rightarrow \pm\sqrt[4]{\frac{5}{4}}$

12. (a) $\frac{x^3-2x^2+x+1}{x^3-2x^2-x-1}=\frac{2x^3+x^2+3x-2}{2x^3+x^2-3x+2}$

Applying componendo and dividendo, we get

$\frac{2(x^3-2x^2)}{2(x+1)}=\frac{2(2x^3+x^2)}{2(3x-2)}$

$\Rightarrow \frac{x^3-2x^2}{x+1}=\frac{2x^3+x^2}{3x-2}$

$\Rightarrow 3x^4-2x^3-6x^3+4x^2=2x^4+2x^3+x^3+x^2$

$\Rightarrow x^4-11x^3+3x^2=0$

$\Rightarrow x^2(x^2-11x+3)=0$

Either $x=0$ or $x^2-11x+3=0$

$\Rightarrow x=\frac{11\pm\sqrt{109}}{2}$

Hence $x=0, \frac{11\pm\sqrt{109}}{2}$

(b) $\frac{(a+b)x-(m-n)}{(a-b)x-(m+n)}=\frac{(a+b)x+m+p}{(a-b)x+m-p}$

Applying componendo and dividendo, we get

$\frac{2(ax-m)}{2(bx+n)}=\frac{2(ax+m)}{2(bx+p)}$

$\Rightarrow \frac{ax-m}{bx+n}=\frac{ax+m}{bx+p}$

$\Rightarrow abx^2+axp-bmx-mp=abx^2+anx+mbx+mn$

$\Rightarrow axp-bmx-anx-mbx=mn+mp$

$\Rightarrow x(a^p-bm-an-mb)=m(n+p)$

$\Rightarrow x=\frac{m(n+p)}{ap-bm-an-mb}=\frac{m(n+p)}{a(p-n)-2mb}$

TEXTUAL EXERCISE-14 (SUBJECTIVE)

1. (a) Let us assume that $\sqrt{2}$ is rational

$\Rightarrow \sqrt{2}=\frac{p}{q}$ (p, q are co-prime)

Squaring, we get $\quad p^2=2q^2$

$\Rightarrow 2\mid p \Rightarrow p=2m \quad \Rightarrow q^2=2m^2$

$\Rightarrow 2\mid q$

Hence 2 is the common factor of p and q which were initially assumed to be co-prime

Hence our assumption is wrong $\Rightarrow \sqrt{2}$ is irrational

(b) Let us assume that $\sqrt{3}-\sqrt{2}$ is rational

$\Rightarrow \sqrt{3}-\sqrt{2}=m$

Squaring both sides, we get $5-2\sqrt{6}=m^2$

$\Rightarrow 5-m^2=2\sqrt{6} \quad \Rightarrow \frac{5-m^2}{2}=\sqrt{16}$

Which is a contradiction as a rational number cannot be equal to an irrational number.

$\Rightarrow$ Our assumption is wrong

$\Rightarrow \sqrt{3}-\sqrt{2}$ is irrational

(c) Let us assume $3\sqrt{2}$ to be a rational

$\Rightarrow 3\sqrt{2}=p \quad \Rightarrow \sqrt{2}=\frac{p}{3}$

But we have already proved that $\sqrt{2}$ is irrational

$\Rightarrow 3\sqrt{2}$ cannot be rational

$\Rightarrow 3\sqrt{2}$ is irrational $3\sqrt{2}$ is irrational

(d) Let us assume that $2-\sqrt{3}$ is rational

$\Rightarrow 5-\sqrt{3}=p \quad \Rightarrow 5-p=\sqrt{3}$

But $\sqrt{3}$ is irrational

$\Rightarrow 5-\sqrt{3}$ is irrational

2. (a) yes, the statement is true. The statement goes with the fact: all terminating decimals are rational.

$\Rightarrow x=2.5=\frac{5}{2}$

(b) yes, it is true $\quad \Rightarrow 1.25=\frac{125}{100}=\frac{125}{5^2.2^2}$

(c) True, $x=\frac{3}{7}=0.\overline{427571}$

$\Rightarrow$ Which is non-terminating repeating

(d) True by (b and c)

3. (a) $\frac{375}{50}$

$\Rightarrow$ Denominator 50 can be written as $50=5^2\times 2$, which has only 2 or 5 as its factors.

$\Rightarrow$ Hence the fraction terminates

(b) $\frac{76}{300} \quad \Rightarrow$ Non-terminating repeating

(c) $\frac{54}{280} \quad \Rightarrow$ non-terminating repeating

4. (a) $x=12.475 \quad \Rightarrow 100x=12475$

$\Rightarrow x=\frac{12475}{100}=\frac{499}{4}$

(b) $x=3.25$ (i) and $100x=325.25$ (ii)

(ii) – (i), we get $99x=322$

$\Rightarrow x=\frac{322}{99}$

(c) $x=6.425 \quad \Rightarrow 10x=64.25$

$\Rightarrow 100x=6425.25 \quad \Rightarrow 90x=6361$

$\Rightarrow x=\frac{6361}{90}$

5. (a) True; the set of integer is a subset of rational numbers

(b) True; $\frac{p}{q}$ is rational only when $q \neq 0$

(c) True; $\frac{a}{b} = \frac{c}{d}$ $\Rightarrow ab = cd$ (on cross-multiplication)

(d) True

(e) True

6. (a) True; (as π is defined as the ratio of circumference to diameter)

(b) True

(c) True; e.g., $2+\sqrt{3}$ is irrational

(d) True; e.g., $2\sqrt{3}$ is irrational

(e) True; $\sqrt{2}+(-\sqrt{2})$ is rational

7. (i) Multiplying the denominator and numerator by $3+\sqrt{5}$

$\Rightarrow \frac{2}{(3-\sqrt{5})}\frac{(3+\sqrt{5})}{3+\sqrt{5}} = \frac{2(3+\sqrt{5})}{4} = \left[\frac{3}{2}+\frac{\sqrt{5}}{2}\right]$

(ii) Multiplying the numerator and denominator by $2\sqrt{3}-\sqrt{7}$

$\Rightarrow \frac{2\sqrt{3}-\sqrt{7}}{5} = \left[\frac{2\sqrt{3}}{5}-\frac{\sqrt{7}}{5}\right]$

(iii) $\frac{2}{\sqrt{5}+\sqrt{3}+2} \Rightarrow \frac{2(2+\sqrt{3}-\sqrt{5})}{(2+\sqrt{3}+\sqrt{5})(2+\sqrt{3}-\sqrt{5})}$

$\Rightarrow \frac{2(2+\sqrt{3}-\sqrt{5})}{4+3+4\sqrt{3}-5} = \frac{2(2+\sqrt{3}-\sqrt{5})}{2+4\sqrt{3}}$

$= \frac{2(2+\sqrt{3}-\sqrt{5})}{(4\sqrt{3}+2)} \times \frac{(4\sqrt{3}-2)}{(4\sqrt{3}-2)} = \frac{2(2+\sqrt{3}-\sqrt{5})(4\sqrt{3}-2)}{46}$

(iv) Which can be written as $\frac{12}{(3+\sqrt{5}-2\sqrt{2})}$

$= \frac{3+\sqrt{5}+2\sqrt{2}}{(3+\sqrt{5}+2\sqrt{2})}$

$\Rightarrow \frac{12(3+\sqrt{5}+2\sqrt{2})}{9+5+6\sqrt{5}-8} = \frac{12(3+\sqrt{5}+2\sqrt{2})}{6(1+\sqrt{5})}$

$= \frac{2(3+\sqrt{5}+2\sqrt{2})}{(1+\sqrt{5})} = \frac{2(3+\sqrt{5}+2\sqrt{2})(\sqrt{5}-1)}{4}$

$= 1+\sqrt{5}+\sqrt{10}-\sqrt{2}$

(v) Which can be written as

$\frac{(x+y)}{(\sqrt{x}+\sqrt{y}+\sqrt{x+y})} = \frac{(\sqrt{x}+\sqrt{y}-\sqrt{x+y})}{(\sqrt{x}+\sqrt{y}-\sqrt{x+y})}$

$= \frac{(x+y)(\sqrt{x}+\sqrt{y}-\sqrt{x+y})}{x+y-x-y+2\sqrt{xy}}$

$= \frac{(x+y)(\sqrt{x}+\sqrt{y}-\sqrt{x+y})}{2\sqrt{xy}}$

Which can be further rationalized as

$= \left(\frac{(x+y)(\sqrt{x}+\sqrt{y}-\sqrt{x+y})(\sqrt{xy})}{2xy}\right)$

(iv) $\frac{(\sqrt{3}+\sqrt{5})(\sqrt{5}+\sqrt{2})}{(\sqrt{2}+\sqrt{3}+\sqrt{5})}$

$= \frac{(\sqrt{3}+\sqrt{5})(\sqrt{5}+\sqrt{2})\times(\sqrt{2}+\sqrt{3}-\sqrt{5})}{(\sqrt{2}+\sqrt{3}+\sqrt{5})\times(\sqrt{2}+\sqrt{3}-\sqrt{5})}$

$= \frac{(\sqrt{3}+\sqrt{5})(\sqrt{5}+\sqrt{2})(\sqrt{2}+\sqrt{3}+\sqrt{5})}{5+2\sqrt{6}-5}$

$= \frac{\sqrt{6}(\sqrt{3}+\sqrt{5})(\sqrt{5}+\sqrt{2})(\sqrt{2}+\sqrt{3}-\sqrt{5})}{12}$

8. (i) $3^{1/3}+2^{1/2}$ $\Rightarrow$ L.C.M of the indices = 6

$\Rightarrow x^6 = 3^2 = 9; y^6 = 2^3 = 8$

$\Rightarrow x^6 - y^6 = (x^3+4^3)(x^3-y^3)$

$\Rightarrow (x+y)(x^2+y^2+xy)(x^3-y^3)$

$\Rightarrow$ Rationalizing factor of $(\sqrt[3]{3}+\sqrt{2})$ is $(\sqrt[3]{9}+2+\sqrt[3]{3}.\sqrt{2})$ $(3-\sqrt[2]{2})$

(ii) $\sqrt[6]{5}+\sqrt[3]{2}$ $\Rightarrow$ L.C.M of the indices = 6

$\Rightarrow x^6 = 5; y^6 = 4$

$\Rightarrow x^6 - y^6 = (x^3+y^3)(x^3-y^3) = (x+4)(x^2+y^2+xy)(x^3-y^3)$

Thus, the rationalizing factor for $x + y$ is = $(\sqrt[3]{2}+\sqrt[3]{4}+\sqrt[6]{5}.\sqrt[3]{2})(\sqrt{5}-2)$

(iii) $2+\sqrt[4]{7}$ $\Rightarrow$ L.C.M of indices 4

$\Rightarrow x^4 = 16$ $\Rightarrow y^4 = 7$

$\Rightarrow x^4 - y^4 = (x+y)(x-y)(x^2+y^2)$

The rationalizing factor would be = $(x-y)(x^2+y^2)$ = $(2-\sqrt[4]{7})(4+\sqrt{7})$

9. Which can be written as $\frac{(5+\sqrt{11})}{(3-2\sqrt{11})} = \frac{(3+2\sqrt{11})}{(3+2\sqrt{11})}$

$= \frac{15+10\sqrt{11}+3\sqrt{11}+22}{9-44} = \frac{(37+13\sqrt{11})}{-35} = -\frac{37}{35}-\frac{13}{35}\sqrt{11}$

$\Rightarrow x = -\frac{37}{35}; y = -\frac{13}{35}$

10. $\frac{\sqrt{5}-1}{\sqrt{5}+1}+\frac{\sqrt{5}+1}{\sqrt{5}-1}$; On rationalizing the individual factors, we get $\frac{(\sqrt{5}-1)(\sqrt{5}-1)}{(\sqrt{5}+1)(\sqrt{5}-1)}+\frac{(\sqrt{5}+1)(\sqrt{5}+1)}{(\sqrt{5}-1)(\sqrt{5}+1)}$

$= \frac{6+2\sqrt{5}}{4}+\frac{6+2\sqrt{5}}{4} = 3 \Rightarrow a = 3; b = 0$

11. (i) Let $\sqrt{16-2\sqrt{20}-2\sqrt{28}+2\sqrt{35}} = \sqrt{x}-\sqrt{y}-\sqrt{z}$

Squaring both sides, we get $16-2\sqrt{20}-2\sqrt{28}+2\sqrt{35}$

$= x+y+z-2\sqrt{xy}-2\sqrt{xz}+2\sqrt{yz}$

$\Rightarrow x+y+z = 16; xy = 20; xz = 28; yz = 35$

$\Rightarrow x = \pm 4, y = \pm 5, z = \pm 7$ and $x+y+z = 16$

$\Rightarrow$ Taking positive sign $\Rightarrow$ $x = 4; y = 5; z = 7$

$\Rightarrow$ Square root is $\pm(2-\sqrt{5}-\sqrt{7})$

(ii) Similarly assume $\sqrt{6+\sqrt{12}-\sqrt{24}-\sqrt{8}}$ $= \sqrt{x}-\sqrt{y}+\sqrt{z}$

On squaring both sides, $6+\sqrt{12}-\sqrt{24}-\sqrt{8}$
$= x+y+z-2\sqrt{xy}-2\sqrt{yz}+2\sqrt{xz}$

$\Rightarrow$ $x+y+z=6;\ xy=6;\ yz=2;\ xz=3$

$\Rightarrow$ $x=3;\ y=2;\ z=1$

$\Rightarrow$ Square root is $\pm\sqrt{3}-\sqrt{2}+1$

(iii) $b+z+\sqrt{2bz+z^2}$

Let $\sqrt{(b+z+\sqrt{2bz+z^2})}=\sqrt{p}+\sqrt{q}$

Squaring both sides, we get $b+z+\sqrt{2bz+z^2} = p+q+2\sqrt{pq}$

$\Rightarrow$ $b+q=b+z$ $\quad\Rightarrow$ $2\sqrt{pq}=\sqrt{2bz+z^2}$

$\Rightarrow$ $(p-q)^2=(p+q)^2-4pq=(b+z)^2-(2b^z+z^2)=b^2$

$\Rightarrow$ $p-q=b$

$\Rightarrow$ $p+q=b+z$

$\Rightarrow$ $p=b+\frac{z}{2};q=\frac{z}{2}$

$\Rightarrow$ Square root is $\left(\sqrt{b+\frac{z}{2}}+\sqrt{\frac{z}{2}}\right)$

(iv) $2x-\sqrt{3x^2-2xy-y^2}$

Which can be written as $=\frac{1}{2}\left[2\times 2x-2\sqrt{3x^2-2xy-y^2}\right]$

$=\frac{1}{2}\left[(3x+y)+(x-y)-2\sqrt{(3x+y)(x-y)}\right]$

$=\left[\sqrt{\frac{3x+y}{2}}\right]^2+\left[\sqrt{\frac{x-y}{2}}\right]^2-2\sqrt{\left(\frac{3x+y}{2}\right)\left(\frac{x-y}{2}\right)}$

$=\left[\sqrt{\frac{3x+y}{2}}+\sqrt{\frac{x-y}{2}}\right]^2$

Square root is $=\pm\left[\sqrt{\frac{3x+y}{2}}+\sqrt{\frac{x-y}{2}}\right]$

(v) $1+x^2+(1+x^2+x^4)^{1/2}$

Solving similarly as done in (iv), we get

$\frac{1}{2}[2+2x^2+2\sqrt{1+x^2+x^4}]$

$=\frac{1}{2}[(1+x^2+x)+(1+x^2-x)+2\sqrt{(1+x^2+x)(1+x^2-x)}]$

$=\frac{1}{2}\left[\sqrt{\frac{1+x^2+x}{2}}+\sqrt{\frac{1+x^2-x}{2}}\right]^2$

Square root of is $=\pm\left[\sqrt{\frac{1+x^2+x}{2}}+\sqrt{\frac{1+x^2-x}{2}}\right]$

(vi) $21-4\sqrt{5}+8\sqrt{3}-4\sqrt{15}$

Assuming $\sqrt{21-4\sqrt{5}+8\sqrt{3}-4\sqrt{15}}$
$=(\sqrt{x}-\sqrt{y}-\sqrt{z})$

Squaring both sides, we get $21-4\sqrt{5}+8\sqrt{3}-4\sqrt{15}$
$= x+y+z-2\sqrt{xy}+2\sqrt{yz}-2\sqrt{xz}$

On comparison, we get $x+y+z=21$

$\Rightarrow$ $xy=20$ $\quad\Rightarrow$ $yz=48$

$\Rightarrow$ $xz=60$ $\quad\Rightarrow$ $x=5;\ y=4;\ z=12$

Hence the square root is $\pm(\sqrt{5}-2-2\sqrt{3})$

12. $\sqrt{40\sqrt{2}+\sqrt{57}}-\sqrt{|40\sqrt{2}-57|}$

Let $\sqrt{40\sqrt{2}+57}=\sqrt{a}+\sqrt{b}$

Squaring both sides, we get $40\sqrt{2}+57=a+b+2\sqrt{ab}$

$\Rightarrow$ $a+b=57;\ ab=800$

$\Rightarrow$ $a=25;\ b=32$

Square root is $\pm(5+\sqrt{32})$

Simply $40\sqrt{2}-57<0$

$\Rightarrow$ $|40\sqrt{2}-57|=57-40\sqrt{2}$

Let $\sqrt{57-40\sqrt{2}}=\sqrt{a}-\sqrt{b}$

Squaring both sides, we get $57-40\sqrt{2}=a+b-2\sqrt{ab}$

$\Rightarrow$ $a+b=57;\ ab=400$

$\Rightarrow$ $a=32;\ b=25$ $\quad\Rightarrow$ Square root is $(\sqrt{32}-5)$

Since the difference is an integer
$=(5+\sqrt{32})-(\sqrt{32}-5)=10$

13. $\sqrt{2+\sqrt{3}+\sqrt{7+4\sqrt{3}}} = \sqrt{2+\sqrt{5}+\sqrt{(2+\sqrt{3})^2}}$

$=\sqrt{4+2\sqrt{3}} = \sqrt{(1+\sqrt{3})^2}=1+\sqrt{3}$

14. $\frac{\sqrt{5}+4\sqrt{3}}{\sqrt{5}-4\sqrt{3}}$; which can be written as

$\frac{\sqrt{5}+\sqrt{\sqrt{3}}(\sqrt{5}+\sqrt{\sqrt{3}})}{(\sqrt{5}-\sqrt{\sqrt{3}})(\sqrt{5}+\sqrt{\sqrt{3}})}$

$=\frac{(\sqrt{5}-\sqrt{\sqrt{3}})(\sqrt{5}+\sqrt{\sqrt{3}})(5+\sqrt{3})}{5-\sqrt{3}(5+\sqrt{3})}$

$=\frac{(5+\sqrt{3}+2\sqrt{5\sqrt{3}})(5+\sqrt{3})}{22}$

$=\frac{25+5\sqrt{3}+10\sqrt{75}+5\sqrt{3}+3+2\sqrt{15\sqrt{3}}}{22}$

$=\frac{28+10\sqrt{3}+10\sqrt{75}+2\sqrt{15\sqrt{3}}}{22}$

$=\frac{14+5\sqrt{3}+5\sqrt{75}+\sqrt{15\sqrt{3}}}{11}$

(expression as rational denominator).

15. $x=3.145$

$\Rightarrow$ $10x=31.45$ (i)

$\Rightarrow$ $1000\,x=3145.45$ (ii)

(ii) – (i), we get $990x=3114$

$\Rightarrow$ $x=\frac{314}{990}=\frac{157}{495}$

TEXTUAL EXERCISE–15 (SUBJECTIVE)

1. **(a)** $x > 4$ $\Rightarrow x \in (4, \infty)$
(b) $x < -2$ $\Rightarrow x \in (-\infty, -2)$
(c) $-2 < x < 5$ $\Rightarrow x \in (-2, -5)$
(d) $x \geq 3$ $\Rightarrow x \in [3, \infty)$
(e) $x \geq -5$ $\Rightarrow x \in [-5, \infty)$
(f) $-7 \leq x < 2$ $\Rightarrow x \in [-7, 2)$
(g) $-3 < x \leq 6$ $\Rightarrow x \in (-3, 6]$
(h) $-1 \leq x \leq 4$ $\Rightarrow x \in [-1, 4]$

2. **(i)** $(-3, 3]$ $\Rightarrow -3 < x \leq 3$

–3 –2 –1 0 1 2 3

(ii) $[6, 12)$ $\Rightarrow 6 \leq x < 12$

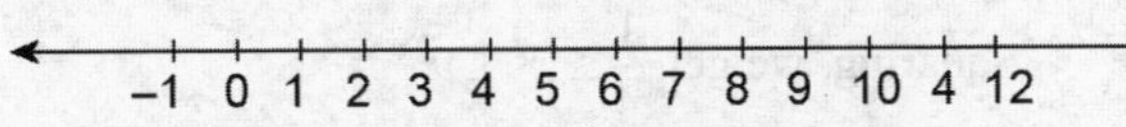

(iii) $[0, 5]$ $\Rightarrow 0 \leq x \leq 5$

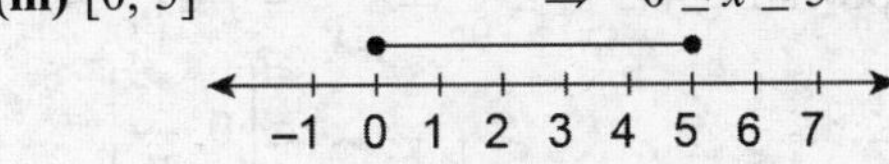

(iv) $\left(\frac{1}{2}, \infty\right)$ $\Rightarrow \frac{1}{2} < x < \infty$

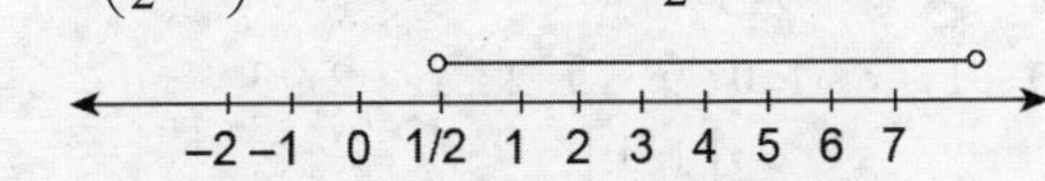

(v) $[-1, \infty)$ $\Rightarrow -1 \leq x < \infty$

–2 –1 0 1 2 3 4 5 6

(vi) $(-\infty, 4]$ $\Rightarrow -\infty < x \leq 4$

–3 –2 –1 0 1 2 3 4

3. **(i)** $\{x : x \in \mathbb{R} \text{ and } x > 3\}$ $\Rightarrow x \in (3, \infty)$
(ii) $\{x : x \in \mathbb{R} \text{ and } x \leq 0\}$ $\Rightarrow x \in (-\infty, 0]$
(iii) $\{x : x \in \mathbb{R} \text{ and } -2 < x < 5\}$ $\Rightarrow x \in (-2, 5)$
(iv) $\{x : x \in \mathbb{R} \text{ and } 3 < x \leq 7\}$ $\Rightarrow x \in (3, 7]$
(v) $\{x : x \in \mathbb{R} \text{ and } 4 \leq x \leq 9\}$ $\Rightarrow x \in [4, 9]$
(vi) $\{x : x \in \mathbb{R} \text{ and } x \leq 7\}$ $\Rightarrow x \in (-\infty, 7]$

TEXTUAL EXERCISE 16 (SUBJECTIVE)

1. **(a)** $30x < 200$

(i) Dividing by 30 both sides

$\Rightarrow x < \frac{20}{3}$

Since x is a natural no. $x = 1$ or 2 or 3 or 4 or 5 or 6

(ii) if x is an integer infinitely many solution.

(b) $5x - 3 < 3x + 1$ $\Rightarrow 2x < 4$

$\Rightarrow x < 2$

(i) x is an integer $x \in [-\infty, ...1, 0, 1]$

(ii) x is a real number $x \in (-\infty, 2)$

2. **(a)** $3x - 7 > x + 1 \Rightarrow 2x > 8 \Rightarrow x > 4$

$\Rightarrow x \in (4, \infty)$

(b) $-(x - 3) + 4 < 5 - 2x \Rightarrow (3 - x) + 4 < 5 - 2x$

$\Rightarrow (7 - x) < 5 - 2x \Rightarrow x < -2$

$\Rightarrow x \in (-\infty, -2)$

(c) $3x - 8 < x + 4 \Rightarrow 2x < 12$

$\Rightarrow x < 6 \Rightarrow x \in (-\infty, 6)$

(d) $2x + 7 \geq 5 - 2x \Rightarrow 4x \geq 5 - 7$

$\Rightarrow 4x \geq -2 \Rightarrow x \geq -\frac{1}{2}$

$\Rightarrow x \in \left[-\frac{1}{2}, \infty\right)$

(e) $\frac{5 - 2x}{3} \leq \frac{x}{6} - 5 \Rightarrow 5 - 2x \leq \frac{x}{2} - 15$

$\Rightarrow 10 - 4x \leq x - 30 \Rightarrow 10 - 5x \leq -30$

$\Rightarrow 5x \geq 40 \Rightarrow x \geq 8$

$\Rightarrow x \in [8, \infty)$

(f) $\frac{x}{5} < \frac{3x - 2}{4} - \left(\frac{5x - 3}{5}\right) \Rightarrow \frac{x}{5} < \frac{15x - 10 - 20x + 12}{20}$

$\Rightarrow 4x < -5x + 2 \Rightarrow 9x < 2$

$\Rightarrow x < \frac{2}{9} \Rightarrow x \in \left(-\infty, \frac{2}{9}\right)$

3. **(a)** $1 < x < 9 \Rightarrow -1 > -x > -9$

$\Rightarrow -1 > y > -9 \Rightarrow y \in (-9, -1)$

(b) $-9 < x < 5 \Rightarrow -9 < x < 0, x < 5$

$\Rightarrow 9 > x > 0, 0 > -x > -5$

$\Rightarrow 9 > y > 0, 0 > y > -5 \Rightarrow y \in (-5, 9)$

(c) $-9 < x < -6 \Rightarrow 9 > -x > 6$

$\Rightarrow 3 > -\frac{x}{3} > 2 \Rightarrow 3 > y > 2$

$\Rightarrow y \in (2, 3)$

(d) $-9 < x < 5 \Rightarrow 9 > -x > -5$

$\Rightarrow 27 > -3x > -15 \Rightarrow 27 > y > -15$

$\Rightarrow y \in (-15, 27)$

4. **(i)** $2 \leq x \leq 5 \Rightarrow 4 \leq x^2 \leq 25 \Rightarrow x^2 = [4, 25]$

(ii) $\frac{1}{2} < x \leq \frac{5}{3} \Rightarrow \frac{1}{4} < x^2 \leq \frac{25}{9}$

$\Rightarrow x^2 \in \left(\frac{1}{4}, \frac{25}{9}\right]$

(iii) $-\frac{1}{2} < x < \frac{3}{2}$

$\Rightarrow -\frac{1}{x} < x < 0 \Rightarrow 0 < x < \frac{3}{2}$

$\Rightarrow -\frac{1}{4} > x^2 > 0 \Rightarrow 0 < x^2 < \frac{9}{4}$

$\Rightarrow x^2 \in \left(0, \frac{9}{4}\right)$

(iv) $-2 < x < 3$

$\Rightarrow -2 < x < 0; 0 < x < 3$

$\Rightarrow 4 > x^2 > 0; 0 < x^2 < 9$

$\Rightarrow x^2 \in (0, 9)$

(iv) $-3 < x < 2$
$\Rightarrow$ $-3 < x < 0;\ 0 < x < 2$
$\Rightarrow$ $9 > x^2 > 0;\ 0 < x^2 < 4$
$\Rightarrow$ $x^2 \in (0, 9)$
(vi) $4 \le x \le 4$
$\Rightarrow$ $-4 \le x \le 0;\ 0 < x \le 4$
$\Rightarrow$ $16 \ge x^2 \ge 0;\ 0 < x^2 \le 16$
$\Rightarrow$ $x^2 \in [0, 16]$

5. (a) $1 \le x \le 5 \Rightarrow 1 \ge \frac{1}{x} \ge \frac{1}{5} \Rightarrow \frac{1}{x} \in \left[\frac{1}{5}, 1\right]$

(b) $2 \le x \le 7 \Rightarrow \frac{1}{2} \ge \frac{1}{x} \ge \frac{1}{7} \Rightarrow \frac{1}{x} \in \left[\frac{1}{7}, \frac{1}{2}\right]$

(c) $0 < x < \infty \Rightarrow \infty > \frac{1}{x} > 0 \Rightarrow \frac{1}{x} \in (0, \infty)$

(d) $0 < x \le 3 \Rightarrow \infty > \frac{1}{x} \ge \frac{1}{3} \Rightarrow \frac{1}{x} \in \left[\frac{1}{3}, \infty\right)$

(e) $-5 \le x \le -1 \Rightarrow -\frac{1}{5} \ge \frac{1}{x} \ge -1 \Rightarrow \frac{1}{x} \in \left[-1, -\frac{1}{5}\right]$

(f) $2 \le x \le 4 \Rightarrow \frac{1}{2} \ge \frac{1}{x} \ge \frac{1}{4} \Rightarrow x \in \left[\frac{1}{4}, \frac{1}{2}\right]$

(g) $-3 \le x \le 5;\ x \ne 0 \Rightarrow -3 \le x < 0$ or $0 < x \le 5$
$\Rightarrow -\frac{1}{3} \ge \frac{1}{x} > -\infty;\ \infty > \frac{1}{x} \ge \frac{1}{5}$
$\Rightarrow \frac{1}{x} \in \left(-\infty, -\frac{1}{3}\right] \cup \left[\frac{1}{5}, \infty\right)$

6. (a) (i) $-8x + 3(x - 2) > -x + 2$
$\Rightarrow$ $-8x + 3x - 6 > -x + 2$ $\Rightarrow -5x + x > 8$
$\Rightarrow$ $-4x > 8$ $\Rightarrow x < -2$
$\Rightarrow$ $x \in (-\infty, -2)$
(ii) $3x + 2 < x - 4$ $\Rightarrow 2x < -6$
$\Rightarrow$ $x < -3$ $\Rightarrow x \in (-\infty, -3)$
(iii) $2x + 5 > 3 - 2x$ $\Rightarrow 4x > -2$
$\Rightarrow$ $x > -\frac{1}{2}$ $\Rightarrow x \in \left(-\frac{1}{2}, \infty\right)$
(iv) $2x + 5 > x + 4 > x - 1$ $\Rightarrow 2x + 5 > x + 4$
$\Rightarrow$ $x > -1$ $\Rightarrow x + 4 > x - 1$
$\Rightarrow$ $0 > -5$ which is always true
$\Rightarrow$ $2x + 5 > x - 1$ $\Rightarrow x > -6$
$\Rightarrow$ $x \in (-1, \infty)$
(v) $3x > 6x + 9$ $\Rightarrow -3x > 9$
$\Rightarrow$ $x < -3$ $\Rightarrow x \in (-\infty, -3)$
(vi) $-3x + 6 < 12x - 9$ $\Rightarrow 15x > 15$
$\Rightarrow$ $x > 1$ $\Rightarrow x \in (1, \infty)$
(b) (i) $1 < x < 6$ $\Rightarrow -1 > x > -6$
$\Rightarrow$ $-1 > y > -6$ $\Rightarrow y \in (-6, -1)$
(ii) $-1 \le x \le 5$ $\Rightarrow -1 \le x \le 0$ or $0 \le x \le 5$
$\Rightarrow$ $1 \ge -x \ge 0$ or $0 \ge -x \ge -5$
$\Rightarrow$ $y \in [-5, 1]$
(iii) $-5 \le x \le -2$ $\Rightarrow 5 \ge -x \ge 2$
$\Rightarrow$ $5 \ge y \ge 2$ $\Rightarrow y \in [2, 5]$
(iv) $-2 \le x < 5$ $\Rightarrow -2 \le x < 0$ or $0 < x < 5$
$\Rightarrow$ $4 \ge x^2 \ge 0$ or $0 < x^2 < 25$ $\Rightarrow y \in [0, 25]$

(v) $-5 < x \le -1$ $\Rightarrow 1 \le x^2 < 25$
$\Rightarrow$ $x^2 = y \in [1, 25)$
(vi) $-2 \le x < 1$ $\Rightarrow -2 \le x < 0$ or $0 < x < 1$
$\Rightarrow$ $-\frac{1}{2} \ge \frac{1}{x} > -\infty$ or $\infty > \frac{1}{x} > 1$
$\Rightarrow$ $y = \frac{1}{x} \in \left[-\infty, -\frac{1}{2}\right) \cup (1, \infty)$
(vii) $-6 \le x \le -1$ $\Rightarrow -\frac{1}{6} \ge \frac{1}{x} \ge -1$
$\Rightarrow$ $y = \frac{1}{x} \in \left[-1, -\frac{1}{6}\right]$
(viii) $2 < x < 3$ $\Rightarrow 8 < x^3 < 27$
$\Rightarrow$ $x^3 = y \in (8, 27)$
(ix) $-3 \le x \le -5$ $\Rightarrow -125 \le x^3 \le -27$
$\Rightarrow$ $y = x^3 \in [-125, -27]$
(x) $\frac{1}{2} \le x \le 3$
Squaring, we get $\frac{1}{4} \le x^2 \le 9$
Reciprocating $4 \ge \frac{1}{x^2} \ge \frac{1}{9} \Rightarrow \frac{1}{x^2} = y \in \left[\frac{1}{9}, 4\right]$
(xi) $-\frac{1}{5} \le x \le \frac{1}{5}$ $\Rightarrow x^2 \in \left[0, \frac{1}{25}\right]$
$\Rightarrow$ $0 \le x^2 \le \frac{1}{25}$ $\Rightarrow \frac{1}{x^2} \in [25, \infty)$
(xii) $-1 \le x \le 1;\ 0 \le x^2 \le 1;\ 2 \le x^2 + 2 \le 3$
$\Rightarrow$ $y = \frac{1}{x^2 + 2} \in \left[\frac{1}{3}, \frac{1}{2}\right]$

7. (a) $x^2 - 3x + 2 < 0$ $\Rightarrow (x - 1)(x - 2) < 0$
$\Rightarrow x \in (1, 2)$
(b) $x^2 - 5x + 4 \ge 0$ $\Rightarrow (x - 4)(x - 1) \ge 0$
$\Rightarrow x \in (-\infty, 1) \cup (4, \infty)$
(c) $x(x - 3) \le 0$ $\Rightarrow x \in [0, 3]$
(d) $x(x - 1)(x - 2) > 0$
It is positive when $x \in (0, 1) \cup (2, \infty)$
(e) $\frac{x}{x - 5} > \frac{1}{2}$ $\Rightarrow 2x > x - 5\ (x \ge 5)$
$\Rightarrow x > -5$ $\Rightarrow x \in (5, \infty)$
If $x \le 5$, then $2x < x - 5$ $\Rightarrow x < -5$
$\Rightarrow x \in (-\infty, -5)$ $\Rightarrow x \in (-\infty, -5) \cup (5, \infty)$
(f) $\frac{1}{x} \le 1$; $x \ge 0;\ 1 \le x$ $\Rightarrow x \in [1, \infty)$
If $x \le 0;\ 1 \ge x$ $\Rightarrow x \in (-\infty, 0)$
Overall $x \in [-\infty, 0) \cup [1, \infty)$
(g) $\frac{x - 5}{x - 9} \le 0$; $x > 9$; $x - 5 \le x - 9$
$\Rightarrow$ $-5 \le -9$, which is not possible
$5 \le x < 9$; $x - 5 \ge x - 9$
$\Rightarrow$ $-5 \ge -9$, which is always true
$x < 5$; both $x - 5$ and $x - 9$ are negative
$\Rightarrow$ $\frac{x - 5}{x - 9} > 0$; Hence not possible
$\Rightarrow$ $x \in [5, 9)$

(h) $\dfrac{5x}{3x-1} \le 0 = \dfrac{\frac{5}{3}x}{x-\frac{1}{3}} \le 0$

$x > \dfrac{1}{3}$;

$\Rightarrow \dfrac{5}{3}x \le x - \dfrac{1}{3} \quad \Rightarrow \dfrac{2x}{3} \le -\dfrac{1}{3}$

$\Rightarrow x \le \dfrac{1}{2}$; which is not possible

$0 \le x < \dfrac{1}{3}$;

$\Rightarrow \dfrac{5}{3}x \ge x - \dfrac{1}{3} \quad \Rightarrow \dfrac{2x}{3} \ge -\dfrac{1}{3}$

$\Rightarrow x \ge -\dfrac{1}{2} \quad \Rightarrow x \in \left[0, \dfrac{1}{3}\right)$

$x < 0$;

$\Rightarrow$ $5x$ and $3x - 1$ are both negative, hence $\dfrac{5x}{3x-1} > 0$.

Hence not possible

(i) $x \le \dfrac{3x-3-1}{x-1} \quad \Rightarrow x \le \dfrac{3x-4}{x-1}; x > 1 \, (\text{clearly} \, x \ne 1)$

$\Rightarrow x^2 - x \le 3x - 4 \quad \Rightarrow x^2 - 4x + 4 \le 0$

$\Rightarrow$ $x = 2$ is the only solution

If $x < 1$, then $x^2 - x \ge 3x - 4$

$\Rightarrow x^2 - 4x + 4 \ge 0$

Hence the solution $x \in (-\infty, 1) \cup \{2\}$

8. **(a)** (i) If $2x + 3 < 3x - 4 \quad \Rightarrow \quad -x < -7$

$\Rightarrow x > 7 \quad \Rightarrow x \in (7, \infty)$

(ii) $3x - 2 > x + 2 \quad \Rightarrow 2x > 4$

$\Rightarrow x > 2 \quad \Rightarrow x \in (2, \infty)$

(iii) $x + 8 > 3x + 1 \quad \Rightarrow 2x < 7$

$\Rightarrow x < \dfrac{7}{2} = 3.5 \quad \Rightarrow x \in (-\infty, 3.5)$

(iv) $5x - 1 < 4x + 6 \quad \Rightarrow x < 7$

$\Rightarrow x \in (-\infty, 7)$

$\Rightarrow x = (7, \infty) \cap (2, \infty) \cap (-\infty, 3.5) \cap (\infty, 7) = \phi$

(b) $x - 1 < 11 - 3x \quad \Rightarrow 4x < 12$

$\Rightarrow x < 3 \quad \Rightarrow x \in (-\infty, 3)$

$x(x - 4) < 0 \quad \Rightarrow x \in (0, 4)$

$\Rightarrow x = (-\infty, 3) \cap (0, 4) \Rightarrow x \in (0, 3)$

9. $\dfrac{x}{8} - \dfrac{x}{4} + \dfrac{x}{2} > x + 5 \Rightarrow \dfrac{x}{8} - \dfrac{x}{4} + \dfrac{x}{2} - x > 5$

$\Rightarrow \dfrac{x - 2x + 4x - 8x}{8} > 5 \Rightarrow -5x > 40$

$\Rightarrow x < -8 \quad \Rightarrow x \in (-\infty, -8)$

$\dfrac{x-2}{8} < \dfrac{2-x}{-7} \quad \Rightarrow 7x - 14 < 16 - 8x$

$\Rightarrow 15x < 30 \quad \Rightarrow x < 2$

$\Rightarrow x \in (-\infty, 2) \quad \Rightarrow x = (-\infty, 0) \cap (-\infty, 2)$

$\Rightarrow (-\infty, -8) \quad \Rightarrow -9$

10. **(a)** $x^3 - 6x \le 0 \Rightarrow \quad x(x + \sqrt{6})(x - \sqrt{6}) \le 0$

$\Rightarrow x \in (-\infty, -\sqrt{6}] \cup [0, \sqrt{6}]$

(b) $x^4 + x^3 - x - 1 > 0 \quad \Rightarrow x(x^3 - 1) + (x^3 - 1) > 0$

$\Rightarrow (x^3 - 1)(x + 1) > 0$

$\Rightarrow (x - 1)(x + 1)(x^2 + 1 - x) > 0$

$\Rightarrow (x - 1)(x + 1) > 0 \quad \Rightarrow x \in (-\infty, -1) \cup (1, \infty)$

(c) $(x^2 - 5x + 6)(x^2 - 3x + 4) < 0$

$\Rightarrow (x - 2)(x - 3)(x^2 - 3x + 4) < 0$

$\Rightarrow x^2 - 3x + 4 > 0$

$\Rightarrow (x - 2)(x - 3) < 0 \quad \Rightarrow x \in (2, 3)$

11. $(x + 3)(x - 3)^2(x - 5)(x - 4)^4(x - 6) < 0$

$\Rightarrow x \in (-\infty, -3) \cup (5, 6) \Rightarrow$ Largest integer $= -4$

12. **(a)** $9 < x < 5 \quad \Rightarrow 25 < x^2 < 81$

$\Rightarrow y \in (25, 81)$

(b) $3 < x < 5 \quad \Rightarrow 9 < x^2 < 25$

$\Rightarrow y \in (9, 25)$

(c) $-9 < x < 5 \quad \Rightarrow x^2 \in [0, 81)$

(d) $4 < x^2 < 9 \quad \Rightarrow 2 < x < 3 \; or \; -3 \le x < -2$

$\Rightarrow y \in (2, 3) \cup (-3, -2)$

(e) $-9 < x < 5 \quad \Rightarrow 0 \le \sqrt{x} < \sqrt{5}$

$\Rightarrow \sqrt{x} = y \in [0, \sqrt{5})$

(f) $9 < x^2 < 25 \quad \Rightarrow 3 < x < 5 \; or -5 < x < -3$

$\Rightarrow x \in (-5, -3) \cup (3, 5)$

13. **(a)** $-9 \le x \le 5 \Rightarrow \; -729 \le x^3 \le 125$

$\Rightarrow y = x^3 \in [-729, 125]$

(b) $27 < x^3 < 125 \quad \Rightarrow 3 < x < 5$

$\Rightarrow y = x \in (3, 5)$

(c) $32 < x^5 < 243$ (Taking fifth roots)

$\Rightarrow 2 < x < 3 \quad \Rightarrow y = x \in (2, 3)$

14. **(a)** $2 < x < 5 \Rightarrow \dfrac{1}{5} < \dfrac{1}{x} < \dfrac{1}{2} \quad \Rightarrow \dfrac{1}{5} < y < \dfrac{1}{2}$

$\Rightarrow y \in \left(\dfrac{1}{5}, \dfrac{1}{2}\right)$

(b) $-6 < x < 6; -6 < x < 0$ or $0 < x < 6$

$\Rightarrow -\dfrac{1}{6} > \dfrac{1}{x} > -\infty$ or $\infty > \dfrac{1}{x} > \dfrac{1}{6}$

$\Rightarrow \dfrac{1}{x} \in \left(-\infty, -\dfrac{1}{6}\right) \cup \left(\dfrac{1}{6}, \infty\right)$

$\Rightarrow \dfrac{1}{x^2} \in \left(\dfrac{1}{36}, \infty\right) \quad \Rightarrow y \in \left(\dfrac{1}{36}, \infty\right)$

(c) $-2 < x < -1 \quad \Rightarrow 1 < \dfrac{1}{x} < \dfrac{-1}{2}$

$\Rightarrow y \in \left(-1, \dfrac{-1}{2}\right)$

(d) $-2 < x < 2, \; y = \dfrac{1}{x^3} \quad \Rightarrow -8 < x^3 < 8$

$\Rightarrow -8 < x^3 < 0$ or $0 < x < 8$

$\Rightarrow -\dfrac{1}{8} > \dfrac{1}{x^3} > -\infty$ or $\infty < \dfrac{1}{x} < \dfrac{1}{8}$

$\Rightarrow -\dfrac{1}{8} > y > -\infty$ or $\infty > y > \dfrac{1}{8}$

$\Rightarrow y \in \left(-\infty, -\dfrac{1}{8}\right) \cup \left(\dfrac{1}{8}, \infty\right)$

15. **(a)** $-2 < x < 4 \Rightarrow -6 < 3x < 12 \Rightarrow -8 < 3x - 2 < 10$

$\Rightarrow \frac{1}{3x-8} \in \left(-\infty, -\frac{1}{8}\right) \cup \left(\frac{1}{10}, \infty\right)$

(b) $y = \frac{x-1}{x+2} = \frac{x+2-3}{x+2} = 1 - \left(\frac{3}{x+2}\right)$

Given $-1 < x < 3 \Rightarrow 1 < x + 2 < 5$

$\Rightarrow 1 > \frac{1}{x+2} > \frac{1}{5} \qquad \Rightarrow 3 > \frac{3}{x+2} > \frac{3}{5}$

$\Rightarrow -\frac{3}{5} > \frac{-3}{x+2} > -3$

$\Rightarrow \frac{2}{5} > 1 - \frac{3}{x+2} > -2 \qquad \Rightarrow y \in \left(-2, \frac{2}{5}\right)$

(c) $y = \frac{1}{x^2+4}$ Given $2 \le x \le 3$

$\Rightarrow 4 \le x^2 \le 9 \qquad \Rightarrow 8 \le x^2 + 4 \le 13$

$\Rightarrow \frac{1}{13} \le \frac{1}{x^2+4} \le \frac{1}{8} \qquad \Rightarrow \frac{1}{x^2+4} \in \left[\frac{1}{13}, \frac{1}{8}\right]$

(d) $y = \frac{x^2-1}{x^2+1} = \frac{x^2+1-2}{x^2+1} = 1 - \frac{2}{x^2+1}; -1 < x < 3$

$\Rightarrow 0 < x^2 < 9 \qquad \Rightarrow 1 < x^2 + 1 < 10$

$\Rightarrow \frac{1}{10} < \frac{1}{x^2+1} < 1 \qquad \Rightarrow -2 < \frac{2}{x^2+1} < \frac{-1}{5}$

$\Rightarrow -1 < 1 - \frac{2}{x^2+1} < \frac{4}{5} \qquad \Rightarrow \frac{x^2-1}{x^2+1} \in \left(-1, \frac{4}{5}\right)$

16. Let us assume that one of the integers in $2n + 1$. The other integer would be $(2n + 3)$

By the question,

$2n + 1 < 10$ (i)

$2n + 3 < 10$ (ii)

and $4n + 4 > 1$ (iii)

By equation (i) $n < \frac{9}{2} = 4.5$

Equation (ii) $n < \frac{7}{2} = 3.5$

Equation (iii) $n < \frac{7}{4} = 1.75 \qquad \Rightarrow 1.75 < n < 3.5$

Obviously n is a an integer $\Rightarrow n = 2$ or 3

If $n = 2$

$2n + 1 = 5 \qquad \Rightarrow 2n + 3 = 7$

$\therefore$ (5, 7)

If $n = 3 \Rightarrow \qquad 2n + 1 = 7$

$\Rightarrow 2n + 3 = 9 \qquad \Rightarrow (7, 9)$

$\Rightarrow$ Possible pairs (5, 7); (7, 9)

17. Let one of the integers be $2n$, the other would be $(2n + 2)$.

By the question $\quad 2n > 5$ (i)

$2n + 2 > 5$ ...(ii) and

$4n + 2 < 23$ ...(iii)

By equation (i) $\quad n > 2.5$

Equation (ii) $\quad n > 1.5 \Rightarrow n < 2.5$

Equation (iii) $\quad n < 5.25 \Rightarrow 2.5 < n < 5.25$

Obviously n is an integer

$\Rightarrow n = 3, 4, 5$

$n = 3 \qquad \Rightarrow (6, 8)$

$n = 4 \qquad \Rightarrow (8, 10)$

$n = 5 \qquad \Rightarrow (10, 12)$

18. Assuming without the loss of any generality $a < b < c$.

By the question $c = 2a$; $b = c - 2 = 3a - 2$

$\Rightarrow a + b + c \le 61 \qquad \Rightarrow a + 3a - 2 + 3a \le 61$

$\Rightarrow 7a - 2 \le 61 \qquad \Rightarrow 7a \le 63$

$\Rightarrow a \le 9$

$\Rightarrow$ Minimum length of shortest side = 9 cm.

TEXTUAL EXERCISE–17: (SUBJECTIVE)

1. **(a)** $(a - 4)x + 5 = a + 1$

$\Rightarrow x = \frac{a-4}{a-4}$; $a \ne 4 \qquad \Rightarrow x = 1$

If $a = 4 \qquad \Rightarrow 0.x + 5 = 5$

$\Rightarrow 0.x = 0$, which is true $\forall\ x \in \mathbb{R}$

(b) $2a(a - 5)x = a - 5$

$a \ne 5, a \ne 0 \qquad \Rightarrow 2ax = 1$

$\Rightarrow x = \frac{1}{2a}$

$a = 5 \qquad \Rightarrow 10.0.x = 0$

$\Rightarrow x \in \mathbb{R}$ (true always)

$a = 0 \qquad \Rightarrow 2.0.(-5).x = -5$

$\Rightarrow$ No solution

(c) $ax + 2x - 6 = 2a - x \Rightarrow ax + 2x + x = 2a + 6$

$\Rightarrow x(a + 3) = 2a + 6$

$a \ne 3 \qquad \Rightarrow x = 2$

$a = -3 \qquad \Rightarrow x.0 = 0$, which is true

$\Rightarrow x \in \mathbb{R}$

(d) $ax + 2x + 3 = 5 - x$; $x(a \ne 3) = 2$

if $a \ne -3 \qquad \Rightarrow x = \frac{2}{a+3}$

If $a = -3 \qquad \Rightarrow x.0 = 8$

Which not possible, hence no solution

2. **(a)** We can be written as, $\frac{x-2+2x+2}{(x+1)(x-2)} = 1$

$\Rightarrow \frac{3x}{(x+1)(x-2)} = 1$

If $x \ne -1$ and $x \ne 2 \qquad \Rightarrow 3x = x^2 - x - 2$

$\Rightarrow x^2 - 4x - 2 = 0$

$\Rightarrow x = \frac{4 \pm \sqrt{16+8}}{2} = (2 \pm \sqrt{6})$

(b) $\frac{x^2-4}{x^2+3x+2} = 0 = \frac{x^2-4}{(x+2)(x+1)} = 0$; $x \ne -2$; $x \ne -1$

$= x^2 - 4 = 0 \qquad \Rightarrow (x + 2)(x + 1) = 0$

$\Rightarrow x = -2$, 2 but $x \ne -2$

$\Rightarrow x = 2$

(c) $\frac{x^2+3x+2}{x^2+4x+3} = 0 = \frac{x^2+3x+2}{(x+3)(x+1)} = 0$; $x \ne -3$, $x \ne = -1$

$\Rightarrow x^2 + 3x + 2 = 0 \qquad \Rightarrow (x + 2)(x + 1) = 0$

$\Rightarrow x = -2$ or $x = -1$ but $x \ne -1$

$\Rightarrow x = -2$

3. **(a)** $\frac{x^2+5x+6}{x^3+3x^2+2x}=0=\frac{x^2+5x+6}{x(x^2+x+2)}=0$

$(x \neq 0, x \neq -2, x \neq -1)$

$\Rightarrow \frac{(x+3)(x+2)}{x(x+2)(x+1)}=0=\frac{x+3}{x(x+1)}=0$

$\Rightarrow x=-3$

(b) $\frac{x}{x+3}+\frac{4}{x+1}=2=\frac{x^2+x+4x+12}{(x+3)(x+1)}=2$

$\Rightarrow \frac{x^2+5x+12}{(x+3)(x+1)}=2 \quad \Rightarrow (x \neq -3 \text{ and } x \neq -1)$

$\Rightarrow x^2+5x+12=2(x^2+4x+3)$

$\Rightarrow x^2+5x+12=2x^2+8x+6$

$\Rightarrow x^2+3x-6=0 \quad \Rightarrow x=\frac{-3\pm\sqrt{9+24}}{2}=\frac{-3\pm\sqrt{33}}{2}$

(c) $\frac{2x-3}{x-1}+1=\frac{6x-x^2-6}{x-1}=\frac{3x-4}{x-1}=-\frac{x^2+6x-6}{x-1};(x\neq1)$

$\Rightarrow x^2-3x+2=0 \quad \Rightarrow (x-2)(x-1)=0$

$\Rightarrow x=2\ (x\neq1)$

4. **(a)** $x^2-y^2=7 \quad \Rightarrow (x+y)(x-y)=7$

Natural solution $\Rightarrow x=4; y=3$

Integral solutions $\Rightarrow x=\pm4, y=\pm3$

(b) $x^2-y^2=21 \quad \Rightarrow (x+y)(x-y)=21$

Integral solution $\Rightarrow x=\pm5, y=\pm2$

Natural solution $\Rightarrow x=\pm11, y=\pm10$

5. $P(x)=px^2+qx+r, p, q, r \in \mathbb{R}$

$P(5)=25p+5q+r$

$P(2)=4p+2q+r$

By the question; $P(5)=-3P(2)$

$\Rightarrow 25p+5q+r=-12p-6q-3r$

$\Rightarrow 37p+11q+4r=0$ (i)

Also $P(3)=0$

$\Rightarrow 9p+3q+r=0$ (ii)

$\Rightarrow 36p+12q+4r=0$ (iii)

(i) – (ii), we get $\quad p-q=0$

$\Rightarrow p=q$

Thus $48p+4r=0 \quad \Rightarrow 12p=-r$

$\Rightarrow -12=\frac{r}{p}$ = product of roots

One root = 3 and other = –4

$\Rightarrow r=48$

If $p=q=0$ equation becomes an identity.

TEXTUAL EXERCISE–18: (SUBJECTIVE)

1. **(a)** $\frac{x}{x-5}>\frac{1}{3}$; which can be written as $\frac{x}{x-5}-\frac{1}{3}>0$

$\Rightarrow \frac{3x-x+5}{3(x-5)}>0 \quad \Rightarrow \frac{(2x+5)}{x-5}>0$

Which can be written as $(2x+5)(x-5)>0$

$\Rightarrow x\in\left(-\infty,\frac{-5}{2}\right)\cup(5,\infty)$

Also $\frac{3}{x}\leq2 \quad \Rightarrow \frac{3}{x}-2\leq0$

$\Rightarrow \frac{3-2x}{x}\leq0 \quad \Rightarrow x(3-2x)\leq0$

$\Rightarrow x\in(-\infty,0]\cup\left[\frac{3}{2},\infty\right)$

Taking $\cap$ we get $x\in\left(-\infty,\frac{-5}{2}\right)\cup(5,\infty)$

(b) $\frac{x+2}{x-6}\leq0$; which is same as $(x+2)(x-6)\leq0$

$\Rightarrow x\in(-2,6)$

(c) $\frac{3x}{5x-4}\geq0$; which can also be written as $3x(5x-4)\geq0$

$(x\neq4/5)$

$\Rightarrow x(5x-4)\geq0$

$\Rightarrow x(x-4/5)\geq0 \quad \Rightarrow x\in(-\infty,0]\cup\left[\frac{4}{5},\infty\right)$

Remember there is an open inequality at 4/5 as the denominator becomes undefined.

(d) $x+\frac{1}{x-1}\leq3 \quad \Rightarrow x+\frac{1}{x-1}-3\leq0$

$\Rightarrow \frac{x^2-x+1-3(x-1)}{x-1}\leq0 \quad \Rightarrow \frac{x^2-x+1-3x+3}{x-1}\leq0$

$\Rightarrow \frac{x^2-4x+4}{x-1}\leq0$

Which can also be written as $(x^2-4x+4)(x-1)\leq0$

$\Rightarrow (x-2)^2(x-1)\leq0$

$\Rightarrow x\in(-\infty,1)\cup\{2\}$

2. **(a)** $x^4-16>0 \quad \Rightarrow (x^2-4)(x^2+4)$

$\Rightarrow (x+2)(x-2)(x^2+4)>0$

Let x^2+4 is always positive

$\Rightarrow (x+2)(x-2)>0 \quad \Rightarrow x\in(-\infty,-2)\cup(2,\infty)$

(b) $x^3-4x<0; x(x^2-4)<0$

$\Rightarrow x(x+2)(x-2)<0 \quad \Rightarrow x\in(-\infty,-2)\cup(0,2)$

(c) $x^6-x^5+x^4-x^3+x^2-x+1>0$

$P(x)=x^6-x^5+x^4-x^3+x^2-x+1$

This can be written as $x^5(x-1)+x^3(x-1)+x(x-1)+1>0$

$\Rightarrow (x-1)(x^5+x^3+x)+1>0$

$\Rightarrow x(x-1)(x^2+x+1)+1>0$

$\Rightarrow x(x-1)\geq0; x\in(-\infty,0]\cup[1,\infty)$

Also $x^2+x+1>0$ (same sign as the leading coefficient)

Hence this expression is always greater that 1.

The only case which remains is when $x\in(0,1)$ in this case what we can write is $x^6<x^5<x^4<x^3<x^2<x<1$

Also $x-1<0$

Hence $x\in\mathbb{R}$

3. $(x^2-16)(x^2+5x+4)(x^2-9)(x^2-7x+12)\leq0$

$\Rightarrow (x+4)(x-4)(x+4)(x+1)(x+3)(x-3)(x-4)(x-3)\leq0$

$\Rightarrow (x+4)^2(x-4)^2(x+1)(x+3)(x-3)^2\leq0$

By wavy curve method

The expression gets negative when $x\in[-3,-1]\cup\{-4, 3, 4\}$

4. (a) As done in previous question the given inequality can be re-written as $(x + 1)^5 (x - 1) (x + 4)^2 (x - 3)^4 (x + 8) (2x - 3) < 0$

By wave curve method

The solution region comes out to be $(-8, -4) \cup (-4, -1) \cup \left(1, \frac{3}{2}\right)$

(b) Similarly as done above $(x + 1) (x - 1) (x - 8) (x - 6)^2 (x - 5)^4 < 0$

By wavy curve method

Thus expression is negative in the region $x \in (-\infty, -1) \cup (1, 8) - (3, 5, 6)$

5. (a) $\frac{(x-1)^2(x+1)^3}{x^4(x-2)} \le 0$

This equation can be written as $(x - 1)^2 (x - 2) (x + 1)^3 \le 0$ $(x \ne 0)$

By wavy curve method $x \in (-1, 0) \cup (0, 2)$

(b) $x^2 + 3x + 2 = (x + 2)(x + 1) > 0$

$\Rightarrow x \in (-\infty, -2) \cup (-1, \infty)$ (i)

Also $\frac{x}{x+1} \le 0$; which can be written as $x(x + 1) \le 0$

$\Rightarrow x \in (-1, 0]$ (ii)

In (i) and (ii) taking intersection $x \in (-1, 0]$

6. (a) $x^2 - 4x - 12 \ge 0 \Rightarrow (x - 6) (x + 2) \ge 0$

$\Rightarrow x \in (-\infty, -2] \cup [6, \infty)$

Largest negative integer: –2

Smallest positive integer: 6

(b) $3x^2 + 5x + 2 \le 0 \Rightarrow 3x^2 + 3x + 2x + 2 \le 0$

$\Rightarrow 3x(x + 1) + 2(x + 1) \le 0$

$\Rightarrow (x + 1) + (3x + 2) \le 0$

Largest negative integer = –1. Smallest positive integer = no positive integer.

(c) $\frac{(x^2-5x+4)}{x^2-1} \le 1$

This can be written as $x \ne 1, -1$

$\Rightarrow \frac{x^2-5x+4}{x^2-1} - 1 \le 0 \Rightarrow \frac{-5x+5}{x^2-1} \le 0$

$\Rightarrow -5(x - 1) (x^2 - 1) \le 0 \Rightarrow (x - 1)^2 (x + 1) \ge 0$

$\Rightarrow (x + 1) \ge 0 \Rightarrow x \ge -1$, but $x \ne 1$ or -1

Hence no negative integer comes in the range.

Smallest positive integer = 2.

7. $x^2 - x - 6 \ge 0 \Rightarrow x^2 - 3x + 2x - 6 \ge 0$

$\Rightarrow x(x - 3) + 2(x - 3) \ge 0$

$\Rightarrow (x + 2) (x - 3) \ge 0$

$\Rightarrow x \in (-\infty, -2] \cup [3, \infty)$ ……(i) and

$|x| \le 10$

$\Rightarrow -10 \le x \le 10$ ……(ii)

Intersection of (i) and (ii), we get $[-10, -2] \cup [3, 10]$

8. (a) $x^4 + 5x^3 + 5x^2 + 5x + 4 \ge 0$

$p(x) = x^4 + 5x^3 + 5x^2 + 5x + 5$

$p(-1) = 1 - 5 + 5 - 5 + 4 = 5 - 5 + 5 - 5 = 0$

Hence $x + 1$ is a factor of $p(x)$

Thus $x^3(x + 1) + 4x^2(x + 1) + x(x + 1) 4(x + 1)$

$= (x + 1) (x^3 + 4x^2 + x + 4) = (x^2 + 1) (x + 1) (x + 4) \ge 0$

Also $x^2 + 1 > 0 \Rightarrow (x + 1) (x + 4) \ge 0$

By wavy curve method, we get $x \in (-\infty, -4] \cup [-1, \infty)$

(b) $x^4 - 2x^3 - x + 2 > 0$; which can written as $x^3(x - 2) - (x - 2) > 0$

$\Rightarrow (x^3 - 1) (x - 2) > 0 \Rightarrow (x - 1) (x^2 + x + 1) (x - 2) > 0$

$\Rightarrow x^2 + x + 1 > 0 \Rightarrow (x - 1) (x - 2) > 0$

By wavy curve method, $x \in (-\infty, 1] \cup [2, \infty)$

9. $y = (x - 2) (6 - x) = 6x - x^2 - 12 + 2x = -x^2 + 8x - 12$

$D = 64 - 4(-1) (-1) (-2) = 64 - 48 = 16$

$\left[\frac{-b}{2a}, -\frac{D}{4a}\right] = \left[\frac{-8}{-2}, \frac{-16}{-4}\right] = [4,4]$

Maximum value of expression = 4

Minimum value = $-\infty$

Graph of the expression is as following

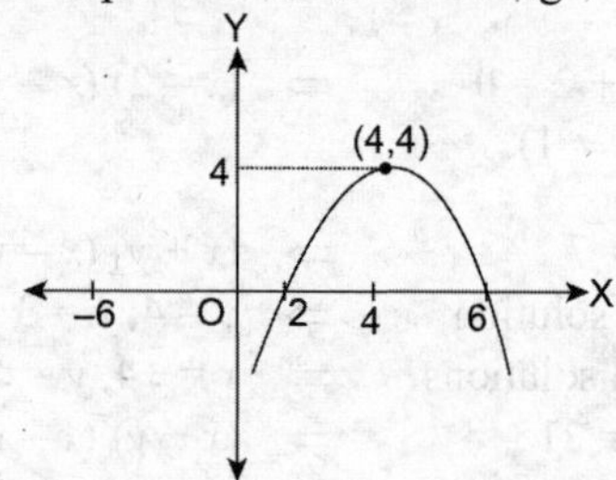

10. (a) $x^2 - 4x + 6$

Consider this quadratic expression $S = 16 - 24 = -8$

$\left(\frac{-b}{2a}, \frac{-D}{4a}\right) \equiv (2,2)$

$\Rightarrow 2 \le x^2 - 4x + 6 < \infty \Rightarrow 0 < \frac{1}{x^2-4x+6} \le \frac{1}{2}$

$\Rightarrow 0 < \frac{3}{x^2-4x+6} \le \frac{3}{2} \Rightarrow \frac{-3}{2} \le \frac{-3}{x^2-4x+6} < 0$

$\Rightarrow \frac{5}{2} \le 4 - \frac{3}{x^2-4x+6} < 4$

$\Rightarrow 4 - \frac{3}{x^2-4x+6} \in \left[\frac{5}{2}, 4\right)$

(b) Consider the quadratic expression $(x - 2) (x - 3) = x^2 - 5x + 6$

$D = 25 - 24 = 1$ $\left(\frac{-b}{2a}, \frac{-D}{4a}\right) = \left(\frac{5}{2}, \frac{-1}{4}\right)$

$\Rightarrow \frac{-1}{4} \le x^2 - 5z + 6 < \infty$

$\Rightarrow \frac{-1}{4} \le x^2 - 5x + 6 < 0$ or $0 \le x^2 - 5x + 6 < \infty$

$\Rightarrow -\infty < \frac{1}{x^2-5x+6} \le -4$ or $0 < \frac{1}{x^2-5x+6} < \infty$

$\Rightarrow -\infty < \frac{2}{x^2-5x+6} \le -8$ or $0 < \frac{2}{x^2-5x+6} < \infty$

$\Rightarrow -\infty < 3 + \frac{2}{x^2-5x+6} \le -5$ or $3 < 3 + \frac{2}{x^2-5x+6} < \infty$

Maximum value and minimum value not specifically defined but $\frac{3+2}{(x-2)(x-1)} \in (-\infty, -5] \cup (3, \infty)$

11. **(a)** $f(x) = ax^2 + bx + c$; $D < 0$, also $a < 0$

$\Rightarrow$ It is an opening upwards parabola which has no real roots.

Obviously $f(1) > 0 \quad \Rightarrow \quad a + b + c > 0$

Hence true.

(b) $f(x) = ax^2 + bx + c$; $a < 0, D < 0$

$\Rightarrow$ It is an opening downward parabola which has no real roots.

$\Rightarrow f(-1) < 0 \quad \Rightarrow \quad a - b + c < 0$

Hence true

(c) $f(x) = ax^2 + bx + c$; $a > 0, D < 0$

$\Rightarrow$ It is opening upward parabola with no real roots.

$\Rightarrow f(x) > 0$

Also $a > 0 \quad \Rightarrow \quad af(x) > 0$

Hence true

(d) $f(x) = ax^2 + bx + c$; $a < 0, D < 0$

$\Rightarrow$ it is opening downward parabola with no real roots

$\Rightarrow f(x) < 0$ also $a < 0$

$\Rightarrow a \neq f(x) > 0 \quad \Rightarrow$ false

12. $f(x) = x^2 + x + 1$

Since a > 0 it is an opening upward parabola

$D = 1 - 4 = -3 < 0$

Hence it has no real roots the graph of the parabola is

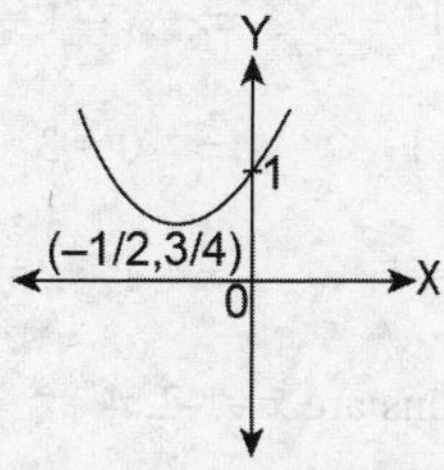

By the graph, it is evident that $f(x)$ never takes negative values $g(x) = x^2 - x + 1$

Here also a > 0. This is also an opening upward parabola $D = 1 - 4 = -3 < 0$

Hence no real roots $g(0) = 1$.

The graph of this parabola is

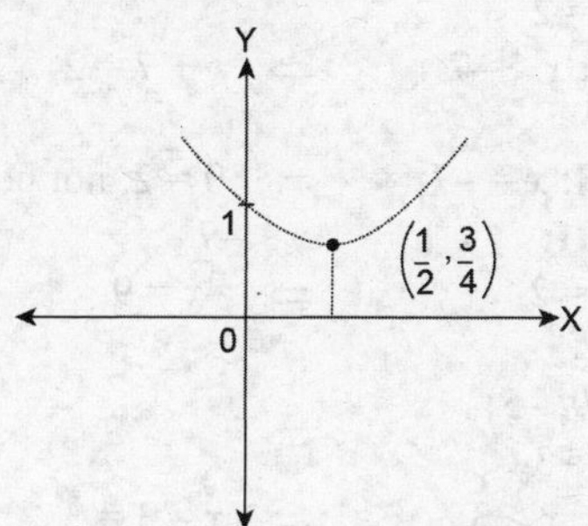

The $g(x)$ also never takes negative value for any real value of x.

TEXTUAL EXERCISE–19: (SUBJECTIVE)

1. **(a)** $|x| = 3 \quad \Rightarrow x = 3$ or -3

(b) $|x| = -5 \quad \Rightarrow$ This is not possible

$\Rightarrow x = \phi$.

2. **(a)** $x - |x| = 0 \quad \Rightarrow x = |x|$

If $x \geq 0 \quad \Rightarrow x = x$, which is true $\forall\, x$

If $x < 0$; $|x| = -x \quad \Rightarrow 2x = 0$

$\Rightarrow x = 0 \quad \Rightarrow x \in [0, \infty)$

(b) $x - |x| = 2x$

Case I: $x \geq 0 \quad \Rightarrow x - x = 2x$

$\Rightarrow x = 0$

Case II: $x < 0 \quad \Rightarrow 2x = 2x$; which is true for all x.

$\Rightarrow x \in (-\infty, 0]$

(c) $x + |x| = 0$

Case I: $x \geq 0 \quad \Rightarrow 2x = 0$

$\Rightarrow x = 0$

Case II: $x < 0 \quad \Rightarrow x - x = 0$

$\Rightarrow 0 = 0$, which is true for all x.

$\Rightarrow x \in (-\infty, 0]$

(d) $x + |x| = 2x$

Case I: $x \geq 0 \quad \Rightarrow 2x = 2x$

$\Rightarrow$ it is true for all x.

Case II: $x < 0 \quad \Rightarrow 0 = 2x$

$\Rightarrow x = 0$

$\Rightarrow x \in [0, \infty)$

3. **(a)** $\dfrac{|x|}{x} = 1$

Case I: $x \geq 0 \quad \Rightarrow \dfrac{x}{x} = 1$; which is true for all x except $x = 0$

Case II: $x < 0 \quad \Rightarrow \dfrac{|x|}{x} = -\dfrac{x}{x} = -1 = 1$ which is not possible

Hence $x \in (0, \infty)$

(b) $\dfrac{x}{|x|} \geq 1$

Case I: $x \geq 0 \quad \Rightarrow \dfrac{x}{x} \geq 1$

$\Rightarrow 1 \geq 1$

Which is true always except at $x = 0$

Case II: $x < 0 \quad \Rightarrow \dfrac{x}{-x} \geq 1$

$\Rightarrow -1 \geq 1$, which is never possible.

Hence $x \in (0, \infty)$

(c) $\dfrac{x}{|x|} = -1$

Case I: $x \geq 0 \quad \Rightarrow \dfrac{x}{\lambda} = -1$, which is not possible

Case II: $x < 0 \quad \Rightarrow \dfrac{x}{|x|} = \dfrac{x}{-x} = -1$. Hence $x \in (-\infty, 0)$

(d) $\dfrac{x}{|x|} \leq 1$

Case I: $x \geq 0 \quad \Rightarrow \dfrac{x}{|x|} = \dfrac{x}{x} = 1 \leq 1$ which is true when $x \in (0, \infty)$

Case II: $x < 0 \quad \Rightarrow \dfrac{x}{|x|} = \dfrac{x}{-x} = -1 \leq 1$ which is also true

Hence $x \in (-\infty, \infty) - \{x\}$

4. (a) $x|x| + x^2 = 0$

Case I: If assume $x \geq 0$

$\Rightarrow |x| = x \quad \Rightarrow x^2 + x^2 = 0$

$\Rightarrow 2x^2 = 0 \quad \Rightarrow x = 0$

Case II: If $x < 0 \quad \Rightarrow |x| = -x$

$\Rightarrow x^2 - x^2 = 0$, which is true for all x.

$\Rightarrow x \in (-\infty, 0]$

(b) $|x| > -x$

Case I: If $x \geq 0 \quad \Rightarrow x > -x$

$\Rightarrow 2x > 0 \quad \Rightarrow x > 0$

$\Rightarrow x \in (0, \infty)$

Case II: If $x < 0 \quad \Rightarrow -x > -x$

$\Rightarrow 0 > 1$ not possible $\Rightarrow x \in (0, \infty)$

(c) $x^2 + |x| = 0$

Case I: $x \geq 0 \quad \Rightarrow |x| = x$

$\Rightarrow x^2 + x = 0 \quad \Rightarrow x(x + 1) = 0$

$\Rightarrow x = 0, -1 \quad \Rightarrow -1$ is not in domain, hence $x = 0$

Case II: $x < 0 \quad \Rightarrow |x| = -x$

$\Rightarrow x^2 - x = 0 \quad \Rightarrow x(x - 1) = 0$

$\Rightarrow x = 1$ or $0 \quad \Rightarrow$ Hence the overall solution is $x = 0$.

(d) $x|x| - x^2 = 0$

Case I: $x \geq 0 \quad \Rightarrow |x| = x$

$\Rightarrow x^2 - x^2 = 0$; which is true

Case II: $x < 0 \quad \Rightarrow |x| = -x$

$\Rightarrow -2x^2 = 0 \quad \Rightarrow x^2 = 0$

$\Rightarrow x = 0$, hence $x \in [0, \infty)$

(e) $|x| < -x$

Case I: $x \geq 0 \quad \Rightarrow |x| = x$

$\Rightarrow x < -x \quad \Rightarrow 2x < 0$

$\Rightarrow x < 0$

Case II: $x < 0 \quad \Rightarrow |x| = -x$

$\Rightarrow -x < -x \quad \Rightarrow 0 < 0$

No solution, hence no solution.

(f) $3x\sqrt{2} = \sqrt{18x^2} \quad \Rightarrow 3x\sqrt{2} = 3\sqrt{2}\,|x|$

$\Rightarrow x = |x|$

Case I: $x \geq 0 \quad \Rightarrow x = x$ which is always true

Case II: $x < 0 \quad \Rightarrow x = -x$

$\Rightarrow 2x = 0 \quad \Rightarrow x = 0$

Hence $x \in [0, \infty)$

5. (a) $x^2 - 3|x| - 4 = 0$

Case I: $x \geq 0 \quad \Rightarrow |x| = x$

Equation reduces to $x^2 - 3x - 4 = 0$

$\Rightarrow (x - 4)(x + 1) = 0 \quad \Rightarrow x = 4, -1$

Hence only solution is domain $x = 4$.

Case II: $x < 0 \quad \Rightarrow |x| = -x$

Equation reduces to $x^2 + 3x - 4 = 0$

$\Rightarrow (x + 4)(x - 1) = 0 \quad \Rightarrow x = 1, -4$

Only solution is domain $x = 4$

$\Rightarrow x = \{-4, 4\}$

(b) $x^2 + 3|x| + 4 = 0$

Case I: $x \geq 0 \quad \Rightarrow |x| = x$

Equation reduces to $x^2 + 3x + 4 = 0$, which has no solution visibly.

Case II: $x < 0 \quad \Rightarrow |x| = -x$

Equation reduces to $x^2 - 3x + 4 = 0$, which also has no solution clearly

$\Rightarrow x \in \phi$

(c) $x^2 - 3|x| + 2 = 0$

Case I: $x \geq 0 \quad \Rightarrow |x| = x$

$\Rightarrow x^2 - 3x + 2 = 0$

$\Rightarrow x^2 - 2x - x + 2 = 0 \quad \Rightarrow x(x - 2) - (x - 2) = 0$

$\Rightarrow (x - 1)(x - 2) = 0$

$\Rightarrow x = 1$ or 2

Case II: $x < 0 \quad \Rightarrow |x| = -x$

$\Rightarrow x^2 + 3x + 2 = 0$

$\Rightarrow x^2 + 2x + x + 2 = 0 \quad \Rightarrow x(x + 2) + (x + 2) = 0$

$\Rightarrow (x + 2)(x + 1) = 0$

$\Rightarrow x = -1$ or -2

Hence $x \in \{-1, 1, -2, 2\}$

(d) $|x| + x^2 + 1 = 0$

Case I: $x \geq 0 \quad \Rightarrow |x| = x$

Equation reduces to $x^2 + x + 1 = 0$, which has no solution clearly

Case II: $x < 0 \quad \Rightarrow |x| = -x$

$\Rightarrow x^2 - x + 1 = 0$

Which has no solution $\quad \Rightarrow x \in \phi$

6. (a) $|x - 1| = 3$

Case I: $x > 1 \quad \Rightarrow x - 1 = 3$

$\Rightarrow x = 4$

Case II: $x = 1 \quad \Rightarrow 0 = 3$

$\Rightarrow$ No solution

Case III: $x < 1 \quad \Rightarrow 1 - x = 3$

$\Rightarrow x = -2$

Hence the solutions are $x = -2, 4$

(b) $|x + 2| = 5$

Case I: $x > -2 \quad \Rightarrow x + 2 = 5$

$\Rightarrow x = 3$

Case II: $x = -2 \quad \Rightarrow 0 = 5$, not possible

Case III: $x < -2 \quad \Rightarrow -x - 2 = 5$, not possible

$\Rightarrow x = -7$

Hence $x \in \{3, -7\}$

(c) $|7 + x| = 2$

Case I: $x > -7 \quad \Rightarrow x + 7 = 2$

$\Rightarrow x = -5$

Case II: $x = -7 \quad \Rightarrow 0 = 2$, not possible

Case III: $\quad x < -7$

$\Rightarrow -x - 7 = 2 \quad \Rightarrow -x = 9$

$\Rightarrow x = -9$

$\Rightarrow x \in \{-9, -5\}$

(d) $|x - 3| = 3$

Case I: $x > 3 \quad \Rightarrow x - 3 = 3$

$\Rightarrow x = 6$

Case II: $x < 3 \quad \Rightarrow 3 - x = 3$

$\Rightarrow x = 0$

Remember in this case $x = 3$ is not possible, so has not been considered.

$\Rightarrow x \in \{0, 6\}$

(e) $|2x - 5| = 3$

Case I: $x > 5/2 \quad \Rightarrow 2x - 5 = 3$

$\Rightarrow x = 4$

Case II: $x < 5/2$ $\Rightarrow$ $5 - 2x = 3$

$\Rightarrow$ $x = 1$

To in above $x = 5/2$ is not possible

$\Rightarrow$ $x \in \{1, 4\}$

(f) $|3x - 5| = 3$

Case I: $x > 5/3$ $\Rightarrow$ $3x - 5 = 3$

$\Rightarrow$ $x = 8/3$

Case II: $x < 5/3$ $\Rightarrow$ $5 - 3x = 3$

$\Rightarrow$ $x = 2/3$

$\Rightarrow$ $x \in \left\{\frac{2}{3}, \frac{8}{3}\right\}$

(g) $|2x + 5| = 3$

Case I: $x < -5/2$ $\Rightarrow$ $-2x - 5 = 3$

$\Rightarrow$ $-2x = 8$ $\Rightarrow$ $x = -4$

Case II: $x > -5/2$ $\Rightarrow$ $2x + 5 = 3$

$\Rightarrow$ $x = -1$ $\Rightarrow$ $x \in \{-4, -1\}$

(h) $|2 - x| = 5$

Case I: $x > 2$ $\Rightarrow$ $x - 2 = 5$

$\Rightarrow$ $x = 7$ $\Rightarrow$ $x = 2$ is not possible

Case II: $x < 2$ $\Rightarrow 2 - x = 5$

$\Rightarrow$ $x = -3$

Hence $x \in \{-3, 7\}$

(i) $|x| = 2x - 1$

Case I: $x > 0$ $\Rightarrow$ $x = 2x - 1$

$\Rightarrow$ $x = 1$

Case II: $x < 0$ $\Rightarrow$ $-x = 2x - 1$

$\Rightarrow$ $x = 1/3$

But $x = 1/3$ is not is the region $x < 0$. Hence $x = \{1\}$

(j) $|x| = x^2 - 1$

Case I: $x > 0$ $\Rightarrow$ $x^2 - x - 1 = 0$

$$\Rightarrow \quad x = \frac{1 \pm \sqrt{1+4}}{2} = \frac{1 \pm \sqrt{5}}{2}$$

$$\Rightarrow \quad x = 1 + \frac{\sqrt{5}}{2}$$

Case II: $x < 0$ $\Rightarrow$ $x^2 + x - 1 = 0$

$$\Rightarrow \quad x = \frac{-1 \pm \sqrt{1+4}}{2} = \frac{-1 \pm \sqrt{5}}{2}$$

$$\Rightarrow \quad x = -1 - \frac{\sqrt{5}}{2}. \text{ Hence } x \in \left\{\pm\left(\frac{1+\sqrt{5}}{2}\right)\right\}$$

(k) $|x^2 - 1| = 2x - 4$

Case I: $x > 1$ $\Rightarrow$ $x^2 - 1 = 2x - 4$

$\Rightarrow$ $x^2 - 2x + 3 = 0$, no solution

Case II: $-1 < x < 1$ $\Rightarrow$ $-x^2 + 1 = 2x - 4$

$\Rightarrow$ $x^2 + 2x - 5 = 0$

$$\Rightarrow \quad x = \frac{-2 \pm \sqrt{4+20}}{2} \quad \Rightarrow \quad \text{No solution in the region.}$$

Case III: $x < -1$ $\Rightarrow$ $x^2 - 1 = 2x - 4$

$\Rightarrow$ $x^2 - 2x + 3 = 0$, again no solution

Hence no solution $\Rightarrow$ $k \in \phi$

(l) $|2x + 3| - 7 = 0$

Case I: $x < -3/2$ $\Rightarrow$ $-2x - 3 - 7 = 0$

$\Rightarrow$ $-2 = 10$ $\Rightarrow$ $x = -5$

Case II: $x > -3/2$ $\Rightarrow$ $(2x + 3) - 7 = 0$

$\Rightarrow$ $2x - 4 = 0$ $\Rightarrow$ $x = 2$

$\Rightarrow$ $x \in \{-5, 2\}$

(m) $|5 - 3x| - 4 = 0$

Case I: $x > 5/3$ $\Rightarrow$ $5 - 3x - 4 = 0$

$\Rightarrow$ $1 - 3x = 0$ $\Rightarrow$ $x = 1/3$

Case II: $x < 5/3$ $\Rightarrow$ $3x - 5 - 4 = 0$

$\Rightarrow$ $x = 3$ $\Rightarrow$ $x \in \left\{\frac{1}{3}, 3\right\}$

7. $\sqrt{x^2 - 2x + 1} - \sqrt{x^2 + 2x + 1} = \sqrt{(x-1)^2} - \sqrt{(x+1)^2} = |x - 1| - |x + 1|$

Case I: $x \le -1$; expression reduces to $-(x - 1) + x + 1 = -x + 1 + x + 1 = 2$

Case II: $x \in (-1, 1)$; expression reduces to $1 - x - (x + 1) = 1 - x - x - 1 = -2x$

Case III: $x \ge 1$ expression reduces to $x - 1 - (x + 1) = -2$

$$\text{Hence } \sqrt{x^2 - 2x + 1} - \sqrt{x^2 + 2x + 1} = \begin{cases} 2; & x \le -1 \\ -2x; & x \in (-1, 1) \\ -2; & x \ge 1 \end{cases}$$

8. (a) $\frac{1}{2}ab\sqrt{8a^3b} + \frac{1}{3}ab\sqrt{18ab^3} - a^2\sqrt{\frac{2b}{a}} - b^2\sqrt{\frac{2a}{b}}$

Given a > 0 and b > 0

$\Rightarrow$ $a^2b\sqrt{2ab} + ab^2\sqrt{2ab} - a^2\sqrt{\frac{2b}{a}} - b^2\sqrt{\frac{2a}{b}}$

$\Rightarrow$ $\sqrt{2ab}\left(a^2b + ab^2\right) - a\sqrt{2ab} - b\sqrt{2ab}$

$\Rightarrow$ $\sqrt{2ab}\left(a^2b + ab^2 - a - b\right)$ $\Rightarrow$ $\sqrt{2ab}(ab - 1)(a + b)$

(b) $x + y + \sqrt{(x-y)^2}$ can be written as $x + y + |x - y|$

If $x \ge y = 2x$

If $x < y = 2y$

(c) $(2-a)\sqrt{\frac{1}{a^2 - 4a + 4}} = (2-a)\sqrt{\frac{1}{(a-2)^2}}$

Case I: $a < 2$ $\Rightarrow$ $\frac{2-a}{|a-2|} = 1$

Case II: $a = 2$ $\Rightarrow$ Expression is undefined

Case II: $a > 2$ $\Rightarrow$ $\frac{2-a}{a-2} = -1$

(d) $x - y - \sqrt{(x-y)^2}$ can be written as $x - y - |x - y|$

If $x \ge y = x - y - x + y = 0$

If $x < y = x - y + x - y = 2x - 2y$

9. $\sqrt{9 - 6a + a^2} + \sqrt{9 + 6a + a^2} = \sqrt{(3-a)^2} + \sqrt{(a+3)^2} = |3 - a| + |a + 3|$

$\Rightarrow$ $a + 3 < 0 = 3 - a - a - 3 = -2a$ (Given $a < -3$)

TEXTUAL EXERCISE–20: (SUBJECTIVE)

1. (a) $|x| > 2$

$\Rightarrow$ Distance of x from 0 is greater than 2 units.

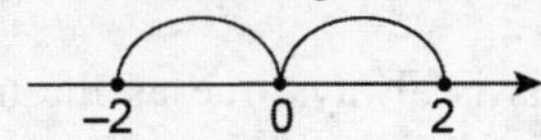

$\Rightarrow$ $x \in (-\infty, -2) \cup [2, \infty)$

(b) $|x - 1| > 3$

$\Rightarrow$ Distance of x from 1 is greater than 3 units.

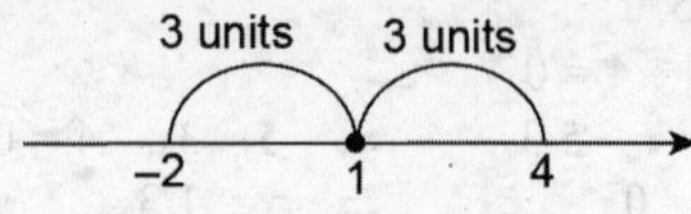

$\Rightarrow x \in (-\infty, -2) \cup (4, \infty)$

(c) $|x - 2| < 1$

$\Rightarrow$ Distance of x from 2 is less than 1

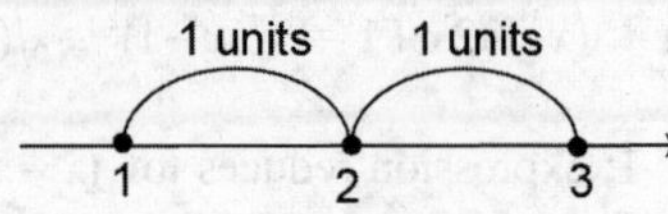

$\Rightarrow x \in (1, 3)$

(d) $|x + 1| \ge 2$

$\Rightarrow$ Distance of x from –1 is greater than or equal to 2.

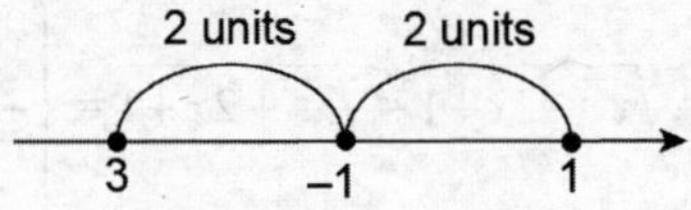

$\Rightarrow x \in (-\infty, -3] \cup [1, \infty)$

(e) $|x - 1| < 5$

$\Rightarrow$ Distance of x from 1 is less than 5

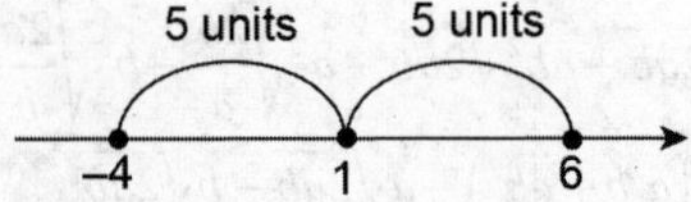

$\Rightarrow x \in (-4, 6)$

(f) $|2x - 3| > 7 \quad \Rightarrow \quad |x - 3/2| > 7/2$

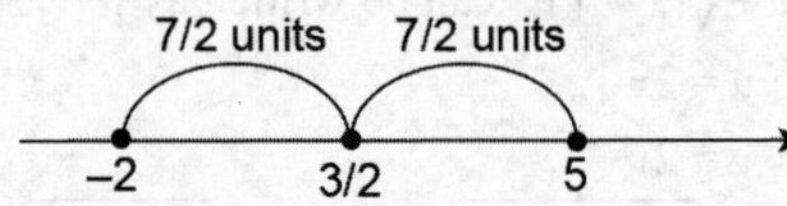

$\Rightarrow x \in (-\infty, -2) \cup (5, \infty)$

(g) $|3x + 5| < 2 \quad \Rightarrow \quad |x + 5/3| < 2/3$

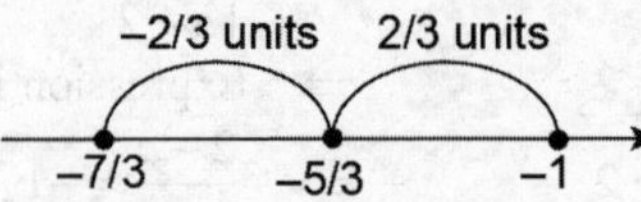

$\Rightarrow x \in \left(-\frac{7}{3}, -1\right)$

(h) $|4x + 6| > 5 \quad \Rightarrow \quad \left|x + \frac{3}{2}\right| > \frac{5}{4}$

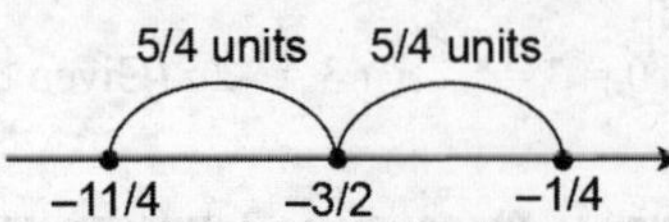

$\Rightarrow x \in \left(-\infty, \frac{-11}{4}\right) \cup \left(-\frac{1}{4}, \infty\right)$

(i) $|2x - 3| > -2$

Clearly this is always true as the number on the left hand side is always positive.

Hence $x \in (-\infty, \infty)$

(j) $|4x - 9| \le 7 \quad \Rightarrow \quad |x - 9/4| \le 7/4$

7/4 units 7/4 units

1/2 9/4 4

$\Rightarrow x \in \left[\frac{1}{2}, 4\right]$

(k) $|3x + 5| \ge 2 \quad \Rightarrow \quad 3|x + 5/3| \ge 2$

$\Rightarrow |x + 5/3| \ge 2/3$

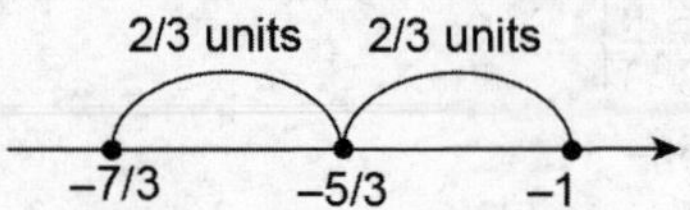

$\Rightarrow x \in \left(-\infty, -\frac{7}{3}\right] \cup [-1, \infty)$

(l) $|2x + 3| \ge 0$

Obviously, the modulus of a number is non-negative. Hence it is always true.

$\Rightarrow x \in (-\infty, \infty)$

(m) $|4 - 3x| < -2$

Modulus is never negative. Hence $x \in \phi$.

(n) $|5 - 3x| \le 0$

Modulus of a number is always non-negative. The only possibility is $|5 - 3x| = 0$ at $x = 5/3$

Hence $x \in \left\{\frac{5}{3}\right\}$

(o) $\left|\frac{x-3}{x-5}\right| > 1$

Case 1: $x < 3$

$\frac{x-3}{x-5} > 1 \quad \Rightarrow \quad \frac{x-3}{x-5} - 1 > 0$

$\Rightarrow \frac{2}{x-5} > 0 \quad \Rightarrow \quad 2(x - 5) > 0$

$\Rightarrow x > 5.$

Hence solution in this region.

Case 2: $3 \le x < 5$

$\frac{x-3}{5-x} - 1 > 0 \quad \Rightarrow \quad (2x - 8)(5 - x) > 0$

$\Rightarrow (x - 4)(5 - x) > 0 \quad \Rightarrow \quad (x - 4)(x - 5) < 0$

$\Rightarrow x \in (4, 5)$

Case 3: $x > 5$ (inclusion of 5 is not admissible)

$\frac{x-3}{x-5} - 1 > 0 \quad \Rightarrow \quad \frac{2}{x-5} > 0$

$\Rightarrow (x - 5) > 0 \quad \Rightarrow \quad x > 5$

Hence the solution region is $x \in (4, \infty) - \{5\}$

(p) $\left|\frac{x+4}{x+2}\right| \le 1$

Case 1: $x < -4$

$\Rightarrow \frac{-(x+4)}{-(x+2)} \le 1 \quad \Rightarrow \quad \text{———} - 1 \le 0$

$\Rightarrow \frac{2}{x+2} \le 0 \quad \Rightarrow \quad (x + 2) \le 0$

$\Rightarrow x \le -2$

Case 2: $-4 \le x < -2$

$\Rightarrow \dfrac{x+4}{-x-2} - 1 \le 0 \quad \Rightarrow \dfrac{2x+6}{-(x+2)} \le 0$

$\Rightarrow (2x+6)(x+2) \ge 0 \quad \Rightarrow x \in (-\infty, -3] \cup [-2, \infty)$

Case 3: $x \ge -2$

Obviously inclusion *of* -2 is not possible according to the domain of function.

$\dfrac{x+4}{x+2} - 1 \le 0 \quad \Rightarrow x \le -2$

Hence the overall solution is $x \in (-\infty, -3]$

(q) $|x^2 - 4x| < 5$

Case 1: $x^2 - 4x \ge 0 \Rightarrow x(x-4) \ge 0$

$\Rightarrow x \in (\infty, 0] \cup [4, \infty) \Rightarrow |x^2 - 4x| = x^2 - 4x$

$\Rightarrow x^2 - 4x < 5 \quad \Rightarrow x^2 - 4x - 5 = 0$

$\Rightarrow (x-5)(x+1) < 0 \quad \Rightarrow x \in (-1, 5)$

Case 2: $x^2 - 4x < 0 \Rightarrow x(x-4) < 0$

$\Rightarrow x \in (0, 4) \quad \Rightarrow |x^2 - 4x| = 4x - x^2$

$\Rightarrow 4x - x^2 < 5 \quad \Rightarrow x^2 - 4x - 5 > 0$, which is true.

$\Rightarrow x \in (-1, 5)$

(r) $|x-3| > -1$

Modulus is always non-negative. Hence this is always true.

$\Rightarrow x \in (-\infty, \infty)$

(s) $|3x - 5/2| \ge 2 \quad \Rightarrow |x - 5/6| \ge 2/3$

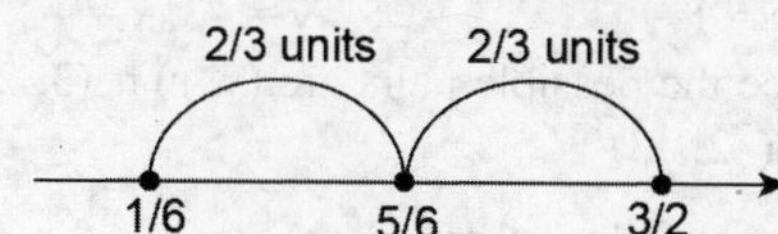

$\Rightarrow x \in \left(-\infty, \dfrac{1}{6}\right] \cup \left[\dfrac{3}{2}, \infty\right)$

(t) $|x-2| - |x+4| \le 0$

Case I: $x < -4$

$\Rightarrow -x + 2 + x + 4 \le 0 \quad \Rightarrow 6 \le 0$ (*not* possible)

Case II: $-4 \le x < 2 \Rightarrow 2 - x - x - 4 \le 0$

$\Rightarrow -2x - 2 \le 0$

$\Rightarrow x + 1 \ge 0 \quad \Rightarrow x \ge -1$

Case III: $x \ge 0 \quad \Rightarrow x - 2 - x - 4 \le 0$

$\Rightarrow -6 \le 0$, which is always true.

$\Rightarrow x \in [-1, \infty)$

2. (a) $|5x^2 - 3| = 2$

Case I: $5x^2 - 3 \ge 0 \quad \Rightarrow x^2 - \dfrac{3}{5} \ge 0$

$\Rightarrow x^2 \ge \dfrac{3}{5} \quad \Rightarrow |5x^2 - 3| = 5x^2 - 3$

$\Rightarrow 5x^2 = 5 \quad \Rightarrow x^2 = 1$

$\Rightarrow x = 1, -1$

Case II: $5x^2 - 3 < 0 \Rightarrow x^2 < 3/5$

$\Rightarrow 3 - 5x^2 = 2 \quad \Rightarrow 5x^2 - 1$

$\Rightarrow x^2 = 1/5 \quad \Rightarrow x = \pm\dfrac{1}{\sqrt{5}}, -\dfrac{1}{\sqrt{5}}$

$\Rightarrow x \in \left\{\pm\dfrac{1}{\sqrt{5}}, \pm 1\right\}$

(b) $\left|\dfrac{x+4}{x+2}\right| = 3$

Case I: $x < -4 \quad \Rightarrow \dfrac{-(x+4)}{-(x+2)} = 3$

$\Rightarrow \dfrac{x+4}{x+2} - 3 = 0$

$\Rightarrow \dfrac{x+4-3x-6}{x+2} = 0 \quad \Rightarrow \dfrac{-2x-2}{x+2} = 0$

$\Rightarrow x + 4 = 3x + 6 \quad \Rightarrow 2x = -2$

$\Rightarrow x = -1$

Case II: $-4 \le x < -2 \Rightarrow \dfrac{x+4}{-(x+2)} = 3$

$\Rightarrow x + 4 = -3x - 6 \quad \Rightarrow 4x = -10$

$\Rightarrow x = -5/2$

Case III: $x > -2 \quad \Rightarrow \dfrac{x+4}{x+2} - 3 = 0$

$\Rightarrow x = -1$

Thus overall $x \in \{-1, -5/2\}$

(c) $|x^2 - 4x| = 5$

Case I: $x^2 - 4x \ge 0 \quad \Rightarrow x(x-4) \ge 0$

$\Rightarrow x \in (\infty, 4] \cup [4, \infty) \quad \Rightarrow |x^2 - 4x| = x^2 - 4x$

$\Rightarrow x^2 - 4x - 5 = 0 \quad \Rightarrow (x-5)(x+1) = 0$

$\Rightarrow x = 5, -1$

Case II: $x^2 - 4x < 0 \Rightarrow x \in (0, 4)$

$\Rightarrow 4x - x^2 = 5$

$\Rightarrow x^2 - 4x + 5 = 0$, which has no solution.

(d) $|x+1| + 2 = 2 \quad \Rightarrow |x+1| = 0$

$\Rightarrow x = -1$

(e) $|3x - 4| = 1/2 \quad \Rightarrow \left|x - \dfrac{4}{3}\right| = \dfrac{1}{2}$

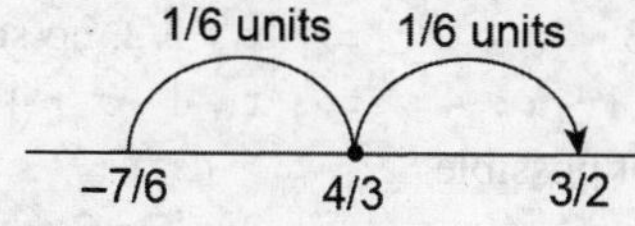

$\Rightarrow x = \dfrac{7}{6}, \dfrac{3}{2}$

(*f*) $|x+2| = 6 - 2x$

Case I: $x < -2$

$\Rightarrow -x - 2 = 6 - 2x$

$\Rightarrow x = 8$, which does not lies in $x < -2$

Case II: $x \ge -2$

$\Rightarrow x + 2 = 6 - 2x \quad \Rightarrow 3x = 4$

$\Rightarrow x = 4/3$

Hence $x = 4/3$

(g) $|x| = -3x - 5$

Case I: $x \ge 0$

$\Rightarrow x + 3x = -5 \quad \Rightarrow x = -5/4$

Case II: $x < 0$

$\Rightarrow -x = -3x - 5 \quad \Rightarrow 2x = -5$

$\Rightarrow x = -5/2$

Hence $x = -5/2$

(h) $x^2 + |x-1| = 1$

Case I: $x \ge 1 \quad \Rightarrow x^2 + x - 2 = 0$

$\Rightarrow x^2 + 2x - x - 2 = 0$

$\Rightarrow x(x+2) - (x+2) = 0 \Rightarrow (x+2)(x-1) = 0$

$\Rightarrow x = 1, -2 \quad \Rightarrow x = 1$

Case II: $x < 1$ $\Rightarrow$ $x^2 - x + 1 = 1$

$\Rightarrow$ $x = 0$ or $x = 1$ $\Rightarrow$ $x = 0$, hence $x = 0, 1$

(i) $|x + 1| - |2x - 3| = x - 4$

$\Rightarrow$ $|x + 1| - 2|x - 3/2| = x - 4$

Case I: $x < -1$ $\Rightarrow$ $-x - 1 + 2x - 3 = x - 4$

$\Rightarrow$ $x - 4 = x - 4$, which is true always

Case II: $-1 \le x < 3/2$ $\Rightarrow$ $x + 1 - (3 - 2x) = x - 4$

$\Rightarrow$ $-x - 2 = x - 4$ $\Rightarrow$ $2x = 2$

$\Rightarrow$ $x = 1$

Case III: $x > 3/2$ $\Rightarrow$ $x + 1 - 2x + 3$

$\Rightarrow$ $-x + 4 = x - 4$ $\Rightarrow$ $2x = 8$

$\Rightarrow$ $x = 4$ $\Rightarrow$ $x \in (-\infty, -1] \cup \{4\}$

3. **(a)** $|x - 1| + |x - 3| = 2$

Case I: $x < 1$ $\Rightarrow$ $1 - x + 3 - x = 2$

$\Rightarrow$ $4 - 2x = 2$ $\Rightarrow$ $2x = 2$

$\Rightarrow$ $x = 1$

Case II: $1 \le x < 3$ $\Rightarrow$ $x - 1 + 3 - x = 2$

$\Rightarrow$ 2= 2, which is true always

Case III: $x \ge 3$ $\Rightarrow$ $x - 1 + x - 3 = 2$

$\Rightarrow$ $2x = 6$ $\Rightarrow$ $x = 3$

$\Rightarrow$ $x \in [1, 3]$

(b) $|x| + |x + 5| = 5$

Case I: $x < -5$ $\Rightarrow$ $-x - x - 5 = 5$

$\Rightarrow$ $-2x = 10$ $\Rightarrow$ $x = -5$

Case II: $-5 \le x < 0$ $\Rightarrow$ $-x + x + 5 = 5$

$\Rightarrow$ 5 = 5, which is always true

Case III: $x \ge 0$ $\Rightarrow$ $x + x + 5 = 5$

$\Rightarrow$ $x = 0$ Hence $x \in [-5, 0]$

(c) $|x - 1| + |x - 4| = 2$

Case I: $x < 1$ $\Rightarrow$ $-x + 1 - x + 4 = 2$

$\Rightarrow$ $-2x = -3$ $\Rightarrow$ $x = 3/2$, no solution

Case II: $1 \le x < 4$ $\Rightarrow$ $x - 1 - x + 4 = 2$

$\Rightarrow$ 3 = 2, not possible

Case III: $x > 4$ $\Rightarrow$ $2x - 5 = 2$

$\Rightarrow$ $x = 7/2 = 3.5$, no solution

Hence $x \in \{\ \}$

(d) $|x^2 - 2x| + |x - 4| = |x^2 - 3x + 4|$

$\Rightarrow$ $|x(x - 2)| + |x - 4| = |x^2 - 3x + 4|$

Clearly $(x^2 - 2x - x + 4) = x^2 - 3x + 4$

Thus the question reduces to $|f(x) - g(x)| = |f(x)| + |g(x)|$

$\Rightarrow$ $f(x).g(x) \le 0$ $(x^2 - 2x)(x - 4)$

$\Rightarrow$ $x(x - 2)(x - 4) \le 0$

$\Rightarrow$ $x \in (-\infty, 0] \cup [2, 4]$

(e) $|x^2 - 2x| + |x - 4| < |x^2 - 3x + 4|$

$\Rightarrow$ $x^2 - 2x - (x - 4) = x^2 - 3x + 4$

Hence the question reduces to $|f(x)| + |g(x)| < |f(x) - g(x)|$, which is never positive.

$\Rightarrow$ $x \in \{\ \}$

(f) $|x^2 - 9| + |16 - x^2| = 7$

Let $f(x) = x^2 - 9$ and $g(x) = 16 - x^2$

$\Rightarrow$ $f(x) + g(x) = 7$

The equation reduces to $|f(x)| + |g(x)| = |f(x) + g(x)|$

$\Rightarrow$ $f(x) . g(x) \ge 0$ $\Rightarrow$ $(x^2 - 9)(16 - x^2) \ge 0$

$\Rightarrow$ $(x + 3)(x - 3)(4 - x)(4 + x) \ge 0$

$\Rightarrow$ $(x + 3)(x - 3)(x + 4)(x - 4) \le 0$

$\Rightarrow$ $x \in [-4, -3] \cup [3, 4]$

4. **(a)** $\begin{cases} |x| + y = 4 \\ x + 3|y| = 6 \end{cases}$

$|x| + y = 4$ $\Rightarrow$ $y = 4 - |x|$

Case I: $x > 0, y > 0$ $\Rightarrow$ $x + y = 4$

$\Rightarrow$ $x + 3y = 6$ $\Rightarrow$ $y = 1, x = 3$

Case II: $x > 0, y < 0$ $\Rightarrow$ $x + y = 4$

$\Rightarrow$ $x - 3y = 6$ $\Rightarrow$ $y = -1/2, x = 9/2$

Case III: $x < 0, y > 0$ $\Rightarrow$ $y - x = 4$

$\Rightarrow$ $x + 3y = 6$ $\Rightarrow$ $x = -3/2, y = 5/2$

Case IV: $x < 0, y < 0$ $\Rightarrow$ $y - x = 4$

$\Rightarrow$ $y = -5, x = -9$

Hence the positive values all $(x, y) = (3, 1)$, $\left(\frac{9}{2}, -\frac{1}{2}\right), \left(-\frac{3}{2}, \frac{5}{2}\right)$, $(-9, -5)$

(b) $\begin{cases} \sqrt{(x+4)^2} = 5 \\ \sqrt{(x-4)^2} = 1 \end{cases} \Rightarrow \begin{cases} |x + 4| = 5 \\ |x - 4| = 1 \end{cases}$

Case I: $0 < y < x$ $\Rightarrow$ $x + y = 5$

$\Rightarrow$ $x - y = 1$ $\Rightarrow$ $x = 3, y = 2$

Case II: $0 < x < y$ $\Rightarrow$ $x + y = 5$

$\Rightarrow$ $y - x = 1$ $\Rightarrow$ $y = 3, x = 2$

Case III: $x < y < 0$ $\Rightarrow$ $-x - y = 5$

$\Rightarrow$ $y - x = 1$ $\Rightarrow$ $x = -3, y = -2$

Case IV: $y < x < 0$ $\Rightarrow$ $-x - y = 5$

$\Rightarrow$ $x - y = 1$ $\Rightarrow$ $y = -3, x = -2$

Hence the possible pairs are $(x, y) = (3, 2), (2, 3), (-3, -2), (-2, -3)$

5. $(4a - 15)x^2 + 2a|x| + 4 = 0$

Clearly there arise two possibilities, $x > 0$ or $x < 0$ (remember $x = 0$ is not a solution here)

Case I: $x > 0$

The equation reduces to $(4a - 15)x^2 + 2ax + 4 = 0$

$$x = \frac{-2a \pm \sqrt{4a^2 - 16(4a - 15)}}{2(4a - 15)}$$

$$= \frac{-2a \pm 2\sqrt{a^2 - 16a + 60}}{2(4a - 15)} = \frac{-a \pm \sqrt{(a-6)(a-10)}}{(4a - 15)}$$

Since $x > 0$

$\Rightarrow$ $\dfrac{-a + \sqrt{(a-6)(a-10)}}{(4a - 15)}$ is positive when $a^2 - 16a + 60 > a^2$

$\Rightarrow$ $16a < 60$ $\Rightarrow$ $a < 15/4$

Case II: $x < 0$

The equation reduces to $(4a - 15)x^2 - 2ax + 4 = 0$

$$\Rightarrow x = \frac{2a \pm \sqrt{4a^2 - 16(4a - 15)}}{2(4a - 15)}$$

$$\Rightarrow x = \frac{2a \pm 2\sqrt{a^2 - 16a + 60}}{2(4a - 15)} \Rightarrow x = \frac{a \pm \sqrt{(a-6)(a-10)}}{4a - 15}$$

Since $x < 0$

$\Rightarrow$ $\dfrac{a - \sqrt{(a-6)(a-10)}}{4a - 15}$ is less than zero for $a < 15/4$ for

$a \ge \frac{15}{4} x \in \phi$

6. $|(x^2 + 2x + 2) + (3x + 7)| < |x^2 + 2x + 2| + |3x + 7|$
Taking $x^2 + 2x + 2 = f(x)$ and $3x^2 + 7 = g(x)$
The equation reduces to $|f(x) + g(x)| < |f(x)| + |g(x)|$
$\Rightarrow f(x).g(x) < 0 \quad \Rightarrow (x^2 + 2x + 2)(3x + 7) < 0$
But $x^2 + 2x + 2 > 0 \quad \Rightarrow 3x + 7 < 0$
$\Rightarrow x < -7/3$

7. (a) $|x + 3| + |x - 3| = 2x$
Case I: $x < -3$
The equation reduces to $-x - 3 + 3 - x = 2x$
$\Rightarrow -2x = 2x$
$\Rightarrow x = 0$, which is not in this region.
Case II: $-3 \le x < 3$
The equation reduces to $x + 3 + 3 - x = 2x$
$\Rightarrow 6 = 2x$
$\Rightarrow x = 3$, which is again not in the region
Case III: $x \ge 3$
The equation is this region reduces to $x + 3 + x - 3 = 2x$
$\Rightarrow 2x = 2x$, which is true for all x. Hence $x \in [3, \infty)$

(b) $|x + 3| + |x - 3| > 2x$, here again we will analyze the solution in three regions.
Case I: $x < -3$
Equation reduces to $-x - 3 - x + 3 > 2x$
$\Rightarrow -2x > 2x \quad \Rightarrow 4x < 0$
$\Rightarrow x < 0$
Hence $x < -3$ (intersection with the region)
Case II: $-3 \le x < 3$
Equation reduces to $x + 3 + 3 - x > 2x$
$\Rightarrow 6 > 2x \quad \Rightarrow x < 3$
$\Rightarrow -3 \le x < 3$
Case III: $x \ge -3$
Equation reduces to $x + 3 + x - 3 > 2x$
$\Rightarrow 2x > 2x$, which is not possible, hence overall $x \in (-\infty, 3)$

8. $|x + 1| + |x - 1| = |2x|$; taking $f(x) = x + 1$; $g(x) = x - 1$
Equation can be written as $|f(x)| + |g(x)| = |f(x) + g(x)|$
$\Rightarrow f(x).g(x) \ge 0 \quad \Rightarrow (x + 1)(x - 1) \ge 0$
$\Rightarrow x \in (-\infty, -1] \cup [1, \infty)$

9. $|x + 1| + |x - 1| > |2x|$
Taking $f(x)$: $x + 1$; $g(x)$: $x - 1$
Inequality reduce to $|f(x)| + |g(x)| > |f(x) + g(x)|$
$\Rightarrow f(x).g(x) < 0 \quad \Rightarrow (x + 1)(x - 1)$
$\Rightarrow x \in (-1, 1)$

10. $|x - 1| + |x - 3| = x - 3$
Case I: $x < 1$
Inequality reduces to $1 - x + 3 - x = x - 3$
$\Rightarrow 4 - 2x = x - 3 \quad \Rightarrow 3x = 7$
$\Rightarrow x = 7/3$, which is not is the region.
Case II: $1 \le x < 3$
Inequality reduces to $x - 1 + 3 - x = x - 3$
$\Rightarrow 2 + 3 = x$
$\Rightarrow x = 5$, which is not in this region.
Case III: $x \ge 3$
Inequality reduces to $x - 1 + x - 3 = x - 3$
$\Rightarrow 2x - 4 = x - 3$, which is also not in the region.
Hence $x \in \{\ \}$ or $n = \phi$

11. $|x - 1| + |x - 2| < x - 3$
Case I: $x < 1$
Inequality reduces to $1 - x + 2 - x < -3$
$\Rightarrow 3 - 2x < x - 3 \quad \Rightarrow 3x > 6$
$\Rightarrow x > 2$
Hence no solution in this region
Case II: $1 \le x < 2$
Inequality reduces to $x - 1 + 2 - x < x - 3$
$\Rightarrow 1 < x - 3 \quad \Rightarrow x - 4 > 0$
$\Rightarrow x > 4$
No solution in this region
Case III: $x > 2$
Inequality reduces to $x - 1 + x - 2 < x - 3$
$\Rightarrow x - 1 + x - 2 < x - 3$
$\Rightarrow 2x - 3 < x - 3 \quad \Rightarrow x < 0$
No solution in this region $x = \phi$.

TEXTUAL EXERCISE–21: (SUBJECTIVE)

1. **(i)** $[x] = 3.9 \quad \Rightarrow$ it is not possible
$\Rightarrow x = \phi$
(ii) $[x] < 3.9 \quad \Rightarrow x \in (-\infty, 4)$
(iii) $[x] > 3.9 \quad \Rightarrow x \in [4, \infty)$
(iv) $[x] > 5 \quad \Rightarrow x \in [6, \infty)$
(v) $2.1 < [x] < 5 \quad \Rightarrow x \in [3, 5)$
(vi) $[x] \le 5 \quad \Rightarrow x \in (-\infty, 6)$
(vii) $-9 \le [x] < -5.3 \quad \Rightarrow x \in [-9, 5)$
(viii) $[x] \ge -5.3 \quad \Rightarrow x \in [-5, \infty)$
(ix) $[x] \le -5.3 \quad \Rightarrow x \in (-\infty, -5)$
(x) $\{x\} = 0$ all integers

2. **(a)** $[\sqrt{x}] = 3 \quad \Rightarrow \sqrt{x} \in [3, 4) \quad \Rightarrow x \in [9, 16)$
(b) $[x^2] = 5 \quad \Rightarrow x^2 \in [5, 6)$
$\Rightarrow x \in (-\sqrt{6}, -\sqrt{5}] \cup [\sqrt{5}, \sqrt{6})$
(c) $[x] + [-x] = 0 \quad \Rightarrow x \in \mathbb{Z}$
(d) $x - [x] = 1/2 \quad \Rightarrow \{x\} = 0.5$
$\Rightarrow x \in n + \frac{1}{2}$ n is any integer.
(e) $[x]^2 - 3[x] + 2 = 0$
$\Rightarrow ([x] - 1)([x] - 2) = 0$
$\Rightarrow [x] = 1$ or $[x] = 2$
$\Rightarrow x \in [1, 2)$ or $x \in [2, 3)$
$\Rightarrow x \in [1, 3)$
(f) $[x]^2 - 5[x] + 6 > 0$; $([x] - 3)([x] - 2) > 0$
$\Rightarrow [x] \in (-\infty, 2) \cup (3, \infty)$
$\Rightarrow x \in (-\infty, 2] \cup [4, \infty)$
(g) $[x]^2 - 3[x] + 2 < 0 \quad \Rightarrow ([x] - 2)([x] - 1) < 0$
$\Rightarrow [x] \in (1, 2) \quad \Rightarrow x \in \phi$
(h) $[3x] = -1 \quad \Rightarrow -1 \le -1/2; x < 0$
$\Rightarrow x \in \left[-\frac{1}{3}, 0\right)$
(i) $[3x] - [-3x] = 0$, which is true if $3x$ = integer = P
$\Rightarrow x = P/3$; $P \in \mathbb{Z}$
(j) $[x]^2 > 9 \quad \Rightarrow ([x] + 3)([x] - 3) > 0$
$\Rightarrow [x] \in (-\infty, -3) \cup (3, \infty)$
$\Rightarrow x \in (-\infty, -3) \cup [4, \infty)$

(k) $[|x|] = 3 \quad \Rightarrow |x| \in [3, 4)$

$\Rightarrow x \in (-4, -3] \cup [3, 4)$

(l) $|[x]| = 2 \quad \Rightarrow [x] = 2$ or $[x] = -2$

$\Rightarrow x \in [2, 3)$ or $x \in [-2, -1)$

$\Rightarrow x \in [-2, -1) \cup [2, 3)$

(m) $4[x] - x = \{x\}$

Which can be written as $4[x] - x = x - [x]$

$\Rightarrow 5[x] - 2x = 0 \quad \Rightarrow [x] = \dfrac{2x}{5}$

$\Rightarrow x = 0$ is the only solution

(n) $[x] \geq n \quad \Rightarrow x \in [n, \infty)$

(o) $[x] < n \quad \Rightarrow x \in (-\infty, n)$

(p) $-2.3 < [x] \leq 3 \quad \Rightarrow x \in [-2, 4)$

(q) $-2 < [x] < 5.3 \quad \Rightarrow x \in [-1, 6)$

3. (a), (b), (c) $[x]^2 = [x + 2]$

$\Rightarrow [x]^2 = [x] + 2 \quad \Rightarrow [x]^2 - [x] - 2 = 0$

$\Rightarrow [x]^2 - 2[x] + [x] - 2 = 0 \Rightarrow [x]([x] - 2) + 1([x] - 2) = 0$

$\Rightarrow ([x] - 2)([x] + 1) = 0 \quad \Rightarrow [x] = 2$ or $[x] = -1$

$\Rightarrow x \in (-1, 0) \cup (2, 3)$

4. (b) $y = 2[x] + 3 = 3[x - 2] + 5$

$\Rightarrow 2[x] + 3 = 3[x - 2] + 5 \Rightarrow 2[x] + 3 = 3[[x] - 2] + 5$

$\Rightarrow 2[x] + 3 = 3[x] - 6 + 5 \Rightarrow [x] = 4$

$\Rightarrow x \in [4, 5) \quad \Rightarrow y = 2[x] + 3 = 11$

$\Rightarrow [x + 4] = 15$

5. (i) Let $[x] = y$

$\dfrac{5y+4}{11y+7} - 3 \geq 0 \quad \Rightarrow \dfrac{5y+4-33y-21}{11y+7} \geq 0$

$\Rightarrow \dfrac{-28y-17}{11y+7} \geq 0 \quad \Rightarrow (11y + 7)(28y + 17) \leq 0$

$\Rightarrow y \in \left[-\dfrac{7}{11}, -\dfrac{17}{28}\right] \quad \Rightarrow [x] \in \left[-\dfrac{7}{11}, -\dfrac{17}{28}\right]$

There is no integer is this region

$\Rightarrow$ No solution

(ii) $[x]^2 - 3[x] + 2 \leq 0 \quad \Rightarrow [x]^2 - 2[x] - [x] + 2 \leq 0$

$\Rightarrow ([x] - 2)([x] - 1) \leq 0$

$\Rightarrow [x] \in [1, 2] \quad \Rightarrow x \in [1, 3]$

6. (d) It can be written as $\left|200 \times \dfrac{1}{4}\right| = 50$

7. (b) $5\{x\} = x + [x] \Rightarrow 5\{x\} = 2[x] + \{x\}$

$\Rightarrow 4\{x\} = 2[x] \quad \Rightarrow [x] = 2\{x\}$ (1)

By equation (1), we get $2\{x\} - \{x\} = 1/2$

$\Rightarrow \{x\} = 1/2$ (2)

$\Rightarrow x \in P + \dfrac{1}{2}$; P is an integer, which is true if $P = 1$

$\Rightarrow x = 3/2$

8. (c) By the questions, $0 < x < 1000$

$\Rightarrow \left[\dfrac{x}{2}\right] + \left[\dfrac{x}{3}\right] + \left[\dfrac{x}{5}\right] = \dfrac{31}{30}x$

which can be written as $\left[\dfrac{x}{2}\right] + \left[\dfrac{x}{3}\right] + \left[\dfrac{x}{5}\right] = \dfrac{x}{2} + \dfrac{x}{3} + \dfrac{x}{5}$

$\Rightarrow \left\{\dfrac{x}{2}\right\} + \left\{\dfrac{x}{3}\right\} + \left\{\dfrac{x}{5}\right\} = 0$

$\Rightarrow x$ must be a multiple of 2, 3, 5

$\Rightarrow x$ must be a multiple of 30.

$\therefore$ Possible number 30, 60, 90,…., 990

$\therefore$ Total number of possible solution = 33

9. (c) $[x + [x] + [x]] \leq 3 \quad \Rightarrow [x + [x] + [x]] \leq 3$

$\Rightarrow [x + 2[x]] \leq 3 \quad \Rightarrow [x] + 2[x] \leq 3$

$\Rightarrow 3[x] \leq 3 \quad \Rightarrow [x] \leq 1$

$\Rightarrow x \in (-\infty, 2)$

10. Let $[x] = y$

$\therefore \dfrac{y+3}{y-2} \geq \dfrac{y+1}{y-3} - 1 \Rightarrow \dfrac{y+3}{y-2} \geq \dfrac{y+1-y+3}{y-3}$

$\Rightarrow \dfrac{y+3}{y-2} \geq \dfrac{4}{y-3} \quad \Rightarrow \dfrac{y+3}{y-2} - \dfrac{4}{(y-3)} \geq 0$

$\Rightarrow \dfrac{(y+3)(y-3)-4y+8}{(y-2)(y-3)} \geq 0$

$\Rightarrow (y - 2)(y - 3)(y^2 - 4y - 1) \geq 0$

$\Rightarrow y = |x| \in \left(-\infty, 2-\sqrt{5}\right] \cup [2,3] \cup \left[2+\sqrt{5}, \infty\right)$

Clearly $|x| = 2$; $|x| = 3$ is not possible

$\Rightarrow |x| \in (-\infty, -0.24) \cup (4.24, \infty)$

$\Rightarrow x \in (-\infty, 0) \cup [5, \infty)$

TEXTUAL EXERCISE–22: (SUBJECTIVE)

1. (i) $(1 - i)^2$ can be written as $= 1 + i^2 - 2i = -2i \; (i^2 = -1)$

(ii) $(1+i)^4 \times \left(1+\dfrac{1}{i}\right)^4$

$= (1+i)^4 \times (1-i)^4 = (1-i^2)^4 = (2)^4 = 16$

2. $\sqrt{\dfrac{-x}{16}} + \sqrt{\dfrac{-x}{25}} - \sqrt{\dfrac{-x}{36}}$ can be written as

$\sqrt{\dfrac{x}{16}}i + \sqrt{\dfrac{x}{25}}i - \sqrt{\dfrac{x}{36}}i$

$= \dfrac{\sqrt{x}}{4}i + \dfrac{\sqrt{x}}{5}i - \dfrac{\sqrt{x}}{6}i = \sqrt{x}i\left(\dfrac{15+12-10}{60}\right) = \dfrac{17}{60}\sqrt{x}i$

3. By the question $3x + 2iy - ix + 5y = 7 + 5i$

$\Rightarrow 3x + 5y + i(2y - x) = 7 + 5i$

$\Rightarrow 3x + 5y = 7$ and $2y - x = 5 \Rightarrow y = 2$ and $x = -1$

4. $(3y - 2) + i(7 + 2x) = 0$

$\Rightarrow 3y - 2 = 0$ and $7 - 2x = 0 \Rightarrow y = 2/3;\; x = 7/2$

5. Sum $= \dfrac{2}{3} + \dfrac{5}{3}i + \left(\dfrac{-2}{3}i\right) - \dfrac{5}{4} - i = \left(\dfrac{2}{3} - \dfrac{5}{4}\right) + i\left(\dfrac{5}{3} - \dfrac{2}{3} - 1\right)$

$= \dfrac{-7}{12} + i\left(\dfrac{0}{3}\right) = \dfrac{-7}{12}$

6. $\left[\dfrac{7+i\sqrt{3}}{7-i\sqrt{3}} + \dfrac{7-i\sqrt{3}}{7+i\sqrt{3}}\right] = \dfrac{\left(7+i\sqrt{3}\right)^2 + \left(7-i\sqrt{3}\right)^2}{\left(7+i\sqrt{3}\right)\left(7-i\sqrt{3}\right)}$

$= \dfrac{49-3+14i\sqrt{3}+49-3-14i\sqrt{3}}{49-i^2 3} = \dfrac{2\times 46}{49+3}$

$= \dfrac{2\times 46}{52} = \dfrac{46}{26} = \dfrac{23}{13} = 1$ which is real.

7. (i) Let $a + ib$ be a complex number $z_1 = a + ib$, then its conjugate is given by $\overline{z_1} = a - ib$

Sum = $z_1 + \overline{z_1} = a + ib + a - ib = 2a$

(ii) Product = $z_1\overline{z_1} = (a + ib)(a - ib) = a^2 - i^2b^2 = a^2 + b^2$.

8. $(1 + 4\sqrt{3}\, i) = (a + ib)^2 \Rightarrow (1 + 4\sqrt{3}\, i) = a^2 - b^2 + 2ib$
$\Rightarrow a^2 - b^2 = 1$ and $2b = 4\sqrt{3}$
$\Rightarrow b = 2\sqrt{3} \qquad \Rightarrow a^2 = 1 + b^2 = 1 + 12 = 13$
$\Rightarrow a^2 - b^2 = 13 - 12 = 1 \Rightarrow \quad ab = \sqrt{13}.2\sqrt{3} = 2\sqrt{39}$

9. Product of these complex numbers = $(3 + 4i)(5 - ki) = (15 - 36i + 20i + 48) = 63 - 16i$

Multiplication inverse of $63 - 16i = \dfrac{1}{16 - 16i}$

$= \dfrac{63+16i}{63^2+16^2} = \dfrac{63+16i}{3969+256} = \dfrac{63+16i}{4225} = \dfrac{63}{4225} + \dfrac{16}{4225}i$

10. Let $\sqrt{3-4i} = a + ib$
Squaring both sides, we get $3 - 4i = a^2 - b^2 + 2iba$
$\Rightarrow a^2 - b^2 = 3$ and $ab = -2$
Also $(a^2 + b^2)^2 = (a^2 - b^2)^2 + 4a^2b^2 = 9 + 16 = 25$
$\Rightarrow a^2 + b^2 = 5 \qquad \Rightarrow a^2 = 4$
$\Rightarrow a = \pm 2$
Similarly $b = \mp 1\ (ab = -2)$
Hence $3 - 4i = \pm(2 - i)$

11. (i) Let $\sqrt{-8-6i} = a + ib$
Squaring both sides, we get $-8 - 6i = a^2 - b^2 + 2abi$
$\Rightarrow a^2 - b^2 = -8$ and $ab = -3$
$\therefore (a^2 + b^2)^2 = (a^2 - b^2)^2 + 4a^2b^2 = 64 + 36 = 100$
$\Rightarrow a^2 + b^2 = 10 \qquad \Rightarrow a^2 = 1$ and $b^2 = 9$
Since $ab = -3$; $a + ib = \pm(1 - 3i)$

(ii) Let $\sqrt{5-12i} = a + ib$
Squaring both sides, we get $5 - 12i = a^2 - b^2 + 2abi$
$\Rightarrow a^2 - b^2 = 5$ and $ab = -6$
$\therefore (a^2 + b^2)^2 = (a^2 - b^2)^2 + 4a^2b^2 = 25 + 144 = 169$
$\Rightarrow a^2 + b^2 = 13$
$\Rightarrow a^2 = 9;\ b^2 = 4$ also since $ab = -6$
$\Rightarrow \sqrt{5-2i} = \pm(3 - 2i)$

(iii) Let $\sqrt{-2+2\sqrt{3}i} = a + ib$
Squaring both sides, we get $-2 + 2\sqrt{3}\ i = a^2 - b^2 + 2abi \quad \Rightarrow \quad a^2 - b^2 = -2$ and $ab = \sqrt{3}$
$\therefore (a^2 + b^2)^2 = (a^2 - b^2)^2 + 4a^2b^2 = 4 + 12 = 16$
$\Rightarrow a^2 + b^2 = 4 \qquad \Rightarrow a^2 = 1,\ b^2 = 3$
Also $ab = \sqrt{3}$
$\Rightarrow \sqrt{-2+2\sqrt{3}i} = \pm\left(1 + \sqrt{3}i\right)$

12. (i) $(1 + \omega)^4$
$\therefore 1 + \omega + \omega^2 = 0 \quad \Rightarrow 1 + \omega^2 = -\omega$
$\Rightarrow (1 + \omega^2)^4 = (-\omega)^4$
$\Rightarrow \omega^3.\omega$
Also $\omega^3 = 1 \qquad \Rightarrow \omega^3\omega = \omega$
Hence $(1 + \omega^2)^4 = \omega$

(ii) $(1 - \omega + \omega^2)(1 + \omega - \omega^2)$ can be written as $(-2\omega)(-2\omega^2)$ {using $1 + \omega + \omega^2 = 0$} $= 4(\omega^3) = 4$
Hence $(1 - \omega + \omega^2)(1 + \omega - \omega^2) = 4$

(iii) $(1 - \omega)(1 - \omega^2)(1 - \omega^4)(1 - \omega^5) = (1 - \omega^2 - \omega + \omega^3)(1 - \omega^4)(1 - \omega^5) = (3)(1 - \omega^4)(1 - \omega^5) = 3(1 - \omega^5 - \omega^4 + \omega^9) = 3(1 - \omega^2 - \omega + 1) = 3(3) = 9$

13. (i) $xyz = (a + b)(a\omega + b\omega^2)(a\omega^2 + b\omega)$
$= (a + b)(a^2\omega^3 + ab\omega^2 + ab\omega^4 + b^2\omega^3)$
$= (a + b)(a^2 + ab\omega^2 + ab\omega + b^2) = (a + b)(a^2 + b^2 - ab)$
$= a^3 + b^3$

(ii) By the question $x^2 = (a + b)^2 = a^2 + b^2 + 2ab$
$\Rightarrow y^2 = (a\omega + b\omega^2)^2 = a^2\omega^2 + b^2\omega^4 + 2ab$
$\Rightarrow z^2 = (a\omega^2 + b\omega)^2 = a^2\omega^4 + b^2\omega^2 + 2ab$
$\Rightarrow x^2 + y^2 + z^2 = 6ab + a^2 + a^2\omega^2 + a^2\omega^4 + b^2 + b^2\omega^4 + b^2\omega^2$
But $1 + \omega^2 + \omega = 0$
$\Rightarrow x^2 + y^2 + z^2 = 6ab + a^2(1 + \omega + \omega^2) + b^2(1 + \omega + \omega^2) = 6ab$

TEXTUAL EXERCISE–23: (SUBJECTIVE)

1. (a) $\sum_{n=1}^{100}(-1)^n = -1 + 1 - 1 + 1 - \ldots. -1 + 1 = 0$

(b) $\sum_{n=1}^{n}(-1)^{2k} = (-1)^2 + (-1)^4 + (-1)^6 + \ldots. + (-1)^{2n} = 1 + 1 + 1 + \ldots..\ n$ times $= n$

(c) $\sum_{k=0}^{80} i^{2k} = i^0 + i^2 + i^4 + i^6 + \ldots. + i^{160} = 1 - 1 + 1 - 1 + 1 - 1 + 1 = 1 + 0 = 1$

(d) $\sum_{k=1}^{4n+3} i^k = 1 + i^2 + i^3 + i^4 + \ldots. + i^{4n+1} + i^{4n+2} + i^{4n+3} = i + i^2 + i^3 + i^4 + \ldots + i + i^2 + i^3 = -1$

2. (a) $5! = 5 \times 4 \times 3 \times 2 \times 1 = 120$
(b) $7! = 7 \times 6 \times 5 \times 4 \times 3 \times 2 \times 1 = 5040$
(c) $8! = 8 \times 7! = 8 \times 5040 = 40320$
(d) $\dfrac{8!}{6!} = \dfrac{8 \times 7 \times 6!}{6!} = 8 \times 7 = 56$
(e) $\dfrac{5!}{2!} = 5 \times 4 \times 3 = 60$
(f) $8! + 7! = 8.7! + 7! = 7!(8 + 1) = 9.7! = 9 \times 5040 = 45360$
(g) $\prod_{k=1}^{n} a = a.a.a\ldots.\ n$ times $= a^n$.
(h) $\prod_{k=1}^{5}(2k - 1) = 1.(3).(5).(7).(9) = 945$
(i) $\prod_{k=1}^{5} ak = a.2a.3a.4a.5a = 120a^5$.
(j) $\prod_{k=1}^{20} 2^k = 2.2^2.2^3.2^4\ldots..\ 2^{20} = 2^{(1+2+3+\ldots+20)} = 2^{210}$.
(k) $\prod_{k=1}^{10} 2k = 2.4.6.8.10 \ldots.\ 20 = 2^{10}(1.2.3.4.5\ldots..10) = 10!.2^{10}$.
(l) $\prod_{k=1}^{5}\left(\dfrac{2^k}{a}\right) = \dfrac{2}{a}.\dfrac{4}{a}.\dfrac{8}{a}.\dfrac{16}{a}.\dfrac{32}{a} = \dfrac{1}{a^5}(2.4.8.16.32) = \dfrac{2^{15}}{a^5}$

3. (a) $\prod_{k=1}^{n+1} k = 1.2.3....n+1 = (n+1)!$

$\Rightarrow \prod_{k=1}^{n} k = 1.2.3....n = n!$

$\Rightarrow (n+1)\prod_{k=1}^{n} k = 1.2.3....n(n+1) = (n+1)!$

$\Rightarrow \prod_{k=1}^{n+1} k = n+1\prod_{k=1}^{n} k$

Also $(n+1)! = (n+1)!$

(b) (i) $\frac{100!}{98!} = \frac{100.99.98!}{98!} = 9900$

(ii) $\frac{n!}{(n-2)!} = \frac{n(n-1)(n-2)!}{(n-2)!} = n(n-1) = n^2 - 1$

(c) $(p-1)! = \frac{p!}{p} = \frac{p!}{p}$

Since p is a prime number $(p-1)!$ will not have any factor of p. Hence p is not divide $(p-1)!$

$\therefore \quad (p-1) = \underbrace{(p-1)(p-2)(p-3)....1}_{\text{out of these factors } p \text{ can divide none. Hence can't divded } (p-1)!}$

(d) $(n-r+1).\frac{n!}{(n-r+1)!} = \frac{(n-r+1)(n!)}{(n-r+1)(n-r)!} = \frac{n!}{(n-r)!}$

(e) $n(n-1)(n-2)....(n-r+1) = \frac{n!}{(n-r)!}$

R.H.S. $= \frac{n!}{(n-r)!} = \frac{n.(n-1)(n-2)...1}{(n-r)(\text{n}-\text{r}-1)....1} = n.(n-1)(n-2)$ $....(n-r+1)$

4. (a) (i) $\sum_{k=1}^{n}(2k-1) = \sum_{k=1}^{n}2k - \sum_{k=1}^{n}1 = 2.\sum_{k=1}^{n}k - \sum_{k=1}^{n}1 = 2(1+2$ $+3+....+n)-(n) = n(n+1) - n = n^2 + n - n = n^2$.

(ii) $\sum_{k=1}^{n} k = 1+2+3+4+....+n$

It is clearly an *A.P.* with common difference 1, first term = 1

$\Rightarrow S_n = \frac{n}{2}(a_1 + a_n) = \frac{(n+1)n}{2}$

(iii) $\sum_{k=1}^{100} k = 1 + 2 + 3 + ... + 100 = \frac{(100+1)(100)}{2}$

$= (101)50 = 5050$

(iv) $\sum_{k=1}^{10} k\lambda = \lambda + 2\lambda + 3\lambda + ... + 10\lambda = \lambda(1+2+3+.....$ $+10) = \lambda.\frac{10.11}{2} = 55\lambda$

(v) $\sum_{j=1}^{n} jk^2 = k^2 + 2k^2 + 3k^2 + ... + nk^2 = k^2(1+2+3+...$ $+n) = \frac{n(n+1)}{2}k^2$

(b) (i) $\sum_{k=1}^{n} k = 1+2+3+4+....+n = \frac{n(n+1)}{2}$

(ii) $\sum_{k=1}^{n} 2k = 2+4+6+....+2n = 2(1+2+3+....+n) =$ $\frac{2.(n(n+1))}{2} = n(n+1)$

(iii) $\sum_{k=1}^{n}(k^2+k) = \sum_{k=1}^{n}k^2 + \sum_{k=1}^{n}k$

$= \frac{n(n+1)(2n+1)}{6} + \frac{n(n+1)}{2}$

$= \frac{n(n+1)(2n+1)+3n(n+1)}{6}$

$= \frac{n(n+1)(2n+4)}{6} = \frac{n(n+1)(n+2)}{3}$

(c) (i) $\sum a^2 = a^2 + b^2 + c^2$

(ii) $\sum(a^2+b^2) = a^2+b^2+b^2+c^2+c^2+a^2$

$= 2(a^2+b^2+c^2)$

(iii) $\sum(a+b) = a - b + b - c + c - a = 0$

(iv) $\sum \text{a}(b-c) = a(b-c) + b(c-a) + c(a-b) = ab - ac +$ $bc - ab + ac - bc = 0$

(v) $\sum \text{a}(b+c) = a(b+c) + b(c+a) + c(a+b) = ab + ac$ $+ bc + ab + ac + bc = 2(ab+bc+ca)$

(vi) $\sum b^2 = a^2 + b^2 + c^2$

(vii) $\sum \text{a}^2(b^2-c^2) = a^2(b^2-c^2) + b^2(c^2-a^2) + c^2(a^2-b^2) =$ $a^2b^2 - a^2c^2 + b^2c^2 - a^2b^2 + a^2c^2 - b^2c^2 = 0$

(viii) $\sum(a^2 - bc) = a^2 - bc + b^2 - ac + c^2 - ab =$ $\frac{1}{2}\sum((a-b)^2)$

TEXTUAL EXERCISE–24: (SUBJECTIVE)

1. (a) $\frac{x}{(x-1)(x-2)} = \frac{A}{(x-1)} + \frac{B}{(x-2)} = \frac{A(x-2)+B(x-1)}{(x-1)(x-2)}$

$= \frac{x(A+B)-2A-B}{(x-1)(x-2)}$

$\Rightarrow A + B = 1$ and $-2A - B = 0$

$\Rightarrow -A = 1 \qquad \Rightarrow A = -1$

$\Rightarrow B = 2$

Hence $\frac{x}{(x-1)(x-2)} = \frac{-1}{(x-1)} + \frac{2}{(x-2)}$

(b) $\frac{x^3-1}{x^3+x} = 1 + \frac{(-x-1)}{x(x^2+1)}$

$= 1 + \frac{Ax+B}{x^2+1} + \frac{c}{x} = 1 + \frac{Ax^2+Bx+Cx^2+C}{x(x^2+1)}$

$= 1 + \frac{x^2(A+C)+\text{B}x+C}{x(x^2+1)}$

$\Rightarrow A + C = 0; B = -1; C = -1$

$\Rightarrow A = 1$

Hence $\frac{x^3-1}{x^3+x} = 1 + \frac{x-1}{x^2+1} - \frac{1}{x}$

(c) $\frac{x^2-x+2}{(x+1)(x-1)} = \frac{(x^2-1)-x+3}{x^2-1}$

$= 1-\frac{(x-3)}{x^2-1} = 1-\left[\frac{A}{x+1}+\frac{B}{x-1}\right]$

$= 1-\left[\frac{Ax-A+Bx+B}{(x+1)(x-1)}\right] = 1-\left[\frac{x(A+B)+B-A}{(x-1)(x+1)}\right]$

$\Rightarrow A+B=1 \qquad \Rightarrow B-A=3$

$\Rightarrow B=-1 \qquad \Rightarrow A=2$

Hence $1-\left[\frac{2}{x+1}-\frac{1}{x-1}\right]$

(d) $\frac{\cos^2\theta}{\cos^2\theta+4\sin^2\theta} = \frac{\cos^2\theta}{\cos^2\theta+4(1-\cos^2\theta)}$

$= \frac{\cos^2\theta}{\cos^2\theta+4-4\cos^2\theta} = \frac{\cos^2\theta}{4-3\cos^2\theta}$

Let $\cos^2\theta = t$

$= \frac{t^2}{4-3t^2} = \frac{-\frac{1}{3}(4-3t^2)+\frac{4}{3}}{4-3t^2} = \frac{-1}{3}+\frac{4}{3(4-3t^2)}$

$= \frac{-1}{3}+\frac{4}{12-9t^2} = \frac{-1}{3}+\frac{4}{12-9\cos^2\theta}$

(e) $\frac{x^3+3x+2}{(x^2+1)^2(x+1)} = \frac{A}{x+1}+\frac{Bx+C}{x^2+1}+\frac{D}{(x^2+1)^2}$

$= \frac{A(x^2+1)^2+(Bx+C)+(x^3+x^2+x+1)+Dx+D}{(x+1)(x^2+1)^2}$

$= \frac{A(x^4+1+2x^2)+Bx^4+Bx^3+Bx^2+Bx+Cx^3+Cx^2+Cx+C+Dx+D}{(x+1)(x^2+1)^2}$

$= \frac{x^4(A+B)+x^3(B+C)+x^2(2A+B+C)+A+C+D}{(x+1)(x^2+1)^2}$

Comparing like coefficients

(i) $A+B=0$ (ii) $B+C=1$

(iii) $2A+B+C=0$ (iv) $A+C+D=2$

On solving, we get $A=\frac{-1}{2}$, $B=\frac{1}{2}$, $C=\frac{1}{2}$, $D=2$

$\Rightarrow \frac{-1}{2(x+1)}+\frac{(x+1)}{2(x^2+1)}+\frac{2}{(x^2+1)^2}$

(f) $\frac{1}{(x^2+a^2)(x^2+b^2)} = \frac{A}{x^2+a^2}+\frac{B}{x^2+b^2}$

$= \frac{(A+B)x^2+Ab^2+Ba^2}{(x^2+a^2)(x^2+b^2)}$

Similarly $A+B=0$ and $Ab^2+Ba^2=1$

$\Rightarrow B=\left(\frac{1}{a^2-b^2}\right); A=\frac{1}{b^2-a^2}$

Hence $\frac{1}{(x^2+a^2)(x^2+b^2)} = \frac{1}{a^2-b^2}\left[\frac{1}{x^2+b^2}-\frac{1}{x^2+a^2}\right]$

2. (a) $\frac{1-3x^2}{(x+3)^2(x-2)} = \frac{A}{(x-2)}+\frac{B}{(x+3)}+\frac{C}{(x+3)^2}$

$= \frac{A(x+3)^2+B(x-2)(x+3)+C(x-2)}{(x-2)(x+3)^2}$

$= \frac{A(x^2+9+6x)+B(x^2+x-6)+(x-2C)}{(x-2)(x+3)^2}$

$= \frac{x^2(A+B)+x(6A+B+C)+9A-2C-6B}{(x-2)(x+3)^2}$

$\Rightarrow A+B=-3 \qquad \Rightarrow 6A+B+C=0$

$\Rightarrow 9A-2C-6B=1$

Solving for A, B, C, we get $A=-\frac{11}{25}, B=\frac{64}{25}, C=\frac{26}{5}$

Hence $\frac{11}{25(x-2)}-\frac{64}{25(x+3)}+\frac{26}{5(x+3)}$

(b) $\frac{2x-1}{(x+1)(x^2+2)} = \frac{A}{x+1}+\frac{Bx+C}{x^2+2}$

$= \frac{Ax^2+2A+Bx^2+Bx+Cx+C}{(x+1)(x^2+2)}$

$= \frac{x^2(A+B)+x((B+C)+2A+C)}{(x+1)(x^2+2)}$

Comparing like coefficients

(i) $A+B=0$ (ii) $B+C=2$

(iii) $2A+C=-1$

$\Rightarrow A=-1, B=1, C=1$

Hence $\frac{2x-1}{(x+1)(x^2+2)} = \frac{-1}{(x+1)}+\frac{x+1}{x^2+2}$

(c) $\frac{3x+4}{(x^2+2x-7)(5x-2)} = \frac{A}{(5x-2)}+\frac{Bx+C}{(x^2+2x-7)}$

$= \frac{Ax^2+2Ax-7A+B5x^2-2Bx+C5x-2C}{(x^2+2x-7)(5x-2)}$

Comparing like coefficients

(i) $A+5B=0$ (ii) $2A-2B+5C=3$

(iii) $-7A-2C=4$

$\Rightarrow B=\frac{26}{151}, A=\frac{-130}{151}, C=\frac{133}{151}$

$= \frac{-130}{151(5x-2)}+\frac{26x+133}{151(x^2+2x+7)}$

(d) $\frac{x^2+3x+6}{x^3-27} = \frac{A}{(x-3)}+\frac{Bx+C}{x^2+3x+9}$

$= \frac{Ax^2+3Ax+9A+Bx^2-3Bx+Cx-3C}{(x-3)(x^2+3x+9)}$

$= \frac{x^2(A+B)+x(3A-3B+C)+9A-3C}{(x^3-27)}$

Comparing like coefficients

(i) $A+B=1$ (ii) $3A-3B+C=3$

(iii) $9A-3C=6$

$\Rightarrow A=\frac{8}{9} \qquad \Rightarrow B=\frac{1}{9}$

$\Rightarrow C=\frac{6}{9}$

Hence $\frac{8}{9(x-3)}+\frac{x+6}{9(x^2+3x+9)}$

(e) $\dfrac{2x-3}{(x-1)(x^2+4)^2}=\dfrac{A}{(x-1)}+\dfrac{Bx+C}{x^2+4}+\dfrac{Dx+E}{(x^2+4)^2}$

$=\dfrac{A(x^2+4)^2+(Bx+C)(x-1)(x^2+4)+(Dx+E)(x-1)}{(x-1)(x^2+4)^2}$

$=\dfrac{A(x^4+16+8x^2)+(Bx+C)(x^3+4x-x^2-4)+Dx^2-D+Ex-E}{(x-1)(x^2+4)^2}$

$=\dfrac{A(x^4+16+8x^2)+Bx^4+4Bx^2-Bx^3-4Bx+Cx^3+4Cx-Cx^2-4C+DC^2-Dx+Ex-E}{(x-1)(x^2+4)^2}$

$=\dfrac{x^4(A+B)+x^3(-B+C)+x^2(8A+4B-C+D)+x(-4B+4C+C-D)+16A+(-4C)-E}{(x-1)(x^2+4)^2}$

Comparing like coefficients

(i) $A+B=0$ (ii) $C-B=0$

(iii) $8A+4B-C+D=0$ (iv) $-4B+4C+C-D=2$

(v) $16A-4C-E=-3$

$\Rightarrow\ A=-\dfrac{1}{25}, B=\dfrac{1}{25}, D=\dfrac{1}{5}, E=\dfrac{11}{5}$

Hence $=\dfrac{-1}{25(x-1)}+\dfrac{x+1}{25(x^2+4)}+\dfrac{x+11}{5(x^2+4)}$

(f) $\dfrac{x^2+x+1}{(x-1)^4}=\dfrac{A}{(x-1)}+\dfrac{B}{(x-1)^2}+\dfrac{C}{(x-1)^3}+\dfrac{D}{(x-1)^4}$

$=\dfrac{A(x-1)^3+B(x-1)^2+C(x+1)+D}{(x-1)^4}$

$=\dfrac{A(x^3-1-3x^2+3x)+Bx^2+B-2Bx+Cx-C+D}{(x-1)^4}$

Comparing like coefficients

(i) $A=0$ (ii) $-3A+B=1$

(iii) $3A-2B+C=1$ (iv) $-A+B-C+D=1$

$\Rightarrow\ B=1, C=3, D=3, A=0$

Hence $\dfrac{x^2+x+1}{(x-1)^4}=\dfrac{1}{(x-1)^2}+\dfrac{3}{(x-1)^3}+\dfrac{3}{(x-1)^4}$

3. (a) $\dfrac{5x-23}{(x-3)(x-7)}=\dfrac{A}{(x-3)}+\dfrac{B}{(x-7)}$

$\Rightarrow\ \dfrac{Ax-7A+Bx-3B}{(x-3)(x-7)}$

$\Rightarrow\ \dfrac{x(A+B)-7A-3B}{(x-3)(x-7)}\ \Rightarrow\ A+B=5$ and $7A+3B=12$

$\Rightarrow\ 7(5-B)+3B=23\quad\Rightarrow\ 35-7B=23$

$\Rightarrow\ 4B=12$

$\Rightarrow\ B=3\quad\Rightarrow\ A=2$

Hence $\dfrac{2}{x-3}+\dfrac{3}{x-7}$

(b) $\dfrac{3x^3-x^2+19x-9}{x^4+18x^2+81}=\dfrac{3x^3-x^2+19x-9}{x^2+9}$

$=\dfrac{Ax+B}{x^2+9}+\dfrac{Cx+D}{(x^2+9)^2}$

$\Rightarrow\ 3x^3-x^2+19x-9=(Ax+B)(x^2+9)+Cx+D$

$\Rightarrow\ 3x^3-x^2+19-9=Ax^3+Bx^2+(9A+C)x+(9B+D)$

Comparing like coefficients

$A=3, B=-1, C=-8, D=0$

$\Rightarrow\ \dfrac{3x^3-x^2+19x-9}{x^4+18x^2+81}=\dfrac{3x-1}{x^2+9}+\dfrac{(-8x)}{(x^2+9)^2}$

(c) $\dfrac{x+1}{x(x+3)(x-2)}=\dfrac{A}{x}+\dfrac{B}{x+3}+\dfrac{C}{x-2}$

$=\dfrac{A(x^2+x-6)+B(x^2-2x)+C(x^2+3x)}{x(x+3)(x-2)}$

Equating like coefficients

$\Rightarrow\ A+B+C=0, A-2B+36C=1, A=-1/6$

Solving, we get $A=-\dfrac{1}{6}, B=\dfrac{-2}{15}, C=\dfrac{3}{10}$

$\Rightarrow\ -\dfrac{1}{6x}-\dfrac{2}{15(x+3)}+\dfrac{3}{10(x-2)}$

(d) $\dfrac{9x}{2(2+3x)(1-3x)}=\dfrac{-9/2x}{(3x+2)(3x-1)}=\dfrac{A}{3x+2}+\dfrac{B}{3x-1}$

$=\dfrac{A.3x-A+B.3x+2B}{(3x+2)(3x-1)}=\dfrac{x(3A+3B)+2B-A}{(3x+2)(3x-1)}$

$\Rightarrow\ 3A+3B=9\quad\Rightarrow\ A+B=3$ and $2B-A=0$

$\Rightarrow\ B=1, A=2$

Hence $\dfrac{9x}{2(2+3x)(1-3x)}=\dfrac{2}{(3x+2)}+\dfrac{1}{(3x-1)}$

(e) $\dfrac{2x+7}{5x^2+12x-32}=\dfrac{2x+7}{5x^2+20x-8x-32}=\dfrac{2x+7}{5x(x+4)-8(x+4)}$

$=\dfrac{2x+7}{(x+4)(5x-8)}=\dfrac{A}{(x+4)}+\dfrac{B}{(5x-8)}$

$=\dfrac{5Ax-8A+Bx+4B}{(x+4)(5x-8)}=\dfrac{x(5A+B)-8A+4B}{(x+4)(5x-8)}$

$\Rightarrow\ 5A+B=2$ and $4B-8A=7$

$\Rightarrow\ A=1/28$ and $B=51/28$

$\Rightarrow\ \dfrac{2x+7}{5x^2+12x-32}=\dfrac{1}{28(x+4)}+\dfrac{51}{28(5x-8)}$

(f) $\dfrac{2x^2}{(x-2)(x+1)^2}=\dfrac{A}{x-2}+\dfrac{B}{(x+1)}+\dfrac{C}{(x+1)^2}$

$=\dfrac{A(x+1)^2+B(x-2)(x+1)+(x-2)}{(x-2)(x+1)^2}$

$=\dfrac{A(x^2+1+2x)+B(x^2-x-2)+Cx-2C}{(x-2)(x+1)^2}$

$=\dfrac{x^2(A+B)+x(2A-B+C)+A-2B-2C}{(x-2)(x+1)^2}$

$\Rightarrow\ A+B=2, 2A-B+C=0, A-2B-2C=0$

$\Rightarrow\ 4B+4C-B+C=0$

$\Rightarrow\ 3B+5C=0\quad\Rightarrow\ 3B+5C=0$

$\Rightarrow\ A=\dfrac{8}{9}, B=\dfrac{10}{9^2}, C=-\dfrac{2}{3}$

$\Rightarrow\ \dfrac{2x^2}{(x-2)(x+1)^2}=\dfrac{8}{9(x-2)}+\dfrac{10}{9(x+1)}+\left(\dfrac{-2}{3(x+1)^2}\right)$

SECTION–III: OBJECTIVE-TYPE (ONLY ONE CORRECT ANSWER)

1. (a) $X \cup \{1, 2\} = \{1, 2, 3, 5, 9\}$

$\Rightarrow X = \{3, 5, 9\}$ or $X = \{1, 3, 5, 9\}$ or $X = \{2, 3, 5, 9\}$ or $X = \{1, 2, 3, 5, 9\}$

$\Rightarrow$ The smallest X is $\{3, 5, 9\}$

2. (d) $n(U) = 20, n(A) = 12, n(B) = 9, n(A \cap B) = 4$

$\therefore\ n(A \cup B) = n(A) + n(B) - n(A \cap B) = 12 + 9 - 4 = 17$

$\Rightarrow n(A \cup B) - 17;\ n(A \cup B)' = 20 - 17 = 3$

3. (b) Case I: $\dfrac{x-1}{x+2} \geq 0 \Rightarrow (x-1)(x+2) \geq 0$

$\Rightarrow x \in (-\infty, -2) \cup [1, \infty)$

Case II: $\dfrac{2x-5}{x-2} \leq 1 \quad \Rightarrow \quad \dfrac{2x-5}{x-2} - 1 \leq 0$

$\Rightarrow \dfrac{x-3}{x-2} \leq 0 \quad \Rightarrow (x-3)(x-2) \leq 0$

$\Rightarrow x \in (2, 3]$ {2 is not in domain}, common region = $(2, 3]$

4. (c) $2x - 7 < 4x - 2 \quad \Rightarrow -2x < 5$

$\Rightarrow x > -\dfrac{5}{2}$ and $5 \leq 2x + 6$

$\Rightarrow 2x \geq -11 \quad \Rightarrow \quad \geq -\dfrac{11}{2}$ and $2x + 6 < 4$

$\Rightarrow x < -1$

Common region to all these solution = $x \in \left(-\dfrac{5}{2}, -1\right)$

5. (b) Case I: $x^2 - x < 6 \quad \Rightarrow x^2 - x - 6 < 0$

$\Rightarrow (x-3)(x+2) < 0 \quad \Rightarrow x \in (-2, 3)$

Case II: $3x^2 - x - 2 > 0 \Rightarrow 3x^2 - 3x + 2x - 2 > 0$

$\Rightarrow 3x(x-1) + 2(x-1) > 0$

$\Rightarrow (x-1)(3x+2) > 0 \quad \Rightarrow x \in \left(-\infty, -\dfrac{2}{3}\right) \cup (1, \infty)$

$\Rightarrow$ Region common to both = $x \in \left(-2, \dfrac{-2}{3}\right) \cup (1, 3)$

6. (a) The option (a) is false as difference of two irrational numbers can be rational also as $(3\sqrt{2} + 1) - (3\sqrt{2}) = 1$

7. (c) $|x^2 - x| + |x + 1| = 5$ can be written as $|x|\,|x - 1| + |x + 1| = 5$

Case I: $x < -1$; equation reduces to $-x(1-x) - (x+1) = 5$

$\Rightarrow -x + x^2 - x - 1 = 5 \quad \Rightarrow x^2 - 2x - 6 = 0$

$\Rightarrow x = \dfrac{2 \pm \sqrt{4+24}}{2} = 1 \pm \sqrt{7} = 1 - \sqrt{7}$

Case II: $-1 \leq x < 0$; equation reduces *to* $-x(1-x) + (x+1) = 5$

$\Rightarrow -x + x^2 + x + 1 = 5 = x^2 = 4$

$\Rightarrow x = 2$ or $x = -2 \quad \Rightarrow$ No solution is this region.

Case III: $0 \leq x < 1$; equation reduces to $x(1-x) + (x+1) = 5$

$\Rightarrow x - x^2 + x + 1 = 5 \quad \Rightarrow x^2 - 2x + 4 = 0$

$\Rightarrow$ Which is not possible.

Case IV: $x \geq 1$; equation becomes $x(x-1) + x + 1 = 5$

$\Rightarrow x^2 - x + x + 1 = 5 \quad \Rightarrow x^2 = 4$

$\Rightarrow x = 2$ or $x = -2 \quad \Rightarrow x = 2$

Hence the solution is $2, 1 - \sqrt{7}$. Thus it has one rational and one irrational root.

8. (b) $\dfrac{x-5}{x^2+5x-14} > 0$, which can be written as $(x-5)(x^2 + 5x - 14) > 0$

$\Rightarrow (x-5)(x+7)(x-2) > 0 \quad \Rightarrow x \in (-7, 2) \cup (5, \infty)$

Smallest integer satisfying the inequality = -6

9. (a) $\dfrac{x^2+6x-7}{|x+4|} < 0$, which can be written as $x^2 + 6x - 7 < 0$ ($|x + 4|$ is always positive)

$\Rightarrow (x+7)(x-1) < 0 \quad \Rightarrow x \in (-7, 1)$

$\Rightarrow$ Number of integer values satisfying the inequality = $6\{-6, -5, -3, -2, -1, 0\}, \{x = -4$ is not in domain$\}$

10. (c) $|x + 4| = 3x - 2$

Case I: $x < -4$, equation can be written as $-x - 4 = 3x - 2$

$\Rightarrow 4x = -2$

$\Rightarrow x = -2$, which is not in the region

Case II: $x \geq -4$, equation reduces to $x + 4 = 3x - 2 = 2x = 6$

$\Rightarrow x = 3$

Hence the overall solution is $x = 3$

11. (b) $2|x + 1| + |x - 3| = 4$

Case I: $x < -1$, equation reduces to $2(-x - 1) + 3 - x = 4$

$\Rightarrow -2x + 1 - x = 4 \quad \Rightarrow -3x = 3$

$\Rightarrow x = -1$, which is not is this region

Case II: $-1 \leq x < 3$, equation reduces to $2(x + 1) + 3 - x = 4$

$\Rightarrow 2x + 2 + 3 - x = 4 \quad \Rightarrow x + 5 = 4$

$\Rightarrow x = -1$

Case III: $x \geq 3$, equation becomes: $2(x + 1) + x - 3 = 4$

$\Rightarrow 3x - 1 = 4$

$\Rightarrow x = 5/3$, which is not in the region.

The complete set of solution is given by $\{-1\}$

12. (c) $\dfrac{x^2+2x-3}{x^2+1} \leq 0 \quad \Rightarrow x^2 + 2x - 3 \leq 0$

$\Rightarrow (x-1)(x+3) \leq 0 \quad \Rightarrow x \in [-3, 1]$

Integer solution = $-3, -2, -1, 0, 1$.

$\therefore$ LCM not defined.

13. (d) $\dfrac{|x-3|}{x^2-5x+6} \geq 2$

Case I: $x < 3$; equation becomes $\dfrac{-(x-3)}{x^2-5x+6} \geq 2$

$\Rightarrow \dfrac{3-x}{x^2-5x+6} - 2 \geq 0 \quad \Rightarrow \dfrac{3-x-2x^2+10x-12}{x^2-5x+6} \geq 0$

$\Rightarrow \dfrac{-2x^2+9x-9}{(x-3)(x-2)} \geq 0$

$\Rightarrow -(2x^2 - 9x + 9)(x-3)(x-2) \geq 0$

$\Rightarrow (2x-3)(x-3)(x-3)(x-2) \leq 0$

$\Rightarrow (2x-3)(x-2) \le 0$

$\Rightarrow x \in \left[\frac{3}{2}, 2\right]$; but 2 is not in the domain

$\Rightarrow x \in \left[\frac{3}{2}, 2\right)$

Case II: $x \ge 3$; equation becomes $\frac{x-3}{x^2-5x+6} \ge 2$

$\Rightarrow \frac{x-3}{x^2-5x+6} - 2 \ge 0$

$\Rightarrow \frac{x-3-2x^2+10x-12}{(x-3)(x-2)} \ge 0$

$\Rightarrow \frac{-2x^2+11x-15}{(x-3)(x-2)} \ge 0$

$\Rightarrow -(2x^2-11x+15)(x-3)(x-2) \ge 0$

$\Rightarrow (x-3)^2(2x-5)(x-2) \le 0$

$\Rightarrow (2x-5)(x-2) \le 0$

$\Rightarrow x \in \left[2, \frac{5}{2}\right]$, but 2 is not in domain

$\Rightarrow x \in \left(2, \frac{5}{2}\right]$

$\Rightarrow$ No solution in this region, hence overall solution is $x \in \left[\frac{3}{2}, 2\right)$

14. (b) $|3x-1| = 2x \quad \Rightarrow \quad \left|x - \frac{1}{3}\right| = \frac{2x}{3}$

Case I: $x \ge 1/3$, equation becomes $x - \frac{1}{3} = \frac{2x}{3}$

$\Rightarrow \frac{x}{3} = \frac{1}{3} \qquad \Rightarrow x = 1$

Case II: $x < \frac{1}{3}$, equation becomes $-x + \frac{1}{3} = \frac{2x}{3}$

$\Rightarrow -\frac{5x}{3} = \frac{-1}{3} \qquad \Rightarrow x = 1/5$

Integral solution on is $x = 1$.

15. (a) $|x^2+x| = 5 \qquad \Rightarrow |x|\,|x+1| = 5$

Case I: $x < -1 \qquad \Rightarrow (-x) - (x+1) = 5$

$\Rightarrow x^2 + x = 5 \qquad \Rightarrow x^2 + x - 5 = 0$

$\Rightarrow x = \frac{-1 \pm \sqrt{1+20}}{2} \qquad \Rightarrow x = -1 - \frac{\sqrt{21}}{20}$ is the region

Case II: $-1 \le x < 0 \quad \Rightarrow -x(x+1) = 5$

$\Rightarrow -x^2 - x = 5 \qquad \Rightarrow -x^2 - x - 5 = 0$

$\Rightarrow x^2 + x + 5 = 0$, which has no real solution.

Case III: $x \ge 0 \qquad \Rightarrow x(x+1) = 5$

$\Rightarrow x^2 + x - 5 = 0 \qquad \Rightarrow x = \frac{-1 \pm \sqrt{1+20}}{2}$

$\Rightarrow x = -1 + \frac{\sqrt{21}}{2}$ is the region.

$\Rightarrow$ The equation has 2 real solutions

16. (c) Let $|x+1| = y \qquad \Rightarrow 2y^2 - y - 3 = 0$

$\Rightarrow 2y^2 - 3y + 2y - 3 = 0 \Rightarrow y(2y-3) + (2y-3) = 0$

$\Rightarrow y = -1$ or $y = 3/2$

Case I: $|x+1| = -1$; which is not positive as modulus is always positive.

Case II: $|x+1| = \frac{3}{2}$

Sub-case I: $x \ge -1 \quad \Rightarrow x = 1/2$

Sub-case I: $x < -1 \quad \Rightarrow -x - 1 = 3/2$

$\Rightarrow x = -5/2$

$\Rightarrow$ There is no negative integer which satisfies the equation.

17. (c) $\frac{(x-1)(x-2)}{x+5} > 1 \quad \Rightarrow \quad \frac{x^2-3x+2}{x+5} - 1 > 0$

$\Rightarrow \frac{x^2-3x+2-x-5}{x+5} > 0$

$\Rightarrow \frac{x^2-4x-3}{x+5} > 0 \qquad \Rightarrow (x^2-4x-3)(x+5) > 0$

$\Rightarrow x \in (-5, 2-\sqrt{7}) \cup (2+\sqrt{7}, \infty)$

18. (c) $x = \sqrt{3+2\sqrt{2}} \Rightarrow x^2 = 3 + 2\sqrt{2}$

$\Rightarrow \frac{1}{x^2} = \frac{1}{(3+2\sqrt{2})} = \frac{3-2\sqrt{2}}{(3+2\sqrt{2})(3-2\sqrt{2})}$

$= \frac{3-2\sqrt{2}}{9-8} = 3 - 2\sqrt{2}$

Hence $x^2 + \frac{1}{x^2} = 3 + 2\sqrt{2} + 3 - 2\sqrt{2} = 6$

19. (c) $y = |2x+1| + 2|x-2|$ in the interval $-\frac{1}{2} \le x < 2$

$\Rightarrow (2x+1) + 2(2-x) = y$

$\Rightarrow 2x + 1 + 4 - 2x = y \quad \Rightarrow y = 5$

20. (d) $|2x+3| - |x-1| = 6$

Case I: $x < -3/2 \qquad \Rightarrow -2x - 3 - (1-x) = 6$

$\Rightarrow -2x - 3 - 1 + x = 6$

$\Rightarrow -x - 4 = 6 \qquad \Rightarrow x = -10$

Case II: $-3/2 \le x < 1 \Rightarrow 2x + 3 - (1-x) = 6$

$\Rightarrow 3x + 2 = 6$

$\Rightarrow x = 4/3$ (not is the region)

Case III: $x > 1 \qquad \Rightarrow 2x + 3 - x + 1 = 6$

$\Rightarrow x + 4 = 6 \qquad \Rightarrow x = 2$

$\Rightarrow x \in \{-10, 2\}$

21. (c) $(x-2)^2 - 3|x-2| + 2 = 0$

Case I: $x \ge 2$; equation reduces to $(x-2)^2 - 3(x-2) + 2 = 0$

$\Rightarrow x^2 + 4 - 4x - 3x + 6 + 2 = 0$

$\Rightarrow x^2 - 7x + 12 = 0 \qquad \Rightarrow x^2 - 4x - 3x + 12 = 0$

$\Rightarrow x(x-4) - 3(x-4) = 0 \Rightarrow (x-4)(x-3)$

$\Rightarrow x = 4$ and $x = 3$

Case II: $x < 2$; equation reduces to $(x-2)^2 - 3(2-x) + 2 = 0$

$\Rightarrow (x-2)^2 - 6 + 3x + 2 = 0$

$\Rightarrow (x-2)^2 + 3x - 4 = 0 \Rightarrow x^2 + 4 - 4x + 3x - 4 = 0$

$\Rightarrow x^2 - x = 0 \qquad \Rightarrow x(x-1) = 0$

$\Rightarrow x = 0, x = 1$

Product of solution $= 0 \times 1 \times 3 \times 4 = 0$

22. (b) $N = \overline{abc} = 100 \times a + 10 \times b + c$

$N_r = \overline{cba} = 100 \times c + 10 \times b + a$

Given $a > c$, by the question $N - Nr = 100(a - c) + c - a$
$= 99(a - c)$
Since last digit is 4 $\Rightarrow$ $a - c = 6$
Hence $N - Nr = 594$
The next two digits from right to left = 9 and 5.

23. (a) Clearly $\sqrt{\pi^2}$ is irrational $\Rightarrow \sqrt[3]{\dfrac{3^3}{10^2}} = \dfrac{3}{\sqrt[3]{100}}$

$= \sqrt[4]{0.00256} = \sqrt[4]{\dfrac{4^4}{10^5}} = \dfrac{4}{10\sqrt[4]{10}}$ $\Rightarrow \sqrt[3]{-8}$ is not real

$\Rightarrow \sqrt{\dfrac{100}{4}} = \dfrac{10}{2} = 5$ is rational.

Out of these only the fourth is rational.

24. (b) $x = 3.1\overline{45}$; 10 $\quad 31.\overline{45}$ $\quad \Rightarrow 11x = 34.5\overline{9}$

$\Rightarrow$ $55x = 172.999....5$
$\Rightarrow$ $55x = 173$ (nearest whole)

25. (b) $x = 3 - \sqrt{8}$; $\dfrac{1}{x} = \dfrac{1}{3-\sqrt{8}} = \dfrac{3+\sqrt{8}}{9-8} = 3 + \sqrt{8}$

$\therefore$ $a^3 + b^3 = (a + b)^3 - 3ab(a + b)$
$\Rightarrow$ $a = x$, $b = 1/x$

$\Rightarrow x^3 + \dfrac{1}{x^3} = \left(x + \dfrac{1}{x}\right)^3 = 3\left(x + \dfrac{1}{x}\right) = (6)^3 - 3(6) = 216 - 18$

$= 198$

26. (b) $\dfrac{3+2\sqrt{2}}{3-\sqrt{2}} = a + b\sqrt{2} \Rightarrow \dfrac{(3+2\sqrt{2})(3+\sqrt{2})}{(3-\sqrt{2})(3+\sqrt{2})}$

$\Rightarrow \dfrac{9+3\sqrt{2}+6\sqrt{2}+4}{7} = \dfrac{13+9\sqrt{2}}{7}$

$\Rightarrow \dfrac{13+9\sqrt{2}}{7} = a + b\sqrt{2} \Rightarrow a = \dfrac{13}{7}$ and $b = \dfrac{9}{7}$

27. (b) $S_1 = (a_1, a_2, a_3, ..., a_n)$
$S_2 = (5a_1 + 80, 5a_2 + 80, ..., 5a_n + 80)$
Sum of numbers is the new set $S_2 = 5(a_1 + a_2 + a_3 + \ldots$
$n) + 80 \times n = 5s + 80n$

28. (b) $x = \sqrt[3]{7+5\sqrt{2}} - \dfrac{1}{\sqrt[3]{7+5\sqrt{2}}}$ which can be written as

$x = \sqrt[3]{y} - \dfrac{1}{\sqrt[3]{y}}$

$\Rightarrow x^3 = y - \dfrac{1}{y} - 3\left(\sqrt[3]{y} - \dfrac{1}{\sqrt[3]{y}}\right)$

$\Rightarrow x^3 = y - \dfrac{1}{y} - 3x \quad \Rightarrow \quad x^3 + 3x = y - \dfrac{1}{y}$

$\Rightarrow x^3 + 3x - 14 = y - \dfrac{1}{y} - 14$

$\Rightarrow 7 + 5\sqrt{2} - \dfrac{1}{(7+5\sqrt{2})} - 14 = 7 + 5\sqrt{2} + 7 - 5\sqrt{2} - 14 =$

$14 - 14 = 0$
$\Rightarrow x^3 + 3x - 14 = 0.$

29. (a) $\dfrac{6x+2a+3b+c}{6x+2a-3b-c} = \dfrac{2x+6a+b+3c}{2x+6a-b-3c}$

By componendo and dividendo $\dfrac{12x+4a}{6b+2c} = \dfrac{4x+12a}{2b+6b}$

$\Rightarrow$ $24bx + 72cx + 8ab + 24ac = 24bx + 72ab + 8cx + 24ac$

$\Rightarrow$ $64x = 64ab$ $\quad \Rightarrow \quad x = \dfrac{ab}{c}$ $(c \neq 0)$

30. (b) $\overline{774958A496B}$ Number is divisible by 8 and 9
(i) $8|B + 12 + 36$
Now $8|B + 48$ $\Rightarrow$ $8|B$
$\Rightarrow$ $B = 8$, also
(ii) $9|55 + A + B$ $\Rightarrow$ $9|63 + A$
$\Rightarrow$ $(A, B) = (0, 8)$ or $(9, 8)$
Hence $(A, B) = (9, 8)$ {non-zero}

31. (c) $\dfrac{x^2(3x-4)^3(x-2)^4}{(x-5)^3(2x-7)^6} < 0$ which can be written as $x^2(x -$
$2)^4 (x - 5) (3x - 4)^3 < 0$
$\Rightarrow$ $(x - 5) (3x - 4)^3 < 0$
$\Rightarrow$ $(x - 5) (x - 4/3)^3 < 0$ $\Rightarrow$ $x \in (4/3, 5)$
Integral (positive solution) = 2, 3, 4 = 3

32. (d) $|x - 1| + |x - 2| + |x - 3| \geq 6$
Case I: $x < 1$; equation reduces to $(1 - x) + (2 - x) + (3 - x) \geq 6$
$\Rightarrow$ $6 - 3x \geq 6$ $\Rightarrow$ $0 \geq 3x$
$\Rightarrow$ $x \leq 0$
Case II: $1 \leq x < 2$; equation reduces to $(x - 1) + (2 - x) + (3 - x) \geq 6$
$\Rightarrow$ $4 - x \geq 6$ $\Rightarrow$ $x \leq -2$
$\Rightarrow$ No solution in this region
Case III: $2 \leq x < 3$; equation reduces to $(1 - x) + (x - 2) + (3 - x) \geq 6$
$\Rightarrow$ $2 - x \geq 6$ $\Rightarrow$ $-4 \geq x$
$\Rightarrow$ No solution in this region.
Case IV: $x \geq 3$; equation reduces to $x - 1 + x - 2 + x - 3 \geq 6$
$\Rightarrow$ $3x - 6 \geq 6$ $\Rightarrow$ $3x \geq 12$
$\Rightarrow$ $x \geq 4$, hence overall solution is $(-\infty, 0] \cup [4, \infty)$

33. (c) $|x^2 + 8x + 7| = |x^2 + 4x + 4| + |4x + 3|$ $x \in \mathbb{R}$
$\Rightarrow$ $|x + 1|\,|x + 7| = (x + 2)^2 + |4x + 3|$
Case I: $x < -7$; equation reduces to $x^2 + 8x + 7 = x^2 + 4x + 4 - 3 - 4x$
$\Rightarrow$ $x^2 + 8x + 7 = x^2 + 1$ $\Rightarrow$ $8x = -6$
$\Rightarrow$ $x = -3/4$
$\Rightarrow$ No solution in the region
Case II: $-7 \leq x < -1$; equation reduces to $(x + 7)(x + 1) = (x + 2)^2 + 4(-3/4 - x)$
$\Rightarrow$ $-x^2 - 8x - 7 = x^2 + 4 + 4x - 3 - 4x$
$\Rightarrow$ $-x^2 - 8x - 7 = x^2 + 1$
$\Rightarrow$ $2x^2 + 8x + 8 = 0$ $\Rightarrow$ $2x(x + 2) + 4(x + 2) = 0$
$\Rightarrow$ $(x + 2)(2x + 4) = 0$
$\Rightarrow$ $(x + 2)^2 = 0$ $\Rightarrow$ $x = -2$
Case III: $-1 \leq x < -3/4$; equation reduces to $(x + 7)(x + 1) - (x + 2)^2 - 4(3/4 + x)$
$\Rightarrow$ $x^2 + 8x + 7 = x^2 + 4 + 4x - 4x - 3$
$\Rightarrow$ $8x + 7 = 1$ $\Rightarrow$ $x = -3/4$ not in the region

Case IV: $x \geq -3/4$; equation reduces to $(x + 7)(x + 1) = (x + 2)^2 + 4(3/4 + x)$

$\Rightarrow$ $x^2 + 8x + 7 = x^2 + 4 + 4x + 4x + 3$

$\Rightarrow$ $8x + 7 = 8x + 7$, which is always true, hence the overall solution is $\{-2\} \cup \left[-\frac{3}{4}, \infty\right)$

34. (d) $\left|1+\frac{1}{x}\right| + |x+1| = \frac{(x+1)^2}{|x|}$

$\Rightarrow$ $\frac{|x+1|}{|x|} + |x+1| = \frac{(x+1)^2}{|x|}$

$\Rightarrow$ clearly $x \neq 0$

Case I: $x < -1$; equation becomes

$$\frac{-(x+1)}{-x} - (x+1) = \frac{(x+1)^2}{-x}$$

$\Rightarrow$ $\frac{x+1}{x} - (x+1) + \frac{(x+1)^2}{x} = 0$

$\Rightarrow$ $\frac{x+1+x^2+1+2x}{x} = x+1$

$\Rightarrow$ $x^2 + 3x + 2 = x^2 + x$ $\Rightarrow$ $2x + 2 = 0$

$\Rightarrow$ $x = -1$ which is not is the region.

Case II: $x \geq -1$ and $x < 0$ equation reduces to

$$\frac{x+1}{-x} + x + 1 = \frac{(x+1)^2}{-x}$$

$\Rightarrow$ $\frac{(x+1)^2}{x} - \frac{x+1}{x} = -(x+1)$

$\Rightarrow$ $x^2 + 1 + 2x - x - 1 = -x^2 - x$

$\Rightarrow$ $x^2 + x = -x^2 - x$ $\Rightarrow$ $2(x^2 + x) = 0$

$\Rightarrow$ $x = 0$ or $x = -1$ $\Rightarrow$ $x = -1$

Case III: $x \geq 0$; equation reduces to

$$\frac{x+1}{x} + x + 1 = \frac{(x+1)^2}{x}$$

$\Rightarrow$ $\frac{(x+1)^2 - (x+1)}{x} = x+1$

$\Rightarrow$ $x^2 + 1 + 2x - x - 1 = x^2 + x$

$\Rightarrow$ $x^2 + x = x^2 + x$ which is true always, hence the overall solution is $\{-1\} \cup (0, \infty)$

35. (d) $x^2 + x + |x| + 1 \leq 0$

Case I: $x \geq 0$; equation reduces to $x^2 + x + x + 1 \leq 0$

$\Rightarrow$ $x^2 + 2x + 1 \leq 0$ $\Rightarrow$ $(x + 1)^2 \leq 0$

$\Rightarrow$ which is not possible.

Case II: $x < 0$; equation reduces to $x^2 + x - x + 1 \leq 0$

$\Rightarrow$ $x^2 + 1 \leq 0$ which is also not possible.

Hence $x = \phi$

36. (a) $|2x^2 - 5x + 3| + (x - 1) = 0$; $|2x^2 - 3x - 2x + 3| + (x - 1) = 0$

$\Rightarrow$ $|x(2x - 3) - (2x - 3)| + (x - 1) = 0$

$\Rightarrow$ $|(x - 1)(2x - 3)| + |x - 1| = 0$

$\Rightarrow$ $|x - 1|\,|2x - 3| + |x - 1| = 0$

$\Rightarrow$ $|x-1|\,2\left|x-\frac{3}{2}\right| + |x-1| = 0$

$\Rightarrow$ $2|x-1|\left[\left|x-\frac{3}{2}\right|+1\right] = 0$

Case I: $x < 1$

$\Rightarrow$ $2(1-x)\left[\frac{3}{2} - x + 1\right] = 0$

$\Rightarrow$ $2(1-x)\left[\frac{5}{2} - x\right] = 0$

$\Rightarrow$ $x = 1$ or $x = 5/2$ which are not region

Case II: $1 \leq x < \frac{3}{2}$ equation becomes

$$2(x-1)\left[\frac{3}{2} - x + 1\right] = 0$$

$\Rightarrow$ $2(x-1)\left[\frac{5}{2} - x\right] = 0$ $\Rightarrow$ $x = 1, x = \frac{5}{2}$

$\Rightarrow$ $x = 1$

Case III: $x \geq \frac{3}{2}$ $\Rightarrow$ $2(x-1)\left[x - \frac{3}{2} + 1\right]$

$\Rightarrow$ $2(x-1)\left(x - \frac{1}{2}\right) = 0$

$\Rightarrow$ $x = 1$, $x = 1/2$ which are not in the region

$\Rightarrow$ Hence the only solution is $x = 1$.

37. (b) $|x^2 + 4|x| + 3| = 11 - 2x$. This can be written as $x^2 + 4|x| + 3 = 11 - 2x$

If $x \geq 0$ $\Rightarrow$ $x^2 + 4x + 3 = 11 - 2x$

$\Rightarrow$ $x^2 + 6x - 18 = 0$

$\Rightarrow$ $\frac{-6 \pm \sqrt{36+32}}{2} - 3 \pm \sqrt{17}$

$\Rightarrow$ $x = \sqrt{17} - 3$ in this region

If $x < 0$ $\Rightarrow$ $x^2 - 4x + 3 = 11 - 2x$

$\Rightarrow$ $x^2 - 2x - 8 = 0$ $\Rightarrow$ $x^2 - 4x + 2x - 8 = 0$

$\Rightarrow$ $x(x - 4) + 2(x - 4) = 0 \Rightarrow (x + 2)(x - 4) = 0$

$\Rightarrow$ $x = -2$ since $x = 4$ is not in this region.

Hence overall $x = 17 - \sqrt{2}, -2$ number of solution = 2

38. (b) $-4x^2 + 12x + 21 = 0$ $\Rightarrow$ $D = b2 - 4ac$

$= (12)^2 - 4(-4)(21) = 144 + 16.21 = 336 + 144 = 480$

$\left[\frac{-b}{2a}, \frac{-D}{4a}\right] = \left[\frac{-12}{-8}, \frac{-480}{-16}\right] = \left[\frac{3}{2}, 30\right]$

On comparison with $ax^2 + bx + ca < 0$

$\Rightarrow$ parabola is opening downward

$\Rightarrow$ Highest value that the parabola takes = 30

39. (c) $\frac{4}{1+x} + \frac{2}{1-x} < 1$ $\Rightarrow$ $\frac{4-4x+2+2x}{1-x^2} < 1$

$\Rightarrow$ $\frac{6-2x}{1-x^2} - 1 < 0$ $\Rightarrow$ $\frac{6-2x+x^2-1}{1-x^2} < 0$

$\Rightarrow$ $\frac{x^2-2x+5}{x^2-1} > 0$ $\Rightarrow$ $(x^2 - 2x + 5)(x^2 - 1) > 0$

$\Rightarrow$ $(x^2 - 1) > 0$ $\Rightarrow$ $(x + 1)(x - 1) > 0$

$\Rightarrow$ $x \in (-\infty, -1) \cup (1, \infty)$

40. (a) $||x - 1| + 2| \leq 2$ this can be written as $|x - 1| + 2 \leq 2$

Case I: $x \geq 1$; equation reduces to $x - 1 + 2 \leq 2$

$\Rightarrow$ $x + 1 \leq 2$ $\Rightarrow$ $x \leq 1$

$\Rightarrow$ $x = 1$ is the only solution on the region.

Case II: $x < 1$; equation reduces to $1 - x + 2 \leq 2$
$\Rightarrow x > 1$ $\Rightarrow$ No solution in this region

41. (d) $(x-1)\sqrt{x^2-x-2} \geq 0$
$\Rightarrow (x-1)\sqrt{x^2-2x+x-2} \geq 0$
$\Rightarrow (x-1)\sqrt{x(x-2)(x-2)} \geq 0$
$\Rightarrow (x-1)\sqrt{(x-2)(x+1)} \geq 0$
$\Rightarrow x - 1 \geq 0$ $\Rightarrow x \geq 1$
$\Rightarrow x \in [1, \infty)$

42. (c) $x^3 - 5x^2 + 4x \leq 0$
$\Rightarrow x^3 - 4x^2 - x^2 + 4x \leq 0 \Rightarrow x^2(x-4) - x(x-4) \leq 0$
$\Rightarrow (x-4)(x^2 - x) \leq 0$ $\Rightarrow x(x-1)(x-4) \leq 0$
$\Rightarrow x \in (-\infty, 0] \cup [1, 4]$ $(x+1)(x-1)2(x-3) \leq 0$
$\Rightarrow x \in [-1, 3]$
$\Rightarrow$ Overall solution is $x \in [-1, 0] \cup [1, 3]$

43. (a) $(3x-4)(x-7) \leq 0$ $\Rightarrow \left(x - \frac{4}{3}\right)(x-7) \leq 0$
$\Rightarrow x \in \left[\frac{4}{3}, 7\right]$
$|3x - 5| \geq 1$ $\Rightarrow \left|x - \frac{5}{3}\right| \geq \frac{1}{3}$

Case I: $x \geq 5/3$, hence the equation reduces to
$x - \frac{5}{3} \geq \frac{1}{3}$
$\Rightarrow x \geq 2$

Case II: $x \leq \frac{5}{3}$, hence the equation reduces to
$\frac{5}{3} - x \geq \frac{1}{3}$
$\Rightarrow x \leq \frac{4}{3}$
Hence the overall solution is $x \in [2, 7] \cup \{4/3\}$

44. (b) $|2^x - 1| + |2^x + 1| = 2$
Let $2^x = y$
$\Rightarrow |y-1| + |y+1| = 2$; which can be compared with $|f(x)| + |g(x)| = |(f(x) - g(x)|$
$\Rightarrow f(x) \,.\, g(x) \leq 0$ $\Rightarrow (y+1)(y-1) \leq 0$
$\Rightarrow y \in [-1, 1]$ $\Rightarrow 2^x \in [-1, 1]$
$\Rightarrow$ Infinity many solutions

45. (c) $|x| + 2|x-1| - 3|x-2| = 4$
Case I: $x < 0$
$-x + 2(1-x) - 3(2-x) = 4$
$\Rightarrow 2 - 2x - x - 6 + 3x = 4$
$\Rightarrow -4 = 4$, which is not possible.
Case II: $0 \leq x < 1$
$x + 2(1-x) - 3(2-x) = 4$
$\Rightarrow x + 2 - 2x - 6 + 3x = 4$
$\Rightarrow 2x - 4 = 4$
$\Rightarrow x = 4$, which is not in the region.
Case III: $1 \leq x < 2$
$x + 2(x-1) - 3(2-x) = 4$
$\Rightarrow x + 2x - 2 - 6 + 3x = 4$
$\Rightarrow 6x - 8 = 4$
$\Rightarrow x = 2$, which is not is the region

Case IV: $x \geq 2$
$x + 2(x-1) - 3(x-2) = 4$
$\Rightarrow x + 2x - 2 - 3x + 6 = 4$
$\Rightarrow 4 = 4$, which is always true
Hence the overall region is $[2, \infty)$

46. (d) $\frac{8x^2+16x-51}{(2x-3)(x+4)} < 3$ $\Rightarrow \frac{8x^2+16x-51}{(2x-3)(x+4)} - 3 < 0$
$\Rightarrow \frac{8x^2+16x-51-3(2x^2+8x-3x-12)}{(2x-3)(x+4)} < 0$
$\Rightarrow \frac{8x^2+16x-51-6x^2-15x+36}{(2x-3)(x+4)} < 0$
$\Rightarrow \frac{2x^2+x-15}{(2x-3)(x+4)} < 0$
$\Rightarrow (2x^2 + 6x - 5x - 15)(2x-3)(x+4) < 0$
$\Rightarrow (2x(x+3) - 5(x+3))(2x-3)(x+4) < 0$
$\Rightarrow (x+3)(2x-5)(2x-3)(x+4) < 0$
$\Rightarrow (x+3)(x-5/2)(x-3/2)(x+4) < 0$
$\Rightarrow x \in \{-4, -3\} \cup \left\{\frac{3}{2}, \frac{5}{2}\right\}$; Largest integer which satisfies the inequality = 2

47. (b) $\left|\frac{y-3}{y+1}\right| < 2$
Case I: $y < -1$, inequation reduces to $\frac{y-3}{y+1} < 2$
$\Rightarrow \frac{y-3}{y+1} - 2 < 0$ $\Rightarrow \frac{y-3-2y-2}{y+1} < 0$
$\Rightarrow \frac{-y-5}{y+1} < 0$ $\Rightarrow (y+5)(y+1) > 0$
$\Rightarrow y \in (-\infty, -5) \cup (-1, \infty)$
In the region, the solution is $y \in (-\infty, -5)$
Case II: $-1 < y < 3$ {-1 is not in domain} inequation reduces to $\frac{3-y}{y+1} < 2$
$\Rightarrow \frac{3-y}{y+1} - 2 < 0$ $\Rightarrow \frac{3-y-2y-2}{y+1} < 0$
$\Rightarrow \frac{-3y+1}{y+1} < 0$ $\Rightarrow -3\left(y - \frac{1}{3}\right)(y+1) < 0$
$\Rightarrow \left(y - \frac{1}{3}\right)(y+1) > 0$ $\Rightarrow y \in (-\infty, -1) \cup (1/3, \infty)$
$\Rightarrow y \in (1/3, \infty)$
Case III: $y > 3$
In equation is same as in case I
$\Rightarrow$ In this region $y \in [3, \infty)$
Overall solution is $y \in (-\infty, -5) \cup (1/3, \infty)$

48. (a) $\frac{x^2+x+1}{(x-1)(x+1)} \geq 0$ inequality reduces to $(x^2 + x + 1)(x - 1)(x + 1) \geq 0$
$\Rightarrow (x-1)(x+1) \geq 0$ {$x^2 + x + 1$ is always positive}

$\Rightarrow$ $(-\infty, -1) \cup (1, \infty)$ {–1, 1 are not in domain}

$\{x\} \le 2$

$\Rightarrow$ $-2 \le x \le 2$ $\Rightarrow$ $[-2, -1) \cup (1, 2]$

49. (b) $\dfrac{x-1}{x+2} \ge 0 \Rightarrow (x-1)(x+2) \ge 0$

$\Rightarrow$ $(-\infty, -2) \cup [1, \infty)$

$\dfrac{2x-5}{x-2} \le 1$ $\Rightarrow$ $\dfrac{2x-5}{x-2} - 1 \le 0$

$\Rightarrow$ $\dfrac{2x-5-x+2}{x-2} \le 0$ $\Rightarrow$ $\dfrac{x-3}{x-2} \le 0$

$\Rightarrow$ $(x-3)(x-2) \le 0$

$\Rightarrow$ $x \in [2, 3]$ $\therefore$ common region (2, 3]

50. (d) $x^3 - \sqrt{x^2} + 4x \le 0$ $\Rightarrow x^3 - |x| + 4x \le 0$

If $x \ge 0$

It reduces to $x^3 - x + 4x \le 0$

$\Rightarrow$ $x^3 + 3x \le 0$ $\Rightarrow$ $x(x+3) \le 0$

If $x < 0$

It reduces to $x^3 + x + 4x \le 0$

$\Rightarrow$ $x^3 + 5x \le 0$ $\Rightarrow$ $x^3 + 5x \le 0$

$\Rightarrow$ $x(x+5) \le 0$

$\Rightarrow$ $y \in [-5, 0]$ $\Rightarrow$ Overall solution $[-5, 0]$

$(x+1)(x-1)2(x-3) \le 0$

$\Rightarrow$ $y \in [-1, 3]$ overall solution for both the equations

$\Rightarrow$ $y \in [1, 0]$

51. (a) $(3x-4)(x-7) \le 0$ $\Rightarrow \left(x - \dfrac{4}{3}\right)(x-7) \le 0$

$\Rightarrow$ $x \in \left[\dfrac{-4}{3}, 7\right]$

$|3x-5| \ge 1$ $\Rightarrow$ $\left|x - \dfrac{5}{3}\right| \ge \dfrac{1}{3}$

If $x \ge \dfrac{5}{3}$ $\Rightarrow$ $x - \dfrac{5}{3} \ge \dfrac{1}{3}$

$\Rightarrow$ $x \ge 2$ $\Rightarrow$ $x \in [2, \infty)$

If $x < \dfrac{5}{3}$ $\Rightarrow$ $\dfrac{5}{3} - x \ge \dfrac{1}{3}$

$\Rightarrow$ $x \le \dfrac{4}{3}$

$\Rightarrow$ $x \in \left(-\infty, \dfrac{4}{3}\right]$ $\Rightarrow$ $x \in \left(-\infty, \dfrac{4}{3}\right] \cup [2, \infty)$

Overall solution is $\left\{\dfrac{4}{3}\right\} \cup [2, 7]$

52. (c) $2x - 7 < 4x - 2$ $\Rightarrow$ $2x > -5$

$\Rightarrow$ $x > -5/2$ $\Rightarrow$ $x > -2.5$

$\Rightarrow$ $-5 \le 2x + 6 \le 4$ $\Rightarrow$ $-11 \le 2x \le -2$

$\Rightarrow$ $-11/2 \le x \le -1$ $\Rightarrow$ $-5.5 \le x \le -1$

$\Rightarrow$ $x \in (-2.5, -1]$

53. (c) $|x-4| = \max\{(x-4), -(x-4)\} + \min\{(x-4), -(x-4)\}$ which can be written as $|x-4| = x - 4 - x + 4 = 0$. which is possible, when $x = 4$

54. (b) $\left|5^{|x|}\right|^{|x|} = 125$ $\Rightarrow$ $5^{|x|^{|x|}} = 125$

$\Rightarrow$ $5^{x^2} = 125$ $\Rightarrow$ $5^{x^2} = 3^3$

$\Rightarrow$ $x^2 = 3$ $\Rightarrow$ $x = \sqrt{3}$ or $-\sqrt{3}$

55. (c) Clearly $6 \le y \le 1$ $\Rightarrow$ $-4 \le y - 10 \le 4$

$\Rightarrow$ $|y - 10| \le 4$

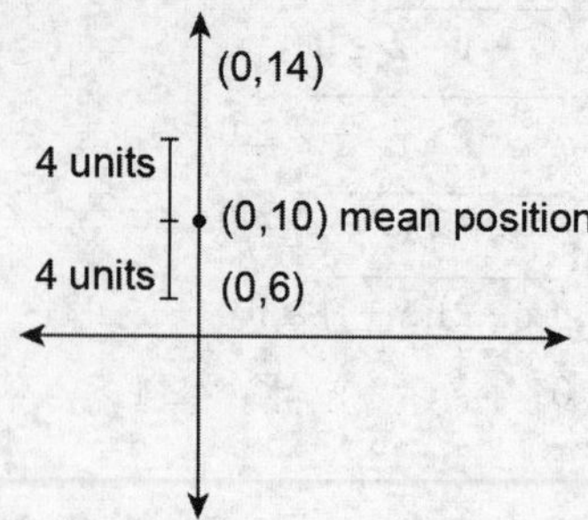

56. (d) Let us assume q_1 is number which when divides 1245 and 920 leaves the same remainder r.

$\Rightarrow$ By division algorithm $1245 = k_1.q_1 + r$

$\Rightarrow$ $920 = k_2\, q_1 + r$

Subtracting the two, we get $325 = q_1(k_1 - k_2)$

Thus q_1 must divide 325 is order to leave the same remainder on division by 1245, 920.

$325 = 5^2 \times 13$ which has total number of divisors = 6

Hence thus are 6 such numbers.

57. (a) $|x+2| + |x-3| = 5$

This equation can be interpreted as the sum of distances from (–2) and (3) is constant and is equal to 5.

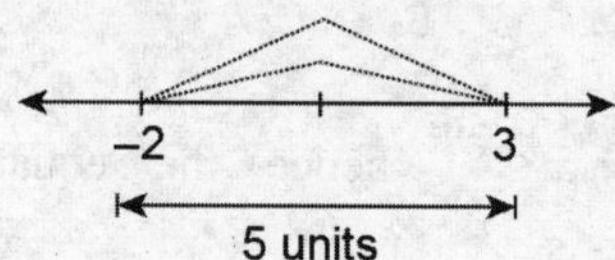

Clearly the point lies on the line joining (–2, 0) and (3, 0)

58. (c) Clearly x coordinate varies from 2 to 4

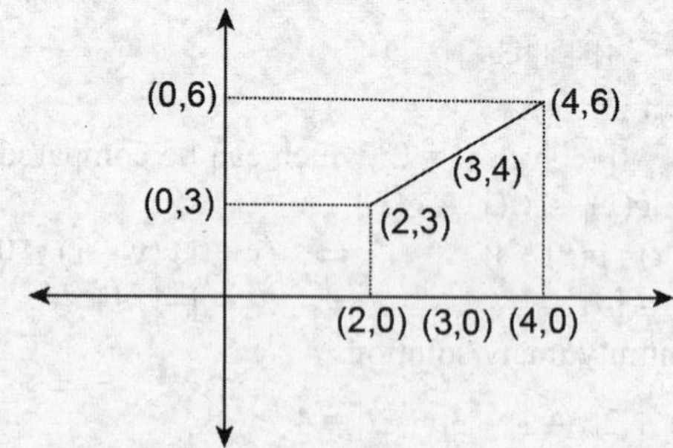

$\Rightarrow$ $|x-2| + |x-4| = 2$ and the ordinate varies from 3 to 6

$\Rightarrow$ $|y-3| + |y-6| = 3$

59. (a) In the region bounded by the rectangle, the abscissa varies from 2 to 6.

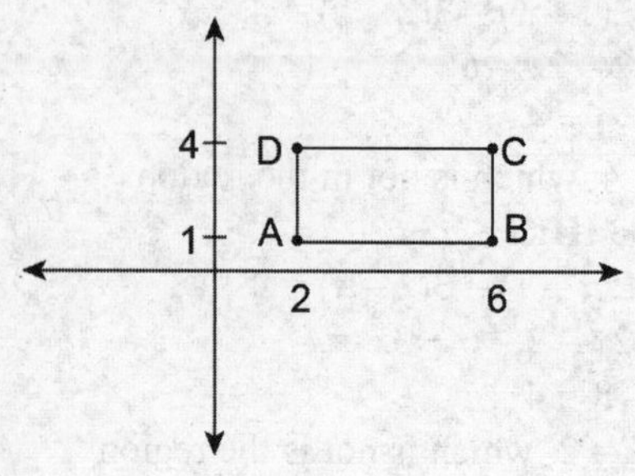

$\Rightarrow$ $|x-2|+|x-6|=4$

Similarly the ordinate varies from 1 to 4

$\Rightarrow$ $|y-1|+|y-4|=3$

Putting them together $|x-2|+|x-6|=4$ and $|y-1|+|y-4|=3$

60. (d) LCM of 2, 3, 4, 5, …, 10 = 2520

This means that all these numbers can divide 2520.

Now, 2520 – 1 = 2519 will give remainder 1 on division by 2, 2 on division by 3 and so on.

$\Rightarrow$ The required number is 2519.

61. (c) $|x-6|\le 8 \Rightarrow -8\le(x-6)\le 8$

$\Rightarrow -2\le x\le 14$

$\Rightarrow A=\{-2,-1,0,1,2,3,\ldots,14\}$

Also $\dfrac{(2x-1)(x-1)^2(x-2)^3}{(x-4)^4}>0$ which we can written as $(x-1)^2(x-2)^3(2x-1)>0$

$\Rightarrow (x-2)(2x-1)>0$

$\Rightarrow x\in\left(-\infty,\dfrac{1}{2}\right)\cup(2,-\infty)-\{4\}$

Out of these the odd integer values which lies in A are {–1, 3, 5, 9, 11, 13}

62. (b) $\sqrt{x^2+12y}+\sqrt{y^2+12x}=33$ and $x+y=23$

$\Rightarrow x=23-y \quad\Rightarrow 12x=12.23-12y$

Similarly $12y=12.23-12x$

$\Rightarrow \sqrt{x^2-12x+12.23}+\sqrt{y^2-12x+12.23}=33$

Which we can write as

$\sqrt{(x-6)^2+240}+\sqrt{(y-6)^2+240}=33$

$\Rightarrow$ Both $x^2-12x+12.23$ and $y^2-12y+12.23$ are perfect squares.

Clearly by observation $x=10$; $y=13$ and $x=13$; $y=10$ are two possible ordered pairs.

63. (c) $\dfrac{(x-5)^2(x+2)^3(x-4)}{(x-3)^4}\le 0$ which can be written as

$(x-5)^2(x+2)^3(x-4)\le 0$

$\Rightarrow x\in[-2,3)\cup(3,4]\cup\{5\}$

Integers which satisfy the inequality –2, –1, 0, 2, 1, 4, 5 = 7

64. (b) $\dfrac{(x-2)(x+2)^2(x-4)^2}{x(x+1)(x-3)}\le 0$

$\Rightarrow x(x+1)(x-3)(x-2)(x+2)^2(x-4)^2\le 0$

Obviously $x\ne 0$ *or* –1 or 3

$\Rightarrow x\in(-1,0]\cup[2,3]$

$\Rightarrow$ Natural numbers = 2, 3

SECTION–IV: (MORE THAN ONE CORRECT)

1. (a), (c) $||x-1|+2|\le 4$; clearly the in-equation reduces to $|x-1|+2\le 4 \Rightarrow |x-1|\le 2$

Case I: $x\ge 1 \quad\Rightarrow x-1\le 2$

$\Rightarrow x\le 3 \quad\Rightarrow x=1,2,3$

Case II: $x<1 \quad\Rightarrow 1-x\le 2$

$\Rightarrow x\ge -1 \quad\Rightarrow x=-1,0$

Hence solutions of x are –1, 0, 1, 2, 3

2. (a), (c) $\left|\dfrac{x^2-1}{x^2+x+1}\right|<1$; which can be reduces to

$\dfrac{|x^2+1|}{x^2+x+1}<1$

$\Rightarrow |x+1|\,|x-1|<x2+x+1$

Case I: $x\ge 1 \quad\Rightarrow x^2-1<x^2+x+1$

$\Rightarrow x>-2 \quad\Rightarrow x\ge 1$

Case II: $-1\le x<1 \quad\Rightarrow (1-x)(x+1)<x^2+x+1$

$\Rightarrow 1-x^2<x^2+x+1 \quad\Rightarrow 2x^2+x>0$

$\Rightarrow x(2x+1)>0$

$\Rightarrow x\in\left(-\infty,\dfrac{-1}{2}\right)\cup(0,\infty)$

$\Rightarrow x=\left(-1,\dfrac{-1}{2}\right)\cup(0,1)$

Case III: $x<-1 \quad\Rightarrow x^2-1<x^2+x+1$

$\Rightarrow x>-2$, which means $x\in(-2,-1)$

$\Rightarrow x\in\left[-2,\dfrac{-1}{2}\right]\cup(0,\infty)$

3. (c), (d) In a triangle sum of any two sides is greater than the third side.

$\Rightarrow 3a^2+2a-3>5a^2-3a-2$

$\Rightarrow a\in\left(\dfrac{5-\sqrt{17}}{4},\dfrac{5+\sqrt{17}}{4}\right)$. Also $7a^2-2a-3>a^2+a-2$

$\Rightarrow 6a^2-3a-1>0$

$\Rightarrow x\in\left(-\infty,\dfrac{3-\sqrt{33}}{12}\right)\cup\left(\dfrac{3+\sqrt{33}}{12},\infty\right)$. Also $6a^2-2a-4>2a^2+a-1$

$\Rightarrow 4a^2-3a-3>0$

$\Rightarrow x\in\left(-\infty,\dfrac{3-\sqrt{57}}{8}\right)\cup\left(\dfrac{3+\sqrt{57}}{8},\infty\right)$

Taking the region common to all of then

$x\in\left(\dfrac{3+\sqrt{57}}{8},\dfrac{5+\sqrt{17}}{4}\right)$

4. (a), (c), (d)

(a) $\sqrt{x^2}=|x|\ \forall\ x\in\mathbb{R}$; which is true as $\sqrt{}$ is the positive square root.

(b) $|x^n|\ne|x|^n$; $x\in\mathbb{R}$ which is false $|-2^4|=|-2|^4$

(c) $(x-a)(x-b)>0 \quad\Rightarrow x\in(-\infty,a)\cup(b,\infty)$

$\Rightarrow$ Statement is true.

(d) True, we have expressed for example $\sqrt{2}$ geometrically.

5. (b), (c) $n(A\times B)=n(A).n(B)=5\times 2=10$

Number of elements in power set of $(A\times B)=2^{10}=1024$.

Which is same as $1+(2^0+2^1+\ldots.+2^9)=$

$1+\dfrac{2^9-1}{8}=1024$

6. (b), (c) By AM-GM inequality AM ≥ GM

$\Rightarrow$ Option (b) is true

If $a = {}^b$, then obviously AM = GM

$\Rightarrow$ Option (c) is true

7. (a), (b), (d)

B: circle of radius R

A: circle of radius r

$Ar(B - A)$ is basically the area of a circular ring without loss of generality let $R > r$

Hence (a) $r = 2, R = 3$

$\Rightarrow Ar \in [5\pi, 9\pi]$

(b) $r = R = 2$ $\Rightarrow Ar \in [0, 9\pi]$

(d) $Ar \in [0, \infty)$ if $r \leq R$ equality holds then area reduces to zero.

8. (a), (b) $\dfrac{2x^3 - 3x^2 + x + 1}{2x^3 - 3x^2 - x - 1} = \dfrac{3x^3 - x^2 + 5x - 13}{3x^3 - x^2 - 5x + 13}$

By componendo and dividendo $\dfrac{4x^3 - 6x^2}{2x + 2} = \dfrac{6x^3 - 2x^2}{10x - 26}$

$\Rightarrow x^2(4x - 6)(10x - 26) = 2(x + 1)(6x^3 - 2x^2)$

$\Rightarrow 4x^2(2x - 3)(5x - 13) = 4(x + 1)(x^3 - x^2)$

$\Rightarrow 4x^2(10x^2 - 26x - 15x + 39) = 4(x^4 - x^3 + x^3 - x^2)$

$\Rightarrow 4x^2(10x^2 - 41x + 39) = 4(x^4 - x^2)$

$\Rightarrow 40x^4 - 164x^3 + 156x^2 = 4x^4 - 4x^2$

$\Rightarrow 36x^4 - 164x^3 + 160x^2 = 0$

$\Rightarrow x^2(36x^2 - 164x + 160) = 0$

$\Rightarrow 4x^2(9x^2 - 41x + 40) = 0$

Clearly one solution is $x = 0$ others are $= \dfrac{-41 \pm \sqrt{241}}{18}$

$\Rightarrow$ it has 3 real solution

9. (a), (c) This curve is simply a parabola which would touch x-axis is both is roots coincides

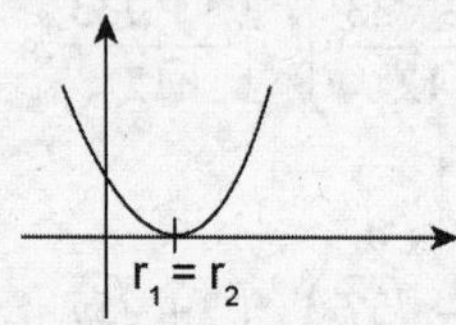

$\Rightarrow$ Discriminate = 0 $\Rightarrow k^2 - 16 = 0$

$\Rightarrow k = +4$ or -4

10. (b), (c)

(a) if $\dfrac{1}{|a|} > \dfrac{1}{b}$ $\Rightarrow 1 > \dfrac{|a|}{b}$ if b is positive

$\Rightarrow b > |a|$ else $b < |a|$

Hence the statement is not true

(b) $\dfrac{1}{a} > \dfrac{1}{|b|}$ $\Rightarrow \dfrac{|b|}{a} > 1$

If $a > 0$ $\Rightarrow |b| > a$ else obviously $|b| > a$

$\Rightarrow$ The statement is true

(c) $\dfrac{1}{(x-y)^2} + \dfrac{1}{(y-z)^2} + \dfrac{1}{(z-x)^2}$

$$\text{R.H.S.} = \left[\frac{1}{x-y} + \frac{1}{y-z} + \frac{1}{z-x}\right]^2$$

$$= \frac{1}{(x-y)^2} + \frac{1}{(y-z)^2} + \frac{1}{(z-x)^2} + \frac{2(z-x) + 2(x-y) + 2(y-z)}{(x-y)(y-z)(z-x)}$$

$$= \frac{1}{(x-y)^2} + \frac{1}{(y-z)^2} + \frac{1}{(z-x)^2}.$$ Hence it is true.

SECTION–V: (ASSERTION & REASON)

1. (a) A: $x < 0$ and $x \in \mathbb{R}$

$\sqrt{x^2}$; which is positive square root of x^2 will be $\sqrt{x^2} = |x| = -x$, hence assertion is true

R: $\sqrt{x^2} = |x|$

Case I: $x \geq 0$

$\Rightarrow \sqrt{x^2} = |x|$ (positive square root of x^2)

Case II: $x < 0$ $\Rightarrow \sqrt{x^2} = -x = |x|$

Hence in either case $\sqrt{x^2} = |x|$

$\Rightarrow$ Hence both reason and assertion are correct and reason correctly explains assertion.

2. (a) A: $A(a + b, a)$ and $B(a - b, a)$, these points are on the same horizontal level.

$\Rightarrow$ Distance between A and $B = |(a + b) - (a - b)| = |2b| = 2|b|$

$\Rightarrow$ Assertion is correct

R: $\sqrt{x^2} = |x|$ and $|xy| = |x| . |y|$

$\sqrt{x^2} = |x|$; Already proved in the previous question $|x.y| = ||x| . |y|| = |x|.|y| \Rightarrow$ Reason is correct

$\Rightarrow$ Hence both reason and assertion are correct and reason correctly explains assertion.

3. (d) A: LCM of $\sqrt{2}$ and 3 does not exist as $\sqrt{2}$ is an irrational number and 3 is not.

$\Rightarrow$ Assertion is incorrect

R: If x and y are co-prime, then we can visualize the multiples of x and y as $x = x.\ 2x, 3x, \ldots\ x.y$ and $y = y, 2y, 3y, \ldots, x.y$

Hence their least common multiple = $x.y$

Reason is correct.

4. (c) A: If $2 \leq x \leq 2$ $\Rightarrow \dfrac{1}{8} \leq \dfrac{1}{x} \leq \dfrac{1}{2}$

$\Rightarrow \dfrac{1}{x} \in \left[\dfrac{1}{8}, \dfrac{1}{2}\right]$ $\Rightarrow$ Assertion is correct

R: If $a \leq x \leq b$, then $\dfrac{1}{x} \in \left[\dfrac{1}{b}, \dfrac{1}{a}\right]$ is true only when a and b are positive

$\Rightarrow$ Reason is incorrect

5. (a) A: $y = \dfrac{(x-3)(x+4)}{(x+5)}$ has the same sign as $(x + 5)(x - 3)(x + 4)$.

Thus, this expression changes sign at 3, –4, –5.

$\Rightarrow$ Assertion is correct

R: If you look carefully at assertion the points of change of sign 3, –4, –5 are also the zeroes of the expression. Thus an expression changes sign at its zero depending on whether the power of monomial is even or odd.

$\Rightarrow$ Reason is correct and is also a correct explanation of assertion

6. (a) A: $0 < a < b$

$\Rightarrow \sqrt{a} < \sqrt{b}$ (law of square roots since a and b are both positive)

⇒ Assertion is correct

R: $|x| < |y|$; since both sides of inequality are positive, squaring both sides, we get $x^2 < y^2$ and other way given $x^2 < y^2$, taking root of both sides, we get $|x| < |y|$.

Hence $|x| < |y| \Leftrightarrow x^2 < y^2$

⇒ Reason is correct

⇒ Reason is a correct explanation of assertion

7. (b) A: $x < x^2$ ⇒ $x - x^2 < 0$

⇒ $x(1 - x) < 0$ ⇒ $x(x - 1) > 0$

⇒ $x \in (-\infty, 0) \cup [1, \infty)$ ⇒ $x > \phi$ and $x < 0$

⇒ Assertion is correct.

R: Square of a real number is never negative.

Case I: Number is positive

⇒ $p \times p = p^2$ is obviously positive

Case II: Number is negative

⇒ $-px - p = p^2$ is also position, hence reason is true.

⇒ Both reason and assertion are true but reason is not a correct explanation to the assertion.

8. (a) A: $|x| < \delta$

$|x| < \delta$ ∀ positive and represent the interior of these concentric circles.

⇒ $x = 0$

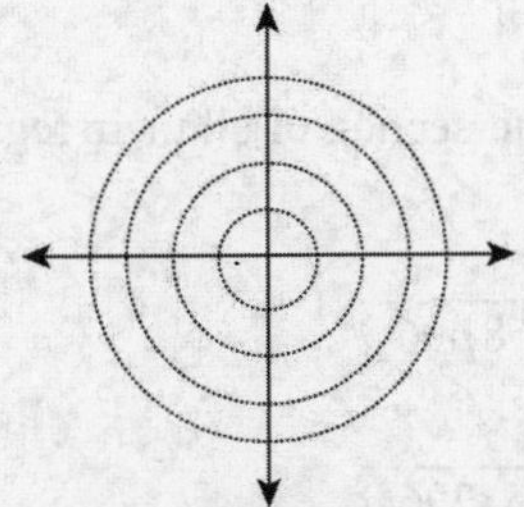

⇒ Assertion is correct

R: $|x| < \delta$ clearly implies $-\delta < x < \delta$

Since δ can be any positive number on real axis

⇒ $\delta \to 0$ and $-\delta \to 0$

⇒ Reason is correct and also is a correct explanation of assertion

9. (a) A : $|x - 1| + |3 - x| = 2$

Case I: $x \geq 3$ ⇒ $x - 1 + x - 3 = 2$

⇒ $2x - 4 = 2$ ⇒ $x = 3$

Case II: $1 \leq x < 3$ ⇒ $x - 1 + 3 - x = 2$

⇒ $2 = 2$; which is always true

⇒ $x \in [1, 3)$

Case III: $x < 1$ ⇒ $1 - x + 3 - x = 2$

⇒ $2 = 2x$ ⇒ $x = 1$

⇒ No solution is this region

Overall solution ⇒ $x \in [1, 3]$

⇒ Assertion is correct

R: $|x| + |y| \geq |x + y|$; Assuming $y > x$

Case I: $0 \leq x < y$ ⇒ $x + y = x + y$ which is true

Case II: $x < 0 \leq y$ ⇒ $-x + y \geq y + x$

⇒ $x < 0$ which is true.

Case III: $x < y < 0$

⇒ $-x - y = -(x + y)$ which is also true

⇒ Reason is correct

It is the same way in which we have analyzed assertion. Hence reason is a correct explanation of the assertion.

10. (a) A: $|x - 3| + |4 - x| > 1$.

Let $f(x) = x - 3$ and $g(x) = 4 - x$

The inequality becomes $|f(x)| + |g(x)| > f(x) + g(x)$

⇒ $f(x) \cdot g(x) < 0$ ⇒ $(x - 3)(4 - x) < 0$

⇒ $(x - 3)(x - 4) > 0$

⇒ $x \in (-\infty, 3) \cup (4, \infty)$ ⇒ Assertion is correct

R: $|x + y| < |x| + |y|$. Without the loss of any generality $y > x$

Case I: $0 \leq x < y$ ⇒ $x + y = x + y$

⇒ Hence no solution

Case II: $x < 0 \leq y$ ⇒ $y + x < -x + y$

⇒ $-x > x$ ⇒ $x < 0$ which is true

Case III: $x < y < 0$

⇒ $-x - y > -x - y$, which is also not true

Hence $|x + y| < |x| + |y|$ holds when x and y are of opposite signs.

⇒ Reason is correct

⇒ Also reason is a correct explanation of assertion

11. (a) A: $x = \{a, b, c\}$

∴ Number of elements in the power set of $x = 2^3 = 8$

⇒ Number of subsets of the power set $= 2^8 = 256$

⇒ Assertion is correct

R: Suppose $x = \{a, b, c\}$

Its subsets are $\{a\}, \{b\}, \{c\}, \{a, b\}, \{b, c\}, \{a, c\}, \phi, \{a, b, c\}$ which is $8 = 2^3$

Power set is the set of all possible subsets of x.

Number of elements is power set = 8

Number of subsets of power set $= 2^8 = 256$

⇒ Reason is correct

⇒ Both reason and assertion are correct and reason is a correct explanation of the assertion.

12. (a) A: *A* set *X* is called a countable set if its element can be listed by counting or labeling with the help of natural number.

Clearly set of prim numbers is a countable set

⇒ Assertion is correct

R: Every subset of a countable set is also countable.

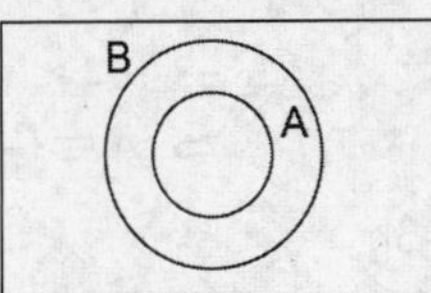

A is a subset of *B*.

Now, if *B* is countable it clearly shows that *A* is also countable.

⇒ Both reason and assertion are true

13. (a) A: $A = \sqrt{2p + 1}$; where p is a prime number.

⇒ *A* contains irrational numbers.

⇒ *A* is uncountable e.g., $\{\sqrt{5}, \sqrt{7}, \sqrt{11}, \sqrt{15}, \sqrt{23}.....\}$

⇒ Assertion is correct

R: Set of irrational number is uncountable as we cannot list all irrational numbers by counting.

⇒ Reason is correct

⇒ Both reason and assertion are correct and reason is a correct explanation of the assertion.

SECTION–VI: (PARAGRAPHS)

Passage A:

1. **(c)** $x = 2^3 . 3^4 . 5^2$
⇒ Number of even divisors = 3 . (5) (3) = 45

2. **(d)** $x = 2^8 . 3^4 . 5^5$
⇒ Number of odd divisors = (4 + 1) (5 + 1) = 30
⇒ Number of odd proper divisor = 30 – 1 = 29

3. **(b)** $x = 2^5 . 3^4 . 6^3$
⇒ Which can be written as $x = 2^8 . 3^7$
⇒ Number of even divisor 8.(8) = 64
⇒ Even proper divisors = 63

4. **(c)** $x = 2^3 . 3^5 . 5^3$
⇒ Odd divisors of $x = 6 \times 4 = 24$
⇒ Odd proper divisors = 24 – 1 = 23

Passage B:

5. **(b)** By the question, $[\phi(x) - \phi(x)]^2 + [\phi(x) - g(x)]^2 = 0$
∴ Sum of two squares cannot be zero until $\phi(x) - f(x) = 0$
⇒ $\phi(x) = f(x)$
And $\phi(x) - g(x) = 0$ ⇒ $\phi(x) = g(x)$
Since $x \geq 0$ ⇒ $\phi(x) = |x|$

6. **(a)** $\phi(x - 2) \leq 2$ ⇒ $|x - 2| \leq 2$
⇒ $-2 \leq x - 2 \leq 2$ ⇒ $0 \leq x \leq 4$
⇒ $x \in [0, 4]$

7. **(c)** $\phi(x - 2) + \phi(x + 2) \leq 4$
⇒ $|x - 2| + |x + 2| \leq 4$
Let $f(x) = x - 2$ and $g(x) = x + 2$
⇒ $|f(x)| + |g(x)| \leq |g(x) - f(x)|$
⇒ $x . y \leq 0$ ⇒ $(x - 2)(x + 2) \leq 0$
⇒ $x \in [-2, 2]$ but $\phi(x)$ is defined for $x \geq 0$
⇒ $x \in [0, 2]$

Passage C:

8. **(a)** $|x + 2| < 4$ ⇒ $-4 < x + 2 < 4$
⇒ $-6 < x < 2$ ⇒ $x \in (-6, 2)$

9. **(b)** $|x - 1| \geq |x - 3|$
Squaring both sides, we get $(x - 1)^2 \geq (x - 3)^2$
⇒ $x^2 + 1 - 2x \geq x^2 + 9 - 6x$
⇒ $4x \geq 8$ ⇒ $x \geq 2$

10. **(d)** $x^2 - 1 \leq 0$ ⇒ $(x + 1)(x - 1) \leq 0$
⇒ $x \in [-1, 1]$
$x^2 - x - 2 = x^2 - 2x + x - 2 \geq 0$
⇒ $x(x - 2) + (x - 2) \geq 0$ ⇒ $(x - 2)(x + 1) \geq 0$
⇒ $x \in (-\infty, -1] \cup [2, \infty)$ ⇒ Overall $\{x\} = \{-1\}$

Passage D:

11. **(b)** $\sqrt{x+14} < (x+2)$
It is equivalent to
(i) $x + 14 \geq 0$ ⇒ $x \geq -14$
(ii) $x + 2 > 0$ ⇒ $x \geq -2$
(iii) $x + 14 < (x + 2)^2$ ⇒ $x + 14 < x^2 + 4x + 4$
⇒ $x^2 + 3x - 10 > 0$
⇒ $x^2 + 5x - 2x - 10 > 0$ ⇒ $x(x + 5) - 2(x + 5) = 0$
⇒ $(x + 5)(x - 2) > 0$
⇒ $x \in (-\infty, -5) \cup (2, \infty)$
Intersection of all three = $(2, \infty)$

12. **(b)** $\sqrt{x+7} < \sqrt{2x+3}$
Squaring both sides, we get $x + 7 < 2x + 3$
⇒ $x > 4$ ⇒ $x \in (4, \infty)$

13. **(a)** $\sqrt{-x^2+4x-3} > 6-2x$
Which is equivalent to
(i) $6 - 2x \geq 0$ ⇒ $x \leq 3$
(ii) $-x^2 + 4x - 3 \geq 0$ ⇒ $x \in [1, 3]$
(iii) $-x^2 + 4x - 3 > (6 - 2x)^2$
⇒ $-x^2 + 4x - 3 > (36 + 4x^2 - 24x)$
⇒ $5x^2 - 28x + 39 < 0$
⇒ $5x^2 - 15x - 13x + 39 < 0$
⇒ $5x(x - 3) - 13(x - 3) < 0$
⇒ $(x - 3)(5x - 13) < 0$
⇒ $x \in \left(\frac{13}{5}, 3\right)$
Overall intersection of all there regions $\left(\frac{13}{5}, 3\right)$

Passage E:

14. **(d)** $N = \overline{774958p96Q}$
If $p = 2$
⇒ $N = \overline{774958296Q}$
$3 \,|a|$
⇒ $3 \mid 57 + Q$ ⇒ $3 \mid Q$
⇒ Q can be 3, 6, 9, 0
⇒ Number of values = 4

15. **(c)** If N is divisible by 4
⇒ Q + 12 is divisible by 4
⇒ $4 \mid Q$ ⇒ $Q = 0, 4, 8$

16. **(b)** $Q + 12 + 36 + 8P$ is divisible by 8
⇒ $8 \mid Q + 8P$ ⇒ $8 \mid e$
For divisibility by 9
⇒ $9 \mid 55 + P + Q$ ⇒ $9 \mid P + Q + 1$
⇒ Possible order pair are $P, Q = (8, 0) = (0, 8)$
⇒ Possible pair = 2

Passage F:

17. **(c)** $\dfrac{3x+4}{(x+1)^2(x-1)} = \dfrac{A}{x-1} + \dfrac{B}{x+1} + \dfrac{C}{(x+1)^2}$

$$= \frac{A(x+1)^2 + B(x^2-1) + C(x-1)}{(x+1)^2(x-1)}$$

$$= \frac{A(x^2+2x+1) + Bx^2 + B + Cx - C}{(x+1)^2(x-1)}$$

$$= \frac{x^2(A+B) + x(A2+C) + A - C - B}{(x+1)^2(x-1)}$$

$\Rightarrow A+B=0$ $\Rightarrow 2A+C=3$

$\Rightarrow C-2B=3$ $\Rightarrow -2B-C=4$

$\Rightarrow B=-\frac{7}{4}$ $\Rightarrow A=\frac{7}{4}$

18. (a) $\frac{3x+7}{x^2-3x+2}=\frac{13x-13+Bx-2B}{(x-2)(x-1)}$

$\Rightarrow 13+B=3$ $\Rightarrow B=-10$

19. (c) $\frac{3x}{(x-6)(x+a)}=\frac{2}{(x-6)}+\frac{1}{(x+a)}$

$=\frac{2x+2a+x-6}{(x-6)(x+a)}=\frac{3x+2a-6}{(x-6)(x+a)}$

By comparison of like terms $2a-6=0 \Rightarrow a=3$

SECTION–VII: (COLUMN MATCHING)

1. (i)→(a, b); (ii) →(b, c); (iii)→(a, b); (iv)→(b, c)

(i) $\{2, 3, 4, 5, 7, 11, 13, 17, 19, 23, 29, 31, 37\}$

$\Rightarrow$ Cardinal number of set = 12

$\Rightarrow$ Obviously is a finite set

(ii) $\{x: x = 4n-1;\ n \in \mathbb{N}, x \in \mathbb{Z} \text{ and } x \le 71\}$

$\Rightarrow \{-1, 3, 7, 11, 15, 19, 23, 27, 31, 39, 43, 47, 51, 55, 59, 63, 71\}$

$\Rightarrow$ Cardinal no = 18

$\Rightarrow$ Obviously the set is finite

(iii) The set is $\{21, 42, 63, 84, 105, 126, 147, 168, 189, 210, 231, 252\}$

$\Rightarrow$ Cardinal no = 12

$\Rightarrow$ Obviously the set is finite

(iv) $\{12, 24, 36, 48, 60, 72, 84, 96, 108, 120, 132, 144, 156, 168, 180, 192, 204, 216\}$

$\Rightarrow$ Cardinal no = 18

$\Rightarrow$ Obviously it is finite

2. (i)→(b); (ii) →(d); (iii)→(a); (iv)→(c)

(i) Proper division of the $pq = 2$ = the lowest prime number

(ii) Number of divisors = $p2q2 = (2+1)(2+1) = 9$, which is the square of prime number 3.

(iii) Number of even proper division of $108 = 2^2 \times 3^3$

Even divisors = $2 \times 4 = 8$

Even proper divisors = $8 - 1 = 7$

HCF of (91, 119) = 7

(iv) Odd divisors of $180 = 2^2 \times 3^3 \times 5 = 3 \times 2 = 6$; which is the lowest composite division of $n(n+1)(n+2)$

3. (i)→(c); (ii) →(a); (iii)→(d); (iv)→(a)

(i) $|x+2|-x<2$

If $x \ge -2$

$\Rightarrow x+2-x<2$ $\Rightarrow 2<2$; no solution

If $x<-2$

$\Rightarrow 2-x-x<2$ $\Rightarrow -2x<0$

$\Rightarrow x>0$; no solution

(ii) $\sqrt{x+1}-\sqrt{x-1}=\sqrt{4x-1}$

Squaring both sides, we get $2x-2\sqrt{x^2-1}=4x-1=$

$-2\sqrt{x^2-1}=2x-1=\sqrt{x^2-1}=\frac{1}{2}-x$

$\Rightarrow x=5/4$; only one solution.

(iii) This has two solutions i.e., x^2-5x+6 and no positive solutions for x^2+5x+6

(iv) $\sqrt{x-5}-\sqrt{9-x}>1$ has only one solution $x=9$

4. (i)→(d); (ii) →(c); (iii)→(b, c); (iv)→(a, d)

(i) $\frac{(x+3)^2(2x+1)^4}{(2x-1)^3(3-x)} \ge 0$; which can be written as $(2x-1)$

$(3-x)(x+3)^2(2x+1)^4 \ge 0$

$\Rightarrow (2x-1)(3-x) \ge 0$ $\Rightarrow (2x-1)(x-3) \le 0$

$\Rightarrow x \in \left(\frac{1}{2}, 3\right)$

(ii) $\frac{(x-5)(x^3-4x^2-4x-5)}{(2x^2+2x+1)} \le 0$; which can be written as

$(x-5)(x^3-4x^2-4x-5) \le 0$

$\Rightarrow x=5$

(iii) $x^2-2x \ge 0$ $\Rightarrow x(x-2) \ge 0$

$\Rightarrow x \in (-\infty, 0] \cup [2, \infty)$ and $x^2-6x+5 \le 0$

$\Rightarrow (x-5)(x-1) \le 0$ $\Rightarrow x \in [1, 5]$

$\Rightarrow x \in [2, 5]$

(iv) $\frac{2x-1}{2x^3+3x^2+x}>0$

$\Rightarrow \frac{2x-1}{x(2x^2+3x+1)}=\frac{2x-1}{x(2x^2+2x+x+1)} \ge$

$\frac{2x-1}{x(2x+1)(x+1)}>0$

$\Rightarrow x(2x+1)(2x-1)(x+1)>0$

$\Rightarrow x \in [-\infty, -1) \cup \left(-\frac{1}{2}, 0\right) \cup \left(\frac{1}{2}, \infty\right)$

5. (i)→(c); (ii) →(a, c); (iii)→(b, d); (iv)→(a, b, c, d)

(i) Even Number is 0

(ii) Rational numbers are $\frac{22}{7}$, (0)

(iii) Irrational numbers π, $\sqrt{2}$

(iv) Real numbers $\frac{22}{7}, \pi, 0, \sqrt{2}$

SECTION–VIII: (INTEGER-TYPE QUESTIONS)

1. $\sqrt{x^2+x-5}+\sqrt{x^2+8x-4}=5$

$\Rightarrow \sqrt{x^2+x-5}=5-\sqrt{x^2+8x-4}$

Squaring both sides, we get $x^2+x-5=25+x^2+8x-4-10\sqrt{x^2+8x-4}$

$\Rightarrow 7x+26=10\sqrt{x^2+8x-4}$

Squaring both sides, we get $49x^2+676+364x=100x^2+800x-400$

$\Rightarrow 51x^2+436x-1076=0$

$\Rightarrow x=2$

2. $(\sqrt{3}+1)^{2x}+(\sqrt{3}-1)^{2x}=2^{3x}$; which can be written as $(4+2\sqrt{3})^x+(4-2\sqrt{3})^x=8^x$

Now, since the surds under the same exponent x are conjugates there is only one solution $x=1 \Rightarrow x=1$

3. Let a, b be two such natural numbers

By the question $a^2 - b^2 = 45$

$\Rightarrow$ $(a + b)(a - b) = 5 \times 3 \times 3$

There arise following possibilities.

(i) $a + b = 9$ (ii) $a + b = 15$
(iii) $a + b = 45$

$a - b = 5$ $a - b = 3$
$a - b = 1$

$\Rightarrow$ $a = 7, b = 2$ $\Rightarrow$ $a = 9, b = 6$
$\Rightarrow$ $a = 23, b = 22$

Hence in all are there are 3 possible pairs $\Rightarrow$ Ans. = 3

4. $497A$ is divisible by 3

$\Rightarrow$ $3|4 + 9 + 7 + A$ $\Rightarrow$ $3|20 + A$
$\Rightarrow$ $3|2 + A$ $\Rightarrow$ $A = \{1\ 4, 7\}$
Also $4|2 \times 2 + B$ $\Rightarrow$ $B = \{0, 4, 8\}$

Total possible ordered pairs = {(1, 0), (1, 4), (1, 8), (4, 0), (4, 4), (4, 8), (7, 0), (7, 4), (7, 8)} = 9

5. By the question $(2x - 1)$ is a factor of $4x^2 - (a - 1)x^3 + ax^2 - 6x + 1 = p(x)$

$\Rightarrow$ $x = 1/2$ must be a root of $p(x) \Rightarrow p(1/2) = 0$

$\Rightarrow$ $\frac{1}{4} - (a-1)\frac{1}{8} + \frac{a}{4} - 3 + 1 = 0$ $\Rightarrow a = 13$

6. $|x-3|^{3x^2-10x+3} = 1 = |x-3|^{(3x-1)(x-3)} = 1$

Following are the possible cases

$\Rightarrow$ $|x - 3| = 1$ $\Rightarrow$ $x = 4$, 2 and
$\Rightarrow$ $3x - 1 = 0$ $\Rightarrow$ $x = 1/3$

Note that case $x = 3$ have not been included as it would reduce base to 0

$\Rightarrow$ Numbers of real solution = 3.

7. $|2x - 4| + |x - 4| = 1$

Here sum of two integers is equal to one, hence there arise four possibilities

Case 1: $2x - y = 0; x - y = 1$ $\Rightarrow$ $x = -1, y = -2$
Case 2: $2x - y = 0; x - y = -1$ $\Rightarrow$ $x = 1, y = 2$
Case 3: $2x - y = 1; x - y = 0$ $\Rightarrow$ $x = 1, y = 1$
Case 4: $2x - y = -1; x - y = 0$ $\Rightarrow$ $x = -1, y = -1$

Hence there are in all four possible solutions.

8. $8(x) = [x^2] - [x]^2$; since $x \in [0, 2]$

If $x = 0$ $\Rightarrow$ $g(x) = 0$
If $0 < x < 1$ $\Rightarrow$ $g(x) = 0$
If $x = 1$ $\Rightarrow$ $g(x) = 0$
If $1 < x < 2$

The possible values of $g(x)$ are 0, 1, 2.

If $x = 2$ $\Rightarrow$ $g(x) = 4 - 2 = 2$

Sum of the possible value of $g(x) = 0 + 1 + 2 = 3$

9. $11 < f(10) < 14$ $\Rightarrow$ $-11 > -f(10) > -14$

$\Rightarrow$ $-1 > 10 - f(10) > -4$

$\Rightarrow$ $-1 > 8\left[\frac{10}{8}\right] - 5\left[\frac{f(10)}{5}\right] > -4$

$\Rightarrow$ $-1 > 8 - 5\left[\frac{f(10)}{5}\right] > -4 \Rightarrow 8 - 5\left[\frac{f(10)}{5}\right] = -2$

$\Rightarrow$ $\left[\frac{f(10)}{5}\right] = 2$ $\Rightarrow$ $f(10) = 12, 13$

Checking it for $x - f(x) = 8\left[\frac{x}{8}\right] - 5\left[\frac{f(x)}{5}\right] = 8 - 10 - 2$

$\Rightarrow$ $f(10) = 12$

10. $\left(a+\sqrt{b}\right)^{x^2-15} + \left(\frac{1}{a+\sqrt{b}}\right)^{x^2-15} = 2a$

Let $\left(a+\sqrt{b}\right)^{x^2-15} = y$ $\Rightarrow$ $y + \frac{1}{y} = 2a$

$\Rightarrow$ $y = a \pm \sqrt{b}$; using $a^2 - b = 1$

$\Rightarrow$ $x^2 - 15 = 1$ or $x^2 - 15 = -1$

Possible values of $x = \pm 4, \pm\sqrt{14}$

Sum of magnitudes of all values = $8 + 2\sqrt{14}$

Comparing it $p + 2\sqrt{q} = 8 + 2\sqrt{14} = 14$

11. p, q, r, are all primes

$\Rightarrow$ $(p + q)(p - q) = r$

Since r is a prime, it must have no factor then 1, r.

$p + q \neq 1$ (sum of no two primes is one)

$\Rightarrow$ $p - q = 1$ $\Rightarrow$ $r = 5$

12. $x + y = 1, x^3 + y^3 = 19$ $\Rightarrow (x + y)(x^2 + y^2 - xy) = 19$

$\therefore$ $x + y = 1$

$\Rightarrow$ $x^2 + y^2 + 2xy = 1$ $\Rightarrow$ $xy = \frac{1 - x^2 - y^2}{2}$

$\Rightarrow$ $(x + 4)\left(\frac{3(x^2 + y^2) - 1}{2}\right) = 19$

$\Rightarrow$ $(x^2 + 4^2)^3 = 39$ $\Rightarrow$ $x^2 + y^2 = 13$

13. $\overline{7A2} - \overline{48B} = \overline{C73}$ $\Rightarrow$ last digit operation $12 - B = 3$

$\Rightarrow$ $B = 9$

$\Rightarrow$ Second last digit operation $A - 8 = \bar{7}$

$\Rightarrow$ $A = 6$

$\Rightarrow$ Third last digit $6 - 4 = C$

$\Rightarrow$ $C = 2$

$\Rightarrow$ $A + B + C = 17$

14. $m^2 = n^2 + 2002 \Rightarrow m^2 - n^2 = 2002$

$\Rightarrow$ $(m + n)(m - n) = 2 \times 1001 = 2 \times 13 \times 7 \times 11$

As done is question (3) section (viii) no possible nature numbers m and exist.

15. $a + b + c = 0, a^2 + b^2 + c^2 = 1$

$\Rightarrow$ $a^2 + b^2 + c^2 + 2(ab + bc + ca) = 0$

$\Rightarrow$ $1 + 2(ab + bc + ca) = 0$

$\Rightarrow$ $ab + bc + ca = -1/2$ (i)

$a^2 + b^2 + c^2 = 1$

Squaring both sides, we get $a^4 + b^4 + c^4 + 2(a^2b^2 + b^2c^2 + c^2a^2) = 1$

Squaring equation (i), we get $a^2b^2 + b^2c^2 + c^2a^2 + 2(ab^2c + bc^2a + a^2bc) = \frac{1}{4}$

$\Rightarrow$ $a^2b^2 + b^2c^2 + c^2a^2 + 2(abc(b + c) + a^2bc) = 1/4$

$\Rightarrow$ $a^2b^2 + b^2c^2 + c^2a^2 + 2(-a^2bc + a^2bc) = 1/4$

$\Rightarrow$ $a^2b^2 + c^2b^2 + c^2a^2 = 1/4$

Putting this, we get $a^4 + b^4 + c^4 + 2(1/4) = 1$

$\Rightarrow$ $a^4 + b^4 + c^4 = 1/2$ $\Rightarrow$ $16(a^4 + b^4 + c^4) = 8$

Exponential Logarithm

CHAPTER 2

■ FUNCTION

A relation 'f' through which each element of set X is related with exactly one element of set Y. Then the rule f is called the function from X to Y and denoted as $f: X \to Y$.
e.g., If $X = \{1, 2, 3, 4\}$ and $Y = \{y : y \in \mathbb{N}$ and $y \le 10\}$ and $f: X \to Y$ is described as $y = f(x) = 2x + 1$.

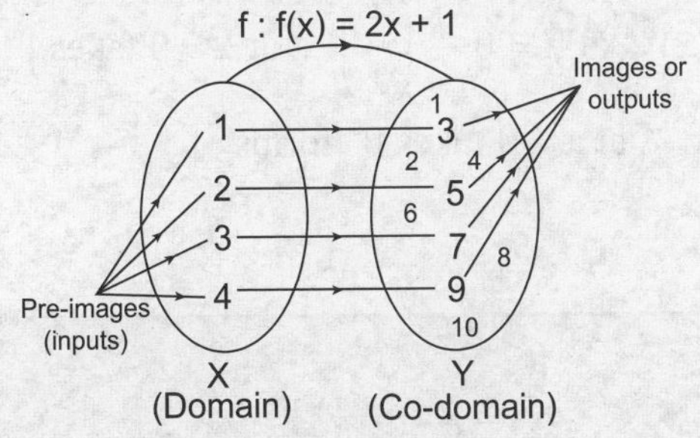

FIGURE 2.1

Thus, relation to be a function, it must satisfy the following two conditions:

(i) $\forall x \in X \; \exists$ *an element* $y \in Y : y = f(x)$
(ii) No two element in Y should have same pre-image in X.

Domain: Set of independent variable x for which $f(x)$ is defined. e.g., X is called domain

Co-domain: Set Y is called co-domain of function f.

Range: Set of images (output) generated corresponding to input $x \in D_f$ is called range of function. e.g., {3, 5, 7 9} is the range of function $f(x)$ defined above.

Machine model of function

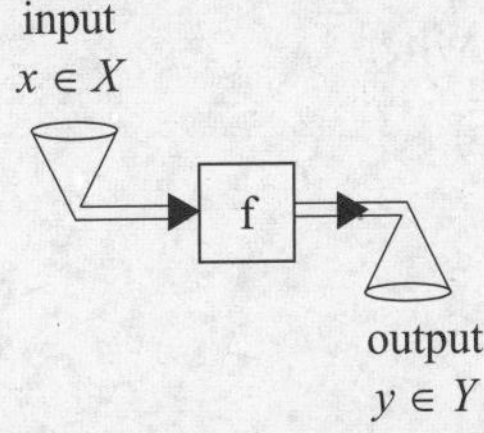

is called as function of x and abbreviated as y is f of x.
If a pre-image is denoted by x and image is denoted by y then we can write:

$y = f(x)$

Image $\in Y$ Pre-image $\in X$

Notations: $f: X \to Y$ or $X \xrightarrow{f} Y$ Which reads as 'f' is a function from X to Y' or 'f maps X to Y. If $x \in X$ is associated with $y \in Y$

$\Rightarrow$ y is f image of x or 'image of x under f' or 'the value of the function f at x'. Also x is called the pre-image of y or argument of y under the function f.

Expression: $y = f(x)$(explicit function) or
$f(x, y) = 0$(Implicit function)

ILLUSTRATION 1: The relation $f: X \to Y$, such that $X = \{1, 4, 9, 16\}$ and $Y = \{y : y \in \mathbb{Z}, |y| \le 10\}$. Mention the images, domain and range for the following definition of f and express it as a set of ordered pairs

(a) $f(x) = \sqrt{x}$ (b) $f(x) = 2x - 5$ (c) $f(x) = 3\sqrt{x} + 1$

SOLUTION: (a) $\because f(x) = \sqrt{x}$; providing the inputs $x \in X$, we get $f(1) = \sqrt{1} = 1 \in Y$, $f(4) = \sqrt{4} = 2 \in Y$, $f(9) = \sqrt{9} = 3 \in Y$, $f(16) = \sqrt{16} = 4 \in Y$

Thus the set of permissible inputs $(D_f) = \{1, 5, 9, 16\}$ and set of all output $(R_f) = \{1, 2, 3, 4\}$

$\therefore f = \{(1, 1), (4, 2), (9, 3), (16, 4)\}$

(b) The relation $f: X \to Y$ is defined such that $f(x) = 2x - 5$

Evaluating the outputs, we get $f(1) = -3 \in Y, f(4) = 3 \in Y, f(9) = 13 \notin Y, f(16) = 27 \notin Y$

$\Rightarrow$ Domain of $f(x)$ is $\{1, 4\}$ and Range of is $\{(1, -3), (4, 3)\}$

(c) $f: x \to Y$ is a relation defined as $f(x) = 3\sqrt{x} + 1$

$f(1) = 4 \in Y, f(4) = 7 \in Y, f(9) = 10 \in Y, f(16) = 13 \notin Y$

$\Rightarrow$ Domain of $f(x)$ is $\{1, 4, 9\}$ and Range is $\{4, 7, 10\}$ and $f = \{(1, 4), (4, 7), (9, 10)\}$.

To find domain of function

We need to know for what inputs expression of f is defined. Hence it is equally necessary to learn.

When does a function become undefined?

A function is said to be undefined when

- Its value tends to infinity (∞)
  e.g., $y = \dfrac{1}{x^2 - 1}$ at $x = \pm 1$
- It takes imaginary value.
  e.g., $y = \sqrt{x - 1}$ at $x \in (-\infty, 1)$
- It takes indeterminate form
  $\dfrac{0}{0}, \dfrac{\infty}{\infty}, 1^\infty, \infty^0, 0^0, \infty - \infty$. *etc*
  e.g., $y = \dfrac{x+1}{x^2 - 1}$ at $x = -1$ takes $\dfrac{0}{0}$ forms
  $y = \dfrac{1}{x^2 - 1} - \dfrac{1}{x^2 - 3x + 2}$ at $x = 1$ takes $\infty - \infty$ forms
  $(1 + x)^{1/x}$ at $x = 0$ $\left(\dfrac{1}{x}\right)^{\sin x}$ at $x = 0$ takes 1^∞ forms
  $\sin x^{\tan x}$ at $x = 0$ takes 0^0 forms

ILLUSTRATION 2: Find the domain of the following functions.

(a) $f(x) = \dfrac{1}{x(x-1)}$ (b) $f(x) = \sqrt{x}$ (c) $f(x) = \dfrac{1}{\sqrt{x-1}}$

(d) $f(x) = \sqrt{x^2 - 1}$ (e) $f(x) = \dfrac{1}{(x-1)\sqrt{x}}$

SOLUTION: (a) $f(x) = \dfrac{1}{x(x-1)}$ to be defined i.e., to be real and finite x should not be zero and one.

Therefore domain set is $(-\infty, 0) \cup (0, 1) \cup (1, \infty)$ or $\mathbb{R} \sim \{0, 1\}$

(b) $f(x) = \sqrt{x}$ will be real and finite only if $x \geq 0$ thus the domain set of square root function will be $[0, \infty)$.

(c) $f(x) = \dfrac{1}{\sqrt{x-1}}$ generates real and finite values only if $\sqrt{x-1}$ is real and non-zero

Consequently, $x - 1 > 0$ thus the domain of function $f(x)$ is $(1, \infty)$.

(d) $f(x) = \sqrt{x^2 - 1}$ to return real and finite values $x^2 - 1 \geq 0$.

$\Rightarrow (x - 1)(x + 1) \geq 0$, applying wavy curve method, we get $x \in (-\infty, -1] \cup [1, \infty)$

(e) $f(x) = \dfrac{1}{(x-1)\sqrt{x}}$ generates real and finite values only if $\sqrt{x}$ is real and non-zero and $x \neq 1$

Consequently, $x > 0$ and $x \neq 1$ thus the domain of function $f(x)$ is $(0, \infty) \sim \{1\}$

ILLUSTRATION 3: Find the set of all values of x for which following functions (expressions) are defined.

(a) $\sqrt{x-4}+\sqrt{7-x}$ (b) $\dfrac{1}{\sqrt{x-4}-\sqrt{6-x}}$ (c) $\sqrt{x-7}-\sqrt{3-x}$

SOLUTION: (a) Let $y = \sqrt{x-4}+\sqrt{7-x}$

Clearly, y to be real and finite $\sqrt{x-4}$ and $\sqrt{7-x}$ both should be real and finite therefore $x-4 \geq 0$ and $7-x \geq 0$

$\Rightarrow x \geq 4$ and $x \leq 7$ $\Rightarrow x \in [4, \infty) \cap (-\infty, 7] \Rightarrow x \in [4, 7]$

(b) $f(x) = \dfrac{1}{\sqrt{x-4}-\sqrt{6-x}}$ to be defined; $\sqrt{x-4}$, $\sqrt{6-x}$ should be real and finite and $\sqrt{x-4} \neq \sqrt{6-x}$.

$\Rightarrow x-4 \geq 0$ and $6-x \geq 0$ and $x-4 \neq 6-x$

$\Rightarrow x \geq 4$ and $x \leq 6$ and $2x \neq 10$ $\Rightarrow x \in [4, \infty) \cap (-\infty, 6]$ but $x \neq 5$

taking intersection of the sets we get $x \in [4, 6] \sim \{5\}$ i.e., $x \in [4, 5) \cup (5, 6]$

(c) $f(x) = \sqrt{x-7}-\sqrt{3-x}$ to be real and finite in value, we must have $x-7 \geq 0$ and $3-x \geq 0$

$\Rightarrow x \geq 7$ and $x \leq 3$

$\Rightarrow x \in [7, \infty) \cap (-\infty, 3]$. Taking intersection we get $x \in \phi$.

TEXTUAL EXERCISE–1 (SUBJECTIVE)

1. Find the set of all values of x for which following functions (expressions) are defined.

(a) $\dfrac{1}{x(x-1)(x-2)}$ (b) $\dfrac{x^2-x}{x^2+x}$

(c) $\dfrac{x+1}{x^2+x+1}$ (d) $\dfrac{1}{\sqrt{x-3}}$

(e) $\sqrt{x-4}$ (f) $\sqrt{x-2}+\sqrt{x+2}$

2. Find the set of all values of x for which following functions (expressions) are defined.

(a) $\dfrac{1}{\sqrt[3]{16x-x^3}}$ (b) $\left(\sqrt{x}-1\right)\left(6-\sqrt{x}\right)$

(c) $\left(\sqrt{x}-1\right)\sqrt{(6-x)}$ (d) $f(x)=\dfrac{\sqrt{x-1}}{\sqrt{6-x}}$

(e) $f(x)=\sqrt{\dfrac{x-1}{6-x}-1}$ (f) $f(x)=\dfrac{\sqrt{x-1}}{6-x}$

3. Find the set of all values of x for which following functions (expressions) are defined.

(a) $\sqrt{x-4}+\sqrt{7-x}$ (b) $\dfrac{1}{\sqrt{x-4}-\sqrt{6-x}}$

(c) $\sqrt{x-7}-\sqrt{3-x}$ (d) $\sqrt{x(x-2)(x-4)}$

(e) $\sqrt{x^3-4x}$ (f) $\sqrt[3]{x^3-9x}$

4. Find the domain of definition of the function.

(a) $f(x)=\sqrt{x-1}\sqrt{6-x}$ (b) $f(x)=\sqrt{(x-1)(6-x)}$

(c) $f(x)=\sqrt{x-x^2}$ (d) $f(x)=\sqrt{x-1}+\sqrt{6-x}$

(e) $f(x)=\sqrt{x-1}(6-x)$ (f) $f(x)=\dfrac{\sqrt{x-1}+\sqrt{6-x}}{\sqrt{1-x}+\sqrt{x-6}}$

Answer Keys

1. (a) $\mathbb{R}-\{0,1,2\}$ (b) $\mathbb{R}-\{0,-1\}$ (c) $\mathbb{R}$ (d) $(3, \infty)$ (e) $[4, \infty)$ (f) $[2, \infty)$

2. (a) $\mathbb{R}-\{-4,0,4\}$ (b) $[0, \infty)$ (c) $[0, 6]$ (d) $[1, 6)$ (e) $[7/2, 6)$ (f) $[1,6)\cup(6,\infty)$

3. (a) $[4, 7]$ (b) $[4,6]$ $\{5\}$ (c) ϕ (d) $[0, 2] \cup [4,\infty)$ (e) $[-2,0]\cup[2,\infty)$ (f) $\mathbb{R}$

4. (a) $[1, 6]$ (b) $[1, 6]$ (c) $[0, 1]$ (d) $[1, 6]$ (e) $[1, \infty)$ (f) $x \in \phi$

■ BOUNDED AND UNBOUNDED FUNCTIONS

A function $f(x)$ whose values lie between two real and finite numbers for all possible inputs that can be given to it is called bounded function. e.g., $f(x)$ = sin$x$, cos$x$, $\frac{1}{x^2+1}, \frac{2x}{x^2+1}, \frac{x^2-1}{x^2+1}$ etc.

An expression of x say $f(x)$ is said to be bounded if we can find two real and finite numbers m and M. such that all the possible values of function satisfy $m \le f(x) \le M$ $\forall x \in D_f$ (domain of $f(x)$). The m is called lower bound of the expression where as M is called upper bound of the expression. The least such number M(sayM_o), is called maximum value of the function and greatest value of m (say m_o). is called minimum value of the function. Following are the properties of lower and upper bound.

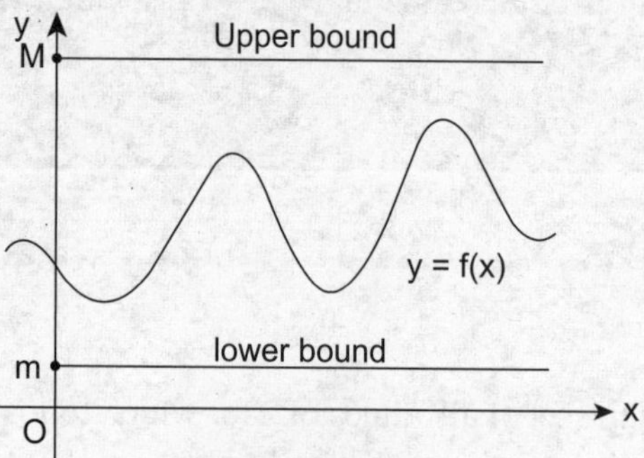

FIGURE 2.2

Existence of one lower bound (m) mean existence of infinitely many lower bounds m_k where $k = 1, 2, 3,....$ i.e., thus if .... $< m_2 < m_1 < m <$ .... $< m_0 \le f(x)$, then $y = m_0$ is greatest of all lower bounds and if for some $x_0 \in D_f, f(x_0) = m_0$, then m_0 is called GLB or minimum value of $f(x)$.

Existence of one upper bound mean existence of infinitly many upper bounds, so if $f(x) \le M_0 < M < M_1 < M_2 < M_3 <$ ....so, $y = M_0$ is least upper bound and if $M_0 = f(x_0)$ for some $x_0 \in D_f$ then M_0 is called maximum value of $f(x)$

Greatest lower bound

The greatest of all lower bounds is called G.L.B. (m_0) and if $f(x) = m_0$ for some $x_0 \in D_f$ then $f(x_0)$ is called minimum value of $f(x)$.

Lowest upper bound

The smallest of all upper bounds is called L.U.B. (M_0) and if $f(x) = M_0$ for some $x_0 \subset D_f$ then $f(x_0)$ is called maximum value of $f(x)$.

E.g., –3, –2, –3/2, ..., –1 etc., are lower bound for the function $f(x)$ = sin$x$ and the greatest of these is –1 (i.e., $m_0 = -1$), because no value of sin$x$ can be smaller than –1 and no such number m larger than –1 posses this property $\left(\text{i.e., } \sin x > m \ \forall x \in \mathbb{R}\right)$ therefore –1 is known as greatest lower bound (GLB) for sin$x$. Also any real number larger than 1 is upper bound for sin$x$ and 1 is the smallest such number called as least upper bound (LUB (M_0) = 1) because no value of sin$x$ can exceed 1 and no number (M) smaller than 1 has this property $\left(\text{i.e., } \sin x < M \ \forall x \in \mathbb{R}\right)$.

Since sin$x$ assumes the above two values, –1 at $x = \left(4k-1\right)\frac{\pi}{2}$ and *at* $x = \left(4k+1\right)\frac{\pi}{2}$ where $k \in \mathbb{Z}$ therefore –1 is called minimum value and 1 is called maximum value of function sin$x$.

Intermediate/extream value theorem

If a function is continuous in its domain and f_{min} = g.l.b $= m$ and f_{max} = l.u.b $= M$ then $f(x)$ must take up all real values between m and M. i.e., $\exists$ at least one $\alpha \in D_f$ where $f(\alpha) = k \ \forall \ k \in [m, M]$

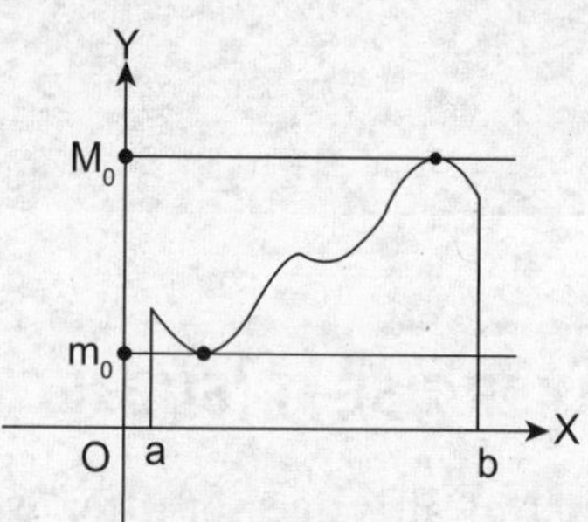

FIGURE 2.3

$\Rightarrow$ Range of f(x) = [m, M] = $[f_{min}, f_{max}]$

If $f(x)$ is throughout increasing or decreasing then it takes up all values between m and M exactly once.

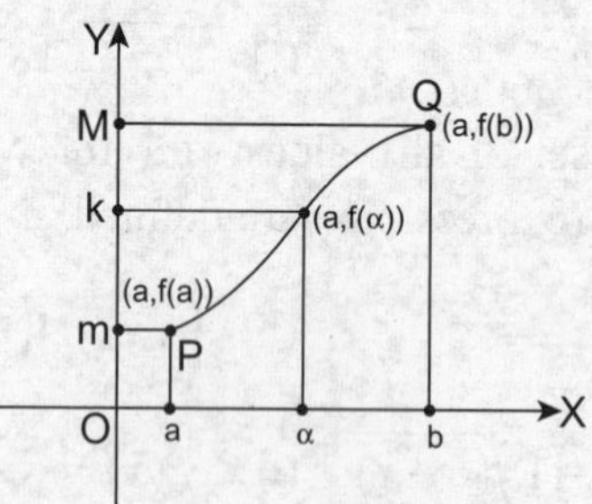

FIGURE 2.4

Range of functions

Range of a function $f(x)$: The range of a function $f(x)$: $A \to B$ is defined as the set of all images corresponding to elements of domain of function i.e., Range of $f(x)$ = {$f(x)$: $x \in$ domain of $f(x)$}

Method to find range of functions

Method to find range of $f(x)$: Let us consider a function $y = f(x)$ (say $y = x^2$), to find out range we follow the given steps.

Step 1: Find the domain of the function say $\alpha < x < \beta$. e.g., $x \in \mathbb{R}$ when $f(x)$ is x^2.

Step 2: Express x in terms of y using given equation of function i.e., $x = f^{-1}(y)$ e.g., $x^2 = y$, $x = \pm\sqrt{y}$

Step 3: Apply the domain restriction to find the set of all possible values of y for which x belongs to the domain of the function. i.e., $\alpha \le x \le \beta \Rightarrow \alpha \le f^{-1}(y) \le \beta$.

For instance, if $f(x) = x^2$ then $x = \pm\sqrt{y}$ x to be real y should be non-negative i.e., $y \ge 0$

$\Rightarrow y \in [0, \infty)$ This is range of $f(x)$

Aliter: $-\infty < x < \infty \Rightarrow -\infty < x \le 0$ or $0 \le x \le \infty$

$\Rightarrow \quad 0 \ge x^2 \ge \infty \qquad \therefore \qquad x^2 \in [0, \infty)$

- Maximum and minimum value, therefore the range of quadratic equation can be obtained by completing the square.
- Maximum and minimum value of any rational expression can be obtained by equating the expression to y and solving the equation obtained for x and applying the condition that x to be real and finite number, find the possible set of values of y.

ILLUSTRATION 4: Prove that the function $f(x) = x^2 - 7x + 5$ is bounded below but unbounded above, hence find its range.

SOLUTION: We know that $y = ax^2 + bx + c$ attains its minimum value equal to $\frac{-D}{4a}$ at $x = \frac{-b}{2a}$

$\therefore \quad (f(x))_{min} = \frac{-D}{4a} = -\frac{(-7)^2 - 4(1)(5)}{4(1)} = \frac{-[49-20]}{4} = -29/4$

But $(f(x))_{max}$ does not exist as it approaches to infinity.

$\Rightarrow$ $f(x)$ is bounded below but unbounded above.

$\therefore$ $f(x)$ is unbounded function and range of $f(x)$ is $\left(-\frac{29}{4}, \infty\right)$

ILLUSTRATION 5: Find domain and range of $y = \frac{x^2-1}{x^2+1}$ and determine the LUB/GLB of the function.

SOLUTION: $\because$ Domain is $\mathbb{R}$

Consider the equation $y = \frac{x^2-1}{x^2+1}$, cross multiplying and rearranging terms

$\Rightarrow \quad yx^2 + y = x^2 - 1 \Rightarrow (y-1)x^2 = -1 - y$

$\Rightarrow \quad x^2 = \frac{(y+1)}{1-y} \qquad \Rightarrow \quad x = \pm\sqrt{\frac{y+1}{1-y}}$

Thus x to be real and finite

$\Rightarrow \quad (y+1)(y-1) < 0$ or $y = -1$ or $\frac{y+1}{y-1} = -\frac{x^2}{1} \le 0 \Rightarrow y \in [-1, 1)$

ILLUSTRATION 6: Determine whether following functions are bounded or not and also find their LUB/GLB and range of function.

(a) $f(x) = \frac{x^2-9}{(x-1)(x-3)}$ (b) $f(x) = \frac{x^2-5x+4}{x^2-7x+12}$

SOLUTION: (a) Consider $f(x) = \frac{x^2-9}{(x-1)(x-3)}$. Domain (D_f) : $\mathbb{R} \sim \{1, 3\}$

with domain restriction it is equivalent to the function

$g(x) = \frac{x+3}{x-1}$ Domain (D_g) : $\mathbb{R} \sim \{1\}$

Now let us find the range of $g(x)$

Let $y = \frac{x+3}{x-1}$; expressing x in terms of y

$\Rightarrow\ yx - x = y + 3$ i.e., $x(y - 1) = y + 3$

$\Rightarrow\ x = \dfrac{(y+3)}{(y-1)}$ x to be real and finite $y \neq 1$

i.e., $y \in \mathbb{R} \sim \{1\}$; notice that range of $g(x)$ contains its value at $x = 3$ that is $g(3)$ and $f(x)$ and $g(x)$ being equivalent functions R_f and R_g are same except $g(3) = 3$ which is an element of R_g but not of R_f becomes $f(x)$ is not defined at $x = 3$

$\Rightarrow\ R_f = R_g \sim \{g(3)\} = \mathbb{R} \sim \{1,3\}$

Clearly, f is not bounded as it neither has lower bound nor upper bound.

(b) Consider $f(x) = \dfrac{x^2-5x+4}{x^2-7x+12}$ i.e., $f(x) = \dfrac{(x-1)(x-4)}{(x-3)(x-4)}$

Domain of $f(x) = \mathbb{R} \sim \{3,4\}$ its equivalent function is $g(x) = \dfrac{x-1}{x-3}$

$D_f = \mathbb{R} \sim \{3\}$ it is important to observe that $R_f = R_g \sim \{g(4)\}$

$\because$ For domain $\mathbb{R} \sim \{3,4\}$ Now, to find range of $g(x)$ let $y = \dfrac{x-1}{x-3}$

$\Rightarrow\ xy - 3y = x - 1$, thus $x(y - 1) = 3y - 1$

$\Rightarrow\ x = \dfrac{3y-1}{y-1}$, therefore x to be real and finite $y \neq 1$

$\Rightarrow\ R_g = \mathbb{R} \sim \{1\}$ $\qquad\qquad \Rightarrow\ R_f = R_g \sim \{g(4)\} = R_g \sim \{3\} = \mathbb{R} \sim \{1,3\}$

$f(x)$ is unbounded function as neither has lower bound nor upper bound.

ILLUSTRATION 7: Find the range of following functions for described domain and hence its LUB and GLB. Also find the maximum/minimum value of $f(x)$.

(a) $f(x) = \dfrac{120-160x^2}{x^2+4}\ \forall\ x \in [-3,6)$ (b) $f(x) = \sqrt{\dfrac{16-x^2}{3x^2+2}}\ \forall\ x \in (-3,3]$

SOLUTION: (a) $f(x) = \dfrac{40(3-4x^2)}{x^2+4} = 40\left(\dfrac{19-4x^2-16}{x^2+4}\right)$; $f(x) = 40\left(\dfrac{19}{x^2+4} - 4\right)$

Now consider the given domain $-3 \leq x < 6$

$\Rightarrow\ 0 \leq x^2 < 36$, thus $4 \leq x^2 + 4 < 40$

Now apply reciprocal property, we get $\dfrac{1}{40} < \dfrac{19}{x^2+4} \leq \dfrac{1}{4}$

Now multiplying by 19, we get $\dfrac{19}{40} < \dfrac{19}{x^2+4} \leq \dfrac{19}{4}$

Adding –4, we get $\dfrac{-141}{40} < \dfrac{3-4x^2}{x^2+4} \leq \dfrac{3}{4}$

Therefore multiplying by 40, we obtain $f(x) \in (-141, 30]$

Clearly, $f(x)$ is bounded function GLB = –141 and LUB = 30

But $f(x)$ cannot take the value –141 for any x

$\Rightarrow\ f_{max} = 30$ but f_{min} does not exist.

(b) Consider $y = \dfrac{x^2-16}{3x^2+2}$; for the domain $-3 < x \leq 3$

$y = \dfrac{1}{3}\left(\dfrac{3x^2+2-50}{3x^2+2}\right)$ $y = \dfrac{1}{3}\left(1 - \dfrac{50}{3x^2+2}\right)$ $\qquad \because\ -3 < x \leq 3,$

Squaring both side and multiplying by 3, we get $0 \leq 3x^2 \leq 27$

Adding 2, we obtained $2 \le 3x^2 + 2 \le 29$; taking reciprocal

$\Rightarrow \frac{1}{29} \le \frac{1}{3x^2+2} \le \frac{1}{2}$; Multiplying by –50

$\Rightarrow -25 \le \frac{-50}{3x^2+2} \le \frac{-50}{29}$; adding 1 and dividing by 3

$\Rightarrow -8 \le \left(\frac{x^2-16}{3x^2+2}\right) \le \frac{-7}{29}$

$\Rightarrow \frac{7}{9} \le \frac{16-x^2}{3x^2+2} \le 8$; taking square root, we get $f(x) \in \left[\frac{\sqrt{7}}{\sqrt{29}}, 2\sqrt{2}\right]$ is the range of function

Clearly, $f(x)$ is bounded function GLB = $\sqrt{\frac{7}{29}}$ and LUB = $2\sqrt{2}$ and $f(x)$ can take both the above values

$\Rightarrow f_{max} = 2\sqrt{2}$ and $f_{min} = \sqrt{\frac{7}{29}}$.

Increasing and decreasing functions

If $f(x)$ is increasing function, then by increasing the input output also increases.

i.e., $x_2 > x_1 \Leftrightarrow f(x_2) > f(x_1)$

$\Rightarrow \Delta x = x_2 - x_1 > 0$

$\Rightarrow \Delta y = f(x_2) - f(x_1) = y_2 - y_1 > 0$

$\Rightarrow \Delta y > 0$

$\Rightarrow$ rate of change (dy/dx) positive.

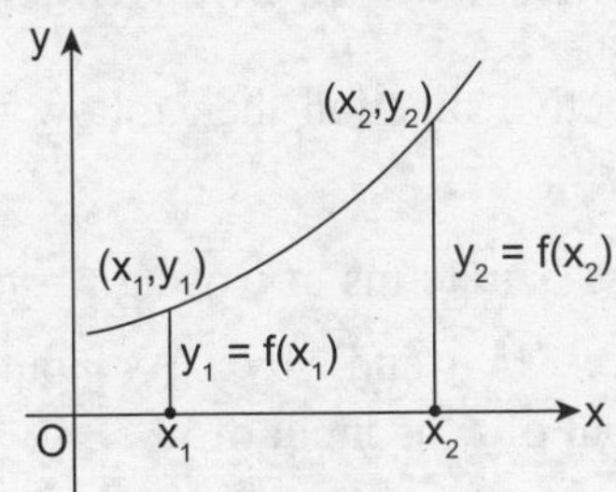

FIGURE 2.5

E.g., $x = 2x + 3, y = x^3, y = 2x$ etc.

If $f(x)$ is decreasing function, then by increasing the input output decreases

i.e., $x_2 > x_1 \Leftrightarrow f(x_2) < f(x_1)$

$\Rightarrow \Delta x = x_2 - x_1 > 0$

$\Rightarrow \Delta y = f(x_2) - f(x_1) = y_2 - y_1 < 0$

$\Rightarrow \Delta y < 0$

$\Rightarrow$ rate of change (dy/dx) negative.

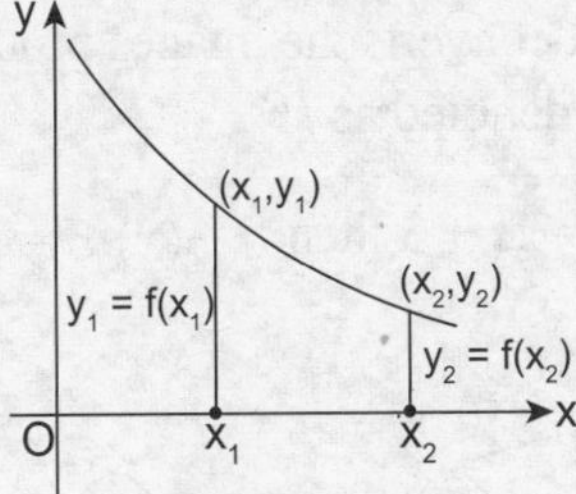

FIGURE 2.6

E.g., $x = 2 - 5x, y = 1/x ; x > 0, y = 2^{-x} ; y = 2 - x^3$ etc

By application of increasing function, the sign of inequality does not change whereas by applying a decreasing function the inequality reverses its sign.

ILLUSTRATION 8: Test whether the following functions are increasing or decreasing or neither.

(a) $f(x) = 4 - 5x ;\ x \in \mathbb{R}$

(b) $f(x) = \frac{1}{2x-3}$; $x \in (2, \infty)$

(c) $f(x) = x^2 - 2x + 3$ where $x \ge 1$

SOLUTION: (a) let $x_1 > x_2$; multiplying by –5

$\Leftrightarrow -5x_1 < -5x_2$; Add 4 to all $\Leftrightarrow 4 - 5x_1 < 4 - 5x_2$

$\Leftrightarrow f(x_1) < f(x_2)$; thus $f(x)$ is a decreasing function.

Aliter: $f(x) = 4 - 5x$, hence $f'(x) = -5 < 0$. Also $f(x)$ is continuous function.

Thus f(x) is decreasing function.

(b) let $2 < x_1 < x_2$; (multiplying by 2)

$\Leftrightarrow\ 4 < 2x_1 < 2x_2$; (subtracting 3) $\Leftrightarrow\ 1 < 2x_1 - 3 < 2x_2 - 3$

$\because$ all are positive so taking reciprocal, we get $\dfrac{1}{2x_1 - 3} > \dfrac{1}{2x_2 - 3} \Leftrightarrow f(x_1) > f(x_2)$

$\Rightarrow$ $f(x)$ is a decreasing function

Aliter: $f(x) = \dfrac{1}{2x-3} \Rightarrow f'(x) = \dfrac{-2}{(2x-3)^2} < 0$

Therefore $f(x)$ is decreasing function, as it is continuous $\forall\ x \geq 1$

(c) $f(x) = x^2 - 2x + 3 = (x - 1)^2 + 2$

$\because\ x_1 > x_2 > 1$ $\Leftrightarrow\ x_1 - 1 > x_2 - 1 > 0$

Squaring, we get $(x_1 - 1)^2 > (x_2 - 1)^2$; (*adding* 2 *to both side*)

$\Leftrightarrow\ (x_1 - 1)^2 + 2 > (x_2 - 1)^2 + 2$

$\Leftrightarrow\ f(x_1) > f(x_2)$; Now $f(x_1) > f(x_2) \Leftrightarrow x_1 > x_2$

Thus the function $f(x)$ is increasing function $\forall\ x \in (2, \infty)$.

Inverse of a function

If a function f is defined from a non empty set A to a non empty set B, then a function from set B to A is called inverse function of f iff it converts the images produced by f back to pre-images. It is denoted as f^{-1}.

E.g., If $f(x) = 2x + 3$ then $f^{-1}(x) = \dfrac{x-3}{2}$

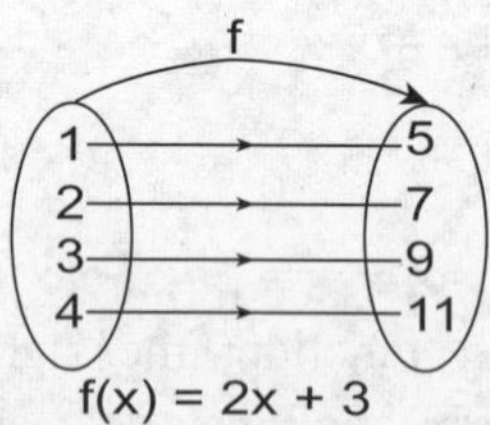

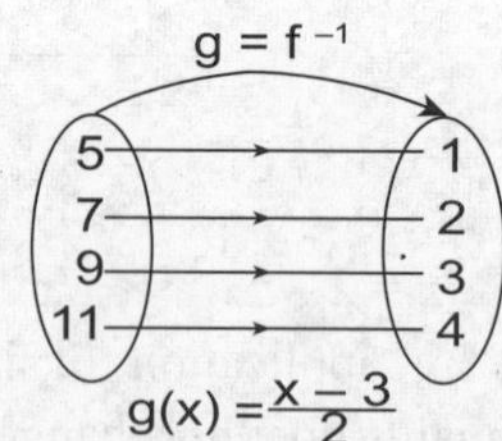

FIGURE 2.7

A function to be invertible it must be one-one (injective) as well as onto (surjective). In the inverse function inputs and outputs interchange their roles, provided the function is bijective.

Method of find inverse of a function

If $f(x)$ is a bijective function then follow the steps given below to write f^{-1}.

Step I: Express x in terms of y using $y = f(x)$.

Step II: Replace x by y and y by x. As input f^{-1} is output of f. Output of f^{-1} is input of x.

For example, given $f: \mathbb{R} \sim \{0\} \to \mathbb{R} \sim \{0\}$ such that $f(x) = 1/x$ $\Rightarrow y = 1/x \Rightarrow x = 1/y$. Now replacing x by y and y by x, we get $y = 1/x$. Thus $f^{-1}(x) = 1/x$, hence it is inverse of itself.

ILLUSTRATION 9: If $f(x) = \dfrac{x-1}{2x+3}$, then find $f^{-1}(x)$.

SOLUTION: Consider $y = \dfrac{3x-4}{7}$ $\Rightarrow 3y+1 = x(1-2y)$ expressing in terms of y

$\Rightarrow 3x = 7y+4 \quad \Rightarrow x = \dfrac{7y+4}{3}$

$\Rightarrow y = \dfrac{7x+4}{3} \quad \Rightarrow f^{-1}(x) = \dfrac{7x+4}{3}$

ILLUSTRATION 10: If $f(x)=\dfrac{x-1}{2x+3}$, then find $f^{-1}(x)$.

SOLUTION: Consider $y=\dfrac{x-1}{2x+3}$ $\Rightarrow 3y+1=x(1-2y)$

Expressing x in terms of y, we get $x=\dfrac{3y+1}{1-2y}$

Now interchanging x and y, we get $y=\dfrac{3x+1}{1-2x}$ $\Rightarrow f^{-1}(x)=\dfrac{3x+1}{1-2x}$

TEXTUAL EXERCISE–2 (SUBJECTIVE)

1. Find the domain of following rational functions and find the maximum/minimum value and range of these functions. Also mention which of these are bounded functions by mentioning there LUB and GLB.

(a) $\dfrac{x-1}{x+1}$ (b) $\dfrac{2x+1}{5x-3}$

(c) $\dfrac{x^2-2}{x^2+4}$

2. Find the domain of following rational functions and find the maximum/minimum value and range of these functions. Also mention which of these are bounded functions by mentioning there LUB and GLB.

(a) $\dfrac{x}{x^2+4}$ (b) $\dfrac{x^2-9}{x^2-4x+3}$

(c) $\dfrac{x^2+1}{2x}$

3. Find the domain of following rational functions and find the maximum/minimum value and range of these functions. Also mention which of these are bounded functions by mentioning there LUB and GLB.

(a) $\dfrac{x^2-5x+4}{x^2-4x+3}$ (b) $\sqrt{x-1}$

(c) $\sqrt{x^2+4}$ (d) $\dfrac{1}{(x-1)(x-5)}$

(e) $\sqrt[3]{x+8}$ (f) $\dfrac{1}{\sqrt[3]{x}}$

(g) $\dfrac{1}{x^2+4}$

4. (i) Find the minimum/maximum value of the following quadratic expressions.

(a) x^2-4x+3 (b) $x^2-6x+12$

(c) $-x^2+4x+5$

(ii) Find the set of all values of parameter k for which the quadratic expression x^2-kx+4 is always positive.

5. (a) If $|x-3|\le 5$, find the range of values of the following:

(i) x^2+4 (ii) $\dfrac{1}{x^2+1}$

(iii) $2x+3$ (iv) $\dfrac{1}{2x+1}$

(b) Find LUB and GLB of s in the following cases.

(i) $s=\dfrac{2-x}{3+x}; -3<x\le 2$

(ii) $s=\dfrac{2}{x^2-1}; -3\le x\le 2$

(iii) $s=\dfrac{3-x}{2+x}; x\ge 0$

(iv) $s=\dfrac{1-x^2}{1+x^2}; x\ge 1$

(v) $s=\dfrac{2x+1}{3x+1}; |x-5|\le 3$

(vi) $s=\sqrt{1-2x^2}; |x|\le\dfrac{\sqrt{3}}{2}$

(vii) $s=\sqrt{4-x^2}; |x|\le\dfrac{1}{2}$

(viii) $s=\dfrac{x}{x+4}; |x-4|<1$

(ix) $s=\dfrac{x-2}{x+2}; |x-3|\le 2$

6. If $f(x) = 3x - 2$. Find out $f^{-1}(x)$ and hence or otherwise
   (a) $f^{-1}(1)$
   (b) $f^{-1}(4)$
   (c) $f^{-1}(-5)$
   (d) $f^{-1}(-2)$
7. Read the following arrow diagram of a function carefully and draw the arrow diagram of $f^{-1}(x)$

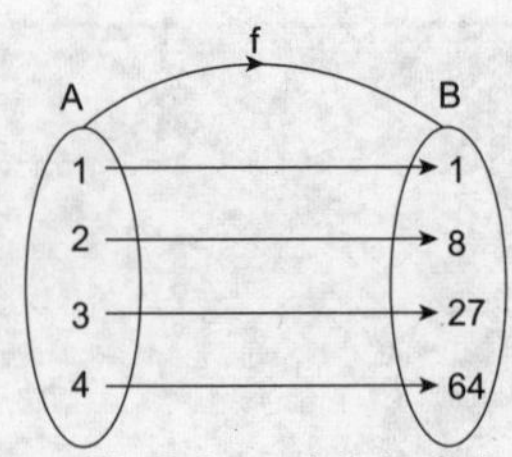

8. Find the value of 'x' for which $f(x) = f^{-1}(x)$ where $f(x) = 10^x + 3$.

Answer Keys

3. (a) $D_f : \mathbb{R} - \{1,3\}$, $R_f : \mathbb{R} - \{1, 3/2\}$ (b) $D_f : [1,\infty)$, $R_f : [0,\infty)$ (c) $D_f : \mathbb{R}$, $R_f : [2,\infty)$ (d) $D_f : \mathbb{R} \sim \{1,5\}$, $R_f : (-\infty,-1/4] \cup (0,\infty)$ (e) $D_f : \mathbb{R}$, $R_f : \mathbb{R}$
   (f) $D_f : \mathbb{R} \sim \{0\}$, $R_f : \mathbb{R} \sim \{0\}$ (g) $D_f : \mathbb{R}$, $R_f : (0,1/4]$
4. (i) (a) $-1; \infty$ (b) $3; \infty$ (c) $-\infty; 9$ (ii) $k \in (-4, 4)$
5. (a) (i) $[4, 68]$ (ii) $\left[\frac{1}{65}, 1\right]$ (iii) $[-1, 19]$ (iv) $\left(-\infty, \frac{-1}{3}\right] \cup \left[\frac{1}{17}, \infty\right)$
   (b) (i) $[0, \infty)$ (ii) $(-\infty, -2 \cup [1/4, \infty)$ (iii) $(-1, 3/2]$ (iv) $(-1, 0]$ (v) $[17/25, 5/7)$
   (vi) $[0, 1]$ (vii) $\left[\frac{\sqrt{15}}{2}, 2\right]$ (viii) $\left[\frac{3}{7}, \frac{5}{9}\right]$ (ix) $\left[-\frac{1}{3}, \frac{3}{7}\right]$
6. (a) 1 (b) 2 (c) -1 (d) 0
8. $-1/3$

■ EXPONENTIAL FUNCTION

There are certain processes in nature where growth/decay of some quantity has very peculiar property e.g., rate of growth of some bacteria, rate of decay of radioactive materials etc. These processes own a typical characteristic which is known as exponential growth/decay and the functions representing them are called exponential functions, denoted by $f(x) = a^x$ where 'a' is known as 'base' and x is called exponent, $a \in \mathbb{R}$, $a > 0$ but $a \neq 1$.

Properties

(i) As we know that $a^n = \underbrace{a \times a \times \ldots \times a}_{n\ times}\ \forall\ n \in \mathbb{N}$ where a is called base and n is index or exponent. Exponential function $f(x) = a^x$ is generalisation of this law to facilitate some useful applications with some imposed functional restrictions i.e., $a > 0$ and $a \neq 1$.

(ii) Domain of $f(x)$ is set of real numbers and range of $f(x)$ is $(0, \infty)$ i.e., $\forall\ x \in \mathbb{R}\ f(x) = a^x$ associates x to some positive real number, uniquely i.e., exponential function $f(x)$ is defined such that it is invertible.

(iii) For $a < 0$ and $a = 0$ the function $f(x) = a^x$ looses its meaning for some values of $x \in \mathbb{R}$.

For instance for $a = -1, -1/2, -3$ etc. $f(x) = a^x$ becomes non real $\forall\ x = \frac{p}{q}$ where p and q are co-prime and q is even integer e.g., $(-3)^{3/2}$, $(-1)^{1/4}$ etc.
Similarly, when base $a = 0$ then $f(x) = 0^x$ does not remain one-to-one function which is required for invertability, same restriction also holds for $a = 1$. Since then $f(x) = 1^x$ again becomes many one function as all inputs x get associated to single output 1.
Therefore we conclude that for $f(x) = a^x$, the base $a > 0$ and $a \neq 1$ and $x \in \mathbb{R}$, thus $y \in (0, \infty)$

(iv) If the base a is Euler number e, then the exponential function e^x is known as natural exponential function.

Laws of indices

(i) a^x is defined and $a^x > 0\ \forall\ x \in \mathbb{R}$

(ii) $a^0 = 1$. We can observe that $\sqrt[n]{a} \to 1$ as n assumes very large value ($n \to \infty$) and it is true for both cases i.e., $a > 1$ or $a \in (0, 1)$, therefore when $n \to \infty$,
$\sqrt[n]{a} = a^{1/n} = a^0 = 1$

(iii) $a^x \cdot a^y = a^{x+y}$

(iv) $\frac{a^x}{a^y} = a^{x-y}$

(v) $(a^x)^y = a^{xy} = (a^y)^x$

(vi) $a^{p/q} = \sqrt[q]{a^p}$; where $q \in \mathbb{N}$ and $q \neq 1$.

(vii) $a^x = a^y \Rightarrow x = y$ or $a = 1$

(viii) $a^x = b^x \Rightarrow$ either $x = 0$ or $a = b$

(ix) $a^x.b^x = (ab)^x$ and $\dfrac{a^x}{b^x} = \left(\dfrac{a}{b}\right)^x$

(x) $a^x \geq a^y \Rightarrow \begin{cases} x \geq y & \text{if } a > 1 \\ x \leq y & \text{if } a \in (0,1) \end{cases}$

REMARKS

1. *a^x, where $a > 1$ behaves as an increasing nature function.*

e.g., when $a = 2$ the value of function 2^x increases as the input x increases. It can be seen from the table given below.

x	–3	–2	–1	0	1	2	3	4	5
a^x	1/8	1/4	1/2	1	2	4	8	16	32

FIGURE 2.8

2. *a^x, where $0 < a < 1$ behaves like a decreasing nature function.*

e.g. when $a = 1/2$ the value of function 2^{-x} decreases as the input x increases which can be seen from the table given below.

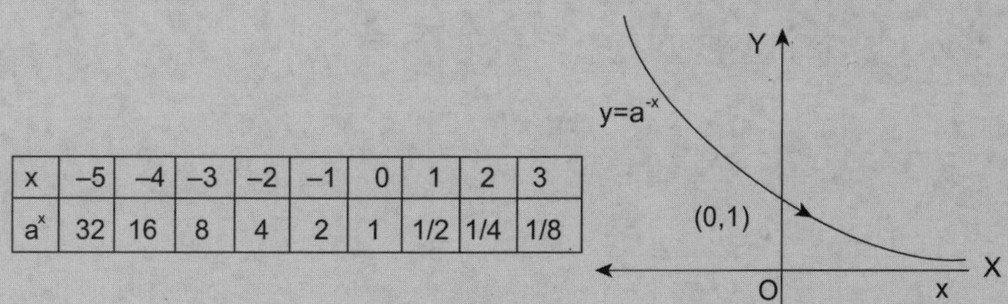

x	–5	–4	–3	–2	–1	0	1	2	3
a^x	32	16	8	4	2	1	1/2	1/4	1/8

FIGURE 2.9

3. *If the base $a > 1$, then $a^x \geq 1$ for all $x \geq 0$ and $a^x < 1$ when $x < 0$, if $0 < a < 1$, then $0 < a^x < 1$ for $x > 0$ and $a^x > 1$ for $x < 0$. The above fact as well as the relative position of graphs of exponential functions with different bases can be understood with the help of following figure.*

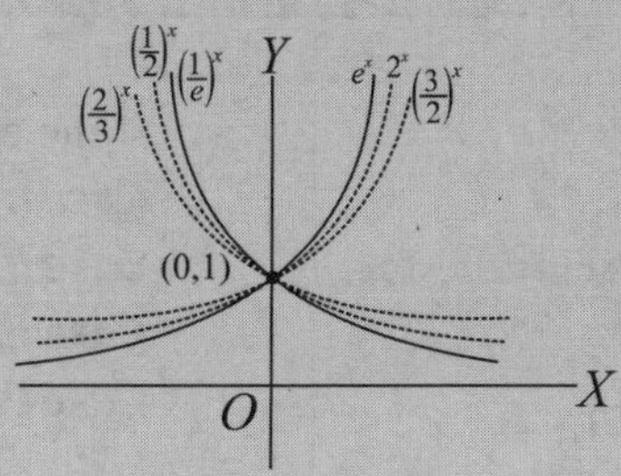

FIGURE 2.10

Composite exponential function

A composite exponential function is a function in which both the base and the exponent are functions of x, for instance, $(\sin x)^{x^2}$, $x^{\tan x}$, x^x, $(\ln x)^x$.

Generally, any function of the form $y = [u(x)]^{v(x)} = u^v$ is a composite exponential function.

This function is also called an exponential power function or a power-exponential function. In calculus, the domain consists of such values of x for which $u(x)$ and $v(x)$ are defined and $u(x) > 0$. e.g., the domain of the function $y = (x+2)^{\frac{1}{x-3}}$ is obtained by the conditions:

$$\left.\begin{matrix} x+2>0 \\ x \neq 3 \end{matrix}\right\} \Rightarrow x \in (-2,3) \cup (3,\infty)$$

Note that the function $g(x) = \sqrt[x]{f(x)}$ has the same meaning as $h(x) = (f(x))^{1/x}$, but their domains are different $g(x)$ is defined under the conditions.

$f(x) > 0$ and $x \in \{2, 3, 4, ...\}$, while $h(x)$ is defined under the conditions $f(x) > 0$ and $x \neq 0$. E.g., to write the domain of $y = \sqrt[x]{4-x}$, we have $4 - x > 0$

$\Rightarrow x < 4$ and $x \in \{2, 3, ...\}$.

Hence the domain is $\{2, 3\}$, while the domain of $y = (4-x)^{\frac{1}{x}}$ is $(-\infty, 4) - \{0\}$.

ILLUSTRATION 11: Simplify and compute the value of the following expression

(a) $\left(\dfrac{(21)^8(49)^{10}(6^{12})}{(42)^{12}(63)^{10}}\right)^{1/3}$ (b) $\sqrt{\dfrac{(70)^6(64)^6(27)^8}{(36)^8(42)^6(192)^2}}$

SOLUTION: (a) Expressing each exponential form to prime bases, we get

$$= \left(\frac{3^8 \times 7^8 \times 7^{20} \times 2^{12} \times 3^{12}}{2^{12} \times 3^{12} \times 7^{12} \times 3^{20} \times 7^{10}}\right)^{1/3} = \left(\frac{7^6}{3^{12}}\right)^{1/3} = \frac{49}{81}.$$

(b) $$\sqrt{\frac{(2\times7\times5)^6(2^6)^6(3^3)^8}{(2^2\times3^2)^8(2\times3\times7)^6(2^6\times3)^2}} = \sqrt{\frac{2^{42}\times3^{24}\times7^6\times5^6}{2^{34}\times3^{24}\times7^6}} = \sqrt{2^8.5^6} = 2000$$

ILLUSTRATION 12: Prove that $\dfrac{4^x.9^y - 9^y - 4^{x+1} + 4}{2^x.3^y + 2^{x+1} + 3^y + 2} = 2^x.3^y - 2^{x-1} - 3^y + 2.$

SOLUTION: $$\frac{4^x.9^y - 9^y - 4^{x+1} + 4}{2^x.3^y + 2^{x+1} + 3^y + 2} = \frac{9^y(4^x-1) - 4(4^x-1)}{2^x(3^y+2) + (3^y+2)} = \frac{(4^x-1)(9^y-4)}{(2^x+1)(3^y+2)}$$

$$= \frac{(2^x-1)(2^x+1)[(3^y)^2-(2)^2]}{(2^x+1)(3^y+2)} = (2^x-1)(3^y-2) = 2^x.3^y - 3^y - 2^{x+1} + 2.$$

ILLUSTRATION 13: Evaluate $\dfrac{\sqrt[4]{xy^4z^3} - xy}{xz - \sqrt[4]{xz^7}} + \dfrac{y}{z}.$

SOLUTION: The given expression is $\dfrac{y(x^{1/4}z^{3/4} - x)}{z(x - x^{1/4}z^{3/4})} + \dfrac{y}{z} = -\dfrac{y}{z} + \dfrac{y}{z} = 0$

Method of solving exponential equation

To solve an exponential equation, we make use of the following facts.

(i) If the equation is of the form $a^x = a^y (a > 0)$
$\Rightarrow x = y$ or $a = 1$

(ii) If the equation is of the form $a^x = b^x (a,b > 0)$
$\Rightarrow$ either $x = 0$ or $a = b$

(iii) If the equation is of the form $a^x = k\ (a > 0)$, then

Case I:	If $k < 0$	$\Rightarrow x \in \{\ \}$
Case II:	If $k > 0, k \neq 1$	$\Rightarrow x = \log_a k$
Case III:	If $a = 1, k \neq 1$	$\Rightarrow x \in \{\ \}$
Case IV:	If $a = 1, k = 1$	$\Rightarrow x \in \mathbb{R}$

(iii) If the equation is of the form $a^{f(x)} = a^{g(x)}$, where $a > 0$ and $a \neq 1$, then the equation will be equivalent to the equation $f(x) = g(x)$

ILLUSTRATION 14: Solve the following equations for x.

(a) $\left(\frac{3}{5}\right)^{2x^2+4x-6} = \left(\frac{5}{3}\right)^{3-2x-x^2}$ (b) $7^{x^3-6x^2+11x} = (343)^2$

SOLUTION: (a) Given equation can be re-written as $\left(\frac{3}{5}\right)^{2x^2+4x-6} = \left(\frac{5}{3}\right)^{3-2x-x^2}$

$\Rightarrow 2x^2 + 4x - 6 = x^2 + 2x - 3$ $\Rightarrow x^2 + 2x - 3 = 0$

$\Rightarrow (x + 3)(x - 1) = 0$ $\Rightarrow x = -3$ or 1 are two solutions.

(b) Consider the equation $7^{x^3-6x^2+11x} \quad 7^6$

$\Rightarrow x^3 - 6x^2 + 11x = 6$

$\Rightarrow x^3 - 6x^2 + 11x - 6 = 0$ $\Rightarrow x = 1, 2, 3$ are solution.

ILLUSTRATION 15: Solve the equation $9^x - 3^{x+1} - 54 = 0$

SOLUTION: Consider the equation $9^x - 3^{x+1} - 54 = 0$

Now let us introduce new variable y for 3^x $\because 9^x = (3^2)^x = (3^x)^2$ and $3^{x+1} = 3 \times 3^x$,

therefore the original equation reduces to $(3^x)^2 - 3 \times 3^x - 54 = 0$

$\Rightarrow y^2 - 3y - 54 = 0$ $\Rightarrow (y - 9)(y + 6) = 0$ $\Rightarrow y = 9$ and $y = -6$ are roots

Re-substituting the values of y, we get, $3^x = 9$; $3^x = -6$

$\Rightarrow \begin{cases} 3^x = 9 \Rightarrow x = 2 \text{ is root} \\ 3^x = -6 \text{ has no roots as } 3^x > 0\ \forall x \in \mathbb{R} \end{cases}$ $\Rightarrow x = 2$ is the only real root.

ILLUSTRATION 16: Solve $2.\left(\sqrt[x-1]{16}\right) - 5\left(\sqrt[x-1]{4}\right) + 2 = 0$

SOLUTION: Consider the equation $2.\left(\sqrt[x-1]{16}\right) - 5\left(\sqrt[x-1]{4}\right) + 2 = 0$

Let $\sqrt[x-1]{4} = z$

$\Rightarrow 2z^2 - 5z + 2 = 0$ $\Rightarrow z = 2$ or $1/2$

$\Rightarrow \sqrt[x-1]{4} = 2$ or $\sqrt[x-1]{4} = \frac{1}{2}$ $\Rightarrow 4^{\overline{\quad}} \quad 4^{-}$ or $4^{\frac{1}{x-1}} = 4^{-\frac{1}{2}}$

$\Rightarrow x = 3, x = -1$

But since x is a natural number greater than 1. Therefore x can't be equal to -1
Hence, $x = 3$ is the only solution.

ILLUSTRATION 17: Solve the equation $3(16)^x - 7(12)^x + 4(9)^x = 0$

SOLUTION: Given equation is $3(16)^x - 7(12)^x + 4(9)^x = 0$

Dividing the equation by 9^x, we get the equivalent equation as, $3\left(\frac{4}{3}\right)^{2x} - 7\left(\frac{4}{3}\right)^x + 4 = 0$

Now let $\left(\frac{4}{3}\right)^x = t$, clearly $t > 0$ $\Rightarrow 3t^2 - 7t + 4 = 0 \Rightarrow t = 1, 4/3$

$\Rightarrow \left(\frac{4}{3}\right)^x = 1$ or $\left(\frac{4}{3}\right)^x = \frac{4}{3}$ $\Rightarrow x = 0$ or 1 are the only solution.

ILLUSTRATION 18: Find the real roots of equations $x^{\sqrt{x-1}} = 4\sqrt{x^{x-1}}$.

SOLUTION: Given equation is $x^{\sqrt{x-1}} = 4\sqrt{x^{x-1}}$ (i)

$\sqrt{x-1}$ to be real $x \geq 1$ and reducing both sides to equal base i.e., x

$\Rightarrow x^{\sqrt{x-1}} = x^{\frac{1}{4}(x-1)}$ that there is number

Now to take care loss of roots. Consider the following cases:

Case I: If $x > 1 \Rightarrow 4\left(\sqrt{x-1}\right) = (x-1) \Rightarrow \sqrt{x-1}\left(\sqrt{x-1}-4\right) = 0 \Rightarrow x = 17$ as $x > 1$

Case II If $x = 1$ then equation reduces to $1^0 = \sqrt{1^0}$; which is true $\Rightarrow x = 1$ is also root

So equation has two roots, $x = 1, 17$

ILLUSTRATION 19: Solve the equation

(a) $4^x + x - 1 = 0$ (b) $2^x + 3^x = 2^{2x+1}$

SOLUTION: (a) $4^x = 1 - x$

As 4^x is an increasing function and takes values from 0 to ∞. Where as $1 - x$ is a decreasing function and takes values from ∞ to $-\infty$, by observation $x = 0$ is solution and their graph can't intersect more than once (see figure).

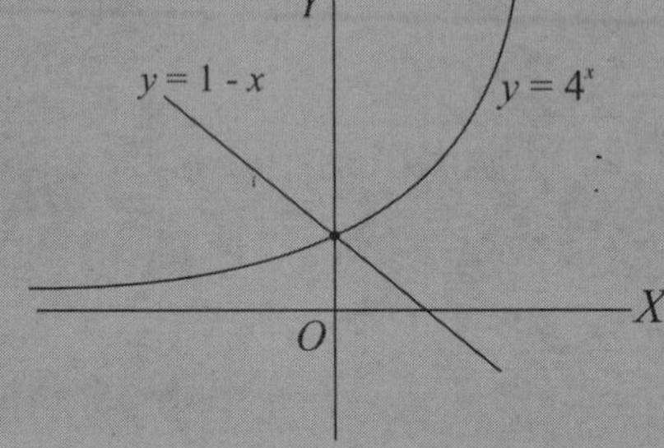

FIGURE 2.11

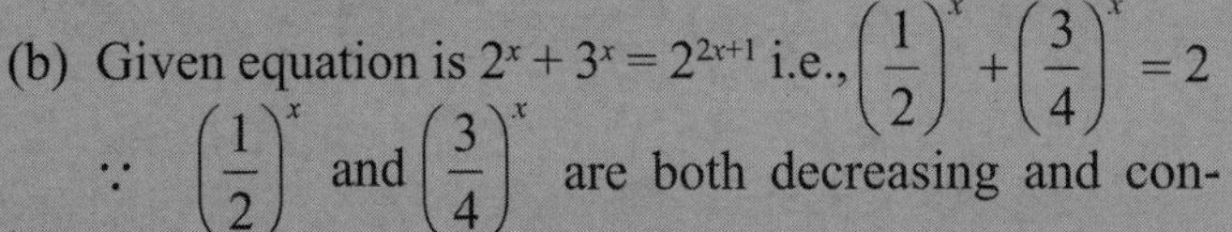

(b) Given equation is $2^x + 3^x = 2^{2x+1}$ i.e., $\left(\frac{1}{2}\right)^x + \left(\frac{3}{4}\right)^x = 2$

$\because \left(\frac{1}{2}\right)^x$ and $\left(\frac{3}{4}\right)^x$ are both decreasing and continuous functions therefore

$\Rightarrow f(x) = \left(\frac{1}{2}\right)^x + \left(\frac{3}{4}\right)^x$ is decreasing and continuous function.

Further $f(-\infty) = \infty$ and $f(\infty) = 0$. Therefore by intermediate value theorem $f(x)$ takes all values between 0 to ∞ exactly once and by trial we find $f(0) = 2$ and therefore $x = 0$ is the only solution.

REMARKS

(i) $a^x = 1 \Rightarrow x = 0$ is an incomplete conclusion it is only true if the base $a \neq 0°$

(ii) If $a = 0$, so equality does not hold as $0°$ is meaningless. Which $a = 1$ then $a^n = 1$.

(iii) When $a = 1$, then $a^x = 1 \Rightarrow 1^x = 1$ which is true $\forall x \in R$

(iv) In case $a = -1$, then $(-1)^x = 1$ is true for $x = p/q$ when p is even and GCD of p and q = 1

TEXTUAL EXERCISE–3 (SUBJECTIVE)

1. Simplify and compute the following expressions:

(a) $\dfrac{(15)^3.(21)^3}{(35)^2.(3)^4}$ (b) $(-1.4)^3.\left(3\dfrac{4}{7}\right)^3$

(c) $\left(\dfrac{\sqrt[4]{ab}-\sqrt{b}}{\sqrt{a}-\sqrt[4]{ab}}\right)^{-4}$

2. Find the number of real values of x satisfying the equation $|x-1|^{x^2-3x} = 1$.

3. Perform the indicated operations and simplify the given expressions:

(a) $\left(\left(x^{\frac{2}{3}}y^{-1}\right)^2\left(x^2y^{-1}\right)^{\frac{1}{2}}\left(y^{\frac{2}{3}}\right)^{\frac{3}{2}}\right)^6$

(b) $\sqrt{\dfrac{a}{b}\sqrt{\dfrac{a}{b}.\sqrt[3]{\dfrac{a}{b}}}}.a^{-\frac{1}{3}}.b^{\frac{1}{3}}$

4. Solve the following exponential equation for x.
(a) $5^{x-1} = 10^x.2^{-x}.5^{x+1}$. (b) $5^{2x-1} + 5^{x+1} = 250$.
(c) $9^x + 6^x = 2.4^x$.

5. Solve the following exponential equation for x.
(a) $4.2^{2x} - 6^x = 18.3^{2x}$.
(b) $2^{\sin^2 x} + 4.2^{\cos^2 x} = 6$.
(c) $7^{x+2} - \frac{1}{7}.7^{x+1} - 14.7^{x+1} + 2.7^x + 48 = 0$

6. Solve the following exponential equation for x.
(a) $64.9^x - 84.12^x + 27.16^x = 0$.
(b) $2^{\frac{3}{\log_2 x}} = \frac{1}{64}$.

7. Solve for equation for x.
(a) $(x-3)^{x^2-4x} = (x-3)^{12}$
(b) $\left(3-2\sqrt{2}\right)^x + \left(3+2\sqrt{2}\right)^x = 6$

Answer Keys

1. (a) 315 (b) –125 (c) $\frac{a}{b}$ **2.** 0, 2, 3 **3.** (a) $x^{14}.y^{-9}$ (b) $\left(\frac{a}{b}\right)^{\frac{1}{2}}$ **4.** (a) –2 (b) 2 (c) 0
5. (a) –2 (b) $\{\pi(2k+1)/2/k \in \mathbb{Z}\}$ (c) 0 **6.** (a) {1, 2} (b) $\{2^{-1/2}\}$ 7. (a) –2, 6 (b) ±1

TEXTUAL EXERCISE–1 (OBJECTIVE)

1. The value of expression $\frac{5(2)^{k-2} + 10(2)^{k-1}}{10^{k+2}}$ is
(a) $(5)^k/8$ (b) $(5)^{2k}/8$
(c) $5^{-k}/16$ (d) None of these

2. The solution of the exponential equation $6^x + 6^{x+1} = 2^x + 2^{x+1} + 2^{x+2}$ is
(a) 1 (b) 0
(c) 2 (d) 3

3. The solution of the exponential equation $9^{|3x-1|} = 3^{8x-2}$ is
(a) 2 (b) 1/7
(c) 0 (d) 2/7

4. The solution set of the exponential equation $3^{|\sin x|} + 4.(3)^{\cos x} = 7$ is
(a) $\{n\pi;\, n \in \mathbb{Z}\}$ (b) $\{2n\pi;\, n \in z\}$
(c) $\{(2n+1)\pi/2 : n \in \mathbb{Z}\}$ (d) None of these

5. The solution set of the exponential equation $2^{[|\sin x|]} + 5 = 6$ is; where |.| is modules and [.] is gint function
(a) $\mathbb{R} - \left\{(2n+1)\frac{\pi}{2};\, n\mathbb{Z}\right\}$
(b) $\mathbb{R}$
(c) $\mathbb{R} - \{n\pi;\, n \in \mathbb{Z}\}$
(d) None of these

6. The solution of equation $9^x - 4(3^x) + 3 = 0$ are
(a) 0, 2 (b) 1, 2
(c) 0, 1 (d) 2, 3

7. If $\sqrt[4]{(2^x - 3)^4} = 16$; then the value of 4^x is
(a) 16 (b) 64
(c) 49 (d) None of these

Answer Keys

1. (c) **2.** (b) **3.** (d) **4.** (c) **5.** (a) **6.** (c) **7.** (c)

■ SOLVING EXPONENTIAL INEQUALITY

To solve an exponential inequality we use following property of exponential function

(i) The value of a^x increases as the value of x increases when base $a \in (1, \infty)$ but the value of a^x decreases as the value of x increases when base $a \in (0, 1)$.

$$a^x \geq a^y \Rightarrow \begin{cases} x \geq y & if\ a > 1 \\ x \leq y & if\ a \in (0,1) \end{cases}$$

(ii) The elementary exponential inequalities are inequalities of form $a^x > k$, $a^x < k$, where a and k are certain numbers ($a > 0$, $a \neq 1$). Depending on the values of the parameters a and k, the set of solutions of the inequality $a^x > k$ can be dealt in the following forms:

(a) $x \in (\log_a k, \infty)$ for $a > 1, k > 0$
(b) $x \in (-\infty, \log_a k)$ for $0 < a < 1, k > 0$;
(c) $x \in \mathbb{R}$ for $a > 0, k \le 0$;
Depending on the values of a and k, the set of solutions of the inequality $a^x < k$ can be in the following forms:

(iii) $\left.\begin{array}{l} f(x+y) = f(x) \,.\, f(y) \\ f(x-y) = f(x)\,/\,f(y) \end{array}\right\} \forall\, x, y \in \mathbb{R}$;
where $f(x) = a^x$; $a > 0, a \ne 1$.

ILLUSTRATION 20: Solve the following exponential inequalities for x.

(a) $9^{x^2} > 6561$ (b) $7^{3x-x^2+1} \ge 343$

SOLUTION: (a) The inequality $9^{x^2} > (3)^8$

$\Rightarrow 3^{2x^2-2} > 3^6$

$\because$ base $3 > 1$ hence functions 3^x is increasing function

$\Rightarrow 2x^2 - 2 > 6 \Rightarrow x^2 > 4 \Rightarrow (x-2)(x+2) > 0 \Rightarrow x \in (-\infty, -2) \cup (2, \infty)$

(b) The inequality $7^{3x-x^2+1} \ge 343$

$\Rightarrow 7^{3x-x^2+1} \ge 7^3$

Functions 7^x is increasing function $\because$ base $7 \ge 1$

$\Rightarrow 3x - x^2 + 1 \ge 3 \Rightarrow x^2 - 3x + 2 \le 0 \Rightarrow (x-1)(x-2) \le 0$

$\Rightarrow x \in [1, 2]$ is the solution set.

ILLUSTRATION 21: Solve the exponential inequalities for x: $(121)^x - 132\,(11^x) + 1331 \ge 0$

SOLUTION: Consider the inequality $(121)^x - 132\,(11^x) + 1331 \ge 0$

Put $11^x = t$

$\Rightarrow t^2 - 132t + 1331 \ge 0$ $\Rightarrow t^2 - 121t - 11t + 1331 \ge 0$

$\Rightarrow (t-121)(t-11) \ge 0$ $\Rightarrow t \in (-\infty, 11] \cup [121, \infty)$

Substituting the value of $t = 11^x$ and keeping in mind that 11^x is positive

$\Rightarrow 0 < 11^x \le 11$ or $121 \le 11^x < \infty$ (Since 11^x is increasing function)

$\Rightarrow x \in (-\infty, 1] \cup [2, \infty)$

ILLUSTRATION 22: Solve the exponential inequalities for x: $\dfrac{4^x - 6(2^x) + 8}{4^x - 24.(2^x) + 128} \le 0$

SOLUTION: Given $\dfrac{4^x - 6(2^x) + 8}{4^x - 24.(2^x) + 128} \le 0$

Let $2^x = y$; substituting in the above inequality, we get, $\dfrac{y^2 - 6y + 8}{y^2 - 24y + 128} \le 0$

$\Rightarrow \dfrac{(y-2)(y-4)}{(y-8)(y-16)} < 0$ or $y = 2, 4$

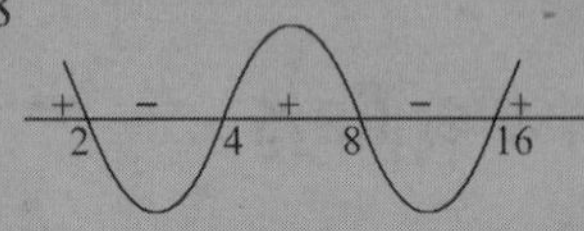

FIGURE 2.12

Applying method of interval

$\Rightarrow y \in (2, 4) \cup (8, 16) \cup \{2, 4\}$ $\Rightarrow y \in [2, 4] \cup (8, 16)$

Now since $y = 2^x$. $\Rightarrow 2 \le 2^x \le 4 \Rightarrow 1 \le x \le 2$

and $8 \le 2^x \le 16$ $\Rightarrow 3 < x < 4 \Rightarrow x \in [1, 2] \cup (3, 4)$

ILLUSTRATION 23: Solve the inequality for $3^{\sqrt{x^4 - 2x^2 + 1}} \ge 3^{2x-1}$

SOLUTION: Consider $\sqrt{x^4 - 2x^2 + 1} \ge 2x - 1$

$\Rightarrow \sqrt{(x^2-1)^2} \ge 2x - 1$ $\Rightarrow |x^2 - 1| \ge 2x - 1$ (i)

Case I: If $-\infty < x < 1/2$

L.H.S. is non–negative where as R.H.S. has -ve values

so $x \in \left(-\infty, \frac{1}{2}\right)$ is solution

Case II: $1/2 \le x < 1$

$2x - 1 \ge 0\ ;\ x^2 - 1 < 0 \Rightarrow |x^2 - 1| = -x^2 + 1 \qquad \Rightarrow -x^2 + 1 \ge 2x - 1$ (using (i))

$\Rightarrow x^2 + 2x - 2 \le 0 \qquad \Rightarrow x \in \left[-1-\sqrt{3}, -1+\sqrt{3}\right] \qquad \Rightarrow x \in \left[\frac{1}{2}, \sqrt{3}-1\right]$

Case III: $x \ge 1$

$\Rightarrow 2x - 1 > 0;\ x^2 - 1 \ge 0 \quad \Rightarrow |x^2 - 1| = x^2 - 1 \Rightarrow x^2 - 1 \ge 2x - 1$ (using (i))

$\Rightarrow x^2 - 2x \ge 0 \Rightarrow x(x-2) \ge 0 \Rightarrow x \le 0$ or $x \ge 2$

$\therefore$ Finally $x \in [2, \infty)$

$\therefore$ Over all $x \in \left(-\infty, \sqrt{3}-1\right] \cup [2, \infty)$

ILLUSTRATION 24: Solve the inequality for $|x|^{x^2-x-2} \ge 1$

SOLUTION: $|x|^{x^2-x-2} \ge |x|^0$

Case I: $0 < |x| < 1$

$\Rightarrow -1 < x < 1, x \ne 0 \Rightarrow (x-2)(x+1) \le 0 \quad \Rightarrow x \in [-1, 2]$

Under the given conditions $-1 < x < 1, x \ne 0$, solution set is $(-1, 1) \sim \{0\}$

Case II: $|x| > 1$

$\Rightarrow x < -1$ and $x > 1 \Rightarrow x^2 - x - 2 \ge 0 \Rightarrow x \le -1, x \ge 2$

Under the given conditions $x < -1, x > 1, x \in (-\infty, -1) \cup [2, \infty)$

Case III: $|x| = 1 \Rightarrow x = \pm 1$, the inequation holds true.

Finally, $x \in (-\infty, 1] \cup [2, \infty) - \{0\}$

ILLUSTRATION 25: Solve the inequality for $\sqrt[3]{(81)^{\left(\frac{3x-1}{2x-2}\right)}} < (729)^{\left(\frac{x-3}{3x-7}\right)}$

SOLUTION: Considering the given inequality $\sqrt[3]{(81)^{\left(\frac{3x-1}{2x-2}\right)}} < (729)^{\left(\frac{x-3}{3x-7}\right)}$

$\Rightarrow \sqrt[3]{9^{\frac{2(3x-1)}{2x-2}}} < 9^{\frac{3(x-3)}{3x-7}} \qquad \Rightarrow 9^{\frac{1}{3}\frac{(3x-1)}{x-1}} < 9^{\frac{3(x-3)}{3x-7}} \qquad \Rightarrow \frac{3x-1}{3(x-1)} < \frac{3x-9}{3x-7}$

$\Rightarrow \frac{3x-1}{3x-3} - \frac{(3x-9)}{3x-7} < 0 \Rightarrow \frac{9x^2 - 3x - 21x + 7 - 9x^2 + 27x + 9x - 27}{(3x-3)(3x-7)} < 0$

$\Rightarrow \frac{12x-20}{(3x-3)(3x-7)} < 0 \qquad \Rightarrow (3x-5)(3x-3)(3x-7) < 0$

Using Wavy Curve Method, we get, $x \in (-\infty, 1) \cup \left(\frac{5}{3}, \frac{7}{3}\right)$

ILLUSTRATION 26: Solve the inequality for $3^x + 6.3^{\sqrt{x^2}} \le 5$.

SOLUTION: Considering the inequality $3^x + 6.3^{\sqrt{x^2}} \le 5$ as we know $\sqrt{x^2} = |x|$

So, problem becomes $3^x + 6.3^{|x|} \le 5$

Case I: If $x \geq 0$

$\Rightarrow 3^x + 6(3^x) \leq 5 \quad \Rightarrow 3^x \leq \frac{5}{7} \quad \Rightarrow x \leq \log_3\left(\frac{5}{7}\right)$

Taking intersection of sets $[0, \infty)$ and $\left(-\infty, \log_3\left(\frac{5}{7}\right)\right)$, we get $x \in \left[0, \log_3 \frac{5}{7}\right]$

Case II: Now if $x < 0 \Rightarrow |x| = -x$ and consequently, inequality reduces to $3^x + 6(3^{-x}) \leq 5$

Put $3^x = y$

$\Rightarrow y^2 - 5y + 6 \leq 0 \Rightarrow (y-2)(y-3) \leq 0 \Rightarrow 2 \leq y \leq 3$

Re-substituting the value of y as $3^x \Rightarrow 3^{\log_3 2} \leq 3^x \leq 3^1 \Rightarrow \log_3 2 \leq x \leq 1$ as 3^x is an ↑ function

$\Rightarrow x \in [\log_3 2, 1]$

Taking the union of set of solutions of both cases, we get $x \in \left[0, \log_3 \frac{5}{7}\right] \cup [\log_3 2, 1]$

TEXTUAL EXERCISE–4 (SUBJECTIVE)

1. Solve the following exponential inequalities for x.
(a) $2^{3-8x} > 1$.
(b) $16^x > 0.125$.
(c) $(0.3)^{2x^2-3x+6} < 0.00243$.

2. Which of the given numbers is greaters?
(a) 2^{300} or 3^{200} (b) 54^4 or 21^{12}
(c) $(0.4)^4$ or $(0.8)^3$ (d) 10^{20} and 40^{10}

3. Solve the following exponential inequalities for x.
(a) $x+1\sqrt{3} > 9$. (b) $2^x + 2^{-x+1} - 3 < 0$
(c) $x^2.5^x - 5^{2+x} < 0$

4. Solve the following exponential inequalities for x.
(a) $\frac{2^{x-1}-1}{2^{x+1}+1} < 2$. (b) $2^{x+2} - 2^{x+1} + 2^{x-1} - 2^{x-2} \leq 9$
(c) $2^{4x^2-6} > 2^3$

5. Solve the following exponential inequalities for x.
(a) $6^x - 2(3^x) - 3(2^x) + 6 > 0$
(b) $2^{x+2} > \left(\frac{1}{4}\right)^{\frac{1}{x}}$ or $2^{x+2} > (2^{-2})^{\frac{1}{x}}$.
(c) $2^x + 2^{|x|} \geq 2\sqrt{2}$

6. Solve the inequality for $3^{\sqrt{x^6-2x^3+1}} \geq 3^{1-x}$

7. Solve the exponential inequality $\sqrt{9^x + 3^x - 2} \geq 9 - 3^x$ for x.

8. Solve the following exponential inequalities for x.
(a) $4^x - 2^{x+2} - 6^x + 4.3^x \leq 0$
(b) $\left(\sqrt{x^2}\right)^{x^2-5x+9} \geq x^3$

Answer Keys

1. (a) $(-\infty, 3/8)$ (b) $(-3/4, \infty)$ (c) $(-\infty, 1/2) \cup (1, \infty)$
2. (a) 3^{200} (b) 21^{12} (c) $(0.8)^3$ (d) 10^{20}
3. (a) $x \in \phi$, (b) $(0, 1)$ (c) $(-5, 5)$
4. (a) $x \in \mathbb{R}$ (b) $(-\infty, 2]$ (c) $(-\infty, -3/2) \cup (3/2, \infty)$
5. (a) $x \in \mathbb{R} \sim \{1\}$ (b) $x \in (0, \infty)$ (c) $(-\infty, \log_2(\sqrt{2}-1)] \cup [1/2, +\infty)$
6. $\mathbb{R} \sim (-1, 0)$ **7.** $\left[\log_3 \frac{83}{19}, \infty\right)$ **8.** (a) $(-\infty, 0] \cup [2, \infty)$ (b) $\mathbb{R} - ((0, 1) \cup (2, 3))$

TEXTUAL EXERCISE–2 (OBJECTIVE)

1. Which of the following is/are correct?
(a) $(0.2)^7 > (0.8)^4$ (b) $(0.2)^7 < (0.8)^4$
(c) $(10)^{30} < (500)^{10}$ (d) $(10)^{30} > (500)^{10}$

2. Solution of the exponential inequality $\left(\frac{1}{3}\right)^{\sqrt{x+2}} > 3^{-x}$ is
(a) $(-\infty, 2)$ (b) $(2, \infty)$
(c) $(-2, 2)$ (d) None of these

3. Solution of the exponential inequality $\left(\frac{2}{5}\right)^{\frac{6-5x}{2+5x}} < \left(\frac{25}{4}\right)$ is
(a) $(-\infty, -2)$ (b) $(-2/5, \infty)$
(c) $(-2, -2/5)$ (d) $(-\infty, -2) \cup (-2/5, \infty)$

4. Solution set of the exponential inequality $\frac{2^{1-x} - 2^x + 1}{2^x - 1} \le 0$ is
(a) $(-\infty, 0) \cup [1, \infty)$ (b) $[0, 1] \cup [1, \infty)$
(c) $(-\infty, 0)$ (d) $[1, \infty)$

5. Solution set of the exponential inequality $12^x - 2(3^x) - 3(4^x) + 6 < 0$ is
(a) $\left(\frac{1}{4}, \frac{1}{2}\right)$ (b) $\left(\frac{1}{2}, 1\right)$
(c) $(1, 3/2)$ (d) $(1/2, 2)$

6. Solution set of the exponential inequality $(1.25)^{1-x} < (0.64)^{2(1+\sqrt{x})}$ is
(a) $(0, 25)$ (b) $(0, 1)$
(c) $(25, \infty)$ (d) Nonc of these

7. Solution set of the exponential inequality $(1/3)^{x+\frac{1}{2}-\frac{2}{x}} > \frac{1}{\sqrt{27}}$ is
(a) $(-\infty, -1) \cup (0, 2)$ (b) $(1, 2)$
(c) $(2, 3)$ (d) $(2, \infty)$

8. Solution set of the exponential inequality $8^{\sqrt{8^x}} > 4096$ is
(a) $(1/3, \infty)$ (b) $(4/3, \infty)$
(c) $(1/3, 4/3)$ (d) None of these

Answer Keys

1. (b, d) **2.** (b) **3.** (d) **4.** (a,c,d) **5.** (b) **6.** (c) **7.** (a) **8.** (b)

■ LOGARITHMIC FUNCTION

"Logarithmic function is defined as inverse function of exponential function". All the properties of logarithms are consequences of the corresponding properties of the exponential function, i.e., "Principles of Indices".

Definition

The logarithm of any number N to the given base a is the exponent or index or the power to which the base must be raised to obtain the number N. Thus if $a^x = N$, x is called the logarithm of N to the base a. It is denoted by $\log_a N$.

$\therefore \log_a N = x \Leftrightarrow a^x = N, a > 0, a \neq 1 \text{ and } N > 0$

NOTES

(a) The logarithm of a number is unique i.e., no number can have two different logarithms to a given base.

(b) The base ***'a'*** *is positive real number, but excluding 1, i.e.,* $\mathbf{a > 0, a \neq 1}$. *As a consequence of the definition of exponential function, we exclude* $\mathbf{a = 1}$,
Since for $\mathbf{a = 1}$, $\mathbf{\log_a x = y \Rightarrow x = a^y = 1^y}$ *which has no relevance to the cases of* $\mathbf{\log_a x}$ *when* $\mathbf{x \neq 1}$ *i.e., for all values of exponent, the value of* $\mathbf{x}$ *remains 1.*

(c) The number ***'x'*** *represents result of exponentiation i.e.,* $\mathbf{a^y}$, *therefore it is also a positive real number i.e.,* $\mathbf{x = a^y > 0}$

*(d) The exponent '**y**', i.e., logarithm of '**x**' is a real number and neither **a** nor **x** equals to zero.*

(d) Domain of function $\mathbf{y = \log_a x}$ *is* $\mathbf{(0, \infty)}$ *and the range* $\mathbf{(-\infty, \infty)}$.

when $\mathbf{x \to 0}$, *then* $\mathbf{\log_a x \to -\infty}$ **(for a > 1) and** $\mathbf{\log_a x \to \infty}$ **(for 0 < a < 1)**

because $\mathbf{y = \log_a x \Rightarrow x = a^y}$ *which approaches to zero iff* $\mathbf{y \to -\infty}$ as $\mathbf{a^{-\infty} = 0\ \forall\ a > 1}$

and when $\mathbf{a \in (0, 1), x = a^y}$ *approaches to zero iff* $\mathbf{y \to \infty}$ $\because \mathbf{a^{\infty} = 0}$ *if* $\mathbf{0 < a < 1}$.

(e) ***Common Logarithms and Natural Logarithms:*** *The base of logarithm can be any positive number other than 1, but basically two bases are mostly used. They are 10 and e (= 2.718 approximately). Logarithm of numbers to the base 10 are named as* ***common logarithms****; whereas the logarithms of the numbers to the base e are called as* ***natural or Napierian logarithms.***

If a = 10, then we write log b instead of $\log_{10} b$.

If a = e, then we write ℓnb *instead of* $\log_e b$.

$\therefore$ *we find* $\log_e a = \log_{10} a . \log_e 10$ *or* $\log_{10} a = \dfrac{\log_e a}{\log_e 10} = 0.434 \log_e a$ *(this transformation is used to convert natural logarithm to common logarithm)*

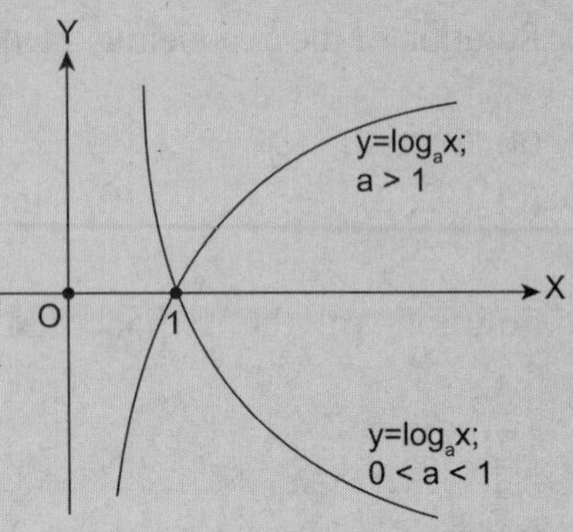

FIGURE 2.13

ILLUSTRATION 27: Find the log of 81 to the base 3.

SOLUTION: Let the logarithm of 81 to the base 3 is $x \Rightarrow \log_3 81 = x$

$\Rightarrow 3^x = 81 \Rightarrow 3^x = (3)^4 \Rightarrow x = 4$

ILLUSTRATION 28: Find the logarithm of $32\sqrt[5]{4}$ to base $2\sqrt{2}$.

SOLUTION: Let x be the required logarithm; then by definition, $(2\sqrt{2})^x = 32\sqrt[5]{4}$

$\therefore\ (2.2^{1/2})^x = 2^5 . 2^{2/5} \Rightarrow 2^{(3/2)x} = 2^{5+2/5}$ $\Rightarrow \dfrac{3}{2}x = \dfrac{27}{5} \Rightarrow x = \dfrac{18}{5} = 3.6$

ILLUSTRATION 29: Evaluate the following:

(a) $\log_4 256$ (b) $5^{\log_5 625}$ (c) $9^{\log_3 625}$

SOLUTION: (a) Let $\log_4 256 = x$ $\Rightarrow 4^x = 256 = 4^4$ $\Rightarrow x = 4$

(b) Since $a^{\log_a N} = N$; taking $N = 625$ and $a = 5$ $\Rightarrow 5^{\log_5 625} = 625$

(c) Similarly, $9^{\log_3 625} = (3^2)^{\log_3 625} = (3^{\log_3 625})^2 = (625)^2 = 390625$

ILLUSTRATION 30: Express log of x to the base 5 in each of the following cases:

(a) $(25)^{-\frac{1}{5}} = 125x$ (b) $(625)^{\frac{4}{9}} = 25x$

SOLUTION: (a) $\because\ 125x = (25)^{-1/5}$ $\Rightarrow$ $x = \dfrac{(5)^{-2/5}}{125} = 5^{-\frac{2}{5}-3}$ $\Rightarrow$ $x = 5^{-\frac{17}{5}}$

Now applying definition of logarithm i.e., $a^y = x \Leftrightarrow \log_a x = y$, we get $\log_5 x = \dfrac{-17}{5}$

(b) Given $(625)^{4/9} = 25x$

$\Rightarrow \dfrac{5^{16/9}}{25} = x \Rightarrow 5^{\frac{16}{9}-2} = x \Rightarrow 5^{-\frac{2}{9}} = x \Rightarrow \log_5 x = -\dfrac{2}{9}$

ILLUSTRATION 31: If $\log_3 x = a$, $\log_7 y = b$ and $\log_2 z = c$, then find the value of $\frac{(27)^a + (343)^b}{(512)^c}$ in terms of x, y and z.

SOLUTION: Given $\log_3 x = a$; $\log_7 y = b$ and $\log_2 z = c$

$\Rightarrow x = 3^a$, $7^b = y$ and $2^c = z$ $\Rightarrow x^3 = (3^a)^3 = 27^a$, $y^3 = (7^b)^3 = (7^3)^b = (343)^b$ and $(512)^c = z^9$

Replacing these value in the expression $\frac{(27)^a + (343)^b}{(512)^c} = \frac{x^3 + y^3}{z^9}$

TEXTUAL EXERCISE–5 (SUBJECTIVE)

1. Find the domain of the following functions:
   (a) $y = \log_3(9 - x^2)$ (b) $y = \log_2(x^2 - 4)$
2. Let $a^{\sin x} = a^{|x|+2}$, then evaluate $\log_2 a$.
3. Evaluate the following:
   (a) $\log_{5\sqrt{5}} 5$ (b) $\log_{\sqrt{7}} 343\sqrt{7}$
   (c) $\log_8 1024$
4. If $\log_7 x = a$ then evaluate $7(2401)^{3a+\frac{1}{4}}$ in terms of x
5. Find the domain of the following functions:
   (a) $f(x) = \log_7(x^2 - 4x + 3)$
   (b) $f(x) = \log_2(4 - x^2) + \log_{10}(x^2 - 1)$
   (c) $f(t) = \log \frac{t^2 + 5t + 9}{t^2 - 5t + 6}$
6. Solve the equation $|x - 5| > 2$ for which $\log(x - 1)$ is defined.
7. Solve the equation $x^4 + 1 = 2x^2$ for which $\log(x + x^{-1})$ as a real value.

Answer Keys

1. (a) $x \in (-3, 3)$ (ii) $x \in (-\infty, -2) \cup (2, \infty)$
2. 0
3. (a) 2/3 (b) 7 (c) 10/3
4. $49(x^{12})$
5. (a) $x \in (-\infty, 1) \cup (3, \infty)$ (b) $x \in (-2, -1) \cup (1, 2)$ (c) $x \in (-\infty, 2) \cup (3, \infty)$
6. $(1, 3) \cup (7, \infty)$
7. 1

■ PROPERTIES OF LOGARITHM

Let a and b be arbitrary positive numbers such that $a > 0$, $a \neq 1$, $b > 0$, $b \neq 1$, then

1. $\log_a 1 = 0$ because 0 is the power to which a must be raised to obtain 1.

Proof: Let $\log_a 1 = x \Rightarrow a^x = 1 = a^0 \Rightarrow x = 0$ i.e., $\log_a 1 = 0$

2. $\log_a a = 1$ since 1 is the power to which a must be raised to obtain a.

Proof: Let $\log_a a = x \Rightarrow a^x = a = a^1 \Rightarrow x = 1$ i.e., $\log_a a = 1$

3. $a^{\log_a N} = N$ and $\log_a a^N = N$, as N is the power to which a must be raised to obtain a^N.

Proof: Let $\log_a N = x \Rightarrow a^x = N$ or, $a^{\log_a N} = N$ [$\because x = \log_a N$]

4. $\log_m(a.b) = \log_m |a| + \log_m|b|$; $a.b > 0$)

Logarithm of the product of two numbers to a certain base is equal to the sum of the logarithms of the numbers to the same base.

Proof: Let $\log_m |a| = x \Rightarrow m^x = |a|$ and $\log_m |b| = y \Rightarrow m^y = |b|$.

$\therefore$ $|a|.|b| = m^x.m^y = m^{x+y}$ $\Rightarrow a.b = m^{x+y}$ (i)

Also let $\log_m (a.b) = z \Rightarrow m^z = a.b = |ab|$ (ii)

From (i) and (ii), we have $m^z = m^{x+y} \Rightarrow z = x + y$

[$\because m \neq 1$]

i.e., $\log_m(a.b) = \log_m|a| + \log_m|b|$.

Note that for $a, b > 0$, $\log_m(ab) = \log_m a + \log_m b$

5. $\log_m (a/b) = \log_m|a| - \log_m|b|$; where $(a/b) > 0$ i.e., logarithm of the quotient of two numbers of same signs is

equal to the difference of their magnitudes logarithms, base remaining the same throughout.

Proof: Let $\log_m|a| = x \Rightarrow m^x = |a|$ (i)

$\log_m|b| = y \Rightarrow m^y = |b|$ (ii)

and $\log_m(a/b) = z \Rightarrow m^z = a/b.$ (iii)

From (i) and (ii), $\frac{a}{b} = \left|\frac{a}{b}\right| = \frac{|a|}{|b|} = \frac{m^x}{m^y} = m^{x-y}$

Now, from (iii) and (iv), we have $m^z = m^{x-y} \Rightarrow z = x - y$ $(\because m \neq 1)$

i.e., $\log_m(a/b) = \log_m|a| - \log_m|b|$

Note that for $a, b > 0$, $\log_m(a/b) = \log_m a - \log_m b$

ILLUSTRATION 32: Prove that $\log_{abc}\left(\frac{ab}{c}\right) + \log_{abc}\left(\frac{bc}{a}\right) + \log_{abc}\left(\frac{ca}{b}\right) = 1$; $a, b, c > 0$.

PROOF: LHS $= \left\{\log_{abc}\left(\frac{ab}{c}\right) + \log_{abc}\left(\frac{bc}{a}\right)\right\} + \log_{abc}\left(\frac{ca}{b}\right)$

$= \log_{abc}\left(\frac{ab^2c}{ca}\right) + \log_{abc}\left(\frac{ca}{b}\right) = \log_{abc}\left(\frac{a^2b^2c^2}{abc}\right) = \log_{abc}(abc) = 1$ $[\because \log_a a = 1]$

ILLUSTRATION 33: Evaluate

(i) $\log_3\left(\frac{\sqrt{3}}{81}\right)$ **(ii)** $\log_{1/2}(0.125)$

SOLUTION: **(i)** $\log_3\left(\frac{\sqrt{3}}{81}\right) = \log_3\sqrt{3} - \log_3 81 = \frac{1}{2}\log_3 3 - 4\log 3 = \frac{1}{2} - 4 = -\frac{7}{2}$

(ii) $\log_{1/2}(0.125) = \log_{1/2}\left(\frac{125}{1000}\right) = \log_{1/2}\left(\frac{1}{8}\right) = 3\log_{1/2}\frac{1}{2} = 3$

ILLUSTRATION 34: For $x \geq 4$, find the least possible value of the expression $\ln(x^3 - 13x^2 + 65x - 105) - \ln(x - 3)$.

SOLUTION: $\ln\left[\frac{x^3 - 13x^2 + 65x - 105}{(x-3)}\right] = \ln\left[\frac{(x^2 - 10x + 35)(x-3)}{(x-3)}\right] = \ln(x^2 - 10x + 35)$ (as $x \geq 4 \Rightarrow x \neq 3$)

$= \ln[x^2 - 10x + 25 + 10] = \ln[(x-5)^2 + 10] \geq \ln 10.$

6. $\log_a N^k = k\log_a|N|$ ($\forall k \in \mathbb{R}$ for $N > 0$ or k is such that $N^k > 0$ if $N < 0$)

i.e., Logarithm of the permissible (power of a number) is equal to the product of the power and logarithm of the magnitude of the number (base remaining the same).

Proof: Let $\log_a|N| = x \Rightarrow a^x = |N|$

Also let $\log_a(N^k) = y$

$\therefore a^y = N^k = |N|^k = (a^x)^k = a^{kx}$

$\Rightarrow y = kx$. i.e., $\log_a(N^k) = k.\log_a|N|$

7. $\log_{a^k} N = (1/k).\log_{|a|} N$; $a^k > 0$

Proof: $\log_{a^k} N = \frac{\log N}{\log a^k} = \frac{\log N}{\log|a|^k} = \frac{1}{k}.\frac{\log N}{\log a} = \frac{1}{k}\log_{|a|} N$

ILLUSTRATION 35: Express logarithm of $\frac{\sqrt{a^3}}{c^5b^2}$ in terms of $\log a$, $\log b$ and $\log c$.

SOLUTION: $\log\frac{\sqrt{a^3}}{c^5b^2} = \log\frac{a^{3/2}}{c^5b^2} = \log a^{3/2} - \log(c^5b^2) = \frac{3}{2}\log a - (\log c^5 + \log b^2) = \frac{3}{2}\log a - 5\log c - 2\log b$

ILLUSTRATION 36: Find x from the equation $a^x c^{-2x} = b^{3x+1}$.

SOLUTION: Taking log on both sides, $x \log a - 2x \log c = (3x + 1) \log b$

$\therefore \quad x(\log a - 2\log c - 3\log b) = \log b \qquad \Rightarrow x = \dfrac{\log b}{\log a - 2\log c - 3\log b}$

ILLUSTRATION 37: Solve $\log_{ab}\dfrac{\sqrt[3]{a}}{\sqrt{b}}$ if $\log_{ab}a = 4$.

SOLUTION: $\log_{ab}\dfrac{\sqrt[3]{a}}{\sqrt{b}} = \dfrac{1}{3}\log_{ab}a - \dfrac{1}{2}\log_{ab}b = \dfrac{4}{3} - \dfrac{1}{2}\log_{ab}b$

It remains to find the quantity $\log_{ab} b$. Since

$1 = \log_{ab}ab = \log_{ab}a + \log_{ab}b = 4 + \log_{ab}b$

It follows that $\log_{ab}b = -3$ and so $\log_{ab}\dfrac{\sqrt[3]{a}}{\sqrt{b}} = \dfrac{4}{3} - \dfrac{1}{2}.(-3) = \dfrac{17}{6}$

ILLUSTRATION 38: Solve $\log_6 16$ if $\log_{12}27 = a$.

SOLUTION: The chain of transformations $\log_6 16 = 4 \log_6 2 = \dfrac{4}{\log_2 6} = \dfrac{4}{1+\log_2 3}$

shows us that we have to know $\log_2 3$ in order to find $\log_6 16$.

We find it from the condition $\log_{12}27 = a$ (given)

$\Rightarrow a = \log_{12}27 = 3\log_{12}3 = \dfrac{3}{\log_3 12} = \dfrac{3}{1+2\log_3 2} = \dfrac{3}{1+\dfrac{2}{\log_2 3}} = \dfrac{3\log_2 3}{2+\log_2 3}$

which means that $\log_2 3 = \dfrac{2a}{3-a}$ $(a \neq 3)$, we finally have $\log_6 16 = \dfrac{4(3-a)}{3+a}$

ILLUSTRATION 39: Solve $x + \log_{10}(1 + 2^x) = x \log_{10}5 + \log_{10}6$.

SOLUTION: Transposing $x \log_{10}5$ to the left member of the equation and utilizing the laws of logarithms, we get, $x + \log_{10}(1 + 2^x) - x \log_{10}5 = x \log_{10}10 - x \log_{10}5 + \log_{10}(1 + 2^x) = \log_{10}2^x(1 + 2^x)$

The equation can thus be rewritten as $\log_{10}2^x(1 + 2^x) = \log_{10}6$, hence

$(2^x)^2 + 2^x - 6 = 0$

Denoting $z = 2^x$, we arrive at the quadratic eqution $z^2 + z - 6 = 0$ which has the roots $z_1 = -3$, $z_2 = 2$. Since the equation $2^x = -3$ is impossible (because 2^x is positive for all values of x), it remains to solve the equation $2^x = 2$. It has the root $x = 1$, which is the sole root of the original equation.

8. $\log_b a = \log_c a \log_b c$

Proof: Let $\log_b a = x \quad \Rightarrow \quad b^x = a$

$\log_c a = y \quad \Rightarrow \quad c^y = a$

and $\log_b c = z \quad \Rightarrow \quad b^z = c$

Now $b^x = a = c^y = (b^z)^y = b^{yz} \Rightarrow \quad x = yz, \qquad [\because b \neq 1]$

i.e., $\log_b a = \log_c a.\log_b c$.

ILLUSTRATION 40: Evaluate $\log_2 5 \log_{25} 2 \log_{100} 25 \log_{625} 100$

SOLUTION: $\log_2 5 \log_{25} 2 \log_{100} 25 \log_{625} 100 = \log_{25} 5 \log_{625} 25$

$= \log_{625} 5 = 1/4 \qquad [(\because 625)^{1/4} = 5]$

9. $\log_b a = \dfrac{\log_c a}{\log_c b} = \dfrac{\log a}{\log b}$ (base remaining the same in numerator and denominator)

Proof: Cross-multiplying, we get $\log_b a.\ \log_c b = \log_c a$ (*which is true by property* 8)

ILLUSTRATION 41: If $\log_{12} 18 = \alpha$ and $\log_{24} 54 = \beta$, prove that $\alpha\beta + 5(\alpha - \beta) = 1$.

SOLUTION: $\alpha = \log_{12} 18 = \dfrac{\log 18}{\log 12} = \dfrac{\log(3^2.2)}{\log(3.2^2)} = \dfrac{2\log 3 + \log 2}{\log 3 + 2\log 2}$ and

$\beta = \log_{24} 54 = \dfrac{\log 54}{\log 24} = \dfrac{\log(3^3.2)}{\log(3.2^3)} = \dfrac{3\log 3 + \log 2}{\log 3 + 3\log 2}$

If $x = \log 2$ and $y = \log 3$, then $\alpha = \dfrac{x+2y}{2x+y}$, $\beta = \dfrac{x+3y}{3x+y}$

By substituting the value of α and β in the given expression and simplifying, we get $\dfrac{6x^2+5xy+y^2}{6x^2+5xy+y^2} = 1$

ILLUSTRATION 42: If $\log_{12} 81 = a$, then find the value of $\log_3 24$ in terms of a.

SOLUTION: $\log_{12} 81 = 4\log_{12} 3$

$\Rightarrow \dfrac{4\log_3 3}{\log_3 12} = \dfrac{4}{2\log_3 2 + 1} = a \qquad \Rightarrow \log_3 2 = \dfrac{1}{2}\left(\dfrac{4}{a} - 1\right) = \dfrac{4-a}{2a}$

$\Rightarrow \log_3 24 = \log_3 8 + \log_3 3 = 3\log_3 2 + 1 = 3\left(\dfrac{4-a}{2a}\right) + 1 = \dfrac{12-a}{2a}$

10. $\log_b a . \log_a b = 1$

$\Rightarrow \log_b a = \dfrac{1}{\log_a b}$

Proof: Let $\log_b a = x$

$\Rightarrow \qquad b^x = a$ and $\log_a b = y \Rightarrow a^y = b$

Now $\qquad a = b^x = (a^y)^x = a^{xy} \Rightarrow xy = 1$

ILLUSTRATION 43: Find $\log_{54}(168)$ in terms of x and y, if $\log_7 12 = x$ and $\log_{12} 24 = y$

SOLUTION: $168 = 24 \times 7$, $\log_{12} 168 = \log_{12} 24 + \log_{12} 7 = y + 1/x = \dfrac{xy+1}{x}$

and $\log_{12} 54 = \dfrac{\log_2 3^3.2}{\log_2 2^2.3} = \dfrac{3\log_2 3 + 1}{2 + \log_2 3}$

$y = \dfrac{\log_2 2^3.3}{\log_2 2^2.3} = \dfrac{3 + \log_2 3}{2 + \log_2 3} \quad \therefore \log_2 3 = \dfrac{3-2y}{y-1}$

Hence $x = 1$ is only root of the original equation. Thus

$$\log_{12} 54 = \frac{3\left(\frac{3-2y}{y-1}\right)+1}{2+\left(\frac{3-2y}{y-1}\right)} = (8-5y)\text{. Hence } \log_{54} 168 = \frac{\log_{12} 168}{\log_{12} 54} = \frac{xy+1}{x(8-5y)}$$

ILLUSTRATION 44: Solve the system of equations 5 ($\log_y x + \log_x y$) = 26 and $xy = 64$.

SOLUTION: It is clear that it must be true that $x > 0$, $y > 0$, $x \neq 1$, $y \neq 1$. Denoting $z = \log_x y$, we find that the first equation of the system can be rewritten as $5(z + 1/z) = 26$, whence $z_1 = 5$, $z_2 = 1/5$. This means that the solutions of the original system must be sought among the solutions of the system $\log_x y = 5$ and $xy = 64$ and of the system $\log_x y = 1/5$ and $xy = 64$.

Solving these systems and choosing those solutions which satisfy the conditions $x > 0$, $x \neq 1$, $y > 0$, $y \neq 1$, we obtain the answer. The original system has two solutions: $x_1 = 2$, $y_1 = 32$, $x_2 = 32$, $y_2 = 2$

ILLUSTRATION 45: If $x = \log_{2a}\left(\frac{bcd}{2}\right); y = \log_{3b}\left(\frac{acd}{3}\right); z = \log_{4c}\left(\frac{abd}{4}\right); w = \log_{5d}\left(\frac{abc}{5}\right)$, then

$\frac{1}{x+1}+\frac{1}{y+1}+\frac{1}{z+1}+\frac{1}{w+1} = \log_{abcd} N + 1$, then evaluate N.

SOLUTION: $x = \log_{2a}\left(\frac{bcd}{2}\right) \Rightarrow x+1 = \log_{2a}\left(\frac{2abcd}{2}\right) = \log_{2a}(abcd)$

$y = \log_{3b}\left(\frac{acd}{3}\right) \Rightarrow y+1 = \log_{3b}\left(\frac{3abcd}{3}\right) = \log_{3b}(abcd)$

Similarly $z + 1 = \log_{4c}(abcd)$ and $w + 1 = \log_{5d}(abcd)$

$$\therefore \frac{1}{x+1}+\frac{1}{y+1}+\frac{1}{z+1}+\frac{1}{w+1} = \log_{abcd}(2a \times 3b \times 4c \times 5d)$$

$= \log_{abcd}(120\ abcd) = \log_{abcd}(120) + 1 = \log_{abcd} N + 1$ (given) $\Rightarrow N = 120$

11. $a^{\log_m b} = b^{\log_m a}$

Proof: Let $a^{\log_m b} = y$. Taking log to the base m, $\log_m y = \log_m b \cdot \log_m a$

$\Rightarrow \frac{\log_m y}{\log_m b} = \log_m a$

$\Rightarrow \log_b y = \log_m a$

$\Rightarrow y = b^{\log_m a}$

ILLUSTRATION 46: Evaluate (i) $8^{\log_2 3}$ (ii) evaluate $(81)^{\log_3 (2/3)}$ (iii) $(49)^{\log_7 (25/49)}$

SOLUTION: (i) $8^{\log_2 3} = (3)^{\log_2 8} = (3)^3 = 27$ $[\because a^{\log_N b} = b^{\log_N a}]$

(ii) $(81)^{\log_3(2/3)} = (81)^{(\log_3 2-\log_3 3)} = (81)^{\log_3 2}(81)^{-1} = (2)^{\log_3 81}\frac{1}{81} = (2)^4\frac{1}{81} = 16/81$

(iii) $(49)^{\log_7(25/49)} = (49)^{(\log_7 25-\log_7 49)} = (49)^{(\log_7 25-2)} = (49)^{\log_7 25}.(49)^{-2}$

$$= (25)^{\log_7 49}\frac{1}{(49)^2} = (25)^2.\frac{1}{(49)^2} = \left(\frac{25}{49}\right)^2 = \frac{625}{2401}$$

ILLUSTRATION 47: Solve the following:

(a) $\log_{3\sqrt{3}} 27$ (b) $2^{(\log_{2\sqrt{2}} 15)}$ (c) $\log_3 5.\log_{25} 27$

SOLUTION: (a) Let $\log_{3\sqrt{3}} 27 = x \Rightarrow (3\sqrt{3})^x = 27$

$\Rightarrow (3)^{\frac{3}{2}x} = 3^3 \Rightarrow x = 2$

(b) $\log_{2\sqrt{2}} 15 = \log_{2^{3/2}} 15 = \frac{2}{3}\log_2 15$, Applying the fundamental logarithmic identity, we get

$2^{\log_{2\sqrt{2}} 15} = 2^{2/3 \log_2 15} = (2^{\log_2 15})^{2/3} = 15^{2/3} = \sqrt[3]{225}$

(c) $\log_3 5.\log_{25} 27 = \log_3 5.\log_{5^2} 3^3 = \frac{3}{2}\log_3 5.\log_5 3$

but $\log_3 5.\log_5 3 = 1$, it follows that $\log_3 5.\log_{25} 27 = 3/2$

TEXTUAL EXERCISE–6 (SUBJECTIVE)

1. Express log of x to the base 2 in each of the following cases:
   (a) $32^{\frac{1}{3}} = 4x$ (b) $64^{\frac{1}{4}} = 8x$
2. Evaluate the following logarithms:
   (a) $\log_8 512$ (b) $\log_{2\sqrt{2}}(32)$
   (c) $\log_8 128$
3. Evaluate the following logarithms:
   (a) $\log_2 8.\log_3 2.\log_4 5.\log_3 4\log_8 2.\log_5 3.\log_2 3$
   (b) $\log_2 48$, where $\log_2 3 = \lambda$
   (c) $\log_9 27 - \log_{27} 9$
4. Evaluate the following logarithms:
   (a) $\frac{\log_3 12}{\log_{36} 3} - \frac{\log_3 4}{\log_{108} 3}$ (b) $\log_5 \frac{\sqrt[4]{25}}{625}$
   (c) $\log_2 \log_2 \log_3 81$
5. Evaluate the following logarithms:
   (a) $\log_5 \frac{(125)(625)}{25}$
   (b) $\frac{(\log_{100} 10)(\log_2(\log_4 2))(\log_4(\log_2(256)^2))}{\log_4 8 + \log_8 4}$
   (c) $81^{\left(\frac{1}{\log_5 3}\right)} + 27^{\log_9 36} + 3^{\frac{4}{\log_7 9}}$
6. Prove that
   (a) log (1 + 2 + 3) = log1 + log2 + log3
   (b) log360 = 3log2 + 2log3 + log5
7. Prove that
   (a) $\log\left(\frac{x^2}{yz}\right) + \log\left(\frac{y^2}{zx}\right) + \log\left(\frac{z^2}{xy}\right) = 0$
   (b) $\frac{\log_2 24}{\log_{96} 2} - \frac{\log_2 192}{\log_{12} 2} = 3.$
8. Prove that $\frac{\log_a N}{\log_{ab} N} = 1 + \log_a b$ and indicate the permissible values of the letters.
9. Let A denotes the value of
   $\log_{10}\left(\frac{ab + \sqrt{(ab)^2 - 4(a+b)}}{2}\right) + \log_{10}\left(\frac{ab - \sqrt{(ab)^2 - 4(a+b)}}{2}\right)$.
   When $a = 43$ and $b = 57$ and B denotes the value of the expression $(2^{\log_6 18}).(3^{\log_6 3})$. Find the value of $(A. B)$.
10. (a) If $x = \log_5 4$ and $y = \log_5 3$, find the value of $\log_3 10$ and $\log_3(1.2)$ in terms of x and y.
    (b) If $K^{\log_2 5} = 16$, find the value of $K^{(\log_2 5)^2}$.

Answer Keys

1. (a) –1/3 (b) –3/2 2. (a) 3 (b) 10/3 (c) 7/3. 3. (a) 1 (b) 4 + λ (c) 5/6
4. (a) 2 (b) –7/2 (c) 1 5. (a) 5 (b) $-\frac{6}{13}$ (c) 890 9. 12 10. (a) $\frac{x}{2} + \frac{1}{y}$, $1 + \frac{x}{2} - \frac{1}{y}$ (b) 625

TEXTUAL EXERCISE–3 (OBJECTIVE)

1. The logarithmic representation of equation $(256)^{1/10} = 8x$ is

(a) $\log_2 x = 2/5$ (b) $\log_2 x = 8/5$

(c) $\log_2 x = -11/5$ (d) $\log_2 x = 3/5$

2. The value of $\dfrac{\log_8 32}{\log_{64} 8}$ is

(a) 5/6 (b) 10/3

(c) 6/5 (d) 2/5

3. The value of $\log_\lambda 625$ where $\lambda = \log_5 \dfrac{(125)(625)}{25}$ is

(a) 2 (b) 3

(c) 4 (d) 5

4. The value of $\log_4 \log_4 \log_4 256$ is

(a) 0 (b) 1

(c) 2 (d) 3

5. If the value of $\log_{0.01} 10000$ is λ then the value of $\log_{1/2} \lambda^4$ is

(a) 4 (b) –4

(c) 2 (d) Not defined

6. The value of $(\log_2 24)(\log_{96} 2)^{-1} - (\log_2 192)(\log_{12} 2)^{-1}$ is

(a) 2 (b) 3

(c) 4 (d) 5

7. If $7\log\dfrac{16}{15} + 5\log\dfrac{25}{24} + 3\log\dfrac{81}{80} = \log\lambda$; then the value of $\log_{1/2}\lambda$ is

(a) 0 (b) 1

(c) 2 (d) –1

8. The value of $a^{\frac{\log_b \log_b N}{\log_b a}}$ is equal to

(a) $\log_b N$

(b) $\log_a N$

(c) $\log_b a$

(d) None of these

Answer Keys

1. (c) **2.** (b) **3.** (c) **4.** (a) **5.** (b) **6.** (b) **7.** (d) **8.** (a)

■ LOGARITHMIC EQUATIONS

if we have an equation of the form $\log_a f(x) = b$, $(a > 0)$, $a \neq 1$ is equivalence to the equation $f(x) = a^b$; $f(x) > 0$.

ILLUSTRATION 48: Solve the equation $\log_3 (5 + 4 \log_3 (x - 1)) = 2$.

SOLUTION: $\log_3(5 + 4 \log_3(x - 1)) = 2$ is equivalent to the equation

$\therefore\ 5 + 4 \log_3 (x - 1) = 3^2 \Rightarrow \log_3 (x - 1) = 1 \Rightarrow x - 1 = 3 \Rightarrow x = 4$

ILLUSTRATION 49: Solve the equation $2x^{\log_4 3} + 3^{\log_4 x} = 27$.

SOLUTION: The domain of the admissible values of the equation is $x > 0$. The given equation is equivalent to $2.3^{\log_4 x} + 3^{\log_4 x} = 27 \Rightarrow 3.3^{\log_4 x} = 27$

$\Rightarrow 3^{\log_4 x} = 9 \Rightarrow 3^{\log_4 x} = 3^2 \Rightarrow \log_4 x = 2 \Rightarrow x = 4^2 = 16$ is its only root

Some standard forms to solve logarithmic equations

Type 1: An equation of the form $\log_x a = b$, $a > 0$ has

(a) only root $x = a^{1/b}$, if $a \neq 1$ and $b \neq 0$

(b) Any positive root different from unity if $a = 1$ and $b = 0$

(c) No roots if $a = 1$, $b \neq 0$

(d) No roots if $a \neq 1$, $b = 0$

ILLUSTRATION 50: Solve the equation $\log_{(\log_5 x)} 5 = 2$.

SOLUTION: We have $\log_{(\log_5 x)} 5 = 2$. Base of logarithm should be > 0 and $\neq 1$

$\Rightarrow \log_5 x > 0$ and $\log_5 x \neq 1 \Rightarrow x > 1$ and $x \neq 5$

$\therefore$ The original equation is equivalent to $\log_5 x = 5^{1/2} = \sqrt{5}$ $\Rightarrow x = 5^{\sqrt{5}}$

Hence $5^{\sqrt{5}}$ is the only root of the original equation.

Type 2: Equations of the form

(i) $f(\log_a x) = 0$, $a > 0, a \neq 1$

(ii) $g(\log_x a) = 0, a > 0$

Then equation (i) is equivalent to $f(t) = 0$ where $t = \log_a x$

If $t_1, t_2, t_3, \ldots t_k$ are the roots of $f(t) = 0$, then $\log_a x = t_1$, $\log_a x = t_2, \ldots, \log_a x = t_k$

$\Rightarrow x = a^{t_1}, a^{t_2}, \ldots\ldots, a^{t_k}$ and equation (ii) is equivalent to $g(y) = 0$; where $y = \log_x a$

If $y_1, y_2, y_3, \ldots y_k$ are the roots of $g(y) = 0$, then $\log_x a = y_1, \log_x a = y_2, \ldots, \log_x a = y_k$

$\Rightarrow x = a^{1/y_1}, a^{1/y_2}, \ldots\ldots, a^{1/y_k}$

ILLUSTRATION 51: Solve the equation $\log_x^3 10 - 6\log_x^2 10 + 11\log_x 10 - 6 = 0$.

SOLUTION: Putting $\log_x 10 = t$ in the given equation, we get $t^3 - 6t^2 + 11t - 6 = 0$

$\Rightarrow (t-1)(t-2)(t-3) = 0$, then $t \in \{1,2,3\} \Rightarrow \log_x 10 \in \{1,2,3\} \Rightarrow x \in \{10, \sqrt{10}, \sqrt[3]{10}\}$

$\therefore x_1 = 10, x_2 = \sqrt{10}$ and $x_3 = \sqrt[3]{10}$ are the roots of the original equation

Type 3: Equation of the form

(i) $\log_a f(x) = \log_a g(x)$; $a > 0, a \neq 1$ is equivalent to systems of simultaneous equations and inequations as given below:

System 1: $\begin{cases} g(x) > 0 \text{ and} \\ f(x) = g(x) \end{cases}$

System 2: $\begin{cases} f(x) > 0 \text{ and} \\ f(x) = g(x) \end{cases}$

(Any one of the two systems can be used)

(ii) $\log_{f(x)} A = \log_{g(x)} A$, $A > 0$ is equivalent to the systems of simultaneous equations and inequations as given below:

System 1: $\begin{cases} g(x) > 0, \\ g(x) \neq 1 \text{ and} \\ f(x) = g(x) \end{cases}$

System 2: $\begin{cases} f(x) > 0, \\ f(x) \neq 1 \text{ and} \\ f(x) = g(x) \end{cases}$

(Any one of the two systems can be used)

ILLUSTRATION 52: Solve the equation $\log_{1/3}(2(1/2)^x - 1) = \log_{1/3}((1/4)^x - 4)$.

SOLUTION: The given equation is equivalent to $\begin{cases} 2(1/2)^x - 1 > 0 \text{ and} \\ 2(1/2)^x - 1 = (1/4)^x - 4 \end{cases}$

$\Rightarrow \begin{cases} (1/2)^x > (1/2)^1 \text{ and} \\ (1/2)^{2x} - 2(1/2)^x - 3 = 0 \end{cases}$ $\Rightarrow \begin{cases} x < 1 \text{ and} \\ [(1/2)^x - 3][(1/2)^x + 1] = 0 \end{cases}$

$\Rightarrow \begin{cases} x < 1 \text{ and} \\ (1/2)^x = 3 \text{ or } (1/2)^x + 1 = 0 \end{cases}$ $\Rightarrow \begin{cases} x < 1 \text{ and} \\ x = -\log_2 3 \text{ or } (1/2)^x \neq -1 \end{cases}$

Hence $x = -\log_2 3$ is the root of the original equation

ILLUSTRATION 53: Solve the equation $\log_{\left(\frac{2+x}{10}\right)} 7 = \log_{\left(\frac{2}{x+1}\right)} 7$.

SOLUTION: The given equation is equivalent to $\begin{cases} \dfrac{2}{x+1} > 0, \\ \dfrac{2}{x+1} \neq 1 \text{ and} \\ \dfrac{2+x}{10} = \dfrac{2}{x+1} \end{cases} \Rightarrow \begin{cases} x+1 > 0, \\ x \neq 1 \text{ and} \\ x = -6, 3 \end{cases} \Rightarrow \begin{cases} x > -1 \\ x \neq 1 \\ x = -6, 3 \end{cases}$

$\Rightarrow$ $x = 3$ is the only root of the original equation.

Type 4: Equation of the form

(i) $\log_{f(x)} g(x) = \log_{f(x)} h(x)$ is equivalent to two systems of simultaneous equations and inequations.

System 1: $\begin{cases} g(x) > 0, \\ f(x) > 0 \text{ and} \\ g(x) = h(x) \end{cases}$

System 2: $\begin{cases} h(x) > 0, \\ f(x) > 0 \text{ and} \\ g(x) = h(x) \end{cases}$

(Any one of the two systems can be used)

(ii) $\log_{g(x)} f(x) = \log_{h(x)} f(x)$ is equivalent to two systems of simultaneous equations and inequations.

System 1: $\begin{cases} f(x) > 0, \\ g(x) > 0, \\ g(x) \neq 1 \text{ and} \\ g(x) = h(x) \end{cases}$

System 2: $\begin{cases} f(x) > 0, \\ h(x) > 0, \\ h(x) \neq 1 \text{ and} \\ g(x) = h(x) \end{cases}$

(Any one of the two systems can be used)

ILLUSTRATION 54: Solve $\log_{(x^2-1)}(x^3+6) = \log_{(x^2-1)}(2x^2+5x)$

SOLUTION: This equation is equivalent to the system of simultaneous equation

$$\begin{cases} 2x^2+5x > 0, \\ x^2-1 > 0, \\ x^2-1 \neq 1 \text{ and} \\ x^3+6 = 2x^2+5x \end{cases} \Rightarrow \begin{cases} x < -1 \text{ or } x > 1, \\ x < -5/2 \text{ or } x > 0, \\ x \neq \pm\sqrt{2} \text{ and} \\ x \in \{-2, 1, 3\} \end{cases}$$

Hence $x = 3$ is only root of the original equation.

ILLUSTRATION 55: Solve the equation $\log_{(x^3+6)}(x^2-1) = \log_{(2x^2+5x)}(x^2-1)$

SOLUTION: This equation is equivalent to the system of simultaneous equation

$$\begin{cases} x^2-1 > 0, \\ 2x^2+5x > 0, \\ 2x^2+5x \neq 1 \text{ and} \\ x^3+6 = 2x^2+5x \end{cases} \Rightarrow \begin{cases} x < -1 \text{ or } x > 1, \\ x < -5/2 \text{ or } x > 0, \\ x \neq \dfrac{-5 \pm \sqrt{33}}{4} \text{ and} \\ x \in \{-2, 1, 3\} \end{cases}$$

Hence $x = 3$ is the only root of the original equation.

Type 5: An equation of the form $\log_{h(x)}[\log_{g(x)} f(x)] = 0$ is equivalent to the system $\begin{cases} h(x) > 0, \\ h(x) \neq 1, \\ g(x) > 0, \\ g(x) \neq 1 \text{ and} \\ f(x) = g(x) \end{cases}$

ILLUSTRATION 56: Solve the equation $\log_{x^2-6x+8}[\log_{2x^2-2x-8}(x^2+5x)] = 0$

SOLUTION: This equation is equivalent to the system

$$\begin{cases} x^2-6x+8>0, \\ x^2-6x+8 \neq 1, \\ 2x^2-2x-8>0, \\ 2x^2-2x-8 \neq 1 \text{ and} \\ x^2+5x = 2x^2-2x-8 \end{cases} \Rightarrow \begin{cases} x<2 \text{ or } x>4, \\ x \neq 3 \pm \sqrt{2}, \\ x < \dfrac{1-\sqrt{17}}{2} \text{ or } x > \dfrac{1+\sqrt{17}}{2}, \\ x \neq \dfrac{1 \pm \sqrt{19}}{2} \text{ and} \\ x \in \{-1, 8\} \end{cases}$$

$x = -1$ does not satisfy the third relation of this system. Hence $x = 8$ is the only root of the original equation.

Type 6: An equation of the form $2m \log_a f(x) = \log_a g(x)$, $a > 0$; $a \neq 1$, $m \in N$ is equivalent to the system $\begin{cases} f(x) > 0 \text{ and} \\ [f(x)]^{2m} = g(x) \end{cases}$

ILLUSTRATION 57: Solve the equation $2 \log 2x = \log(7x - 2 - 2x^2)$.

SOLUTION: The equation is equivalent to the system

$$\begin{cases} 2x > 0 \text{ and} \\ (2x)^2 = 7x-2-2x^2 \end{cases} \Rightarrow \begin{cases} x>0 \text{ and} \\ 6x^2-7x+2=0 \end{cases}$$

$$\begin{cases} x > 0 \text{ and} \\ (x-1/2)(x-2/3)=0 \end{cases} \Rightarrow \begin{cases} x = 1/2 \text{ and} \\ x = 2/3 \end{cases}$$

Hence $x = 1/2$ and $x = 2/3$ are the roots of the original equation.

Type 7: An equation of the form $(2m + 1) \log_a f(x) = \log_a g(x)$, $a > 0$ $a \neq 1$, $m \in \mathbb{N}$ is equivalent to the system $\begin{cases} f(x) > 0 \text{ and} \\ [f(x)]^{2m+1} = g(x). \end{cases}$

ILLUSTRATION 58: Solve the equation $\log(3x^2 + x - 2) = 3\log(3x - 2)$.

SOLUTION: This equation is equivalent to the system

$$\begin{cases} 3x^2+x-2>0 \text{ and} \\ 3x^2+x-2 = (3x-2)^3 \end{cases} \Rightarrow \begin{cases} (x-2/3)(x+1)>0 \text{ and} \\ (x-2/3)(9x^2-13x+3)=0 \end{cases}$$

$$\Rightarrow \begin{cases} x<-1 \text{ or } x>2/3 \text{ and} \\ x=2/3 \text{ or } x=\dfrac{13\pm\sqrt{61}}{18} \end{cases}$$

Original equation has only root $x=\dfrac{13+\sqrt{61}}{18}$ (rejecting $x=\dfrac{2}{3}$ and $x=\dfrac{13-\sqrt{61}}{18}$.

Type 8: An equation of the form $\log_a f(x)+\log_a g(x)=\log_a m(x);\ a>0\ a\neq 1$ is equivalent to the system $\begin{cases} f(x)>0, \\ g(x)>0 \text{ and} \\ f(x)g(x)=m(x) \end{cases}$

ILLUSTRATION 59: Solve the equation $2\log_3 x+\log_3(x^2-3)=\log_3 0.5+5^{\log_5(\log_3 8)}$.

SOLUTION: This equation can be written as $\log_3 x^2+\log_3(x^2-3)=\log_3 0.5+\log_3 8$

$\log_3 x^2+\log_3(x^2-3)=\log_3(4)$

This is equivalent to the system $\begin{cases} x>0, \\ x^2-3>0 \text{ and} \\ x^2(x^2-3)=4 \end{cases} \Rightarrow \begin{cases} x>0, \\ x<-\sqrt{3} \text{ or } x>\sqrt{3} \text{ and} \\ (x^2-4)(x^2+1)=0 \end{cases}$

$\Rightarrow x^2-4=0 \Rightarrow x=\pm 2$ but $x>0$

Consequently, $x=2$ is the only root of the original equation.

Type 9: An equation of the form $\log_a f(x)-\log_a g(x)=\log_a h(x)-\log_a t(x),\ a>0,\ a\neq 1$ is equivalent to the equation $\log_a f(x)+\log_a t(x)=\log_a g(x)+\log_a h(x)$

which is equivalent to the system $\begin{cases} f(x)>0, \\ t(x)>0, \\ g(x)>0, \\ h(x)>0 \text{ and} \\ f(x).t(x)=g(x).h(x) \end{cases}$

ILLUSTRATION 60: Solve the equation $\log_2(3-x)=\log_2\left(\dfrac{\sin 3\pi/4}{5-x}\right)+\dfrac{1}{2}+\log_2(x+7)$.

SOLUTION: This equation is equivalent to

$$\log_2(3-x)=\log_2\left(\frac{\sin 3\pi/4}{5-x}\right)+\frac{1}{2}\log_2 2+\log_2(x+7)$$

$$\log_2(3-x)=\log_2\left(\frac{1}{\sqrt{2}(5-x)}\right)+\log_2\sqrt{2}+\log_2(x+7)$$

which is equivalent to the system $\begin{cases} 3-x>0, \\ \dfrac{1}{\sqrt{2}(5-x)}>0, \\ x+7>0 \text{ and} \\ (3-x)=\dfrac{\sqrt{2}(x+7)}{\sqrt{2}(5-x)} \end{cases} \Rightarrow \begin{cases} x<3, \\ x<5, \\ x>-7 \text{ and} \\ (x-1)(x-8)=0 \end{cases}$

Hence $x=1$ is the only root of the original equation.

TEXTUAL EXERCISE–7 (SUBJECTIVE)

1. Solve the following equations for x:
   (a) $\log_2 (x-1) = 3$ (b) $\log_{\sqrt{\ }}(x-2x) = 2$
   (c) $\log_2 (x^2-3) = 2^2$

2. Solve the following equations for x:
   (a) $\log (x+1) - \log (x-1) = 1$
   (b) $(0.125)\, 4^{2x-6} = \left(\frac{0.25}{\sqrt{2}}\right)$
   (c) $a^{2x}b^{3x} = c^5$

3. Solve the following equations for x:
   (a) $9^{1+\log x} - 3^{1+\log x} - 210 = 0$; (where base of log is 3)
   (b) $\log_{10} (x^2 - 12x + 36) = 2$

4. Solve the following equations for x:
   (a) $\log_x 3.\ \log_{x/3} 3 + \log_{x/81} 3 = 0$
   (b) $\log_2 x = (1/3).\ \log_2 8 - 2\log_2 \sqrt{3}$

5. Solve the following equations for x:
   (a) $\frac{\log_{10}(x-3)}{\log_{10}(x-1)} = \frac{1}{2}$
   (b) $\log(\log x) + \log (\log x^3 - 2) = 0$; (where base of log is 10 everywhere.)
   (c) $\log(_{(\log 5^x)} 5 = 2$

6. Solve the equation for x: $\frac{\log\left(\sqrt{x+2}+1\right)}{\log \sqrt[5]{x-2}} = 5$

7. Solve the following equation $\sqrt{(3+\log_x 9)}\ \log_3 x + 1 = 0$

8. Find the ordered pairs (u, v) satisfying the equations $3(\log_v u + \log_u v) = 10$ and uv = 81

9. Solving graphically, find the number of solutions of equation $x^2 \ln|\mathbf{x}| - 1 = 0$

Answer Keys

1. (a) 9 (b) –1, 3 (c) $x = \pm\sqrt{19}$
2. (a) 4/9 (b) 25/8 (c) $x = \log_{a2\ b3} c^5$
3. (a) $x = 5$ (b) $x = 16, -4$
4. (a) $x = 9, 1/9$ (b) 2/3
5. (a) 5 (b) 10 (c) $x = 5^{\sqrt{5}}$
6. $\frac{7+\sqrt{21}}{2}$
7. $x = \frac{1}{3}, \sqrt[3]{3}$
8. $(27,3);(3,27)$
9. 2

TEXTUAL EXERCISE–4 (OBJECTIVE)

1. The solution of logarithmic equation $\log_{x^2}(2x^2-4)=1$ is
   (a) 2 (b) –2
   (c) 3 (d) 4

2. The solution of logarithmic equation $\log_4 \log_3 \log_2 x = 0$ is
   (a) 4 (b) 6
   (c) 8 (d) None of these

3. The solution of logarithmic equation $\frac{a^{x+1}}{b^{x-1}} = c^{2x}$ is
   (a) $\frac{\log ab}{\log\left(\frac{c^2b}{a}\right)}$ (b) $\log_{\left(\frac{c^2b}{a}\right)} ab$
   (c) $\log_{C^2} ab$ (d) None of these

4. The solution of logarithmic equation $\log_x 2.\log_{2x} 2 = \log_{4x} 2$
   (a) $2^{\sqrt{2}}$ (b) $\sqrt{2}$
   (c) $2^{-\sqrt{2}}$ (d) None of these

5. The solution of logarithmic equation $5^{\log x} + 5\ x^{\log 5} = 3$ $(a > 0)$ [Base of log is a] is
   (a) $2^{\log_5 a}$ (b) $2^{-\log_5 a}$
   (c) $a^{\log_5 2}$ (d) None of these

6. Solution of the logarithmic equation $\log_{\left(\frac{2+x}{10}\right)} 7 = \log_{\left(\frac{2}{x+1}\right)} 7$ is
   (a) 1 (b) –2
   (c) 4 (d) 3

7. Solution of the logarithrmic equation $2 \log 2x = \log (7x - 2 - 2x^2)$ is
   (a) 1 (b) 1/2
   (c) 2/3 (d) 2

8. The value x in the equation $9^{\log_3(1-2x)} = 5x^2 - 5$ is equal to
   (a) $2-\sqrt{10}$ (b) $1-2\sqrt{10}$
   (c) $-2-\sqrt{10}$ (d) None of these

9. The number of solutions of $\log_4(x-1) = \log_2(x-3)$ is

(a) 3 (b) 5

(c) 2 (d) 0

10. The number of solutions of $\dfrac{\log 5 + \log(x^2+1)}{\log(x-2)} = 2$ is

(a) 1 (b) 2

(c) 3 (d) None of these

Answer Keys

1. (a, b) **2.** (c) **3.** (a, b) **4.** (a, c) **5.** (b) **6.** (d) **7.** (b, c) **8.** (c) **9.** (b) **10.** (d)

Logarithmic inequality

When base $a > 1$, then $\log_a x$ is an increasing function, whereas when $0 < a < 1$, then $\log_a x$ is decreasing nature function

We can observe this by simply taking $\log_2 x$ and $\log_{1/2} x$ and evaluating their values for various positive inputs and thus plotting the approximate graph of both functions.

x	1/16	1/8	1/4	1/2	1	2	4	8
$\log_2 x$	-4	-3	-2	-1	0	1	2	3
$\log_{1/2} x$	4	3	2	1	0	-1	-2	-3

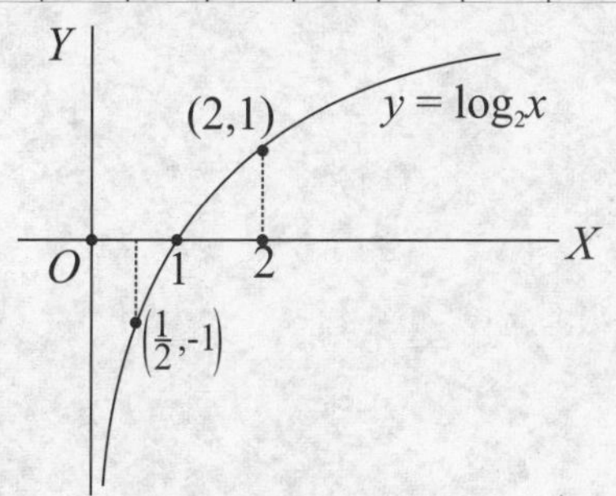

FIGURE 2.14

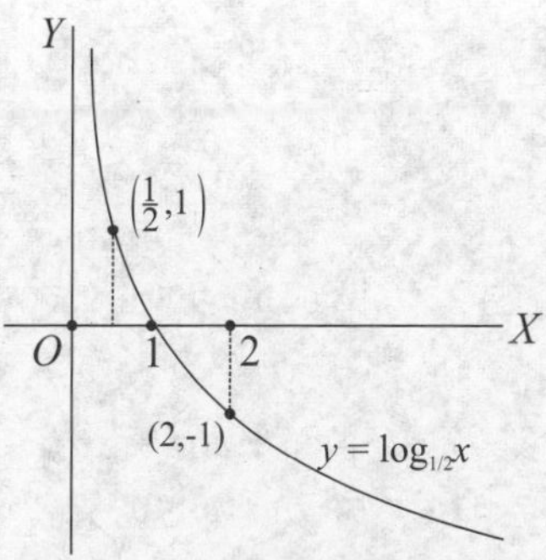

FIGURE 2.15

To solve a logarithmic inequality, following facts must be kept in mind:

Given a be any positive real number, then

(a) For $a > 1$, the inequality $\log_a x > \log_a y \Rightarrow x > y$
(Since, for $a > 1$, $\log_a x$ is an increasing function)
$\Rightarrow$ If $a > 1$, then $\log_a x < \alpha \Rightarrow 0 < x < a^\alpha$
and $\log_a x > \alpha \Rightarrow x > a^\alpha$

(b) For $0 < a < 1$, the inequality $0 < x < y \Rightarrow \log_a x > \log_a y$
($\because$ for $0 < a < 1$; $\log_a x$ is a decreasing function)
$\Rightarrow$ If $0 < a < 1$, then $\log_a x < \alpha \Rightarrow x > a^\alpha$
and $\log_a x > \alpha \Rightarrow 0 < x < a^\alpha$

ILLUSTRATION 61: Solve the logarithmic inequality: $\log_{1/5} \dfrac{4x+6}{x} \geq 0$

SOLUTION: Since $\log_{1/5} 1 = 0$ the given inequality can be written as $\log_{1/5} \dfrac{4x+6}{x} \geq \log_{1/5} 1$

When the domain of the function is taken into account, the inequality is equivalent to the system of inequalities
$$\begin{cases} \dfrac{4x+6}{x} > 0 \text{ and} \\ \dfrac{4x+6}{x} \leq 1 \end{cases}$$

Solving the inequalities by using method of intervals $x \in [-2, -3/2)$

ILLUSTRATION 62: Solve the following inequalities:

(i) $\log_{1/3}(5x-1) > 0$ (ii) $\log_8(x^2 - 4x + 3) \leq 1$ (iii) $(\log_x 2)(\log_{2x} 2)(\log_2 4x) > 1$

SOLUTION: (i) By using the basic property of logarithm

$$\begin{cases} 5x-1<1 \text{ and} \\ 5x-1>0 \end{cases} \Rightarrow \begin{cases} 5x<2 \text{ and} \\ 5x>1 \end{cases} \Rightarrow \begin{matrix} x<2/5 \text{ and} \\ x>1/5 \end{matrix}$$

$\Rightarrow$ The solution of the inequality is (1/5, 2/5).

(ii) By using the basic property of logarithm

$$\Rightarrow \begin{cases} x^2-4x+3>0 \\ x^2-4x+3 \le 8 \end{cases} \Rightarrow \begin{cases} (x-1)(x-3)>0 \\ (x+1)(x-5) \le 0 \end{cases} \Rightarrow \begin{cases} x \in (-\infty,1) \cup (3,\infty) \text{ and} \\ x \in [-1,\ 5] \end{cases} \Rightarrow \in [-1, 1) \cup (3, 5]$$

(iii) By using the basic property of logarithm $\dfrac{\log_2 4x}{\log_2 x \log_2 2x} > 1$ (i)

Now let us assume that $\log_2 x = y$

$\therefore$ The equation (i) changes to $\dfrac{2+y}{y(1+y)} > 1 \Rightarrow \dfrac{y^2-2}{y(1+y)} < 0$

Now solving the inequalities, we get $-\sqrt{2} < y < -1$ and $0 < y < \sqrt{2}$. Recalling that $y = \log_2 x$

$\therefore$ The solution of the first inequality consists of the x in the interval $2^{-\sqrt{2}} < x < 2^{-1}$; and the solution of second inequality consists of the values of x located in the interval $1 < x < 2^{+\sqrt{2}}$.

$\therefore\ x \in (2^{-\sqrt{2}}, 2^{-1}) \cup (1, 2^{\sqrt{2}})$

ILLUSTRATION 63: Given x and y as two real numbers such that ($x \ge 0$ and $y > 0$); $(\log_{10}(x+1))^2 + 4(\log_2 y)^2 = 1$, find the range of values of x and y satisfying the above relation.

SOLUTION: Rearranging the given equation $4(\log_2 y)^2 - 1 = -(\log_{10}(x+1))^2$; where $y = x + 1$

$\Rightarrow (2\log_2 y - 1)(2\log_2 y + 1) \le 0$ $\qquad \Rightarrow -\dfrac{1}{2} \le \log_2 y \le \dfrac{1}{2}$

$\Rightarrow 2^{-\frac{1}{2}} \le y \le 2^{\frac{1}{2}}$ $\qquad \Rightarrow y \in \left[\dfrac{1}{\sqrt{2}}, \sqrt{2}\right]$

Similarly expressing x in terms of y $\qquad \Rightarrow (\log_{10}(x+1))^2 - 1 = -(2\log_2 y)^2 \le 0$

$\Rightarrow (\log_{10}(x+1)-1)(\log_{10}(x+1)+1) \le 0$ $\qquad \Rightarrow -1 \le \log_{10}(x+1) \le 1$

$\Rightarrow \dfrac{}{10} \le \ +1 \le 10$ $\qquad \Rightarrow \dfrac{}{10} \le \ \le$

But given $x \ge 0$

$\Rightarrow x \in [0, 9]$

Thus domain $x \in [0, 9]$ and range $y \in \left[\dfrac{1}{\sqrt{2}}, \sqrt{2}\right]$.

TEXTUAL EXERCISE–8 (SUBJECTIVE)

1. Solve the following inequalities for x:
   (a) $\log_a x \ge 0$; $a > 1$ (b) $\log_a x > 0$ where $a < 1$
2. Solve the following inequalities for x:
   (a) $\log_2 x^2 - 1 \le 0$ (b) $\log_a (x^2 - 1) < 0$ if $0 < a < 1$
3. Solve the following inequalities for x:
   (a) $\log_a (x - 7) > 0$ where $a > 1$
   (b) $\log_{1/2} (x - 1) > 0$
4. Solve the following inequalities for x:
   (a) $\log_2 (x^2 - 2x) > 1$ (b) $\log_{1/5} \dfrac{4x+6}{x} \ge 0$
5. Solve the following inequalities for x:
   (a) $\log_{1/3} (5x - 1) > 0$ (b) $\log_8 (x^2 - 4x + 3) \le 1$
6. What can be said about the number x if it is known that for every real $a \ne 0$; $\log_x (a^2 + 1) < 0$?

7. Which is greater of the following?
(a) $\log_2 3$ and $\log_{1/4} 5$ (b) $\log_5 7$ and $\log_8 3$
(c) 2 and $(\log_\pi 2 + \log_2 \pi)$ (d) $\log_3 2$ and $\log_2 3$

8. Solve the following inequalities for x:
(a) $3^{\log x+2} < 3^{\log x^2+5} - 2$ (b) $\left(\frac{1}{3}\right)^{\log_{1/3}(3.(1/2)^x+5)} < 2^{1+x}$

9. Solve the following inequalities for x:
(a) $\log_5 (3x - 1) < 1$ (b) $\log_7 \frac{2x-6}{2x-1} > 0$
(c) $\log_3 \frac{1-2x}{x} \le 0$

10. Solve the following inequalities for x: $\log_{x^2} \frac{4x-5}{|x-2|} \ge \frac{1}{2}$

Answer Keys

1. (a) $x \in [1, \infty)$ (b) $x \in (0, 1)$ 2. (a) $x \in \left[-\sqrt{2}, \sqrt{2}\right]$ (b) $x \in (-\infty, -\sqrt{2}) \cup (\sqrt{2}, \infty)$
3. (a) $x \in (8, \infty)$ (b) $x \in (1, 2)$ 4. (a) $(-\infty, 1-\sqrt{3}) \cup (1+\sqrt{3}, \infty)$ (b) $x \in [-2, -3/2)$
5. (a) (1/5, 2/5) (b) $x \in [-1, 1) \cup (3, 5]$ 6. $0 < x < 1$.
7. (a) $\log_2 3$ (b) $\log_5 7$ (c) $(\log_\pi 2 + \log_2 \pi)$ (d) $\log_2 3$ 8. (a) $(10^{-2}, \infty)$ (b) $(\log_2 3, \infty)$
9. (a) (1/3, 2) (b) $(-\infty, 1/2)$ (c) [1/3, 1/2) 10. (a) $\left[\sqrt{6}-1, 5\right] - \{2\}$

TEXTUAL EXERCISE–5 (OBJECTIVE)

1. The solution set of logarithmic inequality $\log_2 (x^2 - 2x) < 0$ is
(a) $(1 - \sqrt{2}, 1 + \sqrt{2})$ (b) $(1 - \sqrt{2}, 0) \cup (2, 1 + \sqrt{2})$
(c) $(-\infty, 0) \cup (2, \infty)$ (d) None of these

2. The solution set of the logarithmic inequality $\log_a (x^2 - 1) > 0$; $a < 1$ is
(a) $(\sqrt{2}, \infty)$ (b) $(-\infty, -\sqrt{2}) \cup (\sqrt{2}, \infty)$
(c) $(-\sqrt{2}, -1) \cup (1, \sqrt{2})$ (d) None of these

3. The solution set of the logarithmic inequality $\log_2 \left(\frac{x^2-4x}{3}\right) > \log_2 1$ is
(a) $(-\infty, 2 - \sqrt{7}) \cup (2 + \sqrt{7}, \infty)$
(b) $(2 - \sqrt{7}, 2 + \sqrt{7})$
(c) $(-\infty, 0) \cup (4, \infty)$
(d) None of these

4. Which of the following is/are correct?
(a) $\log_4 5 > \log_{1/6} 1/25$ (b) $\log_4 5 < \log_{1/16} 1/25$
(c) $\log_4 5 = \log_{1/16} 1/25$ (d) $\log_4 5 > \log_6 5$

5. Solution set of the logarithmic inequality $\left(\frac{1}{2}\right)^{\log_2 (x^2-1)} > 1$
(a) $(-\sqrt{2}, -1) \cup (1, \sqrt{2})$
(b) $(-\sqrt{2}, \sqrt{2})$
(c) $(-\infty, -\sqrt{2}) \cup (\sqrt{2}, \infty)$
(d) None of these

6. Solution set of the logarithmic inequality $\log_{0.5} (x^2 - 4x + 3) \le 1$ is
(a) $(-\infty, 1) \cup (3, \infty)$
(b) (1, 3)
(c) $\left(-\infty, 2-\sqrt{\frac{3}{2}}\right) \cup \left(2+\sqrt{\frac{3}{2}}, \infty\right)$
(d) None of these

7. Solution set of the logarithmic inequality $\log_{1/3} \frac{2-3x}{x} \ge -1$ are contained in the set
(a) [1/3, 2/3] (b) $\left[\frac{2}{3}, \infty\right)$
(c) $\left(\frac{1}{3}, \frac{2}{3}\right)$ (d) $\left[\frac{1}{3}, \frac{2}{3}\right)$

8. Solution set of the logarithmic inequality $\log_3 \frac{1+2x}{1+x} < 1$ is
(a) $\left(-2, \frac{-1}{2}\right)$ (b) $(-\infty, -2)$
(c) $(-2, 0)$ (d) $(-\infty, -2) \cup (-1/2, \infty)$

9. Solution set of logarithmic inequality $\log_{0.2}(x^2 - x - 2) > \log_{0.2}(-x^2 + 2x + 3)$ is

(a) (2, 5/2) (b) (5/2, ∞)

(c) (–∞ , 2) (d) None of these

10. Solution of set of inequality $\log_{\frac{x+6}{3}}\left(\log_2 \dfrac{x-1}{x-2}\right) > 0$ is

(a) (–6, – 3) (b) (–6, – 5)

(c) (–6, –5) ∪ (–3, – 2) (d) None of these

Answer Keys

1. (b) **2.** (c) **3.** (a) **4.** (c, d) **5.** (a) **6.** (c) **7.** (a, d) **8.** (d) **9.** (a) **10.** (d)

■ IMPORTANT DISCUSSION

Characteristic and Mantissa

Generally, the logarithm of a number is partially integral and partially fractional. The integral part to the logarithm of a number is called characteristic and the decimal part is known as mantissa.

Characteristic and mantissa

(a) Given a number N, Logarithms can be expressed as $\log_{10} N$

= Integer + fraction (+ *ve*)

↓ ↓

Characteristics Mantissa

(i) The mantissa part of log of a number is always kept positive, the characteristic may be positive or negative. e.g., if $\log_e x = -1.4 = -2 + 0.6$ written as $\bar{2}.6$.

(ii) If the characteristics of $\log_{10} N$ be n, then the number of digits in N before decimal is $(n + 1)$.

(iii) If the characteristics of $\log_{10} N$ be $(-n)$ then there exists $(n - 1)$ number of zeros after decimal point of N and before first significant digit.

(b) The number of positive integers having base a and characteristic $\boldsymbol{n = a^{n+1} - a^n}$.

(c) If the number and base are on the same side of the unity, then the logarithm is positive; and if the number and the base are on opposite sides of unity, then the logarithm is negative.

(d) Characteristic of the common logarithm of

(i) any number greater than 1 is positive.

(ii) any positive number less than 1 is negative.

ILLUSTRATION 64: Find the number of digits in 12^{12}, without actual computation, where log 2 = .301 and log 3 = .477.

SOLUTION: We will make use of the result that, if n; where n is positive be the characteristic of $\log y$, then number of digits in $y = n + 1$. Let $y = 12^{12}$

$\therefore \log y = 12 \log 12 = 12 \log (2^2 \times 3) = 12 [2 \log 2 + \log 3] = 12 (2 \times .301 + .477)$

$= 12 \times 1.08$ (approx.) $= 12.96 = 12 + 0.96$

⇒ Characteristic of $\log y = 12$. Hence number of digits in $y = 13$.

ILLUSTRATION 65: If log 2 = .301 and log 3 = .477, then find the value of logx, where x satisfies the equation $\log_2(x^2 - 4x - 32) = 6$

SOLUTION: $\log_2(x^2 - 4x - 32) = 6 \Rightarrow x^2 - 4x - 32 = (2)^6 \Rightarrow x^2 - 4x - 32 = 64$

$\Rightarrow x^2 - 4x - 96 = 0 \Rightarrow (x - 12)(x + 8) = 0 \Rightarrow x = 12$ or $x = -8$

but for $\log x$; $x > 0 \Rightarrow \log x = \log 12 = \log(2)^2(3)$

$= 2\log 2 + \log 3 = 2(.301) + (.477) = .602 + .477 = 1.0798.$

ILLUSTRATION 66: If log 2 = .301 and log 3 = .477, $\log x = 20.301$, $\log y = 15.477$, then find the number of positive integer divisors of x and y.

SOLUTION: $\log x = 20.301 = 20 + .301 = \log_{10}(10)^{20} + \log_{10}2 = \log_{10}(2 \times 10^{20})$

$= \log_{10}(2) \times (2 \times 5)^{20} = \log_{10}(2)^{21}(5)^{20}$

$\Rightarrow x = (2)^{21} \times (5)^{20}$

Similarly, $\log y = 15.477 = \log_{10}(3 \times (10)^{15}) = \log_{10}(3 \times 2^{15} \times 5^{15})$

$\Rightarrow y = (2)^{15}(3)^1(5)^{15}$

$\because$ Number of positive integer divisors of $x = (22) \times (21) = 462$

$\therefore$ Number of positive integer divisors of $y = (16) \times (2) \times (16) = 512$

ILLUSTRATION 67: If log 2 = .301 and log 3 = .477, then evaluate x for which $20^x = 15$.

SOLUTION: Here $x = \log_{20}15 = \dfrac{\log_{10}15}{\log_{10}20} = \dfrac{\log_{10}(3\times5)}{\log_{10}(2^2\times5)} = \dfrac{\log_{10}3+\log_{10}5}{2\log_{10}2+\log_{10}5} = \dfrac{\log_{10}3+\log_{10}\left(\frac{10}{2}\right)}{2\log_{10}2+\log\left(\frac{10}{2}\right)}$

$$= \frac{\log_{10}3+\log_{10}10-\log_{10}2}{2\log_{10}2+\log_{10}10-\log_{10}2} = \frac{.477+1-.301}{2(.301)+1-(.301)} = \frac{1.176}{1.301} = \frac{1176}{1301} = 0.9039$$

TEXTUAL EXERCISE–9 (SUBJECTIVE)

1. Prove the following results:

(a) $8\log_a x^3 \log_b y^3 . \log_c z^3 = 27$ where $a = y^2$, $b = z^2$, $c = x^2$.

(b) $a^a.b^b.c^c = 1$ where $\dfrac{\log a}{b-c} = \dfrac{\log b}{c-a} = \dfrac{\log c}{a-b}$.

(c) $xyz = xy + yz + zx$. where $x = 1 + \log_a bc$, $y = 1 + \log_b ca$, $z = 1 + \log_c ab$

2. Show the following:

(a) $pqr = p + q + r + 2$ where $p = \log_a bc$, $q = \log_b ca$, $r = \log_c ab$

(b) $\log\dfrac{a+b}{5} = \dfrac{1}{2}(\log a + \log b)$ where $a^2 + b^2 = 23ab$

(c) $xyz + 1 = 2yz$. where $x = \log_{2a} a$, $y = \log_{3a} 2a$ and $z = \log_{4a} 3a$

3. If $\log_b a . \log_c a + \log_a b . \log_c b + \log_a c . \log_b c = 3$ (where a, b, c are different positive real numbers $\neq 1$) then find the value of abc.

4. Given $a^2 + b^2 = c^2$ and $a > 0$; $b > 0$; $c > 0$, $c - b \neq 1$, $c + b \neq 1$.
Prove that $\log_{c+b} a + \log_{c-b} a = 2.\log_{c+b} a.\log_{c-b} a$.

5. Solve the system of the equations $(ax)^{\log a} = (by)^{\log b}$; $b^{\log x} = a^{\log y}$ where $a > 0$, $b > 0$ and $a \neq b$, $ab \neq 1$.

6. If $0 < x < 1$, prove that $\log(1 + x) + \log(1 + x^2) + \log(1 + x^4) + \ldots$ to $\infty = -\log(1 - x)$

7. Find the sum of the series $\dfrac{1}{\log_2 a} + \dfrac{1}{\log_4 a} + \dfrac{1}{\log_8 a} + \ldots$ up to n terms.

8. Prove that $\log_3 5$ and $\log_2 7$ are both irrational numbers.

9. Evaluate the value of x in the following:

(i) $\log_7 \log_5\left(\sqrt{x+5}+\sqrt{x}\right) = 0$

(ii) $\log_{3/4}\log_8(x^2 + 7) + \log_{1/2}\log_{1/4}(x^2 + 7)^{-1} = -2$

10. Determine the value of k in $\log_e 2 . \log_k 625 = \log_{10}16 . \log_e 10$.

Answer Keys

3. $abc = 1$ **5.** $x = 1/z$; $y = 1/b$ **7.** $\dfrac{n(n+1)}{2}\log_a 2$ **9.** (i) 4 (ii) ±3 **10.** 5

TEXTUAL EXERCISE–6 (OBJECTIVE)

1. The number of digits in $(81)^{24}$ is (given $\log_{10}3 = 0.477$)
   (a) 44 (b) 45
   (c) 46 (d) None of these

2. The value of $\log_{10}(36)$ is (Given $\log_{10}2 = 0.301$ and $\log_{10}3 = 0.477$)
   (a) 1.256 (b) 1.556
   (c) 2.566 (d) None of these

3. If '*a*' is the characterstic of logarithm of number 0.0005798 and '*b*' is the characterstic of logarithm of number. 352.526, then the value of $a + b$ is
   (a) –2 (b) 2
   (c) 3 (d) None of these

4. The characterstic of $\log_{10} \log_2 \log_3 \log_3 19683$ is
   (a) –1 (b) 0
   (c) 1 (d) 2

5. If $\log_{10} \overline{abc}\,.\,\overline{pqrst}$ has mantissa 0.4971, then the value of $\log_{10} \bar{a}\,.\,\overline{bcpqrst}$ will be (where *a, b, c, p, q, r, s, t* are digits and $a \neq 0$)
   (a) 2.4791 (b) 1.4971
   (c) 0.4971 (d) None of these

6. The characterstic of number $\log_y x \log_z y \log_p z \log_{x^2} p$ is
   (a) –2 (b) –1
   (c) 0 (d) 1

7. If $\log_{10}3 = 0.477$ and and $\log_{10}2 = 0.301$; then which of the following is true?
   (a) $(3)^{21} > (2)^{48}$
   (b) $(3)^{21} < (2)^{48}$
   (c) $(3)^{21} = (2)^{48}$
   (d) None of these

Answer Keys

1. (c) 2. (b) 3. (a) 4. (b) 5. (c) 6. (c) 7. (b)

MULTIPLE-CHOICE QUESTIONS

SECTION–I

OBJECTIVE-TYPE SOLVED EXAMPLES

1. The value of $(a^{\alpha})^{-\beta \log_{a^5} N^{\gamma}}$ is equal to

(a) $N^{-\frac{\alpha\beta\gamma}{5}}$ (b) $N^{\frac{\alpha\beta\gamma}{5}}$

(c) $N^{5\alpha\beta\gamma}$ (d) None of these

Sol. (a) Given expression $= \left(a^{\alpha}\right)^{-\beta \log_{a^5} N^{\gamma}}$

$$= \left(a^{\alpha}\right)^{-\frac{\beta\gamma}{5}\log_a N} = \left(a^{-\frac{\alpha\beta\gamma}{5}}\right)^{\log_a N}$$

$$= \left(a^{\log_a N}\right)^{\frac{-\alpha\beta\gamma}{5}} = N^{\frac{-\alpha\beta\gamma}{5}}$$

2. The value of $\log_{1/3} \sqrt[4]{\sqrt{729 . \sqrt[3]{9^{-1} 27^{-4/3}}}}$ is equal to

(a) 4 (b) 1/4

(c) –1/4 (d) None of these

Sol. (c) The expression $= \log_{1/3} \sqrt[4]{\sqrt{729 . \sqrt[3]{9^{-1} 27^{-4/3}}}}$

$$= \log_{1/3}\left(\sqrt[4]{\sqrt{\sqrt{729}\sqrt[3]{9^{-1}(27)^{-4/3}}}}\right)$$

$$= \log_{1/3}\left(3^{6/8}\left(3^{-2}.3^{-4}\right)^{1/12}\right)$$

$$= \log_{1/3}\left(3^{6/8-1/2}\right) = \log_{(3^{-1})} 3^{2/8} = \frac{1/4}{-1}\log_3 3 = -\frac{1}{4}$$

3. Complete set of solution of the inequality $(\log_x 2)(\log_{2x} 2)(\log_2 4x) > 1$ is given as

(a) 4 (b) 1/4

(c) –1/4 (d) None of these

Sol. (c) Consider the inequality $\log_x 2 \log_{2x} 2 \log_2 4x > 1$ clearly, $x > 0$ and $x \neq 1, \neq 1/2$

$$\Rightarrow \frac{\log_2(4x)}{(\log_2 x)(\log_2 2x)} > 1; \text{ put } \log_2 x = y$$

$$\Rightarrow \frac{2+y}{y(y+1)} - 1 > 0 \quad \Rightarrow \frac{y+2-y^2-y}{y(y+1)} > 0$$

$$\Rightarrow \frac{y^2-2}{y(y+1)} < 0 \Rightarrow \left(y-\sqrt{2}\right)\left(y+\sqrt{2}\right)y(y+1) < 0$$

Applying Wavy Curve Method

+ − + − +
$-\sqrt{2}$ -1 0 $\sqrt{2}$

$$\Rightarrow y \in \left(-\sqrt{2}, -1\right) \cup \left(0, \sqrt{2}\right)$$

$$\Rightarrow -\sqrt{2} < \log_2 x < -1 \text{ or } 0 < \log_2 x < \sqrt{2}$$

$$\Rightarrow 2^{-\sqrt{2}} < x < \frac{1}{2} \text{ or } 1 < x < 2^{\sqrt{2}}$$

$$\Rightarrow x \in \left(\frac{1}{2^{\sqrt{2}}}, \frac{1}{2}\right) \cup \left(1, 2^{\sqrt{2}}\right)$$

4. If $\dfrac{\left(\log_{1/x}\sqrt{x^2-4}\right)^2 . \log_x \sqrt{x^2-4}}{\log_{x^2}\sqrt{x^2-4} . \log_{\sqrt[3]{x}} \sqrt[6]{x^2-4}} = 1$, then the value of x satisfying the equation is

(a) $\dfrac{\sqrt{17}+1}{2}$ (b) $\dfrac{\sqrt{17}-1}{2}$

(c) $\dfrac{1-\sqrt{17}}{2}$ (d) None of these

Sol. (a) Given equation is

$$\frac{\left(\log_{1/x}\sqrt{x^2-4}\right)^2 . \log_x \sqrt{x^2-4}}{\log_{x^2}\sqrt{x^2-4} . \log_{\sqrt[3]{x}} \sqrt[6]{x^2-4}} = 1$$

Domain of the expression on LHS is $x \in (2, \infty) \sim \{\sqrt{5}\}$

$$\Rightarrow \frac{\left(\log_{1/x}\sqrt{x^2-4}\right)^2 . \log_x \sqrt{x^2-4}}{\frac{1}{2}\log_{|x|}\sqrt{x^2-4} . \frac{3}{3}\log_x \sqrt{x^2-4}} = 1$$

(using property $\log_{a^{\alpha}} x = \alpha \log_{|a|} x$)

$$\Rightarrow \log_x \sqrt{x^2-4} = \frac{1}{2} \quad \Rightarrow \sqrt{x^2-4} = \sqrt{x}$$

$$\Rightarrow x^2 - x - 4 = 0 \qquad \Rightarrow x = \frac{1 \pm \sqrt{17}}{2}$$

but x can't be negative so rejecting the negative value of x.

$$\Rightarrow x = \frac{\sqrt{17}+1}{2}$$

5. The value of expression

$y.x^{\frac{2}{\log_y x}+1} + 2x^{\log_x y+1}.y^{\log_y x+1} + x.y^{\frac{2}{\log_x y}+1}$ is given by

(a) $x^2y\,(x+y)^2$ (b) $xy\,(x-y)^2$

(c) $xy\,(x+y)^2$ (d) None of these

Sol. (c) Given expression is

$$x.y.x^{\frac{2}{\log_y x}}+2x^{\log_x y}.x.y.y^{\log_y x}+x.y.y^{\frac{2}{\log_x y}}$$

$$=xy\left(x^{\log_x y}\right)^2+2(xy)^2+xy(x)^2$$

$$=xy\left(y^2+2xy+x^2\right)=xy(y+x)^2$$

6. The number of solution of the equation $\log_x 3.\ \log_{x/3} 3 + \log_{x/81} 3 = 0$ is given by

(a) $x = 8, 2/8$ (b) $x = 5, 1/9$

(c) $x = 9, 1/9$ (d) None of these

Sol. (c) Let $\log_3 x = y$; substituting in the equation gives $\frac{1}{\log_3 x}.\frac{1}{\log_3 x-1}+\frac{1}{\log_3\left(\frac{x}{81}\right)}=0$

$$\Rightarrow \frac{1}{y(y-1)}+\frac{1}{(y-4)}=0 \Rightarrow y^2-y+y-4=0$$

$$\Rightarrow y=2,-2 \qquad \Rightarrow \log_3 x=2,\ \log_3 x=-2$$

$$\Rightarrow x=9 \text{ or } \frac{1}{9}.$$

7. The number of solution of the equation $9^{1+\log x} - 3^{1+\log x} - 210 = 0$; (where base of log is 3) is

(a) 1 (b) 5

(c) 4 (d) None of these

Sol. (b) $9^{1+\log x} - 3^{1+\log x} - 210 = 0$

$\Rightarrow 9\left(3^{\log x}\right)^2-3\left(3^{\log x}\right)-210=0$; Let $3^{\log_3 x}=z$

$\Rightarrow 9z^2 - 3z - 210 = 0 \quad \Rightarrow 3z^2 - z - 70 = 0$

$\Rightarrow (z - 5)(3z + 14) = 0 \Rightarrow z = 5$ or $\frac{-14}{3}$

But z can't be negative, as $z = 3^{\log x} > 0$. So $z = 5$ is only solution i.e., $3^{\log x} = 5$

$\Rightarrow \log_3 x = \log_3 5 \Rightarrow \quad x = 5$

8. The number of solution of the equation $\log(\log x) + \log(\log x^3 - 2) = 0$; (where base of log is 10 everywhere.) is given as

(a) 10 (b) 12

(c) 11 (d) None of these

Sol. (a) Substituting $\log_{10} x = z$ in the equation, the equation reduces to $\log_{10} z + \log_{10}(3z - 2) = 0$ notice that $z > 2/3$

$\Rightarrow \log(3z^2 - 2z) = 0 \quad \Rightarrow 3z^2 - 2z = 1$

$\Rightarrow 3z^2 - 2z - 1 = 0 \quad \Rightarrow 3z^2 - 3z + z - 1 = 0$

$\Rightarrow (3z + 1)(z - 1)$

$\Rightarrow z = 1$ or $-1/3$ $\left(z=-\frac{1}{3} \text{ is rejected}\right)$

$\Rightarrow \log_{10} x = 1 \qquad \Rightarrow x = 10$ is only solution.

9. The number of solution of the equation $5^{\log x} + 5x^{\log 5} = 3 (a > 0)$; (base of log = a) is given as

(a) $x=a^{\log_5 2}$ (b) $x=-a^{\log_4 1}$

(c) $x=a^{-\log_5 2}$ (d) none

Sol. (c) Given $5^{\log_a x}+5.x^{\log_a 5}=3$; $a>0$

Applying the property $a^{\log_x b}=b^{\log_x a}$, we get

$\Rightarrow 5^{\log_a x}+5\left(5^{\log_a x}\right)=3 \quad \Rightarrow 5^{\log_a x}=\frac{3}{6}=\frac{1}{2}$

Taking log on both sides to the base 5, we have

$(\log_a x)\log_5 5 = -\log_5 2 \quad \Rightarrow \log_a x = -\log_5 2$

$\Rightarrow x=a^{-\log_5 2}$

10. The inequality $\sqrt{x^{\log_2 \sqrt{x}}}\ge 2$ is satisfied by

(a) only one value of x (b) $x\in\left(0,\frac{1}{4}\right]$

(c) $x > 1/4$ (d) $1 < x < 2$

Sol. (b) LHS > 0

Squaring we get, $x^{\log_2\sqrt{x}}\ge 4$

Clearly, $x > 0$ for log to be defined.

Case I: $x \in (0, 1)$

Taking $\log_{10}$ on both sides, we get

$\log_2\sqrt{x}\times\log_{10}x\ge\log_{10}4$

$\Rightarrow (\log_{10}x)^2\ge(\log_{10}4)^2$; But $\log x < 0$

$\Rightarrow \log_{10} x \le -\log_{10} 4 \quad \Rightarrow x \le 1/4$

$\Rightarrow x \in (0, 1/4]$

Case II $x \in [1, \infty)$

taking $\log_{10}$ on both sides; we get

$\Rightarrow \log_2\sqrt{x}\times\log_{10}x\ge\log_{10}4$

$\Rightarrow (\log_{10}x)^2 \ge (\log_{10} 4)^2 \because \log_{10}x \ge 0$

$\Rightarrow \log_{10}x \ge \log_{10}4 \quad \Rightarrow x \ge 4$

$\Rightarrow x \in (0, 1/4] \cup [4, \infty)$

So option (b) is correct.

11. Find the solution of the inequality:

$$\left(2(\log_3 x)^2-3\log_3 x-8\right)\left(2(\log_3 x)^2-3\log_3 x-6\right)\ge 3$$

(a) $\left(0,\frac{1}{\sqrt{27}}\right]\cup\left[\frac{1}{3},\sqrt{243}\right]\cup[27,\infty)$

(b) $\left(0,\frac{1}{27}\right]\cup\left[\frac{1}{3},\sqrt{243}\right]\cup[27,\infty)$

(c) $\left(0,\frac{1}{\sqrt{21}}\right]\cup\left[\frac{1}{3},\sqrt{142}\right]\cup[21,\infty)$

(d) None of these

Sol. (a) Put $\log_3 x = y$ and $2y^2 - 3y = z$

$\Rightarrow (z-8)(z-6) \geq 3$

$\Rightarrow (z-9)(z-5) \geq 0$

$\Rightarrow z \in (-\infty, 5] \cup [9, \infty)$

Case I: $z \in (-\infty, 5]$

$\Rightarrow 2y^2 - 3y \leq 5 \quad \Rightarrow (2y-5)(y+1) \leq 0$

$\Rightarrow y \geq -1$ and $y \leq 5/2$

$\Rightarrow \log_3 x \geq -1$ and $\log_3 x \leq 5/2$

$\Rightarrow x \geq 1/3$ and $x \leq 9\sqrt{3}$ (i)

Case II: $z \in [9, \infty)$

$\Rightarrow 2y^2 - 3y \geq 9 \quad \Rightarrow (2y \mid 3)(y-3) \geq 0$

$\Rightarrow y \leq -3/2$ and $y \geq 3$

$\Rightarrow \log_3 x \leq -3/2$ and $\log_3 x \geq 3$

$\Rightarrow x \leq \dfrac{1}{\sqrt{27}}$ or $x \geq 27$ (ii)

taking the union of (i) and (ii); we get

$$x \in \left(0, \frac{1}{\sqrt{27}}\right] \cup \left[\frac{1}{3}, 9\sqrt{3}\right] \cup [27, \infty)$$

12. The solution set of the equation, $(x+1)(\log_3 x)^2 + 4x \log_3 x - 16 = 0$ is

(a) an empty set

(b) a singleton

(c) a set consisting of exactly two elements

(d) a set consisting of more than two elements.

Sol.(c) $(x+1)(\log_3 x)^2 + 4x \log_3 x - 16 = 0$

$\Rightarrow$ x $(\log_3 x)^2 + 4x \log_3 x + (\log_3 x)^2 - 16 = 0$

$\Rightarrow$ (x $\log_3 x + \log_3 x - 4)(\log_3 x + 4) = 0$

either $\log_3 x + 4 = 0 \Rightarrow x = 1/81$ is one of the solution or $x\log_3 x + \log_3 x - 4 = 0$

Now $y = x \log_3 x + \log_3 x - 4$ is an increasing function and it will have atmost one solution. And $x = 3$ is a solution to this equation

$\therefore$ The solution set of the given equation is a set contianing exactly two element {3, 1/81}.

13. Find out the values of 'a' for which any solution of the inequality, $\dfrac{\log_3(x^2-3x+7)}{\log_3(3x+2)} < 1$ is also a solution of the inequality, $x^2 + (5-2a)x \leq 10a$

(a) $a \leq 3/2$ (b) $a \geq 1/3$

(c) $a \geq 5/2$ (d) None of these

Sol. (c) $x^2 - 3x + 7 > 0$ is satisfied $\forall x \in \mathbb{R}$

$3x + 2 > 0 \quad \Rightarrow x > -2/3$

Case I: when $\log_3(3x+2) < 0 \Rightarrow 3x + 2 < 1$

$\Rightarrow x < -1/3$

$\Rightarrow \log_3(x^2 - 3x + 7) > \log_3(3x+2)$

$\Rightarrow x^2 - 3x + 7 > 3x + 2$

$\Rightarrow x^2 - 6x + 5 > 0$

$\Rightarrow (x-1)(x-5) > 0 \Rightarrow x \in (-\infty, 1) \cup (5, \infty)$

$\Rightarrow$ x $\in (-2/3, -1/3)$

Case II: when $\log_3(3x+2) > 0 \Rightarrow 3x + 2 > 1$

$\Rightarrow x > -1/3$

$\Rightarrow \log_3(x^2 - 3x + 7) < \log_3(3x+2)$

$\Rightarrow x^2 - 3x + 7 < 3x + 2$

$\Rightarrow (x-1)(x-5) < 0 \quad \Rightarrow x \in (1, 5)$

Now $x^2 + 5x - 2ax \leq 10a$

$\Rightarrow x^2 + 5x - (10 + 2x)a \leq 0$

For $x \in \left(-\dfrac{2}{3}, -\dfrac{1}{3}\right) \cup (1,5)$; $10 + 2x > 0$

$\Rightarrow a \geq \dfrac{x^2+5x}{10+2x} = \dfrac{x(x+5)}{2(5+x)} \Rightarrow a \geq \dfrac{x}{2}$

$\Rightarrow a \geq \dfrac{5}{2}$ ($\because$ maximum value that x can have is 5)

14. The number of solution of the equation, $\log(-2x) = 2\log(x+1)$ is

(a) zero (b) 1

(c) 2 (d) none of these

Sol. (b) $\log(-2x) = 2\log(x+1)$

$\Rightarrow x < 0$ and $x + 1 > 0 \Rightarrow x > -1$

$\Rightarrow x \in (-1, 0)$

Now $-2x = (x+1)^2$ (by taking antilog on both sides)

$\Rightarrow -2x = x^2 + 1 + 2x$

$\Rightarrow x^2 + 4x + 1 = 0 \quad \Rightarrow x = \dfrac{-4 \pm \sqrt{12}}{2}$

$\Rightarrow x = -2 \pm \sqrt{3}$

Clearly $x = -2 - \sqrt{3} \notin (-1, 0) \quad \therefore$ rejected

but $x = -2 + \sqrt{3} \notin (-1, 0) \quad \therefore$ accepted

Therefore the above equation has only one root.

Linked Comprehension type

Part 'A' For $\log_x y > 0$, the necessary and sufficient conditions are

(i) $x > 1$ and $y > 1$

or

(ii) $0 < x < 1$ and $0 < y < 1$

Part 'B' For $\log_x y < 0$, the necessary and sufficient conditions are

(i) $x > 1$ and $0 < y < 1$

or

(ii) $0 < x < 1$ and $y > 1$

15. Which of the following comes under the Part 'A'?

(a) $\log_2 t < 0; \dfrac{1}{2} < t < 0.8$

(b) $\log_t 0.6 < 0; 1 < t < 5$

(c) $\log_3 t > 0$; $1 < t < 2$

(d) $\log_t 7 < 0$; $\frac{1}{4} < t < \frac{1}{2}$

16. Which of the following comes under the part 'B'?

(a) $\ln \pi > 0$

(b) $\log_\pi e > 0$

(c) $\log_t \sqrt{2} < 0$; $0 < t < 1$

(d) $\log_a 0.2 > 0$; $0 < a < 1$

17. Let $y = \log_3 2.\log_4 3........ \log_{10} 9.\log_{11} 10.\log_{12} 11$; then

(a) y will be less than 1

(b) $y = \log_{12} 2$

(c) $y > 2$

(d) y lies between 1 and 2

18. The set of real values of x satisfying $\log_{1/2}(x^2 - 6x + 6) > 0$ is

(a) $(-\infty, 3-\sqrt{3})$ (b) $(1, 3-\sqrt{3}) \cup (3+\sqrt{3}, 5)$

(c) $(1, 3-\sqrt{3})$ (d) None of these

Solution 15. From part (c) $\log_3 t > 0$ for $1 < t < 2$

It comes under part(A) as base = 3 and t lies on same side of 1 i.e., greater than 1

16. From part (c), $\log_t \sqrt{2} < 0$ for $0 < t < 1$

It comes under part (B) as t and $\sqrt{2}$ lie on opposite side of 1 i.e., $t < 1$ and $\sqrt{2} > 1$

17. $y = \log_3 2 \log_4 3 ..... \log_{10} 9 \log_{11} 10. \log_{12} 11$

$= \log_{12} 2 > 0$ [as 12, 2 >1]

Now for $a > 1$; $\log_a x$ is an increasing function

$\Rightarrow \log_{12} 2 < \log_{12} 12 = 1$

$\therefore \log_{12} 2 \in (0, 1) \Rightarrow y \in (0, 1) \Rightarrow$ options (a) and (b) are correct

18. $\log_{1/2}(x^2 - 6x + 6) > 0$

$\because$ of part (A); $x^2 - 6x + 6 \in (0, 1)$

$\Rightarrow 0 < x^2 - 6x + 6 < 1 \Rightarrow x^2 - 6x + 5 < 0$ (i)

and $x^2 - 6x + 6 > 0$ (ii)

For sol. of inequality (i): $(x - 1)(x - 5) < 0$

$\Rightarrow x \in (1, 5)$ (iii)

For sol. of inequality

(ii) $x \in (-\infty, 3-\sqrt{3}) \cup (3+\sqrt{3}, \infty)$ (iv)

$\therefore$ Sol. of given inequation will be intersection of (iii) and (iv)

i.e., $(1, 3-\sqrt{3}) \cup (3+\sqrt{3}, 5)$

$\therefore$ **(b) and (c) are correct options**

Assertion and Reason type

19. A: If $\ln(x + z)$, $\ln(x - z)$ and $\ln(x - 2y + z)$ are in A.P., then x, y, z are in H.P

R: $\ln k + \ln p = \ln(kp)$ for $k, p > 0$ and $2b = a + c$ if a, b, c are in A.P

Sol: $\because \ln(x + z)$, $\ln(x - z)$, $\ln(x - 2y + z)$ are in A.P

$\Rightarrow 2\ln(x - z) = \ln(x + z) + \ln(x - 2y + z)$

$\Rightarrow \ln(x - z)^2 = \ln(x + z)(x - 2y + z) \Rightarrow (x - z)^2 = (x + z)(x + z - 2y)$

$\Rightarrow x^2 + z^2 - 2xz = x^2 + z^2 + 2xz - 2xy - 2yz$

$\Rightarrow 4xz = 2xy + 2yz \Rightarrow 2xz = xy + yz$

$\Rightarrow y = \frac{2xz}{x+z} \Rightarrow x, y, z$ are in H.P

$\Rightarrow$ Assertion is correct

$\therefore$ Clearly, the reason is correct and well defining the assertion.

$\therefore$ **Ans (a)**

20. A: If p, q satisfy the equation $x^{\sqrt{x}} = (\sqrt{x})^x$, then $\log_q p$ defined $\Rightarrow \log_p q$ is not defined

R: Base of a logarithmic function is always positive

Sol: $x^{\sqrt{x}} = (\sqrt{x})^x$ (i)

Clearly, $x = 1$ satisfy the given equation (1)

Let $x \neq 1$ and $x > 0$(as for $x \leq 0$; L.H.S and R.H.S. are not defined)

$\Rightarrow x^{\sqrt{x}} = (x^{1/2})^x \Rightarrow x^{\sqrt{x}} = (x)^{x/2} \Rightarrow \sqrt{x} = x/2 \Rightarrow x = x^2/4$

$\Rightarrow x^2 - 4x = 0 \Rightarrow x(x - 4) = 0 \Rightarrow x = 4$ ($\because x \neq 0$)

$\therefore x = 1$, or $x = 4$ $\therefore p, q \in \{1, 4\}$

$\Rightarrow p, q$ are relatively prime and if $\log_4 1$ is defined then $\log_1 4$ is not defined

$\therefore$ Assertion is correct. Also reason is correct, but not a proper reason for assertion.

$\therefore$ **Ans (b)**

Column Matching

21. Column I

(A) If x_1 and x_2 satisfy the equation $x^{\log_{10} x} = 100x$, then the value of x_1x_2 equals

(B) Sum of the squares of the roots of equation $\log_2(9 - 2^x) = 3 - x$ is

(C) If $\log_{1/8}(\log_{1/4}(\log_{1/2} x)) = 1/3$, then x is

(D) If $\log_b a = 3$, $\log_b c = -4$ and if the value of x satisfying the equation $a^{3x} = c^{x-1}$ is expressed in the form p/q, where p and q are relatively prime, then $p + q$ is

Column II

(P) irrational

(Q) rational

(R) prime

(S) Composite

Ans. (A) → Q, S (B) → Q, S (C) → P (D) → Q, R

Sol. (A) $x^{\log_{10} x} = 100x$

$\Rightarrow \log_{10}(x^{\log_{10} x}) = \log_{10}(100x) \Rightarrow (\log_{10}x)^2 = 2 + \log_{10}x$

$\Rightarrow (\log_{10}x)^2 - (\log_{10}x) - 2 = 0 \Rightarrow [\log_{10}x - 2][\log_{10}x + 1] = 0$

$\Rightarrow \log_{10}x = 2$ or $\log_{10}x = -1 \Rightarrow x = 100$ or $x = 1/10$

$\therefore\ x_1.x_2 = (100)\left(\frac{1}{10}\right) = 10$ which is rational and composite $\Rightarrow$ **A → Q, S**

(B) Given equation is $\log_2(9 - 2^x) = 3 - x$

$\Rightarrow 9 - 2^x = (2)^{3-x} \qquad \Rightarrow 9 - 2^x = \frac{8}{2^x}$

$\Rightarrow 9.(2^x) - (2^x)^2 = 8 \Rightarrow (2^x)^2 - 9(2^x) + 8 = 0$

$\Rightarrow (2^x - 1)(2^x - 8) = 0 \Rightarrow 2^x = 1;\ 2^x = 8$

$\Rightarrow x = 0;\ x = 3$

$\therefore$ Sum of square of roots = 9 which is rational as well as composite.

$\Rightarrow$ **B → Q, S**

(C) $\log_{1/8}(\log_{1/4}(\log_{1/2}x)) = 1/3$

$\Rightarrow \log_{1/4}[\log_{1/2}x] = (1/8)^{1/3} \Rightarrow \log_{1/4}[\log_{1/2}x] = 1/2$

$\Rightarrow \log_{1/2}x = (1/4)^{1/2} \Rightarrow \log_{1/2}x = 1/2$

$\Rightarrow x = (1/2)^{1/2} = 1/\sqrt{2}$ which is an irrational number.

$\Rightarrow$ **(C) → P**

(D) $\log_b a = 3,\ \log_b c = -4$

$\Rightarrow a = b^3;\ c = b^{-4}$; Given equation is $a^{3x} = c^{x-1}$

$\Rightarrow (b^3)^{3x} = (b^{-4})^{x-1} \Rightarrow b^{9x} = b^{-4x+4}$

$\Rightarrow 9x = -4x + 4 \Rightarrow x = 4/13 = p/q$

$\Rightarrow p = 4,\ q = 13$

$\therefore\ p + q = 17$ which is rational and prime

$\Rightarrow$ **(D) → Q, R**

SECTION–II

SUBJECTIVE-TYPE SOLVED EXAMPLES

1. Prove that $(zx)^{\log\frac{z}{x}}(xy)^{\log\frac{x}{y}}(zy)^{\log\frac{y}{z}} = 1$

Sol. Let $A = (zx)^{\log\frac{z}{x}}(xy)^{\log\frac{x}{y}}(zy)^{\log\frac{y}{z}}$

Then $\log A = \log(zx)^{\log\frac{z}{x}} + \log(xy)^{\log\frac{x}{y}} + \log(zy)^{\log\frac{y}{z}}$

$\Rightarrow \log A = \log\frac{y}{z}\log(yz) + \log\frac{z}{x}\log(zx) + \log\frac{x}{y}.\log(xy)$

$= (\log y - \log z)(\log y + \log z) + (\log z - \log x)(\log z + \log x) + (\log x - \log y)(\log x + \log y)$

$= (\log y)^2 - (\log z)^2 + (\log z)^2 - (\log x)^2 + (\log x)^2 - (\log y)^2 = 0$

$\therefore\ \log A = 0$; so $A = 1$ i.e., L.H.S. = R. H. S.

2. Solve the following:

(a) $2^{\log_3 5} - 5^{\log_3 2}$

(b) $\log_{10}\tan 1° + \log_{10}\tan 2° + \ldots + \log_{10}\tan 89°$

Sol. (a) $2^{\log_3 5} = 2^{\log_2 5 \log_3 2} = \left(2^{\log_2 5}\right)^{\log_3 2} = 5^{\log_3 2}$

$\therefore\ 2^{\log_3 5} - 5^{\log_3 2} = 5^{\log_3 2} - 5^{\log_3 2} = 0$

(b) $\log_{10}\tan 1° + \log_{10}\tan 2° + \ldots + \log_{10}\tan 89°$

$= \log_{10}(\tan 1° \tan 2° \ldots \tan 44° \tan 45° \tan 46° \ldots \tan 89°)$

$= \log_{10}[(\tan 1° \tan 89°)(\tan 2° \tan 88°) \ldots (\tan 44° \tan 46°) \tan 45°]$

$= \log_{10}[(\tan 1° \cot 1°)(\tan 2° \cot 2°) \ldots (\tan 44° \cot 44°) \tan 45°] = \log_{10} 1 = 0$

3. If $\frac{\log x}{y-z} = \frac{\log y}{z-x} = \frac{\log z}{x-y}$, prove that $x^{y+z}y^{z+x}z^{x+y} = 1$ also prove that $x^{y+z} + y^{z+x} + z^{x+y} \geq 3$

Sol. For $\log x, \log y, \log z$ to be defined $x > 0, y > 0, z > 0$

Now $\frac{\log x}{y-z} = \frac{\log y}{z-x} = \frac{\log z}{x-y} = k$ (say)

$\Rightarrow x = 10^{k(y-z)},\ y = 10^{k(z-x)},\ z = 10^{k(x-y)}$

$\Rightarrow (x)^{y+z}(y)^{z+x}(z)^{x+y} = 10^{k(y^2-z^2+z^2-x^2+x^2-y^2)} = 10^0 = 1$

i.e., $x^{y+z}y^{z+x}z^{x+y} = 1$ (i)

Again take the positive number x^{y+z}, y^{z+x} and z^{x+y}

$\therefore$ A.M $\geq$ G.M

$\Rightarrow \frac{x^{y+z} + y^{z+x} + z^{x+y}}{3} \geq \sqrt[3]{x^{y+z}y^{z+x}z^{x+y}} = 1$

$\therefore\ x^{y+z} + y^{z+x} + z^{x+y} \geq 3$ hence proved.

4. Solve the equation $\log_{x^2+6x+8}\log_{2x^2+2x+3}(x^2 - 2x) = 0$

Sol. Base of logarithm $> 0, \neq 1$

$\therefore\ x^2 + 6x + 8$ and $2x^2 + 2x + 3 > 0$

$\therefore\ (x + 4)(x + 2) > 0$ and $(x + 1/2)^2 + 5/4 > 0$

$\Rightarrow x \in (-\infty, -4) \cup (-2, \infty)$ (i)

and $x^2 - 2x > 0$, then $x(x - 2) > 0$

$\therefore\ x \in (-\infty, 0) \cup (2, \infty)$ (ii)

Then the given equation reduced in the form

$\log_{2x^2+2x+3}(x^2 - 2x) = (x^2 + 6x + 8)^0$

$\Rightarrow \log_{2x^2+2x+3}(x^2-2x) = 1$

$\Rightarrow x^2 - 2x = (2x^2 + 2x + 3)^1 \Rightarrow x^2 + 4x + 3 = 0$

$\therefore$ $x = -1, -3$

$x = -3$ is not satisfying (i)

$\therefore$ $x = -3$ is not a solution of the given equation

But $x = -1$ is satisfying both conditions (i) and (ii)

$\therefore$ $x = -1$ is the only solution of the given equation.

5. How many positive integers have characteristic 2 when base is 3?

Sol. Here, we use the result that the number of positive integers having base a and characteristic n is $a^{n+1} - a^n$. In this problem $a = 3$ and $n = 2$.

$\therefore$ number of positive integers having base 3 and characteristic $2 = 3^{2+1} - 3^2 = 18$

6. If n is a natural number such that $n = p_1^{a_1}.p_2^{a_2}.p_3^{a_3}.....p_k^{a_k}$ and $p_1, p_2, p_3,..., p_k$ are distinct primes, then show that $\log n \geq k \log 2$.

Sol. Since n is a natural number and $p_1, p_2, p_3 ...p_k$ are prime numbers, therefore $a_1, a_2, a_3, ...,a_k$ are also natural numbers.

Now, $\because n = p_1^{a_1}.p_2^{a_2}.p_3^{a_3}.....p_k^{a_k}$

$\therefore$ $\log n = a_1 \log p_1 + a_2 \log p_2 + ... + a_k \log p_k \geq a_1 \log 2 + a_2 \log 2 + ... + a_k \log 2$

[$\because$ smallest (+) ve prime number is 2]

$\geq \log 2 + \log 2 + \log 2 + ...$ up to to k terms

[$\because a_1 \geq 1, a_2 \geq 1, a_3 \geq 1......., a_k \geq 1] \geq k \log 2$

7. Prove that $\log_4 18$ is an irrational number.

Sol. $\text{Log}_4 18 = \log_4 (3^2 \times 2) = 2 \log_4 3 + \log_4 2 = 1/2 + \log_2 3$

It is sufficient to prove that $\log_2 3$ is an irrational number. Suppose if possible that $\log_2 3$ is a rational number. Let $\log_2 3 = p/q$ where p and q are integers

$\Rightarrow 2^{p/q} = 3 \Rightarrow 2^p = 3^q$

Since $\log_2 3 > 0$

$\therefore$ p and q may be regarded as positive integers. Clearly, 2^p is an even number where as 3^q is an odd number. Hence $2^p = 3^q$ is never satisfied.

Hence our supposition that $\log_2 3$ is a rational number is wrong

$\Rightarrow \log_2 3$ is an irrational number

$\Rightarrow 1/2 + \log_2 3$ is an irrational number.

$\Rightarrow \log_4 18$ is an irrational number.

8. Solve the inequality $\log_{10}(x^2 - 16) \leq \log_{10}(4x - 11)$

Sol. $\log_{10}(x^2 - 16) \leq \log_{10}(4x - 11)$

$\Rightarrow x^2 - 16 \leq 4x - 11 \quad \Rightarrow x^2 - 4x - 5 \leq 0$

$\Rightarrow -1 \leq x \leq 5$ (i)

Also $\log_{10}(x^2 - 16)$ is defined if and only if $x^2 - 16 > 0$

Now $x^2 - 16 > 0 \quad \Rightarrow x < -4$ or $x > 4$ (ii)

Again for $\log_{10}(4x - 11)$ to be defined $4x - 11 > 0$

$\Rightarrow x > 11/4$ (iii)

(i), (ii) and (iii) will simultaneously hold if $4 < x \leq 5$

$\therefore$ solution set = (4, 5]

9. Prove that from the equalities $\dfrac{x(y+z-x)}{\log x} = \dfrac{y(z+x-y)}{\log y} = \dfrac{z(x+y-z)}{\log z}$ follows $x^y y^x = y^z z^y = z^x x^z$.

Sol. Put $\dfrac{x(y+z-x)}{\log x} = \dfrac{1}{t}$

$\Rightarrow \log x = tx(y+z-x) \Rightarrow y \log x = txy(y+z-x)$

Similarly, $x. \log y = tyx(z+x-y)$

$\Rightarrow y \log x + x \log y = txy(2z) = 2xyzt$

$\Rightarrow \log x^y. y^x = 2xyzt$

Similarly, for others.

10. Solve the inequality; $\dfrac{(x-0.5)(3-x)}{\log_2|x-1|} > 0$

Sol. Let $x > 1$ and $x \neq 2$

$\Rightarrow \dfrac{(x-1/2)(3-x)}{\log_2(x-1)} > 0$

Case I: For $1 < x < 2$, $\log_2(x-1)$ is negative (number and base on different sides of unity)

$\Rightarrow \left(x - \dfrac{1}{2}\right)(3-x) < 0 \quad \Rightarrow$ No solution

Case II: For $x > 2$, $\log_2(x-1)$ is positive

$\Rightarrow \left(x - \dfrac{1}{2}\right)(3-x) > 0 \Rightarrow x \in (1/2, 3) \Rightarrow x \in (2, 3)$

Again let $x < 1, x \neq 0$ we have $\dfrac{(x-1/2)(3-x)}{\log_2(1-x)} > 0$

Case I: for $0 < x < 1$, $\log_2(1-x)$ is negative

$\Rightarrow \left(x - \dfrac{1}{2}\right)(3-x) < 0 \quad \Rightarrow x \in \left(0, \dfrac{1}{2}\right)$

Case II: for $x < 0$, $\log_2(1-x)$ is positive

$\Rightarrow \left(x - \dfrac{1}{2}\right)(3-x) > 0 \quad \Rightarrow$ No solution.

Hence final solution is $\left(0, \dfrac{1}{2}\right) \cup (2,3)$

11. Solve the inequation $(x^2 + x + 1)^x < 1$.

Sol. Taking logarithm both sides with base 10, then $x \log(x^2 + x + 1) < 0$ which is equivalent to the collection of systems

$\Rightarrow \begin{cases} x>0, & \log(x^2+x+1)<0 \\ x<0, & \log(x^2+x+1)>0 \end{cases}$ or

$\Leftrightarrow \begin{cases} x>0, & x^2+x+1<1 \\ x<0, & x^2+x+1>1 \end{cases}$ or

$\Leftrightarrow \begin{cases} x>0, & x(x+1)<0 \\ x<0, & x(x+1)>0 \end{cases}$ or

$\Leftrightarrow \left[\begin{cases} x>0, & -1<x<0 \\ x<0, & x>0 \text{ or } x<-1 \end{cases}\right.$

$\Leftrightarrow \begin{cases} x\in\phi \\ x<-1 \end{cases}$ or

Consequently, the interval $x \in (-\infty, -1)$ is the set of all solutions of the original inequation.

12. Solve the inequation $3^{72}\left(\frac{1}{3}\right)^x\left(\frac{1}{3}\right)^{\sqrt{x}}>1$

Sol. The given inequation is valid only when $x \geq 0$ (i)

The given inequation can be written in the form

$\Rightarrow 3^{72-x-\sqrt{x}}>1 \quad \Rightarrow 72-x-\sqrt{x}>0 \; (\because 3>1)$

$\Rightarrow x+\sqrt{x}-72<0 \quad \Rightarrow (\sqrt{x}+9)(\sqrt{x}-8)<0$

But $(\sqrt{x}+9)>0$ for all $x \geq 0$

$\therefore (\sqrt{x}-8)<0 \quad \Rightarrow \sqrt{x}<8$

$\therefore 0 \leq x < 64$ from (i)

Thus the interval $x \in [0, 64]$ is the set of all solutions of the given inequation.

13. Solve the system of inequations $\begin{cases} \log_{(2-x)}(2-y)>0 \\ \log_{(4-y)}(2x-2)>0 \end{cases}$.

Sol. If the numbers x and y satisfy this system, then they also satisfy the conditions $2-x>0$, $2-x \neq 1$, $2x-2>0$, $4-y>0$, $4-y \neq 1$, $2-y>0$

i.e., $x \in (1, 2)$ and $y \in (-\infty, 2)$

For the bases of the logarithms of the initial system we have $0<2-x<1$; $0<2-y<1$ (but $y<2$)

$\Leftrightarrow 1<x<2$, $2<4-y<3$. Thus the original system is equivalent to the system

$\Leftrightarrow \begin{cases} 1<x<2 \\ y<2 \\ 2<4-y<3 \\ 2x-2>1 \end{cases} \Leftrightarrow \begin{cases} 1<x<2 \\ y<2 \\ 1<y<2 \\ x>3/2 \end{cases} \Leftrightarrow \begin{cases} 3/2<x<2 \\ 1<y<2 \end{cases}$

Consequently, the set of all solutions of the original system is the set of pairs (x, y), when $x \in (3/2, 2)$ and $y \in (1, 2)$

14. Find the values of 'p' for which the inequality $\left(2-\log_2\left(\frac{p}{p+1}\right)\right) x^2 + 2x\left(1+\log_2\frac{p}{p+1}\right) - 2\left(1+\log_2\frac{p}{p+1}\right)>0$ is valid for all real x.

Sol. $(2-t)x^2+2(1+t)x-2(1+t)>0$

when $t = 2$, $6x-6>0$ which is not true $\forall x \in R$.

Let $t \neq 2$; $t<2$ (i)

and $4(1+t)^2+8(1+t)(2-t)<0$ (for given inequality to be valid)

$\Rightarrow (t-5)(t+1)>0$

$\Rightarrow t>5$ or $t<-1$ (ii)

From (i) and (ii); $t<-1$

$\Rightarrow \log_2\frac{p}{p+1}<-1 \quad \Rightarrow \frac{p}{p+1}<\frac{1}{2}$

$\Rightarrow \frac{p-1}{p+1}<0 \quad \Rightarrow -1<p<1$

but $\frac{p}{p+1}>0 \quad \Rightarrow p>0$ or $p<-1$.

Common solution is $p \in (0, 1)$

15. Determine all positive integers n for which 2^n+1 is divisible by 3.

Sol. 2^n+1 can be written as $(3-1)^n+1$

$= [3^n + (-1)^n + \text{a multiple of } 3] + 1$

$= (-1)^n + 1 + \text{a multiple of } 3$.

Therefore 2^n+1 is divisible by 3 if and only if $(-1)^n + 1$ divisible by 3.

If n is even $(-1)^n+1 = 2$ which is not divisible by 3

If n is odd $(-1)^n+1 = 0$ which is divisible by 3.

Therefore 2^n+1 is divisible by 3 if and only if n is odd.

16. Prove that the function $f(x) = 3\sin x - 4\cos x + 5$ is a bounded function and hence find its range.

Sol. $f(x) = 3\sin x - 4\cos x + 5$

We know that $a\sin x + b\cos x + c \in \left[c-\sqrt{a^2+b^2}, c+\sqrt{a^2+b^2}\right]$

$\therefore 3\sin x - 4\cos x + 5 \in \left[5-\sqrt{9+16}, 5+\sqrt{9+16}\right]$

$= [0, 10] \quad \Rightarrow f(x)$ is bounded function

with g.l.b $f_{min}(x) = 0$ and l.u.b $= f_{max}(x) = 0$

and range of $f(x) = [0, 10]$

17. Show that the function $f(x) = \frac{x-2}{\sqrt{x-4}}$ is bounded and hence find its l.u.b and g.l.b.

Sol. $f(x) = \frac{x-2}{\sqrt{x-4}}$

Domain of $f(x) = \mathbb{R} \sim \{x : x-4 \leq 0\} = \mathbb{R} \sim \{x : x \leq 4\}$

$= (4, \infty)$

Let $y = \dfrac{x-2}{\sqrt{x-4}}; x > 4$

Squaring: $y^2 = \dfrac{x^2+4-2x}{x-4} \Rightarrow xy^2 - 4y^2 = x^2 - 2x + 4$

$\Rightarrow x^2 - (y^2 + 2)\, x + 4y^2 + 4 = 0$

for $x \in \mathbb{R}$; $(y^2 + 2)^2 - 4\,(1)\,(4y^2 + 4) \geq 0$

$\Rightarrow y^4 + 4y^2 + 4 - 16y^2 - 16 \geq 0 \Rightarrow y^4 - 12y^2 - 12 \geq 0$

$\Rightarrow y^2 \leq 6 - 4\sqrt{3}$ or $\geq 6 + 4\sqrt{3}$

But $y^2 \geq 0$ and $6 - 4\sqrt{3} < 0 \Rightarrow y^2 \geq 6 + 4\sqrt{3}$

$\therefore\; y \leq -\sqrt{6+4\sqrt{3}}$ or $y \geq \sqrt{6+4\sqrt{3}}$

But $y = \dfrac{x-2}{\sqrt{x-4}} > 0$ for $x > 4$

$\therefore\; y \geq \sqrt{6+4\sqrt{3}}$

$\therefore\; [f(x)]_{\min} = \sqrt{6+4\sqrt{3}}$; but $[f(x)]_{\max} \to \infty$

$\therefore\; [f(x)]_{\min} = \text{g.}l.b = \sqrt{6+4\sqrt{3}}$

and $[f(x)]_{\max}$ and l.u.b does not exit

and Range of $f(x) = \left[\sqrt{6+4\sqrt{3}}, \infty\right)$

18. Find the g.l.b, l.u.b, of function $f(x) = \sqrt{x-2} + \sqrt{5-x}$ and hence find its range.

Domain of function $f(x) = [2, 5]$

Let $y = \sqrt{x-2} + \sqrt{5-x} \Rightarrow y - \sqrt{x-2} = \sqrt{5-x}$

Squaring, we get, $y^2 + (x - 2) - 2y\sqrt{x-2} = 5 - x$

$\Rightarrow y^2 + 2x - 7 = 2y\sqrt{x-2}$

Squaring again, $\left(y^2+2x-7\right)^2 = 4y^2(x-2)$

$\Rightarrow y^4 + 4x^2 + 49 + 4xy^2 - 28x - 4xy^2 + 8y^2 - 14y^2 = 0$

$\Rightarrow 4x^2 - 28x + (y^4 - 6y^2 + 49) = 0$ for $x \in \mathbb{R}$; $D \geq 0$

$\Rightarrow (-28)^2 - (4)(4)(y^4 - 6y^2 + 49) \geq 0$

$\Rightarrow 49 - (y^4 - 6y^2 + 49) \geq 0$

$\Rightarrow -y^4 + 6y^2 \geq 0 \;\Rightarrow y^4 - 6y^2 \leq 0$

$\Rightarrow y^2(y^2 - 6) \leq 0 \Rightarrow y^2 \in [0, 6]$

$\Rightarrow y \in \left[\sqrt{-6}, \sqrt{6}\right]$

But $y > 0 \Rightarrow y \in (0, \sqrt{6}]$

$\therefore\; [f(x)]_{\min}$ = does not exist

But g.l.b = 0 and $[f(x)]_{\max}$ = l.u.b = $\sqrt{6}$

$\therefore$ Range of $f(x) = (0, \sqrt{6}]$

19. Evaluate $(0.16)^{\log_{2.5}\left(\frac{1}{3}+\frac{1}{3^2}+\frac{1}{3^3}+.....\infty\right)}$

Sol. $(0.16)^{\log_{2.5}\left(\frac{1}{3}+\frac{1}{3^2}+\frac{1}{3^3}+.....\infty\right)}$

$= (0.16)^{\log_{2.5}\left[\frac{1/3}{1-1/3}\right]} = (0.16)^{\log_{2.5}\left[\frac{1}{2}\right]} = (0.16)^{\log_{5/2}\left(\frac{1}{2}\right)}$

$= (0.16)^{\log_{2/5}\left(\frac{1}{2}\right)^{-1}} = (0.16)^{\log_{0.4}(2)} = \left[(0.4)^2\right]^{\log_{0.4}(2)}$

$= (0.4)^{\log_{0.4}(2)^2} = 4$

20. If the solution of equation $a^{2x-3}\, b^{2x} = a^{6-x}\, b^{5x}$ is given by $k \log_{a/b} a$; then evaluate k

Sol. Given equation is $a^{2x-3}\, b^{2x} = a^{6-x}\, b^{5x}$. Taking log on both sides, we get

$(2x - 3) \log a + 2x \log b = (6 - x) \log a + 5x \log b$

$\Rightarrow (\log a)\,[2x - 3 - 6 + x] = (\log b)\,[5x - 2x] \Rightarrow (\log a)\,(3x - 9) = (\log b)\,(3x)$

$\Rightarrow 3x \log a - 9 \log a = 3x \log b \Rightarrow 3x\,[\log a - \log b] = 9 \log a$

$\Rightarrow x \log(a/b) = 3 \log a \Rightarrow x = \dfrac{3\log a}{\log a/b}$

$\Rightarrow x = 3 \log_{a/b} a \qquad \Rightarrow k = 3$

21. If the solutions of logarithmic inequality $\log_{1/\sqrt{2}}(x - 1) > 2$ is $\left(k-2, \dfrac{k}{k-1}\right)$, then evaluate k

Sol. $\log_{1/\sqrt{2}}(x - 1) > 2 \Rightarrow (x - 1) < (1\sqrt{2})^2 \Rightarrow x - 1 < 1/2$

$x < 3/2$; But $x > 1$ (for validity of given inequation)

$\Rightarrow x \in (1, 3/2) \equiv \left(3-2, \dfrac{3}{3-1}\right) \Rightarrow k = 3$

22. Find the solution of logarithmic equation $(\log_2 x)\left(\log_2 \dfrac{x}{16}\right) + 4 = 0$.

Sol. $(\log_2 x)\,[\log_2 x - 4] + 4 = 0$. let $\log_2 x = t$

$\Rightarrow t^2 - 4t + 4 = 0 \qquad \Rightarrow (t - 2)^2 = 0$

$\Rightarrow \log_2 x = 2 \qquad \Rightarrow x = 4$

23. Solution of the equation $x^{0.25\log_{\sqrt[4]{x}}\left(x^2-x\right)} = (3)^{\log_3 2}$

Sol. Given equation is $x^{0.25\log_{\sqrt[4]{x}}\left(x^2-x\right)} = (3)^{\log_3 2}$

$\Rightarrow (x)^{\frac{1}{4}\log_{(x)^{1/4}}(x^2-x)} = 2$ [$\because a^{\log_a x} = x$]

$\Rightarrow x^{4\cdot\frac{1}{4}\log_x\left(x^2-x\right)} = 2 \Rightarrow x^{\log_x\left(x^2-x\right)} = 2 \Rightarrow x^2 - x = 2$

$\Rightarrow x^2 - x - 2 = 0 \Rightarrow (x - 2)\,(x + 1) = 0$

$\Rightarrow x = 2, x = -1$

But $x = -1$ rejected $\Rightarrow x = 2$

24. If the solution of inequality $\log_3 \dfrac{|x^2-4x|+3}{x^2+|x-5|} \geq 0$ is $\left(-\infty, \dfrac{-\lambda}{\lambda+1}\right) \cup \left[\dfrac{1}{\lambda}, \lambda\right]$; then evaluate λ.

Sol. $\log_3 \dfrac{|x^2-4x|+3}{x^2+|x-5|} \geq 0 \Rightarrow \dfrac{|x^2-4x|+3}{x^2+|x-5|} \geq 1$

$\Rightarrow |x^2 - 4x| + 3 \geq x^2 + |x - 5|$

$\Rightarrow |x|\,|x - 4| + 3 \geq x^2 + |x - 5| \qquad (1)$

Case (i) for $x \le 0$

(1) gives $(-x)(-x+4)+3 \ge x^2 - x + 5$

$\Rightarrow x^2 - 4x + 3 \ge x^2 - x + 5$

$3x \le -2$

$\Rightarrow x \le -2/3 \Rightarrow x \in (-\infty, -2/3]$

Case (ii) $0 < x \le 4$

(1) gives $(x)(-x+4)+3 \ge x^2 - x + 5$

$\Rightarrow -x^2 + 4x + 3 \ge x^2 - x + 5 \Rightarrow 2x^2 - 5x + 2 \le 0$

$\Rightarrow (2x-1)(x-2) \le 0 \Rightarrow x \in [1/2, 2]$

Case (iii) $4 < x \le 5$

(1) gives $x(x-4)+3 \ge x^2 - x + 5$

$\Rightarrow x^2 - 4x + 3 \ge x^2 - x + 5 \Rightarrow 3x \le -2 \Rightarrow x \le -2/3$

which is not in the domain of this case

Case (iv) $x > 5$

$x(x-4)+3 \ge x^2 + x - 5$

$\Rightarrow x^2 - 4x + 3 \ge x^2 + x - 5 \Rightarrow 5x \le 8 \Rightarrow x \le 8/5$

which is not in the domain of this case

Final solution is $x \in \left(-\infty, \frac{-2}{3}\right] \cup \left[\frac{1}{2}, 2\right] \Rightarrow \lambda = 2$

SECTION–III

OBJECTIVE-TYPE (ONLY ONE CORRECT ANSWER)

1. The value of $\log_{3\sqrt{3}} 27$ is equal to

(a) 3 (b) 1

(c) 2 (d) None of these

2. The value of $-\log_8 \log_4 \log_2 16$ is equal to

(a) -1 (b) 0

(c) 1 (d) None of these

3. The value of $\log_3 2 . \log_4 3 ... \log_{10} 9 . \log_{11} 10 . \log_2 11$ is equal to

(a) 1 (b) 0

(c) $\log^2_{10}$ (d) $\log_{11} 2$

4. The value of $(\sqrt[3]{9})^{\frac{1}{5\log_5 3}}$ is equal to

(a) $\sqrt[3]{25}$ (b) $\sqrt[9]{25}$

(c) $\sqrt[5]{25}$ (d) $\sqrt[15]{25}$

5. The value of $\sqrt{\left(\frac{1}{\sqrt{27}}\right)^{2-\frac{\log_5 13}{2\log_5 9}}}$ is equal to

(a) $13/3\sqrt{3}$ (b) $39\sqrt{3}$

(c) $3^{-3/2}.\ 13^{3/16}$ (d) None of these

6. If $7^{\log_7(x^2-4x+5)} = (x-1)$, then x may have value(s)

(a) 2, 3 (b) 7

(c) $-2, -3$ (d) $2, -3$

7. The equation $5^{1+\log_5 \cos x} = 2.5$ has

(a) no solution (b) one solution

(c) two solutions (d) infinite solutions

8. Number of digits in the number $(243)^{10}$ is

(a) 23 (b) 24

(c) 25 (d) None of these

9. The value of $\log_3 \left[\frac{\log_{\sqrt[3]{3}} 729}{2}\right]$ is

(a) 1 (b) 3

(c) 2 (d) None of these

10. The value of

$\frac{1}{\log_2 N} + \frac{1}{\log_3 N} + \frac{1}{\log_4 N} + ... + \frac{1}{\log_{1988} N}$ is;

$(N > 0$ and $N \ne 0)$

(a) $\frac{1}{\log_{1988!}(1/N)}$ (b) $\log_N (1988)!$

(c) $\log_N 1988$ (d) None of these

11. The value of $\log_{10} \tan 1° + \log_{10} \tan 2° + ... + \log_{10} \tan 89°$ is equal to

(a) 1 (b) 0

(c) ∞ (d) None of these

12. If $4^{\log_9 3} + 9^{\log_2 4} = 10^{\log_x 83}$ then x is equal to

(a) 3 (b) 4

(c) 2 (d) 10

13. If $x^{\log_3 x^2 + (\log_3 x)^2 - 10}$ $1/x$, then $x =$

(a) 3 (b) 9

(c) 27 (d) 81

14. The number of real solutions of the equation $\log(-x) = 2\log(x+1)$ is

(a) none (b) 1

(c) 2 (d) 3

15. Let $\log_{ab} a = 4$ then the value of $\log_{ab}\left(\frac{\sqrt[3]{a}}{\sqrt{b}}\right)$ is equal to

(a) $\frac{6}{17}$ (b) $\frac{13}{17}$

(c) $\frac{17}{6}$ (d) None of these

16. If $\log_{12} 27 = a$ then $\log_6 16$ has a value

(a) $3\left(\frac{4-a}{4+a}\right)$ (b) $\left(\frac{3-a}{3+a}\right)$

(c) $4\left(\frac{3-a}{3+a}\right)$ (d) None of these

17. If $a = \log_7 12$ and $b = \log_{12} 24$ than the value of $\frac{1+ab}{a(8-5b)}$ is equal to

(a) $\log_7 168$ (b) $\log_{54} 168$

(c) $\log_7 54$ (d) None of these

18. The value of

$$\frac{81^{\frac{1}{\log_5 9}}+3^{\frac{3}{\log_{\sqrt{6}} 3}}}{409}\cdot\left(\left(\sqrt{7}\right)^{\frac{2}{\log_{25} 7}}-(125)^{\log_{25} 6}\right)$$ is equal to

(a) 1 (b) 409

(c) 2 (d) None of these

19. The value of $(81)^{1/\log_5 3}+(27)^{\log_9 36}+3^{4/\log_7 9}$ is

(a) 860 (b) 870

(c) 880 (d) 890

20. For $x \geq 0$, the smallest possible value of the expression, $\log_2 (x^3 - 4x^2 + x + 26) - \log_2 (x + 2)$is

(a) 1 (b) 2

(c) 5 (d) None of these

21. The value of $4^{5\log_{4\sqrt{2}}(3-\sqrt{6})-6\log_8(\sqrt{3}-\sqrt{2})}$ is equal to

(a) 3 (b) 6

(c) 9 (d) None of these

22. The value of $7^{\log_3 5}+3^{\log_5 7}-5^{\log_3 7}-7^{\log_5 3}$ is equal to

(a) 1 (b) $2(7^{\log_3 5}+3^{\log_5 7})$

(c) 0 (d) None of these

23. If $2 \log_{16} (x^2 + x) - \log_4 (x + 1) = 2$, then $x =$

(a) – 1 (b) 16

(c) 2 (d) None of these

24. One of the roots of the equation $9^{\log_3(\log_2 x)} = \log_2 x - (\log_2 x)^2 + 1$ is equal to

(a) 2 (b) 4

(c) 6 (d) 8

25. The value of x satisfying the equation

$|x-1|^{\log_3 x^2-2\log_x 9}=(x-1)^7$ is

(a) 3 (b) 9

(c) 27 (d) 81

26. If we have $x = \sqrt{\log_a b}$ and $y=\sqrt{\log_b a}$ then the value of $a^x - b^y$ is equal to

(a) ba (b) a

(c) 0 (d) None of these

27. $\log_{(2x+3)} (6x^2 + 23x + 21) = 4 - \log_{(3x+7)} (4x^2 + 12x + 9)$, then $x =$

(a) –4 (b) –2

(c) –1/4 (d) –4

28. Let $[x]$ denote the greatest integer function. The number of solution of the equation $x^3 - 3x + [x] = 0$ in $[0, 3]$ is

(a) 4 (b) 3

(c) 2 (d) 1

29. The number of solutions of the equation

$2x^{\log_{10} x}+3x^{\log_{10}(1/x)}=5$ is

(a) 1 (b) 2

(c) 3 (d) None of these

30. $\frac{6}{5}a^{\log_a x\log_{10} a\log_a 5}-3^{\log_{10}(x/10)}=\log_{100}\ \log_4$, then x is equal to

(a) 10^0 (b) 10^1

(c) 10^2 (d) None of these

31. If $p = \log_{245} 175$ and $q = \log_{1715} 875$, then $\frac{1-pq}{p-q} =$

(a) 1 (b) 2

(c) 3 (d) 5

32. The solution set of the equation $\log_{1/5} (2x + 5) + \log_5(16 - x^2) \leq 1$ is

(a) $\left(-\frac{5}{2},1\right)$ (b) $[-1, 4)$

(c) $(1, 4]$ (d) $\left[-\frac{5}{2},4\right]$

33. If $\log_2 a = s$, $\log_4 b = s^2$ and $\log_{c^2} 8 = \frac{2}{s^3+1}$ then $\log_2 \frac{a^2b^5}{c^4}$ is equal to ($a, b, c > 0, c \neq 1$)

(a) $s - 10s^2 - 4(s^3 + 1)$

(b) $2s + 10s^2 - 2 (s^3 + 1)$

(c) $2s + 10s^2 - 3(s^3 + 1)$

(d) None of these

34. Let $N = \frac{4^5+4^5+4^5+4^5}{3^5+3^5+3^5}\cdot\frac{6^5+6^5+6^5+6^5+6^5+6^5}{2^5+2^5}$

then the value of $\log_2 N =$

(a) 10 (b) 11

(c) 12 (d) 14

35. If $x=\prod_{n=1}^{2000} n$, then the value of expression,

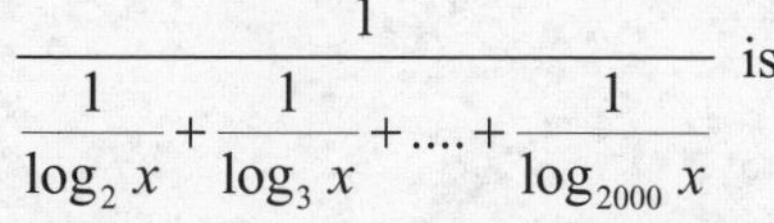

$\dfrac{1}{\dfrac{1}{\log_2 x}+\dfrac{1}{\log_3 x}+....+\dfrac{1}{\log_{2000} x}}$ is

(a) 2 (b) 3
(c) 1 (d) none of these

36. If $\log_{10}(x-1)^3 - 3\log_{10}(x-3) = \log_{10}8$, then $\log_x 625$ has the value equal to

(a) 5 (b) 4
(c) 3 (d) 2

37. The expression $\left[\sqrt[3]{\sqrt[6]{a^9}}\right]^4\left[\sqrt[6]{\sqrt[3]{a^9}}\right]^4$ is simplified to

(a) a^{16} (b) a^{12}
(c) a^8 (d) a^4

38. The number of solutions of $\log_2(x+5) = 6 - x$ is

(a) 2 (b) 0
(c) 3 (d) none of these

39. If $\log_4 5 = a$ and $\log_5 6 = b$, then $\log_3 2$ is equal to

(a) $\dfrac{1}{2a+1}$ (b) $\dfrac{1}{2b+1}$
(c) $2ab+1$ (d) $\dfrac{1}{2ab-1}$

40. If x, y, z are real numbers greater than 1 and 'w' is a positive real number. If $\log_x w = 24$, $\log_y w = 40$ and $\log_{xyz} w = 12$ then $\log_w z$ has the value equal to

(a) $\dfrac{1}{120}$ (b) $\dfrac{2}{120}$
(c) $\dfrac{3}{120}$ (d) $\dfrac{5}{120}$

SECTION–IV

OBJECTIVE-TYPE (MORE THAN ONE CORRECT ANSWER)

1. If $x^{[(\log_2 x)^2-6\log_2 x+11]} = 64$, then $x =$

(a) 2 (b) 4
(c) 8 (d) 16

2. The equations $x^{(3/4)(\log_2 x)^2+\log_2 x-5/4} = \sqrt{2}$ has

(a) at least one real solution
(b) exactly three real solutions
(c) exactly one irrational solution
(d) complex roots

3. The equation $x^{[(\log_3 x)^2-(9/2)\log_3 x+5]} = 3\sqrt{3}$ has

(a) at least one real solution
(b) exactly three real solutions
(c) exactly one irrational solution
(d) None of these

4. The solution of the equation $5^{\log_a x} + 5x^{\log_a 5} = 3, (a > 0)$ is

(a) $a^{-\log_5 2}$ (b) $a^{\log_5 2}$
(c) $2^{-\log_5 a}$ (d) $2^{\log_5 a}$

5. If $\log_2 xy = 5$, $\log_{1/2}(x/y) = 1$, then the values of x, y are

(a) (4, 8) (b) (–4, 8)
(c) (4, – 8) (d) (–4, – 8)

6. For $a > 0 \neq 1$, the roots of the equation $\log_{ax} a + \log_x a^2 + \log_{a^2 x} a^3 = 0$ are given by

(a) $a^{-3/4}$ (b) $a^{-4/3}$
(c) $a^{-1/2}$ (d) None of these

7. If $\log_k x \,.\, \log_{10} k = |\log_{10} 5|$, $k \neq 1$, $k > 0$, then x is equal to

(a) k (b) 1/5
(c) 5 (d) None of these

8. If $\dfrac{1}{2} \le \log_{0.1} x \le 2$ then

(a) the maximum value of x is $\dfrac{1}{\sqrt{10}}$
(b) x lies between $\dfrac{1}{100}$ and $\dfrac{1}{\sqrt{10}}$
(c) x does not lie between $\dfrac{1}{100}$ and $\dfrac{1}{\sqrt{10}}$
(d) the minimum value of x is $\dfrac{1}{100}$

9. The solution of the logarithmic inequality $\log_{2x+3} x^2 < 1$ are contained in the set

(a) (–∞, – 3/2) (b) (–3/2, – 1)
(c) (–1, 0) (d) (0, 3)

10. Solution of equation $x^{\sqrt{x}} = \sqrt{x^x}$ are

(a) 1 (b) 2
(c) 3 (d) 4

11. Solution of equation $\log_{0.5x} x^2 - 14\log_{16x} x^3 + 40\log_{4x} \sqrt{x} = 0$ are
(a) $-1/\sqrt{2}$ (b) 1
(c) 4 (d) $1/\sqrt{2}$

12. Which of the following when simplified reduces to unity?
(a) $\log_{1.5}\log_4\log_{\sqrt{3}} 81$ (b) $\log_2\sqrt{6}+\log_2\sqrt{\frac{2}{3}}$
(c) $-\frac{1}{6}\log_{\frac{\sqrt{3}}{2}}\left(\frac{64}{27}\right)$ (d) $\log_{3.5}(1+2+3\div 6)$

13. Which of the following statement(s) is/are incorrect?
(a) $\log_2 \operatorname{cosec}\frac{5\pi}{6}+\log_{\frac{1}{2}}\sec\frac{7\pi}{3}=2$
(b) $\frac{1}{4}<\log_{100} 4<\frac{1}{3}$
(c) the maximum value of $\log_2(\sin^2 x - 4\sin x + 1)$ is 4
(d) the equation $\log\sqrt{x-1}+\sqrt{1-x}=1$ has only one solution

SECTION–V

ASSERTION AND REASON TYPE

The questions given below consist of an assersion (A) and the reason (R). Use the following key to choose the appropriate answer.

(a) If both assertion and reason are correct and reason is the correct explanation of the assertion.
(b) If both assertion and reason are correct but reason is not correct explanation of the assertion.
(c) If assertion is correct, but reason is incorrect
(d) If assertion is incorrect, but reason is correct

Now consider the following statements:

1. **A:** $\sqrt{\log_{\frac{1}{2}}(2x-3)}$ is real and finite number if $x\in\left(\frac{3}{2},2\right]$
R: $\log_a x$ is defined only if $x > 0$ and $a > 0$, $\neq 1$ and $\log_a x > \log_a y \Leftrightarrow x < y$ if $a \in (0, 1)$

2. **A:** If $\log_2(\log_{1/2}(\log_4 x)) > 0$ then $x \in (0, 2)$
R: $\log_a x$ is defined for $x > 0$, $a > 0$ and $a \neq 1$ and $\log_a x > \log_a y \Leftrightarrow \begin{cases} x>y & \text{if } a>1 \\ x<y & \text{if } a\in(0,1)\end{cases}$

3. **A:** The equation $3\log_4(x^2 + 2x + 1) + 7\log_4(x + 4) = 5 - \log_4(4x - x^2 - 4)$ has no real solution
R: $\log_a x$ is defined iff $a > 0$, $a \neq 1$ and $x > 0$ and solution of any equation must confirm the domain restriction conditions of equation.

4. **A:** If $\log_2 a = s$, $\log_4 b = s^2$ and $\log_{c^2} 8 = \frac{2}{s^3+1}$ where $a, b, c > 0$ and $c \neq 1$ then $\log_2\frac{a^2b^5}{c^4} = 10s^2 - 3s^3 + 2s - 3$
R: $\log_a x^\alpha = \alpha\log_a |x|$ and $\log_{a^\beta} x = \frac{1}{\beta}\log_{|a|} x$ and $\log_b a = \frac{1}{\log_a b}$ $(a \neq 1, a > 0 \text{ and } b > 0, b \neq 1)$

5. **A:** The square of the sum of the roots of the equation $\log_3 x\log_4 x\log_5 x = \log_3 x\log_4 x + \log_4 x\log_5 x + \log_5 x \,.\, \log_3 x$ is 3721
R: $\log_a x = \frac{1}{\log_x a}$; $x > 0$ and $a > 0$,

6. **A:** $2^{\log_2(x^2-1)} = 8$ has two real solutions.
R: a^x and $\log_a x$ are inverse operator of each other.

SECTION–VI

LINKED COMPREHENSION TYPE

A: An eq^n of the form $2n\log_a f(x) = \log_a g(x)$; $a > 0$, $a \neq 1$; $n \in \mathbb{N}$ is equivalent to the system $f(x) > 0$ and $f(x)^{2n} = g(x)$. With the above information, answer the following questions:

1. The solution of the equation $\log x = \frac{1}{2}\log(x+1)$ is
(a) $\frac{1}{2}(\sqrt{5}-1)$ (b) $\frac{1}{2}(\sqrt{5}+1)$
(c) $\left\{\frac{1}{2},\frac{1}{3}\right\}$ (d) $\frac{1}{2}(\sqrt{5}+\sqrt{7})$

2. The number of real solutions of $\log_{0.3}(x-1) = \log_{0.09}(x-2)$ is

(a) 1 (b) 2
(c) 3 (d) None of these

3. The solution of the equation $\log_7 \log_5(\sqrt{x+5}+\sqrt{x}) = 0$ is

(a) 4 (b) 5
(c) 7 (d) None of these

5. Which is/are true in the following?

(a) $\log_a(1/x) = -\log_a x \quad \forall x > 0;\ a > 0;\ a = 1$

(b) If $0 < x < y$ then $\log x < \log y$ (i.e., $\log x$ is an increasing function)

(c) If $0 < \phi(x) < 1;\quad \log_{\phi(x)} f(x) \geq \log_{\phi(x)} g(x) \Leftrightarrow 0 < f(x) \leq g(x)$

(d) None of these.

B: Let a and b real number greater than 1 for which $\exists$ a positive real number. c; different from 1. Such that $2(\log_a c + \log_b c) = 9 \log_{ab} c$

5. The quadratic equation whose two roots have positive value of $\log_b a$ and $\log_a b$ respectively has the following characterstics:

(a) roots of equation are reciprocal to each other

(b) equation has atleast one imaginary root

(c) Sum of roots of the equation is $\frac{5}{2}$

(d) None of these

6. The possible relation between a and b are as under.

(a) $a = \sqrt{b}$ (b) $b = \sqrt{a}$
(c) $a = b$ (d) None of these

7. Largest possible value of $\log_a b$ is equal to

(a) 2 (b) $\frac{3}{2}$
(c) $\frac{5}{2}$ (d) $\frac{1}{2}$

C: If $\log_2 x + \log_4 y + \log_4 z = 2$; $\log_3 y + \log_9 x + \log_9 z = 2$ and $\log_4 z + \log_{16} x + \log_{16} y = 2$. With this information answer the following problems:

8. State the nature of the ratio $\frac{x}{y}$.

(a) A perfect square (b) An irrational number
(c) A real number (d) None of these

9. The ratio of the number $\frac{y}{z}$ will be

(a) $\frac{81}{256}$ (b) $\frac{81}{124}$
(c) $\frac{16}{81}$ (d) None of these

10. Which of the following is correct regarding the above informations?

(a) y is a multiple of x same as x is a multiple of z

(b) z is a sixteen times multiple of x

(c) x, y, z maintain the sum ratio in cyclic order

(d) None of these

D: Consider the equation $2^{|x+1|} - 2^x = |2^x - 1| + 1$ With this information answer the following problems:

11. The least value of x satisfying the equation is

(a) 0 (b) 2
(c) 4 (d) None of these

12. Number of integers less than 15 satisfying the equation are

(a) 14 (b) 15
(c) 16 (d) None of these

13. Number of composite numbers less than 20 which are co-prime with 4 satisfying the given equation is/are

(a) 2 (b) 3
(c) 4 (d) 5

SECTION–VII

MATRIX MATCH TYPE

1. Column - I

(i) In the equation $\log_3 x \log_x 2x \log_{2x} y = \log_x x^2$; then y is

(ii) The value of square root of inverse of x in $4^{\log_{10} x+1} - 6^{\log_{10} x} - 2.3^{\log_{10} x^2+2} = 0$ is

(iii) If $\log_b a = 10$ then $\log_{b^5}(a^3)$ is

(iv) The expression $4^{5\log_{4\sqrt{2}}(3-\sqrt{6})-2\log_2(\sqrt{3}-\sqrt{2})}$ has a value

Column - II

(a) 10

(b) is a perfect square

(c) is a multiple of 3

(d) 6

2. Column - I

(i) In the expression $\frac{1}{3}^{\log_{\frac{1}{9}}\left(x^2-\frac{10}{3}x+1\right)} \le 1$, the value of x belongs to

(ii) The set of real values of x satisfying $\log_{\frac{1}{2}}(x^2-6x+12) \ge -2$, is a subset of

(iii) If $\log_{0.7}(x^2+1) < \log_{0.7} 2x$; $x > 0$, then values of x (with $x \ne 1$) belong to

(iv) Let $f(x) = \sqrt{\log_{10} x^2}$ then set of all values of x for which $f(x)$ is real is

Column - II

(a) $(-\infty, -1] \cup [1, \infty)$

(b) the set of non-negative real numbers.

(c) an uncountable set

(d) $[0, 4]$

3. Column - I

(i) $\log_{\sqrt{2}} 1024$

(ii) $\log_5 2 + \log_5 15 - \log_5 6$

(iii) $\log_{3-2\sqrt{2}}\left(3+2\sqrt{2}\right)$

(iv) $\log_{1.\bar{6}}(1+2\div 3)$

(v) $-\log_8 \log_4 \log_2 16$

Column - II

(a) 1

(b) –1

(c) 20

(d) 0

4. Column - I

(i) If $\log_4(x+1) + \log_4(x+8) = \frac{3}{2}$, then value(s) of x is (are)

(ii) If $|x| + |x-5| = 6$ and $x < 0$, then $\left(x+\frac{3}{2}\right)$ is equal to

(iii) The value of $4\left(3\log_2\frac{81}{80}+5\log_2\frac{25}{24}+7\log_2\frac{16}{15}\right)$ is

(iv) The remainder when $2x^5 - x^3 + x^2 + 1$ is divided by $(2x+1)$ is k. Then $\frac{16k+11}{16}$ is equal to

Column - II

(a) 1

(b) 4

(c) 0

(d) 2

SECTION–VIII

INTEGER-TYPE QUESTIONS

1. Find the solution of equation $\log_3(x^2 - 3x - 5) = \log_3(7 - 2x)$.

2. Find the solution of the equation $\log(x + 4) + \log(2x + 3) = \log(1 - 2x)$.

3. If α, β are the roots of equation $\log_5(5^{1/x} + 125) = \log_5 6 + 1 + 1/2x$ then evaluate the sum $\left(\frac{1}{\alpha}+\frac{1}{\beta}\right)$.

4. Find the number of solutions of the equation $x^{\log_{10} x} + 6x^{\log_{10}\left(\frac{1}{x}\right)} = 5$

5. If the values of x for which 1, $\log_3\sqrt{3^{1-x}+2}$, $\log_3(4.3^x - 1)$ are in $A.P$ is given by $(1 - \log_3 K)$ then evaluate k.

6. The expression $(0.05)^{\log_{\sqrt{20}}(0.\bar{1})}$ is a perfect square of the natural number ______.

7. Find the total number of digits in the number 6^{100} (given $\log_{10}2 = 0.3010$; $\log_{10}3 = 0.4771$)

8. Find the total number of zero immediately after the decimal in 6^{-200}

9. Find the value of log tan 1° + log tan2° + log tan3° + ... + log tan 89°.

10. Find the value of $\frac{1}{\log_2 N}+\frac{1}{\log_3 N}+...+\frac{1}{\log_{2007} N}$, where $N = 1.2.3.....2007$.

11. Find the solution of the following equation $|2 - \log_{1/2} x| - 3 = \log_2(x - 1)$

12. Find the value of $2^{\log_3 5} - 5^{\log_3 2}$

Answer Keys

SECTION–III

1. (c) **2.** (b) **3.** (a) **4.** (d) **5.** (c) **6.** (a) **7.** (d) **8.** (b) **9.** (c) **10.** (b)
11. (b) **12.** (d) **13.** (b) **14.** (b) **15.** (c) **16.** (c) **17.** (b) **18.** (a) **19.** (d) **20.** (b)
21. (c) **22.** (c) **23.** (b) **24.** (a) **25.** (d) **26.** (c) **27.** (c) **28.** (c) **29.** (c) **30.** (c)
31. (a) **32.** (b) **33.** (c) **34.** (c) **35.** (c) **36.** (b) **37.** (d) **38.** (d) **39.** (d) **40.** (b)

SECTION–IV

1. (a, b, c) **2.** (a, b, c) **3.** (a, b, c) **4.** (a, c) **5.** (a, d) **6.** (b, c) **7.** (b, c) **8.** (a, b, d) **9.** (b, c, d)
10. (a, d) **11.** (b, c, d) **12.** (a, b, c, d) **13.** (a, b)

SECTION–V

1. (a) **2.** (a) **3.** (a) **4.** (a) **5.** (c) **6.** (a)

SECTION–VI

1. (b) **2.** (d) **3.** (a) **4.** (b, c) **5.** (a, c) **6.** (a, b) **7.** (a) **8** (a, c) **9.** (a) **10.** (b)
11. (d) **12.** (c) **13.** (a)

SECTION–VII

1. (i) → b, c (ii) → a (iii) → c, d (iv) → b, c
2. (i) → b, c, d (ii) → c (iii) → b, c (iv) → a, c
3. (i) → c (ii) → a (iii) → b (iv) → a (v) → d
4. (i) → c (ii) → a (iii) → b (iv) → d

SECTION–VIII

1. –3 **2.** –1 **3.** 6 **4.** 4 **5.** 4 **6.** 9 **7.** 78 **8.** 155 **9.** 0 **10.** 1
11. 2 **12.** 0

HINTS AND SOLUTIONS

TEXTUAL EXERCISE–1: (SUBJECTIVE)

1. (a) Given $f(x)=\dfrac{1}{x(x-1)(x-2)}$. Since the denominator can not be equal to zero, so $x \neq 0, x-1 \neq 0$ and $x-2 \neq 0$
Hence, x can not have values 0, 1 or 2. So the function is defined when $x \in (-\infty, 0) \cup (0, 1) \cup (1 \cup 2) \cup (2, \infty)$ or $\mathbb{R}-\{0,1,2\}$

(b) Given $f(x)=\dfrac{x^2-x}{x^2+x} = \dfrac{x^2-x}{x(x+1)}$. The function becomes undefined, when $x=-1$ and 0.
So the values of x for which function is defined.
$\Rightarrow \mathbb{R}-\{0,-1\}$

(c) Given $f(x)=\dfrac{x+1}{x^2+x+1}$. To find the points where the function is not defined, we can solve the following equation $x^2+x+1=0$
$\Rightarrow \quad x=\dfrac{-1\pm\sqrt{1-4}}{2}=\dfrac{-1\pm i\alpha\sqrt{3}}{2}$
Both the roots are imaginary. Hence the function is defined for all real values of x.

(d) Given $f(x)=\dfrac{1}{\sqrt{x-3}}$; $x-3>0$, for all function to defined.
Since the roots can not have negative values inside and $x-3=0$ is not possible because the denominator can not be zero.
Hence $x>3 \quad \Rightarrow x \in (3, \infty)$

(e) Given $f(x)=\sqrt{x-4}$. The value inside the under root sign can not be negative.
Hence $x-4 \geq 0 \quad \Rightarrow x \geq 4$
$\Rightarrow x \in [4, \infty)$

(f) Given $f(x)=\sqrt{x-2}+\sqrt{x+2}$
Domain for $\sqrt{x-2} \quad \Rightarrow x-2 \geq 0$
$\Rightarrow x \geq 2 \quad \Rightarrow x \in [2, \infty)$
Domain for $\sqrt{x+2} \quad \Rightarrow x+2 \geq 0$
$\Rightarrow x \geq -2 \quad \Rightarrow x \in [-2, \infty)$
So, the entire function will be valid only for $[2, \infty)$

2. (a) Given $f(x)=\dfrac{1}{\sqrt[3]{16x-x^3}}=\dfrac{1}{\sqrt[3]{x(16-x^2)}}=$
$\dfrac{1}{\sqrt[3]{x(4-x)(4+x)}}$. The cube roots can be negative, so we only need to check for the value of x for which denominator becomes zero
$\Rightarrow x(4-x)(4+x)=0 \quad \Rightarrow x=0, x=4, x=-4$
$\therefore \; x \in \mathbb{R}-\{-4, 0, 4\}$

(b) Given $f(x)=\left(\sqrt{x}-1\right)\left(6-\sqrt{x}\right)$; $x \geq 0$ (as the only constraint is $\sqrt{x}$)
The range for x for function to be defined is $[0, \infty)$.

(c) Given $f(x)=\left(\sqrt{x}-1\right)\sqrt{(6-x)}$; $x \geq 0$ and $6-x \geq 0$
$\Rightarrow 6 \geq x \quad \Rightarrow x \in [0, \infty)$ and $x \in (-\infty, 6]$
So the valid value of x are $[0, 6]$

(d) Given $f(x)=\dfrac{\sqrt{x-1}}{\sqrt{6-x}}$
$\Rightarrow x-1 \geq 0$ and $6-x>0$ (denominator can not be zero)
$\Rightarrow x \geq 1$ and $6>x$
Hence, the values of x arc $[1, 6]$

(e) Given $f(x)=\sqrt{\dfrac{x-1}{6-x}-1}=\sqrt{\dfrac{x-1-6+x}{6-x}}=\sqrt{\dfrac{2x-7}{6-x}}$
$\Rightarrow 2x-7 \geq 0$ and $6-x>0$ (denominator can not be zero)
$\Rightarrow 2x \geq 7$ and $6>x$
$\Rightarrow x \geq 7/2$
Hence the values of x are $[7/2, 6)$

(f) Given $f(x)=\dfrac{\sqrt{x-1}}{6-x} \Rightarrow x-1 \geq 0$ and $6-x \neq 0$
$\Rightarrow x \geq 1$ and $x \neq 6$
Hence, the value of x are $[1, 6) \cup (6, \infty)$

3. (a) Given $f(x)=\sqrt{x-4}+\sqrt{7-x}$
$\Rightarrow x-4 \geq 0$ and $7-x \geq 0$
$\Rightarrow x \leq 4$ and $x \leq 7$
$\therefore$ The values of x for function to be defined are $x \in [4, 7]$

(b) Given $f(x)=\dfrac{1}{\sqrt{x-4}-\sqrt{6-x}}$
$\Rightarrow \sqrt{x-4}-\sqrt{6-x} \neq 0$ [Since denominator can not be zero)
$\Rightarrow \sqrt{x-4} \neq \sqrt{6-x} \quad \Rightarrow x-4 \neq 6-x$
$\Rightarrow 2x \neq 6+4$
$\Rightarrow x \neq 5$ and also $x-4 \geq 0$ and $6-x \geq 0$
$\Rightarrow x \geq 4$ and $6 \geq x$
So, the values of x are $[4, 6] \sim \{5\}$

(c) Given $f(x)=\sqrt{x-7}-\sqrt{3-x}$
$\Rightarrow x-7 \geq 0$ and $3-x \geq 0$
$\Rightarrow x \geq 7$ and $x \leq 3$
There is no possible value of x, which is greater than 7 and smaller than 3.
Hence, no possible value of x for function to be defined.

(d) The desired range for which the function $f(x)=\sqrt{x(x-2)(x-7)}$ has positive values is $[0, 2] \cup (21, \infty)$ (By Wavy curve method)

(e) Given $f(x)=\sqrt{x^3-4x}$
$\Rightarrow \sqrt{x(x^2-4)} \quad \Rightarrow \sqrt{x(x-2)(x+2)}$
Hence the required values of x are $[-2, 0] \cup [2, \infty)$

(f) Given $f(x)=\sqrt[3]{x^3-9x}=\sqrt[3]{x(x^2-9)}$
$=\sqrt[3]{x(x-3)(x+3)}$

The cube root can be negative or positive or even zero, so any value of x can make the function defined.

$\Rightarrow$ $x \in \mathbb{R}$

4. (a) Given $f(x)=\sqrt{(x-1)}\,\sqrt{(6-x)}$

$\Rightarrow$ $x-\geq 0$ $\qquad\Rightarrow$ $x \geq 0$

$\Rightarrow$ $6-x \geq 0$

$\Rightarrow$ $6 \geq 0$ [values inside roots sign must be greater than equal to zero]

$\therefore$ The required values of x are [1, 6]

(b) Given $f(x)=\sqrt{(x-1)(6-x)}$

$\Rightarrow$ $f(x)=\sqrt{(x-1)}\sqrt{(6-x)}$

The function is similar to question 4(*a*)

$\therefore$ The required values of x are [1, 6]

(c) Given $f(x)=\sqrt{x-x^2}$ $\qquad\Rightarrow \sqrt{x-x^2}$

$\therefore$ $x-x^2 \geq 0$ $\qquad\Rightarrow$ $x(1-x) \geq 0$

$\Rightarrow$ $x \geq 0$ and $1 \leq x$

$\therefore$ The domain of the function is [0, 1]

(d) Given $f(x)=\sqrt{x-1}+\sqrt{6-x}$

$\Rightarrow$ $x-1 \geq 0$ $\qquad\Rightarrow$ $x \geq 1$ and

$\Rightarrow$ $6-x \geq 0$ $\qquad\Rightarrow$ $6 \geq x$

The domain for the function is [1, 6]

(e) Given $f(x)=\sqrt{(x-1)(6-x)}$

$\Rightarrow$ $x-1 \geq 0$ $\qquad\Rightarrow$ $x \geq 1$

The domain for the function is $[1, \infty)$

(f) Given $f(x)=\dfrac{\sqrt{x-1}+\sqrt{6-x}}{\sqrt{1-x}+\sqrt{x-6}}$

$\Rightarrow$ $x-1 \geq 0$ and $6-x \geq 0$ and $1-x > 0$ and $x-6 > 0$

$\Rightarrow$ $x \geq 1$ and $6 \geq x$ and $1 > x$ and $x > 6$

There is not value satisfying all the above inequities

$\therefore$ The domain is nil. $\qquad\Rightarrow$ $x \in \phi$.

TEXTUAL EXERCISE–2: (SUBJECTIVE)

1. (a) Given $f(x)=\dfrac{x-1}{x+1}$; $x+1 \neq 0$; $x \neq -1$

The domain of the function is $x \in \mathbb{R}-\{-1\}$

Now for range $y=\dfrac{x-1}{x+1}$

$\Rightarrow$ $yx+y=x-1$ $\qquad\Rightarrow$ $y+1=x(1-y)$

$\Rightarrow$ $\dfrac{y+1}{1-y}=x-g(y)$

The domain for g will be the range for $\dfrac{x-1}{x+1}$

For g, domain is $\mathbb{R}-\{1\}$

Hence, the range of the function is $\mathbb{R}-\{1\}$

From the range, we can see the minimum value for the function is $-\infty$ and the maximum is $+\infty$, the function is not bounded.

(b) Given $f(x)=\dfrac{2x+1}{5x-3}$; $5x-3 \neq 0$; $5x \neq 3$; $6x \neq 3/5$

The domain of the function is $\mathbb{R}-\{3/5\}$

$\Rightarrow$ $\dfrac{2x+1}{5x-3}$ $\qquad\Rightarrow$ $y=\dfrac{2x+1}{5x-3}$

$\Rightarrow$ $5yx-3y=2x+1$ $\qquad\Rightarrow$ $5yx-2x=1+3y$

$\Rightarrow$ $x(5y-2)=1+3y$ $\qquad\Rightarrow$ $x=\dfrac{1+3y}{5y-2}$

The domain for $\dfrac{1+3y}{5y-2}$ is $\mathbb{R}-\{2/5\}$, which is range for the given function.

The maximum value is $+\infty$

Minimum value is $-\infty$

There is no LUB or GUB, as the function is not bounded

(c) Given $f(x)=\dfrac{x^2-2}{x^2+4}$. The domain of the function is $\mathbb{R}$

$\Rightarrow$ $x^2+4 \neq 0$ $\qquad\Rightarrow$ $x^2 \neq -4$

$\therefore$ Whose $\mathbb{R}$ is the domain

$\Rightarrow$ $y=\dfrac{x^2-2}{x^2+4}$ $\qquad\Rightarrow$ $yx^2+4y=x^2-2$

$\Rightarrow$ $x^2(y-1)=-4y-2$

$\Rightarrow$ $x^2=\dfrac{4y+2}{1-y}$ $\qquad\Rightarrow$ $x=\pm\sqrt{\dfrac{4y+2}{1-y}}$

Range is $1-y > 0$ $\qquad\Rightarrow$ $1 > y$ and

$4y-12 \geq 0$ $\qquad\Rightarrow$ $4y \geq -2$

$\Rightarrow$ $y \geq -1/2$ $\qquad\Rightarrow$ $y \in [-1/2, 1)$

The range is $[-1/2, 1)$

$\Rightarrow$ LUB = 1, GLB = –1/2

$\Rightarrow$ Maximum is not there and minimum is –1/2

2. (a) Given $f(x)=\dfrac{x}{x^2+4}$. The domain for the function is $\mathbb{R}$, since $x^2 \neq -4$ is always true

$\Rightarrow$ $y=\dfrac{x}{x^2+4}$ $\qquad\Rightarrow$ $yx^2+4y=x$

$\Rightarrow$ $yx^2+4y-x=0$ $\qquad\Rightarrow$ $yx^2-x+4y=0$

$\Rightarrow$ $x=\dfrac{1\pm\sqrt{1-16y^2}}{2y}=\dfrac{1\pm\sqrt{1-16y^2}}{2y}$

$\Rightarrow$ $2y \neq 0$ $\qquad\Rightarrow$ $y \neq 0$

$\Rightarrow$ $1-16y^2 \geq 0$ $\qquad\Rightarrow$ $1 \geq 16y^2$

$\Rightarrow$ $\dfrac{1}{16} \geq y^2$ $\qquad\Rightarrow$ $\dfrac{1}{4} \geq y \geq \dfrac{1}{4}$

The function is bounded between –1/4 and 1/4.

LUB = 1/4 and GLB = –1/4; maximum = 1/4 and GLB = –1/4

The range for the function is $\left(-\dfrac{1}{4},0\right] \cup \left(0,\dfrac{1}{4}\right]$

(b) Given $f(x)=\dfrac{x^2-9}{x^2-4x+3}$

$\Rightarrow$ $\dfrac{x^2-9}{x^2-3x-x+3}$ $\qquad\Rightarrow$ $\dfrac{x^2-9}{x(x-3)-1(x-3)}$

$\Rightarrow$ $\dfrac{x^2-9}{(x-3)(x-3)}$

The domain the function the function is $\mathbb{R}-\{1, 3\}$

The equivalent function for the above function i.e., $\dfrac{x+3}{x-1}$ [but $x \neq 3$]

$\Rightarrow$ $y=\dfrac{x+3}{x-1}$ $\qquad\Rightarrow$ $yx-y=x+3$

$\Rightarrow x(y-1) = y+3 \qquad \Rightarrow x = \dfrac{y+3}{y-1}$

$y \neq 1$ and since $x \neq 3$, so $3 \neq \dfrac{y+3}{y-1}$

$\Rightarrow 3y-3 \neq y+3;\ 2y \neq 6;\ y \neq 3$

So $y \neq 1$ and $y \neq 3$

$\therefore$ The range of the function is $\mathbb{R} - \{1, 3\}$

(c) Given $f(x) = \dfrac{x^2+1}{2x}$; $2x \neq 0$; $x \neq 0$

The domain of the function is $\mathbb{R} - \{0\}$

$\Rightarrow y = \dfrac{x^2+1}{2x} \qquad \Rightarrow 2xy = x^2+1$

$\Rightarrow x^2 - 2xy + 1 = 0 \qquad \Rightarrow x = \dfrac{2y \pm \sqrt{4y^2-4}}{2}$

$\Rightarrow y \pm \sqrt{y^2-1} \qquad \Rightarrow y^2 - 1 \geq 0$

$\Rightarrow y^2 \geq 1 \qquad \Rightarrow -1 \geq y$ and $y \geq 1$

$\Rightarrow y \in (-\infty, -1] \cup [1, \infty)$

3. (a) Given $f(x) = \dfrac{x^2-5x+4}{x^2-4x+3}$

$\Rightarrow \dfrac{x^2-4x-x+4}{x^2-3x-x+3} \qquad \Rightarrow \dfrac{(x-1)(x-4)}{(x-3)(x-1)}$

The domain of the function is $\mathbb{R} - \{1, 3\}$

The equivalent function for the above function is $\dfrac{x-4}{x-3}$

$\Rightarrow y = \dfrac{x-4}{x-3}$; $yx - 3y = x - 4$

$\Rightarrow (y-0)\,x = 3y - 4$

$\Rightarrow x = \dfrac{3y-4}{y-1}$ and also $x \neq 3$

$\Rightarrow 3 \neq \dfrac{3y-4}{y-1}$

$\Rightarrow 3y - 3 \neq 3y - 4$ always true $x \neq 1$

$\Rightarrow \dfrac{3}{} \neq \dfrac{4}{}$

$\Rightarrow y - 1 \neq 3y - 4 \qquad \Rightarrow y \neq 3/2$

$\Rightarrow y \in \mathbb{R} - \{1, 3/2\}$

$\therefore$ The range is $\mathbb{R} - \{1, 3/2\}$

The function is not bounded no LUB, no GLB

(b) Given $f(x) = \sqrt{x-1}$. The domain of the function is $x - 1 \geq 0$; $x \geq 1$

$\Rightarrow D_f$ is $[1, \infty)$

For range $y = \sqrt{x-1} \Rightarrow y^2 = x - 1$

$\Rightarrow y^2 + 1 = x$

The domain for $y^2 + 1$ is $\mathbb{R}$ but y can not be negative since $y = a\sqrt{x-1}$

So R_f is $[0, \infty)$

The function has lower bound GLB = 0, minimum value = 0, no LUB

(c) Given $f(x) = \sqrt{x^2+4}$

$\Rightarrow x^2 + 4 \geq 0 \qquad \Rightarrow x^2 \geq -4$ [always true]

$\therefore$ The D_f is $\mathbb{R}$

$\Rightarrow y = \sqrt{x^2+4} \qquad \Rightarrow y^2 = x^2 + 4$

$\Rightarrow \pm\sqrt{y^2-4} = x$

$\Rightarrow y^2 \geq 4 \qquad \Rightarrow y \leq -2$ or $y \geq 2$

$\therefore y \in (-\infty, -2] \cup [2, \infty)$

But $y = \sqrt{x^2+4}$

So, y can only have positive values

$\therefore$ The R_f is $[2, \infty)$

The function has lower bound. GLB = 2 and minimum value of 2, not LUB.

(d) Given $f(x) = \dfrac{1}{(x-1)(x-5)}$; $(x-1)(x-5) \neq 0$

So $x \neq L$ and $x \neq 5$

The D_f is $\mathbb{R} - \{1, 5\}$

$y = \dfrac{1}{x^2-6x+5} \qquad \Rightarrow yx^2 - 6xy + 5y = 1$

$\Rightarrow yx^2 - 6xy + 5y - 1 = 0$

$\Rightarrow x = \dfrac{6y \pm \sqrt{36y^2 - 4y(5y-1)}}{2y}$

$= \dfrac{6y \pm \sqrt{36y^2 - 20y^2 + 4y}}{2y} = \dfrac{6y \pm 2\sqrt{4y^2+y}}{2y}$

$= \dfrac{3y \pm \sqrt{4y^2+y}}{y}$

So, $y \neq 0$ and $4y^2 + y \geq 0$

$\Rightarrow y(4y+1) \geq 0 \qquad \Rightarrow y \in \left(-\infty, \dfrac{-1}{4}\right) \cup (0, \infty)$

So, the function is $(-\infty, -1/4] \cup (0, \infty)$. There is no GLB or LUB

(e) Given $f(x) = \sqrt[3]{x+8}$. The domain is $\mathbb{R}$

$\Rightarrow y = \sqrt[3]{x+8} \qquad \Rightarrow y^3 = x + 8$

$\Rightarrow y^3 - 8 = x$

The R_f is $\mathbb{R}$. Function is unbounded, no GLB or LUB.

(f) Given $f(x) = \dfrac{1}{\sqrt[3]{x}}$. The domain is $\mathbb{R} - \{0\}$

$\Rightarrow y = \dfrac{1}{\sqrt[3]{x}} \qquad \Rightarrow x = \dfrac{1}{y^3}$.

The rang is $\mathbb{R} - \{0\}$. Function is unbounded, no GLB or LUB.

(g) Given $f(x) = \dfrac{1}{x^2+4}$. The D_f is $\mathbb{R}$, since $x^2 + 4 \neq 0$ is always true .

$\Rightarrow y = \dfrac{1}{x^2+4} \qquad \Rightarrow x^2 + 4 = \dfrac{1}{y}$

$\Rightarrow x^2 = \dfrac{1}{y} - 4 \qquad \Rightarrow x = \pm\sqrt{\dfrac{1}{y} - 4}$

$\Rightarrow x = \pm\sqrt{\dfrac{1-4y}{y}} \qquad \Rightarrow y > 0$ and $1 - 4y \geq 0$

$\Rightarrow 1 \geq 4y \qquad \Rightarrow 1/4 \geq y$

$\therefore$ The R_f is $(0, 1/4]$.

There is no GLB but LUB = 1/4

Maximum value is 1/4

4. (i) (a) $x^2 - 4x + 3$

$y = ax^2 + bx + c$ attained its minimum value at $x = -b/2a$ and is equal to $\dfrac{-D}{4a}$

$$f(x)_{\min} = \frac{-(-4)^2 - 4(1)(3)}{4\times 1} = \frac{-16-12}{4} = -1$$

$\therefore$ The minimum value is –1 and maximum is ∞.

(b) $x^2 - 6x + 12$

Again $f(x)_{\min} = \frac{-D}{4a} = \frac{-[(-6)^2 - 4(12)]}{4\times 1} = \frac{-[36-48]}{4} = 3$

$\therefore$ The minimum value is 3 and maximum value is ∞

(c) $-x^2 + 4x + 5$

Here the maximum value is $\frac{-D}{4a}$ and minimum value is $-\infty$.

$$f(x)_{\max} = \frac{(4^2 - 4(-1)(5))}{4} = \frac{(16+20)}{4} = 9$$

$\therefore$ The minimum value is $-\infty$ and maximum value is 9

(ii) $x^2 - kx + 4$

For $x^2 - kx + 4$ to be always positive, D should be less than 0

$\Rightarrow D = (-k^2) - 4 \times 1 \times 4 < 0$

$\Rightarrow k^2 - 16 < 0$ $\qquad\Rightarrow k^2 < 16$

$\Rightarrow -4 < k < 4$ $\qquad\Rightarrow k \in (-4, 4)$

5. (a) $|x - 3| \le 5 \Rightarrow -5 \le x - 3 \le 5$

$\Rightarrow -5 + 3 \le x \le 5 + 3 \quad -2 \le x \le 8$

$\Rightarrow x \in [-2, 8]$

(i) $x^2 + 4$ $-2 \le x \le 8$ (squaring each term)

$0 \le x^2 \le 64$ (adding 4)

$\Rightarrow 0 + 4 \le x^2 + 4 \le 64 + 4$

$\Rightarrow 4 \le x^2 + 4 \le 68$

$\therefore$ Range is [4, 68]

(ii) $\frac{1}{x^2+1}$

$\Rightarrow -2 \le x \le 8$ (squaring each term)

$\Rightarrow 0 \le x^2 \le 64$ (adding 1)

$\Rightarrow 1 \le x^2 + 1 \le 65$ (Taking reciprocal)

$\Rightarrow \frac{1}{65} \le \frac{1}{x^2 \le 1} \le 1$

$\therefore$ Range is $\left[\frac{1}{65}, 1\right]$

(iii) $2x + 3 \Rightarrow -2 \le x \le 8$ (multiplying by 2))

$-4 \le 2x \le 16$ (Adding 3)

$-4 + 3 \le 2x + 3 \le 16 + 3$ $-1 \le 2x + 3 \le 19$

The range is [–1, 19]

(iv) $\frac{1}{2x+1}$

$\Rightarrow -2 \le x \le -1/2$ and $-1/2 \le x \le 8$ [multiplying 2]

$\Rightarrow -4 \le 2x \le -1$ and $-1 \le 2x \le 16$ [adding 1]

$\Rightarrow -3 \le 2x + 1 \le 0$ and $0 \le 2x + 1 \le 17$ [inverse]

$\Rightarrow -\infty \le \frac{1}{2x+1} \le \frac{-1}{3}$ and $\frac{1}{17} \le \frac{1}{2x+1} \le \infty$

$\therefore$ Range is $(-\infty, -1/3] \cup [1/17, \infty)$

(b) (i) $S = \frac{2-x}{3+x}; -3 < x \le 2$

$$= -\frac{[x-2]}{3+x} = -\frac{[x+3-2-3]}{3+x} = -\left[1 - \frac{5}{3+x}\right]$$

$\Rightarrow -3 < x \le 2$ (Adding 3)

$\Rightarrow -3 + 3 < x + 3 \le 5$

$\Rightarrow 0 < x + 3 \le 5$ (Taking inverse)

$\Rightarrow \frac{1}{5} \le \frac{1}{x+3} < \infty$ (Multiplying –5)

$\Rightarrow -\infty < \frac{-5}{x+3} \le -1$ (Adding 1)

$\Rightarrow -\infty < 1 - \frac{5}{x+3} \le 0$ (Multiplying –1)

$\Rightarrow 0 \le \frac{2-x}{3+x} < \infty$

$\therefore$ The GLB is 0 and no LUB

(ii) $S = \frac{2}{x^2 - 1}$; $-3 \le x \le 2$

$\Rightarrow -3 \le x \le 2$ (squaring)

$0 \le x^? \le 9$ (adding –1)

$\Rightarrow -1 \le x^2 - 1 \le 8$

$\Rightarrow -1 \le x^2 - 1 < 0$ and $0 < x^2 - 1 \le 8$

Taking inverse $-\infty < \frac{1}{x^2-1} \le -1$ and $\frac{1}{8} \le \frac{1}{x^2-1} < \infty$

$\Rightarrow -\infty < \frac{2}{x^2-1} \le -2$ and $\frac{2}{8} \le \frac{2}{x^2-1} < \infty$ (Multiplying by 2)

The range is $(-\infty, -2] \cup \left[\frac{1}{4}, \infty\right)$

There is no GLB or LUB.

(iii) $S = \frac{3-x}{2+x}; x \ge 0$

$\Rightarrow 0 \le x < \infty$ (adding 2)

$\Rightarrow 2 \le x + 2 < \infty$

Taking reciprocal $0 < \frac{1}{x+2} \le \frac{1}{2}$ (Multiplying –5)

$\Rightarrow \frac{-5}{2} \le \frac{-5}{x+2} < 0$ (Adding 1)

$\Rightarrow \frac{-3}{2} \le 1 - \frac{5}{x+2} < 1$ (Multiplying – 1)

$\Rightarrow -1 < \frac{3-x}{2+x} \le \frac{3}{2}$

The range is $\left(-1, \frac{3}{2}\right]$

The GLB is –1 and LUB is 3/2

(iv) $S = \frac{1-x^2}{1+x^2}; x \ge 1$

$\Rightarrow 1 \le x < \infty$ (squaring)

$\Rightarrow 1 \le x^2 < \infty$ (adding)

$\Rightarrow 2 \le 1 + x^2 < \infty$

Taking inverse $0 < \frac{1}{1+x^2} \le \frac{1}{2}$

$\Rightarrow S = \frac{-1[x^2-1]}{1+x^2} = -1\left[1 - \frac{2}{1+x^2}\right]$ (Multiplying –2)

$\Rightarrow -1 \le \frac{-2}{1+x^2} < 0$ (Adding 1)

$\Rightarrow -1 + 1 \le 1 - \frac{2}{1+x^2} < 1$

$\Rightarrow 0 \le 1 - \frac{2}{1+x^2} < 1$ (Multiplying – 1)

$\Rightarrow -1 < \frac{1-x^2}{1+x^2} \le 0$

$\therefore$ The GLB is –1 & LUB is 0

(v) $S = \frac{2x+1}{3x+1}; |x-5| \le 3$

$\Rightarrow$ $|x-5| \le 3$ $\Rightarrow$ $-3 \le x-5 \le 3$

$\Rightarrow$ $-3+5 \le x \le 3+5$ $\Rightarrow$ $2 \le x \le 8$

$\Rightarrow$ $S = \frac{2x+1}{3x+1}$

$\Rightarrow$ $s = \frac{2}{3}\frac{[3x+3/2]}{3x+1} = \frac{2}{3}\frac{[3x+1+1/2]}{3x+1} = \frac{2}{3}\left[1+\frac{1}{2}\frac{1}{(3x+1)}\right]$

$\Rightarrow$ $2 \le x \le 8$

$\Rightarrow$ $6 \le 3x \le 24$ (multiplying by 3)

$\Rightarrow$ $7 \le 3x+1 \le 25$ (adding 1)

$\Rightarrow$ $14 \le 2(3x+1) \le 50$ (Multiplying 2)

$\Rightarrow$ $\frac{1}{50} \le \frac{1}{2(3x+1)} \le \frac{1}{14}$

$\Rightarrow$ $\frac{2}{3}\left(1+\frac{1}{50}\right) \le \frac{2}{3}\left(1+\frac{1}{2(3x+1)}\right) \le \frac{2}{3}\left(1+\frac{1}{14}\right)$

$\therefore$ Range is $\left[\frac{17}{25}, \frac{5}{7}\right]$. The function is bounded.

(vi) $S = \sqrt{1-2x^2}; |x| \le \sqrt{3}/2$

$\Rightarrow$ $-\frac{\sqrt{3}}{2} \le x \le \frac{\sqrt{3}}{2}$ (Squaring)

$\Rightarrow$ $0 \le x^2 \le 3/4$ (multiplying 2)

$\Rightarrow$ $0 \le 2x^2 \le 3/2$ (multiplying –1)

$\Rightarrow$ $-3/2 \le -2x^2 \le 0$ (adding 1)

$\Rightarrow$ $-1/2 \le 1-2x^2 \le 1$ (taking square roots)

$\Rightarrow$ $0 \le \sqrt{1-2x^2} \le 1$

$\therefore$ Range is [0, 1]; The GLB is 0; The LUB is 1

(vii) $S = \sqrt{4-x^2}; |x| \le \frac{1}{2}$

$\Rightarrow$ $-1/2 \le x \le 1/2$ (Squaring)

$\Rightarrow$ $0 \le x^2 \le 1/4$ (Multiplying –1)

$\Rightarrow$ $\frac{-1}{4} \le x^2 \le 0$ (Adding 4)

$\Rightarrow$ $4-\frac{1}{4} \le 4-x^2 \le 4$

$\Rightarrow$ $\frac{15}{4} \le 4-x^2 \le 4$ (Square rooting)

$\Rightarrow$ $-2 \le \sqrt{4-x^2} \le \frac{-\sqrt{15}}{2}$ and $\frac{\sqrt{15}}{2} \le \sqrt{4-x^2} \le 2$

$\therefore$ Range is $\left[\frac{\sqrt{15}}{2}, 2\right]$; GLB is $\sqrt{15}/2$; LUB is 2.

(viii) $S = \frac{x}{x+4}; |x-4| < 1$

$|x-4| < 1$ $\Rightarrow$ $-1 < x-4 < 1$

$\Rightarrow$ $3 < x < 5$

$S = \frac{x}{x+4}$ $\Rightarrow$ $1-\frac{4}{x+4}$

$\Rightarrow$ $3 < x < 5$ (Adding 4)

$\Rightarrow$ $7 < x+4 < 9$ (Taking inverse)

$\Rightarrow$ $\frac{1}{9} < \frac{1}{x+4} < \frac{1}{7}$ (Multiplying –4)

$\Rightarrow$ $\frac{-4}{7} < \frac{-4}{x+4} < \frac{-4}{9}$ (Adding 1)

$\Rightarrow$ $\frac{3}{4} < \frac{x}{x+4} < \frac{5}{9}$.

$\therefore$ Range is $\left(\frac{3}{4}, \frac{5}{9}\right)$; GLB = 3/4; LUB = 5/9

(ix) $S = \frac{x-2}{x+2}; |x-3| \le 2$

$|x-3| \le 2$

$\Rightarrow$ $-2 \le x-3 \le 2$ (adding 3)

$\Rightarrow$ $-1 \le x \le 5$

$S = \frac{x-2}{x+2} = 1-\frac{4}{x+2}$ $\Rightarrow$ $-1 \le x \le 5$ (adding 2)

$\Rightarrow$ $3 \le x+2 \le 7$ (Taking inverse)

$\Rightarrow$ $\frac{1}{7} \le \frac{1}{x+2} \le \frac{1}{3}$ (Multiplying – 4)

$\Rightarrow$ $\frac{-4}{3} \le \frac{-4}{x+2} \le \frac{-4}{7}$ (Adding 1)

$\Rightarrow$ $\frac{-1}{3} \le \frac{x-2}{x+2} \le \frac{3}{7}$

$\therefore$ Range is $\left[\frac{-1}{3}, \frac{3}{7}\right]$; GLB is –1/3; LUB is 3/7

6. $f(x) = 3x-2$ $\Rightarrow$ $y = 3x-2$

$\Rightarrow$ $y+2 = 3x$ $\Rightarrow$ $\frac{y+2}{3} = x$

$\Rightarrow$ $f^{-1}(x) = \frac{x+2}{3}$

(a) $f^{-1}(1)$ $\Rightarrow$ $\frac{1+2}{3}$ $\Rightarrow$ 1

(b) $f^{-1}(4)$ $\Rightarrow$ $\frac{4+2}{3}$ $\Rightarrow$ 2

(c) $f^{-1}(-5)$ $\Rightarrow$ $\frac{-5+2}{3}$ $\Rightarrow$ –1

(d) $f^{-1}(2)$ $\Rightarrow$ $\frac{-2+2}{3}$ $\Rightarrow$ 0

7.

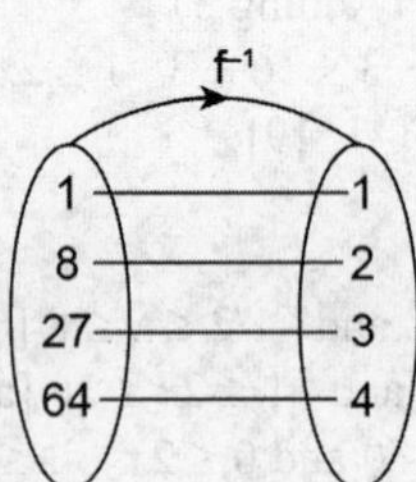

8. $f(x) = 10x+3$ $\Rightarrow$ $y = 10x+3$

$\Rightarrow$ $y-3 = 10x$ $\Rightarrow$ $\frac{y-3}{10} = x$

$\Rightarrow$ $\frac{x-3}{10} = f^{-1}(x)$

$f(x) = f^{-1}(x)$ (given) $\Rightarrow$ $10x+3 = \frac{x-3}{10}$

$\Rightarrow$ $100x+30 = x-3$ $\Rightarrow$ $99x = -33$

$\Rightarrow$ $x = \frac{-33}{99}$ $\Rightarrow$ $x = \frac{-1}{3}$

TEXTUAL EXERCISE–3: (SUBJECTIVE)

1. (a) $\frac{(15)^3.(21)^3}{(35)^2.(5)^4} = \frac{3^3\times5^3\times3^3\times7^3}{5^2\times7^2\times3^4} = 32\times5\times7 = 315$

(b) $(-\ 1.4)^3.\left(3\frac{4}{7}\right)^3 = \left(-\frac{147}{165}\right)^3.\left(\frac{25}{7}\right)^3 = -1\times\frac{7^3}{5^3}\times\frac{5^6 5^3}{7^3}$
$= -125$

(c) $\left(\frac{\sqrt[4]{ab}-\sqrt{b}}{\sqrt{a}-\sqrt[4]{ab}}\right)^{-4} = \left[\frac{\sqrt[4]{b}\left[\sqrt[4]{a}-\sqrt[4]{b}\right]}{\sqrt[4]{a}\left[\sqrt[4]{a}-\sqrt[4]{b}\right]}\right]^{-4} = \left[\left(\frac{b}{a}\right)^{1/4}\right]^{-4}$

$\Rightarrow \left[\frac{b}{a}\right]^{-1} \Rightarrow \frac{a}{b}$

2. $|x-1|^{x^2-3x} = 1$

$\Rightarrow$ $a^b = 1$ is the case when either $b = 0$ or $a = 1$, when either $b = 0$ or $a = 1$

Case 1: $x^2 - 3x = 0$

$\Rightarrow x(x-3) = 0 \qquad \Rightarrow x = 0$ or $x = 3$

Case 2: $|x-1| = 1$

$\Rightarrow x - 1 = -1$ or $x - 1 = 1$

$\Rightarrow x = 0$ or $x = 2$

So the roots are 0, 2, 3. Hence there are three roots

3. (a) $\left(\left(x^{2/3}y^{-1}\right)\left(x^2y^{-1}\right)^{1/2}\left(y^{2/3}\right)^{3/2}\right)^6 = \left(x^{4/3}y^{-2}.x^{2/2}y^{-1/2}.y\right)^6$

$= \left(x^{4/3+1}.y^{-5/2+1}\right)^6 = \left(x^{7/3}.\,y^{-3/2}\right)^6 = x^{(7/3)\times6}.y^{(-3/2)\times6}$

$= x^{14}.y^{-9}$

(b) $\sqrt{\frac{a}{b}\sqrt{\frac{a}{b}.\sqrt[3]{\frac{a}{b}}}}\,.\,a^{-\frac{1}{3}}.b^{\frac{1}{3}} = \sqrt{\frac{a}{b}\sqrt{\frac{a}{b}\times\left(\frac{a}{b}\right)^{1/3}}}\times(a)^{-1/3}\times(b)^{1/3}$

$= \sqrt{\frac{a}{b}\sqrt{\left(\frac{a}{b}\right)^{4/3}}}\times(a)^{-1/3}\times(b)^{1/3}$

$= \sqrt{\frac{a}{b}\times\left(\frac{a}{b}\right)^{2/3}}\times(a)^{-1/3}\times(b)^{1/3}$

$= \left(\frac{a}{b}\right)^{5/6}\times\left(\frac{a}{b}\right)^{-1/3} = \left(\frac{a}{b}\right)^{\frac{1}{2}}$

4. (a) $5^{x-1} = 10^x.\,2^{-x}\,5^{x+1}$

$\Rightarrow 5^{x-1} = 2^x.5^x.2^{-x}.5^{x+1} \qquad \Rightarrow 1 = \frac{5^x.5^{x+1}}{5^{x-1}}$

$\Rightarrow 1 = 5^x\times5^2 \qquad \Rightarrow \frac{1}{25} = (5)^x$

$\Rightarrow (5)^{-2} = 5^x = -2$

(b) $5^{2x-1} + 5^{x+1} = 250 \qquad \Rightarrow \frac{5^{2x}}{5} + 5.5^x = 250$

$\Rightarrow \frac{5^{2x}}{5} + 5.5^x - 250 = 0 \Rightarrow 5^{2x} + 25.5^x - 1250 = 0$

$\Rightarrow 5^x = \frac{-25\pm\sqrt{625+5000}}{2}$

$\Rightarrow \frac{-25\pm\sqrt{5625}}{2} \qquad \Rightarrow \frac{-25\pm75}{2}$

$\Rightarrow 5^x = \frac{50}{2}$ or $5^x = \frac{-100}{2}$

$\Rightarrow 5^x = 25$ or $5^x = -50$ (not possible) $\Rightarrow x = 2$

(c) $9^x + 6^x = 24^x = \frac{9^x}{4^x} + \frac{6^x}{4^x} = 2 = \left(\frac{3}{2}\right)^{2x} + \left(\frac{3}{2}\right)^x - 2 = 0$

$= \left(\frac{3}{2}\right)^x = -\frac{1\pm\sqrt{1+8}}{2} = \frac{-1\pm\sqrt{9}}{2} = \frac{-1\pm3}{2} = \left(\frac{3}{2}\right)^x = 1$

or $\left(\frac{1}{2}\right)^x = -2$ (not possible)

$\Rightarrow x = 0$

5. (a) $4.2^{2x} - 6^x = 18.3^{2x} = \frac{4.2^{2x}}{3^{2x}} - \frac{2^x}{3^x} - 18 = 0$

$= 4\left(\frac{2}{3}\right)^{2x} - \left(\frac{2}{3}\right)^x - 18 = 0$

$\Rightarrow \left(\frac{2}{3}\right)^x = \frac{1\pm\sqrt{1+4\times4\times18}}{8} = \frac{1\pm\sqrt{1+288}}{8} = \frac{1\pm\sqrt{289}}{8}$

$= \frac{1\pm17}{8}$

$\Rightarrow \left(\frac{2}{3}\right)^x = -2$ (Not possible) or $\left(\frac{2}{3}\right)^x = \frac{9}{4} = \left(\frac{2}{3}\right)^x = \left(\frac{2}{3}\right)^{-2}$

$\Rightarrow x = -2$

(b) $2^{\sin^2x} + 4.2^{\cos^2x} = 6 \quad \Rightarrow \quad 2^{\sin^2x} + 4.2^{1-\sin^2x} = 6$

$\Rightarrow 2^{\sin^2x} + \frac{4.2}{2^{\sin^2x}} = 6$

$\Rightarrow \left(2^{\sin^2x}\right)^2 - 6\times2^{\sin^2x} + 8 = 0$

$\Rightarrow 2^{\sin^2x} = \frac{6\pm\sqrt{36-32}}{2} = \frac{6\pm\sqrt{4}}{2} = \frac{6\pm2}{2}$

$\Rightarrow 2^{\sin^2x} = 4$ or $2^{\sin^2x} = 2$

$\Rightarrow \sin^2x = 2$ (not possible) or $\sin^2x = 1$

$\Rightarrow \sin x = \pm1 \qquad \Rightarrow x = \frac{(2n+1)}{2}\pi, \forall x\in\mathbb{Z}$

(c) $7^{x+2} - 7^x - 2.7^{x+2} + 2.7^x + 48 = 0$

$\Rightarrow -7^{x+2} + 7^x + 48 = 0 \quad \Rightarrow \quad -7^2 + 1 + \frac{48}{7^x} = 0$

$\Rightarrow -48 + \frac{48}{7^x} = 0 \qquad \Rightarrow 1 = 7^x$

$\Rightarrow x = 0$

6. (a) $64.9^x - 84.12^x + 27.16^x = 0$

$\Rightarrow 27.16^x - 84.12^x + 64.9^x = 0$

$\Rightarrow 27\left(\frac{4}{3}\right)^{2x} - 84\left(\frac{4}{3}\right)^x + 64 = 0$

$\Rightarrow \left(\frac{4}{3}\right)^x = \frac{84\pm\sqrt{(84)^2-4\times27\times64}}{54}$

$= \frac{84\pm\sqrt{7056-6912}}{54} = \frac{84\pm\sqrt{144}}{54} = \frac{84\pm12}{59}$

$\Rightarrow \left(\frac{4}{3}\right)^x = \frac{16}{9}$ or $\left(\frac{4}{3}\right)^x = \frac{4}{3}$

$\Rightarrow x = 2$ and $x = 1$

(b) $2\frac{3}{\log_2 x} = \frac{1}{64} \qquad \Rightarrow 2^{\frac{3}{\log_2 x}} = (2)^{-6}$

$\Rightarrow \frac{3}{\log_2 x} = -2 \qquad \Rightarrow -\frac{1}{2} = \log_2 x$

$\Rightarrow 2^{-1/2} = x$

7. (a) $(x-3)^{x^2-4x} = (x-3)^{12}$

$\Rightarrow x^2 - 4x = 12 \qquad \Rightarrow x^2 - 4x - 12 = 0$

$\Rightarrow x^2 - 6x + 2x - 12 = 0$

$\Rightarrow x(x-6) + 2(x-6) = 0$

$\Rightarrow (x+2)(x-6) = 0 \qquad \Rightarrow x = -2 \text{ or } x = 6$

(b) $\left(3-2\sqrt{2}\right)^x + \left(3+2\sqrt{2}\right)^x = 6$

$\because \ 3-2\sqrt{2} = \dfrac{1}{3+2\sqrt{2}}$

$\Rightarrow \dfrac{1}{y} + y = 6$; where $y = (3+2\sqrt{2})^x$

$\Rightarrow y^2 - 6y + 1 = 0$

$\Rightarrow y = \dfrac{6 \pm \sqrt{36-4}}{2} = 3 \pm 2\sqrt{2}$

$\Rightarrow (3+2\sqrt{2})^x = (3+2\sqrt{2})^{\pm 1}$

$\Rightarrow x = \pm 1$

TEXTUAL EXERCISE–1: (OBJECTIVE)

1. (c) $\dfrac{5(2)^{k-2} + 10(2)^{k-1}}{10^{k+2}} = 5.2^{k-2}\left[\dfrac{1+2^2}{2^{k+2}.5^{k+2}}\right] = \dfrac{1}{2^4} \times \dfrac{5^2}{5^{k+2}}$

$= \dfrac{1}{16} \times (5)^{-k}$

2. (b) $6^x + 6^{x+1} = 2^x + 2^{x+1} + 2^{x+2}$

$\Rightarrow 2^x\,[3^x + 2.3^{x+1}] = 2^x[1 + 2 + 2^2]$

$\Rightarrow 3^x + 2.3^{x+1} = 7$

$\Rightarrow 3^x + 2.(3).3^x = 7 \qquad \Rightarrow 7(3^x) = 7$

$\Rightarrow 3^x = 1 \qquad \Rightarrow x = 0$

3. (d) $9^{|3x-1|} = 3^{8x-2} \qquad \Rightarrow (3)^{2|3x-1|} = 3^{8x-2}$

$\Rightarrow |3x-1| = \dfrac{8x-2}{2} \qquad \Rightarrow |3x-1| = 4x-1$

$\Rightarrow 3x - 1 = -4x + 1$ or $3x - 1 = 4x - 1$

$\Rightarrow 7x = 2$ or $0 = x$

$\Rightarrow x = 2/7$ or 0

Although we are getting $x = 0$, as solution, but it is not acceptable as it does not satisfy the equation.

4. (c) $3^{|\sin x|} + 4.3^{\cos x} = 7$

In the given equation $|\sin x| = 1$ and $\cos x = 0$ will satisfy the equation as it will leave $3^1 + 4.3^0 = 7$ $\cos x = 0$

$x = \dfrac{(2n+1)}{2}\pi, \forall n \in \mathbb{Z}$. This also satisfies $|\sin x| = 1$

5. (a) $2^{[|\sin x|]} + 5 = 6 \qquad \Rightarrow 2^{[|\sin x|]} = 1$

$\Rightarrow 2^{[|\sin x|]} = 2^0 \qquad \Rightarrow [|\sin x|] = 0$

$\Rightarrow 0 \le |\sin x| < 1 \qquad \Rightarrow x \in \mathbb{R} - (2n+1)\dfrac{\pi}{2} \forall n \in \mathbb{Z}$

6. (c) $9^x - 4(3^x) + 3 = 0 \qquad \Rightarrow 3^{2x} - 4(3^x) + 3 = 0$

$\Rightarrow 3^x = \dfrac{4 \pm \sqrt{16-12}}{2} = \dfrac{4 \pm 2}{2}$

$\Rightarrow 3^x = 3$ or $3^x - 1\ x - 1$ or $x = 0$

7. (c) $\sqrt{(2^x - 3)^4} = 16$

$\Rightarrow (2^x - 3)^2 = 4^2 \qquad \Rightarrow 2^x - 3 = \pm 4$

$\Rightarrow 4^x = 49$

TEXTUAL EXERCISE–4: (SUBJECTIVE)

1. (a) $2^{3-8x} > 1 = 2^{3-8x} > 2^0 \quad 3 - 8x > 0$

$\Rightarrow 3 > 8x \qquad \Rightarrow 3/8 > x$

$\Rightarrow x \in (-\infty, 3/8)$

(b) $16^x > 0.125 = 4^{2x} > \dfrac{125}{1000} = 4^{2x} > \dfrac{1}{8}$

$\Rightarrow 4^{2x} > (4)^{-3/2} \qquad \Rightarrow 2x > -3/2$

$\Rightarrow x > -3/4 \qquad \Rightarrow x \in (-3/4, \infty)$

(c) $(0.3)^{2x^2-3x+6} < 0.00243 = (0.3)^{2x^2-3x+6} > (0.3)^5$

$\Rightarrow 2x^2 - 3x + 6 > 5 \qquad \Rightarrow 2x^2 - 3x + 1 > 0$

$\Rightarrow 2x^2 - 2x - x + 1 > 0 \quad \Rightarrow 2x(x-1) - 1(x-1)$

$\Rightarrow (2x-1)(x-1) > 0 \qquad \Rightarrow x \in (-\infty, 1/2) \cup (1, \infty)$

2. (a) 2^{300} or $3^{200} = (2^3)^{100}$ or $(3^2)^{100}$

$\Rightarrow 8^{100} < 9^{100} \qquad \therefore 3^{200}$ is greater

(b) 54^4 or $21^{12} \qquad \Rightarrow (54)^4$

$\Rightarrow 27^4 \times 2^4 \qquad \Rightarrow 3^{12} \times 2^4$

$21^{12} \qquad \Rightarrow 3^{12} \times 7^{12}$

$\Rightarrow 3^{12}7^{12} > 3^{12}\,2^4 \qquad \therefore 21^{12} > 54^4$

(c) $(0.4)^4$ or $(0.8)^3 \qquad \Rightarrow (0.4)^4$

$\Rightarrow \dfrac{(4)^4}{10^4} \qquad \dfrac{2^8}{10^4}$

$\Rightarrow (0.8)^3 \qquad \Rightarrow \dfrac{8^3}{10^3}$

$\Rightarrow \dfrac{2^9}{10^3}$

$\dfrac{2^9}{10^3} > \dfrac{2^8}{10^4} \qquad \therefore (0.8)^3 > (0.4)^4$

(d) 10^{20} and $40^{10} \qquad \Rightarrow 10^{20}$

$\Rightarrow 2^{20} \times 5^{20} \qquad \Rightarrow 40^{10}$

$\Rightarrow 8^{10} \times 5^{10} \qquad \Rightarrow 2^{30} \times 5^{10}$

$\Rightarrow 5^{10} > 2^{10}$

Multiplying $2^{20}.5^{10}$ both sides, we gets $2^{20}.5^{20} > 2^{30}.5^{10}$

$\therefore 10^{20} > 40^{10}$

3. (a) $\sqrt[(x+1)]{3} > 9 \Rightarrow (3)^{1/(x+1)} > 9 = (3)^2$

$\Rightarrow \dfrac{1}{x+1} > 2 \qquad (\because a^x > a^y \Rightarrow x > y \text{ for } a > 1)$

$\Rightarrow \dfrac{1}{x+1} - 2 > 0 \qquad \Rightarrow \dfrac{1-2x-2}{x+1} > 0$

$\Rightarrow \dfrac{-2x-1}{x+1} > 0 \qquad \Rightarrow \dfrac{2x-1}{x+1} < 0$

$\Rightarrow (2x+1)(x+1) < 0 \qquad \Rightarrow x \in \left(-1, -\dfrac{1}{2}\right)$

But $x + 1 \ge 1$ and $x + 1 \in \mathbb{N}$

$\Rightarrow x \ge 0 \qquad \Rightarrow x \in \phi$

(b) $2^x + 2^{-x+1} - 3 < 0 \qquad \Rightarrow 2^x + \dfrac{2}{2^x} - 3 < 0$

$\Rightarrow 2^{2x} - 3.2^x + 2 < 0 \qquad \Rightarrow 2^{2x} - 2.2^x - 2^x + 2 < 0$

$\Rightarrow 2^x(2^x \ \ 2) \ \ 1(2^x - 2) < 0$

$\Rightarrow (2^x - 1)(2^x - 2) < 0 \quad \Rightarrow 2^x \in (1, 2)$

$\Rightarrow x \in (0, 1)$

(c) $x^2.\,5^x - 5^{2+x} < 0 \qquad \Rightarrow x^2.\,5^x - 25.\,5^x < 0$

$\Rightarrow 5^x(x^2 - 25) < 0 \qquad \because 5^x$ is always greater than 0

$\therefore\ x^2 - 25 < 0 \quad \Rightarrow (x+5)(x-5) < 0$

$\Rightarrow x \in (-5, 5)$

4. (a) $\dfrac{2^{x-1}-1}{2^{x+1}+1} < 2 \quad \Rightarrow 2^{x-1} - 1 < 2.\, 2^{x+1} + 2$

$\Rightarrow 2^{x-1} - 1 < 2^{x+2} + 2 \quad \Rightarrow 2^{x-1} - 2^{x+2} < 3$

$\Rightarrow 2^{x-1}(1-8) < 3 - 2^{x-1} \times 7 < 3$

$\Rightarrow 2^{x-1} > -3/7$

This is always true

Since $2^{x-1} > 0$ for $\forall\, x \in \mathbb{R}$

$\therefore\ x \in \mathbb{R}$

(b) $2^{x+2} - 2^{x+1} + 2^{x-1} - 2^{x-2} \le 9$

$\Rightarrow 2^{x-2}\,[2^4 - 2^3 + 2 - 1] \le 9$

$\Rightarrow 2^{x-2}[16 - 8 + 2 - 1] \le 9$

$\Rightarrow 2^{x-2}\,[9] \le 9 \quad \Rightarrow 2^{x-2} \le 1$

$\Rightarrow 2^{x-2} \le 2^0 \quad \Rightarrow x - 2 \le 0$

$\Rightarrow x \le 2 \quad \Rightarrow x \in (-\infty, 2]$

(c) $2^{4x^2-6} > 2^3 \quad \Rightarrow 4x^2 - 6 > 3$

$\Rightarrow 4x^2 > 9 \quad \Rightarrow x^2 > 9/4$

$\Rightarrow |x| > 3/2 \quad \Rightarrow x \in \left(-\infty, -\dfrac{3}{2}\right) \cup \left(\dfrac{3}{2}, \infty\right)$

5. (a) $6^x - 2(3^x) - 3(2^x) + 6 > 0$

$\Rightarrow 3^x.2^x - 2(3^x) - 3(2^x) + 3.2 > 0$

$\Rightarrow 3^x(2^x - 2) - 3(2^x - 2) > 2$

$\Rightarrow (3^x - 3)(2^x - 2) > 0$

For the satisfaction of above inequality, any value except $x = 1$ will work.

$\Rightarrow x \in \mathbb{R} - \{1\}$

(b) $2^{x+2} > \left(\dfrac{1}{4}\right)^{1/x}$ or $2^{x+2} > (2^{-2})^{1/x}$

$\Rightarrow 2^{x+2} > (2^{-2})^{1/x} \quad \Rightarrow 2^{x+2} > (2)^{-2/x}$

$\Rightarrow x + 2 > -2/x \quad \Rightarrow x + 2 + \dfrac{2}{x} > 0$

$\Rightarrow \dfrac{x^2 + 2x + 2}{x} > 0$

$\Rightarrow [(x+1)^2 + 1]x > 0 \quad \Rightarrow x > 0$

$\Rightarrow x \in (0, \infty)$

(c) $2^x + 2^{|x|} \ge 2\sqrt{2} \quad \Rightarrow 2^x + 2^{|x|} \ge (2)^{3/2}$

Case 1: if $x > 0$

$2^x + 2^x \ge (2)^{3/2} \quad \Rightarrow 2.2^x \ge (2)^{3/2}$

$\Rightarrow 2^{x+1} \ge (2)^{3/2} \quad \Rightarrow x + 1 \ge 3/2$

$\Rightarrow x \ge 1/2 \quad \Rightarrow x \in [1/2, \infty)$

Case 2: if $x < 0$

$2x + \dfrac{1}{2^x} \ge (2)^{3/2} \quad \Rightarrow 2^{2x} + 1 \ge (2)^{3/2}.2^x$

$\Rightarrow 2^{2x} - (2)^{3/2}.\, 2^x + 1 \ge 0 \Rightarrow y^2 - 2\sqrt{2}.y + 1 \ge 0$

$\Rightarrow \left(y - \dfrac{\left(2\sqrt{2} + \sqrt{8-4}\right)}{2}\right)\left(y - \dfrac{(2\sqrt{2} \quad 2)}{2}\right) \ge$

$\Rightarrow \left(y - \left(\sqrt{2}+1\right)\right)\left(y - \sqrt{2} - 1\right) \ge 0$

$\Rightarrow y = \sqrt{2} + 1 \quad$ or $\quad y = \sqrt{2} - 1$

$\Rightarrow 2^x = \sqrt{2} + 1 \quad$ or $\quad 2^x = \sqrt{2} - 1$

$\Rightarrow \sqrt{2} + 1 > 2$ (not possible because $x < 0$) or $x = \log_2\left(\sqrt{2} - 1\right)$

$\Rightarrow y \in \left(-\infty, \sqrt{2} - 1\right) \cup \left[\sqrt{2} + 1, \infty\right]$

$\Rightarrow x \in \left(-\infty, \log_2(\sqrt{2} - 1)\right) \cup [1/2, \infty)$

6. $3\sqrt{x^6 - 2x^3 + 1} \ge 3^{1-x}$

$\Rightarrow \sqrt{x^6 - 2x^3 + 1} \ge 1 - x$; clearly $x \ge 1$ is satisfies

Now for $x < 1$; $x^6 - 2x^3 + 1 \ge (1 - x)^2$

$\Rightarrow (x^3 - 1)^2 \ge (x - 1)^2 \quad \Rightarrow (x-1)^2[(x^2 + x + 1)^2 - 1] \ge 0$

$\Rightarrow (x-1)^2[x^4 + x^2 + 2x^3 + 2x^2 + 2x] \ge 0$

$\Rightarrow x(x-1)^2[x^3 + 2x^2 + 3x + 2] \ge 0$

$\Rightarrow x(x-1)^2(x+1)(x^2 + x + 2) \ge 0$

$\Rightarrow x^2 + x + 2$ has real roots.

$\Rightarrow (x-1)^2$ is always positive or zero.

$\Rightarrow x^2 + x + 2$ is always positive.

$\Rightarrow x \in (-\infty, -1) \cup (0, \infty)$

$\Rightarrow x \in \mathbb{R} \sim (-1, 0)$

7. $\sqrt{9^x + 3^x - 2} \ge 9 - 3^x \quad \Rightarrow \sqrt{3^{2x} + 3^x - 2} \ge 9 - 3^x$

$\Rightarrow 3^{2x} + 3^x - 2 \ge 81 + 3^{2x} - 18.3^x$

$\Rightarrow 19.3^x \ge 81 + 2 \quad \Rightarrow 19.3^x \ge 83$

$\Rightarrow 3^x \ge 83/19$

$\Rightarrow x \ge \log_3(83/19) \quad \Rightarrow x \in \left[\log_3 \dfrac{83}{19}, \infty\right)$

8. (a) $4^x - 2^{x+2} - 6^x + 4.3^x \le 0$

$\Rightarrow 2^{2x} - 4.2^x - 2^x.3^x + 4.3^x \le 0$

$\Rightarrow 2^x\,[2^x - 4] - 3^x\,[2^x - 4] \le 0$

$\Rightarrow [2^x - 3^x]\,[2^x - 4] \le 0$

Case 1: $2^x \le 3^x\ \forall\, x \in [0, \infty)$

$\Rightarrow 2^x \ge 4\ \forall\, x \in [2, \infty) \quad \Rightarrow x \in [2, \infty)$

Case 2: $2^x \ge 3^x$ and $2x \le 4$

$\Rightarrow 2^x \ge 3^x\ \forall\, x \in (-\infty, 0]$

$\Rightarrow 2^x \le 4\ \forall\, x \in (-\infty, 2] \Rightarrow x \in (-\infty, 0]$

$\therefore$ The range of x is $(-\infty, 0] \cup [2, \infty)$

(b) $\left(\sqrt{x^2}\right)^{x^2 - 5x + 9} \ge x^3$

$\Rightarrow \left|(-x)\right|^{x^2 - 5x + 9} \ge x^3 \qquad (1)$

Case 1: For $x < 0$, L.H.S. > 0, whereas R.H.S. < 0

$\therefore$ Inequality (1) holds.

Case 2: For $x > 0$, Inequality (1) becomes $(x)^{x^2 - 5x + 9} \ge (x)^3 \qquad (2)$

Sub case 1: $x \in (0, 1)$

$\Rightarrow x^2 - 5x + 9 \le 3 \quad \Rightarrow x^2 - 5x + 6 \le 0$

$\Rightarrow (x-2)(x-3) \le 0$

$\Rightarrow x \in [2, 3]$ but it is out of sub-case restriction.

Sub case 2: $x \in [1, \infty)$

$\Rightarrow x^2 - 5x + 9 \ge 3 \quad \Rightarrow x^2 - 5x + 6 \ge 0$

$\Rightarrow (x-2)(x-3) \ge 0$

$x \in (-\infty, 2] \cup [3, \infty) \quad \Rightarrow x \in (1, 2] \cup [3, \infty)$

Sub case 2: $x = 1$ or $x = 0$

Obviously, L.H.S. = R.H.S. = 1 for $x = 1$ and L.H.S. = R.H.S. = 0 for $x = 0$

$\therefore$ Concluding from above case analysis, we have solution set $\mathbb{R} - ((0, 1) \cup (2, 3))$

TEXTUAL EXERCISE-2: (OBJECTIVE)

1. **(b), (d)**

(a) $(0.2)^7 > (0.8)^4 \Rightarrow (0.2)^7 > (4 \times 0.2)^4$

$\Rightarrow (0.2)^7 > 256 \times (0.2)^4 \quad \therefore \quad (0.8)^4 > (0.2)^7$

$\Rightarrow$ False

(b) $(0.2)^7 . (0.8)^4$ as shown above it is correct

$\Rightarrow$ True

(c) $(10)^{30} < (500)^{10} \Rightarrow 2^{30} \times 5^{30}$

$\Rightarrow 2^{10} \times 2^{10} \times 5^{10} \times 5^{10} \times 5^{10}$

$\Rightarrow 2^{20} \times 5^{30} \quad \therefore \quad (500)^{10} < 10^{30}$

$\Rightarrow$ False

(d) $(10)^{30} > (500)^{10}$ as shown above is correct option

$\Rightarrow$ True

2. **(b)** $\left(\frac{1}{3}\right)^{\sqrt{x+2}} > 3^{-x} \Rightarrow (3)^{-\sqrt{x+2}} > 3^{-x}$

$\Rightarrow -\sqrt{x+2} > -x \Rightarrow \sqrt{x+2} < x$

$\Rightarrow x + 2 < x^2$

($\because$ if $x < 0$, then inequality does not hold, $\Rightarrow x \geq 0$)

$\Rightarrow x^2 - x - 2 > 0 \Rightarrow x \in (-\infty, -1) \cup \in (2, \infty)$

$\Rightarrow x \in (2, \infty)$

3. **(d)** $\left(\frac{2}{5}\right)^{\frac{6-5x}{2+5x}} < \frac{25}{4}$

$\Rightarrow \left(\frac{2}{5}\right)^{\frac{6-5x}{2+5x}} < \left(\frac{2}{5}\right)^{-2}$ where $x \neq -2/5$

$\Rightarrow \frac{6-5x}{2+5x} > -2$

[2/5 lies between 0 and 1 $\therefore$ greater the power of 2/5 smaller is the number]

$\Rightarrow \frac{6-5x+4+10x}{2+5x} > 0 \Rightarrow \frac{10+5x}{2+5x} > 0$

$\Rightarrow 5(2 + x)(2 + 5x) > 0$

$\Rightarrow x \in (-\infty, -2) \cup \{-2/5, \infty\}$

4. **(a), (c), (d)** $\frac{2^{1-x} - 2^x + 1}{2^x - 1} \leq 0$; Put $2^x = y > 0 \ \forall x \in \mathbb{R}$

$\Rightarrow \frac{\frac{2}{y} - y + 1}{y - 1} \leq 0 \Rightarrow \frac{2 - y^2 + y}{y(y-1)} \leq 0$

$\Rightarrow \frac{y^2 - y - 2}{y(y-1)} \geq 0 \Rightarrow \frac{(y-2)(y+1)}{y(y-1)} \geq 0$

$\Rightarrow y(y - 1)(y - 2)(y + 1) \geq 0; y \neq 0, 1$

$\Rightarrow (y - 1)(y - 2) \geq 0; y \neq 1$ ($\because$ $y, y + 1 > 0$)

$\Rightarrow 2^x = y \in (-\infty, 1) \cup [2, \infty)$ but $y > 0$

$\Rightarrow 2^x \in (0, 1) \cup [2, \infty) \Rightarrow x \in (-\infty, 0) \cup [1, \infty)$

5. **(b)** $12^x - 2(3^x) - 3(4^x) + 6 < 0$

$\Rightarrow 3^x.4^x - 2(3^x) - 3(4^x) + 6 < 0$

$\Rightarrow 3^x(4^x - 2) - 3(4^x - 2) < 0$

$\Rightarrow (3^x - 3)(4^x - 2) < 0$

For the above inequality so hold true one item must be positive and other should be negative

Case: (i) $3^x - 3 < 0$ and $4^x - 2 > 0$

$\Rightarrow 3^x < 3^1 \qquad \Rightarrow 4^x - 2 > 0$

$x < 1 \qquad \Rightarrow 4^x > 2$

$\Rightarrow 4^x > (4)^{1/2} \qquad \Rightarrow x > 1/2$

The range for x is $\left(\frac{1}{2}, 1\right)$

Case: (ii) $3^x - 3 > 0$ and $4^x - 2 < 0$

$\Rightarrow 3^x - 3 > 0 \qquad \Rightarrow 4^x - 2 < 0$

$\Rightarrow 3^x > 3 \qquad \Rightarrow 4^x < 2$

$\Rightarrow x > 1 \qquad \Rightarrow 4x < 4^{1/2}$

$\Rightarrow x < 1/2$

No x possible satisfying both inequality.

(c) $(1.5)^{1-x} < (0.64)^{2(1+\sqrt{x})}$

$\Rightarrow \left(\frac{125}{100}\right)^{1-x} < \left(\frac{64}{100}\right)^{2(1+\sqrt{x})}$

$\Rightarrow \left(\frac{5}{4}\right)^{1-x} < \left(\frac{16}{25}\right)^{2(1+\sqrt{x})} \Rightarrow \left(\frac{4}{5}\right)^{x-1} < \left(\left(\frac{4}{5}\right)^2\right)^{2(1+\sqrt{x})}$

$\Rightarrow \left(\frac{4}{5}\right)^{x-1} < \left(\frac{4}{5}\right)^{4(1+\sqrt{x})} \Rightarrow x - 1 > 4(1 + \sqrt{x})$

$\Rightarrow (\sqrt{x}+1)(\sqrt{x}-1) > 4(1+\sqrt{x})$

$\Rightarrow (\sqrt{x}-1) > 4 \qquad \Rightarrow \sqrt{x} > 5$

$\Rightarrow x > 25 \qquad \Rightarrow x \in (25, \infty)$

7. **(a)** $\left(\frac{1}{3}\right)^{x+\frac{1}{2}-\frac{2}{x}} > \frac{1}{\sqrt{27}} \Rightarrow \left(\frac{1}{3}\right)^{\frac{2x^2+x-4}{2x}} > \frac{1}{(3)^{3/2}}$

$\Rightarrow \frac{2x^2+x-4}{2x} < \frac{3}{2} \Rightarrow \frac{2x^2+x-4}{x} < 3$

$\Rightarrow \frac{2x^2+x-4-3x}{x} < 0 \Rightarrow \frac{2x^2-2x-4}{x} < 0$

$\Rightarrow \frac{x^2-x-2}{x} < 0 \qquad \Rightarrow x(x - 2)(x + 1) < 0$

$\Rightarrow x \in (-\infty, -1) \cup (0, 2)$

8. **(b)** $8^{\sqrt{8^x}} > 4096 \qquad \Rightarrow 8^{\sqrt{8^x}} > 8^4$

$\Rightarrow \sqrt{8^x} > 4 \qquad \Rightarrow 2^{3x/2} > 2^2$

$\Rightarrow 3x/2 > 2 \qquad \Rightarrow 3x > 4$

$\Rightarrow x \in 4/3 \qquad \Rightarrow x \in (4/3, \infty)$

TEXTUAL EXERCISE-5 (SUBJECTIVE)

1. **(a)** $y = \log_3 (9 - x^2)$

In any logarithm $\log_x y$; $x \neq 1$ or negative and $y > 0$. So, in the given logarithm

$\Rightarrow 9 - x^2 > 0 \qquad \Rightarrow 9 > x^2$

$\Rightarrow -3 < x < 3 \qquad \Rightarrow x \in (-3, 3)$

(b) $y = \log_2 (x^2 - 4) \qquad \Rightarrow x^2 - 4 > 0$

$\Rightarrow x^2 > 4 \qquad \Rightarrow x < -2$ or $x > 2$

$\Rightarrow x \in (-\infty, -2) \cup (2, \infty)$

2. $a^{\sin x} = a^{|x|+2}$

Taking logarithm on base a on both sides

$\Rightarrow \sin x \log_a a = (|x| + 2) \log_a a \qquad [\because \log m^n = n \log m]$

$\Rightarrow \sin x = |x| + 2 \ [\log_a a = 1]$

$\Rightarrow$ The above equation can be solved graphically.

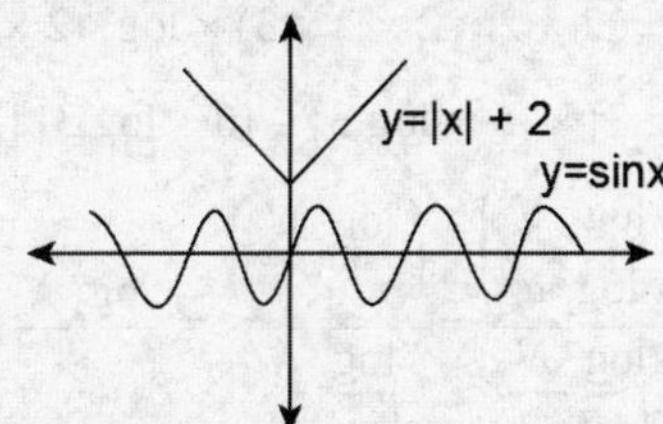

Since there is no intersection point between the two curves, hence $\sin x \neq |x| + 2 \ \forall \in \mathbb{R}$

So $a^{\sin x} = a^{|x|+2}$ can be equal in case only when $a = 0$ or 1. $\log_2 a$ will be undefined if $a = 0$

$\Rightarrow \log_2 1 = 0$

3. (a) $\log_{5\sqrt{5}} 5 \quad \Rightarrow \log_{5\sqrt{5}} 5 = x$

$\Rightarrow 5\sqrt{5}^{\log_{5\sqrt{5}} 5} = (5\sqrt{5})^x \Rightarrow 5 = (5\sqrt{5})^x$

$\Rightarrow 5^1 = ((5)^{3/2})^x \quad \Rightarrow 5^1 = (5)^{3/2x}$

$\Rightarrow 1 = 3/2x \quad \Rightarrow x = 2/3$

(b) $\log_{\sqrt{7}} 343\sqrt{7} \quad \Rightarrow \log_{(7)} 1/2 (7)^3 (7)^{1/2}$

$\Rightarrow \log_{(7)} 1/2\ (7)^{3+1/2} \quad \Rightarrow \log_{(7)} 1/2\ (7)^{7/2}$

$\Rightarrow \log_{(7)^{1/2}} \left((7)^{1/2}\right)^7 \quad \Rightarrow 7\log_{(7)^{1/2}} (7)^{1/2} = 7$

(c) $\log_8 1024 \quad \Rightarrow \log_8 2^{10}$

$\Rightarrow \log_{2^3} (2^3)^{10/3} \quad \Rightarrow 10/3 \log_{2^3} (2)^3$

$\Rightarrow 10/3$

4. $\log_7 x = a = 7(2401)^{3a+\frac{1}{4}} = 7(7^4)^{3a+\frac{1}{4}} = 7 \times (7^4)^{3a} \times (7^4)^{1/4} =$

$7^2 \times (7)^{12a} = 7^2 \times (7)^{12\log_7 x} = 7^2 \times (7)^{\log_7 x^{12}} = 49 \times x^{12}$

5. (a) $f(x) = \log_7 (x^2 - 4x + 3) \quad \Rightarrow x^2 - 4x + 3 >$

$\Rightarrow x^2 - 3x - x + 3 > 0 \quad \Rightarrow x(x - 3) - 1\ (x - 3) > 0$

$\Rightarrow (x - 1)(x - 3) > 0\ x < 1$ or $x > 3$

$\Rightarrow x \in (\infty, 1) \cup (3, \infty)$

(b) $f(x) = \log_2 (4 - x^2) + \log_{10} (x^2 - 1)$

$(4 - x^2) > 0\ 4 > x^2 \quad \Rightarrow -2 < x < 2$ and

$x^2 - 1 > 0 \quad \Rightarrow x^2 > 1$

$\Rightarrow x < -1$ or $x > 1$

The common range for $4 - x^2$ and $x^2 - 1$ is $(-2, -1) \cup (1, 2)$

(c) $f(x) = \log \dfrac{t^2 + 5t + 9}{t^2 - 5t + 6} \quad \Rightarrow \dfrac{t^2 + 5t + 9}{t^2 - 5t + 6} > 0$

$\Rightarrow t^2 + 5t + 9 > 0$

$\Rightarrow t^2 + 5t + 9 > 0$ has no real roots hence it is always positive for any $t \in \mathbb{R}$ and $t^2 - 5t + 6$ can not be negative in order to make whole expression positive as $t^2 + 5t + 9$ is always positive.

$\Rightarrow t^2 - 3t - 2t + 6 > 0 \quad \Rightarrow t(t - 3) - 2\ (t - 3) > 0$

$\Rightarrow (t - 2)(t - 3) > 0 \quad \Rightarrow t \in (-\infty, 2) \cup (3, \infty)$

6. $x - 1 > 0 \quad \Rightarrow x > 1$

$\Rightarrow x \in (1, \infty)$ and $|x - 5| > 2\backslash$

$\Rightarrow -2 < x - 5 \quad \Rightarrow x - 5 > 2$

$\Rightarrow -2 + 5 < x \quad \Rightarrow x > 2 + 5$

$\Rightarrow 3 < x \quad \Rightarrow x > 7$

Hence, the range for x is $x \in (1, 3) \cup (7, \infty)$

7. $x^4 + 1 = 2x^2 \quad \Rightarrow x^4 - 2x^2 + 1 = 0$

$\Rightarrow (x^2 - 1)^2 = 0 \quad \Rightarrow x^2 = 1$

$\Rightarrow x = \pm 1\ \log(x + x^{-1})$ should be defined

$\Rightarrow x + x^{-1} = 0 \quad \Rightarrow x + \dfrac{1}{x} > 0$

$\Rightarrow \dfrac{x^2 + 1}{x} > 0 \quad \Rightarrow (x^2 + 1)(x) > 0$

$\Rightarrow x > 0 \quad \Rightarrow x \in (0, \infty)$

So, the value that can satisfy $x^4 + 1 = 2x^2$ is 1.

TEXTUAL EXERCISE–6: (SUBJECTIVE)

1. (a) $32^{1/3} = 4x$; Taking log both sides, we get

$\log_2 32^{1/3} = \log_2 4x$

$\Rightarrow \dfrac{1}{3}\log_2 32 = \log_2 4x \quad [\because \log mn = \log m + \log n]$

$\Rightarrow \dfrac{1}{3}\log_2 2^5 = \log_2 4 + \log_2 x$

$\Rightarrow \dfrac{5}{3}\log_2 2 = \log_2 2^2 + \log_2 x$

$\Rightarrow \dfrac{5}{3} = 2\log_2 2 = \log_2 x \Rightarrow \dfrac{5}{3} = 2 + \log_2 x$

$\Rightarrow \dfrac{5}{3} - 2 = \log_2 x \quad \Rightarrow -\dfrac{1}{3}\log_2 x$

(b) $64^{1/4} = 8x$; Taking log both sides, we get $\log_2 64^{1/4} = \log_2 8x$

$\Rightarrow \dfrac{1}{4}\log_2 2^6 = \log_2 8x \quad \Rightarrow \dfrac{6}{4}\log_2 2 = \log_2 8 + \log_2 x$

$\Rightarrow \dfrac{3}{2} = 3 + \log_2 x \quad \Rightarrow \dfrac{3}{2} - 3 = \log_2 x$

$\Rightarrow \dfrac{-3}{2} = \log_2 x$

2. (a) $\log_8 512 = \log_8 (8)^3$ (Using property $\log a^4 = n \log a$) $= 3\log_8 8\ [\log_8 8 = 1] = 3 \times 1 = 3$

(b) $\log_{2\sqrt{2}} (32) = \log_{(2)^{3/2}} (2)^5 = \log_{(2)^{3/2}} (2^{3/2})^{5\times\frac{2}{3}}$

$= \log_{(2)^{3/2}} (2^{3/2})^{10/3} = \dfrac{10}{3}\log_{(2)^{3/2}} (2)^{3/2} = \dfrac{10}{3}$

(c) $\log_8 128 = \log_{2^3} 2^7 = \log_{2^3} (2^3)^{7/3} = \dfrac{7}{3}\log_{2^3} (2^3) = \dfrac{7}{3}$

3. (a) $\log_2 8.\ \log_3 2\ .\ \log_4 5.\ \log_3 4\ .\ \log_8 2.\ \log_5 3.\ \log_2 3$

$\Rightarrow \dfrac{\log 8}{\log 2}.\dfrac{\log 2}{\log 3}.\dfrac{\log 5}{\log 4}.\dfrac{\log 4}{\log 3}.\dfrac{\log 2}{\log 8}.\dfrac{\log 3}{\log 5}.\dfrac{\log 3}{\log 2}$

$\left[\text{using properly} \log m^n = \dfrac{\log n}{\log m}\right] \Rightarrow 1$

(b) $\log_2 48$ where $\log_2 3 = A$

$\Rightarrow \log_2 3 \times 2^4 \quad \Rightarrow \log_2 3 + \log_2 2^4$

$\Rightarrow \lambda + 4\log_2 2 \quad \Rightarrow \lambda + 4$

(c) $\log_9 27 - \log_{27} 9 \quad \left[\because \log m^n = \dfrac{\log_x n}{\log_x m}\right]$

$= \dfrac{\log_3 27}{\log_3 9} - \dfrac{\log_3 9}{\log_3 27} = \dfrac{\log_3 3^3}{\log_3 3^2} = \dfrac{\log_3 3^2}{\log_3 3^3}$

$= \dfrac{3\log_3 3}{2\log_3 3} - \dfrac{2\log_3 3}{3\log_3 3} = \dfrac{3}{2} - \dfrac{2}{3} = \dfrac{5}{6}$

4. (a) $\dfrac{\log_3 12}{\log_{36} 3} - \dfrac{\log_3 4}{\log_{108} 3} = \dfrac{\log 12}{3} \times \dfrac{\log 36}{\log 3} - \dfrac{\log 9}{\log 3} \times \dfrac{\log 108}{\log 3}$

$= \log_3 12 \times \log_3 36 - \log_3 4 \times \log_3 108$

$= \log_3(3\times4) \times \log_3 (3^2 \times 4) - \log_3 4 \times \log_3 3^3 \times 4$

$= [1 + \log_3 4]\,[2 + \log_3 4] - \log_3 4\,[3 + \log_3 4]$

$= 2 + 3\log_3 4 + (\log_3 4)^2 - 3\log_3 4 - (\log_3 4)^2 = 2$

(b) $\log_5 \dfrac{\sqrt[4]{25}}{625} = \log_5 \dfrac{(5^2)^{1/4}}{5^4} = \log_5 (5)^{1/2-4} = \log_5 5^{-7/2}$

$= -7/2 \log_5 5 = -7/2$

(c) $\log_2 \log_2 \log_3 81 \Rightarrow \log_2 \log_2 \log_3 3^4$

$\Rightarrow \log_2 \log_2 4\log_3 3 \Rightarrow \log_2 \log_2 4$

$\Rightarrow \log_2 \log_2 2^2 \Rightarrow \log_2 2\log_2 2$

$\Rightarrow \log_2 2 \Rightarrow 1$

5. (a) $\log_5 \dfrac{(125)(625)}{25} \Rightarrow \log_5 \dfrac{5^3 \times 5^4}{5^2}$

$\Rightarrow \log_5 5^5 \Rightarrow 5 \log_5 5$

$\Rightarrow 5$

(b) $\dfrac{(\log_{100} 10)(\log_2(\log_4 2))(\log_4(\log_2(256)^2))}{\log_4 8 + \log_8 4}$

$= \dfrac{(\log_{100}(100)^{1/2})(\log_2 \log_4 (4)^{1/2})(\log_4 2 \times \log_2 2^8)}{\log_4 (4)^{3/2} + \log_8 (8)^{2/3}}$

$= \dfrac{\left(\frac{1}{2}\right) \times \left(\log_2 \frac{1}{2}\right)(\log_4 16)}{\frac{3}{2} + \frac{2}{3}} = \dfrac{\frac{1}{2} \times -1 \times 2}{\frac{9+4}{6}} = \dfrac{-6}{13}$

(c) $(81)^{\left(\frac{1}{\log_5 3}\right)} + 27^{\log_9 36} + 3^{\frac{4}{\log_7 9}}$

$= (3^4)^{\frac{\log_3 5}{\log_3 3}} + (3^3)^{\frac{\log_6 36}{\log_6 9}} + (3)^{\frac{4 \times \log_3 7}{\log_3 9}}$

$= (3^4)^{\log_3 5} + (3^3)^{2/\log_6 9} + (3)^{\frac{4 \times \log_3 7}{2}}$

$= (3^{\log_3 5})^4 + (3^3)^{2 \times \frac{\log_3 6}{\log_3 9}} + \left((3)^{\log_3 7}\right)^2$

$= (5)^4 + (3^3)^{\frac{2}{2}\log_3 6} + (7)^2 = 625 + (6)^3 + 49$

$= 625 + 216 + 49 = 890$

6. (a) $\log(1 + 2 + 3) = \log 1 + \log 2 + \log 3 = \log (1 + 2 + 3) = \log (6) = \log(2 \times 3) = \log 2 + \log 3 = \log 1 + \log 2 + \log 3$

$[\because \log 1 = 0]$

(b) $\log(360) = 3\log 2 + 2\log 3 + \log 5$

$\Rightarrow \log(2 \times 2 \times 2 \times 3 \times 3 \times 5)$

$\Rightarrow \log(2^3) + \log(3^2) + \log 5 \Rightarrow 3 \log 2 + 2 \log 3 + \log 5$

7. (a) $\log\left(\dfrac{x^2}{yz}\right) + \log\left(\dfrac{y^2}{zx}\right) + \log\left(\dfrac{z^2}{xy}\right) = 0$

$\Rightarrow \log\left(\dfrac{x^2\, y^2}{(yz)(zx)}\right) + \log\left(\dfrac{z^2}{xy}\right) = 0$

$\Rightarrow \log\left(\dfrac{x^2.y^2.z^2}{(yz)(zx)(xy)}\right) \Rightarrow \log\left(\dfrac{x^2y^2z^2}{x^2 + y^2z^2}\right)$

$\Rightarrow \log(1) = 0$

(b) $\dfrac{\log_2 24}{\log_{96} 2} - \dfrac{\log_2 192}{\log_{12} 2} = 3$

$\Rightarrow \log_2 24 \times \log_2 96 - \log_2 192 \log_2 12$

$\Rightarrow \log_2 (2 \times 2 \times 2 \times 3) \times \log_2 (2 \times 2 \times 2 \times 2 \times 2 \times 3) - \log_2(2 \times 2 \times 2 \times 2 \times 2 \times 2 \times 3) \times \log_2 (2 \times 2 \times 3)$

$\Rightarrow [3 + \log_2 3] \times [5 + \log_2 3] - [6 + \log_2 3]\,[2 + \log_2 3] = 3$

8. $\dfrac{\log_a N}{\log_{ab} N} = \dfrac{\left(\dfrac{\log_a N}{\log_a a}\right)}{\dfrac{\log_a N}{(\log_a ab)}} = \dfrac{\left(\dfrac{\log_a N}{1}\right)}{\dfrac{\log_a N}{\log_a ab}} = \dfrac{\log_a N}{1} \times \dfrac{\log_a ab}{\log_a N} = \log_a$

$ab = \log_a a + \log_a b = 1 + \log_a b$

9. $A = \log_{10}$

$\left(\dfrac{ab + \sqrt{(ab)^2 - 4(a+b)}}{2}\right) + \log_{10}\left(\dfrac{ab - \sqrt{(ab)^2 - 4(a+b)}}{2}\right)$

$= \log_{10}\left[\left(\dfrac{ab + \sqrt{(ab)^2 - 4(a+b)}}{2}\right)\left(\dfrac{ab - \sqrt{(ab)^2 - 4(a+b)}}{2}\right)\right]$

$= \log_{10}\left[\dfrac{(ab)^2 - ((ab)^2 - 4(a+b))}{4}\right] = \log_{10}\left[\dfrac{4(a+b)}{4}\right]$

$= \log_{10}(a + b) = \log_{10}(43 + 57) = \log_{10} 100 = 2 = A = 2$

$B = \left(2^{\log_6 18}\right)\left(3^{\log_6 3}\right) = 2^{1+\log_6 3}.3^{\log 6^3}$

$= 2.(2.3)^{\log_6 3} = 2.(6)^{\log_6 3} = 2(3) = 6$

$\Rightarrow$ A.B $\Rightarrow 2 \times 6$

$\Rightarrow 12$

10. (a) $x = \log_3 4$ and $y = \log_5 3$; $\log_3 10$ and $\log_3 (1.2)$

$\Rightarrow x = \log_3 4,\ y = \log_5 3 \Rightarrow y = \dfrac{1}{\log_3 5}$

$\Rightarrow \log_3 10 \Rightarrow \log_3 (2 \times 5)$

$\Rightarrow \log_3 2 + \log_3 5 \Rightarrow \dfrac{1}{2}\log_3 4 + \log_3 5$

$\Rightarrow \dfrac{1}{2}x + \dfrac{1}{y} = \log_3 10 \Rightarrow \log_3 (1.2)$

$\Rightarrow \log_3\left(\dfrac{12}{10}\right) \Rightarrow \log_3 (12) - \log_3 10$

$\Rightarrow \log_3 3 + \log_3 4 - \left(\dfrac{1}{2}x + \dfrac{1}{y}\right)$

$\Rightarrow 1 + x - \dfrac{x}{2} - \dfrac{1}{4} \Rightarrow 1 + \dfrac{x}{2} - \dfrac{1}{y} = \log_3(1.2)$

(b) $k^{\log_2 5} = 16 \Rightarrow \log_2 (k)^{\log_2 5} = \log_2 16$

$\Rightarrow (\log_2 5)(\log_2 k) = \log_2 2^4$

Multiplying $\log_2 5$ both sides, we get

$(\log_2 5)^2 (\log_2 k) = (\log_2 16)(\log_2 5)$

$\Rightarrow (\log_2 5)^2 (\log_2 k) = 4\log_2 5$

$\Rightarrow (\log_2 5)^2 (\log_2 k) = \log_2 5^4$

$\Rightarrow \log_2 (k)^{(\log_2 5)^2} = \log_2 625 \Rightarrow k^{(\log_2 5)^2} = 625$

TEXTUAL EXERCISE–3 (OBJECTIVE)

1. (c) $(256)^{1/10} = 8x \Rightarrow (2^8)^{1/10} = 2^3 x$

$\Rightarrow 2^{(4/5)} \times 2^{(-3)} = x \Rightarrow (2)^{4/5-3} = x$

$\Rightarrow (2)^{-11/5} = x \Rightarrow -\dfrac{11}{5} = \log_2 x$

2. (b) $\dfrac{\log_8 32}{\log_{64} 8} \Rightarrow \log_8 32 \times \log_8 64$

$\Rightarrow \log_8(8\times4)\times\log_8(8^2) \Rightarrow 2\times[\log_8 8+\log_8 4]$

$\Rightarrow 2\times[1+\log_8(8)^{2/3}] \Rightarrow 2\times\left[1+\dfrac{2}{3}\right]$

$\Rightarrow 2\times\dfrac{5}{3} \Rightarrow 10/3$

3. (c) $\lambda = \log_5\dfrac{(125)(625)}{25} \Rightarrow \lambda = \log_5\dfrac{5^3\times5^45^2}{5^2}$

$\Rightarrow \lambda = \log_5 5^5 \Rightarrow \lambda = 5$

$\therefore \log_\lambda 625 \Rightarrow \log_5 625$

$\Rightarrow \log_5 5^4 \Rightarrow 4$

4. (a) $\log_4\log_4\log_4 256 \Rightarrow \log_4\log_4\log_4 4^4$

$\Rightarrow \log_4\log_4 4 \Rightarrow \log_4 1 = 0$

5. (b) $\log_{0.01}10000 = \lambda \Rightarrow \dfrac{\log 10000}{\log 0.01} = \lambda$

$\Rightarrow \dfrac{\log 10^4}{\log 10^{-2}} = \lambda \Rightarrow \dfrac{4}{-2} = \lambda$

$\Rightarrow -2 = \lambda$

$\therefore \log_{1/2}(-2)^4 \Rightarrow \log_{1/2} 16$

$\Rightarrow \log_{1/2}\left(\dfrac{1}{2}\right)^{-4} \Rightarrow -4$

6. (b) $\dfrac{\log_2 24}{\log_{96} 2} - \dfrac{\log_2 192}{\log_{12} 2} = \log_2 24\ \log_2 96 - \log_2 192\ \log_2 12$

$= \log_2(2^3\times3)\log_2(2^5\times3) - \log_2(2^6\times3)\log_2(2^2\times3)$

$= [3+\log_2^3][5+\log_2^3]-[6+\log_2^3][2+\log_2^3]$

$= 15+8\log_2 3+(\log_2 3)^2-12-8\log_2 3-(\log_2 3)^2 = 3$

7. (d) $7\log\dfrac{16}{15}+5\log\dfrac{25}{24}+3\log\dfrac{81}{80} = \log\lambda$

$= \log\left(\dfrac{16}{15}\right)^7+\log\left(\dfrac{25}{24}\right)^5\log\left(\dfrac{81}{80}\right)^3$

$= \log\left(\dfrac{16}{15}\right)^7\times\left(\dfrac{25}{24}\right)^5\times\left(\dfrac{81}{80}\right)^3$

$= \log\dfrac{4^{14}}{3^7\times5^7}\times\dfrac{5^{10}}{3^5\times2^{15}}\times\dfrac{3^{12}}{5^3\times2^{12}} = \log\dfrac{2^{18}\times5^{10}\times3^{12}}{3^{12}\times5^{10}\times2^{27}}$

$= \log 2$

$\Rightarrow \log 2 = \log\lambda \Rightarrow 2 = A$

$\Rightarrow \log_{1/2} 2 \Rightarrow \log_{1/2}(1/2)^{-1} = -1$

8. (a) $a^{\frac{\log_b\log_b N}{\log_b a}} \Rightarrow (a)^{(\log_b\log_b N)(\log_a b)}$

$\Rightarrow \left(a^{\log_a b}\right)^{(\log_b\log_b N)} \Rightarrow (b)^{\log_b(\log_b N)}$

$\Rightarrow \log_b N$

TEXTUAL EXERCISE–7: (SUBJECTIVE)

1. (a) $\log_2(x-1) = 3 \Rightarrow 2^{\log_2(x-1)} = 2^3$

$\Rightarrow x-1 = 8 \Rightarrow x = 8+1$

$\Rightarrow x = 9$

(b) $\log_{\sqrt{3}}(x^2-2x) = 2 \Rightarrow \sqrt{3}^{\log_{\sqrt{3}}(x^2-2x)} = (\sqrt{3})^2$

$\Rightarrow x^2-2x = 3 \Rightarrow x^2-2x-3 = 0$

$\Rightarrow x^2-3x+x-3 = 0 \Rightarrow x(x-3)+1(x-3) = 0$

$\Rightarrow (x+1)(x-3) = 0 \Rightarrow x = -1$ or $x = 3$

(c) $\log_2(x^2-3) = 2^2 \Rightarrow \log_2(x^2-3) = 4$

$\Rightarrow 2^{\log_2(x^2-3)} = 2^4 \Rightarrow x^2-3 = 16$

$\Rightarrow x^2 = 19 \Rightarrow x = \pm\sqrt{19}$

2. (a) $\log(x+1)-\log(x-1) = 1 \Rightarrow \log((x+1)/(x-1)) = 1$

$\Rightarrow \dfrac{x+1}{x-1} = 10 \Rightarrow x+1 = 10x-10$

$\Rightarrow 11-9x \Rightarrow x = 11/9$

(b) $(0.125)4^{2x-6} = \left(\dfrac{0.25}{\sqrt{2}}\right)$

$\Rightarrow \dfrac{(0.125)}{(0.25)}4^{2x-6} = 2^{-1/2} \Rightarrow \dfrac{4^{2x-6}}{2} = -2^{1/2}$

$\Rightarrow 2^{4x-12-1} = 2^{-1/2} \Rightarrow 4x-13 = -1/2$

$\Rightarrow 8x-26 = -1 \Rightarrow x = 25/8$

(c) $(a^2b^3)^x = c^5 \Rightarrow \log(a^2b^3)^x = \log c^5$

$\Rightarrow x\log(a^2b^3) = \log c^5 \Rightarrow \dfrac{\log c^5}{\log(a^2b^3)} = \log_{(a^2b^3)} c^5$

3. (a) $9^{1+\log x}-3^{1+\log x}-210 = 0$

$\Rightarrow 9.9^{\log x}-3.3^{\log x}-210 = 0$

$\Rightarrow 9.(3^{\log x})^2-3.3^{\log x}-210 = 0$

$9t^2-3t-210 = 0$; where $t = 3^{\log x}$

$\Rightarrow (t-5)(9t+42) = 0 \Rightarrow t = 5$ or $t = -42/9$

$\Rightarrow 3^{\log_3 x} = 5$ or $-42/9$(impossible)

$\Rightarrow x = 5$

(b) $\log_{10}(x^2-12+36) = 2$

$\Rightarrow x^2-12x+36 = 10^2 = 100$

$\Rightarrow x^2-12x-64 = 0$

$\Rightarrow x^2-16x+4x-64 = 0$

$\Rightarrow x(x-16)+4(x-16) = 0$

$\Rightarrow (x+6)(x+4) = 0$

$\Rightarrow x = 16, x = -4$

4. (a) $\log_x 3\ .\ \log_{x/3} 3+\log_{x/81} 3 = 0$

$\Rightarrow \dfrac{\log 3}{\log x}.\dfrac{\log 3}{\log x/3}+\dfrac{\log 3}{\log x/81} = 0$

$\Rightarrow \dfrac{\log 3}{\log x.\log x/3}+\dfrac{1}{\log x/81} =$

$\Rightarrow \log 3\ .\ \log x/81+\log x\ .\ \log x/3 = 0$

$\Rightarrow \log 3(\log x-\log 81)+\log x.\ \log\dfrac{x}{3} = 0$

$\Rightarrow \log 3(\log x)-\log 3.\log 81+\log x(\log x-\log 3) = 0$

$\Rightarrow \log x\log 3-4\log^2 3+\log^2 x-\log x\log 3 = 0$

$\Rightarrow \log^2 x = 4\log^2 3 \Rightarrow x = 3^2 = 9$ or $x = \dfrac{1}{9}$

(b) $\log_2 x = \dfrac{1}{3}.\log_2 8-2\log_2\sqrt{3}$

$\Rightarrow \log_2 x = 1-\log_2 3 \Rightarrow \log_2 x+\log_2 3 = 1$

$\Rightarrow \log_2 3x = 1 \Rightarrow 3x = 2$

$\Rightarrow x = 2/3$

5. (a) $\dfrac{\log_{10}(x-3)}{\log_{10}(x-1)} = \dfrac{1}{2}$ $\Rightarrow$ $2\log_{10}(x-3) = \log_{10}(x-1)$

$\Rightarrow$ $\log_{10}(x-3)^2 = \log_{10}(x-1)$

$\Rightarrow$ $(x-1) = (x-3)^2$ $\Rightarrow$ $x^2 - 6x + 9 = x - 1$

$\Rightarrow$ $x^2 - 7x + 10 = 0$ $\Rightarrow$ $(x-5)(x-2) = 0$

$\Rightarrow$ $x = 5, 2$

x can not take the value 2 as it is not included in the domain of $\log_{10}(x-3)$.

$\therefore$ $x = 5$

(b) $\log(\log x) + \log(\log x^3 - 2) = 0$

$\Rightarrow$ $\log(\log x(3\log x - 2) = 0$

$\Rightarrow$ $3\log x.\log x - 2\log x = 1$

$\Rightarrow$ $3(\log x)^2 - 2\log x - 1 = 0$

Let $\log x = 4$

$\Rightarrow$ $3y^2 - 2y - 1 = 0$ $\Rightarrow$ $3y^2 - 3y + y - 1 = 0$

$\Rightarrow$ $3y(y-1) + (y-1) = 0$

$\Rightarrow$ $y = 1$ or $y = -1/3$ $\Rightarrow$ $x = 10$ as $\log x \neq -1/3$

(c) $\log_{\log_5 x}(5) = 2$ $\quad 5(\log_5 x)^2$

$\Rightarrow$ $\sqrt{5} = \log_5 x$ $\Rightarrow$ $x = 5^{\sqrt{5}}$

6. $\dfrac{\log\left(\sqrt{x+2}+1\right)}{\log\sqrt[5]{x-2}} = 5$ $\qquad \log\left(\sqrt{x+2}+1\right) = 5\log\sqrt[5]{x-2}$

$\Rightarrow$ $\log\left[(x-2)^{1/5}\right]^5 = \log(x-2)$

$\Rightarrow$ $\sqrt{x+2}+1 = x-2$ $\Rightarrow$ $\sqrt{x+2} = x-3$

$\Rightarrow$ $x+2 = x^2+9-6x$ $\Rightarrow$ $x^2-7x+7=0$

$\Rightarrow$ $x = \dfrac{7\pm\sqrt{49-28}}{2} = \dfrac{7\pm\sqrt{21}}{2}$; But $x > 2$

$\Rightarrow$ $x = \dfrac{-7+\sqrt{21}}{2}$

7. $\sqrt{(3+\log_x 9)\log_3 x + 1} = 0$

$\Rightarrow$ $\sqrt{3(\log_3 x)^2 + 2\log x^3(\log_3 x)^2 + 1} = 0$

$\Rightarrow$ $\sqrt{3(\log_3 x)^2 + 2\log_3 x + 1} = 0$

$\Rightarrow$ $3(\log_3 x)^2 + 2\log_3 x = 1$

Let $\log_3 x = y$

$\Rightarrow$ $3y^2 + 2y - 1 = 0$ $\Rightarrow$ $3y^2 + 3y - y - 1 = 0$

$\Rightarrow$ $3y(y+1) - (y+1) = 0$

$\Rightarrow$ $y = -1$ or $y = 1/3$ $\Rightarrow$ $x = (3)^{1/3}$

or $x = (1/3)$ $\Rightarrow$ $x = 1/3, 3\sqrt{3}$

8. $3(\log_v u + \log_u v) = 10$ $\quad \therefore$ $\log_v u = \dfrac{1}{\log_u v} = y$

$3\left(y + \dfrac{1}{y}\right) = 10$

$\Rightarrow$ $3y^2 + 3 - 10y = 0$ $\Rightarrow$ $3y^2 - 9y - y + 3 = 0$

$\Rightarrow$ $3y(y-3)(y-3) = 0$ $\Rightarrow$ $(y-3)(3y-1) = 0$

$\Rightarrow$ $y = 3, y = 1/3$

$\Rightarrow$ $\log_v u = 3$ or $\dfrac{1}{3}$ $\Rightarrow$ $u = v^3$ or $v^{1/3}$ (Given uv – 81)

$\therefore$ $v^3 = u$

$\Rightarrow$ $v = 3$; $u = 27$ $\Rightarrow$ $(u, v) = (27, 3)$

$\Rightarrow$ $u = 3$; $v = 27$ $\Rightarrow$ $(u, v) = (3, 27)$

9. $x^2\ell n|x| - 1 = 0$ $\Rightarrow$ $x^2\ell n|x| = 1$

$\Rightarrow$ $\ell n|x| = 1/x^2$ $\Rightarrow$ $\ell n|x| = x^{-2}$

$\Rightarrow$ $e^{x-2} = |x|$

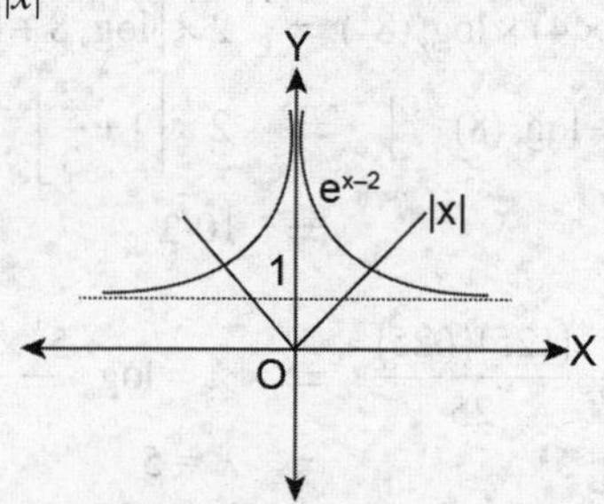

$\therefore$ Clearly there will be two points of intersection and hence two solutions.

TEXTUAL EXERCISE–4: (OBJECTIVE)

1. (a), (b) $\log_{x^2}(2x^2-4) = 1 \Rightarrow x^2 = 2x^2 - 4$

$\Rightarrow$ $x^2 = 4$ $\Rightarrow$ $x = 2, -2$

2. (c) $\log_4 \log_3 \log_2 x = 0$ $\Rightarrow$ $\log_3(\log_2 x) = 1$

$\Rightarrow$ $\log_2 x = 3$ $\Rightarrow$ $x = 2^3 = 8$

3. (a), (b) $\dfrac{a^{x+1}}{b^{x-1}} = c^{2x}$; Taking log of both sides, we get

$\log\left(\dfrac{a^{x+1}}{b^{x-1}}\right) = \log c^{2x}$

$\Rightarrow$ $\log a^{x+1} - \log b^{x-1} = \log c^{2x}$

$\Rightarrow$ $x + 1(\log a) - (x-1)\log b = 2x \log c$

$\Rightarrow$ $x(\log a - \log b) + \log a + \log b = 2x \log c$

$\Rightarrow$ $x(2\log c - \log a + \log b) = \log(ab)$

$\Rightarrow$ $x(2\log c + \log b/a) = \log(ab)$

$\Rightarrow$ $x.\log\left(c^2.\dfrac{b}{a}\right) = \log ab \Rightarrow x = \dfrac{\log(ab)}{\log\left(c^2\dfrac{b}{a}\right)} = \log_{bc^2/a}(ab)$

4. (a), (c) $\log_x 2 . \log_{2x} 2 = \log_{4x} 2$

$\Rightarrow$ $\dfrac{\log 2}{\log x}.\dfrac{\log 2}{\log 2x} = \dfrac{\log 2}{\log 4x}$

$\Rightarrow$ $\log 2(\log 4x) = \log x.(\log 2x)$

$\Rightarrow$ $\log 2(\log 4 + \log x) = \log x(\log 2 + \log x)$

$\Rightarrow$ $\log 2.\log 4 + \log 2.\log x = \log 2.\log x + (\log x)^2$

$\Rightarrow$ $(\log x)^2 = 2(2\log 2)^2$

$\Rightarrow$ $108x = \sqrt{2}\log 2$ or $\log x = -\sqrt{2}\log 2$

$\Rightarrow$ $x = 2^{\sqrt{2}}, 2^{-\sqrt{2}}$

5. (b) $5^{\log_a x} + 5x^{\log 5} = 3$ $\Rightarrow$ $x^{\log_a 5} + 5x^{\log_a 5} = 3$

$\Rightarrow$ $6.x^{\log_a 5} = 3$ $\Rightarrow$ $2 = (x^{\log_a 5})^{-1}$

$\Rightarrow$ $x = 2^{-x^{\log_5 a}}$

6. (d) $\log_{\left(\frac{2+x}{1}\right)} 7 = \log_{\left(\frac{2}{x+1}\right)} 7$. The selection are subject to following constrains

(i) $\dfrac{2}{x+1} > 0$ $\Rightarrow$ $(x+1) > 0$

$x > -1$

(ii) $\dfrac{2}{x+1} \neq 1$ $\Rightarrow$ $x \neq 1$

(iii) $\frac{2+x}{10} = \frac{2}{x+1}$ $\Rightarrow$ $2x + 2 + x^2 + x = 20$

$\Rightarrow$ $x^2 + 3x - 18 = 0$ $\Rightarrow$ $x^2 + 6x - 3x - 18 = 0$

$x(x + 6) - 3(x + 6) = 0$

$\Rightarrow$ $(x - 3)(x + 6) = 0$ $\Rightarrow$ $x = 3$

7. (b), (c) $2\log 2x = \log(7x - 2 - 2x^2)$

$\Rightarrow$ $\log(2x)^2 = \log(7x - 2 - 2x^2)$

$\Rightarrow$ $7x - 2 - 2x^2 = 4x^2$ $\Rightarrow$ $6x^2 - 7x + 2 = 0$

$\Rightarrow$ $6x^2 - 4x - 3x + 2 = 0$ $\Rightarrow$ $2x(3x - 2) - (3x - 2) = 0$

$\Rightarrow$ $(3x - 2)(2x - 1) = 0$ $\Rightarrow$ $x = 2/3, x = 1/2$

8. (c) $9^{\log_3(1-2x)} = 5x^2 - 5$

Taking log both sides, we get $\log_3(1 - 2x)\log 9 = \log(5x^2 - 5)$

$\Rightarrow$ $2\log_3(1-2x) = \frac{\log(5x^2-5)}{\log_3}$

$\Rightarrow$ $\log_3(1 - 2x)^2 = \log_3(5x^2 - 5)$

$\Rightarrow$ $(5x^2 - 5) = (1 - 2x)^2$

$\Rightarrow$ $5x^2 - 5 = (1 - 2x)^2$ $\Rightarrow$ $5x^2 - 5 = 1 + 4x^2 - 4x$

$\Rightarrow$ $x^2 + 4x - 6 = 0$

$\Rightarrow$ $x = \frac{-4 \pm \sqrt{16+24}}{2} = \frac{-4 \pm \sqrt{40}}{2} = -2 \pm \sqrt{10}$

$\Rightarrow$ Options (c) is correct $\because x < 1/2$

9. (b) $\log_4(x - 1) = \log_2(x - 3)$ $\Rightarrow$ $\frac{\log(x-1)}{\log 4} = \frac{\log(x-3)}{\log 2}$

$\Rightarrow$ $\log(x - 1) = 2\log(x - 3)$

$\Rightarrow$ $(x - 3)^2 = x - 1$

$\Rightarrow$ $x^2 + 9 - 6x = x - 1$ $\Rightarrow$ $x^2 - 7x + 10 = 0$

$\Rightarrow$ $(x - 5)(x - 2) = 0$ $\Rightarrow$ $x = 5, x = 2$

But $x \neq 2$ as $\log_2(x - 3)$ does not have 2 in its domain

$\Rightarrow$ $x = 5$

10. (d) $\frac{\log 5 + \log(x^2+1)}{\log(x-2)} = 2$

$\Rightarrow$ $\log 5 + \log(x^2 + 1) = \log(x - 2)^2$

$\Rightarrow$ $\log(x^2 + 1) - \log(x - 2)^2 = -\log 5$

$\Rightarrow$ $\frac{x^2+1}{(x-2)^2} = \frac{1}{5}$ $\Rightarrow$ $x^2 + 4 - 4x = 5x^2 + 5$

$\Rightarrow$ $4x^2 + 4x + 1 = 0$ $\Rightarrow$ $(2x + 1)^2 = 0$

$\Rightarrow$ $x = -1/2$

TEXTUAL EXERCISE–8: (SUBJECTIVE)

1. (a) $\log_a x \geq a$; given $a > 1$

$\Rightarrow$ $x \geq a^\circ$ $\Rightarrow$ $x \geq 1$

$\Rightarrow$ $x \in [1, \infty)$

(b) $\log_a x > 0$; given $a < 1$

$\Rightarrow$ $x < a^\circ$ $\Rightarrow$ $x < 1$

$\Rightarrow$ $x > 0$ $\Rightarrow$ $x \in (0, 1)$

2. (a) $\log_2 x^2 - 1 \leq 0$ $\Rightarrow$ $\log_2 x^2 \leq \log_2 2$

$\Rightarrow$ $x^2 \leq 2$ $\Rightarrow$ $(x-\sqrt{2})(x+\sqrt{2}) \leq 0$

$\Rightarrow$ $x \in [-\sqrt{2}, \sqrt{2}]$

(b) $\log_a(x^2 - 1) < 0$; given $0 < a < 1$

$\Rightarrow$ $\log_a(x^2 - 1) < \log_a 1$ $(x^2 - 1) > 1$

$\Rightarrow$ $x^2 - 2 > 0$ $\Rightarrow$ $(-\infty, -\sqrt{2}) \cup (\sqrt{2}, \infty)$

3. (a) $\log_a(x - 7) > 0$; given $a > 1$

$\Rightarrow$ $(x - 7) > a$ $\Rightarrow$ $x > a + 7$

$\Rightarrow$ $x > 8$ $x \in (8, \infty)$

(b) $\log_{1/2}(x - 1) > 0$ $\Rightarrow$ $\log_{1/2}(x - 1) > \log_{1/2} 1$

$\Rightarrow$ $x - 1 < 1$ $\Rightarrow$ $x < 2$

But $x - 1 > 0$

$\Rightarrow$ $x > 1$ $\Rightarrow$ $x \in (1, 2)$

4. (a) $\log_2(x^2 - 2x) > 1$ $\Rightarrow$ $\log_2(x^2 - 2x) < \log_2 2$

$\Rightarrow$ $x^2 - 2x > 2$, also $x^2 - 2x > 2$

$\Rightarrow$ $x^2 - 2x - 2 > 0$ $\Rightarrow$ $(-\infty, 1-\sqrt{3}) \cup (1+\sqrt{3}, \infty)$

(b) $\log_{1/5}\frac{4x+6}{x} \geq 0$ $\log_{1/5}\frac{4x+6}{x} \geq \log_{1/5} 1$

The selection is rejected to the following equations

(i) $\frac{4x+6}{x} \leq 1$ $\Rightarrow$ $\frac{4x+6}{x} - 1 \leq 0$

$\Rightarrow$ $(3x + 6) \leq 0$ $\Rightarrow$ $(x + 2)x \leq 0$

$\Rightarrow$ $x \in [-2, 0]$

(ii) $\frac{4x+6}{x} > 0$ $\Rightarrow$ $x(4x + 6) > 0$

$\Rightarrow$ $x(2x + 3) > 0$ $\Rightarrow$ $x(x + 3/2) > 0$

$\Rightarrow$ $\Rightarrow$ $(-\infty, -3/2) \cup (0, \infty)$

Taking intersection above two sets

$\Rightarrow$ $x \in [-2, -3/2]$

5. (a) $\log_{1/13}(5x - 1) > 0$ $\Rightarrow$ $\log_{1/3}(5x - 1) > \log_{1/3} 1$

$\Rightarrow$ $5x - 1 < 1$ $\Rightarrow$ $x < 2/3$

Also $5x - 1 > 0$

$\Rightarrow$ $x > 1/5$ $\Rightarrow$ $x \in (1/5, 2/5)$

(b) $\log_8(x^2 - 4x + 3) \leq 1$ $\Rightarrow$ $\log_8(x^2 - 4x + 3) \leq \log 8^8$

$\Rightarrow$ $x^2 - 4x + 3 \leq 8$ $\Rightarrow$ $x^2 - 4x - 5 \leq 0$

$\Rightarrow$ $x^2 - 5x + x - 5 \leq 0$ $\Rightarrow$ $x(x - 5) + (x - 5) \leq 0$

$\Rightarrow$ $(x - 5)(x + 1) \leq 0$ $\Rightarrow$ $x \in [-1, 5]$ (i)

Also $x^2 - 4x + 3 > 0$ $\Rightarrow$ $x \in (-\infty, 1) \cup (3, \infty)$ (ii)

Taking intersection of above two, we get $[-1, 1) \cup (3, 5]$

6. $\log_x(a^2 + 1)$ $\Rightarrow$ $\frac{1}{\log_{a^2+1} x} < 0$

$\Rightarrow$ $\log_{a^2+1} x < 0$ $\Rightarrow$ $\log_{a^2+1} x < \log_{a^2+1} 1$

Obviously $a^2 + 1 > 0$

$\Rightarrow$ $x < 1$ and also $x > 0$ $\Rightarrow$ $x \in (0, 1)$

7. (a) $\log_2 3$ and $\log_{1/4} 5$ $\Rightarrow$ $\frac{\log 3}{\log 2}$ and $\frac{\log 5}{\log 1/4}$

$\Rightarrow$ $\frac{\log 3}{\log 2}$ and $\frac{\log 5}{-2\log 2}$

Clearly $\frac{\log 3}{\log 2} > \frac{-\log 5}{2\log 2}$ $\Rightarrow$ $\log_2 3$ is greater

(b) $\log_5 7$ and $\log_8 3$ $\Rightarrow$ $\frac{\log 7}{\log 5}$ and $\frac{\log 3}{\log 8}$

$\Rightarrow$ $\log 7 > \log 3$ $\Rightarrow$ $\frac{\log 7}{\log 5} > \frac{\log 3}{\log 8}$

$\Rightarrow$ $\log_5 7$ is greater

(c) 2 and $\log_\pi 2 + \log_2\pi$ $\Rightarrow$ 2 and $\frac{1}{\log_2\pi} + \log_2\pi$

$\therefore$ $\log 2\pi$ is a positive number, let us call it y

$\Rightarrow$ $\frac{1}{y} + y$ is always greater than or equal to 2

$\Rightarrow$ $\frac{1}{y} + y - 2$ $\Rightarrow$ $y^2 - 2y + 1 = (y-1)^2 \geq 0$

Hence clearly, $\log_\pi 2 + \log_2\pi$ is greater

(d) $\log_3 2$ and $\log_2 3$ $\Rightarrow$ $\frac{\log 2}{\log 3}$ and $\frac{\log 3}{\log 2}$

$\because$ $\log 3 > \log 2$ $\frac{\log 3}{\log 2} > 1$ $\Rightarrow$ $\log_2 3$ is greater

8. (a) $3^{\log x+2} < 3^{\log x^2+5} - 2$

If $3^{\log x} = y$

The equation reduces to $9y < 3^5y^2 - 2$

$\Rightarrow$ $y^2 3^5 - 9y - 2 > 0$ $\Rightarrow$ $\left(y+\frac{2}{27}\right)\left(y-\frac{1}{9}\right) > 0$

Note that y is always positive

$\Rightarrow$ $y \in \left(\frac{1}{9}, \infty\right)$ $\Rightarrow$ $\frac{1}{9} < 3^{\log x} < \infty$

$\Rightarrow$ $-2 < \log x < \infty$ $\Rightarrow$ $10^{-2} < x < \infty$

$\Rightarrow$ $x \in (10^{-2}, \infty)$

(b) $\left(\frac{1}{3}\right)^{\log_{1/3}\left(3\left(\frac{1}{2}\right)^x + 5\right)} < 2^{1+x}$ $\Rightarrow$ $3\left(\frac{1}{2}\right)^x + 5 < 2^{1+x}$

$\Rightarrow$ $3.2^{-x} + 5 < 2^{1+x}$

$\Rightarrow$ $3.2^{-x} - 2^{1+x} + 5 < 0$ $\Rightarrow$ $3.2^{-x} - 2.2^x + 5 < 0$

Let $2^x = y$

$\Rightarrow$ $\frac{3}{y} - 2y + 5 < 0$ $\Rightarrow$ $3y - 2y^3 + 5y^2 < 0$

$\Rightarrow$ $-2y^3 + 5y^2 + 3y < 0$

$\Rightarrow$ $y(-2y^2 + 5y + 3) < 0$ $\Rightarrow$ $y(-2y^2 + 6y - y + 3) < 0$

$\Rightarrow$ $y(-2y\,(y-3)(y-3)) < 0$

$\Rightarrow$ $y(y-3)\,(-2y-1) < 0$

$\Rightarrow$ $y(y-3)\,(y + 1/2) > 0$

$\Rightarrow$ $(y-3)\,(y+1/2) > 0$ $\because$ $[2x > 0]$

$\Rightarrow$ $y \in (-\infty, -1/2) \cup (3, \infty)$

But $2^x > 0$ $\Rightarrow$ $2^x \in (3, \infty)$

$\Rightarrow$ $\pi \in (\log_2 3, \infty)$

9. (a) $\log_5(3x-1) < 1$ $\Rightarrow$ $\log_5(3x-1) < \log_5 5$

$\Rightarrow$ $3x - 1 < 5$ $\Rightarrow$ $x < 2$

Also $3x - 1 > 0$ $\Rightarrow$ $x > 1/3$

$\Rightarrow$ $x \in (1/3, 2)$

(b) $\log_7\frac{2x-6}{2x-1} > 0$ $\Rightarrow$ $\log_7\frac{2x-6}{2x-1} > \log_7 1$

$\Rightarrow$ $\frac{2x-6}{2x-1} > 1$ $\Rightarrow$ $\frac{2x-6}{2x-1} - 1 > 0$

$\Rightarrow$ $\frac{-5}{2x-1} > 0$ $\Rightarrow$ $5(2x-1) < 0\; x < 1/2$

Also $\frac{2x-6}{2x-1} > 0$

$\Rightarrow$ $(x-3)\,(x-1/2) > 0$ $\Rightarrow$ $x \in (-\infty, 1/2) \cup (3, \infty)$

$\Rightarrow$ $x \in (-\infty, 1/2)$

(c) $\log_3\frac{1-2x}{2x} \leq 0$ $\Rightarrow$ $\log_3\frac{1-2x}{x} \leq \log_3 1$

$\Rightarrow$ $\frac{1-2x}{x} \leq 1$ $\Rightarrow$ $\frac{1-2x}{x} - 1 \leq 0$

$\Rightarrow$ $(1-3x)x \leq 0$ $\Rightarrow$ $x(x-1/3) \geq 0$

$\Rightarrow$ $x \in (-\infty, 0] \cup [1/3, \infty)$

Also $\frac{1-2x}{x} > 0$ $\Rightarrow$ $x\,(x-1/2) < 0$

$\Rightarrow$ $x \in \left(0, \frac{1}{2}\right)$ $\Rightarrow$ $x \in [1/3, 1/2]$

10. $\log_{x^2}\frac{4x-5}{|x-2|} \geq 1/2$

For log to be defined $\left(\frac{4x-5}{|x-2|}\right) > 0$

$\Rightarrow$ $4x - 5 > 0$ $\Rightarrow$ $x > 5/4$ (i)

The inequality reduces to $\left(\frac{4x-5}{|x-2|}\right) \geq x$

Case 1: $x \in [2, \infty)$ $\Rightarrow$ $4x - 5 \geq x^2 - 2x$

$\Rightarrow$ $x^2 - 6x + 5 \leq 0$ $\Rightarrow$ $x \in [1, 5]$ (ii)

Case 1: $x < 2$

$\Rightarrow$ Inequality becomes $x^2 + 2x - 5 > 0$

$\Rightarrow$ $x \in \left(\sqrt{6} - 1, 2\right)$ (iii)

The taking intersection of (i), (ii), (iii) $\left(\sqrt{6}-1, 5\right) \sim \{2\}$

TEXTUAL EXERCISE-5: (OBJECTIVE)

1. (b) $\log_2(x^2 - 2x) < 0$ $\Rightarrow$ $\log_2(x^2 - 2x) < \log_2(1)$

$\Rightarrow$ $x^2 - 2x < 1$ $\Rightarrow$ $x^2 - 2x - 1 < 0$

$\Rightarrow$ $x \in \left(1-\sqrt{2}, 1+\sqrt{2}\right)$

But $x^2 - 2x < 0$ $\Rightarrow$ $x\,(x-2) > 0$

$\Rightarrow$ $x \in (-\infty, 0) \cup (2, \infty)$

$\Rightarrow$ $x \in (1-\sqrt{2}, 0) \cup (2, 1+\sqrt{2})$

2. (c) $\log_a(x^2 - 1) > 0$; given $a < 0$; $a < 1$

$\Rightarrow$ $\log_a(x^2 - 1) < \log_a 1$ $\Rightarrow$ $x^2 - 1 < 1$

$\Rightarrow$ $x^2 - 1 > 0$ $\Rightarrow$ $1 < x^2 < 2$

$\Rightarrow$ $x \in \left(-\sqrt{2}, 1\right) \cup \left(1, \sqrt{2}\right)$

3. (a) $\log_2\left(\frac{x^2-4x}{3}\right) > \log_2 1$ $\Rightarrow$ $\frac{x^2-4x}{3} > 1$

$\Rightarrow$ $x^2 - 4x - 3 > 0$

$\Rightarrow$ $x \in \left(-\infty, 2-\sqrt{7}\right) \cup \left(2+\sqrt{7}, \infty\right)$

But $\frac{x^2-4x}{3} > 0$ $\Rightarrow$ $x\,(x-4) > 0$

$\Rightarrow$ $(-\infty, 0) \cup (4, \infty)$

Making intersection, we get $x \in (-\infty, 2-\sqrt{7}) \cup (2+\sqrt{7}, \infty)$

4. (c), (d)

(a) $\log_4 5 > -\log_{1/6} 25$ $\Rightarrow$ $\log_4 5 > -2\log_{1/6} 5$

$\frac{\log 5}{\log 4} > \frac{2.\log 5}{\log 6}$ $\Rightarrow$ $\log 6 > \log 8$ (False)

(b) $\log_4 5 < \log_{1/15} 1/25 \Rightarrow \frac{\log 5}{\log 4} < \frac{\log 25}{\log 16}$

$\Rightarrow \frac{\log 5}{\log 4} < \frac{2\log 25}{2\log 16} \Rightarrow$ (False)

(c) As proved in the above questions $\log_4 5 = \log_{1/16} 1/25$

$\Rightarrow$ True

(d) $\log_4 5 > \log_6 5 \Rightarrow \frac{\log 5}{\log 4} > \frac{\log 5}{\log 6}$

$\Rightarrow \log_4 < \log 6 \Rightarrow$ True

5. (a) $\left(\frac{1}{2}\right)^{\log_2(x^2-1)} > 1 \Rightarrow \frac{1}{2^{\log_2(x^2-1)}} > 1$

$\Rightarrow 1 > (x^2 - 1) \Rightarrow x^2 - 2 < 0$

$\Rightarrow \left(x+\sqrt{2}\right)\left(x-\sqrt{2}\right) < 0$

$\Rightarrow x \in \left(-\sqrt{2}, \sqrt{2}\right)$

But $x^2 - 1 > 0$

$\Rightarrow (x + 1)(x - 1) > 0$ (i)

$\Rightarrow x \in (-\infty, -1) \cup (1, \infty)$ (ii)

Making intersections of both $\left(-\sqrt{2}, -1\right) \cup \left(1, \sqrt{2}\right)$

6. (c) $\log_{0.5}\left(x^2 - 4x + 3\right) \le 1$

$\Rightarrow \log_{0.5}\left(x^2 - 4x + 3\right) \le \log_{0.5} 0.5$

$\Rightarrow x^2 - 4x + 3 \ge 1/2 \Rightarrow 2x^2 - 8x + 6 \ge 1$

$\Rightarrow 2x^2 - 6x - 2x + 5 \ge 0 \quad 2x^2 - 8x + 5 \ge 0$

$\Rightarrow x \in \left(-\infty, 2 - \sqrt{\frac{3}{2}}\right) \cup \left(2 + \sqrt{\frac{3}{2}}, \infty\right)$

But $x^2 - 4x + 3 > 0 \Rightarrow (x - 3)(x - 1) > 0$

$\Rightarrow x \in (-\infty, 1) \cup (3, \infty)$

Hence the solutions set is taking intersection of above two intervals $\left(-\infty, 2 - \sqrt{\frac{3}{2}}\right) \cup \left(2 + \sqrt{\frac{3}{2}}, \infty\right)$

7. (a), (d) $\log_{1/3}\left(\frac{2-3x}{x}\right) \ge -1$

which can be written as $\log_{1/3}\left(\frac{2-3x}{x}\right) \ge \log_{1/3}(3)$

$\Rightarrow 0 < \frac{2-3x}{x} \le 3$

$\Rightarrow x(2 - 3x) > 0$ and $\frac{2-3x-3x}{x} \le 0; x \ne 0$

$\Rightarrow x \in \left(0, \frac{2}{3}\right)$ and $(2-6x)x \le 0; x \ne 0$

$\Rightarrow x \in \left(0, \frac{2}{3}\right)$ and $x \in (-\infty, 0) \cup \left[\frac{1}{3}, \infty\right)$

$\Rightarrow x \in \left[\frac{1}{3}, \frac{2}{3}\right) \subseteq \left[\frac{1}{3}, \frac{2}{3}\right]; \left[\frac{1}{3}, \frac{2}{3}\right)$

8. (d) $\log_3\left(\frac{1+2x}{1+x}\right) < 1$

Which ca be written as $\log_3\left(\frac{1+2x}{1+x}\right) < \log_3 3$

$\Rightarrow \left(\frac{1+2x}{1+x}\right) < 3 \Rightarrow \frac{1+2x}{1+x} - 3 < 0$

$\Rightarrow \frac{1+2x-3-3x}{1+x} < 0 \Rightarrow (-2 - x)(1 + x) < 0$

$\Rightarrow (1 + x)(x + 2) > 0 \Rightarrow x \in (-\infty, -2) \cup (-1, \infty)$

But $\frac{1+2x}{1+x} > 0$

$\Rightarrow (1 + x)(1 + 2x) > 0 \Rightarrow (x + 1)(x + 1/2) > 0$

$\Rightarrow x \in (-\infty, -1) \cup (-1/2, \infty)$

Solution set $(-\infty, -2) \cup (-1/2, \infty)$

9. (a) $\log_{0.2}\left(x^2 - x - 2\right) > \log_{0.2}\left(-x^2 + 2x + 3\right)$

Case 1: $x^2 - x - 2 < -x^2 + 2x + 3$

$\Rightarrow -2x^2 + 2x + x + 5 > 0$

$\Rightarrow -2x^2 + 3x + 5 > 0$

$\Rightarrow -2x^2 + 5x - 2x + 5 > 0$

$\Rightarrow -x(2x - 5) - (2x - 5) > 0$

$\Rightarrow (2x - 5)(x + 1) < 0$

$\Rightarrow x \in (-1, 5/2)$

Case 2: $x^2 - x - 2 > 0$

$\Rightarrow x^2 - 2x + x - 2 > 0 \Rightarrow x(x - 2) + (x - 2) > 0$

$\Rightarrow (x - 2)(x + 1) > 0 \Rightarrow x \in (-\infty, -1) \cup (2, \infty)$

Case 3: $-x^2 + 2x + 3 > 0$

$\Rightarrow x^2 - 2x - 3 < 0 \Rightarrow x^2 - 3x + x - 3 < 0$

$\Rightarrow x(x - 3) + 1(x - 3) < 0$

$\Rightarrow (x - 3)(x + 1) < 0 \Rightarrow x \in (-1, 3)$

$\Rightarrow$ Overall solution $x \in \left(2, \frac{5}{2}\right)$

10. (d) $\log_{\frac{x+6}{3}}\left(\log_2 \frac{x-1}{x-2}\right) > 0$ (i)

Clearly, $\log_2\left(\frac{x-1}{x-2}\right) > 0$ and $\frac{x-1}{x-2} > 0$

$\Rightarrow \frac{x-1}{x-2} > 1 \Rightarrow \frac{x-1-x+2}{x-2} > 0$

$\Rightarrow \frac{1}{x-2} > 0 \Rightarrow x > 2$ (ii)

Now, for $x > 2$, $\frac{x+6}{3} > \frac{8}{3} > 1$

Again from (i), $\log_2\left(\frac{x-1}{x-2}\right) > \left(\frac{x+6}{3}\right)^0 = 1$

$\Rightarrow \left(\frac{x-1}{x-2}\right) > 2 \Rightarrow \frac{x-1-2x+4}{x-2} > 0$

$\Rightarrow \frac{3-x}{x-2} > 0 \Rightarrow (x - 3)(x - 2) < 0$

$\Rightarrow x \in (2, 3)$ (iii)

$\therefore$ From (ii) and (iii), $x \in (2, 3)$

TEXTUAL EXERCISE–9: (SUBJECTIVE)

1. (a) $8\log_a x^3 \log_b y^3 \log_c z^3$

$\Rightarrow 8.27.\log_a x.\log_b y.\log_c z$

$\Rightarrow \frac{8.27}{\log_x y^2.\log_y z^2.\log_z x^2}$

$\Rightarrow \dfrac{27}{\log_x y.\log_y z.\log_z x} \Rightarrow \dfrac{27\log x.\log y.\log z}{\log y \log z \log x}$

$\Rightarrow 27 \Rightarrow$ L.H.S. = R.H.S.

(b) $a^a.b^b.c^c$; given $\dfrac{\log a}{b-c} = \dfrac{\log b}{c-a}$

$\Rightarrow \log_b a = \dfrac{b-c}{c-a} \Rightarrow b^{\left(\frac{b-c}{c-a}\right)} = a$

Similarly $\dfrac{\log b}{c-a} = \dfrac{\log c}{a-b}$

$\Rightarrow \log_c b = \dfrac{c-a}{a-b} \Rightarrow b = c^{\left(\frac{c-a}{a-b}\right)}$

Also $\dfrac{\log c}{\log a} = \dfrac{a-b}{b-c} \Rightarrow c = a^{\left(\frac{a-b}{b-c}\right)}$

Similarly $b = a^{\left(\frac{c-a}{b-c}\right)}$

$\Rightarrow a^a.\ b^b.\ c^c = a^a.a^{\left(\frac{c-a}{b-c}\right)b}.a^{\left(\frac{a-b}{b-c}\right)c} = a^{a+\frac{bc-ab}{b-c}+\frac{ac-bc}{b-c}} = a^0 = 1$

Hence $a^a.b^b.c^c = 1$

(c) $xyz = xy + zy + zx$

$\Rightarrow x = 1 + \log_a bc = \log_a b + \log_a c + 1$

$\Rightarrow y = 1 + \log_b ca = \log_b c + \log_b a + 1$

$\Rightarrow z = 1 + \log_c ab - \log_c a + \log_a b + 1$

$\Rightarrow x = \dfrac{\log b}{\log a} + \dfrac{\log c}{\log a} + 1$

$\Rightarrow y = \dfrac{\log c}{\log b} + \dfrac{\log a}{\log b} + 1$

$\Rightarrow z = \dfrac{\log b}{\log c} + \dfrac{\log a}{\log c} + 1$

x, y, z can be re-written as $x = \dfrac{\log b + \log c + \log a}{\log a}$ (i)

$y = \dfrac{\log c + \log a + \log b}{\log b}$ (ii)

$z = \dfrac{\log a + \log b + \log c}{\log c}$ (iii)

To prove: $xyz = xy + yz + zx$

Which is true iff $xy\,(z-1) = yz + zx$

Which is true iff $\dfrac{(z-1)}{z} = \dfrac{x+y}{xy}$

$\Rightarrow \dfrac{1}{x} + \dfrac{1}{y} + \dfrac{1}{z} = 1$

By (i), (ii), (iii), we get $\dfrac{1}{x} + \dfrac{1}{y} + \dfrac{1}{z} = 1$

$\Rightarrow xyz = xy + yz + zx$

2. (a) $p = \log_a bc = \dfrac{\log b + \log c}{\log a}$; $q = \log_b ca = \dfrac{\log c + \log a}{\log b}$;

$r = \log_c ab = \dfrac{\log a + \log b}{\log c}$

$\Rightarrow p + q + r$

$= \dfrac{\log b}{\log a} + \dfrac{\log a}{\log b} + \dfrac{\log c}{\log a} + \dfrac{\log a}{\log c} + \dfrac{\log c}{\log b} + \dfrac{\log b}{\log c}$ (i)

$\Rightarrow pqr\left(\dfrac{\log b}{\log a} + \dfrac{\log c}{\log a}\right)\left(\dfrac{\log c}{\log b} + \dfrac{\log a}{\log b}\right)\left(\dfrac{\log a}{\log c} + \dfrac{\log b}{\log c}\right)$

$\Rightarrow \left(1 + \dfrac{\log c}{\log a} + \dfrac{\log c.\log c}{\log a.\log b} + \dfrac{\log c}{\log b}\right)\left(\dfrac{\log a}{\log c} + \dfrac{\log b}{\log c}\right)$

$\Rightarrow \left(\dfrac{\log a}{\log c} + 1 + 1 + \dfrac{\log c}{\log b} + \dfrac{\log a}{\log b} + \dfrac{\log b}{\log c} + \dfrac{\log c}{\log a} + 1 + 1 + \dfrac{\log b}{\log a}\right)$

Now pqr can be written as

$ppr = \dfrac{\log a}{\log c} + \dfrac{\log c}{\log b} + \dfrac{\log a}{\log b} + \dfrac{\log b}{\log c} + \dfrac{\log c}{\log a} + 2$

By (i) $\Rightarrow pqr = p + q + r + 2$

(b) $\log\dfrac{a+b}{5} = \dfrac{1}{2}(\log a + \log b)$; where $a^2 + b^2 = 23ab =$

$\log\left(\dfrac{a+b}{5}\right)^2 = \log a + \log b$

Which is true if $\log\left(\dfrac{a+b}{5}\right)^2 - \log a = \log b$

L.H.S. $= \log\left(\dfrac{a+b}{5}\right)^2 - \log a = \log b$

$= \log\left(\dfrac{a^2 + 2ab + b^2}{25a}\right)$ ($\because a^2 + b^2 = 23at$ (given))

$= \log\left(\dfrac{25ab}{25a}\right) = \log b$

$\Rightarrow$ L.H.S = R.H.S

(c) $xyz + 1 = 2yz \Rightarrow x = \log_{2a} a,\ y = \log_{3a} 2a,$

$z = \log_{4a} 3a$

$2yz = 2\log_{3a} 2a.\log_{4a} 3a = \dfrac{2\log 2a}{\log 3a}.\dfrac{\log 3a}{\log 4a}$

$= \dfrac{2\log 2a}{\log 4a}$ (i)

$\Rightarrow xyz = \dfrac{\log a}{\log 2a}.\dfrac{\log 2a}{\log 3a}.\dfrac{\log 3a}{\log 4a} = \dfrac{\log a}{\log 4a}$

$\Rightarrow xyz + 1 = \dfrac{\log a + \log 4a}{\log 4a} = \dfrac{\log 4a^2}{\log 4a} = \dfrac{2\log 2a}{\log 4a}$ (ii)

By (i) and (ii), we get $xyz + 1 = 2yz$

3. $\log_b a.\ \log_c a + \log_a b\ \log_c b + \log_a c\ .\ \log_b c = 3$

$\Rightarrow \dfrac{(\log a)^2}{\log b.\log c} + \dfrac{(\log b)^2}{\log a.\log c} + \dfrac{(\log c)^2}{\log a.\log b} = 3$

$\Rightarrow \dfrac{(\log a)^3 + (\log b)^3 + (\log c)^3}{\log a.\log b.\log c} = 3$

$\Rightarrow (\log a)^3 + (\log b)^3 + (\log c)^3 = 3\log a.\log b.\log c$

We know that $a^3 + b^3 + c^3 = (a + b + c)\,(a^2 + b^2 + c^2 - ab - bc - ca) - 3abc$

$\Rightarrow a^3 + b^3 + c^3 = 3abc$ if $a + b + c = 0$

$\Rightarrow \log a + \log b + \log c = 0$

$\Rightarrow \log(abc) = 0 \Rightarrow abc = 1$

4. $a^2 + b^2 = c^2$

Now $\log_{c+b} a + \log_{c-b} a = \dfrac{1}{\log_a c+b} + \dfrac{1}{\log_a c-b}$

$$= \frac{\log a\left(c^2 - b^2\right)}{\log_a (c+b)\log_a (c-b)}$$

Using $c^2 - b^2 = a^2$, we get $\dfrac{2}{\log_a (c+b)\log_a (c-b)}$

$\Rightarrow 2\log_{c+b} a \log_{c-b} a$

5. $(ax)^{\log a} = (by)^{\log b}$ (i)

$b^{\log x} = a^{\log y}$ (ii)

Taking log on both sides in equation (ii), we get $\log x \log b = \log y . \log a$

$\Rightarrow \log x = \log y \log_b a$ (iii)

By taking log on both sides in equation (i), we get $\log a . | \log ax = \log b . \log by$

$\Rightarrow \log a\left(\log a + \log y \dfrac{\log a}{\log b}\right) = \log b . \log by$

$\Rightarrow (\log a)^2 + \dfrac{\log y (\log a)^2}{\log b} = (\log b)^2 + \log b . \log y$

$\Rightarrow \log y\left(\dfrac{(\log a)^2}{\log b} - \log b\right) = (\log b)^2 - (\log a)^2$

$\Rightarrow \log y\left(\dfrac{(\log a)^2 - (\log b)^2}{\log b}\right) = (\log b)^2 - (\log a)^2$

$\Rightarrow \log y = -\log b \qquad \Rightarrow y = 1/b$

Similarly $x = 1/z$

6. $x \in (0, 1)$ $\log(1+x) + \log(1+x^2) + \log(1+x^4) + \ldots \infty$

$\Rightarrow \log((1+x)(1+x^2)(1+x^4) \ldots\ldots) = \log((1+x^2+x+x^3)(1+x^4)\ldots) = \log(1+x^4+x^2+x^6+x+x^5+x^3+x^7\ldots) = \log(1+x+x^2+x^7+x^4+x^5) = \log\left(\dfrac{1}{1-x}\right) = -\log(1-x)$

Note that the infinite G.P. coverage only because $x \in (0, 1)$ otherwise at would have not converged.

7. $\dfrac{1}{\log_2 a} + \dfrac{1}{\log_4 a} + \dfrac{1}{\log_8 a} + ..$

This can written as $\log_a 2 + \log_a 4 + \log_a 8 + \ldots$

$\Rightarrow \log_a (2.4.8\ldots 2^n) \quad \Rightarrow \log_a (2^{(1+2+3+\ldots n)}) = \log_a 2^{\frac{n(n+1)}{2}}$

$\Rightarrow \dfrac{n(n+1)}{2}\log_a 2$

8. Let $\log_3 5 = \dfrac{p}{q}$; where $p, q \in \mathbb{Z}$ s.t. g.c.d $(p,q) = 1$

$\Rightarrow 5 = (3)^{\frac{p}{q}} \Rightarrow 5^q = 3^p$

Which is impossible as unit digit of 5^q is $5 \ \forall\ q \in \mathbb{Z}$ and 3^p has its unit digit $\in \{3, 9, 7, 1\}$

$\therefore$ $\log_3 5$ is an irrational number

Now, let $\log_2 7 = \dfrac{p}{q}$; $p, q \in \mathbb{N}$ and g.c.d $(p,q) = 1$

$\Rightarrow 7 = (2)^{p/q} \qquad \Rightarrow (2)^p = (7)^q$

Which is impossible as L.H.S. is an even natural number, whereas R.H.S. is an odd natural number.

(i) $\log_7 \log_5\left(\sqrt{x+5} + \sqrt{x}\right) = 0$

$\Rightarrow \log_5\left(\sqrt{x+5} + \sqrt{x}\right) = 1$

$\Rightarrow \sqrt{x+5} + \sqrt{x} = 5 \quad \Rightarrow x = 4$

(ii) $\log_{\frac{3}{4}} \log_8 (x^2+7) + \log_{\frac{1}{2}} \log_{\frac{1}{4}} (x^2+7)^{-1} = -2$

$\Rightarrow \log_{\frac{3}{4}} \dfrac{1}{3}\log_2 (x^2+7) + \log_{\frac{1}{2}} \dfrac{1}{2}\log_2 (x^2+7) = -2$

$\Rightarrow \log_{\frac{3}{4}} \dfrac{4}{3}.\dfrac{1}{4}\log_2(x^2+7) + 1 + \log_{\frac{1}{2}} \log_2(x^2+7) = -2$

$\Rightarrow \log_{\frac{3}{4}} \dfrac{1}{4}\log_2 (x^2+7) + \log_{\frac{1}{2}} \log_2(x^2+7) = -2$

$\Rightarrow \log_{\frac{3}{4}} \dfrac{k}{4} + \log_{\frac{1}{2}} k = -2$; where $k = \log_2(x^2+7)$

$\Rightarrow \log_{\frac{3}{4}} k + \log_{\frac{1}{2}} k = -2 + \log_{\frac{3}{4}} 4$

$\Rightarrow \log_{\frac{3}{4}} k + \log_{\frac{3}{4}} k.\log_{\frac{1}{2}} \dfrac{3}{4} = -2 + \log_{\frac{3}{4}} 4 = -2\log_{\frac{3}{4}} \dfrac{3}{4} + \log_{\frac{3}{4}} 4$

$\Rightarrow \log_{\frac{3}{4}} k\left(1 + \log_{\frac{1}{2}} \dfrac{3}{4}\right) = \log_{\frac{3}{4}} 4 - \log_{\frac{3}{4}} \dfrac{9}{16} = \log_{\frac{3}{4}} \dfrac{4 \times 16}{9}$

$\Rightarrow \left(\log_{\frac{3}{4}} k\right)\left(\log_{\frac{1}{2}} \dfrac{3}{8}\right) = \log_{\frac{3}{4}}\left(\dfrac{64}{9}\right) = 2\log_{\frac{3}{4}} \dfrac{8}{3} = -2\log_{\frac{3}{4}} \dfrac{3}{8}$

$\Rightarrow \log_{\frac{3}{4}} k \log_{\frac{3}{4}} \dfrac{3}{8}.\log_{\frac{1}{2}} \dfrac{3}{4} = -2\log_{\frac{3}{4}} \dfrac{3}{8}$

$\Rightarrow \log_{\frac{3}{4}} k = -2\log_{\frac{3}{4}} \dfrac{1}{2} = \log_{\frac{3}{4}}\left(\dfrac{1}{2}\right)^{-2}$

$\Rightarrow k = 4 \qquad \Rightarrow \log_2(x^2+7) = 4$

$\Rightarrow x^2 = 9 \qquad \Rightarrow x \pm 3$

10. $\log_e 2 . \log_k 625 = \log_{10} 16 . \log_e 10$

$\Rightarrow \log_e 2 . 4\log_k 5 = 4\log_{10} 2 . \log_e 10$

$\Rightarrow \log_e 2 . \log_k 5 = \log_{10} 2 . \log_e 10$

$\Rightarrow \log_{10} 2 = \log_{10} 2 . \log_5 k$

$\Rightarrow k = 5$

TEXTUAL EXERCISE–6 (OBJECTIVE)

1. (c) $\therefore$ If the characteristic of $\log_{10} N$ is n, then the number of digits in N is $(n+1)$

$\Rightarrow \log_{10}(81)^{24} = 24\log_{10}3^4 = 96\log_{10}3$ (Given $\log_{10}3 = 0.477$)

$\Rightarrow \log_{10}(81)^{24} = 96 \times 0.477 = 45.792$

Characteristic = 45 $\Rightarrow$ Number of digits = 46

2. (b) $\log_{10}36 = \log_{10}9 + \log_{10}4 = 2\log_{10}3 + 2\log_{10}2 = 2 \times 0.477 + 2 \times 0.301 = 1.556$

3. (a) By the question, char [log (0.0005798)] = a and char [log (352.526] = b; where char [] means characteristic of the number

$\Rightarrow \log(0.0005798) = -4 + 0.8$

$\Rightarrow \log(352.526) = 2 + 0.54$

$\Rightarrow a + b = -4 + 2 = -2$

4. (b) $\log_{10}\log_2\log_3 19683 = \log_{10}\log_2\log_3 .9 = \log_{10}\log_2 2 = \log_{10}1 = 0$

5. $\log_{10}\overline{abc}.\overline{pqrst}$ has mantissa 0.4971

$\Rightarrow \log_{10}\overline{abc}.\overline{pqrst} = \log_{10}\overline{abcpqrst}$

Similarly $\log_{10}\overline{a}\overline{bcpqrst}$

$\Rightarrow \log_{10}\overline{abcpqrst} - 7$

Clearly mantissa for $\log_{10}\bar{a}\ \overline{bcpqrst} = 0.4971$

Now characteristic for $\log_{10}\overline{abc}\ \overline{pqrst} = 2$

$\Rightarrow \log_{10}\overline{a}\overline{bcpqrst} = 0 \quad \Rightarrow \log_{10}\bar{a}\ \overline{bcpqrst} = 0.4971$

6. (c) $\log_y x \log_z y \log_p z \log_{x^2} p$

$= \frac{\log x}{\log y}.\frac{\log y}{\log z}.\frac{\log z}{\log p}.\frac{\log p}{2\log x} = \frac{1}{2} = 0.5$ having characteristic $= -1$

7. (b) Given $\log_{10}3 = 0.477$ and $\log_{10}2 = 0.301$

(a) $3^{21} = x$

$\Rightarrow \log x = 21\log 3 = 21 \times 0.477 = 10.017$

(b) $2^{48} = y$ $\quad\Rightarrow 108y = 48 \times \log 2 = 14.448$

Now Base > 1 $\quad\Rightarrow \log x$ is increasing function

$\therefore \log y > \log x \quad \Rightarrow y > x$

$\Rightarrow 2^{48} > 3^{21}$

SECTION–III: OBJECTIVE-TYPE (ONLY ONE CORRECT ANSWER)

1. (c) $\log_{3\sqrt{3}}27 = x \quad \Rightarrow (3\sqrt{3})^x = 3^3$

$\Rightarrow 3^{3/2}x = 3^3 \quad \Rightarrow \frac{3}{2}x = 3$

$\Rightarrow x = 2$

2. (b) $-\log_8\log_4\log_2 16 \quad \Rightarrow -\log_8\log_4 4$

$\Rightarrow \log_8(1)^{-1} \quad \Rightarrow 0$

3. (a) $\log_3 2.\log_4 3..\log_{10}9.\log_{11}10.\log_2 11$

$\Rightarrow \log_3 2.\ \log_4 3.\ \log_5 4\ \log_6 5\log_7 6.\log_8 7\log_9 10......\log_{10}9.\ \log_{11}10\ \log_2 11$

$\log_3 2.\log_4 3\ ......\ \log_{10}9.\ \log_2 10$

$\Rightarrow \log_3 2.\ \log_4 3....\frac{\log_{10}9}{\log_{10}2}$

$\Rightarrow \log_3 2.\ \log_4 3......\ \log_9 8\ .\ \log_2 9$

$\log_3 2.\ \log_4 3.....\log_8 7\ .\log_2 8$

$\Rightarrow \log_3 2.\ \log_4 3\ ....\ \log_7 6\ .\ \log_2 7$

$\log_3 2.\ \log_4 3.....\log_5 5\ \log_2 6$

$\Rightarrow \log_3 2\ .\ \log_4 3\ \log_5 4\ \log_2 5$

$\Rightarrow \log_3 2\ .\ \log_4 3\ .\ \log_2 4 \quad \Rightarrow \log_3 2\ \log_2 3 = 1$

4. (d) $\left(\sqrt[3]{9}\right)^{\frac{1}{5\log_5 3}}$. This can be re-written as $\left(3^{2/3}\right)^{\frac{\log_3 5}{5}}$

$= 3^{\log_3 5^{2/3}.5} = 15\sqrt{5^2} = \sqrt[15]{25}$

5. (c) $\sqrt{\left(\frac{1}{\sqrt{27}}\right)^{2-\frac{\log_5 13}{2\log_5 9}}}$

Let $\left(\frac{1}{\sqrt{27}}\right)^{2-\frac{\log_5 13}{2\log_5 9}} = x^2$

$\Rightarrow \left[\frac{1}{\sqrt{27}}\right]^{2-\log_{81}{}^{13} = x^2}$

Taking log both sides, we get

$\left[2 - \frac{\log_5 13}{\log_5 81}\right]\log\left[\frac{1}{5}\right]^{3/2} = 2\log x$

$\Rightarrow 3\log\frac{1}{3} - \log\left(\frac{1}{3}\right)^{3/2}\log 81^{13} = 2\log x$

$\Rightarrow \log x = \frac{-3}{2}\log 3 + \frac{3}{16}\log 13$

$\Rightarrow \log x = \log 3^{-3/2}.13^{3/16} \Rightarrow x = 3^{-3/2}.13^{3/16}$

6. (a) $7^{\log_7(x^2-4x+5)} = (x-1)$. Which reduces to $x^2 - 4x + 5 = x - 1$

$\Rightarrow x^2 - 5x + 6 = 0 \quad \Rightarrow (x-3)(x-2) = 0$

$\Rightarrow x = 2, 3$

7. (d) $5^{1+\log_5\cos x} = \frac{5}{2} \quad \Rightarrow \quad 5.5^{\log_5\cos x} = \frac{5}{2}$

$\Rightarrow 5^{\log_5\cos x} = \frac{1}{2} \quad \Rightarrow \cos = 1/2$

$\therefore$ Which has infinitely many solution.

8. (b) $(243)^{10}$

Characteristic of $\log_{10}(243)^{10} = 10\log_{10}(3)^5 = 10 \times 5\ \log 10^3 = 50\log_{10}3$

$\because \log_{10}3 = 0.477$

$\Rightarrow 50 \times 0.477 = 2389$

$\Rightarrow$ Number of digits in $(243)^{10} = 23 + 1 = 24$

9. (c) $\log_3\left[\frac{\log_{3\sqrt{3}}3^6}{2}\right] \quad \Rightarrow \log_3\left[\frac{\log_{3^{1/3}}3^6}{2}\right]$

$\Rightarrow \log_3\frac{6\log_{3^{1/3}}3}{2} = \log_3\frac{6\times 3}{2} = \log_3 9 = 2$

10. (b) $\frac{1}{\log_2 N} + \frac{1}{\log_3 N} + \frac{1}{\log_4 N} + ... + \frac{1}{\log_{199}N}$

$= \log_N(2.3.4.5....19998)$

Which can also be written as $\log_N[(1998)(1997)......(2)(1)] = \log_N(1998)!$

11. (b) $\log_{10}\tan^{10} + \log_{10}\tan^{20} + ... + \log_{10}\tan 89^o$

Which can be rewritten as $\log_{10}(\tan 1°.\tan 2°....\tan 89°)$

$= \log_{10}(\tan 1°.\tan 89°.\tan 2°.\tan 88°...)$

$= \log_{10}(\tan 1°.\cot 1°.\tan 2°.\cot 2°....\tan 45)$

$= \log_{10}(\tan 45°) = \log_{10}(1) = 0$

12. (d) $4^{\log_9 3} + 9^{\log_2 4} = 10^{\log_x 83}$

$\therefore \log_9 3 = 1/2 \quad \therefore \log_2 4 = 2$

$\Rightarrow 4^{1/2} + 9^2 = 10^{\log_x 83} \quad \Rightarrow 2 + 81 = 10^{\log_x 83}$

$\Rightarrow 83 = 10^{\log_x 83} \quad \Rightarrow 10^{\log_{10}83} = 10^{\log_x 83}$

$\Rightarrow x = 10$

13. (b) $x^{\log_3 x^2 + (\log_3 x)^2 - 10} = x^{-2}$

Let $\log_3 x = t$

$\Rightarrow 2t + t^2 - 10 = -2 \quad \Rightarrow t^2 + 2t - 8 = 0$

$\Rightarrow t(t+4) - 2(t+4) = 0 \Rightarrow (t+4)(t-2) = 0$

$\Rightarrow t = -4$, which is not possible

$\Rightarrow t = 2\ \log_3 x = 2 \quad \Rightarrow x = 3^2 = 9$

14. (b) $\log(-x) = 2\log(1+x) \Rightarrow \log(-x) = \log(1+x)^2$

$\Rightarrow -x = (1+x)^2 \quad \Rightarrow -x = 1 + x^2 + 2x$

$x^2 + 1 + 3x = 0$

$\Rightarrow$ Discriminate for the above quadratic equation $= \sqrt{9-4} = \sqrt{5}$ means that this has two real relation.

$\Rightarrow x = \dfrac{-3 \pm \sqrt{5}}{2}$

For $\log(-x)$ to be defined $x < 0$ similarly $1 + x > 0$

$\Rightarrow x > -1 \quad \Rightarrow x \in (-1, 0)$

$\Rightarrow$ only one solution $x = \dfrac{-3+\sqrt{5}}{2}$

15. (c) $\log_{ab} a = 4 \quad \Rightarrow (ab)^4 = a$

$\Rightarrow a^4 b^4 = a \quad \Rightarrow a^3 b^4 = 1$

$\Rightarrow b^4 = a^{-3} \quad \Rightarrow b^{1/2} = a^{-3/8}$

$\therefore \log_{ab}\left(\dfrac{\sqrt[3]{a}}{\sqrt{b}}\right) = \log_{ab}(\sqrt[3]{a}) - \log_{ab}(\sqrt{b})$

$\Rightarrow \dfrac{4}{3} - \log_{ab}\left(a^{-3/8}\right) \quad \Rightarrow \dfrac{4}{3} - 4\left(\dfrac{-3}{8}\right) = \dfrac{17}{6}$

16. (c) $\log_{12} 27 = a \quad \Rightarrow 12a = 27$ (Given $\log_{12} 27 = a$)

$\Rightarrow \dfrac{\log 27}{\log 12} = a \quad \Rightarrow \dfrac{3\log 3}{2\log 2 + \log 3} = a$

$\Rightarrow \log_6 16 = \dfrac{\log 16}{\log 6} = \dfrac{4\log 2}{\log 2 + \log 8}$

$\Rightarrow 4\left(\dfrac{\log 2}{\log 2 + \log 3}\right) = 4\left(\dfrac{3-a}{3+a}\right)$

17. (b) $a = \log_7 12$; $b = \log_{12} 24 \quad \Rightarrow a = \dfrac{\log 12}{\log 7}, b = \dfrac{\log 24}{\log 12}$

$\Rightarrow \dfrac{1+ab}{a(8-5b)} = \dfrac{1 + \dfrac{\log 12}{\log 7} \cdot \dfrac{\log 24}{\log 12}}{\dfrac{\log 12}{\log 7}\left(8 - \dfrac{5\log 24}{\log 12}\right)}$

$\Rightarrow \dfrac{1 + \dfrac{\log 24}{\log 7}}{8 \cdot \dfrac{\log 12}{\log 7} - \dfrac{5\log 24}{\log 7}} \quad \Rightarrow \dfrac{\log 7 + \log 24}{8\log 12 - 5\log 24}$

$\Rightarrow \dfrac{\log 168}{\log \dfrac{128}{245}} = \dfrac{\log 168}{\log 54} = \log_{54} 168$

18. (a) $\dfrac{1}{409}\left\{(81)^{\log_9 5} + (3)^{3\log_3 \sqrt{6}}\right\} \cdot \left[\left(\sqrt{7}\right)^{2\log_7 25} - (125)^{\log_{25} 6}\right]$

$= \dfrac{1}{409}\left\{(9)^{\log_9 25} + (3)^{\log_3 (\sqrt{6})^3}\right\} \cdot \left[7^{\log_7 25} - (5)^{\frac{3}{2}\log_5 6}\right]$

$= \dfrac{1}{409}\left\{25 + 6\sqrt{6}\right\} \cdot \left\{25 - 6\sqrt{6}\right\} = \dfrac{625 - 216}{409} = 1$

19. (d) $(81)^{\log_3 5} + (27)^{\log_9 36} + 3^{4\log_9 7} = 5^4 + 9^{3/2\log_9 36} + 9^{\log_9 7^2} = 5^4$

$+ 36^{3/2} + 7^2 = 5^4 + 216 + 49 = 890$

20. (b) $\log_2(x^3 - 4x^2 + 26) - \log_2(x+2)$; which can be written as

$\log_2\left(\dfrac{x^3 + 4x^2 + x + 26}{x+2}\right) = \log_2\left(\dfrac{(x^2 - 6x + 13)(x+2)}{(x+2)}\right)$.

Since $x \geq 20$

$\Rightarrow \log_2(x^2 - 6x + 13)$

$\Rightarrow$ Minimum value at $x = 3[-b/2a]$

$\Rightarrow \log_2(x^2 - 6x + 1) = 2$

21. (c) $4^{5\log_{4\sqrt{2}}(3-\sqrt{6}) - \log_8(\sqrt{3}-\sqrt{2})^6} = \dfrac{4^{5\log_{4\sqrt{2}}(3-\sqrt{6})}}{4^{\log_8(\sqrt{3}-\sqrt{2})^6}}$

$= \dfrac{\left(4\sqrt{2}\right)^{4\log_{4\sqrt{2}}(3-\sqrt{6})}}{(8)^{\frac{2}{3}\log(\sqrt{3}-\sqrt{2})^6}} = \dfrac{\left(3-\sqrt{6}\right)^4}{\left(\sqrt{3}-\sqrt{2}\right)^4}$

$= \left(\dfrac{3-\sqrt{6}\ (\sqrt{3}+\sqrt{2})}{\left(\sqrt{3}-\sqrt{2}\right)\left(\sqrt{3}+\sqrt{2}\right)}\right)^4$

$= \left(3\sqrt{3} + 3\sqrt{2} - 3\sqrt{2} - 2\sqrt{3a}\right)^4 = 9$

22. (c) $7^{\log_3 5} + 3^{\log_5 7} - 5^{\log_3 7} - 7^{\log_5 3}$; Which can be written as $7^{\log_3 5} + 3^{\log_5 7} - 5^{\log_3 7} - 3^{\log_5 7} = 7^{\log_3 5} - 5^{\log_6 7}$

On further simplification $= 7^{\log_3 5} - 7^{\log_3 5} = 0$

23. (b) $2\log_{16}(x^2 + x) - \log_4(x+1) = 2 = \log_{16}(x^2 + x)^2 - \log_{16}(x+1)^2 = 2$

$\Rightarrow \log 16 \dfrac{(x^2+x)^2}{(x+1)^2} = \log_{16} 25^6$

$\Rightarrow \dfrac{x^2(x+1)^2}{(x+1)^2} = 256 \quad \Rightarrow x = 16, -16$

But $x + 1 > 0$

$\Rightarrow x = 16$ (-16 is not permissible)

24. (a) $9^{\log_3(\log_2 x)} = \log_2 x - (\log_2 x)^2 + 1$

$\Rightarrow 3^{\log_3(\log_2 x)^2} = \log_2 x - (\log_2 x)^2 + 1$

$\Rightarrow (\log_2 x)^2 = \log_2 x - (\log_2 x)^2 + 1$

Let $\log_2 x = t$.

$\Rightarrow 2t^2 - t - 1 = 0 \quad \Rightarrow 2t^2 - 2t + t - 1 = 0$

$\Rightarrow 2t(t-1) + (t-1) = 0$

$\Rightarrow (t-1)(2t+1) = 0 \quad \Rightarrow t = 1, -1/2$

Clearly $-1/2$ is not permissible

$\Rightarrow t = 1 \quad \Rightarrow \log_2 x = 1$

$\Rightarrow x = 2$

25. (d) $|x-1|^{\log_3 x^2 - 2\log x^9} = (x-1)^7 = |x-1|^{\log_3 x^2 - \log_x 9^2} = (x-1)^7$

Case I: $x \geq 1$

$\Rightarrow (x-1)^{\log_3 x^2 - \log_x 9^2} = (x-1)^7$

$\Rightarrow \log_3 x^2 - \log x 9^2 = 7 \Rightarrow \dfrac{2}{\log x^3} - 4\log_x 3 = 7$

Let $\log_x 3 = a$

$\Rightarrow -4a + \dfrac{2}{a} = 7 \quad \Rightarrow -4a^2 - 7a + 2 = 0$

$\Rightarrow -4a^2 - 8a + a + 2 = 0$

$\Rightarrow -4a(a+2) + (a+2) = 0$

$\Rightarrow (a+2)(1-4a) = 0 \Rightarrow a = 1/4$

$\Rightarrow (x)^{1/4} = 3 \quad \Rightarrow x = 3^4 = 81$

26. (c) $x = \sqrt{\log_a b}$; $y = \sqrt{\log_b a}$

Let $x = \sqrt{k} \quad \Rightarrow y = \sqrt{\dfrac{1}{k}}$

Now $\log_a b = k \quad \Rightarrow \quad a^k = b$

Also $a = b^{1/k}$ (i)

$\Rightarrow \; a^x - b^y = a^{\sqrt{k}} - b^{\sqrt{1/k}}$

By equation (i), we get $a^x - b^y = (b)^{\frac{1}{\sqrt{k}}} - (b)^{\frac{1}{\sqrt{k}}} = 0$

$\Rightarrow \; a^x - b^4 = 0$

27. (c) $\log_{2x+3}\left(6x^2 + 23x + 21\right) = 4 - \log_{(3x+7)}\left(4x^2 + 12x + 9\right)$

$= \log_{2x+3}(2x+3)(3x+7) = 4 - \log_{3x+7}(2x+3)^2$

$= \log_{2x+3}(3x+7) + 2\log_{3x+7}(2x+3) = 3$

$= \log_{2x+3}(3x+7) = Y = Y + \dfrac{2}{Y} = 3$

$\Rightarrow Y^2 + 2 - 3Y = 0 \quad \Rightarrow \quad (Y^0 - 2)(Y - 1) = 0$

$\Rightarrow Y = 1, 2$

$\log_{(2x+3)} 3x + 7 = 1$

$\Rightarrow 2x + 3 = 3x + 7$

$\Rightarrow x = -4$; which is not permissible or $Y = 2$

$\Rightarrow \log_{(2x+3)} 3x + 7 = 2 \quad \Rightarrow \quad (2x + 3)^2 = 3x + 7$

$\Rightarrow 4x^2 + 9 + 12x = 3x + 7$

$\Rightarrow 4x^2 + 9x + 2 = 0 \quad \Rightarrow \quad 4x^2 + 8x + x + 2 = 0$

$\Rightarrow 4x(x + 2) + (x + 2) = 0$

$\Rightarrow (x + 2)(4x + 1) = 0 \quad \Rightarrow \quad x = -2, x = -1/4$

Only permissible value of $x = -1/4$

28. (c) $x^3 - 3x + [x] = 0, x \in [0, 3]$

$\Rightarrow x^3 - 3x = -[x] \quad \Rightarrow \quad x(x^2 - 3) = -[x]$ (i)

Let us draw the graph of $y = x(x^2 - 3)$ and $y = -[x]$ on same frame of reference as shown below.

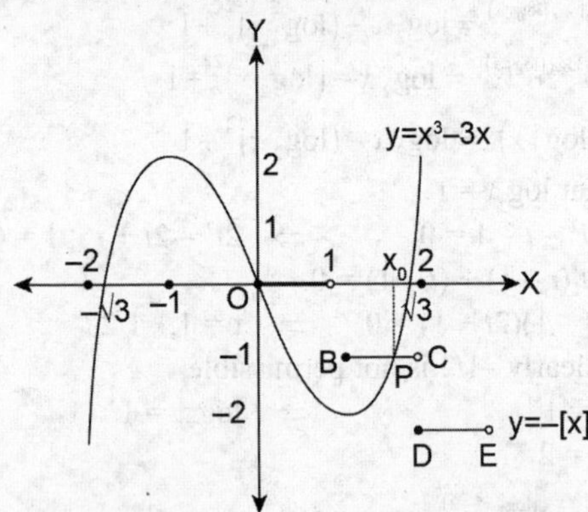

Clearly in [0, 3]; $y = x^3 - 3x$ and $y = -[x]$ intersect each other only at two points i.e., $O(0, 0)$ and $P(x_0, -1)$.

29. (c) $2x^{\log_{10} x} + 3x^{\log_{10}\left(\frac{1}{x}\right)} = 5$; Can be written as

$2x\log_{10} x + 3\left(\dfrac{1}{x}\right)^{\log_{10} x} = 5$

Let $x^{\log_{10} x} = y$

$\Rightarrow 2y + \dfrac{3}{y} = 5 \quad \Rightarrow \quad 2y^2 + 3 - 5y = 0$

$\Rightarrow 2y^2 - 2y - 3y + 3 = 0$

$\Rightarrow 2y(y - 1) - 3(y - 1) = 0$

$\Rightarrow (y - 1)(2y - 3) = 0 \quad \Rightarrow \quad y = 1$ or $y = 3/2$

$\Rightarrow x\log_{10} x = 1 \quad \Rightarrow \quad \log_{10}x . \log x = 0$

$\Rightarrow x = 1$

$x^{\log_{10} x} = 3/2 \quad \Rightarrow \quad \log_{10} x . \log x = \log 3 - \log 2$

$\Rightarrow \log_{10} x = \sqrt{\log\dfrac{3}{2}} \quad \Rightarrow \quad x = 10\sqrt{\log^{3/2}}$

This has another solution viz $x = \left(\dfrac{1}{10}\right)^{\sqrt{\log 3/2}}$

$\Rightarrow$ Overall the equation has three solutions

30. (c) $\dfrac{6}{5}a^{\log_a x . \log_{10} a \log_a 5} - 3^{\log_{10}\left(\frac{x}{10}\right)} = (3)^{2\left[\frac{1}{2}\log_{10} x + \frac{1}{2}\right]} = (3)^{(\log_{10} x + 1)}$

$= 3.(3)^{\log_{10} x}$

$\Rightarrow \dfrac{2}{5}(x)^{\log_{10} 5} - 3^{[\log_{10} x - \log_{10} 10] - 1} = 3^{\log_{10} x}$

$\Rightarrow \dfrac{2}{5}(5)^{\log_{10} x} - 3^{\log_{10} x} . 3^{-2} = 3^{\log_{10} x}$

$\Rightarrow \dfrac{2}{5}(5)^{\log_{10} x} = 3^{\log_{10} x}\left(1 + \dfrac{1}{9}\right)$

$\Rightarrow \dfrac{2}{5}(5)^{\log_{10} x} = \dfrac{10}{9}(3)^{\log_{10} x}$

$\Rightarrow \dfrac{9}{25} = \left(\dfrac{3}{5}\right)^{\log_{10} x} \quad \log_{10} x = 2$

$\Rightarrow x = 100 = 10^2$

31. (a) $p = \log_{245} 175$ and $q = \log_{1715} 875$ (given)

$\Rightarrow 245^p = 175$ and $1715^q = 875$

$\Rightarrow \dfrac{1 - pq}{p - q} = \dfrac{1 - \dfrac{\log 175}{\log 245} . \dfrac{\log 875}{\log 1715}}{\dfrac{\log 175}{\log 245} - \dfrac{\log 875}{\log 1715}}$

$\dfrac{1 - \dfrac{(\log 25 + \log 7)}{(\log 5 + 2\log 7)} . \dfrac{(\log 125 + \log 7)}{(\log 5 + 3\log 7)}}{\dfrac{(\log 25 + \log 7)}{(\log 5 + 2\log 7)} - \dfrac{(\log 125 + \log 7)}{(\log 5 + 3\log 7)}} = 1$

32. (b) $\log_{1/5}(2x + 5) + \log_5(16 - x^2) \le 1$

$\Rightarrow \log_5(2x + 5)^{-1} + \log_5(16 - x^2) \le 1$

$\Rightarrow \log_5 \dfrac{(16 - x^2)}{2x + 5} \le 1 \qquad 0 < \dfrac{16 - x^2}{2x + 5} \le 5$

$\Rightarrow (16 - x^2)(2x + 5) > 0$ and $(x + 1)(x + 9)(2x + 5) \ge 0$; $x \ne -5/2$

$\Rightarrow x \in [-9, -4) \cup [-1, 4)$ (i)

Also $2x + 5 > 0$ and $16 - x^2 > 0$

$\Rightarrow x > \dfrac{-5}{2}$ and $x \in (-4, 4)$

$\Rightarrow x \in \left(\dfrac{-5}{2}, 4\right)$ (ii)

From (i) and (ii), we get $x \in [-1, 4)$

33. (c) $\log_2 a = s$, $\log_4 b = s^2$ and $\log_{c^2} 8 = \dfrac{2}{s^3 + 1}$ (given)

$\Rightarrow 2^s = a \quad \Rightarrow \quad 4^{s^2} = b$

$\Rightarrow c^{2\left(\frac{2}{s^3+1}\right)} = 8 \quad \Rightarrow \quad c = 8^{\left(\frac{s^3+1}{4}\right)}$

Let $\log_2 \dfrac{a^2 b^5}{c^4} = y \quad \Rightarrow \quad 2^y = \dfrac{a^2 b^5}{c^4}$

$\Rightarrow\ a^2 = 2^{2s} \quad \Rightarrow\ b^5 = \left(4^{s^2}\right)^5$

$\Rightarrow\ c^4 = 8^{s^3+1} \quad \Rightarrow\ \dfrac{a^2.b^5}{c^4} = \dfrac{2^{2s}.(4^{s^2})^5}{c^4} = \dfrac{2^{2s}.4^{s^{10}}}{8^{s^3+1}}$

$\Rightarrow\ \dfrac{a^2.b^5}{c^4} = \left(\dfrac{2^{2s}.(2^{2^s})^{10}}{2.^{3(s^3+1)}}\right) = 2^{(2s+10s^2-3(s^3+1))}$

$\Rightarrow\ y = 2s + 10s^2 - 3(s^3 + 1)$

34. (c) $N = \dfrac{4.4^5}{3.3^5}.\dfrac{6.6^5}{2.2^5} = \dfrac{4^6.6^6}{3^6.2^6} = (4)^6$

$\Rightarrow\ \log_2 N = 12$

35. (c) $x = 1.2.3.4.\ldots.2000$

$\Rightarrow\ N = \dfrac{1}{\dfrac{\log 2}{\log x} + \dfrac{\log 3}{\log x} + \ldots + \dfrac{\log 2000}{\log x}}$

Clearly $\log(x) = \log(2) + \log(3) + \ldots + \log(2000)$

$\Rightarrow\ N = \dfrac{1}{\dfrac{\log 2 + \log 3 + \ldots + \log 2000}{\log x}} = 1$

36. (b) $\log_{10}(x-1)^3 - 3\log_{10}(x-3) = \log_{10} 8$; which can be written as $\log_{10}\dfrac{(x-1)^3}{(x-3)^3} = \log_{10}(8)$

$\Rightarrow\ \left(\dfrac{x-1}{x-3}\right)^3 = 8 \quad \Rightarrow\ \dfrac{x-1}{x-3} = 2$

$\Rightarrow\ x = 5 \quad \Rightarrow\ \log_x 625 = 4$

37. (d) $\left[\sqrt[3]{\sqrt[6]{a^9}}\right]^4\left[\sqrt[6]{\sqrt[3]{a^9}}\right]^4 \quad \Rightarrow\ \left[a^{9\times\frac{1}{6}\times\frac{1}{3}}\right]^4\left[a^{9\times\frac{1}{3}\times\frac{1}{6}}\right]^4$

$\Rightarrow\ a^2.a^2 = a^4$

38. (d) $\log_2(x + 5) = 6 - x \quad \Rightarrow\ (x + 5) = 2^{6-x}$

$\Rightarrow\ x = 3$ is the only solution

39. (d) $\log_4 5 = a$ and $\log_5 6 = b$

$\Rightarrow\ 4^a = 5$ and $5^b = 6$

Let $\log_3 2 = y \quad 3^4 = 2$

$\Rightarrow\ ab = \dfrac{\log 5.\log 6}{\log 4.\log 5} = \dfrac{\log 2 + \log 3}{2\log 2}$

$\Rightarrow\ 2ab = 1 + \dfrac{\log 3}{\log 2} = 1 + \log_2 3$

$\Rightarrow\ 2ab - 1 = \log_2 3 \quad \Rightarrow\ \dfrac{1}{2ab-1} = \log_3 2$

40. (b) By the question $x, y, z > 1$

$\log_x w = 24 \quad \Rightarrow\ w = x^{24}$

Similarly, $w = y^{40}$, $w = (xyz)^{12}$

$\Rightarrow\ w = (w^{1/24}.w^{1/40}.z)^{12}$

$\Rightarrow\ w = (w^{1/2}.w^{3/10}.z)^{12}$

$\Rightarrow\ \dfrac{w}{w^{\frac{8}{10}}} = z^{12}$

$\Rightarrow\ w^{2/10} = z^{12} \quad \Rightarrow\ w^{1/60} = z$

$\log_w z = 1/10 = 2/120$

SECTION-VI: OBJECTIVE-TYPE (MORE THAN ONE CORRECT ANSWER)

1. (a), (b), (c) $x^{\left[(\log_2 x)^2 - 6\log_2 x + 11\right]} = 64$

Let $\log_2 x = y \quad \Rightarrow\ x = 2^y$

Expression reduce to $2^{y(y^2-6y+11)} = 2^6$

$\Rightarrow\ y^3 - 6y^2 + 11y - 6 = 0$

Clearly $y = 1$ is a solution

$\Rightarrow\ y^2(y-1) - 5y(y-1) + 6(y-1) = 0$

$\Rightarrow\ (y-1)(y^2 - 5y + 6) = 0$

$\Rightarrow\ (y-1)(y-3)(y-2) = 0$

$\Rightarrow\ y = 1, y = 2$ or $y = 3$

$\Rightarrow\ x = 2, 4, 8$

2. (a), (b), (c) $x^{\frac{3}{4}(\log_2 x)^2 + \log_2 x - \frac{5}{4}} = \sqrt{2}$

Let $\log_2 x = y$

$\Rightarrow\ x^{\frac{3}{4}y^2 + y - \frac{5}{4}} = 2^{1/2} \quad \Rightarrow\ 2^{y.\left(\frac{3}{4}y^2 + y - \frac{5}{4}\right)} = 2^{1/2}$

$\Rightarrow\ \dfrac{3}{4}y^3 + y^2 - \dfrac{5}{4}y = \dfrac{1}{2}$

$\Rightarrow\ \dfrac{3}{2}y^3 + 2y^2 - \dfrac{5}{2}y - 1 = 0$

$\Rightarrow\ 3y^3 + 4y^2 - 5y - 2 = 0$

Clearly $y = 1$ is a root

$\Rightarrow\ 3y^2(y-1) + 7y(y-1) + 2(y-1) = 0$

$\Rightarrow\ (y-1)(3y^2 + 7y + 2) = 0$

$\Rightarrow\ (y+2)(3y+1)(y-1) = 0$

$\Rightarrow\ y = 1, -2, -1/3 \quad \Rightarrow\ x = 2, 1/4, 2^{-1/3}$

3. (a), (b), (c) $x^{\left[(\log_3 x)^2 - \frac{9}{2}\log_3 x + 5\right]} = 3\sqrt{3}$

Let $\log_3 x = y$

$x = 3^y$

$\Rightarrow\ x^{\left[y^2 - \frac{9}{2}y + 5\right]} = 3^{3/2} \quad \Rightarrow\ 3^{y\left(y^2 - \frac{9}{2}y + 5\right)} = 3^{3/2}$

$\Rightarrow\ y^3 - \dfrac{9}{2}y^2 + 5y = \dfrac{3}{2}$

$\Rightarrow\ y^3 - \dfrac{9}{2}y^2 + 5y - \dfrac{3}{2} = 0$

$\Rightarrow\ 2y^3 - 9y^2 + 10y - 3 = 0$

Clearly $y = 1$ is a solution

$\Rightarrow\ 2y^2(y-1) - 7y(y-1) + 3(y-1) = 0$

$\Rightarrow\ (y-1)(2y^2 - 7y + 3) = 0$

$\Rightarrow\ (y-1)(2y^2 - 6y - y + 3) = 0$

$\Rightarrow\ (y-1)(2y(y-3) - (y-3)) = 0$

$\Rightarrow\ (y-1)(y-3)(2y-1) = 0$

$\Rightarrow\ y = 1$ or 3 or $1/2$

$\Rightarrow\ x = 3, 3^3, 3^{1/2}$

4. (a), (c) $5^{\log_a x} + 5^{x^{\log_a 5}} = 3\ (a > o)$ can be written as

$x^{\log_a 5} + 5x^{\log_a 5} = 3$

$\Rightarrow\ y + 5y = 3 \quad \Rightarrow\ y = 1/2$

Hence $x^{\log_a 5} = \dfrac{1}{2} \quad x = \left(\dfrac{1}{2}\right)^{\frac{1}{\log_a 5}} = \left(\dfrac{1}{2}\right)^{\log_5 a}$

$\Rightarrow\ x = 2^{-\log_5 a}$

5. (a), (d) $\log_2 xy = 5,\ \log_{1/2}\left(\frac{x}{y}\right) = 1$

$\Rightarrow\ xy = 2^5$ and $\frac{x}{y} = \frac{1}{2}$ $\quad\Rightarrow\ xy = 2^5$ and $2x = y$

$\Rightarrow\ 2x^2 = 2^5 \qquad x^2 = 2^4 \qquad x = 4, -4$

$\Rightarrow\ y = 8, -8$

6. (b), (c) $\log_{ax} a + \log_x a^2 + \log_{a^2x} a^3 = 0$ can be written as

$\log_{ax} a + 2\log_x a + 3\log_{a^2x} a = 0$

$\Rightarrow\ \frac{1}{\log_a ax} + \frac{2}{\log_a x} + \frac{3}{\log_a a\, x} =$

$\frac{1}{\log_a a + \log_a x} + \frac{2}{\log_a x} + \frac{3}{2 + \log_a x} = 0$

$\Rightarrow\ \frac{1}{1 + \log_a x} + \frac{2}{\log_a x} + \frac{3}{2 + \log_a x} = 0$

$\Rightarrow\ \frac{1}{1+y} + \frac{2}{y} + \frac{3}{2+y} = 0$

$\Rightarrow\ \frac{2y + y^2 + 2(y^2 + 3y + 2) + 3(y^2 + y)}{(y+2)(y+1)y} = 0$

$\Rightarrow\ 6y^2 + 11y + 4 = 0$

$\Rightarrow\ 6y^2 + 8y + 3y + 4 = 0 \quad 2y(3y + y) + (3y + 4) = 0$

$\Rightarrow\ (3y + 4)(2y + 1) = 0 \quad y = -\frac{1}{2}, y = -\frac{4}{3}$

$\Rightarrow\ x = a^{-\frac{1}{2}}, x = a^{-\frac{4}{3}}$

7. (b), (c) $\log_k x.\log_{10} k = |\log_{10} 5|, k \neq 1, k > 0$ can be written as

$\frac{\log_k x}{\log_k 10} = |\log_{10} 5|$

$\Rightarrow\ \log_{10} x = |\log_{10} 5| \qquad x = 5$ or $\frac{1}{5}$

8. (a), (b), (d) $\frac{1}{2} \leq \log_{0.1} x \leq 2$

$\log_{0.1} x$ is clearly a decreasing function

$\Rightarrow\ f(x_1) \leq f(x_2) \qquad x_1 \geq x_2$ if f is decreases

$\Rightarrow\ (0.1)^2 \leq x \leq (0.1)^{\frac{1}{2}} \quad\Rightarrow\ \frac{1}{100} \leq x \leq \frac{1}{\sqrt{10}}$

9. (b), (c), (d) $\log_{2x+3} x^2 < 1$

Clearly $2x + 3 \neq 1 \qquad\Rightarrow\ x \neq -1$ and

$2x + 3 > 0 \qquad\Rightarrow\ x > -3/2$

Case 1: $2x + 3 > 1 \qquad\Rightarrow\ x > -1$

$\Rightarrow\ x^2 < 2x + 3 \qquad\Rightarrow\ x^2 - 2x - 3 < 0$

$\Rightarrow\ (x - 1)(x + 1) < 0$

Case 2: $x^2 > 2x + 3 \qquad\Rightarrow\ x < -1$

$\Rightarrow\ x^2 - 2x - 3 > 0 \qquad\Rightarrow\ x \in (-\infty, -1) \cup (3, \infty)$

In the region $x \in \left(-\frac{3}{2}, -1\right)$

10. (a), (d) $x^{\sqrt{x}} \quad \sqrt{x^x} \qquad\Rightarrow\ \log_2 x\sqrt{x} = \log_2 \sqrt{x^x}$

$\Rightarrow\ \sqrt{x}\ \log_2 x = \frac{x}{2}\ \log_2 x$

$\Rightarrow\ \log_2 x\left(\sqrt{x} - \frac{x}{2}\right) = 0 \ \Rightarrow\ x = 1, x = 4$

11. (b), (c), (d) $\log_{0.5x} x^2 - 14\log_{16x} x^3 + 40\log_{4x} \sqrt{x}$

This can be written as

$\frac{\log_2(x^2)}{\log_2\left(\frac{x}{2}\right)} - \frac{14\log_2 x^2,}{\log_2 16x} + \frac{40\log_2 \sqrt{x}}{\log_2 4x} = 0$

$\Rightarrow\ \frac{2\log_2 x}{\log_2 x - 1} - \frac{14.3\log_2 x}{\log_2 x + 4} + \frac{20\log_2 x}{2 + \log_2 x} = 0$

Let as assume $\log_2 x = y$

The equation reduces to $\frac{2y}{y-1} - \frac{42y}{y+4} + \frac{20y}{2+y} = 0$

$\Rightarrow\ \frac{2y}{y-1} + \frac{20y}{2+y} = \frac{42y}{y+4} \quad \frac{2y^2 + 4y + 20y^2 - 20y}{(y-1)(y+2)} = \frac{42y}{y+4}$

$\Rightarrow\ (22y^2 - 16y)(y + 4) = 42y(y - 1)(y + 2)$

$\Rightarrow\ y(22y^2 + 72y - 64) - 42y(y^2 + y - 2) = 0$

$\Rightarrow\ y(22y^2 + 72y - 64 - 42y^2 - 42y + 8) = 0$

$\Rightarrow\ y(-20y^2 + 30y + 20) = 0$

Solutions to this cubic equation are $y = 0,\ y = 2,\ y = -\frac{1}{2}$

Corresponding values of $x = 1, 4, \frac{1}{\sqrt{2}}$

12. (a), (b), (c), (d)

(a) $\log_{\frac{3}{2}} \log_4 \log_{\sqrt{3}} 81 = \log_{\frac{3}{2}} \log_4 \left(2\log_3 (3)^4\right)$

$= \log_{\frac{3}{2}} \log_4 (8) = \log_{\frac{3}{2}}\left(\frac{1}{2}(3)\right) = \log_{\frac{3}{2}}\left(\frac{3}{2}\right) = 1$

(b) $\log_2 \sqrt{6} + \log_2 \sqrt{\frac{2}{3}} = \log_2\left(\sqrt{6} \times \sqrt{\frac{2}{3}}\right) = \log_2 2 = 1$

(c) $-\frac{1}{6} \log_{\frac{\sqrt{}}{}} \left[\frac{64}{27}\right] = \log_{\frac{\sqrt{3}}{2}} \left[\frac{64}{27}\right]^{-\frac{1}{6}} = \log_{\frac{\sqrt{3}}{2}} \left[\frac{27}{64}\right]^{\frac{1}{6}}$

$= \log_{\frac{\sqrt{3}}{2}} \left[\frac{3}{4}\right]^{\frac{1}{2}} = \log_{\frac{\sqrt{3}}{2}} \left[\frac{3}{2}\right] = 1$

(d) $\log_{3.5}(1 + 2 + 3 \div 6) = \log_{3.5}\left(1 + 2 + \frac{1}{2}\right) = \log_{3.5}\left(\frac{7}{2}\right) =$ $\log_{3.5}(3.5) = 1$

13. (a), (b)

(a) $\log_2 \text{cosec}\frac{5\pi}{6} + \log_{\frac{1}{2}} \sec\left(\frac{7\pi}{3}\right) = 2$

$\Rightarrow\ 1 + 1 = 2 \qquad \therefore$ L.H.S. = R.H.S.

$\therefore$ Yes, the statement is correct

(b) $\frac{1}{4} < \log_{100} 4 < \frac{1}{3} \qquad\Rightarrow\ \frac{1}{4} < \log_{100} 4 < \log\frac{1}{3}$

$\Rightarrow\ \log_{100} 4\sqrt{100} < \log_{100} 4 < \log_{100} 3\sqrt{100}$

Which is true if $4\sqrt{100} < 4 < 3\sqrt{100}$

Which is true if $100 < 256$ and $64 < 100$

$\therefore$ Yes, the statement is correct

(c) $\log_2(\sin^2 x - 4\sin x + 1)$ is maximum when

$(\sin^2 x - 4\sin x + 1)$ is maximum

$\max\left((\sin x - 2)^2 - 3\right)$ is maximum when $|\sin x - 2|$ is maximum

$\max\left((\sin x-2)^2-3\right)=6$
$\max\log_2(\sin^2 x-4\sin x+1)\neq 4$
∴ No, the statement is incorrect

(d) $\log\sqrt{x-1}=1-\sqrt{1-x}$
This has no solution rather as $1-x>0 \Rightarrow 1>x$
But at the same time $x-1>0 \Rightarrow x>1$
Which is not possible simultaneously.
⇒ The statement is not correct

SECTION–V: ASSERTION REASON

1. A: $\sqrt{\log_{\frac{1}{2}}(2x-3)}$ for this to be real and finite
$\log_{\frac{1}{2}}(2x-3)\geq 0$
$\Rightarrow (2x-3)\leq 1 \quad \Rightarrow \quad 2x\leq 4$
$x\leq 2$ but $2x-3\geq 0 \Rightarrow \quad x>\frac{3}{2}$
For $\sqrt{\log_{\frac{1}{2}}(2x-3)}$ to be real and finite $x\in\left(\frac{3}{2},2\right]$

R: $\log_a x$ is defined only for $x>0$ and $a>0, \neq 1$ $\log_a x>\log_a y \Leftrightarrow x<y$ if $a\in(0,1)$
Which is true according to the domain of log function and since $\log_a x$ is decreasing function for $a\in(0,1)$
∴ Option (a) is correct

2. A: $\log_2\left(\log_{\frac{1}{2}}(\log_4 x)\right)>0 \quad \Rightarrow \log_{\frac{1}{2}}(\log_4 x)>1$
$\Rightarrow \log_4(x)<\frac{1}{2} \quad \Rightarrow \quad x<(4)^{\frac{1}{2}}=2$
$\Rightarrow x\in(0,2)$ as $\log_a x$ is defined for $x>0$.

R: $\log_a x$ is defined for $x>0$, $a>0$ and $a\neq 0$
$\Rightarrow \log_a x>\log_a y \Leftrightarrow \begin{cases} x>y \text{ if } a>1 \\ x<y \text{ if } a\in(0,1)\end{cases}$
⇒ log x is increasing for base greater then one which is true.
⇒ Both reason and assertion are correct and reason is also correct explanation to assertion.
∴ Option (a) is correct

3. A: $3\log_4(x^2+2x+1)+7\log_4(x+4)=5-\log(4x-x-4)$
Which is same as $\log_4(x^2+2x+1)^3+\log_4(x+4)^7=5-\log_4(-(x-2)^2)$
This number $(4x-x^2-4)=-(x^2-4x+4)=-(x-2)^2<0$ but for the domain of log x
This is not permissible, hence no real solution are possible
⇒ Assertion is corrects.

R: Also reason is the correct explanation of assertion.
∴ Option (a) is correct

4. A: $\log_2 a=S=\frac{\log a}{\log 2}$ (i)
$\log_4 b=S^2=\frac{\log b}{\log 4}$ (ii)
$\log_{c^2} 8=\frac{2}{s^3+1}=\frac{3\log 2}{2\log c}=\frac{2}{s^3+1}$ (iii)

$\Rightarrow \log_2\frac{a^2b^5}{c^4}=\log_2 a^2b^5-\log_2 c^4$
$=\frac{\log a^2}{\log 2}+\frac{\log b^5}{\log 2}-\frac{4\log c}{\log 2}=\frac{2\log a}{\log 2}+\frac{5\log b}{\log 2}-\frac{4\log c}{\log 2}$
Using (i), (ii) and (iii), we get $2s+10s^2-4.\frac{3}{4}(s^3+1)$
$=10s^2+2s-3s^3-3$
⇒ Assertion is correct

R: $\log_a x^\alpha=\alpha\log_a|x|$, $\log_{a^\beta}(x)=\frac{1}{\beta}\log_{|a|}x$
$\log_a x^a=a\log_a|x|$ which is correct.
$\log_{a^\beta}(x)=\frac{\log x}{\log a^\beta}=\frac{\log x}{\beta\log|a|}=\frac{1}{\beta}\log_{|a|}x$ and similarly $\log_b a=\frac{\log a}{\log b}=\frac{1}{\frac{\log b}{\log a}}=\frac{1}{\log_a b}$
⇒ Reason is correct and reason is the correct explanation of assertion.
∴ Option (a) is correct

5. A: $\log_3 x\log_4 x\log_5 x=\log_3 x\log_4 x+\log_4 x\log_5 x+\log_5 x\log_3 x$
Let $\log x=y$
$\Rightarrow \frac{y^3}{\log 3.\log 4.\log 5}=\frac{y^2}{\log 3.\log 4}+\frac{y^2}{\log 4.\log 5}+\frac{y^2}{\log 3.\log 5}$
$\Rightarrow y=\log 5+\log 3+\log 4=\log(5\times 3\times 4)=\log(60)$
$(\because y\neq 0)$
$\Rightarrow \log(x)=\log(60) \quad \Rightarrow x=60$
But for the case $\log x=y=0$
$\Rightarrow x=1$
Sum of the roots $=60+1=61$
⇒ Square = 3721
⇒ Assertion is correct

R: $\log_a x=\frac{1}{\log_x a}$ which is not possible if $x=1$ or $a=1$
because $\frac{1}{\log 1}$ is not defined
⇒ Reason is correct
⇒ Option (c) is correct.

6. A: $2^{\log_2(x^2-1)}=8$
∴ $2^{\log_2(x^2-1)}=(x^2-1)=8$
$\Rightarrow x^2=9 \quad \Rightarrow x=3$ or -3
⇒ Assertion is correct

R: a^x and $\log_a x$
∴ $a^{\log_a x}=x$ and $\log_a(a^x)=x$
Hence they are inverse operate of each other.
⇒ Option (a) is correct.

SECTION-VI: PASSAGE

Passage – A:

1. (b) $\log x=\frac{1}{2}\log(x+1)=\log(x+1)^{1/2}$
By the information in the comprehension $x=\sqrt{x+1}$

$\Rightarrow$ x has to be positive.

$\Rightarrow x^2 = x + 1 \qquad \Rightarrow x^2 - x - 1$

$\Rightarrow x = \dfrac{1 \pm \sqrt{1+4}}{2} = \dfrac{1 \pm \sqrt{5}}{2}$

$\Rightarrow$ Positive $x = \dfrac{1+\sqrt{5}}{2}$

2. (d) $\log_{\frac{3}{10}}(x-1) = \log_{\frac{9}{100}}(x-2) \quad \dfrac{\log(x-1)}{\log\left(\frac{3}{10}\right)} = \dfrac{\log(x-2)}{\log\left(\frac{9}{100}\right)}$

$\Rightarrow \dfrac{\log(x-1)}{\log\left(\frac{3}{10}\right)} = \dfrac{\log(x-2)}{2\left(\log\left(\frac{3}{10}\right)\right)}$

$\Rightarrow (x-1)^2 - (x-2)^2$

$\Rightarrow x^2 + 1 - 2x = x - 2$

$\Rightarrow x^2 - 3x + 3 = 0 \qquad \Rightarrow$ Which has no solution

3. (a) $\log_7 \log_5 \left(\sqrt{x+5} + \sqrt{x}\right) = 0$

$\Rightarrow \log_5 \left(\sqrt{x+5} + \sqrt{x}\right) = 1$

$\Rightarrow \sqrt{x+5} = 5 - \sqrt{x}$

Squaring, we get $x + 5 = 25 + x - 10\sqrt{x}$

$\Rightarrow 10\sqrt{x} = 20 \qquad \Rightarrow \sqrt{x} = 2$

$\Rightarrow x = 4$

4. (b), (c)

(a) $\log_a\left(\dfrac{1}{x}\right) = \dfrac{\log(1) - \log x}{\log a} = -\log_a a$

But a = 1

$\Rightarrow \log 1 = 0 \qquad \Rightarrow \dfrac{1}{\log a}$ is not defined.

Hence the statement is false.

(b) if $0 < x < y$

$\log x < \log y$

$\Rightarrow x < y$ which is true

(c) $0 < \phi(x) < 1$

$\log_{\phi(x)} f(x) \geq \log_{\phi(x)} g(x)$

$\Rightarrow \dfrac{\log f(x)}{\log \phi(x)} \geq \dfrac{\log g(x)}{\log \phi(x)}$ but since $\phi(x) < 1$

$\Rightarrow \log \phi(x) < 0$

$\Rightarrow 0 < f(x) \leq g(x)$ which is true

Passage – B:

5. (a), (c) $2\left(\dfrac{\log c}{\log a} + \dfrac{\log c}{\log b}\right) = \dfrac{9 \log c}{\log ab}$

$\Rightarrow 2\log c\left(\dfrac{\log a + \log b}{\log a.\log b}\right) - \dfrac{9 \log c}{\log a + \log b}$

Excluding $\log c = 0$

$\Rightarrow 2(\log a + \log b)^2 = 9. \log a. \log b$

$\Rightarrow 2(\log a)^2 + 2(\log b)^2 + 4 \log a. \log b = 9 \log a. \log b$

$\Rightarrow \dfrac{(\log a)^2 + (\log b)^2}{\log a - \log b} = \dfrac{5}{2}$ (i)

If a quadratic equation has $\log_a b$ and $\log_b a$ as its roots.

$\Rightarrow \log_a b = \dfrac{1}{\log_b a}$

Sum of the roots $= \log_a b + \log_b a = \dfrac{\log b}{\log a} + \dfrac{\log a}{\log b}$

$= \dfrac{(\log b)^2 + (\log a)^2}{\log a.\log b} = \dfrac{5}{2}$

6. (a), (b) Let $\log_a b = x$

$\Rightarrow \log_a b + \log_b a = x + \dfrac{1}{x}$

We have already proved that $x + \dfrac{1}{x} = \dfrac{5}{2}$

$\Rightarrow x - \dfrac{5}{2} + \dfrac{1}{x} = 0 \qquad \Rightarrow 2x^2 - 5x + 2 = 0$

$\Rightarrow 2x^2 - 4x - x + 2 = 0$

$\Rightarrow (2x - 1)(x - 2) = 0 \qquad \Rightarrow x = 2$ or $x = \dfrac{1}{2}$

$\Rightarrow b = a^2 \qquad \Rightarrow a = \sqrt{b}$ or $b = \sqrt{a}$

7. (a) We have proved above that $\log_a b = 2$ or $\dfrac{1}{2}$

$\Rightarrow$ Maximum value of $\log_a b = 2$

Passage – C:

$\log_2 x + \log_4 y + \log_4 z = 2$; $\log_3 y + \log_9 x + \log_9 z = 2$ and $\log_4 z + \log_{16} x + \log_{16} y = 2$

(i) $\dfrac{\log x}{\log z} + \dfrac{\log y}{2\log z} + \dfrac{\log z}{2\log z} = z$

$\Rightarrow 2\log x + \log y + \log z = 4 \log z$ (i)

(ii) $\dfrac{\log y}{\log 3} + \dfrac{\log x}{\log 9} + \dfrac{\log z}{\log 9} = z$

$2\log y + \log x + \log z = 4 \log 3$ (ii)

(iii) $\dfrac{\log z}{\log 4} + \dfrac{\log x}{\log 16} + \dfrac{\log y}{\log 16} = z$

$\Rightarrow 2\log z + \log x + \log y = 4 \log z$ (iii)

Equation (iii) – (i), we get $\log z - \log x = 4 \log z$

$\Rightarrow \log\left(\dfrac{z}{x}\right) = \log(z)^4 \qquad \Rightarrow \dfrac{z}{x} = 2^4$ (a)

Equation (ii) – (i), we get $\log y - \log x = 4 \log\left(\dfrac{3}{2}\right)$

$\Rightarrow \left(\dfrac{y}{x}\right) = \left(\dfrac{3}{2}\right)^4$ (b)

Equation (iii) – (ii), we get $\log z - \log y = \log\left(\dfrac{2^8}{3^4}\right)$

$\Rightarrow \dfrac{z}{y} = \dfrac{2^8}{3^4}$ (c)

8. (a), (c) $\dfrac{x}{y} = \left(\dfrac{2}{3}\right)^4$

$\Rightarrow$ a real number and a perfect square.

9. (a) $\dfrac{y}{2} = \dfrac{3^4}{2^8} = \dfrac{81}{256}$

10. (b) $z = 2^4 x$ (a) $\qquad \Rightarrow \qquad z = 16x$

Passage – D:

$2^{|x+1|} - 2^x = |2^x - 1| + 1$

Case – 1: $x < 0$

$\Rightarrow 2^{|x+1|} - 2^x = 1 - 2^x + 1 \Rightarrow \quad 2^{|x+1|} = 2$

$\Rightarrow |x + 1| = 1 \qquad \Rightarrow x = -2$ is the region.

Case – 2: $x \geq 0$

$\Rightarrow\ 2^{|x+1|} - 2^x = 2^x + 1 - 1 \Rightarrow\ 2^{|x+1|} = 2^{x+1}$

$\Rightarrow\ |x+1| = x+1$, which is true $\forall\ x;\ x \geq 0$

11. (d) Least value of x satisfying the equation = –2

12. (c) Integers less than fifteen satisfying are, –2, 0, 1,.....,14 = 16 integers

13. (a) Composite numbers less than 20 co-prime to 4 satisfying the equation are 9, 15 = 2

SECTION–VII: (COLUMN MATCHING)

1. (i) → (b), (c); (ii) → (a); (iii) → (c), (d); (iv) → (b), (c)

(i) $\log_3 x \log_x 2x \,.\, \log_{2x} y = \log_x x^2$

$\Rightarrow\ \dfrac{\log x}{\log 3}\cdot\dfrac{\log 2x}{\log x}\cdot\dfrac{\log y}{\log 2x} = 2\ \Rightarrow \log y = 2.\log^3 y = 9$

(ii) $4^{\log_{10} x+1} - 4^{\log_{10} x} - 2.34^{\log_{10} x^2 + 2} = 0$

$= 4.4^{\log_{10} x} - 6^{\log_{10} x} - 2.3^2 \cdot 3^{2\log_{10} x}$

Let $\log_{10} x = y$

$\Rightarrow\ 4.\ 4^y - 6^y - 18.3^{2y} = 0$

$\Rightarrow\ 4.4^y - 6^y = 18.3^{2y}$

$\Rightarrow\ 4.\ 4^y - 2^y.\ 3^y = 2.3^{2(y+1)}$

Which is possible iff $y = -2$ as $4.4^y = 2.3^{2y+2} + 2^y \cdot 3^y$

$\Rightarrow \log_{10} x = -2\ \Rightarrow\ x = \dfrac{1}{100}$

$\therefore$ Square root of $\dfrac{1}{x} = \sqrt{100} = 10$

(iii) $\log_b a = 10\ \Rightarrow\ a = b^{10}$

Let $\log_{b^5} a^3 = y\ \Rightarrow\ b^{5y} + a^3$

$\Rightarrow\ b^{5y} = b^{30}\ \Rightarrow\ y = 6$

(iv) $4^{5\log_{4\sqrt{2}}(3-\sqrt{6}) - 2\log_2(\sqrt{3}-\sqrt{2})}$

$\Rightarrow\ 2^{\left(10\times\frac{1}{5}\right)\log_{\sqrt{2}}(\sqrt{3})(\sqrt{3}-\sqrt{2})}.(2)^{-4\log_2(\sqrt{3}-\sqrt{2})}$

$\Rightarrow\ 2^{4\log_2(\sqrt{3})(\sqrt{3}-\sqrt{2})}.(2)^{\log_2(\sqrt{3}-\sqrt{2})^{-4}}$

$\Rightarrow\ 9(\sqrt{3}-\sqrt{2})^4.(\sqrt{3}-\sqrt{2})^{-4} = 9$

2. (i) → (b), (c), (d); (ii) → (c); (iii) → (b), (c); (iv) → (a), (c)

(i) $\left(\dfrac{1}{3}\right)^{\log_{\frac{1}{9}}\left(x^2 - \frac{10}{3}x + 1\right)} \leq 1\quad 0 \leq \left(x^2 - \dfrac{10}{3}x + 1\right)^{\frac{1}{2}} \leq 1$

$\Rightarrow\ 0 \leq 3x^2 - 10x + 3$ and $3x^2 - 10x \leq 0$

$\Rightarrow\ x \in \left(-\infty, \dfrac{1}{3}\right] \cup [3, \infty)$ and $x \in \left[0, \dfrac{10}{3}\right]$

$\Rightarrow\ x \in \left[0, \dfrac{1}{3}\right] \cup \left[3, \dfrac{10}{3}\right]$

(ii) $\log_{\frac{1}{2}}(x^2 - 6x + 12) \geq -2$

$\Rightarrow\ 0 \leq (x^2 - 6x + 2) \leq \left(\dfrac{1}{2}\right)^{-2}$

$\Rightarrow\ 0 \leq x^2 - 6x + 2 \leq 4$

$\Rightarrow\ x^2 - 6x - 2 \leq 0$ and $x^2 - 6x + 2 \geq 0$

$\Rightarrow\ x \in \left(3 - \sqrt{11}, 3 + \sqrt{11}\right)$ and

$x \in \left(-\infty, 3 - \sqrt{7}\right] \cup \left[3 + \sqrt{7}, \infty\right)$

$\Rightarrow\ x \in \left(3 - \sqrt{11}, 3 - \sqrt{7}\right] \cup \left[3 + \sqrt{7}, 3 + \sqrt{11}\right)$

(iii) $\log_{0.7}(x^2 + 1) < \log_{0.7} 2x;\ x > 0$

$\Rightarrow\ x^2 + 1 > 2x\qquad \Rightarrow\ x^2 - 2x + 1 > 0$

$\Rightarrow\ (x-1)^2 > 0$, which is true $\forall\ x > 0$

$\Rightarrow\ x \in (0, \infty)$

(iv) $f(x) = \sqrt{\log_{10} x^2}$; Which is real when $\log_{10} x^2 \geq 0$

$\Rightarrow\ x^2 \geq 1\qquad \Rightarrow\ x \in (-\infty, -1] \cup [1, \infty)$

3. (i) → (c); (ii) → (a); (iii) → (b); (iv) → (a); (v) → (d)

(i) $\log_{\sqrt{2}} 1024 = 2\log_2 2^{10} = 20$

(ii) $\log_5 2 + \log_5 15 - \log_5 6$

$= \dfrac{\log 2}{\log 5} + \dfrac{\log 15}{\log 5} - \dfrac{\log 6}{\log 5} = \dfrac{\log 30 - \log 6}{\log 5} = 1$

(iii) $\log_{3-2\sqrt{2}}\left(3 + 2\sqrt{2}\right)$

$\therefore\ 3 - 2\sqrt{2} = \dfrac{\left(3-2\sqrt{2}\right)\left(3+2\sqrt{2}\right)}{\left(3+2\sqrt{2}\right)} = \dfrac{9-8}{3+2\sqrt{2}} = \left(3+\sqrt{2}\right)^{-1}$

$\Rightarrow\ \log_{(3-2\sqrt{2})}\left(3+2\sqrt{2}\right) = -1$

(iv) $\log_{(1.\bar{6})}\left(1 + \dfrac{2}{3}\right) = \log_{(1.\bar{6})}\left(\dfrac{5}{3}\right) = 1$

(v) $-\log_8 \log_4 .\ 4\qquad \Rightarrow\ -\log_8 1$

$\Rightarrow\ 0$

4. (i) → (c); (ii) → (a); (iii) → (b); (iv) → (d)

(i) $\log_4(x+1) + \log_4(x+8) = \dfrac{3}{2}$

$\Rightarrow\ \log_4 (x+1)(x+8) = \dfrac{3}{2}$

$\Rightarrow\ (x+1)(x+8) = (4^{\frac{1}{2}})^3 = 8$

$\Rightarrow\ x^2 + 9x + 8 = 8\qquad \Rightarrow\ x(x+9) = 0$

$\Rightarrow\ x = 0$ or $x = -9\qquad \Rightarrow\ x$ cannot $\neq -9$

$\Rightarrow\ x = 0$

(ii) $|x| + |x-5| = 6;\ x < 0$

$\Rightarrow\ -x + |x-5| = 6\qquad \Rightarrow\ -x + 5 - x = 6$

$\Rightarrow\ 5 - 2x = 6\qquad \Rightarrow\ -2x = 1$

$\Rightarrow\ x = -\dfrac{1}{2}\qquad \Rightarrow\ x + \dfrac{3}{2} = 1$

(iii) $4\left(3\log_2\dfrac{81}{80} + 5\log_2\dfrac{25}{24} + 7\log_2\dfrac{16}{15}\right)$

$= 4\left(\log_2\left(\dfrac{81^3 \times 25^5 \times 16^7}{80^3 \times 24^5 \times 15^7}\right)\right) = 4\log_2(2) = 4$

(iv) $2x^5 - x^3 + x^2 + 1$ is divided by $(2x+1)$. The remainder is $\dfrac{21}{16}\qquad \Rightarrow\ k = \dfrac{21}{16}$

$\Rightarrow\ \dfrac{16k + 11}{16} = \dfrac{21 + 11}{16} = \dfrac{32}{16} = 2$

SECTION –VIII: INTEGER TYPE

1. $\log_3(x^2 - 3x - 5) = \log_3(7 - 2x)$

$\Rightarrow\ (x^2 - 3x - 5) = (7 - 2x)$

$\Rightarrow\ x^2 - 3x + 2x - 12 = 0$

$\Rightarrow\ x^2 - x - 12 = 0\qquad \Rightarrow\ x^2 - 4x + 3x - 12 = 0$

$\Rightarrow\ x(x-4) + 3(x-4) = 0$

$\Rightarrow$ $(x+3)(x+4)=0$

$\Rightarrow$ $x=-3, x=4$, but $x=4$ is not in the domain of $\log_3(7-2x)$

$\Rightarrow$ $x=-3$

2. $\log(x+4)+\log(2x+3)=\log(1-2x)$

$\log((x+4)(2x+3))=\log(1-2x)$

$\Rightarrow$ $2x^2+3x+8x+12=1-2x$

$\Rightarrow$ $2x^2+13x+11=0 \quad 2x^2+11x+2x+11=0$

$\Rightarrow$ $(2x+11)(x+1)=0 \Rightarrow x=-\frac{11}{2},-1$

$\therefore$ In the domain of the function $x=-1$

3. $\log_5\left(5^{\frac{1}{x}}+125\right)=\log_5 6+1+\frac{1}{2x}$

$\Rightarrow$ $5^{\frac{1}{x}}+125=5^{\log_5 6}.5.5^{\frac{1}{2x}} \Rightarrow 5^{\frac{1}{x}}+125=30.5^{\frac{1}{2x}}$

Let $5^{\frac{1}{2x}}=y$

$\Rightarrow$ $y^2+125=30y \quad \Rightarrow y^2-30y+125=0$

$\Rightarrow$ $(y-25)(y-5)=0$

$\Rightarrow$ $y=5$ or $y=25 \quad \Rightarrow x=\frac{1}{2}$ or $\frac{1}{4}$

$\frac{1}{\alpha}+\frac{1}{\beta}=4+2=6$

4. $x^{\log_{10}x}+6x^{\log_{10}\left(\frac{1}{x}\right)}=5 \qquad x^{\log_{10}x}+6x^{-\log_{10}x}=5$

$\Rightarrow$ $x^{\log_{10}x}+\frac{6}{x^{\log_{10}x}}=5$

Put $x^{\log_{10}x}=y \quad \Rightarrow y+\frac{6}{y}=5$

$\Rightarrow$ $y^2-5y+6=0$

$\Rightarrow$ $(y-2)(y-3)=0 \quad \Rightarrow y=2$ or $y=3$

$\Rightarrow$ $x^{\log_{10}x}=2,3$

$\Rightarrow$ $\log_{10}x.\ \log_{10}2, \log_{10}3 \Rightarrow (\log_{10}x)^2=(\log_{10}2), (\log_{10}3)$

$\Rightarrow$ $\log_{10}x=\pm(\log_{10}2)^{1/2}, \pm(\log_{10}3)^{1/2}$

$\Rightarrow$ $x=10^{\pm(\log_{10}2)^{\frac{1}{2}}}, 10^{\pm(\log_{10}3)^{\frac{1}{2}}}$

$\Rightarrow$ Four solutions

5. By the question 1, $\log_3\sqrt{3^{1-x}+2}$, $\log_3\left(4.3^x-1\right)$ are in A.P.

$\Rightarrow$ $1+\log_3(4.3^x-1)=2\log_3\sqrt{3^{1-x}+2}$

$1+\log_3(4.3^x-1)=\log_3(3^{1-x}+2)$

$\Rightarrow$ $1=\log_3\left(\frac{3^{1-x}+2}{4.3^x-1}\right) \Rightarrow 3=\frac{3^{1-x}+2}{4.3^x-1}$

$\Rightarrow$ $4.3^{1+x}-3=3^{1-x}+2$

$\Rightarrow$ $3.4.\ 3^x=3.3^{-x}+5$

Let $3^x=y$

$\Rightarrow$ $12y=\frac{3}{y}+5 \quad \Rightarrow 12y^2-3-5y=0$

$\Rightarrow$ $12y^2-9y+4y-3=0$

$\Rightarrow$ $3y(4y-3)+(4y-3)=0$

$\Rightarrow$ $(4y-3)(3y+1)=0 \Rightarrow y=-\frac{1}{3},\frac{3}{4}$

$\therefore$ The only possibility is $y=\frac{3}{4}$

$\Rightarrow$ $3^x=\frac{3}{4}$

By the question $x=1-\log_3 k$

$\Rightarrow$ $3^{x-1}=\frac{1}{4} \qquad \Rightarrow 3^{-\log_3 k}=\frac{1}{4}$

$\Rightarrow$ $k=4$

6. $y=(0.05)^{\log_{\sqrt{20}}\left(\frac{1}{9}\right)} \qquad y=\left(\frac{1}{20}\right)^{\log_{20}\left(\frac{1}{9}\right)^2}$

$\Rightarrow$ $y=\frac{1}{\left(\frac{1}{9}\right)^2}=9^2 \qquad \Rightarrow 9$

7. $y=6^{100}=2^{100}.\ 3^{100}$

$\log_{10}y=\log_{10}(2^{100}-3^{100})$

$\log_{10}y=100\log_{10}2+100\log_{10}3$

$=30.10+47.71=77.81$

$\Rightarrow$ Characteristic of $\log_{10}y=77$

$\therefore$ Number of digits $=77+1=78$

8. $y=6^{-200}$

$y=2^{-200}.3^{-200}$

$\log_{10}y=200\log_{10}(2^{-1})+200\log(3^{-1})$

$=200(-0.30.10-0.4771)=200(-0.7781)=100(-1, 5562)$

$=-155.6\ 2$

Number of zeroes immediately after decimal point

$\Rightarrow$ 155

9. $\log\tan 1°+\log\tan 2°+\log\tan 3°+\ldots\ldots.+\log\tan 89°$

$=\log(\tan 1^0.\ \tan 2^0.\ \tan 3^0\ \ldots\ldots:\tan 89^0)$

Since $\tan 89^0=\tan(90-1)=\cot(1)$

Simply expression reduces to $=\log(1)=0$

10. $\frac{1}{\log_2 N}+\frac{1}{\log_3 N}+\ldots\ldots+\frac{1}{\log_{2007}N}$

$=\frac{\log 2}{\log N}+\frac{\log 3}{\log N}\ldots\ldots\ldots.+\frac{\log 2007}{\log N}$

$=\frac{\log 2+\log 3+\ldots\ldots.+\log 2007}{\log N}$

By the question $N=1.2.3\ldots\ldots\ldots2002$

$\Rightarrow$ $\frac{\log 2+\log 3+\ldots\ldots.+\log 2007}{\log 2+\log 3\ldots\ldots.+\log 2007}=1$

11. $|2-\log_{\frac{1}{2}}x|-3=\log_2(x-1)$

Due to domain restriction $x-1>0$

$\Rightarrow$ $x>1 \qquad \Rightarrow \log_{\frac{1}{2}}x<0$

$\Rightarrow$ $-\log_{\frac{1}{2}}x>0$

$\Rightarrow$ $2-\log_{\frac{1}{2}}x-3=\log_2(x-1)=-1+\frac{\log x}{\log 2}=\log_2(x-1)$

$=-1=\log_2(x-1)-\log_2(x)=-1=\log_2\left(\frac{x-1}{x}\right)$

$\Rightarrow$ $\frac{1}{2}=1-\frac{1}{x} \qquad \Rightarrow \frac{1}{x}=\frac{1}{2}$

$\Rightarrow$ $x=2$

12. Let $N=2^{\log_3 5}-5^{\log_3 2}$

$\Rightarrow$ $2^{\log_3 5}=2^{\log_2 5.\log_3 2}=(2^{\log_2 5})^{\log_3 2}=5^{\log_3 2}$

$\Rightarrow$ $N=5^{\log_3 2}-5^{\log_3 2}=0$

Sequence and Progression

CHAPTER 3

INTRODUCTION

A series or a group of numbers which follow certain characteristics which are exclusive only to numbers of that groups, then that group of numbers is said to be in a sequence. Informally, a sequence is an ordered list of objects but in this topic the objects usually be numbers.

Now, if the characteristic is such that the consecutive terms bear fixed relation, then the sequence is known as a progression and further if the two consecutive numbers of the group have constant difference between them, then such numbers are said to be in "Arithmetic progression". If the numbers are such that the square of one number is equal to product of the number before it and after it, then such numbers are said to be in "Geometric progression". If the characteristic is that the reciprocals of the given numbers are in Arithmetic Progression, then such numbers are said to be in "Harmonic Progression".

SEQUENCE DEFINITION

"Sequence is a set of numbers each of which is derived according to a definite law and whose general term is expressible in terms of n", where is the number of terms. Sometimes this law/pattern is easy to observe and sometimes quiet difficult to make out.

A sequence $S_n: \mathbb{N} \to \mathbb{C}$ is a function defined from set of natural number to the set of real numbers (or complex numbers). If the range is real numbers then it is known as real sequence, otherwise non-real complex sequence. It is denoted by $<a_n>$; where a_n is the general term of the sequence.

e.g., $<n> = <1, 2, 3, 4....>$; $<n^2> = <1^2, 2^2, 3^2....>$

ILLUSTRATION 1: Write 5th term of following sequences whose n^{th} term is given by

(a) $x^2\cos(n\pi/2)$ (b) $u_{n+1} = 2u_n - u_{n-1}$ if $u_0 = 2$ and $u_1 = 3$

SOLUTION: (a) Let $t_n = x^2\cos(n\pi/2) \Rightarrow T_5 = 25.\ \cos 5\pi/2 = 0$

(b) Substituting $n = 1$ in the relation $\Rightarrow u_2 = 2u_1 - u_0 = 2 \times 3 - 2 = 4$

Substituting $n = 2$ in the relation $\Rightarrow u_3 = 2u_2 - u_1 = 2 \times 4 - 3 = 5$

Substituting $n = 3$ in the relation $\Rightarrow u_4 = 2u_3 - u_2 = 2 \times 5 - 4 = 6$

Substituting $n = 4$ in the relation $\Rightarrow u_5 = 2u_4 - u_3 = 2 \times 6 - 5 = 7$

Self effort

Enquiry 1: Is it possible that every sequence be expressed by an algebraic formula?

Ans. No. Consider sequence of primes.

Enquiry 2: Does every sequence follow certain fixed pattern?

Ans. No, only progressions follow.

Classification of sequences

It is very obvious that there is no limit to the kind of such pattern of numbers, therefore infinite types of sequences can be generated but broadly, they can be categorized in following types:

Increasing/Decreasing sequence $<a_n>$ is called increasing sequence iff $a_{n+1} > a_n$, $n \in \mathbb{N}$

i.e., $a_1 < a_2 < a_3 < a_4$......... and $<a_n>$ is called decreasing sequence iff $a_{n+1} < a_n$, $n \in N$

e.g., $<2n-1>$: 1, 3, 5, 7, 9, 11.................is increasing sequence; $< 10 - 2n >$:8, 6, 4, ... is decreasing sequence.

Converging sequence A sequence is called converging sequence iff its term at $n \to \infty$ is a finite real number. i.e., T_n = finite when $n \to \infty$.

e.g., $\frac{1}{2}, \frac{1}{4}, \frac{1}{8}, \frac{1}{16}$,..... is converging as $T_\infty \to \frac{1}{2^\infty} \to 0$

Diverging sequence A sequence is called diverging sequence iff $T_n \to \infty$, when $n \to \infty$.

e.g., $<2^n>$: $2^1, 2^2, 2^3, 2^4$, ... $T_\infty \to 2^\infty \to \infty$

Oscillating sequence A sequence is called oscillating sequence iff its terms oscillates between two numbers e.g., $<(-1)^n>$: – 1, 1, – 1, 1, – 1, 1 . . . .

Periodic sequence If the terms of a sequence repeat after a fixed constant interval, then the sequence is called periodic sequence.

e.g., $\left[\sin\frac{n\pi}{2}\right]$: $\underbrace{1,\ 0,\ -1,\ 0}_{\text{Periodically repeating terms}}$, 1, 0, –1, 0,.....

Monotonic sequence

A sequence $<a_n>$ is said to be monotonic if it is either increasing or decreasing.

ILLUSTRATION 2: Show that the sequence $<a_n>$: $a_n = \dfrac{n}{2n+1}$ is monotonically increasing.

SOLUTION: $a_n = \dfrac{n}{2n+1}$.

Now $a_{n+1} - a_n = \dfrac{n+1}{2n+3} - \dfrac{n}{2n+1} = \dfrac{1}{(2n+3)(2n+1)} > 0\ \forall n \in \mathbb{N}$

$\therefore$ $<a_n>$ is monotonically increasing.

ILLUSTRATION 3: Prove that $<a_n>$: $a_n = \cos \pi n$ is non-monotonic; $\forall n \in \mathbb{N}$

SOLUTION: $a_{n+1} - a_n = \cos \pi(n+1) - \cos \pi(n)$

$= \cos(\pi + \pi n) - \cos \pi n$

$= -\cos \pi n - \cos \pi n = -2\cos \pi n$

$= -2(-1)^n > 0$ for 'n' odd and < 0 for 'n' even.

$\therefore$ $a_{n+1} - a_n$ does not hold a single sign throughout:

$\therefore$ $<a_n>$ is non-monotonic.

ILLUSTRATION 4: Test whether the sequence $<a_n>$ where

$a_n = \dfrac{1}{n+1} + \dfrac{1}{n+2} + \dfrac{1}{n+3} + ... + \dfrac{1}{3n}$ is monotonic or not.

SOLUTION: $a_{n+1} - a_n = \left(\dfrac{1}{n+2} + \dfrac{1}{n+3} + \dfrac{1}{n+4} + ... + \dfrac{1}{3n+3}\right) - \left(\dfrac{1}{n+1} + \dfrac{1}{n+2} + \dfrac{1}{n+3} + ... + \dfrac{1}{3n}\right)$

$\dfrac{1}{3n+1} + \dfrac{1}{3n+2} + \dfrac{1}{3n+3} - \dfrac{1}{n+1} > \dfrac{1}{3n+3} + \dfrac{1}{3n+3} + \dfrac{1}{3n+3} - \dfrac{1}{n+1}$

$= \dfrac{1}{n+1} - \dfrac{1}{n+1} = 0$

$\therefore a_{n+1} - a_n > 0\ \forall n \in \mathbb{N}$

$\Rightarrow$ $<a_n>$ is a monotonically increasing sequence.

TEXTUAL EXERCISE–1 (SUBJECTIVE)

1. (a) Write down the first three terms of the following sequences whose nth term is given as:

   (i) $\frac{1}{n^3}\sin\frac{n\pi}{6}$

   (ii) $(-1)^n (2n + 1) \cos\frac{n\pi}{3}$

   (iii) $\frac{n}{(2n-1)^2}$

   (iv) $a_n = (-1)^{n-1} 5^{n+1}$.

   (v) $a_n = \frac{n^2}{2^n}$

   (b) The Fibonacci sequence is defined by $a_1 = a_2 = 1$ and $a_n = a_{n-1} + a_{n-2}$, $n > 2$, then

   Find $\frac{a_{n+1}}{a_n}$, for $n = 2, 3, 4$.

2. Let (a_n) be a finite sequence with 9 terms defined as:

$$a_n = \begin{cases} 1, \text{if the digits '}n\text{' occurs infinitely many times} \\ \text{in decimal expansion of } 7/3 \\ 2, \text{ if digits '}n\text{' occurs odd number of times} \\ \text{in decimal expansion of } 7/3 \\ 3, \text{ if digits '}n\text{' occurs even number of times} \\ \text{in decimal expansion of } 7/3, \end{cases}$$

   then evaluate $\sum_{n=1}^{6} a_n$

3. Find the first five terms of the sequence and write the corresponding series given by

   (a) $a_1 = 1,\ a_n = a_{n-1} + \cos\left(\frac{n\pi}{2}\right), n \geq 2$

   (b) $t_1 = 1, t_2 = 2, t_n = \frac{t_{n-1}}{t_{n-2}}, n \geq 3$

Answer Keys

1. (i) $\frac{1}{2}, \frac{\sqrt{3}}{16}, \frac{1}{27}$ (ii) $\frac{-3}{2}, \frac{-5}{2}, 7$ (iii) $1, \frac{2}{9}, \frac{3}{25}$

   (iv) 25, – 125, 625 (v) 1/2, 1, 9/8 (b) 2, 3/2, 5/3

2. 15 3. (a) 1 + 0 + 0 + 1 + 1 + ... (b) 1, 2, 2, 1, 1/2, ...

TEXTUAL EXERCISE–1 (OBJECTIVE)

1. Find which of the following sequence $<a_n>$ are increasing:

   (a) $a_n = 3n + 2$ (b) $a_n = 3 - 2n$

   (c) $a_n = 2 - 3n$ (d) None of these

2. Find the converging sequence $<a_n>$ out of the following:

   (a) $a_n = \frac{n^2-1}{2n}$ (b) $a_n = \frac{n^2-1}{n^2+2}$

   (c) $a_n = \frac{2n}{n^2+1}$ (d) None of these

3. Which of the following sequences $<a_n>$ is diverging?

   (a) $a_n = \frac{n^2-1}{n^2}$ (b) $a_n = \frac{5n^2+2n+7}{n+5}$

   (c) $a_n = \frac{n^3+n^2-5}{2n^3-5}$ (d) None of these

4. Which of the following sequences $<a_n>$ are oscillating?

   (a) $a_n = (-1)^n.n$ (b) $a_n = (-1)^{2n}.n^2$

   (c) $a_n = 2n \cos\left(\frac{n\pi}{2}\right)$ (d) None of these

5. Which of the following sequences $<a_n>$ is periodic?

   (a) $a_n = (-1)^n \sin\left(\frac{n\pi}{2}\right)$ (b) $a_n = (-1)^n n \sin\left(\frac{n\pi}{2}\right)$

   (c) $a_n = \left[\cos\frac{n\pi}{2}\right]$ (d) None of these

6. Which of the following sequences $<a_n>$ are monotonic?

   (a) $a_n = \frac{1}{n^2}$ (b) $a_n = (-1)^n$

   (c) $a_n = n^{th}$ prime (d) $a_n = \frac{(-1)^n}{n}$

7. With which term onwards the sequence $<T_n>$; $T_n = n^2 - 5n + 6$ is monotonic?
(a) 3 (b) 5
(c) 7 (d) None of these

8. The third term of the sequence $\left\langle (-1)^n \frac{2n}{n^2-6} \sin\frac{n\pi}{2} \right\rangle$ is
(a) 2 (b) –3
(c) -3/2 (d) None of these

Answer Keys

1. (a) 2. (b), (c) 3. (b) 4. (*a*, *c*) 5. (*a*, *c*) 6. (*a*, *c*) 7. (a) 8. (a)

■ PROGRESSION AND SERIES

Progression is a sequence in which each succeeding term bears a fixed relation with its preceding one.

A set of numbers connected by a sign of addition or subtraction and each of which is derived from the preceding one according to some definite law is called a *series*.

NOTE

*A **series** therefore is nothing but summation of terms of a progression.*

Types of progression

Progressions are of the following types:

1. Arithmetic Progression
2. Geometric Progression
3. Harmonic Progression
4. Arithmetico – Geometric Progression

■ ARITHMETIC PROGRESSION

Arithmetic Progression is the progression in which the difference of successive terms remains constant and this constant is known as *common difference.* e.g., sequence of odd natural numbers 1, 3, 5, 7, ...

General terms of AP

If a is the first term and d is the common difference of the AP then AP can be written as $a, a + d, a + 2d, \ldots\ldots, a + (n-1)d, \ldots\ldots$

General terms: nth term from beginning: $t_n = a + (n - 1 d$
where $d = t_n - t_{n-1}$ (common difference)
n^{th} term from last $t'_n = \ell + (n-1)(-d)$

ILLUSTRATION 5: Find the indicated terms of the given sequences:
(a) 19, 30, 41, 52….; t_{20} (b) $27, 27\frac{1}{3}, 27\frac{2}{3}, 28, 28\frac{1}{3}, \ldots; t_{15}$
(c) $x^2 - x + 2, x^2 - 3x + 5, x^2 - 5x + 8, \ldots; t_{17}$

SOLUTION: (a) 19, 30, 41, 52,……;
Here first term a = 19 and common difference $d = 11$
$\therefore\ t_{20} = [a + (n-1)d] = 19 + (20 - 1)(11) = 19(1 + 11) = 228$

(b) $27, 27\frac{1}{3}, 27\frac{2}{3}, 28, \ldots$
Here first term $a = 27$ and common difference $d = 1/3$
$\therefore\ t_{15} = [a + (n-1)d] = 27 + (14)(1/3) = 27 + \frac{14}{3} = \frac{95}{3}$

(c) $x^2 - x + 2, x^2 - 3x + 5, x^2 - 5x + 8, \ldots$

Here first term $a = x^2 - x + 2$ and common difference $d = -2x + 3$

$\therefore\ t_{17} = a + 16d = (x^2 - x + 2) + 16(-2x + 3) = x^2 - x + 2 - 32x + 48 = x^2 - 33x + 50$

ILLUSTRATION 6: If $(x + 1)$, $3x$ and $(4x + 2)$ are first three terms of an AP, then find its 5th term.

SOLUTION: $(x + 1), 3x, (4x + 2)$ are in AP

$\Rightarrow 3x - (x + 1) = (4x + 2) - 3x \qquad \Rightarrow x = 3$

$\Rightarrow$ The terms are 4, 9, 14

$\therefore\ a = 4, d = 9 - 4 = 5 \qquad \Rightarrow t_5 = 4 + 4(5) = 24$

ILLUSTRATION 7: Find the first negative term of the sequence 2000, 1995, 1990, 1985, ...

SOLUTION: Let the nth term be the first negative term

$\therefore\ n^{th}$ term $(t_n) < 0 \qquad \therefore\ a + (n-1)d < 0\ (\because t_n = a + (n-1)d)$

or, $2000 + (n-1)(-5) < 0$ or $-5n + 2005 < 0$ or, $5n > 2005$

$\therefore\ n > \frac{2005}{5} \Rightarrow n > 401$

$\therefore\ n = 402$ (least values on n for which $n > 401$ and $t_n < 0$)

Hence 1st negative term, i.e., 402nd *term* $= 2000 + (402 - 1)(-5) = 2000 - 2005 = -5$

ILLUSTRATION 8: If u times the vth term of an AP is equal to v times its uth term, show that $t_{(u-v)} : t_{(u+v)} = u - v : u + v$.

SOLUTION: Let us proceed backwards.

We require $t_{u-v} : t_{u+v}$ in terms of u and v only

If we assume the first term as *'a'* and common difference as *'d'*, then we must obtain a relation between them to get the required ratio in that form.

Now, $\frac{t_{u-v}}{t_{u+v}} = \frac{a+(u-v-1)d}{a+(u+v-1)d}$

But from the given condition, $ut_v = vt_u$

$\Rightarrow u[a + (v-1)d] = v[a + (u-1)d] \qquad \Rightarrow (u - v)a = (uv - v - uv + u)d$

$\Rightarrow a = d\quad (\because u \neq v)$

Hence, $\frac{t_{u-v}}{t_{u+v}} = \frac{a+(u-v-1)a}{a+(u+v-1)a} = \frac{u-v}{u+v}$

Sum of first *n* terms of AP

Sum of first n terms: $S_n = \frac{n}{2}[2a + (n-1)d] = \frac{n}{2}[a + l]$

Proof: Let *'a'* be the first term and *'d'* be the common difference of given AP, then $S_n = a + (a + d) + (a + 2d) + (a + 3d) + \ldots\ [a + (n-2)d] + [a + (n-1)d]$

Let $a + (n - 1)d = l$ (last term), then the given sequence taken in reverse order will also be an AP with first term l and common difference $(-d)$

$\therefore\ S_n = l + (l - d) + (l - 2d) + (l - 3d) + \ldots + [l - (n-2)d] + [l - (n-1)d]$

Adding above two equations, we get

$2S_n = (a+l) + (a+l) + (a+l) + \ldots + (a+l) \ldots = n(a+l)$ [n-terms]

$\Rightarrow\ S_n = \frac{n}{2}(a+l) = \frac{n}{2}(2a+(n-1)d)$

ILLUSTRATION 9: Find the sum of series given below upto indicated terms:

(a) $3 + 10 + 17 + 24 + 31 + \ldots\ldots; S_{15}$

(b) $4 - 8 + 11 - 16 + 18 - 24 + 25 - 32 + \ldots; S_{20}, S_{13}$

(c) $\log_{a^{1/2}} 5 + \log_{a^{1/5}} 5 + \log_{a^{1/8}} 5 + \log_{a^{1/11}} 5 + \ldots;\ S_{30};\ S_{50}$

(d) $\log_a 5 + \log_a 25 + \log_a 125 + \ldots;\ S_{10};\ S_{20}$

SOLUTION: (*a*) $3 + 10 + 17 + \ldots\ldots$; first terms $a = 3$; common difference; $d = 7$

$\therefore\ S_{15} = \frac{15}{2}[2(3) + (15-1)(7)] = \frac{15}{2}[104] = 780$

(b) $4 - 8 + 11 - 16 + 18 - 24 + \ldots\ldots; = (4 + 11 + 18 + \ldots) - (8 + 16 + 24 + \ldots)$

$\therefore\ S_{20} = (4 + 11 + 18 + .. + \text{upto 10 terms}) - (8 + 16 + 24 + \ldots \text{ upto 10 terms})$

$= \frac{10}{2}[2(4) + (10-1)(7)] - \frac{10}{2}[2(8) + (10-1)(8)] = 5[71] - 5[88] = -85$

$S_{13} = (4 + 11 + 18 + \ldots + \text{upto 7 terms}) - (8 + 11 + 18 + \ldots\ldots \text{ upto 6 terms})$

$= \frac{7}{2}[2(4) + (7-1)(7)] - \frac{6}{2}[2(8) + (6-1)(3)] = \frac{7}{2}[8 + 42] - 3(16 + 15)] = 82$

(c) $\log_{a^{1/2}} 5 + \log_{a^{1/5}} 5 + \log_{a^{1/8}} + \ldots$

$\therefore\ S_{30} = 2\log_a 5 + 5\log_a 5 + 8\log_a 5 + \ldots \quad \left[\because \log_{a^N} x = \frac{1}{N}\log_a x\right]$

$\Rightarrow\ S_{30} = (\log_a 5)[2 + 5 + 8 + \ldots \text{upto 30 terms}] = (\log_a 5)\left(\frac{30}{2}\right)[2(2) + (29)(3)] = 1365 \log_a 5$

Similarly, $S_{50} = (\log_a 5)\left(\frac{50}{2}\right)[4 + 49(3)] = 3775 \log_a 5$

(d) $\log_a 5 + \log_a 25 + \log_a 125 + \ldots = \log_a 5 + 2\log_a 5 + 3\log_a 5 + \ldots.$

$\Rightarrow\ S_{10} = \frac{10}{2}[2(\log_a 5) + (9)\log_a 5)] = 55 \log_a 5;$

Similarly, $s_{20} = 10[21 \log_a 5] + 19[\log_a 5] = 210 \log_a 5$

ILLUSTRATION 10: The interior angles of a convex polygon form an arithmetic progression with a common difference of 4°. Determine the number of sides of the polygon if its largest interior angle is 172°.

SOLUTION: Let n be the number of sides of polygon. Thus n[th] angle is given by $t_n = a + [n - 1]\, d = 172$

or $a + (n - 1)4 = 172$

or $a = 172 - 4(n - 1)$ (1)

and $\frac{n}{2}[a + 172] = (n - 2)\,180$ (2)

Substring the value of a from equation (1) in (2), we get $\frac{n}{2}[172 - 4(n-1) + 172] = (n - 2)\,180$

$\Rightarrow\ \frac{n}{2}[2 \times 172 - 4(n - 1)] = (n - 2)\,180$

or $86n - n^2 + n = 90n - 180$ or $n^2 + 3n - 180 = 0$

or $(n + 15)(n - 12) = 0$ or $n = 12$

ILLUSTRATION 11: Show that $\ell n(4 \times 12 \times 36 \times 108 \times \ldots\ldots\ldots \text{up to } n \text{ terms}) = 2n\,\ell n\,2 + \frac{n(n-1)}{2}\ell n3$

SOLUTION: $\ell n(4 \times 12 \times 36 \times 108 \ldots\ldots\ldots \text{upto } n \text{ terms}) = \ell n\,4 + \ell n12 + \ell n\,36 + \ell n\,108 + \ldots.. + \ell n(t_n)$

The above series is an AP with common difference (d) = ln12 – ln4

$$= \frac{n}{2}[2a + (n-1)d] = \frac{n}{2}[2.2\,\ell n2 + (N-1)\,\ell n3]$$

$$= 2n\ell n2 + \frac{n(n-1)}{2}\,\ell n3$$

ILLUSTRATION 12: Find the co-efficient of x^{99} in $(x-1)(x-2)(x-3)\ldots(x-100)$.

SOLUTION: Given polynomial can be written as $x^{100} + x^{99}(-1-2-3\ldots-100) + \ldots$

$\therefore$ Co-efficient of $x^{99} = -(1+2+3+\ldots+100) = -\frac{100}{2}(1+100) = -5050$

ILLUSTRATION 13: Let the sum of n terms of a series be $n(2n-1)$. Find its nth term.

SOLUTION: Let S_n and S_{n-1} denote the sum of first m and $(n-1)$ terms respectively,

$S_n = t_1 + t_2 + t_3 + \ldots\ldots + t_{n-1} + t_n$

$S_{n-1} = t_1 + t_2 + t_3 + \ldots\ldots + t_{n-1}$

subtracting $S_n - S_{n-1} = t_n$

$\Rightarrow t_m = n(2n-1) - (n-1)[2(n-1)-1)] = (2n^2 - n) - (2n^2 - 5n + 3) = 4n - 3$

ILLUSTRATION 14: Find the sum of the series $1 - 3 + 5 - 7 + 9 - 11 + \ldots\ldots +$ upto n terms.

SOLUTION: This problem can be solved by different approaches, of course some are tricky, some are little bit lengthy. Now you have to judge which one is suitable for you.

Method 1:

Case 1: **when n is even**

i.e., $n = 2m$, Now the given series can be broken into two series like

$(1 + 5 + 9 + 13 + \ldots +$ upto m terms$) - (3 + 7 + 11 + \ldots +$ upto m terms$)$

$$= \frac{m}{2}[2+(m-1)4] - \frac{m}{2}[2\times 3+(m-1)4] = \frac{m}{2}(-4) = -2m = -n$$

Case 2: **when n is odd**

i.e., $n = 2m + 1$

$[1 + 5 + 9 + \ldots\ldots +$ upto $(m+1)$ terms$] - [3 + 7 + 11 + \ldots +$ upto m terms$]$

$$= \frac{m+1}{2}[2+4m] - \frac{m}{2}[6+(m-1)4] = \frac{m}{2}[2+4m-6-4m+4] + 1 + 2m = 2m + 1 = n$$

Method 2:

$1 - 3 + 5 - 7 + 9 \ldots\ldots +$ upto n terms

Case 1: **When n is even i.e., $n = 2m$**

Taking two terms of given series at a time, then the above series becomes

$(-2) + (-2) + (-2) + \ldots\ldots$ upto m times

so, sum of series $= -2m = -n$

Case 2: **When n is odd i.e., $n = 2m + 1$**

$1 + (2 + 2 + 2 + \ldots\ldots$ upto m times$)$

$= 1 + 2m = n$

Method 3:

$1 - 3 + 5 - 7 + 9 - 11 + . . .$ upto n terms

This series can also be written as

$1 + 3.(-1) + 5.(-1)^2 + 7.(-1)^3 + 9.(-1)^4 + ...+$ upto n terms

$1 + [3.(-1) + 5.(-1)^2 + 7.(-1)^3 + 9.(-1)^4 + . . +$ upto $(n - 1)$ terms] and seeing clearly, it is Arithmetico-geometric series and common difference is 2 and the first term of geometric series is -1 and common ratio is (-1).

$S_n = 1 + [3.(-1) + 5(-1)^2 + 7.(-1)^3 + ... + (2n - 1).(-1)^{n-1}]$

Let $S_{n-1} = 3.(-1) + 5(-1)^2 + ... + (2n - 1).(-1)^{n-1}$

$-S_{n-1} = 3.(-1)^2 + ... + (2n - 3)(-1)^{n-1} + (2n - 1).(-1)^n$

Subtracting, we get

$2S_{n-1} = -3 - 2[(-1) + (-1)^2 + ... + (-1)^{n-2}] - (2n - 1)(-1)^n$

Case 1: **When n is even**

$2S_{n-1} = -3 - 2n + 1 = -2(n + 1)$

$S_{n-1} = -(n + 1)$

$S_n = 1 + S_{n-1} = -n$

Case 2: **When n is odd**

$2S_{n-1} = -3 + 2 + (2n - 1) = 2n - 2$

$S_{n-1} = n - 1$

$S_n = 1 + S_{n-1} = n$

REMARKS

- For any series *(progression) nth* term can be written as, $t_n = S_n - S_{n-1}$
- For arithmetic progression $d = T_n - T_{n-1}$

ILLUSTRATION 15: The sequence N of natural numbers is divided into classes as follows:

1
2 3 4
5 6 7 8 9
10 11 12 13 14 15 16
---- ---- ---- ---- ---- ---- ---- ---- ----
---- ---- ---- ---- ---- ---- ---- ---- ---- ---- ----

Find the sum of the numbers of jth row.

SOLUTION: Numbers of elements in j^{th} row = $(2j - 1)$, so number of elements in first j rows

$$\sum(2j-1) = 2\sum j - \sum 1 = 2\times\frac{j(j+1)}{2} - j = j(j + 1 - 1) = j^2$$

so number of elements in first $(j - 1)$ class = $(j - 1)^2$

so first element of jth class = $(j - 1)^2 + 1$, so sum of $(2j - 1)$ terms of AP with first term, $(9j - 1)^2 + 1$ and common difference 1.

$$1 = \frac{(2j-1)}{2}[2\{(j-1)^2+1\}+(2j-1-1).1] = (2j - 1)(j^2 - 2j + 2 + j - 1) = (2j - 1)(j^2 - j + 1).$$

TEXTUAL EXERCISE–2 (SUBJECTIVE)

1. Find the sum of 1st n odd natural numbers.
2. Get the sum of all two-digit numbers.
3. Find the sum of 1st n numbers that leaves remainder 3 when divided by 4.
4. Find 5th term of sequence whose sum of 1st n terms is given as $2n^3 - 7n + 5$.
5. Is 307 a term of the AP 3, 8, 13, 18, ...?
6. Which term of the AP $8 - 6i, 7 - 4i, 6 - 2i, \ldots$ is
   (a) Purely imaginary? (b) Purely real?
7. Find the 20th term from the end of AP 2, 7, 12, 17,......, 222.
8. If T_r denotes r[th] terms of an AP *s. t.*
   (i) If n^{th} term of a series is $3n - 5$. Then show that it is an AP and find its common difference.
   (ii) $t_m = n, t_n = m$. Then prove that $t_r = m + n - r$ and find the $(m + n)^{th}$ terms.
   (iii) $t_m = 1/n, t_n = 1/m$, then find the $(mn)^{th}$ term of the AP
9. For the AP $a_1, a_2, a_3, \ldots\ldots$, if $\frac{a_4}{a_7} = \frac{2}{3}$, find $\frac{a_6}{a_8}$.
10. Given that $(p + 1)^{th}$ terms of an AP is twice the $(q + 1)^{th}$ term. Prove that $(3p + 1)^{th}$ term is twice the $(p + q + 1)^{th}$ term.
11. For what values of the parameter a . $5^{1+x} + 5^{1-x}, a/2, 25^x + 25^{-x}$ are three consecutive terms of an AP?
12. Find the sum of the following series:
    (a) $\sqrt{2} + \sqrt{8} + \sqrt{18} + \ldots\ldots +$ upto n terms
    (b) $\frac{n-1}{n} + \frac{n-2}{n} + \frac{n-3}{n} + \ldots\ldots +$ upto n terms
    (c) $\frac{1}{1+\sqrt{a}} + \frac{1}{1-a} + \frac{1}{1-\sqrt{a}} + \ldots\ldots +$ upto n terms
    (d) $1/2 + 1/3 + 1/6 + \ldots +$ upto 9 terms
    (e) $1 - 2 + 3 - 4 + 5 - 6 + 7 - \ldots\ldots - (2n)$
    (f) $1^2 - 2^2 + 3^2 - 4^2 + 5^2 - 6^2 + \ldots\ldots - (2n)^2$
13. How many terms of the sequence 18, 15, 12, ... are needed to give the sum 45? Also explain the double answer.
14. Find the sum of all natural numbers between 100 and 300 (not including 100 and 300) which are neither divisible by 4 nor by 6.
15. Find the rth term of an AP, the sum of whose first n terms is $2n + 3n^2$.
16. (a) "If sum of n-terms of a series is given by $s_n = an^2 + bn + c$, where a, b, c are constants, then the series is an AP with common difference $2a$". Is the above statement true, prove it. If not modify the statements?
    (b) Sum of first n terms of a series is $4n^2 + 3$, then find its 1st and 5th term. Is this series an AP?
17. Certain numbers appear in both AP's 17, 21, 25 .. and 16, 21, 26 ..... Find the sum of first hundred numbers appearing in both progressions.

Answer Keys

1. n^2 **2.** 4905 **3.** $2n^2 + n$ **4.** 115 **5.** no **6.** (a) 9th (b) 4th **7.** 127

8. (i) 3 (*ii*) zero (*iii*) 1 **9.** 4/5 **11.** $[12, \infty)$

12. (a) $S_n = \frac{n(n+1)}{\sqrt{2}}, T_n = n\sqrt{2}$ (b) $S_n = \frac{n-1}{2}, T_n = 0$ (c) $\frac{n}{2(1-a)}\left(2+(n-3)\sqrt{a}\right)$

(d) $-3/2$ (e) $(-n)$ (f) $-n(2n + 1)$

13. n = 3, 10; upto 7th term summation increases, then start decreasing because 8th terms onward are negative and therefore summation repeated its previous values.

14. 26634 **15.** $6r - 1$ **16.** (b) $t_1 = 4, t_5 =$ **17.** 101100.

TEXTUAL EXERCISE–2 (OBJECTIVE)

1. If the numbers a, b, c, d, e are in AP, then the value of $a - 4b + 6c - 4d + e$ is
   (a) 1 (b) 2
   (c) 0 (d) $16c$
2. In an AP, the pth term is q and the $(p + q)^{th}$ term is 0, then the qth term is
   (a) $-p$ (b) p
   (c) $p + q$ (d) $p - q$

3. The number of terms common to two APs 3, 7, 11,...., 407 and 2, 9, 16, ..., 709 is
(a) 21 (b) 28
(c) 14 (d) None of these

4. The largest term common to the sequences 1, 11, 21, 31, ... upto 100 terms and 31, 36, 41, 46, ... upto 100 terms is
(a) 381 (b) 471
(c) 281 (d) None of these

5. Let x_1, x_2...be positive integers in AP, such that $x_1 + x_2 + x_3 = 12$ and $x_4 + x_6 = 14$. Then x_5 is
(a) 7 (b) 1
(c) 4 (d) None of these

6. In the sequence 1, 2, 2, 3, 3, 3, 4, 4, 4, 4.....; where n consecutive terms have the value n, the 150th term is
(a) 17 (b) 16
(c) 18 (d) None of these

7. Six numbers are in AP such that their sum is 3. The first number is four times the third number. The fifth number is equal to
(a) –15 (b) –3
(c) 9 (d) –4

8. The sum of the first n terms ($n > 1$) of an AP is 153 and the common difference is 2. If the first term is an integer, the number of possible values of n is
(a) 3 (b) 4
(c) 5 (d) 6

9. If s_r denotes the sum of the first r terms of an AP, then $\frac{s_{3r} - s_{r-1}}{s_{2r} - s_{2r-1}}$ is equal to
(a) $2r - 1$ (b) $2r + 1$
(c) $4r + 1$ (d) $2r + 3$

10. Let s_n denote the sum of the first n terms of an AP If $s_{2n} = 3s_n$, then $s_{3n}:s_n$ is equal to
(a) 4 (b) 6
(c) 8 (d) 10

11. The mth term of an arithmetic progression is x and the nth term is y. Then the sum of the first $(m + n)$ terms is
(a) $\frac{m+n}{2}\left[(x+y)+\frac{x-y}{m-n}\right]$
(b) $\frac{m+n}{2}\left[(x-y)+\frac{x+y}{m-n}\right]$
(c) $\frac{1}{2}\left[\frac{x+y}{m+n}+\frac{x+y}{m-n}\right]$
(d) $\frac{1}{2}\left[\frac{x+y}{m+n}-\frac{x-y}{m-n}\right]$

12. If s_r denotes the sum of r terms of an AP and $\frac{S_a}{a^2} = \frac{S_b}{b^2} = c$, then s_c is
(a) c^3 (b) c/ab
(c) abc (d) $a + b + c$

13. The sum of the series: $1^2 - 2^2 + 3^2 - 4^2 + 5^2 - 6^2 + ... - 100^2$ is
(a) –10100 (b) –5050
(c) –2525 (d) None of these

Answer Keys

1. (c) **2.** (b) **3.** (c) **4.** (d) **5.** (a) **6.** (a) **7.** (d) **8.** (c) **9.** (b) **10.** (b)
11. (a) **12.** (a) **13.** (b)

Properties of arithmetic progression

(a) n^{th} term can also be written as, $t_n = s_n - s_{n-1}$

(b) Summation of equidistant terms from beginning and end of an AP is always constant and is equal to sum of first and last term

$$\Rightarrow s_n = \frac{n}{2}(t_1 + t_n) = \frac{n}{2}(t_2 + t_{n-1}) = ...$$

Proof: $\frac{n}{2}(t_1 + t_n) = \frac{n}{2}[a + a + (n-1)d] = \frac{n}{2}[2a + (n-1)d]$

Similarly,

$$\frac{n}{2}(t_2 + t_{n-1}) = \frac{n}{2}[a + d + a + (n-2)d] = \frac{n}{2}[2a + (n-1)d]$$

and so on. Hence the result.

(c) If n^{th} term $t_n = an + b$, then the series so formed is an AP (with common difference a)

Proof: $t_n = an + b$

$\Rightarrow t_{n+1} = a(n + 1) + b$

$\Rightarrow t_{n+1} - t_n = a$ constant independent of n.

$\Rightarrow$ given sequence is an AP.

(d) If sum of first n terms of a series $s_n = an^2 + bn + c$, then series so formed is an AP (with common difference $2a$) provided ($c = 0$).

Proof: $t_1 = S_1 = a + b + c$

$t_2 = S_2 - S_1 = (4a + 2b + c) - (a + b + c) = 3a + b$

$t_3 = S_3 - S_2 = (9a + 3b + c) - (4a + 2b + c) = 5a + b$

Now, $t_n = S_n - S_{n-1} = a[n^2 - (n-1)^2] + b[n - (n-1)]$
$= a(2n-1) + b;\ n \geq 2$

$\Rightarrow t_n - t_{n-1} = a[2n-1] - a[2(n-1) - 1] = 2a$ for $n \geq 3$

$\Rightarrow t_2, t_3, t_4, \ldots$ are in AP. But $t_2 - t_1 = 2a - c$

$t_1, t_2, t_3, t_4, \ldots$, will be in AP Provided $c = 0$

(e) If every term of an AP is increased or decreased by the same quantity, the resulting terms will also be in AP with no change in common difference.

Proof: Let the AP be $a, a + d, a + 2d, a + 3d, \ldots$ Let each term be changed by $\pm k$, then new sequence is $a \pm k, a + d \pm k, a + 2d \pm k, \ldots$ which is again an AP with common difference d.

(f) If every term of an AP ($C.D. = d$) is multiplied or divided by the same non-zero quantity k, then resulting terms will be in AP with new common difference equal to $d.k$ or d/k.

Proof: On multiplying each term by k or $1/k$ we get ka, k($a + d$), k($a + 2d$), k($a + 3d$), ... or a/k, ($a+d$)/k, ($a + 2d$)/k, ... which are clearly in AP with common difference kd and d/k respectively.

(g) $\langle T_n \rangle$ is an AP $\Rightarrow \langle T_{n-k+1} \rangle$ is also an AP $\forall k \in 1, 2, \ldots, n$ with common difference $= (-d)$

(h) $\langle a_n \rangle$ and $\langle b_n \rangle$ are two APs, then $\langle a_n \pm b_n \rangle$ is also an AP with common difference $= d_a \pm d_b$.

(i) If equal number of terms (say k terms of an AP) are dropped alternately, the resulting terms lie in AP with common difference $= (k + 1)\, d$. e.g. $a, a + d, a + 2d, a + 3d, a + 4d, a + 5d, a + 6d$, then for sequence $a, a, 3d, a + 6d$, number of terms dropped = 2; so common difference $= (2 + 1)\, d = 3d$

(*j*) If equal number of terms say 'k' terms of an AP are grouped together and sum of terms in each group is obtained; then the sums are in AP with common difference k^2d e.g.,

$$\underbrace{a+a+d+a+2d}_{S_1=3a+3d},\ \underbrace{a+3d+a+4d+a+5d}_{S_2=3a+12d},$$

$$\underbrace{a+6d+a+7d+a+8d}_{S_3=3a+21d}$$

$\Rightarrow S_1, S_2, S_3, \ldots$ are in AP

with common difference of sums $= 9d$ i.e., $(3)^2 d = 9d$.

(*k*) If terms $a_1, a_2, \ldots, a_n, a_{n+1}, \ldots, a_{2n+1}$ are in AP Then sum of these terms will be equal to $(2n + 1)a_{n+1}$. Here total number of terms in the series is $(2n + 1)$ and middle term is a_{n+1}.

Proof: $s_{2n+1} = \dfrac{2n+1}{2}[a_1 + a_{2n+1}]$ (terms have their usual meanings)

$$= \frac{(2n+1)}{2}[2a_1 + (2n)\, d] = (2n + 1)\, [a_1 + nd]$$

$$= (2n + 1)\, a_{n+1} = (2n + 1) \text{ (middle term)}$$

(*l*) If terms $a_1, a_2, \ldots, a_{2n-1}, a_{2n}$ are in AP The sum of these terms will be equal to $(2n)\left(\dfrac{a_n + a_{n+1}}{2}\right)$, where $\dfrac{a_n + a_{n+1}}{2}$ = AM of middle terms.

Proof: $s_{2n} = \dfrac{2n}{2}[a_1 + a_{2n}] = \dfrac{2n}{2}[2a_1 + (2n - 1)d]$ (terms have their usual meanings)

$$= \frac{2n}{2}[\{a_1 + (n-1)d\} + \{a_1 + nd\}] = \frac{2n}{2}[a_n + a_{n+1}]$$

$$= (2n)\left[\frac{a_n + a_{n+1}}{2}\right] = 2n \times (\text{AM of two middle terms})$$

(*m*) If for two different AP's ratio of sum of 1st n terms is $\dfrac{S_n}{S'_n} = \dfrac{f(n)}{\phi(n)}$, then $\dfrac{t_n}{t'_n} = \dfrac{f(2n-1)}{\phi(2n-1)}$

Proof: (i) Given $\dfrac{S_n}{S'_n} = \dfrac{f(n)}{\phi(n)}$

$$\Rightarrow \frac{\frac{n}{2}[2a+(n-1)d]}{\frac{n}{2}[2a'+(n-1)d']} = \frac{f(n)}{\phi(n)}$$

$$\Rightarrow \frac{a+(n-1)d/2}{a'+(n-1)d'/2} = \frac{f(n)}{\phi(n)}$$

Put $\dfrac{n-1}{2} = (m-1) \Rightarrow n = 2m-1$

$$\therefore \frac{a+(m-1)d}{a'+(m-1)d'} = \frac{f(2m-1)}{\phi(2m-1)} \Rightarrow \frac{T_m}{T_m'} = \frac{f(2m-1)}{\phi(2m-1)}$$

$\therefore$ **In general,** $\dfrac{T_n}{T_n'} = \dfrac{f(2n-1)}{\phi(2n-1)}$

(*n*) If for two AP's, ratio of nth term is given by

$$\frac{T_n}{T_n'} = \frac{F_1(n)}{F_2(n)} \Rightarrow \frac{S_n}{S_n'} = \frac{F_1\left(\frac{n+1}{2}\right)}{F_2\left(\frac{n+1}{2}\right)}$$

Proof: Given $\dfrac{T_n}{T_n'} = \dfrac{a+(n-1)d}{a'+(n-1)d'} = \dfrac{F_1(n)}{F_2(n)}$

$$\Rightarrow \frac{S_n}{S_n'} = \frac{\frac{n}{2}[2a+(n-1)d]}{\frac{n}{2}[2a'+(n-1)d']} = \frac{a+\left(\frac{n-1}{2}\right)d}{a'+\left(\frac{n-1}{2}\right)d'} = \frac{F_1\left(\frac{n+1}{2}\right)}{F_2\left(\frac{n+1}{2}\right)}$$

POINTS TO REMEMBER

(i) 3 numbers in AP be taken as $a - d, a, a + d$ *[c.d. = d]*

(ii) 4 numbers in AP be taken as $a - 3d, a - d, a + d, a + 3d$ *[c.d = 2d]*

(iii) 5 numbers in AP be taken as $a - 2d, a - d, a, a + d, a + 2d$ *[c.d. = d]*

NOTE

In general, if we have to take (2r + 1) terms in AP, we take them as $a - rd, a - (r - 1)d, \ldots, a - d, a, a + d, \ldots, a + rd$ *and if we have to take 2r terms in AP, we take them as* $(a - (2r - 1)d), (a - (2r - 3)d), \ldots, (a + (2r - 3)d), (a + (2r - 1)d)$.

ILLUSTRATION 16: If the roots of the equation $x^3 - 12x^2 + 39x - 28 = 0$ are in AP, then find its common difference.

SOLUTION: Let roots be α, β, γ and $\alpha = a - d, \beta = a, \gamma = a + d$

then $\alpha + \beta + \gamma = 3a = -(-12) \Rightarrow a = 4$

$\alpha\beta\gamma = a(a^2 - d^2) = -(-28) \Rightarrow d = \pm 3$

ILLUSTRATION 17: If the ratio of the sum of n terms of two AP's is $(3n + 1): (2n + 3)$, then find the ratio of their 11th term.

SOLUTION: Here $\frac{(S_n)_1}{(S_n)_2} = \frac{3n+1}{2n+3} \Rightarrow \frac{n/2[2a_1 + (n-1)d_1]}{n/2[2a_2 + (n-1)d_2]} = \frac{3n+1}{2n+3}$

$$\Rightarrow \frac{2a_1 + (n-1)d_1}{2a_2 + (n-1)d_2} = \frac{3n+1}{2n+3}$$

$$\Rightarrow \frac{a_1 + \frac{(n-1)}{2}d_1}{a_2 + \frac{(n-1)}{2}d_2} = \frac{3n+1}{2n+3} \quad \text{(i)}$$

$$\therefore \frac{T_{11}}{T_{11}'} = \frac{a_1 + 10d_1}{a_2 + 10d_2} \quad \text{(ii)}$$

$\frac{n-1}{2} = 10 \Rightarrow n = 21$; putting the values of n in (i),

$$\frac{a_1 + 10d_1}{a_2 + 10d_2} = \frac{3 \times 21 + 1}{2 \times 21 + 3} = \frac{64}{45}$$

ILLUSTRATION 18: The sum of four integers in AP is 24 and their product is 945. Find the numbers.

SOLUTION: Let the numbers are $a - 3d, a - d, a + d, a + 3d$

given $a - 3d + a - d + a + d + a + 3d = 24$

or $4a = 24 \quad \therefore \quad a = 6$

and $(a - 3d)(a - d)(a + d; (a + 3d) = 945$

$\Rightarrow (a^2 - 9d^2)(a^2 - d^2) = 945 \Rightarrow (36 - 9d^2)(36 - d^2) = 945$

$\Rightarrow d^4 - 40d^2 + 144 = 105 \Rightarrow d^4 - 40d^2 + 39 = 0$

or $(d^2-1)(d^2-39)=0$

Since numbers are integers

$\therefore\ d^2 \neq 39 \Rightarrow d^2-1=0 \Rightarrow d=\pm 1$

Hence the four integers are 3, 5, 7, 9 or 9, 7, 5, 3

ILLUSTRATION 19: If $\frac{b+c-a}{a}, \frac{c+a-b}{b}, \frac{a+b-c}{c}$ are in AP, then show that $1/a$, $1/b$, $1/c$ are also in AP.

SOLUTION: $\frac{b+c-a}{a}, \frac{c+a-b}{b}, \frac{a+b-c}{c}$, are in AP.

$\therefore\ \frac{b+c-a}{a}+2, \frac{c+a-b}{b}+2, \frac{a+b-c}{c}+2$ are in AP (adding 2 in each term)

or $\frac{a+b+c}{a}, \frac{c+a+b}{b}, \frac{a+b+c}{c}$, are in AP.

(dividing by $(a+b+c)$ each term) $1/a$, $1/b$, $1/c$ are in AP

ILLUSTRATION 20: (a) If $a^2+ab+bc+ca,\ b^2+ab+bc+ca,\ c^2+ab+bc+ca$ are in AP, then show that $\frac{1}{b+c}, \frac{1}{c+a}, \frac{1}{a+b}$ are in AP

(b) If $\frac{a}{b+c}, \frac{b}{c+a}, \frac{c}{a+b}$ are in AP, then prove that $\frac{1}{b+c}, \frac{1}{c+a}, \frac{1}{a+b}$ are in AP

SOLUTION: (a) $a^2+ab+bc+ca,\ b^2+ab+bc+ca,\ c^2+ab+bc+ca$ are in AP

$\Rightarrow (a+b)(a+c), (b+c)(b+a), (c+a)(c+b)$ are in AP

$\Rightarrow \frac{1}{b+c}, \frac{1}{c+a}, \frac{1}{a+b}$ are in AP (dividing each term by $(a+b)(b+c)(c+a)$)

Hence proved.

(b) $\frac{a}{b+c}, \frac{b}{c+a}, \frac{c}{a+b}$ are in AP.

$\Rightarrow \frac{a}{b+c}+1, \frac{b}{c+a}+1, \frac{c}{a+b}+1$ are in AP (adding 1 to each term)

$\Rightarrow \frac{a+b+c}{b+c}, \frac{a+b+c}{c+a}, \frac{a+b+c}{a+b}$ are in AP.

$\Rightarrow \frac{1}{b+c}, \frac{1}{c+a}, \frac{1}{a+b}$ are in AP] (dividing each term by $(a+b+c)$)

Hence proved.

ILLUSTRATION 21: The sequence $a_1, a_2, a_3, \ldots\ldots a_{98}$ satisfies the relation $a_{n+1}=a_n+1$ for $n = 1, 2, 3, \ldots\ldots 97$ and has the sum equal to 4949. then, evaluate $\sum_{k=1}^{49} a_{2k}$.

SOLUTION: Given recurrence equation is $a_{n+1}=a_n+1$

$\Rightarrow a_2=a_1+1;\ a_3=a_2+1$ and so on.

$\therefore$ the series is $\Rightarrow a_1+(a_1+1)+(a_1+1+1)+\ldots\ldots\ldots(a_1+97)$

$\Rightarrow 4949=\frac{98}{2}(a_1+a_1+97)$

$\Rightarrow 2a_1=101-97$ $\qquad \Rightarrow a_1=2, a_2=3, a_4=5$, and so on

$\therefore$ Required sum $=a_2+a_4+\ldots\ldots+a_{98}=3+5+7\ldots\ldots+99$

$S_n=\frac{49}{2}(3+99)=49\times 51=2499$

ILLUSTRATION 22: If x, y and z are real numbers satisfying the equation $25(9x^2 + y^2) + 9z^2 - 15(5xy + yz + 3zx) = 0$, then prove that x, y, z are in AP.

SOLUTION: $25(9x^2 + y^2) + 9z^2 - 15(5xy + yz + 3zx) = 0$

$\Rightarrow (15x)^2 + (5y)^2 + (3z)^2 - (15x)(5y) - (5y)(3z) - (15x)(3z) = 0$

$\Rightarrow 1/2\,[(15x - 5y)^2 + (5y - 3z)^2 + (3z - 15x)^2] = 0$

[since, $a^2 + b^2 + c^2 - ab - bc - ac = \frac{1}{2}(a-b)^2 + (b-c)^2 + (c-a)^2$]

Also all the three terms being squares are ≥ 0 and the sum of the terms being zero, we have

$(15x - 5y)^2 = (5y - 3z)^2 = (3z - 15x)^2 = 0$

$\Rightarrow 15x = 5y = 3z \qquad \Rightarrow \frac{x}{1} = \frac{y}{3} = \frac{z}{5} = k$ (say)

$\Rightarrow x = k, y = 3k, z = 5k$. Hence x,y and z are in AP

ILLUSTRATION 23: Show that the sequence $\log a$, $\log\left(\frac{a^2}{b}\right)$, $\log\left(\frac{a^3}{b^2}\right)$, $\log\left(\frac{a^4}{b^3}\right)$,....forms an AP

SOLUTION: We have $a_n = \log\left(\frac{a^n}{b^{n-1}}\right)$ and $a_{n+1} = \log\left(\frac{a^{n+1}}{b^n}\right)$

Now, $a_{n+1} - a_n = \log\left(\frac{a^{n+1}}{b^n}\right) - \log\left(\frac{a^n}{b^{n-1}}\right) = \log\left(\frac{a^{n+1}}{b^n} \times \frac{b^{n-1}}{a^n}\right) = \log\left(\frac{a}{b}\right)$

Clearly, $a_{n+1} - a_n$ is a constant for all values of n. i.e., the difference between the two terms is independent of n.

Hence the given sequence is an AP with common difference $\log\left(\frac{a}{b}\right)$.

ILLUSTRATION 24: If $a_1, a_2,..........,a_n$ are in arithmetic progression, where $a_i > 0$ for all i, show that

$$\frac{1}{\sqrt{a_1}+\sqrt{a_2}} + \frac{1}{\sqrt{a_2}+\sqrt{a_3}} + ... + \frac{1}{\sqrt{a_{n-1}}+\sqrt{a_n}} = \frac{1}{\sqrt{a_1}+\sqrt{a_n}}$$

SOLUTION: $\text{L.H.S.} = \frac{1}{\sqrt{a_1}+\sqrt{a_2}} + \frac{1}{\sqrt{a_2}+\sqrt{a_3}} + ... + \frac{1}{\sqrt{a_{n-1}}+\sqrt{a_n}}$

$$= \frac{\left(\sqrt{a_1}-\sqrt{a_2}\right)}{\left(\sqrt{a_1}+\sqrt{a_2}\right)\left(\sqrt{a_1}-\sqrt{a_2}\right)} + \frac{\left(\sqrt{a_2}-\sqrt{a_3}\right)}{\left(\sqrt{a_2}+\sqrt{a_3}\right)\left(\sqrt{a_2}-\sqrt{a_3}\right)} + ... + \frac{\left(\sqrt{a_{n-1}}-\sqrt{a_n}\right)}{\left(\sqrt{a_{n-1}}+\sqrt{a_n}\right)\left(\sqrt{a_{n-1}}-\sqrt{a_n}\right)}$$

$$= \frac{\sqrt{a_1}-\sqrt{a_2}}{a_1 - a_2} + \frac{\sqrt{a_2}-\sqrt{a_3}}{a_2 - a_3} + ... + \frac{\left(\sqrt{a_{n-1}}-\sqrt{a_n}\right)}{(a_{n-1} - a_n)}$$

Since a_1, a_2, a_3, ...a_n are in AP

So $a_2 - a_1 = a_3 - a_2 = ... = a_n - a_{n-1} = d$ (say)

Adding all terms, we have $a_n - a_1 = (n - 1)\, d$ (i)

$$\text{So L.H.S.} = \frac{\sqrt{a_1}-\sqrt{a_2}}{-d} + \frac{\sqrt{a_2}-\sqrt{a_3}}{-d} + ... + \frac{\left(\sqrt{a_{n-1}}-\sqrt{a_n}\right)}{-d}$$

$$= -\frac{1}{d}\left[\sqrt{a_1}-\sqrt{a_2}+\sqrt{a_2}-\sqrt{a_3}+....+\sqrt{a_{n-1}}-\sqrt{a_n}\right]$$

$$= \frac{\sqrt{a_n}-\sqrt{a_1}}{d} = \frac{\sqrt{a_n}-\sqrt{a_1}}{(a_n - a_1)/(n-1)} = \frac{(n-1)\left(\sqrt{a_n}-\sqrt{a_1}\right)}{\left(\sqrt{a_n}+\sqrt{a_1}\right)\left(\sqrt{a_n}-\sqrt{a_1}\right)} \text{ (from (i))} = \frac{n-1}{\sqrt{a_n}+\sqrt{a_1}} = \text{R.H.S.}$$

TEXTUAL EXERCISE–3 (SUBJECTIVE)

1. An AP consists of 60 terms. If the first and the last terms be 7 and 125 respectively, find the 25th term.
2. How many two-digit numbers are divisible by 3?
3. Find four numbers in AP whose sum is 6 and sum of whose squares is 14.
4. Find three numbers in AP, whose sum and product are 21 and 315 respectively.
5. Prove or disprove if a, b, c are in AP then a^2, b^2, c^2 also in AP.
6. Prove or disprove if a_1, a_2, a_3 are in AP, b_1, b_2, b_3 are in AP and k is any real constant, then $a_1 \pm kb_1$, $a_2 \pm kb_2$ and $a_3 \pm kb_3$ are also in AP.
7. Each term of an AP $a, a + d, a + 2d, \ldots,$ is tripled. Is the resulting sequence also an AP? If so, write its first term, common difference and the general term.
8. If a, b, c are in AP then prove that the following are also in AP.
   (a) $a\left[\frac{1}{b}+\frac{1}{c}\right], b\left[\frac{1}{c}+\frac{1}{a}\right], c\left[\frac{1}{a}+\frac{1}{b}\right]$
   (b) $b + c, c + a, a + b$
   (c) $a^2 (b + c), b^2 (c + a), c^2 (a + b)$ $[\Sigma ab \neq 0]$
   (d) $1/bc, 1/ca, 1/ab$
9. If $\frac{1}{a}, \frac{1}{b}, \frac{1}{c}$ are in AP Prove that $\frac{a}{c} = \frac{a-b}{b-c}$.
10. If a, b, c, d are in AP, show that $b + c + d, c + d + a, d + a + b, a + b + c$ are also in AP?
11. (a) If the numbers a^2, b^2, c^2 are in AP, then prove that $\frac{1}{b+c}, \frac{1}{c+a}, \frac{1}{a+b}$ are also in AP.
    (b) If $\frac{c^2}{(a+b)^2}, \frac{a^2}{(b+c)^2}, \frac{b^2}{(c+a)^2}$ are in AP, then show that $\frac{(s-c)}{(2s-c)^2}, \frac{(s-a)}{(2s-a)^2}, \frac{(s-b)}{(2s-b)^2}$ in AP, where s = semiperimeter of ΔABC having sides a, b and c.
12. The sum of n terms of two arithmetic series are in the ratio of $\frac{7n+14}{4n+7}$. Find the ratio of their 11th terms.
13. The ratio between the sum of n terms of two AP's is $(3n + 8)$: $(7n + 15)$. Find the ratio of their 7th terms.

Answer Keys

1. 55 **2.** 30 **3.** 0, 1, 2, 3 or 3, 2, 1, 0 **4.** 5, 7, 9 or 9, 7, 5
7. $t_n = 3[a + (n - 1)d]$ **12.** 23/13 **13.** 47/106

TEXTUAL EXERCISE–3 (OBJECTIVE)

1. If the sum of three numbers in AP is 12 and sum of their cubes is 408. Then.
   (a) middle numbers is 4
   (b) the product of extreme numbers is 7
   (c) the product of 3 numbers is 28
   (d) None of these
2. If sum of four integers in AP is 72 and their product is 92160. Then
   (a) middle numbers are 16, 20
   (b) the product of extreme numbers is 288
   (c) the sum of middle numbers is 36
   (d) None of these
3. If s_r and t_r denotes the sum of first r terms and rth term of an AP and given that $\frac{s_p}{s_q} = \frac{p^2}{q^2}$, then $\frac{t_p}{t_q}$ is
   (a) $(p + 1)/(p - 1)$ (b) $(p - 1)/(p - 1)$
   (c) $(2p + 1)/(2p + 1)$ (d) $(2p - 1)/(2q - 1)$
4. If 1, $\log_y x$, $\log_z y$, $- 15 \log_x z$ are in AP; then
   (a) $z^3 = x$ (b) $x = 1/y$
   (c) $z^{-3} = y$ (d) None of these
5. If a, b, c, d, e, f are in AP, then $e - c$ is equal to:
   (a) $2 (c - a)$ (b) $2 (d - c)$
   (c) $2(f - d)$ (d) $(d - c)$
6. In an AP, the sum of terms equidistant from the beginning and end is equal to
   (a) first term
   (b) second term
   (c) sum of the first and last term
   (d) last term

7. If three positive real numbers a, b, c are in AP such that $abc = 4$, then the minimum possible value of b is

(a) $2^{3/2}$ (b) $2^{2/3}$
(c) $2^{1/3}$ (d) $2^{5/2}$

8. If the length of sides of a right triangle are in AP, then the sines of the acute angle are

(a) 3/5, 4/5 (b) $\sqrt{2/3}, \sqrt{1/3}$

(c) $\sqrt{\frac{\sqrt{5}-1}{2}}, \sqrt{\frac{\sqrt{5}+1}{2}}$ (d) $\sqrt{\frac{\sqrt{3}-1}{2}}, \sqrt{\frac{\sqrt{3}+1}{2}}$

9. If 2 and 31 appear as two terms in an AP, then

(a) common difference of the AP is a rational number
(b) all the terms of the AP must be rational
(c) all the terms of the AP must be integers
(d) sum of any finite number of terms of the AP must be rational

10. If 1, $\log_3(3^x - 2)$, $2\log_9(3^x - 8/3)$ are in AP, the value of x can be

(a) $\log(4/3)$ (b) $\frac{\log 4}{\log 3}$
(c) 1 (d) $\log_3 4$

Answer Keys

1. (a, b, c) **2.** (a, b, c) **3.** (d) **4.** (a, b, c) **5.** (b) **6.** (c) **7.** (b) **8.** (a) **9.** (a, b, d) **10.** (b, c)

ARITHMETIC MEAN

Arithmetic means of numbers

(a) If A be mean between two numbers a and b then it is also known as arithmetic mean of a and b.
$\Rightarrow a, A, b$ in $A.P \Rightarrow A = (a + b)/2$

(b) Arithmetic mean for any n positive numbers $a_1, a_2, a_3, \ldots\ldots a_n$ is AM $= \frac{a_1 + a_2 + a_3 + \ldots\ldots + a_n}{n}$

Insertion of *n AM*'s between two numbers

Let a and b be two given numbers and $A_1, A_2, A_3, \ldots, A_n$ are AM's between them.

Then $a, A_1, A_2, A_3, \ldots\ldots, A_n, b$ will be in AP

Now $b = (n + 2)$th term

$$b = a + (n + 2 - 1)\,d \Rightarrow d = \left(\frac{b-a}{n+1}\right)$$

(where d = common difference)

$\therefore\ A_1 = a + d, A_2 = a + 2d, \ldots, A_n = a + nd$

$$\Rightarrow A_1 = a + \left(\frac{b-a}{n+1}\right),$$

$$A_2 = a + 2\left(\frac{b-a}{n+1}\right), \ldots,$$

$$A_k = a + k\left(\frac{b-a}{n+1}\right)\quad k \in \mathbb{N}$$

NOTE

Sum of n AM's between a and b is equal to n times single AM between a and b. i.e., $\sum_{i=1}^{n} A_i = \frac{n}{2}(a+b)$

Proof: Let as $a, A_1, A_2, \ldots, A_{n-1}, A_n$ is an AP

$\Rightarrow a + b = A_1 + A_n = A_2 + A_{n-1} = \ldots\ldots$ so on and

$$A_1 + A_2 + \ldots. A_n = \frac{n}{2}(A_1 + A_n) = \frac{n}{2}(a+b) = n\left(\frac{a+b}{2}\right)$$

$= (n$ Single AM between a and $b)$

ILLUSTRATION 25: If x, y, z are in AP, a is AM between x and y and b is AM between y and z; then find the AM of a and b.

SOLUTION: Since a is AM between x and y and b is AM between y and z

$\Rightarrow x, a, y, b, z$ must be in AP. $\Rightarrow a, y, b$ are in AP.

$\Rightarrow y$ is arithmetic mean between a and b

ILLUSTRATION 26: n AM's are inserted between 2 and 38. If third AM is 14, then evaluate n.

SOLUTION: Here $2 + 3d = 14 \Rightarrow d = 4$

$$\therefore\ 4 = \frac{38-2}{n+1}$$

$$\Rightarrow 4n + 4 = 36$$

$$\Rightarrow n = 8$$

ILLUSTRATION 27: Insert 20 AM between 2 and 86 and also find their sum.

SOLUTION: 2 is the first term and 86 is the 22nd term of AP $\Rightarrow a = 2$ and $t_{22} = 86 \Rightarrow 2 + (21)d = 86$

$\Rightarrow d = 4$

So the series is 2,6,10,14…82,86

required arithmetic means are 6, 10,14,….,82.

ILLUSTRATION 28: Between two numbers whose sum is $\frac{13}{6}$, an even number of AM's are inserted, the sum of these means exceeds the number of means by unity. Find the number of means.

SOLUTION: Let a and b be two numbers and $2n$ AM's are inserted between a and b, then

$$\frac{2n}{2}(a+b) = 2n + 1 \left[\text{given } a+b=\frac{13}{16}\right]$$

$$n\left(\frac{13}{6}\right) = 2n+1$$

$$\Rightarrow n = 6$$

$\therefore$ Number of means = 12

TEXTUAL EXERCISE–4 (SUBJECTIVE)

1. If a, b, c are in AP and p is the AM between a and b, q is the AM between b and c, show that b is the AM between p and q.

2. If A is the AM between a and b, prove that

(a) $(A - a)^2 + (A - b)^2 = \frac{1}{2}(a - b)^2$

(b) $4(a - A)(A - b) = (a - b)^2$

(c) $\frac{A+2a}{A-b} + \frac{A+2b}{A-a} = 4$

3. Insert 6 arithmetic means between 3 and 24 and also find their sum.

4. There are n AM's between 3 and 54 s.t. 8th mean is to $(n - 2)^{th}$ mean as 3 to 5. Find n.

5. The sum of two numbers is 13/6. An even number of AM's are being inserted between them and their sum exceeds the sum of numbers by 13. Find the number of means inserted.

6. n AM's are inserted in between x and $2y$ and then between $2x$ and y. In case r^{th} means in each case be equal, then find the ratio x/y.

7. Between 1 and 31, m numbers have been inserted in such a way that the resulting sequence is in an AP and the ratio of 7th and $(m - 1)^{th}$ numbers is 5 : 9. Find the value of m.

Answer Keys

3. 6, 9,..., 21 and sum = 81 **4.** $n = 16$ **5.** 14 **6.** $\frac{r}{n-r+1}$ **7.** $m = 14$

TEXTUAL EXERCISE–4 (OBJECTIVE)

1. If $c = (a^{n+1} + b^{n+1})/(a^n + b^n)$ is arithmetic mean of a and b, then n is
(a) 0 (b) 1
(c) –1 (d) None of these

2. Given two numbers a and b. Let A denote the single AM and S denote the sum of n APs between a and b, then $\frac{S}{A}$ depends on
(a) n, a, b (b) n, b
(c) n, a (d) n

3. If the AM between p^{th} and q^{th} terms of an AP be equal to the AM between r^{th} and s^{th} terms of an AP, then
(a) $p + q = r + s$
(b) $p - q = r - s$
(c) $p - q = s - r$
(d) None of these

4 If 11 AM's be inserted between 28 and 10. Find the middle term in the series.
(a) 24 (b) 20
(c) 19 (d) None of these

5. If 14 AM's are inserted between 5 and 8. And if their sum is n times the AM then n is.
(a) 5 (b) 8
(c) 14 (d) None of these

6. Let n AM's are inserted between 1 and 51, if the 4th mean: 7th mean = 3: 5 Find n.
(a) 25 (b) 24
(c) 26 (d) None of these

Answer Keys

1. (a) 2. (d) 3. (a) 4. (c) 5. (c) 6. (b)

■ GEOMETRIC PROGRESSION

Geometric Progression is a progression in which the ratio of the successive terms remains constant. Such ratio is known as **common ratio.**

(a) **General term of G.P.:** If a is the first term and r is the common ratio, then GP can be written as a, ar, ar^2, ar^3, ar^4, ..., ar^{n-1}, ... ***n^th^* term from beginning:**
$T_n = ar^{n-1} = l$ (last term) where $r = \frac{T_n}{T_{n-1}}$

n^th^ term from last: $T'_n = \frac{\ell}{r^{n-1}}$

(b) **Sum of first n–terms of GP:** $S_n = \frac{a(1-r^n)}{(1-r)} = \frac{a-lr}{1-r}$; a = first terms, r = common ratio, l = last terms (n^{th} terms), when $r \neq 1$ and $= na$ for $r = 1$.

Proof: Let $S_n = a + ar + ar^2 + ar^3 + ... + ar^{n-1}$
$\Rightarrow rS_n = ar + ar^2 + ar^3 + ... + ar^{n-1} + ar^n$
On subtracting, we get $(1 - r) S_n = a - ar^n$

$$\Rightarrow S_n = \frac{a(1-r^n)}{1-r} = \frac{a-ar^n}{1-r} = \frac{a-(ar^{n-1})r}{1-r} = \frac{a-lr}{1-r}$$

$$\therefore S_n = \frac{a(1-r^n)}{1-r} = \frac{a-lr}{1-r}; r \neq 1$$

For $r = 1$, $S_n = a + a + ...+ a$ (constant sequence)
$\Rightarrow S_n = na$

(c) **Sum of infinitely many terms of *G.P*:-** As the GP is convergent only for $r \in (-1, 1) \sim \{0\}$, i.e., $S_n \to a$ finite number as $n \to \infty$ Iff $r \in (-1, 1)$, otherwise sequence is either oscillating or diverging, therefore we can find s_∞ only for those sequence for which $r \in (-1, 1) \sim \{0\}$ and is given by $s_\infty = \frac{a}{1-r}$;

Proof: Let $S_\infty = a + ar + ar^2 + ar^3 + ...$
$rS_\infty = ar + ar^2 + ar^3 + ...$
On subtraction $(1 - r) s_\infty = a$

$$\Rightarrow S_\infty = \frac{a}{1-r}$$

Aliter: $S_n = \frac{a}{1-r} - \frac{ar^n}{1-r}$

$$\Rightarrow S_\infty = \lim_{n\to\infty} S_n = \lim_{n\to\infty} \frac{a}{1-r} - \frac{ar^n}{1-r}$$

$$= \frac{a}{1-r} \text{ as } r \in (-1,1)$$

$$\therefore S_\infty = \frac{a}{1-r} \text{ for } 0 < |r| < 1$$

Aliter: *S_∞ is not sum of infinite terms but it is* $\lim_{n\to\infty} S_n$

ILLUSTRATION 29: If first, second and eighth terms of a GP are respectively $(n)^{-4}$, $(n)^{n}$, $(n)^{52}$ then find the value of n.

SOLUTION: Here $\left(\frac{T_2}{T_1}\right)^{\frac{1}{2-1}} = \left(\frac{T_8}{T_2}\right)^{\frac{1}{8-2}}$

$\therefore \frac{n^n}{n^{-4}} = \left(\frac{n^{52}}{n^n}\right)^{1/6}$ or $n^{n+4} = n^{(52-n)/6}$ or $n + 4 = \frac{52-n}{6} \Rightarrow n = 4$

ILLUSTRATION 30: If the first term of a GP be 5 and common ratio be 5, then find which term is 3125.

SOLUTION: $3125 = 5\,(5)^{n-1} \Rightarrow 625 = (5)^{n-1}$

$\Rightarrow (5)^4 - (5)^{n-1} \Rightarrow n - 1 = 4$ $\Rightarrow n - 1 = 4 \Rightarrow n = 5$ $\therefore$ 5th term

ILLUSTRATION 31:. The first term of an infinite GP is 1 and any term is equal to the sum of all of its succeeding terms. Find the progression.

SOLUTION: Let the GP be $1, r, r^2, r^3, \ldots$

According to given condition $r = \frac{r^2}{1-r}$ $\Rightarrow r = \frac{1}{2}$,

Hence the progression is $1, \frac{1}{2}, \frac{1}{4}, \frac{1}{8}, \ldots \infty$

ILLUSTRATION 32: If $S = 1 + \frac{1}{2} + \frac{1}{4} + \frac{1}{8} + \ldots$, then find the sum of

(i) first 20 terms of the series (ii) infinite terms of the series

SOLUTION: (i) sum of first 20 terms is given by $S_{20} = \frac{a(1-r^{20})}{(1-r)} = \frac{\left(1-\left(\frac{1}{2}\right)^{20}\right)}{1-\frac{1}{2}} = \frac{2^{20}-1}{2^{19}}$

(ii) sum of infinite terms is given by $S_\infty = \frac{a}{1-r} = \frac{1}{1-\frac{1}{2}} = 2$

ILLUSTRATION 33: Let a, b and c form a GP of common ratio r, with $0 < r < 1$. If a, $2b$ and $3c$ form an AP, then find r.

SOLUTION: Let $b = ar$ and $c = ar^2$, where $0 < r < 1$. Now a, $2b$ and $3c$ form an AP

$\therefore 4b = a + 3c \Rightarrow 4ar = a + 3ar^2 \Rightarrow 3r^2 - 4r + 1 = 0$

$\Rightarrow (3r-1)(r-1) = 0 \Rightarrow r = 1/3$ $[\because 0 < r < 1]$

ILLUSTRATION 34: If the sum of an infinitely decreasing GP is 3, and the sum of the squares of its terms is 9/2, then find the sum of the cubes of the terms.

SOLUTION: Let the GP be $a, ar, ar^2, \ldots$ where $0 < r < 1$. Then

$a + ar + ar^2 + \ldots = 3$ and $a^2 + a^2r^2 + a^2r^4 + \ldots = 9/2$

$\Rightarrow \frac{a}{1-r} = 3$ and $\frac{a^2}{1-r^2} = \frac{9}{2} \Rightarrow \frac{9(1-r)^2}{1-r^2} = \frac{9}{2} \Rightarrow \frac{1-r}{1+r} = \frac{1}{2} \Rightarrow r = 1/3$

Putting $r = 1/3$ in $\frac{a}{1-r} = 3$ we get $a = 2$

Now the required sum of the cubes is

$$a^3 + a^3r^3 + a^3r^6 + \ldots = \frac{a^3}{1-r^3} = \frac{8}{1-(1/27)} = \frac{108}{13}$$

ILLUSTRATION 35: The sum of three numbers in GP is 21 and the sum of their squares is 189, find the numbers.

SOLUTION: Let the three numbers be a, ar, ar^2

Given $a + ar + ar^2 = 21$ or $a(1 + r + r^2) = 21$ (i)

and $a^2 + a^2r^2 + a^2r^4 = 189$ or $a^2(1 + r^2 + r^4) = 189$ (ii)

dividing (*ii*) by square of (*i*), we get $\frac{a^2(1+r^2+r^4)}{a^2(1+r+r^2)^2} = \frac{189}{441} = \frac{3}{7}$

or $\frac{1+2r^2+r^4-r^2}{(1+r+r^2)^2} = \frac{3}{7}$ or $\frac{(1+r^2)^2-r^2}{(1+r+r^2)^2} = \frac{3}{7}$

or $\frac{1+r^2-r}{1+r+r^2} = \frac{3}{7}$ or $7(1 + r^2 - r) = 3(1 + r + r^2)$

or $4r^2 - 10r + 4 = 0$ or $2r^2 - 5r + 2 = 0$ $\therefore r = 2, 1/2$

When $r = 2$ from (*i*) $a = \frac{21}{1+2+2^3} = 3$ when $r = 1/2$, $a = 12$

Hence the three numbers are 3, 6, 12 or 12, 6, 3

ILLUSTRATION 36: If S be the sum to infinite terms of a GP, having first term as A, then prove that the sum of the first n terms is $\left[1-\left(1-\frac{A}{S}\right)^n\right]S$.

SOLUTION: If R be the common ratio, we have $S = \frac{A}{1-R}$

$$S_n = A\left[\frac{1-R^n}{1-R}\right] = A\left[\frac{1-\left(1-\frac{A}{S}\right)^n}{1-\left(1-\frac{A}{S}\right)}\right] = \frac{A\left[1-\left(1-\frac{A}{S}\right)^n\right]}{\frac{A}{S}}$$

$$S_n = \left[1-\left(1-\frac{A}{S}\right)^n\right]S$$

ILLUSTRATION 37: If a, b, c are in GP and the equations $ax^2 + 2bx + c = 0$ and $dx^2 + 2ex + f = 0$ have a common root, then show that $\frac{d}{a}, \frac{e}{b}, \frac{f}{c}$ are in AP.

SOLUTION: If a, b, c are in GP then $b^2 = ac$. The first quadratic equation becomes

$ax^2 + 2\sqrt{ac}x + c = 0 \Rightarrow (\sqrt{a}x + \sqrt{c})^2 = 0$

Which has exactly one root $-\frac{\sqrt{c}}{\sqrt{a}}$. Therefore if the two equations have a common root, we must have $d\left(-\frac{\sqrt{c}}{\sqrt{a}}\right)^2 + 2e\left(\frac{-\sqrt{c}}{\sqrt{a}}\right) + f = 0 \Rightarrow \frac{dc}{a} - 2e\frac{\sqrt{c}}{\sqrt{a}} + f = 0$

$\Rightarrow \frac{d}{a} - \frac{2e}{\sqrt{ac}} + \frac{f}{c} = 0$ (on dividing by c)

$\Rightarrow \frac{d}{a} + \frac{f}{c} = \frac{2e}{b}$ $(\because \sqrt{ac} = b)$

$\Rightarrow \frac{d}{a}, \frac{e}{b}, \frac{f}{c}$ are in AP.

ILLUSTRATION 38: Evaluate 3 + 33 + 333 + ... upto n terms.

SOLUTION: Let S = 3 + 33 + 333 + ... upto n terms.

$$=\frac{3}{9}[9+99+999+....+\text{ upto } n \text{ terms}] =\frac{3}{9}[(10-1)+(10^2-1)+(10^3-1)+...+\text{upto } n \text{ terms}]$$

$$=\frac{1}{3}[10+10^2+10^3+....+10^n-n] =\frac{1}{3}\left(\frac{10(10^n-1)}{9}-n\right)=\frac{1}{27}[10^{n+1}-9n-10]$$

ILLUSTRATION 39: Show that $\underset{n\text{ digits}}{(66......6)^2}+\underset{n\text{ digits}}{(88......8)}=\underset{2n\text{ digits}}{(44......4)}$.

SOLUTION: LHS $=\left[\frac{6}{9}(999...9)\right]^2+\frac{8}{9}[999....9]$

$$=\frac{36}{81}(10^n-1)^2+\frac{8}{9}(10^n-1)=\frac{4}{9}[10^{2n}-1]\left[\because \underbrace{999....9}_{n-\text{times}}=(10)^n-1\right]=\frac{4}{9}(99......2n \text{ times})=\underbrace{44...4}_{2n-\text{digits}}$$

TEXTUAL EXERCISE–5 (SUBJECTIVE)

1. Write down the series whose n^{th} term is $(5)^{\frac{3}{5}-3n}$. What type of this series is? Write down it's 7th term.
2. Find the indicated terms in the following GP 's:
   (a) $a^{x-y}+a^x+a^{x+y}$ ....;$10^{th}, n^{th}$
   (b) $3\sqrt{2}+\frac{3}{\sqrt{2}}+\frac{3}{2\sqrt{2}}+..;5^{th}$ terms.
3. Which term of the sequence $\frac{2}{27}+\frac{2}{9}+\frac{2}{3}+$.......... is 1458?
4. The third term of a GP is 9. Find the product of its first five terms.
5. Evaluate for what values of k are $2k$, $5k + 2$, $20k - 4$ consecutive terms of a GP?
6. The 4th, 7th and 10th terms of a GP are a, b and c respectively. Show that $b^2 = ac$.
7. The lengths of the sides of the triangle from a GP If the perimeter of the triangle is 37 cm and the shortest side is 9 cm find the lengths of the other two sides of the triangle.
8. Find three numbers in GP whose sum is 13 and product is 27.
9. Find three numbers in GP whose sum is 13 and sum of whose square is 91.
10. If $\frac{1}{x+y},\frac{1}{2y},\frac{1}{y+z}$ are in AP. Prove that x, y, z are in GP.
11. The sum of n terms of a progression is $\frac{2^n-1}{3}$. Show that it is a GP and find its common ratio.
12. The sum of the first three terms of a GP is 39/10 and their product is 1. Find the first term, common ratio and three numbers.
13. If $1 + 2 + 2^2 +$ .... $+ 2^{n-1} = 511$, then find n.
14. How many terms of the series $\sqrt{3}+3\sqrt{2}+6\sqrt{3}+$........ will amount to $21\sqrt{2}+7\sqrt{3}$?
15. Find the S_n and hence sum of infinite number of term of the following sequences ....
    (a) .5, .05, . 005, ...
    (b) 0.6 + 0.66 + 0.666 + ...
16. The sum of the first three terms of a GP is to the sum of the first six terms is 125 : 152. Find the common ratio of the GP.
17. The first term of a GP exceeds the second term by 2 and sum to infinity is 50, find the GP.
18. The sum of an infinite number of terms of a GP is 4 and the sum of their cubes is 192, find the GP.
19. Evaluate the following:
    (a) $\sum_{j=1}^{9}(2+3^j)$ (b) $\sum_{n=1}^{13}(2^n-1)$
    (c) $\sum_{j=1}^{n}(2^j+3^j+5)$

20. One side of an equilateral triangle is 24 cm. The mid-points of its sides are joined to form another triangle whose mid-points, in turn are join to form still another triangle. This process continues indefinitely. Find the sum of the perimeters of all the triangles.

21. What happens to S_∞ if $r = 1$ and $r = -1$?

22. What happens to S_∞ if $|r| > 1$?

Answer Keys

1. G.P, $\sqrt[5]{5^{-102}}$ **2.** (a) $a^{x+(n-2)y}$ and a^{x+8y} (b) $\frac{3}{8\sqrt{2}}$ **3.** 10 **4.** 9^5 **5.** $k = 2, -2/15$ **7.** 9, 12, 16 **8.** 1, 3, 9 or 9, 3, 1 **9.** 1, 3, 9 or 9, 3, 1 **11.** 2 **12.** $\frac{5}{2}, 1, \frac{2}{5}$ **13.** 9 **14.** $n = 4$

15. (a) $\frac{5}{9}\left[1-10^{-n}\right]$ (b) $\frac{2}{3}\left[n-\frac{\left[1-10^{-n}\right]}{9}\right]$ **16.** 3/5 **17.** $a = 10, r = 4/5$ **18.** $a = 6, r = -1/2$

19. (a) $\frac{3}{2}(11+3^9)$ (b) $2^{14} - 15$ (c) $2(2^n-1)+\frac{3}{2}(3^n-1)+5n$ **20.** 144 cm

21. If $r = 1$ then S_∞ is ∞ for $a > 0$ and $-\infty$ for $a < 0$, if r is -1 then S_∞ oscillates and takes value 0 for even number of terms sum and takes value a for odd number of terms sum.

22. Series does not converge i.e., oscillates for $r < -1$ and $\to\infty$ for $a > 0$; $\to -\infty$ for $a < 0$.

TEXTUAL EXERCISE–5 (OBJECTIVE)

1. If sum of three numbers in GP is 21 and the sum of their squares is 189, then the common ratio of the GP is
(a) 2, 1/2 (b) 3, 1/3
(c) 4, 1/4 (d) None of these

2. If the product of three numbers in GP be 216 and their sum is 19, then the numbers are
(a) 4, 6, 9 (b) 4, 7, 8,
(c) 3, 7, 9 (d) None of these

3. Six numbers are in GP such that their product is 512. If the fourth number is 4, then the second number is
(a) $\frac{1}{2}$ (b) 1
(c) 2 (d) None of these

4. If a, b, c are in GP then
(a) $a(b^2 + a^2) = c(b^2 + c^2)$
(b) $a(b^2 + c^2) = c(a^2 + b^2)$
(c) $a^2(b + c) = c^2(a + b)$
(d) None of these

5. If $\log_x a$, $a^{x/2}$ and $\log_b x$ are in GP, then x is equal to
(a) $\log_a(\log_b a)$
(b) $\log_a(\log_e a) + \log_a(\log_e b)$
(c) $\log_a(\log_a b)$
(d) $\log_a(\log_e b) - \log_a(\log_e a)$

6. The value of $(0.2)^{\log_{\sqrt{5}}\left(\frac{1}{4}+\frac{1}{8}+\frac{1}{16}+.....\infty\right)}$ is:
(a) 1 (b) 2
(c) $\frac{1}{2}$ (d) 4

7. If $1 + a + a^2 + a^3 + ...a^n = (1 + a)(1 + a^2)(1 + a^4)$, then n is
(a) 3 (b) 5
(c) 7 (d) 9

8. The value of $\sum_{n=1}^{m}\log\frac{a^{2n-1}}{b^{m-1}}(a \neq 0,1; b \neq 0,1)$ is
(a) $m\log\frac{a^{2m}}{b^{m-1}}$ (b) $\log\frac{a^{2m}}{b^{m-1}}$
(c) $m\log\left(\frac{a^m}{b^{m-1}}\right)$ (d) $\frac{m}{2}\log\frac{a^{2m}}{b^{m+1}}$

9. The second term of a geometric progression (*of positive numbers*), is 54 and the fourth term is 24. Then the fifth term is
(a) 12 (b) 15
(c) 16 (d) None of these

10. The sum of the series 1 + 11 + 111 + ... to n terms is
(a) $\frac{1}{9}\left[\frac{10}{9}(10 -1)+\right]$ (b) $\frac{1}{9}\left[\frac{10}{9}(10^n-1)-n\right]$;
(c) $\frac{10}{9}\left[\frac{1}{9}(10^n-1)-n\right]$ (d) $\frac{10}{9}\left[\frac{1}{9}(10^n-1)+n\right]$;

11. The first term of an infinite geometric series is a and its common ratio is r. If its sum is 4 and its second term is 3/4, then

(a) $a = \frac{7}{4}, r = \frac{3}{4}$ (b) $a = 2, r = \frac{3}{8}$

(c) $a = \frac{3}{2}, r = \frac{1}{2}$ (d) $a = 3, r = \frac{1}{4}$

12. Let $f(x) = 2x + 1$. Then the number of real values of x for which the three unequal numbers $f(x), f(2x), f(4x)$ are in GP is

(a) 1 (b) 2

(c) 0 (d) None of these

13. An infinite GP has first term 'x' and sum '5', then x belongs to

(a) $x < -10$ (b) $-10 < x < 0$

(c) $0 < x < 10$ (d) $x > 10$

14. If $(1 + p)(1 + 3x + 9x^2 + 27x^3 + 81x^4 + 243x^5) = 1 - p^6$, $p \neq 1$, then the value of $\frac{p}{x}$ is

(a) 1/3 (b) –3

(c) 1/2 (d) 2

Answer Keys

1. (a)	**2.** (a)	**3.** (b)	**4.** (b)	**5.** (a)	**6.** (d)	**7.** (c)	**8.** (c)	**9.** (c)	**10.** (b)
11. (d)	**12.** (c)	**13.** (c)	**14.** (b)						

Points to Remember

If we are given product of terms in GP, then

- ❑ Three numbers in GP are generally taken as a/r, a, ar so that their product is a^3 and common ratio is r.
- ❑ Four numbers in GP are generally taken as a/r^3, a/r, ar, ar^3 so that their product is a^4 and common ratio is r^2.
- ❑ Five numbers in GP are generally taken as a/r^2, a/r, a, ar, ar^2 so that product is a^5 and common ratio is r.
- ❑ In general, if we have to take $(2k + 1)$ terms in GP we take them as $\frac{a}{r^k}, \frac{a}{r^{k-1}}, \ldots\ldots, \frac{a}{r}, a, ar, \ldots\ldots ar^k$

and if we have to take $2k$ terms in GP, we take them $\frac{a}{r^{2k-1}}, \frac{a}{r^{2k-3}}, \frac{a}{r^{2k-5}}, \ldots, \frac{a}{r}, ar, ar^3, \ldots\ ar^{2k-3}, ar^{2k-1}$.

ILLUSTRATION 40: If product of three terms of a GP is 216 and sum of their products taken in pairs is 156, then find the greatest term.

SOLUTION: Let the terms are a/r, a, ar

then $a/r \times a \times ar = 216$

$\Rightarrow a = 6$, and $a/r \times a + a \times ar + ar \times a/r = 156$

$\Rightarrow a^2 (1/r + r + 1) = 156$

$\Rightarrow 36 (r^2 + r + 1) = 156 r$ $(\because a = 6)$

$\Rightarrow 3r^2 - 10r + 3 = 0$ $\Rightarrow (3r - 1)(r - 3) = 0$

$\Rightarrow r = 3, 1/3$

Terms are 2, 6, 18.

$\therefore$ The greatest term is 18.

Properties of geometric progression

(a) Product of the equidistant terms of a GP is always constant and equal to product of first term and last term.

(b) If every term of GP is increased or decreased by the same non-zero quantity, the resulting series may not be in GP.

(c) If every term of GP is multiplied or divided by the same non-zero quantity, the resulting series is in GP with same common ratio.

ILLUSTRATION 41: If a, b, c, d are in GP, then prove that $a^n + b^n, b^n + c^n, c^n + d^n$ are also in GP.

SOLUTION: Given a, b, c, d are in GP.

$\Rightarrow a^n, b^n, c^n, d^n$ are also in GP.

Let the common ratio is k

$\Rightarrow b^n = k a^n, c^n = k^2a^n, d^n = k^3 a^n$

Now $a^n + b^n, b^n + c^n, c^n + d^n = a^n + ka^n, ka^n + k^2a^n, k^2a^n + k^3a^n$

$= a^n(k + 1), ka^n (k + 1), k^2 a^n (k + 1)$

$\Rightarrow 1, k, k^2$ (dividing each by $a^n (k + 1)$

$\therefore$ given terms are in GP.

(d) If a_1, a_2, a_3, ... and b_1, b_2, b_3, ... are two GP's having common ratios r_1 and r_2 respectively, then a_1b_1, a_2b_2, ... and $\frac{a_1}{b_1}, \frac{a_2}{b_2}, \frac{a_3}{b_3}$ will also form GP and their common ratios will be r_1r_2 and $\frac{r_1}{r_2}$ respectively.

(e) If each term of a GP (with common ratio r) be raised to the *same* power k (*say*), then the resulting one is also a GP with common ratio $(r)^k$.

(f) If a_1, a_2, a_3, ... be a GP of positive terms, then $\log a_1$, $\log a_2$, $\log a_3$, ... will be in AP and conversely

Proof: Let $a_1 = a, a_2 = ar, a_3 = ar^2, a^4 = ar^3$, ... then $\log a_1 = \log a, \log a_2 = \log a + \log r, \log a_3 = \log a + 2\log r$, ...

In general, $\log a_k = \log a + (k - 1)\log r$ and $\log a_{k+1} = \log a + k \log r$

$\Rightarrow \log a_{k+1} - \log a_k = \log r$ (*independent of k*)

$\Rightarrow$ (*log* a_1, $\log a_2$, $\log a_3$, ..., are in AP)

(g) **Value of a recurring decimal:** Let X denote the figure which do not reoccur, and suppose it contains x number of digits; let Y denote the recurring number consisting of y figures, let R denote the value of the recurring decimal; then $R = 0..XYYY.....;$

Proof: Let $R = 0..XYYY.....;$

$\therefore\ 10^x \times R = X.YYY .....;$ and $10^{x+y} \times R = XY.YYY .....;$

$\therefore$ therefore by subtraction $R = \dfrac{XY - X}{(10^{x+y} - 10^x)}$

Aliter: Let $R = 0\,.\,XYYY$...; let $X = a_1a_2a_3 \ldots a_x\}$ and $Y = b_1b_2b_3 \ldots b_y\}$

$\Rightarrow R = 0\,.\,(a_1a_2a_3\ldots a_x)\,(b_1b_2b_3 \ldots b_y)\,(b_1b_2b_3 \ldots b_y)$

$\Rightarrow R = 0.a_1a_2a_3 \ldots a_x + \underbrace{0.000\ldots.0}_{x \text{ times}}b_1b_2b_3\ldots.b_y$

$+\underbrace{0.0000\ldots.00\ldots.0}_{(x+y)\text{ times}}b_1b_2b_3\ldots.b_y$

$+\underbrace{0.0000\ldots.00\ldots.0}_{(x+2y)\text{ times}}b_1b_2b_3\ldots.b_y$

$\Rightarrow R = 0.a_1a_2a_3 \ldots a_x + (b_1b_2b_3 \ldots b_y)\,\{10^{-(x+y)} + 10^{-(x+2y)} + 10^{-(x+3y)} + \ldots\}$

$\Rightarrow R = 0.a_1a_2a_3 \ldots a_x + (b_1b_2b_3 \ldots b_y)\left\{\dfrac{10^{-(x+y)}}{1-(10)^{-y}}\right\}$

$\Rightarrow\ R = 0.X + Y\left\{\dfrac{1}{10^{x+y} - 10^x}\right\} \Rightarrow R = \dfrac{X}{10^x} + \dfrac{Y}{10^{x+y} - 10^x}$

$\Rightarrow\ R = \dfrac{X(10^y - 1) + Y}{10^{x+y} - 10^x} \Rightarrow R = \dfrac{X(10^y) + Y - X}{10^{x+y} - 10^x}$

$\Rightarrow\ R = \dfrac{a_1a_2a_3\ldots a_x\underbrace{00000\ldots.0}_{y\text{ times}} + b_1b_2b_3\ldots b_y - X}{10^{x+y} - 10^x}$

$\Rightarrow\ R = \dfrac{XY - X}{10^{x+y} - 10^x}$

ILLUSTRATION 42: Prove that 0. 423232323..... is a rational number.

SOLUTION: This problem could be solved by either using progression or without progression.

Let S =0. 423232323..........

Method 1.

$$S = \frac{4}{10} + \frac{23}{1000} + \frac{23}{100000} + \ldots. = \frac{4}{10} + \frac{23}{10^3} + \frac{23}{10^5} + \ldots.$$

$$= \frac{4}{10} + \frac{23}{10^3}\left[1 + \frac{1}{10^2} + \frac{1}{10^4} + \ldots\right] = \frac{4}{10} + \frac{23}{10^3}\left[\frac{1}{1 - 1/10^2}\right]$$

$$= \frac{4}{10} + \frac{23}{10^3} \times \frac{100}{99} = \frac{4}{10} + \frac{23}{990} = \frac{419}{990}$$

So, S is a rational number

Method 2. Let S = 0.4232323......

$1000\,S = 423.\,232323......$ (i)

$10S = 4.\,232323.........$ (ii)

On subtracting, we get $990\,S = 419 \Rightarrow S = \dfrac{419}{990}$

So, S is rational number.

ILLUSTRATION 43: Express $0.25\overline{78239}$ as a rational number.

SOLUTION: Let $X = 0.25782398239$ ....

$\Rightarrow\ 10^3 X = 257.82398239......$ (1)

$\Rightarrow\ 10^7 X = 2578239.82398239.......$ (2)

Equation (2) – (1) gives

$10^7X - 10^3X = 2578239 - 257$

$$\Rightarrow X = \frac{2578239 - 257}{10^7 - 10^3} = \frac{2577982}{9999000}$$

■ GEOMETRIC MEAN

Single geometric mean between two numbers *a* and *b*: A number G is said to be a geometric mean between a and b if a, G, b are in GP.

$$\frac{G}{a} = \frac{b}{G}$$

$$G^2 = ab$$

$$\left(G - \sqrt{ab}\right)\left(G + \sqrt{ab}\right) = 0$$

$$G = \sqrt{ab} \text{ or } -\sqrt{ab} \text{ or } G = (ab)^{1/2} = \pm\sqrt{ab}$$

i.e., any one of $\sqrt{ab}$ and $-\sqrt{ab}$ can serve as a single geometric mean between a and b.

REMARK

From above definition, it is clear that geometric mean between two numbers a and b of opposite signs never exists. In fact, there exists no real number G for which a, G, b are in GP. If $a.b \le 0$. Thus from above we conclude that between two real numbers either there is no single GM or two GM's.

ILLUSTRATION 44: Find the single geometric mean between the given numbers a and b.

(i) $a = 4, b = 9$

(ii) $a = -9, b = -16$

(iii) $a = -4, b = 9$

(iv) $a = 10\log_3(4), b = 20\log_4(9)$

(v) $a = 5\log_{1/2}(4), b = 5\log_{20}(10)$

SOLUTION: (i) Single GM's between a and b = $\pm\sqrt{ab} = \pm\sqrt{36} = \pm 6$

(ii) Single GM's between a and b = $\pm\sqrt{(-9)(-16)} = \pm\sqrt{144} = \pm 12$

(iii) Single GM's between a and b does not exist as $a.b = (-4)\ (9) = -36 < 0$

(iv) Single GM's between a and b = $\pm\sqrt{10(\log_3 4)(20\log_4 9)} = \pm\sqrt{200(\log_3 4)(2\log_4 3)}$

$= \pm\sqrt{400(\log_3 4)(\log_4 3)} = \pm\sqrt{400} = \pm\ 20$

(v) $a = 5\log_{1/2}4 < 0$ as $\log_b a < 0$ for a and b at opposite sides of 1.

Where as $b = 5\log_{20}10 > 0$ as $\log_b a > 0$ for a and b on same side of 1

$\Rightarrow$ $a.b < 0$

Single GM between a and b does not exist.

Remarks: In above Illustration (i) and (ii) any one real number out of two possible can serve as a single geometric mean between a and b.

Geometric mean of two numbers *a* and *b*

Geometric mean of two numbers a and b is the principal square root (positive square root) of (ab) i.e., GM of a and $b = \sqrt{ab}$

Thus GM of a and b exist only when $ab \geq 0$

e.g. (*i*) if $a = 5$, $b = 4$, then

GM of a and $b = \sqrt{ab} = \sqrt{20} = 2\sqrt{5}$

(*ii*) if $a = 0$, $b = 6$, then

GM of a and $b = \sqrt{(0)(6)} = \sqrt{0} = 0$

(*iii*) If $a = -2$ and $b = -8$, then GM of a and $b = \sqrt{(-2)(-8)} = \sqrt{16} = 4$

(*iv*) If $a = -2$, $b = 8$, then GM of a and $b = \sqrt{(-2)(8)} = \sqrt{-16}$

which is not real i.e., does not exist.

REMARK

Single GM between a and b does not exist for a.b ≤ 0, where as GM of a and b does not exist for a.b < 0.

Geometric mean of *n* numbers: Geometric mean of n-numbers $a_1, a_2, a_3, \ldots, a_n$ is the principal n^{th} root of their product.

i.e., GM of $a_1, a_2, a_3, \ldots, a_n = \sqrt[n]{a_1, a_2, a_3, \ldots, a_n}$

Thus GM of even number of real numbers would exist only when their product is non-negative where as GM of odd number of real numbers would always exist.

E.g., (*i*) GM of numbers $-2, 5, 10, \frac{1}{4}, 125$

$= \sqrt[5]{-2\times5\times10\times\frac{1}{4}\times125} = \sqrt[5]{-5\times5\times5^3}$

$= \sqrt[5]{(-5)^5} = -5$

E.g., (ii) GM of numbers $2, 7, 3, \frac{128}{21}$

$= \sqrt[4]{(2)(7)(3)\left(\frac{128}{21}\right)} = \sqrt[4]{256} = \sqrt[4]{(4)^4} = 4$

e.g. (*iii*) GM of numbers $2, -3, 7, 8$

$= \sqrt[4]{(2)(-3)(7)(8)} = \sqrt[4]{-336}$

which does not exist in set of real numbers.

Insertion of *n* geometric means between two numbers

Let a and b be two given numbers and $G_1, G_2, G_3, \ldots G_n$ are GM's between them.

Then $a, G_1, G_2, G_3, \ldots, G_n, b$ will be in GP.

$T_{n+2} = b = ar^{n+1}$ (where r is the common ratio of above G.P.)

$\Rightarrow r = (b/a)^{\frac{1}{n+1}}$

$G_1 = ar, G_2 = ar^2, \ldots, G_n = ar^n$

$G_1 = a(b/a)^{\frac{1}{n+1}}, G_2 = a\ (b/a)^{\frac{2}{n+1}}, \ldots,$

$G_k = a(b/a)^{\frac{k}{n+1}}$

NOTE

Product of n GM's between a and b is equal to the nth power of single GM between a and b.

Prove: *As* $a, G_1, G_2, G_3, \ldots, G_{n-1}, G_n$, b *in GP.*

$\Rightarrow G_1.G_n = G_2.G_{n-1} = a^2r^{n+1} = ab$

$\Rightarrow (G_1.G_2G_3.....G_n)^2 = (G_1.G_n)(G_2.G_{n-1}).... (G_n.G_1) = (a.b)^n$

$\Rightarrow \prod_{k=1}^{n} G_k = (ab)^{n/2} = \left[(ab)^{1/2}\right]^n$

$\Rightarrow$ n^{th} *power of single geometric mean between a and b.*

ILLUSTRATION 45: Insert 4 GMs between 2 and 486.

SOLUTION: Let G_1, G_2, G_3, G_4, be four GM's between 2 and 486

$\Rightarrow$ 2, G_1, G_2, G_3, G_4, 486 are in GP.

$\Rightarrow$ First term = a = 2 and t_6 = 486

$\Rightarrow ar^5 = 486$ $\qquad \Rightarrow 2(r)^5 = 486$

$\Rightarrow r^5 = 243$ $\qquad \Rightarrow (r) = (243)^{1/5} = 3$

$\Rightarrow G_1 = t_2 = ar = (2)\ (3) = 6$ $\qquad \Rightarrow G_2 = t_3 = ar^2 = (2)(3)^2 = 18$

$\Rightarrow G_3 = t_3 = ar^3 = (2)\ (3)^3 = 54$ $\qquad \Rightarrow G_4 = t_5 = ar^4 = (2)\ (3)^4 = (2)\ 81 = 162$

$\Rightarrow$ four GM's between 2 and 486 are 6, 18, 54 and 162

ILLUSTRATION 46: If A_1, A_2 be two AM's and G_1, G_2 be two GM's between two numbers a and b, then evaluate $\dfrac{A_1 + A_2}{G_1G_2}$.

SOLUTION: By the property of AP and GP we have

$A_1 + A_2 = a + b$ (i)

$G_1\ G_2 = ab$ (ii)

$\therefore \dfrac{A_1 + A_2}{G_1G_2} = \dfrac{a+b}{ab}$

ILLUSTRATION 47: If the AM and GM between two numbers be 5 and 3 respectively, find the numbers.

SOLUTION: Let a and b be the two numbers.

Given AM between a and b is 5

$\therefore \dfrac{a+b}{2} = 5$ (i)

$\because$ 3 is the GM between a and b

$\therefore$ a, 3, b will be in GP.

If r be common ratio of this GP then $3 = ar$ and $b = ar^2$ (ii)

Now, from (*i*) $\frac{a+ar^2}{2} = 5$ (*iii*) Also $ar = 3$ (iv)

Dividing (*iii*) by (*iv*), we get $\frac{1+r^2}{2r} = \frac{5}{3}$ or $3r^2 - 10r + 3 = 0$

or $3r^2 - 9r - r + 3 = 0$ or $(r - 3)(3r - 1) = 0$

$\therefore$ $r = 3$ or $1/3$

From (*iv*) when $r = 3$, $a = 1$ and $b = ar^2 = 9$

When $r = 1/3$, $a = 9$ and then $b = ar^2 = 9.1/9 = 1$

Thus the two numbers are 1 and 9 or 9 and 1.

ILLUSTRATION 48: If three geometric means be inserted between 2 and 32, then, find the third geometric mean.

SOLUTION: Let G be the geometric mean, then

$G_3 = 2\,(32/2)^{3/4} = 2.(2)^3 = 16.$

TEXTUAL EXERCISE–6 (SUBJECTIVE)

1. If a, b, c, d are in GP, show that
   (a) $a + b$, $b + c$, $c + d$ are also in GP.
   (b) $a^2 + b^2$, $b^2 + c^2$, $c^2 + d^2$ are also in GP.
   (c) $a^2 + b^2 + c^2$, $ab + bc + cd$, $b^2 + c^2 + d^2$ are also in GP.
2. Find Geometric means of the numbers $3, 3^2, 3^3, ..., 3^n$.
3. Prove that the product of the n GM's between two given numbers is the nth power single GM.
4. Insert two GM's between a, b and show that their sum is $a^{1/3}.b^{1/3}(a^{1/3} + b^{1/3})$.
5. Find n so that $\frac{a^{n+1}+b^{n+1}}{a^n+b^n}$ may be the GM between a and b.
6. Insert three geometric means between 2 and 162 and find their product as well as their summation.
7. If 'a' be one AM and G_1, G_2 be two GMs between b and c. Prove that $G_1^3 + G_2^3 = 2abc$.
8. Solve system of equation $2x^4 = y^4 + z^4$, $xyz = 8$, knowing that $\log_y x$, $\log_z y$ and $\log_x z$ form a geometric progression.

Answer Keys

2. $3^{\frac{(n+1)}{2}}$ **5.** $n = -1/2$ **6.** 6, 18, 54; – 6, 18, – 54; Product: $(324)^{3/2}$; Sum: 78, – 42

8. $x = y = z = 2$

TEXTUAL EXERCISE–6 (OBJECTIVE)

1. If 1, x, y, z, 2 are in GP, then xyz is equal to
   (a) $2\sqrt{2}$ (b) 4
   (c) 8 (d) None of these
2. If $n!$, $3 \times n!$ and $(n + 1)!$ are in GP, then $n!$, $5 \times n!$ and $(n + 1)!$ are in
   (a) AP
   (b) GP
   (c) HP
   (d) None of these
3. Three numbers are in GP, whose sum is 70, if the extremum be each multiplied by 4 and the mean by 5, they will be in AP The numbers are
   (a) 10, 20, 40 (b) 10, 30, 40
   (c) 20, 30, 40 (d) None of these
4. If a, b, c, are in GP then $(a - c)^2 + (c - b)^2 + (b - d)^2 - (d - a)^2$ is
   (a) –1 (b) 2
   (c) 0 (d) None of these

Answer Keys

1. (a) **2.** (a) **3.** (a) **4.** (c)

HARMONIC PROGRESSION

A sequence is said to be a harmonic progression, if and only if the reciprocal of its terms form an arithmetic progression.

i.e., $\frac{1}{a}+\frac{1}{a+d}+\frac{1}{a+2d}+.....$ are in HP e.g., 1/2, 1/4, 1/6 ...... form a HP because 2, 4, 6, ... are in AP.

ILLUSTRATION 49: Three terms are in HP, if the sum of their reciprocals is equal to the first term and if the sum of reciprocals of the first and third terms is equal to third term. Find the terms.

SOLUTION: Let three terms in HP be $\frac{1}{a-d},\frac{1}{a},\frac{1}{a+d}$

According to the question $(a-d)+(a)+(a+d)=\frac{1}{a-d}$

$\Rightarrow\ 3a=\frac{1}{a-d}\Rightarrow 3a^2-3ad=1$ (i)

Also , $(a-d)+(a+d)=\frac{1}{a+d}\Rightarrow 2a^2+2ad=1$ (ii)

Solving (i) and (ii), we get, $a^2=\frac{5}{12}$

From equation (ii), $2ad=1-\frac{5}{6}=\frac{1}{6}>0$ i.e. 'a' and 'd' are of same sign

$\Rightarrow\ a=\sqrt{\frac{5}{12}}$ and $d=\frac{1}{\sqrt{60}}$ or $a=-\sqrt{\frac{5}{12}}$ and $d=-\frac{1}{\sqrt{60}}$

when $a=\sqrt{\frac{5}{12}}$ and $d=\frac{1}{\sqrt{60}}$. Terms of HP are $\frac{\sqrt{15}}{2},2\sqrt{\frac{3}{5}},\sqrt{\frac{5}{3}}$

when $a=\sqrt{\frac{5}{12}}$ and $d=-\frac{1}{\sqrt{60}}$. Terms of HP are $-\frac{\sqrt{15}}{2},-2\sqrt{\frac{3}{5}},-\sqrt{\frac{5}{3}}$

ILLUSTRATION 50: If m^{th} term of HP is n, while n^{th} term is m, find its $(m+n)^{th}$ term.

SOLUTION: Given $t_m=n$, or $\frac{1}{a+(m-1)d}=n$; where a is the first term and d is the common difference of the corresponding A.P.

So $a+(m-1)d=\frac{1}{n}$ and $a+(n-1)d=1/m$

$\Rightarrow\ d=\frac{1}{mn}$ and $a=\frac{1}{n}-\frac{(m-1)}{mn}=\frac{1}{mn}$

Hence $t_{(m+n)}=\frac{}{a+(m+n-1)d}=\frac{mn}{1+m+n-1}=\frac{mn}{m+n}$

ILLUSTRATION 51: If s_n denotes the sum of first (2^n-1) terms of HP $1,\frac{1}{2},\frac{1}{3},\frac{1}{4},.....$, then show that $s_n<n$.

SOLUTION: We have $S_1=1;S_2=1+\frac{1}{2}+\frac{1}{3};S_3=1+\frac{1}{2}+\frac{1}{3}+\frac{1}{4}+\frac{1}{5}+\frac{1}{6}+\frac{1}{7};$

$\therefore$ In general, $S_n = 1 + \frac{1}{2} + \frac{1}{3} + \frac{1}{4} + \ldots + \frac{1}{2^n - 1}$

$$\Rightarrow S_n = 1 + \left(\frac{1}{2} + \frac{1}{3}\right) + \left(\frac{1}{4} + \ldots + \frac{1}{7}\right) + \left(\frac{1}{8} + \ldots + \frac{1}{15}\right) + \ldots + \left(\frac{1}{2^{n-1}} + \frac{1}{2^{n-1}+1} + \ldots + \frac{1}{(2^n) - 1}\right)$$

$$< 1 + \frac{2}{2} + \frac{4}{4} + \frac{8}{8} + \ldots + \frac{2^{n-1}}{2^{n-1}} = n$$

$\Rightarrow S_n < n \ \forall \ n \in \mathbb{N}$.

ILLUSTRATION 52: If S_n denotes the sum of first $(2^n - 1)$ terms of HP $1, \frac{1}{2}, \frac{1}{3}, \frac{1}{4}, \ldots.,$ then show that $S(2n) > n$.

SOLUTION: We have $S_n = 1 + \frac{1}{2} + \frac{1}{3} + \frac{1}{4} + \frac{1}{5} + \ldots$; Let us put terms in grouping as follows:

$$S_n = 1 + \frac{1}{2} + \left(\frac{1}{3} + \frac{1}{4}\right) + \left(\frac{1}{5} + \ldots + \frac{1}{8}\right) + \ldots + \left(\frac{1}{2^{n-1}+1} + \ldots + \frac{1}{2^n}\right) - \frac{1}{2n}$$

$$> \left(1 + \frac{1}{2} + \frac{2}{4} + \frac{4}{8} + \ldots. + \frac{2^{n-1}}{2^n} - \frac{1}{2^n}\right) > \underbrace{\frac{1}{2} + \frac{1}{2} + \ldots. + \frac{1}{2}}_{n \text{ times}} = \frac{n}{2}$$

Thus $S(n) > \frac{n}{2}$

$\Rightarrow S(2n) > n$

Properties of harmonic progression

1. **General Term:** If a, b are first two terms of an HP

then $t_n = \dfrac{1}{\frac{1}{a} + (n-1)\left(\frac{1}{b} - \frac{1}{a}\right)}$.

Proof: Let $a, b \ldots t_n \ldots$ be a HP

$\Rightarrow \frac{1}{a}, \frac{1}{b}, \ldots\ldots \frac{1}{t_n}, \ldots\ldots.$ are in AP,

with first term $1/a$, and common difference

$\Rightarrow d = 1/b - 1/a$

$$\therefore \ \frac{1}{t_n} = \frac{1}{a} + (n-1).d$$

$$= \frac{1}{a} + (n-1)\left[\frac{1}{b} - \frac{1}{a}\right]$$

$$\therefore \ t_n = \frac{1}{\frac{1}{a} + (n-1)\left[\frac{1}{b} - \frac{1}{a}\right]}$$

2. If all the terms of HP are multiplied or divided by a constant non-zero quantity the resulting, series remains in HP.

(a) If terms are given in HP then the terms could be picked up in the following way:

For three terms: $\frac{1}{a-d}, \frac{1}{a}, \frac{1}{a+d}$

For four terms: $\frac{1}{a-3d}, \frac{1}{a-d}, \frac{1}{a+d}, \frac{1}{a+3d}$

(b) In general, if we are to take $(2r + 1)$ terms in HP we take them as

$\frac{1}{a-rd}, \frac{1}{a-(r-1)d}, \ldots, \frac{1}{a}, \frac{1}{a+d}, \ldots, \frac{1}{a+rd}$ similarly,

$2r$ terms can be taken as

$$\frac{1}{a-(2r-1)d}, \frac{1}{a-(2r+1)d}, \ldots\ldots,$$

$$\frac{1}{a-d}, \frac{1}{a+d}, \ldots, \frac{1}{a+(2r-1)d}.$$

ILLUSTRATION 53: If p^{th}, q^{th}, r^{th} terms of an HP be a, b, c respectively, then prove that $(q-r)bc + (r-p)\,ac + (p-q)\,ab = 0$

SOLUTION: Let a' be the first term and d be the common difference of the corresponding AP.

$$\therefore \ t_p = \frac{1}{a} = a' + (p-1)d \qquad \text{(i)}$$

$t_q = \frac{1}{b} = a' + (q-1)d$ (ii)

and $t_r = \frac{1}{c} = a' + (r-1)d$ (iii)

(i) – (ii) $\Rightarrow ab\,(p-q)\,d = b - a$ (iv)

(ii) – (iii) $\Rightarrow bc\,(q-r)\,d = c - b$ (v)

(iii) – (i) $\Rightarrow ca\,(r-p)\,d = (a-c)$ (vi)

(iv) + (v) + (vi) gives

$bc\,(q-r) + ac\,(r-p) + ab\,(p-q) = 0$

ILLUSTRATION 54: If a, b, c, d are in HP then prove that $ab + bc + cd = 3ad$

SOLUTION: $\because$ a, b, c, d are in HP.

$\therefore$ $1/a, 1/b, 1/c, 1/d$ are in AP.

Let k be its c.d

Now $1/b - 1/a = k$

$\therefore$ $\frac{a-b}{ab} = k \Rightarrow ab = 1/k\,(a-b)$

Thus $ab = 1/k\,(a-b)$ (i)

Similarly, $bc = 1/k(b-c)$ (ii)

and $cd = 1/k\,(c-d)$ (iii)

Adding (i), (ii) and (iii), we get

$$ab + bc + cd = \frac{1}{k}(a-d) = \frac{3ad(a-d)}{a-d} = 3ad \quad \left[\because \frac{1}{d} = \frac{1}{a} + 3k \Rightarrow k = \frac{a-d}{3ad}\right]$$

HARMONIC MEAN

If three or more than three terms are in HP, then all the numbers lying between first and last term are called harmonic means between them.

Harmonic mean of numbers

(a) H of any two numbers a and b is given by $H = \frac{2ab}{a+b}$ where a, b are two non-zero numbers.

(b) Also $H = \frac{n}{\frac{1}{a_1} + \frac{1}{a_2} + \ldots\ldots + \frac{1}{a_n}}$

$= \frac{n}{\sum_{j=1}^{n} \frac{1}{a_j}}$

the harmonic mean of n non-zero numbers $a_1, a_2, a_3, .., a_n$.

ILLUSTRATION 55: If A be the AM and H the HM between two quantities a and b, prove that $\frac{a-A}{a-H} \times \frac{b-A}{b-H} = \frac{A}{H}$.

SOLUTION: Given $A = \frac{a+b}{2}$ and $H = \frac{2ab}{a+b}$

$$\text{Now, } \frac{a-A}{a-H} \times \frac{b-A}{b-H} = \frac{a - \left(\frac{a+b}{2}\right)}{a - \frac{2ab}{a+b}} \times \frac{b - \left(\frac{a+b}{2}\right)}{b - \frac{2ab}{a+b}} = \frac{(a-b)(b-a)(a+b)^2}{4(a^2+ab-2ab)(ab+b^2-2ab)}$$

$$= \frac{(a-b)(b-a)(a+b)^2}{4.a(a-b).b(b-a)} = \frac{(a+b)^2}{4ab} = \frac{(a+b)/2}{\frac{2ab}{a+b}} = \frac{A}{H}$$

ILLUSTRATION 56: Find harmonic mean of

(a) $\frac{1}{3}, \frac{1}{7}, \frac{1}{11}, \frac{1}{15}, , ...$ n-terms (b) $\log_2 k, \log_3 k, \log_4 k, ...\log_n k$

(c) $\log_a k, \log_{a^2} k, \log_{a^3} k, ...\log_{a^n} k$

SOLUTION: Harmonic mean of $a_1, a_2, a_3, ...a_n$ is given by $\frac{n}{\left(\frac{1}{a_1}+\frac{1}{a_2}+\frac{1}{a_3}+....+\frac{1}{a_n}\right)}$

$\therefore$ HM of $\frac{1}{3}, \frac{1}{7}, \frac{1}{11}, \frac{1}{15}$, ...n-terms is given by $\frac{n}{(3+7+11+15+....\text{upto } n\text{-terms})}$

$$= \frac{n}{\frac{n}{2}\left[2(3)+(n-1)(4)\right]} = \frac{1}{(3+2n-2)} = \frac{1}{(2n+1)}$$

(b) HM of $\log_2 k$, $\log_3 k$, $\log_4 k$, ...$\log_n k$ $= \frac{(n-1)}{\log_k 2+\log_k 3+\log_k 4+...+\log_k n}$

$$= \frac{(n-1)}{\log_k (2.3.4....n)} = \frac{(n-1)}{\log_k (n!)} = (n-1)\log_{n!} k$$

(c) HM $\log_a k$, $\log_{a^2} k, \log_{a^3} k, ...\log_{a^n} k$

$$= \frac{n}{\log_k a+\log_k a^2+\log_k a^3+....+\log_k a^n} = \frac{n}{(\log_k a)(1+2+3+...n)}$$

$$= \frac{n}{\frac{n(n+1)}{2}\left[\log_k a\right]} = \frac{2}{(n+1)\log_k a} = \frac{2}{(n+1)}\log_a k$$

ILLUSTRATION 57: A boy goes from his home to school and travels part of distance by uniform speed 'u' and rest with speed 'v'. Find the ratio of both distances such that average speed of journey is

(a) AM of u and v (b) GM of u and v

(c) HM of u and v

SOLUTION: Let the boy starts his journey from point A and upto point B with uniform speed 'u' and let the time taken be t_1 and $AB = x$ .Now let he further travels from B to C with uniform speed v covering a distance $d-x$ in time t_2 as shown Figure 3.1:

FIGURE 3.1

$\therefore \quad t_1 = \frac{x}{u}$ and $t_2 = \frac{d-x}{v}$

$\therefore$ Average speed $= \frac{\text{Total distance travelled}}{\text{Total time taken}}$

i.e., $A_v = \frac{d}{\left(\frac{x}{u}+\frac{d-x}{v}\right)}$ (i)

(a) When average speed = AM of u and v

$$\Rightarrow A_v = \frac{u+v}{2} \Rightarrow \frac{d}{\left(\frac{x}{u}+\frac{d-x}{v}\right)} = \frac{u+v}{2} \Rightarrow (u+v)\left(\frac{x}{u}+\frac{d-x}{v}\right) = 2d$$

$$\Rightarrow x+\frac{u}{v}(d-x)+\frac{v}{u}x+(d-x)=2d \Rightarrow \frac{u}{v}(d-x)+\frac{v}{u}x=d \Rightarrow x\left(\frac{v}{u}-\frac{u}{v}\right)=d\left(1-\frac{u}{v}\right)$$

$$\Rightarrow x\left[\frac{v^2-u^2}{uv}\right]=d\left[\frac{v-u}{v}\right] \Rightarrow x\left(\frac{v+u}{u}\right)=d \Rightarrow \frac{x}{d}=\frac{u}{u+v} \Rightarrow \frac{d}{x}=\frac{u+v}{u} \Rightarrow \frac{d-x}{x}=\frac{v}{u}$$

$$\Rightarrow \frac{x}{d-x}=\frac{u}{v} \text{ Now } A_v=\sqrt{uv} \Rightarrow \frac{d}{\left(\frac{x}{u}+\frac{d-x}{v}\right)}=\sqrt{uv} \Rightarrow \frac{duv}{(vx+ud-ux)}=\sqrt{uv}$$

$$\Rightarrow d\sqrt{uv}=vx+ud-ux \Rightarrow d\left(\sqrt{uv}-u\right)=x(v-u)$$

$$\Rightarrow \frac{d}{x}=\frac{v-u}{\sqrt{uv}-u}=\frac{v-u}{\sqrt{u}\left(\sqrt{v}-\sqrt{u}\right)}=\frac{\sqrt{v}+\sqrt{u}}{\sqrt{u}} \Rightarrow \frac{d-x}{x}=\frac{\sqrt{v}}{\sqrt{u}} \Rightarrow \frac{x}{d-x}=\frac{\sqrt{u}}{\sqrt{v}}=\sqrt{\frac{u}{v}}$$

(c) Now $A_v=\frac{2uv}{u+v} \Rightarrow \frac{duv}{(vx+ud-ux)}=\frac{2uv}{u+v} \Rightarrow d(u+v)=2v_x+2ud-2ux$

$\Rightarrow d[u+v-2u]=x(2v-2u) \Rightarrow d(v-u)=2x(v-u)$

$\Rightarrow d=2x \Rightarrow \frac{d}{x}=2 \Rightarrow \frac{d-x}{x}=1 \Rightarrow \frac{x}{d-x}=\frac{1}{1}$ i.e., 1:1

Insertion of *n* harmonic mean between two numbers

Let a and b be two given numbers and $H_1, H_2, H_3, \ldots H_n$ are HM's between them. Then $a, H_1, H_2, H_3, \ldots, H_n, b$ will be in HP. If d is the common difference of the corresponding AP.

$\therefore\ b=(n+2)$th term of HP

$$=\frac{1}{(n+2)th \text{ term of corresponding A.P.}}$$

$$\Rightarrow b=\frac{1}{(1/a)+(n+2-1)d} \Rightarrow a/b=1+ad(n+1)$$

$$\Rightarrow \frac{a-b}{b}=ad(n+1)$$

$$\Rightarrow d=\frac{(a-b)}{(n+1)ab}$$

$$\therefore \frac{1}{H_1}=\frac{1}{a}+d;\ \frac{1}{H_2}=\frac{1}{a}+2d;\ \ldots\ldots;\frac{1}{H_n}=\frac{1}{a}+nd$$

$$\Rightarrow \frac{1}{H_1}=\frac{1}{a}+\frac{(a-b)}{(n+1)ab},\ \frac{1}{H_2}=\frac{1}{a}+\frac{2(a-b)}{(n+1)ab},\ldots\ldots,$$

$$\frac{1}{H_n}=\frac{1}{a}+\frac{n(a-b)}{(n+1)ab}$$

$$\frac{1}{H_r}=\frac{1}{a}+rd \text{ where } d=\frac{n(a-b)}{(n+1)ab}$$

ILLUSTRATION 58: Insert 4 HM between $\frac{2}{3}$ and $\frac{2}{13}$

SOLUTION: Let d be the common difference of corresponding AP.

$$\Rightarrow d=\frac{\frac{13}{2}-\frac{3}{2}}{5}=1$$

$$\therefore \frac{1}{H_1}=\frac{3}{2}+1=\frac{5}{2} \Rightarrow H_1=\frac{2}{5};\ \frac{1}{H_2}=\frac{3}{2}+2=\frac{7}{2}\ ;\Rightarrow H_2=\frac{2}{7}$$

$$\frac{1}{H_3}=\frac{3}{2}+3=\frac{9}{2} \Rightarrow H_3=\frac{2}{9};\text{ and } \frac{1}{H_4}=\frac{3}{2}+4=\frac{11}{2} \Rightarrow H_4=\frac{2}{11}$$

Thus 4 H.M's are $\frac{2}{5},\frac{2}{7},\frac{2}{9},\frac{2}{11}$

TEXTUAL EXERCISE-7 (SUBJECTIVE)

1. Find the nth term of the sequences.
   (a) $\frac{1}{3}, \frac{3}{10}, \frac{3}{11}, \frac{1}{4}, \ldots$ (b) $\frac{5}{2}, \frac{20}{13}, \frac{10}{9}, \frac{20}{23}, \ldots$
2. Find the HP whose 3rd and 14th terms are respectively 6/7 and 1/3.
3. If the sum of reciprocals of three numbers in HP be 18 and their product be 120. Find the numbers.
4. The mth term of a series in HP is n and n^{th} term is m. Then find:
   (a) $(m+n)^2$ term (b) $(mn)^{th}$ term
5. In an HP the pth term is qr and q^{th} term is pr. Prove that the rth term is pq.
6. The sum of three numbers in HP is 11 and the sum of their reciprocals 1. Find the numbers.
7. If the roots of the equation $a(b-c)x^2 + b(c-a)x + c(a-b) = 0$ be equal, then prove that a, b, c are in HP.
8. Solve the equation $6x^3 - 11x^2 + 6x - 1 = 0$, if its root are in HP.
9. If the roots of $10x^3 - cx^2 - 54x - 27 = 0$ are in HP, then find c and all the roots.
10. If a, b, c are in HP show that $\frac{a}{b+c}, \frac{b}{c+a}, \frac{c}{a+b}$ are also in HP.
11. Find n so that $\frac{a^{n+1}+b^{n+1}}{a^n+b^n}$ may be the harmonic means between a and b.
12. If x, y, z are in HP, then show that $\log(x+z) + \log(x-2y+z) = 2\log(x-z)$. when $x > z$
13. If H be HM of a and b, then find the value of $\frac{H}{a}+\frac{H}{b}-2$.
14. If $H_1, H_2 \ldots\ldots H_n$ be n HM's between a and b, then show that..... $[H_1 + a)/(H_1 - a)] + [H_n + b)/(H_n - b)] = 2n$
15. (a) If a, b, c be in HP, prove that
    (i) $[b+a)/(b-a)] + [(b+c)/(b-c)] = 2$
    (ii) $[(1/a) + (1/b) - (1/c)]\,[(1/b) + (1/c) - (1/a)] = (4/ac) - (3/b^2)$
    (iii) $[a/(b+c-a)], [b/(c+a-b)], [c/(a+b-c)]$ are in HP.
    (iv) $\{(1/a) + [1/(b+c)]\}, \{(1/b) + [1/(c+a)]\}, \{1/c) + 1/(a+b)]\}$
    (b) If $b+c, c+a, a+b$ are in HP, then prove that .... $[(b+c)/a], [(c+a)/b], [(a+b)/c]$ are in HP.

Answer Keys

1. (a) $\frac{3}{8+n}$ (b) $t_n = \frac{20}{5n+3}$ **2.** $\frac{6}{4+n}$ **3.** $\frac{1}{2}, \frac{1}{6}, \frac{1}{10}$ **4.** (a) $\frac{mn}{m+n}$ (b) 1 **6.** 6, 3, 2
8. $1, \frac{1}{2}, \frac{1}{3}$ **9.** $c = 9; \frac{-3}{5}, \frac{-3}{2}, 3$ **11.** $n = -1$ **13.** zero

TEXTUAL EXERCISE-7 (OBJECTIVE)

1. If a, b, c and d are in HP then $ab + bc + cd =$
   (a) ad (b) $2ad$
   (c) $3ad$ (d) None of these
2. If a, b, c are in HP, then the value of $\left(\frac{1}{b}+\frac{1}{c}-\frac{1}{a}\right)\left(\frac{1}{c}+\frac{1}{a}-\frac{1}{b}\right)$ is
   (a) $\frac{2}{bc}-\frac{1}{b^2}$ (b) $\frac{1}{4}\left(\frac{3}{c^2}+\frac{2}{ca}-\frac{1}{a^2}\right)$
   (c) $\frac{3}{b^2}-\frac{2}{ab}$ (d) None of these
3. If $H_n = 1 + \frac{1}{2} + \ldots + \frac{1}{n}$, then value of $1 + \frac{3}{2} + \frac{5}{3} + \ldots + \frac{2n-1}{n}$ is
   (a) $H_n + n$ (b) $2^n - H_n$
   (c) $(n-1) + H_n$ (d) $H_n + 2^n$
4. If 0.272727 ......, x and 0.727272.... are in HP, then x must be
   (a) rational (b) integer
   (c) irrational (d) None of these

Answer Keys

1. (c) **2.** (a) **3. (b)** **4.** (c)

ARITHMETICO GEOMETRIC PROGRESSION

A series formed by multiplying the corresponding terms of an AP and GP is called an Arithmetic Geometric progression. e.g., $1 + 3 + 5 + 7 + ...$ is an AP.

$1 + x + x^2 + x^3 + ...$ is a GP.

Multiplying together the terms of these series, we get, $1 + 3x + 5x^2 + 7x^3 + ...$ which is an Arithmetico Geometric Series.

Standard form: $ab + (a + d)br + (a + 2d)\, br^2 + ... + [a + (n - 1)d]br^{n-1}$

Sum to n terms of an Arithmetico Geometric Series:

Let the series be $ab + (a + d)br + (a + 2d)\, br^2 + ... + [a + (n - 1)d]br^{n-1}$

Let S_n denote the sum to n terms, then

$S_n = ab + (a + d)br + (a + 2d)\, br^2 + ... + [a + (n - 1)d]br^{n-1}$ (i)

Multiplying both sides of (*i*) by *r* we get

$r\, S_n = arb + (a + d)br^2 + (a + 2d)\, br^3 + ... + [a + (n - 2)dbr^{n-1} + [a + (n -1)d]br^n$ (ii)

Subtracting (*ii*) from (*i*) $S_n\,(1 - r) = ab + dbr + dbr^2 + ... dbr^{n-1} - [a + (n -1)\, d].br^{\,n}$

$S_n\,(1 - r) = ab + db(r + r^2 + r^3 + ... + r^{n-1}; - [a + (n - 1)\, d].br^{\,n}$

$S_n\,(1 - r) = ab + [dbr\,(1 - r^{n-1})/(1 - r)\,] - [a + (n -1)\, d].\, br^n$

$$S_n = \frac{ab}{1-r} + \frac{dbr(1-r^{n-1})}{(1-r)^2} - \frac{[a+(n-1)d]}{1-r}br^n$$

Sum to infinity terms: When $|\, r \,| < 1$

$$\therefore \quad S_\infty = \frac{ab}{1-r} + \frac{dbr}{(1-r)^2}$$

- If rth term of an AP is $T_r = Ar^3 + Br^2 + Cr + D$, then sum of n term of AP is $S_n = \sum_{r=1}^{n} T_r = A\sum_{r=1}^{n} r^3 + B\sum_{r=1}^{n} r^2 + C\sum_{r=1}^{n} r + D\sum_{r=1}^{n} 1 = A\left[\frac{n(n+1)}{2}\right]^2 + B\left[\frac{n(n+1)(2n+1)}{6}\right] + C\frac{n(n+1)}{2} + D_n$
- $\sum_{r=1}^{n} r^4 = \frac{n}{30}(n+1)(2n+1)(3n^2+3n-1)$

ILLUSTRATION 59: Find the sum of the series $1 + 2x + 3x^2 + 4x^3 + ...$

(a) to n terms (b) to infinity

SOLUTION: (a) Let sum of n terms of the series is denoted by S_n.

Then $S_n = 1 + 2x + 3x^2 + 4x^3 + ... + T_{n-1} + T_n$ (i)

$\therefore \quad xS_n = 0 + x + 2x^2 + 3x^3 + ... + xT_{n-1} + xT_n$ (ii)

Subtracting (*ii*) from (*i*), $(1-x)\, S_n = 1 + x + x^2 + x^3 + ... + (T_n - x\, T_{n-1}) - x\, T_n$ (iii)

where T_n = [nth term of 1, 2, 3, 4, ...] × [nth term of 1, x, x^2. ...] $= n.x^{n-1}$

then from (*iii*), we get $(1-x)\, S_n = 1 + x + x^2 + ... + x^{n-1} - nx^n \Rightarrow (1-x)\, S_n = \frac{1.(1-x^n)}{(1-x)} - nx^n$

$$\text{Hence } S_n = \frac{(1-x^n)}{(1-x)^2} - \frac{nx^n}{(1-x)}$$

(b) $S_\infty = 1 + 2x + 3x^2 + 4x^3 + ...+\infty$ (i)

$xS_\infty = 0 + x + 2x^2 + 3x^3 + ...+\infty$ (ii)

Subtracting (*ii*) from (*i*) we get $(1 - x)S_\infty = 1 + x + x^2 + x^3 + ...\infty = \frac{1}{1-x}$

$$\text{Hence } S_\infty = \frac{1}{(1-x)^2}$$

ILLUSTRATION 60: Find the sum of the series $1.2 + 2.2^2 + 3.2^3 + .. + 100.2^{100}$.

SOLUTION: $S = 1.2. + 2.2^2 + 3.2^3 + .. + (100).2^{100}$. (i)

$2S = 1.2^2 + 2.2^3 + .. + (99).2^{100} + (100).2^{101}$. (ii)

Subtracting (*ii*) from (*i*)

$\Rightarrow -S = 1.2 + 1.2^2 + 1.2^3 + ... + 1.2^{100} - (100).2^{101}$

$\Rightarrow -S = 1.2\left(\frac{2^{100}-1}{2-1}\right) -100.2^{101}$

$\Rightarrow S = -2^{101} + 2 + (100).2^{101} = 99.(2^{101}) + 2$

TEXTUAL EXERCISE–8 (SUBJECTIVE)

1. Sum the series upto infinite terms.

(a) $1+\frac{3}{2}+\frac{5}{2^2}+\frac{7}{2^3}+...$ (b) $1+\frac{2}{3}+\frac{1}{3}+\frac{4}{27}+...$

(c) $3+\frac{5}{4}+\frac{7}{4^2}+\frac{9}{4^3}+...$ (d) $1-\frac{3}{2}+\frac{5}{4}-\frac{7}{8}+...$

(e) $1-\frac{2}{3}+\frac{3}{3^2}-\frac{4}{3^3}+\frac{5}{3^4}-...$

2. Evaluate the following:

(a) $1 + 3x + 5x^2 + 7x^3 + ...$up to n terms. Hence find the sum to infinity when $|x| < 1$.

(b) $1 + 2x + 3x^2 + 4x^3 + ...$ up to n terms. Hence find the sum to infinity when $| x | < 1$.

(c) $2^{1/4}. 4^{1/8}.8^{1/16}.16^{1/32}$ ... up to infinite factors

3. If the sum to infinity of the series $1 + 2r + 3r^2 + 4r^3 +$ .... is 9/16 . Find r.

4. If the sum to infinity of the series $1 + (1 + d)\frac{1}{3} + (1 + 2d)\frac{1}{9}+(1+3d)\frac{1}{27}+$........ is $\frac{9}{16}$. Find d.

5. Sum of the series to n terms

(a) $1+\frac{4}{5}+\frac{7}{5^2}+\frac{10}{5^3}+...$ (b) $1+\frac{2}{5}+\frac{3}{5^2}+\frac{4}{5^3}+...$

(c) $1+\frac{2}{3}+\frac{3}{3^2}+\frac{4}{3^3}+...$

6. If $\log_a x$, $\log_a y$, $\log_a z$ are in AP, prove that x, y, z are in GP.

7. If p^{th}, q^{th} and r^{th} terms of a GP are themselves in GP show that p, q and r are in AP.

8. (a) The sum of four numbers in GP is 60 and AM of first and last is 18. Find the numbers.

(b) The AM of the two numbers exceeds the GM by 8 and the ratio of the numbers is 4. Find the numbers.

9. The sum of three numbers which are consecutive terms of an AP is 21. If the second number is reduced by 1 while the third is increased by 1, three consecutive terms of a GP result. Find these numbers.

10. (a) The first and the last two terms of an AP are a, b, c respectively. Find its sum.

(b) If $(b + c)$, $(c + a)$, $(a + b)$ are in HP show that a^2, b^2, c^2 are in AP.

(c) If the pth, qth and rth terms of an AP are in GP, then find the common ratio of the GP.

11. If A_1, A_2 be the AM's, G_1, G_2 be the GM's and H_1, H_2 be the HM's between any two numbers, then show that $\frac{G_1G_2}{H_1H_2} = \frac{A_1+A_2}{H_1+H_2}$.

12. (a) If p^{th}, q^{th}, r^{th} and s^{th} terms of an AP are in GP, then show that $(p - q)$, $(q - r)$, $(r - s)$ are also in GP.

(b) If a, b, c are in GP and $a^{\frac{1}{x}} = b^{\frac{1}{y}} = c^{\frac{1}{z}}$, prove that x, y, z are in AP.

Answer Keys

1. (a) 6 (b) 9/4 (c) 44/9 (d) 2/9 (e) 9/16

2. (a) $\frac{1}{1-x}+\frac{2x(1-x^{n-1})}{(1-x)^2}-\frac{(2n-1)x^n}{(1-x)};\frac{1}{1-x}+\frac{2x}{(1-x)^2}$ (b) $\frac{1}{1-x}+\frac{x(1-x^{n-1})}{(1-x)^2}-\frac{nx^n}{1-x};\frac{1}{1-x}+\frac{x(1-x^{n-1})}{(1-x)^2}$ (c) 2

3. –1/3 **4.** –5/4 **5.** (a) $\frac{35}{16}-\frac{(12n+7)}{16(5)^{n-1}}$ (b) $\frac{25}{16}-\frac{(4n+5)}{16}\frac{1}{(5)^{n-1}}$ (c) $\frac{9}{4}-\frac{(2n+3)}{4}\frac{1}{(3)^{n-1}}$

8. (a) 4, 8, 16, 32 (b) 64, 16

9. 3, 7, 11 or 12, 7, 2 **10.** (a) $\frac{(2c-a-b)(a+c))}{2(c-b)}$ (c) $\frac{r-q}{q-p}$

TEXTUAL EXERCISE–8 (OBJECTIVE)

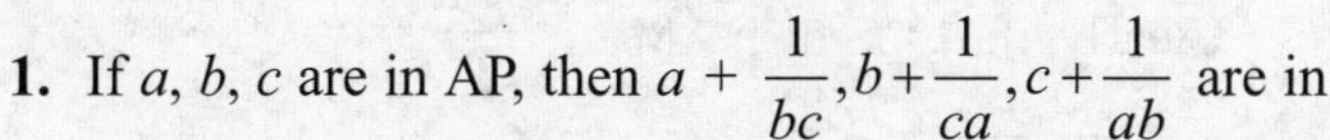

1. If a, b, c are in AP, then $a+\frac{1}{bc}, b+\frac{1}{ca}, c+\frac{1}{ab}$ are in

(a) AP (b) GP
(c) HP (d) None of these

2. If $\frac{a+b}{1-ab}, b, \frac{b+c}{1-bc}$ are in AP, then a^{-1}, b, c^{-1} are in

(a) AP (b) GP
(c) HP (d) None of these

3. If x, $2y$, $3z$ are in AP, where the distinct numbers x, y, z are in GP, then the common ratio of the GP is

(a) 3 (b) $\frac{1}{3}$
(c) 2 (d) $\frac{1}{2}$

4. If a, b, c, are in AP then $3^a, 3^b, 3^c$ are in

(a) GP (b) HP
(c) AP (d) None of these

5. If $a - b$, $ax - by$, $ax^2 - by^2 (a, b, \neq 0)$ are in GP, then x, y, $\frac{ax-by}{a-b}$ are in

(a) AP only (b) GP only
(c) AP and GP (d) None of these

6. If a, b, c, are in AP, a mb, c are in GP, then a, m^2b, c are in

(a) HP (b) GP
(c) AP (d) None of these

7. If a, b, c are in GP then $a + b$, $2b$, $b + c$ are in

(a) AP (b) GP
(c) HP (d) None of these

8. If $x > 1$, $y > 1$, $z > 1$ are in GP, then $\frac{1}{1+In\,x}, \frac{1}{1+In\,y}, \frac{1}{1+In\,z}$ are in:

(a) AP (b) GP
(c) HP (d) None of these

9. Suppose a, b, c are in AP and a^2, b^2, c^2 are in GP If $a < b < c$ and $a + b + c = \frac{3}{2}$, then the value of a is

(a) $\frac{1}{2\sqrt{2}}$ (b) $\frac{1}{2\sqrt{3}}$
(c) $\frac{1}{2}-\frac{1}{\sqrt{3}}$ (d) $\frac{1}{2}-\frac{1}{\sqrt{2}}$

10. The sum to infinity of the series $1 - 3x + 5x^2 - 7x^3 + \ldots \infty$, $|x| < 1$, is

(a) $\frac{(1-x)}{(1+x)^2}$ (b) $\frac{1+x}{(1+x)^2}$
(c) $\frac{(1-x)}{(1-x)^2}$ (d) None of these

11. If $3+\frac{1}{4}(3+d)+\frac{1}{4^2}(3+2d)+\ldots+up\ to\ \infty = 8$, then the value of d is

(a) 9 (b) 5
(c) 1 (d) None of these

12. The sum of $0.2 + 0.004 + 0.00006 + 0.0000008 + \ldots + \infty$; is

(a) $\frac{200}{891}$ (b) $\frac{2000}{9801}$
(c) $\frac{1000}{9801}$ (d) None of these

13. Let a, b be two positive numbers, where $a > b$ and $4 \times GM = 5 \times HM$ for the numbers, then a is

(a) $4b$ (b) 1/4
(c) $2b$ (d) b

14. If the first and the $(2n - 1)$ th terms of an AP, a GP and HP, are equal and their nth terms are a, b and c respectively, then

(a) $a = b = c$ (b) $a < b < c$
(c) $a + c = b$ (d) $ac - b^2 = 0$

Answer Keys

1. (a) **2.** (a) **3.** (b) **4.** (a) **5.** (c) **6.** (a) **7.** (c) **8.** (c) **9.** (d) **10.** (a)
11. (a) **12.** (b) **13.** (a) **14.** (d)

Inequality of means

If A, G and H are respectively AM, GM and HM, of a and b both being unequal and positive, then

$\Rightarrow$ $G^2 = AH$

and $A \geq G \geq H$ and every mean must lie between the minimum and the maximum terms.

$A = G = H$ iff all terms whose mean is taken are equal otherwise $A > G > H$.

$\Rightarrow$ If sum of the given positive numbers is constant, then their product will be maximum if numbers are equal and it the product of given positive numbers is constant then, their sum will be minimum, if the numbers are equal.

Proof: Let a and b be two positive numbers and A, G, H be AM, GM, HM, of these two numbers, then AM = $\frac{a+b}{2}$ and GM = $\sqrt{ab}$, HM = $\frac{2ab}{a+b}$ $\Rightarrow G^2 = ab$ and $AH = ab \Rightarrow G^2 = AH$. Since $(\sqrt{a} - \sqrt{b})^2 \geq 0 \Rightarrow a + b \geq 2\sqrt{ab} \Rightarrow \frac{a+b}{2} \geq \sqrt{ab}$ (i)

In (i) replacing a by 1/a, b by 1/b, we get

$$\frac{1/a+1/b}{2} \geq \sqrt{\frac{1}{a}\cdot\frac{1}{b}} \Rightarrow \frac{a+b}{2ab} \geq \frac{1}{\sqrt{ab}} \quad \text{(ii)}$$

$$\Rightarrow \frac{2ab}{a+b} \leq \sqrt{ab} \quad \text{(ii)}$$

Thus from (i) and (ii) we note that

$$\frac{a+b}{2} \geq \sqrt{ab} \geq \frac{2ab}{a+b} \quad \text{(iii)}$$

and $\frac{2ab}{a+b} \geq a$ as $\Rightarrow 1+\frac{a}{b} \leq 2$ for $a \leq b$

$$\Rightarrow \frac{b+a}{b} \leq 2$$

$$\Rightarrow \frac{2b}{a+b} \geq 1 \Rightarrow \frac{2ab}{a+b} \geq a \quad \text{(iv)}$$

and $\frac{a+b}{2} \leq b$ as $a \leq b \Rightarrow a+b \leq 2b$

$$\frac{a+b}{2} \leq b \quad \text{(v)}$$

from (iii), (iv) and (v) we note that

$$a \leq \frac{2ab}{a+b} \leq \sqrt{ab} \leq \frac{a+b}{2} \leq b$$

Thus AM $\geq$ GM $\geq$ HM and all means lie between a and b i.e., minimum and maximum terms.

$\Rightarrow$ AM $\geq$ GM $\geq$ HM

Clearly, if $a = b$, then AM = $\frac{a+a}{2} = a$,

GM = $\sqrt{a.a} = \sqrt{a^2} = |a| = a$ as a > 0

HM = $\frac{2a.a}{a+a} = \frac{2a^2}{2a} = a$

$\therefore$ AM = GM = HM for $a = b$ and AM > GM > HM for $a \neq$ b. If sum $a + b$ is constant = $S(say)$, then GM $\leq$ AM

$$\Rightarrow \sqrt{ab} \leq \frac{S}{2} \Rightarrow ab \leq \left(\frac{S}{2}\right)^2$$

$\Rightarrow$ Product of terms is maximum = $\left(\frac{S}{2}\right)^2$, provided both a and b are equal to S/2

Now if the product of terms is constant = $P(say)$, then

AM $\geq$ GM $\Rightarrow \frac{a+b}{2} \geq \sqrt{ab}$

$\Rightarrow a+b \geq 2\sqrt{P} \Rightarrow a+b \geq \sqrt{P}+\sqrt{P}$

$\Rightarrow$ sum of terms is minimum if each of the terms are equal to $\sqrt{P}$.

Conditions

Inequality $A \geq G \geq H$ can be used only for n positive terms $(n \geq 2)$ (think why?) and generally subjected to following conditions:

(a) If sum of terms is given and maximum value of product is to be obtained.

(b) If product of terms is given and minimum value of sum is to be obtained.

(c) For negative real numbers a, and b. AM $\leq$ GM $\leq$ HM

ILLUSTRATION 61: If $a,b,c > 0$, then prove that $\frac{a}{b}+\frac{b}{c}+\frac{c}{a} \geq 3$.

SOLUTION: Using the relation AM $\geq$ GM, we have

$$\frac{\frac{a}{b}+\frac{b}{c}+\frac{c}{a}}{3} \geq \left(\frac{a}{b}\cdot\frac{b}{c}\cdot\frac{c}{a}\right)^{1/3} \Rightarrow \frac{a}{b}+\frac{b}{c}+\frac{c}{a} \geq 3$$

ILLUSTRATION 62: If $a_i > 0 \ \forall \ i \in \mathbb{N}$ such that $\prod_{i=1}^{n} a_i = 1$, then prove that $(1+a_1)(1+a_2)(1+a_3)\ldots\ldots(1+a_n) \geq 2^n$

SOLUTION: Using AM ≥ GM on a_i and 1, we get

$$1+a_1 \geq 2\sqrt{a_1}$$
$$1+a_2 \geq 2\sqrt{a_2}$$
$$\vdots$$
$$1+a_n \geq 2\sqrt{a_n}$$

$\Rightarrow (1+a_1)(1+a_2)\ldots\ldots(1+a_n) \geq 2^n (a_1a_2a_3\ldots a_n)^{1/2}$

As $a_1 a_2 a_3 \ldots\ldots a_n = 1$

Hence $(1+a_1)(1+a_2)\ldots\ldots(1+a_n) \geq 2^n$

ILLUSTRATION 63: If $n > 0$, then prove that $2^n > 1 + n\sqrt{2^{n-1}}$

SOLUTION: Using the relation AM ≥ GM on the numbers $1, 2, 2^2, 2^3 \ldots\ldots, 2^{n-1}$ we have,

$$\frac{1+2+2^2+\ldots+2^{n-1}}{n} \geq \left(1.2.2^2.2^3\ldots..2^{n-1}\right)^{1/n}$$

Equality does not hold as all the numbers are not equal

$$\Rightarrow \frac{2^n-1}{2-1} > n\left(2^{\frac{(n-1)n}{2}}\right)^{\frac{1}{n}} \qquad \Rightarrow 2^n - 1 > n\, 2^{\frac{(n-1)}{2}}$$

$$\Rightarrow 2^n > 1 + n\, 2^{\frac{(n-1)}{2}}$$

ILLUSTRATION 64: Find the greatest value of uvw for positive value of u,v,w subject to the condition $uv + vw + wu = 12$

SOLUTION: Using the relation AM ≥ GM

$$\frac{uv+vw+wu}{3} \geq \left(u^2v^2w^2\right)^{1/3}$$

$\Rightarrow 4 \geq (uvw)^{2/3} \Rightarrow uvw \leq 8$

∴ The greatest value of uvw is 8.

ILLUSTRATION 65: If $xyz = 3$, then find $(xy + yz + zx)_{min}$.

SOLUTION: $\frac{xy+yz+zx}{3} \geq \sqrt[3]{(xyz)^2} \Rightarrow xy + yz + zx \geq 3\sqrt[3]{9} \quad \therefore \quad (xy + yz + zx)_{min} = 3\sqrt[3]{9}$

ILLUSTRATION 66: If $x \in (0, 3)$, find $[x(3-x)]_{max}$

SOLUTION: As $x \in (0, 3)$, it implies $x, 3 - x > 0$ therefore by using AM ≥ GM we get,

$$\frac{x+3-x}{2} \geq [x(3-x)]^{1/2} \Rightarrow [x(3-x)]^{1/2} \leq \frac{3}{2}$$

$$\Rightarrow x(3-x) \leq \left(\frac{3}{2}\right)^2 = \frac{9}{4} \qquad \therefore \ [x(3-x)]_{max} = \frac{9}{4}$$

ILLUSTRATION 67: If a, b, c are the sides of a triangle and $s = \frac{a+b+c}{2}$, then prove that $8(s-a)(s-b)(s-c) \leq abc$.

SOLUTION: Let $x = s - a$, $y = s - b$, $z = s - c$, then $a = y + z$, $b = x + z$, $c = x + y$

then the inequality reduces to $8xyz \leq (x + y)(y + z)(x + z)$ for all $x, y, z \geq 0$

which follows easily from AM ≥ GM inequality i.e.,

$x + y \geq 2\sqrt{xy}$, $y + z \geq 2\sqrt{yz}$, $x + z \geq 2\sqrt{xz}$ $\quad\therefore\quad (x + y)(y + z)(x + z) \geq 8xyz$

ILLUSTRATION 68: Show that $x + 1/x \geq 2$, if $x > 0$ and $x + 1/x \leq -2$, if $x < 0$.

SOLUTION: Since $x > 0$, $\frac{1}{2}(x+1/x) \geq \sqrt{x.\frac{1}{x}}$ (AM ≥ GM)

$\Rightarrow x + 1/x \geq 2$

If $x < 0$, let $y = -x$, then $y > 0$ and $y + 1/y \geq 2$

$\Rightarrow -x - 1/x \geq 2 \Rightarrow x + 1/x \leq -2$

ILLUSTRATION 69: If a_i's are all positive real numbers, then prove that $(1 + a_1 + a_1^2)(1 + a_2 + a_2^2) \ldots (1 + a_n + a_n^2) \geq 3^n a_1 a_2 \ldots a_n$

SOLUTION: $\frac{1+a_i+a_i^2}{3} \geq (1.a_i.a_i^2)^{1/3} = a_i$ $(i = 1, 2, 3, \ldots, n)$

$\Rightarrow 1+a_i+a_i^2 \geq 3a_i$ $\quad \Rightarrow (1 + a_1 + a_1^2)(1 + a_2 + a_2^2) \ldots (1 + a_n + a_n^2) \geq 3^n a_1 a_2 \ldots a_n$

ILLUSTRATION 70: If x, y, z are positive real numbers, such that $x + y + z = a$, then prove that $\frac{1}{x}+\frac{1}{y}+\frac{1}{z} \geq \frac{9}{a}$.

SOLUTION: Since AM ≥ HM $\frac{x+y+z}{3} \geq \frac{3}{x^{-1}+y^{-1}+z^{-1}}$ $\quad \Rightarrow \frac{1}{x}+\frac{1}{y}+\frac{1}{z} \geq \frac{9}{a}$

ILLUSTRATION 71: By inequality of means show that

(a) $2^n(n!) \leq (n + 1)^n$; $n \in \mathbb{N}$

(b) $(n + 1)(2n + 1)^n \geq 6^n(n!)^2$; $n \in \mathbb{N}$

(c) $n^n\left(\frac{n+1}{2}\right)^{2n} > (n!)^3$; $n \in \mathbb{N}$

SOLUTION: (a) Applying AM ≥ GM for 1st n natural numbers we get,

$$\frac{\sum_{k=1}^{n} k}{n} \geq \left(\prod_{k=1}^{n} k\right)^{\frac{1}{n}}$$

$$\Rightarrow \frac{n+1}{2} \geq (n!)^{\frac{1}{n}}$$

$\Rightarrow 2^n(n!) \leq (n + 1)^n$

(b) Applying AM ≥ GM for square of 1st n natural numbers we get,

$$\frac{\Sigma k^2}{n} \geq ((n!)^2)^{\frac{1}{n}} \quad \Rightarrow \left[\frac{(n+1)(2n+1)}{6}\right]^n \geq (n!)^2$$

$\Rightarrow ((n + 1)(2n + 1))^n \geq 6^n (n!)^2$

(c) Applying AM ≥ GM of $1^3, 2^3, 3^3, \ldots\ldots, n^3$ we get,

$$\frac{\left(\frac{n(n+1)}{2}\right)^2}{n} \geq (n!)^{\frac{3}{n}} \quad \Rightarrow \frac{n(n+1)^2}{4} \geq (n!)^{\frac{3}{n}}$$

$$\Rightarrow n^n\left(\frac{n+1}{2}\right)^{2n} \geq (n!)^3$$

ILLUSTRATION 72: If a, b, c are positive real numbers such that $a + b + c = 18$ find the maximum value of $a^k b^m c^n$.

SOLUTION: $a + b + c = 18 \Rightarrow k.\frac{a}{k} + m\frac{b}{m} + n.\frac{c}{n} = 18$

$$\Rightarrow \left(\left(\frac{a}{k}\right)^k \cdot \left(\frac{b}{m}\right)^m \cdot \left(\frac{c}{n}\right)^n\right)^{1/k+m+n} \leq \frac{1}{k+m+n}\left(k.\frac{a}{k} + m\frac{b}{m} + n.\frac{c}{n}\right) \text{ (by using AM} \geq \text{GM)}$$

$$\Rightarrow \left(\frac{a^k b^m c^n}{k^k m^m n^n}\right)^{\frac{1}{k+m+n}} \leq \frac{18}{k+m+n}$$

$$\Rightarrow a^k\, b^m\, c^n \leq l^{k+m+n}\,.\, k^k\,.\, m^m.n^n$$

Where $l = 18/(k+m+n)$

Thus the maximum value of $a^k b^m c^n$ is $l^{k+m+n} . k^k . m^m.n^n$, where $l = 18/(k+m+n)$.

Here, equality will hold when $a^k b^m c^n \leq k^k m^m n^n \left(\frac{18}{k+m+n}\right)$

$$\Rightarrow a = a^k b^m c^n \leq (k)^{k+m+n} k^k .m^m .n^n \text{ where } l = \frac{18}{k+m+n}$$

TEXTUAL EXERCISE–9 (SUBJECTIVE)

1. If a, b, c are positive real numbers, prove that $a^3 + b^3 + c^3 \geq 3abc$.
2. If a, b, c are all positive sides of Δ, prove that $abc \geq (a + b - c)(b + c - a)(c + a - b)$.
3. If a, b, c are distinct positive real numbers, then show that $\frac{b^3+c^3}{b+c} + \frac{c^3+a^3}{c+a} + \frac{a^3+b^3}{a+b} > ab + bc + ca$.
4. If a, b, c, x, y, z are all positive, prove that
   (a) $(a + b + c)(ab + bc + ca) \geq 9abc$
   (b) $(x+y+z)\left(\frac{1}{x}+\frac{1}{y}+\frac{1}{z}\right) \geq 9$
   (c) $\left(\frac{x}{a}+\frac{y}{b}+\frac{z}{c}\right)\left(\frac{a}{x}+\frac{b}{y}+\frac{c}{z}\right) \geq 9$
   (d) $(a + b)(b + c)(c + a) \geq 8abc$
5. If $x + y + z = a$ and x, y, z are positive numbers, then show that $(a - x)(a - y)(a - z) \geq 8xyz$.
6. If a, b, c, be lengths of sides of a Δ then prove that $(a + b + c)^3 \geq 27(a + b - c)(b + c - a)(c + a - b)$
7. If A, B, C are acute angles, then prove that cotA . cotB. cotC $\leq 1/3\sqrt{3}$.
8. If a, b, c are sides of a triangle then show that area of triangle Δ satisfies following inequalities:
   (a) $\Delta < s^2/4$ (b) $\Delta \leq s^2/3\sqrt{3}$
9. Using a fixed length (l cm) a rectangle has to be formed, what should be the dimension of rectangle so that its area enclosed is maximum?
10. Find the minimum perimeter rectangle out of all the rectangles of area 100 cm^2.
11. If sum of the lengths of all edges of cuboids is given as 12cm. Then find the dimension of that cuboid which is of maximum volume.
12. Prove that for all cuboids of a given volume (v) the one having minimum surface area is a cube and find the minimum surface area of a cuboid out of all such cuboids having volume 10,00 cm^3.
13. Find the least value of $(3x + 4y)$, when $x^2y^3 = 6$, where x, y are positive real numbers.
14. Find the greatest value of x^2y^3, when $x + y = c\ \forall$ positive and real real x and y.
15. (a) Find the maximum value of the product $x.(1 - x)$ $\forall\, x \in (0, 1)$.
    (b) Find the minimum value of the
    (*i*) $\frac{x^3+x^2+2x}{x^2}$; $x > 0$
    (*ii*) $\frac{x^3+x+2}{x}$; $x > 0$

(c) If $x + y + z = 10$; where x, y, z are + *ve* real numbers, then evaluate

(*i*) $(xyz)_{max}$

(*ii*) $(x^2 y^3 z)_{max}$

16. (a) If the three positive unequal quantities a, b, c be in HP then prove that $a^n + c^n > 2b^n, n \in \mathbb{N}$.

(b) If the three positive unequal quantities a, b, c be in GP, then prove that $a^n + c^n > 2b^n, n \in \mathbb{N}$

Answer Keys

9. $A_{max} = l^2/16$ cm^2, length = breadth = $l/4$ cm **10.** 40 cm **11.** $V_{max} = 1$ cm^3; $l = b = h = 1$ cm

12. 600 cm^2 **13.** 10 **14.** $\dfrac{108c^5}{3125}$

15. (a) 1/4 at $x = 1/2$ (b) (*i*) $1+2\sqrt{2}$ (*ii*) 4

(c) (*i*) 1000/27 at $x = y = z = 10/3$ (*ii*) $\dfrac{4\times5^6}{27}$ at $x = 10/3$; $y = 5$; $z = 5/3$

TEXTUAL EXERCISE–9 (OBJECTIVE)

1. If $a + b + c = 3$; $a > 0, b > 0, c > 0$, then the greatest value of $a^2b^3c^2$ is

(a) $\dfrac{3^{10}.2^4}{7^7}$ (b) $\dfrac{3^9.2^4}{7^7}$

(c) $\dfrac{3^8.2^4}{7^7}$ (d) None of these

2. The least value of $2\log_{100}a - \log_a 0.0001$, $a > 1$, is

(a) 2 (b) 3

(c) 4 (d) None of these

3. x, y, z are positive then the minimum value of $x^{(\log y - \log z)} + y^{(\log z - \log x)} + z^{(\log x - \log y)}$ is

(a) 3 (b) 1

(c) 9 (d) 16

4. If $a > 0, b > 0, c > 0$ and the minimum value of $a(b^2 + c^2) + b(c^2 + a^2) + c(a^2 + b^2)$ is λabc, then λ is

(a) 2 (b) 1

(c) 6 (d) 3

5. If three positive real numbers a, b, c are in A.P. such that $abc = 4$, then the minimum possible value of b is

(a) $2^{3/2}$ (b) $2^{2/3}$

(c) $2^{1/3}$ (d) $2^{5/2}$

6. If x, y, z are three real numbers of the same sign, then the value of $\dfrac{x}{y}+\dfrac{y}{z}+\dfrac{z}{x}$ lies in the interval

(a) $[2, \infty)$ (b) $[3, \infty)$

(c) $(3, \infty)$ (d) $(-\infty, 3)$

7. If a, b, c are three positive real numbers such that $b + c - a$, $c + a - b$ and $a + b - c$ are positive, the expression $(a + b - c)(b + c - a)(c + a - b) - abc$ is

(a) positive (b) negative

(c) non-positive (d) non-negative

Answer Keys

1. (a) **2.** (c) **3.** (a) **4.** (c) **5.** (b) **6.**(b) **7.** (b)

■ (Σ) SIGMA NOTATION

The symbol Σ(*sigma*) represents the sum of similar terms. Usually, sum of n terms of any series is represented by placing S before the nth term of the series. But if we have to find the sum of k terms of a series whose nth term is u_n then this will be represented by $\sum_{n=1}^{k} u_n$.

NOTE

Shortly S is written in place of $\sum_{1}^{n}$.

- If nth term of sequence is given by $T_n = an^3 + bn^2 + cn + d$ when a, b, c, d are constants, then sum of n terms $S_n = \Sigma T_n = a\,\Sigma n^3 + b\Sigma n^2 + c\Sigma n + \Sigma d$

Properties

(a) $\sum_{r=1}^{n}(a_r \pm b_r) = \sum_{r=1}^{n} a_r \pm \sum_{r=1}^{n} b_r$

(b) $\sum_{r=1}^{n} ka_r = k\sum_{r=1}^{n} a_r$

(c) $\sum_{i=1}^{m} a = a + a + a + \ldots m \text{ terms} = am$

(d) $\sum_{r=1}^{n} r = 1 + 2 + 3 + \ldots + n = \dfrac{n(n+1)}{2}$

(e) $\sum_{r=1}^{n} r^2 = 1^2 + 2^2 + 3^2 + \ldots n^2 = \dfrac{n(n+1)(2n+1)}{6}$

(e) ***Proof:*** Consider the identity $(x + 1)^3 - x^3 = 3x^2 + 3x + 1$

Putting $x = 1, 2, 3, \ldots, (n - 1), n$ successively, we get

$2^3 - 1^3 = 3.1^2 + 3.1 + 1$

$3^3 - 2^3 = 3.2^2 + 3.2 + 1$

$4^3 - 3^3 = 3.3^2 + 3.3 + 1$

....

$n^3 - (n - 1)^3 = 3.(n - 1)^2 + 3.(n - 1) + 1$

and $(n + 1)^3 - n^3 = 3.n^2 + 3.n + 1$

Adding vertically $(n + 1)^3 - 1^3 = 3.(1^2 + 2^2 + \ldots n^2) + 3(1 + 2 + 3 + \ldots + n) + \underbrace{1 + 1 + \ldots + 1}_{n \text{ terms}}$

$$\Rightarrow n^3 + 3n^2 + 3n = 3\left(\sum_{k=1}^{n} k^2\right) + 3\frac{n(n+1)}{2} + n$$

$$\left[\because \sum_{k=1}^{n} k = \frac{n(n+1)}{2}\right]$$

$$\Rightarrow 3\left(\sum_{k=1}^{n} k^2\right) = n^3 + 3n^2 + 3n - \left[\frac{3n(n+1)}{2} + n\right]$$

$$\Rightarrow 3\left(\sum_{k=1}^{n} k^2\right) = \frac{2n^3 + 3n^2 + n}{2} = \frac{n(n+1)(2n+1)}{2}$$

$$\Rightarrow \sum_{k=1}^{n} k^2 = \frac{n(n+1)(2n+1)}{6}$$

Hence, $S_n = \sum_{k=1}^{n} k^2 = 1^2 + 2^2 + \ldots + n^2 = \dfrac{n(n+1)(2n+1)}{6}$

(f) $\sum_{r=1}^{n} r^3 = \left[\dfrac{n(n+1)}{2}\right]^2$

(f) ***Proof:*** Consider the sequence of cubes of the natural numbers,

viz., $1^3, 2^3, 3^3, \ldots, n^3, (n + 1)^3, \ldots$

Let S_n denote the sum to n terms of this sequence i.e.,

$S_n = 1^3 + 2^3 + 3^3 + \ldots + n^3 = \sum_{k=1}^{n} k^3$

Consider the identity $(x + 1)^4 - x^4 = 4x^3 + 6x^2 + 4x + 1$ (i)

Putting $x = 1, 2, 3, \ldots, (n - 1), n$ successively, we get

$2^4 - 1^4 = 4.1^3 + 6.1^2 + 4.1 + 1$

$3^4 - 2^4 = 4.2^3 + 6.2^2 + 4.2 + 1$

$4^4 - 3^4 = 4.3^3 + 6.3^2 + 4.3 + 1$

... ...

$n^4 - (n - 1)^4 = 4(n - 1)^3 + 6(n - 1)^2 + 4(n - 1) + 1$

$(n + 1)^4 - n^4 = 4.n^3 + 6.n^2 + 4.n + 1$

Adding column wise, we get $(n + 1)^4 - 1^4 = 4.(1^3 + 2^3 + \ldots + n^3) + 6(1^2 + 2^2 + 3^2 + \ldots + n^2) + 4(1 + 2 + 3 + \ldots + n) + \underbrace{1 + 1 + \ldots + 1}_{n \text{ terms}}$

$$\Rightarrow n^4 + 4n^3 + 6n^2 + 4n = 4\left(\sum_{k=1}^{n} k^3\right) + 6\left(\sum_{k=1}^{n} k^2\right) + 4\left(\sum_{k=1}^{n} k\right) + n$$

$$\Rightarrow n^4 + 4n^3 + 6n^2 + 4n = 4\left(\sum_{k=1}^{n} k^3\right) + 6\left(\frac{n(n+1)(2n+1)}{6}\right) + 4\left(\frac{n(n+1)}{2}\right) + n$$

$$\Rightarrow 4\left(\sum_{k=1}^{n} k^3\right) = n^4 + 4n^3 + 6n^2 + 4n - n(n + 1)(2n + 1) - 2n(n + 1) - n$$

$$\Rightarrow 4\left(\sum_{k=1}^{n} k^3\right) = n^4 + 2n^3 + n^2 = n^2(n + 1)^2$$

$$\Rightarrow \sum_{k=1}^{n} k^3 = \frac{n^2(n+1)^2}{4} \Rightarrow \sum_{k=1}^{n} k^3 = \left(\frac{n(n+1)}{2}\right)^2 = \left(\sum_{k=1}^{n} k\right)^2$$

Hence,

$$\sum_{k=1}^{n} k^3 = 1^3 + 2^3 + \ldots + n^3 = \left(\frac{n(n+1)}{2}\right)^2 = \left(\sum_{k=1}^{n} k\right)^2$$

(g) $\sum_{r=1}^{n} r^4 = \dfrac{n}{30}(n+1)(2n+1)(3n^2 + 3n - 1)$

(h) $\sum_{n=1}^{n} n^a$ or $Sn^a = 1^a + 2^a + 3^a + \ldots + n^a$

(*i*) If rth term of an AP is given by

$T_r = Ar^3 + Br^2 + Cr + D$, then sum of n terms of AP is

$$S_n = \sum_{r=1}^{n} T_r = A\sum_{r=1}^{n} r^3 + B\sum_{r=1}^{n} r^2 + C\sum_{r=1}^{n} r + D\sum_{r=1}^{n} 1$$

NOTE

If nth term of sequence is given by $T_n = an^3 + bn^2 + cn + d$ *when a, b, c, d are constants, then sum of n terms* $S_n = \Sigma T_n = a\,\Sigma n^3 + b\Sigma n^2 + c\Sigma n + \Sigma d$

ILLUSTRATION 73: Find the sum of n terms of series 1.3 + 3.5 + 5.7 + ...

SOLUTION: T_n = [n^{th} term of 1.3.5...] × [n^{th} term of 3, 5, 7...]

or $T_n = [\,1 + (n-1) \times 2] \times [3 + (n-1) \times 2]$

or $T_n = (2n-1)(2n+1) = (4n^2-1)$ $\qquad \therefore\ S_n = \Sigma\, T_n = \Sigma\,(4n^2-1)$

$= 4.\Sigma\, n^2 - \Sigma\, 1 = \dfrac{4\times n(n+1)(2n+1)}{6} - n = \dfrac{2}{3}\, n\,(n+1)\,(2n+1) - n$

ILLUSTRATION 74: Find the sum of the series $1.n + 2.(n-1) + 3.(n-2) + .. + n\,.1$

SOLUTION: Here n occurs in each term, therefore for general we will find the rth term

Since r^{th} term of the sequence 1, 2, 3 ... = $1 + (r-1).1 = r$

and r^{th} term of the sequence $n, n-1, n-2, ... = n + (r-1)(-1)$

Now r^{th} term $t_r = \{1 + (r-1).1\}\ \{\,n + (r-1)(-1)\}$

$= r\,(n - r + 1) = nr - r^2 + r \;\therefore\; S_n = \sum_{r=1}^{n} t_r = \sum_{r=1}^{n} (nr - r^2 + r)$

$= n\sum_{r=1}^{n} r - \sum_{r=1}^{n} r^2 + \sum_{r=1}^{n} r = \dfrac{n(n+1)}{2}\left(n - \dfrac{2n+1}{3} + 1\right) = \dfrac{n(n+1)}{2}.\dfrac{(3n-2n-1+3)}{3} = \dfrac{n(n+1)(n+2)}{6}$

Double sigma notation

$\sum_{j=1}^{m}\sum_{i=1}^{n} a_{ij}$ stands for summation of elements of two dimentional array (arrangement) $m \times n$ of terms (i.e., arranged along n-horizontal rows and n-vertical columns) the sum of elements a_{ij} where a_{ij}, is function of two variables i and j such that i and $j \in \mathbb{N}$. " It can also be regarded as summation of summation of series".

Notation Since Double Sigma $\left(\sum_{j=1}^{m}\sum_{i=1}^{n} T_{ij}\right)$ represents the summation of summation of series and theorefore it can be represented as dimensional array of numbers on a rectagular Matrix ($m \times n$) and in which the **general** term is represented by T_{ij} where i denotes the row index (*row position*) and j denotes the column index (*column position*) of the term.

ΣΣ (Double Sigma) has following properties.

P1. **General element:** T_{ij} (i → Row index, j → Column index) is the element placed in i^{th} row and j^{th} column. e.g.,

T_{14} is element placed in 1st row and 4th column, T_{41} is element placed in 4th row and 1st column.

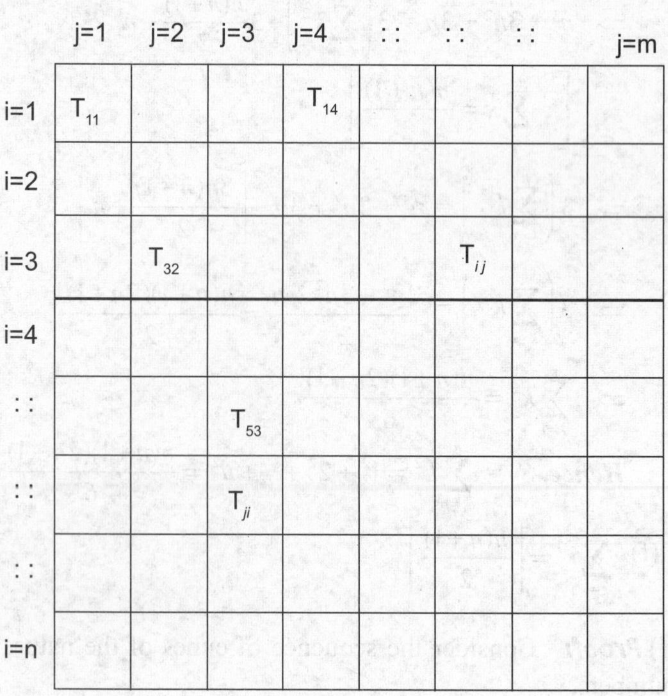

	j=1	j=2	j=3	j=4	: :	: :	: :	j=m
i=1	T_{11}			T_{14}				
i=2								
i=3		T_{32}				T_{ij}		
i=4								
: :			T_{53}					
: :			T_{ji}					
: :								
i=n								

FIGURE 3.2

ILLUSTRATION 75: Evaluate : $\sum\sum_{1\le i<j\le n} i.j$

SOLUTION: Let us first understand the equation.

It means sum of product of n-numbers taken two at a time

i.e., $1.2 + 1.3 + 1.4 + 1.5 + ...+ 1.n$

$+ 2.3 + 2.4 + 2.5 + ...+ 2n$

$+ 3.4 + 3.5 + ...+ 3.n$

....

$+ (n-1).n$

Method 1: $$\sum\sum_{1\le i<j\le n} i.j = \sum j\sum_{i=1}^{j-1} i = \sum_{j=2}^{n}\frac{j(j-1)j}{2} = \frac{1}{2}\sum_{j=1}^{n}(j^3 - j^2)$$

$$= \frac{1}{2}\left[\left(\frac{n(n+1)}{2}\right)^2 - \frac{n(n+1)(2n+1)}{6}\right] = \frac{n(n-1)}{24}(3n^2 - n - 2) = \frac{n(n+1)(3n^2+2)(n-1)}{24}$$

Method 2: We know that, $(a + b + c + d)^2 = a^2 + b^2 + c^2 + d^2 + 2(ab + ac + ab + bc + bd + cd)$

$(1 + 2 + 3 + ... + n)^2 = (1^2 + 2^2 + ... + n^2) + 2\,[1.2 + 1.3 + 1.4 + ... + 1.n$

$+ 2.3 + 2.4 + ... + 2.n$

....

$+ (n-1)\,n\,]$

$$\left(\sum_{r=1}^{n} r\right)^2 = \sum_{r=1}^{n} r^2 + 2\,(\text{Required sum})$$

$\Rightarrow$ 2 (Required sum)

$$= \left(\frac{n(n+1)}{2}\right) - \frac{n(n+1)(2n+1)}{6} = \frac{n(n+1)}{2}\left[\frac{n(n+1)}{2} - \frac{2n+1}{3}\right] = \frac{n(n+1)(3n+2)(n-1)}{24}$$

ILLUSTRATION 76: Evaluate the following double summations.

(i) $\sum_{j=1}^{10}\sum_{i=1}^{20} k$

(ii) $\sum_{j=1}^{10}\sum_{i=1}^{20} (i+j)$

SOLUTION: $$\sum_{j=1}^{10}\sum_{i=1}^{20} k = \sum_{j=1}^{10}(k+k+k+...+k) = \sum_{j=1}^{10} 20k$$

$$= 20\sum_{j=1}^{10} k = 20\,(k + k + k + ... + k)\ (10 \text{ times}) = 20\,(10\,k) = 300\,k.$$

(ii) $$\sum_{j=1}^{10}(i+j) = \sum_{j=1}^{10}(1+j)+(2+j)+(3+j)+....+(20+j)....[j \text{ braces}]$$

$$= 10 + \sum_{j=1}^{10} j + 20 + \sum_{j=1}^{10} j + 30 + \sum_{j=1}^{10} j + ... + 200\sum_{j=1}^{10} j = 10\left\{\frac{(20)(21)}{2}\right\} + 20\sum_{j=1}^{10} j$$

$$= 2100 + \frac{20(10)(11)}{2} = 2100 + 1100 = 3200.$$

P.2. Now consider square of size $n \times n$ ($n \times n$ matrix). The elements on the principal diagonal are addressed with $i = j$ and above the principal diagonal are addressed $i < j$, whereas those below the principal diagonal are by $i > j$, and hence

T_{ij} ; $i < j$ the term lies above the Principal Diagonal.
T_{ij} ; $i > j$ the term lies below the Principal Diagonal.
T_{ij} ; $i = j$ the term lies on the Principal Diagonal.

P.3. It is very simple to observe the following facts on the above square matrix.

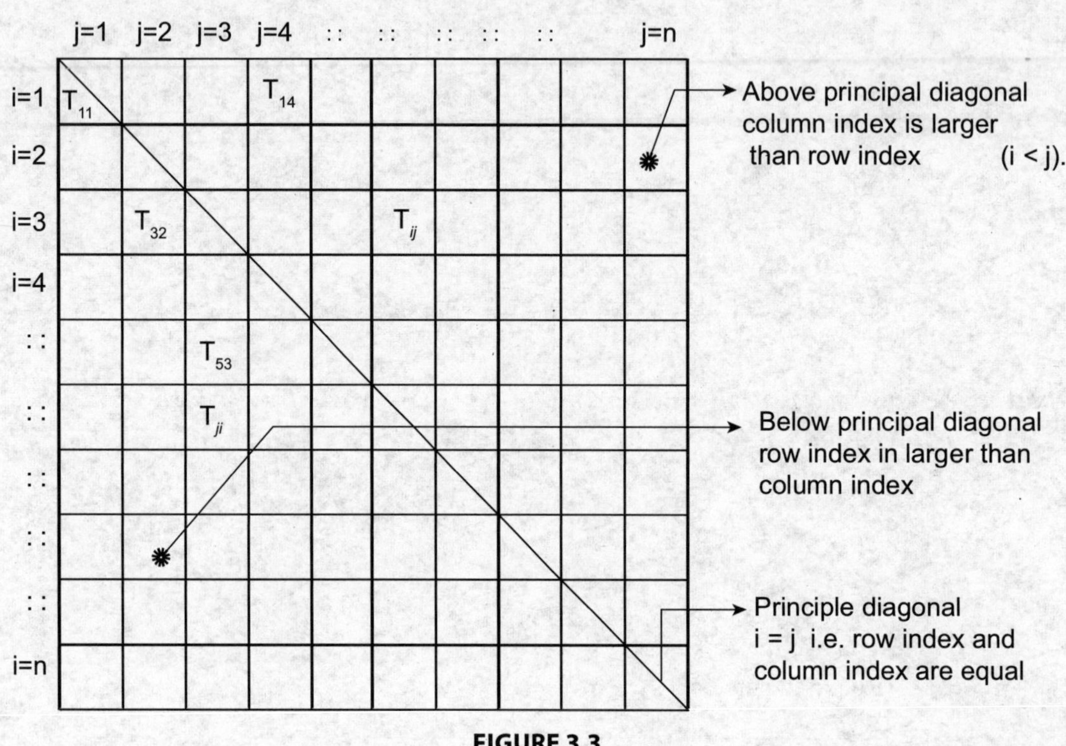

FIGURE 3.3

- Total number of unit squares = $n \times n = n^2$
- Total number of squares on the diagonal line = n
- Since the total number of square above PD = *total* number of squares below PD = k (*say*) (Think why) !

$\Rightarrow k + k + n = n^2$

$\Rightarrow 2k = n^2 - n$

$\Rightarrow k = \dfrac{n(n-1)}{2}$

Aliter:

Number of terms on or above diagonal

= number of terms on or below diagonal

$= 1 + 2 + 3 + \ldots\ldots + n$

$= \dfrac{n(n+1)}{2}$

= *no.* of term above/below the principal diagonal.

$= \dfrac{n(n+1)}{2} - n = \dfrac{n(n-1)}{2}$.

- Total number of squares above/below the principal diagonal line $= \dfrac{n(n-1)}{2} = {}^nC_2$.
- Total number of squares on or below diagonal (on or above diagonal)

$$= \frac{n^2 - n}{2} + n = \frac{n^2 + n}{2} = \frac{n(n+1)}{2} = {}^{n+1}C_2.$$

P.4. $$\sum_{j=1}^{n}\sum_{i=1}^{n} a = \sum_{j=1}^{n}\left(\sum_{i=1}^{n} a\right) = \sum_{j=1}^{n}\sum_{i=1}^{n} a = \sum_{j=1}^{n} na = na\sum_{j=1}^{n} 1$$

$$= na \,.\, n = n^2 a.$$

$$or = \sum_{\substack{i=1\\j=1}}^{n} a + \sum_{\substack{i=1\\j=2}}^{n} a + \ldots\ldots\ldots = \sum_{\substack{i=1\\j=n}}^{n} a$$

$$= \underset{na}{\overset{j=1}{\downarrow}} + \underset{na}{\overset{j=2}{\downarrow}} + \underset{na}{\overset{j=3}{\downarrow}} + \ldots\ldots + \underset{na}{\overset{j=n}{\downarrow}} = (n)(na) = n^2 a.$$

$\therefore \sum_{j=1}^{n}\sum_{i=1}^{n} a = n^2 a$ (i.e., summation of $a, a, a, \ldots\ldots\ldots$ in n^2 places on array/matrix).

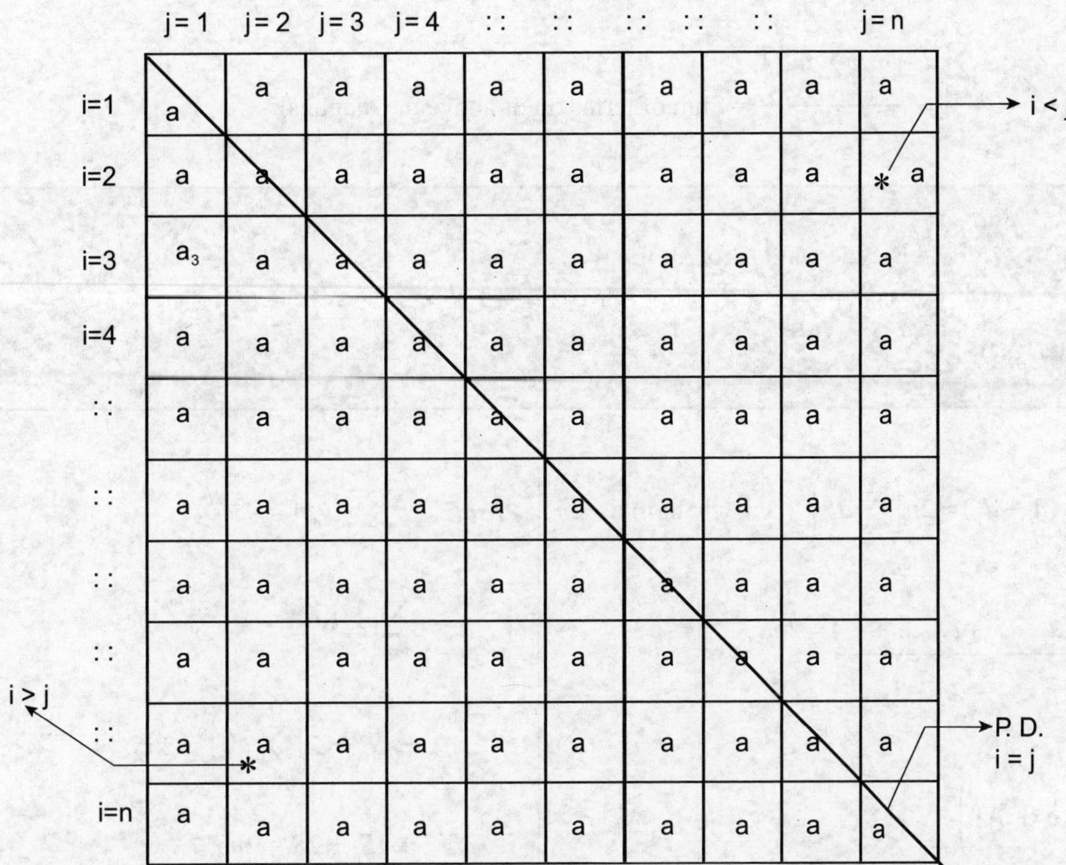

FIGURE 3.4

P.5. $\sum\sum_{1\le i<j\le n} a = \sum_{\substack{j=2\\i=1}}^{n} a + \sum_{\substack{j=3\\i=2}}^{n} a + ... + \sum_{\substack{j=n\\i=n-1}}^{n} a$

$= (n-1)a + (n-2)a + ... + a$

$= a(1 + 2 + 3 + ... + (n-1))$

$= \dfrac{an(n-1)}{2}.$

Aliter: $\sum\sum_{1\le i<j\le n} a$ = (No. of terms above P.D).a = k.

$a = \dfrac{an(n-1)}{2}.$

P.6. $\sum\sum_{1\le i\le j\le n} a = \dfrac{(n^2+n)a}{2} = {}^{n+1}C_2 . a$

$\left(\because a\left(\dfrac{n^2-n}{2}\right) + na = na\left(\dfrac{n-1}{2}+1\right) = na\dfrac{(n+1)}{2}\right)$

Aliter: Look at the sum of all term on or above $P.D.$ = (no. of terms) . $a = {}^{n+1}C_2 . a$.

P.7. $\sum_{j=1}^{n}\sum_{i=1}^{n} a_i\, a_j = \sum_{i=1}^{n}\left(a_j \sum_{i=1}^{n} a_i\right)$

$= \sum_{j=1}^{n} S\, a_j$ $(Let \sum_{j=1}^{n} a_j = a_1 + a_2 + a_3 + ... + a_n = S)$

$= S\sum_{j=1}^{n} a_j$

$= S . S = S^2 = \left(\sum_{k=1}^{n} a_k\right)^2$

P.8. Summation of product taken two at a time of any set of given n numbers $a_1, a_2, a_3, ..., a_n$. numbers is given by $\sum\sum_{1\le i<j\le n} a_i\, a_j = S_0$ (say) [sum of products above/below principal diagonal]

$\Rightarrow \quad 2S_0 + \sum_{i=1}^{n} a_i^2 = \left(\sum_{k=1}^{n} a_k\right)^2$

$\left(\because \sum\sum_{1\le i<j\le n} a_i\, a_j = \sum\sum_{n\ge i>j\ge 1} a_i\, a_j = S_0\right)$

$\Rightarrow \; S_0 = \dfrac{\left(\sum_{k=1}^{n} a_k\right)^2 - \left(\sum_{k=1}^{n} a_k^{\,2}\right)}{2}.$

P.9. $\sum\sum_{1\le j\le j\le n} a_i\, a_j = \dfrac{\left(\sum_{k=1}^{n} a_k\right)^2 + \left(\sum_{k=1}^{n} a_k^{\,2}\right)}{2}$ = Sum of terms on or above the diagonal.

ILLUSTRATION 77: Evaluate the summation of number $\sum_{j=1}^{n}\sum_{i=1}^{n} i.j$.

SOLUTION: $\sum_{j=1}^{n}\sum_{i=1}^{n} i\, j = \left(\sum_{k=1}^{n} k\right)^2 = \left(\dfrac{n(n+1)}{2}\right)^2 = \sum_{k=1}^{n} k^3$

P.10. $\sum_{i=1}^{n}\sum_{j=1}^{n}(a_i + a_j) = 2n\left(\sum_{k=1}^{n} a_k\right)$ [∵ each term is $2n$ times]

$$= \underbrace{2n(a_1 + a_2 + a_3 + \dots\dots\dots + a_n)}_{S} = 2nS$$

Proof.

$$= \sum_{i=1}^{n}\left(\sum_{j=1}^{n}(a_i + a_j)\right)$$

$$= \sum_{j=1}^{n}\left(\sum_{i=1}^{n} a_i + \sum_{j=1}^{n} a_j\right) = \sum_{i=1}^{n}(S+S) = \sum_{j=1}^{n} 2S = 2nS$$

P.11. $\sum\sum_{1\le i<j\le n}(a_i + a_j) = (n-1)\sum_{k=1}^{n} a_k$

Proof. $\sum\sum_{1\le i<j\le n}(a_i + a_j) = S_0$

$$\sum\sum_{n\ge i>j\ge i}(a_i + a_j) = S_0$$

$$\Rightarrow 2S_0 + 2\left(\sum_{k=1}^{n} a_k\right) = 2nS$$

$$\Rightarrow 2S_0 + 2S = 2nS$$

$$\Rightarrow 2S_0 = (2n-2)S$$

$$\Rightarrow S_0 = (n-1)S$$

$$\Rightarrow \sum\sum_{1\le i<j\le n}(a_i + a_j) = (n-1)\sum_{k=1}^{n} a_k$$

NOTE

Since each variable repeats 2n times on the matrix whereas it occurs 2 times on the diagonal. Therefore it occurs total (2n – 2) times above or below diagonal. As we know every variable occurs equal number of times below the diagonal as it occurs above the diagonal. Therefore number of times the variable repeat es in the summation of elements above/below is equal to $\dfrac{2n-2}{2} = n-1$ *times.*

P.12. $\sum\sum_{i\le i\le j\le n}(a_i + a_j) = (n+1)\sum_{k=1}^{n} a_k$

Proof. $\sum\sum_{1\le i\le j\le n}(a_i + a_j) = \sum\sum_{1\le i\le j\le n}(a_i + a_j) + \sum_{i=n}^{n}(a_i + a_j)$

$$= (n-1)\sum_{k=1}^{n} a_k + 2\sum_{k=1}^{n} a_k = (n+1)\sum_{k=1}^{n} a_k$$

P.13. A constant factor can always be factored out of double sigma. i.e.

$$\sum\sum_{i\le i<j\le n}(a_i + a_j)\lambda = \lambda\sum\sum_{i\le i<j\le n}(a_i + a_j)$$

P.14. Double sigma distributes on sum and difference of elements provided the elements are symmetric in the variable i and j.

$$\sum\sum(i+j+ij) = \sum\sum((i+j)+ij) = \sum\sum(i+j) + \sum\sum ij$$

ILLUSTRATION 78: Find the value of the expression $\sum_{u=1}^{n}\sum_{v=1}^{u}\sum_{w=1}^{v}1$.

SOLUTION: $\sum_{u=1}^{n}\sum_{v=1}^{u}\sum_{w=1}^{v}1=\sum_{u=1}^{n}\sum_{v=1}^{u}j=\sum_{u=1}^{n}\frac{u(u+1)}{2}=\frac{1}{2}\left[\sum_{i=1}^{n}i^2+\sum_{i=1}^{n}i\right]$

$$=\frac{1}{2}\left[\frac{n(n+1)(2n+1)}{6}+\frac{n(n+1)}{2}\right]=\frac{n(n+1)}{12}[2n+4]=\frac{n(n+1)(n+2)}{6}$$

TEXTUAL EXERCISE–10 (SUBJECTIVE)

1. Obtain n^{th} term and the sum of following series upto n-terms.

(i) $1+\frac{1+2}{2}+\frac{1+2+3}{3}+.......$

(ii) $\frac{1^3}{1}+\frac{1^3+2^3}{2}+\frac{1^3+2^3+3^3}{3}+.......$

(iii) 1.2.3 + 2.3.4 + 3.4.5. + ...

2. Find the sum to n terms of the series.

(a) $\frac{1}{1\times4}+\frac{1}{4\times7}+\frac{1}{7\times10}+......$

(b) $\frac{1}{1\times6}+\frac{1}{6\times11}+\frac{1}{11\times16}+......$

3. Sum the series $1+\frac{1}{1+2}+\frac{1}{1+2+3}+......$ upto n terms.

4. Series of natural numbers is divided into groups as {1}, {2, 3}, {4, 5, 6}, {7, 8, 9, 10}, ... and so on. Prove that the sum of the numbers in the nth group is $\frac{n(n^2+1)}{2}$.

5. The sum to n terms of the series $\frac{3}{1^2.2^2}+\frac{5}{2^2.3^2}+\frac{7}{3^2.4^2}$ +...... is ______.

6. Find the sum of n terms of the following series...........

(a) $[3/(1.2)](1/2) + [4/(2.3)].(1/2^2) + [5/(3.4)](1/2^3) + [6/(4.5)].(1/2^4) + ...$

(b) $[2(1.2)] + 2[5/(2.3)] + 2^2.[10/(3.4)] + 2^3.[17/(4.5)]$ + ...

(c) $[1^2/(2.3)]\ 4 + [2^2/(3.4)]\ 4^2 + [(3)^2/(4.5)]\ .4^3 + [4^2/(5.6)].4^4 +$ ....

7. Evaluate the sum [3/(1.2.4)] + [4/(2.3.5)] + [5/(3.4.6)] + ... upto n terms.

8. Find the sum of n terms of the series whose n^{th} term is ....

(i) $(n^2 + 5n + 4)(n^2 + 5n + 8)$

(ii) $[n^2(n^2 - 1)]/(4n^2 - 1)$

9. Find the sum of n terms of the series.

(a) 3. 4 + 8. 11 + 15.20 + 24.31 + 35.44 +............

(b) 1. 3 + 4.7 + 9.13 + 16. 21 + 25. 31 +...............

10. Find the summation of following series:

(a) $\sum\sum_{1\le i<j\le n}(i+j)$ (b) $\sum\sum_{1\le i<j\le n}(i\,j)$

(c) $\sum\sum_{1\le i<j\le n}(i+j)^2$

Answer Keys

1. (i) $\frac{n+1}{2}$ (ii) $\frac{n(n+1)^2}{4}$ (iii) $n(n + 1)(n + 2)$ **2.** (a) $\frac{n}{3n+1}$ (b) $\frac{n}{5n+1}$ **3.** $\frac{2n}{n+1}$ **5.** $\frac{n(n+2)}{(n+1)^2}$

6. (a) $1-\frac{1}{(n+1)2^n}$ (b) $\frac{n.2^n}{n+1}$ (c) $\frac{4^{n+1}-4}{3}-\frac{4^{n+1}}{n+2}+2$ **7.** $\frac{29}{36}-\frac{1}{n+3}-\frac{3}{2(n+2)(n+3)}-\frac{4}{3(n+1)(n+2)(n+3)}$

8. (i) $\frac{1}{15}(n-1)(n+2)(3n^2+36n^2+151n+240)-32$ (ii) $\frac{n(n+1)(n-1)(n+2)}{6(2n+1)}$

9. (a) $\frac{n(n+1)(3n^3+27n^2+58n+2)}{15}$ (b) $\frac{n(n+1)(12n^3+33n^2+37n+8)}{60}$

10. (a) $n^2 - n$ (b) $\frac{1}{2}\left[\left(\frac{n(n+1)}{2}\right)^2-\frac{n(n+1).(2n+1)}{6}\right]$ (c) $(n - 1)\Sigma k^2 + 2\sum\sum_{1\le i<j\le n}(i\,j)$

TEXTUAL EXERCISE–10 (OBJECTIVE)

1. The value of 1.3.5 + 3.5.7 + 5.7.9 +.. + 17.19.21 equals
(a) 12270 (b) 17220
(c) 12720 (d) 19503

2. If the sum of n terms of an AP is $cn(n + 1)$ where $c \neq 0$. The sum of the squares of these terms is
(a) $c^2n^2(n + 1)^2$
(b) $\frac{2}{3}c^2n(n + 1)(2n + 1)$
(c) $\frac{2c^3}{3}n(n + 1)(2n + 1)$
(d) None of these

3. Let $t_n = n.(n!)$.Then $\sum_{n=1}^{15} t_n$ is equal to
(a) 15! – 1 (b) 15! + 1
(c) 16! – 1 (d) None of these

4. The sum of the series $\frac{1}{1.4}+\frac{1}{4.7}+\frac{1}{7.10}+$............. to n terms is
(a) $\frac{n}{3n+1}$ (b) $\frac{n}{2n+1}$
(c) $\frac{2n}{3n+1}$ (d) None of these

5. The sum of the series 1.1! + 2.2! + 3.3! +..... to n terms is
(a) $(n - 1)! - 1$ (b) $(n + 1)! - 1$
(c) $(n - 1)! + 1$ (d) None of these

6. The sum of all the numbers of the form n^3 which lie between 100 and 10, 000 is
(a) 43261 (b) 53261
(c) 63261 (d) None of these

Answer Keys

1. (d) **2.** (b) **3.** (c) **4.** (a) **5.** (b) **6.** (b)

■ METHODS OF DIFFERENCE

If the differences of the successive terms of a series are in AP, or GP, we can find n^{th} term of the series by the following steps:

Step1: Denote the nth term and the sum of the series upto n terms of the series by T_n and S_n respectively.

Step2: Rewrite the given series with each term shifted by one place to the right.

Step3: Then subtract the second expression of S_n from the first expression to obtain T_n.

NOTES

$x_1, x_2, x_3, x_4, x_5, x_6$ is given series and

(i) Difference of successive terms is constant then nth term is given by
$T_n = a + bn$ (where a and b are constants)

(ii) If difference of difference is constant then
$T_n = an^2 + bn + c$ (where a, b, c are constants)

(iii) If difference of difference of difference is constant then
$T_n = an^3 + bn^2 + cn + d$ (where a, b, c, d are constants)

ILLUSTRATION 79: Find the sum of the series

7 + 12 + 20 + 31 + 45 + 62 +.....upto n-terms.

SOLUTION: Let $S_n = 7 + 12 + 20 + 31 + 45 + 62 + ... + t_n$

Also $S_n = 7 + 12 + 20 + 31 + 45 + ... + t_{n-1} + t_n$

On subtracting

$= 7 + 5 + 8 + 11 + 14 + 17 + \ldots\ldots (t_n - t_{n-1})t_n$

$\Rightarrow t_n = 7 + (5 + 8 + 11 + 14 + 17 + \ldots\ldots\ldots\ldots$ upto $(n - 1)$ terms)

$\Rightarrow t_n = 7 + \left(\frac{n-1}{2}\right)[2(5) + (n-2)(3)]$ $\Rightarrow t_n = \frac{14+(n-1)(3n+4)}{2}$

$\Rightarrow t_n = \frac{14(3n^2+4n-3n-4)}{2}$ $\Rightarrow t_n = \frac{3n^2+n+10}{2}$

$\therefore S_n = \sum t_n = \frac{3}{2}\sum n^2 + \frac{1}{2}\sum n + 5\sum 1 = \frac{1}{4}n(n+1)(2n+1) + \frac{1}{4}n(n+1) + 5n$

$= \frac{n}{4}\left[(n+1)(2n+1)+n+1+20\right] = \frac{n}{4}\left[2n^2+4n+22\right] = \frac{n}{2}\left(n^2+2n+11\right)$

Aliter:

First differences are 5,8,11,14,17..................
which are in AP;
Second differences are 3,3,3..........which are constant
So Let $T_n = an^2 + bn + c$

$\Rightarrow T_1 = a + b + c = 7$

$T_2 = 4a + 2b + c = 12$

$T_3 = 9a + 3b + c = 20$

Solving for a,b,c we get $a = 3/2$, $b = 1/2$, $c = 5$

$\therefore T_n = \frac{3}{2}n^2 + \frac{1}{2}b + 5$

After that we can proceed to find S_n as above.

ILLUSTRATION 80: Find the sum of the series 50 + 70 + 106 + 162 + 242 +..........upto n-terms.

SOLUTION: Let $S_n = 50 + 70 + 106 + 162 + 242 + \ldots\ldots\ldots\ldots + t_n$

$\Rightarrow S_n = 50 + 70 + 106 + 162 + 242 + \ldots\ldots\ldots\ldots + t_{n-1} + t_n$

$\Rightarrow 0 = (50 + 20 + 36 + 56 + 80 + \ldots\ldots n\text{-terms}) - t_n$

$\Rightarrow t_n = 50 + 20 + 36 + 56 + 80 + \ldots\ldots\ldots\ldots n$-terms (i)

Let $S'_n = 50 + 20 + 36 + 56 + 80 + \ldots\ldots\ldots\ldots + t'_n$ (ii)

$\Rightarrow S_n' = 50 + 20 + 36 + 56 + \ldots\ldots\ldots\ldots + t'_{n-1} + t_n'$

$\Rightarrow 0 = [50 + (-30) + 16 + 20 + 24 + \ldots\ldots\ldots\ldots + n\text{-terms}] - t'_n$

$\Rightarrow t'_n = 20 + (16 + 20 + 24 + \ldots\ldots\ldots\ldots + (n-2)$ terms] for $n \ge 3$

$\Rightarrow t'_n = 20 + \frac{n-2}{2}\left[2(16)+(n-3)(4)\right]$

$\Rightarrow t'_n = 20 + (n-2)[16 + 2n - 6]$

$\Rightarrow t'_n = 20 + (n-2)[2n + 10]$

$\Rightarrow t'_n = 20 + 2n^2 + 10n - 4n - 20$

$\Rightarrow t'_n = 2n^2 + 6n;\ n \ge 3$

$\therefore S'_n = 2\sum n^2 + 6\sum n - (t_1' + t_2') + (t_1 + t_2)$

$\Rightarrow S'_n = \frac{2n(n+1)(2n+1)}{6} + \frac{6n(n+1)}{2} - (8+20) + (50+20)$

$\Rightarrow S'_n = \frac{n(n+1)(2n+1)}{3} + 3n(n+1) + 42$ (iii)

$\therefore$ From (i), (ii) and (iii), $t_n = s'_n = \frac{1}{3}[2n^3 + 12n^2 + 10n] + 42$

$$\therefore \quad S_n \sum t_n = \frac{2}{3}\sum n^3 + 4\sum n^2 + \frac{10}{3}\sum n + 42n$$
$$= \frac{2}{3}\left(\frac{n(n+1)}{2}\right]^2 + 4\left[\frac{n(n+1)(2n+1)}{6}\right] + \frac{10}{3}\frac{n(n+1)}{2} + 42n$$
$$= \frac{1}{6}n^2(n+1)^2 + \frac{2}{3}\ n\ (n+1)\ (2n+1) + \frac{5}{3}n\ (n+1) + 42n$$
$$= \frac{1}{6}n(n+1)\ [n^2 + 9n + 14) + 42n = \frac{1}{6}n(n+1)\ (n+2)\ (n+7) + 42n \textbf{ Ans}$$

ILLUSTRATION 81: Find the sum of n–terms 3 + 7 + 13 + 21 +.....

SOLUTION: Let $S = 3 + 7 + 13 + 21 + ... + T_n$ (i)

$S = 3 + 7 + 13 + ... + T_{n-1} + T_n$ (ii)

$(i) - (ii) \Rightarrow T_n = 3 + 4 + 6 + 8 + ... + (T_n - T_{n-1})$

$= 3 + \frac{n-1}{2}[8 + (n-2)2] = 3 + (n-1)(n+2) = n^2 + n + 1$

Hence $S = \Sigma(n^2+n+1) = \Sigma n^2 + \Sigma n + \Sigma 1 = \frac{n(n+1)(2n+1)}{6} + \frac{n(n+1)}{2} + n = \frac{n}{3}(n^2 + 3n + 5)$

ILLUSTRATION 82: Find the sum to n-terms 1 + 4 + 10 +22 +...

SOLUTION: Let $S = 1 + 4 + 10 + 22 + ... + T_n$ (i)

$S = 1 + 4 + 10 + ... + T_{n-1} + T_n$ (ii)

$(i) - (ii) \Rightarrow T_n = 1 + (3 + 6 + 12 + ... + T_n - T_{n-1})$

$T_n = 1 + 3\left(\frac{2^{n-1} - 1}{2-1}\right)$

$T_n = 3.\ 2^{n-1} - 2$

So $S = \Sigma\ T_n = 3\ \Sigma\ 2^{n-1} - \Sigma 2 = 3\left(\frac{2^n - 1}{2-1}\right) - 2n = 3.2^n - 2n - 3$

ILLUSTRATION 83: Find the nth term and sum of n terms of the series 1 + 3 + 7 + 15 + 31 +.....

SOLUTION: Let nth term and sum of n terms of the series be denoted by T_n and S_n respectively.

$\Rightarrow \quad S_n = 1 + 3 + 7 + 15 + 31 + ... + T_{n-1} + T_n$ (i)

Also, $S_n = 1 + 3 + 7 + 15 + ... + T_{n-2} + T_{n-1} + T_n$ (ii)

Subtracting (*ii*) from (*i*) we get

$0 = 1 + 2 + 4 + 8 + 16 + ... + (T_n - T_{n-1}) - T_n$

$T_n = 1 + 2 + 4 + 8 + 16 + ...n \text{ terms} = 1.\frac{(2^n - 1)}{2-1}$

Hence, $T_n = (2^n - 1)$

$\therefore$ Sum of n terms $S_n = \Sigma T_n = \Sigma\ (2^n - 1) = \Sigma\ 2^n - \Sigma 1 = (2 + 2^2 + 2^3 + ...2^n) - n$

Hence $S_n = 2.\frac{(2^n - 1)}{2-1} - n = 2(2^n - 1) - n$

ILLUSTRATION 84: Find the sum of n-terms of the series 1 + 4 + 13 + 40 + 121 +.......

SOLUTION: $S_n = 1 + 4 + 13 + 40 + 121 + ... + t_n$

Also, $S_n = 1 + 4 + 13 + 40 + ... + t_{n-1} + t_n$

On subtracting $0 = (1 + 3 + 9 + 27 + 81 + ... \text{up } n\text{-terms}) - t_n$

$\Rightarrow t_n = (1 + 3 + 9 + 27 + 81 + ...\text{upto } n\text{-term})$

$= 1.\frac{((3)^n - 1)}{(3-1)} = \frac{1}{2}(3^n - 1)$

$$\therefore\ S_n=\sum t_n=\frac{1}{2}\sum 3^n-\frac{1}{2}\sum 1=\frac{3}{2}\left[\frac{(3)^n-1}{(3-1)}\right]-\frac{1}{2}n=\frac{3}{4}\left(3^n-1\right)-\frac{1}{2}n=\frac{3^{n+1}}{4}-\frac{1}{2}n-\frac{3}{4}$$
$$=\frac{1}{4}\left(3^{n+1}-2_n-3\right)$$

ILLUSTRATION 85: Find the sum of n-terms of the series 14 + 20 + 28 + 40 60 +96 +……

SOLUTION: Let S_n = 14 + 20 + 28 + 40 + 60 + 96 + …… + t_n (i)

Also, S_n = 14 + 20 + 28 + 40 + 60 + …… + t_{n-1} + t_n (ii)

(*i*) – (*ii*) gives 0 = (14 + 6 + 8 + 12 + 20 +36+ …………upto n-terms) – t_n; $n \geq 2$

$\Rightarrow t_n$ = 14 + 6 + 8 + 12 + 20 + …. + upto n terms; $n \geq 2$

$\Rightarrow t_n$ = 14 + (6 + 8 + 12 + 20 + …. + upto (n – 1) terms) for $n \geq 2$

Let S'_n = 6 + 8 + 12 + 20 +……..+ upto (n – 2) terms + t'_{n-1}; $n \geq 3$

On subtracing; 0 = 6 + 2 + 4 + 8 + 16 +…..upto (n–1) terms – t'_{n-1}; $n \geq 3$

$\Rightarrow t'_{n-1}$ = 6 + (2 + 4 + 8 + 16 +..........upto (n–2) terms); $n \geq 3$

Let $n - 1 = m$; $\therefore n \geq 3 \Rightarrow n - 1 \geq 2 \Rightarrow m \geq 2$

$\therefore\ t'_m = 6 + (2)\,[(2)m - 1 - 1];\ m \geq 2 = 6 + (2)^m - 2;\ m \geq 2$

$\Rightarrow\ t'_m = (2)^m + 4;\ m \geq 2$

$$\therefore\ S'_n=6+\sum_{m=2}^{n-1}t'_m=6+\sum_{m=2}^{n-1}(2)^m+4=(2)^n+4n-6;n\geq 2$$

$\therefore\ S'_n = (2)^n + 4n - 6;\ n \geq 2$

$\therefore\ t_n = 14 + [2^n + 4n - 6];\ n \geq 2$

$$\therefore\ S'_n=14n+\sum 2^n+4+\sum n-6\sum 1=14n+(2)\left[2^n-1\right]+4\frac{n(n+1)}{2}-6n$$

$= 14n + 2^{n+1} - 2 + 2n^2 + 2n - 6n = (2)^{n+1} + 10n - 2n^2 - 2$ **Ans**

ILLUSTRATION 86: Find the nth term of the series 1 + 2 + 5 + 12 + 25 + 46 +....

SOLUTION: Let the sum of the series be S_n and nth term of the series be T_n

Then S_n = 1 + 2 + 5 + 12 + 25 + 46 +........ + T_{n-1} + T_n (i)

Also, S_n = 1 + 2 + 5 + 12 + 25 + 46 +... + T_{n-2} + T_{n-1} + T_n (ii)

Subtracting (*ii*) from (*i*), we get

T_n = 0 + 1 + 1 + 3 + 7 + 13 + 21 + ... + ($T_n - T_{n-1}$) (iii)

$\Rightarrow$ T_n = 1 + 1 + 3 + 7 + 13 + 21 + ... + t_{n-1} + t_n (iv)

(*Here nth* term *of* T_n is t_n)

Subtracting (iv) from (iii) we get

0 = 1 + 0 + 2 + 4 + 6 + 8 +....+ upto (n – 1) terms – t_n

$\Rightarrow t_n$ = 1 + 2 + 4 + 6 + 8 +.....(n–1) terms = 1 + (2 + 4 + 6 + 8 + (n –2) terms)

$$= 1 + \frac{(n-2)}{2}\{2.2 + (n-2-1)2\} = 1 + (n-2)(2 + n - 3)$$

$t_n = n^2 - 3n + 3$

then $T_n = \sum t_n = \sum n^2 - 3\sum n + 3\sum 1 = \dfrac{n(n+1)(2n+1)}{6} - \dfrac{3n(n+1)}{2} + \dfrac{3n}{1}$

$$= \frac{n}{6}\{2n^2 + 3n + 1 - 9n - 9 + 18\}$$

$T_n = \dfrac{n}{6}(2n^2 - 6n + 10)$. Hence, n^{th} terms of series is $= \dfrac{n}{3}(n^2 - 3n + 5)$

■ V_n METHODS

This method is used to find the sum of series $t_1 + t_2 + t_3 + \ldots\ldots$ up to n-terms, when each term t_n can be expressed as the difference of two consecutive terms of a new series i.e., $t_n = V_n - V_{n-1}$

$$\Rightarrow S_n = \sum t_n = (V_1 - V_0) + (V_2 - V_1) + (V_3 - V_2) + \ldots (V_n - V_{n-1})$$
$$= (V_n - V_0)$$

Let us find the sum of two types of series up to n-terms

(*i*) $\dfrac{1}{a_1a_2\ldots a_r} + \dfrac{1}{a_2a_3\ldots a_{r+1}} + \dfrac{1}{a_3a_4\ldots a_{r+2}} + \ldots + \dfrac{1}{a_n\,a_{n+1}\,a_{n+2} + \ldots\ldots a_{n+r-1}}$

(*ii*) $a_1.a_2.a_3\ldots.a_r + a_2.a_3\ldots a_{r+1} + a_3.a_4\ldots.a_{r+2} + \ldots + a_n\,a_{n+1}\,a_{n+2}\ldots.a_{n+r-1}$; where a_1, a_2, a_3 ....are in AP

Case (i):

Let $S_n = \dfrac{1}{a_1a_2\ldots a_r} + \dfrac{1}{a_2a_3\ldots a_{r+1}} + \dfrac{1}{a_3a_4\ldots a_{r+2}} + \ldots + \dfrac{1}{a_n\,a_{n+1}\,a_{n+2}\ldots\ldots a_{n+r-1}}$;

where a_1, a_2, a_3 ....are in AP with common difference 'd'

and let $V_m = \dfrac{1}{a_{m+1}a_{m+2}a_{m+3}\ldots a_{m+r-1}}$

$$\Rightarrow V_{m-1} = \frac{1}{a_m a_{m+1} a_{m+2}\ldots a_{m+r-2}}$$

$$\therefore V_{m-} - V_{m-1} = \frac{a_m - a_{m+r-1}}{a_m.a_{m+1}a_{m+2}\ldots a_{m+r-1}} = t_m = (a_m - a_{m+r-1})$$

$$\Rightarrow t_m = \frac{V_m - V_{m-1}}{a_m - a_{m+r-1}} = \frac{V_m - V_{m-1}}{(m-1)d - (m+r-2)d}$$

$$\Rightarrow t_m = \frac{V_m - V_{m-1}}{(1-r)d} = \frac{V_{m-1} - V_m}{(r-1)d}$$

$$\therefore S_n = \sum_{m=1}^{n} t_m = \frac{1}{(r-1)}\begin{bmatrix}(V_0 - V_1) + (V_1 - V_2) \\ + (V_2 - V_3) + \ldots + (V_{n-1} - V_n)\end{bmatrix}$$

$$= \frac{V_0 - V_n}{(r-1)d}$$

$$\therefore S_n = \frac{1}{(r-1)d}\left[\frac{1}{a_1a_2a_3\ldots\ldots\ldots a_{r-1}} - \frac{1}{a_{n+1}\,a_{n+2}\ldots\ldots a_{n+r-1}}\right]$$

E.g., (*i*) $\dfrac{1}{3.4} + \dfrac{1}{4.5} + \dfrac{1}{5.6} + \ldots\ldots$ up to n-terms

$$= \frac{1}{(2-1)(1)}\left[\frac{1}{3} - \frac{1}{(n+3)}\right] = \frac{n+3-3}{3(n+1)} = \frac{(n)}{3(n+1)}$$

(*ii*) $\dfrac{1}{2.4.6} + \dfrac{1}{4.6.8} + \dfrac{1}{6.8.10} + \ldots + \dfrac{1}{(2n)(2n+2)(2n+4)}$

$$= \frac{1}{(3-1)(2)}\left[\frac{1}{2.4} - \frac{1}{(2n+2)(2n+4)}\right]$$

$$= \frac{1}{4}\left[\frac{1}{8} - \frac{1}{(2n+2)(2n+4)}\right]$$

Case (ii): Let $S_n = a_1\,a_2\ldots.a_r + a_2a_3a_4\ldots..a_{r+1} + \ldots\ldots\ldots + a_n.a_{n+1}.a_{n+2}\ldots\ldots a_{n+r-1}$

Now, let $V_m = a_n a_{n+1}.a_{m+2}\ldots.a_{m+r-1}.a_{m+r}$

$$\Rightarrow V_m - V_{m-1} = (a_m.a_{m+1}\ldots.a_{m+r-1})\,[a_{m+r} - a_{m-1}]$$
$$= t_m\,[(m+r+1)d - (m-2)d] = t_m\,(r+1)d$$

$$\Rightarrow t_m = \frac{1}{(r+1)d}[V_m - V_{m-1}]$$

$$\Rightarrow S_n = \sum_{m=1}^{n} t_m = \frac{1}{(r+1)d}$$
$$[(V_1 - V_0) + (V_2 - V_1) + \ldots.(V_n - V_{n-1})]$$

$$= \frac{1}{(r+1)d}[V_n - V_0] = \frac{1}{(r+1)d}$$
$$[a_n.a_{n+1}\ldots.a_{n+r} - a_0, a_1, a_2\ldots\ldots.a_r]$$

Take $a_0 = (a_1 - d)$

E.g., (*i*) 3.4.5 + 4.5.6 + ….up to n terms.

$$\Rightarrow S_n = 3.4.5 + 4.5.6 + \ldots..+(n+2)\,(n+3)\,(n+4)$$

$$= \frac{1}{(3+1)(1)}\,[(n+2)\,(n+3)\,(n+4)(n+5) - (3-1)\,(3)\,(4)\,(5)]$$

$$= \frac{1}{4}\,[(n+2)\,(n+3)\,(n+4)(n+5) - (2)\,(3)\,(4)\,(5)]$$

$$= \frac{1}{4}[(n+2)\,(n+3)\,(n+4)(n+5) - 120]$$

(*ii*) 3.5.7.9 + 5.7.9.11 + 7.9.11.13 +… up to n terms

$$= \frac{1}{(4+1)d}\,[(2n+1)\,(2n+3)\,(2n+5)(2n+7)\,(2n+9) - (1)\,(3)\,(5)\,(7)\,(9)]$$

$$= \frac{1}{5(2)}[(2n+1)\,(2n+3)\,(2n+5)(2n+7)\,(2n+9) - 945]$$

$$= \frac{1}{10}\,[(2n+1)\,(2n+3)\,(2n+5)(2n+7)\,(2n+9) - 945]$$

ILLUSTRATION 87: Show that $\dfrac{1}{1.2} + \dfrac{1}{2.3} + \dfrac{1}{3.4} + \ldots. + \dfrac{1}{n(n+1)} = \dfrac{n}{n+1}$.

SOLUTION: n^{th} term $T_n = \dfrac{1}{n(n+1)} = \dfrac{1}{n} - \dfrac{1}{n+1}$

$S_n = T_1 + T_2 + T_3 + ... + T_{n-1} + T_n$

$= (1 - 1/2) + (1/2 - 1/3) + (1/3 - 1/4) + ... + \left(\frac{1}{n-1} - \frac{1}{n}\right) + \left(\frac{1}{n} - \frac{1}{n+1}\right) = 1 - \frac{1}{n+1} = \left(\frac{n}{n+1}\right)$

ILLUSTRATION 88: Show that

$$\frac{1}{1.2.3} + \frac{1}{2.3.4} + \frac{1}{3.4.5} + ... + \frac{1}{n(n+1)(n-2)} = \frac{1}{2}\left[\frac{1}{1.2} - \frac{1}{(n+1)(n+2)}\right] = \frac{1}{4} - \frac{1}{2(n+1)(n+2)}.$$

SOLUTION: n^{th} term $T_n = \frac{1}{n(n+1)(n+2)} = \frac{1}{2}\left[\frac{(n+2)-n}{n(n+1)(n+2)}\right] = \frac{1}{2}\left[\frac{1}{n(n+1)} - \frac{1}{(n+1)(n+2)}\right]$

$$S_n = \sum_{k=1}^{n} T_k = \frac{1}{2}\left[\frac{1}{1.2} - \frac{1}{(n+1)(n+2)}\right] = \frac{1}{4} - \frac{1}{2(n+1)(n+2)}$$

ILLUSTRATION 89: Sum to n terms of the series $\frac{1}{(1+x)(1+2x)} + \frac{1}{(1+2x)(1+3x)} + \frac{1}{(1+3x)(1+4x)} + ...$

SOLUTION: Let T_r be the general term of the series

$$\therefore \quad T_r = \frac{1}{x}\left[\frac{[1+(r+1)x]-(1+rx)}{(1+rx)(1+(r+1)x)}\right]$$

$$= \frac{1}{x}\left[\frac{1}{1+rx} - \frac{1}{1+(r+1)x}\right]; \; T_r = f(r) - f(r+1) \text{ where } f(r) = \frac{1}{x(1+rx)}$$

$$S_n = f(1) - f(n+1) = \frac{1}{x}\left[\frac{1}{1+x} - \frac{1}{1+(x+1)x}\right] = \frac{x}{(1+x)[1+(x+1)x]}$$

ILLUSTRATION 90: Sum to n terms of the series $\frac{4}{1.2.3} + \frac{5}{2.3.4} + \frac{6}{3.4.5} + ...$

SOLUTION: Let $T_r = \frac{r+3}{r(r+1)(r+2)} = \frac{1}{(r+1)(r+2)} + \frac{3}{r(r+1)(r+2)}$

$$= \left[\frac{1}{r+1} - \frac{1}{r+2}\right] + \frac{3}{2}\left[\frac{1}{r(r+1)} - \frac{1}{(r+1)(r+2)}\right]$$

$$\therefore \quad S = \left[\frac{1}{2} - \frac{1}{n+2}\right] + \frac{3}{2}\left[\frac{1}{2} - \frac{1}{(n+1)(n+2)}\right]$$

$$= \frac{5}{4} - \frac{1}{n+2}\left[1 + \frac{3}{2(n+1)}\right] = \frac{5}{4} - \frac{1}{2(n+1)(n+2)}[2n+5]$$

ILLUSTRATION 91: Show that $\frac{1}{1.2.3.4} + \frac{1}{2.3.4.5} + \frac{1}{3.4.5.6} + ... + \frac{1}{n(n+1)(n+2)(n+3)} = \frac{1}{3}$

$= \left[\frac{1}{1.2.3} - \frac{1}{(n+1)(n+2)(n+3)}\right] = \frac{1}{18} - \frac{1}{3(n+1)(n+2)(n+3)}$, and hence evaluate S_∞.

SOLUTION: n^{th} term $T_n = \frac{1}{n(n+1)(n+2)(n+3)} = \frac{1}{3}\left[\frac{(n+3)-n}{n(n+1)(n+2)(n+3)}\right]$

$$= \frac{1}{3}\left[\frac{1}{n(n+1)(n+2)} - \frac{1}{(n+1)(n+2)(n+3)}\right]$$

$$S_n = \frac{1}{3}\left[\frac{1}{1.2.3} - \frac{1}{(n+1)(n+2)(n+3)}\right] = \frac{1}{18} - \frac{1}{3(n+1)(n+2)(n+3)}$$

if $n \to \infty$ then $s_n = 1/18 - 1/\infty = 1/18$

ILLUSTRATION 92: Find the sum of the series 1.2.3.4 + 2.3.4.5 + 3.4.5.6 +...........up to n-terms.

SOLUTION:

Method 1: (*By* $\mathbf{V_n}$**-method)**

Here $T_n = n(n+1)(n+2)(n+3)$

Consider $V_m = m(m+1)(m+2)(m+3)(m+4)$

$\therefore\ V_{m-1} = (m-1)(m)(m+1)(m+2)(m+3)$

$\therefore\ V_m - V_{m-1} = m(m+1)(m+2)(m+3)[(m+4)-(m-1)] = 5m(m+1)(m+2)(m+3) = 5T_m$

$\Rightarrow\ T_m = \frac{1}{5}[V_m - V_{m-1}]$

$\therefore\ S_n = \sum_{m=1}^{n} T_m = \frac{1}{5}\left[(V_1 - V_0) + (V_2 - V_1) + (V_3 - V_2) + \ldots\ldots + (V_n - V_{n-1})\right]$

$= \frac{1}{5}[V_n - V_0] = \frac{1}{5}[n(n+1)(n+2)(n+3)(n+4) - 0]$

Thus $S_n = \frac{1}{5}n(n+1)(n+2)(n+3)((n+4)$

Method 2:

$T_n = n(n+1)(n+2)(n+3)$ (i)

$\Rightarrow\ T_{n+1} = (n+1)(n+2)(n+3)(n+4)$ (ii)

$\therefore$ (*ii*) $\div$ (*i*) gives, $\frac{T_{n+1}}{T_n} = \frac{n+4}{n}$

$\Rightarrow\ nT_{n+1} = (n+4)T_n$

$\Rightarrow\ nT_{n+1} = (n-1+5)T_n$

$\Rightarrow\ nT_{n+1} = (n-1)T_n + 5T_n$

$\Rightarrow\ 5T_n = nT_{n+1} - (n-1)T_n$

$\Rightarrow\ 5T_n = V_n - V_{n-1}$; where $V_n = nT_{n+1}$

$\Rightarrow\ T_n = 1/5\,[V_n - V_{n-1}]$

$\Rightarrow\ S_n = \sum_{m=1}^{n} T_m = \frac{1}{5}\left[(V_1 - V_0) + (V_2 - V_1) + (V_3 - V_2) + \ldots\ldots + (V_n - V_{n-1})\right]$

$= \frac{1}{5}[V_n - V_0] = \frac{1}{5}[nT_{n+1} - 0] = \frac{1}{5}\ n(n+1)(n+2)(n+3)(n+4)$

Method 3: (Fastest method)

$T_n = n(n+1)(n+2)(n+3) = \frac{1}{5}n(n+1)(n+2)(n+3)[(n+4)-(n-1)]$

[$(n+4)$ is next to $(n+3)$ and $(n-1)$ is preceding to n]

$\Rightarrow\ T_n = \frac{1}{5}[n(n+1)(n+2)(n+3)(n+4) - (n-1)(n)(n+1)(n+2)(n+3)]$

$\therefore\ S_n = T_1 + T_2 + T_3 + T_4 + \ldots\ldots + T_n$

$= \frac{1}{5}[(1.2.3.4.5 - 0) + (2.3.4.5.6 - 1.2.3.4.5) + (3.4.5.6.7 - 2.3.4.5.6)\ldots.+n(n+1)(n+2)(n+3)(n+4) - (n-1)(n)(n+1)(n+2)(n+3)] = \frac{1}{5}\ n(n+1)(n+2)(n+3)(n+4)$ [$\because$ remaining terms cancel out in pairing diagonally]

ILLUSTRATION 93: Evaluate the sum of the series $\frac{1}{2.4}+\frac{1.3}{2.4.6}+\frac{1.3.5}{2.4.6.8}+......+$ up to n-terms.

SOLUTION: $S_n=\frac{1}{2.4}+\frac{1.3}{2.4.6}+\frac{1.3.5}{2.4.6.8}+......+\frac{1.3.5..........(2n-1)}{2.4.6.8.(2n+2)}$

Here $T_n=\frac{1.3.5......(2n-1)}{2.4.6.....(2n+2)}=\frac{1.3.5......(2n-1)[(2n+2)-(2n+1)]}{2.4.6........(2n+2)}$

$\Rightarrow T_n=\frac{1.3.5.......(2n-1)}{2.4.6........2n}-\frac{1.3.5......(2n-1).(2n+1)}{2.4.6......(2n+2)}$

$$\therefore\ S_n=\sum_{m=1}^{n}T_m=\left[\begin{array}{l}\left(\frac{1}{2}-\frac{1.3}{2.4}\right)+\left(\frac{1.3}{2.4}-\frac{1.3.5}{2.4.6}\right)+\left(\frac{1.3.5}{2.4.6}-\frac{1.3.5.7}{2.4.6.8}\right)\\+.........\left(\frac{1.3.5....(2n-1)}{2.4.6.....2n}-\frac{1.3.5....(2n-1)(2n+1)}{2.4.6....(2n+2)}\right)\end{array}\right]$$

Thus $S_n=\left[\frac{1}{2}-\frac{1.3.5....(2n+1)}{2.4.6.......(2n+2)}\right]$

TEXTUAL EXERCISE–11 (SUBJECTIVE)

1. Obtain n^{th} term and find the sum of the series up to n terms: $\frac{1}{1.2.3.4.5}+\frac{1}{2.3.4.5.6}+\frac{1}{3.4.5.6.7}+....$

2. Find the sum of n terms of the series
   (a) $\frac{1}{1\times4}+\frac{1}{4\times7}+\frac{1}{7\times10}+......$
   (b) $\frac{1}{1\times6}+\frac{1}{6\times11}+\frac{1}{11\times16}+......$

3. Find the summation of the following series up to n terms:
   (a) $1+2+4+7+11+16+.....$
   (b) $3+4+6+10+18+34+66+....$
   (c) $1+4+8+14+24+42+76+....$
   (d) $1+4+10+21+39+......$

4. Evaluate the sum of following series
   (a) $\frac{1}{1.3}+\frac{2}{1.3.5}+\frac{3}{1.3.5.7}+....$
   (b) $\frac{3}{1^2.2^2}+\frac{5}{2^2.3^2}+\frac{7}{3^2.4^2}+.....$ up to n terms
   (c) If $1-1/2+1/3-1/4....\infty=ln\ 2$, then evaluate $\frac{1}{1.3}+\frac{1}{2.5}+\frac{1}{3.7}+....\ \infty$
   (d) If $\frac{1}{1^2}+\frac{1}{3^2}+\frac{1}{5^2}+....\infty=\frac{\pi^2}{8}$ then evaluate $\frac{1}{1^2}+\frac{1}{2^2}+\frac{1}{3^2}+....\infty$

5. Evaluate the sum of following series up to n terms.
   (a) $\frac{1}{1!(n-1)!}+\frac{1}{3!(n-3)!}+....$; $n!$ called n factorial and is equal to $1\times2\times3\times....\times n$.
   (b) $1+\frac{1}{1+2}+\frac{1}{1+2+3}+...+\frac{1}{1+2+...+n}$
   (c) $\frac{2}{3}+\frac{8}{9}+\frac{26}{27}+\frac{80}{81}+....$
   (d) $\cot^{-1}3+\cot^{-1}7+\cot^{-1}13+....$

6. Sum to n terms of the following series:
   (*i*) $\frac{1}{t^3}+\frac{1+2}{1^3+2^3}+\frac{1+2+3}{1^3+2^3+3^3}+...$
   (*ii*) $1.5.9+2.6.10+3.7.11+....$
   (*iii*) $4+14+30+52+82+114+....$
   (*iv*) $2+5+12+31+86+....$

Answer Keys

1. $\left[\frac{1}{96}-\frac{1}{4(n+1)(n+2)(n+3)(n+4)}\right]$ **2.** (a) $\frac{n}{3n+1}$ (b) $\frac{n}{5n+1}$ **3.** (a) $\frac{n(2n^2+10)}{12}$ (b) $2n + 2^n - 1$

(c) $n^2 + 2^n - n - 1$ (d) $\frac{n^4+11n^2}{12}$ **4.** (a) 1/2 (b) $\frac{n^2+2n}{(n+1)^2}$ (c) $2 - ln_e 2$ (d) $\pi^2/6$

5. (a) $2^{n-1}/n!$ (b) $2n/(n+1)$ (c) $\frac{2n.3^n-(3^n-1)}{2(3^n)}$ (d) $\cot^{-1}\left(\frac{n+2}{n}\right)$

6. (i) $\frac{2n}{n+1}$ (ii) $\frac{n}{4}(n+1)(n+8)(n+9)$ (iii) $n(n+1)^2$ (iv) $\frac{3^n+n^2+n-1}{2}$

TEXTUAL EXERCISE–11 (OBJECTIVE)

1. The next term of the sequence 1, 5, 14, 30, 55,.....is:
(a) 91 (b) 5
(c) 90 (d) 95

2. The next term of the sequence 1, 3, 6, 10,.... is
(a) 16 (b) 3
(c) 15 (d) 14

3. The value of $\frac{1}{1.3.5}+\frac{1}{3.5.7}+...+\frac{1}{11.13.15}$ equals
(a) $\frac{32}{195}$; (b) $\frac{16}{195}$;
(c) $\frac{64}{195}$; (d) None of these

4. The sum of n terms of 1.2.3 + 2.3.4. +... will
(a) $\frac{n(n+1)(n+2)(n+3)}{4}$ (b) $\frac{2n(n+1)(n+2)(n+3)}{3}$
(c) $\frac{(n+2)(n+1)(n+3)}{4}$ (d) $\frac{n(n-1)(n-2)(n-3)}{4}$

5. The value of $100\left[\frac{1}{1.2}+\frac{1}{2.3}+\frac{1}{3.4}+....+\frac{1}{99.100}\right]$
(a) is 99
(b) lies between 50 and 98
(c) is 100
(d) is different from values specified in the foregoing statements

Answer Keys

1. (a) **2.** (c) **3.** (b) **4.** (c) **5.** (a) **6.** (a)

MULTIPLE-CHOICE QUESTIONS

SECTION–I

OBJECTIVE-TYPE SOLVED EXAMPLES

1. If a, b, c are positive real numbers in GP then $a + b$, $2b$, $b + c$ are in

(a) AP (b) GP
(c) HP (d) None of these

Solution: (c) a, b, c in GP $\Rightarrow b^2 = ac$

$T_1 = a + b = \sqrt{a}\left(\sqrt{a}+\sqrt{c}\right)$ and

$T_3 = b + c = \sqrt{c}\left(\sqrt{a}+\sqrt{c}\right)$

Now HM of T_1 and

$$T_3 = \frac{2T_1T_3}{T_1+T_3} = \frac{2\sqrt{a}\sqrt{c}\left(\sqrt{a}+\sqrt{c}\right)^2}{\left(\sqrt{a}+\sqrt{c}\right)^2} = 2\sqrt{a}\,c$$

But $T_2 = 2b = 2\sqrt{ac}$ $\therefore$ T_1, T_2, T_3 are in HP.

2. If $x^2 + 9y^2 + 25z^2 = xyz\left(\frac{15}{x}+\frac{5}{y}+\frac{3}{z}\right)$, then x, y, z are in

(a) AP (b) GP
(c) HP (d) None of these

Solution: (c) $x^2 + 9y^2 + 25z^2 = xyz\left(\frac{15}{x}+\frac{5}{y}+\frac{3}{z}\right)$

$\Rightarrow x^2 + 9y^2 + 25z^2 - 15yz - 5xz - 3xy = 0$

$\Rightarrow (x)^2 + (3y)^2 + (5z)^2 - (3y)(5z) - x.(5z) - x(3y) = 0$

$\Rightarrow (x - 3y)^2 + (3y - 5z)^2 + (5z - x)^2 = 0$

It is possible only when $x = 3y = 5z$. So x, y, z in HP.

3. Let x be the AM and y, z be two GMs between two positive numbers Then $\frac{y^3+z^3}{xyz}$ is equal to

(a) 1 (b) 2
(c) 1/2 (d) None of these

Solution: (b) Let two numbers be a and b, then a, x, b in AP $\Rightarrow x = \frac{a+b}{2}$ and a, y, z, b in GP $\Rightarrow y = a^{2/3}.b^{1/3}$, $z = a^{1/3}.b^{2/3}$ Now $\frac{y^3+z^3}{xyz} = \frac{a^2b+ab^2}{\left(\frac{a+b}{2}\right).ab} = 2$

4. The sum of the series $\frac{1}{\log_2 4}+\frac{1}{\log_4 4}+\frac{1}{\log_8 4}+\ldots..+\frac{1}{\log_{2^n} 4}$ is

(a) $\frac{n(n+1)}{2}$ (b) $\frac{n(n+1)(2n+1)}{12}$
(c) $\frac{1}{n(n+1)}$ (d) $\frac{n(n+1)}{4}$

Solution: (d) $\frac{1}{\log_2 4}+\frac{1}{\log_4 4}+\frac{1}{\log_8 4}+\ldots+\frac{1}{\log_{2^n} 4}$

$= \log_4 2 + \log_4 4 + \log_4 8 + \ldots + \log_4 2^n$

$= \frac{1}{2}+1+\frac{3}{2}+\ldots+\frac{n}{2} = \frac{1+2+3+4+\ldots\ldots\ldots+n}{2}$

$= \frac{n(n+1)}{4}$

5. If a, b, c are in HP, then the value of $\left(\frac{1}{b}+\frac{1}{c}-\frac{1}{a}\right)\left(\frac{1}{c}+\frac{1}{a}-\frac{1}{b}\right)$ is

(a) $\frac{2}{bc}-\frac{1}{b^2}$ (b) $\frac{1}{4}\left(\frac{3}{c^2}+\frac{2}{ca}-\frac{1}{a^2}\right)$
(c) $\frac{3}{b^2}-\frac{2}{ab}$ (d) None of these

Solution: (a, b, c) As a, b, c are in HP $1/a$, $1/b$, $1/c$ are in AP.

$$\Rightarrow \frac{1}{b}-\frac{1}{a}=\frac{1}{c}-\frac{1}{b} \text{ or } \frac{2}{b}=\frac{1}{a}+\frac{1}{c} \quad (1)$$

Therefore, $\left(\frac{1}{b}+\frac{1}{c}-\frac{1}{a}\right)\left(\frac{1}{c}+\frac{1}{a}-\frac{1}{b}\right) = \left(\frac{1}{c}+\frac{1}{c}-\frac{1}{b}\right)\left(\frac{1}{c}+\frac{1}{b}-\frac{1}{c}\right)$ [using (1)] $= \left(\frac{2}{c}-\frac{1}{b}\right)\left(\frac{1}{b}\right) = \frac{2}{bc}-\frac{1}{b^2}$

Also, $\left(\frac{1}{b}+\frac{1}{c}-\frac{1}{a}\right)\left(\frac{1}{c}+\frac{1}{a}-\frac{1}{b}\right)$

$= \left(\frac{1}{2a}+\frac{1}{2c}+\frac{1}{c}-\frac{1}{a}\right)\left(\frac{1}{c}+\frac{1}{a}-\frac{1}{2a}-\frac{1}{2c}\right)$

$= \left(\frac{3}{2c}-\frac{1}{2a}\right)\left(\frac{1}{2c}+\frac{1}{2a}\right) = \frac{1}{4}\left(\frac{3}{c^2}+\frac{2}{ca}-\frac{1}{a^2}\right)$

Lastly, $\left(\frac{1}{b}+\frac{1}{c}-\frac{1}{a}\right)\left(\frac{1}{c}+\frac{1}{a}-\frac{1}{b}\right)$

$= \left(\frac{1}{b}+\frac{2}{b}-\frac{1}{a}-\frac{1}{a}\right)\left(\frac{1}{b}-\frac{1}{a}+\frac{1}{a}\right)$

$= \left(\frac{3}{b}-\frac{2}{a}\right)\frac{1}{b} = \frac{3}{b^2}-\frac{2}{ab}$

6. For what values of the parameter 'a' are there real values of x such that $5^{1+x}+5^{1-x}, \frac{a}{2}, 25^x+25^{-x}$ are three consecutive terms of an AP?
(a) 11 (b) 12
(c) 10 (d) 9

Solution: (b) We have $2\,(a/2) = (5^{1+x} + 5^{1-x}) + (25^x + 25^{-x})$

$\Rightarrow a = 5(5^x + 5^{-x}) + (5^{2x} + 5^{-2x})$

$$\left\{\because t+\frac{1}{t} \geq 2 \text{ since } t+\frac{1}{t} = \left(\sqrt{t}-\frac{1}{\sqrt{t}}\right)^2 + 2 \geq 2\right\}$$

$$\Rightarrow a = 5\left(5^x + \frac{1}{5^x}\right) + \left(5^{2x} + \frac{1}{5^{2x}}\right) \geq 5(2) + (2) = 12$$

Hence, $a \geq 12$

7. The sum of the following series 5 + 55 + 555 +.... to n terms is

(a) $\frac{5}{81}[10^{n-1} - 10 - 9n]$ (b) $\frac{5}{81}[10^n - 10 - 9n]$

(c) $\frac{5}{9}[10^{n-1} - 10 - 9n]$ (d) None of these

Solution: (a) 5 + 55 + 555....... to n

terms $= \frac{5}{9}(9+99+999+.........\text{to n terms})$

$= \frac{5}{9}[(10-1)+(100-1)+(1000-1)+...(10^n-1)]$

$= \frac{5}{9}[(10+10^2+10^3+..........10^n)-n]$

$$= \frac{5}{9}\left[\frac{10(10^n-1)}{10-1} - n\right] = \frac{5}{81}\left[10^{n+1} - 10 - 9n\right]$$

8. If $\sqrt[x]{a} = \sqrt[y]{b} = \sqrt[z]{c}$ and if a, b, c are in GP, then x, y, z are in
(a) AP (b) GP
(c) HP (d) AGP

Solution: (a) $\sqrt[x]{a} = \sqrt[y]{b} = \sqrt[z]{c}$

$\Rightarrow (a)^{1/x} = (b)^{1/y} = (c)^{1/z}$

$\Rightarrow \frac{1}{x}\log a = \frac{1}{y}\log b = \frac{1}{z}\log c$

Since, a, b, c are in GP, we can write $b = ar, c = ar^2$

$\Rightarrow \frac{1}{x}\log a = \frac{1}{y}\log(ar) = \frac{1}{z}\log(ar^2) = k\,(say)$

$$\Rightarrow x = \frac{\log a}{k}, y = \frac{\log a}{k} + \frac{\log r}{k}, z = \frac{\log a}{k} + \frac{2\log r}{k}$$

Hence, x, y, z are in AP with common difference $\frac{\log r}{k}$

9. If a, b, c, d are positive real numbers such that $a + b + c + d = 2$, then $M = (a + b)(c + d)$ satisfies the relation:
(a) $0 \leq M \leq 1$ (b) $1 \leq M \leq 2$
(c) $2 \leq m \leq 3$ (d) $3 \leq M \leq 4$

Solution: (a) Since, AM ≥ GM, we have,

$$\frac{(a+b)+(c+d)}{2} \geq \sqrt{(a+b)(c+d)}$$

$\Rightarrow M \leq 1$

Also, $(a + b) + (c + d) > 0$ ($\because a, b, c, d > 0$)

10. Let α, β be the roots of $x^2 - x + p = 0$ and γ, δ be the roots of $x^2 - 4x + q = 0$. If $\alpha, \beta, \gamma, \delta$ are in GP, then the integral values of p and q respectively, are
(a) –2, – 32 (b) –2, 3
(c) –6, 3 (d) –6, – 32

Solution (a)

$$\alpha, \beta \text{ are roots of } x^2 - x + p = 0 \Rightarrow \left.\begin{matrix}\alpha+\beta=1\\ \alpha\beta=p\end{matrix}\right\};$$

$$\gamma, \delta \text{ are roots of } x^2 + 4x + q = 0 \Rightarrow \left.\begin{matrix}\gamma+\delta=4\\ \lambda\delta=q\end{matrix}\right\}$$

Let r be the common ratio.

Since, α, β, γ and δ are in GP. Therefore

$\beta = ar, \gamma = ar^2$ and $\delta = ar^3$

Then, $\alpha + ar = 1 \Rightarrow \alpha(1 + r) = 1$ (i)

and $ar^2 + ar^3 = 4 \Rightarrow ar^2(1 + r) = 4$ (ii)

From Eqs. (*i*) and (*ii*), $r^2 = 4 \Rightarrow r = \pm 2$

Now, $\alpha.\ ar = p$ and $ar^2.\ ar^3 = q$; On putting $r = -2$, we get $\alpha = -1, p = -2$ and $q = -32$

Again putting $r = 2$, we get $\alpha = 1/3$, and $p = \frac{2}{9}$

Since, $q, p\ r$ are integers,

Therefore, we take $p = -2$ and $q = -32$

11. If the sum of the first $2n$ terms of the AP 2, 5, 8,......... is equal to the sum of the first n terms of the AP 57,59,61,......., then n equals
(a) 10 (b) 12
(c) 11 (d) 13

Solution: (c) According to given condition, $S_{2n} = S'_n$ where S_n and S'_n denotes the sum of first n-terms of AP 2,5,8.... and 57,59,61... respectively

$$\Rightarrow \frac{2n}{2}[2\times 2 + (2n-1)\times 3] = \frac{n}{2}[2\times 57 + (n-1)\times 2]$$

$$\Rightarrow (4 + 6n - 3) = \frac{1}{2}(114 + 2n - 2)$$

$\Rightarrow 6n + 1 = 57 + n - 1 \Rightarrow 5n = 55 \Rightarrow n = 11$

12. Let the positive numbers *a, b, c, d* be in AP. Then *abc*, *abd*, *acd*, *bcd* are

(a) not in AP/GP/HP (b) in AP
(c) in GP (d) HP

Solution: (d) Since, *a*, *b*, *c*, *d* are in AP.

$\Rightarrow \dfrac{a}{abcd}, \dfrac{b}{abcd}, \dfrac{c}{abcd}, \dfrac{d}{abcd}$ are in AP.

(dividing each terms by abcd)

$\Rightarrow \dfrac{1}{bcd}, \dfrac{1}{cda}, \dfrac{1}{abd}, \dfrac{1}{abc}$ are in AP.

$\Rightarrow$ *bcd, cda, abd, abc* are in HP.

$\Rightarrow$ *abc, abd, cda, bcd* are in HP.

13. Suppose *a*, *b*, *c* are in AP and a^2, b^2, c^2 are in GP. If $a < b < c$ and $a + b + c = \dfrac{3}{2}$, then the value of *a* is

(a) $\dfrac{1}{2\sqrt{2}}$ (b) $\dfrac{1}{2\sqrt{3}}$

(c) $\dfrac{1}{2} - \dfrac{1}{\sqrt{3}}$ (d) $\dfrac{1}{2} - \dfrac{1}{\sqrt{2}}$

Solution: (d) Since, *a*, *b*, *c* are in AP.

Let $a = A - D$, $b = A$, $c = A + D$

Given, $a + b + c = \dfrac{3}{2}$

$\Rightarrow (A - D) + A + (A + D) = \dfrac{3}{2}$

$\Rightarrow 3A = \dfrac{3}{2} \Rightarrow A = \dfrac{1}{2}$

$\therefore$ The number are $\dfrac{1}{2} - D, \dfrac{1}{2}, \dfrac{1}{2} + D$.

Also, $\left(\dfrac{1}{2} - D\right)^2, \dfrac{1}{4}, \left(\dfrac{1}{2} + D\right)^2$ are in GP.

$\Rightarrow \left(\dfrac{1}{4}\right)^2 = \left(\dfrac{1}{2} - D\right)^2 \left(\dfrac{1}{2} + D\right)^2$

$\Rightarrow \dfrac{1}{16} = \left(\dfrac{1}{4} - D^2\right)^2 \quad \Rightarrow \dfrac{1}{4} - D^2 = \pm\dfrac{1}{4}$

$\Rightarrow D^2 = \dfrac{1}{2} \quad \Rightarrow D = \pm\dfrac{1}{\sqrt{2}}$

$\therefore a = \dfrac{1}{2} \pm \dfrac{1}{\sqrt{2}}$

So, out of the given values, $a = \dfrac{1}{2} - \dfrac{1}{\sqrt{2}}$ is the right choice.

14. If $0 < x < 1$ and $y > 1$; then evaluate $\left(x + \dfrac{1}{y}\right) + \left(x^2 + \dfrac{1}{y^2}\right) + \left(x^3 + \dfrac{1}{y^3}\right) + \ldots$ is

(a) $\dfrac{xy + 1}{(x-1)(y-1)}$ (b) $\dfrac{xy - 2x + 1}{(1-x)(y-1)}$

(c) $\dfrac{(x-y)(1+x)}{(1-x)(y-1)}$ (d) None of these

Solution: (b) Let

$$S_\infty = \left(x + \frac{1}{y}\right) + \left(x^2 + \frac{1}{y^2}\right) + \left(x^3 + \frac{1}{y^3}\right) + \ldots$$

$$= (x + x^2 + x^3 + \ldots) + \left(\frac{1}{y} + \frac{1}{y^2} + \frac{1}{y^3} + \ldots\right) \quad \text{(i)}$$

$\because\ 0 < x < 1; y > 1 \Rightarrow \dfrac{1}{y^n} < 1\ \forall\ n \in \mathbf{N}$

$\Rightarrow$ Sum of both series in (*i*) exists

$$\therefore S_\infty = \frac{x}{1-x} + \frac{1/y}{1 - 1/y} \quad \left(\because S_\infty = \frac{a}{1-r}\right)$$

$$= \frac{x}{1-x} + \frac{1}{y-1} = \frac{xy - x + 1 - x}{(1-x)(y-1)} = \frac{xy - 2x + 1}{(1-x)(y-1)}$$

15. The sum of series $\left(x + \dfrac{1}{x}\right)^2 + \left(x^2 + \dfrac{1}{x^2}\right)^2 + \left(x^3 + \dfrac{1}{x^3}\right)^2 + \ldots$ *n*-terms is

(a) $\dfrac{(1 + x^{2n})}{x^n(1 + x^2)}$ (b) $\dfrac{(1 - x^{2n})(1 + x)}{x^n(1 - x^2)}$

(c) $\dfrac{(1 - x^{2n})(1 + x^{2n+2})}{x^{2n}(1 - x^2)}$ (d) None of these

Solution: (c) Let

$$S_n = \left(x + \frac{1}{x}\right)^2 + \left(x^2 + \frac{1}{x^2}\right)^2 + \left(x^3 + \frac{1}{x^3}\right)^2 + \ldots$$

up to *n*-terms

$$= \left(x^2 + \frac{1}{x^2} + 2\right) + \left(x^4 + \frac{1}{x^4} + 2\right) + \left(x^6 + \frac{1}{x^6} + 2\right) + \ldots$$

up to *n*-terms

$$= (x^2 + x^4 + x^6 + \ldots\text{up to } n\text{-terms}) + \left(\frac{1}{x^2} + \frac{1}{x^4} + \frac{1}{x^6} + \ldots\text{up to } n\text{-terms}\right)$$

$$= \frac{x^2(1 - x^{2n})}{1 - x^2} + \frac{\frac{1}{x^2}\left[1 - \frac{1}{x^{2n}}\right]}{1 - \frac{1}{x^2}}$$

$$= \frac{x^2(1 - x^{2n})}{1 - x^2} + \frac{x^{2n} - 1}{(x^2 - 1).x^{2n}}$$

$$= \left(\frac{1 - x^{2n}}{1 - x^2}\right)\left[x^2 + \frac{1}{x^{2n}}\right] = \frac{(1 - x^{2n})(1 + x^{2n+2})}{x^{2n}(1 - x^2)}$$

16. The sum of series

$$\left(2^{19}+\frac{1}{2^{19}}\right)+2\left(2^{18}+\frac{1}{2^{18}}\right)+3\left(2^{17}+\frac{1}{2^{17}}\right)+\ldots\ldots\ldots$$

$+ (19)\left(2+\frac{1}{2}\right)+20$ is

(a) $2^{21}-4+\frac{1}{2^{19}}$ (b) $2^{21}-16\frac{1}{2^{18}}$

(c) $2^{21}+24-\frac{1}{2^{19}}$ (d) None of these

Solution (a) Let

$$S_{\infty}=\left(2^{19}+\frac{1}{2^{19}}\right)+2\left(2^{18}+\frac{1}{2^{18}}\right)+3\left(2^{17}+\frac{1}{2^{17}}\right)+\ldots\ldots\ldots$$

$$+19\left(2+\frac{1}{2}\right)+20$$

$= [1.(2)^{19} + 2(2)^{18} + 3(2)^{17}+\ldots+19(2)^{1}]$

$+\left[1.\left(\frac{1}{2^{19}}\right)+2\left(\frac{1}{2^{18}}\right)\right]+3\left[\frac{1}{2^{17}}+\ldots+19\left(\frac{1}{2}\right)\right]+20$

$= S_1 + S_2 + 20$ (*say*) (i)

Now, $S_1 = 1.(2)^{19} + 2(2)^{18} + 3(2)^{17}+\ldots..19(2)'$ (AGP)

$\Rightarrow \frac{1}{2}S_1 = 1.(2)^{18} + 2(2)^{17} + 3(2)^{17}+\ldots..18(2)'+19$

Subtracting,

$$\Rightarrow \frac{1}{2}S_1 = (2)\frac{\left[(2)^{19}-1\right]}{2-1}-19$$

$\Rightarrow S_1 = 4(2^{19}-1)-38 = 2^{21}-42$

Now $S_2 = 1.\frac{1}{2^{19}}+2.\frac{1}{2^{18}}+3.\frac{1}{2^{17}}+\ldots19.\frac{1}{2^{1}}$ (A.G.P)

$\Rightarrow 2S_2 = 1.\frac{1}{2^{18}}+2.\frac{1}{2^{17}}+\ldots18.\frac{1}{2}+19.$

On subtracting, $-S_2=\frac{1}{2^{19}}+\frac{1}{2^{18}}+\frac{1}{2^{17}}+\ldots.+\frac{1}{2}-19$

$$\Rightarrow S_2=19-\left(\frac{1}{2^{19}}+\frac{1}{2^{18}}+\frac{1}{2^{17}}+\ldots.+\frac{1}{2}\right)$$

$$=19-\frac{\left(\frac{1}{2}\right)\left(1-\left(\frac{1}{2}\right)^{19}\right)}{1-\frac{1}{2}}$$

$$=19-1+\frac{1}{2^{19}}=18+\frac{1}{2^{19}}$$

$\therefore$ From (i) $S_{\infty} = 2^{21}-42+18+\frac{1}{2^{19}}+20$

$$=2^{21}+\frac{1}{2^{19}}-4$$

17. If $v_n=\sum_{m=1}^{n}\frac{1}{(3)^m}$, then the value of $v_n=\sum_{m=1}^{n}v_m$ equals

(a) $\frac{n}{2}+\frac{1}{4(3)^n}+\frac{1}{4}$ (b) $\frac{n}{2}+\frac{1}{4(3)^n}-\frac{1}{4}$

(c) $\frac{n}{2}-\frac{1}{4(3)^n}$ (d) None of these

Solution: (b) $v_n=\sum_{m=1}^{n}\frac{1}{(3)^m}=\left(\frac{1}{3}+\frac{1}{3^2}+\frac{1}{3^3}+\ldots+\frac{1}{3^n}\right)$

$$=\frac{\frac{1}{3}\left[1-\left(\frac{1}{3}\right)^n\right]}{1-\frac{1}{3}}=\frac{1}{2}\left[1-\frac{1}{3^n}\right]$$

$$\therefore \sum_{m=1}^{n}v_m=\sum_{m=1}^{n}\frac{1}{2}\left(1-\frac{1}{3^m}\right)=\frac{1}{2}\sum_{m=1}^{n}\left(1-\frac{1}{3^m}\right)$$

$$=\frac{1}{2}\left[n-\sum_{m=1}^{n}\frac{1}{3^m}\right]=\frac{1}{2}\left[n-\frac{1}{2}+\frac{1}{2(3^n)}\right]$$

$$=\frac{n}{2}-\frac{1}{4}+\frac{1}{4(3)^n}=\frac{n}{2}+\frac{1}{4(3)^n}-\frac{1}{4}$$

18. If $\sqrt{x^{1/x}.(2x)^{1/2x}.(4x)^{1/4x}.(8x)^{1/8x}\ldots..\infty}=\frac{32}{3125}$, then x equals

(a) 1/4 (b) 1/3

(c) 1/5 (d) None of these

Solution: (c) $x^{1/2x}.(2x)^{1/4x}.(4x)^{1/8x}.(8x)^{1/16x}\ldots\ldots\infty$

$$=\frac{32}{3125} \quad \text{(i)}$$

$$\text{LHS}=\left(x^{\frac{1}{2x}+\frac{1}{4x}+\frac{1}{8x}+\frac{1}{16x}+\ldots\infty}\right).\left(2^{\left(\frac{1}{4x}+\frac{2}{8x}+\frac{3}{16x}+\ldots\infty\right)}\right)$$

$$=x^{\frac{1}{x}\left(\frac{1}{2}+\frac{1}{4}+\frac{1}{8}+\frac{1}{16}+\ldots\infty\right)}.(2)^{\frac{1}{4x}\left(1+\frac{2}{2^1}+\frac{3}{2^2}+\frac{4}{2^3}+\ldots\infty\right)} \quad \text{(i)}$$

Now $1+\frac{2}{2^1}+\frac{3}{2^2}+\frac{4}{2^3}+\ldots.\infty=S$

$$\Rightarrow 1.\frac{1}{2}+2.\frac{1}{2^2}+3\left(\frac{1}{2^3}\right)+\ldots\infty=\frac{1}{2}S$$

On subtraction, $\frac{1}{2}S=1+1.\frac{1}{2}+1.\frac{1}{2^2}+1.\frac{1}{2^3}+\ldots\infty$

$$\Rightarrow S=2\left(1+\frac{1}{2}+\frac{1}{2^2}+\frac{1}{2^3}+\ldots\infty\right)$$

$$\Rightarrow S=2\left[\frac{1}{1-1/2}\right]=4$$

∴ From (i)

$$\text{LHS} = x^{\frac{1}{x}}.(2)^{\frac{1}{4x}(4)} = x^{\frac{1}{x}}.(2)^{\frac{1}{x}} = \frac{32}{3125}(\text{Given})$$

$$\Rightarrow (x)^{1/x}.(2)^{1/x} = \frac{(2)^5}{(5)^5} = \left(\frac{1}{5}\right)^5(2)^5 \Rightarrow x = \frac{1}{5}$$

19. The sum of the series $\frac{1}{2}+\frac{1}{3}+\frac{1}{4}-\frac{1}{6}+\frac{1}{8}+\frac{1}{9}+\frac{1}{16}-\frac{1}{12}+......+\infty$ is

(a) $\frac{1}{2}-\log\sqrt[3]{2}$ (b) $1+\log\sqrt[3]{2}$

(c) 3/2 (d) None of these

Solution: (b) Let $S_\infty = \frac{1}{2}+\frac{1}{3}+\frac{1}{4}-\frac{1}{6}+\frac{1}{8}+\frac{1}{9}+...\infty$

$$= \left(\frac{1}{2}+\frac{1}{4}+\frac{1}{8}+...\infty\right)+\left(\frac{1}{3}-\frac{1}{6}+\frac{1}{9}...\infty\right)$$

$$= \left(\frac{1}{2}+\frac{1}{2^2}+\frac{1}{2^3}+...\infty\right)+\frac{1}{3}\left[1-\frac{(1)^2}{2}+\frac{(1)^3}{3}...\infty\right]$$

$$= 1+\frac{1}{3}\log(2)$$

$$= \left[\because \log(1+x) = x-\frac{x^2}{2}+\frac{x^3}{3}-\frac{x^4}{4}+...\infty\right]$$

$$= 1+\log\sqrt[3]{2}$$

20. The sum of the series $x+\frac{1}{3}+3x-\frac{1}{6}+5x+\frac{1}{12}+...$ to $2n$ terms is

(a) $n^2x+\frac{2}{9}\left(1-\frac{(-1)^n}{2^n}\right)$ (b) $2n^2x+\frac{2}{1}\left(1-\frac{(-1)^n}{2^n}\right)$

(c) $nx+1-\frac{(-1)^n}{2^n}$ (d) None of these

Solution: (a) S_{2n} = (x + 3x + 5x + up to n-terms) + $\left(\frac{1}{3}-\frac{1}{6}+\frac{1}{12}+...\text{up to } n \text{ terms}\right)$

$$= \frac{n}{2}[2(x)+(n-1)(2x)]+\frac{1}{3}\frac{\left(1-\left(-\frac{1}{2}\right)^n\right)}{1-\left(-\frac{1}{2}\right)}$$

$$= n^2x+\frac{2}{9}\left(1-\frac{(-1)^n}{2^n}\right)$$

21. The sum of the series $1+\frac{3}{2}+\frac{5}{4}+\frac{7}{8}+...+\frac{2n-1}{(2)^{n-1}}$ is f(n), then f(8) is

(a) $4+\frac{12}{(2)^5}$ (b) $5+\frac{13}{(2)^7}$

(c) $6-\frac{19}{(2)^7}$ (d) None of these

Solution: (c) $S_n = 1+\frac{3}{2}+\frac{5}{4}+\frac{7}{8}+....+\frac{2n-1}{(2)^{n-1}}$ (i)

Clearly, it is an A.G.P

With common ratio ½

$$\Rightarrow \frac{1}{2}S_n = \frac{1}{2}+\frac{3}{4}+\frac{5}{8}+...+\frac{2n-3}{(2)^{n-1}}+\frac{2n-1}{(2)^n} \quad \text{(ii)}$$

(i) –(ii) gives

$$\frac{1}{2}S_n = 1+2\left(\frac{1}{2}+\frac{1}{4}+\frac{1}{8}+...\text{up to}(n-1)\text{ terms}\right)-\frac{(2n-1)}{(2)^n}$$

$$\Rightarrow \frac{1}{2}S_n = 1+2\frac{\left(\frac{1}{2}\right)\left[1-\left(\frac{1}{2}\right)^{n-1}\right]}{\left(1-\frac{1}{2}\right)}-\frac{(2n-1)}{(2)^n}$$

$$\Rightarrow \frac{1}{2}S_n = 1+2\left[1-\frac{1}{(2)^{n-1}}\right]-\frac{(2n-1)}{(2)^n}$$

$$\Rightarrow \frac{1}{2}S_n = 1+2-\frac{1}{(2)^{n-1}}-\frac{(2n-1)}{(2)^n} = 3-\frac{1}{(2)^{n-2}}-\frac{(2n-1)}{(2)^n}$$

$$\Rightarrow S_n = 6-\frac{1}{(2)^{n-3}}-\frac{n}{(2)^{n-2}}+\frac{1}{2^{n-1}}$$

Aliter: $S_n = \frac{ab}{1-r}+\frac{dbr(1-r^{n-1})}{(1-r)^2}-\frac{[a+(n-1)d]r^n}{1-r}$

$$= \frac{1}{1/2}+\frac{(2)(1)\frac{1}{2}\left[1-\frac{1}{2^{n-1}}\right]}{(1-1/2)^2}-\frac{[1+(n-1)(2)]\left(\frac{1}{2}\right)^n}{1-1/2}$$

$$= 2+4\left(1-\frac{1}{2^{n-1}}\right)-2(1+2n-2)\frac{1}{2^n}$$

$$= 2+4-\frac{1}{2^{n-3}}-2(2n-1)\frac{1}{2^n}$$

$$= 6-\frac{1}{2^{n-3}}-\frac{n}{2^{n-2}}+\frac{1}{2^{n-1}}$$

$$\therefore f(n) = 6-\frac{1}{2^{x-3}}-\frac{n}{2^{n-2}}+\frac{1}{2^{n-1}}$$

$$\Rightarrow f(8) = 6-\frac{1}{(2)^5}-\frac{8}{(2)^6}+\frac{1}{(2)^7}$$

$$\Rightarrow f(8) = 6-\left[\frac{4+16-1}{2^7}\right] = 6+\frac{19}{2^7}$$

22. Sum of the series $\frac{3}{2}+\frac{3}{4}+\frac{9}{8}+\frac{15}{16}+$.... up to 2*n*-terms is

(a) $2n+\frac{1}{(3)^{2n}}-\frac{1}{3}$ (b) $2n-\frac{1}{3(2)^{2n}}+\frac{1}{3}$

(c) $n+\frac{1}{3(2)^{2n}}+\frac{1}{3}$ (d) None of these

Solution: (b) $S_n=\frac{3}{2}+\frac{3}{4}+\frac{9}{8}+\frac{15}{16}+\ldots$up to $2n$ – terms

$=\left(1+\frac{1}{2}\right)+\left(1-\frac{1}{4}\right)+\left(1+\frac{1}{8}\right)+\left(1-\frac{1}{16}\right)+\ldots\ldots$ upto

2*n*-terms $=2n+\frac{1}{2}+\frac{1}{2^2}+\frac{1}{2^3}-\frac{1}{2^4}+\ldots$ up to $2n$ –terms

$$= 2n+\frac{1}{2}\left[\frac{1-\left(-\frac{1}{2}\right)^{2n}}{1-\left(-\frac{1}{2}\right)}\right]$$

$$= 2n+\frac{1}{3}\left[1-\frac{1}{(2)^{2n}}\right]=2n-\frac{1}{3(2)^{2n}}+\frac{1}{3}$$

23. A person starts his job with salary Rs 15000 and gets an increment every month so that the salary he gets in ith month is i thousand more than that in $(i-1)^{\text{th}}$ month. Then his annual income is (k = 1000)

(a) 530 k (b) 531k

(c) 532 k (d) None of these

Solution: (c) Let a_i denotes the salary of person for ith month of the year

Thus $a_1 = 15000$ and $a_i = i(1000) + a_{i-1}$

$\Rightarrow a_2 = 2000 + a_1 = 17000 = 17k$

$a_3 = 3000 + a_2 = 20000 = 20k$

$a_4 = 4000 + a_3 = 24000 = 24k$ and so on

Thus we get a sequence

$15k, 17k, 20k, 24k, \ldots$, where $k = 1000$

∴ Annual income

$= 15k + 17k + 20k + 24k + \ldots +$ upto n-terms where $n = 12$

First differences are $2k, 3k, 4k, 5k, \ldots\ldots$

Second differences are $k, k, k, \ldots.$, (constant)

∴ Let $t_n = an^2 + bn + c$

$\Rightarrow t_1 = a + b + c = 15k;$

$\Rightarrow t_2 = 4a + 2b + c = 17k$

and $t_3 = 9a + 3b + c = 20k$

$\Rightarrow 3a + b = 2k$ and $5a + b = 3k$

$\Rightarrow a = k/2;\ b = k/2;\ c = 14k$

$\therefore\ t_n=\frac{k}{2}n^2+\frac{k}{2}n+14k$

$\therefore\ S_n=\frac{k}{2}\sum n^2+\frac{k}{2}\sum n+14k\sum 1;\ n=12$

$=\frac{k}{2}\frac{n(n+1)(2n+1)}{6}+\frac{k}{2}\frac{n(n+1)}{2}+14k(n);\ n=12$

$=\frac{k}{2}(12)(13)(25)+\frac{k}{4}(12)(13)+14\times 12k$

$= 325k + 39k + 168k = 532k.$

24. The sum of first 10 terms of the series $\frac{5}{1.2.3}+\frac{7}{2.3.9}+\frac{9}{3.4.27}+\ldots$ is

(a) $2+\frac{1}{(3)^{10}}$ (b) $1+\frac{1}{11(3)^{10}}$

(c) $2-\frac{1}{11(3)^{10}}$ (d) $1-\frac{1}{11(3)^{10}}$

Solution: (d) $T_n=\frac{\text{n}^{\text{th}}\text{ terms of sequence }5,7,9,\ldots\ldots}{(\text{n})(\text{n}+1)(3)^{\text{n}}}$

$=\frac{5+(\text{n}-1)(2)}{n(n+1)(3)^n}=\frac{2n+3}{n(n+1)(3)^n}$

Let $\frac{2n+3}{n(n+1)}=\frac{A}{n}+\frac{B}{(n+1)}$

$\Rightarrow (2n+3) = A(n+1) + B(n)$

$\Rightarrow 1 = -B;\ 3 = A$

$\therefore\ T_n=\left[\frac{3}{n}-\frac{1}{(n+1)}\right]\cdot\frac{1}{(3)^n}=\frac{1}{n(3)^{n-1}}-\frac{1}{(n+1)(3)^n}$

$\therefore\ S_n=\sum T_n$

$$=\left[\left(1-\frac{1}{2(3)}\right)+\left(\frac{1}{2(3)}-\frac{1}{(3)(3)^2}\right)+\left(\frac{1}{3(3)^2}-\frac{1}{4(3)^3}\right)+\ldots\right.$$

$$\left.+\left(\frac{1}{n(3)^{n-1}}-\frac{1}{(n+1)(3)^n}\right)\right]=\left[1-\frac{1}{(n+1)(3)^n}\right]$$

$\therefore\ \text{S}_{10}=1-\frac{1}{11(3)^{10}}$

25. The value of $\sum_{i=1}^{n}\sum_{j=1}^{i}\sum_{k=1}^{j}n$ is

(a) $\frac{n^2(n+1)(n+2)}{6}$ (b) $\frac{n(n+1)(n+2)}{6}$

(c) $\frac{n^2(n+2)}{12}$ (d) None of these

Solution: (a) $\sum_{i=1}^{n}\sum_{j=1}^{i}(n)\sum_{k=1}^{j}1=\sum_{i=1}^{n}\sum_{j=1}^{i}n(j)$

$$=\sum_{i=1}^{n}n\left(\frac{i(i+1)}{2}\right)=\frac{n}{2}\sum_{i=1}^{n}(i^2+i)$$

$$=\frac{n}{2}\left[\sum_{i=1}^{n}i^2+\sum_{i=1}^{n}i\right]$$

$$=\frac{n}{2}\left[\frac{n(n+1)(2n+1)}{6}+\frac{n(n+1)}{2}\right]$$

$$=\frac{n}{2}\frac{n(n+1)}{2}\left[\frac{(2n+1)}{3}+1\right]=\frac{n^2(n+1)}{12}[2n+4]$$

$$=\frac{n^2(n+1)}{6}[n+2]$$

SECTION–II

SUBJECTIVE-TYPE SOLVED EXAMPLES

1. The fourth power of the common difference of an arithmetic progression with integer entries added to the product of any four consecutive terms of it. Prove that the resulting sum is the square of an integer.

Solution: Let four consecutive terms of the AP are $a-3d$, $a-d$, $a+d$, $a+3d$ which are integers.

Again

Product, $P=(a-3d)(a-d)(a+d)(a+3d)+(2d)^4$ (by given condition)

$=(a^2-9d^2)(a^2-d^2)+16d^4=(a^2-5d^2)^2$

Now, $a^2-5d^2=a^2-9d^4+4d^2$

$=(a-3d)(a+3d)+(2d)^2$

$=I$ (where I is any integer)

Therefore, $P=(I)^2=$ Integer

2. Find the nth term and the sum of n term of the sequence 2,12,36,80,150,252.

Solution: Let

$S=2+12+36+80+150+252+\ldots\ldots+T_n$ (i)

$S=2+12+36+80+150+252+\ldots+T_{n-1}+T_n$ (ii)

(i) – (ii) $\Rightarrow T_n=2+10+24+44+70+102+(T_n-T_{n-1})$ (iii)

$T_n=2+10+24+44+70+102+\ldots+(T_{n-1}-T_{n-2})+(T_n-T_{n-1})$ (iv)

(iii) – (iv) $\Rightarrow T_n-T_{n-1}=2+8+14+20+26+\ldots$up to n-terms

$$=\frac{n}{2}[4+(n-1)6]=n[3n-1]\Rightarrow T_n-T_{n-1}=3n^2-n$$

$\therefore$ general term of given sequence $\Sigma\, T_n-T_{n-1}=\Sigma\, 3n^2-n=n^3+n^2$

Hence sum of this series is $S=\Sigma n^3+\Sigma n^2$

$$=\frac{n^2(n+1)^2}{4}+\frac{n(n+1)(2n+1)}{6}$$

$$=\frac{n(n+1)}{12}(3n^2+7n+2)=\frac{1}{12}n(n+1)(n+2)(3n+1)$$

3. Find the number of terms common to the two APs 3, 7, 11,...........407 and 2, 9,16,...........,709.

Solution: Let the number of terms in two APs be 'm' and 'n' respectively.

Then, $407=3+(m-1).4$ and $709=2+(n-1).7$

$\Rightarrow m=102$ and $n=102$.

$\Rightarrow$ each AP consists of 102 terms.

Let the pth term of 1st AP be equal to q^{th} term of 2nd AP.

Then, $3+(p-1).4=2+(q-1).7$

$\Rightarrow 4(p+1)=7q$

$\Rightarrow \frac{p+1}{7}=\frac{q}{4}=k$ (say)

$\Rightarrow p=7k-1$ and $q=4k$ Since, $p\le 102$ and $q\le 102$

$\Rightarrow 7k-1\le 102$ and $4k\le 102$

$\Rightarrow k\le 14\frac{5}{7}$ and $k\le 25\frac{1}{2}$

$\Rightarrow k\le 14$ corresponding to each value of k, we get a pair of identical terms.

Hence, there are14 identical terms in two APs.

4. If the sum of m terms of an AP is equal to the sum of either the next n terms or the next p terms, prove that $(m+n)\left(\frac{1}{m}-\frac{1}{p}\right)=(m+p)\left(\frac{1}{m}-\frac{1}{n}\right)$.

Solution: Let 'a' and 'd' be the first term and common difference respectively.

Then, $S_m=S_{m+n}-S_m$ and $S_m=S_{m+p}-S_m$

$\Rightarrow S_{m+n}=2S_m$ and $S_{m+p}=2S_m$

$\Rightarrow \dfrac{(m+n)}{2}[2a+(m+n-1)d] = 2.\dfrac{m}{2}[2a+(m-1)d]$

$\Rightarrow \dfrac{m-n}{m+n} = \dfrac{nd}{2a+(m-1)d}$ (i)

Similarly, $\dfrac{m-p}{m+p} = \dfrac{pd}{2a+(m-1)d}$ (ii)

Dividing (*i*) by (*ii*), we get $\dfrac{m-n}{m+n} \cdot \dfrac{m+p}{m-p} = \dfrac{n}{p}$

$\Rightarrow \dfrac{(m-n)(m+p)}{n} = \dfrac{(m+n)(m-p)}{p}$

$\Rightarrow (m+n)\left(\dfrac{1}{m}-\dfrac{1}{p}\right) = (m+p)\left(\dfrac{1}{m}-\dfrac{1}{n}\right)$

5. The $(m+n)^{th}$ and $(m-n)^{th}$ terms of a GP are p and q respectively. Show that the mth and n^{th} terms are $\sqrt{pq}$ and $p\left(\dfrac{q}{p}\right)^{m/2n}$ respectively.

Solution: Let 'a' and 'r' be the first term and common ratio respectively .

Then, $t_{m+n} = ar^{m+n-1} = p$ and $t_{m-n} = ar^{m-n-1} = q$

$\dfrac{t_{m+n}}{t_{m-n}} = \dfrac{ar^{m+n-1}}{ar^{m-n-1}} = r^{2n} = \dfrac{p}{q} \Rightarrow r = \left(\dfrac{p}{q}\right)^{\frac{1}{2n}}$

$t_{m+n}\,t_{m-n} = (ar^{m+n-1})\,(ar^{m-n-1}) = a^2r^{2m-2} = pq$ (i)

$\Rightarrow ar^{m-1} = \sqrt{pq}$

Hence, m^{th} term $= t_m = \sqrt{pq}$.

Putting the value of r in (i), we get

$a\left(\dfrac{p}{q}\right)^{\frac{m-1}{2n}} = (pq)^{1/2} = p\left(\dfrac{q}{p}\right)^{1/2}$

$a = p\left(\dfrac{q}{p}\right)^{1/2}\left(\dfrac{q}{p}\right)^{\frac{m-1}{2n}} = p\left(\dfrac{q}{p}\right)^{\frac{m+n-1}{2n}}$

Hence, n^{th} term $= t_n = ar^{n-1}$

$= p\left(\dfrac{q}{p}\right)^{\frac{m+n-1}{2n}}\left(\dfrac{p}{q}\right)^{\frac{n-1}{2n}} = p\left(\dfrac{q}{p}\right)^{\frac{m}{2n}}$

6. The sum of the squares of three distinct real numbers which are in GP is S^2. If there sum is αS, prove that $\alpha^2 \in (1/3, 1) \cup (1, 3)$.

Solution: Let the three numbers be $\dfrac{a}{r}, a, ar$

Then, $\dfrac{a}{r}+a+ar = \alpha S$ and $\dfrac{a^2}{r^2}+a^2+a^2r^2 = S^2$

$\Rightarrow a\left(\dfrac{1}{r}+1+r\right) = \alpha S$ and $a^2\left(\dfrac{1}{r^2}+1+r^2\right) = S^2$

Putting $r+\dfrac{1}{r} = x$, we get $a(1-x) = \alpha S$ and

$a^2\left[\left(\dfrac{1}{r}+r\right)^2-1\right] = S^2$

$\Rightarrow a^2(1+x)^2 = \alpha^2S^2$ and $a^2(x^2-1) - S^2$

$\Rightarrow \dfrac{a^2(1+x)^2}{a^2(x^2-1)} = \dfrac{\alpha^2S^2}{S^2} \Rightarrow \dfrac{(1+x)^2}{(x^2-1)} = \alpha^2$

$\Rightarrow (1+x)^2 = \alpha^2(x^2-1)$

$\Rightarrow (x+1) = \alpha^2(x-1) \Rightarrow x = r+\dfrac{1}{r} = \dfrac{\alpha^2+1}{\alpha^2-1}$

$\Rightarrow r^2(\alpha^2-1) - (\alpha^2+1)r + (\alpha^2-1) = 0$

Since r is real, Discriminant ≥ 0

$\Rightarrow (\alpha^2+1)^2 - 4(\alpha^2-1)^2 \geq 0$

$\Rightarrow [\alpha^2+1) - 2(\alpha^2-1)][(\alpha^2+1) + 2(\alpha^2-1)] \geq 0$

$\Rightarrow (3-\alpha^2)(3\alpha^2-1) \geq 0$

$\Rightarrow (\alpha^2-3)(\alpha^2-1/3) \leq 0$

$\Rightarrow \dfrac{1}{3} \leq \alpha^2 \leq 3$

But for $\alpha^2 = 3$, $x = \dfrac{\alpha^2+1}{\alpha^2-1} = \dfrac{3+1}{3-1} = 2 = r+\dfrac{1}{r} \Rightarrow r = 1$

for $\alpha^2 = 1/3$, $x = \dfrac{1/3+1}{1/3-1} = -2 = r+\dfrac{1}{r} \Rightarrow r = -1$

for $\alpha^2 = 1$, x does not exist.

Since, the three numbers are distinct, $r \neq \pm 1$

$\Rightarrow \alpha^2 \neq -1, +1, \dfrac{1}{3}, 3.$

Hence, $\Rightarrow \alpha^2 \in (1/3, 1) \cup (1, 3)$

7. If $|x| < 1$ and $|y| < 1$, find the sum to infinity of the series $(x+y) + (x^2+xy+y^2) + (x^3+x^2y+xy^2+y^3)$ ....∞

Solution: $(x+y) + (x^2+xy+y^2) + (x^3+x^2y+xy^2+y^3) + ...\infty$

$= \dfrac{(x^2-y^2)}{x-y} + \dfrac{(x^3-y^3)}{x-y} + \dfrac{(x^4-y^4)}{x-y} + ...\infty$

$= \dfrac{1}{x-y}[(x^2+x^3+x^4+....) - (y^2+y^3+y^4+....)]$

$\dfrac{1}{x-y}\left[\dfrac{x^2}{1-x} - \dfrac{y^2}{1-y}\right] = \dfrac{x^2(1-y) - y^2(1-x)}{(x-y)(1-x)(1-y)}$

$= \dfrac{(x-y)(x+y-xy)}{(x-y)(1-x)(1-y)}$

$= \dfrac{x+y-xy}{(1-x)(1-y)}$

8. If p be the first of n AMs between 2 numbers, q be the first of n HMs between the same numbers, prove that the value of q cannot lie between p and $\left(\frac{n+1}{n-1}\right)^2 p$.

Solution: Let the two numbers be a and b. Then,

$$p = a + \frac{(b-a)}{n+1} = \frac{b+an}{n+1} \quad \text{(i)}$$

$$\frac{1}{q} = \frac{1}{a} + \frac{\frac{1}{b} - \frac{1}{a}}{n+1} \Rightarrow q = \frac{ab(n+1)}{bn+a} \quad \text{(ii)}$$

Dividing (*ii*) by (*i*), we get

$$\frac{q}{p} = \frac{ab(n+1)^2}{(bn+a)(b+an)} = \frac{(n+1)^2}{n^2+1+n\left(\frac{a}{b}+\frac{b}{a}\right)}$$

We know that the sum of a number and its reciprocal cannot lie between −2 and 2.

$$\Rightarrow \frac{a}{b}+\frac{b}{a} \geq 2 \text{ or } \frac{a}{b}+\frac{b}{a} \leq -2$$

$$\Rightarrow n\left(\frac{a}{b}+\frac{b}{a}\right) \geq 2n \text{ or } n\left(\frac{a}{b}+\frac{b}{a}\right) \leq -2n$$

$$\Rightarrow n\left(\frac{a}{b}+\frac{b}{a}\right) + n^2 + 1 \geq 2n + n^2 + 1 = (n+1)^2$$

$$\text{or } n\left(\frac{a}{b}+\frac{b}{a}\right) + n^2 + 1 \leq -2n + n^2 + 1 = (n-1)^2$$

$$\Rightarrow \frac{(n+1)^2}{n^2+1+n\left(\frac{a}{b}+\frac{b}{a}\right)} \leq 1 \text{ or}$$

$$\frac{(n+1)^2}{n^2+1+n\left(\frac{a}{b}+\frac{b}{a}\right)} \geq \frac{(n+1)^2}{(n-1)^2}$$

$$\Rightarrow \frac{q}{p} \leq 1 \text{ or } \frac{q}{p} \geq \frac{(n+1)^2}{(n-1)^2} \Rightarrow q \leq p$$

$$\text{or } q \geq \left(\frac{n+1}{n-1}\right)^2 p$$

Hence, q cannot lie between p and $\left(\frac{n+1}{n-1}\right)^2 p$

9. If $a > 0$, $b > 0$, $c > 0$, prove that

$$\frac{1}{s-a} + \frac{1}{s-b} + \frac{1}{s-c} > \frac{9}{s} \text{ where } 2s = a+b+c.$$

Solution: For three positive numbers x, y, z, we have, Arithmetic mean $A = \frac{x+y+z}{3}$,

Harmonic mean $H = \frac{1}{(1/x+1/y+1/z)/3}$ and $A > H$.

Here, $s - a$, $s - b$, $s - c$ are positive (follows from triangle inequality)

$$\therefore \frac{s-a+s-b+s-c}{3} > \frac{1}{\frac{\frac{1}{s-a}+\frac{1}{s-b}+\frac{1}{s-c}}{3}}$$

$$\Rightarrow \frac{3s-(a+b+c)}{3} > \frac{3}{\frac{1}{s-a}+\frac{1}{s-b}+\frac{1}{s-c}}$$

$$\Rightarrow \frac{3}{s} < \frac{\frac{1}{s-a}+\frac{1}{s-b}+\frac{1}{s-c}}{3}$$

$$\therefore \frac{1}{s-a}+\frac{1}{s-b}+\frac{1}{s-c} > \frac{9}{s}$$

10. Find the coefficient of x^{98} in the expansion of $(x+1)(x+2)(x+3)......(x+100)$.

Solution: $(x+a_1)(x+a_2)(x+a_3)......(x+a_n)$; n = 100

$$= x^{100} + \left(\sum a_1\right)x^{99} + \left(\sum a_1 a_2\right)x^{98} + \left(\sum a_1 a_2 a_3\right) x^{97} + ... + (a_1 a_2 .....a_n)$$

⇒ The coefficient of x^{98} in the expansion of $(x+1)(x+2)(x+3)......(x+100)$ is sum of the products of 1, 2, 3 .....100 taken two at a time, denote it as by S.

Now $(1+2+3+....100)^2 = 1^2+2^2+3^2+.....100^2+2S$

$$\Rightarrow \left[\frac{100}{2}(1+100)\right]^2 = \frac{100(100+1)(200+1)}{6} + 2S$$

$$\Rightarrow \left(\frac{10100}{2}\right)^2 = \frac{201(10100)}{6} + 2S \quad \text{(required sum)}$$

∴ Required Sum (S)

$$= \frac{1}{2}\left[\left(\frac{10100}{2}\right)^2 - \frac{201(10100)}{6}\right] = 12582075$$

11. The sum of three consecutive terms in AP is 27 and the sum of their squares is 293, then find all three terms.

Solution: If we take three terms of an AP like a, $a + d$. and $a + 2d$ then

$a + (a + d) + (a + 2d) = 27$

$(a + d) = 3$ and $a^2 + (a + d)^2 + (a + 2d)^2 = 293$

In this way, calculation is very long, so we take the terms like $a - b$, a, $a + b$ are the required numbers.

So $(a - b) + a + (a + b) = 27$ or $3a = 27 \Rightarrow a = 9$

Now $(a - b)^2 + a^2 + (a + b)^2 = 293$.

or $a^2 + b^2 - 2ab + a^2 + a^2 + b^2 + 2ab = 293$.

or $3a^2 + 2b^2 = 293$.

or $2b^2 = 293 - 3a^2 = 293 - 3(9^2) = 293 - 243 = 50$.

or $b^2 = 25$ or $b = 5$

So the number are 4, 9, 14. Negative values will just reverse the order.

12. Find the common difference of an AP whose first term is 100 and the sum of whose first six terms is five times the sum of the next six terms.

Solution: Let the common difference is d.

$\therefore\ S_n = \frac{n}{2}[\,2a + (n-1)\,d\,]$

$S_6 = \frac{6}{2}[2 \times 100 + (6-1)\,d\,] = 3\,[\,200 + 5d]$ (i)

also $S_{7\text{ to }12} = \frac{7^{th}\text{ term} + 12^{th}\text{ term}}{2} \times 6$ (according to question;

$= \frac{100 + 6d + 100 + 11d}{2} \times 6 = (200 + 17\,d)\,3$ (ii)

According to question 5 × eq. (ii) = equation (i)

so $5 \times (200 + 17d)3 = 3\,(200 + 5d)$

$\Rightarrow 1000 + 85d = 200 + 5d$

$\Rightarrow 80\,d = -800 \Rightarrow d = -10$

13. The sum of three consecutive numbers in GP is 39 and their product is 729, then find all three numbers.

Solution: Let a/b, a, ab are required numbers. Product $= a^3 = 729 = 9^3 \Rightarrow a = 9$

Now, $a/b + a + ab = 39$ (given) $\Rightarrow a\left(\frac{1}{b} + 1 + b\right) = 39$

Multiplying each term by b, $9\,(1 + b + b^2) = 39\,b$

or $9\,b^2 + 9b + 9 - 39b = 0$ or $9b^2 - 30b + 9 = 0$

$$b = \frac{30 \pm \sqrt{900 - 324}}{18} = \frac{30 \pm \sqrt{576}}{18}$$

$$\Rightarrow\ b = \frac{30 \pm 24}{18} = \frac{54}{18}, \frac{6}{18} = 3, \frac{1}{3}$$

so numbers are 3, 9, 27 or 27, 9, 3.

14. If the AM between 'a' and 'b' is twice the GM, show that $a/b = 7 \pm 4\sqrt{3}$

Solution: AM $= \frac{a+b}{2}$; GM $= \sqrt{ab}$

We are given AM = 2 GM

$\Rightarrow \frac{a+b}{2} = 2\sqrt{ab} \Rightarrow a + b - 4\,(ab)^{1/2} = 0$

Dividing each term by 'b' gives $\left(\frac{a}{b}\right) + 1 - 4\left(\frac{a}{b}\right)^{1/2} = 0$

or $\left(\sqrt{\frac{a}{b}}\right)^2 - 4\sqrt{\frac{a}{b}} + 1 = 0$

$\because\ \sqrt{\frac{a}{b}} = \frac{4 \pm \sqrt{16-4}}{2} = \frac{4 \pm 2\sqrt{3}}{2} = 2 \pm \sqrt{3}$

Squaring both sides, we get,

$$\frac{a}{b} = \left(2 \pm \sqrt{3}\right)^2 = 4 + 3 \pm 4\sqrt{3} = 7 \pm 4\sqrt{3}$$

15. If S be the sum, P the product and R the sum of the reciprocals of n terms of a GP. Prove that $\left(\frac{S}{R}\right)^n = P^2$

Solution: Given $S = a + ar + ar^2 + \ldots\ldots + ar^{n-1}$;

$P = a.\ ar.\ ar^2 \ldots\ldots\ldots\ ar^{n-1}$;

$$R = \frac{1}{a} + \frac{1}{ar} + \frac{1}{ar^2} + \ldots. + \frac{1}{ar^{n-1}}$$

So, $S = \frac{a(1-r^n)}{1-r}$; $P = a^n.r^{\frac{n(n-1)}{2}}$

$R = \frac{(1/a)(1-1/r^n)}{1-1/r}$;

So L.H.S. $= \left(\frac{S}{R}\right)^n$

$$= \left[\frac{a(1-r^n)}{(1-r) \times \left[(1/a)(1-1/r^n)\right]/(1-1/r)}\right]^n$$

$$= \left[\frac{a^2(1-r^n)\left(\frac{r-1}{r}\right)}{(1-r)\left(\frac{r^n-1}{r^n}\right)}\right]^n = \left[\frac{a^2(1-r^n)(1-r)r^n}{r(1-r)(1-r^n)}\right]^n$$

$$= \left[a^2 r^{n-1}\right]^n = \left[a^n r^{\frac{n(n-1)}{2}}\right]^2$$

$= P^2 =$ R.H.S.

16. If a, b and c are in HP and $a > c$, show that $\frac{1}{b-c} + \frac{1}{a-b} > \frac{4}{a-c}$

Solution: a, b, and c are in HP.

$\Rightarrow\ \frac{1}{a}, \frac{1}{b}$ and $\frac{1}{c}$ are in AP.

$$\Rightarrow\ \frac{1}{b} - \frac{1}{a} = \frac{1}{c} - \frac{1}{b} = \frac{1}{2}\left(\frac{1}{c} - \frac{1}{a}\right)$$

$\left(\because \text{ if } x = y \text{ then } x = y = \frac{x+y}{2}\right)$

$\Rightarrow \frac{a-b}{ab} = \frac{b-c}{bc} = \frac{a-c}{2ac}$

$\Rightarrow \frac{1}{b-c} = \frac{2a}{b}.\frac{1}{a-c}$ and $\frac{1}{a-b} = \frac{2c}{b}.\frac{1}{a-c}$

LHS of given expression $= \frac{1}{b-c} + \frac{1}{a-b}$

$= \frac{2(a+c)}{b(a-c)} = \frac{4ac}{b^2(a-c)} \quad \left(\because b = \frac{2ac}{a+c}\right)$

$> \frac{4}{a-c}$ (As GM of a and c > HM of a and c i.e., $\sqrt{ac} > b$)

17. In an AP of which 'a' is the first term, if the sum of the first p terms is equal to zero, show that the sum of the next q terms is $-\left(\frac{aq(p+q)}{p-1}\right)$.

Solution: Sum of first p terms = 0

or $\frac{p}{2}$ [2a + (p – 1) d] = 0

or $d = -\frac{2a}{p-1}$ (1)

sum of next q terms = (sum of first p terms = 0)

Now, sum of next q terms

= sum of $(p + q)$ terms

$= \frac{p+q}{2}$ [2a + (p + q – 1)d]

Putting value of d from equation (1)

$= \frac{p+q}{2}\left[2a+(p+q-1)\frac{(-2a)}{p-1}\right]$

$= (p+q)\left[a+\frac{(-ap)+(-aq)+}{p-1}\right]$

$= (p+q)\left[\frac{ap-a-ap-aq+a}{p-1}\right]$

$= -aq\frac{(p+q)}{p-1}$ **proved.**

18. There are nAM's between 1 and 31 such that 7th mean: $(n-1)^{th}$ mean = 5 : 9, then find the value of n.

Solution: $d = \frac{31-1}{n+1} = \frac{30}{n+1}$ (1)

According to the question, $\frac{a+7d}{a+(n-1)d} = \frac{5}{9}$

or $9a + 63d = 5a + 5nd - 5d$

or $4 = 5nd - \frac{68\times 30}{n+1}$

or $4 = \frac{5n(30)}{n+1} - \frac{68\times 30}{n+1}$

or $4n + 4 = 150n - 2040$

or $2044 = 146n$

or $n = 14$

19. Prove that the average of the numbers n sin n°, n = 2, 4, 6,......, 180, is cot 1°.

Solution: Sum = 2 sin 2° + 4 sin 4° +.......+ 180° sin 180° (90° terms)

= 2 sin 2° + 4 sin 4° +....+ 90 sin 90°+.......+ 178 sin 178° + 180 sin 180°

= 2 sin 2° + 4 sin 4° +....+ 178 sin 178° + 0

= (2 sin 2° + 4 sin 4° +.....+ 176 sin 176° + 178 sin 178°) + 90

= (2 sin 2° + 4 sin 4°+....+ 176 sin 4° + 178 sin 2°) + 90°

= 180 [sin 2° + sin 4° +.....+ sin 88°] + 90

$= 180\left[\frac{\sin\frac{88°}{2}}{\sin\frac{2°}{2}} \times \sin\left(\frac{2°+88°}{2}\right)\right] + 90$

$= 180\left[\frac{\sin 44° \sin 45°}{\sin 1°}\right] + 90$

$= 90\ \frac{[\cos 1° - \cos 89°]}{\sin 1°} + 90$

= 90 [cot 1° – 1] + 90 = 90 cot 1° – 90 + 90

or sum = 90 cot 1°

Since there are 90 terms, therefore average of 90 terms will be $= \frac{\text{sum}}{\text{total no. of terms}} = \frac{90\cot 1°}{90} = \cot 1°$

∴ average = cot1° **proved.**

20. Find the value of the sum $\sum_{k=0}^{359} k.\cos k°$.

Solution: $\sum_{k=0}^{359} k.\cos k°$ = 0 cos0° + 1 cos 1° + 2 cos 2° +....+ 359 cos 359°

= {1 cos 1° + 2 cos 2° +........+ 89 cos 89°}

+ {91 cos 91° + 92 cos 92° +....+ 179 cos 179°}

+ {181 cos 181° +.....+ 269 cos 269°} + {271 cos 271° + ... + 359 cos 359°}

+ 90 cos 90° + 180 cos 180° + 270 cos 270° + 0 cos 0

$\left.\begin{aligned} &= 1\cos 1° + 2\cos 2° + ... + 89\cos 89° \\ &-91\sin 1° - 92\sin 2° ..... - 179 \sin 89° \\ &-181\cos 1° - 182\cos 2° .... - 269\cos 89° \\ &+271\sin 1° + 272\sin 2° .... 359\sin 89° \end{aligned}\right\}$ 359 terms

= – 180

= (– 180 cos 1° – 180 cos2°.....–180 cos 89°) + (180 sin 1° + 180 sin 2° +....+ 180 sin 89°)

$= -180 [\cos 1° + \cos 2° + ... + \cos 89°] + 180 [\sin 1° + \sin 2° + ... \sin 89°] - 180$

$$= -180\left(\frac{\sin\frac{89}{2}.\cos 45}{\sin\frac{1}{2}}\right)+180\frac{\sin\frac{89°}{2}\sin 45°}{\sin\frac{1°}{2}}-180$$

$= -180$

21. In a set of four integers, the first three are in GP and the last three are in AP, with common difference 6. If the first number is the same as the fourth, find the four numbers.

Solution: Let α, β, γ....are in GP & β, γ, δ are in AP and let $\alpha = \frac{a}{r}, \beta = a; \gamma = ar$

and β, γ, δ........are in AP, so let

$\beta = A - d, \gamma = A, \delta = A + d$

$\Rightarrow A - d = a$ and $A = ar;\ \delta = A + d$ and $\delta = \frac{a}{r}; d = 6$

$\Rightarrow A - 6 = a;\ A + 6 = \frac{a}{r}$

or $r = \frac{A-6}{A+6}$ Also $\frac{A}{A-d} = r$

$\Rightarrow A = \frac{(A-6)(A-6)}{A+6}$

or $A^2 + 6A = A^2 + 36 - 12A$

$\therefore A = 2; r = -1/2$

$\Rightarrow a = A - 6 = 2 - 6 = -4$

$\therefore$ set of numbers are

$\Rightarrow 8, -4, 2, 8$

22. The 1st, 2nd and 3rd terms of an arithmetic series are a, b and a^2 where 'a' is negative. The 1st, 2nd and 3rd terms of a geometric series are a, a^2 and b find the

(a) value of a and b

(b) sum of infinite geometric series if it exists. if no then find the sum to n terms of the GP.

(c) sum of the 40 terms of the arithmetic series.

Solution: (a) a, b, a^2.....are in AP.

$b - a = a^2 - b$

or $2b = a^2 + a$ (1)

and $a^3 = b$ (2)

or $(a^2 + a)^3 = (2b)^3$

$(a^2)^3 + a^3 + 3a^3(a^2 + a) = 8b^3$

or $b^2 + b + 6b^2 = 8b^3$

or $8b^2 - 7b^2 - b = 0 \Rightarrow 8b^2 - 8b + b - 1 = 0$

or $8b^2 - 7b - 1 = 0 \Rightarrow 8b(b - 1) + 1(b - 1) = 0$

$\Rightarrow (8b + 1)(b - 1) = 0 \Rightarrow b = -\frac{1}{8}, 1$

and $a = -\frac{1}{2}, 1$

given that a is negative $\therefore$ a cannot be 1

$\therefore\ a = -\frac{1}{2}$ and $b = -\frac{1}{8}$

(b) a, a^2, b..are in GP, then putting $a = -\frac{1}{2}$ and $b = -\frac{1}{8}$ we get $-\frac{1}{2}, \frac{1}{4}, -\frac{1}{8}$.. are in GP. Sum of infinite

$$\text{GP} = \frac{a}{1-r} = \frac{\left(-\frac{1}{2}\right)}{1-\left(\frac{\frac{1}{4}}{\frac{-1}{2}}\right)} = \frac{-1}{3} \textbf{ Ans}$$

(c) sum of 40 terms of AP $= \frac{n}{2}[2a + (n-1)d]$

$$= \frac{40}{2}\left[2\left(\frac{-1}{2}\right)+(40-1)\times\left(-\frac{1}{8}+\frac{1}{2}\right)\right]$$

$$= 20\left[-1+39\times\frac{3}{8}\right] = \frac{545}{2}$$

23. If $S_1, S_2, S_3,...S_n,...$ are the sums of infinite geometric series whose first terms are 1, 2, 3,...n,... and whose common ratios are $\frac{1}{2}, \frac{1}{3}, \frac{1}{4}, ..., \frac{1}{n+1}, ...$ respectively, then find the value of $\sum_{r=1}^{2n-1} S_r^2$

Solution: $S_1 = \frac{1}{1-\frac{1}{2}} = 2,$

$S_2 = \frac{2}{1-\frac{1}{3}} = 3$

$\sum_{r=1}^{2n-1} S_r^2 = (S_1)^2 + (S_2)^2 + (S_3)^2 + ...(S_{2n-1})^2$

$= 2^2 + 3^2 + 4^2 + ...(2n)^2$

$=$ (sum of squares of first $2n$ natural numbers) $- 1$

$= 1^2 + 2^2 + 3^2 + 4^2 + ... + (2n)^2 - 1^2$

$= \frac{(2n)(2n+1)(4n+1)}{6} - 1$

24. Sum the following series to n terms and to infinity:

(*i*) $\frac{1}{1.4.7} + \frac{1}{4.7.10} + \frac{1}{7.10.13} + ...$

(*ii*) $\sum_{r=1}^{n} r(r+1)(r+2)(r+3)$

(*iii*) $\sum_{r=1}^{n} \frac{1}{4r^2 - 1}$

(*iv*) $\frac{1}{4} + \frac{1.3}{4.6} + \frac{1.3.5}{4.6.8} + ...$

Solution: (i) $\frac{1}{1.4.7}+\frac{1}{4.7.10}+\frac{1}{7.10.13}+..........$

$$T_n=\frac{1}{(3n-2)\,(3n+1)\,(3n+4)}$$

$$S_n=\sum\frac{1}{6}\frac{[(3n+4)-(3n-2)]}{(3n-2)\,(3n+1)\,(3n+4)}$$

or $S_n=\frac{1}{6}\left[\frac{1}{(3n-2)\,(3n+1)}-\frac{1}{(3n+1)\,(3n+4)}\right]$

$$=\frac{1}{6}\left[\frac{1}{4}-\frac{1}{28}+\frac{1}{28}-......-\frac{1}{(3n+1)\,(3n+4)}\right]$$

or $S_n=\frac{1}{6}\left[\frac{1}{4}-\frac{1}{(3n+1)\,(3n+4)}\right]$

$\Rightarrow S_\infty=\frac{1}{6}\left[\frac{1}{4}-0\right]=\frac{1}{24}$ **Ans.**

(ii) $\sum_{r=1}^{n}r(r+1)(r+2)\,(r+3)$

$$=\sum_{r=1}^{n}r(r+1)\,(r+2)(r+3)\times\left[\frac{(r+4)-(r-1)}{5}\right]$$

$$=\sum_{r=1}^{n}\frac{r(r+1)\,(r+2)\,(r+3)\,(r+4)}{5}-\frac{(r-1)(r)(r+1)\,(r+2)(r+3)}{5}$$

$$=\frac{1.2.3.4.5}{5}-0+\frac{2.3.4.5.6}{5}-\frac{1.2.3.4.5}{5}-\frac{3(4).5.6.7}{5}-\frac{2.3.4.5.6}{5}.......+\frac{n(n+1)\,(n+2)\,(n+3)\,(n+4)}{5}-\frac{(n-1)n(n+1)(n+2)}{5}$$

$\Rightarrow S_n=\frac{n(n+1)(n+2)(n+3)\,(n+4)}{5}$ **Ans.**

(iii) $\sum_{r=1}^{n}\frac{1}{4r^2-1}=\sum_{r=1}^{4}\frac{1}{(2r-1)\,(2r+1)}$.

$$=\sum_{r=1}^{n}\frac{1}{2}\left[\frac{(2r+1)-(2r-1)}{(2r-1)\,(2r+1)}\right]=\sum_{r=1}^{n}\frac{1}{2}\left[\frac{1}{2r-1}-\frac{1}{2r+1}\right]$$

$$=\frac{1}{2}\left[\frac{1}{1}-\frac{1}{3}+\frac{1}{3}-\frac{1}{5}+\frac{1}{5}.......-\frac{1}{2n+1}\right]$$

$$=\frac{1}{2}\left[1-\frac{1}{2n+1}\right]=\frac{n}{2n+1}\Rightarrow S_\infty=\frac{1}{2}$$

(iv) $\frac{1}{4}+\frac{1.3}{4.6}+\frac{1.3.5}{4.6.8}+..........$ up to n-terms

$$=\frac{2}{2}\times\frac{1}{4}+\frac{1.3}{4.6}+\frac{1.3.5}{4.6.8}+.......\text{ up to n-terms}$$

$$=2\left[\frac{1}{2.4}+\frac{1.3}{2.4.6}+\frac{1.3.5}{2.4.6.8}+......+\frac{1.3....(2n-1)}{2.4.6.....(2n+2)}\right]$$

$$\Rightarrow T_n=2\left[\frac{1.3.5.7.......(2n-1)}{2.4.6.8........(2n+2)}\{(2n+2)-(2n+1)\}\right]$$

$$\Rightarrow T_n=2\left[\frac{1.3.5.......(2n-1)}{2.4.6.8.....2n}-\frac{1.3.5......(2n+1)}{2.4.6....(2n+2)}\right]$$

$$\Rightarrow S_n=2\left[\left(\frac{1}{2}-\frac{1.3}{2.4}\right)+\left(\frac{1.3.....1.3.5}{2.4....2.4.6}\right)+...+(T_n)\right]$$

$\Rightarrow S_n=2\left[\frac{1}{2}-\frac{1.3.5....(2n+1)}{4.6....(2n+12)}\right]$ and $S_\infty=1$

25. Find the sum of the n terms of the sequence $\frac{1}{1+1^2+1^4}+\frac{2}{1+2^2+2^4}+\frac{3}{1+3^2+3^4}+..........$

Solution: $\frac{1}{1+1^2+1^4}+\frac{2}{1+2^2+2^4}+\frac{3}{1+3^2+3^4}+......$ upto n-terms

Now, $T_n=\frac{n}{1+n^2+n^4}=\frac{n}{n^4+n^2+1}$

$$=\frac{1}{2}\left[\frac{(n^2+n+1)-(n^2-n+1)}{(n^2+n+1)\,(n^2-n+1)}\right]$$

$$S_n=\frac{1}{2}\left[\frac{1}{n^2-n+1}-\frac{1}{n^2+n+1}\right]$$

$$=\frac{1}{2}\left[\frac{1}{1}-\frac{1}{3}+\frac{1}{3}-\frac{1}{7}+.....-\frac{1}{n^2+n+1}\right]=\frac{1}{2}\left[\frac{n^2+n}{n^2+n+1}\right]$$

26. If 'K' denotes the sum of the infinite series $\sum_{n=1}^{\infty}\left(\frac{n^2+2n+3}{2^n}\right)$. Compute the value of ($1^3+2^3+3^3$ +......+ K^3).

Solution: $K=\sum_{n=1}^{\infty}\left(\frac{n^2+2n+3}{2^n}\right)$.

$$K=\frac{6}{2}+\frac{11}{4}+\frac{18}{8}+\frac{27}{16}+...\frac{n^2+2n+3}{2^n}+..... \quad (1)$$

dividing in equation (1) by 2, we get,

$$\frac{K}{2}=\frac{6}{4}+\frac{11}{8}+\frac{18}{16}.....+\frac{n^2+2n+3}{2^{n+1}}+.... \quad (2)$$

subtracting equation (2) from (1), we get

$$\frac{K}{2}=\frac{6}{2}+\frac{5}{4}+\frac{7}{8}+\frac{9}{16}+....+\frac{n^2+2n+1}{2^{n+1}}+.... \quad (3)$$

now dividing equation (3) by 2 again, we get

$$\frac{K}{4}=\frac{6}{4}+\frac{5}{8}+\frac{7}{16}+.......\frac{n^2+2n+1}{2^{n+2}}+.... \quad (4)$$

equation (4) – equation (3) gives,

or $\frac{K}{4}=\frac{6}{4}+\frac{5}{4}+\underbrace{\frac{2}{8}+\frac{2}{16}+\frac{2}{32}+.....\text{up to } \infty}_{G.P.}$

or $\frac{K}{4}=\frac{11}{4}+2\left[\frac{1}{8}+\frac{1}{16}+\frac{1}{32}+.....\infty\right]$

or $\frac{K}{4}=\frac{13}{4}$

or $K = 13$ Now $S = 1^3 + 2^3 + 3^3+.......(13)^3$

$$=\sum_{n=1}^{13} n^3=\left(\frac{13\times 14}{2}\right)^2=(13\times 7)^2=8281$$

27. If the sum

$\sqrt{1+\frac{1}{1^2}+\frac{1}{2^2}}+\sqrt{1+\frac{1}{2^2}+\frac{1}{3^2}}+\sqrt{1+\frac{1}{3^2}+\frac{1}{4^2}}+......+\sqrt{1+\frac{1}{(2012)^2}+\frac{1}{(2013)^2}}$

equal to $n-\frac{1}{n}$; where $n \in \mathbb{N}$. Find $\sqrt{n+12}$.

Solution:

$\sqrt{1+\frac{1}{1^2}+\frac{1}{2^2}}+\sqrt{1+\frac{1}{2^2}+\frac{1}{3^2}}+\sqrt{1+\frac{1}{3^2}+\frac{1}{4^2}}+......+\sqrt{1+\frac{1}{(2012)^2}+\frac{1}{(2013)^2}}$

$=\frac{3}{2}+\frac{7}{6}+\frac{13}{12}+.......$ up to 2012th term

$T_n=\frac{n(n+1)+1}{n(n+1)}=1+\frac{1}{n(n+1)}$

Now $\Sigma T_n = n + \Sigma\frac{(n+1)-n}{n(n+1)} = n+\Sigma\left[\frac{1}{n}-\frac{1}{n+1}\right]$

or $\Sigma T_n = n+\frac{n}{n+1}$

or $\Sigma T_{2012} = 2012 + \frac{2012}{2013}$

$= 2013 - 1 + \frac{2013-1}{2013} = 2013 - 1 + 1 - \frac{1}{2013}$

or $\Sigma T_{2012} = 2013-\frac{1}{2013} = n-\frac{1}{n}$

therefore $n = 2013$

$\Rightarrow \sqrt{n+12}=\sqrt{2025}=45$

28. The pth term T_p of HP is $q(p + q)$ and q[th] term T_q is $p(p + q)$ when $p > 2$, $q > 2$. Prove that

(a) $T_{p+q} = pq$; (b) $T_{pq} = p + q$;

(c) $T_{p+q} > T_{pq}$.

Solution: T_p of HP $= q(p + q)$

$\Rightarrow T_p$ of corresponding AP $=\frac{1}{q(p+q)}$

$\Rightarrow a + (p-1)\, d=\frac{1}{q(p+q)}$ (1)

T_q of HP $= p(p + q)$

$\Rightarrow T_q$ of corresponding AP $=\frac{1}{p(p+q)}$

$\Rightarrow a + (q - 1)d = \frac{1}{p(p+q)}$ (2)

(1)–(2) gives

$(p - q)d = \frac{1}{q(p+q)}-\frac{1}{p(p+q)}=\frac{(p-q)}{pq(p+q)}$

$\Rightarrow d = \frac{1}{pq(p+q)}$

$\therefore\ a + \frac{(p-1)}{pq(p+q)}=\frac{1}{q(p+q)}$ [from (i)]

$\Rightarrow a = \frac{1}{q(p+q)}-\frac{(p-1)}{pq(p+q)}$

$\Rightarrow a = \frac{p-p+1}{pq(p+q)}=\frac{1}{pq(p+q)}$

(a) Now, $t(p + q)$ of AP $= a + (p + q - 1)\, d$

$=\frac{1}{pq(p+q)}+(p+q-1)\frac{1}{pq(p+q)}$

$=\frac{1+p+q-1}{pq(p+q)}=\frac{1}{pq}$

T_{p+q} of HP $= pq$

(b) t_{pq} of AP $= a + (pq - 1)$d

$=\frac{1}{pq(p+q)}+(pq-1)\frac{1}{pq(p+q)}$

$=\frac{1+pq-1}{pq(p+q)}=\frac{1}{p+q}$

T_{pq} of HP $= p + q$

(c) We have to prove pq > $p + q$ for p > 2, q > 2

$\Rightarrow \frac{1}{p}<\frac{1}{2};\ \frac{1}{q}<\frac{1}{2}$

$\Rightarrow \frac{1}{p}+\frac{1}{q}<1 \Rightarrow p+q<pq \Rightarrow T_{p+q}>T_{pq}$

29. Two distinct, real, infinite geometric series each have a sum of 1 and have the same second term. The third term of one of the series is 1/8. If the second term of both the series can be written in the form $\frac{\sqrt{m}-n}{p}$, where m, n and p are positive intergers and m is not divisible by the square of any prime, find the value of $100m + 10n + p$.

Solution: Let the two infinite GP's be a_1, a_2, a_3..... and b_1, b_2, b_3....... with common ratios r_1 and r_2 respectively.

$\therefore$ According to the question.

$$\Rightarrow \frac{a_1}{1-r_1} = 1; \frac{b_1}{1-r_2} = 1$$

$\Rightarrow a_1 = 1 - r_1$

$\Rightarrow a_1 + r_1 = 1$ (1)

Similarly, $b_1 + r_2 = 1$ (2)

Also, $a_1 r_1 = b_1 r_2$ (given) (3)

Let, $a_1 r_1^2 = \frac{1}{8}$ (Considering third terms of first G.P. = 1/8)

$\Rightarrow (1 - r_1)(r_1^2) = 1/8$

or $8(-r_1^3 + r_1^2) = 1$ or $8r_1^3 - 8r_1^2 + 1 = 0$

or $r_1^3 - r_1^2 + 1/8 = 0$ or $r = \frac{1}{2}, \frac{1-\sqrt{5}}{4}, \frac{1+\sqrt{5}}{4}$

$\Rightarrow a = \frac{1}{2}, \frac{3+\sqrt{5}}{4}, \frac{3-\sqrt{5}}{4}$

$T_2 = \frac{1}{4}; \frac{-2-2\sqrt{5}}{16}; \frac{\sqrt{5}-1}{8}$

Clearly, $\frac{\sqrt{5}-1}{8}$ is of the required form $\frac{\sqrt{m}-n}{p}$

so $m = 5, n = 1, p = 8$

$\therefore$ value of $100m + 10n + p = 518$

30. One of the roots of the equation $2000x^6 + 100x^5 + 10x^3 + x - 2 = 0$ is of the form $\frac{m+\sqrt{n}}{r}$, where m is non zero integer and n and r are relatively prime natural numbers. Find the vlaue of $2m+\sqrt{n-r}$.

Solution: $2(1 - 1000x^6) = x(1 + 10x^2 + 100x^4)$

$$2(1 - 1000x^6) = x\left[\frac{1-(10x^2)^3}{1-10x^2}\right]$$

$2 = \frac{x}{1-10x^2}$ or $2 - 20x^2 = x$

or $20x^2 + x - 2 = 0$

or $x = \frac{-1\pm\sqrt{161}}{40}$; Thus $x = \frac{-1+\sqrt{161}}{40}$ is of the form $\frac{m+\sqrt{n}}{p}$

$\Rightarrow m = -1, n = 161, r = 40$

$\Rightarrow 2m+\sqrt{n-r} = -2+\sqrt{161-40} = 9$

31. Find the condition that the roots of the equation $x^3 - px^2 + qx - r = 0$ are in AP and hence solve the equation $x^3 - 12x^2 + 39x - 28 = 0$.

Solution: Let the roots of the given cubic be

$(a - d), (a), (a + d)$

sum of roots is $= a - d + a + a + d = p$ or $a = p/3$

product of roots is $= (a^2 - d^2)a = r$

or $d = \sqrt{\frac{p^3-27r}{9p}}$

Also, $a(a - d) + a(a + d) + a^2 - d^2 = q$

$\Rightarrow a^2 - ad + a^2 + ad + a^2 - d^2 = q$

or $\frac{3p^2}{9} - \left(\frac{p^3-27r}{9p}\right) = q$ or $\frac{2p^3+27r}{9p} = q$

$\Rightarrow 2p^3 + 27r - 9pq = 0$

Now comparing the equation $x^3 - 12x^2 + 39x - 28 = 0$ with $x^3 - px^2 + qx - r = 0$

we get $p = 12, q = 39, r = 28$

these values satisfy condition $zp^3 + 27r - 9pq = 0$

$\Rightarrow a = \frac{p}{3} = 4$; a, d

$d = \sqrt{\frac{p^3-27r}{9p}} = \sqrt{\frac{1728-756}{108}} = 3$

$\therefore$ Roots are 1, 4, 7.

32. If a, b, c, d, e be 5 numgers such that a, b, c are in AP; b, c, d are in GP and c, d, e are in HP, then:

(i) Prove that a, c, e are in GP.

(ii) Prove that $e = (2b - a)^2/a$.

(iii) If $a = 2$ and $e = 18$, find all possible values of b, c, d.

Solution: Given that a, b, c are in AP therefore

$\Rightarrow 2b = a + c$ (1)

and b, c, d are in GP.

$\Rightarrow c^2 = bd$ (2)

Also, c,d,e are in HP.

$\Rightarrow d = \frac{2ce}{c+e}$ (3)

from (*1*) $c^2 = b.d$

$\Rightarrow c^2 = b.\left(\frac{2ec}{e+c}\right)$ ...(using (3) equation)

$\Rightarrow c = \frac{2be}{e+c} = \frac{(2b)e}{e+c}$ (4)

$\Rightarrow c = \frac{(a+c)e}{(e+c)}$ (using equation (1))

$\Rightarrow ce + c^2 = ae + ce$

$\Rightarrow c^2 = ae \Rightarrow a, c, e$ are in GP.

(*ii*) we have equation no. (4)

$$c = \frac{2be}{e+c}$$

putting $c = 2b - a$ (using equation (1))

$$(2b-a) = \frac{2be}{e+(2b-a)}$$

or $(2b-a)e + (2b-a)^2 = 2be$

or $e = \frac{(2b-a)^2}{a}$ (5)

(*iii*) If $a = 2$, $e = 18$ from equation (5) $e = \frac{(2b-a)^2}{a}$

or $ae = (2b-a)^2$

$\Rightarrow 2 \times 18 = (2b-2)^2$

or $b - 1 = \pm 3$ or $b = 4, -2$ when $b = 4$

$\Rightarrow c = 2b - a = 8 - 2 = 6$

When b = – 2; $c = 2b - a = -4 - 2 = -6$

Now, $d = \frac{c^2}{b}$

$= 9$ for $b = 6$; and -18 for $b = -2$

b, c, d are given by (4, 6, 9) and (–2, –6, –18)

33. A computer solved several problems in succession. The time it took to solve each successive problem was the same number of times smaller than the time it took to solve the preceding problem. How many problems were suggested to the computer if it spent 63.5 min to solve all the problems except for the first, 127 min to solve all the problems except for the last one, and 31.5 min to solve all the problems except for the first two?

Solution: Let there be n-problems. According to questions, the times taken to solve the problems forms a GP and let it be..... a, ar, ar^2, ar^3............ar^{n-1}

$ar + ar^2 + ... + ar^{n-1} = 63.5$

$$\Rightarrow ar\left(\frac{r^{n-1}-1}{r-1}\right) = 63.5 \quad (1)$$

and $a + ar + ... + ar^{n-2} = 127$

$$\Rightarrow a\left(\frac{r^{n-1}-1}{r-1}\right) = 127 \quad (2)$$

Also, $ar^2 + ar^3 + ... + ar^{n-1} = 31.5$

$$\Rightarrow ar^2\left(\frac{r^{n-2}-1}{r-1}\right) = 31.5 \quad (3)$$

(2) ÷ (3) gives,

$$\Rightarrow \frac{a\left(\frac{r^{n-1}-1}{r-1}\right)}{ar^2\left(\frac{r^{n-2}-1}{r-1}\right)} = \frac{127}{31.5}$$

$$\Rightarrow \frac{1}{r^2}\left(\frac{r^{n-1}-1}{r^{n-2}-1}\right) = \frac{127}{31.5} \quad (4)$$

Also dividing (2) by (1) we get $\frac{1}{r} = 2 \Rightarrow r = \frac{1}{2}$

$$\therefore \text{ from (4) } \frac{1}{\left(\frac{1}{2}\right)^2}\left(\frac{\left(\frac{1}{2}\right)^{n-1}-1}{\left(\frac{1}{2}\right)^{n-2}-1}\right) = \frac{127}{31.5}$$

$$\Rightarrow 4\left(\frac{2\left(\frac{1}{2}\right)^n-1}{4\left(\frac{1}{2}\right)^n-1}\right) = \frac{127}{31.5}$$

$\Rightarrow \frac{2x-1}{4x-1} = \frac{127}{126}$; where $x = \left(\frac{1}{2}\right)^n$

$\Rightarrow 252x - 126 = 508x - 127$

$\Rightarrow 1 = 256x \Rightarrow x = \frac{1}{256}$

$\Rightarrow x = \left(\frac{1}{2}\right)^8 \therefore \left(\frac{1}{2}\right)^n = \left(\frac{1}{2}\right)^8$

$\Rightarrow n = 8$

34. If n is a root of the equation $x^2(1 - ac) - x(a^2 + c^2) - (1 + ac) = 0$ and if n HM's are inserted between a and c, show that the difference between the first and the last mean is equal to $ac(a - c)$.

Solution: Given equation is

$x^2(1 - ac) - x(a^2 + c^2) - (1 + ac) = 0$

$$\Rightarrow x^2 - x\frac{(a^2+c^2)}{1-ac} - \frac{(1+ac)}{1-ac} = 0$$

since n is a root of this equation, therefore

$$n^2 - n\left(\frac{a^2+c^2}{1-ac}\right) - \left(\frac{1+ac}{1-ac}\right) = 0 \quad (1)$$

n HM's are inserted between a and c

$$\Rightarrow H_1 = \frac{ac(n+1)}{cn+a};\ H_n = \frac{ac(n+1)}{an+c}$$

$$\Rightarrow H_1 - H_n = \frac{ac(a-c)(n^2-1)}{acn^2+n(a^2+c^2)+ac} \quad (2)$$

from equation (1), we have

$n^2 - acn^2 - na^2 - nc^2 - 1 - ac = 0$

or $n^2 - 1 = acn^2 + n(a^2 + c^2) + ac$

putting this value in equation (2), we get

$\therefore H_1 - H_n = ac(a - c)$

35. Given that the cubic $ax^3 - ax^2 + 9bx - b = 0$ $(a \neq 0)$ has all three positive roots. Find the harmonic mean of the roots independent of a and b, hence deduce that the roots are equal. Find also the minimum value of $(a + b)$ if a and $b \in \mathbb{N}$.

Solution: $ax^3 - ax^2 + 9bx - b = 0$ (1)

$\Rightarrow x^3 - x^2 + 9\frac{b}{a}x - \frac{b}{a} = 0$

let its three roots be α, β, γ, then

$\alpha + \beta + \gamma = -\frac{(-1)}{1} = 1 \Rightarrow \alpha\beta\gamma = \frac{b}{a}$

$\Rightarrow \alpha\beta + \beta\gamma + \gamma\alpha = 9b/a$

dividing by $\alpha\beta\gamma$ on both sides, we get

$\frac{1}{\gamma} + \frac{1}{\beta} + \frac{1}{\alpha} = +\frac{9b}{a} \times \frac{a}{b} = +9$

$\therefore \text{HM}(\alpha, \beta, \gamma) = \frac{3}{\frac{1}{\alpha} + \frac{1}{\beta} + \frac{1}{\gamma}} = \frac{3}{9} = \frac{1}{3}$

Also, $\text{AM} = \frac{\alpha + \beta + \gamma}{3} = \frac{1}{3}$

$\therefore$ AM = HM $\Rightarrow$ Roots must be equal

[$\because$ AM $\geq$ HM are equally holds for equal possible numbers]

so the roots are $\alpha = \beta = \gamma = 1/3$

putting in equation (1)

$\frac{a}{27} - \frac{a}{9} + 3b - b = 0$

$-\frac{2a}{27} + 2b = 0 \Rightarrow 2b = \frac{2a}{27}$

$\Rightarrow 27b = a$ minimum value of $(a + b)$ = minimum value of $28b = 28$ as $b \in \mathbb{N}$

36. In a right angled triangle, S_a and S_b denote the medians to the legs of the triangle, the median belonging to the hypotenuse is S_c. Find the maximum value of the expression $\left(\frac{S_a + S_b}{S_c}\right)^2$.

(You may use the fact that RMS $\geq$ AM)

Solution: Let a,b,c, denote the base, perpendicular and hypotenuse of right angled ΔABC as shown below;

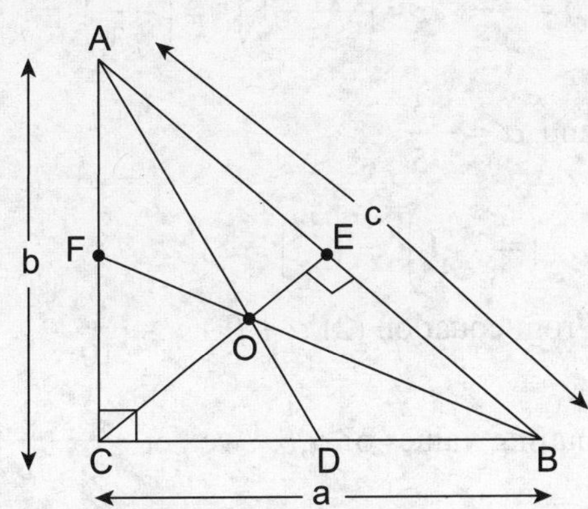

then, AD = S_a, BF = S_b, CE = S_c, then

$S_a = \sqrt{b^2 + \frac{a^2}{4}} = \sqrt{\frac{4b^2 + a^2}{4}}$; $S_b = \sqrt{\frac{4a^2 + b^2}{4}}$;

and $S_c = \frac{c}{2}$ and $c^2 = a^2 + b^2$

$\Rightarrow \frac{c^2}{4} = \frac{a^2 + b^2}{4} \quad \Rightarrow \frac{c}{2} = \sqrt{\frac{a^2 + b^2}{4}}$

$\Rightarrow S_c = \sqrt{\frac{a^2 + b^2}{4}}$

now $\frac{S_a + S_b}{S_c} = \frac{\sqrt{\frac{4b^2 + a^2}{4}} + \sqrt{\frac{4a^2 + b^2}{4}}}{\sqrt{\frac{a^2 + b^2}{4}}}$

let $\sqrt{\frac{4b^2 + a^2}{4}} = \alpha, \sqrt{\frac{4a^2 + b^2}{4}} = \beta$

and $\sqrt{\frac{a^2 + b^2}{4}} = \gamma$

now using the fact that RMS $\geq$ AM we have

$\sqrt{\frac{\alpha^2 + \beta^2}{2}} \geq \frac{\alpha + \beta}{2}$

or $\frac{\alpha + \beta}{2} \leq \frac{1}{2}\sqrt{\frac{5b^2 + 5a^2}{2}} \Rightarrow \alpha + \beta \leq \sqrt{\frac{5b^2 + 5a^2}{2}}$

or $\frac{\alpha + \beta}{\gamma} \leq \sqrt{\frac{4}{2}\frac{(5b^2 + 5a^2)}{a^2 + b^2}}$

or $\frac{\alpha + \beta}{\gamma} \leq \sqrt{10} \Rightarrow \left(\frac{\alpha + \beta}{\gamma}\right)^2 \leq 10$

$\Rightarrow \left(\frac{Sa + Sb}{Sc}\right)^2_{max} = 10$

37. (a) The value of $x + y + z$ is 15 if a, x, y, z, b are in AP while the value of (1/x) + (1/y) + (1/z) is 5/3 if a, x, y, z, b are in HP. Find a and b.

(b) The values of xyz is 15/2 or 18/5 according as the series a, x, y, z, b are an AP or HP. Find the values of a and b assuming them to be positive integers.

Solution: (a) a, x, y, z, b........are in AP.

given that $x + y + z = 15$ (1)

Let $x = A - d$

$\Rightarrow y = A$

$\Rightarrow z = A + d$

putting in relation $x + y + z = 15$, we get

$\Rightarrow (A - d) + A + (A + d) = 15$

$\Rightarrow 3A = 15$

$\Rightarrow A = 5 = y$

so $y = 5$, $\because$ a, x, y, z, b are in AP.

$\therefore\ y = \dfrac{a+b}{2}$

or $a + b = 2y = 10$ (2)

given that a, x, y, z, b are in HP.

and $\dfrac{1}{x}+\dfrac{1}{y}+\dfrac{1}{z}=\dfrac{5}{3}$ (3)

then $\dfrac{1}{a},\dfrac{1}{x},\dfrac{1}{y},\dfrac{1}{z},\dfrac{1}{b}$ will be in AP.

Let

$\therefore\ \dfrac{1}{x}=A-d;\dfrac{1}{y}=A;\dfrac{1}{z}=A+d$

putting in (3), we get

$(A-d)+A+(A+d)=\dfrac{5}{3}$

$\Rightarrow 3A = \dfrac{5}{3}$ $\qquad \Rightarrow A=\dfrac{5}{9}=\dfrac{1}{y}\Rightarrow y=\dfrac{9}{5}$

so $\dfrac{1}{a}+\dfrac{1}{b}=\dfrac{2}{y}=\dfrac{10}{9}$ or $\dfrac{a\quad b}{ab}\quad\dfrac{10}{}$

or $ab = 9$ (using equation (2))

solving equation (2) and (4) we get

$a = 1, 9, b = 9$ or $a = 9, b = 1$

i.e., the two numbers are 1 and 9

(b) Now, it is given that $xyz = \dfrac{15}{2}$ if x, y, z are in AP.

and $xyz = \dfrac{18}{5}$ if x, y, z are in HP.

If d is the common difference AP a, x, y, z, b, then

$\Rightarrow d=\dfrac{b-a}{n+1}=\dfrac{b-a}{4}$

Also, $y = \dfrac{a+b}{2}$

$\Rightarrow x=\dfrac{3a+b}{4}$ and $z=\dfrac{3b+a}{4}$

$\therefore\ xyz=\dfrac{15}{2}=\left(\dfrac{3a+b}{4}\right)\left(\dfrac{a+b}{2}\right)\left(\dfrac{3b+a}{4}\right)$ (1)

If a, x, y, z, b are in HP.

$\Rightarrow \dfrac{1}{a},\dfrac{1}{x},\dfrac{1}{y},\dfrac{1}{z},\dfrac{1}{b}$ are in AP.

$\Rightarrow$ y = HM of a and $b \Rightarrow y=\dfrac{2ab}{a+b}$

$\Rightarrow \dfrac{1}{y}=\dfrac{a+b}{2ab}$

$\dfrac{1}{x}=\dfrac{\left(\dfrac{3}{a}\right)+\left(\dfrac{1}{b}\right)}{4}\Rightarrow\dfrac{4ab}{3b+a}=x$ and $z=\dfrac{4ab}{3a+b}$

Now, given that $xyz=\dfrac{18}{5}=\left(\dfrac{4ab}{3b+a}\right)\left(\dfrac{2ab}{a+b}\right)\left(\dfrac{4ab}{3a+b}\right)$ (2)

multiplying equations (1) and (2) we get,

$a^3b^3=\dfrac{18}{5}\times\dfrac{15}{2}=27$

or $ab = 3$; but a and b are positive integers

$\Rightarrow a = 1, b = 3$, or $a = 3, b = 1$

38. If the roots of $10x^3 - cx^2 - 54x - 27 = 0$ are in harmonic progression, then find c and all the roots.

Solution: Let the roots of equations

$10x^3 - cx^2 - 54x - 27 = 0$ (1)

be α,β,γ then, $\dfrac{1}{\alpha},\dfrac{1}{\beta},\dfrac{1}{\gamma}$ ....are in AP.

So, let $\dfrac{1}{\alpha}=a-d,\ \dfrac{1}{\beta}=a,\dfrac{1}{\gamma}=a+d$

$\Rightarrow \dfrac{2}{\beta}=\dfrac{1}{\alpha}+\dfrac{1}{\gamma}$

from equation (1) $\alpha+\beta+\gamma=\dfrac{c}{10}$ (sum of roots) (2)

$\Rightarrow \alpha\beta+\beta\gamma+\alpha\gamma=-\dfrac{54}{10}$ (3)

$\Rightarrow \alpha\beta\gamma=\dfrac{27}{10}$ (4)

now $\dfrac{1}{\alpha}+\dfrac{1}{\beta}+\dfrac{1}{\gamma}=\dfrac{\Sigma\alpha\beta}{\alpha\beta\gamma}=\left(\dfrac{-54}{10}\right)\div\left(\dfrac{27}{10}\right)=-2$

$\Rightarrow (a-d)+a+(a+d)=-2$

$\Rightarrow 3a=-2$

$\Rightarrow a=-\dfrac{2}{3}$

now $\dfrac{1}{\alpha}\times\dfrac{1}{\beta}\times\dfrac{1}{\gamma}=(a^2-d^2)a=\left(\dfrac{4}{9}-d^2\right)\left(\dfrac{-2}{3}\right)=\dfrac{10}{27}$

$\Rightarrow (4-9d^2)(-2)=10$

or $d=\pm1$; for $d=1$

$\Rightarrow \beta=-\dfrac{3}{2},\ \alpha=\left(-\dfrac{2}{3}-1\right)^{-1}=\left(-\dfrac{5}{3}\right)^{-1}=-\dfrac{3}{5}$

and $\alpha=-\dfrac{3}{5}$

$\Rightarrow \gamma=\left(\dfrac{-2}{3}+1\right)^{-1}=\left(\dfrac{1}{3}\right)^{-1}=3$

From equation (2) $\alpha+\beta+\gamma=\dfrac{c}{10}$

putting values of α,β,γ we get $-\dfrac{3}{5}-\dfrac{3}{2}+3=\dfrac{c}{10}$

$\Rightarrow c=9$

39. If a, b, c be in GP and $\log_c a$, $\log_b c$, $\log_a b$ be in AP, then show that the common difference of the AP must be 3/2.

Solution: Given that a, b, c are in GP then let $a = \frac{b}{r}$, $b = b$, $c = br$ given that $\log_c a$, $\log_b c$, $\log_a b$ are in AP

$\Rightarrow$ common difference $d = \log_b c - \log_c a = \log_a b - \log_b c$

$$\Rightarrow d = \frac{\log_{10} c}{\log_{10} b} - \frac{\log_{10} a}{\log_{10} c} = \frac{\log_{10} b}{\log_{10} a} - \frac{\log_{10} c}{\log_{10} b}$$

$$\Rightarrow d = \frac{\log_{10}^2 c - \log_{10} a \log_{10} b}{\log_{10} b \log_{10} c}$$

$$= \frac{\log_{10}^2 b - \log_{10} a \log_{10} c}{\log_{10} a \log_{10} b}$$

$$\Rightarrow d = \frac{X}{Y} = \frac{Z}{Q} = \frac{X - Z}{Y - Q}$$

$$\Rightarrow \text{d} = \frac{\log^2 c - \log a \log b - \log^2 b + \log c \log a}{\log b \log c - \log a \log b}$$

[base of log is 10]

$$= \frac{(\log c - \log b)(\log c + \log b + \log a)}{\log b(\log c - \log a)}$$

$$= \frac{\log \frac{c}{b} . \log abc}{\log \frac{c}{a} . \log b} = \frac{\log r}{\log r^2} . \frac{\log b^3}{\log b} = \frac{3}{2}$$

40. In a GP the ratio of the sum of the first eleven terms to the sum of the last eleven terms is 1/8 and the ratio of the sum of all the terms without the first nine the sum of all the terms without the last nine is 2. Find the number of terms in the GP.

Solution: Let the GP be $a, ar, ar^2.....ar^{n-1}$; then

$$S_{11} = \frac{a(1-r^{11})}{1-r} \text{ and } S'_{11} \text{ (from last)} = ar^{n-11}\frac{(1-r^{11})}{1-r}$$

$$\therefore \frac{S_{11}}{S'_{11}} = \frac{a}{ar^{n-11}} = \frac{1}{8} \text{ (given)}$$

$$\Rightarrow \frac{1}{r^{n-11}} = \frac{1}{8} \text{ (given)}$$

$\Rightarrow r^{n-11} = 8$

and $S = ar^9 + ...+ ar^{n-1}$

$$\Rightarrow S = ar^9 . \frac{(1-r^{n-9})}{1-r}; \; S' = \frac{a.(1-r^{n-9})}{1-r}$$

$$\therefore \frac{S}{S'} = r^9 = 2 \qquad \text{or} \quad r^9 = 2$$

and $r^{n-11} = 8$

$\Rightarrow n = 38$ **Ans.**

41. The sum of roots of the equation $ax^2 + bx + c = 0$ is equal to the sum of squares of their reciprocals. Find whether bc^2, ca^2 and ab^2 are in AP, GP or HP.

Solution: Given equation is $ax^2 + bx + c = 0$

Let its roots be α and β

$\Rightarrow \alpha + \beta = -\frac{b}{a}; \alpha\beta = \frac{c}{a}$; According to the question

$$\Rightarrow \alpha + \beta = \frac{1}{\alpha^2} + \frac{1}{\beta^2} = \frac{\beta^2 + \alpha^2}{(\alpha\beta)^2}$$

$$\Rightarrow (\alpha + \beta) = \frac{(\alpha+\beta)^2 - 2\alpha\beta}{(\alpha\beta)^2}$$

$$\Rightarrow \left(-\frac{b}{a}\right) = \frac{\left(-\frac{b}{a}\right)^2 - 2\times\frac{c}{a}}{\left(\frac{c}{a}\right)^2}$$

$$\Rightarrow -\frac{b}{a} = \frac{b^2 - 2ac}{c^2} \quad - bc^2 = ab^2 - 2a^2 c$$

$\Rightarrow 2a^2c = ab^2 + bc^2$

$\Rightarrow bc^2, a^2c, ab^2$ are in AP.

42. Solve the following simultaneous equations for x and y.

(i) $\log_2 x + \log_4 x + \log_{16} x$............... $= y$

(ii) $\dfrac{5+9+13+........+(4y+1)}{1+3+5+........+(2y-1)} = 4\log_4 x$

Solution: (i) $\log_2 x + \log_4 x + \log_{16} x +$............... $= y$

$$\Rightarrow \log_2 x + \frac{1}{2}\log_2 x + \frac{1}{4}\log_2 x + ...\infty = y$$

$$\Rightarrow (\log_2 x)\left(\frac{1}{1-\frac{1}{2}}\right) = y$$

$\Rightarrow y = 2\log_2 x$

$$\text{Also, } 4\log_4 x = \frac{5+9+13+.......+(4y+1)}{1+3+5+.......+(2y-1)}$$

(each series in numerator and denominator contains y terms)

$$= \frac{\frac{y}{2}(5+4y+1)}{\frac{y}{2}(1+2y-1)} = \frac{4y+6}{2y} = \frac{2y+3}{y}$$

$$\therefore \quad 2\log_2 x = \frac{2y+3}{y}$$

$$\Rightarrow 2 \times \left(\frac{y}{2}\right) = \frac{2y+3}{y}$$

$\Rightarrow y^2 = 2y + 3$

$\Rightarrow y = 3$

$\Rightarrow \log_2 x = \left(\frac{3}{2}\right)$

$\Rightarrow x = 2^{\frac{3}{2}}$

$\Rightarrow x = 2\sqrt{2}$

43. Let a, b be positive real numbers. If a, A_1, A_2, b are in AP a, G_1, G_2, b are in GP and a, H_1, H_2, b are in HP, show that $\frac{G_1G_2}{H_1H_2} = \frac{A_1 + A_2}{H_1 + H_2} = \frac{(2a+b)(a+2b)}{9ab}$.

Solution: Since, a, A_1, A_2, b are in AP

$\Rightarrow A_1 + A_2 = a + b$

Also, a, G_1, G_2, b are in GP

$\Rightarrow G_1G_2 = ab$

and a, H_1, H_2, b are in HP

$\Rightarrow H_1 = \frac{3ab}{2b+a}$,

$\Rightarrow H_2 = \frac{3ab}{b+2a}$

$\therefore \frac{1}{H_1} + \frac{1}{H_2} = \frac{1}{a} + \frac{1}{b}$

$\Rightarrow \frac{H_1 + H_2}{H_1H_2} = \frac{A_1 + A_2}{G_1G_2} = \frac{1}{a} + \frac{1}{b}$ (i)

Now, $\frac{G_1G_2}{H_1H_2} = \frac{ab}{\left(\frac{3ab}{2b+a}\right)\left(\frac{3ab}{b+2a}\right)}$

$= \frac{(2a+b)(a+2b)}{9ab}$ (ii)

From equations (i) and (ii), we get

$\frac{G_1G_2}{H_1H_2} = \frac{A_1 + A_2}{H_1 + H_2} = \frac{(2a+b)(a+2b)}{9ab}$

44. If $A_n = \left(\frac{3}{4}\right) - \left(\frac{3}{4}\right)^2 + \left(\frac{3}{4}\right)^3 + \ldots\ldots + (-1)^{n-1}\left(\frac{3}{4}\right)^n$ and $B_n = 1 - A_n$, then find the minimum natural number n_0 such that $B_n > A_n$. $\forall\, n > n_0$.

Solution: $B_n = 1 - A_n > A_n \Rightarrow A_n < \frac{1}{2}$

Now, $A_n = \frac{\frac{3}{4}\left(1 - \left(-\frac{3}{4}\right)^n\right)}{1 + \frac{3}{4}} < \frac{1}{2} \Rightarrow \left(-\frac{3}{4}\right)^n > -\frac{1}{6}$

Obviously, it is true for all even values of n.

But, for $n = 1$, $\frac{3}{4} < \frac{1}{6}$ (false);

for $n = 3$, $\frac{27}{64} < \frac{1}{6}$ (false);

for $n = 5$, $\frac{243}{1024} < \frac{1}{6}$ (false)

for n = 7, $\frac{2187}{16384} < \frac{1}{6}$ (true)

which is true for $n = 7$.

Also, $\left(\frac{3}{4}\right)^n \le \left(\frac{3}{4}\right)^7 < \frac{1}{6} \forall n \ge 7 \Rightarrow n_0 = 7$

45. If $S_1, S_2, S_3, \ldots\ldots S_p$ are the sums of n terms of 'p' arithmetic series whose first terms are 1, 2, 3, 4........ and whose common difference are 1, 3, 5, 7, ...; prove that

$S_1 + S_2 + S_3 + \ldots\ldots + S_p = \frac{np}{2}(np+1)$

Solution: $S_1 = \frac{n}{2}[2 + (n-1)] = \frac{n(n+1)}{2}$

$S_2 = \frac{n}{2}[4 + \overline{n-1}\ 3] = \frac{n(3n+1)}{2}$

$S_p = \frac{n}{2}[2p + \overline{n-1}\ (2p-1)] = \frac{n}{2}\left[\frac{(2p-1)n+1}{2}\right]$

$\therefore\ S_1 + S_2 + \ldots. + S_p = \frac{n}{2}$

$[n + 3n + 5n + \ldots\ldots + (2p-1)n + p]$

$= \frac{n}{2}\ [n(1 + 3 + 5 + \ldots. + 2p - 1) + p]$

$= \frac{n}{2}[np^2 + p] = \frac{np}{2}(np+1)$

46. A number sequence $a_1, a_2, a_3 \ldots\ldots\ a_n$ is such that $a_1 = 0$; $|a_2| = |a_1 + 1|$; $|a_3| = |a_2 + 1|$ ......; $|a_n| = |a_{n-1} + 1|$.

Prove that the arithmetic mean of $a_1, a_2, \ldots\ldots\ a_n$ is not less than $-\frac{1}{2}$.

Solution: Given $a_1 = 0$; $|a_2| = |a_1 + 1|$; $|a_3| = |a_2 + 1|$ .... $|a_n| = |a_{n-1} + 1|$

also let $a_{n+1} = |a_n + 1|$

now squaring $a_1^2 = 0$

$a_2^2 = a_1^2 + 2a_1 + 1$

$a_3^2 = a_2^2 + 2a_2 + 1$

$a_4^2 = a_3^2 + 2a_3 + 1$

$\vdots$

$a_{n+1}^2 = a_n^2 + 2a_n + 1$

adding above equation, we get

$a_1^2+a_2^2+.....+a_n^2+a_{n+1}^2$

$= a_1^2+a_2^2+.....+a_n^2+2(a_1+a_2+.....+a_n)+n$

$\Rightarrow a_{n+1}^2=2(a_1+a_2+.....+a_n)+n$

$\Rightarrow 2(a_1+a_2+......+a_n)=a_{n+1}^2-n$

hence, $2(a_1+a_2+......+a_n)\geq -n$

$\therefore \dfrac{a_1+a_2+....+a_n}{n}\geq -\dfrac{1}{2}$

47. If $\log_3 2$, $\log_3(2^x-5)$ and $\log_3\left(2^x-\dfrac{7}{2}\right)$ are in AP, then determine x.

Solution: $\log_3 2, \log_3(2^x-5); \log_3\left(2^x-\dfrac{7}{2}\right)$

(are in AP)

$\Rightarrow \log_3(2^x-5)-\log_3 2=$

$\log_3\left(2^x-\dfrac{7}{2}\right)-\log_3(2^x-5)$

$\Rightarrow \log_3\left(\dfrac{2^x-5}{2}\right)=\log_3\left(\dfrac{2^x-\frac{7}{2}}{2^x-5}\right)$

$\Rightarrow \dfrac{2^x-5}{2}=\dfrac{2^x-\frac{7}{2}}{2^x-5}; (2^x-5)^2=2^{x+1}-7$

$\Rightarrow 2^{2x}-10.2^x+25=2.2^x-7$; put $2^x=y$

$\Rightarrow y^2-12y+32=0$

$\Rightarrow y=8$ or 4; hence $x=3$ (as $x=2$ is rejected as otherwise $\log_3(2^x-5)$ is not defined)

48. Prove that $\sqrt{2},\sqrt{3},\sqrt{5}$ can not be the terms of an AP (not necessarily adjacent).

Solution: Let if possible $\sqrt{2},\sqrt{3},\sqrt{5}$ be p^{th}, q^{th} and r^{th} terms of an AP.

Hence $\sqrt{2}=a+(p-1)d$; $\sqrt{3}=a+(q-1)d$; $\sqrt{5}=a+(r-1)d$

$\therefore \dfrac{\sqrt{5}-\sqrt{3}}{\sqrt{3}-2}=\dfrac{r-q}{q-p}$; RHS is rational and LHS is irrational, hence our assumption was wrong so $\sqrt{2},\sqrt{3},\sqrt{5}$ cannot be the terms of any AP.

49. In a GP with a_n

$a_1+a_2+a_3=13$ and $a_1^2+a_2^2+a_3^2=91$. Find S_n.

Solution: first term of GP $a_1=a$ and common ratio be 'r' then given $a_1+a_2+a_3=13$

$\Rightarrow a(1+r+r^2)=13$ (i)

and $a_1^2+a_2^2+a_3^2=91\Rightarrow a^2(1+r^2+r^4)=91$ (ii)

squaring both side of equation (i) and dividing by (ii) we get $\dfrac{a^2(1+r+r^2)}{a^2(1+r^2+r^4)}=\dfrac{13\times13}{13\times7}$

$\Rightarrow \dfrac{(1+r+r^2)^2}{(r^2+r+1)(r^2-r+1)}=\dfrac{13}{7}$

$\Rightarrow 13(r^2-r+1)=7+7r+7r^2$

$\Rightarrow 6r^2-20r+6=0 \quad \Rightarrow r=3$ or $\dfrac{1}{3}$

Case I: of $r=3\Rightarrow a=1$ (from equation *i*)

Thus the sum of 'n' terms

$s_n=1+3+3^2+.....+3^{n-1}=\dfrac{1}{2}(3^n-1)$

Case II: of $r=\dfrac{1}{3}\Rightarrow$ a = 9 (from equation (i))

consequently the series formed is decreasing GP.

$s_n=9+3+1+$ ....; up to n terms

$=\dfrac{9\left(1-\left(\frac{1}{3}\right)^n\right)}{1-\frac{1}{3}}=\dfrac{27}{2}\left(1-\dfrac{1}{3^n}\right)$

50. If sum of two positive numbers a and b is n times their GM then show that $\sqrt{a}:\sqrt{b}=\dfrac{n\pm\sqrt{n^2-4}}{2}$

Solution: $a+b=n\sqrt{ab}\Rightarrow \sqrt{\dfrac{a}{b}}+\sqrt{\dfrac{b}{a}}=n$

let $\sqrt{\dfrac{a}{b}}=y$; $\Rightarrow y+\dfrac{1}{y}=n\Rightarrow y^2-ny+1=0$

$\Rightarrow y=\dfrac{n\pm\sqrt{n^2-4}}{2} \quad \Rightarrow \sqrt{a}:\sqrt{b}=\dfrac{n\pm\sqrt{n^2-4}}{2}$

51. If *a, b, c* are in GP and *x, y* are respectively the AM's between *a, b* and *b, c* then prove that $\dfrac{1}{x}+\dfrac{1}{y}=\dfrac{2}{b}$ and $\dfrac{a}{x}+\dfrac{c}{y}=2$

Solution: Let $a=a$; $b=ar$; $c=ar^2$ as *a,b,c,* are in GP. also *a, x, b* are in A.P and *b y* c are in AP.

$\Rightarrow 2x=a+b=a(1+r)$ (1)

and $2y=b+c=ar(1+r)$ (2)

now $\dfrac{1}{x}+\dfrac{1}{y}=\dfrac{2}{a(1+r)}+\dfrac{2}{ar(1+r)}$

$=\dfrac{2(1+r)}{ar(1+r)}=\dfrac{2}{ar}=\dfrac{2}{b}$

again $\frac{a}{x}+\frac{c}{y}=\frac{2}{1+r}+\frac{(ar^2)2}{ar(1+r)}$ [from (1) and (2)]

$$=\frac{2}{1+r}+\frac{2r}{(1+r)}=2$$

52. Prove that a Δ ABC is equilateral if and only $\tan A+\tan B+\tan C=3\sqrt{3}$

Solution: ***Case 1:*** Let ABC is an equilateral then $\tan A+\tan B+\tan C=3\sqrt{3}$ is obviously true as $\tan A=\tan B=\tan C=\sqrt{3}$

Case 2: Let $\tan A+\tan B+\tan C=3\sqrt{3}$ be true

$\Rightarrow \frac{\tan A+\tan B+\tan C}{3}=\sqrt{3}$

$\Rightarrow$ AM of $\tan A$, $\tan B$, $\tan C=\sqrt{3}$

Now GM of $\tan A$, $\tan B$, $\tan C=(\tan A\tan B\tan C)^{1/3}=\left(3\sqrt{3}\right)^{1/3}=\left(3^{3/2}\right)^{1/3}=\sqrt{3}$ as in a Δ $\tan A+\tan B+\tan C=\tan A\cdot\tan B\cdot\tan C$

Hence AM = GM;

$\Rightarrow \tan A=\tan B=\tan C$

$\Rightarrow \angle A=\angle B=\angle C$

$\Rightarrow \Delta$ is equilateral

53. Find the value(s) of the positive integer n for which the quadratic equation, $\sum_{k=1}^{n}((x+k-1)(x+k))=10n$ has solutions α and $\alpha+1$ for some α.

Solution: Given equation is $\sum_{K=1}^{n}\left((x+K)^2-(x+K)\right)=10n$

$\Rightarrow \sum_{K=1}^{n}\left(x^2+(2K-1)x+K(K-1)\right)=10n$

$\Rightarrow nx^2+n^2x+\frac{n(n+1)(2n+1)}{6}-\frac{n(n+1)}{2}-10n=0$

$\Rightarrow 3x^2+3nx+(n^2-31)=0$; its roots are α, $\alpha+1$

$$\left.\begin{aligned}&\alpha+(\alpha+1)=-n\\&\alpha,(\alpha+1)=\frac{n^2-31}{3}\end{aligned}\right]$$

$\Rightarrow n=11$ or $-11\Rightarrow n=11$

54. If $a_1, a_2, a_3......a_n$ are in HP then prove that $a_1a_2+a_2a_3+a_3a_4+......+a_{n-1}\cdot a_n=(n-1)a_1a_n$

Solution: $\frac{1}{a_1},\frac{1}{a_2},\frac{1}{a_3}.....\frac{1}{a_n}$ are in AP.

$$d=\frac{a_1-a_2}{a_1a_2}=\frac{a_2-a_3}{a_2a_3}=.....\frac{a_{n-1}-a_n}{a_na_{n-1}}$$

now LHS $=\frac{1}{d}[(a_1-a_2)+(a_2-a_3)+......+(a_{n-1}-a_n)]$

$$=\frac{a_1-a_n}{d}$$

now $\frac{1}{a_n}=\frac{1}{a_1}+(n-1)d\Rightarrow(n-1)d=\frac{a_1-a_n}{a_na_1}$

$d=\frac{a_1-a_n}{(a_na_1)(n-1)}$;

$\therefore$ LHS $=(n-1)a_1a_n=$ RHS

55. If $\frac{a-x}{px}=\frac{a-y}{qy}=\frac{a-z}{rz}$ and p, q, r are in AP, then prove that x, y, z are in HP.

Solution: $\frac{\frac{a}{x}-1}{p}=\frac{\frac{a}{y}-1}{q}=\frac{\frac{a}{z}-1}{r}=\frac{\frac{a}{x}-\frac{a}{y}}{p-q}=\frac{\frac{a}{y}-\frac{a}{z}}{q-r}$

$\left(\because \frac{a}{b}=\frac{c}{d}=\frac{a-c}{b-d}\right)$

Since p, q, r are in AP $\Rightarrow p-q=q-r$

$\therefore \frac{a}{x}-\frac{a}{y}=\frac{a}{y}-\frac{a}{z}$

$\Rightarrow \frac{1}{x},\frac{1}{y},\frac{1}{z}$ are in AP $\Rightarrow x, y, z$ in HP]

56. If $a^x=b^y=c^z=d^w=....$ and $a, b, c, d,.....$ are in GP then prove that x, y, z, w... are in HP.

Solution: If $a^x=b^y=c^z=d^w=.......=k$

$\Rightarrow a=k^{\frac{1}{x}}; b=k^{\frac{1}{y}}; c=k^{\frac{1}{z}}; d=k^{\frac{1}{w}}$

$\therefore a, b, c, d,....$ are in GP $\Rightarrow \frac{b}{a}=\frac{c}{b}=\frac{d}{c}=......$

$\Rightarrow \frac{k^{1/y}}{k^{1/x}}=\frac{k^{1/z}}{k^{1/y}}=\frac{k^{1/w}}{k^{1/z}}=.........$

$\Rightarrow k^{\frac{1}{y}-\frac{1}{x}}=k^{\frac{1}{z}-\frac{1}{y}}=k^{\frac{1}{w}-\frac{1}{z}}$

$\Rightarrow \frac{1}{y}-\frac{1}{x}=\frac{1}{z}-\frac{1}{y}=\frac{1}{w}-\frac{1}{z}$

$\Rightarrow \frac{1}{x},\frac{1}{y},\frac{1}{z},\frac{1}{w},....$ are in AP.

$\Rightarrow x, y, z, w.....$ are in HP.

57. If a, b, c are in AP, p, q, r are in HP and ap, bq, cr are in GP, then prove that $\frac{p}{r}+\frac{r}{p}=\frac{a}{c}+\frac{c}{a}$.

Solution: As a,b,c, are in AP

$\Rightarrow b=\frac{a+c}{2}$

$\Rightarrow$ As p,q,r in HP

$\Rightarrow\ q = \dfrac{2pr}{p+r}$ and *ap, bq, cr* are in GP.

$\Rightarrow\ apcr = b^2q^2$

$\therefore\ apcr = \left(\dfrac{a+c}{2}\right)^2 \cdot \left(\dfrac{2pr}{p+r}\right)^2 = \dfrac{(a+c)^2.p^2r^2}{(p+r)^2}$

$\Rightarrow\ \dfrac{(p+r)^2}{pr} = \dfrac{(a+c)^2}{ac}$

$\Rightarrow\ \dfrac{p}{r} + \dfrac{r}{p} = \dfrac{a}{c} + \dfrac{c}{a}$

$\Rightarrow$ Hence proved.

58. The AM, GM and HM of first and last term of the series 100, 101, 102,......, n are also terms of this series, then the value of $n(100 \le n \le 500)$ is

Solution: AM = $\dfrac{100+n}{2}$, GM = $\sqrt{100.n}$,

HM = $\dfrac{200n}{100+n}$

Let $n = 4k^2$ as for AM and GM we need a even perfect square

$\Rightarrow$ HM = $\dfrac{800k^2}{100+k^2} = \dfrac{200k^2}{25+4k^2}$

$\Rightarrow 100 \le \dfrac{200k^2}{25+k^2} \le 500$

$2500 + 100k^2 \le 200k^2 \le 12500 + 500k^2 \Rightarrow k^2 \ge 25$

$\Rightarrow k^2 = 25, 36, 49, 64, 81, 100, 121,144,$

$\Rightarrow 4k^2 = 100,144,196,256,400,484,576,...$

But $n = 4k^2 \le 500$

$\Rightarrow n = 100, 144, 196, 256, 400, 484$

But HM is an integer only for $n = 400$

59. If $b_{n+1} = \dfrac{1}{1-b_n}$ for $n \ge 1$ and $b_1 = b_3$, then $\sum_{r=1}^{2001} b_r^{2001}$ is

Solution: $b_2 = \dfrac{1}{1-b_1}$;

$b_3 = \dfrac{1}{1-b_2} = \dfrac{1}{1-\dfrac{1}{1-b_1}} = \dfrac{1-b_1}{-b_1} = \dfrac{b_1-1}{b_1}$

as $b_1 = b_3 \Rightarrow b_1^2 - b_1 + 1 = 0$

$\Rightarrow b_1 = -\omega$ or $-\omega^2$

$\Rightarrow b_1 = b_2 = b_3 = ...-\omega$ or $-\omega^2$

$\Rightarrow \sum_{r=1}^{2001} b_r^{2001} = 2001(-1)^{2001} = -2001$

Comprehension passage

A: Sum of four terms which are in AP is 44, and product of extreme terms is 40.

60. The sum of two mid-terms of sequence are

(a) 22 (b) 32

(c) 42 (d) None of these

61. Common difference of AP is

(a) ± 5 (b) ± 4

(c) ± 6 (d) all of the above

62. If the above AP is multiplied by 4, the common difference of the new AP obtained will be

(a) ± 20 (b) ± 16

(c) ± 24 (d) None of these

Solution:

60. Let the four terms in AP be, $a - 3d, a - d, a + d, a + 3d$

$\therefore$ A.T.Q. $(a-3d) + (a-d) + (a+d) + (a+3d) = 44$

$\Rightarrow 4a = 44 \Rightarrow a = 11$

Also $(a-3d)(a+3d) = 40$

$\Rightarrow a^2 - 9d^2 = 40 \Rightarrow 9d^2 = a^2 - 40 \Rightarrow 9d^2 = 121 - 40$

$\Rightarrow 9d^2 = 81 \Rightarrow d^2 = 9 \Rightarrow d = \pm 3$

$\therefore$ Terms will be 11 – 3 (3), 11 – 3, 11 + 3, 11 + 3 (3)

or 11 – 3 (–3), 11 – (–3), 11 + (–3), 11 + 3(–3)

i.e., 2, 8, 14, 20 or 20, 14, 8, 2

$\therefore$ The sum of two middle terms = 8 + 14 = 22

$\therefore$ **Ans.** (a)

61. Common difference = $2d = 2 (\pm 3) = \pm 6$

$\therefore$ **Ans.** (c)

62. On multiplying the AP by 4, common difference also gets multiplied by 4

$\therefore$ It will become ± 24

$\therefore$ **Ans.** (c)

B. The infinite series $1 + x + x^2 + x^3 +....(|x| <1)$ has the sum $\dfrac{1}{1-x}$. The infinite series $1 + 2x + 3x^2 + 4x^3$ +...can be added with the help of previous one.

Let us study this. If $S = 1 + 2x + 3x^2 + 4x^3 +........$, then $xS = x + 2x^2 + 3x^3 +.....$

$\Rightarrow S(1-x) = 1 + x + x^2 + x^3 +... = \dfrac{1}{1-x}$

$\Rightarrow S = \dfrac{1}{(1-x)^2}\ (|x| < 1)$

We note that coefficient of x^n in the expansion of $(1-x)^{-2}$ is $n + 1$

The infinite series may be used to find the number of ways of distributing identical objects into distinct boxes. For example, the number of ways in which 5 identical balls can be distributed in 3 different boxes must be equal to the co-efficient of x^5 in the infinite product $(x^0 + x^1 + x^2 + ...)$ $(x^0 + x^1 + x^2 + ...)$ $(x^0 + x^1 + x^2 + ..)$. For any way in which x^5 is obtained is one of the ways in which 5 identical balls can be distributed in 3 distinct boxes. While finding the number of ways, the condition $|x| < 1$ may be insignificant.

63. The co-effcient of y^n in the expression $\left(\frac{1+y}{1-y}\right)^2$ must be

(a) $4n$ (b) $4n + 1$

(c) $4n - 1$ (d) None of these

64. The sum of the series $1 + 3x + 6x^2 + 10x^3 + 15x^4 + ... + (|x| < 1)$ must be

(a) $\frac{1}{(1-x)^3}$ (b) $\frac{1}{1-x^3}$

(c) $\frac{1}{1-3x}$ (d) None of these

65. The co-efficient of x^n in the expansion of $(1 - x)^{-3}$ must be

(a) $\frac{n(n+1)}{2}$ (b) $\frac{n(n-2)}{2}$

(c) $\frac{(n+1)(n+2)}{2}$ (d) None of these

66. The number of ways in which 20 identical sweets can be distributed among 3 childern, when there is no restriction on the number of sweets, given to a child

(a) 225 (b) 231

(c) 230 (d) None of these

Solution:

63. Co-efficient of y^n in the expression $\left(\frac{1+y}{1-y}\right)^2$

$= (1 + y)^2(1 - y)^{-2}$

$= (1 + y^2 + 2y)(S) = (1 + y^2 + 2y)(1 + 2y + 3y^2 + 4y^3 + ...)$

$\therefore$ Co-efficient of $y^n = (n + 1) + (n - 1) + 2(n) = 4n$

$\therefore$ **Ans.** (a)

64. Let, $S' = 1 + 3x + 6x^2 + 10x^3 + 15x^4 + ...$

$\Rightarrow xS' = x + 3x^2 + 6x^3 + 10x^4 + ...$

$\Rightarrow (1 - x)S' = 1 + 2x + 3x^2 + 4x^3 + 5x^4 + ...$

$\therefore (1 - x)S' = S$

$\Rightarrow S' = \frac{S'}{(1-x)} = \frac{1}{(1-x)^3}$

$\therefore$ **Ans.** (a)

65. $(1 - x)^{-3} = 1 + 3x + 6x^2 + 10x^3 + 15x^4 + ...$

$\therefore$ Co-efficient of $x^n = t_{n+1}$ of sequence 1, 3, 6, 10, 15...........

Let $S_n = 1 + 3 + 6 + 10 + 15 + ...t_n$

Also $S_n = 1 + 3 + 6 + 10 + ... + t_{n-1} + t_n$

$\therefore 0 = 1 + 2 + 3 + 4 + 5 + ... + -t_n$

$\therefore t_n = 1 + 2 + 3 + 4 + ... + n$

$\Rightarrow t_n = \frac{n(n+1)}{2} \Rightarrow t_{n+1} = \frac{(n+1)(n+2)}{2}$

$\Rightarrow$ **Ans** (c)

66. Consider $(1 - x)^3 = (1 - x)^{-1}(1 - x)^{-1}(1 - x)^{-1}$

$= (1 + x + x^2 + x^3 + ...)(1 + x + x^2 + x^3 + ...)(1 + x + x^2 + x^3 + ...)$

$= (1 - x)^{-1}(1 - x)^{-2} = (x^0 + x^1 + x^2 + x^3 + ...)(x^0 + x^1 + x^2 + x^3 + ...)(x^0 + x^1 + x^2 + ...)$

$= (1 + x + x^2 + x^3 + ...)(1 + 2x + 3x^2 + 4x^3 + ...) = (x^0 + x^1 + x^2 + ...)(x^0 + x^1 + x^2 + ...)$

$(x^0 + x^1 + x^2 + ...)$

= Number of ways distributing 20 sweets among 3 children

= co-efficients of x^{20} in LHS expression $= 21 + 20 + 19 + ... + 2 + 1 = \frac{(21)(22)}{2} = 231$

Ans is (b).

C: Consider a sequence of equilateral ΔS as shown below, where each outer Δ is obtained by shifting the sides of inner Δ by 1 cm parallelly, If each side of ΔABC is *'a'* units, then answer the following questions.

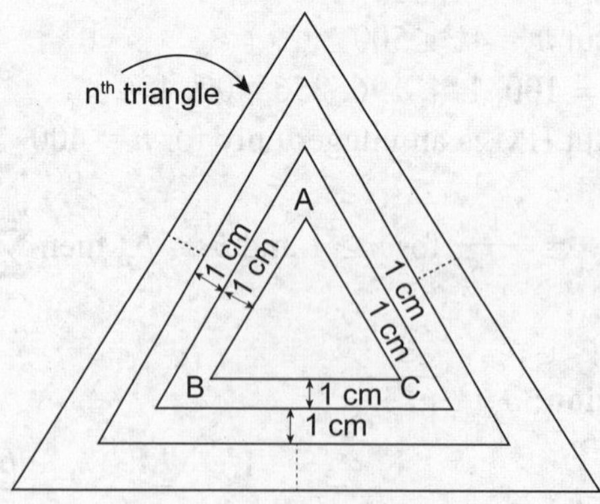

67. Increment in length of each side of triangle during each step of expansion of triangle is

(a) $\sqrt{2}$ (b) $\sqrt{3}$

(c) $2\sqrt{3}$ (d) None of these

68. Length of side of nth Δ is (counting from inner to outer)

(a) $a+(n-1)\sqrt{3}$ (b) $a+(n-1)2\sqrt{3}$

(c) $a+\sqrt{2}\,n$ (d) None of these

69. Area of 5th triangle is

(a) $\frac{\sqrt{3}}{4}\left(a+8\sqrt{3}\right)^2$ (b) $\frac{\sqrt{3}}{4}\left(a+\sqrt{3}\right)^2$

(c) $\sqrt{3}\left(a+2\sqrt{3}\right)^2$ (d) None of these

70. Sum of perimeter of first 10 Δs is

(a) $10a+\sqrt{3}$ (b) $10a+2\sqrt{2}$

(c) $30a+270\sqrt{3}$ (d) None of these

Solution:

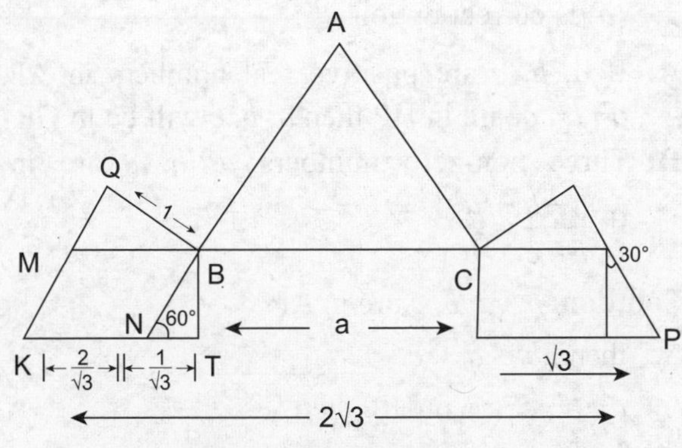

$\Rightarrow MB = \sec 30° = 2/\sqrt{3}$ Cot 60° = NT/BT

$\therefore$ $KN = 2\sqrt{3}$; $NT = 1/\sqrt{3}$

$\therefore$ $KT = KN + NT = \frac{2}{\sqrt{3}}+\frac{1}{\sqrt{3}}=\sqrt{3}$

$\therefore$ $KP = a + 2\sqrt{3}$

$\therefore$ Each time side of Δ increases by $2\sqrt{3}$

$\therefore$ $a_1 = a$; $a_2 = a + 2\sqrt{3}$

$a_3 = a + 4\sqrt{3}$ $a_4 = a + 6\sqrt{3}$

$a_n = a + 2(n-1)\sqrt{3}$

Perimeter of $\Delta_1 = 3a$

Perimeter of $\Delta_2 = 3(a + 2\sqrt{3})$;

Perimeter of $\Delta_3 = 3[a + \sqrt{3}]$

Perimeter of $\Delta_4 = 3[a + 6\sqrt{3}]$

Perimeter of $\Delta_n = 3[a+(n-1)(2\sqrt{3})]$

It is an AP with first term $3a$, and c.$d = 6\sqrt{3}$

$\therefore$ $S_n = \frac{n}{2}\left[2(3a)+(n-1)\left(6\sqrt{3}\right)\right]=n\left[3a+(n-1)\left(3\sqrt{3}\right)\right]$

$\therefore$ $S_{10} = 10[3a + (9)(3\sqrt{3})] = 30a + 270\sqrt{3}$

67. From above, clearly increment in length $= 2\sqrt{3}$

68. From above length of side of nth triangle $=a+(n-1)2\sqrt{3}$

69. Area $=\frac{\sqrt{3}}{4}\left[a+(5-1)\left(2\sqrt{3}\right)\right]^2=\frac{\sqrt{3}}{4}\left[a+8\sqrt{3}\right]^2$

70. Perimeter are forming an AP with first term $= 3a$ and common difference $= 6\sqrt{3}$

$\therefore$ $S_n = n/2\,[6a + (n-1)\,6\sqrt{3}]$

$\therefore$ $S_{10} = 5[6a + 54\sqrt{3}] = 30a + 270\sqrt{3}$

Assertion and Reason

The questions given below consist of an Assertion (A) and the reason (R). Use the following key to choose the appropriate answer.

(a) If both assertion and reason are correct and reason is the correct explanation of the assertion.

(b) If both assertion and reason are correct but reason is not correct explanation of the assertion.

(c) If assertion is correct, but reason is incorrect

(d) If assertion is incorrect, but reason is correct

Now consider the following statements:

71. Suppose four distinct positive numbers a_1, a_2, a_3, a_4 are in GP Let $b_1 = a_1$, $b_2 = b_1 + a_2$, $b_3 = b_2 + a_3$ and $b_4 = b_3 + a_4$.

Statement-1: The numbers b_1,b_2,b_3,b_4 are neither in AP nor in GP.

Statement-2: The numbers b_1, b_2, b_3, b_4 are in HP.

Solution: (b) Let $a_1 = 1$, $a_2 = 2$, $a_3 = 4$, $a_4 = 8$ in GP.

$\therefore$ $b_1 = 1$, $b_2 = 3$, $b_3 = 7$, $b_4 = 15$

Clearly, b_1, b_2, b_3, b_4 are not in HP.

Statement II is false.

Statement I is already true.

72. A: If a, b, c are the sides of a triangle then $(a + b + c)^2 \geq 3(ab + bc + ca)$

R: $a, b, c \in R^+$then $\frac{a+b+c}{3}\geq\frac{3}{\frac{1}{a}+\frac{1}{b}+\frac{1}{c}}$

Solution: $(a + b + c)^2 = a^2 + b^2 + c^2 + 2ab + 2bc + 2ca$

$\therefore$ $(a + b + c)^2 - 3(ab + bc + ca) = 1/2\,[(a-b)^2 + (b-c)^2 + (c-a)^2] \geq 0$

$\therefore$ $(a + b + c)^2 \geq 3[ab + bc + ca]$

Here equality will hold if $a = b = c$

$\therefore$ Assertion is correct.

Also for $a, b, c \in \mathbb{R}^+$,

$A.M \geq H.M$

$\Rightarrow$ $\frac{a+b+c}{}\geq\frac{}{\frac{1}{a}+\frac{1}{b}+\frac{1}{c}}$

$\therefore$ Reason is also correct.

But reason has no connectivity with the assertion

$\therefore$ **Ans** (b)

73. A: In a triangle ABC, $\sin A + \sin B + \sin C \leq \frac{3\sqrt{3}}{2}$

R: If a, b, c are the real, then $\frac{a+b+c}{3}\geq\sqrt[3]{abc}$.

Solution: Let $f(x) = \sin x$

Consider the graph of $f(x) = \sin x$ for $x \in [0, \pi/2]$

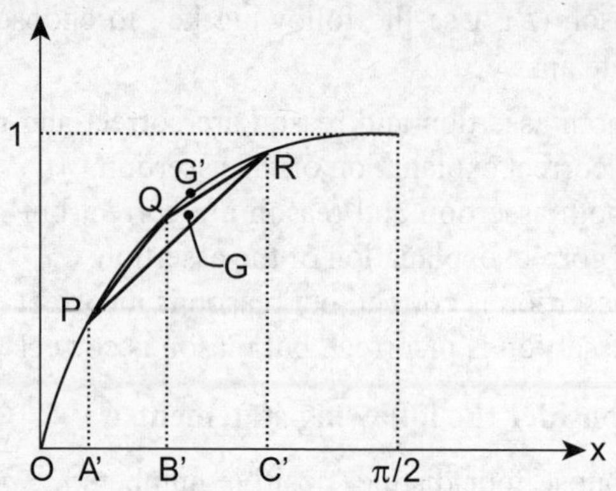

Let P, Q, R be three points on $y = f(x)$

Whose projections on X-axis are A', B' and C', having their co-ordinates (A, O), (B, O) and (C, O) respectively, then the co-ordinates of centroid will be $G \left(\frac{A+B+C}{3}, \frac{\sin A+\sin B+\sin C}{3}\right)$; and that of G' will be $\left(\frac{A+B+C}{3}, \sin\left(\frac{A+B+C}{3}\right)\right)$ as shown in figure (ii)

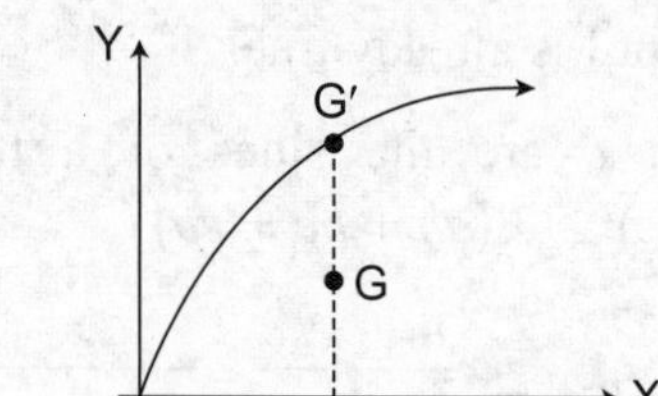

Clearly, $GL \le G'L$ [equality holds when $A = B = C$]

$$\Rightarrow \frac{\sin A+\sin B+\sin C}{3} \le \sin\left(\frac{A+B+C}{3}\right)$$

$$= \sin\frac{\pi}{3} = \frac{\sqrt{3}}{2} \text{ for } A = B = C$$

$\therefore$ $\sin A + \sin B + \sin C \le \frac{3\sqrt{3}}{2}$

$\therefore$ Assertion is correct.

Also reason is correct, but it is not the correct of explanation of reason.

$\therefore$ **Ans** (b)

74. A: If three positive numbers in GP represent sides of a triangle, then the common ratio of the GP must lie between $\frac{\sqrt{5}-1}{2}$ and $\frac{\sqrt{5}+1}{2}$.

R: Three positive real numbers can form a triangle if sum of any two is greater than the third.

Solution: Let $\frac{a}{r}$, a, ar be three sides of a triangle.

$$\Rightarrow \frac{a}{r}+a > ar; \frac{a}{r}+ar > a \ ; \ a + ar > a/r$$

$$\Rightarrow \frac{1}{r}+r > r; \frac{1}{r}+r > 1; \ 1 + r > 1/r$$

$$\Rightarrow r^2 - r - 1 < 0, r^2 - r + 1 > 0; r^2 + r - 1 > 0$$

$$\Rightarrow r \in \left(0, \frac{(1+\sqrt{5})}{2}\right) \cap \left(\frac{\sqrt{5}-1}{2}, \infty\right) = \left(\frac{\sqrt{5}-1}{2}, \frac{\sqrt{5}+1}{2}\right)$$

$\Rightarrow$ Assertion is correct also reason is correct.

$\Rightarrow$ (*a*) is correct option.

75. A: If a, b, c are positive real numbers in AP and a^2, b^2, c^2 are in HP then a, b, c will be in GP.

R: Three non-zero numbers a, b, c are in GP If $\frac{a-b}{b-c} = \frac{a}{b}$.

Solution: $\because$ a, b, c are in AP.

then $2b = a + c$ ______________ (1)

$\because$ a^2, b^2, c^2 are in HP, then

$$b^2 = \frac{2a^2c^2}{a^2+c^2}$$

$$b^2 = \frac{2a^2c^2}{(a+c)^2 - ac} \quad \frac{2a^2c^2}{4b^2 \quad 2ac} \quad \text{[from 1]}$$

$\Rightarrow$ $4b^4 - 2acb^2 - 2a^2c^2 = 0$

$\Rightarrow$ $2b^4 - acb^2 - a^2c^2 = 0$

$$\Rightarrow b^2 = \frac{ac \pm \sqrt{9a^2c^2}}{4} = \frac{ac \pm 3ac}{4}$$

$\Rightarrow$ $b^2 = ac$ or $- 1/2\ ac$

$\therefore$ $b^2 = ac$ [$\because$ $ac > 0$]

then, a, b, c will be G.P

$\therefore$ Assertion is correct.

if, a, b, c are in G.P

then $b = ar$, $c = ar^2$ [r being common ratio]

$\therefore$ $\frac{a-b}{b-c} = \frac{a-ar}{ar-ar^2} = \frac{a(1-r)}{ar(1-r)} = \frac{a}{b}$ (*whenever* left side is defined)

$\therefore$ Reason is also correct, having no connection with assertion.

$\therefore$ **Ans** (b)

76. A: If a, b, c are in GP and $a^{\frac{1}{x}} = b^{\frac{1}{y}} = c^{\frac{1}{z}}$, then x, y, z are in AP

R: Whenever $a^u = b^v = c^w$, then $\frac{1}{u}, \frac{1}{v}, \frac{1}{w}$ are in AP

Solution: Let $b = ar$, $c = ar^2$; r being common ratio, then $a^{1/x} = b^{1/y} = c^{1/z}$

$\Rightarrow a^{1/x} = (ar)^{1/y} = (ar^2)^{1/z}$

$\Rightarrow a^{1/x} = a^{1/y} r^{1/y} = a^{1/z} r^{2/z}$

$\Rightarrow a^{\frac{1}{x}-\frac{1}{y}} = r^{1/y}$ and $a^{\frac{1}{x}-\frac{1}{z}} = r^{\frac{2}{z}}$

$\Rightarrow r = a^{y\left(\frac{1}{x}-\frac{1}{y}\right)} = a^{\frac{z}{2}\left(\frac{1}{x}-\frac{1}{z}\right)}$

$\Rightarrow \frac{y}{x} - 1 = \frac{z}{2x} - \frac{1}{2}$ $\quad\Rightarrow \frac{y}{x} - \frac{z}{2x} = \frac{1}{2}$

$\Rightarrow 2y - z = x$ $\quad\Rightarrow 2y = x + z$

$\Rightarrow x, y, z$ are in $A.P$

∴ Assertion is correct.

Now consider:

$(64)^2 = (8)^4 = (2)^{12}$

But $\frac{1}{2}, \frac{1}{4}, \frac{1}{12}$ are not in AP.

∴ Reason is not correct.

∴ **Ans.** (c)

Match the column type:

77. Match the following sum of the sequences with their suitable alternatives:

Column-I

(a) $3 + 5 + 9 + 17 + 33 + \ldots\ldots$ upto 9 terms

(b) $1 - 2 + 3 - 4 + 5 \ldots\ldots\ldots$ upto 1001 terms

(c) $1 + 3 + 5 + 7 + \ldots\ldots\ldots$ upto 100 terms

(d) $1^2 + 2^2 + 3^2 + 4^2 + 5^2 \ldots\ldots\ldots$ upto 20 terms

Column-II

(i) 100^2

(ii) 2870

(iii) 1031

(iv) 501

Solution: (a) → iii $\quad (b) \to$ iv $\quad (c) \to (i) \quad (d) \to$ ii

(a) $S_n = 3 + 5 + 9 + 17 + 33 + \ldots$ up to n terms

Also $S_n = 3 + 5 + 9 + 17 + \ldots\ldots\ t_{n+1} t_n$

on subtraction, $= 3 + (2 + 4 + 8 + 16 + \ldots$ + up to $(n - 1) - Tn$

$\Rightarrow t_n = 3 + [2 + 4 + 8 + 16 + \ldots$ + up to $(n - 1)$ terms]

$= 3 + \frac{2\left((2)^{n-1} - 1\right)}{(2) - 1}$

$\Rightarrow t_n = 3 + 2^n - 2 \Rightarrow t_n = 1 + 2^n$

$\therefore S_n = \sum t_n = n + \sum (2)^n$

$\therefore S_9 = \sum t_9 = 9 + \sum_{n=1}^{9} (2)^n$

$= 9 + (2)^1 \frac{\left[(2)^9 - 1\right]}{(2) - 1} = 9 + 2^{10} - 2$

$= 7 + 2^{10} = 7 + 1024 = 1031$

$\therefore (a) \to (iii)$

(b) $1 - 2 + 3 - 4 + 5 \ldots$ up to 1001 terms

$= [1 + 3 + 5 + \ldots$ 501 term]

$-2[1 + 2 + 3 + \ldots$ 500 terms]

$= (501)^2 - \frac{2.(500) \times 501}{2} = (501)[501 - 500] = 501$

Aliter:

$(1 - 2) + (3 - 4) + (5 - 6) + \ldots\ldots + (999 - 1000) + 1001 = (-1) + (-1) + (-1) + \ldots$ 500 times + 1001 = 501

(c) $1 + 3 + 5 + 7 + \ldots\ldots$ up to 100 terms

$= (100)^2$ [∵ Sum of first n odd terms $= n^2$]

$\therefore (c) \to (i)$

(d) $1^2 + 2^2 + 3^2 + 4^2 + 5^2 + \ldots$ up to 20 terms

$= \frac{(20)(20+1)\left[2(20)+1\right]}{6} = \frac{20 \times 21 \times 41}{6} = 2870$

$\therefore d \to (ii)$

Questions for example 15 – 19: Each question contains Assertion (A) and Reason (R). Each question has 4 choices (a), (b), (c) and (d) out of which **only one** is correct.

SECTION–III

OBJECTIVE-TYPE (ONLY ONE CORRECT ANSWER)

1. An AP whose first term is unity and in which the sum of the first half of any even number of terms to that of the second half of the same number of the same set of terms is in constant ratio, the common difference d is given by

(a) 1 (b) 2

(c) 3 (d) 4

2. The number of natural numbers less than 400 that are not divisible by 17 or 23 is

(a) 382 (b) 359

(c) 360 (d) 376

3. If the sum of the first 11 terms of an arithmetical progression equals that of the first 19 terms, then the sum of the first 30 terms, is

(a) equal to 0 (b) equal to –1

(c) equal to 1 (d) non-unique

4. Consider the pattern shown below:

Row 1 1
Row 2 3 5
Row 3 7 9 11
Row 4 13 15 17 19 etc.

The number at the end of rows 80 is
(a) 6479 (b) 6319
(c) 6481 (d) 6531

5. If the arithmetic mean between a and b is twice their geometric mean, then a/b is
(a) $\left(\frac{\sqrt{2}-\sqrt{3}}{\sqrt{2}+\sqrt{3}}\right)$ (b) $\left(\frac{2-\sqrt{3}}{2+\sqrt{3}}\right)$
(c) $\left(\frac{\sqrt{2}+\sqrt{3}}{\sqrt{2}-\sqrt{3}}\right)$ (d) $\sqrt{3/2}$

6. The sum of the infinite series $\frac{1}{7}+\frac{2}{7^2}+\frac{1}{7^3}+\frac{2}{7^4}$...... is
(a) 13/24 (b) 14/47
(c) 3/16 (d) 9/49

7. The consecutive odd integers whose sum is $45^2 - 21^2$ are:
(a) 43, 45,...75 (b) 43, 45,..79
(c) 43, 45,......85 (d) 43, 45,...89

8. If $(1 + x)(1 + x^2)(1 + x^4)....(1 + x^{128}) = \sum_{r=0}^{n} x^r$, then n is
(a) 255 (b) 127
(c) 60 (d) None of these

9. Let $S_k = \lim_{n\to\infty}\sum_{i=0}^{n}\frac{1}{(k+1)^i}$, then $\sum_{k=1}^{n} k\,S_k$ equals
(a) $\frac{n(n+1)}{2}$ (b) $\frac{n(n-1)}{2}$
(c) $\frac{n(n+2)}{2}$ (d) $\frac{n(n+3)}{2}$

10. In a sequence, if the sum of the first n terms is given by $S_n = 2^{np} - 1$, when 'p' is fixed real number. The nature of the sequence, is
(a) AP (b) GP
(c) HP (d) AGP

11. The minimum number of terms of 1 + 3 + 5 + 7 +... that add up to a number exceeding 1357 is
(a) 15 (b) 37
(c) 35 (d) 17

12. If first, fifth and last terms of an AP is l, m, p respectively and sum of the AP is $\frac{(l+p)(4p+m-5l)}{k(m-l)}$, then k is
(a) 2 (b) 3
(c) 4 (d) 5

13. The number of terms common between the series 1 + 2 + 4 + 8 +....to 100 terms and 1 + 4 + 7 + 10 +....to 100 terms is
(a) 6 (b) 4
(c) 5 (d) None of these

14. If a, b, c, d are in GP, then $(a \pm b)^2$;$(b \pm c)^2$, $(c \pm d)^2$ are in
(a) AP (b) GP
(c) HP (d) None of these

15. If a, b, c are non-zero real numbers such that $3(a^2 + b^2 + c^2 + 1) = 2(a + b + c + ab + bc + ca)$; then a, b, c are in
(a) AP only (b) GP only
(c) AP and GP (d) None of these

16. The lengths of three unequal edges of a rectangular solid block are in GP. The volume of the block is 216 cm³ and the total surface area is 252 cm². The length of the longest edge is
(a) 12 cm (b) 6 cm
(c) 18 cm (d) 3 cm

17. If $m = \sum_{r=0}^{\infty} a^r, n = \sum_{r=0}^{\infty} b^r$, where $0 < a, b < 1$, then quadratic equation whose roots are a and b is
(a) $mnx^2 + (m + n - 2mn)x + mn - m - n + 1 = 0$
(b) $mnx^2 + (2mn - m - n)x + mn - m - n + 1 = 0$
(c) $mnx^2 + (2mn + m - n)x + mn - m - n + 1 = 0$
(d) $mnx^2 + (2mn + m + n)x + mn + m - n + 1 = 0$

18. Suppose a, b, c are in GP and $a^p = b^q = c^r$, then
(a) p, q, r are in GP.
(b) p, q, r are in AP.
(c) $\frac{1}{p}, \frac{1}{q}, \frac{1}{r}$ are in AP
(d) None of the foregoing statements is true

19. If $A = 1 + r^a + r^{2a} + r^{3a} +......\infty$ and $B = 1 + r^b + r^{2b} + r^{3b} +...\infty$, (given $|r| < 1$), then $\frac{a}{b}$ is equal to
(a) $\log_B A$ (b) $\log_{1-B}(1 - A)$
(c) $\log_{\frac{B-1}{B}}\left(\frac{A-1}{A}\right)$ (d) None of these

20. The sum of first n terms of the series $1^2 + 2.2^2 + 3^2 + 2.4^2 + 5^2 + 2.6^2 + ...$is $\frac{n(n+1)^2}{2}$ when n is even. When n is odd, the sum is

(a) $\frac{n^2(n+1)}{2}$ (b) $\frac{n(n+1)^2}{2}$

(c) $\left[\frac{n(n+1)}{2}\right]^2$ (d) $\frac{n(n+1)}{2}$

21. Sum of series 4 + 18 + 48 + 100 +....... to n terms is

(a) $\Sigma(n^3 + 2n^2 + n)$ (b) $\Sigma(2n^3 - n^2 + n)$
(c) $\Sigma(n^3 + n^2 + 2n)$ (d) None of these

22. Along a road lies an odd number of stones placed at intervals of 10 m. These stones have to be assembled around the middle stone. A person can carry only one stone at a time. A man carried out the job starting with the stone in the middle, carrying stones in succession, thereby covering a distance of 4.8 km. Then the number of stones is

(a) 15 (b) 29
(c) 31 (d) 35

23. $(1 + x)(1 + x + x^2)(1 + x + x^2 + x^3)$............$(1 + x + x^2 +........ x^{100})$ when written in the ascending power of x, then highest exponent of x is

(a) 4950 (b) 5050
(c) 5150 (d) None of these

24. The sum of the infinite series,

$$1^2 - \frac{2^2}{5} + \frac{3^2}{5^2} - \frac{4^2}{5^3} + \frac{5^2}{5^4} - \frac{6^2}{5^5} + ... \text{ is}$$

(a) $\frac{1}{2}$ (b) $\frac{25}{24}$

(c) $\frac{25}{54}$ (d) $\frac{125}{252}$

25. If $4a^2 + 9b^2 + 16c^2 = 2(3ab + 6bc + 4ca)$, where a, b, c are non-zero numbers, then a, b, c are in

(a) AP (b) GP
(c) HP (d) None of these

26. If three numbers are in HP, then the numbers obtained by subtracting half of the middle number from each of them are in

(a) AP (b) GP
(c) HP (d) None of these

27. $L = \lim_{n\to\infty} \frac{1.2.3 + 2.3.4 + 3.4.5 + .. + \text{up to n terms}}{n(1.2 + 2.3 + 3.4 + ... + \text{up to n terms})}$ is equal to

(a) $\frac{3}{4}$ (b) $\frac{1}{4}$

(c) $\frac{1}{2}$ (d) $\frac{5}{4}$

28. An infinite GP has 2nd term x and its sum is 4, then x belongs to

(a) (0, 2] (b) (1, 8)
(c) (–8, 1] (d) None of these

29. If the sides of a right angled triangle are in GP, then the cosines of the acute angles of the triangle are

(a) $\frac{\sqrt{5}-1}{2}, \sqrt{\frac{\sqrt{5}-1}{2}}$ (b) $\frac{\sqrt{5}-1}{2}, \frac{\sqrt{\sqrt{5}-1}}{2}$

(c) 1/2, 1/4 (d) None of these

30. Let $a_1, a_2, a_3,........., a_n$ are in GP such that $3a_1 + 7a_2 + 3a_3 - 4a_5 = 0$, then common ratio of GP can be

(a) 2 (b) $\frac{3}{2}$

(c) $\frac{5}{2}$ (d) $\frac{1}{2}$

31. If the expression $\exp\{(\sin^2 x + \sin^4 x + \sin^6 x + ... + \text{up to } \infty) \log_e 2\}$ satisfies the equation $t^2 - 17t + 16 = 0$, then the value of $\frac{2\cos x}{\sin x + 2\cos x}$; where $(0 < x < \pi/2)$ is

(a) 1/2 (b) 3/2
(c) 5/2 (d) None of these

32. If a, b, c, d are distinct integers in AP such that $d = a^2 + b^2 + c^2$, then $a + b + c + d$ is

(a) 0 (b) 1
(c) 2 (d) None of these

33. Let $f(n) = \left[\frac{1}{2} + \frac{n}{100}\right]$, where $[x]$ denotes the integral part of x. Then the value of $\sum_{n=1}^{100} f(n)$ is

(a) 50 (b) 51
(c) 1 (d) None of these

34. $\lim_{n\to\infty}(1+3^{-1})(1+3^{-2})(1+3^{-4})(1+3^{-8}) .... (1 + 3^{-2n})$ is equal to

(a) 1 (b) $\frac{1}{2}$

(c) $\frac{3}{2}$ (d) None of these

35. The sum of the products taken two at a time of the numbers $1, 2, 2^2, 2^3,....2^{n-2}, 2^{n-1}$ is

(a) $\frac{1}{3}2^{2n} + \frac{2}{3}$ (b) $\frac{1}{3}2^{2n} - 2^2 + \frac{1}{3}$

(c) $\frac{1}{3}2^{2n} - \frac{1}{3}$ (d) $\frac{1}{3}2^{2n} - 2^{2n} + \frac{2}{3}$

36. If the ratio of AM between two positive real numbers a and b to their HM is m: n; then a: b is equal to

(a) $\frac{\sqrt{(m-n)}+\sqrt{n}}{\sqrt{(m-n)}-\sqrt{n}}$ (b) $\frac{\sqrt{n}+\sqrt{(m-n)}}{\sqrt{n}-\sqrt{(m-n)}}$

(c) $\frac{\sqrt{m}+\sqrt{(m-n)}}{\sqrt{m}-\sqrt{(m-n)}}$ (d) $\frac{\sqrt{m}-\sqrt{(m-n)}}{\sqrt{m}+\sqrt{(m-n)}}$

37. The product of the arithmetic mean of the lengths of the sides of a triangle and harmonic mean of the lengths of the altitudes of the triangle is equal to:
(a) Δ (b) 2Δ
(c) 3Δ (d) 4Δ

38. Concentric circles of radii 1, 2, 3.....100 cm are drawn. The interior of the smallest circle is coloured red and the angular regions are coloured alternately green and red, so that no two adjacent regions are of the same colour. The total area of the green regions in cm² is equal to
(a) 1000π (b) 5050π
(c) 4950π (d) 5151π

39. The minimum value of the expression $\frac{9x^2\sin^2 x+4}{x\sin x}$ for $x\in(0,\pi)$ is
(a) $\frac{16}{3}$ (b) 6
(c) 12 (d) $\frac{8}{3}$

40. Let C be a circle with centre P_0 and AB be a diameter of C. Suppose P_1 is the mid-point of the line segment P_0P_1, P_2 is the mid-point of the line segment P_1B and so on. Let C_1, C_2, C_3.....be circles with diameters P_0P_1, P_1P_2, P_2P_3......... respectively. Suppose the circles C_1, C_2, C_3.....are all shaded. The ratio of the area the unshaded portion of C to that of the original circle C is
(a) 8: 9 (b) 9: 10
(c) 10: 11 (d) 11: 12

41. A circle of radius r is inscribed in a square. The mid points of sides of the square have been connected by line segments and a new square resulted. The sides of the resulting square were also connected by segments so that a new square was obtained and so on, then the radius of the circle inscribed in the nth square is

(a) $\left(2^{\frac{1-n}{2}}\right)r$ (b) $\left(2^{\frac{3-3n}{2}}\right)r$

(c) $\left(2^{-\frac{n}{2}}\right)r$ (d) $\left(2^{\frac{5-3n}{2}}\right)r$

42. The sum of the series
$(1^2+1).1!+(2^2+1).2!+(3^2+1).3!+.....+(n^2+1).n!$ is:
(a) $(n+1).(n+2)!$ (b) $n.(n+1)!$
(c) $(n+1).(n+1)!$ (d) None of these

43. If x, y, z are real numbers satisfing the expression $25(9x^2+y^2)+9z^2-15(5xy+yz+3zx)=0$, then x, y, z are in
(a) AP (b) GP
(c) HP (d) None of these

44. 15 should be split into how many parts show that 243 is the maximum value of their product
(a) 9 (b) 10
(c) 5 (d) None of these

45. Let a_1, a_2.........a_{10} be in AP and h_1, h_2, h_{10} be in HP If $a_1=h_1=2$ and $a_{10}=h_{10}=3$ then $[a_5\ h_5]$ where [.] gint function is
(a) 2 (b) 3
(c) 5 (d) 6

46. Suppose a, b, c are in AP and a^2, b^2, c^2 are in GP. If $a<b<c$ and $a+b+c=3/2$, then the value of a is
(a) $\frac{1}{2\sqrt{2}}$ (b) $\frac{1}{2\sqrt{3}}$
(c) $\frac{1}{2}-\frac{1}{\sqrt{3}}$ (d) $\frac{1}{2}-\frac{1}{\sqrt{2}}$

47. Let $\sum_{r=1}^{n} r^4=f(n)$, then $\sum_{r=1}^{n}(2r-1)^4$ is equal to
(a) $f(2n)-16f(n)$ (b) $f(n)-7f(n)$
(c) $f(2n-1)-8f(n)$ (d) None of these

48. If three positive real numbers a, b, c are in AP such that $abc=4$, then the minimum possible value of b is
(a) $2^{3/2}$ (b) $2^{2/3}$
(c) $2^{1/3}$ (d) $2^{5/2}$

49. If A,G and H are respectively the AM,GM and HM of three positive number a, b and c, then the equation whose roots are a, b, c is given by
(a) $x^3-3Ax^2+3G^3x-G^3=0$
(b) $x^3-3Ax^2+3(G^3/H)x-G^3=0$
(c) $x^3+3Ax^2+3(G^3/H)x-G^3=0$
(d) $x^3-3Ax^2-3(G^3/H)x+G^3=0$

50. The sum $\sum_{r=2}^{\infty}\frac{1}{r^2-1}$ is equal to
(a) 1 (b) 3/4
(c) 4/3 (d) None of these

51. If p is positive, then the sum to infinity of the series, $\frac{1}{1+p}-\frac{1-p}{(1+p)^2}+\frac{(1-p)^2}{(1+p)^3}\ldots$is

(a) 1/2 (b) 3/4
(c) 1 (d) None of these

52. In a GP of positive terms, any term is equal to the sum of the next two terms. The common ratio of the GP is

(a) 2 cos 18° (b) sin18°
(c) cos 18° (d) 2 sin 18°

53. If 's' be the sum of 'n' positive unequal quantities a,b,c ,..........then $\frac{s}{s-a}+\frac{s}{s-b}+\frac{s}{s-c}+$.......*is*

(a) $>\frac{n^2}{n+1}$ (b) $<\frac{n^2}{n-1}$
(c) $\frac{n^2}{n-1}$ (d) None of these

54. The sum of the series $\frac{5}{13}+\frac{55}{(13)^2}+\frac{555}{(13)^3}+\frac{5555}{(13)^4}+\ldots$up to ∞ ...is

(a) $\frac{65}{36}$ (b) $\frac{65}{37}$
(c) $\frac{65}{38}$ (d) none of these

55. If $0<x<\pi$ and the expression exp$\{(1+|\cos x|+\cos^2 x+|\cos^3 x|+\cos^4 x+\ldots$up to ∞$)\log_e 4\}$ satisfies the quadratic equation $y^2-20y+64=0$ then the value of x is

(a) $\frac{\pi}{2},\frac{2\pi}{3},\frac{\pi}{3}$ (b) $\frac{\pi}{4},\frac{3\pi}{4},\frac{2\pi}{3}$
(c) $\frac{\pi}{6},\frac{2\pi}{9},\frac{4\pi}{3}$ (d) None of these

56. Given that α , γ are roots of the equations, $Ax^2-4x+1=0$ and β ,δ the roots of the equation, $Bx^2-6x+1=0$, then the values of A and B is such that α,β,γ and δ are in H.P

(a) $A=3$; $B=8$ (b) $A=2$; $B=6$
(c) $A=4$; $B=8$ (d) None of these

57. If $a_1, a_2 \ldots a_n$ are in AP with common difference $d\neq 0$, then the sum of the series (sin d) [cosec a_1 cosec a_{2+} cosec a_2 cosec a_3+.... +cosec a_{n-1} cosec a_n] is

(a) sec a_1 – sec a_n (b) cosec a_1 – cosec a_n
(c) cot a_1 – cota_n (d) tan a_1 – tan a_n

58. If $H_n=1+\frac{1}{2}+\frac{1}{3}+\ldots+\frac{1}{n}$ then value of $1+\frac{3}{2}+\frac{5}{3}+\ldots+\frac{2n-1}{n}$ is

(a) $2n-H_n$ (b) $2n+H_n$
(c) H_n-2n (d) H_n+n

59. If S_1, S_2, S_3 are the sums of first n natural numbers, their squares, their cubes respectively, then $\frac{S_3(1+8S_1)}{S_2^2}$ is equal to

(a) 1 (b) 3
(c) 9 (d) 10

60. Sum of n terms of the series $1+\frac{x}{a_1}+\frac{x(x+a_1)}{a_1a_2}+\frac{x(x+a_1)(x+a_2)}{a_1a_2a_3}+\ldots$is

(a) $\frac{x(x+a_1)\ldots(x+a_{n-1})}{a_1a_2\ldots..a_n}$

(b) $\frac{x(x+a_1)(x+a_2)\ldots..(x+a_{n-1})}{a_1a_2\ldots..a_{n-1}}$

(c) $\frac{x(x+a_1)\ldots(x+a_n)}{a_1a_2\ldots..a_n}$

(d) None of these

61. If a_1,a_2,a_3 ,..........a_n are positive real numbers whose product is a fixed number c, then the minimum value of $2(a_1+a_2+a_3+\ldots a_{n-1}+a_n)$ is

(a) $n(2c)^{1/n}$ (b) $(n+1)c^{1/n}$
(c) $2nc^{1/n}$ (d) $(n+1)(2c)^{1/n}$

62. If a, b, c are in AP, then $a+\frac{1}{bc},b+\frac{1}{ca},c+\frac{1}{ab}$ are in

(a) AP (b) GP.
(c) HP (d) None of these

63. If x,y,z are in A.P, then $\frac{1}{\sqrt{y}+\sqrt{z}},\frac{1}{\sqrt{z}+\sqrt{x}},\frac{1}{\sqrt{x}+\sqrt{y}}$ will be in

(a) AP (b) GP
(c) HP (d) None of these

64. If 'n' arithmetic means are inserted between 20 and 80, such that first mean : the last mean 1 :3, the value of 'n' is

(a) 8 (b) 9
(c) 10 (d) 11

65. The sum of all the 12 arithmetic means inserted between $-3\frac{1}{2}$and $-42\frac{1}{2}$is

(a) 276 (b) –276
(c) –23 (d) None of these

SECTION–IV

OBJECTIVE-TYPE (MORE THAN ONE CORRECT ANSWER)

1. Let $a_n = \underbrace{(111....1)}_{n \text{ times}}$, then

(a) a_{912} is not prime (b) a_{951} is not prime
(c) a_{480} is not prime (d) a_{91} is not prime

2. $11^2 + 12^2 + 13^2 + ... + 20^2$ is

(a) an odd integer divisible by 5
(b) an even integer
(c) multiple of 10
(d) odd integer but not multiple of 10.

3. If the first and $(2n - 1)$th terms of an AP, a GP and a HP are equal and their nth terms are a, b and c respectively, then.

(a) $a = b = c$ (b) $a + c = b$
(c) $a \geq b \geq c$ (d) $ac = b^2$

4. In a GP, the product of the first four terms is 4 and the second term is the reciprocal of the fourth term. The sum of the GP up to infinite terms is

(a) 8 (b) –8
(c) 8/3 (d) –8/3

5. Let a, x, b be in AP; a, y, b be in GP and a, z, b be in HP. If $x = y + 2$ and $a = 5z$ then

(a) $y^2 = xz$ (b) $x > y > z$
(c) $a = 9, b = 1$ (d) $a = \frac{1}{4}, b = \frac{9}{4}$

6. Three positive numbers form a GP. If the middle number is increased by 8, the three numbers form an AP. If the last number is also increased by 64 along with the previous increase in the middle number, the resulting numbers form a GP again. Then

(a) common ratio = 3 (b) first number = 4/9
(c) common ratio = –5 (d) first number = 4

7. Let $a_1, a_2, ...$ be in $A.P$ and $q_1, q_2, ..., q_n$ be in GP if $a_1 = q_1 = 2$ and $a_{10} = q_{10} = 3$ then

(a) $a_7 q_{19}$ is not an integer
(b) $a_{19} q_7$ is an integer
(c) $a_7 q_{19} = a_{19} q_{10}$
(d) None of these

8. If $S_n = \sum_{r=1}^{n} \frac{2r+1}{r^4 + 2r^3 + r^2}$, then

(a) $S_{15} = \frac{255}{256}$ (b) $S_{10} = \frac{120}{121}$
(c) $S_{20} = \frac{439}{221}$ (d) $S_{20} = \frac{440}{441}$

9. If a, b, c, d are four unequal positive numbers which are in AP then

(a) $\frac{1}{a} + \frac{1}{d} = \frac{1}{b} + \frac{1}{c}$ (b) $\frac{1}{a} + \frac{1}{d} < \frac{1}{b} + \frac{1}{c}$
(c) $\frac{1}{a} + \frac{1}{d} > \frac{1}{b} + \frac{1}{c}$ (d) $\frac{1}{b} + \frac{1}{c} > \frac{4}{a+d}$

10. The sum to 'n' terms of the series $\tan^{-1}\left(\frac{1}{2}\right) + \tan^{-1}\left(\frac{2}{5}\right) + \tan^{-1}\left(\frac{1}{8}\right) + \tan^{-1}\left(\frac{2}{25}\right) + \tan^{-1}\left(\frac{1}{18}\right) + ... n$ terms is

(a) $\tan^{-1} 3$ (b) $\cot^{-1}\left(\frac{1}{3}\right)$
(c) $\tan^{-1}\left(\frac{1}{3}\right)$ (d) None of these

11. If $\cos(x - y)$, $\cos x$ and $\cos(x + y)$ are in HP, then $\cos x \sec\left(\frac{y}{2}\right)$ is equal to

(a) $\sqrt{2}$ (b) $\frac{1}{\sqrt{2}}$
(c) $\frac{-1}{\sqrt{2}}$ (d) $-\sqrt{2}$

12. If a, b, c, d and p are distinct real numbers such that $(a^2 + b^2 + c^2)p^2 - 2(ab + bc + cd)p + b^2 + c^2 + d^2 \leq 0$, then

(a) $b^2 = ac$ (b) $c^2 = bd$
(c) $ad = bc$ (d) a, b, c, d are in GP

13. If $\sum_{r=1}^{n} r(r+1) = \frac{(n+a)(n+b)(n+c)}{3}$, where $a < b < c$. then

(a) $2b = c$ (b) $a^3 - 8b^3 + c^3 = 8abc$
(c) c is prime number (d) $(a + b)^2 = 0$

14. If $\sum_{r=1}^{n} r(r+1)(2r+3) = an^4 + bn^3 + cn^2 + dn + e$, then
(a) $a - b = d - c$
(b) $e = 0$
(c) a, $b - 2/3$, $c - 1$ are in AP
(d) (a, b, c) are in GP

15. If b_1, b_2, b_3 $(b_1 > 0)$ are three successive terms of a GP with common ratio r, the value of r for which the inequality $b_3 > 4b_2 - 3b_1$ holds is given by
(a) $r > 3$ (b) $r < 1$
(c) $r = 3.5$ (d) $r = 5.2$

16. If a, b, c are in AP, and a^2, b^2, c^2 are in HP, then
(a) $a = b = c$ (b) $a, b, -\frac{1}{2}c$ are in GP
(c) a, b, c are in HP (d) $-\frac{1}{2}a, b, c$ are in GP

17. If 2 and 31 apppear as two terms in an AP, then
(a) Common diference of the AP is a rational number
(b) all the terms of the AP must be rational
(c) all the terms of the AP must be integers.
(d) Sum to any finite number of terms of the AP must be rational

18. The numbers 1, 5, 25 can be three terms (not necessarily consecutive) of
(a) at least one AP
(b) at least one GP
(c) infinite number of AP's
(d) infinite number GP's

19. The terms of an infinitely decreasing GP in which all the terms are positive, the first term is 4, and the difference between the third and fifth term is 32/81, then
(a) $r = 1/3$ (b) $r = 2\sqrt{2}/3$
(c) $s_\infty = 6$ (d) None of these

20. The sides of a right triangles form a GP. The tangent of the smallest angle is
(a) $\sqrt{\frac{\sqrt{5}+1}{2}}$ (b) $\sqrt{\frac{\sqrt{5}-1}{2}}$
(c) $\sqrt{\frac{2}{\sqrt{5}+1}}$ (d) $\sqrt{\frac{2}{\sqrt{5}-1}}$

SECTION–V

LINKED COMPREHENSION TYPE

A: Let A_1, G_1, H_1 denote the arithmetic, geometric and harmonic means, respectively, of two distinctpositive numbers for $n \geq 2$, let A_{n-1} and H_{n-1} have arithmetic, geometric and harmonic means as A_n, G_n, H_n respectively.

1. Which one of the following statements is correct?
(a) $G_1 > G_2 > G_3 >$..........
(b) $G_1 < G_2 < G_3 <$.........
(c) $G_1 = G_2 = G_3 =$.........
(d) $G_1 < G_3 < G_5 <$.... and $G_2 > G_4 > G_6 >$......

2. Which one of the following statements is correct?
(a) $A_1 > A_2 > A_3$......
(b) $A_1 < A_2 < A_3 <$....
(c) $A_1 > A_3 > A_5 >$...... and $A_2 < A_4 < A_6 <$.....
(d) $A_1 < A_3 < A_5 <$...... and $A_2 > A_4 > A_6 >$.....

3. Which one of the following statements is correct?
(a) $H_1 > H_2 > H_3 >$....
(b) $H_1 < H_2 < H_3 <$....
(c) $H_1 > H_3 < H_5 >$.... and $H_2 < H_4 < H_6 <$.....
(d) $H_1 < H_3 < H_5 <$.... and $H_2 > H_4 > H_6 >$.......

B: Consider two different infinite geometric progressions with their sums S_1 and S_2 as $S_1 = a + ar + ar^2 + ar^3 + \ldots\ldots\infty$; $S_2 = b + bR + bR^2 + bR^3 + \ldots\ldots\infty$
If the sum of both the series are equal to 1 and their 2nd terms are equal i.e., $S_1 = S_2 = 1$, $ar = bR$ and $ar^2 = \frac{1}{8}$

4. The sum of their common ratios is
(a) $\frac{1}{2}$ (b) $\frac{3}{4}$
(c) 1 (d) $\frac{3}{2}$

5. The sum of their first terms is

(a) 1 (b) 2
(c) 3 (d) None of these

6. Common ratio of the first GP is

(a) $\frac{1}{2}$ (b) $\frac{1-\sqrt{5}}{4}$
(c) $\frac{\sqrt{5}-1}{4}$ (d) $\frac{\sqrt{5}+1}{4}$

7. Common ratio of the second GP is

(a) $\frac{3+\sqrt{5}}{4}$ (b) $\frac{3-\sqrt{5}}{4}$
(c) $\frac{1}{2}$ (d) None of these

C: For any positive integer n, let (n) denote the integer nearest to √n: for example (1) = 1, (2) = 1, (3) = 2, (4) = 2, (5) = 2, (6) = 2 $\left(\because \sqrt{6} \cong 2.449\right)$, (7) = 3 etc.

8. Let k be a given integer then number of solutions of the equation $(n) = k$ must be

(a) $2k$ (b) $2k + 1$
(c) $2k - 1$ (d) integer part of $\sqrt{k}$

9. In the infinite summation $S = \sum_{n=1}^{\infty} \frac{2^{(n)} + 2^{-(n)}}{2^n}$ The number of terms of the type $\frac{2^2 + 2^{-2}}{2^k}$ must be

(a) 3 (b) 1
(c) 6 (d) None of these

10. The value of S must be

(a) 3 (b) 9/2
(d) 4 (d) Infinity

D: Let A_r be the coefficient of x^r in the expansion of $(1 + x)^2 \left(1+\frac{x}{2}\right)^2 \left(1+\frac{x}{2^2}\right)^2 \left(1+\frac{x}{2^3}\right)^2$ .... up to infinity (It is being assumed that the infinite product converges. Answer the following questions:

11. The recurance relation satisfied by A_r must be

(a) $A_r \frac{2}{2^r-1}(A_{r-1} + A_{r-2})$

(b) $A_r = \frac{4}{2^r-1}(A_{r-1} + A_{r-2})$

(c) $A_r = \frac{1}{2^r-1}(A_{r-1} + A_{r-2})$

(d) None of these

12. The value of A_1 must be

(a) 1 (b) 2
(c) 3 (d) 4

13. The value of A_2 must be

(a) 5/13 (b) 7/61
(c) 128/21 (d) None of these

E: If $a_1, a_2....a_n$ are in AP and $h_1, h_2 ...... h_n$ are in HP and d is the common difference of the AP. Then answer the following questions:

14. $\tan^{-1}\left(\frac{d}{1+a_1a_2}\right) + \tan^{-1}\left(\frac{d}{1+a_2a_3}\right) + ... + \tan^{-1}\left(\frac{d}{1+a_1a_n}\right)$ equals

(a) $\tan^{-1}\left(\frac{nd}{1+a_1a_n}\right)$ (b) $\tan^{-1}\left(\frac{(n-1)d}{1+a_1a_n}\right)$

(c) $\tan^{-1}\left(\frac{d}{1+a_1a_n}\right)$ (d) None of these

15. If each $h_i > 0$, then the value of

$$\frac{\sqrt{h_1h_2}}{\sqrt{h_1}+\sqrt{h_2}} + \frac{\sqrt{h_2h_3}}{\sqrt{h_2}\sqrt{h_3}} + ... + \frac{\sqrt{h_{n-1}h_n}}{\sqrt{h_{n-1}}+\sqrt{h_n}}$$ is

(a) $\frac{(1-n)\sqrt{h_1h_2}}{\sqrt{h_1}+\sqrt{h_n}}$ (b) $\frac{(n-1)\sqrt{h_1h_2}}{\sqrt{h_1}+\sqrt{h_n}}$

(c) $\frac{(1-n)\sqrt{h_1h_2}}{\sqrt{h_1}+\sqrt{h_n}}$ (d) None of these

16. If $a_1 = h_1 = 2$ and $a_{10} = h_{10} = 3$, then $a_4\, h_7$ is

(a) 3 (b) 2
(c) 6 (d) 5

F: Four different integers form an increasing AP. One of these numbers is equal to the sum of the squares of the other three numbers Then

17. The smallest number is

(a) –2 (b) 0
(c) –1 (d) 2

18. The common difference of the four numbers is

(a) 2 (b) 1
(c) 3 (d) 4

19. The sum of all the four numbers is

(a) 10 (b) 8
(c) 2 (d) 6

G: There are two sets A and B each of which consists of three numbers in AP whose sum is 15 and where D and d are the common differences such that $D - d = 1$. If $p/q = 7/8$ where p and q are the product of the numbers respectively and $d > 0$, in the two sets.

20. Value of p is
(a) 100 (b) 120
(c) 105 (d) 110

21. Value of q is
(a) 100 (b) 120
(c) 105 (d) 110

22. Value of $D + d$ is
(a) 1 (b) 2
(c) 3 (d) 4

H: Two arithmetic progressions have the same numbers. The ratio of the last term of the first progression to first term of the second progression is equal to the ratio of the last term of the second progression to the first term of the first progression and is equal to 4, the ratio of the sum of the n terms of the first progression to the sum of the n terms of the second progression is equal to 2.

23. The ratio of their common difference is
(a) 12 (b) 24
(c) 26 (d) 9

24. The ratio of their nth term is
(a) 6/5 (b) 7/2
(c) 9/5 (d) None of these

25. Ratio of their first term is
(a) 2/7 (b) 3/5
(c) 4/7 (d) 2/5

SECTION–VI

COLUMN MATCHING

Directions: For questions 1 and 3: Each question contains statements given in two columns which have to be matched. Statements (*i*, ii, iii, *iv*) in **column** A have to be matched with statements (*a*, *b*, c, *d*) in **column B**. The answers to these questions have to be apropriately bubbled as illustrated in the following example. If the correct matches are i-*a*, *d*, ii-*b*, c, iii-*a*, *b*, iv-*d*, then the correctly bubbled 4 *x* 4 matrix should be as follows:

1. Column-I

(i) If $a^x = b^y = c^z$ and a, b, c are in GP then x, y, z are in

(ii) If $\frac{x+y}{2}, y, \frac{y+z}{2}$ are in HP then x, y, z in

(iii) If a, b, c are in AP b, c, d are in GP and c, d, e are in HP the a, c, e in

(iv) If $(y - x)$, $2(y - a)$, $(y - z)$ are in HP then $x - a$, $y - a$, $z - a$ are in

Column-II

(a) AP
(b) GP
(c) HP

2. For $a, b, c > 0$

Column I

(i) $A = \frac{1}{a}+\frac{1}{b}+\frac{1}{c}$

(ii) $A = (a + b)(a + c)(b + c)$

(iii) $A = a^{\frac{a}{a+b+c}} b^{\frac{b}{a+b+c}} c^{\frac{c}{a+b+c}}$

Column II

(a) $A \geq \frac{1}{3}(a+b+c)$

(b) $A \geq \frac{3}{2}$

(c) $A \geq \frac{9}{a+b+c}$

(d) $A \geq 8abc$

3. Match the following:

Column-I

(i) The sum of n-terms of series is $a2^n - b$, where a, b are constants and $n \geq 2$, then series is

(ii) $\frac{a+be^y}{a-be^y} = \frac{b+ce^y}{b-ce^y} = \frac{c+de^y}{c-de^y}$ then a, b, c, d are in

(iii) If roots of equation $x^3 - 6x^2 + 11x - 6 = 0$ are in AP then root of equation $6x^3 - 11x^2 + 6x - 1 = 0$ are in

Column-II

(a) AP
(b) GP
(c) HP

SECTION–VII

ASSERTION AND REASON TYPE

The questions given below consist of an Assertion (A) and the Reason (R). Use the following key to choose the appropriate answer.

(a) If both assertion and reason are correct and reason is the correct explanation of the assertion.

(b) If both assertion and reason are correct but reason is not correct explanation of the assertion.

(c) If assertion is correct, but reason is incorrect

(d) If assertion is incorrect, but reason is correct

Now consider the following statements:

1. A: Three exists an $A.P$ whose terms $\sqrt{2}$, $\sqrt{3}$, $\sqrt{5}$.

R: There exists distinct real number p, q, r satisfying $\sqrt{2} = A + (p-1)d$, $\sqrt{3} = A + (q-1)d$, $\sqrt{5} = A\,(r-1)d$

2. A: If the nth term of a series is $n^3 + n^2 + 1$, then the second order differences must be in AP

R: If the nth term of a series is a polynomial of degree r, then rth order differences of the series are constant

3. A: If the sides of a right angled triangle are in GP then the common ratio of the GP can take two and only two values

R: The common ratio is either greater than 1 or less than 1

4. A: The maximum number of acute angles in a convex polygon of n sides is 3

R: The sum of internal angles of any convex polygon is $(n–2).180°$

5. A: If the arithmetic mean of two numbers is 5/2, geometric mean of the numbers, is 2, then the harmonic mean will be 8/5.

R: For a group of positive numbers $(GM)^2 = (AM) \times (HM)$

SECTION-VIII

INTEGER-TYPE QUESTIONS

1. The first term of an AP $a_1, a_2, a_3 \ldots\ldots\ldots a_n$ is unity. If the common difference is $-5/\lambda$, for which the value of expression $a_1a_3 + a_2a_3$ is minimum, then find the value of λ.

2. Given a, b, c are positive integers forming an increasing GP, $b - a$ is a prefect square of a natural number, and $\log_6 a + \log_6 b + \log_6 c = 6$. Find the value of $a + b + c$.

3. Let x, y, z be three positive real numbers such that $x + y + z = 1$, then find the maximum vlaue of the expression $[(1-x)(2-y)(3-z)]$; where [.] is greatest integer function.

4. If $f(x)$ is a function such that $f(x-1) + f(x+1) = \sqrt{3}\,f(x)$ and $f(5) = 10$, then find the value of $\sum_{r=0}^{19} f(5+12r)$.

5. Evaluate the sum $1^2 + (1^2 + 2^2) + (1^2 + 2^2 + 3^2) + \ldots\ldots$ upto 22nd term.

6. If in an AP, $d = \dfrac{\ell^2 - a^2}{\lambda s - (\ell + a)}$ then find λ, where ℓ = last term, s = sum of all terms (n), a = first term.

7. If $\sqrt{3} + \dfrac{1}{\sqrt{3}} + \dfrac{1}{3\sqrt{3}} + \ldots\ldots = \dfrac{3\sqrt{\lambda}}{2}$; then find λ

8. In an increasing GP, the sum of the first and the last term is 66, the product of the second and the second last term is 128 and the sum of the terms is 126. How many terms are there in the progression?

9. If 2 be the first term of an AP and the sum of its first 10 terms is equal to zero. If the sum of the next 15 terms is $= \dfrac{-\lambda}{3}$, then find λ.

10. If one geomteric mean G and two Arithmetic means p and q be inserted between two quantities, then $G^2 = (kp - q)(kq - p)$ then find k.

11. If $(1 + 5^{-1})(1 + 5^{-2})(1 + 5^{-4})(1 + 5^{-8})\ldots\ldots(1 + 5^{-2n})$ $\dfrac{\lambda}{\mu}(1 - 5^{-4n})$; such that gcd $(\lambda, \mu) = 1$ then evaluate $\lambda\mu$.

12. If $\sum_{k=1}^{10}(3+2^k) = 28 + 2^k$, then find k.

13. If $\sum_{k=2}^{15}(1+3^{k-1}) = 1/2\ [25 + (3)^{\lambda}]$ then find λ.

14. If $\sum_{k=1}^{10}([1/2]^{k-1}+[1/5]^{k+1}) = 2-(2)^{-9}+1/20\ [1-5^{-\lambda}]$; find λ

15. The inventor of the chess board suggested a reward of one grain of wheat for the first square, 2 grains for the second, 4 grains for the third and so on, doubling the number of the grains for subsequent squares. If then, the number of grains would have to be given is $2^{\lambda}-1$; then find λ (There are 64 squares in the chess board).

16. 25 trees are planted in a straight line at interval of 5 metres To water them, the gardener must bring water for each tree separately from a well 10 metres from the first tree in line with the trees. How far he will have to cover in order to water all the trees beginning with the first if he starts from the well?

17. If the value of series $\sum_{i=0}^{\infty}\sum_{j=0}^{\infty}\sum_{\substack{k=0 \\ (i\neq j\neq k)}}^{\infty}\frac{1}{3^i 3^j 3^k}$ is S, then integer part of $5S$ is equal to

18. If $a=\sum_{n=1}^{\infty}\frac{1}{n^n}$, then find [a], where [x] denoted the greatest integer $\leq a$.

19. If the sum of the series $\sum_{k=1}^{\infty}\frac{k.6^k+2^{k+1}.3^k}{3^k.2^{2k+1}.(k+1).k}=\frac{1}{S}$, then find S

20. Find the value of 2550 S, where $S=\sum_{k=1}^{\infty}\frac{k}{k^4+k^2+1}$.

21. The harmonic mean of two numbers is 4. The arithmetic mean A and the geometric mean G satisfy the relation $2A + G^2 = 27$. Find the square root of sum of numbers.

22. If $S_1, S_2, S_3, \ldots, S_n$ are the sums of infinite geometric series whose first terms are 1, 2, 3, .., n and whose ratios are $\frac{1}{2},\frac{1}{3},\frac{1}{4},\ldots,\frac{1}{n+1}$ respectively, then find the value of $S_1^2+S_2^2+S_3^2+\ldots+S_{2n-1}^2$ for $n = 10$.

23. Let $a_1, a_2, \ldots, a_n$ be an AP with common difference $\pi/6$ and assume sec a_1 sec a_2 + sec a_2 sec a_3 + ... + sec a_{n-1} sec $a_n = k(\tan a_n - \tan a_1)$ find the value of k.

Answer Keys

SECTION–III

1. (b)	**2.** (c)	**3.** (a)	**4.** (a)	**5.** (b)	**6.** (c)	**7.** (d)	**8.** (a)	**9.** (d)	**10.** (b)
11. (b)	**12.** (a)	**13.** (c)	**14.** (b)	**15.** (c)	**16.** (a)	**17.** (a)	**18.** (c)	**19.** (c)	**20.** (a)
21. (a)	**22.** (c)	**23.** (b)	**24.** (c)	**25.** (c)	**26.** (b)	**27.** (a)	**28.** (c)	**29.** (a)	**30.** (b)
31. (a)	**32.** (c)	**33.** (b)	**34.** (c)	**35.** (d)	**36.** (c)	**37.** (b)	**38.** (b)	**39.** (c)	**40.** (d)
41. (a)	**42.** (b)	**43.** (a)	**44.** (c)	**45.** (c)	**46.** (d)	**47.** (a)	**48.** (b)	**49.** (b)	**50.** (b)
51. (a)	**52.** (d)	**53.** (a)	**54.** (a)	**55.** (a)	**56.** (a)	**57.** (c)	**58.** (a)	**59.** (c)	**60.** (b)
61. (a)	**62.** (a)	**63.** (a)	**64.** (d)	**65.** (b)					

SECTION–IV

1. (a, b, c, d) **2.** (a, d) **3.** (c, d) **4.** (a, b, c, d) **5.** (a, c) **6.** (a, d)
7. (c) **8.** (a, b, d) **9.** (c, d) **10.** (a, b) **11.** (a, d) **12.** (a, b, c, d) **13.**(a, b, c)
14. (a, b, c) **15.** (a, b, c) **16.** (a, b, c) **17.** (a, b, d)
18. (a, b, c, d) **19.** (a, b, c) **20.** (b, c)

SECTION–V

1. (c)	**2.** (a)	**3.** (b)	**4.** (c)	**5.** (a)	**6.** (d)	**7.** (b)	**8.** (a)	**9.** (d)
10. (a)	**11.** (b)	**12.** (d)	**13.** (d)	**14.** (b)	**15.** (b)	**16.** (c)	**17.** (c)	**18.** (b)
19. (c)	**20.** (c)	**21.** (b)	**22.** (c)	**23.** (c)	**24.** (b)	**25.** (a)		

SECTION–VI

1. (i) → (c) (ii) → (b) (iii) → (b) (iv) → (b)
2. (i) → (c) (ii) → (d) (iii) →(a)
3. (i) → (b) (ii) → (b) (iii) → (c)

SECTION–VII

1. (d) **2.** (a) **3.** (b) **4.** (b) **5.** (a)

SECTION–VIII

1. 4	**2.** 111	**3.** 4	**4.** 200	**5.** 23276	**6.** 2	**7.** 3	**8.** 6	**9.** 250	**10.** 2
11. 20	**12.** 11	**13.** 15	**14.** 10	**15.** 64	**16.** 3370	**17.** 1	**18.** 1	**19.** 1	
20. 1275	**21.** 3	**22.** 2869	**23.** 2						

HINTS AND SOLUTIONS

TEXTUAL EXERCISE–1: (SUBJECTIVE)

1. (a) (i) $n = 1 \Rightarrow \frac{1}{1}\sin\frac{\pi}{6} = \frac{1}{2}$

$n = 2 \Rightarrow \frac{1}{2^3} = \sin\frac{2\times n}{6} = \frac{1}{8}\times\frac{\sqrt{3}}{2} = \frac{\sqrt{3}}{16}$

$n = 3 \Rightarrow \frac{1}{3^3}\sin\frac{3\pi}{6} = \frac{1}{27}$

(ii) $n = 1 \Rightarrow (-1)^1 (2 + 1) \cos\frac{\pi}{3}$

$\Rightarrow -1 \times 3 \times 1/2 \Rightarrow -3/2$

$n = 2 \Rightarrow (-1)^2 (2 \times 2 + 1) \cos\frac{2\pi}{3}$

$\Rightarrow 5 \times -1/2 \Rightarrow -5/2$

$n = 3 \Rightarrow (-1)^3 (2 \times 3 + 1) \cos\frac{3\pi}{3}$

$\Rightarrow -1 \times 7 \times -1 \Rightarrow 7$

(iii) $n = 1 \Rightarrow \frac{1}{(2\times1-1)^2} = \frac{1}{1} = 1$

$n = 2 \Rightarrow \frac{2}{(2\times2-1)^2} = \frac{2}{3^2} = \frac{2}{9}$

$n = 3 \Rightarrow \frac{3}{(2\times3-1)^2} = \frac{3}{5^2} = \frac{3}{25}$

(iv) $a_n = (-1)^{n-1} 5^{n+1}$

$\Rightarrow n = 1$ $\qquad \Rightarrow n = 2$

$\Rightarrow n = 3$

$= (-1)^{1-1} \times 5^{1+1}$ $\qquad = (-1)^{2-1} \times 5^{2+1}$

$= (-1)^{3-1} \times 5^{3+1}$

$= 1 \times 5^2$ $\qquad = -1 \times 5^3$

$= (-1)^2 \times 5^4$

$= 25$ $\qquad = -125$

$= 625$

(v) $a_n = n^2 / 2n^2$

$\Rightarrow n = 1$ $\qquad \Rightarrow n = 2$

$\Rightarrow n = 3$

$= (1)^2 /2^1$ $\qquad = (2)^2 /2^2$

$= (3)^2/2^3$

$= 1/2$ $\qquad = 1 = 9/8$

(b) $a_1 = 1, a_2 = 1$

$a_3 = a_1 + a_2 = 1 + 1 = 2$

$a_4 = a_2 + a_3 = 1 + 2 = 3$

$a_5 = a_3 + a_4 = 2 + 3 = 5$

$\Rightarrow n = 2$ $\qquad \Rightarrow n = 3$

$\Rightarrow n = 4$

$= \frac{a_3}{a_2}$ $\qquad = \frac{a_4}{a_3}$

$= \frac{a_5}{a_4}$

$= 2 = 3/2$ $\qquad = 5/3$

2. Decimal expansion of 7/3 = 2.333 ….

2 occurs once (odd)

$\therefore\ a_1 = 3; a_2 = 2; a_3 = 1; a_4 = 3; a_5 = 3$

3 occurs infinitely times

All other occurs zero times $= \sum_1^6 a_n = a_1 + a_2 + a_3 + a_4 + a_5 + a_6 = 3 + 2 + 1 + 3 + 3 + 3 = 15$

3. (a) $a_1 = 1, a_n = a_{n-1} + \cos\frac{(n\pi)}{2}, n \ge 2$

$\Rightarrow a_2 = a_1 + \cos\left(2\times\frac{\pi}{2}\right) = 1 + (-1) = 0$

$\Rightarrow a_3 = a_2 + \cos\left(\frac{3\pi}{2}\right) = 0 + 0 = 0$

$\Rightarrow a_4 = a_3 + \cos\left(\frac{4\pi}{2}\right) = 0 + 1 = 1$

$\Rightarrow a_5 = a_4 + \cos\left(\frac{5\pi}{2}\right) = 1 + 0 = 1$

$\therefore$ The sequence is 1 + 0 + 0 + 1 + 1 + ...

(b) $t_1 = 1, t_2 = 2, t_n = \frac{t_{n-1}}{t_{n-2}}, n \ge 3$

$t_3 = \frac{t_1}{t_2} = \frac{2}{1} = 2;\ t_4 = \frac{t_3}{t_2} = \frac{2}{2} = 1;\ t_5 = \frac{t_4}{t_3} = \frac{1}{2}$

$\therefore$ The sequence is 1 + 2 + 2 + 1 + 1/2 + …

TEXTUAL EXERCISE–1: (OBJECTIVE)

1. (a) $a_n = 3n + 2$

$= a_n - a_{n-1} = 3n + 2 - [(n - 1) + 2] = 3n + 2 - [3n - 3 + 2] = 3n + 2 - [3n - 1] = 3n - 3n + 2 + 1 = 3$ which is clearly positive.

$\Rightarrow \langle a_n\rangle$ is increasing

Similarly check for (b),(c), (d) $a_n - a_{n-1} < 0$. Hence not increasing

2. (b), (c) $a_n = \frac{n^2-1}{n^2+2} = \frac{1-\frac{1}{n^2}}{1+\frac{2}{n^2}}$, As $n \to \infty$, term a_n approaches to 1

$a_n = \frac{2n}{n^2+1} = a = \frac{\frac{2}{n}}{1+\frac{1}{n^2}}$, As $n \to \infty$, term a_n approaches to 0.

3. (b) $a_n = \frac{5n^2+2n+7}{n+5} = \frac{5+\frac{2}{n}+\frac{7}{n^2}}{\frac{1}{n}+\frac{5}{n^2}}$ as $n \to \infty$

The denominator tends to zero making the whole term approaching infinity. Hence the sequence by definition is diverging.

4. (a), (c) (a) $a_n = (-1)^n n = -1, 2, -3, 4, -5, 6$ …….. , which is an oscillating sequence.

(b) $a_n = (-1)^{2n} n^2 = 1, 4, 9, 16$, which is not oscillating sequence

(c) $a_n = 2n\cos\left(\frac{n\pi}{2}\right) = 2\cos\frac{\pi}{2}$, $4\cos\pi$, $6\cos\frac{3\pi}{2}$, 8 cos2π,……

= 0, –4, 0, 8, 0…….., which is an oscillating sequence.

5. (a), (c) $(-1)^n \sin\left(\frac{n\pi}{2}\right)$

The series is $-1 + 0 + 1 + 0 + (-1) + ... \Rightarrow$ periodic

(c) $a_n = \left[\cos\frac{n\pi}{2}\right]$

This series is $0 - 1 + 0 + 1 + 0 - 1 + ...$

$\Rightarrow$ periodic

6. (a), (c) $a_n = \frac{1}{n^2} \quad \Rightarrow \quad \frac{1}{n^2} - \frac{1}{(n-1)^2}$

$\Rightarrow \frac{(n-1)^2 - n^2}{n^2(n-1)^2} \quad \Rightarrow \quad \frac{n^2+1-2n-n^2}{n^2(n-1)^2}$

$\Rightarrow \frac{1-2n}{n^2(n-1)^2}$ for all $n > 1$, $1 - 2n < 0$

$\therefore$ The difference of two consecutive terms in series is negative. So, the series is always decreasing & hence, monotonic.

(c) $a_n = n^{th}$ prime no.

The prime no S are 1, 3, 5, 7, 11, 13, ...

We can see with increasing n, a_n also increases, Hence the series is monotonic.

7. (a) $n^2 - 5n + 6 = n^2 - 2n - 3n + 6 = n(n-2) - 3(n-2) = (n-3)(n-2)$

So, when $n > 3$, the term $(n^2 - 5n + 6)$ is always increasing and hence the series is monotonic for n > 3

8. (a) $(-1)^n \frac{2n}{n^2-6}\sin\frac{n\pi}{2} \quad = (-1)^3\frac{2\times3}{3^2-6}\sin\left(\frac{3\pi}{2}\right)$

$= (-1)\times\frac{6}{9-6}\times(-1) = 1\times\frac{6}{3} = 2$

TEXTUAL EXERCISE–2: (SUBJECTIVE)

1. $1 + 3 + 5 + 7 + 9 + 11$ ......

$\Rightarrow$ Sum $= \frac{n}{2}\left[2\times1+(n-1)^2\right] = \frac{n}{2}[2+2n-2]$

$= \frac{n}{2}\times2n = n^2$

2. $10 + 11 + 12 + 13 + ... + 99$

$\Rightarrow$ Sum $= \frac{90}{2}\left[2\times10+(90-1)\times1\right] = 45\,[20 + 89] = 45 \times 109 = 4905$

3. General term $= 4n - 1$

$\Rightarrow 3 + 7 + 11 + 15 + 19 + ...$

$\Rightarrow$ Sum $= \frac{n}{2}\left[2\times3+(n-1)4\right] = \frac{n}{2}[6+4n-4]$

$= \frac{n}{2}[4n+2] = n(2n+1)$

$\Rightarrow 2n^2 + n$

4. Given $S_n = 2n^3 - 7n + 5$

5th term of the sequence $S_5 - S_4$

$= 2(5)^3 - 7(5) + 5 - (2(4)^3 - 7(4) + 5) = 2.125 - 35 + 5 - (128 - 28 + 5) = 250 - 35 + 5 - 128 + 28 - 5 = 215 + 5 - 5 - 10 = 0 = 115$

5. Let 307 be the nth term of the sequence $a_n = a + (n-1)d$

$\Rightarrow 307 = 3 + (n-1)5 \quad \Rightarrow 304 = (n-1)5$

$\Rightarrow \frac{304}{5} + 1 = n$; which is not possible

Hence 307, is not a term of the given A.P.

6. $8 - 6i$, $7 - 4i$, $6 - 2i$, + ...

Common difference $= -(8-6i) + (7-4i) = -(1-2i)$

(a) So, the purely imaginarily term will be $a + (n-1)d = iy$ [Purely imaginary]

$\Rightarrow 8 - 6i + (n-1)(-1+2i) = iy$

$\Rightarrow 8 - 6i - n + 1 + 2ni - 2i = iy$

$\Rightarrow 9 - n - (8-2n)i = iy \Rightarrow 9 - n = 0$ [$\because$ real part is zero]

$\Rightarrow 9 = n$

(b) Purely real term

$\Rightarrow 8 - 6i + (n-1)(-1+2i) = x$

$\Rightarrow 8 - 6i - n + 1 + 2ni - 2i = x$

$\Rightarrow (9-n) - (8-2n)i = x$

$\Rightarrow 8 - 2n = 0$ [$\because$ imaginably part is zero]

$\Rightarrow 2n = 8$

$\Rightarrow n = 4$

7. 2, 7, 12, 17,...222

Common difference $= 2 - 7 = -5$ (from the end it is a decreasing A.P.)

So, the 20th term from the end is $222 + (20-1)(-5) = 222 + 19 \times -5 = 222 - 96 = 127$

8. (i) n^{th} term $= 3n - 5$

$\Rightarrow (n-1)^{th}$ term $= 3(n-1) - 5$

$\Rightarrow (n-2)^{th}$ term $= 3(n-2) - 5$

If $2(n-1)^{th}$ term $= n^{th}$ term $+ (n-2)^{th}$ term

The series is A.P.

$\Rightarrow 2(3(n-1) - 5) \quad \Rightarrow 3n - 5 + 3(n-2) - 5$

$\Rightarrow 2(3n - 8) \quad \Rightarrow 3n - 5 + 3n - 6 - 5$

$\Rightarrow 6n - 16 \quad \Rightarrow 6n - 16$

$\Rightarrow$ L.H.S = R.H.S.

Hence the series is A.P.

The common difference is $3n - 5 - (3(n-1) - 5) = 3n - 5 - 3n + 3 + 5 = 3$

(ii) $t_m = n$; $t_n = m$

Let a be the first term of A.P. and d be difference

$a(m-1)d = n$ (i)

$a + (n-1) = m$ (ii)

Subtracting (ii) from (i), we get $(m-n)d = (n-m)d$

$\Rightarrow d = 1$

Putting $d = -1$ in equation (i), we get $a + (m-1) - 1 = n$

$\Rightarrow a - m + 1 = n \quad \Rightarrow a + 1 = n + m$

The rth term will bc $t_r = a + (r-1)d$

$\Rightarrow a + (r-1) - 1 \quad \Rightarrow a + 1 - r$

$\therefore t_r = n - m - r$

The $(m+n)^m$ term

$\Rightarrow (n + m - 1) + (n + m - 1)(-1)$

$\Rightarrow (n + m - 1) - n - m + 1 = 0$

(iii) $t_m = 1/n$, $t_n = 1/m$

Let a be me first term of A.P. and d be me difference, than $a + (m-1)d = 1/n$ (i)

$a+(n-1)d=1/m$ (ii)

Subtracting (ii) from (i), we get $(m-n)d=\dfrac{(m-n)}{mn}$

$\Rightarrow$ $d = 1/mn$

Putting $d = 1/mn$ in equation (1), we get

$a+(m-1)\dfrac{1}{mn}=1/n$

$\Rightarrow$ $a+\dfrac{1}{n}-\dfrac{1}{mn}=\dfrac{1}{n}$ $\Rightarrow$ $a=\dfrac{1}{mn}$

$\therefore$ The $(mn)^{th}$ terms will be $t_{mn}=\dfrac{1}{mn}+(mn-1)\dfrac{1}{mn}$

$=\dfrac{1}{mn}+1-\dfrac{1}{mn}=1$

9. $\dfrac{a_4}{a_7}=\dfrac{2}{3}$ $\Rightarrow$ $\dfrac{a_1+(4-1)d}{a_1+(7-1)d}=\dfrac{2}{3}$

$\Rightarrow$ $\dfrac{a_1+3d}{a_1+6d}=\dfrac{2}{3}$ $\Rightarrow$ $3a_1+9d=2a_1+12d$

$\Rightarrow$ $a_1=3d$ $\dfrac{a_6}{a_8}$ $\dfrac{a_1+(6-1)d}{a_1(8-1)d}$

$\Rightarrow$ $\dfrac{a_1/d+5}{a_1/d+7}$ $\dfrac{3+5}{3+7}\Rightarrow\dfrac{8}{10}\Rightarrow\dfrac{4}{5}$

10. Let a is the first term of A.P. and d is the common difference. According to question $(p+1)^{th}$ term = $2(q+1)^{th}$ term

$\Rightarrow$ $a+(p+1-1)d=2[a+(q+1-1)d]$

$\Rightarrow$ $a+pd=2[a+qd]$ $\Rightarrow$ $a=(p-2q)d$

$\Rightarrow$ $a/d=p-2q$

$\Rightarrow$ $\dfrac{(3p+1)^{th}\text{ term}}{(p+q+1)^{th}\text{ term}}$ $\Rightarrow$ $\dfrac{a+(3p+1-1)d}{a+(p+q+1-1)d}$

$\Rightarrow$ $\dfrac{a+(3p)d}{a+(p+q)d}$ $\dfrac{a/d+3p}{a/d+p+q}$

$\Rightarrow$ $\dfrac{p-2q+3p}{p-2q+p+q}$ $\Rightarrow$ $\dfrac{4p-2q}{2p-q}$

$\dfrac{2(2p-q)}{2p-q}$ $\Rightarrow$ 2

$\therefore$ The $(3p+1)^{th}$ term is twice me $(p+q+1)^{th}$ term.

11. $5^{1+x}+5^{1-x}+25^x+25^{-x}=2\times a/2$

$\Rightarrow$ $5.5^x+5.5^{-x}+5^{2x}+5^{-2x}=a\Rightarrow 5(5^x+5^{-x})+(5^{2x}+5^{-2x})=a$

$\because$ A.M. $\geq$ G.M.

$\Rightarrow$ $\dfrac{5^x+5^{-x}}{2}\geq\sqrt{5^x\times 5^{-x}}$

$\Rightarrow$ $5^x+5^{-x}\geq 2$ and $5^{2x}+5^{-2x}\geq 2$

$\therefore$ The minimum value can have is $5\times 2+2=12$ and the maximum can be infinite $a\in[12,\infty)$

12. (a) $\sqrt{2}+\sqrt{8}+\sqrt{18}+\ldots$ to n terms $=\sqrt{2}+2\sqrt{2}+3\sqrt{2}+\ldots$

Sum $=\dfrac{n}{2}\left[\dfrac{2(n-1)}{n}+(n-1)-\dfrac{1}{n}\right]=\dfrac{n}{\sqrt{2}}[2+n-1]=\dfrac{n(n+1)}{\sqrt{2}}$

(b) $\dfrac{n-1}{n}+\dfrac{n-2}{n}+\dfrac{n-3}{n}+\ldots$ upto n terms

First term $=\dfrac{n-1}{n}$.

Common difference $=\dfrac{-1}{n}$

Sum $=\dfrac{n}{2}\left[\dfrac{2(n-1)}{n}+(n-1)-\dfrac{1}{n}\right]=\dfrac{n}{2}\left[\dfrac{n-1}{n}\right]=\dfrac{n-1}{2}$

(c) $\dfrac{1}{1+\sqrt{a}}+\dfrac{1}{1-a}+\dfrac{1}{1-\sqrt{a}}+\ldots$ up to n terms

First term $=\dfrac{1}{1+\sqrt{a}}$.

Common difference $=\dfrac{1}{1-a}-\dfrac{1}{1+\sqrt{a}}$

$=1-\dfrac{(1-\sqrt{a})}{1-a}=\dfrac{\sqrt{a}}{1-a}$

Sum $=\dfrac{n}{2}\left[\dfrac{2}{1+\sqrt{a}}+\dfrac{(n-1)\sqrt{a}}{1-a}\right]$

$=\dfrac{n}{2}\left[\dfrac{2(1-\sqrt{a})+(n-1)\sqrt{a}}{1-a}\right]$

$=\dfrac{n}{2(1-a)}\left[2+(n-3)\sqrt{a}\right]$

(d) $\dfrac{1}{2}+\dfrac{1}{3}+\dfrac{1}{6}+\ldots$ to 9 terms

First term = 1/2

Common difference = –1/6

Sum$=\dfrac{9}{2}\left[2\times\dfrac{1}{2}-(9-1)\times\left(-\dfrac{1}{6}\right)\right]=\dfrac{9}{2}\left[1-\dfrac{4}{3}\right]=-\dfrac{3}{2}$

(e) $1-2+3-4+5-6+7\ldots\ldots(2n)=(1+3+5+7+2n-1)-(2+4+6+8+\ldots\ldots+2n)$

$=\dfrac{n}{2}[2\times 1(n-1)2]-\dfrac{n}{2}[2\times 2+(n-1)2]$

$=\dfrac{n}{2}[2+2n-2]-\dfrac{n}{2}[4+2n-2]=\dfrac{n}{2}[2n]-\dfrac{n}{2}[2n+2]$

$=n^2-(n^2+n)=-n$

(f) $1^2-2^2+3^2-4^2+5^2-6^2+7^2+\ldots+(2n)^2$

$1^2-2^2=-3$

$3^2-4^2=-7$

$5^2-6^2=-11$

.

.

.

$=1^2-2^2+3^2-4^2+5^2-6^2+\ldots\ldots+=-3-7-11-\ldots$ n terms

$=\dfrac{n}{2}[2(-3)+(n-1)(-4)]$

$=\dfrac{n}{2}[-6-4n+4]=\dfrac{n}{2}[-4n-2]=-n(2n+1)$

13. $\dfrac{n}{2}[2\times 18+(n-1)(-3)]=45=\dfrac{n}{2}[36-3n+3]=45$

$\Rightarrow$ $n[39-3n]=90$ $\Rightarrow$ $3n^2-39n+90=0$

$\Rightarrow$ $n^2-13n+30=0$

$\Rightarrow$ $n^2-10n-3n+30=0$

$\Rightarrow$ $n(n-10)-3(n-10)=0$

$\Rightarrow$ $(n-3)(n-10)=0$

For $n=3$ and $n=10$, the sum is 45, and the double answer we get is due to the fact that from the 7th term onwards negative terms add up to previous to equalize it to 45 again.

14. To find the sum of all natural number between 100 and 300 not divisible by 4 or 6. We can find the sum of 101 to 299 and subtract the multiples of 4 and 6 and as same of the no. have 4 and 6 as common multiples, we have to add multiplies of 12.

(*a*) Sum of no of 100 – 300 (excluding 100 and 30)

$= \frac{199}{2}(2 \times 10^1 (199-1)1) = 199 \times 20 = 39800$

(b) Sum of multiplies of 4; 100 – 300

$= \frac{49}{2}[2 \times 104 + (49-1)4] = \frac{49}{2}[400] = 9800$

(c) Multiples of G b/w 100 – 300

$= \frac{33}{2}[2 \times 102 + (33-1)6] = 6534$

(d) Sum of multiplies of 12 (LCM (4, 6)) between 100 – 30

= 16/2 [108 + 288] = 8 × 396 = 3168

Required area = 39800 – (9800 + 6534 – 3168)

= 26,634

15. $2n + 3n^2$ [Rearranging the given sum]

$= n[3n+2] = \frac{n}{2}[6n+4] = \frac{n}{2}[6(n-1)+6+4]$

$= \frac{n}{2}[10+(n-1)6]$

$a = 5, d = 6, r^{th}$ term $= 5 + 6r - 6 = 6r - 1$

16. **(a)** $S_{n-1} = a(n-1)^2 + b(n-1) + c = a[n^2 + 1 - 2n] + b[n - 1] + c = an^2 + a - 2an + bn - b + c = an^2 + (b-2a)n + (a - b + c)$

$T_n = S_n - S_{n-1}$

$= (an^2 + bn + c) - [an^2 + (b-2a)n + (a - b + c] = -2a_n + b - a$

$\therefore \; T_{n-1} = 2a(n-1) + b - a = (2a_n + b - a) - 2a = T_n - 2a$

∴ The statement is true

(b) $S_n = 4n^2 + 3 \quad \Rightarrow \quad S_{n-1} = 4(n-1)^2 + 3$

$\Rightarrow 4n^2 + 4 - 8n + 3 \quad \Rightarrow \quad (4n^2 + 3) - 8n + 4$

$\Rightarrow S_n - 8n + 4 \quad \Rightarrow \quad 8n - 4 = S_n - S_{n-1}$

$\Rightarrow 8n - 4 = S_n - S_{n-1} \quad \Rightarrow \quad 8n - 4 = T_n$

$[\because S_n - S_{n-1} = T_n]$ where T_n is the nth term

So, the first term is = 8 × 1 – 4 = 4

5th term is = 8 × 5 – 4 = 36

17. Series 1: 17, 21, 25 .....

n^{th} term of this series is $17 + (n-1)4$ (i)

Series 2: 16, 21 , 25, ...

m^{th} term of this series is $= 16 + (m-1)5$ (ii)

The common difference for series 1 is 4 and for series 2 is 5

The common difference for series of common term is 1 cm of 4 & 5 i.e., 20

Now a = 21, *d* = 20, n = 100

Sum $= \frac{100}{2}[2 \times 21 \; (100-1)20] = 50\,[42 + 1980] = 50 \times 2022 = 101100$

TEXTUAL EXERCISE–2: (OBJECTIVE)

1. **(c)** *a, b, c, d, e* are in A.P

$= a - 4b + 6c - 4d + c$

$= a - b - 3b + 3c - 3d - d + e$

$= (a-b) - 3(b-c) + 3(c-d) - 1(d-e)$

$= a - b = b - c = c - d = d - e =$ Common difference of A.P. x

$= x - 3x + 3x - x = 0$

2. **(b)** $a + (p-1)d = q$ (i)

$a + (p + q - 1)d = 0$ (ii)

Subtracting (i) from (ii), we get $qd = -q$

$\Rightarrow d = -1$

Now, $a + (p + q - 1)\,d = 0$

$= a + (q-1)d + pd = 0$

Putting d = –1, we get $a + (q-1)d - p = 0$

$= a + (q-1)\,d = p$

3. **(c)** 3, 7, 11,...,407 → series 1 and common difference = 4

2, 9, 16,...,709 → series 2 and common difference = 7

The first common term of both series = 23

Common difference for the series of common terms = l.c.m of 4 & 7 = 28

So, no of common terms $= 23 + (n-1)\,28 \le 407 = 23 + 28n - 28 \le 407 = 28n - 5 \le 407 = 28n \le 412 = n \le 103/7 = n \le 14\frac{5}{7}$

∵ n should be integer

∴ 14 terms are common

4. **(d)** Series 1: 1, 11, 21, 31.... upto 100 terms

Series 2: 31, 36, 41, 46 … upto 100 terms

Common difference of series 1: 10

Common difference of series 2: 5

Common difference of series of common terms = l.c.m of 5 & 10 = 10

The largest term of series 2 = 31 + (100 – 1) 5 = 31 + 99 × 5 = 31 + 495 = 526

The nth term of series of common terms is $= 31 + (n-1)\,10$

The largest term should be smaller than 526 $= 31 + (n-1)10 \le 526 = 31 + 10n - 10 \le 526 = 10n + 21 \le 526 = 10n \le 505 = n \le 50\frac{1}{2}$

So, the 50th term is largest term = 31 + (50 – 1)10 = 31 + 490 = 521

5. **(a)** x_1, x_2, x_3 … are in A.P

$x_1, x_2, x_3 = 12$ (i)

$x_4 + x_6 = 14$ (ii)

$\because x_4, x_5, x_6$ are consecutive terms

$\Rightarrow x_5 - x_4 = x_6 - x_5 \quad \Rightarrow \quad 2x_5 = x_4 + x_6$

Putting this value in (ii), we get $2x_5 = 14$

$\Rightarrow x_5 = 7$

6. **(a)** The given series can be represented in following way

	1	
2	2	
3	3	3
4	4	4
.	.	.
.	.	.

In each line number of terms is one more man the previous line. So this is an A.P. of no of terms in each line.

The term that will be 150th the sequence can be formed by finding the value of in for which

$= \frac{n}{2}[2\times1+(n-1)1] \le 150 = n[2+n-1]\ 0 \le 300 = n[n+1] \le 300$

In the above relation, for n = 16, the relation holds true that means the sum of terms of each line is smaller than 150, and when

n = 17, its greater than 150

∴ The 150th terms of the sequence lies in the 17th line in which all terms are 17.

7. **(d)** $a_1, a_2, a_3 \ldots, a_6$ be the number

Sum $= \frac{6}{2}[2a_1+(6-1)d] = 3$

$= 3[2a_1 + 5d] = 3 = 2a_1 + 5d = 1$ (i)

$a_2 - a_1 = a_3 - a_2 = a_4 - a_3 = a_5 - a_4 = a_6 - a_5 = d$ (ii)

$a_1 = 4a_3$ (iii)

$\Rightarrow a_1 = 4[a_1 + (2d)] \quad \Rightarrow a_1 = 4a_1 + 8d$

$\Rightarrow 3a_1 = -8d$ (iv)

$\Rightarrow a_1 = \frac{-8d}{3}$

Putting $a_1 = \frac{-8d}{3}$ in equation (i), we get 2

$\times\left(-\frac{8d}{3}\right)+5d = 1 = -16d + 15d = 3 = d = -3$

This gives us $a_1 = 8 \Rightarrow$ Fifth term $= 8 + 4(-3) = -4$

8. **(c)** $S_n \Rightarrow 153 = \frac{n}{2}(2a+(n-1)2)$

$\Rightarrow 306 = n(2a + (n-1)2) \quad \Rightarrow 306 = n(2n + 2a - 2)$

$\Rightarrow 2n^2 + (2a-2)n - 306 = 0 \Rightarrow n^2 + (a-1)n - 153 = 0$

Factors of 153 = 3 × 3 × 17

So $(a - 1)$ can have values

(i) 17 – 9 or 9 –17

(ii) 51 –3 or –3 + 51

(iii) 513 –1 or 1 –153

First case gives $n = 9$ or 17

Second case $n = 51$ or 3

Third case $n = 153$ or 1

$n = 1$ is not possible (given)

So, 5 values are possible

9. **(b)** S_r = Sum of first r terms of an A.P.

a_r (r^{th} term of A.P.) $= S_r - S_{r-1}$

Similarly $S_{2r} - S_{2r-1} = a_{2r} = a + (2r-1)d$

a: first term of A.P.

D: common difference

A.T.Q. $\frac{S_{3r}-S_{r-1}}{S_{2r}-S_{2r-1}} = \frac{S_{3r}-S_{r-1}}{a+(2r+1)d}$

$= \frac{\frac{3r}{2}[2a+(3r-1)d]-\frac{(r-1)}{2}[2a+(r-2)d]}{a+(2r-1)d}$

$= \frac{a(2r+1)+d(4r^2-1)}{a(2r-1)d} = \frac{(2r+1)(a+(2r-1))}{a+(r-1)d} = 2r+1$

10. **(b)** $S_{2n} = 3s_n$

$\Rightarrow \frac{2n}{2}[2a+(2n-1)d] = \frac{3n}{2}[2a+(n-1)d]$

$\Rightarrow 4a + 2(n-1)d = 6a + 3(n-1)d$

$\Rightarrow 4a + 4n - 2d = 6a + 3nd - 3d$

$\Rightarrow nd + d = 2a \qquad \Rightarrow (n+1)d = 2a$

$\Rightarrow \frac{S_{3n}}{S_n} \qquad \Rightarrow \frac{\frac{3n}{2}[2a+(3n-1)d]}{\frac{n}{2}[2a+(n-1)d]}$

$\frac{3\left[\frac{2a}{d}+(3n-1)\right]}{\left[\frac{2a}{d}+(n-1)\right]} \qquad \Rightarrow \frac{3[n+1+3n-1]}{n+1+n-1}$

$\Rightarrow \frac{3[4n-d]}{2n} \Rightarrow 6$

11. **(a)** By the question,

$x = a(m-1)d \qquad (a_m)$ (i)

$y = a + (n-1)d \qquad (a_n)$ (ii)

$S_{m+n} = \frac{m+n}{2}(2a+(m+n-1)d)$

Rearranging this, we get

$S_{m+n} = \frac{m+n}{2}(a+(m-1)d+a+nd)$

$= \frac{m+n}{2}(x+a+nd)$

By equation (i), we get $a + nd = y + d$

Subtracting (i) – (ii), we get $x - y = (m-n)d$

$\Rightarrow d = \frac{x-y}{m-n}$

$\Rightarrow S_{m+n} = \frac{m+n}{2}\left(y+x+\frac{x-y}{m-n}\right)$

12. **(a)** $\frac{S_a}{a^2} = \frac{S_b}{b^2} = c \quad S_a = a^2c$

$\Rightarrow \frac{a}{2}[2x+(a-1)y] = a^2c$

$\Rightarrow 2x + (a-1)y = 2ac$ (i)

$\Rightarrow 2x + (b-1)y = 2bc$ (ii)

Using (i) and (ii), we get $(a-b)y = 2(a-b)c$

$\Rightarrow y = 2c$

Putting $y = 2c$ in (i), we get $2x + (a-1)y = 2ac$

$\Rightarrow 2x + (c-1)y + ay - cy = 2ac$

$\Rightarrow 2x + (c-1)y = 2ac - (a-c) \times 2c$

$\Rightarrow 2x - 1(c-1)y = 2c^2$

$\Rightarrow -[2x+(c-1)y] = c$

13. **(b)** $1^2 - 2^2 + 3^2 - 4^2 + 5^2 - 6^2 + \ldots\ldots$

$\Rightarrow -3 - 7 - 11 - 15 - \ldots\ldots$

$\Rightarrow \frac{50}{2}[-6+(50-1)-4]$

$\Rightarrow \frac{50}{2}[-6-196] \qquad \Rightarrow 25 \times -202$

$\Rightarrow -5050$

TEXTUAL EXERCISE-3: (SUBJECTIVE)

1. $a_1 = 7$ and $a_{60} = 125$ (given)

$\Rightarrow a_1 + (60 - 1)d = 125 \Rightarrow 7 + 59d = 125$

$\Rightarrow 59d = 125 - 7 \qquad \Rightarrow 59d = 118$

$\Rightarrow d = 2$

$\Rightarrow a_{25} = 7 + (25 - 1)2 = 7 + 48 = 55$

2. First two digit number divisible by 3 = 12

Last two digits no divisible by 3 = 99

Let number of terms be n

$\Rightarrow 12 + (n - 1)3 = 99 \qquad \Rightarrow (n - 1)3 = 87$

$\Rightarrow (n - 1) = 29 \qquad \Rightarrow n = 30$

3. $a - 3d, a - d, a + d, a + 3d$

$\Rightarrow a - 3d + a - d + a + d + a + 3d = 6$

$\Rightarrow 4a = 6 \qquad \Rightarrow a = 3/2$

$\Rightarrow (a - 3d)^2 + (a - d)^2 + (a + d)^2 + (a + 3d)^2 = 14$

$\Rightarrow a^2 + 9d^2 - 6ad + a^2 + d^2 - 2ad + a^2 + d^2 + 2ad + a^2 + 9d^2 + 6da = 14$

$\Rightarrow 4a^2 + 20d^2 = 14 \qquad \Rightarrow 4\times\frac{9}{4}+20d^2=14$

$20d^2 = 5 \qquad \Rightarrow d^2 = 1/4$

$\Rightarrow d = \pm 1/2$

So, the series is 0, 1, 2, 3, or 3, 2, 1, 0.

4. $a - d, a, a + d$, b, the numbers

$\Rightarrow a - d + a + a + d = 21$

$\Rightarrow 3a = 21 \qquad \Rightarrow a = 7$

$\Rightarrow (a - d)(a)(a + d) = 315$

$\Rightarrow (a^2 - d^2)a = 315 \qquad \Rightarrow (49 - d^2) \times 7 = 315$

$\Rightarrow 49-\frac{315}{7}=d^2 \qquad \Rightarrow 49 - 45 = d^2$

$\Rightarrow 4 = d^2 \qquad \Rightarrow \pm 2 = d$

$\therefore$ The series is 5, 7, 9 or 9, 7, 5

5. If a, b, c are in A.P., then $2b = a + c$

Squaring both sides, we get $4b^2 = a^2 + c^2 + 2ac$ (i)

Assuming a^2, b^2, c^2 are in A.P.,

then we can have $2b^2 = a^2 + c^2$ (ii)

Solving (i) & (ii), we get $2b^2 = 2ac$

$\Rightarrow b^2 = ac$

Putting $b^2 = ac$ in equation (i), we get $4ac = a^2 + c^2 + 2ac$

$\Rightarrow 0 = (a - c)^2 \qquad \Rightarrow a = c$

$\therefore$ The terms a^2, b^2, c^2 will not be in A.P.

6. a_1, a_2, a_3 are in A.P.

$\therefore\ 2a_2 = a_1 + a_3$ (i)

b_1, b_2, b_3 are in A.P.

$\therefore\ 2b_2 = b_1 + b_3$ (ii)

Now if $a_1 \pm kb_1, a_2 \pm kb_2, a_3 \pm kb_3$ are in A.P., then $2(a_2 \pm kb_2) = a_1 \pm kb_1 + a_3 \pm kb_3$ should hold true

L.H.S. = $2a_2 \pm 2kb_2$

R.H.S. = $a_1 \pm kb_1 + a_3 \pm kb_3 = (a_1 + a_3) \pm k(b_1 + b_3) = a_2 \pm kb_2$

$\therefore$ L.H.S. = R.H.S.

So, for all a_1, a_2, a_3 in A.P. and b_1, b_2, b_3 in A.P. $a_1 \pm kb, a_2 \pm kb_2, a_3 \pm kb_3$ will be in A.P.

7. The nth term of given A.P. will be $a + (n - 1)d$

If each term is tripled, then the nth term will be $3(a + (n - 1)d) = 3a + (n - 1)3d$

$\therefore$ The resulting sequence is an A.P. as well with $3a$ as first term and $3d$ will be common difference

$1_n = 3a + (n - 1)3a = 3(a + (n - 1)d)$

8. (a) $a\left[\frac{1}{b}+\frac{1}{c}\right], b\left[\frac{1}{c}+\frac{1}{a}\right], c\left[\frac{1}{a}+\frac{1}{b}\right]$ for the terms to be in A.P.

$\Rightarrow 2b\left[\frac{1}{c}+\frac{1}{a}\right]=a\left[\frac{1}{b}+\frac{1}{c}\right]+c\left[\frac{1}{a}+\frac{1}{b}\right]$ (Given $2b = a + c$)

L.H.S. = $\frac{b}{c}\ \frac{b}{a}$

R.H.S. = $\frac{a}{b}+\frac{a}{c}+\frac{c}{a}+\frac{c}{b}=\frac{a^2c+a^2b+b^2c+ac^2}{abc}$

$=\frac{1}{b}(a+c)+\frac{a^2+c^2}{ac}=\frac{2ac+a^2+c^2}{ac}$

$=\frac{(a+c)^2}{ac}=2b\left(\frac{a+c}{ac}\right)=2b\times\left[\frac{1}{a}+\frac{1}{c}\right]$

= L.H.S = R.H.S

(b) $b + c, c + a, a + b$, To prove $2(c + a) = (b + c) + (a + b)$

L.H.S = $2(c + a) = 2c + 2a$

R.H.S = $b + c + a + b$

$= a + c + 2b = a + c + (a + c) = 2(a + c)$

(c) $a^2(b + c), b^2(c + a), c^2(a + b)$;

(Given : $2b = a + c \Rightarrow ab + bc + ca \neq 0$)

To prove: $2b^2(c + a) = a^2(b + c) + c^2(a + b)$

L.H.S. = $2b^2(c + a) = 2b^2 \times 2b = 4b^3$

R.H.S. = $a^2(b + c) + c^2(a + b) = b(a^2 + c^2) + a^2c + ac^2 = b(a^2 + c^2) + ac(a + b) = b(a^2 + c^2) + ac(2b) = b[a^2 + c^2 + 2ac]$

$\Rightarrow b[a + c]^2 \qquad \Rightarrow b \times 4b^2$

$\Rightarrow 4b^3 \qquad \Rightarrow$ L.H.S. = R.H.S.

(d) $1/bc, 1/ca, 1/ab$; To proof $\frac{2}{ca}=\frac{1}{bc}+\frac{1}{ab}$ (given: $2b = a + c$)

L.H.S. = $2/ca$

R.H.S. = $\frac{1}{b}\left[\frac{1}{c}+\frac{1}{a}\right]=\frac{1}{b}\left[\frac{a+c}{ac}\right]=\frac{2b}{b\times ac}=\frac{2}{ac}$

$\therefore$ L.H.S. = R.H.S.

9. Given $\frac{2}{b}=\frac{1}{a}+\frac{1}{c} \qquad \Rightarrow 1+1=\frac{b}{a}+\frac{b}{c}$

$\Rightarrow \frac{b}{c}-1=1-\frac{b}{a}$ (i)

L.H.S. = $\frac{a}{c}$

R.H.S = $\frac{a-b}{b-c}=\frac{a\left[1-\frac{b}{a}\right]}{c\left[\frac{b}{c}-1\right]}$ (using (i))

$=\frac{a}{c}$ $\therefore$ L.H.S. = R.H.S.

10. Given a, b, c, d are in A.P.

$\therefore\ b-a=c-b=d-c$

To prove, $b+c+d, c+d+a, d+a+b, a+b+c$

$\Rightarrow (c+d+a)-(b+c+d)=(d+a+b)-(c+d+a)=(a+b+c)-(d+a+b)$

$\Rightarrow a-b=b-c=c-d$ as already given

$\Rightarrow b-a=c-b=d-c$

$\Rightarrow a-b=b-c=c-d$ terms are in A.P.

11. **(a)** a^2, b^2, c^2 are in A.P. (given)

$2b^2=a^2+c^2$ (i)

$$\text{R.H.S.}=\frac{1}{b+c}+\frac{1}{a+b}=\frac{a+2b+c}{(a+b)(b+c)}$$

$$=\frac{a+2b+c}{(ab+b^2+ac+bc)}=\frac{(a+2b+c)^2}{a^2+b^2+2bc+2ab+2ca}\text{ (by (i))}$$

$$\Rightarrow \frac{(a+2b+c)^2}{((a+b)^2+2b(a+c))}$$

$$\Rightarrow \frac{2(a+2b+c)}{(a+c)(a+2b+c)}\Rightarrow \frac{2}{a+c}=\text{L.H.S.}$$

$$\Rightarrow \frac{1}{b+c},\frac{1}{c+a},\frac{1}{a+b}\text{ are in A.P.}$$

(b) $\because \dfrac{c^2}{(a+b)^2},\dfrac{a^2}{(b+c)^2},\dfrac{b^2}{(c+a)^2}$ are in A.P.

$$\Rightarrow 1-\frac{c^2}{(a+b)^2},1-\frac{a^2}{(b+c)^2},1-\frac{b^2}{(c+a)^2}\text{ are in A.P.}$$

$$\Rightarrow \frac{(a+b+c)(a+b-c)}{(a+b)^2},\frac{(b+c+a)(b+c-a)}{(b+c)^2},\frac{(c+a+b)(c+a-b)}{(c+a)^2}\text{ are in A.P.}$$

$$\Rightarrow \frac{a+b-c}{(a+b)^2},\frac{b+c-a}{(b+c)^2},\frac{c+a-b}{(c+a)^2}\text{ are in A.P.}$$

$$\Rightarrow \frac{2(s-c)}{(2s-c)^2},\frac{2(s-a)}{(2s-a)^2},\frac{2(s-b)}{(2s-b)^2}\text{ are in A.P.}$$

$$\Rightarrow \frac{(s-c)}{(2s-c)^2},\frac{(s-a)}{(2s-a)^2},\frac{(s-b)}{(2s-b)^2}\text{ are in A.P.}$$

12. $$\frac{7n+14}{4n+7}=\frac{21+(n-1)7}{11+(n-1)4}=\frac{\frac{n}{2}[21+(n-1)7]}{\frac{n}{2}[11+(n-1)4]}$$

The given ratio gives us two series where we can assume the first term for series 1 as 10.5

The first for series 2 as 5.5

Common difference for series 1 as 7 and for series 2 as 4

So the 11th term ratio can be given as $\dfrac{10.5+(11-1)7}{5.5+(11-1)4}=\dfrac{10.5+70}{5.5+40}=\dfrac{80.5}{45.5}=\dfrac{23}{13}$

13. Like the previous question, the ratio can be reduced to

$$\frac{3n+8}{7n+15}=\frac{\frac{n}{2}[11+3(n-1)]}{\frac{n}{2}[22+7(n-1)]}$$

So, the ratio of 7th term can be given as $\dfrac{5.5+(7-1)3}{11+(7-1)7}=\dfrac{5.5+18}{11+42}=\dfrac{235}{530}=\dfrac{47}{106}$

TEXTUAL EXERCISE-3: (OBJECTIVE)

1. **(a), (b), (c)** Let $a-d, a, a+d$ be the numbers in A.P.

$a-d+a+a+d=12$

$\Rightarrow 3a=12 \quad\Rightarrow a=4$

$\Rightarrow (a-d)^3+a^3+(a+d)^3=408$

$\Rightarrow a^3-d^3+3ad^2-3a^2d+a^3+a^3+d^3+3a^2d+3ad^2=408$

$\Rightarrow 3a^3+6ad^2=408 \quad\Rightarrow 3\times 64+24d^2=408$

$\Rightarrow 24d^2=408-192 \quad\Rightarrow 24d^2=216$

$\Rightarrow d^2=9 \quad\Rightarrow d=\pm 3$

$\therefore$ The series is 1, 4, 7 or 7, 4, 1

2. **(a), (b), (c)** Let the numbers be $a-3d, a-d, a+d, a+3d$

$\Rightarrow 4a=72 \quad\Rightarrow a=18$

$\Rightarrow (a-3d)(a-d)(a+d)(a+3d)=92160$

$\Rightarrow (a^2-9d^2)(a^2-d^2)=92160$

$\Rightarrow a^4-10a^2d^2+9d^4=92160$

$\Rightarrow (18)^4-10\times 18^2\times d^2+9d^4=92160$

$\Rightarrow 104976-3240d^2+9d^4=92160$

$\Rightarrow d^4-360d^2+1424=0$

$\Rightarrow d^4-356d^2-4d^2+1424=0$

$\Rightarrow d^2(d^2-356)-4(d^2-356)=0$

$\Rightarrow (d^2-4)(d^2-356)=0$

$\Rightarrow d=\pm 2$ [$\because$ d can have only integral values]

$\therefore$ The numbers are 12, 16, 20, 24; middle numbers be 16, 20; Product of 12; 288

Sum of middle numbers 36

3. **(d)** $$\frac{S_p}{S_q}=\frac{p^2}{q^2}\Rightarrow \frac{\frac{p}{2}[2a+(p-1)d]}{\frac{q}{2}[2a+(q-1)d]}=\frac{p^2}{q^2}$$

$$\Rightarrow \frac{[2a+(p-1)d]}{[2a+(q-1)d]}=\frac{p}{q}$$

$$\Rightarrow q\left[\frac{2q}{d}+p-1\right]=p\left[\frac{2a}{d}+q-1\right]\ (q-p)\left[\frac{2a}{d}\right]=q-p$$

$$\Rightarrow \left[\frac{2a}{d}\right]=1 \quad\Rightarrow \frac{a}{d}=\frac{1}{2}$$

$$\Rightarrow \frac{t_p}{t_q}=\frac{a+(p-1)d}{a+(q-1)d}=\frac{a/d+(p-1)}{a/d+(q-1)}=\frac{\frac{1}{2}+(p-1)}{\frac{1}{2}(q-1)}$$

$$=\frac{2p-1}{2q-1}$$

4. **(a), (b), (c)** Let $\log_y x=m$ and $\log_z y=n$

$\Rightarrow x=y^m$ and $y=z^n \quad\Rightarrow x=z^{mn}$

$\therefore$ 1, m, n, $-15/mn$ are in A.P.

$$\Rightarrow 2m=1+n\text{ and }2n=m-\frac{15}{mn}$$

$$4m-2=\frac{2m^3-m^2-15}{m(2m-1)}$$

$\Rightarrow 6m^3-7m^2+2m+15=0$ which is satisfied for $m=-1$

$\Rightarrow (m + 1)(6m^2 - 13m + 15) = 0$
$\Rightarrow m = -1$ as $6m^2 - 13m + 15 > 0$
$\therefore m = -1, n = -3 \quad \Rightarrow x = y^{-1}; y = z^{-3}$ and $x = z^3$

5. (b) Let D be the common difference
Here, $e - c = (a + 4D) - (a + 2D) = 2D$
Clearly, $2(c - a) = 4D$, $2(d - c) = 2D$, $2(f - d) = 4D$ and $(d - c) = D$

6. (c) Let an AP be
$S = a + (a + d) + (a + 2d) + ... + a + (n - 1)d$
$S = a + (n - 1)d + a + (n - 2)d + ... + a$ [reversing the order of terms]
Adding the, we get $2s = 2a + (n - 1)d + 2a + (n - 1)d + ... + 2a(n - 1)d$
From the above equation we can see sum of each term equidistant from beginning and the end becomes the sum of first and last term.

7. (b) $abc = 4$ (i)
and $2b = a + c$ (ii)

$\Rightarrow ac = 4/b \quad \Rightarrow b = \dfrac{a+c}{2}$

$\Rightarrow b = \dfrac{a+c}{2} \ge \sqrt{ac}$; $b \ge \sqrt{ac}$; $\ge \sqrt{\ }$

$\Rightarrow b^2 \ge \dfrac{4}{b} \quad \Rightarrow b^4 \ge \dfrac{16}{b^2}$

$\Rightarrow b^6 \ge 16 \quad \Rightarrow b \ge (2^4)^{1/16}$

$\Rightarrow b \ge (2)^{2/3}$

8. (a) Let the sides be $a - d, a, a + d$
By Pythagoras theorem, $(a + d)^2 = a^2 + (a + d)^2$
$\Rightarrow a^2 + d^2 + 2ad = a^2 + a^2 + d^2 - 2ad$
$\Rightarrow 4ad = a^2 \quad \Rightarrow 4d = a$

$$\Rightarrow \sin A \Rightarrow \frac{a-d}{a+d} \Rightarrow \frac{\frac{a}{d}-1}{\frac{a}{d}+1} \Rightarrow \frac{4-1}{4+1} \Rightarrow \frac{3}{5}$$

$$\Rightarrow \sin C \Rightarrow \frac{a}{a+d} \Rightarrow \frac{a}{a+d} \Rightarrow \frac{1}{1+\frac{d}{a}} \Rightarrow \frac{1}{1+\frac{1}{4}} \Rightarrow \frac{4}{5}$$

9. (a), (b), (d) Since, 2 of the terms in A.P. are rational
$\therefore$ The common difference can never be irrational so, (a) is correct.
Now all the terms are of form
$\Rightarrow a + (n - 1)d$ for n^{th} term
Since all a, d and n are rational number
$\therefore$ All the terms of A.P. are rational, So, (b) is also correct
Since all the terms in A.P. are rational
$\therefore$ Sum of finite numbers of A.P. will be rational, So, (d) is also correct

10. (b), (c) $2\log_3(3^x - 2) = 1 + 2\log_9(3^x - 8/3)$

$$\Rightarrow \frac{2\log(3^x-2)}{\log 3} = \frac{\log 3}{\log 3} + \frac{2\log(3^x - 8/3)}{2\log 3}$$

$\Rightarrow 2\log(3^x - 2) = \log 3 + \log(3^x - 8/3)$
$\Rightarrow \log(3^x - 2)^2 = \log(3.3^x - 8)$
$\Rightarrow 3^{2x} + 4 - 4.3^x = 3.3^x - 8$
$\Rightarrow 3^{2x} - 7.3^x + 12 = 0$
$\Rightarrow 3^{2x} - 4.3^x - 3.3^x + 12 = 0$
$\Rightarrow 3^x(3^x - 4) - 3(3^x - 4) = 0$
$\Rightarrow (3^x - 4)(3^x - 3) = 0$
$\Rightarrow 3^x = 4$ or $3^x = 3$
$\Rightarrow x\log 3 = \log 4$ or $x = 1$
$\Rightarrow x = \dfrac{\log 4}{\log 3}$

TEXTUAL EXERCISE-4: (SUBJECTIVE)

1. $b = \dfrac{a+c}{2}$ (i)

$p = \dfrac{a+b}{2}$ (ii)

$q = \dfrac{b+c}{2}$ (iii)

$\Rightarrow p + q = \dfrac{a+2b+c}{2}$

$\Rightarrow (p+q) = \dfrac{2(a+c)}{2}$

$\Rightarrow \left(\dfrac{p+q}{2}\right) = \left(\dfrac{a+c}{2}\right) \Rightarrow \dfrac{p+q}{2} = b$

$\therefore$ Proved b is the AM between p and q.

2. (a) $(A - a)^2 + (A - b)^2 = 1/2\,(a - b)^2$ where $A = \dfrac{a+b}{2}$

$\Rightarrow \left(\dfrac{a+b}{2} - a\right)^2 + \left(\dfrac{a-b}{2} - b\right)^2$

$\Rightarrow \left(\dfrac{b-a}{2}\right)^2 + \left(\dfrac{a-b}{2}\right)^2$

$\Rightarrow \dfrac{b^2}{4} + \dfrac{a^2}{4} - \dfrac{ab}{2} + \dfrac{b^2}{4} + \dfrac{a^2}{4} - \dfrac{ab}{2}\ \dfrac{a^2}{2} + \dfrac{b^2}{2} - ab$

$\Rightarrow \dfrac{1}{2}(a-b)^2$

(b) $4(a - A)(A - b) = (a - b)^2$ where $A = \dfrac{a+b}{2}$

$\Rightarrow 4\left(a - \left(\dfrac{a+b}{2}\right)\right)\left(\dfrac{a+b}{2} - b\right)$

$\Rightarrow 4\left(\dfrac{a-b}{2}\right)\left(\dfrac{a-b}{2}\right) \quad \Rightarrow \dfrac{4(a-b)^2}{4}$

(c) $\dfrac{A+2a}{A-b} + \dfrac{A+2b}{A-b} = 4$ where $A = \dfrac{(a+b)}{2}$

$$\Rightarrow \frac{\left(\frac{a+b}{2}\right)+2a}{\frac{a+b}{2}-b} + \frac{\left(\frac{a+b}{2}\right)+2b}{\left(\frac{a+b}{2}\right)-a}$$

$\Rightarrow \dfrac{5a+b}{a-b} + \dfrac{(a+5b)}{b-a} \quad \Rightarrow \dfrac{1}{a-b}[5a+b-(a-5b)]$

$\Rightarrow \dfrac{1}{a-b}(4a-4b) \quad \Rightarrow 4$

3. $a=3, b=24$

$\Rightarrow A_1 = 3+\frac{(24-3)}{(7)}=3+\frac{21}{7}=6$

$\Rightarrow A_2=3+2\frac{(24-3)}{7}=3+2\times\frac{21}{7}=3+6=9$

$\Rightarrow A_3=3+3\frac{(24-3)}{7}=3+3\times\frac{21}{7}=3+9=12$

$\Rightarrow A_4=3+4\frac{(24-3)}{7}=3+4\times\frac{21}{7}=3+12=15$

$\Rightarrow A_5=3+5\frac{(24-3)}{7}=3+5\times\frac{21}{7}=3+15=18$

$\Rightarrow A_6=3+6\times\frac{(24-3)}{7}=3+6\times\frac{21}{7}=3+18=21$

Sum $=\frac{6}{2}[2\times6+(6-1)3]$ = 3 [12 + 15] = 81

4. $a=3, b=54$

8th mean $= 3+8\times\left(\frac{54-3}{h+1}\right)=3+\frac{8\times51}{n+1}$

$(n-2)^{th}$ mean $=3+8(n-2)\frac{(54-3)}{(n+1)}=3+\frac{(n-2)51}{(n+1)}$

$\Rightarrow \frac{3+\frac{408}{(n+1)}}{3+\frac{(51n-102)}{n+1}}=\frac{3}{5}$

$\Rightarrow \frac{3n+3+408}{3n+3+51n-102}=\frac{3}{5}$

$\Rightarrow 15n + 2055 = 162n - 297$

$\Rightarrow 2055 + 297 = 162n - 15n$

$\Rightarrow 2352 = 147\,n \quad \Rightarrow 16 = n$

5. $a+b=13/6$

Let $2n$ be the number of A.M. inserted

$\Rightarrow \frac{2n}{2}(a+b)=(a+b)+13$

$\Rightarrow n\times\frac{13}{6}=\frac{13}{6}+13 = \frac{n}{6}=\frac{7}{6}$

$\Rightarrow n=7$

So, the no. of means inserted are 2 × 7 = 14

6. The rth mean between x and $2y = x+r\frac{(2y-x)}{n+1}$

The rth mean between $2x$ and $y = 2x+r\frac{(y-2x)}{n+1}$

$\Rightarrow x+r\frac{(2y-x)}{n+1}=2x+r\frac{(y-2x)}{n+1}$

$\Rightarrow \frac{r}{n+1}[2y-x-y+2x]=x$

$\Rightarrow \frac{r}{n+1}[x+y]=x \quad \Rightarrow \frac{r}{n+1}\left[\frac{bx}{y}+1\right]=\frac{x}{y}$

$\Rightarrow \frac{r}{n+1}=\left[1-\frac{r}{n+1}\right]\frac{x}{y} \quad \Rightarrow \frac{r}{n+1}=\frac{(n+1-r)}{(n+1)}\frac{x}{y}$

$\Rightarrow \frac{r}{n+1-r}=\frac{x}{y}$

7. $\frac{1+7\left(\frac{31-1}{m+1}\right)}{1+(m-1)\frac{(31-1)}{m+1}}=\frac{5}{9} \quad \Rightarrow \frac{m+1+210}{m+1+30m-30}=\frac{5}{9}$

$\Rightarrow 9m+1899=155m-145$

$\Rightarrow 2044 = 146m \quad \Rightarrow 14 = m$

TEXTUAL EXERCISE-4: (OBJECTIVE)

1. **(a)** $c=\frac{a^{n+1}+b^{n+1}}{a^n+b^n}=\frac{a+b}{2}$ [C is the arithmetic mean of a and b]

The only value that satisfies the relation is 0.

2. **(d)** $A=\frac{a+b}{2}$; $S=(a+b)$

$\Rightarrow \frac{S}{A}=\frac{n(a+b)}{(a+b)}=n$

3. **(a)** A.M between p and q = $\frac{p+q}{2}$

A.M. between r and s = $\frac{r+s}{2}$

$\Rightarrow \frac{p+q}{2}=\frac{r+s}{2}$ [Given] $\quad\therefore\ p+q=r+s$

4. **(c)** $a = 28$, b = 10, $n = 11$.

6th A.M. is the middle term = $28+6\times\frac{(10-28)}{(11+1)}$ = 28 $+6\times\frac{(-18)}{(12)}$ = 28 – 9 = 19

5. **(c)** $A_1+A_2+A_3+\ldots\ldots..+A_{14}=n\left(\frac{5+8}{2}\right)$

$\Rightarrow \frac{14}{2}\left[10+\frac{1}{15}(8-5)+5+\frac{14}{15}(8-5)\right]=\frac{13n}{2}$

$\Rightarrow 7\left[10+\frac{1}{15}(3+42)\right]=\frac{13n}{2}$

$\Rightarrow 7[10+3]=\frac{13n}{2} \quad \Rightarrow n=14$

Aliter: It is a property that the sum of n-arithmetic means between two numbers a and b is n-times the single arithmetic mean between the numbers a and b.

$\therefore\ A_1+A_2+A_3+\ldots\ldots..+A_{14}=14\left(\frac{a+b}{2}\right)=n\left(\frac{a+b}{2}\right)$ (Given)

$\Rightarrow n=14$; where a = 5, b = 8

6. **(b)** 4th mean $=1+4\times\frac{(51-1)}{n+1}=\frac{1+200}{n+1}$

7th mean $=1+7\times\frac{(51-1)}{n+1}=1+\frac{350}{n+1}$

$\Rightarrow \frac{\frac{1+200}{n+1}}{1+\frac{350}{n+1}}=\frac{3}{5} \quad \Rightarrow \frac{n+201}{n+351}=\frac{3}{5}$

$\Rightarrow 5n + 1005 = 3n + 1053$

$\Rightarrow 2n = 48 \quad \Rightarrow n = 24$

TEXTUAL EXERCISE–5: (SUBJECTIVE)

1. n^{th} term = $(5)^{3/5-3n} = \frac{(5)^{3/5}}{5^{3n}}$. The series is G.P.

7th term = $\frac{(5)^{3/5}}{(5)^{21}} = (5)^{-102/5} = \sqrt[5]{5^{-102}}$

2. (a) $a^{x-4}, a^x, a^{x+4}, \ldots; 10^m, n^{th}$

n^{th} term = $a^{x+(n-2)y}$

10th term = a^{x+8y}

(b) $3\sqrt{2}+\frac{3}{\sqrt{2}}+\frac{3}{2\sqrt{2}}+\ldots; 5^{th}$

5th term = $3\times\sqrt{2}\times\left(\frac{1}{2}\right)^{(5-1)} = \frac{1}{2} = 3\times\sqrt{2}\times\frac{1}{16} = \frac{3}{8\sqrt{2}}$

3. $a=\frac{2}{27}; r=3$

Let $T_n = 1458$

$\Rightarrow a(r)^{n-1} = 1458 \qquad \Rightarrow \frac{2}{27}(3)^{n-1} = 1458$

$\Rightarrow (3)^{n-4} = 729 = (3)^6 \qquad \Rightarrow n = 10$

4. $a \times r^2 = 9$

Product of first 5 terms = $a \times ar \times ar^2 \times ar^3 \times ar^4 = a^5r^{10} = (ar^2)^5 = (9)^5$

5. $(5k+2)^2 = 2k \times (20k-4)$

$\Rightarrow 25k^2 + 4 + 20\,k = 40k^2 - 8k$

$\Rightarrow 15k^2 - 28k - 4 = 0 \qquad \Rightarrow 15k^2 - 30k + 2k - 4 = 0$

$\Rightarrow 15k(k-2) + 2(k-2) = 0$

$\Rightarrow (15k+2)(k-2) = 0$

$\therefore$ The values of k are –2/15 and 2.

6. $ar^3 = a$ (4th term); $ar^6 = b$ (7th term); $ar^9 = c$ (10th term)

$\Rightarrow b^2 = (ar)^2 = a^2r^{12}$

$\Rightarrow ac = (ar^3)(ar^9) = a^2r^{12}$

$\therefore b^2 = ac$

7. Let the sides be $9, 9\times r, 9\times r^2$

$\Rightarrow 9 + 9r + 9r^2 = 37 \qquad \Rightarrow 9(1+r+r^2) = 37$

$\Rightarrow 1 + r + r^2 = 37/9$

$\Rightarrow 9 + 9r + 9r^2 = 37 \qquad \Rightarrow 9r^2 + 9r - 28 = 0$

$\Rightarrow r = \frac{-9\pm\sqrt{9^2+4\times9\times28}}{18} = \frac{-9\pm\sqrt{33}}{18} = \frac{-9+33}{18}$

$= \frac{24}{18} = 4/3$

(Neglecting negative value of r since each side has to be of positive length)

$\therefore$ The sides are 9, 12, 16

8. Let a^{r-1}, a, a^r be the terms

$\Rightarrow a^{r-1}\times a\times ar = 27 \qquad \Rightarrow a^3 = 27$

$\Rightarrow a = 3$

$\Rightarrow \frac{a}{r}+a+ar = 13 \qquad \Rightarrow 3[1+r^2+r] = 13r$

$\Rightarrow 3r^2 - 10r + 3 = 0 \qquad \Rightarrow 3r^2 - 9r - r + 3 = 0$

$\Rightarrow 3r(r-3) - 1(r-3) = 0$

$\Rightarrow (3r-1)(r-3) = 0 \qquad \Rightarrow r = 1/3$ or 3

$\therefore$ The series is 9, 3, 1 or 1, 3, 9

9. Let the numbers be a, ar, ar^2, then

$a + ar + ar^2 = 13$ (i)

$a^2 + a^2r^2 + a^4r^4 = 13$ (ii)

Dividing (ii) by (i)^2, we get $\frac{a^2(1+r^2+r^4)}{a^2(1+r+r^4)} = \frac{91}{(13)^2}$

$\Rightarrow \frac{(r^4+2r^2+1-r^2)}{(r^2+r+1)^2} = \frac{7}{13}$

$\Rightarrow \frac{(r^2+1+r)(r^2+1-r)}{(r^2+r+1)^2} = \frac{7}{13}$

$\Rightarrow \frac{r^2+1-r}{r^2+r+1} = \frac{7}{13}$

$\Rightarrow 6r^2 - 20r + 6 = 0 \qquad \Rightarrow r = 3$ or 1/3

For $= r = 3, a = 1 \qquad \Rightarrow$ terms are 1, 3, 9 and

For $= r = 1/3, a = 9 \qquad \Rightarrow$ terms are 9, 3, 1

10. $\frac{1}{2y}-\frac{1}{x+y} = \frac{1}{y+z}-\frac{1}{2y} \Rightarrow \frac{x-y}{x+y} = \frac{y-z}{y+z}$

$\Rightarrow xy + xz - y^2 - yz = xy - xz + y^2 - yz$

$\Rightarrow y^2 = xz \qquad \Rightarrow x, y, z$ are in G.P.

11. Sum of n terms = $\frac{2^n-1}{3}$

$\Rightarrow$ Sum of $(n-1)$ terms = $\frac{2^{n-1}-1}{3}$

$\Rightarrow n^{th}$ term = $\frac{2^n-1}{3} - \frac{(2^{n-1}-1)}{3} = \frac{2^n-2^{n-1}}{3} = \frac{2^{n-1}}{3}$

$\therefore$ The series is $\frac{1}{3}+\frac{2}{3}+\frac{4}{3}+\frac{8}{3}+\ldots$

We can clearly see that the relation $b^2 = ac$ is valid on any three consecutive terms. The common ratio is 2.

12. Let the numbers be $\frac{a}{r}, a, ar \qquad \Rightarrow \frac{a}{r}\times a\times ar = 1$

$\Rightarrow a^3 = 1 \qquad \Rightarrow a = 1$

$\Rightarrow \frac{a}{r}+a+ar = \frac{31}{10} \qquad \Rightarrow 1\left[\frac{1}{r}+1+r\right] = \frac{39}{10}$

$\Rightarrow 10(r^2+r+1) = 39r$

$\Rightarrow 10r^2 - 29r + 10 = 0 \quad \Rightarrow 10r^2 - 25r - 4r + 10 = 0$

$\Rightarrow 5r(2r-5) - 2(2r-5) = 0$

$\Rightarrow (5r-2)(2r-5) = 0 \Rightarrow r = 2/5$ or 5/2

$\therefore$ The forms are $\frac{2}{5}, 1, \frac{5}{2}$ or $\frac{5}{2}, 1, \frac{2}{5}$

13. $1 + 2 + 2^2 \ldots + 2^{n-1} = 511$

$\Rightarrow \frac{1(2^n-1)}{2-1} = 511 \qquad \Rightarrow 2^n - 1 = 511$

$\Rightarrow 2^n = 512 \qquad \Rightarrow 2^n = 2^9$

$\Rightarrow n = 9$

14. $\sqrt{3}+3\sqrt{2}+6\sqrt{3}+\ldots = \sqrt{3}\frac{(\sqrt{6}^n-1)}{(\sqrt{6}-1)} = 21\sqrt{2}+7\sqrt{3}$

$= \sqrt{3}\left(\sqrt{6}^n-1\right) = 42+\sqrt{3}+21\sqrt{2}-21\sqrt{2}-7\sqrt{3}$

$= \sqrt{3}\left(\sqrt{6}^n-1\right) = 35\sqrt{3}$

$= \sqrt{6}^4 - 1 = 35 = \sqrt{6}^n = 36 = \left(\sqrt{6}\right)^n = \left(\sqrt{6}\right)^4 = n = 4$

15. **(a)** 0.5, 0.05, 0.005 …. $\Rightarrow S_n = 0.5 + 0.05 + 0.005 + \ldots$

$= 0.5\left[1+\frac{1}{10}+\frac{1}{100}+\ldots\right] = 0.5\left[1+10^{-1}+10^{-2}+10^{-3}+\ldots\right]$

$= 0.5\times\frac{\left[1-10^{-n}\right]}{1-10^{-1}} = \frac{5}{9}\times\left[1-10^{-n}\right]$

$\Rightarrow \lim_{n\to\infty} S_n = \lim_{n\to\infty}\frac{5}{9}\left[1-10^{-n}\right] = \lim_{n\to\infty}\frac{5}{9}\left[1-\frac{1}{10^n}\right] = \frac{5}{9}$

(b) 0.6 + 0.66 + 0.666 + ….

$\Rightarrow S_n = 0.6 + 0.66 + 0.666 + \ldots$

$= 6[0.1+0.11+0.111+\ldots] = \frac{6}{9}[0.9+0.99+0.999+\ldots]$

$= \frac{6}{9}[1-0.1+1-0.01+1-0.01+\ldots]$

$= \frac{6}{9}\left[(1+1+\ldots\text{n times})-(0.1+0.01+0.001+\ldots)\right]$

$= \frac{6}{9}\left[n-0.1\times\frac{(1-0.1^n)}{1-0.1}\right] = \frac{6}{9}\left[n-0.1\frac{(1-10^{-n})}{0.9}\right]$

$= \frac{6}{9}\left[n-\frac{1}{9}\left[1-10^{-n}\right]\right] = \frac{2}{3}\left[n-\frac{\left[1-10^{-n}\right]}{9}\right]$

16. Sum of first three terms $= \frac{a(1-r^3)}{1-r}$

Sum of first six terms $= \frac{a(1-r^6)}{1-r} = \frac{125}{152}$

$\Rightarrow 152 = 125 + 125r^3 \quad \Rightarrow 27 = 125r^3$

$\Rightarrow \left(\frac{3}{5}\right)^3 = r^3 \quad \Rightarrow 3/5 = r$

17. $a - ar = 2$

$\Rightarrow a(1-r) = 2$ (i)

$\Rightarrow \frac{a}{1-r} = 50$ (ii)

Equation (i) divided by equation (ii), we get $(1-r)^2 = 1/25$

$\Rightarrow 1 - r = \pm\frac{1}{5} \quad \Rightarrow r = \frac{4}{5}\text{ or }\frac{6}{5}$

$\because \frac{6}{5}$ will be neglected because the equation (ii) is valid only for r smaller than 1

$\Rightarrow a\left(1-\frac{4}{5}\right) = 2 \quad \Rightarrow a\times\frac{1}{5} = 2$

$a = 10,\ r = 4/5$

18. $\frac{a}{1-r} = 4$ (i)

$\frac{a^3}{1-r^3} = 142$ (ii)

Cubing equation (i) and dividing by equation (ii), we get

$\frac{\frac{a^3}{(1-r)^3}}{\frac{a^3}{1-r^3}} = \frac{64}{192} = \frac{1-r^3}{(1-r)^3} = \frac{1}{3} = (1+r+r^2)\times 3 = (1-r)^2$

$= 3 + 3r + 3r^2 = 1 + r^2 - 2r = 2r^2 + 5r + 2 = 0 = 2r^2 + 4r + r + 2 = 0 = 2r(r+2) + 1(r+2) = 0 = (2r+1)(r+2) = 0$

$r = -1/2$ or $r = -2$

$\because$ r must be smaller than 1

$\therefore$ $r = -1/2$

$\Rightarrow \frac{a}{1+1/2} = 4 \quad \Rightarrow a\times\frac{2}{3} = 4$

$a = 6$

19. **(a)** $\sum_1^9\left(2+3^i\right) = 2+3+2+3^2+2+3^3+\ldots+2+3^9 = 9\times 2 + 3 + 3^2 + 3^3 + \ldots 3^9 = 18 + 3\frac{(3^9-1)}{3-1}$

$= 18 + \frac{3}{2}(3^9-1) = \frac{3}{2}\left(11+3^9\right)$

(b) $\sum_{n=1}^{13}(2^n-1) = 2^1 - 1 + 2^2 - 1 + 2^3 - 1 + \ldots + 2^{13} - 1$

$= 2^1 + 2^2 + \ldots + 2^{13} - 1\times 13 = \frac{2(-1+2^{13})}{2-1} - 13 = 2^{14} - 2 - 13 = 2^{14} - 15$

(c) $\sum_{j=1}^{n}\left(2^i+3^j+5\right) = 2+3+5+2^2+3^2+5+\ldots+2^n+3^n + 5 = 5\times n + 2 + 2^2 + \ldots + 2^n + 3 + 3^2 + 3^3 + \ldots + 3^n$

$= 5\times n + 2\frac{(2^n-1)}{2-1} + 3\frac{(3^n-1)}{3-1} = 5^n + 2^{n+1} - 2 + \frac{3}{2}(3^n-1)$

20. Perimeter of first triangle = 3 × 24

Perimeter of second triangle $= 3\times\frac{24}{2}$

. . . .

. .

Perimeter of nth triangle $= 3\times\frac{24}{2^{n-1}}$

Sum of perimeter $= 3\times 24 + 3\times\frac{24}{2} + \frac{3\times 24}{4} + \ldots + 3\times\frac{24}{2^{n-1}} + \ldots\infty$

$= \frac{3\times 24}{\left(1-\frac{1}{2}\right)} = 3\times 24\times 2 = 144$ cm

21. Let us take a general G.P.

$S_n = a + ar + ar^2 + ar^3 + \ldots + ar^n$

$S_\infty = a + ar + ar^2 + ar^3 + \ldots + \infty$ terms

If $r = 1$

$S_\infty = a + a + a + \ldots \infty$ times

Now if $a > 0 \quad \Rightarrow S_\infty = +\infty$

If $a < 0 \quad \Rightarrow S_\infty = -\infty$

If $r = -1 \quad \Rightarrow S_\infty = a - a + a - a + \ldots$

If even numbers of terms $S_\infty = 0$

If odd numbers of terms $S_\infty = a$

22. $S_n = \frac{a(r^n-1)}{(r-1)} \quad \Rightarrow \quad \lim_{n\to\infty} S_n \lim_{n\to\infty}\frac{a(r^n-1)}{(r-1)}$

If $a > 0$

Series will oscillate $r < -1$ and ∞

If $a < 0$

Series will oscillate $r < -1$ and $-\infty$

Note: series no longer is a converging series.

TEXTUAL EXERCISE–5: (OBJECTIVE)

1. (a) Let the 3 numbers be a, ar, ar^2

By the questions $a + ar + ar^2 = 21$

$\Rightarrow a(1 + r + r^2) = 21$ (i)

Squaring equation (i), we get

$a^2 (1 + r^2 + r^4) = 189$ (ii)

$\Rightarrow \dfrac{a(1-r^3)}{(1-r)} = 21$ and $\dfrac{a^2(1-r^6)}{(1-r^2)} = 189$

$\Rightarrow 9a\left[\dfrac{1-r^3}{1-r}\right] = a^2\left[\dfrac{1-r^6}{1-r^2}\right]$

$\Rightarrow a\left[\dfrac{1+r^3}{1+r}\right] = 9 \quad \Rightarrow a[1 + r^2 - r] = 9$

$\Rightarrow$ By (i) $\dfrac{(1+r^2-r)}{(1+r^2+r)} = \dfrac{9}{21} = \dfrac{3}{7}$

By componendo and dividendo, we get $\dfrac{1+r^2}{r} = \dfrac{5}{2}$

$\Rightarrow 2r^2 - 5r + 2 = 0 \quad \Rightarrow r = 2, 1/2$

2. (a) Let the numbers be $\dfrac{a}{r}, a, ar$

$\Rightarrow a^3 = 216 \quad \Rightarrow a = 6$

$\dfrac{a}{r} + a + ar = 19 \quad \Rightarrow a[1 + r + r^2] = 19r$

$\Rightarrow 6[1 + r + r^2] = 19r \quad \Rightarrow 6r^2 - 13r + 6 = 0$

$\Rightarrow 6r^2 - 9r + 4r + 6 = 0 \Rightarrow (3r - 2)(2r - 3) = 0$

$\Rightarrow r = 2/3$ or $3/2$

$\therefore$ The numbers are 4, 6, 9

3. (b) Let the numbers be $\dfrac{a}{r^2}, \dfrac{a}{r}, a, ar, ar^2, ar^3$

Product = 512

$\Rightarrow \dfrac{a}{r^2} \times \dfrac{a}{r} \times a \times ar \times ar^2 \times ar^3 = 512$

$\Rightarrow a^6 r^3 = 512$

$\Rightarrow a^2 r = 8$ (i)

Fourth term $\Rightarrow ar = 4$

Solving (i) and (ii), we get $r = 2$, a = 2

$\therefore$ Second terms = $\dfrac{a}{r} = 1$

4. (b) Let $b = ar$ and $c = ar^2$

(a) $a(b^2 + a^2) = a(a^2r^2 + a^2) = a^3 (1 + r^2)$ and $c(b^2 + c^2) = ar^2 (a^2r^2 + a^2r^4) = a^3r^4 (1 + r^2)$; which are not equal

(b) $a(b^2 + c^2) = a(a^2r^2 + a^2r^4) = a^3r^2 (1 + r^2)$ and $c (b^2 + a^2) = ar^2 (a^2r^2 + a^2) = r^2a^3 (1 + r^2)$; which are equal

(c) $a^2(b + c) = a^2(ar + ar^2) = a^3r (1 + r)$ and $c^2 (a + b) = a^2r^4 (a + ar) = a^3r^4 (1 + r)$; which are not equal

5. (a) $(a^{x/2})^2 \log_x a \times \log_b x$

$\Rightarrow a^x = \dfrac{\log a}{\log x} \times \dfrac{\log x}{\log b} \quad \Rightarrow a^x = \dfrac{\log a}{\log b} = a^x = \log_b a$

$\therefore x = \log_a (\log_b a)$

6. (d) $(0.2)^{\log_{\sqrt{5}}\left(\frac{1}{4}+\frac{1}{8}+\frac{1}{16}+....\infty\right)} = (0.2)^{\log_{\sqrt{5}}\left(\frac{\frac{1}{4}}{\left(1-\frac{1}{2}\right)}\right)}$

$= (0.2)^{\log_{(5)^{1/2}}\left(\frac{1}{2}\right)} = (5^{-1})^{\log_5\left(\frac{1}{2}\right)^2} = \left(\dfrac{1}{2}\right)^{-2} = 4$

7. (c) $1 + a + a^2 + ... a^n = (1 + a)(1 + a^2)(1 + a^4)$

$\Rightarrow \dfrac{1(a^{n+1}-1)}{(a-1)} = (1+a)(1+a^2)(1+a^4)$

$\Rightarrow a^{n+1} - 1 = (a^2 - 1)(a^2 + 1)(a^4 + 1)$

$\Rightarrow a^{n+1} - 1 = (a^4 - 1)(a^4 + 1)$

$\Rightarrow a^{n+1} - 1 = a^8 - 1$

$\Rightarrow a^{n+1} = a^8 \quad \Rightarrow$ n = 7

8. (c) $\sum_{n=1}^{m} \log \dfrac{a^{2n-1}}{b^{m-1}}$

$\Rightarrow \log\dfrac{a}{b^{m-1}} + \log\dfrac{a^3}{b^{m-1}} + ... + \log\dfrac{(a^{2m-1})}{b^{m-1}}$

$\Rightarrow \log\dfrac{a \times a^3 \times a^5 \times .... \times a^{2m-1}}{b^{(m)(m-1)}}$

$\Rightarrow \log\dfrac{a^{1+3+5+7+......+2m-1}}{b^{m(m-1)}} \quad \Rightarrow \log\dfrac{a^{m^2}}{(b)^{(m-1)(m)}} \quad m\log\dfrac{a^m}{b^{m-1}}$

9. (c) Second term = $ar = 54$ (i)

Fourth term = $ar^3 = 24$ (ii)

Equation (i) divided by equation (ii), we get

$\dfrac{1}{r^2} = \dfrac{54}{24} = \dfrac{9}{4}$

$\dfrac{1}{r} = \pm\dfrac{3}{2}$ [$\because$ G.P. is of positive terms $r > 0$]

$\Rightarrow r = 2/3 \quad \Rightarrow a \times 2/3 = 54$

$\Rightarrow a = 81$

$\therefore$ Fifth term = $81 \times \dfrac{2^4}{3^4} = 16$

10. (b) 1 + 11 + 111 + ... n terms

$= \dfrac{1}{9}[9 + 99 + 999 + ... n \text{ terms}]$

$= \dfrac{1}{9}[10.1 + 100 - 1 + 1000 - 1 + ... n \text{ terms}]$

$= \dfrac{1}{9}\left[10 + 10^2 + 10^3 + ... n \text{ terms} - 1(1 + 1 + ... n \text{ terms})\right]$

$= \dfrac{1}{9}\left[\dfrac{10(10^n - 1)}{10-1} - 1 \times n\right] = \dfrac{1}{9}\left[\dfrac{10}{9}(10^n - 1) - n\right]$

11. (d) $\dfrac{a}{1-r} = 4 \Rightarrow a = 4 - 4r$

$\Rightarrow a + 4r = 4$ (i)

$ar = 3/4 \quad \Rightarrow r = 3/4a$ (ii)

$\Rightarrow a + 4 \times \dfrac{3}{4a} = 4 \quad \Rightarrow a^2 - 4a + 3 = 0$

$\Rightarrow (a - 3)(a - 1) = 0$

$\Rightarrow a = 3$ or $1 \quad \Rightarrow r = \dfrac{1}{4}$ or $\dfrac{3}{4}$

12. (c) $f(x), f(2x), f(4x)$ to be in G.P.

$[f(2x)^2] = f(x).f(4x)$

$\Rightarrow (4x + 1)^2 = (2x + 1)(8x + 1)$

$\Rightarrow 16x^2 + 8x + 1 \quad \Rightarrow 16x^2 + 10x + 1$

$\Rightarrow 2x = 0 \quad \Rightarrow x = 0$

$\therefore$ There is only one value of x for which $f(x), f(2x), f(3x)$ are in G.P. but are equal.

$\therefore$ No real x exists for unequal terms in G.P.

13. (c) $\frac{x}{1-r}=5$ $x=5-5r \Rightarrow r=1-x/5$

$\Rightarrow |r|<1$ for infinite G.P.

$\Rightarrow -1<r<1 \qquad \Rightarrow -1<1-x/5<1$

$\Rightarrow -2<-x/2<2 \qquad \Rightarrow 0<x/5<2$

$\Rightarrow 0<x<10$

14. (b) $(1+p)(1+3x+9x^2+27x^3+81x^4+243x^5)=1-p^6$

$\Rightarrow (1+p)(1+3x+(3x)^2+(3x^3)+(3x)^4+(3x)^5)=1-p^6$

$\Rightarrow (1+p)\frac{\left(1\left((3x)^6-1\right)\right)}{(3x-1)}=1-p^6$; for $x\neq 1/3$

$\Rightarrow (1+p)\left(\frac{(3x)^6-1}{3x-1}\right)=1-p^6$

$\Rightarrow (1+p)\frac{\left((3x)^3-1\right)(3x^3+1)}{(3x-1)}=1-p^6$

$\Rightarrow (1+p)(9x^2+1+3x)((3x)^3+1)=(1-p^6)$

$\Rightarrow (9x^2+3x+1)((3x)^3+1)=(1-p^3)(1+p^2-p)$

By comparison $p=-3x$

$\Rightarrow p/x=-3$

TEXTUAL EXERCISE–6: (SUBJECTIVE)

1. **(a, b, c, d)** are in G.P. Let $b=ar$; $c=ar^2$; $d=ar^3$

(a) $(b+c)^2=(a+b)(c+d)$

L.H.S. $=(b+c)^2$

$\Rightarrow (ar+ar^2)^2 \qquad \Rightarrow a^2r^2(1+r)^2$

R.H.S. $=(a+b)(c+d)$

$\Rightarrow (a+ar)(ar^2+ar^3)$

$\Rightarrow a(1+r)\,ar^2(1+r) \qquad \Rightarrow a^2r^2(1+r)^2$

$\therefore$ L.H.S. = R.H.S.

(b) $(b^2+c^2)^2=(c^2+d^2)(a^2+b^2)$

L.H.S. $=(b^2+c^2)^2 \qquad \Rightarrow (a^2r^2+a^2r^4)^2$

$\Rightarrow a^4r^4(1+r^2)^2$ R.H.S. $=(c^2+d^2)(a^2+b^2)$

$\Rightarrow (a^2r^4+a^2r^6)(a^2+a^2r^2) \qquad \Rightarrow a^2r^4(1+r^2)a^2(1+r^2)$

$\Rightarrow a^4r^4(1+r^2)^2$

$\therefore$ L.H.S. = R.H.S.

(c) $(ab+bc+cd)^2=(a^2+b^2+c^2)(b^2+c^2+d^2)$

L.H.S. $=(a^2r+a^2r^3+a^2r^5)^2$

$\Rightarrow a^4r^2(1+r^2+r^4)^2$

R.H.S. $=(a^2+b^2+c^2)(b^2+c^2+d^2)$

$\Rightarrow (a^2+a^2r^2+a^2r^4)(a^2r^2+a^2r^4+a^2r^6)$

$\Rightarrow a^2(1+r^2+r^4)\,a^2r^2(1+r^2+r^4)$

$\Rightarrow a^4r^2(1+r^2r^4) \qquad \therefore$ L.H.S. = R.H.S.

2. G.M. of these n numbers is $\sqrt[n]{3^1.3^2.3^3.....3^n}=\sqrt[n]{3^{1+2+3+...+n}}$

$=\left[3^{\frac{n(n+1)}{2}}\right]^{1/n}=3^{\frac{(n+1)}{2}}$

3. Let a and b be the number. If we insert n G.M.S between a and b series will look like.

$\Rightarrow a, G_1, G_2, G_3 ......G_n$

$\Rightarrow b=a.r^{n+1} \qquad \Rightarrow \left(\frac{b}{a}\right)^{1/n+1}=r$

$\Rightarrow$ Product of $G_1, G_2, G_3,....$ and G_n

$\Rightarrow G_1\times G_2\times G_3\times G_4\times .....\times G_n$

$\Rightarrow ar\times ar^2\times ar^3\times ar^4\times a\times r^n$

$\Rightarrow a^n\ r^{1+2+3+4+....+n} \qquad \Rightarrow a^n\ r^{\frac{n(n+1)}{2}}$

$\Rightarrow a^n\times\left(\left(\frac{b}{a}\right)^{\frac{1}{n+1}}\right) \Rightarrow a^n\times\left(\frac{b}{a}\right)^{n/2}$

Single G.M. between a & $b=2\sqrt{ab}$

n^{th} power of single G.M. $=\left((ab)^{1/2}\right)^n$

4. Let GM'S be G_1 and G_2, So $b=ar^3$

$\Rightarrow \left(\frac{b}{a}\right)^{1/3}=r \qquad \Rightarrow G_1+G_2$

$\Rightarrow ar+ar^2 \qquad \Rightarrow a(r+r^2)$

$\Rightarrow a\left(\left(\frac{b}{a}\right)^{1/3}+\left(\frac{b}{a}\right)^{2/3}\right) \qquad \Rightarrow a^{2/3}b^{1/3}+a^{1/3}b^{2/3}$

$\Rightarrow a^{1/3}b^{1/3}(a^{1/3}+b^{1/3})$

5. $\frac{a^{n+1}+b^{n+1}}{a^n+b^n}=\sqrt{ab}$

$\Rightarrow a^{n+1}+b^{n+1}=a^{(n+1/2)}b^{1/2}+a^{1/2}b^{(n+1/2)}$

$\Rightarrow a^{(n+1/2)}(a^{1/2}-b^{1/2})=b^{(n+1/2)}(a^{1/2}-b^{1/2})$

$\Rightarrow a^{(n+1/2)}=b^{(n+1/2)}$

$\Rightarrow \left(\frac{a}{b}\right)^{n+1/2}=1 \qquad \Rightarrow n+1/2=0$

$\Rightarrow n=-1/2$

6. Let the series be 2, G_1, G_2, G_3, 162

$\Rightarrow 2\times r^4=162 \qquad \Rightarrow r^4=81$

$\Rightarrow r=\pm 3$

$\therefore$ $G_1=2\times r=6$ *or* -6

$G_2=2\times r^2=18$ (*both cases*)

$G_3=2\times r^3=54$ *or* -54

Product $=6\times 18\times 59=(18)^3=(18^2)^{3/2}=(324)^{3/2}$

Summation $=G_1+G_2+G_3=6+18+54$ *or* $-6+18-54=78$ *or* -42

7. $a=\frac{b+c}{2} \qquad \Rightarrow b\times r^3=c \Rightarrow r=\left(\frac{c}{b}\right)^{1/3}$

$\Rightarrow G_1=b\times\left(\frac{c}{b}\right)^{1/3}=(b)^{2/3}(c)^{1/3}$

$\Rightarrow G_2=b\times\left(\frac{c}{b}\right)^{2/3}=(b)^{1/3}(c)^{2/3}$

$\Rightarrow G_1^3+G_2^3 \qquad \Rightarrow \left((b^{2/3})(c)^{1/3}\right)^3+\left(b^{1/3}(c)^{2/3}\right)^3$

$\Rightarrow b^2\times c+bc^2 \qquad \Rightarrow 2bc\frac{(b+c)}{2}$

$\Rightarrow 2abc$

8. $2x^4=y^4+z^4$ (i)

$xyz=8$ (ii)

Since $\log_y x$, $\log_z y$, $\log_x z$ are in G.P.

$=(\log_z y)^2=\frac{\log x}{\log y}.\frac{\log z}{\log x}=\frac{\log z}{\log y}$

$\Rightarrow (\log_z y)^2=\left(\frac{1}{\log_z y}\right) \Rightarrow (\log_z y)^3=1$

$\Rightarrow y=z$

$\Rightarrow 2x^4=2y^4 \qquad \Rightarrow x=y$ or $-y$

$\{x, y, z\}=\{2, 2, 2\}$

TEXTUAL EXERCISE-6: (OBJECTIVE)

1. (a) 1, x, y, z, $21 \times r^4 = 2$

$\Rightarrow r^4 = 2$ $\quad\Rightarrow r(2)^{1/4}$

$\Rightarrow xyz$ $\quad\Rightarrow r \times r^2 \times r^3$

$\Rightarrow (r)^6$ $\quad\Rightarrow (2)^{6/4}$

$\Rightarrow (2)^{3/2}$ $\quad\Rightarrow 2\sqrt{2}$

2. (a) $n!$, $3 \times n!$ and $(n + 1)!$ are in G.P.

$\Rightarrow (3 \times n!)^2 = n! \times (n + 1)!$

$\Rightarrow 9 \times (n!)^2\ (n!)^2 \times (n + 1)$

$\Rightarrow 9 = n + 1$ $\quad\Rightarrow 8 = n$

$\Rightarrow$ 8!, 5 × 8! and 9 × 8!

These three terms are in A.P. with common difference 4 × 8!

3. (a) $\dfrac{a\left(r^3-1\right)}{r-1} = 70\ a(1 + r + r^2) = 70$

Now, by the questions $4a$, $5ar$, $4ar^2$ are in A.P.

$\Rightarrow 10ar = 4\ (a + r^2)$ $\quad\Rightarrow 10r = 4(1 + r^2)$

$\Rightarrow 4r^2 - 10r + 4 = 0$

$\Rightarrow 4r^2 - 8r - 2r + 4 = 0 \Rightarrow (4r - 1)\ (r - 2) = 0$

$\Rightarrow r = 2$ or $r = 1/4$

$\Rightarrow a = 10$ $\quad\Rightarrow$ 10, 20, 40 are terms

4. (c) a, b, c are in G.P. Let $b = ar$ and $c = ar^2$ [r is common multiple]

$\Rightarrow (a - c)^2 + (c - b)^2 + (b - d)^2 - (d - a)^2$

$\Rightarrow (a - ar^2)^2 + (ar^2 - ar)^2 + (ar - ar^3)^2 - (ar^3 - a)^2 = 0$

TEXTUAL EXERCISE-7: (SUBJECTIVE)

1. (a) $\dfrac{1}{3}, \dfrac{3}{10}, \dfrac{3}{11}, \dfrac{1}{4}, \ldots$

Common difference $= \dfrac{10}{3} - 3 \Rightarrow \dfrac{1}{3}$

n^{th} term $= \dfrac{1}{a+(n-1)d} = \dfrac{1}{3+(n-1)1/3} = \dfrac{3}{8+n}$

(b) $\dfrac{5}{2}, \dfrac{20}{13}, \dfrac{10}{9}, \dfrac{20}{23}, \ldots$

Common difference $= \dfrac{13}{20} - \dfrac{2}{5} = \dfrac{13-8}{20} = \dfrac{1}{4}$

n^{th} terms $= \dfrac{1}{\dfrac{2}{5}+(n-1)1/4} = \dfrac{1}{\dfrac{2}{5}-\dfrac{1}{4}+\dfrac{n}{4}} = \dfrac{20}{3+5n}$

2. $a + (3 - 1)d = 7/6$

$a + 2d = 7/6$ (i)

$a + 13d = 3$ (ii)

Subtracting (i) from (ii), we get $11d = 3 - \dfrac{7}{6}$

$\Rightarrow 11d = \dfrac{11}{6}$ $\quad\Rightarrow d = 1/6, a = 5/6$

General term of H.P.$= \dfrac{1}{\dfrac{5}{6}+(n-1)\dfrac{1}{6}} = \dfrac{6}{4+n}$

3. Let the numbers be $\dfrac{1}{a-d}, \dfrac{1}{a}, \dfrac{1}{a+d}$ in H.P.

$\Rightarrow a - d + a + a + d = 18$

$\Rightarrow 3a = 18$ $\quad\Rightarrow a = 6$

$\Rightarrow (a - d)\ (a)\ (a + d) = 120$

$\Rightarrow (a^2 - d^2)\ a = 120$ $\quad\Rightarrow a^3 - d^2a = 120$

$\Rightarrow 216 - 6d^2 = 120$ $\quad\Rightarrow 96 = 6d^2$

$\Rightarrow d = \pm 4$

So, the numbers are $\dfrac{1}{2}, \dfrac{1}{6}, \dfrac{1}{10}$

4. $a + (m - 1)d = \dfrac{1}{n}$ (i)

$a + (n - 1)d = \dfrac{1}{m}$ (ii)

Subtracting (i) from (ii), we get $(n-m)d = \dfrac{(n-m)}{nm}$

$\Rightarrow d = \dfrac{1}{nm}$

$\Rightarrow a+(m-1)\dfrac{1}{mn} = \dfrac{1}{n}$ $\quad\Rightarrow a+\dfrac{1}{n}-\dfrac{1}{mn} = \dfrac{1}{n}$

$\Rightarrow a = \dfrac{1}{mn}$

(a) $(m+n)^2$ + term $\quad\Rightarrow \dfrac{1}{a+((m+n)^2-1)d}$

$\Rightarrow \dfrac{1}{\dfrac{1}{mn}+(m^2+n^2+2mn-1)\dfrac{1}{mn}}$

$\Rightarrow \dfrac{mn}{(m+n)^2}$

(b) $(mn)^{\text{th}}$ term $\quad\Rightarrow \dfrac{1}{a+(mn-1)d}$

$\Rightarrow \dfrac{1}{\dfrac{1}{mn}+(mn-1)\dfrac{1}{mn}}$ $\quad\Rightarrow \dfrac{mn}{mn} \Rightarrow 1$

5. $a + (p - 1)d = \dfrac{1}{qr}$ (i)

$a + (q - 1)d = \dfrac{1}{pr}$ (ii)

(–) (–) (–)

$= (p-q)d = \dfrac{1}{r}\left(\dfrac{p-q}{pq}\right)$ $\quad\Rightarrow d = \dfrac{1}{pqr}$

$\Rightarrow$ Putting value of d in equation (i), we get

$a+(p-1)\dfrac{1}{pqr} = \dfrac{1}{qr}$

$\Rightarrow a = \dfrac{1}{pqr}$

r^{th} term $= \dfrac{1}{\dfrac{1}{pqr}+(r-1)\dfrac{1}{pqr}}$

$\Rightarrow \dfrac{pqr}{r} \Rightarrow pq$

6. Let the numbers be $\dfrac{1}{a-d}, \dfrac{1}{a}, \dfrac{1}{a+d}$

$3a = 1$ [∵ Sum of reciprocals = 1]

$\Rightarrow a = 1/3$

$\Rightarrow \frac{1}{\frac{1}{3}-d}+\frac{1}{\frac{1}{3}}+\frac{1}{\frac{1}{3}+d}=11$

$\Rightarrow \frac{3}{1-3d}+3+\frac{3}{1+3d}=11$

$\Rightarrow 3\left[\frac{1+3d+1-3d}{1-9d^2}\right]=8$

$\Rightarrow \frac{2}{1-9d^2}=\frac{8}{3}$ $\quad\Rightarrow 3 = 4 - 36d^2$

$\Rightarrow 36d^2 = 1$ $\quad\Rightarrow d^2 = \frac{1}{36}\ \pm\frac{1}{6}$

∴ The numbers are 6, 3, 2.

7. $a(b-c)x^2 + b(c-a)x + c(a-b) = 0$

The sum of coefficients is zero

∴ $x = 1$ is the roots

∴ $\frac{-b(c-a)}{2a(b-c)}=1$

$\Rightarrow -bc + ab = 2ab - 2ac \Rightarrow \quad 2ac = ab + bc$

$\Rightarrow \frac{1}{b}=\frac{1}{a}+\frac{1}{c}$ $\quad$ ∴ a, b, c are in H.P.

8. $6x^3 - 11x^2 + 6x - 1 = 0$

$\Rightarrow 6x^3 - 6x^2 - 5x^2 + 5x + x - 1 = 0$

$\Rightarrow 6x^2(x-1) - 5x(x-1) + 1(x-1) = 0$

$\Rightarrow (x-1)(6x^2 - 5x + 1) = 0$

$\Rightarrow (x-1)(6x^2 - 3x - 2x + 1) = 0$

$\Rightarrow (x-1)(3x(2x-1) - 1(2x-1)) = 0$

$\Rightarrow (x-1)(2x-1)(3x-1) = 0$

∴ Solutions are 1, 1/2, 1/3

Aliter: Let α, β, γ be the roots and also they are in H.P.

$\alpha\beta + \beta\gamma + \gamma\alpha = 1$ (i)

$\alpha\beta\gamma = 1/6$ (ii)

$\alpha + \beta + \gamma = 11/6$ (iii)

Divided by (ii), we get $\frac{1}{\alpha}+\frac{1}{\beta}+\frac{1}{\gamma}=6$ (iv)

Let $\alpha=\frac{1}{a-d}$; $\beta=\frac{1}{a}$; $\gamma=\frac{1}{a+d}$

∴ (iv) gets reduced to $3a = 6$

$\Rightarrow a = 2$

Using the values of α, β, γ and $a = 2$ in (ii), we get

$\left(\frac{1}{a-d}\right)\left(\frac{1}{a}\right)\left(\frac{1}{a+d}\right)=\frac{1}{6} \Rightarrow \quad \frac{1}{a(a^2-d^2)}=\frac{1}{6}$

$\Rightarrow \frac{1}{2(4-d^2)}=\frac{1}{3}$ $\quad\Rightarrow 4 - d^2 = 3$

$\Rightarrow d^2 = 1$ $\quad\Rightarrow d = \pm 1$

∴ The numbers are $1, \frac{1}{2}, \frac{1}{3}$

9. $10x^3 - cx^2 - 54x - 27 = 0$

Let the roots be $\frac{1}{a-d}, \frac{1}{a}, \frac{1}{a+d}$

Now $\frac{1}{a-d}+\frac{1}{a}+\frac{1}{a+d}=\frac{c}{10}$ (i)

$\Rightarrow \frac{1}{(a-d)(a+d)(a)}=\frac{27}{10}$ (ii)

$\Rightarrow \frac{1}{(a-d)(a)}+\frac{1}{a(a+d)}+\frac{1}{(a+d)(a-d)}=-\frac{54}{10}$ (iii)

Dividing (iii) by (ii), we get $a - d + a + a + d = \frac{54}{27}$

$\Rightarrow 3a = -2$ $\quad\Rightarrow a = -2/3$

Putting a = –2/3 in (ii), we get

$\frac{1}{\left(-\frac{2}{3}-d\right)\left(d-\frac{2}{3}\right)\left(-\frac{2}{3}\right)}=\frac{27}{10}$

$\Rightarrow \frac{1}{\left(\frac{4}{3}-d^2\right)\frac{2}{3}}=-\frac{27}{10}$

$\Rightarrow 5 = -4 + 9d^2$ $\quad\Rightarrow 9 = 9d^2$

$\Rightarrow d = \pm 1$

∴ The roots are $-\frac{3}{5}, \frac{-3}{2}, 3$

$\Rightarrow \frac{c}{10}=\frac{-3}{5}\frac{-3}{2}+3$ $\quad\Rightarrow \frac{c}{10}=\frac{-6-15+30}{10} \Rightarrow c = 9$

10. a, b, c are in H.P. To prove $\frac{2(c+a)}{b}=\frac{(b+c)}{a}+\frac{(a+b)}{c}$

L.H.S. $=\left(\frac{1}{a}+\frac{1}{c}\right)(a+c) \Rightarrow \quad \frac{(a+c)^2}{ac}$

R.H.S. $= b\left(\frac{1}{a}+\frac{1}{c}\right)+\frac{c}{a}+\frac{a}{c}$

$\Rightarrow 2+\frac{c}{a}+\frac{a}{c}$ $\quad\Rightarrow 1+\frac{c}{a}+1+\frac{a}{c}$

$\Rightarrow \frac{(a+c)}{a}+\frac{(a+c)}{c}$ $\quad\Rightarrow (a+c)\left[\frac{1}{a}+\frac{1}{c}\right]$

$\Rightarrow \frac{(a+c)^2}{ac}$

∴ L.H.S. = R.H.S.

11. $\frac{a^{n+1}+b^{n+1}}{a^n+b^n}=\frac{2ab}{a+b}$

$= a^{n+2} + b^{n+2} + a^{n+1}b + ab^{n+1} = 2a^{n+1}b + 2ab^{n+1}$

$= a^{n+2} + b^{n+2} = a^{n+1}b + ab^{n+1}$

$= a^{n+1}(a-b) = b^{n+1}(a-b)$

$= a^{n+1} = b^{n+1}$

Possible iff $a = b$; $n + 1 = 0$; $n = -1$

Since a and b are distinct numbers. The possible values of n = – 1.

12. $\log(x + z - y + y) + \log(x + z - y - y) = 2\log(x - z)$

$\Rightarrow \log[(x + z - y)^2 - y^2] = \log(x - z)^2$

$\Rightarrow (x + z - y)^2 - y^2 = (x - z)^2 =$ L.H.S.

$\Rightarrow x^2 + z^2 + y^2 + 2xz - 2zy - 2xy - y^2$

$\Rightarrow x^2 + z^2 + 2xz - 2zy - 2xy$

$\Rightarrow x^2 + z^2 + 2xz - 2y(x + z)$

$\Rightarrow x^2 + z^2 + 2xz - \frac{-4(x+z)}{\frac{2}{y}}$

$\Rightarrow x^2 + z^2 + 2xz - \frac{4(x+z)}{\left(\frac{1}{x}+\frac{1}{z}\right)}$

$\Rightarrow\ x^2+z^2+2xz-\dfrac{4(x+z)}{(x+z)}\times x^z$

$\Rightarrow\ x^2+z^2-2xz \qquad \Rightarrow\ (x-z)^2$

$\therefore$ L.H.S. = R.H.S.

13. H.M. of ab $\Rightarrow\ n=\dfrac{2ab}{a+b}\ \Rightarrow \dfrac{H}{a}+\dfrac{H}{b}-2$

$\Rightarrow\ n\left(\dfrac{1}{a}+\dfrac{1}{b}\right)-2 \qquad \Rightarrow\ \dfrac{2ab}{(a+b)}\times\dfrac{(a+b)}{ab}-2$

$\Rightarrow\ 0$

14. $\dfrac{1}{H_1}=\dfrac{1}{a}+\dfrac{(a-b)}{(n+1)(ab)}=\dfrac{a}{H_1}=1+\dfrac{(a-b)}{(n+1)b}$

$\Rightarrow\ \dfrac{1}{H_n}=\dfrac{1}{a}+\dfrac{n(a-b)}{(n+1)(ab)}\Rightarrow\dfrac{b}{H_n}=\dfrac{b}{a}+\dfrac{n(a-b)}{(n+1)a}$

To prove $[(H_1+a)/(H_1-a)]+[(H_n+b)/(H_n-b)]=2n$

L.H.S $=\dfrac{\left[1+\dfrac{a}{H_1}\right]}{\left[1-\dfrac{a}{H_1}\right]}+\dfrac{\left[1+\dfrac{b}{H_n}\right]}{\left[1-\dfrac{b}{H_n}\right]}$

$\Rightarrow\ \dfrac{\left[1+1+\dfrac{(a-b)}{(n+1)b}\right]}{\left[1-1+\dfrac{(b-a)}{(n+1)b}\right]}+\dfrac{\left[1+\dfrac{b}{a}+\dfrac{n(a-b)}{(n+1)a}\right]}{\left[1-\dfrac{b}{a}-\dfrac{n(a-b)}{(n+1)a}\right]}$

$\Rightarrow\ \left[\dfrac{2(n+1)b+(a-b)}{(b-a)}\right]+\left[\dfrac{(n+1)a+b(n+1)+n(a-b)}{(n+1)a-b(n+1)-n(a-b)}\right]$

$\Rightarrow\ \left[\dfrac{2nb+a+b}{(b-a)}\right]+\left[\dfrac{2na+a+b}{a-b}\right]$

$\Rightarrow\ \left[\dfrac{2nb+a+b}{b-a}\right]-\left[\dfrac{2na+a+b}{b-a}\right]$

$\Rightarrow\ 2n\left[\dfrac{b-a}{b-a}\right] \qquad \Rightarrow\ 2n$

$\therefore$ L.H.S. = R.H.S.

15. (a) a, b, c be in H.P.

$\Rightarrow\ \dfrac{2}{b}=\dfrac{1}{a}+\dfrac{1}{c} \qquad \Rightarrow\ 2ac=ab+ac$

$\Rightarrow\ 2=\dfrac{b}{a}+\dfrac{b}{c} \qquad \Rightarrow\ \dfrac{b}{a}-1=-\left[\dfrac{b}{c}-1\right]$

(i) $\left[\dfrac{b+a}{b-a}+\dfrac{b+c}{b-c}\right]=2\ \Rightarrow\ \left[\dfrac{\dfrac{b}{a}+1}{\dfrac{b}{a}-1}+\dfrac{\dfrac{b}{c}+1}{\dfrac{b}{c}-1}\right]=2$

$\Rightarrow\ \left[-\dfrac{\left(\dfrac{b}{a}+1\right)}{\left(\dfrac{b}{c}-1\right)}+\dfrac{\left(\dfrac{b}{c}+1\right)}{\left(\dfrac{b}{c}-1\right)}\right]\Rightarrow\left[\dfrac{-\dfrac{b}{a}-1+\dfrac{b}{c}+1}{\left(\dfrac{b}{c}-1\right)}\right]$

$\Rightarrow$ L.H.S = R.H.S

(ii) $\left[\dfrac{1}{a}+\dfrac{1}{b}-\dfrac{1}{c}\right]\left[\dfrac{1}{b}+\dfrac{1}{c}-\dfrac{1}{a}\right]=\dfrac{4}{ac}-\dfrac{3}{b^2}=$ L.H.S.

$\Rightarrow\ -\dfrac{1}{a^2}+\dfrac{1}{b^2}-\dfrac{1}{c^2}+\dfrac{2}{ac}\ \Rightarrow\ \dfrac{1}{b^2}-\left[\dfrac{1}{a^2}+\dfrac{1}{c^2}+\dfrac{2}{ac}\right]+\dfrac{4}{ac}$

$\Rightarrow\ \dfrac{1}{b^2}-\left(\dfrac{1}{a}+\dfrac{1}{c}\right)^2+\dfrac{4}{ac}\ \Rightarrow\ \dfrac{1}{b^2}-\left(\dfrac{2}{b}\right)^2+\dfrac{1}{ac}\Rightarrow\dfrac{4}{ac}-\dfrac{3}{b^2}$

$\therefore$ L.H.S. = R.H.S.

(iii) $\dfrac{2(c+a-b)}{b}=\dfrac{b+c-a}{a}+\dfrac{(a+b-c)}{c}$

L.H.S. $=\left[\dfrac{1}{a}+\dfrac{1}{c}\right][c+a-b]$

$\Rightarrow\ \left[\dfrac{a+c}{ac}\right][(a-b)]$

$\Rightarrow\ \dfrac{\left[ac+a^2-ab+c^2+ac-bc\right]}{ac}$

$\Rightarrow\ \dfrac{a^2+c^2}{ac} \qquad [\because\ 2ac=ab+bc]$

R.H.S. $=\dfrac{bc+c^2-ac+a^2+ab-ac}{ac}$

$\Rightarrow\ \dfrac{a^2+c^2+bc+ab-2ac}{ac} \qquad [\because\ 2ac=ab+bc]$

$\Rightarrow\ \dfrac{a^2+c^2}{a+c} \qquad \therefore$ L.H.S. = R.H.S.

(iv) $\dfrac{2}{\left(\dfrac{1}{b}+\dfrac{1}{c+a}\right)}=\dfrac{1}{\dfrac{1}{a}+\dfrac{1}{b+c}}+\dfrac{1}{\dfrac{1}{c}+\dfrac{1}{a+b}}$

$\Rightarrow\ \dfrac{2b(c+a)}{a+b+c}=\dfrac{(b+c)a}{a+b+c}+\dfrac{c(a+b)}{a+b+c}$

$\Rightarrow\ 2b(c+a)=(b+c)\,a+c\,(a+b)$

$\Rightarrow\ 2ab+2ab \qquad [\because\ 2ac=ab+bc]$

$\Rightarrow\ 4ac=$ L.H.S.

$\Rightarrow\ ab+ac+ac+bc \qquad [\because\ 2ac=ab+bc]$

$\Rightarrow\ 2ac+2ac \qquad \Rightarrow 4ac$

$\therefore$ L.H.S. = R.H.S.

(b) $\dfrac{2}{c+a}=\dfrac{1}{b+c}+\dfrac{1}{a+b}\ \Rightarrow\ 2=\dfrac{c+a}{(b+c)}+\dfrac{(c+a)}{(a+b)}$

$\Rightarrow\ 2=\dfrac{a}{(b+c)}+\dfrac{c}{(a+b)}+\dfrac{c}{b+c}+\dfrac{a}{a+b}$

$\Rightarrow\ 1-\dfrac{c}{b+c}+1-\dfrac{a}{a+b}=\dfrac{a}{b+c}+\dfrac{c}{a+b}$

$\Rightarrow\ \dfrac{b}{b+c}+\dfrac{b}{a+b}=\dfrac{a}{b+c}+\dfrac{c}{a+b}$

$\Rightarrow\ b\left[\dfrac{1}{b+c}+\dfrac{1}{a+b}\right]=\dfrac{a}{b+c}+\dfrac{c}{a+b}$

$\Rightarrow\ b\left[\dfrac{2}{c+a}\right]=\dfrac{a}{b+c}+\dfrac{c}{a+b}\ \Rightarrow\ \dfrac{2b}{c+a}=\dfrac{a}{b+c}+\dfrac{c}{a+b}$

$\therefore$ Proved $\dfrac{b+c}{a},\dfrac{c+a}{b}$ and $\dfrac{a+b}{c}$ are in H.P.

TEXTUAL EXERCISE-7: (OBJECTIVE)

1. (c) a, b, c, d are in H.P.

Let a be $\dfrac{1}{x-y}$; b be $\dfrac{1}{x}$; c be $\dfrac{1}{x+y}$; d be $\dfrac{1}{x+2y}$

$\Rightarrow\ \dfrac{1}{(x-y)x}+\dfrac{1}{x(x+y)}+\dfrac{1}{(x+y)(x+2y)}$

$\Rightarrow \frac{1}{x}\times\left[\frac{2x}{(x-y)(x+y)}\right]+\frac{1}{(x+y)(x+2y)}$

$\Rightarrow \frac{1}{x+y}\left[\frac{2}{(x-y)}+\frac{1}{[(x+2y)]}\right]$

$\Rightarrow \frac{1}{x+y}\left[\frac{3x+3y}{(x-y)(x+2y)}\right]$

$\Rightarrow \frac{3}{(x-y)(x+2y)} \quad \Rightarrow 3ad$

2. **(a)** $\frac{2}{b}=\frac{1}{a}+\frac{1}{c} \quad \Rightarrow \quad \left(\frac{1}{b}+\frac{1}{c}-\frac{1}{a}\right)\left(\frac{1}{c}+\frac{1}{a}-\frac{1}{b}\right)$

$\Rightarrow \frac{1}{bc}+\frac{1}{c^2}-\frac{1}{ac}+\frac{1}{ab}+\frac{1}{ac}-\frac{1}{a^2}-\frac{1}{b^2}-\frac{1}{bc}+\frac{1}{ab}$

$\Rightarrow -\frac{1}{a^2}-\frac{1}{b^2}+\frac{2ab}{ab}+\frac{1}{c^2}$

$\Rightarrow -\frac{1}{b^2}-\frac{1}{a^2}+\frac{1}{c^2}+\frac{1}{a}\left[\frac{1}{a}+\frac{1}{c}\right]$

$\Rightarrow -\frac{1}{b^2}-\frac{1}{a^2}+\frac{1}{c^2}+\frac{1}{a^2}+\frac{1}{ac}$

$\Rightarrow -\frac{1}{b^2}+\frac{2}{bc}$

3. **(b)** $H_n=1+\frac{1}{2}+...+\frac{1}{n} \quad \Rightarrow \quad 1+\frac{3}{2}+\frac{5}{3}+....+\frac{2n-1}{n}$

$\Rightarrow 1+2-\frac{1}{2}+2-\frac{1}{3}+...+2-\frac{1}{n}$

$\Rightarrow 2(n-1)+2-1\left[1+\frac{1}{2}+\frac{1}{3}+...+\frac{1}{n}\right]$

$\Rightarrow 2^n - H^n$

4. **(a)** $y = 0.272727.....$

$100y = 27.2727$

$99y = 27 \quad \Rightarrow \quad \frac{27}{99}$

Similarly, $p = 0.727272.......$

$100p = 72.7272.....$

$99p = 72 \quad \Rightarrow \quad \frac{72}{99}$

$\frac{99}{27},\frac{1}{x},\frac{99}{72}$ are in A.P. (Given)

$\Rightarrow \frac{1}{x}=\frac{1}{2}\left(\frac{99}{27}+\frac{99}{72}\right) \quad \Rightarrow \quad x=2\left(\frac{27}{99}+\frac{72}{99}\right)$

[∵ Harmonic mean of two rational is rational.]

$\Rightarrow$ x is rational

TEXTUAL EXERCISE–8: (SUBJECTIVE)

1. **(a)** $S_\infty=1+\frac{3}{2}+\frac{5}{2^2}+\frac{7}{2^5}+... \quad \Rightarrow \frac{S_\infty}{2}=0+\frac{1}{2}+\frac{3}{2^2}+\frac{5}{2^3}+...$

Subtracting, we get $\frac{S_n}{2}=1+1+\frac{1}{2}+\frac{1}{2^2}+\frac{1}{2^3}+...$

$\Rightarrow S_n=1+2\left[\frac{1}{2}+\frac{1}{2^2}+\frac{1}{3^3}+...\right]$; which is a G.P. with infinite number of terms and $|r| < 1$

$\Rightarrow S_n=1+2\left[\frac{\frac{1}{2}}{1-\frac{1}{2}}\right] \quad \Rightarrow S_n = 6$

(b) $S_n=1+\frac{2}{3}+\frac{1}{3}+\frac{4}{27}+.....$

Which can be written as : $S_n=1+\frac{2}{3}+\frac{3}{9}+\frac{4}{27}+...$

$\Rightarrow \frac{S_n}{3}=0+\frac{1}{3}+\frac{2}{9}+\frac{3}{27}+..$

$\Rightarrow \frac{2S_n}{3}=1+\frac{1}{3}+\frac{1}{9}+\frac{1}{3^3}+\frac{1}{3^4}+..$

$\Rightarrow \frac{2}{3}S_n=\frac{1}{1-\frac{1}{3}} \quad \Rightarrow \quad S_n=\frac{3}{2}\left(\frac{3}{2}\right)=\frac{9}{4}$

(c) $3+\frac{5}{4}+\frac{7}{4^2}+\frac{9}{4^3}+.. \quad \Rightarrow \quad S_n=3+\frac{5}{4}+\frac{7}{4^2}+\frac{9}{4^3}+...$

$\Rightarrow \frac{S_n}{4}=0+\frac{3}{4}+\frac{5}{4^2}+\frac{7}{4^3}+\frac{9}{4^4}+...$

Subtracting, we get $\frac{3S_n}{4}=3+2\left[\frac{1}{4}+\frac{1}{4^2}+\frac{1}{4^3}+..\right]$

$\Rightarrow \frac{3S_n}{4}=3+2\left[\frac{\frac{1}{4}}{1-\frac{1}{4}}\right]$

$\Rightarrow \frac{3}{4}S_n=\frac{11}{3} \quad \Rightarrow \quad S_n=\frac{44}{9}$

(d) $1-\frac{3}{2}+\frac{5}{4}-\frac{7}{8}+...$

$\Rightarrow S_n=1-\frac{3}{2}+\frac{5}{4}-\frac{7}{8}+..$ and $\frac{S_n}{2}=\frac{1}{2}-\frac{3}{4}+\frac{5}{8}+..$

Adding both, we get $\frac{3S_n}{2}=\frac{2}{4}-\frac{2}{8}+\frac{2}{16}..$

$\Rightarrow \frac{3S_n}{2}=2\left[\frac{1}{4}-\frac{1}{8}+\frac{1}{16}..\right]$

$\Rightarrow \frac{3S_n}{2}=2\left[\frac{\frac{1}{4}}{1+\frac{1}{2}}\right]$

$\Rightarrow \frac{\frac{1}{2}}{\frac{3}{2}}=\frac{1}{3} \quad S_n=\frac{2}{9}$

(e) $S_n=1-\frac{2}{3}+\frac{3}{3^2}-\frac{4}{3^3}+\frac{5}{3^4}-...$

$\Rightarrow \frac{S_n}{3}=0+\frac{1}{3}-\frac{2}{3^2}+\frac{3}{3^3}-\frac{4}{3^4}+..$

$\Rightarrow \frac{4S_n}{3}=1-\frac{1}{3}+\frac{1}{3^2}-\frac{1}{3^3}+\frac{1}{3^4}+..$

$\Rightarrow \frac{4S_n}{3}=1-\left[\frac{1}{3}-\frac{1}{3^2}+\frac{1}{3^3}-\frac{1}{3^4}+..\right]$

$\Rightarrow \quad \frac{4S_n}{3} = 1 - \left[\frac{\frac{1}{3}}{1+\frac{1}{3}}\right] = 1 - \frac{1}{4}$

$\Rightarrow \quad S_n = \frac{9}{16}$

2. (a) $S = 1 + 3x + 5x^2 + 7x^3 + \ldots..$

$\Rightarrow xS = x + 3x^2 + 5x^3 + \ldots.$

Subtracting, we get $(1-x)S_n = 1 + 2x + 2x^2 + \ldots. -x.T_n$

$\Rightarrow (1-x)S_n = 1 + 2\left[\frac{x(1-x^{n-1})}{1-x}\right] - (2n-1)x^0$

$\Rightarrow \quad = \quad + \frac{2x(1 \quad x \quad)}{(1-x)^2} - \frac{(2n \quad 1)x}{(1-x)^2}$

For $n \to \infty$

$S_n = \frac{1+2x+2x^2+2x^3+\ldots}{1-x} = \frac{1+2\left(\frac{x}{1-x}\right)}{1-x}$

$\Rightarrow \quad S_n = \frac{1}{1-x} + \frac{2x}{(1-x)^2}$

(b) $S = 1 + 2x + 3x^2 + 4x^3 + \ldots.$

$xS = x + 2x^2 + 3x^3 + \ldots.$

$(1-x)S = 1 + x + x^2 + x^3 + \ldots.. - nx^n = 1 + x\frac{(1-x^{n-1})}{(1-x)} - nx^n$

$\Rightarrow S = \frac{1}{1-x} + \frac{x(1-x^{n-1})}{(1-x)^2} - \frac{nx^n}{(1-x)}$

For $n \to \infty \qquad \Rightarrow S_n \frac{1}{1-x} + \frac{x}{(1-x)^2}$

(c) $2^{1/4}, 4^{1/8}, 8^{1/6}, 16^{1/32}$

Which can be written as $2^{1/4} . 2^{1/4} . 2^{3/16} . 2^{4/32}$

$\Rightarrow \quad 2^{\left(\frac{1}{4}+\frac{2}{8}+\frac{3}{16}+\frac{4}{32}+\ldots\right)} \qquad \Rightarrow \quad S_n = \frac{1}{4} + \frac{2}{8} + \frac{3}{16} + \frac{4}{32} + \ldots$

$\frac{S_n}{2} = \frac{1}{8} + \frac{2}{16} + \frac{3}{32} + ..$

$\Rightarrow \quad \frac{S_n}{2} = \frac{1}{4} + \frac{1}{8} + \frac{1}{16} + \frac{1}{32} + ..$

$\Rightarrow \quad \frac{S_n}{2} = \frac{1}{2^2} + \frac{1}{2^3} + \frac{1}{2^4} + \frac{1}{2^5} + \ldots$

$\Rightarrow \quad \frac{S_n}{2} = \frac{\frac{1}{4}}{1-\frac{1}{2}} = \frac{1}{2} \qquad \Rightarrow \quad S_n = 1$

$\Rightarrow \quad 2^{S_n} = 2 \qquad \Rightarrow \quad 2$

3. $S_\infty = 1 + 2r + 3r^2 + 4r^3 + \ldots$

$\Rightarrow \quad rS_\infty = r + 2r^2 + 3r^3 + \ldots..$

$\Rightarrow \quad S_\infty(1-r) = 1 + r + r^2 + \ldots$

$\Rightarrow \quad \frac{9}{16} = \frac{1}{(1-r)^2} \qquad \Rightarrow \quad (1-r)^2 = \frac{16}{9}$

$\Rightarrow \quad r = -1/3$

4. $S_\infty = 1 + (1+d)\frac{1}{3} + (1+2d)\frac{1}{9} + \ldots.$

$\Rightarrow \quad \frac{S_\infty}{3} = \frac{1}{3} + (1+d)\frac{1}{9} + \ldots$

$\Rightarrow \quad \frac{2S_\infty}{3} = 1 + \frac{d}{3} + \frac{d}{3^2} + \frac{d}{3^3} + ..$

$\Rightarrow \quad \frac{2S_\infty}{3} = 1 + d\left(\frac{\frac{1}{3}}{\frac{2}{3}}\right) \qquad \Rightarrow \quad \frac{2S_\infty}{3} = 1 + \frac{d}{2}$

$\Rightarrow \quad \frac{3}{8} - 1 = \frac{d}{2} \qquad \Rightarrow \quad d = \frac{-5}{8} \times 2 = \frac{-5}{4}$

5. (a) $S_n = 1 + \frac{4}{5} + \frac{7}{5^2} + \frac{10}{5^3} + ..$

$\Rightarrow \quad \frac{S_n}{5} = \frac{1}{5} + \frac{4}{5^2} + \frac{7}{5^3} + \ldots$

Subtracting, we get

$\frac{4S_n}{5} = 1 + \frac{3}{5} + \frac{3}{5^2} + \frac{3}{5^3} + \ldots \frac{-(3n-2)}{5^n}$

$\Rightarrow \quad \frac{4S_n}{5} = 1 + 3\left[\frac{\frac{1}{5}\left(1-\left(\frac{1}{5}\right)\right)^{n-1}}{\frac{4}{5}}\right] + \frac{2-3n}{5^n}$

$\Rightarrow \quad \frac{4S_n}{5} = 1 + 3\left[\frac{1}{4}\left[1 - \frac{1}{5^{n-1}}\right]\right] + \frac{2-3n}{5^n}$

$\Rightarrow \quad \frac{4S_n}{5} = 1 + \frac{3}{4} - \frac{3}{4.5^{n-1}} + \frac{2-3n}{5^n}$

$\Rightarrow \quad \frac{4S_n}{5} = \frac{7}{4} - \frac{3}{4.5^{n-1}} + \frac{2-3n}{5^n}$

$\Rightarrow \quad S_n = \frac{35}{16} - \frac{15}{16.5^{n-1}} + \frac{10-5.3n}{4.5^n} = \frac{35}{16} - \frac{(15-8+12n)}{16.5^{n-1}}$

$= \frac{35}{16} - \frac{(7+12n)}{16.5^{n-1}}$

(b) $S_n = 1 + \frac{2}{5} + \frac{3}{5^2} + \frac{4}{5^3} + \ldots$

$\Rightarrow \quad \frac{S_n}{5} = \frac{1}{5} + \frac{2}{5^2} + \frac{3}{5^3} + \ldots$

$\Rightarrow \quad \frac{4S_n}{5} = 1 + \frac{1}{5} + \frac{1}{5^2} + \frac{1}{5^3} + \ldots - \frac{n}{5^n}$

$\Rightarrow \quad \frac{4S_n}{5} = 1 + \left[\frac{\frac{1}{5}\left(1-\left(\frac{1}{5}\right)\right)^{n-1}}{\frac{4}{5}}\right] - \frac{n}{5^n}$

$\Rightarrow \quad \frac{4S_n}{5} = \frac{5}{4} - \frac{1}{4.5^{n-1}} - \frac{n}{5^n}$

$\Rightarrow \quad S_n = \frac{25}{16} - \frac{1}{16.5^{n-2}} - \frac{n}{4.5^{n-1}} = \frac{25}{16} - \frac{(4n+5)}{16.5^{n-1}}$

(c) $S_n = 1 + \frac{2}{3} + \frac{3}{3^2} + \frac{4}{3^3} + \ldots$

$\Rightarrow \quad \frac{S_n}{3} = \frac{1}{3} + \frac{2}{3^2} + \frac{3}{3^2} + \frac{4}{3^4}$

$\Rightarrow \quad \frac{2S_n}{3} = 1 + \frac{1}{3} + \frac{1}{3^2} + \ldots \frac{1}{3^{n-1}} - \frac{n}{3^n}$

$\Rightarrow \frac{2S_n}{3} = \frac{\left(1-\left(\frac{1}{3}\right)^n\right)}{\frac{2}{3}} - \frac{n}{3^n}$

$\Rightarrow S_n = \frac{9}{4} - \frac{9}{4.3} - \frac{3n}{2.3^n} = \frac{9}{4} - \frac{(2n+3)}{4.3^{n-1}}$

6. Given $\log_a x$, $\log_a y$, $\log_a z$ are in A.P.

$\Rightarrow 2\log_a y = \log_a x + \log_a z = \log_a(xz)$

$\Rightarrow \log_a(y^2) = \log_a(xz)$

$\Rightarrow y^2 = xz$

$\Rightarrow$ x, y, z form a geometric

7. a, ax, ax^2

p^{th} term of a G.P.= $a.x^{p-1}$

$q^{th} = a.x^{q-1}$

$r^{th} = ax^{r-1}$

By the question $(ax^{q-1})^2 = ax^{10-1} \times ax^{r-1}$

$= a^2.x^{2(q-1)} = a^2.x^{p+r-2} \quad \Rightarrow p + r = 29$

$\Rightarrow$ p, q, r are in A.P.

8. (a) By the questions: $\frac{a(r^4-1)}{r-1} = 60$ (i)

$\Rightarrow \frac{a+ar^3}{2} = 18 \quad \Rightarrow \frac{a(1+r^3)}{2} = 18$

$\Rightarrow a(1 + r^3) = 36$ (ii)

$\Rightarrow \frac{(r^4-1)}{(r-1)(r^3+1)} = \frac{60}{36} \quad \Rightarrow \frac{r^2+1}{r^2+r+1} = \frac{5}{3}$

$\Rightarrow 3r^2 + 3 = 5r^2 + 5r + 5$

$\Rightarrow 2r^2 + 5r + 2 = 0 \quad \Rightarrow 2r^2 + 4r + r + 2 = 0$

$\Rightarrow (2r + 1)(r + 2) = 0 \quad \Rightarrow r = -1/2$ or $r = 2$

Putting value of r on (ii), we get $\frac{a}{2}\left(1+\frac{1}{8}\right) = 18$ or $\frac{a}{2}(1+0) = 18$

$\Rightarrow$ a = 32 or a = 4

$\therefore$ Numbers are 4, 8, 16, 32

(b) Let us assume that the numbers are x and $4x$

By the questions, A.M. = $5x/2$; G.M. = $2x$; AM – G.M. = 0

$\Rightarrow 5x - 4x = 16 \quad \Rightarrow x = 16$

$\Rightarrow$ Number are 16, 64

9. Let the numbers be $a - d, a, a + d$

$\Rightarrow 3a = 21 \quad \Rightarrow a = 7$

$\Rightarrow (7 - 1)^2 = (7 - d)(7 + d + 1)$

$\Rightarrow 36 = 56 - 8d + 7d - d^2$

$\Rightarrow d^2 + d - 20 = 0 \quad \Rightarrow d^2 + 5d - 4d - 20 = 0$

$\Rightarrow d(d + 5) - 4(d + 5) = 0$

$\Rightarrow (d + 5)(d - 4) = 0 \quad \Rightarrow d = 4$ or -5

$\Rightarrow$ The numbers are 3, 7, 11 or 12, 7, 2

10. (a) Let d be the common difference $b = a + (n - 2)d$

$\Rightarrow b - a = (n - 2)d$ (i)

$c = a + (n - 1)d$

$\Rightarrow c - a = (n - 1)d$ (ii)

Solving (i) and (ii), we get $(b-a) = \frac{(n-2)(c-a)}{n-1}$

$\Rightarrow n(b - a) - (b - a) = n(c - a) - 2(c - a)$

$\Rightarrow n[\,b - a - c + a\,] = b - a - 2c + 2a$

$\Rightarrow n = \frac{b+a-2c}{b-c}$

Sum $= \frac{n}{2}[a+c] = \frac{b+a-2c}{2(b-c)}.(a+c)$

$= \frac{(2c-b-a)(a+c)}{2(c-b)}$

(b) $(b + c), (c + a), (a + b)$ are in H.P.

$\Rightarrow \frac{2}{c+a} = \frac{1}{a+b} + \frac{1}{b+c}$

$\Rightarrow 2(b + c)(a + b) = (c + a)(a + b) + (c + a)(b + c)$

$\Rightarrow 2(ab + ac + bc) + 2b^2 = 2(ac + bc + ab) + a^2 + ac$

$\Rightarrow 2b^2 = a^2 + c^2$

$\Rightarrow a^2, b^2, c^2$ in A.P.

(c) $a_p = a + (p - 1)d$

$a_q = a + (q - 1)d$

$a_r = a + (r - 1)d$

Since they are in G.P.

$\Rightarrow [a + (q - 1)d]^2 = (a + (p - 1)d)(a + (r - 1)d)$

$\Rightarrow a^2 + (q + 1)^2d^2 + 2ad(q - 1) = a^2 + ad(r - 1) + ad(p - 1) + (p - 1)(r - 1)d^2$

$= (q - 1)^2 d^2 + 2ad(q - 1) = ad(p + r - 2) + d^2(p - 1)(r - 1)$

$\Rightarrow ad(2q - 2 - p + r + 2) = d^2(pr - p - r + 1 - q^2 + 1 + 2q)$

$\Rightarrow ad(2q - p - r) = d^2(-q^2 - p + pr + 2q) - r$

$\Rightarrow d = \frac{a(2q-p-r)}{(-q^2-p-r+2q+pr)}$

Common ratio $= \frac{a_q}{q_p} = \frac{a+(q-1)d}{a+(p-1)d}$ (i)

Putting value of d from (i), we get

$\frac{1+\frac{(q-1)(2q-p-r)}{(pr+2q-p-r-q^2)}}{1+\frac{(p-1)(2q-p-r)}{(pr+2q-p-r-q^2)}}$

$\Rightarrow \frac{q^2-pq-qr+pr}{-(p-q)^2} \quad \Rightarrow \frac{q(q-p)-r(q-p)}{(q-p)(p-q)}$

$\Rightarrow \frac{(p-q)(r-q)}{(p-q)(q-p)} \quad \Rightarrow \frac{(r-q)}{(q-p)}$

11. Let a and be the two numbers $A_1 = a + \frac{(b-a)}{3} = \frac{2a+b}{3}$;

$A_2 = a + \frac{2(b-a)}{3} = \frac{a+2b}{3}$; $G_1 = a\left(\frac{b}{a}\right)^{1/3} \Rightarrow a^{2/3}.b^{1/3}$;

$G_2 = a^{1/3}.b^{2/3}$

Similarly, $\frac{1}{H_1} = \frac{1}{a} + \frac{(a-b)}{3ab} = \frac{2b+a}{3ab}$;

$\frac{1}{H_2} = \frac{1}{a} + \frac{2(a-b)}{3ab} = \frac{b+2a}{3ab}$

L.H.S. $= \frac{G_1G_2}{H_1H_2}$

Using value from above: $\dfrac{ab}{\left(\dfrac{3ab}{2b+a}\right)\left(\dfrac{3ab}{2a+b}\right)}$

$= \dfrac{(2b+a)(2a+b)}{9ab}$

R.H.S. $= \dfrac{A_1 + A_2}{H_1 + H_2} \Rightarrow \dfrac{\dfrac{2a+b}{3} + \dfrac{a+2b}{3}}{\dfrac{3ab}{a+2b} + \dfrac{3ab}{2a+b}}$

$\Rightarrow \dfrac{(a+b)(2a+b)(2b+a)}{9ab\,(a+b)}$

$\Rightarrow \dfrac{(2b+a)(2a+b)}{9ab}$

L.H.S = R.H.S

12. (a) p^{th}, q^{th}, r^{th} and s^{th} terms of A.P. can be written as :
$a_p = a + (p-1)d$; $a_q = a + (q-1)d$; $a_r = a + (r-1)d$; $a_s = a + (s-1)d$

By the question a_p, a_q, a_r, a_s are in G.P.

Let us compare this G. P. with x, xr, xr^2, xr^3

$\Rightarrow a_p - a_q = (p-q)d$

$\Rightarrow x(1-x) = (p-q)d$

$\Rightarrow p - q = \dfrac{x(1-r)}{d}$ (i)

Similarly, $a_q - a_r = (q-r)d$

$\Rightarrow q - r = \dfrac{rx(1-r)}{d}$ (ii)

$\Rightarrow r - s = \dfrac{r^2x(1-r)}{d}$ (iii)

Clearly the terms obtained by the equation (i), (ii), (iii) haves $\dfrac{x(1-r)}{d}, \dfrac{rx(1-r)}{d}, \dfrac{r^2x(1-r)}{d}$ is a G.P.

(b) Given a, b, c are in G.P.

$\Rightarrow a, ar, ar^2$ can be written as this $(a)^{1/x} = (ar)^{1/y} = (ar^2)^{1/2} = k$

$\Rightarrow a = k^x \qquad \Rightarrow ar = k^y$

$\Rightarrow ar^2 = k^z$

$\Rightarrow x = \log_k a;\ y = \log_k ar;\ z = \log_k ar^2$

$\Rightarrow x + z = \log_k a + \log_k ar^2 = \log_k (ar)^2 = 2\log_k(ar)$

$\Rightarrow y = \log_k(ar)$

Clearly, $\dfrac{x+z}{2} = y$

$\Rightarrow x, y, z$ are in A.P.

TEXTUAL EXERCISE-8: (OBJECTIVE)

1. (a) Given a, b, c are in A.P.

$2b = a + c$

$\Rightarrow b + \dfrac{1}{ca}$

$\Rightarrow \dfrac{c+a}{2} + \dfrac{1}{2b}\left(\dfrac{c+a}{ac}\right) \dfrac{1}{2}\left[(a+c) + \dfrac{1}{b}\left(\dfrac{1}{a} + \dfrac{1}{c}\right)\right]$

$\Rightarrow \dfrac{1}{2}\left[(a+c) + \dfrac{1}{ab} + \dfrac{1}{bc}\right] \Rightarrow \dfrac{1}{2}\left[\left(a + \dfrac{1}{bc}\right) + \left(c + \dfrac{1}{ab}\right)\right]$

$\Rightarrow$ These terms are in A.P.

2. (a) $\dfrac{a+b}{1-ab}, b, \dfrac{b+c}{1-bc}$ are in A.P.

$\Rightarrow 2b = \dfrac{a+b}{a-ab} + \dfrac{b+c}{1-bc}$

$\Rightarrow 2b = \dfrac{(a+b)(1-bc) + (b+c)(1-ab)}{1 - ab - bc + ab^2c}$

$\Rightarrow 2b - 2ab^2 - 2b^2c + 2ab^3c = a + b - abc - b^2c + b + c - ab^2 - abc$

$\Rightarrow 2ab^3c + 2a\pi + 2a\pi = b^2c + ab^2 + a + c$

$\Rightarrow 2bca = a + c$

$\Rightarrow 2b = \dfrac{1}{a} + \dfrac{1}{c} \qquad \Rightarrow a^{-1}, b, c^{-1}$ are in A.P.

3. (b) By the questions, $y^2 = xz \quad \Rightarrow 2y = \dfrac{x+3z}{z}$

Let r be the common ratio

$\Rightarrow 4xr = x + 3xr^2 \qquad \Rightarrow 3r^2 - 4r + 1 = 0$

$\Rightarrow (3r-1)(r-1) \qquad \Rightarrow r = 1/3$ or 1

4. (a) By the questions $2b = a + c$

$\Rightarrow 3^{2b} = 3^{a+5} \qquad \Rightarrow (3b)^2 = 3^a . 3^c$

$\Rightarrow 3^a, 3^b\ 3^c$ are in G.P.

5. (c) $a - b, ax - by, ax^2 - by^2$ are in G.P.

$\Rightarrow (ax - by)^2 = (a-b)(ax^2 - by^2)$

$\Rightarrow a^2x^2 + b^2y^2 = 2axby = a^2x^2 - abx^2 - aby^2 + b^2y^2$

$\Rightarrow -2abxy = -abx^2 - y^2ab$

$\Rightarrow 2ab = x^2 + y^2$

$\Rightarrow (x-y)^2 = 0 \qquad \Rightarrow x = y$

$\Rightarrow x, x, \left(\dfrac{a-b}{a-b}\right)^x \qquad \Rightarrow x, x, x$

It is an A.P. with zero common difference and H.P. with common ratio.

6. (a) By the questions $2b = a + c$ and $ac = m^2b^2$

$\Rightarrow m^2 = \dfrac{ac}{b^2} \qquad \Rightarrow m^2b = \dfrac{ac}{b^2}.b$

$\Rightarrow 2\left[\dfrac{ac}{a+c}\right] = m^2\,b$ is the H.P. of a and c

$\Rightarrow a_1, m^2b, c$ are in H.P.

7. (c) By the questions $b^2 = ac$

Let $b = ar$ and $c = ar^2$

$\Rightarrow a + b, b + b, b + c$

$\Rightarrow a(1+r) + 2ar, ar(r+1)$

$\Rightarrow \dfrac{1}{a(1+r)} + \dfrac{1}{a^r(r+1)} = \dfrac{r+1}{ar(1+r)} = \dfrac{1}{ar} = \dfrac{2}{2ar}$

$\Rightarrow \dfrac{1}{a(1+r)}, \dfrac{1}{2ar}, \dfrac{1}{ar(r+1)}$ are in A.P

$\Rightarrow a(1+r), 2ar, ar(r+1)$ are in H.P.

8. (c) x, y, z are in G.P.

$\Rightarrow y^2 = xz$

Taking ℓnx operator

$\Rightarrow 2\ell ny = \ell nx + \ell nz$

$\Rightarrow \ell ny = \dfrac{\ell nx + \ell nz}{2}$

$\Rightarrow$ $\ell nx, \ell ny, \ell nz$ are in A.P.

$\Rightarrow$ $1 + \ell nx, 1 + \ell ny, 1 + \ell nz$ are also A.P.

$\Rightarrow$ $\frac{1}{1+\ell nx}, \frac{1}{1+\ell ny}, \frac{1}{1+\ell nz}$ are H,P,

9. (d) By the questions $2b = a + c$, $b^4 = a^2.c^2$; $a + b + c = 3/2$

$\Rightarrow$ $b + 2b = 3/2$ $\quad 3b = 3/2$

$\Rightarrow$ $b = 1/2$

$\Rightarrow$ $a + c = 1$ $\quad \Rightarrow a^2c^2 = 1/16$

$\Rightarrow$ $ac = \pm 1/4$

$\Rightarrow$ $a + \frac{1}{4a} = 1$ or $a - \frac{1}{4a} = 1$

$\Rightarrow$ $4a^2 - 4a + 1 = 0$ or $4a^2 - 4a - 1 = 0$

$\Rightarrow$ $a = 1/2$ or $a = 1/2 - \sqrt{2}/2$

$\Rightarrow$ $a - 1/2 - \sqrt{2}/2$

10. (a) $1 - 3x + 5x^2 - 7x^3 + \ldots. \alpha$

$\Rightarrow$ $S = 1 - 3x + 5x^2 - 7x^3 + \ldots.$

$\Rightarrow$ $-xs = -x + 3x^2 - 5x^3$

$\Rightarrow$ $(1 + x)S = 1 - 2x + 2x^2 - 2x^3 \ldots$

$\Rightarrow$ $S = \frac{1-x}{(1+x)^2}$

11. (a) $S = 3 + \frac{(3+d)}{4} + \frac{(3+2d)}{4^2} + \ldots$

$\Rightarrow$ $\frac{S}{4} = \frac{3}{4} + \frac{(3+d)}{4^2} + \frac{(3+2d)}{4^3} + \ldots$

Subtracting the above equations

$\frac{3S}{4} = 3 + \frac{d}{4} + \frac{d}{4^2} + \frac{d}{4^3} + \ldots.\infty$

$\Rightarrow$ $\frac{3S}{4} = 3 + d\left[\frac{1}{4} + \frac{1}{4^2} + \ldots\right]$

$\Rightarrow$ $\frac{3S}{4} = 3 + d\left[\frac{\frac{1}{4}}{1-\frac{1}{4}}\right]$ $\quad \Rightarrow \frac{3S}{4} = 3 + \frac{d}{3}$

Given $S = 8$

$\Rightarrow$ $6 = 3 + d/3$ $\quad 3 = d/3$

$\Rightarrow$ $d = 9$

12. (b) $S = 0.2 + 0.004 + 0.0006 + \ldots$

$\Rightarrow$ $S = \frac{2}{10} + \frac{4}{1000} + \frac{6}{10000} + \ldots$

$\Rightarrow$ $\frac{S}{100} = \frac{2}{1000} + \frac{4}{100000} + \ldots$

Subtracting the above two equations, we get

$\frac{99S}{1000} = \frac{2}{10} + \frac{2}{1000} + \frac{2}{100000} + \ldots$

$\Rightarrow$ $\frac{99S}{100} = \frac{\frac{2}{10}}{1-\frac{1}{100}}$ $\quad \frac{99S}{100} = \frac{2}{10} \times \frac{100}{99}$ $\quad S = \frac{2600}{9801}$

13. (a) $4 \times$ G.M. $= 5$ H.M. $\quad \Rightarrow 4\sqrt{ab} = 5 \times \frac{2ab}{a+b}$

$\Rightarrow$ $a + b = 5/2\ \sqrt{ab}$

$\Rightarrow$ $a^2 + b^2 + 2ab = \frac{25}{4}(ab)$

$\Rightarrow$ $4a^2 + 4b^2 + 8ab = 25ab$

$\Rightarrow$ $4a^2 - 17ab - 4b^2 = 0$

$\Rightarrow$ $(4a - b)(a - 4b) = 0 \Rightarrow a = b/4$ or $4b$

$\because$ $a = b/a$ not possible, as $a > b$ $a = 4b$

14. (d) Let x be the first term and d be the common difference of A.P.

If $(2n - 1)^{th}$ term of all A.P., G.P., H.P. is p

$\Rightarrow$ $p = x + 2(n - 1)d$

$\Rightarrow$ $d = \frac{p-x}{2(n-1)}$ (n^{th} term of A.P. $= a$)

$\Rightarrow$ $x + (n - 1)d = a$ $\quad \Rightarrow x + \frac{p-x}{2} = a$

$\Rightarrow$ $a = \frac{p+x}{2}$ (i)

Similarly for G.P.

$P = x \,.\, r^{2(n-1)}$ $\quad \Rightarrow r = \left(\frac{p}{x}\right)^{\frac{1}{2(n-1)}}$

$\Rightarrow$ $b = x.r^{n-1} = x.\left(\frac{p}{x}\right)^{\frac{1}{2}} = \sqrt{px}$ (ii)

For H.P.; $\quad c = \frac{2px}{p+x}$ (iii)

$\therefore$ From (i), (ii) and (iii), we get $b^2 = ac$

TEXTUAL EXERCISE–9: (SUBJECTIVE)

1. Given a, b, c are positive numbers

$\Rightarrow$ a^3, b^3, c^3 also positive reals

$\Rightarrow$ $\frac{a^3+b^3+c^3}{3} \geq \left(a^3b^3c^3\right)^{1/3}$

$\Rightarrow$ $a^3 + b^3 + c^3 \geq 3abc$

2. a, b, c are positive real

By A.M. G.M. inequality

$(a + b)(b + c)(c + a) \geq 8\,abc$ (i)

Or without the loss of generality $(p + q)(q + r)(r + p) \geq 8pqr$

Let $p + q = 2a$; $q + r = 2b$; $r + p = 2c$

Putting these values in (i), $abc \geq (a + b - c)(b + c - a)(a + c - b)$

3. $\frac{b^3+c^3}{b+c} + \frac{c^3+a^3}{c+a} + \frac{a^3+b^3}{a+b}$

Since a, b, c are distinct positive real $\frac{a^2+b^2}{2} > ab$

$\Rightarrow$ $a^2 + b^2 > 2ab$ (i)

Similarly

$\Rightarrow$ $b^2 + c^2 < 2ac$ (ii)

$\Rightarrow$ $c^2 + a^2 < ac$ (iii)

Adding (i), (ii) and (iii), we get $2(a^2 + b^2 + c^2) > 2(ab + bc + ca)$

Further, this can be written as $2(a^2 + b^2 + c^2) - ab - bc - ca > ab + bc + ca$

$\Rightarrow$ $a^2 + b^2 - ab + b^2 + c^2 - bc + c^2 + a^2 - ca > ab + bc + ca$

$\Rightarrow$ $\frac{a^3+b^3}{a+b} + \frac{b^3+c^3}{b+c} + \frac{c^3+a^3}{c+a} > ab + bc + ca$

4. (a) $(a + b + c)(ab + bc + ca) \geq 9abc$

a, b, c are positive real

Hence by AM-GM $\frac{a+b+c}{3} \geq (abc)^{1/3}$ (i)

Similarly AM-GM on ab, bc, ca gives $\frac{ab+bc+ca}{3} \geq (a^2+b^2+c^2)^{1/3}$

$\Rightarrow$ $(ab+bc+ca) \geq 3(abc)^{2/3}$ (ii)

Multiplying (i) and (ii), we get $(a + b + c)(ab + bc + ca) \geq 9(abc)$

(b) $(x+y+z)\left[\frac{1}{x}+\frac{1}{y}+\frac{1}{z}\right] \geq 9$; Since x, y, z are positive real.

$\Rightarrow$ $\frac{x+y+z}{3} \geq (xyz)^{1/3}$

$\Rightarrow$ $x+y+z \geq 3(xyz)^{1/3}$ (i)

Similarly $\frac{1}{x}+\frac{1}{y},\frac{1}{z}$

$\Rightarrow$ $\frac{1}{x}+\frac{1}{y}+\frac{1}{z} \geq \left(\frac{1}{xyz}\right)^{1/3}$ (ii)

Multiplying equation (i) and (ii), we get $(x + y + z)\left(\frac{1}{x}+\frac{1}{y}+\frac{1}{z}\right) \geq 9$

(c) $\left[\frac{x}{a}+\frac{y}{b}+\frac{z}{c}\right]\left[\frac{a}{x}+\frac{b}{y}+\frac{c}{z}\right] \geq 9$; since x, a, y, b, z, c are positive real

$\Rightarrow$ $\frac{x}{a}+\frac{y}{b}+\frac{z}{c} \geq 3\left(\frac{xyz}{abc}\right)^{1/3}$

Similarly the other way $\frac{a}{x}+\frac{b}{y}+\frac{c}{z} \geq 3\left(\frac{abc}{xyz}\right)^{1/3}$

Multiplying the above two equations, we get $\left(\frac{x}{a}+\frac{y}{b}+\frac{z}{c}\right)\left\{\frac{a}{x}+\frac{b}{y}+\frac{c}{z}\right\} \geq 9$

(d) $(a + b)(b + c)(a + c) \geq 8abc$; since a, b, c are positive real

Applying A.M.-G.M. pair wise, we get

$a + b \leq 2ab$; $b + c \geq 2bc$; $a + c \geq 2ac$

Multiplying all, we get $(a + b)(b + c)(c + a) \geq 8abc$

5. $x + y + z = a$ (given), to prove $(a - x)(a - y)(a - z) \geq 8xyz$

Which is equivalent to $(y + z)(x + z)(z + y) \geq 8xyz$

Which has already been proceed is 4 – (d)

6. $(a + b + c)^3 \geq 27(a + b - c)(b + c - a)(a + c - b)$

By A.M. $\geq$ G.M., we get $\frac{(a+b-c)+(b+c-a)+(a+c-b)}{3}$

$> \{(a + b - c) + (b + c - a)(a + c + b)^{1/3}\}$

$\Rightarrow$ $(a + b + c) > 3\{(a + b + c)(b + c - a)(a + c + b)\}$

Taking cube of both sides $(a + b + c)3 \geq 27(a + b - c)(b + c - a)(c + a - b)$

7. To prove $\cot A.\cot B.\cot C \leq 1/3\sqrt{3}$

Applying A.M.-G.M. for $\tan A$, $\tan B$, $\tan C$

$\Rightarrow$ $\frac{\tan A+\tan B+\tan C}{3} \geq (\tan A.\tan B.\tan C)$

$\Rightarrow$ $(\tan A.\tan B.\tan C)^{2/3} \geq 3$

$\Rightarrow$ $\cot A.\cot B.\cot C \leq 1/3\sqrt{3}$

8. **(a)** If a, b, c are the sides of the triangle

Area of the triangle is given by

$\Delta = \sqrt{s(s-a)(s-b)(s-c)}$

Squaring both sides, we get $\Delta^2 = s(s - a)(s - b)(s - c)$

Applying AM-GM inequality on s, $s - a$, $i - b$, $s - c$

$\Rightarrow$ $(s(s - a)(s - b)(s - c)]^{1/4} \leq \frac{s+s-a+s-b+s-c}{4}$

$\Rightarrow$ $(\Delta)^{1/2} \leq s/2$

Squaring, we get $\Delta < s^2/4$

(b) By AM-GM inequality

$[(s-a)(s-b)(s-c)]^{1/3} \leq \frac{3s-(a+b+c)}{3}$

$\Rightarrow$ $[(s-a)(s-b)(s-c)]^{1/3} \leq \frac{s}{3}$

$\Rightarrow$ $s^{1/3}[(s-a)(s-b)(s-c)]^{1/3} \leq \frac{s^{4/3}}{3}$

$\Rightarrow$ $[s(s-a)(s-b)(s-c)] \leq \frac{s^4}{(3)^3}$

$\Rightarrow$ $\Delta^2 \leq \frac{s^4}{(3)^3}$ $\qquad \Rightarrow$ $\Delta \leq \frac{s^2}{3\sqrt{3}}$

9. Length of the rectangle $= \ell_1$ cm

Let x be the breadth of the rectangle area $= \ell_1 x$

$\therefore$ $\frac{\ell_1+x}{2} \geq (\ell x)^{1/2}$ $\qquad \Rightarrow$ $\frac{(\ell_1+x)^2}{4} \geq (\ell_1 x)$

For minimum area $\frac{(\ell_1+x)^2}{4} = \ell_1 x$

$\Rightarrow$ $\ell_1^2 + x^2 + 2\ell x = 4\ell x$ $\qquad \Rightarrow$ $\ell_1^2 + x^2 - 2\ell x = 0$

$\Rightarrow$ $(\ell_1 - x)^2 = 0$ $\qquad \Rightarrow$ $\ell_1 = x$

Also $2(\ell_1 + x) = \ell$ $\qquad \Rightarrow$ $4\ell_1 = \ell$

$\Rightarrow$ $\ell_1 = \ell/a = x$

Area maximum $= \frac{\ell}{4} \times \frac{\ell}{4} = \frac{\ell^2}{16}$ cm^2

10. Let ℓ be the length (cm) and b be the breadth of the rectangle.

By the questions $\ell b = 100$

Since ℓ and b are positive reals $\frac{\ell+b}{2} \geq (\ell b)^{1/2}$

$\Rightarrow$ $\ell + b \geq 2(\ell b)^{1/2}$ $\qquad \Rightarrow$ $2(\ell + b) \geq 4(\ell b)^{1/2}$

$\Rightarrow$ $2(\ell + b) \geq 40$ $\qquad \Rightarrow$ $p \geq 40$ cm

$\Rightarrow$ Minimum value of the perimeter for this rectangle is 40 cm^2

11. By the questions $4(\ell + b + h) = 12$ cm

$\Rightarrow$ $\ell + b + h = 3$cm

Volume of cube $= \ell bh$ cm^3

By AM-GM Inequality $\frac{\ell+b+h}{3} \geq (\ell bh)^{1/3}$

Volume will be maximum when $\ell = b$

$\Rightarrow$ $\frac{3}{3} \geq (\ell)$ $\qquad \Rightarrow$ $\ell \leq 1$

$\Rightarrow$ Maximum volume $= 1 \times 1 \times 1 = 1$ cm^3

Length = 1 cm; Breath = 1cm; Height = 1cm

12. Volume $= \ell bh = v$

Surface area $= 2(\ell b + bh + h\ell)$

By AM-GM inequity, we get $\frac{(\ell b+bh+h\ell)}{3} \geq \ell bh$

$\Rightarrow \ell b + bh + h\ell \geq 3v \quad \Rightarrow 2(\ell b + bh + h\ell) \geq 6v$

Surface area is minimum when $\ell b = bh = h\ell$

$\Rightarrow \ell b = b = h$

$\Rightarrow$ It is a cube if $u = 1000$ cm^3

Minimum surface area will be of a cube of edge $= 3\sqrt{1000} = 10cm$

Surface area = 2(300) = 600 cm^2

13. We can write $3x + 4y$ as $3\left[\frac{x}{2}+\frac{x}{2}\right]+4\left[\frac{y}{3}+\frac{y}{3}+\frac{y}{3}\right]$

Applying A.M-G.M. on this 5 numbers

$\Rightarrow \frac{3x+4y}{5} \geq \left(\frac{4^3x^2}{2^2}\cdot\frac{y^33^2}{3^3}\right)^{1/5}$

Given $x^2y^3 = 6$

$\Rightarrow \frac{3x+4y}{5} \geq \left(\frac{4^3}{2}\right)^{1/5} \quad \Rightarrow \frac{3x+4y}{5} \geq (32)^{1/5}$

$\Rightarrow 3x + 4y \geq 2 \times 5 = 10$

$\Rightarrow$ Minimum value of $3x + 4y$ is 10

14. $x + y = c$ (given)

$\Rightarrow \left[\frac{x}{2}+\frac{x}{2}\right]+\left[\frac{y}{3}+\frac{y}{3}+\frac{y}{3}\right] = c$

x and y being positive reals applying AM-GM

$\frac{\left[\frac{x}{2}+\frac{x}{2}\right]+\left[\frac{y}{3}+\frac{y}{3}+\frac{y}{3}\right]}{5} \geq \sqrt[5]{\frac{x^2}{4}\cdot\frac{y^3}{27}}$

$\Rightarrow \frac{x+y}{5} \geq \left[\frac{x^2}{4}\cdot\frac{y^3}{27}\right]^{1/5} \quad \Rightarrow \left[\frac{c}{5}\right](4.27)^{1/5} \geq \left[x^2y^3\right]^{1/5}$

Taking 5th power on both sides, we get

$\frac{(c)^5}{5^5}4.27 \geq x^2y^3 \quad \Rightarrow \frac{108c^5}{3125} \geq x^2y^3$

$\Rightarrow$ Maximum value of x^2y^3 is $\frac{108x^5}{3125}$

15. (a) $x(1 - x)$ (given)

Applying AM-GM on x and $1 - x$

$\Rightarrow \frac{x+1-x}{2} \geq (x(1-x))^{1/2}$

$\Rightarrow \frac{1}{2} \geq (x(1-x))^{1/2}$

Squaring both sides as they are positive $\frac{1}{4} \geq x(1-x)$

Maximum value of $x(1 - x) = 1/4$ at $x = 1 - x + x = 1/2$

(b) (i) Appling AM-GM inequality relation on x^3 and $2x$

$\Rightarrow x^3 + 2x \geq 2.\ (2x^4)^{1/2}$

$\Rightarrow x^3 + 2x \geq 2\sqrt{2}x^2$

Adding x^2 (always positive) to both sides of inequality $x^3 + 2x + x^2 \geq x^2\ (1 + 2\sqrt{2})$

$\Rightarrow \frac{x^3+x^2+2x}{x^2} \geq \left(1+2\sqrt{2}\right)$

$\Rightarrow$ Minimum value of $\frac{x^3+x^2+2x}{x^2}$ is $1 + 2\sqrt{2}$

(ii) $\frac{x^3+x+2}{x}; x > 0$

Consider 4 number x^2, x, 1

Applying AM-GM, we get $\frac{x^3+x+1+1}{4} \geq (x^4)^{1/4}$

$\Rightarrow x^2 + x + 2 \geq 4x \quad \Rightarrow \frac{x^3+x+2}{x} \geq 4$

$\Rightarrow$ Maximum value of $\frac{x^2+x+2}{x}$ is 4

(c) (i) Given $x + y + z = 10$

x, y, z are positive real

$\Rightarrow \frac{x+y+z}{3} \geq (xyz)^{1/3}$

By AM-GM inequality

$\Rightarrow \frac{10}{3} \geq (xyz)^{1/3}$

$\Rightarrow (xyz)_{max} = \frac{1000}{27}$ at $x = y = z = 10/3$

(ii) Consider $\frac{x}{2},\frac{x}{2},\frac{y}{3},\frac{y}{3},\frac{y}{3},z$ all of these are positive real

$\Rightarrow$ By A.M.-G.M. $\frac{x+y+z}{6} \geq \left(\frac{x^2y^3z}{4.27}\right)^{1/6}$

$\Rightarrow (x^2y^3z)_{max} = \frac{10^6.4.27}{6^6} = \frac{5^6-4.27}{3^6} = \frac{5^6.4}{27}$

16. (a) a, b, c are in H.P.

$\Rightarrow \frac{1}{a},\frac{1}{b},\frac{1}{c}$ are in A.P.

$\Rightarrow \frac{1}{a}+\frac{1}{c}=\frac{2}{b} \quad \Rightarrow b = \frac{2ac}{a+c}$

$\therefore$ A.M. $\geq$ G.M. > H.M.

Applying this inequality on a^n and c^n

$\Rightarrow \frac{a^n+c^n}{2} > (ac)^{n/2}$

Applying G.M. > H.M. on a, c

$\Rightarrow (ac)^{1/2} = \frac{2ac}{a+c} = b \quad \Rightarrow \quad a^n \quad c^n \quad 2.$

(b) a, b, c are in G.P.

$\Rightarrow b^2 = ac$

$\therefore \frac{a^n+c^n}{2} > (ac)^{n/2}$

Simply substituting, we get $ac = b^2$

$\Rightarrow \frac{a^n+c^n}{2} > b^n$

$\Rightarrow a^n + c^n > 2b^n$

TEXTUAL EXERCISE-9: (OBJECTIVE)

1. (a) $a + b + c = 3;\ a > 0,\ b > 0$

Consider the numbers $\frac{a}{2},\frac{a}{2},\frac{b}{3},\frac{b}{3},\frac{b}{3},\frac{c}{2},\frac{c}{2}$

By AM-GM $\frac{a+b+c}{7} \geq \left(\frac{a^2b^3c^2}{2^4.3^3}\right)^{1/7}$

Taking 7th power on both sides $\left(\frac{a+b+c}{7}\right)^7 \geq \frac{a^2b^3c^2}{2^4.3^3}$

Putting $a + b + c = 3$, we get $\frac{3^7}{7^7} \geq \frac{a^2b^3c^2}{2^4.3^3}$

$\Rightarrow \quad a^2b^3c^2 \leq \frac{3^{10}.2^4}{7^7}$

2. (c) $2\log_{100}a - \log_a 0.0001;\ a > 1$

$\Rightarrow \quad 2\log_{100} a - \log_a\left(\frac{1}{10000}\right)$

$\Rightarrow \quad 2\log_{100} a + \log_a(10)^4$

$\Rightarrow \quad \log_{100} a^2 + \log a(10)^4$

By A.M.-G.M.,

$$\frac{\log_{100} a^2 + \log a(10)^4}{2} \geq \left(2\log_{100} a.4\log_a 10\right)^{1/2}$$

$$\Rightarrow \quad \frac{\log_{100} a^2 + \log_a(10)^4}{2} \geq \left(2\frac{1}{2.\log_a 100}.4\log_a 10\right)^{1/2}$$

$\Rightarrow \quad \log_{100} a^2 + \log_a(10)^4 \geq 2(4)^{1/2}$

$\Rightarrow \quad \log_{100} a^2 + \log_a(10)^4 \geq 4$

3. (a) $x^{(\log y - \log z)} + y^{(\log z - \log x)} + z^{(\log x - \log y)}$ (given)

Consider the numbers $\frac{x^{\log y}}{x^{\log z}}, \frac{y^{\log z}}{y^{\log x}}, \frac{z^{\log x}}{z^{\log y}}$

Applying AM-GM

$$= \frac{x^{\log y - \log z} + y^{\log z - \log x} + z^{\log x - \log y}}{3} \geq \left(\frac{x^{\log y}}{x^{\log z}}.\frac{y^{\log z}}{y^{\log x}}.\frac{z^{\log x}}{z^{\log y}}\right)^{1/3}$$

$$\Rightarrow \quad \frac{x^{\log y - \log z} + y^{\log z - \log x} + z^{\log z - \log y}}{3} \geq (1)^{1/3}$$

$\Rightarrow$ Minimum value of required exp = 3

4. (c) $a(b^2 + c^2) + b(c^2 + a^2) + c(a^2 + b^2)$

Consider the numbers $ab^2, c^2a, bc^2, ba^2, ca^2, cb^2$

All of these real and positive.

$$\text{By AM-GM} = \frac{ab^2 + c^2a + bc^2 + ba^2 + ca^2 + cb^2}{6} \geq ((abc)^6)^{1/6}$$

$\Rightarrow \quad a(b^2 + c^2) + b(c^2 + a^2) + c(a^2 + b^2) \geq 6abc$

$\Rightarrow \quad x = 6$

5. (b) a, b, c are in A.P. $\quad \Rightarrow \quad 2b = a + c;\ abc = 4$

By AM-GM inequality $\frac{a+b+c}{3} \geq (abc)^{1/3}$

$\Rightarrow \quad \frac{3b}{3} \geq (abc)^{1/3} \quad \Rightarrow \quad b \geq 2^{2/3}$

Minimum value of $b = 2^{2/3}$

6. (b) By A.M.-G.M. on $\frac{x}{y}, \frac{y}{z}, \frac{z}{x}$

$$\Rightarrow \quad \frac{x}{y} + \frac{y}{z} + \frac{z}{x} \geq 3\left(\frac{x}{y}.\frac{y}{z}.\frac{z}{x}\right)^{1/3}$$

$\Rightarrow \quad \frac{x}{y} + \frac{y}{2} + \frac{z}{x} \geq 3 \quad \Rightarrow \quad \frac{x}{y} + \frac{y}{z} + \frac{z}{x} \in [3, \infty)$

7. (b) $a, b, c > 0$ and $b + c - a > 0,\ c + a - b > 0,\ a + b - c > 0$ (given)

$\therefore$ By A.M.-G.M.;

$$\frac{(b+c-a)+(c+a-b)}{2} \geq \sqrt{(b+c-a)(c+a-b)}$$

$\Rightarrow \quad c \geq \sqrt{(b+c-a)(c+a-b)}$ (i)

Similarly, $b \geq \sqrt{(b+c-a)(a+b-c)}$ (ii)

and $a \geq \sqrt{(a+c-b)(a+b-c)}$ (iii)

Multiplying (i), (ii) and (iii), we get $abc \geq (a + b - c)(b + c - a)(c + a - b)$

$\Rightarrow \quad (a + b - c)(b + c - a)(c + a - b) - abc \leq 0$

But equality would hold when $b + c - a = c + a - b = a + b - c$ i.e., $a = b = c$ but a, b, c are different positive real numbers.

$\Rightarrow \quad (a + b - c)(b + c - a)(c + a - b) - abc < 0$ i.e., negative

TEXTUAL EXERCISE–10: (SUBJECTIVE)

1. (i) $1 + \frac{1+2}{3} + \frac{1+2+3}{3} + \ldots\ldots$

$$T_n = \frac{n + (n-1) + (n-2) + \ldots + 1}{n} = \frac{n(n+1)}{n \times 2} = \frac{n+2}{2}$$

(ii) $\frac{1^3}{1} + \frac{1^3+2^3}{2} + \frac{1^3+2^3+3^3}{3} + \ldots\ldots$

n^{th} is given by $T_n = \frac{1^3 + 2^3 + \ldots\ldots + n^3}{n}$

$$T_n = \frac{(n[n+1])^2}{2^2 n} = \frac{n^2(n+1)^2}{4n} = \frac{n(n+1)^2}{4}$$

(iii) $1.2.3 + 2.3.4 +$

$T_n = n(n + 1)(n + 2) \Rightarrow T_n = n^3 + 3n^2 + 2n$

2. (a) $\frac{1}{1 \times 4} + \frac{1}{4 \times 7} + \frac{1}{7 \times 10} + \ldots$

The nth term (T_n) can be written as

$$T_n = \frac{1}{n^{th}\text{term of }(1,4,7\ldots) \times n^{th}\text{of }(4,7,10\ldots.)}$$

n^{th} term of an A.P. = (1, 4, 7) is given by $a_n = 1 + (n - 1)3$

Similarly n^{th} term of (4, 7, 10,….) is $4 + (n - 1)3$

$$\Rightarrow \quad T_n = \frac{1}{(3n-2)(3n+1)}$$

$$\Rightarrow \quad S_n = \Sigma\, T_n = \frac{1}{3}\left(1 - \frac{1}{4} + \frac{1}{4} - \frac{1}{7} + \frac{1}{7} + \ldots.\right)$$

$$\Rightarrow \quad \frac{1}{3}\left(1 - \frac{1}{3n+1}\right) = \frac{n}{3n+1}$$

(b) $\frac{1}{1 \times 6} + \frac{1}{6 \times 11} + \frac{1}{11 \times 16} + \ldots..$

The nth term of the equation =

$$\frac{1}{n^{th}\text{ term of }(1,6,11) \times (n^{th})\text{ term of }6,11,16)}$$

$\Rightarrow \quad n^{th}$ term of 6, 11, 16 = $1+(n - 1)5 = 5n - 4$

$\Rightarrow \quad n^{th}$ term of 6, 11, 16 = $6 + (n - 1)5 = 5n + 1$

$$\Rightarrow \quad T_n = \frac{1}{(5n-4)(5n+1)}$$

$$S_n = \sum T_n = \frac{1}{5}\left[1 - \frac{1}{6} + \frac{1}{6} - \frac{1}{11} \ldots \frac{-1}{5n+1}\right]$$

$$= \frac{1}{5}\left[1 - \frac{1}{5n+1}\right] = \frac{n}{5n+1}$$

3. $1+\frac{1}{1+2}+\frac{1}{1+2+3}+......$

$T_n=\frac{1}{n+(n-1)+.....+1}$

$=\frac{1}{(n\ \ 1)}=\frac{2}{(n\ \ 1)}$

$S_n=\sum T_n=\sum\frac{2}{n(n+1)}=2\sum\frac{1}{n(n+1)}=2\sum\left(\frac{1}{n}-\frac{1}{n+1}\right)=2$

$\left\{\sum\frac{1}{n}-\sum\frac{1}{n+1}\right)$

$=2\left[1+\frac{1}{2}+\frac{1}{3}+\frac{1}{4}.....\frac{1}{n}-\left(\frac{1}{2}+\frac{1}{3}+\frac{1}{4}+..+\frac{1}{n+1}\right)\right]$

$=2.\left[1-\frac{1}{n+1}\right]=\frac{2n}{n+1}$

4. {1}, {2, 3}, {4, 5, 6}, {7, 8, 9, 10}; number of elements in n^{th} group = n

Number of elements before the nth group = $\frac{n(n-1)}{2}$

First element of the nth group = $\frac{n^2-n}{2}+1$

Last element in the nth group = $\frac{n^2-n}{2}+1+n-1=\frac{n^2+n}{2}$

Sum of numbers in the nth group = $\frac{n}{2}\left[\frac{n^2-n}{2}+1+\frac{n^2+n}{2}\right]$

$=\frac{n}{2}\left[n^2+1\right]$

5. $\frac{3}{1^2.2^2}+\frac{5}{2^2.3^2}+\frac{7}{3^2.4^2}+....$

The series can be re- written as

$1-\frac{1}{2^2}+\frac{1}{2^2}-\frac{1}{3^2}+\frac{1}{3^2}-\frac{1}{4^2}+....$

$\Rightarrow\ 1-\frac{1}{(n+1)^2}\qquad\Rightarrow\ \frac{n^2+1+2n-1}{(n+1)^2}=\frac{n(n+2)}{(n+1)^2}$

6. (a) $\left[\frac{3}{1.2}\right]\left(\frac{1}{2}\right)+\frac{4}{2.3}\left(\frac{1}{2^2}\right)+....$

$T_n=\frac{1}{2^n}\left[\frac{n+2}{n(n+1)}\right]=\frac{1}{2^n}\left[\frac{2}{n}-\frac{1}{n+1}\right]$

$T_n=\frac{1}{n-2^{n-1}}-\frac{1}{(n+1)2^n}$

$T_{n-1}=\frac{1}{(n-1)2^{n-2}}-\frac{1}{n\,2^{n-1}}$

$T_{n-2}=\frac{1}{(n-2)2^{n-3}}-\frac{1}{(n-1)2^{n-2}}$

....

....

$T_1=\frac{1}{2^0}-\frac{1}{2.2^1}$

$S_n=1-\frac{1}{(n+1)2^n}$

(b) $2\ (\ 1.2)+\ 2.\left[\frac{5}{2.3}\right]+2^2\left[\frac{10}{3.4}\right]+\left[\frac{2^3.17}{4.5}\right]$

$U_n=\frac{n^2+1}{n(n+1)}2^{n-1}=\left[\frac{2n}{n+1}-\frac{n-1}{n}\right]2^{n-1}$ as in 6 (*a*)

$S_n=\sum U_n=\frac{n.2^n}{n+1}$

(c) $\frac{1^2.4}{2.3}+\frac{2^2.4^2}{3.4}+\frac{3^2.4^3}{4.5}+...$

$U_n=\frac{n^2}{(n+1)(n+2)}.4^n=\left[\frac{n^2+1-1}{(n+1)(n+2)}\right]4^n$

$=\left(\frac{n-1}{n+2}+\frac{1}{n+1}-\frac{1}{n+2}\right)4^n$

$\Rightarrow\ \left(1-\frac{4}{n+2}+\frac{1}{n+1}\right)4^n$

$T_n=4^n-\frac{4^{n+1}}{n+1}+\frac{4^n}{n+1}$

$T_1=4-\frac{4^2}{3}+2$

$T_2=4^2-\frac{4^3}{4}+\frac{4^2}{3}$

....

....

$T_n=4^n-\frac{4^{n+1}}{n+2}+\frac{4^n}{n+1}$

$\Rightarrow\ S_n=\left(4+4^2+....4^n\right)-\frac{4^{n+1}}{n+2}+2$

$\Rightarrow\ \frac{4^{n+1}-4}{3}-\frac{4^{n+1}}{n+2}+2$

7. $\frac{3}{1.2.4}+\frac{4}{2.3.5}+\frac{5}{3.4.6}+...$

$U_n=\frac{(n+2)}{n(n+1)(n+3)}$

$\Rightarrow\ U_n=\frac{(n+2)^2}{n(n+1)(n+2)(n+3)}$

$=\frac{1}{(n+2)(n+3)}+\frac{3}{(n+1)(n+2)(n+3)}$

$+\frac{4}{n(n+1)(n+2)(n+3)}$

$\Rightarrow\ S_n=\frac{29}{36}-\frac{1}{n+3}-\frac{3}{2(n+2)(n+3)}-\frac{4}{3(n+1)(n+2)(n+3)}$

8. (i) Sum of n terms when $T_n=(n^2+5n+4)\ (n^2+5n+8)$

$=(n+1)\ (n+4)\ [(n+2)\ (n+3)+2]$

$=(n+1)\ (n+4)\ (n+2)\ (n+3)+2\ (n+1)\ (n+4)$

Further

$(n+1)\ (n+2)\ (n+3)\ (n+4)+2\ (n+1)\ (n+2)+(n+1)$

$\Rightarrow$ $(n+1),\ (n+2),\ (n+3),\ (n+4)$ are in A.P.

Also $(n+1)\ (n+2)$ are in A.P

Hence

$S_n=\frac{1}{15}(n-1)(n+2)\left(3n^2+36n^2+151n+240\right)-32$

(ii) Given $T_n = \frac{n^2(n^2-1)}{4n^2-1}$

$\Rightarrow \frac{n^2}{4}\left[\frac{4n^2-3-1}{4n^2-1}\right] \Rightarrow \frac{n^2}{4} - \frac{4n^2}{4-(4n^2-1)}$

$\frac{n^2}{4} - \frac{3}{16}\left(1+\frac{1}{4n^2-1}\right)$

$\Rightarrow \frac{n^2}{4} - \frac{3}{16} - \frac{3}{16(4n^2-1)}$

$S_n = \sum T_n$

$= \left(\frac{n(n+1)(2n+1)}{24}\right) - \frac{3}{16}n - \frac{3}{16}\left[\frac{1}{2} - \frac{1}{2(2n+1)}\right]$

$\Rightarrow \frac{n(n+1)(2n+1)}{24} - \frac{3}{16}\left[\frac{4n^2+4n}{2(2n+1)}\right]$

On simplification, we get $\frac{n(n+1)(n-1)(n+2)}{6(2n+1)}$

9. (a) 3.4 + 8.11 + 15 .20 + 24.31 + 35.44 +......

First terms of the series 3, 8, 15, 24, 35......

$T_n = n^2 + 2n$

Second terms of 4, 11, 20, ...

$T_n = n^2 + 4n - 1$

For the series $T_n = (n^2 + 2n)(n^2 + 4n - 1)$

$= n(n + 2)((n + 1)(n + 3) - 4)$

$= n(n + 2)(n + 1)(n + 3) - 4n(n + 2)$

$= n(n + 1)(n + 2)(n + 3) - 4(n + 1)n - 4n$

As proceeded in Q. No. 8

$\Rightarrow \frac{n(n+1)(n+3)(n+4)}{5} - \frac{4n(n+1)(n+2)}{3} - \frac{4n(n+1)}{2}$

$\Rightarrow \frac{n(n+1)(3n^3+27n^2+58n+2)}{15}$

(b) 1.3 + 4.7 + 9.13 + 16.21

As done in 9 (*a*)

$U_n = n^2(n^2 + n + 1) = (n^2 - 1 + 1)(n^2 + n + 1)$

$= \{(n + 1)(n - 1) + 1\}\{n^2 + n + 1\}$

$= (n - 1)(n + 1)n(n + 2) - (n - 1)n(n + 1) + (n + 1)(n - 1) + (n + 2)n - n + 1$

On simplification

$= n(n + 1)(n - 1)(n + 2) - n(n - 1)(n + 1) + n(2n + 1)$

$S_n = \frac{n(n-1)(n+1)(n+2)(n+3)}{5}$

$- \frac{n(n-1)(n+1)(n+2)}{4} + \frac{2n(n+1)(n+2)}{3} - \frac{n(n+1)}{2}$

$= \frac{n(n+1)(12n^3+33n^2+37n+8)}{60}$

10. (a) $\sum_{1\le i<j\le n}\sum (i+j)$

$\Rightarrow \sum_{1\le i<j\le n}\sum (a_i + a_j) = n - 1\sum_{k=1}^{n} a_k$

$\because a_i \sim i; a_j \sim j$

$\Rightarrow (n - 1)n = n^2 - n$

(b) $\sum_{1\le i<j\le n}\sum (i.j) = \frac{\left(\sum_{k=1}^{n} k\right)^2 - \sum_{k=1}^{n} k^2}{2}$

$= \frac{1}{2}\left(\frac{n(n+1)}{2}\right)^2 - \frac{n(n+1)(2n+1)}{12}$

(c) $\sum_{1\le i<j\le n}\sum (i+j)^2 \Rightarrow \sum_{1\le i<j\le n}\sum (i^2 + j^2 + 2ji)$

$\Rightarrow \sum_{1\le i<j\le n}\sum (i^2 + j^2) + 2\sum_{1\le i<j\le n}\sum (ji)$

$\Rightarrow (n-1)\sum k^2 + 2\sum_{1\le i<j<n}\sum (i.j)$

(Symmetric distribution of j, i)

Hence can be distributed)

TEXTUAL EXERCISE–10: (OBJECTIVE)

1. (d) 1.3.5 + 3.5.7 + 5.7.9.+

Let us calculate the sum to n terms, $T_n = (2n - 1)(2n + 1)(2n + 3)$

$S_n = \frac{(2n-1)(2n+1)(2n+3)(2n+5)}{8} + \frac{15}{8} =$

$\Rightarrow n = 9$

$S_9 = \frac{17.19.21.23}{8} + \frac{15}{8} = \frac{17.19.21.23+15}{8} = 19503$

2. (b) $S_n = cn(n + 1)$. Let us takes first n natural numbers which are also in A.P. with common difference = 1

$\Rightarrow S_n = \frac{n(n+1)}{2} = \frac{c(n+1)n}{2} \Rightarrow 1/2$

We also have sum of squares

of n natural numbers as $\sum n^2 = \frac{n(n+1)(2n+1)}{6}$

$\Rightarrow \frac{2}{3}c^2(n+1)(2n+1)$

3. (c) $S_n = 1! + 2.2! + 3.3! + \ldots\ldots$

General term $T_n = n.n!$

Which be written as $T_n = ((n + 1) - 1)n! = (n + 1)n! - n!$

$\Rightarrow T_n = (n + 1)! - n!$

$\Rightarrow T_1 = 2! - 1!$

$T_2 = 3! - 2!$

....

....

$T_n = (n + 1)! - n!$

Adding all, we get $S_n = (n + 1)! - 1!$

$\Rightarrow S_{15} = 16! - 1$

4. (a) $\frac{1}{1.4} + \frac{1}{4.7} + \frac{1}{7.10} + \ldots\ldots n$

$T_n = \frac{1}{(3n-2)(3n+1)}$

$S_n = \frac{1}{3} - \frac{1}{3(3n+1)}$

$\Rightarrow \frac{n}{3n+1}$

5. (b) $1.1! + 2.2! + 3.3! + \ldots$

$T_n = n.\,n! = ((n+1)-1)\,n! = (n+1)n! - n! = (n+1)! - n!$

$T_1 = 2! - 1!$

$T_2 = 3! - 2!$

....

....

$T_n = (n+1)! - n!$

$\Rightarrow S_n = (n+1)! - 1!$

6. (b) $100 < n^3 < 1000$

$S < n < 2 \qquad 1.5$

$\Rightarrow S_n = 5^3 + 6^3 + \ldots\ldots + 21^3$

$\Rightarrow S_{21} = \dfrac{21^2.(22)^2}{4}$

$\Rightarrow S_4 = \dfrac{4^2.5^2}{4}$

$S_n = \dfrac{(22.21)^2 - (20)^2}{4} = \dfrac{213444 - 400}{4} = \dfrac{213044}{4} = 53261$

TEXTUAL EXERCISE-11: (SUBJECTIVE)

1. $\dfrac{1}{1.2.3.4.5} + \dfrac{1}{2.3.4.5.6} + \dfrac{1}{3.4.5.6.7} + \ldots + \dfrac{1}{n(n+1)(n+2)(n+3)(n+4)}$

$= \dfrac{1}{4}\left[\dfrac{1}{1.2.3.4} - \dfrac{1}{2.3.4.5} + \dfrac{1}{2.3.4.5} - \dfrac{1}{3.4.5.6} + \dfrac{1}{3.4.5.6} - \dfrac{1}{4.5.6.7} + \ldots + \dfrac{1}{n(n+1)(n+2)(n+3)} - \dfrac{1}{n(n+1)(n+2)(n+3)(n+4)}\right]$

$= \dfrac{1}{4}\left[\dfrac{1}{1.2.3.4} - \dfrac{1}{n(n+1)(n+2)(n+3)(n+4)}\right]$

$= \left[\dfrac{1}{96} - \dfrac{1}{4(n+1)(n+2)(n+3)(n+4)}\right]$

2. (a) $\dfrac{1}{1\times4} + \dfrac{1}{4\times7} + \dfrac{1}{7\times10} + \ldots$ which can also written as

$\dfrac{1}{3}\left(1 - \dfrac{1}{4} + \left(\dfrac{1}{4} - \dfrac{1}{7}\right) + \left(\dfrac{1}{7} - \dfrac{1}{10}\right)\right)\ldots\ldots$

$\Rightarrow S_n = \dfrac{1}{3}\left(1 - \dfrac{1}{3n+1}\right)$

$\Rightarrow \dfrac{1}{3}\left(\dfrac{3n}{3n+1}\right) \qquad \Rightarrow \dfrac{n}{3n+1}$

(b) $\dfrac{1}{1\times6} + \dfrac{1}{6\times11} + \dfrac{1}{11\times16}$

$\Rightarrow T_n = \dfrac{1}{(5n-4)(5n+1)}$

$\Rightarrow S_n = \dfrac{1}{5}\left(1 - \dfrac{1}{6} + \dfrac{1}{6} - \dfrac{1}{11} + \dfrac{1}{16} - \dfrac{1}{16}\right)$

$\Rightarrow \dfrac{1}{5}\left(1 - \dfrac{1}{5n+1}\right) \qquad \Rightarrow \dfrac{n}{5n+1}$

3. (a) $S_n = 1 + 2 + 4 + 7 + 11 + 16\ldots.$

$S_n = 1 + 2 + 4 + 7 + 11\ldots$

$0 = 1 + 1 + 2 + 3 + 4 + 5 + \ldots\ldots + t_n$

$\Rightarrow t_n = \dfrac{1 + (n-1).n}{2} = 1 + \dfrac{n^2}{2} - \dfrac{n}{2}$

$S_n = \Sigma t_n = \Sigma 1 + \Sigma\dfrac{n^2}{2} - \Sigma\dfrac{n}{2}$

$= n + \dfrac{n(n+1)(2n+1)}{12} - \dfrac{n(n+1)}{4}$

$= \dfrac{12n + n(n+1)(2n+1) - 3n(n+1)}{12}$

$= \dfrac{n(12 + 2n^2 + 3n + 1 - 3n - 3)}{12} = \dfrac{n(2n^2+10)}{12}$

(b) $S_n = 3 + 4 + 6 + 10 + 18 + 34 + \ldots$

$S_n = 3 + 4 + 6 + 10 + 18 + \ldots.$

$0 = 3 + 1 + 2 + 4 + 8 + 16 + \ldots - t_n$

$\Rightarrow t_n = 3 + 1 + 2 + 4 + 8 + \ldots\ (n-1)^{\text{th}}$ term

$\Rightarrow t_n = 3 + 2^{n-1} - 1 = 2 + 2^{n-1}$

$\Rightarrow T_1 = 2 + 1 = 3$; $T_2 = 2 + 2 = 4$; $T_3 = 2 + 4 = 6$; $T_4 = 2 + 8 = 10$

$\Rightarrow S_n = \Sigma t_n = \Sigma 2 + \Sigma 2^{n-1} = 2n + 2^n - 1$

(c) $S_n = 1 + 4 + 8 + 14 + 24 + 42 + \ldots.$

$S_n = 1 + 4 + 8 + 14 + 24 + \ldots\ldots$

$\Rightarrow t_n = 1 + 3 + 4 + 6 + 10 + 18 + \ldots.$

Using the result of part (b)

$\Rightarrow t_n = 1 + 2^{n-1} + 2n - 3 = -2 + 2n + 2^{n-1}$

$S_n = \Sigma t_n = -2n + n(n+1) + 2^n - 1$

$= 2^n - 2n + n^2 + n - 1 = n^2 + 2^n - n - 1$

(d) $S_n = 1 + 4 + 10 + 21 + 39 + \ldots.$

First difference = 3, 6, 11, 18

Second difference = 3, 5, 7.....

Third difference = 2, 2... constant

$T_n = A + Bn + Cn^2 + Dn^3$

$1 = A + B + C + D$

$4 = A + 2B + 4C + 8D$

$10 = A + 3B + 9C + 27D$

$21 = A + 4B + 16C + 64D$

$\Rightarrow T_n = -1 + \dfrac{13n}{6} - \dfrac{n^2}{2} + \dfrac{n^3}{3}$

$S_n = \Sigma T_n = -n + \dfrac{13}{6}\left(\dfrac{n(n+1)}{2}\right) - \dfrac{n(n+1)(2n+1)}{12} + \dfrac{n^2(n^2+1+2n)}{12}$

$= \dfrac{-12n + 13n^2 + 13n - n(2n^2+3n+1) + n^4 + n^2 + 2n^3}{12}$

$= \dfrac{-12n + 13n^2 + 13n - 2n^3 - 3n^2 - n + n^4 + n^2 + 2n^3}{12}$

$= \dfrac{n^4 + 11n^2}{12}$

4. (a) $\dfrac{1}{1.3} + \dfrac{2}{13.5} + \dfrac{3}{1.3.5.7} + \ldots$

Clearly the nth term is $t_n = \dfrac{n}{1.3.5.7\ldots(2n-1)(2n+1)} =$

$\dfrac{1}{1.3\ldots(2n-1)} - \dfrac{1}{2}\dfrac{1}{(1.3\ldots2n+1)}$

$$t_1 = \frac{1}{2} - \frac{1}{2} + \frac{1}{3}$$

$$t_2 = \frac{1}{2}.\frac{1}{1.3} - \frac{1}{2}.\frac{1}{1.3.5}$$

.

.

.

$$= \frac{1}{1.3....(2n-1)} - \frac{1}{2}\frac{1}{1.3....(2n+1)}$$

Summation of the above terms $S_n = \frac{1}{2} - \frac{1}{2}\frac{1}{1.3.5...(2n+1)}$

$$\Rightarrow \quad S_\infty = \frac{1}{2}$$

(b) $\frac{3}{1.2^2} + \frac{5}{2^2.3^2} + \frac{7}{3^2.4^2} + ...$

$$T_n = \frac{2n+1}{n^2(n+1)^2} = \frac{n}{b^2(n+1)^2} + \frac{n+1}{n^2(n+1)^2}$$

$$= \frac{1}{n(n+1)^2} + \frac{1}{n^2(n+1)}$$

$$= \frac{1}{n} - \frac{-(n+2)}{(n+1)^2} + \frac{1-n}{n^2} + \frac{1}{n+1} = \frac{1}{n^2} - \frac{1}{(n+1)^2}$$

$$T_1 = 1 - \frac{1}{2^2}$$

$$T_2 = \frac{1}{2^2} - \frac{1}{3^2}$$

$$T_3 = \frac{1}{3^2} - \frac{1}{4^2}$$

....

....

Adding are, we get $S_n = 1 - \frac{1}{(n+1)^2} = \frac{n^2+2n}{(n+1)^2}$

(c) $1 - \frac{1}{2} + \frac{1}{3} - \frac{1}{4}$ ......$\infty = \ell n 2$ and $\frac{1}{1.3} + \frac{1}{2.5} + \frac{1}{3.7} + ...\infty$

(given)

$$T_n = \frac{1}{n(2n+1)} = \frac{-2}{2n+1} + \frac{1}{n}$$

$$T_1 = 1 - \frac{2}{3} = 1 - \frac{1}{3} - \frac{1}{3}$$

$$T_2 = \frac{1}{2} - \frac{2}{5} = \frac{1}{2} - \frac{1}{5} - \frac{1}{5}$$

$$T_3 = \frac{1}{3} - \frac{2}{7} = \frac{1}{3} - \frac{1}{7} - \frac{1}{7}$$

$S_n = T_1 + T_2 + T_3 + \quad + T_\infty$

Adding add the terms above, we get

$$1 + \frac{1}{2} - \frac{1}{3} + \frac{1}{4} - \frac{1}{5} + \frac{1}{6} - \frac{1}{7} + ...\infty$$

$$= 1 - \left(\frac{1}{2} + \frac{1}{3} + \frac{1}{4} + \frac{1}{5} .....\infty\right) = 1 - (\ell n\, 2 - 1) = 2 - \ell n\, 2$$

(d) $\frac{1}{1^2} + \frac{1}{3^2} + \frac{1}{5^2} + ...\infty = \frac{\pi^2}{8}$ and $S_n = \frac{1}{1^2} + \frac{1}{2^2} + \frac{1}{3^2} + ...\infty$

Given $\sum \frac{1}{(2n-1)^2} = \frac{\pi^2}{8}$ and $S_n = \sum \frac{1}{n^2} = ?$

We can easily write

$$\sum \frac{1}{n^2} = \sum \frac{1}{(2n-1)^2} + \frac{1}{2^2} + \frac{1}{4^2} + \frac{1}{6^2} + ...$$

$$= \sum \frac{1}{(2n-1)^2} + \frac{1}{2^2}\left(1 + \frac{1}{2^2} + \frac{1}{3^2} + \frac{1}{4^2} ..\right)$$

$$\Rightarrow R = \frac{\pi^2}{8} + \frac{1}{4}(R) \qquad \Rightarrow \frac{3R}{4} = \frac{\pi^2}{8}$$

$$\Rightarrow R = \frac{\pi^2.4}{8.3} \qquad \Rightarrow R = \frac{\pi^2}{6}$$

When R was takes to represent the require sum.

5. (a) $S_n = \frac{1}{n!}\left[\frac{n!}{1!(n-1)!} + \frac{n!}{3!(n-3)!} + \frac{n!}{5!(n-3)!} + ... + \right]$

$$\frac{1}{n!}\left[{}^nC_1 + {}^nC_3 + {}^nC_5 + ...\right]$$

$$\frac{1}{n!}\left[(2)^{n-1}\right] = \frac{2^{n-1}}{n!}$$

(b) $1 + \frac{1}{1+2} + \frac{1}{1+2+3} + ...$

$$T_n = \frac{1}{1+2+3+....n}$$

$$\Rightarrow T_n = \frac{2}{n(n+2)}$$

$$\Rightarrow T_n = \frac{1}{n} - \frac{1}{n+2}$$

$$\Rightarrow S_n = \Sigma T_n = \Sigma \frac{1}{n} - \frac{1}{n+2}$$

$$T_1 = 1 - \frac{1}{3}$$

$$T_2 = \frac{1}{2} - \frac{1}{4}$$

$$T_3 = \frac{1}{3} - \frac{1}{5}$$

$$T_{n-1} = \frac{1}{n-1} - \frac{1}{n+1}$$

$$T_n = \frac{1}{n} - \frac{1}{n+2}$$

$$S_n\left(1 + \frac{1}{2} + \frac{1}{3} + ... + \frac{1}{n} - \left(\frac{1}{3} + \frac{1}{4} + \frac{1}{5} + \frac{1}{6} - \frac{1}{n+2}\right)\right)$$

$$= \left(1 + \frac{1}{2} - \frac{1}{n+1} - \frac{1}{n+2}\right) = \frac{2n}{n+1}$$

(c) $\frac{2}{3} + \frac{8}{9} + \frac{26}{27} + \frac{80}{81}$

$$T_n = \frac{3^n - 1}{3^n} = 1 - \frac{1}{3^n}$$

$$S_n = n - \left(\frac{1}{3} + \frac{1}{3^2} + \frac{1}{3^3} + ...\frac{1}{3^n}\right)$$

$$= n - \left(\frac{1/3\left(1-\left(\frac{1}{3}\right)^n\right)}{2/3} \right) = n - \left(\frac{3^n - 1}{2.3^n}\right)$$

$$S_n = \frac{2n.3^n - 3^n + 1}{2.3^n}$$

(d) $\cot^{-1}3 + \cot^{-1} 7 + \cot^{-1} 13 + \ldots = (\cot^{-1}1 + \cot^{-1} 3 + \cot^{-1} 7 + \ldots) - \pi/4$

$$= \sum_{k=1}^{(n+1)} \cot^{-1}(k^2 - k + 1) - \frac{\pi}{4}$$

$$= \sum_{k=1}^{(n+1)} \cot^{-1}\left[\frac{k(k-1)+1}{k-(k-1)}\right] - \frac{\pi}{4}$$

$$= \sum_{k=1}^{(n+1)} -\left[\cot^{-1} k - \cot^{-1}(k-1)\right] - \frac{\pi}{4}$$

$$= -\left[\begin{matrix}(\cot^{-1}1 - \cot^{-1}0) + (\cot^{-1}2 - \cot^{-1}1) + \\ (\cot^{-1}3 - \cot^{-1}2) + \ldots + (\cot^{-1}(n+1) - \cot^{-1}n))\end{matrix}\right] - \frac{\pi}{4}$$

$$= -\cot^{-1}(n+1) + \cot^{-1}0 - \frac{\pi}{4} = -\cot^{-1}(n+1) + \frac{\pi}{2} - \frac{\pi}{4}$$

$$= -\cot^{-1}(n+1) + \frac{\pi}{4} = -\cot^{-1}(n+1) + \cot^{-1}1$$

$$= \cot^{-1}\left(\frac{n+2}{n}\right)$$

6. (i) $T_n = \dfrac{1+2+3+\ldots\ldots+n}{1^3+2^3+3^3+\ldots+n^3} = \dfrac{2n(n+1)}{n^2(n+1)^2}$

$$T_n = \frac{2}{n(n+1)} = \left(\frac{2}{n} - \frac{2}{n+1}\right)$$

$$S_n = \Sigma T_n \qquad = \frac{2n}{n+1}$$

(ii) $1.5.9 + 2.6.10 + 3.7.11 + \ldots$

$t_n = n(n+4)(n+8) = n^3 + 12n^2 + 32n$

$S_n = \Sigma t_n = \Sigma n^3 + 12\Sigma n^2 + 32\Sigma n$

$$= \left[\frac{n(n+1)}{2}\right]^2 + \frac{12n(n+1)(2n+1)}{6} + 16n(n+1)$$

$$= \frac{n(n+1)}{4}\left[n^2 + 7n + 72\right] = \frac{n(n+1)(n+8)(n+9)}{4}$$

(iii) $4 + 14 + 30 + 52 + 82 + 114 + \ldots$

Let $T_n = A + Bn + Cn^2$

$\Rightarrow 4 = A + B + C$

$14 = A + 2B + 4C$

$30 = A + 3B + 9C$

$\Rightarrow A = 0, B = 1, C = 3$

$\Rightarrow T_n = 3n^2 + n$

$\Rightarrow S_n = \Sigma T_n = \dfrac{n(n+1)}{2}[2n+1+1] = n(n+1)^2$

(iv) $S_n = 2 + 5 + 12 + 31 + 86$

First set of differences = 2, 5, 12, 31, 86

Second = 3, 7, 19, 55

Third = 4, 12, 16

Let nth term be $T_n = a.3^{n-1} + bn + c$

By equation solving for n = 1, 2, 3, we get $T_n = 3^{n-1} + n$

$\Rightarrow S_n = \Sigma(3^{n-1} + n) = \Sigma 3^{n-1} + \Sigma n = \dfrac{3^n - 1 + n(n+1)}{2}$

$$= \frac{3^n + n^2 + n - 1}{2}$$

TEXTUAL EXERCISE–11: (OBJECTIVE)

1. (a) 1, 5, 14, 30, 55

First difference = 4, 9, 16, 25…

Second difference = 5, 7, 9…

Which is a AP

$\Rightarrow T_n = A + Bn + Cn^2 + Dn^3$

$\Rightarrow A + B + C + D = 1 \qquad \Rightarrow A + 2B + 4C + 8D = 5$

$\Rightarrow A + 3B + 9C + 27D = 14$

$\Rightarrow A + 4B + 16 + 64D = 30$

Hence $T_n = \dfrac{n^3}{3} + \dfrac{n^2}{2} + \dfrac{n}{6} = 55 + 6^2 = 91$

2. (c) Next term of 1, 3, 6, 10…..

$T_n = \dfrac{n^2+n}{2} \qquad \Rightarrow T_5 = \dfrac{25+5}{2} = 15$

3. (b) $S_n = \dfrac{1}{13.5} + \dfrac{1}{3.5.7} + \ldots + \dfrac{1}{11.13.15}$

$\Rightarrow T_n = \dfrac{1}{(2n-1)(2n+1)(2n+3)}$

$\Rightarrow S_n = \Sigma T_n = \dfrac{1}{12} - \dfrac{1}{4(2n+1)(2n+3)}$

$\Rightarrow S_6 = \dfrac{1}{12} - \dfrac{1}{4.13.15} = \dfrac{16}{195}$

4. (a) $T_n = n(n+1)(n+2)$

$T_n = n^3 + 3n^2 + 2n$

$S_n = \Sigma T_n$

$\Rightarrow \sum n^3 + 3\sum n^2 + 2\sum n$

$\Rightarrow \dfrac{3.n(n+1)(2n+1)}{6} + \dfrac{n^2(n+1)^2}{4} + \dfrac{2.n(n+1)}{2}$

$= \dfrac{n(n+1)(n+2)(n+3)}{4}$

5. (a) $100\left[\dfrac{1}{1.2} + \dfrac{1}{2.3} + \dfrac{1}{3.4} + \ldots + \dfrac{1}{99.100}\right]$

$T_n = \dfrac{1}{n(n+1)} = \dfrac{1}{n} - \dfrac{1}{n+1}$

$T_1 = 1 - \dfrac{1}{2}$

$T_2 = \dfrac{1}{2} - \dfrac{1}{3}$

$T_{99} = \dfrac{1}{99} - \dfrac{1}{100}$

Summation of $T_1 + T_2 + \ldots + T_{99}$ gives $1 - \dfrac{1}{100}$

By the questions

$\Rightarrow$ 100 [summation]

$\Rightarrow 100\left[1 - \dfrac{1}{100}\right] = 100\left[\dfrac{99}{100}\right] = 99$

SECTION-III: (SINGLE CORRECT ANSWER)

1. (b) By the equation $a_1 = 1$

Consider first $2n$ terms

First half of n terms $\Rightarrow S_n = \frac{n}{2}(2+(n-1)d)$

$a_{n+1} = 1 + nd$

$a_{2n} = 1 + 2nd - d$

Sum of second half of these $2n$ terms $= \frac{n}{2}(1 + nd + 1 + 2nd - d) = \frac{n}{2}(2 + 3nd - d)$

By the question-: $\dfrac{\frac{n}{2}(2+(n-1)d)}{\frac{n}{2}(2+3nd-d)}$ = constant

This means that the impression must be independent of n

$\Rightarrow d = 2 \quad \Rightarrow \frac{2n}{6n} = \frac{1}{3}$

2. (c) The number of natural numbers in this range divisible by 17 $= \left[\frac{400}{17}\right] = 23$

The number of natural numbers in the range divisible by 23 $= \left[\frac{400}{23}\right] = 17$

The number of natural numbers in this range divisible by both 17 and 23 = 1 (394)

Required number =399 – (23 + 17 – 1) = 360

3. (a) Sum of first 11 terns of an A.P $= \frac{11}{2}(2a_1 + 10d)$

Sum of first 19 terms of A.P $= \frac{19}{2}(2a_1 + 18d)$

By the question: $\frac{11}{2}(2a_1 + 10d) = \frac{19}{2}(2a_1 + 18d)$

$\Rightarrow 8a_1 = -116d$

Sum of first 30 terms $= 15(2a_1 + 29d) = (-29d + 29d) = 0$

4. (a) First row has 1 number, second row has 2 numbers

$\Rightarrow$ 80th row has 80 numbers.

Total numbers including the last number in 80th row $= \frac{80}{2}(80 + 1) = 3240$

The 3240th term in the series 1, 3, 5, 7....

$a_{3240} = 1 + (3239).2 = 1 + 6478 = 6479$

5. (b) A.M $= \frac{a+b}{2}$; G.M $= \sqrt{ab}$

By the question $\frac{a+b}{2} = 2\sqrt{ab}$

$\Rightarrow a + b = 4\sqrt{ab} \quad \Rightarrow a^2 + b^2 + 2ab = 16ab$

$\Rightarrow a^2 + b^2 - 14ab = 0$

Let $\frac{a}{b} = x \quad \Rightarrow x + \frac{1}{x} - 14 = 0$

$\Rightarrow x = 7 \pm \sqrt{192} = \left(\frac{2-\sqrt{3}}{2+\sqrt{3}}\right)$

6. (c) Sum $= \frac{1}{7} + \frac{2}{7^2} + \frac{1}{7^3} + \frac{2}{7^4} + \ldots\ldots$

$= \left(\frac{1}{7} + \frac{1}{7^3} + \frac{1}{7^5} + \ldots\right) + 2\left(\frac{1}{7^2} + \frac{1}{7^4} + \frac{1}{7^6}\ldots\ldots\right)$

$= \dfrac{\left(\frac{1}{7}\right)}{\left(1-\frac{1}{7^2}\right)} + 2\left(\dfrac{\left(\frac{1}{7^2}\right)}{\left(1-\frac{1}{7^2}\right)}\right) = \frac{3}{16}$

7. (d) Sum of consecutive odd integer $= 45^2 - 21^2 = (45 + 21)(45 - 21) = 66.\ 24.$

Out of the available options-: 43, 45, ...,89 (24 terms)

Sum = 12 (32) = 66. 24.

8. (a) $(1 + x)(1 + x^2) \ldots\ldots(1 + x^{128}) = \sum_{r=0}^{n} x^r$

n is the maximum power of x in the expression.

$n = 1 + 2 + 4 + \ldots\ldots + 128$

$ar^{n'-1} = 128$

$r^{n'-1} = 128$

$2^{n'-1} = 2^7$

$n' \le 8$

$S_{n'} = 2^8 - 1 = 255$

9. (d) $S_k = 1 + \frac{1}{k+1} + \frac{1}{(k+1)^2} + \frac{1}{(k+1)^3} + \ldots\ldots$

$= \dfrac{1}{1-\left(\frac{1}{k+1}\right)} = \frac{k+1}{k} = 1 + \frac{1}{k}$

$\sum_{k=1}^{n} kS_k = 1 + 1 + 2\left(1+\frac{1}{2}\right) + 3\left(1+\frac{1}{3}\right) + \ldots\ldots + n\left(1+\frac{1}{n}\right)$

$= n + 1 + 2 + 3 + \ldots\ldots + n$

$= n + \frac{n(n+1)}{2} = \frac{n(n+3)}{2}$

10. (b) By the question $S_n = 2^{np} - 1$

$S_1 = 2^p - 1$

$S_2 = 2^{2p} - 1$

$S_3 = 2^{3p} - 1$

$\Rightarrow a_1 = 2^p - 1;\ a_2 = 2^{2p} - 2^p = 2^p(2^p - 1);\ a_3 = a^{3p} - a^{2p} = a^{2p}(a^p - 1)$

$\Rightarrow$ The sequence was a G.P.

11. (b) Let the minimum number of required terms be n.

$\Rightarrow S_n = \frac{n}{2}(2 + (n - 1)2) > 1357$

$\Rightarrow n^2 > 1357 \quad \Rightarrow n > 37$

12. (a) By the question $a_1 = l;\ a_5 = l + (5 - 1)d = m$

$a_n = p$ (n is the total number of terms)

Given $m = l + 4d \quad \Rightarrow \mathbf{d} = \frac{m-\ell}{4}$ (i)

$S_n = \frac{p}{2}\left(2\ell + (n-1)\frac{(m-\ell)}{4}\right)$ (ii)

$p = \ell + (n-1)\frac{(m-\ell)}{4}$

$\Rightarrow\ (n-1)=\dfrac{(p-\ell)4}{(m-\ell)}$ (iii)

Putting (iii) in (i), we get

$S_n=\dfrac{p}{2}(\ell+p)=\dfrac{(4p+m-5\ell)}{2(m-\ell)}\times(\ell+p)$

$\Rightarrow\ k=2$

13. (c) By the question

$S_1 = 1+2+4+8+16$ .....to 100 terms

$S_2 = 1+4+7+10$ ....to 100 terms

Clearly 1 is common to both S_1 and S_2

a_{100} for $S_2 = 1+(99).\ 3 = 298$

The task is to find the powers of 2 with in 298. Which include $2^0, 2^1, 2^2, 2^3, 2^4, 2^5, 2^6, 2^7, 2^8$,

Out of these the terms which are terms of S_2

$\Rightarrow\ 2^6 = 64 = 1+(n\ \ 1)\ 3$

$\Rightarrow$ 64 is a terms of S_2

$\Rightarrow$ Such terms are $2^0, 2^2, 2^4, 2^6, 2^8$, = 5 terms are common between S_1 and S_2

14. (b) Given a, b, c, d are in G.P

Let $b = ar$; $c = ar^2$; $d = ar^3$

$\Rightarrow\ (a+b) = a+ar = a(1+r)$

$\Rightarrow\ (b+c) = ar+ar^2 = ar(1+r)$

$\Rightarrow\ (c+d) = ar^2+ar^3 = ar^2(1+r)$

$\Rightarrow\ (a+b),(b+c),(c+d)$ are in G.P with common ratio r.

Similarly $(a-b), (b-c), (c-d)$ are also in G.P.

15. (c) By the question, $3(a^2+b^2+c^2+1) = 2(a+b+c+ab+bc+ca)$

$\Rightarrow\ a^2+b^2-2ab+b^2+c^2-2bc+c^2+a^2-2ac = -1-a^2+2a-1-b^2+2b-1-c^2+2c$

$\Rightarrow\ (a-b)^2+(b-c)^2+(c-a)^2 = -((1-a)^2+(1-b)^2+(1-c)^2)$

$\Rightarrow\ (a-b)^2+(b-c)^2+(c-a)^2+(1-a)^2+(1-b)^2+(1-c)^2 = 0$

Which is possible only when $a = b = c = 1$

$\Rightarrow$ $a.\ b,\ c$, are in A.P. as well as G.P.

16. (a) Let the length of edges be a, ar, ar^2

By the question volume $= a^3 r^3 = 216$

$\Rightarrow\ ar = 6$

Total surface area $= 2(lb+nl+nl) = 2(a^2r+a^2r^3+a^2r^2)$

$\therefore\ 2(a^2r+a^2r^3+36) = 252$

$\Rightarrow\ a^2r(1+r^2) = 90$

$\Rightarrow\ r = 2, a = 3$

$\Rightarrow$ Length of longest side = 12cm.

17. (a) By the question, $m=\sum_{r=0}^{\infty}a^r=1+a+a^2+......=\dfrac{1}{1-a}$

and $n=\sum_{r=0}^{\infty}b^r=1+b+b^2+.......=\dfrac{1}{1-b}$

$\Rightarrow\ a=1-\dfrac{1}{m}$ and $b=1-\dfrac{1}{n}$

Equation whose roots are a and b: $a'x^2+b'x+c'$

$\Rightarrow\ \dfrac{-b'}{a'}=2-\dfrac{1}{m}-\dfrac{1}{n}=\dfrac{2mn-n-m}{mn}$

$\Rightarrow\ \dfrac{b'}{a'}=m+n-2mn$ and

$\dfrac{c'}{a}=\left(1-\dfrac{1}{m}\right)\left(1-\dfrac{1}{n}\right)=1-\dfrac{1}{n}-\dfrac{1}{m}+\dfrac{1}{mn}=\dfrac{mn-m-n+1}{mn}$

$\Rightarrow$ The equation becomes $= mnx^2+(m+n-2mn)x+mn-m-n+1=0$

18. (c) Let $a^p = b^q = c^r = z$

By the question a, b, c are in G.P.

$\Rightarrow\ ac = b^2$

Taking logarithm, we get $\log_z a + \log_z b = 2\log_z b$

$\Rightarrow\ \dfrac{1}{p}+\dfrac{1}{q}=\dfrac{2}{r}$

$\Rightarrow\ \dfrac{1}{p},\dfrac{1}{q},\dfrac{1}{r}$ are in A.P.

19. (c) $A = 1+r^a+r^{2a}+r^{3a}+....\infty$ and $B = 1+r^b+r^{2b}+r^{3b}+.....\infty$

We can write $A=\dfrac{1}{1-r^a}$

$\Rightarrow\ 1-r^a=\dfrac{1}{A}$ $\Rightarrow\ r^a=\dfrac{A-1}{A}$

$\Rightarrow\ a=\log_r\left(\dfrac{A-1}{A}\right)$

Similarly, $b=\log_r\left(\dfrac{B-1}{B}\right)$

$\Rightarrow\ \dfrac{a}{b}=\dfrac{\log_r\left(\dfrac{A-1}{A}\right)}{\log_r\left(\dfrac{B-1}{B}\right)}=\log_{\left(\frac{B-1}{B}\right)}\left(\dfrac{A-1}{A}\right)$

20. (a) $S_n = 1^2+2.2^2+3^2+2.4^2+5^2+2.6^2+$ ....

If n is even, say $n = 2p$

$\Rightarrow\ S_{2p} = [1^2+3^2+5^2+.....(2p-1)^2]+2.2^2+2.4^2+....+2.(2p)^2$

Obviously if n is odd

Let us say $n = (2p-1)$

$\Rightarrow\ S_{2p-1} = S_{2p}-2(2p)^2$ (i)

By the question $S_{2p}=\dfrac{2p(2p+1)^2}{2}=p(2p+1)^2$

Putting this in equation (i), we get $S_{2p-1} = S_{2p}-2(2p)^2 = p(2p+1)^2-2(2p)^2$

Putting $p=n+\dfrac{1}{2}$ $\Rightarrow\ S_n=\dfrac{n^2(n+1)}{2}$

21. (a) $S_n = 4+18+48+1000+...$

Let the nth term of the series be an^3+bn^2+cn (i)

$\Rightarrow\ a+b+c = 4$

$\Rightarrow\ 8a+4b+2c = 18$

$\Rightarrow\ 27a+9b+3c = 48$

Solving the above three equations for three variables

$\Rightarrow\ a = 1;\ b = 2;\ c = 1$

$\Rightarrow\ S_n = \Sigma(n^3+2n+n)$

22. (c) $2n+1 = m$ stones

Let the number of stones be $m = 2n+1$, $(n+1)^{th}$ stone is the middle stone

A man will hence start from $(n + 1)^{th}$ stone and move towards left end .

$P_1 = 20 + 40 + 60 + \ldots + 20n = 20(1 + 2 + 3 + \ldots + n)$
$= 10\,n\,(n + 1)$

Now for the right half of the stones

$D_2 = 10\,n\,(n + 1)$

Total distance $20\,n\,(n + 1) = 4800$

$\Rightarrow n(n + 1) = 240 \quad \Rightarrow n^2 + n - 240 = 0$

$\Rightarrow n^2 + 16n - 15n - 240 = 0$

$\Rightarrow n(n + 16) - 15(n + 16) = 0$

$\Rightarrow (n + 16)(n - 15) = 0 \Rightarrow n = 15$

Total number of stones m $= 2n + 1 = 2 \times 15 + 1 = 31$

23. (b) $(1 + x)(1 + x + x^2)(1 + x + x^2 + x^3) \ldots (1 + x + \ldots + x^{100})$

Clearly the highest exponent is achieved by $100 + 99 + 98 + \ldots + 1 = \dfrac{100\,(101)}{2} = 50 \times 101 = 5050$

24. (c) $S_n = 1^2 - \dfrac{2^2}{5} + \dfrac{3^2}{5^2} - \dfrac{4^2}{5^3}$

$\therefore \quad \dfrac{1}{1-x} = \sum_{n=0}^{\infty} x^n$; $|x| < 1$ (infinite G.P.)

Differentiating both sides, we get $\dfrac{1}{(1-x)^2} = \sum_{n=1}^{\infty} n\,x^{n-1}$

Multiplying by x, we get $\dfrac{x}{(1-x)^2} = \sum_{n=1}^{\infty} n.x^n$

Differentiating again, we get $\dfrac{1+x}{(1-x)^3} = \sum_{n=1}^{\infty} n^2\,x^{(n-1)}$

if $x = -\dfrac{1}{5}$ (as $|x| < 1$)

$\Rightarrow \sum_{n=1}^{\infty} n^2 \left(\dfrac{-1}{5}\right)^{n-1} = \dfrac{25}{54}$

25. (c) $4a^2 + 9b^2 + 16c^2 = 2(3ab + 6bc + 4ac)$

$\Rightarrow 4a^2 + 9b^2 + 16c^2 - 6ab - 12bc - 8ac = 0$

$\Rightarrow (2a + 3b + 4c)^2 = 4(3ab + 6bc + 4ca)$

$\Rightarrow (2a - 3b)^2 + (3b - 4c)^2 + (4c - 2a)^2 = 0$

$\Rightarrow 2a = 3b = 4c$

As sum of positive numbers is zero only when each of them are individually zero.

$\Rightarrow b = \dfrac{2ac}{a+c} = \dfrac{4c^2}{3c} = \dfrac{4c}{3}$

$\Rightarrow a, b, c$ are in H.P

26. (b) Let a, b, c be in H.P.

New set of numbers $p = a - \dfrac{b}{2}$; $q = \dfrac{b}{2}$; $r = c - \dfrac{b}{2}$

By the question $b = \dfrac{2ac}{a+b}$

$pr = \left(ac - \dfrac{b}{2}(a+c) + \dfrac{b^2}{4}\right)$

$= \left(\dfrac{(a+c)b}{2} - (a+c)\dfrac{b}{2} + \dfrac{b^2}{4}\right) = \dfrac{b^2}{4} = q^2$

$\Rightarrow p, q, r$ are in G.P.

27. (a) $\lim_{n\to\infty} \dfrac{1.2.3 + 2.3.4 + \ldots + n}{n(1.2 + 2.3 + 3.4 + \ldots + n)}$

$S_n = 1.\,2.\,3 + 2.\,3.\,4 + \ldots + n$ terms
$= \Sigma\, n(n + 1)(n + 2)(n + 3)$

As already evaluated in previous exercise

$S_n = \dfrac{n(n+1)(n+2)(n+3)}{4}$

Similarly $S'_n = 1.2 + 2.3 + 3.4 + \ldots + n$ terms

$S'_n = \Sigma\, n(n + 1) = \Sigma(n^2 + n) = \Sigma n^2 + \Sigma n$

$= \dfrac{n(n+1)(2n+1)}{6} + \dfrac{n(n+1)}{2} = \dfrac{n(n+1)(2n+1) + 3n^2 + 3}{6}$

$= \dfrac{(n+1)(2n^2+n+n)}{6} = \dfrac{n(n+1)(2n+2)}{6} = \dfrac{n(n+1)^2}{3}$

Required $= \lim_{n\to\infty} \dfrac{S_n}{nS'_n} = \dfrac{n(n+1)(n+2)(n+3)}{4n.n(n+1)^2}.3$

$= \dfrac{3(n+2)(n+3)}{4n(n+1)} = \dfrac{3(n^2+5n+6)}{4(n^2+n)} = \dfrac{3}{4}\dfrac{\left(1+\dfrac{5}{n}+\dfrac{6}{n^2}\right)}{\left(1+\dfrac{1}{n^2}\right)}$

Putting $n \to \infty$

$= \dfrac{3}{4}$

28. (c) Let r be the common ratio of the G.P.

$\Rightarrow S_n : \dfrac{x}{r}, x, xr, xr^2, \ldots \infty$

Without loss of generality $|r| < 1$

$\Rightarrow S_n = \dfrac{\dfrac{x}{r}}{1-r} = \dfrac{x}{r(1-r)} = 4$

$\Rightarrow x = 4(r - r^2) = 4r(1 - r)$

Already $r \in (-1, 1)$

Similarly $-4 < 4r - 4r^2$ and $x = 4r(1 - r) = 4r - 4r^2$

$\therefore \quad -1 < r < 1$

$\Rightarrow 0 < r^2 < 1$ (i)

$\Rightarrow 0 < 4r^2 < 4$ (ii)

Also $-4 < 4r < 4$ (iii)

$\Rightarrow -4 < -4r^2 < 0$

Adding, we get $-8 < 4r - 4r^2 < 4$ (iv)

But for the quadratic to give real possible solution $b^2 - 4ac \geq 0$

$\Rightarrow 16 - 16x \geq 0$

$\Rightarrow x \leq 1$ (v)

Taking intersection of (iv) and (v), we get $x \in (-8, 1]$

29. (a) Let us assume the sides to be a, ar, ar^2

By Pythagoras theorem, $a^2 + a^2r^2 = a^2r^4$

$\Rightarrow 1 + r^2 = r^4 \quad \Rightarrow r^4 - r^2 - 1 = 0$

$\Rightarrow r^2 = \dfrac{1 \pm \sqrt{1+4}}{2} \quad \Rightarrow r^2 = \dfrac{1 \pm \sqrt{5}}{2}$

$\cos A = \dfrac{1}{r}$; $\cos C = \dfrac{1}{r^2}$

Taking the feasible value of r, we get $\cos A = \sqrt{\dfrac{\sqrt{5}-1}{2}}$ and $\cos C = \dfrac{\sqrt{5}-1}{2}$

30. (b) Let $a_1, a_2, a_3, \ldots\ldots, a_n$ be in G.P.
Given $3a_1 + 7a_2 + 3a_3 - 4a_5 = 0$
Let r be the common ratio of G.P.
$\Rightarrow a_2 = a_1 r;\ a_3 = a_1 r^2;\ a_4 = a_1 r^3;\ a_5 = a_1 r^4$
$\Rightarrow 3a_1 + 7a_1 r + 3a_1 r^2 - 4a_1 r^4 = 0$
$\Rightarrow (3 + 7r + 3r^2 - 4r^4) = 0$ of the given options $r = \frac{3}{2}$ satisfies the above equation

31. (a) $\{(\sin^2 x + \sin^4 x + \sin^6 x + \ldots.. + \infty))\log_e 2\}$ satisfies $t^2 - 17t + 16 = 0$
$\sin^2 x + \sin^4 x + \sin^6 x \ldots\ldots\infty$ is a G.P. with common ratio $= \sin^2 x$

$$\text{Sum} = \frac{\sin^2 x}{1-\sin^2 x} = \tan^2 x$$

$t^2 - 17t + 16 = 0$
$\Rightarrow (t - 16)(t - 1) = 0 \quad \Rightarrow \quad t = 16$ or $t = 1$

$$\frac{2\cos x}{\sin x + 2\cos x} = \frac{2}{\tan x + 2}$$

$\exp((\sin^2 x + \sin^4 x + \ldots.\infty)\log_e 2)$

$$= e^{\ln\left(2^{\tan^2 x}\right)} = 2^{\tan^2 x} = 2^4 = \tan^2 x = 4$$

$\Rightarrow \tan x = 2$ (in the region $\left(0, \frac{\pi}{2}\right)$)

$$\Rightarrow \frac{2\cos x}{\sin x + 2\cos x} = \frac{2}{\tan x + 2} = \frac{2}{4} = \frac{1}{2}$$

32. (c) Let $x - 3r, x - r, x + r, x + 3r$
$\Rightarrow x + 3r = (x - 3r)^2 + (x - r)^2 + (x + r)^2$
$\Rightarrow x + 3r = 3x^2 + 11r^2 - 6xr$
$\Rightarrow 11r^2 - (3 + 6x)r + 3x^2 - x = 0;\ x \in \mathbb{R}$
$\Rightarrow (3 + 6x)^2 - 44(3x^2 - x) > 0$
$\Rightarrow 9 + 36x^2 + 36x - 132x^2 + 44x > 0$
$\Rightarrow -96x^2 + 80x + 9 > 0$
$\Rightarrow 96x^2 - 80x - 9 < 0$

$$\Rightarrow x \in \left(\frac{10-\sqrt{154}}{24}, \frac{10+\sqrt{154}}{24}\right)$$

$$\Rightarrow 2x \in \left(\frac{10-\sqrt{154}}{12}, \frac{10+\sqrt{154}}{12}\right)$$

$\Rightarrow$ Only possible values of integers of $2x$ are 0 and 1.
$\Rightarrow 2x = 1 \qquad \Rightarrow 4x = 2$
$\Rightarrow a + b + c + d = 2$
(As for $x = 0$, $r = 0$ or $r = 3/11$
$\Rightarrow$ A.P. is constant or terms are non-integer))

33. (b) $f(n) = \left[\frac{1}{2} + \frac{n}{100}\right]$

$$S_n = \sum_{n=1}^{100} f(n) = \left[\frac{1}{2} + \frac{1}{100}\right] + \left[\frac{1}{2} + \frac{2}{100}\right] + \ldots.$$

This is equivalent to summing up values [[0.5 + 0.01] + [0.5 +0.02] +.....+ [0.5 + 0.1]]
Now the integer part of the expression remains zero till [0.5 + 0.49] for the rest of the terms the integer part is 1
$\Rightarrow$ [0.5 + 0. 01] = 0
[0.5 + 0.02] = 0
.
.
.
[0. 5 + 0.49] = 0
[0.5 + 0.51] = 1
.
.
.
[0.5 + 1] = 1
$\Rightarrow$ Total of = 51

34. (c) $\lim\limits_{n\to\infty}(1+3^{-1})(1+3^{-2})(1+3^{-4})(1+3^{-8})\ldots(1+3^{-2^n})$

$$= \lim_{n\to\infty}\left[1+\frac{1}{3}+\frac{1}{3^2}+\frac{1}{3^3}+\ldots+\frac{1}{3^{(1+2+4+8+\ldots+2^n)}}\right]$$

$$= \lim_{n\to\infty}\left[1+\frac{1}{3}+\frac{1}{3^2}+\frac{1}{3^3}+\ldots+\frac{1}{3^{\{(2^{n+1}-1)/(2-1)\}}}\right]$$

$$= \lim_{n\to\infty}\left[\frac{1\left(1-\left(\frac{1}{3}\right)^{(2^{n+1})}\right)}{\left(1-\frac{1}{3}\right)}\right] = \lim_{n\to\infty}\left\{\frac{3}{2}\left[1-\frac{1}{(3)^{2^{n+1}}}\right]\right\} = \frac{3}{2}$$

35. (d) $(1 + 2 + 2^2 + 2^3 + \ldots + 2^{n-2} + 2^{n-1})^2 = 1^2 + 2^2 + 2^4 + 2^6 + 2^8 + \ldots + 2^{2(n-2)} + 2^{2(n-1)} + 2S$; where S is the required sum

$$\Rightarrow \left[\frac{1((2)^n - 1)}{(2-1)}\right]^2 = \frac{1((2^2)^n - 1)}{((2)^2 - 1)} + 2S$$

$$\Rightarrow (2^n - 1)^2 = \frac{(2)^{2n} - 1}{3} + 2S$$

$$\Rightarrow 2 = (2 \ -1) - \left[\frac{(2) \quad 1}{}\right]$$

$$\Rightarrow S = \frac{(2^n - 1)^2}{2} - \left[\frac{(2)^{2n} - 1}{6}\right]$$

$$\Rightarrow \left[\frac{(2^{2n} + 1 - 2^{n+1})}{2}\right] - \left[\frac{(2)^{2n} - 1}{6}\right]$$

$$\Rightarrow \frac{3.(2)^{2n} + 3 - 3(2)^{n+1} - (2)^{2n} + 1}{6}$$

$$\Rightarrow \frac{2.(2)^{2n} - 3(2)^{n+1} + 4}{6}$$

$$\Rightarrow \frac{(2)^{2n} - 3(2)^n + 2}{3}$$

$$\Rightarrow \frac{1}{3}(2)^{2n} - (2)^n + \frac{2}{3}$$

36. (c) A.M. $= \frac{a+b}{2}$ and H.M. $= \frac{2ab}{a+b}$

By the question, $\frac{a.m}{H.M} = \frac{m}{n} = \frac{(a+b)}{2.2ab}(a+b)$

$$\Rightarrow \frac{m}{n} = \frac{(a+b)^2}{4ab} \qquad \text{(i)}$$

$\Rightarrow \quad \frac{\sqrt{m}}{\sqrt{n}} = \frac{a+b}{2\sqrt{ab}}$

$\therefore \quad \frac{(a+b)^2}{2ab} = \frac{2m}{n}$

Applying componendo and divedendo after dividendo, we get $\frac{a^2+b^2}{2ab} = \frac{2m-n}{n}$

$\Rightarrow \quad \frac{(a+b)^2}{(a-b)^2} = \frac{m}{m-n} \quad \Rightarrow \quad \frac{a+b}{a-b} = \frac{\sqrt{m}}{\sqrt{m-n}}$

$\Rightarrow \quad \frac{a}{b} = \frac{\sqrt{m}+\sqrt{m-n}}{\sqrt{m}-\sqrt{m-n}}$

(by componendo and dividendo again)

37. (b) Consider the triangle

$\therefore \quad \frac{1}{2}a.ha = \Delta = \frac{1}{2}b.hb = \frac{1}{2}c.hc$

$\Rightarrow ha = \frac{2\Delta}{a}, hb = \frac{2\Delta}{b}, hc = \frac{2\Delta}{c}$; where Δ = area of the triangle

A.M of sides = $\frac{a+b+c}{3}$

H.M of altitudes = $\frac{3(2\Delta)}{a+b+c}$

Product = 2 Δ

38. (b) Area in smallest circle $C_1 = \pi$

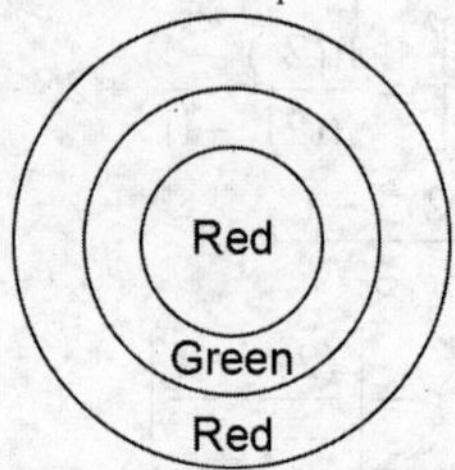

Area in $C_2 = 4\pi$
Area in $C_3 = 9\pi$
Area in $C_4 = 16\pi$
Area in $C_5 = 25\pi$
Area in $C_6 = 36\pi$
Total area in green = $3\pi + 7\pi + 11\pi + \ldots.. 199\pi$
Which is an A.P with first term 3π and common difference $= 2\pi$

$\Rightarrow$ Sum = π (3 + 7 + ….+ 199) = 25π (202) = 5050π

39. (c) Expression = $\frac{9x^2\sin^2 x+4}{\sin x} = 9x^2 \sin x + \frac{4}{x\sin x}$

$\Rightarrow \quad \frac{9x^2 \times \sin^2 x+4}{\sin x} \geq (2.(36.x^2)^{1/2})$

$\therefore \quad \frac{9x^2 \times \sin^2 x+4}{\sin x} \geq 2.6x = 12x$

$\Rightarrow$ Minimum value = 12

Note here we applied A.M.-G.M. because $x \in (0, \pi)$ for which the two numbers are positive

40. (d) Let the radius of C be r with area A.

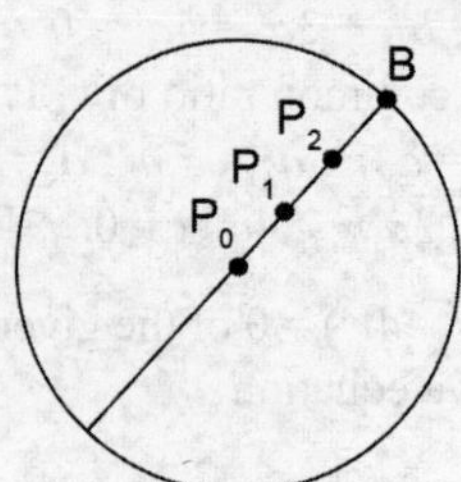

$P_0P_1 = \frac{r}{2}$

Radius of $C_1 = \frac{r}{4}$; Area = $\frac{A}{64}$

Radius of $C_2 = \frac{r}{8}$; Area = $\frac{A}{64}$

Radius of $C_3 \rightarrow \frac{r}{16}$; Area = $\frac{A}{256}$

Shaded area = $A\left(\frac{1}{16}+\frac{1}{64}+\frac{1}{256}+\ldots\right) = \frac{\frac{A}{16}}{1-\frac{1}{4}} = \frac{A}{12}$

Unshaded area = $A - \frac{A}{12} = \frac{11}{12}A$

$\Rightarrow$ 11: 12

41. (a) Let S_1 be the original square with side length S.

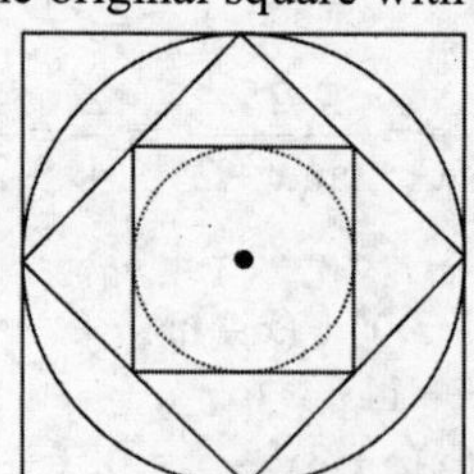

Side length of $S_2 = \sqrt{\left(\frac{5}{2}\right)^2+\left(\frac{5}{2}\right)^2} = \sqrt{\frac{(25)^2}{4}} = \frac{5}{\sqrt{2}}$

Side length of $S_3 = \sqrt{\frac{5^2}{8}+\frac{5^2}{8}} = \sqrt{\frac{(25)^2}{8}} = \frac{5^2}{2}$

$\therefore \quad S, \frac{5}{\sqrt{2}}, \frac{5}{2}, \frac{5}{2\sqrt{2}}, \ldots$

Radii of the respective circle follow the sequence

$\frac{5}{2}, \frac{5}{2\sqrt{2}}, \frac{5}{4}, \frac{5}{8}, \ldots$ which is same as $r_1 \frac{r}{\sqrt{2}}, \frac{r}{2}, \ldots$

Radius of the circle inscribed in the nth circle = $\left(2^{\frac{1-n}{2}}\right)r$

42. (b) $T_r = (r^2+1)\,r! = (r^2+1+r-r)\,r! = r\,(r+1)! - (r-1)\,r!$

$\Rightarrow \quad T_r = r\,(r+1)! - (r-1)\,r!$

$\Rightarrow \quad \sum_{r=1}^{n} T_r = S_n = n\,(n+1)\,!$

43. (a) $25(9x^2 + y^2) + 9z^2 - 15\,(5xy + yz\ 3zx) = 0$

Which can be written as $(15x - 5y)^2 + (5y - 3z)^2 + (3z - 15x)^2 = 0$

$\Rightarrow \quad 15x = 5y = 3z \qquad \Rightarrow \quad \frac{x}{1} = \frac{4}{3} = \frac{z}{5} = k$

$\Rightarrow \quad x = k, y = 3k, z = 5k$

$\Rightarrow \quad x, y, z$ are in A.P

44. (c) Let the number of required parts be $n = a_1 + a_2 \dots a_n$

By the question, Applying A.M.-G.M., we get

$$\left(\frac{a_1 + a_2 + \dots + a_n}{n}\right)^n \ge (a_1 a_2 \dots a_n)$$

$$\Rightarrow \left(\frac{15}{n}\right)^n \ge 243$$

Clearly $n = 5$ will make the maximum value of product $= 243$

45. (c) $a_1, a_2, \dots\dots, a_{10}$ are in A.P.

$h_1, h_2, \dots\dots, h_{10}$ are in H.P.

$a_{10} = 3 = 2 + 9\, d_1$

$$\Rightarrow d_1 = \frac{1}{9} \qquad \text{(i)}$$

$$\Rightarrow \frac{1}{h_{10}} = \frac{1}{3} = \frac{1}{2} + 9d_2$$

$$\Rightarrow d_2 = \frac{-1}{54}$$

$$\Rightarrow a_5 = 2 + \frac{4}{5} = \frac{22}{9} \qquad \Rightarrow h_5 = \frac{1}{\frac{1}{2} - \frac{2}{27}} = \frac{54}{23}$$

$$\therefore a_5 . h_5 = \frac{22}{9} \times \frac{54}{23} = \frac{6.22}{23} = 5.78$$

$\therefore [a_5 . h_5] = 5$

46. (d) Since a, b, c are in A.P.

$b = a + d,\ c = a + 2d$

Again a^2, b^2, c^2 are in G.P.

$\therefore a^2, (a + d)^2, (a + 2d)^2$ are in G.P.

$\Rightarrow a^2 + d^2 + 2ad = \pm (a^2 + 2ad)$

Taking positive sign, $d = 0$

Taking negative sign, $2a^2 + 4ad + d^2 = 0$

$$\Rightarrow 2a^2 + 4a\left(\frac{1}{2} - a\right) + \left(\frac{1}{2} - a\right)^2 = 0$$

$$\Rightarrow 4a^2 - 4a - 1 = 0 \qquad \Rightarrow a = \frac{1}{\sqrt{2}} \pm \frac{1}{\sqrt{2}}$$

Here $d = a = \frac{1}{2} - a > 0 \qquad \Rightarrow a < \frac{1}{2}$

Hence $a = \frac{1}{2} - \frac{1}{\sqrt{2}}$

47. (a) $\sum_{r=1}^{n} r^4 = f(n)$

$$\therefore \sum_{r=1}^{n} (2r - 1)^4$$

$= 1^4 + 3^4 + 5^4 + \dots + (2n - 1)^4$

$= [1^4 + 2^4 + 3^4 + 4^4 + \dots + (2n)^4] - [2^4 + 4^4 + 6^4 + \dots + ((2n)^4]$

$= f(2n) - 16f(n)$

48. (b) Given a, b, c are in A.P.

$\Rightarrow 2b = a + c$

By A.M.-G.M., we get $\frac{3b}{3} \ge (abc)^{1/3}$

$\Rightarrow b \ge (4)^{1/3} = (2)^{2/3}$

49. (b) If the equation is $A_1 x^3 + B_1 x^2 + C_1 x + 4 = 0$

Sum of the roots $= a + b + c = 3.A = -\frac{B_1}{A_1}$

Product of roots $= abc = (G)^3 = \frac{-D}{A_1}$

If $A_1 = 1 \qquad \Rightarrow B_1 = -3A$

$\Rightarrow D = -G^3$

50. (b) $$\sum_{r=2}^{\infty}\left(\frac{1}{r^2 - 1}\right) = \sum_{r=2} \frac{1}{(r+1)(r-1)} = \sum_{r=2}^{\infty} \frac{1}{2}\left(\frac{-1}{r+1} + \frac{1}{r-1}\right)$$

$$= \sum_{r=2}^{\infty} \frac{1}{2}\left(\frac{1}{r-1} - \frac{1}{r+1}\right) = \frac{1}{2}\left(1 - \frac{1}{3}\right) + \frac{1}{2}\left(\frac{1}{2} - \frac{1}{4}\right)$$

$$+ \frac{1}{2}\left(\frac{1}{3} - \frac{1}{5}\right) + \dots$$

$$= \frac{1}{2}\left(1 - \frac{1}{3} + \frac{1}{2} - \frac{1}{4} + \frac{1}{3} - \frac{1}{5} \dots\right) = \frac{1}{2}\left(\frac{3}{2}\right) = \frac{3}{4}$$

51. (a) $$\frac{1}{1+p} - \frac{(1-p)}{(1+p)^2} + \frac{(1-p)^2}{(1+p)^3} + \dots$$

This series can be thought of as a G.P. with first term $\frac{1}{1+p}$ and common ratio $= \frac{-(1-p)}{(1+p)}$

Given $p > 0$

$\Rightarrow -p < 0$

$\Rightarrow 1 - p < 1$, clearly $1 + p > 1$

$$\Rightarrow \left|\frac{1-p}{1+p}\right| < 1$$

Hence the sum to infinite number of terms $= \dfrac{\frac{1}{1+p}}{1 + \frac{1-p}{1+p}} = \frac{1}{2}$

52. (d) Consider a G.P. of positive terms $a, ar, ar^2 \dots$

if $a = ar + ar^2 \qquad \Rightarrow r^2 + r - 1 = 0$

$$\Rightarrow r = \frac{-1 \pm \sqrt{5}}{2}$$

We are taking G.P. with positive terms

$$\Rightarrow r = \frac{\sqrt{5} - 1}{2} = \left(\frac{\sqrt{5} - 1}{4}\right)^2 = 2 \sin 18$$

53. (a) $S = \underbrace{a + b + c + \dots}_{n \text{ terms}}$

By A.M. > G.M., we get $[(s - a) + (s - b) + (s - c) + \dots] > n[(s - a)(s - b) \dots]^{1/n}$

$$\Rightarrow \left[\frac{1}{s-a} + \frac{1}{s-b} + \frac{1}{s-c} + \dots\right] > n\left[\frac{1}{(s-a)(s-b)(s-c)\dots}\right]^{1/n}$$

Multiplying $[(s - a) + (s - b) + \dots]$, we

get $\left[\frac{1}{s-a} + \frac{1}{s-b} + \frac{1}{s-c} + \dots\right] > n^2$ or

$$\left[\frac{s-a}{s} + \frac{s-b}{s} + \frac{s-c}{s} + \dots\right]$$

$$\left[\frac{s}{s-a} + \frac{s}{s-b} + \frac{s}{s-c} + \dots\right] > n^2$$

$\Rightarrow \left[\frac{s}{s-a}+\frac{s}{s-b}+\frac{s}{s-c}+.....\right]\left(\frac{ns-s}{s}\right)>n^2$

$\Rightarrow \left[\frac{s}{s-a}+\frac{s}{s-b}+.....\right]>\frac{n^2}{n-1}$

54. (a) $S_n = \frac{5}{13}+\frac{55}{(13)^2}+....$

$S_n = \frac{5}{9}\sum_{n=1}^{\infty}\frac{10^n-1}{13^n} = \frac{5}{9}\left(\sum_{n=1}^{\infty}\left(\frac{10}{13}\right)^n-\sum_{n=1}^{\infty}\left(\frac{1}{13}\right)^n\right)$

$= \frac{5}{9}\left(\frac{10}{3}-\frac{1}{12}\right)=\frac{65}{36}$

55. (a) $e^{\{(1+|\cos x|+\cos^2 x+|\cos^3 x|+...)\log_e 4)}$

$= e^{\left(\frac{1}{1-|\cos x|}\right)\log_e 4} = e^{\log_e 4^{\frac{1}{1-|\cos x|}}} = 4^{\frac{1}{1-|\cos x|}}$

$\Rightarrow y^2 - 20y + 64 = 0 \quad \Rightarrow y = 16$ or 4

$\Rightarrow \frac{1}{1-|\cos x|} = 1$ or $2 \Rightarrow |\cos x| = 0, \frac{1}{2}$

$\Rightarrow \frac{\pi}{3},\frac{2\pi}{3},\frac{\pi}{2}$

56. (a) α, γ are the roots of $Ax^2 - 4x + 1 = 0$

$\Rightarrow \alpha+\gamma = \frac{4}{A}, \alpha\gamma = \frac{1}{A}$

Similarly β, δ are the roots of $Bx^2 - 6x + 1 = 0$

$\Rightarrow \beta+\delta = \frac{6}{B}; \beta\delta = \frac{1}{B}$

$\because$ α, β,γ,δ are in H.P.

$\Rightarrow \beta = \frac{2\alpha\gamma}{\alpha+\gamma} = \frac{2A}{A(4)} = \frac{1}{2}$

$\Rightarrow \gamma = \frac{2B\delta}{\beta+\delta} = \frac{2.\frac{1}{B}}{\frac{6}{B}} = \frac{1}{3}$

$\Rightarrow \alpha = 1, \delta = \frac{1}{4} \quad \Rightarrow A = 3$ and $B = 8$

57. (c) sin d [cosec a_1 . cos sec a_2 + cosec a_2 cosec a_3 +….]

$= \frac{\sin(a_2-a_1)}{\sin a_2.\sin a_1}+\frac{\sin(a_3-a_2)}{\sin a_3-\sin a_2}+\frac{\sin(a_4-a_3)}{\sin a_4.\sin a_3}+...$

$= \frac{\cos a_1}{\sin a_1}-\frac{\cos a_2}{\sin a_2}+\frac{\cos a_2}{\sin a_2}+... = \cot a_1 - \cot a_n$

58. (a) $1+\frac{3}{2}+\frac{5}{3}+.....+2-\frac{1}{n}$

$= (2-1)+\left(2-\frac{1}{2}\right)+\left(2-\frac{1}{3}\right)+....\left(2-\frac{1}{n}\right)$

$= 2n-\left(1+\frac{1}{2}+\frac{1}{3}+...\frac{1}{n}\right) = 2n - H_n$

59. (c) By the question, $S_1 = \frac{n(n+1)}{2}; S_2 = \frac{n(n+1)(2n+1)}{6}$;

$S_3 = n^2(n+1)$

$\Rightarrow \frac{S_3(1+8S_1)}{S_2^{\,2}} = \frac{\frac{n^2(n+1)^2}{4}(1+4n(n+1))}{\frac{n^2(n+1)^2(2n+1)^2}{36}} = \frac{9(1+4n(n+1))}{(2n+1)^2}$

$= 9$

60. (b) $1+\frac{x}{a_1}+\frac{x(x+a_1)}{a_1.a_2}+\frac{x(x+a_1)(x+a_2)}{a_1.a_2.a_3}+.....$

$= \underbrace{\left(\frac{x+a_1}{a_1}\right)+\frac{x(x+a_1)}{a_1.a_2}}_{\text{combine}}+\frac{x(x+a_1)(x+a_2)}{a_1.a_2.a_3}+...+\frac{x(x+a_1)(x+a_2)...(x+a_{n-2})}{a_1.a_2.a_3...a_{n-1}}$

$= \left(\frac{x+a_1}{a_1}\right)\left(1+\frac{x}{a_2}\right)+\frac{x(x+a_1)(x+a_2)}{a_1.a_2.a_3}+...+\frac{x(x+a_1)(x+a_2)...(x+a_{n-2})}{a_1.a_2.a_3...a_{n-1}}$

$= \underbrace{\frac{(x+a_1)(x+a_2)}{a_1.a_2}+\frac{x(x+a_1)(x+a_2)}{a_1.a_2.a_3}}_{\text{combine}}+...+\frac{x(x+a_1)(x+a_2)...(x+a_{n-2})}{a_1.a_2.a_3...a_{n-1}}$

$= \frac{(x+a_1)(x+a_2)(x+a_3)}{a_1.a_2.a_3}+...+\frac{x(x+a_1)(x+a_2)...(x+a_{n-2})}{a_1.a_2.a_3...a_{n-1}}$

Counting combining terms, we finally get

$\frac{(x+a_1)(x+a_2)(x+a_3)...(x+a_{n-1})}{a_1.a_2.a_3....a_{n-1}}$

61. (a) $a_1 . a_2 . a_3 ...a_n = c$

$2(a_1 . a_2 . a_3 ....a_n) = 2c$

By A.M.-G.M., we get $\frac{2(a_1+a_2+a_3+......+a_n)}{n} > (2c)^{1/n}$

$\Rightarrow 2(a_1 + a_2 + ...+ a_n) > n(2c)^{1/n}$

62. (a) a, b, c are in A.P.

$\Rightarrow 2b = a + c$

$\Rightarrow a+\frac{1}{bc}+c+\frac{1}{ab} = a+c+\frac{1}{b}\left(\frac{a+c}{ac}\right) = 2b+\frac{2}{ac}$

$= 2\left(b+\frac{1}{ac}\right)$

$\Rightarrow a+\frac{1}{bc}, b+\frac{1}{ac}, c+\frac{1}{ab}$ are in A.P

63. (a) x, y, z are in A.P.

$\Rightarrow x + z = 2y$

$\Rightarrow \frac{1}{\sqrt{y}+\sqrt{z}} = \frac{\sqrt{y}-\sqrt{z}}{y-z}, \frac{\sqrt{z}-\sqrt{x}}{z-x}, \frac{\sqrt{y}-\sqrt{x}}{y-x}$

$xz = a - d; y = a; z = a + d$

The terms be become $\frac{\sqrt{y}-\sqrt{z}}{-d}, \frac{\sqrt{z}-\sqrt{x}}{2d}, \frac{\sqrt{y}-\sqrt{x}}{d}$

$= \frac{\sqrt{z}-\sqrt{y}}{d}, \frac{\sqrt{z}-\sqrt{x}}{2d}, \frac{\sqrt{y}-\sqrt{x}}{d}$

Which are in A.P as $\frac{\sqrt{z}-\sqrt{y}+\sqrt{y}-\sqrt{x}}{2d} = \sqrt{z}-\frac{\sqrt{x}}{2d}$

64. (d) Let Arithmetic means be inserted between 20 and 80.

$A_1 = 20 + \frac{60}{n+1}$ and $A_n = 20 + \frac{n60}{n+1}$

By the question, $\frac{A_1}{A_n} = \frac{1}{3}$

$\Rightarrow \frac{20+\frac{60}{n+1}}{20+\frac{n60}{n+1}} = \frac{1}{3} \Rightarrow 60n + 60 + 180 = 80n + 20$

$\Rightarrow 20n = 220 \quad \Rightarrow n = 11$

65. (b) Sum of n A.M 'S between a and b is equal to $= \frac{n}{2}(a + b)$

$= \frac{12}{2}\left(-\frac{7}{2} - \frac{85}{2}\right) = 6\left(-\frac{92}{2}\right) = -276$

SECTION–IV: (MORE THAN ONE CORRECT ANSWER)

1. (a), (b), (c), (d) $a_n = (111\ldots1)$

a_{12}, a_{951}, a_{480} are divisible by 3, none of them are prime.

For $a_1 = \frac{1}{9}(\underbrace{999....9}_{91\,times}) = \frac{1}{9}(10^{91} - 1) = \frac{[(10^7)^{13} - 1]}{9}$

$= \left[\frac{(10^7)^{13} - 1}{10^7 - 1}\right]\left[\frac{10^7 - 1}{10 - 1}\right]$

$= [(10^7)^{12} + (10^7)^{11} + ...+1] \times [10^6 + 10^5 + ...+ 1]$

$\Rightarrow a_{91}$ is not prime

2. (a), (d) $11^2 + 12^2 + 13^2 + ...+ 20^2$

$\sum_{n=1}^{20} n^2 - \sum_{n=1}^{10} n^2 = \frac{20.21.41}{6} - \frac{10.11.21}{6} = \frac{14910}{6} = 2485$

3. (c), (d) Let there first terms be x and $(2n - 1)$th terms be y

$\Rightarrow 2a = x + y$ (i)

$\Rightarrow b^2 = xy$ (ii)

$\Rightarrow \frac{2}{c} = \frac{1}{x} + \frac{1}{y}$ (iii)

$\Rightarrow c = \frac{2xy}{x+y} = \frac{2b^2}{2a} \quad \Rightarrow b^2 = ac$

Also, $a \geq b \geq c$

4. (a), (b), (c), (d)

Let the G.P. be a ar, ar^2, ar^3 .....

Product of first 4 terms $= a^4 . r^6$

$\Rightarrow a^4 . r^6 = 4 \quad \Rightarrow a^2 r^3 = +2$ or -2 and $ar = \frac{1}{ar^3}$

$\Rightarrow a^2 r^4 = 1 \quad \Rightarrow ar^2 = 1$ or -1

$\Rightarrow a, ar, ar^2 . \frac{1}{ar} = 4 \quad \Rightarrow a = 4 / -4$

$\Rightarrow r = \frac{1}{2}$ or $\frac{-1}{2}$

$\Rightarrow S_\infty = \frac{4}{\frac{1}{2}} = 8$ or $S_\infty = -8$ or $S_\infty = \frac{8}{3}$ or $-\frac{8}{3}\left(r = -\frac{1}{2}\right)$

5. (a), (c) $x = \frac{a+b}{2}$; $y = \sqrt{ab}$; $z = \frac{2ab}{a+b}$

$\Rightarrow xz = y^2$ (i)

$\Rightarrow ax = 5y^2$

$\Rightarrow a(y + 2) = 5y^2$ (ii)

Satisfying (i) and (ii), we get $a = 9$, $b = 1$

6. (a), (d) Let a, ar, ar^2 be the three terms.

By the question, $ar + 8 = b_2$

$\Rightarrow a, b_2, ar^2$ are in A.P

$\Rightarrow ar + 8 = \frac{a(1 + r^2)}{2}$ (i)

Also, a $ar + 8$, $ar^2 + 64$ are in G.P.

$\Rightarrow a(ar^2 + 64) = (ar + 8)^2$

$\Rightarrow a(ar^2 + 64) = \frac{a^2(1+r^2)^2}{4}$

$\Rightarrow \frac{a(1+r^2)^2}{4} = ar^2 + 64$

$\Rightarrow a(1 + r^4 + 2r^2) = 4ar^2 + 64.4$

$\Rightarrow a + ar^4 - 2ar^2 = 64.4$

$\Rightarrow a(1 + r^4 - 2r^2) = 64.4$

$\Rightarrow a(1 - r^2)^2 = 64.4 = 4.(8)^2$

$\Rightarrow a = 4$ and $r = 3$

7. (c) By the question, 2, a_2, a_3 ......are in A.P.

2, q_2, q_3, ..., are in G.P.

$a_{10} = 2 + 9. d = 3$

$\Rightarrow d = \frac{1}{9}$ (i)

$q_{10} = 2r^9 = 3$

$\Rightarrow r^9 = \frac{3}{2}$ (ii)

$a_7 = 2 + 6d = 2 + \frac{2}{3} = \frac{8}{3}$

$a_{19} = 4$

$q_{19} = \frac{9}{2}$

$q_{10} = 3$

$a_7 . q_{19} = \frac{8}{3} \times \frac{9}{2} = 12$

$a_{19} \times q_{10} = 4 \times 3 = 12$

8. (a), (b), (d) $S_n = \sum_{r=1}^{n} \frac{2r+1}{r^4 + 2r^3 + r^2}$

$\therefore r^4 + 2r^3 + r^2 = r^2(r^2 + 2r + 1) = r^2(r + 1)^2$

$\Rightarrow S_n = \sum_{r=1}^{n} \frac{2r+1}{r^2(r+1)^2} = S_n = \sum_{r=1}^{n}\left[\frac{1}{r^2} - \frac{1}{(r+1)^2}\right]$

$\Rightarrow S_{20} = \frac{440}{441} \quad \Rightarrow S_{15} = \frac{255}{256}$

$\Rightarrow S_{10} = \frac{126}{121}$

9. (c), (d) a, b, c, d are in A.P.

$\Rightarrow 2b = a + c$ (i)

$\Rightarrow 2c = b + d$ (ii)

Adding (i) and (ii), we get $2(b + c) = (a + d) + (b + c)$

$\Rightarrow (b + c) = (a + d)$ (iii)

$\Rightarrow \frac{1}{a} + \frac{1}{d} = \frac{b+c}{ad} \quad \Rightarrow \frac{1}{b} + \frac{1}{c} = \frac{b+c}{bc}$

Now, $bc > ad \quad \Rightarrow \frac{1}{ad} > \frac{1}{bc}$

$\Rightarrow \quad \frac{a+d}{ad} > \frac{b+c}{bc} \quad (a + d = b + c)$

$\Rightarrow \quad \frac{1}{a}+\frac{1}{d}>\frac{1}{b}+\frac{1}{c} \qquad \Rightarrow \quad \frac{1}{b}+\frac{1}{c}>\frac{4}{a+d}$

$\Rightarrow \quad (a + d)^2 > 4bc \qquad \Rightarrow \quad (b + c)^2 > 4bc$

$\Rightarrow \quad b^2 + c^2 - 2bc > 0$

$\Rightarrow \quad (b - c)^2 > 0$, which is always true.

10. (a), (b) The General term $T_r = \tan^{-1}\left[\frac{\sqrt{2}}{r+1}\right]^2$

$$S_n = \sum_{r=1}^{n} \tan^{-1}\left[\frac{2}{r^2+2r+1}\right] = \sum_{r=1}^{n} \tan^{-1}\left[\frac{r+2-r}{1+r(r+2)}\right]$$

$= \tan^{-1}(r + 2) - \tan^{-1}$

$S_n = \tan^{-1}(3) = \cot^{-1}\left(\frac{1}{3}\right)$

11. (a), (d) $\cos(x - y)$, $\cos x$, $\cos(x + y)$ are in H.P.

$\cos(x - y) = \cos x . \cos y + \sin x . \sin y$

$\Rightarrow \quad \sec(x - y), \sec x, \sec(x + y)$ are in A. P.

$\Rightarrow \quad \sec(x - y) + \sec(x + y) = 2 \sec x$

$\Rightarrow \quad \frac{\cos(x-y)+\cos(x+y)}{2\cos(x-y).\cos(x+y)} = \frac{1}{\cos x}$

$\Rightarrow \quad \frac{2\cos x.\cos y}{2\cos(x-y).\cos(x+y)} = \frac{1}{\cos x}$

$\Rightarrow \quad \cos^2 x . \cos y = \cos^2 x - \sin^2 y$

$\Rightarrow \quad \cos^2 x = 2\cos^2 (y/2)$

$\Rightarrow \quad \cos^2 x / \cos^2(y/2) = 2 \Rightarrow \quad \cos^2 x . \sec^2\left(\frac{y}{2}\right) = 2$

Taking positive square root, we get $\left|\cos x \sec\left(\frac{y}{2}\right)\right| = \sqrt{2}$ and other solution is $-\sqrt{2}$

12. (a), (b), (c), (d)

$(a^2 + b^2 + c^2)p^2 - 2(ab + bc + cd)p + b^2 + c^2 + d^2 \le 0$

$(ap)^2 - 2abp + b^2 + (bp)^2 + c^2 - 2cbp + (pc)^2 + d^2 - 2pcd \le 0$

$\Rightarrow \quad (ap - b)^2 + (bp - c)^2 + (pc - d)^2 \le 0$

Which is possible only when $ap - b = bp - c = pc - d = 0$

$\Rightarrow \quad b = ap \qquad \Rightarrow \quad c = bp$

$\Rightarrow \quad d = pc$

$\Rightarrow \quad b^2 = ap \times \frac{c}{p} = ac \qquad \therefore \quad c^2 = bp \times \frac{d}{p} = bd$

$\Rightarrow$ Similarly $ad = bc$

By (a), (b) $\qquad \Rightarrow \quad a, b, c, d$ are in G.P.

13. (a), (b), (c)

$$\sum_{r=1}^{n} r(r+1) = \sum_{r\pm1}^{n}(r^2+r) = \sum_{r=1}^{n} r^2 + \sum_{r=1}^{n} r$$

$$= \frac{n(n+1)(2n+1)}{6} + \frac{n(n+1)}{2} = \frac{2n(n+1)(n+2)}{6}$$

$$= \frac{n(n+1)(n+2)}{3}$$

On comparison $a = 0$; $b = 1$; $c = 2$;

$\Rightarrow \quad 2b = c = 2$

$\Rightarrow \quad a^3 - 8b^3 + c^3 = 0 = 8abc$

$\Rightarrow \quad c$ is a prime number $\Rightarrow \quad (a + b)^2 = 1$

14. (a), (b), (c)

$$\sum_{r=1}^{n} r(r+1)(2r+3) = an^4 + bn^3 + cn^2 + dn + e$$

$$\Rightarrow \quad \sum_{r=1}^{n} (2r^3 + 5r^2 + 3r) = an^4 + bn^3 + cn^2 + dn + e$$

$$\Rightarrow \quad \frac{2.n^2(n+1)^2}{4} + \frac{5n(n+1)(2n+1)}{6} + \frac{3n(n+1)}{2}$$

$$= \frac{3n^2(n^2+1+2n)+5n(2n^2+3n+1)+3n^2+3n}{6}$$

$$= \frac{3n^4+3n^2+6n^3+10n^3+15n^2+5n+3n^2+3}{6}$$

$$= \frac{3n^4+16n^3+21n^2+5n+3n}{6}$$

$a = \frac{1}{2}$; $b = \frac{8}{3}$; $c = \frac{7}{2}$; $d = \frac{8}{6} = \frac{4}{3}$; $e = 0$

$a - b = \frac{-13}{6} = \frac{4}{3} - \frac{7}{2} = \frac{-13}{6} = d - c$

$e = 0$

$\frac{1}{2}, 2, \frac{5}{2}$ are in A.P.

15. (a), (b), (c)

b_1, b_2, b_3 are three successive terms of a G.P. with common ratio r such that $b_3 > 4b_2 - 3b_1$

Hence we can write $ar^2 > 4ar - 3a$

$\Rightarrow \quad ar^2 > a(4r - 3) \qquad \Rightarrow \quad r^2 > 4r - 3 \; (a > 1)$

$\Rightarrow \quad r^2 - 4r + 3 > 0 \qquad \Rightarrow \quad (r - 3)(r - 1) > 0$

16. (a), (b), (c)

a, b, c are in A.P.

$\Rightarrow \quad 2b = a + c$ (i)

a^2, b^2, c^2 are in H.P.

$\Rightarrow \quad \frac{2}{b^2} = \frac{1}{a^2} + \frac{1}{c^2}$ (ii)

$\Rightarrow \quad \frac{8}{(a+c)^2} = \frac{a^2+c^2}{a^2c^2}$

$\Rightarrow \quad (a - c)^2(a^2 + 4ac + c^2) = 0$

Either $a - c = 0 \qquad \Rightarrow \quad a = b = c$

$a^2 + c^2 + 4ac \qquad \Rightarrow \quad (a + c)^2 + 2ac = 0$

$\Rightarrow \quad 2b^2 + ac = 0$

$\Rightarrow \quad a, b, -\frac{c}{2}$ are in G.P. and also a, b, c are in H.P.

17. (a), (b), (d)

Let a be the first term of the A.P.

$\Rightarrow \quad a + (n_1 - 1)d = 2 \qquad \Rightarrow \quad a + (n_2 - 1)d = 31$

$\Rightarrow \quad (n_2 - n_1)d = 29 \Rightarrow \quad d = \frac{29}{n_2 - n_1}$ which is ration.

$\Rightarrow$ All the terms are rational

$\Rightarrow$ Sum to any finite number of terms of the A.P. must be rational.

18. (a), (b), (c), (d)

Let 1, 5, 25 be the pth, q^{th}, r^{th} terms of an A.P. with common difference d, then $(q - p)d = 5 - 1$ and $(r - p)d = 25 - 1$

Let $\frac{q-p}{1} = \frac{r-p}{6} = k$

$\Rightarrow\ q = p + k, r = p + 6k; k \in \mathbb{N}$

Let 1, 5, 25 be P^{th}, q^{th}, r^{th} terms of a G.P. with common k, then $k^{q-p} = 5$ and $k^{r-p} = 25$

$\Rightarrow\ r - p = 2q - 2p$; which can be true for many triplets

19. (a), (b), (c)

Let the G.P. be a, ar, ar^2, ar^3, ar^4

By the question $a = 4$

$\therefore\ a(r^2 - r^4) = \dfrac{32}{81}$

$\Rightarrow\ 4r^2(1 - r^2) = \dfrac{32}{81} \quad \Rightarrow\ r^2(1 - r^2) = \dfrac{8}{81}$

$\Rightarrow\ r = \dfrac{1}{3}$ or $r = \dfrac{2\sqrt{2}}{3} \quad \therefore\ S_\infty = \dfrac{a}{1-r}\ (|r| < 1)$

$\Rightarrow\ S_\infty = 6$

20. (b), (c) Let a, ar, ar^2 be the sides of the right triangles

$\therefore\ (ar^2)^2 = a^2 + a^2 r^2$

$\Rightarrow\ a^2r^4 = a^2 + a^2 r^2 \quad \Rightarrow\ r^4 = r^2 + 1$

$\Rightarrow\ r^4 - r^2 - 1 = 0 \quad \Rightarrow\ r^2 = \dfrac{1 \pm \sqrt{5}}{2}$

$\tan(\theta) = \dfrac{1}{r} = \sqrt{\dfrac{2}{\sqrt{5}+1}} = \sqrt{\dfrac{\sqrt{5}-1}{2}}$

SECTION–V: (COMPREHENSION)

Passage: A

1. (c) Let two distinct positive numbers be a and b.

$A_1 = \dfrac{1}{2}(a + b);\ G_1 = \sqrt{ab}\ ;\ H_1 = \dfrac{2ab}{a+b}$

$A_n = \dfrac{1}{2}(A_{n-1} + G_{n-1});\ G_n = \sqrt{A_{n-1} + G_{n-1}}\ ;\ H_n = \dfrac{2A_{n-1}G_{n-1}}{A_{n-1} + G_{n-1}}$

For $n \ge 2$

$A_n H_n = A_{n-1} \cdot G_{n-1} \quad \Rightarrow\ G_1^2 = G_2^2 = G_3^2$

$\Rightarrow\ G_1 = G_2 = G_3$

2. (a) As a and b are distinct, $A_1 > H_1$

$\Rightarrow\ A_1 > A_2 > H_2 > H_1$

$\Rightarrow\ A_1 > A_2 > A_3 > H_3 > H_2 > H_1$

Thus $A_1 > A_2 > A_3$

3. (b) As Proved in Q. no. (2).

$H_3 > H_2 > H_1$

Passage: B

4. (c) $S_1 = \dfrac{a}{1-r}\ (|r| < 1); \qquad S_2 = \dfrac{b}{1-R}\ (|R| < 1)$

$\therefore\ S_1 = S_2 = 1$

$\Rightarrow\ \dfrac{a}{1-r} = \dfrac{b}{1-R} \quad \Rightarrow\ \dfrac{a}{b} = \dfrac{1-r}{1-R}$

$\Rightarrow\ r + R = 1$ as $ar = bR$ (given)

5. (a) Since $r = 1 - a$ and $R = 1 - b$

$\Rightarrow\ a + b = 2 - (R + r) = 1$

6. (d) $ar^2 = 1/8$

$\Rightarrow\ (1 - r)r^2 = 1/8 \quad \Rightarrow\ 8r^3 - 8r^2 + 1 = 0$

$\Rightarrow\ (2r - 1)(4r^2 - 2r - 1) = 0$

$\Rightarrow\ r = R = 1/2$ (impossible as in this case two series will be same)

$\Rightarrow\ r = \dfrac{1+\sqrt{5}}{4}, \dfrac{1-\sqrt{5}}{4}$

If $r = \dfrac{1-\sqrt{5}}{4}$, then $R = 1 - \left(\dfrac{1-\sqrt{5}}{4}\right) = \dfrac{3+\sqrt{5}}{4} > 1$

$\Rightarrow\ r = \dfrac{1+\sqrt{5}}{4}$

7. (b) $R = 1 - r \ \Rightarrow\ R = 1 - \left(\dfrac{1+\sqrt{5}}{4}\right) = \dfrac{3-\sqrt{5}}{4}$

Passage: C

(n) = integer nearest to $\sqrt{n}$

$\Rightarrow\ n \in \left[k - \dfrac{1}{2}, k + \dfrac{1}{2}\right)$

For the equation $(n) = k$

8. (a) The number of solution of $(n) = k$ is $2k$

9. (d) $S = \displaystyle\sum_{n=1}^{\infty} \dfrac{2^{(n)} + 2^{-(n)}}{2^n}$ will contain a term like $\dfrac{2^2 + 2^{-2}}{2^k}$; whenever $(n) = 2$

$\Rightarrow$ 4 terms

10. (a) $S = \displaystyle\sum_{n=1}^{\infty} \dfrac{2^{(n)} + 2^{-(n)}}{2^n} = \dfrac{2^{(1)} + 2^{-(1)}}{2} + \dfrac{2^{(2)} + 2^{-(2)}}{2^2} + \ldots.$

$\Rightarrow\ 1 + \dfrac{1}{4} + \dfrac{1}{2} + \dfrac{1}{8} + \dfrac{1}{2} + \dfrac{1}{32} + \dfrac{1}{4} + \dfrac{1}{48} + \dfrac{1}{8} + \dfrac{1}{128} + \ldots. = 1 + 1 + 1 = 3$

Passage: D

11. (b) Let $(1 + x)^2\left(1 + \dfrac{x}{2}\right)^2\left(1 + \dfrac{x}{2^2}\right)^2 \ldots\infty = a_0 + a_1x + a_2x_2 + \ldots$

Replacing x by $\dfrac{x}{2}$, we get $\left(1 + \dfrac{x}{2}\right)^2\left(1 + \dfrac{x}{2^2}\right)^2\left(1 + \dfrac{x}{2^3}\right)^2 \ldots.\infty$

$= a_0 + a_1\dfrac{x}{2} + a_2\left(\dfrac{x}{2}\right)^2 + \ldots + a_3\left(\dfrac{x}{2}\right)^3$

$\Rightarrow\ (1 + x)^2\left(a_0 + a_1\dfrac{x}{2} + a_2\left(\dfrac{x}{2}\right)^2 + \ldots\right)$

$= a_0 + \left(2a_0 + \dfrac{a_1}{2}\right)x + \ldots..$

Equating coefficient of x^r in the expression $(r \ge 2)$

$A_r = \dfrac{4}{2^r - 1}(A_{r-1} + A_{r-2})$

12. (d) $A_1 = \dfrac{A_1}{2} + 290; \qquad A_0 = 1$

$\Rightarrow\ A_1\left(\dfrac{1}{2}\right) = 2 \qquad \Rightarrow\ A_1 = 4$

13. (d) $a_2 = \dfrac{4}{4-1}(4 + 1) = \dfrac{20}{3}$

Passage: E

14. (b) $a_1, a_2, \ldots a_n$ are in A.P.

$\tan^{-1}\left(\dfrac{d}{1 + a_1a_2}\right) = \tan^{-1}\dfrac{(a_2 - a_1)}{1 + a_1a_2} = \tan^{-1} a_2 - \tan^{-1} a_1$

Similarly, $\tan^{-1}\left(\dfrac{d}{a_2a_3+1}\right)=\dfrac{\tan^{-1}(a_3-a_2)}{1+a_2a_3}=\tan^{-1}a_3-\tan a_2$

....

....

Summing all the terms $=\tan^{-1}a_n-\tan^{-1}a_1=\dfrac{\tan^{-1}(a_n-a_1)}{(1+a_1a_n)}$

$=\tan^{-1}\left(\dfrac{(n-1)d}{1+a_1a_n}\right)$

15. (b) $\dfrac{\sqrt{h_1h_2}}{\sqrt{h_1}+\sqrt{h_2}}+\dfrac{\sqrt{h_2h_3}}{\sqrt{h_2}+\sqrt{h_3}}+\ldots+\dfrac{\sqrt{h_{n-1}.h_n}}{\sqrt{h_{n-1}}+\sqrt{h_n}}$

$$=\frac{\sqrt{h_1h_2}\left(\sqrt{h_1}-\sqrt{h_2}\right)}{(h_1-h_2)}+\frac{\sqrt{h_2h_3}\left(\sqrt{h_2}-\sqrt{h_3}\right)}{(h_2-h_3)}+\ldots+\frac{\sqrt{h_{n-1}.h_n}\left(\sqrt{h_{n-1}}-\sqrt{h_n}\right)}{(h_{n-1}-h_n)}$$

$$=\frac{\sqrt{h_1h_2}\left(\sqrt{h_1}-\sqrt{h_2}\right)}{h_1.h_2}\left(\frac{h_1.h_2}{h_1-h_2}\right)+\frac{\sqrt{h_2h_3}\left(\sqrt{h_2}-\sqrt{h_3}\right)}{h_2.h_3}\left(\frac{h_2.h_3}{h_2-h_3}\right)+\ldots+\frac{\sqrt{h_{n-1}.h_2}\left(\sqrt{h_{n-1}}-\sqrt{h_n}\right)}{(h_{n-1}-h_n)}\left(\frac{h_{n-1}.h_n}{h_{n-1}-h_n}\right)$$

$$=\left[\left(\frac{1}{\sqrt{h_2}}-\frac{1}{\sqrt{h_1}}\right)+\left(\frac{1}{\sqrt{h_3}}-\frac{1}{\sqrt{h_2}}\right)+\ldots+\left(\frac{1}{\sqrt{h_n}}-\frac{1}{\sqrt{h_{n-1}}}\right)\right]\left(\frac{1}{D}\right)$$

$$\left(\because\ \frac{h_1-h_2}{h_1h_2}=\frac{h_2-h_3}{h_2h_3}=D(\text{say})\right)$$

$$=\frac{1}{D}\left(\frac{1}{\sqrt{h_n}}-\frac{1}{\sqrt{h_1}}\right)=\frac{1}{D}\left(\frac{\sqrt{h_1}-\sqrt{h_n}}{\sqrt{h_1}.\sqrt{h_n}}\right)$$

$$=\frac{1}{D}.\left(\frac{(h_1-h_n)}{\sqrt{h_1}.\sqrt{h_n}}\right)\times\frac{1}{\left(\sqrt{h_1}+\sqrt{h_n}\right)}=\left(\frac{1}{h_n}-\frac{1}{h_1}\right).\left(\frac{\sqrt{h_1}.\sqrt{h_n}}{\sqrt{h_1}+\sqrt{h_n}}\right).\frac{1}{D}$$

$$=\left((n-1).\left(\frac{\sqrt{h_1}.\sqrt{h_n}}{\sqrt{h_1}+\sqrt{h_n}}\right)\right)$$

16. (c) $a_1=h_1=2$

$a_{10}=h_{10}=3$

$a_{10}=a_1+9d$

$\Rightarrow 3=2+9d \qquad \Rightarrow d=\dfrac{1}{9}$ (i)

Similarly $\dfrac{1}{h_{10}}=\dfrac{1}{h_1}+(9).d_1 \Rightarrow 9d_1=\dfrac{1}{3}-\dfrac{1}{2}=-\dfrac{1}{6}$

$\Rightarrow d=-\dfrac{1}{54}$ (ii)

$a_4=a_1+3d=2+\dfrac{1}{3}=-\dfrac{7}{3}$

$\dfrac{1}{h_7}=\dfrac{1}{h_1}+6d=\dfrac{1}{2}-\dfrac{1}{9}=\dfrac{7}{18}$

$\Rightarrow a_4\,h_7=\dfrac{7}{3}\times\dfrac{18}{7}=6$

Passage: F

Let the four integers be $a-d$, a, $a+d$, $a+2d$; where $d>0$

$\therefore\ a+2d=(a-d)^2+a^2+(a-d)^2$

$\Rightarrow 2d^2-2d+3a^2-a=0$

$\Rightarrow d=\dfrac{1}{2}\left[1\pm\sqrt{1+2a-6a^2}\right]$

Since d is a positive integer, then $1+2a-6a^2>0$

$\Rightarrow \dfrac{1-\sqrt{7}}{6}<a<\dfrac{1+\sqrt{7}}{6}$

$\Rightarrow a=0 \qquad \Rightarrow d=1$ or 0

But since it is an increasing A.P. $\Rightarrow d=1$

Numbers are –1, 0, 1, 2

17. (c) Smallest number = – 1

18. (b) Common difference = 1

19. (c) Sum of the 4 no.s = 2

Passage: G

$A=a_1, a_2, a_3\ (D)$

$B=b_1, b_2, b_3\ (d)$

$S_A=\dfrac{3}{2}(a_1+a_3)=15$

$\Rightarrow a_1+a_3=10$ (i)

Similarly $b_1+b_3=10$ (ii)

Replacing, we get

$a_3=a_1+2D$

$b_3=b_1+2d$

$\Rightarrow 2a_1+2D=10$ (iii)

$\Rightarrow 2b_1+2d=10$ (iv)

(iii) – (iv), we get $(a_1-b_1)+(D-d)=0$

$\Rightarrow a_1-b_1=-1 \qquad \Rightarrow b_1-a_1=-1$ (v)

$\Rightarrow a_1=a_1 \qquad \Rightarrow a_2=5$

$\Rightarrow a_3=10-a_1$

$\Rightarrow b_1=a_1+1 \qquad \Rightarrow b_2=5$

$\Rightarrow b_3=9-a_1$

By the question, we get $\dfrac{(10-a_1)a_1.5}{(1+a_1).5.(9-a_1)}=\dfrac{7}{8}$

$\Rightarrow \dfrac{(10-a_1)a_1}{(1+a_1)(9-a_1)}=\dfrac{7}{8} \quad \Rightarrow a_1^2-24a_1+63=0$

$\Rightarrow a_1=21$ or 3

But $d>0\Rightarrow \qquad A=3, 5, 7$

$\Rightarrow B=4, 5, 6$

20. (c) $P=105$

21. (b) $q=120$

22. (c) $D+d=2+1=3$

Passage: H

Let $a_1, a_2, \ldots\ldots a_n$ be first A.P. and $b_1, b_2, \ldots, b_n$ be second A.P.

$\therefore\ \dfrac{a_n}{b_1}=\dfrac{b_n}{a_1}=4$

$\therefore\ \dfrac{\frac{n}{2}(a_1+a_n)}{\frac{n}{2}(b_1+b_n)}=2$

$\Rightarrow \dfrac{a_1+4b_1}{b_1+4a_1}=2 \qquad \Rightarrow \dfrac{a_1}{b_1}=\dfrac{2}{7}$

$\Rightarrow \dfrac{b_n}{a_n} = \dfrac{a_1}{b_1} = \dfrac{2}{7} \Rightarrow \dfrac{a_n}{b_n} = \dfrac{7}{2}$

$\Rightarrow \dfrac{a_n}{b_1} = \dfrac{7b_n}{2b_1} = 4 = \dfrac{7}{2}\left(\dfrac{b_1+(n-1)d_2}{b_1}\right)$

$\Rightarrow \dfrac{7(n-1)d_2}{2b_1} = \dfrac{1}{2}$ (i)

Similarly $\dfrac{2(n-1)d_1}{a_1} = 13$ (ii)

Dividing (i) by (iii), we get $\dfrac{d_1}{d_2} = 13 \times 7 \times \dfrac{2}{7} = 26$

23. **(c)** $\dfrac{d_1}{d_2} = 26$

24. **(b)** $\dfrac{a_n}{b_n} = \dfrac{7}{2}$

25. **(a)** $\dfrac{a_1}{b_1} = \dfrac{2}{7}$

SECTION–VI: (COLUMN MATCHING)

1. **(i)→(c); (ii)→(b); (iii)→(b); (iv)→(b)**

(i) $a^x = b^y = c^z$

a, b, c are in G.P.

$\Rightarrow b = ar$ and $c = ar^2$

$(a)^x = (ar)^y = (ar^2)^z = k$

$\Rightarrow k^{\frac{1}{x}}.k^{\frac{1}{z}}.k^{\frac{1}{2y}} \quad \Rightarrow \dfrac{1}{x} + \dfrac{1}{z} = \dfrac{2}{y}$

$\Rightarrow x, y, z$ are in H.P.

(ii) $\dfrac{x+y}{2}, y, \dfrac{y+2}{z}$ are in H.P.

$\Rightarrow \dfrac{2}{x+y}, \dfrac{1}{y}, \dfrac{2}{y+z}$ are in A.P.

$\Rightarrow \dfrac{1}{x+y} + \dfrac{1}{y+z} = \dfrac{1}{y}$

$\Rightarrow y(2y + z + x) = (x + y)(y + z)$

$\Rightarrow xy + 2y^2 + yz = xy + xz + y^2 + zy$

$\Rightarrow y^2 + xz$

$\Rightarrow x, y, z$ are in G.P.

(iii) Given a, b, c are in A.P.

$b = \dfrac{a+c}{2}$ (i)

$c^2 = bd$ (ii)

Similarly $d = \dfrac{2ce}{c+e}$ (iii)

$c^2 = \left(\dfrac{a+c}{2}\right)\left(\dfrac{2ce}{c+e}\right)$

$\Rightarrow c^2 + ce = ae + ce$

$\Rightarrow a, c, e$ are in G.P.

(iv) $\dfrac{1}{2(y-b)} - \dfrac{1}{(y-x)} = \dfrac{1}{y-z} - \dfrac{1}{2(y-b)}$

which can be written as $\dfrac{y-x-2(y-b)}{2(y-b)(y-x)} = \dfrac{2(y-b)-(y-z)}{2(y-z)(y-b)}$

$\Rightarrow \dfrac{y+x-2b}{x-y} = \dfrac{y+z-2b}{y-z}$

$\Rightarrow \dfrac{(x-b)+(y-b)}{(x-b)-(y-b)} = \dfrac{(y-b)+(z-b)}{(y-b)-(z-b)}$

$\Rightarrow \dfrac{x-b}{y-b} = \dfrac{y-b}{z-b}$

$\Rightarrow (x - b)(y - b)(z - b)$ are in G.P

2. **(i)→(c); (ii) → (d); (iii) → (a)**

(i) $A = \dfrac{1}{a} + \dfrac{1}{b} + \dfrac{1}{c}$

Applying A.M.-G.M. inequality on $\dfrac{1}{a}, \dfrac{1}{b}, \dfrac{1}{c}$

$\Rightarrow \dfrac{1}{a} + \dfrac{1}{b} + \dfrac{1}{c} \geq 3\left(\dfrac{1}{abc}\right)^{1/3}$ (i)

and clearly $a + b + c \geq 3(abc)^{1/3}$

$\Rightarrow \left[\dfrac{1}{(abc)}\right]^{1/3} \geq \dfrac{3}{(a+b+c)}$

Putting in (i), we get $\dfrac{1}{a} + \dfrac{1}{b} + \dfrac{1}{c} \geq \dfrac{9}{a+b+c}$

(ii) $A = (a + b)(b + c)(c + a)$

$a + b \geq 2\sqrt{ab}$ (i)

$a + b \geq 2\sqrt{ac}$ (ii)

$b + c \geq 2\sqrt{bc}$ (iii)

Multiplying (i), (ii) and (iii), we get $(a + b)(a + c)(b + c) \geq 8$ abc $\quad \therefore$ (ii) → (d)

(iii) $A = a^{\frac{a}{a+b+c}}.b^{\frac{b}{a+b+c}}.c^{\frac{c}{a+b+c}}$

This we can arrange as $A = (a^a b^b c^c)^{\frac{1}{a+b+c}}$

Applying G.M. ≥ H.M., We get $\left[\underbrace{(a.a.a...)}_{a\text{ times}}\underbrace{(b.b.b...)}_{b\text{ times}}\underbrace{(c.c.c...)}_{c\text{ times}}\right]^{\frac{1}{a+b+c}}$ is greater than or

equal to $\dfrac{a+b+c}{1+1+1}$

$\Rightarrow A \geq \dfrac{1}{3}$

3. **(i) → (b); (ii) → (b); (iii) → (c)**

(i) $S_n = a2^n - b$ for $n \geq 2$

$S_2 = 4a - b$

$S_3 = 8a - b$

$S_4 = 16a - b$

$S_5 = 32\,a - b$

$S_3 = 4a$

$S_4 = 8a$

$S_5 = 16a$

$\Rightarrow$ The series is a G.P.

(ii) $\dfrac{a+be^y}{a-be^y} = \dfrac{b+ce^y}{b-ce^y} = \dfrac{c+de^y}{c-de^y}$

Using componendo and dividendo $\dfrac{2a}{2be^y} = \dfrac{2b}{2ce^y} = \dfrac{2c}{2de^y}$

$\Rightarrow \dfrac{a}{b} = \dfrac{b}{c} = \dfrac{c}{d}$

$\Rightarrow a, b, c, d$ are in G.P.

(iii) $x^3 - 6x^2 + 11x - 6 = 0$

One of the root is $x = 1$

$\Rightarrow x^2(x-1) - 5x(x-1) + 6(x-1) = 0$

$\Rightarrow (x-1)(x-2)(x-3) = 0$

$\Rightarrow$ Roots are 1, 2, 3.

$6x^2 - 11x^2 + 6x - 1 = 0$

$\Rightarrow 6x^2(x-1) - 5x(x-1) + (x-1) = 0$

$\Rightarrow (x-1)(6x^2 - 5x + 1) = 0$

$\Rightarrow (x-1)(6x^2 - 3x - 2x + 1) = 0$

$\Rightarrow (x-1)(3x(2x-1) - (2x-1)) = 0$

$\Rightarrow (x-1)(3x-1)(2x-1) = 0$

$\Rightarrow x = 1, \frac{1}{3}, \frac{1}{2} \Rightarrow$ which are in H.P

$\therefore$ (iii) $\to$ (c)

SECTION–VII: (ASSERTION AND REASON)

1. A: Suppose $\sqrt{2}, \sqrt{3}, \sqrt{5}$ are pth qth and rth terms of an A.P. whose common difference is d.

$t_r - t_p = (r-p)d$

$t_q - t_p = (q-p)d$

$\Rightarrow \frac{t_r - t_p}{t_q - t_p} = \frac{r-p}{q-p}$; which is a rational number

$\Leftrightarrow \frac{(\sqrt{5}-\sqrt{2})}{(\sqrt{3}-\sqrt{2})}$ is a rational number

$\Rightarrow (\sqrt{15} - \sqrt{6} + \sqrt{10} - 3)$ is rational.

$\Leftrightarrow \sqrt{15} - \sqrt{6} + \sqrt{10}$ is rational say r

$\Rightarrow \sqrt{6} - \sqrt{10} = \sqrt{15} - r$

$\Rightarrow \sqrt{15}$ is rational; which is a contradiction

$\Rightarrow \sqrt{2}, \sqrt{3}, \sqrt{5}$ can't be terms of an A.P.

R: Already explained in Assertion

$\therefore$ option (d) is correct.

2. A: $a_n = n^3 + n^2 + 1$

$a_1 = 3$

$a_2 = 13$

$a_3 = 37$

$a_4 = 81$

$a_5 = 151$

First order difference = 10, 24, 44, 70

Second order difference = 14, 20, 26

Which are in A.P.

$\Rightarrow$ Assertion is correct.

R: a_n = a polynomial of degree n

$\Rightarrow (n-1)^{th}$ order difference from an A.P

$\Rightarrow n^{th}$ order difference are constant

$\therefore$ option (a) is correct

3.A: Let a, b, c be sides of a right Δ

By Pythagoras $c^2 = a^2 + b^2$

$\Rightarrow \frac{c^2}{b^2} = \frac{a^2}{b^2} + 1 \qquad \Rightarrow r^2 = \frac{1}{r^2} + 1$

$\Rightarrow r^4 - r^2 - 1 = 0 \qquad \Rightarrow r^2 = \frac{1+\sqrt{5}}{2}, \frac{1-\sqrt{5}}{2}$

Only possible values can take two and only 2 values.

R: Clearly $r = 1$ will not satisfy the Pythagoras theorem

$\Rightarrow$ Common ratio is either greater than or less than one.

$\therefore$ Option (b) is correct

4. A: Sum of all angles of a convex polygon = $Sn = (n-2) \times 180^0$. If an angle is acute, then the corresponding exterior angle is greater than 90^0. Let us assume that a convex polygon has four or more acute angles. Since polygon is convex, all exterior angles are positive.

$\Rightarrow$ Sum of exterior angles > 360^0, which is impossible

$\Rightarrow$ Largest number of acute angles in a convex polygon is 3.

R = Sum of all angles of a polygon (n-sides) = sum of all angles of $(n-2)$ triangles = $(n-2) \times 180^0$

$\Rightarrow$ Reason is correct

$\therefore$ option (b) is correct

5. A: A.M. of 2 numbers = $\frac{5}{2}$; G.M. = 2

$\Rightarrow$ H. M = $\frac{8}{5}$; $\qquad a + b = 5$

$ab = 4$

$\Rightarrow \frac{2ab}{a+b} = \frac{8}{5} \qquad \Rightarrow$ Assertion is correct.

R: (G.M.)^2 = (A.M.) × (H.M.)

For 2 numbers A.M. = $\frac{a+b}{2}$

H.M. = $\frac{2ab}{a+b}$

$\Rightarrow$ A.M. × H.M. = ab

$\Rightarrow$ G.M. = $\sqrt{ab}$

$\Rightarrow$ (G.M)^2 + (A.M) × (H.M)

$\therefore$ option (a) is correct

SECTION–VIII: (INTEGER TYPE)

1. $a_1, a_2 \ldots a_n$ are in A.P.

$a_1 = 1$; $d = -\frac{5}{\lambda}$

$\Rightarrow a_2 = 1 - \frac{5}{\lambda} \qquad \Rightarrow a_3 = \frac{1-10}{\lambda}$

Expression = $\left(1 - \frac{10}{\lambda}\right) + \left(1 - \frac{10}{\lambda}\right)\left(1 - \frac{5}{\lambda}\right) = \frac{2\lambda^2 - 25\lambda + 50}{\lambda^2}$

$= \left(2 - \frac{25}{\lambda} + \frac{50}{\lambda^2}\right)_{min}$ when $\left(\frac{25}{\lambda^2} - \frac{100}{\lambda^3}\right) = 0$

$\Rightarrow \frac{1}{\lambda^2} = \frac{4}{\lambda^3} \qquad \Rightarrow \lambda = 4$

2. a, b, c are in G.P. $\Rightarrow b^2 = ac$

$\log_6 a + \log_6 b + \log_6 c = 6$

$\Rightarrow abc = 6^6 \qquad \Rightarrow b^3 = 6^6$

$\Rightarrow b = 36$

$\Rightarrow ac = 36 \times 36 \qquad \Rightarrow b - a = N^2$

$\Rightarrow 36 - a = N^2$

$\therefore a$ is a factor of $2^4 3^4 \quad \Rightarrow a = 27$ is a possibility

$\Rightarrow a + b + c = 111$

3. $x, y, z > 0$ such that $x + y + z = 1$

Clearly, $1 - x = y + z > 0$,

$2 - y = 2 - (1 - x - z) = 1 + x + z > 0$ and

$3 - z = 3 - (1 - x - y) = 2 + x + y > 0$

$\therefore$ BY A.M. ≥ G.M., $(1 - x)(2 - y)(3 - z) \le \left[\frac{(1-x)+(2-y)+(3-z)}{3}\right]^3$

$$= \left[\frac{6-(x+y+z)}{3}\right]^3 = \left[\frac{6-1}{3}\right]^3 = \frac{125}{27}$$

$$\Rightarrow [(1-x)(2-y)(3-z)]_{\max} = \left[\frac{125}{27}\right] = 4$$

4. $f(x - 1) + f(x + 1) = \sqrt{3}\, f(x)$ (i)

Replacing x by $(x + 1)$, we get $f(x) + f(x + 2) = \sqrt{3}\, f(x + 1)$ (ii)

Multiplyiug (i) by $\sqrt{3}$, we get $\sqrt{3}\, f(x + 1) + \sqrt{3}\, f(x + 1) = 3f(x)$

$\Rightarrow \sqrt{3}\, f(x + 1) = 3f(x) - \sqrt{3}\, f(x - 1)$ (iii)

$\therefore$ From (ii) and (iii), we get $f(x) + f(x + 2) + 3f(x) - \sqrt{3}\, f(x - 1)$

$\Rightarrow f(x) + f(x + 2) = 3f(x) - [f(x - 2) + f(x)]$

$\Rightarrow f(x) + f(x + 2) = 2f(x) - f(x - 2)$

$\Rightarrow f(x) = f(x + 2) + f(x - 2)$

$\Rightarrow f(x) = f(x + 2) + [f(x) + f(x - 4)]$

$\Rightarrow f(x + 2) = -f(x - 4) \Rightarrow f(x) = -f(x - 6)$

$\Rightarrow f(x) = -[-f(x - 12)] \Rightarrow f(x) = f(x - 12)$

$\Rightarrow f(x) = f(x + 12)$

$\Rightarrow f(x)$ is periodic with period 12

$\Rightarrow f(5 + 12r) = f(5) = 10$ " $0 \le r \le 19$

$$\Rightarrow \sum_{r=0}^{19} f(5+12r) = 20\,(10) = 200$$

5. $S_n = 1^2 + (1^2 + 2^2) + (1^2 + 2^3 + 3^2) + \ldots$

First sum has 1 term, second sum = 2 term, ….. and so on.

6 term will have $S_6 = \frac{6\,(6+1)}{2} = 21$

$$S_{21} = \sum_{n=1}^{6} \frac{n(n+1)\,(2n+1)}{6}$$

$$= \sum_{n=1}^{6} \frac{(n^2+n)\,(2n+1)}{6} = \sum_{n=1}^{6} \frac{2n^3+3n^2+n}{6}$$

Using $\sum n^3 = \frac{n^2(n+1)^2}{4} = \sum n^2 = n\frac{(n+1)\,(2n+1)}{6}$

$$= \sum_{n=1}^{6} \frac{(2n^3+3n^2+n)}{6} = 23276$$

6. $d = \frac{\ell^2 - a^2}{\lambda S - (\ell + a)}$

By the question $l = a + (n - 1)\, d$

$\Rightarrow S = \left(\frac{a+\ell}{2}\right)^n \quad \Rightarrow \left(\frac{\ell - a}{d}\right) + 1 = \frac{2s}{a+1}$

$\Rightarrow ((l - a) + d)(1 + a) = 2$ ds

$\Rightarrow (l^2 - a^2) + d(1 + a) = 2$ ds

$\Rightarrow (l^2 - a^2) = d[25 - p(l + a)]$

$\Rightarrow \frac{\ell^2 - a^2}{2s - (\ell + \text{a})} = d$; $\lambda = 2$

7. $S_n = \sqrt{3} = \frac{1}{\sqrt{3}} + \frac{1}{3\sqrt{3}} + \ldots$ is a G.P. with $r = \frac{1}{3}$

$S_n = \frac{\sqrt{3}}{1-\frac{1}{3}} = \frac{3\sqrt{3}}{2} \quad \Rightarrow \lambda = 3$

8. Let the G.P. be $a, ar, \ldots ar^n$

By the question

$ar \,.\, ar^{n-2} = 128$ (i)

$a(1 + r^{n-1}) = 66$ (ii)

$\frac{a(r^n - 1)}{r - 1} = 126$ (iii)

By (i), (ii) and (iii), we get $66 = a\left(1 + \frac{128}{a^2}\right)$

$\Rightarrow a^2 + 128 - 66a = 0 \Rightarrow a = 2, 64$

$\Rightarrow 66 = a(1 + r^{n-1})$ or $66 = 64(1 + r^{n-1})$

$\Rightarrow r = 1/2, n = 6$ Or $66 = 2(1 + r^{n-1})$

$\Rightarrow r^{n-1} = 32 \Rightarrow r = 2, n = 6$

9. $a_1 = 2$

$S_{10} = 5(4 + 9d) = 0 \quad \Rightarrow d = -\frac{4}{9}$

Sum of next 15 terms $= S_{25} - S_{10} = S_{25} = \frac{25}{2}\left(4 + 24\left(\frac{-4}{9}\right)\right)$

$$= \frac{25}{2}\left(4 - \frac{32}{3}\right) = \frac{-20.25}{6} = \frac{-250}{3} = -\frac{\lambda}{3}$$

$\Rightarrow \lambda = 250$

10. Let the two quantities be a and b

$G = \sqrt{ab}$; $p = a + \frac{b-a}{3}$; $q = a + \frac{2(b-a)}{3}$

$(kp - q) = ka + \frac{k(b-a)}{3} - a$

$-2\,\frac{(b-a)}{3} = a(k-1) + \frac{b-a}{3}(k-2)$

$kq - p = ak + \frac{2k(b-a)}{3} - a - \frac{(b-a)}{3}$

$\Rightarrow a(k-1) + \frac{b-a}{3}\,(2k-1)$

$\therefore (kp - q)(kq - p) = ab \;\therefore\; k = 2$

11. Let $X = \lim_{n\to\infty} (1 + 5^{-1})(1 + 5^{-2}) \ldots (1 + 5^{-2n})$

$\Rightarrow \left(1 - \frac{1}{3}\right)X = \lim_{n\to\infty} (1 - 5^{-1})(1 + 5^{-1})(1 + 5^{-2}) \ldots (1 + 5^{-2n})$

$= \lim_{n\to\infty} (1 - 5^{-2})(1 + 5^{-2}) \ldots (1 + 5^{-2n})$

$X = \frac{5}{4}(1 - 5^{-4n})$

$\Rightarrow \lambda = 5, \mu = 4 \quad \Rightarrow \lambda\mu = 20$

12. $\sum_{k=1}^{10}(3 + 2^k) = 30 + (2 + 2^2 + \ldots + 2^{10}) = 30 + 2\,\frac{(2^{10} - 1)}{2 - 1} = 28 + 2^{11} = 28 + 2^k \quad \Rightarrow k = 11$

13. $\sum_{k=2}^{15}(1 + 3^{k-1}) = (1 + 3) + (1 + 3^2) + \ldots + (1 + 3^3) + \ldots + (1 + 3^{14}) = 14 + 3\,\frac{(3^{14} - 1)}{2} = \frac{1}{2}(25 + 3^{15}) \Rightarrow \lambda = 15$

14. $\sum_{k=1}^{10}\left(\left(\frac{1}{2}\right)^{k-1}+\left(\frac{1}{5}\right)^{k+1}\right)$

$= 1+\frac{1}{2}+\frac{1}{2^2}+....+\frac{1}{2^9}+\frac{1}{5^2}+\frac{1}{5^3}+....+\frac{1}{5^{11}} = 2-2^{-9}+\frac{1}{20}$

$(1-5^{-10})$

On comparison $\lambda = 10$

15. The total number of grains $= 1 + 2 + 4 + ...+ 2^{63}$

Sum $= 2^{64-1} = 2^{\lambda-1}$ $\Rightarrow \lambda = 64$

16. To water $T_1 = 10$

To water $T_2 = 25$

To water $T_3 = 35$

To water $T_4 = 45$

$\Rightarrow$ 10, 25, 35, 45, 55, ...

$\Rightarrow T_{25} = 25 + 23.10 = 255$

Total distance = 10 + 12 (280) = 3370 meters

17. $S_1=\sum_{i=0}^{\infty}\sum_{j=0}^{\infty}\sum_{k=0}^{\infty}\frac{1}{3^i3^j3^k}=\left(\frac{3}{2}\right)^3=\frac{27}{8}$

Let $i \neq j = k$ and $i, j, k \in \{0, 1, 2, 3, ..\}$

$S_2 = \sum_{i=0;i\neq j}^{\infty}\sum_{j=0}^{\infty}\frac{1}{3^i(3)^{2j}}=\sum_{j=0i\neq j}^{\infty}\sum_{j=0}^{\infty}\frac{1}{3^i(9)^j}$

$=\left(\frac{1}{1-\frac{1}{3}}\right)\left(\frac{1}{1-\frac{1}{9}}\right)-\sum_{i=0}^{\infty}\frac{1}{3^i(9)^i}$

$=\left(\frac{3}{2}\right)\left(\frac{9}{8}\right)-\sum_{i=0}^{\infty}\frac{1}{(27)^i}=\frac{27}{16}-\frac{1}{\left(1-\frac{1}{27}\right)}=\frac{27}{16}-\frac{27}{26}=27\left(\frac{10}{16\times 26}\right)$

$=\frac{135}{208}$

Let $i = j = k$

$S_3=\sum_{i=0}^{\infty}\frac{1}{3^{3i}}=\sum_{i=0}^{\infty}\frac{1}{(27)^i}=\frac{1}{1-\frac{1}{27}}=\frac{27}{26}$

$\therefore$ Required sum $(S) = S_1 - 3S_2 - S_3$

$=\frac{27}{8}-\frac{405}{208}-\frac{27}{26}=\frac{702-405-216}{208}=\frac{81}{208}$

$\Rightarrow 5S = \frac{405}{208}\in(1,2)$

$\Rightarrow [5S] = 1$

18. $a=\sum_{x=1}^{\infty}\frac{1}{n^n}=\frac{1}{1}+\frac{1}{2^2}+\frac{1}{3^3}+\frac{1}{4^4}+...$

Clearly $a > 1$.

Now $a < 1+\frac{1}{2}+\frac{1}{2^2}+\frac{1}{2^2}+\frac{1}{2^3}+....$

$\Rightarrow a<\frac{1}{1-\frac{1}{2}}=2$

$\Rightarrow 1<a<2$ $\Rightarrow [a]=1$

19. $S=\sum_{k=1}^{\infty}\frac{k+2}{2^{k+1}.k.(k+1)}=\sum_{k=1}^{\infty}\frac{1}{2^{k+1}}\left[\frac{2}{k}-\frac{1}{k+1}\right]$

$=\sum_{k=1}^{\infty}\left[\frac{1}{2^k.k}-\frac{1}{2^{k+1}(k+1)}\right]$

$=\lim_{k\to\infty}\left[\left(\frac{1}{2.1}-\frac{1}{2^2.2}\right)\right]+\left[\frac{1}{2^2.2}-\frac{1}{2^3.3}\right]+...+\left[\frac{1}{2^k.k}-\frac{1}{2^{k+1}(k+1)}\right]$

$=\lim_{k\to\infty}\left[\frac{1}{2}-\frac{1}{2^{k+1}.(k+1)}\right]=\frac{1}{2}$

$\Rightarrow \frac{1}{S}=\frac{1}{2}\Rightarrow S=2$

$\Rightarrow 5S=\frac{405}{208}\in(1,2)$ $\Rightarrow [5S] = 1$

20. $S=\sum_{k=1}^{\infty}\frac{k}{(k^4+2k^2+1-k^2)}=\sum_{k=1}^{\infty}\frac{k}{(k^2+1)^2-(k)^2}$

$=\sum_{k=1}^{\infty}\frac{k}{(k^2+1+k)(k^2+1-k)}=\sum_{k=1}^{\infty}\frac{(k^2+1+k)-(k^2-k+1)}{(k^2+k+1)(k^2-k+1)}$

$=\lim_{n\to\infty}\frac{1}{2}\sum_{k=1}^{n}\left(\frac{1}{k^2-k+1}-\frac{1}{k^2+k+1}\right)$

$=\frac{1}{2}\lim_{x\to\infty}\left[\left(\frac{1}{1}-\frac{1}{3}\right)+\left(\frac{1}{3}-\frac{1}{7}\right)+\left(\frac{1}{7}-\frac{1}{13}\right)+...+\left(\frac{1}{n^2-n+1}-\frac{1}{n^2+n+1}\right)\right]$

$=\frac{1}{2}\lim_{x\to\infty}\left(1-\frac{1}{n^2+n+1}\right)=\frac{1}{2}$

$\Rightarrow$ (2550) (S) = (2550) $\left(\frac{1}{2}\right)$ = 1275

21. $\frac{2ab}{a+b}=4$ $\Rightarrow a+b+ab=27$

$\Rightarrow \frac{3}{2}ab=27$ $\Rightarrow ab=18, a+b=9$

$\Rightarrow$ The two numbers are 6 and 3

Squares root of the sum of the number $=\sqrt{9}=3$

22. $S_1=\frac{1}{1-\frac{1}{2}}$ and $S_2=\frac{2}{1-\frac{1}{3}}$

Similarly $S_n=\frac{n}{1-\frac{1}{n+1}}=n+1$

Required sum $=\sum_{n=1}^{19}(n+1)^2=\sum_{n=1}^{19}(n^2+2n+1)$

$=\frac{19.20+39}{6}$ + 19.20 + 19 = 2869

23. Let $d=\frac{\pi}{2}$

$L = \sin d\,(\sec a_1 \sec a_2 + ...+ \sec a_{n-1} \sec a_n)$

$=\frac{\sin(a_2-a_1)}{\cos a_2\, a_1}+\frac{\sin(a_3-a_2)}{\cos a_2.\cos a_3}+..... = \tan A_n - \tan A_1$

$\Rightarrow$ Required sum $=\frac{\tan a_n-\tan a_1}{\sin\left(\frac{\pi}{6}\right)}=2(\tan a_n-\tan a_1)$

$\Rightarrow k=2$

Inequalities

CHAPTER 4

■ INTRODUCTION

Theory of inequality has been introduced to understand the comparative analysis of two quantities. e.g., weight of two cricket balls may be equal, but the weight of a tennis ball or a football is not equal to that of a cricket ball. This is the concept of inequality used in mathematics and it basically arises from our habit of comparing two things.

For solving complicated inequality problems, some theories have been introduced that will be dealt in this chapter. For our convenience, some signs have been introduced. For greater than " > ", for less than " < " and for equality " = ".

A number 'a' is said to be greater than another number 'b', when $a - b$ is positive. We write this as $a > b$. Also b is said to be less than a ($b < a$) when $b - a$ is negative.

Inequalities have been discussed in various chapters in a discrete manner. Students are suggested a brief review of these topics before they proceed further in this chapter.

1. Foundation Mathematics: Rational Inequalities, Irrational Inequalities, Modulus Inequalities
2. Exponential Logarithm: Exponential Inequalities, Logarithmic Inequalities
3. Sequence and Series: Inequality of Mean

This chapter will provide a chassis of theory of inequality

■ LINEAR INEQUATIONS

(i) The law of trichomy of real numbers asserts that any pair of real numbers x and y bear one of the three relation: $x = y$, $x > y$ or $x < y$ the 2nd and third relations are signs of inequality.

These are the fundamental laws of inequalities. The statement of inequality can be defined as below:

An inequation is a statement involving a sign of inequality. The signs of inequality are given as: $<, >, \leq, \geq, \nless, \ngtr, \neq$.

(ii) An inequation can have one or more variables e.g., $ax + b \geq 0$, $ax + by + c \geq 0$

(iii) The values of the unknown for which an inequation holds good are called the solutions of the inequation.

■ PROPERTIES OF THE INEQUALITIES

1. Same number can be added or subtracted to both sides of an inequation.

   If $a > b$, then (i) $a + c > b + c \quad \forall c \in \mathbb{R}$

   (ii) $a - c > b - c \quad \forall c \in \mathbb{R}$

   If $a_1 > b_1, a_2 > b_2, a_3 > b_3 \ldots\ldots a_n > b_n$

   then $a_1 + a_2 + a_3 + \ldots\ldots + a_n > b_1 + b_2 + b_3 + \ldots\ldots + b_n$

2. If both sides of an inequality are multiplied (*or divided*) by a positive number, inequality does not change but inequality gets reversed when both of its sides are multiplied (*or divided*) by a negative number.

   If $a > b$, then

   $$\left.\begin{array}{ll}\text{(i)} & ac > bc \\ \text{(ii)} & a/c > b/c\end{array}\right\} \forall c > 0$$

   $$\left.\begin{array}{ll}\text{(iii)} & ac < bc \\ \text{(iv)} & a/c < b/c\end{array}\right\} \forall c < 0$$

   Also if $a/b \geq c/d$, then

   (a) $ad \geq bc$ if b and d are of same sign

   (b) $ad \leq bc$ if b and d are of opposite sign.

3. If $a_1 > b_1 > 0, a_2 > b_2 > 0, a_3 > b_3 > 0, \ldots\ldots, a_n > b_n > 0$; $a_1 a_2 a_3 \ldots\ldots a_n > b_1 b_2 b_3 \ldots\ldots b_n$

4. If $a > b > 0 \Rightarrow 1/a < 1/b$
5. If $0 < a < 1$ and $r \in \mathbb{R}^+$ (*set of positive real numbers*), then $0 < a^r \le a^{-r}$.
6. Again if a and b are any two positive numbers and $a > b$ then $a^r > b^r$ if $r > 0$ and $a^r < b^r$ if $r < 0$.
7. Most of the inequalities are based on the fact that "sum of squares of real numbers is always non-negative". e.g., if $x^2 + y^2 + z^2 \ge 0$ for all $x, y, z \in \mathbb{R}$ and equality holds only when $x = y = z = 0$
8. $x^2 \le a^2 \Leftrightarrow |x| \le a$, '$a$' being a positive real constant. i.e., $-a \le x \le a$

   Similarly, $x^2 \ge a^2 \Leftrightarrow |x| \ge a$, i.e., $x \le -a, x \ge a$

   Again $x^2 < a^2 \Leftrightarrow |x| < a \Leftrightarrow -a < x < a$

   and $x^2 > a^2 \Leftrightarrow |x| > a \Leftrightarrow x < -a, x > a$
9. $||x|-|y|| \le |x \pm y| \le |x| + |y|$. This is also known as *Triangle inequality*.

   $|x+y| = |x| + |y|$ if x and y are either of same sign or atleast one is zero $\Rightarrow x.y \ge 0$

   $|x-y| = |x| + |y|$ if x and y are either of opposite sign or at least one is zero $\Rightarrow x.y \le 0$
10. If $x > y > 0$ then

    (i) $\log_a x > \log_a y$, if $a > 1$

    (ii) $\log_a x < \log_a y$, if $0 < a < 1$
11. If $x > y > 0$ then

    (i) $a^x > a^y$, if $a > 1$

    (ii) $a^x < a^y$, if $0 < a < 1$

NOTE

Above two results follow from the fact that logarithmic and exponential function to the base a > 1 are increasing function and when base lies between 0 and 1 then they become decreasing function.

ILLUSTRATION 1: Find which one is greater, $3ab^2$ or $a^3 + 2b^3$.

SOLUTION: Since $a^3 + 2b^3 - 3ab^2 = a^3 - ab^2 + 2b^3 - 2ab^2 = a(a^2 - b^2) + 2b^2(b - a)$

$= a(a-b)(a+b) - 2b^2(a-b) = (a-b)(a^2 + ab - 2b^2)$

But $(a^2 + ab - 2b^2) = a^2 - b^2 + ab - b^2 = (a-b)(a+b) + b(a-b) = (a-b)(a+2b)$

$\therefore\ a^2 + 2b^2 - 3ab^2 = (a-b)^2(a+2b)$

$$\begin{cases} = 0; \text{if } a + 2b = 0 \\ > 0; \text{if } a + 2b > 0 \\ < 0; \text{if } a + 2b < 0 \end{cases}$$

ILLUSTRATION 2: Prove that $a^3b + ab^3 < a^4 + b^4$.

SOLUTION: Since $a^4 + b^4 - (a^3b + ab^3) = a^4 - a^3b + b^4 - ab^3$

$= a^3(a-b) - b^3(a-b) = (a-b)(a^3 - b^3)$

$= (a-b)^2(a^2 + ab + b^2)$ which is always positive

$\therefore\ a^4 + b^4 - a^3b - ab^3 > 0$

or $a^4 + b^4 > a^3b + ab^3$

ILLUSTRATION 3: Which is greater x^3 or $x^2 + x + 2$ for positive values of x?

SOLUTION: $x^3 - x^2 - x - 2 = x^2(x-2) + x(x-2) + (x-2) = (x-2)(x^2 + x + 1)$

which is positive or negative according as x is greater or less than 2

i.e., $x^3 > x^2 + x + 2$ for $x > 2$

and $x^3 < x^2 + x + 2$ for $x < 2$

ILLUSTRATION 4: Show that $x^3 + 13a^2x > 5ax^2 + 9a^3$ if $x > a$.

SOLUTION: Since $x^3 - 5ax^2 + 13a^2x - 9a^3$

$= x^2(x - a) - 4ax(x - a) + 9a^2(x - a) = (x - a)(x^2 - 4ax + 9a^2)$

$= (x - a)\{(x^2 - 4ax + 4a^2) + 5a^2\} = (x + a)\{(x - 2a^2) + 5a^2\}$

By hypothesis, $x > a$ or $x - a > 0$ i.e., $(x - a)$ is positive

and $(x - 2a)^2 + 5a^2$ is always positive

$\therefore\ x^3 - 5ax^2 + 13a^2x - 9a^3 > 0$ or $x^3 + 13a^2x > 5ax^2 + 9a^3$

ILLUSTRATION 5: If x,y,z denote real quantities, then which is greater $x^2 + y^2 + z^2$ or $xy + yz + zx$?

SOLUTION: $x^2 + y^2 > xy \quad \because (x - y)^2 \geq 0$

Similarly, $y^2 + z^2 \geq 2yz$ and $z^2 + x^2 \geq 2zx$

Hence, by addition; we get $x^2 + y^2 + z^2 \geq xy + yz + zx$ (equality occurs when $x = y = z$)

ILLUSTRATION 6: If x,y,z denote positive quantities, then which one is greater $2(x^3 + y^3 + z^3)$ or $xy(x + y) + yz(y + z) + zx(z + x)$?

SOLUTION: $\because x^2 + y^2 > 2xy$

$\Rightarrow x^2 + y^2 - xy > xy$

Multiplying $(x + y)$ on both sides; we get

$x^3 + y^3 \geq xy(x + y)$

Similarly, $y^3 + z^3 \geq yz(y + z)$

and $x^3 + z^3 \geq xz(x + z)$

Hence, by addition; we get

$2(x^3 + y^3 + z^3) \geq xy(y + x) + yz(y + z) + zx(x + z)$

(equality occurs $x = y = z$)

ILLUSTRATION 7: If $a^2 + b^2 = 1$ and $p^2 + q^2 = 1$; then show that $ap + bq \leq 1$

SOLUTION: ***Method I:*** $a^2 + b^2$ (i) and $p^2 + q^2 = 2$ (ii)

Adding of (i), (ii), we get $(a^2 + p^2) + (b^2 + q^2) = 2$

Subtracting $2ap + 2bq$ from both sides; we get

$(a - p)^2 + (b - q)^2 = 2(1 - (ap + bq))$

LHS $\geq 0 \Rightarrow$ RHS ≥ 0

$\Rightarrow ap + bq \leq 1$

Method II: Put $a = \cos\theta$, $b = \sin\theta$, $p = \cos\phi$, $q = \sin\phi$

$ap + bq = \cos\theta\cos\phi + \sin\theta\sin\phi = \cos(\theta - \phi) \leq 1 \Rightarrow ap + bq \leq 1$

ILLUSTRATION 8: If $a^2 + b^2 + c^2 + d^2 = 1$ and $p^2 + q^2 + r^2 + s^2 = 1$ then show that $ap + bq + cr + d \leq 1$.

SOLUTION: Adding the two equations; we get, $(a^2 + b^2 + c^2 + d^2) + (p^2 + q^2 + r^2 + s^2) = 2$

$\Rightarrow 2ap + 2bq + 2cr + 2ds$ on both sides; we get

$\Rightarrow (a - p)^2 + (b - q)^2 + (c - r)^2 + (d - s)^2 = 2(1 - (ap + bq + cr + dr))$

$\because$ LHS $\geq 0 \Rightarrow$ RHS ≥ 0

$\Rightarrow ap + bq + cr + dr \leq 1$

TEXTUAL EXERCISE–1 (SUBJECTIVE)

1. Prove that $x^2 + 5y^2 + z^2 - 2yz + 4xy \geq 0$ for all $x, y, z \in \mathbb{R}$.
2. Prove that $x^2 + y^2 + z^2 - 2x - 4y - 6z + 14 < 0$ for no real values of all x, y, z.
3. Prove that $x^2 - 4x + 7 \geq 3$ for all $x \in \mathbb{R}$.
4. Find the greatest integral value of x in order that $7x^2 + 11$ may be greater than $x^3 + 17x$.
5. Solve for x, y the inequality $x^2 - 4xy + 5y^2 + 2y + 1 \leq 0$.
6. Prove that $(x + y)(y + z)(z + x) \geq 8xyz \ \forall\ x, y, z \in \mathbb{R}^+$.
7. Prove that $(ab + cd)(ac + bd) \geq 4abcd$.

Answer Keys

4. $x = 0$ **5.** $x = -2$ and $y = -1$

LINEAR INEQUATIONS IN TWO VARIABLES AND THEIR SOLUTION BY GRAPHICAL METHOD

Let $L \equiv ax + by + c = 0$ be a line then $by = -ax - c$

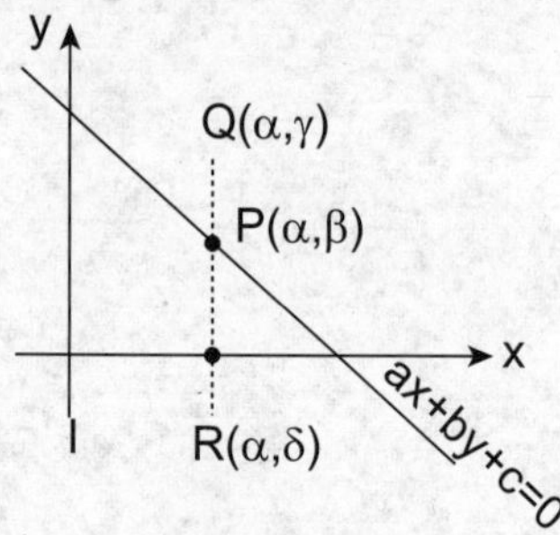

FIGURE 4.1

Since P point satisfies the equation of the line

$\therefore \quad a\alpha + b\beta + c = 0$

From the above diagram, we interpret that $\gamma > \beta$

$\therefore \quad b\gamma > b\beta \qquad \Rightarrow a\alpha + b\gamma > a\alpha + b\beta$

$\Rightarrow \quad a\alpha + b\gamma + c > a\alpha + b\beta + c$

$\Rightarrow \quad a\alpha + b\gamma + c > 0$

Thus all the points lying in the half plane II above the line $ax + by + c = 0$ satisfy the inequality $ax + by + c > 0$.

Similarly, in case $b < 0$, we can prove that point satisfying $ax + by + c$ lies in the half plane I.

Hence, we infer that all points satisfying $ax + by + c > 0$ lies in one of the half plane II or I according as $b > 0$ or $b < 0$ and conversely.

ALGORITHM TO FIND SOLUTION SPACE OF LINEAR INEQUALITY

1. A linear equation in two variables x and y is of the form $ax + by + c \leq 0$ or $ax + by + c \geq 0$ or $ax + by + c < 0$ or $ax + by + c > 0$, where $a \neq 0$ and $b \neq 0$.
2. The graphical representation of these types of inequations will be studied with the help of an equality i.e., with the help of an equation.
3. Since every equation of the form $ax + by + c = 0$ where a and b are not zero, represent a straight line in the plane. So, replace the inequality sign by equality in inequations (1) and plot the line. In case of strict inequalities $>$ or $<$ draw the line dotted and in case of $\geq$ or $\leq$, the line must be thick.
4. A straight line $ax + by + c = 0$ (if $c > 0$) divides the xy plane in to three regions (set of points).

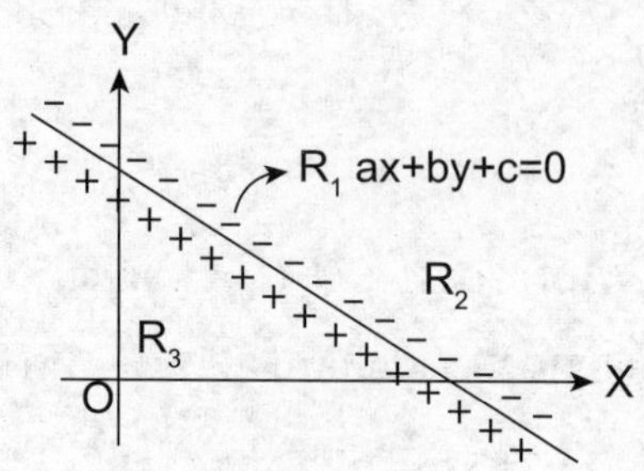

FIGURE 4.2

$R_1 = \{(\alpha, \beta) : a\alpha + b\beta + c = 0\}$

i.e., set of all points on the line.

$R_2 = \{(\alpha, \beta) : a\alpha + b\beta + c < 0\}$

i.e., set of all points on non-origin side of line.

$R_3 = \{(\alpha, \beta) : a\alpha + b\beta + c > 0\}$

i.e., set of all points on origin side of line.

$R_4 = \{(\alpha, \beta) : a\alpha + b\beta + c \leq 0\} = R_1 \cup R_2$

$R_5 = \{(\alpha, \beta) : a\alpha + b\beta + c \geq 0\} = R_1 \cup R_3$

- The region containing all the solutions of an inequality is called the solution region.

Solving linear inequality

In order to identify the half plane represented by the given inequality $ax + by + c \geq 0$

Step I: Consider the equation from the inequality.

Step II: Draw the straight line representing the equation.

Step III: Consider a point P (α, β) (not on the line) and find the sign of linear expression for P (α,β).

Step IV: Check whether it satisfies the inequality or not. If it satisfies, then the inequality represents the half plane which contains the point and shade the region.

Step V: Otherwise, the inequality represents that half plane which does not contain the point within it.

- For convenience, the point (0, 0) is preferred.

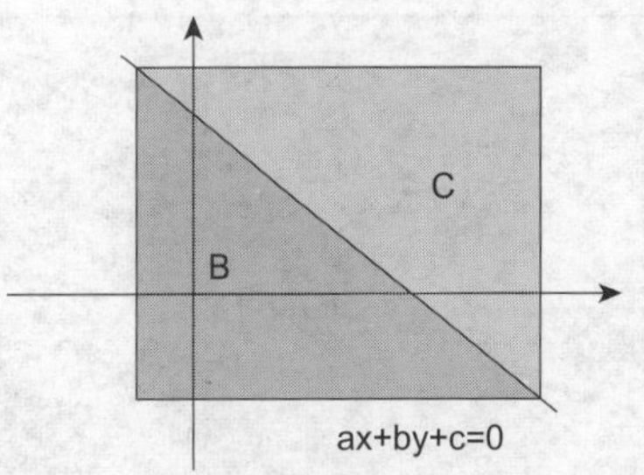

FIGURE 4.3

6. The set A is a straight line while the sets B and C are called open half planes. The set $A \cup B$ represent the points, whose co-ordinates satisfy $ax + by \leq c$ and $A \cup C$ represent the points whose co-ordinates satisfying $ax + by \geq c$.
7. The shaded region (feasible region) represents the solution space or solution set. The dotted line is not a part of the shaded region but the thick line is a part of the solution set.

ILLUSTRATION 9: Draw the graph of

(i) $4x + 3y = 12$ (ii) $4x + 3y < 12$

(iii) $4x + 3y > 12$ (iv) $4x + 3y \leq 12$

(v) $4x + 3y \geq 12$

SOLUTION: (i)

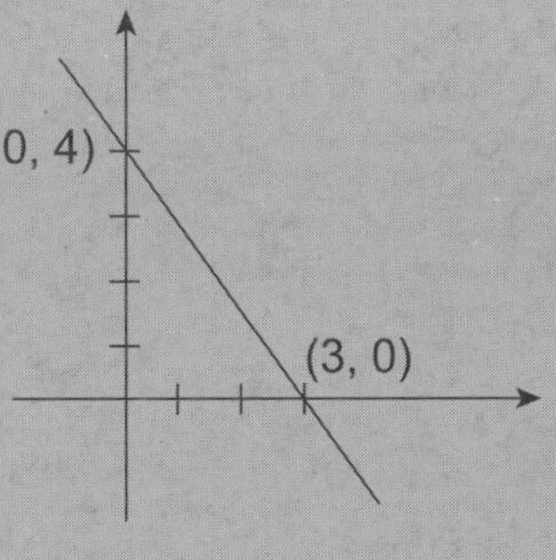

(0, 4) (3, 0)

FIGURE 4.4

(ii)

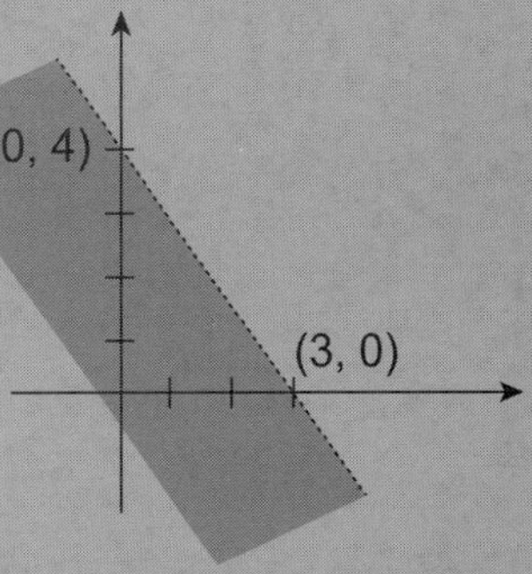

(0, 4) (3, 0)

FIGURE 4.5

(iii)

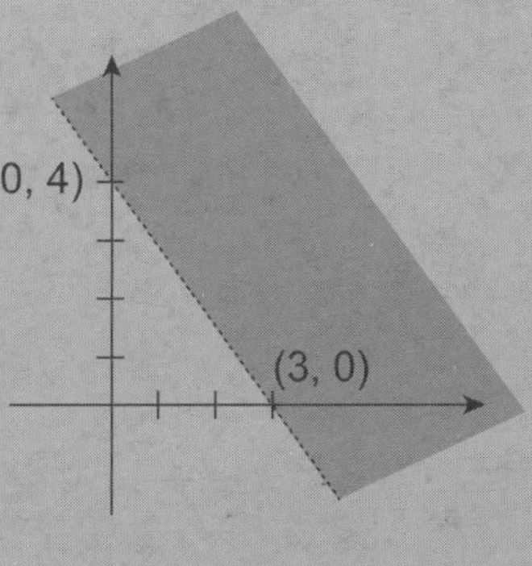

(0, 4) (3, 0)

FIGURE 4.6

(iv)

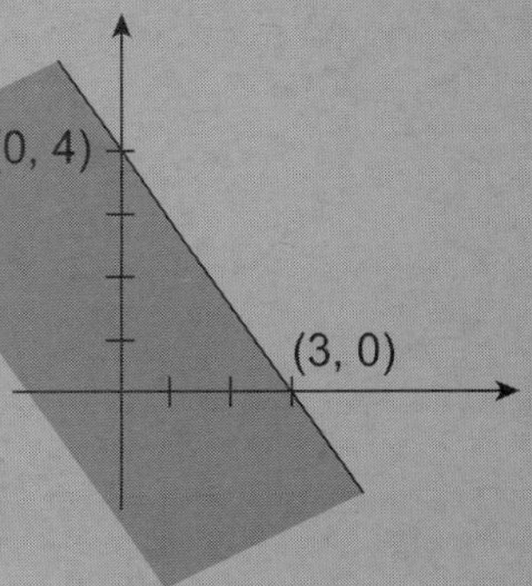

(0, 4) (3, 0)

FIGURE 4.7

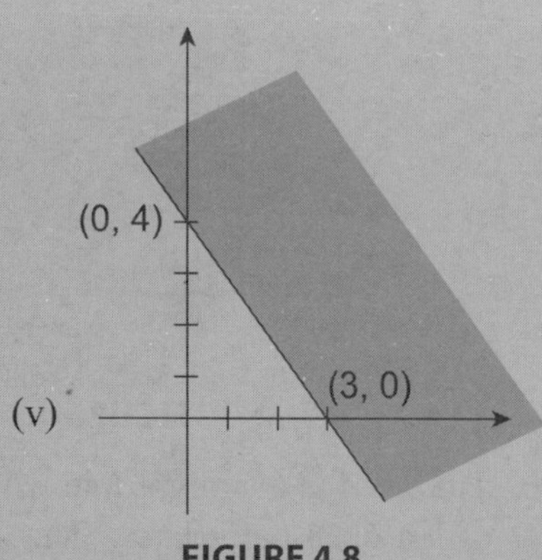

FIGURE 4.8

ILLUSTRATION 10: Shade the region which satisfies the system of inequalities $5x + 4y \leq 20$; $x \geq 1$ and $y \geq 2$ and hence, find the integral values of (x,y) which satisfy the above region.

SOLUTION: Clearly, the integral pts (x,y) lying in the above region are (1,2), (2,2), (1,3), (1,4) and (2,2).

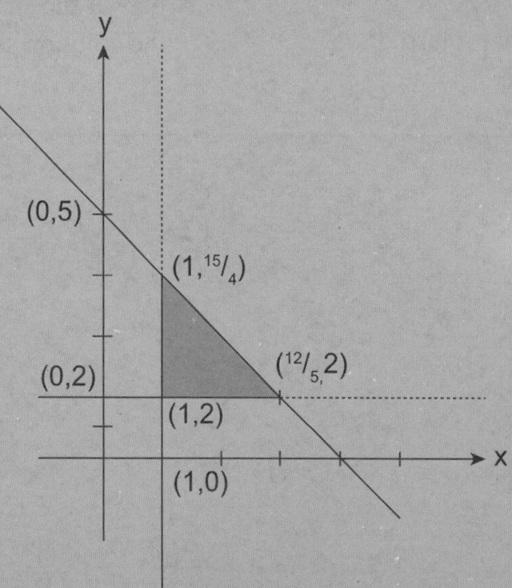

FIGURE 4.9

ILLUSTRATION 11. Solve the following system of in equations graphically $x + 2y \leq 4$, $x + y \geq 1$, $x - y \leq 0$, $x \geq 0$ and $y \geq 0$.

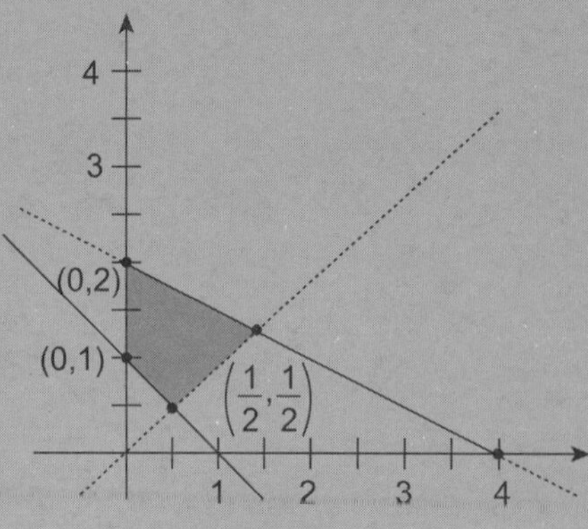

FIGURE 4.10

ILLUSTRATION 12: A cottage industry manufactures pedestal lamps and wooden shades, each requiring the use of a grinding machine and a sprayer. It takes two hours on the grinding machine and three hours on the sprayer to manufacture a pedestal lamp. It takes one hour on the grinding machine and two hour on the sprayer to manufacture a shade. On any day, the sprayer is available for at the most twenty hours and the grinding machine for at the most twelve hours. Write inequalities representing the daily schedule of production. Show all possible solutions graphically.

SOLUTION: Let x be the number of lamps manufactured.

$\Rightarrow$ $2x$ is the amount of time for which the grading machine is occupied due to lamps and $3x$ is amount of time which sprayer is occupied due to lamps.

Similarly, let y be the no of wooden shades manufactured

$\Rightarrow$ y and $2y$ are the time for which the grinding machine and sprayer are occupied due to wooden shades

Now: total time of grinding machine ≤ 12, total time of grinding sprayer ≤ 20

$\therefore$ $2x + y \leq 12$ and $3x + 2y \leq 20$

Also $x \geq 0$ and $y \geq 0$ ($\because$ x and y represent the no of items manufactured)

Region $OABC$ denotes the possible values of (x,y)

Coordinates of point B can be calculated by simultaneously solving $2x + y = 12$ and $3x + 2y = 20$

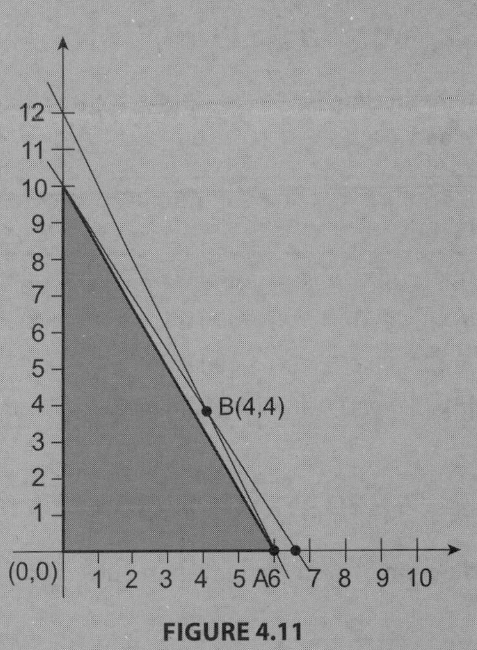

FIGURE 4.11

TEXTUAL EXERCISE–2 (SUBJECTIVE)

1. Find the solution set of the following in the interval notations.

(a) $\dfrac{1}{1-2x} < 0$

(b) $\dfrac{2}{3+x} > 5$

(c) $\dfrac{x}{x-5} > \dfrac{1}{2}$

(d) $(x + 5)(x - 3) < 2$

(e) $3x - 2 \geq 0$ and $5x - 1 < 0$

(f) $3 + x \leq 5x - 2 \leq 7 + x$

(g) $\dfrac{2}{x-2} < \dfrac{x+2}{x-2} < 1$

2. If x,y,z are real and satisfy the following set of inequalities $4x + 2 < \dfrac{8y-4}{5}$, and $3 - y > \dfrac{7-4z}{3}$ and $y > 0$ then prove that $x <$ z.

3. There are two plans A and B for phone usage. Plan A charges a fixed rental of Rs 250 and charges calls at 75 p per min. Plan B has a fixed rental of Rs 175 and charges Rs 1per min for every call. What should be the minimum number of minutes (integrals) consumed so that plan B proves expensive than A?

4. Write the number of integral pairs (x,y) satisfying the inequalities $3x + 2y \leq 12$, $x^2 - x - 6 \leq 0$ and $y > 0$.

Answer Keys

1. (a) $x \in \left(\frac{1}{2}, \infty\right)$ (b) $x \in \left(-\frac{13}{5}, -3\right)$ (c) $(-\infty,-5)\cup(5,\infty)$ (d) $\left(-\sqrt{18}-1, \sqrt{18}-1\right)$

(e) ϕ (f) $\left[\frac{5}{4}, \frac{9}{4}\right]$ (g) $(-\infty,0)$ **3.** 301 **4.** 30

INEQUALITIES CONTAINING MODULUS FUNCTIONS

By definition, $|x| < a \Rightarrow -a < x < a (a > 0)$ and $|x| > a \Rightarrow x < -a$ and $x > a$

Modular Inequality	Test Condition–1	Test Condition–2
f(|x|) < g(x)	**f(x) < g(x) if x ≥ 0**	**f(–x) < g(x) if x < 0**
|f(x)| < g(x)	**f(x) < g(x) if f(x) ≥ 0**	**–f(x) < g(x) if f(x) < 0**
|f(x)| > g(x)	**f(x) > g(x) if f(x) ≥ 0**	**–f(x) > g(x) if f(x) < 0**
|f(|x|)| > g(x)	**|f(x)| > g(x) if x ≥ 0**	**|f(–x)| > g(x) if x < 0**

THEOREM OF WEIGHTED MEAN

Theorem of weighted mean implies

$$\frac{m_1a_1 + m_2a_2 + \dots\dots + m_na_n}{m_1 + m_2 + \dots + m_n} \geq (a_1^{m_1} a_2^{m_2} a_3^{m_3} \dots\dots a_n^{m_n})^{\frac{1}{m_1+m_2+\dots\dots m_n}}$$

or $\dfrac{\sum m_i a_i}{\sum m_i} \geq \left(\prod a_i^{m_i}\right)^{\frac{1}{\sum m_i}}$ equality holds where a_i's are equal.

Here $a_1, a_2, a_3 \dots\dots a_n$ are positive real numbers and $m_1, m_2 \dots\dots m_n$ are positive rational numbers.

Proof: ***Case I:*** Let $(m_1, m_2, m_3, \dots m_n)$ be the set of 'n' positive integers. We may consider some number of the type

$$\underbrace{a_1 \dots\dots a_1 \dots\dots a_1}_{m_1\ no's}; \underbrace{a_2, a_2 \dots a_2}_{m_2\ no's}, \dots\dots\dots\dots \underbrace{a_n, a_n \dots a_n \dots\dots an}_{m_n\ number}$$

then applying AM ≥ GM on these $(m_1 + m_2 + \dots m_n)$ numbers; we get

$$\frac{m_1a_1 + m_2a_2 + \dots m_na_n}{m_1 + m_2 \dots\dots\dots m_n} \geq \left(a^{m_1} a_2^{m_2} \dots\dots a_n^{m_n}\right)^{\frac{1}{m_1+m_2+\dots\dots m_n}}$$

Case II: If $m_1, m_2, m_3, \dots\dots, m_n$ are positive rational numbers but not all integers; we can find out a positive number k for, which $km_1, km_2, \dots\dots\dots\dots, km_n$ are all integers

∴ By case I, we get

$$\frac{km_1a_1 + km_2a_2 + km_na_n}{km_1 + km_2 + km_3 + \dots km_n} \geq \left(a_1^{km_1}, a_2^{km_2}, \dots\dots, a_n^{km_n}\right)^{\frac{1}{km_1+km_2+km_2}}$$

$$\Rightarrow \frac{m_1a_1 + m_2a_2}{m_1 + m_2 + \dots\dots m_n} \geq \left(a_1^{m} a_2^{m_2}, \dots\dots, a_n^{m_n}\right)^{\frac{1}{m_1+m_2+\dots\dots m_n}}$$

NOTE

The proof is also valid for positive irrational numbers as well. Hence, the above theorem is valid for all m_i's > 0

ILLUSTRATION 13: If x and any positive number except 1 and a, b, c one distinct rationals which may be positive or negative then prove that $x^a(b-c) + x^b(c-a) + x^c(a-b) > 0$

SOLUTION: Without loss of generality we can assume that $a > b > c$ now $a - b$ and $b - c$ are positive

∴ By the theorem of weighted mean, we get $\dfrac{x^a(b-c) + x^c(a-b)}{b-c+a-b} > \left[x^{a(b-c)} + x^{c(a-b)}\right]^{\frac{1}{a-c}}$

$$\Rightarrow \frac{(b-c)x^a + (a-b)x^c}{a-c} > x^b$$

$$\Rightarrow (b-c)x^a + (c-a)x^b + (a-b)x^c > 0$$

MEAN OF M^TH POWER > M^TH POWER OF MEAN

If $a, b > 0$ be two real numbers then

$$\frac{a^m + b^m}{2} > \left(\frac{a+b}{2}\right)^m \quad \text{If } m < 0 \text{ or } m > 1$$

$$\frac{a^m + b^m}{2} < \left(\frac{a+b}{2}\right)^m \quad \text{if } 0 < m < 1$$

equality holds when $a = b$ when $m \in \{0, 1\}$

In general, if there are 'n' positive real number $a_1, a_2, \ldots a_n$ then

$$\begin{cases} \dfrac{\sum a_i^m}{n} > \left(\dfrac{\sum a_i}{n}\right)^m & \text{if } m \in (-\infty, 0) \cup (1, \infty) \\ \dfrac{\sum a_i^m}{n} < \left(\dfrac{\sum a_i}{n}\right)^m & \text{if } m \in (0,1) \\ \dfrac{\sum a_i^m}{n} = \left(\dfrac{\sum a_i}{n}\right)^m & \text{if either } a_1 = a_2 = \ldots a_n \text{ OR } m = 0 \text{ or } 1 \end{cases}$$

ILLUSTRATION 14: Prove that if a, b, c are distinct $+ve$ and in $H.P.$ and $n \notin (0, 1)$; then $a^n + c^n > 2b^n$

SOLUTION: $\dfrac{a^n + c^n}{2} > \left(\dfrac{a+c}{2}\right)^n \Rightarrow a^n + c^n > 2\left(\dfrac{a+c}{2}\right)^n$

$\therefore \; A > G > H$

$\Rightarrow AM > HM = \dfrac{a+c}{2} > \dfrac{2ac}{a+c} = b \qquad \Rightarrow 2\left(\dfrac{a+c}{2}\right)^n > 2b^n$ (i)

$\Rightarrow a^n + c^n > 2b^n$

ILLUSTRATION 15: Prove that arithmetic mean of (1/2)th power $< \dfrac{1}{2}$th power of $A.M.$

SOLUTION: $\Rightarrow \dfrac{(x^2)^{1/2} + (y^2)^{1/2}}{2} \le \left(\dfrac{x^2 + y^2}{2}\right)^{1/2} \qquad \Rightarrow \dfrac{x+y}{2} \le \left(\dfrac{x^2+y^2}{2}\right)^{1/2}$ (squaring)

$\Rightarrow \dfrac{x^2 + y^2}{2} \ge \left(\dfrac{x+y}{2}\right)^2 \qquad \Rightarrow 16 \ge (x+y)^2 \qquad \Rightarrow x + y \le 4$

$$\frac{\sum a_i^m}{n} > \left(\frac{\sum_{i=1}^{n} a_i}{n}\right)^m \text{ If } m < 0 \text{ or } m > 1 \text{ and } \frac{\sum_{i=1}^{n} a_i^m}{n} < \left(\frac{\sum_{i=1}^{n} a_i}{n}\right)^m \text{ if } 0 < m < 1$$

ILLUSTRATION 16: Show that sum of mth power of 1st n odd numbers is greater than n^{m+1} for $m > 1$.

SOLUTION: $\dfrac{1^m + 3^m + \ldots + (2n-1)^m}{n} > \left(\dfrac{1+3+5\ldots+(2n-1)}{n}\right)^m$

$1^m + 3^m + \ldots + (2n-1)^m > n\,(n)^{1/m} = n^{m+1}$

ILLUSTRATION 17: If $C_r = \dfrac{n!}{r!(n-r)!}$ then show that $\sqrt{C_1} + \sqrt{C_2} + \ldots + \sqrt{C_n} < \sqrt{n(2^n - 1)}$.

SOLUTION: $\dfrac{(C_1)^{1/2} + (C_2)^{1/2} + (C_3)^{1/2} + \ldots + (C_n)^{1/2}}{n} < \left(\dfrac{C_1 + C_2 + C_3 + \ldots + C_n}{n}\right)^{1/2} = \left(\dfrac{2^n - 1}{n}\right)^{1/2}$

$\Rightarrow \sqrt{C_1} + \sqrt{C_2} + \ldots + \sqrt{C_n} < \sqrt{n}\sqrt{(2^n - 1)}$

WEIGHTED POWER MEAN INEQUALITY

If $a_1, a_2, ... a_n, b_1, b_2, ... b_n$ are two sets of n rationals a_i's are not all equal $m \in Q$ (rational).

Then,

$$\frac{b_1a_1^m + b_2a_2^m + ... + b_na_n^m}{b_1 + b_2 + ... + b_n} > \left(\frac{b_1a_1 + b_2a_2 + ... + b_na_n}{b_1 + b_2 + ... + b_n}\right)^m$$

when $m \notin (0,1)$

and $\frac{b_1a_1^m + ... + b_na_n^m}{b_1 + b_2 + ... + b_n}$

$$< \left(\frac{b_1a_1 + b_2a_2 + ... + b_na_n}{b_1 + b_2 + ... + b_n}\right)^m \quad \text{when } m \in (0, 1)$$

Equality occurs when either $a_1 = a_2 = ... = a_n$ or $m \in \{0,1\}$

ILLUSTRATION 18: If $a^2 + b^2 = 1$ and $x^2 + y^2 = 1$ show that $ax + by \leq 1$

SOLUTION: We know that arithmetic mean of two quantities is greater than their geometic mean.

$$\Rightarrow \frac{a^2 + x^2}{2} > (a^2x^2)^{1/2} = ax \qquad \text{or} \quad (a^2 + x^2) > 2ax \qquad \text{(i)}$$

$$\text{Similarly, } \frac{b^2 + y^2}{2} > (b^2y^2)^{1/2} = by \qquad \text{or} \quad b^2 + y^2 > 2by \qquad \text{(ii)}$$

On adding (i) and (ii), we get $a^2 + b^2 = 1$ and $x^2 + y^2 = 1$

$y^2 + a^2 + b^2 + x^2 > 2ax + 2by$

$\therefore\ 2 > 2ax + 2by$ or $ax + by < 1$ $\{\because a^2 + b^2 = 1$ and $x^2 + y^2 = 1)$

ILLUSTRATION 19: If n be a positive integer, greater than 2, show that $2^n > 1 + n\sqrt{2^n - 1}$

SOLUTION: If n is positive integer and greater than 2, then to show that $2^n > 1 + n\sqrt{2^n - 1}$ or $2^{n-1/n} > \sqrt{2^{n-1} - 1}$

We know that arithmetic mean of any number of quantities is greater than their geometric mean

$$\therefore \frac{1 + 2 + 2^2 + ...2^{n-1}}{n} > (1.2.2^2.....2^{n-1})^{1/n}$$

$$\text{i.e., } \frac{2^n - 1}{n(2-1)} > \{2^{1+2+3+.....(n-1)}\}^{1/n} \qquad \text{or} \quad \frac{2^n - 1}{n} > \{2^{n(n-1)/2}\}^{1/n}$$

$$\text{or} \quad \frac{2^n - 1}{n} > \sqrt{2^{n-1}} \qquad \text{or} \quad 2^n > 1 + n\sqrt{2^{n-1}}$$

ILLUSTRATION 20: Show that $27(a^4 + b^4 + c^4) > (a + b + c)^4$.

SOLUTION: The arithmetic mean of the mth powers of n positive quantities is greater than the mth power of their arithmetic mean except when m lies between 0 and 1.

$$\therefore \frac{(a^4 + b^4 + c^4)}{3} > \left(\frac{a + b + c}{3}\right)^4 \qquad \text{or} \quad 27(a^4 + b^4 + c^4) > (a + b + c)^4$$

ILLUSTRATION 21: Show that the sum of the mth powers of the first even numbers is greater than $n(n + 1)^m$ if $m > 1$.

SOLUTION: The arithmetic mean of the mth powers of n positive quantities is greater than the mth power of their arithmetic mean except when m lies between 0 and 1.

$$\therefore \frac{2^m + 4^m + 6^m + ...(2n)^m}{n} > \left(\frac{2 + 4 + 6 + ...2n}{n}\right)^m$$

$$\text{or} \quad \frac{2^m + 4^m + 6^m + ...(2n)^m}{n} > \left\{\frac{2n(n+1)}{2.n}\right\}^m$$

or $2^m + 4^m + 6^m + ...(2n)^m > n(n + 1)^m$

TEXTUAL EXERCISE–3 (SUBJECTIVE)

1. Show that the sum of any real positive quantity and its reciprocal is never less than two.
2. If $a^2 + b^2 + c^2 = 1$ and $x^2 + y^2 + z^2 = 1$, show that $ax + by + cz < 1$.
3. Prove that $6abc < bc(b + c) + ca(c + a) + ab(a + b)$.
4. Show that $n(n + 1)^3 \le 8(1^3 + 2^3 + 3^3 + ... + n^3)$ for $n \ge 1$.
5. Let $a_1, a_2,.....,a_m$ are positive real number and not all equal. also $s = a_1 + a_2 + ... + a_m$; then show that $\left(\frac{s}{a_1}-1\right)^{a_1}\left(\frac{s}{a_2}-1\right)^{a_2}.....\left(\frac{s}{a_m}-1\right)^{a_m} = (m-1)^s$
6. If a, b, c are positive real numbers such that $a + b + c = 3$, show that $a^b b^c c^a \le 1$.
7. Let $a, b, c > 0$ such that $a + b + c = 1$, prove that $a^a b^b c^c + a^b b^c c^a + c^c b^a c^b \le 1$.

SPECIAL TYPE OF INEQUALITIES

Cauchy–Schwarz inequality

If $a_1, a_2,.....,a_n$ and $b_1, b_2,.....,b_n$ are two sets of n real numbers, then $(a_1 b_1 + a_2 b_2 +...... + a_n b_n)^2 \le (a_1^2 + a_2^2 +... + a_n^2)(b_1^2 + b_2^2 +....b_n^2)$. with the equality holding if and only if $\frac{a_1}{b_1} = \frac{a_2}{b_2} = ... = \frac{a_n}{b_n}$.

Proof If $x \in R$, then $(a_1x - b_1)^2 + (a_2x - b_2)^2 +.... + (a_nx - b_n)^2 \ge 0$

$\Rightarrow (a_1^2 + a_2^2 +.... + a_n^2)x^2 - 2(a_1b_1 + a_2b_2 +.... + a_nb_n)x + (b_1^2 + b_2^2 +.... + b_n^2) \ge 0$

We know that $at^2 - 2bt + c \ge 0$ for each $t \in R$ if and only if $b^2 - ac \le 0$ and $a > 0$.

Thus, (1) holds for all $x \in R$ if and only if $(a_1 b_1 + a_2b_2 +.... + a_nb_n)^2 \le (a_1^2 +... + a_m^2)(b_1^2 +....b_n^2)$

Another proof we have

$= (a_1^2 + a_2^2 +..... + a_n^2)(b_1^2 + b_2^2 +.... + b_n^2) - (a_1b_1 + a_2b_2 +..... + a_nb_n)^2$

$= (a_2^2b_1^2 + a_1^2b_2^2 - 2a_1b_1a_2b_2) + (a_3^2b_1^2 + a_1^2b_3^2 - 2a_1a_3b_1b_3) +....$

$= (a_2b_1 - a_1b_2)^2 + (a_3b_1 - a_1b_3)^2 +....... \ge 0$

Thus, $(a_1b_1 + a_2b_2 +.... + a_nb_n)^2 \le (a_1^2 + a_2^2 +.... + a_n^2)(b_1^2 + b_2^2 +... + b_n^2)$

Also, the equality holds if and only if $a_2b_1 - a_1b_2 = 0$, $a_3b_1 - a_1b_3 = 0$

that is if and only if $\frac{a_1}{b_1} = \frac{a_2}{b_2} = \frac{a_3}{b_3} = ...$

ILLUSTRATION 22: Prove that $\sqrt{1} + \sqrt{2} +....+ \sqrt{n} \le \sqrt{\frac{n^2(n+1)}{2}}$.

SOLUTION: Take $a_1 = \sqrt{1},\ a_2 = \sqrt{2},......, a_n = \sqrt{n}$ and $b_1 = b_2 = ...b_n = 1$

$\Rightarrow (1^2+1^2+.....+1^2)(1+2+3+....+n) \ge (\sqrt{1}+\sqrt{2}+....+\sqrt{n})^2$

$\Rightarrow \sqrt{\frac{n(n(n+1))}{2}} \ge (\sqrt{1}+\sqrt{2}+....+\sqrt{n})$

ILLUSTRATION 23: If a,b,c be positive real numbers such that $a^2 + b^2 + c^2 = 27$; then show that $a^2 + b^2 + c^2 \ge 81$.

SOLUTION: Applying Cauchy–Schwartz inequality to the two sets of numbers $a^{3/2}, b^{3/2}, c^{3/2}$ and $a^{1/2}, b^{1/2}, c^{1/2}$ we have, $(a^2 + b^2 + c^2)^2 \le (a^3 + b^3 + c^3)(a + b + c)$ (1)

Again applying Cauchy–Schwartz inequality to the two sets of number a,b,c; 1,1,1

we have, $(a + b + c)^2 \le 3(a^2 + b^2 + c^2)$ (2)

Squaring both sides of (1); we have, $(a^2 + b^2 + c^2)^4 \le (a^3 + b^3 + c^3)^2 (a + b + c)$

On using (2); the above inequality yields $(a^2 + b^2 + c^2)^4 \leq 3\,(a^3 + b^3 + c^3)^2\,(a^2 + b^2 + c^2)$ ...(3)

Since $a^2 + b^2 + c^2 = 27$

Therefore from equation (3); we get, $(a^3 + b^3 + c^3)^2 \geq (81)^2$

Taking positive roots; we roots $a^3 + b^3 + c^3 \leq 81$

ILLUSTRATION 24: Prove that for all $a_i > 0$, $\left(\sum_{i=1}^{n} a_i\right)\left(\sum_{i=1}^{n}\frac{1}{a_i}\right) \geq n^2$

SOLUTION: Let two sets of numbers are $\sqrt{a_1}, \sqrt{a_2}, ..., \sqrt{a_n}$ and $\frac{1}{\sqrt{a_1}}, \frac{1}{\sqrt{a_2}}, ..., \frac{1}{\sqrt{a_n}}$ then Cauchy -Schwarz

inequality we have, $(\sqrt{a_1})^2 + (\sqrt{a_2})^2 + ... + (\sqrt{a_n})^2 \left(\left(\frac{1}{\sqrt{a_1}}\right)^2 + \left(\frac{1}{\sqrt{a_2}}\right)^2 + ... + \left(\frac{1}{\sqrt{a_n}}\right)^2\right)$

$$\geq \left(\sqrt{a_1}.\frac{1}{\sqrt{a_1}} + \sqrt{a_2}.\frac{1}{\sqrt{a_2}} + ... + \sqrt{a_n}.\frac{1}{\sqrt{a_n}}\right)^2$$

or $(a_1 + a_2 + ... + a_n)\left(\frac{1}{a_1} + \frac{1}{a_2} + ... + \frac{1}{a_n}\right) \geq (1 + 1 + 1 + ... + 1)^2$

or $(a_1 + a_2 + ... + a_n)\left(\frac{1}{a_1} + \frac{1}{a_2} + ... + \frac{1}{a_n}\right) \geq n^2$

TCHEBYSHEFF'S INEQUALITY

If $x_1,....x_n$ and $y_1,...., y_n$ are real numbers such that $x_1 \leq x_2 \leq .... \leq x_n$ and $y_1 \leq y_2 \leq .... \leq y_n$, then $n(x_1y_1 + .. + x_ny_n) \geq (x_1 + .. + x_n)(y_1 + .. + y_n)$. For $i \neq j$, $x_i - x_j$ and $y_i - y_i$ are both non-positive or non-positive.

$\therefore\ (x_i - x_j)(y_i - y_j) \geq 0$

$\Rightarrow\ x_iy_i + x_jy_j \geq x_iy_j + x_jy_i$

There are ${}^nC_2 = \frac{1}{2}n(n-1)$ such types of inequalities.

Adding the corresponding sides of these inequalities, we get

$(n-1)(x_1y_1 + ... + x_ny_n) \geq (x_1 + ... + x_n)(y_1 + ... + y_n) - (x_1y_1 + ... + x_ny_n)$

$\Rightarrow\ n(x_1y_1 + ... + x_ny_n) \geq (x_1 + ... + x_n)(y_1 + ... + y_n)$

For the equality to hold, at least one in every pair of $x_i - x_j$ and $y_i - y_j$ must be zero. This certainly happens if $x_1 = x_2 = ... = x_n$, or if $y_1 = y_2 = ... = y_n$, and these are the only possibilities.

Corollary: If $x_1,......x_n$ and $y_1,......y_n$ are any real numbers such that $x_1 \leq x_2 \leq ..... \leq x_n$ and $y_1 \leq y_2 \leq ...... \leq y_n$, then

$$\frac{x_1y_1 + ...x_ny_n}{n} \geq \left(\frac{x_1 + ... + x_n}{n}\right).\left(\frac{y_1 + ... + y_n}{n}\right)$$

ILLUSTRATION 25: Prove that $\sqrt{1} + \sqrt{2} + ... + \sqrt{n} \leq n\sqrt{\frac{(n+1)}{2}}$.

SOLUTION: Let $x_1, x_2, x_3,.....x_n$ and $y_1, y_2,.....y_n$ be two set of real numbers such that

$x_1 = y_1 = \sqrt{1},\ x_2 = y_2 = \sqrt{2},\ x_3 = y_3 = \sqrt{3},\ ......,\ x_n = y_n = \sqrt{n}$

then $\frac{x_1y_1 + ... + x_ny_n}{n} \geq \left(\frac{x_1 + x_2 + ... + x_n}{n}\right)\left(\frac{y_1 + y_2 + ... + y_n}{n}\right)$

$$\Rightarrow\ \frac{1 + 2 + ... + n}{n} \geq \left(\frac{\sqrt{1} + \sqrt{2} + ... + \sqrt{n}}{n}\right)^2$$

$$\Rightarrow\ \frac{\sqrt{1} + \sqrt{2} + ... + \sqrt{n}}{n} \leq \sqrt{\frac{n(n+1)}{2n}} \qquad \Rightarrow\ \sqrt{1} + \sqrt{2} + ... + \sqrt{n} \leq n\sqrt{\frac{(n+1)}{2}}$$

REARRANGEMENT INEQUALITY

Let $<a_i>$ and $<b_i>$ be sequences of n positive numbers increasing or decreasing in the same direction.

That is either $a_1 \geq a_2 \geq \ldots.. \geq a_n$ and $b_1 \geq b_2 \geq \ldots..\geq b_n$ *or* $a_1 \leq a_2 \ldots \leq a_n$ and $b_1 \leq b_2 \ldots\ldots \leq b_n$, then for any permutation (C_n) of the (b_n).

we have $\sum_{i=1}^{n} a_i b_i \geq \sum_{i=1}^{n} a_i c_i \geq \sum_{i=1}^{n} a_i b_{n-i+1}$

⇒ Maximum of the sum occurs when two sequences are similarly sorted and minimum occurs when they are oppositely sorted.

Proof: $S = a_1 b_1 + a_2 b_2 + \ldots\ldots + a_n b_n$

$S' = a_1 b_1 + a_2 b_2 + \ldots..+ a_x b_y + \ldots..+ a_y b_x + \ldots..+ a_n b_n$

$S - S' = a_x b_x + a_y b_y - a_x b_y - a_y b_x = (a_x - a_y)(b_x - b_y) \geq 0$

Since both of $a_x - a_y$ and $b_x - a_y$ and $b_x - b_y$ are either positive or negative.

ILLUSTRATION 26: Let a, b, c be positive reals, then prove that $a^3 + b^3 + c^3 \geq a^2 b + b^2 c + c^2 a$

SOLUTION: By rearrangement inequality, for (a^2, b^2, c^2) and (a, b, c)

We conclude that $a^2 . a + b^2 . b + c^2 . c \geq a^2 . b + b^2 . c + c^2 . a$

JENSEN'S INEQUALITY

A function $f(x)$ is called convex if the line segment joining any two points of the curve of function lies above the curve.

e.g., $f(x) = x^2$ and $f(x) = e^x$

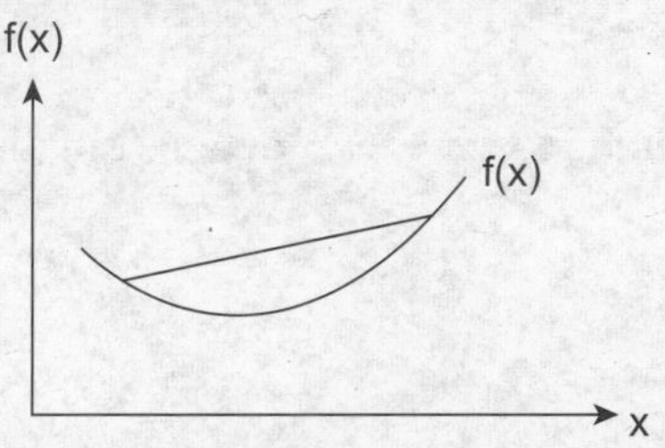

FIGURE 4.12

Example of a convex function

- A convex function is convex downward or concave upward.
- $f(x)$ is concave if $-f(x)$ is convex.

Jensen's inequality says that if f is a continuous and convex function on an interval I, if $x_1, x_2, \ldots\ldots, x_n$ are in I and $0 < t_1, t_2, \ldots., t_n < 1$ with $t_1 + t_2 + t_3 + \ldots + t_n = 1$, then $f(x_1 t_1 + x_2 t_2 + \ldots.. + x_n t_n) \leq t_1 f(x_1) + t_2 f(x_2) + \ldots\ldots + t_n f(x_n)$

- Basically Jensen's inequality says that for a convex function average of the function ≥ function of the average.
- Jensen's inequality generalizes the fact that a secant line of a convex function lies above the curve.

ILLUSTRATION 27: Use Jensen's inequality to show that for a ΔABC, $\sin A + \sin B + \sin C \leq \frac{3\sqrt{3}}{2}$.

SOLUTION: Let $f(x) = \sin x$

$\sin x$ is concave on $[0, \pi]$

$\Rightarrow \sin A + \sin B + \sin C \leq 3f\left(\frac{A+B+C}{3}\right)$

$\Rightarrow \sin A + \sin B + \sin C \leq \frac{3\sqrt{3}}{2}$

ILLUSTRATION 28: If $a, b, c > 0$ and $a + b + c = 1$, then find the minimum of $\left[a+\frac{1}{a}\right]^{10} + \left[b+\frac{1}{b}\right]^{10} + \left[c+\frac{1}{c}\right]^{10}$

SOLUTION: Let $f(x) = \left(x+\frac{1}{x}\right)^{10}$ on $1 = (0, 1)$

$\Rightarrow f$ is strictly convex on 1

By Jensen's inequality, $\frac{10^{10}}{3^9} = 3f\left(\frac{a+b+c}{3}\right) \leq f(a)+f(b)+f(c) = \left(a+\frac{1}{a}\right)^{10} + \left(b+\frac{1}{b}\right)^{10} + \left(c+\frac{1}{c}\right)^{10}$

So the minimum is $\frac{10^{10}}{3^9}$ achieved at $a = b = c = \frac{1}{3}$

■ WEIERSTRASS INEQUALITY

For all $a_i \in IR^+$ *and* $n > 1$ and $a_i < 1$. If $S_n = a_1 + a_2 + a_3 + ...a_n$ then

$(1 + S_n) < (1 + a_1)(1 + a_2)(1 + a_3)......(1 + a_n) < \left(\frac{1}{1-S_n}\right)$ if $\{S_n < 1\}$

otherwise $(1 - S_n) < (1 - a_1)(1 - a_2)(1 - a_3)......(1 - a_n) < \left(\frac{1}{1+S_n}\right)$

Proof: We prove this by mathematical induction.

Step: 1 for $n = 2$: $L.H.S = (1 + a_1)(1 + a_2)$
$= 1 + a_1 + a_2 + a_1 a_2$
$R.H.S = 1 + a_1 + a_2$

a_1, a_2 are real positive number then $a_1 a_2 > 0$. So L.H.S > R.H.S

Step: 2 for $n = m$: $P(m)$: $(1 + a_1)(1 + a_2)...(1 + a_m) > 1 + a_1 + a_2 + ... + a_m$

Step: 3 We have to prove that for $n = m + 1$.

$P(m + 1)$: $(1 + a_1)(1 + a_2)....(1 + a_m) > 1 + a_1 + a_2 + ... + a_m + a_{m+1}$

L.H.S. $(1 + a_1)(1 + a_2)... (1 + a_m)(1 + a_{m+1}) > (1 + a_1 + a_2 + ...a_m)(1 + a_m)$

$= 1 + a_1 + a_2 + ... + a_m + a_{m+1} + a_{m+1}(a_1 + a_2 + ... + a_m)$

i.e., $(1 + a_1)(1 + a_2)... (1 + a_m)(1 + a_{m+1}) > 1 + a_1 + a_2 + ... + a_m + a_{m+1}$

This inequality is known as Weierstrass inequality.

ILLUSTRATION 29: If $x, y, z \in R + x + y + z = 1/2$ apply Weierstrass inequality to show that

(i) $1/2 < (1 - x)(1 - y)(1 - z) < 2/3$

(ii) $3/2 < (1 + x)(1 + y)(1 + z) < 2$

SOLUTION: (i) Since $x + y + z = 1/2$ and $x, y, z > 0$ so all numbers are + *ve* fractions smaller than one and $S = 1/2$

$$\because (1 - S) < (1 - x)(1 - y)(1 - z) < \frac{1}{1+S}$$

$$\frac{1}{2} < (1 - x)(1 - y)(1 - z) < \frac{2}{3}$$

(ii) $$(1 - S_n) < (1 + a_1)(1 + a_2)(1 + a_3)...(1 + a_n) < \frac{1}{1-S_n}$$

$$\Rightarrow (1 + 1/2) < (1 + x)(1 + y)(1 + z) < \frac{1}{1-1/2}$$

$$\Rightarrow \frac{3}{2} < (1 + x)(1 + y)(1 + z) < 2$$

■ FOR ALL POSITIVE *A, B, X*; $\begin{cases} \frac{a+x}{b+x} > \frac{a}{b} \text{ IF } a < b \\ \frac{a+x}{b+x} < \frac{a}{b} \text{ IF } a > b \end{cases}$

Proof: $\frac{a+x}{b+x} > a/b \quad \Rightarrow \quad ab + bx > ab + ax \quad \Rightarrow bx > ax \quad \Rightarrow \quad b > a$

which is true. Similarly, 2nd can be proved

ILLUSTRATION 30: Prove the inequality $\frac{1}{2\sqrt{n+1}} < 1/2.\ 3/4.\ 5/6.....\frac{2n-1}{2n} < \frac{1}{\sqrt{2n+1}}$.

SOLUTION: Let $S_n = 1/2.\ 3/4.5/6.\ \frac{2n-1}{2n} < 2/3.4/5.6/7......\frac{2n}{2n+1}$ (i)

$\Rightarrow S_n < \left(\frac{2}{1}.\frac{4}{3}.\frac{6}{5}.\frac{8}{7}.......\frac{2n}{2n-1}\right).\frac{2n}{2n-1} = \frac{1}{S_n}\frac{2n}{2n-1}$

$\Rightarrow S_n^2 < \frac{1}{2n+1}$ $\Rightarrow S_n < \frac{1}{\sqrt{2n+1}}$ (ii)

from (i) $(2n+1)\,S_n = 2n+1\left(\frac{1}{2}.\frac{3}{4}.\frac{5}{6}.......\frac{2n-1}{2n}\right)$

$= \left(\frac{3}{2}.\frac{5}{4}.\frac{7}{6}.......\frac{2n+1}{2n}\right) > \frac{4}{3}.\frac{6}{5}.\frac{8}{7}.......\frac{2n+2}{2n+1}\ \frac{2}{1}.\frac{4}{3}.\frac{6}{5}.......\frac{n+1}{2n+1}$

$\Rightarrow (2n+1)S_n > \frac{n+1}{S_n(2n+1)}$ $\Rightarrow S_n^2 > \frac{n+1}{(2n+1)^2}$

$\Rightarrow S_n > \frac{\sqrt{n+1}}{(2n+1)} > \frac{1}{2\sqrt{n+1}}$ $\Rightarrow S_n > \frac{1}{2\sqrt{n+1}}$ (iii)

From (ii) and (iii), $\frac{1}{2\sqrt{n+1}} < S_n < \frac{1}{2\sqrt{n+1}}$. Hence proved.

TEXTUAL EXERCISE–4 (SUBJECTIVE)

1. By Cauchy's inequality, prove that $\frac{b+c}{a}+\frac{c+a}{b}+\frac{a+b}{c} \geq 6$ where a, b, c are all positive.
2. If ${}^nC_r = \frac{n!}{r!(n-r)!}$ then prove by Cauchy's Inequality that $\sqrt{C_1}+\sqrt{C_2}+.....+\sqrt{C_n} < \sqrt{n\ (2^n-1)}$.
3. If $a_1, a_2,.....,a_n$ and $b_1, b_2,.....,b_n$ be any two sets of positive numbers, use of Tcheychef's inequality to show that $\left(\frac{a_1}{b_1}+\frac{a_2}{b_2}+...+\frac{a_n}{b_n}\right)\left(\frac{b_1}{a_1}+\frac{b_2}{a_2}+...+\frac{b_n}{a_n}\right) \leq n^2$
4. Show that $a_1, a_2, a_3, ...a_n$ are real numbers such that $a_1 + a_2 + ...+ a_n = 1$, then $a_1^2 + a_2^2 + ...a_n^2 \geq \frac{1}{n}$
5. Let a, b, c be positive real numbers such that $abc = 1$, prove that $\frac{1}{a^3(b+c)}+\frac{1}{b^3(c+a)}+\frac{1}{c^3(a+b)} \geq \frac{3}{2}$

■ APPLICATION TO PROBLEMS OF MAXIMA AND MINIMA

Suppose that $a_1, a_2, a_3,......\ a_n$ are n positive variables and k is constant, then

(a) If $a_1 + a_2 + a_3 +......+ a_n = k$ (constant), the value of $a_1.\ a_2.\ a_3.......a_n$ is greatest when $a_1 = a_2 = a_3 =...... = a_n$ so that the greatest value of $a_1, a_2, a_3,......\ a_n$ is $(k/n)^n$

(b) If $a_1.\ a_2.\ a_3.......a_n = k$ (constant), the value of $a_1 + a_2 + a_3 +......+ a_n$ is least when $a_1 = a_2 = a_3 =...... = a_n$. So the least value of $a_1 + a_2 + a_3 +......+ a_n$ is $n\,(k)^{1/n}$.

(c) If $a_1 + a_2 + a_3 +......+ a_n = k$ (constant) then according as m does not or does lie between 0 and 1, the least or the greatest value of $a_1^m + a_2^m + a_3^m + ...+ a_n^m$ occurs when $a_1 = a_2 = a_3 =...... = a_n$, the value in question being $n^{1-m}.k^m$.

(d) If $a_1^m + a_2^m + a_3^m + ...+ a_n^m = k$, then according as m does not or does lie between 0 and 1 the greatest or the least value of $a_1 + a_2 + a_3 +......+ a_n$ occurs when $a_1 = a_2 = a_3 =...... = a_n$, the value in question being $n^{1-1/m}.k^{1/m}$.

ILLUSTRATION 31: Find the greatest value of x^3y^4 if $2x + 3y = 7$ and $x \geq 0, y \geq 0$.

SOLUTION: To find the greatest value of $x^3 y^4$ or $x\,x\,x\,y\,y\,y\,y$

Here x repeat three times and y repeat four times

Given $2x + 3y = 7$

(then multiplying and dividing coefficient of x and y by 3 and 4 respectively)

Rewrite $3\left(\frac{2x}{3}\right)+4\left(\frac{3y}{4}\right)=7$ or $\underbrace{\frac{2x}{3}+\frac{2x}{3}+\frac{2x}{3}+\frac{3y}{4}+\frac{3y}{4}+\frac{3y}{4}+\frac{3y}{4}}_{1\ 2\ 3\ 4\ 5\ 6\ 7}=7$

Here $k = 7$ and $n = 7$

Hence greatest value of $\left(\frac{2x}{3}\right)\left(\frac{2x}{3}\right)\left(\frac{2x}{3}\right)\left(\frac{3y}{4}\right)\left(\frac{3y}{4}\right)\left(\frac{3y}{4}\right)\left(\frac{3y}{4}\right)$ is $\left(\frac{7}{7}\right)^7$

or greatest value of $\frac{2^3.3^4}{3^3.4^4}x^3y^4$ is 1; Thus greatest value of $x^3 y^4$ is 32/3.

ILLUSTRATION 32: If $a > 0, b > 0, c > 0$ and $a^4b^2c^2 = \frac{1}{9.4^8}$; then find the minimum value of $2a + 4b + 3c$.

(a) 4 (b) 1

(c) 2 (d) None of these

SOLUTION: Consider the positive numbers $\frac{2a}{4},\frac{2a}{4},\frac{2a}{4},\frac{2a}{4},2b,2b,\frac{3c}{2},\frac{3c}{2}$.

Now these numbers are considered, so that the sum of these numbers give $2a + 4b + 3c$ and the product of these number give a number of the form k $a^4\ b^2\ c^3$. Where k is a constant

Applying AM ≥ GM on these numbers;

We get, $$\frac{4\left(\frac{2a}{4}\right)+2(2b)+2\left(\frac{3c}{2}\right)}{8} \geq \sqrt[8]{\left(\frac{2a}{4}\right)^4\times(2b)\times\left(\frac{3c}{2}\right)^2}$$

$$\Rightarrow \frac{2a+4b+3c}{8} \geq \sqrt[8]{\frac{1}{2^4}\times 2^2\times\frac{3^2}{2^2}\times a^4\times b^2\times c^2}$$

$$\Rightarrow 2a + 4b + 3c \geq 8\times\sqrt[8]{3^2\times\frac{1}{9\times4^8}} \quad \left(\because\ a^4b^2c^2=\frac{1}{a\times4^8}\right)$$

$\Rightarrow 2a + 4b + 3c \geq 8 \times 1/4 = 2$ $\therefore$ minimum value of $2a + 4b + 3c = 2$

ILLUSTRATION 33: Find the minimum value of $bcx + cay + abz$ when $xyz = abc$.

SOLUTION: To find the minimum value of $bcx + cay + abz$ write $xyz = abc$

or $(bcx)(cay)(abz) = a^3b^3c^3 = k$ (constant)

Here $n = 3$. Hence minimum value of $bcx + cay + abz = n\,(k)^{1/n} = 3(a^3b^3c^3)^{1/3} = 3abc$

ILLUSTRATION 34: Find the least value of $x^{-1} + y^{-1} + z^{-1}$ for possible values of x, y, z which satify the condition $x + y + z = 9$.

SOLUTION: Given $x + y + z = 9 = k$ (constant). Here $m = -1$ and $n = 3$; $\therefore$ value $= n^{1-m} . k^m$

Hence the least value of $x^{-1} + y^{-1} + z^{-1}$ is $3^{1-(-1)}.\ 9^{-1}$ i.e., $9/9 = 1$

ILLUSTRATION 35: Find the least value of $a + b + c + d + e + f + g + h$ for possible values of a, b, c, d, e, f, g and h which satisfy the condtion $a^{2/3} + b^{2/3} + c^{2/3} + d^{2/3} + e^{2/3} + f^{2/3} + g^{2/3} + h^{2/3} = 4$.

SOLUTION: Given $a^{2/3} + b^{2/3} + c^{2/3} + d^{2/3} + e^{2/3} + f^{2/3} + g^{2/3} + h^{2/3} = 4$ (constant)

Here $m = 2/3$ and $n = 8$ $(0 < m < 1)$

Hence the least value of $a+b+c+d+e+f+g+h$ is $8^{1-3/2}.4^{3/2} = 2^{-3/2} \times 2^3$

Thus the required least value is $2^{3/2}$

ILLUSTRATION 36: Find the maximum value of $(7-x)^4(2+x)^5$, when x lies between 7 and –2.

SOLUTION: $(7-x)^4(2+x)^5$ is maximum when $\left(\frac{7-x}{4}\right)^4\left(\frac{2+x}{5}\right)^5$ is maximum when it satisfies the following conditions:

$$\therefore \quad 4\left(\frac{7-x}{4}\right)+5\left(\frac{2+x}{5}\right)=\text{constant} \qquad \text{(i)}$$

$$\text{and } \frac{7-x}{4}=\frac{2+x}{5} \qquad \text{(ii)}$$

From (i) we see that the sum of the two factors = 9 i.e., a constant

From (ii) $35-5x=8+4x \Rightarrow 27=9x$ or $x=3$

Thus the maximum value is $4^4.5^5$.

Theorem 1: If α, β are two angles in 1st quadrant with given constant sum φ then maximum value of sinαsinβ = $\frac{1-\cos\phi}{2}$. i.e., $\sin^2\frac{\phi}{2}$ and that of sinα +sinβ = $2\sin\frac{\phi}{2}$ and it occurs when $\alpha=\beta=\frac{\phi}{2}$ and similar result also holds good for cosine.

Proof: Given α + β = φ

$\Rightarrow$ 2 sinα sinβ = cos(α –β) – cos(α + β)

$\Rightarrow$ sinα sinβ $= \frac{\cos(\alpha-\beta)-\cos\phi}{2}$

then sin α sin β will be maximum when cos(α–β) is maximum, i.e., 1 and it happens when $\alpha-\beta=2n\pi$ i.e., $\alpha=2n\pi+\beta$ and for 1st quadrant α = β

$\Rightarrow$ Therefore maximum value $=\sin^2\frac{\phi}{2}$

$\Rightarrow$ Similarly, $\sin\alpha+\sin\beta=2\sin\frac{\alpha+\beta}{2}\cos\frac{\alpha-\beta}{2}=2\sin\frac{\phi}{2}\cos\frac{\alpha-\beta}{2}$ which is maximum when α = β = φ/2 and equal to $2\sin\frac{\phi}{2}$.

ILLUSTRATION 37: If α and β are two angles in the first quadrant such that α + β = 2π/3; then find maximum values of

(i) sinα sinβ (ii) sinα + sinβ

SOLUTION: (i) Max value of sinα sinβ $=\frac{1-\cos\left(\frac{\alpha+\beta}{2}\right)}{2}=\frac{1-\cos(\pi/3)}{2}=\frac{1}{4}$

(ii) Max value of sinα + sinβ $=2\sin\left(\frac{\alpha+\beta}{2}\right)=2\times\sin(\pi/3)=\sqrt{3}$

Theorem 2: If $\alpha_1,\alpha_2,\alpha_3$ are n angles each lying between (0,π/2) whose sum is constant A. To find maximum value of $\prod_{K=1}^{n}\sin\alpha_k$ and $\sum_{k=1}^{n}\sin\alpha_k$

Suppose that any two of the angles (say) α_1 and α_2 are unequal then if we replace two unequal factors sin α_1 and sin α_2 in the given product by two equal factors $\sin\frac{\alpha_1+\alpha_2}{2}$, $\sin\frac{\alpha_1+\alpha_2}{2}$ the value of product is increasing but the sum of angles remains unaltered so so as long as any two of the angles are unequal the product is not max^m this indicalies that the product is max^n when all the angles are equal so each angle is A/n. Therefore $\left(\prod_{k=1}^{n}\sin\alpha_k\right)_{\max}=\sin^n\frac{A}{n}$, $\left(\sum_{k=1}^{n}\sin\alpha_k\right)_{\max}=n\sin\frac{A}{n}$

ILLUSTRATION 38: If $\alpha_1, \alpha_2, \ldots\ldots\ldots\ldots \alpha_8$ are 8 angles lying in first quadrant such that $\prod_{i=1}^{8} \alpha; = 3\pi$, then find the maximum value of

(i) $\prod_{i=1}^{8} \sin \alpha_i$ (ii) $\sum_{i=1}^{8} \sin \alpha_i$

SOLUTION: (i) Maximum value of $\prod_{i=1}^{8} \sin \alpha_i = \sin^8 \frac{A}{n}$

$$= \sin^8\left(\frac{3\pi}{8}\right) = \left(\sin^2\left(\frac{3\pi}{8}\right)\right)^4 = \left(\frac{1-\cos(3\pi/4)}{2}\right)^4 = \left(\frac{1-(-1/\sqrt{2})}{2}\right)^4$$

$$= \left(\frac{\sqrt{2}+1}{(2\sqrt{2})^4}\right)^4 = \frac{(\sqrt{2}+1)^4}{64}$$

(ii) Maximum of value $\sum_{i=1}^{8} \sin \alpha_i = 8 \times \sin\left(\frac{A}{n}\right) = 8 \times \sin\left(\frac{3\pi}{8}\right) = 8 \times \cos\left(\frac{\pi}{8}\right)$

$$= 8 \times \frac{\sqrt{1-\cos\pi/4}}{2} = 8 \times \sqrt{\frac{1-\frac{1}{\sqrt{2}}}{2}} = 8\sqrt{\frac{\sqrt{2}-1}{2\sqrt{2}}}$$

ILLUSTRATION 39: To find the greatest and least value of $a\cos(\theta + \alpha) + b\cos(\theta + \beta)$

SOLUTION: $y = a(\cos\theta \cos\alpha - \sin\theta \sin\alpha) + b(\cos\theta \cos\beta - \sin\theta \sin\beta)$

$= (a\cos\alpha + b\cos\beta) \cos\theta - \sin\theta(a\sin\alpha + b\sin\beta)$

$\Rightarrow |y| \le \sqrt{a^2 + b^2 + 2ab\cos(\alpha - \beta)} \le |a + b|$

ILLUSTRATION 40: To find greatest and least value of $a^2\tan^2\theta + b^2\cot^2\theta$

SOLUTION: $(a\tan\theta - b\cot\theta)^2 \ge 0 \ \forall \theta \in \mathbb{R}$

$\Rightarrow a^2\tan^2\theta + b^2\cot^2\theta \ge 2ab \ \forall \theta \in \mathbb{R}$

$\Rightarrow$ least value $= 2ab$ ie when $a\tan\theta = b\cot\theta$

i.e., $\tan^2\theta = \frac{b}{a}$.

ILLUSTRATION 41: To find the maximum value of

(a) $a\sec\theta - b\tan\theta$ (b) $a^2\sec^2\theta + b^2\mathrm{cosec}^2\theta$

SOLUTION: (a) Let $y = a\sec\theta - b\tan\theta$ i.e. $y + b\tan\theta = a\sec\theta$

Squaring $y^2 + b^2\tan^2\theta + 2by\tan\theta = a^2 - \sec^2\theta$

$\Rightarrow (b^2 - a^2)\tan^2\theta + 2by\tan\theta + y^2 - a^2 = 0, \ D \ge 0$

$\Rightarrow 4b^2y^2 \ge 4(y^2 - a^2)(b^2 - a^2)$

$\Rightarrow y^2 \ge a^2 - b^2$

$\Rightarrow |y| \ge \sqrt{a^2 - b^2}$ similarly, for part (b)

(b) $y = a^2\sec^2\theta + b^2\mathrm{cosec}^2\theta = a^2 + b^2 + a^2\tan^2\theta + b^2\cot^2\theta$

$= (a^2 + b^2 + 2ab) + (a^2\tan^2\theta + b^2\cot^2\theta - 2ab) = (a + b)^2 + (a\tan\theta - b\cot\theta)^2$

$\Rightarrow y \ge (a + b)^2$

■ USE OF CALCULUS IN PROVING INEQUALITIES

Mono tonicity

A function f is defined on an interval $[a, b]$ said to be

(a) Monotonically increasing function: If $x_2 \geq x_1 \Rightarrow f(x_2) \geq f(x_1)$ for all $x_1, x_2 \in [a, b]$.

(b) Strictly increasing function: If $x_2 > x_1 \Rightarrow f(x_2) > f(x_1)$ for all $x_1, x_2 \in [a, b]$.

(c) Monotonically decreasing function: If $x_2 \geq x_1 \Rightarrow f(x_2) \leq f(x_1)$ for all $x_1, x_2 \in [a, b]$.

(d) Strictly decreasing function: If $x_2 > x_1 \Rightarrow f(x_2) < f(x_1)$ for all $x_1, x_2 \in [a, b]$.

Test of mono tonicity

(a) The function $f(x)$ is monotonically increasing in the interval $[a, b]$.if $f'(x) \geq 0$ in$[a, b]$.

(b) The function $f(x)$ is strictly increasing in the interval $[a, b]$. if $f'(x) > 0$ in $[a, b]$..

(c) The function $f(x)$ is monotonically decreasing in the interval $[a, b]$. if $f'(x) \leq 0$ in $[a, b]$..

(d) The function $f(x)$ is strictly decreasing in the interval $[a, b]$. if $f'(x) < 0$ in $[a, b]$.

ILLUSTRATION 42: Prove that In $(1 + x) < x;\ x > 0$

SOLUTION: Let $f(x) = \text{In}(1 + x) - x$

$$\therefore\quad f'(x) = \frac{1}{1+x} - 1 = -\frac{x}{1+x} < 0 \qquad (\because\ x > 0)$$

or $f'(x) < 0$

Therefore $f(x)$ is strictly decreasing $x > 0$

$\because\ f(x) < f(0)$ or $\text{In}(1 + x) - x < 0$ or $\text{In}(1 + x) < x$

ILLUSTRATION 43: Prove that $e^x + e^{-x} > 2 - x^2$ $(x > 0)$ (use of infinite series not allowed)

SOLUTION: Since $(e^{x/2} - e^{x/2})^2 > 0)$

$\therefore\ e^x - e^{-x} - 2 > 0$ (i)

and $x^2 > 0$ (ii)

adding (i) and (ii), we get $e^x - e^{-x} + x^2 - 2 > 0$.

Hence $e^x - e^{-x} > 2 - x^2$

TEXTUAL EXERCISE–5 (SUBJECTIVE)

1. Given that $m + n = 1$, $m > 0$, $n > 0$ without using A.M.-G.M. prove that $\left[x+\frac{1}{x}\right]^2 + \left[y+\frac{1}{y}\right]^2 \geq \frac{25}{2}$

2. Prove the following inequality

$$\frac{1}{n}+\frac{2}{n-1}+\frac{3}{n-2}+.....+n \geq \frac{n+1}{2}\left[\frac{1}{n}+\frac{1}{n-1}+.....+1\right]$$

3. Prove that

(i) ${}^4C_0 + {}^4C_1 + {}^4C_2 + ...{}^4C_n > \frac{2^{4n}}{n^3}$

(ii) $\tan A + \tan B + \tan C \geq 3\sqrt{3}$; where $A, B, C \in \left[0, \frac{\pi}{2}\right]$

4. Prove that if the number x_1 and x_2 does not exceed 1 in absolute value, then $\sqrt{1-x_1^2} + \sqrt{1-x_2^2} \leq 2\sqrt{1-\left(\frac{x_1+x_2}{2}\right)^2}$

MULTIPLE-CHOICE QUESTIONS

SECTION–I

OBJECTIVE-TYPE SOLVED EXAMPLES

1. If A, B, C are angles of a triangle and C is obtuse then
(a) $\tan A \tan B < 1$ (b) $\tan A \tan B > 1$
(c) $\tan A \tan B = 1$ (d) None of these

Solution: (a) Since C is obtuse angle therefore other two angles A and B must be acute $(A + B + C = \pi)$
So, $\tan A > 0$ and $\tan B > 0$ and $\tan A + \tan B > 0$
Now, $\tan (A + B) = \tan (\pi - C) = -\tan C > 0$

$$\Rightarrow \frac{\tan A + \tan B}{1 - \tan A \tan B} > 0$$

$\Rightarrow 1 - \tan A \tan B > 0 \Rightarrow \tan A \tan B < 1$

2. Let $a_1, a_2, \ldots, a_n$ be non-negative real numbers such that $a_1 + a_2 + \ldots + a_n = m$ and let $S = \sum_{i<j} a_i a_j$ then
(a) $S \le m^2/2$ (b) $S > m^2/4$
(c) $S < m/2$ (d) $S > m^2/2$

Solution: (a) $\because \left(\sum_{i=1}^{n} a_i\right)^2 = \left(\sum_{i=1}^{n} a_i^2\right) + 2\sum_{i<j} a_i a_j$ (i)

E.g., $(a + b + c)^2 = a^2 + b^2 + c^2 + 2(ab + bc + ca)$

$\Rightarrow (m)^2 = \left(\sum_{i=1}^{n} a_i^2\right) + 2S$

$\Rightarrow 2S < m^2 \quad \Rightarrow S < m^2/2$

3. The least value of $6 \tan^2\phi + 54 \cot^2\phi + 18$ is
I. 54 when $A.M. \ge G.M.$ is applicable for $6 \tan^2\phi$, $54 \cot^2\phi$, 18
II. 54 when $A.M. \ge G.M.$ is applicable for $6 \tan^2\phi$, $54 \cot^2\phi$ and 18 is added further.
III. 78 when $\tan^2\phi = \cot^2\phi$
(a) I is correct
(b) I and II are correct
(c) III is correct
(d) None of the above are correct

Solution: (b) Applying $A.M. \ge G.M.$ on $6 \tan^2\phi$, $54 \cot^2\phi$, 18

$$\Rightarrow \frac{6\tan^2\phi + 54\cot^2\phi + 18}{3} \ge (6.54.18)^{1/3} \ge 18$$

$\Rightarrow \tan^2\phi = 3$ and $\cot^2\phi = \frac{1}{3}$

$\Rightarrow$ I and II are correct.

4. If p,q and r are any real numbers, then
(a) $\max (p, q) < \max (p, q, r)$
(b) $\min (p, q) + \frac{1}{2} (p + q - |p - q|)$
(c) $\min (p, q) < \min (p, q, r)$
(d) None of these

Solution: (b) If we take $r < p, q$ then (a) and (c) cannot hold. For (b), if $p \ge q$, then $|p - q| = p - q$

$\therefore \frac{1}{2}(p+q-|p-q|)$

$= \frac{1}{2}(p+q-p+q) = q = \min(p,q)$

If $p < q$ then $|p - q| = q - p$

$\therefore (p+q-|p-q|)$

$= \frac{1}{2}(p+q-q+p) = p = \min(p,q)$

5. If $x \in \mathbb{R}$ and $\alpha = \frac{x^2}{1+x^4}$ then
(a) $0 \le \alpha \le 2$ (b) $0 \le \alpha \le 1$
(c) $0 \le \alpha \le \alpha$ (d) $0 \le \alpha \le 1/2$

Solution: (d) For real x, we have $\frac{x^2}{1+x^4} \ge 0$

Also $1 + x^4 - 2x^2 = (1 - x^2)^2 \ge 0$
$\Rightarrow 1 + x^4 \ge 2x^2$

Therefore $\frac{x^2}{1+x^4} \le \frac{1}{2}$

6. The inequality $n! > 2^{n-1}$ is true for
(a) all $n \in \mathbb{N}$ (b) $n > 1$
(c) $n > 2$ (d) $n \notin \mathbb{N}$

Solution: (c) For $n = 1$ and $n = 2$
$\Rightarrow n! = 2^{n-1}$

For $n \ge 3$, $n! = 1.2.3......n > 1.\underbrace{2.2.....2}_{(n-1)\,times} = 2^{n-1}$

7. If a, b and c are three positive real number such that $a + b \geq c$, then

(a) $\frac{a}{1+a}+\frac{b}{1+b}\geq\frac{c}{1+c}$

(b) $\frac{a}{1+a}+\frac{b}{1+b}<\frac{c}{1+c}$

(c) $\frac{a}{1+a}+\frac{b}{1+b}\leq\frac{c}{1+c}$

(d) None of these

Solution:

We have, $\frac{a}{1+a}+\frac{b}{1+b}\geq\frac{a}{1+a+b}+\frac{b}{1+a+b}=\frac{1}{\frac{1}{a+b}+1}$

Now, since $a + b \geq c$, we get

$\frac{a}{1+a}+\frac{b}{c}\Rightarrow 1+\frac{1}{a+b}\leq 1+\frac{1}{c}$

$\Rightarrow\frac{1}{\frac{1}{a+b}+1}\geq\frac{1}{\frac{1}{c}+1}$

Thus, $\frac{a}{1+a}+\frac{b}{1+b}\geq\frac{c}{a/c+1}=\frac{c}{1+c}$

8. If $a,b,c > 0$ and $a(1-b) > \frac{1}{4}, b(1-c) > \frac{1}{4}$ and $c(1-a) > \frac{1}{4}$, is

(a) never possible

(b) always true

(c) cannot be discussed

(d) None of these

Solution: First we find the max value of $x(1-x) = x - x^2$

Maximum value occurs at $x = 1//2$

and maximum value is equal to 1/4

$\therefore$ $x(1-x) \leq 1/4$

$\therefore$ we can get a $(1-a) \leq 1/4$; $b(1-b) \leq 1/4$ and $c(1-c) \leq 1/4$

Multiplying we get,

$abc(1-a)(1-b)(1-c) \leq 1/64$ (1)

And from the question; we have

$a(1-b) > 1/4$; $b(1-c) > 1/4$ and $c(1-a) > 1/4$

multiplying; we get

$abc(1-a)(1-b)(1-c) > 1/64$, which is a contradiction to inequation (1) and hence is never possible.

9. If a,b,c are the sides of a triangle, then $\frac{1}{b+c},\frac{1}{c+a},\frac{1}{a+b}$ are also the sides of the triangle is

(a) always true

(b) some times true

(c) can not be discussed

(d) never true

Solution: Without loss of generality, we may assume $a \geq b \geq c > 0$

$\therefore$ $a + b \geq b + c$ and $a + b \geq c + a$

$\therefore$ $\frac{1}{a+b}\leq\frac{1}{b+c}$ and $\frac{1}{a+b}\leq\frac{1}{c+a}$

$\Rightarrow\frac{1}{b+c}\leq\frac{1}{c+a}+\frac{1}{a+b}$

$\Rightarrow\frac{2a+b+c}{ac+a^2+bc+ab}-\frac{1}{b+c}\geq 0$

$\Rightarrow\frac{2ab+b^2+bc+2ac+bc+c^2-ac-a^2-bc-ab}{(a+b)(b+c)(c+a)}\geq 0$

$\Rightarrow ab + b^2 + c^2 - a^2 + ac + bc \geq 0$

Now $ab > bc$ and $ac > bc$

$\Rightarrow b^2 + c^2 + ac + bc + ab > b^2 + c^2 + 3bc$

$\Rightarrow (b^2 + c^2 + 2ab) + bc > a^2$

$\because a < b + c$

Hence $ab + b^2 + c^2 - a^2 + ac + bc \geq 0$

Hence $\frac{1}{b+c}\leq\frac{1}{c+a}+\frac{1}{a+b}$

$\therefore$ $\frac{1}{b+c},\frac{1}{c+a},\frac{1}{a+b}$ are the sides of the triangle and hence the answer is option (a)

10. If $x_1, x_2, \ldots\ldots\ldots, x_n$ are any real number and n is any positive integer, then

(a) $n\sum_{i=1}^{n}x_i^2\leq\left(\sum_{i=1}^{n}x_i\right)^2$ (b) $n\sum_{i=1}^{n}x_i^2\geq\left(\sum_{i=1}^{n}x_i\right)^2$

(c) $\sum_{i=1}^{n}x_i^2\geq n\left(\sum_{i=1}^{n}x_i\right)^2$ (d) None of these

Solution:

$Let\ \overline{x}=\frac{x_1+x_2+x_3\ldots\ldots\ldots x_n}{n}=\frac{1}{n}\left(\sum_{i=1}^{n}x_i\right)$

Now, $\sum_{i=1}^{n}x_i(\overline{x}_i-\overline{x})^2\geq 0 \Rightarrow\sum_{i=1}^{n}(x_i^2-2x_i\overline{x}+\overline{x}^2)\geq 0$

$\Rightarrow\sum_{i=1}^{n}x_i^2-2\overline{x}\sum_{i=1}^{n}x_i+n\overline{x}^2\geq 0$

$\Rightarrow\sum_{i=1}^{n}x_i^2-2\overline{x}\overline{x}+n\overline{x}^2=\sum_{i=1}^{n}x_i-n\overline{x}^2\geq 0$

$\Rightarrow\sum_{i=1}^{n}x_i^2-n^2\left(\frac{1}{n}\sum_{i=1}^{n}x_i\right)^2\geq 0\Rightarrow n\sum_{i=1}^{n}x_i^2\leq\left(\sum_{i=1}^{n}x_i\right)^2$

11. A straight line through the vertex P of a triangle PQR intersects the side QR at the point S and the circumcircle of the triangle PQR at the point T. If S is not the centre of the circumcircle, then

(a) $\frac{1}{PS}+\frac{1}{ST}<\frac{2}{\sqrt{QS\times SR}}$

(b) $\frac{1}{PS}+\frac{1}{ST}>\frac{2}{\sqrt{QS\times SR}}$

(c) $\frac{1}{PS}+\frac{1}{ST}<\frac{4}{QR}$

(d) $\frac{1}{PS}+\frac{1}{ST}>\frac{4}{QR}$

Solution: As S is not the centre of the circumcircle, therefore $PS \neq ST$ and $QS \neq SR$.

Also $(PS)(ST) = (QS)(SR)$ (From the properties of two intersecting chords in a circle)

Applying, AM > GM on two numbers $\frac{1}{PS}$ and $\frac{1}{ST}$;

we get, $\frac{1}{2}\left(\frac{1}{PS}+\frac{1}{ST}\right)>\frac{1}{\sqrt{(PS)(ST)}}$

$\Rightarrow \frac{1}{PS}+\frac{1}{ST}>\frac{2}{\sqrt{(QS)(SR)}}$

$[\because (PS)(ST)=(QS)(SR)]$

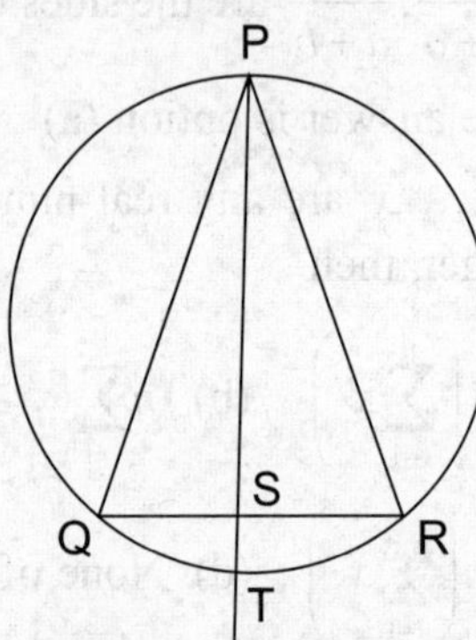

We know that if $x + y = \lambda$, a constant, then xy is maximum if $x = y = \lambda/2$

Thus, $(QS)(SR) < \frac{1}{4}(QR)^2$

$\Rightarrow \frac{1}{(QS)(SR)}>\frac{4}{(QR)^2}$

Thus, $\frac{1}{PS}+\frac{1}{ST}>2\sqrt{\frac{4}{(OR)^2}}=\frac{4}{QR}$

$\therefore$ (b) and (d) are correct.

12. Let S be a square of unit area. Consider any quadrilateral which has one vertex on each side of S, If a,b,c and d denote the lengths of the sides of the quadrilateral, then which of the following is correct

(a) $a^2 + b^2 + c^2 + d^2 \leq 4$

(b) $a^2 + b^2 + c^2 + d^2 \leq 3$

(c) $a^2 + b^2 + c^2 + d^2 \geq 2$

(d) $a^2 + b^2 + c^2 + d^2 \geq 1/4$

Solution: Let us consider the square S with boundary lines as $x = \pm 1/2$ and $y = \pm 1/2$

We have

$a^2 = (x_1 - 1/2)^2 + (-1/2 - y_1)^2$

[By use of distance formula]

$= x_1^2 + y_1^2 - x_1 + y_1 + 1/2$

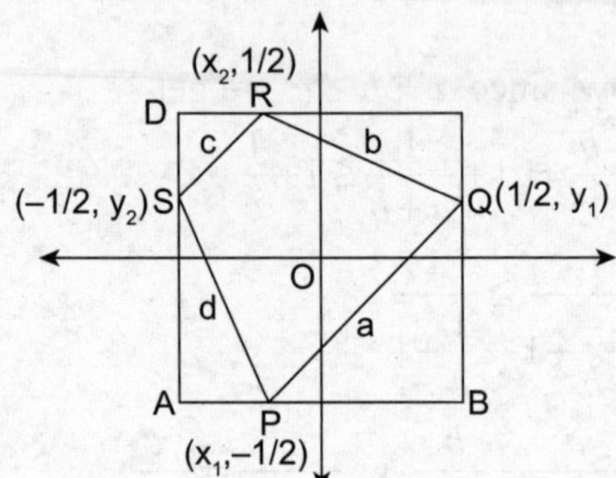

Similarly,

$b^2 = x_2^2 + y_1^2 - x_2 - y_1 + 1/2$

$c^2 = x_2^2 + y_2^2 + x_2 - y_2 + 1/2$

and $d^2 = x_1^2 + y_2^2 + x_1 - y_2 + 1/2$

$\therefore\ a^2 + b^2 + c^2 + d^2 = 2\left(x_1^2 + y_1^2 + x_2^2 + y_2^2\right) + 2 \quad (1)$

As $0 \leq x_1^2, y_1^2, x_2^2, y_2^2 \leq 1/4$, we get

$0 \leq x_1^2 + y_1^2 + x_2^2 + y_2^2 \leq 1$

Thus, from (1), we get, $2 \leq a^2 + b^2 + c^2 + d^2 \leq 4$

$\therefore$ Option (a) and (c) are correct.

13. If $a_1, a_2, \ldots\ldots a_n$ are real number such that $(a_1 - 8)(a_2 - 8)\ldots(a_n - 8) = 12^n$ and $a_i > 8$ for $i = 1,2,3,\ldots.n$; then find the least value of $\prod_{i=1}^{n} a_i$.

(a) 16^n (b) 20^n

(c) 18^n (d) None of these

Solution: We have,

$$\frac{(12)\left(\frac{a_i-8}{12}\right)+8.1}{8+12} \geq \left(\left(\frac{x_i-8}{12}\right)^{12}.1^6\right)^{\frac{1}{20}}$$

$$\Rightarrow \frac{a_i}{20} \geq \left(\frac{x_i-8}{12}\right)^{\frac{12}{20}}$$

$$\therefore \quad \frac{a_i.a_2.a_3......a_n}{20^n} \geq \left(\frac{x_1-8}{12} \times \frac{x_2-8}{12} \times \frac{x_n-8}{12}\right)^{\frac{12}{20}}$$

$$\Rightarrow a_i...a_2...........a_n \geq 20^n \left(\frac{x_i-8}{12} \times \frac{x_2-8}{12} \times \frac{x_n-8}{12}\right)^{\frac{12}{20}}$$

$$\Rightarrow a_1.....a_2.........a_n \geq 20^n$$

$\therefore$ the least value of $a_1 . a_2 ....a_n = 20^n$

14. If x,y,z be any three positive real number and $A = \frac{x+y}{x^2+y^2} + \frac{y+z}{y^2+z^2} + \frac{x_1+z}{x^2+z^2}$ and $B = \frac{1}{x} + \frac{1}{y} + \frac{1}{z}$; then which of the following is true?

(a) $A \geq B$ (b) $A < B$
(c) $A = B$ (d) $A < B$

Solution: $\frac{x+y}{x^2+y^2} - \frac{1}{2}\left(\frac{1}{x} + \frac{1}{y}\right)$

$$= \frac{x+y}{x^2+y^2} - \frac{x+y}{2xy} = (x+y)\left(\frac{1}{x^2+y^2} - \frac{1}{2xy}\right)$$

$$= (x+y)\left(\frac{2xy-(x^2+y^2)}{(x^2+y^2)(2xy)}\right)$$

and $= (x+y)\left(\frac{-(x-y)^2}{(x^2+y^2)2xy}\right) \leq 0$

Similarly, $\frac{y+z}{y^2+z^2} \leq \frac{1}{2}\left(\frac{1}{y} + \frac{1}{z}\right)$

and $\frac{x+z}{x^2+z^2} \leq \frac{1}{2}\left(\frac{1}{x} + \frac{1}{z}\right)$

$\therefore$ Adding; we get

$\frac{x+y}{x^2+y^2} + \frac{y+z}{y^2+z^2} + \frac{z+x}{z^2+x^2} \leq \frac{1}{x} + \frac{1}{y} + \frac{1}{z}$ and

Hence $A \leq B$

15. If $a_1, a_2 .....a_n$ are 'n' distinct odd natural number not divisible by any prime greater than 7; then find the maximum value of $\frac{1}{a_1} + \frac{1}{a_2} + \frac{1}{a_3} + ... \frac{1}{a_n}$.

(a) 1 (b) 2
(c) 3 (d) None of these

Solution: Since each a_i is an odd number and not divisible by a prime number greater than 7; a_i can be written in the form of

$a_i = 3^\alpha 5^\beta 7^\gamma$ where α, β, γ are non-negative integer

Thus for all $n \in N$

$$\frac{1}{a_1} + \frac{1}{a_2} + \frac{1}{a_3} + ... \frac{1}{a_0} < \left(1 + \frac{1}{3} + \frac{1}{3^2} + ...\right)$$

$$\left(1 + \frac{1}{5} + \frac{1}{5^2} + ...\right)\left(1 + \frac{1}{7} + \frac{1}{7^2} + ...\right)$$

$$= \left(\frac{1}{1-\frac{1}{3}}\right) \times \left(\frac{1}{1-\frac{1}{5}}\right) \times \left(\frac{1}{1-\frac{1}{7}}\right) = \frac{3}{2} \times \frac{5}{4} \times \frac{7}{6} = \frac{35}{16} < 3$$

max integral value of $\frac{1}{a_1} + \frac{1}{a_2} + \frac{1}{a_3} + ... \frac{1}{a_n}$ is 2

16. If a and b are positive real numbers such that $a + b = 1$; then find the minimum value of $\left(a + \frac{1}{a}\right)^2 + \left(b + \frac{1}{b}\right)^2$.

(a) 16 (b) 27/2
(c) 25/2 (d) None of these

Solution: Let S = $\left(a + \frac{1}{a}\right)^2 + \left(b + \frac{1}{b}\right)^2$

Then S = $(a^2 + b^2) + \left(\frac{1}{a^2} + \frac{1}{b^2}\right) + 4$

$$= (a^2 + b^2) + \left(\frac{a^2+b^2}{a^2b^2}\right) + 4$$

$$= (a^2 + b^2) \times \left(1 + \frac{1}{a^2b^2}\right) + 4 \quad (1)$$

Now $a^2 + b^2 = 1/2\left((a+b)^2 - (a-b)^2\right) \geq \frac{1}{2}(a+b)^2$

$\Rightarrow a^2 + b^2 \geq 1/2$ $(\because a + b = 1)$

Also, since a,b are positive numbers, therefore

$$\frac{a+b}{2} \geq (ab)^{1/2}$$

or $(ab)^{1/2} \leq 1/2$ or $ab \leq ¼$

$$\Rightarrow \frac{1}{ab} \geq 4 \Rightarrow \frac{1}{a^2b^2} \geq 16$$

$\therefore$ Substituting these values of $a^2 + b^2$ and $\frac{1}{a^2b^2}$ in equation (1); we get

$$\Rightarrow S \geq \left(\frac{1}{2}\right) \times (1+16) + 4 = \frac{25}{2}$$

Hence $\left(a + \frac{1}{a}\right)^2 + \left(b + \frac{1}{b}\right)^2 \geq \frac{25}{2}$

SECTION–II

SUBJECTIVE-TYPE SOLVED EXAMPLES

1. Show that if $n \in \mathbb{N}$,

then $2\sqrt{n}-2<1+\frac{1}{\sqrt{2}}+\frac{1}{\sqrt{3}}+.....+\frac{1}{\sqrt{n}}<2\sqrt{n}-1$

Solution: We first show that if $m \in N$, then

$$2\sqrt{m+1}-2\sqrt{m}<\frac{1}{\sqrt{m}}<2\sqrt{m}-2\sqrt{m-1}$$

Now, $2\sqrt{m+1}-2\sqrt{m}=\frac{2(\sqrt{m+1}-\sqrt{m})(\sqrt{m+1}+\sqrt{m})}{\sqrt{m+1}+\sqrt{m}}$

$$=\frac{2}{\sqrt{m+1}+\sqrt{m}}<\frac{2}{2\sqrt{m}}=\frac{1}{\sqrt{m}} \quad [\because \sqrt{m+1}>\sqrt{m}]$$

Also $2\sqrt{m}-2\sqrt{m-1}=\frac{2(\sqrt{m}-\sqrt{m-1})(\sqrt{m}+\sqrt{m-1})}{\sqrt{m}+\sqrt{m-1}}$

$$=\frac{2}{\sqrt{m}+\sqrt{m-1}}>\frac{2}{2\sqrt{m}}=\frac{1}{\sqrt{m}}$$

Thus $2\sqrt{m+1}-2\sqrt{m}<\frac{1}{\sqrt{m}}<2\sqrt{m}-2\sqrt{m-1}$ (i)

Putting $m = 2, 3,......, n$ in (i)

we get, $2\sqrt{3}-2\sqrt{2}<\frac{1}{\sqrt{2}}<2\sqrt{2}-2\sqrt{1}$

$$2\sqrt{4}-2\sqrt{3}<\frac{1}{\sqrt{3}}<2\sqrt{3}-2\sqrt{2}$$

$$\vdots$$

$$2\sqrt{n+1}-2\sqrt{n}<\frac{1}{\sqrt{n}}<2\sqrt{n}-2\sqrt{n-1}$$

Adding the above inequalities, we get

$$2\sqrt{n+1}-2\sqrt{2}<\frac{1}{\sqrt{2}}+\frac{1}{\sqrt{3}}+....+\frac{1}{\sqrt{n}}<2\sqrt{n}-2\sqrt{1}$$

Adding 1 to both sides, we get

$$2\sqrt{n+1}+1-2\sqrt{2}<1+\frac{1}{\sqrt{2}}+....+\frac{1}{\sqrt{n}}<2\sqrt{n}+1-2\sqrt{1}$$

We also have, $\sqrt{n}<\sqrt{n+1}$ and $2\sqrt{2}<3$

$\Rightarrow 2\sqrt{n}+1-3<2\sqrt{n+1}+1-2\sqrt{2}$

Thus $2\sqrt{n}-2<1+\frac{1}{\sqrt{2}}+\frac{1}{\sqrt{3}}+....+\frac{1}{\sqrt{n}}<2\sqrt{n}-1$

2. If a and b are two distinct positive real numbers, show that $(ab^n)^{1/(n+1)}<\frac{a+nb}{n+1}$ and hence prove that $\left(1+\frac{1}{n+1}\right)^{n+1}>\left(1+\frac{1}{n}\right)^n$ for $n \in \mathbb{N}$.

Solution: We have

$$\frac{a+\overbrace{b+...+b}^{n\ times}}{n+1}>(a\underbrace{bb.....b}_{n\ times})^{1/(n+1)} \Rightarrow \frac{a+nb}{n+1}>(ab^n)^{1/(n+1)}$$

Now, taking $a = 1$ and $b = 1 + (1/n)$, where n is positive integer, we get

$$\frac{1+n(1+1/n)}{n+1}>\left[1.(1+1/n)^n\right]^{1/(n+1)}$$

$$\Rightarrow 1+\frac{1}{n+1}>\left[(1+1/n)^n\right]^{1/(n+1)}$$

$$\Rightarrow \left(1+\frac{1}{n+1}\right)^{n+1}>(1+1/n)^n$$

3. If $C_r=\frac{n!}{r!(n-r)!}$, prove that

$$\sqrt{C_1}+\sqrt{C_2}+......+\sqrt{C_n}\le 2^{n-1}+\frac{1}{2}(n-1)$$

Solution: We have,

$$(\sqrt{C_1}-1)^2+(\sqrt{C_2}-1)^2+......+(\sqrt{C_n}-1)^2\le 0$$

$$\Rightarrow 2\sqrt{C_1}+2\sqrt{C_2}+......+2\sqrt{C_n}\le C_1+C_2+.....+C_n+n=2^n-1+n$$

$$\Rightarrow \sqrt{C_1}+\sqrt{C_2}+......+\sqrt{C_n}\le \frac{2^n-1+n}{2}=2^{n-1}+\frac{1}{2}(n-1)$$

4. If $C_r=\frac{n!}{r!(n-r)!}$, prove that for $n \ge 2$, $\sqrt{C_1}+\sqrt{C_2}+........+\sqrt{C_n}\le\{n(2^n-1)\}^{1/2}$.

Solution: For $x \in R$, we have

$$\Rightarrow (x\sqrt{C_1}-1)^2+(x\sqrt{C_2}-1)^2+........+(x\sqrt{C_n}-1)^2\ge 0$$

$$\Rightarrow x^2(C_1+C_2+.....+C_n)-2x(\sqrt{C_1}+\sqrt{C_2}+........+\sqrt{C_n})+n\ge 0$$

$$\Rightarrow (2^n-1)x^2-2(\sqrt{C_1}+\sqrt{C_2}+........+\sqrt{C_n})x+n\ge 0$$

We know that $ax^2+2bx+c\ge 0$ for each $x \in R$ if $b^2-ac\le 0$ and $a>0$.

Since $2^n-1>0$, then inequality in (i) will hold if and only if $(\sqrt{C_1}+\sqrt{C_2}+........+\sqrt{C_n})^2\ge n(2^n-1)$

$$\Rightarrow \sqrt{C_1}+\sqrt{C_2}+........+\sqrt{C_n}\le[n(2^n-1)]^{1/2}$$

5. If *a*, *b* and *c* are the sides of a triangle, show that

$$\frac{1}{b+c-a}+\frac{1}{c+a-b}+\frac{1}{a+b-c}>\frac{1}{a}+\frac{1}{b}+\frac{1}{c}.$$

Solution: Since *a*, *b* and *c* are the sides of a triangle, $b + c - a$, $c + a - b$ and $a + b - c$ are positive.

We have $\frac{1}{b+c-a}+\frac{1}{c+a-b}=\frac{2c}{(b+c-a)(c+a-b)}$ (i)

We know that, $c^2 > c^2 - (a-b)^2 = (c-a+b)(c+a-b)$

$\Rightarrow \frac{1}{c^2}<\frac{1}{(c-a+b)(c+a-b)}$ (ii)

From (i) and (ii), we get,

$\frac{1}{b+c-a}+\frac{1}{c+a-b}>\frac{2c}{c^2}=\frac{2}{c}$ (iii)

Similarly, $\frac{1}{c+a-b}+\frac{1}{a+b-c}>\frac{2}{a}$ (iv)

and $\frac{1}{a+b-c}+\frac{1}{b+c-c}>\frac{2}{b}$ (v)

Adding (iii) and (iv) and (v) we get the required inequality

6. In a triangle with base *a*, the ratio of the other two sides is r (< 1). Show that the altitude of the triangle is less than or equal to $ar/(1 - r^2)$.

Solution: We have $\frac{1}{2}ap=\frac{1}{2}bc\sin A$ (*p* is length of altitude)

$$\Rightarrow p=\frac{bc\sin A}{a}=\frac{abc(\sin^2 B-\sin^2 C)\sin A}{a^2(\sin^2 B-\sin^2 C)}$$

$$=\frac{abc\sin(B+C)\sin(B-C)\sin A}{a^2(\sin^2 B-\sin^2 C)}$$

We know that in ΔABC, $a \sin B = b \sin A$, $a \sin C = c \sin A$ and $\sin(B + C) = \sin(p - A) = \sin A$. Therefore

$$=\frac{abc\sin(B-C)\sin^2 A}{(b^2-c^2)\sin^2 A}=\frac{abc}{(b^2-c^2)}\sin(B-C)$$

$$=\frac{abbr}{(b^2-b^2r^2)}\sin(B-C) \quad [\because c=br]$$

$$=\frac{ar}{1-r^2}\sin(B-C)\le\frac{ar}{1-r^2} \quad [\because \sin(B-C)\le 1]$$

7. Prove that $2n > 1 + n\sqrt{(2^{n-1})}$.

Solution: Since arithmetic mean > geometric mean

$$\therefore \frac{1+2+2^2+...+2^{n-1}}{n}>(1.2.2^2...2^{n-1})^{1/n}$$

or $\frac{1.(2^n-1)}{(2-1)n}>\{2^{1+2+3+...+(n-1)}\}^{1/n}$

or $\left(\frac{2^n-1}{n}\right)>\left[2^{\frac{(n-1)n}{2}}\right]^{1/n}$

or $\left(\frac{2^n-1}{n}\right)>2^{(n-1)/2}$ or $2^n-1>n\sqrt{(2^{n-1})}$

Hence $2^n > 1 + n\sqrt{(2^{n-1})}$

8. If *a*, *b*, *c*, *d* be positive and not all equal to one another, prove that $\frac{3}{b+c+d}+\frac{3}{c+d+a}+\frac{3}{d+a+b}+\frac{3}{a+b+c}>\frac{16}{a+b+c+d}$.

Solution: Since *A*.M of $(-1)^{th}$ powers > $(-1)^{th}$ power of *A.M.*

$$\therefore \frac{\left(\frac{b+c+d}{3}\right)^{-1}+\left(\frac{c+d+a}{3}\right)^{-1}+\left(\frac{d+a+b}{3}\right)^{-1}+\left(\frac{a+b+c}{3}\right)^{-1}}{4}$$

$$>\left(\frac{\frac{b+c+d}{3}+\frac{c+d+a}{3}+\frac{d+a+b}{3}+\frac{a+b+c}{3}}{4}\right)^{-1}$$

or $\frac{3}{b+c+d}+\frac{3}{c+d+a}+\frac{3}{d+a+b}+\frac{3}{a+b+c}>\left(\frac{3a+3b+3c+3d}{12}\right)^{-1}$

or $\frac{3}{b+c+d}+\frac{3}{c+d+a}+\frac{3}{d+a+b}+\frac{3}{a+b+c}>\frac{48}{3a+3b+3c+3d}$

Hence $\frac{3}{b+c+d}+\frac{3}{c+d+a}+\frac{3}{d+a+b}+\frac{3}{a+b+c}>\frac{16}{a+b+c+d}$

9. If *a*, *b*, *c* are the sides of the triangle, then $\frac{ab+bc+ca}{a^2+b^2+c^2}$ cannot be greater than 1 or less than 1/2.

Solution: Since $(a-b)^2 + (b-c)^2 + (c-a)^2 \ge 0$

$\therefore a^2 + b^2 + c^2 \ge ab + bc + ca$

or $\frac{ab+bc+ca}{a^2+b^2+c^2}\le 1$

i.e., $\frac{ab+bc+ca}{a^2+b^2+c^2}\not> 1$, again *a*, *b*, *c* are the sides of the triangle

$\therefore\ a > 0, b > 0, c > 0$
and $b + c > 0, c + a > b, a + b > c$
or $b + c - a > 0, c + a - b > 0, a + b - c > 0$
or $a(b + c - a) + b(c + a - b) + c(a + b - c) \geq 0$
or $a^2 + b^2 + c^2 \leq 2(ab + bc + ca)$
or $\dfrac{ab+bc+ca}{a^2+b^2+c^2} \geq \dfrac{1}{2}$. Hence $\dfrac{ab+bc+ca}{a^2+b^2+c^2} \not< \dfrac{1}{2}$

10. If $x > 0$, $y > 0$, $z > 0$, prove that $x^{\log_e y - \log_e z} + y^{\log_e z - \log_e x} + z^{\log_e x - \log_e y} \geq 3$.

Solution: Let $\log_e x = a$, $\log_e y = b$, and $\log_e z = c$
$x = e^a, y = e^b$, and $z = e^c$ then given inequality becomes
$e^{a(b-c)} + e^{b(c-a)} + e^{c(a-b)} \geq 3$
Since AM ≥ GM

$$\therefore \frac{e^{a(b-c)}+e^{b(c-a)}+e^{c(a-b)}}{3} \geq [e^{a(b-c)}.e^{b(c-a)}.e^{c(a-b)}]^{1/3}$$

or $e^{a(b-c)} + e^{b(c-a)} + e^{c(a-b)} \geq 3\,[e^0]^{1/3}$
or $e^{a(b-c)} + e^{b(c-a)} + e^{c(a-b)} \geq 3$
Hence $x^{\log_e y - \log_e z} + y^{\log_e z - \log_e x} + z^{\log_e x - \log_e y} \geq 3$

11. If $a_1^2 + a_2^2 + a_2^3 + ... + a_n^2 = A$ then prove that $nA > (a_1 + a_2 + ... + a_n)^2 > A$.

Solution: Since AM of 2nd powers > 2nd power of AM.

then $\dfrac{a_1^2+a_2^2+.......+a_n^2}{n} > \left(\dfrac{a_1+a_2+....+a_n}{n}\right)^3$

or $\dfrac{A}{n} > \dfrac{(a_1+a_2+....+a_n)^n}{n^2}$

$\therefore\ nA > (a_1 + a_2 + ... + a_n)^2$ (i)
Taking all $a_1, a_2, ...a_n$ are + *ve* or – ve, then
$(a_1 + a_2 + ... + a_n)^2 = a_1^2 + a_2^2 + ... + a_n^2$
$+ 2(a_1a_2 + a_1a_3 + ... + a_1 a_n + a_2a_3 + ... + ... + a_{n-1}a_n) = A + 2[S a_1 a_2] > A$
$\therefore\ (a_1 + a_2 + ... + a_n)^2 > A$
from (i) and (ii),
we get $nA > (a_1 + a_2 + ... + a_n)^2 > A$

12. Prove that the cube is the rectangular parallelopiped of maximum volume for given surface and of minimum surface for given volume.

Solution: Let a, b, c be the edges of the rectangular parallelopiped. Let volume and surface denoted by V and S respectively. $V = abc$ and $s = 2(ab + bc + ca)$

First Part: Surface given
Here S = constant ⇒ $2(ab + bc + ca)$ = constant
or $2ab + 2bc + 2ca$ = constant
$\therefore$ Volume $V = abc$

$$V^2 = a^2 b^2 c^2 = \frac{1}{8}(2ab)(2bc)(2ca)$$

or $8V^2 = (2ab)(2bc)(2ca)$
The product $(2ab)(2bc)(2ca)$ will be maximum when all the factors are equal.
i.e., when $2ab = 2bc = 2ca$
⇒ $1/c = 1/a = 1/b$
or $a = b = c$, hence parallelopiped is cube.

Second part: Volume given
Here V = constant
⇒ abc = constant
or $8a^2b^2c^2$ = constant
or $(2ab)(2bc)(2ca)$ = constant
$\therefore$ Surface $S = 2ab + 2bc + 2ca$
will be minimum when all the factors are equal
i.e., $2ab = 2bc = 2ca$
or $1/c = 1/a = 1/b$ or $a = b = c$
Hence parallelopiped is a cube

13. If a, b, x, y are positive natural numbers such that $1/x + 1/y = 1$ then prove that $\dfrac{a^x}{x} + \dfrac{b^y}{y} \geq ab$.

Solution: Consider the positive numbers $a^x, a^x, ...ky$ times and $b^y, b^y, ...kx$ times.
For all these numbers

$$AM = \frac{\{a^x + a^x + ...ky\ times\}\{b^x + b^x + ...kx\ times\}}{kx+ky}$$

$$= \frac{kya^x + kya^x}{k(x+y)} = \frac{ya^x + ya^x}{(x+y)}$$

$GM = \{(a^x.\ a^x.....ky \text{ times})(b^y.b^y....kx \text{ times})\}^{1/x\,(x+y)}$
$= (a^{x(ky)}.\ b^{y(kx)})^{1/x\,(x+y)} = (ab)^{kxy/k(x+y)} = (ab)^{xy/(x+y)}$ (i)

As $1/x + 1/y = 1$, $(x + y)/xy = 1$, *i.e.*, $x + y = xy$

$\therefore$ (i) becomes $\dfrac{ya^x + xa^y}{xy} \geq ab$

or $a^x/x + a^y/y \geq ab$

14. For positive real numbers x, y, z prove that

$$\left(\frac{x^2+y^2+z^2}{x+y+z}\right)^{(x+y+z)} \geq x^x y^y z^z \geq \left(\frac{x+y+z}{3}\right)^{(x+y+z)}$$

Solution: Let x, y, z be three numbers with weights x, y, z respectively. Then $\left(\dfrac{x.x+y.y+z.z}{x+y+z}\right) \geq (x^x.y^y.z^z)^{\frac{1}{(x+y+z)}}$

(weighted A.M ≥ weighted $G.M.$)

$$\left(\frac{x^2+y^2+z^2}{x+y+z}\right)^{(x+y+z)} \geq (x^x.y^y.z^z) \quad \text{(i)}$$

Again let $1/x$, $1/y$, $1/z$ be three numbers with weights x, y, z respectively then

$$\Rightarrow \frac{x.\frac{1}{x}+y.\frac{1}{y}+z.\frac{1}{z}}{x+y+z} \geq (1/x^x.1/y^y.1/z^z)^{\frac{1}{(x+y+z)}}$$

(weighted $A.M \geq$ weighted $G.M.$)

$$\Rightarrow \left(\frac{1}{x+y+z}\right)^{x+y+z} \geq (1/x^x y^y z^z)$$

$$\Rightarrow x^x y^y z^z \geq \left(\frac{x+y+z}{3}\right)^{x+y+z} \quad \text{(ii)}$$

Using (i) and (ii), we get the result

15. Let a, b, c be three distinct positive real numbers in $G.P.$, then prove that $a^2 + 2bc - 3ac > 0$.

Solution: Since $a, b, c \in R^+$ and distinct

$\Rightarrow AM > GM > \text{HM}$

since $b = \sqrt{ac}$ and consider AM and HM of a and c

$$\Rightarrow \frac{a+c}{2} > b > \frac{2ac}{a+c}$$

From first inequality $(a + c) > 2b$

$\Rightarrow a^2 + ac - 2ab > 0$

From second inequality $b(a + c) > 2ac$

$\Rightarrow 2ab + 2bc - 4ac > 0$

Adding the two inequalities $a^2 + 2bc - 3ac > 0$

16. If $1 + \log_2(1 + \cos 2x) > \log_4 2$ then find x.

Solution: $1 + \log_2 (2\cos^2 x) > \frac{1}{2}\log_2 2 = \frac{1}{2}$

or $2 + \log_2 \cos^2 x > 1/2$

or $2\log_2 \cos x > -3/2$

$\therefore \log_2 \cos x > -3/4$

$\Rightarrow \cos x > 2^{-3/4} = \frac{1}{2^{3/4}}$

Let $\cos\alpha = \frac{1}{2^{3/4}}$, i.e., $\alpha = \cos^{-1}\frac{1}{2^{3/4}}$

So, from the value scheme we get $2n\pi - \alpha < x < 2n\pi + \alpha$

$\therefore 2n\pi - \cos^{-1}\frac{1}{2^{3/4}} < x < 2n\pi + \cos^{-1}\frac{1}{2^{3/4}}$ where $n \in \mathbb{Z}$

17. Solve the inequation $\log\left(\frac{25-x^2}{16}\right)^{\left(\frac{24-2x-x^2}{14}\right)} > 1$

Solution: The given inequation is valid for

$$\frac{24-2x-x^2}{14} > 0 \text{ and } \frac{25-x^2}{16} > 0$$

$\therefore x^2 + 2x - 24 < 0$ and $x^2 - 25 < 0$

$\Rightarrow (x - 6)(x - 4) < 0$ and $-5 < x < 5$

$\Rightarrow -6 < x < 4$ and $-5 < x < 5$

Combining both inequalities $-5 < x < 4$ (i)

Now consider the following cases:

Case I: If $0 < \frac{25-x^2}{16} < 1$

$\Rightarrow 9 < x^2 < 25$ (ii)

$\therefore x \in (-5, -3) \cup (3, 5)$

The given inequation converts in the form

$$\Rightarrow \frac{24-2x-x^2}{14} < \frac{25-x^2}{16}$$

$\Rightarrow x^2 + 16x - 17 > 0$ (iii)

Combining (ii) and (iii), we get

$\therefore x \in (3, 5)$ but $-5 < x < 4$

$\therefore x \in (3, 4)$ (iv)

Case II: If $\frac{25-x^2}{16} > 1$

$\Rightarrow x \in (-3, 3)$ (v)

The given inequation convert in then form

$$\frac{24-2x-x^2}{14} > \frac{25-x^2}{16}$$

$\Rightarrow x^2 + 16x - 17 > 0$ (vi)

$\therefore x \in (-17, 1)$

Combining (v) and (vi), we get

$x \in (-3, 1)$ but $-5 < x < 4$

$\therefore x \in (-3, 1)$ (vii)

Now combining (iv) and (vii), the inequation have the final solution is $x \in (-3, 1) \cup (3, 4)$

18. Solve the following inequations:

(a) $\log_{\left(\frac{x^2-12x+30}{10}\right)}\left(\log_2 \frac{2x}{5}\right) > 0$

(b) $\log_{(x-3)} \{2(x^2 - 10x + 24)\} \geq \log_{(x-3)} (x^2 - 9)$

Solution: (a) This inequation is equivalent to the collection of following system:

$$\begin{cases} \left(\frac{x^2-12x+30}{10}\right) > 1 \\ \left(\log_2 \frac{2x}{5}\right) > 0 \end{cases} \begin{cases} 0 < \left(\frac{x^2-12x+30}{10}\right) > 1 \\ 0 < \log_2\left(\frac{2x}{5}\right) > 1 \end{cases};$$

Solving the first system, we have

$$\begin{cases} x^2 - 12x + 20 > 0 \\ \frac{2x}{5} > 2 \end{cases} \Leftrightarrow \begin{cases} (x-10)(x-2) > 0 \\ x > 2 \end{cases}$$

$$\Leftrightarrow \begin{cases} x < 2 \text{ and } x > 10 \\ x > 5 \end{cases}$$

Therefore the system has solution $x > 10$

Solving the second system, we have

$$\Rightarrow \begin{cases} 0 < x^2 - 12x + 30 < 10 \\ 1 < \dfrac{2x}{5} < 2 \end{cases}$$

$$\Leftrightarrow \begin{cases} x^2 - 12x + 30 < 0 \text{ and } x^2 - 12x + 20 < 0 \\ \dfrac{5}{2} < x < 5 \end{cases}$$

$$\Rightarrow \begin{cases} x < 6 - \sqrt{6} \text{ and } x < 6 + \sqrt{6} \text{ and } 2 < x < 10 \\ 0 < x < 5 \end{cases}$$

Therefore the system has solution $2 < x < 6 - \sqrt{6}$ combining both systems, then solution of the original inequations is $x \in (2,\ 6-\sqrt{6}) \cup (10,\ \infty)$

(b) This inequation is equivalent to the collection of systems:

$$\begin{cases} 2(x^2 - 10x + 24) \geq x^2 - 9 \\ x^2 - 9 > 0 \\ x - 3 > 1 \end{cases}$$

$$\begin{cases} 2(x^2 - 10x + 24) \leq x^2 - 9 \\ 2(x^2 - 10x + 24) > 0 \\ 0 < x - 3 > 1 \end{cases}$$

Solving the first system, we have $\begin{cases} x^2 - 10x + 43 \geq 0 \\ (x+3)(x-3) > 0 \\ x > 4 \end{cases}$

$$\Leftrightarrow \begin{cases} x \in (-\infty, 10 - \sqrt{43}] \cup [10 + \sqrt{43}, \infty) \\ x \in (-\infty, -3) \cup (3,\ \infty) \\ x \in (4,\ \infty) \end{cases}$$

Therefore the system, has solution $x \geq 10 + \sqrt{43}$

i.e., $x \in [10 + \sqrt{43}, \infty)$

Solving the second system, we have

$$\Leftrightarrow \begin{cases} x^2 - 10x + 43 \leq 0 \\ (x-6)(x-4) > 0 \\ 3 < x < 4 \end{cases}$$

$$\Leftrightarrow \begin{cases} x \in [10 - \sqrt{43},\ 10 + \sqrt{43}) \\ x \in (-\infty, 4) \cup (6, \infty) \\ x \in (3, 4) \end{cases}$$

Therefore the system has solution $10 - \sqrt{43} \leq x < 4$

i.e., $x \in [10 - \sqrt{43},\ 4)$

Combining the both systems, then solution of the original inequation is

$x \in [10 - \sqrt{43},\ 4) \cup [10 + \sqrt{43},\ \infty)$

19. Solve the inequality, $\sqrt{\log_{1/2}^2 x + 4\log_2 \sqrt{x}} < \sqrt{2}\,(4 - \log_{16} x^4)$.

Solution: Given inequality is

$\sqrt{\log_2^2 x + 2\log_2 x} < \sqrt{2}\,(4 - \log_2 x)$

Let $\log_2 x = y$ $\quad\Rightarrow \sqrt{y^2 + 2y} < \sqrt{2}(4 - y)$

This will be true if; $y^2 + 2y \geq 0$; $4 - y \geq 0$ and $y^2 + 2y < 4(4 - y)^2$ i.e., $(y - 16)(y - 2) > 0$

Hence solution set is $y \in [0, 2) \cup (-\infty, -2]$

Hence $\log_2 x < 2 \quad\Rightarrow x < 4$

$\log_2 x \geq 0 \quad\Rightarrow x \geq 1.$

Solution is $[1, 4)$;

again $\log_2 x \leq -2 \quad\Rightarrow x \in 1/4$

and $\log_2 x > -\infty \quad\Rightarrow x > 0$

$\Rightarrow x \in (0,\ 1/4]$

Therefore final solution is $[1, 4) \cup (0, 1/4]$.

20. Show that $(n!)^3 < n^n \cdot \left(\dfrac{n+1}{2}\right)^{2n}$.

Solution: $\dfrac{1^3 + 2^3 + 3^3 + \ldots n^3}{n} > (1^3 . 2^3 . 3^3 \ldots\ldots x^3)^{1/n}$

$\{\because A.M. > G.M.\}$

or $\left\{\dfrac{n(n+1)}{2}\right\}^2 . \dfrac{1}{n} > \{(n!)^3\}^{1/n}$

or $n\dfrac{(n+1)^2}{4} > \{(n!)^3\}^{1/n}$

Raising each side to the nth power, we have

$n^n \left(\dfrac{(n+1)}{4}\right)^{2n} > (n!)^3$

or $(n!)\quad n\,.\left(\dfrac{\quad}{\quad}\right)$

21. Find the minimum value of $\dfrac{(5+x)(2+x)}{(1+x)}$.

Solution: Let $\dfrac{(5+x)(2+x)}{(1+x)} = u$

Then we have to find the minimum value of u.

Put $(1 + x) = a$

$\therefore \quad u = \dfrac{(4+a)(1+a)}{a}$ or $u = \dfrac{4}{a} + 5 + a$

$= \left(\dfrac{4}{a} + 5 + a\right) + 9$ or $u = \left(\dfrac{2}{\sqrt{a}} - \sqrt{a}\right)^2 + 9$

Hence u is minimum when square term is zero:

i.e., when $\dfrac{2}{\sqrt{a}} - \sqrt{a} = 0$ i.e., when a = 2 or when $x = 1$

Thus the required minimum value is 9.

22. If a,b and c are in descending order of magnitude, show that $\left(\frac{a+c}{a-c}\right)^a \le \left(\frac{b+c}{b-c}\right)^b$.

Solution: Given that $a > b > c$ to show that $\left(\frac{a+c}{a-c}\right)^a \le \left(\frac{b+c}{b-c}\right)^b$

Put $c = ay$ and $c = bx$ then $\left(\frac{a+c}{a-c}\right)^a > \left(\frac{b+c}{b-c}\right)^b$

if $\left(\frac{a+ay}{a-ay}\right)^{c/y} < \left(\frac{b+bx}{b-bx}\right)^{c/n}$

i.e., if $\left(\frac{1+y}{1-y}\right)^{1/y} < \left(\frac{1+x}{1-x}\right)^{1/x}$

It is possible when $x > y$.

Since a, b, c are in descending order of magnitude hence $a > b > c$

or $c/y > c/x$ or $x > y$

23. If n is a positive integer and $x < 1$, show that $\frac{1-x^{n+1}}{n+1} < \frac{1-x^n}{n}$.

Solution: If $x < 1$, show that $\frac{1-x^{n+1}}{n+1} < \frac{1-x^n}{n}$.

$$\Rightarrow \frac{1-x^{n+1}}{1+x^n} = 1 + \frac{x^n(1-x)}{1-x^n}$$

$$= 1 + \frac{x^n}{1+x+x^2+\ldots x^{n-1}} = \frac{1}{\frac{1}{x^n}+\frac{1}{x^{n-1}}+\frac{1}{x^{n-2}}+\ldots+\frac{1}{x}}$$

Since $x < 1$, each of the n terms

$\frac{1}{x}, \frac{1}{x^2}, \frac{1}{x^3}, \ldots\ldots \frac{1}{x^n}$ is greater than 1, and hence their sum is greater than n.

$$\therefore \frac{1-x^{n+1}}{1-x^n} < 1 + \frac{1}{n} \ldots\ldots \text{ i.e., } \frac{1-x^{n+1}}{1-x^n} < \frac{n+1}{n}$$

$$\therefore \frac{1-x^{n+1}}{n+1} > \frac{1-x^n}{n}$$

24. If x is positive, show that $\log(1+x) < x$ and $> \frac{x}{1+x}$.

Solution: If $1 + x > e^x$

Since x is positive $e^x = 1 + x + \frac{x^2}{2!} + \frac{x^3}{3!} + \ldots\ldots$

$\therefore$ $1 + x < e^x$

Hence $\log(1 + x) < x$

Again $\log(1+x) > \frac{x}{1+x}$

if $(1+x) > \frac{x}{e^{1+x}}$

Now $1+x = \frac{1}{\frac{1}{1+x}} = \frac{1}{1-\frac{x}{1+x}} + \left(1-\frac{x}{1+x}\right)^{-1}$

or $(1+x)^{-1} = 1 + \frac{x}{1+x} + \frac{x^2}{(1+x)^2} + \frac{x^3}{(1+x)^3} + \ldots\ldots$

$> 1 + \frac{x}{1+x} + \frac{x^2}{2!(1+x)^2} + \frac{x^3}{3!(1+x)^3} + \ldots\ldots$

that is $(1+x) > \frac{x}{e^{1+x}}$ or $e^{(1+x)} > \frac{x}{1+x}$

25. Show that $(x^m + y^m)^n < (x^n + y^n)^m$ if $m > n$ and $x \ne y$

Solution: Dividing both sides by y^{mn}, we have to show that $\left(1+\frac{x^m}{y^m}\right)^n < \left(1+\frac{x^n}{y^n}\right)^m$

Let us first suppose that $x/y < 1$. Since $m > n$

$\therefore$ $\left(\frac{x}{y}\right)^m < \left(\frac{x}{y}\right)^n$

or $1+\frac{x^m}{y^m} < 1+\frac{x^n}{y^n}$ and hence $\left(1+\frac{x^m}{y^m}\right)^n < \left(1+\frac{x^n}{y^n}\right)^m$

Hence the inequality holds for $\frac{x}{y} < 1$ or $x < y$;

Again suppose $x/y > 1$

Since $m > n$

$\therefore$ $\left(\frac{x}{y}\right)^m > \left(\frac{x}{y}\right)^n$ or $\frac{y^m}{x^m} < \frac{y^n}{x^n}$

or $1+\frac{y^m}{x^m} < 1+\frac{y^n}{x^n}$ and hence $\left(1+\frac{y^m}{x^m}\right)^n < \left(1+\frac{y^n}{x^n}\right)^m$

On multiplying both sides of the inequality by $(x/y)^{mn}$

we have $\left(1+\frac{x^m}{y^m}\right)^n < \left(1+\frac{x^n}{y^n}\right)^m$ and hence the inequality still holds.

26. Show that for any triangle with sides a,b and c. $3(bc + ca + ab) \le (a+b+c)^2 < 4(bc + ca + ab)$. When are the first two expression equal?

Solution: Considering $(a + b + c)^2 - 3(bc + ca + ab)$

$= a^2 + b^2 + c^2 - bc - ca - ab$

$$= \frac{1}{2}\left[(b-c)^2 + (c-a)^2 + (a-b)^2\right] \ge 0 \quad (1)$$

$$\therefore \quad (a + b + c)^2 \ge 3(bc + ca + ab) \quad (2)$$

Also, As a,b,c are the sides of a triangle, we have,

$a < b + c \Rightarrow a^2 < ab + ac$

Similarly, $b^2 < bc + ca$ and $c^2 < ca + ab$

Adding the above inequalities,

we get $a^2 + b^2 + c^2 < 2(bc + ca + ab)$

Adding 2 $(bc + ca + ab)$ to both the sides, we get $(a + b + c)^2 < (bc + ca + ab)$ … (3)

∴ From (2) and (3); we get,

$3(bc + ca + ab) \le (a + b + c)^2 < 4(bc + ca + ab)$ (4)

From (1), we get the first two expressions in (4) will be equal if

$b - c = 0,\ c - a = 0$ and $b - b = 0$

$\Leftrightarrow a = b = c$

27. If $ax^2 + \frac{b}{x} \ge c$ for all positive x where $a > 0$ and $b > 0$, show that $27ab^2 \ge 4c^3$

Solution: Applying $AM \ge GM$ on three numbers $ax^2, \frac{b}{2x}, \frac{b}{2x}$; we get, $\frac{1}{3}\left(ax^2 + \frac{b}{x}\right) = \frac{1}{3}\left(ax^2 + \frac{b}{2x} + \frac{b}{2x}\right)$

$\ge \left(ax^2 \cdot \frac{b}{2x} \cdot \frac{b}{2x}\right)^{1/3}$

$\Rightarrow \frac{1}{3}\left(ax^2 + \frac{b}{x}\right) \ge \left(\frac{ab^2}{4}\right)^{1/3}$

Thus, least value of $ax^2 + \frac{b}{x}$ is $3\left(\frac{ab^2}{4}\right)^{1/3}$.

Therefore we must have

$3\left(\frac{ab^2}{4}\right)^{1/3} \ge c \Rightarrow 27b^2 \ge 4c^3$

28. If Δ is the area of a triangle with sides of lengths a,b,c then show that $\Delta \le \frac{1}{4}\sqrt{(a+b+c)abc}$

Also show that the equality occurs in the above inequality if and only if $a = b = c$.

Solution:

We have $a^2 \ge a^2 - (b - c)^2 = (a + b + c)(a - b + c)$

$\Rightarrow a^2 \ge (2s - 2c)(2s - 2b) = 4(s - b)(s - c)$

$\left(s = \frac{a+b+c}{2}\right)$

Similarly, $b^2 \ge 4(s - c)(s - a)$ and $c^2 \ge 4(s - c)(s - b)$

Multiplying the above inequalities, we get,

$a^2b^2c^2 \ge 64(s - a)^2(s - b)^2(s - c)^2$ $abc \ge 8(s - a)(s - b)(s - c)$

$\Rightarrow abc(a + b + c) \ge 16s(s - a)(s - b)(s - c)$

$\Rightarrow \Delta \le \frac{1}{4}\sqrt{(a+b+c)abc}$

The equality holds if and only if $(b - c)^2 = 0$, $(c - a)^2 = 0$ and $(a - b)^2 = 0$ that is, if and only if $a = b = c$

29. Show that if $a,b,c > 0$; $[(1+a)(1 + b)(1+c)]^7 \ge 7^7 a^4 b^4 c^4$.

Solution: We have, $(1 + a)(1 + b)(1+c)$

$= 1 + a + b + c + bc + ca + ab + abc$

Applying A.M ≥ G.M, on 7 numbers; a, b, c, bc, ca, ab, abc;

we get, $\frac{a+b+c+bc+ca+ab+abc}{7} \ge \sqrt[7]{a^4b^4c^4}$

$\Rightarrow [(1+a)(1 + b)(1+c)]^7 \ge 7^7(a^4 b^4 c^4)$

30. Find the least value of $3x + 4y$ if $x^5 y^7 = k$.

Solution: To find the least value of $3x + 4y$ where $x,y \ge 0$.

We rewrite $3x + 4y$ as

$$3\left(\frac{x}{5}+\frac{x}{5}+\frac{x}{5}+\frac{x}{5}+\frac{x}{5}\right)+4\left(\frac{y}{7}+\frac{y}{7}+\frac{y}{7}+\frac{y}{7}+\frac{y}{7}+\frac{y}{7}+\frac{y}{7}\right)$$

Now taking AM ≥ GM of these 12 numbers;

we get, $\frac{3\left(\frac{x}{5}+\dots\frac{x}{5}\right)+4\left(\frac{y}{7}+\dots\frac{y}{7}\right)}{12} \ge \sqrt[12]{\left(\frac{x}{5}\right)^5 \times \left(\frac{y}{7}\right)^7}$

$\Rightarrow \frac{3x+4y}{12} \ge \sqrt[12]{\frac{x^5y^7}{5^5 \times 7^7}}$

$\Rightarrow 3x + 4y \ge 12 \times \left(\frac{k}{5^5 \times 7^7}\right)^{1/12}$

31. If $x_1, x_2 \ldots\ldots x_n$ are all positive and distinct real number; then show that the AM of the numbers $\sqrt{x_1,x_2}, \sqrt{x_1,x_3}, \sqrt{x_1,x_4} \ldots\ldots \sqrt{x_1,x_n}$

$\sqrt{x_2,x_3} \ldots\ldots\ldots\ldots \sqrt{x_2,x_n} \ldots\ldots\ldots\ldots \sqrt{x_{n-1}x_n}$

is less than the AM of the numbers $x_1, x_2, x_3 \ldots\ldots\ldots x_n$

Solution: There are ${}^nC_2 = \frac{n(n-1)}{2}$ number of the form $\sqrt{x_ix_j}$ where $1 \le i < j \le n$ and we have, $\sqrt{x_1 x_2} < \frac{x_1+x_2}{2}$

and $\sqrt{x_1 x_3} < \frac{x_1+x_3}{2}$ $\sqrt{x_{n-1}x_n} < \frac{x_{n-1}+x_n}{2}$

By addition; we get, $\sum\sqrt{x_i x_j} < \left(\frac{n-1}{2}\right)\sum xi$

(∵ each of $x_1, x_2, \ldots x_n$ occur $(n - 1)$ times)

$\Rightarrow \frac{\sum\sqrt{x_ix_j}}{\frac{n(n-1)}{2}} < \frac{\sum x_i}{n}$

32. Prove that following inequality

$$\frac{1}{\sqrt{1}}+\frac{1}{\sqrt{2}}+\frac{1}{\sqrt{3}}+\ldots\frac{1}{\sqrt{n}} > 2\sqrt{n+1}-2$$

Solution: For $r > 0$; we get, $\sqrt{r} < \sqrt{r+1}$

$\Rightarrow \sqrt{r} + \sqrt{r} < \sqrt{r} + \sqrt{r+1}$

$\Rightarrow 2\sqrt{r} < \sqrt{r} + \sqrt{r+1} \Rightarrow \frac{1}{2\sqrt{r}} > \frac{1}{\sqrt{r+1}+\sqrt{r}}$

$\Rightarrow$ rationalizing the RHS; we get, $\frac{1}{2\sqrt{r}} > \sqrt{r+1} - \sqrt{r}$

$\Rightarrow \frac{1}{\sqrt{r}} > 2\left(\sqrt{r+1} - \sqrt{r}\right)$

For $r = 1$; $\frac{1}{\sqrt{1}} > 2\left(\sqrt{2} - \sqrt{1}\right)$

For $r = 2$; $\frac{1}{\sqrt{2}} > 2\left(\sqrt{3} - \sqrt{2}\right)$

For $r = 3$; $\frac{1}{\sqrt{3}} > 2\left(\sqrt{4} - \sqrt{3}\right)$

⋮

For $r = n$; $\frac{1}{\sqrt{n}} > 2\left(\sqrt{n+1} - \sqrt{n}\right)$

Adding; we get, $\frac{1}{\sqrt{1}} + \frac{1}{\sqrt{2}} + \ldots\ldots \frac{1}{\sqrt{n}} > 2\sqrt{n+1} - 2$

SECTION–III

OBJECTIVE-TYPE (ONLY ONE CORRECT ANSWER)

1. The solution set of $4^{-x+0.5} - 7.2^{-x} < 0$ ($\forall x \in \mathbb{R}$) is

(a) $(-\infty, \infty)$ (b) $\left(-\log_2 \frac{7}{2}, \infty\right)$
(c) $(2, \infty)$ (d) $(2, 7/2)$

2. The number of integral solutions of $\frac{x+2}{x^2+1} > \frac{1}{2}$ is

(a) 4 (b) 5
(c) 3 (d) None of these

3. If $x^2 - 3x < 4$ then the number of possible integral values of x is

(a) 3 (b) 4
(c) 6 (d) None of these

4. If the product of n positive number is unity, then their sum is

(a) a positive integer (b) divisible by n
(c) equal to $n + 1/n$ (d) never less than n

5. Let $a_1, a_2, .., a_n$ be non-positive real numbers such that $a_1 + a_2 + ... + a_n = m$ and let $S = \sum_{i<j} a_i a_j$ then

(a) $S \le m^2/2$ (b) $S > m^2/4$
(c) $S < m/2$ (d) $S > m^2/2$

6. If $-\pi/2 < \theta < \pi/2$, then then minimum value of $\cos^3\theta + \sec^3\theta$ is

(a) 1 (b) 2
(c) 0 (d) None of these

7. If $a > 1$, $b > 1$ then the minimum value of $\log_b a + \log_a b$ is

(a) 0 (b) 1
(c) 2 (d) None of these

8. If a, b, c are distinct positive real numbers then the expression $(b + c - a)(c + a - b)(a + b - c) - abc$ is

(a) positive (b) negative
(c) non-positive (d) non-negative

9. If x and y are postive real numbers and m, n are any positive integer and $E = \frac{x^n y^m}{(1+x^{2n})(1+y^{2m})}$ then

(a) $E \ge \frac{1}{4}$ (b) $E > \frac{1}{2}$
(c) $E \le \frac{1}{4}$ (d) $E < \frac{1}{8}$

10. For a positive integer n let $a(n) = 1 + \frac{1}{2} + \frac{1}{3} + \frac{1}{4} + ... + \frac{1}{2^n - 1}$ then

(a) $a(100) < 100$ (b) $a(100) > 100$
(c) $a(200) \le 100$ (d) $a(200) = 100$

11. If a, b, c, d are positive real numbers such that $a + b + c + d = 2$ and $m = (a + b)(c + d)$ then

(a) $0 \le m \le 1$ (b) $0 \le m \le 2$
(c) $2 \le m \le 3$ (d) $3 \le m \le 4$

12. Suppose n is a positive integer. Then the least value of N for which $\left|\frac{n^2+n+1}{3n^2+1} - \frac{1}{3}\right| < \frac{1}{10}$ when $n \ge N$ is

(a) 4 (b) 5
(c) 100 (d) 1000

13. The number of solutions of the inequality $2^{1/\sin^2 a_2} \cdot 3^{1/\sin^2 a_3} \cdot 4^{1/\sin^2 a_4} \ldots\ldots n^{1/\sin^2 a_n} \le n!$ where $a_i \in (-\pi, \pi)$ for $i = 1, 2, 3, \ldots\ldots, n$ is

(a) 0 (b) 2^{n-1}

(c) 3^{n-1} (d) infinite

14. If $a_n > 1$ for all $n \in \mathbb{N}$ then $\log_{a_2} a_1 + \log_{a_3} a_2 + \ldots \log_{a_n} a_{n-1} + \log_{a_1} a_n$ has the minimum value

(a) 1 (b) 2

(c) 0 (d) None of these

15. The inequality $n! > 2n - 1$ is true for

(a) $\forall\, n \in \mathbb{N}$ (b) $n > 1$

(c) $n > 2$ (d) None of these

16. If x, y, z are positive numbers in AP then

(a) $y^2 \ge xz$

(b) $y \ge 2\sqrt{xz}$

(c) $\dfrac{x+y}{2y-x} + \dfrac{y+z}{2y-z}$ has the minimum value 2.

(d) $\dfrac{x+y}{2y-x} + \dfrac{y+z}{2y-z} \ge 4$

17. If $3^{x/2} + 2^x > 25$ then the solution set is

(a) R (b) $(2, \infty)$

(c) $(4, \infty)$ (d) None of these

18. If a, b and c are three positive real numbers, then the minimum value of the expression $\dfrac{b^n + c^n}{a^n} + \dfrac{c^n + a^n}{b^n} + \dfrac{a^n + b^n}{c^n}$ is

(a) 1 (b) 2

(c) 3 (d) 6

19. Let $a_n = 1000^n/n!$ for $n \in \mathbb{N}$. Then a_n is greatest when

(a) $n = 999$ (b) $n = 1000$

(c) $n = 1001$ (d) None of these

20. The largest interval for which $x^{12} - x^9 + x^4 - x + 1 > 0$ is

(a) $-4 < x \le 0$ (b) $-100 < x < 100$

(c) $0 < x < 1$ (d) $-\infty < x < \infty$

21. Let a, b, c be distinct real numbers such that $a^2 + b^2 + c^2 = 1$. Then the quantity $(ab + bc + ca)$ satisfies the condition

(a) $(ab + bc + ca)$ is constant

(b) $-\dfrac{1}{2} < (ab + bc + ca) < 1$

(c) $-\dfrac{1}{4} < (ab + bc + ca) < 1$

(d) $-1 < (ab + bc + ca) < \dfrac{1}{2}$

22. If a and b are positive numbers and c and d are real numbers, positive or negative then $a^c \le b^d$

(a) if $a \le b$ and $c \le d$

(b) if either $a \le b$ or $c \le d$

(c) if $a \ge 1$ $b \ge 1$ $d \ge c$

(d) is not implied by one of the foregoing conditions

23. If x, y, z are arbitrary real numbers satisfying the condition $x\,y + yz + zx < 0$ and if $u = \dfrac{x^2 + y^2 + z^2}{xy + yz + zx}$ then only one of the following statements is always correct. Which one is it?

(a) $-1 \le u < 0$

(b) u takes all negative real values

(c) $-2 < u \le -1$

(d) $u \le -2$

24. If $x\,y\,z = 10$ $(x, y, z > 0)$ the minimum value of $x + y + z$ must be

(a) 10 (b) $\sqrt{10}$

(c) $10^{1/3}$ (d) $3\sqrt[3]{10}$

25. If $x\,y\,z = 10$ $(x, y, z > 0)$ the minimum value of $x + 2y + 3z$ must be

(a) $10^{/3}$ (b) $20^{1/3}$

(c) $60^{1/3}$ (d) $3 \times 60^{1/3}$

26. It is given that the numbers $a \ge 0$, $b \ge 0$, and $c \ge 0$ are such that $a + b + c = 4$ and $(a + b)(b + c)(c + a) = 24$, then only one of the following statements is correct. Which is one is it?

(a) More information is needed to determine the values of a, b and c.

(b) Even when a is given to be 1, more information is needed to determine the values of b and c.

(c) These two equations are inconsistent.

(d) There exist values of a and b from which the value of ac could be determined.

27. A collections of points (x, y) of the plane is said to be convex, if whenever two points $P = (u, v)$ and $Q = (s, t)$ belong S, every point one the line segment PQ also belongs to S. Let S_1 be the collection of all points (x, y) for which $1 < x^2 + y^2 < 2$ and let S_2 be the collection of all points (x, y) for which x and y have the same sign. Then

(a) S_1 is convex and S_2 is not convex

(b) S_1 and S_2 are both convex

(c) neither S_1 nor S_2 is convex

(d) S_1 is not convex and S_2 is convex

28. Solution set of the inequality $\frac{1}{2^x - 1} > \frac{1}{1 - 2^{x-1}}$ is

(a) $(1, \infty)$ (b) $\left(0, \log_2\left(\frac{4}{3}\right)\right)$

(c) $(-1, \infty)$ (d) $\left(0, \log_2\left(\frac{4}{3}\right)\right) \cup (1, \infty)$

29. What is the number of values that λ can take, if $\left[\sqrt{n^2+1}\right] = \left[\sqrt{n^2+\lambda}\right]$ when n, $\lambda \in \mathbb{N}$

(a) $2n+1$ (b) $2n$

(c) $3n$ (d) $3n+1$

30. If $\alpha \in \left(0, \frac{\pi}{2}\right)$, then the expression $\sqrt{x^2+x} + \frac{\tan^2 \alpha}{\sqrt{x^2+x}}$ is always greater than or equal to

(a) 2 tan α (b) 2

(c) 1 (d) $\sec^2\alpha$

31. If a,b,c are all +ve real numbers, which one of the following is true?

(a) $(b+c)(c+a)(a+b) \geq 8abc$

(b) $(b+c)(c+a)(a+b) < 8abc$

(c) $\left(\frac{a}{e}+\frac{b}{f}+\frac{c}{g}\right)\left(\frac{e}{a}+\frac{f}{b}+\frac{g}{c}\right) < 9$

(d) $(a+b)\left(\frac{1}{a}+\frac{1}{b}\right) < 4$

32. If a and b are two positive quantities whose sum is λ, then the minimum value of $\sqrt{\left(1+\frac{1}{a}\right)\left(1+\frac{1}{b}\right)}$ is

(a) $\lambda - \frac{1}{\lambda}$ (b) $\lambda - \frac{2}{\lambda}$

(c) $1 + \frac{2}{\lambda}$ (d) —

33. If a, b, c are positive distinct reals, then $a^4 + b^4 + c^4$ is greater than

(a) $(a+b+c)3$ (b) 49

(c) 25 (d) $abc(a+b+c)$

34. $\frac{\sqrt{1}+\sqrt{\frac{1}{2}}+....+\sqrt{\frac{1}{n}}}{\sqrt{n}}$ is always less than or equal to

(a) $(2n-1)^{1/4}$ (b) $(2n-1)$

(c) $(2n+1)^{1/4}$ (d) $(2n)^{1/4}$

35. The greatest value of $(a+x)^3(a-x)^4$ for any real value of x numerically less then a is

(a) $\frac{6^2.8^2}{7}a^7$ (b) $\frac{6^3.8^2}{7^7}.a^7$

(c) $\frac{6^3.8^4}{7^7}.a^7$ (d) $\frac{6.8^4}{7}.a^7$

SECTION–IV

OBJECTIVE-TYPE (MORE THAN ONE CORRECT ANSWER)

1. If a, b, c are three positive real numbers, which one of the following holds?

(a) $a^2 + b^2 + c^2 \geq bc + ca + ab$

(b) $a^3 + b^3 + c^3 \geq 3abc$

(c) $(a+b)(c+a)(a+b) \geq 8abc$

(d) $bc/a + ca/b + ab/c \geq a + b + c$

2. If $R \geq r > 0$ and $d > 0$, then $0 < \frac{d^2+R^2-r^2}{2dR} \leq 1$

(a) is satisfied if $|d - R| \leq r$

(b) is satisfied if $-r \leq d - R < r$

(c) is satisfied if $|d - R| \geq r$

(d) is not satisfied at all

3. $y = \sqrt{x^8 - x^5 + x^2 - x + 1}$ is real and finite for x belonging to

(a) $x \in [1, \infty)$ (b) $x \in (-\infty, 0)$

(c) $x \in (0, 1)$ (d) $x \in \mathbb{R}$

4. Which of the following is true for the function $f(x) = \tan x + \cot x$?

(a) $f(x)$ is bounded function

(b) $f(x)$ is unbounded function

(c) $\forall x \in \left(0, \frac{\pi}{2}\right)$ $f_{\min} = 2$

(d) $\forall x \in \left(-\frac{\pi}{2}, 0\right)$ $f_{\max} = -2$

5. Which of the following is true about the function $a^4\sec^2x + b^4\mathrm{cosec}^2x$?

(a) $f_{\min} = (a^2 - b^2)^2$

(b) $f_{\min} = (a^2 + b^2)^2$

(c) $f_{\max} \to \infty$

(d) $f(x)$ is bounded below but not bounded above

6. If $y = \sin^4x - 6\sin^2x + 5$ where $x \in \mathbb{R}$ then which of the following is true about y?

(a) $y \in [0, 5]$ (b) $y_{min} = 4$ & $y_{max} = 9$

(c) $y_{min} = 0$ & $y_{max} = 5$ (d) None of the above

7. What is the minimum value of $x^2 - 12x + 40$
(a) 4 (b) 6
(c) 0 (d) 10

8. The value $a^3b + ab^3 - a^4 - b^4$ is
(a) positive (b) negative
(c) undefined (d) zero

9. If $-2 < x < 7$, then the maximum value of $(7 - x)^4(2 + x)^5$ is
(a) $4^4.5^5$ (b) 2^2
(c) 0 (d) $4^2.5$

SECTION–V

ASSERTION AND REASON TYPE

1. **A:** If a,b,c are three distinct number in HP, then $\left(\frac{a+b}{2a-b}\right)+\left(\frac{c+b}{2c-b}\right)>4$
R: A.M. > G.M.

2. **A:** $a + b + c = 12(a, b, c > 0)$, then maximum value of abc is 64.
R: Maximum value occurs when $a = b = c$; where $a + b + c =$ constants

3. **A:** If $x^2 + y^2 = 1$, then $|x + y| \leq \sqrt{2}$
R: $AM \geq GM$

4. **A:** For $n \in \mathbb{N}$, $2^n \geq 1 + n\sqrt{(2^{n-1})}$
R: GM > HM and (AM)(HM) = $(GM)^2$

5. **A:** For $n \in \mathbb{N}$; $(n!)^3 < n^n\left(\frac{n+1}{2}\right)^{2n}$
R: $(n!)^2 > n^n$

6. **A:** If positive number a^{-1}, b^{-1}, c^{-1} are in AP, then product of roots of equation $x^2 - \lambda x - 2b^{101} - a^{101} - c^{101} = 0$ $(\lambda \in R)$ has -ve sign.
R: If a, b, c are in HP, then $\frac{a^n+c^n}{2}<b^n$ $(\because AM > HM)$

7. **A:** $1!\ 3!\ 5!\ ....(2n - 1)! > (n!)^n$
R: $(x^m + y^m)^n < (x^n + y^n)^m$ if $m < n$

SECTION–VI

LINKED COMPREHENSION TYPE

A: We are giving the concept of arithmetic mean of mth power. Let $a, b > 0$ and $a \neq b$ and let m be a real number then $\frac{a^m+b^m}{2}>\left(\frac{a+b}{2}\right)^m$, If $m \in \mathbb{R} \sim [0, 1]$.

However, if $m\in(0, 1)$, then $\frac{a^m+b^m}{2}<\left(\frac{a+b}{2}\right)^m$.

Obviously, if $m\in\{0,1\}$, then $\frac{a^m+b^m}{2}=\left(\frac{a+b}{2}\right)^m$. On the basis of above information, answer the following questions:

1. If a, b be positive and $a + b = 1$ $(a \neq b)$ and if $A = \sqrt[3]{a} + \sqrt[3]{b}$ then the correct statment is
(a) $A > 2^{2/3}$ (b) $A = \frac{2^{2/3}}{3}$
(c) $A < 2^{2/3}$ (d) $A = 2^{2/3}$

2. If x, y be positive real numbers such that $x^2 + y^2 = 8$, then the maximum value of $x + y$ is
(a) 2 (b) 4
(c) 6 (d) 8

3. If a and b are positive $(a \neq b)$ and $a + b = 1$ and if $A = \left(a+\frac{1}{a}\right)^2+\left(b+\frac{1}{b}\right)^2$, then the correct statment is
(a) $A > 8$ (b) $A < 8$
(c) $A > \frac{25}{2}$ (d) $A < \frac{25}{2}$

4. If a, b, c be positive and in Harmonic progression and if $\lambda = \frac{a^n+c^n}{b^n}, \forall n \notin (0,1)$, then the correct statement is
(a) $\lambda < 2$ (b) $\lambda > 2$
(c) $\lambda = 2$ (d) None of these

B: We are giving the concept of arithmatic mean of mth power, Let $a_1, a_2, a_3, \ldots\ldots, a_n$ be n positive real numbers (not all equal) and let m be real number.

Then $\dfrac{a_1^m + a_2^m + a_3^m + \ldots\ldots + a_n^m}{n} >$

$\left(\dfrac{a_1 + a_2 + a_3 \ldots\ldots\ldots + a_n}{n}\right)^m$;

if $m \in \mathbb{R} \sim [0,1]$. However, if $m \in (0, 1)$,

then $\dfrac{a_1^m + a_2^m + a_3^m + \ldots\ldots\ldots\ldots + a_n^m}{n} <$

$\left(\dfrac{a_1 + a_2 + a_3 \ldots\ldots\ldots\ldots + a_n}{n}\right)^m$.

Obviously, if $m \in \{0, 1\}$, then

$\dfrac{a_1^m + a_2^m + a_3^m + \ldots\ldots\ldots\ldots + a_n^m}{n}$

$= \left(\dfrac{a_1 + a_2 + a_3 \ldots\ldots\ldots\ldots + a_n}{n}\right)^m$.

On the basis of the above information, answer the following question:

5. If sum of the mth power of first n odd natural number is λ, $\forall\, m > 1$ then

(a) $\lambda < n^m$ (b) $\lambda > n^m$
(c) $\lambda < n^{m+1}$ (d) $\lambda > n^{m+1}$

6. If a, b, c be positive real numbers, then the possible best option of values $\dfrac{a}{b+c} + \dfrac{b}{c+a} + \dfrac{c}{a+b}$ lies between

(a) $(1, \infty)$ (b) $(0, \infty)$
(c) $\left[-\infty\right)$ (d) $[2, \infty)$

7. If $x > 0$, $y > 0$, $z > 0$ and $x + y + z = 1$, then the minimum value of $\dfrac{x}{2-x} + \dfrac{y}{2-y} + \dfrac{z}{2-z}$ is

(a) $\dfrac{9}{5}$ (b) $\dfrac{8}{5}$
(c) $\dfrac{3}{5}$ (d) $\dfrac{2}{5}$

8. If $a_1, a_2, a_3, \ldots\ldots, a_n$ are all positive such that $a_1^2 + a_2^2 + a_3^2 + \ldots\ldots\ldots\ldots + a_n^2 = A$ and if greatest and least values of $(a_1 + a_2 + a_3 + \ldots\ldots\ldots\ldots + a_n)^2$ are G and L respectively, then

(a) $G - L = 2A$ (b) $G - L = nA$
(c) $G - L = (n-1)A$ (d) $G - L = (n-2)A$

9. a, b, c, d be positive and not all equal to one another such that $a + b + c + d = 4/3$, then the minimum value of $\sqrt{\left(\dfrac{1}{b+c+d}\right)} + \sqrt{\left(\dfrac{1}{c+d+a}\right)} + \sqrt{\left(\dfrac{1}{d+a+b}\right)} + \sqrt{\left(\dfrac{1}{a+b+c}\right)}$ is

(a) 2 (b) 4
(c) 6 (d) 8

C: It is easy to show that A.M.-G.M. inequality is a special case of the Jensen's inequality.

Let $a_1, a_2, \ldots, a_m$ be positive real numbers.

$\Rightarrow x_i = \log a_i$ for i = 1, 2, …, m

Take $[p, q]$ be any interval containing x_i's if $f(x) = e^x$ $(f''(x) > 0)$

By Jensen's inequality:

$e^{\frac{x_1 + x_2 + \ldots + x_m}{m}} \le \dfrac{e^{x_1} + a^{x_2} + \ldots\ldots + e^{x_m}}{m}$

$\Rightarrow e^{xi} = a_i$ for $i \in \{1, 2, \ldots, m\}$

$\Rightarrow (a_1\ a_2\ \ldots a_m)^{1/m} \le \dfrac{a_1 + a_2 + \ldots + a_m}{m}$ which is the A.M.-G.M. inequality.

10. What is the greatest value of $f(x) = \dfrac{x}{ax^2 + b}$ $(a > 0$, $b > 0$ and $x > 0)$

(a) $2ab$ (b) 0
(c) ∞ (d) $\dfrac{1}{2\sqrt{ab}}$

11. If $a_1, a_2, a_3, \ldots, a_n$ are real numbers and $(a_1 - 6)(a_2 - 6)\ldots(a_n - 6) = 8n$ and $a_i > 6$ (i = 1, 2,…n) . What is the least value of $\prod_{i=1}^{n} a_i$

(a) 3^n (b) 6^n
(c) 14^n (d) $6n$

12. If a, b, c are real numbers such that $0 < a < 1$, $0 < b < 1$, $0 < c < 1$. What is the maximum value of $\sqrt{ab} + \sqrt{(1-a)(1-b)}$

(a) 0 (b) 2
(c) abc (d) 1

13. In part (3), what is the maximum of $\sqrt{abc} + \sqrt{(1-a)(1-b)(1-c)}$

(a) 1 (b) 0
(c) 2 (d) –1

SECTION–VII

COLUMN MATCHING

1. Column I

(i) The AM of two positive numbers a and b exceed their GM by 3/2 and the GM exceed their HM by 6/5, such that $a + b = \alpha$, $|a - b| = \beta$, then

(ii) The AM of two positive numbers a and b exceeds their GM by 2 and HM is one fifth of the greater of a and b such that $a + b = \alpha$, $|a - b| = \beta$, then

(iii) The HM of two positive numbers a and b is 4, their AM is A and geometric mean G satisfy the relation $2A + G^2 = 27$. If $a + b = \alpha$, $|a - b| = \beta$, then

Column II

(a) $\alpha + \beta^2 = 96$

(b) $\alpha + \beta^2 = 74$

(c) $\alpha^2 + \beta = 234$

(d) $\alpha^2 + \beta = 84$

(e) $1+\left(\frac{\alpha}{\beta}\right)+\left(\frac{\alpha}{\beta}\right)^2+\ldots\ldots+\left(\frac{\alpha}{\beta}\right)^5=364$

2. Column I

(i) Sum of mth powers of first n even numbers is

(ii) $n!.n!$ is

(iii) If $m = a_1 + a_2 + \ldots + a_n$; $(m < 1)$, then $(1 + a_1)(1 + a_2) \ldots (1 + a_n)$ is

Column II

(a) greater than $n(n + 1)^m$

(b) greater than m^n

(c) greater than n^n

(d) less that 1/1 – m

3. Match the solution regions of the following inequalities, in column I to the corresponding values in column II.

Column I

(i) $3^x\,(0.33333\ldots..)^{x-3} < \left(\frac{1}{27}\right)^x$

(ii) $\log_5 (2x^2 + 3x + 2)^{1/4} = \log_{25} (2x)$, $x > 0$

(iii) $3^{\log_5(x-7)} = \log_5(125)$

Column II

(a) $x = 2$

(b) $x = 12$

(c) $x \le \frac{3}{2}$

SECTION–VIII

INTEGER-TYPE QUESTIONS

1. Given that $n^4 < 10^n$ for a fixed integer $n \ge 2$,and $(n+1)^4 < k^{n+1}$; then find the maximum value of k.

2. If $0 < a,b,c < 1$ and $a + b + c = 1$ and $\frac{(1-a)}{a}\frac{(1-b)}{b}\frac{(1-c)}{c} \ge k$; then find the maximum value of k

3. If $|x - 3| < 2$; and $\frac{x-3}{x+3} \in \left(\frac{-1}{k_1}, \frac{-1}{k_2}\right)$ then find the value of $k_1 + k_2$.

4. If $\frac{1}{11} < \frac{1-x}{1+x} < \frac{5}{7}$ and $\left|x - \frac{1}{2}\right| < \frac{1}{k}$; then find the value of k.

5. If the values of 'a' for which the zeroes x_1 and x_2 of the polynomial $f(x) = 2x^2 - 2(2a + 1)x + a(a - 1)$ satisfy the inequality $x_1 < a < x_2$ are given by $(-\infty, k_1) \cup (k_2, \infty)$; then find the value of $|k_1 + k_2|$.

6. If 'k' be any integer such that the set of all real values of x, satisfy the equation $(\sin 3^x)(\cos 3^x) \le \frac{3x + 3^{-x}}{k}$; then find the minimum value k.

7. If $f(x) = (2^x - 1)(2^x - 2)^2$ is increasing in the interval $\left(-\infty, \log_2 \frac{k}{3}\right) \cup (1, \infty)$ then find the value of k.

8. If $\frac{1}{5}\log(1+a^5) < \frac{1}{k}\log(1 + a^k)$; $0 < a < 1$, then find the maximum value of $[k]$, where [.] denotes the greatest integer function.

9. How many solutions does the equation $\sin^2 x = x^2 + 1/x^2$ have?

10. If r and s are non-negative integers such that $r + s = 2n + 1$, then evaluate $|r - s|$ when $r!\,s!$ is least.

11. Find the value of k for which out of all rectangular parallelopipes with given volume V, the cube has the minimum perimeter k $V^{1/3}$.

12. Find the value of k for which out of all rectangular parallelopipes with given volume V, the cube has the minimum area of faces 6 V^{2}/k.

13. Find the value of k for which out of all triangles with a given semi-perimeter s, equilateral triangle has the maxium area $\frac{s^2}{3.\sqrt{k}}$.

Answer Keys

SECTION–III

1. (b)	**2.** (c)	**3.** (b)	**4.** (d)	**5.** (a)	**6.** (b)	**7.** (c)	**8.** (b)	**9.** (a)	**10.** (a)
11. (a)	**12.** (a)	**13.** (d)	**14.** (d)	**15.** (c)	**16.** (a)	**17.** (c)	**18.** (d)	**19.** (a)	**20.** (d)
21. (b)	**22.** (d)	**23.** (d)	**24.** (d)	**25.** (d)	**26.** (c)	**27.** (c)	**28.** (d)	**29.** (b)	**30.** (a)
31. (a)	**32.** (c)	**33.** (d)	**34.** (a)	**35.** (c)					

SECTION–IV

1. (a,b,c,d) **2.** (a,b) **3.** (a,b,c,d) **4.** (b,c,d) **5.** (b,c,d) **6.** (a,c) **7.** (a) **8.** (b)
9. (a)

SECTION–V

1. (a) **2.** (a) **3.** (a) **4.** (a) **5.** (b) **6.** (c) **7.** (b)

SECTION–VI

1. (c)	**2.** (b)	**3.** (c)	**4.** (b)	**5.** (d)	**6.** (c)	**7.** (c)	**8.** (c)	**9.** (b)	**10.** (d)
11. (c)	**12.** (d)	**13.** (a)							

SECTION–VII

1. (i) → (a),(c) (ii) → (b), (iii) → (d),(e)
2. (i) → (a) (ii) → (c), (iii) → (d)
3. (i) → (c), (ii) → (a), (iii) → (b)

SECTION–VIII

1. 100	**2.** 8	**3.** –2	**4.** 3	**5.** 3	**6.** 4	**7.** 4	**8.** 4	**9.** 0	**10.** 1
11. 2	**12.** 3	**13.** 3							

HINTS AND SOLUTIONS

TEXTUAL EXERCISE–1: (SUBJECTIVE)

1. $x2 + 5y2 + z2 - 2yz + 4xy$ 0
$\therefore\ x^2 + 4y^2 + 4xy = (x + 2y)^2 \geq 0$ (i)
Also, $y^2 + z^2 - 2yz = (y - z)^2 \geq 0$ (ii)
Adding (i) and (ii), we get $x^2 + 5y^2 + z^2 - 2yz + 4xy \geq 0$

2. $x^2 + y^2 + z^2 - 2x - 4y - 6z + 14 = 0$
Consider the following
$x^2 - 2x + 1 = (x - 1)^2 \geq 0$ (i)
$y^2 - 4y + 4 = (y - 2)^2 \geq 0$ (ii)
$z^2 - 6z + 9 = (z - 3)^2 \geq 0$ (iii)
Adding (i), (ii) and (iii), we get $x^2 + y^2 + z^2 - 2x - 4y - 6z + 14 \geq 0$
Hence for no real values of x, y, z. It is negative.

3. $x^2 - 4x + 7 \geq 3$, which is true iff $x^2 - 4x + 4 \geq 0$
$\Rightarrow (x - 2)^2 \geq 0$, which is definitely true.
$\Rightarrow x^2 - 4x + 7 \geq 3$

4. $7x^2 + 11 > x^3 + 17x$
It is true when, $x^3 - 7x^2 + 17 - 11 < 0$
Let us factories $x^3 - 7x^2 + 17x - 11$
$= x^2 (x - 1) - 6x (x - 1) + 11 (x - 1)$
$= (x - 1) (x^2 - 6x + 11)$
Now $x^2 - 6x + 11$ is always positive, as the discriminate $D = 36 - 44 < 0$
Hence, the solution lies in the region, $x - 1 < 0$
$\Rightarrow x < 1$
$\Rightarrow$ First integral value = 0

5. $x^2 - 4xy + 5y^2 + 2y + 1 \leq 0$
Which can be written as $x^2 - 4xy + 4y^2 + y^2 + 2y + 1 \leq 0$
$\Rightarrow (x - 2y)^2 + (y + 1)^2 \leq 0$
Which is true only when $y + 1 = 0$ and $x - 2y = 0$
$\Rightarrow y = -1, x = -2$

6. $(x + y)(y + z)(z + x) \geq 8xyz$
Without loss of generality $x \geq y \geq z$
$\Rightarrow x \geq y$
$\Rightarrow x + y \geq 2y$ (i)
$\Rightarrow y + z \geq 2z$ (ii)
$\Rightarrow x + z \geq 2x$ (iii)
Multiplying (i), (ii), (iii), we get $(x + y)(y + z)(x + z) \geq 8xyz$

7. $(ab + cd)(ac + bd) \geq 4\,abcd$
$\therefore\ ab + cd > 2\,(abcd)^{1/2}$
$\Rightarrow \dfrac{ab+cd}{2} > (abcd)^{1/2}$ (i)
Similarly, $\dfrac{ac+bd}{2} \geq (abc)^{1/2}$ (ii)
Multiplying (i) and (ii), we get $(ab + cd)(ac + bd) \geq 4(abcd)$

TEXTUAL EXERCISE–2: (SUBJECTIVE)

1. (a) $\dfrac{1}{(1-2x)} < 0$
Multiplying the numerator and denominator by$(1 - 2x)$, we get $(1 - 2x) < 0$
$\Rightarrow 2x > 1 \quad \Rightarrow x > \dfrac{1}{2}$
$\Rightarrow x \in \left(\dfrac{1}{2}, \infty\right)$

(b) $\dfrac{2}{3+x} > 5 \quad \Rightarrow \dfrac{2}{3+x} - 5 > 0$
$\Rightarrow \dfrac{2-15-5x}{3+x} > 0 \quad \Rightarrow (-5x - 13)(x + 3) > 0$
$\Rightarrow (5x + 13)(x + 3) < 0 \quad \Rightarrow \left(x + \dfrac{13}{5}\right)(x+3) < 0$
$\Rightarrow x \in \left(-\dfrac{13}{5}, -3\right)$

(c) $\dfrac{x}{x-5} > \dfrac{1}{2} \quad \Rightarrow \dfrac{x}{x-5} - \dfrac{1}{2} > 0$
$\Rightarrow \dfrac{2x-x+5}{(x-5)} > 0 \quad (x + 5)(x - 5) > 0$
$\Rightarrow x \in (-\infty, -5) \cup (5, \infty)$

(d) $(x + 5)(x - 3) < 2 \quad \Rightarrow x^2 + 2x - 15 < 2$
$\Rightarrow x^2 + 2x - 17 < 0 \quad \Rightarrow (x + 1)^2 - 18 < 0$
Clearly$(x + 1) \geq 0$
$\Rightarrow \left(x+1-\sqrt{18}\right)\left(x+1+\sqrt{18}\right) < 0$
Hence the solution set is $x \in \left(-\sqrt{18} - 1, \sqrt{18} - 1\right)$

(e) $3x - 2 \geq 0 \quad \Rightarrow x \geq \dfrac{2}{3}$ and $5x - 1 < 0$
$\Rightarrow x < \dfrac{1}{5} \quad \Rightarrow x \in \phi$

(f) Solving this as two different inequalities $3 + x \leq 5x - 2$
$\Rightarrow 4x \geq 5 \quad \Rightarrow x \geq \dfrac{5}{4}$ and
$5x - 2 \leq 7 + x \quad \Rightarrow 4x \leq 9$
$\Rightarrow x \leq \dfrac{9}{4} \quad \Rightarrow x \in \left[\dfrac{5}{4}, \dfrac{9}{4}\right]$

(g) $\dfrac{2}{x-2} < \dfrac{x+2}{x-2} < 1 \quad \Rightarrow \dfrac{2}{x-2} - \dfrac{(x+2)}{x-2} < 0$
$\Rightarrow x \in (-\infty, 0) \cup (2, \infty)$
The other half of the inequality gives us $\dfrac{x+2}{x-2} < 1$
$\Rightarrow \dfrac{x+2}{x-2} - 1 < 0 \quad \Rightarrow \dfrac{x+2-x+2}{x-2} < 0$
$\Rightarrow 4(x - 2) < 0 \quad \Rightarrow x < 2$
Taking intersection of both the regions $= x \in (-\infty, 0)$

2. $4x+2<\frac{8y-4}{5}$ $\Rightarrow$ $20x + 10 < 8y - 4$

$\Rightarrow$ $20x - 8y + 14 < 0$ (i)

The other point is $3-y>\frac{7-4z}{3}$

$\Rightarrow$ $9 - 3y > 7 - 4z$ $\Rightarrow$ $4z - 3y + 2 > 0$

Multiplying by $\frac{8}{3}$, we get $\frac{32z}{3}-8y+\frac{16}{3}>0$

$\Rightarrow$ $8y-\frac{32z}{3}-\frac{16}{3}<0$ (ii)

Adding (i) and (ii), we get $20x-\frac{32z}{3}+14-\frac{16}{3}$

$\Rightarrow$ $60x - 32z + 42 - 16 < 0$

$\Rightarrow$ $60x - 32z + 26 < 0$

Which is not possible if $x > z$

$\Rightarrow$ $x < z$

3. Let as consider that maximum number of minutes, so required is m,

Change of $A = 250 + \frac{3m}{4}$

Change of $B = 175 + m$

By the question, $175+m > 250+\frac{3}{4}m$

$\Rightarrow$ $\frac{m}{4}>75$ $\Rightarrow$ $m > 300$

Thus maximum of minutes m = 301

4. $3x + 2y \le 12$, $x^2 - x - 6 \le$ and $y > 0$

$x^2 - x - 6 = (x - 3)(x + 2) \le 0$

$\Rightarrow$ $x \in [-2, 3]$ and $y > 0$

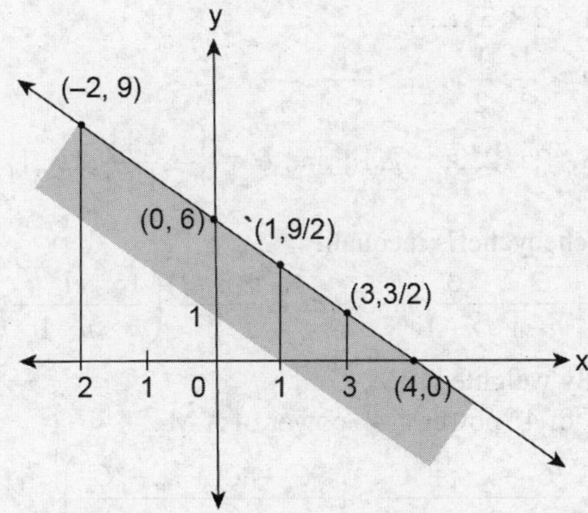

The shaded region gives the region $3x + 2y \le 12$

Total number of integral pairs in the region is equal to = 6 × 5 = 30

TEXTUAL EXERCISE–3: (SUBJECTIVE)

1. Let r be a real positive quantity

By the question, $r+\frac{1}{r}\ge 2\ \forall\ r\in\mathbb{R}^+$

$\Rightarrow$ $r+\frac{1}{r}=\frac{r^2+1}{r}$

Let us try find $\frac{r^2+1}{r}\ge 2$

$\Rightarrow$ $\frac{r^2+1}{r}-2\ge 0$ $\Rightarrow$ $r^2 - 2r + 1 \ge 0$

$\Rightarrow$ $(r - 1)^2 \ge 0$, which is always true

Hence for no real positive value of r

$\Rightarrow$ $r+\frac{1}{r}<2$

2. $a^2 + b^2 + c^2 = 1$

$x^2 + y^2 + z^2 = 1$

Applying A.M-G.M separately on $a^2, x^2, b^2, y^2, c^2, z^2$

We get, $a^2 + x^2 > 2ax$ (i)

$b^2 + y^2 > 2\,by$ (ii)

$c^2 + z^2 > 2\,cz$ (iii)

Applying three equations, we get $a^2 + b^2 + c^2 + x^2 + y^2 + z^2 > 2\,(ax + by + cz)$

$\Rightarrow$ $2 > 2(ax + by + cz)$

$\Rightarrow$ $ax + by + cz < 1$

3. $6\,abc < bc\,(b + c) + ca\,(a + c) + ab\,(a + b)$

Applying A.M-G.M on following quantities $\frac{b}{a},\frac{c}{a},\frac{a}{c},\frac{b}{c},\frac{c}{b},\frac{a}{b}$

$\Rightarrow$ $\frac{\frac{b}{a}+\frac{c}{a}+\frac{c}{b}+\frac{a}{c}+\frac{a}{b}+\frac{b}{c}}{6}\ge (1)^{1/6}$

$\Rightarrow$ $\frac{b}{a}+\frac{c}{a}+\frac{a}{c}+\frac{b}{c}+\frac{a}{b}+\frac{c}{b}\ge 6$

$\Rightarrow$ $bc\,(b + c) + ca\,(a + c) + ab\,(a + b) \ge 6\,abc$ (after taking LCM of abc)

4. $n\,(n + 1)^3 \le (1^3 + 2^3 + 3^3 + \ldots + n^3)$

$\therefore$ $1^3 + 2^3 + 3^3 + \ldots + n^3 = \frac{n^2(n+1)^2}{4}$

$\Rightarrow$ $n\,(n + 1)^3 \le 2n^2\,(n + 1)^2$

$\Rightarrow$ $2n \ge (n + 1)$

$\Rightarrow$ $n \ge 1$, which is true

5. By the weighted power mean inequality

$$\left[\frac{s}{a_1}-1\right]^{a_1}\left[\frac{s}{a_2}-1\right]^{a_2}\ldots\left[\frac{s}{a_n}-1\right]^{a_m}$$

$$<\left[\frac{a_1\left[\frac{s}{a_1}-1\right]+a_2\left[\frac{s}{a_2}-1\right]+\ldots+a_m\left[\frac{s}{a_m}-1\right]}{a_1+a_2+\ldots a_m}\right]^{a_1+a_2+\ldots+a_m}$$

$$<\left[\frac{ms-\sum a_i}{\sum a_i}\right]<\left[\frac{ms-s}{s}\right]^s=(m-1)^s$$

Hence $a_1 + a_2 + \ldots a_m = s$

6. $a + b + c = 3$ (given)

$\frac{a+b+c}{3}\ge\frac{ab+bc+ca}{a+b+c}\ge\left(a^b b^c c^a\right)^{\frac{1}{a+b+c}}$

$\Rightarrow$ $a^b\, b^c\, c^a \le 1$

7. By weighted A.M-G.M $\frac{a^2+b^2+c^2}{a+b+c}\ge\left(a^2\, b^b\, c^c\right)^{\frac{1}{a+b+c}}$

$\Rightarrow$ $a^2 + b^2 + c^2 \ge a^a\, b^b\, c^c$ (i)

Also, $\frac{ab+bc+ca}{a+b+c} \geq \left(a^c b^a c^b\right)^{\frac{1}{a+b+c}}$

$\Rightarrow ab + bc + ca \geq a^a b^b c^c$ (ii)

Similarly, $ab + bc + ca \geq a^c b^a c^b$ (iii)

Adding (i), (ii) and (iii), we get $(a + b + c)^2 \geq a^a b^b c^c + a^b b^c c^a + b^a c^b a^c$

$\Rightarrow a^a b^b c^c + a^b b^c c^a + a^c b^a c^b \leq 1$

TEXTUAL EXERCISE–4: (SUBJECTIVE)

1. $\frac{b+c}{a}+\frac{c+a}{b}+\frac{a+b}{c} \geq 6$

Which can also be written as

$\frac{a+b+c}{a}+\frac{a+b+c}{b}+\frac{a+b+c}{c}-3 \geq 6$

$\Rightarrow (a+b+c)\left(\frac{1}{a}+\frac{1}{b}+\frac{1}{c}\right) \geq 9$, which is true by Cauchy's inequality.

Taking a, b, c, as one set an $\left(\frac{1}{a},\frac{1}{b},\frac{1}{c}\right)$

2. ${}^nc_r = \frac{n!}{r!(n-r)!}$; Clearly ${}^nC_r$ is always a positive integer,

Consider two sets of numbers

(i) $\sqrt{C_1}, \sqrt{C_2}, \sqrt{C_3} \ldots \sqrt{C_n}$

(ii) 1, 1, 1, 1, …,1 → n times

Applying Cauchy's Inequality

$\left(\sqrt{C_1}+\sqrt{C_2}+\ldots.+\sqrt{C_n}\right)^2 < (n)(C_1+C_2+\ldots+C_n)$

$\therefore {}^nC_1 + {}^nC_2 + \ldots + {}^nC_2 = 2^{n-1}$

Replacing this value, we get

$\left(\sqrt{C_1}+\sqrt{C_2}+\sqrt{C_3}+\ldots+\sqrt{C_n}\right)^2 < n(2^n-1)$

$\Rightarrow \sqrt{C_1}+\sqrt{C_2}+\ldots+\sqrt{C_n} < \sqrt{n(2^n-1)}$

3. $\left[\frac{a_1}{b_1}+\frac{a_2}{b_2}+\ldots..+\frac{a_n}{b_n}\right]\left[\frac{b_1}{a_1}\times\frac{b_2}{a_2}\times\ldots.\times\frac{b_n}{a_n}\right] \geq n^2$

Consider two set of numbers

(i) $\left(\frac{a_1}{b_1},\frac{a_1}{b_1},\ldots\ldots,\frac{a_n}{b_n}\right)$

(ii) $\left(\frac{b_1}{a_1},\frac{b_2}{a_2},\ldots,\frac{b_n}{a_n}\right)$

$\frac{n}{n} \geq \frac{1}{n^2}\left(\frac{a_1}{b_1}+\ldots..+\frac{a_n}{b_n}\right)\left(\frac{b_1}{a_1}+\ldots+\frac{b_n}{a_n}\right)$

$\Rightarrow n^2 \geq \left(\frac{a_1}{b_1}+\frac{a_2}{b_2}+\ldots.+\frac{a_n}{b_n}\right)\left(\frac{b_1}{a_1}+\ldots.+\frac{a_n}{a_n}\right)$

4. Using Cauchy-Schwarz with $b_1 = b_2 = \ldots. = b_n = 1$

$(a_1^2 + a_2^2 + \ldots + a_n^2)(1^2 + 1^2 \ldots. + 1^2) \geq (a_1.1 + \ldots. + a_n.1)^2$

$\Rightarrow (a_1^2 + a_2^2 + \ldots + a_n)^2. n \geq (a_1 + a_2 + \ldots. + a_n)^2$

Given $a_1 + a_2 + \ldots. + a_n = 1$

$(a_1^2 = a_2^2 + \ldots a_n^2). n \geq 1$

Which in twin implies that $(a_1^2 + a_2^2 + \ldots.+ a_n^2) \geq \frac{1}{n}$

5. Let $x = \frac{1}{a}, y = \frac{1}{b}, z = \frac{1}{c}$

By the question $xyz = 1$

$\therefore \sum \frac{1}{a^3(b+c)} = \sum \frac{x^2}{y+z}$

Since $\frac{a_1^2}{b_1}+\frac{a_2^2}{b_2}+\ldots..+\frac{a_n^2}{b_n} \geq \frac{(a_1+a_2+\ldots.+a_n)^2}{b_1+b_2+\ldots+b_n}$

$\Rightarrow \sum \frac{x^2}{y+z} \geq \frac{(x+y+z)^2}{2(x+y+z)} = \frac{(x+y+z)}{2} \geq \frac{3\sqrt[3]{xyz}}{2} = \frac{3}{2}$

TEXTUAL EXERCISE–5: (SUBJECTIVE)

1. Let $M = \left[x+\frac{1}{x}\right]^2 + \left[y+\frac{1}{y}\right]^2$

$M = x^2 + y^2 + \frac{1}{x^2}+\frac{1}{y^2}+4 = x^2 + y^2 + \frac{(x^2+y^2)}{x^2y^2}+4$

Consider $x^2 + y^2 \geq \frac{1}{2}$

Similarly $x^2 + y^2 \geq \frac{1}{2}$, $x^2 y^2 \geq \frac{1}{16}$

Multiplying $\frac{x^2+y^2}{x^2y^2} \geq 8$

$\Rightarrow M = x^2 + y^2 - \left(\frac{x^2+y^2}{x^2y^2}\right)+4 \geq \frac{1}{2}+8+4 = \frac{25}{2}$

2. $\because 1 < 2 < 3 \ldots.. < n$

$\Rightarrow 1 > \frac{1}{2} > \frac{1}{2} > \ldots.. > \frac{1}{n-1} > \frac{1}{n}$

For $S = \{1, 2, 3, \ldots..,n\}$ and $U = \left\{\frac{1}{n}, \frac{1}{n-1}, \ldots...,1\right\}$

By Tchebychef's inequality

$n\left(n+\frac{2}{n-1}+\frac{3}{n-1}+\ldots...+n\right) \geq \frac{n(n+1)}{2}\left(\frac{1}{n}+\frac{1}{n-1}+\ldots.+1\right)$

3. (a) By weighted A.M.-G.M.

A.M. of 4th power > 4th power of A.M.

$\frac{{}^4C_0+{}^4C_1+\ldots...+{}^4C_n}{n} > \left(\frac{{}^4C_0+{}^4C_1+\ldots.+{}^4C_n}{n}\right)^4$

$\Rightarrow {}^4C_0 + {}^4C_1 + \ldots...+ {}^4C_n > \left(\frac{2^n}{n}\right)^4$

${}^4C_0 + {}^4C_1 + \ldots...+ {}^4C_n > \frac{2^{4n}}{n^3}$

(b) $\tan A + \tan B + \tan C \geq 3\sqrt{3}$

Assume $f(x) = \tan x$

$\Rightarrow f'(x) = \sec^2 x$

$f'(x) = 2\sec^2 x + \tan x > 0 \ \forall \ x \in \left[0, \frac{\pi}{2}\right)$

$f\left(\frac{A+B+C}{3}\right) \le \frac{f(A)+f(B)+f(c)}{3}$

$\Rightarrow$ $\tan A + \tan B + \tan C \ge 3 \tan\left(\frac{A+B+C}{3}\right)$

$\Rightarrow$ $\tan A + \tan B + \tan C \ge 3\sqrt{3}$

4. Satisfying the inequality criterion of squaring
Squaring both sides, we get $1 - x_1^2 + 1 - x_2^2$
$= 2\sqrt{(1-x_1^2)(1-x_2^2)} \le 4 - (x_1^2 + 2x_1 + x_2 + x_2^2)$
i.e., $2\sqrt{(1-x_1^2)(1-x_2^2)} \le 2 - 2x_1 x_2$
$\Rightarrow$ $\sqrt{(1-x_1^2)(1-x_2^2)} \le 1 - x_1 x_2$
Squaring again, we get $1 - x_1^2 - x_2^2 + x_1^2 x_2^2 \le 1 - 2x_1 x_2 + x_1^2 x_2^2$
$\Rightarrow$ $0 \le (x_1 - x_2)^2$
Equating at $x_1 = x_2$

SECTION–III

1. **(b)** $4^{-x+0.5} - 7.2^{-x} < 0$ $(\forall x \in \mathbb{R})$
$\Rightarrow$ $2^{-2x+1} - 7.2^{-x} < 0 = 2.2^{-2x} - 7.2^{-x} < 0$
Let $2^{-x} = y$
$\Rightarrow$ $2.y^2 - 7y < 0$ $\Rightarrow$ $y\left(y - \frac{7}{2}\right) < 0$
$\Rightarrow$ $y \in \left(0, \frac{7}{2}\right)$ $\Rightarrow$ $0 < y < \frac{7}{2}$
$\Rightarrow$ $0 < 2^{-x} < \frac{7}{2}$ $\Rightarrow$ $-\log_2\left(\frac{7}{2}\right) < x < \infty$

2. **(c)** $\frac{x+2}{x^2+1} - \frac{1}{2} > 0$ $\Rightarrow$ $\frac{2x+4-x^2-1}{2(x^2+1)} > 0$
$\Rightarrow$ $-x^2 + 2x + 3 > 0$
$\Rightarrow$ $x^2 - 2x - 3 < 0$ $\Rightarrow$ $(x-3)(x+1) < 0$
$\Rightarrow$ $x \in (-1, 3)$
Integral solutions are 0, 1, 2

3. **(b)** $x^2 - 3x < 4$
$\Rightarrow$ $x^2 - 3x - 4 < 0$ $\Rightarrow$ $x(x-4) + (x-4) < 0$
$\Rightarrow$ $(x-4)(x+1) < 0$ $\Rightarrow$ $x \in (-1, 4)$
Number of integral values = 0, 1, 2, 3

4. **(d)** Let $a_1, a_2, a_3, a_4, \ldots, a_n$ be n positive integers
By the question $a_1, a_2, \ldots, a_n = 1$
By A.M-G.M
If their sum is S $\Rightarrow$ $\frac{S}{n} \ge (a_1 a_2 \ldots a_n)^{1/n}$
$\Rightarrow$ $S \ge n$

5. **(a)** $a_1 + a_2 + \ldots + a_n = m$ and $S = \sum_{i<j} a_i a_j$
We have $\sqrt{a_1 a_2} \le \frac{a_1 + a_2}{2}$
Equating at $a_1 = a_2 = 0$
$\Rightarrow$ Similarly for all product $(a_i a_j)$ $(i < j)$
$\sqrt{a_i a_j} \le \frac{a_i + a_j}{2}$
Addition and squaring, we get $S \le \frac{m^2}{2}$

6. **(b)** In the region $\frac{-\pi}{2} < \theta < \frac{\pi}{2}$, cos and sec θ are positive
On applying A.M-G.M., we get
$\frac{\cos^3\theta + \sec^3\theta}{2} \ge \sqrt{\cos\theta.\sec\theta}$
$\Rightarrow$ $\cos^3\theta + \sec^3\theta \ge 2$
$\Rightarrow$ Minimum value is 2

7. **(c)** Min $(\log_b a + \log_a b)$
If $\log_b a = x$
$\Rightarrow$ $\log_a b = \frac{1}{x}$
$\therefore$ $x + \frac{1}{x} \ge 2$ $\Rightarrow$ Minimum value is 2

8. **(b)** $(b+c-a)(c+a-b)(a+b-c) - abc$
Without loss of generality we can assume, $a > b > c$
Applying A.M.-G.M. pair wise
$(b+c) > 2\sqrt{bc}$ (i)
$(a+c) > 2\sqrt{ac}$ (ii)
$(a+b) > 2\sqrt{(ab)}$ (iii)
Multiplying equation (i), (ii), (iii), we get
$(a+b)(b+c)(c+a) > 8abc$
Let us put $b + c = 2p$; $c + a = 2q$; $a + b = 2r$
$\Rightarrow$ $a = -p + r + q$; $b = p - q + r$; $c = p + q - r$
$\Rightarrow$ $2p.2q.2r \ge r \ge 8(q + r + p)$; $(p + r - q)$; $(p + q - r)$
$\Rightarrow$ $pqr \ge (q + r - p)(p + r - q)(p + r - r)$
Replacing p, q, r by $a\ b\ c$
Without loss of generality, we get $abc \ge (a + b - c)(b + c - a)(c + a - b)$
$\Rightarrow$ The required expression is always negative

9. **(a)** $E = \frac{x^n y^m}{(1+x^{2n})(1+y^{2m})}$
This expression can be re-arranged $E = \frac{1}{(x^{-n}+x^n)(y^m+y^{-m})}$
$\therefore$ $x + \frac{1}{x} \ge 2$
Hence $x^{-n} + x^n \ge 2$
$\Rightarrow$ $(x^{-n} + x^n)(y^m + y^- m) \ge 4$
$\Rightarrow$ $\frac{1}{(x^n+x^{-n})(y^m+y^{-m})} \ge \frac{1}{4}$ $\Rightarrow$ $E \ge \frac{1}{4}$

10. **(a)** $a(n) = 1 + \frac{1}{2} + \frac{1}{3} + \ldots + \frac{1}{2^n - 1}$
$\therefore$ $1 + \frac{1}{2} + \frac{1}{3} + \ldots + \frac{1}{k} < \ln k + 1$
$\Rightarrow$ $1 + \frac{1}{2} + \frac{1}{3} + \ldots + \frac{1}{2^n - 1} < \ln(2^n - 1) + 1$
$\Rightarrow$ $1 + \frac{1}{2} + \ldots + \frac{1}{2^n - 1} < \ln(2^n - 1) + 1$
$\Rightarrow$ $1 + \frac{1}{2} + \ldots + \frac{1}{2^{100} - 1} < \ln(2^{100} - 1) + 1$, which comes out to be a value near 70.
$\Rightarrow$ $a(100) < 100$

11. (a) $a+b+c+d=2$

$m=(a+b)(c+d)$

Which can be written as $(2-(c+d))(c+d)=m$

Let $x=c+d$

$\Rightarrow (2-x)(x)=m$

$\Rightarrow -x^2+2x=x(-x+2)=m$

Clearly $0\le x\le 2$

$\Rightarrow$ m will range from $0\le m\le 1$

12. (a) $\left|\frac{n^2+n+1}{3n^2+1}-\frac{1}{3}\right|<\frac{1}{10}\quad\left|\frac{3n^2+3n+3-3n^2-1}{3(3n^2+1)}\right|<\frac{1}{10}$

$\Rightarrow \left|\frac{3n+2}{3(3n^2+1)}\right|<\frac{1}{10}\quad\Rightarrow\quad\frac{|3n+2|}{3(3n^2+1)}<\frac{1}{10}$

Solve the above modules inequality

By breaking n into regions around $n=-\frac{2}{3}$

$\Rightarrow$ Minimum possible value of n = 4

13. (d) $\frac{1}{2^{\sin 2a_2}}\frac{1}{3^{\sin 2a_4}}\ldots\frac{1}{n^{\sin 2a_n}}\le n!$

In the region $(-\pi,\pi)$ at $a_i=\frac{\pi}{4}$

L.H.S. = R.H.S.

Then any other value for which $\frac{1}{\sin 2a_i}<0$ is a solution as it will reduce the product on the left hand side.

$\Rightarrow$ Hence there are infinitely many solutions.

14. (d) $\log_{a_2}a_1+\log_{a_3}a_2+\ldots+\log_{a_n}a_{n-1}+\log_{a_1}a_n$

$=\frac{\log a_1}{\log a_2}+\frac{\log a_2}{\log a_3}+\ldots+\frac{\log a_n}{\log a_1}$

Consider numbers $\frac{\log a_1}{\log a_2},\ldots\ldots,\frac{\log a_n}{a_1}$

Since $a_n>1\ \forall\ n\in\mathbb{N}$

$\Rightarrow$ All $\log a_n>0$ $\quad\Rightarrow$ by A.M.-G.M.

$\Rightarrow \frac{\text{sum}}{n}\ge(\log a_n)^{1/n}\quad\Rightarrow$ Sum $\ge n(\log a_n)^1$

15. (c) $n!>2n-1$

$\Rightarrow n!-n>2n-1$

$\Rightarrow n(n-1)!-1)>n-1$

Clearly $(n-1)!>n$ for $n>2$

$\Rightarrow (n-1)!-1>n-1$

$\Rightarrow$ For $\forall\ n>2$ this holds

16. (a) x, y, z are in A.P.

$\Rightarrow 2y=x+z$

Obviously $x+z\ge 2\sqrt{xz}$

$\Rightarrow 2y\ge 2\sqrt{xz}\Rightarrow y\ge\sqrt{xz}\Rightarrow y^2\ge xz$

17. (c) $(3)^{x/2}+(4)^{x/2}>25$

But $(3)^2+(4)^2=25$

$\Rightarrow \frac{x}{2}>2\quad\Rightarrow x\in(4,\infty)$

18. (d) $\frac{b^n+c^n}{a^n}+\frac{c^n+a^n}{b^n}+\frac{a^n+b^n}{c^n}$; which is equal to

$\frac{b^n}{a^n}+\frac{c^n}{a^n}+\frac{c^n}{b^n}+\frac{a^n}{b^n}+\frac{a^n}{c^n}+\frac{b^n}{c^n}$

They are positive real. Hence applying A.M-G.M.

$\Rightarrow \frac{\text{required sum}}{6}\ge(1)^{1/6}$

$\Rightarrow$ Required sum ≥ 6

19. (a) $a_n=\frac{1000^n}{n!}\forall n\in\mathbb{N}\quad\Rightarrow\quad a_n=\frac{(1000)(1000)\ldots.n\text{ times}}{n.(n-1)(n-2)\ldots.1}$

By A.M-G.M, we get

$1000\left(\frac{1}{n}+\frac{1}{n-1}+\frac{1}{n-2}+\ldots\ldots+1\right)\ge n\left(\frac{1000^n}{n!}\right)$

$\Rightarrow 1000\left(\frac{1}{n}+\frac{1}{n-1}+\ldots.+1\right)\ge n\left(\frac{1000^n}{n!}\right)$

$\Rightarrow \frac{1000}{n}\left(\frac{1}{n}+\frac{1}{n-1}+\ldots.+1\right)\ge\left(\frac{1000^n}{n!}\right)$

$\Rightarrow \left(\frac{1000^n}{n!}\right)$ Maximizes when n is minimum

$\Rightarrow$ Out of given options n = 999

20. (d) $x^{12}-x^9+x^4-x+1>0$; which can be written as $x^4(x^8+1)-x(x^8+1)>0$

$\Rightarrow (x^4-x)(x^8+1)+1>0\Rightarrow x(x^3-1)(x^8+1)+1>0$

$\Rightarrow$ which is always positive

21. (b) $a^2+b^2+c^2=1$

$\therefore \frac{a^m+b^m+c^m}{3}>\left[\frac{a+b+c}{3}\right]^m$

$\Rightarrow \frac{a^2+b^2+c^2}{3}>\left[\frac{a+b+c}{3}\right]^2$

$\Rightarrow \frac{1}{3}>\frac{a^2+b^2+c^2+2(ab+bc+ca)}{9}$

$\Rightarrow 3>1+2(ab+bc+ca)$

$\Rightarrow ab+bc+ca<1$

Clearly, $(a+b+c)^2>0$

$\Rightarrow a^2+b^2+c^2+2(ab+bc+ca)>0$

$\Rightarrow 1+2(ab+bc+ca)>0$

$\Rightarrow ab+bc+ca>-\frac{1}{2}$. Hence $\frac{-1}{2}<ab+bc+ca<1$

22. (d) Option (a), $a\le b$ and $c\le d$ does not empty $a^b\le c^d$ as there is a possibility $a<1$ or $b<1$

Option (b) and (c), none of the conditions necessary and sufficient for the inequality $a^c\le b^a$

23. (d) $xy+yz+zx<0$ and $\mu=\frac{x^2+y^2+z^2}{xy+yz+zx}$

$\therefore (x+y+z)^2=x^2+y^2+z^2+2(xy+yz+zx)$

$\therefore (x+y+z)^2\ge 0$

$\Rightarrow x^2+y^2+z^2+2(xy+yz+zx)\ge 0$

$\Rightarrow x^2+y^2+z^2 \ge -2(xy+yz+zx)$

$\Rightarrow \dfrac{x^2+y^2+z^2}{xy+yz+zx} \le -2$

24. (d) Given $xyz = 10$

By A.M-G.M inequality

$\Rightarrow x+y+z \ge 3\,(xyz)^{1/3} \Rightarrow x+y+z \ge 3(10)^{1/3}$

25. (d) $xyz = 10$

Let us apply A.M.-G.M. on numbers

$\dfrac{x}{3},\dfrac{x}{3},\dfrac{x}{3},\dfrac{2y}{3},\dfrac{2y}{3},\dfrac{2y}{3},z,z,z$

By inequality, we get

$$\frac{\frac{x}{3}+\frac{x}{3}+\frac{x}{3}+\frac{2y}{3}+\frac{2y}{3}+\frac{2y}{3}+z+z+z}{9} \ge \left(\frac{8(xyz)^3}{3^6}\right)^{1/9}$$

By the question $xyz = 10$

$$\Rightarrow \frac{x+2y+3z}{9} \ge \left[\left(\frac{8\times 10^3}{3^6}\right)^{1/3}\right]^{1/3}$$

$$\Rightarrow x+2y+3z \ge 9\left[\left[\frac{2\times 10}{3^2}\right]\right]^{1/3}$$

Making 9 inside the exponent

$\Rightarrow x+2y+3z \ge 3 \times (60)^{1/3}$

26. (c) $a+b+c = 4$ and $(a+b)(b+c)(b+c) = 24$

Given a, b, c are all positive

Applying A.M.-G.M. on $(a+b)$, $(b+c)$ and $(c+a)$

$$\Rightarrow \frac{2(a+b+c)}{3} \ge [(a+b)(b+c)(c+a)]^{1/3}$$

$$\Rightarrow \frac{8}{3} \ge [(a+b)(b+c)(c+a)]^{1/3}$$

$$\Rightarrow (a+b)(b+c)(c+a) \le \frac{512}{27}$$

$\Rightarrow (a+b)(b+c)(c+a)$ cannot be equal to 24.

27. (c) If $P, Q \in S$

$\Rightarrow$ all points of $PQ \in S$, the collection of PQ is convex,

Given $1 < x^2 + y^2 < 2$

If $x_1 y_1 \in S_1 \quad \Rightarrow 1 < x_1^2 + y_1^2 < 2$ and

$x_2 y_2 \in S_2 \quad \Rightarrow 1 < x_2^2 + y_2^2 < 2$

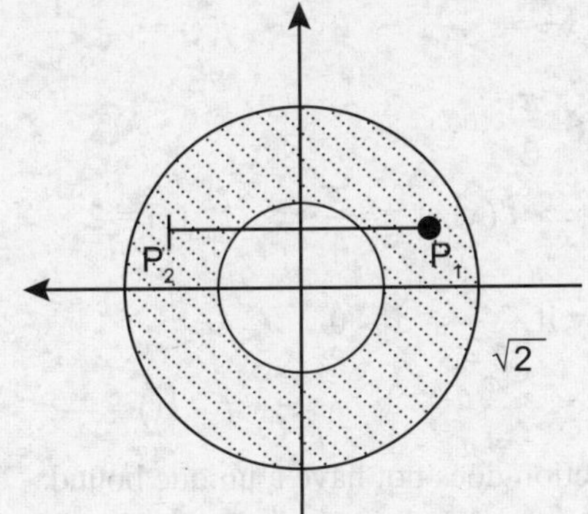

The region S_1 is given by ▨

Now all points between P_1 and P_2 do not belong to S_1

$\Rightarrow S_1$ is not convex and similarly S_2 is not convex

$\Rightarrow xy > 0 \quad \Rightarrow (x, y) \in S_2$

28. (d) $\dfrac{1}{2^x-1} > \dfrac{1}{1-2^{x-1}}$

Let us assume $2^x = y \quad \Rightarrow 2^{x-1} = \dfrac{y}{2}$

Substituting, we get $\dfrac{1}{y-1} > \dfrac{1}{1-\frac{y}{2}}$

$\Rightarrow \dfrac{1}{y-1} > \dfrac{2}{2-y} \quad \Rightarrow \dfrac{1}{y-1} - \dfrac{2}{2-y} > 0$

$\Rightarrow \dfrac{2-y-2y+2}{(y-1)(2-y)} > 0 \quad \Rightarrow (4-3y)(y-1)(2-y) > 0$

$\Rightarrow (3y-4)(y-1)(y-2) > 0$

$\Rightarrow \left(y-\dfrac{4}{3}\right)(y-1)(y-2) > 0$

$\Rightarrow 1 < y < 4/3$ and $2 < y < \infty$

$\Rightarrow 1 < 2^x < 4/3$ and $2 < 2^x < \infty$

$\Rightarrow 0 < x < \log_2\left(\dfrac{4}{3}\right) \cup 1 < x < \infty$

$\Rightarrow \left[0, \log_2\left(\dfrac{4}{3}\right)\right] \cup (1, \infty)$

29. (b) $n^2 + 1 = (n+1)^2 + 2n < (n+1)^2 \ \forall\, n \in \mathbb{N}$

We have $n < \sqrt{n^2+1} < n+1$

$\Rightarrow [n^2+1] = n$

Equation reduces to $\left[\sqrt{n^2+\lambda}\right] = n$

$\Rightarrow n < \sqrt{n^2+\lambda} < n+1$

$\Rightarrow n^2 < n^2 + \lambda < (n+1)^2$

$\Rightarrow 0 < \lambda < 2n+1$

$\Rightarrow \lambda$ can take $2n$ different values .

30. (a) If $\alpha \in \left[0, \dfrac{\pi}{2}\right]$; $0 < \alpha < \dfrac{\pi}{2} \Rightarrow 0 < \tan\alpha < \infty$

$\Rightarrow \sqrt{x^2+x}$ and $\dfrac{\tan^2\alpha}{\sqrt{x^2+x}}$ are positive quantities.

Applying A.M-G.M

$\Rightarrow \sqrt{x^2+x} + \dfrac{\tan^2 x}{\sqrt{x^2+x}} \ge 2\left(\tan^2 x\right)^{1/2}$

$\Rightarrow \sqrt{x^2+x} + \dfrac{\tan^2 x}{\sqrt{x^2+x}} \ge 2\tan\alpha$

31. (a) By A.M.-G.M. inequality

(i) $\dfrac{b+c}{2} \ge (bc)^{1/2}$ **(ii)** $\dfrac{a+c}{2} \ge (ac)^{1/2}$

(iii) $\dfrac{a+b}{2} \ge (ab)^{1/2}$

Multiplying (i), (ii), (iii), we get $(a+b)(a+c)(b+c) \ge 8(abc)$

32. (c) By the question, $a+b = \lambda$

$$\Rightarrow \sqrt{\left(1+\frac{1}{a}\right)\left(1+\frac{1}{b}\right)} = \sqrt{1+\frac{1}{b}+\frac{1}{a}+\frac{1}{ab}} = \sqrt{1+\frac{a+b}{ab}+\frac{1}{ab}}$$

$$\therefore \quad ab \le \left(\frac{a+b}{2}\right)^2 = \frac{\lambda^2}{4}$$

$$\left(\sqrt{1+\frac{\lambda}{ab}+\frac{1}{ab}}\right)_{\min} = \left(\sqrt{1+\frac{\lambda}{(ab)_{\max}}+\frac{1}{(ab)_{\max}}}\right)$$

$$=\left(\sqrt{1+\frac{4\lambda}{\lambda^2}+\frac{4}{\lambda^2}}\right)=\left(\sqrt{\frac{\lambda^2+4\lambda+4}{\lambda^2}}\right)=\sqrt{\left(\frac{\lambda+2}{\lambda}\right)^2}$$

$$\Rightarrow \frac{\lambda+2}{\lambda}=1+\frac{L}{\lambda}$$

33. (d) Without loss of generality, we assume that $a < b < c$

$\Rightarrow a^3 < b^3 < c^3$

By Tchebychef's inequality

$$\frac{a^4+b^4+c^4}{3} > \frac{a^3+b^3+c^3}{3}\cdot\frac{a+b+c}{3}$$

but $\frac{a^3+b^3+c^3}{3} > abc$

$\Rightarrow a^4 + b^4 + c^4 > \text{abc}\,(a + b + c)$

34. (a) Consider two sets of numbers $S_1 = \left[1, \frac{1}{2}, ..., \frac{1}{n}\right]$ and $S_2 = \left[1, \frac{1}{2}, \frac{1}{3}, ..., \frac{1}{n}\right]$

By Tchebychef's inequality,

$$\left(1+\frac{1}{2}+....+\frac{1}{n}\right)^2 \le \left[\frac{1}{1^2}+\frac{1}{2^2}+....\frac{1}{n^2}\right]$$

$$\le\left[1+\frac{1}{1.2}+.....+\frac{1}{n(\text{n}-1)}\right] \le \left[1+1-\frac{1}{2}+....+\frac{1}{n-1}-1\right]$$

$$\le n\left(1+1-\frac{1}{n}\right)$$

$$\Rightarrow \left(1+\frac{1}{2}+....+\frac{1}{n}\right] \le \sqrt{2n-1}$$

By Tchebychef's inequality $S_3 : \left(\sqrt{1}, \sqrt{\frac{1}{2}}, ..., \sqrt{\frac{1}{n}}\right]$ and $S_4 : \left[\sqrt{1}, \sqrt{\frac{1}{2}}, ..., \sqrt{\frac{1}{n}}\right]$

$$\Rightarrow \left(\sqrt{1}+\sqrt{\frac{1}{2}}+....+\sqrt{\frac{1}{n}}\right]^2 \le n\sqrt{2n-1)}$$

$$\Rightarrow \frac{\left(\sqrt{1}+\sqrt{\frac{1}{2}}+....+\sqrt{\frac{1}{n}}\right]}{\sqrt{n}} \le (2\text{n}-1)^{1/4}$$

35. (c) $f(x) = (a + x)^3 (a - x)^4$

$f(x)$ is greatest when $\left(\frac{a+x}{3}\right)^3\left(\frac{a-x}{4}\right)^4$ is greatest, but the sum of the factors of this expression is $3\left[\frac{a+x}{3}\right]+4\left[\frac{a-x}{4}\right]$ or $2a$,

Hence $f(x)$ is greatest when $\frac{a+x}{3}=\frac{a-x}{4} \Rightarrow x = -\frac{a}{7}$

Hence greatest value is $\frac{6^3.8^4}{7^7}.a^7$

SECTION–IV

1. (a), (b), (c), (d) Parts (a), (b), (c), are correct; as we have proved in section III, now let us investigate option (d).

$$\frac{bc}{a}+\frac{ac}{b}+\frac{ab}{c} \ge a+b+c$$

Which is equivalent to $b^2c^2 + a^2c^2 + a^2b^2 \ge abc\,(a + b + c)$

By A.M-G.M on b^2c^2 and a^2c^2

$\Rightarrow b^2 + c^2 \ge 2abc^2$ (i)

Similarly

$a^2\,c^2 + a^2\,b^2 \ge 2\,a^2\,b\,c$ (ii)

$a^2\,b^2 + b^2\,c^2 \ge 2\,ab^2c$ (iii)

Adding (i), (ii) and (iii), we get $b^2c^2 + a^2c^2 + a^2b^2 \ge abc\,(a + b + c)$

$\Rightarrow$ All option (a), (b), (c), (d) are correct

2. (a), (b) Given $R \ge r > 0$ and $d > 0$

$$\Rightarrow 0 < \frac{d^2+R^2-r^2}{2dR} \le 1$$

$\Rightarrow 0 < (d + R - r)\,(d + R + r) \le 2\,dR$; which is true iff $(d^2 + R^2 - r^2) \le 2\,dR$, which is true iff $d^2 + R^2 - 2dR \le r^2$

$\Rightarrow (d - R)^2 \le r^2$

$\Rightarrow |d - R| \le r$; which is also $-r \le (d - R) \le \text{r}$

3. (a), (b), (c), (d)

$y=\sqrt{x^8-x^5+x^2-x+1}$ can be written as

$\sqrt{x^5(x^3-1)+(x^2-x+1)}$

$=\sqrt{(x^5)(x-1)\,(x^2+1+x)+(x^2-x+1)}$

Now, let us analyze the value in various regions.

(i) $[1, \infty]$ $\Rightarrow$ The expression under the root is always positive

$\Rightarrow$ y is real and finite

(ii) $[-, 0)$ $\Rightarrow$ y is real and finite as x^5, $x^3 - 1$ are simultaneously negative

(iii) $x \in (0, 1)$ $\Rightarrow$ $x^2 > x^5$

$\Rightarrow$ $x^2 - x^5 > 0$

Similarly $1 > x$

$\Rightarrow 1 - x > 0$ $\Rightarrow$ $x^8 - x^5 + x^2 + 1 - x > 0$

$\Rightarrow$ y is real and finite

$\Rightarrow$ All the option (a), (b), (c) and (d) are correct

4. (b), (c), (d) $f(x) = \tan x + \cot x$

If $\tan x = y$

$\Rightarrow \cot x = \frac{1}{y}$ $\Rightarrow f(x) = y + \frac{1}{y}$

If $0 < x < \frac{\pi}{2}$

$\Rightarrow f_{\min} \Rightarrow f(x)$ at $x = \frac{\pi}{4} \Rightarrow f_{\min}(x) = 2$

Similarly if $-\frac{\pi}{2} < x < 0$

$\Rightarrow$ at $x = -\frac{\pi}{4}$ $\Rightarrow f_{\min}(x) = -2$

The function does not have a unique bound.

$\therefore$ It is unbounded.

5. (b), (c), (d) $E = a^4\,(1 + \tan^2 x) + b^4\,(1 + \cot^2 x)$

$= a^4 + b^4 + a^4 \tan^2 x + b^4 \cot^2 x \ge a^4 + b^4 + 2\,a^2\,b^2 = (a^2 + b^2)^2$ $\left[\begin{array}{l}\because \text{By } A.M. \ge G.M.\\ a^4\tan^2 x+b^4\cot^2 x \ge 2a^2b^2\end{array}\right]$

$\therefore\ f_{min} = (a^2 + b^2)$ $\Rightarrow$ option (b) is correct.

Clearly As $x \to \frac{\pi}{2}, f(x)\ \infty$

$\therefore$ Range of $f(x) = [(a^2 + b^2)^2, \infty)$

$\Rightarrow f(x)$ is bounded below, but not bounded above

6. (a), (c) $y = \sin^4 x - 6\sin^2 x + 5$

Let $\sin^2 x = p$ $\Rightarrow y = p^2 - 6p + 5 = (p-5)(p-1)$

Clearly $p\ 0$ $\Rightarrow p - 5 \ge -5$

$\Rightarrow p - 1 \ge -1$

$\therefore \sin x \le 1$ $\Rightarrow \sin^2 x \le 1$

$\Rightarrow y_{min} = 0$ and $y_{max} = 5$ $\Rightarrow y \in [0, 5)$

7. (a) $x^2 - 12x + 40 = x^2 - 12x + 36 + 4 = (x-6)^2 + 4$

$\Rightarrow$ Minimum at $x = 6$

$\Rightarrow$ Value = 4

8. (b) $a^3b + ab^3 - a^4 - b^4 = -(a^4 - a^3b + b^4 - ab^3)$

$\Rightarrow -(a^3(a-b) - b^3(a-b))$

$\Rightarrow -(a-b)(a^3 - b^3)$ $\Rightarrow -(a-b)^2(a^2 + ab + b^2)$

which is always negative.

9. (a) $(7-x)^4(x+2)^5|_{max}$ at $4\left(\frac{7-x}{4}\right)+5\left(\frac{x+2}{5}\right)$ is maximum

Which is maximum at $\frac{7-x}{4} = \frac{x+2}{5}$

$\Rightarrow x = 3$ $\Rightarrow$ Value at $x - 3 = 4^4.5^5$

SECTION–V

1. (a) A: Given a, b, c are in H.P.

$\Rightarrow \frac{1}{a}+\frac{1}{c}=\frac{2}{b}$ $\Rightarrow b = \frac{2ac}{a+c}$

Applying A.M.-G.M. on $\left(\frac{a+b}{2a-b}\right)$ and $\left(\frac{c+b}{2c-b}\right)$

$$\Rightarrow \frac{\left(\frac{a+b}{2a-b}\right)+\left(\frac{b+c}{2c-b}\right)}{2} \ge \left(\frac{a+b}{2a-b}\times\frac{b+c}{2c-b}\right)^{\frac{1}{2}}$$

Substituting $b = \frac{2ac}{a+c}$, we get $\frac{a+b}{2a-b}+\frac{b+c}{2c-b} \ge 2.(4)^{1/2}$

Since a, b, c are distinct numbers,

$\Rightarrow \frac{a+b}{2a-b}+\frac{b+c}{2c-b} > 4$

R: A.M. > G.M. Since a, b, c are distinct numbers,

$\Rightarrow \frac{a+c}{2} > \sqrt{ac}$

Which is true as $\left(\sqrt{a}-\sqrt{c}\right)^2 > 0$

$\Rightarrow$ Both assertion and reason are correct and is the correct explanation.

2. (a) A: $a + b + c = 12$

$\therefore$ By A.M-G.M inequality $\frac{a+b+c}{3} \ge (abc)^{1/3}$

$\Rightarrow (4) \ge (abc)^{1/3}$

Cubing both sides, we get $64 \ge (abc)$

Which is at $a = b = c$ $\therefore$ Assertion is correct

R: if $a + b + c$ = constant

Then maximum of abc is when $a = b = c$

$\therefore$ Reason is correct and is the correct explanation

3. (a) A: $x^2 + y^2 = 1 = (x+y)^2 = x^2 + y^2 + 2xy = 1 + 2xy$

Clearly, $(x+y)(x+y) \le (x^2 + y^2)^2$

$\Rightarrow (x+y)^2 \le 2$ $\Rightarrow |x+y| \le \sqrt{2}$

$\therefore$ Assertion is correct is correct

R: Reason is correct as already discussed in reason Q. No. (i)

4. (a) A: $2^n \ge 1 + n\sqrt{2^{n-1}}$

$\Rightarrow$ by A.M $\ge$ G.M

$$\Rightarrow \frac{\left(1+2+2^2+.....+2^{n-1}\right)}{n} > \left(1.2^2.2^3....2^{n-1}\right)^{1/n}$$

$$\Rightarrow \frac{2^{n-1}}{n(1)} > \left[2^{1+2+........+n-1}\right]^{1/n} \Rightarrow \frac{2^n-1}{n} > \left(2^{\frac{n(n-1)}{2}}\right]^{1/2}$$

$\Rightarrow 2^n - 1 > n\sqrt{2^{n-1}}$ $\Rightarrow 2^n > 1 + n\sqrt{2^{n-1}}$

Assertion is correct

R: (A.M). (H.M) = (G.M)^2

Also G.M > H.M

Let us consider 3 nos. a, b, c

$\Rightarrow \sqrt{ac} > \frac{2ac}{a+c}$ $\Rightarrow ac > \frac{4a^2c^2}{(a+b)^2}$

$\Rightarrow (a^2 + c^2 + 2ac)\,ac > 4a^2c^2$

$\Rightarrow a^3c + c^3a - 2a^2c^2 > 0$

$\Rightarrow 2a^2c^2 - 2a^2c^2 = 0$, when $a^3c + c^3a$ is maximum but if a, b, c are distinct

$\Rightarrow a^3c + c^3a > 2a^2c$

$\Rightarrow$ Reason is correct and is the correct explanation

5. (b) A: By A.M > G.M

$$\frac{1^3+2^3+....+n^3}{n} > \left(1^3.2^3.3^3.....x^3\right)^{1/n}$$

$$\Rightarrow \frac{n^2(n+1)^2}{4}.\frac{1}{n} > \left[(n!)^3\right]^{1/n} \Rightarrow n\frac{(n+1)^2}{4} > \left[(n!)^3\right]^{1/n}$$

$$\Rightarrow n^n.\left(\frac{n+1}{2}\right)^{2n} > (n!)^3 \Rightarrow (n!)^3 < n^n\left(\frac{n+1}{2}\right)^{2n}$$

$\Rightarrow$ Assertion is correct

R: For > 1

We can write $r(n - r + 1) > n$ at $r = 1$

$\Rightarrow r(n - r + 1) = n$

$\therefore$ $(n-1) > n$ (i)

$4(n-2) > n$ (ii)

$3(n-1)(n)$ (iii)

$2(n-1) > n$ (iv)

and so on.

Multiplying, we get $(n!)^2 > n^n$ $\Rightarrow$

Reason is correct but not correct explanation of assertion.

6. (c) A: By the question, $\frac{1}{a},\frac{1}{b},\frac{1}{c}$ are in *A.P.*

$\Rightarrow a, b, c,$ are in H.P.

$\Rightarrow b = \frac{2ac}{a+c}$ (i)

Consider the equation $-\lambda x + x^2 - 2b^{101} - a^{101} - c^{101} = 0$

$\Rightarrow x^2 - \lambda x - (2b^{101} + a^{101} + c^{101}) = c$

Product of root $-\left(2b^{101}+a^{101}+c^{101}\right)$

Which has a negative sign as a, b, c are always positive and $b = \frac{2ac}{a+c}$ $\Rightarrow$ Assertion is correct

R: $\frac{a^n+c^n}{2} > \left[\frac{a+c}{2}\right]^n \Rightarrow a^n+c^n > 2\left[\frac{a+c}{2}\right]^n$

$\frac{a+c}{2}$ is the A.M. and A.M. > H.M.

$\Rightarrow a^n + c^n > 2b^n \quad \Rightarrow$ Reason is incorrect.

7. (b) A: $\frac{r!(2n-r)!}{n!} > n! \quad (n>r)$

$\Rightarrow r!\,(2n-r)! > (n!)^2 \quad \Rightarrow 1!\,(2n-1)!\,(n!)^2$

....

....

$(2n-1)!\,1! > (n!)^2$

Multiplying all, we get $1!\,3!\,5!\,.....\,(2n-1)! > (n!)^n$

R: $\left(x^m+y^m\right)^n < \left(x^n+y^n\right)^m$

$\Rightarrow \left[1+\frac{x^m}{y^m}\right]^n < \left[1+\frac{x^n}{y^n}\right]^m$

If $\frac{x}{y}<1 \quad \Rightarrow \left(\frac{x}{y}\right)^m < \left(\frac{x}{y}\right)^n$

$\Rightarrow 1+\frac{x^m}{y^m} < 1+\frac{x^n}{y^n} \quad \Rightarrow \left[1+\frac{x^m}{y^m}\right]^n < \left[1+\frac{x^n}{y^n}\right]^m$

Similarly proceeding for $\frac{x}{y}>1$

We get $\left[1+\frac{x^m}{y^m}\right]^n < \left[1+\frac{x^n}{y^n}\right]^m$

$\Rightarrow$ Reason is correct but not correct explanation of assertion.

SECTION–VI

Passage A:

1. (c) By the question $a+b=1$

$\therefore \frac{a^{1/3}+b^{1/3}}{2} < \left(\frac{a+b}{2}\right)^{1/3}$

$\Rightarrow \frac{A}{2} < \left(\frac{1}{2}\right)^{1/3} \quad \Rightarrow A < \frac{2}{(2)^{1/3}}$

$\Rightarrow A < 2^{2/3}$

2. (b) $x^2+y^2=8$

$\Rightarrow \frac{(x^2)^{1/2}+(y^2)^{1/2}}{2} < \left(\frac{x^2+y^2}{2}\right)^{1/2}$

$\Rightarrow \frac{x+y}{2} < (4)^{1/2} \quad \Rightarrow x+y<4$

$\Rightarrow$ Maximum value is of x + y is 4

3. (c) $a+b=1, A=\left[a+\frac{1}{a}\right]^2+\left[b+\frac{1}{b}\right]^2$

$A=a^2+\frac{1}{a^2}+4+b^2+\frac{1}{b^2} \Rightarrow a^2+b^2>2\left[\frac{1}{2}\right]^2$

$\Rightarrow a^2+b^2>\frac{1}{2}$

Similarly $\frac{1}{a^2}+\frac{1}{b^2} \Rightarrow \left(\frac{a^2+b^2}{a^2b^2}\right)_{max} = \frac{16}{2}$ (as $a+b=1$)

$\Rightarrow A > 4+\frac{16}{2}+\frac{1}{2}=\frac{25}{2}$

4. (b) if a, b, c, are in H.P

$\Rightarrow \frac{a^n+c^n}{2} > b^n \quad \Rightarrow \frac{a^n+c^n}{b^n} > 2$

$\Rightarrow x>2$

Passage B:

5. (d) Given sum of mth power of first n odd numbers = λ

$\Rightarrow \frac{\lambda}{n} > \left[\frac{n^2}{n}\right]^m \quad \lambda > n.\,n^m$

$\Rightarrow \lambda > n^{m+1}$

6. (c) Assuming $b+c \le c+a \le a+b$

$\Rightarrow \frac{1}{b+c} \ge \frac{1}{c+a} \ge \frac{1}{a+b}$

$\Rightarrow (a+b)+(a+c)+(b+c)\left[\frac{1}{b+c}+\frac{1}{c+a}+\frac{1}{a+b}\right] \ge$

$3\left[(b+c)\frac{1}{(b+c)}+(a+c)\frac{1}{(a+c)}+(a+b)\frac{1}{a+b}\right]$

$\Rightarrow \frac{a}{b+c}+\frac{b}{c+a}+\frac{c}{a+b} \ge \frac{3}{2} \Rightarrow \left[\frac{3}{2},\infty\right)$

7. (c) $x+y+z=1$

$\therefore \frac{x}{2-x}+\frac{y}{2-y}+\frac{z}{2-z}$

$\therefore \frac{x}{2-x}+\frac{y}{2-y}+\frac{z}{2-z} \ge 3\left(\frac{xyz}{(2-x)(2-y)(2-z)}\right)^{1/3}$

$\therefore x+y+z=1$

$\Rightarrow (2-x)+(2-x)+(2-z)=5$

$\Rightarrow$ Product maximizes at equality

$\frac{x}{2-x}+\frac{y}{2-y}+\frac{z}{2-z} \ge 3\left(\frac{\frac{1}{27}}{\frac{5^3}{27}}\right)^{1/3} \ge \frac{3}{5}$

8. (c) $a_1, a_2, a_3, ..., a_n$ are all positive

$A = a_1^2 = a_2^2 + a_3^2 + ...+ a_n^2$

Greatest value of $(a_1+a_2+...+a_n)^2$

$\Rightarrow \left(\frac{a_1^2+a_2^2+.....+a_n^2}{n}\right).n^2 \Rightarrow nA$

Least values of $(a_1+a_2+...\,a_n)^2 = A$

$\Rightarrow$ G – L = $nA - A = A(n-1)$

9. (b) $a+b+c+d=\frac{4}{3}$

$\Rightarrow \frac{\text{Required sum}}{4} < \left[\frac{3(a+b+c+d)}{4}\right]^{1/2} \Rightarrow$ RS < 4

Passage-3

10. (d) $\frac{ax^2+b}{2} \le \sqrt{ax^2b} = x\sqrt{ab}$

$\Rightarrow \forall\, x>0\; f(x) = \frac{x}{ax^2+b} \le \frac{x}{2x\sqrt{ab}} = \frac{1}{2\sqrt{ab}}$

11. (c) for all a_i's we can write $\frac{8.\frac{a_i-6}{8}+1}{8+6} \ge \left[\left[\frac{a_i-6}{8}\right]^8.1^6\right]^{1/14}$

$\Rightarrow \frac{a_i}{14} \ge \left[\frac{a_i-6}{8}\right]^{8/14}$

Similarly $a_1, a_2 \ldots a_n \geq 14^n \left\{\frac{a_1-6}{8}\ \frac{a_2-6}{8} \ldots\ldots \frac{a_n-6}{8}\right\}^{8/14}$

$\Rightarrow [a_1\, a_2 \ldots a_n]_{\min} = 14^n$

12. (d) Substitute $a = \sin^2 x$ and $b = \sin^2 y$

$\Rightarrow \sqrt{ab} + \sqrt{(1-a)(1-b)}\ \sin x \,.\, \sin y + \cos y$

$= \cos[x-y] \leq 1$

$\Rightarrow$ Maximum value is 1

13. (a) Given $0 < c < 1 \quad \Rightarrow 0 \sqrt{c} < 1 \Rightarrow 0 < \sqrt{c-1} < 1$

$\Rightarrow \sqrt{abc} + \sqrt{(1-a)(1-b)(1-c)} \leq \sqrt{ab} + \sqrt{(1-a)(1-b)}$

Whichfollowsfrom(c)that $\sqrt{abc} + \sqrt{(1-a)(1-b)(1-c)} \leq 1$

SECTION–VII

1. (i)→(a), (c); (ii)→(b); (iii)→(d), (e)

(i) $A.M = G.M + \frac{3}{2} \quad \Rightarrow \quad \frac{a+b}{2} = \sqrt{ab} + \frac{3}{2}$

$\sqrt{ab} = \frac{2ab}{a+b} + \frac{6}{5} \quad \Rightarrow \quad \frac{a+b}{2} = \frac{2ab}{a+b} + \frac{3}{2} + \frac{6}{5}$

$\Rightarrow \quad \frac{a+b}{2} - \frac{2ab}{a+b} = \frac{15+12}{10} = \frac{27}{10}$

$\Rightarrow \quad \frac{a^2+b^2+2ab-4ab}{2(a+b)} = \frac{27}{10} \Rightarrow \frac{(a-b)^2}{a+b} = \frac{27}{5}$

Which can be written as $\frac{(a-b)^2}{a+b} = \frac{81}{15}$

$\Rightarrow \alpha = 15$ and $\beta^2 = 81$

$\Rightarrow \lambda + \beta^2 = 96 \quad \Rightarrow \lambda^2 + \beta = 225 + 9 = 234$

(ii) a > b

$\frac{a+b}{2} = \sqrt{ab} + 2$ (i)

$\frac{2ab}{a+b} = \frac{a}{5}$ (ii)

$\Rightarrow 2b = \frac{(a+b)}{5} \quad 10b = a + b$

$\Rightarrow 9b = a \quad \Rightarrow 5b = 3b + 2$

$\Rightarrow 2b = 2 \quad \Rightarrow b = 1$

$\Rightarrow a = 9 \quad \Rightarrow a + b = 10 = \alpha$

$\Rightarrow a - b = \beta \quad \Rightarrow \alpha + \beta^2 = 74$

(iii) $\frac{2ab}{a+b} = 4$

$\frac{a+b}{2} = A, \ \sqrt{ab} = G.M = G$

$\Rightarrow a + b + ab = 27 \quad \Rightarrow a + b + 2(a+b) = 27$

$\Rightarrow (a+b) = 9 \quad \Rightarrow$ a = 6 and b = 3

$\Rightarrow \alpha = 9$

$\Rightarrow |a-b| = 3 = \beta \quad \Rightarrow \alpha^2 + \beta = 84$

$\Rightarrow 1 + 6 + 6^2 + 6^5 = 364$

2. (i)→(a); (ii)(c); (iii)→(d)

(i) Required sum is $= \left[\frac{2+4+\ldots\ldots+2n}{n}\right]^m$

$\Rightarrow \quad \frac{2^m+4^m+\ldots.+(2n)^m}{n} > \left[\frac{2n(n+1)}{2.n}\right]^m$

$\Rightarrow \quad 2^m + 4^m + \ldots\ldots.(2n)^m > n(n+1)^m$

(ii) $n = n$

$(n-1) > n$

$4(n-2) > 0$

....

....

$\Rightarrow (n!)^2 > n^n$

(iii) if p is a positive real numbers less than unity, such that $0 < 1 - p^2 < 1$

$\Rightarrow \quad 0 < 1 - p < \frac{1}{1+p}$

Replacing p by $a_1, a_2 \ldots a_n$ one by one and multiplying, we get

$(1+a_1)(1+a_2)\ldots\ldots.(1+a_n) < \frac{1}{(1-a_1)(1-a_2)\ldots.(1-a_n)} < \frac{1}{1-m}$

3. (i)→(c); (ii)→(a); (iii)→(b)

(i) We know that $0.\overline{3} = \frac{1}{3}$

$\Rightarrow 3^x \left(\frac{1}{3}\right)^{x-3} \leq 3^{-2x}$

$\Rightarrow 3^{-3} \leq 3^{-2x} \quad \Rightarrow x \leq \frac{3}{2}$

(ii) Obviously, $x > 0$ and $(2x^2 + 3x + 2) = (2x)^2$

$\Rightarrow 2x^2 - 3x - 2 = 0 \quad \Rightarrow x = 2\ \forall\, x > 0$

(iii) $x - 7 > 0 \quad \Rightarrow x > 7$ (i)

$3^{\log_5(x-7)} = \log_5(125) = \log_5(125) = \log_5(5^3) = 3$

$\Rightarrow \log_5(x-7) = 1$

$\Rightarrow x - 7 = 5 \quad \Rightarrow x = 12$

SECTION–VIII: (INTEGER TYPE)

1. Consider $\left(\frac{n+1}{n}\right)^4 = \left(1+\frac{1}{n}\right)^4$

$n \geq 2 \quad \Rightarrow \frac{1}{n} \leq \frac{1}{2} \Rightarrow 1 + \frac{1}{n} \leq \frac{3}{2}$

$\Rightarrow \left(1+\frac{1}{n}\right)^4 \leq \left[\frac{3}{2}\right]^4 \quad \left(\frac{n+1}{n}\right)^4 < 10$

$\Rightarrow n^4(10) < (n+1)^4 \quad \Rightarrow (n+1)^4 < 10^{n+1}$

$\Rightarrow k = 100$

2. $0 < a, b, c < 1$; Given $a + b + c = 1$

By A.M.-H.M. inequality, $\frac{a+b+c}{3} \geq \frac{3}{\left(\frac{1}{a}+\frac{1}{b}+\frac{1}{c}\right)}$

$\Rightarrow \quad \left(\frac{1}{a}+\frac{1}{b}+\frac{1}{c}\right) \geq 9$

Now $\left(\frac{1-a}{a}\right)\left(\frac{1-b}{b}\right)\left(\frac{1-c}{c}\right) = \left(\frac{1}{a}-1\right)\left(\frac{1}{b}-1\right)\left(\frac{1}{c}-1\right)$

By A.M.-G.M., $\frac{\frac{1}{a}+\frac{1}{b}+\frac{1}{c}-3}{3} \geq$ (Required product)$^{1/3}$

For maximum values $k \leq \left(\frac{9-3}{3}\right)^2 = 8$

$\Rightarrow k = 8$ (max)

3. Given $|x-3| < 2$

$\Rightarrow\ -2 < |x-3| < 2$

$\Rightarrow\ 1 < x < 5$ (i)

$\therefore\ -\dfrac{1}{k_1} < \dfrac{x-3}{x+3} < -\dfrac{1}{k_2}$

Applying componendo and dividendo, we get

$\dfrac{-1+k_1}{-1-k_1} < \dfrac{2x}{-6} < \dfrac{-1-k_2}{-1+k_2} \Rightarrow \dfrac{k_2-1}{1+k_2} < \dfrac{x}{3} < \dfrac{k_1-1}{k_1+1}$

$\Rightarrow$ On comparison $k_2 = -\dfrac{1}{3}, k_1 = -\dfrac{5}{3}$

$\Rightarrow\ k_1 + k_2 = -\dfrac{1}{3} + \left(-\dfrac{5}{3}\right) = -2$

4. $\dfrac{1}{11} < \dfrac{1-x}{1+x} < \dfrac{5}{7}$ By componendo and dividendo, we get

$\dfrac{12}{-10} < \dfrac{2}{-2x} < \dfrac{12}{-2}$

$\Rightarrow\ \dfrac{6}{5} > \dfrac{1}{x} > \dfrac{1}{6} \qquad \Rightarrow\ \dfrac{1}{6} < x < \dfrac{5}{6}$

$\Rightarrow\ -\dfrac{1}{3} < x - \dfrac{1}{2} < \dfrac{1}{3} \qquad \Rightarrow\ \left|x - \dfrac{1}{2}\right| < \dfrac{1}{3}$

$k = 3$

5. $f(x) = 2x^2 - 2(2a+1)x + a(a-1)$

$\Rightarrow\ f(a) < 0$

$\Rightarrow\ 2a^2 - 2(2a+1)a + a(a-1) < 0$

$\Rightarrow\ 2a^2 - 4a^2 - 2a + a^2 - a < 0$

$\Rightarrow\ -a^2 - 3a < 0 \qquad \Rightarrow\ a^2 + 3a > 0$

$\Rightarrow\ a(a+3) > 0 \qquad \Rightarrow\ a \in (-\infty, -3) \cup (0, \infty)$

$\Rightarrow\ k_1 = -3, k_2 = 0 \qquad \Rightarrow\ |k_1 + k_2| = 3$

6. Consider the L.H.S of the equation, $(\sin 3^x)(\cos 3^x) = \dfrac{2\sin 3^x . \cos 3^x}{2} = \dfrac{\sin(2.3^x)}{2} \le \dfrac{1}{2}$

$\Rightarrow\ \dfrac{3^x + 3^{-x}}{k} \le \dfrac{1}{2}$ but $(3^x + 3^{-x}) \ge 2$

$\Rightarrow$ Minimum value of k = 4

7. Given $f(x) = (2^x - 1)(2^x - 2)^2$

Let us assume $2^x = y \Rightarrow f(x) = (y-1)(y-2)^2$

Since $f(x)$ is increasing the started interval

$\Rightarrow\ f'(x) > 0$

$\Rightarrow\ f'(x) = 2(y-1)(y-2) + (y-2)^2 > 0 = 2y^2 - 6y + 4 + y^2 + 4 - 4y > 0 = 3y^2 - 10y + 8 > 0$

Which can be factorials $= 3y^2 - 6y - 4y + 8 > 0$

$\Rightarrow\ 3y(y-2) - 4(y-2) > 0 \ \left(y - \dfrac{4}{3}\right)(y-2) > 0$

Putting in the inequality, we get $2^x \in \left(-\infty, \dfrac{4}{3}\right) \cup (2, \infty)$

$\Rightarrow\ x \in \left(-\infty, \log_2 \dfrac{4}{3}\right) \cup (1, \infty)$

$\Rightarrow$ On comparison k = 4

8. $\dfrac{1}{5}\log(1+a^5) < \dfrac{1}{k}\log(1+a^k)$

$\Rightarrow\ \log(1+a^5)^{1/5} < \log(1+a^k)^{1/k}$

$\Rightarrow\ (1+a^5)^{1/5} < (1+a^k)^{1/k}$ as base of log is e > 1

$\Rightarrow\ (1+a^5)^k < (1+a^k)^5$; Clearly $k \ne 5, k > 0$

Case-(i): $k > 5 \qquad \Rightarrow\ k = 5 + h;\ h > 0$

$\Rightarrow\ (1+a^5)^k < (1+a^k)^5 \qquad \Rightarrow\ (1+a^5)^{5+h} < (1+a^{5+h})^5$

$\Rightarrow\ \left[\dfrac{(1+a^5)}{(1+a^{5+h})}\right]^5 . (1+a^5)^h < 1$ (i)

$\therefore\ 0 < a < 1 \qquad \Rightarrow\ 1 + a^{5+h} < 1 + a^5$

$\Rightarrow\ \left[\dfrac{(1+a^5)}{(1+a^{5+h})}\right] > 1 \qquad \Rightarrow$ L.H.S. of (i) > and R.H.S < 1

$\Rightarrow$ (i) is impossible $\qquad \therefore\ k \in (0, 5)$

$\Rightarrow\ [k] \in \{0, 1, 2, 3, 4\} \qquad \Rightarrow$ Maximum value of $[k] = 4$

9. $\sin^2 x = x^2 + \dfrac{1}{x^2}$

Let us consider the R.H.S. of the equation.

Clearly by A.M.-G.M., $x^2 + \dfrac{1}{x^2} \ge 2$

But $|\sin x| \le 1$

$\Rightarrow$ The equation has zero solutions.

10. r, n, s area non- negative integers.

Let us consider ${}^{2n}C_r$ which is an integer $= \dfrac{n!}{r!s!}$

$\Rightarrow\ {}^{2n}C_r$ maximum where r! s! is least i.e., $r = n$

$\Rightarrow\ r + s = 2r + 1 \qquad \Rightarrow\ |r - s| = 1$

11. Consider a parallelepiped of dimensions l, b, h

$\therefore$ Volume of the parallelepiped $= l . b . h = V$

Applying A.M.-G.M. on l, b, h

$\Rightarrow\ \dfrac{\ell+b+h}{3} \ge (\ell b h)^{1/3} \Rightarrow \dfrac{\ell+b+h}{3} \ge (V)^{1/3}$

Clearly equality holds, when l = b = h = a

$\Rightarrow\ a \ge (V)^{1/3}$

Perimeter of cube = 12 × edge length

$\Rightarrow$ Perimeter $\ge 12\ V^{1/3} \qquad \Rightarrow\ k = 2$

12. Consider a rectangular parallelepiped with dimension l, b, h

By the question, lbh $= V$

By A.M.-G.M. inequality, $\dfrac{\ell+b+h}{3} \ge (V)^{1/3}$

Equality holes when $l = b = h = a$ say

$\Rightarrow\ a \ge (V)^{1/3}$

Area of faces $= 6a^2 \qquad \Rightarrow\ 6a^2 \ge 6\ V^{2/3}$

$\Rightarrow\ k = 3$

13. Here we are fixing the semi-perimeter of the triangle

$\therefore$ Area $= \Delta = \sqrt{s(s-a)(s-b)(s-c)}$

Applying A.M.-G.M. of s, $s-a, s-b, s-c$ (which are positive quantities)

$\Rightarrow\ \dfrac{s+s-a+s-b+s-c}{4} (\Delta^2)^{1/4} = \Delta^{1/2}$

$\Rightarrow$ Equality holds at $s = s - a = s - b = s - c$

$\Rightarrow\ a = b = c$ (equilateral triangle)

Area of equilateral triangle $= \dfrac{\sqrt{3}\,a^2}{4}$

Semi-perimeter $S = \dfrac{3a}{2} \qquad \Rightarrow\ a = \dfrac{2s}{3}$

$\Rightarrow$ Area $= \dfrac{\sqrt{3}.4.s^2}{9.4} = \dfrac{s^2}{3\sqrt{3}}$

$\Rightarrow\ k = 3$

Theory of Equations

5 CHAPTER

■ INTRODUCTION

This chapter is concerned with various methods of finding solution to dependent quantities. Suppose there were two quantities which were dependent on each other and their dependence could be quantified.

Now, you were asked to find out the numerical values which could satisfy both the quantities and give a solution. One way of finding such a solution can be to guess what value can satisfy the quantities and try to find out if they hold true by making simple calculation. Now this can take any amount of time. But all this time could be saved if we have some simple methodology to sort out this problem. In fact, there is a simple methodology to solve such problems. It is well developed and extensively used. This area of mathematics is called Quadratic Equations and Expression. This is extensively used in developing technologies. The basic objective of this chapter is to understand the concept.

The notion of quadratic equation is a ancient one. Can you imagine that the babylonians knew about it some 4000 years back and their clay tablets dating back to 1600 BC contain several quadratic equation. A quadratic equation can also be evident in some geometrical work of Euclid (300 BC). An Indian mathematical text named Sulba Sutra dating back to 800 BC Aryabhatta (476 AD), Brahamgupta (598 AD) Mahavira (850 AD) purposed solutions to many quadratic problems. But Shridharacharya (around 900 AD) was the first to provide an algebraic solution of general equation $ax^2 + bx + c = 0$ where $a \neq 0$ using the method of completing squares and shown the roots to be equal to $x = \dfrac{-b \pm \sqrt{b^2 - 4ac}}{2a}$.

Harriot in 1631 AD provided the solution by factorisation and later on some modern mathematicians Leonard Euler, E. Bezout and Sylvester also contributed greatly to the development of theory of equations.

■ POLYNOMIALS AND EQUATION

The algebraic expression $a_0 + a_1x + a_2x^2 + ...+ a_nx^n$, is called as polynomial in x with degree n, provided power of x in each term is a non negative integer and $a_n \neq 0$. It is also denoted by $P_n(x)$. The constants a_i ($a_i \ \forall\ i = 0, 1,.....n$) are known as Coefficients of polynomial.

Degree(*n*) of polynomial

Degree of the polynomial is defined as power of highest power term in x in the polynomial expression. e.g., $4x^3 - 3x^2 + 2x + 1$ is polynomial of degree 3.

Zeros/roots of polynomial and its geometric significance

'*Roots are values of independent variable x at which the polynomial expression vanishes*'. i.e., if $x = \alpha$ *is a root then* $P_n(\alpha) = a_0 + a_1\alpha + ... + a_n\alpha^n = 0$

A polynomial $P_n(x)$ is said to have roots $x = \alpha_1, \alpha_2, ...$ if $P_n(\alpha_i) = 0$ i.e., it vanishes at $x = \alpha_i$. Since $y = P_n(x)$ is an algebraic function, so it possesses all properties of a function e.g., domain, range, monotonicity, maxima/minima, graph etc.

The *graph* of polynomial is set of all points $(x, P_n(x))$ satisfying polynomial and thus geometrically real roots of polynomial are given by x-coordinate of those points where curve of polynomial intersects x-axis, since at these points the value of polynomial given by y-coordinate vanishes (i.e., $y = P_n(x) = 0$). Clearly $\alpha_1, \alpha_2, \alpha_3, \alpha_4$ the roots of polynomial shown in the figure.

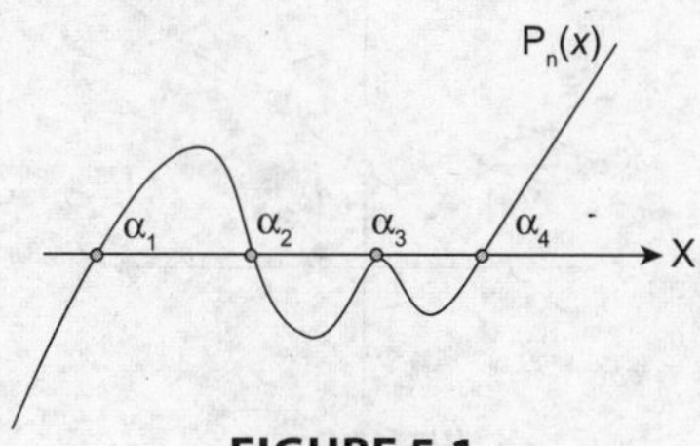

FIGURE 5.1

NOTE

A polynomial of nth degree $y = P_n(x)$ has exactly n root (not necessarily all real) (roots of polynomial are points) (complex number) at which polynomial cuts the Argand plane)

Classification of polynomials

Polynomial can be classified in following two ways:

(a) Based on coefficient
(b) Based on degree

Based on coefficient Since $a_i \in C$ where $i = 0, 1, 2, \ldots n$ therefore all the polynomial are called as *complex polynomials*. If $a_i \in R$ where $i = 0, 1, 2, \ldots n$, then the polynomial is called a *real polynomial.*

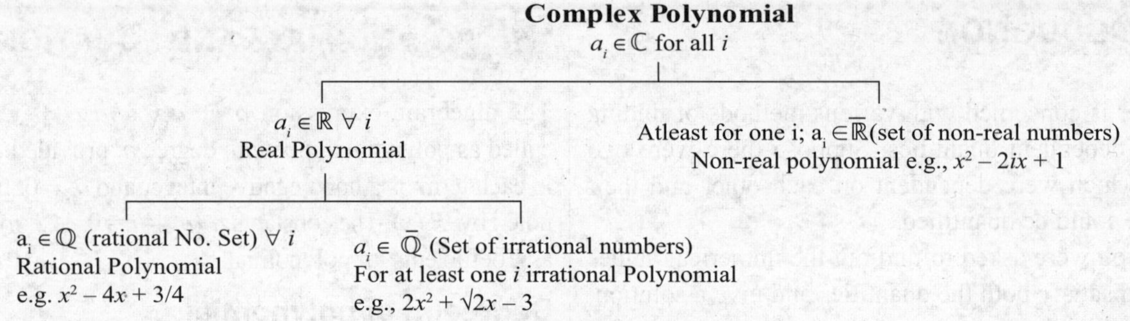

FIGURE 5.2

Based on degree Polynomials can be classified based on degree in following ways:

(a) When $n = 0$ then the polynomial is called *constant polynomial*. It has no real roots. e.g., $y = a_0x^0$

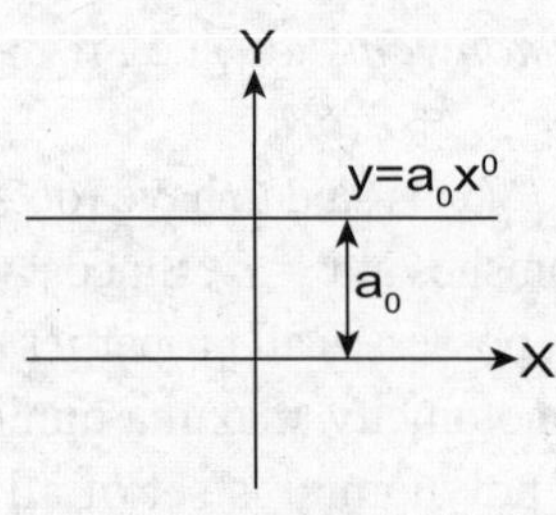

FIGURE 5.3

(b) When $n = 1$ then the polynomial is called *linear polynomial*. e.g., $y = a_0x + a_1$

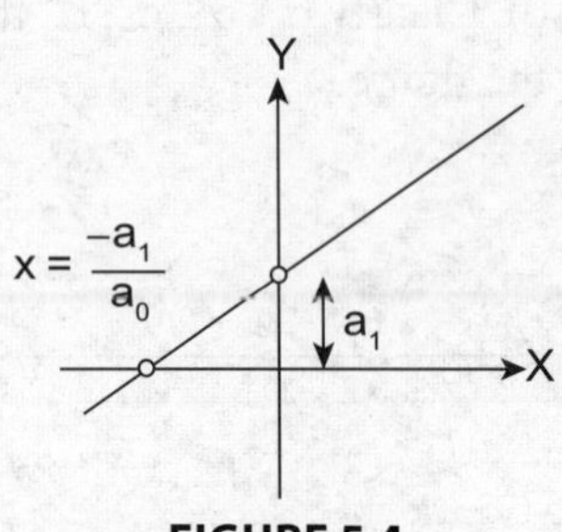

FIGURE 5.4

(c) When $n = 2$, then the polynomial is called *quadratic polynomial* and the degree of the polynomial is 2.

$$y = a_0x^2 + a_1x + a_2 = x^2\left(a_0 + \frac{a_1}{x} + \frac{a_2}{x^2}\right)$$

$$y \approx a_0x^2 \text{ when } x \to \pm\infty, y \to +\infty \text{ if } a > 0 \text{ and } -\infty \text{ if } a < 0$$

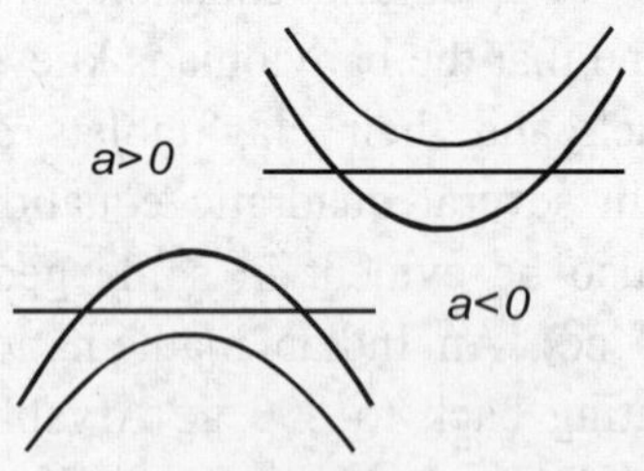

FIGURE 5.5

(d) When $n = 3$, polynomial is called *cubic polynomial* and the degree of the polynomial is 3.

$$y = a_0x^3 + a_1x^2 + a_2x + a_3 = x^3\left(a_0 + \frac{a_1}{x} + \frac{a_2}{x^2} + \frac{a_3}{x^3}\right)$$

$y \approx a_0x^3$ when $x \to \infty$

when $a_0 > 0 : y \to -\infty$ as $x \to -\infty; y \to \infty$ as $x \to \infty$

when $a_0 < 0 : y \to \infty$ as $x \to -\infty; y \to -\infty$ as $x \to \infty$

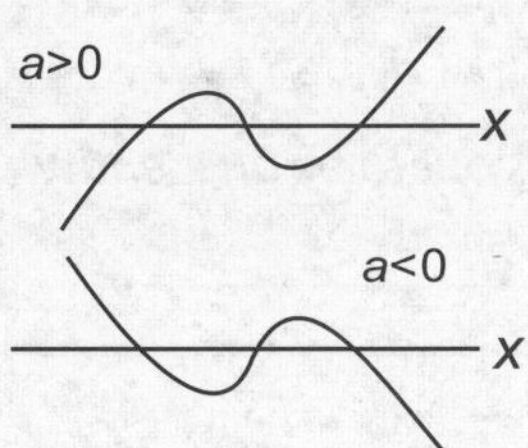

FIGURE 5.6

(e) When $n = 4$, the polynomial is called *Biquadratic polynomial*.

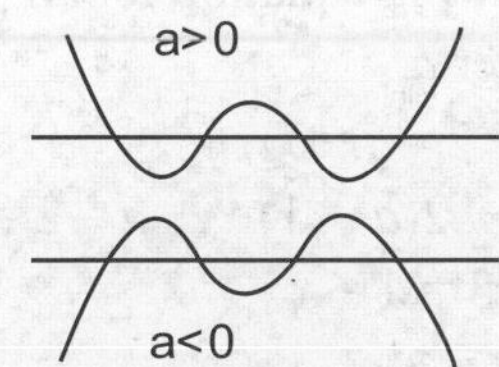

FIGURE 5.7

■ POLYNOMIAL EQUATION AND IDENTITY

When a polynomial expression is equated to zero, it becomes a *polynomial equation*.

e.g., $a_0 + a_1x + a_2x^2 + ... + a_nx^n = 0$, $(a_n \neq 0)$ is an equation of degree n. The roots of this equation are same as the roots of the polynomial expression. So a polynomial equation of nth degree will have exactly n roots *not necessarily all real* because its expression can be factorized into n linear (*real or imaginary*) factors.

A polynomial equation is called an *identity* if it is true for all values of x for which it is defined. The following points must be readily admitted.

(i) If a polynomial equation of nth degree has more than n roots then it will be true for all values of independent variable x, and therefore it becomes an identity in x.

(ii) A polynomial equation $P_n(x) = a_0 + a_1x + a_2x^2 + ... + a_nx^n = 0$ $(a_n \neq 0)$ will be an identity iff each of its coefficients vanish simultaneously.

ILLUSTRATION 1: Find the value of a for which the equation; $(a^2 + 4a + 3)\,x^2 + (a^2 - a - 2)x + (a - 1)a = 0$ has more than two roots.

SOLUTION: Since given equation is quadratic, so it has more than two roots iff it is identity i.e.,

$a^2 - 4a + 3 = 0 \Rightarrow \quad a = 1, 3$

and $a^2 + a - 2 = 0 \quad \Rightarrow \quad a = 1, -2$

and $(a - 1)\,a = 0 \quad \Rightarrow \quad a = 0, 1$

$\Rightarrow$ when $a = 1$ all the coefficient vanish simultaneously.

So equation becomes identity and has infinitely many roots.

ILLUSTRATION 2: Show that the following relation is true for all values of x, $(x - a)^2(b - c) + (x - b)^2(c - a) + (x - c)^2(a - b) = (a - b)(b - c)(a - c)$

SOLUTION: Given equation is quadratic in x so unless it is an identity it will have only two roots.
So to have more than two roots, it must be identity.
Clearly, $x = a \Rightarrow (a - b)^2(c - a) + (a - c)^2(a - b) = (a - b)(b - c)(a - c)$ which is true.

Similarly, putting $x = b$ or $x = c$ we can verify that b and c are also roots. Thus making no of roots more than degree. So it is an identity, so it is true for all values of x.

ILLUSTRATION 3: Prove that the equation $\dfrac{(x-a)(x-b)}{(c-a)(c-b)} + \dfrac{(x-b)(x-c)}{(a-b)(a-c)} + \dfrac{(x-c)(x-a)}{(b-c)(b-a)} - 1 = 0$ has infinitely many roots.

SOLUTION: $f(x)$ is quadratic in nature, so $f(x) = 0$ must have two solutions.
Since $f(a) = f(b) = f(c) = 0$
i.e., a, b, c all are solutions of equation $(x) = 0$
We know that when a polynomial equation of degree n has $(n + 1)$ roots then it becomes an identity. Here a, b, c are distinct and $f(x) = 0$, a quadratic equation has 3 roots therefore $f(x) = 0$ is an identity as $f(x)$ gives constant value (i.e., 0) for any value of x.

NOTE

Whenever a polynomial equation of degree n has more than n roots then it turns out to be an identity.

TEXTUAL EXERCISE-1 (SUBJECTIVE)

1. Classify the following as rational/irrational/real/non-real complex polynomials and also state its degree.
   (a) $(a - \sqrt{2})x^3 + (\sqrt{2} - a)x^2 + x + 1$ at $a = 1 + \sqrt{2}$
   (b) $(k^2 - 5k + 6)x^5 + (k - 2)x^3 + (k + 2)x^2 + (k - 3)x + 1$ at $k = 2, 3$
   (c) $(a_1 + a_2)x^2 + 2i(a_1 - a_2)x + 3$ at $a_1 = 1 + 2i$, $a_2 = 1 - 2i$
2. Find the value of a for which the polymial $\sqrt{a^2 - 4}x^2 + \sqrt{8 - a}\,x + 7$ represents
   (i) Real polynomial (ii) Non-real Polynomial.
3. Find the value of a belonging to set $\{2, 3, 4, 5\}$ for which the equation $\sqrt{a^2 - 9}\,x^2 + \sqrt{14 - a}\,x - 8$ represents
   (i) Real polymial
   (ii) Non-real polynomial
   (iii) Rational Polynomial
   (iv) Irational polynomial.
4. Find the number of values of p for which the equation, $(p^2 - 3p + 2)x^2 - (p^2 - 5p + 4)x + p - p^2 = 0$ possess more than two roots.
5. If $(a^2 - 1)x^2 + (a - 1)x + a^2 - 4a + 3 = 0$ is an identity in x, then find all possible values of a.
6. Solve the equation $2x^2 - (a - 1)x + a + 1 = 0$ for all values of a.
7. Solve the following equation for all permissible values of the parameter a.
   (a) $(a - 1)x + 2 = a + 1$
   (b) $(a + 1)x^2 + 2(a + 1)x + a - 2 = 0$
   (c) $ax + 2x + 3 = 1 - x$
8. Solve the equation, $\dfrac{x - ab}{a + b} + \dfrac{x - bc}{b + c} + \dfrac{x - ca}{c + a} = a + b + c$. What happens if $\dfrac{1}{a+b} + \dfrac{1}{b+c} + \dfrac{1}{c+a} = 0$.
9. Show that $a^2\left\{\dfrac{(x-b)(x-c)}{(a-b)(a-c)}\right\} + b^2\left\{\dfrac{(x-c)(x-a)}{(b-c)(b-a)}\right\} + c^2\left\{\dfrac{(x-a)(x-b)}{(c-a)(c-b)}\right\} = x^2$ is an identity.

Answer Keys

1. (a) Real, Rational, 3 (b) Real, Rational; $D = 2$, when $k = 2$; and $D = 3$, when $k = 3$ (c) Real, 2
2. (i) $(-\infty, -2] \cup [2, 8]$ (ii) $(-2, 2) \cup (8, \infty)$
3. (i) $a = 3, 4, 5$ (ii) $a = 2$ (iii) $a = 5$ (iv) $a = 3, 4$
4. 1
5. 1
6. $x = \dfrac{(a-1) \pm \sqrt{a^2 - 10a - 7}}{4}$ For $(-\infty, 5 - \sqrt{32}) \cup (5 + \sqrt{32}, \infty)$
7. (a) For a not equal to one $x = 1$ and if $a = 1$ it is an identity.
   (b) No real roots for $a \le -1$ and for $a > -1$; $x = -1 \pm \sqrt{\dfrac{3}{a+1}}$ (c) $x = \dfrac{-2}{a+3}\ \forall a \in \mathbb{R} - \{3\}$
8. $x = ab + bc + ca$. If $\dfrac{1}{a+b} + \dfrac{1}{b+c} + \dfrac{1}{c+a} = 0 \Rightarrow$ the given equation becomes an identity and is true for all $x \in R$

TEXTUAL EXERCISE-1 (OBJECTIVE)

1. The number of values of the triplet (a, b, c) for which $a\cos 2x + b\sin^2 x + c = 0$ is satisfied by all real x is
   (a) 0 (b) 2
   (c) 3 (d) infinite
2. The number of values of the pair (a, b) for which $a(x + 1)^2 + b(x^2 - 3x - 2) + x + 1 = 0$ is an identity in x is
   (a) 0 (b) 1
   (c) 2 (d) infinite

3. The value of 'a' for which the polynomial $ax^3 - \sqrt{a^2 - 8}$ $x + 10$ represents a real and rational polynomial is
(a) 1 (b) –1
(c) $\sqrt{-17}$ (d) All of these

4. The value of 'a' for which the polynomial $(\sqrt{a^2 + 5a + 6})x^2 + \sqrt{a - 7}x + \sqrt{a}$ represents a real polynomial belong to
(a) $(-\infty, -3] \cup [-2\infty)$
(b) $(-3, -2)$
(c) $[7, \infty)$
(d) $(-\infty, -3] \cup [-2, \infty) \cup [7, \infty)$

5. The value of 'a' for which the polynomial $ax^2 + \sqrt{a-1}$ $x + a$ is real and has real zeros, belong to
(a) $[1, \infty)$ (b) $(-\infty, -1]$
(c) $(-\infty, -1]$ (d) ϕ

6. The value of a for which the polynomial $\sqrt{a^2 - 7}\, x^2 + \sqrt{a}x + 9$ is non-real polynomial belong to
(a) $[-\sqrt{7}, \sqrt{7}]$ (b) $[-\sqrt{7}, 0)$
(c) $(-\infty, \sqrt{7})$ (d) None of these

Answer Keys

1. (d) **2.** (a),(b) **3.** (a) **4.** (c) **5.** (d) **6.** (c)

■ REMAINDER THEOREM

Division algorithm

When a polynomial $P(x)$ (of degree n) is divided by $f(x)$ where Degree of divisor $f(x) <$ Degree of dividend $P(x)$ i.e., $D_{f(x)} < D_{P(x)}$ then there exist two polynomials $q(x)$ (quotient) and remainder $r(x)$, such that $P(x) = f(x).q(x) + r(x)$, provided $D_{r(x)} < D_{f(x)}$.

Remainder theorem If we divide polynomial $f(x)$ by $(x - \alpha)$, the remainder obtained is $f(\alpha)$.

Since remainder theorem mathematically states, $f(x) = (x - \alpha)\, q(x) + r(x)$; putting $x = \alpha$, we get $P(\alpha) = r(\alpha)$, and we know that degree of $r(x)$ is non negative integer less than 1, so in the above case, degree of $r(x) = 0$ i.e., remainder is constant. Hence $r(x) = P(\alpha)$.

(When $f(x)$ is divided by $(x - a)(x - b)$ then remainder

$$r(x) = \left(\frac{f(a) - f(b)}{a - b}\right)x + \left(\frac{af(b) - bf(a)}{a - b}\right).$$

ILLUSTRATION 4: Find the remainder when $3x^3 + 4x^2 + x + 1$ is divided by $x - 2$.

SOLUTION: Consider $P(x) = 3x^3 + 4x^2 + x + 1$

Remainder $= P(2) = 3(2)^3 + 4(2^2) + 2 + 1 = 43$

ILLUSTRATION 5: Find the remainder when $x^{100} + x + 2$ is divided by
(a) $x - 1$ (b) $x^2 - 1$

SOLUTION: (a) Let $f(x) = x^{100} + x + 2 \Rightarrow$ remainder $f(1) = 4$

(b) when $f(x)$ is divided by $x + 1$ then remainder is $f(-1) = 2$

using $f(1) = 4, f(-1) = 2$ (remainders) (Applying Divisors Algorithm)

We write $\dfrac{f(x)}{x-1} = g(x) + \dfrac{4}{x-1}$; $\dfrac{f(x)}{x+1} = h(x) + \dfrac{2}{x+1}$

On subtracting, we get $\dfrac{2f(x)}{x^2-1} = g(x) - h(x) + \dfrac{2x+6}{x^2-1}$ or $\dfrac{f(x)}{x^2-1} = \dfrac{1}{2}g(x) - \dfrac{1}{2}h(x) + \dfrac{x+3}{x^2-1}$

$\Rightarrow$ The remainder when $f(x)$ is divided by $x^2 - 1$ is $x + 3$

ILLUSTRATION 6: If the expression $mx^4 + nx^3 - x^2 + 2x + 3$ has remainder $4x + 3$ when divided by $x^2 + x - 2$, find the value m and n.

SOLUTION: Let $f(x) = mx^4 + nx^3 - x^2 + 2x + 3$.

Now, $x^2 + x - 2 = (x + 2) . (x - 1)$. Given

$f(-2) = m(-2)^4 + n(-2)^3 - (-2)^2 + 2(-2) + 3 = 4(-2) + 3$

$\Rightarrow 16m - 8n - 5 = -5 \qquad \Rightarrow 2m - n = 0 \qquad$ (i)

Also, $f(1) = m + n - 1 + 2 + 3 = 4(1) + 3$

$\Rightarrow m + n = 3$; From (1) and (2), $m = 1, n = 2$

ILLUSTRATION 7: An unknown polynomial yields remainder 2 and 1 when divided by $x - 1$ and $x - 2$ respectively. Find the remainder when it is divided by $(x - 1).(x - 2)$.

SOLUTION: Let the unknown polynomial be $P(x)$ where deg $P(x) \geq 2$.

From the conditions given in the problem, we have,

$\frac{P(x)}{x-1} = Q(x) + \frac{2}{x-1}, \frac{P(x)}{x-2} = S(x) + \frac{1}{x-2}$ (where $Q(x)$ and $S(x)$ are polynomials).

On subtracting, we get $\frac{P(x)}{(x-1)(x-2)} = S(x) - Q(x) + \frac{3-x}{(x-1)(x-2)}$.

$\Rightarrow P(x) = (S(x) - Q(x))(x - 1)(x - 2) + 3 - x$. Clearly the remainder is $3 - x$.

ILLUSTRATION 8: What is the remainder when $x + x^{11} + x^{19} + x^{43} + x^{71}$ is divided by $x^3 - x$?

SOLUTION: We have $x + x^{11} + x^{19} + x^{43} + x^{71} = x(1 + x^{10} + x^{18} + x^{42} + x^{70})$

$= x[(x^{10} - 1) + (x^{18} - 1) + (x^{42} - 1) + (x^{70} - 1)] + 5x$

$= x(x^{10} - 1) + x(x^{18} - 1) + x(x^{42} - 1) + x(x^{70} - 1) + 5x$

Now $x^3 - x = x(x^2 - 1)$ and we know that each of $x^{10} - 1, x^{18} - 1, x^{42} - 1, x^{70} - 1$ is divisible by $x^2 - 1$

$\Rightarrow x(x^{10} - 1) + x(x^{18} - 1) + x(x^{42} - 1) + x(x^{70} - 1)$ is divisible by $x(x^2 - 1)$

$\therefore$ Remainder is $5x$

ILLUSTRATION 9: Show that the expression $(x - 1)(x + 1)(x + 2)(x + 4) + 9$ is a perfect square of a quadratic expression and hence find the quadratic.

SOLUTION: Let $(x^2 + ax + b)$ be the required quadratic

$\therefore (x^2 + ax + b)^2 = (x - 1)(x + 1)(x + 2)(x + 4) + 9$

$\Rightarrow x^4 + 2ax^3 + (a^2 + 2b)x^2 + 2abx + b^2 = x^4 + 6x^3 + 7x^2 - 6x + 1;$

Comparing the coefficients, we get $2a = 6$; $a^2 + 2b = 7$; $2ab = -6$ and $b^2 = 1$

The value of 'a' and 'b' that satisfy all the above conditions are $a = 3$ and $b = -1$

$\therefore$ The required quadratic expression is $x^2 + 3x - 1$

ILLUSTRATION 10: Find a polynomial in the variable x of the degree three such that the polynomial vanishes when $x = 2$ or $x = -3$ and will have the values 8 and 18 at $x = -2$ and 3 respectively.

SOLUTION: Let the required polynomial be $f(x) = a(x - \alpha)(x - \beta)(x - \gamma)$

$f(2) = 0 \Rightarrow$ either of $\alpha, \beta, \gamma, = 2 \qquad$ Let $\alpha = 2$

Similarly, $f(-3) = 0 \Rightarrow$ either of $\beta, \gamma = -3 \qquad$ Let $\beta = -3$

$\therefore f(x)$ becomes $a(x - 2)(x + 3)(x - \gamma)$

$f(-2) = 8 \Rightarrow a(2 + \gamma) = 2 \qquad$ (i)

Similarly,

$f(3) = 18 \Rightarrow a(3 - \gamma) = 3 \qquad$ (ii)

Dividing (i) and (ii); we get, $\frac{2+\gamma}{3-\gamma} = \frac{2}{3} \Rightarrow \gamma = 0 \Rightarrow a = 1$

$\therefore f(x) = x(x - 2)(x + 3)$ is required polynomial.

Factorization theorem If $(x-\alpha)$ divides $P(x)$ completely then remainder $r(x)$ must be equal to zero (i.e., $r(x) = P(\alpha) = 0$) $\Rightarrow x = \alpha$ is a root, then $x - \alpha$ will be a factor of $P(x)$. It is also known as factorization theorem.

ILLUSTRATION 11: If $ax^3 + bx + c$ has a factor of the form $x^2 + px + 1$, show that $a^2 - c^2 = ab$.

SOLUTION: By actual division we have $\dfrac{ax^3+bx+c}{x^2+px+1} = ax - ap + \dfrac{R(x)}{x^2+p(x)+1}$ where the remainder polynomial is obtained as $R(x) = (b-a+ap^2)x + c + ap$.

Now if ax^3+bx+c has a factor of the form x^2+px+1 then $R(x)$ must be identically zero. Indeed, $R(x)$ is identically zero if $b - a + ap^2 = 0$ and $c + ap = 0$

Eliminating p between these equations, we get $b-a+a\left(-\dfrac{c}{a}\right)^2 = 0$ or $a^2 - c^2 = ab$

ILLUSTRATION 12: Use the factorization theorem to find the value of λ for which $(\alpha + 2\beta)$, where $\alpha, \beta \neq 0$ is a factor of $\alpha^4 + 32\beta^4 + \alpha^3\beta(\lambda + 3)$.

SOLUTION: Let $f(\alpha) = \alpha^4 + 32\beta^4 + \alpha^3\beta(\lambda + 3)$, Now, as $\alpha + 2\beta$ has to be factor thus $\alpha = -2\beta$ shall be root of $f(x)$.

$\Rightarrow f(-2\beta) = (-2\beta)^4 + 32\beta^4 + (-2\beta)^3\beta(\lambda + 3) = 0$

$\Rightarrow 48\beta^4 - 8\beta^4(\lambda + 3) = 0 \Rightarrow 8\beta^4[6 - (\lambda + 3)] = 0$

$\Rightarrow 8\beta^4(3 - \lambda) = 0$

Since $\beta \neq 0$, so, $3 - \lambda = 0$, therefore $\lambda = 3$.

ILLUSTRATION 13: Simplify the equation $(x + y + z)^3 = x^3 + y^3 + z^3$ and show that it holds good if atleast two of the three variable take value equal in magnitude and opposite in sign.

SOLUTION: We have $x^3 + y^3 = (x + y + z)^3 - z^3$

R.H.S. $((x + y + z) - z)((x + y + z)^2 + (z)^2 + (x + y + z)(z))$

$= (x + y)(x^2 + y^2 + z^2 + 2xy + 2yz + 2zx + z^2 + xz + yz + z^2)$

$(x + y)(x^2 + y^2 + 3z^2 + 2xy + 3yz + 3zx)$

L.H.S : $(x + y)(x^2 + y^2 - xy)$

Now L.H.S = R.H.S. $\Rightarrow$ either $x + y = 0$ or $x^2 + y^2 - xy = x^2 + y^2 + 3z^2 + 2xy + 3yz + 3zx$

$\Rightarrow z^2 + zx + yz + xy = 0$

$\therefore (z + x)(x + y) = 0$

$\therefore$ Equation becomes $(x + y)(y + z)(z + x) = 0$

ILLUSTRATION 14: Find the factorization of polynomial $p(x) = (x^2 + 5x + 6)(x^2 + 5x + 7) - 12$.

SOLUTION: $P(x) = (x^2 + 5x + 6)(x^2 + 5x + 7) - 12$

$P(x) = (x^2 + 5x + 6)((x^2 + 5x + 6) + 1) - 12$

Let $x^2 + 5x + 6 = y$

$\Rightarrow P(x) \equiv y(y+1) - 12 = (y + 4)(y - 3)$

Passing from y to x, we get $(x^2 + 5x + 10)(x^2 + 5x + 3)$

$$= \left(x - \left(\frac{-5+\sqrt{13}}{2}\right)\right)\left(x - \frac{-5-\sqrt{13}}{2}\right)(x^2 + 5x + 10)$$

TEXTUAL EXERCISE–2 (SUBJECTIVE)

1. Given that the expression $4x^3 + 5kx^2 - 3x + k$ has a remi-nader of 5 when divided by $x + 1$ find the value of k.

2. If γ, δ are the roots of the equation $(x - \alpha)(x - \beta) - k = 0$, prove that α, β are the roots of the equation $(x - \gamma)(x - \delta) + k = 0$.

3. If $x + 1$ is a factor of $x^4 + (p - 3)x^3 - (3p - 5)x^2 + (2p - 9)x + 6$ then find the remaining factors of the above biquadratic expression.

4. Find the factors of $x^5 - 11x^4 + 33x^3 + 11x^2 - 154x + 120 = 0$.

Answer Keys

1. $k = 1$ **3.** $x - 1, x + 3, x - 2$ **4.** $x - 1, x + 2, x - 3, x - 4, x - 5$

TEXTUAL EXERCISE–2 (OBJECTIVE)

1. If $x^2 + x - 6$ is a factor of $2x^4 + x^3 - \alpha x^2 + \beta x + \beta - 1$, then which of the following is/are correct?
(a) $9\alpha + 2\beta = 134$ (b) $4\alpha - 3\beta = 39$
(c) $7\alpha = 96$ (d) None of these

2. The value of the parametre k for which $x + 4$ is a factor of the polynomial expression $(x + 3)^9 + (3x + k)^3$.
(a) 13 (b) $11 - \omega$
(c) 11 (d) $12 + \omega$

3. A certain polynomial $p(x), x \in \mathbb{R}$ when divided by $x - a$, $x - b$ and $x - c$ leaves remainders a, b and c respectively. Then find the remainder when $P(x)$ is divided by $(x - a)(x - b)(x - c)$ where a, b, c are distinct.
(a) $2x + 1$ (b) $x - 1$
(c) x (d) None of these

4. If $x^2 + ax + 1$ is a factor of $ax^3 + bx + c$, then which of the following conditions are valid?
(a) $a^2 + c = 0$
(b) $b - a = ac$
(c) $c^3 + 2c^2 + c + b^2 = 0$
(d) None of these

Answer Keys

1. (a, b, c) **2.** (a, b, d) **3.** (c) **4.** (a, b, c)

■ QUADRATIC EQUATION

$ax^2 + bx + c = 0$ is known as quadratic equation if a is non-zero $a, b, c \in \mathbb{C}$. The roots of this equation can be obtained by method of completing the square as below:

$$ax^2 + bx + c = 0 \text{ (i)} \Rightarrow a\left(x^2 + \frac{b}{a}x + \frac{c}{a}\right) = 0$$

$$\Rightarrow x^2 + \frac{b}{a}x + \frac{c}{a} = 0 \because a \neq 0$$

$$\Rightarrow x^2 + 2\frac{b}{2a}x + \frac{b^2}{4a^2} - \frac{b^2}{4a^2} + \frac{c}{a} = 0$$

$$\Rightarrow \left(x + \frac{b}{2a}\right)^2 = \frac{b^2 - 4ac}{4a^2} \Rightarrow x = \frac{-b}{2a} \pm \frac{\sqrt{b^2 - 4ac}}{2a}$$

($b^2 - 4ac = D$ is known as **Discriminant** of quadratic)

The above method was first proposed by Shridharacharya in 900AD (approx). That is why it is also called as Shridharacharya Vidhi.

Nature of roots: It is very evident from the following results that roots of quadratic equation are functions of its coefficients.

❑ If $a, b, c \in \mathbb{R}$ and $a \neq 0$, then $\alpha = \dfrac{-b + \sqrt{D}}{2a}$, $\beta = \dfrac{-b - \sqrt{D}}{2a}$ and $ax^2 + bx + c = a(x - \alpha)(x - \beta)$ (ii)

Thus roots depends on nature of coefficients.

- If $D > 0$, then roots of equation (i) are real and distinct.
- If $D = 0$, then roots of equation (i) will be real and equal. i.e., $\alpha = \beta = -\dfrac{b}{2a}$

- If $D < 0$, then roots of equation (i) will be non-real complex conjugate.
- For quadratic with non-real coefficient above con collusion may not hold good.

☐ If $a, b, c \in \mathbb{Q}$ and D is a *perfect square of a rational number*, then the roots are *rational* and in case it is not a perfect square then the roots are irrational. (*conjugate surds*)

☐ If $a, b, c \in \mathbb{R}$ and $p + iq$ is one root of equation (*i*) $(q \neq 0)$ then the other must be the conjugate $p - iq$ and vice versa. $(p, q \subset \mathbb{R}$ and $i = \sqrt{-1})$.

☐ If $a, b, c \in Q$ and $p + \sqrt{q}$ is one root of equation (*i*) then the other must be the conjugate $p - \sqrt{q}$ and vice versa. (where p is a rational and $\sqrt{q}$ is irrational)

☐ $ax^2 + bx + c = 0 \equiv a(x - \alpha)(x - \beta)$ (if α and β are roots of the equation)

$\because$ $a \neq 0$; dividing both side of equation by a and comparing the coefficient

$\alpha + \beta = -\frac{b}{a}$ and $\alpha\beta = \frac{c}{a}$

$\Rightarrow \alpha - \beta$ (difference of roots) $= \frac{\sqrt{D}}{a}$

☐ Let D_1 and D_2 are discriminants of equation $a_1x^2 + b_1x + c_1 = 0$ and $a_2x^2 + b_2x + c_2 = 0$

Case I: $D_1 + D_2 \geq 0$, then at least one of D_1 and $D_2 \geq 0$ (must be greater than or equal to zero) i.e., if $D_1 \leq 0$, then $D_2 \geq 0$ and if $D_2 \leq 0$ then $D_1 \geq 0$, i.e., at least one of the equations has both roots real.

Case II: If $D_1 + D_2 < 0$, then at least one of D_1 and D_2 must be negative i.e., If $D_1 > 0$, then $D_2 < 0$ and if $D_1 < 0$, then $D_1 > 0$ (must be less than zero). At least one of the equation has both roots, non-real complex conjugates.

☐ Irrational roots for rational polynomial and non-real roots for real polynomials always occur in conjugate pairs.

☐ If the equation $ax^2 + bx + c = 0$ has more than two roots, then it will become an identity and this implies $a = b = c = 0$ and it will have infinite real roots.

☐ If $a = 1$ and b, c are integers and the root of equation (i) are rational numbers, i.e., $D > 0$ and perfect square then these roots must be integers.

Proof: If $a = 1$, b and c integer and $D = b^2 - 4c = k^2$ and $k \in \mathbb{R}$

$\therefore\ b^2 - 4c = k^2 \Rightarrow \qquad b^2 - k^2 = 4c$

$\Rightarrow$ b and k have same parity (i.e., either both odd or both even)

$\Rightarrow$ Root α and $\beta = \frac{-b \pm \sqrt{b^2 - 4c}}{2}$

$\Rightarrow \alpha$ and $\beta = \frac{-b \pm \sqrt{k^2}}{2} = \frac{-b \pm |k|}{2}$

$= \frac{-b \pm k}{2} = \frac{-b + k}{2}, \frac{-b - k}{2} \in \mathbb{Z}$

Converse: α and β be integer roots

$\Rightarrow \begin{cases} \alpha + \beta = -b \\ \alpha.\beta = c \end{cases} \quad \therefore$ root $\in \mathbb{Q}$

If sum and product of two rational is integer then they both must be integer.

☐ If $a + b + c = 0$ and a, b, c are rational then 1 is a root of the equation (i) and roots of the equation (ii) are rational.

☐ $a^2 + b^2 + c^2 - ab - bc - ca = \frac{1}{2}\{(a - b)^2 + (b - c)^2 + (c - a)^2\} = -\{(a - b)(b - c) + (b - c)(c - a) + (c - a)(a - b)\}$

ILLUSTRATION 15: For what values of $m \in \mathbb{R}$, the equation $(1 + m)x^2 - 2(1 + 3m)x + (1 + 8m) = 0$ has

(a) both roots imaginary

(b) both roots equal

(c) both roots real and distinct?

SOLUTION: Since discriminant $D = 4(1 + 3m)^2 - 4(1 + m)(1 + 8m)$

(a) roots are imaginary only if $D < 0$ $\qquad \Rightarrow 4m(m - 3) < 0 \Rightarrow \quad m \in (0, 3)$

(b) both roots are equal when $D = 0$ $\qquad \Rightarrow 4m(m - 3) = 0 \Rightarrow \quad m = 0, 3$

(c) both roots are real and distinct when $D > 0$

$\Rightarrow 4m(m - 3) > 0 \quad \Rightarrow \quad m(m - 3) > 0$

$\Rightarrow m \in (-\infty, -1) \cup (-1, 0) \cup (3, \infty) \qquad \because\ m \in \mathbb{R}$

ILLUSTRATION 16: Prove that the roots of the following equations are real:

(a) $x^2 - 2ax + a^2 - b^2 - c^2 = 0$ (b) $(a - b + c)x^2 + 4(a - b)x + (a - b - c) = 0$

SOLUTION: (a) The given equation is $x^2 - 2ax + a^2 - b^2 - c^2 = 0$, the discriminant

$D = 4a^2 - 4(a^2 - b^2 - c^2) = 4a^2 - 4a^2 + 4b^2 + 4c^2 = 4(b^2 + c^2) \Rightarrow D \geq 0$. Hence roots are real.

(b) The given equation is $(a - b + c)x^2 + 4(a - b)x + (a - b - c) = 0$

$D = 16(a - b)^2 - 4(a - b + c)(a - b - c)$

$= 16(a - b)^2 - 4[(a - b)^2 - c^2] = 12(a - b)^2 + 4c^2 \Rightarrow D \geq 0$; Hence both roots are real.

ILLUSTRATION 17: Prove that roots of the equation $\sin^2 \alpha\, x^2 + \cos^2\alpha\, x - 1 = 0$ are rational.

SOLUTION: Sum of coefficient $\sin^2 \alpha + \cos^2 \alpha - 1 = 0$

$\Rightarrow$ $x = 1$ is one root of equation

$\Rightarrow$ Other roots must be rational because the given quadratic has rational coefficients, therefore if irrational roots occur, they must occur in conjugate pairs. So if one root is rational then other root must also be rational.

ILLUSTRATION 18: Prove that the roots of $ax^2 + 2bx + c = 0$ will be real and distinct if and only if the roots of $(a + c)(ax^2 + 2bx + c) = 2(ac - b^2)(x^2 + 1)$ are imaginary.

SOLUTION: Let D_1 be the discriminant of quadratic equation $ax^2 + 2bx + c = 0$ (i)

$\Rightarrow$ $D_1 = 4(b^2 - ac)$; given $D_1 > 0$.

The other equation $(a + c)(ax^2 + 2bx + c) = 2(ac - b^2)(x^2 + 1)$ can be written as

$(a^2 + 2b^2 - ac)x^2 + 2(ab + bc)x + (c^2 + 2b^2 - ac) = 0$ (ii)

Let its discriminant be D_2

$\therefore$ $D_2 = 4(ab + bc)^2 - 4(c^2 + 2b^2 - ac)(a^2 + 2b^2 - ac)$

$= 4(-a^2b^2 - b^2c^2 - 2a^2c^2 + 6ab^2c - 4b^4 + ac^3 + a^3c)$

$= -4[4b^2(b^2 - ac) + a^2(b^2 - ac) + c^2(b^2 - ac) - 2ac(b^2 - ac)]$

$= -4(b^2 - ac)(4b^2 + (a - c)^2)$

Clearly, when $b^2 - ac > 0$, D_2 will be negative.

and if $D_2 < 0 \Rightarrow b^2 - ac > 0$

therefore $D_2 < 0 \Leftrightarrow b^2 - ac > 0$ or, $D_2 < 0 \Leftrightarrow D_1 > 0$,

the roots of (i) are real and distinct if and only if the roots of

(ii) are imaginary.

ILLUSTRATION 19: If the roots of the equation $x^2 - 8x + a^2 - 6a = 0$ are real and distinct, then find all possible value of a.

SOLUTION: Since the roots of the given equation are real and distinct, we must have $D > 0$.

$\Rightarrow$ $64 - 4(a^2 - 6a) > 0 \Rightarrow 4[16 - a^2 + 6a] > 0 \Rightarrow a^2 - 6a - 16 < 0$

$\Rightarrow$ $(a - 8)(a + 2) < 0 \Rightarrow -2 < a < 8$

Hence, the roots of the given equation are real if a lies between -2 and 8.

ILLUSTRATION 20: If $\cos\theta$, $\sin\phi$, $\sin\theta$ are in GP, then check the nature of roots of $x^2 + 2(\cot\phi)x + 1 = 0$.

SOLUTION: We have, $\sin^2\phi = \cos\theta \sin\theta$

The discriminant of the given equation is; $D = 4\cot^2\phi - 4$

$$= 4\left[\frac{\cos^2\phi - \sin^2\phi}{\sin^2\phi}\right] = \frac{4(1 - 2\sin^2\phi)}{\sin^2\phi} = 4\left[\frac{(1 - 2\cos\theta\sin\theta)}{\sin^2\phi}\right]$$

$$= \left[\frac{2(\sin\theta - \cos\theta)}{\sin\phi}\right]^2 \geq 0$$ $\Rightarrow$ Roots of given equation will be real.

ILLUSTRATION 21: Prove that the roots of the equation $(a + b - c)x^2 + 2bx + (b + c - a) = 0$ are rational, provided a, b, c are rational.

SOLUTION: The given equation is $(a + b - c) x^2 + 2bx + (b + c - a) = 0$

$\therefore \quad D = 4b^2 - 4\left[(a+b-c)(b+c-a)\right]$

$= 4b^2 - 4(b^2 - (a - c)^2) = 4(a-c)^2 \qquad \Rightarrow a$ and c are rational

$\Rightarrow D = (2(a - c))^2$ is a perfect square of a rational number.

$\Rightarrow$ Roots must be rational.

Note that if a, b, c are real and coefficient of x is $-2b$ instead of $2b$, then $f(1) = 0 \Rightarrow$ one root (1) is rational $\Rightarrow$ other root must be rational.

ILLUSTRATION 22: If a, b and c are odd integers, then prove that roots of $ax^2 + bx + c = 0$ cannot be rational.

SOLUTION: Discriminant $D = b^2 - 4ac$. Suppose the roots are rational.

Then, D will be perfect square as a, b, c are rational.

Let $b^2 - 4ac = d^2$; since a, b and c are odd integers, clearly, d will be odd.

Now, $b^2 - d^2 = 4ac$

Le $b = 2k + 1$ and $d = 2m + 1$. Then $b^2 + d^2 = (b - d)(b + d) = 2(k - m)\, 2(k + m + 1)$

Now, either $(k - m)$ or $(k + m + 1)$ is always even. Hence $b^2 - d^2$ is always a mutiple of 8. But $4ac$ is only a multiple of 4 (not of 8,) which is a contradiction. Hence, the roots of $ax^2 + bx + c = 0$ cannot be rational.

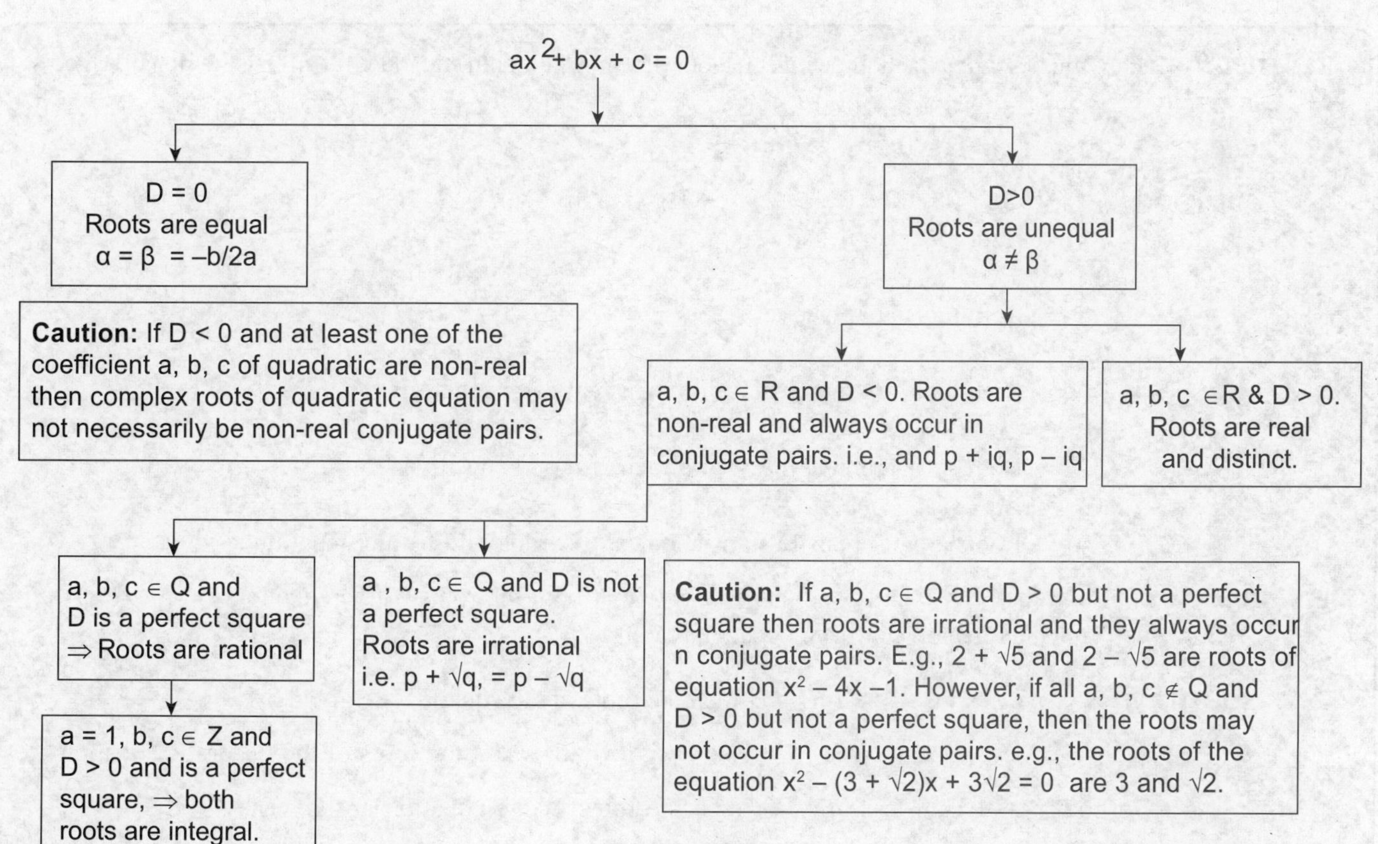

FIGURE 5.8

Determination of sign of roots without solving the Equation:

Given: $ax^2 + bx + c = 0$.

If α, β be roots $\Rightarrow$ $\alpha + \beta = \frac{-b}{a}$

$\Rightarrow \alpha\beta = \frac{c}{a}$

Case 1: D > 0

Sub-case 1: $\alpha.\beta < 0$ and $\alpha + \beta > 0$,

Let $\alpha > 0, \beta < 0 \quad \Rightarrow \quad |\alpha| > ||$.

$\Rightarrow$ α and β of opposite sign and magnitude of positive root is larger than negative root.

Sub-case II: $\alpha.\beta < 0$ and $\alpha + \beta < 0$,

Let $\alpha > 0, \beta < 0 \quad \Rightarrow \quad |\alpha| < |\beta|$.

$\Rightarrow$ α and β of opposite sign and magnitude negative root is larger than positive root.

Sub-case III: $\alpha.\beta < 0$ and $\alpha + \beta = 0$,

Let $\alpha > 0, \beta < 0 \Rightarrow |\alpha| = |\ |$.

$\Rightarrow$ α and β of opposite sign and magnitude of negative root is same as that of positive root.

Sub-case IV: $\alpha.\beta > 0$ and $\alpha + \beta < 0$

$\Rightarrow$ α and β of same sign and both negative.

Sub-case V: $\alpha.\beta > 0$ and $\alpha + \beta > 0$,

$\Rightarrow$ α and β of same sign and both positive.

Sub-case VI: $\alpha.\beta = 0$ and $\alpha + \beta < 0$,

$\Rightarrow$ One of α and β = 0 and other is negative,

Sub-case VII: $\alpha.\beta = 0$ and $\alpha + \beta > 0$,

$\Rightarrow$ One root zero and other positive,

Sub-case VIII: $\alpha.\beta = 0$ and $\alpha + \beta = 0$,

$\Rightarrow$ Both roots zero.

Case (2) : D < 0

Sub-case (I) $\alpha.\beta > 0$; $\alpha + \beta > 0$

$\Rightarrow$ Both roots imaginary with positive real part.

Sub-case (II) $\alpha + \beta = 0$

$\Rightarrow$ Both roots purely imaginary.

Sub-case (III) $\alpha + \beta < 0$

$\Rightarrow$ Both roots imaginary with negative real part.

Case (3) : D = 0

Sub-case (I): $\alpha + \beta > 0$

$\Rightarrow$ Both roots are equal and are positive

Sub-case (II): $\alpha + \beta < 0$

$\Rightarrow$ Both roots are equal and are negative

Sub-case (III): $\alpha + \beta = 0$

$\Rightarrow$ Both roots are equal and are zeros

ILLUSTRATION 23: Without solving the Following equations determine the sum equations determine the sign of its roots.

(a) $x^2 + 5x + 4 = 0$ (b) $x^2 - 6x + 8 = 0$ (c) $x^2 + x + 1 = 0$

(d) $x^2 - 2x + 3 = 0$ (e) $x^2 + 6x - 4 = 0$

SOLUTION: (a) $x^2 + 5x + 4 = 0 \Rightarrow \alpha + \beta = -5, \alpha\beta = 4, D = 9$

$\Rightarrow$ Both roots are negative.

(b) $x^2 - 6x + 8 = 0 \Rightarrow \alpha + \beta = 6, \alpha\beta = 8, D = 4$

$\Rightarrow$ Both roots are positive

(c) $x^2 + x + 1 = 0 \Rightarrow \alpha + \beta = -1, \alpha\beta = 1, D = -3$

$\Rightarrow$ Both roots are imaginary with their real parts negative.

(d) $x^2 - 2x + 3 = 0 \Rightarrow \alpha + \beta = 2, \alpha\beta = \frac{3}{2}, D = -8$

$\Rightarrow$ Both roots are imaginary with their real parts positive.

(e) $x^2 + 6x - 4 = 0 \Rightarrow \alpha + \beta = -6, \alpha\beta = -4, D = 52$

$\Rightarrow$ Roots are of opposite signs and negative root with greater magnitude .

ILLUSTRATION 24: Let $a > 0$, $b > 0$ and $c > 0$. Then prove that both the roots of the equation $ax^2 + bx + c = 0$ are either negative or have negative real parts.

SOLUTION: We have $D = b^2 - 4ac$. If $D \geq 0$, then the roots of the equation are given by $x = \frac{-b \pm \sqrt{D}}{2a}$.

As $D = b^2 - 4ac < b^2$ ($\because$ $a > 0, c > 0$), it follows that the roots of the quadratic equation are both negative. In case $D < 0$, then the roots of the equation are given by $x = \frac{-b \pm i\sqrt{-D}}{2a}$, which have negative real parts.

THINK YOURSELF

1. *Why a quadratic equation cannot have more than two roots?*

TEXTUAL EXERCISE-3 (SUBJECTIVE)

1. Find the nature of roots of equation $x^2 + k = 0$, where $k < 0$.
2. If l, m are real $l \neq m$, find the nature of roots of the equation $(l - m)x^2 - 5(l + m)x - 2(l - m) = 0$.
3. If the roots of $ax^2 + b = 0$ are real and distinct then find the condition for which it is true.
4. Find the value of k ($k > 0$) for which the equation $x^2 + kx + 64 = 0$ and $x^2 - 8x + k = 0$, both will have real roots.
5. If $b \in \mathbb{R}^+$ then find nature of the roots of the equation $(2 + b)x^2 + (3 + b)x + (4 + b) = 0$.
6. For what values of m will the expression $(m + 1)x^2 - 4(m + 2)x + 25$ be a perfect square?
7. Find the set of values of a for which quadratic equation $(a + 1)x^2 + 2(a + 1)x + a - 2 = 0$
   (a) has two distinct real roots
   (b) has no real roots
   (c) has two equal real roots.
8. Find out whether $10 - 2\sqrt{5}$ is a root of equation $x^2 - 20x + 80 = 0$.
9. Without solving the following equations, determine the sign of its roots.
   (a) $x^2 + (3 - 2a)x - 3a + 2 = 0$
   (b) $x^2 + 5x + 4 = 0$
10. Show that the roots of equation $px^2 - 3qx - 4p = 0$ are all real and distinct $\forall\, p, q \in \mathbb{R}$ and also analyses the nature of root when p, q are purely imaginary.
11. Find the roots of the equation $(b - c)x^2 + (c - a)x + (a - b) = 0$.
12. If $a(b - c)x^2 + b(c - a)xy + c(a - b)y^2$ is a perfect square, then prove that a, b, c are in H.P.
13. If $a, b \in \mathbb{R}$ and the quadratic equation $x^2 + (a - b)x - a - b + 1 = 0$ has unequal real roots for all $b \in \mathbb{R}$, then show that $a > 1$.

Answer Keys

1. real and distinct 2. real and unequal 3. $ab < 0$ 4. 16
5. imaginary 6. $m = 3, -3/4$
7. (a) $a \in (-1, \infty)$ (b) $a \in (-\infty, -1)$ (c) $a \in \{\phi\}$ 8. yes
9. (a) both roots negative for $a < 2/3$, one root –ve and other is zero if $a = 2/3$, $a \in (2/3, 3/2)$ opposite sign and –ve root larger, $a = 3/2$
$\Rightarrow$ equal magnitude and opposite sign $a > 3/2$: opposite and + ve roots is larger in magnitude.
(b) both roots negative
11. $\dfrac{a-b}{b-c}, 1$

TEXTUAL EXERCISE-3 (OBJECTIVE)

1. If the roots of the equation $9x^2 + 4ax + 4 = 0$ are imaginary, then
   (a) $a \in (-3, 3)$
   (b) $a \in [-3, 3]$
   (c) $a \in (-\infty, -3] \cup [3, \infty)$
   (d) None of these
2. The value of k for which the expression $x^2 + (2 - k)x + k - 3/4$ will be a perfect square, is
   (a) 1
   (b) 6
   (c) 7
   (d) None of these

3. The equation $x^2 + 3|x| + 2 = 0$ have
(a) 4 real roots (b) no roots
(c) 2 real roots (d) None of these

4. If l, m are real, $l \neq m$, then the roots of the equation $(l - m)x^2 - (l + m)x - 2(l - m) = 0$
(a) real and equal (b) complex
(c) real and unequal (d) None of these

5. The value of m for which the equation $x^2 - x + m^2 = 0$ has no real roots is given as
(a) $m > 1/2$ (b) $m = 0$
(c) $m < 1/2$ (d) $m < 1/2$

6. The equation $x^2 - (2 \tan \alpha)\, x - 1 = 0$ has always
(a) integer roots (b) real roots
(c) equal roots (d) None of these

7. If $x^2 - 4x + \log_{1/2} a^2 = 0$ does not have two distinct real roots, then maximum value of a is
(a) 1/4 (b) 1/16
(c) –1/4 (d) None of these

8. The polynomial $(ax^2 + bx + c)(ax^2 - dx - c) = 0$; $ac \neq 0$, has
(a) four real zeros
(b) at least two real zeros
(c) at most two real zeros
(d) no real zeros

9. If roots of the equation $(a^2 + b^2)y^2 - 2(ac + bd)y + c^2 + d^2 = 0$ are equal, then
(a) $ab = bc$ (b) $ac = bd$
(c) $ad + bc = 0$ (d) $\dfrac{a}{b} = \dfrac{c}{d}$

10. The value of m for which the equation $(1 + m)x^2 - 2(1 + 3m)\, x + (1 + 8m) = 0$ has equal roots, is
(a) 0, 3 (b) 1
(c) 2 (d) 3

11. If the roots of the equation $(b - c)\, x^2 + (c - a)\, x + (a - b) = 0$ are equal, then a, b, c are in
(a) *A.P.* (b) *G.P.*
(c) *H.P.* (d) None of these

12. The roots of the equation $(x - a)(x - b) = abx^2$ are always
(a) real (b) imaginary
(c) cannot be discussed (d) None of these

13. The quadratic equation $8 \sec^2\theta - 6\sec\theta + 1 = 0$ has:
(a) infinitely many roots
(b) exactly two roots
(c) exactly four roots
(d) no real roots

14. Let a, b and c be real numbers such that $4a + 2b + c = 0$ and $ab > 0$. Then the quadratic equation $ax^2 + bx + c = 0$ has:
(a) real roots
(b) complex roots
(c) purely imaginary roots
(d) only one root

15. The condition that the equation $(c^2 + a^2)x^2 - 2(a + b)cx + (b^2 + c^2) = 0$ has equal roots is
(a) $c^2 = ab$ (b) $b^2 = ac$
(c) $2b = a + b$ (d) None of these

Answer Keys

1. (a) **2.** (a), (c) **3.** (b) **4.** (c) **5.** (a) **6.** (b) **7.** (a) **8.** (b) **9.** (d) **10.** (a)
11. (a) **12.** (a) **13.** (d) **14.** (a) **15.** (a)

■ RELATION BETWEEN ROOTS AND COEFFICIENTS

Let the roots of the equation $ax^2 + bx + c$ be given by (α, β), then by factor theorem $(x - \alpha)$ and $(x - \beta)$ are factor.

$$\Rightarrow ax^2 + bx + c = a(x - \alpha)(x - \beta)$$

$$\Rightarrow x^2 + \frac{b}{a}x + \frac{c}{a} = (x - \alpha)(x - \beta)$$

$$\Rightarrow x^2 + \frac{b}{a}x + \frac{c}{a} = x^2 - (\alpha + \beta)x + \alpha\beta$$

Comparing the coefficients of x and constant term, we get $\alpha + \beta = -b/a$ and $\alpha\beta = c/a$.

For cubic polynomial equation

If $ax^3 + bx^2 + cx + d = 0$ has roots α, β, γ then

$\Sigma\alpha = \alpha + \beta + \gamma = -b/a$; $\Sigma\alpha\beta = \alpha\beta + \beta\gamma + \gamma\alpha = c/a$; $\alpha\beta\gamma = -d/a$

Similarity, for biquadratic polynomial

If $ax^4 + bx^3 + cx^2 + dx + e = 0$ has roots $\alpha, \beta, \gamma, \delta$ then

$\Sigma\alpha = -b/a$; $\Sigma\alpha\beta = c/a$; $\Sigma\alpha\beta\gamma = -d/a$; $\Sigma\alpha\beta\gamma\delta = e/a$

For general polynomial equation

In general, if $(a_0 \neq 0)$, then $a_0x^n + a_1x^{n-1} + a_2x^{n-2} + ... + a_n =$ 0 be a polynomial equation of degree n.

Let $\alpha_1.\alpha_2.\alpha_3$ ....α_n be the roots of the above equation. Therefore $a_0(x-\alpha_1)(x-\alpha_2)......(x-\alpha_n)$

$a_0\,[x^n - S_1x^{n-1} + S_2x^{n-2} - S_3x^{n-3} + ... + (-1)^r S_r.x^{n-r} + ...]$

(where S_r denotes sum of product of roots taken r at a time). Comparing the coefficients of L.H.S. and R.H.S. polynomial expression.

$$S_1 = (\alpha_1 + \alpha_2 + \alpha_3 + ...) = \sum \alpha_i = \frac{a_1}{a_{.0}}$$

$$S_2 = (\alpha_1\alpha_2 + \alpha_2\alpha_3 + ...) = \sum \alpha_i\alpha_j = -\frac{a_2}{a_0}$$

....

$$S_n = \alpha_1\alpha_2..............\alpha_n = \prod_{k=1}^{n} \alpha_k = (-1)^n \frac{a_n}{a_0}$$

ILLUSTRATION 25: Find the sum of cubes of roots of equation $x^3 - 12x^3 + 48x - 64 = 0$

SOLUTION: Comparing the given equation with $a_0\,x^3 + a_1\,x^2 + a_2\,x + a_3 = 0$, we have $a_0 = 1$, $a_1 = -12$, $a_2 =$ 48, $a_3 = -64$

$\Rightarrow \sum \alpha = (-1)^1 \frac{a_1}{a_0} = \frac{-(-12)}{1} = 12, \sum \alpha\beta = (-1)^2 \frac{a_2}{a_0} = 48,\ \alpha\beta r = (-1)^3 \frac{a_3}{a_0} = 64$

$\therefore\ f(-t) = -t^3 - 12t^2 - 48t - 64 < 0\ \forall\ t \geq 0$

$\Rightarrow$ All roots of given equation are non- negative.

Further $\alpha + \beta + \gamma = 12$, $\alpha\,\beta\,\gamma = 64$ $\quad\Rightarrow\quad \frac{\alpha+\beta+\gamma}{3} = 4\ 3\sqrt{\alpha\beta\gamma} = 4$

$\Rightarrow$ A.M. of $\alpha, \beta, \gamma = 4$, G.M. of $\alpha, \beta, \gamma = 4$

$\Rightarrow$ A.M. = G.M.

$\Rightarrow \alpha = \beta = \gamma = 4$ $\quad\Rightarrow \alpha^3 + \beta^3 + \gamma^3 = 3\,(4)^3 = 192$

Formation/transformation of quadratic equation

If all the roots of a polynomial are transformed by same function (say f(x)), then the equation obtained can be generated directly as described below:

Step-I: Let the equation $ax^2 + bx + c = 0$ has root α and β.

Step II: To obtain the equation with root $f(\alpha)$ and $f(\beta)$ consider $x = f(\alpha)$

Express α in terms of $x \Rightarrow \quad \alpha = f^1(x)$

Step III: Substitute the value of α in equation $a\alpha^2 + b\alpha + c = 0$

Then we obtain the transformed equation $a(f^1(x))^2 + b\,(f^1(x)) + c = 0$

A quadratic equation whose summation of roots is S and product of roots is P can be written as $x^2 - Sx + P = 0$. Hence α, β be the roots of equation $ax^2 + bx + c = 0$, then to obtain the equation whose roots are

(i) $1/\alpha, 1/\beta$ (ii) $-\alpha, -\beta$
(iii) $k\alpha, k\beta$ (iv) $-1/\alpha, -1/\beta$
(v) $p\alpha + q, p\beta + q$, Now we proceed as:

Since $\alpha + \beta = -b/a$ and $\alpha\beta = c/a$ and the equation whose summation of roots is S and product of roots is P can be written as $x^2 - Sx + P = 0$. Therefore

(i) $S = \frac{\beta+\alpha}{\alpha\beta}, P = 1/\alpha\beta \Rightarrow x^2 - \frac{\beta+\alpha}{\alpha\beta}x + 1/\alpha\beta = 0$

$\Rightarrow \alpha\beta x^2 - (\beta + \alpha)x + 1 = 0 \Rightarrow cx^2 + bx + a = 0$

(The reciprocal equation of $ax^2 + bx + c = 0$ can be obtained by replacing x with 1/x in the later equation i.e., interchanging the coefficients of equidistant terms from beginning and end.)

(ii) $S = -(\alpha + \beta), P = \alpha\beta \Rightarrow x^2 + (\alpha + \beta)x + \alpha\beta = 0$

$\Rightarrow ax^2 - bx + c = 0$

(The equation whose roots are negative of the roots of equation $ax^2 + bx + c = 0$ can be obtained by replacing x with $-x$ is the $ax^2 + bx + c = 0$)

(iii) $S = k(\alpha + \beta), P = k^2\alpha\beta \Rightarrow x^2 - k(\alpha + \beta)x + k^2\alpha\beta = 0$

$\Rightarrow ax^2 + kbx + k^2c = 0$

(The equation whose roots are k times of the roots of $ax^2 + bx + c = 0$ can be obtained by replacing x with x/k in the $ax^2 + bx + c = 0$)

(iv) $S = \frac{-(\beta+\alpha)}{\alpha\beta}, P = 1/\alpha\beta \Rightarrow \alpha\beta x^2 + (\beta + \alpha)x + 1 = 0$

$\Rightarrow cx^2 - bx + a = 0$

(The negative reciprocal of roots of equation $ax^2 + bx + c = 0$ whose roots can be obtained by replacing x by $-1/x$ in the given equation)

(v) $S = p(\alpha + \beta) + 2q,$

$P = p^2\alpha\beta + pq(\alpha + \beta) + q^2$

Hence the required equation

$\Rightarrow x^2 - [p(\alpha+\beta)+2q]x + [p^2\alpha\beta + pq(\alpha+\beta) + q^2] = 0$

$\Rightarrow ax^2 + [pb - 2q]x + [p^2c - pqb + q^2] = 0$

Alternatively, for the new equation $x = p\alpha + q$, $\alpha = \frac{x-q}{p}$.

Therefore the required equation can be obtained by replacing x by $\frac{x-q}{p}$ in the $ax^2 + bx + c = 0$

ILLUSTRATION 26: If α and β are the roots of the equation $ax^2 + bx + c = 0$, find the values of $\alpha^4\beta^7 + \alpha^7\beta^4$.

SOLUTION: The given equation $ax^2 + bx + c = 0$

Since α and β are the roots of the equation $\alpha + \beta = -b/a \Rightarrow \alpha\beta = c/a$

$$\alpha^4\beta^7 + \alpha^7\beta^4 = \alpha^4\beta^4(\alpha^3+\beta^3) = \alpha^4\beta^4[(a+\beta)^3 - 3\alpha\beta(\alpha+\beta)]$$

$$= \frac{c^4}{a^4}\left[-\frac{b^3}{a^3} - 3\frac{c}{a}\cdot\left(-\frac{b}{a}\right)\right] = \frac{c^4}{a^4}\left[\frac{3bc}{a^2} - \frac{b^3}{a^3}\right] = \frac{bc^4}{a^7}(3ac - b^2)$$

ILLUSTRATION 27: For what values of $m \in \mathbb{R}$, the equation $(1+m)x^2 - 2(1+3m)x + (1+8m) = 0$ has

(a) roots, that are opposite in sign?

(b) roots, that are equal in magnitude but opposite in sign?

(c) roots of same sign

SOLUTION: Since discriminant $D = 4(1+3m)^2 - 4(1+m)(1+8m) = 4m^2 - 12m = 4m(m+3)$

For real roots. $D \geq 0 \quad \Rightarrow \quad m \in (-\infty, 0] \cup [3, \infty)$

(a) Roots are opposite in sign means $\alpha\beta < 0$

$\Rightarrow c/a < 0 \quad \Rightarrow \frac{1+8m}{1+m} < 0$

$\Rightarrow (8m+1)(m+1) < 0 \Rightarrow m \in (-1, -1/8)$

(b) Roots are equal in magnitude but opposite in sign then sum of root vanishes

$\Rightarrow \alpha + \beta = 0 \qquad \Rightarrow -b/a = 0$

$\Rightarrow \frac{2(1+3m)}{1+m} = 0 \qquad \Rightarrow m = -1/3$

(c) ab > 0 $\Rightarrow m(-\infty, -1) \cup (-1/8, \infty)$ but for real part $m(-\infty, 0] \cup [3, \infty)$. Taking $\cap$, we get $(-\infty, -1) \cup [3, \infty)$.

ILLUSTRATION 28: Form an equation whose roots are $p/q, -q/p$.

SOLUTION: Here $\alpha = p/q$, $\beta = -q/p$ and $\alpha + \beta = \frac{p^2 - q^2}{pq}$, $\alpha\beta = -1$

Hence the required equation is $x^2 - x\left(\frac{p^2-q^2}{pq}\right) 1 = 0$

or $pqx^2 + x(p^2 - q^2) - pq = 0$

ILLUSTRATION 29: If a, b and c are in $A.P$, and one root of the equation $ax^2 - 2bx + c = 0$ is 3 then find the other root and harmonic mean of both the roots.

SOLUTION: Let α be the other root, then $9a - 6b + c = 0$ and $2b = a + c$

$\Rightarrow 6a - 2c = 0 \qquad \Rightarrow c/a = 3$

Now product of roots $= 3\alpha = c/a = 3$

$\Rightarrow \alpha = 1$

H.M. of the roots $= \dfrac{2(3)(1)}{3+1} = \dfrac{3}{2}$

ILLUSTRATION 30: Find the condition that the one root of $ax^2 + bx + c = 0$ shall be n times of the other.

SOLUTION: Let one root of $ax^2 + bx + c = 0$ is α, the other is $n\alpha$.

$\therefore$ Sum of the roots i.e., $\alpha + n\alpha = -b/a$ or $\alpha(1 + n) = -b/a$ (i)

Product of roots i.e, $\alpha.n\alpha = c/a$ or $n\alpha^2 = c/a$ (ii)

From (i) and (ii), we get $\alpha^2 = \left[\dfrac{-b}{a(1+n)}\right]^2 = \dfrac{c}{an}$

Thus required condition is $b^2n = ac(1+n)^2$

ILLUSTRATION 31: If the roots of the quadratic equation $x^2 + ax + b = 0$ are tan 30° and tan 15°, respectively, then find the value of angle $\phi \in (0, \pi)$ such that $\tan\phi = \dfrac{a+b\sqrt{3}}{(a-b)}$ hence show that $\dfrac{a+b\sqrt{3}}{a-b}$ is a root of given quadratic equation.

SOLUTION: The equation $x^2 + ax + b = 0$ has roots tan 30° and tan 15° therefore,

$\tan 30° + \tan 15° = -a$ (1)

$\tan 30° . \tan 15° = b$ (2)

Now, $\tan 45° = \tan (30° + 15°)$

$\Rightarrow 1 = \dfrac{\tan 30° + \tan 15°}{1 - \tan 30° \tan 15°} \Rightarrow 1 = \dfrac{-a}{1-b}$ (Using (1) and (2))

$\Rightarrow 1 - b = -a \Rightarrow b - a = 1$

$\because$ tan 30° is root of the given equation

$\therefore 1/3 + a/\sqrt{3} + b = 0$

$\Rightarrow a + b\sqrt{3} = -1/\sqrt{3}$

$\therefore \tan\phi = \dfrac{a+b\sqrt{3}}{a-b} = \dfrac{-1/\sqrt{3}}{-1} = 1/\sqrt{3}$

$\Rightarrow \phi = \pi/6$ hence $\dfrac{a+b\sqrt{3}}{a-b}$ is clearly a root of given quadratic equation.

ILLUSTRATION 32: $0 < a < b < c$ and the roots α, β of the equation $ax^2 + bx + c = 0$ are imaginary, then prove that $|\alpha| = |\beta|$ and $|\alpha| > 1$.

SOLUTION: Since roots are imaginary, $D = b^2 - 4ac < 0$

$\Rightarrow \alpha = \dfrac{-b + i\sqrt{4ac - b^2}}{2a}$ and $\beta = \dfrac{-b - i\sqrt{4ac - b^2}}{2a}$

Clearly, $\bar{\beta} = \alpha \Rightarrow |\alpha| = |\bar{\beta}| = |\beta|$

Also $|\alpha| = \sqrt{\dfrac{b^2}{4a^2} + \dfrac{4ac - b^2}{4a^2}} = \sqrt{\dfrac{c}{a}} > 1 \Rightarrow |\alpha| > 1$. (Think how can you solve the problem graphically)

ILLUSTRATION 33: If α and β ($\neq 0$) are the roots of the equation $x^2 + \alpha x + \beta = 0$, then find the least value of $x^2 + \alpha x + \beta$ ($x \in \mathbb{R}$).

SOLUTION: Since α and β are the roots of the equation $x^2 + \alpha x + \beta = 0$ so $\alpha + \beta = -\alpha$, $\alpha\beta = \beta$

Now $\alpha\beta = \beta \Rightarrow (\alpha - 1)\beta = 0 \Rightarrow \alpha = 1$ ($\because \beta \neq 0$)

Puttig $\alpha = 1$ in $\alpha + \beta = -\alpha$, we get $\beta = -2$. Hence

$x^2 + \alpha x + \beta = x^2 + x - 2 = (x + 1/2)^2 - 1/4 - 2 = (x + 1/2)^2 - 9/4$

which has minimum value of $-9/4$

ILLUSTRATION 34: Find the value of 'a' for which one root of the quadratic equation $(a^2 - 3a + 2)x^2 + 2(2a - 1)x + 3 = 0$ is thrice as large as the other.

SOLUTION: Let α and 3α be the roots, then

$$\alpha + 3\alpha = \frac{(2-4a)}{a^2-3a+2};\ \alpha \times 3\alpha = \frac{3}{a^2-3a+2} \Rightarrow 3\left[\frac{1}{16}\frac{(2-4a)^2}{(a^2-3a+2)^2}\right] = \frac{3}{(a^2-3a+2)}$$

$$\Rightarrow \frac{4(1-2a)^2}{16\left[a^2-3a+2\right]} = 1 \Rightarrow 1 + 4a^2 - 4a = 4a^2 - 12a + 8 \Rightarrow 8a = 7 \Rightarrow a = 7/8$$

ILLUSTRATION 35: If the harmonic mean between roots of $(2 + \sqrt{5})x^2 - 3bx + 6 + 2\sqrt{3} = 0$ is 12, then show that $b = \frac{1}{3} + \frac{1}{3\sqrt{3}}$.

SOLUTION: Let α, β be the roots of the equation whose H.M. is 12 then, $12 = \frac{2\alpha\beta}{\alpha+\beta}$.

$$\Rightarrow 6 = \frac{\frac{6+2\sqrt{3}}{2+\sqrt{5}}}{\frac{3b}{2+\sqrt{5}}} \Rightarrow 6 = \frac{6+2\sqrt{3}}{3b} \Rightarrow 3 = \frac{3+\sqrt{3}}{3b}$$

$$\Rightarrow b = \frac{3+\sqrt{3}}{9} = \frac{1}{3} + \frac{1}{3\sqrt{3}}$$ **Hence proved.**

TEXTUAL EXERCISE–4 (SUBJECTIVE)

1. If $f(x) = 2x^3 + mx^2 - 13x + n$ and 2, 3 are roots of the equation $f(x) = 0$, then find the value of m and n.
2. Find the value of m for which the equation $x^3 - mx^2 + 3x - 2 = 0$ has two roots equal in magnitude but opposite in sign.
3. If α, β are roots of equation $2x^2 - 3x - 6 = 0$ then find the equation whose roots are $\alpha^2 + 2$, $\beta^2 + 2$.
4. If α and β are the roots of $ax^2 + bx + c = 0$ then find the roots of the quadratic equation $ax^2 - bx(x - 1) + c(x - 1)^2 = 0$.
5. Find the quadratic equation whose roots are cubes of the roots of $x^2 + bx + c = 0$.
6. Roots of $x^3 - 9x^2 + kx - 24 = 0$ are in *A.P.* then find roots and k.
7. Suppose a, b are complex numbers and $x^3 + ax + b = 0$ has a pair of complex conjugate roots, then show that a and b are real.
8. If $\cot\theta$, $\operatorname{cosec}\theta$ are the roots of the equation $ax^2 + bx + c = 0$ and $\Delta = b^2 - 4ac$, then find the value of a^4.
9. If α, β are the roots of equation $\lambda(x^2 - x) + x + 5 = 0$ and λ_1, λ_2 are two values of λ for which the roots α, β are related by: $\alpha/\beta + \beta/\alpha = 4/5$. Then find the values of $\lambda_1/\lambda_2 + \lambda_2/\lambda_1$.
10. Let [a] denote the greatest integer less than or equal to a. Given that the quadratic equation $x^2 + [a^2 - 5a + b + 4]x + b = 0$ has roots -5 and 1, find all the values of a.

Answer Keys

1. –5, 30
2. 2/3
3. $4x^2 - 49x + 118 = 0$
4. $\frac{\alpha}{\alpha+1}, \frac{\beta}{\beta+1}$
5. $x^2 + b(b^2 - 3c)x + c^3 = 0$
6. 2, 3, 4 and $k = 26$
8. $b^2\Delta$.
9. 254
10. $a \in \left(-1, \frac{5-3\sqrt{5}}{2}\right] \cup a \in \left[\frac{5-3\sqrt{5}}{2}, 6\right)$

TEXTUAL EXERCISE-4 (OBJECTIVE)

1. If α, β are the roots of $9x^2 + 6x + 1 = 0$, then the equation with roots $\frac{1}{\alpha}, \frac{1}{\beta}$ is
(a) $2x^2 + 3x + 18 = 0$ (b) $x^2 + 6x - 9 = 0$
(c) $x^2 + 6x + 9 = 0$ (d) $x^2 - 6x + 9 = 0$

2. If α, β are the roots of the equation $x^2 + px + q = 0$, then $-\frac{1}{\alpha}, -\frac{1}{\beta}$ are the roots of the equation
(a) $qx^2 - px + 1 = 0$ (b) $qx^2 + px + 1 = 0$
(c) $x^2 + px + q = 0$ (d) $x^2 - px + q = 0$

3. The equation formed by decreasing each root of $ax^2 + bx + c = 0$ by 1 is $2x^2 + 8x + 2 = 0$, then:
(a) $a = -b$ (b) $b = -c$
(c) $c = -a$ (d) $b = a + c$

4. If α, β be roots of equation $ax^2 + bx + c = 0$ then equation having roots $\alpha + \beta, \alpha\beta$ is
(a) $a^2x^2 - a(c - b)x + bc = 0$
(b) $a^2x^2 - a(c - b)x - bc = 0$
(c) $a^2x^2 - ab\,x - bc = 0$
(d) None of these

5. If α, β be roots of equation $ax^2 + bx + c = 0$ then equation having roots $1/\alpha^2, 1/\beta^2$ is
(a) $c^2x^2 - (b^2 - 2ac)x + a^2 = 0$
(b) $c^2x^2 + (b^2 - 2ac)x + a^2 = 0$
(c) $c^2x^2 - (b^2 - 2ac)x - a^2 = 0$
(d) None of these

6. If α, β are the roots of the equation $ax^2 + bx + c = 0$, then the equation whose roots are $\frac{1}{a\alpha + b}$ and $\frac{1}{a\beta + b}$ is
(a) $cax^2 - bx + 1 = 0$ (b) $cax^2 + bx + 1 = 0$
(c) $cax^2 + bx - 1 = 0$ (d) None of these

7. If a and b are rational and b is not a perfect square, then the quadratic equation with rational co-efficients whose one root is $\frac{1}{a+\sqrt{b}}$ is
(a) $x^2 - 2ax + (a^2 - b) = 0$
(b) $(a^2 - b)x^2 - 2ax + 1 = 0$
(c) $(a^2 - b)x^2 - 2ax + 1 = 0$
(d) None of these

8. If $2 + i\sqrt{3}$ is a root of $x^2 + px + q = 0$, where p, q are real then (p, q) is equal to
(a) (–4, 7) (b) (4, –7)
(c) (–7, 4) (d) (4, 7)

9. If the roots of $x^2 - p(x + 1) + c = 0$ are α and β, then the value of $\alpha^2 + (2 + p)\alpha\beta + \beta^2$ is
(a) pc (b) $p^2 + pc$
(c) $p^2 - pc$ (d) $-pc$

10. If the roots of $x^3 - 12x^2 + 39x - 28 = 0$ are in *A.P.* then their common difference is
(a) ±1 (b) ±2
(c) ±3 (d) ±4

11 If the roots of $ax^2 - bx - c = 0$ change by the same quantity then the expression in a, b, c that does not change is
(a) $\frac{b^2 - 4ac}{a^2}$ (b) $\frac{b - 4c}{a}$
(c) $\frac{b^2 + 4ac}{a^2}$ (d) None of these

12. The quadratic equation whose roots are *A.M.* and *H.M.* between the roots of the equation $ax^2 + bx + c = 0$ is
(a) $abx^2 + (b^2 + ac)x + bc = 0$
(b) $2abx^2 + (b^2 + 4ac)x + 2bc = 0$
(c) $2abx^2 + (b^2 + ac)x + bc = 0$
(d) None of these

13. If the sum of the roots of the quadratic equation $ax^2 + bx + c = 0$ is equal to the sum of the squares of their reciprocals, then $\frac{b^2}{ac} + \frac{bc}{a^2}$ is

(a) 2 (b) –2

(c) 1 (d) –1

14. If α, β are the roots of the quadratic equation $6x^2 - 6x + 1 = 0$, then $\frac{1}{2}(a + b\alpha + c\alpha^2 + d\alpha^3) + \frac{1}{2}(a + b\beta + c\beta^2 + d\beta^3)$ is equal to

(a) $\dfrac{12d + 6c + 4b + a}{12}$

(b) $12a + 6b + 4c + 9d$

(c) $\frac{1}{12}(12a + 6b + 4c + 3d)$

(d) None of these

15. The set of possible values of λ for which $x^2 - (\lambda^2 - 5\lambda + 5)x + (2\lambda^2 - 3\lambda - 4) = 0$ has roots, whose sum and product are both less than 1, is

(a) $\left(1, \frac{5}{2}\right)$ (b) $(1, 4)$

(c) $\left[1, \frac{5}{2}\right]$ (d) $\left(-1, \frac{5}{2}\right)$

Answer Keys

1. (c)	**2.** (a)	**3.** (b)	**4.** (b)	**5.** (a)	**6.** (a)	**7.** (b)	**8.** (a)	**9.** (a)	**10.** (c)
11. (c)	**12.** (b)	**13.** (a)	**14.** (c)	**15.** (d)					

■ CONDITION FOR COMMON ROOTS

Consider two quadratic equations: $ax^2 + bx + c = 0$ and $a'x^2 + b'x + c' = 0$ (where $aa' \neq 0$ and $ab' - a'b \neq 0$) have a root common

Let α be a common root then

$a\alpha^2 + b\alpha + c = 0$ (i) and $a'\alpha^2 + b'\alpha + c' = 0$ (ii)

Equation (i) and (ii), using cross multiplication method, we get

$$\frac{\alpha^2}{bc' - b'c} = \frac{\alpha}{ca' - c'a} = \frac{1}{ab' - a'b}$$

From first two relations, we get: $\alpha = \dfrac{bc' - b'c}{ca' - c'a}$,

and from the last two relations, we get: $\alpha = \dfrac{ca' - c'a}{ab' - a'b}$

eliminating α, from these two obtained relations we get,

$$\frac{bc' - b'c}{ca' - c'a} = \frac{ca' - c'a}{ab' - a'b}$$

$$\Rightarrow (bc' - b'c)(ab' - a'b) = (ca' - c'a)^2$$

or $\begin{vmatrix} a & b \\ a' & b' \end{vmatrix} \times \begin{vmatrix} b & c \\ b' & c' \end{vmatrix} = \begin{vmatrix} c & a \\ c' & a' \end{vmatrix}^2$

(Remember this is the required condition for one root of two quadratic equations to be common).

This condition can easily be remembered by cross-multiplication method as shown in the following figure:

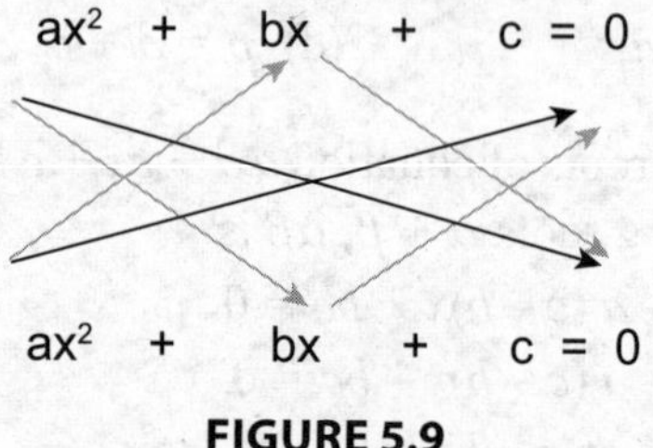

FIGURE 5.9

(Bigger cross product)² = Product of the two smaller crosses.

> **NOTE**
>
> *The common root can also be obtained by making the coefficient of x^2 common to the two given equations and then subtracting the two equations. The other roots of the given equations can be determined by using the relations between their roots and co-efficients.*

Condition for both roots to be common

If $\alpha + \beta = -b/a = -b'/a'$ and $\alpha\beta = c/a = c'/a'$ i.e., $\frac{a}{a'} = \frac{b}{b'} = \frac{c}{c'}$ this is the required condition for both roots of two quadratic equations to be identical.

NOTES

1. *If two quadratic equations with real coefficients have a non-real complex common root then both the roots will be common, i.e., both the equation will be the same. So the co-efficients of the corresponding powers of x will have proportional values.*
2. *If two quadratic equations with rational co-efficients have a common irrational root $p + \sqrt{q}$ then both the roots will be common, i.e., no two different quadratic equations with rational co-efficients can have a common irrational root $p + \sqrt{q}$.*
3. *If any one equation has all coefficients numerically known then find its roots and then proceed.*

ILLUSTRATION 36: Find the value of k, so that the equations $x^2 - x - 12 = 0$ and $kx^2 + 10x + 3 = 0$ may have one root in common. Also find the common root.

SOLUTION: Let α be the common root of two equations then $\alpha^2 - \alpha - 12 = 0$ and $k\alpha^2 + 10\alpha + 3 = 0$

Solving the two equations: $\dfrac{\alpha^2}{117} = \dfrac{\alpha}{-12k-3} = \dfrac{1}{10+k}$

$\Rightarrow (-12k - 3)^2 = 117(10 + k)$ $\qquad \Rightarrow (4k + 1)^2 = 13(10 + k)$

$\Rightarrow 16k^2 - 5k - 129 = 0$

or $(k - 3)(16k + 43) = 0$ $\qquad \therefore\ k = 3$ or $k = -43/16$

from (i) we have $\alpha = \dfrac{-12k-3}{10+k}$ Hence, $\alpha = -3$ or 4

Aliter: Roots of $x^2 - x - 12 = 0$ are 4 and -3, therefore if 4 is common root then $k = -43/16$ and when -3 is common root, then $k = 3$

ILLUSTRATION 37: If every pair of equations $x^2 + ax + bc = 0$, $x^2 + bx + ca = 0$, $x^2 + cx + ab = 0$ have a common root, then find the sum and product of these common roots.

SOLUTION: Let α, β be the roots of the first equation; α, γ the roots of the second and β, γ the roots of the third.

Since α is common root to the first and second equations, we have $\alpha^2 + a\alpha + bc = 0$ and $\alpha^2 + b\alpha + ca = 0$.

One subtracting these, we get $(a - b)\alpha + c(b - a) = 0$ i.e., $\alpha = c$. From the first equation, the product of roots $\alpha\beta = bc$, so $b = \beta$.

Similarly, from the second equation $\alpha\gamma = ca$, so that $\gamma = a$. Hence $\alpha . \beta . \gamma = abc$.

Hence $\alpha + \beta + \gamma = a + b + c$ and $\alpha\beta\gamma = abc$

ILLUSTRATION 38: If the equation $x^3 - 7x^2 + 11x + 3 = 0$ and $x^3 - 8x^2 + 15x = 4 = 0$ has a common root, then find their other roots.

SOLUTION: Let α be the common root of given equations.

$\Rightarrow \alpha^3 - 7\alpha^2 + 11\alpha + 3 = 0$ (i)

and $\alpha^3 - 8\alpha^2 + 15\alpha + 4 = 0$ (ii)

(i) – (ii) gives, $\alpha^2 - 4\alpha - 1 = 0$

$\Rightarrow \alpha = \dfrac{4 \pm \sqrt{16+4}}{2}$

$\Rightarrow \alpha = 2 \pm \sqrt{5}$ i.e., both roots $2 + \sqrt{5}$ and $2 - \sqrt{5}$ are common, as the irrational roots always exists in conjugate pairs.

Thus for equation $x^3 - 7x^2 + 11x + 3 = 0$, roots be $2 \pm \sqrt{5}$ and β

$\Rightarrow \left(2+\sqrt{5}\right)\left(2-\sqrt{5}\right)(\beta) = (-1)^3(3) = -3$

$\Rightarrow \beta = 3$ and for equation $x^3 - 8x^2 + 15x + 4 = 0$, roots be $2 \pm \sqrt{5}$ and γ

$\Rightarrow \left(2+\sqrt{5}\right)\left(2-\sqrt{5}\right)(\gamma) = (-1)^3 (4)$

$\Rightarrow \gamma = 4$

Thus respective roots are $2 \pm \sqrt{5}, 3 \text{ and } 2 \pm \sqrt{5}, 4$

THINK YOURSELF

On subtracting any two quadratic equation after making their leading coefficients same we get some value of x, even if the equations do not have that as a common root. What does that value represents?

ILLUSTRATION 39: If $x^2 + 3x + 5 = 0$ and $ax^2 + bx + c = 0$ have common roots $a, b, c \in \mathbb{N}$, then find the minimum value of $a + b + c$.

SOLUTION: The roots of $x^2 + 3x + 5 = 0$ are non-real. Thus the given equation will have two common roots.

We have $\frac{a}{1} = \frac{b}{3} = \frac{a}{5} = \lambda$.

$\Rightarrow a + b + c = 9\lambda$

Thus minimum value of $a + b + c$ is 9.

ILLUSTRATION 40: The equations $ax^2 + bx + a = 0$ and $x^3 - 2x^2 + 2x - 1 = 0$ have two roots common. Then find the value of $a + b$. Given a, b are real number.

SOLUTION: We have $x^3 - 2x^2 + 2x - 1 = 0$

$\Rightarrow (x - 1)(x^2 - x + 1) = 0$ $\Rightarrow x = 1$ or $x = -\omega, -\omega^2$

Since $ax^2 + bx + a = 0$ and $x^3 - 2x^2 + 2x - 1 = 0$ have two roots in common, therefore, $-\omega$ and $-\omega^2$ are common roots (as both the roots of a real quadratic equation are either real or non-real). Now, $-\omega$ is a root of $ax^2 + bx + a = 0$. Hence, $a(1 + \omega^2) - b\omega = 0$.

$\Rightarrow a(-\omega) - b\omega = 0$ (as $1 + \omega + \omega^2 = 0$)

$\Rightarrow a + b = 0$

ILLUSTRATION 41: If α, β are the roots of $x^2 + px + q = 0$ and γ, δ are the roots of $x^2 + rx + s = 0$, evaluate $(\alpha - \gamma)(\alpha - \delta)(\beta - \gamma)(\beta - \delta)$ in term of p, q, r and s. Deduce the condition that the equation may have a common root.

SOLUTION: $\alpha + \beta = -p; \alpha\beta = q; \gamma + \delta = -r; r\delta = s$

$\Rightarrow (\alpha - \gamma)(\alpha - \delta)(\beta - \gamma)(\beta - \delta) = \{\alpha^2 - \alpha(\gamma + \delta) + \gamma\delta\}\{\beta^2 - \beta(\gamma + \delta) + \gamma\delta\}$

$= (\alpha^2 + \alpha r + s)(\beta^2 + \beta r + s)$

$= (\alpha\beta)^2 + r(\alpha^2\beta + \beta^2\alpha) + s(\alpha^2 + \beta^2) + \alpha\beta r^2 + rs(\alpha + \beta) + s^2$

$= q^2 - prq + s\{p^2 - 2q\} + qr^2 - prs + s^2$

$= (s - q)^2 + q(r - p)^2 - p(s - q)(r - p) = (s - q)^2 + (r - p)(qr - ps)$

If the two equations have a common root, then either $\alpha = \gamma$ or $\alpha = \delta$ or $\beta = \gamma$ or $\beta = \delta$

Hence one of the factors of $(\alpha - \gamma)(\alpha - \delta)(\beta - \gamma)(\beta - \delta)$ must be zero. Therefore $(s - q)^2 + (r - p)(qr - ps) = 0$ is the condition for the equations to have a common root.

Condition for integer roots

If $a = 1$ and b, c are integers and the root of equation (i) are rational numbers, i.e., $D > 0$ and perfect square then these roots must be integers.

$\because \quad \alpha + \beta = -\dfrac{b}{a} \in \mathbb{Z}$ and $\alpha\beta = \dfrac{c}{a} \in \mathbb{Z}$

$\therefore \quad \alpha$ and β must be integers (if α and β are rational).

ILLUSTRATION 42: If $a, b \in \mathbb{Z}$ and $a^2 - 4b$ is perfect square then show that both roots of equation $x^2 + ax + b = 0$.

SOLUTION: Let $a^2 - 4b = k^2$ where $k \in \mathbb{Z}$

$\Rightarrow$ a and k both are integers of some parity i.e., either both odd or both even.

$\Rightarrow$ Roots α, β are given as $\dfrac{-a \pm \sqrt{a^2 - 4b}}{2} = \dfrac{-a \pm |k|}{2} \in \mathbb{Z}$

as a and $|k|$ are integers with same parity so $-a \pm |k|$ is always even.

ILLUSTRATION 43: Find the set of integer values of $a \in [-6, 6]$ for which $x^2 + ax + 1 = 0$ has both roots integer.

SOLUTION: Given equation $x^2 + ax + 1 = 0$.

Roots to be integer $a \in \mathbb{Z} \Rightarrow D$ has to be a perfect square and non-negative.

$\Rightarrow a^2 - 4 \geq 0$ and $a^2 - 4$ is perfect square

$\Rightarrow a \in [-6, -2] \cup [2, 6]$

$\Rightarrow a \in \{-6, -5, -4, -3, -2, 2, 3, 4, 5, 6\}$

$\therefore \quad a^2 - 4$ to be a perfect square; $a \in \{-2, 2\}$

■ APPLICATION OF QUADRATIC EXPRESSION

1. Rational factorization of 2*nd* degree equation

$ax^2 + 2hxy + by^2 + 2gx + 2fy + c$ in x and y may be resolved into two linear rational factors:

Proof: The quadratic expression $ax^2 + 2hxy + by^2 + 2gx + 2fy + c$ can be written in the form of the quadratic equation in x as $ax^2 + 2x(hy + g) + by^2 + 2fy + c = 0$.

Solving for x, we get,

$$x = \frac{-2(hy+g) \pm \sqrt{4(hy+g)^2 - 4a(by^2 + 2fy + c)}}{2a},$$

where $a \neq 0$

The given equation has rational linear factor only when quantity under the square root is perfect square. i.e., quadratic equation in y: $4(hy + g)^2 - 4a(by^2 + 2fy + c) = 0$ has real and equal roots. So its discriminant must be zero. i.e., $abc + 2fgh - af^2 - bg^2 - ch^2 = 0$

$$\text{or} \begin{vmatrix} a & h & g \\ h & b & f \\ g & f & c \end{vmatrix} = 0$$

ILLUSTRATION 44: For what values of m, will the expression $y^2 + 2xy + 2x + my - 3$ be capable of resolution into two rational linear factors?

SOLUTION: Comparing $y^2 + 2xy + 2x + my - 3 = 0$ with $ax^2 + 2hxy + by^2 + 2gx + 2fy + c = 0$, we have $a = 0, b = 1, c = -3, f = m/2, g = 1, h = 1$

The given expression is reducible into linear factors if $abc + 2fgh - af^2 - bg^2 - ch^2 = 0$

$\Rightarrow 0 + 2.m/2\ .1.1 - 0 - 1 + 3 = 0$

$\Rightarrow m + 2 = 0$ $\qquad\qquad \therefore \; m = -2$

Aliter: $\begin{vmatrix} 0 & 1 & 1 \\ 1 & 1 & m/2 \\ 1 & m/2 & -3 \end{vmatrix} = 0 \Rightarrow m = -2$

ILLUSTRATION 45: Show that the expression, $A(x^2 - y^2) - xy(B - C)$ always admits of two real linear factors.

SOLUTION: Equating the expression to zero, we get $A(x^2 - y^2) - xy(B - C) = 0$

$Ax^2 - xy(B - C) - Ay^2 = 0$

It is *a* 2nd degree equation and 2nd degree equation represents two linear factors if $abc + 2fgh - af^2 - bg^2 - ch^2 = 0$.

Thus $A(-A) \times 0 + 2(0) \times 0 \times 0 - A \times 0 + A \times 0 - 0 = 0$

Hence the given expression can be split up into two linear rational factors.

2. To find the domain and range of quadratic expressions

Consider the function $f(x) = ax^2 + bx + c$

If $a > 0$ then domain $= \mathbb{R}$ and Range$=\left[\frac{-D}{4a}, \infty\right)$

If $a < 0$ then domain $= \mathbb{R}$ and Range$=\left(-\infty, \frac{-D}{4a}\right]$

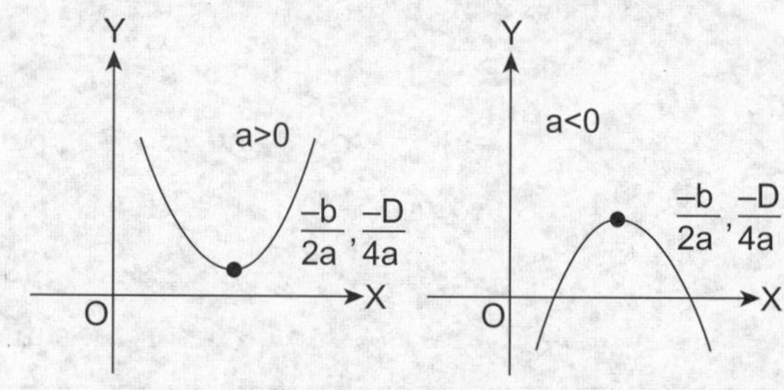

FIGURE 5.10

ILLUSTRATION 46: Find the range of following quadratic expression:

(i) $x^2 + 17x - 13$ $\qquad$ (ii) $-3x^2 + 4x - 5$

SOLUTION: (i) $\because a > 0 \Rightarrow$ Range $\left[\frac{-D}{4a} - \infty,\right)$

$$\frac{-D}{4a} = -\left(\frac{(17)^2 - 4\times(-13)}{4\times 1}\right) = -\left(\frac{289+52}{4}\right) = \frac{-341}{4}$$

$$\text{Range}=\left[\frac{-341}{4}, \infty\right)$$

(ii) For $-3x^2 + 4x - 5$; $a < 0$

$$\Rightarrow \text{Range} = \left(-\infty, \frac{-D}{4a}\right] \quad \frac{-D}{4a} = -\left(\frac{(4)^2 - 4\times(-3)\times(-5)}{-4\times 3}\right)$$

$$= -\left(\frac{16-60}{-4\times 3}\right) = -\left(\frac{-44}{-4\times 3}\right) = 11/3$$

$$\Rightarrow \text{Range} = \left(-\infty, \frac{-11}{3}\right]$$

3. To find the range of quadratic expression $ax^2 + bx + c$ in restricted domain

Consider $f(x) = ax^2 + bx + c$; $x \in [\alpha, \beta]$ and $a > 0$.

Evaluate $f(x)$ at α and β the following points and chose the least and greatest values of $f(x)$ as described below:

Case I: If $\beta < -\dfrac{b}{2a}$: $\because$ $f(x)$ is $\downarrow \forall x \in [\alpha, \beta]$

$\therefore \alpha \le x \le \beta \quad \Rightarrow f(x) \in [f(\beta), f(\alpha)]$

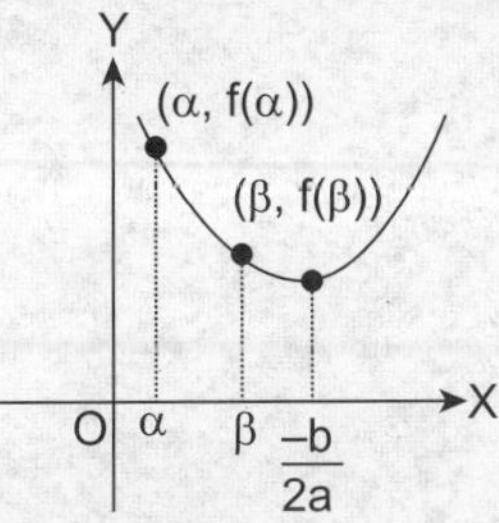

FIGURE 5.11

Case II: If $\alpha > -\dfrac{b}{2a}$: $\quad \because$ $f(x)$ is $\uparrow \forall x \in [\alpha, \beta]$

$\therefore \alpha \le x \le \beta \quad \Rightarrow f(\alpha) \le f(x) \le f(\beta)]$

$\Rightarrow f(x) \in [f(\alpha), f(\beta)]$

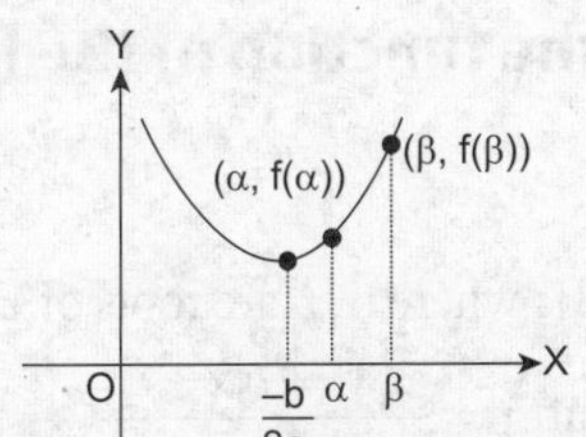

FIGURE 5.12

Case (iii): If $x = -\dfrac{b}{2a} \in (\alpha, \beta)$; then find $f\left(\dfrac{-b}{2a}\right) = \dfrac{-D}{4a}$

Clearly $f(x) \in \left[-\dfrac{D}{4a}, \max\{f(\alpha), f(\beta)\}\right]$

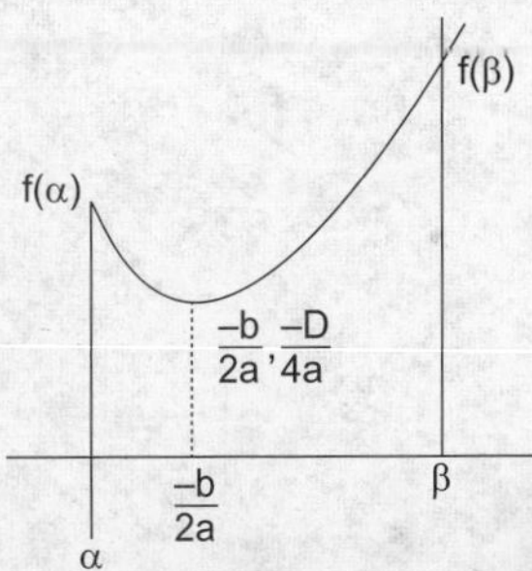

FIGURE 5.13

ILLUSTRATION 47: Find the range of $x^2 + 17x - 13 \ \forall x \in [1,2]$.

SOLUTION: $f(1) = 5$; $f(2) = 25$

Now $-\dfrac{b}{2a} = -\dfrac{17}{2 \times (-13)} = \dfrac{17}{26} \notin [1,2]$ and $-\dfrac{b}{2a} < 1$

$\therefore$ min value = 5 and max = 25

$\therefore$ Range = [5,25]

ILLUSTRATION 48: Find the range of $-3x^2 + 4x - 5 \ \forall x \in (0,2]$.

SOLUTION: $f(0) = -5 \quad \because \quad x \ne 0$ and only approaching towards 0.

$\Rightarrow \lim_{x \to 0} f(x) \to -5$

$f(2) = -3(2)^2 + 4(2) - 5 = -9$

$\dfrac{-b}{2a} = \dfrac{-4}{2 \times (-3)} = \dfrac{2}{3}$ and

$\because \dfrac{2}{3} \in (0,2]$

$\therefore f\left(\dfrac{-b}{2a}\right) = \dfrac{-D}{4a} = \dfrac{-11}{3}$

$\therefore$ min value = −9 and max value = −11/3

$\Rightarrow$ Range [−9,−11/3]

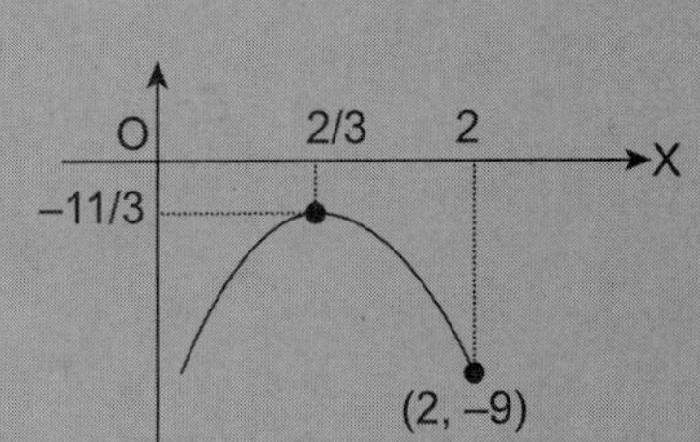

FIGURE 5.14

4. Consider the function of the form $\dfrac{a_1x^2+b_1x+c_1}{a_2x^2+b_2x+c_2}$

domain: $\mathbb{R} \sim \{\alpha, \beta\}$; where α, b are roots of $a_2x^2 + b_2x + c_2 \neq 0$

For range: Put $y=\dfrac{a_1x^2+b_1x+c_1}{a_2x^2+b_2x+c_2}$

Cross-multiply and form a quadratic in x (containing terms of y). And apply the condition x to be real $D \geq 0$.

Which will give a required quadratic inequality in y and from that, we will be able to get the range of the rational function, as set of all possible values of y.

ILLUSTRATION 49: Find the range of rational expression $y=\dfrac{x^2-x+1}{x^2+x+1}$ if x is real.

SOLUTION: $y=\dfrac{x^2-x+1}{x^2+x+1} \Rightarrow (y-1)x^2+(y+1)x+y-1=0$ (1)

Case (i) If $y \neq 1$, then equation (i) is quadratic in x

And $\because$ x is real $\therefore$ $D \geq 0$

$\Rightarrow (y+1)^2-4(y-1)^2 \geq 0 \Rightarrow (y-3)(3y-1) \leq 0$

$\therefore\ y \in \left[\dfrac{1}{3}, 3\right]-\{1\}$

Case (ii) If $y = 1$, then equations becomes $2x = 0 \Rightarrow x = 0$ which is possible as x is real

$\therefore$ Range $\left[\dfrac{1}{3}, 3\right]$

ILLUSTRATION 50: Find the range of $y=\dfrac{x+2}{2x^2+3x+6}$, if x is real.

SOLUTION: $y=\dfrac{x+2}{2x^2+3x+6}$

$\Rightarrow 2yx^2+3yx+6y=x+2$ $\Rightarrow 2yx^2+(3y-1)x+6y-2=0$ (i)

Case (i) If $y \neq 0$, then equation (i) is quadratic in x

$\therefore$ x is real $\Rightarrow D \geq 0$

$\Rightarrow (3y-1)^2-8y(6y-2) \leq 0$ $\Rightarrow (3y-1)^2(13y+1) \leq 0$

$y \in \left[-\dfrac{1}{13}, \dfrac{1}{3}\right]-\{0\}$

Case (ii) If $y = 0$, then equation becomes $x = -2$ which is possible as x is real

$\therefore$ Range $y \in \left[-\dfrac{1}{13}, \dfrac{1}{3}\right]$

ILLUSTRATION 51: Find the range of the expression $\dfrac{x^2-4x+3}{x^2-7x+6}$, for $x \in \mathbb{R}$.

SOLUTION: $\dfrac{x^2-4x+3}{x^2-7x+6}=\dfrac{(x-1)(x-3)}{(x-1)(x-6)}=\dfrac{x-3}{x-6},\ x \neq 1,6$

Let $y=\dfrac{x-3}{x-6} \Rightarrow x-3=xy-6y$ $\Rightarrow x=\dfrac{3-6y}{1-y} \Rightarrow y \in R-\{1\}$

For $x = 1$, $y = \dfrac{1-3}{1-6} \Rightarrow y = \dfrac{2}{5}$; but original expression do not assume this value as 1 does not lie in its domain.

Hence range of expression will be $R - \left\{1, \dfrac{2}{5}\right\}$.

ILLUSTRATION 52: If $\dfrac{x^2+ax+3}{x^2+x+a}$ takes all real values for possible real values of x then prove that $4a^2 + 39 < 0$.

SOLUTION: Let $\dfrac{x^2+ax+3}{x^2+x+a} = y$

$\Rightarrow x^2(1-y) - x(y-a) + 3 - ay = 0$

For x to be real $(y \quad a)^2 \quad 4(1 \quad y)(3 \quad ay) \geq 0$

$\Rightarrow y^2 + a^2 - 2ay - 4(3 - ay - 3y + ay^2) \geq 0$ for all real y

$\Rightarrow y^2(1-4a) + y(4a + 12 - 2a) + a^2 - 12 \geq 0 \ \forall\ y \in \mathbb{R}$

For above expression to be true for all values of y, $1 - 4a > 0$ and $D \leq 0$ i.e.,

$a < 1/4$ and $4(a+6)^2 - 4(a^2-12)(1-4a) \leq 0$

i.e., $(a+6)^2 - (a^2 - 4a^3 - 12 + 48a) \leq 0$

$\Rightarrow a^2 + 12a + 36 - a^2 + 4a^3 + 12 - 48a \leq 0$

or, $4a^3 - 36a + 48 \leq 0$, or $4a^3 \leq 36a - 48$

or, $4a^3 < -39$ (as $< 1/4$) $\Rightarrow 4a^3 + 39 < 0$

ILLUSTRATION 53: If $(y^2 - 5y + 3)(x^2 + x + 1) < 2x$ for all $x \in \mathbb{R}$, then show the interval in which y lies is $\left(\dfrac{5-\sqrt{5}}{2}, \dfrac{5+\sqrt{5}}{2}\right)$.

SOLUTION: $(y^2 - 5y + 3)(x^2 + x + 1) < 2x$ for all $x \in \mathbb{R}$

$\Rightarrow y^2 - 5y + 3 < \dfrac{2x}{x^2+x+1}$ for all $x \in \mathbb{R}$

Let $\dfrac{2x}{x^2+x+1} = p \Rightarrow px^2 + (p-2)x + p = 0$

Since x is real, $(p-2)^2 - 4p^2 \geq 0$

$\Rightarrow -2 \leq p \leq 2/3$

Minimum value of $\dfrac{2x}{x^2+x+1}$ is -2

So, $y^2 - 5y + 3 < -2 \Rightarrow y^2 - 5y + 5 < 0$

$\Rightarrow y \in \left(\dfrac{5-\sqrt{5}}{2}, \dfrac{5+\sqrt{5}}{2}\right)$

ILLUSTRATION 54: If the inequality $\dfrac{mx^2+3x+4}{x^2+2x+2} < 5$ is satisfied for all $x \in \mathbb{R}$, then

(a) $1 < m < 5$
(b) $-1 < m < 5$
(c) $1 < m < 6$
(d) $m < 71/24$

SOLUTION: We have $x^2 + 2x + 2 = (x + 1)^2 + 1 > 0 \, \forall x \in \mathbb{R}$.

Therefore, $\dfrac{mx^2+3x+4}{x^2+2x+2} < 5 \Rightarrow mx^2 + 3x + 4 < 5\,(x^2 + 2x + 2)$

$\Rightarrow (m-5)x^2 - 7x - 6 < 0, \forall x \in \mathbb{R}$

This is possible if $D = b^2 - 4ac = 49 + 24\,(m-5) < 0$ and $m - 5 < 0$

$\Rightarrow$ m < 71/24 and m < 5 $\Rightarrow m \in (-\infty, 71/24)$

Hence (d) is the correct answer

5. To find the value of x and y for where an equation of the type $ax^2 + by^2 + 2gx + 2fy + 2hxy + c = 0$ is valid

Now, the above equation can be written in the terms of a quadratic in x i.e., $ax^2 + x(2g + 2hy) + (by^2 + 2fy + c) = 0$ and $\because$ for real input x the, the discriminant D must be non-negative.

$\Rightarrow D \geq 0$

$\Rightarrow (2g + 2hy)^2 - 4\,(by^2 + 2fy + c)a \geq 0$

Which will give the all posible value of y, that expression can generate.

Similarly, for finding the required value of x; we can also represent the above equation as a quadratic in y.

i.e., $by^2 + y\,(2f + 2hx) + (ax^2 + 2gx + c) = 0$ and here also $D \geq 0$

$\Rightarrow (2f + 2hx)^2 - 4\,(ax^2 + 2gx + c)\,(b) \geq 0$

Which will return all possible values of x which generate real y.

ILLUSTRATION 55: Find the value of x, y for which the equation $x^2 - 3xy + 2y^2 - 2x - 3y - 35 = 0$.

SOLUTION: $x^2 + x\,(-3y - 2) + (2y^2 - 3y - 35) = 0$

$D \geq 0 \Rightarrow (3y + 2)^2 - 4\,(2y^2 - 3y - 35) \geq 0$

$\Rightarrow 9y^2 + 4 + 12y - 8y^2 + 12y + 140 \geq 0$

$\Rightarrow y^2 + 24y + 144 \geq 0$

$\Rightarrow (y + 12)^2 \geq 0$

which is true for all $y \in R$

Similarly, $2y^2 + y\,(-3x - 3) + (x^2 - 2x - 35) = 0$

$D \geq 0 \Rightarrow (3x + 3)^2 - 4\,(x^2 - 2x - 35)\,(2) \geq 0$

$\Rightarrow 9x^2 + 9 + 18x - 8x^2 + 16x + 280 \geq 0$

$\Rightarrow x^2 + 34x + 289 \geq 0 \Rightarrow (x + 17)^2 \geq 0$

which is true for all $x \in \mathbb{R}$. Hence the above equation is valid for all $x, y \in \mathbb{R}$. In other words, we can say that for every real x, there is real value of y and for every real y, there is a real value of x.

TEXTUAL EXERCISE–5 (SUBJECTIVE)

1. Find the value of parameter k so that
   (a) $x^2 - 3x + 2 = 0$ has a common root with $x^2 - (2k + 1)x + k = 0$
   (b) $x^2 - 2kx + 3 = 0$ has a common root with $x^2 - 5x + 4 = 0$.

2. If the roots of $a_1x^2 + b_1x + c_1 = 0$ are α_1, β_1 and those of $a_2x^2 + b_2x + c_2 = 0$ are α_2, β_2, such that $\alpha_1.\alpha_2 = \beta_1.\beta_2 = 1$ then prove that $\dfrac{a_1}{c_2} = \dfrac{b_1}{b_2} = \dfrac{c_1}{a_2}$.

3. Let a, b, c are the sides of ΔABC, predict the nature of triangle if $ax^2 + bx + c$ has a common root with the equations:
   (i) $x^2 + x + 1 = 0$
   (ii) $x^2 + x\sqrt{2} + 1 = 0$
   (iii) $3x^2 + 4x + 5 = 0$
   (iv) $x^2 + 3x + 5 = 0$

4. Prove that if p and q are odd numbers, then the equation $x^{10} + px^9 + q = 0$ does not have integral solutions.

5. If $2x^2 + 3x + 4 = 0$ and $ax^2 + bx + c = 0$, where $a, b, c \in N$ have a common root, then find the least value of $a + b + c$.

6. If $x^2 - bx + c = 0$ has equal integral roots then prove that b and c both are integers where b is even and c is a perfect square.

7. If $ax^2 + bx + c = p$ has both roots integer then show that $ax^2 + bx + c = 2p$ can never have both integral roots where p is a prime number $p \neq a$ and $a \neq 1$.

8. Find all integral values of a for which the quadratic expression $(x - a)(x - 10) + 1$ can be factored as a product $(x + \alpha)(x + \beta)$ of two factors and $\alpha, \beta \in \mathbb{Z}$.

9. If each pair of the following three equations $x^2 + ax + b = 0$, $x^2 + cx + d = 0$ and $x^2 + ex + f = 0$ has exactly one root in common, then show that $(a + c + e)^2 = 4(ac + ce + ea - b - d - f)$.

10. Find k if
    (i) $x^2 + ky^2 + 3xy - x - 2y = 0$
    (ii) $x^2 + 4xy + 4y^2 + 2kx + 4y + 1 = 0$
    can be represented as a product of two rational factors.

11. Find the range of x and y of the equations: $x^2 + 4xy + 4y^2 + 2kx + 4y + 1 = 0$

12. If $x + y + z = 6$, $xy + yz + zx = 7$, find range of x, y, z where $x, y, z \in \mathbb{R}$.

13. Find the range of following quadratic expressions:
    (i) $f(x) = -x^2 + 2x + 3 \quad \forall x \in \mathbb{R}$
    (ii) $f(x) = x^2 - 2x + 3 \quad \forall x \in [0, 2]$
    (iii) $f(x) = x^2 - 4x + 6 \quad \forall x \in [0, 1]$

14. If x be real, then find the range of the following rational expressions:
    (i) $y = \dfrac{x^2 + x + 1}{x^2 + 1}$
    (ii) $y = \dfrac{x^2 - 2x + 9}{x^2 + 2x + 9}$

Answer Keys

1. (a) $k = 2/3, 0$ (b) $k = 2, 19/8$
3. (i) equilateral triangle (ii) Isosceles right angled triangle (iii) right angled triangle (iv) triangle does not exist
5. 9
8. 8, 12
10. (i) 2 (ii) 1
11. (i) $x \in [-\sqrt{5}, \sqrt{5}], y \in [-\sqrt{2}, \sqrt{2}]$ (ii) $x, y, \in \mathbb{R}$
12. $x, y, z \in \left[\dfrac{6-\sqrt{60}}{3}, \dfrac{6+\sqrt{60}}{3}\right]$
13. (i) $(-\infty, 4]$ (ii) $[2, 3]$ (iii) $[3, 6]$
14. (i) $\left[\dfrac{1}{2}, \dfrac{3}{2}\right]$ (ii) $\left[\dfrac{1}{2}, 2\right]$

TEXTUAL EXERCISE–5 (OBJECTIVE)

1. The values of λ so that the following equations $x^2 - x - 12 = 0$ and $\lambda x^2 + 10x + 3 = 0$ a common root is
   (a) 3, 1 (b) 3, –43/16
   (c) 3, –16/43 (d) None of these

2. Let a, b, c are sides of ΔABC then nature of triangle if $ax^2 + bx + c = 0$ has common roots with equation
   (i) $3x^2 + x + 3 = 0$
   (a) right angle triangle
   (b) isosceles triangle
   (c) equilateral triangle
   (d) None of these
   (ii) $5x^2 + 12x + 13 = 0$
   (a) right angle triangle

(b) isosceles triangle
(c) equilateral triangle
(d) None of these

(iii) $2x^2 + 3x + 5 = 0$
(a) right angle triangle
(b) isosceles triangle
(c) scalene triangle
(d) ΔABC does not exists

3. If the quadratic equations $ax^2 + 2cx + b = 0$ and $ax^2 + 2bx + c = 0$ $(b \neq c)$ have a common root, then $a + 4b + 4c$ is equal to
(a) –2 (b) –1
(c) 0 (d) 1

4. The value of k for which the equations $x^3 + x^2 - 4x - k = 0$ and $x^2 + x - 2 = 0$ have a common root
(a) 2 (b) 4
(c) –2 (d) 4

5. If equations $ax^2 + bx + c = 0$ and $x^2 + 2x + 3 = 0$ have a common root, then a: b: c is
(a) 1 : 2 : 3 (b) 3 : 2 : 1
(c) 4 : 9 : 16 (d) None of these

6. If the equation $ax^2 + bx + c = 0$ and $x^3 - 2x^2 + 2x - 1 = 0$ have two common roots, then
(a) $a = b \neq c$ (b) $a = -b = c$
(c) $a = b = c$ (d) None of these

7. For what integral values of a, the eqn. $x^2 - x(1 - a) - (a + 2) = 0$ has integral roots. The roots are
(a) For $a = -2$; (0, 3), for $a = 0$; (–1, 2)
(b) For $a = -2$; (0, 2), for $a = 0$; (–1, 1)
(c) For $a = -2$; (0, 3), for $a = 0$; (–1, 1)
(d) None of these

8. Consider $y = \dfrac{2x}{1+x^2}$, where x is real, then the range of expression $y^2 + y - 2$ is
(a) [–1, 1] (b) [0, 1]
(c) [–9/4, 0] (d) [–9/4, 1]

9. The least value of expression $x^2 + 2xy + 2y^2 + 4y + 7$ is
(a) –1 (b) 1
(c) 3 (d) 7

10. $12x^2 - 10xy + 2y^2 + 11x - 5y + k$ is resolvable into two linear factors. Then k =
(a) 1 (b) 2
(c) 4 (d) –2

Answer Keys

1. (b) **2.** (i) b (ii) (a) (iii) (d) **3.** (c) **4.** (b, c) **5.** (a) **6.** (c) **7.** (a) **8.** (c) **9.** (c) 10. (b)

■ EXPRESSION REDUCIBLE TO QUADRATIC FORM

Involving variable as powers

In these questions, a particular number with some variable power is (exponential function) substituted as a new variable, in order to make the equation quadratic in new variable. Or we can say that, if we have an equation of the form $a^x = b$ $(a > 0)$, then

(i) $x \in \{\ \}$ if $b \leq 0$
(ii) $x = \log_a b$ if $b > 0$, $a \neq 1$
(iii) $x \in \{\ \}$ if $a = 1$, $b \neq 1$
(iv) $x = \mathbb{R}$ if $a = 1$, $b = 1$ Since $(1^x = 1 \forall x \in \mathbb{R})$

These kind of equations may appear in following types:

Type I: An equation of the form $a^{f(x)} = 1$, $a > 0$, $a \neq 1$ is equivalent to the equation $f(x) = 0$

Type II: An equation of the form $f(a^x) = 0$ is equivalent to the equation $f(z) = 0$ when $z = a^x$

If $z_1, z_2, \ldots\ldots, z_k$ are the roots of $f(z) = 0$, then $a^x = z_1$, $a^x = z_2, \ldots\ldots, a^x = z_k$

Type III: An equation of the form $\alpha a^{f(x)} + \beta b^{f(x)} + \gamma c^{f(x)} = 0$ where $\alpha, \beta, \gamma \in R$ and $\alpha, \beta, \gamma \neq 0$ and the bases satisfy the condition $b^2 = ac$ is equivalent to the equation $\alpha z^2 + \beta z + \gamma = 0$ when $z = (b/c)^{f(x)}$. If roots of this equation are z_1 and z_2 then $(b/c)^{f(x)} = z_1$ and $(b/c)^{f(x)} = z_2$

Type IV: An equation of the form $\alpha a^{f(x)} + \beta b^{f(x)} + c = 0$ when $\alpha, \beta, c \in R$ and $\alpha, \beta, c \neq 0$ and $ab = 1$ (a and b are +ve reciprocals) is equivalent to the equation $\alpha z^2 + cz + \beta = 0$ when $z = a^{f(x)}$. If roots of this equation are z_1 and z_2, then $a^{f(x)} = z_1$ and $a^{f(x)} = z_2$ will give the equivalent equations for $f(x)$.

Type V: An equation of the form $a^{f(x)} + b^{f(x)} = c$ where $a, b, c \in \mathbb{R}$ and a, b, c satisfies the condition $a^2 + b^2 = c$, then solution of the equation is $f(x) = 2$ and no other solution of this equation.

Type VI: An equation of the form $\{f(x)\}^{g(x)}$ is equivalent to the equation $\{f(x)\}^{g(x)} = 10^{g(x)\log f(x)}$; where $f(x) > 0$ and $\log_{10}$ used is common log i.e., having base 10..

ILLUSTRATION 56: Solve $2^{\sin^2 x} - 2^{\cos^2 x} = 1$.

SOLUTION: Let $2^{\sin^2 x} = z \Rightarrow 2^{\cos^2 x} = 2/z \Rightarrow z - 2/z = 1$

$\Rightarrow (z-2)(z+1) = 0 \Rightarrow z = 2$ or $z = -1$

$\Rightarrow 2^{\sin^2 x} = 2$ or $2^{\sin^2 x} = -1$ (not possible)

$\Rightarrow \sin^2 x = 1 \Rightarrow x = (2n \pm 1)\dfrac{\pi}{2}$, $n \in \mathbb{Z}$

ILLUSTRATION 57: Solve the equation $64.9^x - 84.12^x + 27.16^x = 0$.

SOLUTION: Here $9 \times 16 = (12)^2$

Then we divide its both sides by 12^x and obtain

$\Rightarrow 64.(3/4)^x - 84 + 27.(4/3)^x = 0$ (i)

Let $(3/4)^x = t$, then equation (i) reduces in the form

$64t^2 - 84t + 27 = 0$ therefore roots are $t = 3/4$ or $9/16$

then $(3/4)^x = (3/4)^1$ or $(3/4)^x = (3/4)^2$ $\Rightarrow x = 1$ or $x = 2$

$\Rightarrow$ Roots of the original equation are 1 and 2.

ILLUSTRATION 58: Solve the equation $15.2^{x+1} + 15.2^{2-x} = 135$.

SOLUTION: $15.2^{x+1} + 15.2^{2-x} = 135 \Rightarrow 30.2^x + \dfrac{60}{2^x} = 135$

Let $t = 2^x$, then $30.t^2 - 135t + 60 = 0$ $\Rightarrow 6.t^2 - 27t + 12 = 0$

$\Rightarrow 6.t^2 - 24t - 3t + 12 = 0$ $\Rightarrow (t-4)(6t-3) = 0$ $\Rightarrow t = 4$ or $t = 1/2$

Thus equation is equivalent to $2^x = 4$ and $2^x = 1/2$ $\Rightarrow x = -1, 2$

Hence roots of the original equation are 2 and -1.

Involving logarithms

By using basic definition of logarithm i.e., $\log_a b = x \Rightarrow a^x = b \; \forall \; a, b > 0$ and $a \neq 1$, we change logarithmic equation to exponential equation and proceed, but if equation or inequation compares two different logarithmic expressions and they have the same base, we use following basic theorem

i.e., $\log_a x > \log_a y$

$\Rightarrow x > y$ if $a > 1$ and $x < y$ if $0 < a < 1$

and $\log_a x = \log_a y$ $\Rightarrow x = y \; \forall \; a > 0, \neq 1$

ILLUSTRATION 59: Solve $\log_3 (3^x - 8) = 2 - x$

SOLUTION: Given equation is $\log_3(3^x - 8) = \log_3(3^{2-x})$

$\Rightarrow 3^x - 8 = 3^{2-x} = \dfrac{9}{3^x}$; put $3^x = z$; $z - 8 = \dfrac{9}{z}$

$\Rightarrow z^2 - 8z - 9 = 0$ $\Rightarrow (z-9)(z+1) = 0$

$\Rightarrow z = 9$ and $z = -1$ $\Rightarrow 3^x = 9$

$\Rightarrow x = 2$ which is the only solution ($\because z = -1 \Rightarrow 3^x = -1$ which is not possible)

Involving modulus

By using the basic definition of modulus i.e.,

$$|f(x)| = \begin{cases} f(x) & \forall x: f(x) > 0 \\ -f(x) & \forall x: f(x) < 0 \end{cases}$$

To find x such that $f(x)$ is > or < 0 we use Wavy curve method if $f(x)$ can be factorized, or any other suitable method. The equation involving modulus may appear in the following types:

Type I: The equation of the form $f(|x|) = g(x)$ is equivalent to the system of equation

$$\begin{cases} f(x) = g(x), & \text{if } x \geq 0 \\ f(-x) = g(x), & \text{if } x < 0 \end{cases}$$

Type II: The equation of the form $|f(x)| = g(x)$ is equivalent to the system of equation

$$\begin{cases} f(x) = g(x), & \text{if } g(x) \geq 0, f(x) \geq 0 \\ -f(x) = g(x), & \text{if } g(x) \geq 0, f(x) \leq 0 \end{cases}$$

e.g., the equation of the type $|f(x)| = k$, $k \in \mathbb{R}$ is equivalent to the system of equation.

$$\begin{cases} \text{no solution;} & \text{when } k < 0 \\ f(x) = 0; & \text{when } k = 0 \\ f(x) = k; & \text{when } k, f(x) < 0 \\ f(x) = -k; & \text{when } k > 0, f(x) < 0 \end{cases}$$

Type III: The equation of the form $h(|f(x)|) = g(x)$ (when h is the function of $|f(x)|$ is equivalent to the system of equation)

$$\begin{cases} h(f(x)) = g(x), & \text{if } f(x) \geq 0 \\ h(-f(x)) = g(x), & \text{if } f(x) < 0 \end{cases}$$

Type IV: The equation of the form $|f_1(x)| + |f_2(x)| + |f_3(x)| + \ldots\ldots + |f_n(x)| = g(x)$ when $f_1(x), f_2(x), \ldots\ldots, f_n(x), g(x)$ are functions of x and $g(x)$ may be a constant. Equations of this form is solved by the method of intervals. We first find all critical points of $f_1(x), f_2(x), \ldots\ldots, f_n(x)$. We pass from equation (i) to a collection of systems which do not contain the modulus sign).

NOTE

If $|f(x) + g(x) + h(x)| = |f(x)| + |g(x)| + |h(x)|$
If f(x), g(x), h(x) are all non-positive or all non-negative

ILLUSTRATION 60: Solve $|x^2 - 3| + |2 - x| = |x^2 - x - 1|$.

SOLUTION: $|x^2 - x - 1| = |(x^2 - 3) + (2 - x)|$ Now, $|a| + |b| = |a + b|$ iff $ab \geq 0$

This is true $\forall x$ which is satisfying the inequality

$\Rightarrow (x^2 - 3)(2 - x) \geq 0$

$\Rightarrow (x - \sqrt{3})(x + \sqrt{3})(x - 2) = 0$

$\Rightarrow x \in (-\infty, -\sqrt{3}] \cup [\sqrt{3}, 2]$

ILLUSTRATION 61: Solve the equation $x^2 - 5|x| + 6 = 0$.

SOLUTION: The given equation is equivalent to the system of equation

$$\Rightarrow \begin{cases} x^2 - 5x + 6 = 0, & \text{if } x \geq 0 \\ x^2 + 5x + 6 = 0, & \text{if } x < 0 \end{cases} \quad \Rightarrow \begin{cases} (x-2)(x-3) = 0 & \text{if } x \geq 0 \\ (x+2)(x+3) = 0 & \text{if } x < 0 \end{cases}$$

Hence the solutions of the given equation are $x_1 = 2$, $x_2 = 3$, $x_3 = -2$, $x_4 = -3$.

Equation of the form $(a+\sqrt{b})^{Q(x)} + (a-\sqrt{b})^{Q(x)-2k} = p$, where $a^2 - b = 1$, $(k \in \mathbb{Z})$

ILLUSTRATION 62: Find the solutions of $(2+\sqrt{3})^{x^2-2x+1}+(2-\sqrt{3})^{x^2-2x-1}=\dfrac{4}{2-\sqrt{3}}$.

SOLUTION: Given equation is $(2+\sqrt{3})^2\times(2+\sqrt{3})^{x^2-2x-1}+\dfrac{1}{(2+\sqrt{3})^{x^2-2x-1}}=4(2+\sqrt{3})$

Let $(2+\sqrt{3})^{x^2-2x-1}=y$

So, equation becomes, $(2+\sqrt{3})^2\,y+\dfrac{1}{y}=4(2+\sqrt{3})$

i.e., $((2+\sqrt{3})^2y^2-4(2+\sqrt{3})y+1=0$, As the sum of the co-efficients $=0 \Rightarrow y=1$ is a root

If the other root is α, then $\alpha.\ 1=\dfrac{c}{a}=\dfrac{1}{(2+\sqrt{3})^2}$

$\Rightarrow y=1$ or $(2+\sqrt{3})^{-2}$. Now $(2+\sqrt{3})^{x^2-2x-1}=1$ and $(2+\sqrt{3})^{x^2-2x-1}=(2+\sqrt{3})^{-2}$

$\Rightarrow x=1\pm\sqrt{2}$ and $x=1$

RATIONAL AND IRRATIONAL EQUATIONS

A rational/irrational expression when equated to zero, is called rational/irrational equation. i.e., $\dfrac{2x-1}{x+3}=0$ is a rational equation whereas $\sqrt{2x+1}=x$ is an irrational equation. While solving such equations, following concepts are needed:

1. **Equivalent equations:** Two equations $f_1(x)=g_1(x)$ and $f_2(x)=g_2(x)$ are equivalent if the sets of all their solutions are coincident or neither of them has a solution. It follows from the definition of the equivalence of equations that instead of solving a given equation, we can solve an equivalent equation.

   The concept of equivalence possesses the property of transitivity, i.e., if the equation $f(x)=g(x)$ is equivalent to $\alpha(x)=\beta(x)$, and the equation $\alpha(x)=\beta(x)$ is equivalent to $m(x)=p(x)$, then the equation $f(x)=g(x)$ is equivalent to $m(x)=p(x)$. A replacement of an equation by an equivalent equation or by an equivalent collection of equations (inequalities system) is an equivalent transition.

2. **Domain of equation and extraneous roots:** Set of the values of independent variables x for which each function used in the equation is defined i.e., it takes up finite real values. While solving an equation one must take care of the fact that, the final solution obtained while solving any equation must satisfy the domain of the parent equation. Consider an equation $\sqrt{5-x}=x+1$ squaring both sides, we get

   $5-x=x^2+2x+1 \Rightarrow x^2+3x-4$

   $\Rightarrow x=\dfrac{-3\pm\sqrt{25}}{2}=\dfrac{-3+5}{2},\dfrac{-3-5}{2}=1,-4.$

   But at $x=-4$ the equation does not remain valid due to RHS being – ve and LHS being + ve quantity. Thus $x=1$ is the only solution.

NOTE

The transformation leading to expansion of domain of equation e.g., squaring etc., should be avoided; if it is not possible then the final solution obtained must be cross-verified to satisfy the original equation.

3. **Misconception and loss of roots:** Cancellation of common factors from both sides of equation or many other such transformation may lead to loss of roots and while writing the answer; proper care should be taken to reaccomodate the roots which are lost in the process e.g., consider an equation

   $x^2-3x=2x-6 \Rightarrow x(x-3)=2(x-3)$

   $\Rightarrow x=2$ is an incomplete solution.

   Correct way of solving it is as floloows:

   $x^2-3x=2x-6 \Rightarrow x(x-3)-2(x-3)=0$

   $\Rightarrow (x-3)(x-2)=0$

   $\Rightarrow x-3=0$ or $x-2=0$ i.e., $x=2$ or 3

Irrational equations

Here we consider equations of the type which contain the unknown under the radical sign and the value under the radical sign is known as radicand. e.g., $\sqrt{2x-3}$, here $2x-3$ is radicand.

NOTES

1. *If radical (i.e., $\sqrt{x}, \sqrt[4]{x}, \sqrt[6]{x}$,...... etc.) of an equation are all even, then equation is defined only for non-negative values of radicand. In other words,*

   if the radicand is negative (i.e., $x < 0$), then the root is imaginary.

   If the radicand is zero, then the root is also zero.

   If the radicand is positive, then the value of the root is positive as well as negative.

2. *If radicals (i.e, ($\sqrt[3]{x}, \sqrt[5]{x}, \sqrt[7]{x}$,.....etc.) of an equation are all odd, then it is defined for all real values of the radicand. If the radicand is negative, then the root is negative.*

If the radicand is zero, then the root is zero.

If the radicand is positive, then the root is positive.

Method of solving irrational equations and inequations

Step 1: Reduce the given irrational (equation or inequality) to an equivalent system of (rational equation or inequalities) including the domains of functions involved.

Step 2: Solve the reduced system of rational equalities and inequalities and find the common solutions.

Some standard formulae to solve irrational equations

If f and g be functions of x and k is a natural number, then following results hold good.

1. $\sqrt[2k]{f}\ \sqrt[2k]{g} = \sqrt[2k]{fg}$ if $f \geq 0, g \geq 0$
2. $\dfrac{\sqrt[2k]{f}}{\sqrt[2k]{g}} = \sqrt[2k]{f/g}$ if $f \geq 0, g > 0$
3. $|f|\sqrt[2k]{g} = \sqrt[2k]{f^{2k}g}$ if $g \geq 0$
4. $\sqrt[2k]{f/g} = \dfrac{\sqrt[2k]{|f|}}{\sqrt[2k]{|g|}}$ if $fg \geq 0, g \neq 0$
5. $\sqrt[2k]{fg} = \sqrt[2k]{|f|}\sqrt[2k]{|g|}$ if $fg \geq 0,$

ILLUSTRATION 63: Solve the irrational equation $\sqrt{3x-2} = 4$.

SOLUTION: Domain of L.H.S. function is $\{x: 3x - 2 \geq 0\} = \{x: x \geq 2/3\} = [2/3, \infty)$

Squaring the given equation, we get, $3x - 2 = 16 \quad \Rightarrow 3x = 18 \Rightarrow x = 6 \in [2/3, \infty)$

ILLUSTRATION 64: Solve $\sqrt{x-2} + \sqrt{7-x} = 3$.

SOLUTION: For the domain of functions involved on L.H.S

We must have, $x - 2 \geq 0 \quad \Rightarrow x \in [2, \infty)$ (i)

and $7 - x \geq 0 \quad \Rightarrow x \leq 7$

$\Rightarrow x \in (-\infty, 7]$ (ii)

From the given equation, we have, $\sqrt{x-2} = 3 - \sqrt{7-x}$

Squaring, $(x - 2) = 9 + (7 - x) - 6\sqrt{7-x}$

$\Rightarrow -18 + 2x = -6\sqrt{7-x} \quad \Rightarrow x - 9 = -3\sqrt{7-x}$

Squaring again, we get $x^2 + 81 - 18x = 63 - 9x \Rightarrow x^2 - 9x + 18 = 0$

$\Rightarrow x = 3$ or $x = 6 \quad \Rightarrow x \in \{3, 6\}$ (iii)

Taking intersection of (i), (ii) and (iii) we must have $x = 3$ or 6

ILLUSTRATION 65: Prove that the following equations has no solution:

(a) $\sqrt{(x-4)} = -5$ (b) $\sqrt{x} + \sqrt{x+16} = 3$ (c) $\sqrt{x-3} + \sqrt{x+9} = \sqrt{x-1}$

SOLUTION: (a) We have $\sqrt{(x-4)} = -5$

Left hand side of the original equation is non-negative but right hand side is negative. Therefore the equation has no root.

(b) Given equation is $\sqrt{x}+\sqrt{x+16}=3$

The equation is defined for $x \geq 0$ and $x + 16 \geq 0 \Rightarrow \begin{cases} x \geq 0 \\ x \geq -16 \end{cases}$

Hence $x \geq 0$. For $x \geq 0$ the left hand side ≥ 4 but right hand side is 3. Therefore the equation has no root.

(c) Given equation is $\sqrt{x-3}-\sqrt{x+9}=\sqrt{x-1}$

This equation is defined for $\begin{cases} x-3 \geq 0 \\ x+9 \geq 0 \\ x-1 \geq 0 \end{cases} \Rightarrow \begin{cases} x \geq 3 \\ x \geq -9 \\ x \geq 1 \end{cases}$. Hence $x \geq 3$

For $x \geq 3$, $\sqrt{x-3} < \sqrt{x+9}$ i.e., $\sqrt{x-3}-\sqrt{x+9} < 0$

Hence for $x > 3$, the left hand side of the original equation is negative and right hand side is positive. Therefore the equation has no root.

Some standard types to solve irrational equations

Type-I: An equation of the type $\sqrt[2n]{f(x)} = \sqrt[2n]{g(x)},\ n \in \mathbb{N}$ is equivalent to $f(x) = g(x)$, $f(x) \geq 0$

Then find the roots of this equation. If a root of this equation satisfies the original equation, then its a root of the original equation otherwise we say that this root is its extraneous root.

ILLUSTRATION 66: Solve the equation $3\sqrt{x+3}-\sqrt{x-2}=7$.

SOLUTION: We have $3\sqrt{x+3}-\sqrt{x-2}=7 \quad \Rightarrow 3\sqrt{x+3}=7+\sqrt{x-2}$

Squaring both sides of the equation, we obtain $9x+27=49+x-2+14\sqrt{x-2}$

$\Rightarrow 8x-20=14\sqrt{x-2} \Rightarrow 4x-10=7\sqrt{x-2}$ Again squaring both sides, we obtain

$\Rightarrow 16x^2+100-80x=49x-98 \quad \Rightarrow 16x^2-129x+198=0$

$\Rightarrow (x-6)\left(x-\frac{33}{16}\right)=0 \quad \Rightarrow x_1=6,\ x_2=\frac{33}{16}$

Hence $x_1 = 6$ satisfies the original equation but $x_2=\frac{33}{16}$ does not satisfy the original equation. Therefore $x_2=\frac{33}{16}$ is the extraneous root.

Type-II: An equation of the type $\sqrt[2n]{f(x)} = g(x),\ n \in N$ is equivalent to the system of equations $\begin{cases} g(x) \geq 0 \\ f(x) = g^{2n}(x) \end{cases}$

ILLUSTRATION 67: Solve the equation $\sqrt{4-6x-x^2}=x+4$.

SOLUTION: We have $\sqrt{4-6x-x^2}=x+4$

This equation is equivalent to the system $\begin{cases} x+4 \geq 0 \Rightarrow x \geq -4 \\ 4-6x-x^2=(x+4)^2 \Rightarrow x^2+7x+6 \\ 4-6x-x^2 \geq 0 \Rightarrow x^2+6x-4 \leq 0 \end{cases}$

$\Rightarrow\ x \in [-3-\sqrt{13}, -3+\sqrt{13}]$, $x \geq -4$ as solution of lower and upper inequality

Solving the equation $x^2+7x+6=0$, we find $x_1 = -1$ and $x_2 = -6$

Only $x_1 = -1$ satisfies the condition $x \geq -4$ and $x \in [-3-\sqrt{13}, -3+\sqrt{13}]$

Consequently, the number -1 is the only solution of the given equation.

Type-III: An equation of the type

$$\sqrt[3]{f(x)} + \sqrt[3]{g(x)} = h(x) \qquad \text{(i)}$$

where $f(x)$, $g(x)$ are the functions of x, but $h(x)$ is either a function of x or constant, can be solved by cubing both sides of the equation and rearranging mentioned below:

$$f(x)+g(x)+3\sqrt[3]{f(x)\,g(x)}\,(\sqrt[3]{f(x)}+\sqrt[3]{g(x)}) = h^3(x)$$

$$\Rightarrow\ f(x)+g(x)+3\sqrt[3]{f(x)\,g(x)}\,(h(x)) = h^3(x)$$

{from (i)}

We find its roots and then substituting into the original equation, we choose those which satisfy the original equation.

ILLUSTRATION 68: Solve the equation $\sqrt[3]{x^2} + \sqrt[3]{x^4} = 2$.

SOLUTION: Given equation is $\sqrt[3]{x^2} + \sqrt[3]{x^4} = 2$. (i)

Cubing both sides, we get $x^2 + x^4 + 3(x^2x^4)^{1/3}\,(\sqrt[3]{x^2} + \sqrt[3]{x^4}) = 8$

$\Rightarrow\ x^2 + x^4 + 6x^2 = 8 \quad \Rightarrow \quad x^4 + 7x^2 - 8 = 0$

$\Rightarrow\ t^2 + 7t - 8 = 0 \quad \Rightarrow \quad (t+8)(t-1) = 0 \quad \Rightarrow\ t = 1, t = -8$

$\Rightarrow\ x^2 = 1$ or $x^2 = -8 \quad \Rightarrow \quad x = \pm 1$ or $\pm 2\sqrt{2}i$

ILLUSTRATION 69: Solve the equation $\sqrt{2x^2+5x-2} - \sqrt{2x^2+5x-9} = 1$.

SOLUTION: Let $u = \sqrt{2x^2+5x-2}$ and $v = \sqrt{2x^2+5x-9}$

$\therefore\ u^2 = 2x^2 + 5x - 2$ and $v^2 = 2x^2 + 5x - 9$

Then the equation reduces to the solution of the system of algebraic equations $u - v = 1$

$u^2 - v^2 = 7 \qquad \Rightarrow\ (u+v)(u-v) = 7$

$\Rightarrow\ u + v = 7 \qquad (\because\ u - v = 1)$, we get $u = 4$, $v = 3$

$\therefore\ \sqrt{2x^2+5x-2} = 4$, $\sqrt{2x^2+5x-9} = 3$

$\Rightarrow\ 2x^2 + 5x - 18 = 0 \qquad \Rightarrow\ x_1 = 2$ and $x_2 = -9/2$

Both roots satisfy the original equation.

Hence $x_1 = 2$ and $x_2 = -9/2$ are the roots of the original equation.

ILLUSTRATION 70: Solve the equation for real 'x', $\sqrt[3]{1-x} + \sqrt[3]{26+x} = 3$.

SOLUTION: Let us assume $u = \sqrt[3]{1-x}$ and $v = \sqrt[3]{26+x}$, then equation $\sqrt[3]{1-x} + \sqrt[3]{26+x} = 3$ (1)

becomes $u + v = 2$ and $u^3 = 1 - x$ and $v^3 = 26 + x \ \Rightarrow\ u^3 + v^3 = 27$

Thus, for finding u, v, we have the following symmetric system of equations

$u + v = 3$ and $u^3 + v^3 = 27$

Solving this system, we find $u_1 = 0$, $v_1 = 3$ or $u_2 = 3$ and $v_2 = 0$

(considering only the real solutions)

$$\Rightarrow \begin{cases} \sqrt[3]{1-x} = 0 \\ \sqrt[3]{26+x} = 3 \end{cases} \text{ or } \begin{cases} \sqrt[3]{1-x} = 3 \\ \sqrt[3]{26+x} = 0 \end{cases}$$

Solving this collection, we find $x_1 = 1$ and $x_2 = -26$

TEXTUAL EXERCISE–6 (SUBJECTIVE)

1. Solve the following irrational equations for x:
   (i) $\sqrt{x-4}+\sqrt{2-x}=2$
   (ii) $\sqrt{x-2}+\sqrt{4-x}=2$
   (iii) $\sqrt{2x-1}=-4$
   (iv) $(x^2-4)\sqrt{x^2-4x+3}=0$
   (v) $\sqrt{x^2-1}=2\sqrt{2}$
   (vi) $\sqrt{x-3}.\sqrt{x-4}=\sqrt{30}$
2. Solve for the value of x.
   (a) $\dfrac{4}{\sqrt{5-x}}-\sqrt{5-x}=\sqrt{2}$
   (b) $x-3=\sqrt{\dfrac{3x}{2}-\dfrac{x^2}{4}-\dfrac{5}{4}}$
   (c) $\sqrt[3]{64-x^3}=8-x$
   (d) $\dfrac{2+\sqrt{19-2x}}{x}=1$
   (e) $\sqrt[4]{1-x}+\sqrt[4]{15+x}=2$
3. Assume that 'a' a real number. Find the value of 'a' so that $\sqrt[3]{x+3a+1}=1+\sqrt[3]{x}$ has real solutions.
4. Find the value of α and β for which the equation $\sqrt{x+\alpha\sqrt{x}+\beta}+\sqrt{x}=4$ has infinitely many real solutions.
5. Find the number of real roots of equation $\sqrt{x}+\sqrt{x-\sqrt{1-x}}=1$
6. Show that the equation $\sqrt{x+3-4\sqrt{x-1}}+\sqrt{x+15-8\sqrt{x-1}}=2$ has infinite number of real roots.
7. Solve the equation for real roots $2x-5+2\sqrt{(x^2-5x)}+2\sqrt{(x-5)}+2\sqrt{x}=48.$
8. Find the real values of x satisfying the $(\sqrt{x^2-5x+6}-\sqrt{x^2-5x+4})^{x/2}+(\sqrt{x^2-5x+6}+\sqrt{x^2-5x+4})^{x/2}=2^{\frac{x+4}{4}}$
9. Solve for all $x, y \in R$ the system of equations reducible to quadratics. $\sqrt{\dfrac{3x-2y}{2x}}+\sqrt{\dfrac{2x}{3x-2y}}=2$ and $4y^2-1=3y(x-1)$

Answer Keys

1. (i) ϕ (ii) {3} (iii) ϕ (iv) {1, – 2, 3} (v) { – 3, 3} (vi) {9}
2. (a) {3} (b) $\left\{3+\dfrac{2\sqrt{5}}{5}\right\}$ (c) $x\in\{\phi\}$ (d) {5} (e) 1, –15
3. $a\in\left[\dfrac{-1}{4},\infty\right)$ **4.** α = –8, β = 16 **5.** $x \in [5, 17]$ **7.** $\dfrac{1681}{144}$ **8.** $x = 0, 4, 1$ **9.** $\left(1,\dfrac{1}{2}\right),(2,1)$

■ SOME IMPORTANT EQUATIONS REDUCIBLE TO QUADRATIC FORM

- **Equation of the form** $(x-a)(x-b)(x-c)(x-d)=A$; where $a<b<c<d$, $a+b=c+d$, can be solved by a change of variable.

i.e., $y=\dfrac{(x-a)+(x-b)+(x-c)+(x-d)}{4}$ or

$$y=x-\frac{(a+b+c+d)}{4}$$

ILLUSTRATION 71: Solve $(x-1)(x-2)(x-3)(x-4)=3$.

SOLUTION: $(x^2-5x+6)(x^2-5x+4)=3$

Let $x^2-5x+6=t \Rightarrow t(t-2)=3 \Rightarrow t^2-2t-3=0 \Rightarrow t=3$ or $t=-1$

$\Rightarrow x^2-5x+6=3$ or $x^2-5x+6=-1$

$\Rightarrow x^2-5x+3=0$ or $x^2-5x+7=0$

$\Rightarrow x=\dfrac{5\pm\sqrt{13}}{2}$ or $x=\dfrac{5\pm i\sqrt{3}}{2}$ i.e., two real and two non-real roots.

- **Equation of the form**

$(x - a)(x - b)(x - c)(x - d) = Ax^2$, where $ab = cd$, can be reduced to a collection of two quadratic equations by a change of variable $y = x + \dfrac{ab}{x}$.

ILLUSTRATION 72: Solve $(x + 2)(x + 3)(x + 8)(x + 12) = 4x^2$.

SOLUTION: We note that $(-2)(-12) = (-3)(-8)$. Multiplying the first bracket by the fourth and the second bracket by the third on the left hand side of this equation, we obtain.

$\Rightarrow (x^2 + 14x + 24)(x^2 + 11x + 24) = 4x^2$

Since $x = 0$ is not a root of this equation, we divide both sides of the equation by x^2 and get an equation $(x + 14 + 24/x)(x + 11 + 24/x) = 4$

which is equivalent to the original one. We make a change of variable $x + 24/x = y$

$\Rightarrow (y + 14)(y + 11) = 4$ or $y^2 + 25y + 150 = 0$ whence $y_1 = -15$ and $y_2 = -10$.

Thus the original equation is equivalent to the collection of equations

$$\begin{cases} x + 24/x = -15 \\ x + 24/x = -10 \end{cases} \text{ i.e., } \begin{cases} x^2 + 15x + 24 = 0 \\ x^2 + 10x + 24 = 0 \end{cases}$$

Solving this collection, we get an answer

$$x_1 = \frac{-15 - \sqrt{129}}{2},\ x_2 = \frac{-15 + \sqrt{129}}{2},\ x_3 = -6,\ x_4 = -4$$

- **Equation of the form: $(x - a)^4 + (x - b)^4 = A$**

It can also be solved by a change of variable, i.e., making a substitution $y = \dfrac{(x-a)+(x-b)}{2}$

ILLUSTRATION 73: Solve the equation $(6 - x)^4 + (8 - x)^4 = 16$

SOLUTION: After a change of variable $y = \dfrac{6 - x + 8 - x}{2} = 7 - x$. This equation reduces to the form $(y + 1)^4 + (y - 1)^4 = 16$ or $y^4 + 6y^2 - 7 = 0$

Solving this biquadratic equation, we get its roots. They are $y_1 = 1$, $y_2 = -1$. Thus the numbers $x_1 = 8$ and $x_2 = 6$ are the roots of this equation.

- **Reciprocal equation of the standard form:**

It can be reduced to an equation of half of its dimensions. Let the equation be $ax^{2m} + bx^{2m-1} + cx^{2m-2} + \ldots + kx^m + \ldots + cx^2 + bx + a = 0$. Dividing by x^m and rearranging the terms, we have

$$a\left(x^m + \frac{1}{x^m}\right) + b\left(x^{m-1} + \frac{1}{x^{m-1}}\right) + c\left(x^{m-2} + \frac{1}{x^{m-2}}\right) + .. + k = 0$$

Now $x^{p+1} + \dfrac{1}{x^{p+1}} = \left(x^p + \dfrac{1}{x^p}\right)\left(x + \dfrac{1}{x}\right) - \left(x^{p-1} + \dfrac{1}{x^{p-1}}\right)$

Hence, writing z for $x + 1/x$, and giving to p in succession the values 1, 2, 3, ... , we obtain $x^2 + 1/x^2 = z^2 - 2$ and $x^3 + 1/x^3 = z(z^2 - 2) - z = z^3 - 3z$ and $x^4 + 1/x^4 = z(z^3 - 3z) - (z^2 - 2) = z^4 - 4z^2 + 2$ and so on; and generally $x^m + 1/x^m$ is of m dimensions in z and therefore, the equations in z is of m dimensions.

ILLUSTRATION 74: Solve the equation $2x^5 + 3x^4 - 5x^3 - 5x^2 + 3x + 2 = 0$.

SOLUTION: This equation has a root $x_1 = -1$, since it is a symmetric equation of an odd degree. Factorizing the left hand side, we obtain $(x + 1)(2x^4 + x^3 - 6x^2 + x + 2) = 0$,
we solve the equation $(2x^4 + x^3 - 6x^2 + x + 2) = 0$
Dividing both sides of this equation by x^2 (since $x = 0$ is not its root)

$$\Rightarrow\ 2x^2 + x - 6 + \frac{1}{x} + \frac{2}{x^2} = 0\ \Rightarrow\ 2\left(x + \frac{1}{x}\right)^2 - 4 + \left(x + \frac{1}{x}\right) - 6 = 0$$

and making the substitution $x + 1/x = t$

$$\Rightarrow 2t^2 + t - 10 = 0 \Rightarrow t = \frac{-1 \pm \sqrt{81}}{4} = \frac{-1 \pm 9}{4} \quad \Rightarrow t = 2, -5/2$$

So we obtain two quadratic equations:
$x^2 - 2x + 1 = 0$ and $2x^2 - 5x + 2 = 0$
Solving, we get the roots as $x_2 = x_3 = 1$, $x_4 = -2$, $x_5 = -0.5$.

- **Trinomial equations:** Equations of the form $ax^{2n} + bx^n + c = 0, a \neq 0, n \geq 2, n \in \mathbb{N}$ (i)

are called trinomial equations. For $n = 2$ the trinomial equation is called a biquadratic equation.

Putting $y = x^n$, we can write equation as $ay^2 + by + c = 0$. If y_1 and y_2 are two different roots of the last equation, then equation is equivalent to the collection of equations $\begin{cases} x^n = y_1 \\ x^n = y_2 \end{cases}$

If $y_1 = y_2$, then equation (i) is equivalent to the equation $x^n = y_1$.
If the equation $ay^2 + by + c = 0$ has no real solution, then equation (i) has no real solution.

ILLUSTRATION 75: Solve the equation $x^8 - 17x^4 + 16 = 0$.

SOLUTION: Designating $x^4 = y$, we get an equation $y^2 - 17y + 16 = 0$, hence we find that $y_1 = 1$ and $y_2 = 16$. Thus the given equation is equivalent to the collection of equations $x^4 = 1$ and $x^4 = 16$

Solving which we find that $x_1 = 1, x_2 = -1, x_3 = 2, x_4 = -2$ are the real roots and $x_5 = i, x_6 = -i$, $x_7 = 2i$ and $x_8 = -2i$ are the imaginary roots.

TEXTUAL EXERCISE–7 (SUBJECTIVE)

1. Solve the following equations for x:
   (i) $(x - 1)(x - 2)(x - 3)(x - 4) = 3$
   (ii) $(x + 2)(x + 3)(x + 8)(x + 12) = 4x^2$
   (iii) $(6 - x)^4 + (8 - x)^4 = -16$

2. Solve the following equation for real roots:
   (i) $x^2 + \left(\frac{x}{x-1}\right)^2 = 8$.
   (ii) $x\{(5-x)/(x+1)\}\{x+[(5-x)/(x+1)\} = 6$

3. Show that $e^{\sin x} - e^{-\sin x} - 4 = 0$ has no real root.

4. Solve the following equations for x:
   (i) $4^x + 6^x = 9^x$ (ii) $\log_3(3^x - 8) = 2 - x$

5. Solve the following quadratic equations reducible for real roots.
   (a) $|x-1|^{\log_3 x^2 - 2\log_x 9} = (x-1)^7$
   (b) $\dfrac{\log_2 x}{\log_4 2x} = \dfrac{\log_8 4x}{\log_8 8x}$
   (c) $\log_x(3x^2 + 10x) = 3$

6. (i) $|x^2 - 2| + |x - 1| = |x^2 - x - 1|$
   (ii) $|x^2 - 2| + |x - 1| = |x^2 + x - 3|$

Answer Keys

1. (i) $\frac{5\pm\sqrt{13}}{2}, \frac{5\pm i\sqrt{3}}{2}$ (ii) –6, –4, $\frac{-15\pm\sqrt{129}}{2}$ (iii) $x = 7+i\sqrt{3}, 7+i\sqrt{3}, 7-i\sqrt{3}, 7-i\sqrt{3}$

2. (i) 2, 2, $-1 \pm \sqrt{3}$ (ii) 1, 2, $1\pm i\sqrt{2}$ **4.** (i) $\log_{2/3}\left(\frac{\sqrt{5}-1}{2}\right)$ (ii) $x = 2$

5. (a) 81, 2 (b) $2^{\frac{-3+\sqrt{17}}{2}}, 2^{\frac{-3-\sqrt{17}}{2}}$ (c) 5 **6.** (i) $(-\infty, \sqrt{-2}]\cup[1,\sqrt{2}]$ (ii) $[-\sqrt{2},1]\cup[\sqrt{2},\infty)$

TEXTUAL EXERCISE–6 (OBJECTIVE)

1. The number of real roots of $(x + 3)^4 + (x + 5)^4 = 16$ is
(a) 0 (b) 2
(c) 4 (d) None of these

2. If $x + \frac{1}{x} = 5$, then $\left(x^3 + \frac{1}{x^3}\right) - 5\left(x^2 + \frac{1}{x^2}\right) + \left(x + \frac{1}{x}\right)$ is equal to
(a) 0 (b) 5
(c) –5 (d) 10

3. If $(2x^2 - 3x + 1)(2x^2 + 5x + 1) = 9x^2$ then equation has
(a) four real roots
(b) two real and two imaginary roots
(c) all imaginary
(d) none of the above

4. If $(x - 2)^6 + (x - 4)^6 = 64$, then equation has
(a) real and irrational roots
(b) real and rational roots
(c) two real and two irrational roots
(d) None of these

5. If $(4 + \sqrt{15})^x + (4 - \sqrt{15})^x = 62$ then x is
(a) ±5 (b) ±4
(c) ±3 (d) ±2

6. Number of roots of the equation $\sqrt{x} + \sqrt{x - \sqrt{1-x}} = 1$ is
(a) 0 (b) 1
(c) 2 (d) 3

7. The solution set of $\log_{1/2}(2x^2 + 2 - 4x) \geq -2$
(a) $[1-\sqrt{2}, 1+\sqrt{2}] \sim \{1\}$ (b) $(-\infty, 2+\sqrt{13})$
(c) $(-\infty, 2)$ (d) None of these

8. Number of integers, which satisfy the inequality $\frac{(16)^{1/x}}{(2^{x+3})} > 1$ is equal to
(a) infinite (b) 0
(c) 1 (d) 4

9. If $\log_2(ax^2 + x + a) \geq 1\ \forall\ x \in \mathbb{R}$, then exhaustive set of value of 'a' is
(a) $\left(0, 1+\frac{\sqrt{5}}{2}\right)$ (b) $\left(1-\frac{\sqrt{5}}{2}, 1+\frac{\sqrt{5}}{2}\right)$
(c) $\left(0, 1-\frac{\sqrt{5}}{2}\right)$ (d) $\left(1+\frac{\sqrt{5}}{2}, \infty\right)$

10. Given the following set of equations:
(i) $x^2 - 2|x| - 3 = 0$
(ii) $|x - 2|^2 + |x - 2| - 2 = 0$
(iii) $|x^2 - x - 6| = x + 2$

Which of the following is true about the above equations?
(a) has only one solution
(b) has atleast two solutions
(c) has more then two solutions
(d) has no solution

11. Solution of the equation $2x^4 + x^3 - 11x^2 + x + 2 = 0$ are
(a) $\frac{-3\pm\sqrt{5}}{2} - 2, -1/2$
(b) $\frac{-3\pm\sqrt{5}}{2}, 2, \frac{1}{2}$
(c) $\frac{-3\pm\sqrt{5}}{2}, \pm 2$
(d) $\frac{-3\pm\sqrt{5}}{2}, \pm\frac{1}{2}$

12. Solution of equation $(5+2\sqrt{6})^{x^2-3} + (5-2\sqrt{6})^{x^2-3} = 10$ are
(a) ± 2 (b) ±1/2
(c) $\pm\sqrt{2}$ (d) None of these

13. Solution of the system of equations $(x+y)^{2/3}+2(x-y)^{2/3}=3(x^2-y^2)^{1/3}$ and $3x-2y=13$ are
(a) $x=13/3, y=0$ (b) $x=9, y=7$
(c) $x=13/3, y=7$ (d) $x=9, y=0$

14. The values of a for which the equation $2(\log_3 x)^2-|\log_3 x|+a=0$ possess four distinct real solutions belong to
(a) $(-\infty, 1/8)$ (b) $(0, 1/8)$
(c) $(1/8, \infty)$ (d) None of these

15. Solution set of the inequality $5^{x+2} > \left(\frac{1}{25}\right)^{1/x}$ is
(a) $(-2, 0)$ (b) $(-2, 2)$
(c) $(-5, 5)$ (d) $(0, \infty)$

Answer Keys

1. (b)	**2.** (a)	**3.** (a)	**4.** (d)	**5.** (d)	**6.** (b)	**7.** (a)	**8.** (a)	**9.** (d)	**10.** (b)
11. (b)	**12.** (a, c)	**13.** (a, b)	**14.** (b)	**15.** (d)					

GEOMETRICAL REPRESENTATION OF A QUADRATIC EXPRESSION

Consider the quadratic expression $y = ax^2 + bx + c$ $(a \neq 0)$ and a, b, c are real numbers.

Thus $y = ax^2 + bx + c = a\left[x^2 + 2.\frac{b}{2a}x + \frac{c}{a}\right]$

$$= a\left[x^2 + 2.\frac{b}{2a}x + \frac{b^2}{4a^2} + \frac{c}{a} - \frac{b^2}{4a^2}\right]$$

$$= a\left[\left(x + \frac{b}{2a}\right)^2 + \frac{4ac - b^2}{4a^2}\right]$$

$$\Rightarrow \left(y + \frac{b^2 - 4ac}{4a}\right) = a\left(x + \frac{b}{2a}\right)^2$$

$$\Rightarrow \left(y + \frac{D}{4a}\right) = a\left(x + \frac{b}{2a}\right)^2$$

Shifting the origin at $(-b/2a, -D/4a)$, i.e., substituting $X = x + \left(\frac{b}{2a}\right)$ and $Y = y + \left(\frac{D}{4a}\right)$, we get, $Y = aX^2$, which is the equation of a parabola having its vertex at $\left(\frac{-b}{2a}, \frac{-D}{4a}\right)$

The parabola opens upwards or downwards according to as $a > 0$ (Figure–5.11) or $a < 0$ (Figure–5.12).

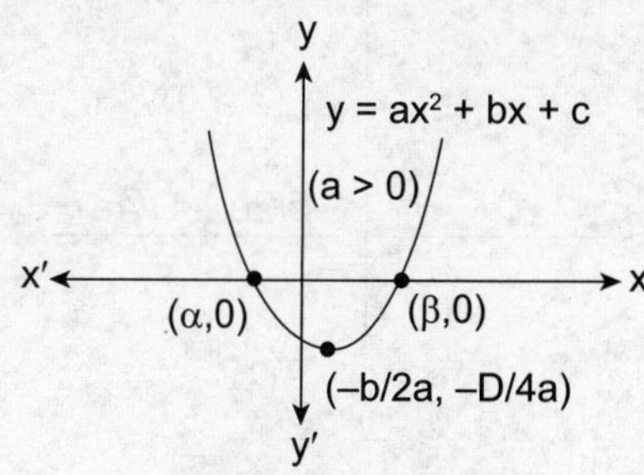

FIGURE 5.15

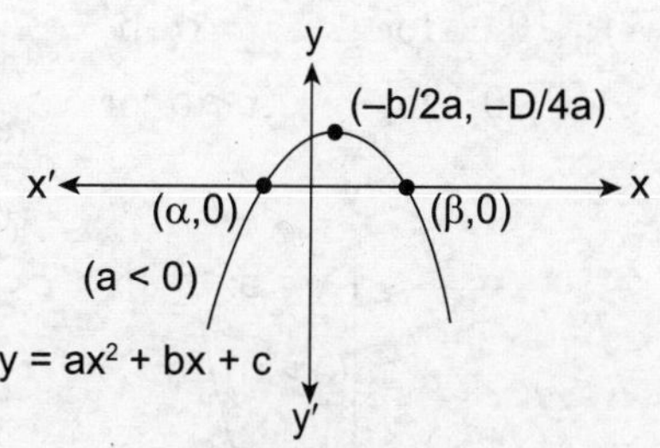

FIGURE 5.16

Maximum/minimum value and sign of quadratic expression:

Extreme value of any quadratic expression $y = ax^2 + bx + c$ is given by y-coordinate of vertex $-D/4a$ of corresponding parabola and it occurs at $x = x$-co-ordinate of vertex. $(-b/2a)$. Consider two cases for $a > 0$ and $a < 0$.

Case (i): For $a > 0$; $D \in \mathbb{R}$: The curve $y = ax^2 + bx + c$ is a parabola opening upwards such that

$$y_{min} = \frac{-D}{4a} \text{ at } x = \frac{-b}{2a} \text{ and } y_{max} \to +\infty$$

as $y = a\left(x + \frac{b}{2a}\right)^2 - \frac{D}{4a}$

Clearly, $y_{max} = \infty$ when $x \to \pm\infty$; $y_{min} = \frac{-D}{4a}$ when $\left(x + \frac{b}{2a}\right)^2 = 0$ i.e., $x = -\frac{b}{2a}$

Case (ii): For $a < 0$; $D \in \mathbb{R}$: The curve $y = ax^2 + bx + c$ is a parabola opening downwards such that

$$y_{max} = \frac{-D}{4a} \text{ at } x = \frac{-b}{2a} \text{ and } y_{min} \to -\infty$$

as $y = a\left(x + \frac{b}{2a}\right)^2 - \frac{D}{4a}$

Clearly, $y_{min} = -\infty$ when $x \to \pm\infty$; $y_{max} = -\frac{D}{4a}$ when $\left(x + \frac{b}{2a}\right)^2 = 0$ i.e., $x = -\frac{b}{2a}$

NOTE

Let α, be a root of the quadratic equation $ax^2 + bx + c$, then $a\alpha^2 + b\alpha + c = 0$. Point (α, 0) lies on $y = ax^2 + bx + c$. "Thus every real root is represented by the point of intersection of the parabola with x-axis and vice versa and the expression can change its sign only at its roots and no where else."

Case (i) D > 0: The parabola will intersect the x-axis in two distinct points iff $D > 0$ (Figure 5.17 and 5.18)

In this case, the parabola meets x-axis at

$$\alpha = \frac{-b-\sqrt{D}}{2a} \quad \text{and} \quad \beta = \frac{-b+\sqrt{D}}{2a}$$

Sub-case I: $a > 0$,

$$\text{Thus } y = f(x): \begin{cases} < 0 & \text{for } \alpha < x < \beta \\ 0 & \text{for } x = \alpha, \beta \\ > 0 & \text{for } x < \alpha \text{ or } x > \beta \end{cases}$$

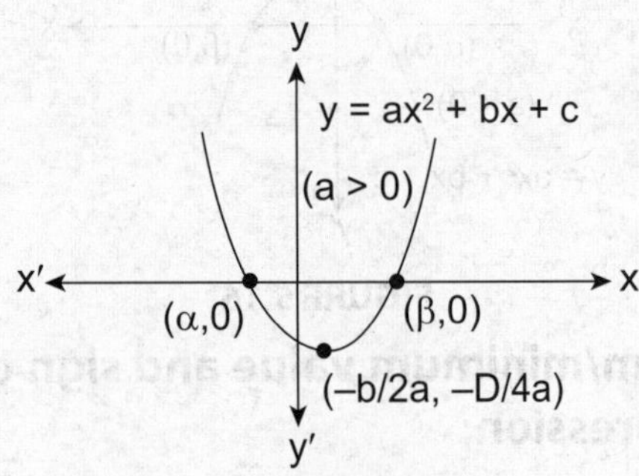

FIGURE 5.17

Sub-case II: $a < 0$,

$$y = f(x): \begin{cases} > 0 & \text{for } \alpha < x < \beta \\ 0 & \text{for } x = \alpha, \beta \\ < 0 & \text{for } x < \alpha \text{ or } x > \beta \end{cases}$$

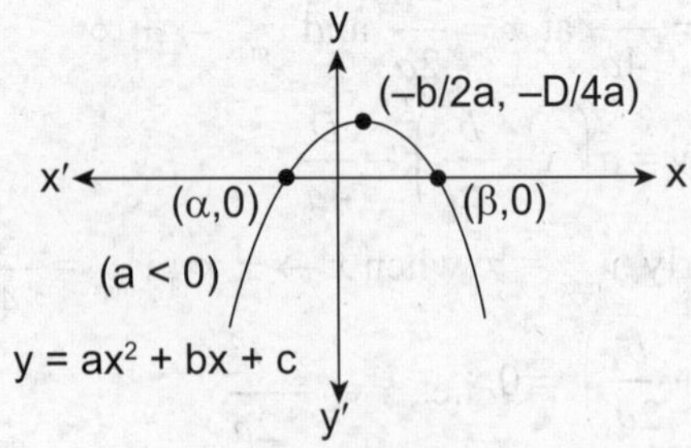

FIGURE 5.18

Case (ii): D = 0: The parabola will just touch the x-axis at one point iff $D = 0$ (Figure 5.19 and 5.20)

In this case, the parabola touches x-axis at $x = -b/2a$

Sub-case I: $a > 0$

$$y = f(x) \begin{cases} > 0 & \text{for } x \neq \alpha \\ 0 & \text{for } x = \alpha \end{cases}$$

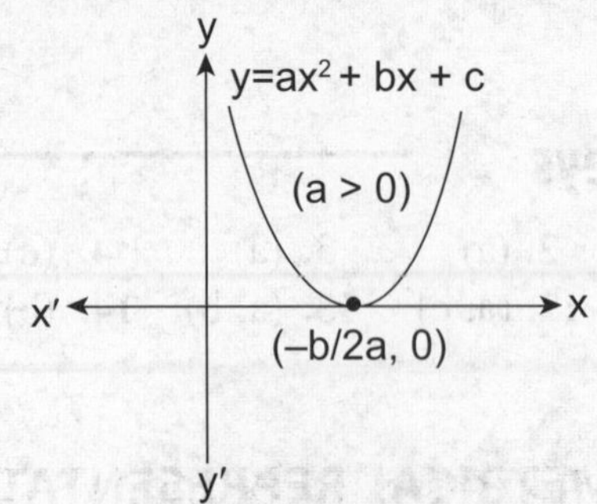

FIGURE 5.19

Sub-case II: $a < 0$:

$$y = f(x): \begin{cases} < 0 & \text{for } x \neq \alpha \\ 0 & \text{for } x = \alpha \end{cases}$$

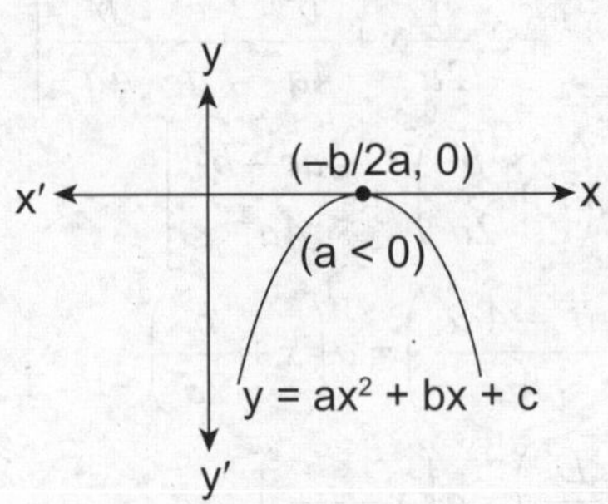

FIGURE 5.20

Case (iii) $D < 0$: The parabola will not intersect x-axis iff $D < 0$: In this case, the parabola will remain either completely above x-axis or completely below x-axis according as $a > 0$ or $a < 0$ respectively.

Sub-case I: $a > 0$: $y = f(x) > 0$ for all x as shown below:

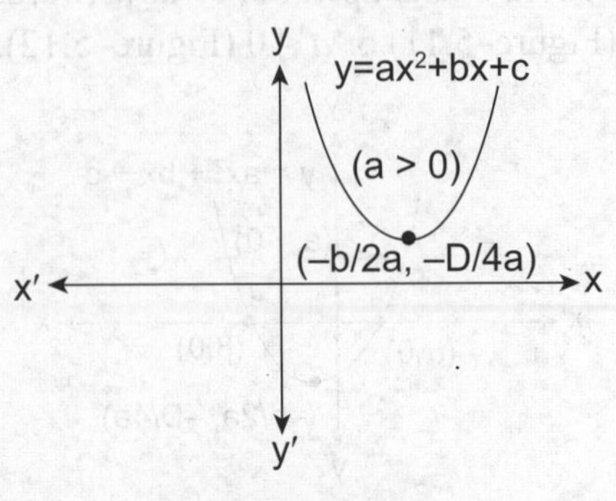

FIGURE 5.21

Case II: $a < 0$, we have

$$y_{max} = \frac{-D}{4a} \text{ at } x = \frac{-b}{2a} \text{ and } y_{min} \to -\infty$$

and $y = f(x) < 0$ for all x as shown below:

Subcase (ii): a< 0

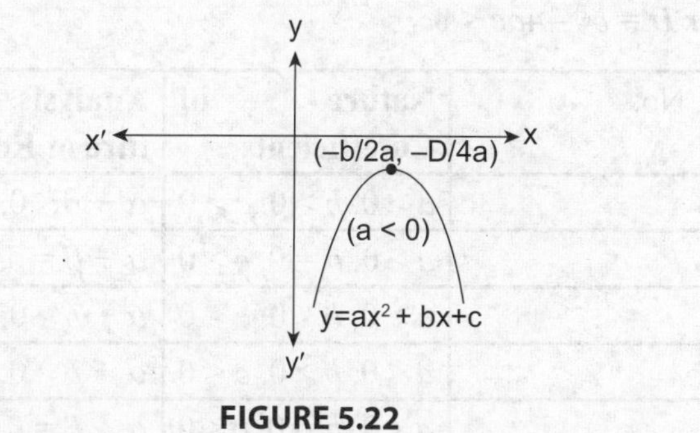

FIGURE 5.22

ILLUSTRATION 76: Prove that the minimum value of $\frac{(a+x)(b+x)}{(c+x)}$ is $(\sqrt{a-c}+\sqrt{b-c})^2$; where $x > -c$ and $a, b > c$

SOLUTION: Let $y = \frac{(a+x)(b+x)}{(c+x)} = \frac{(a-c+c+x)(b-c+c+x)}{(c+x)}$

$$= \frac{(c+x)^2+(a+b-2c)(c+x)+(a-c)(b-c)}{(c+x)} = (c+x) + \frac{(a-c)(b-c)}{(c+x)} + (a+b-2c)$$

$$= (\sqrt{c+x})^2 + \left(\sqrt{\frac{(a-c)(b-c)}{c+x}}\right)^2 - 2\sqrt{(a-c)(b-c)} + [(a-c)+(b-c)] + 2\sqrt{(a-c)(b-c)}$$

$$= \left(\sqrt{c+x} - \sqrt{\frac{(a-c)(b-c)}{c+x}}\right)^2 + (\sqrt{a-c})^2 + (\sqrt{b-c})^2 + 2\sqrt{(a-c)(b-c)}$$

So $y_{min} = (\sqrt{a-c}+\sqrt{b-c})^2$

Detailed analysis of quadratic equation

***For D** = $b^2 - 4ac > 0$,*

Sr. No.	Nature of Co-efficients	Analysis of Nature of Roots
1.	$a > 0, b > 0, c > 0$	$\alpha + \beta < 0, \alpha\beta > 0$
2.	$a > 0, b = 0, c = 0$	$\alpha + \beta < 0, \alpha\beta = 0$
3.	$a > 0, b < 0, c < 0$	$\alpha + \beta < 0, \alpha\beta < 0$
4.	$a > 0, b < 0, c > 0$	$\alpha + \beta > 0, \alpha\beta > 0$
5.	$a > 0, b < 0, c = 0$	$\alpha + \beta > 0, \alpha\beta = 0$
6.	$a > 0, b < 0, c < 0$	$\alpha + \beta > 0, \alpha\beta < 0$

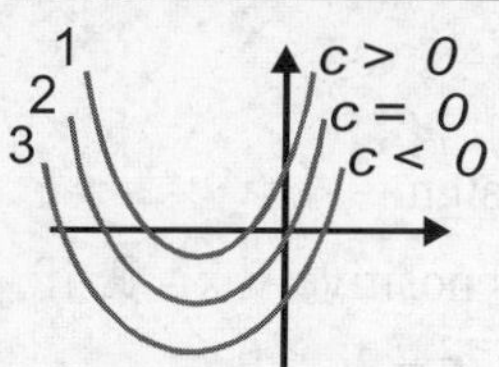

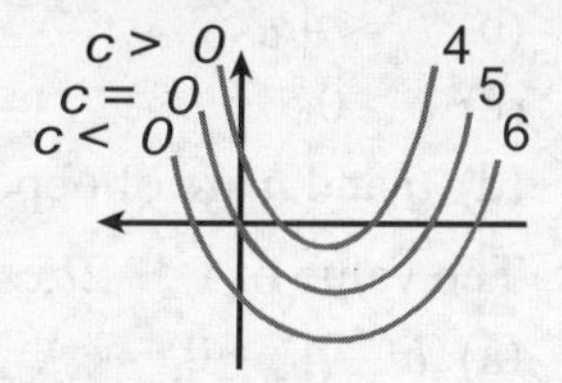

FIGURE 5.23

***For D** = $b^2 - 4ac = 0$,*

Sr.No	Nature of Co-efficients	Analysis of Nature of Roots
1.	$a > 0, b > 0, c > 0$	$\alpha + \beta < 0, \alpha\beta > 0$
2.	$a > 0, b = 0, c = 0$	$\alpha + \beta = 0, \alpha\beta = 0$
3.	$a > 0, b < 0, c > 0$	$\alpha + \beta > 0, \alpha\beta > 0$
4.	$a < 0, b > 0, c < 0$	$\alpha + \beta > 0, \alpha\beta > 0$
5.	$a < 0, b = 0, c = 0$	$\alpha + \beta = 0, \alpha\beta = 0$
6.	$a < 0, b < 0, c < 0$	$\alpha + \beta < 0, \alpha\beta > 0$

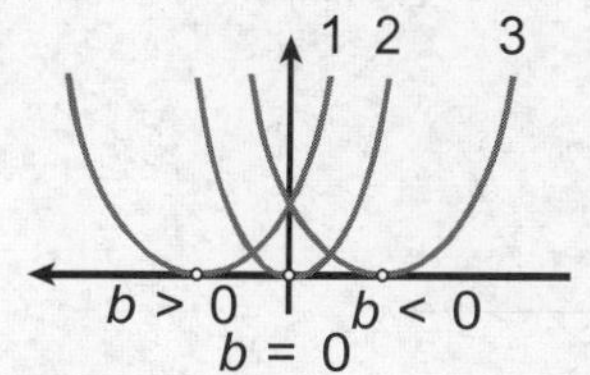

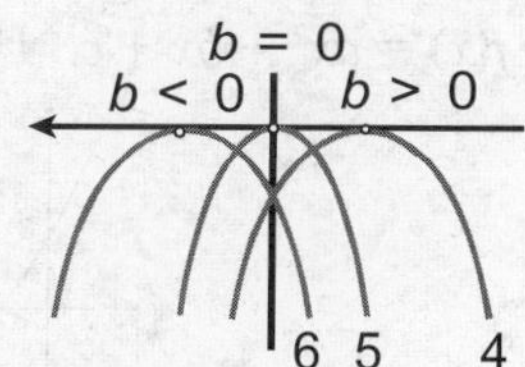

FIGURE 5.24

***For D* = $b^2 - 4ac < 0$;**

S. No.	Nature of Co-efficients	Analysis of Nature of Roots
1.	$a > 0, b > 0, c > 0$	$\alpha + \beta < 0, \alpha\beta > 0$
2.	$a > 0, b = 0, c > 0$	$\alpha + \beta = 0, \alpha\beta > 0$
3.	$a > 0, b < 0, c > 0$	$\alpha + \beta > 0, \alpha\beta > 0$
4.	$a < 0, b > 0, c < 0$	$\alpha + \beta > 0, \alpha\beta > 0$
5.	$a < 0, b = 0, c < 0$	$\alpha + \beta = 0, \alpha\beta > 0$
6.	$a < 0, b < 0, c < 0$	$\alpha + \beta < 0, \alpha\beta > 0$

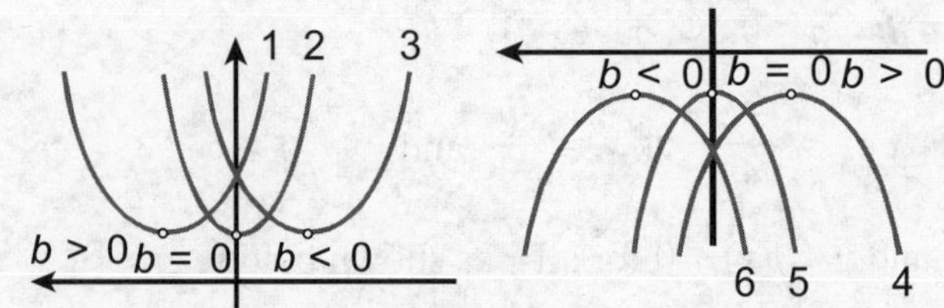

FIGURE 5.25

TEXTUAL EXERCISE–8 (SUBJECTIVE)

1. Find the set of value of k for which entire graph of the equation $y = x^2 + kx - x + 9$ is strictly above the x-axis.
2. Find the values of k if graph of $kx^2 + 2kx - 2$ lies below x-axis and also find k if graph lies above x-axis.
3. If $x \in [2, 4]$, then find the least and greatest value of the expression $x^2 - 6x + 5$.
4. If α and β be the roots of the equation $ax^2 + 2bx + c = 0$ and $\alpha + k$, $\beta + k$ be the roots of $Ax^2 + 2Bx + C = 0$. Then prove that $A^2(b^2 - ac) = a^2(B^2 - AC)$.
5. Given that the equation $ax^2 + bx + c = 0$ has both of its roots non-real ($a, b, c \in \mathbb{R}$) then, state whether the following statements is true/false:
   (i) $a \,.\, c < 0$
   (ii) $a(a + b + c) > 0$
   (iii) $c(4c - 2b + a) > 0$
   (iv) $ac(a + b + c)(a - b + c) > 0$
6. If both roots of $ax^2 + bx + c$ are real (i.e., $b^2 - 4ac > 0$) and given by α and β such that $\beta > \alpha$ such that $0 < \alpha < 1$ and $\beta \geq 5$ then state whether the following is true.
   (i) $a(a + b + c) < 0$
   (ii) $ac(9a + 3b + c) > 0$
   (iii) $(a - b + c)(16a - 4b + c) < 0$
7. If α and β where α is less then β are the roots of equation $x^2 + bx + c = 0$, where c is < 0 and b is greater than 0, $c < 0 < b$, then show that $\alpha < 0 < \beta < |\alpha|$.
8. Find all values of a for which the equation $4^x - a2^x - a + 3 = 0$ has at least one solution.
9. If x be real, then show that the expression $\dfrac{x^2 + 2x - 11}{x - 3}$ can take all values which do not lie in the open interval (4, 12).
10. Show that the value of $\dfrac{\tan x}{\tan 3x}$ wherever it is defined never lies between 1/3 and 3.

Answer Keys

1. $-5 < k < 7$ **2.** $k \in (-2, 0)$, $k \in \{\}$ **3.** Greatest value is -3, Least value -4
5. (i) F (ii) T (iii) T (iv) T **6.** (i) T (ii) F (iii) F **8.** $a \in [2, \infty)$

TEXTUAL EXERCISE–7 (OBJECTIVE)

1. The following figure shows the graph of $f(x) = ax^2 + bx + c$.

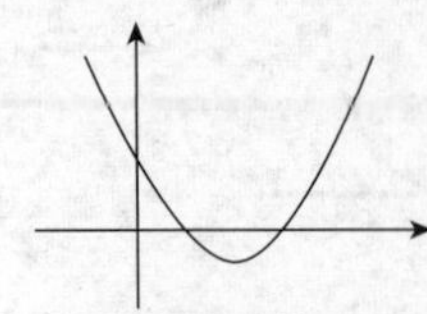

FIGURE 5.26

   (a) $a < 0$
   (b) $b^2 < 4ac$
   (c) $c > 0$
   (d) a and b are of opposite sign
2. The value of $x^2 + 2bx + c$ is positive $\forall\, x \in \mathbb{R}$ if:
   (a) $b^2 - 4c > 0$ (b) $b^2 - 4c < 0$
   (c) $c^2 < b$ (d) $b^2 < c$

3. Given that $ax^2 + bx + c = 0$ has no real root and $a + b + c < 0$ then

(a) $c = 0$ (b) $c > 0$

(c) $c < 0$ (d) $c \leq 0$

4. If $c > 0$ and $4a + c < 2b$ then $ax^2 - bx + c = 0$ has a root in the interval

(a) (0, 2) (b) (2, 4)

(c) (0, 1) (d) (–2, 0)

5. Value of 'a' for which the quadratic equation $3x^2 + 2(a^2 + 1)x + (a^2 - 3a + 2) = 0$ possesses roots of opposite sign, lies in

(a) $(-\infty, 1)$ (b) $(-\infty, 0)$

(c) (1, 2) (d) $\left(\frac{3}{2}, 2\right)$

6. Let $a > 0$, $b > 0$ and $c > 0$. Then both the roots of the equation $ax^2 + bx + c = 0$

(a) are real and negative

(b) have negative real parts

(c) are rational number

(d) None of these

7. If $a \in \mathbb{R}$, $b \in \mathbb{R}$ then the equation $x^2 - abx - a^2 = 0$ has

(a) one positive root and one negative root

(b) both positive roots

(c) both negative roots

(d) none real roots

8. If the equation $ax^2 + 2bx - 3c = 0$ has non-real roots and $(3c/4) < (a + b)$; then c is always

(a) < 0 (b) > 0

(c) ≥ 0 (d) zero

9. If $b > a$, then the equation $(x - a)(x - b) - 1 = 0$, has

(a) both roots in $[a, b]$

(b) both roots in $(-\infty, a)$

(c) both roots in (b, ∞)

(d) one root in $(-\infty, a)$ and other in (b, ∞)

10. Complete set of values of 'a' such that $\frac{x^2 - x}{1 - ax}$ attains all real values, is

(a) $[1, \infty)$ (b) (0, 4]

(c) (0, 1] (d) None of these

11. The expression $-a^2x^2 + bx - c$; $a \neq 0$ is negative for all x if

(a) $b^2 > 4a^2c$

(b) $b^2 < 4a^2c$

(c) $b^2 = 4a^2c$

(d) $4b^2 < a^2c$

12. The greatest negative integer satisfying $x^2 + 3x - 10 < 0$ and $x^2 > 9$ is

(a) –3 (b) –4

(c) –5 (d) –6

13. The greatest positive integral value of x for which $200 - x(10 + x)$ is positive, is

(a) 11 (b) 9

(c) 10 (d) 19

14. For $a \neq b$ and $x \in R$, $x^2 - (a + b)x + a^2 - ab + b^2$

(a) ≥ 0 (b) > 0

(c) ≤ 0 (d) < 0

15. If $4x^2 + kx + 3 \geq 0$ for all x, then $k \in$

(a) $(-4\sqrt{3}, 4\sqrt{3})$ (b) $\left[-4\sqrt{3}, 4\sqrt{3}\right]$

(c) $\left(-\frac{3}{4}, \frac{3}{4}\right)$ (d) $\left[-\frac{3}{4}, \frac{3}{4}\right]$

16. The number of values of the pair (a, b) for which $a(x + a)^2 + b(x^2 - 3x - 2) + x + 1 = 0$ is an identify in x is

(a) 0

(b) 1

(c) 2

(d) infinite

17. The number of real roots of the equation $\sqrt{x-5}\,(x^2 - 5x + 4) = 0$ is

(a) one (b) two

(c) three (d) four

Answer Keys

1. (c, d)	**2.** (d)	**3.** (c)	**4.** (a)	**5.** (c)	**6.** (b)	**7.** (a)	**8.** (b)	**9.** (d)	**10.** (a)
11. (b)	**12.** (b)	**13.** (d)	**14.** (b)	**15.** (b)	**16.** (a)	**17.** (a)			

LOCATION OF ROOTS

Let $f(x) = ax^2 + bx + c$, where $a, b, c \in R$ be a quadratic expression and k, k_1, k_2 be real numbers such that $k_1 < k_2$ and if α, β be the roots of equation $f(x) = 0$.

Then $\alpha = \dfrac{-b-\sqrt{D}}{2a}$ and $\beta = \dfrac{-b+\sqrt{D}}{2a}$; where D is the discriminant of the equation.

(a) ***Conditions for a number k to lie between the roots of a quadratic equation OR under what condition do the roots of $ax^2 + bx + c = 0$ lie on either side of number k? (Figure 5.27 and 5.28)***

If a number k lies between the roots of a quadratic equation $f(x) = ax^2 + bx + c = 0$, then the sign of $f(k)$ is opposite to the sign of 'a'.

Condition are (i) $D > 0$ and

(ii) $a.f(k) < 0 \Rightarrow a.f(k) < 0$

In fact, above two conditions are equivalent to single condition $af(k) < 0$ because sign of a is sign of quadratic expression when $x \to \pm\infty$, so $af(k) > 0$ as $x \to \pm\infty$

So $af(k) < 0 \Rightarrow$ Quadratic expression changes its sign so must have real roots. i.e., $D > 0$

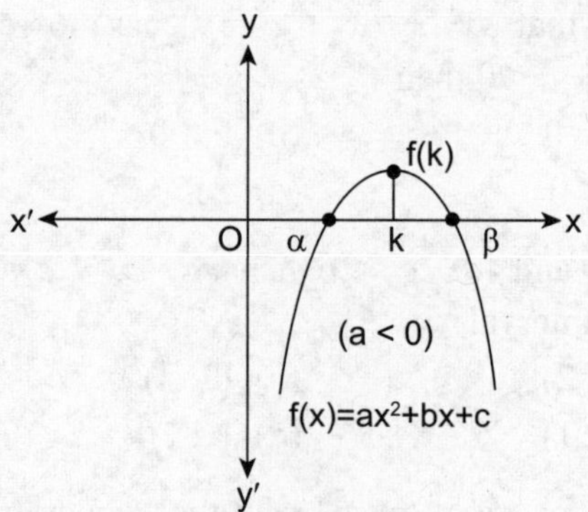

FIGRUE 5.27

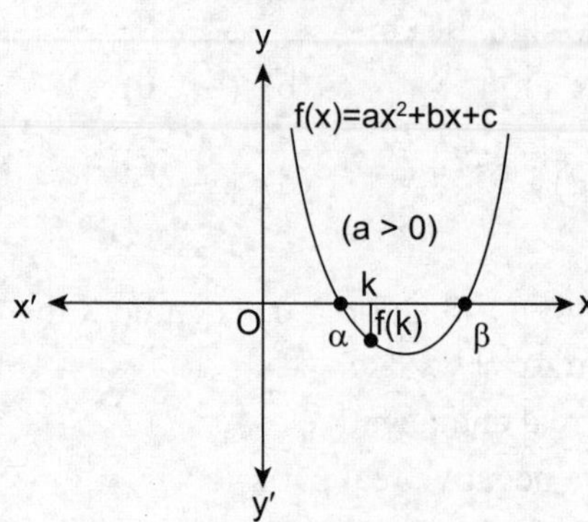

FIGRUE 5.28

ILLUSTRATION 77: Find the value of p, for which 6 lie between the roots of the equation $x^2 + 2(p-3)x + 9 = 0$.

SOLUTION: (a) $D > 0$

$\Rightarrow 4(p-3)^2 - 36 > 0$

$\Rightarrow p(p-6) > 0$

$\Rightarrow p < 0$ or $p > 6$ (i)

(b) $1 . f(6) < 0$

$\Rightarrow 36 + 12(p-3) + 9 < 0$

$\Rightarrow 12p + 9 < 0$

$\Rightarrow p < -3/4$ (ii)

Taking intersection of (i) and (ii), we get $p \in (-\infty, -3/4)$

(b) ***Condition for exactly one root of a quadratic equation to lie in the interval (k_1, k_2); where $k_1 < k_2$ (Figure 5.29 and 5.30)***

If exactly one root of the equation $ax^2 + bx + c = 0$ lies in the interval (k_1, k_2), then $f(k_1)$ and $f(k_2)$ must be of opposite signs.Thus exactly one root of the equation $ax^2 + bx + c = 0$ lies in the interval (k_1, k_2) if

(i) $D > 0$

(ii) $f(k_1) . f(k_2) < 0$

$\Rightarrow f(k_1) . f(k_2) < 0$

In fact, above two conditions are equivalent to single condition $f(k_1). f(k_2) < 0$ because sign of quadratic expression at k_1 and k_2 is opposite. Therefore it must have one real root between k_1 and k_2. So, both roots are real. i.e., $D > 0$

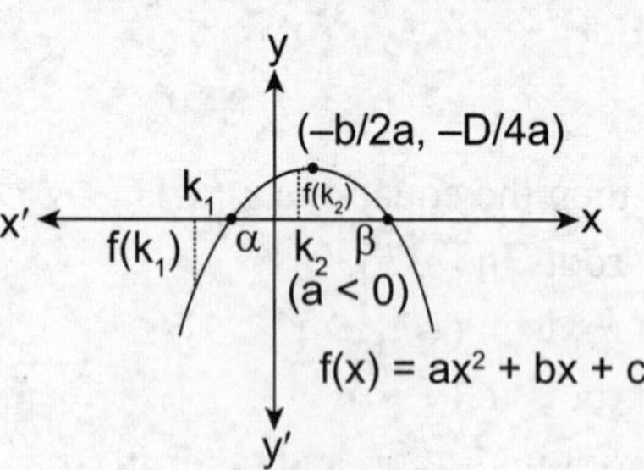

FIGURE 5.29

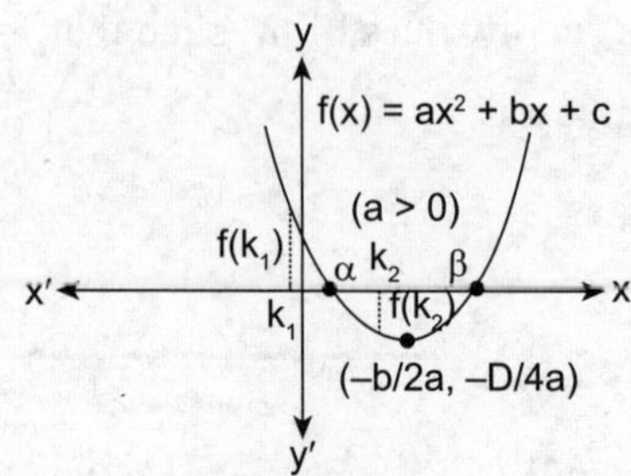

FIGURE 5.30

ILLUSTRATION 78: Find the values of m for which exactly one root of the equation $x^2 - 2mx + m^2 - 1 = 0$ lies in the interval $(-2, 4)$.

SOLUTION: (i) $D > 0$ $\Rightarrow (-2m)^2 - 4.1(m^2 - 1) > 0$

$\Rightarrow 4 > 0 \Rightarrow m \in \mathbb{R}$ (i)

(ii) $f(-2).f(4) < 0$ $\Rightarrow (4 + 4m + m^2 - 1)(16 - 8m + m^2 - 1) < 0$

$\Rightarrow (m + 3)(m + 1)(m - 3)(m - 5) < 0$

$\Rightarrow m \in (-3, -1) \cup (3, 5)$ (ii)

Taking intersection of (i) and (ii) $\Rightarrow (-3, -1) \cup (3, 5)$

(c) ***Conditions for a number k to be less than the roots of a quadratic equation or Under what condition will both roots of $ax^2 + bx + c = 0$ be greater than a certain specified number, k?***

Thus a number k is smaller than both the roots of a quadratic equation $ax^2 + bx + c = 0$ iff

(i) $D \geq 0$ (ii) $a\,f(k) > 0$ (iii) $k < -b/2a$

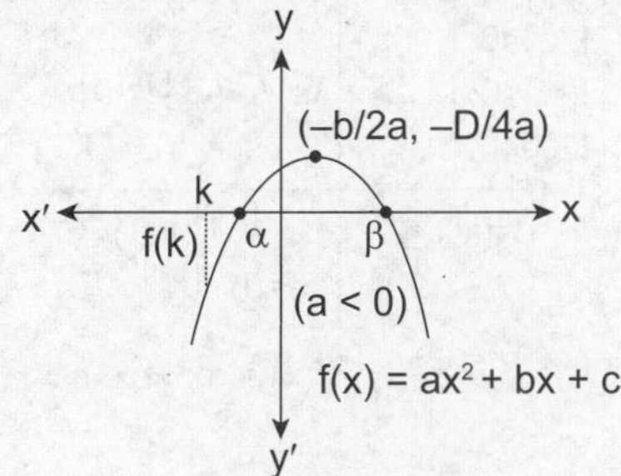

FIGURE 5.31

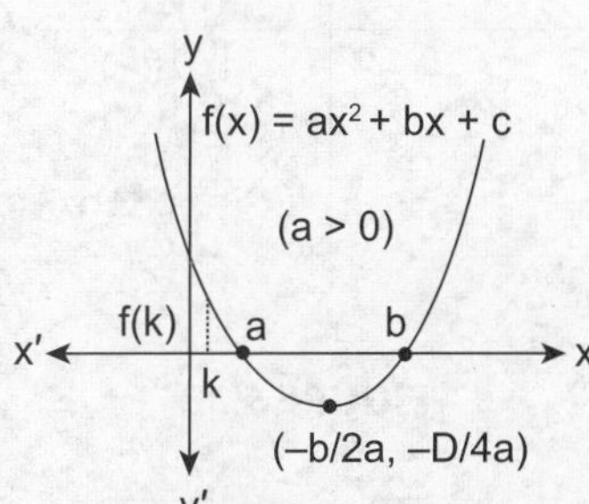

FIGURE 5.32

ILLUSTRATION 79: Find the value of p, for which both the roots of the equation $4x^2 - 20px + (25p^2 + 15p - 66) = 0$ are less than 2.

SOLUTION: (i) $D \geq 0$

(ii) $4\,f(2) > 0$

(iii) $-\dfrac{b}{2a} < 2$

$\Rightarrow 15p - 66 \leq 0;\ 4(16 - 40p + 25p^2 + 15p - 66); \Rightarrow \dfrac{20p}{8} < 2$

$\Rightarrow p \leq 22/5;\ p^2 - p - 2 > 0;\ p < 4/5$ (iii)

$\Rightarrow p \in (-\infty, -1) \cup (2, \infty);\ p \in \left(-\infty, \dfrac{22}{5}\right]$ and $p \in \left(-\infty, \dfrac{4}{5}\right)$ (ii)

Taking intersection, $\Rightarrow p \in (-\infty, -1)$

(e) ***Condition for a number 'k' to be more than the roots of a quadratic equation:*** (Figure–5.33 and 5.34)

If a number k is more than the roots of a quadratic equation $ax^2 + bx + c = 0$, then

(i) $D \geq 0$

(ii) $a f(k) > 0$

(iii) $k > -b/2a$

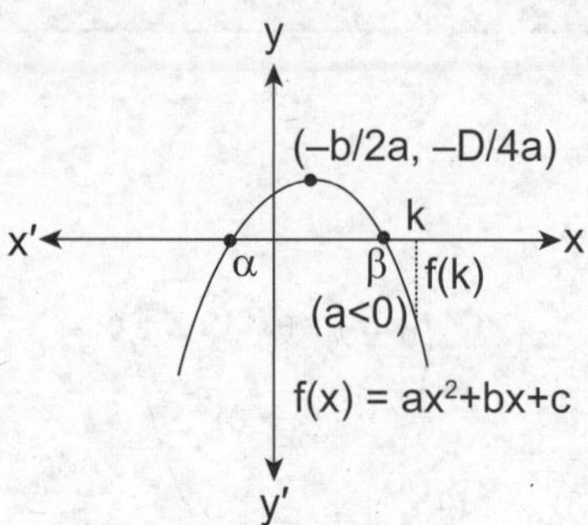

FIGURE 5.33

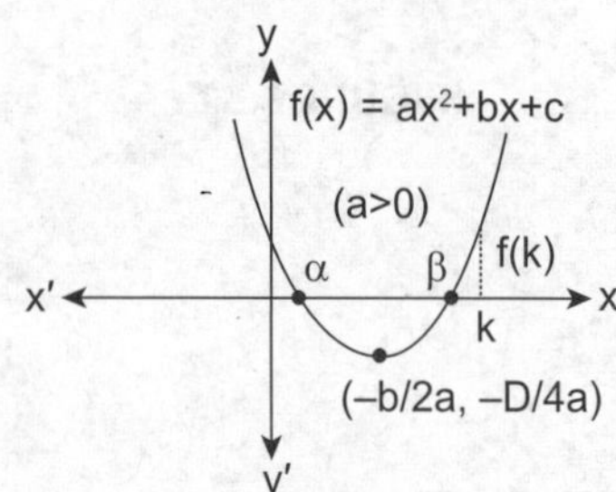

FIGURE 5.34

(f) ***Condition for both the roots of a quadratic equation to lie between numbers k_1 and k_2 or in the interval (k_1, k_2)*** (Figure–5.35 and 5.36): If both the roots a and b of a quadratic equation lie between number k_1 and k_2

(i) $D \geq 0$

(ii) $a f(k_1) > 0$, $a f(k_2) > 0$

(iii) $k_1 < -b/2a < k_2$

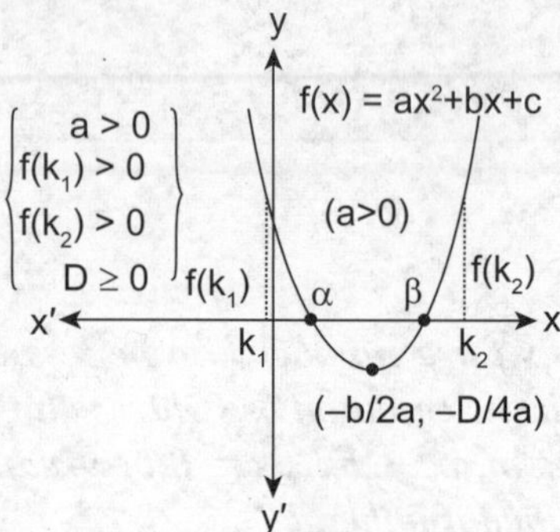

FIGURE 5.35

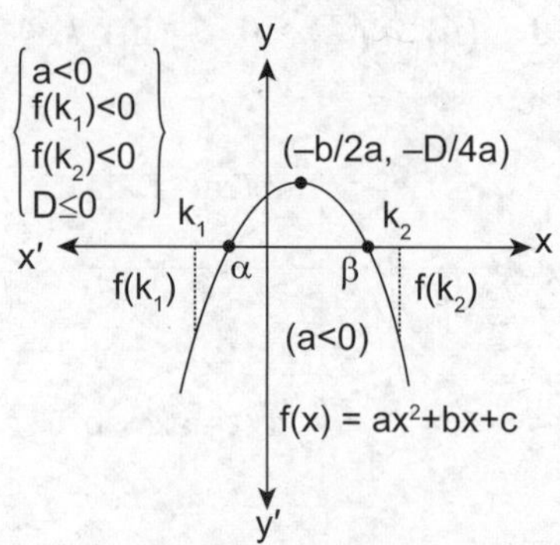

FIGURE 5.36

ILLUSTRATION 80: If both roots of the equation $x^2 - 2ax + a^2 - 1 = 0$ lie between –3 and 4, then evaluate $[a]$. (where [ ] = G.I.F)

SOLUTION: Roots of the equation are $a \pm 1$ $\quad (\because D = \sqrt{4} = 2 > 0)$

Given $a - 1 > -3 \Rightarrow a > -2$ and $a + 1 < 4 \quad \Rightarrow a < 3$

$\Rightarrow -2 < a < 3 \quad \Rightarrow [a] \in \{-1, 0, 1, 2\}$

ILLUSTRATION 81: Find the set of values of m for which the equation $x^2 + 2(m + 1)x + (9m - 5) = 0$ has both roots negative.

SOLUTION: The given equation is $x^2 + 2(m + 1)x + (9m - 5) = 0$

Since, both roots are negative, then $b^2 - 4ac \geq 0$,

Sum of roots < 0 and product of roots > 0

(a) $b^2 - 4ac \geq 0 \quad \Rightarrow 4(m + 1)^2 - 4(9m - 5) \geq 0$

$\Rightarrow m^2 - 7m + 6 \geq 0 \quad \Rightarrow (m - 1)(m - 6) \geq 0 \Rightarrow -\infty < m \leq 1$ or $6 \leq m < \infty$ (i)

(b) Sum of roots < 0

$\Rightarrow -2(m + 1) < 0 \quad \Rightarrow (m + 1) > 0 \quad \Rightarrow m > -1$ (ii)

(c) Product of roots > 0

$\Rightarrow 9m - 5 > 0 \quad \Rightarrow m > 5/9$ (iii)

From equations (i), (ii) and (iii), $\frac{5}{9} < m \leq 1$ or $6 \leq m < \infty \Rightarrow m \in (5/9, 1] \cup [6, \infty)$

ILLUSTRATION 82: Find the values of a for which one root of equation $x^2 - (a + 1)x + a^2 + a - 8 = 0$ is greater than 2 and the other root smaller than 2.

SOLUTION: The given quadratic equation is $f(x) = x^2 - (a + 1)x + a^2 + a - 8 = 0$ (i)

Since, one root of equation (i) is greater than 2 and the other root is smaller than 2, then

$(a + 1)^2 - 4(a^2 + a - 8) \geq 0$ and $f(2) < 0$

(a) $(a + 1)^2 - 4(a^2 + a - 8) \geq 0$

$\Rightarrow a^2 + 2a + 1 \geq 4a^2 + 4a - 32$ $\Rightarrow 3a^2 + 2a - 33 \leq 0$

$\Rightarrow (a - 3)(3a + 11) \leq 0$ $\Rightarrow -11/3 \leq a \leq 3$ (ii)

(b) $f(2) < 0$

$\Rightarrow 4 - 2(a + 1) + a^2 + a - 8 < 0$ $\Rightarrow a^2 - a - 6 < 0$

$\Rightarrow (a - 3)(a + 2) < 0$ $\Rightarrow -2 < a < 3$ (iii)

From equations (i), (ii) and (iii), we get $-2 < a < 3$

ILLUSTRATION 83: Let $x^2 - (m - 3)x + m = 0$; $(m \in \mathbb{R})$ be a quadratic equation. Find the values of $'m'$ for

(i) real and distinct roots
(ii) equal roots
(iii) no real roots
(iv) roots opposite in sign
(v) roots equal in magnitude but opposite in sign
(vi) positive roots
(vii) negative roots
(viii) at least one positive roots
(ix) one root smaller than 2 and other root greater than 2
(x) both the roots greater than 2
(xi) both the roots smaller than 2
(xii) exactly one root lying in the interval (1, 2)
(xiii) both roots lying in the interval (1, 2)
(xiv) at least one root lying in the interval (1, 2)
(xv) one root greater than 2 and the other root smaller than 1.

SOLUTION: Let $f(x) = x^2 - (m - 3)x + m = 0$

(i) Both the roots are real and distinct $\Rightarrow D > 0$

$\Rightarrow (m - 3)^2 - 4m > 0$ $\Rightarrow m^2 - 10m + 9 > 0$

$\Rightarrow (m - 1)(m - 9) > 0$ $\Rightarrow m \in (-\infty, 1) \cup (9, \infty)$

(ii) Both the roots are equal $\Rightarrow D = 0 \Rightarrow m = 9$ or $m = 1$

(iii) Both the roots are imaginary $\Rightarrow D < 0 \Rightarrow (m - 1)(m - 9) < 0 \Rightarrow m \in (1, 9)$

(iv) Both the roots are opposite in sign $\Rightarrow$ product of roots $< 0 \Rightarrow m < 0 \Rightarrow m \in (-\infty, 0)$

(v) Roots are equal in magnitude but opposite in sign

$\Rightarrow$ sum of roots $= 0$ and product of roots < 0

$\Rightarrow m = 3$ and $m < 0$ $\Rightarrow$ no $'m'$ exists

(vi) Both the roots are positive $\Rightarrow D \geq 0$, sum of roots > 0, product of roots > 0

$\Rightarrow m - 3 > 0$, $m > 0$ and $m \in (-\infty, 1] \cup [9, \infty) \Rightarrow m \in [9, \infty)$.

(vii) Both roots are negative $\Rightarrow D \geq 0$; sum is negative but product is positive

$\Rightarrow m - 3 < 0$, $m > 0$, $m \in (-\infty, 1] \cup [9, \infty)$ $\Rightarrow m \in (0, 1]$

(viii) At least one root is positive

$\Rightarrow$ either one root positive or both roots positive.

$\Rightarrow$ union of (*iv*) and (*vi*) $\Rightarrow m \in (-\infty, 0) \cup [9, \infty)$

(ix) One root smaller than 2 and other root greater than 2
$\Rightarrow$ 2 lies between the roots $\Rightarrow f(2) < 0$
$\Rightarrow 4 - 2(m - 3) + m < 0 \Rightarrow m > 10$ i.e., $m \in (10, \infty)$

(x) Both roots greater than 2 $\Rightarrow f(2) > 0, D \geq 0, -b/2a > 4$
$\Rightarrow m < 10$ and $m \in (-\infty, 1] \cup [9, \infty)$ and $m - 3 > 4 \Rightarrow m \in [9, 10)$

(xi) Both the roots are smaller than 2
$\Rightarrow f(2) > 0, D \geq 0, -b/2a < 2$ $\Rightarrow m \in (-\infty, 1]$

(xii) Exactly one root lies in (1, 2) $\Rightarrow f(1).f(2) < 0$
$\Rightarrow 4(10 - m) < 0 \Rightarrow m \in (10, \infty)$

(xiii) Both roots lie in the interval (1, 2). Then $D \geq 0, f(1) > 0, f(2)>0, -b/2a \in (1, 2)$
$\Rightarrow (m - 1)(m - 9) \geq 0, 4 > 0, 10 - m > 0$ and $5 < m < 7$ (iii)
No such m exists

(xiv) Union of (xii) and (xiii) $\Rightarrow m \in (10, \infty)$

(xv) One root greater than 2 and other smaller than 1
$\Rightarrow f(1) < 0$ and $f(2) < 0$ (i)
$4 < 0$ and $10 - m < 0$ which is impossible.
Thus no such m exists.

TEXTUAL EXERCISE–9 (SUBJECTIVE)

1. If the roots of $x^2 - 2ax + a^2 + a - 3 = 0$ are real and less than 3, then show that $a < 2$.
2. Find a
   (i) If both the roots of the equation $x^2 - 6ax + 2 - 2a + 9a^2 = 0$ exceed the real number 3.
   (ii) Exactly one root of $x^2 + 2ax + 2a^2 - 1 = 0$, lies between 0 and 1.
3. Find the values of parameter k of equation $x^2 + (2k - 1)x + 4 = 0$ so that even number of real roots lie in $(-1, 1)$
4. Find all the values of parameter k for which one of the roots of the equation $(k^2 + k + 1)x^2 + (k - 1)x + k^2 = 0$ is greater than 3 and other is less than 3.
5. Find the set of all real value of k.
   (a) $x^2 + 2kx + 1$ has both roots smaller than 1.
   (b) $x^2 + 2kx + 1$ has both roots larger than 0.
6. Find all values of p, so that 6 lies between roots of the equation $x^2 + 2(p - 3)x + 9 = 0$
7. Find the values of m for which both roots of equation $x^2 - mx + 1 = 0$ are less than unity.
8. If $a < b < c < d$ then show that $(x - a)(x - c) + 3(x - b)(x - d) = 0$ has real and distinct roots.
9. If x is real, find the values of k for which
$$\left|\frac{x^2 + kx + 1}{x^2 + x + 1}\right| < 2$$
10. If m is positive but not greater than 3, then show that the roots of the equation $(m - 2)x^2 - (8 - 2m)x - (8 - 3m) = 0$ are real. Find the range of values of m for which one root is positive and the other root is negative.
11. Find the value (s) of a for which the inequality $\tan^2 x + (a + 1)\tan x + 2a - 1 < 0$, is true for at least one $x \in (0, \pi/2)$.
12. Find the value of a for which the inequality $x^2 + ax + a^2 + 6a < 0$ is satisfied for all $x \in (1, 2)$.

Answer Keys

2. (i) $a \in (11/9, \infty)$ (ii) $a \in \left(-1, \frac{-1}{\sqrt{2}}\right) \cup \left(0, \frac{1}{2}\right)$ **3.** $k \in \left(-2, \frac{-3}{2}\right] \cup \left[\frac{5}{2}, 3\right)$ **4.** $k \in \phi$

5. (a) $k \in [1, \infty)$ (b) $k \in (-\infty, -1]$ **6.** $\left(-\infty, -\frac{3}{4}\right)$ **7.** $(-\infty, -2]$

9. $0 < k < 4$ **10.** $2 < m < 8/3$ **11.** $a \in (-\infty, -3 - 2\sqrt{5}) \cup (3, \infty)$ **12.** $\frac{-7 - 3\sqrt{5}}{2} \leq a \leq -4 + 2\sqrt{3}$

TEXTUAL EXERCISE–8 (OBJECTIVE)

1. Values of a for which exactly one root of $5x^2 + (a + 1)x + a = 0$ lies in the interval $1 < x < 3$ is
   (a) $a > 2$ (b) $-12 < a < -3$
   (c) $a > 0$ (d) None of these

2. The value of a for which the equation; $x^2 - 2(a - 1)x + (2a + 1) = 0$ has both roots positive, is
   (a) 1 (b) 2
   (c) 0 (d) None of these

3. All the values of parameter k for which one of the roots of the equation $(k^2 + k + 1)x^2 + (k - 1)x + k^2 = 0$ is less than 4 and other belongs to (1, 3) are
   (a) $k \in (-1, 0)$ (b) $k \in (-1, 1)$
   (c) $k \in (0, 1)$ (d) None of these

4. If the roots of the equation $x^2 - 2ax + a^2 + a - 3 = 0$ are real and less than 3, then
   (a) $a < 2$ (b) $2 \leq a \leq 3$
   (c) $3 < a \leq 3$ (d) $a > 4$

5. If $x^2 - (a - 3)x + a = 0$ has at least one positive root, then
   (a) $a \in (-\infty, 0) \cup [7, 9]$
   (b) $a \in (-\infty, 0) \cup [7, \infty]$
   (c) $a \in (-\infty, 0] \cup [9, \infty)$
   (d) None of these

6. If roots of $x^2 - (a - 3)x + a = 0$ are such that both of them is greater than 2, then
   (a) $a \in [7, 9]$ (b) $a \in [7, \infty)$
   (c) $a \in [9, 10)$ (d) $a \in [7, 9)$

7. Let S denotes the set of real values of 'a for which the roots of the equation $x^2 - ax - a^2 = 0$ exceeds 'a', then S equals to
   (a) $(-\infty, 0)$ (b) $\left(-2, -\frac{1}{2}\right)$
   (c) $\left(-\frac{1}{2}, \frac{1}{4}\right)$ (d) null set

8. The values of a for which the equation $2x^2 - 2(2a + 1)x + a(a - 1) = 0$ has roots α and β satisfying the condition $\alpha < a < \beta$ are:
   (a) $(-3, 0)$ (b) $(0, \infty)$
   (c) $(-\infty, -3) \cup (0, \infty)$ (d) None of these

9. The values of p, for which 6 lie between the roots of the equation $x^2 + 2(p - 3)x + 9 = 0$, is
   (a) $(3/4, \infty)$ (b) $(-\infty, -3/4)$
   (c) $(-3/4, 3/4)$ (d) None of these

10. The values of m, for which exactly one root of the equation $x^2 - 2mx + m^2 - 1 = 0$ lies in the interval $(-2, 4)$ is
    (a) $(-3, -1)$ (b) $(3, 5)$
    (c) $(-\infty, \infty)$ (d) $(-3, -1) \cup (3, 5)$

11. One set of values of 'a' for which the equation $4x^2 - 2x + a = 0$ has two roots belonging to $(-1, 1)$ are
    (a) $-2 < a \leq \frac{1}{4}$ (b) $a > -4$
    (c) $a < 4$ (d) none of these.

12. If α, β be the roots of $x^2 + px + q = 0$ and $\alpha + h$, $\beta + h$ are the roots of $x^2 + rx + s = 0$, then
    (a) $\frac{p}{r} = \frac{q}{s}$ (b) $h = \frac{1}{2}\left[\frac{p}{r} + \frac{q}{s}\right]$
    (c) $p^2 - 4q = r^2 - 4s$ (d) None of these.

13. The co-efficient of x in the equation $x^2 + 13x + q = 0$ was wrongly written as 17 in place of 13 and the roots thus found were -2 and -15. The roots of the correct equation are
    (a) $(-10, -3)$ (b) $(3, 10)$
    (c) $(2, 5)$ (d) $(-2, -15)$

14. If the equation $x^3 + ax^2 + bx - 4 = 0$ has two roots equal to 2, then the ordered pair (a, b) is
    (a) $(-5, 8)$ (b) $(5, -8)$
    (c) $(1, 1)$ (d) $(2, 2)$.

Answer Keys

1. (b) 2. (b) 3. (a) 4. (a) 5. (c) 6. (c) 7. (d) 8. (c) 9. (b) 10. (d)
11. (a) 12. (c) 13. (a) 14. (a)

■ ROLLE'S THEOREM

Let $f(x)$ be a function defined on a closed interval $[a, b]$ such that

(a) $f(x)$ is continuous on $[a, b]$

(b) $f(x)$ is derivable on (a, b)

(c) $f(a) = f(b)$

Then, there exists at least one point $c \in (a, b)$ s.t. $f'(c) = 0$

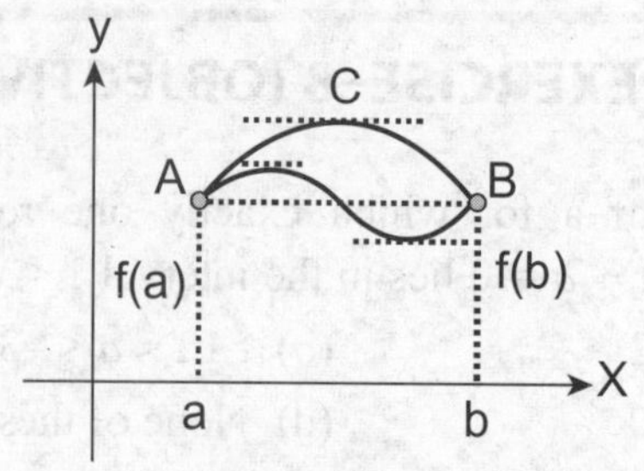

FIGURE 5.37

ILLUSTRATION 84: Check the validity of Rolle's theorem for

(i) $p(x) = x^2 - 3x + 2$ (ii) $p(x) = x^3 - x^2 - 4x + 4$

SOLUTION: (i) $p(1) = p(z) = 0$ and $p(x)$ is continuous on $[1, 2]$

p(x) is derivable on (1, 2)

$\Rightarrow$ Roll's theorem is applicable, $P'(x) = 2x - 3 = 0 \Rightarrow x = 3/2$ which lies between 1 and 2.

Thus Rolle's theorem is verified.

(ii) $p(1) = p(-2) = p(2) = 0$ and $p(x)$ is continous on $[-2, 1]$ and also on $[1, 2]$

Also $p(x)$ is derivable on $(-2, 1)$ and on $(1, 2)$ $\Rightarrow$ Roll's theorem is applicable and

$p'(x) = 3x^2 - 2x - 4 = 0$

$$\Rightarrow x = \frac{2 \pm \sqrt{4+48}}{6} = \frac{2 \pm 2\sqrt{13}}{6} = \frac{1}{3} \pm \frac{\sqrt{13}}{3}$$

Clearly, one root lies in $(-2, 1)$ and other $(1, 2)$

Application of Rolle's theorem

Between any two consecutive roots of $P_n(x) = 0$, the equation $P_n'(x) = 0$ must have atleast one root but vice versa is not true. *If* $P_n(x)$ is a polynomial of degree n such that $P_n(\alpha_1) = P_n(\alpha_2) = ... = P_n(\alpha_n) = 0$, then there exist $\beta_1, \beta_2, \beta_3 ...... \beta_{n-1} : \beta_i \in (\alpha_i, \alpha_{i+1})$ and $p'_n(\beta_i) = 0$.

ILLUSTRATION 85: Show that the equation $x^3 - 3x + c = 0$ can't have two different roots in the interval (0, 1).

SOLUTION: $f(x) = x^3 - 3x + c = 0 \Rightarrow f'(x) = 3x^2 - 3 = 0 \Rightarrow x = \pm 1$

$\Rightarrow f'(x) \neq 0$ in $(0, 1) \Rightarrow f(x) = 0$, can't have any two different roots in (0, 1) as otherwise by Rolle's theorem $f'(x) = 0$ atleast once in (0, 1) which is not the case.

ILLUSTRATION 86: Without finding the derivative of the function $f(x) = (x - 1)(x - 2)(x - 3)(x - 4)$. Find out how many real roots the equation $f'(x) = 0$ has and indicate the intervals in which they lie.

SOLUTION: Applying Rolle's theorem:

$f(x)$ is continuous in the interval [0, 5] and differentiable in the interval (0, 5)

Now $f(1) = 0; f(2) = 0; f(3) = 0; f(4) = 0;$

$f(1) = 0 = f(2) \Rightarrow$ there exist c such that $1 < c < 2$; $f'(c) = 0$

So there exist one root of $f'(x) = 0$ in the interval (1, 2).

Similarly, one root in each of the interval (2, 3) and (3, 4).

ILLUSTRATION 87: If the equation $f(x) = ax^3 + bx^2 + cx + d = 0$ has all roots real, then prove that $b^2 \geq 3ac$.

SOLUTION: Let $f(x) = 0$ has real roots α_1, α_2 and α_3, then by Rolle's theorem $f'(x) = 0$

i.e., $3ax^2 + 2bx + c = 0$ has two real roots, one in each of the intervals $(f(\alpha_1), f(\alpha_2))$ and $(f(\alpha_2), f(\alpha_3))$

$\Rightarrow D \geq 0 \Rightarrow 4b^2 - 12ac \geq 0 \Rightarrow b^2 \geq 3ac$

Application of concept of inverse function in solving equations

Since a function $f(x_i) = \{(x, y): y = f(x)\ \forall\ x \in \text{Domain}\}$, then its inverse $f^{-1}(y) = (x)$ is defined as $\{(y, x) : (x, y) \in f\}$ and therefore graph of $f(x)$ and $f^{-1}(x)$ are mirror reflection of each other in the line $y = x$.

So whenever $f(x)$ and $f^{-1}(x)$ happen to meet they meet on the line $y = x$ or $y = -x + c$ which mathematically means $\Rightarrow f(x) = f^{-1}(x) \Rightarrow f(x) = x$ or $f(x) = -x + c$. However for later case $f(x)$ must contain atleast one pair (α, β) such that $(\beta, \alpha) \in f(x)$

ILLUSTRATION 88: Solve the equation $x^2 - x + 1 = \frac{1}{2} + \sqrt{x - \frac{3}{4}}$ for real values of x.

SOLUTION: The function $y = f(x) = x^2 - x + 1 = (x - 1/2)^2 + 3/4$ increases in the interval $[1/2, \infty)$ and x varying in the indicated interval $y = f(x) \geq 3/4$ i.e., $y \in [3/4, \infty)$. Thus $f(x)$

$$\therefore\ x^2 - x + 1 - y = 0$$

$$\Rightarrow\ x = \frac{1 \pm \sqrt{1 - 4.1.(1-y)}}{2} = \frac{1 \pm \sqrt{(4y-3)}}{2}$$

$$= \frac{1}{2} \pm \sqrt{y - \frac{3}{4}} = \frac{1}{2} + \sqrt{y - \frac{3}{4}} = g(y)$$

$\therefore\ y = g^{-1}(x)$ $\qquad \Rightarrow f(x) = g^{-1}(x)$

Hence $f(x)$ and $g(x)$ are mutually inversion. Again it is given $x^2 - x + 1 = \frac{1}{2} + \sqrt{x - \frac{3}{4}}$ Since the graphs of the original and inverse functions can intersect only on the straight line $y = x$

$\therefore\ x = f(x)$ $\qquad \Rightarrow x = x^2 - x + 1$

$\Rightarrow x^2 - 2x + 1 = 0$ $\qquad \Rightarrow (x - 1)^2 = 0$

$\therefore\ x = 1$

Position of roots of a polynomial equation

Since we know that a polynomial is a continuous function for all $x \in \mathbb{R}$. Therefore if it its expression changes its sign at $x = \alpha$ means $x = \alpha$ is a root of polynomial therefore if sign of expression of the polynomial at a and b $(a < b)$ is opposite then it evidently implies that polynomial has at least one real root larger than a not exceeding b.

Mathematically, if $P(x)$ is a polynomial of degree $n\ (>1)$ and $a, b \in R$

$$\lim_{x \to a^+} P(x) = L_1,\ \lim_{x \to b^-} P(x) = L_2 \text{ such that } L_1, L_2 < 0$$

i.e., L_1 and L_2 are of opposite signs then $P(x)$ must have at least one real root $\in (a, b)$

In view of the above discussion, the truth of the following points can be readily admitted:

(a) If $f(x) = 0$ is an equation and a, b are two real numbers such that $f(a) . f(b) < 0$, then the equation $f(x) = 0$ has at least one real root or an odd number of real roots between a and b.

(b) If $f(a). f(b) > 0$, then either no real root or an even number of real roots of $f(x) = 0$ lies between a and b.

ILLUSTRATION 89: Show that

(a) a polynomial of an odd degree has at least one real root.

(b) a polynomial of an even degree has at least two real roots if it attains at least one value opposite in sign to the co-efficient of its highest-degree term.

SOLUTION: (a) Let $y = a_0x^n + a_1x^{n-1} + ...+ a_n$ where n is odd and let $n = 2m - 1$; $m = 1, 2, 3, ...$

$$\Rightarrow\ y = x^n\left[a_0 + \frac{a_1}{x} + ... + \frac{a_n}{x^n}\right] = x^{2m-1}\left[a_0 + \frac{a_1}{x} + ... \frac{a_n}{x^{2m-1}}\right] = \frac{x^{2m}}{x}\left[a_0 + \frac{a_1}{x} + ... \frac{a_n}{x^{2m-1}}\right]$$

$$\Rightarrow \quad y = \frac{1}{x}[x^{2m}]\left[a_0 + \frac{a_1}{x} + ... \frac{a_n}{x^{2m-1}}\right]$$

$\therefore \lim_{x\to\infty} y \to 0^+$ (approaches zero from right hand side)

and $\lim_{x\to-\infty} y \to 0^-$ (approaches zero from left hand side)

Hence odd degree polynomial has at least one real root

(b) $y = a_0x^n + a_1x^{n-1} + ...+ a_n$ where n is even and let $n = 2m;\ m = 1, 2, 3, ...$

$$\Rightarrow \quad y = x^n\left[a_0 + \frac{a_1}{x} + ... + \frac{a_n}{x^n}\right] = x^{2m}\left[a_0 + \frac{a_1}{x} + ... + \frac{a_n}{x^{2m}}\right]$$

$\Rightarrow \lim_{x\to\pm\infty} y = \infty$ for $a_0 > 0$ and $-\infty$ for $a_0 < 0$

If there is one value of $f(x)$ opposite in sign to the co-efficient of its highest degree then it shows polynomial crosses x-axis at one point, then if we remove the corresponding term (a_0) factor, the polynomial becomes odd degree, but it attains at least one real root, so even degree has at least one real root other than root corresponding to the above factor.

Repeated root and multiplicity of root

If $x = \alpha$ is a root of $P(x) = 0$ repeated r times, then α is said to be root of multiplicity r.

$\Rightarrow \quad P(x) = (x - \alpha)^r.\ Q(x)$:

$Q(\alpha) \neq 0$ where degree of $P(x) = n$

$\therefore \quad$ degree of $Q(x) = n - r$

$$P'(x) = (x - \alpha)^r .Q'(x) + Q(x)r(x - \alpha)^{r-1}$$
$$= (x - \alpha)^{r-1}[r.Q(x) + (x - \alpha)Q'(x)]$$

which clearly shows that α will also be a root of $P'(x) = 0$ repeated $(r - 1)$ times.

So we can say that multiplicity of a root decreases by 1 after each differentiation.

ILLUSTRATION 90: If $f(x) = x^3 + ax + b$ and $f(x)$ is divisible by $(x - 1)^2$, then show that it is also divisible by $(x + 2)$.

SOLUTION: $x = 1$ is repeated root

$\Rightarrow f(1) = 0 \qquad \Rightarrow \ 1 + a + b = 0 \qquad$ (i)

and $x = 1$ is also root of $\frac{d}{dx}(x^3 + ax + b)$ i.e., $y = 3x^2 + a$

$\Rightarrow f'(1) = 0 \ \Rightarrow \ 3(1) + a = 0 \Rightarrow a = -3 \Rightarrow \quad b = -1 - a \quad \Rightarrow \quad b = 2$

$\Rightarrow f(x) = x^3 - 3x + 2 = 0 \qquad \Rightarrow f(-2) = (-2)^3 - 3(-2) + 2 = 0$

$\Rightarrow f(x)$ is completely divisible by $(x + 2)$

ILLUSTRATION 91: Show that the polynomial $x(x^{n-1} - na^{n-1}) + a^n(n - 1)$ is divisible by $(x - a)^2$.

SOLUTION: Let $f(x) = x(x^{n-1} - na^{n-1}) + a^n(n - 1)$,

then $f(a) = a(a^{n-1} - na^{n-1}) + a^n(n - 1) = 0$

Also $f'(x) = nx^{n-1} - na^{n-1} \qquad \Rightarrow f'(a) = 0$

Since both $f(a)$ and $f'(a)$ are zero. The polynomial $f(x)$ must be divisible by $(x - a)^2$.

ILLUSTRATION 92: If $x^3 + 3px + q$ has a factor of the form $(x - a)^2$, show that $q^2 + 4p^3 - 0$.

SOLUTION: By actual division $\frac{x^3 + 3px + q}{(x-a)^2} = x + 2a + \frac{(3p + 3a^2)x - 2a^3 + q}{(x-a)^2}$

proceeding as in the previous Illustration, we must have $3p + 3a^2 = 0$, $2a^3 - q = 0$

Eliminating a, we get the required result

Aliter: Let $f(x) = x^3 + 3px + q$. Now as $(x - a)^2$ is a factor of $f(x)$, we must have $f(a) = 0$, $f'(a) = 0 \Rightarrow a^3 + 3ap + q = 0, f'(a) = 0, 3a^2 + 3p = 0$

From second equation $a^2 = -p$ putting in the first, we get

$\Rightarrow a(a^2 + 3p) = -q$ $\qquad \Rightarrow a(2p) = -q \Rightarrow 4a^2p^2 = q^2$

$\Rightarrow 4p^2(-p) = q^2$ $\qquad \Rightarrow q^2 + 4p^3 = 0$

ILLUSTRATION 93: If the equation $ax^3 + 3bx^2 + 3cx + d = 0$ has 2 equal roots, then show that each of them is equal to $\dfrac{bc-ad}{2(ac-b^2)}$.

SOLUTION: Let α be the root of $ax^3 + 3bx^2 + 3cx + d = 0$ $\Rightarrow a\alpha^3 + 3b\alpha^2 + 3c\alpha + d = 0$ (i)

Also α is a root of $3ax^2 + 6bx + 3c = 0$ $\Rightarrow a\alpha^2 + 2b\alpha + c = 0$ (ii)

Multiply (ii) by α and subtracting from (i), we get $b\alpha^2 + 2c\alpha + d = 0$ (iii)

Multiply (ii) by b and (iii) by a and subtracting, we get,

$ab\alpha^2 + 2b^2\alpha + bc = 0$ and $ab\alpha^2 + 2ac\alpha + ad = 0$

we get, $2(b^2 - ac)\,\alpha = ad - bc \Rightarrow \alpha = \dfrac{bc-ad}{2(ac-b^2)}$

■ GRAPHICAL REPRESENTATION OF CUBIC AND BIQUADRATIC POLYNOMIALS

Cubic polynomials

$f(x) = ax^3 + bx^2 + cx + d$ is a cubic polynomial with leading co-efficient $(a \neq 0)$. Let α, β, γ be the roots of above polynomial, then at least one of them must be real because $f(-\infty)$. $f(\infty) < 0$ so at least one real root must be present between $(-\infty, \infty)$.

Graphical analysis for different combination of roots is given below:

(a) When all roots are real and distinct (α, β, γ) say $(\alpha < \beta < \gamma)$

$f(x) = a(x - \alpha)(x - \beta)(x - \gamma)$

for $x < \alpha$: $f(x) = a(-)(-)(-) = -a$

i.e., sign of expression is opposite to sign of leading co-efficients.

for $\alpha < x < \beta$: $f(x) = a(+)(-)(-) = +a$

i.e., sign is same as that of leading co-efficients.

for $\beta < x < \gamma$: $f(x) = a(+)(+)(-) = -a$ sign is opposite to leading co-efficient. for $x > \gamma$: $f(x) = a(+)(+)(+) = a$ same as that of leading co-efficient.

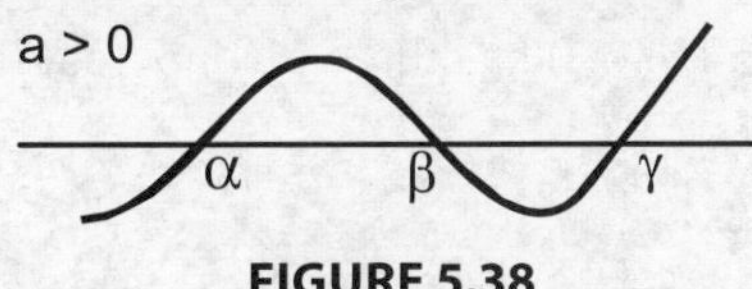

FIGURE 5.38

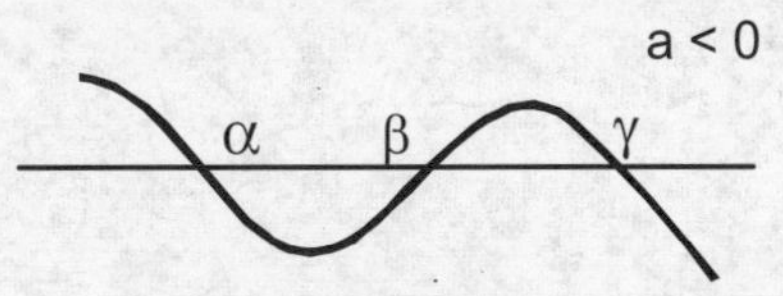

FIGURE 5.39

(b) When two roots are real and repeated (α, α, β)

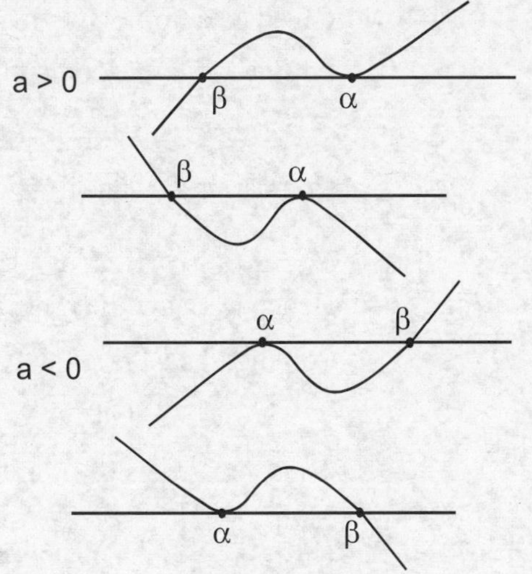

FIGURE 5.40

(c) When all three roots are real and equal: (α, α, α)

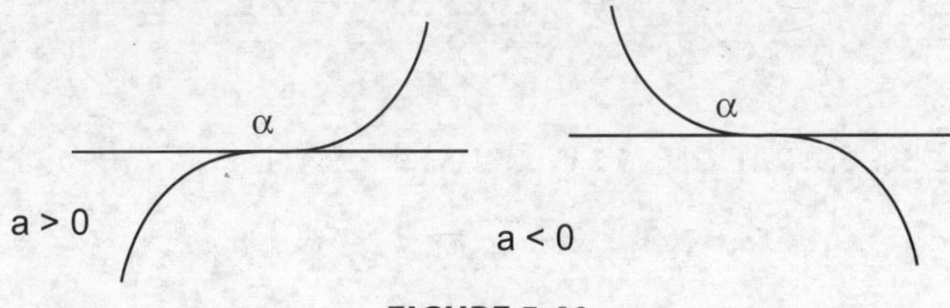

FIGURE 5.41

Solving cubic equation By using factor theorem together with some intelligent guessing, we can factorize polynomials of higher degree. In summary, to solve a cubic equation of the form $ax^3 + bx^2 + cx + d = 0$,

1. Obtain one factor $(x - \alpha)$ by trial and error
2. Factorize $ax^3 + bx^2 + cx + d = 0$ as $(x - \alpha)(hx^2 + kx + s) = 0$
3. Solve the quadratic $hx^2 + kx + s = 0$ for other roots.

Necessary and Sufficient Condition that a cubic equation has all roots real

Necessary Condition:

Let $f(x) = ax^3 + bx^2 + cx + d = 0$ (i)

$\Rightarrow f'(x) = 3ax^2 + 2bx + c = 0$

Let the roots of $f'(x) = 0$ are α and β

$\because f(x) = ax^3 + bx^2 + cx + d = 0$ has all roots real,

$\Rightarrow f'(x) = 3ax^2 + 2bx + c = 0$ also has all roots real

$\Rightarrow 4b^2 - 12ac \geq 0 \quad \Rightarrow \quad b^2 - 3ac \geq 0$

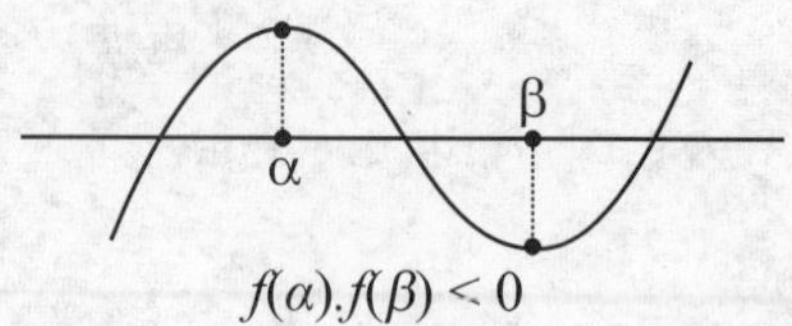

$f(\alpha).f(\beta) < 0$

FIGURE 5.42

Sufficient Condition: Let α, β be the real roots of $f'(x) = 0$, then $f(\alpha).f(\beta) < 0$

$\Rightarrow$ Cubic must have all real roots.

ILLUSTRATION 94: Find the condition that the roots of the equation $x^3 - px^2 + qx - r = 0$ may be in A.P.

SOLUTION: Let the roots of the given equation be $a - d, a, a + d$.

Then, $(a - d) + a + (a + d) = p \quad \Rightarrow a = p/3$

Since, a is a root of the equation, replacing x by a, we get

$$\left(\frac{p}{3}\right)^3 - p\left(\frac{p}{3}\right)^2 + q\left(\frac{p}{3}\right) - r = 0 \quad \Rightarrow \quad \frac{p^3}{27} - \frac{p^3}{9} + \frac{pq}{3} - r = 0$$

$\Rightarrow 2p^3 - 9pq + 27r = 0$ is the required condition

ILLUSTRATION 95: Solve the equation $x^3 - 18x = 35$

SOLUTION: Given equation is $x^3 - 18x = 35$ (i)

Putting $x = y + z$ and cubing both sides, we get

$x^3 = y^3 + z^3 + 3yz(y + z)$ or $x^3 - 3xyz - (y^3 + z^3) = 0$ (ii)

Comparing (i) and (ii), we have

$yz = 6$ or $y^3 z^3 = 216$ and $y^3 + z^3 = 35$

Hence y^3, z^3 are the roots of quadratic equation $t^2 - 35t + 216 = 0$

Solving this $y^3 = 27$ and $z^3 = 8$ [cube roots of 1 are $1, \omega, \omega^2$]

$y = 3, 3\omega, 3\omega^2$ and $z = 2, 2\omega, 2\omega^2$

Thus three roots of (i) are $(2 + 3)$, $(2\omega + 3\omega^2)$, and $(3\omega + 2\omega^2)$

Now $3\omega + 2\omega^2 = \omega + 2(\omega + \omega^2) = \omega + 2(-1) = \dfrac{-1+\sqrt{-3}}{2} - 2 = \dfrac{-5+\sqrt{-3}}{2}$

and $2\omega + 3\omega^2 = -\omega + 3(\omega + \omega^2) = -\omega - 3$ [$\because 1 + \omega + \omega^2 = 0$]

$= \dfrac{+1-\sqrt{-3}}{2} - 3 = \dfrac{-5-\sqrt{-3}}{2}$ thus three roots are 5, $\dfrac{-5\pm\sqrt{-3}}{2}$.

ILLUSTRATION 96: Find the set of values of a for which equation $x^3 - 3x + a = 0$ has three distinct real roots.

SOLUTION: Let $f(x) = x^3 - 3x + a$

$\Rightarrow f'(x) = 3x^2 - 3 = 3\,(x - 1)\,(x + 1)$

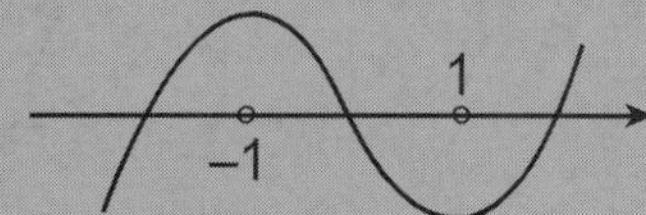

FIGURE 5.43

$\Rightarrow f'(x) = 0$; when $x = \pm 1$ now $f(1) = a - 2, f(-1) = a + 2$

We know the roots would be real and distinct if $f(1)\,f(-1) < 0$

$\Rightarrow (a - 2)\,(a + 2) < 0 \Rightarrow -2 < a < 2$ (using wavy curve method)

Thus the given equation would have real and distinct roots if $a \in (-2, 2)$.

ILLUSTRATION 97: Show that all the roots of the equation $ax^3 + x^2 + x + 1 = 0$ can't be real where a is any real number.

SOLUTION: If $a = 0$, then the all roots are obviously non-real therefore assume $a \neq 0$. Let the roots be x_1, x_2, x_3 then we have $x_1 + x_2 + x_3 = -\dfrac{1}{a}$, $x_1x_2 + x_2x_3 + x_3x_1 = \dfrac{1}{a}$, $x_1x_2x_3 = -\dfrac{1}{a}$

Now if possible, let all the roots be real. Consider the expression

$x_1^2x_2^2 + x_2^2x_3^2 + x_3^2x_1^2 = (x_1x_2 + x_2x_3 + x_3x_1)^2 - 2\,x_1x_2x_3(\,x_1 + x_2 + x_3)$

$= \dfrac{1}{a^2} - 2\left(\dfrac{1}{a}\right)\left(\dfrac{1}{a}\right) = -\dfrac{1}{a^2} < 0$ essentially, which is absurd since $x_1^2x_2^2 + x_2^2x_3^2 + x_3^2x_1^2$ must be essentially non-negative if all the roots be real.

Biquadratic polynomials

$f(x) = ax^4 + bx^3 + cx^2 + dx + e$ is known as biquadratic polynomial and it has exactly four roots $\alpha, \beta, \gamma, \delta$. $\because f(\infty).\,f(-\infty) > 0$ therefore it may or may not have real roots we analyze this polynomial graphically as below:

Case I: *All roots real (say $\alpha < \beta < \gamma < \delta$) and distinct*

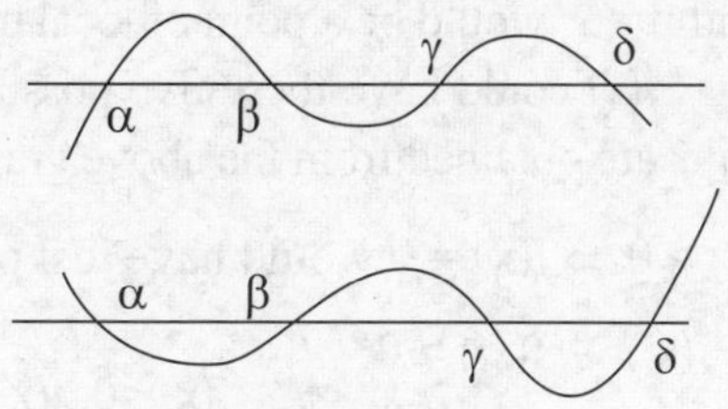

FIGURE 5.44

Case II: *Repeated roots (real)*

(a) $\alpha, \alpha, \beta, \gamma$

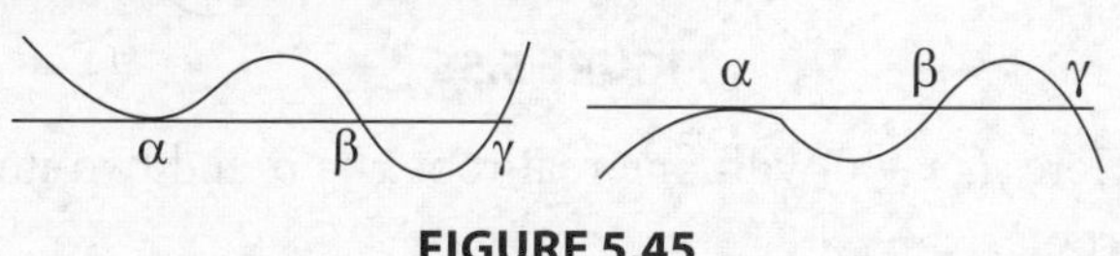

FIGURE 5.45

(b) $\alpha, \beta, \gamma, \gamma$

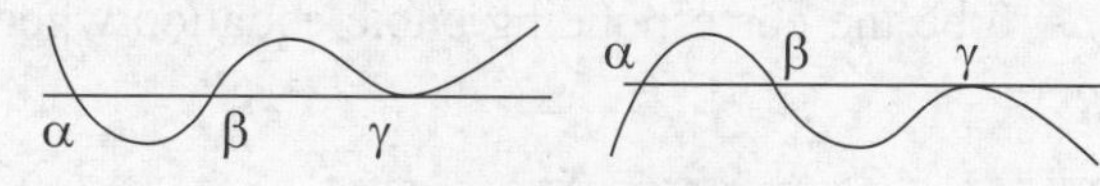

FIGURE 5.46

(c) $\alpha, \beta, \beta, \gamma$

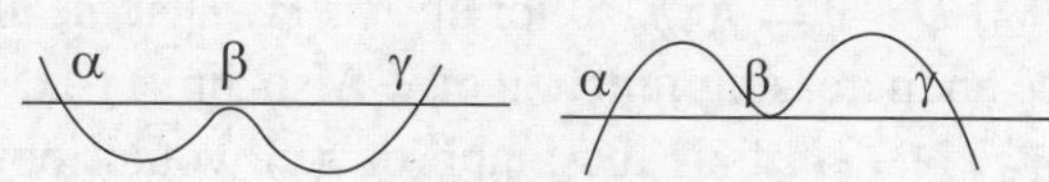

FIGURE 5.47

(d) $\alpha, \alpha, \beta, \beta$

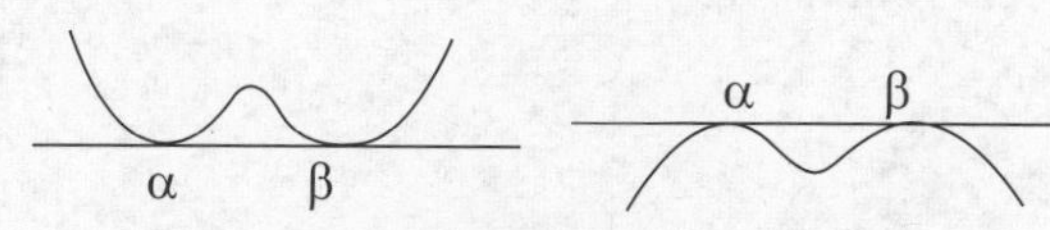

FIGURE 5.48

(e) $\alpha, \alpha, \alpha, \beta$

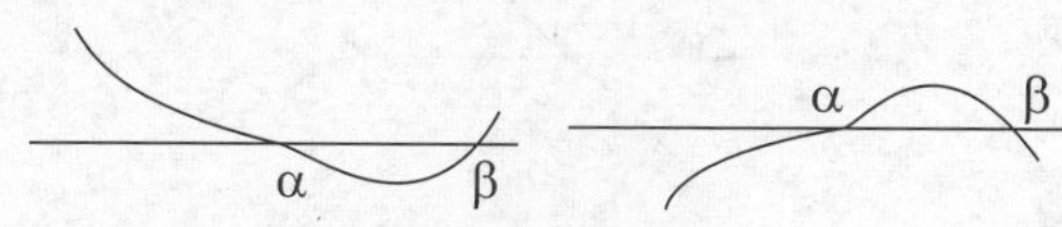

FIGURE 5.49

(f) $\alpha, \alpha, \alpha, \alpha$

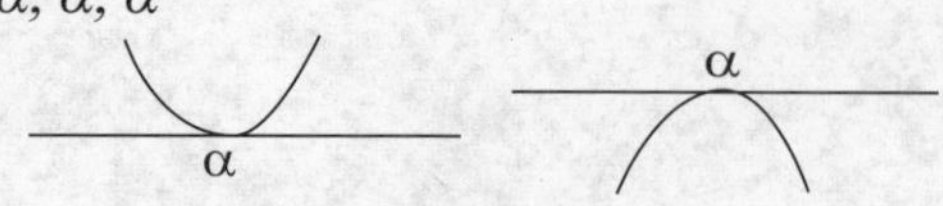

FIGURE 5.50

Case III:

(a) *Two real distinct and two non-real roots. a, b, p + iq, p – iq*

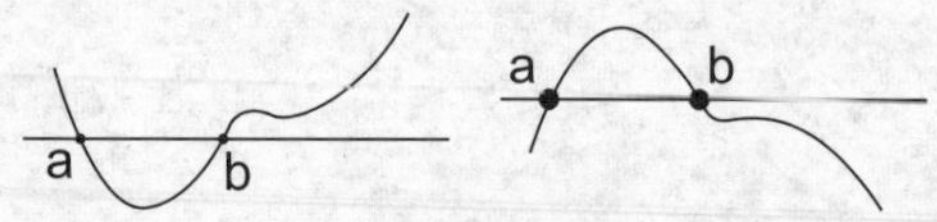

FIGURE 5.51

(b) *Two real repeated and two non-real complex roots.*

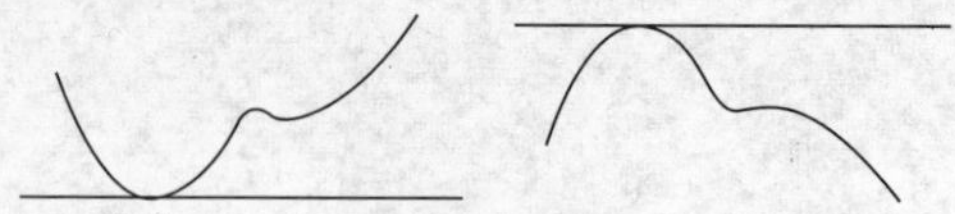

FIGURE 5.52

(c) *All roots non-real complex.*

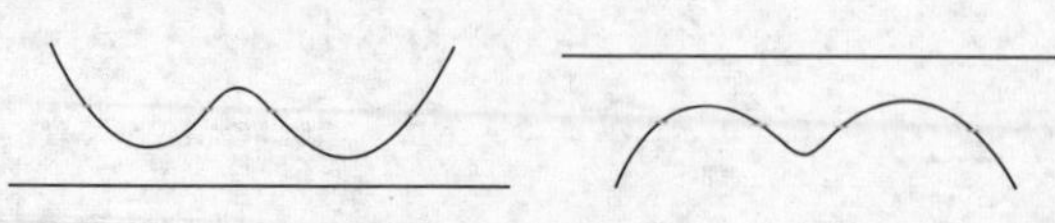

FIGURE 5.53

ILLUSTRATION 98: Find the real values of a, b, c and d for which biquadratic $x^4 + ax^3 + bx^2 + cx - d^2 = 0$ has at least two real roots.

SOLUTION: $f(+\infty) = +\infty > 0$ and $f(0) = -d^2 \le 0$

$\Rightarrow$ $\exists$ a root $\in(-\infty, 0)$

Similarly, $f(0) < 0$ and $f(\infty) > 0$

$\Rightarrow$ $\exists$ a root $\in(0, \infty)$

$\Rightarrow$ The biquadratic has atleast 4 real roots for $a, b, c, d \in \mathbb{R}$

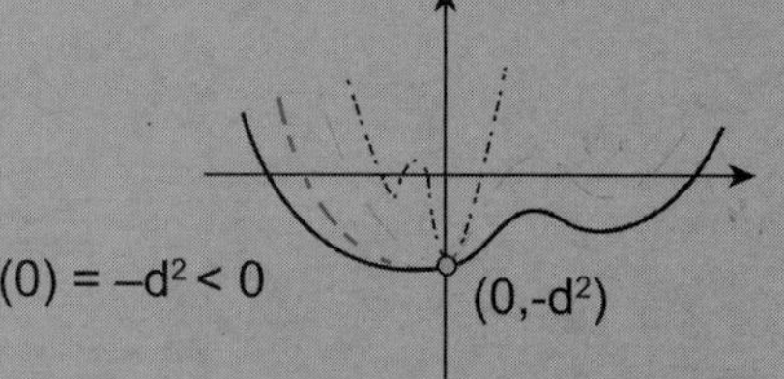

FIGURE 5.54

APPLICATION OF DERIVATIVES TO DETERMINE THE NATURE OF ROOT

Let $f(x) = x^3 + ax^2 + bx + c$ be the given cubic polynomial and $f(x) = 0$ be the corresponding cubic equation where $a, b, c \in R$.

Now $f'(x) = 3x^2 + 2ax + b$.

Let $D = 4a^2 - 12b = 4(a^2 - 3b)$, be the discriminant of the equation $f'(x) = 0$. Then the following cases arise:

Case I: If $D < 0 \Rightarrow f(x) > 0$ for all $x \in \mathbb{R}$. That means $f(x)$ would be an increasing function of x. Also $\lim\limits_{x\to\infty} f(-x) = -\infty$ and $\lim\limits_{x\to\infty} f(x) = \infty$, thus the graph of $f(x)$ would look like given in the figure. It is clear that the graph of $y = f(x)$ would cut the x-axis only once. That means we would have just one real root (say x_0).

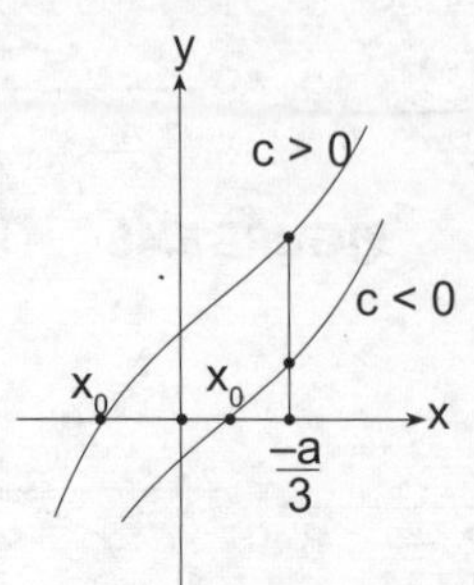

FIGURE 5.55

Clearly, $x_0 > 0$ if $c < 0$ and $x_0 < 0$ if $c > 0$.

Case II: If $D > 0$, then $f'(x) = 0$ would have two real roots (say x_1 and x_2, let $x_1 < x_2$)

$\Rightarrow$ $f'(x) = 3(x - x_1)(x - x_2)$

Clearly, $f'(x) < 0, x \in (x_1, x_2)$;

$f'(x) > 0, x \in (-\infty, x_1) \cup (x_2, \infty)$

That means $f(x)$ would increases in $(-\infty, x_1)$ and (x_2, ∞) and would decrease in (x_1, x_2). Hence $x = x_1$ would be a point of local maxima and $x = x_2$ would be a point of local minima. Thus the graph of $y = f(x)$ could have these five possibilities. Thus following results are obtained from the above graph:

(a) $f(x_1) f(x_2) > 0 \Rightarrow f(x) = 0$ would have just one real root.

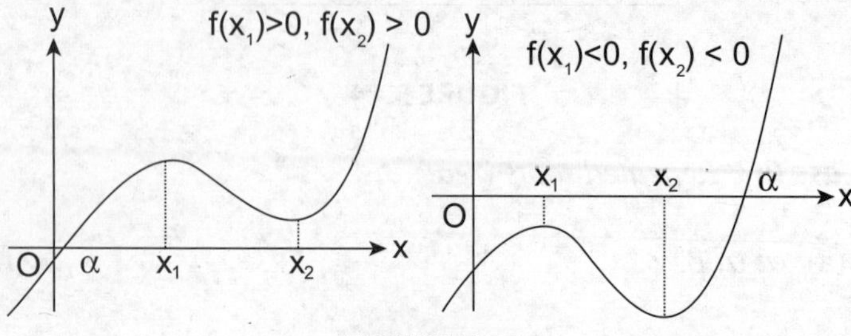

FIGURE 5.56

Here $f(x) = 0$ with one real root $x = \alpha$ and two imaginary roots.

(b) $f(x_1)\, f(x_2) < 0 \Rightarrow f(x) = 0$ would have three real and distinct root.

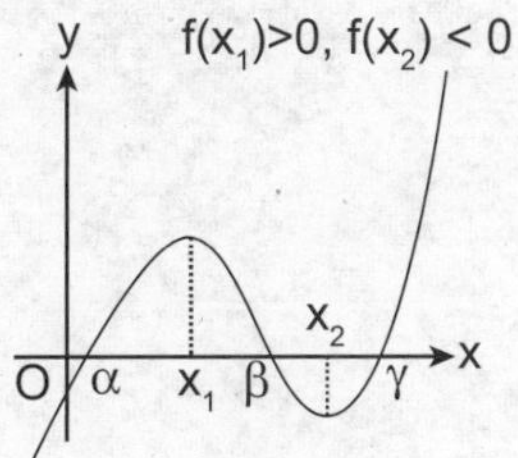

FIGURE 5.57

Here $f(x) = 0$ with three distinct real roots $x = \alpha, \beta, \gamma$

(c) $f(x_1)\, f(x_2) = 0 \Rightarrow f(x) = 0$ would have three real roots but one of the root would be repeated.

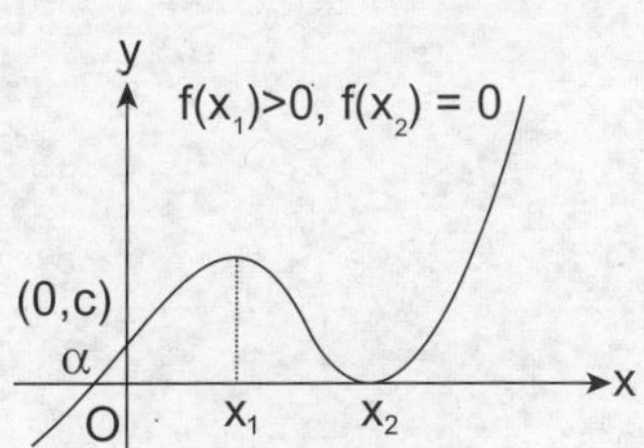

FIGURE 5.58

$f(x) = 0$ with three roots $x = \alpha, x_2, x_2$ (x_2 being repeated root)

Case III: If $D = 0, f'(x) = 3(x - x_1)^2$; where x_1 is root of $f'(x) = 0$

$\Rightarrow$ $f(x) = (x - x_1)^3 + k$. (where k is any constant), Then

$f(x) = 0$ has three real roots if $k = 0$

$f(x) = 0$ have one real root, if $k \neq 0$.

$f(x) = 0$ with three real roots $x = x_1, x_2, \alpha$, (x_1 being repeated root)

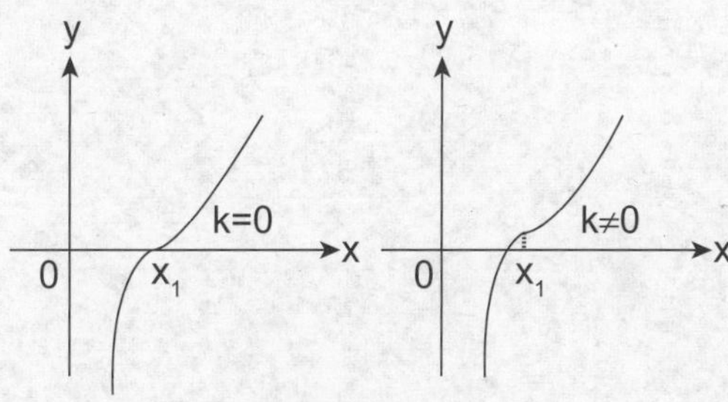

FIGURE 5.59

ILLUSTRATION 99: Find all values of p for which the equation $x^4 + 4x^3 - 8x^2 + p = 0$ has

(a) all real roots (b) two real roots (c) no real roots.

SOLUTION: The given equation is $x^4 + 4x^3 - 8x^2 + p = 0$

$f'(x) = 4x^3 + 12x^2 - 16x = 0 = 4x(x + 4)(x - 1) = 0$

$\Rightarrow$ Horizontal tangents at $x = 0, -4, 1$ and $\lim_{x\to\infty} f(x) = \infty = \lim_{x\to-\infty} f(x)$

(a) For all real roots the graph of $f(x)$ has two possibilities. Now, value of p can be obtained by observing co-ordinate of the following figures.

$f(-4) = p - 128$; $f(0) = p$; $f(1) = p - 3$

From above three conditions, we will write the value(s) of p for all real roots.

Case 1:

$$\left.\begin{array}{l} p - 128 < 0 \\ p > 0 \\ p - 3 = 0 \end{array}\right\} \Rightarrow \left.\begin{array}{l} p < 128 \\ p > 0 \\ p = 3 \end{array}\right\} \Rightarrow p = 3$$

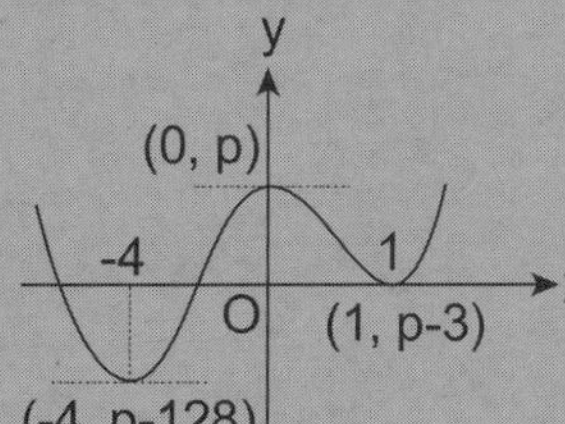

FIGURE 5.60

Case 2:

$$\left.\begin{array}{l} p - 128 < 0 \\ p - 3 < 0 \\ p > 0 \end{array}\right\} \Rightarrow \left.\begin{array}{l} p < 128 \\ p < 3 \\ p > 0 \end{array} \quad \Rightarrow p \in (0, 3)\right\}$$

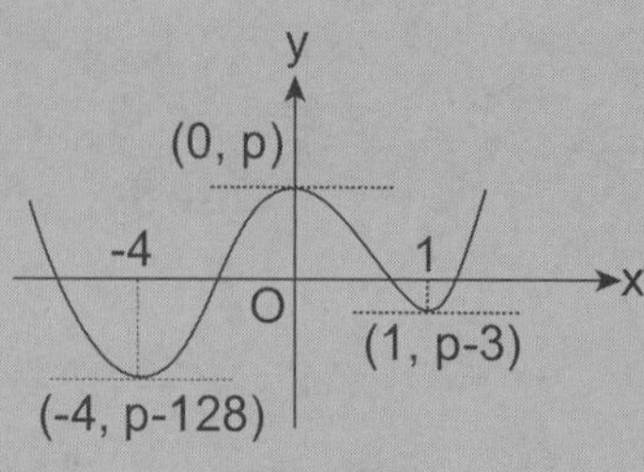

FIGURE 5.61

Case 3: $p - 128 < 0, p = 0, p - 3 = 0$

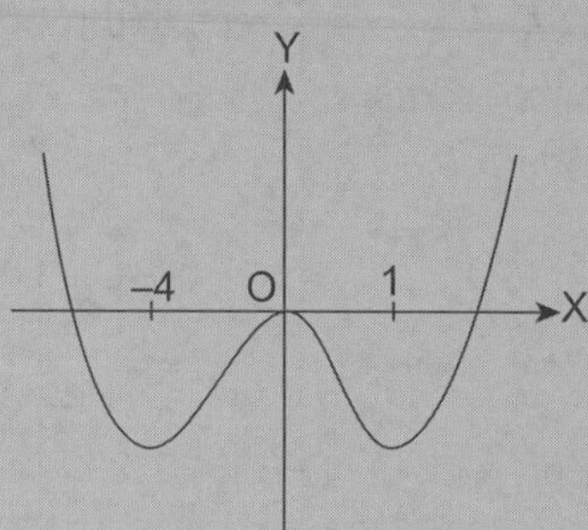

FIGURE 5.62

i.e., $p = 0$. Thus for all four real roots $p \in [0, 3]$

(b) For two real roots the possibilities of $f(x)$ is as follows:

$$\textbf{Case 1: } \left.\begin{aligned} p-128<0 &\Rightarrow p<128 \\ p-3<0 &\Rightarrow p<3 \\ p<0 &\Rightarrow p<0 \end{aligned}\right\} \Rightarrow p<0$$

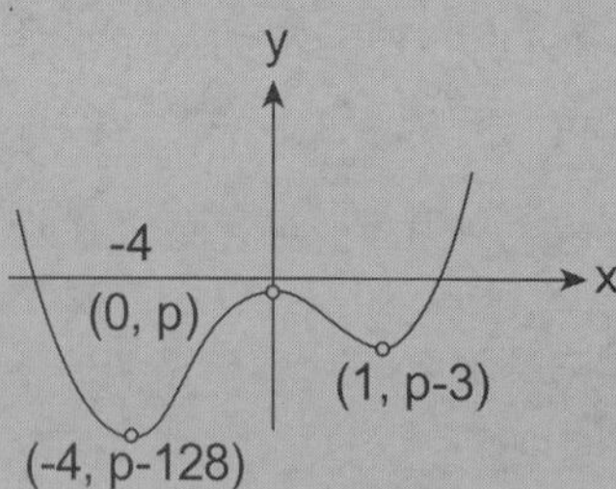

FIGURE 5.63

$$\text{Case II: } \left.\begin{aligned} p-128<0 &\Rightarrow p<128 \\ p-3>0 &\Rightarrow p>3 \\ p>0 &\Rightarrow p>0 \end{aligned}\right\} \Rightarrow 3<p<128$$

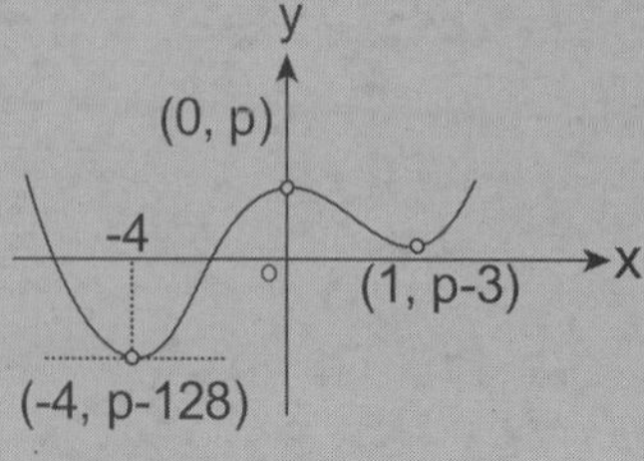

FIGURE 5.64

Case III: $\left.\begin{array}{l} p-3>0 \\ p>0 \\ p-128=0 \end{array}\right\} \Rightarrow p=128$

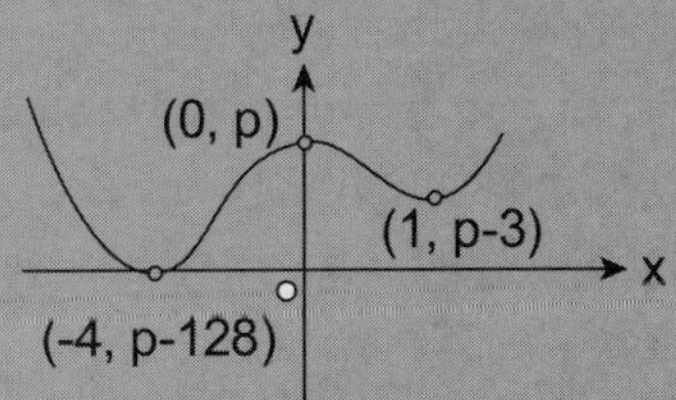

FIGURE 5.65

From above condition, we will write the value p for which two roots real i.e., $p < 0$ or $3 < p \leq 128$

(c) For no real roots, there is only one possibility:
i.e., $p - 128 > 0 \Rightarrow p > 128$

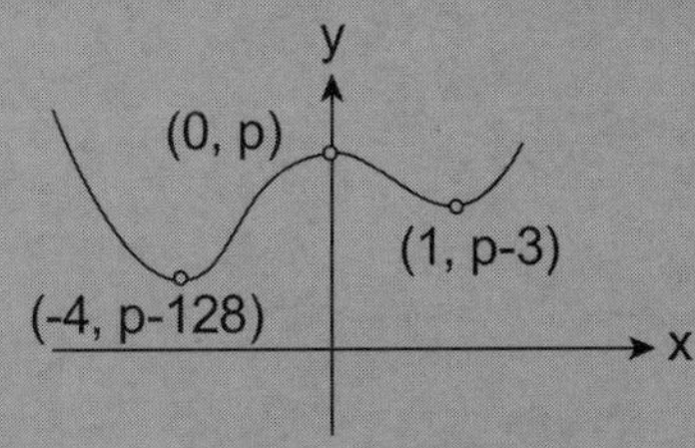

FIGURE 5.66

■ DESCARTES' RULE

An equation $f(x) = 0$ can't have more positive roots than number of changes of sign in $f(x)$, and can't have more negative roots than number of changes of sign in $f(-x)$.

Step 1: To check at most positive roots in $f(x) = 0$
Check change in sign = most number of positive roots
e.g., $f(x) = x^9 + 5x^8 - x^3 + 7x + 2 = 0$

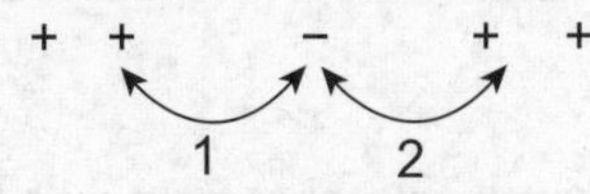

FIGURE 5.67

There are two changes in sign ⇒ at most two positive roots.

Step 2: Check at most negative roots in $f(x) = 0$

The number of changes in sign = most number of negative roots

e.g., $f(x) = x^9 + 5x^8 - x^3 + 7x + 2$

$\Rightarrow \quad f(-x) = -x^9 + 5x^8 + x^3 - 7x + 2$

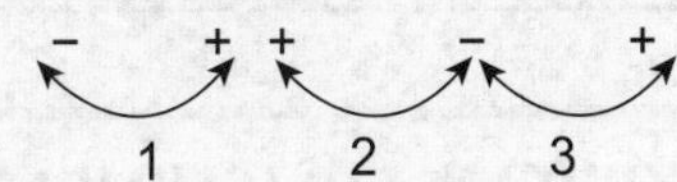

FIGURE 5.68

There are 3 changes in sign
⇒ At most 3 negative roots.

NOTES

1. *If there is no change in sign, then all the roots are imaginary.*
2. *If in the polynomial of degree n, the maximum number of possible positive real roots is k_1 and maximum number of possible negative real roots is k_2 and zero is not the root of polynomial, then the minimum number of complex roots will be equal to $n - (k_1 + k_2)$.*

ILLUSTRATION 100: Find the number of maximum possible positive/negative roots of the eqaution.

$$x^6 - 3x^5 + 4x^3 + 3x^2 + 4 = 0$$

SOLUTION: Let $f(x) = x^6 - 3x^5 + 4x^3 + 3x^2 + 4$

Here $f(x)$ has 2 changes in sign of co-efficients, applying Descartes rule of sign, first change is from positive to negative for x^6 to x^5 and second change is from negative to positive for x^5 to x^3. So $f(x) = 0$ has at most two positive real roots.

$f(-x) = x^6 + 3x^5 - 4x^3 + 3x^2 + 4$ has 2 changes in sign so $f(x) = 0$ has atmost 2 negative real roots.

Since the least degree in $f(x)$ is zero, so $f(x)$ has no root at $x = 0$.

Hence $f(x) = 0$ has at most four real roots, therefore it has at least two complex roots.

ILLUSTRATION 101: Prove that $a^2x^4 + bx^3 - cx^2 + dx - e^2$ has at least two real roots?

SOLUTION: We know that if we have even degree polynomial with positive co-efficient of highest degree, then $f(\infty) = f(-\infty) = \infty$.

The given fourth degree equation becomes negative between $(-\infty, \infty)$ i.e., at $x = 0$ which implies that it has at least two real roots.

Aliter: Mathematically, we can say,

$$f(x) = a^2x^4 + bx^3 - cx^2 + dx - e^2$$

$$\Rightarrow \lim_{x\to\infty} f(x) = \lim_{x\to\infty} x^4\left(a^2 + \frac{b}{x} - \frac{c}{x^2} + \frac{d}{x^3} - \frac{e^2}{x^4}\right) > 0$$

$$\Rightarrow \lim_{x\to-\infty} f(x) = \lim_{x\to-\infty} x^4\left(a^2 + \frac{b}{x} - \frac{c}{x^2} + \frac{d}{x^3} - \frac{e^2}{x^4}\right) > 0$$

and $f(0) = -e^2 < 0$, means $f(x)$ crosses x-axis once between $(-\infty, 0)$ and again between $(0, \infty)$. So equation has at least two real roots.

ILLUSTRATION 102: Prove the number of the + ve real roots of the equation $x^4 - x - 1 = 0$ is one and number of negative real root is also one and show that above equation has exactly two non-real complex root.

SOLUTION: $f(x) = x^4 - x - 1$ has only one change in sign so at most one positive real root.

$f(-x) = x^4 + x - 1$ has only one change in sign so at most one negative real root.

$\Rightarrow$ Above equation has at least two complex real roots.

Since $f(-\infty)$ is positive, $f(\infty)$ is also positive, but $f(0)$ is -1 therefore the above equation has at least one negative real root and at least one positive real root.

Now we can conclude that the above equation has exactly one positive real root, exactly one negative real root and exactly two non-real complex roots.

TEXTUAL EXERCISE–10 (SUBJECTIVE)

1. Show that $f(x) = x^3 + ax^2 + bx + c$ has at least one real root.
2. Show that $f(x) = x^4 - 2x^2 + 3x - 4$ has at least two real roots which are of opposite sign.
3. Show that $f(x) = x^3 - 9x + 1 = 0$ has all roots real.
4. Find the values of k and m so that $x^3 + 3kx^2 + mx + 1$ has $x = 1$ as twice repeated roots.
5. Predict the nature of roots using descarte rule of sign if a, b, c, d are positive real number and $e < 0$. of the polynomial equation $ax^5 + bx^4 + cx^2 + dx + e$.
6. Find the maximum number of positive/negative real roots and minimum number of possible non-real roots of the following equations
   (i) $x^7 - 4x^3 + 3x + 1$ (ii) $x^5 + 3x^3 - 1$
7. Find the set of values of 'a' for which equation $x^3 - 3x + a = 0$ has three distinct real roots.
8. Find the values of parameter k for which all the roots of the equation $x^4 - 4x^3 - 8x^2 + k = 0$ are real.
9. If $a, b, c \in \mathbb{R}$ and $a + b + c = 0$, then prove that the quadratic equation $3ax^2 + 2bx + c = 0$ has at least one root in $(0, 1)$.

Answer Keys

4. $k = -1/3$, $m = -1$, roots are 1, 1, –1, –1
5. one positive, two negative, other two may none real.
6. (i) max: 6; min: 2 (ii) max: 4, min: 4 **7.** (–2, 2) **8.** $0 \le k \le 3$

TEXTUAL EXERCISE–9 (OBJECTIVE)

1. Let a, b, c be three real numbers such that $2a + 3b + 6c = 0$. Then the quadratic equation $ax^2 + bx + c = 0$ has
(a) imaginary roots
(b) at least one roots in (0, 1)
(c) at least one root in (–1, 0)
(d) both roots in (1, 2)

2. $x^4 - 4x - 1 = 0$ has
(a) exactly two postive real root
(b) exatly two negative real root
(c) exactly two real roots
(d) None of these

3. Root of the equation $ax^3 + bx^2 + cx + d = 0$ remain unchanged by increasing each coefficient by one unit, then
(a) $a = b = c = d \neq 0$ (b) $a = b \neq c = d \neq 0$
(c) $a \neq b = c = d \neq 0$ (d) $a = b = c \neq d \neq 0$

4. If $(x - 1)^3$ is a factor of $x^4 + ax^3 + bx^2 + cx - 1$, then the other factor is:
(a) $x - 3$ (b) $x + 1$
(c) $x + 2$ (d) None of these

5. If $16 - x^2 > |x - a|$ is to be satisfied by at least one negative value of x, then complete set of values of 'a' is
(a) $\left(-6, \frac{65}{4}\right)$ (b) $\left(-8, \frac{65}{2}\right)$
(c) (–65/4, 16) (d) (–8, 8)

6. The number of solutions of the equation $|x - 1| = e^x$
(a) 0 (b) 1
(c) 2 (d) 3

7. If α, β, γ are the roots fo $x^3 - px - q = 0$, then the value of $(2\alpha + \beta + \gamma)(2\beta + \gamma + \alpha)(2\gamma + \alpha + \beta)$ is
(a) q (b) $-q$
(c) p (d) $-p$

8. The expression $2x^4 - 7x^3 + 2x^2 - x + 1$ when divided by $x^2 - 1$ leaves a remainder $px + q$. Then the ordered pair (p, q) is
(a) (5, –8) (b) (–8, 5)
(c) (8, 5) (d) (–5, –8).

9. The roots of the equation $x^3 + 7x^2 - 36 = 0$, given that one root is double the other, are
(a) –2, –4, –6 (b) –2, 3, 6
(c) 2, –3, 6 (d) None of these.

10. If the equation $x^3 + ax^2 + bx - 4 = 0$ has two roots equal to 2, then the ordered pair (a, b) is
(a) (–5, 8) (b) (5, –8)
(c) (1, 1) (d) (2, 2)

11. The roots of the equation $4x^3 + 16x^2 - 9x - 36 = 0$, given that sum of two of its roots is zero are
(a) 3, –3, –1 (b) $-4, \frac{3}{2}, -\frac{3}{2}$
(c) $4, \frac{3}{2}, -\frac{3}{2}$ (d) 1, –1, –9

12. If $x - y$ and $y - 2x$ are two factors of the expression $x^3 - 3x^2y + \lambda xy^2 + \mu y^3$, then
(a) $\lambda = 11, \mu = -3$ (b) $\lambda = 3, \mu = -11$
(c) $\lambda = \frac{11}{4}, \mu = -\frac{3}{4}$ (d) None of these

13. If $x + y$ and $y + 3x$ are two factors of the expression $\lambda x^2 - \mu x^2 y + xy^2 + y^3$, then the third factor is
(a) $y + 3x$ (b) $y - 3x$
(c) $y - x$ (d) None of these

Answer Keys

1. (b) **2.** (c) **3.** (a) **4.** (b) **5.** (c) **6.** (b) **7.** (a) **8.** (b) **9.** (d) **10.** (a)
11. (b) **12.** (c) **13.** (b)

REMARKS

The truth of the following statements will be readily admitted

1. *If all the co-efficients are real, then the imaginary roots occur in pairs i.e., number of complex roots is always even.*
2. *If the degree of a polynomial equation is odd, then the number of real roots will also be odd. It follows that at least one of the roots will be real.*
3. *Every equation of an odd degree has at least one real root whose sign is opposite to that of its last term.*
4. *Every equation which is of even degree and has its last term negative has at least two real roots; one positive and one negative.*
5. *If a is repeated roots repeating 'r' times of a polynomial equation f(x) = 0 of degree n i.e.,*

   $f(x) = (x - \alpha)^r g(x)$, where g(x) is a polynmial of degree (n – r) and $g(\alpha) \neq 0$, then $f(\alpha) = f'(\alpha) = f''(\alpha) = ... = f^{(r-1)}(\alpha) = 0$ and $f'(\alpha) \neq 0$ and vice versa.
6. *If a, b, c, ...,k are roots of the equation f(x) = 0, then* $f'(x) = \dfrac{f(x)}{x-a} + \dfrac{f(x)}{x-b} + \dfrac{f(x)}{x-c} + ... + \dfrac{f(x)}{x-k}$
7. *If the co-efficients are all positive, the equation has no positive root; thus the equation $x^5 + x^3 + 2x + 1 = 0$ can't have a positive root.*
8. *If the co-efficients of the even powers of x are all of one sign, and the co-efficients of the odd powers are all of the contrary sign, the equation has no negative root; thus the equation $x^7 + x^5 - 2x^4 + x^3 - 3x^2 + 7x - 5 = 0$ cannot have a negative root.*
9. *If the equation contains only even powers of x and the co-efficients are all of the same sign, the equation has no real root; thus the equation $2x^6 + 3x^4 + x^2 + 7 = 0$ cannot have a real root.*
10. *If the equation contains only odd powers of x and the co-efficients are all of the same sign, the equation has no real root except x = 0; thus the equation $x^9 + 2x^5 + 3x^3 + x = 0$ has no real root except x = 0.*

MULTIPLE-CHOICE QUESTIONS

SECTION–I

OBJECTIVE-TYPE SOLVED EXAMPLES

1. If $\sin\alpha$, $\cos\alpha$ are the roots of the equation $ax^2 + bx + c = 0$, $(c \neq 0)$ then

(a) $a^2 - b^2 + 2ac = 0$ (b) $(a + c)^2 = b^2 + c^2$
(c) $a^2 + b^2 - 2ac = 0$ (d) $(a - c)^2 = b^2 + c^2$

Solution: (a) and (b) Sum and product of the roots

$\sin\alpha + \cos\alpha = -b/a$, $\sin\alpha \cos\alpha = c/a$

$1 = \sin^2\alpha + \cos^2\alpha = (\sin\alpha + \cos\alpha)^2 - 2\sin\alpha\cos\alpha$

$\Rightarrow \quad = \dfrac{b^2}{a^2} - \dfrac{2c}{a}$

$\Rightarrow a^2 = b^2 - 2ac \quad \therefore$ (a) is correct

$\Rightarrow a^2 + c^2 + 2ac = b^2 + c^2 \Rightarrow (a + c)^2 = b^2 + c^2$

Thus (c) also correct.

2. If the sum of roots of the quadratic equation $ax^2 + bx + c = 0$, $(a, b, c \neq 0)$ is equal to sum of the squares of their reciprocals, then a/c, b/a, c/b, are in

(a) arithmetic progression (A.P.)
(b) geometric progression (G.P.)
(c) harmonic progression (H.P.)
(d) None of these

Solution: (c) Let α, β be the roots of quadratic equation $ax^2 + bx + c = 0$

Then $\alpha + \beta = \dfrac{1}{\alpha^2} + \dfrac{1}{\beta^2} = \dfrac{\alpha^2 + \beta^2}{\alpha^2\beta^2}$

$= \dfrac{(\alpha+\beta)^2 - 2\alpha\beta}{\alpha^2\beta^2}$

$\Rightarrow -\dfrac{b}{a} = \dfrac{b^2/a^2 - 2c/a}{c^2/a^2} = \dfrac{b^2 - 2ac}{c^2}$

$\Rightarrow \dfrac{2a}{c} = \dfrac{b^2}{c^2} + \dfrac{b}{a} = \dfrac{ab^2 + bc^2}{ac^2}$

$\Rightarrow 2a^2c = ab^2 + bc^2$

$\Rightarrow \dfrac{2a}{b} = \dfrac{b}{c} + \dfrac{c}{a}$ [dividing by abc]

$\Rightarrow \dfrac{c}{a}, \dfrac{a}{b}, \dfrac{b}{c}$ are in A.P.

$\Rightarrow \dfrac{a}{c}, \dfrac{b}{a}, \dfrac{c}{b}$ are in H.P.

3. If $0 < x < 1000$ and $[x/2] + [x/3] + [x/5] = \dfrac{31}{30}x$, where $[x]$ is the greatest integer less than or equal to x, the number of possible values of x is

(a) 34 (b) 32
(c) 33 (d) None of these

Solution: (c) $[x/2] + [x/3] + [x/5] = \dfrac{31}{30}x$

$= x/2 + x/3 + x/5$

$\Rightarrow x/2, x/3, x/5$ are all integers.

So, x = multiple of the LCM of 2, 3, 5

$\therefore \; x = 30 \times 1, 30 \times 2, 30 \times 3, \ldots 30 \times 33.$

$[0 < x < 1000]$

i.e., 33 values of x are possible.

4. If a, b, c, d are four consecutive terms of an increasing AP, then the roots of the equation $(x - a)(x - c) + 2(x - b)(x - d) = 0$ are

(a) real and distinct (b) non-real complex
(c) real and equal (d) integers

Solution: (a) If k (> 0) be the common difference of A.P., then $b = a + k$, $c = a + 2k$, $d = a + 3k$

Equation is $3x^2 - [(a + c) + 2(b + d)]x + (ac + 2bd) = 0$

$\Rightarrow 3x^2 - (6a + 10k)x + a(a + 2k) + 2(a + k)(a + 3k) = 0$

$\therefore \; D = (6a + 10k)^2 - 4.3.\{a^2 + 2ak + 2a^2 + 8ak + 6k^2\} = 28k^2 > 0 \quad [\because k \neq 0]$

so real and distinct roots

5. If $ax + by = 1$, $cx^2 + dy^2 = 1$ have only one solution, then

(a) $a^2/c + b^2/d = 1$ (b) $x = a/c$
(c) $y = b/d$ (d) None of these

Solution: (a, b, c) $ax + by = 1 \Rightarrow y = \dfrac{1 - ax}{b}$

Putting this value in the second equation,

$cx^2 + \dfrac{d}{b^2}(1 - ax)^2 = 1$

$\Rightarrow (b^2c + a^2d)x^2 - 2adx + d - b^2 = 0$

This quadratic equation will have equal roots if
$D = 4a^2d^2 - 4(b^2c + a^2d)(d - b^2) = 0$
$\Rightarrow a^2d^2 + (b^2c + a^2d)b^2 - b^2cd - a^2d^2 = 0$
$\Rightarrow b^2[b^2c + a^2d - cd] = 0$
$\Rightarrow b^2c + a^2d = cd$
$\Rightarrow \dfrac{b^2}{d} + \dfrac{a^2}{c} = 1$ also, in this case

$$x = \frac{2ad}{2(b^2c + a^2d)} = \frac{ad}{cd} = \frac{a}{c}$$

$$\Rightarrow y = \frac{1 - ax}{b} = \frac{1}{b}\left(1 - \frac{a^2}{c}\right) = \frac{1}{b}\cdot\frac{b^2}{d} = \frac{b}{d}$$

6. The equation $\sqrt{(x+1)} - \sqrt{(x-1)} = \sqrt{(4x-1)}$ has

(a) no solution (b) one solution
(c) two solution (d) more than one solutions

Solution: (a) The domain of admissible values of the equation is given by $x \geq 1$. Squaring both the sides of the equation, we get $(x + 1) + (x - 1) - 2\sqrt{x^2 - 1} = 4x - 1$ or $2\sqrt{x^2 - 1} = 1 - 2x$
Squaring again, we get $4(x^2 - 1) = 1 - 4x + 4x^2$
$\Rightarrow 4x = 5$ or $x = 5/4$

For $x = 5/4$, LHS $= \sqrt{5/4 + 1} - \sqrt{5/4 - 1} = \dfrac{3}{2} - \dfrac{1}{2} = 1$

And the RHS $= \sqrt{4\left(\dfrac{5}{4}\right) - 1} = \sqrt{4} = 2$

$\therefore$ $x = 5/4$ is not a root of the equation. i.e., this equation has no real solution.

7. If the expression $y^2 + 2xy + 2x + my - 3$ can be resolved into two rational linear factors, then m must be

(a) any positive real number
(b) -2
(c) any negative real number
(d) 3

Solution: (b) $abc + 2fgh - af^2 - bg^2 - ch^2 = 0$
$\Rightarrow m = -2$
and $h^2 - ab = 1 > 0$ is satisfied. Hence correct answer is (b).

8. The smallest value of $x^2 - 3x + 3$ in the interval $[-3, 3/2]$ is

(a) 3/4 (b) 5
(c) -15 (d) -20

Solution: (a) $x^2 - 3x + 3 = (x - 3/2)^2 + 3/4$
$\therefore$ Smallest value $= 3/4$ at $x \in 3/2$, which lie in $[-3, 3/2]$.

9. Let $f(x) = 1 + 2x + 3x^2 + \ldots.. + (n + 1)x^n$, where n is even. Then the number of real roots of the equation $f(x) = 0$

(a) 0 (b) 1
(c) n (d) None of these

Solution: (a) For $x > 0, f(x) > 0$
so there is no positive real roots of $f(x) = 0$
Now $f(0) = 1$; so $x = 0$ is not a root
$\Rightarrow f(x) = 1 + 2x + 3x^2 + \ldots + (n + 1)x^n$,
$\Rightarrow x f(x) = x + 2x^2 + \ldots + n x^n + (n + 1)x^{n+1}$
$\Rightarrow (1 - x) f(x) = (1 + x + x^2 + \ldots. + x^n) - (n + 1)x^{n+1}$
$= \dfrac{1 - x^{n+1}}{1 - x} - (n+1)x^{n+1}$
$\Rightarrow f(x) = \dfrac{1 - x^{n+1}}{(1-x)^2} - \dfrac{(n+1)x^{n+1}}{(1-x)}$
$= \dfrac{1 - (n+2)x^{n+1} + (n+1)x^{n+2}}{(1-x)^2}$

$\therefore$ The equation $f(x) = 0$ is equivalent to $P(x) = (n + 1)x^{n+2} - (n + 2)x^{n+1} + 1 = 0$
$P(-x) = (n + 1)x^{n+2} + (n + 2)x^{n+1} + 1 = 0$ which has no change of sign so has no negative real root.
Hence $f(x) = 0$ has no real root.

10. Roots of the quadratic equation $(x^2 - 4x + 3) + \lambda(x^2 - 6x + 8) = 0$, $\lambda \in \mathbb{R}$ will be

(a) always real
(b) real only when λ is positive
(c) real only when λ is negative
(d) always imaginary

Solution: (a) Let $f(x) = (x^2 - 4x + 3) + \lambda(x^2 - 6x + 8)$
$= (x - 1)(x - 3) + \lambda(x - 2)(x - 4)$
Now $f(2).f(4) < 0$, so $f(x) = 0$ has a root in $(2, 4)$.
Thus roots are always real.

11. Suppose $f(x)$ is a quadratic expression which is negative for all real x. If $g(x) = f(x) + f'(x) + f''(x)$, then for any real x

(a) $g(x) < 0$ (b) $g(x) > 0$
(c) $g(x) = 0$ (d) None of these

Solution: (a) Let $f(x) = ax^2 + bx + c$
where $a < 0$ and $b^2 - 4ac < 0$
$g(x) = ax^2 + bx + c + (2ax + b) + 2a$
$= ax^2 + x(2a + b) + 2a + b + c$
Consider,
$(2a + b)^2 - 4a(2a + b + c) = (b^2 - 4ac) - 4a^2 < 0$
$\Rightarrow g(x) < 0 \ \forall x \in \mathbb{R}$

12. The equation $(\sqrt{5}+2)^{|x|} + (\sqrt{5}-2)^{|x|} = 18$ has
(a) only one solution
(b) no solution
(c) any number of solutions
(d) two solutions

Solution: (d) Since $(\sqrt{5}+2) + (\sqrt{5}-2) = 1$, on taking $a = (\sqrt{5}+2)^{|x|} = (\sqrt{5}-2)^{-|x|}$, the equation reduces to
$\Rightarrow a^2 - 18a + 1 = 0$
$\Rightarrow a = \dfrac{18 \pm \sqrt{324-4}}{2} = 9 \pm 4\sqrt{5}$
Thus $|x| = 2 \Rightarrow x = \pm 2$

13. The values of a and b such that $x^4 + 12x^3 + 46x^2 + ax + b = 0$ is square of a quadratic expression are
(a) $a = 30, b = 25$ (b) $a = 60, b = 25$
(c) $a = 60, b = 100$ (d) $a = 60, b = 64$

Solution: (b) Let $x^4 + 12x^3 + 46x^2 + ax + b = (x^2 + \alpha x + \beta)^2$
$\Rightarrow x^4 + 12x^3 + 46x^2 + ax + b = x^4 + 2\alpha x^3 + (2\beta + \alpha^2) x^2 + 2\alpha\beta x + \beta^2$
$\Rightarrow 12 = 2\alpha \qquad \Rightarrow \alpha = 6$
and $46 = 2\beta + \alpha^2 \quad \Rightarrow \beta = 5$
Now $a = 2\alpha\beta = 60 \Rightarrow b = \beta^2 = 25$

14. If the equation $x^2 + 2(k+1)x + 9k - 5 = 0$ has only negative roots, then
(a) $k \le 0$ (b) $k \ge 0$
(c) $k \le 6$ (d) $k \ge 6$ or $k \in (5/9, 1]$

Solution: (d) Let $f(x) = x^2 + 2(k+1)x + 9k - 5 = 0$
$\Rightarrow f(0) > 0, -\dfrac{b}{2a} < 0, D \ge 0 \Rightarrow k \ge 6$ or $k \in (5/9, 1]$

15. Let $x, y \in [0, 10]$, then number of solutions (x, y) of the inequation $3^{\sec^2 x - 1}\sqrt{9y^2 - 6y + 2} \le 1$ is
(a) 4 (b) 2
(c) 1 (d) infinite

Solution: (a) Given equation can be rewritten as
$3^{\sec^2 x}\sqrt{y^2 - \dfrac{2y}{3} + \dfrac{2}{9}} \le 1$
$\Rightarrow 3^{\sec^2 x}\sqrt{\left(y - \dfrac{1}{3}\right)^2 + \dfrac{1}{9}} \le 1$
Now, $3^{\sec^2 x} \ge 3$ and $\sqrt{\left(y - \dfrac{1}{3}\right)^2 + \dfrac{1}{9}} \ge \dfrac{1}{3}$
so we should have $\sec^2 x = 1, y = \dfrac{1}{3}$
$\Rightarrow x = 0, \pi, 2\pi, 3\pi.$

16. The number of real solutions of the equation $\tan^{-1}\sqrt{x^2 - 3x + 2} + \cos^{-1}\sqrt{4x - x^2 - 3} = \pi$ is equal to
(a) one (b) two
(c) zero (d) infinite

Solution: (c) Since $\sqrt{x^2 - 3x + 2} \ge 0$
$\Rightarrow 0 \le \tan^{-1}\sqrt{x^2 - 3x + 2} < \dfrac{\pi}{2}$
$\because \sqrt{4x - x^2 - 3} \ge 0$
and $\cos^{-1}\sqrt{4x - x^2 - 3} \in \left[0, \dfrac{\pi}{2}\right]$
$\Rightarrow 0 <$ L.H.S. $< \pi$
$\Rightarrow$ The given equation has no solution.

17. The values of 'a' for which the equation $2x^2 - 2(2a+1)x + a(a-1) = 0$ has roots α and β, where $\alpha < a < \beta$ are such that
(a) $a > -3$ (b) $a < 0$
(c) $a > 0$ or $a < -3$ (d) None of these

Solution: (c) Let $f(x) = 2x^2 - 2(2a+1)x + a(a-1)$ has roots α, β such that $\alpha < a < \beta$
$\Rightarrow f(a) < 0$
$\Rightarrow 2a^2 - 2(2a+1)a + a(a-1) < 0$
$\Rightarrow a(a+3) > 0 \Rightarrow a < -3$ or $a > 0$

18. If $ax^2 + bx + c = 0, a \ne 0, a, b, c \in \mathbb{R}$ has distinct real roots belonging to (1, 2), then signs of 'a' and $5a + 2b + c$ are;
(a) of same type (b) of opposite type
(c) undetermined (d) None of these

Solution. (a) Let the roots be x_1 and x_2
Now $a(5a + 2b + c) = a^2\left(5 + 2\dfrac{b}{a} + \dfrac{c}{a}\right)$
$\Rightarrow a^2(5 + x_1(x_2 - 2) - 2(x_2 - 2) - 4)$
$\Rightarrow a^2((x_2 - 2)(x_1 - 2) + 1) =$ Positive number
$\Rightarrow$ signs of a and $5a + 2b + c$ are same

19. If a and b are distinct positive real numbers such that $a, a_1, a_2, a_3, a_4, a_5, b$ are in A.P.; $a, b_1, b_2, b_3, b_4, b_5, b$ are in G.P. and $a, c_1, c_2, c_3, c_4, c_5, b$ are in H.P., then roots of $a_3x^2 + b_3x + c_3 = 0$ are;
(a) real and distinct (b) real and equal
(c) imaginary (d) None of these

Solution: (c) Clearly, a_3, b_3 and c_3 are A.M., G.M. and H.M. respectively of a and b. Thus $b_3^2 = a_3c_3$. Now discriminant of the given equation is $b_3^2 - 4a_3c_3$, which is negative.

20. If a, b, c are positive and $a = 2b + 3c$, then roots of the equation $ax^2 + bx + c = 0$ are real for

(a) $\left|\frac{a}{c} - 11\right| \geq 4\sqrt{7}$ (b) $\left|\frac{c}{a} - 11\right| \geq 4\sqrt{7}$

(c) $\left|\frac{b}{c} - 4\right| \geq 2\sqrt{7}$ (d) $\left|\frac{c}{b} - 4\right| \geq 2\sqrt{7}$

Solution: (a, c) $ax^2 + bx + c = 0$

For real roots, $b^2 - 4ac \geq 0$

$\Rightarrow \left(\frac{a-3c}{2}\right)^2 - 4ac \geq 0$

Solving it, $a^2 - 22ac + 9c^2 \geq 0$

Dividing by c^2; $\left(\frac{a}{c}\right)^2 - 22\left(\frac{a}{c}\right) + 9 \geq 0$ (1)

$\therefore$ We have $\frac{a}{c} \leq 11 - 4\sqrt{7}$ or $\frac{a}{c} \geq 11 - 4\sqrt{7}$

$\Rightarrow \left|\frac{a}{c} - 11\right| \geq 4\sqrt{7}$, similarly $\left|\frac{b}{c} - 4\right| \geq 2\sqrt{7}$

21. If $a, b, c \in R$, and quadratic equation $x^2 + (a + b)x + c = 0$ has no real root, then

(a) $c(a + b + c) > 0$

(b) $c + c(a + b + c) > 0$

(c) $c - c(a + b - c) > 0$

(d) $c\,(a + b + c) > 0$

Solution: (b, c) Since $f(x) = 0$ has no real roots. Hence $f(x)$ have same sign $\forall\, x \Rightarrow f(0).\,f(1) > 0, f(0).\,f(-1) > 0$.

22. If ${}^6C_k + 2\,{}^6C_{k+1} + {}^6C_{k+2} > {}^8C_3$, then the quadratic equation whose roots are α, β and $\alpha^{k-1}, \beta^{k-1}$ have

(a) no common root (b) 1 common root

(c) 2 common root (d) imaginary roots

Solution: (c) Given ${}^6C_k + 2\,{}^6C_{k+1} + {}^6C_{k+2} > {}^8C_3$

$\Rightarrow ({}^6C_k + {}^6C_{k+1}) + ({}^6C_{k+1} + {}^6C_{k+2}) > {}^8C_3$

$\Rightarrow {}^7C_{k+1} + {}^7C_{k+2} > {}^8C_3$

$\Rightarrow {}^8C_{k+2} > {}^8C_3$ $(\because {}^8C_4 > {}^8C_3)$

$\therefore k + 2 = 4$ $\Rightarrow k = 2$

$\therefore \alpha^{k-1} = \alpha, \beta^{k-1} = \beta$.

Hence quadratic equations having roots α and β and α^{k-1} and β^{k-1} are identical. Hence they have both roots common.

23. Let $f(x) = x^3 + 3x^2 + 6x + 9 \sin x$, then roots of equation $\frac{1}{z - f(1)} + \frac{2}{z - f(2)} + \frac{3}{z - f(3)} = 0$ has

(a) no real root (b) 1 real root

(c) 2 real root (d) more than 2 real roots

Solution:(c) $f'(x) \geq 0$, increasing function

$\therefore f(1) < f(2) < f(3)$

Let $f(1) = a, f(2) = b, f(3) = c$, then $a < b < c$

Given equation is $\frac{1}{z-a} + \frac{2}{z-b} + \frac{3}{z-c} = 0$

$\Rightarrow g(z) = (z - b)(z - c) + 2(z - a)(z - c) + 3(z - a)(z - b)$

$\Rightarrow g(a) > 0, g(b) < 0,$

Hence $g(z) = 0$ has one real root between a and b and other lies between b and c as $g(c) > 0$.

24. The solution of equation $3^{(2-2\cos 2x)} + 3^{(2+2\cos 2x)} = 30$ for $x \in \left[0, \frac{\pi}{2}\right]$

(a) $\pi/3$ (b) $\pi/4$

(c) π (d) None of these

Solution: Given $\frac{9}{3^{2\cos 2x}} + 9.3^{2\cos 2x} = 30$, put $3^{2\cos 2x} = t$

$\Rightarrow \frac{9}{t} + 9t = 30 \Rightarrow t = \frac{1}{3}, 3 \Rightarrow 3^{2\cos 2x} = \frac{1}{3}, 3$

$\Rightarrow \cos 2x = -\frac{1}{2}, \frac{1}{2} \Rightarrow x = \frac{\pi}{3}, \frac{\pi}{6}$

25. If $a^2 + b^2 + c^2 = 1$, then $ab + bc + ca$ lies in

(a) [1/2, 2] (b) [–1, 2]

(c) [–1/2, 1] (d) [1, 1/2]

Solution: (c) We have $(a + b + c)^2 \geq 0$

$\Rightarrow a^2 + b^2 + c^2 + 2\,(ab + bc + ca) \geq 0$

$\Rightarrow ab + bc + ca \geq -1/2$

Again $(a - b)^2 + (b - c)^2 + (c - a)^2 \geq 0$

$\Rightarrow 2\,(a^2 + b^2 + c^2) - 2\,[ab + bc + ca] \geq 0$

$\Rightarrow ab + bc + ca \leq 1$

$\therefore ab + bc + ca \in \left[-\frac{1}{2}, 1\right]$

26. Let a, b, c be the sides of a triangle. No two of them are equal and $\lambda \in \mathbb{R}$. If the roots of the equation $x^2 + 2(a + b + c)x + 3\lambda(ab + bc + ca) = 0$ are real, then

(a) $\lambda < \frac{4}{3}$ (b) $\lambda > \frac{5}{3}$

(c) $\lambda \in \left(\frac{1}{3}, \frac{5}{3}\right)$ (d) $\lambda \in \left(\frac{1}{3}, \frac{5}{3}\right)$

Solution: (a) $x^2 + 2(a + b + c)x + 3\lambda(ab + bc + ca) = 0$, since roots are real.

$D \geq 0$

$\Rightarrow 4(a + b + c)^2 - 4.3\lambda(ab + bc + ca) \geq 0$

$\Rightarrow (a+b+c)^2 - 3\lambda(ab+bc+ca) \geq 0$

$\Rightarrow a^2+b^2+c^2+2ab+2bc+3ca-3\lambda(ab+bc+ca) \geq 0$

$\Rightarrow a^2+b^2+c^2+(2-3\lambda)(ab+bc+ca) \geq 0$

$\Rightarrow a^2+b^2+c^2 \geq (3\lambda-2)(ab+bc+ca)$

$$\Rightarrow \frac{a^2+b^2+c^2}{ab+bc+ca} \geq 3\lambda - 2 \quad (\because a, b, c > 0) \qquad \text{(i)}$$

In ΔABC, $\cos A = \dfrac{b^2+c^2-a^2}{2bc} < 1$

$\Rightarrow b^2+c^2-a^2 < 2bc$

Similarly, $c^2+a^2-b^2 < 2ca$, and

$a^2+b^2-c^2 < 2ab$

Adding the above equations, we get

$a^2+b^2+c^2 < 2(ab+bc+ca)$

$$\Rightarrow \frac{a^2+b^2+c^2}{ab+bc+ca} < 2$$

Hence from equation (i), $3\lambda - 2 < 2$

$\Rightarrow 3\lambda < 4$

$$\Rightarrow \lambda < \frac{4}{3}$$

SECTION–II

SUBJECTIVE-TYPE SOLVED EXAMPLES

1. If $\dfrac{a_1}{a_2}, \dfrac{b_1}{b_2}, \dfrac{c_1}{c_2}$ are in A.P. and the equations $a_1x^2+2b_1x+c_1=0$ and $a_2x^2+2b_2x+c_2=0$ have a common root, prove that a_2, b_2, c_2 are in G.P.

Solution: Let α be the common root.

Then, $a_1\alpha^2+2b_1\alpha+c_1=0$ and $a_2\alpha^2+2b_2\alpha+c_2=0$

$$\Rightarrow \frac{\alpha^2}{2(b_1c_2-b_2c_1)} = \frac{-\alpha}{a_1c_2-a_2c_1} = \frac{1}{2(a_1b_2-a_2b_1)}$$

$$\Rightarrow \alpha = \frac{c_1a_2-a_1c_2}{2(a_1b_2-a_2b_1)} = \frac{2(b_1c_2-b_2c_1)}{c_1a_2-a_1c_2}$$

$$\Rightarrow (c_1a_2-a_1c_2)^2 = 4(b_1c_2-b_2c_1)(a_1b_2-a_2b_1)$$

$$\Rightarrow (a_2c_2)^2\left(\frac{c_1}{c_2}-\frac{a_1}{a_2}\right)^2 = 4a_2b_2^2c_2\left(\frac{b_1}{b_2}-\frac{c_1}{c_2}\right)\left(\frac{a_1}{a_2}-\frac{b_1}{b_2}\right)$$

Since, $\dfrac{a_1}{a_2}, \dfrac{b_1}{b_2}, \dfrac{c_1}{c_2}$ are in A.P,

$$\Rightarrow \frac{a_1}{a_2}-\frac{b_1}{b_2} = \frac{b_1}{b_2}-\frac{c_1}{c_2} = \frac{1}{2}\left[\frac{a_1}{a_2}-\frac{c_1}{c_2}\right]$$

$\Rightarrow (a_2c_2)^2 = a_2b_2^2c_2$

$\Rightarrow a_2c_2 = b_2^2$

Hence, a_2, b_2, c_2 are in G.P.

2. If a,b,c are real and $ax^2+bx+c=0$ has two real roots α and β where $\alpha < -1$ and $\beta > 1$, then show that $1+\dfrac{c}{a}+\left|\dfrac{b}{a}\right| < 0$.

Solution: It can be seen that

if $a > 0$, $f(-1) < 0$ and $f(1) < 0$

if $a < 0$, $f(-1) > 0$ and $f(1) > 0$

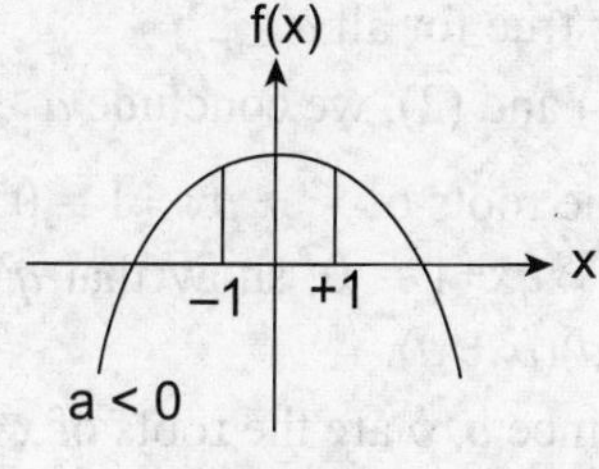

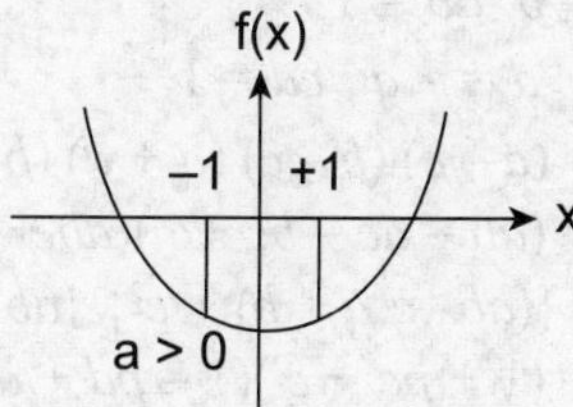

If $a > 0$, $a-b+c < 0$ and $a+b+c < 0$

$$\Rightarrow 1-\frac{b}{a}+\frac{c}{a} < 0 \text{ and } 1+\frac{b}{a}+\frac{c}{a} < 0 \qquad (1)$$

and if $a < 0$; $a-b+c > 0$ and $a+b+c > 0$

$$\Rightarrow 1-\frac{b}{a}+\frac{c}{a} < 0 \text{ and } 1+\frac{b}{a}+\frac{c}{a} < 0 \qquad (2)$$

From (1) and (2) (i.e., in both cases)

$1-\dfrac{b}{a}+\dfrac{c}{a} < 0$ and $1+\dfrac{b}{a}+\dfrac{c}{a} < 0$.

Therefore, $1+\dfrac{c}{a}+\left|\dfrac{b}{a}\right| < 0$

3. For what values of the parameter 'a', the equation $x^4+2ax^3+x^2+2ax+1=0$ has at least two distinct negative roots?

Solution. Dividing the equation by x^2, we get,

$$\left(x^2+\frac{1}{x^2}\right)+2a\left(x+\frac{1}{x}\right)+1=0$$

Let $x+\frac{1}{x}=t$

Then, for two distinct negative real roots of x, $t<-2$. (Since sum of a number and its reciprocal is greater than or equal to 2 or less than or equal to –2)

The equation now becomes $(t^2-2)+2at+1=0$

$\Rightarrow\ t^2+2at-1=0$

$\Rightarrow\ t=\frac{-2a\pm\sqrt{4a^2+4}}{2}=-a\pm\sqrt{a^2+1}$

$\Rightarrow$ For two distinct negative real roots of x,

$\Rightarrow\ -a-\sqrt{a^2+1}<-2\ \Rightarrow\ \sqrt{a^2+1}>2-a$

If $a<2$, R.H.S. is +ve $\Rightarrow a^2+1>4+a^2-4a$

$\Rightarrow\ 4a>0\ \Rightarrow\ a>3/4$ (1)

If $a\geq 2$, R.H.S. ≤ 0 and L.H.S. >0

which is true for all $a\geq 2$, (2)

From (1) and (2), we conclude $a>3/4$

4. If a, b are the roots of $x^2+px+1=0$ and c, d are the roots of $x^2+qx+1=0$, show that $q^2-p^2=(a-c)(b-c)(a+d)(b+d)$.

Solution: Since a, b are the roots of $x^2+px+1=0$

So $a+b=-p;\ ab=1$ (i)

Similarly, $c+d=-q;\ cd=1$

$\therefore$ R.H.S. $=(a-c)(b-c)(a+d)(b+d)$

$=(ab-ac-bc+c^2)(ab+ad+bd+d^2)$

$=\{(ab-c(a+b)+c^2\}\{ab+d(a+b)+d^2\}$

$=(1+pc+c^2)(1-pd+d^2)$ (from (i))

$=(cd+pc+c^2)(cd-pd+d^2)$

$(\because ab=cd=1)$

$=c\{(d+c)+p\}d\{(c+d)-p\}$

$=cd(-q+p)(-q-p)$

$=-(p-q)(p+q)=q^2-p^2$

5. Find the set of values of 'a' for which the equation, $(1+a)\left(\frac{x^2}{x^2+1}\right)^2-3a\frac{x^2}{x^2+1}+4a=0$ has real roots.

Solution: Put $\frac{x^2}{1+x^2}=y\Rightarrow y\in[0,1)$

$\Rightarrow\ (a+1)y^2-3ay+4a=0$

Find 'a' for which the equation has at least one solution, for $y=0$; $a=0$ i.e., $x=0$ for $a=0$ (1)

Case I: Exactly one root between 0 and 1

for $a=-1;\ y=\frac{4}{3}\notin(0,1)$

for $a\neq-1;\ y^2-\frac{3a}{a+1}y+\frac{4a}{a+1}=0$

(i) $D>0$ and (ii) $f(0).f(1)<0$

$\Rightarrow\ a\in(-1/2,0)$ combining with (1) $\Rightarrow a\in(-1/2,0]$

Case II: when both roots lie in (0, 1)

(i) $f(0)>0$; (ii) $f(1)>0$;

(iii) $D\geq 0$; (iv) $0<-\frac{b}{2a}<1$

No solution in this case.

Therefore the values of 'a' are given by $-\frac{1}{2}<a\leq 0$.

6. Solve the equation $x^4-3x^2-42x-40=0$

Solution: Given equation is $x^4-3x^2-42x-40=0$

Let, $x^4-3x^2-42x-40\equiv(x^2+px+q)(x^2-px+q')$

Comparing the co-efficients, we get

$\Rightarrow\ q+q'-p^2=-3$ or $q+q'=p^2-3$ (i)

and $p(q'-q)=-42$ or $q'-q=\frac{-42}{p}$ (ii)

and $qq'=-40$

Now $(q-q')^2=(q+q')^2-4qq'$

$\Rightarrow\ (-42/p)^2=(p^2-3)^2+160$

$\Rightarrow\ p^6-6p^4+169p^2-1764=0$

Putting $p^2=t$, we get $t^3-6t^2+169t-1764=0$

Here $t=9$ satisfies the above equation

$\therefore\ p^2=9\ \therefore\ p=3$ or -3

$\therefore\ q=-4$ and $q=10, p=3$ (without loss of generality)

Hence $x^4-3x^2-42x-40\equiv(x^2+3x+10)(x^2-3x-4)=0$

$\therefore\ x^2+3x+10=0$ or $x=\frac{-3\pm\sqrt{-31}}{2}$

and when $x^2-3x-4=0$

$\Rightarrow\ x=4,-1$

$\therefore\ 4,-1,-\frac{1}{2}(3\pm\sqrt{-31})$ are the roots.

7. Solve the equation $(12x-1)(6x-1)(4x-1)(3x-1)=5$.

Solution: The given equation can be written as

$$\left(x-\frac{1}{12}\right)\left(x-\frac{1}{6}\right)\left(x-\frac{1}{4}\right)\left(x-\frac{1}{3}\right)=\frac{5}{12.6.4.3}$$

Since, $1/12 < 1/6 < 1/4 < 1/3$
and $1/6 - 1/12 = 1/3 - 1/4$

$$\Rightarrow y = \frac{1}{4}\left[\left(x - \frac{1}{12}\right) + \left(x - \frac{1}{6}\right) + \left(x - \frac{1}{4}\right) + \left(x - \frac{1}{3}\right)\right]$$

$\Rightarrow y = x - 5/24$

Substituting $x = y + 5/24$ in (i), we get

$$\Rightarrow \left(y + \frac{3}{24}\right)\left(y + \frac{1}{24}\right)\left(y - \frac{1}{24}\right)\left(y - \frac{3}{24}\right) = \frac{5}{12.6.4.3}$$

$$\Rightarrow \left[y^2 - \left(\frac{1}{24}\right)^2\right]\left[y^2 - \left(\frac{3}{24}\right)^2\right] = \frac{5}{12.6.4.3}$$

Hence we find that $y^2 = \dfrac{49}{(24)^2}$

$\Rightarrow y_1 = 7/24$ and $y_2 = -7/24$

$\therefore$ The corresponding roots of the original equation are $-\dfrac{1}{12}$ and $\dfrac{1}{2}$.

8. Find all possible parameters 'a' for which $f(x) = (a^2 + a - 2)x^2 - (a + 5)x - 2$ is non-positive for every $x \in [0, 1]$.

Solution: $f(x) = (a + 2)(a - 1)x^2 - (a + 5)x - 2 \le 0$
for $a = -2$; $f(x) = -3x - 2$ which is negative in [0, 1]
for $a = 1$; $f(x) = -6x - 2$ which is negative in [0, 1]
Now analyse the following cases:

Case I: for $a^2 + a - 2 > 0$ i.e., $a > 1$ or $a < -2$ (1)
(i) $f(0) \le 0$ always true
(ii) $f(1) \le 0$
$\Rightarrow a \in [-3, 3]$ (2)
from (1) and (2), $a \in [-3, -2) \cup (1, 3]$

Case II: $a^2 + a - 2 < 0$ i.e., $-2 < a < 1$
In this case:
(i) $D \ge 0 \Rightarrow (a + 2)^2 \ge 0 \Rightarrow a \in \mathbb{R}$
(ii) $f(1) < 0$ and $f(0) < 0$ (always true)
$\Rightarrow a \in (-3, 3)$
Common solution is $(-2, 1)$
Thus, the final solution set is given by $a \in [-3, 3]$

9. Solve the following equation $1 + 3^{x/2} = 2^x$.

Solution: We have $1 + 3^{x/2} = 2^x$
Dividing both sides by 2^x, we obtain

$$\Rightarrow \frac{1}{2^x} + \frac{3^{x/2}}{2^x} = 1 \; (\because 2^x > 0)$$

$$\Rightarrow \left(\frac{1}{2}\right)^x + \left(\frac{3}{4}\right)^{x/2} = 1 \Rightarrow \left(\frac{1}{2}\right)^x + \left(\frac{\sqrt{3}}{2}\right)^x = 1$$

$\Rightarrow (\cos \pi/3)^x + (\sin \pi/3)^x = 1$
which is possible only when $x = 2$

10. If each pair of the following three equations $x^2 + ax + b = 0$, $x^2 + cx + d = 0$, and $x^2 + ex + f = 0$ has exactly one root in common, then show that $(a + c + e)^2 = 4\,(ac + ce + ea - b - d - f)$.

Solution: Given equations arc $x^2 + ax + b = 0$ (i)
$x^2 + cx + d = 0$ (ii)
$x^2 + ex + f = 0$ (iii)
Let α, β be the roots of (i), β, γ be the roots of (ii) and γ, δ be the roots of (iii)
$\Rightarrow \alpha + \beta = -a$, $\alpha\beta = b$ (iv)
$\beta + \gamma = -c$, $\beta\gamma = d$ (v)
$\gamma + \alpha = -e$, $\gamma\alpha = f$ (vi)
L.H.S. $= (a + c + e)^2 = (-\alpha - \beta - \beta - \gamma - \gamma - \alpha)^2$
(Using (iv), (v) and (vi))
$= 4(\alpha + \beta + \gamma)^2$ (vii)
R.H.S. $= 4(ac + ce + ea - b - d - f)$
$= 4\{(\alpha + \beta)(\beta + \gamma)(\gamma + \alpha) + (\gamma + \alpha)(\alpha + \beta) - \alpha\beta - \beta\gamma - \gamma\alpha\}$
(Using (iv), (v) and (vi))
$= 4(\alpha^2 + \beta^2 + \gamma^2 + 2\alpha\beta + 2\beta\gamma + 2\gamma\alpha)$
$= 4(\alpha + \beta + \gamma)^2$ (viii)
From (vii) and (viii), we get
$(a + c + e)^2 = 4(ac + ce + ea - b - d - f)$

11. Show that the equation

$$\frac{A^2}{x-a} + \frac{B^2}{x-b} + \frac{C^2}{x-c} + \ldots + \frac{K^2}{x-k} = x + \ell$$

has no imaginary root, where $A, B, C, \ldots K, a, b, c, \ldots, k$ and ℓ are real.

Solution: Assume $\alpha + i\beta$ is an imaginary root of the given equation, then conjugte of this root $\alpha - i\beta$ is also root of this equation. Putting $x = \alpha + i\beta$ and $x = \alpha - i\beta$ in the given equation, we have

$$\frac{A^2}{\alpha + i\beta - a} + \frac{B^2}{\alpha + i\beta - b} + \frac{C^2}{\alpha + i\beta - c} + \ldots + \frac{K^2}{\alpha + i\beta - k} = \alpha + i\beta + \ell \quad \text{(i)}$$

and

$$\frac{A^2}{\alpha - i\beta - a} + \frac{B^2}{\alpha - i\beta - b} + \frac{C^2}{\alpha - i\beta - c} + \ldots + \frac{K^2}{\alpha - i\beta - k} = \alpha - i\beta + \ell \quad \text{(ii)}$$

Subtracting (i) from (ii), we get

$$\Rightarrow 2i\beta\left\{\begin{matrix}\dfrac{A^2}{(\alpha-a)^2+\beta^2}+\dfrac{B^2}{(\alpha-b)^2+\beta^2}+\\ \dfrac{C^2}{(\alpha-c)^2+\beta^2}+.....+\dfrac{K^2}{(\alpha-k)^2+\beta^2}\end{matrix}\right\}=-2i\beta$$

$$\Rightarrow 2i\beta\left\{\begin{matrix}1+\dfrac{A^2}{(\alpha-a)^2+\beta^2}+\dfrac{B^2}{(\alpha-b)^2+\beta^2}+\\ \dfrac{C^2}{(\alpha-c)^2+\beta^2}+.....+\dfrac{K^2}{(\alpha-k)^2+\beta^2}\end{matrix}\right\}=0$$

The expression in bracket $\neq 0$

($\because$ it is sum of non-negative quantities)

$\therefore$ $2i\beta = 0 \Rightarrow \beta = 0$

Hence all roots of the given equation are real.

12. Find the real roots of the equation $x^2+2ax+\frac{1}{16}=-a+\sqrt{\left(a^2+x-\frac{1}{16}\right)}$; $0 < a < 1/4$

Solution: We have

$$x^2+2ax+\frac{1}{16}=-a+\sqrt{(a^2+x-1/16)}$$

Let $y=x^2+2ax+\frac{1}{16}$ (i)

and $y_1=-a+\sqrt{(a^2+x-1/16)}$ (ii)

$\therefore$ $y=y_1$ (iii)

From (ii) $y_1+a=\sqrt{a^2+x-1/6}$

$\Rightarrow$ $x=y_1^2+2ay_1+1/16$ (iv)

(from (iii), equations (i) and (iv) represents parabolas, both parabolas symmetrical about the line)

$\Rightarrow$ $y=x$ (v)

From (i) and (v), we get,

$$\Rightarrow x=x^2+2ax+\frac{1}{16}\Rightarrow x^2-(1-2a)x+\frac{1}{16}=0$$

$$\Rightarrow x=\frac{(1-2a)\pm\sqrt{(1-2a)^2-1/4}}{2}$$

Hence $x_1=\dfrac{1-2a}{2}+\sqrt{\left(\dfrac{1-2a}{2}\right)^2-\dfrac{1}{16}}$

and $x_2=\dfrac{1-2a}{2}-\sqrt{\left(\dfrac{1-2a}{2}\right)^2-\dfrac{1}{16}}$

13. If α is a root of the equation $ax^2+bx+c=0$, β is a root of the equation $-ax^2+bx+c=0$ and γ is a root of the equation $\frac{a}{2}x^2+bx+c=0$, then prove that γ lies between α and β.

Solution: For $a = 0$, the three given equations become linear in x and have a single root.

i.e., $\alpha=\beta=\gamma$

For $c = 0$, the three given equations have roots $0, -\frac{b}{a}$; $0, \frac{b}{a}$ and $0, -\frac{2b}{a}$ respectively because in this case, the root $\gamma = 0$ lies between any root of $ax^2 + bx + c = 0$ and any root of $-ax^2 + bx + c = 0$

Again, $a\alpha^2+b\alpha+c=0$ as α is a root (i)

then, $\frac{a}{2}\alpha^2+b\alpha+c=(a\alpha^2+b\alpha+c)-\frac{a\alpha^2}{2}$

$=0-\frac{a\alpha^2}{2}=-\frac{a\alpha^2}{2}$ [(from (i)]

Also, $-a\beta^2+b\beta+c=0$ as β is a root,

then $\frac{a}{2}\beta^2+b\beta+c=-a\beta^2+b\beta+c+\frac{3}{2}a\beta^2$

$=0+\frac{3}{2}a\beta^2=\frac{3}{2}a\beta^2$

Consequently, the expressions

$\frac{a}{2}\alpha^2+b\alpha+c=-\frac{a\alpha^2}{2}$ and $\frac{a}{2}\beta^2+b\beta+c=\frac{3a\beta^2}{2}$

are of different signs.

$\because$ $y=f(x)=\frac{a}{2}x^2+bx+c$ is a parabola and $(\alpha, f(\alpha))$ and $(\beta, f(\beta))$ belonging to the parabola on opposite side of x-axis and the parabola intersect x-axis at $(\gamma, 0)$. Hence γ is an intermediate point i.e., $\alpha\le\gamma\le\beta$ or $\alpha\ge\gamma\ge\beta$.

14. Find a quadratic equation whose sum and product of the roots are the values of the expressions (cos 10° – $\sqrt{3}$ sec 10°) and (0.5 cosec 10° – 2 sin 70°) respectively. Also express the roots of this quadratic in terms of tangent of an angle lying in $(0, \pi/2)$.

Solution. (cosec 10° – $\sqrt{3}\sec 10^\circ$)

$$=2\left[\frac{1}{2\sin 10^\circ}-\frac{\sqrt{3}}{2\cos 10^\circ}\right]$$

$$=2\left[\frac{\sin 30^\circ}{\sin 10^\circ}-\frac{\cos 30^\circ}{\cos 10^\circ}\right]=\frac{2\times 2\sin 20^\circ}{2\sin 10^\circ\cos 10^\circ}=4$$

and 0.5 cosec 10° – 2 sin 70°

$$=\frac{\sin 30^\circ}{\sin 10^\circ}-\frac{\sin 70^\circ}{\sin 30^\circ}=\frac{2\sin^2 30^\circ-2\sin 10^\circ\sin 70^\circ}{2\sin 10^\circ\sin 30^\circ}$$

$$= \frac{\frac{1}{2} - (\cos 60^\circ - \cos 80^\circ)}{2\sin 10^\circ \sin 30^\circ}$$

$$= \frac{\frac{1}{2} - \frac{1}{2} + \sin 10^\circ}{2\sin 10^\circ \sin 30^\circ} = \frac{1}{2\times\frac{1}{2}} = 1$$

$\therefore$ Required quadratic equation is $x^2 - 4x + 1$

$\Rightarrow$ Roots $= 2-\sqrt{3}, 2+\sqrt{3} = \alpha, \beta$ (say), then

$\alpha = \tan\frac{\pi}{12}$, $\beta = \tan\frac{5\pi}{12}$

15. If the range of the function $f(x) = \frac{x^2+ax+b}{x^2+2x+3}$ is $[-5, 4]$; $a, b \in \mathbb{N}$, then find the value of $(a^2 + b^2)$.

Solution: $y = \frac{x^2+ax+b}{x^2+2x+3}$

$\Rightarrow (y-1)x^2 + (2y-a)x + (3y-b) = 0$

$\Rightarrow (2y-a)^2 - 4(y-1)(3y-b) \geq 0$ as $x \in \mathbb{R}$

$\Rightarrow -8y^2 + (-4a + 4b + 12)y + a^2 - 4b \geq 0$

$\Rightarrow y^2 + \left(\frac{4a-4b-12}{8}\right)y + \frac{4b-a^2}{8} \leq 0$

As $-5 \leq y \leq 4$ $\quad \Rightarrow (y+5)(y-4) \leq 0$

$y^2 + y - 20 \leq 0$

$\Rightarrow \frac{4a-4b-12}{8} = 1 \quad \Rightarrow a - b = 5$

and $\frac{4b-a^2}{8} = -20 \quad \Rightarrow 4b - (b+5)^2 = -160$

$\Rightarrow b^2 + 6b - 135 = 0 \quad \Rightarrow (b-9)(b+15) = 0$

$\Rightarrow b = 9$ and $a = 14$

$\Rightarrow a^2 + b^2 = 9^2 + 14^2 = 81 + 196 = 277$

16. (a) If α, β are the roots of the quadratic equation $ax^2 + bx + c = 0$, then which of the following expressions in α, β will denote the symmetric functions of roots? Give proper reasoning.

(i) $f(\alpha, \beta) = \alpha^2 - \beta$ (ii) $f(\alpha, \beta) = \alpha^2\beta + \alpha\beta^2$

(iii) $f(\alpha,\beta) = \ln\frac{\alpha}{\beta}$ (iv) $f(\alpha, \beta) = \cos(\alpha - \beta)$

(b) If α, β are the roots of the equation $x^2 - px + q = 0$, then find the quadratic equation the roots of which are $(\alpha^2 - \beta^2).(\alpha^3 - \beta^3)$ and $\alpha^3\beta^2 + \alpha^2\beta^3$.

Solution: (a) $\beta = -\alpha + p$

(i) $f(\alpha, \beta) = \alpha^2 - \beta = \alpha^2 + \alpha - p$

$f(\beta, \alpha) = \beta^2 - \alpha = (-\alpha + p)^2 - \alpha = \alpha^2 + p^2 - 2\alpha p - \alpha$

$\because f(\alpha, \beta) \neq f(\beta, \alpha) \Rightarrow f$ is not symmetric function

(ii) $\left.\begin{array}{l} f(\alpha,\beta) = \alpha^2\beta + \alpha\beta^2 \\ f(\beta,\alpha) = \beta^2\alpha + \beta\alpha^2 \end{array}\right\} \Rightarrow f(\alpha, \beta) = f(\beta, \alpha)$

$\Rightarrow f$ is symmetric function

(iii) $\left.\begin{array}{l} f(\alpha,\beta) = \ln\frac{\alpha}{\beta} \\ f(\beta,\alpha) = \ln\frac{\beta}{\alpha} \end{array}\right\} \Rightarrow f(\alpha, \beta) \neq f(\beta, \alpha)$

$\Rightarrow f$ is not symmetric function

(iv) $f(\alpha, \beta) = \cos(\alpha - \beta)$ and

$f(\beta, \alpha) = \cos(\beta - \alpha) = \cos(\alpha - \beta)$

$\therefore f(\alpha, \beta) = f(\beta, \alpha) \Rightarrow f$ is symmetric function

(b) Given equation is $x^2 - px + q = 0$

$\because$ α, β are the roots of this equation, $\alpha + \beta = p$, $\alpha\beta = q$

Now finding the equation whose roots are

$\underbrace{(\alpha^2-\beta^2).(\alpha^3-\beta^3)}_{\Downarrow}$ and $\underbrace{(\alpha^3\beta^2+\alpha^2\beta^3)}_{\Downarrow}$

or $(\alpha - \beta)^2 (\alpha + \beta) ((\alpha + \beta)^2 - \alpha\beta)$ and $\alpha^2\beta^2 (\alpha + \beta)$

i.e., $(p^2 - 4q)(p)(p^2 - q)$ and $q^2 p$

i.e., $(p^4 - 5qp^2 + 4q^2)(p)$ and $q^2 p$

$\therefore$ The required equation is $x^2 - p(p^4 - 5p^2q + 5q^2)x + p^2q^2(p^2 - 4q)(p^2 - q) = 0$

17. A quadratic polynomial $y = f(x)$ satisfies $f(x) = \left[\frac{f(x+1)-f(x-1)}{2}\right]^2$ for all real x. Find the leading co-efficient of the quadratic polynomial and hence find the value of $[f(0) - f(-1)] + [f(0) - f(1)]$

Solution: $f(x) = ax^2 + bx + c$; $a \neq 0$

$\therefore ax^2 + bx + c = f(x) = \left[\frac{f(x+1)-f(x-1)}{2}\right]^2$

$= \left[\frac{a(x+1)^2 + b(x+1) + c - a(x-1)^2 - b(x-1) - c}{2}\right]^2$

$= \left[\frac{a[(x+1)^2 - (x-1)^2] + b[(x+1) - (x-1)]}{2}\right]^2$

or $ax^2 + bx + c = \left(\frac{4ax+2b}{2}\right)^2 = 4a^2x^2 + 4abx + b^2$

On comparing, $4a^2 = a$, $\Rightarrow a = 1/4$

Now $[f(0) - f(-1)] + [f(0) - f(1)]$

$= [c - (a - b + c)] + [c - (a + b + c)] = -2a = -\frac{1}{2}$

18. If the quadratic equations $x^2 + bx + ca = 0$ and $x^2 + cx + ab = 0$ have a common root, prove that the equation containing their other root is $x^2 + ax + bx = 0$.

Solution: Let $x^2 + bx + ca = 0$; $x^2 + cx + ab = 0$ have roots α, β and α, γ respectively

$\Rightarrow \alpha^2 + b\alpha + ca = 0; \alpha^2 + c\alpha + ab = 0$ (i)

$\Rightarrow \alpha^2 = -(b\alpha + ca)$

Putting the value of α^2 in equation (i), we have

$-b\alpha - ca + c\alpha + ab = 0$

$\Rightarrow \alpha(c-b) + a(b-c) = 0 \Rightarrow \alpha - a = 0 \Rightarrow \alpha = a$

Also, $\alpha.\beta = ca$ and $\alpha.\gamma = ab$

$\Rightarrow a.\beta = ca$ and $a\gamma = ab$

$\Rightarrow \beta = c$ and $\gamma = b$

$\because \alpha^2 + b\alpha + ca = 0$

($\because \alpha$ is a root of equation $x^2 + bx + ca = 0$)

$\Rightarrow a^2 + ba + ca = 0 \quad \Rightarrow a + b + c = 0$ (ii)

$\therefore$ A quadratic equation whose roots are β, γ is given by $x^2 - (\beta + \gamma)x + \beta\gamma = 0$

$\Rightarrow x^2 - (b + c)x + bc = 0$

$\therefore x^2 + ax + bc = 0$ (from equation (ii)) is the equation having roots β and γ.

19. We call 'p' a good number if the inequality $\frac{2x^2+2x+3}{x^2+x+1} \le p$ is satisfied for every real x. Find the smallest integral good number.

Solution: Let $y = \frac{2x^2+2x+3}{x^2+x+1}$

$\Rightarrow yx^2 + yx + y = 2x^2 + 2x + 3$

$\Rightarrow x^2(y-2) + x(y-2) + (y-3) = 0; x \in \mathbb{R}$

$\Rightarrow (y-2)^2 - 4(y-2)(y-3) \ge 0$

$\Rightarrow 3y^2 - 16y + 20 \le 0$

$\Rightarrow (y-2)(3y-10) \le 0$

$\Rightarrow y \in \left(2, \frac{10}{3}\right)$

$\Rightarrow \frac{2x^2+2x+3}{x^2+x+1} \le p \Rightarrow \frac{10}{3} \le p \Rightarrow p \ge 4$ if $p \in \mathbb{Z}$

$\Rightarrow$ smallest integer $p = 4$

20. Find all real numbers x such that,

$$\left(x-\frac{1}{x}\right)^{\frac{1}{2}} + \left(1-\frac{1}{x}\right)^{\frac{1}{2}} = x.$$

Solution: Given that, $\sqrt{\left(x-\frac{1}{x}\right)} + \sqrt{\left(1-\frac{1}{x}\right)} = x$ (1)

Using rationalization,

$$\frac{\left(\sqrt{\left(x-\frac{1}{x}\right)}\right)^2 - \left(\sqrt{1-\frac{1}{x}}\right)^2}{\sqrt{x-\frac{1}{x}} - \sqrt{1-\frac{1}{x}}} = x$$

$$\Rightarrow \frac{x-\frac{1}{x}-1+\frac{1}{x}}{\sqrt{x-\frac{1}{x}} - \sqrt{1-\frac{1}{x}}} = x$$

$$\Rightarrow \frac{(x-1)}{x} = \sqrt{x-\frac{1}{x}} - \sqrt{1-\frac{1}{x}} \quad (2)$$

$$(1) + (2) \Rightarrow \left(1-\frac{1}{x}\right) + x = 2\sqrt{x-\frac{1}{x}}$$

Putting $\sqrt{x-\frac{1}{x}} = t$, we have $1 + t^2 = 2t$

or $(t-1)^2 = 0 \Rightarrow t = 1$ or $\sqrt{x-\frac{1}{x}} = 1 \Rightarrow x^2 - x - 1 = 0$

$\Rightarrow x = \frac{1+\sqrt{5}}{2}$ as (–)ve value is rejected.

21. Find the minimum value of $\frac{\left(x+\frac{1}{x}\right)^6 - \left(x^6+\frac{1}{x^6}\right) - 2}{\left(x+\frac{1}{x}\right)^3 + x^3 + \frac{1}{x^3}}$ for $x > 0$.

Solution: $y = \frac{\left[\left(x+\frac{1}{x}\right)^3\right]^2 - \left[x^3+\frac{1}{x^3}\right]^2}{\left(x+\frac{1}{x}\right)^3 + \left(x^3+\frac{1}{x^3}\right)}$

$= \left(x+\frac{1}{x}\right)^3 - x^3 - \frac{1}{x^3} \quad \Rightarrow 3\left(x+\frac{1}{x}\right)$

$\Rightarrow y_{min} = 6 \left(\text{since } x+\frac{1}{x} \ge 2 \text{ for } x > 0\right)$

22. Find the product of the real roots of the equation, $x^2 + 18x + 30 = 2\sqrt{x^2+18x+45}$.

Solution: $x^2 + 18x + 45 - 15 = 2\sqrt{x^2+18x+45}$ (1)

Putting $\sqrt{x^2+18x+45} = t$, we get $t^2 - 15 = 2t$

$\Rightarrow t^2 - 2t - 15 = 0 \quad \Rightarrow (t-5)(t+3) = 0$

$\Rightarrow t = -3, 5 \quad \Rightarrow t = 5$ (– 3 is rejected)

$\therefore t = \sqrt{x^2+18x+45} = 5 \Rightarrow x^2 + 18x + 20 = 0$

$\Rightarrow$ product of roots for this equation = 20

23. Let $x^2 + y^2 + xy + 1 \ge a(x + y)\ \forall\ x, y \in \mathbb{R}$. Find the possible integer(s) in the range of a.

Solution: $x^2 + y^2 + xy + 1 \ge a(x + y)$

$\Rightarrow x^2 + x(y - a) + y^2 - ay + 1 \ge 0 \Rightarrow D \le 0$

$\Rightarrow (y - a)^2 - 4(y^2 - ay + 1) \le 0$

$\Rightarrow -3y^2 + 2ay + a^2 - 4 \le 0 \Rightarrow 3y^2 - 2ay + 4 - a^2 \ge 0$

$\Rightarrow D \leq 0 \Rightarrow 4a^2 - 12(4 - a^2) \leq 0$

$\Rightarrow 4a^2 - 48 + 12a^2 \leq 0 \Rightarrow a \in [-\sqrt{3}, \sqrt{3}]$

$\Rightarrow$ Integers values of $a \in \{-1, 0, 1\}$

24. Solve the following for $x \in \mathbb{R}$.

(a) $(x - 1)|x^2 - 4x + 3| + 2x^2 + 3x - 5 = 0$

(b) $3|x^2 - 4x + 2| = 5x - 4$

(c) $|x^3 + 1| + x^2 - x - 2 = 0$

(d) For $a \leq 0$, determine all real roots of the equation $x^2 - 2a|x - a| - 3a^2 = 0$.

Solution: (a) $(x - 1)|x^2 - 4x + 3| + 2x^2 + 3x - 5 = 0$

when $x^2 - 4x + 3 \geq 0$, then $x \in (-\infty, 1] \cup [3, \infty)$

$\Rightarrow (x - 1)(x^2 - 3x - x + 3) + 2x^2 + 5x - 2x - 5 = 0$

$\Rightarrow (x - 1)(x^2 - 3x - x + 3 + 2x + 5) = 0$

$\Rightarrow (x - 1)(x^2 - 2x + 8) = 0$

$\Rightarrow x - 1 = 0 \qquad \Rightarrow x = 1$

when $x^2 - 4x + 3 < 0 \Rightarrow x \in (1, 3)$

$(x - 1)(-x^2 + 4x - 3 + 2x + 5) = 0$

$\Rightarrow (x - 1)(-x^2 + 6x + 2) = 0$

$\Rightarrow -x^2 + 6x + 2 = 0$ as $x \neq 1$

$x^2 - 6x - 2 = 0 \qquad \Rightarrow x = 3 \pm \sqrt{11}$

Both values will not satisfy

$\Rightarrow x = 1$ is the only solution

(b) $3|x^2 - 4x + 2| = 5x - 4$

For $x^2 - 4x + 2 \geq 0$ i.e., $x \in (-\infty, 2 - \sqrt{2}) \cup [2 + \sqrt{2}, \infty)$

$\therefore 3x^2 - 12x + 6 = 5x - 4 \Rightarrow 3x^2 - 17x + 10 = 0$

$\Rightarrow x = 5, \frac{2}{3}$, but $x \neq \frac{2}{3} \Rightarrow x = 5$

For $x^2 - 4x + 2 < 0$ i.e., $x \in (2 - \sqrt{2}, 2 + \sqrt{2})$

$\therefore -3x^2 + 12x - 6 = 5x - 4 \Rightarrow x = \frac{1}{3}, 2$

$\Rightarrow x = 2$ as $x \neq \frac{1}{3}$

Thus $x = 2$ and $x = 5$ are the only possible roots.

(c) $|x^3 + 1| + x^2 - x - 2 = 0$

when $x^3 + 1 \geq 0$ i.e., $x \geq -1$,

$x^3 + 1 + x^2 - x - 2 = 0$

$\Rightarrow (x + 1)(x - 1)(x + 1) = 0 \Rightarrow x = -1, 1$

when $x^3 + 1 < 0$ i.e., $x < -1$

$-x^3 - 1 + x^2 - x - 2 = 0$

$\Rightarrow (x + 1)(x^2 - 2x + 3) = 0$

But $x \neq -1$ and $x^2 - 2x + 3 > 0$

so $x = -1, 1$ are the only roots.

(d) For $a \geq 0 \Rightarrow x^2 - 2a|x - a| - 3a^2 = 0$

for $x - a \geq 0$; for $x - a < 0 \Rightarrow x \geq 0; x < a$

$\Rightarrow x^2 - 2ax + 2a^2 - 3a^2 = 0; x^2 + 2ax - 2a^2 - 3a^2 = 0$

$\Rightarrow x = a \pm a\sqrt{2}\ ;\ x = -a \pm \sqrt{6}\,a$

but $a - a\sqrt{2}$ will be rejected since, then $x < a$

Also $x \neq -a(1 - \sqrt{6})$, since then $x > a$.

Thus $x = a(1 + \sqrt{2})$ and $x = -a(\sqrt{6} + 1)$

25. If α, β are the roots of the equation, $x^2 - 2x - a^2 + 1 = 0$ and γ, δ are the roots of the equation, $x^2 - 2(a + 1)x + a(a - 1) = 0$ such that $\alpha, \beta \in (\gamma, \delta)$, then find the values of 'a'.

Solution:

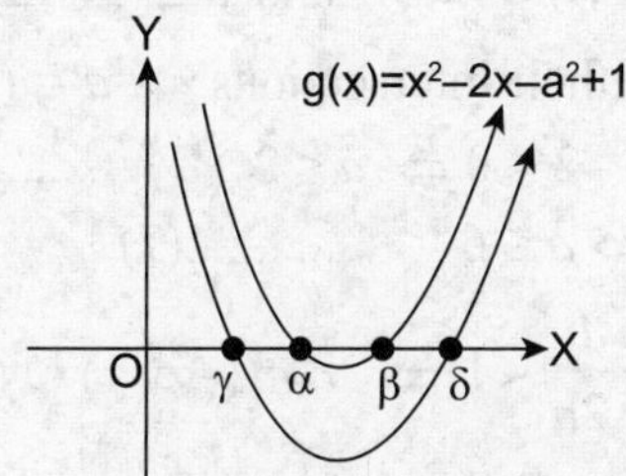

$g(x) = x^2 - 2x + 1 - a^2 = 0$

$\Rightarrow \alpha + \beta = 2$ and $\alpha\beta = (1 - a)(1 + a)$

$\Rightarrow \alpha = 1 - a, \beta = 1 + a$

$\Rightarrow f(\alpha) < 0 \qquad \Rightarrow f(1 - a) < 0$

$\Rightarrow (1 - a)^2 - 2(1 + a)(1 - a) + a(a - 1) < 0$

$\Rightarrow (1 - a)[1 - a - 2(1 + a) - a] < 0$

$\Rightarrow (1 - a)(1 - a - 2 - 2a - a) < 0$

$\Rightarrow (a - 1)(4a + 1) < 0$

$\Rightarrow a \in \left(-\frac{1}{4}, 1\right)$ (1)

Also $f(\beta) < 0 \qquad \Rightarrow f(a + 1) < 0$

$\Rightarrow (a + 1)^2 - 2(a + 1)(a + 1) + a(a - 1) < 0$

$\Rightarrow a^2 + 1 + 2a - 2a^2 - 2 - 4a + a^2 - a < 0$

$\Rightarrow -3a - 1 < 0 \qquad \Rightarrow 3a + 1 > 0$

$\Rightarrow a \in \left(\frac{-1}{3}, \infty\right)$ (2)

From (1) ∩ (2), we have $a \in \left(-\frac{1}{4}, 1\right)$

26. At what values of 'a' do all the zeroes of the function, $f(x) = (a - 2)x^2 + 2ax + a + 3$ lie on the interval $(-2, 1)$?

Solution: $f(x) = (a - 2)x^2 + 2ax + a + 3$

Case-I: $(a - 2) > 0 \qquad \Rightarrow a > 2$ (i)

(i) $D \geq 0 \Rightarrow 4a^2 - 4(a - 2)(a + 3) \geq 0$

$\Rightarrow 4a^2 - 4(a^2 + a - 6) \geq 0 \Rightarrow -4a \geq -24 \Rightarrow a \leq 6$ (2)

(ii) $f(-2) > 0$

$\Rightarrow (a-2)(-2)^2 + 2a(-2) + a + 3 > 0$

$\Rightarrow a - 5 > 0 \quad \Rightarrow a > 5$ (3)

(iii) $f(1) > 0 \Rightarrow a - 2 + 2a + a + 3 > 0$

$\Rightarrow a > -\dfrac{1}{4}$ (4)

(iv) $-2 < \dfrac{-b}{2a} < 1 \Rightarrow -2 < \dfrac{-2a}{2(a-2)} < 1$

$\Rightarrow \dfrac{(a-4)}{(a-2)} > 0$ and $(a-1)(a-2) > 0$

$\Rightarrow a \in (-\infty, 1) \cup (2, \infty)$ and $a \in (-\infty, 2) \cup (4, \infty)$ ...(5)

From all of their intersections $\Rightarrow a \in (5, 6]$

Case II $a - 2 < 0 \Rightarrow a < 2$ ....(6)

$D \geq 0 \Rightarrow a \leq 6$ ....(7)

and $-2 < -\dfrac{b}{2a} < 1 \Rightarrow a \in (-\infty, 1) \cup (4, \infty)$....(8)

$\Rightarrow f(-2) < 0 \Rightarrow a < 5$ ....(9)

Also $f(1) < 0 \Rightarrow a < \dfrac{-1}{4} \Rightarrow a \in \left(-\infty, \dfrac{-1}{4}\right)$.....(10)

$\therefore$ In this case (ii), $a \in \left(-\infty, \dfrac{-1}{4}\right)$

Case III when $a = 2$; $x = -1.25 \in (-2, 1)$

$\Rightarrow a = 2$ is possible

which lies between -2 and 1

$\therefore$ we have $a \in \left(-\infty, \dfrac{-1}{4}\right) \cup (5, 6] \cup \{2\}$

27. Suppose a cubic polynomial $f(x) = x^3 + px^2 + qx + 72$ is divisible by both $x^2 + ax + b$ and $x^2 + bx + a$ (where a, b, p, q are constants and $a \neq b$). Find the sum of the squares of the roots of the cubic polynomial.

Solution: Let the roots of $x^2 + ax + b$ be α, β and that of $x^2 + bx + a$ be α, γ

$\Rightarrow \alpha^2 + a\alpha + b = 0, \alpha^2 = -(a\alpha + b)$ (1)

and $\alpha^2 + b\alpha + a = 0$ (2)

$\Rightarrow -a\alpha - b + b\alpha + a = 0$ (from (1) and (2))

$\Rightarrow (\alpha - 1)(b - a) = 0 \Rightarrow \alpha = 1$ as $a \neq b$

$\Rightarrow \alpha = 1, \begin{cases} \beta = b, & \alpha\beta = b \\ \gamma = a, & \alpha\gamma = a \end{cases}$ as $\alpha = 1$

Since $f(x)$ is divisible by both the equations, so $1, \alpha, \beta$ are roots of $f(x) = 0$

$\Rightarrow (1)^2 + \beta^2 + \gamma^2 = (1 + \beta + \gamma)^2 - (2\beta + 2\gamma + 2\beta\gamma)$

$= (1 + b + a)^2 - (2b + 2a + 2ab)$

Also, when $\alpha = 1, \Rightarrow a + b + 1 = 0 \Rightarrow 1 + \beta^2 + \gamma^2$
$= (0)^2 - [2(a + b) + 2ab] = -(-2 - 144) = 146$

28. Find the complete set of real values of 'a' for which both roots of the quadratic equation $(a^2 - 6a + 5)x^2 - \sqrt{a^2 + 2a}\, x + (6a - a^2 - 8) = 0$ lie on either side of the origin.

Solution: $(a^2 - 6a + 5)x^2 - \sqrt{a^2 + 2a}\, x + (6a - a^2 - 8) = 0$, $D_f = \mathbb{R} - (-2, 0)$

$\because$ Both roots lie on either side of origin, $Af(0) < 0$

$\Rightarrow (a^2 - 6a + 5)(6a - a^2 - 8) < 0$

$\Rightarrow (a^2 - 6a + 8)(a^2 - 6a + 5) > 0$

$\Rightarrow (a - 4)(a - 2)(a - 1)(a - 5) > 0$

+ 1 − 2 + 4 − 5 +

$\Rightarrow a \in (-\infty, 1) \cup (2, 4) \cup (5, \infty)$

$\Rightarrow a \in (-\infty, -2] \cup (0, 1) \cup (2, 4) \cup (5, \infty)$

29. Given $x, y \in \mathbb{R}$, $x^2 + y^2 > 0$. If the maximum and minimum value of the expression $E = \dfrac{x^2 + y^2}{x^2 + xy + 4y^2}$ are M and m, and A denotes the average value of M and m, compute $(2007)A$.

Solution: $E = \dfrac{1 + \left(\dfrac{y}{x}\right)^2}{1 + \dfrac{y}{x} + 4\left(\dfrac{y}{x}\right)^2}$; putting $\dfrac{y}{x} = t$

$\Rightarrow E = \dfrac{1 + t^2}{1 + t + 4t^2} \quad \Rightarrow E + Et + 4Et^2 = 1 + t^2$

$\Rightarrow t^2(4E - 1) + t(E) + E - 1 = 0$, for $t \in \mathbb{R}$, $D \geq 0$

$\Rightarrow E^2 - 4(4E^2 - 5E + 1) \geq 0 \Rightarrow 15E^2 - 20E + 4 \leq 0$

$\Rightarrow E \in \left(\dfrac{10 - 2\sqrt{10}}{15}, \dfrac{10 + 2\sqrt{10}}{15}\right)$

$\Rightarrow \dfrac{M + m}{2} = \dfrac{10 - 2\sqrt{10} + 10 + 2\sqrt{10}}{15 \times 2} = \dfrac{10}{15} = A$

$\therefore 2007A = 2007 \times \dfrac{10}{15} = 1338$

30. Find the range of values of t for which $2\sin t = \dfrac{1 - 2x + 5x^2}{3x^2 - 2x - 1}$, $t \in \left[-\dfrac{\pi}{2}, \dfrac{\pi}{2}\right]$.

Solution: $2\sin t = \dfrac{1 - 2x + 5x^2}{3x^2 - 2x - 1}$

consider, $y = \dfrac{5x^2 - 2x + 1}{3x^2 - 2x - 1}$

$\Rightarrow 3yx^2 - 2yx - y = 5x^2 - 2x + 1$

$\Rightarrow 3yx^2 - 2yx - y - 5x^2 + 2x - 1 = 0$

$\Rightarrow x^2(3y-5) - 2(y-1)x - (y+1) = 0 \Rightarrow D \geq 0; x \in \mathbb{R}$

$\Rightarrow 4(y-1)^2 + 4(y+1)(3y-5) \geq 0$

$\Rightarrow (y-1)^2 + (y+1)(3y-5) \geq 0$

$\Rightarrow y^2 - y - 1 \geq 0$

$\Rightarrow y \in \left(-\infty, \frac{1-\sqrt{5}}{2}\right] \cup \left[\frac{1+\sqrt{5}}{2}, \infty\right)$

$\because 2\sin t = y \in [-2, 2]$

$\Rightarrow 2\sin t \in \left[-2, \frac{1-\sqrt{5}}{2}\right] \cup \left[\frac{1+\sqrt{5}}{2}, 2\right]$

$\Rightarrow \sin t \in \left[-1, \frac{1-\sqrt{5}}{4}\right] \cup \left[\frac{1+\sqrt{5}}{4}, 1\right]$

$\Rightarrow t \in \left[\frac{-\pi}{2}, \frac{-\pi}{10}\right] \cup \left[\frac{3\pi}{10}, \frac{\pi}{2}\right]$

31. Prove that the equation

$$2\cos^2\left(\frac{x}{2}\right)\sin^2 x = x^2 + x^{-2}, 0 < x \leq \pi/2$$

has no real solution.

Solution: For $0 < x \leq \pi/2$, $x^2 + x^{-2} \geq 2$.

$\Rightarrow 2\cos^2\left(\frac{x}{2}\right) \sin^2 x \geq 2$ (1)

But $2\cos^2\left(\frac{x}{2}\right) \sin^2 x \leq 2$ (2)

$\therefore \cos^2\left(\frac{x}{2}\right) \sin^2 x = 1$ [from (1) and (2)]

But this is possible if and only if

$\cos^2\left(\frac{x}{2}\right) = 1$ and $\sin^2 x = 1$, which is impossible

Hence given equation no real solution.

32. Let a, b, c be non-zero real numbers such that

$$\int_0^1 (1+\cos^8 x)(ax^2+bx+c)dx = \int_0^2 (1+\cos^8 x)(ax^2+bx+c)dx,$$

then prove that the quadratic equation $ax^2 + bx + c = 0$ has at least one real root in [1, 2].

Solution: The given relation gives

$$\Rightarrow \int_1^2 (1+\cos^8 x)(ax^2+bx+c)dx = 0$$

Case I If $ax^2 + bx + c > 0$ for $1 \leq x \leq 2$, then

Since $1 + \cos^8 x \geq 1$, we get

$$\int_1^2 (1+\cos^8 x)(ax^2+bx+c)dx > 0$$

which is a contradiction and hence no solution.

Case II Similarly, if $ax^2 + bx + c < 0$ for $1 \leq x \leq 2$, then

$$\int_1^2 (1+\cos^8 x)(ax^2+bx+c)dx < 0$$

Which is a contradiction and hence no solution again. Thus, $ax^2 + bx + c$ assumes both positive and negative values in [1,2], therefore, by the intermediate value theorem there exists $\alpha \in [1,2]$ such that $a\alpha^2 + b\alpha + c = 0$

33. Let a,b,c be real numbers, $a \neq 0$. If α is a root of $a^2x^2 + bx + c = 0$, β is a root of $a^2x^2 - bx - c = 0$ and $0 < \alpha < \beta$, then prove that the equation $a^2x^2 + 2bx + 2c = 0$ has a root γ that always satisfy $\alpha < \gamma < \beta$.

Solution: We have $a^2\alpha^2 + b\alpha + c = 0$ (i)

and $a^2\beta^2 - b\beta - c = 0$ (ii); where $0 < \alpha < \beta$, and $a \neq 0$

Let $f(x) = a^2x^2 + 2bx + 2c$

Since f is a polynomial function, f is continuous on $\mathbb{R}$ and hence on $[\alpha, \beta]$.

Also, $f(\alpha) = a^2\alpha^2 + 2b\alpha + 2c$

$= 2(a^2\alpha^2 + b\alpha + c) - a^2\alpha^2$

$= 2(0) - a^2\alpha^2 = -a^2\alpha^2 < 0$ [Using (1)]

And $f(\beta) = a^2\beta^2 + 2b\beta + 2c$

$= 3a^2\beta^2 - 2(a^2\beta^2 - b\beta - c)$

$= 3a^2\beta^2 - 2(0) = 3a^2\beta^2 > 0$ [Using (2)]

Since f is continuous on $[\alpha, \beta]$ and $f(\alpha) < 0$, $f(\beta) > 0$

$\Rightarrow f$ must vanish at least once in (α, β) say at γ.

34. Let $f(x)$ be a quadratic expression which is positive for all real x. If $g(x) = f(x) + f'(x) + f''(x)$, then for all real x prove that $g(x) > 0$.

Solution: Let $f(x) = ax^2 + bx + c$

As $f(x) > 0 \ \forall x \in \mathbb{R}$, $a > 0$ and $b^2 - 4ac < 0$

Now, $g(x) = ax^2 + bx + c + (2ax + b) + 2a$

$= ax^2 + (b + 2a)x + 2a + b + c$

Here $a > 0$ and $(b + 2a)^2 - 4a(2a + b + c)$

$= (b^2 - 4ac) - 4a^2 < 0$. Thus $g(x) > 0 \ \forall x \in \mathbb{R}$

35. If the roots of the equation $x^2 - 2ax + a^2 + a - 3 = 0$ are real less than 3, then prove that $a < 2$.

Solution: The equation can be written as $(x - a)^2 = 3 - a$

Thus $3 - a \geq 0$ and $x = a \pm \sqrt{3-a}$

Both the roots will be less than 3 if the larger of the two is less than 3 $\Rightarrow a + \sqrt{3-a} < 3$

$\Rightarrow \sqrt{3-a} < 3 - a \Rightarrow \sqrt{3-a} > 1 \Rightarrow 3 - a > 1$ or $a < 2$.

36. Let a, b, c be the sides of a triangle, where $a \neq c$ and $\lambda \in \mathbb{R}$. If the roots of the equation $x^2 + 2(a + b + c)x + 3\lambda(ab + bc + ca) = 0$ are real, then find the values of λ.

Solution: As roots are real,

$D = 4 (a + b + c)^2 - 12\lambda (bc + ca + ab) \geq 0$

$\Rightarrow \lambda \leq \dfrac{(a+b+c)^2}{3(bc+ca+ab)}$ (1)

As a, b, c are the sides of a triangle $b + c > a$, $c + a > b$ and $a + b > c$

$\Rightarrow a(b + c) + b (c + a) + c (a + b) > aa + bb + cc$

$\Rightarrow 4(bc + ca + ab) > (a + b + c)^2$ (2)

From (1) and (2), we get

$\lambda < 4/3 \Rightarrow \lambda \in (-\infty, 4/3)$

37. For real x, prove that the function $\dfrac{(x-a)(x-c)}{(x-b)}$ will assume all real values, provided b lie between a and c.

Solution: Let $y = \dfrac{(x-a)(x-c)}{x-b} = \dfrac{x^2-(a+c)x+ac}{x-b}$

$\Rightarrow x^2 - (a + c + y) x + ac + by = 0$........ (1)

Since x is real, the discriminant of (1) ≥ 0

$\Rightarrow (a + c + y)^2 - 4(ac + by) \geq 0$

$\Rightarrow y^2 + 2 (a + c) y + (a + c)^2 - 4ac - 4by \geq 0$

$\Rightarrow y^2 + 2 (a + c - 2b) y + (a + c)^2 \geq 0$ (2)

Since y takes all real values, (2) is possible if and only if $4(a + c - 2b)^2 - 4 (a - c)^2 < 0$

$\Leftrightarrow (a + c - 2b + a - c) (a + c - 2b - a + c) \leq 0$

$\Leftrightarrow (2a - 2b) (2c - 2b) \leq 0 \Leftrightarrow b$ lies between a and c.

38. Prove that if $(x - r)$ is a factor of the polynomial $f(x) = a_0x^n + a_1x^n + ... + a_n$ repeated m times. $(1 < m \leq n)$, then r is a root of $f'(x) = 0$, repeated $(m - 1)$ times.

Solution: As $x - r$ is a factor of

$f(x) = a_0x^n + a_1x^{n-1} + ... + a_n$

repeated m times, we can write $f(x) = (x - r)^m p(x)$, where $p(x)$ is a polynomial of degree $n - m$ and $p(r) \neq 0$

$\Rightarrow f'(x) = m (x - r)^{m-1} .p(x) + (x - r)^m p'(x) = (x - r)^{m-1} .q(x)$; where $q(x) = mp(x) + (x - r) p'(x)$

$\Rightarrow q(r) = mp (x) \neq 0$

$\Rightarrow r$ is a root of $f'(x) = 0$, repeated $(m - 1)$ times.

39. Let a, b, c, p, q be real numbers. Suppose α, β are the roots of the equation $x^2 + 2px + q = 0$ and — are the roots of the equation $ax^2 + 2bx + c = 0$, where $\beta^2 \notin \{-1, 0, 1\}$

Assertion: $(p^2 - q) (b^2 - ac) \leq 0$

Reason: $b \neq pa$ or $c \neq qa$

Solution: (b) Suppose $\alpha \notin \mathbb{R}$

As $a, b, c, p, q \in \mathbb{R}$, the other root of $x^2 + 2px + q = 0$ and $ax^2 + 2bx + c = 0$ must be $\bar{\alpha}$. Thus $\bar{\alpha} = \beta = 1/\beta \Rightarrow \beta^2 = 1$ But $\beta^2 \notin \{-1, 0, 1\}$ (given)

$\Rightarrow \alpha \in \mathbb{R} \Rightarrow \beta, 1/\beta \in \mathbb{R}$

$\Rightarrow D_1 = 4(p^2 - q) \geq 0$ and $D_2 = 4(b^2 - ac) \geq 0$

Thus, Assertion is correct.

Next let $b = pa$ and $c = qa$, then

$ax^2 + 2bx + c = a (x^2 + 2px + q)$

$\Rightarrow$ both the roots of the two equations are common

$\Rightarrow \beta = 1/\beta \quad \Rightarrow \beta^2 = 1$. (a contradiction)

Thus $b \neq pa$ or $c \neq qa$

$\therefore$ Reason is true but is not the correct explanation Assertion

40. Find the smallest value of $k \in \mathbb{Z}$, for which both the roots of the equation $x^2 - 8kx + 16 (k^2 - k + 1) = 0$ are real, distinct and have value at least 4.

Solution: As $x^2 - 8kx + 16 (k^2 - k + 1) = 0$ (1)

has real and distinct roots,

$(-8k)^2 - (4) (16) (k^2 - k + 1) > 0 \Rightarrow k - 1 > 0$

As k is an integer, $k \geq 2$

If α,β are roots of (1), then $\alpha, \beta \geq 4$.

$\Rightarrow \alpha + \beta \geq 8$ and $\alpha . \beta \geq 16$

$\Rightarrow 8k \geq 8$ and $16 (k^2 - k + 1) \geq 16$

$\Rightarrow k \geq 1$ and $k(k - 1) \geq 0 \Rightarrow k \geq 1$

Thus, smallest value of k is 2.

41. If α, β are roots of $x^2 + px + q = 0$ and γ, δ are the roots of $x^2 + rx + s = 0$, then evaluate $E = (\alpha - \gamma) (\beta - \gamma) (\alpha - \delta) (\beta - \delta)$ in terms of p, q, r and s. Deduce the condition that equations have a common root.

Solution: $x^2 + px + q = (x - \alpha) (x - \beta)$

Now, $E = (\gamma - \alpha) (\gamma - \beta)(\delta - \alpha) (\delta - \beta)$

$= (\gamma^2 + p\gamma + q)(\delta^2 + p\delta + q)$

$= (- r\gamma - s + p\gamma + q)(-r\delta - s + p\delta + q)$

Thus, $E = [(q - s) - (r - p)\gamma][(q - s) - (r - p)\delta]$

$= (r-p)^2\left[\left(\dfrac{q-s}{r-p}\right)-\gamma\right]\left[\left(\dfrac{q-s}{r-p}\right)-\delta\right]$

$= (r-p)^2\left[\left(\dfrac{q-s}{r-p}\right)^2+r\left(\dfrac{q-s}{r-p}\right)+s\right]$

$= (q - s)^2 + r(q - s) (r - p) + s (r - p)^2$

The two equations have a common root if and only if $E = 0$

$\Leftrightarrow (q - s)^2 + r(q - s) (r - p) + s(r - p)^2 = 0$

42. For $a \le 0$ determine all real roots of the equation $x^2 - 2a|x - a| - 3a^2 = 0$.

Solution: Put $|x - a| = y$

$\Rightarrow y \ge 0$ and $x = a \pm y$

Putting in given equation, we get

$(a \pm y)^2 - 2ay - 3a^2 = 0$

$\Rightarrow y^2 - 2a^2 = 0$ or $y^2 - 4ay - 2a^2 = 0$

$\Rightarrow y = -\sqrt{2}\,a$ or $y = a(2 - \sqrt{6})$ as $y \le 0$

$\Rightarrow x = (1 \pm \sqrt{2})a, (3 - \sqrt{6})a, (\sqrt{6} - 1)a$

But $x = (1 + \sqrt{2})a$ and $x = a(3 - \sqrt{6})$ do not satisfy the given equation.

$\therefore\ x = (1 - \sqrt{2})a$ and $x = (\sqrt{6} - 1)a$

43. Let α_1, α_2 and β_1, β_2 be the roots of $ax^2 + bx + c = 0$ and $px^2 + qx + r = 0$ respectively. If the system of equations $\alpha_1 y + \alpha_2 z = 0$ and $\beta_1 y + \beta_2 z = 0$ has non-trivial solutions, then prove that $\dfrac{b^2}{q^2} = \dfrac{ac}{pr}$.

Solution: $\alpha_1 y + \alpha_2 z = 0$ and $\beta_1 y + \beta_2 z = 0$ has non-trivial solution if and only if $\begin{vmatrix} \alpha_1 & \alpha_2 \\ \beta_1 & \beta_2 \end{vmatrix} = 0 \Leftrightarrow \dfrac{\alpha_1}{\alpha_2} = \dfrac{\beta_1}{\beta_2}$

Applying dividendo and componendo, we get

$$\frac{\alpha_1 - \alpha_2}{\alpha_1 + \alpha_2} = \frac{\beta_1 - \beta_2}{\beta_1 + \beta_2} \Rightarrow \frac{(\alpha_1 - \alpha_2)^2}{(\alpha_1 + \alpha_2)^2} = \frac{(\beta_1 - \beta_2)^2}{(\beta_1 + \beta_2)^2}$$

$$\Rightarrow 1 - \frac{4\alpha_1\alpha_2}{(\alpha_1 + \alpha_2)^2} = 1 - \frac{4\beta_1\beta_2}{(\beta_1 + \beta_2)^2}$$

$$\Rightarrow \frac{\alpha_1\alpha_2}{(\alpha_1 + \alpha_2)} = \frac{\beta_1\beta_2}{(\beta_1 + \beta_2)^2}$$

$$\Rightarrow \frac{c/a}{(-b/a)^2} = \frac{r/p}{(-q/p)^2} \Rightarrow \frac{b^2}{q^2} = \frac{ac}{pr}$$

44. A function $f: \mathbb{R} \to \mathbb{R}$, where $\mathbb{R}$ is the set of real number, is defined by $f(x) = \dfrac{\alpha x^2 + 6x - 8}{\alpha + 6x - 8x^2}$. Find the interval of values of α for which f is onto. Is the function one to one for $\alpha = 3$? Justify your answer.

Solution: Let $y \in \mathbb{R}, f(x) = y$

$\Rightarrow (\alpha + 8y)x^2 + 6(1 - y)x - (8 + \alpha y) = 0$

As x is real, $36(1 - y)^2 + 4(\alpha + 8y)(8 + \alpha y) \le 0$

$\Rightarrow (9 + 8\alpha)y^2 + (46 + \alpha^2)y + (9 + 8\alpha) \le 0$

This is true for each $y \in \mathbb{R}$. Therefore,

$9 + 8a > 0$ and $(46 + \alpha^2)^2 - 4(9 + 8\alpha)^2 \le 0$

$\Rightarrow \alpha > -9/8$ and $(\alpha^2 + 16\alpha + 64)(\alpha^2 - 16\alpha + 28) \le 0$

$\Rightarrow \alpha > -9/8$ and $(\alpha + 8)^2(\alpha - 2)(\alpha - 14) \le 0$

$\Rightarrow 2 \le \alpha \le 14$

For $\alpha = 3, f(x) = \dfrac{3x^2 + 6x - 8}{3 + 6x - 8x^2}$

And $f(1) = f(-1) = 1 \Rightarrow f$ is not one one for $\alpha = 3$

45. Find the set of all solutions of the equations $2^{|y|} - |2^{y-1} - 1| = 2^{y-1} + 1$.

Solution: When $y < 0$, $|y| = -y$ and $|2^{y-1} - 1| = 1 - 2^{y-1}$

In this case, the equation can be written as

$2^{-y} - (1 - 2^{y-1}) = 2^{y-1} + 1 \Rightarrow 2^{-y} = 2^1$

$\Rightarrow -y = 1$ or $y = -1$

When $0 \le y < 1$, the equation becomes

$2^y - (1 - 2^{y-1}) = 2^{y-1} + 1 \Rightarrow 2^y = 2 \Rightarrow y = 1$

Not possible

When $y \ge 1$, the equation becomes

$2^y - (2^{y-1} - 1) = 2^{y-1} + 1$

$\Rightarrow 2^y = 2^{y-1} + 2^{y-1}$

which is an identity.

Thus, the solution set is $\{-1\} \cup [1, \infty)$.

46. Let $f(x) = Ax^2 + Bx + C$ where A, B, C are real numbers. Prove that if $f(x)$ is an integer whenever x is an integer, then the numbers $2A$, $A + B$ and C are all integers. Conversely, prove that if the numbers $2A$, $A + B$ and C are integers, then $f(x)$ is an integer whenever x is an integer.

Solution: Assume $f(x) = Ax^2 + Bx + C$ is an integer whenever x is an integer.

$\Rightarrow f(-1), f(0)$ and $f(1)$ are integers.

$\Rightarrow A - B + C$, C and $A + B + C$ are integers

$\Rightarrow A - B$, $A + B$ and C are integers.

$\Rightarrow 2A$, $A + B$ and C are integers.

Conversely, assume $2A$, $A + B$ and C are integers.

Let $x = 2m$, where m is an integer;

Then $f(x) = 4Am^2 + 2Bm + C = 2Am(2m - 1) + 2(A + B)m + C$

As $2A$, $A + B$, C and m are integers, $f(x)$ is an integer.

Next, let $x = 2m + 1$, where m is an integer, then

$f(x) = A(2m + 1)^2 + B(2m + 1) + C = 2Am(2m + 1) + (A + B)(2m + 1) + C$

As $2A$, $A + B$, C and m are integers, $f(x)$ is also an integer.

Thus, $f(x)$ is an integer whenever x is an integer.

47. Let a, b, c, d be real numbers in G.P. If u, v, w satisfy the system of equations: $u + 2v + 3w = 6$; $4u + 5v + 6w = 12$ and $6u + 9v = 4$, then show that the roots of the equation $\left(\frac{1}{u}+\frac{1}{v}+\frac{1}{w}\right)x^2+[(b-c)^2+(c-a)^2+(d-b)^2]x+u+v+w=0$ and $20x^2+10(a-d)^2x-9=0$ are reciprocal of each other.

Solution: Solving for u, v and w, we get $u=-1/3$, $v=2/3$ and $w=5/3$

Now, $(b-c)^2+(c-a)^2+(d-b)^2$

$=a^2+2b^2+2c^2+d^2-2bc-2ca-2bd$

As a, b, c, d are in G.P. $bc=ad$, $ca=b^2$ and $bd=c^2$

$\therefore\ (b-c)^2+(c-a)^2+(d-b)^2=(a-d)^2$

$\therefore$ The quadratic equation

$\left(\frac{1}{u}+\frac{1}{v}+\frac{1}{w}\right)x^2+[(b-c)^2+(c-a)^2+(d-b)^2]x+u+$

$v+w=0$, becomes $\left(-\frac{9}{10}\right)x2+(a-d)2x+2=0$

or $-9x^2+(10)(a-d)^2+20=0$ whose roots are reciprocal of those of $20x^2+10(a-d)2x-9=0$

48. Let $-1\leq\ \ \leq 1$. Show that the equation $4x^3-3x-p=0$ has a unique root in the interval [1/2, 1] and identify it.

Solution: Let $f(x)=4x^3-3x-p$

We have, $f\left(\frac{1}{2}\right)=-1-p\leq 0$ and $f(1)=1-p\geq 0$

By the intermediate value theorem, $f(x)=0$ has a root in the interval [1/2,1].

Suppose $\alpha, \beta \in [1/2, 1]$ are $\alpha<\beta$ are such that $f(\alpha)=f(\beta)=0$

By Rolle's theorem, there exists $\gamma\in(\alpha,\beta)\subset(1/2,1)$ such that $f'(\gamma)=0\Rightarrow 4\gamma^2-1=0$

$\Rightarrow \gamma=\pm 1/2\notin(1/2,1)$

Thus, there is a unique root of $4x^3-3x-p=0$ in the interval [1/2,1]

Let $x=\cos\theta\in[1/2,1]\Rightarrow\theta\in[0,\pi/3]$

Putting $x=\cos\theta$ in $4x^2-3x-p=0$, we get $4\cos^3\theta-3\cos\theta-p=0$

$\Rightarrow p=\cos(3\theta)\Rightarrow\theta=\frac{1}{3}\cos^{-1}(p)$

49. Let a and b be the roots of the equation $x^2-10cx-11d=0$ and those of $x^2-10ax-11b=0$ are c, d, then find the value of $a+b+c+d$, assuming that a, b, c, d are distinct.

Solution: $a+b=10c$, $ab=-11d$

$\Rightarrow c+d=10a$, $cd=-11b$

$\Rightarrow a+b+c+d=10(a+c)$ and $abcd=121bd$

$\Rightarrow b+d=9(a+c)$ and $ac=121$

Also $a^2-10ac-11d=0$

And $c^2-10ac-11b=0$

$\Rightarrow a^2+c^2-20ac-11(b+d)=0$

$\Rightarrow (a+c)^2-(11)(9)(a+c)-22ac=0$

$\Rightarrow (a+c)^2-99(a+c)-22.(121)=0\Rightarrow(a+c-121)(a+c+22)=0$

$\Rightarrow a+c=121,-22$

But $a+c=-22$, $ac=121\Rightarrow a=c=-11$

$\therefore\ a+c\neq-22\ (\because a\neq c)$

Thus, $a+c=121$

$\therefore\ a+b+c+d=10(a+c)=1210$

50. Solve for integer x, y, z; $x+y=1-z$, $x^3+y^3=1-z^2$.

Solution: $(1-z^2)=(1-z)(1+z)=(x^3+y^3)$

$\Rightarrow (1+z)=\frac{x^3+y^3}{x+y}=x^2+y^2-xy$

Now $1-z=x+y$

$\Rightarrow z=1-x-y$

$\therefore\ 1+z=x^2+y^2-xy$

$\Rightarrow 1+1-x-y=x^2+y^2-xy$

$\Rightarrow x^2+y^2-xy+x+y-2=0$

$\Rightarrow x^2+x(1-y)+(y^2+y-2)=0$

$\Rightarrow x=\frac{-(1-y)\pm\sqrt{(1-y)^2-4(y^2+y-2)}}{2}$

$\Rightarrow x=\frac{-(1-y)\pm\sqrt{-3(y+3)(y-1)}}{2}$

Now, $-3(y+3)(y-1)\geq 0$

$\Rightarrow (y+3)(y-1)\leq 0\ \Rightarrow y\in[-3,1]$

$\Rightarrow y\in\{-3,-2,-1,0,1\}$ as $y\in\mathbb{Z}$

For $y=-3$; $x=-2$ and $z=6$

For $y=-2$; $x=0$ and $z=3$ or $x=-3$, $z=6$

For $y=-1$; $x\notin\mathbb{Z}$ $\Rightarrow y\neq-1$

For $y=0$; $x=1$ and $z=0$ or $x=-2$; $z=3$

For $y=1$; $x=0$ and $z=0$

$\therefore$ Required solution are (–2, –3, 6), (0, –2, 3), (–3, –2, 6), (1, 0, 0), (–2, 0, 3) and (0, 1, 0)

Match the column:

51. Let $f(x)=\frac{x^2-6x+5}{x^2-5x+6}$.

Column I

(i) If $-1<x<1$, then $f(x)$ satisfies

(ii) If $1<x<2$, then $f(x)$ satisfies

(iii) If $3<x<5$, then $f(x)$ satisfies

(iv) If $x>5$, then $f(x)$ satisfies

Column II

(p) $0 < f(x) < 1$

(q) $f(x) < 0$

(r) $f(x) > 0$

(s) $f(x) < 1$

Solution: (b) $f(x) = \dfrac{x^2-6x+5}{x^2-5x+6} = -\dfrac{x+1}{x^2-5x+6}$

$\Rightarrow f'(x) = 0 - \dfrac{1.(x^2-5x+6)-(x+1)(2x-5)}{(x^2-5x+6)^2}$

$= -\dfrac{(-x^2-2x+11)}{(x^2-5x+6)^2} = \dfrac{x^2+2x-11}{(x^2-5x+6)^2}$

$= \dfrac{(x-(-1-2\sqrt{3}))\,(x-(-1+2\sqrt{3}))}{(x^2-5x+6)^2}$

sign of $f'(x)$

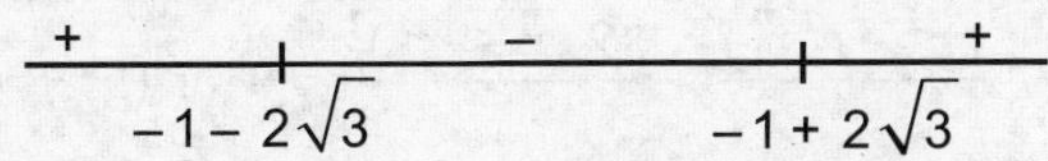

Also, $f(x) = \dfrac{x^2-6x+5}{x^2-5x+6} = \dfrac{(x-1)\,(x-5)}{(x-2)\,(x-3)}$

Further, $\lim\limits_{x\to 2^+} f(x) = +\infty; \lim\limits_{x\to 2^-} f(x) = -\infty$

and $\lim\limits_{x\to 3^+} f(x) = -\infty;\ \lim\limits_{x\to 3^-} f(x) = +\infty$;

and $f(1) = 0, f(5) = 0$

Next, $\lim\limits_{x\to\mp\infty} f(x) = \lim\limits_{x\to\mp\infty} \dfrac{x^2-6x+5}{x^2-5x+6}$

$= \lim\limits_{x\to\mp\infty} \dfrac{1-6/x+5/x^2}{1-5/x+6/x^2} = 1$

∴ Graph of $f(x)$ will be as shown below

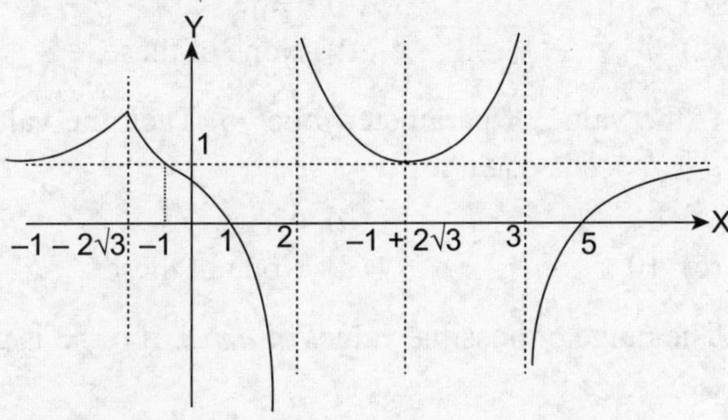

(i) For $-1 < x < 1$ (∵ $f(x)$ decreasing)

$\Rightarrow f(1) < f(x) < f(-1)$

$\Rightarrow f(x) \in (0, 1)$ $\Rightarrow$ **(i)→(P), (R), (S)**

(ii) For $1 < x < 2$ (∵ $f(x)$ decreasing)

$\Rightarrow f(2) < f(x) < f(1)$ $\Rightarrow -\infty < f(x) < 0$

$\Rightarrow f(x) \in (-\infty, 0)$ $\Rightarrow$ **(ii)→(Q), (S)**

(iii) For $3 < x < 5$ (∵ $f(x)$ increasing)

$\Rightarrow f(3) < f(x) < f(5)$ $\Rightarrow -\infty < f(x) < 0$

$\Rightarrow$ **(iii)→(Q), (S)**

(iv) For $x > 5$ (∵ $f(x)$ increasing)

$\Rightarrow f(5) < f(x) < f(\infty)$ $\Rightarrow 0 < f(x) < 1$

$\Rightarrow f(x) \in (0, 1)$ $\Rightarrow$ **(iv)→(P), (R), (S)**

52. The set of value (s) of $\lambda \in \mathbb{R}$ for which

Column–I

(i) $\lambda x^2 - (\lambda + 1)x + 3\lambda - 1 = 0$ has no real roots

(ii) $x^2 - 2(4\lambda - 1)x + 15\lambda^2 - 2\lambda - 7 \geq 0$ for each real x.

(iii) Sum of the roots of $x^2 + (6 - \lambda - \lambda^2)x - \lambda^2 = 0$ is zero.

(iv) The roots of $x^2 + (2\lambda - 1)x + \lambda^2 + 2 = 0$ are in the ratio 1 : 2.

Column–II

(a) $\{-3, 2\}$

(b) $(-\infty, -1/5) \cup (2, \infty)$

(c) $\{-4\}$

(d) $[2, 4]$

Solution: (i) $(\lambda + 1)^2 - 4\lambda(3\lambda - 1) < 0$

$\Rightarrow \lambda^2 + 2\lambda + 1 - 12\lambda^2 + 4\lambda < 0$

$\Rightarrow -11\lambda^2 + 6\lambda + 1 < 0$

$\Rightarrow 11\lambda^2 - 6\lambda - 1 > 0$

$\Rightarrow \lambda \in \left(-\infty, \dfrac{6-\sqrt{80}}{22}\right) \cup \left(\dfrac{6+\sqrt{80}}{22}, \infty\right)$

$\Rightarrow \lambda \in \left(-\infty, \dfrac{3-2\sqrt{5}}{11}\right) \cup \left(\dfrac{3+2\sqrt{5}}{11}, \infty\right)$

Clearly, range set of λ is a super set of sets given in options (a), (b), (c) and (d).

(ii) Disc. ≤ 0

$(4\lambda - 1)^2 - (15\lambda^2 - 2\lambda - 7) \leq 0$

$(\lambda - 2)(\lambda - 4) \leq 0$

$\Rightarrow \lambda \in [2, 4] \Rightarrow$ (ii) → (d)

(iii) Sum of roots $= -(6 - \lambda - \lambda^2) = 0$

$\Rightarrow \lambda^2 + \lambda - 6 = 0$ $\Rightarrow (\lambda + 3)(\lambda - 2) = 0$

$\Rightarrow \lambda = -3, 2$ ∴ (iii) → (a)

(iv) Let the roots be α and 2α

∴ $\alpha + 2\alpha = -(2\lambda - 1)$ and $\alpha . 2\alpha = \lambda^2 + 2$

$\Rightarrow 9/2 = \dfrac{(2\lambda-1)^2}{(\lambda^2+2)} \Rightarrow (\lambda + 4)^2 = 0 \Rightarrow \lambda = -4$

∴ (iv) → c

53. If $ax^2 + bx + c = 0$, where $a \neq 0$ is satisfied by α, β, α^2 and β^2, then:

Column–I

(a) The value of $\alpha+\beta$ can be

(b) The number of unordered pairs (α, β) is (where $\alpha\beta \neq 0$)

(c) The value of $\alpha\beta$ can be

(d) The value of $\alpha^2+\beta^2$ can be

Column–II

(p) 3

(q) 1

(r) 2

(s) –1

Solution: (a) → (q, r, s), (b) → (p), (c) → (q, s), (d) → (q, r, s)

Since $ax^2+bx+c=0$ is satisfied by α, β, α^2 and β^2

$\Rightarrow$ α^2 and β^2 must belong to $\{\alpha, \beta\}$

Let $\alpha^2=\alpha, \beta^2=\beta$

$\Rightarrow$ (α, β) is (0, 1) or (1, 1) or (0, 0) or (1, 0)

or $\alpha^2=\beta, \beta^2=\alpha \Rightarrow \alpha^4=\alpha$

$\Rightarrow$ (α, β) is (1, 1) or (ω, ω^2)

or $\alpha^2=\beta, \beta^2=\beta \Rightarrow \alpha^2=\beta^2 \Rightarrow \alpha=\pm\beta$

$\Rightarrow$ (α, β) is (–1, 1)

$\Rightarrow$ $\alpha+\beta$ can be equal to 1, 2, 0 or – 1

also number of un-ordered pairs α, β such that $\alpha\beta \neq 0$ is (1, 1), (–1, 1) or (ω, ω^2)

$\alpha\beta$ can be equal to 0, 1 or –1.

The value of $\alpha^2+\beta^2$ can be equal to 0, 1, 2 or –1.

54. If α, β be the roots of the equation $px^2+3qx+r=0$. The equation whose roots are

Column–I

(i) $\pm3\alpha, \pm3\beta$

(ii) $\pm1/\alpha, \pm1/\beta$

(iii) $\pm\alpha^2, \pm\beta^2$

(iv) $\pm1/\alpha^2, \pm1/\beta^2$

Column–II

(a) $(r^2x^2+p^2)^2-(2pr-9q^2)^2x^2=0$

(b) $(p^2x^2+r^2)^2-(2pr-9q^2)^2x^2=0$

(c) $p^2x^4+9(2pr-9q^2)x^2+81r^2=0$

(d) $r^2x^4+(2pr-9q^2)x^2+p^2=0$

Solution:

(i) $3\alpha, 3\beta$ are roots of $p\left(\frac{x}{3}\right)^2+3q\left(\frac{x}{3}\right)+r=0$

$\Rightarrow px^2+9qx+9r=0$ and $-3\alpha, -3\beta$ are roots of $p(x^2)-9qx+9r=0$

$\therefore$ Required equation is $(px^2+9r)^2-81q^2x^2=0$

or $p^2x^4+(18pr-81q^2)x^2+81r^2=0$

or $p^2x^4+9(2pr-9q^2)x^2+81r^2=0 \therefore$ (i) → (c)

(ii) $1/\alpha, 1/\beta$ are roots of equation $rx^2+3qx+p=0$; $-1/\alpha, -1/\beta$ are roots of equation $rx^2-3qx+p=0$

$\therefore$ Required equation is $(rx^2+p)^2-9q^2x^2=0$

or $r^2x^4+(2pr-9q^2)x^2+p^2=0 \therefore$ (ii) → (d)

(iii) α^2, β^2 are roots of $px+3q\sqrt{x}+r=0$

or $(px+r)^2=9q^2x$ or $p^2x^2+r^2+2prx-9q^2x=0$

or $p^2x^2+(2pr-9q^2)x+r^2=0$ and $-\alpha^2$ and $-\beta^2$ are roots of $p^2x^2-(2pr-9q^2)x+r^2=0$

$\Rightarrow$ The required equation is $(p^2x^2+r^2)^2-(2pr-9q^2)^2x^2=0 \therefore$ (iii) → (b)

(iv) $\pm\alpha^2, \pm\beta^2$ are roots of equation $(p^2x^2+r^2)^2-(2pr-9q^2)^2x^2=0$

$\therefore$ $\pm1/\alpha^2, \pm1/\beta^2$ will be the roots of equation

$$\left(\frac{p^2}{x^2}+r^2\right)^2-(2pr-9q^2)^2\frac{1}{x^2}=0$$

or $\frac{(p^2+r^2x^2)^2}{x^4}-\frac{(2pr-9q^2)^2}{x^2}=0$ or $(p^2+r^2x^2)^2-(2pr-9q^2)^2x^2=0 \therefore$ (iv) → (a)

Comprehension passage

A: Sometimes, the concept of theory of equation and symmetric functions of roots and their relations with co-efficients of equation can be applied in evaluation optimization of real valued function of several variable parameters. Given three distinct real numbers a, b, c satisfying the relation $a^2(a+p)=b^2(b+p)=c^2(c+p)=k$, where $p \in \mathbb{R}$.

Based on above discussion, answer the following questions:

55. The values of $ab+bc+ca$ is

(a) $2\sqrt{3}$ (b) $-2\sqrt{3}$

(c) 0 (d) None of these

56. If the value of parameter p be –5. Then the value of $a+b+c$ is equal to

(a) –5 (b) 5

(c) 10 (d) None of these

57. The range of possible values of a, b, c if $p=3$ is given as

(a) $k \in (-4, 0)$ (b) $k \in (0, 4)$

(c) $k \in (0, 2)$ (d) None of these

Solution: 55. $\because$ $a^2(a+p)=b^2(b+p)=c^2(c+p)=k$ holds for three distinct real values a, b and c; $p \in \mathbb{R}$

$\Rightarrow$ $x^2(x+p)=k$ has 3 real and different roots a, b, c, where $p \in \mathbb{R}$

$\Rightarrow$ $x^3+px^2-k=0$ has 3 real and different roots a, b, c, where $p \in \mathbb{R}$

$\Rightarrow \Sigma a = a + b + c = -p,$

$\Sigma ab = ab + bc + ca = 0, abc = k$

$\Rightarrow$ The value of $ab + bc + ca = 0$

$\therefore$ **Ans.** (c)

56. The value of $a + b + c = -p$

$\therefore$ If $p = -5$, then $a + b + c = -(-5) = 5$

$\therefore$ **Ans.** (b)

57. Let $f(x) = x^3 + px^2 - k$

$\Rightarrow f'(x) = 3x^2 + 2px = 0 \Rightarrow x = 0$ or $x = -2p/3$

for 3 distinct real roots

$$f(0).f\left(\frac{-2p}{3}\right) < 0$$

$\Rightarrow f(0).f(-2) < 0$ ($\because$ $p = 3$)

$\Rightarrow (-k)(-8 + (+12) - k) < 0$

$\Rightarrow (-k)(-k + 4) < 0 \Rightarrow k(k - 4) < 0$

$\Rightarrow k \in (0, 4)$

$\therefore$ **Ans.** (b)

B: Consider the biquadratic equation $(x^2 + 2x + 3)^2 - (\lambda - 3)(x^2 + 2x + 3) + \lambda = 0$, where λ is a parameter. This biquadratic equation can be transferred to $f(t) = t^2 - (\lambda - 3)t + \lambda = 0$ by substituting $x^2 + 2x + 3 = t$. Then find

58. All the values of λ for which the given biquadratic equation has all 4 roots real form the set

(a) $(-\infty, 1] \cup [9, \infty)$ (b) $[9, 10]$

(c) $[9, \infty)$ (d) None of these

59. All the values of λ for which the given biquadratic equation has two real roots form the set

(a) $(-\infty, 1] \cup [9, \infty)$ (b) $(-\infty, 10]$

(c) $[10, \infty)$ (d) None of these

60. All the values of λ for which the given biquadratic equation has no real root form the set

(a) $(-\infty, 1)$ (b) $(-\infty, 1) \cup (9, \infty)$

(c) $(9, \infty)$ (d) None of these

Solution: Let $x^2 + 2x + 3 = t$

$\therefore$ $f(t) = t^2 - (\lambda - 3)t + \lambda = 0$ (ii)

is a quadratic in t

Also, minimum value of $x^2 + 2x + 3 = -D/4a$

$$= -\frac{(4-12)}{4} = 2$$

$\therefore$ $t \in [2, \infty)$

Solution 58. The given biquadratic would have all real roots if (ii) has both real roots and both are greater than or equal to 2

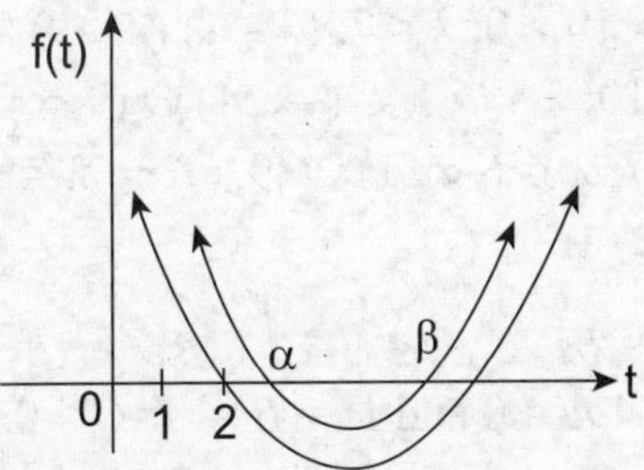

$\therefore$ Let they be α and β. If we put $t = \alpha$ i.e, $x^2 + 2x + 3 = \alpha$

We would get two real roots and if we put $t = \beta$ i.e, $x^2 + 2x + 3 = \beta$ We would get two real roots.

$\therefore$ we will get all four real roots, so for all 4 real roots, we must have disc. of (ii) ≥ 0;

$$f(2) \geq 0; \frac{(\lambda-3)}{2} > 2$$

$\therefore$ $(\lambda - 3)^2 - 4\lambda \geq 0; 4 - (\lambda - 3)(2) + \lambda \geq 0; \lambda > 7$

$\Rightarrow \lambda^2 - 10\lambda + 9 \geq 0; -2\lambda + \lambda + 10 \geq 0; \lambda > 7$

$\Rightarrow (\lambda - 9)(\lambda - 1) \geq 0; \lambda \leq 10; \lambda > 7$

$\Rightarrow \lambda \in [9, 10]$

Ans. (b)

59. The given biquadratic equation has 2 roots real if one root of equation (ii) is < 2 and other is greater than or equal to 2.

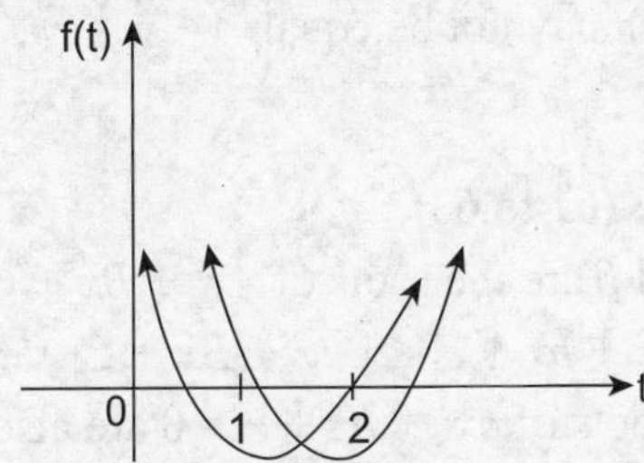

$\Rightarrow f(2) \leq 0 \Rightarrow 4 - (\lambda - 3)(2) + \lambda \leq 0$

$\Rightarrow 4 - 2\lambda + \lambda + 6 \leq 0$

$\Rightarrow -\lambda + 10 \leq 0 \Rightarrow \lambda \geq 10 \Rightarrow \lambda \in [10, \infty)$

$\therefore$ **Ans.** (c)

60. The given biquadratic equation has no real root if both the roots are less than 2.

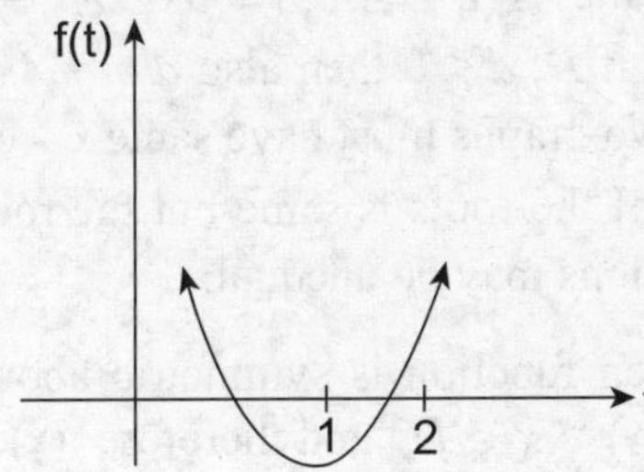

$$\Rightarrow f(2) > 0; \frac{(\lambda-3)}{2} < 2; \text{Disc} > 0$$

$\Rightarrow -\lambda + 10 > 0;\ \lambda < 7;\ (\lambda - 1)(\lambda - 9) > 0$

$\Rightarrow \lambda < 10;\ \lambda < 7;\ \lambda \in (-\infty, 1) \cup (9, \infty)$

$\Rightarrow \lambda < 7;\ \lambda \in (-\infty, 1) \cup (9, \infty) \Rightarrow \lambda \in (-\infty, 1)$

$\therefore$ **Ans.** (a)

C: If $|ax^2 + bx + c| \le |Ax^2 + Bx + C|\ \forall\ x \in \mathbb{R}$ and $d = b^2 - 4ac > 0$ and $D = B^2 - 4AC > 0$, then

61. Which of the following must be true?

(a) $|a| \ge |A|$ (b) $|a| \le |A|$

(c) $|a| = |A|$ (d) all the above

Ans. (b)

62. Which of the following must be true?

(a) $d \le D$ (b) $d \ge D$

(c) $d = D$ (d) none of these

Ans. (a)

63. If D and d are not necessarily positive, then which of the following must be true?

(a) the roots of $ax^2 + bx + c = 0$ and $Ax^2 + Bx + C = 0$ are equal

(b) the roots of $ax^2 + bx + c = 0$ and $Ax^2 + Bx + C = 0$ are equal only when they are real

(c) the roots of $ax^2 + bx + c = 0$ and $Ax^2 + Bx + C = 0$ are equal only when they are imaginary

(d) the roots of $ax^2 + bx + c = 0$ and $Ax^2 + Bx + C = 0$ may not be equal

Ans. (d)

Solution: (61 to 63)

Let α and β are the roots of $Ax^2 + Bx + C = 0$

since $|ax^2 + bx + c| \le |Ax^2 + Bx + C|\ \forall\ x \in R$

$\Rightarrow$ the roots of $ax^2 + bx + c = 0$ are also α and β

$\Rightarrow |ax^2 + bx + c| = |a|\ |x - \alpha|\ |x - \beta|$

and $|Ax^2 + Bx + C| = |A||x - \alpha|\ |x - \beta|$

$\Rightarrow |a| \le |A|$; Also difference of roots is same

$$\Rightarrow \frac{b^2 - 4ac}{a^2} = \frac{B^2 - 4AC}{A^2}$$

since $|a| \le |A|$

$\Rightarrow (b^2 - 4ac) \le (B^2 - 4AC) \Rightarrow d \le D$

Now, if D, $d < 0$ then also $a/b = A/B$ (vertices of the two graphs must have same x – coordinate)

$\Rightarrow$ sum of the roots is same but the roots of the two equations may be unequal.

D: Every even function is symmetric about y-axis. [i.e, $f(-x) = f(x)\ \forall\ x \in D_f$] and therefore $f(x)$ possess same properties (continuity, diff, value of function, roots extremities) at x and $x - x\ \forall\ x \in D_f$. If $f(x)$ is an even function, then $f(x) = 0$ always has even no. of real roots unless $x = 0$ is one of its root (because if $f(\alpha) = 0$, then $f(-\alpha) = 0$). Graph of $f(|x|)$ can be drawn by deleting the portion of $f(x)$ for $x < 0$ and reflecting the retained portion of $f(x)$ for $x \ge 0$ in y-axis. Using these facts answer the following problems, related to equation $x^2 - (2|a| + 1)|x| + a^2 - 4 = 0$ (i)

64. The set of real values of 'a' for which equation (i) has exactly three real roots is

(a) $\{2, -2\}$ (b) $\{2\}$

(c) $\{-2\}$ (d) $\{1, 2\}$

65. The set of values 'a' for which equation (i) has four real roots is

(a) $(-\infty, -2)$ (b) $(-\infty, -2) \cup (2, \infty)$

(c) $(-2, 2)$ (d) None of these

66. The set of values of 'a' for which equation(i) has two real roots is

(a) $(-1, 1)$ (b) $(-\infty, -2) \cup (2, \infty)$

(c) $(-2, 2)$ (d) None of these

67. The set of values 'a' for which equation (i) has no real roots is

(a) $(-1, 1)$ (b) $(-\infty, -1)$

(c) $(1, \infty)$ (d) $\{\}$

Solution: 64. Given equation is $x^2 - (2|a| + 1)|x| + a^2 - 4 = 0$

Put $|x| = y$

$\Rightarrow y^2 - (2|a| + 1)y + a^2 - 4 = 0$ (ii)

Disc. $= [2|a| + 1]^2 - 4(1)(a^2 - 4)$

$= 4|a|^2 + 1 + 4|a| - 4a^2 + 16$

$= 4|a| + 17 > 0$

$\therefore$ equation (ii) must have two different roots

(i) will have three real roots if

$y = 0$ is a root of (ii)

then, $f(y) = 0 \Rightarrow a^2 - 4 = 0 => a = \pm 2$. Also;

we have, $y^2 - (2|a| + 1)y = 0$

$\Rightarrow y[y - (2|a| + 1)] = 0$

$\Rightarrow y = 0$ or $y = 2|a| + 1 > 0$

$\therefore y = 0$ and $y = 2|a| + 1 > 0$ are roots of (ii)

$\Rightarrow |x| = 0$ and $|x| = 2|a| + 1 = 5$

$\Rightarrow x = 0$ and $x = \pm 5$ are three real roots

$\therefore a = \pm 2$ **Ans.** (a, b, c)

65. Equation (i) would have four real roots if both the roots of (ii) are + ve and different.

$\Rightarrow$ sum of roots > 0; product of roots > 0

$\Rightarrow 2|a| + 1 > 0;\ a^2 - 4 > 0$

$\Rightarrow$ always true; $a \in (-\infty, -2) \cup (2, \infty)$

$\therefore$ **Ans.** (a, b)

66. The given equation (i) will have 2 real roots, if roots of equation (ii) are of opposite signs i.e, $a^2 - 4 < 0$

$\Rightarrow a \in (-2, 2)$

$\therefore$ **Ans.** (a, c)

67. The given equation (i) will have no real roots, if both roots of equation (ii) are – ve

$\Rightarrow 2|a| + 1 < 0$ and $a^2 - 4 > 0$, which is impossible

$\Rightarrow a \in \{\}$

$\therefore$ **Ans.** (d)

Assertion/Reason

68. A: If all the four roots of $x^4 - 8x^3 + ax^2 - bx + 16 = 0$ are positive, then $a = 24$ and $b = 32$

R: If polynomial equation $p(x) = 0$ has 'n' positive roots, then $p'(x) = 0$ has $(n - 1)$ positive roots.

Ans. (d)

Solution: Let $\alpha, \beta, \gamma, \delta$ be the four roots, then $\alpha + \beta + \gamma + \delta = (-1)^1 . \frac{a_1}{a_0} = -\frac{(-8)}{1} = 8$

and $\alpha . \beta . \gamma . \delta = \frac{(-1)^4 a_4}{a_0} = \frac{a_4}{a_0} = \frac{16}{1} = 16$

$\therefore \quad \frac{\alpha + \beta + \gamma + \delta}{4} = 2$ and $(\alpha.\beta\,\gamma.\delta)^{1/4} = (16)^{1/4} = 2$

$\therefore$ A.M. = G.M $\quad \Rightarrow \alpha = \beta = \gamma = \delta = 2$

Now, $\Sigma\, \alpha\beta = \frac{(-1)^2 a_2}{a_0} = a$

$\Rightarrow a = {}^4C_2(4) = \frac{4 \times 3}{2 \times 1} \times 4 = 24$

and $\Sigma\, \alpha\beta\gamma = \frac{(-1)^3 a_3}{a_0} = -\frac{(-b)}{1} = b$

$\Rightarrow b = {}^4C_3(8) = 32$

$\therefore$ Assertion is correct.

Reason follows from Rolle's theorm but has no connection with Assertion.

$\therefore$ **Ans.** (b)

69. A: $a + b + c > 0, ab + bc + ca > 0, abc > 0 \Leftrightarrow a > 0, b > 0, c > 0$

R: If $p, q, r > 0$, then equation $x^3 - px^2 + qx - r = 0$ can't have negative roots.

Solution: (a) If $x < 0$, then

$x^3 - px^2 + qx - r < 0$, as $p, q, r > 0$

$\therefore$ $x^3 - px^2 + qx - r = 0$ can't have negative roots.

$\therefore$ Reason is correct.

Now, let a, b, c be the roots of a cubic given by $(x - a)(x - b)(x - c) = 0$

or $x^3 - (a + b + c)x^2 + (ab + bc + ca)x - abc = 0$ (1)

Let $a + b + c = p, ab + bc + ca = q, abc = r$

$\therefore$ (1) becomes, $x^3 - px^2 + qx - r = 0$ (2)

Clearly, if $a, b, c > 0$, then

$a + b + c > 0, ab + bc + ca > 0, abc > 0$

and conversely, if $a + b + c > 0, ab + bc + ca > 0$ and $abc > 0$

i.e., $p > 0, q > 0, r > 0$, then from (2) and by reason we find roots of (2) can't be negative and $abc > 0$

$\Rightarrow a, b, c \neq 0$

$\Rightarrow a > 0, b > 0, c > 0$

$\therefore$ Assertion and reason both are correct and reason is the correct explanation of reason.

$\therefore$ **Ans.** (a)

70. Consider the function $f(x) = ln\,(ax^3 + (a + b)x^2 (b + c)x + c)$; where $a > 0, b^2 - 4ac = 0$

A: Domain of the function is $(-1, \infty) \sim \{(-b/2a)\}$

R: $ax^2 + bx + c = 0$ has equal roots when $b^2 - 4ac = 0$.

Solution: (a) $ax^3 + (a + b)x^2 + (b + c)x + c > 0$

$\Rightarrow ax^2(x + 1) + bx(x + 1) + c(x + 1) > 0$

$\Rightarrow (x + 1)(ax^2 + bx + c) > 0$

$\Rightarrow a(x+1)\left(x + \frac{b}{2a}\right)^2 > 0$ as $b^2 = 4ac$

$\Rightarrow x > -1$ and $\neq -\frac{b}{2a}$

71. A: If $a, b, c \in \mathbb{Z}$ and $ax^2 + bx + c = 0$ has an irrational root, then $|f(\lambda)| \geq 1/q^2$, where $\lambda \in Q$ and $f(x) = ax^2 + bx + c$.

R: If $a, b, c \in Q$ and $b^2 - 4ac$ is positive but not a perfect square, then roots of equation $x^2 + bx + c = 0$ are irrational and always occur in conjugate pair like $2 + \sqrt{3}$ and $2 - \sqrt{3}$.

Solution: (a) Let $f(x) = ax^2 + bx + c$. Since co-efficient are integers and one root is irrational so both the roots are irrational. Hence, for any $\lambda \in Q; f(\lambda) \neq 0 \Rightarrow |f(\lambda)| > 0$

$\Rightarrow \left|\frac{ap^2}{q^2} + \frac{bp}{q} + c\right| > 0$, where $\lambda = p/q\ p; q \in \mathbb{Z}, q \neq 0$

$\Rightarrow \frac{1}{q^2}\left|ap^2 + bpq + cq^2\right| > 0 \Rightarrow |ap^2 + bpq + cq^2| > 0$

Now $a, b, c, p, q \in \mathbb{Z}$. Hence, $|ap^2 + bpq + cq^2| \geq 1$

$\Rightarrow |f(\lambda)| \geq \frac{1}{q^2}$

72. **A:** If equations $ax^2 + bx + c = 0$ and $x^2 - 3x + 4 = 0$ have exactly one root common, then at least one of a, b, c is imaginary.

R: If a, b, c are not all real, then equation $ax^2 + bx + c = 0$ can have one root real and one root imaginary.

Solution: (a) $ax^2 + bx + c = 0$ has two complex conjugate roots only if all the coefficients are real. If all the co-efficients are not real, then it is not necessary that both the roots are imaginary, Hence, statement 1 is true. Now, equation $x^2 - 3x + 4 = 0$ has two complex conjugate roots. If $ax^2 + bx + c = 0$ has all co-effcients real, then there will be two common roots. But if there is only one root common, then at least one of a, b, c must be non-real.

SECTION–III

OBJECTIVE-TYPE (ONLY ONE CORRECT ANSWER)

1. Let α, β be the roots of the equation $(x - a)(x - b) = c, c \neq 0$. Then the roots of the equation $(x - \alpha)(x - \beta) + c = 0$ are

(a) (a, c) (b) (b, c)
(c) (a, b) (d) $(a + c, b + c)$

2. If $x \in \mathbb{R}$, the expression $\frac{x^2+2x-11}{x-3}$ takes all values which do not lie between a and b; then the values of a, b are

(a) 12, 16 (b) 4, 12
(c) 3, 9 (d) 8, 16

3. The number of real solutions of the equation $(9/10)^x = -3 + x - x^2$ is

(a) none (b) one
(c) two (d) more than two

4. The value of $\sqrt{8+2\sqrt{8+2\sqrt{8+2\sqrt{8}}}}$ .... is

(a) 10 (b) 6
(c) 8 (d) 4

5. If the roots of the equation $(a^2 + b^2)x^2 - 2b(a + c)x + (b^2 + c^2) = 0$ are equal then a, b, c are in

(a) GP (b) AP
(c) HP (d) None of these

6. The two equation $x^2 - cx + d = 0$ and $x^2 - ax + b = 0$ have a common root and the second has equal roots, then $2(b + d)$ is equal to

(a) $a + c$ (b) $3a + 2a$
(c) ac (d) None of these

7. If the quadratic equations $ax^2 + 2bx + c = 0$ and $ax^2 + 2cx + b = 0$ $(b \neq c)$ have a common root, then $a + 4b + 4c$ is

(a) 0 (b) $-1/2$
(c) 2 (d) 1

8. If α, β are the roots of the equation $ax^2 + bx + c = 0$, then $(1 + \alpha + \alpha^2)(1 + \beta + \beta^2)$ is equal to

(a) 0 (b) positive
(c) negative (d) None of these

9. The value of m for which the equation $\frac{a}{(x+a+m)} + \frac{b}{(x+b+m)} = 1$, has roots equal in magnitude but opposite in sign is

(a) $\frac{a+b}{a-b}$ (b) 0
(c) $\frac{a-b}{a+b}$ (d) $\frac{2(a-b)}{a+b}$

10. If $a > 1$, roots of the equation $(1 - a)x^2 + 3ax - 1 = 0$ are

(a) one positive and one negative
(b) both non-real complex
(c) both negative
(d) both positive

11. If the quadratic equation $x^2 + ax + b = 0$ and $x^2 + bx + a = 0$ $(a \neq b)$ have a common root, then numerical value of $a + b$ is

(a) 1 (b) -1
(c) 0 (d) None of these

12. The real roots of the equation, $5^{\log_5 (x^2 - 4x + 5)} = x - 1$ are

(a) 1 and 2 (b) 2 and 3
(c) 3 and 4 (d) 4 and 5

13. If the quadratic equations $ax^2 + 2cx + b = 0$ and $ax^2 + 2bx + c = 0$ $(b \neq c)$ have a common root, then $\frac{b+c}{a}$ is equal to

(a) 0 (b) 1

(c) $\frac{1}{4}$ (d) $-\frac{1}{4}$

14. Given that tan A and tan B are the roots of $x^2 - px + 2 = 0$, then the value of $\cos^2(A + B)$ is equal to

(a) $\frac{1}{p^2-1}$ (b) $\frac{p^2}{p^2+1}$

(c) $\frac{1}{p^2+1}$ (d) None of these

15. If x is real, then $\frac{x^2+2x+c}{x^2+4x+3c}$ can take all values if

(a) $0 < c < 2$ (b) $0 < c < 1$

(c) $-1 < c < 1$ (d) None of these

16. The number of solutions of $\log_x 3 = 2x - 3$ is

(a) 3 (b) 1

(c) 2 (d) 0

17. Let $a > 0$, $b > 0$ and $c > 0$. Then both the roots of the equation $ax^2 + bx + c = 0$

(a) are real and negative

(b) have negative real parts

(c) are rational numbers

(d) None of these

18. If the quadratic equations, $x^2 + abx + c = 0$ and $x^2 + acx + b = 0$ have a common root, then the equation containing their other roots is/are:

(a) $x^2 + a(b + c)x - a^2bc = 0$

(b) $x^2 + a(b + c)x + a^2bc = 0$

(c) $a(b + c)x^2 - (b + c)x + abc = 0$

(d) $a(b + c)x^2 + (b + c)x - abc = 0$

19. If α, β are the roots of the equation $x^2 - 2x + 4 = 0$, then the value of $\alpha^n + \beta^n$ is

(a) $2^{n+1}\cos\frac{n\pi}{3}$ (b) $2^n\cos\frac{2n\pi}{3}$

(c) $2^{n+1}\cos\frac{n\pi}{4}$ (d) None of these

20. If $\tan x \tan y = a$ and $x + y = \pi/6$, then tan x and tan y satisfy the equation

(a) $x^2 - \sqrt{3}(1 - a)x + a = 0$

(b) $\sqrt{3}x^2 - (1 - a)x + a\sqrt{3} = 0$

(c) $x^2 + \sqrt{3}(1 + a)x - a = 0$

(d) $\sqrt{3}x^2 + (1 + a)x - a\sqrt{3} = 0$

21. If α, β are the roots of $ax^2 - 2bx + c = 0$, then $\alpha^3\beta^3 + \alpha^2\beta^3 + \alpha^3\beta^2 =$

(a) $c^2(c + 2b)/a^3$ (b) $c^3/a^3(c - 2b)$

(c) bc^3/a^3 (d) None of these

22. The number of real solutions of $x - \frac{1}{x^2-4} = 2 - \frac{1}{x^2-4}$ is

(a) 0 (b) 1

(c) 2 (d) infinite

23. The value of a for which the sum of the squares of the roots of the equation $x^2 - (a - 2)x - a - 1 = 0$ assume the least value is

(a) 0 (b) 1

(c) 2 (d) 3

24. The number of values of the triplet (a, b, c) for which $a\cos 2x + b\sin^2 x + c = 0$ is satisfied by all real x is

(a) 2 (b) 4

(c) 6 (d) infinite

25. If α, β are the roots of the equation $8x^2 - 3x + 27 = 0$, then the value of $[(\alpha^2/\beta)^{1/3} + (\beta^2/\alpha)^{1/3}]$ is equal to

(a) 1/3 (b) 1/4

(c) 1/5 (d) 1/6

26. If the roots of the equation $x^2 + a^2 = 8x + 6a$ are real, then

(a) $a \in (-\infty, -2)$ (b) $a \in (-2, 8)$

(c) $a \in (8, \infty)$ (d) None of these

27. If the roots of $(b - c)x^2 + (c - a)x + (a - b) = 0$ are equal, then $a + c$ is equal to

(a) b^2 (b) b

(c) $2b$ (d) $3b$

28. If $ax^2 + bx + c = a(x - \alpha)(x - \beta)$, then $a(\alpha x + 1)(\beta x + 1)$ is equal to

(a) $cx^2 - bx - a$ (b) $cx^2 + bx + a$

(c) $cx^2 - bx + a$ (d) $cx^2 + bx + c$

29. The quadratic equation $8\sec^2\theta - 6\sec\theta + 1 = 0$ has

(a) exactly two roots (b) exactly four roots

(c) inifinitly many roots (d) no real roots

30. If the ratio of the roots of $x^2 + bx + c = 0$ and $x^2 + qx + r = 0$ be the same, then

(a) $r^2c = b^2q$ (b) $r^2b = c^2q$

(c) $rb^2 = cq^2$ (d) $rc^2 = bq^2$

31. If $a.3^{\tan x} + a.3^{-\tan x} - 2 = 0$ has only real solution, $\neq \pi/2$, $0 \le x \le \pi$, then the set of the values of parameter a is

(a) $[-1, 1]$ (b) $[-1, 0]$

(c) $(0, 1]$ (d) $[0, \infty)$

32. If α, β are the roots of $ax^2 + c = bx$ then the equation $(a + cy)^2 = b^2y$ in y has the roots

(a) α^{-1}, β^{-1} (b) α^2, β^2

(c) $\alpha\beta^{-1}, \alpha^{-1}\beta$ (d) α^{-2}, β^{-2}

33. If a and b are odd integers, then the roots of the equation $2ax^2 + (2a + b)x + b = 0; a \neq 0$, will be
(a) rational (b) irrational
(c) non-real (d) equal

34. If S is the set of all real x such that $\frac{2x-1}{2x^3+3x^2+x}$ is positive, then S contains
(a) $(-\infty, -3/2)$ (b) $(1/4, 3/2)$
(c) $(-1/4, 1/2)$ (d) None of these

35. If the roots of the equation $x^2 - 2ax + a^2 + a - 3 = 0$ are real and less than 3
(a) $a < 2$ (b) $2 \leq a \leq 3$
(c) $3 < a \leq 4$ (d) $a > 4$

36. If the product of the roots of the equation $x^2 + 3kx + (2e^{2\ln k} - 1) = 0$ is 7, then the roots are real only if
(a) $k = 2$ (b) $k = -2$
(c) $k = 4$ (d) $k = -4$

37. The given equation $\sqrt{x+3-4\sqrt{x-1}} + \sqrt{x+8-6\sqrt{x-1}} = 1$ has
(a) no solution (b) only one solution
(c) only two solution (d) more than two solution

38. Both the roots of the equation $(x - b)(x - c) + (x - a)(x - c) + (x - a)(x - b) = 0$ are always
(a) positive (b) negative
(c) real (d) None of these

39. If α, β are the roots of $ax^2 + bx + c = 0$, then the equation $ax^2 - bx(x - 1) + c(x - 1)^2 = 0$ has roots
(a) $\frac{\alpha}{1-\alpha}, \frac{\beta}{1-\beta}$ (b) $\frac{1-\alpha}{\alpha}, \frac{1-\beta}{\beta}$
(c) $\frac{\alpha}{\alpha+1}, \frac{\beta}{\beta+1}$ (d) $\frac{\alpha+1}{\alpha}, \frac{\beta+1}{\beta}$

40. The value of p for which both the roots of the equation $4x^2 - 20px + (25p^2 + 15p - 66) = 0$, are less than 2, lies in
(a) $(4/5, 2)$ (b) $(2, \infty)$
(c) $(-1, -4/5)$ (d) $(-\infty, -1)$

41. If the equation $ax^2 + 2bx - 3c = 0$ has non-real roots and $(3c/4) < (a + b)$; then
(a) $c < 0$ (b) $c > 0$
(c) $c \geq 0$ (d) $c = 0$

42. If $a > b > 0$ are two real nos., the value of, $\sqrt{ab + (a - b)\sqrt{ab + (a - b)\sqrt{ab + (a - b)\ldots}}}$ is equal to:
(a) independent of b
(b) independent of a
(c) independent of both a and b
(d) dependent on both a and b

43. If the sum of the squares of the roots of a quadratic equation is equal to twice the product of those roots. Then the discriminant of the quadratic equation is:
(a) negative
(b) positive
(c) neither negative nor positive
(d) nothing definite can be said

44. The roots of the equation $(3 - x)^4 + (2 - x)^4 = (5 - 2x)^4$ are
(a) all real
(b) all imaginary
(c) two real and two imaginary
(d) None of these

45. The roots α and β of the equation $ax^2 + bx + c = 0$ are real and of opposite sign. Then the roots of the equation $\alpha(x - \beta^2) + \beta(x - \alpha)^2 = 0$ are
(a) positive
(b) negative
(c) real and of opposite sign
(d) imaginary

46. If the absolute value of the difference of roots of the equation $x^2 + px + 1 = 0$ exceeds $\sqrt{3p}$ then p cannot take the integer values.
(a) $0, \pm1, 2, 3, 4$ (b) $0, \pm1, \pm2, \pm3, \pm4$
(c) that are positive (d) none of these

47. If $f(x) = x^2 + 2bx + 2c^2$ and $g(x) = -x^2 - 2cx + b^2$ are such that min $f(x) >$ max $g(x)$, then relation between b and c, is
(a) no relation (b) $0 < c > \frac{b}{2}$
(c) $|x| < \sqrt{2}|b|$ (d) $|c| > \sqrt{2}|b|$

48. The equation $x + \frac{1}{x} = 2x^2$ has a root $x = 1$ Therefore, it will have
(a) no other root
(b) one more root only that is real
(c) two more roots only which are both non real
(d) two more roots which are also real.

49. The number of +ve integral pairs (x,y) satisfying the equation $x^2 - y^2 = 35370$ is
(a) 0 (b) 1
(c) 2 (d) none of these

50. The number of real roots of the equation $(3/5)^x + 7/5 = 2^x$
(a) 0 (b) 1
(c) 2 (d) 3

51. Number of ordered pairs , (x,y) satisfying $x^2 + 1 = y$ and $y^2 + 1 = x$, is

(a) 0 (b) 1
(c) 2 (d) 4

52. The number of positive integral solutions of $x^4 - y^4 = 3789108$ is
(a) 0 (b) 1
(c) 2 (d) 4

53. If x and y are real numbers such that $x^2 + xy - y^2 + 2x - y + 1 = 0$, then
(a) y cannot be between 0 and 8/5
(b) y cannot be between –8/5 and 8/5
(c) y cannot be between –8/5 and 0
(d) none of the foregoing statments is correct

54. If a, b, c are non-zero, unequal rational numbers then the roots of the equation $abc^2 x^2 + 2(3a^2 + b^2)cx - 6a^2 - ab - 2b^2 = 0$
(a) rational (b) imaginary
(c) irrational (d) none

55. The equation $(a+2)x^2 + (a-3)x = 2a - 1$, $a \neq -2$ has roots rational for:
(a) all rational values of a except $a = -2$
(b) all real values of a except $a = -2$
(c) rational values of $a > 1/2$
(d) none of these

56. The value of 'a', for which the equations $x^3 + ax + 1 = 0$ and $x^4 + ax + 1 = 0$ have a common root, then a is
(a) 2 (b) –2
(c) 0 (d) none of these

57. Total number of roots of the equation $3^{\cos x} = |\sin x|$, belonging to $[-2\pi, 2\pi]$, are:
(a) 6 (b) 8
(c) 10 (d) 12

58. Let a, b and c are real numbers, $a \neq 0$. If α is a root of $a^2 x^2 + bx + c = 0$, β is a root of $a^2x^2 - bx - c = 0$ and $0 < \alpha < \beta$, then the equation $a^2x^2 + 2bx + 2c$ has a root γ that always satisfies
(a) $\gamma = \dfrac{\alpha + \beta}{2}$ (b) $\gamma = \alpha + \dfrac{3}{2}$
(c) $\gamma = \alpha$ (d) $\alpha < \beta < \gamma$

59. In a triangle ABC, if a, b and A are given, then one of the roots of the equation
$x^2 - 2bx \cos A + b^2 - a^2 = 0$ is
(a) $x = a$ (b) $x = b$
(c) $x = c$ (d) None of these

60. If every pair from among the equations $x^2 + px + pr = 0$, $x^2 + qx + rq = 0$ and $x^2 + rx + pq = 0$ has a common root, then the product of the common roots is
(a) pqr (b) $2pqr$
(c) $p^2q^2r^2$ (d) None of these

61. The set of all real numbers a such that $a^2 + 2a$, $2a + 3$ and $a^2 + 3a + 8$ are the sides of a triangle is
(a) $[5, \infty)$ (b) $(5, \infty)$
(c) $(-\infty, 5)$ (d) $(-\infty, 5]$

62. If α and β are the roots of $x^2 + px + q = 0$ and α^4 and β^4 are roots of $x^2 - rx + ps = 0$, then the equation $x^2 - 4qx + 2q^2 - r = 0$ has always
(a) two real roots
(b) two negative roots
(c) two positive roots
(d) one positive and one negative root.

63. The number of real solutions of $1 + |e^x - 1| = e^x(e^x - 2)$ is
(a) 0 (b) 1
(c) 2 (d) 4

64. If the roots of the equation, $x^2 + 2ax + b = 0$, are real and distinct and they differ by at most $2m$, then b lies in the interval
(a) $(a^2 - m^2, a^2)$ (b) $[a^2 - m^2, a^2)$
(c) $(a^2, a^2 + m^2)$ (d) None of these

65. If a, b, c be positive real numbers, the following system of equations in x, y and z: $\dfrac{x^2}{a^2} + \dfrac{y^2}{b^2} - \dfrac{z^2}{c^2} = 1$, $\dfrac{x^2}{a^2} - \dfrac{y^2}{b^2} + \dfrac{z^2}{c^2} = 1$, $-\dfrac{x^2}{a^2} + \dfrac{y^2}{b^2} + \dfrac{z^2}{c^2} = 1$, has:
(a) no solution
(b) unique solution
(c) infinitely many solution
(d) finitely many solutions

66. If $a < 0$, the positive root of the equation $x^2 - 2a|x - a| - 3a^2 = 0$ is
(a) $a(-1 - \sqrt{6})$ (b) $a(1 - \sqrt{2})$
(c) $a(-1 + \sqrt{6})$ (d) $a(1 + \sqrt{2})$

67. The set of real value(s) of p for which the equation, $|2x + 3| + |2x - 3| = px + 6$ has more than two solutions is:
(a) [0, 4} (b) (–4, 4)
(c) $R - \{4, -4, 0\}$ (d) {0}

68. The maximum value of the expression, $f(x, y, z) = xyz(4d - ax - by - cz)$ where a, b, c, d are positive constants, x, y, z are positive variables and $4d - ax - by - cz > 0$ is

(a) $\frac{abc}{d}$ (b) $\frac{d^2}{abc}$

(c) $\frac{abc}{d^3}$ (d) $\frac{d^4}{abc}$

69. If α and β are two distinct roots of $x^2 + px + q = 0$ and α^4, β^4 are the roots of $x^2 - rx + s = 0$, then the equation $x^2 - 4qx + 2q^2 - r = 0$ has always ($p, q, r, s \in \mathbb{R}$):

(a) two real roots

(b) two positive roots

(c) two negative roots

(d) one positive and one negative root.

70. If $\cos^2 \frac{\pi}{8}$ is a root of the equation, $x^2 + bx + c = 0$ where $b, c \in \mathbb{Q}$, then the ordered pair (b, c) is:

(a) (1, 1/8) (b) (–1, 1/8)

(c) (1, –1/8) (d) (–1, –1/8)

71. If α, β and γ are the roots of the equation, $x^3 - x - 1 = 0$ then, $\frac{1+\alpha}{1-\alpha} + \frac{1+\beta}{1-\beta} + \frac{1+\gamma}{1-\gamma}$ has the value equal to:

(a) zero (b) –1

(c) –7 (d) 1

72. Let $[a]$ denote the greatest integer less than or equal to a. The set of all values of x satisfying the inequality, $|2x^2 - 4x - 7| < \left[1 + \frac{1}{2}\left(\frac{\cos\theta}{\cos\theta/2 - \sin\theta/2}\right)^2\right]$, $-\frac{\pi}{2} \le \theta < \frac{\pi}{2}$ is:

(a) (–1, 3)

(b) $(1 - \sqrt{5}, 1 + \sqrt{5})$

(c) $(1 - \sqrt{5}, -1) \cup (3, 1 + \sqrt{5})$

(d) None of these

73. If a, b, c, x, y and z are real and $a^2 + b^2 + c^2 = 16$, $x^2 + y^2 + z^2 = 9$ and $ax + by + cz = 12$, then the value of $\frac{a+b+c}{x+y+z}$ is equal to

(a) 4/3 (b) 16/9

(c) 1 (d) None of these

74. If the quadratic equations, $3x^2 + ax + 1 = 0$ and $2x^2 + bx + 1 = 0$ have a common root, then the value of the given expression $5ab - 2a^2 - 3b^2$ is

(a) 0 (b) 1

(c) –1 (d) None of these

75. If a, b, c are real numbers satisfying the condition $a + b + c = 0$, then the roots of the quadratic equation $3ax^2 + 5bx + 7c = 0$ are

(a) positive (b) negative

(c) real and distinct (d) imaginary

76. Let $f(x)$, $g(x)$ and $h(x)$ be quadratic polynomials having positive leading co-efficients and real and distinct roots. If each pair of them has a common root, then the roots of $f(x) + g(x) + h(x) = 0$ are

(a) always real and distinct

(b) always real and may be equal

(c) may be imaginary

(d) always imaginary

77. The range of value of a so that all the roots of the equation $2x^3 - 3x^2 - 12x + a = 0$ are real and distinct belong to

(a) (7, 20) (b) (–7, 20)

(c) (–20, 7) (d) (–7, 7)

78. The number of integral value(s) of x satisfying $\sqrt{-x^2 + 10x - 16} < x - 2$ is

(a) 0 (b) 1

(c) 2 (d) 3

79. If $x^2 + ax - 3x - (a + 2) = 0$ has real and distinct roots, then minimum value of $\frac{a^2+1}{a^2+2}$ is

(a) 1 (b) 0

(c) 1/2 (d) 1/4

80. The set of values of a for which inequation $(a - 1)x^2 - (a + 1)x + a - 1 \ge 0$ is true for all $x \ge 2$

(a) $\left[1, \frac{7}{3}\right]$ (b) $(-\infty, 1)$

(c) $\left[\frac{7}{3}, \infty\right)$ (d) None of these

81. Suppose $f(x)$ is a quadratic expression which is positive for all real x and $g(x) = f(x) + f'(x) + f''(x)$ where $f'(x)$ and $f''(x)$ are the derivatives of $f(x)$ of first and second order, then $g(x)$ is

(a) 0 (b) positive

(c) negative (d) non-positive

82. If $ax^2 + bx + 8 = 0$ does not have 2 distinct real roots, then the minimum value of $2a + b$ is

(a) 4 (b) 2

(c) –4 (d) 6

SECTION–IV

OBJECTIVE-TYPE (MORE THAN ONE CORRECT ANSWER)

1. Let $a > 0, b > 0, c > 0$, then both roots of the equation $ax^2 + bx + c = 0$
   (a) are real and negative
   (b) have negative real parts
   (c) have positive real parts
   (d) None of these

2. If a, b, c are in G.P. where a, c are positive, then the equation $ax^2 + bx + c = 0$ has
   (a) real roots
   (b) imaginary roots
   (c) ratio of roots $= 1 : \omega$ where ω is a non-real cube root of unity
   (d) ratio of roots $= b : ac$

3. The common roots of the equations $x^3 + 2x^2 + 2x + 1 = 0$ and $1 + x^{130} + x^{1988} = 0$ are (where ω is a non-real cube root of unity)
   (a) ω (b) ω^2
   (c) -1 (d) $\omega - \omega^2$

4. For $a > 0 \neq 1$, the roots of the equation $\log_{ax} a + \log_x a^2 + \log_{a^2x} a^3 = 0$, are given by
   (a) $a^{-4/3}$ (b) $a^{-3/4}$
   (c) $a^{-1/2}$ (d) a^{-1}

5. The real value of λ for which the equation $3x^3 + x^2 - 7x + \lambda = 0$ has two distinct real roots in $[0, 1]$ lie in the interval(s)
   (a) $(3, 833/243)$ (b) $[3, 4]$
   (c) $[1, 2]$ (d) $(-\infty, \infty)$

6. If $0 < a < b < c$, and the roots α, β of the equation $ax^2 + bx + c = 0$ are non-real complex numbers, then
   (a) $|\alpha| = |\beta|$ (b) $|\alpha| > 1$
   (c) $|\beta| < 1$ (d) None of these

7. If $a, b, c \in \mathbb{R}$ and the equation $ax^2 - bx + c = 0$ has complex roots which are reciprocal of each other, then
   (a) $|b| \leq |a|$ (b) $|b| \leq |c|$
   (c) $a = c$ (d) $b \leq a$

8. If $a, b, c \in \mathbb{R}$ and $a + b + c = 0$, then the equation $3ax^2 + 2bx + c = 0$ has
   (a) at least one root in $[0, 1]$
   (b) at least one root in $[-1, 1]$
   (c) at least one root in $[0, 2]$
   (d) None of these

9. If the equation $ax^2 + bx + c = 0$ $(a > 0)$ has two roots α and β such that $\alpha < -2$ and $\beta > 2$, then
   (a) $b^2 - 4ac > 0$ (b) $c < 0$
   (c) $a + |b| + c < 0$ (d) $4a + 2|b| + c < 0$

10. The value of c for which $x^4 + cx^3 + x - 2 = 0$ must have at least two real roots are
    (a) 2 (b) 3
    (c) 4 (d) None of these

11. The roots of the equation $(a^2 + b^2)x^2 + 2x(ac + bd) + c^2 + d^2 = 0$, are real, then these are equal. This statement is $(a, b, c, d \in \mathbb{R})$
    (a) true (b) false
    (c) true if $a, b, c, d \in \mathbb{R}^+$ (d) true if $a, b, c, d \in \mathbb{R}^-$

12. If the quadratic equaiton $(ab - bc)\, x^2 + (bc - ca)\, x + ca - ab = 0$, has equal root then
    (a) both roots are equal to 0
    (b) both roots are equal to 1
    (c) a, c, b are in harmonic progression
    (d) $ab^2c^2, b^2a^2c, a^2c^2b$ are in arithmetic progression

13. If $a, b, c \in \mathbb{R}$ $(a \neq 0)$ and $a + 2b + 4c = 0$, then equation $ax^2 + bx + c = 0$ has
    (a) at least one positive root
    (b) at least one non integral root
    (c) no irrational root if a/b is rational
    (d) no irrational root

14. Let p and q be roots of the equation $x^2 - 2x + A$ and let r and s be the roots of the equation $x^2 - 18x + B = 0$. If $p < q < r < s$ are in AP, then
    (a) $p + q + r + s = 20$ (b) $q = 3, r = 7$
    (c) $A = -83, B = -3$ (d) $A = -3, B = 77$

15. If $x^2 - 2x + \sin^2\alpha = 0$, then
    (a) $x \in [-2, 2]$ (b) $x \in [0, 2]$
    (c) $x \in [1, 2]$ (d) $x \in [-1, 1]$

16. The quadratic equation $x^4 - (m - 3)x^2 + m = 0$
    (a) has no real roots iff $m \in (0, 1)$
    (b) has four real roots iff $m > 9$.
    (c) has no real roots iff $m \in (0, 9)$
    (d) has root as zero iff $m = 0$

17. If the roots of the equation $ax^2 + b(2x + 1) = 0$ are imaginary, then those of the equation $bx^2 + (b - c)x = c + a - b$ will not be
    (a) real and unequal (b) real and equal
    (c) imaginary (d) real

18. Consider the quadratic equation $(a + c - b)x^2 + 2cx + (b + c - a) = 0$, where a, b, c are distinct real numbers and $a + c - b \neq 0$. Suppose that both the roots of the equation are rational, then

(a) a, b and c are rational

(b) $\frac{c}{(a-b)}$ is rational

(c) $\frac{b}{(c-a)}$ is rational

(d) None of these

19. If the system of inequations $x^2 + 2x + k \leq 0$, $x^2 - 4x - 6k \leq 0$ has a unique solution, then

(a) $k = 0$ (b) $k = 48/49$

(c) $k = -1$ (d) $k \in [0, 1)$

SECTION—V

ASSERTION AND REASON TYPE

1. A: If $\cos^2 \pi/8$ is a root of the equation $x^2 + ax + b = 0$ where $a, b \in \mathbb{Q}$ (set of rational numbers) then ordered pair (a, b) is $(-1, (1/8))$.

R: If $a + mb = 0$ and m is irrational, then $a, b = 0$.

2. A: $ix^2 + (i - 1)x - (1/2) - i = 0$ has imaginary roots.

R: If $a = i$, $b = i - 1$ and $c = (-1/5) - i$, then $b^2 - 4ac < 0$.

3. A: If $f(x)$ is a quadratic polynomial satisfying $f(2) + f(4) = 0$. If unity is a root of $f(x) = 0$, then the other root is 3.5.

R: If $g(x) = px^2 + qx + r = 0$ has roots α, β, then $a + \beta = -q/p$ and $\alpha\beta = (r/p)$.

4. A: If $px^2 + qx + r = 0$ is a quadratic equation $(p, q, r \in \mathbb{R})$ such that its roots are α, β and $p + q + r < 0$, $p - q + r < 0$ and $r > 0$, then $[\alpha] + [\beta] = -1$, where [.] denotes G.I.F

R: If for any two real numbers a and b, function $f(x)$ is such that $f(a) f(b) < 0 \Rightarrow f(x)$ has at least one real root lying in (a, b); when f is continuous in (a, b).

5. A: If equation $ax^2 + bx + c = 0$; $(a, b, c \in \mathbb{R})$ and $2x^2 + 3x + 4 = 0$ have a common root, then $a: b: c = 2: 3: 4$.

R: Roots of $2x^2 + 3x + 4 = 0$ are imaginary.

6. A: If α, β are the roots of equation $x^2 + 2(a - 3)x + 9 = 0$; $a \in \mathbb{R}$ and $\alpha < 6 < \beta$, then $a < -3/4$

R: If $f(x) = x^2 + 2(a - 3)x + 9$, then $f(6) < 0 \Rightarrow a < -3/4$.

7. A: If $a < b < c < d$, then $(x - a)(x - c) + 3(x - b)(x - d) = 0$ has real and distinct root

R: Let $f(x) = (x - a)(x - c) + 3(x - b)(x - d)$ and let λ and μ be two real numbers. If $f(\lambda)$ and $f(\mu)$ are of opposite signs, then one root of $f(x)$ lie between λ and μ.

8. A: The minimum possible number complex roots of $x^6 - 3x^5 + 4x^3 + 3x^2 + 4 = 0$ is two.

R: Let $f(x) = x^6 - 3x^5 + 4x^3 + 3x^2 + 4 \Rightarrow f(x)$ has two changes in sign.

9. A: The greatest integral value of λ for which $(2\lambda - 1)x^2 - 4x + (2\lambda - 1) = 0$ has real roots is 2.

R: For real roots of $ax^2 + bx + c = 0$ $D \geq 0$.

10. A: If $a + b + c > 0$ and $a < 0 < b < c$, then the roots of the equation $a(x - b)(x - c) + b(x - c)(x - a) + c(x - a)(x - b) = 0$ are of both negative.

R: If both roots are negative, then sum of roots < 0 and product of roots > 0.

11. A: If $a^3 + b^3 + c^3 = 3abc$, then the equation $ax^2 + bx + c = 0$ has one positive and one negative real root always.

R: If roots of opposite nature, then product of roots < 0 and |sum of roots| ≥ 0.

12. A: Let $(a_1, a_2, a_3, a_4, a_5)$ denote a re-arrangement of $(1, -4, 6, 7, -10)$. Then the equation $a_1x^4 + a_2x^3 + a_3x^2 + a_4x + a_5 = 0$ has at least two real roots

R: If $ax^2 + bx + c = 0$ and $a + b + c = 0$, then $x = 1$ is root of $ax^2 + bx + c = 0$

13. A: The maximum number of non-real roots of the equation $2x^{100} + 7x^{99} + 7x^{98} + 7x^{97} + .. + 7x^3 + 7x^2 + 7x - 5 = 0$ is 98.

R: If $ax^2 + bx + c = 0$ has real roots, then $D = b^2 - 4ac \geq 0$.

14. A: The equation $ax^2 + bx + c = 0$ cannot have rational roots if a, b, c are odd integers.

R: If an odd number does not leave remainder 1 when divided by 8, then it cannot be a perfect square.

15. A: The equation $(x - a)(x - c) + \lambda(x - b)(x - d) = 0$ where $a < b < c < d$ has non-real roots, if $\lambda > 0$.

R: The equation $(a, b, c \in \mathbb{R})$ $ax^2 + bx + c = 0$ has non-real roots, if $b^2 - 4ac < 0$.

16. A: If $x^4 + px^3 + qx^2 + rx + s = 0$ has four positive roots then $pr - 16s \le 0, r > 0$.

R: AM $\ge$ GM for positive numbers.

17. Let $a_1x^2 + b_1x + c_1 = 0$ and $a_2x^2 + b_2x + c_2 = 0$ be the quadratic equations such that $\Delta_1 = b_1^2 - 4a_1c_1$ and $\Delta_2 = b_2^2 - 4a_1c_1$.

A: At least one of the given equations have real roots if and only if $\Delta_1 + \Delta_2 \ge 0$ because

R: If $\Delta_1 + \Delta_2 \ge 0$, then at least one of the Δ_1 and Δ_2 is non-negative.

SECTION–VI

LINKED COMPREHENSION TYPE

A: If roots of the biquadratic equation $x^4 - 12x^3 + 2bx^2 + 3cx + 81 = 0$ are positive, then

1. Value of b is

(a) –54 (b) 54

(c) 27 (d) –27

2. Value of c is

(a) 108 (b) –108

(c) 54 (d) –36

3. Root of equation $2bx + c = 0$ is

(a) –1/2 (b) 1/2

(c) 2/3 (d) –1

B: In the given figure, vertices of ΔABC lie on the curve $y = f(x) = ax^2 + bx + c$. Let the triangle, ABC is right angled isosceles whose hypotaneous $AC = 6\sqrt{3}$ units, then

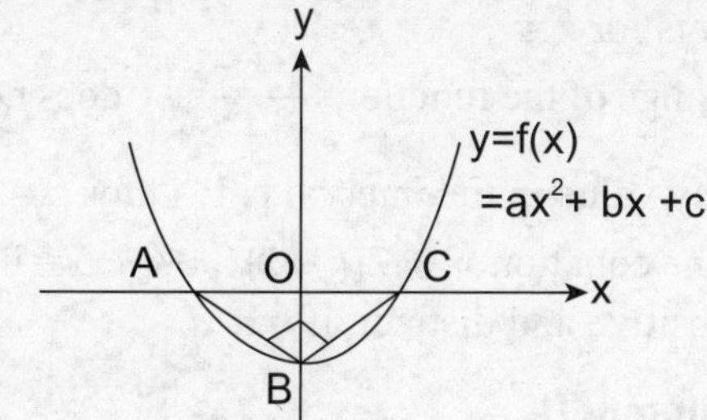

4. $y = f(x)$ is given by

(a) $y = \dfrac{x^2}{3\sqrt{3}} - 3\sqrt{3}$

(b) $y = \dfrac{x^2}{3} - 3$

(c) $y = x^2 - 27$

(d) $y = x^2 - 3\sqrt{3}$

5. Minimum value of $y = f(x)$ is

(a) $3\sqrt{3}$ (b) $-3\sqrt{3}$

(c) 3 (d) –3

6. Number of integral value of k for which $k/2$ lies between the roots of $f(x) = 0$, is

(a) 19 (b) 20

(c) 21 (d) 22

C: $a.g(\lambda) < 0$' is the necessary and sufficient condition for a particular real λ to lie between the roots of a quadratic equation $g(x) = 0$, where $g(x) = ax^2 + bx + c$. Again if $g(\lambda_1)g(\lambda_2) < 0$, then exactly one of the roots will lie between λ_1 and λ_2.

7. If $|2b| > |4a + c|$, then

(a) one root of $g(x) = 0$ is positive, the other is negative

(b) exactly one of the root of $g(x) = 0$ lies in $(-2, 2)$

(c) 1 lies between the roots of $g(x) = 0$

(d) both the roots of $g(x) = 0$ are less than 1

8. If $a(a - b + c) < 0 < (a - b + c)\,c$, then

(a) one root is less than – 1 the other is greater than 0

(b) exactly one of the roots lies in $(-1, 0)$

(c) both the roots lie outside $(-1, 0)$

(d) at least one of the roots lies in $(-1, 0)$

9. If $(a + b + c)\,c < 0 < a\,(a + b + c)$, then

(a) one root is less than 0, the other is greater than 1

(b) one root lies in $(-\infty, 0)$ and other in $(0, 1)$

(c) both the roots lie in $(0, 1)$

(d) one roots lies in $(0, 1)$ and other in $(1, \infty)$

D: Let $f(x) = ax^2 + bx + c$ be a quadratic expression and $y = f(x)$ has graph as shown in figure.

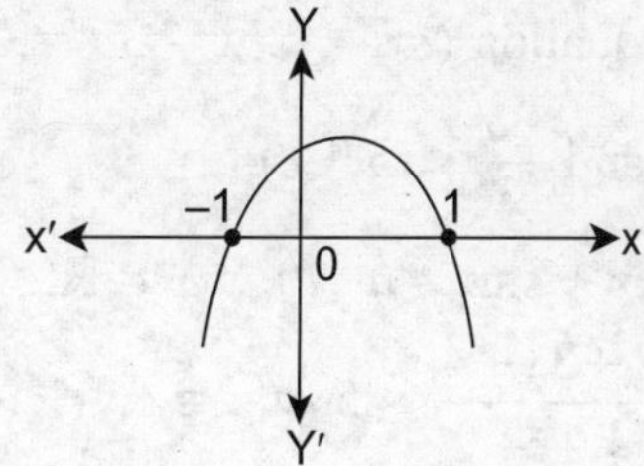

10. Which of the following is false?

(a) $ab > 0$ (b) $abc < 0$
(c) $ac < 0$ (d) $bc < 0$

11. Which of the following is true?

(a) $a + b + c > 0$ (b) $a - b + c > 0$
(c) $a + 3b + 9c < 0$ (d) $a - 3b + 9c > 0$

12. If $f(x)$ is an integer whenever x is an integer, then which of the following is always correct?

(a) a is an integer (b) $2a$ is an integer
(c) b is an integer (d) $c/2$ is an integer

E: Consider two quadratic polynomials $f(x) = x^2 + b_1x + c_1$ and $g(x) = x^2 + b_2x + c_2$. Let α and β be two real roots of equation $f(x) = 0$. Let the roots of the equation $g(x) = 0$ exceeds the roots of $f(x) = 0$ by same quantity. If least value of $f(x)$ *is* $-1/8$ and that for $g(x)$ occurs at $x = 7/4$, then

13. The least value of $g(x)$ is

(a) -1 (b) $-1/2$
(c) $-1/8$ (d) $-1/3$

14. The value of b_2 is

(a) $3/2$ (b) $-7/2$
(c) $7/2$ (d) 0

15. The product of the root of $g(x) = 0$ is

(a) 42 (b) 45/16
(c) 47/16 (d) None of these

SECTION—VII

COLUMN MATCHING

1. Column–I

(i) Number of real solutions of $a^2 + b^2 + c^2 = x^2$ is
(ii) The number of non-negative real roots of $2x^3 - x - 1 = 0$ equals
(iii) Let p and q be the roots of the quadratic equation $x^2 - (\alpha - 2)x - \alpha - 1 = 0$. What is the minimum possible value of $p^2 + q^2$ when $a \neq 0$.
(iv) The value of 'c' for which $|\alpha^2 - \beta^2| = \frac{7}{4}$, where α and β are the roots of $2x^2 + 7x + c = 0$

Column–II

(a) 2
(b) ∞
(c) 6
(d) 5

2. Column–I

(i) α, β are the roots of $x^2 - 3x + a = 0$, $a \in \mathbb{R}$ and $\alpha < 1 < \beta$.
(ii) The equation $(cx^2 + 2bx - 3a = 0)$ has non-real roots and $\frac{3a}{4} < (b + c)$.
(iii) If $\sin^2 x + \sin x - a = 0$, $\forall\, x \in \mathbb{R}$.
(iv) If $\frac{ax^2 + 3x + 4}{x^2 + 2x + 2} < 5$, $\forall\, x \in \mathbb{R}$

Column–II

(a) $a \in (-\infty, 0)$
(b) $a \in \left[-\frac{1}{4}, 2\right]$
(c) $a \in (-\infty, 2)$
(d) $a \in \left(-\infty, \frac{71}{24}\right)$

3. Column–I

(i) $(x - 1)(x - 3) + k(x - 2)(x - 4) = 0$ $(k \in R)$, has real roots for $k \in$
(ii) Range of the function $\frac{x - 1}{x^2 - k + 1}$ does not contain any value in the interval $[-1, 1]$ for $k \in$
(iii) The equation $x^2 + 2(k - 1)x + k + 5 = 0$ has roots positive and distinct, if $k \in$

Column–II

(a) $(-5, -1)$
(b) ϕ
(c) $(-\infty, \infty)$
(d) $[2\sqrt{2}, \infty)$

4. Column–I

(i) If $x^2 + ux + v = 0$ has roots α, β and $x^2 + mx + n = 0$ has roots $-2/\alpha, \gamma$, then
(ii) If $x^2 + ux + v = 0$ has roots α, β and $x^2 + mx + n = 0$ has roots $-\alpha, \gamma$, then

(iii) If $x^2 + ux + v = 0$ has roots α, β and $x^2 + mx + n = 0$ has roots $1/\alpha, \gamma$, then

Column–II

(a) $(4 - vn)^2 = (4u + 2mv)(-2m - un)$

(b) $(1 - vn)^2 = (u - mv)(m - un)$

(c) $(n - v)^2 = (un + vm)(m - u)$

(d) $(1 - 4vn)^2 = (u + 2vm)(-2m - 4un)$

5. Column–I

(i) If p, q, r and s are four non-zero real numbers such that $(s + p - q)^2 + (s + q - r)^2 = 0$ and the roots of the equation $p(q - r)x^2 + q(r - p)x + r(p - q) = 0$ are real and equal then

(ii) If the roots of the equation $(p^2 + q^2)x^2 - 2q(p + r) + (q^2 + r^2) = 0$ are real and equal, then

(iii) If the equation $px^2 + qx + r = 0$ and $x^3 - 3x^2 + 3x - 1 = 0$ have a common real root, then

(iv) Let p, q, r be positive real numbers such that the expression $qx^2 + (\sqrt{(p+r)^2 + 4q^2})x + (p+r)$ is non-negative $\forall \in \mathbb{R}$, then

Column II

(a) $p + q + r = 0$

(b) p, q, r are in A.P.

(c) p, q, r in G.P.

(d) p, q, r in H.P.

SECTION–VIII

INTEGER-TYPE QUESTIONS

1. Given α, β as the roots of the equation $6x^2 - 6x + 1 = 0$, If $1/2(a + b\alpha + c\alpha^2 + d\alpha^3) + 1/2(a + b\beta + c\beta^2 + d\beta^3) = a/k_1 + b/k_2 + c/k_3 + d/k_4$, then evaluate $\sum_{i=1}^{4} k_i$.

2. If the sum of the roots of the equation $1/(x - h) + 1/(x - k) = 1/m$ is zero, and the product of the roots is $-1/\alpha(h^2 + k^2)$; then find the value of α.

3. If the sum of the roots of the equation $(a + 1)x^2 + (2a + 7)x + (3a + 4) = 0$ is -3, then find the value of $[P]$; where P denotes the product of roots and [.] is gint function.

4. If the values of the parameter $\lambda \in (a, b)$ for which the roots α, β of the equation $3x^2 + 6x - \lambda = 0$ satisfy the inequality $0 < (\alpha/\beta + \beta/\alpha) < 2$; then find the value of $|a| + |b|$.

5. Let α and β are the abscissa of the pts. of intersection of parabola $y = x^2$ and the st. line $y = 4x - 1$, then the equation whose roots are α/β and β/α be $x^2 - kx + 1 = 0$, then find the value of k.

6. If the roots of $x^2 + bx + c = 0$ are both real and greater then unity, then $(b + c) \in (k, \infty)$ then find the value of k.

7. If p, q, r are positive and are in A.P, then the roots of the quadratic equation $px^2 + qx + r = 0$ are real for $\left|\frac{r}{p} - 7\right| \geq k\sqrt{3}$ then find the value of k.

8. The sum of the integral values of $a \in \{5, 6, 7, 12\}$ for which the equation $ax^2 + (2a - 1)x + (a - 2) = 0$ has rational roots.

9. If the expression $ax^4 + bx^3 - x^2 + 2x + 3$ has remainder $4x + 3$ when divided by $x^2 + x - 2$, find the value of $|a + b|$.

10. If $a \in \left[-\sqrt{k}, \frac{-1-\sqrt{\lambda}}{2}\right] \cup \left[\frac{-1+\sqrt{\lambda}}{2}, \sqrt{k}\right]$ for which both the roots of the equation $2x^2 + ax + a^2 - 5 = 0$ are less than unity, then evaluate λ.

11. If $m \in (a, b)$, so that the inequality $\left|\frac{x^2 + mx + 1}{x^2 + x + 1}\right| < 3$ holds for all $x \in \mathbb{R}$, then evaluate $\log_{|ab|} 625$.

12. Let $y = \sqrt{\frac{2}{x^2 - x + 1} - \frac{1}{x + 1} - \frac{(2x + 1)}{x^3 + 1}}$. If all the real values of x for which y takes real values are given by x $(-\infty, -\lambda) \cup [0, 1]$, then find x.

13. Suppose x_1 and x_2 are the roots of the equation $x^2 + 2(k - 3)x + 9 = 0$. If the greatest integral value of k for which both 6 and 3 lie between x_1 and x_2 is λ, then evaluate λ.

14. Find the least integral value of parameter 'a', for which the equation $x^4 + 2ax^3 + x^2 + 2ax + 1 = 0$ has at least two distinct negative roots.

15. Find the least integeral solution of the equation $2^{|x+1|} - 2^x = |2^x - 1| + 1$

16. If k_1 and k_2 are such that $[k_1, k_2]$ are the value of a for which $(1 + a)y^2 - 3ay + 4a = 0$ has real roots. Evaluate $\sqrt{k_1 . k_2}$.

17. Solve the equation $5^x \sqrt[x]{8^{x-1}} = 500$ and find the positive root.

18. Find the least positive integral value of a for which the equation $4^x - a2^x - a + 3 = 0$ has at least one solution.

19. Solve the inequation $3^{72}\left(\dfrac{1}{3}\right)^x\left(\dfrac{1}{3}\right)^{\sqrt{x}} > 1$ and find the greatest integer value satisfying the given inequality.

Answer Keys

SECTION–III

1. (c)	**2.** (b)	**3.** (a)	**4.** (d)	**5.** (a)	**6.** (c)	**7.** (a)	**8.** (b)	**9.** (a)	**10.** (d)
11. (b)	**12.** (b)	**13.** (d)	**14.** (c)	**15.** (b)	**16.** (c)	**17.** (b)	**18.** (d)	**19.** (a)	**20.** (b)
21. (a)	**22.** (a)	**23.** (d)	**24.** (d)	**25.** (b)	**26.** (b)	**27.** (c)	**28.** (c)	**29.** (d)	**30.** (c)
31. (c)	**32.** (d)	**33.** (a)	**34.** (a)	**35.** (a)	**36.** (a)	**37.** (d)	**38.** (c)	**39.** (c)	**40.** (d)
41. (a)	**42.** (a)	**43.** (c)	**44.** (c)	**45.** (c)	**46.** (a)	**47.** (d)	**48.** (c)	**49.** (a)	**50.** (b)
51. (a)	**52.** (a)	**53.** (c)	**54.** (a)	**55.** (a)	**56.** (b)	**57.** (b)	**58.** (d)	**59.** (c)	**60.** (a)
61. (b)	**62.** (a)	**63.** (b)	**64.** (b)	**65.** (d)	**66.** (b)	**67.** (d)	**68.** (d)	**69.** (d)	**70.** (b)
71. (c)	**72.** (c)	**73.** (a)	**74.** (b)	**75.** (c)	**76.** (a)	**77.** (b)	**78.** (d)	**79.** (c)	**80.** (c)
81. (b)	**82.** (c)								

SECTION–IV

1. (a, b) **2.** (b, c) **3.** (a, b) **4.** (a, c) **5.** (a, b, d) **6.** (a, b) **7.** (a, b, c) **8.** (a, b, c)

9. (a, b, c, d) **10.** (a, b, c) **11.** (a, c, d) **12.** (b,c , d) **13.** (a, b, c) **14.** (a, b, d) **15.** (a, b)

16. (a, b, c, d) **17.** (b, c) **18.** (b) **19.** (a, b, d)

SECTION–V

1. (a)	**2.** (c)	**3.** (a)	**4.** (a)	**5.** (b)	**6.** (b)	**7.** (a)	**8.** (b)	**9.** (d)	**10.** (d)
11. (d)	**12.** (a)	**13.** (b)	**14.** (a)	**15.** (d)	**16.** (b)	**17.** (d)			

SECTION–VI

1. (c)	**2.** (d)	**3.** (c)	**4.** (a)	**5.** (b)	**6.** (b)	**7.** (b)	**8.** (a, c)	**9.** (b)	**10.** (b)
11. (d)	**12.** (b)	**13.** (c)	**14.** (b)	**15.** (c)					

SECTION–VII

1. (i) → (b), (ii) → (a), (iii) → (d), (iv) → (c)
2. (i) → (c), (ii) → (a), (iii) → (b), (iv) → (d)
3. (i) → (c), (ii) → (b), (iii) → (a)
4. (i) → (a), (ii) → (c), (iii) → (b)
5. (i) → (b, c, d), (ii) → (c), (iii) → (a), (iv) → (b)

SECTION–VIII

1. 10	**2.** 2	**3.** 3	**4.** 3	**5.** 14	**6.** –1	**7.** 4	**8.** 18	**9.** 3	**10.** 13
11. 4	**12.** –1	**13.** –1	**14.** –2	**15.** 0	**16.** 3	**17.** 2	**18.** 64		

HINTS AND SOLUTIONS

TEXTUAL EXERCISE-1: (SUBJECTIVE)

1. **(a)** $\because a = 1 + \sqrt{2}$, thus $a - \sqrt{2} = 1$ and $\sqrt{2} - a = -1$.
   Thus the polynomial $f(x) = x^3 - x^2 + x + 1$, clearly has real rational coefficients and degree 3.
   (b) For $k = 2$, the polynomial because $4x^2 - x + 1$ which is real/rational quadratic polynomial and for $k = 3$, it is $f(x) = x^3 + 5x^2 + 1$ which is real/rational cubic polynomial.
   (c) $\because a_1 + a_2 = 2$ and $a_1 - a_2 = 4i$, therefore $f(x) = 2x^2 - 4x + 3$ is real rational quadratic polynomial.

2. Given $f(x) = \sqrt{a^2 - 4}x^2 + \sqrt{8 - a}x + 7$ represents.
   (i) Real polynomial iff $a^2 - 4 \geq 0$ and $8 - a \geq 0$
   $\Rightarrow a \in (-\infty, -2] \cup [2, \infty)$ and $a \leq 8$
   $\Rightarrow a \in (-\infty, -2] \cup [2, 8]$
   (ii) Hence for $a \in (-2, 2) \cup (8, \infty)$ the above polynomial is non-real polynomial.

3. $a \in \{2, 3, 4, 5\}$; $f(x) = \sqrt{a^2 - 9}x^2 + \sqrt{14 - a}x - 8$
   (i) For real polynomial $a \in [3, 14]$
   $\Rightarrow a = 3, 4, 5$
   (ii) For non-real polynomial $a = 2$
   (iii) For rational polynomial $a = 5$
   (iv) For irrational polynomial $a = 3, 4$

4. If $(p^2 - 3p + 2)x^2 - (p^2 - 5p + 4)x + p - p^2 = 0$ has more than two roots
   $\Rightarrow$ Above said must be identity and thus $p^2 - 3p + 2 = 0$, $p^2 - 5p + 4 = 0$ and $p(1 - p) = 0$
   $\Rightarrow p = \{1, 2\} \cap \{1, 4\} \cap \{0, 1\}$
   $\Rightarrow p = \{1\}$

5. $(a^2 - 1)x^2 + (a - 1)x + a^2 - 4a + 3 = 0$ to be identity in x.
   $a^2 - 1 = 0$, $a - 1 = 0$ and $a^2 - 4a + 3 = 0$
   $\Rightarrow a^2 - 4a + 3 = 0 \quad \Rightarrow a = 1$

6. Given equation $2x^2 - (a - 1)x + a + 1 = 0$
   $$\Rightarrow x = \frac{a-1 \pm \sqrt{(a-1)^2 - 8(a+1)}}{4} = \frac{a-1 \pm \sqrt{a^2 - 10a - 7}}{4}$$
   For $a^2 - 10a - 7 \geq 0$ i.e., $a \in (-\infty, 5 - \sqrt{32}) \cup (5 + \sqrt{32}, \infty)$

7. **(a)** $(a - 1)x + 2 = a + 1 \quad \Rightarrow (a - 1)x - (a - 1) = 0$
   $\Rightarrow$ For $a = 1$ it is identity and thus has infinite solution and for $a \neq 1$; $x = 1$ is only root.
   (b) Consider the quadratic equation $(a + 1)x^2 + 2(a + 1)x + a - 2 = 0$
   $$\Rightarrow x = \frac{-2(a+1) \pm \sqrt{4(a+1)^2 - 4(a+1)(a-2)}}{2(a+1)}$$
   $$\Rightarrow x = \frac{-(a+1) \pm \sqrt{(a+1)3}}{(a+1)} = -1 \pm \frac{\sqrt{3}}{\sqrt{a+1}}$$
   Hence for $a = -1$ above equation has no solution.
   For $a \in (-\infty, 1)$, it has two non-real roots given as $-1 \pm i\sqrt{\frac{-3}{a+1}}$
   For $a \in (-1, \infty)$, the equation has two distinct real roots.
   (c) Given equation is $ax + 2x + 2 + x = 0$
   $\Rightarrow (a + 3)x = -2 \qquad \Rightarrow$ For $a = -3$; it has no solution
   $\Rightarrow$ For $a \neq -3$; $x = \dfrac{-2}{a+3}$ is only solution

8. Consider equation $\dfrac{x-ab}{a+b} + \dfrac{x-bc}{b+c} + \dfrac{x-ca}{c+a} = a + b + c$
   Rearranging the expression, we get
   $$\left(\frac{x-ab}{a+b} - c\right) + \left(\frac{x-bc}{b+c} - a\right) + \left(\frac{x-ca}{c+a} - b\right) = 0$$
   $$\Rightarrow (x - ab - bc - ca)\left(\frac{1}{a+b} + \frac{1}{b+c} + \frac{1}{c+a}\right) = 0$$
   Therefore if $\dfrac{1}{a+b} + \dfrac{1}{b+c} + \dfrac{1}{c+a} = 0$, the equation turns out to be identity and thus has infinite many solutions.
   If $\dfrac{1}{a+b} + \dfrac{1}{b+c} + \dfrac{1}{c+a} \neq 0$
   $\Rightarrow x = ab + bc + ca$ is single roots.

9. Given quadratic equation is $a^2\left(\dfrac{(x-b)(x-c)}{(a-b)(a-c)}\right) + b^2\left(\dfrac{(x-c)(x-a)}{(b-c)(b-a)}\right) + c^2\left(\dfrac{(x-a)(x-b)}{(c-a)(c-b)}\right) = x^2$ Clearly $x = a$ is one root and thus by symmetry of three terms one can also observe other two roots as $x = b$ and $x = c$.
   $\because$ no of roots exceeds degree of equation therefore we conducts that it is an identity and therefore has infinitely many roots.

TEXTUAL EXERCISE-1: (OBJECTIVE)

1. **(d)** Consider the equation $a\cos 2x + b\sin^2 x + c = 0$
   $a(1 - 2\sin^2 x) + b\sin^2 x + c = 0$
   $\Rightarrow (b - 2a)\sin^2 x + (c + a) = 0$, to be an identity $b = 2a$ and $c + a = 0$
   $\Rightarrow b = 2a$ and $c = -a$
   $\Rightarrow$ The triplet (a, b, c) is of the type $(a, 2a, -a)$ a $\mathbb{R}$
   Clearly, infinitely many triplets possible.

2. **(a)** $a(x + 1)^2 + b(x^2 - 3x - 2) + x + 1 = 0$
   $\Rightarrow (a + b)x^2 + (2a - 3b + 1)x + a - 2b + 1 = 0$
   To be an identity $a + b = 0$ and $2a - 3b + 1 = 0$ and $a - 2b + 1 = 0$
   Clearly no value of a, b possible to satisfy the above three equations simultaneously

3. **(a), (b)** $ax^3 - \sqrt{a^2 + 18}x + 10$ to be real and rational polynomial $a \in Q$ and $a^2 + 8$ must be perfect square of a rational number, clearly for $a = \pm 1$ both condition hold good.

4. **(c)** $\left(\sqrt{a^2 + 5a + 6}\right)x^2 + \sqrt{a - 7}x + \sqrt{a}$ represents a real polynomial if $a^2 + 5a + 6 \geq 0$, $a - 7 \geq 0$ and $a \geq 0$
   $\Rightarrow (a + 2)(a + 3) \geq 0$ and $a \geq 7$
   $\Rightarrow a \in (-\infty, -3] \cup [-2, \infty)$ and $a \in [7, \infty)$
   $\Rightarrow a \in [7, \infty)$

5. (d) $ax^2+\sqrt{a-1}x+a$ is real polynomial and has roots real

$\Rightarrow a \geq 1$ and $D \geq 0$

$\Rightarrow a$ 1 and $a-1-4a^2 \geq 0$

$\Rightarrow a \in [1, \infty)$ and $-(4a^2-a+1) \geq 0$

$\Rightarrow a \in [1, \infty)$ and $-\left(\left(a-\frac{1}{8}\right)^2+\frac{15}{64}\right) \geq 0$

$\Rightarrow a \in [1, \infty)$ and $a \in \phi$

6. (c) $\sqrt{a^2-7x^2}+\sqrt{ax}+9$ to be non real polynomial $a^2-7 \leq 0$ or $a<0$

$\Rightarrow (a-\sqrt{7})(a+\sqrt{7})<0$ or $a \in (-\infty, 0)$

$\Rightarrow (-\sqrt{7}, \sqrt{7}) \cup (\infty, 0) \quad \Rightarrow \quad a \in (-\infty, \sqrt{7})$

TEXTUAL EXERCISE–2: (SUBJECTIVE)

1. By division algorithm $4x^3+5kx^2-3x+k=(x+1)g(x)+5$

Subtracting $x=-1$, we get $-4+5k+3+k=5$

$\Rightarrow 6k=6 \qquad \Rightarrow k=1$

2. $f(x)=(x-\alpha)(x-\beta)-k=0$ has roots γ and δ

$\Rightarrow (x-\alpha)(x-\beta)-k=(x-\gamma)(x-\delta)$

$\Rightarrow (x-\alpha)(x-\beta)=(x-\gamma)(x-\delta)+k$

$\Rightarrow g(x)=(x-\gamma)(x-)+k=0$ is therefore

$\Rightarrow (x-\alpha)(x-\beta)=0$ thus clearly have roots α and β.

$\Rightarrow g(x)$ has roots α, β.

3. $(x+1)$ is factor of $f(x)=x^4+(p-3)x^3-(3p-5)x^2+(2p-9)x+6$

$\Rightarrow$ f(–1) = 0 i.e., $1+3-p-3p+5+9-2p+6=0$

$\Rightarrow 6p=24 \qquad \Rightarrow p=4$

Thus $f(x)=x^4+x^3-7x^2-x+6$

Clearly $x=1$ is a root as sum of coefficient is zero

$\Rightarrow f(x)=(x^2-1)(x^2+kx-6)$

Comparing the coefficient, we get $k=1$

$\Rightarrow f(x)=(x^2-1)(x^2+x-6)=(x-1)(x+1)(x+3)(x-2)$

4. Given $f(x)=x^5-11x^4+33x^3+11x^2-154x+120=0$

As sum of coefficients zero thus are root shall be 1 and observing product of roots as 120 = 1.2.3.4.5 by trials and errors one can conclude that $x=-2$ and $x=3$, $x=4$, $x=5$ are also roots.

TEXTUAL EXERCISE–2: OBJECTIVE

1. (a), (b), (c)

$\because$ x^2+x-6 is factor of $f(x)=2x^4+x^3-\alpha x^2+\beta x+\beta-1$

$\Rightarrow f(-3)=0$ i.e., $2(81)-27-9\alpha-3\beta+\beta-1=0$ i.e., $9\alpha+2\beta=134$ and

$\Rightarrow f(2)=0$ i.e., $32+8-4\alpha+2\beta+\beta-1=0$ i.e., $4\alpha-3\beta=39$

Solving above $\dfrac{\alpha}{\begin{vmatrix}134 & 2\\ 39 & -3\end{vmatrix}}=\dfrac{\beta}{\begin{vmatrix}9 & 134\\ 4 & 39\end{vmatrix}}=\dfrac{1}{\begin{vmatrix}9 & 2\\ 4 & -3\end{vmatrix}}$

$\Rightarrow \dfrac{\alpha}{-480}=\dfrac{\beta}{-215}=\dfrac{1}{-35} \Rightarrow \alpha=\dfrac{480}{35}=\dfrac{96}{7}, \beta=\dfrac{37}{7}$

2. (a), (b), (d) $\quad f(x)=(x+3)^9+(3x+k)^3$ has $x+4$ as factor

$\Rightarrow f(-4)=0 \qquad \Rightarrow -1+(k-12)^3=0$

$\Rightarrow (k-12)=(1)^{1/3} \qquad \Rightarrow k-12=1, \omega, \omega^2$

$\Rightarrow k=13, 12+\omega, 12+\omega^2$

$\Rightarrow k=13, k=12+\omega$ or $k=11+(1+\omega^2)=11-\omega$

3. (c) Given $P(x)$ is a polynomial such that

$P(x)=(x-a).\,q_1(x)+a \qquad$ (i)

$P(x)=(x-b).\,q_2(x)+b \qquad$ (ii)

$P(x)=(x-c).\,q_3(x)+c \qquad$ (iii)

Now

$p(x)=(x-a)(x-b)(x-c).\,Q(x)+Ax^2+Bx+C \qquad$ (iv)

$\Rightarrow \begin{cases} a=Aa^2+Ba+C\\ b=Ab^2+Bb+C\\ c=Ac^2+Bc+C\end{cases} \Rightarrow \begin{cases}(b+a)A+B=1\\ (c+b)A+B=1\end{cases}$

$\Rightarrow A=0, B=1$ and $C=0$.

$\Rightarrow$ Thus remainder is clearly x.

4. (a), (b), (c)

$\because$ x^2+ax+1 is factor of ax^3+bx+c

$\Rightarrow ax^3+bx+c=(x^2+ax+1)(ax+c)$

$\Rightarrow ax^3+bx+c=ax^3+(c+a^2)x^2+(ac+a)x+c$

Comparing the coefficients of L.H.S. and R.H.S., we get

$c+a^2=0 \qquad$ (i)

$ac+a=0 \qquad$ (ii)

$\because$ $a=\dfrac{b}{c+1}$, now eliminating a from (i) and (ii), we get

$c=-\left(\dfrac{b}{c+1}\right)^2$

$\Rightarrow c(c+1)^2=-b^2 \qquad \Rightarrow c^3+2c^2+c+b^2$

TEXTUAL EXERCISE–3: (SUBJECTIVE)

1. $x^2+k=0 \qquad \Rightarrow \quad x=\pm\sqrt{-k}$

$\because$ $k<0$ i.e., $-k>0$, thus both roots are real and distinct.

2. $(l-m)x^2-5(l+m)x-2(l-m)=0$

$D=25(l+m)^2+8(l-m)^2>0$

Thus equation has pair of real and distinct roots.

3. $ax^2+b=0$ to have real distinct roots, b and a must have opposite sign and therefore ab < 0.

4. Given $k>0$ and $x^2+kx+64=0$, $x^2-8x+k=0$ both have real roots $k^2-(16)^2 \geq 0$ and $(64-4k) \geq 0$

$\Rightarrow k \in [16, \infty)$ and $k \leq 16$

$\Rightarrow k=16$ only

5. $b \in \mathbb{R}^+$ and discriminate of equation

$D=(3+b)^2-4(2+b)(4+b)$

$=-3b^2-12b-23<0\ \forall\ b \in \mathbb{R}^+$

Hence both roots of equation are imaginary.

6. Consider quadratic polynomial $f(x)=(m+1)x^2-4(m+2)x+25$; to be perfect square its $D=0$

$\Rightarrow 16(m+2)^2-100(m+1)=0$

$\Rightarrow 4(m^2+4m+4)-25m-25=0$

$\Rightarrow 4m^2-9m-9=0 \qquad \Rightarrow (4m+3)(m-3)=0$

$\Rightarrow m=3, -3/4$

7. Consider the equation $(a + 1)x^2 + 2(a + 1)x + a - 2 = 0$
$D = 4(a + 1)^2 - 4(a + 1)(a - 2) = 12(a + 1)$
Case (a): if $a > -1$ $\Rightarrow D > 0$
$\Rightarrow$ both roots are real and distinct
Case (b): if $a < -1$ $\Rightarrow D < 0$
$\Rightarrow$ both roots are non-real.
Case (c): if $a = -1$, the equation because $0.x^2 + 0.x - 3 = 0$
$\Rightarrow$ roots can't be finite real numbers both roots must lie as ∞.

8. $x^2 - 20x + 80 = 0$ has roots $\alpha = 10 - 25$, then other root must be $\beta = 10 + 2\sqrt{5}$
$\Rightarrow \alpha + \beta = 20$ and $\alpha\beta = 100 - 20$, which is clearly true.

9. **(a)** Given equation $x^2 + (3 - 2a)x - 3a + 2 = 0$
$a + \beta = 2a - 3$ (i)
$\alpha\beta = 2 - 3a$ (ii)
$D = (3 - 2a)^2 - 4(2 - 3a) = 9 + 4a^2 - 12a + 12a - 8 = 1 + 4a^2 > 0$
Thus roots are real $\forall$ a $\in \mathbb{R}$
If $a \in \left(-\infty, \frac{2}{3}\right)$; $\alpha\beta > 0$ and $\alpha + \beta < 0$ thus both roots are negative
If $a \in \left(\frac{2}{3}, \frac{3}{2}\right)$; $\alpha\beta < 0$ and $\alpha + \beta < 0$
$\Rightarrow$ Both roots of opposite sign and negative root has larger magnitude.
If $a \in \left(\frac{3}{2}, \infty\right)$; $\alpha\beta < 0$ and $\alpha + \beta > 0$
$\Rightarrow$ Both roots of opposite sign and positive root has larger magnitude.
If $a = 2/3$, then $\alpha\beta = 0$ and $\alpha + \beta < 0$
$\Rightarrow$ One roots zero and other negative
If $a = 3/2$, then $\alpha\beta < 0$ and $\alpha + \beta = 0$
$\Rightarrow$ One roots have equal magnitude but opposite sign.
(b) $x^2 + 5x + 4 = 0$ $\Rightarrow \begin{cases} \alpha + \beta = -5 & < 0 \\ \alpha\beta = 4 & > 0 \end{cases}$ and $D > 0$
Thus both roots are negative as they have same sign and their sum is negative.

10. $\because$ $px^2 - 3qx - 4p = 0$; $D = 9p^2 + 16p^2 > 0 \ \forall\ p, q \in \mathbb{R}$
Thus roots are real and distinct but if $p = ai$ and $q - bi$, $a, b \in \mathbb{R}$
$\Rightarrow D = -(9a^2 + 16b^2) < 0$
Roots must not be predicted on the basis of D, rather by solving equation, we get roots as
$$x = \frac{3bi \pm i\sqrt{9a^2 + 16b^2}}{2ai} = \frac{3b \pm \sqrt{9a^2 + 16b^2}}{2a}$$. Both roots real and distinct

11. $(b - c)x^2 + (c - a)x + (a - b) = 0$
$\because$ Sum of coefficient = 0
$\Rightarrow x = 1$ is one root. Let other roots be α
$\Rightarrow 1.\alpha = \frac{a-b}{b-c}$
$\Rightarrow$ Roots are 1 and $\left(\frac{a-b}{b-c}\right)$

12. Consider the expression $a(b - c)x^2 + b(c - a)xy + c(a - b)y^2$
$= y^2\left(a(b-c)\left(\frac{x}{y}\right)^2 + b(c-a)\frac{x}{y} + c(a-b)\right)$ to be perfect square: $a(b - c)t^2 + b(c - a)t + c(a - b)$ where $t = x/y$
$\because$ Sum of coefficient = 0
$\Rightarrow$ One root is one therefore other roots must be 1.
$\Rightarrow$ Product of roots $= \frac{c(a-b)}{a(b-c)} = 1$
$\Rightarrow ca - bc = ab - ac$ $\Rightarrow 2ac = b(a + c)$
$\Rightarrow b = \frac{2ac}{a+c}$ $\Rightarrow a, b, c$ are in H.P.

13. $a, b \in \mathbb{R}$ and $x^2 + (a - b)x - a - b + 1 = 0$ has unequal roots (real) $\forall\ b \in \mathbb{R}$.
$\Rightarrow (a - b)^2 + 4(a + b - 1) > 0 \ \forall\ b \in \mathbb{R}$.
$\Rightarrow b^2 + (4 - 2a)b + a^2 + 4x - 4 > 0 \ \forall\ b \in \mathbb{R}$.
$\Rightarrow D < 0$ i.e., $(4 - 2a)^2 - 4(a^2 + 4a - 4) < 0$
$\Rightarrow 16 + 4a^2 - 16a - 4a^2 - 16a + 16 < 0$
$\Rightarrow 32(1 - a) < 0$
$\Rightarrow a > 1$

TEXTUAL EXERCISE-3: (OBJECTIVE)

1. **(a)** $9x^2 + 4ax + 4 = 0$ for imaginary roots
$D = 16a^2 - 144 < 0 \Rightarrow (a - 3)(a + 3) < 0$
$\Rightarrow a \in (-3, 3)$

2. **(a), (c)** For $f(x) = x^2 + (2 - k)x + k - 3/4$ to be perfect square; $D = 0$
$\Rightarrow 4 + k^2 - 4k - 4k + 3 = 0$
$\Rightarrow k^2 - 8k + 7 = 0$ $\Rightarrow k = 1, 7$

3. **(b)** Consider equation $x^2 + 3|x| + 2 = 0$
$\Rightarrow (|x| + 1)(|x| + 2) = 0 \Rightarrow |x| = -1, -2$ not possible.
$\Rightarrow$ No roots

4. **(c)** Given l, $m \in \mathbb{R}$
Consider the real quadratic equation $(l - m)x^2 - (1 + m)x - 2(l - m) = 0$
Clearly, $D = 4(1 + m)^2 + 4(l - m)^2 > 0$
$\Rightarrow$ Real an unequal roots.

5. **(a)** $x^2 - x + m^2 = 0$ has no real roots
$\Rightarrow D = 1 - 4m^2 < 0$
$\Rightarrow (1 - 2m)(1 + 2m) < 0$
$\Rightarrow m \in \left(-\infty, -\frac{1}{2}\right) \cup \left(\frac{1}{2}, \infty\right)$

6. **(b)** $x^2 - (2\tan\alpha)x - 1 = 0$ has $D = 4\tan^2\alpha + 4 = 4\sec^2 4$
Thus equation has real roots.

7. **(a)** $x^2 - 4x + \log_{1/2}(a^2) = 0$ doesn't have two distinct real root.
$\Rightarrow D \leq 0$ $16 - 4\log_{1/2}(a^2) \leq 0$
$\Rightarrow 8\log_{1/2}|a| \geq 16$
$\Rightarrow \log_{1/2}|a| \geq 2$ $\log_{1/2}|a| \geq \log_{1/2}(1/4)$
$\Rightarrow |a| \leq 1/4$
$\Rightarrow a \in \left[-\frac{1}{4}, \frac{1}{4}\right]$ $\Rightarrow a_{max} = 1/4$

8. **(b)** $(ax^2 + bx + c)(ax^2 - dx - c) = 0;\ ac \neq 0$
$\Rightarrow D_1 = b^2 - 4ac$ and $D_2 = d^2 + 4ac$
$\Rightarrow D_1 + D_2 = b^2 + d^2 \geq 0$
$\Rightarrow$ Atleast one of D_1 or D_2 positive.
$\Rightarrow$ Atleast two real zeros.

9. **(d)** $(a^2 + b^2)y^2 - 2(ac + bd)y + c^2 + d^2 = 0$ have equal roots.
$\Rightarrow D = 0$
$\Rightarrow 4(a^2c^2 + b^2d^2 + 2abcd) - 4(a^2 + b^2)(c^2 + d^2) = 0$
$2abcd - a^2d^2 - b^2c^2 = 0$
$\Rightarrow (ad - bc)^2 = 0$
$\Rightarrow ad = bc \qquad \Rightarrow \dfrac{a}{b} = \dfrac{c}{d}$

10. **(a)** $(1 + m)x^2 - 2(1 + 3m)x + (1 + 8m) = 0$ has equal roots.
$\Rightarrow D = 0$
$\Rightarrow 4(9m^2 + 6m + 1) - 4(1 + m)(1 + 8m) = 0$
$\Rightarrow 9m^2 + 6m + 1 - 8m^2 - 9m - 1 = 0$
$\Rightarrow m^2 - 3m = 0 \qquad \Rightarrow m(m - 3) = 0$
$\Rightarrow m = 0, 3$

11. **(a)** $(b - c)x^2 + (c - a)x + (a - b) = 0$
$\because$ Sum of coefficient = 0, thus one of the roots is 1. Other roots also one as roots are equal
$\Rightarrow \dfrac{a-c}{b-c} = 2 \qquad \Rightarrow a - c = 2b - 2c$
$\Rightarrow a + c = 2b \qquad \Rightarrow a, b, c$ are in A.P.

12. **(a)** The roots of the equation $(x - a)(x - b) = abx^2$
$\Rightarrow x^2(1 - ab) - (a + b)x + ab = 0$
$\Rightarrow D = a^2b^2 + 2ab - 4ab(1 - ab)$
$\Rightarrow (a - b)^2 + 4a^2b^2 \geq 0 \quad \Rightarrow$ Roots are real

13. **(d)** $8\sec^2\theta - 6\sec\theta + 1 = 0$
$\Rightarrow \sec\theta = \dfrac{6 \pm \sqrt{36-32}}{16} = \dfrac{6 \pm 2}{16} = \dfrac{1}{2}, \dfrac{1}{4}$
$\Rightarrow$ Both not possible $\quad \Rightarrow$ No real roots

14. **(a)** Given $a, b, c \in \mathbb{R}$ and $4a + 2b + c = 0$ and $ab > 0$
Now $4D = 4b^2 - 16ac = (4a + c)^2 - 16ac$
$= 16a^2 + c^2 - 8ac = (4a - c)^2 \geq 0$
$\Rightarrow D \geq 0$, clearly roots are real

15. **(a)** $(c^2 + a^2)x^2 - 2(a + b)cx + b^2 + c^2 = 0$ to have equal roots.
$\Rightarrow D = 0$
$\Rightarrow 4(a^2 + b^2 + 2ab)c^2 - 4(a^2 + c^2)(b^2 + c^2) = 0$
$\Rightarrow a^2c^2 + b^2c^2 + 2abc^2 - a^2b^2 - a^2c^2 - b^2c^2 - c^4 = 0$
$\Rightarrow 2abc^2 - a^2b^2 - c^4 = 0$
$\Rightarrow -(c^2 - ab)^2 = 0 \qquad \Rightarrow c^2 = ab$

TEXTUAL EXERCISE–4: (SUBJECTIVE)

1. $f(x) = 2x^3 + mx^2 - 13x + n$ have roots 2, 3, α.

$2 + 3 + \alpha = -\dfrac{m}{2}$ (i)

$6 + 3\alpha + 2\alpha = \dfrac{-13}{2}$ (ii)

$6\alpha = -\dfrac{n}{2}$ (iii)

Therefore $5\alpha = \dfrac{-13}{2} - 6 = \dfrac{-25}{2}$; $\alpha = \dfrac{-5}{2}$

$\Rightarrow \dfrac{-m}{2} = 5 + \alpha = 5 - \dfrac{5}{2} \quad \Rightarrow m = -5$

Also $n = -12 = -12(-5/2) = 30 \quad \Rightarrow m = -5$ and $n = 30$

2. $x^3 - mx^2 + 3x - 2 = 0$ have roots $\alpha, -\alpha, \beta$
$\alpha + (-\alpha) + \beta = m$ (i)
$-\alpha - \alpha\beta + \alpha\beta = 3$ (ii)
$-\alpha^2\beta = 2$ (iii)
$\Rightarrow \alpha^2 = -3,\ \beta = m$ and $3\beta = 2$
$\Rightarrow 3m = 2 \qquad \Rightarrow m = 2/3$

3. α, β are roots of equation $2x^2 - 3x - 6 = 0$ (i)
For the equation with root $\alpha^2 + 2$ and $\beta^2 + 2$
$x = \alpha^2 + 2;\ \alpha = \pm\sqrt{x-2}$
Replacing in (i), we get $2(x-2) \mp 3\sqrt{x-2} - 6 = 0$
$\Rightarrow 2(x-2) \mp 3\sqrt{x-2}$; squaring both side, we get $4x^2 + 100 - 4x = 9x - 18$
$\Rightarrow 4x^2 - 49x + 118 = 0$ is the required equation.

4. $ax^2 + bx + c = 0$ has root α, β the given equation is $a\left(\dfrac{x}{x-1}\right)^2 - b\left(\dfrac{x}{x-1}\right) + c = 0$ and $a\left(\dfrac{x}{x-1}\right)^2 + b\left(\dfrac{x}{1-x}\right) + c = 0$

$\because x \to \dfrac{x}{1-x} \qquad \Rightarrow \alpha = \dfrac{x}{1-x}$

$\Rightarrow \dfrac{1}{\alpha} = \dfrac{1}{x} - 1$

$\Rightarrow \dfrac{1}{x} = \dfrac{1+\alpha}{\alpha} \qquad \Rightarrow x = \left(\dfrac{\alpha}{\alpha+1}\right)$

Therefore the roots of given equation is must be $\dfrac{\alpha}{\alpha+1}, \dfrac{\beta}{\beta+1}$.

5. Let α, β be roots of equation $x^2 + bx + c = 0$ for equation with roots α^3, β^3
$\Rightarrow \alpha = x^{1/3} \qquad \because x = {}^3$
The transformed equation shall be $x^{2/3} + bx^{1/3} + c = 0$
$\Rightarrow (x^{2/3} + bx^{1/3})^3 = -c^3$
$\Rightarrow x^2 + b^3x + 3bx(x^{2/3} + bx^{1/3}) = -c^3$
$\Rightarrow x^2 + b^3x + 3bx(-c) = -c^3$
$\Rightarrow x^2 + (b^3 - 3bc)x + c^3 = 0$

6. $x^3 - 9x^2 + kx - 24 = 0$, let the roots be $\alpha - \beta, \alpha, \alpha + \beta$
$\Rightarrow 3\alpha = 9 \qquad \Rightarrow \alpha = 3$ and $\alpha(\alpha^2 - \beta^2) = 24$
$\Rightarrow 3(9 - \beta^2) = 24 \qquad \Rightarrow 9 - \beta^2 = 8$
$\Rightarrow \beta^2 = 1$
$\Rightarrow \beta = \pm 1$, thus roots are therefore 2, 3, 4 and $k = 6 + 12 + 8 = 26$.

7. $a, b \in \mathbb{C}$ and $x^3 + ax + b = 0$ has pair of conjugate roots $\alpha + i\beta, \alpha - i\beta$
Clearly the third root must be -2α
$\Rightarrow$ Roots are $\alpha + i\beta, \alpha - i\beta, 2\alpha$
$\Rightarrow a = \alpha^2 + \beta^2 + 2\alpha(\alpha - i\beta) + 2\alpha(\alpha + i\beta) = \alpha^2 + \beta^2 + 4\alpha^2 \in \mathbb{R}$ and $b = -(\alpha + i\beta)(\alpha - i\beta)(2\alpha) = -2\alpha(\alpha^2 + \beta^2) \in \mathbb{R}$
$\Rightarrow$ Both a and b are real.

8. $ax^2 + bx + c = 0$ has roots cotθ, cosecθ.

$\cot\theta + \text{cosec}\theta = -\dfrac{b}{a}$

$\cot\theta \,.\, \text{cosec}\theta = c/a$

$\because\ \text{cosec}^2\theta - \cot^2\theta = 1$

$\Rightarrow\ (\text{cosec}\theta - \cot\theta)(\text{cosec}\theta + \cot\theta) = 1$

$\Rightarrow\ \sqrt{(\text{cosec}\,\theta + \cot\theta)^2 - 4\text{cosec}\,\theta\cot\theta}(\text{cosec}\,\theta.\cot\theta) = 1$

$\Rightarrow\ \sqrt{\dfrac{b^2}{a^2} - 4\left(\dfrac{c}{a}\right)}\left(-\dfrac{b}{a}\right) = 1$

$\Rightarrow\ \sqrt{b^2 - 4ac}\left(-\dfrac{b}{a^2}\right) - 1$

$\Rightarrow\ a^2 = -b\sqrt{\Delta} \qquad \Rightarrow\ a^4 = b^2\Delta.$

9. $\lambda(x^2 - x) + x + 5 = 0$

$\Rightarrow\ \lambda x^2 + (1 - \lambda)x + 5 = 0$ has roots α, β

$\Rightarrow\ \alpha + \beta = \dfrac{\lambda - 1}{\lambda}$ (i)

$\Rightarrow\ \alpha\beta = \dfrac{5}{\lambda}$ (ii)

Now $\dfrac{\alpha}{\beta} + \dfrac{\beta}{\alpha} = \dfrac{4}{5} \qquad \Rightarrow\ 5(\alpha^2 + \beta^2) = 4\alpha\beta$

$\Rightarrow\ 5\left(\left(\dfrac{\lambda - 1}{\lambda}\right)^2 - \dfrac{10}{\lambda}\right) = \dfrac{20}{\lambda}$

$\Rightarrow\ (\lambda - 1)^2 - 10\lambda = 4\lambda \quad \Rightarrow\ (\lambda - 1)^2 - 14\lambda = 0$

$\Rightarrow\ \lambda^2 - 16\lambda + 1 = 0$ has roots λ_1 and λ_2.

$\Rightarrow\ \begin{cases}\lambda_1 + \lambda_2 = 16 \\ \lambda_1\lambda_2 = 1\end{cases}$

Therefore $\dfrac{\lambda_1}{\lambda_2} + \dfrac{\lambda_2}{\lambda_1} = \dfrac{(\lambda_1 + \lambda_2)^2 - 2\lambda_1\lambda_2}{\lambda_1\lambda_2} = \dfrac{(16)^2 - 2}{1}$

$= 256 - 2 = 254$

10. $x^2 + [a^2 - 5a + b + 4]x + b = 0$ has roots –5, 1.

$\Rightarrow\ -[a^2 - 5a + b + 4] = -4$ and $b = -5$

$\Rightarrow\ [a^2 - 5a - 1] = 4$

$\Rightarrow\ [a^2 - 5a] = 5$

$\Rightarrow\ 5 \le a^2 - 5a < 6$

$\Rightarrow\ a^2 - 5a - 5 \ge 0$ and $a^2 - 5a - 6 < 0$

$\Rightarrow\ a \in \left(-\infty, \dfrac{5 - 3\sqrt{5}}{2}\right] \cup \left[\dfrac{5 + 3\sqrt{5}}{2}, \infty\right)$ and $a \in (-1, 6)$

$\Rightarrow\ a \in \left(-1, \dfrac{5 - 3\sqrt{5}}{2}\right] \cup \left[\dfrac{5 + 3\sqrt{5}}{2}, 6\right)$

TEXTUAL EXERCISE–4: (OBJECTIVE)

1. (c) $9x^2 + x + 1 = 0$ has roots α, β

$\Rightarrow$ For equation with roots 1/α, 1/β replacing x by $1/x$

$\Rightarrow\ x^2 + 6x + 9 = 0$

2. (a) Replacing $x \to -1/x$

We get the required equation $9x^2 - px + 1 = 0$

3. (b) Given $ax^2 + bx + c = 0$ having roots α, β and $2x^2 + 8x + 2 = 0$ with roots α – 1, β – 1

$a(x + 1)^2 + b(x + 1) + c = 0$ is same as $2x^2 + 8x + 2 = 0$

$\Rightarrow\ \begin{cases}ax^2 + (2a + b)x + a + b + c = 0 \\ x^2 + 4x + 1 = 0\end{cases}$ are similar equation.

$\Rightarrow\ \dfrac{a}{1} = \dfrac{2a + b}{4} = \dfrac{a + b + c}{1}$

$\Rightarrow\ 2a = b = -c$

4. (b) $ax^2 + bx + c = 0$ has roots α, β

$\Rightarrow\ \alpha + \beta = \dfrac{-b}{a}$ and $\alpha\beta = \dfrac{c}{a}$ thus the equation with roots α + β and α is $x^2 - (\alpha + \beta + \alpha\beta)x + (\alpha + \beta)\alpha\beta = 0$

$\Rightarrow\ x^2 - \left(-\dfrac{b}{a} + \dfrac{c}{a}\right)x + \dfrac{(-bc)}{a^2} = 0$

$\Rightarrow\ a^2x^2 + a(b - c)x - bc = 0$

5. (a) $ax^2 + bx + c = 0$ have roots α, β, then equation with roots $\dfrac{1}{\alpha^2}, \dfrac{1}{\beta^2}$ is $x^2 - \left(\dfrac{\alpha^2 + \beta^2}{\alpha^2\beta^2}\right)x + \dfrac{1}{(\alpha\beta)^2} = 0$

$\Rightarrow\ x^2 - \left(\dfrac{\left(-\dfrac{b}{a}\right)^2 - \dfrac{2c}{a}}{\dfrac{c^2}{a^2}}\right)x + \dfrac{a^2}{c^2} = 0$

$\Rightarrow\ c^2x^2 - (b^2 - 2ac)x + a^2 = 0$

6. (a) For equation with root $\dfrac{1}{a\alpha + b}, \dfrac{1}{a\beta + b}$

$\because\ \alpha + \beta = \dfrac{-b}{a}$ and $\alpha\beta = \dfrac{c}{a}$

$a\alpha + b = -a\beta$

$a\beta + b = -a\alpha$

$\Rightarrow$ Sum of roots $= \dfrac{1}{a\alpha + b} + \dfrac{1}{a\beta + b} = -\left(\dfrac{1}{a\beta} + \dfrac{1}{a\alpha}\right)$

$= -\dfrac{1}{a}\left(\dfrac{\alpha + \beta}{\alpha\beta}\right) = \dfrac{b}{ac}$

$\Rightarrow$ Product of roots $= \left(\dfrac{1}{a\alpha + b}\right)\left(\dfrac{1}{a\beta + b}\right) = \dfrac{1}{a^2\alpha\beta} = \dfrac{1}{ac}$

Equation is $x^2 - \dfrac{b}{ac}x + \dfrac{1}{ac} = 0$

$\Rightarrow\ acx^2 - bx + 1 = 0$

7. (b) $a, b \in \mathbb{Q}$ and b is not a perfect squares $\dfrac{1}{a + \sqrt{b}}$ is one root.

So other roots $\dfrac{1}{a - \sqrt{b}}$, thus equation is

$x^2 - \dfrac{2a}{a^2 - b}x + \dfrac{1}{a^2 - b} = 0$

$\Rightarrow\ (a^2 - b)x^2 - 2ax + 1 = 0$

8. (a) $x^2 + px + q = 0$ has roots $2 + i\sqrt{3}$; so other roots is $2 - i\sqrt{3}$ using sum and product of roots.

$\Rightarrow\ -p = 4$ and $q = 7 \qquad \Rightarrow\ (p, q)$ is (–4, 7)

9. (a) $x^2 - p(x + 1) + c = 0$ have roots α, β then $\alpha^2 + (2 + p)\alpha\beta + \beta^2 = (\alpha + \beta)^2 + p\alpha\beta = p^2 + p(c - p) = pc$

10. (c) $x^3 - 12x^2 + 39x - 28 = 0$ have roots α – β, α, α + β

$\Rightarrow\ 3\alpha = 12$ thus $\alpha = 4$ and $\alpha(\alpha^2 - \beta^2) = 28$

$\Rightarrow\ 4(16 - \beta^2) = 28 \qquad \Rightarrow\ 16 - \beta^2 = 7$

$\Rightarrow\ \beta^2 = 9 \qquad \Rightarrow\ \beta = \pm 3$

11. (c) $ax^2 - bx - c = 0$ has root α, β and if root change by same quantity k i.e., $\alpha + k$, $\beta + k$

Clearly difference of root does not change $|\alpha - \beta| = |(\alpha + k) - (\beta + k)| = \dfrac{\sqrt{b^2 + 4ac}}{a}$ does not change.

12. (b) α, β be roots of $ax^2 + bx + c = 0$

$$\alpha + \beta = \frac{-b}{a}; \alpha\beta = \frac{c}{a}$$

Equation with roots $\dfrac{\alpha+\beta}{2}, \dfrac{2\alpha\beta}{\alpha+\beta}$ i.e., $\dfrac{-b}{2a}, \dfrac{-2c}{b}$ is

$$x^2 + \left(\frac{b}{2a} + \frac{2c}{b}\right)x + \frac{c}{a} = 0$$

$$\Rightarrow x^2 + \left(\frac{b^2 + 4ac}{2ab}\right)x + \frac{c}{a} = 0$$

$\Rightarrow 2abx^2 + (b^2 + 4ac)x + 2bc = 0$

13. (a) $ax^2 + bx + c = 0$ with roots α, β

$$\because \alpha + \beta = \frac{1}{\alpha^2} + \frac{1}{\beta^2}$$

$$\Rightarrow -\frac{b}{a} = \frac{\left(\frac{-b}{a}\right)^2 - \frac{2c}{a}}{\frac{c^2}{a^2}} \qquad \Rightarrow -\frac{b}{a} = \frac{b^2 - 2ac}{c^2}$$

$$\Rightarrow \frac{-b}{a}\left(\frac{c}{a}\right) = \frac{b^2}{c^2}\left(\frac{c}{a}\right) - \frac{2a}{c}\cdot\frac{c}{a}$$

$$\Rightarrow \frac{b^2}{ac} + \frac{bc}{a^2} - 2 = 0 \qquad \Rightarrow \frac{b^2}{ac} + \frac{bc}{a^2} = 2$$

14. (c) $6x^2 - 6x + 1 = 0$; α, β

$$\begin{cases} \alpha + \beta = 1 \\ \alpha\beta = 1/6 \end{cases}, \text{ then}$$

$$\frac{1}{2}(a + b\alpha + c\alpha^2 + d\alpha^3) + \frac{1}{2}(a + b\beta + c\beta^2 + d\beta^2)$$

$$= \frac{1}{2}(2a + b(\alpha+\beta) + c(\alpha^2 + \beta^2) + d(\alpha^3 + \beta^3))$$

$$= \frac{1}{2}\left(2a + b + c\left(1 - \frac{1}{3}\right) + d(\alpha+\beta)(\alpha^2 + \beta^2 - \alpha\beta)\right)$$

$$= \frac{1}{2}\left(2a + b + \frac{2c}{3} + d\left(1 - \frac{1}{2}\right)\right)$$

$$= \frac{1}{2}\left(2a + b + \frac{2c}{3} + \frac{d}{2}\right) = \frac{12a + 6b + 4c + 3d}{12}$$

15. (d) $x^2 - (\lambda^2 - 5\lambda + 5)x + 2\lambda^2 - 3\lambda - 4 = 0$ has sum of roots < 1

Product of roots < 1

$\Rightarrow \lambda^2 - 5\lambda + 5 < 1$ and $2^2 - 3\lambda - 4 < 0$

$\Rightarrow \lambda^2 - 5\lambda + 4 < 0$ and $2\lambda^2 - 3\lambda - 5 < 0$

$$\Rightarrow \begin{cases} (\lambda - 1)(\lambda - 4) < 0 \\ \text{and} \\ (2\lambda - 5)(\lambda + 1) < 0 \end{cases}$$

$$\Rightarrow \lambda \in (1, 4) \cap \left(-1, \frac{5}{2}\right)$$

TEXTUAL EXERCISE–5: (SUBJECTIVE)

1. (a) $x^2 - 3x + 2 = 0$ and $x^2 - (2k + 1)x + k = 0$

Have a common root then the common root is either 1 or 2.

$$\Rightarrow \begin{cases} 1 - 2k - 1 + k = 0 \\ \text{or} \\ 4 - 4k - 2 + k = 0 \end{cases} \Rightarrow k = 0 \text{ or } 2/3$$

(b) $x^2 - 2kx + 3 = 0$ has a root common with $x^2 - 5x + 4 = 0$

$$\Rightarrow \begin{cases} 1 - 2k + 3 = 0 \\ \text{or} \\ 16 - 8k + 3 = 0 \end{cases} \Rightarrow k = 2, \frac{19}{8}$$

2. $a_1x^2 + b_1x + c_1 = 0$ has roots α_1, β_1 and $a_2x^2 + b_2x + c_2 = 0$ has roots α_2, β_2

$$\Rightarrow \alpha_1\alpha_2 = \beta_1\beta_2 = 1 \qquad \Rightarrow \alpha_2 = \frac{1}{\alpha_1} \text{ and } \beta_2 = \frac{1}{\beta_1}$$

$$\Rightarrow \begin{cases} a_1x^2 + b_1x + c_1 = 0 \\ \text{and} \\ a_2x^2 + b_2x + c_2 = 0 \end{cases}$$

Have both roots common $\dfrac{a_1}{c_1} = \dfrac{b_1}{b_2} = \dfrac{c_1}{a_2}$

3. (i) $ax^2 + bx + c = 0$ has a root common with $x^2 + x + 1 = 0$

$\Rightarrow$ Both roots common as 2nd equation has roots non real

$$\Rightarrow \frac{a}{1} = \frac{b}{1} = \frac{c}{1} \qquad \Rightarrow \Delta ABC \text{ is equilateral.}$$

(ii) $D < 0$ thus both roots must be common

$$\Rightarrow \frac{a}{1} = \frac{b}{\sqrt{2}} = \frac{c}{1}$$

$\Rightarrow$ Isosceles right angled triangle

(iii) Similarly here as well $\dfrac{a}{3} = \dfrac{b}{4} = \dfrac{c}{5}$

$\Rightarrow \Delta ABC$ is right angled triangle.

(iv) Also here as $D < 0$

$\Rightarrow$ Both roots should be common

$$\Rightarrow \frac{a}{1} = \frac{b}{3} = \frac{c}{5} \qquad \Rightarrow a = k, b = 3k, c = 5k$$

$\Rightarrow a + b < c$, which is impossible therefore no ΔABC shall be possible.

4. p, q are odd integer $f(x) = x^{10} + px^9 + q$

Let $f(x)$ has an odd integer root

$\Rightarrow f(\alpha) = 0 \qquad \Rightarrow \alpha^{10} + p\alpha^9 + q = 0$

$\Rightarrow$ odd integer = 0 (not possible)

Let $f(x)$ has β as even integer root

$\Rightarrow f(\beta) = 0 \qquad \Rightarrow \beta^{10} + p\beta^9 + q = 0$

$\Rightarrow$ even + even + odd = 0

$\Rightarrow$ odd integer = 0 (not possible)

Thus $f(x)$ has no integer root.

5. $\because$ $2x^2 + 3x + 4 = 0$ and $ax^2 + bx + c = 0$ have a common root and both roots of 1st equation are non real both roots are common.

$$\Rightarrow \frac{a}{2} = \frac{b}{3} = \frac{c}{4}$$

⇒ $a = 2k, b = 3k, c = 4k$ but $a, b, c \in \mathbb{N}$

⇒ $(a + b + c)_{min} = 2 + 3 + 4 = 9$

6. $x^2 - bx + c = 0$ has equal integral root say α, α

⇒ $2\alpha = b; \alpha^2 = c$

⇒ b is even integer and c is perfect square of an integer.

7. Given $x^2 + \frac{b}{a}x + \frac{c-p}{a} = 0$ has both integer roots

⇒ $\frac{b}{a} \in \mathbb{Z}, \frac{c-p}{a} \in \mathbb{Z}$ and $\frac{b^2 - 4(c-p)a}{a^2}$ is perfect square.

Let $x^2 + \frac{b}{a} + \frac{c-2p}{a} = 0$ has both roots integer

⇒ $\frac{b}{a} \in \mathbb{Z}, \frac{c-2p}{a} \in \mathbb{Z}$ and D is perfect square

⇒ $\frac{c-p}{a} - \frac{p}{a} \in \mathbb{R}$ ⇒ $\frac{p}{a} \in \mathbb{R}$

⇒ Either $p = a$ or $a \backslash p$ or $a = 1$ all of which is false

⇒ $ax^2 + bx + c = 2p$ can never have both roots integer.

8. $(x - a)(x - 10) = -1$ has two integer roots where $a \in \mathbb{Z}$

Case (i): $x - a = 1$ and $x - 10 = -1$ i.e., $x = 9$ and $a = 8$

Case (ii): $x - a = -1$ and $x - 10 = 1$ i.e., $x = 11$ and $a = 12$

⇒ $a = 8, 12$

9. $x^2 + ax + b = 0$ (i)

$x^2 + cx + d = 0$ (ii)

$x^2 + ex + f = 0$ (iii)

(i) – (ii); let α be the common root, $\frac{\alpha^2}{ad - bc} = \frac{\alpha}{b - d} = \frac{1}{c - a}$

⇒ $\frac{ad - bc}{b - d} = \frac{b - d}{c - a}$

⇒ $(b - d)^2 = (c - a)(ad - bc)$ (iv)

Similarly for (ii) – (iii)

$\gamma^2 + c\gamma + d = 0$

$\gamma^2 + e\gamma + f = 0$

⇒ $\frac{\gamma^2}{cf - ed} = \frac{\gamma}{d - f} = \frac{1}{e - c}(ce - ed)(f - d) = (e - c)^2$ (iv)

For (i) – (ii), we get $\frac{\beta^2}{af - eb} = \frac{\beta}{b - f} = \frac{1}{e - a}$

⇒ $(af - eb)(e - a) = (b - f)^2$ (v)

Adding equations (i), (ii) and (iii), we get $2a^2 + 2c^2 + 2e^2 - 4b - 4f - 4d - 4ac - 4ea - 4ce$

$= -2ac - 2ce - 2ea$ (vi)

Consider $(a + c + e)^2 = 4(ac + ce + ae - b - d - f)$

$= a^2 + c^2 + e^2 + 2ae + 2ce + 2ea = 4ac + 4ce + 4ae - 4b - 4d - 4f$

⇒ $a^2 + c^2 + e^2 - 2ac - 2ce - 2ae = -4(b + d + f)$ (vii)

Equation (vi) is same as (vii)

⇒ Hence proved.

10. **(i)** $x^2 + ky^2 + 3xy - x - 2y = 0$

$x^2 + (3y - 1)x + ky^2 - 2y = 0$ to be resolved in to two rational linear factors.

$(3y - 1)^2 - 4(ky^2 - 2y)$ must be perfect square.

⇒ $(9 - 4k)y^2 + 2y + 1$ has $D = 0$

⇒ $4 - 4(9 - 4k) = 0$ ⇒ $-32 + 16k = 0$

⇒ $k = 2$

(ii) $x^2 + (4y + 2k)x + 4y^2 + 4y + 1 = 0$ to have two rational linear factors.

Its D must be perfect square.

⇒ $(4y + 2k)^2 - 4(4y^2 + 4y + 1)$

⇒ $(16k - 16)y + 4k^2 - 4$ has equal roots

⇒ $k = 1$

11. $x^2 + 4xy + 4y^2 + 2x + 4y + 1 = 0$; x to be real $(4y + 2)^2 - 4(4y^2 + 4y + 1) > 0$

⇒ which is always true $\forall\, y \in \mathbb{R}$

Similarly y to be real the quadratic in 'y' must have $D \geq 0$

⇒ $4y^2 + 4(x + 1)y + x^2 + 2x + 1 = 0$ has $D \geq 0$

⇒ $16(x^2 + 2x + 1) - 8(x^2 + 2x + 1) \geq 0$

⇒ $2x^2 + 4x + 2 - x^2 - 2x - 1 \geq 0$

⇒ $x^2 + 2x + 1 \geq 0$ ⇒ $(x + 1)^2 \geq 0$

⇒ $x \in \mathbb{R}$ ⇒ $x, y \in \mathbb{R}$.

12. $x + y + z = 6$; $xy + yz + zx = 7$; given $x, y, z \in \mathbb{R}$

∵ $z = 6 - (x + y)$ substituting in second equation, we get

$xy + (x + y)(6 - (x + y)) = 7$

⇒ $xy + 6(x + y) - (x + y)^2 - 7 = 0$

⇒ $x^2 + y^2 + xy - 6x - 6y + 7 = 0$

Considering as quadratic in 'x' and applying x to be real $D \geq 0$

⇒ $(y - 6)^2 - 4(y^2 - 6y + 7) \geq 0$

⇒ $-3y^2 + 12y + 8\ 0$ ⇒ $y \in \left[\frac{6 - \sqrt{60}}{3}, \frac{6 + \sqrt{60}}{3}\right]$

And since both expression are symmetric in variables x, y and z thus ranges of all three variable must be same.

⇒ $x, y, z \in \left[\frac{6 - \sqrt{60}}{3}, \frac{6 + \sqrt{60}}{3}\right]$

13. **(i)** $f(x) = -x^2 + 2x + 3 = -(x^2 - 2x - 3) = -(x^2 - 2x + 1 - 4)$

$= 4 - (x - 1)^2$

Clearly $f(x)\ (-\infty, 4]\ \forall\, x \in \mathbb{R}$

(ii) $f(x) = x^2 - 2x + 3 = (x - 1)^2 + 2$

Thus $\forall\, x \in \mathbb{R}$

$f(x) \in [2, \infty)$ but as $x \in [0, 2]$

$-1 \leq x - 1 \leq 1$

$0 \leq (x - 1)^2 \leq 1$

$2 \leq (x - 1)^2 + 2 \leq 3$

⇒ $f(x) \in [2, 3]$

(iii) $f(x) = x^2 - 4x + 6 = (x - 2)^2 + 2$

Now since $x\ (0, 1)$

$x - 2 \in (-2, -1)$ ⇒ $(x - 2)^2 \in [1, 4]$

$(x - 2)^2 + 2 \in [3, 6]$ ⇒ $f(x) \in [3, 6]$

14. **(i)** $y = \frac{x^2 + x + 1}{x^2 + 1} = 1 + \frac{x}{x^2 + 1}$

Let $y_1 = \frac{x}{x^2 + 1}$

⇒ $y_1x^2 - x + y_1 = 0$ for x to be real

⇒ $1 - 4y_1^2 \geq 0$ ⇒ $y_1 \in \left[-\frac{1}{2}, \frac{1}{2}\right]$

⇒ $1 + y_1 \in \left[\frac{1}{2}, \frac{3}{2}\right]$ ⇒ $y \in \left[\frac{1}{2}, \frac{3}{2}\right]$

(ii) $y = \frac{x^2 - 2x + 9}{x^2 + 2x + 9}$ $\Rightarrow$ $y = 1 - \frac{4x}{x^2 + 2x + 9}$

For $y_f = \frac{4x}{x^2 + 2x + 9}$

$yx^2 + (2y - 4)x + 9y = 0$; x to be real D 0

$\Rightarrow$ $4(y^2 - 4y + 4) - 36y^2 \geq 0$

$\Rightarrow$ $y^2 - 4y + 4 - 9y^2 \geq 0$ $\Rightarrow$ $8y^2 + 4y - 4 \leq 0$

$\Rightarrow$ $2y^2 + y - 1 \leq 0$ $\Rightarrow$ $(2y - 1)(y + 1) \leq 0$

$\Rightarrow$ $y \in \left[-1, \frac{1}{2}\right]$ $\Rightarrow$ $\frac{4x}{x^2 + 2x + 9} \in \left[-1, \frac{1}{2}\right]$

$\Rightarrow$ $-\frac{4x}{x^2 + 2x + 9} \in \left[-\frac{1}{2}, 1\right]$

$\Rightarrow$ $y = 1 - \frac{4x}{x^2 + 2x + 9} \in \left[\frac{1}{2}, 1\right]$

TEXTUAL EXERCISE–5: (OBJECTIVE)

1. (b) If $x^2 - x - 12 = 0$ and $\lambda x^2 + 10x + 3 = 0$ have common root thus the common root must be either $x = 4$ or -3

$\Rightarrow$ Either $16\lambda + 43 = 0$ or $9\lambda - 27 = 0$

$\Rightarrow$ $\lambda = -\frac{43}{16}$ or 3

2. (i) (b) $a, b, c \in (0, \infty)$

$ax^2 + bx + c = 0$ has a common root with $3x^2 + x + 3 = 0$

Since 2nd equation has non real roots thus both roots must be common

$\Rightarrow$ $\frac{a}{3} = \frac{b}{1} = \frac{c}{3}$ $\Rightarrow$ ΔABC is isosceles triangle.

(ii) (a) By similar logic $ax^2 + bx + c = 0$ and $5x^2 + 12x + 13 = 0$ must also have both root common and thus $\frac{a}{5} = \frac{b}{12} = \frac{c}{13} = k$

$\Rightarrow$ $a = 5k$, $b = 12k$, $c = 13k$

$\Rightarrow$ $c^2 = a^2 + b^2$

$\Rightarrow$ ΔABC is right angle triangle.

(iii) (d) Also if $ax^2 + bx + c = 0$ has a root common with $x^2 + 3x + 5 = 0$

$\Rightarrow$ $\frac{a}{2} = \frac{b}{3} = \frac{c}{5}$ $\Rightarrow$ $a = 2k$, $b = 3k$, $c = 5k$

$\Rightarrow$ $a + b = c$ $\Rightarrow$ ΔABC does not exist.

3. (c) $ax^2 + 2cx + b = 0$ and $ax^2 + 2bx + c = 0$ ($b \neq c$) have a common roots α.

$\Rightarrow$ $\begin{cases} a\alpha^2 + 2c\alpha + b = 0 \\ a\alpha^2 + 2b\alpha + c = 0 \end{cases}$; subtracting we get $2\alpha(c - b) = c - b$

$\Rightarrow$ $\alpha = 1/2$

$\Rightarrow$ $a\left(\frac{1}{2}\right)^2 + 2c\left(\frac{1}{2}\right) + b = 0$

$\Rightarrow$ $a + 4c + 4b = 0$

4. (b), (c) $x^3 + x^2 - 4x - k = 0$ has a common root with $x^2 + x - 2 = 0$ say 'α'

$\alpha^3 + \alpha^2 - 4\alpha - k = 0$ and $\alpha^3 + \alpha^2 - 2\alpha - 2\alpha = 0$

$\Rightarrow$ $-2\alpha - k = 0$ $\Rightarrow$ $\alpha = -k/2$

And since $\alpha^2 + \alpha - 2 = 0$

$\Rightarrow$ $\frac{k^2}{4} - \frac{k}{2} - 2 = 0$ $\Rightarrow$ $k^2 - 2k - 8 = 0$

$\Rightarrow$ $(k - 4)(k + 2) = 0$ $\Rightarrow$ $k = -2, 4$

5. (a) $ax^2 + bx + c = 0$ and $x^2 + 2x + 3 = 0$ has one root common

$\Rightarrow$ $\frac{a}{1} = \frac{b}{1} = \frac{c}{3}$ $\Rightarrow$ $a : b : c$ is $1 : 2 : 3$

6. (c) $x^3 - 2x^2 + 2x - 1 = 0$, roots of the cubic equation $1, -\omega, -\omega^2$

$\Rightarrow$ Roots of the quadratic are $-\omega, -\omega^2$

$\Rightarrow$ $a\omega^2 - b\omega + c = 0$ $\Rightarrow$ $-a - a\omega - b\omega + c = 0$

$\Rightarrow$ $a = b = c$

7. (a) $x^2 - x(1 - a) - (a + 2) = 0$ has integer roots.

$\Rightarrow$ $(1 - a) \in \mathbb{Z}$ and $a + 2 \in \mathbb{Z}$ and D perfect square

$\Rightarrow$ $a \in \mathbb{Z}$ and $(1 - a)^2 + 4(a + 2)$ is perfect square

$\Rightarrow$ $a^2 + 2a + 9$ is perfect square

$\Rightarrow$ $a(a + 2) + 9$ is perfect square

$\Rightarrow$ $a = 0, -2$ clearly for $a = 0$; $x^2 - 3x = 0$ has roots -1 and 2.

For $a = -2$; $x^2 - 3x = 0$ has roots 0, 3

8. (c) $\because$ $y = \frac{2x}{1 + x^2}$ $\forall x \in \mathbb{R}$ $\Rightarrow$ $y \in [-1, 1]$

Now the expression $y^2 + y - 3 = \left(y + \frac{1}{2}\right)^2 - \frac{9}{4}$

$\because$ $y + \frac{1}{2} \in \left[-\frac{1}{2}, \frac{3}{2}\right]$ $\Rightarrow$ $\left(y + \frac{1}{2}\right)^2 \in \left[0, \frac{9}{4}\right]$

$\Rightarrow$ $\left(y + \frac{1}{2}\right)^2 - \frac{9}{4} \in \left[-\frac{9}{4}, 0\right]$

$\Rightarrow$ $y^2 + y - 2 \in \left[-\frac{9}{4}, 0\right]$

9. (c) $f(x, y) = x^2 + 2xy + 2y^2 + 4y + 7 = (x + y^2)^2 + (y + 2)^2 + 3$

Therefore $f(x, y)_{\min} = 3$; when $x = -y = 2$

10. (b) $12x^2 - 10xy + 2y^2 + 11x - 5y + k$ can be resolved in to two linear factors iff $abc + 2fgh - af^2 - bg^2 - ch^2 = 0$

$\Rightarrow$ $(12)(2)k + 2\left(\frac{-5}{2}\right)\left(\frac{11}{2}\right)(-5)$

$-12\left(\frac{-5}{2}\right)^2 - 2\left(\frac{11}{2}\right)^2 - k(-5)^2 = 0$

$\Rightarrow$ $24k + \frac{275}{2} - 75 - \frac{121}{2} - 25k = 0$

$k = \frac{154 - 150}{2} = 2$

TEXTUAL EXERCISE–6: (SUBJECTIVE)

1. (i) $\sqrt{x - 4} + \sqrt{2 - x} = 2$ domain of expression is ϕ thus $\forall x \in \mathbb{R}$

L.H.S. is an imaginary number whereas R.H.S. is 2 which is real therefore equation has no real solution.

(ii) $\sqrt{x - 2} + \sqrt{4 - x} = 2$ domain of expression [2, 4] within domain restriction squaring, we get $x - 2 + 4 - x + 2\sqrt{(x - 2)(4 - x)} = 4$

$\Rightarrow$ $\sqrt{(x-2)(4-x)}=1$ $\Rightarrow$ $-(x^2-6x+8)=1$
$\Rightarrow$ $x^2-6x+9=0$ $\Rightarrow$ $(x-3)^2=0$
$\Rightarrow$ $x=3\in[2,4]$
$\Rightarrow$ $x=3$ is only solution of equation.

(iii) $\sqrt{2x-1}=-4$ the above equation has no solution becomes $\forall x\in\left[\frac{1}{2},\infty\right)$
L.H.S. is non negative, whereas R.H.S. is negative therefore no solution
Also for $x\in\left(-\infty,\frac{1}{2}\right)$, L.H.S. is imaginary thus equality does not hold good.

(iv) $(x^2-4)\sqrt{x^2-4x+3}=0$; Domain : $x\in(-\infty,1]\cup[3,\infty)$
Now solving, we get $(x-2)(x+2)\sqrt{(x-1)(x-3)}=0$
Thus $x=-2, 2, 1, 3$ are roots but $x=2\notin$ domain thus discarded leading to exactly three roots. i.e., $x=-2, 1, 3$.

(v) $\sqrt{x^2-1}=2\sqrt{2}$ Domain of L.H.S. expression $D_f=(-\infty,-1]\cup[1,\infty)$
Squaring, we get $x^2-1=8$
$\Rightarrow$ $x=-3, 3\in D_f$ $\Rightarrow$ $x=-3, 3$ are two roots.

(vi) $\sqrt{x-3}\sqrt{x-4}=\sqrt{30}$ Domain of L.H.S. is $[4,\infty)$
Squaring, we get $x^2-7x+12=30$
$\Rightarrow$ $x^2-7x-18=0$ $\Rightarrow$ $(x-9)(x+2)=0$
$\Rightarrow$ $x=-2, 9$
Clearly -2 does not satisfies the domain restriction and hence is not root.
$\Rightarrow$ $x=9$ is only root

2. (a) $\frac{4}{\sqrt{5-x}}-\sqrt{5-x}=\sqrt{2}$ (1)
Clearly $D_f:(-\infty,5)$, now multiplying by $\sqrt{5-x}$, we get $4-(5-x)=\sqrt{2}\sqrt{5-x}$
$\Rightarrow$ $x-1=\sqrt{10-2x}$ (2)
Squaring both ways, we get $x^2-2x+1=10-2x$
$\Rightarrow$ $x^2=9$
$\Rightarrow$ $x=-3, 3$ but $x=-3$ is discarded as it does not satisfy equation (2) and (1)
$\Rightarrow$ $x=3$ is only root
Caution: Students must notice the appearance of extraneous root due to squaring both side of equation.

(b) $x-3=\sqrt{\frac{3x}{2}-\frac{x^2}{4}-\frac{5}{4}}$
$\Rightarrow$ $2x-6=\sqrt{6x-x^2-5}$
Domain of R.H.S. function: $x\in[1,5]$
Case I: If $x\in[1,3)$
$2x-6<0$ whereas R.H.S. is positive thus equation has no root lying in the interval $[1,3)$
Case II: If $x\in[3,5]$
Squaring, we get $4x^2+36-24x=6x-x^2-5$
$\Rightarrow$ $5x^2-30x+41=0$
$\Rightarrow$ $x=\frac{30\pm\sqrt{80}}{10}$ $\Rightarrow$ $x=3+\frac{2\sqrt{5}}{5}, 3-\frac{2\sqrt{5}}{5}$

$\Rightarrow$ Rejecting the negative root, we get $x=3+\frac{2}{\sqrt{5}}$ is only root of equation.

(c) $\sqrt[3]{64-x^3}=8-x$
Domain of expression: $x\in\mathbb{R}$
Cubing both sides, we get $64-x^3=512-x^3-24x(8-x)$
$\Rightarrow$ $24x^2-192x+448=0$
$\Rightarrow$ $3x^2-24x+56=0$ $\Rightarrow$ No real root as $D<0$

(d) Since $\frac{2\sqrt{19-2x}}{x}=1$
Domain restriction: $x\in\left(-\infty,\frac{19}{2}\right]\sim\{0\}$ rearranging the expression, we get $19-2x=x-2$
Thus solution must lie in $\left[2,\frac{19}{2}\right]$; squaring, we get $19-2x=x^2-4x+4$
$\Rightarrow$ $x^2-2x-15=0$ $\Rightarrow$ $x=\frac{2\pm\sqrt{64}}{2}=1\pm4$
$\Rightarrow$ $x=5, -3$ rejecting the negative root as it does not satisfy the parent equation.
$\Rightarrow$ $x=5$ is only root.

(e) $\sqrt[4]{1-x}-\sqrt[4]{15-x}=2$
Domain of L.H.S. expression $[-15, 1]$
$\sqrt[4]{15-x}=2-\sqrt[4]{1-x}$; Raising 4th power both side, we get $15+x=16-32(1-x)^{1/4}+24(1-x)^{1/2}-8(1-x)^{3/4}+1-x$
Let $(1-x)^{1/4}=y$
$\Rightarrow$ $2y^4-8y^3+24y^2-32y=0$
$\Rightarrow$ $y(y^3-4y^2+12y-16)=0$
$\Rightarrow$ $y=0$ or $y^3-4y^2+12y-16=0$
$\Rightarrow$ $y=0$ is one solution
$\Rightarrow$ $\sqrt{1-x}=0$
$\Rightarrow$ $x=1$ is a root by trial and error other root is $x=-15$
Thus roots are $x=1$ and -15.

3. $\sqrt[3]{x^3+3a+1}=1+\sqrt[3]{x}$
Cubing both side, we get $x+3a+1=1+x+3(x)^{1/3}(1+x^{1/3})$
$\Rightarrow$ $a=x^{1/3}(1+x^{1/3})$
Let $x^{1/3}=y\in\mathbb{R}$
$\Rightarrow$ $y^2+y-a=0$ for real roots $D\ge0$
$\Rightarrow$ $1+4a\ge0$ $\Rightarrow$ $a\ge-1/4$, thus $a\in\left(-\frac{1}{4},\infty\right)$

4. Clearly $x>0$ $\sqrt{x+\alpha\sqrt{x}+\beta}=4-\sqrt{x}$
Squaring, we get $x+\alpha\sqrt{x}+\beta=16+x-8\sqrt{x}$
$\Rightarrow$ $(\alpha+8)\sqrt{x}=16-\beta$
Clearly to have infinitely many roots above equation must turn out to be identity
$\Rightarrow$ $\alpha+8=0$ and $16-\beta=0$
$\Rightarrow$ $\alpha=-8$ and $\beta=16$

5. $\sqrt{x}+\sqrt{x-\sqrt{1-x}}=1$
For domain of L.H.S. expression $x\ge0$ and $x\ge\sqrt{1-x}$
$x\ge0$ and $x^2\ge1-x$

$\Rightarrow\ x \geq \dfrac{\sqrt{5}-1}{2}$

Now $\sqrt{x-\sqrt{1-x}} = 1-\sqrt{x}$

$\Rightarrow\ x-\sqrt{1-x} = 1+x-2\sqrt{x}$

$\Rightarrow\ 2\sqrt{x} = 1+\sqrt{1-x}$ $\quad\Rightarrow\ 4x = 1+1-x+2\sqrt{1-x}$

$\Rightarrow\ 5x-1 = 2\sqrt{1-x}$ $\quad\Rightarrow\ 25x^2+1-10x = 4-4x$

$\Rightarrow\ 25x^2-6x-3=0$

$\Rightarrow\ x = \dfrac{6\pm\sqrt{36+300}}{50}$; But $x > \dfrac{\sqrt{5}-1}{2}$ thus rejecting the negative root we get only solution as $x = \dfrac{6+2\sqrt{21}}{25}$.

6. $\sqrt{x+3-4\sqrt{x-1}}+\sqrt{x+15-8\sqrt{x-1}} = 2$

$\Rightarrow\ \sqrt{x-1+4-2.2\sqrt{x-1}}+\sqrt{x-1+16-2(4)\sqrt{x-1}} = 2$

$\Rightarrow\ \sqrt{\left(\sqrt{x-1}-2\right)^2}+\sqrt{\left(\sqrt{x-1}-4\right)^2} = 2$

$\Rightarrow\ \left|\sqrt{x-1}-2\right|+\left|\sqrt{x-1}-4\right| = 2$

Let $\sqrt{x-1}-2$ and $\sqrt{x-1}-4 = b$

$\Rightarrow\ |a|+|b| = |a-b|$; which is true iff $a.b \leq 0$

$\Rightarrow\ \left(\sqrt{x-1}-2\right)\left(\sqrt{x-1}-4\right) \leq 0$

$\Rightarrow\ 2 \leq \sqrt{x-1} \leq 4$

$\Rightarrow\ 4 \leq x-1 \leq 16$ $\quad\Rightarrow\ 5 \leq x \leq 17$

$\Rightarrow\ x \in [5, 17]$ is set of solution.

7. $2x-5+2\sqrt{x(x-5)}+2\sqrt{x-5}+2\sqrt{x} = 48$

We can solve the *problem* by two ways

Approach 1: Rearranging expression, we get $x+x-5+2\sqrt{x}\sqrt{x-5}+2\left(\sqrt{x-5}+\sqrt{x}\right) = 48$

Adding 1 both side we observe L.H.S. becomes perfect square $\left(\sqrt{x}+\sqrt{x-5}+1\right)^2 = 49$

$\Rightarrow\ \sqrt{x}+\sqrt{x-5}+1 = 7$ $\quad\Rightarrow\ \sqrt{x}+\sqrt{x-5} = 6$

$\Rightarrow\ x-5 = 36+x-12\sqrt{x}$ $\Rightarrow\ 41 = 12\sqrt{x}$

$\Rightarrow\ x = \left(\dfrac{41}{12}\right)^2 = \dfrac{1681}{144}$

Approach 2: Completing square of L.H.S., we get $\left(\sqrt{x}+\sqrt{x-5}\right)^2+2\left(\sqrt{x}+\sqrt{x-5}\right)+1 = 49$

Let $\sqrt{x}+\sqrt{x-5} = y$; $(y+1)^2 = 49$

$\Rightarrow y+1 = 7$ $\qquad\because\ y+1>0$

$\Rightarrow y = 6$ thus follows the result.

8. Let $\left(\sqrt{x^2-5x+6}-\sqrt{x^2-5x+4}\right)^{x/2} = A$;

$\left(\sqrt{x^2-5x+6}+\sqrt{x^2-5x+4}\right)^{x/2} = B$

$\Rightarrow\ A+B = 2^{\frac{x+4}{4}}$ and $A.B = 2^{x/2}$

Therefore $A-B = \sqrt{(A+B)^2-4AB} = \sqrt{2^{\frac{x+4}{2}}-2^{\frac{x+4}{2}}} = 0$

$\Rightarrow\ A = B$ which is possible iff – or $\sqrt{x^2-5x+4} = 0$

$\Rightarrow\ x = 0$ or $x = 1, 4$ $\qquad\Rightarrow$ roots are 0, 1, 4.

9. $\sqrt{\dfrac{3x-2y}{2x}}+\sqrt{\dfrac{2x}{3x-2y}} = 2$ $\qquad$ (1)

and $4y^2-1 = 3y(x-1)$ $\qquad$ (2)

Clearly from equation (1), we get $\dfrac{3x-2y}{2x} = 1$

$\Rightarrow\ 3x-2y = 2x$ $\qquad x = 2y$

Substituting in (2), we get $4y^2-1 = 3y(2y-1)$

$\Rightarrow\ 4y^2-1 = 6y^2-3y$ $\quad\Rightarrow\ 2y^2-3y+1 = 0$

$\Rightarrow\ (2y-1)(y-1) = 0$

$\Rightarrow\ y = 1, \tfrac{1}{2}$, thus $x = 2, 1$

$\Rightarrow$ (2, 1) and (1, 1/2) are solution.

TEXTUAL EXERCISE–7: (SUBJECTIVE)

1. (i) Given equation $(x-1)(x-2)(x-3)(x-4) = 3$

$\Rightarrow\ (x-1)(x-4)(x-2)(x-3) = 3$

Let $x^2+5x+4 = y$

$\Rightarrow\ y(y+2) = 3$ $\qquad\Rightarrow\ y^2+2y-3 = 0$

$\Rightarrow\ (y+3)(y-1) = 0$ $\quad\Rightarrow\ y = -3, 1$

$$\Rightarrow \left\{\begin{array}{l} x^2-5x+4=-3 \\ \text{or} \\ x^2-5x+4=1 \end{array}\right.$$

$$\Rightarrow \left\{\begin{array}{l} x^2-5x+7=0 \Rightarrow x=\dfrac{5\pm i\sqrt{3}}{2} \\ \text{or} \\ x^2-5x+3=0 \Rightarrow x=\dfrac{5\pm\sqrt{13}}{2} \end{array}\right.$$

$\Rightarrow\ x = \dfrac{5\pm i\sqrt{3}}{2}, \dfrac{5\pm\sqrt{3}}{2}$ are root

(ii) Given equation $(x+2)(x+12)(x+3)(x+8) = 4x^2$

$\Rightarrow\ (x^2+14x+24)(x^2+11x+24) = 4x^2$

$\Rightarrow\ \left(x+\dfrac{24}{x}+14\right)\left(x+\dfrac{24}{x}+11\right) = 4$

Let $x+\dfrac{24}{x}+14 = y$ thus equations becomes

$\Rightarrow\ y(y-3) = 4$ $\qquad\Rightarrow\ y^2-3y-4 = 0$

$\Rightarrow\ (y-4)(y+1) = 0$ i.e., $y = -1, 4$

$\Rightarrow\ x+\dfrac{24}{x}+14 = -1 \text{ or } 4$

$$\Rightarrow \left\{\begin{array}{l} x^2+15x+24=0 \Rightarrow x=\dfrac{-15\pm\sqrt{129}}{2} \\ \text{or} \\ x^2+10x+24=0 \Rightarrow x=-6,-4 \end{array}\right.$$

$\Rightarrow\ x \in \left\{-6, -4, \dfrac{-15\pm\sqrt{129}}{2}\right\}$

(iii) Consider equation $(6-x)^4 + (8-x)^4 = -16$ (i)

Let $y = \dfrac{6-x+8-x}{2} = 7-x$

Equation (i) become $(y-1)^4 + (y+1)^4 = -16$

$\Rightarrow\ 2\left({}^4C_0y^4 + {}^4C_2y^2 + 1\right) = -16$

$\Rightarrow\ y^4 + 6y^2 + 1 = -8 \quad \Rightarrow\ y^4 + 6y^2 + 9 = 0$

$\Rightarrow\ (y^2+3)^2 = 0 \quad \Rightarrow\ y^2 = -3$

$\Rightarrow\ y = \pm i\sqrt{3}$. Now as $x = 7 - y$

$\Rightarrow\ x = 7 \mp i\sqrt{3}$ each root repeated twice.

2. (i) Given equation $x^2 + \left(\dfrac{x}{x-1}\right)^2 = 8$ as

$x\left(\dfrac{x}{x-1}\right) = x + \dfrac{x}{x-1}$ thus completing the square on L.H.S.

$$\left(x + \frac{x}{x-1}\right)^2 - 2\left(x\left(\frac{x}{x-1}\right)\right) = 8$$

Let $\dfrac{x^2}{x-1} = y$ (i)

$\Rightarrow\ y^2 - 2y - 8 = 0 \quad \Rightarrow\ (y-4)(y+2) = 0$

$\Rightarrow\ y = -2, 4$

Substituting (i), we get $\dfrac{x^2}{x-1} = 4, -2$

$$\Rightarrow \begin{cases} x^2 - 4x + 4 = 0 \Rightarrow (x-2)^2 = 0 \\ \text{or} \\ x^2 + 2x - 2 = 0 \Rightarrow x = \dfrac{-2 \pm \sqrt{12}}{2} \end{cases}$$

$\Rightarrow\ x = 2, 2, -1+\sqrt{3}, -1-\sqrt{3}$ are 4 real roots.

(ii) Given equation $\underbrace{x\left(\dfrac{5-x}{x+1}\right)}_{A}\underbrace{\left\{x + \dfrac{5-x}{x+1}\right\}}_{B} = 6$

Clearly AB = 6 (i)

$A + B = x + (x+1)\left(\dfrac{5-x}{x+1}\right)$

$A + B = x + 5 - x = 5$

$A + B = 5$ (ii)

Solving (i) and (ii), we get A = 3 and $B = 2$ or A = 2, $B = 3$

$$\Rightarrow \begin{cases} \dfrac{5x - x^2}{x+1} = 3 \text{ and } \dfrac{x^2+5}{x+1} = 2 \\ \text{or} \\ \dfrac{5x - x^2}{x+1} = 2 \text{ and } \dfrac{x^2+5}{x+1} = 3 \end{cases}$$

$$\Rightarrow \begin{cases} x^2 - 2x + 3 = 0 \Rightarrow x = \dfrac{2 \pm \sqrt{-8}}{2} \\ \text{or} \\ x^2 - 3x + 2 = 0 \Rightarrow x = 1, 2 \end{cases}$$

$\Rightarrow\ x = 1, 1, 1 \pm \sqrt{2}$ are four roots.

3. Let $e^{\sin x} = y \in \left[\dfrac{1}{e}, e\right]$ the equations becomes $y^2 - 4y - 1 = 0$

$\Rightarrow\ y = \dfrac{4 \pm \sqrt{20}}{2} = 2 \pm \sqrt{5}$

$\Rightarrow\ y = 2 - \sqrt{5}, 2 + \sqrt{5}$ both does not belong to $\left[\dfrac{1}{e}, e\right]$ therefore no. real value of x can satisfy the equation.

4. (i) $4^x + 6^x = 9^x$, dividing by 9^x we get $\left(\dfrac{4}{9}\right)^x + \left(\dfrac{6}{9}\right)^x = 1$

$\Rightarrow\ \left(\left(\dfrac{2}{3}\right)^x\right)^2 + \left(\dfrac{2}{3}\right)^x = 1$

Let $\left(\dfrac{2}{3}\right)^x = y > 0 \quad \Rightarrow\ y^2 + y - 1 = 0$

$\Rightarrow\ y = \dfrac{-1 \pm \sqrt{5}}{2}$

$\Rightarrow\ y = \dfrac{\sqrt{5}-1}{2} \quad \Rightarrow\ \left(\dfrac{2}{3}\right)^x = \dfrac{\sqrt{5}-1}{2}$

$\Rightarrow\ x = \log_{2/3}\left(\dfrac{\sqrt{5}-1}{2}\right)$ is only root

(ii) $\text{Log}_3(3^x - 8) = 2 - x \Rightarrow\ 3^x - 8 = 3^{2-x}$

$\Rightarrow\ (3^x)^2 - 8(3^x) = 9$

Let $3^x = y > 0 \quad \Rightarrow\ y^2 - 8y - 9 = 0$

$\Rightarrow\ (y-9)(y+1) = 0$

$\Rightarrow\ y = 9 \quad \Rightarrow\ 3^x = 9$

$\Rightarrow\ x = 2$ is only root.

5. (a) $|x-1|^{\log_3 x^2 - 2\log_x 9} = (x-1)^7$

Clearly solution may exist iff $x > 1$, thus

$(x-1)^{2\log_3 x - 4\log_x 3} = (x-1)^7$

$\Rightarrow\ 2\log_3 x - \dfrac{4}{\log_3 x} = 7$

Let $\log_3 x = y$

$2y^2 - 7y - 4 = 0$

$\Rightarrow\ y = \dfrac{7 \pm \sqrt{49+32}}{4} = \dfrac{7 \pm 9}{4}$

$\Rightarrow\ y = 4$ or $-1/2$

$\log_3 x = 4$ or $-1/2$

$\Rightarrow\ x = 81$ or $1/\sqrt{3}$, but $x = 1/\sqrt{3}$ rejected

Also $x = 2$ is obvious solution when base become 1

$\Rightarrow\ x \in \{2, 81\}$

(b) $\log_2 x = y$

$$\frac{y}{\frac{1}{2}(1+y)} = \frac{\frac{1}{3}(2+y)}{1+\frac{y}{3}} \Rightarrow \frac{2y}{1+y} = \frac{2+y}{3+y}$$

$\Rightarrow\ 6y^2 + 2y^2 = y^2 + 3y + 2$

$\Rightarrow\ y^2 + 3y - 2 = 0 \quad \Rightarrow\ y = \dfrac{-3 \pm \sqrt{17}}{2}$

$\Rightarrow\ \log_2 x = y = \dfrac{-3 \pm \sqrt{17}}{2}$

$\Rightarrow\ 2^{\frac{-3\pm\sqrt{17}}{2}}$

(c) $\because\ \log_x(3x^2 + 10x) = 3$

$\Rightarrow\ 3x^2 + 10x = x^3 \quad \Rightarrow\ x^3 - 3x - 10x = 0$

$\Rightarrow\ x(x^2 - 3x - 10) = 0$

$\Rightarrow\ x(x-5)(x+2) = 0 \quad \Rightarrow\ x = 0, -2, 5$

But $\log_x (3x^2 + 10x)$ is defined iff $x > 0$ and $x(3x + 10) > 0$ i.e., $x \in (0, \infty)$ thus $x = 0$ and -2 are rejected.
$\Rightarrow$ $x = 5$ is only root.

6. (i) Given equation $|x^2 - 2| + |x - 1| = |x^2 - x - 1| = |(x^2 - 2) - (x - 1)|$
Therefore $(x^2 - 2)$ and $(x - 1)$ must opposite same sign or atleast one of zero

$\Rightarrow (x^2 - 2)(x - 1) \le 0 \quad \Rightarrow \left(x+\sqrt{2}\right)(x-1)\left(x-\sqrt{2}\right) \le 0$

$x \in \left(-\infty, -\sqrt{2}\right] \cup \left[1, \sqrt{2}\right]$

(ii) Consider the equation $|x^2 - 2| + |x - 1| = |x^2 + x - 3| = |(x^2 - 2) + (x - 1)|$
Then $(x^2 - 2)(x - 1) \ge 0$ $(x + \sqrt{2})(x - 1)(x - \sqrt{2}) \ge 0$

$\Rightarrow x \in \left[-\sqrt{2}, 1\right] \cup \left[\sqrt{2}, \infty\right)$

TEXTUAL EXERCISE–6: (OBJECTIVE)

1. (b) Let $\dfrac{x+3+x+5}{2} = y$

$\Rightarrow y = x + 4$
$\Rightarrow y - 1 = x + 3$ and $y + 1 = x + 5$
Therefore equation becomes $(y - 1)^4 + (y + 1)^4 = 16$
$\Rightarrow y^4 + 6y^2 + 1 = 8 \quad \Rightarrow y^4 + 6y^2 - 7 = 0$
$\Rightarrow (y^2 + 7)(y^2 - 1) = 0 \quad \because y^2 + 7 \ne 0$
$\Rightarrow y^2 = 1 \quad \Rightarrow x + 4 = -1, 1$
$\Rightarrow x = -5, -3$
Therefore two real roots

2 (a) Given $x + \dfrac{1}{x} = 5$

$$x^3 + \frac{1}{x^3} + \left(x + \frac{1}{x}\right) - 5\left(x^2 + \frac{1}{x^2}\right)$$

$$= \left(x + \frac{1}{x}\right)\left(x^2 + \frac{1}{x^2} - 1\right) + 5 - 5\left(x^2 + \frac{1}{x^2}\right)$$

$$= 5\left(x^2 + \frac{1}{x^2}\right) - 5 + 5 - 5\left(x^2 + \frac{1}{x^2}\right) = 0$$

3. (a) Given equation $(2x^2 - 3x + 1)(2x^2 + 5x + 1) = 9x^2$

Divided by x^2, we get $\left(2x - 3 + \dfrac{1}{x}\right)\left(2x + 5 + \dfrac{1}{x}\right) = 9$

Let $2x + \dfrac{1}{x} = y \quad \Rightarrow (y - 3)(y + 5) = 9$

$\Rightarrow y^2 + 2y - 24 = 0 \quad \Rightarrow (y + 6)(y - 4) = 0$

$\Rightarrow 2x + 1/x = -6$ or $2x + \dfrac{1}{x} = 4$

$\Rightarrow 2x^2 + 6x + 1 = 0$ or $2x^2 - 4x + 1 = 0$

$\Rightarrow x = \dfrac{-6 \pm \sqrt{28}}{4}$ or $x = 1/2, 1/2$

Thus four real root.

4 (d) Let $\dfrac{(x-2)+(x-4)}{2} = y$ i.e., $y = x - 3$ the equation becomes $(y + 1)^6 + (y - 1)^6 = 64$

${}^6C_6 . y^6 + {}^6C_2 . y^4 + {}^6C_4 y^2 + 1 = 32$

Let $y^2 = z$
$z^3 + 15z^2 + 15z - 31 = 0$
Sum of coefficient zero, thus $z = 1$ is root
$(z^3 - 1) + 15(z^2 - 1) + 15(z - 1) = 0$
$\Rightarrow (z - 1)(z^2 + z + 1 + 15(z + 1) + 15) = 0$
$\Rightarrow (z - 1)(z^2 + 16z + 31) = 0$

$\Rightarrow z = 1, \dfrac{-16 \pm \sqrt{256 - 124}}{2}$

$\Rightarrow z = 1, -8 \pm \sqrt{33}$
$y^2 = 1, y^2 = -8 \pm \sqrt{33}$
$\Rightarrow x - 3 = \pm 1$ or $x - 3 = \pm\sqrt{-8 \pm \sqrt{33}}$
Thus two real root and 4 non real roots.

5. (d) $\left(4+\sqrt{15}\right)^x + \left(4-\sqrt{15}\right)^x = 62$

Let $\left(4+\sqrt{15}\right)^x = A, \left(4-\sqrt{15}\right)^x = B$

$\Rightarrow A + 1/A = 62$

$\Rightarrow A^2 - 62A + 1 = 0$

$\Rightarrow A = \dfrac{62 \pm \sqrt{62 - 4}}{2}$

$\Rightarrow A = 31 \pm 8\sqrt{15}$

$$\Rightarrow \begin{cases} A = \left(4+\sqrt{15}\right)^2 \\ \text{or} \\ A = \left(4-\sqrt{15}\right)^2 \end{cases}$$

$\Rightarrow \left(4+\sqrt{15}\right)^x = \left(4+\sqrt{15}\right)^2$ or $\left(4-\sqrt{15}\right)^{-2}$

$\Rightarrow x = 2$ or -2

6. (b) The equation $\sqrt{x} + \sqrt{x - \sqrt{1-x}} = 1$

Clearly $x \in \left[\dfrac{\sqrt{5}-1}{2}, 1\right]$

$\sqrt{x - \sqrt{1-x}} = 1 - \sqrt{x}$; Squaring both sides, we get $x + \sqrt{1-x} = 1 + x - 2\sqrt{x}$

$\Rightarrow \sqrt{1-x} = 1 - 2\sqrt{x}$; Squaring both sides, we get $1 - x = 1 + 4x - 4\sqrt{x}$
$5x - 4\sqrt{x} = 0$
$\sqrt{x}\left(5\sqrt{x} - 4\right) = 0$

$\Rightarrow x = 0, \dfrac{16}{25}$

Clearly '0' must be rejected, thus only one real roots

7. (a) $\log_{1/2}(2x^2 + 2 - 4x) \ge 2 \quad \Rightarrow 0 < 2x^2 + 2 - 4x \le 4$
$\Rightarrow x^2 - 2x + 1 > 0$ and $x^2 - 2x - 1 \le 0$
$\Rightarrow x \in \mathbb{R} \sim \{1\}$ and $(x - 1 + \sqrt{2})(x - 1 - \sqrt{2}) \le 0$

$\Rightarrow x \in \mathbb{R} \sim \{1\} \cap \left[1-\sqrt{2}, 1+\sqrt{2}\right]$

$\Rightarrow x \in [1 - \sqrt{2}, 1) \cup (1, 1 + \sqrt{2}]$

8. (a) Given inequality $\dfrac{16^{\frac{1}{x}}}{2^{x+3}} > 1 \quad \because 2^{x+3} > 0 \ \forall \ x \in \mathbb{R}$

$\Rightarrow 2^{4/x} > 2^{x+3} \quad \Rightarrow \dfrac{4}{x} > x + 3$

$\Rightarrow \dfrac{4}{x} - x - 3 > 0 \quad \Rightarrow \dfrac{4 - x^2 - 3x}{x} > 0$

$\Rightarrow \dfrac{x^2 + 3x - 4}{x} < 0 \quad \Rightarrow \dfrac{(x+4)(x-1)}{x} < 0$

$\Rightarrow x \in (-\infty, -4) \cup (0, 1)$

Clearly infinite may integers satisfy the above inequity.

9. (d) $\log_2 (ax^2 + x + a) \geq 1 \ \forall x \in \mathbb{R}$

$\Rightarrow ax^2 + x + a \geq 2 \ \forall x \in \mathbb{R}$

$\Rightarrow ax^2 + x + (a - 2) \geq 0 \ \forall x \in \mathbb{R}$

$\Rightarrow a > 0$ and $D \leq 0$

$\Rightarrow a > 0$ and $1 - 4a(a - 2) \leq 0$

$\Rightarrow a > 0$ and $4a^2 - 8a - 1 \geq 0$

$\Rightarrow a > 0$ and $a \in \left(-\infty, 1 - \dfrac{\sqrt{5}}{2}\right] \cup \left[1 + \dfrac{\sqrt{5}}{2}, \infty\right)$

$\Rightarrow a \in \left[1 + \dfrac{\sqrt{5}}{2}, \infty\right)$

10. (b) For Equation (i), $|x|^2 - 2|x| - 3 = 0$

$\Rightarrow (|x| - 3)(|x| + 1) = 0 \quad \Rightarrow |x| = 3$ as $|x| + 1 \neq 0$

$\Rightarrow x = -3, 3$ the solution

For equation (ii), $|x - 2|^2 + |x - 2| - 2 = 0$

$\Rightarrow (|x - 2| + 2)(|x - 2| - 1) = 0$

$\Rightarrow |x - 2| = 1$ as $|x - 2| + 2 \neq 0$

$\Rightarrow x = 1$ or 3

Also equation (iii), $|x^2 - x - 6| = x + 2$ i.e., $|(x - 3)(x + 2)| = x + 2$ (iii)

Solution exist only for $x \geq -2$ if $x \in [-2, 3)$, equation (iii) becomes $(3 - x)(x + 2) = (x + 2)$

$\Rightarrow (x + 2)(2 - x) = 0$

$\Rightarrow x = -2, 2$ are two solution but if $x \geq 3$

$\Rightarrow (x - 3)(x + 2) = (x + 2)$

$\Rightarrow (x + 2)(x - 4) = 0$

$\Rightarrow x = -2, 4$ are solution

$\Rightarrow x \in \{-2, 2, 4\}$ is set of solutions.

Thus all three equations have atleast three solutions.

11. (b) $2x^4 + x^3 - 11x^2 + x + 2 = 0$ is self reciprocal equation, thus dividing by x^2, we get $2\left(x^2 + \dfrac{1}{x^2}\right) + \left(x + \dfrac{1}{x}\right) - 11 = 0$

Let $x + \dfrac{1}{x} = y$, then equation becomes $2(y^2 - 2) + y - 11 = 0$

$\Rightarrow 2y^2 + y - 15 = 0 \quad \Rightarrow y = \dfrac{-1 \pm \sqrt{121}}{4} = \dfrac{5}{2}, -3$

$$\Rightarrow \begin{cases} x + \dfrac{1}{x} = \dfrac{5}{2} \\ \text{or} \\ x + \dfrac{1}{x} = -3 \end{cases} \Rightarrow \begin{cases} 2x^2 - 5x + 2 = 0 \\ \text{or} \\ x^2 + 3x + 1 = 0 \end{cases}$$

$\Rightarrow x \in \left\{\dfrac{1}{2}, 2\right\} \cup \left\{\dfrac{-3 + \sqrt{5}}{2}, \dfrac{-3 - \sqrt{5}}{2}\right\}$

$\Rightarrow$ Roots are $2, \dfrac{1}{2}, \dfrac{-3 \pm \sqrt{5}}{2}$

12. (a), (c) Let $\left(5 + 2\sqrt{6}\right)^{x^2 - 3} = y$, thus $\left(5 - 2\sqrt{6}\right)^{x^2 - 3} = \dfrac{1}{y}$

Thus equation becomes $y^2 - 10y + 1 = 0$

$\Rightarrow y = 5 \pm 2\sqrt{6}$

$\Rightarrow \left(5 + 2\sqrt{6}\right)^{x^2 - 3} = 5 + 2\sqrt{6}$ or $\left(5 + 2\sqrt{6}\right)^{-1}$

$\Rightarrow x^2 - 3 = 1, -1 \quad \Rightarrow x = \pm\sqrt{2}, \pm 2$

13. (a), (b) Set of equation given $(x + y)^{2/3} + 2(x - y)^{2/3} = 3(x^2 + y^2)^{1/3}$

Let $\left(\dfrac{x + y}{x - y}\right) = z$

Dividing $(x - y)^{2/3}$, we get $z^2 + 2 = 3z$

$\Rightarrow z^2 - 3z + 2 = 0 \quad \Rightarrow (z - 1)(z - 2) = 0$

$\Rightarrow \left(\dfrac{x + y}{x - y}\right) = 1, 2$

$\Rightarrow \dfrac{x + y}{x - y} = 1$ or 8, But $3x - 13 = 2y$

$\Rightarrow \dfrac{2x + 3x - 13}{2x - (3x - 13)} = 1$ or 8

$$\Rightarrow \begin{cases} 5x - 13 = 13 - x \\ \text{or} \\ 5x - 13 = 104 - 8x \end{cases} \Rightarrow x = \frac{13}{3} \text{ or } 9$$

$$\Rightarrow \begin{cases} \text{if } x = \dfrac{13}{3}, \text{ then } y = 0 \\ \text{or} \\ \text{if } x = 9, \text{ then } y = 7 \end{cases}$$

14. (b) Let $|\log_3 x| = z \geq 0$

The equation becomes $2z^2 - z + a = 0$

$\Rightarrow z = \dfrac{1 \pm \sqrt{1 - 8a}}{4}$ for four real roots of original equations both above value must be positive real numbers

$1 - 8a > 0$ and $\sqrt{1 - 8a} < 1$

$\Rightarrow a < \dfrac{1}{8}$ and $-a < 0 \quad \Rightarrow a \in \left(0, \dfrac{1}{8}\right)$

15. (d) $5^{x+2} > \left(\dfrac{1}{25}\right)^{1/x} \quad \Rightarrow 5^{x+2} > 5^{-2/x}$

$\Rightarrow x + 2 > -2/x \quad \Rightarrow \dfrac{x^2 + 2x + 2}{x} > 0$

$\Rightarrow \dfrac{(x+1)^2 + 1}{x} > 0 \quad \Rightarrow x > 0$

$\Rightarrow x \in (0, \infty)$ is set of solution

TEXTUAL EXERCISE-8: (SUBJECTIVE)

1. $y = x^2 + kx - x + 9$ lies entirely above x-axis iff $D < 0$ and $a > 0$, thus $(k - 1)^2 - 36 < 0$

$\Rightarrow (k - 7)(k + 5) < 0 \quad \Rightarrow k \in (-5, 7)$

2. If $y = kx^2 + 2kx - 2$ lies below x–axis, then $a < 0$ and $D < 0$

$\Rightarrow k < 0$ and $4k^2 + 8k < 0$

⇒ $k < 0$ and $4k(k + 2) < 0$

⇒ $k \in (-\infty, 0) \cap (-2, 0)$

⇒ $k \in (-2, 0)$

If $y = kx^2 + 2kx - 2$ lies entirely above x–axis $a > 0$ and $D < 0$

⇒ $k > 0$ and $4k(k + 2) < 0$

⇒ $k \in (0, \infty) \cap (-2, 0)$

⇒ $k \in \{\}$

3. $y = x^2 - 6x + 5;\ x \in [2, 4]$

⇒ $y = (x - 3)^2 - 4 \quad \because\ 2 \le x \le 4$

$-1 \le x - 3 \le 1$

$0 \le (x - 3)^2 \le 1$

$-4 \le (x - 3)^2 - 4 \le -3$

⇒ $y \in [-4, -3]$, therefore $y_{min} = -4$ and $y_{max} = -3$

4. Given α, β be root of equation $ax^2 + 2bx + c = 0$ and $\alpha + k$, $\beta + k$ for $Ax^2 + 2Bx + C = 0$

Clearly differences of root is same for both equations

⇒ $\dfrac{\sqrt{D}}{a}$ must be same for both

⇒ $\dfrac{\sqrt{4b^2 - 4ac}}{a} = \dfrac{\sqrt{4B^2 - 4AC}}{A}$

⇒ $a^2(B^2 - AC) = A^2(b^2 - ac)$

5. Given $f(x) = ax^2 + bx + c = 0$ has both roots non real then $af(x) > 0\ \forall\ x \in \mathbb{R}$

⇒ For $x = 0$; $af(0) = ac > 0$; statement (i) is False

∴ $cf(x) > 0\ \forall\ x \in \mathbb{R}$ for $x = 1$; $af(1) = a(a + b + c) > 0$; statement (ii) is true

Similarly $cf(-1/2) > 0$

⇒ $c(a - 2b + 4c) > 0 \quad ⇒\ af(1) > 0$ and $cf(-1) > 0$

⇒ $ac(a + b + c)(a - b + c) > 0$; statement (iii) and (iv) also true

6.

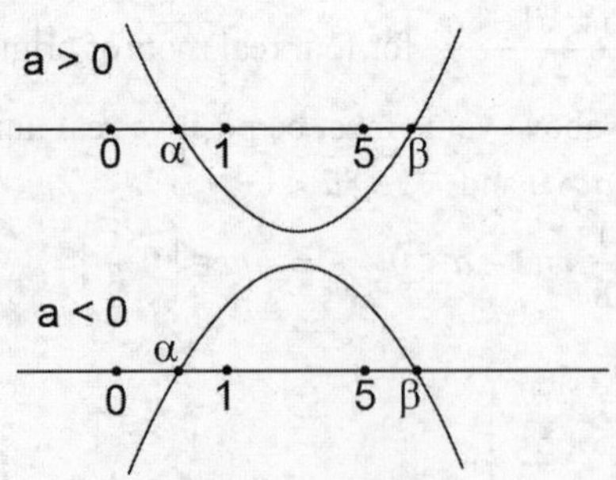

Above two are the possible graphs of $y = ax^2 + bx + c$

Clearly $af(1) < 0$ as $1 \in (\alpha, \beta)$

⇒ $a(a + b + c) < 0$; Statement (i) correct

Also -1 lies outside and 4 lies between the roots $af(-1) > 0$ and $af(4) < 0$

⇒ $f(-1).f(4) < 0$

⇒ $(a - b + c)(16a - 4b + c) < 0$; Statement (iii) is correct

∵ zero lies outside and 3 lies between roots

⇒ $af(0) > 0$ thus $ac > 0$

$af(3) < 0$ therefore $a(9a + 3b + c) < 0$

⇒ Thus sign of $(9a + 3b + c)$ depends on sign of a, so ac $(9a + 3b + c) < 0$ if $a > 0$ and > 0 if $a < 0$

∴ Statement (iii) is incorrect

7. ∵ $c < 0 < b$ and $\alpha, \beta\ (\alpha < \beta)$ be roots of $x^2 + bx + c = 0$

$\alpha + \beta = -b < 0$ and $\alpha\beta = c < 0$

Thus both roots are of opposite sign (as $\alpha\beta < 0$) and negative root is larger in magnitude (as $\alpha + \beta < 0$)

⇒ $\alpha < 0 < \beta$ & $|\alpha| > |\beta| = \beta$

⇒ $\alpha < 0 < \beta < |\alpha|$

Aliter:

As per graph ∵ $f(0) = c < 0$ and vertex lies in 3rd quadrant

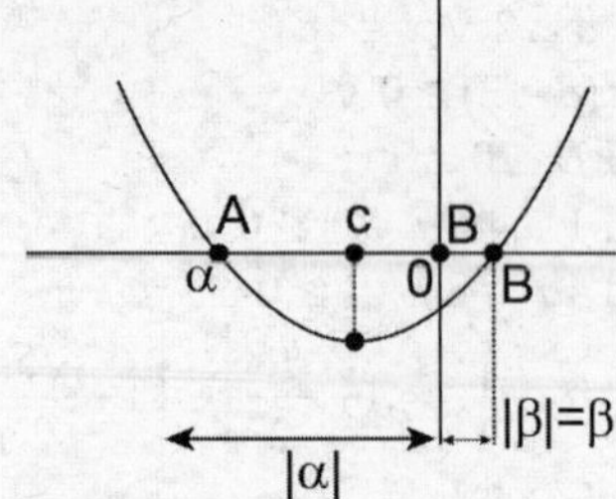

Clearly $\alpha < 0 < \beta$, Also $AC = CB$

⇒ $OA > OB \qquad ⇒\ |\alpha| > |\beta| = \beta$

8. Consider the function $4^x - a.2^x - a + 3$ to have at least one real root. Let $2^x = t \in (0, \infty)$

$f(t) = t^2 - at - a + 3$ must have atleast one positive real root therefore both roots of $f(t)$ should not be non positive

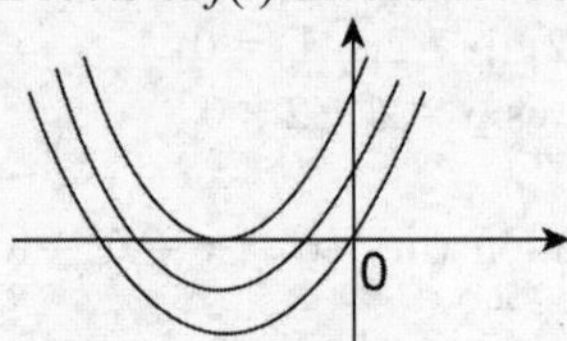

For real root (both non positive)

$$⇒ \begin{cases} D = a^2 + 4(a - 3) \ge 0\ \& \\ f(0) \ge 0 \text{ i.e.,} -a + 3 \ge 0\ \& \\ \dfrac{a}{2} < 0 \end{cases}$$

$$⇒ \begin{cases} (a + 6)(a - 2) \ge 0\ \& \\ a \le 3\ \& \\ a < 0 \end{cases}$$

Taking intersection, we get $a \in (-\infty, -6]$

⇒ $a \in [2, \infty)$ for atleast one root positive root.

9. $y = \dfrac{x^2 + 2x - 11}{x - 3}$

$= x^2 + (2 - y)x + 3y - 11 = 0$ has real roots $(2 - y)^2 - 4(3y - 11) \ge 0$

⇒ $y^2 - 16y + 48 \ge 0$

⇒ $(y - 12)(y - 4) \ge 0$

⇒ $y \in (-\infty, 4] \cup [12, \infty)$

Thus range of function is $(-\infty, 4] \cup [12, \infty)$, so clearly it can take values that does not lie in the interval (4,12)

10. Consider $f(x) = \dfrac{\tan x}{\tan 3x}$

⇒ $y = \dfrac{\tan x}{\dfrac{3\tan x - \tan^3 x}{1 - 3\tan^2 x}} \quad ⇒\ y = \dfrac{1 - 3\tan^2 x}{3 - \tan^2 x}$

$\Rightarrow$ $3y - y\tan^2 x = 1 - 3\tan^2 x$

$\Rightarrow$ $3y - 1 = (y - 3)\tan^2 x$ $\Rightarrow$ $\tan^2 x = \dfrac{3y-1}{y-3}$

$\because$ $\tan^2 x \in [0, \infty)$ $\Rightarrow$ $\dfrac{3y-1}{y-3} \geq 0$

$\Rightarrow$ $y \in \left(-\infty, \dfrac{1}{3}\right) \cup (3, \infty)$

Therefore clearly $f(x)$ never takes value between 1/3 and 3.

TEXTUAL EXERCISE-7: (OBJECTIVE)

1. (c), (d) The graph opening upward, thus a > 0 and roots are real, so $D > 0$ and $b^2 > 4ac$

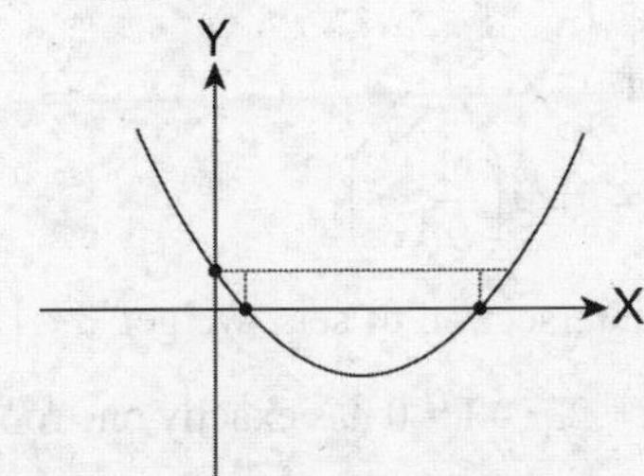

Also y intercept positive implies $c > 0$ and vertex has positive abscissa, therefore $-\dfrac{b}{2a} > 0$

$\Rightarrow$ $\dfrac{b}{a} < 0$ $\Rightarrow$ $b < 0$

$\because$ $a > 0$

Thus a and b are of opposite sign

2. (d) $x^2 + 2bx + c > 0\ \forall\ x \in \mathbb{R}$ iff leading coefficient is positive and $D < 0$

$\Rightarrow$ $4b^2 - 4c < 0$

$\Rightarrow$ $b^2 - c < 0$

$\Rightarrow$ $b^2 < c$

3. (c) $\because$ $ax^2 + bx + c = 0$ has no real root

$\Rightarrow$ $af(x) > 0\ \forall\ x \in \mathbb{R}$

Also given $a + b + c < 0$

$\Rightarrow$ $f(1) < 0$

$\Rightarrow$ $a < 0$

$\because$ $af(1) > 0$ and as $af(0) > 0$

$\Rightarrow$ $ac > 0$ $\Rightarrow$ $c < 0$

$\because$ $a < 0$

4. (a) $f(x) = ax^2 - bx + c$ $\because$ $c > 0$

$\Rightarrow$ $f(0) > 0$ and $4a + c < 2b$ $4a + c - 2b < 0$

$\Rightarrow$ $f(-2) < 0$

$\Rightarrow$ $f(x)$ changes its sign between 0 and 2

$\Rightarrow$ $f(x) = 0$ has a root between 0 and 2

5. (c) $3x^2 + 2(a^2 + 1)x + a^2 - 3a + 2 = 0$ posses roots α, β of opposite sign

$\Rightarrow$ $\alpha\beta < 0$ $\Rightarrow$ $\dfrac{a^2 - 3a + 2}{3} < 0$

$\Rightarrow$ $(a-1)(a-2) < 0$ $\Rightarrow$ $a \in (1, 2)$

6. (b) $f(x) = ax^2 + bx + c$

$a > 0, b > 0, c > 0$

$\Rightarrow$ $\alpha\beta = ->$ and $\alpha + \beta = \dfrac{-b}{a} < 0$

$D = b^2 - 4ac$ can be positive or negative, thus roots are not necessary real

$\Rightarrow$ $\alpha + \beta = 2R(\alpha) = -b/a < 0$

$\Rightarrow$ Real part of root must be negative

7. (a) Given $a, b \in \mathbb{R}$ and the equation $x^2 - abx - a^2 = 0$

$\Rightarrow$ $D = a^2b^2 - a^2 = 0$ and product of root $= -a^2 \leq 0$, thus both roots are real and of opposite sign

8. (b) Given $f(x) = ax^2 + 2bx - 3c$ has non real root i.e., $D < 0$ and $f(2) = 4(a + b) - 3c > 0$

Therefore $f(x) > 0\ \forall\ x \in \mathbb{R}$

$\Rightarrow$ $f(0) > 0$ $\Rightarrow$ $c > 0$

9. (d) From the graph it is clear that $f(x) = 0$ has one root $\in (-\infty, a)$ and other $\in (b, \infty)$

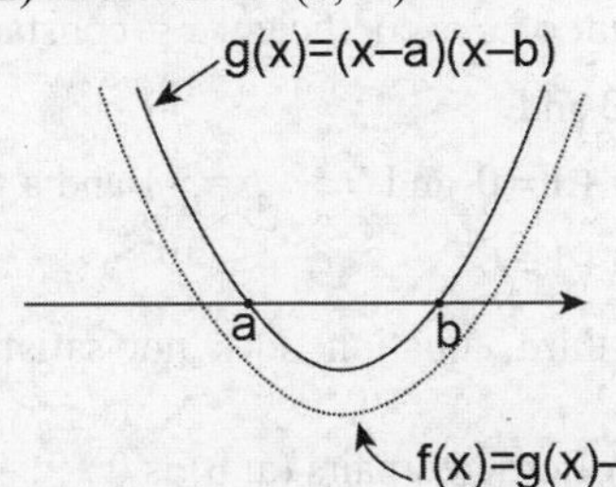

Aliter: $f(-\infty) \to \infty$; $f(0) = -1$; $f(b) = -1$; $f(\infty) \to \infty$

$\Rightarrow$ $f(-\infty)\ f(a) < 0$ thus one root lies in $(-\infty, a)$

$\Rightarrow$ $f(b)\ f(\infty) < 0$ therefore one root lies (b, ∞)

10. (a) $y = \dfrac{x^2 - x}{1 - ax}$ attains all real values

$\Rightarrow$ $y - ayx = x^2 - x$

$\Rightarrow$ $x^2 + (ay - 1)x - y = 0$

$\Rightarrow$ $D \geq 0$

$\Rightarrow$ $(ay - 1)^2 + 4y \geq 0\ \forall\ y \in \mathbb{R}$

$\Rightarrow$ $a^2y^2 + (4 - 2a)y + 1 \geq 0\ \forall\ x \in \mathbb{R}$

$\Rightarrow$ $D \leq 0$

$\Rightarrow$ $(4 - 2a)^2 - 4a^2 \leq 0$

$\Rightarrow$ $(4 - 2a - 2a)(4 - 2a + 2a) \leq 0$

$\Rightarrow$ $16(1 - a) \leq 0$

$\Rightarrow$ $a \geq 1$ i.e., $a \in [1, \infty)$

11. (b) $\because$ $f(x) = -a^2x^2 + bx - c$

$\therefore$ $f(x) < 0\ \forall\ \mathbb{R}$ is true iff $-a^2 < 0$ and $D < 0$

$\Rightarrow$ $a \in \mathbb{R} \sim \{0\}$ and $b^2 - 4a^2c < 0$

$\Rightarrow$ $a \in \mathbb{R} \sim \{0\}$ and $b^2 < 4a^2c$

12. (b) $x^2 + 3x - 10 < 0$ and $x^2 > 9$

$\Rightarrow$ $(x + 5)(x - 2) < 0$ and $(x - 3)(x + 3) > 0$

$\Rightarrow$ $x \in (-5, 2)$ and $c\ (-\infty, -3) \cup (3, \infty)$

$\Rightarrow$ $x \in (-5, -3)$ $\Rightarrow$ $x \in \{-4\}$

Clearly the greatest negative integer $x = -4$

13. (d) $200 - x(10 + x) > 0$

$\Rightarrow$ $x^2 + 10x - 200 < 0$

$\Rightarrow$ $(x - 20)(x + 10) < 0$

$\Rightarrow$ $x \in (-10, 20)$ $\because$ x is integer

$\Rightarrow$ $x \in \{-9, -8, \ldots, 19\}$ $\Rightarrow$ $x_{max} = 19$

14. (b) Given $a \neq b$ and $x \in \mathbb{R}$

$f(x) = x^2 - (a + b)x + a^2 - ab + b^2$

Clearly leading coefficient > 0

$D = (a + b)^2 - 4(a^2 - ab + b^2)$

$= -(3a^2 + 3b^2 - 6ab)$

$= -3(a - b)^2 < 0$

Thus $f(x)$ has same sign as it leading coefficient.

$\therefore\ f(x) > 0\ \forall\ x \in \mathbb{R}$

15. (b) $4x^2 + k + 3 \ge 0\ \forall\ x \in \mathbb{R}$

$\Rightarrow D \le 0$

$\Rightarrow k^2 - 48 \le 0$

$\Rightarrow (k - 4\sqrt{3})(k + 4\sqrt{3})$

$\Rightarrow k \in [-4\sqrt{3}, 4\sqrt{3}]$

16. (a) Consider the equation $(x + a)^2 + b(x^2 - 3x - 2) + x + 1 = 0$ to be an identity in x

Coefficient of x^2 = coefficient x = constant term = 0

$$\Rightarrow \begin{cases} 1 + b = 0 \text{ and} \\ 2a - 3b + 1 = 0 \text{ and } \Rightarrow\ b = -1 \text{ and } a = -2 \\ a^2 - 2b + 1 = 0 \end{cases}$$

But the third equation does not satisfying for these value

$\Rightarrow$ Number of ordered pairs (a, b) is 0

17. (a) Given equation is $\sqrt{x-5}\left(x^2 - 5x + 4\right) = 0$

Solving, we get $x = 5, 4$ but for $x = 4$, $\sqrt{x-5}$ become imaginary thus only root of equation in set of real number is $x = 5$.

TEXTUAL EXERCISE–9: (SUBJECTIVE)

1. $x^2 - 2ax + a^2 + a - 3 = 0$ has both roots real and less than 3.

$\because$ leading coefficient positive graph is *parabola* opening upward

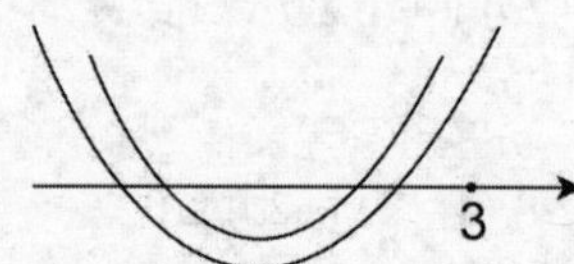

$\Rightarrow D \ge 0,\ f(3) > 0, \dfrac{-b}{2a} < 3$

$$\Rightarrow \begin{cases} 4a^2 - 4\left(a^2 + a - 3\right) \ge 0 \\ \text{and} \\ 9 - 6a + a^2 + a - 3 > 0 \\ \text{and} \\ \dfrac{2a}{2} < 3 \end{cases} \Rightarrow \begin{cases} a - 3 \le 0 \\ \text{and} \\ a^2 - 5a + 6 > 0 \\ \text{and} \\ a < 3 \end{cases}$$

$\Rightarrow (a - 2)(a - 3) > 0$ and $a < 3$

$\Rightarrow a \in (-\infty, 2) \cup (3, \infty)$ and $a < 3$

$\Rightarrow a \in (-\infty, 2)$

2. (i) Given both roots of $x^2 - 6ax + 2 - 2a + 9a^2 = 0$

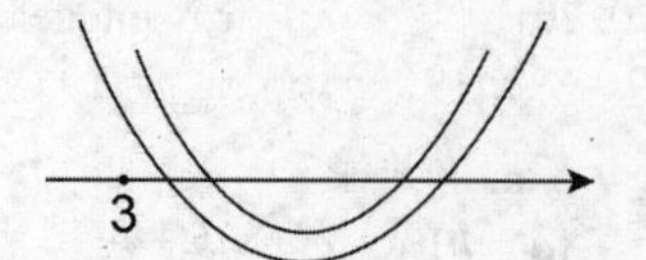

$\Rightarrow D = 36a^2 - 4(2 - 2a + 9a^2) \ge 0$ and $f(3) = 9 - 18a + 2 - 2a + 9a^2 > 0$ and abscissa of vertex > 3 i.e., $\dfrac{6a}{2} > 3$

$$\Rightarrow \begin{cases} 8(a-1) \ge 0 & \text{....}(i) \\ 9a^2 - 20a + 11 > 0 & \text{.....}(ii) \\ a > 1 & \text{....}(iii) \end{cases}$$

$$\Rightarrow \begin{cases} a \in (1, \infty) \\ \text{and} \\ (9a - 11)(a - 1) > 0 \end{cases}$$

$$\Rightarrow \begin{cases} a \in (1, \infty) \\ \text{and} \\ a \in (-\infty, 1) \cup \left(\dfrac{11}{9}, \infty\right) \end{cases}$$

Taking intersection of sets, we get $a \in \left(\dfrac{11}{9}, \infty\right)$

(ii) $x^2 + 2ax + 2a^2 - 1 = 0$ has exactly one root in the interval (0, 1)

$\Rightarrow f(0).f(1) < 0$

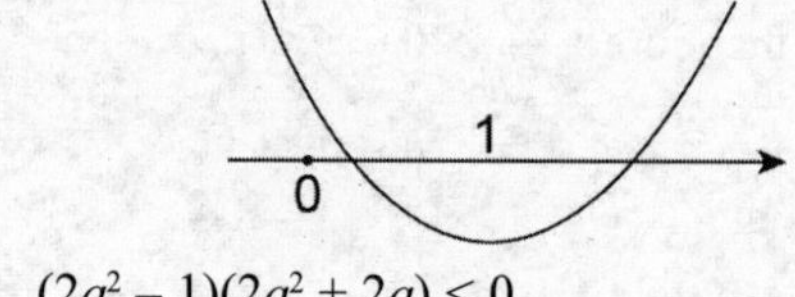

$\Rightarrow (2a^2 - 1)(2a^2 + 2a) < 0$

$\Rightarrow \left(a\sqrt{2} - 1\right)\left(a\sqrt{2} + 1\right)a(a + 1) < 0$

+ − + − +

−1 −1/√2 0 1/√2

$\Rightarrow a \in \left(-1, \dfrac{-1}{\sqrt{2}}\right) \cup \left(0, \dfrac{1}{\sqrt{2}}\right)$

3. $f(x) = x^2 + (2k - 1)x + 4$ has both root $\in (-1, 1)$

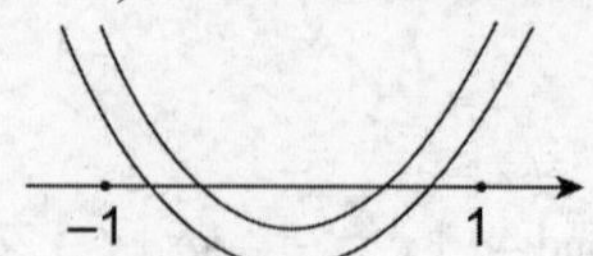

$\Rightarrow D \ge 0$, $f(-1) > 0$ and $f(1) > 0$

$$\Rightarrow \begin{cases} (2k-1)^2 - 4^2 \ge 0\ \& \\ 1 + 1 - 2k + 4 > 0\ \&\ 1 + 2k - 1 + 4 > 0 \end{cases}$$

$$\Rightarrow \begin{cases} (2k-5)(2k+3) \ge \text{i.e., } k \in \left(-\infty, \dfrac{3}{2}\right] \cup \left[\dfrac{5}{2}, \infty\right)\ \& \\ x \in (-2, 3) \end{cases}$$

$\Rightarrow \left(-2, \dfrac{-3}{2}\right] \cup \left[\dfrac{5}{2}, 3\right)$

4. $f(x) = (k^2 + k + 1)x^2 + (k - 1)x + k^2$ has one root greater than 3 and other less than 3

$\Rightarrow$ Real number 3 lies between the root

$\because$ graph opening upwards on $k^2 + k + 1 > 0 \ \forall \ x \in \mathbb{R}$

$\Rightarrow$ $f(3) < 0$

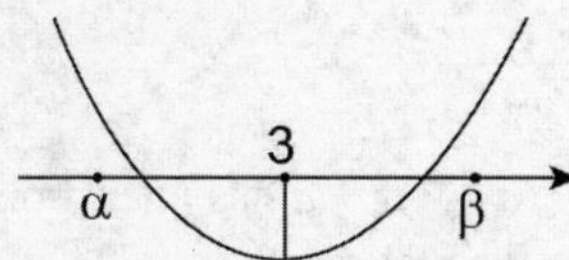

$\Rightarrow$ $9(k^2 + k + 1) + 3\,(k - 1) + k^2 < 0$

$\Rightarrow$ $10k^2 + 12k + 6 < 0$

$\Rightarrow$ $5k^2 + 6k + 3 < 0$, never true because leading coefficient $5 > 0$ and $D = 36 - 60 < 0$

Thus $5k^2 + 6k + 3 > 0 \ \forall \ x \in \mathbb{R}$

$\Rightarrow$ $k \in \{\}$

5. **(a)** $f(x) = x^2 + 2kx + 1$ has both root < 1

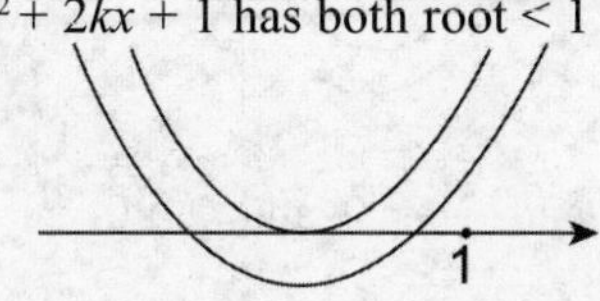

$\Rightarrow$ $D \geq 0,\ f(1) > 0\ ,\ \dfrac{-b}{2a} < 1$

$\Rightarrow$ $(4k - 4^2) \geq 0$ and $2(1 + k) > 0$ and $-k < 1$

$$\Rightarrow \begin{cases} k \in (-\infty, -1] \cup [1, \infty) \\ \quad \text{and} \\ k \in (-1, \infty) \end{cases}$$

Taking intersection of solutions we get $k \in [1, \infty)$

(b) $f(x) = x^2 + 2kx + 1$ has both roots positive

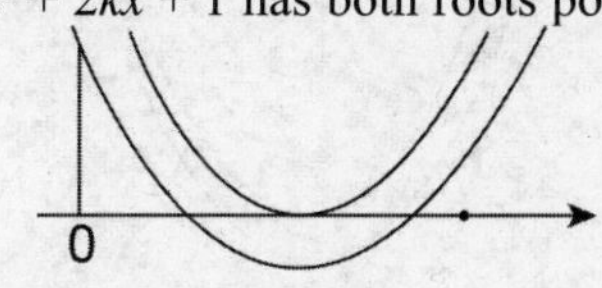

$\Rightarrow$ $D \geq 0,\ f(0) > 0,\ -\dfrac{b}{2a} > 0$

$\Rightarrow$ $k^2 - 1 \geq 0,\ 1 > 0,\ -k > 0$

$\Rightarrow$ $k \in (-\infty, -1] \cup [1, \infty)$ & $k \in \mathbb{R}$ and $x \in (-\infty\ ,\ 0)$

Taking intersection of the above three sets, we get $k \in (-\infty, -1]$

6. Given that 6 lie between root of $f(x) = x^2 + 2(p - 3)\,x + 9$

$\Rightarrow$ $af(6) < 0$ $\qquad \because \ a = 1$

$\Rightarrow$ $f(6) < 0$ $\qquad 36 + 12(p - 3) + 9 < 0$

$\Rightarrow$ $12p + 9 < 0$ $\qquad \Rightarrow \ p < -3/4$

$\Rightarrow$ $p \in \left(-\infty, -\dfrac{3}{4}\right)$

7. $\because$ Both roots of $f(x) = x^2 - mx + 1$ are less than 1

$$\Rightarrow \begin{cases} D \geq 0 \\ f(1) > 0 \\ \dfrac{-b}{2a} < 1 \end{cases}$$

f(1)>0

1

8. Given $a < b < c < d$ and let $f(x) = (x - a)\,(x - c) + 3(x - b)\,(x - d)$

$f(a) = 0 + 3\,(a - b)\,(a - d) > 0$

$f(b) = (b - a)\,(b - c) < 0$

$f(c) = 0 + 3\,(c - b)\,(c - d) < 0$

$f(d) = (d - a)\,(d - c) > 0$

$\Rightarrow$ One root lie in (a, b) and other lie in (c, d)

$\Rightarrow$ $f(x)$ has both roots real and distinct

9. Given $\left|\dfrac{x^2 + kx + 1}{x^2 + x + 1}\right| < 2$

$\Rightarrow$ $-2 < \dfrac{x^2 + kx + 1}{x^2 + x + 1} < 2$

$\Rightarrow$ $-2x^2 - 2x - 2 < x^2 + kx + 1 < 2x^2 + 2x$

$$\Rightarrow \begin{cases} 3x^2 + (k + 2)x + 3 > 0 \\ \quad \& \\ x^2 + (2 - k)x + 1 > 0 \forall x \in \mathbb{R} \end{cases}$$

$\Rightarrow$ Discriminant of both quadratic functions must be negative

$(k + 2)^2 - 36 < 0$ and $(2 - k)^2 - 4 < 0$

$\Rightarrow$ $(k - 4)\,(k + 8) <$ and $k(k - 4) < 0$

$\Rightarrow$ $k \in (-8, 4)$ and $k \in (0, 4)$

10. Given $m \in (0, 3)$

$f(x) = (m - 2)x^2 - (8 - 2m)\,x - (8 - 3m)$

$D = (8 - 2m)^2 + 4\,(8 - 3m)\,(m - 2)$

$= 64 + 4m^2 - 32m + 4\,(14m - 16 - 3m^2)$

$= -8m^2 + 24m = -8m\,(m - 3)$

Clearly for $D > 0$; $m\,(m - 3) < 0$ i.e., $m \in (0, 3)$

$\therefore$ both roots of $f(x) = 0$ are real as $m \in (0, 3)$ given

Now for one positive other negative root

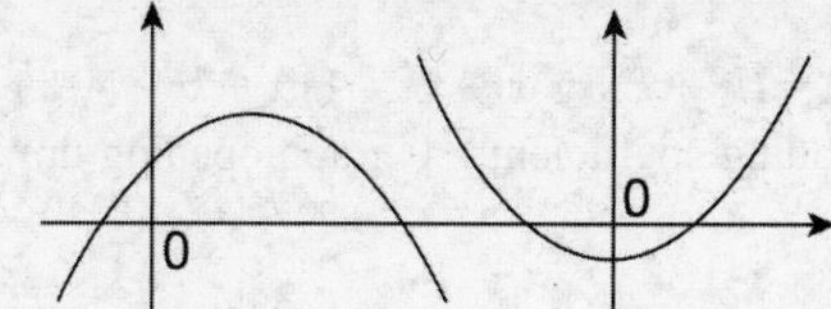

$af(0) < 0$

$\Rightarrow$ $(m - 2)\,(3m - 8) < 0 \Rightarrow \ m \in \left(2, \dfrac{8}{3}\right)$

11. $\tan^2 x + (a + 1)\tan x + 2a - 1 < 0$

Let $\tan^2 x = p$

$p^2 + (a + 1)p + 2a - 1 < 0$

$\Rightarrow$ $-(a + 1)^2 + 4\,(2a - 1) < 0$

$\Rightarrow$ $-a^2 - 1 - 2a + 8a - 4 < 0$

$\Rightarrow$ $-a^2 + 6a - 5 < 0$

$\Rightarrow$ $a^2 - 6a + 5 < 0$

$\Rightarrow$ $(a - 1)\,(a - 5) < 0$

For at least one root $x \in \left(0 < \dfrac{\pi}{2}\right)$

$\Rightarrow$ $a \in (-\infty, 1) \cup (5, \infty)$

12. $x^2 + ax + a^2 + 6a < 0$
This means that for $x \in (1, 2)$
The above inequation always holds.
$a^2 + a(x + 6) + 1 < 0$ in which $x \in (1, 2)$
$\Rightarrow\ a = \{\ \}$

TEXTUAL EXERCISE–8: (OBJECTIVE)

1. **(b)** Exactly one root of $f(x) = 5x^2 + (a + 1)x + a$ lie in interval (1, 3)
$\Rightarrow\ f(1)\ f(3) < 0$

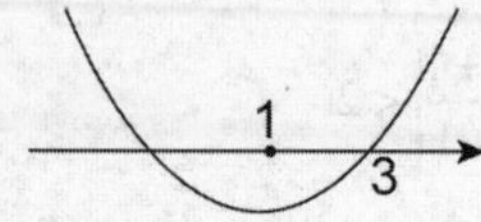

$\Rightarrow\ (2a + 6)(4a + 48) < 0$
$\Rightarrow\ (a + 3)(a + 12) < 0$
$\Rightarrow\ a \in (-12, -3)$

2. **(b)** $f(x) = x^2 - 2(a - 1)x + (2a + 1)$ has both root positive

$$\Rightarrow \begin{cases} D \geq 0 \text{ and } f(0) > 0 \\ \text{and} \\ \text{abscissa of vertex postive} \end{cases}$$

$$\Rightarrow \begin{cases} 4(a-1)^2 - 4(2a+1) \geq 0 \\ \text{and} \\ (2a+1) \geq 0 \\ \text{and} \\ (a-1>0) \end{cases}$$

$$\Rightarrow \begin{cases} a^2 - 4a - 3 \geq 0 \\ \& \\ a - 1/2 \\ \& \\ a > 1 \end{cases}$$

3. **(a)** $f(x) = (k^2 + k + 1)x^2 + (x - 1)x + k^2$
$\because$ Leading coefficient > 0 graph opening upward

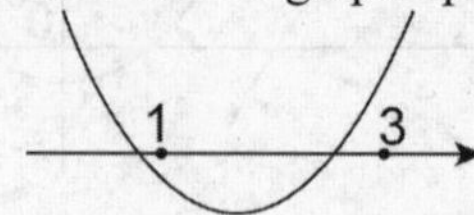

$\because$ Given that 1 and 3 both lie between roots $f(1) < 0$ and $f(3) > 0$
$\Rightarrow\ 2k^2 + 2k < 0$ and $10k^2 + 12k + 6 > 0$
$\Rightarrow\ k(k + 1) < 0$ and $k \in \mathbb{R}$
$\Rightarrow\ k \in (-1, 0)$

4. **(a)** $f(x) = x^2 - 2ax + a^2 + a - 3$ has both roots less than 3

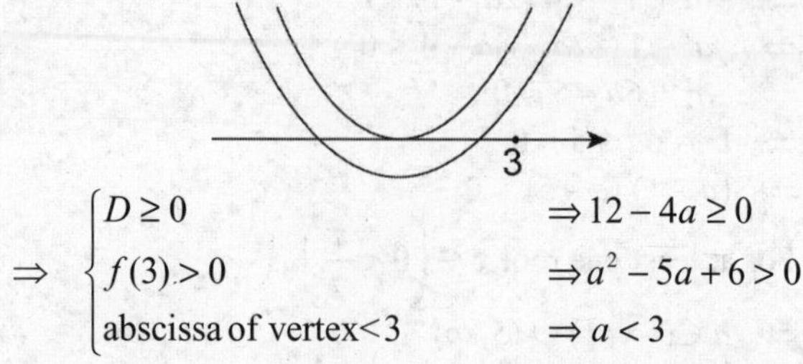

$$\Rightarrow \begin{cases} D \geq 0 \\ f(3) > 0 \\ \text{abscissa of vertex} < 3 \end{cases} \quad \begin{matrix} \Rightarrow 12 - 4a \geq 0 \\ \Rightarrow a^2 - 5a + 6 > 0 \\ \Rightarrow a < 3 \end{matrix}$$

$$\Rightarrow \begin{cases} a \in (-\infty, 3] \\ a \in (-\infty, 2) \cup (3, \infty) \\ a \in (-\infty, 3) \end{cases}$$

$\Rightarrow\ a \in (-\infty, 2)$

5. **(c)** $f(x) = x^2 - (a - 3)x + a$ has atleast one positive root
$\because$ Condition for real root
$D \geq 0 \qquad \Rightarrow\ (a - 1)(a - 9) \geq 0$
$\Rightarrow\ a \in (-\infty, 1] \cup [9, \infty)$
Condition for both root non positive.

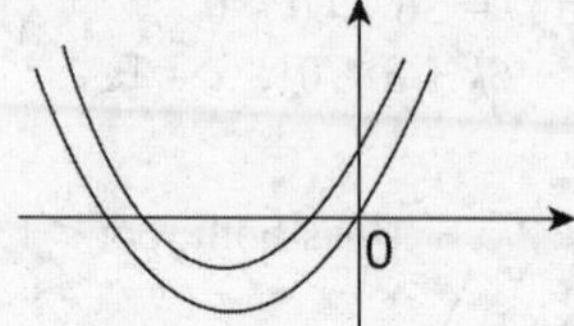

$F(0) \geq 0$ and $\dfrac{-b}{2a} < 0$ and $D \geq 0$

$\Rightarrow\ a \geq 0$ and $\dfrac{a-3}{2} < 0$ and $(a-1)(a-9) \geq 0$
$\Rightarrow\ a \in [0, 3)$ and $a \in (-\infty, 1] \cup (9, \infty)$
$\Rightarrow\ a \in [0, 1]$
Thus condition for atleast one root be positive is $a \in (-\infty, 0) \cup [9, \infty)$

6. **(c)** Given both roots of $f(x) = x^2 - (a - 3)x + a$ are greater than 2.

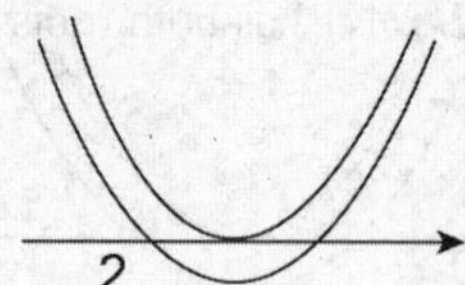

$$\Rightarrow \begin{cases} D \geq 0 \\ f(2) > 0 \\ \dfrac{-b}{2a} > 2 \end{cases} \Rightarrow \begin{cases} a^2 - 10a + 9 \geq 0 \\ 10 - a > 0 \\ \dfrac{2-3}{2} > 2 \end{cases}$$

$\Rightarrow\ a \in (-\infty, 1] \cup [9, \infty)$ and $a < 10$ and $a > 7$
$\Rightarrow\ a \in [9, 10)$

7. **(d)** $f(x) = x^2 - ax - a^2$ has both roots larger than a.

$$\Rightarrow \begin{cases} D \geq 0 \\ f(a) > 0 \\ \text{abscissa of vertex} > a \end{cases}$$

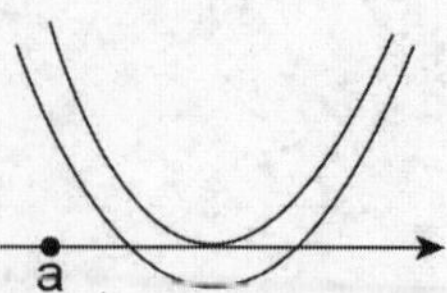

$$\Rightarrow \begin{cases} a^2 + 4a^2 \geq 0\ \& \\ -a^2 > 0\ \& \\ a/2 > a \end{cases} \Rightarrow \begin{cases} a \in \{0\}\ \&\ a \in \{\ \}\ \& \\ a \in (-\infty, 0) \end{cases}$$

The intersection of above sets {}

8. (c) Consider equation $f(x) = 2x^2 - 2(2a + 1)x + a(a - 1)$
Given α, β as roots such that $\alpha < a < \beta$

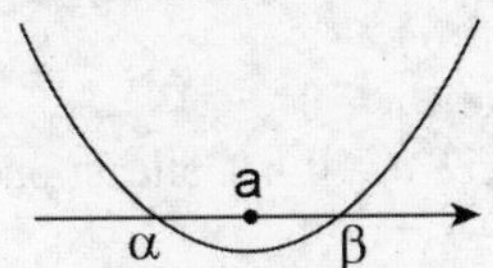

$\Rightarrow f(a) < 0$
$\Rightarrow 2a^2 - 2(2a + 1)a + a^2 - a < 0$
$\Rightarrow -a^2 - 3a < 0$
$\Rightarrow a(d + 3) > 0$
$\Rightarrow a \in (-\infty, -3) \cup (0, \infty)$

9. (b) Given that 6 lies between the roots of $f(x) = x^2 + 2(p - 3)x + 9$
$\Rightarrow f(6) < 0$
$\Rightarrow 36 + 12(p - 3) + 9 < 0$
$\Rightarrow 12p < -9$ i.e., $p < -3/4$
$\Rightarrow p \in (-\infty, -3/4)$

10. (d) $f(x) = x^2 - 2mx + m^2 - 1$ has exactly one root in (–2, 4)
$f(-2). f(4) < 0$
$\Rightarrow (4 + 4m + m^2 - 1)(16 - 8m + m^2 - 1) < 0$
$\Rightarrow (m + 1)(m + 3)(m - 3)(m - 5) < 0$
$\Rightarrow m \in (-3, -1) \cup (3, 5)$

11. (a) $f(x) = 4x^2 - 2x + a$ has two roots $\in (-1, 1)$

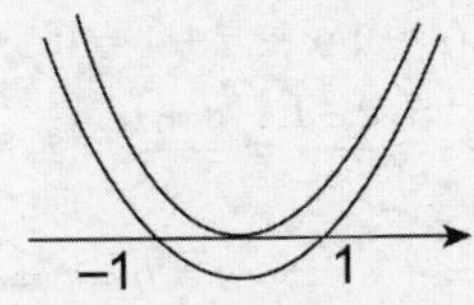

$$\Rightarrow \begin{cases} D \geq 0 \;\&\; f(-1) > 0, f(1) > 0 \\ \& -\dfrac{b}{2a} \in (-1,1) \end{cases}$$

$$\Rightarrow \begin{cases} 4 - 16a \geq 0 \;\& \\ 6 + a > 0 \;\&\; 2 + a > 0 \;\& \\ \dfrac{1}{4} \in (-1,1) \end{cases}$$

$$\Rightarrow a \in \left(-\infty, \frac{1}{4}\right] \cap (-6, \infty) \cap (-2, \infty)$$

$$\Rightarrow a \in \left(-2, \frac{1}{4}\right]$$

12. (c) Equation $x^2 + px + q = 0$ has root α, β and $x^2 + rx + s = 0$ has root $\alpha + h$, $\beta + h$
Difference of root is same for both $|\alpha - \beta| = |\alpha + h - (\beta + h)|$

$$\Rightarrow \frac{\sqrt{p^2 - 4a}}{1} = \frac{\sqrt{r^2 - 4s}}{1}$$

$\Rightarrow p^2 - 4q = r^2 - 4s$

13. (a) $x^2 + 13x + q = 0$; considering coefficients of x as it roots were –2, –15
$\Rightarrow q = (-2)(-15) = 30$

Let correct roots be α, β

$$\Rightarrow \begin{cases} \alpha + \beta = -13 \\ \alpha\beta = 30 \end{cases}$$

$\Rightarrow \alpha = -10, \beta = -3$

14. (a) $f(x) = x^3 + ax^2 + bx - 4 = 0$ has two repeated real root each equal to 2.
$\Rightarrow f(2) = 0$ $\Rightarrow 8 + 4a + 2b - 4 = 0$
$\Rightarrow f'(2) = 0$ $\Rightarrow 12 + 4a + b = 0$
$\Rightarrow 4a + b = -12$ (i)
$\Rightarrow 4a + 2b = -4$ (ii)
Subtracting, we get $b = 8$, $a = -5$

TEXTUAL EXERCISE–10: (SUBJECTIVE)

1. $f(x) = x^3 + ax^2 + bx + c = x^3\left(1 + \dfrac{a}{x} + \dfrac{b}{x^2} + \dfrac{c}{x^3}\right)$
$f(-\infty) = -\infty$
$f(\infty) = \infty$
$\Rightarrow f(x)$ changes its sign
$\Rightarrow f(x)$ has atleast one real root.

2. $f(x) = x^4 - 2x^2 + 3x - 4$

$$\Rightarrow f(x) = x^4\left(1 - \frac{2}{x^2} + \frac{3}{x^3} - \frac{4}{x^4}\right)$$

$f(-\infty) \to \infty$; $f(\infty) \to \infty$; $f(0) \to -4$

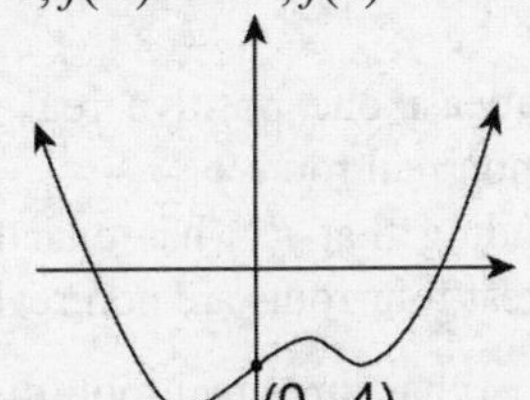

$\Rightarrow$ Clearly one root $\in(-\infty, 0)$ and other $(0, \infty)$, therefore two real roots of opposite sign.

3. $f(x) = x^3 - 9x + 1$
$f'(x) = 3x^2 - 9$
$f'(x) = 3(x - \sqrt{3})(x + \sqrt{3})$

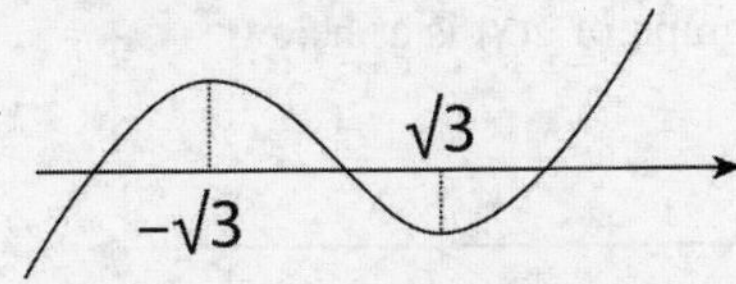

$f(x)$ has maxima at $x = \sqrt{-3}$ and minima at $x = \sqrt{3}$
$f(-\sqrt{3}) = -3\sqrt{3} + 9\sqrt{3} + 1 = 6\sqrt{3} + 1$
$f(\sqrt{3}) = 1 - 6\sqrt{3}$ $\because f(-\sqrt{3}) f(\sqrt{3}) < 0$
$\Rightarrow f(x)$ must have all three real roots

4. $f(x) = x^3 + 3kx^2 + mx + 1$ has $x = 1$ as root repeated twice.
$f(1) = 0$ and $f'(1) = 0$

$$\Rightarrow \begin{cases} 3k + m + 2 = 0 \\ \& \\ 6k + m + 3 = 0 \end{cases} \Rightarrow 3k = -1, \text{ thus } k = -1/3$$

$\Rightarrow m = -1$
$f(x) = x^3 - x^2 - x + 1$
$\Rightarrow$ Clearly roots are 1, 1, –1, –1

5. $\because$ a, b, c, d are positive and $e < 0$
$f(x) = ax^5 + bx^4 + cx^2 + dx + e$
$\Rightarrow$ $f(x)$ has almost one +ve real root
$f(-x) = -ax^5 + bx^4 + cx^2 - dx + e$
$\Rightarrow$ $f(x)$ has almost two negative real root
$\Rightarrow$ $f(x)$ has almost 3 real root thus atleast two non real root
But $f(x)$ has atleast one negative and are positive real root.
$\Rightarrow$ $f(x)$ has exactly one negative and at least one positive root but $f(x)$ can't have even number of real root as its degree is odd and non real root occur in pairs (conjugate)
$\Rightarrow$ $f(x)$ has at least two positive real root but decants rule of sign concludes atmost two positive real root thus confirming the existence of exactly two positive real root.
So we finally conclude that $f(x)$ exactly one negative exactly two positive & exactly two non real roots.

6. **(i)** $f(x) = x^7 - 4x^3 + 3x + 1$ has two change in sign of coefficient, thus has at most two positive real root
$f(x) = -x^7 + 4x^3 - 3x + 1$
Thus $f(x)$ has at the most three negative real root
$\Rightarrow$ Atmost 5 real root thus atleast two non-real roots.
(ii) $f(x) = x^5 + 3x^3 - 1$
$f(-x) = -x^5 - 3x^3 - 1$
$f(x)$ has atmost one positive real root and no negative real root.
$f(x)$ has atleast one positive real root as it can have atmost 4 non real roots.
So concluding that $f(x)$ has exactly one positive real root and rest four roots are non real complex conjugate

7. $f(x) = x^3 + 3x + a$ has three real root (distinct).
Iff $f'(x)$ has two real root α and β and $f(\alpha) f(\beta) < 0$
$\therefore$ $f'(x) = 3x^2 - 3 = 0$ $\Rightarrow x = \pm 1$ and $f(-1) f(1) < 0$
$\Rightarrow$ $(a - 2)(a + 2) < 0$ $\Rightarrow$ $a \in (-2, 2)$

8. $f(x) = x^4 - 4x^3 - 8x^2 + k = g(x) + k$ (say)
Thus $g(x) = x^4 - 4x^3 - 8x^2 = x^2(x^2 - 4x - 8)$
$g'(x) = 4x^3 - 12x^2 - 16x = 4x(x^2 - 3x - 4) = 4x(x - 4)(x + 1)$, thus the graph of $g(x)$ is as below.

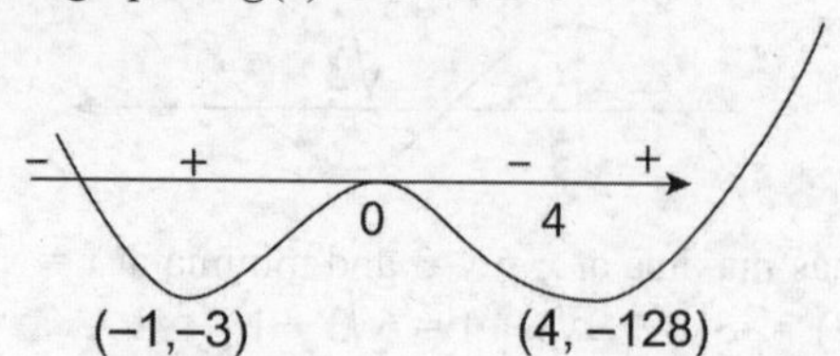

$g(-1) = -3$, $g(0) = 0$, $g(4) = -128$
$\because$ $f(x)$ is obtained by shifting graph of $g(x)$ by $|k|$ unit vertically, thus $\forall\, k \in (0, 3)$
$f(x)$ has 4 real and distinct roots and for $k \in [0, 3]$, it has 4 real roots.

9. Consider $f'(x) = 3ax^2 + 2bx + c$
$\Rightarrow$ $f(x) = ax^3 + bx^2 + cx + d$
Clearly $f(0) = d$ and $f(1) = a + b + c + d = d$
$\because$ $a + b + c = 0$ (given)
$\because$ f is continuous and differentiable function $\forall\, x \in \mathbb{R}$
$f(0) = f(1)$ thus by Rolles theorem $\exists$ at least one $\alpha \in (0, 1)$
Such that $f'(\alpha)$
$\Rightarrow$ $3a\alpha^2 + 2b\alpha + c = 0$
$\Rightarrow$ $3ax^2 + 2bx + c = 0$ has atleast one real root in interval $(0, 1)$

TEXTUAL EXERCISE-9: (OBJECTIVE)

1. **(b)** Let $f'(x) = ax^2 + bx + c$
$\Rightarrow$ $f(x) = \dfrac{ax^3}{3} + \dfrac{bx^2}{2} + cx + d \Rightarrow f(0) = d$
$\Rightarrow$ $f(1) = \dfrac{a}{3} + \dfrac{b}{2} + c + d = \dfrac{2a + 3b + 6c}{6} + d = 0$
$\because$ f is continuous and differentiable in $[0, 1]$ and $f(0) = f(1)$
By Rolles theorem $f'(x)$ has atleast one real root $\in (0, 1)$

2. **(c)** $f(x) = x^4 - 4x - 1$
By Decart's rule of sign $f(x)$ has atmost one positive and one negative real root.
$\because$ $f(-\infty)\, f(0) < 0$ and $f(0)\, f(\infty) < 0$; thus $f(x)$ has atleast one negative and one positive real root.
Therefore $f(x)$ has exactly one negative root, one positive root and exactly two non-real complex roots.

3. **(a)** $\because$ $ax^3 + bx^2 + cx + d = 0$ has same root as $(a + 1)x^3 + (b + 1)x^2\ (c + 1)x + d + 1 = 0$
$\Rightarrow$ $\dfrac{a+1}{a} = \dfrac{b+1}{b} = \dfrac{c+1}{c} = \dfrac{d+1}{d}$
$\Rightarrow$ $\dfrac{1}{a} = \dfrac{1}{b} = \dfrac{1}{c} = \dfrac{1}{d}$ $\Rightarrow a = b = c = d \neq 0$

4. **(b)** $(x - 1)^3$ is factor of $f(x) = x^4 + ax^3 + bx^2 + cx - 1$
$\Rightarrow$ $f(1) = 0, f'(1) = 0, f''(1) = 0$
$$\Rightarrow \begin{cases} a + b + c = 0 & \text{...(i)} \\ 3a + 2b + c = -4 & \text{...(ii)} \\ 6a + 2b = -12 & \text{...(iii)} \end{cases}$$
$$\Rightarrow \begin{cases} 2a + b = 4 & \text{...(iv) from (i) (ii)} \\ 3a + b = -6 & \text{...(v) from (iii)} \end{cases}$$
$\Rightarrow$ $a = -2, b = 0, c = 2$
$\Rightarrow$ $f(x) = x^4 - 2x^3 + 2x - 1$ has roots 1, 1, 1, α (say)
$\Rightarrow$ $3 + \alpha = 2$ $\Rightarrow \alpha = -1$
$\therefore$ Clearly fourth factor is $(x + 1)$

5. **(c)** Consider inequation $16 - x^2 > |x - a|$
Sketching graph of $y = 16 - x^2$ and $y = |x - a|$ as below

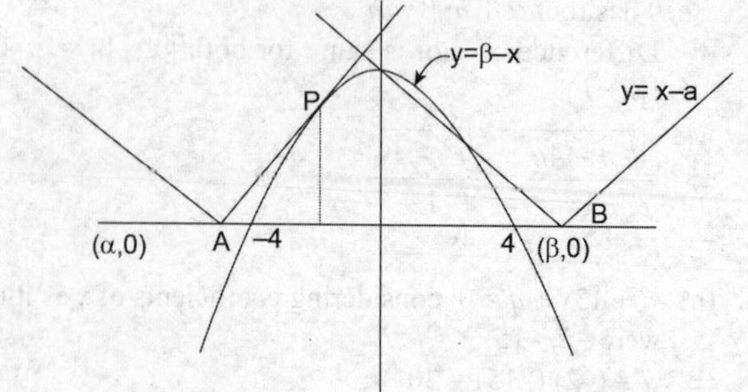

Clearly the inequality to be satisfied by atleast one negative 'x' i.e., $\alpha < a < \beta$

For α: $y = x - \alpha$ touches and $y = 16 - x^2$

$\Rightarrow -2x = 1$ i.e., $x = -1/2$

Point of contact $\left(-\frac{1}{2}, \frac{63}{4}\right)$

$\Rightarrow \alpha = -\frac{1}{2} - \frac{63}{4} = -\frac{65}{4}$

For β: $y = \beta - x$ pass through (0, 16)

$\Rightarrow \beta = 16$

$\Rightarrow a \in \left(-\frac{65}{4}, 16\right)$

6 (b) $y = |x - 1|$ and $y = e^x$

Sketching the graph on some frame of reference

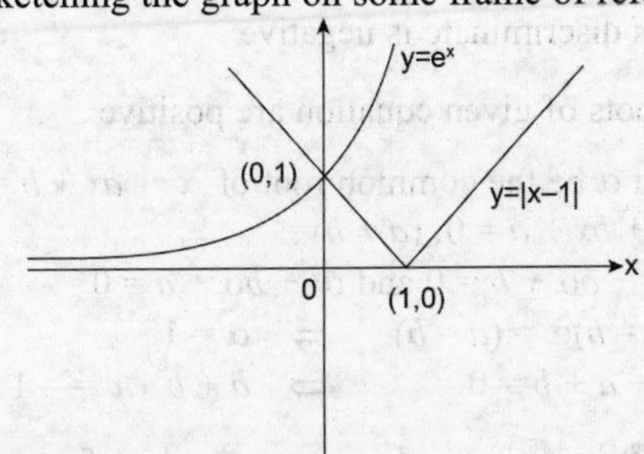

Clearly $|x - 1| = e^x$ has exactly one real root i.e., $x = 0$

7. (a) α, β, γ be roots of equation $f(x) = x^3 - px - q = 0$

$\alpha + \beta + \gamma = 0$ (i)

$\alpha\beta + \beta\gamma + \gamma\alpha = -p$ (ii)

$\alpha\beta\gamma = q$ (iii)

$(2\alpha + \beta + \gamma)(2\beta + \gamma + \alpha)(2\gamma + \alpha + \beta) = \alpha\beta\gamma = q$

8. (b) $f(x) = 2x^4 - 7x^3 + 2x^2 - x + 1$, leave reminder $px + q$ when divided by $x^2 - 1$

$f(x) = (x^2 - 1)\, g(x) + px + q$

Putting $x = -1, 1$, we get

$f(-1) = a - p = 13$ (i)

$f(1) = p + q = -3$ (ii)

Adding, we get $q = 5$ and $p = -8$

Ordered pair (p, q) is $(-8, 5)$

9. (d) Given $x^3 + 7x^2 - 36 = 0$ has one root double of other.

Let α, $2\alpha + \beta$ be roots

$\Rightarrow 3\alpha + \beta = -7$ (i)

$2\alpha^2\beta = 36$ (ii)

$2\alpha^2 + 3\alpha\beta$ (iii)

$\alpha(2\alpha + 3\beta) = 0$

$\Rightarrow$ Either $\alpha = 0$ or $\alpha = -\frac{3\beta}{2}$ but $\alpha \neq 0$

$\Rightarrow 2\alpha = -3\beta$ put in (iii), we get $3\left(\frac{-3\beta}{2}\right) + \beta = -7$

$\Rightarrow -7\beta = -14 \quad \Rightarrow \beta = 2$ and $\alpha = 3$

$\Rightarrow$ Roots are $-3, -6, 2$

10. (a) $f(x) = x^3 + ax^2 + bx - 4$ has two roots equal to 2

Let α be third root

$f(2) = 0 \quad \Rightarrow 2a + b = -2$ (i)

$f'(2) = 0 \quad \Rightarrow 4a + b = -12$ (ii)

From (i) and (ii), we get $a = -5$ and $b = 8$

11. (b) Let α, β, γ be roots of equation $4x^3 + 16x^2 - 9x - 36 = 0$

$\alpha + \beta + \gamma = -4$ (i)

$\alpha\beta + \beta\gamma + \gamma\alpha = -9/4$ (ii)

$\alpha\beta\gamma = 9$ (iii)

$\because \alpha + \beta = 0$ (given)

$\Rightarrow \gamma = -4$ from (i)

From equation (ii) or (iii), we get $\alpha\beta = \frac{-9}{4}$

Clearly $\alpha = \frac{3}{2}$ satisfies the equation $f(3/2) = 0$, thus roots are $\frac{3}{2}, -\frac{3}{2}, -4$

12. (c) Let $f(x, y) = x^3 - 3x^2y + \lambda xy^2 + y^3$

$\because x - y$ is factor, thus $y = x$ is root

$f(x, x) = x^3 - 3x^3 + \lambda x^3 + \mu x^3 = 0$

$\Rightarrow (\lambda + \mu - 2)\, x^3 = 0 \ \forall\, x$

$\Rightarrow \lambda + \mu = 2$ (i)

Also $f(x, 2x) = 0$

$\Rightarrow x^3 - 6x^3 + 4\lambda x^3 + 8\mu x^3 = 0$

$\Rightarrow 4\lambda + 8\mu = 5\sim$ (ii)

Solving (i) and (ii), we get $4\lambda = 11$

$\Rightarrow \lambda = \frac{11}{4}$

Therefore $\mu = 2 - \lambda = 2 - 11/4 = -3/4$

13 (b) $(x + y)$ and $(y + 3x)$ are factors of expression $f(x, y) = \lambda x^3 + \mu x^2y + xy^2 + y^3$

$$\Rightarrow \begin{cases} f(x,-x) = 0 & \Rightarrow (\lambda + \mu + 1 - 1)x^3 = 0 \\ & \Rightarrow \lambda + \mu = 0 \quad \text{...(i)} \\ & \text{and} \\ f(x,-3x) = 0 & \Rightarrow \lambda x^3 + 3\mu x^3 + 9x^3 - 27x^3 = 0 \\ & \Rightarrow \lambda + 3\mu = 18 \quad \text{...(ii)} \end{cases}$$

Solving (i) and (ii), we get $\mu = 9$ and $\lambda = -9$

$\Rightarrow f(x, y) = y^3 - 9x^3 - 9x^2y + xy^2 = y^3 - 9x^2y + xy^2 - 9x^3$

$= y(y^2 - 9x^2) + x(y^2 - 9x^2) = (y + x)(y - 3x)(y + 3x)$

Thus the third factor is $(y - 3x)$

SECTION–III: (SINGLE CORRECT)

1. (c) α, β are the root of equation $(x - a)(x - b) = c$; $c \neq 0$ (i)

$\Rightarrow x^2 - (a + b)\, x + ab - c = 0$

$\Rightarrow \alpha + \beta = (a + b)$; $\alpha\beta = ab - c$

Now, $(x - \alpha)(x - \beta) + c = 0$ (ii)

$\Rightarrow x^2 - (\alpha + \beta)x + \alpha\beta + c = 0$

$\Rightarrow x^2 - (a + b)\, x + ab - c + c = 0$

$\Rightarrow x = a, x = b$ are roots of equation (ii)

2. (b) Let $y = \frac{x^2 + 2x - 11}{x - 3}; x \neq 3$

$\Rightarrow x^2 + (2 - y)\, x + (3y - 11) = 0$

$\therefore x \in \mathbb{R}$

$\Rightarrow (2 - y)^2 - 4\,(1)\,(3y - 11) \geq 0$

$\Rightarrow y^2 - 16\, y + 48 \geq 0$

$\Rightarrow (y-4)(y-12) \geq 0$

$\Rightarrow y \notin (4, 12)$ $\Rightarrow a = 4, b = 12$

3. (a) $\left(\frac{9}{10}\right)^x = -(x^2 - x + 3) = -\left(\left(x-\frac{1}{2}\right)^2 + \frac{11}{4}\right)$

$= -\frac{11}{4} - \left(x - \frac{1}{2}\right)^2$

L.H.S. > 0 where as R.H.S. < 0

Clearly, no solution.

4. (d) Let $y = \sqrt{8+2\sqrt{8+2\sqrt{8+2\sqrt{8+....}}}}$

$\Rightarrow y = \sqrt{8+2y}\ ; y > 0$

$\Rightarrow y^2 = 2y + 8$ $\Rightarrow y^2 - 2y - 8 = 0$

$\Rightarrow (y-4)(y+2) = 0$ $\Rightarrow y = 4$ as $y > 0$

5. (a) Roots of equation $(a^2 + b^2)x^2 - 2b(a+c)x + (b^2 + c^2) = 0$ are equal

$\Rightarrow 4b^2(a+c)^2 - 4(a^2+b^2)(b^2+c^2) = 0$

$\Rightarrow b^2(a+c)^2 - (a^2+b^2)(b^2+c^2) = 0$

$\Rightarrow 2ac\,b^2 - b^4 - a^2c^2 = 0$

$\Rightarrow (b^2 - ac)^2 = 0$ $\Rightarrow b^2 = ac$

$\Rightarrow a, b, c$ are in G.P.

6. (c) Let α, β be the roots of equation $x^2 - cx + d = 0$ (i)

And α, α be that of equation $x^2 - ax + b = 0$ (ii)

$\Rightarrow \alpha^2 - c\alpha + d = \alpha^2 - a\alpha + b = 0$

$\Rightarrow \alpha(a - c) = b - d$

$\Rightarrow \alpha = \frac{(b-d)}{(a-c)}$ $\Rightarrow 2\alpha = a;\ \alpha^2 = b$

$\Rightarrow 2\left(\frac{b-d}{a-c}\right) = a$ and $a^2 = 4b$

$\Rightarrow 2(b-d) = a^2 - ac$ $\Rightarrow 2(b-d) = 4b - ac$

$\Rightarrow 2b - 2d = 4b - ac$ $\Rightarrow 2b + 2d = ac$

7. (a) Let α be the common root

$\Rightarrow a\alpha^2 + 2b\alpha + c = 0$ and $a\alpha^2 + 2c\alpha + b = 0$

$\Rightarrow 2\alpha(b-c) = (b-c)$ $\Rightarrow \alpha = \frac{1}{2}$ as $b \neq c$

$\Rightarrow \frac{a}{4} + \frac{2b}{2} + c = 0$ $\Rightarrow 4c + 4b + a = 0$

8. (b) $(1 + \alpha + \alpha^2)(1 + \beta + \beta^2)$

$= 1 + (\alpha+\beta)(\alpha\beta) + (\alpha\beta)^2 + \alpha\beta(\alpha+\beta) + (\alpha+\beta)^2 - 2\alpha\beta$

$= 1 + (\alpha+\beta) + (\alpha+\beta)^2 - (\alpha\beta) + (\alpha\beta)^2 + (\alpha\beta)(\alpha+\beta)$

$= 1 + \left(\frac{-b}{a}\right) + \left(\frac{-b}{a}\right)^2 - \frac{c}{a} + \frac{c^2}{a_2} + \frac{c}{a}\left(\frac{-b}{a}\right)$

$= 1 - \frac{(b+c)}{a} + \frac{b^2+c^2}{a^2} - \frac{bc}{a^2}$

$= \frac{a^2 - ab - ac + b^2 + c^2 - bc}{a^2}$

$= \frac{(a^2+b^2+c^2) - (ab+bc+ca)}{a^2}$

$= \frac{(a-b)^2 + (b-c)^2 + (c-a)^2}{2a^2} > 0$ for a, b and c distinct

Note that if α, β were real roots, then $\alpha^2 + \alpha + 1$, $\beta^2 + \beta + 1$ were positive

9. (a) Let $x + m = y$

∴ If α, – α are roots of given equation, then $\alpha + m$, $-\alpha + m$ will be the roots of equation $\frac{a}{(x+a)} + \frac{b}{(x+b)} = 1$

$\Rightarrow x(a+b) + 2ab = x^2 + x(a+b) + ab$

$\Rightarrow x^2 = ab$

$\Rightarrow (m+\alpha)(m-\alpha) = ab$

$\Rightarrow m^2 - \alpha^2 = ab$ and $(m+\alpha) + (m-\alpha) = 0$

$\Rightarrow 2m = 0$ $\Rightarrow m = 0$

10. (d) $\alpha + \beta = \frac{-3a}{1-a}, \alpha\beta = \frac{-1}{1-a}; a > 1$

$\Rightarrow \alpha + \beta = \frac{3a}{a-1} > 0; \alpha\beta = \frac{1}{a-1} > 0$

Disc. $= 9a^2 + 4(1-a) = 9a^2 - 4a + 4 > 0\ \forall\ a \in \mathbb{R}$ as it's discriminate is negative

$\Rightarrow$ Roots of given equation are positive.

11. (b) Let α be the common root of $x^2 + ax + b = 0$ and $x^2 + bx + a = 0$; $(a \neq b)$.

$\Rightarrow \alpha^2 + a\alpha + b = 0$ and $\alpha^2 + b\alpha + a = 0$

$\Rightarrow (a-b)\alpha = (a-b)$ $\Rightarrow \alpha = 1$

$\Rightarrow 1 + a + b = 0$ $\Rightarrow a + b + c = -1$

12. (b) $5^{\log_5(x^2-4x+5)} = x - 1$ $\Rightarrow x^2 - 4x + 5 = x - 1$

$\Rightarrow x^2 - 5x + 6 = 0$ $\Rightarrow x = 2$ or 3

13. (d) Let α be the common root $a\alpha^2 + 2c\alpha + b = 0$ and $a\alpha^2 + 2b\alpha + c = 0$ $(b \neq c)$

$\Rightarrow 2(c-b)\alpha = (c-b)$ $\Rightarrow \alpha = \frac{1}{2}$

$\Rightarrow \frac{a}{4} + \frac{2c}{2} + b = 0$ $\Rightarrow b + c = -\frac{a}{4}$

$\Rightarrow \frac{b+c}{a} = \frac{-1}{4}$

14. (c) $\tan A + \tan B = p$, $\tan A \cdot \tan B = 2$

∴ $\cos^2(A+B) = \frac{1}{1+\tan^2(A+B)} = \frac{1}{1+\left[\frac{p}{1-2}\right]^2} = \frac{1}{1+p^2}$

15. (b) Let $y = \frac{x^2+2x+c}{x^2+4x+3c}$

$\Rightarrow x^2(1-y) + (2-4y)x + c(1-3y) = 0$

For $y = 1$; $-2x + c(-2) = 0$

$\Rightarrow x + c = 0$ $\Rightarrow x = -c$

$\Rightarrow y = \frac{c^2-c}{c^2-c} = 1$; provided $c \neq 0, 1$

∴ $y = 1$ at $x = -c$; $c \neq 0, 1$

∴ $c \neq 0, 1$ and for $y \neq 1$, Disc. ≥ 0 for $x \in \mathbb{R}$

$\Rightarrow (2-4y)^2 - 4(1-y)c(1-3y) \geq 0\ \forall\ y \in \mathbb{R}; y \neq 1$

$\Rightarrow (1-2y)^2 - (1-y)c(1-3y) \geq 0\ \forall\ y \in \mathbb{R} - \{1\}$

$\Rightarrow y^2(4-3c) \quad (4-4c)y + 1 - c \geq \forall\ y \in \mathbb{R} - \{1\}$

$\Rightarrow 4(1-c)^2 - (4 - 7c + 3c^2) \leq 0$

$\Rightarrow 4 - 8c + 4c^2 - 4 + 7c - 3c^2 \leq 0$

$\Rightarrow c^2 - c \leq 0$

$\Rightarrow c \in [0, 1]$, but $c \neq 0, 1$

$\Rightarrow c \in (0, 1)$

16. (c) $\log x^3 = 2x - 3; x > 0; x \neq 1$

$\Rightarrow \dfrac{\ell n3}{\ell n} = 2x - 3 \quad \Rightarrow \left(\dfrac{1}{\ell nx}\right) = \dfrac{2x-3}{\ell n3}$

$\Rightarrow \dfrac{1}{\ell nx} = \left(\dfrac{2}{a}\right)x - \dfrac{3}{a}$; Where $a = \ln 3 \in (1, 2)$

$\Rightarrow \dfrac{1}{\ell nx} = bx - \dfrac{3b}{2}$; $b = \dfrac{2}{a} \in (1, 2)$

$\Rightarrow (\ln x)^{-1} = \left(bx - \dfrac{3b}{2}\right); x > 0$

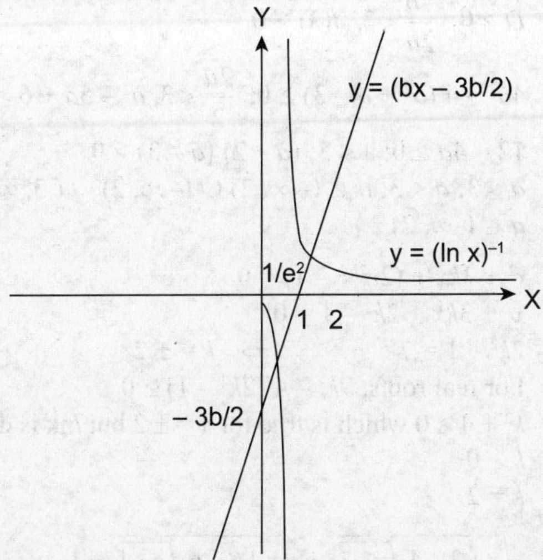

Drawing the graphs of $y = (\ln x)^{-1}$ and $y = bx - \dfrac{3b}{2}$ on same frame of reference as shown above.

Clearly, there are two points of intersection and hence two solutions.

17. (b) $a > 0, b > 0, c > 0$

$\alpha + \beta < 0$ and $\alpha\beta = c/a > 0$

So if $D > 0$ both roots are negative of when $D < 0$ both root have negative real part.

$\Rightarrow$ Both roots have negative real part irrespective of $D > 0$ or $D < 0$.

18. (d) Let α be the common root

$\Rightarrow \alpha^2 + ab\alpha + c = 0$ (i) and

$\alpha^2 + ac\,\alpha + b = 0$ (ii)

and β and γ be their other roots respectively.

$\Rightarrow \alpha + \beta = -ab, \alpha\beta = c$ and $\alpha + \gamma = -ac, \alpha\gamma = b$

$\Rightarrow \beta - \gamma = ac - ab = a(\alpha\beta - \alpha\gamma)$

$\Rightarrow (\beta - \gamma) = a\alpha(\beta - \gamma)$

$\Rightarrow \alpha = \dfrac{1}{a}, \beta = ca, \lambda = ba$

$\therefore$ The equation containing other two roots β and γ is given by $x^2 - (ca + ba)x + a^2 bc = 0$ or $x^2 - a(b + c)x + a^2 bc = 0$

$\Rightarrow \dfrac{1}{-a}x^2 + (b + c)x - abc = 0$ (iii)

From (i), we get $\dfrac{1}{a^2} + \dfrac{ab}{a} + c = 0$

$\Rightarrow \dfrac{1}{a^2} = -(b+c) \quad \Rightarrow -\dfrac{1}{a} = a(b+c)$ (iv)

Using (iv) in (iii), we get $a(b + c)x^2 (b + c)x - abc = 0$

19. (a) $\alpha, \beta = \dfrac{2 \pm \sqrt{4-16}}{2} \Rightarrow \alpha, \beta = 1 \pm \sqrt{3}i$

$\Rightarrow \alpha, \beta = -2\left(\dfrac{-1 \mp \sqrt{3}i}{2}\right) \Rightarrow \alpha, \beta = -2\omega, -2\omega^2$

$\Rightarrow \alpha^n + \beta^n = (2)^n\left[(-\omega)^n + (-\omega^2)^n\right]$

$= (2)^n\left[\left(-\cos\dfrac{2\pi}{3} - i\sin\dfrac{2\pi}{3}\right)^n + \left(-\cos\dfrac{2\pi}{3} + i\sin\dfrac{2\pi}{3}\right)^n\right]$

$= (2)^n\left[\left(\cos\left(\dfrac{-\pi}{3}\right) + i\sin\left(\dfrac{-\pi}{3}\right)\right)^n + \left(\left(\cos\dfrac{\pi}{3}\right) + i\sin\left(\dfrac{\pi}{3}\right)\right)^n\right]$

$= (2)^n\left[\cos\dfrac{n\pi}{3} - i\sin\dfrac{n\pi}{3} + \cos\dfrac{n\pi}{3} + i\sin\dfrac{n\pi}{3}\right]$

$= (2)^n\left(2\cos\dfrac{n\pi}{3}\right) = (2)^{n+1} \cdot \cos\left(\dfrac{n\pi}{3}\right)$

20. (b) $\tan x \cdot \tan y = a, x + y = \dfrac{\pi}{6}$

$\Rightarrow \tan(x + y) = \dfrac{\tan x + \tan y}{1 - a}$

$\Rightarrow \tan x + \tan y = (1 - a) \cdot \dfrac{1}{\sqrt{3}}$

$\Rightarrow \tan x$ and $\tan y$ satisfy the equation $x^2 - \dfrac{(1-a)}{\sqrt{3}}x + a = 0$ i.e., $\sqrt{3}x^2 - (1-a)x + \sqrt{3}a = 0$

21. (a) $\alpha + \beta = \dfrac{2b}{a}, \alpha\beta = \dfrac{c}{a}$

$\Rightarrow \alpha^3\beta^3 + \alpha^2\beta^3 + \alpha^3\beta^2 = (\alpha\beta)^3 + \alpha^2\beta^2(\beta + \alpha) = \dfrac{c^3}{a^3} + \dfrac{c^2}{a^2}\left(\dfrac{2b}{a}\right) = \dfrac{2bc^2 + c^3}{a^3} = \dfrac{c^2(c+2b)}{a^3}$

22. (a) Clearly domain of equation ($\mathbb{R} \sim \{-3, 2\}$) and equally $\dfrac{1}{x^2-4}$ from both side $x = 2$ is solution but it does not $\in$ Domain.

23. (d) $x^2 - (\alpha - 2)x - (\alpha + 1) = 0$; let roots be γ and β.

$\gamma + \beta = \alpha - 2$ and $\gamma\beta = (\alpha + 1)$

$\Rightarrow \gamma^2 + \beta^2 = (\gamma + \beta)^2 - 2\gamma\beta = (\alpha - 2)^2 - 2(\alpha + 1) = \alpha^2 - 4\alpha + 4 - 2\alpha - 2 = \alpha^2 - 6\alpha + 2 = (\alpha - 3)^2 - 7$

Clearly min occurs at $\alpha = 3$.

24. (d) $a\cos 2x + b\sin^2 x + c = 0\ \forall x \in \mathbb{R}$

$\Rightarrow a(1 - 2\sin^2 x) + b\sin^2 x + c = 0$

$\Rightarrow (b - 2a)\sin^2 x + (a + c) = 0\ \forall x \in \mathbb{R}$

$\Rightarrow b - 2a = 0$ and $a + c = 0$

$\Rightarrow b = 2a, c = -a \Rightarrow (a, b, c) = (a, 2a, -a); a \in \mathbb{R}$

$\Rightarrow$ Infinitely many triplets

25. (b) $\alpha + \beta = 3/8, \alpha\beta = 27/8$

$\therefore \left(\dfrac{\alpha^2}{\beta}\right)^{1/3} + \left(\dfrac{\beta^2}{\alpha}\right)^{1/3} = \dfrac{\alpha^{2/3}}{\beta^{1/3}} + \dfrac{\beta^{2/3}}{\alpha^{1/3}} = \dfrac{\alpha + \beta}{\alpha^{1/3}\beta^{1/3}}$

$= \dfrac{(\alpha+\beta)}{(\alpha\beta)^{1/3}} = \dfrac{3/8}{(27/8)^{1/3}} = \dfrac{3/8}{3/2} = \dfrac{3}{8} \times \dfrac{2}{3} = \dfrac{1}{4}$

26. (b) equation $x^2 - 8x + a^2 - 6a = 0$; $D \geq 0$

$\Rightarrow 64 - 4a^2 + 24a \geq 0 \quad \Rightarrow a^2 - 6a - 16 \leq 0$

$\Rightarrow (a-8)(a+2) \leq 0 \quad \therefore a \in [-2, 8]$

27. (c) $(b-c)x^2 + (c-a)x + a - b = 0$, roots are equal and one root is one and sum of coefficient = 0

$\Rightarrow \dfrac{a-c}{b-c} = 2$ and $1 = \dfrac{a-b}{b-c}$

$\Rightarrow a - c = 2b - 2c$ and $b - c = a - b$

$\Rightarrow 2b = a + c$

28. (c) $ax^2 + bx + c = a(x-\alpha)(x-\beta)$

$\Rightarrow a(\alpha x + 1)(\beta x + 1) \quad \Rightarrow a\alpha\beta\,(x + 1/\alpha)(x + 1/\beta)$

$= \dfrac{c}{a}\left(a\left(x+\dfrac{1}{\alpha}\right)\left(x+\dfrac{1}{\beta}\right)\right) = c\left(x^2 - \dfrac{b}{c}x + \dfrac{a}{c}\right) = 0$

$= cx^2 - bx + a = 0$

29. (d) $8\sec^2\theta - 6\sec\theta + 1 = 0$

$\sec\theta = \dfrac{6 \pm \sqrt{36-32}}{16} = \dfrac{6 \pm 2}{16} = \dfrac{1}{2}, \dfrac{1}{4}$ both never possible

$\because \quad |\sec\theta| \geq 1$

30. (c) $x^2 + bx + c = 0$ and $x^2 + qx + r = 0$

$\Rightarrow \dfrac{\alpha+\beta}{\alpha-\beta} = \dfrac{r+\delta}{r\delta} \quad \Rightarrow \dfrac{-b}{\sqrt{b^2-4c}} = \dfrac{-q}{\sqrt{q^2-4r}}$

$\Rightarrow b^2(q^2 - 4r) = q^2(b^2 - 4c)$

$\Rightarrow b^2q^2 - b^2(4r) = q^2b^2 - q^2.4c$

$\Rightarrow b^2r = q^2c$

31. (c) Let $3^{\tan x} = y > 0 \quad \Rightarrow ay + a/y - 2 = 0$

$\Rightarrow ay^2 - 2y + a = 0$ has positive real roots

$0 \leq x \leq \pi \quad \Rightarrow \tan x \in \mathbb{R};\ y > 0$

$\Rightarrow D \geq 0;\ 4 - 4a^2 \geq 0 \quad \Rightarrow a \in [-1, 1]$ and $af(k) > 0$

$\Rightarrow a^2 > 0 \quad \Rightarrow a \in \mathbb{R} \sim \{0\}$

$\Rightarrow -b/2a > 0 \quad \Rightarrow 1/a > 0$

$\Rightarrow a > 0 \quad \Rightarrow a \in (0, 1]$

32. (d) $ax^2 - bx + c = 0$ has roots α, β then $(a + cy)^2 = b^2y$

$\Rightarrow cy + a = \pm b\sqrt{y}$

$\Rightarrow c(\pm\sqrt{y})^2 - b(\pm\sqrt{y}) + a = 0$

Clearly the transformation is $x \to \pm 1/\sqrt{x}$

$\Rightarrow \alpha \to \pm 1/\sqrt{x}$

$\Rightarrow \alpha^2 \to 1/x$

$\Rightarrow x \to 1/\alpha^2$. So roots of new equation $1/\alpha^2, 1/\beta^2$

33. (a) Given equation is $2ax^2 + (2a + b)x + b = 0$; $a \neq 0$

Disc. $= (2a+b)^2 - 4(2a)(b)$

$= 4a^2 + b^2 + 4ab - 8ab$

$= 4a^2 + b^2 - 4ab$

$= (2a - b)^2 \neq 0$ as $b \neq 2a$;

$\Rightarrow$ Roots will be $-\dfrac{(2a+b) \pm (2a-b)}{4a}$

$\Rightarrow -\dfrac{b}{2a}, 1$; which are rational and unequal

34. (a) $S = \left\{x : \dfrac{2x-1}{2x^3 + 3x^2 + x} > 0; x \in \mathbb{R}\right\}$

$= \left\{x : \dfrac{2x-1}{x(2x^2 + 3x + 1)} > 0; x \in \mathbb{R}\right\}$

$= \left\{x : \dfrac{2x-1}{x(x+1)(2x+1)} > 0; x \in \mathbb{R}\right\}$

$\Rightarrow x \in (-\infty, -1) \cup \left(\dfrac{-1}{2}, 0\right) \cup \left(\dfrac{1}{2}, \infty\right)$

$\Rightarrow$ Which contains $\left(-\infty, -\dfrac{3}{2}\right)$.

35. (a) $x^2 - 2ax + a^2 + a - 3 = 0$ (i)

$\alpha, \beta < 3$

$\Rightarrow D \geq 0,\ \dfrac{-b}{2a} < 3,\ f(3) > 0$

$\Rightarrow 4a^2 - 4(a^2 + a - 3) \geq 0;\ \dfrac{2a}{2} < 3,\ a^2 - 5a + 6 > 0$

$\Rightarrow 12 - 4a \geq 0;\ a < 3;\ (a-2)(a-3) > 0$

$\Rightarrow a \leq 3;\ a < 3;\ a \in (-\infty, 2) \cup (-\infty, 2) \cup (3, \infty)$

$\Rightarrow a \in (-\infty, 2)$

36. (a) $x^2 + 3kx + (2e^{2\ln k} - 1) = 0$

$\Rightarrow x^2 + 3kx + 2k^2 - 1 = 0$

$\Rightarrow 2k^2 - 1 = 7 \quad \Rightarrow k = \pm 2$

For real roots, $9k^2 - 4(2k^2 - 1) \geq 0$

$\Rightarrow k^2 + 4 \geq 0$ which is true for $k = \pm 2$ but $\ln k$ is defined for $k > 0$

$\Rightarrow k = 2$

37. (d) $\sqrt{x+3-4\sqrt{x-1}} + \sqrt{x+8-6\sqrt{x-1}} = 1$

$\sqrt{\left(\sqrt{x-1}\right)^2 + 2^2 - 2(2)\sqrt{x-1}} + \sqrt{\left(\sqrt{x-1}\right)^2 + 3^2 - 2(3)\sqrt{x-1}} = 1$

$\sqrt{\left(\sqrt{x-1}-2\right)^2} + \sqrt{\left(\sqrt{x-1}-3\right)^2} = 1$

$|\sqrt{x-1} - 2| + |\sqrt{x-1} - 3| = 1$

$\left|\sqrt{x-1}-2\right|\left|\sqrt{x-1}-3\right| = \left|\left(\sqrt{x-1}-2\right) - \left(\sqrt{x-1}-3\right)\right|$

$\Rightarrow \left(\sqrt{x-1}-2\right)\left(\sqrt{x-1}-3\right) \leq 0$

$\Rightarrow 2 \leq \sqrt{x-1} \leq 3 \quad \Rightarrow 4 \leq x - 1 \leq 9$

$5 \leq x \leq 10$, infinitely many solutions.

38. (c) $(x-b)(x-c) + (x-a)(x-c) + (x-a)(x-b) = 0$

$\Rightarrow 3x^2 - 2(a+b+c)x + (ab+bc+ca) = 0$

Disc. $= 4(a+b+c)^2 - 12(ab+bc+ca)$

$= 4[a^2 + b^2 + c^2 - ab - bc - ca]$

$= 2[(a-b)^2 + (b-c)^2 + (c-a)^2] \geq 0$

$\Rightarrow$ Roots are real, not necessary both positive or both negative

$\therefore \quad \alpha\beta = \dfrac{ab+bc+ca}{3}, \alpha+\beta = \dfrac{2(a+b+c)}{3}$

Now $\dfrac{ab+bc+ca}{3} > 0, \dfrac{2(a+b+c)}{3} > 0$

For $a, b, c > 0$ and $\dfrac{ab+bc+ca}{3} > 0, \dfrac{2(a+b+c)}{3} < 0$ for $a, b, c < 0$

39. (c) α, β are roots of equation $ax^2 + bx + c = 0$

$\Rightarrow \alpha + \beta = \dfrac{-b}{a}, \alpha\beta = \dfrac{c}{a}$

Also equation $ax^2 - bx(x-1) + c(x-1)^2 = 0$ can be rearranged as $a\left(\frac{x}{x-1}\right)^2 - b\left(\frac{x}{x-1}\right) + c = 0$ or

$a\left(\frac{x}{1-x}\right)^2 + \left(\frac{x}{1-x}\right) + c = 0$

$\Rightarrow \alpha, \beta = \frac{x}{1-x}$ [$\because$ α, β satisfy $ax^2 + bx + c = 0$)

$\Rightarrow x = \frac{\alpha}{\alpha+1}, \frac{\beta}{\beta+1}$

40. (d) For both roots to be less than 2, (i) Disc. ≥ 0 (ii) $\frac{-b}{2a} <$ 2, (iii) f(2) > 0

$\Rightarrow 400p^2 - 16(25p^2 + 15p - 66) \geq 0$, $\frac{20p}{8} < 2$ and $16 - 40p + 25p^2 + 15p - 66 > 0$

$\Rightarrow 15p - 66 \leq 0; p < \frac{4}{5}$ and $25p^2 - 25p - 50 > 0$

$\Rightarrow p \leq \frac{22}{5}; p < \frac{4}{5}$ and $p^2 - p - 2 > 0$

$\Rightarrow p < \frac{4}{5}$ and $p \in (-\infty, -1) \cup (2, \infty)$ $p(-\infty, -1)$

41. (a) $ax^2 + 2bx - 3c = 0$ has non real roots and $(3c/4) < (a + b)$

$\Rightarrow 4b^2 + 12ac < 0$

$\Rightarrow b^2 + 3ac < 0$

$\Rightarrow ac < \frac{-b^2}{3} < 0$ $\Rightarrow ac < 0$

Now $\frac{3c}{4} < a + b$

$\Rightarrow 4a + 4b - 3c > 0$ $\Rightarrow f(2) > 0$

$\Rightarrow a > 0$ $\Rightarrow c < 0$

42. (a) Given $a > b > 0$ (i)

Let $y = \sqrt{ab + (a-b)\sqrt{ab + (a-b)\sqrt{ab + (a-b)}}}$

$\Rightarrow y = \sqrt{ab + (a-b)y}$

$\Rightarrow y^2 - (a-b)y - ab = 0 \Rightarrow y^2 - ay + by - ab = 0$

$(y - a)(y + b) = 0$

$\Rightarrow y = a$ or $y = -b$ but $y > 0$

$\Rightarrow y = a$

43. (c) Let α, β be the roots of quadratic equation $ax^2 + bx + c = 0$

$\Rightarrow \alpha^2 + \beta^2 = 2\alpha\beta$

$\Rightarrow (\alpha + \beta)^2 = 4\alpha\beta$

$\Rightarrow \frac{b^2}{a^2} = \frac{4c}{a} \Rightarrow \frac{b^2 - 4ac}{a^2} = 0$

$\Rightarrow$ Disc. = 0

which is neither positive nor negative.

44. (c) Given equation is $(3 - x)^4 + (2 - x)^4 = (5 - 2x)^4$

Let $\frac{5}{2} - x = y$

$\Rightarrow \left(\frac{1}{2} + \frac{5}{2} - x\right)^4 + \left(\frac{5}{2} - x - \frac{1}{2}\right)^4 = \left(2\left(\frac{5}{2} - x\right)\right)^4$

$\Rightarrow \left(\frac{1}{2} + y\right)^4 + \left(y - \frac{1}{2}\right)^4 = (2y)^4$

$\Rightarrow 112y^4 - 24y^2 - 1 = 0$

$\Rightarrow y^2 = \frac{24 \pm \sqrt{576 + 448}}{224}$

$\Rightarrow$ One root $y^2 > 0$ and there root $y^2 < 0$

$\Rightarrow \left(x - \frac{5}{2}\right)^2 > 0$ and $\left(x - \frac{5}{2}\right)^2 < 0$

$\Rightarrow x_1, x_2$ real and x_3, x_4 imaginary

45. (c) We have $\alpha\beta = \frac{c}{a} < 0$ (i)

Now, $\alpha(x - \beta)^2 + \beta(x - \alpha)^2 = 0$ (ii)

$\Rightarrow (\alpha + \beta)x^2 - 4\alpha\beta x + \alpha\beta^2 + \beta\alpha^2 = 0$

$\Rightarrow (\alpha + \beta)x^2 - 4\alpha\beta x + (\alpha\beta)(\alpha + \beta) = 0$

$\Rightarrow \alpha'\beta' = \alpha\beta < 0$

$\Rightarrow$ Roots of (ii) are real and of opposite sign.

46. (a) $x^2 + px + 1 = 0$

Given $|\alpha - \beta| > \sqrt{3p}$ $\Rightarrow \frac{\sqrt{D}}{|a|} > \sqrt{3p}$

$\Rightarrow \frac{\sqrt{p^2 - 4}}{1} > \sqrt{3P}$ $\Rightarrow p^2 - 4 - 3p > 0$

$\Rightarrow p^2 - 3p - 4 > 0$ $\Rightarrow (p - 4)(p + 1) > 0$

$\Rightarrow p^2 \in (-\infty, -1) \cup (4, \infty)$

$\Rightarrow p \neq 0, \pm 1, 2, 3, 4.$

47. (d) $f(x) = x^2 + 2bx + 2c^2$

$\Rightarrow f_{\min} = \frac{-D}{4a} = -\frac{4(b^2 - 2c^2)}{4} = 2c^2 - b^2$

$\Rightarrow g_{\max} = \frac{-(4c^2 + 4b^2)}{-4} = b^2 + c^2$

$\Rightarrow f_{\min} > g_{\max}$

$\Rightarrow 2c^2 - b^2 > b^2 + c^2$

$\Rightarrow c^2 > 2b^2$ $\Rightarrow |c| > \sqrt{2}\,|b|$

48. (c) The equation $x + 1/x = 2x^2$

Clearly only one real solution

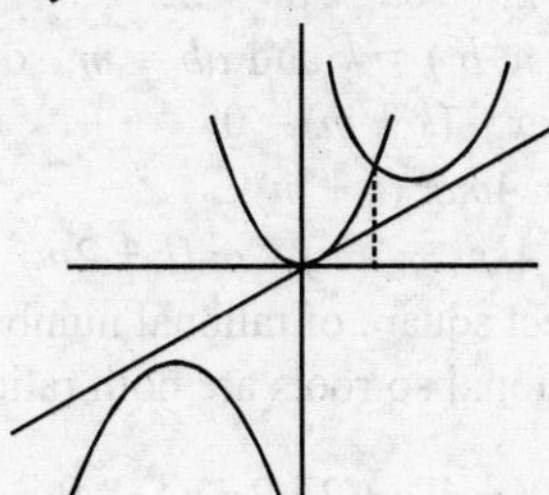

Aliter: $f(x) = 2x^3 - x^2 - 1 = 0$

Atmost one positive roots no negative root

$\because$ $f(x) = ---$

Atleast two non real roots.

$\Rightarrow$ one real and two non-real roots.

49. (a) $x^2 - y^2 = 35370$

$(x - y)(x + y) = 35370 = 2(17685)$

$\because$ $x - y$ and $x + y$ have same parity, so $x - y$ and $x + y$ both must be even, thus L.H.S. divided by whereas R.H.S. only by 2, hence no real solution.

50. (b) $2^x - (3/5)^x = 7/5$

Let $f(x) = 2^x - (3/5)^x$

f is an increasing function and continuous function for all $x \in \mathbb{R}$.
$f(-\infty) \to -\infty$ and $f(\infty) \to \infty$.
So by IMVT, $f(x)$ takes all real values exactly once, so $\exists$ exactly are $\alpha \in \mathbb{R}$.
$f(\alpha) = 7/5$

51. (a) $x^2 + 1 = y$ and $y^2 + 1 = x$

$\Rightarrow \dfrac{x^2+1}{x} = \dfrac{y}{y^2+1} \quad \Rightarrow \quad x + \dfrac{1}{x} = \dfrac{1}{y + \dfrac{1}{y}}$

$\Rightarrow x + 1/x \in (-\infty, -2] \cup [2, \infty)$
$\Rightarrow y + 1/y \in (-\infty, -2] \cup [2, \infty)$

$\Rightarrow \dfrac{1}{y + \dfrac{1}{y}} \in [-1/2, 0) \cup (0, 1/2]$

$\Rightarrow x + 1/x = \dfrac{1}{y + \dfrac{1}{y}}$ has no real solution (no ordered pair possible).

52. (a) $(x - y)(x + y)(x^2 + y^2) = 4(947277)$
$\because$ $x - y, x + y, x^2 + y^2$ have same purity.
So L.H.S. divided by 8 where as R.H.S. is not dividing by 8 only by 4.
So no integer solution.

53. (c) Considering quadratic in x, $x^2 + (y + 2)x + 1 - y - y^2 = 0$
Now x to be real $D \geq 0$
$\Rightarrow y^2 + 4y + 4 - 4(1 - y - y^2) \geq 0$
$\Rightarrow 5y^2 + 8y \geq 0$
$\Rightarrow y(5y + 8) \geq 0 \qquad \Rightarrow y \in (-\infty, -8/5] \cup (0, \infty)$
$\Rightarrow$ can't lie between $-8/5$ to zero.

54. (a) a, b, c non-real unequal rational numbers, then $abc^2x^2 + 2(3a^2 + b^2)cx - 6a^2 - ab - 2b^2 = 0$
Let $3(3a^2 + b^2) = k$ and $ab = m$, so equation becomes $mc^2x^2 + kcx - (k + m) = 0$
$D = k^2c^2 + 4mc^2(k + m)$
$= c^2(k^2 + 4km + 4m^2) = c^2(k + 2m)^2$
D is perfect square of rational numbers and coefficients are all rational so roots are both rational.

55. (a) $D = (a - 3)^2 + 4(a + 2)(2a - 1) = 9a^2 + 6a + 1 = (3a + 1)^2$
So equation has rational roots for all rational values of a except of $a = -2$.

56. (b) $x^3 + ax + 1 = 0$ (i)
$x^4 + ax + 1 = 0$ (ii)
$x^4 + ax^2 + x = 0$ (iii)
From Equation (i), (ii) and (iii), we get $ax^2 + (1 - a)x - 1 = 0$
Let α be the roots common $\alpha^3 + a\alpha + 1 = 0$
$\alpha^4 + a\alpha + 1 = 0 \qquad \Rightarrow \alpha^4 - \alpha^3 = 0$
$\Rightarrow \alpha = 0, 1$
If $\alpha = 0$ is never true
$\Rightarrow \alpha = 1 \qquad \Rightarrow 1 + a + 1 = 0$
$\Rightarrow a = -2$

57. (b) $3^{\cos x} = |\sin x|, x \in [-2\pi, 2\pi]$
The graphs of $y = 3^{\cos x}$ and $y = |\sin x|$ drawn on same frame of reference are as shown below.

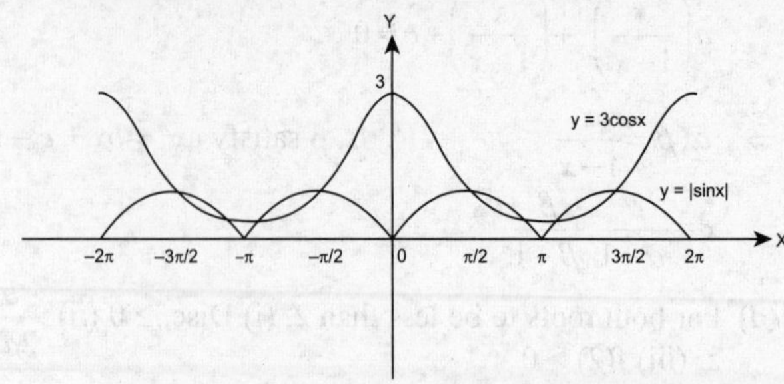

Clearly, there are 8 roots.

58. (d) $a, b, c \in \mathbb{R}$; $a \neq 0$
α is a root of $ax^2 + bx + c = 0$ (i)
and β is a root of $a^2x^2 - bx - c = 0$ (ii)
and $0 < \alpha < \beta$.
$\Rightarrow a^2\alpha^2 + b + c = 0$ (iii)
and $a^2\beta^2 - b\beta - c = 0$ (iv)
Adding equation (iii) and (iv), we get $a^2(\alpha^2 - \beta^2) + b(\alpha - \beta) = 0$
$\Rightarrow a^2(\alpha + \beta) + b = 0 \qquad (\because \alpha \neq \beta)$
$\Rightarrow b = -a^2(\alpha + \beta)$
Similarly
$\therefore a^2x^2 + 2bx + 2c = 0$
$\Rightarrow a^2x^2 - 2a^2(\alpha + \beta)x + 2c = 0$
If γ is its root, then $a^2\gamma^2 - 2a^2(\alpha + \beta)\gamma + a^2(\alpha^2 - \beta^2) + b(\alpha + \beta)$
$\Rightarrow a^2\gamma^2 - 2a^2(\alpha + \beta)\gamma + a^2(\alpha^2 - \beta^2) - a^2(\alpha + \beta)^2 = 0$
$\Rightarrow \gamma^2 - 2(\alpha + \beta)\gamma + (\alpha^2 - \beta^2) - \alpha^2 - \beta^2 - 2\alpha\beta = 0$
$\Rightarrow \gamma^2 - 2(\alpha + \beta)\gamma - 2\beta^2 - 2\alpha\beta = 0$

$\Rightarrow \gamma = \dfrac{2(\alpha+\beta) \pm \sqrt{4(\alpha+\beta)^2 + 8(\beta^2 + \alpha\beta)}}{2}$

$\Rightarrow \gamma = (\alpha+\beta) \pm \sqrt{\alpha^2 + \beta^2 + 2\alpha\beta + 2\beta^2 2\alpha\beta}$

$\Rightarrow \gamma = (\alpha+\beta) \pm \sqrt{\alpha^2 + 3\beta^2 + 4\alpha\beta}$

$\Rightarrow \gamma = (\alpha+\beta) \pm \sqrt{(\alpha+\beta)(\alpha+3\beta)}$

$\Rightarrow \gamma = (\alpha+\beta) + \sqrt{(\alpha+\beta)(\alpha+3\beta)}$

Such that $\alpha < \beta < \gamma$

59. (c) $x^2 - 2bx\cos A + (b^2 - a^2) = 0$ (i)
$\Rightarrow 2bx\cos A = x^2 + b^2 - a^2$

$\Rightarrow \cos A = \dfrac{x^2 + b^2 - a^2}{2bx}$

Also $\cos A = \dfrac{c^2 + b^2 - a^2}{2bc}$

$\Rightarrow$ one root of (i) must be c

60. (a) Let α, β be roots of $x^2 + px + pr = 0$
β, γ be roots of $x^2 + qx + rq = 0$ and γ, α roots of $x^2 + rx + pq = 0$
Clearly $(\alpha\beta)(\beta\gamma)(\gamma\alpha) = (pr)(rq)(pq)$
$\Rightarrow (\alpha\beta\gamma)^2 = p^2q^2r^2 \qquad \Rightarrow (\alpha\beta\gamma) = \pm pqr$

61. (b) $a^2 + 2a, 2a + 3, a^2 + 3a + 8$ will be the sides of Δ, if sum of two sides > third side

$\Rightarrow a^2 + 4a + 3 > a^2 + 3a + 8 > 0$ (i)

$\Rightarrow a^2 + 5a + 11 > a^2 + 2 + 2a > 0$ (ii)

and $2a^2 + 5a + 8 > 2a + 3 > 0$ (iii)

$\Rightarrow a > 5, a \in \left(\frac{-11}{3}, -2\right) \cup (0, \infty), a \in \left(\frac{-3}{2}, \infty\right)$

$\Rightarrow a \in (5, \infty)$

62. (a) α, β are roots of $x^2 + px + q = 0$

$\alpha + \beta = -p$ and $\alpha\beta = q$

α^4, β^4 are roots $x^2 - rx + 5 = 0$

$\alpha^4 + \beta^4 = r$ and $\alpha^{4\,4} = r$

Equation of $x^2 - 4qx + 2q^2 - r$

$D = 16q^2 - 4(2q^2 - r) = 8q^2 + 4r$

$= 8\alpha^2\beta^2 + 4(\alpha^4 + \beta^4) = 4(\alpha^2 + \beta^2)^2$

$= 4((\alpha + \beta)^2 - 2\alpha\beta)^2 > 0$ if $\alpha\beta \in \mathbb{R}$

$= 4((2R(\alpha))^2 - 2|\alpha|^2)^2$ if α, β non real

So $D \geq 0$, so roots are real.

63. (b) $1 + |e^x - 1| = e^x(e^x - 2)$

Case (i): for $x \geq 0$; $1 + e^x - 1 = (e^x)^2 - 2e^x$

$\Rightarrow (e^x)^2 - 3e^x$

$\Rightarrow e^x = 3$ as $e^x \neq 0$ $\Rightarrow x = \ln 3 > 0$

Case (ii): for $x < 0$; $1 - e^x + 1 = (e^x)^2 - 2e^x$

$\Rightarrow (e^x)^2 - e^x - 2 = 0$ $\Rightarrow (e^x - 2)(e^x + 1) = 0$

$\Rightarrow e^x = 2$ as $e^x \neq -1$

$\Rightarrow x = \ln 2 > 0$ and hence rejected

∴ There is only one solution $x = \ln 3$

64. (b) Given equation $x^2 + 2ax + b = 0$

$\Rightarrow |\alpha - \beta| \leq 2m, D > 0$

$\Rightarrow \sqrt{D} \leq 2m, 4a^2 - 4b > 0$

$\Rightarrow \sqrt{4a^2 - 4b} \leq 2m, 4a^2 - 4b > 0$

$\Rightarrow 4a^2 - 4b \leq 4m^2, b < a^2$

$\Rightarrow b \geq a^2 - m^2, b < a^2$

$\Rightarrow b \in [a^2 - m^2, a^2)$

65. (d) Let $\frac{1}{a^2} = A, \frac{1}{b^2} = B, \frac{1}{c^2} = C$

$\Rightarrow Ax^2 + By^2 - Cz^2 = 1$ (i)

$\Rightarrow Ax^2 - By^2 + Cz^2 = 1$ (ii)

and $-Ax^2 + By^2 + Cz^2 = 1$ (iii)

Adding (i) and (ii), we get $2Ax^2 = 2$

$\Rightarrow x^2 = \frac{1}{A} = a^2$ (iv)

Adding (i) and (iii), we get $y^2 = \frac{1}{B} = b^2$ (v)

Using (iv) and (v) in (iii), we get $Cz^2 = 1 + Ax^2 - By^2$

$= 1 + 1 - 1 = 1$ $\Rightarrow z^2 = \frac{1}{c} = c^2$

∴ $x^2 = a^2, y^2 = b^2, z^2 = c^2$ satisfy the equation (i), (ii) and (iii)

$\Rightarrow x = \pm a, y = \pm b, z = \pm c$ gives us (8) triplets (x, y, z)

66. (b) Given equation is $x^2 - 2a|x - a| - 3a^2 = 0$

$\Rightarrow x^2 - 2a(x - a) - 3a^2 = 0$ for $x \geq a$ and $x^2 + 2a(x - a) - 3a^2 = 0$ for $x < a$

$\Rightarrow x^2 - 2ax - a^2 = 0$ for $x \geq a$ and $x^2 + 2ax - 5a^2 = 0$ for $x < 0$

$\Rightarrow (x - a)^2 = 2a^2$ for $x \geq a$ and $(x + a)^2 = 6a^2$ for $x < a$

$\Rightarrow x = a \pm\sqrt{2}|a|$ for $x \geq a$ and $x = -a \pm \sqrt{6}|a|$ for $x < a$

∴ $a < 0$ (given), $|a| = -a$

$\Rightarrow x = a \pm\sqrt{2}a$ for $x \geq a$ and $x = -a \pm\sqrt{6}a$ for $x < a < 0$

$\Rightarrow x = a(1 - \sqrt{2})$ for $x \geq a$ and $x = a(\sqrt{6} - 1)$ for $x < a$

∴ Possible root of given equation is $x = a(1 - \sqrt{2})$ as $a < 0$

67. (d) Given equation is $|2x + 3| + |2x - 3| = px + 6$

Case (i): For $x \leq -3/2$

$\Rightarrow -2x - 3 - 2x + 3 = px + 6$

$\Rightarrow (4 + p)x = -6$

$\Rightarrow$ unique solution for every $p \neq -4$

Case (ii): $\frac{-3}{2} < x \leq \frac{3}{2}$

$\Rightarrow 2x + 3 - 2x + 3 = px + 6$

$\Rightarrow px = 0$

$\Rightarrow x = 0$ if $p \neq 0$ i.e., unique solution for $p \neq 0$ and $x \in \left[\frac{-3}{2}, \frac{3}{2}\right]$ for $p = 0$

i.e., more than 2 solution for $p = 0$

Case (iii): $x > \frac{3}{2}$, $2x + 3 + 2x - 3 = px + 6$

$\Rightarrow (4 - p)x = 6$

$\Rightarrow$ unique solution $\forall\, p \neq 4$

68. (d) $f(x, y, z) = xyz(4d - ax - by - cz)$; where $a, b, c, d > 0$ (constants) and $x, y, z > 0$ (variable) and $4d - ax - by - cz > 0$

$ax, by, cz, 4d - ax - by - cz > 0$

∴ By A.M. ≥ G.M. we have $(ax.by.cz)(4d - ax - by - cz)$

$\leq \left[\frac{(ax + by + cz) + (4d - ax - by - cz)}{4}\right]^4$

$\Rightarrow (abc)(xyz)(4d - ax - by - cz) \leq (d)^4$

$\Rightarrow (xyz)(4d - ax - by - cz) \leq \frac{d^4}{abc}$

69. (d) $\alpha + \beta = -p, \alpha\beta = q, \alpha^4 + \beta^4 = r, \alpha^4 . \beta^4 = s; \alpha \neq \beta$

Now Disc. of given equation $= 16q^2 - 4(2q^2 - r)$

$= 8q^2 + 4r = 8\alpha^2\beta^2 + 4(\alpha^4 + \beta^4)$

$= 4(\alpha^2 + \beta^2)^2 > 0$

$\Rightarrow$ Two real roots and product of two given equation $= \alpha'.\beta'$

$= 2q^2 - r = 2(\alpha\beta)^2 - (\alpha^4 + \beta^4)$

$= -[\alpha^4 + {}^4 - 2\alpha^2\beta^2]$

$= -(\alpha^2 - \beta^2)^2 < 0$ as $\alpha \neq \beta$

$\Rightarrow$ Roots will be are of opposite signs.

70. (b) $\cos^2\frac{\pi}{8} = \frac{1 + \cos\frac{\pi}{4}}{2} = \frac{1 + \frac{1}{\sqrt{2}}}{2} = \frac{1}{2} + \frac{1}{2\sqrt{2}}$

$\Rightarrow \frac{1}{2} - \frac{1}{2\sqrt{2}}$ will also be a root

$\Rightarrow \alpha + \beta = 1, \alpha.\beta = \frac{1}{4} - \frac{1}{8} = \frac{1}{8}$

$\Rightarrow$ Required equation is $x^2 - x + \frac{1}{8} = 0$ which is identical to $x^2 + bx + c = 0$

$\Rightarrow b = -1, c = \frac{1}{8}$

71. (c) $\frac{1+\alpha}{1-\alpha} = \frac{1-\alpha+2\alpha}{1-\alpha} = 1 + \frac{2\alpha}{1-\alpha}$

$\therefore$ Equation having its roots $1+\frac{2\alpha}{1-\alpha}$, $1+\frac{2\beta}{1-\beta}$, $1+\frac{2r}{1-r}$ can be obtained by replacing x by y such that

$y = 1+\frac{2x}{1-x} \quad \Rightarrow \quad (y-1)(1-x) = 2x$

$\Rightarrow (y-1) = (2+y-1)x$

$\Rightarrow x = \frac{y-1}{y+1}$ i.e., $\left(\frac{y-1}{y+1}\right)^3 - \left(\frac{y-1}{y+1}\right) - 1 = 0$

i.e., $(y-3)^3 - (y-1)(y+1)^2 - (y+1)^3 = 0$

i.e., $-y^3 - 7y^2 + y - 1 = 0$ or $y^3 + 7y^2 - y + 1 = 0$

$\Rightarrow \frac{1+\alpha}{1-\alpha} + \frac{1+\beta}{1-\beta} + \frac{1+\gamma}{1-\gamma} = \frac{(-1)^1(7)}{1} = -7$

72. (c) $|2x^2 - 4x - 7| < \left[1 + \frac{1}{2}\left(\frac{\cos\theta}{\cos\frac{\theta}{2} - \sin\frac{\theta}{2}}\right)^2\right]$

$\Rightarrow |2x^2 - 4x - 7| < 1 + \left[\frac{1}{2}\frac{\cos^2\theta}{\left(\cos\frac{\theta}{2} - \sin\frac{\theta}{2}\right)^2}\right]$

$\Rightarrow |2x^2 - 4x - 7| < 1 \left[\frac{1}{4}\cdot\frac{\left(\cos^2\frac{\theta}{2} - \sin^2\frac{\theta}{2}\right)^2}{\left(\cos\frac{\theta}{2} - \sin\frac{\theta}{2}\right)^2}\right]$

$= 1 + \left[\frac{1}{4}\left(\frac{\cos\frac{\theta}{2} + \sin\frac{\theta}{2}}{\cos\frac{\theta}{2} - \sin\frac{\theta}{2}}\right)\right] = 1 + \left[\frac{1}{4}\tan\left(\frac{\pi}{4} + \frac{\theta}{2}\right)\right]$ ...(i)

Now, $-\frac{\pi}{2} \le \theta < \frac{\pi}{2} \Rightarrow -\frac{\pi}{4} \le \frac{\theta}{2} < \frac{\pi}{4}$

$\Rightarrow 0 \le \left(\frac{\pi}{4} + \frac{\theta}{2}\right) < \frac{\pi}{2} \Rightarrow \frac{1}{4}\tan\left(\frac{\pi}{4} + \frac{\theta}{2}\right) \in [0, \infty)$

$\Rightarrow \left[\frac{1}{4}\tan\left(\frac{\pi}{4} + \frac{\theta}{2}\right)\right] \in \{0, 1, 2, 3, \ldots\}$

$\Rightarrow 1 + \left[\frac{1}{4}\tan\left(\frac{\pi}{4} + \frac{\theta}{2}\right)\right] \in \{1, 2, 3, \ldots\}$

$\therefore$ Inequality (i) holds if $|2x^2 - 4x - 7| < 1$

$\Rightarrow -1 < 2x^2 - 4x - 7 < 1$

$\Rightarrow 2x^2 - 4x - 6 > 0$ and $2x^2 - 4x - 8 < 0$

$\Rightarrow x^2 - 2x - 3 > 0$ and $x^2 - 2x - 4 < 0$

$\Rightarrow (x+1)(x-3) > 0$ and $x \in \left(1-\sqrt{5}, 1+\sqrt{5}\right)$

$\Rightarrow x \in (-\infty, -1) \cup (3, \infty)$ and $x \in \left(1-\sqrt{5}, 1+\sqrt{5}\right)$

$\Rightarrow x \in \left(1-\sqrt{5}, -1\right) \cup \left(3, 1+\sqrt{5}\right)$

73. (a) $a, b, c, x, y, z \in \mathbb{R}$

$a^2 + b^2 + c^2 = 16$, $x^2 + y^2 + z^2 = 9$, $ax + by + cz = 12$,

$\frac{a+b+c}{z+y+z} = t$ (say)

Consider $(a - xt)^2 + (b - yt)^2 + (c - zt)^2 \ge 0$

$\Rightarrow (x^2 + y^2 + z^2)t^2 - 2(ax + by + cz)t + (a^2 + b^2 + c^2) \ge 0$

$\Rightarrow$ Disc. ≤ 0

$\Rightarrow 4(ax + by + cz)^2 - 4(x^2 + y^2 + z^2)(a^2 + b^2 + c^2) \le 0$

$\Rightarrow 4(12)^2 - 4(9)(16) \le 0$

$\Rightarrow$ Disc. $= 0$

$\Rightarrow (x^2 + y^2 + z^2)t^2 - 2(ax + by + cz)t + (a^2 + b^2 + c^2) = 0$

$\Rightarrow 9t^2 - 24t + 16 = 0$

$\Rightarrow (3t - 4) = 0 \quad \Rightarrow t = \frac{4}{3}$

74. (b) Let α be the common root of $3x^2 + ax + 1 = 0$ and $2x^2 + bx + 1 = 0$

$\Rightarrow 3\alpha^2 + a\alpha + 1 = 0$ (i)

$\Rightarrow 2\alpha^2 + b\alpha + 1 = 0$ (ii)

$\Rightarrow a\alpha - \frac{3}{2}b\alpha + 1 - \frac{3}{2} = 0$

$\Rightarrow \left(a - \frac{3}{2}b\right)\alpha = \frac{1}{2}$

$\Rightarrow \alpha = \left(\frac{1}{2a - 3b}\right)$

$\therefore$ From (i), we get $3\left(\frac{1}{2a-3b}\right)^2 + a\left(\frac{1}{2a-3b}\right) + 1 = 0$

$\Rightarrow 3 + a(2a - 3b) + (2a - 3b)^2 = 0$

$\Rightarrow 3 + 2a^2 - 3ab + 4a^2 + 9b^2 - 12ab = 0$

$\Rightarrow 3 + 6a^2 + 9b^2 - 15ab = 0$

$\Rightarrow 1 + 2a^2 + 3b^2 - 5ab = 0$

$\Rightarrow 5ab - 2a^2 - 3b^2 = 1$

75. (c) $a, b, c \in \mathbb{R}$ such that $a + b + c = 0$ (i)

Given quadratic equation is $3ax^2 + 5bx + 7c = 0$

$\Rightarrow$ Disc. $= 25b^2 - 84ac$ (ii)

From (i), $ax^2 + bx + c = 0$ has a real root $x = 1$ and hence both real roots

$\Rightarrow b^2 - 4ac \ge 0$ (iii)

Now, from (ii), Disc. $= 4b^2 + 21b^2 - 84a$

$= 4b^2 + 21(b^2 - 4ac) > 0$ (using (ii), otherwise $D = 0$

$\Rightarrow a = b = c = 0$

$\Rightarrow$ Given quadratic equation has a real and distinct root.

76. (a) Let $f(x) = a(x - \alpha)(x - \beta)$; $a > 0$

$g(x) = b(x - \beta)(x - \gamma)$; $b > 0$, $h(x) = c(x - \gamma)(x - \alpha)$; $c > 0$, $\alpha \ne \beta \ne \gamma$.

$F(x) = f(x) + g(x) + h(x)$, then $F(\alpha) = g(\alpha) = b(\alpha - \beta)(\alpha - \gamma)$, $F(\beta) = h(\beta) = c(\beta - \gamma)(\beta - \alpha)$ and $F(\gamma) = f(\gamma) = a(\gamma - \alpha)(\gamma - \beta)$

Without loss of generality let $\alpha < \beta < \gamma$

$\Rightarrow F(\alpha) > 0, F(\beta) < 0, F(\gamma) > 0$

$\Rightarrow F(x) = 0$ has one real root between α and β and other real root between β and γ

77. (b) $f(x) = 2x^2 - 3x^2 - 12x + a = 0$

$f'(x) = 6x^2 - 6x - 12$

$\because f'(x) = 0 \quad \Rightarrow x^2 - x - 2 = 0$

$\Rightarrow$ $(x-2)(x+1)=0$ $\Rightarrow$ $x=-1$ or $x=2$

$\therefore$ For real and distinct roots, $f(-1)>0$ and $f(2)<0$

$\Rightarrow$ $(-2-3+12+a)>0$ and $(16-12-24+a)<0$

$\Rightarrow$ $a>-7$ and $a<20$ $\Rightarrow$ $a\in(-7, 20)$

78. (d) $\sqrt{-x^2+10x-16}<(x-2)$ (i)

For above inequality to hold R.H.S > 0, i.e., $x>2$

Also, squaring (i) gives, $0\le -x^2+10x-16<x^2-4x+4$

$\Rightarrow$ $2x^2-14x+20>0$ and $x^2-10x+16\le 0$

$\Rightarrow$ $x^2-7x+10x>0$ and $(x-2)(x-8)$

$\Rightarrow$ $(x-2)(x-5)>0$ and $(x-2)(x-8)$

$\Rightarrow$ $x\in(-\infty, 2)\cup(5,\infty)$ and $x\in[2, 8]$ and $x\in(2,\infty)$

$\therefore$ Finally, taking intersection, $x\in(5, 8]$ integer solution are 6, 7 and 8 i.e., 3 in counting

79. (c) $x^2+ax-3x-(a+2)=0$ has real and distinct roots.

$\Rightarrow$ Disc. > 0

$\Rightarrow$ $(a-3)^2+4(a+2)>0$

$\Rightarrow$ $a^2-2a+17>0$

$\Rightarrow$ $a^2-2a+1+16>0$

$\Rightarrow$ $(a-1)^2+16>0$ which is true $\forall\ a\in\mathbb{R}$

Now, $\dfrac{a^2+1}{a^2+1}=1-\dfrac{1}{a^2+2};a\in\mathbb{R}$

Now, $a^2+2\in[2,\infty)\Rightarrow\dfrac{1}{a^2+2}\in\left(0,\dfrac{1}{2}\right]$

$\Rightarrow$ $\dfrac{1}{a^2+2}\in\left[-\dfrac{1}{2},0\right)$ $\Rightarrow$ $1-\dfrac{1}{a^2+2}\in\left[\dfrac{1}{2},1\right)$

$\Rightarrow$ Minimum value of $\dfrac{a^2+1}{a^2+1}$ is $\dfrac{1}{2}$

80. (c) $(a-1)x^2-(a+1)x+(a-1)\ge 0\ \forall\ x\ge 2$

For $a=1$, $-2x\ge 0\ \forall\ x\le 2$

$\Rightarrow$ $a\ne 1$

$\Rightarrow$ $a>1$ and $f'(x)\ge 0\ \forall\ x\ge 2$, $f(2)\ge 0$

$\Rightarrow$ $2(a-1)x-(a+1)\ge 0\ \forall\ x\ge 2, f(2)\ge 0$

$\Rightarrow$ $2(a-1)x\ge(a+1)\ \forall x\ge 2,\ 3a-7\ge 0$

$\Rightarrow$ $x\ge\dfrac{a+1}{2(a-1)}\ \forall\ x\ge 2, x\ge\dfrac{7}{3}$

$\Rightarrow$ $\dfrac{a+1}{2(a-1)}\le 2;\ a\ge\dfrac{7}{3}$

$\Rightarrow$ $a+1\le 4a-4;\ a\ge\dfrac{7}{3};\ a>1$

$\Rightarrow$ $a\ge\dfrac{5}{3};\ a\ge\dfrac{7}{3};\ a>1\Rightarrow\ a\in\left[\dfrac{7}{3},\infty\right)$

81. (b) Let $f(x)=ax^2+bx+c$

$f(x)>0\ \forall\ x\in\mathbb{R}$

$\Rightarrow$ Disc. < 0 $\Rightarrow$ $b^2-4ac<0$

$g(x)=f(x)+f'(x)+f''(x)$ (given)

$\Rightarrow$ $g(x)=(ax^2+bx+c)+(2ax+b)+(2a)=ax^2+(b+2a)$ $x+(2a+b+c)$

Its Disc. $=(b+2a)^2-4ac\,(2a+b+c)=(b^2-4ac)-4ac^2<0$

$\Rightarrow$ $g(x)>0\ \forall\ x\in\mathbb{R}$

82. (c) By given condition, $D\le 0$

$\Rightarrow$ $b^2-32a\le 0$ $\Rightarrow$ b^2-32 a

$\Rightarrow$ $2a\ge\dfrac{b^2}{16}$ $\Rightarrow$ $2a+b\ge\dfrac{b^2}{16}+b\ge -4$

$\Rightarrow$ Minimum value of $(2a+b)$ *is* -4

SECTION–IV: (ONE OR MORE THAN ONE ARE CORRECT)

1. (a), (b) $a>0, b>0, c>0$

$\alpha+\beta=\dfrac{-b}{a}<0, \alpha\beta=\dfrac{c}{a}>0$

$\Rightarrow$ Both roots are negative or both are imaginary with their negative real parts.

2. (b), (c) a, b, c are in G.P., $a, c>0$

Disc. $=b^2-4ac=ac-4ac$

$=-3ac<0$ as $a, c>0$

$\Rightarrow$ Both roots will be imaginary.

Let $b=ar$, $c=ar^2$

$\Rightarrow$ $ax^2+ar\,x+ar^2=0$ $\Rightarrow$ $x^2+rx+r^2=0$

$\Rightarrow$ $x=\dfrac{-r\pm\sqrt{r^2-4r^2}}{2}$

$\Rightarrow$ $x=\dfrac{-r\pm r\sqrt{3}}{2}$ $\Rightarrow$ $\alpha, \beta=r\left(\dfrac{-1\pm\sqrt{3}i}{2}\right)$

$\Rightarrow$ $\alpha, \beta=r\omega, r\omega^2$ $\Rightarrow$ $\dfrac{\alpha}{\beta}=1:\omega$

3. (a), (b) $x^3+2x^2+2x+1=0$

$\Rightarrow$ $(x^3+1)+2x(x+1)=0$

$\Rightarrow$ $(x+1)[x^2+x+1)=0$

$\Rightarrow$ $x=-1$ or $x=\omega, \omega^2$

$\Rightarrow$ $x=-1$, does not satisfy $1+x^{130}+x^{1988}=0$

$\Rightarrow$ $x=\omega$, and $x=\omega^2$ satisfy $1+x^{130}+x^{1988}=0$

4. (a), (c) $a>0$, $\log_{ax}a+\log_x a^2+\log_{a^2x}a^3=0$

$$\frac{\log a}{\log a+\log x}+\frac{2\log a}{\log x}+\frac{3\log a}{2\log a+\log x}=0$$

$\Rightarrow$ $\dfrac{1}{\log a+\log x}+\dfrac{2}{\log x}+\dfrac{3}{2\log a+\log x}=0$ $(\because\ a\ne 1)$

$\Rightarrow$ $6(\log x)^2+11(\log a)(\log x)+4(\log a)^2=0$

$\Rightarrow$ $(2\log x+\log a)(3\log x+4\log a)=0$

$\Rightarrow$ $x=a^{-1/2}$ or $x=a^{-4/3}$

5. (a), (b), (d)

Let $g(x)=3x^2+x^2-7x+\lambda$

If $\lambda=0$, $3x^2+x^2-7x=0$

$\Rightarrow$ $x(3x^2+x-7)=0$

$\Rightarrow$ $x=0$ or $\dfrac{-1\pm\sqrt{85}}{6}$

$\Rightarrow$ $x=0, \dfrac{-1-\sqrt{85}}{6}, \dfrac{-1+\sqrt{85}}{6}$

If $f(x)=3x^3+x^2-7x$

$\Rightarrow$ $f'(x)=9x^2+2x-7$

$\therefore$ $f'(x)=0$ $\Rightarrow$ $x=\dfrac{-2\pm\sqrt{256}}{18}$

$\Rightarrow$ $x=-1, \dfrac{7}{9}$

$\Rightarrow f(-1) = -3 + 1 + 7 = 5, f\left(\frac{7}{9}\right) = \frac{-833}{243}$

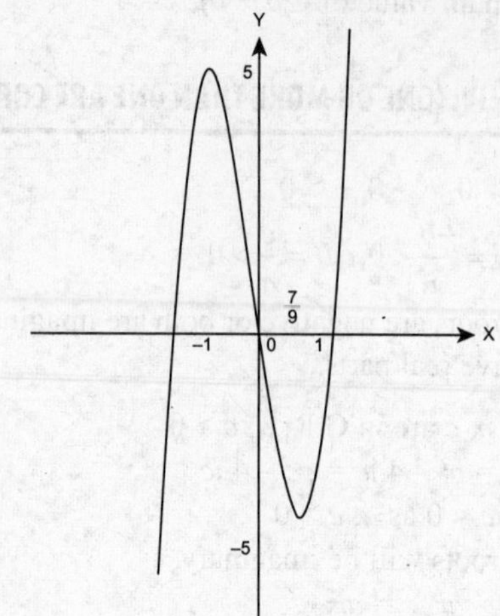

If we transform the graph in upwards direction from the situation g(1) = 0 to $g\left(\frac{7}{9}\right) = 0$ i.e., as shown below.

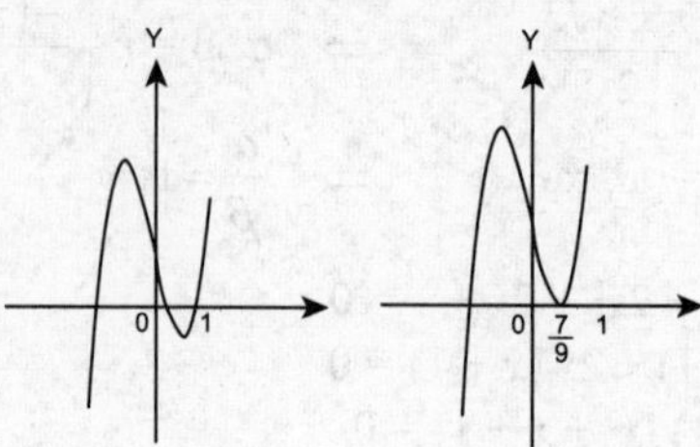

When g (1) = 0 $\Rightarrow -3 + \lambda = 0$

$\Rightarrow \lambda = 3$

When $g\left(\frac{7}{9}\right) = 0 \Rightarrow f\left(\frac{7}{9}\right) + \lambda = 0$

$\Rightarrow \lambda = \frac{833}{243} \Rightarrow \lambda \in \left[3, \frac{833}{243}\right]$

6. (a), (b) If $0 < a < b < c$

Sum of roots = $\frac{-b}{a} < 0$; Product of roots = $\frac{c}{a} > 0$

$\Rightarrow$ Roots are imaginary with their real parts negative and as they occur in conjugate pairs

$\Rightarrow |\alpha| = |\beta|$ and $\alpha, \beta = \frac{-b \pm \sqrt{b^2 - 4ac}}{2a} = \frac{-b}{2a} \pm \frac{\sqrt{4ac - b^2}\, i}{2a}$

$\Rightarrow |\alpha| = |\beta| = \sqrt{\frac{b^2}{4a^2} + \frac{4ac - b^2}{4a^2}} = \sqrt{\frac{c}{a}} > 1$ as $c < a$

7. (a), (b), (c)

Let $\alpha + i\beta$ and $\frac{1}{\alpha + i\beta}$ be two imaginary roots but $\frac{1}{\alpha + i\beta} = \alpha + i\beta$

$\Rightarrow \frac{1}{\alpha + \beta} = \alpha - i\beta \Rightarrow \alpha^2 + \beta^2 = 1$

Product of roots = 1 $\Rightarrow \frac{c}{a} = 1$

$\Rightarrow c = a$

Also $\alpha^2 + {}^2 = 1 \Rightarrow (\alpha + \beta)^2 - 2\alpha\beta = 1$

$\Rightarrow \left(\frac{b^2}{a^2}\right) - 2\frac{c}{a} = 1 \Rightarrow \frac{b^2}{a^2} - 2 = 1$

$\Rightarrow b^2 = 3a^2$

$\Rightarrow |b| < \sqrt{3}\ |a| < |a| = |c|$

$\Rightarrow |b| < |a|, |b| < |c|$

8. (a), (b), (c) $3ax^2 + 2bx + c = 0$

Let $f'(x) = 3ax^2 + 2bx + c$

$\Rightarrow f(x) = ax^3 + bx^2 + cx + d$

$\Rightarrow f(0) = d$ and $f(1) = a + b + c + d = d$

$(\because a + b + c = 0)$

$\therefore$ By Roll's theorem f '(x) must have at least one root in (0, 1)

9. (a), (b), (c), (d) Clearly $f(0) = c < 0$,

Being two real roots, $b^2 - 4ac > 0, f(-1), f(1) < 0$

$\Rightarrow a - b + c, a + b + c < 0$

$\Rightarrow a + |b| + c < 0$, Also $f(-2), f(2) < 0$

$\Rightarrow 4a + 2|b| + c < 0$

10. (a), (b), (c) Since $f(x)$ is a biquadratic with leading coefficient positive.

It has either no root real i.e., $f(x) > 0\ \forall \in \mathbb{R}$ or at least two real roots i.e., $f(x) \le 0$ at least for one real x.

Note that $f(0) = -2 < 0$

$\Rightarrow f(x)$ would have at least 2 real roots for every $c \in \mathbb{R}$

11. (a), (c), (d) $(a^2 + b^2)x^2 + 2x(ac + bd) + c^2 + d^2 = 0$

$D = 4\{ac + bd)^2 - 4(a^2 + b^2)(c^2 + d^2)$

$= 4\{a^2c^2 + b^2 d^2 + 2abcd - a^2c^2 - b^2c^2 - b^2d^2 - a^2d^2 - b^2c^2\}$

$= -4\{(ad)^2 + (bc)^2 - 2(ad)(bd)\}$

$= -4(ad - bc)^2 \le 0$

$\Rightarrow$ Roots are real iff. $D = 0$

12. (b), (c), (d) $(ab - bc)x^2 + (bc - ca)x + ca - ab = 0$ has clearly $x = 1$ as roots, so it has equal root

$\Rightarrow$ Both roots must be 1

$\Rightarrow$ Option (a) is false and (b) is correct

Product of root = 1 = $\frac{ca - ab}{ab - bc}$

$\Rightarrow 2ab = ca + bc = \frac{2ab}{a + b} = c$

$\Rightarrow a, c, b$ are in H.P. $\Rightarrow$ option (c) is correct

$\Rightarrow \frac{1}{a}, \frac{1}{c}, \frac{1}{b}$ in A.P.

13. (a), (b), (c) $a + 2b + 4c = 0$

Let $f(x) = ax^2 + bx + c$

$f(1/2) = a/4 + b/2 + c = 1/4\,(a + 2b + 4c) = 0$

$\Rightarrow x = 1/2$ is one root i.e., positive root

$\Rightarrow$ Atleast one positive non-integer root and so other root cannot be irrational, if coefficient had been rational but given the coefficient are real numbers.

$\therefore D = b^2 - 4ac$

$= \left(\frac{4c + a}{2}\right)^2 - 4ac = \frac{16c^2 + a^2 - 8ac}{4} = \left(\frac{4c - a}{2}\right)^2$

$\therefore$ Roots are given as $x = \dfrac{b \pm \dfrac{4c-a}{2}}{2a}$

$= \dfrac{4c-a-2b}{4a}; \left(\dfrac{2b+4c-a}{4a}\right); -\dfrac{1}{2}-\dfrac{b}{a}; \dfrac{1}{2}$

Other root can be irrational, if b/a is irrational e.g., $b = a\sqrt{2}$

14. (a), (b), (d) $x^2 - 2x + A = 0$ has roots p, q

$p + q = 2$ (i)

$pq = A$ (ii)

$x^2 - 18x + B = 0$ and r, s are roots

$r + s = 18$ (iii)

$rs = B$ (iv)

p, q, r, s are in A. P. and $p < q < r < s$

Also from (i) and (iii), we get $(r - p) + (s - q) = 16$

$\Rightarrow 2d + 2d = 16 \qquad \Rightarrow d = 4$

$\Rightarrow q = p + 4, r = p + 8, s = p + 12$

$\because p + q = 2 \qquad \Rightarrow p + q + 4 = 2$

$2P = -2 \qquad \Rightarrow p = -1$

$\Rightarrow p = -1, q = 3, r = 7, s = 11$

$\Rightarrow A = -3$ and $B = 77$

15. (a), (b) $x^2 - 2x + \sin^2\alpha = 0$

$\Rightarrow x^2 - 2x + 1 = 1 - \sin^2\alpha$

$\Rightarrow (x - 1)^2 = \cos^2\alpha$

$\Rightarrow x - 1 = \pm \cos\alpha$

$\Rightarrow x = 1 \pm \cos\alpha$

$\Rightarrow x = 2\sin^2\dfrac{\alpha}{2}$ or $2\cos^2\dfrac{\alpha}{2}$

$\Rightarrow x \in [0, 2] \leq [-2, 2]$

16. (a), (b), (c), (d) $x^4 - (m - 3)x^2 + m = 0$ (i)

Let $x^2 = y$

$y^2 - (m - 3)y + m = 0$ (ii)

(a) Equation (i) has no real root if equation (ii) has both roots negative

$\Rightarrow D \geq 0, f(0) > 0, \dfrac{-b}{2a} < 0$

$\Rightarrow (m - 3)^2 - 4m \geq 0$ and $m > 0$, $\dfrac{m-3}{2} < 0$

$\Rightarrow m^2 - 10m + 9 \geq 0$ and $m > 0, m < 3$

$\Rightarrow (m - 1)(m - 9) \geq 0, m < 3$

$\Rightarrow m \in (0, 1]$

(b) Equation (i) has four roots, and then equation (ii) has both root positive

$\Rightarrow D \geq 0, m \in (-\infty, 1] \cup [9, \infty)$

$\Rightarrow f(0) \geq 0, m \geq 0$

$\Rightarrow \dfrac{-b}{2a} > 0, m - 3 > 0$

$\Rightarrow m \in [9, \infty)$

Similarly no real root if $m \in (0, 9)$

if $m = 0$, then $x^4 + 3x^2 = 0$

$\Rightarrow x^2(x^2 + 3) = 0$

$\Rightarrow x^2 = 0 \qquad \Rightarrow x = 0$

17. (b), (c) $ax^2 + 2bx + b = 0$ has imaginary root.

$D = 4b^2 - 4ab < 0 \qquad \Rightarrow b(b - a) = 0$

Then, $bx^2 + (b - c)x + b - c - a = 0$

$D = (b - c)^2 - 4b(b - c - a)$

$= b^2 + c^2 - 2bc - 4b^2 + 4bc + 4ab$

$= c^2 - 3b^2 - 2bc + 4ab$

$= (c^2 + b^2 + 2bc) + 4ab - 4b^2$

$= (c + b)^2 + 4(ab - b^2)$

$D > 0 \ \forall \ a, b, c \in \mathbb{R}$

$\Rightarrow$ Roots are real and unequal $\forall \ a, b, c, \in \mathbb{R}$

18. (b) $(a + c - b)x^2 + 2cx + (b + c - a) = 0$; $a, b, c \in \mathbb{R}$ and distinct and $(a + c - b) \neq 0$, (given both roots α and β rational).

$\Rightarrow \alpha + \beta = \dfrac{2c}{b-c-a} \in \mathbb{Q}$ and $\alpha\beta = \dfrac{b+c-a}{a+c-b} \in \mathbb{Q}$

$\Rightarrow \dfrac{2}{\dfrac{b-a}{c}-1} \in \mathbb{Q} \qquad \Rightarrow \dfrac{b-a}{c} \in \mathbb{Q}$

$\Rightarrow \dfrac{c}{a-b} \in \mathbb{Q}$

Now, consider the following counter example

Let $c = 3, a = \sqrt{3}, b = 2 + \sqrt{3}$

Clearly, $D = 4(2)^2 = 16$ i.e., perfect square of rational

and $\dfrac{c}{a-b} = \dfrac{3}{2} \in \mathbb{Q}$, $\dfrac{b}{c-a} = \dfrac{2+\sqrt{3}}{3-\sqrt{3}} \notin \mathbb{Q}$

Now, given equation becomes $x^2 + 6x + (5) = 0$

$\Rightarrow (x + 1)(x + 5) = 0$

Clearly, both roots are rational.

Thus if both roots are rational, then it is not necessary that a, b, c are rational and $\dfrac{b}{c-a}$ is rational.

19. (a), (b), (d) The system of equation $x^2 + 2x + k \leq 0$ and $x^2 - 4x - 61k \leq 0$ have unique solution.

$x \in \left[-1-\sqrt{1-k}, -1+\sqrt{1-k}\right]$ and $x \in \left[2-\sqrt{4+6k}, 2+\sqrt{4+6k}\right]$, both solution set have only one common element

$-1 + \sqrt{1-k} = 2 - \sqrt{4+6k}$

$\sqrt{1-k} + \sqrt{4+6k} = 3$

$1 - k + 4 + 6k + 2\sqrt{1-k}\sqrt{4+6k} = 9$

$2\sqrt{1-k}\sqrt{4+6k} = 4 - 5k\,2$

$4(1 - k)(4 + 6k) = 16 + 25k^2 - 40k$

$4(4 + 6k - 4k - 6k^2) = 16 + 25k^2 - 40k$

$k(49k - 48) = 0$

$k = 0$ or $k = 48/49$

SECTION–V: (ASSERTION AND REASON)

1. A: Given $\cos^2\dfrac{\pi}{8}$ is a root of $x^2 + ax + b = 0$ (i)

$\therefore \cos 2x = \cos^2 x - \sin^2 x$

$\Rightarrow \cos 2x = 2\cos^2 x - 1$

$\Rightarrow \cos^2 x = \dfrac{1+\cos 2x}{2}$

$\Rightarrow \cos^2\left(\frac{\pi}{8}\right) = \frac{1+\cos\left(\frac{\pi}{4}\right)}{2}$

$\Rightarrow \cos\left(\frac{\pi}{4}\right) = \left(\frac{1}{\sqrt{2}}\right) \Rightarrow \cos^2\left(\frac{\pi}{8}\right) = \frac{1}{2} + \frac{1}{2\sqrt{2}}$

By (i), we get $\left(\cos^2\frac{\pi}{8}\right) + a\left(\cos^2\frac{\pi}{8}\right) + b = 0$

$\Rightarrow \frac{1}{4} + \frac{1}{8} + \frac{1}{2\sqrt{2}} + a\left(\frac{1}{2} + \frac{1}{2\sqrt{2}}\right) + b = 0$

$\Rightarrow \left(b + \frac{3}{8} + \frac{a}{2}\right) + \frac{1}{2\sqrt{2}}(a+1) = 0$

$\Rightarrow a = -1, b = \frac{1}{8}$

$\Rightarrow (a, b) = \left(-1, \frac{1}{8}\right)$ $\Rightarrow$ assertion is correct.

R: $a + mb = 0$; m is irrational

$\Rightarrow mb$ $\Rightarrow$ irrational.

$a + mb$ = rational

$\Rightarrow a = 0$ and $b = 0$ $\Rightarrow$ R is correct

$\Rightarrow$ option (a) is correct.

2. A: Given that $ix^2 + (i-1)x - \frac{1}{2} - i = 0$ has imaginary roots

$\Rightarrow$ Discriminant of the equation must be negative

$\Rightarrow (i-1)^2 + 4\left(\frac{1}{2} + i\right) < 0$

Which is true iff $i^2 + 1 - 2i + 2i + 4i^2 < 0$

$\Rightarrow 4i^2 < 0 \Rightarrow -4 < 0$, which is true

$\Rightarrow$ Imaginary roots $\Rightarrow$ Assertion is correct

R: $a = i$, $b = i - 1$ and $c = \frac{-1}{5} - i$

$\Rightarrow b^2 - 4ac = (i-1)^2 - 4i\left(\frac{-1}{5} - i\right) = i^2 + 1 - 2i + \frac{4}{5}i + 4i^2$

$= -2i + \frac{4}{5}i - 4 = \frac{-6i}{5} - 4$

Which is not subject to order relation

$\Rightarrow$ Reason is incorrect $\Rightarrow$ option (c) is correct

3. A: Let us assume $f(x) = ax^2 + bx + c$

$\Rightarrow f(2) = 4a + 2b + c$

$f(4) = 16a + 4b + c$

$f(2) + f(4) = 20a + 6b + 2c = 0$

$\Rightarrow 10a + 3b + c = 0$ (i)

Given that f(1) = 0

$\Rightarrow a + b + c = 0$ (ii)

Equation (i) – (ii), we get $9a + 2b = 0$

$\Rightarrow \frac{a}{b} = -\frac{2}{9}$ (iii)

$\therefore$ Sum of the roots of $f(x) = 0$

$= 1 + \text{root} - 2 = -\frac{b}{a}$

$= 1 + \text{root} - 2 = \frac{9}{2}$

$= \text{root} - 2 = \frac{9}{2} - 1 = \frac{7}{2} = 3.5$

$\Rightarrow$ The other root is 3.5 $\Rightarrow$ Assertion is correct.

R: $g(x) = px^2 + qx + r = 0$, if α is the root

$p\alpha^2 + q\alpha + r = 0$ (i)

Similarly $p\beta^2 + q\beta + r = 0$ (ii)

Equation (i) – (ii), we get $p(\alpha^2 - \beta^2) + q(\alpha - \beta) = 0$

$\Rightarrow p(\alpha + \beta)(\alpha - \beta) + q(\alpha - \beta) = 0$

$\Rightarrow (\alpha - \beta)((\alpha + \beta)p + q) = 0$

Taking the case of distinct roots

$\Rightarrow (\alpha + \beta)p + q = 0$

$\Rightarrow \alpha + \beta = -\frac{q}{p}$

Similarly $\beta(\text{i}) - \alpha(\text{ii}) = 0$

$\Rightarrow p\alpha^2\beta - p\beta^2\alpha + r(\beta - \alpha) = 0$

$\Rightarrow p\alpha\beta(\alpha - \beta) + r(\beta - \alpha) = 0$

$\Rightarrow (\beta - \alpha)(r - p\alpha\beta) = 0$

Again taking the case of distinct roots $\beta \neq \alpha$

$\therefore r - p\alpha\beta = 0$

$\Rightarrow \alpha\beta = \frac{r}{p}$ $\Rightarrow$ Reason is correct.

$\Rightarrow$ option (a) is correct.

4. A: $f(x) = px^2 + qx + r$; $p, q, r \in \mathbb{R}$

Given that $f(1) < 0$; $f(-1) < 0$; $f(0) = r > 0$

This means one of the roots say α

$\Rightarrow -1 < \alpha < 0$ and the other root β

$\Rightarrow 0 < \beta < 1$

$\Rightarrow [\alpha] = -1$ and $[\beta] = 0 \Rightarrow [\alpha] + [\beta] = -1$

$\Rightarrow$ assertion is correct.

R: $f(a).f(b) < 0$

$\Rightarrow f(a)$ and $f(b)$ have opposite signs

$\Rightarrow$ Between a and b iff the function continuous, then it must cross the $x = 0$ axis

$\Rightarrow$ There lives one root of $f(x)$ is (a, b)

$\Rightarrow$ Reason is correct $\Rightarrow$ option (a) is correct.

5. A: $ax^2 + bx + c = 0$

$2x^2 + 3x + 4 = 0$

Given that they have a common root.

$\Rightarrow$ Let the common root be α but since the roots of $2x^2 + 3x + 4 = 0$ are imaginary

$\Rightarrow$ Both roots will be common

$\Rightarrow \frac{a}{2} = \frac{b}{3} = \frac{c}{4}$ $\Rightarrow$ a: b: c = 2: 3: 4

$\Rightarrow$ assertion is correct .

R: Roots of $2x^2 + 3x + 4$ are imaginary as $D = (3)^2 - 4(4)(2) = 9 - 32 = -23 < 0$

$\Rightarrow$ Roots are imaginary $\Rightarrow$ Reason is correct

$\Rightarrow$ option (b) is correct.

6. A: α, β are the roots of equation $x^2 + 2(a-3)x + 9 = 0$

$\Rightarrow$ The roots of this equation lie on either side of 6.

$\Rightarrow D > 0$ $\Rightarrow f(k) < 0$

$D = 4(a-3)^2 - 36 > 0 = 4(a^2 + 9 - 6a) - 36 > 0 = 4a^2 + 36 - 24a - 36 > 0 = a(a-6) > 0$ (i)

$\Rightarrow f(6) < 0$

⇒ $36 + 2(a - 3)\,6 + 9 < 0$
⇒ $36 + 12a - 36 + 9 < 0$
⇒ $12a + 9 < 0$
⇒ $a < -3/4$ (ii)
By (i) and (ii), we get $a < -3/4$
⇒ assertion is correct
R: $f(x) = x^2 + 2(a - 3)x + 9$
$f(6) = 36 + 12a - 36 + 9$
⇒ $f(6) < 0$ ⇒ $12a + 9 < 0$
⇒ $a < 3/4$
⇒ Reason is correct ⇒ option (b) is correct

7. A: Let us consider $a < b < c < d$
$f(x) = (x - a)(x - c) + 3(x - b)(x - d)$
∴ $f(a) = 3(a - b)(a - d)$
$a - b < 0$
$a - d < 0$
⇒ $f(a) < 0$
Similarly,
$f(b) = (b - a)(b - c) < 0$
$f(c) = 3(c - b)(c - d) < 0$
$f(d) = (d - a)(d - c) > 0$
Let us plot the values that $f(x)$ takes in (a, d)
This means $f(x)$ changes sign from a to b and c to d
⇒ Real and distinct root
⇒ Assertion is correct.
R: if $(\lambda).(\mu) > 0$
⇒ $f(x)$ crosses x-axis between λ and μ at least once. This means there exist a root between λ and μ.
⇒ which is true ⇒ Reason is correct
⇒ option (a) is correct.

8. A: $f(x) = x^6 - 3x^5 + 4x^3 + 3x^2 + 4$, changes in sign of $f(x)$ $x^6 \to x^5$ and $x^5 \to x^3 = 2$
Similarly, $f(-x) = x^6 + 3x^5 - 4x^3 + 3x^2 + 4$, changes in sign of $f(-x) = x^5 \to x^3$ and $x^3 \to x^2 = 2$
Minimum number of complex roots $= 6 - (2 + 2) = 6 - 4 = 2$
⇒ Assertion is correct.
R: $f(x) = x^6 - 3x^5 + 4x^3 + 3x^2 + 4$, we have already proved in (A) that there are 2 changes in sign of $f(x)$ $x^6 \to x^5$ and $x^5 \to x^3$ but to explain the assertion we need to account for sign changes of $f(-x)$ also
⇒ option (b) is correct.

9. A: For $(2\lambda - 1)x^2 - 4x + (2\lambda - 1) = 0$ to have real roots
⇒ $D \ge 0$
⇒ $16 - 4(2\lambda - 1)^2 \ge 0$ ⇒ $16 \ge 4(2\lambda - 1)^2$
⇒ $(2\lambda - 1)^2 \le 4$ ⇒ $\lambda \le \frac{3}{2}$
⇒ Greatest possible integral value of $\lambda = 1$
⇒ Assertion is correct
R: For real roots of $ax^2 + bx + c$
$D \ge 0$; which is correct.
Hence reason is correct
⇒ option (d) is correct.

10. A: Consider the equation $H(x) = a(x - b)(x - c) + b(x - c) + c(x - a) + c(x - a)(x - b)$
$H(x) = x^2$ can be rewritten as $H(x) = x^2(a + b + c) - 2x(ab + bc + ca) + 3abc$
$H(x) = 0$
Sum of roots $= \dfrac{2(ab+bc+ca)}{a+b+c}$
Product of roots $= \dfrac{3abc}{a+b+c}$
It is given that $a + b + c > 0$, but $a < 0$
⇒ $abc < 0$
⇒ Product of roots < 0
⇒ Roots can't be both negative
⇒ Assertions is incorrect
R: If both roots are negative say $\alpha < 0$ and $\beta < 0$
⇒ $\alpha\beta > 0$ ⇒ $\alpha + \beta < 0$
⇒ Reason is correct ⇒ option (d) is correct.

11. A: $a^3 + b^3 + c^3 - 3abc = (a + b + c)(a^2 + b^2 + c - ab - bc - ca)$
Given $a^3 + b^3 + c^3 - 3abc = 0$
⇒ $a + b + c = 0$ as the other factor is a perfect square which cannot be zero unless $a = b = c$
$a + b + c = 0$
⇒ $f(x) = ax^2 + bx + c = 0$
⇒ $f(1) = 0$
⇒ 1 is one of the roots.
If the other root is negative r
⇒ $1 + r = -b/a$
⇒ $1 + r = \dfrac{a+c}{a} = 1 + \dfrac{c}{a}$
⇒ $r = \dfrac{c}{a}$
⇒ $\dfrac{c}{a} < 0$, but there is a possibility that c and a have the same sign.
⇒ Assertion is incorrect.
R: If roots are of opposition nature says $\alpha > 0, \beta < 0$
⇒ $|\alpha + \beta| \ge 0$ and $\alpha\beta < 0$
⇒ Reason is correct ⇒ option (d) is correct

12. A: $f(x) = a_1x^4 + a_2x^3 + a_3x^2 + a_4x + a_5$
Now, $f(1) = a_1 + a_2 + a_3 + a_4 + a_5 = (1 - 4 + 6 + 7 - 10) = 0$
$f(1) = 0$ ⇒ 1 is a root of $f(x)$
Now degree of $f(x) = 4$
⇒ At least one more real root will exist
⇒ At least two real roots exist
⇒ Assertion is correct
R: $f(x) = ax^2 + bx + c$
⇒ $f(1) = a + b + c$ ⇒ $f(1) = a + b + c$
⇒ $a + b + c = 0$ ⇒ 1 is a root of $f(x)$
⇒ Reason is correct ⇒ option (a) is correct

13. A: $f(x) = 2x^{100} + 7x^{99} + \ldots + 7x + 5 = 0$
$f(x)$ is an even degree polynomial with positive coefficient of highest degree, then $f(\infty) + f(-\infty) = \infty$
⇒ $\lim_{x\to\infty} f(x) > 0$

$\lim_{x \to -\infty} f(x) = >0$

$f(0) = -5$

$\Rightarrow$ There are at least two real roots

$\Rightarrow$ Assertion is correct

R: $f(x) = ax^2 + bx + c \quad \Rightarrow f(x)$ has real roots

$\Rightarrow$ Reason is correct $\quad \Rightarrow$ option (b) is correct

14. A: $f(x) = ax^2 + bx + c$

$D = b^2 = 4ac$

Suppose roots are rational.

Let $b^2 - 4ac = d^2$; since a, b, c are odd

$\Rightarrow d$ will be odd

Now $b^2 - d^2 = 4ac$

Let $b = 2k + 1, d = 2m + 1$

$\Rightarrow b^2 - d^2 = 2(k - m)^2 (k + m - 1)$ but either of $(k - m)$ and $(k + m - 1)$ is even

$\Rightarrow b^2 - d^2$ is a multiple of 8, but $4ac$ is multiple of 4

$\Rightarrow$ Roots of $ax^2 + bx + c$ cannot be rational

$\Rightarrow$ Assertion is correct

R: As proved above as $b^2 - d^2$ is a multiple of 8

$\Rightarrow$ if the odd number cannot be written $8m + 1$

$\Rightarrow b^2 - 4ac$ is not a perfect square $\Rightarrow b^2 - 4ac \neq d^2$

$\Rightarrow$ Reason is correct $\quad \Rightarrow$ option (a) is correct

15. A: $f(x) = (x - a)(x - c) + \lambda(x - b)(x - d)$

$f(a) = \lambda(a - b)(a - d)$

if $\lambda < 0 \quad \Rightarrow f(a) < 0$

Similarly $f(c) = > 0$

$f(b) > 0$

$f(d) < 0$; which has real – roots by the Roll's theorem

$\Rightarrow$ Assertion is incorrect

R: $ax^2 + bx + c = 0$ has non – real roots iff **D** < 0; which is correct

$\Rightarrow$ option (d) is correct

16. A: Let x_1, x_2, x_3, x_4, be 4 roots of the given equation

$\Rightarrow x_1 + x_2 + x_3 + x_4 = -p$

$\Rightarrow x_1 x_2 x_3 x_4 = s$

$= -\frac{p}{4} \geq (s)^{1/4} = -p > 4\ (5)1/4$

H.M. of $x_1, x_2, x_3, x_4 = \dfrac{4}{-\frac{r}{s}}$

Since A.M $\geq$ H.M $\quad \frac{-p}{4} \geq \frac{-4s}{r}$

$\Rightarrow -pr \geq -16s \Rightarrow pr - 16s \leq 0$

$\Rightarrow$ Assertion is correct

R: A.M. $= \frac{a+b}{2}$; G.M. $= \sqrt{ab}$

Clearly A.M $\geq$ G.M $\forall$ positive numbers

$\Rightarrow$ Reason is correct $\quad \Rightarrow$ option (b) is correct.

17. A: For an equation to have real roots clearly $\Delta \geq 0$, if one of the equations has real roots.

$\Rightarrow \Delta_1 \geq 0$ or $\Delta_2 \geq 0$ atleast, but there is a possibility $\Delta_2 \leq 0$ and $\Delta_1 \geq 0$

$\Rightarrow$ It is not necessary that $\Delta_1 + \Delta_2\ 0$

$\Rightarrow$ Assertion is incorrect

R: $\Delta_1 + \Delta_2 \geq 0$

If both $\Delta_1 < 0, \Delta_2 < 0$

$\Rightarrow \Delta_1 + \Delta_2$ cannot be greater than zero

This means that at least one of Δ_1 and Δ_2 must be greater that zero

$\Rightarrow$ Reason is correct $\quad \Rightarrow$ option (d) is correct.

SECTION–VI: (PASSAGE)

Passage A:

$x^4 - 12x^3 + 2bx^2 + 3cx + 81 = 0$

Let $\alpha, \beta, \gamma, \delta$ be roots $\alpha + \beta + \gamma + \delta = 12$ (i)

$\alpha\beta + \beta\gamma + \gamma\delta + \delta\alpha + \alpha\gamma + \gamma\beta = 2b$

$\alpha\beta\gamma + \beta\gamma\delta + \alpha\beta\delta + \alpha\gamma\delta = -3c$

$\alpha\beta\gamma = 81$

A.M. of roots $= \frac{12}{4} = 3$

G.M. of root $= (\alpha\beta\gamma\delta)^{1/4} = (81)^{1/4} = 3$

$\Rightarrow$ Roots are all equal = 3 i.e., $\alpha = \beta = \gamma = \delta = 3$

1. (c) $2b = \sum \alpha\beta = {}^4C_2\,(\alpha\beta) = {}^4C_2 \times 9 = 54$

$\Rightarrow b = 27$

2. (d) $3c = -\left(\sum \alpha\beta\gamma\right) = -{}^4C_3\,(\alpha\beta\gamma) = -4(27) = -108$

$\Rightarrow c = -36$

3. (c) Roots of equation $2bx + c = 0$ is $x = \frac{-c}{2b} = \frac{18}{27} = \frac{2}{3}$

Passage B:

$AC = 6\sqrt{3}$

$\therefore$ By symmetry of parabola about the axis $AO = OC = 3\sqrt{3}$

$\angle OAB = \angle OCB = \pi/4$

$AB = BC$ and $\angle ABO = \pi/2$

$\Rightarrow OB = OC = 3\sqrt{3}$, B has co-ordinate $(0, -3\sqrt{3})$ and A $(-3\sqrt{3}, 0)$

$\Rightarrow f(x) = a(x - 3\sqrt{3})(x + 3\sqrt{3})$ and $f(x) = a(x^2 - 27)$ but $f(0) = -3\sqrt{3} \quad \Rightarrow -27a = -3\sqrt{3}$

$\Rightarrow a = 1/3\sqrt{3}$

4. (a) $f(x) = \frac{1}{3\sqrt{3}}(x^2 - 27) = \frac{1}{3\sqrt{3}}x^2 - 3\sqrt{3}$

5. (b) $f(x)_{\min} = -3\sqrt{3}$

6. (b) $k/2 \in (-3\sqrt{3}, 3\sqrt{3})$

$k \in (-6\sqrt{3}, 6\sqrt{3})$ as $k \in \mathbb{Z}$

$\Rightarrow k = \pm 10, \pm 9, \ldots\ldots, \pm 1$

Number of integer values of k is 20.

Passage C:

7. (b) Consider $g(x) - ax^2 + bx + c$

$g(2) = 4a + 2b + c$

$g(-2) = 4a - 2b + c$

Given $|2b| > |4a + c|$

$\Rightarrow$ g(2) and g(– 2) are of opposite sign

$\Rightarrow$ exactly one root of $g(x) = 0$ lies $(-2, 2)$

8. (a), (c) $g(x) = ax^2 + bx + c$

$g(-1) = a - b + c$

$a. 8 (-1) < 0$

$\Rightarrow$ -1 lies between both roots of $g(x)$

Also $g(0) = c$

Given $g(-1) . g(0) > 0$

$\Rightarrow$ No root will be in $(-1, 0)$

$\Rightarrow$ One root is less than -1 and other is greater than 0

9. (b) Consider $g(x) = ax^2 + bx + c$

$g(1) = a + b + c$

$g(0) = c$

Given that $g(1).g(0) < 0$

$\Rightarrow$ Exactly one root will lie between (0, 1). Also $a.f(1) > 0$

$\Rightarrow$ Both roots will lie on same side of 1

$\Rightarrow$ One root will exist between (0, 1) and the other $(-\infty, 0)$

Passage D:

10. (b) $f(x) = ax^2 + bx + c$

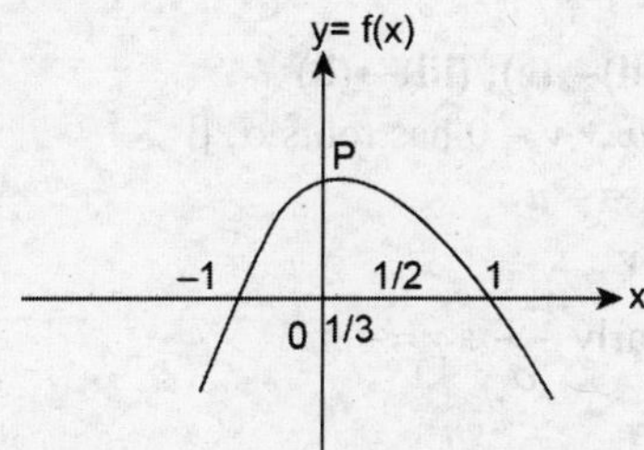

The first conclusion from the graph is $a < 0$ (i)

And $f(0) > 0 \quad \Rightarrow \quad c > 0$ (ii)

By equation (i) and (ii), we get $ac < 0$

$\therefore$ Coordinates of $p = \left[\frac{-b}{2a}, \frac{-D}{4a}\right]$

$\Rightarrow b < 0$ (since $a < 0$)

$\Rightarrow ab > 0 \qquad \Rightarrow ac < 0$

$\Rightarrow bc < 0$

$\Rightarrow abc > 0$

11. (d) $f(x) = ax^2 + bx + c$

$\Rightarrow f(1) = a + b + c = 0$

$\Rightarrow f(-1) = a - b + c = 0$

$\Rightarrow f\left(\frac{1}{3}\right) = \frac{a}{9} + \frac{b}{3} + c < 0$

$\Rightarrow a + 3b + 9c > 0$

$\Rightarrow f\left(-\frac{1}{3}\right) = \frac{a}{9} - \frac{b}{3} + c > 0$

$\Rightarrow a - 3b + 9c > 0$

12. (b) $f(x) = ax^2 + bx + c = k$

$\Rightarrow ax^2 - bx + c - k = 0$ has real roots $\forall x \in \mathbb{Z}$

$\Rightarrow \frac{b \pm \sqrt{b^2 - 4a(c-k)}}{2a} =$ integer

$\Rightarrow 2a$ has to be an integer

Passage E:

$f(x) = x^2 + b_1 x + c_1$

$g(x) = x^2 + b_2 x + c_2$

α, β are the roots of $f(x)$

$\alpha + k, \beta + k$ are roots of $g(x)$

Least value of $f(x) = -\frac{D}{4a}$

$\Rightarrow -\frac{D}{4} = -\frac{1}{8} \qquad \Rightarrow D = \frac{1}{2}$

$\Rightarrow b_1^2 - 4c_1 = \frac{1}{2}$ (i)

From the picture below

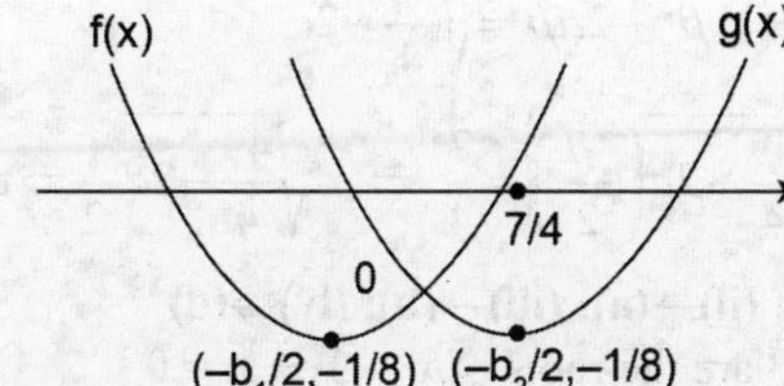

Minimum value of $g(x) = -\frac{1}{8}$ at $x = \frac{7}{4}$

13. (c)

14. (b) As stated in question no. (13)

Minimum at g (x) occur when $x = \frac{7}{4}$ but $\frac{-b_2}{2a} = \frac{7}{4} = \frac{-b_2}{2}$

$\Rightarrow b_2 = -\frac{7}{2}$

15. (c) Product of roots of $g(x) = c_2$

$-\frac{D}{4} = -\frac{1}{8} \qquad \Rightarrow D = \frac{1}{2}$

$\Rightarrow b_2^2 - 4c_2 = \frac{1}{2} \qquad \Rightarrow \frac{49}{4} - 4c_2 = \frac{1}{2}$

$\Rightarrow c_2 = \frac{1}{4}\left(\frac{49-2}{4}\right) = \frac{47}{16}$

$\Rightarrow$ Product of roots of $g(x) = c_2 = \frac{47}{16}$

SECTION–VII: (COLUMN MATCHING)

1. (i)→(b); (ii) →(a); (iii) →(d); (iv) →(c)

(i) $x^2 - a^2 - b^2 - c^2 = 0$, this can have infinitely many real solutions

(ii) $f(x) = 2x^3 - x - 1 = 0$, this clearly has a 3 roots say a, b, c,

$\therefore abc < 0$

$\therefore f(1) = 2 - 1 - 1 = 0$

$\Rightarrow$ 1 is a root

$\therefore b^2 - 3ac = 0 - 3(2)(-1) = 6 > 0$

$\Rightarrow$ All roots are real

$\Rightarrow bc < 0$; b, c must be of opposite side

$\Rightarrow$ 2 non negative roots are there

(iii) Given that p, q are the roots of equation $x^2 - (\alpha - 2)x - \alpha - 1$

$\Rightarrow p + q = \alpha - 2$

$\Rightarrow pq = -\alpha - 1$

$\Rightarrow p^2 + q^2 - 2\alpha - 2 = \alpha^2 + 4 - 4\alpha$

$\Rightarrow p^2 + q^2 = \alpha^2 + 6 - 2\alpha$

$\Rightarrow$ Minimum value $P^2 + q^2 = 1 + 6 - 2 = 5$.

(iv) α, β are the roots of $2x^2 + 7x + c = 0$

$\alpha + \beta = -7/2$

$\alpha\beta = c/2$

$\alpha^2 - \beta^2 (\alpha + \beta)(\alpha - \beta)$

$\alpha^2 + \beta^2 = \frac{49}{4} - c$

$\alpha^2 +^2 - 2\alpha\beta = \frac{49}{4} - 2c$

$\sqrt{\alpha^2+\beta^2-2\alpha\beta} = \sqrt{\frac{49}{4} - 2c}$

$\Rightarrow \left|\sqrt{\frac{49}{4} - 2c}\left(\frac{-7}{2}\right)\right| = \frac{7}{4} \Rightarrow \sqrt{\frac{49}{4} - 2c} = \frac{1}{2} \Rightarrow c = 6$

2. (i)→(c); (ii)→(a); (iii)→(b); (iv)→(d)

(i) α, β are the roots of $x^2 - 3x + a = 0$

$\alpha < 1 < \beta$

$\Rightarrow f(1) < 0 \qquad \Rightarrow a - 2 < 0$

$\Rightarrow a \in (-\infty, 2)$

(ii) The equation $cx^2 + 2bx - 3a = 0$ has non real roots

$\Rightarrow D < 0$

$\Rightarrow 4b^2 + 12ac < 0$

$\Rightarrow b^2 + 3ac < 0$ (ii)

Also $\frac{3a}{4} < (b + c)$

$\Rightarrow 3a < 4b + 4c$ (ii)

By (i) and (ii), we get $a \in (-\infty, 0)$

(iii) $\sin^2 x + \sin x - a = 0$

Let $\sin x = y$

$\Rightarrow y^2 + y - a = 0$

$\Rightarrow D \geq 0$

$\Rightarrow 1 + 4a \geq 0$

$\Rightarrow a \geq -\frac{1}{4}$ (i)

$f(1) \cdot f(-1) \leq 0$

$\Rightarrow (1 - 1 - a)(2 - a) \leq 0$

$\Rightarrow a(a - 2) \leq 0$

$\Rightarrow a \in [0, 2]$ (ii)

By (i) and (ii), we get $a \in \left[-\frac{1}{4}, 2\right]$

(iv) $\frac{ax^2+3x+4}{x^2+2x+2} < 5$

$x^2 + 2x + 2$ has imaginary roots

$\Rightarrow x^2 + 2x + 2 > 0$

$\Rightarrow ax^2 + 3x + 4 < 5x^2 + 10x + 10$

$\Rightarrow x^2(5 - a) + 7x + 6 > 0$

$\Rightarrow \frac{49}{24} < 5 - a$

$\Rightarrow a \in \left[-\infty, \frac{71}{24}\right]$

3. (i)→(c); (ii)→(b); (iii)→(a)

(i) $f(x) = (x - 1)(x - 3) + k(x - 2)(x - 4)$

$= x^2(k + 1) - x(6k + 4) + 8k + 3$

For real roots $D \geq 0$

$\Rightarrow (6k + 4)^2 - 4(k + 1)(8k + 3) \geq 0$

$\Rightarrow 36k^2 + 16 + 48k - 32k^2 - 44k - 12 \geq 0$

$\Rightarrow k^2 + k + 1 \geq 0 \qquad \Rightarrow k \in (-\infty, \infty)$

(ii) By the question $\frac{x-1}{x^2-k+1} < -1$ and $\frac{x-1}{x^2-k+1} > 1$

$\Rightarrow \frac{x^2-k+x}{x^2-k+1} < 0$ and $\frac{-x^2+x+k-2}{x^2-k+1} > 0$

$\Rightarrow (x^2 - k + 1)(x^2 - k - x + 2) < 0$ (i)

Also $(x^2 - k + 1)(x^2 + x - k) < 0$ (ii)

Adding (i) and (ii), we get $(x^2 - k + 1)(2x^2 - 2k + 2) < 0$

$\Rightarrow (x^2 \;\; k + 1)(x^2 - k + 1) < 0$

$\Rightarrow (x^2 - k + 1)^2 < 0$; which is never possible

(iii) The equation $x^2 + 2(k - 1)x + k + 5 = 0$, for positive and distinct roots

$\Rightarrow D > 0 \qquad \Rightarrow 4(k - 1)^2 - 4(k + 5) > 0$

$\Rightarrow k^2 + 1 - 2k - k - 5 > 0$

$\Rightarrow k^2 - 3k - 4 > 0 \qquad \Rightarrow (k - 4)(k + 1) > 0$

$\Rightarrow k \in (-\infty, -1)(4, \infty)$

$\Rightarrow k \in (-5, -1)$

4. (i)→(a); (ii)→(c); (iii)→(b)

(i) $x^2 + ux + v = 0$ has roots α, β

$\Rightarrow \alpha + \beta = -u$ (i)

$\Rightarrow \alpha\beta = v$ (ii)

Similarly $\frac{-2}{\alpha} + \gamma = -m$ (iii)

$\frac{-2\gamma}{\alpha} = n$ (iv)

From (i), (ii), (iii), (iv), we get $(4u + 2mv)(-2m - un)$

$= \left[(-\alpha-\beta) - 2\alpha\beta.\left(\frac{2}{\alpha} - \gamma\right)\right]\left[\frac{-4}{\alpha} + 2\gamma + (\alpha+\beta)\left(\frac{-2\gamma}{\alpha}\right)\right]$

$= \left(2 - \frac{2\gamma\alpha\beta}{\alpha} + 2\right)^2 = (4 - 2\gamma\beta)^2 = (4 - vn)^2$

(ii) $x^2 + ux + v = 0$; since α, β are the roots

$\Rightarrow \alpha + \beta = -u$ (i)

$\Rightarrow \alpha\beta = v$ (ii)

Similarly $-\alpha + \gamma = -m$ (iii)

$\Rightarrow -\alpha\gamma = n$ (iv)

From (i), (ii), (iii), (iv), we get $(un + vm)(m - u) = (\alpha\gamma(\alpha + \beta) + \alpha\beta(\alpha - \gamma))(\gamma - \alpha + \alpha + \beta)$

$= (\alpha^2 + \alpha\beta\gamma + \alpha^2\beta - \alpha\beta\gamma)(\gamma + \beta) = -\alpha^2(\gamma + \beta)^2 = (n - v)^2$ $\quad \therefore$ (ii)→(c)

(iii) $x^2 + ux + v = 0$ has roots α and β

$\Rightarrow \alpha + \beta = -u$ (i)

$\Rightarrow \alpha\beta = v$ (ii)

Similarly $\frac{1}{\alpha} + \gamma = -m$ (iii)

$\frac{\gamma}{\alpha} = n$ (iv)

From (i), (ii), (iii), (iv), we get $(u - mv) = (-\alpha - \beta + \alpha\beta\left(\frac{1}{\alpha} + \gamma\right))$

$\Rightarrow (u - mv) + \left(-\frac{1}{2} - \gamma + (\alpha+\beta)\frac{\gamma}{2}\right) = (u - mv)(m - un) = (1 - \gamma\beta)^2 = (1 - vn)^2$

5. (i) → (b, c, d); (ii) → (c); (iii) → (a); (iv) → (b)

(i) Roots of $p(q-r)x^2 + q(r-p)x + r(p-q) = 0$ are real and equal

$\Rightarrow D = 0$

$\Rightarrow q^2(r-p)^2 - 4rp(q-r)(p-q) = 0$ (i)

Also, $(s+p-q)^2 + (s+q-r)^2 = 0$

$\Rightarrow s^2 + p^2 + q^2 + 2sp - 2pq - 2qs + s^2 + q^2 + r^2 + 2sq - 2qr - 2rs = 0$ (ii)

$\Rightarrow$ By (i) and (ii), we get $p = 0, q = 0, r = 0$

(ii) $(p^2+q^2)x^2 - 2q(p+r) + (q^2+r^2) = 0$, for real and equal roots

$\Rightarrow D = 0$

$\Rightarrow 4q^2(p+r)^2 - 4(p^2+q^2)(q^2+r^2) = 0$

$\Rightarrow q^2 = pr$

(iii) The equation $px^2 + qx + r = 0$ and $x^3 - 3x^2 + 3x - 1 = 0$ have a common real root

Clearly 1 is a root of $x^3 - 3x^2 + 3x - 1 = 0$

$x^3 - 3x^2 + 3x - 1 = x^2(x-1) - 2x(x-1) + (x-1) = (x-1)(x^2 - 2x + 1)$

This means 1 is also a root of $px^2 + qx + r = 0$

$\Rightarrow p + q + r = 0$

(iv) Given that $qx^2 + \sqrt{(p+r)^2 + 4q^2}\,x + (p+r)$ is non-negative

This equation has no real roots

$\Rightarrow (p+r)^2 + 4q^2 - 4q(p+q) \le 0$

$\Rightarrow p^2 + r^2 + 2pr + 4q^2 - 4qp - 4qr \le 0$

$\Rightarrow (p + r - 2q)^2 \le 0$; which is possible only when $p + r = 2q$

$\Rightarrow p, q, r$ are in A.P.

SECTION–VIII (INTEGER TYPE)

1. $6x^2 - 6x + 1 = 0$, for the given if α and β are the roots

$\alpha + \beta = 1$ (i)

$\alpha\beta = \frac{1}{6}$ (ii)

Squaring (i), we get $\alpha^2 + \beta^2 + 2\alpha\beta = 1$

$\Rightarrow \alpha^2 + \beta^2 + \frac{1}{3} = 1 \quad \Rightarrow \alpha^2 + {}^2 = \frac{2}{3}$ (iii)

Required sum

$= \frac{1}{2}(2a) \frac{b}{2}(\alpha+\beta) + \frac{c}{2}(\alpha^2+\beta^2) + \frac{d}{2}(\alpha^3+\beta^3)$

$= a + \frac{b}{2} + \frac{c}{3} + \frac{d}{4}$

Sum $= k_1 + k_2 + k_3 + k_4 = 1 + 2 + 3 + 4 = 10$

2. Consider the equation $\frac{1}{x-h} + \frac{1}{x-k} = \frac{1}{m}$

This can be re-written as $x^2 - hx - kx + hm = m(2x - h - k)$

By the equation $-2m = h + k$ (i)

Product of roots $= hk + m(h+k) = hk + \frac{(h+k)^2}{2}$

$= \frac{-1(h^2+k^2)}{2} \quad \Rightarrow \alpha = 2$

3. $(a+1)x^2 + (2a+7)x + (3a+4) = 0$

Sum of the roots $= \frac{-(2a+7)}{a+1} = -3$

$\Rightarrow 2a + 7 = 3a + 3 \quad \Rightarrow a = 4$

Product of root $= \frac{(3a+4)}{a+1} = \frac{16}{5} = p$

$\Rightarrow [p] = 3$

4. Consider the equation $3x^2 + 6X - \lambda = 0$. If α and β are the roots.

$\Rightarrow \alpha + \beta = -2 \quad \Rightarrow \alpha\beta = -\frac{\lambda}{3}$

$\Rightarrow \alpha^2 + \beta^2 - 2\frac{\lambda}{3} = 4 \quad \Rightarrow 0 < \frac{\alpha^2+\beta^2}{\alpha\beta} < 2$

$\Rightarrow 0 < \frac{4 + \frac{2\lambda}{3}}{-\frac{\lambda}{3}} < 2 \quad \Rightarrow \lambda \in (-3, 0)$

$\Rightarrow a = -3, b = 0 \quad \Rightarrow |a| + |b| = 3$

5. $y = 4x - 1$

$\Rightarrow x = y + \frac{1}{4}$

Putting in the equation $y = x^2$

$\Rightarrow x^2 = 4x - 1$

$\Rightarrow x^2 - 4x + 1$

$\Rightarrow$ The roots of the equation will be the abscissa say α, β

$\Rightarrow \alpha + \beta = 4 \quad \Rightarrow \alpha\beta = 1$

$\Rightarrow \alpha^2 + \beta^2 = 14 \quad \Rightarrow \frac{\alpha^2+\beta^2}{\alpha\beta} = 14$

$\Rightarrow k = 14$

6. If $x^2 + bx + c = 0$ has real roots greater than unity

$\Rightarrow b^2 - 4c > 0$

$\Rightarrow f(1) \quad \Rightarrow 1 + b + c > 0$

$\Rightarrow b + c > -1 \quad \Rightarrow b + c \in (-1, \infty)$

$\Rightarrow k = -1$

7. If p, q, r are in A.P. $p + r = 2q$

Since $D \ge 0$

$\Rightarrow \frac{p^2 + r^2 + 2pr}{4} - 4pr \ge 0$

$\Rightarrow p^2 + r^2 - 14\,pr > 0$

$\Rightarrow \frac{p}{r} + \frac{r}{p} > 14 \quad \Rightarrow \left|\frac{r}{p} - 7\right| \ge 4\sqrt{3}$

$\Rightarrow k = 4$

8. For rational roots, the D = perfect square

$\Rightarrow (2a-1)^2 - 4a^2 + 8a$ = perfect square

$\Rightarrow 4a + 1 = a$ perfect square possible values from the set a $= 6, 12$

$\Rightarrow$ Sum $= 6 + 12 = 18$

9. $p(x) = ax^4 + bx^3 - x^2 + 2x + 3$

$q(x) = (x+2)(x-1)$

Remainder $= \frac{p(-2) - p(1)}{-3} + \frac{-2p(1) - p(-2)}{-3} = 4x + 3$

Comparing, we get $-5a + 3b + 3 = 4$ (i)

$\Rightarrow 6a - 2b + 1 = 2$

$\Rightarrow a = 1, b = 2 \quad \Rightarrow |a + b| = 3$

10. Consider the equation $2x^2 + ax + a^2 - 5 = 0$ for both roots less that unity

$2(2 + a + a^2 - 5) > 0$

$\Rightarrow a^2 + a - 3 > 0$ (i)

and $a > -4$

$\Rightarrow$ By (i) $a = \dfrac{-1 \pm \sqrt{13}}{2}$ $\Rightarrow \lambda = 13$

11. Consider the inequality $\left|\dfrac{x^2+mx+1}{x^2+x+1}\right| < 3$

$\Rightarrow -3 < \dfrac{x^2+mx+1}{x^2+x+1} < 3$

$\therefore$ $x^2 + x + 1 > 0$ (no real roots, opening upwards), when

$\dfrac{x^2+mx+1}{x^2+x+1} > -3$

$\Rightarrow -2x^2 + x(m-3) - 2 < 0$

$\Rightarrow (m-3)^2 < 16$

$\Rightarrow (m-7)(m+1) < 0$ and $\dfrac{x^2+mx+1}{x^2+x+1} > -3$

$\Rightarrow m^2 + 6m - 55 < 0$ $\Rightarrow (m+11)(m-5) < 0$

$\Rightarrow m \in (-1, 5)$ $\Rightarrow |ab| = 5$

$\Rightarrow \log_{|ab|} 625 = 4$

12. $y = \sqrt{\dfrac{2}{x^2-x+1} - \dfrac{1}{x+1} - \dfrac{(2x+1)}{x^3+1}}$ for y to take real values

$\therefore$ $\dfrac{2}{x^2-x+1} - \dfrac{1}{x+1} - \dfrac{(2x+1)}{x^3+1} \geq 0$

$\Rightarrow$ $\dfrac{2x+2-x^2+x-1-2x-1}{x^3+1} > 0$

$\Rightarrow$ $\dfrac{x^2+x}{x^3+1} < 0$

$\Rightarrow$ $\dfrac{x(x+1)}{x^3+1} < 0$

$\Rightarrow \lambda \in (-\infty, -1) \cup [0, 1]$ $\lambda = -1$

13. Given x_1, x_2 are roots of $x^2 + 2(k-3)x + 9 = 0$

$\Rightarrow$ 6 and 4 lie between x_1 and x_2

$\Rightarrow f(6) = 36 + 12k - 36 + 9 < 0$

$\Rightarrow 12k + 9 < 0$ $\Rightarrow k < -\dfrac{3}{4}$

$\Rightarrow f(3) = 9 + 6k - 18 + 9 < 0$

$\Rightarrow k < 0$

$\Rightarrow$ Greatest integral value of k = – 1

14. Solving the equation in the region $x < -1$

$\Rightarrow \dfrac{2^{-x}}{2} - 2^x = 1 - 2^x - 1$

$\Rightarrow 2^{-x} = 2^2$

$\Rightarrow x = -2$, this is the least integral solution of the equation.

15. The equation $(1 + a)y^2 - 3ay + 4a = 0$ has real roots.

$\Rightarrow 9a^2 - 4(4a)(1 + a) \geq 0$

$\Rightarrow 9a^2 - 16a(1 + a) \geq 0$

$\Rightarrow 9a^2 - 16a - 16a^2 \geq 0 \Rightarrow -16a - 7a^2 \geq 0$

$\Rightarrow a(7a + 16) \leq 0$ $\Rightarrow a\left(a + \dfrac{16}{7}\right) \leq 0$

$\Rightarrow k \in \left[\dfrac{-16}{7}, 0\right]$ $\Rightarrow \sqrt{k_1 k_2} = 0$

16. $5^x\, 8^{1-1/x} = 500 = 5^3 . 8^{2/3}$

On comparing $1 - \dfrac{1}{x} = 1 - \dfrac{1}{3}$

$\Rightarrow x = 3$

17. $4^x - a2^x - a + 3 = 0$

Let $2^x = y$

$\Rightarrow y^2 - ay - a + 3 = 0$

For solution (real)

$\Rightarrow a^2 - 4(-a + 3) > 0$

$\Rightarrow (a - 2)(a + 6) \geq 0$

$\Rightarrow$ Least positive integral solution

$\Rightarrow a = 2$

18. $3^{72}\left(\dfrac{1}{3}\right)^x \cdot \left(\dfrac{1}{3}\right)^{\sqrt{x}} > 1$ $\Rightarrow$ $3^{72-x\sqrt{x}} > 1$

$\Rightarrow 3^{72-x-\sqrt{x}} > 3^0$

Let $x = y^2$ $\Rightarrow 3^{72-y^2-y} > 3^0$

$\Rightarrow 72 - y^2 - y > 0$

$\Rightarrow y^2 + y - 72 < 0$ $\Rightarrow y \in (-9, 8)$

Greatest integer value $= (-8)^2 = x = 64$

Permutation and Combination

CHAPTER 6

■ INTRODUCTION

Permutation and combinations are also known as counting without counting i.e., we count the number of ways without actually counting it.

This chapter is concerned with various methods of counting and choosing. Suppose in your colony there are twenty-five lanes and each lane has 20 houses. Now you and your friend have been asked to count them up. Your friend goes in each and every lane and starts counting them one by one, but you just multiply 20 and 25 and conclude that there are 500 houses in your colony. With a simple trick, a good amount of time is saved. Likewise, suppose there is a party of 25 persons which you go to attend. The question is if every person shakes hand with the rest of 25, then how many hand-shakes will take place?

Mr X forgot his four digit ATM access code and he only remembers that the digits were 1,3,5,9 (but do not remember the order) Utmost how many trials would be necessary to him to obtain the correct code.

Above and all such simulating questions, can be answered by use of concepts of Permutation and Combination. We can use "Permutation and Combination" in every kind of problems, where many possibilities of different events exist. These concepts are now used to solve many problems that we come across in modern subjects like Meterology, Astronomy, Botany, Zoology, Software industries etc.

■ COMBINATORICS

'Combinatorics' is an art (or technique) of counting without counting. This involves numerous methods to perform the process of counting without actually counting the each possibility. e.g., Addition and multiplication rule, bijection rule, Inclusion-Exclusion Principle (IEP) etc. Here we are going to discuss some of the above methods in particular.

■ FUNDAMENTAL PRINCIPLE OF COUNTING

Addition rule

If an operation W_1 can be performed in m ways and W_2 (which is independent of W_1) is performed in n ways, then either of the two operations (W_1 or W_2) can be performed in $(m + n)$ ways. This can be extended to any finite number of mutually exclusive operations. The Addition Principle assumes that there are

n_1 ways for the event E_1 to occur

n_2 ways for the event E_2 to occur

.....

.....

n_k ways for the event E_k to occur,

Where $k \geq 1$. If these ways for the different events to occur are pairwise disjoint, then the number of ways for at least one of the events E_1, E_2, ..., or E_k to occur is $n_1 + n_2 + ... + n_k = \sum_{i=1}^{k} n_i$

Let $A_1, A_2, ..., A_k$ be any k finite sets, where $k \geq 1$. If the given sets are pairwise disjoint, i.e., $A_i \cap A_j = \phi$ for $i, j \in \{1, 2, ..., k\}, i \neq j$, then $\left|\bigcup_{i=1}^{k} A_i\right| = |A_1 \cup A_2 \cup ... \cup A_k| = \sum_{i=1}^{k} |A_i|$

■ COMPLEMENTARY PRINCIPLE

If a work is to be done under some restriction (s), then the number of ways of doing that work. (the total number of ways doing the work without restrictions) – (the number of ways to do that work under opposite restrictions)

Example:

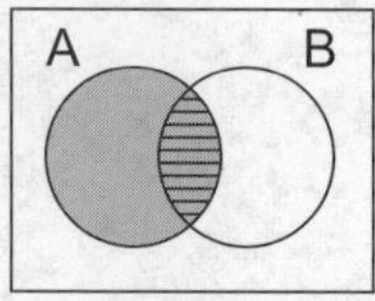

FIGURE 6.1

$$n(A\cap B') = n(A) - n(A\cap B)$$

ILLUSTRATION 1: There are 50 soldiers in a guard in which there are 30 Sikhs and remaining 20 are Gurkhas. The captain wants to select one of them as the Commander of the guards. How many different ways he can do it?

SOLUTION: There are 30 ways to select a commander from Sikh soldiers and 20 from Gurkhas. Hence the total number of ways = 30 + 20 = **50 ways**

ILLUSTRATION 2: There are three trains, four buses and two planes to travel from Chandigarh to Delhi. How many different ways a passenger can travel from Chandigarh to Delhi?

SOLUTION: The passenger can travel either by bus or by train or by plane.

Hence the total number of ways = 3 + 4 + 2 = **9 ways**

ILLUSTRATION 3: Find the number of numbers from 1 to 150 (both inclusive) which are divisible by 2 but not by 5.

SOLUTION: Number of numbers divisible by 2 without any restriction = 75

Number of numbers divisible by both 2 and 5 = 15

∴ Required number of numbers i.e. number of numbers from 1 to 150 (both inclusive) which are divisible by 2 but not by 5.

= (number of numbers divisible by 2 without any restriction) – (number of numbers divisible by both 2 and 5) (using complementary principle) = 75 – 15 = 60.

ILLUSTRATION 4: Let A = $\{x : x \in \mathbb{N} \; \& \; x \leq 50\}$. Find the number of ways in which ordered triplet $\{(a, b, c)$: $(a, b, c \in A)\}$ can be chosen so that a, b, c are in an increasing AP.

SOLUTION: Let the there numbers be a, $a + d$, $a + 2d$ (with $d \in \mathbb{N}$)

If $a = 1,\ 3 \leq a + 2d \leq 50 \quad \Rightarrow \quad 2 \leq 2d \leq 49$

$\Rightarrow \ 1 \leq d \leq 24.5 \qquad \Rightarrow \ 1 \leq d \leq 24$

$\Rightarrow$ d can be chosen in 24 ways

$\Rightarrow$ 24 ways to choose the triplet (a, b, c)

If $a = 2,\ 4 \leq 2 + 2d \leq 50 \Rightarrow 1 \leq d \leq 24$

Again 24 again

If $a = 3,\ 5 \leq 3 + 2d \leq 50 \Rightarrow 1 \leq d \leq 23.5$

$\Rightarrow$ 23 ways to select the triplet

Similarly, proceeding ahead in this manner.

If a =46, $48 \leq 46 + 2d \leq 50;\ 1 \leq d \leq 2$

$\Rightarrow$ 2 ordered triplets (46, 47, 48) and (46, 48, 50)

If a =. 47; $49 \leq 47 + 2d \leq 50,\ \ 1 \leq d \leq 1.5$

$\Rightarrow$ only one tripled (47, 48, 49)

And for a = 48; again only the triplet (48, 49, 50)

∴ Total number of triplets:

$$24 + 24 + 23 + 23 + \ldots.. + 2 + 2 + 1 + 1 = 2\,(1 + 2 + 3 + \ldots\ldots + 24) = 2\times\left(\frac{24\times 25}{2}\right) = 600$$

ILLUSTRATION 5: Find the number of integral points (x, y) such that $x^2 + y^2 \le 9$.

SOLUTION: Let $x^2 + y^2 = k$, where $k \in \{0, 1, 2, 3, ..., 9\}$

Let us defined a set $S_k = \{(x, y): x^2 + y^2 = k;\ x, y \in \mathbb{R}\ \}$

Since $S_0, S_1, S_2, ..., S_9$ are disjoint sets

$\therefore$ Total number of point $= n(S) = \sum_{k=0}^{9} n(S_k)$

i.e., $n(S) = n(S_0) + n(S_1) + n(S_2) + ... + n(S_9)$

$S_0 \Rightarrow x^2 + y^2 = 0 \Rightarrow (x, y) \in \{(0, 0)\} \Rightarrow n(S_0) = 1$

$S_1 \Rightarrow x^2 + y^2 = 1 \Rightarrow (x, y) \in \{(0, \pm1) \text{ or } (\pm1, 0)\} \Rightarrow n(S_1) = 4$

$S_2 \Rightarrow x^2 + y^2 = 2 \Rightarrow (x, y) \in \{(\pm1, \pm1)\} \Rightarrow n(S_2) = 4$

$S_3 \Rightarrow x^2 + y^2 = 3 \Rightarrow (x, y) \in \phi \Rightarrow n(S_3) = 0$

$S_4 \Rightarrow x^2 + y^2 = 4 \Rightarrow (x, y) \in \{(\pm2, 0), (0, \pm2)\} \Rightarrow n(S_4) = 4$

$S_5 \Rightarrow x^2 + y^2 = 5 \Rightarrow (x, y) \in \{(\pm2, \pm1), (\pm1, \pm2)\} \Rightarrow n(S_5) = 8$

$S_6 \Rightarrow x^2 + y^2 = 6 \Rightarrow (x, y) \in \phi \Rightarrow n(S_6) = 0$

$S_7 \Rightarrow x^2 + y^2 = 7 \Rightarrow (x, y) \in \phi \Rightarrow n(S_7) = 0$

$S_8 \Rightarrow x^2 + y^2 = 8 \Rightarrow (x, y) \in \{(\pm2, \pm2)\} \Rightarrow n(S_8) = 4$

$S_9 \Rightarrow x^2 + y^2 = 9 \Rightarrow (x, y) \in \{(0, \pm3), (\pm3, 0)\} \Rightarrow n(S_9) = 4$

$\Rightarrow$ n(S) = 29

Aliter: $x^2 + y^2 \le 9$

$\Rightarrow x, y \in \{-3, -2, -1, 0, 1, 2, 3\}$

Maximum number of possible ordered pairs of $(x, y) = 49$

Now when $x = \pm3$; $y^2 = 0$ i.e., $y = 0$

$\Rightarrow y \ne \pm3, \pm2, \pm1$

$\therefore$ These 12 cases are not possible

Similarly, when $x = \pm2 \Rightarrow y \ne \pm3$

$\Rightarrow$ 4 more cases rejected

And when $x = \pm1 \Rightarrow y \ne \pm3$

$\Rightarrow$ 4 more cases rejected.

$\therefore$ ordered pairs of $(x, y) = 49 - (12 + 4 + 4) = 29$.

MULTIPLICATION RULE

If an operation W_1 can be performed in m ways and W_2 is performed in n ways, then W_1 and W_2 can be performed in succession in $m.n$ ways. The multiplication principle assumes that an event E can be decomposed into r ordered events $E_1, E_2, ..., E_r$ and there are

n_1 ways for the event E_1 to occur,

n_2 ways for the event E_2 to occur

.....

n_r ways for the event E_r to occur.

Then the total number of ways for the event E to occur is given by:

$$n_1 \times n_2 \times ... \times n_r = \prod_{i=1}^{r} n_i$$

Let $\prod_{i=1}^{r} A_i = A_1 \times A_2 \times ... \times A_r = \{(a_1, a_2, ..., a_r) \mid a_i \in A_i,$ $i = 1, 2, ..., r\}$ denote the cartesian product of the finite sets $A_1, A_2, ..., A_r$. Then

$$\left|\prod_{i=1}^{r} A_i\right| = |A_1| \times |A_2| \times ... \times |A_r| = \prod_{i=1}^{r} |A_i|$$

ILLUSTRATION 6: There are three trains, four buses and two planes to travel from Chandigarh to Delhi. In how many different ways a passenger can travel from Chandigarh to Delhi and return back?

SOLUTION: Number of ways of travelling Chandigarh to Delhi is $(2 + 3 + 4) = 9$ ways. He can return by any of three modes. So number of ways of returning Delhi to Chandigarh is $(2 + 3 + 4) = 9$ ways. Complete journey includes travelling Chandigarh to Delhi and coming back which thus can be done in $= 9 \times 9 = 81$ ways.

ILLUSTRATION 7: A conference room has 10 different entrance doors and 5 different exit doors. In how many different ways delegates can enter into the hall and come out once?

SOLUTION: Delegates have 10 ways to enter into the conference hall and since they can come out only through exit door. So number of ways of exist = 5

So total number of ways of entering and exit $= 10 \times 5 = 50$ ways

ILLUSTRATION 8: The number of ways in which 6 rings can be worn on the four fingers of one hand is:

(a) 4^6 (b) 360

(c) 6^4 (d) None of these

SOLUTION: Each ring have 4 options to go, so required number of ways = 4^6

ILLUSTRATION 9: One has 10 different shirts, 5 different trousers, 5 different ties, 3 different pair of shoes. In how many different ways can he wear them if

(a) wearing all the items necessary (b) wearing shirt and trousers is compulsory

SOLUTION: (a) Number of ways of wearing all items = n (shirt, trouser, tie and shoes)

$= 10 \times 5 \times 5 \times 3 = 50 \times 15 = 750$

(b) In second case, there will be following four possible.

(i) n (Shirt and Trouser) = 50

(ii) n (shirt, Trouser and Tie) = 250

(iii) n (shirt, Trouser and Shoes) = 150

(iv) n (Shirt, Trouser, Shoes and Tie) = 750

$\Rightarrow$ Hence total number of ways = 1200

ILLUSTRATION 10: How many numbers between 10 and 10,000 can be formed by using the digits 1, 2, 3, 4, 5 if

(i) No digit is repeated in any number?

(ii) Digits can be repeated?

SOLUTION: (i) Number of two digit numbers $= 5 \times 4 = 20$

Number of three digit numbers $= 5 \times 4 \times 3 = 60$

Number of four digit numbers $= 5 \times 4 \times 3 \times 2 = 120$

$\therefore$ Total number of numbers formed $= 20 + 60 + 120 = 200$

(ii) Number of two digit numbers $= 5 \times 5 = 25$

Number of three digit numbers $= 5 \times 5 \times 5 = 125$

Number of four digit numbers $= 5 \times 5 \times 5 \times 5 = 625$

$\therefore$ Total number of numbers formed $= 25 + 125 + 625 = 775$

ILLUSTRATION 11: Find the number of ways in which 3 distinct numbers can be selected from the set $\{3^1, 3^2, 3^3, \ldots\ldots 3^{100}, 3^{101}\}$ so that they form a G.P.

SOLUTION: Let the three number be $a = 3^m$, $b = 3^n$ and $c = 3^p$; $m, n, p \in (1, 2, 3, \ldots\ldots, 10\}$

Since a, b, c are in GP $\Rightarrow b^2 = ac$ $\Rightarrow$ $3^{2n} = 3^{m+p}$

$\because$ $(m + p)$ must be even $\Rightarrow$ Either both m and n are odd or both even.

$\Rightarrow$ $a, c \in$ either $\{3^1, 3^3, 3^5....3^{101}\}$ or $\{3^2, 3^4, ... 3^{100}\}$

$\Rightarrow$ Required no. of ways of selection of a and $c = (51 \times 50 + 50 \times 49) = 50(51 + 49) = 5000$ and b is automatically selected as $b = \sqrt{ac}$.

ILLUSTRATION 12: To reach city D from city A; one has to pass through any of the ways as shown in the diagram (movement allowed in forward direction only), find.

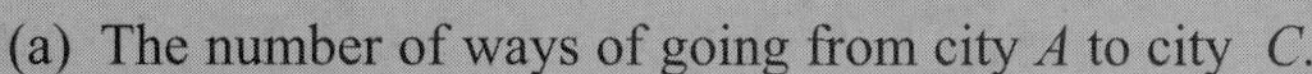

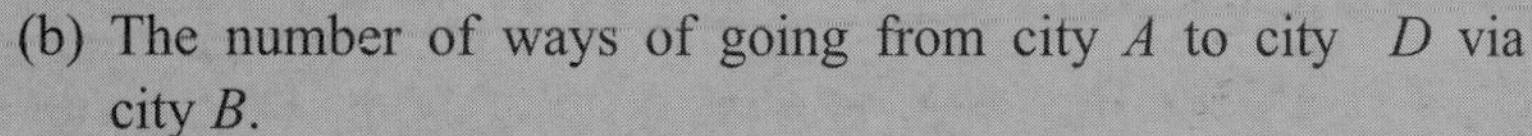

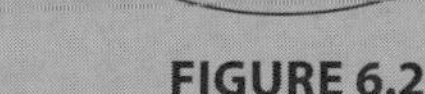

FIGURE 6.2

(a) The number of ways of going from city A to city C.

(b) The number of ways of going from city A to city D via city B.

(c) Find the number of ways of going from city A to city D

SOLUTION: (a) A person can go either directly from A to C or can go from A to C via B.

If he goes directly then, two ways are there. If he goes via B; then he must first go from A to B and then go from B to C. Number of ways from A to $B = 2$ and number of ways from B to $C = 4$

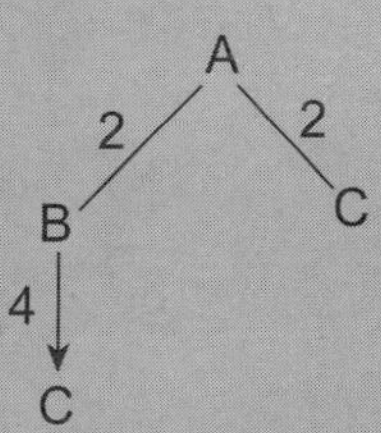

FIGURE 6.3

$\therefore$ Number of ways from A to C via B

= (number of ways from A to B) $\times$ (number of ways from B to C)

$= 2 \times 4 = 8$

$\therefore$ Total number of ways to go from A to C

= Number of ways to go from A to C directly + Number of ways to go from A to C via B.

$= 2 + 8 = 10$

(b) Number of ways of going from city A to city D via city B.

A person has to go to city B and then go from city B to city D. One can go from A to B in 2 ways.

To go from B to D; one has two alternatives.

He can go directly from B to D or go to D via C.

To go directly B to D; he has 2 ways.

To go via C; he will first have to go to C by any of the 4 ways and then from C to D by any of the 3 ways.

$\therefore$ 12 ways of going from B to D via C.

$\therefore$ Total number of ways of going from city A to city D via city B is

$2 \times (2 + 12) = 2 \times 14 = 28$.

(c) Number of ways of going from A to D

A person can go from A to D either via B or without visiting B.

For A to D via B; we already know there are 28 ways.

For A to D without visiting B

$A \to C \to D$ or $A \to D$

$A \to C$ and $C \to D$ or $A \to D$

$= 2 \times 3 + 1 = 7$

$\therefore$ total number of ways = 35.

Aliter:

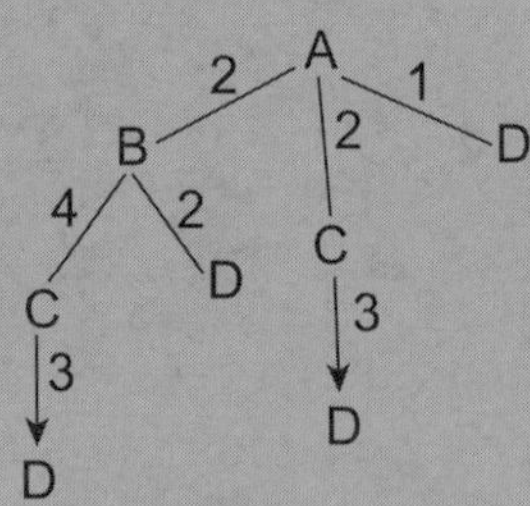

FIGURE 6.5

$\because$ Total number of ways $A \to B \to C \to D = 2 \times 4 \times 3$

or $A \to B \to D = 2 \times 2$ or $A \to C \to D = 2 \times 3$ or $A \to D = +1$

Adding these cases; we get total number of cases = 35.

ILLUSTRATION 13: The number of ordered quadruples (*x*, *y*, z, *w*) such that (*x*, *y*, z, *w*) ∈ [0, 10π] and which satisfy the inequality. $2^{\sin^2 x}.3^{\cos^2 y}.4^{\sin^2 z}.5^{\cos^2 w} \geq 120$

(a) 14641 (b) 10000 (c) 12100 (d) infinite

SOLUTION: Maximum value of $2^{\sin^2 x} = 2$ when $\sin^2 x = 1$

Maximum value of $3^{\cos^2 y} = 3$ when $\cos^2 y = 1$

Maximum value of $4^{\sin^2 z} = 4$ when $\sin^2 z = 1$

Maximum value of $5^{\cos^2 w} = 5$ when $\cos^2 w = 1$

$\therefore$ Maximum value of $2^{\sin^2 x}.3^{\cos^2 y}.4^{\sin^2 z}.5^{\cos^2 w} = 2 \times 3 \times 4 \times 5 = 120$

$\therefore$ $\sin^2 x = 1 \Rightarrow x = n\pi \pm \frac{\pi}{2} \Rightarrow x \in \left\{\frac{\pi}{2}, \frac{3\pi}{2}, \frac{5\pi}{2}, ..., \frac{19\pi}{2}\right\}$

$\sin^2 z = 1 \Rightarrow z = n\pi \pm \frac{\pi}{2} \Rightarrow z \in \left\{\frac{\pi}{2}, \frac{3\pi}{2}, \frac{5\pi}{2}, ..., \frac{19\pi}{2}\right\}$

$\cos^2 y = 1 \Rightarrow y = n\pi \Rightarrow y \in \{0, \pi, 2\pi, ..., 10\pi\}$

$\cos^2 w = 1 \Rightarrow w = n\pi \Rightarrow w \in \{0, \pi, 2\pi, ..., 10\pi\}$

$\therefore$ Number of possible values of x = 10

Number of possible values of z = 10

Number of possible values of *y* = 11

Number of possible values of w = 11

$\therefore$ Number of possible values of quadruples (*x*, *y*, z, *w*) = 12100

ILLUSTRATION 14: Given that 'n' is odd, the number of ways in which three numbers in A.P. can be formed from 1, 2, 3, 4, …., n is

(a) $\frac{(n-1)^2}{2}$ (b) $\frac{(n+1)^2}{4}$ (c) $\frac{(n+1)^2}{2}$ (d) $\frac{(n-1)^2}{4}$

SOLUTION: Let the three numbers in AP be *a*, *b*, *c*

$\therefore$ $2b = a + c$

Now $\because$ $b \in \mathbb{Z}$

$\Rightarrow$ $2b$ is an even integer

$\Rightarrow$ $a + c$ is an even integer

$\Rightarrow$ Either both *a* and *c* are odd integer or both are even integers.

Case I: Both a and c are odd integers. Number of ways of selecting two odd numbers from $\left(\frac{n+1}{2}\right)$ odd numbers. $=\frac{\left(\frac{n+1}{2}\right)\left(\frac{n+1}{2}-1\right)}{2}=\frac{(n+1)(n-1)}{8}=\frac{n^2-1}{8}$ (i)

Case II: Both a and c are even integers

$\therefore$ Number of ways of selecting two even numbers from $\left(\frac{n-1}{2}\right)$ even numbers is

$$=\frac{\left(\frac{n-1}{2}\right)\left(\frac{n-1}{2}-1\right)}{2}=\frac{(n-1)(n-3)}{2} \quad \text{(ii)}$$

Adding (i) and (ii); we get $N=\frac{n^2-1}{8}+\frac{(n-1)(n-3)}{8}=\frac{(n-1)^2}{4}$

And in all of there $\frac{(n-1)^2}{4}$ cases; (the middle term will be selected automatically, depending upon the values of 'a' and 'c').

Also 'a' and 'c' can interchange their values in 2! ways.

$\Rightarrow$ Total number of ways of selecting three terms in an AP is $\frac{(n-1)^2}{4}\times 2!=\frac{(n-1)^2}{2}$.

ILLUSTRATION 15: Given a balance and weights $2^0, 2^1, 2^2, 2^3, \ldots, 2^n$. Find the number of ways in which all these weights can be arranged on the balance so that the net weight on right side is never greater than that on the left side. $= 2^n - 1$

SOLUTION: Since, we know that $2^0 + 2^1 + 2^2 + \ldots + 2^{n-1} = \frac{2^0(2^n-1)}{2-1}=2^n-1$

$\therefore$ Since the net weight on the right side is never to be greater than that on the left side therefore the weight '2^n' is to be always point on the left side.

Therefore for each of the weights $2^0, 2^1, \ldots, 2^{n-1}$; we have 2 options

i.e., either we can put it on the left side or the right side.

Whereas, for the weight 2^n, we have only one option the left side

$\therefore$ By the law of multiplication, the number of ways of arranging these weights on the balance is $\underbrace{2\times2\times2\times\ldots..2}_{\text{n times}}\times1=2^n$

ILLUSTRATION 16: Find the number of distinct ways in which a mouse can enter and come out of the cage once, if movement is allowed in the direction of the arrow only and path once traced by mouse remains closed till the mouse comes out of the cage.

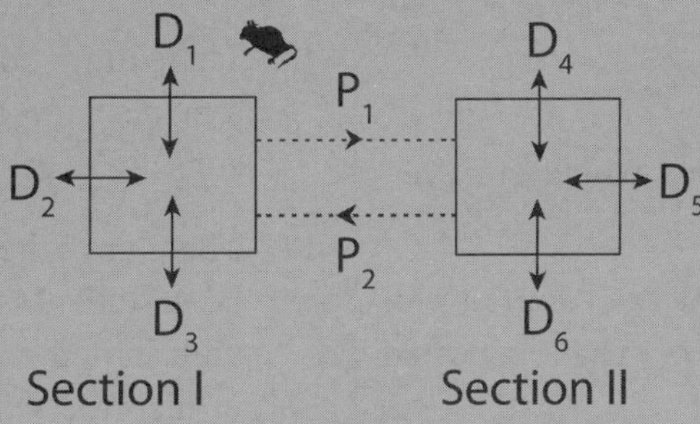

FIGURE 6.6

SOLUTION: The mouse can enter in 6 ways (through either of D_1, D_2, D_3, D_4, D_5 OR D_6) and all the cases will be alike (due to symmetry).

Let us suppose the mouse enters through D_1.

Now the mouse has the following options

(i) To come out of either D_2 or D_3 (i.e., 2 ways)

(ii) or to travel through P_1 towards section II of the cage

Now if the mouse moves to section II; then it has the following options

(i) To come out of the cage via D_4, D_5 or D_6

(ii) or to come back to section I via path P_2 and then come out of cage via D_2 or D_3 (i.e., 2 ways)

$\therefore$ Number of ways $= 6(2 + 1 \times (3 + 1 \times 2)) = 6\ (2 + 5) = 42$

NOTES

- *AND stands for intersection ($\cap$) or multiplication.*
- *OR stands for union ($\cup$) or addition.*

TEXTUAL EXERCISE–1 (SUBJECTIVE)

1. Find the number of ways of wearing 10 shirts, 5 different trousers and 4 ties, when:
   (a) all three items are necessarily to be used
   (b) wearing tie is not necessary
2. A hall has 12 gates. In how many ways can a man enter the hall through one gate and come out of the hall if
   (a) he can come out through any gate?
   (b) he comes out through different gate?
3. To reach city D from city A, one has to pass through city B and then city C as shown in figure. Then number of ways of travelling from city A to city D (when movement only in forward direction is allowed).

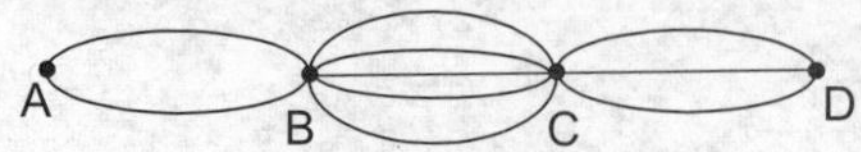

FIGURE 6.7

4. Find the number of 2-digit numbers which are even and have different digits.
5. How many numbers can be formed from some or all of the digits 2, 3, 4, 5 if no number is to have repeated digits?
6. In how many ways 5 letters can be posted in 6 letter boxes available in the locality?
7. A coin is tossed three times and the outcomes are recorded. How many possible outcomes are there? How many possible outcomes if the coin is tossed four times? Five times? n times?
8. In a city, telephone numbers consist of 8-digits and none of them begins with 0. How many telephone numbers could be possible in that city?
9. How many 3-digit numbers are there, with distinct digit, whose each digit is odd?
10. Find the number of all even 2-digit numbers, not having 0 at the unit's place?
11. Find the number of positive divisors of 600, inclusive of 1 and 600 itself.
12. Let $X = \{1, 2, ..., 100\}$ and let $S = \{(a, b, c) |\ a, b, c \in X, a < b \text{ and } a < c\}$. Find $| S |$.
13. There are 6 colleges in a city. In how many ways can a man send 3 of his sons to a college, if no two of his sons are to read in the same college?
14. There are 5 items in column A and 5 items in column B. A student is asked to match each item in column A with an item in column B. How many possible (correct or incorrect) answers are there to this question? What is the answer if there will be multiple matching?
15. How many arithmetic progressions with 10 terms are there whose first term is in the set {1, 2, 3} and... whose common difference is in the set {2, 3, 4}?

16. Find the number of five digit numbers that can be generated by arranging digits from 0 to 9 (where leading zeros i.e., 00235 are not allowed) when
(a) Repetition of digits are allowed
(b) Repetition of digits are not allowed
(c) How many of them are odd in both cases (a) and (b)?

17. Find the total number of increasing AP's consisting of three terms that can be formed out of first $(2n + 1)$ natural numbers.

18. Find the number of distinct ways in which a mouse can enter and come out of the cage once, in the case (a) and (b) if movement only in the direction of arrow is allowed and path once traced by mouse remains closed till the mouse comes out of the cage.

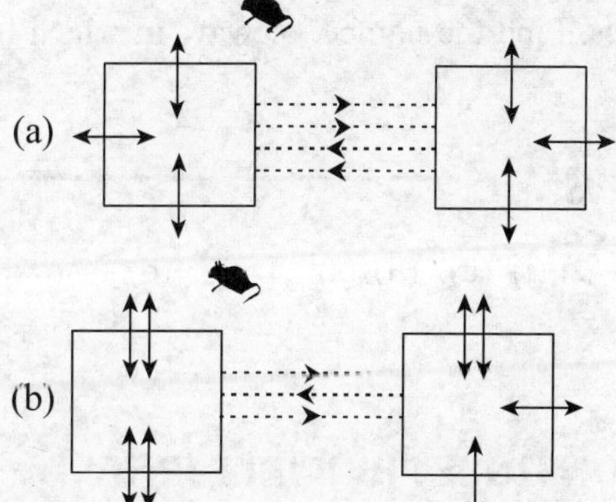

Answer Keys

1. (a) 200 (b) 250 2. (a) 144 ways (b) 132 ways 3. 30 4. 41 5. 64 6. 6^5
7. $2^3, 2^4, 2^5, 2^n$ 8. 9×10^7 9. 60 10. 36 11. 24 12. 328350
13. 120 14. $5!, 5^5$ 15. 9 16. (a) 9×10^4 (b) 27216
(c) 45000, 13440 17. n^2 18. (a) 216 ways (b) 152 ways

TEXTUAL EXERCISE–1 (OBJECTIVE)

1. Mr Amar has 5 shirts, 4 trousers and 3 shoes. In how many different ways can he wear them?
(a) 12 (b) 60
(c) 23 (d) None of these

2. A hall has 5 doors, in how many ways a person can enter and leave if
(i) Entry and exit should be from different doors?
(a) 25 (b) 10
(c) 16 (d) 20
(ii) Entry and exit may be from same doors?
(a) 25 (b) 10
(c) 16 (d) 20

3. A tyre store carries 10 different sizes of tyres each in with tube and tubeless variety each with red side wall or plain black. How many different kinds of tyres does the store has?
(a) 17 (b) 43
(c) 120 (d) None of these

4. How many four different digited natural numbers are there having each digit a prime number?
(a) 10 (b) 12
(c) 24 (d) None of these

5. The number of terms in the product $(a)\,(b+c)\,(d+e+f)\,(g+h+i+j)$.....(last factor of the sequence) (remaining alphabets)
(a) 120 (b) 840
(c) 3600 (d) None of these

6. The number of 4-digit even numbers that can be formed by using the digits 0, 1, 2, 3, 4, 5, 6 is
(a) 2201 (b) 1176
(c) 1372 (d) None of these

7. A teacher has 5 books. In how many ways he can arrange the books in a row?
(a) 120 (b) 3125
(c) 15 (d) None of these

8. A lady has 4 rings of different materials. She wants to wear three of them in 3 fingers, one in each finger. In how many different ways she can wear them?
(a) 12 (b) 64
(c) 24 (d) None of these

9. How many different digited 4-digits numbers are there?
(a) 4532 (b) 4537
(c) 4536 (d) None of these

10. A prize distribution is to be hold in a class of 8 students for the following results: first, second and third position in chemistry; first and second in maths; first in physics. Find the number of ways in which it can be done.

(a) $2^{10}3^{1}7^{2}$
(b) 820
(c) 56
(d) None of these

Answer Keys

1. (b) **2.** (i) (d), (ii) (a) **3.** (d) **4.** (c) **5.** (c) **6.** (b) **7.** (a) **8.** (c) **9.** (c)
10. (a)

PIGEON HOLE PRINCIPLE (PHP)

The Pigeon hole principle is stated (by famous mathematician Dirichlet) as below:

If more than n objects are distributed in n boxes, then at least one box should contain more than one object in it.

It can also be stated as if m pigeons are placed in n pigeon holes, where $m > n$, then there will be more than one pigeon in at least one pigeon-hole.

Generalized Pigeon Hole Principle

If $mn + 1$ or more number of pigeons are kept into m pigeon holes, then some pigeon hole must contain at least $n + 1$ pigeons.

Bijection principle Generally, it is not easy to count the numbers belonging to a very large collection (set) directly. Let us assume that we have a set X and we want to count $n(X)$ (number of elements in X). And we have another set Y and $n(Y)$ can be easily counted. Now if there exists one-one and onto relationship from set X to set Y (popularly called as bijection), then $n(X) = n(Y)$.

Alternatively, if X and Y are two finite sets such that there is a bijection (i.e., one-one onto mapping) from X to Y, then $n(X) = n(Y)$

e.g., The sitting capacity of a class is 30. On a particular day, the class is full then, without actual counting, we can say that the total number of the students present in the class is 30 as there is one-one onto correspondence between the set of students and set of seats.

INCLUSION-EXCLUSION PRINCIPLE

Let U be a finite set of m elements and $x_1, x_2, x_3, \ldots, x_r$ be some properties which the elements of U may or may not have. If the subset of U having the property x_i (where $i = 1, 2, 3, \ldots, r$) is X_i and those having the property x_i and x_j is denoted by $X_i \cap X_j$ and those having the property x_i, x_j and x_k is denoted by $X_i \cap X_j \cap X_k$ and so on.

Then the number of elements of U which have at least one of the properties $x_1, x_2, x_3, \ldots x_r$ is given by $n\left(\bigcup_{i=1}^{r} X_i\right) = s_1 - s_2 + s_3 - s_4 + \ldots + (-1)^{r-1} s_r$ and the number of elements of U which have none of the properties $x_1, x_2, x_3, \ldots x_r$ is given by $n\left(\bigcup_{i=1}^{r} X_i^c\right) = m - s_1 + s_2 - s_3 + \ldots + (-1)^r s_r$ where $s_1 = \sum_{i=1}^{r} n(X_i)$; $s_2 = \sum\sum_{1 \le i < j \le r} n(X_i \cap X_j)$

i.e., $s_1 = n(X_1) + n(X_2) + \ldots + n(X_r)$; $s_2 = n(X_1 \cap X_2) + n(X_1 \cap X_3) + \ldots + n(X_1 \cap X_r) + n(X_2 \cap X_3) + \ldots + n(X_2 \cap X_r) + \ldots + n(X_{r-1} \cap X_r)$

In particular case:

For $r = 2$, $n(X_1 \cup X_2) = n(X_1) + n(X_2) - n(X_1 \cap X_2)$

For $r = 3$,

$n(X_1 \cup X_2 \cup X_3) = n(X_1) + n(X_2) + n(X_3) - n(X_1 \cap X_2) - n(X_1 \cap X_3) - n(X_2 \cap X_3) + n(X_1 \cap X_2 \cap X_3)$

For $r = 4$,

$n(X_1 \cup X_2 \cup X_3 \cup X_4) = n(X_1) + n(X_2) + n(X_3) + n(X_4) - n(X_1 \cap X_2) - n(X_1 \cap X_3) - n(X_1 \cap X_4) - n(X_2 \cap X_3) - n(X_2 \cap X_4) - n(X_3 \cap X_4) + n(X_1 \cap X_2 \cap X_3) + n(X_1 \cap X_2 \cap X_4) + n(X_1 \cap X_3 \cap X_4) + n(X_2 \cap X_3 \cap X_4) - n(X_1 \cap X_2 \cap X_3 \cap X_4)$

ILLUSTRATION 17: Find the number of integers between 1 and 1000 both inclusive
(a) which are divisible by atleast one of the integers 10, 15 and 25.
(b) which are divisible by none of the integers 10, 15 and 25.

SOLUTION: Let U denote the set of numbers from 1 and 1000.

So that $n(U) = 1000$.

Let X, Y and Z denote the sets of integers divisible by 10, 15 and 25 respectively. Then n (X)

$= \left[\frac{1000}{10}\right] = 100$, $n(Y) = \left[\frac{1000}{15}\right] = 66$ and $n(Z) = \left[\frac{1000}{25}\right] = 40$

$S_1 = n(X) + n(Y) + n(Z) = 100 + 66 + 40 = 206$

Considering two of the three sets X, Y, Z, we have

$X \cap Y$ = set of integers divisible by 10 and 15

= set of integers divisible by 30 (L.C.M. of 10 and 15)

$\Rightarrow n(X \cap Y) = \left[\frac{1000}{30}\right] = 33$

Similarly, $(Y \cap Z)$ = set of integers divisible by 15 and 25

= set of integers divisible by 75 (L.C.M. of 15 and 25)

$\Rightarrow n(Y \cap Z) = \left[\frac{1000}{75}\right] = 13$

Similarly, $(X \cap Z)$ = set of integers divisible by 10 and 25

= set of integers divisible by 50 (L.C.M. of 10 and 25)

$\Rightarrow n(X \cap Z) = \left[\frac{1000}{50}\right] = 20$

$\Rightarrow S_2 = 33 + 13 + 20 = 66$

Now we can say, $(X \cap Y \cap Z)$ = set of integers divisible by 10, 15 and 25

= set of integers divisible by 150 (L.C.M. of 10, 15 and 25)

$\Rightarrow n(X \cap Y \cap Z) = \left[\frac{1000}{150}\right] = 6 \qquad \Rightarrow S_3 = 6$

(a) We have to find the number of integers which are divisible by at least one of 10, 15 and 25.
i.e., $n(X \cup Y \cup Z) = S_1 - S_2 + S_3 = 206 - 66 + 6 = 146$

(b) The number of integers divisible by neither none of 10, 15 and 25.
$= n(U) - n(X \cup Y \cup Z) = 1000 - 146 = 854$

ILLUSTRATION 18: Total number of integers 'n' such that $2 \le n \le 2000$ and H.C.F. of n and 36 is one, is equal to

(a) 666 (b) 667 (c) 665 (d) None of these

SOLUTION: If HCF of n and 36 = 1

$\Rightarrow$ n and 36 must be co-prime

So n must be co-prime with prime factors of 36 i.e., 2 and 3

Hence n cannot be multiple of 2 or 3

Number of Natural numbers less than equal to 2000 which are divisible by $2 = \left[\frac{2000}{2}\right] = 1000$

and that by $3 = \left[\frac{2000}{3}\right] = 666$

and those which are divisible by $6 = \left[\frac{2000}{6}\right] = 333$

So number of natural numbers which are multiple of 2 or 3 = 1000 + 666 - 333 = 1333

Now we have (2000 - 1) = 1999 numbers

Options to select 'n'; $\{2 \le n \le 2000\}$ of which we can't take 1333 values, so required number of options = 1999 – 1333 = 666.

REMARKS

(a) *The number of integers from 1 to n which are divisible by k is [n/k]; where [] is greatest integer function.*

(b) *The number of natural numbers from 1 to n which are perfect k^{th} powers is $[n^{1/k}]$.*

TEXTUAL EXERCISE-2 (SUBJECTIVE)

1. Consider two sets A {2, 3, 4, 5, 6} and B = {7, 8}. Let the products a.b, where (a,b) ∈ A × B are being put in each of the boxes of the figure shown below.

FIGURE 6.8

Considering each box can accommodate only single product, prove that either there are atleast three boxes having the same product or there exist two pairs of boxes, each pair having same product but different from other pair.

2. A store has slippers of sizes 6, 7, 8, 9. If 201 pairs are available in store, then show that there is a size having at least 51 pairs.

3. A book contains 12 chapters and has 305 pages. Then show that there must be a chapter having at least 26 pages and the maximum number of such chapters can be 5.

4. 45 packets of diamonds were delivered to a jewellery shop. These diamonds are of four different types and all the diamonds in each packet are identical then show that among these packets, at least 12 packet contain same type of diamonds.

5. In the given arrangement of 9 squares, each square is filled by exactly one of the number –1, 0 or 1. Prove that out of eight possible ways of addition (three along columns, three along rows and two across diagonals) at least two sums must be equal.

6. Find the number of elements in the set A where A = $\{x : x, x^4 \in \mathbb{N} \text{ and } 1 \le x^4 \le 4096\}$.

7. Find the number of 2 digits numbers (having different digits), which are divisible by 5.

8. Find the number of integers from 73 to 241 which are
   (i) Divisible by 2
   (ii) Divisible by 5
   (iii) Divisible by either 2 or 5
   (iv) Divisible by exactly one of 2 and 5
   (v) Divisible by both 2 and 5
   (vi) Divisible by neither 2 nor 5
   (vii) Divisible by 2 but not 5
   (viii) Divisible by 5 but not 2.

Answer Keys

6. 8 **7.** 17 **8.** (i) 84 (ii) 34 (iii) 101 (iv) 84 (v) 17 (vi) 68 (vii) 67 (viii) 17

TEXTUAL EXERCISE-2 (OBJECTIVE)

1. A survey shows that 65 % of the Americans like cheese, whereas 75% like apples. If x per cent of the Americans like both cheese, and apples, the range of the value of x is
   (a) [40, 65] (b) [30, 60]
   (c) [0, 40] (d) none

2. A box contains 25 different coloured balls blue, black, red, white and green, 5 of each colour. The minimum number of balls to be drawn out of the box without looking, so that at least two drawn balls are of indentical colour are.
   (a) 5 (b) 4
   (c) 3 (d) 6

3. Out of (m + 1) consecutive given integers two of them can always be chosen such that there
   (a) Difference is divisible by m.
   (b) Sum is divisible by m.
   (c) Product is divisible by m.
   (d) None of these

4. 17 ants are roaming over the chess board of the area of 8 × 8 (i.e., 64 square inches) then at least two of them must always be closer than
   (a) 2 inches (b) $2\sqrt{2}$ inches
   (c) $\sqrt{2}$ inches (d) None of these

5. A sentence contains 10 words each containing 4 different letters of english alphabet. At least how

many words should be selected so that at least two words among the selected words have at least one common letter.

(a) 6 (b) 7
(c) 8 (d) 9

6. There are 60 lottery tickets, out of which 30 tickets have prizes whereas remaining 30 are blank. Then least number of tickets purchased to ensure the prize is

(a) 40 (b) 32
(c) 31 (d) 30

7. How many least number of different positive integers should be chosen so that the difference of at least two integers divisible by 23?

(a) 22 (b) 23
(c) 24 (d) 25

8. 8 couples are invited in a party by Mr Ravinder Tiwari. How many people should be invited to dance, so that at least one man and one woman are included in dancing group?

(a) 7 (b) 8
(c) 9 (d) 10

9. There are three machines in a factory having production 70%, 20%, 10% respectively. From a lot of products containing 500 items, least number of products that should be selected, so that not all the items are produced by a single machine are

(a) 51 (b) 101
(c) 351 (d) None of these

Answer Keys

1. (a) **2.** (d) **3.** (*a, b, c*) **4.** (b) **5.** (b) **6.** (c) **7.** (c) **8.** (d) **9.** (c)

FACTORIAL

An efficient way of writing a product of finite number of consecutive positive integers integers is the factorial notation. The number $n!$ (read as "*n*-factorial") is defined as follows: For any positive integer *n*,

$$n! = n\,(n-1)\,(n-2).....(3)(2)(1) \text{ and } 0! = 1$$

For instance, $4! = 4.3.2.1 = 24$

ILLUSTRATION 19: The ten's digit in $1! + 4! + 7! + 10! + 12! + 13! + 15! + 16! + 17!$ is divisible by

(a) 4 (b) 3! (c) 5 (d) 7

SOLUTION: As we know the last two digits of 10! and above factorials will be 00.

$\therefore\ 1! + 4! + 7! + 10! + 12! + 13! + 15! + 16! + 17!$

$= 1 + 24 + 5040 + 10! + 12! + 13! + 15! + 16! + 17!$

$= 5065 + 10! + 12! + 13! + 15! + 16! + 17! =$ abcd......65; where *a, b, c, d* are digits i.e., 0 to 9.

Thus, in the sum of this series, the digit in the ten place is 6 which is divisible by 3!.

NOTES

(i) *Factorials of negative integers are not defined.*
(ii) *0! = 1 (by definition of factorial)*
(iii) $n! = n.(n-1)!,\ n \in \mathbb{N}$
(iv) $(2n)! = 2^n n!\,[1.\,3.\,5.\,7...\,(2n-1)]$
(v) *Whereas the reader is asked to evaluate or compute such numbers as 5! and 8!, he would not be expected to compute (say) 20! If such a number is the answer to a question, it should be left in precisely that form.*

■ INTRODUCTION TO PERMUTATION AND COMBINATION

Combinatorics means counting of things by using combinations and permutations.

Let us define combination and permutation as given below.

Combination

Combination is a process of selection where order of selection has no importance e.g., combinations of four numbers 6, 7, 8, 9 taking two at a time are:

(6, 7); (6, 8); (6, 9); (7, 8); (7, 9); (8, 9)

∴ Number of combinations is 6

Number of combinations of *n* thing taking *r* at *a* time is denoted by ^nC_r.

Thus in view of above example, $^4C_2 = 6$

Permutation

Permutation of given number of object is a process of selecting the objects where the orders of selection is important. (It is also called as arrangement/array) e.g., permutations of four numbers 6, 7, 8, 9 taking two a time are:

(6, 7), (6, 8), (6, 9), (7, 8), (7, 9), (8, 9), (7, 6), (8, 6), (9, 6), (8, 7), (9, 7), (9, 8).

∴ Number of permutations is 12

No of permutation of n-things taking *r* at a time is denoted by ^nP_r.

Thus $^4P_2 = 12$.

ILLUSTRATION 20: Write all combinations of four players Dhoni, kohli, Rahane and Gambhir taking at a time.

SOLUTION: Combinations

(Dhoni, Kholi, Rahane), (Dhoni, Rahane, Gambhir), (Kohli, Rahane, Gambhir), (Dhoni, Kohli, Gambhir).

$\therefore$ No of combinations $= 4 = {}^4C_3 = \dfrac{4!}{3!(4-3)!} = \dfrac{4!}{3!1!}$

ILLUSTRATION 21: Write all permutations of the letters a, e, i, o using three at a time.

SOLUTION: Permutations

(a, e, i), (a, i, o), (e, i, o), (a, e, o),
(a, i, e), (a, o, i), (e, o, i), (a, o, e),
(e, i, a), (o, a, i), (i, o, e), (o, e, a),
(e, a, i), (o, i, a), (i, e, o), (o, a, e),
(i, a, e), (i, a , o), (o, e, i,),(e, a, o),
(i, e, a), (i , o, a), (o, i, e), (e, o, a).

$\therefore$ Number of permutations $= 24 = {}^4P_3 = \dfrac{4!}{(4-3)!} = \dfrac{4!}{1!}$

NOTES

- *From above, we conclude,* $^nC_r = \dfrac{n!}{r!(n-r)!}$ *and* $^nP_r = \dfrac{n!}{(n-r)!}$
- *The proof of above two formulae will given in the fourth coming articles PERMUTATION and there after COMBINATION.*

■ PERMUTATION

Each of the arrangements which can be made by taking some or all of a number of things is called **permutation.** So it can be defined as a selection when order of selection matters.

e.g., Permutation which can be made by taking the letters *a, b, c, d* two at a time are twelve in number, namely,

ab,	*ac,*	*ad,*	*bc,*	*bd,*	*cd*
ba,	*ca,*	*da,*	*cb,*	*db,*	*dc;*

Permutations of different objects

Number of permutations of n distinct things taken r at a time ($0 \le r \le n$) is denoted by ${}^nP_r = n(n-1)(n-2)....(n-r+1)$

$$= \frac{n!}{(n-r)!} = r!.\frac{n!}{r!(n-r)!}$$

$$= {}^nC_r \times r!; \text{where } {}^nC_r = \frac{n!}{r!(n-r)!}$$

(so permutation includes selection first, then arrangement)

This is equivalent to filling up of r vacancies by n different person, 1st place can be filled in n ways and after which 2nd place can be filled in $(n-1)$ ways and 3rd place can be filled in $(n-2)$ ways and similarly, rth place can be filled in $(n-r+1)$ ways. Hence the total number of ways of filling the vacancies will be

$$= n(n-1)(n-2)....(n-r+1) = \frac{n!}{(n-r)!}$$

Hence the number of permutaions of n distinct objects taken all at a time $= n!$

NOTE

The words indicating permutation are arrangement, standing in a line, seated in a row, problems on digits, word formation and rank of word etc. In problems related to word formation using the given letters, we consider meaningful as well as meaningless words if not stated.

ILLUSTRATION 22: How many 9 letter words can be formed using the letters of the word PRODUCING?

SOLUTION: (a) PRODUCING has all 9 different letters

∴ Number of words formed $= {}^9P_9 = 9! = 362880$.

ILLUSTRATION 23: (a) Find the number of words made by using the letters of the word COMBINE and also obtain the number of words which begin and end with vowel.

(b) How many of the words formed above contain vowels and consonants occupying the same relative positions as in the word COMBINE?

SOLUTION: (a) The total number of words

= arrangement of seven letters taken all at a time $= {}^7P_7 = 7! = 5040$

The corresponding choices for all the places are as follows:

Places	Vowel	–	–	–	–	–	Vowel
Number of choices	3	5	4	3	2	1	2

As there are three vowels (O, I, E) first place can be filled in three ways and the last place can be filled in two ways. The rest of the places can be filled in 5! ways using five remaining letters. Number of words $= 3 \times 5! \times 2 = 720$

(b) Vowels should be at second, fifth and seventh positions

{same position of constant in the word COMBINE}

They can be arranged in 3! ways

Consonants should be at first, third, fourth and sixth positions

{same position of vowel in the word COMBINE}

They can be arranged here in 4! ways. Total number of words $= 3! \times 4! = 144$

ILLUSTRATION 24: How many words can be formed using the letters of the word TRIANGLE so that

(a) A and N are always together (b) T, R, I are always together?

SOLUTION: (a) Assume (AN) as a single letter.

Now there are seven letters in all: (AN), T, R, I, G, L, E

Seven letters can be arranged in 7! ways

All these 7! words will contain A and N together.

A and N can now be arranged among themselves in 2! ways (AN and NA)

Hence total number of words = 7! . 2! = 10080

(b) Assume (TRI) as a single letter

The letters: (TRI), A, N, G, L, E can be arranged in 6! ways

TRI can be arranged among themselves in 3! ways

Total number of words = 6! . 3! = 4320

ILLUSTRATION 25: From 6 different novels and 3 different dictionaries, 4 novels and 1 dictionary are to be selected and arranged in a row on the shelf so that the dictionary is always in the middle. Then the number of such arrangements is

(a) at least 500 but less than 750
(b) at least 750 but less than 1000
(c) at least 1000
(d) less than 500

SOLUTION: The number of ways in which 4 novels can be selected $= {}^6C_4 = 15$

The number of ways in which 1 dictionary can be selected $= {}^3C_1 = 3$

4 novels can be arranged in 4! ways.

The total number of ways = 15 × 4! × 3 = 15 × 24 × 3 = 1080.

ILLUSTRATION 26: Find the total number of signals that can be made by five flags of different colours when any number of them may be used in any signal.

SOLUTION: ***Case I:*** When only one flag is used.

No. of signals made $= {}^5P_1 = 5$.

Case II: When only two flags are used.

Number of signals made $= {}^5P_2 = 5.4 = 20$.

Case III: When only three flags are used.

Number of signals made $= {}^5P_3 = 5.4.3 = 60$.

Case IV: When only four flags are used.

Number of signals made $= {}^5P_4 = 5.4.3.2 = 120$.

Case V: When five flags are used.

Number of signals made $= {}^5P_5 = 5! = 120$.

Hence required number = 5 + 20 + 60 + 120 + 120 = 325.

ILLUSTRATION 27: m men and n women are to be seated in a row so that no two women sit together. If $m > n$, then show that the number of ways is which they can be seated, is $\dfrac{m!(m+1)!}{(m-n+1)!}$

SOLUTION: Since, m men and n women are to be seated in a row so that no two women sit together. This can be shown as $\times M_1 \times M_2 \times M_3 \times .... \times M_m \times$,

which shows that there are (m + 1) places for n women.

Number of ways in which they can be arranged $= (m)!\,{}^{m+1}P_n = \dfrac{(m)!(m+1)!}{(m+1-n)!}$

NOTES

(a) *The number of all permutations of n different objects taken r at a time, when a particular object is to be always included in each arrangement is* $r!\,{}^{n-1}C_{r-1}$

(b) *Number of permutations of n different things, taken all at a time, when m specified things always come together is m! (n–m +1)!*

(c) *Number of permutations of n different things, taken all at a time, when m specified things never come together is n! – m! (n– m +1) !*

TEXTUAL EXERCISE–3 (SUBJECTIVE)

1. Evaluate the following:

(i) $\dfrac{12!-10!}{9!}$

(ii) $\dfrac{n!}{r!\times(n-r)!}$, when $n = 15, r = 12$.

(iii) $(n - r + 1).\dfrac{n!}{(n-r+1)!}$

(iv) $n(n - 1)(n - 2)\ldots\ldots\ldots(n - r + 1)$

2. Find the value of r if

(i) $P(15, r) = 2730$

(ii) $P(15, r - 1)$: $P(16, r - 2) = 3: 4$

(iii) $P(2r - 1, r)$: $P(2r + 1, r - 1) = 22: 7$

3. Raju wants to arrange 3 English, 4 History and 5 Mathematics books on a book shelf. If the books on the same subject are different. Determine the number of all possible arrangements, if the books on same subject are always together.

4. Find the number of different 7-letter words (may be meaningless) that can be formed from the letter of the word, NUMBERS' so that vowels always occupy the present position.

5. Ten students are participating in a race. In how many ways can the first three prizes and the next three consolation prizes be given so that all the prizes go to different students?

6. How many words can be formed from the letters of the word, 'DAUGHTER' so that?

(i) D is always next to E but before G

(ii) D occurs after E

(iii) the vowels occupy even places

(iv) the vowels always come together

(v) All the vowels are never together

(vi) the vowels are separated

(vii) the vowels occupy odd prime positions.

(viii) D occurs before E and E occurs before R.

(ix) D occurs before E and E occurs after R.

(x) D and R occupy extreme positions.

7. In how many ways can 6 balls of different colours, namely, white, black, blue, red, green and yellow be arranged in a row in such a way that white and black balls are never together?

8. How many different 6-digit numbers can be formed with the digits 0, 1, 3, 5, 7 and 9? How many of them are divisible by 10? (repetitions is not allowed)

9. (a) How many numbers greater than 40000 can be formed using the digits 1, 2, 3, 4 and 5 if each digit is used only once in each number?

(b) How many odd numbers greater than 80000 can be formed using the digits 2, 3, 4, 5 and 8 if each digits used only once in a number?

10. How many numbers divisible by 5 and lying between 3000 and 4000 can be formed by using the digits 3, 4, 5, 6, 7, 8 when no digit is repeated in any such number?

11. Out of 5 ladies and 5 gents ($L_1, L_2, L_3, L_4, L_5, G_1, G_2, G_3, G_4, G_5$) in how many ways they can be arranged in a row?

(i) If no restriction applied

(ii) If all ladies are together.

(iii) iff all ladies are together as well as gents are also together.

(iv) If no two ladies are together

(v) If neither two ladies nor two gents together.

(vi) if L_1 L_2 together

(vii) if G_1 G_2 are never together
(viii) if L_1 L_2 together and G_1 G_2 also together
(ix) if L_1 L_2 together and G_1, G_2 never together
(x) L_1 L_2 not together and G_1 G_2 not together

12. The letters of the word FLOWER are taken 4 at a time and arranged in all possible ways. The number of arrangements that contain the letter 'F' is 240 and which do not contain F is ______.

Answer Keys

1 (i) 1310 (ii) 455 (iii) ${}^nP_r$ (iv) ${}^nP_r$ **2.** (i) 3 (ii) $r = 14$ (iii) 10 **3.** (3! × 4! × 5!) × 3!
4. 5! **5.** ${}^{10}P_6$ or ${}^{10}P_3 \times {}^7P_3$
6. (i) 7! /2! (ii) 4.(7!) (iii) ${}^4P_{3.}{}^5P_5$ (iv) ${}^3P_{3.}{}^6P_6$ (v) ${}^8P_{8.} - ({}^3P_{3.} \times {}^6P_6)$ (vi) ${}^5P_{5.}{}^6P_3$ (vii) 720 (viii) 6720
(ix) 13440 (x) 1440 **7.** ${}^6P_{6.} - 2.({}^5P_5)$ **8.** 600, 120
9. (a) 48 (b) 12 **10.** 12
11. (i) 10! (ii) 6! 5! (iii) 2! (5!)^2 (iv) 6! 5! (v) 2! (5!)^2 (vi) 2! 9! (vii) 10! – 2!9! (viii) 2! 2! 8!
(ix) 9! 2!–2! 2! 8! (x) 58 (8!) **12.** 120

TEXTUAL EXERCISE–3 (OBJECTIVE)

1. The value of $\frac{51! - 50!}{25}$ is
(a) $\frac{51}{25}$ (b) $\frac{1}{25}$
(c) 2(50)! (d) (100)!

2. The value of expression $\frac{n!}{(n-3)!} + \frac{(2n)!}{4(2n-3)!}$ is
(a) $n(n-1)^2$ (b) $3n(n-1)^2$
(c) $n^2(n-1)^2$ (d) $n^2(3n-1)$

3. Let $f(x) = \frac{3.6.9.12...(3n)}{(3)^n}$ be a function of natural number then evaluate $f(50)$.
(a) 25! (b) 75!
(c) 100! (d) 50!

4. If general term of a sequence is given $t_n = n!.\ n$, then the sum of first n terms will be
(a) $(n + 1)! - n!$ (b) $(n+1)! - 1$
(c) $(n + 1)!$ (d) None of these

5. If $\frac{{}^nP_{r-1}}{a} = \frac{{}^nP_r}{b} = \frac{{}^nP_{r+1}}{c}$, then
(a) ab, b, ac are in $A.P.$ (b) ab, b, ac are is $G.P.$
(c) $b^2 = a(b + c)$ (d) None of these

6. ${}^1P_1 + 2.{}^2P_2 + 3.\ {}^3P_3 + ... + n.\ {}^nP_n$ is equal to
(a) ${}^{n+1}P_{n+1}$
(b) $\frac{1}{(n+2)}\ {}^{n+2}P_{n+2} - 1$
(c) $\frac{1}{(n+2)(n+3)}\ {}^{n+3}P_{n+3} + 1$
(d) None of these

7. If $\frac{{}^nP_{r-1}}{a} = \frac{{}^nP_r}{b} = \frac{{}^nP_{r+1}}{c}$, then $\frac{b^2}{a(b+c)}$ is equal to
(a) 1 (b) 2
(c) 1/2 (d) None of these

8. Which of the following statement is false?
(a) ${}^nP_n = {}^nP_{n-1} = {}^{n-1}P_{n-1}$
(b) ${}^nP_r = {}^{n-1}P_r + r = {}^{n-1}P_{r-1}$
(c) ${}^nP_r = n\ .\ {}^{n-1}P_{r-1}$
(d) ${}^nP_n = 2.\ {}^nP_{n-2} = 3.{}^nP_{n-3}$

9. If ${}^{56}P_{r+6} : {}^{54}P_{r+3} = 30800{:}1$, then the values or r is
(a) 40 (b) 41
(c) 42 (d) None of these

10. The value of $\sum_{r=1}^{10} r\ .\ {}^rP_r$ is
(a) ${}^{11}P_{11}$ (b) ${}^{11}P_{11} - 1$
(c) ${}^{11}P_{11} + 1$ (d) None of these

11. If ${}^{2n+1}P_{n-1} : {}^{2n-1}P_n = 3 : 5$, then n is equal to
(a) 4 (b) 6
(c) 3 (d) 8

12. In a class of 50 students, in how many ways 1st, 2nd and 3rd prizes be given, so that no student gets more than one prize?

(a) ${}^{50}P_3$ (b) 53!

(c) $\frac{50!}{3!}$ (d) None of these

13. How many integers less than 1000, are there, having each digit distinct and odd?

(a) 5 (b) 20

(c) 60 (d) 85

14. A lady has three rings. In how many ways she can wear them if no finger carries more than one ring?

(a) $10P_3$ (b) $\frac{10!}{3!}$

(c) $\frac{10!}{7!}$ (d) None of these

15. How many opening order pairs can be made in a cricket team of 11 players?

(a) $10P_2$ (b) $10C_2$

(c) $\frac{10!}{8!}$ (d) 90

16. A flag contains 5 strips. In how many different ways colours can be filled in flag, out of 8 given colours, so that no two different strips have same colour?

(a) $8P_5$ (b) $8C_5$

(c) 8!/5! (d) None of these

17. How many different words can be formed having 4 different letters of English alphabet?

(a) 26! (b) $\frac{26!}{22!}$

(c) $26P_4$ (d) $\frac{10!}{2!}$

18. On a railway there are 10 stations. The number of types of tickets required in order that it may be possible to book a passenger from every station to every other is

(a) $\frac{10!}{2!}$ (b) 10! 2!

(c) $\frac{10!}{8!}$ (d) $\frac{10!}{8!2!}$

19. The number of ways in which 9 pictures can be hung on 6 picture nails (in a row) is (Here, it is obvious that only 6 pictures out of 9 will be hung and 3 will be left out).

(a) 9^6 (b) 6^9

(c) ${}^9P_6$ (d) None of these

20. In a group of boys, the number of arrangements of 4 boys is 12 times the number of arrangements of 2 boys. The numbers of boys in the group is

(a) 10 (b) 8

(c) 6 (d) None of these

21. The number of ways in which $m + n$ $(n \le m + 1)$ different things can be arranged in a row such that no two of the n things may be together is

(a) $\frac{(m+n!)}{m!n!}$ (b) $\frac{m!(m+1)!}{(m+n)!}$

(c) $\frac{m!n!}{(m-n+1)!}$ (d) None of these

22. The number of arrangements which can be made using all the letters of the word LAUGH, if vowels occur together.

(a) 48 (b) 96

(c) 24 (d) None of these

23. The number of ways in which four particular persons *A, B, C, D* and six more persons can stand in a queue so that A always stands before *B*, *B* before *C* and *C* before *D*., is

(a) 7! 4! (b) 10! – 7! 4!

(c) 10!/4! (d) None of these

24. The total number of words which can be formed out of the letters *a, b, c, d, e, f* taken 3 together, such that each word contains at least one vowel, is

(a) 72 (b) 48

(c) 96 (d) None of these

25. The number of different ways in which 8 persons can stand in a row so that between two particular persons A and *B*, there are always two persons, is

(a) 60(5!) (b) 15(4!) × (5 1)

(c) 4! × 5! (d) None of these

26. The greatest possible number of points of intersection of 8 straight lines and 4 circles is

(a) 32 (b) 4

(c) 76 (d) 104

Answer Keys

1. (c)	**2.** (b)	**3.** (d)	**4.** (b)	**5.** (c)	**6.** (b)	**7.** (a)	**8.** (a),(b)	**9.** (b)	**10.** (b)
11. (b)	**12** (a)	**13.** (d)	**14.** (a), (c)	**15.** (a)	**16.** (a)	**17.** (b),(c)	**18.** (c)	**19.** (c)	**20.** (c)
21. (d)	**22.** (a)	**23.** (c)	**24.** (c)	**25.** (a)	**26.** (d)				

Permutation of identical objects, taking all of them at a time

Number of permutations of 'n' things taken all at a time when 'p' are of one kind, 'q' of a second kind, 'r' of a third kind and so on.

Let N be the required number of permutations. From any one of these, if the p like things were different we could make $p!$ new permutations. Thus if the p like things were all different, we would have got $N(p!)$ new permutations. Similarly, if the q like things were different, we would get N ($q!$) new permutations from each of the second set of permutations.

Thus if the p like things and the q like things were all different, we would have got $N.p!q!$ permutations in all. The process is continued until all the sets of like things are different, and we then get the number of permutations of n things taken all at a time when they are all different.(which is $n!$)

$$\therefore \quad N.p!.q!.r! = n!$$

$$\therefore \quad N = \frac{n!}{p!q!r!}$$

ILLUSTRATION 28: How many 9 letter words can be formed using the letters of the word?

(a) ALLAHABAD (b) INTERMEDIATE

(c) ARRANGE (d) MATHEMATICS

SOLUTION: (a) Number of total letters = 9;

Number of A's = 4

Number of L's = 2

$\therefore$ Total number of word that can be formed from ALLAHABAD is $= \dfrac{9!}{4!\,2!} = 7560$

(b) Total number of word that can be formed from INTERMEDIATE having $2I$, $3E$, $2T$, A, N, D, M, R occurs $= \dfrac{12!}{2!\,3!\,2!}$

(c) Total number of words that can be formed from ARRANGE having $2A$, $2R$, N, G, E $= \dfrac{7!}{2!2!}$

(d) Total number of words that can be formed from MATHEMATICS having $2M$, $2T$, $2A$, H, I, C, $S = \dfrac{10!}{(2!)^3}$

ILLUSTRATION 29: How many different words can be formed with the letters of the word ORDINATE so that

(i) All vowels occupy odd places

(ii) Beginning with O

(iii) Beginning with O and endings with E?

SOLUTION: 'ORDINATE' has 8 letters having 4 vowels and 4 consonants.

(i) Required number of words $= 4! \times 4! = 24 \times 24 = 576$, because 4 vowels are to be adjusted in 4 odd places and the 4 consonants in the remaining 4 even places.

(ii) 7! ways, O being fixed

(iii) 6! ways, O fixed in 1st and E fixed in last places.

ILLUSTRATION 30: Find the number of ways in which 5 boys and 5 girls be seated in a row so that

(i) No two girls will sit together

(ii) All the girls sit together and all the boys sit together

(iii) All the girls are never together

SOLUTION: (i) 5 boys can be seated in a row in ${}^5P_5 = 5!$ ways. Now in 6 gaps, 5 girls can be arranged in ${}^6P_5$ ways

Hence the number of ways in which no two girls sit together $= 5! \times {}^6P_5 = 5! \times 6!$

(ii) The two groups of girls and boys can be arranged in 2! ways. 5 girls can be arranged among themselves in 5! ways. Similarly, 5 boys can be arranged among themselves in 5! ways. Hence by the fundamental principle of counting, the total number of requisite seating arrangements $= 2!\,(5! \times 5!) = 2(5!)^2$

(iii) The total number of ways in which all the girls are never together = total number of arrangements – Total number of arrangements in which all the girls are always together = $10! - 5! \times 6!$

ILLUSTRATION 31: There are 21 balls which are either white or black and the ball of the same colour are alike. Find the number of white balls so that the number of arrangements of these balls in a row be maximum.

SOLUTION: Let there be r white (alike) balls so that the number of black balls is $(21- r)$ (These are also alike)

Number of arrangements of these 21 balls is $A = \dfrac{21!}{r!(21-r)!} = {}^{21}C_r$

Again $A = {}^{21}C_r$, will be maximum when $r = \dfrac{21+1}{2}$ or $\dfrac{21-1}{2}$ i.e., 10 or 11

ILLUSTRATION 32: In how many ways we can arrange 3 red flowers, 4 yellow flowers and 5 white flowers in a row? In how many ways this is possible if the white flowers are to be separated in any arrangement (Flowers of same colour are identical)?

SOLUTION: We have 12 flowers consisting of 3 red, 4 yellow and 5 white flowers.

Number of arrangements $= \dfrac{12!}{3!4!5!} = 27720.$

For the second part, first arrange 3 red and 4 yellow

This can be done in $\dfrac{7!}{3!4!} = 35$ ways

Now select 5 places from among 8 places (including extremes) and put the white flowers there. This can be done in ${}^8C_5 = 56$.

$\therefore$ The number of ways for the 2nd part $= 35 \times 56 = 1960$.

IMPORTANT RESULTS

1. *The number of permutations of n different things, taking all at a time, when r particular things always remain together* $= r! \times (n-r+1)!$
2. *Number of permutations of n different things, taken all at a time, when r particular things don't remain together* $= n! - r! \times (n-r+1)!$
3. *The number of permutations of n different things, taken all at a time, when no two of the r particular things come together is* ${}^{n-r+1}C_r\,(n-r)!\,r!;\ n-r \geq r-1$

TEXTUAL EXERCISE-4 (SUBJECTIVE)

1. In how many ways can the letters of the word 'INSURANCE' be arranged, so that
   (i) the vowels occur together?
   (ii) the vowels never occur together?

2. How many words can be formed by using all the letters of the word 'ALLAHABAD'? How many these words will not contain both L together?

3. How many different signals can be made from 4 red, 2 white and 3 green flags by arranging all of them vertically on a flagstaff?

4. How many five digit numbers can be formed with the help of the digits 5, 4, 3, 5, 3, using all at a time?

5. How many 7 digit numbers can be formed using the digits 1, 2, 0, 2, 4, 2, 4 using all at a time?

6. (a) How many 7 digit numbers can be formed using the digits 1, 2, 3, 4, 3, 2, 1 so that the odd digits always occupy the odd places?
   (b) Find number of 7 digit numbers formed using digits 3, 3, 5, 4, 4, 6, 6 such that even digits always occupy odd places.

7. (a) Find the total number of permutations of n kind of objects, each kind having unlimited objects, taken not more than r at a time when each object may be repeated any number of times in the arrangement.
   (b) Find the number of possible outcomes in a throw of n ordinary dice in which at least one dice shows an odd number.

8. Find number of five-digit numbers formed using 0, 1, 2, ..., 9
   (a) When repetition of digit is allowed
   (b) When repetition of digit is not allowed
   (c) No two consecutive digits are same
   (d) At least two consecutive digit are same

9. Find the number of ways in which 4 friends can stay in 10 hotels such that all the friends do not stay in the same hotel.

10. Find the number of permutations of the letters of the following mentioned words taking all the letters at a time.
    (a) 'DADDY DID A DEADLY DEED'
    (b) 'INTERMEDIATE'
    (c) 'CALCULATOR'

11. In the given figure, you have the road plan of a city. A man standing at X wants to reach the cinema hall at Y by the shortest path.
    (a) What is the number of different paths that he can take?
    (b) Find the number of shortest routes from X to Y via B.

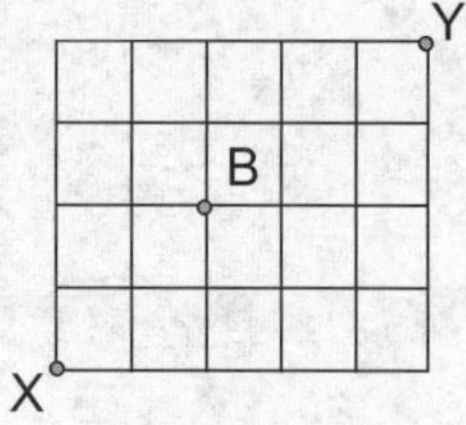

FIGURE 6.9

12. (a) An n-bit string is n-digit "word", each digit of which is either 0 or 1. Find the number of n-bit strings containing
    (i) at least one zero.
    (ii) both the digit zero and one.
    (b) How many strictly increasing sequences of positive integers begin with 1 and end with 1000?

Answer Keys

1. (i) 8640 (ii) 172800 **2.** $\frac{9!}{2!4!}$ & $\frac{9!}{2!4!} - \frac{8!}{4!}$ **3.** 9!/4!.3!.2! **4.** $\frac{5!}{2!2!}$ **5.** $\frac{7!}{3!2!} - \frac{6!}{2!3!}$

6. (a) $\frac{4!}{2!2!} \times \frac{3!}{2!}$ (b) 18 **7.** (a) $\frac{n(n^r - 1)}{n-1}$ (b) $6^n - 3^n$ **8.** (a) 9×10^4 (b) 27216 (c) 9^5

(d) $9(10^4 - 9^4)$ **9.** 9990 **10.** (a) $\frac{19!}{9! \times 3! \times 2! \times 3!}$ (b) $\frac{12!}{2!3!2!}$ (c) $\frac{10!}{(2!)^3}$

11. (a) $\frac{9!}{5! \times 4!}$ (b) 60 ways **12.** (a) (i) $2^n - 1$ (ii) $2^n - 2$ (b) 2^{98}

TEXTUAL EXERCISE–4 (OBJECTIVE)

1. How many 4-digited numbers are there?
(a) $(10)^4$ (b) $9 \times (10)^3$
(c) 4! (d) $10P_4$

2. A question paper consists of 10 single answer correct multiple choice questions, each having 4 options. How many different sequences of wrong answers are possible?
(a) $4^{(10)}$ (b) $(10)^4-1$
(c) $(4)^{10}-1$ (d) $10\,P_4$

3. A number lock can be unlocked by using a 5 digited code. How many maximum attempts should be made to unlock?
(a) $(10)^5$ (b) 10^5-1
(c) $(5)^{10}$ (d) None of these

4. How many integers between 100 and 1000 have each digit odd?
(a) $(5)^3$ (b) $(3)^5$
(c) 5! (d) None of these

5. In how many ways 5 delegates can be put in 6 offices of a city if there is no restriction?
(a) $(5)^6$ (b) $(6)^5$
(c) $6P_5$ (d) $\frac{6!}{5!}$

6. A safe is unlocked by a drive consisting of five rings with the digits 0, 1, 2, 3.....9. The safe can be unlocked by dialing a particular code. If it required 5 second to dial any codes and each working day lasts for 12 hours on which day is the safe opened if it is unlocked in the last attempt.
(a) 10 th (b) 11th
(c) 12th (d) None of these

8. Five persons entered the lift cabin on the ground floor of an 8-floor house. Suppose each of them can leave the cabin independent at any floor beginning with the first. The total number of ways in which all five persons can leave the cabin
(i) at any one of the 7 floors.
(a) 5^7 (b) 7^5
(c) 7×5 (d) None of these
(ii) at different floors.
(a) 5^7 (b) 7!
(c) 7!/2! (d) None of these

9. The number of ways in which Mr X can give 5 banglow to his 3 daughters is?
(a) 3^5 (b) 5^3
(c) 15 (d) None of these

10. The number of signals that can be made by using 6 flags of different colours when any number of them may be hoisted at a time is
(a) 720 (b) 1956
(c) 2^6-1 (d) None of these

11. The number of possible outcomes in a throw of n ordinary dice in which at least one of the die shows an odd number is
(a) 6^n-1 (b) 3^n-1
(c) 6^n-3^n (d) None of these

12. Three dice are rolled. The number of possible outcomes in which at least one die shows 5 is
(a) 215 (b) 36
(c) 125 (d) 91

13. In an examination, there are three multiple-choice questions and each question has four choices. Number of sequences in which a student can fail to get all answers correct is
(a) 11 (b) 15
(c) 80 (d) 63

14. In a club election, the number of contestants is one more than number of maximum candidates for which a voter can vote. If the total number of ways in which a voter can vote be 62, then the number of candidates is (voter has to cast atleast one vote)
(a) 7 (b) 5
(c) 6 (d) None of these

15. Consider a set P consisting of n elements. A subset 'A' of P is chosen thereafter set P is reconstructed by replacing the elements of A and finally another subset 'B' of P is chosen. The number of ways of choosing 'A' and 'B' such that $(A \cup B)$ is proper subset of P is
(a) 4^n (b) 4^n-3^n-1
(c) 4^n-2^n (d) None of these

16. If m be the number of different words that can be formed with the letters of the word BHARAT in which B and H are never together and n be number of different words that can be formed with the letters of the words BHARAT in which words always begin with B and end with T. Then m/n is
(a) 10 (b) 20
(c) 1 (d) 2

Answer Keys

1. (b) **2.** (c) **3.** (a) **4.** (a) **5.** (b) **6.** (c) **7.** (i) (b) (ii) (c) **8.** (a) **9.** (b)
10. (c) **11.** (d) **12.** (d) **13.** (c) **14.** (b) **15.** (b)

CIRCULAR PERMUTATION

Consider four persons *A, B, C* and *D,* who are to be arranged along a circle. One such circular arrangement is shown here.

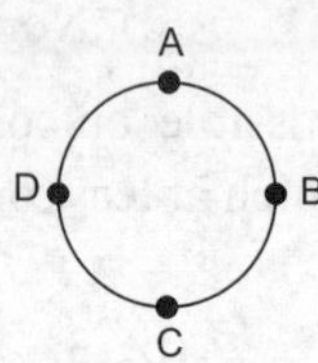

Shifting *A, B, C, D* one position in anti-clockwise direction, we will get arrangements as follows (**fig-6.10a, fig-6.10b, fig-6.10c.**) and shifting *A, B, C, D* one position in clockwise direction we will get arrangements as follows: (**fig-6.10d, fig-6.10e, fig-6.10f.**)

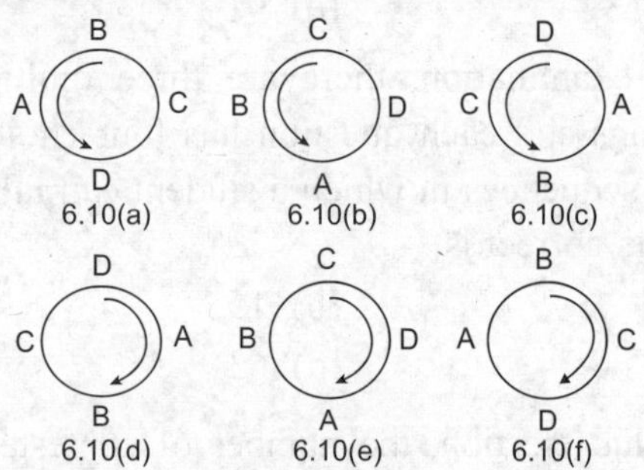

FIGURE 6.10

Arrangements as shown in **fig:** 6.10 and 6.10(a), 6.10(b) and 6.10(c) are not different as relative position of none of the four persons *A, B, C, D* is changed. Similarly those of fig. 6.10 and 6.10(d), 6.10(e), 6.10(f) are same. But in case of linear arrangements the four arrangements are.

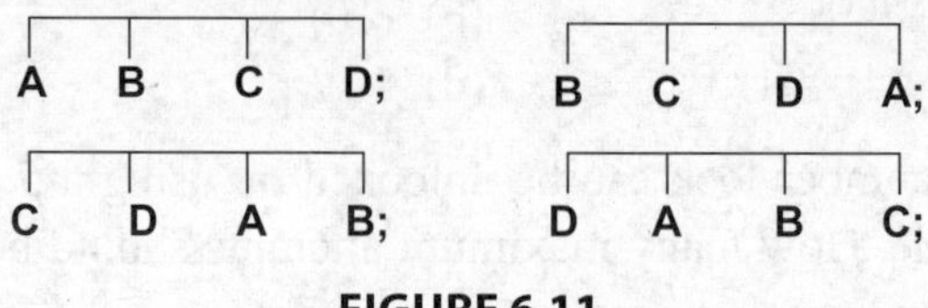

FIGURE 6.11

Thus it is clear that corresponding to a single circular arrangement of four different things there will be 4 different linear arrangements.

Let the number of different things be n and the number of their circular permutations be x. Now for one circular permutation number of linear arrangements is n. If x be the number of circular arrangements, then number of linear arrangements $= nx$ (1)

But number of linear arrangements of n different things $= n!$ (2)

From (1) and (2), we get $nx = n! \Rightarrow x = \frac{n!}{n} = (n-1)!$

ILLUSTRATION 33: In how many ways can we arrange 6 different flowers in a circle. In how many ways we can form a garland using these flowers.

SOLUTION: The number of circular arrangements of 6 different flowers $= (6 - 1)! = 120$
When we form a garland, clockwise and anti-clockwise arrangements are similar. Therefore, the number of ways of forming garland $= \frac{1}{2}(6-1)! = 60$.

ILLUSTRATION 34: In how many ways 6 persons can sit at a round table, if two of them prefer to sit together.

SOLUTION: Let $P_1, P_2, P_3, P_4, P_5, P_6$ be the persons, where P_1, P_2 want to sit together. Regarding (P1, P2) together as a single object and other persons as different objects, we have total 5 objects. They can be arranged in a circle in $(5 - 1)! = 24$. Now P_1P_2 can be arranged in 2! ways. Thus the total number of ways $= 24 \times 2 = 48$.

ILLUSTRATION 35: In how many different ways can five boys and five girls form a circle such that the boys and girls alternate?

SOLUTION: After fixing up one boy on the table the remaining can be arranged in 4! ways, but boys and girls are to alternate.
There will be 5 places, one place each between two boys these five places can be filled with 5 girls in 5! ways
Hence by the principle of multiplication, the required number of ways $= 4! \times 5! = 2880$

NOTES

1. *(a) The number of circular permutations of n different things taking x at a time equals.*

(i) ${}^nP_x/x$, when clockwise and anti-clockwise orders are treated as different.

(ii) ${}^nP_x/2x$, when the above two orders are treated as same.

(b) The number of circular permutations of n different things all at a time equals.

(i) ${}^nP_n/n = (n-1)!$ when clockwise and anti clockwise orders are treated as different.

(ii) ${}^nP_n/2n = \frac{1}{2}(n-1)!$, when above two orders are treated as same.

(c) In a garland of flowers or a necklace of beads. it is difficult to distinguish clockwise and anti-clockwise orders of things, so a circular permutation under both these orders is considered to be the same. Therefore the number of ways of arranging n beads along a circular wire is $\frac{(n-1)!}{2}$.

2. *In a circular permutation, the relative position among the things is important whereas the place of a thing has no significance. Thus in a circular permutation first thing can be placed anywhere. This operation can be done only in one way, then relative order begins. Thus the ways for performing remaining parts of the operation can be calculated just like the calculation of linear permutation for example to place 8 different things round a circle, first we place any one thing at any place, there will be only one way, thus required number of circular permutations is 7!.*

ILLUSTRATION 36: How many necklaces of 12 beads each can be made from 18 beads of various colours?

SOLUTION: In this case of necklace, there is no distinction between the clockwise and anti-clockwise arrangements, thus the required number of circular permutations

$$= \frac{{}^{18}P_{12}}{2\times 12} = \frac{18!}{6!\times 24}$$

ILLUSTRATION 37: There are 20 persons among whom two are brothers. Find the number of ways in which they can be arranged round a circle so that there is exactly one person between the two brothers.

SOLUTION: Let among the 20 persons, B_1 and B_2 be two brothers and M be the person between them. Now, considering B_1MB_2 as one person, we have a total of 18 persons.

No. of ways to arrange these, 18 persons round a circle = 17!

No. of ways to arrange B_1MB_2 among themselves

$= 2$ {i.e., $B_1\,M\,B_2$ and $B_2\,M\,B_1$}

No.of ways to select M among 18 persons = 18

∴ Total number of ways $17! \times 2 \times 18 = 2 \times 18!$

■ RANK OF WORDS

When all the letters of a word are arranged to form different words and the words are arranged now as per dictionary. The position occupied by that word is the rank of that word.

ILLUSTRATION 38: Find the rank of the word CRICKET.

SOLUTION: (a) In alphabetic order, the letters are $C, C, E, I\,K, R, T.$ Words beginning with C will come first. Our word also begins with C. The number of words beginning with C and having C or E or I or K in the second place $= 4 \times 5!$

$$C\begin{cases} C \times \times \times \times \times \\ E \times \times \times \times \times \\ I \times \times \times \times \times \\ K \times \times \times \times \times \end{cases} \quad CR\begin{cases} C \times \times \times \times \\ E \times \times \times \times \end{cases} \quad CRIC\begin{cases} E \times \times \\ K\ E\ T \end{cases}$$

The number of words beginning with CR and having C or E in the third place = $2 \times 4!$

The number of words beginning with CRIC and having E in the fifth place = 2!

After printing all these words, the word CRICKET will be printed

∴ the required place of the word CRICKET

$= (4 \times 5! + 2 \times 4! + 2!) + 1 = 531$

∴ the word will be printed in the 531th place. Thus rank of word CRICKET = 531

ILLUSTRATION 39: From the letters of the word AMERICA, find the rank of the word if all the permutations are alphabetically arranged in a dictionary.

SOLUTION: The words starting with AA are 5! = 120

The words starting with AC are 5! = 120

The words starting with AE are 5! = 120

The words starting with AI are 5! = 120

The words starting with AMA are 4! = 24

The words starting with AMC are 4! = 24

The words starting with AMEA are 3! = 6

The words starting with AMEA are 3! = 6

The words starting with AMEI are 3! = 6

The words starting with AMERA are 2! = 2

The words starting with AMERC are 2! = 2

Next word is AMERIAC i.e., 1

Next word is AMERICA i.e., 1

Adding all these, rank of the word America = 552

ILLUSTRATION 40: Shortcut method of finding rank:

This can be understood by following Illustration.

Find the rank of following [when none of the alphabet is repeated]

(a) LARGE (b) MOTHER

SOLUTION: (a) LARGE

Step 1: First of all write, the alphabet in alphabetical order A E G L R } 5 letters

Step (2) write

Rank = $(x_1)4! + (x_2)3! + (x_3)2! + (x_4)1! + 0!$

Where x_1, x_2, x_3, x_4 are obtained as follows

For x_1, see which letter we here first, here, it is "L"

Now, counting the number of letters on the left on L = 3

So $x_1 = 3$

Since "L" is used so cross it

i.e., A E G ~~L~~ R

For x_2, the next letter we want is A, No of letters on the left of A = 0

So $x_2 = 0$, Now cross "*A*" i.e., ~~A~~ E G ~~L~~ R
For x_3, the next letter we want is *R*
Number of uncrossed letters on the left of $R = 2$
So $x_3 = 2$; Now cross "*R*" i.e., ~~A~~ E G ~~L~~ ~~R~~
For x_4, the next letter we want is *G*
Number of uncrossed letters on the left of "*G*" = 1 so $x_4 = 1$
Hence rank of LARGE = 3 x 4! + 0.3! + 2.2! + 1.1! + 0! = 78

(b) MOTHER

Writing alphabetical order; we have, E H M O R T} 6 letters
So rank = $(x_1)5! + (x_2)4! + (x_3)3! + (x_4)2! + (x_5)1! + 0!$
Now, $x_1 = 2$
because there are two uncrossed letters on the left of M.
Now we cross M
i.e., E H ~~M~~ O R T
Similarly, $x_2 = 2$ (Since there are two uncrossed letters on the left of *O)*
Crossing O ⇒ E H ~~M~~ ~~O~~ R T
and, $x_3 = 3$ (Since there are 3 uncrossed letters on the left of *T)*
Crossing T ⇒ E H ~~M~~ ~~O~~ R ~~T~~
and, $x_4 = 1$ (Since there is just one uncrossed letter on the left of *H)*
Crossing H ⇒ E ~~H~~ ~~M~~ ~~O~~ R T
and, $x_5 = 0$ (Since there is no uncrossed letter on the left of *E)*
Crossing E ⇒ ~~E~~ H ~~M~~ ~~O~~ R T
So rank = 2 × 5! + 2 × 4 ! + 3.3! + 1 × 2! + 0.1! + 0! = 240 + 48 + 18 + 2 + 0 + 1 = 309

ILLUSTRATION 41: Find the rank of the following (when one or more alphabets are repeated).
(a) BANANA (b) TITANIC

SOLUTION: BANANA

Step I: Write all the alphabets in alphabetical order
⇒ AABNN] 6 letters

Step II: Write rank $(x_1)5! + (x_2)4! + (x_3)3! + (x_4)2! + (x_5)1! + 0!$
Where x_1, x_2, x_3, x_4, x_5 are obtained as follows:

Step 2.1 $x_1 = \dfrac{3}{3!2!}$ (Here the 3 in the numerator is because there are 3 letters on the left of B on the left of B in the above sequence Also 3! is because the 3 A's are identical and 2! is because the 2*N*'s are identical)

Step 2.1: Now since B has been used, therefore cut B from the sequence; we get *AAA*~~*B*~~*NN* = AAANN

Step 2.2: $x_2 = 0$ (Since the first preference will be A so no other alternative permutation possible)

Step 2.2′: Since one A has been used, therefore we cut one A from the sequence and hence get ~~*A*~~*AA*~~*B*~~*NN* = AANN

Step 2.3: $x_3 = \dfrac{2}{2!2!}$ (2 because of two letters on left on N and 2! 2! Because of 2 identical A's and 2 identical N's)

Step:2.3′ Sequence = $\cancel{A}AA\cancel{B}\cancel{N}N = AAN$

Step 2.4 $x_4 = 0$ ($\because$ no other alternative) (as no letter on left of A)

Step 2.4′: sequence $\equiv$ $\cancel{A}\cancel{A}A\cancel{B}\cancel{N}N = AN$

Step 2.5: $x_5 = \dfrac{1}{1!}$ (one letters on left of N)

Step 2.5′: Sequence $\equiv$ $\cancel{A}\cancel{A}A\cancel{B}\cancel{N}\cancel{N} = A$

Therefore, Rank = $5!\times\left(\dfrac{3}{3!2!}\right)+3!\times\left(\dfrac{2}{2!2!}\right)+1!\times\left(\dfrac{1}{1!}\right)+0! = 35$

(b) TITANIC

Step 1: ACIINTT } 7 letters

Step 2: Rank = $(x_1) \times 6! + (x_2) \times 5! + (x_3) \times 4! + (x_4) \times 3! + (x_5) \times 2! + (x_6) \times 1! + 0!$

Step 2.1: $x_1 = \dfrac{5}{2!2!}$

Step 2.1′: Sequence = ACIIN$\cancel{\text{T}}$T = ACIINT

Step 2.2: $x_2 = \dfrac{2}{2!}$

Step 2.2′: Sequence = AC$\cancel{\text{I}}$INT = ACINT

Step 2.3: $x_3 = 4$ (As there are 4 letters on left of T)

Step 2.3′: Sequence $\equiv$ ACIN$\cancel{\text{T}}$ = ACIN

Step 2.4: $x_4 = 0$ (As there are no letters on left of A)

Step 2.4′: Sequence $\equiv$ $\cancel{\text{A}}$CIN = CIN

Step 2.5: $x_5 = 2$ (As there are 2 letters on left of N)

Step 2.5′: Sequence $\equiv$ CI$\cancel{\text{N}}$ = CI

Step 2.6: $x_6 = 1$ (As there is only 1 letters on left of I).

Step 2.6′: Sequence $\equiv$ C$\cancel{\text{I}}$ = C

$\therefore$ Rank = $6!\times\left(\dfrac{5}{2!2!}\right)+5!\times\left(\dfrac{2}{2!}\right)+4!\times(4)+2!\times(2)+1!\times(1)+0! = 1122$

TEXTUAL EXERCISE–5 (SUBJECTIVE)

1. In how many different ways can 25 different pearls be arranged to form a necklace?
2. In how many different ways can a garland of 21 different flowers be made?
3. Consider 23 different coloured beads in a necklace. In how many ways can the beads be placed in the necklace so that 3 specific beads always remain together?
4. In how many ways can 15 members of a committee sit at a round table so that secretary and the joint secretary are always the neighbours of the president?
5. In how many ways the letters of the word 'MONDAY' can be written around a circle if the vowels are to be separated in any arrangement?
6. In how many ways we can form a garland using 3 different red flowers, 5 different yellow flowers and 4 different blue flowers, if flowers of same colour must be together.
7. Three boys and three girls are to be seated around a table in a circle. Among them, the boy X does not want any girl neighbor and the girl Y does not want

any boy neighbor. How many such arrangements are possible?

8. In how many ways 5 boys (b_1, b_2, ..., b_5) and 5 girls (g_1, g_2, ..., g_5) can sit around a circular table so that
(a) no two girls sit together
(b) neither two girls nor two boys sit together
(c) all boys are sitting together
(d) b_1 b_2 sit together and g_1 g_2 sit together.
(e) b_1 b_2 together but g_1 g_2 not together.
(f) neither b_1, b_2 nor g_1, g_2 sit together

9. There are 20 persons including two brothers. In how many ways can they be arranged on a round table if:
(a) There is exactly one person between the two brothers.
(b) The two brothers are always separated.
(c) What will be the corresponding answers of part (a) and (b) if the two brothers were twins (alike in all respects)?

10. Find the rank of the following words as per the order of an ordinary dictionary.

(a) 'RATNA'	(b) 'FATHER'
(c) SHRUTI	(d) ARRANGE
(e) 'TOPOLOGY'	(f) TATTOO.

Answer Keys

1. $\frac{24!}{2}$ **2.** $\frac{20!}{2}$ **3.** (1/2). 20!. 3! **4.** (12!)2! **5.** 72 **6.** 17280 **7.** 4

8. (a) 4! 5! (b) 4! 5! (c) 5! 5! (d) $(2!)^2 7!$ (e) $8!\,2! - (2!)^2 7!$ (f) (44)7!

9. (a) 2(18!) (b) 17(18)! (c) 18!, $\frac{17(18!)}{2}$. **10.** (a) 42 (b) 261 (c) 372 (d) 342 (e) 5553 (f) 36

TEXTUAL EXERCISE–5 (OBJECTIVE)

1. Six boys and six girls sit along a line alternately in x ways; and along a circle (again alternatively) in y ways, then
(a) $x = y$
(b) $y = 12x$
(c) $x = 10y$
(d) $x = 12y$

2. A round table conference is to be held between 20 delegates of 20 countries. The number of ways, they can be seated if two particular delegates always sit together, is
(a) 2 × 17!
(b) 2 × 19!
(c) 2 × 18!
(d) None of these

3. In the above problem, the number of ways, can the delegates be seated if two particular delegates never sit together, is
(a) 17. 18!
(b) 19!
(c) 18. 18!
(d) None of these

4. The number of ways in which 20 different pearls of two colours can be set alternately on a necklace, there being 10 pearls of each colour, is
(a) 9! × 10!
(b) $5(9!)^2$
(c) $(9!)^2$
(d) None of these

5. If all permutations of the letters of the word AGAIN are arranged as in dictionary, then fiftieth word is
(a) NAAGI
(b) NAGAI
(c) NAAIG
(d) NAIAG

6. If the permutations of a, b, c, d, e taken all together be written down in alphabetical order as in dictionary and numbered, then the rank of the permutation 'debac' is
(a) 90
(b) 91
(c) 92
(d) 93

7. If all the permutations of the letters of the word 'TACKLE' are written in the dictionary, then the rank of the word 'TACKLE' is
(a) 602
(b) 603
(c) 604
(d) 605

8. If the letters of the word LATE be permuted and the words so formed be arranged as in a dictionary. Then the rank of LATE is
(a) 12
(b) 13
(c) 14
(d) 15

Answer Keys

1. (d) **2.** (c) **3.** (a) **4.** (b) **5.** (c) **6.** (d) **7.** (c) **8.** (c)

■ COMBINATION

Each of the groups or selections (ignoring order) which can be made by taking some or all of a number of things is called a **combination.** To understand the concept of combination, let us consider the combinations which can be made by the letters *a, b, c* and *d,* two at a time as given below.

ab, **ac,** **ad,**
bc, **bd,**
cd; (*they are six in number.*)

NOTE

From the above, it is amply clear that in combinations we are only concerned with the number of things each selection contains without taking into account the order in which the objects are being selected.

Properties of combination

1. The number of combinations of n different things taken r at a time is denoted by

${}^nC_r$ or $C(n, r)$ or $\binom{n}{r}$ and it is empirically calculated as:

$${}^nC_r = \frac{n!}{r!(n-r)!};\ (0 \le r \le n)$$

[where $n \in N$ and $r \in W$ {whole numbers}]
$= 0$ (if $r > n$)

2. ${}^nC_r$ is always an whole number.

Following important conclusions can be made out of the above statement:

(a) Product of r consecutive integers is always divisible by $r!$

$$\because\ {}^nC_r = \frac{n(n-1)(n-2)(n-3).....(n-r+1)}{r!} \in \mathbb{Z}$$

Clearly, the numerator is completely divisible by $r!$

(b) $0! = 1$; $\left\{ {}^nC_0 = {}^nC_n = \frac{n!}{n!\,0!} = 1 \right\}$ and ${}^nC_1 = n$

(c) $k! = \infty$ if $k < 0$ (Think why?)

3. ${}^nC_r = {}^nC_{n-r}$

Proof: $\text{LHS} = {}^nC_r = \frac{n!}{r!(n-r)!}$

$$\text{RHS} = {}^nC_{n-r} = \frac{n!}{(n-r)!(n-(n-r))!} = \frac{n!}{(n-r)!r!}$$

Choosing r things out of n given things ≡ choosing $(n - r)$ things out of given n things because when r things are chosen, remaining $(n - r)$ things automatically get selected.

4. ${}^nC_x = {}^nC_y \Rightarrow x = y$ or $x + y = n$

5. Pascal Rule: ${}^nC_r + {}^nC_{r-1} = {}^{n+1}C_r\ (1 < r \le n)$

Proof: $\text{LHS} = \frac{n!}{r!(n-r)!} + \frac{n!}{(r-1)!\,(n-r+1)!}$

$$= n!\left[\frac{1}{r(r-1)!(n-r)!} + \frac{1}{(r-1)!\,(n-r+1)(n-r)!}\right]$$

$$= \frac{n!}{(r-1)!(n-r)!}\left[\frac{1}{r} + \frac{1}{n-r+1}\right] = \frac{(n+1)!}{r!(n-r+1)!}$$

$$= \frac{n!}{(r-1)!(n-r)!}\left[\frac{n+1}{(n-r+1)r}\right]$$

$= {}^{n+1}C_r = \text{R.H.S.}$

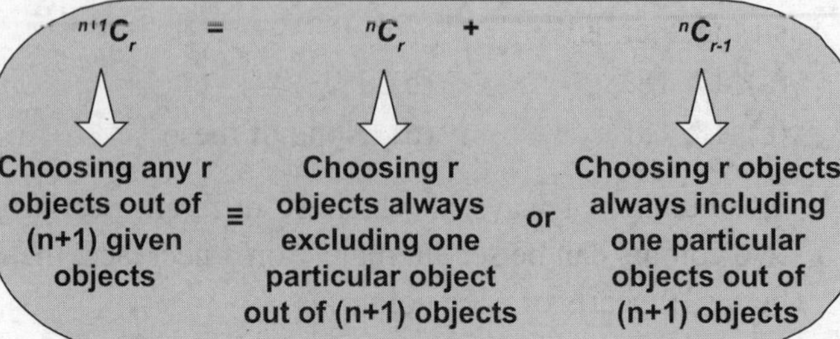

FIGURE 6.12

ILLUSTRATION 42: Evaluate ${}^nC_r + \sum_{J=0}^{3} {}^{n+j}C_{r+1+j}$

SOLUTION: $({}^nC_r + {}^nC_{r+1}) + {}^{n+1}C_{r+2} + {}^{n+2}C_{r+3} + {}^{n+3}C_{r+4} = ({}^{n+1}C_{r+1} + {}^{n+1}C_{r+2}) + {}^{n+2}C_{r+3} + {}^{n+3}C_{r+4}$

$= ({}^{n+2}C_{r+2} + {}^{n+2}C_{r+3}) + {}^{n+3}C_{r+4} = + {}^{n+3}C_{r+3} + {}^{n+3}C_{r+4} = {}^{n+4}C_{r+4}$

ILLUSTRATION 43: Given that ${}^nC_{n-r} + 3\,{}^nC_{n-r+1} + 3.\,{}^nC_{n-r+2} + {}^nC_{n-r+3} = {}^xC_r$. Find x.

SOLUTION: We have ${}^nC_{n-r} + 3\,{}^nC_{n-r+1} + 3\,{}^nC_{n-r+2} + {}^nC_{n-r+3} = {}^xC_r$

$\Rightarrow ({}^nC_{n-r} + {}^nC_{n-r+1}) + 2({}^nC_{n-r+1} + {}^nC_{n-r+2}) + ({}^nC_{n-r+2} + {}^nC_{n-r+3}) = {}^xC_r$

$\Rightarrow {}^{n+1}C_{n-r+1} + 2.\,{}^{n+1}C_{n-r+2} + {}^{n+1}C_{n-r+3} = {}^xC_r$

$\Rightarrow ({}^{n+1}C_{n-r+1} + {}^{n+1}C_{n-r+2}) + ({}^{n+1}C_{n-r+2} + {}^{n+1}C_{n-r+3}) = {}^xC_r \Rightarrow {}^{n+2}C_{n-r+2} + {}^{n+2}C_{n-r+3} = {}^xC_r$

$\Rightarrow {}^{n+3}C_{n-r+3} = {}^xC_r \qquad \Rightarrow {}^{n+3}C_r = {}^xC_r \quad (\because {}^nC_r = {}^nC_{n-r})$

Hence, $x = n + 3$.

6. $r.{}^nC_r = n.{}^{n-1}C_{r-1} \qquad \Rightarrow {}^nC_r =$

$\frac{n}{r}\left({}^{n-1}C_{r-1}\right) = \frac{n}{r}\left(\frac{n-1}{r-1}\right){}^{n-2}C_{r-2} = \ldots\ldots\ldots$

Proof: $\text{LHS} = r \times \frac{n!}{r!(n-r)!} = \frac{n!}{(r-1)!(n-r)!}$

$\text{RHS} = n \times \frac{(n-1)!}{(r-1)!(n-r)!} = \frac{n!}{(r-1)!(n-r)!}$

Choosing r MP's from n citizens (${}^nC_r$ ways)		Choosing 1 PM from n citizens (n ways)
and		and
Choosing 1 PM from r choosen MPs (r ways) $r \times {}^nC_r$	≡	Choosing remaining $(r-1)$ MP's from remaining $(n-1)$ citizens (${}^{n-1}C_{r-1}$) ways
MP: Member of Parliament		PM: Prime Minister

ILLUSTRATION 44: If ${}^nC_{n-4}, {}^nC_{n-5}, {}^nC_{n-6}$ are in A.P., then n is equal to

(a) 7 (b) 14 (c) 6 (d) 12

SOLUTION: ${}^nC_{n-4}, {}^nC_{n-5}, {}^nC_{n-6}$ are in AP. So $2.{}^nC_{n-5} = {}^nC_{n-4} + {}^nC_{n-6}$

$2 \times \frac{n!}{(n-5)!5!} = \frac{n!}{(n-4)!4!} + \frac{n!}{(n-6)!6!}$

$\Rightarrow \frac{2}{(n-\ )(n-\ )} = \frac{1}{(n-\ )(n-\ )(n-\ )} + \frac{1}{(n-\ )}$

$\Rightarrow \frac{2}{(n-5)5 \times 4!} = \frac{1}{(n-4)(n-5)4!} + \frac{1}{6 \times 5 \times 4!} \Rightarrow \frac{2}{(n-5)5} = \frac{1}{(n-4)(n-5)} + \frac{1}{30}$

$\Rightarrow n^2 - 21n + 98 = 0 \qquad \Rightarrow n = 14$ or $n = 7$.

ILLUSTRATION 45: **(i)** If ${}^{n+1}C_{r+1} : {}^nC_r : {}^{n-1}C_{r-1} = 11 : 6 : 3$, then find the values of n and r.

(ii) If $\frac{{}^nP_{r-1}}{a} = \frac{{}^nP_r}{b} = \frac{{}^nP_{r+1}}{c}$, then prove that $b^2 = a(b + c)$.

SOLUTION: **(i)** We have ${}^{n+1}C_{r+1} : {}^nC_r : {}^{n-1}C_{r-1} = 11 : 6 : 3$

or $\frac{{}^{n+1}C_{r+1}}{11} = \frac{{}^nC_r}{6} = \frac{{}^{n-1}C_{r-1}}{3} = k$ (let), from relation I and II $\frac{{}^{n+1}C_{r+1}}{11} = \frac{{}^nC_r}{6}$

$$\Rightarrow \frac{\left(\frac{n+1}{r+1}\right){}^nC_r}{11} = \frac{{}^nC_r}{6};\ 6\left(\frac{n+1}{r+1}\right) = 11 \qquad (\because {}^nC_r \neq 0)$$

$\Rightarrow 6n - 11r = 5$ (i)

Now from relation II and III $\frac{{}^nC_r}{6} = \frac{{}^{n-1}C_{r-1}}{3}$

$$\Rightarrow \frac{n}{r}.\frac{{}^{n-1}C_{r-1}}{2} = \frac{{}^{n-1}C_{r-1}}{1} \Rightarrow \frac{n}{2r} = 1 \qquad (\because {}^{n-1}C_{r-1} \neq 0)$$

$\therefore\ n = 2r.$ (ii)

Solving (i) and (ii), we get, $r = 5$ and $n = 10$

(ii) Given $\frac{{}^nP_{r-1}}{a} = \frac{{}^nP_r}{b} = \frac{{}^nP_{r+1}}{c}$

$$\therefore\ \frac{1}{a}\left\{\frac{n!}{(n-r+1)!}\right\} = \frac{1}{b}\left\{\frac{n!}{(n-r)!}\right\} = \frac{1}{c}\left\{\frac{n!}{(n-r-1)!}\right\}$$

$$\Rightarrow \frac{1}{a}\left\{\frac{n!}{(n-r+1)(n-r)!}\right\} = \frac{1}{b}\left\{\frac{n!}{(n-r)!}\right\} = \frac{1}{c}\left\{\frac{n!}{(n-r-1)!}\right\}$$

From first two relations, $\frac{b}{a} = n-r+1$ (i)

and from last two relations, $\frac{c}{b} = n-r$ (ii)

From (i) and (ii), we get $\frac{b}{a} = \frac{c}{b}+1$

$\Rightarrow b^2 = a(b+c).$

7. ${}^nC_r = {}^{n+1}C_{r+1}\cdot\left(\frac{r+1}{n+1}\right) = \frac{(r+1)(r+2)}{(n+1)(n+2)}\,{}^{n+2}C_{r+2}$

8. ${}^nC_r\,{}^rC_s = {}^nC_s\cdot{}^{n-s}C_{r-s}\ (n \geq r \geq s).$

Proof: LHS $= \frac{n!}{r!(n-r)!}\times\frac{r!}{s!(r-s)!}$

$$= \frac{n!}{s!(r-s)!(n-r)!}$$

RHS $= \frac{n!}{s!(n-s)!}\times\frac{(n-s)!}{(r-s)!((n-s)-(r-s))!}$

$$= \frac{n!}{s!(r-s)!(n-r)!}$$

From n-citizens		From n-citizens
choosing r MP's (${}^nC_r$ ways)		choosing s ministers (${}^nC_s$ ways)
and	≡	and
Choosing s ministers out of r		Choosing remaining $(r-s)$ MP's out of remaining (n–s) citizens (${}^{n-s}C_{r-s}$ ways)
MP's (${}^rC_s$ ways)		
∴ Total ways = ${}^nC_r \times {}^nC_s$		∴ Total ways = ${}^nC_s.{}^{n-s}C_{r-s}$

9. $\frac{{}^nC_r}{{}^nC_{r-1}} = \frac{n-r+1}{r}$

ILLUSTRATION 46: If ${}^nC_{r-1} = 36$, ${}^nC_r = 84$ and ${}^nC_{r+1} = 126$, then find the values of n and r.

SOLUTION: We know, $\frac{{}^nC_r}{{}^nC_{r-1}} = \frac{n-r+1}{r} \Rightarrow \frac{84}{36} = \frac{7}{3} = \frac{n-r+1}{r}$ (given)

$\Rightarrow 3n - 10r + 3 = 0$ (i)

Also given, $\frac{{}^nC_r}{{}^nC_{r+1}} = \frac{84}{126} \Rightarrow \frac{r+1}{n-r} = \frac{2}{3}$

$\Rightarrow 2n - 5r - 3 = 0$ (ii)

On solving eq. (i) and (ii), we get $r = 3$ and $n = 9$

ILLUSTRATION 47: If ${}^{n+1}C_{r+1} : {}^nC_r : {}^{n-1}C_{r-1} = 11 : 6 : 3$, then find the value of nr.

SOLUTION: Given $\frac{{}^{n+1}C_{r+1}}{{}^nC_r} = \frac{11}{6} \Rightarrow \frac{n+1}{r+1} = \frac{11}{6}$

$\Rightarrow 6n + 6 = 11 + 11 \Rightarrow 6n - 11r = 5$ (1)

Also $\frac{{}^nC_r}{{}^{n-1}C_{r-1}} \Rightarrow \frac{\frac{n}{r} \times {}^{n-1}C_{r-1}}{{}^{n-1}C_{r-1}} = \frac{6}{3} \Rightarrow n = 2r$

From (1) and (2); $r = 5$ and $n = 10$

$\Rightarrow nr = 50$

10. ${}^nC_0 + {}^nC_1 + {}^nC_2 + ... + {}^nC_n = 2^n$

Proof: We consider the following binomial expansion

$(1 + x)^n = {}^nC_0 + {}^nC_1x + {}^nC_2x^2 + ... + {}^nC_{n-1}x^{n-1} + {}^nC_nx^n$

Putting $x = 1$ on both sides, we get $2^n = {}^nC_0 + {}^nC_1 + {}^nC_2 + .. + {}^nC_{r-1} + {}^nC_n$

11. ${}^nC_0 + {}^nC_2 + {}^nC_4 + ... = {}^nC_1 + {}^nC_3 + {}^nC_5 + ... = 2^{n-1}$

12. ${}^nC_n + {}^{n+1}C_n + {}^{n+2}C_n + {}^{n+3}C_n + ... + {}^{2n+1}C_n = {}^{2n+2}C_{n+1}$

13. The greatest value of ${}^nC_r$ is ${}^nC_{n/2}$ if n is even and ${}^nC_{\frac{n-1}{2}}$ or ${}^nC_{\frac{n+1}{2}}$ if n is odd

Proof: $\frac{{}^nC_{r+1}}{{}^nC_r} = \frac{n!}{(r+1)!(n-r-1)!} \times \frac{r!(n-r)!}{n!}$

$= \frac{n-r}{r+1}$

Case I: If n is even ${}^nC_{r+1} \geq {}^nC_r$ if $n - r \geq r + 1$

if $n - 1 \geq 2r$ if $r \leq \frac{n}{2} - \frac{1}{2}$

$\because r \in \mathbb{Z} \therefore {}^nC_r \leq {}^nC_{r+1}$ upto $r = n/2 - 1$

Hence ${}^nC_0 \leq {}^nC_1 \leq {}^nC_2 \leq ... \leq {}^nC_{\frac{n}{2}-1}$

$\leq {}^nC_{\frac{n}{2}} \geq {}^nC_{\frac{n}{2}+1} \geq {}^nC_{\frac{n}{2}+2} \geq ...$

$\therefore$ The greatest values of ${}^nC_r$ is ${}^nC_{n/2}$

Case II: If n is odd ${}^nC_{r+1} \geq {}^nC_r$ if $r \leq \frac{n-1}{2}$; equality holds for $r = \frac{n-1}{2}$

$\therefore {}^nC_0 \leq {}^nC_1 \leq {}^nC_2 \leq .... \leq {}^nC_{\frac{n+1}{2}} \geq {}^nC_{\frac{n+3}{2}} \geq .... \geq {}^nC_n$

$\therefore$ The greatest value is ${}^nC_{\frac{n-1}{2}}$ or ${}^nC_{\frac{n+1}{2}}$

ILLUSTRATION 48: A class has 21 students. The class teacher has been asked to make groups of r students each and go to zoo taking one group at a time. Find the size of group for which the teacher goes the maximum number of times to the zoo.

SOLUTION: Number of groups of r students each $= {}^{21}C_r$

Number of times the teacher can go to the zoo =

Number of groups she can form $= {}^{21}C_r$

$\therefore$ It is maximum when $r = \frac{21-1}{2}$ or $\frac{21+1}{2}$; i.e., $r = 10$ or 11

ILLUSTRATION 49: By joining the vertices of a hexagon, number of triangles are formed

(a) 18 (b) 21 (c) 20 (d) 19

SOLUTION: A triangle is formed by selecting 3 points out of six and joining these points.

$\Rightarrow$ Number of triangles that can be formed $= {}^6C_3 = 20$

ILLUSTRATION 50: Number of diagonals in a polygon with n sides is

(a) $\frac{n(n-3)}{2}$ (b) $\frac{n(n-2)}{2}$ (c) $\frac{(n-2)}{2}$ (d) None of these

SOLUTION: Diagonals are formed by selecting any two points out of n points and joining them. But we should exclude n sides.

$\therefore$ Number of diagonals $= {}^nC_2 - n = \frac{n(n-1)}{2} - n = \frac{n(n-3)}{2}$

TEXTUAL EXERCISE–6 (SUBJECTIVE)

1. (i) If ${}^nC_r = {}^nC_{3r-4}$ then find all possible values of r and show that if the above equation has solution then r is 2 or $n + 4$ is divisible by 4.
   (ii) Solve ${}^nC_r = {}^nC_{r^2-r}$ then show that if the equation has solution then $r = 0$, 2 or n is perfect square of some integer.
   (iii) Solve ${}^nC_r = {}^nC_{r^2+2r}$ for all possible values of r.
2. (a) Find the values of n and r if it is given that ${}^nC_{r-1} = 28$ and ${}^nC_{r+1} = 70$ and ${}^nC_r = 56$.
   (b) ${}^{n+1}C_{r+1} : {}^nC_r : {}^{n-1}C_{r-1} = 56 : 35 : 20$ find n and r.
   (c) Prove the identity $\sum_{r=1}^{n} r\left(\frac{{}^nC_r}{{}^nC_{r-1}}\right) = \sum_{k=1}^{n} k$
   (d) Evaluate the series $\sum_{r=1}^{n} r^2\left(\frac{{}^nC_r}{{}^nC_{r-1}}\right)$.
3. Prove that the greatest value of ${}^{2n}C_r = {}^{2n}C_n$
4. Prove the following identities:
   (a) $\sum_{r=0}^{n} r\binom{n}{r} = n.2^{n-1}$
   (b) $\sum_{r=2}^{n} r(r-1)\,{}^nC_r = n.(n-1)2^{n-2}$
   (c) $\sum_{r=1}^{n} r^2\,{}^nC_r = n.(n+1)2^{n-2}$
   (d) $\sum_{r=1}^{n} r^3\,{}^nC_r = n^2.(n+3)2^{n-3}$
5. Evaluate the following
   (i) ${}^8C_3 + {}^7C_3 + {}^6C_3 + {}^5C_3 + {}^4C_3$
   (ii) ${}^{13}C_6 + {}^{12}C_6 + {}^{11}C_6 + {}^{10}C_6 + {}^9C_6$

Answer Keys

1. (i) $r = 2$ (iii) $r = 0\ \forall\ n \in \mathbb{N}$ and $r = k \in \mathbb{N}$, when $n = \frac{(2k+3)^2 - 9}{4}$
2. (a) $n = 8, r = 3$ (b) $n = 7, r = 4$ (d) $\frac{n(n+1)(n+2)}{6}$
5. (a) ${}^9C_4 - 1$ (b) ${}^{14}C_7 - {}^9C_7$

TEXTUAL EXERCISE–6 (OBJECTIVE)

1. ${}^{52}C_{26} \div {}^{51}C_{25}$ is
   (a) 3 (b) 2
   (c) 4 (d) None of these
2. If ${}^mC_{{}^kC_r} = {}^mC_{{}^kC_{r-1}}$ then m is
   (a) ${}^{k+1}C_{r-1}$ (b) ${}^kC_r$
   (c) ${}^{k+1}C_r$ (d) None of these

3. The least +ve integer n for which ${}^{n-1}C_5 + {}^{n-1}C_6 < {}^{n}C_7$, is
   (a) 12 (b) 13
   (c) 14 (d) 15

4. The total number of selections of at most n things from $(2n + 1)$ different things is 63; where atleast one thing is selected. Then the value of n is
   (a) 3 (b) 2
   (c) 4 (d) None of these

5. The value of ${}^{40}C_8 + \sum_{j=1}^{7} {}^{47-j}C_{40-j}$ is
   (a) ${}^{47}C_7$ (b) ${}^{47}C_8$
   (c) ${}^{46}C_7$ (d) ${}^{46}C_8$

6. The domain of definition of the function $f(x) = {}^{2x-8}C_{x+1}$ is
   (a) $[9, \infty)$ (b) $\{-1, 0, 1, 2, 3.....\}$
   (c) $\{9, 10, 11, 12...\}$ (d) None of these

7. Solution of inequality ${}^{10}C_{x-1} > 2\ {}^{10}C_x$ is
   (a) $\{8, 9, 10, 11...\}$ (b) $\{8, 9, 10\}$
   (c) $\{9, 10, 11\}$ (d) None of these

8. Solution of incquality $8\,{}^{105}C_x < 3\,{}^{105}C_{x+1}$ is
   (a) $\{0, 1, 2, 3.....27\}$ (b) $\{0, 1, 2, 3,.....10\}$
   (c) $x \in \{27, 28...10\}$ (d) None of these

9. Solution of inequality ${}^{x-1}C_4 - {}^{x-1}C_3 - \frac{5}{4}(x-2)(x-3) < 0$ is
   (a) $\{5, 6, 7\}$ (b) $\{7, 8, 9\}$
   (c) $\{8, 9, 10\}$ (d) $\{5, 6, 7, 8, 9, 10\}$

Answer Keys

1. (b) **2.** (c) **3.** (c) **4.** (a) **5.** (b) **6.** (c) **7.** (b) **8.** (a) **9.** (d)

SELECTION OF DISTINCT OBJECTS

Combination of objects taking any number of them at a time (all possible selections):

Number of selections of objects when any number of them can be selected is given as ${}^{n}C_0 + {}^{n}C_1 + ... + {}^{n}C_n = 2^n$ where ${}^{n}C_r$ correspond to the case when r objects are selected out of n different objects. In above case, r varies from 0 to n.

Proof: In other ways, we can say that any object can be dealt in two ways

1. when it is selected
2. when it is not selected

So the total number of ways of selection = $2 \times 2 \times 2....... \times 2$($n$ times) = 2^n

NOTES

- *Number of selections of objects (at least one) out of n different objects equals* ${}^{n}C_1 + {}^{n}C_2 + ... + {}^{n}C_n = 2^n - 1$
- *Number of selections of at least two objects out of n =* $2^n - {}^{n}C_0 - {}^{n}C_1$

ILLUSTRATION 51: Raj has 10 friends and wants to invite them on dinner party. In how many ways can it be done if

(a) any number of friends can be invited? (b) at least one friend must be invited?

SOLUTION: (a) Number of ways in which dinner party can be arranged when any number of friends are invited = ${}^{10}C_0 + {}^{10}C_1 + {}^{10}C_2 + ... + {}^{10}C_{10} = 2^{10}$

(b) Number of ways in which dinner party can be arranged when one or more friends are invited = ${}^{10}C_1 + {}^{10}C_2 + ... + {}^{10}C_{10} = 2^{10} - 1$

ILLUSTRATION 52: From 10 candidates of *N.C.C*, 7 to be chosen for a *N.C.C.* Camp. In how many ways can this be done?

SOLUTION: The total number of ways of selecting 7 candidates out of 10 is ${}^{10}C_7 = \dfrac{10!}{7! \times 3!} = 120$ (where n is total number of candidates and r is the number of candidates to be chosen)

ILLUSTRATION 53: (a) How many triangles can be formed by joining the vertices of a hexagon?
(b) How many diagonals are there in a polygon with n sides?

SOLUTION: (a) A triangle is formed by selecting 3 points out of six and joining these points.
$\Rightarrow$ Number of triangles that can be formed $= {}^6C_3 = 20$.
(b) Diagonals are formed by selecting any two points out of n points and joining them. But we should exclude n sides.
$\therefore$ Number of diagonals $= {}^nC_2 - n = \dfrac{n(n-1)}{2} - n = \dfrac{n(n-3)}{2}$

ILLUSTRATION 54: A committee of 12 is to be formed from 9 women and 8 men. In how many ways can this be done if at least five women have to be included in the committee?

SOLUTION: Total number of women = 9 and Total number of men = 8
Number of ways to form committee of 12 with at least 5 women is the sum total
Number of ways to have 5 women and 7 men $= {}^9C_5 \times {}^8C_7 = 1008$
Number of ways to have 6 women and 6 men $= {}^9C_6 \times {}^8C_6 = 2352$
Number of ways to have 7 women and 5 men $= {}^9C_7 \times {}^8C_5 = 2016$
Number of ways to have 8 women and 4 men $= {}^9C_8 \times {}^8C_4 = 630$
Number of ways to have 9 women and 3 men $= {}^9C_9 \times {}^8C_3 = 56$
on adding terms, we get 6062 = required number of ways.

ILLUSTRATION 55: A student is allowed to select atmost n books from a collection of $(2n + 1)$ books. If the total number of ways in which he can select at least one book is 63, find the value of n.

SOLUTION: Since, student is allowed to select at most n books out of $(2n + 1)$ books

$\therefore \quad {}^{2n+1}C_1 + {}^{2n+1}C_2 + \ldots\ldots + {}^{2n+1}C_n = 63$ (i)

we know ${}^{2n+1}C_0 + {}^{2n+1}C_1 + {}^{2n+1}C_2 + \ldots\ldots + {}^{2n+1}C_{2n+1} = 2^{2n+1}$

$\Rightarrow 2\left({}^{2n+1}C_0 + {}^{2n+1}C_1 + {}^{2n+1}C_2 + \ldots\ldots + {}^{2n+1}C_n\right) = 2^{2n+1}$

$\Rightarrow \quad {}^{2n+1}C_1 + {}^{2n+1}C_2 + \ldots\ldots + {}^{2n+1}C_n = \left(2^{2n} - 1\right)$ (ii)

From eq. (i) and (ii), we get
$\Rightarrow 2^{2n} - 1 = 63 \Rightarrow 2^{2n} = 64 \Rightarrow 2n = 6 \Rightarrow n = 3$.

Restricted combinations

The number of combinations of n different things taking r at a time

(a) When p particular things are always to be excluded $= {}^{n-p}C_r$

Method to solve

Consider the objects $A_1, A_2, A_3, \ldots\ldots A_p, A_{p+1}, \ldots\ldots A_n$

If the p objects $A_1, A_2, \ldots\ldots, A_p$ are to be excluded, then we will have to select r objects from the remaining $n - p$ objects $A_{p+1}, A_{p+2}, \ldots\ldots A_n$. Hence required number of ways $= {}^{n-p}C_r$

(b) When p particular things are always to be included $= {}^{n-p}C_{r-p}$

Method to solve

Consider the objects $A_1, A_2, A_3, \ldots\ldots A_p, A_{p+1}, \ldots\ldots A_n$

If the p particular objects $A_1, A_2, \ldots\ldots A_p$ must be included in the selection, then to complete the selection, we must select $(r - p)$ more things to complete the selection. From the remaining $n - p$ things $(A_{p+1}, A_{p+2}, \ldots\ldots, A_n)$.

Hence required number of ways $= {}^{n-p}C_{r-p}$

(c) When p particular things are always included and q particular things are always excluded $= {}^{n-p-q}C_{r-p}$ (can be explained as in case (a) and (b))

(d) Number of ways of choosing from the objects of two or more different categories, counting in these cases can be simplified by using tree diagram.

NOTE

The things included are always subtracted from availability and requirement both, while, the things excluded are subtracted only from availability.

ILLUSTRATION 56: Fifteen players are selected for a cricket match.

(i) In how many ways the playing 11 can be selected?

(ii) In how many ways the playing 11 can be selected including a particular player?

(iii) In how many ways the playing 11 can be selected excluding two particular players?

SOLUTION: (i) 11 players are to be selected from 15

Number of ways = ${}^{15}C_{11} = 1365$

(ii) Since one player is already included, we have to select 10 from the remaining 14

Number of ways = ${}^{14}C_{10} = 1001$.

(iii) Since two players are to be excluded, we have to select 11 from the remaining 13.

Number of ways = ${}^{13}C_{11} = 78$

ILLUSTRATION 57: A regular polygon has 20 sides. How many triangles can be drawn by using the vertices, but not using the sides?

SOLUTION: The first vertex can be selected in 20 ways. The remaining two are to be selected form 17 vertices so that they are not consecutive. This can be done in ${}^{17}C_2 - 16$ ways.

∴ The total number of ways = $20 \times ({}^{17}C_2 - 16)$

But in this method, each selection is repeated thrice.

∴ Number of triangles = $\dfrac{20 \times ({}^{17}C_2 - 16)}{3} = 800$.

ILLUSTRATION 58: In how many ways we can select 4 letters from the letters of the word MISSISSIPPI?

SOLUTION: M IIII SSSS PP

Number of ways of selecting 4 alike letters = ${}^{2}C_1 = 2$.

Number of ways of selecting 3 alike and 1 different letters = ${}^{2}C_1 \times {}^{3}C_1 = 6$

Number of ways of selecting 2 alike and 2 alike letters = ${}^{3}C_2 = 3$

Number of ways of selecting 2 alike and 2 different = ${}^{3}C_1 \times {}^{3}C_2 = 9$

Number of ways of selecting 4 different = ${}^{4}C_4 = 1$

∴ Total numbers of ways of selection = 2 + 6 + 3 + 9 + 1 = 21

ILLUSTRATION 59: A group of students consists of 4 boys and 5 girls. Find the number of ways of selecting a team of at least 3 boys and 4 girls.

SOLUTION: Every branch of above tree diagram gives us the constitutions of the team which are as follows:

	Constitution of team	Number of ways of choosing
	3 boys and 4 girls	${}^4C_3 \times {}^5C_4$
or	3 boys and 5 girls	${}^4C_3 \times {}^5C_5$
or	4 boys and 4 girls	${}^4C_4 \times {}^5C_4$
or	4 boys and 5 girls	${}^4C_4 \times {}^5C_5$

Total number of ways of choosing a team $= {}^4C_3 \times {}^5C_4 + {}^4C_3 \times {}^5C_5 + {}^4C_4 \times {}^5C_4 + {}^4C_4 \times {}^5C_5$

$= 4 \times 5 + 4 \times 1 + 1 \times 5 + 1 \times 1 = 30$

ILLUSTRATION 60: The straight lines l_1, l_2, l_3 are parallel and lie in the same plane. A total number of m points are taken on l_1, n points on l_2, k points on l_3. Find the maximum number of triangles formed with vertices at these points are.

SOLUTION: Maximum number of triangles = selection of 3 points out of $m + n + k$ points – {selection of 3 points out of m collinear point's} – {selection of 3 points out of n collinear points} – {selection of 3 points out of p collinear points} $= {}^{m+n+k}C_3 - {}^mC_3 - {}^nC_3 - {}^pC_3$

ILLUSTRATION 61: In an election, a voter may vote for any number of candidates not greater than the number of candidates to be elected. There are 10 candidates and 4 are to be elected. If a voter votes for at least one candidate, then find the number of ways in which he can vote.

SOLUTION: Total number of ways $= {}^{10}C_1 + {}^{10}C_2 + {}^{10}C_3 + {}^{10}C_4$

$= 10 + 45 + 120 + 210 = 385.$

ILLUSTRATION 62: The number of triangles which can be formed by using the vertices of a regular polygon of (n + 3) sides is 220, then find n

SOLUTION: Number of triangles $= {}^{n+3}C_3 = 220$

$$\Rightarrow \frac{(n+3)!}{3!n!} = 220$$

$\Rightarrow$ (n + 1) (n + 2) (n + 3) = 1320 = 10 × 11 × 12 $\quad \Rightarrow \quad n = 9$

ILLUSTRATION 63: In how many ways can a pack of 52 cards be

(a) divided equally among four players in order

(b) divided into four groups of 13 cards each

(c) divided in 4 sets, three of them having 17 cards each and the fourth just one card?

SOLUTION: (a) The number of ways in which 52 cards be divided equally among four players in order

$$= {}^{52}C_{13} \times {}^{39}C_{13} \times {}^{26}C_{13} \times {}^{13}C_{13} = \frac{(52)!}{(13!)^4}$$

(b) The number of ways in which a pack of 52 cards can be divided equally into four groups of 13 cards each

$$= \frac{{}^{52}C_{13} \times {}^{39}C_{13} \times {}^{26}C_{13} \times {}^{13}C_{13}}{4!} = \frac{(52)!}{4!(13!)^4}$$

(c) The number of ways in which a pack of 52 cards be divided into 4 sets, three of them having 17 cards each and the fourth just one card

$$= \frac{{}^{52}C_{17} \times {}^{35}C_{18} \times {}^{18}C_{17} \times {}^{1}C_{1}}{3!} = \frac{(52)!}{3!(17)^3}$$

ILLUSTRATION 64: Five balls of different colours are to be placed in three boxes of different sizes. Each box can hold all five. In how many different ways can we place the balls so that no box remains empty?

SOLUTION: Since, each box can hold five balls.

Number of ways in which balls could be distributed so that none is empty are (2, 2, 1) or (3, 1, 1).

i.e., $\left(\dfrac{{}^5C_2\,{}^3C_2\,{}^1C_1}{2!} + \dfrac{{}^5C_3\,{}^2C_1\,{}^1C_1}{2!}\right) \times 3! = 300$

ILLUSTRATION 65: 7 relatives of a men comprises 4 ladies and 3 gentlemen, his wife has also 7 relatives; 3 of them are ladies and 4 gentlemen. In how many ways can they invite a dinner party of 3 ladies and 3 gentlemen so that there are 3 of man's relative and 3 of the wife's relatives?

SOLUTION: The possible cases are

Case I: Man invites 3 ladies and women invites 3 gentlemen.

Number of ways = ${}^4C_3.{}^4C_3 = 16$

Case II: Man invites (2 ladies, 1 gentleman) and women invites (2 gentlemen, 1 lady).

Number of ways = $({}^4C_2.{}^3C_1).({}^3C_1.{}^4C_2) = 324$

Case III: Man invites (1 lady, 2 gentlemen) and women invites (2 ladies, 1 gentleman).

Number of ways = $({}^4C_1.{}^3C_2).({}^3C_2.{}^4C_1) = 144$

Case IV: Man invites (3 gentlemen) and women invites (3 ladies)

Number of ways = ${}^3C_3.{}^3C_3 = 1$

Total number of ways = 16 + 324 + 144 + 1 = 485.

ILLUSTRATION 66: A box contains two white balls, three black balls and four red balls. In how many ways can three balls be drawn from the box, if at least one black ball is to be included in the draw?

SOLUTION: ***Case I:*** When one black and two others balls are drawn

$\Rightarrow$ Number of ways = ${}^3C_1.{}^6C_2 = 45$

Case II: When two black and one other balls are drawn

$\Rightarrow$ Number of ways = ${}^3C_2.{}^6C_1 = 18$

Case III: When all three black balls are drawn

$\Rightarrow$ Number of ways = ${}^3C_3 = 1$

Total number of ways = 45 + 18 + 1 = 64

ILLUSTRATION 67: A committee of 12 is to be formed from 9 women and 8 men. In how many ways this can be done if at least five women have to be included in the committee? In how many of these committees

(a) the women are in majority? (b) the men are in majority?

SOLUTION: Given that there are 9 women and 8 men, a committee of 12 is to be formed including at least 5 women.

This can be done in the following ways

= (5 women and 7 men) + (6 women and 6 men) + (7 women and 5 men) + (8 women and 4 men) + (9 women and 3 men)

Total number of ways of forming committee

$= ({}^9C_5.{}^8C_7) + ({}^9C_6.{}^8C_6) + ({}^9C_7.{}^8C_5) + ({}^9C_8.{}^8C_4) + ({}^9C_9.{}^8C_3)$

$= 1008 + 2352 + 2016 + 630 + 56$

$= 6062$ ways

(a) The women are in majority $= 2016 + 630 + 56$

$= 2702$ ways

(b) The men are in majority $= 1008$

ILLUSTRATION 68: There are n points in a plane out of these points no three are in the same straight line except p points which are collinear. How many

(i) straight lines and

(ii) triangles can be formed by joining them?

SOLUTION: **(i)** Number of lines formed by joining any two points out of given n points $= {}^nC_2$ and number of lines formed by joining any two points out of p collinear points $= {}^nC_2$, but these collinear points giving exactly one straight line passing through all of them.

Hence, required number of straight lines $= {}^nC_2 - {}^pC_2 + 1$.

(ii) Number of triangles formed by joining any three points out of given n points $= {}^nC_3$ and number of triangles formed by joining any three points out of p collinear points $= {}^pC_3$, but not triangle would be formed by joining any three points out of these p collinear points. Hence, the number of triangles formed $= {}^nC_3 - {}^pC_3$.

ILLUSTRATION 69: There are ten points in a plane. Of these ten points, four points are in a straight line and no other three points are in the same straight line. Find

(i) the number of straight lines formed.

(ii) the number of triangles formed.

(iii) the number of quadrilaterals formed by joining these ten points.

SOLUTION: **(i)** For straight line, we need 2 points

Number of points selected out of 4 collinear points	Number of points selected out of remaining 6 points	Number of straight lines formed
0	2	${}^4C_0 \times {}^6C_2 = 15$
1	1	${}^4C_1 \times {}^6C_1 = 24$
2	0	1

(In last case, only one straight line is formed)

$\therefore$ Required number $= 15 + 24 + 1 = 40$

(ii) For triangle, we need 3 points

Number of points selected out of 4 collinear points	Number of points selected out of remaining 6 points	Number of triangles formed
0	3	${}^4C_0 \times {}^6C_3 = 20$
1	2	${}^4C_1 \times {}^6C_2 = 60$
2	1	${}^4C_2 \times {}^6C_1 = 36$
3	0	0

(In last case, number of triangles formed is 0)

$\therefore$ required number $= 20 + 60 + 36 + 0 = 116$

(iii) For a quadrilateral we need 4 points

Number of points selected out of 4 collinear points	Number of points selected out of remaining 6 points	Number of quadrilaterals formed
0	4	${}^4C_0 \times {}^6C_4 = 15$
1	3	${}^4C_1 \times {}^6C_3 = 80$
2	2	${}^4C_2 \times {}^6C_2 = 90$
3	1	0
40	0	0

(In the last two cases, no quadrilateral is formed)

∴ Required number = 15 + 80 + 90 = 185.

SELECTION OF IDENTICAL OBJECTS

Combination when some objects are identical

1. All possible selections of n identical objects:

As we know there is only one way to select only particular number of things out of given available identical things irrespective of number of available things and required things (provided availability ≥ Requirement) so all possible selections of n identical things = $\underbrace{1+1+1....1}_{n+1 \text{ times}} = n+1$.

2. To find the total number of ways in which it is possible to make a selection taking some or all out of $(p + q + r + s)$ things, where p are alike of one kind, q are alike of second kind and r alike of third kind and s are different.

Out of p alike things, we may select none or one or two or three,...........or all p. Hence they may be disposed of in $(p + 1)$ ways. Similarly, q alike things may be disposed of in $(q + 1)$ ways, similarly for r. And s different things may be disposed of in 2^s ways. (This includes the case in which all of them are rejected).

∴ the total number of selection = $(p + 1)(q + 1) .... (r + 1)\, 2^s$

NOTES

- *Number of ways if atleast one object is to be selected* = $(p+1)(q+1)(r+1)\,2^s - 1$
- *Number of ways if atleast one from s different objects is to be selected* = $(p+1)(q+1)(r+1)(2^s - 1)$
- *Number of ways if atleast one object of each alike type is i.e., p-alike, q-alike,.....,is to be selected)* = $(p.\, q.\, r)\, 2^s$

ILLUSTRATION 70: How many combinations you can make from 5 pairs of (identical) shoes out of which 2 are brown and the remaining three are black?

SOLUTION: Since the shoes are alike in combinations 1 pair shoe or 2 pair shoe (for brown shoes) and 1, 2, 3 pair of shoes (for black).

Hence number of combinations = (2 + 1) (3 + 1) = 12

ILLUSTRATION 71: Find the number of ways in which one or more digits can be selected from the following: 11111 2222 333 44 567.

SOLUTION: Here five 1's are alike, four 2's, are alike three 3's are alike, two 4's are alike and 5, 6, 7 are different.

Selection from (11111) can be made by 6 ways {such include no 1, include one 1, two 1, three 1, four 1, five 1}. Similarly, selections from (2222) can be made in 5 ways, selection from (333) can be made in 4 ways, selection from (44) can be made in 3 ways and selections from 5, 6, 7 can be made in $2 \times 2 \times 2$ ways.

Then total number of combinations

$= (5+1)(4+1)(3+1)(2+1)\,2^3 - 1 = 6.5.4.3.\,8 - 1$

$= 2879$ (excluding the case when no letter is selected)

Combination when some objects are identical

(taking specific number of them at a time)

Method: 1 If a group has n things in which p are identical, then the number of ways of selecting r things from group = $\sum_{k=0}^{r} {}^{n-p}C_{r-k}$ or $\sum_{k=r-p}^{r} {}^{n-p}C_k$ according as $r \le p$ or $r > p$

It can be obtained in following manner:

Split the question into following cases:

Case I: No object is selected from identical objects Number of ways $= {}^{n-p}C_r$

Case II: 1 object is selected from identical objects, Number of ways $= {}^{n-p}C_{r-1}$

Case III: 2 objects are selected from identical objects, Number of ways $= {}^{n-p}C_{r-2}$ and so on, finally p identical objects are selected. Number of ways $= {}^{n-p}C_{r-p}$

NOTES

- *The number of ways of selecting r objects out of n identical objects is* 1.
- *The number of ways of selecting any number of objects out of n identical objects is* n+1.

ILLUSTRATION 72: How many 3 letter words can be formed from the letters of the word CALCUTTA?

SOLUTION: CALCUTTA has letters CC, AA, TT, U, L. There are different number of cases where 3 letter words can be formed.

I. 3 alike NOT POSSIBLE II. 2 alike, 1 different. III. 3 different.

For case (II), the number of ways it can be done in ${}^3C_1 \,.\, {}^4C_1$, since there are 3 pairs of identical letters and 2 other different letters. Now, these 3 letters can be arranged in 3!/2! ways since 2 of them are identical. Hence, the total number for case (II) is ${}^3C_1 \,.\, {}^4C_1 \,.\, (3!/2!) = 36$.

For case (III), the number of ways we can choose 3 different letters from 5 different letters is ${}^5C_3$. These 3 letters can be arranged in 3! ways, so that the number of ways $= {}^5C_3 \,.\, 3! = 60$

Hence the total number of words that can be formed $= 36 + 60 = 96$

TEXTUAL EXERCISE–7 (SUBJECTIVE)

1. Out of 5 boys and 3 girls, find the number of 4 member committee formed containing:
   (i) At least
   (a) 2 girls (b) 2 boys and 1 girl:
   (ii) At most
   (a) 3 boys (b) 2 girls
2. Out of the 10 persons named $P_1, P_2, P_3, \ldots\ldots P_{10}$. Find the number of committees of three people formed.
   (a) If no restriction is applied.
   (b) If a person (P_1) is always selected in the committee.
   (c) If P_2 refuses to be in the committee with P_1.
   (d) If P_1 agrees to be in the committee only if P_2 is selected.
   (e) If P_1 and P_2 have decided to be in the committee together.

3. Show that total number of subsets of a set S with n element is 2^n and Also find the total number of non empty subsets of S as well as total number of proper subsets.

4. A father has eight children. He takes three out of them at a time to zoo and never takes the same group again. If all the children has to visit zoo equal number of times, then:
   (a) how many times father will go to zoo?
   (b) how many times each child will go to zoo?
   (c) how many times father will go to zoo if C_1 C_2 decide to always go together?
   (d) how many times father will go to zoo if C_7 C_8 decide never to go together?
   (e) how many times father will go to zoo C_1 C_2 decide to go together and C_7 C_8 decide never to go together?

5. If n people shake hands with each other in a Party then find the number of hand shakes, if no two people shake hand more than once.

6. (a) Out of two sets of equispaced parallel lines containing m and n lines respectively; when lines of first set are non-parallel to lines of second sets, then find number of parallelogram formed.
   (b) Find the number of squares and rectangles formed on a chess board.

7 There are n points in a plane and six out of them are collinear, find the total number of distinct lines, line segments, directed line segments formed by joining them.

8. (a) How many diagonals are there in an n -sided convex polygon ($n > 3$)?
   (b) How many triangles can be formed by joining the vertices of an n -sided convex polygon? How many of these triangles have:
      (i) exactly one side common with that of the polygon
      (ii) exactly two sides common with that of the polygon
      (iii) no sides common with that of the polygon?

9. (a) In how many ways can two unit squares be selected from an 8-by-8 chessboard so that they are not in the same row or the same column?
   (b) In how many ways can four unit squares, not all in the same row or column, be selected from an 8-by-8 chessboard to form a rectangle?

10. Applying the combinatorial arguments (without using binomial theorem) prove the following mathematical statements:
   (a) ${}^nC_0 + {}^nC_1 + {}^nC_2............ {}^nC_n = 2^n$
   (b) $1.\,{}^nC_1 + 2.\,{}^nC_2 + ... + n.\,{}^nC_n = n.2^{n-1}$.
   (c) $2^0.\,{}^nC_0 + 2^1.\,{}^nC_1 + 2^2.\,{}^nC_2 + ... + 2^n.\,{}^nC_n = 3^n$.
   (d) $({}^nC_0)^2 + ({}^nC_1)^2 + ({}^nC_2)^2 + ... + ({}^nC_n)^2 = {}^{2n}C_n$
   (e) $({}^mC_0)({}^nC_r) + ({}^mC_1)({}^nC_{r-1}) + ({}^mC_2)({}^nC_{r-2}) + ... + ({}^mC_r)({}^nC_0) = {}^{m+n}C_r$

11. Find the number of ways in which nine speakers(S_1, S_2, ...S_9) can address an assembly such that
   (a) S_1 and S_2 speak together
   (b) S_1 speaks just before S_2.
   (c) S_1 speaks before S_2.
   (d) speaker S_1 wants to address the assembly before speaker S_2 and S_2 wants to address before speaker S_3.

12. Find the number of ways in which 8 members committee can be formed out of 15 people (including five senior citizens), so that.
   (a) All senior citizens are included
   (b) No senior citizen is included.

13. Find the number of ways in which 15 peoples (including five senior citizens) can be seated on 10 chairs arranged in a row, so that
   (a) All senior citizens are always occupying the chair
   (b) None of them occupying the chair.

14. From a class containing $2n$ students of which n are boys and remaining n are girls. Find the number of ways of choosing students such that
   (a) number of boys is one more than number of girls.
   (b) number of boys is 2 more than number of girls.
   (c) number of boys is k more than number of girls.

15. A cricket eleven has to be chosen from 15 players of whom 6 can bowl and 3 keep wicket, while none can bowl and keep wicket. In how many ways can the eleven be chosen so as to contain at least 4 bowlers and 2 wicket keepers?

16. How many numbers of n digits can be made with the non-zero digits in which no two consecutive digits are the same?

17. Find the number of elements in the set $X = \{x: x \in Q,\ 0 < x < 1,\ x = p/q$. where p and q are to be chosen from the set $\{1, 2, 3, 4, 5, 6\}$ }.

18. Imagine a piece of graph paper. Starting at the origin draw a path to the point (n, n) that stays on the grid lines (which are one unit apart) and has a total length of $2n$. For example, one path is to go from (0, 0) to $(0, n–k)$ to $(5, n–k)$ to $(5, n)$ to (n, n). Another path goes from (0, 0) to $(n, 0)$ to (n, n). How many possible different paths are there?

Answer Keys

1. (i) (a) 35 (b) 60 (ii) (a) 65 (b) 65 **2.** (a) 120 (b) 36 (c) 112 (d) 92 **(e)** 64

3. 2^n-1 **4.** (a) ${}^8C_3$ (b) ${}^7C_2$ (c) ${}^6C_3+{}^6C_1$ (d) ${}^6C_2+{}^7C_3$ (e) ${}^6C_1+{}^4C_2+{}^5C_3$

5. ${}^nC_2$ **6.** (a) ${}^mC_2\times{}^nC_2$ (b) 204, $({}^9C_2)^2$

7. $\dfrac{n^2-n-28}{2}$, ${}^nC_2$, $2.{}^nC_2$

8. (a) $\dfrac{n(n-3)}{2}$ (b) ${}^nC_3$ (i) $n(n-4)$ (ii) n (iii) $\dfrac{n(n-4)(n-5)}{6}$

9. (a) 1568 (b) 49

11. (a) 8! 2! (b) 8! (c) ${}^9C_2$. 7! (d) 84× 6! **12.** (a) ${}^{10}C_3$ (b) ${}^{10}C_2$

13. (a) ${}^{10}P_5$ 10! (b) 10! × 5! **14.** (a) $\dfrac{(2n)!}{(n+1)!(n-1)!}$ (b) $\dfrac{(2n)!}{(n+2)!(n-2)!}$ (c) ${}^{2n}C_{n-k}$

15. 960 **16.** $9\times 8^{n-1}$

17. 11 **18.** ${}^{2n}C_n$

TEXTUAL EXERCISE–7 (OBJECTIVE)

1. From 4 gentlemen and 6 ladies, a committee of five is to be selected. The number of ways, in which the committee can be formed so that gentlemen are in majority, is

(a) 66 (b) 156
(c) 60 (d) None of these

2. From a class containing 25 boys and 25 girls, some students are chosen such that number of girls is one more than the number of boys. Total number of ways of choosing the students under above restriction is

(a) ${}^{50}C_{25}$ (b) ${}^{50}C_{24}$
(c) ${}^{50}C_{23}$ (d) None of these

3. An urn contains 3 red pens, 4 green pens and 6 yellow pens. The number of ways of drawing 4 pens from the urn, if at least one red pen is to be included in the draw is (All the pens are different from each other)

(a) 500 (b) 505
(c) 510 (d) None of these

4. There are 20 questions in a question paper. If no two students solve the same combination of question but solve equal number of questions then the maximum number of students who appeared in the examination is

(a) ${}^{20}C_9$ (b) ${}^{20}C_{11}$
(c) ${}^{20}C_{10}$ (d) None of these

5. Out of 10 consonants and four vowels, the number of words that can be formed using six consonants and three vowels is

(a) ${}^{10}P_6\times{}^9P_3$ (b) ${}^{10}C_6\times{}^6C_3$
(c) ${}^{10}C_6\times{}^4C_3\times 9!$ (b) ${}^{10}P_6\times{}^4P_3$

6. The number of all three elements subsets of the set $\{a_1, a_2, a_3,.......a_n\}$ which contain a_3 is

(a) ${}^nC_3$ (b) ${}^{n-1}C_3$
(c) ${}^{n-1}C_2$ (d) None of these

7. A lady gives a dinner party to 5 guests to be selected from nine friends. The number of ways of forming the party of 5 given that two of the friends will not attend the party together is

(a) 56 (b) 126
(c) 91 (d) None of these

8. Let T_n denote the number of triangles which can be formed by using the vertices of a regular polygon of n sides. If $T_{n+1}-T_n=21$, then n equals

(a) 5 (b) 7
(c) 6 (d) 4

9. The number of triangles whose vertices are at the vertices of the octagon but none of whose sides happen to come from the octagon is

(a) 16 (b) 18
(c) 36 (d) 70

10. If 7 points out of 12 are in the same straight line, then the number of triangles formed is

(a) 19 (b) 158
(c) 185 (d) 201

11. The number of sides of a polygon having p diagonal, is given by the equation (let number of sides $= n$)

(a) ${}^nP_2 - {}^nC_2 = p$ (b) ${}^nC_2 - n = p$

(c) ${}^nC_2 + n = p$ (d) None of these

12. In a cricket tournament, n teams participated. Before semi-finals every team played a match with every other team. If total number of matches played before semi-finals was 91, then n is

(a) 11 (b) 12

(c) 13 (d) 14

13. The number of ways in which we can select four numbers from 1 to 30 as to exclude every selection of four consecutive numbers is

(a) 27378 (b) 27405

(c) 27399 (d) None of these

14. A class has n students. We have to form a team of the students including at least two students and also excluding at least two students. The number of ways of forming the team is

(a) $2^n - 2n$ (b) $2^n - 2n - 2$

(c) $2^n - 2n - 4$ (d) None of these

15. Given that n is odd, the number of ways in which three numbers in A.P. can be selected from 1, 2, 3, ..., n is

(a) $\frac{(n+1)^2}{4}$ (b) $\frac{(n-1)^2}{4}$

(c) $\frac{(n+1)^2}{2}$ (d) $\frac{(n-1)^2}{2}$

16. The number of integral points (both co-ordinates integers) that lie exactly in the interior of the triangles with vertices (0, 0), (0, 21) and (21, 0) is

(a) 133 (b) 190

(c) 233 (d) 105

17. The number of different triangles formed by joining the points A, B, C, D, E, F and G as shown in the figure below will be:

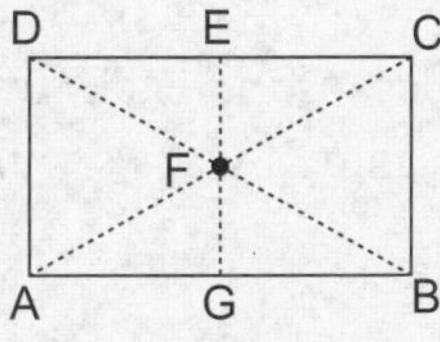

(a) 20 (b) 24

(c) 25 (d) 30

Answer Keys

1. (a)	**2.** (b)	**3.** (b)	**4.** (c)	**5.** (c)	**6.** (c)	**7.** (c)	**8.** (b)	**9.** (a)	**10.** (c)
11. (b)	**12.** (d)	**13.** (a)	**14.** (b)	**15.** (b)	**16.** (b)	**17.** (d)			

DISTRIBUTION

Distribution among unequal groups

To find the number of ways in which $m + n$ things can be divided into two groups containing m and n things respectively.

This is clearly equivalent of finding the number of combinations of $m + n$ things taking m at a time, as for every time we select one group of m things we leave a group of n things behind.

Thus the required number $= \frac{(m+n)!}{m!n!}$

To find the number of ways in which $m + n + p$ things can be divided into three groups containing m, n, p things separately.

First divide $m + n + p$ things into two groups containing m and $n + p$ things respectively; the number of ways in which this can be done $= {}^{m+n+p}C_m = \frac{(m+n+p)!}{m!(n+p)!}$ (i)

And the number of ways in which the group of $n + p$ things can be divided into two groups containing n and p things respectively $= {}^{n+p}C_n = \frac{(n+p)!}{n!p!}$

Hence the number of ways in which the subdivision into three groups containing m, n, p things can be made is

$$\frac{(m+n+p)!}{m!(n+p)!} \times \frac{(n+p)!}{n!p!} = \frac{(m+n+p)!}{m!n!p!}$$

e.g., If alphabets a, b, c, d are to be distributed among two groups containing three and one alphabets respectively. The number of divisions will actually be equal to number of ways of selecting three alphabets out of four (or one out of four) for Ist group, because the remaining will automatically go to second group. So the number of ways will be equal to ${}^4C_3 = 4$ and the groups formed will be:

{a, b, c} {d}

{a, b, d} {c}

{a, c, d} {b}

{b, c, d} {a}

ILLUSTRATION 73: Find the number of ways of dividing 50 students into

(a) three groups containing 10, 15, 25 students respectively.

(b) two groups containing 30 and 20 students respectively.

SOLUTION: (a) number of divisions $= {}^{50}C_{10}\,{}^{40}C_{15}\,{}^{25}C_{25} = \dfrac{50!}{10!15!25!}$

(b) number of ways $= {}^{50}C_{30}\,{}^{20}C_{20} = \dfrac{50!}{30!20!}$

Distribution among equal groups

Case I: When groups are identical to be distributed among two identical groups equally (containing m objects each), then it can be done in $\dfrac{(m+m)!}{m!m!2!} = \dfrac{(2m)!}{(m!)^2\,2!}$

Dividing by 2! because in each division it is possible to arrange the groups into 2! ways's without obtaining new distribution

Case II: when groups are distinct (name of group is specified)

If the name of group among which objects are distributed are specified (e.g., distribution of books among student, dividing soldiers into regiment, distributing student into section etc.)

We put $n = p = m$ in equation (i),

we get $\dfrac{3m!}{m!m!m!} = \dfrac{(3m)!}{(m!)^3}$

Note: **Problem solving trick**

Consider the following situation:

Case I: Groups are identical or distinct having m, n and p such that $m \neq n \neq p$.

Since we can recognize the groups easily so no degeneracy and no division by 3!

Hence number of ways $= \dfrac{(m+n+p)!}{m!n!p!}$

Case II: Groups are identical each having m-objects.

Here we cannot recognize the groups so there is degeneracy by 3!

Hence, No. of ways $= \dfrac{(m+m+m)!}{m!m!m!3!}$

Case III: Groups are distinct (name specified) and number of things to be distributed are equal.

Here any of the arrangement can be recognized easily [as the groups are specified]. So no degeneracy by 3! Hence the number of ways are $= \dfrac{(m+m+m)!}{m!m!m!}\ \dfrac{(3m)!}{(\ \ )}$

ILLUSTRATION 74: Find the number of ways in which 15 recruits can be divided into three equal groups and also obtain the number of ways in which they can be divided equally into three regiments.

SOLUTION: Simple division into three equal groups can be done is $\dfrac{15!}{5!5!5!3!}$ and the number of ways in which they can be drafted equally into three different regiments $= \dfrac{15!}{5!5!5!}$.

NOTE

*The number of ways of dividing pq objects among **p** groups of same size, each group containing **q** objects* $= \dfrac{(pq)!}{(q!)^p.p!}$

ILLUSTRATION 75: In how many ways can a pack of 52 cards be distributed into 4 groups each containing 13 cards ?

SOLUTION: Here order of group is not important, thus the number of ways in which 52 different cards can be divided equally into 4 groups is $\dfrac{52!}{(13!)^4.4!}$ (groups are identical and things are equal)

NOTE

The number of ways of distributing ***pq*** *objects among* ***p*** *persons, each getting* ***q*** *objects* $= \dfrac{(pq)!}{(q!)^p}$

ILLUSTRATION 76: In how many ways can a pack of 52 cards be equally distributed among 4 players in order?

SOLUTION: Here order of group is important, then the numbers of ways in which 52 different cards can be divided equally into 4 players is $\dfrac{52!}{(13!)^4}$

ILLUSTRATION 77: The set S = {1, 2, 3, ..., 12} is to be partitioned into three sets *A, B, C* of equal size.
Thus, $A \cup B \cup C = S$
$A \cap B = B \cap C = A \cap C = \phi$
The number of ways to partition S is

(a) $12!/3!(4!)^3$ (b) $12!/3!(3!)^4$
(c) $12!/(4!)^3$ (d) $12!/(3!)^4$

SOLUTION: Required number of ways $= {}^{12}C_4 \times {}^{8}C_4 \times {}^{4}C_4 = \dfrac{12!}{8! \times 4!} \times \dfrac{8!}{4! \times 4!} \times 1 = \dfrac{12!}{(4!)^3}$

ILLUSTRATION 78: The number of ways in which 20 different things can be divided into three sets of 7, 7 and 6 things

(a) $\dfrac{20!}{7!\,7!\,6!\,2!}$ (b) $\dfrac{20!}{7!\,7!\,6!}$ (c) 1 (d) $\dfrac{20!}{7!\,7!\,6!\,3!}$

SOLUTION: First select '6' things out of '20' and it can be done in ${}^{20}C_6$ ways

After that, '14' things are to be divided into two groups of '7' each. This can be done in $\dfrac{{}^{14}C_7}{2!}$

Hence the total number of ways $= \dfrac{{}^{20}C_6 \times {}^{14}C_7}{2!} = \dfrac{20!}{7!\,7!\,6!\,2!}$

TEXTUAL EXERCISE–8 (SUBJECTIVE)

1. There are two boys B_1 and B_2. B_1 has n_1 different toys and B_2 has n_2 different toys. Find the number of ways in which B_1 and B_2 can exchange their toys in such a way that after exchanging they still have same number of toys but not the same set.

2. (a) Out of 35 distinct pink shirts, 10 distinct white shirts and 15 distinct trousers. In how many ways shopping can be done
   (i) if you have previously decided to buy at least one pink shirt?
   (ii) If at least one item from each lot has to be bought?

   (b) Let a person have 3 identical coins of 25 paise, 4 identical coins of 50 paise and 2 identical coins of 1 rupee. Then, in how many ways can he give none or some coins to a begger? Further, find the number of ways so that
   (i) he gives at least one coin of one rupee.
   (ii) he gives at least one coin of each kind.

3. In a city, no two persons have identical set of teeth and no person has no teeth. If any person can have maximum thirty-two teeth. Find maximum possible population of city disregarding the shape and size of teeth and considering only positions of the teeth.

4. Out of the letters of the word ARRANGEMENT.
   (i) How many ways one or more letters are selected?
   (ii) If at least one letter of each type is selected.
   (iii) If all E's are selected.

5. Find the number of ways into which 6 books can be:
   (i) divided into groups each having two books.
   (ii) can be divided into groups such that one group is containing exactly 4 books.
   (iii) can be distributed amongst three persons such that each is getting exactly two books.

6. (i) Find the number of ways in which 15 recruits can be divided into three equal groups.
   (ii) Find the number of ways in which they can be drafted into three different regiments of five each.
   (iii) Distribute m subject books having n different volumes of each subject into:
   (a) n equal groups
   (b) m equal groups
   (c) into n persons equally
   (d) into m persons equally

7. A is a set containing 'n' elements a subset P of A is chosen and set A is reconstructed by replacing the elements into it and subset Q is again chosen and this process continues. Find the number of ways of choosing P and Q such that $P \cap Q = \phi$. In the above question, find the number of ways of choosing P and Q such that
   (i) $P \cup Q$ contains exactly 2 elements.
   (ii) If $P \cap Q = A$ and $P \cap Q = \phi$.

8. In how many ways 10 scientist can be assigned to 5 different research projects so that equal number of scientists work on each project?

9. Suppose we have three different toys and we want to give them away to two girls and one boy (one toy per child). The children will be selected from 4 boys and 6 girls. In how many ways can this be done?

Answer Keys

1. ${}^{n_1+n_2}C_{n_1} - 1$ **2.** (a) (i) $(2^{35} - 1)2^{25}$ (ii) $(2^{35} - 1)(2^{10} - 1)(2^{15} - 1)$
(b) 60 ways (i) 40 ways (ii) 24 ways **3.** $2^{32} - 1$ **4.** (i) 647 (ii) 16 (iii) 216

5. (i) $\frac{6!}{(2!)^3.3!}$ (ii) $2\left(\frac{6!}{(4!)(1!)^2.2!}\right)$ (iii) $\frac{6!}{(2!)^3}$ **6.** (i) $\frac{15!}{3!\,(5!)^3}$ (ii) $\frac{15!}{(5!)^3}$

(iii) (a) $\frac{(mn)!}{(m!)^n\, n!}$ (b) $\frac{(mn)!}{(n!)^m\, m!}$ (c) $\frac{(mn)!}{(m!)^n}$ (d) $\frac{(mn)!}{(n!)^m}$ **7.** 3^n ways (i) ${}^nC_2(3^{n-2})$ (ii) 2^n ways

8. 113400 **9.** 360

TEXTUAL EXERCISE–8 (OBJECTIVE)

1. The total number of ways of distributing n different balls among k different boxes if each box can hold any number of balls is
   (a) k^n (b) n^k
   (c) $\frac{(k+n-1)!}{(k-1)!n!}$ (d) $\frac{(k-n+1)!}{k!(n-1)!}$

2. The number of ways in which 8 distinct toys can be distributed among 5 children is
   (a) 5^8 (b) 8^5
   (c) ${}^8P_5$ (d) 40

3. The number of ways in which one can post 5 letters in 7 letter boxes is
   (a) 35 (b) ${}^7P_5$
   (c) 7^5 (d) 5^7

4. **Comprehension passage:** Five balls are to be placed in three boxes. Each can hold all the five balls.

Now answer the following questions:

(i) In how many ways balls can be placed in boxes so that no box remains empty, if balls and boxes are all different?
   (a) 100 (b) 150
   (c) 200 (d) None of these

(ii) In how many ways balls can be placed in boxes so that no box remains empty, if balls are identical but boxes are different?
   (a) 4 (b) 5
   (c) 6 (d) None of these

(iii) In how many ways balls can be placed in boxes so that no box remains empty, if balls are different but boxes are identical?
   (a) 25 (b) 30
   (c) 50 (d) 60

(iv) In how many ways balls can be placed in boxes so that no box remains empty? If balls as well as boxes are identical.

(a) 5 (b) 6

(c) 3 (d) 2

(v) In how many ways balls can be placed in boxes so that no box remains empty. If balls as well as boxes are identical but boxes are kept in a row?

(a) 3 (b) 4

(c) 5 (d) 6

5. In how many ways 50 different things can be divided in 5 sets, three of them having 12 things each and two of them having 7 things each?

(a) $\frac{50!}{12!\,7!\,3!\,2!}$ (b) $\frac{50!}{(12!)^2(7!)^2\,3!\,2!}$

(c) $\frac{50!}{(12!)^3(7!)^2\,3!\,2!}$ (d) None of these

6. In how many ways 50 different things can be distributed among 5 persons so that, three of them get 12 things each and two of them get 7 things each?

(a) $\frac{50!}{12!\,7!\,3!\,2!}$ (b) $\frac{50!}{(12!)^3(7!)^2\,3!\,2!}5!$

(c) $\frac{50!}{(12!)^3(7!)^2\,3!\,2!}$ (d) None of these

Answer Keys

1. (a) **2.** (a) **3.** (c) **4.** (i) (b) (ii) (c) (iii) (a) (iv) (d) (v) (d) **5.** (c) **6.** (b)

■ FORMATION OF NUMBERS

There are two methods to form numbers of certain digits with the help of given digits or using all digits.

(a) when the repetition of digits is allowed

(b) when the repetition of digits is not allowed

The process is mentioned taking following examples:

Number of numbers

To find the number of numbers formed we have to obtain total number of ways of filling all the places of the number, applying the given restrictions:

ILLUSTRATION 79: Find the total number of four digit numbers formed using all digits from 0 to 9.

(a) with repetition (b) without repetition

SOLUTION: (a) ∵ zero can not be at 4th place otherwise number will be of 3 digits.

So number of ways filling 4th place = 9 (placing any of digits from 1, 2, 3,.......9) since repetition of digits is allowed so each of the remaining places can be filled in 10 ways. So total number of numbers formed = 9 × 10 ×10 × 10 = 9000

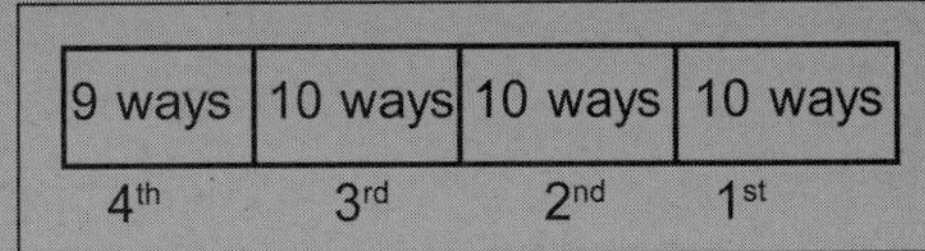

FIGURE 6.13

However, this question can be answered even by a child as he will find out total number of 4 digits numbers as 9999 – 999 = 9000

(b) ∵ zero can not be at 4th place otherwise number will be of 3 digits. Therefore,

4th place can be filled in 9 ways

3rd place can be filled in 9 ways (dropping 4th place digit and including 0)

2nd place can be filled in 8 ways

1st place can be filled in 7 ways

Thus the total numbers formed = 9 × 9 × 8 × 7 = 4536 ways

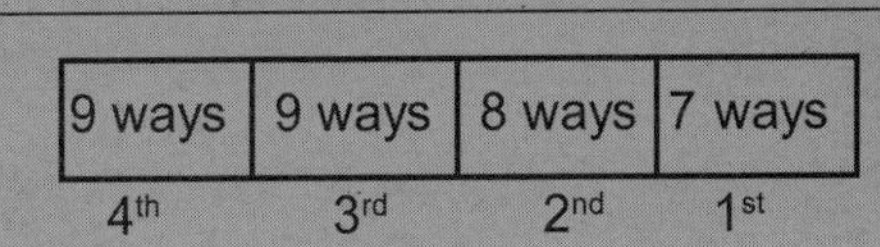

FIGURE 6.14

ILLUSTRATION 80. Number of integers greater than 7000 and divisible by 5 that can be formed using the digits 3, 5, 7, 8 and 9, no digit being repeated is

(a) 46 (b) 48 (c) 72 (d) 42

SOLUTION: Since the number is divisible by 5, the unit place must be 5.

Now we may have 4 digit numbers as well as 5 digit numbers.

case 1: 4 digit numbers divisible by 5 and greater than 7000

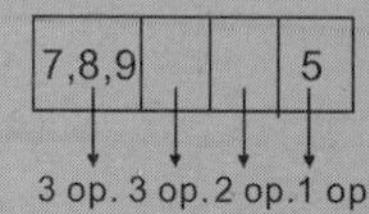

FIGURE 6.15

$= 3 \times 3 \times 2 \times 1 = 18$

case 2: 5 digit numbers divisible by 5 and greater than 7000

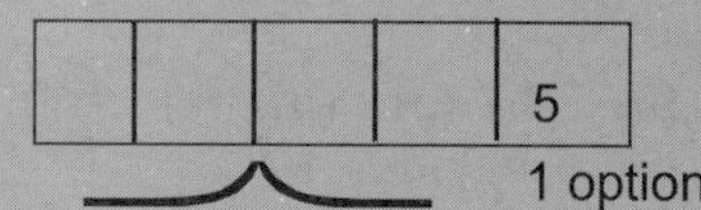

FIGURE 6.16

4! ways to arrange remaining because a 5 digit number is always greater than 7000.
$= 4! \times 1 = 24$. Total number of numbers $= 18 + 24 = 42$.

ILLUSTRATION 81: How many 5-digit and 3-digit numbers can be formed by using the digits 1, 2, 4, 6 and 8 without any repetition of digits?

SOLUTION: **5 digit numbers:**

Places	A	B	C	D	E
Number of choices	5	4	3	2	1

Number of ways to fill place $A = 5$ { Any of the digits 1, 2, 4, 6, 8 }
Number of ways to fill place $B = 4$ { Since, digits cannot be repeated}
Similarly, number of ways to fill places C, D and E, = 3, 2 and 1 respectively.

$\therefore$ Total no of ways $= 5 \times 4 \times 3 \times 2 \times 1 = 120$

3-digit numbers:

Places	A	B	C
Number of choices	5	4	3

$\therefore$ Total number of ways $= 5 \times 4 \times 3 = 60$

ILLUSTRATION 82: How many 5-digit and 3-digit numbers can be formed by using the digits 1, 2, 4, 6, 8, if the digits can be repeated?

SOLUTION: **5-digit numbers**

Places	A	B	C	D	E
Number of choices	5	5	5	5	5

Number of ways to fill place $A = 5$ { any of the digits 1, 2, 4, 6 and 8}
Number of ways to fill place $B = 5$ { Since, digits can be repeated}
Similarly, number of ways to fill places C, D and $E = 5$ each

$\therefore$ Total no.of ways $= 5 \times 5 \times 5 \times 5 \times 5 = 5^5$

3-digit numbers

Places	A	B	C
Number of choices	5	5	5

$\therefore$ Total number of ways $= 5 \times 5 \times 5 = 5^3$

ILLUSTRATION 83: How many 5 digit numbers can be formed by using the digit 0, 1, 3, 5 and 7 if (a) the digits can't be repeated? (b) the digits can be repeated?

SOLUTION: (a) The digits can't be repeated

Places	A	B	C	D	E
Number of choices	4	4	3	2	1

Number of ways to fill place A = 4 {any of the digits 1, 3, 5 and 7 can be used except for 0}

Number of ways to fill place $B = 4$ {any of the digits 0, 1, 3, 5, 7 except for the digit already used in place A}

Similarly, number of ways to fill places C, D and $E = 3$, 2 and 1 respectively.

$\therefore$ Total number of ways $= 4 \times 4 \times 3 \times 2 \times 1 = 96$

(b) The digits can be repeated

Places	A	B	C	D	E
Number of choices	4	5	5	5	5

$\therefore$ Total number of ways $= 4 \times 5 \times 5 \times 5 \times 5 = 4 \times 5^4$

■ SUM OF NUMBERS

Case I: Sum of numbers formed using the digits D_1, D_2,....., D_r all at a time when none of the digits is zero.

Every digit will occur at a place $(r-1)!$

Sum of column = (summation of digits) $(r-1)!$

or $\left[\sum_{k=1}^{r} D_k\right](r-1)!$

Sum of all numbers

$$= \left[\sum_{k=1}^{r} D_k\right](r-1)!\,[10^{r-1} + 10^{r-2} + ...10 + 1]$$

$$= \left(\sum_{k=1}^{r} D_k\right)(r-1)!\underbrace{(11111....1)}_{r\text{ times}} = \left(\frac{10^r - 1}{9}\right)\left[\sum_{k=1}^{r} D_k\right](r-1)!$$

Case II: When one of the digit is zero,

then $\sum_{k=1}^{r} D_k \left[(r-1)!\underbrace{(11111...1)}_{r\text{ times}} - (r-2)!\underbrace{(11111...1)}_{(r-1)\text{ times}}\right]$

Example: Find the sum of numbers formed by the digit 0,1,2,3 and 4 (using all at a time).

Solution: $S = 10\,[24 \times 11111 - 6 \times 1111] = 2599980$

Case III: Sum of r digit numbers formed using the digits $D_1, D_2, D_3, \ldots, D_r$ when repetition of digits is allowed

1. When none of the digits is zero

$$\text{Sum} = \left(\sum_{i=1}^{r} D_i\right) r^{r-1} \underbrace{(\pm\pm\pm\pm\pm\pm\pm\ )}_{r\text{ times}}$$

2. When one of the digits is zero

Sum

$$= \sum_{i=1}^{r} D_i \left[r^{r-1}\underbrace{(11111.........1)}_{r\text{ times}} - (r-1)^{r-2}\underbrace{(11111.........1)}_{(r-1)\text{ times}} \right]$$

ILLUSTRATION 84: Find the sum of all 4 digit numbers formed by using 2,3,7 and 8 when

(a) repetition is not allowed (b) repetition of digits is allowed

SOLUTION: (a) Sum of all 4 digit numbers formed by using 2,3,7 and 8 (without repetition)

$= (2 + 3 + 7 + 8)\,(4 - 1)!\,(1111) = 20 \times 6 \times 1111 = 133320$

(b) Sum of all 4 digit numbers formed by using 2,3,7 and 8 (with repetition)
$= (2 + 3 + 7 + 8)4^{4-1}\,(1111) = 1422080$

ILLUSTRATION 85: Find summation of numbers formed using digits 1, 3, 4, 5 and 7 (all at a time without repetition).

SOLUTION: $S = \dfrac{10^r - 1}{9}\left[\sum_{k=1}^{r} D_k\right][r-1!] = \dfrac{10^5 - 1}{9}\,[1 + 3 + 4 + 5 + 7]\,4!$

$= \dfrac{10^5 - 1}{9}\,[20] \times 24 = 480 \times 11111 = 5333280$

TESTS OF DIVISIBILITY

1. **Divisibility by 2:** A number is divisible by 2 if and only if its last digit is divisible by 2
2. **Divisibility by 3:** A number is divisible by 3 if and only if the sum of all digits is divisible by 3
3. **Divisibility by 4:** A number is divisible by 4 if its unit's place digit plus twice its ten's place, e.g. 35784 digit is divisible by 4 or last two digit number is divisible by 4.
4. **Divisibility by 5:** A number is divisible by 5 if and only if its last digit is divisible by 5 (i.e., if it ends in 0 or 5).
5. **Divisibility by 6:** A number is divisible by 6 if and only if its units's place digit is even and the sum of its digits is divisible by 3
6. **Divisibility by 7:** A number is divisible by 7 if and only if 1 × unit's digit + 3 × ten's digit + 2 × hundred's digit – 1 × thousand's digit –3 × ten thousand's digit –2 × hundred thousand's digit is divisible by 7. If there are more digits present, the sequence of multipliers 1, 3, 2, –1, –3, –2 is repeated as often necessary.

   Example: to test the divisibility of (2018289) by 7

   $(1 \times 9 = 9) + (3 \times 8 = 24) + (2 \times 2 = 4) + (-1 \times 8 = -8) + (-3 \times 1 = -3) + (-2 \times 0 = 0) + (1 \times 2 = 2)\,) = 28$ (7 divides 28)

   since 28 is divisible by 7, so the given number is divisibly by 7.
7. **Divisibility by 8:** A number is divisible by 8 if and only if its units's place digit + 2 × ten's place digit + 4 × hundred's is divisible by 8 or last three digit number is divisible by 8.
8. **Divisibility by 9:** A number is divisible by 9 if and only if the sum of its digits is divisible by 9.
9. **Divisibility by 10:** A number is divisible by 10 if and only if the last digit is 0.
10. **Divisibility by 11:** A number is divisible by 11 if and only if the difference between the sum of the digits in the odd places (starting from the right) and the sum of the digits in the even places (starting from the right) is a multiple of 11
11. **Divisibility by 13:** A number is divisible by 13 if and only if 1 × units's digit – 3 × ten's digit – 4 × hundred's digit – 1 × thousand's digit + 3 × ten thousand's digit + 4 × hundred thousand's digit is divisible by 13. If there are more digits present, the sequence of multipliers 1, –3, –4, –1, 3, 4 is repeated as often as necessary. e.g., if N = 512473, then (1 × 3) – (3 × 7) – (4 × 4) – (1 × 2) + (3 × 1) + (4 × 5) = –13 which is divisible by 13, hence the given number is divisible by 13.

ILLUSTRATION 86: All possible two factors products are formed from numbers 1, 2, 3, 4, ... ,200. The number of factors out of the total obtained which are multiples of 5 is:

(a) 5040 (b) 7180

(c) 8150 (d) None of these

SOLUTION: Out of 1, 2, 3, 4, ...,200.

We have $\left[\dfrac{200}{5}\right] = 40$ numbers which are multiple of 5.

Now all possible two factor products which are multiple of 5 = Total no. of two factor products – Those two factor products which are not divisible by 5.

$$= {}^{200}C_2 - {}^{160}C_2 = \frac{200 \times 199}{2} - \frac{160 \times 159}{2} = 19900 - 12720 = 7180.$$

ILLUSTRATION 87: How many number of 4 digits can be made with the digits 0, 1, 2, 3, 4 and 5 which are divisible by 3, digits being unrepeated in the same number? How many of these will be divisible by 6?

SOLUTION: We know that a number is divisible by 3 if the sum of the digits in the number is divisible by 3.

Here 0 + 1 + 2 + 3 + 4 + 5 = 15; so two digits are to be omitted whose sum is 3 or 6 or 9.

Hence the number of four digits can be made by using the digits of sets

$A = \{1, 2, 4, 5\}$ or $B = \{0, 3, 4, 5\}$ or $C = \{0, 1, 3, 5\}$ or $D = \{0, 2, 3, 4\}$ or $E = \{0, 1, 2, 3\}$

The number of 4-digit numbers that can be made using set $A = {}^4P_4 = 4!$

The number of 4-digit numbers that can be made by the digits in any one of the remaining four sets (each containing 0) = 4! – 3!

($\because$ The number of numbers beginning with $0 = {}^3P_3 = 3!$)

$\therefore$ The required number of 4-digit numbers divisible by 3

$= 4! + 4(4! - 3!) = 24 + 4(24 - 6) = 96$

Now, a number is divisible by 6 if it is even as well as divisible by 3.

So, the number of 4-digit numbers divisible by 6 that can be made by using set $A = 2 \times 3!$

($\because$ The numbers should have an even digit in the units place)

The number of numbers of 4 digits, divisible by 6, that can be made by using set B and set E = (3! – 2!) + 3! for each set

($\because$ The numbers should have 4 or 2 or 0 in units place and 0 should not appear in thousands place.)

The number of 4-digits numbers divisible by 6 that can be made by using set $C = 3!$

The numbers of 4 digits, divisible by 6, that can be made by using set $D = (3! – 2!) + (3! – 2!) + 3!$

($\because$ The numbers should have 4 or 2 or 0 in units place and 0 should not appear in thousands place)

$\therefore$ The number of required 4-digit numbers divisible by 6

$= 2 \times 3! + 2[(3! - 2!) + 3!] + 3! + (3! - 2!) + (3! - 2!) + 3! = 52$

TEXTUAL EXERCISE–9 (SUBJECTIVE)

1. Find out the total number of 4 digit numbers formed when repetition of digits is allowed and
(a) how many of them are odd
(b) how many of them are even
(c) how many of them have sum of digits as even
(d) how many of them are divisible by 5.

2 Find the number of 4 digit numbers formed without repetition of digits and also find how many of them are even.

3. (a) How many 3 digit numbers can be formed using the digits 0, 1, 2, 3, 4 and 5 such that:
(i) digits may not be repeated?
(ii) digits may be repeated?
(b) Find the numbers between 300 and 3000 that can be formed with the digits 0, 1, 2, 3, 4 and 5 no digit being repeated in any number.

4. Find the sum of all 4-digit numbers which can be using the digits 1, 2, 3 and 4 such that
(i) each digit may be repeated up to 4 times;
(ii) each digit may be used only once.

5. Number plates of cars must contain 3 letters of the alphabet denoting the place and area to which its owner belongs. This is to be followed by a three-digit number (in which leading zeros not allowed). How many number plates can be printed if
   (a) repetition of letters and digits is not allowed?
   (b) repetition of letters and digits is allowed?

6. How many 7 digit numbers are there which are, divisible by 8 and formed by using the digits 1, 2, 3, 4, 5, 6, 7 (repetition of digits not allowed)?

7. (a) A five digit number is formed by the digits 1, 2, 3, 4, 5 without repetition. Find the number of the numbers, thus formed which are divisible by 4.
   (b) Find the number of 5 digit numbers divisible by 4 using digit 1, 2, 3, 4, 5, 6, 7, 8, when
   (i) without repetition
   (ii) with repetition

8. A five digit number divisible by 3 is to be formed using the numerals 0, 1, 2, 3, 4, 5, without repetition of digits. Find the total number of ways in which this can be done.

Answer Keys

1. 9000 (a) 4500 (b) 4500 (c) 4500 (d) 1800 **2.** 4536, 2296
3. (a) (i) 100 (ii) 180 (b) 180 **4.** (i) 711040 (ii) 66660
5. (a) 10108800 (b) 15818400 **6.** 528 ways
7. (a) 24 (b) (i) 1680 (ii) $16(8^3)$ **8.** 216

TEXTUAL EXERCISE–9 (OBJECTIVE)

1. The sum of all five digit numbers that can be formed using the digits 1, 2, 3, 4, 5, when repetition of digits is not allowed, is
   (a) 366000 (b) 660000
   (c) 360000 (d) 3999960

2. Consider seven digit number $x_1, x_2......x_7$, where $x_1, x_2,......x_7 \neq 0$ having the property that x_4 is the greatest digit and digits towards the left and right of x_4 are in decreasing order. Then total number of such numbers in which all digits are distinct, is
   (a) ${}^9C_7.{}^6C_3$ (b) ${}^9C_6, {}^5C_3$
   (c) ${}^{10}C_7, {}^6C_3$ (d) None of these

3. The number of six-digit odd numbers, greater than 6, 00, 000 can be formed from the digits 5, 6, 7, 8, 9, 0 if repetition of digits is allowed is
   (a) 15120 (b) 15100
   (c) 16000 (d) None of these

4. In the above problems, if repetition of digits is not allowed, then number of such number is
   (a) 120 (b) 24
   (c) 10 (d) 240

5. How many numbers greater then 1000 can be formed from the digits 1, 1, 2, 3, 4, 0, taken 4 at a time?
   (a) 159 (b) 160
   (c) 161 (d) 162

6. The number of positive integers which can be formed by using any numbers of digits from 0, 1, 2, 3, 4, 5 but using each digit not more then once in each number. Also find how many of these integers are greater then 3000?
   (a) 1630, 1380 (b) 1200, 960
   (c) 900, 300 (d) None of these

7. The total number of natural numbers of six digits that can be made with digits 1, 2, 3, 4 if all digits are to appear in the same number at least once, is
   (a) 1560 (b) 840
   (c) 1080 (d) 480

8. The total number of seven-digit numbers the sum of whose digits is even is
   (a) 9000000 (b) 4500000
   (c) 8100000 (d) None of these

9. All possible four-digit numbers are formed using the digits 0, 1, 2, 3 so that no number has repeated digits. The number of even numbers among them is
   (a) 9 (b) 18
   (c) 10 (d) None of these

10. The total number of numbers greater then 1000, but not greater than 4000, that can be formed with the digits 0, 1, 2, 3 when the repetition of digits allowed is
    (a) 191 (b) 374
    (c) 375 (d) None of these

11. The number of all four digit numbers which are divisible by 4 that can be formed from the digits 1, 2, 3, 4 and 5 is
(a) 125 (b) 30
(c) 95 (d) None of these

12. The number of numbers, that can be formed by using all digits 1, 2, 3, 3, 3, 2, 1 so that odd digits always occupy odd places, is
(a) 3! 4! (b) 34
(c) 30 (d) 12

13. The number of times the digit 5 will be written when listing the integers from 1 to 1000 is
(a) 271 (b) 272
(c) 300 (d) None of these

Answer Keys

1. (d) **2.** (a) **3.** (d) **4.** (d) **5.** (a) **6.** (a) **7.** (a) **8.** (b) **9.** (c)
10. (a) **11.** (a) **12.** (c) **13.** (c)

■ DIVISORS OF COMPOSITE NUMBER

Unique factorization theorem

Let n be any integer such that $|n| > 1$. Then $|n|$ is expressible as a product of a unit and finitely many prime numbers. Moreover, such an expression is unique except as to the order in which the various factors occur. Any natural number N can be written as $N = p^a q^b r^c s^d$ ..... where p, q, r, s are prime numbers and a, b, c, d are non-negative integers. e.g., $225 = 3^2 \times 5^2$; $345 = 3 \times 5 \times 23$

Given a natural number $N = p^a.q^b.r^c$ and a number $x = p^\alpha q^\beta r^\gamma$ is called divisor of N. If N is completely divisible by x i.e., $N = x.m$ where $m \in \mathbb{Z}$. In other words, that will be divisor of N iff all the prime factors of x are present in N (but not necessarily all prime factors of N are in x). This condition can be mathematically expressed as $0 \le \alpha \le a$; $0 \le \beta \le b$; $0 \le \gamma \le c$; where α, β, γ are integers.

Number of positive integer divisors

If the number N is the given positive integer such that:

$N = a^p\, b^q\, c^r$.......... where a, b, c are different prime numbers and $p, q, r \in W$ (whole numbers set)

The number of positive integer divisors of N = total number of selections out of p number of 'a', q number of 'b', r number of 'c' etc.

= number of positive integer divisors are given by number of distinct terms in the product

$= (1 + a + a^2 + ... + a^p)(1 + b + b^2 + ... + b^q)(1 + c + c^2 + ... + c^r)......$

$= (p+1)(q+1)(r+1)......$ (which includes 1 and the N it self)

Example

(i) Number of positive integer divisors of 420 including 1 and itself $420 = 2^2 . 3^1 . 5^1\, 7^1 \Rightarrow 3 \times 2 \times 2 \times 2 = 24$

(ii) Total number of proper positive integer divisors of $2^p\, 6^q\, 15^r\ (= 2^{p+q}\, 3^{q+r}\, 5^r)$
$= (p + q + 1)(q + r + 1)(r + 1) - 2$

(iii) Find the number of proper positive integer divisor of 1800 which are also divisible by 10
$1800 = 2^3 \times 3^2 \times 5^2$
= total number of proper positive integer divisors having at least one 2 and one 5 from set {2, 2, 2, 3, 3, 5, 5} $= 3 \times 3 \times 2 = 18$

Proper and improper positive integer divisors

As unity (1) is a divisor of every natural number (N) and every natural number N is divisor of itself. These two numbers are called the improper divisors of (N) and remaining divisors are known as proper divisors.

∴ Number of proper positive divisors divisors of (N) $= (a + 1)(b + 1)(c + 1) - 2.$

Sum of positive integer divisors of N(= $a^p.b^q.c^r.d^s$)

Since each individual positive integer divisor is given as term of the expansion,

$(a^0 + a^1 + a^2 + ... + a^p)(b^0 + b^1 + b^2 + ... + b^q)(c^0 + c^1 + c^2 + ... + c^r)(d^0 + d^1 + d^2 + ... + d^s)$,

therefore the sum of all positive integer divisors is

$= 1 + a + b + c + d + a^2 + b^2 + c^2 + d^2 + ab + ac + ... + a^p b^q c^r d^s$

$$= \left(\frac{a^{p+1}-1}{a-1}\right)\left(\frac{b^{q+1}-1}{b-1}\right)\left(\frac{c^{r+1}-1}{c-1}\right)\left(\frac{d^{s+1}-1}{d-1}\right) \quad \text{(i)}$$

NOTE:

From now, whenever we ask about divisors, it must be taken as positive integers divisors.

ILLUSTRATION 88: Find the sum of divisors of number 420.

SOLUTION: Divisors of 420 is $2^2 . 3^1 . 5^1\ 7^1$

$\therefore$ Sum of divisors $= (1 + 2 + 2^2)(1 + 3)(1 + 5)(1 + 7) = 1344$

ILLUSTRATION 89: Find the sum of all the proper divisors of $N = 2^p.3^q.5^r$ where p,q,r, are positive integers. Also find the sum of all the proper divisors that are multiples of 3.

SOLUTION: If we multiply three geometric series

$(2^0+2^1+2^2+....+2^p)(3^0+3^1+3^2+...+3^q)(5^0+5^1+5^2+...+5^r)$, then we get the sum of all the terms of the form $2^i3^j5^k$; where $i = 0, 1, 2, ..., p; j = 0, 1, 2,.....q; k = 0, 1, 2, ..., r$.

Clearly, each term is a divisor of $2^p.3^q.5^r$ of which $2^0.3^0.5^0$ and $2^p.3^q.5^r$are not proper divisors. Therefore, the sum of all the proper divisors of $2^p.3^q.5^r$ is

$$= (2^0+2^1+2^2+...+2^p)(3^0+3^1+3^2+...+3^q)(5^0+5^1+5^2+...+5^r)-(2^0.3^0.5^0+2^p.3^q.5^r)$$

$$= \left(\frac{2^{p+1}-1}{2-1}\right).\left(\frac{3^{q+1}-1}{3-1}\right).\left(\frac{5^{r+1}-1}{5-1}\right)-\left(1+2^p3^q5^r\right) = \frac{1}{8}.(2^{p+1}-1)\ (3^{q+1}-1)(5^{r+1}-1)\ -1-2^p3^q5^r$$

The sum of all proper divisors of $2^p.3^q.5^r$ that are multiples of 3 is

$$= \left(2^0+2^1+2^2+.....2^p\right)\left(3^1+3^2+3^3+...3^q\right)\left(5^o+5^1+5^2+...5^r\right)-2^p3^q5^r$$

$$= \left(\frac{2^{p+1}-1}{2-1}\right).\left(\frac{3\left(3^q-1\right)}{3-1}\right).\left(\frac{5^{r+1}-1}{5-1}\right)-2^p3^q5^r = \frac{3}{8}(2^{p+1}-1)(3^q-1)\ (5^{r+1}-1)\ -2^p3^q5^r$$

Number of specific divisor

If one is asked to find out the number of divisors of distinct property e.g., odd divisors, even divisors, the divisors which are divisible by certain number, then we will proceed as below:

(i) Number of odd proper divisors of $3^p\ 6^m\ 21^n\ (= 2^m\ 3^{p+m+n}.\ 7^n)$ equals

The number of ways of selections of 3 and 7 except rejcting both $= (p + m + n + 1)\ (n + 1) - 1$; subtracting 1 as 1 is odd improper divisor

(ii) number of even proper divisor of 1008 $(= 2^4 \times 3^2 \times 7^1)$

= total number of ways of selections of at least one 2 and any number of 3's or 7's from set {3, 3. 7} except for selecting all 2's, all 3's and 7's.

$= (4)\ (2 + 1)\ (1 + 1) -1 = 23$

Number and sum of divisors of n (= $p^a.q^b.r^c$) divisible by a natural number $y = p^{a_1}.q^{b_1}.r^{c_1}$

Let $x = p^\alpha . q^\beta . r^\gamma$ be such divisors

$\because y \mid x \Rightarrow p^{a_1}.q^{b_1}.r^{c_1} \mid p^\alpha.q^\beta.r^\gamma$ also x|n

$\Rightarrow a_1 \le \alpha \le a;\ b_1 \le \beta \le b$ and $c_1 \le \gamma \le c$

$\Rightarrow$ number of such divisors

$= (a - a_1 + 1)\ (b - b_1 + 1)\ (c - c_1 + 1)$

Sum of such divisors $S_y = \left(p^{a_1}+p^{a_1+1}+....+p^a\right).\left(q^{b_1}+q^{b_1+1}+....+q^b\right).\left(r^{c_1}+r^{c_1+1}+....+r^c\right)$

$$= y\left(1+p+p^2+...+p^{a-a_1}\right)\left(1+q+q^2+...+q^{b-b_1}\right)\left(1+r+...+r^{c-c_1}\right)$$

$$= y\left(\frac{p^{a-a_1+1}-1}{p-1}\right)\left(\frac{q^{b-b_1+1}-1}{q-1}\right)\left(\frac{r^{c-c_1+1}-1}{r-1}\right)$$

ILLUSTRATION 90: Find the number of factors (excluding 1 and the expression itself) of the product $a^7b^4c^3def$ where a, b, c, d, e, f are all prime numbers.

SOLUTION: The total number of factors is equal to the number of ways of selecting at the most 7 a's, 4 b's, 3 c's, one d, one e and one f minus 2 (Since selection of all or none of a, b, c, d, e, f is to be excluded)

$\therefore$ Number of factors = (7 + 1) (4+ 1)(3 + 1) (1+ 1) (1 + 1) (1 + 1) – 2 = 1278.

ILLUSTRATION 91: Find the number and sum of all divisors of 129600 that are divisible by 180.

SOLUTION: $129600 = 2^6 \times 5^2 \times 3^4$

Any divisor of 129600 divisible by 180 is of the form 180. $(2^a\ 3^b\ 5^c)$

i.e., $2^{a+2}\ 3^{b+2}\ \ 5^{c+1}$ where $a, b, c \in W$ (whole number set)

$\Rightarrow$ Number of such divisors = (number of possible values of a) × (number of possible values of b) × (number of possible values of c)

$= 5 \times 3 \times 2$, since $0 \le a + 2 \le 6$; $0 \le b + 2 \le 4$; $0 \le c + 1 \le 2$; $a, b, c \in W$

Sum of these divisors $= 180\ (2^0 + 2^1 + 2^2 + 2^3 + 2^4)\ (3^0 + 3^1 + 3^2)\ (5^0 + 5^1)$

$= 180 \times 31 \times 13 \times 6 = 435240$

To find the number of ways in which a composite number can be resolved into two factors

Consider the natural number $N = p^a q^b r^c$ .... As the number of divisors of N is $(a + 1)(b + 1)(c + 1)$, among these divisors we can always find a pair of two divisors x, y such that their product $x.y = N$.

Therefore number of ordered pairs (x, y) satisfying above equation $x.y = N$ is equal to number of divisors.

Case I: Every unordered pair of such divisors represents one way of resolving N into two factors. Therefore, the number of ways of resolving N into two factors is half the total number of divisors. Number of such pair of factors $= \frac{1}{2}(a+1)(b+1)(c+1)$... But, this is true only if N is not a perfect square (*i.e., at least one of the quantities a, b, c, ... is an odd natural number*).

Hence, the **product of all the divisors of N is** $N^{1/2\{(a+1)(b+1)(c+1)\ .....\}}$

Case II: N being a perfect square, one of the possible resolution into factors is $x = \sqrt{N}$ and $y = \sqrt{N}$, and corresponding to this there will be only one unordered pair of solution. While counting number of (x, y) as $(a + 1)(b + 1)(c + 1)$ the above $\left(\sqrt{N}, \sqrt{N}\right)$ has been counted only once. So to find number of unordered pair of solutions it should be counted twice and then the total must be factored by two.

Hence, number of ways of resolution is $\frac{1}{2}$ $[\{(a + 1)(b + 1)(c + 1)\ ......\} + 1]$

If N is a perfect square, one way of resolution into two factors in $\sqrt{N} \times \sqrt{N}$ and to this way, there corresponds only one divisors $\sqrt{N}$, so in the product $N^{\frac{1}{2}[\{(a+1).(b+1).(c+1)......\}+1]}$

We must divide it by $\sqrt{N}$.

Hence again the product of all the divisors of N is $N^{\frac{1}{2}\{(a+1)(b+1)+(c+1)+...\}}$

ILLUSTRATION 92: To find the product of all the factors of the following numbers
(i) 12960 (ii) 129600

SOLUTION: (i) $12960 = 2^5 \times 5^1 \times 3^4$, here this is not a perfect square

and Product of all the factors $= 12960^{\left(\frac{1}{2}\times 6\times 2\times 5\right)} = 12960^{(3\times 2\times 5)} = (12960)^{30}$

(ii) $129600 = 2^6 \times 5^2 \times 3^4$, here 129600 is a perfect square

and Product of all the factors $= (129600)^{\frac{1}{2}\{(6+1)(2+1)(4+1)\}} = (129600)^{\frac{1}{2}\times 7\times 3\times 55} = (129600)^{52.5} = 360^{105}$

To find the number of ways in which a composite number can be resolved into two factors which are co-prime

Let $N = p^a q^b r^c \ldots$

Now one of the factors must contain p^a or else, there would be some power of 'p' in the second factor. Therefore p^a has only two options, similarly, for q^b and r^c and so on.

⇒ The required number is equal to the number of ways in which all the prime factors can be resolved into two factors.

⇒ Number of ways

$$= \frac{1}{2}(1+1)(1+1)(1+1)\ldots = \frac{1}{2}\times 2^n = 2^{n-1}$$

Where 'n' is the number of different prime factors of N

ILLUSTRATION 93: Find the number of ways in which the number $(1001)^{33} \times (999)^{22}$ can be resolved into two co-prime factors.

SOLUTION: $1001 = 7 \times 11 \times 13$ and $999 = 27 \times 37 = 3^3 \times 37$ = Prime factor of $(1001)^{33} \times (999)^{22}$

$N = 7^{33} \times 11^{33} \times 13^{33} \times 3^{66} \times 37^{22}$

∴ Number of ways of resolving N into two

co-prime factor $= \frac{1}{2}\times(1+1)(1+1)(1+1)(1+1)(1+1) = 2^4 = 16$

To find the number of ordered pairs (x,y) such that LCM of x and y is a composite number 'N'

Let $N = p^a q^b r^c$

Of the two factors (x and y) ; one must contains p^a or else the LCM would have smaller power of

'p'.Now if x contains p^a ; y can have any of the factors $1, p, p^2, p^3 \ldots p^a$ .Also, if y contains p^a ; x can have any one of the factors $1\ p, p^2, p^3 \ldots p^a$

Hence, the number of ways to distribute powers of p to x and y to ensure that the LCM contains p^a is $(2a+1)$. Similarly, for q^b is $(2b+1)$ and for r^c is $(2c+1)$

Therefore, the total number of ways is $(2a+1)(2b+1)(2c+1)\ldots$.

ILLUSTRATION 94: Find the number of ordered pair (x, y) such that the number 274400 can be resolved into two factors x and y such that the LCM of x and y is equal to 274400.

SOLUTION: $274400 = 2^5 \times 5^2 \times 7^3$

⇒ Number of ordered pairs $= (2 \times 5 + 1)(2 \times 2 + 1)(2 \times 3 + 1) = 11 \times 5 \times 7 = 385$

ILLUSTRATION 95: In how many ways the number 18900 can be shifted into two factors which are relatively prime (or coprime)?

SOLUTION: Here $N = 18900 = 2^2.3^3.\ 5^2.\ 7^1$. Here primes are 2, 3, 5, 7

∴ $n = 4$(number of different prime factors in N)

Hence number of ways in which a composite number N, can be resolved into two factors which are relatively prime (or coprime) $= 2^{n-1} = 2^{4-1} = 2^3 = 8$

ILLUSTRATION 96: The number of positive integral solutions of the equation $xyz = 3000$ are

(a) 200 (b) 300 (c) 3000 (d) 50

SOLUTION: $xyz = 3 \times 2^3 \times 5^3$

Now the power of 3 i.e., 1 can be distributed among three variables in 3 ways. Similarly, the power of 2 i.e., 3 can be distributed among x, y and z in 10 ways {(0, 0, 3), (0, 3, 0), (3, 0, 0), (1, 2, 0), (1, 0, 2), (0, 1, 2), (2, 1, 0), (2, 0, 1), (0, 2, 1), (1, 1, 1)} and same is the case of 5^3.

Hence total ways $= 3 \times 10 \times 10 = 300$

ILLUSTRATION 97: Number of ways in which four digit numbers divisible by 4 can be formed by using digit 1, 2, 3, 4, 5, if the repetition of digits is not allowed is

(a) 42 (b) 24 (c) 28 (d) None of these

SOLUTION: A number is divisible by 4 if the last two digit is divisible by 4.

Number of ways to fill last two places digits = 4 i.e.,12, 32, 52, 24.

Now, last two places are already filled and we are left with only 3 digits filled in first two places.

Number of ways to fill first two places = $3 \times 2 = 6$

$\therefore$ Total number of ways = $4 \times 6 = 24$

ILLUSTRATION 98: Number of even divisors of 504 is

(a) 12 (b) 24 (c) 6 (d) 18

SOLUTION: $504 = 2^3 \times 3^2 \times 7$. Any even divisor of 504 is of the form $2^i \times 3^j \times 7^k$,

where $1 \le i \le 3, 0 \le j \le 2, 0 \le k \le 1$.

Thus total number of even divisors is $3 \times 3 \times 2 = 18$

ILLUSTRATION 99: Let p be a prime number such that $p \ge 3$. Let $n = p! + 1$. The number of primes in the list $n + 1$, $n + 2$, $n + 3$,.... $n + p - 1$ is

(a) p –1 (b) 2

(c) 1 (d) Zero

SOLUTION: (d) For $1 \le k \le p-1$, $n + k = p! + k + 1$, is clearly divisible by $k + 1$ as $2 \le k + 1 \le p$

$\Rightarrow n + k = (1.2.3....k + 1...p) + (k + 1)$

Therefore, there is no prime number in the given list

ILLUSTRATION 100: (a) How many divisors are there of the number $x = 21600$. Find also the sum of these divisors?

(b) In how many ways the number 7056 can be resolved as a product of 2 factors?

(c) Find the number of ways in which the number 300300 can be splitted into 2 factors which are relatively prime.

(d) Find the number of positive integers that are divisors of at least one of the numbers 10^{10}; 15^7; 18^{11}.

SOLUTION: (a) $21600 = 216 \times 100 = 2^5 . 3^3 . 5^2$

total no. of divisors = $(5 + 1)(3 + 1)(2 + 1) = 6 \times 4 \times 3 = 72$

sum of all divisors = $(3^0 + 3^1 + 3^2 + 3^3)(5^0 + 5^1 + 5^2)(2^0 + 2^1 + 2^2 + 2^3 + 2^4 + 2^5)$

$$= \left(\frac{2^6 - 1}{2 - 1}\right)\left(\frac{3^4 - 1}{3 - 1}\right)\left(\frac{5^3 - 1}{5 - 1}\right) = 63 \times \frac{80}{2} \times \frac{124}{4} = 78120$$

(b) $7056 = 2^4 . 3^2 . 7^2$, no. of divisors = $(4 + 1)(2 + 1)(2 + 1) = 5 \times 3 \times 3 = 45$

No. of ways of resolving into 2 factors = $\frac{45 + 1}{2} = 23$

(c) $300300 = 2^2 \times 3^1 \times 5^2 \times 7^1 \times 11^1 \times 13^1$

Now we have to make two factors x and y of 300300, which are relatively prime i.e., $x.y = 300300$, but g.c.d $(x, y) = 1$

$\Rightarrow 2^2, 3^1, 5^2, 7^1, 11^1, 13^1$ should behave as single entities

So number of unordered pairs divisors = $\{(1 + 1)(1 + 1)(1 + 1)(1 + 1)(1 + 1)(1 + 1)\} = 2^5 = 32$

$\therefore$ No. of ways of splitting into 2 factors = 32

(d) I $\rightarrow 10^{10} = 2^{10}.5^{10}$

II $\rightarrow 15^7 = 3^7.5^7$

III $\rightarrow 18^{11} = 2^{11}.3^{22}$

No. of divisors of at least one of the numbers = (No. of divisors of no. I) + (No. of divisors of no. II) + (No. of divisors of no. III) – (No. of of divisors common to I and II) – (No. of divisors common to I and III) – (No. of divisors common to II and III) + (No. of divisors common to all I, II, III)

$= 11 \times 11 + 8 \times 8 + 12 \times 23 - 8 - 11 - 8 + 1 = 435$

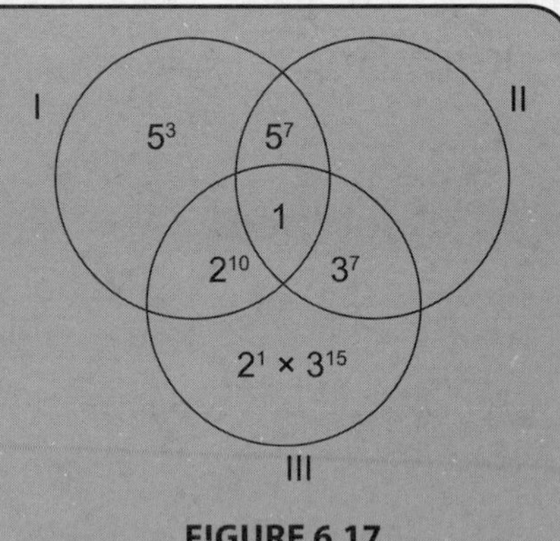

FIGURE 6.17

TEXTUAL EXERCISE–10 (SUBJECTIVE)

1. Suppose we have three different toys and we want to give them away to two girls and one boy (one toy per child). The children will be selected from 4 boys and 6 girls. In how many ways can this be done?
2. Find the number of positive integer divisors
   (a) of the number 420 including 1 and itself (also find the sum of all divisors).
   (b) of the number 1008 which are even and proper.
   (c) of the number 1800 which are proper and divisible by 10.
3. Find the number of positive integer
   (a) proper divisors of $2^p. 6^q. 15^r$.
   (b) odd proper divisors of $3^p. 6^m. 21^n$.
4. Find the number of positive integer divisors of 420 and also find the sum of divisors in each case.
   (a) Which are even
   (b) Which are divisible by 6
   (c) Which are of the type $4m + 2$; $m \in W$ (whole number set)

Answer Keys

1. 360 **2.** (a) 24, 1344 (b) 23 (c) 17
3. (a) $(p + q + 1)(q + r + 1)(r + 1) - 2$ (b) $(p + m + n + 1)(n + 1) - 1$
4. (a) 16, 1152 (b) 8, 864 (c) 8, 384

TEXTUAL EXERCISE–10 (OBJECTIVE)

1. The number and sum of positive integer divisors of the number 12600 including 1 and itself is
   (a) 72, 48360 (b) 72, 36360
   (c) 36, 38360 (d) None of these
2. The number of positive integer divisor of the number 1008 which are even and proper.
   (a) 19 (b) 21
   (c) 23 (d) None of these
3. The number and sum of positive integer divisors of the number 1800 which are proper and divisible by 6.
   (a) 15, 2064 (b) 17, 2046
   (c) 17, 3408 (d) None of these
4. The number of proper positive integer divisors of 1260 is
   (a) 42 (b) 26
   (c) 34 (d) None of these
5. The number of proper positive integer divisors of 2520 is
   (a) 46 (b) 52
   (c) 64 (d) None of these
6. The sum of proper positive integer divisors of 72 is equal to
   (a) 195 (b) 122
   (c) 194 (d) None of these

7. Number of even divisors of 504 is

(a) 12 (b) 24

(c) 6 (d) 18

8. The number of proper positive integer divisors of 2^p. 6^q. 15^r divisible by 30 and greater than 30 is

(a) $(p + q + 1)(q + r + 1)(r + 1)$

(b) $(p + q + 1)(q + r + 1)(r + 1) - 2$

(c) $(p + q)(q + r) r - 2$

(d) None of these

Answer Keys

1. (a) **2.** (c) **3.** (c) **4.** (c) **5.** (a) **6.** (b) **7.** (d) **8.** (c)

■ MULTINOMIAL THEOREM

The expansion of $[x_1 + x_2 + x_3 + ... + x_n]^r$ where n and r are integers ($0 < r \le n$) is a homogenous expression of 'r' degree in $x_1, x_2, x_3 ... x_n$ and is given as below: $[x_1 + x_2 + x_3 + ... + x_n]^r$

$$= \sum\left(\frac{r!}{\lambda_1!.\lambda_2!.\lambda_3!.......\lambda_n!}\right) x_1^{\lambda_1}.x_2^{\lambda_2}.x_3^{\lambda_3}....x_n^{\lambda_n}.$$

where $\lambda_1, \lambda_2, ..., \lambda_n$ are non negative integers, such that $\lambda_1 + \lambda_2 + ... + \lambda_n = r$ (valid only if $x_1, x_2, x_3, ... x_n$ are independent of each other).

Coefficient of $x_1^{\lambda_1} x_2^{\lambda_2} x_3^{\lambda_3}$ .... = total number of arrangements of r objects out of which λ_1 number of x_1s are identical, λ_2 number of x_2s are identical and so on.

$$= \frac{(\lambda_1 + \lambda_2 + \lambda_3 + ... + \lambda_n)!}{\lambda_1!\lambda_2!\lambda_3!...\lambda_n!} = \frac{r!}{\lambda_1!\lambda_2!\lambda_3!...\lambda_n!}$$

Number of distinct terms (seperator method)

Since $(x_1 + x_2 + x_3 + .. + x_n)^r$ is multiplication of $(x_1 + x_2 + x_3 + .. + x_n)$, r times and will be a homogeneous expression of rth degree in $x_1, x_2, ... x_n$ So in each term sum of powers of variables must be r.

So number of distinct terms will be total number of non-negative integral solution of equation $\lambda_1 + \lambda_2 + \lambda_3 + ... + \lambda_n = r$ = Number of ways of distributing r identical objects among n persons

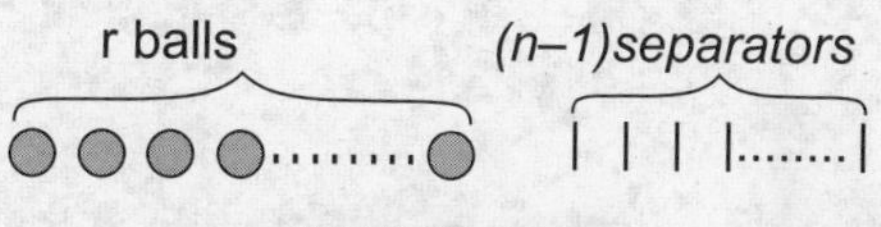

FIGURE 6.19

= number of ways of distributing r balls among n people

= number of arrangements of r balls and n–1 identical separators $= \frac{(n-1+r)!}{(n-1)!r!} = {}^{n+r-1}C_r = {}^{n+r-1}C_{n-1}$

ILLUSTRATION 101: Find the number of ways in which 16 identical toys are to be distributed among 3 children such that each child does not receive less than 3 toys.

SOLUTION: Let x_1, x_2, x_3 be the no. of toys received by the three children.

Then, $x_1, x_2, x_3 \ge 3$ and $x_1 + x_2 + x_3 = 16$

Let $u_1 = x_1 - 3$, $u_2 = x_2 - 3$ and $u_3 = x_3 - 3$

Then, $u_1, u_2, u_3 \ge 0$ and $u_1 + u_2 + u_3 = 7$. Here, $n = 7$ and $r = 3$; $u_i \ge 0$

∴ Number of ways $= {}^{n+r-1}C_{r-1} = {}^9C_2 = 36$

ILLUSTRATION 102: Find the number of non-negative integral solutions of $x_1 + x_2 + x_3 + 4x_4 = 20$

SOLUTION: Here, clearly, $0 \le x_4 \le 5$, $x_1, x_2, x_3 \ge 0$ and $x_1 + x_2 + x_3 = 20 - 4x_4$

$\Rightarrow r = 3$ and $n = 20 - 4x_4$

If $x_4 = 0$, number of ways ${}^{20+3-1}C_{3-1} = {}^{22}C_2$

If $x_4 = 1$, number of ways ${}^{16+3-1}C_{3-1} = {}^{18}C_2$

Similarly, if $x_4 = 2, 3, 4, 5$, no. of ways $= {}^{14}C_2, {}^{10}C_2, {}^6C_2, {}^2C_2$ respectively

∴ Total number of ways $= {}^{22}C_2 + {}^{18}C_2 + {}^{14}C_2 + {}^{10}C_2 + {}^6C_2 + {}^2C_2 = 536$

Applications of multinomial theorem

Case I: If we want to distribute n identical objects in r different groups under the condition that empty groups are not allowed.

$a_1 + a_2 + a_3 + ... + a_r = n$. Boundary conditions are $1 \le a_1, a_2, ..., a_r \le n$

(As each box contains at least one object)

Number of ways = coefficient of x^n in $(x^1 + x^2 + ... + x^n)^r$

$= $ coefficient of x^n in $(1 + x + x^2 + ... + x^{n-1})^r . x^r$

$= $ coefficient of x^{n-r} in $(1 + x + x^2 + ... + x^{n-1})^r$

$= $ coefficient of x^{n-r} in $(1 + x + x^2 + ... + \infty)^r$

$= {}^{n-r+r-1}C_{r-1} = {}^{n-1}C_{r-1}$

ILLUSTRATION 103: In how many ways 5 identical balls can be distributed into 3 different boxes so that no box remains empty?

SOLUTION: The required number of ways $= {}^{5-1}C_{3-1} = {}^4C_2 = \dfrac{4.3}{1.2} = 6$

Aliter Each box must contain at least one ball since no box remains empty. Boxes can have balls in the following system:

Box	I	II	III
Number of balls	1	1	3

or

Box	I	II	III
Number of balls	1	2	2

Here balls are identical but boxes are different the number of combinations will be 1 in each system.

$\therefore$ Required number of ways $= 1 \times \dfrac{3!}{2!} + 1 \times \dfrac{3!}{2!} = 3 + 3 = 6$

ILLUSTRATION 104: In a bakery, four types of biscuits are available. In how many ways a person can buy 10 biscuits if he decides to take at least one biscuit of each variety?

SOLUTION: Let x be the number of biscuits the person select from first variety, y from the second, z from the third and w from the fourth variety. Then the number of ways = number of solutions of the equations $x + y + z + w = 10$.

where $x \in \{1, 2, ..., 7\}$

$y \in \{1, 2, ..., 7\}$

$z \in \{1, 2, ..., 7\}$

$w \in \{1, 2, ..., 7\}$

This is equal to = coefficient of x^{10} in $(x + x^2 + ... + x^7)^4$

$= $ coefficient of x^6 in $(1 + x + ... + x^6)^4$

$= $ coefficient of x^6 in $(1 - x^7)^4 (1 - x)^{-4}$

$= $ coefficient x^6 in $(1 - x)^{-4} = {}^{4+6-1}C_6 = {}^9C_3 = 84$

Case II: If there are a_1 objects of one kind, a_2 objects of 2nd kind, a_3 of 3rd kind, ..., a_n of the nth kind, and we want to choose r objects out of these, then $t_1 + t_2 + t_3 + ... + t_n = r$

Boundary conditions are $0 \le t_1 \le a_1$, $0 \le t_2 \le a_2$, ..., $0 \le t_n \le a_n$,

(here t_i is number of objects chosen from i[th] kind and any number of objects ranging from 0 to a_1; can be chosen from i[th] kind). Number of ways = coefficient of x^r in

$(1 + x + x^2 + ... + x^{a_1})(1 + x + x^2 + ... + x^{a_2})$ ....$(1 + x + x^2 + ... + x^{a_n})$

Also same will be the numbers of ways of distribution of r-identical things among n-distinct persons such that first gets a maximum of a_1 object, second person gets a maximum of a_2 objects, so on.

ILLUSTRATION 105: In how many ways can 10 identical toys be distributed among 3 children such that the first receives a maximum of 6 toys, the second receives a maximum of 7 toys and the third receives a maximum of 8 toys.

SOLUTION: Let x_1, x_2 and x_3 be the number of toys received by the three children.

Then, $x_1 + x_2 + x_3 = 10, 0 \le x_1 \le 6, 0 \le x_2 \le 7, 0 \le x_3 \le 8$

$\Rightarrow$ Required no. of ways = coeff. of x^{10} in

$(x^0 + x^1 + x^2 + ...+ x^6)(x^0 + x^1 + x^2 + ...+ x^7)(x^0 + x^1 + x^2 + ...+ x^8)$

= coeff of x^{10} in $(1 - x^7)(1 - x^8)(1 - x^9)(1 - x)^{-3}$ = coeff of x^{10} in

$(1 - x^7 - x^8 - x^9)(1 + {}^3C_1x + {}^4C_2x^2 + {}^5C_3x^3 + ... + {}^{12}C_{10}x^{10} + ...)$

{Note that powers >10 are unimportant and hence ignored}

$= {}^{12}C_{10} - {}^5C_3 - {}^4C_2 - {}^3C_1 = 66 - 10 - 6 - 3 = 47$

ILLUSTRATION 106: Find the number of combinations of 4 letters taken from the letters of the word MATHEMATICS.

SOLUTION: Word 'MATHEMATICS' contains 11 letters 2*M*'s, 2*A*'s, 2*T*'s, 1*H*, 1*E*, 1*I*, 1*C*, 1*S*

Now total number of combinations are given by coefficient of x^4 in $(1 + x + x^2)^3(1 + x)^5$

= Coefficient of x^4 in $[(1 + x)^3 + x^6 + 3(1 + x)^2x^2 + 3(1 + x)x^4]\{1 + {}^5C_1x + {}^5C_2x^2 + {}^5C_3x^3 + {}^5C_4x^4 + {}^5C_5x^5\}]$

= Coefficient x^4 in $[(1 + x^3 + 3x^2 + 3x + x^6 + 3x^4 + 3x^2 + 6x^3 + 3x^4 + 3x^5)(1 + 5x + 10x^2 + 10x^3 + 5x^4 + x^5)]$

= Coefficient x^4 in $[5x^4 + 5x^4 + 30x^4 + 30x^4 + 3x^4 + 30x^4 + 30x^4 + 3x^4]$

= 5 + 5 +30 +30 +3 + 30 +30 +3 = 136

ILLUSTRATION 107: The number of ways in which a student can answer four questions from a paper containing '3' sections, five questions in each section is

(a) 12 (b) 53

(c) 15 (d) 5! / 4!

SOLUTION: A student can attempt any number of questions ranging from 0 to 4 from each section, but the total questions answered should be equal to four. This is equivalent of finding coefficient of x^4 in $(1 + x + ... + x^5)(1 + x + ... + x^5)(1 + x + ... + x^5)$ or, x^4 in $(1 + x + ... + x^5)^3 = (1 - x^6)^3(1 - x)^{-3}$

= Coefficient of x^4 in $(1 - x)^{-3} = {}^{3+4-1}C_4 = {}^6C_4 = 15$

Case III: If there are a_1 objects of one kind, a_2 objects of 2nd kind, a_3 of 3rd kind, ..., a_n of the nth kind, and we want to choose *r* objects out of these under the condition that at least one object of every kind should be chosen $t_1 + t_2 + t_3 + ... + t_n = r$ Boundary conditions are $1 \le t_1 \le a_1, 1 \le t_2 \le a_2, ..., 1 \le t_n \le a_n$,

Number of ways = coefficient of x^r in $(x + x^2 + ... + x^{a_1})(x + x^2 + ... + x^{a_2}) .... (x + x^2 + ... + x^{a_n})$

Case IV: For the equation $\alpha + 2\beta + 3\gamma + ... + q\theta = n$ (i)

(a) If zero is included, then number of solutions of (i) = coefficient of x^n in

$(1 + x + x^2 + ...)(1 + x^2 + x^4 + ...)(1 + x^3 + x^6 + ...)...(1 + x^q + x^{2q} + ...)$

= coefficient of x^n in $(1 - x)^{-1}(1 - x^2)^{-1}(1 - x^3)^{-1}...(1 - x^q)^{-1}$

(b) If zero is excluded, then number of solutions of (i) = coefficient of x^n in

$(x + x^2 + x^3 + ...)(x^2 + x^4 + x^6 ...)(x^3 + x^6 + x^9 ...)....(x^q + x^{2q} + ...)$

= coefficient of x^n in $x^{1+2+3+...+q}(1 - x)^{-1}(1 - x^2)^{-1}(1 - x^3)^{-1}...(1 - x^q)^{-1}$

= coefficient of $x^{n - \frac{q(q+1)}{2}}$ in $(1 - x)^{-1}(1 - x^2)^{-1}(1 - x^3)^{-1}...(1 - x^q)^{-1}$

Case V: The number of ways in which *n* identical objects can be distributed in *r* different groups so that all groups contain minimum of a objects and maximum of b objects is coefficient of x^n in $(x^a + x^{a+1} + x^{a+2} + ... x^b)^r$.

Case VI: If there are l objects of one kind, m objects of 2nd kind, n of 3rd kind and so on; then the number of possible arrangement/permutations of r objects out of these objects (i.e., $l + m + n + ...$) is the coefficient of x^r in the expansion of

$$r!\left(1+\frac{x}{1!}+\frac{x^2}{2!}+....+\frac{x^l}{l!}\right)\left(1+\frac{x}{1!}+\frac{x^2}{2!}+....+\frac{x^m}{m!}\right)\left(1+\frac{x}{1!}+\frac{x^2}{2!}+....+\frac{x^n}{n!}\right)....$$

ILLUSTRATION 108: Find the number of Permutation of 4 letters taken from the word EXAMINATION.

SOLUTION: Number of Permutations are:

$$= \text{coefficient of } x^4 \text{ in } 4!\left(1+\frac{x}{1!}+\frac{x^2}{2!}\right)^3\left(1+\frac{x}{1!}\right)^5 = \text{coefficient of } x^4 \text{ in } 4!\left(1+x+\frac{x^2}{2!}\right)^3(1+x)^5$$

$$= \text{coefficient of } x^4 \text{ in } 4!\left\{(1+x)^3+\frac{x^6}{8}+\frac{3}{2}(1+x)^2x^2+\frac{3}{4}x^4(1+x)\right\}.(1+x)^5$$

$$= \text{coefficient of } x^4 \text{ in } 4!\left\{(1+x)^8+\frac{x^6}{8}(1+x)^5+\frac{3}{2}x^2(1+x)^7+\frac{3}{4}x^4(1+x)^6\right\}$$

$$= 4!\left\{{}^8C_4+0+\frac{3}{2}{}^7C_2+\frac{3}{4}\right\} = 24\left\{\frac{8.7.6.5}{1.2.3.4}+\frac{3}{2}\times\frac{7.6}{1.2}+\frac{3}{4}\right\}$$

$$= 8.7.6.5 + 6(3.7.6) + 6.3 = 1680 + 756 + 18 = 2454$$

ILLUSTRATION 109: Find the number of combination of the letters taken from the words

(i) EXAMINATION, 4 at a time (ii) PROPORTION 6 at a time

SOLUTION: (i) The word EXAMINATION contains; *AA, I I, N N, E, X, M, T,* O

Then number of combinations = coefficient of x^4 in $(1+x+x^2)^3(1+x)^5$

($\because$ 2*A*'s, 2*I*'s, 2*N*'s, *E*, 1*X*, 1*M*, 1*T* and 1*O*)

$= \text{coefficient of } x^4 \text{ in } \{(1+x)^3 + x^6 + 3(1+x)^2x^2 + 3(1+x)x^4\}(1+x)^5$

$= \text{coefficient of } x^4 \text{ in } \{(1+x)^8 + x^6(1+x)^5 + 3x^2(1+x)^7 + 3x^4(1+x)^5\}$

$$= {}^8C_4 + 0 + 3.{}^7C_2 + 3 = \frac{8.7.6.5}{1.2.3.4} + 3.\frac{7.6}{1.2} + 3 = 70 + 63 + 3 = 136$$

(ii)

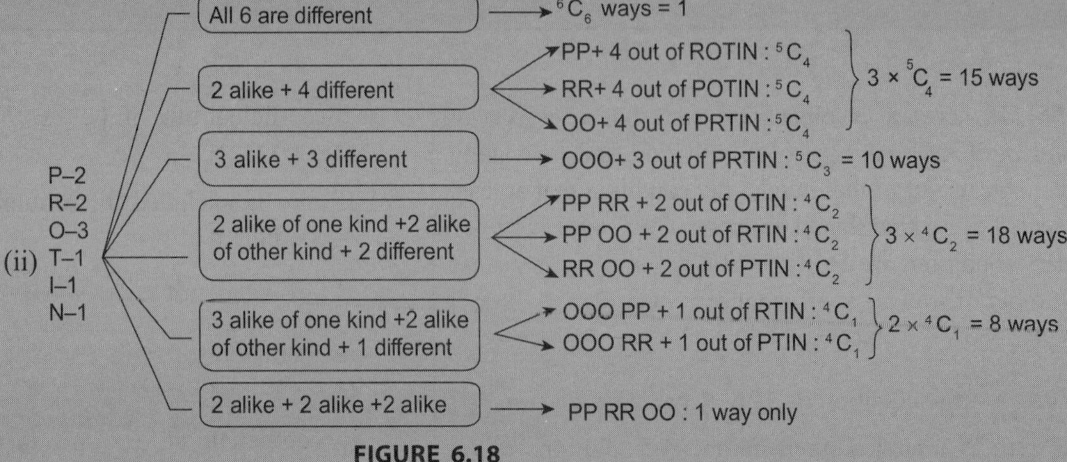

FIGURE 6.18

Total number of combinations: 1 + 15 + 10 + 18 + 8 + 1 = 53

ILLUSTRATION 110: Show that the number of ways of selecting n things out of $3n$ things, of which n are of one kind and alike, and n are of a second kind and alike and the rest n are unlike, is $(n+2)(2)^{2n-1}$

SOLUTION: The required number of selections

$$= \text{coefficient of } x^n \text{ is } \left[(1+x+...+x^n)(1+x+......+x^n)\underbrace{(1+x)......(1+x)}_{n\,times}\right]$$

$= \text{coefficient of } x^n \text{ in } (1-x^{n+1})^2 (1-x)^{-2} (1+x)^n$

$= \text{coefficient of } x^n \text{ in } (1-x)^{-2} [2-(1-x)]^n$

$= \text{coefficient of } x^n \text{ in } (1-x)^{-2} [2^n - {}^nC_1(1-x)2^{n-1} + {}^nC_2 (1-x)^2 2^{n-2} - {}^nC_3 (1-x)^3 2^{n-3} + ... + (-1)^n(1-x)^n$.

$= \text{coefficient of } x^n \text{ in } [2^n(1-x)^{-2} - n.\, 2^{n-1} (1-x)^{-1} + {}^nC_2\, 2^{n-2} - {}^nC_3\, 2^{n-3} (1-x).... + (-1)^n (1-x)^{n-2}]$

$= \text{coefficient of } x^n \text{ in } [2^n (1-x)^{-2} - n.\, 2^{n-1} (1-x)^{-1}]$

$= \text{coefficient of } x^n \text{ in } [2^n (1 + {}^2C_1x + {}^3C_2x^2 + ...) - n\, 2^{n-1} (1 + x + x^2 + ...)]$

$= 2^n (n+1) - n.2^{n-1} = 2^{n-1} (n+2)$

TEXTUAL EXERCISE–11 (SUBJECTIVE)

1. (i) In how many ways can a selection of 10 balls be made from an unlimited number of Red, White, Blue and Green balls?

(ii) How many of these contain balls of all 4 colours?

2. 3 unbiased dice are thrown. Find the number of ways of obtaining a sum
(i) 10
(ii) 11

3. Find the number of ways of distributing twenty 'one rupee coins' among 5 beggars, when
(a) any number of coins can be given to baggers.
(b) at least one coin to each beggar must be given.
(c) beggar 1 and beggar 2 will take at least two coins.
(d) each beggar wants even number of coins.
(e) senior beggar is not ready to take less than 3 coins.
(f) no one gets less than three coins.

4. In how many ways can 10 identical toys be distributed among 3 children such that first receives maximum of 6 toys second receives maximum 7 toys and third receives maximum 8 toys?

5. (i) Find the number of integral solutions for the following equations
(a) $x_1 + x_2 + x_3 = 0$ where $x_1, x_2, x_3 \geq -5$
(b) $x_1 + x_2 + x_3 + 4x_4 = 20$ where $x_1, x_2, x_3, x_4 \geq 0$
(c) $x_1 + x_2 + x_3 + x_4 + x_5 = 20$, $x_1 + x_2 = 15$, and $x_k \geq 0$ for all k

(ii) Find the integral solution of
(a) $x\,y\,z = 24$ where x, y, z are non-zero integer
(b) $x_1\ x_2\, x_3\ x_4 = 360$ and also find its negative integral solution.

6. Find the number of non-negative integral solutions of $x_1 + x_2 + x_3 + x_4 \leq n$ (where n is a positive integer)

7. Find the number of non-negative integer solutions of the inequality $3x + y + z \leq 30$.

8. A conference attended by 200 delegates is held in a hall. The hall has 7 doors, marked $A, B, ...G$. At each door, an entry book is kept and the delegates entering through that door sign it in the order in which they enter. If each delegate is free to enter any time and through any door he likes, how many different sets of seven lists would arise in all? (Assume that every person signs only at his first entry.)

9. How many different ordered triplets (a, b, c) of non-negative integers are there such that $a + b + c = 50$? What if the three integers had to be positive?

Answer Keys

1. (i) ${}^{13}C_{10}$ (ii) ${}^{9}C_{6}$

2. (i) 27 (ii) 27

3. (a) ${}^{24}C_{4}$ (b) ${}^{19}C_{4}$ (c) ${}^{20}C_{4}$ (d) ${}^{14}C_{4}$ (e) ${}^{21}C_{4}$ (f) ${}^{9}C_{4}$ **4.** 47

5. (i) (a) ${}^{17}C_{2}$ (b) 536 (c) 336 (ii) (a) 120 (b) 1600, 1400

6. ${}^{n+4}C_{4} - 1$ **7.** 1991 **8.** ${}^{206}P_{200}$ **9.** ${}^{52}C_{2}$, ${}^{49}C_{2}$

TEXTUAL EXERCISE–11 (OBJECTIVE)

1. The number of integer solutions for the equation $x + y + z + t = 20$, where x, y, z, t are all ≥ -1 is

(a) ${}^{20}C_{4}$ (b) ${}^{23}C_{3}$
(c) ${}^{27}C_{4}$ (d) ${}^{27}C_{3}$

2. The number of non-negative integral solutions of $x + y + z \leq n$, where $n \in \mathbb{N}$ is

(a) ${}^{n+3}C_{3} - 1$ (b) ${}^{n+4}C_{4}$
(c) ${}^{n+5}C_{5}$ (d) None of these

3. If there are 4 oranges, five apples and six mangoes in a fruit basket, then the number of ways, a person make a selection of fruits among the fruits in the basket, is

(a) 210 (b) 209
(c) 211 (d) None of these

4. The number of ways, in which 12 identical coins can be put into 5 different purse, if none of the purse remains empty, is

(a) 660 (b) 110
(c) 165 (d) 330

5. If $x + y + z + w = 20$, then the number of positive integral solutions

(a) 960 (b) 969
(c) 320 (d) 333

6. If $x_1 + x_2 + x_3 + x_4 + x_5 = 22$; $x_1 + x_2 + x_3 = 5$; $x_1, x_2, x_3 \geq 0$, then the number of solutions for positive integer values of x_4 and x_5 is

(a) ${}^{7}C_{5} \times {}^{16}C_{15}$ (b) ${}^{7}C_{5}$
(c) ${}^{16}C_{5}$ (d) None of these

7. If $x + y + z + w = 20$, the number of positive integral solutions, if each variable is an odd number, is

(a) 160 (b) 162
(c) 163 (d) 165

8. In a, b, c, d are even natural numbers such that $a + b + c + d = 24$, then the number of values of the ordered quadruplet (a, b, c, d) is

(a) 165 (b) 455
(c) 310 (d) None of these

Answer Keys

1. (d) **2.** (a) **3.** (b) **4.** (d) **5.** (b) **6.** (a) **7.** (d) **8.** (a)

■ DEARRANGEMENTS

Any change in the order of the things in a group is called a dearrangment. If n things are arranged in a row, the number of ways in which they can be dearranged so that none of them occupies its original position is

$$n!\left\{1-\frac{1}{1!}+\frac{1}{2!}-\frac{1}{3!}+\frac{1}{4!}-......+(-1)^n\frac{1}{n!}\right\}$$

Proof: If n things are arranged in a row, the number of ways this can be done $= n!$ and of these the number in which a_1 stands 1st (i.e., in situ) $= (n-1)!$

$\Rightarrow$ a_1 is not in 1st (situation) $= n! - (n-1)!$.

Of the last number in which a_2 is in situ $= a_2$ in situation a_1, a_2 in situation

$= (n-1)! - (n-2)!$

$\Rightarrow$ number of ways in which a_1, a_2 are not in situation.

$= n! - (n-1)! - [(n-1)! - (n-2)!]$

$= n! - 2(n-1)! + (n-2)!$

$\Rightarrow$ number of ways in which a_3 is in situation but a_1, a_2 are not in situation.

$= (n-1)! - [2(n-2)! - (n-3)!]$

$\therefore$ The number of ways in which a_1, a_2, a_3 are not in situation = $\{n! - 2(n-1)! + (n-2)!\} - \{(n-1)! - 2(n-2)! + (n-3)!\}$

$= n! - 3(n-1)! + 3(n-2)! - (n-3)! = {}^3C_0(n-0)! - {}^3C_1(n-1)! + {}^3C_2(n-2)! - {}^3C_3(n-3)!$

Hence the number of arrangement in which no one of x letters are in situation $= n! - {}^xC_1(n-1)! + {}^xC_2(n-2)! - .... + (-1)^x(n-x)!$

REMARK

If each of r objects out of n are wrongly placed and remaining (n – r) objects occupy their original position, then let Δ_r denotes the number of such dearrangements. Further if Δ_r' denotes the number of dearrangements when none of given r objects occupy their correct places, then $\Delta_r = {}^nC_r \Delta'_r$; where

$$\Delta'_r = r!\left\{1 - \frac{1}{1!} + \frac{1}{2!} - \frac{1}{3!} + \frac{1}{4!} - ...... + (-1)^r \frac{1}{r!}\right\}$$

Alternatively

$A_i \to A_i$ is in situ, $A_i \cap A_j \Rightarrow i^{th}$ and j^{th} in situation

$$n\left(\bigcup_{i=1}^{x} A_i\right)$$

$$= \sum_{i=1}^{x} n(A_i) - \sum\sum_{1 \le i < j \le x}(A_i \cap A_j) + \sum\sum\sum_{1 \le i < j < k \le x} n(A_i \cap A_j \cap A_k) - ...$$

Now, $n(A_i) = (n-1)!$ and $n(A_i \cap A_j) = (n-2)!$

$$\Rightarrow \quad n\left(\bigcup_{i=1}^{x} A_i\right) = \sum_{i=1}^{x} n(A_i) - \sum\sum_{1 \le i < j \le x} n(A_i \cap A_j) + ...$$

$= {}^xC_1\,(n-1)! - {}^xC_2\,(n-2)! + {}^xC_3\,(n-3)! - ..... + (-1)^x(n-x)!$

$$\Rightarrow \quad \left(n\left(\overline{\bigcup_{i=1}^{x} A_i}\right)\right) = n! - {}^xC_1\,(n-1)! + {}^xC_2\,(n-2)! - {}^xC_3\,(n-3)! + ...$$

$\therefore$ For x = n,

$$n\left(\bigcup_{i=1}^{n} A_i\right) = n! - {}^nC_1(n-1)! + {}^nC_2(n-2)! - ... + (-1)^n$$

$$= n!\left(1 - \frac{1}{1!} + \frac{1}{2!} - \frac{1}{3!} + ... + (-1)^n . \frac{1}{n!}\right)$$

ILLUSTRATION 111: Suppose 4 letters are placed in 4 different envelopes, in how many ways can they be taken out from their envelopes and distributed again among the envelopes so that no letter goes to in its original envelope?

SOLUTION: Using the formula for the number of dearrangements so that no object goes to its original place that are possible out of 4 letters in 4 envelopes, we get the number of ways

$$= 4!\left(1 - \frac{1}{1!} + \frac{1}{2!} - \frac{1}{3!} + \frac{1}{4!}\right) = 24\left(1 - 1 + \frac{1}{2} - \frac{1}{6} + \frac{1}{24}\right) = 9$$

ILLUSTRATION 112: Four slips of paper with the numbers 1, 2, 3, 4 written on them are put in a box. They are drawn one by one (without replacement) at random. In how many ways it can happen that the ordinal number of atleast one slip coincide with its own number?

SOLUTION: Total number of ways = 4! = 24.

The number of ways in which ordinal number of no slip coincides with its own number is the number of dearrangements of 4 objects $= 4!\left(\frac{1}{2!} - \frac{1}{3!} + \frac{1}{4!}\right) = 9$

Thus the required number of ways = 24 – 9 = 15

ILLUSTRATION 113: A person writes letters to six friends and addresses the corresponding envelopes. In how many ways can the letters be placed in the envelopes so that

(i) at least two of them are in the wrong envelopes?

(ii) all the letters are in the wrong envelopes?

SOLUTION: (i) The number of ways in which at least two of them are in the wrong envelopes

$$= \sum_{r=2}^{6} {}^6C_r \Delta'_r = {}^6C_2\,\Delta'_2 + {}^6C_3\,\Delta'_3 + {}^6C_4\,\Delta'_4 + {}^6C_5\,\Delta'_5 + {}^6C_6\,\Delta'_6$$

$$= {}^6C_2 .\ 2!\left(1-\frac{1}{1!}+\frac{1}{2!}\right) + {}^6C_3 .\ 3!\left(1-\frac{1}{1!}+\frac{1}{2!}-\frac{1}{3!}\right) +$$

$${}^6C_4 .\ 4!\left(1-\frac{1}{1!}+\frac{1}{2!}-\frac{1}{3!}+\frac{1}{4!}\right) + {}^6C_5 .\ 5!\left(1-\frac{1}{1!}+\frac{1}{2!}-\frac{1}{3!}+\frac{1}{4!}-\frac{1}{5!}\right) +$$

$${}^6C_6 .6!\left(1-\frac{1}{1!}+\frac{1}{2!}-\frac{1}{3!}+\frac{1}{4!}-\frac{1}{5!}+\frac{1}{6!}\right) = 15 + 40 + 135 + 264 + 265 = 719$$

(ii) The number of ways in which all letters be placed in wrong envelopes

$$= 6!\left(1-\frac{1}{1!}+\frac{1}{2!}-\frac{1}{3!}+\frac{1}{4!}-\frac{1}{5!}+\frac{1}{6!}\right) = 720\left(\frac{1}{2}-\frac{1}{6}+\frac{1}{24}-120+\frac{1}{720}\right)$$

$$= 360 - 120 + 30 - 6 + 1 = 265$$

DISTRIBUTION IN PARCELS

Distribution in parcels when empty parcels are allowed

The number of ways in which n different objects can be distributed in r different groups (here distributed means order of objects inside a group is not important) under the condition that empty groups are allowed $= r^n$

Take anyone of objects. This object can be put in anyone of groups in r ways.

Similarly, each of the objects can be put in any one of groups in r ways.

So number of ways $= r.\ r.\ r......(n \text{ times}) = r^n =$ coefficient of x^n in $n!\,(e^x)^r$

Distribution in parcels when empty parcels are not allowed

The number of ways in which n different things can be distributed into r different parcels such that no parcel is blank $= r^n - {}^rC_1\,(r-1)^n + {}^rC_2\,(r-2)^n + ... + (-1)^n\,(r-x)^n$ which is $n!$ times the coefficient of x^n in expansion of $(e^x - 1)^r$

Denoting parcels by $a_1, a_2, ..., a_r$ and consider the distribution in which blank parcels are allowed. Number in which a_1 is blank $= (r-1)^n$

Number in which a_1 is not blank $= r^n - (r-1)^n$.

Of the last, number in which a_2 is not blank $= (r-1)^n - (r-2)^n$

$\therefore$ number in which a_1, a_2 not blank $= r^n - (r-1)^n - [(r-1)^n - (r-2)^n] = r^n - 2(r-1)^n + (r-2)^n$.

Of the last, number in which a_3 is blank (a_1 and a_2 not blank) $= (r-1)^n - [(r-2)^n + (r-2)^n - (r-3)^n] = (r-1)^n - 2(r-2)^n + (r-3)^n$.

$\Rightarrow$ number of ways in which $a_1\ a_2\ a_3$ not blank

$= r^n - 3(r-1)^n + 3(r-2)^n - (r-3)^n$ (subtracting last two expressions)

Alternatively

Let A_i be the case when i^{th} parcel is blank

Let $A_i \cap A_j$ be the case when i^{th} and j^{th} parcels are blank

Let $A_i \cap A_j \cap A_k$ be the case when i^{th}, j^{th} and k^{th} parcels are blank

$\Rightarrow\ n(A_i) = (r-1)^n$ and $n(A_i \cap A_j) = (r-2)^n$

So number of cases when at least one parcel is blank is equal to

$$n\left(\overline{\bigcup_{i=1}^{x} A_i}\right) = \sum_{i=1}^{x} n(A_i) - \sum\sum_{1\le i< j\le x} n(A_i \cap A_j)$$
$$+\sum\sum\sum_{1\le i<j<k\le x} n(A_i \cap A_j \cap A_k) + \ldots$$
$$= {}^rC_1(r-1)^n - {}^rC_2(r-2)^n + {}^rC_3(r-3)^n - \ldots$$

∴ Total number of cases when no parcel is blank

$$= r^n - \left(n\left(\overline{\bigcup_{i=1}^{x} A_i}\right)\right)$$
$$= r^n - {}^rC_1(r-1)^n + {}^rC_2(r-2)^n - {}^rC_3(r-3)^n + \ldots$$

NOTES

(i) *The number of ways in which n different things can be arranged into r different group is r(r+1) (r + 2)....(r + n – 1) or* $n!\,{}^{n-1}C_{r-1}$ *according as blank groups are or are not admissible.*

(ii) *The number of ways in which n different things can be distributed into r different places, blank lots being admissible is* r^n.

(iii) *The number of ways in which n different things can be distributed into r different parcels there being no blank lot is* $r^n - {}^rC_1(r-1)^n + \ldots (-1)^{r-1}({}^rC_{r-1})$. *Which is n! times the coefficient of* x^n *in the expansion of* $(e^x - 1)^r$.

ILLUSTRATION 114: In how many ways can three persons, each throwing a single die once, make a total score of 11?

SOLUTION: The required number is equal to the

$= $ coefficient of x^{11} in $(x + x^2 + x^3 + \ldots + x^6)^3$

$= $ coefficient of x^{11} in $x^3 (1 - x^6)^3 (1 - x)^{-3}$

$= $ coefficient of x^8 in $(1 - x^6)^3 (1 - 3x^6) = 45 - 18 = 27$

ILLUSTRATION 115: In how many ways 5 different balls can be distributed into 3 boxes so that no box remains empty?

SOLUTION: The required number of ways

$= 3^5 - {}^3C_1(3-1)^5 + {}^3C_2(3-2)^5 - {}^3C_3(3-3)^5 = 243 - 96 + 3 - 0 = 150$

■ EXPONENT OF A PRIME IN '*n!*'

Exponent of prime p in $n!$ is denoted by $E_p(n!)$, where n is natural number, so the last integer amongst 1, 2,.....$(n - 1)$, n which is divisible by p is $[n/p]\,p$ when $[n] \le x$

$$\Rightarrow E_p(n!) = E_p(1.2.3.....(n-1).\,n)$$
$$= E_p(p.2p.3p.....([n/p]-1)p.[n/p]\,p)$$

now the last integer out of 1, 2, 3,......$[n/p]$ which is divisible by p is

$$= [n/p] + E_p(1.2.3.....[n/p]])$$
$$= [n/p] + E_p(p.2p.3p.....[n/p^2]p) \text{ as } \left[\frac{[x]}{n}\right] = \left[\frac{x}{n}\right]$$
$$= [n/p] + [n/p^2] + E_p(1.2.3......[n/p^3])$$
$$\Rightarrow E_p(n!) = [n/p] + [n/p^2] + \ldots\ldots + [n/p^s]$$

where s is the largest number such that $p^s \le n < p^{s+1}$

ILLUSTRATION 116: Number of zeros at the end of 300! is equal to

(a) 75 (b) 89

(c) 74 (d) 98

SOLUTION: Exponent of 2 in 300! has to be greater than exponent of 5 in 300!

⇒ exponent of 5 in 300! will decide the number of zero's at the end of 300!

Number of zeros at end of 300! = Exponent of 5 in (300)!

$$= \left[\frac{300}{5}\right] + \left[\frac{300}{25}\right] + \left[\frac{300}{125}\right] = 60 + 12 + 2 = 74.$$

ILLUSTRATION 117: What is the largest integer n such that 33! is divisible by 2^n?

SOLUTION: $33! = 1 \times 2 \times 3 \times 4 \times .... \times 33$

$= (2 \times 4 \times 6 \times .... \times 32)(1 \times 3 \times 5 \times .... \times 33)$

$= 2^{16}(1 \times 2 \times 3 \times .... \times 16)(1 \times 3 \times .... \times 33)$

$= 2^{16}(2 \times 4 \times .... \times 16)(1 \times 3 \times ...... \times 15)(1 \times 3 \times .... \times 33)$

$= 2^{16} \times 2^8 \times (1 \times 2 \times ...... \times 8)(1 \times 3 \times .... \times 15)(1 \times 3 \times .... \times 33)$

$= 2^{16} \times 2^8 \times (2 \times 4 \times 6 \times 8)(1 \times 3 \times 5 \times 7)(1 \times 3 \times .... \times 15)(1 \times 3 \times .... \times 33)$

$= 2^{16} \times 2^8 \times 2^4(1 \times 2 \times 3 \times 4)(1 \times 3 \times 5 \times 7)(1 \times 3 \times ... \times 15)(1 \times 3 \times .... \times 33)$

$= 2^{16} \times 2^8 \times 2^4 \times 2^2(1 \times 2)(1 \times 3)(1 \times 3 \times 5 \times 7)(1 \times 3 \times ... \times 15)(1 \times 3 \times .... \times 33)$

$= 2^{16} \times 2^8 \times 2^4 \times 2^2 \times 2^1(1 \times 3)(1 \times 3 \times 5 \times 7)(1 \times 3 \times ... \times 15)(1 \times 3 \times .... \times 33)$

$= 2^{31} \times P$ Where $P = (1 \times 3)(1 \times 3 \times 5 \times 7)(1 \times 3 \times ... \times 15)(1 \times 3 \times .... \times 33)$

$\therefore$ Maximum value of n for which 33! is divisible by 2^n is 31.

ILLUSTRATION 118: What is the largest integer 'n' for which 300! is divisible by 160^n?

SOLUTION: Exponent of 2 in 300! =

$$\left[\frac{300}{2}\right]+\left[\frac{300}{2^2}\right]+\left[\frac{300}{2^3}\right]+\left[\frac{300}{2^4}\right]+\left[\frac{300}{2^5}\right]+\left[\frac{300}{2^6}\right]+\left[\frac{300}{2^7}\right]+\left[\frac{300}{2^8}\right]+\left[\frac{300}{2^9}\right]+....$$

$= 150 + 75 + 37 + 18 + 9 + 4 + 2 + 1 = 296$

Exponent of 5 in 300!

$$=\left[\frac{300}{5}\right]+\left[\frac{300}{5^2}\right]+\left[\frac{300}{5^3}\right]+\left[\frac{300}{5^4}\right]+... = 60 + 12 + 2 = 74$$

$\Rightarrow$ $300! = 2^{296} \times 5^{74} \times k$; where k is an integer (not a multiple of 2 or 5)

Now $160 = 2^5 \times 5$ $\Rightarrow$ $300! = (2^5)^{59}.2^1.(5)^{59}.(5)^{15} \times k = (2^5.5)^{59}(2.5^{15})k = (160)^{59}.k_1$;

where $k_1 = 2.5^{15}.k$ and is not divisible by 160

$\Rightarrow$ Largest value of n = 59

ILLUSTRATION 119: Find the number of zero's at the end of $(100!)^{100!}$

(a) $24^{100!}$ (b) 24^2

(c) $24 \times 100!$ (d) None of these

SOLUTION: Number of zeros at the end of 100! = exponent of 5 in 100!

$$=\left[\frac{100}{5}\right]+\left[\frac{100}{5^2}\right]+\left[\frac{100}{5^3}\right]+\left[\frac{100}{5^4}\right]+... = 20 + 4 = 24$$

Now number of zeros at the end of $(100!)^2$ = Number of zeros in (100!) + Number of zeros in 100! = 2×24

Similarly, number of zeros at the end of $(100!)^3 = 3 \times 24$ and thereby, number of zeros at the end of $(100!)^{100!} = 24 \times 100!$

Number of ways of selecting r letters of k letters of first type, m letters of second type, n letters of third type and so on

= Coefficient of x^r in $(1 + x + x^2 + ... + x^k)(1 + x + x^2 + ... + x^m)(1 + x + x^2 + ...x^n)$

Number of ways of arragements of r letters out of k letters of first type, m leteers of second type, n letters of third type on so on

Coefficient of x^r in

$$r!\left(1+x+\frac{x^2}{2!}+\frac{x^3}{3!}+...+\frac{x^k}{k!}\right)\times\left(1+x+\frac{x^2}{2!}+\frac{x^3}{3!}+...+\frac{x^m}{m!}\right)$$

$$\times\left(1+x+\frac{x^2}{2!}+\frac{x^3}{3!}+...+\frac{x^n}{n!}\right)$$

TEXTUAL EXERCISE–12 (SUBJECTIVE)

1. There are 5 letters and 5 directed envelopes:
   (a) In how many ways can all the letters be kept into wrong envelopes?
   (b) In how many ways can 2 letters be rightly placed and 3 letters wrongly placed?

2. There are 4 balls of different colours and four boxes of colours same as those of the balls. Find the numbers of ways in which the balls one each in the box, could be placed such that a ball does not go to the box of its own colour.

3. Find the number of ways in which 100 students can be distributed into three classrooms if
   (i) empty classrooms are permissible
   (ii) empty classrooms are not permissible

4. (a) Find the number of combinations of four letters of the word
   (i) EXAMINATION (ii) ALLAHABAD
   (b) Find the number of combinations of the letters of the word PROPORTION taken 6 letters at a time.

5. Find the number of arrangement of letters of word EXAMINATION taken four at a time.

6. Find the number of different selection of 5 letters which can be made from 5*a*'s, 4*b*'s, 3*c*'s, 2*d*'s and one 1*e*.

7. Find the number of ways of displaying 5 different flags on 4 masts if all the flags are to be used,
   (i) one or more of the masts need not be used;
   (ii) all the masts are to be used.

8. If n objects are arranged in row, then find the number of ways of selecting 3 of these objects so that no two of them are next to each other.

9. In n distinct things are arranged in a circle, show that the number of ways of selecting 3 of these things so that no two of them are next to each other is $\frac{n(n-4)(n-5)}{6}$.

10. (i) (a) If the prime factorisation of $10! = 2^p . 3^q\ 5^r\ 7^s$, then find p, q, r and s.
    (ii) (a) Find the number of zeroes at the end of
    (i) 100! (ii) 50! (iii) 25!
    (b) If $l = LCM$ of 8!, 10! and 12 ! and h be HCF of 8!, 10! and 12! then evaluate l/h.
    (c) Find the exponent of 2 in $x = 20 \times 19 \times 18 \times ..... \times 11$.
    (d) If 250! is divisible by5^p, then find the maximum value of p.
    (e) Find the exponent of 12 in ${}^{100}C_{30}$.

Answer Keys

1. (a) 44 (b) 20
2. 9
3. (i) 3^{100} (ii)$3^{100} - 100(2)^{100} + 4950$
4. (a) (i) 136 (ii) 23 (b) 53
5. 2454
6. 71
7. (i) 6720 (ii) 480
8. ${}^{n-2}C_3$
10. (i) $p = 8, q = 4, r = 2, s = 1$ (ii) (a) (i) 24 zeros (ii) 12 zeros (iii) 6 zeros
    (b) 11880 (c) 10 (d) 62 (e) 2

TEXTUAL EXERCISE–12 (OBJECTIVE)

1. The number of times the digit 5 will be written when listing the integers from 1 to 1000 is
   (a) 256 (b) 280
   (c) 300 (d) None of these

2. The number of ways in which n distinct objects can be put into two identical boxes so that no box remains empty, is
   (a) $2^n - 2$ (b) $2^n - 1$
   (c) $2^{n-1} - 1$ (d) $n^2 - 2$

3. We have 4 balls of different colours and 4 boxes with colours the same as those of the balls. The number of ways in which the balls can be arranged in the boxes so that no ball goes into a box of its own colour
   (a) 4! (b) 9
   (c) 4! –4 (d) None of these

4. A person writes letter to 6 friends and addresses the corresponding envelopes. In how many ways can the

letters be placed in the envelopes so that at least 4 of them are in wrong envelopes?
(a) 72
(b) 719
(c) 664
(d) None of these

5. Exponent of 12 in 50! is
(a) 20 (b) 21
(c) 22 (d) None of these

6. The number 24! is divisible by
(a) 6^{24} (b) 24^6
(c) 12^{12} (d) 48^5

7. The number of zero's at the end of 60! is
(a) 14 (b) 15
(c) 16 (d) None of these

8. The exponent of 7 in ${}^{100}C_{50}$ is
(a) 8 (b) 16
(c) 0 (d) 2

9. The exponent of 2 in ${}^{50}P_{10}$ is:
(a) 8 (b) 9
(c) 12 (d) 11

10. The largest integer n for which 45! is divisible by 3^n is
(a) 16 (b) 20
(c) 21 (d) 28

Answer Keys

1. (c) **2.** (c) **3.** (b) **4.** (c) **5.** (c) **6.** (b), (d) **7.** (a) **8.** (c) **9.** (b) **10.** (c)

MULTIPLE-CHOICE QUESTIONS

SECTION–I

OBJECTIVE-TYPE SOLVED EXAMPLES

1. A letter lock consists of three rings each marked with 10 different letters. Number of ways it is possible to make an unsuccessful attempt to open the lock is

(a) 1000 (b) 999
(c) 998 (d) None of these

Solution: (b) Two rings may have same letter at a time but same ring cannot have two letters at a time, therefore, we must proceed ringwise.
Each of the three rings can have any one of the 10 different letters in 10 ways.

∴ Total number of attempts = 10 × 10 × 10 = 1000. But out of these 1000 attempts only one attempt is successful

∴ Required number of unsuccessful attempts are = 1000 – 1= 999.

2. Three travellers arrive at a town where there are four hotels; Number of ways they take up their quarters, each at a different hotel is:

(a) 24 (b) 25
(c) 20 (d) None of these

Solution: (a) The first traveller has choice of four hotels, and when he has made his selection in any one way, the second traveller has a choice of three; therefore the first two can make their choice in 4 × 3 ways; and with any one such choice the third traveller can select his hotel in 2 ways; hence the required number of ways is = (4 × 3 × 2) = 24.

3. (a) In how many ways can three persons be selected from amongst 10 persons?

(b) How many times will a particular person be always selected?

(c) How many committees can be formed if Rajan refuses to be in committee with Neeraj?

(d) How many committees can be formed if Rajan says that he should be selected in committee only if Neeraj is selected in committee?

(e) How many committees can be formed if Rajan and Neeraj say that they both should be there in committee together, if selected?

Solution: (a) Selection of three persons from amongst ten persons can be made in ${}^{10}C_3$ ways $= \dfrac{10.9.8}{3.2.1.} = 120$ ways.

(b) If a particular person is always selected, then we have to select two more person from the remaining nine person and this can be done in ${}^{9}C_2$ ways $= \dfrac{9\times 8}{2} = 36$ ways

(c) There will be two sets of committees, one in which Neeraj is selected and other in which Neeraj is not selected. Adding these two sets of committees, we will get the total number of committees.
i.e., ${}^{8}C_2 + {}^{9}C_3 = 112$

Alternatively, required ways = Total number of ways – Number of ways when both Ranjan and Neeraj are selected $= {}^{10}C_3 - {}^{8}C_1 = 112$

(d) Here we should concentrate ourselves on Neeraj.

Case I: Neeraj is selected. In this case, Ranjan may or may not be selected. Thus we are left to select two persons from remaining nine persons. This can be done is ${}^{9}C_2$ ways = 36 ways.

Case II: Neeraj is not selected. In this case Ranjan will refuse to be selected. i.e., we have to select three person from the remaining eight persons and this can be done in ${}^{8}C_3$ ways $= \dfrac{8\times 7\times 6}{3\times 2\times 1} = 56$ ways

Total number of ways = 36 + 56 = 92.

(e) Since Rajan and Neeraj both decided to be together.

Case I: Rajan and Neeraj both are selected. Then we are to select one person from remaining eight persons, which can be done in ${}^{8}C_1$ ways i.e., 8 ways.

Case II: Rajan and Neeraj are not selected. So we have to choose three people from remaining 8 which can be done in ${}^{8}C_3$ ways i.e., $\dfrac{8\times 7\times 6}{3\times 2\times 1} = 56$ ways.

∴ Total number of committees fromed = 8 + 56 = 64.

4. The number of ways in which 3 boys and 4 girls be seated around a circular table if no two boys sit together is

(a) 36 (b) 3! 4!
(c) 7! – 3! × 4! (d) 18

Solution: (b) First make the 4 girls sit around a circular table.

This can be done in $(4 - 1)! = 3! = 6$.

After that 3 boys can occupy any three out of 4 blank spaces.

This can be done in $^4p_3 = 4!$ ways.

Hence total number of ways $= 3! \times 4!$

5. The number of ways of selecting at least one fruit out of 4 apples, 3 bananas and 1 each of mango, pineapple and guava is

(a) 159 (b) 12
(c) $4! \times 3! - 1$ (d) None of these

Solution: (a) Among 4 apples, we can none, either 1, 2, 3 or all the four apples i.e., we have total 5 choices. Similarly, for 3 bananas, we have four choices and for 3 other fruits, we have 2 choices each. Hence total ways $= 5 \times 4 \times 2 \times 2 \times 2 = 160$. But this includes a case of selecting 0 apples 0 banana and 0 of every other fruits which means that no fruit is selected.

Hence total number of ways $= 160 - 1 = 159$ ways

6. The number of ways in which 7 different books can be given to 5 students if each can recieve none, one or more thing are

(a) 5^7 (b) 7^5
(c) $^{11}C_5$ (d) 12!

Solution: (a) First book can be given to any of the five students, similarly, each one of other six books also have 5 choices. Hence the total number of ways $= 5^7$

7. Number of times digit 0 is used in writing the number from 1 to 1000 is

(a) 189 (b) 300
(c) 192 (d) None of these

Solution: (c) Consider the number from 000, 001 to 999. since each digit has equal likelihood of coming and digits used are 3×1000. Hence 0 appear = 300 times. But since 000, 001, 002....099, have some unwanted zeros, we subtract these zero's, i.e., $3 + 2 \times 9 + 1 \times 90 = 111$.

Thus total number of times 0 appears $= 300 - 111 = 189 +$ (3 zero's in 1000) $= 192$

8. A room has 6 doors. Number of ways a man enter the room through one door and come out through a different door is

(a) 31 (b) 30
(c) 29 (d) None of these

Solution: (b) Number of ways in which the man can enter the room = 6.

Number of ways in which he can leave the room = $6 - 1 = 5$. {Since, the man has to come out through a different door, number of choices left with him to come out is 5}

$\therefore$ Total no.of ways $= 6 \times 5 = 30$

9. Total numbers between 100 and 1000 having it every digit either 2 or 9 is

(a) 6 (b) 7
(c) 8 (d) 9

Solution: (c) All digits between 100 and 1000 are 3 digit numbers. Since each of the three digits is 2 or 9, each digit can be filled up in 2 ways i.e., 2 or 9

$\therefore$ Total number of ways $= 2 \times 2 \times 2 = 8$

10. The letters of the word 'RANDOM' are written in all posible orders and these 6 letter words are written out as in a dictionary. The rank of the word 'RANDOM' is

(a) 614 (b) 416
(c) 164 (d) None of these

Solution: (a) The alphabetical order of the letters in the word 'RANDOM' is *A, D, M, N, O, R.*

Number of words starting with *A, D, M, N,* or $O = 5 \times 5! = 600$

No.of words with *R* in Ist place, A in 2nd place and (*D* or *M* in third place). $= 2(3!) + 2$.

$\therefore$ Rank of the word RANDOM is 614 $(= 600 + 12 + 2)$.

11. Number of different garlands using 3 flowers of one kind and 12 flowers of second kind is

(a) 19 (b) $11! \times 2!$
(c) $^{14}C_2$ (d) None of these

Solution: (a) Let x, y, z be the number of flowers of second kind between first and second flowers of first kind, second and third flowers of first kind and third and first flower of first kind respectively., as shown below.

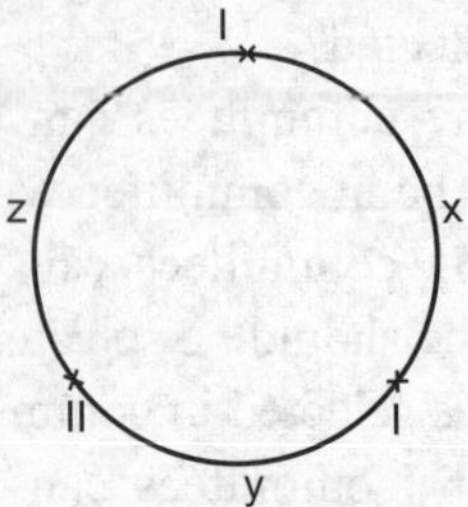

Now, $x + y + z = 12$; x, y, $z \geq 0$

Total number of solutions $= {}^{14}C_2 = 91$

Case 1: Number of solution (x = y = z) = 1 i.e., (4, 4, 4)

Case 2: Number of solution (x = y ≠ z) = Number of solution 2x + z = 12

$$6 \times 3 = 18$$

Number of garlands = 6 as x = y ≠ z, y = z ≠ x, z = x ≠ y would give same garlands.

Case 3: Number of solution (x ≠ y ≠ z) = 91 – 1 – 18 = 72

Number of garlands = $\frac{72}{6} = 12$ (as 72 possibilities x ≠ y ≠ z contains 3! times the actual number of garlands in this case)

∴ Total numbers of possible garlands = 1 + 6 + 12 = 19

12. Let A = { $x \mid x$ is a prime number and $x < 30$}. The number of different rational numbers whose numerator and denominator belong to A is

(a) 90 (b) 180
(c) 91 (d) None of these

Solution: (c) $A = \{2, 3, 5, 7, 11, 13, 17, 19, 23, 29\}$. A rational number is made by taking any two in any order. So, the required number of rational numbers = ${}^{10}P_2$ +1(including 1) = 91

13. The number of ways in which 10 gentlemen can sit around a table so that the gentlemen are not to have the same two neighbours, is

(a) 181400 (b) 181440
(c) 18220 (d) None of these

Solution: (b) As the gentlemen are not to have the same two neighbours, clockwise and anti-clockwise arrangements will be CAB or BAC treated as identical.

∴ required number of arrangements

$$= \frac{1}{2}(10-1)! = \frac{1}{2}9! = 181440$$

14. Number of ways in which 6 different toys can be distributed among two brothers in ratio 1: 2, is

(a) 30 (b) 60
(c) 20 (d) 40

Solution: (a) We have to distribute 6 toys among two brothers in 1: 2

So if one of them get a no. of toys, then second one will get $2a$ toys

∴ $a + 2a = 6$ ⇒ $a = 2$

There are two ways of selection of brothers for ratio 1:2

Two toys can be allocated to second in ${}^6C_2$ ways

So required number of ways = 2 × ${}^6C_2$ = 30 ways.

15. Number of ways in which AAA B B B can be placed in the squares of the figure as shown, so that no row remains empty, is

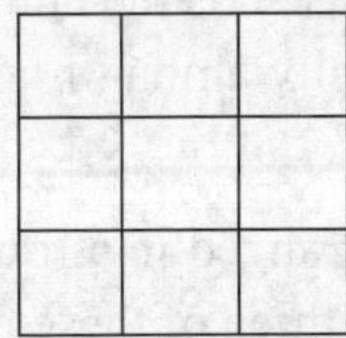

(a) 2430 (b) 2160
(c) 1620 (d) None of these

Solution: We have to arrange *A, A, A, B, B, B* in the squares of the fig.

So that no row remains empty.

First of all the total no. of ways of filling 9 squares with 6 things {of which 3 are identical and other three are also identical}

$$= {}^9C_6 \times \frac{6!}{3!3!} = 1680$$

Now counting the ways in which any of row remain empty.

For this we have the situation when the given '6' alphabet's occupy exactly two rows completely and this will happen in

$$= {}^3C_2 \times \frac{6!}{3!3!} = 60$$

{selecting two rows out of '3'}

So required number of ways in which no rows remain empty = 1680 - 60 = 1620.

16. If n and m are +ve integers, which of the following is/are an integer

(a) $\frac{(mn)!}{m!(n!)^m}$

(b) $\frac{(n^2)!}{(n!)^{n+1}}$

(c) $\frac{n \times (n+1) \times (n+2) \times .... (n+r-1)}{(r+n!)!}$

(d) $\frac{m!+n!}{(m!+n!)!}$

Solution: (a), (b) If n and m are both integer, then

$\frac{(mn)!}{m!(n!)^m}$ is an integer because

$\frac{(mn)!}{m!(n!)^m}$ is the no. of ways

of dividing 'mn' things equally in 'm' identical groups of 'n' objects each.

Also, $\frac{(n^2)!}{(n!)^{n+1}}$

is an integer because it is the number of ways of dividing n^2 things equally among n identical groups of 'n' objects each.

17. If n objects are arranged in a row, then the number of ways of selecting three of these objects so that no two of them are next of each other is

(a) $\frac{(n-2)(n-3)(n-4)}{6}$ (b) ${}^{n-2}C_2$

(c) ${}^{n-3}C_3 + {}^{n-3}C_2$ (d) ${}^{n}C_2$

Solution: (a) Let O_1, O_2, O_3 are selected objects. Now let us arrange the given n object as G_1 O_1 G_2 O_2 G_3 O_3 G_4; where G_1, G_2, G_3, G_4 are groups of unselected objects positioned w.r.t. O_1, O_2, O_3 such that

$$n(G_1) \geq 0, n(G_2) \geq 1, n(G_3) \geq 1, n(G_4) \geq 0$$

and $x_1 + x_2 + x_3 + x_4 = n-3$; where $x_i = n(G_i)$

Req. number of ways = coefficient of x^{n-3} in

$$(x^0 + x^1 + x^2 + ...)^2 (x^1 + x^2 + x^3 + ...\infty)^2$$

$$= {}^{n-3+1}C_3 = \frac{(n-2)(n-3)(n-4)}{6}$$

Aliter: $x_1 + x_2 + x_3 + x_4 = n-3$

$x_1 \geq 0, x_2 \geq 1, x_3 \geq 1, x_4 \geq 0$

Let $x_2 - 1 = y_2 \Rightarrow x_2 = y_2 + 1$

and $x_3 - 1 = y_3 \Rightarrow x_3 = y_3 + 1; y_2, y_3 \geq 0$

$\Rightarrow x_1 + y_2 + y_3 + x_4 = n-3-2 = n-5$

$\Rightarrow x_1 + y_2 + y_3 + x_4 = n-5$ where $x_1, y_2, y_3, x_4 \geq 0$

$\Rightarrow$ Number of non-negative integral solution = ${}^{5+3}C_3$ = ${}^{n-2}C_3$.

$$= \frac{(n-2)(n-3)(n-4)}{6}$$

18. Total number of positive integral solutions of $15 < x_1 + x_2 + x_3 \leq 20$, is equal to

(a) 1125 (b) 1150

(c) 1245 (d) 685

Solution: Considering the equations $15 < x_1 + x_2 + x_3 \leq 20$; $x_1 \geq 1, x_2 \geq 1, x_3 \geq 1$ adding a new variable $y_4 \geq 0$ on left hand side, the inequality $x_1 + x_2 + x_3 \leq 20$ becomes

$x_1 + x_2 + x_3 + y_4 = 20$;

$x_1 \geq 1, x_2 \geq 1, x_3 \geq 1, y_4 \geq 0$

$\Rightarrow y_1 + y_2 + y_3 + y_4 = 20 - 3; y_i = x_i - 1; i = 1, 2, 3$

Number of non-negative integral solution = ${}^{20}C_3$

Now $x_1 + x_2 + x_3 > 15 \Rightarrow x_1 + x_2 + x_3 \not\leq 15$

Now; find the integral solution of $x_1 + x_2 + x_3 \leq 15$

Again adding $y_4 \geq 0$ we have $x_1 + x_2 + x_3 + y_4 = 15$

$\Rightarrow y_1 + y_2 + y_3 + y_4 = 15 - 3; y_i = x_i - 1; i = 1, 2, 3; y_i \geq 0$

Number of non-negative integral solution = ${}^{15}C_3$

Required number of solutions $= {}^{20}C_3 - {}^{15}C_3$ = 1140 – 455 = 685.

19. Total number of polynomials of the form $x^3 + ax^2 + bx + c$ that are divisible by $x^2 + 1$, where a, b, $c \in \{1, 2, 3, ..., 9, 10\}$ is equal to

(a) 10 (b) 15

(c) 5 (d) 8

Solution: (a) Considering the equation $x^3 + ax^2 + bx + c$; dividing by $x^2 + 1$, we have $x^3 + ax^2 + bx + c = (x^2 + 1)(x + a)(b - 1)x + c - a$

For complete divisibility, reminder = 0

$\Rightarrow b = 1$, and $c = a$

Since $a, c \in \{1, 2, 3, ...,10\}$

So we have 10 options to select a or c and ony one option to select b.

$\therefore$ Total number of polynomials = 10 × 1 × 1 = 10.

20. Total number of positive integral solutions of the equation $x_1 . x_2 . x_3 = 60$, is equal to

(a) 27 (b) 54

(c) 64 (d) None of these

Solution: Considering the equation $x_1\ x_2\ x_3 = 60 = (2)^2.(3)^1.(5)^1$

Let $x_i = 2^{\alpha i}, 3^{\beta i}, 5^{\gamma i}$; $\alpha i, \beta i, \gamma i \geq 0$

$\Rightarrow (2)^{\alpha_1+\alpha_2+\alpha_3}.(3)^{\beta_1+\beta_2+\beta_3}.(5)^{\gamma_1+\gamma_2+\gamma_3} = (2)^2.(3)^1.(5)^1$

$\Rightarrow \alpha_1 + \alpha_2 + \alpha_3 = 2; \beta_1 + \beta_2 + \beta_3 = 1; \gamma_1 + \gamma_2 + \gamma_3 = 1;$

Total number of positive integral solutions = ${}^4C_2.{}^3C_2.{}^3C_2 = 6 \times 3 \times 3 = 54$

21. Total number of divisors of $n = 3^5.5^7.7^9$ that are of the form $4\lambda + 1, \lambda \geq 0$ is equal to

(a) 240 (b) 30

(c) 120 (d) 15

Solution: (a) Considering $n = 3^5 5^7 7^9$ For number of divisors of form $4\lambda + 1$; $\lambda \geq 0$. Let us examine 3, 5, 7 and behaviour of its powers.

$$\left.\begin{array}{l} 3 \Rightarrow 4\lambda - 1 \text{ form} \\ 3^2 = 9 \Rightarrow 4\lambda + 1 \text{ form} \\ 3^3 = 27 \Rightarrow 4\lambda - 1 \text{ form} \\ 3^4 = 81 \Rightarrow 4\lambda + 1 \text{ form} \end{array}\right\} \lambda \in \mathbb{N}$$

So even powers of 3 are of 4λ + 1 form and odd powers are 4λ – 1 form.

Now each of 5, 5^2, 5^3,......,5^7 is of (4λ + 1) form

Considering '7'

$7' = 7$; 4λ – 1 form

$7^2 = 49$; 4λ + 1 form

$7^3 = 343$; 4λ – 1 form

$7^4 = 2401$; 4λ + 1 form

So even powers of 7 are of 4λ + 1 form and odd powers are of 4λ – 1 form.

We also have to notice that $(4\lambda-1)(4\lambda-1)=16\lambda^2+1-8\lambda \Rightarrow 4\lambda+1$ form

So, for divisors of 4λ + 1 form

We have to consider all possible ways to select powers of 5, [even powers of 3 even power of 7 + odd powers of 3 odd powers of 7]

= 8[3 × 5 + 3 × 5] = 8[30] = 240.

22. Total number of divisors of $n=2^5.3^4.5^{10}.7^6$ that are of the form $4\lambda+2, \lambda\ge1$ is equal to

(a) 385 (b) 55

(c) 384 (d) 54

Solution: (c) Considering $n=2^5.3^4.5^{10}.7^6$

We have to find number of divisors of the form = $4\lambda+2, \lambda\ge1$

i.e., = 2[2λ + 1] {but 2λ + 1 is odd no}

So for that we have to select exactly one '2' and all possible powers of 3, 5, 7

Which can be done in

= 1 × (4 + 1) (10 + 1) (6 + 1) = 5 × 11 × 7 = 385

But these divisor carries a divisor '2' {when 3^0, 5^0, 7^0 is selected} but $4\lambda+2\ge6, \lambda\ge1$

So this divisor must be excluded

Hence, number of divisors = 385 – 1 = 384.

23. A person predicts the outcome of 20 cricket matches of his home team. Each match can result either in a win, loss or tie for the home team. Total number of ways in which he can make the predictions so that exactly 10 predictions are correct, is equal to

(a) ${}^{20}C_{10} \cdot 2^{10}$ (b) ${}^{20}C_{10} \cdot 3^{20}$

(c) ${}^{20}C_{10} \cdot 3^{10}$ (d) ${}^{20}C_{10} \cdot 2^{20}$

Solution: (a) In order to predict exactly 10 correct predictions,

⇒ We have to select 10 matches out of 20 in ${}^{20}C_{10}$ ways

⇒ Ways of making correct prediction for each match is 1 so for 10 matches it is equal to $(1)^{10} = 1$

⇒ Remaining 10 predictions will must be wrong so for each incorrect prediction we have 2 choice out of 3 this can be done in 2^{10} ways.

Required of ways = ${}^{20}C_{10}(1).2^{10} = {}^{20}C_{10}\times2^{10}$

24. The total number of six digit numbers $\overline{x_1x_2x_3x_4x_5x_6}$ having the property that $x_1 < x_2 \le x_3 < x_4 < x_5 \le x_6$ is equal to

(a) ${}^{10}C_6$ (b) ${}^{12}C_6$

(c) ${}^{11}C_6$ (d) None of these

Solution: (c) We have to form six digit number $x_1x_2x_3x_4x_5x_6$ having $x_1 < x_2 \le x_3 < x_4 < x_5 \le x_6$

So here arises following cases:

Case I: $x_1 < x_2 < x_3 < x_4 < x_5 < x_6$

Now single order is already fixed so we just need to select 6 numbers out of 9 possible numbers {1, 2, 3, 4, 5, 6, 7, 8,9}

{zero is neglected because it can't be placed at any place}

This can be done in ${}^9C_6$ ways

Case II: $x_1 < x_2 = x_3 < x_4 < x_5 < x_6$

Now we have to select 5 digits

No. of ways = ${}^9C_5$

Case III: $x_1 < x_2 = x_3 < x_4 < x_5 = x_6$

Now we have to select 4 digits done in ${}^9C_4$ ways.

Case IV: $x_1 < x_2 < x_3 < x_4 < x_5 = x_6$

We have select 5 digits

which is done in = ${}^9C_5$ ways.

Total no. ways = ${}^9C_6 + 2 \,.\, {}^9C_5 + {}^9C_4 = {}^9C_6 + {}^9C_5 + {}^9C_5 + {}^9C_4 = {}^{10}C_6 + {}^{10}C_5 = {}^{11}C_6$

25. Total number of integral solutions (*a, b, c*) such that *abc* = 105 is

(a) 108

(b) 135

(c) equivalent to total number of integral solution of *abc* = 1001

(d) equivalent to total number of integral solution of *abc* = 343

Solution: (*b, c*) For the integral solution of abc = 105 we, write 105 = 3 × 5 × 7 ⇒ abc = 3 × 5 × 7

1. Positive integral solution

= no. of ways of allotment of 3, 5, 7 among 3 distinct groups = 3 x 3 x 3 = 27

2. Negative integral solution

= No. of positive x no of ways of allotment of -ve sign to any one out of a,b,c or to all of them

$= 27\left[{}^3C_1 + {}^3C_3\right] = 27 \times [3+1] = 27 \times 4 = 108$

Total integral solution = 27 + 108 = 135.

26. Number of ways in which 15 identical coins can be put into 6 different bags, if no bag remains empty

(a) is co-efficient of x^{15} in $x^6\ (1+x+x^2+......\infty)^6$

(b) is coefficient of x^9 in $(1-x)^{-6}$

(c) is same as number of positive integral solutions of $a+b+c+d+e+f=15$

(d) is same as number of non-negative integral solutions of $\sum_{i=1}^{6} x_i = 15$

Solution: (a), (b), (d)

No. of ways of distributing 15 identical coin into 6 different bags.

$\Rightarrow\ B_1 + B_2 + B_3 + B_4 + B_5 + B_6 = 15;$

where $B_i \geq 0\ \ \forall i \in \{1,2,3,4,5,6\}$

coeff. of x^{15} in $\left(x^0 + x^1 + x^2 + ...\infty\right)^6$ if any bag can have any number of coin.

coeff. of x^{15} in $\left(x^1 + x^2 + ...\infty\right)^6$ if no bag remain empty.

27. The number of seven digit integers, with sum of the digits equal to 10 and formed by using the digits 1, 2 and 3 only, is

(a) 55 (b) 66

(c) 77 (d) 88

Solution: (c) There are two possible cases:

Case I Five 1's, one 2's, one 3's

Number of numbers = $\dfrac{7!}{5!} = 42$

Case II Four 1's, three 2's

Number of numbers = $\dfrac{7!}{4!3!} = 35$

Total number of numbers = 42 + 35 = 77.

28. If $P(n, r) = 1680$ and $C(n, r) = 70$, then $69n + r!$ is equal to

(a) 128 (b) 576

(c) 256 (d) 625

Solution: $\because\ {}^nP_r = 1680$

$$\Rightarrow \frac{n!}{(n-r)!} = 1680 \qquad \text{(i)}$$

and ${}^nC_r = 70$

$$\Rightarrow \frac{n!}{(n-r)!r!} = 70 \qquad \text{(ii)}$$

From equations (i) and (ii), we get

$$r! = \frac{1680}{70} = 24 = 4! \Rightarrow r = 4$$

On putting the value of r in equation (i), we get

$$\frac{n!}{(n-4)!} = 1680$$

$\Rightarrow n(n-1)(n-2)(n-3) = 1680$

$\Rightarrow n(n-1)(n-2)(n-3) = 8(8-1)(8-2)(8-3)$

$\Rightarrow$ n = 8

$\therefore\ \ 69n + r! = 69 \times 8 + 24 = 576$

29. A crew of an eight oar boat has to be chosen out of 11 men, five of whom can row on stroke side only, four on the bow side only, and the remaining two on either side. How many different selections can be made?

(a) 145 (b) 146

(c) 147 (d) 148

Solution: (a)

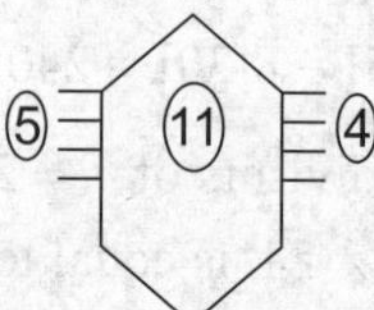

Total – when all 5 of stroker are selected.

$= {}^{11}C_8 - ({}^5C_5 \cdot {}^6C_3) = 165 - 20 = 145$

30. In how many ways can a team of 6 horses be selected out of a stud of 16, so that there shall always be 3 out of ABCA'B'C', but never AA', BB' or CC' together?

(a) 496 (b) 960

(c) 1024 (d) None of these

Solution: (b) ${}^{10}C_3 \times 8$ (corresponding to A four and A' also 4) total = 120 × 8 = 960

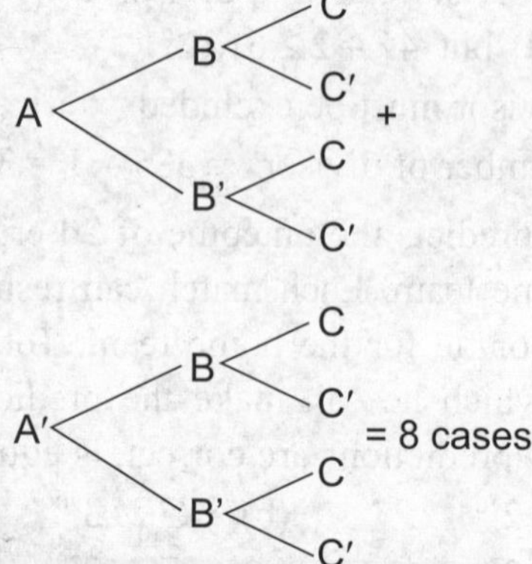

31. During a draw of lottery, tickets bearing numbers 1, 2, 3,.....,40, 6 tickets are drawn out and then arranged in the descending order of their numbers. In how many ways, it is possible to have 4th ticket bearing number 25?

(a) ${}^{15}C_3 \times {}^{24}C_2$ (b) ${}^{12}C_3 \times {}^{20}C_2$

(c) ${}^{15}C_3 + {}^{24}C_2$ (d) None of these

Solution: (a) Arrangement does not matter because of descending order there should be only one arrangement

∴ Required number of ways = ${}^{15}C_3 \times {}^{24}C_2$

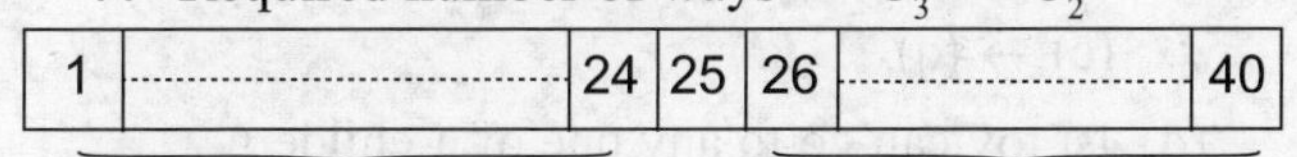

Selecting any 2 out of 1 to 24 = ${}^{24}C_2$ Selecting any 3 from 26 to 40 = ${}^{15}C_3$

32. Find the number of distinct natural numbers upto a maximum of 4 digits and divisible by 5, which can be formed with the digits 0, 1, 2, 3, 4, 5, 6, 7, 8, 9 each digit not occuring more than once in each number.

(a) 1100 (b) 1106

(c) 1050 (d) None of these

Solution: (b) A number *abcde* to be divisible by 5; e = 0 or 5

⇒ number of one digit natural number = 1 i.e., 5,

number of two digit natural number = 9 + 8 = 17

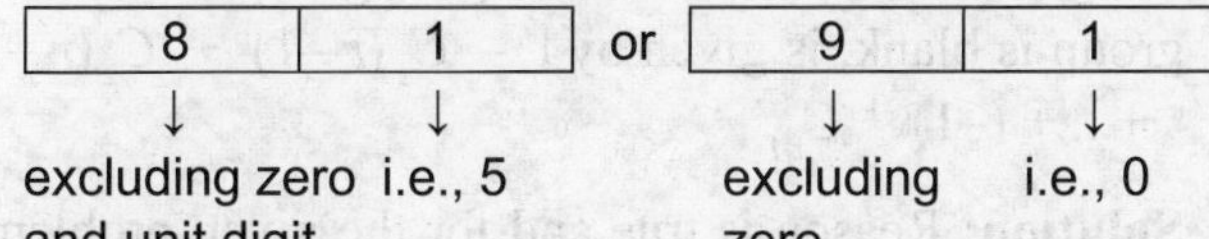

number of three digit natural number = 64 + 72 = 136

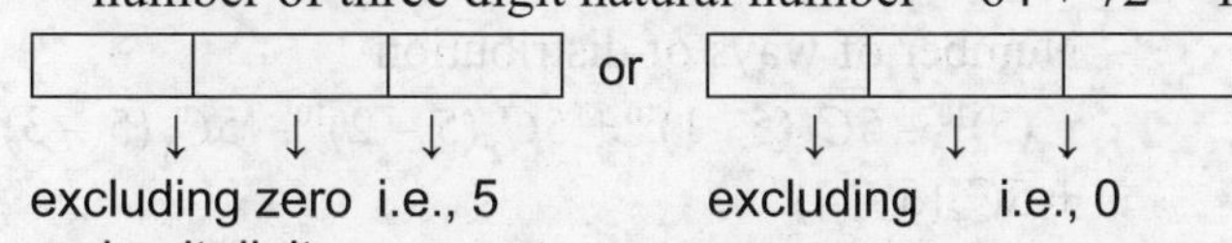

number of four digit natural number = 448 + 504 = 952

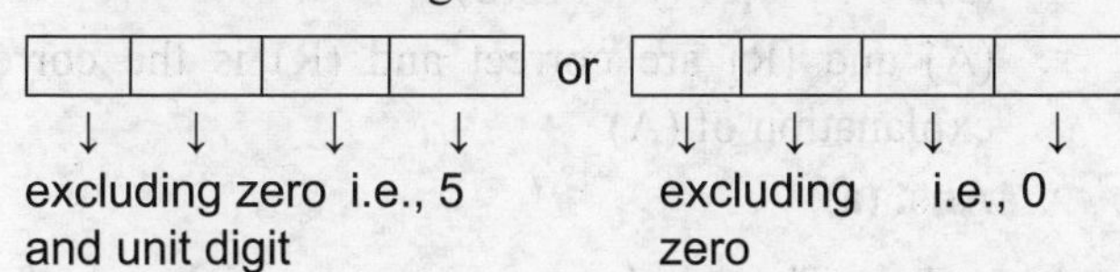

∴ Total numbers of number = 1 + 17 + 136 + 952 = 1106

33. Let T_n denote the number of triangles which can be formed using the vertices of regular polygon of '*n*' sides. If $T_{n+1} - T_n = 21$, then '*n*' equals:

(a) 5 (b) 7

(c) 6 (d) 4

Solution: $T_n = {}^nC_3$

$\Rightarrow T_{n-1} - T_n = {}^{n+1}C_3 - {}^nC_3 = 21$

$$\Rightarrow \frac{(n+1)\,(n)\,(n-1)}{1.2.3} - \frac{n(n-1)\,(n-2)}{1.2.3} = 21$$

$\Rightarrow n(n-1)\,[n+1-n+2] = 126 \Rightarrow 7$

Comprehension Passage

A: In a meeting of P.M.'s of 24 nations, 3 round tables are there which can accommodate 7, 8 and 9 persons respectively. Then answer the following questions:

34. The number of ways in which the P.M.'s can sit in the meeting

(a) $\frac{24!}{7!8!9!}$ (b) $\frac{24!\times 6!}{9!}$

(c) 24! × 6! × 7! × 8! (d) None of these

Solution: (b) For first round table 7 PM's can be selected out of 24 in ${}^{24}C_7$ ways

Now for second round table 8 PM's can be selected in ${}^{17}C_8$ ways and for third round table 9 PM's can be selection ${}^9C_9$ ways

∴ Number of ways of dividing 24 PM's into three groups

$${}^{24}C_7 \times {}^{17}C_8 \times {}^9C_9 = \frac{24!}{7!\,17!} \times \frac{17!}{8!\,9!} \times 1 = \frac{24!}{7!8!9!}$$

⇒ Number of arrangements of 24 PM's around 3 round tables

$$= \frac{24!}{7!8!9!} \times (6)! \times (7)! \times (8)! = \frac{24! \times 6!}{9!}$$

35. If PM's of India and Pakistan wants to sit on table I and adjacent to each other, then the number of ways of sitting will be

(a) $\frac{24!}{36}$ (b) $\frac{22!}{72}$

(c) $\frac{22!}{6!}$ (d) None of these

Solution: (a) Let us consider the PM's of India and Pakistan always together, when they sit on table 1, then number of ways ${}^{22}C_5 \times {}^{17}C_8 \times {}^9C_9 \times 5! \times 2! \times 7! \times 8!$

$$= \frac{22!}{5!17!} \times \frac{17!}{8!9!} \times 5! \times 2! \times 7! \times 8!$$

$$= \frac{22! \times 2! \times 7!}{9!} = \frac{22! \times 2}{72} = \frac{22!}{36}$$

36. If PM of India wants to sit on table 1 and PM of Pakistan wants to sit on table 3, the the number of ways will be

(a) $\frac{22!}{8}$ (b) $\frac{24!}{8}$

(c) $\frac{22!}{6!7!8!}$ (d) None of these

Solution: (a) If PM of India sits on take 1 and PM of Pakistan sits on table 2, then number of ways ${}^{22}C_6 \times {}^{16}C_8 \times {}^8C_8 \times 6! \times 7! \times 8!$

$$= \frac{22!}{6!16!} \times \frac{16!}{8!8!} \times 6! \times 7! \times 8! = \frac{22! \times 7!}{8!} = \frac{22!}{8}$$

Column Matching

37. **Column-A**

(a) Number of increasing permutations of m numbers from the set of n numbers $\{a_1, a_2, a_3,.., a_{n-1}, a_r\}$ is

(b) There are m-men and n-monkeys. Numbers of ways in which every monkey has a master if a man can have any number of monkeys is

(c) Number of ways in which n- red balls and $(m-1)$ black balls can be arranged in a line, so that no two red balls are together $(n \le m-1)$ (balls of same colour are alike).

(d) Number of ways in which m-different toys can be distributed in n-children if every child may receive any number of toys.

Column-B

(p) n^m

(q) ${}^mC_n$

(r) ${}^nC_m$

(s) m^n

Solution: Let us select any 'm' numbers out of given n- numbers $a_1, a_2, a_3......a_n$

This can be done in ${}^nC_m$ ways

Now corresponding to each selection, there is a unique increasing sequence.

∴ Number of increasing sequence of m-numbers $= {}^nC_m$

∴ (a) → (r)

(b) 1st monkey has m choices

IInd monkey has m choices

.

.

n^{th} monkey has m choices

∴ Total number of ways $= m \times m \times m \times .... \times m$ (n-terms) $= (m)^n$

∴ (b) → (s)

(c) 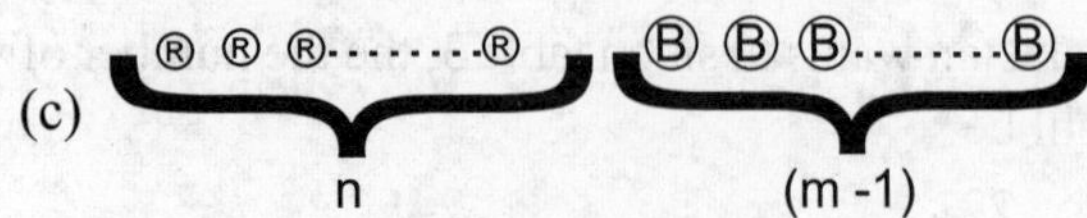

Here $n \le (m-1)$

Let us first of all arrange $(m-1)$ black balls in a row, which can be done in 1 way as shown below (as balls of same color are identical).

X Ⓑ X Ⓑ X Ⓑ.............. X Ⓑ X

we are left with 'm' spaces in between the black balls.

Now, if we place red balls in places marked with X, then no two red balls will be together, and this can be done in ${}^mC_n$ ways

∴ (c) → (q)

(d) Ist toy can go to any one of n-childern

IInd toy can go to any one of n-chlidern

and so on, i.e., every toy out of (m) have n choices

∴ Total no of ways $= n \times n \times n \times ..... \times n$ (m– factors) $= (n)^m$.

∴ Ans (d) → (p)

Assertion Reason Type

38. **Assertion:** The number of ways in which 10 different toys can be given to 5 chlidern so that every child gets at least one toys is $[5^{10} + 10(3)^{10} + 5] - [5(4)^{10} + 10(2)^{10}]$

Reason: The number of ways in which n – different things can be distributed among r – groups, So, that no group is blank, is given by $r^n - {}^rC_1(r-1)^n + {}^rC_2(r-2)^n + ... + (-1)^{r-1}\,{}^rC_{r-1}$

Solution: Reason is true and for the given problem $r = 5$ and $n = 10$

∴ Number of ways of distribution

$= (5)^{10} - 5C_1(5-1)^{10} + 5C_2(5-2)^{10} - 5C_3(5-3)^{10} + 5C_4(5-4)^{10}$

$= 5^{10} - 5(4)^{10} + 10(3)^{10} - 10(2)^{10} + 5 = [5^{10} + 10(3)^{10} + 5] - [5(4)^{10} + 10(2)^{10}]$

∴ (A) and (R) are correct and (R) is the correct explanation of (A)

∴ **Ans.** (a)

39. **Assertion:** The number of ways in which out of 10 letters goes to correct envelopes and 3 goes to in correct envelopes is 280. (given that exactly one letter goes in each of 10 envelopes)

Reason: The number ways in which $(n-r)$ things go to original places and r things go to wrong places is given by ${}^nC_{n-r} D_r$ where

$$D_r = r!\left(1 - \frac{1}{1!} + \frac{1}{2!} - \frac{1}{3!} + ... + (-1)^r \frac{1}{r!}\right)$$

Solution: Reason is correct as, $(n-r)$ things going to original places can be selected in ${}^nC_{n-r}$ ways. Now the remaining r things go to wrong places in $r!\left(1 - \frac{1}{1!} + \frac{1}{2!} - \frac{1}{3!} + ... + (-1)^r \frac{1}{r!}\right) = D_r$ ways.

∴ Total no of ways $= {}^nC_{n-r} \times D_r$

Out of 10 letters the number of selections of 7 letters, which go to correct envelopes $= 10C_7$

Now, 3 letters which go to incorrect envelopes can be put in

$$3!\left(1-\frac{1}{1!}+\frac{1}{2!}-\frac{1}{3!}\right)=3!\left(\frac{1}{2}-\frac{1}{6}\right)=6\left(\frac{3-1}{6}\right)=2$$

∴ Total no of ways $= {}^{10}C_7 \times 2$

$$=\frac{10!}{7!(3)!}\times 2=\frac{10\times 9\times 8\times 2}{6}=240$$

∴ Assertion is incorrect by reason is correct

∴ **Ans.** (d)

40. Assertion: The sum of the numbers formed by using the digits 2, 4, 6, 7, 9 without repetition is $\frac{(10^5-1)(4!)(28)}{9}$

Reason: The sum of the numbers formed by using the digits $d_1, d_2, d_3, \ldots, d_n$ without repetition $= n!\left(\sum_{i=1}^{n} d_i\right)\left[\frac{10^n-1}{9}\right]$

Solution: We know that sum of the numbers formed by using the digits $d_1, d_2, d_3, \ldots, d_n$ is

$$=(n-1)!\left(\sum_{i=1}^{n} d_i\right)\left[\frac{10^n-1}{9}\right]$$

∴ Reason is incorrect

∴ If $d_1 = 2, d_2 = 4, d_3 = 6, d_4 = 7, d_5 = 9$, then required sum is

$$\left(\frac{(10)^5-1}{9}\right)(4!)[2+4+6+7+9]=\frac{(10^5-1)(4!)(28)}{9}$$

∴ Assertion is correct.

∴ **Ans.** (c)

41. Assertion: The number of 4 letters words that can be formed by using the letters of the word PARALLEL is 286.

Reason: The number of ways of permutations of r things out of n things of which 'p' things are of one kind, q things are of second kind and so on.

= coefficient of x^r in

$$r!\left(1+\frac{x}{1!}+\frac{x^2}{2!}+\ldots+\frac{x^p}{p!}\right)\left(1+\frac{x}{1!}+\frac{x^2}{2!}+\ldots+\frac{x^q}{q!}\right)\ldots$$

Solution: Reason is correct. In the given problem $r = 4$ and $n = 8$ and P occurs 1 times, A occurs 2 times, R occurs 1 times, L occurs 3 times and E occurs 1 times.

∴ Total number of 4 letters words that can be formed

= Coefficient of x^4 in

$$4!\left(1+\frac{x}{1!}\right)\left(1+\frac{x}{1!}\right)\left(1+\frac{x}{1!}\right)\left(1+\frac{x}{1!}+\frac{x^2}{2!}\right)\left(1+\frac{x}{1!}+\frac{x^2}{2!}+\frac{x^3}{3!}\right)$$

= Coefficient of x^4 in

$$4!(1+x)^3\left(1+x+\frac{x^2}{2}\right)\left(1+x+\frac{x^2}{2}+\frac{x^3}{6}\right)$$

= Coefficient of x^4 in

$$4!\left(1+x^3+3x+3x^2\right)\left[\left(1+x+\frac{x^2}{2}\right)^2+\left(1+x+\frac{x^2}{2}\right)\frac{x^3}{6}\right]$$

= Coefficient of x^4 in 4! $[1 + x^3 + 3x^2 + 3x]$

$$\left[1+x^2+\frac{x^4}{4}+2x+x^3+x^2+\frac{x^3}{6}+\frac{x^4}{6}+\frac{x^5}{12}\right]$$

= Coefficient of x^4 in

$$4!\left[\frac{1}{4}x^4+\frac{1}{6}x^4+2x^4+3x^4+3x^4+3x^4+\frac{1}{2}\right]$$

$$=4!\left(\frac{1}{4}+\frac{1}{6}+\frac{1}{2}+11\right)=286$$

∴ Both assertion and reason are correct.

∴ **Ans.** (a)

SECTION–II

SUBJECTIVE-TYPE SOLVED EXAMPLES

1. Consider a set $A = \{(x, y): x, y \in \{1, 2, 3, \ldots, 70\}$. Then find the number of elements of A i.e., (x, y) such that at least one of x, y is divisible by 3.

Solution: $n(A) = {}^{70}C_2$

Number from 1 to 70, which are multiples of 3 are 3, 6, 9, 12,.......,69 which are 23

∴ Number of numbers from 1 to 70, which are not multiples of 3 = 70 – 23 = 47

∴ Number of elements of A having both numbers not multiples of 3 = ${}^{47}C_2$

∴ Number of elements of A having at least one number multiple of 3 = ${}^{70}C_2 - {}^{47}C_2$

$$=\frac{70\times 69}{2}-\frac{47\times 46}{2}=(35\times 69-47\times 23)$$

= 23 [35 × 3 – 47] = 23 × 58 = 1334

2. How many triangles can be constructed by connecting the vertices of an octagon, so that the Δ's have at the most one side common with octagon?

Solution: Total number of Δ's that can be constructed $= {}^8C_3 = 56$ out of which, there can be drawn 8 TRIANGLES having two sides common with octagon as shown below:

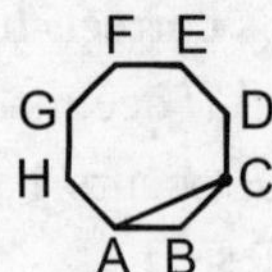

∴ Reqd. Δ's = 56 – 8 = 48

3. How many integers between 10^2 and 10^4 having the sum of their digits equal to 14?

Solution: Let us first of all find the number of digits between 0 and 10^4 having sum of their digits 14.

These numbers have 4 digits say x_1, x_2, x_3, x_4, then x_1, x_2, x_3, x_4 are integers and $0 \le x_i \le 9 \ \forall \ i$. The number of such numbers

= Coefficient of x^{14} in $(1 + x + x^2 + x^3 + ...x^9)^4$

= Coefficient of x^{14} in $\left[\dfrac{1-x^{10}}{1-x}\right]^4$

= Coefficient of x^{14} in $(1 - x^{10})^4 (1 - x)^{-4}$

= coefficient of x^{14} in

$[1 - {}^4C_1x^{10} + {}^4C_2x^{20} - {}^4C_3x^{30} + {}^4C_4x^{40}]$

$\times (1 + {}^4C_1x + {}^5C_2x^2 + {}^6C_3x^3 + ...)$

$= {}^{17}C_{14} - {}^4C_{1.}\ {}^7C_4 = {}^{17}C_3 - 4.({}^7C_3)$

$= \dfrac{17\times16\times15}{3\times2\times1} - \dfrac{4\times7\times6\times5}{3\times2\times1} = 680 - 140 = 540$

Also the numbers less than or equal to 10^2 having sum of their digits 14 are 59, 68, 77, 86, 95 which are 5

∴ The required number of numbers = 540 – 5 = 535

4. Given a matrix $A = [a_{ij}]_{3\times3}$; $a_{ij} \in \{0, 1, 2, 3\}$. Find the number of such matrices A in which the sum of digits of each Row/Column remain divisible by 4.

Solution: Total number of 3 × 3 matrices formed using $a_{ij} \in \{0, 1, 2, 3\} = 4^9$

a_{11}	a_{12}	a_{13}
a_{21}	a_{22}	a_{23}
a_{31}	a_{32}	a_{33}

⇒ $a_{11} + a_{12} + a_{13} \in \{0, 4, 8\}$

⇒ elements in any row/column can be (0, 0, 0); (0, 1, 3); (0, 2, 2); (1, 1, 2); (2, 3, 3) and all their permutations.

Let $\sum a_1 \quad 4n_1,\ \sum_{k=1}^{3} a_{k1} = 4m_1$

$\sum_{k=1}^{3} a_{2k} = 4n_2,\ \sum a\ _2 \quad m_2$

$\sum_{k=1}^{3} a_{3k} = 4n_3,\ \sum_{k=1}^{3} a_{k3} = 4m_3$

For each way of choosing a_{11}; a_{12}; a_{21} and a_{22} can be chosen in 4 ways each i.e. number of ways of filling these places is 4 × 4 × 4 × 4 $= 4^4 = 256$ ways.

On the basis of above determined triplets.

∵ As a_{11} and a_{12} are chosen, a_{13} is determined automatically; a_{11} and a_{21} are chosen, a_{31} is determined automatically on the basis of above determined triplets and their permutation.

⇒ If $a_{11}, a_{12}, a_{21}, a_{22}$ are chosen independently then $a_{31}, a_{32}, a_{33}, a_{13}, a_{23}$ are determined automatically.

5. (a) There are five points in a plane such that line joining no two of these are parallel, perpendicular or coincident. From each point perpendiculars are drawn to all the lines joining other four points (taken 2 at a time). Find the total number of points of intersection.

Solution: No of lines through $A_2 A_3 A_4 A_5 = {}^4C_2$

From each of A_1, A_2, A_3, A_4, A_5 we can draw ${}^4C_2$ perpendiculars i.e., 6 perpendiculars each

⇒ Total number of perpendiculars = 30

⇒ Total number of points of intersection

$= {}^{30}C_2 = \dfrac{30\times29}{2} = 435$

∵ We have over-counted point of intersections of 6 concurrent perpendiculars from each point i.e., ${}^6C_2$ × 5 points

⇒ Points = 435 – 75 + 5 = 365

⊥ for 3 point to any one line are || so three such ⊥ for each line will not intersect.

⇒ ${}^3C_2$ of point of intersection were counted extra for each line.

⇒ ${}^5C_2\left({}^3C_2\right)$ number of points are to be subtracted i.e., 30 points.

Now, as we see, any three altitudes intersect at only one point (orthocentre) and not ${}^3C_2$ points.

⇒ $\left(10\times{}^3C_2 - 10\right)$ to be subtracted

⇒ Actual point of intersection = 365 – 30 – 30 + 10 = 315

6. Prove using the first principle that ${}^nP_r = (n - r + 1) \times {}^nP_{r-1}$ and hence deduce the value of ${}^nP_r$ as a product.

Solution: We know ${}^nP_r$ is the total number of permutations of n things taken r at a time. If we fill up $(r - 1)$ places by these n things, then number of permutations ${}^nP_{r-1}$ and the remaining $n - (r - 1)$ i.e., $(n - r + 1)$ things can be filled after $(r - 1)$ places.

∴ By the principle of multiplication, the total number of ways to fill the r places by n things.

$= (n - r + 1) \times {}^nP_{r-1}$

Hence, ${}^nP_r = (n - r + 1) \times {}^nP_{r-1}$ (i)

Hence, by replacing r by $r - 1, r - 2, r - 3, ..., 3, 2, 1$ successively in (i), we get

${}^nP_{r-1} = (n-r+2) \times {}^nP_{r-2}$

${}^nP_{r-2} = (n-r+3) \times {}^nP_{r-3}$

${}^nP_{r-3} = (n-r+4) \times {}^nP_{r-4}$

....

${}^nP_3 = (n-2) \times {}^nP_2$

${}^nP_2 = (n-1) \times {}^nP_1$

${}^nP_1 = n$

Multiplying the vertical columns together each side, we get

${}^nP_{r-1} . {}^nP_{r-2} . {}^nP_{r-3} .... {}^nP_3 . {}^nP_2 . {}^nP_1 =$

$n(n-1)(n-2)...(n-r+2)$

∴ ${}^nP_1 . {}^nP_2 . {}^nP_3 .... {}^nP_{r-r} . {}^nP_{r-3} . {}^nP_{r-2}$

∴ ${}^nP_{r-1} = n(n-1)(n-2)........(n-r+2)$

∴ from (i) we get ${}^nP_r = n(n - 1)(n - 2)....(n - r + 2)(n - r + 1)$.

7. In how many ways 3 boys and 15 girls can sit together in a row such that between any 2 boys at least 2 girls sit?

Solution: Let x_1 girls sit before first boy, x_2 girls between the first and second boy, x_3 girls between second and third boy and x_4 after the third boy.

Now number of ways in which we can choose the places for boys is same as the number of solution of the equation. $x_1 + x_2 + x_3 + x_4 = 15$

Subject to condition $x_1 \geq 0, x_2 \geq 2, x_3 \geq 2, x_4 \geq 0$

∴ Required number of ways = coefficient of x^{15} in

$(1+x+x^2+...)(x^2+x^3+...)(x^2+x^3+...)$

$(1+x+x^2+...)$

$=$ coefficient of x^{11} in $(1 - x)^{-4} = {}^{4+11-1}C_{4-1} = {}^{14}C_3$

Now 3 boys can be permuted in their places in 3! ways and 15 girls can be permuted in 15! ways. So required number of ways $= {}^{14}C_3$ (3!) (15!).

8. In how many ways can a mixed doubles game in tennis be arranged from 5 married couples, if no husband and wife play in the same game?

Solution: Now let sides of game be A and B. Given 5 married couples, i.e., 5 husbands and 5 wives. Now 2 husbands for two sides A and B be selected out of $5 = {}^5C_2 = 10$ ways.

After choosing the two husbands their wives are to be excluded (since, no husband and wife play in the same game). So, we are to choose 2 wives out of remaining $5 - 2 = 3$ wives i.e., ${}^3C_2 = 3$ ways

Again two wives can interchange their sides A and B in $2! = 2$ ways.

∴ By the principle of multiplication, the required number of ways $= 10 \times 3 \times 2 = 60$.

9. There are p intermediate stations on a railway line from one terminus to another. In how many ways a train can stop at 3 of these intermediate stations if number of two of these stopping stations are to be consecutive?

Solution: Let there be p intermediate stations between two terminus stations A and B as shown below.

$S_1 \; S_2 \; S_3 .... S_p$

A ● ● ● ● ● ● B

No. of ways the train can stop in three intermediate stations $= {}^pC_3$

These are comprised of two exclusive cases viz.,

(i) At least two stations are consecutive.

(ii) Now two of which is consecutive.

No there are $(p - 1)$ pairs of consecutive intermediate stations.

In order to get a station trio in whch at least two stations are consecutive, each pair can be associated with a third station in $(p - 2)$ ways. Hence, total number ways in which 3 stations consisting of least two consecutive stations can be chosen in $(p - 1)(p - 2)$ ways. The number of three consecutive stations trio should be subtracted.

Now, no. of these three consecutive stations trio $(p - 2)$.

Hence, the number of ways the triplet of stations consisting of at least two consecutive stations can be chosen in

$= \{(p - 1)(p - 2) - (p - 2)\}$ ways $= (p - 2)^2$ ways

Hence, the number of ways the train can stop in three consecutive stations is

$$= {}^pC_3 - (p - 2)^2 = \frac{p(p-1)(p-2)}{1.2.3} - (p-2)^2$$

$$= (p-2)\left[\frac{p^2 - p - 6p + 12}{6}\right]$$

$$= \frac{(p-2)(p-3)(p-4)}{1.2.3} = {}^{(p-2)}C_3.$$

10. Find the number of ways of distribution of 12 identical balls in three identical boxes.

Solution: Let number of balls inside the boxes are a, b and c

So, $a + b + c = 12, a \geq 0, b \geq 0, c \geq 0$ (1)

Since boxes are identical so number of ways will not be equal to the number of solutions of (1) as 1 + 3 + 8 and 3 + 8 + 1 are two different solutions of (1) but this will give the same distribution.

To avoid the duplication, we do as follows:

Total number of solutions of (1) is coefficient of t^{12} in $(1 - t)^{-3} = {}^{14}C_2 = 91$

Now in 91, we have three types of solutions:

(1) All a, b, c are same. Corresponding to this, we have one distribution.

(2) Exactly two are same. We have 6 × 3 = 18 solutions and

(3) All are different. We have 91 – (1 + 18) = 72 solutions and corresponding to these, we have 72/6 = 12 distributions.

So number of total distributions is 1 + 6 + 12 = 19.

11. There are 15 seats in a row numbered as 1 to 15. In how many ways 4 persons can sit such that seat number 6 is always occupied if no two persons sit in adjacent seats.

Solution: Since seat number '6' is always occupied remaining 3 can sit in the following ways:

Case - I: 2 left to 6 and 1 right to 6.

Two can sit in the ways.

(1, 3) or (1, 4) or (2, 4) and one who is sitting right to 6 can sit in the 8 ways. Hence total number of ways in this case = 3 × 8 = 24.

Case - II: 1 left to 6 and 2 right to 6

The person sitting left can sit in 4 ways.

Number of ways in which two person can sit right to 6 is same as number of integral solution of $x_1 + x_2 + x_3 = 7, x_1 \geq 1, x_2 \geq 1, x_3 \geq 0$

i.e., coefficient of t^5 in $(1 - t)^{-3} = {}^{5+3-1}C_{3-1} = {}^7C_2 = 21$

Hence total number of ways = 21 × 4 = 84 ways.

Case - III: No one sits left to 6 and 3 sit right to 6.

Number of ways = number of solution to $x_1 + x_2 + x_3 + x_4 = 6 (x_1 \geq 1, x_2 > 1, x_3 \geq 1, x_4 \geq 0)$

= coefficient of t^3 in $(1 - t)^{-4} = {}^{4+3-1}C_{4-1} = {}^6C_3 = 20$

Hence total number of ways in this case = 20

Hence number of ways of selection of seats = 24 + 84 + 20 = 128

Total number of ways of arrangement of 4 person on these seats = 128 × 4! = 3072.

12. In an examination, the maximum marks for each of the three papers is 50. Maximum marks for the fourth paper is 100. Find the number of ways in which the candidate can score 60% marks in the aggregate.

Solution: Aggregate of marks 50 ×3 + 100 = 250

$\therefore$ 60% of the aggregate $= \frac{3}{5} \times 250 = 150$

Now the number of ways of getting 150 marks in the aggregate

= coefficient of x^{150} in $(x^0 + x^1 + ...+ x^{50})^3 (x^0 + x^1 + x^2 +....+ x^{100})$

$= \text{coeff. of } x^{150} \text{ in } \left(\frac{1-x^{51}}{1-x}\right)^3 \left(\frac{1-x^{101}}{1-x}\right)$

= coeff. of in x^{150} in $(1 - x^{51})^3 (1 - x^{101}) (1 - x)^{-4}$

= coeff. of x^{150} in $(1 - 3x^{51} + 3.x^{102} - x^{153}) (1 - x^{101}) (1 - x)^{-4}$

= coeff. of x^{150} in $(1 - 3.x^{51} - x^{101} + 3.x^{102} + 3x^{152} + ...\infty) \times (1 + 4x + ... + {}^{(r+3)}C_r x^r)$

$$= 1.\frac{151.152.153}{6} - 3\frac{100.101.102}{6} - 1$$

$$= \frac{50.51.52}{6} + 3.\frac{49.50.51}{6} = 110551$$

13. You are given the responsiblity of organizing a freshers welcome party at IIT-Delhi. Total 496 students will join IIT-D. Six restaurants A, B, C, D, E and F are booked. Capacity of each is 120, 146, 46, 72, 72, 80 persons at a time respectively. You have to group them in such a way that each group has least possible number of students. How would you do so?

Solution: We know that equal division minimizes the number of students in each group.

But: $\frac{496}{6} = 82.6 > 46$

$\therefore$ C has least capacity of 46 and is not capable to accommodate 82 students. Hence let us group for it first i.e., 46 students get accommodated.

Student left	Restaurant left
450	$A\ B\ D\ E$ and F

But 450/5 = 90 > 72

Next D and E each require smallest group 72, 72

D → 72 E → 72

Students left Restaurant left

306 *A B* and *F*

Now 306/3 = 102 > 80

Next *F* is least left for grouping, so assigning 80 to F.

Students left Restaurant left

226 A and B

Now therefore $\frac{226}{2}$ =113 < 120 and each of A and *B* is capable of accommodating to this.

Hence A → 113

or B → 113

Hence we grouped 496 students into 46, 72, 72, 80, 113 and 113 each.

$$\text{No. of ways of doing so} = \frac{496!}{46!(72!)^2.2!80!(113!)^2.2!}$$

14. In how many ways can (2*t* + 1) identical balls be placed in 3 distinct boxes so that any two boxes together will contain more balls than the third.

Solution: Since, any two boxes together should contain more balls than the third, any box should contain a maximum of *t* balls.

Let x_1, x_2, x_3 be the no. of balls contained in the three boxes.

Then, $x_1 + x_2 + x_3 = 2t + 1$

and $0 \le x_1, x_2, x_3 \le t$

$= \text{coeff of } x^{2t+1} \text{ in } (x^0 + x^1 + x^2 + \ldots\ldots\ldots.x^t)^3$

$= \text{coeff of } x^{2t+1} \text{ in } (1 - x^{t+1})^3 (1 - x)^{-3}$

$= \text{coeff of } x^{2t+1}$ in

$(1 - 3x^{t+1})(1 + {}^3C_1 x + {}^4C_2 x^2 + \ldots\ldots\ldots {}^{t+2}C_t x^t + \ldots\ldots {}^{2t+3}C_{2t+1} x^{2t+1} + \ldots\ldots\ldots)$

{Powers > 2*t* +1 are ignored}

$= {}^{2t+3}C_{2t+1} - 3\ {}^{t+2}C_t = {}^{2t+3}C_2 - 3\ {}^{t+2}C_2$

$= \frac{(2t+3)(2t+2)}{2} - \frac{3.(t+2)(t+1)}{2}$

$= \frac{t^2 + t}{2} = \frac{t}{2}(t+1)$

15. How many integral solutions are there to the system of equations $x_1 + x_2 + x_3 + x_4 + x_5 = 20$ and $x_1 + x_2 = 15$ when $x_k \ge 0$?

Solution: We have $x_1 + x_2 + x_3 + x_4 + x_5 = 20$ (i)

$x_1 + x_2 = 15$ (ii)

from (i) and (ii), we get $x_3 + x_4 + x_5 = 5$ (iii)

$x_1 + x_2 = 15$ (iv)

and given $x_1 \ge 0, x_2 \ge 0, x_3 \ge 0, x_4 \ge 0$ and $x_5 \ge 0$

Then number of solutions of equation (iii) $= {}^{5+3-1}C_{3-1}$

$= {}^7C_2 = \frac{7.6}{1.2} = 21$

Then number of solutions of equation (iv) $= {}^{15+2-1}C_{2-1}$

$= {}^{16}C_1 = 16$

Hence total number of solutions of the given system of equations = 21 × 16 = 336

16. Find the number of non-negative integral solutions of $3x + y + z = 24$.

Solution: We have $3x + y + z = 24$ and given $x \ge 0$, $y \ge 0, z \ge 0$

let $x = k$

$\therefore\ y + z = 24 - 3k$ (i)

Here $24 \ge 24 - 3k \ge 0$ ($\because x \ge 0$)

Hence $0 \le k \le 8$

The total number of integral solution of (i) is ${}^{24-3k+2-1}C_{2-1} = {}^{25-3k}C_1 = 25 - 3k$

∴ Total number of non-negative integers solutions=

$$\sum_{k=0}^{8}(25 - 3k) = 25\sum_{k=0}^{8}1 - 3\sum_{k=0}^{8}k$$

$= 25.\ 9.- 3\ .\ \frac{8.9}{2} = 225 - 108 = 117$

17. There are 2*n* guests at a dinner party. Supposing that the master and mistress of the house have fixed seats opposite one another, and that there are two specified guests who must not be placed next to one another, find the number of ways in which the company can be placed.

Solution: Let the *M* and *M*′ represent seats of the master and mistress respectively, and let $a_1, a_2, a_3, a_3, a_4, \ldots\ldots, a_{2n}$ represent the 2*n* seats

Let the guests not be placed next to one another be called *P* and Q.

Put *P* at a_1 and *Q* at any place, other than a_2, say at a_3, then remaining 2*n* – 2 guests can be arranged in the remaining (2*n* – 2) positions in (2*n* – 2) ! ways. Hence there will be altogether (2*n* – 2) (2*n* – 2)! arrangements of the guests when *P* is at a_1.

The same number of arrangements when *P* is at a_n or a_{n+1} or a_{2n}. Hence for these positions $(a_1, a_n, a_{n+1}, a_{2n})$ of *P* there are altogether 4(2*n* – 2) (2*n* – 2) ! ways (i)

If *P* is at a_2 there are altogether (2*n* – 3) positions for *Q*, hence there will be altogether (2*n* – 3) (2*n* – 2)! arrangements of the guests when *P* is at a_2. The same number of arrangements can be made when *P* is at any other position excepting the four positions a_1, a_n, a_{n+1}, a_{2n}

Hence for these $(2n-4)$ positions of P there will be altogether $(2n-4)(2n-3)(2n-2)!$ arrangements of the guests. (ii)

Hence from (i) and (ii), the total number of ways of arranging the guests

$= 4(2n-2)(2n-2)! + (2n-4)(2n-3)(2n-2)!$

$= (4n^2 - 6n + 4)(2n-2)!$

18. Show that if $a_1, a_2, ..., a_m$ are distinct prime numbers, the number of solutions in integers of the equation $x_1 x_2 x_3 .... x_n = a_1 a_2 a_3 ....a_n$ is n^m. Show also that the number of solutions in which at least one x is unity is ${}^nC_1(n-1)^m \times {}^nC_2(n-2)^m + ... + (-1)^{n-1}\,{}^nC_{n-1} \cdot 1^m$

Solution: $x_1 x_2 x_3 ....x_n = a_1 a_2 a_3 ....a_m$

Number of positive integral solutions of the above equation = number of ways in which we can distribute m distinct balls in n distinct boxes (where order is not consider inside the boxes)

Note that here boxes are representing $x_1, x_2, x_3, ...x_n$ and balls are representing $a_1, a_2, a_3, ...a_m$. If in any box say in x_i there is no ball, then we are assuming that the value of x_i is 1 and if in any box say x_j there is three balls say a_1, a_5, a_7, then the value of x_j is $a_1.a_5.a_7$.

Now number of ways to distribute the ball a_1 is n. (since there are n boxes)

Similarly, number of ways to distribute the ball a_2 is n.

Number of ways to distribute the ball a_m is n.

Hence total number of ways is n^m

We know that the number of ways to distribute m balls in n boxes so that none of the box remain blank is

$n^m - {}^nC_1(n-1)^m + {}^nC_2(n-2)^m - {}^nC_3(n-3)^m + .. (-1)^{n-1}\,{}^nC_{n-1}(1)^m$

= Number of solutions in which atleast one one x_i's is unity

$= n^m - \{n^m - {}^nC_1(n-1)^m + {}^nC_2(n-2)^m - {}^nC_3(n-3)^m + ... (-1)^{n-1}\,{}^nC_{n-1}(1)^m\} = {}^nC_1(n-1)^m - {}^nC_2(n-2)^m + ...+ (-1)^{n-1}.{}^nC_{n-1}(1)$

19. How many integers between 1 and 1000000 have the sum of their digits equal to 18?

Solution: We must count the number of solutions of

$x_1 + x_2 + ..+ x_6 = 18$ (i)

satisfying $0 \le x_i \le 9$, $i \in \{1, 2, ..., 6\}$. The number of solutions of (i)

= coefficient of x^{18} in $(1 + x + x^2 + ... + x^9)^6$

= coefficient of x^{18} in $(1 - x^{10})^6 (1 - x)^{-6}$

$= {}^{23}C_{18} - 6.{}^{13}C_8 = \dfrac{23!}{18!\,5!} - 6\dfrac{13!}{8!\,5!}$

$= 33649 - (6)(1287) = 25927$

20. Find the number of natural numbers which are smaller than 2.10^8 and are divisible by 3 and which can be written by means of the digits 0, 1 and 2.

Solution: A natural number which is smaller than 2.10^8 and which can be written by means of the digits 0, 1 and 2 is of the form $\overline{a_1 a_2 a_3 ....a_9}$; where $0 \le a_1 \le 1$ and $0 \le a_i \le 2$ where $i = 2,3,....,9$ and where all $a_1, a_2, ..., a_9$ cannot be equal to zero.

We can choose a_i in two ways (0 or 1) and a_i for i = 2, 3, ...8 in three ways (0, 1 or 2). After choosing a_1, a_2, ...a_8 we find the sum $s = a_1 + a_2 + ... + a_8$ is of the form $3m$ -2, $3m$ -1 or $3m$. We can now choose a_9 in just one way. In fact a_9 = 2, 1 or 0 depending on whether $s = 3m - 2$, $3m - 1$ or $3m$. Therefore, we can choose the number in $(2)(3)^7(1)$ ways. But this includes a choice in which each of $a_i = 0$. Thus, the required number of numbers $= (2)(3)^7 - (1) = 4373$

21. How many different 7 digit numbers are there sum of whose digits is even?

Solution: Let us consider the seven digit numbers as $\overline{a_1 a_2 a_3 a_4 a_5 a_6 a_7}$

The first digit a_1 can assume 9 different values and each of the digits a_2, a_3, a_4, a_5, a_6 can assume 10 different values.

The last digit a_7 can assume only 5 different values of which the sum of all digits is even (if sum of $a_1, a_2, a_3, ..., a_6$ is odd, then a_7 is odd and if sum is even, then a_7 is even).

∴ There are $9 \times 10^5 \times 5 = 4500000$

22. In a certain test, there are n questions. In this test, 2^{n-i} students gave wrong answers to at least i questions where i = 1,2,3,.., n. If the total number of wrong answers is 2047, prove that n = 11.

Solution: Number of students who answer exactly i questions wrong $(1 \le i \le n-1)$

= Number of students answering at least i questions wrong – number of students answering at least $(i+1)$ questions wrong

$= 2^{n-i} - 2^{n-(i+1)} = 2^{n-i-1}$

Also, the number of students who answered all n questions wrong

$= 2^{n-n} = 1$ (writing $i = n$)

$\therefore$ Total number of wrong answers $= \sum_{i=1}^{n-1} i.2^{n-i-1} + n.2^0$

$= 2^{n-2} + 2.\ 2^{n-3} + 3.\ 2^{n-4} + ... + (n-1)\ 2^0 + n$

$\therefore$ $2047 = 2^{n-2} + 2.\ 2^{n-3} + 3.\ 2^{n-4} + ... + (n-1) + n$

$\Rightarrow$ $2047 - n = 2^{n-2} + 2.\ 2^{n-3} + 3.\ 2^{n-4} + ... + (n-1)$

$\Rightarrow$ $2047 - n = 2^n - n - 1$ [since the series on RHS is an AGP series]

$\Rightarrow$ $2^n = 2048 = 2^{11}$ $\Rightarrow n = 11$

23. Consider forming teams of various sizes from group of n persons and selecting a captain and a vice-captain from each team, prove using the principle of permutations and combinations that $2.1\ .^nC_2 + 3.2\ ^nC_3 + ... + n(n-1).^nC_n = 2^{n-2}.n(n-1)$

Solution: Quesion can be divided into following cases:

Case - I: For 2 member team

Select 2 people in $^nC_2$ ways. Captain would be any one of the two i.e., 2 ways. Other would be vice captain. So the number of ways $2.1.\ ^nC_2$

Case - II: For 3 member team

Select 3 people in $^nC_3$ ways. Captain would be any one of the three i.e., 3 ways. Vice captain would be anyone of the remaining 2 i.e., 2 ways

Number of ways $3.2.\ ^nC_3$

Case - III: For 4 member team

Number of ways $4.3.\ ^nC_4$ and proceeding similarly

so number of ways $= 2 \times 1.\ ^nC_2 + 3 \times 2\ ^nC_3 + ... + n(n-1)\ ^nC_n$ (i)

Alternatively: There is another way of doing the question. Select a captain for the team in $^nC_1$ ways. From the remaining people, select a vice-captain in $^{n-1}C_1$ ways. each one of the remaining people have 2 choices i.e., they may be in the team or they may not be in the team. So 2 choices for each one

$\Rightarrow$ 2^{n-2} choices overall for the remaining $(n-2)$ people.

So number of ways $= 2^{n-2}\ n(n-1)$ (ii)

$\therefore$ From (i) and (ii) result follows.

24. In how many ways, two distinct natural numbers can be selected which are less than or equal to 100 and differ at most 10?

Solution: If the selected numbers differ by atmost 10, the complements of two numbers differing by at least 11.

$\therefore$ If $x = 1$, $y = 11, 12, 13, ..., 100$

If $x = 2$, $y = 13, 14, ..., 100$

If $x = 3$, $y = 14, 15, ..., 100$

If $x = 89$, $y = 100$

$\therefore$ Number of ways of choosing two numbers having there difference atleast $11 = 1 + 2 + 3 + ... + 89 = {}^{90}C_2$ and total number of ways $= {}^{100}C_2$

$\therefore$ Required number of ways $= {}^{100}C_2 - {}^{90}C_2$

25. A flight of stairs has 10 steps. A person can go up the steps one at a time, two at a time, or any combination of 1's and 2's. Find the total number of ways in which the person can go up the stairs.

Solution: only one step = (1) $\to$ 10

only two step = (2) $\to$ 5

$\Rightarrow$ one and two = (2) $\to$ 4 (times); (1) $\to$ 2 (times)

similarly (2) $\to$ 3; (1) $\to$ 4; (2) $\to$ 2; (1) $\to$ 6; (2) $\to$ 1; (1) $\to$ 8

$$\text{Total ways} = 1 + 1 + \frac{6!}{4!2!} + \frac{7!}{3!4!} + \frac{8!}{2!6!} + \frac{9!}{8!1!}$$

$$= 2 + 15 + \frac{7 \times 6 \times 5}{2.3} + \frac{8 \times 7}{1.2} + 9 = 89$$

26. In how many other ways can the letters of the word **MULTIPLE** be arranged;

(i) without changing the order of the vowels

(ii) keeping the position of each vowel fixed and

(iii) without changing the relative order/position of vowels and consonants? (i.e., places occupied by consonants and vowels remain same as in original)

Solution: |M| U |L| T |(I)|P| L |(E)|

(i) $\left({}^8C_3.\frac{5!}{2}\right) - 1$ = (number of ways of selecting 3 places for vowels × number of arrangements of consonants) – 1

Here 1 is subtracted corresponding to given arrangement

(ii) No. of arrangements in which vowels are not changed – 1

$= \frac{5!}{2!} - 1 = 59;$

	U			I			E

(iii) consonants and vowels come at same positions but they can change mutually

$\Rightarrow$ Total numbers of ways $= \frac{5!}{2!} \times 3! - 1 = 359$

27. How many 15 letter arrangements of 5 A's, 5B's and 5C's have no A's in the first 5 letters, no B's in the next 5 letters, and no C's in the last 5 letters?

Solution:

Ist 5 letters -----			Middle 5 letters -----			last 5 letters -----		
letters which can come B,C			letters which can come A,C			letters which can come A,B		
Cases		No. of ways	Cases		No. of ways	Cases		No. of ways
$5B$	$0C$	${}^5C_0$	$0A$	$5C$	${}^5C_0$	$5A$	$0B$	${}^5C_0$
$4B$	$1C$	${}^5C_1$	$1A$	$4C$	${}^5C_1$	$4A$	$1B$	${}^5C_1$
$3B$	$2C$	${}^5C_2$	$2A$	$3C$	${}^5C_2$	$3A$	$2B$	${}^5C_2$
$2B$	$3C$	${}^5C_3$	$3A$	$2C$	${}^5C_3$	$2A$	$3B$	${}^5C_3$
$1B$	$4C$	${}^5C_4$	$4A$	$1C$	${}^5C_4$	$1A$	$4B$	${}^5C_4$
$0B$	$5C$	${}^5C_5$	$5A$	$0C$	${}^5C_5$	$0A$	$5B$	${}^5C_2$

total no. of ways

$= ({}^5C_0)^3 + ({}^5C_1)^3 + ({}^5C_2)^3 + ({}^5C_3)^3 + ({}^5C_4)^3 + ({}^5C_5)^3$

$= 1^3 + 5^3 + 10^3 + 10^3 + 5^3 + 1^3$

$= 2 + 2(125) + 2(1000)$

$= 2252$

28. How many different ways can 15 Candy bars be distributed between Ram, Shyam, Ghanshyam and Balram, if Ram can't have more than 5 candy bars and Shyam must have at least two? Assume all Candy bars to be alike.

Solution:

R S G B

(not more than 5) (at least 2) (any no. of candies)

$\therefore$ Total no. of ways = coefficient of x^{15} in $(x^0 + x^1 + x^2 + x^3 + x^4 + x^5) \times (x^2 + x^3 + \ldots\infty) \times (x^0 + x^1 + x^2 + \ldots + \infty)^2$

Coefficient of x^{15} in $\left(\dfrac{1-x^6}{1-x}\right) \cdot \dfrac{x^2}{(1-x)} \cdot \dfrac{1}{(1-x)^2}$

Coefficient of x^{15} in $x^2(1 - x^6)(1 - x)^{-4}$

Coefficient of x^{13} in $(1 - x^6)(1 - x)^{-4}$

$= {}^{16}C_3 - {}^{10}C_3$

$= \dfrac{16.15.14 - 10.9.8}{3!} = 440$

29. For each positive integer k, let S_k denotes the increasing arithmetic sequence of integers whose first term is 1 and whose common difference is k. For example, S_3 is the sequence 1, 4, 7, 10....Find the number of values of k for which S_k contains the term 361.

Solution: $S_k = 1 + (n - 1)k = 361$

$(n - 1)k = 360$

$360 = 2^3.3^2.5^1$

No. of factors of 360 including 1 and 360 = (3 + 1) (2 + 1) (1 + 1) = 4 × 3 × 2 = 24

No. of ways in which 360 can be factorized into 2 factors considering the order 24.

30. All the 7 digit numbers containing each of the digits 1, 2, 3, 4, 5, 6, 7 exactly once, and not divisible by 5 are arranged in the increasing order. Find the (2004)th number in this list.

Solution: Number should not be divisible by 5. It implies that the unit place does not contain 5.

The number of such numbers

$= 6 \times 6 \times 5 \times 4 \times 3 \times 2 \times 1 = 4320$

The number of numbers starting with

$1 \to n(1) = 5 \times 5 \times 4 \times 3 \times 2 = 600$

$2 \to n(2) = 5 \times 5 \times 4 \times 3 \times 2 = 600$

$3 \to n(3) = 5 \times 5 \times 4 \times 3 \times 2 = 600$

$4 \to n(4) = 5 \times 5 \times 4 \times 3 \times 2 = 600$

Total = 2400

$\because$ $n(1) + n(2) + n(3) < 2004$

and $n(1) + n(2) + n(3) + n(4) > 2004$

$\therefore$ 2004th term must be starting with 4

$\therefore$ Now we consider the numbers starting with 4

Number of numbers starting with

$41 \to n(41) = 4 \times 4 \times 3 \times 2 = 96$

$42 \to n(42) = 4 \times 4 \times 3 \times 2 = 96$; $n(1) + n(2) + n(3) + n(41) + n(42) = 1992$

$431 \to n(431) = 3 \times 3 \times 2 \times 1 = 18$

But $n(1) + n(2) + n(3) + n(41) + n(42) + n(431) = 2010 > 2004$

$\therefore$ Number of must start with 431

$\Rightarrow$ Number of numbers starting with

$4312 \to n(4312) = 2 \times 2 = 4$

$4315 \to n(4315) = 2 \times 3 = 6$

Total numbers rejected till now
= 1800 + 96 + 96 + 4 + 6 = 2002
2003rd number will be 4316257
and 2004th number will be 4316527.

31. 12 persons are to be seated at a square table, three on each side. 2 persons wish to sit on the north side and two wish to sit on the east. One other person insists on occupying the middle seat (which may be on any side). Find the number of ways they can be seated.

Solution: Let twelve persons be N_1,N_2,E_1,E_2,M, P_1,P_2,P_3,P_4, P_5,P_6, and P_7

Let N_1 N_2 be the persons who wish to sit on north side of the table and E_1, E_2 be the persons who wants to sit on the east side of the table and M be person who wants to sit in the middle seat (which may be on any side)

Case I: When 'M' sits on south or west side of the table

⇒ Number of ways = 2

N_1 and N_2 can occupy their seats in $\left({}^3C_2 \times 2!\right)$ ways

Similarly, for E_1, E_2

Rest of the persons (P_1, P_2,…,P_7) can be arranged in the remaining 7 chairs in 7! ways

⇒ No of ways = ${}^3C_2 \times 2! \times {}^3C_2 \times 2! \times 2 \times 7!$ (i)

Case II: When 'M' sits on either North or East side

Lets consider north side

⇒ N_1 and N_2 will have to take the corner seats on north side

⇒ 2! Ways

Number of ways of arrangement of E_1 and E_2 = ${}^3C_2 \times 2!$ ways

Rest of the persons (P_1, P_2…P_7) can be arranged remaining 7 places in 7 ! ways

Similarly, if 'M' sits on east side

∴ No of ways = $2 \times 2! \times {}^3C_2 \times 2! \times 7!$ …(2)

∴ Adding (1) and(2) ; we get

Total number of ways = 96 × 7!

32. How many integers between 1000 and 9999 have exactly one pair of same digit such as 4049 or 9902 but not 4449 or 4040?

Solution: The following cases arise:

Case I: When unit and ten's (or hundred and ten's or units and hundred) place digits are identical and rest are different

N = yzxx; when x is a non-zero digit = 64 × 9 = 576

when x is zero, number of numbers = 9 × 8 = 72

Thus total numbers = 576 + 72 = 648

Similarly, if units and hundred's places are identical

Also, similarly if ten's and hundred's places are identical

∴ Total no of numbers 648 × 3 = 1994 (i)

Case II: When thousand's and hundred's (or thousand and unit or thousand and ten's) place digit are identical xyxz

Number of ways = 9 × 9 × 8 = 648

Similarly, thousand's and ten's placed are identical

And also if thousand's and units placed are identical

∴ Number of number 648 × 3= 1944 ways (ii)

Adding (i) and (ii); we get

Total no. of such numbers = 2 + 1944 = 3888

33. A man has 3 friends. In how many ways he can invite one friend everyday for dinner on 6 successive? nights so that no friend is invited more than 3 times?

Solution: The following cases arise

(i) Each friend invited 2 times

(ii) One friend (F_1) is invited 3 times, F_2 is invited 2 times and F_3 invited just once

(iii) Two friends invited 3 times each and the third friend is not invited

Case (i) No of ways $= \dfrac{6!}{2!2!2!}$

Case (ii) No of ways $= 3! \times \dfrac{6!}{3!2!}$

Case (iii) No of ways $= {}^3C_2 \times \dfrac{6!}{3!3!}$

∴ Adding; we get, total number of case = 510

34. Let (x,y,z) be points with integer coordinates satisfying the system of homogenous equations

$3x - y - z = 0$

$-3x + z = 0$

$-3x + 2y + z = 0$

Then find the number of such points for which $x^2 + y^2 + z^2 \le 100$.

Solution:

Given equations are

$3x - y - z = 0$

$-3x + z = 0$

$-3x + 2y + z = 0$

Solving above equations, we get

$y = 0$, $z = 3x$

Now $x^2 + y^2 + z^2 \le 100$

$\Rightarrow 10x^2 \ge 100 \Rightarrow x^2 \le 10$

$\Rightarrow x = 0, \pm 1, \pm 2, \pm 3.$

∴ the required points are (0,0,0), (1,0,3), (-1,0,-3), (2,0,6), (-2,0,-6),(3,0,9), (-3,0,-9)

Thus there are 7 such points

35. Let S_k ; k ∈ {1, 2100}, denote the sum of infinite geometric series whose first term is $\frac{k-1}{k!}$ and the common ratio is $\frac{1}{k}$. Then find the value of $\frac{100^2}{100!}+\sum_{k=1}^{100}|\left(k^2-3k+1\right)S_k|$

Solution: We have

$$S_k=\frac{(k-1)/k!}{1-1/k}=\frac{1}{(k-1)!}\forall k\geq 1$$

Now, $|k^2 - 3k + 1|\, S_k$

$$=|(k-2)(k-1)-1|\,\frac{1}{(k-1)!}$$

$$=\left|\frac{1}{(k-3)!}-\frac{1}{(k-1)!}\right|\forall k\geq 3$$

Therefore $\sum_{k=1}^{100}\left|\left(k^2-3k+1\right)S_k\right|$

$$=\frac{1}{0!}+\frac{1}{1!}+\sum_{k=3}^{100}\left(\frac{1}{(k-3)!}-\frac{1}{(k-1)!}\right)$$

$$=1+1+1+1-\frac{1}{98!}-\frac{1}{99!}=4-\frac{100}{99!}$$

Thus $\frac{100}{100!}+\sum^{100}|\left(k\ -3k+1\right)S\ |=\frac{100}{99!}+4-\frac{100}{99!}=4$

36. Find the number of points with integral co-ordinates that lie inside a triangle whose co-ordinates are (0, 0), (0, 102) and (102, 0).

Solution: $x + y < 102;\ x \in \mathbb{N},\ y \in \mathbb{N}$

i.e., $x + y \leq 101$; let z be slack variable.

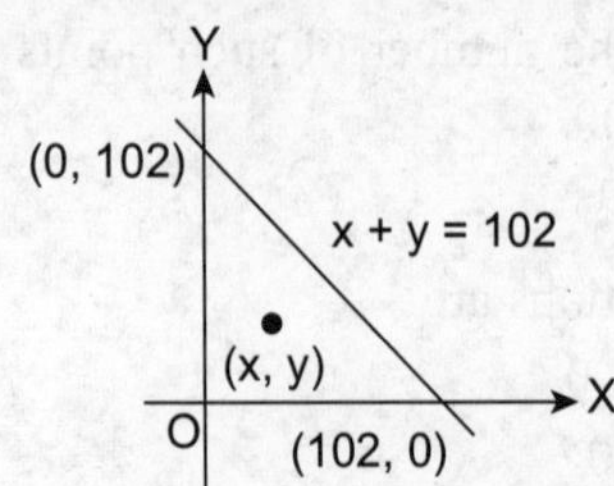

⇒ $x + y + z = 101;\ x \geq 1, y \geq 1, z \geq 0$

⇒ $(x - 1) + (y - 1) + z = 101 - 2;\ x - 1 \geq 0;\ y - 1 \geq 0;\ z \geq 0$

⇒ $x' + y' + z = 99;\ x', y', z \geq 0$

⇒ ${}^{101}C_2=\frac{101.100}{2}=5050$

37. A bag contains $6n$ tickets numbered from 0, 1, 2, ... $6n–1$. In how many ways, 3 tickets can be selected so that the sum of the numbers shown on them is equal to $6n$?

Solution: Number of ways = coefficient of x^{6n} in $(1 + x + x^2 + ... + x^{6n-1})^3 - R$

where R = number of cases to be rejected

or coefficient of x^{6n} in $\left(\frac{1-x^{6n}}{1-x}\right)^3$

coefficient of x^{6n} in $(1 - x)^{-3} = {}^{6n+2}C_2$

$$\text{now } R=\begin{bmatrix}1 & 1 & 6n-2\\ 2 & 2 & 6n-4\\ \vdots & \vdots & \vdots\\ 2n & 2n & 2n\\ \vdots & \vdots & \vdots\\ 3n & 3n & 0\end{bmatrix}$$

= $(3n - 1)$ ways. (excluding $2n, 2n, 2n$)

But each of such cases repeated 3 times + one case $2n, 2n, 2n$

$R = 3(3n - 1) + 1$

required number of ways $\frac{{}^{6n+2}C_2-3(3n-1)-1}{3!}$

38. An 8 oared boat to be manned from a crew of eleven of whom 3 can only steer but can not row. 8 can row but can not steer. In how many ways the staff can be arranged if 2 of the men can only row on bow side.

Solution:

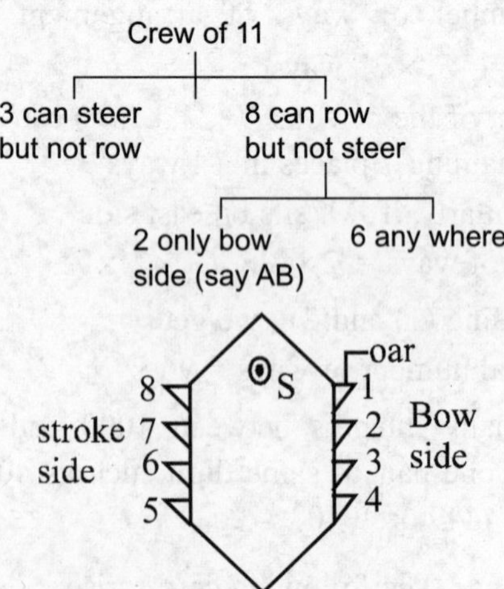

- Position for steering can be selected in ${}^3C_1$ ways.
- Two positions on the bow side can be selected in ${}^4C_2$ ways and AB can be arranged in 2! ways .
- Remaining 6 people on 6 positions can be seated in 6! ways.

Hence using FPC, total ways = ${}^3C_1 . {}^4C_2 .2! . 6!$ = 25920.

Alternatively: 2 out of 6 people can be selected in ${}^6C_2$ ways. Now (${}^6C_2$ + AB)
i.e., 4 persons on bow side can be seated in 4! ways.
Total ways = ${}^3C_1 . {}^6C_2 . 4! . 4!$ = 25920

39. Find the number of 7 digit numbers if the sum of their digits is 59, how many of these are divisible by 11, if the digits to be used are 5, 6, 7, 8, 9?

Solution: Possible digits are 5, 6, 7, 8, 9

Category	Number of 7 digit number	Divisible by 11
9999995	$\frac{7!}{6!} = 7$	×
9999977	$\frac{7!}{5!\cdot 2!} = 21$	×
9999968	$\frac{7!}{5!} = 42$	$\frac{4!}{3!}\ \frac{3!}{2!} = 12$
9999887	$\frac{7!}{4!\cdot 2!} = 105$	$\frac{4!}{3!} . 3! = 24$
9998888	$\frac{7!}{3!\cdot 4!} = 35$	$\frac{4!}{3!} \cdot 1! = 4$
Total	210	40

40. There are $6n$ flowers of one kind and 3 flowers of another kind. How many different garlands can be made using all the flowers?

Solution:

when '0'0 is always taken	'1' is always taken	'2' is always taken	$(2n-1)$ always taken	'$2n$' is always taken
0 0 $6n$	1 1 $6n-2$	2 2 $6n-4$		
0 1 $6n-1$	1 2 $6n-3$	2 3 $6n-5$		
0 2 $6n-2$	1 3 $6n-4$	⋮ ⋮ ⋮	$2n-1$ $2n-1$ $2n+2$	$2n$ $2n$ $2n$
⋮ ⋮ ⋮	⋮ ⋮ ⋮	2 $3n-2$ $3n$	$2n-1$ $2n$ $2n+1$	
0 $3n$ $3n$	1 $3n-1$ $3n$	2 $3n-1$ $3n-1$		
$(3n+1)$ ways	$(3n-1)$ ways	$(3n-2)$ ways	2ways	1 way

Total = 1 + (2 + 4) + (5 + 7) + (8 + 10) ... ((3n – 1) + (3n + 1))

$= 1 + 6\,[1 + 2 + 3 + ... + n]$

$= 1 + 6 \times \frac{n(n+1)}{2}$

$= 3n^2 + 3n + 1$

Note: '0' is always taken means all $6n$ flowers on the same side of the extreme G.

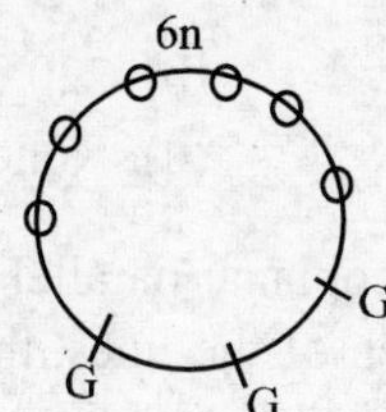

Similarly, 1 is always taken means at least 1 different flower between two successive G's.

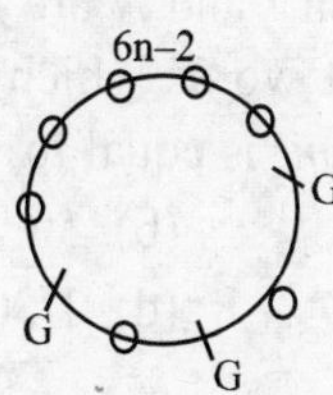

41. Find the number of functions $f:\{1, 2, 3, 4, 5, 6\} \to \{7, 8, 9, 10\}$ such that the sum $\sum_{i=1}^{6} f(i)$ is odd.

Solution: Odd number of odds + any number of even = odd numbers, therefore we can have

(i) one output odd and 5 outputs even in $2^6 \times {}^6C_1$ ways

(ii) three outputs odd and three output even in $2^6 \times {}^6C_3$ ways

(iii) five outputs odd and one outputs even in $2^6 \times {}^6C_5$ ways

therefore total number of ways = $2^6\,({}^6C_1 + {}^6C_3 + {}^6C_5) = 2^{11}$

SECTION–III

OBJECTIVE-TYPE (ONLY ONE CORRECT ANSWER)

1. The number of different matrices that can be formed with elements 0, 1, 2 or 3 each matrix having 4 elements is
(a) 3×2^4 (b) 2×4^4
(c) 3×4^4 (d) None of these

2. The number of ways in which 52 cards can be divided into 4 sets, three of them having 17 cards each and the fourth one having just one card, is
(a) $\frac{52!}{(17!)^3}$ (b) $\frac{52!}{(17!)^3 3!}$
(c) $\frac{51!}{(17!)^3}$ (d) $\frac{51!}{(17!)3!}$

3. There were two women participating in a chess tournament. Every participant played two games with the other participants. The number of games that the men played between themselves proved to exceed by 66 the number of games that the men played with the women. The number of participants is
(a) 6 (b) 11
(c) 13 (d) None of these

4. We are required to form different words by using all letters of the word INTEGER. Let m_1 be the number of words in which I and N are never together and m_2 be the number of words which begin with I and end with R, then m_1 / m_2 is equal to
(a) 42 (b) 30
(c) 6 (d) 1/30

5. The total number of ways in which six '+' and four '–' signs can be arranged in a line such that no two '–' signs occur together is
(a) 35 (b) 15
(c) 30 (d) None of these

6. Let S be a set having 18 elements. The number of subsets of S having number of elements a multiple of 3 is
(a) $\frac{2^{18}-1}{3}$ (b) $\frac{2^{18}-2}{3}$
(c) $\frac{2^{18}+1}{3}$ (d) $\frac{2^{18}+2}{3}$

7. The number of non-negative integral solutions of $x_1 + x_2 + x_3 + x_4 \leq n$ (where n is a non-negative integer) is
(a) ${}^{n+3}C_3$ (b) ${}^{n+4}C_4$
(c) ${}^{n+5}C_5$ (d) ${}^{n+4}C_n$

8. The number of three digit numbers having only two consecutive digits identical is
(a) 153 (b) 162
(c) 180 (d) 161

9. In a unique hockey series between India and Pakistan, they decide to play on till a team wins 5 matches. The number of ways in which the series can be won by India, if no match ends in a draw is
(a) 126 (b) 252
(c) 225 (d) None of these

10. Number of 7-digit numbers, which doesn't change on reversing the order of digit is
(a) 9×10^6 (b) 10^4
(c) 9×10^3 (d) 10^7

11. How many factors of 3780 are either divisible by 3 or 2 or both?
(a) 44 (b) 45
(c) 46 (d) None of these

12. With 17 consonants and 5 vowels. words of 4 letters are formed having two different vowels in the middle and one consonant (repeated/different) at each end. The number of words thus formed is
(a) 5780 (b) 5365
(c) 3400 (d) None of these

13. Let A = $\{x \mid x$ is a prime number and $x < 30\}$. The number of different rational numbers whose numerator and denominator belong to A is
(a) 90 (b) 180
(c) 91 (d) None of these

14. $ABCD$ is a convex quadrilateral 3, 4, 5 and 6 points are marked on the sides AB, BC, CD, and DA respectively. The number of triangles with vertices on different sides is
(a) 270 (b) 220
(c) 282 (d) None of these

15. There are three coplanar parallel lines. If any p points are taken on each of the lines, the maximum number of triangles with vertices at these points is
(a) $3p^2(p-1)+1$ (b) $3p^2(p-1)$
(c) $p^2(4p-3)$ (d) None of these

16. All possible two factor products are formed using the numbers 1, 2, 3, 4, ... 200. The number of products of the total thus obtained which are mulltiple of 5 is

(a) 5040 (b) 7180
(c) 8150 (d) None of these

17. The number of ways in which four letters can be selected from the word 'degree' is

(a) 7 (b) 6
(c) 6! /3! (d) None of these

18. In a plane, there are two families of lines $y = x + r$, $y = -x + r$, whcrc $r \in \{0, 1, 2, 3, 4\}$. The number of squares of diagonals of the length 2 formed by the lines is

(a) 9 (b) 16
(c) 25 (d) None of these

19. A class has 21 students. The class teacher has been asked to make n groups of r students each and go to zoo taking one group at a time. The size of group (i.e., the value of r) for which the teacher goes to the maximum number of times is (no group can go to the zoo twice)

(a) 9 or 10 (b) 10 or 11
(c) 11 or 12 (d) 12 or 13

20. A teacher takes 3 children from her class to the zoo at a time as often as she can, but she does not take the same three children to the zoo more than once he finds than she goes to the zoo 84 times more than a particular child goes to the zoo. The number of children in her class is

(a) 12 (b) 10
(c) 60 (d) None of these

21. The number of different ways in which five 'dashes' and eight 'dots' can be arranged, using only seven of these 13 'dashes' and 'dots' is

(a) 1287 (b) 119
(c) 120 (d) 1235520

22. The value of ${}^{40}C_{31} + \sum_{j=0}^{10} {}^{40+j}C_{10+j}$

(a) ${}^{51}C_{20}$ (b) $2.\,{}^{50}C_{20}$
(c) $2.{}^{45}C_{15}$ (d) None of these

23. The number of ways in which 9 identical balls can be placed in three identical boxes is (a box can have any number of balls)

(a) 55 (b) $\dfrac{9!}{(3!)^4}$
(c) $\dfrac{9!}{(3!)^3}$ (d) 12

24. The number of words that can be made by writing down the letters of the word CALCULATE such that each word starts and ends with a consonant is

(a) $\dfrac{5(7!)}{2}$ (b) $\dfrac{3(7!)}{2}$
(c) 2(7!) (d) None of these

25. The number of points (x, y, z) in space, whose each coordinate is a negative integer such that $x + y + z + 12 = 0$ is

(a) 358 (b) 55
(c) 110 (d) None of these

26. Let A be the set of 4-digit numbers $a_1 a_2 a_3 a_4$; where $a_1 > a_2 > a_3 > a_4$, then $n(A)$ is equal to

(a) 126 (b) 84
(c) 210 (d) None of these

27. The number of numbers divisible by 3 that can be formed by four different even digits is

(a) 18 (b) 36
(c) 0 (d) None of these

28. Two teams are to play a series of 5 matches between them. A match ends in a win or loss or draw for a team. A number of people forecast the result of each match and no two people make the same forecast for the series of matches. The smallest group of people in which one person forecasts correctly for all the matches will contain n people, where n is

(a) 81 (b) 243
(c) 486 (d) None of these

29. A person goes in for an examination in which there are four papers with maximum of m marks from each paper. The number of ways in which one can get $2m$ marks is

(a) ${}^{2m+3}C_3$

(b) $\frac{1}{3}(m+1)(2m^2+4m+1)$

(c) $\frac{1}{3}(m+1)(2m^2+4m+3)$

(d) None of these

30. In the next World Cup of cricket, there will be 12 teams, divided equally in two groups. Teams of each group will play a match against each other. From each group 3 top teams will qualify for the next round. In this round, each team will play against others once. Four top teams of this round will qualify for the semifinal round, where each team will play against the others once. Two top teams of this round will go to the final round, where they will play the best of three matches. The minimum number of matches in the next World Cup will be

(a) 54 (b) 53
(c) 38 (d) None of these

31. The number of ordered 4–tuple (x, y, z, w); $x, y, z, w \in [0, 10]$) which satisfies the inequality, $2^{\sin^2 x} . 3^{\cos^2 y} . 4^{\sin^2 z} . 5^{\cos^2 w} . \geq 120$ is

(a) 0 (b) 144
(c) 81 (d) infinite

32. Given 11 points, of which 5 lie on one circle, other than these 5, no 4 lie on one circle. Then the maximum number of circles that can be drawn so that each contains at least three of the given points is

(a) 216 (b) 156
(c) 172 (d) None of these

33. Seven different coins are to be divided amongst three persons. If no two of the persons receive the same number of coins but each receives at least one coin and none is left over, then the number of ways in which the division may be made is

(a) 420 (b) 630
(c) 710 (d) None of these

34. Sum of all the numbers that can be formed using all the digits 2, 3, 3, 4, 4, 4 is

(a) 22222200 (b) 11111100
(c) 55555500 (d) 20333280

35. The number of numbers less than or equal to 10^{12} which are niether perfect squares, nor perfect cubes, nor perfect 4th power is

(a) 999998990100 (b) 999998999000
(c) 999998999100 (d) None of these

36. A gentleman invites a party of m + n (3 ≠ n) friends to a places m at one table and n at another, the table being round. If the clockwise and anti-clockwise arrangements are not to be distinguished and assuming sufficient space on both tables, then the number of ways in which he can arrange the guest is

(a) $\frac{(m+n)!}{4mn}$ (b) $\frac{1}{2}\frac{(m+n)!}{4mn}$
(c) $2\frac{(m+n)!}{4mn}$ (d) None of these

37. Number of numbers divisible by 25 that can be formed using only the digits 1, 2, 3, 4, 5 and 0 taken five different digits at a time is

(a) 2 (b) 32
(c) 42 (d) 52

38. Six cards are drawn one by one from a set of unlimited number of cards, each card is marked with numbers –1, 0 or 1. Number of different ways in which they can be drawn if the sum of the numbers shown by them vanishes, is

(a) 111 (b) 121
(c) 141 (d) None of these

39. The number of 5 digit numbers of the form x y z y x in which x < y is

(a) 350 (b) 360
(c) 380 (d) 390

40. Let P_n denotes the number of ways of selecting 3 people out of 'n' sitting in a row, if no two of them are consecutive and Q_n is the corresponding figure when they are in a circle. If $P_n - Q_n = 6$, then 'n' is equal to

(a) 8 (b) 9
(c) 10 (d) 12

41. For some natural N the number of positive integers 'x' satisfying the equation, $1! + 2! + 3! + ... + (x!) = (N)^2$ is

(a) infinite (b) one
(c) two (d) None of these

42. Messages are conveyed by arranging 4 white, 1 blue and 3 red flags on a pole. Flags of the same colour are alike. If a message is transmitted by the order in which the colours are arranged, then the total number of messages that can be transmitted if exactly 6 flags are used is

(a) 45 (c) 65
(c) 125 (d) 185

43. Number of different words that can be formed using all letters of the word ''ELEVEN'' if each word neither begins nor ends in E, is

(a) 24 (b) 36
(c) 48 (d) None of these

44. Three digit numbers in which the middle one is a perfect square are formed using the digits 1 to 9. Their sum is

(a) 134055 (b) 270540
(c) 170055 (d) None of these

45. Number of numbers greater than a million and divisible by 5 which can be formed by using all the digits 1, 2, 1, 2, 0, 5 and 2 at a time is

(a) 120 (b) 110
(c) 90 (d) None of these

46. In a shooting competition, a man can score 0, 2 or 4 points for each shot. Then the number of different ways in which he can score 14 points in 5 shots, is

(a) 20 (b) 24
(c) 30 (d) None of these

47. Sum of all the digits used in writting all the numbers from 1 to 1000 is

(a) 12741 (b) 13946
(c) 4996 (d) 13501

48. A set 'A' consists of 6 and the set B consists of 3 distinct elements. The total number of functions form A → B which are surjective is

(a) 240 (b) 540
(c) 960 (d) None of these

49. A box contains 6 balls which may be all of different colours or three each of two colours or two each of three different colours. The number of ways of selecting 3 balls from the box is

(a) 60 (b) 31
(c) 30 (d) None of these

50. Number of positive integral solutions or the equation $20 \le x + y + z \le 50$ is

(a) ${}^{50}C_3 - {}^{20}C_3$ (b) ${}^{51}C_3 - {}^{19}C_3$
(c) ${}^{50}C_3 - {}^{19}C_3$ (d) ${}^{51}C_3 - {}^{21}C_3$

51. A question paper on mathematics consists of twelve questions divided into three parts A, B and C, each containing four questions. In how many ways can an examinee answer five questions, selecting at least one from each part?

(a) 623 (b) 624
(c) 625 (d) 626

52. Six married couple are sitting in a room. Number of ways in which 4 people can be selected so that there is exactly one married couple among the four is

(a) 240 (b) 255
(c) 360 (d) 480

53. The result of 21 football match (win, lose or draw) are to be predicted. The number of different forecasts which contain exactly 18 correct results is

(a) ${}^{21}C_3$ (b) $3.{}^{21}C_3$
(c) $8.{}^{21}C_3$ (d) $27.{}^{21}C_3$

54. Let there be 9 fixed points on the circumference of a circle. Each of these points is joined to every one of the remaining 8 points by a straight line and the points are so positioned on the circumference that atmost 2 straight lines meet in any interior point of the circle. The number of such interior intersection points is

(a) 126 (b) 351
(c) 756 (d) None of these

55. A student has to answer 10 out of 13 questions in an examination. The number of ways in which he can answer if he must answer at least 3 of the first five questions is

(a) 276 (b) 267
(c) 80 (d) None of these

56. The number of ways selecting 8 books from a library which has 10 books each of Mathematics, Physics, Chemistry and English, if books of same subject are alike, is

(a) ${}^{13}C_4$ (b) ${}^{13}C_3$
(c) ${}^{11}C_4$ (d) ${}^{11}C_3$

57. Number of ways in which 12 identical coins can be distributed in 6 different purses, if not more than 3 and not less than 1 coin goes in each purse is

(a) 131 (b) 141
(c) 247 (d) None of these

58. Number of ways in which 2 Indians, 3 Americans, 3 Italians and 4 Frenchmen can be seated on a circle, if the people of the same nationality sit together is

(a) $2.(4!)^2(3!)^2$ (b) $2.(3!)^3.4!$
(c) $2.(3!)(4!)^3$ (d) None of these

59. Number of ways in which two Americans, two British, one Chinese, one Dutch and one Egyptian can sit on a round table so that persons of the same nationality are separated is

(a) 48 (b) 240
(c) 336. (d) None of these

60. Number of ways in which 4 girls and 4 boys can sit around in circular table if the boys and girls are alternate and a particular boy and a girl are never together in any arrangement is

(a) 108 (b) 96
(c) 84 (d) 72

61. Number of ways in which 9 different prizes be given to 5 students if one particular boy receives 4 prizes and the rest of the students can get any numbers of prizes, is

(a) ${}^{9}C_4 . 2^{10}$ (b) ${}^{9}C_5 . 5^4$
(c) $4. 4^5$ (d) None of these

62. There are 5 balls of different colours and 5 boxes of colours same as those of the balls. The number of ways in which the balls, could be placed such that exactly 2 balls go to the box of its own colour is:

(a) 31 (b) 30
(c) 20 (d) None of these

63. Number of ways in which *p* identical white balls, *q* identical black balls and *r* identical red balls can be put in n different bags, if none, one or more of the bags remain empty is

(a) ${}^{n+p-1}C_p \cdot {}^{n+q-1}C_q \cdot {}^{n+r-1}C_r$
(b) ${}^{n+p-1}C_{p-1} \cdot {}^{n+q-1}C_{q-1} \cdot {}^{n+r-1}C_{r-1}$
(c) ${}^{n+p}C_p \cdot {}^{n+q}C_q \cdot {}^{n+r}C_r$
(d) None of these

64. Number of ways in which all the letters of the word "ALASKA" can be arragnged in a circle distinguishing between the clockwise and anti-clockwise arrangement is

(a) 60 (b) 40
(c) 20 (d) None of these

65. 6 white and 6 black balls are distributed among ten identical urns so that there is atleast one ball in each urn. Balls are all alike except for the colour and each box can hold any number of balls. The number of different distributions of the balls is:

(a) 26250 (b) 132
(c) 12 (d) 10

66. There are $(p + q)$ differnet books on different topics in Mathematics. $(p \neq q)$

If L = The number of ways in which these books are distributed between two students X and Y such that X get p books and Y gets q books.

M = The number of ways in which these books are distributed between two students X and Y such that one of them gets p books and another gets q books.

N = The number of ways in which these books are divided into two groups of p books and q books then,

(a) L = M = N (b) L = 2M = 2N
(c) 2L = M = 2N (d) L = M = 2N

67. Number of different ways in which 8 different books can be distributed among 3 students, if each student receives at least 2 books is

(a) 2940 (b) 2980
(c) 3042 (d) None of these

68. The number of ways of distributing 12 identical oranges among 4 children so that every child gets at least one and no child more than 4 is:

(a) 29 (b) 31
(c) 39 (d) None of these

69. In an eleven storey building, 9 people enter a lift cabin. It is known that they will leave the lift in groups of 2, 3 and 4 at different residential storeys. Number of ways in which they can get down is:

(a) $\dfrac{(12)!}{2!(3!)^2.4!}$ (b) $\dfrac{10!}{4}$
(c) $\dfrac{12!}{4}$ (d) None of these

70. A committee of 10 is to be formed from 8 teachers and 12 students of whom 4 are girls. In how many ways this can be done so that the committee contains atleast four of either groups (teachers and students) and atleast 2 girls and at least 2 boys are in the committee?

(a) 76832 (b) 78598
(c) 76840 (d) None of these

71. A train time-table must be compiled for various days of the week so that two trains a day depart for three days, one train a day for two days and three trains a day for two days. How many different time-table can be compiled?

(a) 140 (b) 210
(c) 133 (d) 72

72. The number of times the digit 3 will be written when listing the integers from 1 to 1000 is

(a) 300 (b) 269
(c) 271 (d) 302

73. The number of non-negative integral solution of the equation, x + y + 3z = 33 is

(a) 120 (b) 135
(c) 210 (d) 520

74. In an examination, the marks for physics and chemistry papers are 25 each, whereas maximum marks for maths paper is 100. The number of ways in which a student can score 50 marks is [assume that the marks are awarded in non-negative integral values]

(a) 716 (b) 676
(c) 605 (d) None of these

75. The number of ways in which 5 X's can be placed in the squares of the figure so that no row remains empty is

(a) 56 (b) 44
(c) 98 (d) 40

76. Number of ways in which AAABBB can be placed in the squares of the figure as shown so that no row remains empty, is

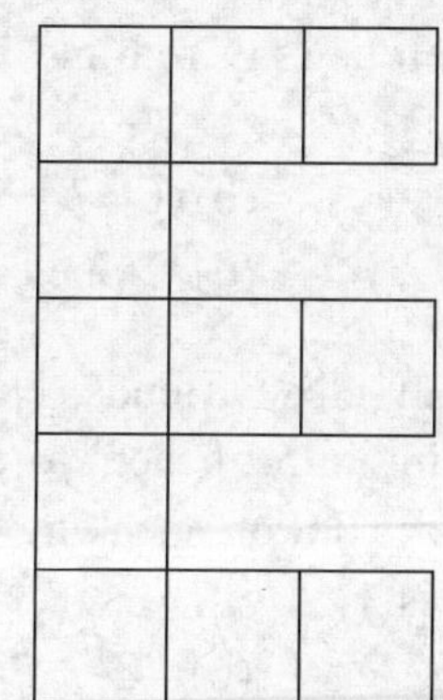

(a) 2430 (b) 2160
(c) 1620 (d) None of these

77. The number of ways in which 5 X's can be placed in the squares of the figure so that no row remains empty is

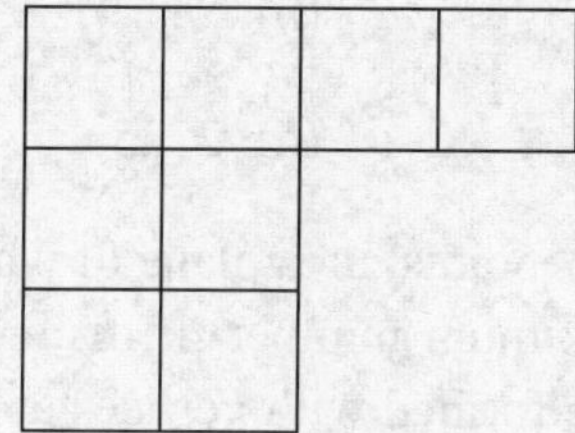

(a) 97 (b) 44
(c) 100 (d) 126

78. A regular polygon has 104 diagonals. The number of sides is
(a) 8 (b) 10
(c) 16 (d) None of these

79. Number of sub parts into which 'n' straight lines in a plane can divide it is

(a) $\frac{n^2+n+2}{2}$ (b) $\frac{n^2+n+4}{2}$

(c) $\frac{n^2+n+6}{2}$ (d) None of these

80. All the 7 digit numbers containing each of the digits 1, 2, 3, 4, 5, 6, 7 exactly once, and not divisible by 5 are arranged in the increasing order. Find the (2001)st number in this list.
(a) 4315726 (b) 4315658
(c) 4254789 (d) None of these

81. There 6 pairs of different gloves. In how many different ways can each of 6 persons be distributed a pair of left and right gloves, if at least 3 persons get a complete pair?
(a) 10! (b) 8!
(c) 45! (d) None of these

82. From 25 tickets numbered from 1 to 25, number of ways in which 3 tickets can be chosen such that the numbers on them are in A.P. with even common difference, is:
(a) 66 (b) 88
(c) 85 (d) None of these

83. The sum of all the four digit even numbers which can be formed by using the digits 0,1,2,3,4, and 5 if repetiton of digits is allowed is:
(a) 1765980 (b) 1756980
(c) 1769580 (d) 1759680

84. The Reserve Bank of India prints currency notes in denominations of Five rupees, Ten rupees, Twenty rupees, Fifty rupees, One hundred rupee, Five hundred rupees and One thousand rupees. In how many ways can it display in a set order ten currency notes not necessarily of different denominations? How many of these will have currency notes of all denominations?

(a) $7^{10};\left(\frac{49}{6}\right)10!$ (b) $7^{10};\left(\frac{49}{6}\right)20!$

(c) $10^{10};\left(\frac{49}{6}\right)10!$ (d) None of these

85. How many 5 digit numbers are there which contains not more than two different digits?
(a) 1224 (b) 1248
(c) 1325 (d) None of these

86. There are 2n guests at a dinner party. Supposing that the master and mistress of the house have fixed seats opposite one another, and that there are two specified guests who must not be placed next to one another. Find the number of ways in which the company can be placed around a circular table.
(a) $(2n – 1)!. (4n^2 – 6n + 4)$.
(b) $(2n – 2)!. (4n^2 – 6n + 2)$.
(c) $(2n – 2)!. (4n^2 – 6n + 4)$.
(d) None of these

87. Number of ways in which we can choose 2 distinct integers form 1 to 100 such that the difference between them is atmost 10 is
(a) 945 (b) 975
(d) 956 (d) None of these

SECTION–IV

OBJECTIVE-TYPE (MORE THAN ONE CORRECT ANSWER)

1. Let N denote the number of ways of selecting r objects out of n distinct objects $(r \geq n)$ with unlimited repetition but with each object included at least once in selection. Then N is

(a) ${}^{r-1}C_{r-n}$ (b) ${}^{r-1}C_{n-1}$
(c) ${}^{r-1}C_{n}$ (d) None of these

2. If $P = n(n^2 - 1^2)(n^2 - 2^2)(n^2 - 3^2).......(n^2 - r^2)$, $n > r$, $n \in \mathbb{N}$, then P is divisible by

(a) $(2r + 2)!$ (b) $(2r - 1)!$
(c) $(2r + 1)!$ (d) None of these

3. For the equation $x+y+z+w = 19$, the number of positive integral solutions is equal to

(a) The number of ways in which 15 identical things can be distributed among 4 persons.
(b) the number of ways in which 19 identical things can be distributed among 4 persons.
(c) coefficient of x^{19} in $(x^0+x^1+x^2+.+x^{19})^4$
(d) coefficient of x^{19} in $(x+x^2+x^3+....x^{19})^4$

4. The number of ways in which 200 things can be divided into groups of 100 pairs is

(a) $\dfrac{200!}{2^{100}}$
(b) $\left(\dfrac{101}{2}\right)\left(\dfrac{102}{2}\right)\left(\dfrac{103}{2}\right)....\left(\dfrac{200}{2}\right)$
(c) $\dfrac{200!}{2^{100}(100)!}$
(d) (1. 3. 5...... 199)

5. The maximum number of permutations of 2n letters in which there are only a's and b's, taken all at a time is given by:

(a) ${}^{2n}C_n$
(b) $\dfrac{2}{1}\cdot\dfrac{6}{2}\cdot\dfrac{10}{3}\cdots\cdots\dfrac{4n-6}{n-1}\cdot\dfrac{4n-2}{n}$
(c) $\dfrac{n+1}{1}\cdot\dfrac{n+2}{2}\cdot\dfrac{n+3}{3}\cdot\dfrac{n+4}{4}\cdots\dfrac{2n-1}{n-1}\cdot\dfrac{2n}{n}$
(d) $\dfrac{2^n\cdot[1.3.5 ...... (2n-3)(2n-1)]}{n!}$

6. You are given 8 balls of different colours (black, white, ...) . The number of ways in which these balls can be arranged in a row so that the two balls of particular colour (say red and white) may never come together is

(a) 8 ! - 2.7 ! (b) 6 . 7 !
(c) $2 . 6 ! . {}^7C_2$ (d) None of these

7. A women has 11 close friends. Number of ways in which she can invite 5 of them to dinner, if two particular of them are not on speaking terms and will not attend together is

(a) ${}^{11}C_5 - {}^9C_3$ (b) ${}^9C_5 + 2\,{}^9C_4$
(c) $3\,{}^9C_4$ (d) 378

8. Number of quadrilaterals which can be constructed by joining the vertices of a convex polygon of 20 sides if none of the side of the polygon is also the side of the quadrilateral is

(a) ${}^{17}C_4 - {}^{15}C_2$ (b) $\dfrac{{}^{15}C_3 . 20}{4}$
(c) 2275 (d) 2125

9. There are 12 points in a plane of which 5 are collinear. The maximum number of distinct quadrilaterals which can be formed with vertices at these points is

(a) $2 . {}^7P_3$ (b) ${}^7P_3$
(c) $10 . {}^7C_3$ (d) 420

10. The number of non-negative integer solutions of x + y + z + w = 10 must be same as

(a) Number of ways of distributing 10 identical objects in four distinct boxes.
(b) Number of selections of 10 objects from a lot containing four varieties of objects
(c) Number of selections of four objects from a lot containing 10 distinct objects.
(d) Number of results of a 10 match series between two countries if a match ends either in a win or loss or a draw.

11. On the normal chess board I_1 and I_2 are two insects which starts moving towards each other. I_1 starts from extreme left bottom and I_2 starts with extreme right top. Each insect moving with the same constant speed. Insect I_1 can move only to the right or upward along the lines while the insect I_2 can move only to the left or downward along the lines of the chess board. The total number of ways the two insects can meet at same point during their trip is:

(a) $\left(\frac{9}{8}\right)\left(\frac{10}{7}\right)\left(\frac{11}{6}\right)\left(\frac{12}{5}\right)\left(\frac{13}{4}\right)\left(\frac{14}{3}\right)\left(\frac{15}{2}\right)\left(\frac{16}{1}\right)$

(b) $2^8\left(\frac{1}{1}\right)\left(\frac{3}{2}\right)\left(\frac{5}{3}\right)\left(\frac{7}{4}\right)\left(\frac{9}{5}\right)\left(\frac{11}{6}\right)\left(\frac{13}{7}\right)\left(\frac{15}{8}\right)$

(c) $\left(\frac{2}{1}\right)\left(\frac{6}{2}\right)\left(\frac{10}{3}\right)\left(\frac{14}{4}\right)\left(\frac{18}{5}\right)\left(\frac{22}{6}\right)\left(\frac{26}{7}\right)\left(\frac{30}{8}\right)$

(d) C(16, 8)

12. There are 10 seats in the first row of a theatre of which 4 are to be occupied. The number of ways of arranging 4 persons so that no two persons sit side by side is

(a) ${}^7C_4$ (b) $4.{}^7P_3$
(c) ${}^7C_3.4!$ (d) 840

13. Find the number of ways in which 3 numbers in A.P. can be selected from 1, 2, 3, ... n.

(a) $\frac{(n-1)^2}{4}$ if n is odd (b) $\frac{n(n-2)}{4}$ if n is even
(c) $\frac{(n+1)^2}{4}$ if n is odd (d) $\frac{n(n+2)}{4}$ if n is even

14. The number of triplets (a, b, c) such that $a \le b < c$, where $a, b, c \in \{1, 2, 3,.....n\}$ is

(a) ${}^nC_3 + {}^nC_2$ (b) ${}^{n+1}C_3$
(c) ${}^{n-1}C_3$ (d) ${}^{n-1}C_2 + {}^{n-1}C_3$

15. A man is at the origin on the x-axis and takes a unit step either to the left or to the right. He stops after 5 steps or if he reaches 3 or –2. Number of ways in which he

(a) reaches –2 is 3
(b) reaches 3 is 4
(c) stop exactly after walking 5 steps is 12
(d) can perform the experiment is 20

16. The kindergarden teacher has 25 kids in her class. She takes 5 of them at a time, to zoological garden as often as she can, without taking the same 5 kids more than once. Then the number of visits, the teacher makes to the garden exceeds that of a kid by:

(a) ${}^{25}C_5 - {}^{24}C_4$ (b) ${}^{24}C_5$
(c) ${}^{25}C_5 - {}^{24}C_5$ (d) ${}^{24}C_4$

SECTION–V

ASSERTION AND REASON TYPE

1. A: The maximum number of points of intersection of 8 circles is 56.

R: The maximum number of points into which 4 circles and 4 straight lines intersect, is 50.

2. A: $\frac{n!}{(n-3)!}$ is divisible by 6.

R: Product of 3 consecutive integers is divisible by 3!.

3. A: If there are six letters $L_1, L_2, L_3, L_4, L_5, L_6$ and their corresponding six envelopes $E_1, E_2, E_3, E_4, E_5, E_6$. Letters having odd value can be put into odd value envelopes and even value letters can be put into even value envelopes, so that no letter goes into the right envelopes, the number of arrangement will be equal to 4.

R: If P_n number of ways in which n letter can be put in 'n' corresponding envelopes such that no letters goes to correct envelopes, then $P_n = n!\left(1-\frac{1}{1!}+\frac{1}{2!}+....+\frac{(-1)^n}{n!}\right)$.

4. A: The maximum value of K such that $(50)^k$ divides 100! is 2

R: If P is any prime number, then power of P in $n!$ is equal to $\left[\frac{n}{P}\right]+\left[\frac{n}{P^2}\right]+\left[\frac{n}{P^3}\right]$..... where [.] represents greatest integer function.

5. A: A five digit number divisible by 3 is to be formed using the digits 0, 1, 2, 3, 4, and 5 with repetition. The total number formed are 216.

R: If sum of digits of any number is divisible by 3, then the number must be divisible by 3.

6. A: If f {a, b, c, d, e} → {a, b, c, d, e} f is onto and $f(x) \ne x$ for each $x \in$ {a, b, c, d, e} is 44

R: The number of dearrangement for n object is n! $\left(1-\frac{1}{1!}+\frac{1}{2!}+....+\frac{(-1)^n}{n!}\right)$.

7. A: The one's, ten's and hundred's digit in 1! + 2! + 3! + 4! + 5! + 6! + 7! + 8! + 9! + 20! + 21! + 22! +....... + 49! is/are 3, 1, 1 respectively.

R: 1! + 2! + 3! + 4! + 5! + 6! + 7! + 8! + 9! = 409113. and n! is divisible by 1000 for $n \ge 20$.

8. A: The total number of ways in which 4 Mathematics and 5 Biology teachers can be seated on a table for a meeting, so that all the teachers of Maths dept. are not together is 4! (5!)^2.

R: Number of permutations of n different things taken all at a time when all m, specific things never come together is $n! - m! \times (n - m + 1)!$.

9. A: Sum of all the odd divisors of 720, which are not a perfect square is 78.

R: The sum of the positive integer divisior of $N = p_1^{\alpha_1} . p_2^{\alpha_2} . p_3^{\alpha_3} \ldots p_k^{\alpha_k}$, when $p_1, p_2, p_3 \ldots$ are different primes and $\alpha_1, \alpha_2, \ldots\ldots, \alpha_k$ are natural numbers is given by $(p_1^0 + p_1^1 + \ldots + p_1^{\alpha_1})$ $(p_2^0 + p_2^1 + \ldots + p_2^{\alpha_2}) \ldots (p_k^0 + \ldots + p_k^{\alpha_k})$.

10. A: The sum of all the five digit numbers that can be formed using digits 1, 2, 3, 4, 0 is (repetition of digits not allowed) 240×11111.

R: The sum of all numbers that can be formed using all the non-zero digits $a_1, a_2, \ldots a_n$ is $\lfloor(n-1)$. $(a_1 + a_2 + \ldots + a_n). \dfrac{10^n - 1}{9}$.

11. A: 4 points out of 8 points in a plane are collinear. Number of different quadrilaterals that can be formed by joining them is 53.

R: If 'm' points out of 'n' points in a plane are collinear, then the number of different quadrilaterals, that can be formed by joining these points is ${}^nC_4 - {}^mC_4 + 1$.

SECTION–VI

LINKED COMPREHENSION TYPE

A: If 25 identical things be distributed among 5 persons then

1. The number of ways each receives at least one is

(a) ${}^{24}C_4 - 5$ (b) ${}^{24}C_4 - 5^{13}C_4$
(c) ${}^{24}C_4 - 5^{13}C_4$ (d) ${}^{24}C_4$

2. The number of ways each receives odd number of things

(a) ${}^{14}C_4$ (b) ${}^{15}C_4$
(c) ${}^{16}C_4$ (d) None of these

3. The number of ways each receives at least one thing but not more than eleven is

(a) ${}^{24}C_4 - 5^{12}C_4$ (b) ${}^{24}C_4 - 5$
(c) ${}^{24}C_4 - 5^{13}C_4$ (d) None of these

B: Number of ways of distributing n different things into r different groups is r^n, when blank groups are taken into account. But when blank groups ar not permitted, then the number of ways of distribution are $r^n - {}^rC_1 (r-1)^n + {}^rC_2(r-2)^n - \ldots + (-1)^{r-1}\,{}^rC_{r-1}$

4. 4 candidates are competing for two managerial posts, in how many ways can the candidates be selected?

(a) 4^2 (b) ${}^4C_2$
(c) 2^4 (d) None of these

5. 8 different balls can be distributed among 3 children so that every child receives at least 1 ball is

(a) 3^8 (b) ${}^8C_3$
(c) 8^3 (d) None of these

6. 5 letters can be posted into 3 letter boxes in

(a) 3^5 ways (b) 5^3 ways
(c) ${}^5C_3$ ways (d) None of these

C: We have to choose 11 players for cricket team from 8 batsmen, 6 bowlers, 4 all-rounders and 2 wicket-keepers, in the following conditions:

7. The number of sections when at most 1 all-rounder and 1 wicket-keeper will play

(a) ${}^4C_1.\,{}^{14}C_{10} + {}^2C_1.\,{}^{14}C_{10} + {}^4C_1.\,{}^2C_1.\,{}^{14}C_9 + {}^{14}C_{11}$
(b) ${}^4C_1.\,{}^{15}C_{11} + {}^{15}C_{11}$
(c) ${}^4C_1.\,{}^{15}C_{10} + {}^{15}C_{11}$
(d) None of these

8. Number of selections when 2 particular batsmen don't want to play, if a particular bowler will play

(a) ${}^{17}C_{10} + {}^{19}C_{11}$ (b) ${}^{17}C_{10} + {}^{19}C_{11} + {}^{17}C_{11}$
(c) ${}^{17}C_{10} + {}^{20}C_{11}$ (d) ${}^{19}C_{10} + {}^{19}C_{11}$

9. Number of selections when a particular bastsman and a particular wicke-tkeeper don't want to play together

(a) $2\ {}^{18}C_{10}$ (b) ${}^{19}C_{11} + {}^{18}C_{10}$
(c) ${}^{19}C_{10} + {}^{19}C_{11}$ (d) None of these

D: Consider the letters of the word MATHEMATICS. There are eleven letters some of them are identical. Letters are classified as repeating and non-repeating letters: Set of repeating letter = $\{M, A, T\}$. Set of non-repeating letters = $\{H, E, O, C, S\}$

10. Possible number of words taking all letters at a time such that at least one repeating letter is at odd position in each word, is

(a) $\frac{9!}{2!.2!.2!}$ (b) $\frac{11!}{2!.2!.2!}$

(c) $\frac{11!}{2!.2!.2!}\frac{9!}{2!.2!}$ (d) $\frac{9!}{2!2!}$

11. Possible number of words taking all letters at a time such that in each word both M's are together and both T's are together but both *A's* are not together is

(a) 7!, ${}^8C_2$ (b) $\frac{11!}{2!.2!.2!}-\frac{10!}{2!.2!}$

(c) $\frac{6!.4!}{2!.2!}$ (d) $\frac{9!}{2!.2!.2!}$

12. Possible number of words in which no two vowels are together, is

(a) $\frac{7!}{2!2!}.{}^8C_4.\frac{4!}{2!}$ (b) $\frac{7!}{2!}.{}^8C_4.\frac{4!}{2!}$

(c) $7!.{}^8C_4.\frac{4!}{2!}$ (d) $\frac{7!}{2!2!2!}.{}^8C_4.\frac{4!}{2!}$

E: There are 8 official, 4 non-official members, out of these 12 members, a committee of 5 members is to be formed, the answer the following questions.

13. Number of committees consisting of 3 official and 2 non-official members, are

(a) 363 (b) 336
(c) 236 (d) 326

14. Number of committees consisting of at least two non-official members, are

(a) 456 (b) 546
(c) 654 (d) 466

15. Number of committees in which a particular official member is never included are

(a) 264 (b) 642
(c) 266 (d) 462

SECTION–VII

MATRIX MATCH TYPE

1. **Column-I**

(i) The number of 6-digit natural numbers, where each digit appears at least twice.
(ii) In how many ways can five different books be dedup in three bundles?
(iii) How many non-empty collections are possible by using 5*P*'s and 6*Q*'s?
(iv) How many students do you need in a school to guarantee that there are at least 2 students, who have the same first two initials?

Column-II

(a) 41
(b) 677
(c) 11754
(d) 25

2. **Column-I**

(i) The number of five-digit numbers having the product of digits 20 is
(ii) A man took 5 space plays out of an engine to clean them. The number of ways in which he can place at least two plays in the engine from where they came out is
(iii) The number of integers from 1 to 1000 in which at least two consecutive digits are equal is
(iv) The value of $\frac{1}{15}\sum_{1\le i\le j\le 9}\sum i.j$

Column-II

(a) 77
(b) 31
(c) 50
(d) 181

3. **Column-I**

(i) The number of arrangements that can be made taking 4 letters, at a time, out of the letters of the word ''PASSPORT'' is
(ii) The number of ways of forming a 4 letter word using the letters of the word MATHEMATICS, is
(iii) The number of selection of four letters from the letters of the word ASSASSINATION is
(iv) If there are 9 students in section I of a class and 8 students in section II of a class. A students council having 2 seats with one student from each section can be formed in ways is

Column-II

(a) 2454
(b) 606

(c) 72
(d) 2424

4. **Column-I**

(i) The total number of selections of fruits which can be made from 3 bananas, 4 apples and 2 oranges is
(ii) If 7 points out of 12 are in the same straight line, then the number of triangles formed is
(iii) The number of ways of selecting 10 balls from unlimited number of red, blacks, white and green balls is
(iv) The total number of proper positive integer divisors of 38808 is

Column-II

(a) greater than 50
(b) greater than 100
(c) Greater than 150
(d) Greater than 200

5. Consider all possible permutations of the letters of the word ENDEANOEL

Match the statement/expression in **Column-I** with the statements/expressions in **Column-II.**

Column-I

(i) The number of permutations containing the word ENDEA
(ii) The number of permutations in which the letter *E* occurs in the first and the last position is
(iii) The number of permutations in which none of the letters *D,* L, *N* occurs in the last five positions is
(iv) The number of permutations in which the letters *A,* E, *O* occurs only in odd positions is

Column-II

(a) 5!
(b) $2 \times 5!$
(c) $7 \times 5!$
(d) $21 \times 5!$

6. If repetitions are not allowed

Column I

(i) How many 3 digit numbers can be formed from the six digits 2, 3, 5, 6, 7 and 9?
(ii) How many of these are less than 400?
(iii) How many are even?
(iv) How many are odd?
(v) How many are multiples of 5?

Column II

(a) 120
(b) 40
(c) 80
(d) 20

SECTION–VIII

INTEGER-TYPE QUESTIONS

1. Find the sum of all natural numbers n such that $100 \leq n \leq 4000$, that can be made with the digits 0, 1, 2, 3, 4 if repetition of digits in the same number is allowed.

2. How many sides are there in a polygon which has 35 diagonals?

3. Find the number of combinations of the letters of the word PROPORTION taken six at a time.

4. If $x \in N$ and ${}^{x-1}C_4 - {}^{x-1}C_3 - \frac{5}{4} \cdot {}^{x-2}P_2 < 0$, then find greatest possible value of x.

5. 6 balls marked as 1, 2, 3, 4, 5, and 6 are kept in a box. Two players A and *B* start to take out 1 ball at a time from the box one after another without replacing the ball till the game is over. The number marked on the ball is added each time to the previous sum to get the sum of numbers marked on the balls taken out. If this sum is even, then 1 point is given to the player. The first player to get 2 points is declared winner. At the start of the game, the sum is 0. If A starts to take out the ball, then find the number of ways in which the game can be won by A.

6. Find the number of integral solutions to the equation $2x + y + z = 20$ with $x, y, z \geq 0$.

7. Find the number of non-negative integral solutions of $3x + y + z \leq 30$.

8. How many integral solutions are there to the system of equation? $x_1 + x_2 + x_3 + x_4 + x_5 = 20$ and $x_1 + x_2 + x_3 = 5$ when $x_k \geq 0$

9. A number of four different digits is formed using the digits 1, 2, 3, 4, 5, 6, 7 in all possible ways. Find

(a) how many of them are exactly divisible by 25?

(b) how many of them are exactly divisible by 4?

10. In a single correct match the column question, Column I contain 10 questions and Column II contain 10 answers written in some arbitrary order. In how many ways a student can answer this question so that exactly 6 of his matchings are correct.

11. In how many ways we can put 5 letters into 5 corresponding envelopes so that at least one letter go to wrong envelope.

12. Let A = {1, 2, 3, 4, 5} if '*f*' be a one-one onto function from $A \to A$ and number of such functions for which $f(k) \neq k;\ \forall\ k \in \{1, 2, 3, 4, 5\}$ is $11p$, find p.

13. Let S = {1,2,3,4}. Then find the number of unordered pairs of disjoint subsets of S.

Answer Keys

SECTION–III

1. (c)	**2.** (b)	**3.** (c)	**4.** (b)	**5.** (a)	**6.** (d)	**7.** (b)	**8.** (b)	**9.** (a)	**10.** (c)
11. (a)	**12.** (a)	**13.** (c)	**14.** (d)	**15.** (c)	**16.** (b)	**17.** (a)	**18.** (a)	**19.** (b)	**20.** (b)
21. (c)	**22.** (a)	**23.** (d)	**24.** (a)	**25.** (b)	**26.** (c)	**27.** (b)	**28.** (b)	**29.** (c)	**30.** (b)
31. (b)	**32.** (b)	**33.** (b)	**34.** (a)	**35.** (a)	**36.** (c)	**37.** (c)	**38.** (c)	**39.** (b)	**40.** (c)
41. (c)	**42.** (d)	**43.** (a)	**44.** (a)	**45.** (b)	**46.** (c)	**47.** (d)	**48.** (b)	**49.** (b)	**50.** (c)
51. (b)	**52.** (a)	**53.** (c)	**54.** (a)	**55.** (a)	**56.** (d)	**57.** (b)	**58.** (b)	**59.** (c)	**60.** (d)
61. (a)	**62.** (c)	**63.** (a)	**64.** (c)	**65.** (d)	**66.** (c)	**67.** (a)	**68.** (b)	**69.** (b)	**70.** (a)
71. (b)	**72.** (a)	**73.** (c)	**74.** (b)	**75.** (b)	**76.** (c)	**77.** (b)	**78.** (c)	**79.** (a)	**80.** (a)
81. (b)	**82.** (a)	**83.** (c)	**84.** (a)	**85.** (a)	**86.** (c)	**87.** (a)			

SECTION–IV

1. (a, b)	**2.** (b, c)	**3.** (a,d)	**4.** (b,c,d)	**5.** (a,b,c,d)	**6.** (a, b, c)
7. (a, b, c, d)	**8.** (a, b, c)	**9.** (a,d)	**10.** (c,d)	**11.** (a,b,c,d)	**12.** (b,c,d)
13. (a,b)	**14.** (a,b)	**15.** (a,b,c)	**16.** (a,b)		

SECTION–V

1. (b)	**2.** (a)	**3.** (a)	**4.** (d)	**5.** (d)	**6.** (a)	**7.** (a)	**8.** (a)	**9.** (d)	**10.** (d)
11. (c)									

SECTION–VI

1. (d)	**2.** (a)	**3.** (c)	**4.** (b)	**5.** (d)	**6.** (a)	**7.** (a)	**8.** (a)	**9.** (b)	**10.** (b)
11. (a)	**12.** (a)	**13.** (b)	**14.** (a)	**15.** (d)					

SECTION–VII

1. (i) → (c)	(ii) → (d)	(iii) → (a)	(iv) → (b)	
2. (i) → (c)	(ii) → (b)	(iii) → (d)	(iv) → (a)	
3. (i) → (b)	(ii) → (a)	(iii) → (c)	(iv) → (c)	
4. (i) → (a)	(ii) → (a, b, c)	(iii) → (a, b, c, d)	(iv) → (a)	
5. (i) → (a)	(ii) → (d)	(iii) → (b)	(iv) → (b)	
6. (i) → (a)	(ii) → (b)	(iii) → (b)	(iv) → (c)	(v) → (d)

SECTION–VIII

1. 94700	**2.** 10	**3.** 53	**4.** 10	**5.** 168	**6.** 121	**7.** 1991	**8.** 336	**9.** **(i)** 40
(ii) 200	**10.** 1890	**11.** 119	**12.** 4	**13.** 41				

HINTS AND SOLUTIONS

TEXTUAL EXERCISE–1: (SUBJECTIVE)

1. (a) Shirt can be choosen in 10 ways
Trouser can be choosen in 5 ways
Tie can be choosen in 4 ways
∴ Total number of ways = 10 × 5 × 4 = 200

(b) ∵ Wearing tie is not necessary, tie can be choosen in 4 ways if weared and there is 1 extra way when it is not weared
∴ Total ways = 10 × 5 × 5 = 250

2. (a) Number of ways of entering = 12
Number of ways of coming out = 12
As there is no restriction on the gate through which entry or exit are being made.
∴ Total ways = 12 × 12 = 144.

(b) As the exist is to be done through *a* different gate, we are left with 11 ways to exist leaving the gate through which entry is done.
∴ Total number of ways = 12 × 11 = 132

3. Number of ways to go from A to B = 2
Number of ways to go from B to C = 5
Number of ways to go from C to D = 3

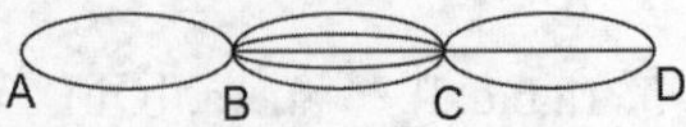

∴ Total number of ways = 2 × 5 × 3 = 30

4. Unit place digit has 5 choice i.e., 0, 2, 4, 6, 8 and ten's place digit has 9 choices i.e., 1, 2, 3, 4, 5, 6, 7, 8 or 9
∴ Total number of possible two digit even numbers = 5 × 9 = 45
Out of these 45, than are four numbers having same digits i.e., 22, 44, 66, 88
∴ Required number of two digits even numbers having different digits = 45 – 4 = 41
Aliter: Unit place digit has 5 choices i.e., 0, 2, 4, 6, 8
Now if unit place digit is 0, then ten's place digit has 9 choices i.e., 1, 2, 3, 4, 5, 6, 7, 8, 9 i.e., 9 ways.
If unit place digit is any one of 2, 4, 6, 8 the ten's place digit has 8 choice (excepting it self)
∴ Total ways = 9 + (4 × 8) = 41

5. Given digits are 2, 3, 4, 5
Number of one digit numbers = 4
Number of two digit numbers = 4 × 3 = 12
Number of three digit numbers = 4 × 3 × 2 = 24
Number of four digit number = 4 × 3 × 2 × 1 = 24
∴ Total number of possible different digit number = 4 + 12 + 24 + 24 = 64

6. Since each letter can be posted into any are of the letter boxes, so each liter has 6 choices.
∴ Number of ways = 6 × 6 × 6 × 6 × 6 = $(6)^5$

7. Each toss has two possible outcomes head or tail
∴ Total number of possible outcomes = 2 × 2 × 2 = 8 = $(2)^3$
If the coin is tossed 4 times, five times, n times, then the respective number of outcome will be 2^4, 2^5, 2^n
∴ Required outcomes 2^3, 2^4, 2^5, 2^n

8. First place digit has 9 choices (except for 0)
Second place digit has 10 choices (any digit)
Third place digit has 10 choices (any digit)
Eight place digit has 10 choices (any digit)
∴ Total number of possible telephone numbers = 9 × $(10)^7$

9. Since each digit is odd and we have 5 odd digits i.e., 1, 3, 5, 7 or 9
Also given that each number has distinct digits.
First place has 5 choices, second place has 4 choices and third place has 3 choices
∴ Total number of such numbers = 5 × 4 × 3 = 60

10. Unit place has 4 choices i.e., 2, 4, 6 or 8 and ten's place has 9 choices i.e., 1, 2, 3, 4, 5, 6, 7, 8 or 9
∴ Total number of such numbers = 4 × 9 = 36

11. $600 = (2)^3 \times (3)^1 \times (5)^2$
Now any factor x of 600 is composed of any four of 2, 3 and 5 i.e., $x = (2)^a (3)^b (5)^c$; where $a \in \{0, 1, 2, 3\}$; $b \in \{0, 1\}$; $c \in \{0, 1, 2\}$
∴ Total number of factors = 4 × 2 × 3 = 24

12. X = {1, 2, 3, ...,100} and S = $\{(a, b, c) : a, b, c, d \in X, a < b, a < c\}$
Since $a < b$ and $a < c$ and $b, c \le 100$
⇒ $a < 100$
⇒ a has 99 choices i.e., 1, 2 , 3 99
Now if $a = 1$, b has 99 choices i.e., 2, 3, 4 100
Similarly C has 99 choices i.e., 2, 3, 4........100
($\because b \ne c$ or $b = c$)
If $a = 2$, b and c both has 99 choices
If $a = 3$, b and c both has 97 choices
If $a = 99$, b and c both has 1 choice
∴ Total number of ways of constructing a member of S = 99 × 99 + 98 + 98 + 97 + 97 + ... + 1 × 1

$$= \sum_{n=1}^{99} n^2 = \left[\frac{n(n+1)(2x+1)}{6}\right]_{n=99}$$

$$= \frac{99 \times 100 \times 199}{6} = 328350$$

13. I[st] son has 6 options to get admission; IInd son has 5 options to get admission and IIIrd son has 4 options to get admission
∴ Total number of ways = 6 × 5 × 4 = 120

14. I[st] item of column A has 5 choices to be matched in column B
IInd item of column has 4 choices to be matched in column B
Similarly, IIIrd, IVth and V[th] item of column A has respectively 3 choices, 2 choice and 1 choice in column B

$\therefore$ Total number of matching = $5 \times 4 \times 3 \times 2 \times 1 = 5! = 120$
Further, if there are multiple matching, then each item of column A has 5 choice in column B.
Thus total number of ways of matching = $5 \times 5 \times 5 \times 5 \times 5 = (5)^5$

15. An ordered pair (a, d); where a = first term $\in \{1, 2, 3\}$ and d = common difference $\in \{2, 3, 4\}$
Represent an arithmetic progression (having 10 terms)
$\therefore$ Total number of arithmetic progressions = Total number of ordered pairs $(a, d) = 3 \times 3 = 9$

16. (a) Repetition of digits are allowed: First place has 9 choice (non-zero) and each of the next 4 places has 10 choices (any digit)
$\therefore$ Total number of such numbers = $9 \times 10 \times 10 \times 10 \times 10 = 9 \times (10)^4$

(b) Repetition of digits are not allowed: First place has 9 choices second, third, fourth, fifth place has 9, 8, 7 and 6 choices respectively.
Thus total number of numbers = $9 \times 9 \times 8 \times 7 \times 6 = 27216$

17. We are to form A.P.'s containing 3 terms from the set $\{1, 2, 3, \ldots, 2n + 1\}$
Let the terms be a, $a + b$, $a + 2d$, then $a \geq 1$ and $a + 2d \leq 2x + 1$
$\Rightarrow 2d \leq (2x + 1) - a \leq (2x + 1) - 1 \quad (\because a \geq 1 \Rightarrow -a \leq -1)$
$\Rightarrow 2d \leq 2n \quad \Rightarrow d \leq n$
Thus, whatever may be $a \geq 1$; $d \leq$ n.
If $d = 1$; then it forms following sets of AP's $\{1, 2, 3\}$; $\{2, 3, 4\}$; $\{3, 4, 5\}$; ……$\{2n - 1, 2n, 2n + 1\}$
If $d = 2$; then it for as following sets of AP's $\{1, 3, 5\}$; $\{2, 4, 6\}$; $\{3, 5, 7\}$; …. $\{2n - 3, 2n - 1, 2n - 1\}$
If $d = 3$; then it forms following sets of AP's $\{1, 4, 7\}$; $\{2, 5, 8\}$; $\{3, 6, 9\}$;……$\{2n - 5, 2n - 2, 2n + 5\}$
And so on
Finally, If d = n; then the sets of AP's are $\{1, n + 1, 2n + 1\}$
Thus, we get $(2n - 1) + (2n - 3) + (2n - 5) + \ldots + (1)$ AP's
i.e., $1 + 3 + 5 + \ldots, (2n - 3) + (2n - 1)$ = sum of first n-odd natural numbers = n^2

18. (a) By symmetry of two boxes, number of ways in which mouse can enter box 1 and come out in any way is the same as that of entering second box and come out in any way,

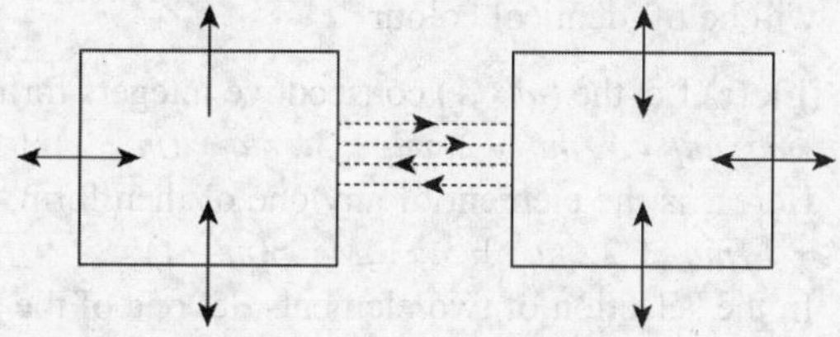

$\therefore$ It is sufficient to find the number of ways when mouse enters through box 1 and we twice it.
Now corresponding to each of 3 ways of entering the box 1, mouse can come out leaving it in 2 ways or can enter second box in 2 ways.
If it enters box 2, then it can come out leaving it in 3 ways or go back to box 1 in two ways. Now it can come out leaving box 1 in 2 ways or can enter box 2 in 1 way and come out leaving box 2 in 3 ways or go back to box 1 in one way and come out leaving it in 2 ways.
$\therefore$ Required number of ways = $2[3 \times \{2 + 2 (3 + 2(2 + 1 (3 + 1 \times 2))))\}] = 2[3 \times \{36\}] = 216$ ways.

(b) Natural ways corresponding to through box 1 and box 2 are not same due to non-symmetricity

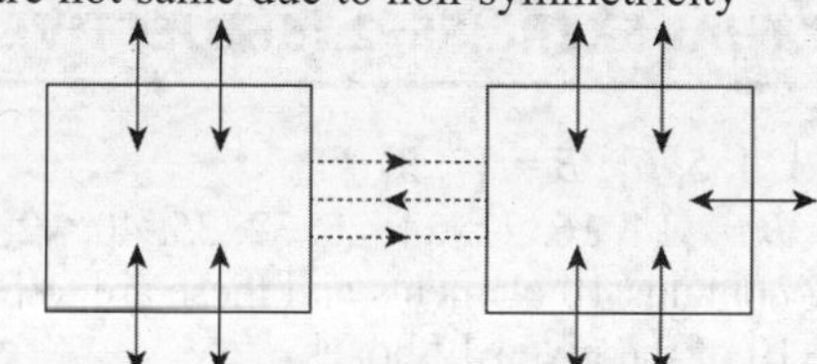

$\therefore$ Required number of ways = $4 [3 + 2 \times (4 + 1 (3 + 1 \times 4))]$ (entry through box 1) + $4 [3 + 1 \times (4 + 2 \times 3)]$ (Entry through box 2)
$= 100 + 52 = 152$

TEXTUAL EXERCISE–1: (OBJECTIVE)

1. (b) $5 \times 4 \times 3 = 60$

2. (i) (d) $5 \times 4 = 20$
(ii) (a) $5 \times 5 = 25$

3. (d) $\underbrace{10}_{size} \times \underbrace{2}_{tube/tubeless} \times \underbrace{2}_{redside/plain\ black} = 40$

4. (c) Prime number digits are 2, 3, 5, 7
$\therefore$ Number of number having four different digits having each digit are prime number = $4 \times 3 \times 2 \times 1 = 24$

5. (c) (a) $(b + c)(d + e + f)(g + h + i + j)$ ……… (Last factor of the sequence) (Remaining alphabets)
= (1) (2) (3) (4) (5) (6) (5) = 3600
($\because$ Remaining alphabets are v, w, x, y, z)

6. (b) Given digits are 0, 1, 2, 3, 4, 5, 6
Units place digit has 4 choices i.e., 0, 2, 4 and 6
Now first place has 6 choices, where as second and third place each has 7 choices
$\therefore$ Total number of possible even 4 digit numbers = $6 \times 7 \times 7 \times 4 = 1176$

7. (b) First book can be placed in any of the 5 places
Second book can be placed in any of the remaining 4 places
Third book can be placed in any of the remaining 3 places
Fourth book can be placed in any of the remaining 2 places,
Finally, fifth book has only one option left.
$\therefore$ Total number of ways in which, the teacher can arrange 5 book in allow = $5 \times 4 \times 3 \times 2 \times 1 = 120$

8. (c) First figure has 4 choices of rings
Second figure has 3 choices of rings
Third figure has 2 choices of rings
$\therefore$ Total number of ways = $4 \times 3 \times 2 = 24$

9. (c) 1st place has 9 choices.
2nd place has 9 choices
3rd place has 8 choices
4th place has 7 choices
$\therefore$ Total number of different digited 4-digits numbers $= 9 \times 9 \times 8 \times 7 = 4536$

10. (a) Number of ways $= (8 \times 7 \times 6)(8 \times 7) \times (8) = (2)^{10}(3)^1(7)^2$

TEXTUAL EXERCISE-2: (SUBJECTIVE)

1. $A = \{2, 3, 4, 5, 6\}$; $B = \{7, 8\}$
$\therefore$ $A \times B = \{14, 16, 21, 24, 28, 32, 35, 40, 42, 48\}$ i.e., $A \times B$ contains 10 elements and these are to be placed in any 10 of the given 12 boxcs.
The two boxes which are left either accommodate different products of $(A \times B)$ or same product of $(A \times B)$. In the former case, there will be two pairs of boxes each pair having same product but different from other and in later case there will be three boxes each having same product.

2. Store has slippers of 4 different sizes i.e., 6, 7, 8 and 9
Total slippers available = 201.
If we assume that store contains 51 or more slippers of any size, then we have nothing to prove. So, trying to contradict, let each type of slipper be less than 51, then if we assume that each type of slipper be 50, then we are left with one more slipper, naturally, the least one will be one of the size 6, 7, 8, or 9.
Thus the store must accommodate at least 51 slippers.

3. Trying to contradict if each chapter contains 25 pages, then there will be $12 \times 25 = 300$ pages. Still 5 pages are left. Now then 5 pages belong to any one or more of 12 chapters. Thus we find that there will be at least 1 chapter having at least 26 pages. For maximum number of such chapters if out of 5 page left, if each page belong to *a* different chapter, then there will be 5 chapters having 26 pages. Thus there will be maximum 5 chapters having at least 26 pages.

4. Trying to contradict, if it is assumed that the number of packets of each type of diamonds be 11, then total packets will be 44. One packet is still left. That last packet contains diamonds of any one of the four types. Thus there will be at least 12 packets having diamonds of same type.

5. Possible sums are –3, –2, –1, 0, 1, 2, or 3. If there sum are pigeon holds and boxes are pigeons, then by pigeon hole

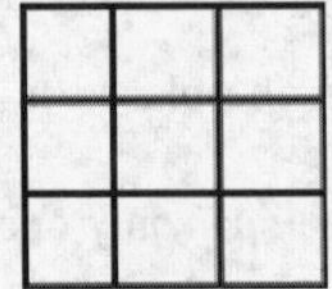

principle at least two boxes must have same sum.

6. $A = \{x: x, x^4 \in \mathbb{N}$ and $1 \le x^4 \le 4096\}$
$\because$ $4096 = (2)^{12} = (2^3)^4 = (8)^4$
$\therefore$ $A = \{1, 2, 3, 4, 5, 6, 7, 8\}$
$\Rightarrow$ A contains 8 elements.

7. For *a* number to be disable by 5, its unit place digits must be either 0 or 5. If unit place digit is 0, then ten's places digit has 9 choices and if unit place digit is 5, then ten's place digit has 8 choices.
$\therefore$ Total possible numbers $= 9 + 8 = 17$

8. (i) $\left[\frac{241}{2}\right] - \left[\frac{73}{2}\right]$; [.] is greatest inter function.
$= 120 - 36 = 84$

(ii) $\left[\frac{241}{5}\right] - \left[\frac{73}{5}\right] = 48 - 14 = 34$

(iii) Let A = set of numbers between 73 and 241 which are divisible by 2 and
B = set of numbers between 73 and 241 which are divisible by 5
$\therefore$ $n(A \cup B) = n(A) + n(B) - n(A \cap B)$
$= 84 + 34 - \left(\left[\frac{241}{10}\right] - \left[\frac{73}{10}\right]\right)$
$= 84 + 34 - (24 - 7) = 101$

(iv) $n(A \Delta B)$
$n(A \cup B) - n(A \cap B)$
$= 101 - \left(\left[\frac{241}{10}\right] - \left[\frac{73}{10}\right]\right)$
$= 101 - (24 - 7) = 101 - 17 = 84$

(v) $n(A \cap B) = \left[\frac{241}{10}\right] - \left[\frac{73}{10}\right] = 24 - 7 = 17$

(vi) $n(\bar{A} \cap \bar{B}) = n(\overline{A \cup B}) = n(X) - n(A \cup B)$
$= (241 - 72) - 101 = 169 - 101 = 68$

(vii) $n(A \cap \bar{B}) = n(A) - n(A \cap B)$
$= 84 - 17 = 67$

(viii) $n(\bar{A} \cap B) = n(B) - n(A \cap B)$
$= 34 - 17 = 17$

TEXTUAL EXERCISE-2: (OBJECTIVE)

1. (a) $\max\{n(A) + n(B) - n(x), 0\} \le n(A \cap B) \le \min\{n(A), n(B)\}$
$\Rightarrow$ $\max\{65 + 75 - 100, 0\} \le n(A \cap B) \le \min\{65, 75\}$
$\Rightarrow$ $40 \le x \le 65$
$\therefore$ $\mathbf{x} \in [40, 65]$

2. (d) Since there are 5 balls of each colour
If we draw any 6 balls, then by pigeon-hole principle at least two will be of identical colour

3. (a), (b), (c) Let the $(m + 1)$ consecutive integers form the set $A = \{mq, mq + 1, mq + 2, mq + 3.. mq + (m + 1)x\}$
Here x is the element of any one of then form $\in \{mq', mq' + 1, mq' + 2, mq' + 3, \ldots, M' + (m - 1)\}$
In the selection of two elements, let one of the selected element be x,
If $x = mq'$; then select the other number $y = mq$
$\Rightarrow$ $x + y = m(q' + q)$ which is divisible by m
If $x = mq' + r$; $1 \le r \le m - 1$, then $-m + 1 \le -r \le -1$ and hence $1 \le (m - r) \le m - 1$

Select $y = mq + (m - r) \in A$

$\therefore$ $x, y \in A$ such that $x + y = m(q' + q) + m$, divisible by m.

Similarly if $x = mq + 2;\ 0 \le r \le m - 1$

Select $y = mq + r;\ 0 \le 1 \le m - 1$;

$\Rightarrow$ $x - y = m(q' - q)$ which is divisible by m.

If $x = mq' + r;\ 0 \le r \le m - 1$, then $y = mq$

$\Rightarrow$ $xy = mq\ (mq' + l)$ which is divisible by m.

4. **(b)** In *a* chess board of area 64 sq. inches (8 × 8); there are 16 square each of side 2 inches of area 4 square inches. The maximum distance between any two ants with in a square of side 2 inches is $2\sqrt{2}$ inches. If we put two ants in each square of side 2 inches, then out of 17 ants, one ant is left and hence by pigeon hole principle there must be *a* square of 2 inches having 3 ants.
If out of these three ants two are placed at end points of *a* diagonal, then the distance of third ant from the first two ants will be less than $2\sqrt{2}$ inches. Thus there will be at least two ants close than $2\sqrt{2}$ inches.

5. **(b)** Since each word contains 4 letters, and we have total 26 letters of English alphabet. So if we selected at least 7 words, i.e., 28 letters. Thus there will be atleast two words having atleast one common letter.

6. **(c)** 31 lotteries should be purchased as 30 are blank and 30 have prizes. So if all 30 blank are among the purchased lotteries, then still 1 purchased lotery must have *a* prize.

7. **(c)** If we select 24 positive integers, then on dividing by 23, we get 24 remainders, but only23 remainder are possible i.e., {0, 1, 2, 3.......,22}. It means by pigeon hole principle atleast two integers must have same remainder. Let they be $a = 23q_1 + r$ and $b = 23q_2 + r$. Then $a - b = 23(q_1 - q_2)$ which is divisible be 23.

8. **(d)** Including Mr. Ravindra Tiwari, there are 9 men and 8 women. Thus if we invite atleast 10 people to dance, then by pigeon hole principle atleast one man and one women will be there in dancing group.

9. **(c)** Total items in lot = 500
Production of first machine = 70% of 500 = 350
So, if we select 351 items, then all the selected product are not made by *a* single machine.

TEXTUAL EXERCISE-3: (SUBJECTIVE)

1. **(i)** $\dfrac{12! - 10!}{9!} = \dfrac{10!(132-1)}{9!} = 10 \times 131 = 1310$

(ii) $\dfrac{n!}{r! \times (n-r)!} = \dfrac{15!}{12! \times 3!} = \dfrac{15 \times 14 \times 13 \times 12!}{12! \times 3 \times 2} = 455$

(iii) $(n-r+1) \times \dfrac{n!}{(n-r+1)!}$

$= (n-r+1) \times \dfrac{n!}{(n-r+1)(n-r)!} = \dfrac{n!}{(n-r)!} = {}^nP_r$

(iv) $n(n-1)(n-2) \ldots\ldots (n-r+1)$
$= n(n-1)(n-2) \ldots\ldots (n-(r-1))$

$= \dfrac{n(n-1)(n-2)\ldots(n-(r-1))(n-r)(n-(r+1))\ldots..3.2.1}{(n-r)[n-(r+1)][n-(r+2)]\ldots..3.2.1}$

$= \dfrac{n!}{(n-r)!} = {}^nP_r$

2. **(i)** $P(15, r) = 2730$

$\Rightarrow$ ${}^{15}P_r = 2730$ $\quad\Rightarrow\quad \dfrac{15!}{(15-r)!} = 2730$

$\Rightarrow$ $\dfrac{(15)(15-1)(15-2)\ldots(15-(r-l))(15-r)!}{(15-r)!} = 2730$

$\Rightarrow$ $15 \times 14 \times 13 \times \ldots. \times [15 - (r - l)] = 2730$

Now, $\because$ $15 \times 14 \times 13 = 2730$

$\Rightarrow$ $15\ (r - l) = 13$

$\Rightarrow$ $r - l = 2$ $\quad\Rightarrow\quad r = 3$

(ii) $P(15, r - 1) : P(16, r - 2) = 3 : 4$

$\Rightarrow$ $\dfrac{15!}{(15-r+1)!} : \dfrac{16!}{(16-r+2)!} = 3:4$

$\Rightarrow$ $\dfrac{15!}{(16-r)!} \times \dfrac{(18-r)!}{16!} = \dfrac{3}{4}$

$\Rightarrow$ $\dfrac{(18-r) \times (17-r)}{16} = \dfrac{3}{4}$

$\Rightarrow$ $(18 - r) \times (17 - r) = 12 = 4 \times 3$

$\Rightarrow$ $18 - r = 4$ $\quad\Rightarrow\quad$ r = 14

(iii) $P(2r - 1, r) : \mathbf{P}(2r + 1, r - 1) = 22 : 7$

$\Rightarrow$ $\dfrac{(2r-1)!}{(r-1)!} \times \dfrac{(r+2)!}{(2r+1)!} = \dfrac{22}{7}$

$\Rightarrow$ $\dfrac{(2r-1)!}{(r-1)!} \times \dfrac{(r+2)(r+1)r(r-1)!}{(2r+1)(2r)(2r-1)!} = \dfrac{22}{7}$

$\Rightarrow$ $7(r + 2)(r + 1) = 44(2r + 1)$

$\Rightarrow$ $7[r^2 + 3r + 2] = 88r + 44$

$\Rightarrow$ $7r^2 - 67r - 30 = 0$ $\quad\Rightarrow\quad 7r^2 - 70r + 3r - 30 = 0$

$\Rightarrow$ $7r(r - 10) + 3(r - 10) = 0$

$\Rightarrow$ $(r - 10)(7r + 3) = 0$

$\Rightarrow$ $r = 10$ or $r = -\dfrac{3}{7}$ $\therefore$ r = 10 as r is *a* +ve integer

3. 3 English books can be allayed among the selves in 3! = 6 ways.
4 History books can be arranged among themselves in 4! = 24 ways.
5 mathematics books can be arranged among themselves in 5! = 120 ways.
Now these three sets of English, History and Mathematics can be arranged on a shelf in 3! Ways.
Thus total number of ways = (3! × 4! × 5!) × 3!

4. Here vowels are U, and E. The consonants are N, M, B, R, S keeping the positions of vowels fixed; the consonants can be arranged among themselves in 5! Ways.

5. Three prizes can be given in ${}^{10}P_3$ ways
Next there consolation prizes can be given in ${}^7P_3$ ways

$\therefore$ Total number of ways $= {}^{10}P_3 \times {}^7P_3 = \dfrac{10!}{7!} \times \dfrac{7!}{4!} = \dfrac{10!}{4!} = {}^{10}P_6$

= Permutation of 10 taking 6 at a time

$\Rightarrow$ ${}^{10}P_3 \times {}^7P_3$ or ${}^{10}P_6$

6. **(i)** We are to find the number of possible words of the type having *a* pair **ED** and D is before a, not necessarily

just before *G*. So we permute (*ED*), *A*, *U*, *G*, *H*, *T*, *R* which can be done in 7! Ways. Now half are those ways in which *D* comes before *G*. Thus required number of words = $\frac{7!}{2!}$

(ii) Similarly, if we permute the letters *D, A, U, G, H, T, E, R*, then half are those ways when *D* occurs after *E*.

∴ Required ways = $\frac{8!}{2} = 4 \times 7!$

(iii) There are four even places i.e., 2nd, 4th, 6th, and 8th, and we have three vowels i.e., *A, U* and *E*.
Thus these vowels can be arranged in even places in ${}^4P_3 = \frac{4!}{1!} = 24$ ways. Now the remaining five places can be occupied by 5 consonants i.e., *D, G, H, T, R* in 5! = 120 ways.
Thus, the required number of ways = 24 × 120 or ${}^4P_3 \times {}^5P_5$ ways.

(iv) Considering the vowels group (*A, U, E*) as a single and permuting along with the letters, *D, G, H, T, R,* the number of ways = 6!, but (*A, U, E*) can be arranged among themselves in 3! Ways.
Thus total number of ways = $6! \times 3! = {}^3P_3 \times {}^6P_3$

(v) All the vowels are never together = (Number of ways of permutation of letters of word DAUGHTER) – (Number of ways when vowels are together) = 8! – (6! × 3!) = ${}^8P_8 - ({}^6P_6 \times {}^3P_3)$

(vi) First of all arrange the five consonant among themselves, and it can be done in 5! Ways.

Ⓧ C. Ⓧ C Ⓧ C Ⓧ C Ⓧ C Ⓧ

Now the vowels can be arranged in any three of the six places in between/before/after consonants represented by cross marks as shown above. It can be done in ${}^6P_3$ ways.
∴ Total number of ways = $5! \times {}^6P_3 = {}^5P_5 \times {}^6P_3$

(vii) Odd prime positions are 3rd, 5th, and 7th, three vowels can be arranged in these places in ${}^3P_3$ ways.
Now the consonants can be arranged in remaining 5 places i.e., 1st, 2nd, 4th, 6th, and 8th, in ${}^5P_5$ ways.
∴ Required number of ways = ${}^3P_3 \times {}^5P_5 = 3! \times 5! = 720$

(viii) Total number of permutations = 8!. Now in these 8! Permutations *D, E, R* can be permuted in 3! i.e., 6 ways out of which only one specific arrangement is desirable which is when *D* occurs before *E* and E occur before R.
Thus required number of ways = $\frac{8!}{3!} = 8 \times 7 \times 6 \times 5 \times 4 = 56 \times 120 = 6720.$

(ix) Following patterns are desirable
……… *D* ……….. *R* ……….. *S*
And
……… *R* ……….. *D* ……… *E*
∴ Required number of ways = $2\left(\frac{8!}{3!}\right) = 2 \times 6720 = 13440$

(x) There are two possible types of permutation for whose case
(a) When *D* …… *R* occure
(b) When *R* ……. *D* occure
∴ Required ways = 2 × 6! = 2 × 720 = 1440.

7. White and black balls are never together
= (Total number of ways) – (Number of ways white and black balls are together)
= 6! – (5! × 2!) = ${}^6P_6 - 2({}^5P_5)$

8. Number of 6 digit number formed using the digits 0, 1, 3, 5, 7, 9 = $\underset{\text{(except for 0)}}{5} \times 5 \times 4 \times 3 \times 2 \times 1 = 600$

For disability by 10, unit plane digit must be 0. Remaining places can be filled up in 5 × 4 × 3 × 2 × 1 i.e., 120 ways.

9. **(a)** For *a* number to be greater then 40,000, first place digit has two choices 4 or 5, 2nd place digit has 4 choices 3rd place has choices 2nd place only one choice.
∴ Required number of numbers = 2 × 4 × 3 × 2 × 1 = 48
(b) Odd number greater than 80,000, first place has only one choice i.e., 8 units place has two choices i.e., 3 & 5 Now 2nd, 3rd and 4th places has 3, 2 and 1 choice respectively.
Thus total number of ways = 1 × 2 × 3 × 2 × 1 = 12 numbers

10. Any number between 3000 and 4000 has its first place digit 3. It will be divisible by 5 if its unit place digit is 5.
Now 2nd and 3rd place has 4 and 3 choices respectively. Thus required number of numbers = 1 × 4 × 3 × 1 = 12 ways.

11. **(i)** Total 10 persons can be arranged in a row in ${}^{10}P_{10} = 10!$
(ii) Taking the graph of ladies as a single object, this group and 5 gents can be arranged in 6! Ways.
Now corresponding to each of 6! Ways, 5 ladies can be arranged among themselves in 5! Ways.
Thus the total number of ways = 6! × 5! Ways.
(iii) Required number of ways = 2! × 5! × 5!, as ladies group and gent group can be arranged in 2! Ways. i.e., (ladies) (gents) or (gents) (ladies) corresponding to each ways 5 ladies and 5 gents can be arranged in 5! × 5! Ways.
∴ Total ways = $2! \times 5! \times 5! = 2! \times (5!)^2$
(iv) Number two ladies are together i.e., ladies cases separated first of all arrange the gents in 5! Ways.
Now in between the gents, before and after total 6 vacancies are generated in which 5 ladies can be arranged in ${}^6P_5$ ways.
Thus total ways = $5! \times {}^6P_5 = 5! \times 6!$
(v) First permuting ladies and arranging gents in between them staring from second position i.e., Lm_1 Gn_1 Lm_2 Gn_2 Lm_3 Gn_3 Lm_4 Gn_4 Lm_5 Gn_5; where $m_i, n_i \leftarrow \{1, 2, 3, 4, 5\}$
Number of ways = 5! × 5!
Similarly first permuting ladies and arranging gents in between, then starting from first position i.e., Gn_1 Lm_1 Gn_2, Lm_2, $Gn_3 Lm_3$ Gn_4 Lm_4 Gn_5 Lm_5
Number of ways = 5! × 5!
∴ Total number of ways = $2! \times (5!)^2$
(vi) Considering (L_1, L_2) on single group and permuting along with L_3, L_4, L_5, G_1, G_2, G_3, G_4 and G_5, number of ways = 2! × 9!
(vii) G_1, G_2 re nor together = Total ways – number of ways when $\mathbf{G}_1$ and G_2 are together
= 10! – 2! × 9!

(viii) L_1, L_2 together and G_1, G_2 together = Number of ways = $2! \times 2! \times 8!$

(xi) L_1 L_2 together and G_1 G_2 never together = (L_1 L_2 together) – (G_1 G_2 together and L_1 L_2 together)
$= 2! \times 9! - 2! \times 2! \times 8!$

(x) L_1 L_2 not together and G_1G_2 not together
= Total ways – (number of ways when either L_1 L_2 together or G_1 G_2 together)
$= 10! - [(L_1\ L_2 \text{ together}) + (G_1\ G_2 \text{ together}) - (L_1\ L_2 \text{ and } G_1\ G_2 \text{ together})]$
$= 10! - [2! \times 9! + 2! \times 9! - 2! \times 2! \times 8!]$
$= 10! - [2! \times 2! \times 9! - 2! \times 2! \times 8!]$
$= 10! - 2! \times 2! \times 8!\ (9 - 1) = 8!\ (10 \times 9 - 2 \times 2 \times 8) = (58) \times 8!$

12. Number of arrangement that do not contain F
= Total arrangements – number of arrangements units which contains F
$= {}^6P_4 - 240$
$= \frac{6!}{2!} - 240 = 360 - 240 = 120$

TEXTUAL EXERCISE–3: (OBJECTIVE)

1. (c) $\frac{51! - 50!}{25} = \frac{(51-1)\times 50!}{25} = 2(50!)$

2. (b) $\frac{n!}{(n-3)!} + \frac{(2n)!}{4(2n-3)!}$
$= n(n-1)(n-2) + \frac{(2n)(2n-1)(2n-2)}{4}$
$= n(n-1)\ (n-2) + n(2n-1)\ (n-1)$
$= n(n-1)\ [n - 2 + 2n - 1] = 3n\ (n-1)^2$

3. (d) $f(n) = \frac{36.9.12....(3n)}{(3)^n} = \frac{(3)^n (1.2.3....n)}{(3)^n} = n!$
$\therefore\ f(50) = 50!$

4. (b) Given $t_n = n!.n$
$= n!\ (n + 1 - 1) = (n + 1)! - n!$
$\therefore\ S_n = t_1 + t_2 + ... + t_n$
$= (2! - 1!) + (3! - 2!) + ... + [(n + 1)! - n!] = (n + 1)! - 1!$

5. (c) $\frac{{}^nP_{r-1}}{a} = \frac{{}^nP_r}{b} = \frac{{}^nP_{r+1}}{c}$
$\Rightarrow \frac{n!}{a(n-r+1)!} = \frac{n!}{(n-r)!b} = \frac{n!}{(n-r-1)!c}$
$\Rightarrow \frac{1}{a(n-r+1)(n-r)} = \frac{1}{(n-r)b} = \frac{1}{c} = \frac{1}{k}$ (say)
$\Rightarrow a = \frac{k}{(n-r+1)(n-r)}$; $b = \frac{k}{(n-r)}; c = k$
$\Rightarrow ab = \frac{k^2}{(n-r+1)(n-r)^2}$;
$b = \frac{k}{(n-r)}; ac = \frac{k^2}{(n-r+1)(n-r)}$

Clearly ab, b, ac can't be in G.P. and A.P.
Now, $b^2 = \frac{k^2}{(n-r)^2}$;
$ab + ac = \frac{k^2}{(n-r+1)(n-r)}\left[\frac{1}{(n-r)} + 1\right]$
$= \frac{k^2}{(n-r+1)(n-r)}\left[\frac{(1+n-r)}{(n-r)}\right] = \frac{k^2}{(n-r)^2}$
$\therefore\ b^2 = a\ (b + c)$

6. (b) ${}^1P_1 + 2\ .{}^2P_2 + 3\ .{}^3P_3 + ... + n\ .{}^nP_n$
$= (1)\ 1! + 2(2!) + 3(3!) + ... + n(n!)$
$= \sum_{r=1}^{n} r(r!) = \sum_{r=1}^{n} (r+1-1)r! = \sum_{r=1}^{n} [(r+1)! - r!]$
$= (n + 1)! - 1!$
$= \frac{(n+2)!}{(n+2)} - 1$ or $\frac{(n+3)!}{(n+3)(n+2)} - 1$
$= \frac{1}{(n+2)}.{}^{(n+2)}P_{(n+2)} - 1$ or $\frac{1}{(n+3)(x+2)}.{}^{n+3}P_{n+3} - 1$

7. (a) $\frac{{}^nP_{r-1}}{a} = \frac{{}^nP_r}{b} = \frac{{}^nP_{r+1}}{c}$;
As in solution of question number (5), $b^2 = a(b + c)$
$\Rightarrow \frac{b^2}{a(b+c)} = 1$

8. (a), (b) ${}^nP_n = n!;\ {}^nP_{n-1} = \frac{n!}{1!} = n!$
${}^{n-1}P_{n-1} = (n-1)!$
$\Rightarrow$ (a) is false.
Now ${}^{n-1}P_{r-1} = \frac{(n-l)!}{(n-r)!} \neq {}^nP_r$
$\Rightarrow$ (b) is false.
Now $n\ .{}^{n-1}P_{r-1} = n.\left(\frac{(n-1)!}{(n-r)!}\right) = \frac{n!}{(n-l)!} = {}^nP_r$
$\Rightarrow$ (c) is true.
Now $2.{}^nP_{n-2} = 2\left(\frac{n!}{2!}\right) = {}^nP_n$
Also $3.{}^nP_{n-3} = 3\left(\frac{n!}{3!}\right) = {}^nP_n$
$\Rightarrow$ (d) is true.

9. (b) Given ${}^{56}P_{r+6} : {}^{54}P_{r+3} = 30800 : 1$
$\Rightarrow \frac{56!}{(50-r)!} \times \frac{(51-r)!}{54!} = 30800$
$\Rightarrow 56 \times 55 \times (51 - r) = 30800$
$\Rightarrow 51 - r = 10 \qquad \Rightarrow r = 41$

10. (b) $\sum_{r=1}^{10} r.{}^rP_r = \sum_{r=1}^{10} r.r! = \sum_{r=1}^{10} [(r+1)! - r!] = 11! - 1 = {}^{11}P_{11} - 1$

11. (a) ${}^{2n+1}P_{n-1} : {}^{2n-1}P_n = 3 : 5$
$\Rightarrow \frac{(2n+1)!}{(n+2)!} \times \frac{(n-1)!}{(2n-1)!} = \frac{3}{5}$
$\Rightarrow \frac{(2n+1)(2n)}{(n+2)(n+1)(n)} = \frac{3}{5}$

$\Rightarrow$ $10(2n+1) = 3(n+2)(n+1)$

$\Rightarrow$ $20n + 10 = 3n^2 + 9n + 6$

$\Rightarrow$ $3n^2 - 11n - 4 = 0 \quad \Rightarrow \quad 3n^2 - 12n + n - 4 = 0$

$\Rightarrow$ $3n(n-4) + 1(n-4) = 0$

$\Rightarrow$ $(n-4)(3n+1) = 0$

$\Rightarrow$ $n = 4$

12. **(a)** Ist price has 50 choices
IInd price has 49 choices
IIIrd price has 48 choices

$\therefore$ Total $= 50 \times 49 \times 48 = \dfrac{50!}{47!} = {}^{50}P_3$

13. **(d)** Let any number less than 1000 be of three digits.
If 1st and 2nd place digits are zeros, then 3rd place has 5 choices 1, 3, 5, 7 and 9
If 1st place digits are zeros, then 3rd place has 5 choices i.e., 1,3,5,7 or 9 and 2nd place hove 4 choices

$\therefore$ Two digits odd numbers having different digits $= 5 \times 4 = 20$
If no place have zero, 3rd place has 5 choices
2nd place has 4 choices and 1st place has 3 choices

$\therefore$ Total 3 digit odd numbers $= 5 \times 4 \times 3 = 60$

$\therefore$ Total nos. $= 5 + 20 + 60 = 85$

14. **(a, c)** 1st ring has 10 choices
2nd ring has 9 choices
3rd ring has 8 choices

$\therefore$ Total ways $= 10 \times 9 \times 8 = \dfrac{10!}{7!} = {}^{10}P_3$

15. **(a)** Number of opening order pairs $= {}^{11}P_2$

16. **(a)** 1st, 2nd, 3rd, 4th, and 5th strips can be coloured Respectively in 8, 7, 6, 5 and 4 ways.

$\therefore$ Total ways $= 8 \times 7 \times 6 \times 5 \times 4 = {}^8P_3 = {}^8P_5$

17. **(b, c)** Number of different 4 letter $= {}^{26}P_4 = \dfrac{26!}{22!}$

18. **(c)** Every ticket corresponds to an ordered pair of two stations.

Thus number of tickets required $= {}^{10}P_2 = \dfrac{10!}{8!}$

19. **(c)** Number of ways = permutation of 9 taking 6 at *a* time $= {}^9P_6$

20. **(c)** ${}^nP_4 = 12\,({}^nP_2)$

$\Rightarrow \dfrac{n!}{(n-4)!} = 12\left(\dfrac{n!}{n-2!}\right)$

$\Rightarrow \dfrac{1}{(n-4)!} = \dfrac{12}{(n-2)(n-3)(n-4)!}$

$\Rightarrow 1 = \dfrac{12}{(n-2)(n-3)}$

$\Rightarrow (n-2)(n-3) = 12 \quad \Rightarrow \quad n = 6$

21. **(d)** Number of ways of arranging m things = m!
Now we have $(m+1)$ places to fill and n thing to be placed so that they are separated out by m thins.
This can be done in ${}^{m+1}P_n$ ways.

$\therefore$ Total ways $= m!\,({}^{m+1}P_n)$ ways $= m!\left[\dfrac{(m+1)!}{(m+1-n)!}\right]$

22. **(a)** (AU), *L*, *G*, *H* can be arranged in $4! \times 2! = 48$ ways.

23. **(c)** …….. *A* …….. *B* ……….. *C* ………… *D* …………
Total ways = 10!
But required ways $= \dfrac{10!}{4!}$
Since order (*A*, *B*, *C*, *D*) is desired.

24. **(c)** Required ways = (Total words) – (Numbers of words having no vowel)
$= {}^6P_3 - ({}^4P_3)$
$= \dfrac{6!}{3!} - \dfrac{4!}{1!} = 120 - 24 = 96$

25. **(a)** *A X Y B*
Let between the two particular persons *A* and *B*, two persons be identified by *X* and *Y* and they can be selected in ${}^6C_2$ ways and they can be arranged in between *A* and *B* in $\underbrace{2!}_{AB \text{ or } BA} \times \underbrace{2!}_{XY \text{ or } YX} \times {}^6C_2$ ways
Now each of this group consisting of *A*, *B*, *X* and *Y* along with other 4 persons can be arranged in 5! Ways

$\therefore$ Total ways $= 2! \times 2! \times {}^6C_2 \times 5! = 60\,(5!)$

26. **(d)** 8 straight lines can intersect each other at ${}^8C_2$ points
4 circles can intersect each other at $2[{}^4C_2]$ ways
Also 8 straight lines and 4 circles can intersect each other at $2(8 \times 4)$ points
Thus greatest number of points of intersection $= {}^8C_2 + 2({}^4C_2) + 2\,(8 \times 4)$
$= 28 + 12 + 64 = 104$ points

TEXTUAL EXERCISE–4: (SUBJECTIVE)

1. **(i)** $\underbrace{(IUAE)}_{(1)\text{ vowels}}\overset{}{N}SRNC$ (2 3 4 5 6)

Number of ways $= 4! = \dfrac{6!}{2!}$ ($\because$ *N* is repeated twice)
$= 360 \times 24 = 8460$

(ii) Vowels never occur together = (Total number of ways) – (Number of ways when vowels occur together)

$= \dfrac{9!}{2!} - \dfrac{4! \times 6!}{2!} = \dfrac{6!}{2!}[9 \times 8 \times 7 - 4 \times 3 \times 2 \times 1]$

$= \dfrac{6!}{2!} \times 8(60) = 172800$

2. *A L L A H A B A D* (1 2 3 4 5 6 7 8 9)

Total number of words formed $= \dfrac{9!}{4!2!}$

($\because$ *A* is repeated 4 times, *L* is repeated 2 times)

Number of ways when both L are not together = (total number of ways) – (number of ways when both L are together)

$= \dfrac{9!}{4!2!} - \dfrac{8!}{4!} \qquad \left(\because \underbrace{(LL)}_{1} A A H A B A D \;\; 2\;3\;4\;5\;6\;7\;8\right)$

3. 4 red, 2 white and 3 green flags.
Required number of ways = Number of permutation of

$\underbrace{RRRR}_{4 \text{ red flags}}\ \underbrace{WW}_{2 \text{ white flags}}\ \underbrace{GGG}_{3 \text{ green flags}} = \dfrac{9!}{4!2!3!}$

4. Given digits are 5, 4, 3, 5, 3
Number of numbers formed using all at *a* time = number of permutations of 5, 4, 3, 5, 3
$= \frac{5!}{2!2!}$ ($\because$ 5 and 3 are repeated twice)

5. Given digits are 1, 2, 0, 2, 4, 2, 4
Number of 7 digit numbers formed = (Total number of permutations) – (Number of permutations when 0 is at Ist place)
$= \frac{7!}{3!2!} - \frac{6!}{3!2!} = \frac{6!}{3!2!}(7-1) = \frac{6!}{2!} = 360$

6. **(a)** Given digits are 1, 2, 3, 4, 3, 2, 1
It is require to arrange the odd digits at odd places i.e., at 1st, 3rd, 5th and 7th place odd digits are 1, 3, 3, 1 and hence they can be arranged in $\frac{4!}{2!2!}$ ways.
The remaining digits 2, 4, 2 can be arranged at 2nd, 4th, and 6th place in $\frac{3!}{2!}$ ways
$\therefore$ Total ways $= \frac{4!}{2!2!} \times \frac{3!}{2!} = 18$

(b) Given digits are 3, 3, 5, 4, 4, 6, 6.
Even digits are 4, 4, 6, 6 and they are to be placed at odd places i.e., at 1st, 3rd, 5th and 7th places.
This can be done in $\frac{4!}{2!2!}$ ways. The remaining digits 3, 3, 5 can be placed at 2nd, 4th and 6th places in $\frac{3!}{2!}$ ways.
$\therefore$ Total ways $= \frac{4!}{2!2!} \times \frac{3!}{2!} = 18$

7. **(a)** When 1 object is chosen, number of ways = n
When 2 objects are chosen, number of ways = $n \times n = n^2$
When 3 objects are chosen, number of ways = $n \times n \times n = n^3$
When r objects are chosen, number of ways = n^r
$\therefore$ Total ways $= n + n^2 + n^3 + ... + n^r = \frac{n(n^r - 1)}{(n-1)}$

(b) Required number of ways = (Total out comes) – (Number of out comes when no die shown an odd number)
$= \underbrace{(6\times6\times6\times...\times6)}_{n-time} - \underbrace{(3\times3\times3\times...\times3)}_{n-time} = (6)^n - (3)^n$

8. Given digits are 0, 1, 2, 3,....,9
(a) Required numbers = $9 \times 10 \times 10 \times 10 \times 10$, as first place has 9 choices except for 0. $= 9 \times (10)^4$
(b) Required numbers = $9 \times 9 \times 8 \times 7 \times 6 = 27216$
(c) Required numbers = $\underset{\text{(except for 0)}}{9} \times \underset{\text{(except for 1st place digit)}}{9} \times \underset{\text{(Except for IInd place digits)}}{9} \times 9 \times 9 = (9)^5$
(d) Required numbers = (Total number of ways when repetition is allowed) – (number of ways when no two consecutive digits are same)
$= 9 \times (10)^4 - (9)^5 = 9(10^4 - 9^4)$

9. Required ways = (Total number of ways when a hotel can accommodate one or more friends) – (Number of ways when all friends stay in the same hotel) $= (10)^4 - 10 = 10(10^3 - 1) = 9990$

10. **(a)** Permutations of $\underbrace{D....D}_{9\text{ times}}\underbrace{AAA}_{3\text{ times}}\underbrace{YY}_{2\text{ times}}\underbrace{EEE}_{3\text{ times}}IL = \frac{19!}{9!3!2!3!}$
(b) Permutation of $\underbrace{II}_{2\text{ times}}\underbrace{TT}_{2\text{ times}}\underbrace{EEE}_{3\text{ times}}NRMDA = \frac{12!}{2!2!3!}$
(c) Permutations of $\underbrace{CC}_{2\text{ times}}\underbrace{AA}_{2\text{ times}}\underbrace{LL}_{2\text{ times}}UTOR = \frac{10!}{2!2!2!} = \frac{10!}{(2!)^3}$

11. **(a)** To reach from X to Y the man requires to take 5 horizontal steps and 4 verticle steps.
$\therefore$ Required number of ways $= \frac{(5+4)!}{5!\cdot4!}$ i.e., number of permutations of *HHHHHVVVV*. i.e., $\frac{9!}{5!4!}$
(b) To go for X to B, number of ways $= \frac{(2+2)!}{2!2!}$ i.e., permutation of *HHVV* and to go from B to Y, number of ways $= \frac{(3+2)!}{3!\cdot2!}$ i.e., permutation of *HHHVV*.
$\therefore$ Total number of ways to go form X to Y, via $B = \frac{4!}{2!2!} \times \frac{5!}{3!2!} = \frac{24\times120}{4\times12} = 60$ ways.

12. Each n-bit sting corresponds to an n-digit word. The bit has value 1 corresponding to digit occurring in the word and 0 corresponding to digit not occurring in the word.
So to represent all possible permutations of n-digits, we require $\underbrace{2\times2\times2\times....\times2}_{n-times} = (2)^n$ string.
Out of these string only one string is the having no zero i.e., $\underbrace{111...1}_{n-times}$
(a) Thus number of strings having at least one zero $= (2)^n - 1$
(b) Similarly there are two strings having either all 1's or all 0's, thus the numbers of strings having both 1's and zeros $= (2)^n - 2$

TEXTUAL EXERCISE-4: (OBJECTIVE)

1. **(b)** First place has 9 choices (except for 0)
Second place, 3rd place and 4th place each has 10 choices.
$\therefore$ Total number of 4 digits numbers $= 9 \times 10^3$
Aliter: Largest 4 digits numbers = 9999
Largest 3 digit number = 999
$\therefore$ Total 4 digit numbers $= 9000 = 9 \times 10^3$

2. **(c)** Since each question can be answered in 4 ways
$\therefore$ 10 questions can be answered in $4 \times 4 \times 4 \times .... \times 4 = (4)^{10}$ ways
Out of these $(4)^{10}$ ways only one sequence of answers is correct.
So number of wrong answer sequences $= (4)^{10} - 1$

3. **(a)** Each digit of 5 digited code has 10 choices (0 to 9)
$\therefore$ Maximum number of attempts require to unlock $= 10 \times 10 \times 10 \times 10 \times 10 = (10)^5$

4. (a) Each number between 100 and 1000 is 3 digit number. Now for each digit to be odd, each digit of number has 5 choices i.e., 1, 3, 5, 7 or 9

$\therefore$ Total number of such type = $5 \times 5 \times 5 = (5)^3$

5. (b) Since each delegate has 6 choices for office

$\therefore$ 5 delegates has $6 \times 6 \times 6 \times 6 \times 6 = (6)^5$ choices.

6. (c) Obviously there are five rings and hence the unlocking code is 5 digited, with each digit on each ring.

Now each digit of code has 10 choices

So maximum number of attempted require = $(10)^5$

Now, dialing 1 code require 5 seconds

$\therefore$ Total time requires to attempted all codes = $\dfrac{(10)^5 \times 5}{3600} = \dfrac{5\times 10^3}{36}$ = 138.8 has $\simeq 11.56 \times 12$ hrs.

i.e., 12th day

7. (i) (b) Each person can leave the cabin at any one of the 7floors

$\therefore$ 5 persons can leave the cabin in $7 \times 7 \times 7 \times 7 \times 7 = (7)^5$ ways

(ii) (c) 1st person can leave the cabin at any one of the 7 floors

2nd person can leave the cabin at any of 6 floors and so on.

$\therefore$ Number of ways in which 5 persons can leave the cabin at different floors

$= 7 \times 6 \times 5 \times 4 \times 3 = \dfrac{7!}{2!}$

Aliter: Number of ways = ${}^7P_5 = \dfrac{7!}{2!}$

8. (a) Each of 5 bungalow can be given to any one of the 3 daughters

$\therefore$ Number of ways = $3 \times 3 \times 3 \times 3 \times 3 = (3)^5$ ways

9. (b) ${}^6P_6 + {}^6P_5 + {}^6P_4 + {}^6P_3 + {}^6P_2 + {}^6P_1$ (using any 6, any 5, any 4,...,any 1)

$= \dfrac{6!}{0!} + \dfrac{6!}{1!} + \dfrac{6!}{2!} + \dfrac{6!}{3!} + \dfrac{6!}{4!} + \dfrac{6!}{5!} = 720 + 720 + 360 + 120 + 30 + 6 = 1956$

10. (c) Required ways = (Total ways) – (Number of ways when no die shows an odd numbers) = $(6)^n - (3)^n$

11. (d) Required number of ways = (Total number of ways) – (Number of ways when no die shows *a* 5)

$= (6 \times 6 \times 6) - (5 \times 5 \times 5) = 216 - 125 = 91$

12. (d) Number of ways in which *a* student can fail to get all answer correct

= (Total number of sequences) – 1(correct sequences) = $(4)^3 - 1 = 63$

13. (c) Let the number of candidates = n

$\therefore$ a votes can vote for maximum $(n - 1)$ candidate

$\therefore$ A voter can vote in ${}^nC_1 + {}^nC_2 + {}^nC_3 + ... + {}^nC_{n-1}$ ways

$\Rightarrow (2)^n - 2 - 62 \quad \Rightarrow (2)^n = 64$

$\Rightarrow$ n = 6

14. (b) Required ways = (Number of ways of forming subsets *A* and *B*) – (Number of ways of for subsets *A* and *B*) such that $A \cup B = \phi$ or $A \cup B = \mathbf{p}$

= [number of ways in which n elements can be distributed among four places $A \cap B^c, B \cap A^c, A \cap B, (A \cup B)^c$]

– [number of ways in which n elements can be distributed among three places i.e., $(A \cap B^c), (B \cap A^c), (A \cap B)$]

– 1 (when $A = \phi, B = \phi, P = (A \cup B)^c = \phi^c$)

Remark: (A non-empty set having at least one element less than the number of elements of set *A* is called proper subset of *A*) = $(4)^n - (3)^n - 1$

15. (b) m = Number of permutations of letters of the word BHARAT, when *B* and *H* are never together

$= \dfrac{6!}{2!} - \dfrac{51}{2!} \times 2!$ (keeping (**BH**) together and permuting with *A, R, A, T*)

= 360 – 120 = 240 and n = number of permutations of the letters of the word BHARAT when each word begins with *B* and ends with $T = \dfrac{4!}{2!} = 12$

$\therefore \dfrac{m}{n} = \dfrac{240}{12} = 20$

TEXTUAL EXERCISE–5: (SUBJECTIVE)

1. Number of ways = $\dfrac{(25-1)!}{2!} = \dfrac{24!}{2}$

2. Number of ways = $\dfrac{(21-1)!}{2} = \dfrac{20!}{2}$

3. Consider the group of 3 specific beads as *a* single article and hence the total articles to be permuted in circular way are 21. Also group of 3 specific beads can be arranged in 3! ways and corresponding to each of 3! ways, we have $\dfrac{(21-1)!}{2} = \dfrac{20!}{2}$ circular arrangements.

$\therefore$ Total ways = $\dfrac{3! \times 20!}{2}$

4. Group of secretary, president, and joint secretary can be formed in following two ways.

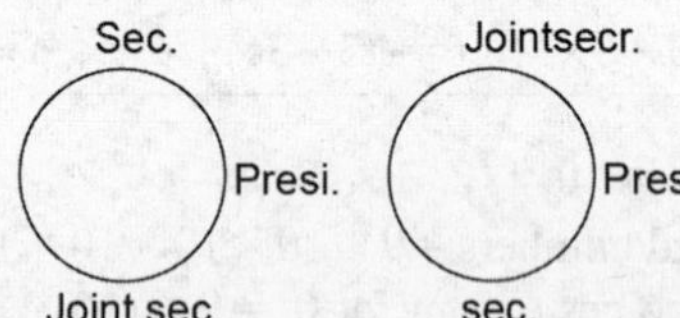

Considering the group of above three specific persons as *a* single article, we have total 13 articles to be permuted around round articles.

$\therefore$ Number of ways = $2(13 - 1)! = 2(12!)$

5. The consonant *M, N, D, Y* can be permuted around the circle in $(4 - 1)!$ i.e., 3! Ways.

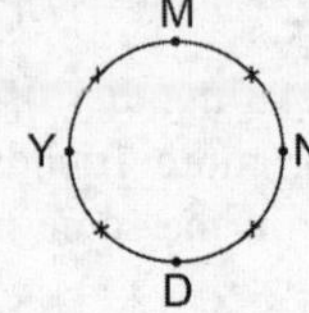

Now in between the consonants 4 gaps are there, in which we can arrange the vowels O and A, which can be done in ${}^4P_2$ ways.

∴ Total number of circular arrangements $= 3! \times {}^4P_2$

$$= \frac{3! \times 4!}{2!} = \frac{6 \times 24}{2} = 72 \text{ ways.}$$

6. There are 3 different red flowers} → 1st article
5 different yellow flowers} → 2nd article
and 4 different blue flowers} → 3rd article

Required number of ways $= \frac{(3-1)!}{2} \times 3! \times 5! \times 4! = 17280$

7. Girl Y can have two girls in her neighborhood in two ways i.e., $G_1\,Y\,G_2$ or $G_2\,Y\,G_1$
Similarly corresponding to each of two arrangements of girls group, boy X can have two boys in his neighborhood in two ways i.e., $B_1 \times B_2$ or $B_2 \times B_1$

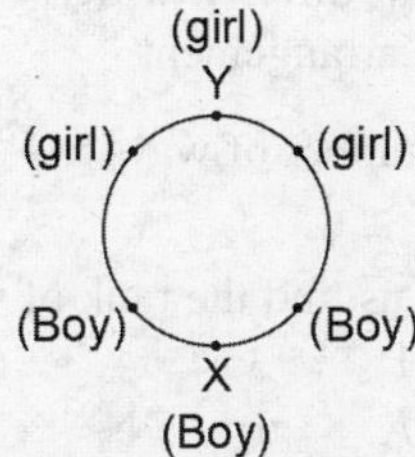

∴ Total ways $= 2 \times 2 = 4$

8. (a) No two girls sit together i.e., girls are separated. First of all arranging boys around table in $(5-1)! = 4!$ ways. Now to separate the girls arrange then in 5 places in between the boys and it can be done in 5! Ways

∴ Total ways $= 4! \times 5!$

(b) Neither two girls, nor two boys together means girls and boys are separated i.e., they are alternately.
As in part (a), number of ways $= 4! \times 5!$

(c) All boys are sitting together: means all girls are also sitting together. Therefore number of ways $= 5! \times 5!$

(d) b_1b_2 sit together and g_1g_2 sit together: we have following articles to be permuted around the circle (b_1b_2), (g_1g_2), $b_3, b_4, b_5, g_3, g_4, g_5$

∴ Number of ways $= (8-1)! \times 2! \times 2! = (2!)^2 \times 7!$

(e) b_1b_2 together but g_1g_2 not together = Number of ways when b_1b_2 are together –
Number of ways when b_1b_2 as well as g_1g_2 are together $= (9-1)! \times 2! - (2!)^2 \times 7! = 8! \times 2! - (2!)^2 \times 7!$

(f) Neither b_1, b_2 nor g_1, g_2 sit together
= (Total number of ways) – [$(b_1\ b_2$ together) + $(g_1\ g_2$ together) – $(b_1b_2$ aswell as g_1g_2 together)]
$= (10-1)! - [(9-1)! \times 2! + (9-1)! \times 2! - (2!)^2 \times 7!]$
$= 9! - [8! \times 2! \times 2 - (2!)^2 \times 7!] = 7!\,[72 - 32 + 4] = 44(7!)$

9. (a) Between B_1 and B_2 one person X can be selected in ${}^{18}C_1 = 18$ ways and the group of two brothers and X can be arranged in 2 ways i.e., $B_1 \times B_2$ or $B_2 \times B_1$. Now these groups along with other 17 persons can be arranged on round table in $2 \times (18-1)!$ Ways
$= 18 \times 2 \times 17! = 2(18!)$ ways

(b) First of all arranging the 18 people around the table in 17! Ways.
Now two brothers can be arranged in between the 18 people in ${}^{18}P_2$ ways.

∴ Total ways $= 17! \times {}^{18}P_2 = 17! \times \frac{18!}{16!} = 17(18!)$

(c) When exactly one person sits in between the twins $\underbrace{B \times B}_{1}, P_1, P_2, P_3 \ldots P_{17}$
Number of ways $= {}^{18}C_1 \times (18-1)! = 18 \times 17! = 18!$
The two brothers are always separated
Number of ways $= (18-1)! \times {}^{18}C_2 = \frac{17! \times 18!}{2!\,16!} = \frac{17 \times 18!}{2}$

10. To find the rank of a word we have two methods
(i) Exhaustive method
(ii) Short cut method
We shall find rank of word 'RATNA' by using both methods and by short cut method for the remaining words.

(a) Rank of 'RATNA' by using exhaustive method:
Let less of word RATNA are A, A, N, R, T

Number of words starting with A: $A\underbrace{(ANRT)}_{\text{permute}} = 4! = 24$

Number of words starting with N: $N\underbrace{(AART)}_{\text{permute}} = \frac{4!}{2!} = 12$

Number of words starting with RAA: $RAA\underbrace{(TN)}_{\text{permute}} = 2! = 2$

Number of words starting with RAN: $RAN\underbrace{(TA)}_{\text{permute}} = 2! = 2$

Number of words starting with RATA: $RATA\underbrace{(N)}_{\text{permute}} = 1! = 1$

Number of words starting with RATN: RATNA = 1! = 1

∴ Rank of RATNA = 24 + 12 + 2 + 2 + 1 + 1 = 42

RANK of RATNA by short cut method:

Step I: Write the letters of the word RATNA and above them number according to their order in English alphabet, keeping same number for same letter as shown below

3	1	4	2	1
R	A	T	N	A

Step II: Rank will be $(4! \times x_1 + 3! \times x_2 + 2! \times x_3 + 1! \times x_4 + 0! \times x_5 + 1)$;
Where x_i = (number of letters on the right of ith letter having numbers less than that on ith letter)/(factors having factorials of number of times each letter repeats)

$$\therefore\ x_1 = \frac{3}{2!};\ x_2 = \frac{0}{2!};\ x_3 = \frac{2}{0!};\ x_4 = \frac{1}{0!};\ x_5 = \frac{0}{0!}$$

$$\therefore\ \text{Rank} = 4! \times \frac{3}{2!} + 3! \times \frac{0}{2!} + 2! \times \frac{2}{0!} + 1! \times \frac{1}{0!} + 0! \times \frac{0}{0!} + 1$$

$= 26 + 0 + 4 + 1 + 1 = 42$

(b) RANK of word Father

3	1	6	4	2	5
F	A	T	H	E	R

$\therefore$ Rank = 5! (x_1) + 4! (x_2) + 3! (x_3) + 2! (x_4) + 1! (x_5) + 0! (x_6) + 1;

Where $x_1 = \frac{2}{0!}; x_2 = \frac{0}{0!}; x_3 = \frac{3}{0!}; x_4 = \frac{1}{0!}; x_5 = \frac{0}{0!}; x_6 = \frac{0}{0!}$

$\therefore$ Rank = $5! = \frac{2}{0!} + 4! \times \frac{0}{0!} + 3! \times \frac{3}{0!} +$

$2! \times \frac{1}{0!} + 1! \times \frac{0}{0!} + 0! \times \frac{0}{0!} + 1 = 240 + 18 + 2 + 1 = 261$

(c) Rank of word SHRUTI

4	1	3	6	5	2
S	H	R	U	T	I

Rank: $5!\left(\frac{3}{0!}\right) + 4! \times \left(\frac{0}{0!}\right) + 3! \times \left(\frac{1}{0!}\right) +$

$2! \times \left(\frac{2}{0!}\right) + 1! \times \left(\frac{1}{0!}\right) + 0! \times \left(\frac{0}{0!}\right) + 1$

$= 360 + 0 + 6 + 4 + 1 + 0 + 1 = 372$

(d) Rank of word ARRANGE:

1	5	5	1	4	3	2
A	R	R	A	N	G	E

Rank: $6!\left(\frac{0}{2!2!}\right) + 5!\left(\frac{4}{2!}\right) + 4!\left(\frac{4}{0!}\right) + 3!\left(\frac{0}{0!}\right) +$

$2!\left(\frac{2}{0!}\right) + 1!\left(\frac{1}{0!}\right) + 0!\left(\frac{0}{0!}\right) + 1$

$= 0 + 240 + 96 + 0 + 4 + 1 + 1 = 342$

(e) Rank of word TOPOLOGY

5	3	4	3	2	3	1	6
T	O	P	O	L	O	G	Y

Rank: $7!\left(\frac{6}{3!}\right) + 6!\left(\frac{2}{3!}\right) + 5!\left(\frac{4}{2!}\right) + 4!\left(\frac{2}{2!}\right) +$

$3!\left(\frac{1}{0!}\right) + 2!\left(\frac{1}{0!}\right) + 1!\left(\frac{0}{0!}\right) + 0!\left(\frac{0}{0!}\right) + 1$

$= 7! + 240 + 240 + 24 + 6 + 2 + 1 = 5040 + 513 = 5553$

(f) Rank of word JATTO:

3	1	3	3	2	2
T	A	T	T	O	O

Rank = $5!\left(\frac{3}{3!2!}\right) + 4!\left(\frac{0}{2!2!}\right) + 3!\left(\frac{2}{2!2!}\right) +$

$2!\left(\frac{2}{2!}\right) + 1!\left(\frac{0}{2!}\right) + 0!\left(\frac{0}{0!}\right) + 1$

$= 30 + 0 + 3 + 2 + 0 + 0 + 1 = 36$

TEXTUAL EXERCISE–5: (OBJECTIVE)

1. (d) Permuting 6 boys along line in 6! Ways.

$X\ B_1\ X\ B_2\ X\ B_3\ X\ B_4\ X\ B_5\ X\ B_6$

Or $B_1\ X\ B_2\ X\ B_3\ X\ B_4\ X\ B_5\ X\ B_6\ X$

Now in space in between boys, 6 girls can be arranged in 6! × 2 ways.

$\therefore$ Total ways = 6! × 6! × 2 = x (i)

Permuting 6 boys along circle in 5! Ways.

Now in 6 spaces in between the boys, 6 girls can be arranged in 6! Ways.

$\therefore$ Total ways = 5! × 6! = y (ii)

$\therefore \frac{x}{y} = \frac{6! \times 6! \times 2}{5! \times 6!} = 12 \Rightarrow x = 12y$

2. (c) $\left.\begin{matrix}(XY)(D_1D_2D_3....D_{18})\\(YX)(D_1D_2D_3....D_{18})\end{matrix}\right\}$; permutations = 2 × (19 – 1)!

= 2 × 18!

3. (a) Required ways = Total ways – number of ways when two particular delegates sit together

= (20 – 1)! — 2 × 18!

= 19! – 2 × 18! = 18! (19 – 2) = 17(18!)

4. (b) Let there be 10 red colored pearls (different) and 10 white colored pearls (different).

Now 10 Red colored pearls can be arranged along the circle in (10 – 1)! = 9! Ways.

After that 10 spaces are created in between the red colored pearls, in which 10 white colored pearls can be arranged in 10! Ways.

But there is no difference between the clockwise and anticlockwise arrangement

So required number of ways = $\frac{9! \times 10!}{2} = (9!)^2 \times 5$

5. (c) First of all let us find the rank of word 'AGAIN'

1	2	1	3	4
A	G	A	I	N

$\therefore$ Rank = $4!\left(\frac{0}{2!}\right) + 3!\left(\frac{1}{0!}\right) + 2!\left(\frac{0}{0!}\right) + 1!\left(\frac{0}{0!}\right) + 0!\left(\frac{0}{0!}\right) + 1$

$= 0 + 6 + 0 + 0 + 0 + 1 = 7$

It means fiftieth word is not starting with A.

Now, all words starting with A = 4! = 24

All words starting with $G = \frac{4!}{2!} = 12$

All words starting with $I = \frac{4!}{2} = 12$

Till now, we reached upto 24 + 12 + 12 = 48 words.

$\therefore$ Clearly, 49th word will start with N it will be NAAGI and 50th word will be NAAIG

6. (d)

4	5	2	1	3
D	E	B	A	C

Rank = $4!\left(\frac{3}{0!}\right) + 3!\left(\frac{3}{0!}\right) + 2!\left(\frac{1}{0!}\right) + 1!\left(\frac{0}{0!}\right) + 0!\left(\frac{0}{0!}\right) + 1$

$= 72 + 18 + 2 + 1 = 93$

7. (c)

6	1	2	4	5	3
T	A	C	K	L	E

$\therefore$ Rank = $5!\left(\frac{5}{0!}\right) + 4!\left(\frac{0}{0!}\right) + 3!\left(\frac{0}{0!}\right) +$

$2!\left(\frac{1}{0!}\right) + 1!\left(\frac{1}{0!}\right) + 0!\left(\frac{0}{0!}\right) + 1$

$= 600 + 2 + 1 + 1 = 604$

8. (c)

3	1	4	2
L	A	T	E

$\therefore$ Rank = $3!\left(\frac{2}{0!}\right) + 2!\left(\frac{0}{0!}\right) + 1!\left(\frac{1}{0!}\right) + 0!\left(\frac{0}{0!}\right) + 1 = 14$

TEXTUAL EXERCISE–6: (SUBJECTIVE)

1. (i) ${}^nCr = {}^nC_{3r-4}$

$\Rightarrow$ $r = 3r - 4$ or $r + 3r - 4 = x$ $\quad (\because {}^nC_r = {}^nC_{n-r})$

$\Rightarrow$ $r = 2$ or $r = \dfrac{n+4}{4}$; thus for a solution

$\Rightarrow$ $r = 2$ or $n + 4$ is divisible by 4

(ii) ${}^nC_r = {}^nC_{r^2-r}$

$\Rightarrow$ $r = r^2 - r$ or $r + r^2 - r = n$

$\Rightarrow$ $r^2 - 2r = 0$ or $r^2 = n$

$\Rightarrow$ $r = 0$ or 2 or $n = r^2$

$\Rightarrow$ $r = 0$ or 2 or n is a perfect square of some integer

(iii) ${}^nC_r - {}^nC_{r^2+2r}$

$\Rightarrow$ $r^2 + 2r = r$ or $r^2 + 2r + r = n$

$\Rightarrow$ $r^2 + r = 0$ or $r^2 + 3r = n$

$\Rightarrow$ $r = 0$ or -1 but $r \neq -1$

$\Rightarrow$ $r = 0$ or $r^2 + 3r = n$

$\Rightarrow$ $r = 0$ or $r = \dfrac{-3 \pm \sqrt{9+4n}}{2}$

$\Rightarrow$ $r = 0$ or $r = \dfrac{-3 + \sqrt{9+4n}}{2}$

Let $r = k \in \{1, 2, 3, ...\}$, then $k = \dfrac{-3+\sqrt{9+4n}}{2}$

$\Rightarrow$ $\sqrt{9+4n} = 2k+3$

$\Rightarrow$ $n = \dfrac{(2k+3)^2-9}{4}$

$\Rightarrow$ $r = 0$ is a solution □ $n \in \mathbb{N}$ and $r = k \in \mathbb{N}$ when $n = \dfrac{(2k+3)^2-9}{4}$

2. (a) ${}^nC_{r-1} = 28$ (i)

${}^nC_{r+1} = 70$ (ii)

${}^nC_r = 56$ (iii)

$\therefore \quad \dfrac{C}{C} = \dfrac{n-r+l}{r} = \dfrac{56}{28} =$

$\Rightarrow$ $n = 3r - 1$ (iv)

Also by same formula, replacing r by $r + 1$, we get

$\dfrac{{}^nC_{r+1}}{{}^nC_r} = \dfrac{n-(r+1)+1}{r+1} = \dfrac{70}{56} = \dfrac{5}{4}$

$\Rightarrow$ $n = \dfrac{5}{4}(r+1)+r$ (v)

Solving (iv) and (v), we get $r = 3$, $n = 8$

(b) ${}^{n+1}C_{r+1} : {}^nC_r : {}^{n-1}C_{r-1} = 56 : 35 : 20$

$\Rightarrow$ $\dfrac{x+1}{r+1}\cdot\dfrac{n}{r}\cdot{}^{n-1}C_{r-1} : \dfrac{n}{r}\cdot{}^{n-1}C_{r-1} : {}^{n-1}C_{r-1} = 56 : 30 : 20$

$\left(\because {}^nC_r = \dfrac{n}{r}\cdot{}^{n-1}C_{r-1}\right)$

$\Rightarrow$ $\dfrac{n+1}{r+1}\cdot\dfrac{n}{r} : \dfrac{n}{r} : 1 = 56 : 35 : 20$

$\Rightarrow$ $\dfrac{n}{r} = \dfrac{35}{20} = \dfrac{7}{4}$ (i)

And $\dfrac{n+1}{r+1} = \dfrac{56}{35} = \dfrac{8}{5}$ (ii)

Solving (i) and (ii), we get $x = 7$, $r = 4$

(c) To proved: $\displaystyle\sum_{r=1}^{n} r\left(\frac{{}^nC_r}{{}^nC_{r-1}}\right) = \sum_{k=1}^{n} k$

L.H.S $= \displaystyle\sum_{r=1}^{n} r\left(\frac{{}^nC_r}{{}^nC_{r-1}}\right) = \sum_{r=1}^{n} r\left(\frac{n-r+1}{r}\right)$

$= \displaystyle\sum_{r=1}^{n}(n+1-r) = \sum_{r=1}^{n}(n+1) - \sum_{r=1}^{n} r = n(n+1) - \frac{n(n+1)}{2}$

$= \dfrac{n(n+1)}{2} = \displaystyle\sum_{k=1}^{n} k =$ R.H.S.

(d) $\displaystyle\sum_{r=1}^{n} r^2\left(\frac{{}^nC_r}{{}^nC_{r-1}}\right) = \sum_{r=1}^{n} r^2\left(\frac{n-r+1}{r}\right) = \sum_{r=1}^{n} r(n-r+1)$

$= n\displaystyle\sum_{r=1}^{n} r - \sum_{r=1}^{n} r^2 + \sum_{r=1}^{n} r$

$= \dfrac{n^2(n+1)}{2} - \dfrac{n(n+1)(2n+1)}{6} + \dfrac{n(n+1)}{2}$

$= \dfrac{n(n+1)}{2}\left[n - \dfrac{(2n+1)}{3} + 1\right]$

$= \dfrac{n(n+1)}{2}\left[\dfrac{n+2}{3}\right] = \dfrac{n(n+1)(n+2)}{6}$

3. $\dfrac{{}^{2n}C_r}{{}^{2n}C_{r-1}} = \dfrac{2n-r+1}{r}; r \geq 1$

Now ${}^{2n}C_r > {}^{2n}C_{r-1}$

$\Leftrightarrow$ $2n - r + 1 > r$

$\Leftrightarrow$ $2n + 1 > 2r$

$\Leftrightarrow$ $r < n + \dfrac{1}{2}$

$\Leftrightarrow$ $r \leq n$

$\therefore$ ${}^{2n}C_r > {}^{2n}C_{r-1}$ for $r = 1, 2, 3, ..., n$

$\Rightarrow$ ${}^{2n}C_0 < {}^{2n}C_1 < {}^{2n}C_2 < {}^{2n}C_3 .... < {}^{2n}C_{n-1} < {}^{2n}C_n$ (i)

Now ${}^{2n}C_r < {}^{2n}C_{r-1}$

$\Leftrightarrow$ $2n - r + 1 < r$

$\Leftrightarrow$ $2n + 1 < 2r$

$\Rightarrow$ $r > n + \dfrac{1}{2}$

$\Rightarrow$ $r \geq (n + 1)$

$\Rightarrow$ ${}^{2n}C_n > {}^{2n}C_{n+1} > {}^{2n}C_{n+2} > {}^{2n}C_{n+3} > ... > {}^{2n}C_{2n+2} < {}^{2n}C_n$ (ii)

Combining (i) and (ii), we see that ${}^{2n}C_n$ is the greatest value.

Among ${}^{2n}C_r : r \in \{0, 1, 2,...,2n\}$.

4. (a) $\displaystyle\sum_{r=0}^{n} r({}^nC_r) = \sum_{r=1}^{n} r({}^nC_r) = \sum_{r=1}^{n} r\cdot\frac{n}{r}\cdot{}^{n-1}C_{r-1}$

$= \displaystyle\sum_{r=1}^{n} n\cdot{}^{n-1}C_{r-1} = n\sum_{r=1}^{n}{}^{n-1}C_{r-1} = n((2)^{n-1})$

(b) $\displaystyle\sum_{r=2}^{n} r(r-1)\,{}^nC_r = \sum r(r-1)\cdot\frac{n}{r}\frac{n}{r}\cdot\quad C$

$= n(n-1)\displaystyle\sum_{r=2}^{n}{}^{n-2}C_{r-2} = n(n-1)\,(2)^{n-2}$

(c) $\displaystyle\sum_{r=1}^{n} r^2\cdot{}^nC_r = \sum_{r=1}^{n} r^2\cdot\frac{n}{2}\cdot{}^{n-1}C_{r-1} = n\sum_{r=1}^{n} r\cdot{}^{n-1}C_{r-1}$

$= n\displaystyle\sum_{r=1}^{n}(r-1+1)^{n-1}C_{r-1}$

$= n\sum_{r=1}^{n}(r-1)\cdot {}^{n-1}C_{r-1} + n\sum_{r=1}^{n} {}^{n-1}C_{r-1}$

$= n\sum_{r=2}^{n}(r-1)\frac{(n-1)}{(r-1)}\cdot {}^{n-2}C_{r-2} + n(2)^{n-1}$

$= n(n-1)\sum_{r=2}^{n} {}^{n-2}C_{r-2} + n(2)^{n-1}$

$= n(n-1)(2)^{n-2} + n(2)^{n-1} = n[(n-1)+2](2)^{n-2} = n(n+1)(2)^{n-2}$

(d) $\sum_{r=1}^{n} r^3 \cdot {}^nC_r$

$= n\sum_{r=1}^{n} r^2 \cdot {}^{n-1}C_{r-1}$

$= n\sum_{r=1}^{n}[(r^2-1)+1]\cdot {}^{n-1}C_{r-1}$

$= n\sum_{r=1}^{n}(r-1)(r+1)\cdot {}^{n-1}C_{r-1} + n\sum_{r=1}^{n} {}^{n-1}C_{r-1}$

$= n\sum_{r=2}^{n}(r+1)(n-1)^{n-2}C_{r-2} + n(2)^{n-1}$

$= n(n-1)\sum_{r=2}^{n}(r-2+3)^{n-2}C_{r-2} + n(2)^{n-1}$

$= n(n-1)\sum_{r=2}^{n}(r-2)\cdot\frac{(n-2)}{(r-2)}\cdot^{n-3}C_{r-3} + 3n(x-1)(2)^{n-2} + n(2)^{n-1}$

$= n(n-1)(n-2)\sum_{r=3}^{n} {}^{n-3}C_{r-3} + 3n(n-1)(2)^{n-2} + n(2)^{n-1}$

$= n(n-1)(n-2)(2)^{n-3} + n(2)^{n-1} + 3n(n-1)(2)^{n-2}$

$= n(2)^{n-3}[(n-1)(n-2) + 4 + 3(n-1)(2)]$

$= n(2)^{n-3}[n^2 - 3n + 6 + 6n - 6]$

$= n(2)^{n-3}[n^2 + 3n]$

$= n^2(n+3)(2)^{n-3}$

5. (i) ${}^8C_3 + {}^7C_3 + {}^6C_3 + {}^5C_3 + {}^4C_3$

$(\because {}^nC_r + {}^nC_{r-1} = {}^{n+1}C_r$ and ${}^nC_r = {}^nC_{n-r})$

$= {}^4C_3 + {}^5C_3 + {}^6C_3 + {}^7C_3 + {}^8C_3$

$= {}^4C_1 + {}^5C_2 + {}^6C_3 + {}^7C_4 + {}^8C_5$

$= ({}^4C_0 + {}^4C_1 + {}^5C_2 + {}^6C_3 + {}^7C_4 + {}^8C_5) - {}^4C_0$

$= {}^5C_1 + {}^5C_2 + {}^6C_3 + {}^7C_4 + {}^8C_5 - {}^4C_0$

$= {}^6C_2 + {}^6C_3 + {}^7C_4 + {}^8C_5 - {}^4C_0$ and so on ……

$= {}^9C_5 - 1 = {}^9C_4 - 1$

(ii) ${}^{13}C_6 + {}^{12}C_6 + {}^{11}C_6 + {}^{10}C_6 + {}^9C_6$

$= {}^9C_6 + {}^{10}C_6 + {}^{11}C_6 + {}^{12}C_6 + {}^{13}C_6$

$= {}^9C_3 + {}^{10}C_4 + {}^{11}C_5 + {}^{12}C_6 + {}^{13}C_7$

$= ({}^9C_2 + {}^9C_3 + {}^{10}C_4 + {}^{11}C_5 + {}^{12}C_6 + {}^{13}C_7) - {}^9C_2$

$= ({}^{10}C_3 + {}^{10}C_4 + {}^{11}C_5 + {}^{12}C_6 + {}^{13}C_7) - {}^9C_2$

$= ({}^{11}C_4 + {}^{11}C_5 + {}^{12}C_6 + {}^{13}C_7) - {}^9C_2$ and so on ……

$= {}^{14}C_7 - {}^9C_2 = {}^{14}C_7 - {}^9C_7$

TEXTUAL EXERCISE–6: (OBJECTIVE)

1. (b) ${}^{52}C_{26} \div {}^{51}C_{25} = \frac{52!}{26!26!} \times \frac{25!26!}{51!} = 2$

2. (c) ${}^mC_{{}^kC_r} = {}^mC_{{}^kC_{r-1}}$

$\Rightarrow {}^kC_r + {}^kC_{r-1} = m$ or $r = r - 1 \Rightarrow {}^{k+1}C_r = m$

3. (c) ${}^{n-1}C_5 + {}^{n-1}C_6 < {}^nC_7$

$\Rightarrow {}^nC_6 < {}^nC_7 \qquad \Rightarrow \frac{{}^nC_7}{{}^nC_6} > 1$

$\Rightarrow \frac{n-7+1}{7} > 1 \qquad \left(\because \frac{{}^nC_r}{{}^nC_{r-1}} = \frac{n-r+1}{r}\right)$

$\Rightarrow n - 6 > 7 \qquad \Rightarrow n > 13$

$\Rightarrow n \geq 14$

Thus 14 is the least positive integer

4. (a) ${}^{2n+1}C_1 + {}^{2n+1}C_2 + \ldots + {}^{2n+1}C_n = 63$ (i)

$\because {}^{2n+1}C_0 + {}^{2n+1}C_1 + {}^{2n+1}C_2 + \ldots + {}^{2n+1}C_n$

$= {}^{2n+1}C_{2n+1} + {}^{2n+1}C_{2n} + \ldots + {}^{2n+1}C_{n+1} = (2)^{2n}$

$\therefore (2)^{2n} - 1 = 63$

$\Rightarrow (2)^{2n} = 64 = (2)^6 \qquad \Rightarrow$ n = 3

5. (b) ${}^{40}C_8 + \sum_{j=1}^{7} {}^{47-j}C_{40-j}$

$= {}^{40}C_8 + {}^{46}C_{39} + {}^{45}C_{38} + {}^{44}C_{37} + \ldots + {}^{40}C_{33}$

$= {}^{40}C_8 + {}^{46}C_7 + {}^{45}C_7 + {}^{44}C_7 + \ldots + {}^{40}C_7$

$= ({}^{40}C_8 + {}^{40}C_7) + {}^{41}C_7 + {}^{42}C_7 + {}^{43}C_7 + {}^{44}C_7 + {}^{45}C_7 + {}^{46}C_7$

$= {}^{41}C_8 + {}^{41}C_7 + {}^{42}C_7 + {}^{43}C_7 + {}^{44}C_7 + {}^{45}C_7 + {}^{46}C_7$ and so on

Using ${}^nC_r + {}^nC_{r-1} = {}^{n+1}C_r = {}^{47}C_8$

6. (c) $f(x) = {}^{2x-8}C_{x+1}$

For domain, $2x - 8 \geq x + 1 \geq 0$; $2x - 8 \neq 0$

$\Rightarrow x \geq 9$ and $x \geq -1$; $x \neq 0$

$\Rightarrow x \geq 9$ also, $x \in \mathbb{Z} \qquad \Rightarrow x \in \{9, 10, 11, \ldots\}$

7. (b) ${}^{10}C_{x-1} > 2\,({}^{10}C_x)$; $x \geq 1$ (clearly)

$\Rightarrow \frac{{}^{10}C_x}{{}^{10}C_{x-1}} < \frac{1}{2}$

$\Rightarrow \frac{10-x+1}{x} < \frac{1}{2}$

$\Rightarrow 20 - 2x + 2 < x \qquad (\because x \geq 1)$

$\Rightarrow 3x > 22 \qquad \Rightarrow x > 7\cdot\overline{3}$

$\Rightarrow x \geq 8$ (i)

Also $10 \geq x - 1$ and $10 \geq x$

$\Rightarrow x \leq 11$ and $x \leq 10$ (ii)

$\therefore$ From (i) and (ii), we get $x \in \{8, 9, 10\}$

8. (a) $8\,.\,{}^{105}C_x < 3\,.\,{}^{105}C_{x+1}$; $x + 1 \geq 1$

$\Rightarrow \frac{8}{3} < \frac{{}^{105}C_{x+1}}{{}^{105}C_x}$

$\Rightarrow \frac{8}{3} < \frac{105-x-1+1}{x+1}$

$\Rightarrow \frac{8}{3} < \frac{105-x}{x+1}$

$\Rightarrow 8x + 8 < 315 - 3x \qquad (\because x + 1 \geq 1)$

$\Rightarrow 11x < 307$

$\Rightarrow x < 27.9$

$\Rightarrow x \leq 27$ (i)

Also $105 \geq x$ and $105 \geq x + 1$

$\Rightarrow x \leq 105$ and $x \leq 104$

$\Rightarrow x \leq 104$ (ii)

Also $x \in \mathbb{Z}$ and $x \geq 0$

$\therefore x \in \{0, 1, 2, 3, \ldots, 27\}$

9. (d) $^{x-1}C_4 - {}^{x-1}C_3 - \frac{5}{4}(x-2)(x-3) < 0$

$\Rightarrow \frac{(x-1)!}{4!(x-5)!} - \frac{(x-1)!}{3!(x-4)!} - \frac{5}{4}(x-2)(x-3) < 0$

$\Rightarrow \frac{(x-1)!}{3!(x-5)!}\left[\frac{1}{4} - \frac{1}{(x-4)}\right] - \frac{5}{4}(x-2)(x-3) < 0$

$\Rightarrow \frac{(x-1)!}{3!(x-5)!}\left[\frac{x-4-4}{4(x-4)}\right] - \frac{5}{4}(x-2)(x-3) < 0$

$\Rightarrow \frac{(x-1)(x-2)(x-3)(x-4)(x-8)}{4\times 6(x-4)} - \frac{5}{4}(x-2)(x-3) < 0$

$\Rightarrow (x-2)(x-3)[(x-1)(x-8) - 30] < 0$

$\Rightarrow (x-2)(x-3)(x^2 - 9x - 22) < 0$

$\Rightarrow (x-2)(x-3)(x-11)(x+2) < 0$

$\Rightarrow x \in (-2, 2) \cup (3, 11)$

Also $x - 1 \geq 4$ and $x - 1 \geq 3$ and $x \in \mathbb{Z}$ (combination restriction)

$\Rightarrow x \geq 5$ and $x \geq 4$ and $x \in \mathbb{Z}$ (ii)

$\therefore$ From (i) and (ii), we get $x \in \{5, 6, 7, 8, 9, 10\}$

TEXTUAL EXERCISE-7: (SUBJECTIVE)

1. (i) (a) At least 2 girls

$\Rightarrow$ Select $\begin{cases} 2 \text{ girls} + 2 \text{ boys} \\ 3 \text{ girls} + 1 \text{ boy} \end{cases}$

$\therefore$ Number of ways $= {}^3C_2 \times {}^5C_2 + {}^3C_3 + {}^5C_1 = 3 \times 10 + 1 \times 5 = 35$

(b) At least 2 boys and 1 girl

$\Rightarrow$ Select $\begin{cases} 2 \text{ boys} + 2 \text{ girls} \\ \text{or } 3 \text{ boys} + 1 \text{ girl} \end{cases}$

$\therefore$ Number of ways $= {}^5C_2 \times {}^3C_2 + {}^5C_3 \times {}^3C_1 = 30 + 30 = 60$

(ii) (a) At most 3 boys

$\Rightarrow$ Select $\begin{cases} 1 \text{ boy } 3 \text{ girls} \\ \text{or } 2 \text{ boys } 2 \text{ girls} \\ \text{or } 3 \text{ boys } 1 \text{ girl} \end{cases}$

$\therefore$ Number of ways $= {}^5C_1 \times {}^3C_3 + {}^5C_2 \times {}^3C_2 + {}^5C_3 \times {}^3C_1$
$= 5 \times 1 + 10 \times 3 + 10 \times 3 = 65$

(b) At most 2 girls

$\Rightarrow$ Select $\begin{cases} 2 \text{ boys} + 2 \text{ girls} \\ \text{or } 3 \text{ boys} + 1 \text{ girls} \\ \text{or } 4 \text{ boys} \end{cases}$

$\therefore$ Number of ways $= {}^5C_2 \times {}^3C_2 + {}^5C_3 \times {}^3C_1 + {}^5C_4$
$= 10 \times 3 + 10 \times 3 + 5 = 65$

2. (a) $^{10}C_3 = 120$

(b) Since P_1 is already selected, other two can be selected out of remaining 9

$\therefore$ Number of ways $= {}^9C_2 = 36$

(c) Two possible cores are there $\begin{cases} P_1 \text{ selected}, P_2 \text{ refuses} \\ P_1 \text{ rejected} \end{cases}$

$\therefore$ Number of ways $= {}^8C_2 + {}^9C_3 = 28 + 84 = 112$

(d) Two possible cases are there, $\begin{cases} P_2 \text{ selected}, \\ P_2 \text{ rejected}, P_1 \text{ refuses} \end{cases}$

$\therefore$ Number of ways $= {}^9C_2 + {}^8C_3 = 36 + 56 = 92$

(e) Two possible cases are there $\begin{cases} P_1, P_2 \text{ selected} \\ P_1, P_2 \text{ rejected} \end{cases}$

$\therefore$ Number of ways $= {}^8C_1 + {}^8C_3 = 8 + 56 = 64$

3. Let $S = \{a_1, a_2, a_3, \ldots, a_n\}$, then every element of set s has two choices, either it is in *a* given subset or not.

Thus two possible subsets $= 2 \times 2 \times 2 \times \ldots \times 2 = (2)^n$

Aliter: We have subsets having no element, 1 elements, 2 elements, ..., n elements

$\therefore$ Total possible subsets $= {}^nC_0 + {}^nC_1 + {}^nC_2 + \ldots + {}^nC_n = (2)^n$

Since ϕ and S are improper subsets, $(2)^n - 1$ are proper subsets.

4. (a) Father will go to zoo as many times as is the number of groups of three children out of eight i.e., $^8C_3 = 56$

(b) Each child will accompany the group of two children out of other 7

$\therefore$ Number of ways each child visit the zoo $= {}^7C_2 = 21$

(c) Either C_1C_2 go together or both do not go

$\therefore$ Number of ways $= {}^6C_1 + {}^6C_3 = 26$

(d) Following cases arise: $\begin{cases} C_7 \text{ goes}, C_8 \text{ refuses} \\ C_7 \text{ do not go} \end{cases}$

$\therefore$ Number of ways $= {}^6C_2 + {}^7C_3$

(e) Following cases arise:

$\begin{cases} C_1, C_2 \text{ goes} \\ C_1, C_2 \text{ do not go}, C_7 \text{ goes}, C_8 \text{ refuse} \\ C_7, C_1, C_2 \text{ do not go} \end{cases}$

$\therefore$ Number of ways $= {}^6C_1 + {}^4C_2 + {}^5C_3$

5. Number of hand shakes $= {}^nC_2$

6. (a) A parallelogram require two pairs of parallel lines, lines of first pair non-parallel to lines of second pair.

$\therefore$ Number of parallelogram formed $= {}^mC_2 \times {}^nC_2$

(b) A chess board contains

Square $= (8)^2 + (7)^2 + (6)^2 + \ldots + (7)^2$

↓ unit length ↓ 2units length ↓ 8 units length

$= \sum_{n=1}^{8} n^2 = \frac{8\times 9\times 17}{6} = 204$

Next, chess board contains rectangles $= {}^9C_2 \times {}^9C_2$ as each side contains 9 lines $= ({}^9C_2)^2$

7. Since every pair of two points forms *a* straight line

$\therefore$ Total $^nC_2$ lines are formed but 6 collinear points represent *a* single strongest line.

$\therefore$ Required number of lines $= {}^nC_2 - {}^6C_2 + 1$

$= \frac{n(n-1)}{2} - \frac{6\times 5}{2} + 1$

$= \frac{n(x-1)}{2} - 14 = \frac{n^2 - n - 28}{2}$

Required number of line segments: $= {}^nC_2$

Number of directed line segments $= 2 \times {}^nC_2$ as each line segment gives rise to two directed line segment one along formed and other backward.

8. (a) number of diagonals; $(n > 3) = (^nC_2 - n)$

$$= \frac{n(n-1)}{2} - n = n\left[\frac{n-1}{2} - 1\right] = n\left(\frac{n-3}{2}\right)$$

(b) Total $^nC_3$ triangles can be formed by joining the vertices of n-sided convex polygon.

(i) If one side is common in triangle and polygons, then except for four points (two end points of common side and two points, each next to end points); total $(n - 4)$ triangles can be formed by joining the end points of common side with remaining of common side with remaining $(n - 4)$ points.

$\therefore$ Total $n(n - 4)$ triangles can be formed with one side common

(ii) Let the sides be numbered 1, 2, 3,....n, then the common two sides can be (1, 2); (2, 3), (3, 4) .... $(n - 1, n)$; $(n, 1)$

Thus there will be n such triangles.

(iii) No side common with that of the polygon

= Total triangles – [(Number of triangles with one side common) + (Number of triangles with two sides common)]

$= {}^nC_3 - [n(n-4) + n]$

$$= \frac{n(n-1)(n-2)}{3\times2\times1} - [n^2 - 3n]$$

$$= n\left[\frac{(n-1)(n-2)}{6} - (n-3)\right]$$

$$= n\left[\frac{n^2 - 9n + 20}{6}\right] = \frac{n(n-4)(n-5)}{6}$$

9. (a) If we select any one square, then we can't select other 14 squares lying on the same row and same column, So we are left with (64 – 15) = 49 squares for the selecting of 2nd square.

$\therefore$ Total ways $= \frac{64\times49}{2} = 1568$

Here divided by 2 since we have counted (A, B) and (B, A) both pairs of 4 units squares in 64 × 49.

(b) Four units square forming a rectangle has its area 4 square units = 1 × 4 or 4 × 1 or 2 × 2.

But 1 × 4 or 4 × 1 lie along a column and along a low respectively. Thus we require to find 2 × 2 rectangles i.e., squares of 2 units number of such squares are 7 × 7 = 49

10. (a) $^nC_0 + {}^nC_1 + {}^nC_2 + \ldots.. + {}^nC_n = (2)^n$

L.H.S. can be expressed as the number of ways of selections of none or more things out of n-different things. Further the same process can be dealt with other method i.e., each element has two choices i.e., either selected or rejected.

Thus number of ways $= \underbrace{2\times2\times2\times\ldots\times2}_{n\text{-times}} = (2)^n$

(b) To form a committee having 1 chairman = select r persons in committee and there will be r choices to select a chairman; $1 \le r \le n$

$= 1\times{}^nC_1 + 2\times{}^nC_2 + 3\times{}^nC_3 + \ldots. + n\times{}^nC_n =$ L.H.S.

Aliter: Select a chairman and the remaining persons have two choices each i.e., include in committee or not $= n(2)^{n-1} =$ R.H.S.

(c) To form a committee and from it a subcommittee.

In a committee select r persons and from these r persons $(2)^r$ ways of forming a subcommittee $= (2)^0.{}^nC_0 + (2)^1.{}^nC_1 + (2)^2.{}^nC_2 + (2)^3.{}^nC_3 + \ldots. + (2)^n.{}^nC_n =$ L.H.S.

Also, every person has three choice i.e.,

(i) He is in committee but not subcommittee

(ii) He is in committee as well as in subcommittee

(iii) Neither in committee nor in subcommittee

$\therefore$ Number of ways of forming committee and subcommittee out of n-persons $= (3)^n$.

(d) $^nC_0\times{}^nC_n + {}^nC_1\times{}^nC_{n-1} + {}^nC_2\times{}^nC_{n-2} + \ldots.. + {}^nC_n\times{}^nC_0$

= Number of ways of selecting n persons out of n men and n women

= Number of ways of selecting n persons out of $2n$ persons $= {}^{2n}C_n$

(e) $^mC_0\times{}^nC_r + {}^mC_1\times{}^nC_{r-1} + \ldots. + {}^mC_r\times{}^nC_0$

= Number of ways of selecting $r\ (\le m, n)$ persons out of (m) men and (n) women

= Number of ways of selecting r persons out of $(m + n)$ persons $= {}^{m+n}C_r$

11. (a) (S_1S_2), S_3, S_4, ... S_9 can be permuted in 8! Ways but S_1 and S_2 can address in the same order of S_2 after S_1

$\therefore$ Total ways = 2! × 8!

(b) (S_1, S_2), S_3, S_4, S_5, ... S_9 can be permuted in 8! ways.

(c) S_1 ....S_2 ....i.e., S_1 speaks before S_2

If we permute S_1, S_2, S_3, ... S_9,

Number of ways = 9!

Half of these are the ways when S_1 speaks before S_2,

$\therefore$ Required ways $= \frac{9!}{2!}$

Aliter: Choose any two positions out of 1st, 2nd, 3rd, ...9th and in 1st selected position, let S_1 to speak and in second selected position, let S_2 to speak.

Now in remaining 7 positions, 7 speakers can speak in 7! ways.

$\therefore$ Total number of ways $= {}^9C_2\times 7!$

(d) .... S_1 ....S_2 ....S_3 .... out of 9! arrangement each of 3! orders of group (S_1, S_2, S_3) occurs equal number of times. Thus (S_1, S_2, S_3) order occurs in $\frac{9!}{3!}$ ways.

Aliter: Selecting 3 positions for S_1, S_2, S_3 in this order, and permuting the remaining, number of ways $= {}^9C_3\times 6! = 84(6!)$

12. (a) 5 square citizens + 3 out of 10 $= {}^{10}C_3$ ways.

(b) 8 members out of 10 (square citizens are excluded) $= {}^{10}C_8$ or $^{10}C_2$ ways.

13. (a) 5 square citizens can be arranged in 10 chairs in $^{10}P_5$ ways and the remaining 5 chairs can be occupied by 5 other persons in $^{10}P_5$ ways and remaining 5 persons can stand in 5! Ways.

$\therefore$ Total number of ways $= {}^{10}P_5\times{}^{10}P_5\times 5!$

$$= \frac{10!}{5!}\times\frac{10!}{5!}\times5! = {}^{10}P_5\times5!$$

Aliter: Out of 10 chairs 5 can be occupied by 5 senior citizens in $^{10}P_5$ ways. The remaining 10 persons can be arranged in 10! Ways.

$\therefore$ Total number of ways = $^{10}P_5 \times 5!$

(b) None of senior citizen occupy the chair: 10 people other than senior citizens can sit in chairs in 10! ways and the 5 senior citizens can stand in 5! ways.

$\therefore$ Total number of ways = 10! × 5!

14. (a)

Number of boys	Number of girls
1	0
2	1
3	2
⋮	⋮
n	$(n-1)$

$\therefore$ Total number of ways = $^nC_1 \times {}^nC_0 + {}^nC_2 \times {}^nC_1 + {}^nC_3 \times {}^nC_2 + ... + {}^nC_n \times {}^nC_{n-1}$

$= {}^nC_1 \times {}^nC_n + {}^nC_2 \times {}^nC_{n-1} + {}^nC_3 \times {}^nC_{n-2} + ... + {}^nC_n \times {}^nC_1$

= Number of ways of selecting $(n+1)$ things out of $2n$

$= {}^{2n}C_{n+1} = \dfrac{2n!}{(n+1)!(n-1)!}$

(b)

Number of boys	Number of girls
2	0
3	1
4	2
5	3
n	$(n-2)$

$\therefore$ Total number of ways = $^nC_2 \times {}^nC_0 + {}^nC_3 \times {}^nC_1 + {}^nC_4 \times {}^nC_2 + ... + {}^nC_n \times {}^nC_{n-2}$

$= {}^nC_2 \times {}^nC_n + {}^nC_3 \times {}^nC_{n-1} + {}^nC_4 \times {}^nC_{n-2} + ... + {}^nC_n \times {}^nC_2$

$= {}^{2n}C_{n+2}$

$= \dfrac{(2n)!}{(x+2)!(x-2)!}$

(c) $^nC_0 \times {}^nC_k + {}^nC_1 \times {}^nC_{k+1} + {}^nC_2 \times {}^nC_{k+2} + ... + {}^nC_{n-k} \times {}^nC_n$

$= {}^nC_0 \times {}^nC_{n-k} + {}^nC_1 \times {}^nC_{(n-k-1)} + {}^nC_2 \times {}^nC_{n-k-2} + ... + {}^nC_{n-k} \times {}^nC_0 = {}^{2n}C_{n-k}$

15. 6 → bowl

3 → keep wicket

None can bowl and keep wicket

Total 15 players are there, and to choose 11 containing at least 4 bowlers and 2 wicket keeps

$$= \begin{cases} 4 \text{ bowler} + 2 \text{ wicket keeper} \\ 5 \text{ bowler} + 2 \text{ wicket keeper} \\ 6 \text{ bowler} + 2 \text{ wicket keeper} \\ 4 \text{ bowler} + 3 \text{ wicket keeper} \\ 5 \text{ bowler} + 3 \text{ wicket keeper} \\ 6 \text{ bowler} + 3 \text{ wicket keeper} \end{cases}$$

$= {}^6C_4 \times {}^3C_2 \times {}^6C_5 + {}^6C_5 \times {}^3C_2 \times {}^6C_4 + {}^6C_6 \times {}^3C_2 \times {}^6C_3 + {}^6C_4 \times {}^3C_3 \times {}^6C_4 + {}^6C_5 \times {}^3C_3 \times {}^6C_3 + {}^6C_6 \times {}^3C_3 \times {}^6C_2$

= (15 × 3 × 6) + (6 × 3 × 15) + (1 × 3 × 20) + (15 × 1 × 15) + (6 × 1 × 20) + (1 × 1 × 15)

= 270 + 270 + 60 + 225 + 120 + 15 = 960

16. Digits are non-zeros i.e., 1, 2, 3.....,9

1st place digit has 9 choices (Except for zero)

2nd place digit has 8 choices (Except for 1st place digit)

3rd place digit has 8 choices

⋮

nth place digit has 8 choice

$\therefore$ Total number of possible numbers of n digits = $9 \times \underbrace{8 \times 8 \times ..... \times 8}_{(n-1)\text{ times}} = 9 \times (8)^{n-1}$

17. Clearly for $0 < x < 1$; $x = \dfrac{p}{q}; p < q$

If $p = 1$, q has 5 choices

If $p = 2$, q has 4 choices

If $p = 3$, q has 3 choices

If $p = 4$, q has 2 choices

If $p = 5$, q has 1 choices

$p = 6$ is impossible as q has no choice for it

$\therefore$ We have total = 5 + 4 + 3 + 2 + 1 = 15

Number $x = \dfrac{p}{q} \in (0, 1)$ but $\dfrac{1}{2} = \dfrac{2}{4} = \dfrac{3}{6}$ and $\dfrac{1}{3} = \dfrac{2}{6}$ and $\dfrac{2}{3} = \dfrac{4}{6}$

$\therefore$ Neglecting $\dfrac{2}{4}, \dfrac{3}{6}, \dfrac{2}{6}$ and $\dfrac{4}{6}$, we are left with (15 – 4) = 11 numbers

18. For a path of length $2n$ starting from origin to point (n, n), we are to take n horizontal step of unit length and n vertical steps of unit length.

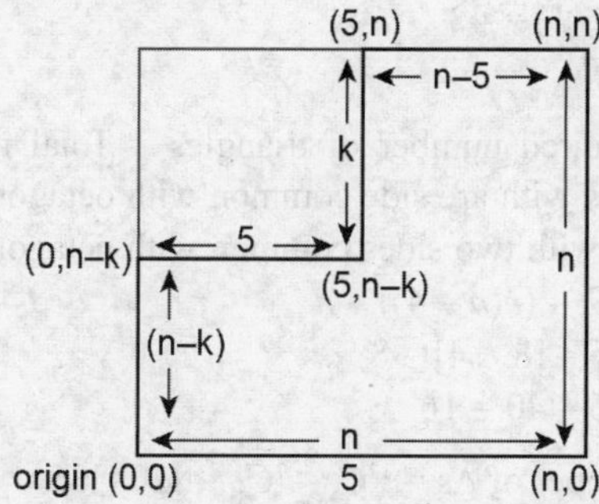

i.e., number of permutations of $\underbrace{HHH....H}_{(n\text{ times})}\underbrace{VVVV.....V}_{(n\text{ times})} = \dfrac{2n!}{n!n!} = {}^{2n}C_n$

TEXTUAL EXERCISE–7: (OBJECTIVE)

1. (a)

Gentle men	Ladies
3	2
4	1

$\therefore$ Number of ways = ${}^4C_3 \times {}^6C_2 + {}^4C_4 \times {}^6C_1$ = 4 × 15 + 1 × 6 = 66

2. (b) $\underbrace{{}^{25}C_0}_{boys} \times \underbrace{{}^{25}C_1}_{girls} + {}^{25}C_1 \times {}^{25}C_2 + {}^{25}C_2 \times {}^{25}C_3 + ... + {}^{25}C_{24} \times {}^{25}C_{25}$

$= {}^{25}C_0 \times {}^{25}C_{24} + {}^{25}C_1 \times {}^{25}C_{23} + ... + {}^{25}C_{24} \times {}^{25}C_0 = {}^{50}C_{24}$

3. (b) $\begin{cases} 1 \text{ red} + 3 \text{ out of } 10 \text{ (green + yellow)} \\ 2 \text{ red} + 2 \text{ out of } 10 \\ 3 \text{ red} + 1 \text{ out of } 10 \end{cases}$

$= {}^3C_1 \times {}^{10}C_3 + {}^3C_2 \times {}^{10}C_2 + {}^3C_3 \times {}^{10}C_1$
$= 3 \times 120 + 3 \times 45 + 1 \times 10 = 505$

4. (c) Let each student attempt r questions.
$=$ Number of combinations of r questions $= {}^nC_r = {}^{20}C_r$
$\therefore$ Students will be maximum if ${}^{20}C_r$ is maximum $= {}^{20}C_{10}$

5. (c) 6 consonants can be selected out of 10 in ${}^{10}C_6$ ways and 3 vowels can be selected out of 4 vowels in ${}^4C_3$ ways and 9 letters can be arranged in 9!ways.
$\therefore$ Total number of ways $= {}^{10}C_6 \times {}^4C_3 \times 9!$

6. (c) Since a_3 is included, the remaining 2 elements can be selected out of $(n-1)$ (Except for a_3) in ${}^{n-1}C_2$ ways.

7. (c) Since 2 friends are not attending the party together we are to select 5 out of 7 when both are not invited
$\therefore$ Number of ways $= {}^7C_5 = {}^7C_2 = 21$
Also when any one is invited the other is not attending
$\therefore$ Number of ways $= 2 \times {}^7C_4 = 70$
$\Rightarrow$ Total ways $= 21 + 70 = 91$

8. (b) Clearly $T_n = {}^nC_3$
$\therefore$ $T_{n+1} - T_n = 21$
$\Rightarrow$ ${}^{n+1}C_3 - {}^nC_3 = 21$
$\Rightarrow$ $\dfrac{(n+1)(n)(n-1) - n(n-1)(n-2)}{3!} = 21$
$\Rightarrow$ $n(n-1)[n+1-n+2] = 126$
$\Rightarrow$ $n(n-1)(3) = 126$
$\Rightarrow$ $n(n-1) = 42$
$\Rightarrow$ $n = 7$

9. (a) Required number of triangles = Total no of triangles – (Δs with are side common with octagon) – (Δs with two sides common with octagon)
$= {}^8C_3 - (n(n-4)) - n$
$= 56 - [8 \times 4] - 8$
$= 56 - 40 = 16$

10. (c) Number of Δs $= {}^{12}C_3 - {}^7C_3 = 220 - 35 = 185$

11. (b) Number of diagonals $= {}^nC_3 - n$
$\Rightarrow$ $P = {}^nC_3 - n$

12. (d) ${}^nC_2 = 91$
$\Rightarrow$ $n(n-1) = 18^2 = 14 \times 13$
$\Rightarrow$ $n = 14$

13. (a) Four consecutive nos. are (1, 2, 3, 4); (2, 3, 4, 5) ..... (27, 28, 29, 30) i.e., 27
Now total number of ways of selecting 4 out of 30 = ${}^{30}C_4$
$\therefore$ Required number of ways $= {}^{30}C_4 - 27$
$= \dfrac{30 \times 29 \times 28 \times 27}{4 \times 3 \times 2 \times 1} - 27 = 27378$

14. (b) Let the number of selected students = n out of n such that at least 2 are selected and atleast 2 are excluded
$\Rightarrow$ $2 \le n \le (n-2)$
$\Rightarrow$ Number of ways $= {}^nC_2 + {}^nC_3 + {}^nC_4 + \ldots + {}^nC_{n-2}$
$= (2)^n - ({}^nC_0 + {}^nC_1 + {}^nC_{n-1} + {}^nC_n)$
$= 2^n - [1 + n + n + 1] = (2)^n - 2n - 2$

15. (b) Let $n = (2m+1)$; $m \in \{0, 1, 2, 3, \ldots\}$
Let the numbers be a, $a+d$, $a+2d$
$\Rightarrow$ $a \ge 1$; $a + 2d \le 2m + 1$
$\Rightarrow$ $2d \le 2m + 1 - a \le 2m + 1 - 1$
$\Rightarrow$ $d \le m$
For $d = 1$
AP's → (1, 2, 3); (2, 3, 4)... $(2m-1, 2m, 2m+1)$;
For $d = 2$
AP's → (1, 3, 5); (2, 4, 6); (3, 5, 7) .... $(2m-3, 2m-1, 2m+1)$
For $d = 3$,
AP's → (1, 4, 7); (2, 5, 8); .....$(2m-5, 2m-2, 2m+1)$
For $d = m$,
AP's → $(1, 1+m, 2m+1)$
$\therefore$ Total number of AP's $= (2m-1) + (2m-3) + (2m-5)$ ...... 1 or $= 1 + 3 + 5 + \ldots + (2m-1)$
= sum of first m odd numbers $= m^2 = \left(\dfrac{n-1}{2}\right)^2$

16. (b) Total integer points including boundary = 22 + 21 + 20 + ... + 1 $= \dfrac{22 \times 23}{2} = 253$

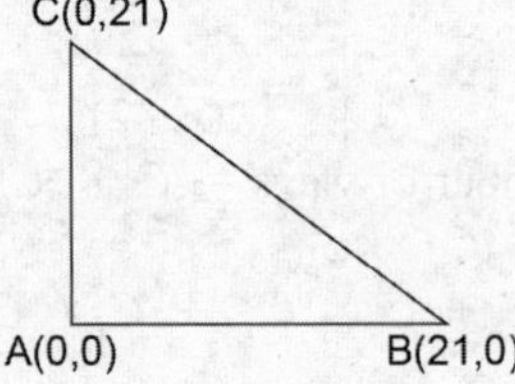

Out of these points, number of point lying on boundary
$= \underbrace{22}_{\text{on } AB} + \underbrace{21}_{\text{on } AC} + \underbrace{20}_{\text{on } BC} = 63$
$\therefore$ Number of integer points in the interior of $D = 253 - 63 = 190$

17. (d) There are total 7 points out of which AGB; DEC; AFC; BFD; EFA are collinear

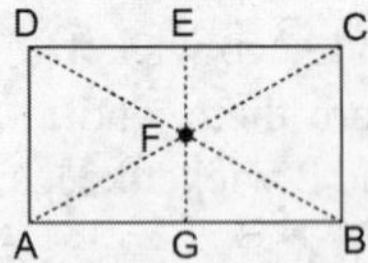

$\therefore$ Required number of Δ's formed $= {}^7C_3 - 5 = 35 - 5 = 30$

TEXTUAL EXERCISE–8: (SUBJECTIVE)

1. $(B_1 + B_2)$ has $(n_1 + n_2)$ toys.
Now, after mixing them, if n_1 toys are given to B_1, in ${}^{n_1+n_2}C_{n_1}$ ways, n_2 toys are left which goes to B_2. But there is a ways of selecting n_1 toys for B_1, which exactly match, with the original one.
$\therefore$ Required number of ways $= {}^{n_1+n_2}C_{n_1} - 1$ or ${}^{n_1+n_2}C_{n_2} - 1$

2. (a) (i) Required number of ways = Total number of ways – (Number of ways when no pink shirt is purchased).
$= ({}^{60}C_0 + {}^{60}C_1 + {}^{60}C_2 + ... + {}^{60}C_{60}) - ({}^{25}C_0 + {}^{25}C_1 + {}^{25}C_2 + ... + {}^{25}C_{25}) = (2)^{60} - (2)^{25} = ((2)^{35} - 1)\,(2)^{25}$

(ii) $= ({}^{35}C_1 + {}^{35}C_2 + ... + {}^{35}C_{35}) \times ({}^{10}C_1 + {}^{10}C_2 + ... + {}^{10}C_{10}) \times ({}^{15}C_1 + {}^{15}C_2 + ... + {}^{15}C_{15})$
$= ((2)^{35} - 1)\,(2^{10} - 1)\,(2^{15} - 1)$

(b) 3 identical coins of 25 paisa; 4 identical coins of 50 paisa; 2 identical coins of 1 rupee Total number of ways = (Number 25 paisa coin or 1, 25 paisa coin, 2, 25 paisa coin...) × (Number 50 paisa coin or 1, 50 paisa coin ....) × (Number 1 rupee coin, or 1, rupee coin ....) = 4 × 5 × 3 = 60 ways.

(i) He can give either 1 coin of 1 rupee coin or 2 coin of 1 rupee along with other coins.
∴ Number of ways = 2 × 4 × 5 = 40

(ii) He can give 25 paisa coins in 3 ways, 50 paisa coins in 4 ways and 1 rupee coins in 2 ways, when atleast one coin of each type is given
∴ Number of ways = 3 × 4 × 2 = 24

3. Total population persons having one tooth + persons having 2 teeth + 2 cases having 3 teeth +........+ Persons having 32 teeth $= {}^{32}C_1 + {}^{32}C_2 + {}^{32}C_3 + ... + {}^{32}C_{32}$
($\because {}^{32}C_r$ represents the combinations of 32 positions taking r at a time) $= (2)^{32} - 1$

4. There are 2 A's; 2*R*'s; 2*N*'s; 2*E*'s; 1*G*; 1*M*; 1*T*

(i) One or more letters can be selected i.e., not all rejected = 3 × 3 × 3 × 3 × 2 × 2 × 2 – 1 = 647
(∵ *A* can be rejected, one *A* selected or 2 *A* selected and so on)

(ii) If at least one letter of each type is selected, then after selecting 1*A*, 1*R*, 1*N*, 1*E*, 1*G*, 1*M* and 1*T*, we are left with 1*A*, 1*R*, 1*N* and 1*E*, each of there can be selected in two ways.
∴ Required number of ways of selective = 2 × 2 × 2 × 2 = 16

(iii) After selecting all E's we are left with 2 A's, 2 R's, 2 N's, 1*G*, 1*M*, 1*T*
∴ Number of ways of selection = 3 × 3 × 3 × 2 × 2 × 2 = 216

5. (i) It is the distribution of 6 different things equally among 3 unnamed groups.
$$\therefore \text{ Number of ways} = \frac{(2+2+2)!}{(2!)^3.3!} = \frac{6!}{(2!)^3.3!}$$

Aliter: $\text{Number of ways} = \dfrac{{}^6C_2 \times {}^4C_2 \times {}^2C_2}{3!}$
$$= \frac{15 \times 6 \times 1}{6} = 15$$

(ii) Case (i): 3 groups; containing 4, 1 and 1 book
Case (ii): 2 groups containing 4 and 2 books.
$$\therefore \text{ Required number of ways} = \frac{6!}{4!1!1!2!} + \frac{6!}{4!2!} = 2\left(\frac{6!}{4!2!}\right)$$

Aliter: Required number of ways
$$= \frac{{}^6C_4 \times {}^2C_1 \times {}^1C_1}{2!} + {}^6C_4 \times {}^2C_2 = 30$$

(iii) $\dfrac{6!}{2!2!2!} = \dfrac{6!}{(2!)^3}$

Aliter: ${}^6C_2 \times {}^4C_2 \times {}^2C_2 = \dfrac{6!}{4!2!} \times \dfrac{4!}{2!2!} = \dfrac{6!}{(2!)^3}$

(We don't divide by 3! as distribution is amongst persons i.e., naming groups)

6. (i) It is the distribution of 15 thins into three unnamed groups
$$\therefore \text{ Number of ways} = \frac{15!}{5!5!5!\cdot 3!} = \frac{15!}{(5!)^3\cdot 3!}$$

(ii) Now the distribution is among the naming groups, therefore the number of ways $= \dfrac{15!}{5!5!5!} = \dfrac{15!}{(5!)^3}$

(iii) There are m subject and there are n different volumes of each subject. Thus total books = mn.

(a) There (mn) books are to be divided into n unnamed groups equally.
Thus each groups having m books.
$$\therefore \text{ Number of ways} = \frac{(mn)!}{(m!)^n\,.\,n!}$$

(b) To distribute (*mn*) books into m unnamed groups each containing n books.
$$\therefore \text{ Number of ways} = \frac{(mn)!}{(n!)^m\, m!}$$

(c) To distribute (*mn*) book among n persons i.e., n naming groups equally.
$$\therefore \text{ Number of ways} = \frac{(mn)!}{(m!)^n}$$

7. We are to find the numbers of ordered pairs (*P*, *Q*) such that $P, Q \subseteq A$ and $P \cap Q = \phi$.

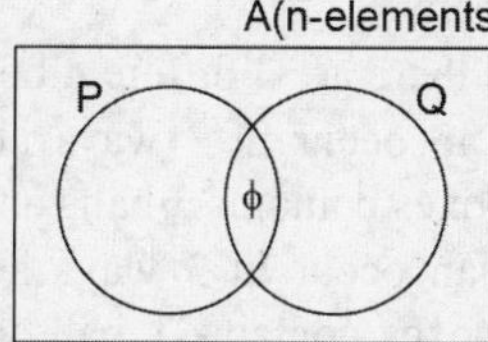

Each element of *A* has three choices i.e., $P \cap Q'$ or $Q \cap P'$ or $(P \cup Q)'$
∴ Total number of ways = $(3)^n$

(i) $(P \cap Q)$ contains exactly two elements. These two elements can be selected in ${}^nC_2$ ways and the remaining $(n - 2)$ can be distributed among $(P \cap Q')$; $(Q \cap P')$; $(P \cup Q)'$ in $(3)^{(n-2)}$ ways.
∴ Total number of ways = ${}^nC_2\,(3)^{n-2}$

(ii) Each element has two choices i.e., $P \cap Q'$ or $Q \cap P'$
∴ Required number of ways = $(2)^n$

8. It is the distribution of 10 thins among 5 naming groups each having equal things
$$\therefore \text{ Number of ways} = \frac{10!}{(2!)^5} = 113400$$

9. Two girls and one boy can be selected out of 4 boys and 6 girls in ${}^6C_2 \times {}^4C_1$ ways.
Now, we are to distribute 3 toys among three persons (naming group) equally

$\therefore$ corresponding to each selection of 2 girls and 1 boy

$\therefore$ Number of ways $= \dfrac{3!}{(1!)^3} = 6$

$\therefore$ Total ways $= {}^6C_2 \times {}^4C_1 \times 6 = 15 \times 4 \times 6 = 360$

TEXTUAL EXERCISE-8: (OBJECTIVE)

1. (a) Each of n-different balls has k choices i.e., each can go to any of the k different boxes.

$\therefore$ Number of ways $= (k)^n$.

2. (a) Each toy has 5 choices

$\therefore$ Total number of ways $= (5)^8$

3. (c) Each letter has 7 choices

$\therefore$ Total number of ways $= (7)^5$

4. (i) (b) Total number of ways $= (3)^5$

($\because$ Each ball has 3 choices)

Number of ways unwanted

(a) When all balls goes to only one box.

Number of ways = 3

(b) When all balls goes to two boxes.

Number ways $= {}^3C_2 \times [(2)^5 - 2]$ when all balls go to *a* single out of two boxes

$\therefore$ Required ways $= (3)^5 - [3 + 3(30)] = 243 - 93 = 150$

(ii) (c) 5 identical balls and 3 different boxes, no box remains empty.

Following can one possible

Case (i): 1 box → 3 balls; 2 box → 1 ball; 3 box → 1 ball

Case (ii): 1 box → 2 balls; 2 box → 2 balls; 3 box → 1 balls

Now, since there are 3 different boxes

Case (i): Can occur in 3 ways i.e., any one of three boxes contains 3 balls and other two 1 ball.

Case (ii): can occur in 3 ways i.e., any one of there boxes contains 1 ball and other two 2 balls each

$\therefore$ Total ways $= 3 + 3 = 6$

(iii) 5 different balls, 3 identical boxes, no box remains empty.

Following cases are possible

Case (i): One box contains 3 balls and other two one ball each.

Number of ways $= {}^5C_3 = 10$ ways

Case (ii): Two boxes contain 2 balls each and *a* third box contains 1 ball.

Number of ways $= \dfrac{{}^5C_1 \times {}^4C_2}{2!} = 15$ ways

$\therefore$ Total ways $= 10 + 15 = 25$

(iv) 5 identical balls and 3 identical boxes:

Now cases depend on the number of balls contained in boxes.

$\therefore$ following cases are possible

(a) 3, 2, 1 (b) 2, 2, 1

$\therefore$ 2 ways

(v) Balls as will as boxer are identical but boxes are placed on *a* low: Following cases are there

	Box 1	Box 2	Box 3
Number of balls	2	2	1
	2	1	2
	1	2	2
	3	1	1
	1	3	1
	1	1	3

$\therefore$ Total ways = 6

5. (c) It is the distribution of 50 different things among 5 unnamed groups, 3 groups containing 12 things each, and 2 groups containing 7 things each

$\therefore$ Number of ways $= \dfrac{50!}{(12!)^3\,(7!)^2 \cdot 3! \cdot 2!}$

6. (b) 3 persons for giving 12 balls each can be selected in ${}^5C_3$ ways and remaining two would get 7 balls each.

Let first 3 persons get 12 each and next 2 persons get 7 each

1st	2nd	3rd	4th	5th
12	12	12	7	7

$\Rightarrow {}^{50}C_{12} \times {}^{38}C_{12} \times {}^{26}C_{12} \times {}^{14}C_7 \times {}^7C_7$

$\therefore$ Required number of ways $= {}^5C_3 \times {}^2C_2 \times {}^{50}C_{12} \times {}^{38}C_{12} \times {}^{26}C_{12} \times {}^{14}C_7 \times {}^7C_7$

$$= \frac{5!}{3!2!} \times 1 \times \frac{50!}{12!38!} \times \frac{38!}{12!26!} \times \frac{26!}{12!14!} \times \frac{14!}{7!7!} \times 1$$

$$= \frac{50! \cdot 5!}{(12!)^3\,(7!)^2 \cdot 3!2!}$$

TEXTUAL EXERCISE-9: (SUBJECTIVE)

1. Ist place has 9 choices (except for 0)

IInd place has 10 choices

IIIrd and IVth place has 10 choices each

$\therefore$ Total possible numbers of 4 digits $= 9 \times 10 \times 10 \times 10 = 9000$

Aliter: Largest number of 3 digits = 999 and largest number of 4 digits = 9999

$\therefore$ Total number of 4 digit numbers $= 9999 - 999 = 9000$

(a) We know that out of $(2n)$ constantly natural numbers n are odd and n are even

$\Rightarrow$ 4500 are odd

(b) 4500 are even.

(c) Sum of digits will be odd if exactly one digit is odd, other 3 are even

Or three digits are odd and 1 is even.

Case (i): 1 digit odd, 3 even.

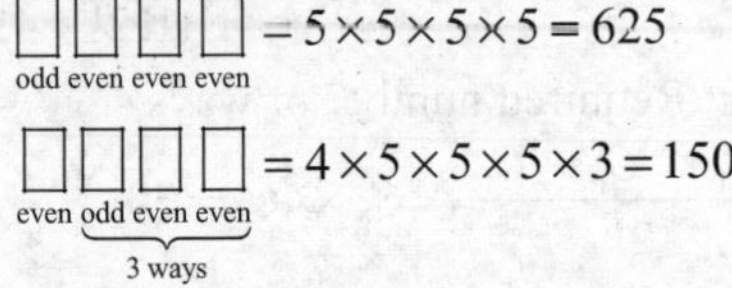

Case (ii): 3 digits odd, 1 even

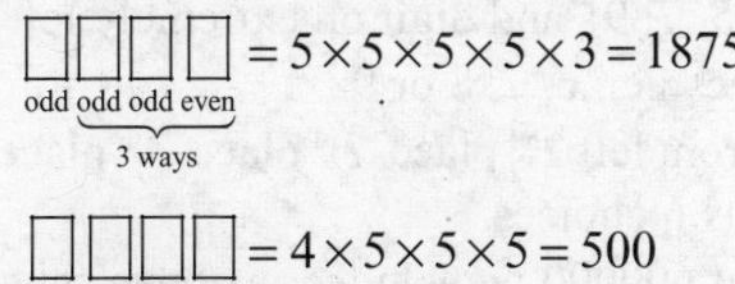

$\square\square\square\square = 5 \times 5 \times 5 \times 5 \times 3 = 1875$

odd odd odd even (3 ways)

$\square\square\square\square = 4 \times 5 \times 5 \times 5 = 500$

even odd odd odd

$\therefore$ Total number of numbers having sum of digits odd $= 4500$

$\therefore$ Total number of numbers having sum of digits even $= 9000 - 4500 = 4500$

(d) For divisibility by 5, unit place digit must be 5 or 0

$\therefore$ Number of numbers divisibly by $5 = 9 \times 10 \times 10 \times 2 = 1800$

2. ${}^{10}P_4 - {}^{9}P_3$ (Numbers with first digit = 0)

$$= \frac{10!}{6!} - \frac{9!}{6!} = \frac{9!}{6!}(10-1) = 9 \times 8 \times 7 \times 9 = 4536$$

For even numbers:

Unit place digit has 5 choices i.e., 0,2,4,6 or 8

Now thousand place would have 8 choices (except for 0 and units place digit if unit place digit is non-zero) and *a* choices (except for 0 which is in unit place)

Hundred place would have 8 choice and ten's place would have 7 choice

$\therefore$ Total number of even numbers of 4 digits $= 8 \times 8 \times 7 \times 4 + 9 \times 8 \times 7 \times 1 = 2296$

3. (a) (i) First place has 5 choices (Except for 0)

Second place has 5 choices

Third place has 4 choices

$\therefore$ Total number of number formed $= 5 \times 5 \times 4 = 100$

(ii) First place has 5 choices

Second place has 6 choices

Third place has 6 choices

$\therefore$ Total number of numbers formed $= 5 \times 6 \times 6 = 180$

(b) Three digit numbers greater than 300.

Hundred place has 3 choices i.e., 3, 4 or 5

Ten's place has 5 choices (Except for hundred place digit) and unit's place has 4 choices

$\therefore$ Total number of 3 digit numbers greater than $300 = 3 \times 5 \times 4 = 60$

Four digit numbers less than 3000

Thousand place has 2 choices (1 or 2)

Hundred place has 5 choices (except for thousand place digit)

Ten's place has 4 choice

Unit place has 3 choice

$\therefore$ Total number of four digit number less than $3000 = 2 \times 5 \times 4 \times 3 = 120$

$\therefore$ Total number or required numbers $= 60 + 120 = 180$

4. (i) $\left(\sum_{i=1}^{4} di\right)(4)^3(10^3 + 10^2 + 10 + 1) = (1 + 2 + 3 + 4)\ (64)$ $(1111) = (640)\ (1111) = 711040$

(ii) $\left(\sum_{i=1}^{4} di\right)(3!)(10^3 + 10^2 + 10 + 1) = (10)\ (6)\ (1111)$ $= 66660$

5. (a) Possible number of plates without repetition of alphabets and digits $= 26 \times 25 \times 24 \times 9 \times 9 \times 8 = 10108800$

(b) Number of plates with repetition of alphabets and digits $= 26 \times 26 \times 26 \times 9 \times 10 \times 10 = 15818400$

6. For divisibility by 8, *a* 7 digit number $\overline{gfedcba}$ must be such that $(4c + 2b + a)$ is divisible by 8; where $a, b, c, d, e, f, g, \in \{1, 2, 3, 4, 5, 6, 7\}$ and are all different.

But for divisibility by 8, *a* must be even.

$\therefore\ a \in \{2, 4, 6\}$

Now $(4c + 2b + a) = 8k;\ k \in \mathbb{N}$

$$\Rightarrow \left(2c + b + \frac{a}{2}\right) = 4k \qquad \text{(i)}$$

Let $a = 2$; then $2c + b + 1 = 4k;\ k \in \mathbb{N}$

$\Rightarrow$ *b* must be odd $\quad \Rightarrow b \in \{1, 3, 5, 7\}$

$$\Rightarrow \begin{cases} \text{For } b = 1, 2c + 2 = 4k \Rightarrow c = 2k - 1 \Rightarrow c \in \{3, 5, 7\} \\ \text{For } b = 3, 2c + 4 = 4k \Rightarrow c = 2k - 2 \Rightarrow c \in \{4, 6\} \\ \text{For } b = 5, 2c + 6 = 4k \Rightarrow c = 2k - 3 \Rightarrow c \in \{1, 3, 7\} \\ \text{For } b = 7, 2c + 8 = 4k \Rightarrow c = 2k - 4 \Rightarrow c \in \{4, 6\} \end{cases}$$

Now, let $a = 4$; $2c + b + 2 = 4k$

$\Rightarrow$ b must be even $\quad \Rightarrow b \in \{2, 6\}$

For $b = 2$; $2c + 4 = 4k$

$\Rightarrow 2c = 4k - 4 \quad \Rightarrow c = 2k - 2$

$\Rightarrow c \in \{6\}$

For $b = 6$; $2c + 8 = 4k$

$\Rightarrow 2c = 4k - 8 \quad \Rightarrow c = 2k - 4$

$\Rightarrow c \in \{2\}$

Now, Let $a = 6$; $2c + b + 3 = 4k$

$\Rightarrow$ *b* must be odd $\quad \Rightarrow b \in \{1, 3, 5, 7\}$

For $b = 1$; $2c + 4 = 4k$

$\Rightarrow c = 2k - 2 \quad \Rightarrow c \in \{2, 4\}$

For $b = 3$; $2c + 6 = 4k$

$\Rightarrow c = 2k - 3 \quad \Rightarrow c \in \{1, 5, 7\}$

For $b = 5$; $2c + 8 = 4k$

$\Rightarrow c = 2k - 4 \quad \Rightarrow c \in \{2, 4\}$

For $b = 7$; $2c + 10 = 4k$

$\Rightarrow c = 2k - 5 \quad \Rightarrow c \in \{1, 3, 5\}$

$\therefore$ There are 22 triplets (a, b, c) for which $\overline{g\,f\,e\,d\,c\,b\,a}$ is divisible by 8. Now after fixing a, b, c; d, e, f, g must belong to set of remaining 4 digits; which can be permuted in 4! ways.

$\therefore$ Total numbers $= 4! \times 22 = 24 \times 22 = 528$

7. (a) A five digit number $\overline{e\,d\,c\,b\,a}$; where a, b, c, d, e are different and belong to set $\{1, 2, 3, 4, 5\}$ would be divisible by 4 if $2b + a = 4k;\ k \in \mathbb{N}$

$\Rightarrow$ a must be even $\quad \Rightarrow a \in \{2, 4\}$

For $a = 2$; $2b + 2 = 4k$

$\Rightarrow b = 2k - 1 \quad \Rightarrow b \in \{1, 3, 5\}$

For $a = 4$; $2b + 4 = 4k$

$\Rightarrow b = 2k - 2 \quad \Rightarrow b \in \{2\}$

$\therefore$ There are 4 pairs of $(a, b) \in \{(2, 1), (2, 3), (2, 5), (4, 2)\}$ for which the number $\overline{ed\,c\,b\,a}$ is divisible by 4 after fixing b and a; the digits e, d, c belong to set of other three digits and can be permuted in 3! Ways.

∴ Total number of required numbers = 3! × 4 = 24

(b) Let $\overline{edcba}$ be a five digit number divisible by 4; where $a, b, c, d, e \in \{1, 2, 3, 4, 5, 6, 7, 8\}$, then

$2b + a = 4k;\ k \in \mathbb{N} \Rightarrow$ a must be even

$\Rightarrow a \in \{2, 4, 6, 8\}$

For $a = 2$; $2b = 4k - 2$

$\Rightarrow b = 2k - 1 \qquad \Rightarrow b \in \{1, 3, 5, 7\}$

For $a = 4$; $2b = 4k - 4$

$\Rightarrow b = 2k - 2 \qquad \Rightarrow b \in \{2, 4, 6, 8\}$

When repetition is allowed and {2, 6, 8} when repletion is not allowed.

For $a = 6$; $2b = 4k - 6$

$\Rightarrow b = 2k - 3 \qquad \Rightarrow b \in \{1, 3, 5, 7\}$

For $a = 8$; $2b = 4k - 8$

$\Rightarrow b = 2k - 4 \qquad \Rightarrow b \in \{2, 4, 6, 8\}$

When repletion is allowed and {2, 4, 6} when repetition is not allowed.

(i) When repetition is not allowed;

From above, we have 14 pairs (a, b) for which the number $\overline{edcba}$ is divisible by 4

∴ Number of required number $= {}^6P_3 \times (14) = \frac{6!}{3!} \times 14 = 1680$

(ii) When repetition is allowed:

From above, we have 16 pairs (a, b) for which the number $\overline{edcba}$ is divisible by 4.

Now each of e, d, and c have 8 choices.

∴ Number of required number $= (8)^3 \times 16 = 8192$

8. Let $\overline{abcde}$ be a fine digit number divisible by 3 where a, b, c, d, e are different and belong to set {0, 1, 2, 3, 4, 5}

$\Rightarrow a + b + c + d + e = 3k$

$\Rightarrow a, b, c, d, e \in \{1, 2, 3, 4, 5\}$ or $\{0, 1, 2, 4, 5\}$

$\Rightarrow$ Required number of numbers formed = 5! + 4 × 4! = 120 + 96 = 216

TEXTUAL EXERCISE–9: (OBJECTIVE)

1. (d) $\left(\sum_{i=1}^{5} Di\right)(4!)(10^4 + 10^3 + 10^2 + 10^1 + 1) = (15)(24)$ $(11111) = 3999960$

2. (a) $x_1 < x_2 < x_3 < x_4 < x_5 < x_6 < x_7$; x_i's are different and non-zeros.

$x_i \in \{1, 2, 3, 4, 5, 6, 7, 8, 9\}$

Now 7 digits out of 9 can be selected in ${}^9C_7 = {}^9C_2 = 36$ ways.

Now each of 36 groups of 7 digits has a greatest digit not giving the value for x_4.

Now, select any 3 out of remaining 6 from each group they can be arranged either in left of x_4 or right of x_4 in a unique way as desired the other three will be automatically arranged in other side of x_4.

∴ Total number of required numbers formed $= 36 \times {}^6C_3 = {}^9C_7 . {}^6C_3$

3. (d) For a six digit odd number, unit place digit must belong to set {5, 7, 9} and digit on extremely left has 4 choices i.e., 6, 7, 8 or 9

Now, from left 2nd place, 3rd place, 4th place and 5th place each has 6 choices.

Not that 600000 is included in above scheme

∴ Total number of numbers formed $= 4 \times (6)^4 \times 3 - 1 = 15552 - 1 = 15551$

4. (d) If the number is greater than 600000, then first place digit has 4 choices i.e., 6, 7, 8 and 9.

But the number should be odd and digits are different.

Case (i): [box diagram: first place has 2 choices 6 or 8; (filled with 4 different digits); last place has 3 choices 5, 7 or 9]

∴ Number of ways = 2 × 4! × 3 = 144

Case (ii): [box diagram: first place has 2 choices 7 or 9; (filled with 4 different digits); last place has 2 choices our of 5, 7 or 9]

∴ Number of ways = 2 × 4! × 2 = 96

∴ Total ways = 144 + 96 = 240

5. (a) Case (i): When two 1's and two non-zeros are selected e.g., (1123)

Number of ways $= \quad \times \frac{4!}{2!} = 36$

Case (ii): When two 1's, one zero and one non-zero are selected (e.g., 1103)

Number of ways $= {}^3C_1 \times \left(\frac{4!}{2!} - \frac{3!}{2!}\right) = 27$

Case (iii): When all four digits are different and non-zeros (e.g., 1234)

Number of ways = 4! = 24

Case (iv): When one 1, one zero and two non-zeros are selected (e.g., 1023)

Number of ways $= {}^3C_1\,(4! - 3!) = 3 \times 18 = 54$

Case (v): When three non-zeros and one zero is selected (i.e., 2040)

Number of ways = (4! – 3!) = 18

∴ Total numbers = 36 + 27 + 24 + 54 + 18 = 159

6. (a) One digit numbers = 5

Two digit numbers = 5 × 5

Three digit numbers = 5 × 5 × 4

Four digit numbers = 5 × 5 × 4 × 3

Five digit numbers = 5 × 5 × 4 × 3 × 2

Six digit numbers = 5 × 5 × 4 × 3 × 2 × 1

∴ Total numbers formed = 5 + 25 + 100 + 300 + 600 + 600 = 1630

Number of numbers greater than 3000 $= 3 \times 5 \times 4 \times 3 + \underbrace{600}_{\text{four digit numbers}} + \underbrace{600}_{\text{five digit numbers}} = 1380$

7. (a) Each of these numbers will be of the type 12341 or 123412 i.e., with a digit repeating 3 times or two digits repeating twice.

∴ Required number of ways $= \frac{6!}{3!} \times 4 + \frac{6!}{2! \times 2!} \times {}^4C_2 = 1560$

8. (b) The smallest 7 digit numbers is 1000000. The sum of its digits = 1 = odd. Thus the sum of digits of next numbers will be 2 i.e., even. The sum of digit would be odd and even alternatively. The greatest 7 digit number is 9999999; the sum of its digits is odd. From 1000000 to 9999999 we have total 9000000.

9. (c) For even number the unit place digit has two choices 0 or 2

Case (i): If unit place digit is 0, other three places can be filled up in 3! = 6 ways.

Case (ii): If unit place digit is 2, Thousand's place has 2 choices, hundred place has 2 choices, Ten's place has only 1 choice

∴ Total number of ways = 6 + 2 × 2 × 1 = 10

10. (a) First place (from left) has 3 choice i.e., 1, 2 or 3

Second place has 4 choices

Third place has 4 choices

Fourth place has 4 choices

∴ Total number of numbers formed = (3 × 4 × 4 × 4) – 1 (∵ 1000 is included)

= 192 – 1 = 191

11. (a) For divisibility by 4, the number $\overline{abcd}$ must be such that $2c + d = 4k$; $k \in \mathbb{N}$ and $a, b, c, d \in \{1, 2, 3, 4, 5\}$

Also clearly d must be even

$\Rightarrow d \in \{2, 4\}$

For $d = 2$; $2c = 4k - 2$

$\Rightarrow c = 2k - 1 \qquad \Rightarrow d \in \{1, 3, 5\}$

For $d = 4$; $2c = 4k - 4$

$\Rightarrow c = 2k - 2 \qquad \Rightarrow c \in \{2, 4\}$

a and b have 5 choices each

⇒ Total number of required numbers = 5 × 5 (3 + 2) = 125

12. (c) Out of digits 1, 2, 3, 3, 3, 2, 1 a seven digit number can be formed with 1st, 3rd, 5th and 7th odd places.

Further we have 5 odd digits i.e., 1, 3, 3, 3, 1.

Thus arise two cases.

Case (i): Using 1, 3, 3, 3 for odd places

Number of ways $= \frac{4!}{3!} \times \underbrace{\frac{3!}{2!}}_{\text{(for 2,2,1)}}$

Case (ii): Using 1, 1, 3, 3 for odd places

Number of ways $= \frac{4!}{2!2!} \times \underbrace{\frac{3!}{2!}}_{\text{(for 2,2,3)}}$

∴ Total number of required numbers = 12 + 18 = 30

13. (c) From 000 to 999 each digit will occur equal number of times but from 000 to 999, we have 1000 numbers.

Thus number of digits = 1000 × 3 = 3000. Thus each digit will occur = 300 times.

Thus from 000 to 999, 5 will occur 300 times.

It implies from 1 to 1000, 5 will also occur 300 times.

TEXTUAL EXERCISE–10: (SUBJECTIVE)

1. Number of ways of selecting 2 girls and one boy out of 6 girls and 4 boys = ${}^6C_2 \times {}^4C_1$ = 60 ways.

Now 3 toys can be given to 3 children in 3! ways (Permutation of T_1, T_2, T_3)

∴ Total ways = 60 × 6 = 360

2. (a) $420 = 2 \times 2 \times 3 \times 5 \times 7 = (2)^2 \times 3^1 \times 5^1 \times 7^1$

∴ Number of positive integer devises of 420 = (3) (2) (2) (2) = 24

Future, Sum of positive integer devises = $(1 + 2 + 2^2)(1 + 3)(1 + 5)(1 + 7) = 1344$

(b) $1008 = 2 \times 2 \times 2 \times 2 \times 3 \times 3 \times 7 = (2)^4 \times (3)^2 \times (7)^1$

Number of even proper devises = (4 × 3 × 2) – 1 = 23

(c) $1800 = 2 \times 2 \times 2 \times 3 \times 3 \times (5) \times (5) = (2)^3 \times (3)^2 \times (5)^2$

For divisibility by 10, factor must contain at least one 2 and at least one 5.

∴ Number of proper devisors and divisible by 10 = 3 × 3 × 2 – 1 = 17

3. (a) Number of positive integer proper devises of $2^p \cdot 6^q\ 15^r$ i.e., of $(2)^{p+q}\ (3)^{q+r}\ (5)^r$

$= (p + q + 1)(q + r + 1)(r + 1) - 2$

(b) Number of positive odd proper divisors of $3^p \cdot 6^m \cdot 21^n$ i.e., of $(2)^m \cdot (3)^{p+m+n} \cdot (7)^n = (p + m + n + 1)(n + 1) - 1$

4. $420 = 2 \times 2 \times 3 \times 5 \times 7 = (2)^2 \times 3^1 \times (5)^1 \times (7)^1$

(a) Number of even positive integer devisers = 2 × 2 × 2 × 2 = 16

Sum of even positive integer devisers = $(2^1 + 2^2)(1 + 3)(1 + 5)(1 + 7) = 1152$

(b) A factor will be divisible by 6 if it contains at least one 2 and one 3.

∴ Number of such divisors = (2) (1) (2) (2) = 8

Sum of such divisors = $(2 + 2^2)(3)(1 + 5)(1 + 7) = 6 \times 3 \times 6 \times 8 = 864$

(c) Divisors of the form $(4m + 2) = 2(2m + 1)$; $m \in W$ i.e., having exactly one 2

∴ Number of sub divisors = (1) (2) (2) (2) = 8 and sum of divisors = (2) (1 + 3) (1 + 5) (1 + 7)

= 2 × 4 × 6 × 8 = 384

TEXTUAL EXERCISE–10: (OBJECTIVE)

1. (a) $12600 = 2 \times 2 \times 2 \times 3 \times 3 \times 5 \times 5 \times 7 = (2)^3 \times (3)^2 \times (5)^2 \times (7)^1$

∴ Number of divisors = 4 × 3 × 3 × 2 = 72

Sum of divisors = $(1 + 2 + 2^2 + 3^3)(1 + 3 + 3^2)(1 + 5 + 5^2)(1 + 7)$

$= \left(\frac{2^4 - 1}{2 - 1}\right)\left(\frac{3^3 - 1}{3 - 1}\right)\left(\frac{5^3 - 1}{5 - 1}\right)(8)$

= 15 × 13 × 31 × 8 = 48360

2. (c) $1008 = 2 \times 2 \times 2 \times 2 \times 3 \times 3 \times 7 = (2)^4 \times (3)^2 \times (7)^1$

∴ Number of positive even proper divisors = 4 × 3 × 2 – 1 = 23

3. (c) $10800 = 2 \times 2 \times 2 \times 3 \times 3 \times 5 \times 5 = (2)^3 \times (3)^2 \times (5)^2$

A positive integer divisor of 1800 will be divisible by 6 if it contains at least one 2 and one 3 in its prime factorization 1800 is also *a* divisor of such type, but improper.

∴ Number of such divisions = (3 × 2 × 3 – 1) = 17

Sum of such divisor = $(2 + 2^2 + 2^3)(3 + 3^2)(1 + 5 + 5^2)$ = (14) (12) (31) = 3408

4. (c) $1260 = 2 \times 2 \times 3 \times 3 \times 5 \times 7 = (2)^2 \times (3)^2 \times (5)(7)$

∴ Number of positive integer divisors which have proper $= (3 \times 3 \times 2 \times 2) - (2) = 34$

5. (a) $2520 = (2)^3 \times (3)^2 \times (5) \times (7)$

∴ Number of proper positive integer divisors $= 4 \times 3 \times 2 \times 2 - 2 = 46$

6. (b) $72 = 2 \times 2 \times 2 \times 3 \times 3 = (2)^3 (3)^2$

∴ Sum of proper positive integer divisors $= (1 + 2 + 2^2 + 2^3)(1 + 3 + 3^2) - (1 + 72) = (15)(13) - 73 = 122$

7. (d) $504 = 2 \times 2 \times 2 \times 3 \times 3 \times 7 = (2)^3 \times (3)^2 \times (7)$

∴ Number of even divisors $= 3 \times 3 \times 2 = 18$

8. (c) $(2)^p . (6)^q . (15)^r = (2)^{p+q} . (3)^{q+r} . (5)^r$

A number to be divisible by 30 must contain at least one 2, one 3 and one 5.

∴ Number of positive integer divisors divisible by 30 = $(p + q)(q + r)(r)$.

But these positive integer divisors include 30 and the number it self (improper)

Thus the proper positive integer divisors divisible by 30 and greater than 30 = $(p + q)(q + r)(r) - 2$

TEXTUAL EXERCISE-11: (SUBJECTIVE)

1. (i) Number of ways = coefficient of x^{10} in the expansion of $(1 + x + x^2 + x^3 + ...)^4$

$= \text{Coefficient of } x^{10} \text{ in } \left[\frac{1}{1-x}\right]^4$

$= \text{Coefficient of } x^{10} \text{ in } (1 - x)^{-4}$

$= \frac{(-4)(-5)(-6)....(-4-10+1)}{(10)!}$

$= \frac{(-1)^{10}(4 \cdot 5 \cdot 6....13)}{10!} = \frac{13!}{3!10!} = {}^{13}C_{10} \text{ or } {}^{13}C_3$

(Also coefficient of x^r in $(1 + x + x^2 + x^3 + ...)^n$ is ${}^{r+n-1}C_{n-1}$)

(ii) Number of ways = Coefficient of x^{10} in $(x + x^2 + x^3 + ...)^4$ = Coefficient of x^6 in $(1 + x + x^2 + ...)^4 = {}^{6+(4-1)}C_{4-1} = {}^9C_3$ or ${}^9C_6$

Aliter: Required number of ways = Number of solutions of equation $x_1 + x_2 + x_3 + x_4 = 10; x_i \geq 1$ or $(x_1 - 1) + (x_2 - 1) + (x_3 - 1) + (x_4 - 1) = 6$ or $y_1 + y_2 + y_3 + y_4 = 6; y_i \geq 0 = {}^{6+3}C_3 = {}^9C_3$

2. (i) Required number of ways = Number of solutions of equation $x_1 + x_2 + x_3 = 10; 6 \geq x_i \geq 1$ or $y_1 + y_2 + y_3 = 7; 5 \geq y_i \geq 0; y_i = x_i - 1 = {}^{7+2}C_2 = {}^9C_2 = 36$

But there include the cases when $y_i = 6$ and 7 i.e., the undesired cares $y_i \in \{6, 1, 0\}$; and $y_i \in \{7, 0, 0\}$ i.e., (3! + 3) cases

∴ Required number of ways = 36 – 9 = 27

Aliter: Required number of ways = coefficient of x^{10} in the expansions of $(x + x^2 + ... + x^6)^3$

= Coefficient of x^7 in $(1 + x + x^2 + ... + x^5)^3$ = Coefficient x^7 in $\left[\frac{1-x^6}{1-x}\right]^3$

= Coefficient of x^7 in $(1 - x^6)^3 (1 - x)^{-3}$

= Coefficient of x^7 in $({}^3C_0 + {}^3C_1(-x^6)^1 + {}^3C_2(-x^6)^2 + {}^3C_3(-x^6)^3)\left(1 + 3x + \frac{12x^2}{2!} + ...\right)$

= Coefficient of x^7 in $(1 - 3x^6)(1 + 3x + 6x^2 + ...) = \frac{(-3)(-4)(-5)(-6)(-7)(-8)(-9)(-1)}{7!} - 9 = {}^9C_2 - 9 = 27$

(ii) Required no of ways = Number of solution of equation $x_1 + x_2 + x_3 = 11; 1 \leq x_i \leq 6$

Or $y_1 + y_2 + y_3 = 8; 0 \leq y_i \leq 5; y_i = x_i - 1$

= Coefficient of x^8 in $(1 + x + x^2 + ... + x^5)^3$

Aliter: Required number of ways = ${}^{8+2}C_2$ – number of undesired cases

Undesired cases are when $y_i = 6, 7$ or 8

$y_i \in \{6, 1, 1\}; y_i \in \{6, 2, 0\}; y_i \in \{7, 1, 0\}; y_i \in \{8, 0, 0\}$

∴ Number of undesired cases = 3 + 3! + 3! + 3 = 18

∴ Required number of ways = ${}^{10}C_2 - 18 = 45 - 18 = 27$

3. (a) $x_1 + x_2 + x_3 + x_4 + x_5 = 20; x_i \geq 0$

Number of ways = ${}^{20+4}C_4 = {}^{24}C_4$

(b) $x_1 + x_2 + x_3 + x_4 + x_5 = 20; x_i \geq 1$

Or $(x_1 - 1) + (x_2 - 1) + (x_3 - 1) + (x_4 - 1) + (x_5 - 1) = 15; x_i - 1 \geq 0$

Or $y_1 + y_2 + y_3 + y_4 + y_5 = 15; y_i \geq 0; y_i = x_i - 1$

∴ Number of ways = ${}^{15+4}C_4 = {}^{19}C_4$

(c) $x_1 + x_2 + x_3 + x_4 + x_5 = 20; x_1, x_2, \geq 2$ and $x_i \geq 0$ for $i \geq 3$

Or $(x_1 - 2) + (x_2 - 2) + x_3 + x_4 + x_5 = 16$

Or $y_1 + y_2 + x_3 + x_4 + x_5 = 16; y_i, x_i \geq 0$

∴ Number of ways = ${}^{16+4}C_4 = {}^{20}C_4$ ways

(d) $2x_1 + 2x_2 + 2x_3 + 2x_4 + 2x_5 = 20; x_i \geq 0$

Or $x_1 + x_2 + x_3 + x_4 + x_5 = 10; x_i \geq 0$

∴ Number of ways = ${}^{10+4}C_4 = {}^{14}C_4$ ways

(e) Let x_5 be the senior beggar; then $x_5 \geq 3$

$x_1 + x_{2+1} x_3 + x_4 + x_5 = 20; x_i \geq 0$ for $i \neq 5$ and $x_5 \geq 3$

⇒ $x_1 + x_2 + x_3 + x_4 + (x_5 - 3) = 17$

⇒ $x_1 + x_2 + x_3 + x_4 + y_5 = 17; x_i, y_i \geq 0$

⇒ Number of ways = ${}^{17+4}C_4 = {}^{21}C_4$

(f) $x_1 + x_2 + x_3 + x_4 + x_5 = 20; x_i \geq 3$

$\Rightarrow \sum_{i=1}^{5}(x_i - 3) = 5$

$\Rightarrow \sum_{i=1}^{5} y_i = 5; y_i = x_i - 3 \geq 0$

⇒ Number of ways = ${}^{5+4}C_4 = {}^9C_4$

4. $x_1 + x_2 + x_3 = 10; x_1 \leq 6; x_2 \leq 7; x_3 \leq 8$

Total number of ways = ${}^{10+2}C_2$ – Number of undesirable cases (i)

Now, undesirable cases are

Case (i): $x_1 = 7; x_2 + x_3 = 3; x_2, x_2 \geq 0$

Number of ways = ${}^{3+1}C_1 = {}^4C_1 = 4$

Case (ii): $x_1 = 8; x_2 + x_3 = 2; x_2, x_3 \geq 0$

Number of ways $= {}^{2+1}C_1 = {}^{3}C_1 = 3$

Case (iii): $x_1 = 9; x_2 + x_3 = 1$

Number of ways $= {}^{1+1}C_1 = {}^{2}C_1 = 2$

Case (iv): $x_1 = 10; x_2 - x_3 = 0$

Number of ways = 1

$\therefore$ Total ways = 4 + 3 + 2 + 1 = 10

Similarly for x_2 = 8, 9, or 10

Number of undesirable cases = 3 + 2 + 1 = 6 and for x_3 = 9, 10

Number of undesirable cases = 2 + 1 = 3

$\therefore$ Total number of undesirable cases = 10 + 6 + 3 = 19

$\therefore$ Required number of ways $= {}^{12}C_2 - 19 = 66 - 19 = 47$

5. (i) (a) $x_1 + x_2 + x_3 = 0;\ x_1, x_2, x_3 \geq -5$

$\Rightarrow \sum_{i=1}^{3}(x_i + 5) = 15$

$\Rightarrow \sum_{i=1}^{3} y_i = 15; y_i = x_i + 5 \geq 0$

$\Rightarrow$ Number of ways $= {}^{15+2}C_2 = {}^{17}C_2$

(b) $x_1 + x_2 + x_3 + 4x_4 = 20; x_i \geq 0$

Here, $0 \leq 4x_4 \leq 20 \quad \Rightarrow \quad 0 \leq x_4 \leq 5$

For $x_4 = 0; x_1 + x_2 + x_3 = 20$

For $x_4 = 1; x_1 + x_2 + x_3 = 16$

For $x_4 = 2; x_1 + x_2 + x_3 = 12$

For $x_4 = 3; x_1 + x_2 + x_3 = 8$

For $x_4 = 4; x_1 + x_2 + x_3 = 4$

For $x_4 = 5; x_1 + x_2 + x_3 = 0$

Number of ways $= {}^{22}C_2 + {}^{18}C_2 + {}^{14}C_2 + {}^{10}C_2 + {}^{6}C_2 + {}^{2}C_2$
$= (11 \times 21) + (9 \times 17) + (7 \times 13) + (5 \times 9) + (3 \times 5) + 1 = 231 + 153 + 91 + 45 + 15 + 1 = 536$

Aliter: $x_1 + x_2 + x_3 = 20 - {}^4x_4$

$\Rightarrow \sum_{t=0}^{5} {}^{20-4t+2}C_2$

$\Rightarrow {}^{22}C_2 + {}^{18}C_2 + {}^{14}C_2 + {}^{10}C_2 + {}^{6}C_2 + {}^{2}C_2 = 536$

(c) $x_1 + x_2 + x_3 + x_4 + x_5 = 20; x_1 + x_2 = 15$ and $x_k \geq 0$ □ k

$x_1 + x_2 + 15$; $\mathbf{x_i} \geq 0$ has ${}^{15+1}C_1 = {}^{16}C_1 = 16$ solutions

Now corresponding to each of 16 solutions, $x_3 + x_4 + x_5 = 5; x_i \geq 0$ can be solved in ${}^{5+2}C_2 = {}^{7}C_2$ way

$\therefore$ Total number of solutions $= {}^{16\times 7}C_2 = 16 \times 21 = 336$

(ii) To find integer solution of

(a) xyz = 24; where x, y, z are non-zero integers

$\Rightarrow$ xyz $= (2)^3 \times (3)^1$

Let $x = (2)^{\alpha_1}(3)^{\beta_2}; y = (2)^{\alpha_2}(3)^{\beta_2}$ and $z = (2)^{\alpha_3}(3)^{\beta_3}$

$\therefore (2)^{\alpha_1+\alpha_2+\alpha_3} \cdot (3)^{\beta_1+\beta_2+\beta_3} = (2)^3 \cdot (3)^1$

$\Rightarrow \left.\begin{matrix}\alpha_1 + \alpha_2 + \alpha_3 \text{ and} \\ \beta_1 + \beta_2 + \beta_3\end{matrix}\right\}$

$\Rightarrow$ Number of ways $= {}^{5}C_2 \times {}^{3}C_2 = 10 \times 3 = 30$

Now, above 30 solutions are for $x, y, z > 0$.

Also $x \,.y \,. z = 24$ can be obtained when any 2 of x, y and z are we –ve and other is +ve.

$\therefore$ There are 3 more ways.

Thus total number of possible solutions = 30 × 4 = 120

(b) $x_1 \,.\, x_2 \,.\, x_3 \,.\, x_4 = 360 = (2)^3 \times (3)^2 \times (5)^1$

Let $x_i = (2)^{\alpha_i}(3)^{\beta_i}(5)^{\gamma_i}; x_i > 0$

$\therefore x_1 \,.\, x_2 \,.\, x_3 \,.\, x_4 \,. = (2)^{\sum\alpha_i} \cdot (3)^{\sum\beta_i} \cdot (5)^{\sum\gamma_i}; 1 \leq i \leq 4$
$= (2)^3 \,.\, (3)^2 \,.\, (5)^1$

$\Rightarrow \Sigma\alpha_i = 3; \Sigma\beta_i = 2; \Sigma\gamma_i = 1$

$\Rightarrow \alpha_1 + \alpha_2 + \alpha_3 + \alpha_4 = 3; \alpha_i \geq 0$

$\beta_1 + \beta_2 + \beta_3 + \beta_4 = 2; \beta_i \geq 0$

$\gamma_1 + \gamma_2 + \gamma_3 + \gamma_4 = 1; \gamma_i \geq 0$

$\Rightarrow$ Number of positive integer solutions ${}^{6}C_3 \times {}^{5}C_3 \times {}^{4}C_3 = 20 \times 10 \times 1 = 200$

Same number of solutions can be obtained if we take (i) all x is –ve, (ii) $2x$'s +ve and $2x$'s –ve (${}^{4}C_2$ ways)

$\therefore$ Total number of solution + ve or $-ve$ = 200 × 8 = 1600

Here negative integeral solutions means solutions having atleast one of x_i's $-ve$.

$\therefore$ Negative integral solution = 200 × 7 = 1400

6. Non-negative integral solution of $x_1 + x_2 + x_3 + x_4 \leq n; n \in \mathbb{Z}$ and $n \geq 0$

$= {}^{4}C_3 + {}^{5}C_3 + {}^{6}C_3 + {}^{7}C_3 + ... + {}^{n+2}C_3 + {}^{n+3}C_3$

$= {}^{4}C_1 + {}^{5}C_2 + {}^{6}C_3 + {}^{7}C_4 + ... + {}^{n+2}C_{n-1} + {}^{n+3}C_n$

$= -{}^{4}C_0 + ({}^{4}C_0 + {}^{4}C_1) + {}^{5}C_2 + {}^{6}C_3 + {}^{7}C_4 + ... + {}^{n+3}C_n$

$= -{}^{4}C_0 + ({}^{5}C_1 + {}^{5}C_2) + {}^{6}C_3 + {}^{7}C_4 + ... + {}^{n+3}C_n$

$= -{}^{4}C_0 + {}^{6}C_2 + {}^{6}C_3 + {}^{7}C_4 + ... + {}^{n+3}C_n$

And so on, finally,

$= -{}^{4}C_0 + {}^{n+3}C_{n-1} + {}^{n+3}C_n = -{}^{4}C_0 + {}^{n+4}C_n = {}^{n+4}C_4 - 1$

7. $3x + y + z \leq 30; x, y, z > 0$

$\Rightarrow y + z \leq 30 - 3x$

$\Rightarrow y + z + u = 30 - 3x; 0 \leq u \leq 30; 0 \leq x \leq 10$

$\therefore {}^{32}C_2 + {}^{29}C_2 + {}^{26}C_2 + {}^{23}C_2 + ... + {}^{5}C_2 + {}^{2}C_2$

$= \frac{1}{2}(32\times31 + 29\times28 + 26\times25 + ... + 2\times1)$

$= \frac{1}{2}(1\times2 + 4\times5 + 7\times8 + ... + 31\times32)$

$= \frac{1}{2}\sum_{n=1}^{11}[1 + (n-1)(3)] \times [2 + (n-1)(3)]$

$= \frac{1}{2}\sum_{n=1}^{11}(3n-2)(3n-1) = \frac{1}{2}\sum_{n=1}^{11}(9n^2 - 9n + 2)$

$= \frac{1}{2}\times 9\sum_{n=1}^{11} n^2 - \frac{9}{2}\sum_{n=1}^{11} n + 11$

$= \frac{9}{2}\left(\frac{11\times12\times23}{6}\right) - \frac{9}{2}\times 66 + 11 = 2277 - 297 + 11$

$= 1991$

8. Let x_λ be the number of delegates entering through door λ; where $\lambda \in \{A, B, C, D, E, F, G\}$

$\therefore x_A + x_B + x_C + x_D + x_E + x_F + x_G = 200; x_\lambda \geq 0$

Number of solution $= {}^{200+6}C_6 = {}^{206}C_6$

Now corresponding to each of above solution, the delegates can be permeated in 200! Ways.

$\therefore$ Total number of possible 7 lists (each list having names of delegates entering one of the seven gates) $= {}^{206}C_6 \times 200! = {}^{206}P_{200}$

9. $a + b + c = 50$; $a, b, c, \geq 0$ and $a, b, c, \in \mathbb{Z}$
Number of possible ordered triplets $= {}^{50+2}C_2 = {}^{52}C_2$
If $a, b, c > 0$; then $(a-1) + (b-1) + (c-1) = 47$
$\Rightarrow$ $d + e + f = 47$; $d = a - 1 \geq 0$ as $a \geq 1$
Similarly e, f ≥ 0
$\therefore$ Number of different ordered triplets $= {}^{47+2}C_2 = {}^{49}C_2$

TEXTUAL EXERCISE-11: (OBJECTIVE)

1. (d) $x + y + z + t = 20$; $x, y, z \geq -1$
$\Rightarrow$ $(x+1) + (y+1) + (z+1) + (t+1) = 24$
$\Rightarrow$ $x' + y' + z' + t' = 24$; $x' = x + 1 \geq 0$; $y', z', t' \geq 0$
$\therefore$ Number of integer solution $= {}^{27}C_3$

2. (a) $x + y + z \leq n$; $x, y, z \in W$ and $x \in \mathbb{N}$
$\therefore$ Number of solution $= {}^3C_2 + {}^4C_2 + {}^5C_2 + \ldots + {}^{n+2}C_2$
$= {}^3C_1 + {}^4C_2 + {}^5C_3 + \ldots + {}^{n+2}C_n$
$= -{}^3C_0 + {}^3C_0 + {}^3C_1 + {}^4C_2 + {}^5C_3 + \ldots + {}^{n+2}C_n$
$= -{}^3C_0 + {}^4C_1 + {}^4C_2 + {}^5C_3 + \ldots + {}^{n+2}C_n$
$= -{}^3C_0 + {}^{n+2}C_{n-1} + {}^{n+2}C_n$
$= -{}^3C_0 + {}^{n+3}C_n = {}^{n+3}C_n - 1 = {}^{n+3}C_3 - 1$

3. (b) 4 oranges + 5 apples + 6 mangoes
Number of ways $= (4+1)(5+1)(6+1) = 5 \times 6 \times 7 = 210$
But there is *a* way when no fruit is selected i.e., all rejected
$\therefore$ Number of ways of selection of fruits $= 210 - 1 = 209$.

4. (d) Number of ways of putting 12 identical coins into 5 different purses is the number of positive integer solutions of equation $x_1 + x_2 + x_3 + x_4 + x_5 = 12$ or $y_1 + y_2 + y_3 + y_4 + y_5 = 7$; $y_i \geq 0$
i.e., ${}^{11}C_4 = \dfrac{11 \times 10 \times 9 \times 8}{24} = 330$

5. (b) $x + y + z + w = 20$; $x, y, w \in \mathbb{N}$ or $x' + y' + z' + w' = 16$; $x' = x - 1 \geq 0$ etc.
Number of solution $= {}^{19}C_3 = 969$

6. (a) $x_1 + x_2 + x_3 + x_4 + x_5 = 22$; (i)
$x_1 + x_2 + x_3 = 5$; $x_k \geq 0$ (ii)
From equation (ii), we get $x_1 + x_2 + x_3 = 5$; $x_k \geq 0$
$\Rightarrow$ Number of solutions $= {}^7C_2 = {}^7C_5$
Now from (i), $x_1 + x_2 + x_3 + x_4 + x_5 = 22$
$\Rightarrow$ $5 + x_4 + x_5 = 22$ $\Rightarrow$ $x_4 + x_5 = 17$; $x_4, x_5 \geq 1$
$\Rightarrow$ $y_4 + y_5 = 15$; $y_4, y_5 \geq 0$
Number of solution $= {}^{16}C_1 = {}^{16}C_{15}$
$\Rightarrow$ Required number of solutions $= {}^7C_5 \times {}^{16}C_{15}$

7. (d) $x + y + z + w = 20$
Let $x = 2u + 1$; $y = 2v + 1$; $z = 2s + 1$; $w = 2t + 1$; where $u, v, s, t \in W$ (whole number)
$\therefore$ $2u + 2v + 2s + 2t + 4 = 20$
$\Rightarrow$ $u + v + s + t = 8$; $u, v, s, t, \in W$
$\Rightarrow$ Number of solution $= {}^{11}C_3 = 165$

8. (a) $a + b + c + d = 24$ and a, b, c, d are even natural numbers.
$\Rightarrow$ $a, b, c, d \in \mathbb{N}$ and each ≥ 2
Let $a = 2u$, $b = 2v$, $c = 2w$, $d = 2t$; $u, v, w, t, \in \mathbb{N}$
$\Rightarrow$ $2u + 2v + 2w + 2t = 24$
$\Rightarrow$ $u + v + w + t = 12$; $u, v, w, t \in \mathbb{N}$
$\Rightarrow$ $(u-1) + (v-1) + (w-1) + (t-1) = 8$
$\Rightarrow$ $u' + v' + w' + t' = 8$; $u', v', w', t' \geq 0$
$\Rightarrow$ Number of solution $= {}^{11}C_3 = 165$

TEXTUAL EXERCISE-12: (SUBJECTIVE)

1. (a) $\Delta_5 = 5!\left(1 - \dfrac{1}{1!} + \dfrac{1}{2!} - \dfrac{1}{3!} + \dfrac{1}{4!} - \dfrac{1}{5!}\right) = 44$

(b) $\Delta_3 = 3!\left(1 - \dfrac{1}{1!} + \dfrac{1}{2!} - \dfrac{1}{3!}\right) \times \underbrace{{}^5C_2}_{\text{Number of ways of selecting 2 letter which are correctly placed.}} = 2 \times 10 = 20$

2. $\Delta_4 = 4!\left(1 - \dfrac{1}{1!} + \dfrac{1}{2!} - \dfrac{1}{3!} + \dfrac{1}{4!}\right) = 9$

3. (i) Each student has three choices for classrooms.
$\therefore$ Number of ways of distribution $= (3)^{100}$

(ii) Number of ways of distribution when empty classrooms are not allowed
$= (3)^{100} - {}^{100}C_1 (2)^{100} + {}^{100}C_2 (1)^{100}$
$= (3)^{100} - 100(2)^{100} + \dfrac{100 \times 99}{2}$
$= (3)^{100} - 100(2)^{100} + 4950$

4. (a) (i) Required number of combinations of four letters
= coefficient of x^4 in $(1+x)^5 (1 + x + x^2)^3$ (for E, X, M, T, O) (for A, I, N)
= Coefficient of x^4 in $(1+x)^5 (1 + x + x^2)^3$
= Coefficient x^4 in $({}^5C_0 + {}^5C_1 x + {}^5C_2 x^2 + {}^5C_3 x^3 + {}^5C_4 x^4)$
$\times ({}^3C_0 (1+x)^3 + {}^3C_1 (1+x)^2 (x^2)^1 + {}^3C_2 (1+x)(x^2)^2)$
= Coefficient of x^4 in $(1 + 5x + 10x^2 + 10x^3 + 5x^4) \times (1 + x^3 + 3x^2 + 3x + 3(1 + x^2 + 2x)x^2 + 3(1+x)(x^4))$
= coefficient of x^4 in $(1 + 5x + 10x^2 + 10x^3 + 5x^4) \times (1 + 3x + 6x^2 + 7x^3 + 6x^4)$
$= 6 + 35 + 60 + 30 + 5 = 136$

(ii) Number of required condition as
= Coefficient of x^4 in
$\underbrace{(1+x)^3}_{\text{(For H, B, D)}} \underbrace{(1+x+x^2)}_{\text{(For } L)} \underbrace{(1+x+x^2+x^3+x^4)^1}_{\text{(For } A)}$
$= (1 + x^3 + 3x^2 + 3x)(1 + x + x^2)(1 + x + x^2 + x^3 + x^4)$
$= 1 + 1 + 1 + 1 + 1 + 3 + 3 + 3 + 3 + 3 + 3 = 23$

(b) Number of required combinations
= Coefficient of x^6 in
$\underbrace{(1+x)^3}_{\text{(For } T, I, N)} \times \underbrace{(1+x+x^2)^2}_{\text{(For } P, R)} \times \underbrace{(1+x+x^2+x^3)}_{\text{(For } O)}$
= Coefficient of x^6 in $(1 + x^3 + 3x^2 + 3x) \times (1 + x^2 + x^4 + 2x + 2x^3 + 2x^2) \times (1 + x + x^2 + x^3)$
$= (1 + 2 + 1 + 1 + 2 + 2 + 2 + 3 + 3 + 6 + 6 + 6 + 3 + 3 + 6 + 6) = 53$

5. Required number of arrangements = coefficient of x^4 in $4!\left(1 + \dfrac{x}{1!}\right)^5 \left(1 + \dfrac{x}{1!} + \dfrac{x^2}{2!}\right)^3$

$= \text{coefficient } x^4 \text{ in } 4!\ (1 + 5x + 10x^2 + 10x^3 + 5x^4) \times \left(1+3x+\frac{9}{2}x^2+4x^3+\frac{9}{4}x^4\right)$

$= 4!\left[\frac{9}{4}+20+45+30+5\right] = 24\left(\frac{409}{4}\right) = 2454$

6. Required number of selections of 5 letters
$= \text{coefficient of } x^5 \text{ in } (1 + x)(1 + x + x^2) \times (1 + x + x^2 + x^3)(1 + x + x^2 + x^3 + x^4) \times (1 + x + x^2 + x^3 + x^4 + x^5)$
$= \text{coefficient of } x^5 \text{ in}$
$(1+x)\left[\frac{x^3-1}{x-1}\right]\left[\frac{x^4-1}{x-1}\right]\left[\frac{x^5-1}{x-1}\right]\times\left[\frac{x^6-1}{x-1}\right]$
$= \text{coefficient of } x^5 \text{ in } (x^3 - 1)(x^4 - 1)(x^5 - 1)(x^6 - 1) \times (x - 1)^{-4}(1 + x)$
$= \text{coefficient of } x^5 \text{ in } (x^3 - 1)(x^4 - 1)(x^5 - 1)(x^6 - 1)(1 + x) \times (1 + 4x + 10x^2 + 20x^3 + 35x^4 + \ldots. +)$
$= \text{coefficient of } x^5 \text{ in } (-x^3 - x^4 - x^4 - x^5 - x^5 + 1 + x)(1 + 4x + 10x^2 + 20x^3 + 35x^4 + 56x^5)$
$= (-10 - 8 - 2 + 56 + 35) = 71$

7. **(i)** Let x_i = number of flags displayed on i^{th} mast; $i \in \{1, 2, 3, 4\}$
$\Rightarrow x_1 + x_2 + x_3 + x_4 = 5;\ x_i \geq 0$
Number of ways $= {}^{5+3}C_3 = {}^8C_3 = 56$
Now each of the above 56 distributions of 5 different flags can be permuted in 4 groups (masts) in
$56 \times 5! = 6720$ ways.

(ii) $x_1 + x_2 + x_3 + x_4 = 5;\ x_i \geq 1$
$\Rightarrow y_1 + y_2 + y_3 + y_4 = 1;\ y_i = x_i - 1 \geq 0$
$\therefore$ Number of ways $= {}^{1+3}C_3 = {}^4C_3 = 4$ ways and each way of distribution can be permuted in $4 \times 5! = 480$ ways.

8. ${}^nC_3$ – [Number of ways when 3 consecutives are selected] – [Number of ways when 2 consecutives are selected]
$= {}^nC_3 - (n - 2) - [2(n - 3) + (n - 3)(n - 4)] = {}^{n-2}C_3$

9. Number of ways $= {}^nC_3$ – [Number of ways when 3 consecutive are selected] – [Number of ways when 2 consecutive are selected] $= {}^nC_3 - n - n(n-4) = \frac{n(n-4)(n-5)}{6}$

10. **(i)** $10! = 2^p \cdot 3^q \cdot 5^r \cdot 7^s$

$P = \text{Exponent of 2 in } 10! = \left[\frac{10}{2}\right]+\left[\frac{10}{2^2}\right]+\left[\frac{10}{2^3}\right] = 5 + 2 + 1 = 8$

$q = \text{Exponent of 3 in } 10! = \left[\frac{10}{3}\right]+\left[\frac{10}{3^2}\right]+\left[\frac{10}{3^3}\right] = 3+1 = 4$

$r = \text{exponent of 5 in } 10! = \left[\frac{10}{5}\right]+\left[\frac{10}{5^2}\right] = 2$

$s = \text{exponent of 7 in } 10! = \left[\frac{10}{7}\right]+\left[\frac{10}{7^2}\right]+\ldots = 1$

$\therefore p = 8, q = 4, r = 2, s = 1$

Aliter: $10! = 1 \times 2 \times 3 \times 4 \times 5 \times 6 \times 7 \times 8 \times 9 \times 10$
$= 1 \times 2 \times 3 \times 2^2 \times 5 \times 2 \times 3 \times 7 \times 2^3 \times 3^2 \times 2 \times 5$
$= (2)^8 \times (3)^4 \times (5)^2 \times (7)^1$
$= p = 8, q = 4, r = 2, s = 1$

(ii) **(a)** **(i)** Number of zeros at the end of 100!

Exponent of 2 in $100! = \left[\frac{100}{2}\right]+\left[\frac{100}{2^2}\right]+\left[\frac{100}{2^3}\right]+\left[\frac{100}{2^4}\right] + \left[\frac{100}{2^5}\right]+\left[\frac{100}{2^6}\right] = 50 + 25 + 12 + 6 + 3 + 1 = 97$

Exponent of 5 in 100!

$= \left[\frac{100}{5}\right]+\left[\frac{100}{5^2}\right]+\left[\frac{100}{5^3}\right] = 20 + 4 = 24$

$\therefore$ Exponent of 10 in 100! = common exponent of 2 and 5 = 24

$\therefore$ There will be 24 zeros at the end of 100!

(ii) Exponent of 2 in $50! = \left[\frac{50}{2}\right]+\left[\frac{50}{2^2}\right]+\left[\frac{50}{2^3}\right]+\left[\frac{50}{2^4}\right]+\left[\frac{50}{2^5}\right]$
$= 25 + 12 + 6 + 3 + 1 = 47$

Exponent of 5 in $50! = \left[\frac{50}{5}\right]+\left[\frac{50}{5^2}\right] = 10 + 2 = 12$

$\therefore$ There will be 12 zero at the end of 50!

(iii) $\because$ Exponent of 2 > exponent of 5
$\therefore$ It is sufficient to find the exponent of 5

$\therefore$ Exponent of 5 in $25! = \left[\frac{25}{5}\right]+\left[\frac{25}{5^2}\right] = 5 + 1 = 6$

$\Rightarrow$ There will be 6 zero at the end of 25!

(b) l = L.C.M. of 8!, 10! and 12! = 12!
h = H.C.F. of 8! 10! and 12! = 8!
$\therefore \frac{l}{h} = \frac{12!}{8!} = 12 \times 11 \times 10 \times 9 = 11880$

(c) Exponent of 2 in $x = 20 \times 19 \times 18 \times \ldots. \times 11$

$\Rightarrow$ Exponent of 2 in $x = \frac{20!}{10!}$

= Exponent of (2 in 20!) – (Exponent of 2 in 10!)

$= \left(\left[\frac{20}{2}\right]+\left[\frac{20}{2^2}\right]+\left[\frac{20}{2^3}\right]+\left[\frac{20}{2^4}\right]\right) - \left(\left[\frac{10}{2}\right]+\left[\frac{10}{2^2}\right]+\left[\frac{10}{2^3}\right]\right) = (10 + 5 + 2 + 1) - (5 + 2 + 1)$
$= 10$

(d) 250! is divisible by 5^p, to find maximum value of p means to find exponent of 5 in 250!

$= \left[\frac{250}{5}\right]+\left[\frac{250}{5^2}\right]+\left[\frac{250}{5^3}\right] = 50 + 10 + 2 = 62$

(e) Exponent of 12 in ${}^{100}C_{30} = \frac{100!}{30!\,70!}$

Exponent of 2 in ${}^{100}C_{30}$
= (exponent of 2 in 100!) – (exponent of 2 in 30! + exponent of 2 in 70!)
$= (50 + 25 + 12 + 6 + 3 + 1) - (15 + 7 + 3 + 1 + 35 + 17 + 8 + 4 + 2 + 1) = 97 - 73 = 4$

Exponent of 3 in ${}^{100}C_{30} = \frac{100!}{30!\,70!}$
= (exponent of 3 in 100!) – (exponent of 3 in 30! + exponent of 3 in 70!)
$= (99 + 11 + 3 + 1) - (10 + 3 + 1 + 23 + 7 + 2) = 114 - 46 = 68$

$\therefore\ {}^{100}C_{30} = (2)^4 \times (3)^{68} \times (5)^1 \times (7)^m \times ......$
$= (4)^2 \times (3)^{68} \times (5)^1 \times (7)^m \times .....$
$= (12)^2 (3)^{66} \times (5)^1 \times (7)^m \times ......$
$\Rightarrow$ Exponent of 12 in ${}^{100}C_{30} = 2$

TEXTUAL EXERCISE–12: (OBJECTIVE)

1. (c) From 000 to 999, each integer is repeated equal number of times i.e., $\dfrac{1000\times 3}{10} = 300$ times

$\therefore$ 5 also occurs 300 times from 000 to 999, and hence 300 times from 12 to 1000

2. (c) Each of n district objects has two choices

$\therefore$ Total number of ways = 2^n

Now number of ways when either of two boxes is empty = $2^n - 2$

But due to identical boxes is a duplication of each case

$\therefore$ Required number of cases = $\dfrac{2^n-2}{2} = (2)^{n-1} - 1$

3. (b) Number of ways = $4!\left(1-\dfrac{1}{1!}+\dfrac{1}{2!}-\dfrac{1}{3!}+\dfrac{1}{4!}\right)$

$= 4!\left(\dfrac{1}{2!}-\dfrac{1}{3!}+\dfrac{1}{4!}\right) = 12 - 4 + 1 = 9$

4. (c) Number of ways = 4 wrong + 5 wrong + 6 wrong

$= {}^6C_2 \cdot 4!\left[1-\dfrac{1}{1!}+\dfrac{1}{2!}-\dfrac{1}{3!}+\dfrac{1}{4!}\right] +$

${}^6C_1 \cdot 5!\left[1-\dfrac{1}{1!}+\dfrac{1}{2!}-\dfrac{1}{3!}+\dfrac{1}{4!}-\dfrac{1}{5!}\right] +$

$6!\left[1-\dfrac{1}{1!}+\dfrac{1}{2!}-\dfrac{1}{3!}+\dfrac{1}{4!}-\dfrac{1}{5!}+\dfrac{1}{6!}\right]$

$= 15 \times (12 - 4 + 1) + 6 \times (60 - 20 + 5 - 1) + (360 - 120 + 30 - 6 + 1) = 135 + 264 + 265 = 664$

5. (c) Exponent of 12 in 50!

Exponent of 2 in 50! = $\left[\dfrac{50}{2}\right]+\left[\dfrac{50}{2^2}\right]+\left[\dfrac{50}{2^3}\right]+\left[\dfrac{50}{2^4}\right]+\left[\dfrac{50}{2^5}\right]$

$= 25 + 12 + 6 + 3 + 1 = 47$

Exponent of 3 in 50! = $\left[\dfrac{50}{3}\right]+\left[\dfrac{50}{3^2}\right]+\left[\dfrac{50}{3^3}\right]+\left[\dfrac{50}{3^4}\right] = 16$

$+ 5 + 1 + 0 = 22$

$\therefore\ 50! = (2)^{47} \times (3)^{22} \times (5)^l \times (7)^m \times .....$
$= (2)^{46} \times (2) \times (3)^{22} \times (5)^l \times (7)^m \times .....$
$= [(2)^2]^{23} \times (2) (3)^{22} \times (5)^l \times (7)^m \times .....$
$= (4)^{23} \times (3)^{22} \times (2) \times (5)^l \times (7)^m \times .....$
$= (4 \times 3)^{22} \times (4) (2) \times (5)^l \times (7)^m \times ......$
$\Rightarrow$ Exponent of 12 in 50! = 22

6. (b), (d) Exponent of 2 in 24!

$= \left[\dfrac{24}{2}\right]+\left[\dfrac{24}{2^2}\right]+\left[\dfrac{24}{2^3}\right]+\left[\dfrac{24}{2^4}\right] = 12 + 6 + 3 + 1 = 22$

Exponent of 3 in 24! = $\left[\dfrac{24}{3}\right]+\left[\dfrac{24}{3^2}\right]+\left[\dfrac{24}{3^3}\right] = 8 + 2 = 10$

$\therefore\ 24! = (2)^{22} \times (3)^{10} \times (5)^l \times (7)^m \times .....$
$= (2 \times 3)^{10} \times (2)^{12} \times (5)^l \times (7)^m \times .....$
$\Rightarrow$ Divisible by $(6)^{10}$
$= (2^3)^7 \times (2) (3)^7 \times (3)^3 \times (5)^l \times (7)^m \times ......$
$\Rightarrow$ Divisible by $(24)^6$
$= (2^2)^{10} \times (2)^2 \times (3)^{10} \times (5)^l \times (7)^m$ ....
$= (4 \times 3)^{10} \times (2)^2 \times (5)^l \times (7)^m$ ......
$\Rightarrow$ Divisible by $(12)^{10}$
$= (2^4)^5 \times (2)^2 \times (3)^{10} \times (5)^l \times (7)^m \times ......$
$= (2^4 \times 3)^5 \times (2)^2 \times (3)^5 \times (5)^l \times (7)^m \times .....$
$= (48)^5 \times (2)^2 \times (3)^5 \times (5)^l \times (7)^m \times .....$
$\Rightarrow$ divisible by $(48)^5$

7. (a) Exponent of 2 in 60! = $\left[\dfrac{60}{2}\right]+\left[\dfrac{60}{2^2}\right]+\left[\dfrac{60}{2^3}\right]+\left[\dfrac{60}{2^4}\right]+\left[\dfrac{60}{2^5}\right]$

$= 30 + 15 + 7 + 3 + 1 = 56$

Exponent of 5 in 60! = $\left[\dfrac{60}{5}\right]+\left[\dfrac{60}{5^2}\right]+\left[\dfrac{60}{5^3}\right] = 12 + 2 = 14$

$\therefore$ Exponent of 10 in 60! = (14)

$\Rightarrow$ There will be 14 zeros at the end of 60!

8. (c) Exponent of 7 in ${}^{100}C_{50}$ i.e., $\dfrac{100!}{50!\,50!}$

= (Exponent of 7 in 100!) – 2(Exponent of 7 in 50!)= (14 + 2) – 2 (7 + 1) = 0

9. (b) Exponent of 2 in ${}^{50}P_{10}$ i.e., $\dfrac{50!}{40!}$ = (Exponent of 2 in 50!) – (Exponent of 2 in 40!)

= (25 + 12 + 6 + 3 + 1) – (20 + 10 + 5 + 2 + 1) = 9

10. (c) Largest integer n = exponent of 3 in 45! =

$\left[\dfrac{45}{3}\right]+\left[\dfrac{45}{3^2}\right]+\left[\dfrac{45}{3^3}\right] = 15 + 5 + 1 = 21$

SECTION–III: (SINGLE CORRECT)

1. (c) A matrix having 4 elements can be of order 1 × 4; 2 × 2 or 4 × 1;

Now in each matrix each element has 4 choices.

$\therefore$ Total number of different possible matrices = $3 \times (4)^4$

2. (b) $\dfrac{{}^{52}C_{17} \times {}^{35}C_{17} \times {}^{18}C_{17} \times {}^1C_1}{3!}$

$= \dfrac{\dfrac{52!}{17!35!} \times \dfrac{35!}{17!\times 18!} \times \dfrac{18!}{17!\times 1!} \times 1}{3!} = \dfrac{52!}{(17!)^3.3!}$

3. (c) Let the number of men = n

Number of women = 2

$\therefore$ Total participants = $(n + 2)$

Now number of games played by men among the m selves = $2({}^nC_2)$

Number of games men played with women = $4n$

According to question $2({}^nC_2) = 4n + 66$

$\Rightarrow n(n - 1) = 4n + 66 \quad \Rightarrow n^2 - 5n - 66 = 0$

$\Rightarrow (n - 11)(n + 6) = 0$

$\Rightarrow n = 11$ or $n = -6$

$\therefore$ Total number of participants = 11 + 2 = 13

4. (b) $m_1 = \frac{7!}{2!} - \frac{6!}{2!} \times 2! = 2520 - 720 = 1800$

$m_2 = \frac{5!}{2!} = 60 \quad \therefore \quad \frac{m_1}{m_2} = 30$

5. (a) In between the + signs or on their left or right there are 7 places, out of which any 4 can be used to put –ve signs in ${}^7C_4$ ways $= \frac{7!}{4!3!} = 35$

6. (d) Number of subsets $= {}^{18}C_0 + {}^{18}C_3 + {}^{18}C_6 + {}^{18}C_9 + \ldots + {}^{18}C_{18}$

$(1+x)^{18} = {}^{18}C_0 + {}^{18}C_1 x + {}^{18}C_2 x^2 + {}^{18}C_3 x^3 + \ldots + {}^{18}C_{18} x^n$

Put x = cube roots of unity i.e., 1, w, w^2

$\Rightarrow (2)^{18} = {}^{18}C_0 + {}^{18}C_1 + {}^{18}C_2 + {}^{18}C_3 + \ldots + {}^{18}C_{18}$ (i)

$\Rightarrow (1+w)^{18} = {}^{18}C_0 + {}^{18}C_1 w + {}^{18}C_2 w^2 + {}^{18}C_3 w^3 + \ldots + {}^{18}C_{10} w^{18}$ (ii)

$\Rightarrow (1+w^2)^{18} = {}^{18}C_0 + {}^{18}C_1 w^2 + {}^{18}C_2 w^4 + {}^{18}C_3 w^6 + \ldots + {}^{18}C_{18} w^{36}$ (iii)

$\Rightarrow (2)^{18} + (1+w)^{18} + (1+w^2)^{18} = 3[{}^{18}C_0 + {}^{18}C_3 + \ldots + {}^{18}C_{18}]$

$\Rightarrow \frac{(2)^{18} + (-w^2)^{18} + (-w)^{18}}{3} = {}^{18}C_0 + {}^{18}C_3 + \ldots + {}^{18}C_{18}$

$\Rightarrow \frac{(2)^{18} + 1 + 1}{3} = {}^{18}C_0 + {}^{18}C_3 + \ldots + {}^{18}C_{18} \Rightarrow \frac{2^{18} + 2}{3}$

7. (b) $x_1 + x_2 + x_3 + x_4 = 0$ or 1 or 2 or 3 or … n and each $x_i \geq 0$

$\therefore$ Number of solutions $= {}^3C_3 + {}^4C_3 + {}^5C_3 + {}^6C_3 + \ldots + {}^{n+3}C_3$

$= {}^4C_0 + {}^4C_1 + {}^5C_2 + {}^6C_3 + \ldots + {}^{n+3}C_n \; (\because {}^3C_3 = {}^4C_0 = 1)$

$= {}^5C_1 + {}^5C_2 + {}^6C_3 + \ldots + {}^{n+3}C_n$

$= {}^6C_2 + {}^6C_3 + \ldots + {}^{n+3}C_n$

$= {}^{n+3}C_{n-1} + {}^{n+3}C_n = {}^{n+4}C_n = {}^{n+4}C_4$

8. (b) Case (i): First two places have identical digits.

Number of ways = 9 × 9 = 81

Case (ii): Last two places have identical digits (non-zeros)

Number of ways = 9 × 8 = 72

Case (iii): Last two places have identical digits (zeros)

Number of ways = 9 × 1 = 9

$\therefore$ Total number of ways = 81 + 72 + 9 = 162

9. (a) India can won if

(i) India wins first 5 matches

(ii) Indian wins 5 matches and loses 1

(iii) Wins 5 matches and loses 2

(iv) Wins 5 matches and loses 4

(v) Wins 5 matches and loses 4

In above cases the 5th winning should be at last match.

$\therefore$ Number of ways $= {}^4C_4 + {}^5C_4 + {}^6C_4 + {}^7C_4 + {}^8C_4$

As the first 4 winnings should be from any four of the matches played except for the last (reserved for last win) = 1 + 5 + 15 + 35 + 70 = 126

10. (c) If a 7 digit number does not change on reversing the order, then it should have same digits at equidistant places from left and right ends.

Thus if we first fix fourth place, then it can be done in 10 ways.

Now (first and last) have a choices (Second and second last)

(Third and third last) have 10 choices each

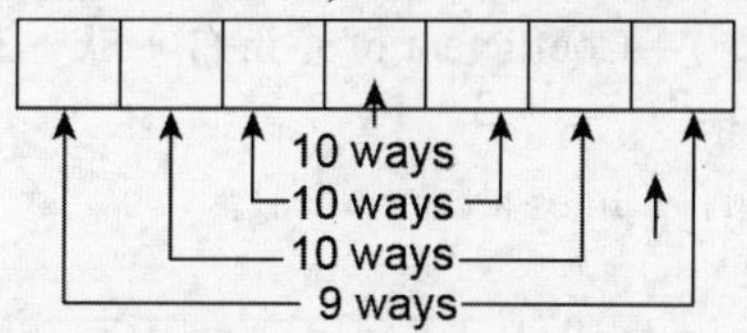

$\therefore$ Total number of 9×10^3

11. (a) $3780 = 2 \times 2 \times 3 \times 3 \times 3 \times 5 \times 7 = (2)^2 \times (2)^3 \times 5 \times 7$

Number of facts divisible by 2 or 3 or both

= Total facts – factors neither divisible by 2 nor by 3

= (3 × 4 × 2 × 2) – (1 × 1 × 2 × 2) = 48 – 4 = 44

12. (a) Number of ways $= \underbrace{17}_{\text{first letter}} \; \underbrace{{}^4P_2}_{\text{for middle 2 vowels}} \times \underbrace{17}_{\text{last letter}}$

$= 17 \times \frac{5!}{3!} \times 17 = 5780$

13. (c) $A = \{x : x \text{ is prime and } x < 30\}$

$A = \{2, 3, 5, 7, 11, 13, 17, 19, 23, 29\}$

Let $\frac{p}{q}$ be any rational number when $p, q \in A$,

Then the number of such rational numbers = (10 × 10 – 9) = 91

(We subtracted 9 as if numerator and denominator are same, we get 1, 10 times, retaining 1 times and removing 9 times).

14. (d) For forming a Δ we can use (AB, BC, CD) or (BC, CD, DA) or (CD, AD, AB) or (AB, BC, AD)

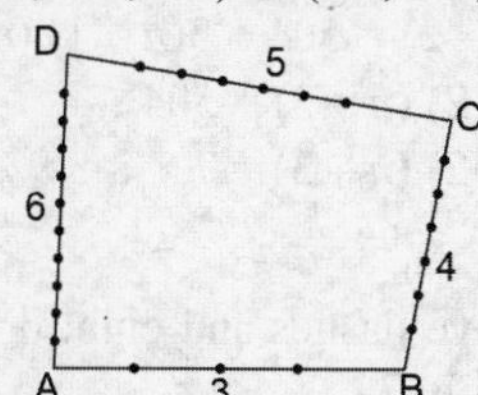

$\therefore$ Number of triangles = (3 × 4 × 5) + (4 × 5 × 6) + (5 × 6 × 3) + (3 × 4 × 6)

= 60 + 120 + 90 + 72 = 342

15. (c) Required number of Δs $= {}^{3p}C_3 - 3({}^pC_3)$

$= \frac{(3p)(3p-1)(3p-2)}{3!} - \frac{3(p)(p-1)(p-2)}{3!}$

$= \frac{3p}{3!}[(3p-1)(3p-2) - (p-1)(p-2)]$

$= \frac{p}{2}[8p^2 - 6p] = p^2(4p-3)$

16. (b) Let $A = \{1, 2, 3, 4, \ldots 200\}$; $B = \{5, 10, 15, \ldots 200\}$ and $C = A - B$, then the product of two factors will be divisible by 5 if atleast one of two factors is a multiple of 5.

Case (ii): When exactly one factor is a multiple of 5

Number of product = 40 × 160 = 6400

Case (ii): When both factors are multiple of 5.

Number of product $= {}^{40}C_2 = \frac{40 \times 39}{2} = 780$

$\therefore$ Total numbers = 6400 + 780 = 7180

17. (a) Number of ways = Coefficient of x^4 in $(1 + x)^3 (1 + x + x^2 + x^3)$ = Coefficient of x^4 in $(1 + 3x + 3x^2 + x^3)(1 + x + x^2 + x^3) = 3 + 3 + 1 = 7$

18. (a) Family of lines are $y = x + r$ (i) and
$y = -x + r$ (ii);
where $r \in \{0, 1, 2, 3, 4\}$

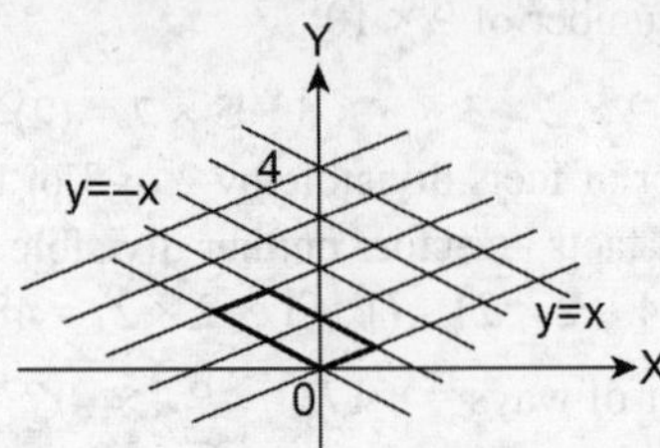

Total 16 squares of unit diagonal length are obtained from the intersection of two given families of straight lines. Out of these squares of 2 units diagonal length are $3 \times 3 = 9$

19. (b) $n = {}^{21}C_r$

For n to be maximum, $r = \dfrac{21-1}{2}$ or $\dfrac{21+1}{2}$ i.e., $r = 10$ or 11

20. (b) Let the number of children in the class = n.

Number of groups of 3 children = ${}^nC_3$

Each child would go to zoo ${}^{n-1}C_2$ times.

$\therefore$ According the question: ${}^nC_3 = 84 + {}^{n-1}C_2$

$\Rightarrow \dfrac{n(n-1)(n-2)}{6} = 84 + \dfrac{(n-1)(n-2)}{2}$

$\Rightarrow n(n-1)(n-2) = 504 + 3(n-1)(n-2)$

$\Rightarrow (n-1)(n-2)(n-3) = 504$

$\Rightarrow (n-1)(n-2)(n-3) = 7 \times 8 \times 9$

$\Rightarrow x = 10$

21. (c) These are five dashes and eight dots, out of which we are to use only 7.

$= \text{Coefficient of } x^7 \text{ in } 7!\left(1+\dfrac{x^1}{1!}+\dfrac{x^2}{2!}+\dfrac{x^3}{3!}+\dfrac{x^4}{4!}+\dfrac{x^5}{5!}\right) \times \left(\dfrac{x^2}{2!}+\dfrac{x^3}{3!}+\dfrac{x^4}{4!}+\dfrac{x^5}{5!}+\dfrac{x^6}{6!}+\dfrac{x^7}{7!}\right)$

$= 7!\left(\dfrac{1}{7!}+\dfrac{1}{6!}+\dfrac{2}{2!5!}+\dfrac{2}{3!4!}\right) = 1 + 7 + 42 + 70 = 120$

22. (a) ${}^{40}C_{31} + \sum\limits_{j=0}^{10} {}^{40+j}C_{10+j} = {}^{40}C_{31} + \sum\limits_{j=0}^{10} {}^{40+j}C_{30}$

$= {}^{40}C_{31} + {}^{40}C_{30} + \sum\limits_{j=1}^{10} {}^{40+j}C_{30} = {}^{41}C_{31} + {}^{41}C_{30} + \sum\limits_{j=2}^{10} {}^{40+j}C_{30}$

$= \underbrace{{}^{42}C_{31} + \sum\limits_{j=2}^{10} {}^{40+j}C_{30}}_{\text{Proceeding similarly using parcals value}} = {}^{50}C_{31} + {}^{50}C_{30} = {}^{51}C_{31} = {}^{51}C_{20}$

23. (d) All possible ways are (0, 0, 9), (0, 1, 8), (0, 2, 7), (0, 3, 6), (0, 4, 5), (1, 1, 7), (1, 2, 6), (1, 3, 5), (1, 4, 4), (2, 2, 5), (2, 3, 4), (3, 3, 3) i.e., 12 ways.

Aliter: Let a, b, c be the number of balls in box 1, 2 and 3.

$\therefore a + b + c = 9$ (i)

Number of solutions of (1) = ${}^{9+2}C_2 = {}^{11}C_2 = 55$

But these are not the actual solutions i.e., duplication is there e.g., $a = 1, b = 2, c = 6$, or $a = 2, b = 1, c = 6$

These two solutions are same as the boxes are identical. We have following three types of distribution.

(i) When all the boxes, have equal number of balls. Number of solutions = 1 i.e., all boxes have 3 balls.

(ii) Two boxes have same balls: i.e., (1, 1, 7); (2, 2, 5); (4, 4, 1); (0, 0, 9)
Number of solutions of (1) arising from this case = $4 \times 3 = 12$

(iii) All boxes have unequal number of balls:
Number of solutions of (1) arising from this case = $55 - (1 + 12) = 42$

$\therefore$ For our problem, number of ways = $1 + 4 + \dfrac{42}{3!} = 1 + 4 + 7 = 12$

24. (a) Case (i): First and last uses the consonants C, L
Required ways = 2! × (Number of permutations of C, L, T, A, U, A, E) = $2! \times \dfrac{7!}{2!} = 7!$

Case (ii): First and last uses the consonants C, C,
Required ways = (Number of permutations of L, L, T, A, U, A, E) = $\dfrac{7!}{2!2!}$

Case (iii): First and last uses (L, L)
Number of ways = $\dfrac{7!}{2!2!}$

Case (iv): First and last uses (L, T)
Number of ways = 2! × (Number of permutations of C, L, C, A, U, A, E) = $2! \times \dfrac{7!}{2!2!} = \dfrac{7!}{2!}$

Case (v): First and last uses (C, T)
Number of ways = $\dfrac{7!}{2!}$

$\therefore$ Total number of ways = $7! + 2\left(\dfrac{7!}{2!2!}\right) + 2\left(\dfrac{7!}{2!}\right)$

$= 2(7!) + \dfrac{7!}{2} = \dfrac{5}{2}(7!)$

25. (b) $x, y, z < 0; x + y + z + 12 = 0$

$\Rightarrow x + y + z = -12 \qquad \Rightarrow (-x) + (-y) + (-z) = 12$

$\Rightarrow x' + y' + z' = 12$; (where $x' = -x$ etc.

$\Rightarrow x' > 0 \Rightarrow x' \geq 1$)

$\Rightarrow (x' - 1) + (y' - 1) + (z' - 1) = 9$

$\Rightarrow x'' + y'' + z'' = 9$

(where $x'' = x' - 1$ etc. and $x'' \geq 0$)

$\Rightarrow$ Number of solutions = ${}^{9+2}C_2 = {}^{11}C_2 = 55$

26. (c) Out of 10 digits 4 digits can be selected in ${}^{10}C_4$ ways and can be arranged in a unique way $a_1 > a_2 > a_3 > a_4$

$\therefore n(A) = {}^{10}C_4 = 210$

27. (b) Even digits are 0, 2, 4, 6, 8 out of these 5 we are to use any 4 so that their sum is divisible by 3

$\therefore$ We can choose (0, 4, 6, 8) or (0, 2, 4, 6)

$\therefore$ Number of numbers divisible by 3 and having each digit even is = $2 \times (4! - 3!) = 36$

28. (b) Smallest group having n-people implies n is the total number of different predictions
$= 3 \times 3 \times 3 \times 3 \times 3 = 243$

29. (c) Let a_1, a_2, a_3, a_4 be the marks obtained in paper 1st, 2nd, 3rd, and 4th respectively.
Then $0 \le a_i \le m$ and $a_1 + a_2 + a_3 + a_4 = 2m$
Number of ways $= {}^{2m+3}C_3$ .... (i)
But here those cases are also included when any one of a_i's attain value greater then m i.e.,
$m + 1, m + 2, \ldots\ldots\ldots, 2m$.
We are to exclude those cases:
When $a_i = m + 1$; $a_j + a_k + a_l = m - 1$
$\Rightarrow$ Number of ways $= 4({}^{m+1}C_2)$
When $a_i = m + 2$; $a_j + a_k + a_l = m - 2$
$\Rightarrow$ Number of ways $= 4({}^{m}C_2)$
When $a_i = m + 3$; $a_j + a_k + a_l = m - 3$
$\Rightarrow$ Number of ways $= 4({}^{m-1}C_2)$ and so on.
Finally when $a_i = 2m$; $a_j + a_k + a_l = 0$;
$\Rightarrow$ Number of ways $= {}^2C_2$
Thus total number of undesirable cases $= 4[{}^2C_2 + {}^3C_2 + {}^4C_2 + \ldots\ldots + {}^mC_2 + {}^{m+1}C_2]$
$= 4[{}^3C_3 + {}^3C_2 + {}^4C_2 + \ldots\ldots + {}^mC_2 + {}^{m+1}C_2] = 4[{}^{m+1}C_3 + {}^{m+1}C_2] = 4({}^{m+2}C_3)$
$\therefore$ Required number of ways $= {}^{2m+3}C_3 - 4\ ({}^{m+2}C_3) = \dfrac{(m+1)}{3}(2m^2+4m+3)$

30. (b) Each group would consists of 6 teams and they play against each other a total of ${}^6C_2 = 15$ matches
$\therefore$ Total matches played by two groups $= 2 \times 15 = 30$
Now after selecting 3 top teams from each group, total 6 teams would play each other a total of ${}^6C_2 = 15$ matches. Further, after selecting 4 teams for semi-final, they would play ${}^4C_2 = 6$ matches
$\therefore$ Before final match, there will be $30 + 15 + 6 = 51$ matches.
Now two top teams play in the final for best of three matches means a team winning two matches, would be declared world champion. For this at least two matches would be played as if a team wins two matches consecutively is no need for third match.
$\therefore$ Minimum number of matches played $= 51 + 2 = 53$

31. (b) $2^{\sin^2 x} \cdot 3^{\cos^2 y} \cdot y^{\sin^2 z} \cdot 5^{\cos^2 w} \ge 120$ (i)
$\because\ 0 \le \sin^2\theta, \cos^2\phi \le 1$
$\Rightarrow\ 1 \le a^{\sin^2\theta}, a^{\cos^2\phi} \le a$ for $a > 1$
$\Rightarrow\ 1 \le 2^{\sin^2 x} \le 2 \qquad \Rightarrow\ 1 \le 3^{\cos^2 y} \le 3$
$\Rightarrow\ 1 \le 4^{\sin^2 z} \le 4$ and $1 \le 5^{\cos^2 w} \le 5$
$\Rightarrow\ 1 \le 2^{\sin^2 x} \cdot 3^{\cos^2 y} \cdot 4^{\sin^2 z} \cdot 5^{\cos^2 w} \le 120$ (ii)
$\therefore$ From (i) and (ii), we get $2^{\sin^2 x} \cdot 3^{\cos^2 y} \cdot 4^{\sin^2 z} \cdot 5^{\cos^2 w} = 120$
$\Rightarrow\ \sin^2 x = \cos^2 y = \sin^2 z = \cos^2 w = 1$
$\Rightarrow\ \sin x = \pm 1, \cos y = \pm 1, \sin z = \pm 1, \cos w = \pm 1$
$\Rightarrow\ x, y, z, w \in [0, 10] \subseteq \left[0, 3\pi + \dfrac{\pi}{2}\right) \Rightarrow\ z, x \in \left\{\dfrac{\pi}{2}, \dfrac{3\pi}{2}, \dfrac{5\pi}{2}\right\}$
$\Rightarrow\ w, y \in \{0, \pi, 2\pi, 3\pi\}$
$\Rightarrow$ Required number of 4-tables $(x, y, z, w) = 3 \times 4 \times 3 \times 4 = 144$

32. (b) 5 points lying on a circle represent a circle.
We have total 11 points, any three of these represent a circle and no four points except for give 5 are concylic.
$\therefore$ Total number of circles formed $= {}^{11}C_3 - {}^5C_3 + 1 = 156$

33. (b) Let a_1, a_2, a_3 be the number of coins received by 1st, 2nd and 3rd person respectively.
Then $a_i \ge 1$ and $a_i \ne a_j$ for $i \ne j$ and $a_1 + a_2 + a_3 = 7$
Number of cases: (1, 2, 4); i.e., a persons get 1, 2nd person 2 and 3rd person 4 coins.
$\therefore$ Required ways $= 3! \times ({}^7C_1 \times {}^6C_2 \times {}^4C_4) = 3! \times 7 \times 15 \times 1 = 630$ ways.

34. (a) Required sum $= \left(2 \times \dfrac{5!}{2!\,3!} + 3 \times \dfrac{5!}{3!} + 4 \times \dfrac{5!}{2!2!}\right) \times (10^5 + 10^4 + 10^3 + 10^2 + 10^1 + 1)$
$= (20 + 60 + 120) \times (111111) = 22222200$

35. (a) Number of numbers lass than or equal to 10^{12} which are perfect squints $= \sqrt{10^{12}} = 10^6$
Number of numbers lass than or equal to 10^{12} which are perfect cubes $= \sqrt[3]{10^{12}} = 10^4$
Number of numbers less than or equal to 10^{12} which are perfect 4th powers $= \sqrt[4]{10^{12}} = 10^3$
Number of numbers which are perfect square as well as perfect cubes $= \sqrt[6]{10^{12}} = 10^2$
Number of numbers which are perfect cubes are well as perfect forth powers $= \sqrt[12]{10^{12}} = 10^1$
Number of numbers which are perfect square as well as perfect 4th powers $= \sqrt[4]{10^{12}} = 10^3$
Number of numbers which are perfect square cubes as well as perfect 4th powers $= \sqrt[12]{10^{12}} = 10$
$\therefore$ Number of numbers which are neither perfect square, cubes and 4th powers and less than of equal to 10^{12} $= 10^{12} - [10^6 + 10^4 + 10^3 - 10^2 - 10 - 10^3 + 10] = 999998990100$

36. (c) For first table m gentlemen can be selected and permuted in ${}^{(m+n)}C_m \times \dfrac{(m-1)!}{2}$ ways.
The remaining n gentlemen can be permuted in $\dfrac{(n-1)!}{2}$ ways
$\therefore$ Total number of ways $= {}^{(m+n)}C_m \times \dfrac{(m-1)!}{2}\dfrac{(n-1)!}{2}$
$= \dfrac{(m+n)!}{n!m!} \times \dfrac{(m-1)!}{2} \times \dfrac{(n-1)!}{2} = \dfrac{(m+n)!}{4mn}$
But m gentleman and n gentleman can also be arranged in 2nd and 1st table respectively
$\therefore$ Required number of ways $= 2\left(\dfrac{(m+n)!}{4m}\right)$

37. (c) Let the five digit number be $\overline{a\,b\,c\,d\,e}$
$= \overline{a\,b\,c\,0\,0} + \overline{de}$ is divisible by 25 if $\overline{de}$ is divisible by 25

$\Rightarrow \overline{de} \in \{00, 25, 50, 75\}$

$\therefore$ $\overline{de} = 25$ or 50 (others impossible)

$\therefore$ For $\overline{de} = 25$, a has 3 choices i.e., 1, 3, 4; b has 3 choice; c has 2 choice

$\therefore$ Required number = 4 × 3 × 2 = 24

$\therefore$ Number of numbers divisible by 25 and of given form = 18 + 24 = 42

38. (c) Sum of six numbers $\in \{-1, 0, 1\}$ vanishes if
(i) All are zeros
(ii) 2 zeros; two (1's) and two (–1's)
(iii) 4 zeros; one 1 and one –1
(iv) Three 1's and three –1's

$\therefore$ Required number of ways $= 1 + \frac{6!}{(2!)^3} + \frac{6!}{4!} + \frac{6!}{(3!)^2}$
= 1 + 90 + 30 + 20 = 141

39. (b) $x\,y\,z\,y\,x$; $x < y$; clearly $x \neq 0$

$\Rightarrow x \in \{1, 2, 3, ... 9\}$ and $x < y$

$\Rightarrow x \neq y \Rightarrow x \in \{1, 2, 3, 4, 5,.... 8\}$ and $y \in \{2, 3, 4,....9\}$

$\Rightarrow$ Number of choices for $y = 8 + 7 + 6 +.....+ 1 = 36$
Also z has 10 choices (any digit)

$\Rightarrow$ Total number of numbers = 36 × 10 = 360

40. (c) Number of ways when two consecutives are selected = $2(n-3) + (n-3)(n-4)$
Number of ways when three consecutives are selected $= (n-2)$

P_1 P_2 P_3 P_{n-1} P_n

$\therefore$ Number of ways when no two are consecutives $= {}^nC_3 - [(n-3)(n-2) + (n-2)] = {}^nC_3 - (n-2)^2 = P_n$

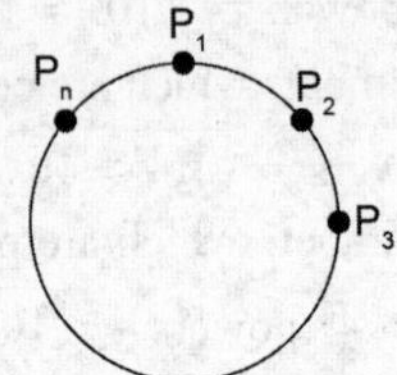

Number of ways when 2 consecutives are selected = $n(n-4)$
Number of ways when 3 consecutives are selected = n

$\therefore$ Total number of ways when 2 or 3 are consecutive = $n(n-4) + n = n(n-3)$

$\therefore$ Number of ways when number of two are consecutive $= {}^nC_3 - n(n-3) = Q_n$

$\therefore$ $P_n - Q_n = 6$

$\Rightarrow -(n-2)^2 + n(n-3) = 6$

$\Rightarrow -n^2 - 4 + 4n + n^2 - 3n = 6 \Rightarrow n = 10$

41. (c) For $x = 1$, and $x = 3$, the equation is satisfied for $x = 4$
L.H.S = 9 + 4!; R.H.S = $(N)^2$
$1! = 1 = (1)^2$
$1! + 2! = 3 \neq (N)^2$
$1! + 2! + 3! = 9 = (3)^2$
$1! + 2! + 3! + 4! = 33 \neq (N)^2$
$1! + 2! + 3! + 4! + 5! = 153$
From 5! Onwards, the sum 1! + 2! + 3! + 4! + 5! + 6! + ..., would have 3 at its unit place, and there is no natural number whose square has unit place digit 3.

$\therefore$ There are exactly two solutions $x = 1$ and $x = 3$

42. (d) A signal having 6 flags can have
(i) 4 white, 1 blue, 1 red flag.
(ii) 3 white, 1 blue, 2 red flags
(iii) 2 white, 1 blue, 3 red flags
(iv) 4 white, 2 red
(v) 3 white, 3 red
A signal is identified by the order of columns.

$\therefore$ Total number of signals formed

$$= \frac{6!}{4!} + \frac{6!}{3!2!} + \frac{6!}{2!3!} + \frac{6!}{4!2!} + \frac{6!}{3!3!}$$

$$= 6!\left[\frac{1}{4!} + \frac{1}{3!2!} + \frac{1}{2!3!} + \frac{1}{4!2!} + \frac{1}{3!3!}\right] = 185$$

43. (a) Required number of words $= \frac{6!}{3!}$ – [(Number of words starting with E) + (Number of words ending with E) – (Number of words starting with E and ending with E)] =

$$\frac{6!}{3!} - \left[\frac{5!}{2!} + \frac{5!}{2!} - 4!\right] = 24$$

44. (a) Let the three digit number be $\overline{abc}$; $b \in \{1, 4, 9\}$
Corresponding to each choice of b, a has 9 choices i.e., $a \in \{1, 2, 3,....,9\}$ and corresponding to each choice of pair (a, b), c has 9 choices i.e., $c \in \{1, 2, 3,....,9\}$

$\therefore$ Sum of numbers

$$= 3 \times 9 \sum_{k=1}^{9} k \times 10^2 + (1+4+9) \times 10 \times 81 + 9\sum_{k=1}^{9} k$$

$= 27 \times 45 \times 10^2 + 14 \times 810 + 1215 = 121500 + 11340 + 1215 = 134055$

45. (b) 1 million = 10,00000, thus 1 million is smallest 7 digit number and we are two find 7 digits numbers greater than 1 million and formed by using the digits 1, 2, 1, 2, 0, 5, 2 and divisible by 5.
Clearly unit place digit should be 0 or 5.
If the unit place digit is 0, the other digits can be permuted in $\frac{6!}{3!2!} = 60$ ways.
If the unit place digit is 5, the other digits can be permuted in $\left[\frac{6!}{3!2!} - \frac{5!}{3!2!}\right] = 50$

$\therefore$ Required number of number = 60 + 50 = 110

46. (c) Required number of ways = coefficient of x^{14} in $(1 + x^2 + x^4)^5$

$= $ Coefficient of x^{14} in $\left[\frac{(x^2)^3 - 1}{x^2 - 1}\right]^5$

$= $ Coefficient of x^{14} in $[x^6 - 1]^5 (x^2 - 1)^{-5}$

$= $ Coefficient of x^{14} in $(1 - x^6)^5 (1 - x^2)^{-5}$

$= $ Coefficient of x^{14} in $({}^5C_0 - {}^5C_1 x^6 + {}^5C_2 x^{12}) \times (1 + 5x^2 + 70x^8 + 330x^{14})^2 = 330 - 350 + 50 = 30$

47. (d) From 000 to 999, (writing 2 as 002 and 12 as 012 etc.). There are 1000 numbers having 1000 × 3 = 3000 digits in which each digits occur equal number of times i.e., 300 times.

$\therefore$ Sum of all digits from 000 to 999 = 300 (1 + 2 + 3 + ... + 9) = 13500

$\therefore$ Sum of digits from 1 to 1000 = 13500 + 1 = 13501

48. (b) $n(A) = 6$; $n(B) = 3$

$\therefore$ Number of onto function = $(3)^6 - {}^3C_1\,(2)^6 + {}^3C_2\,(1)^6 =$ 729 – 192 + 3 = 540

49. (b) Case (i): All 6 are different

Number of ways of selecting 3 balls = ${}^6C_3 = 20$

Case (ii): Three each of two columns (say) R R R B B B

Number of ways of selecting 3 balls = Coefficient of x^3 in $(1 + x + x^2 + x^3)^2$

= Coefficient of x^3 in $\left[\dfrac{1-x^4}{1-x}\right]^2$

= Coefficient of x^3 in $(1 - x^4)^2\,(1 - x)^{-2}$

= Coefficient of x^3 in $(1 + x^8 - 2x^4)$

$\left(1+2x+\dfrac{2(3)x^2}{2!}+\dfrac{2(3)(4)x^3}{3!}+....\right)=4$

(These four ways are RRR, BBB, RRB, RBB) one can also write directly

Case (iii): Two each of three columns (say) RR BB WW

Number of ways = Coefficient of x^3 in $(1 + x + x^2)^3$

= coefficient of x^3 is $(1 - x^3)^3\,(1 - x)^{-3}$

= Coefficient of x^3 in $(1 - x^9 - 3x^3 + 3x^6)\,(1 + 3x + 6x^2 + 10x^3 + ...)$

= 10 – 3 = 7, these 7 ways are (RRB), (RRW), (BBR), (BBW), (WWR), (WWB), (BRW)

(one can write directly)

$\therefore$ Total number of ways = 20 + 4 + 7 = 31

50. (c) $20 \le x + y + z \le 50$; $x, y, z \in \mathbb{N}$

Required number of solutions = (Number of solutions of $x + y + z \le 50$) – (Number of solutions of $x + y + z \le 19$); $x, y, z \in \mathbb{N}$

= (Number of solution of $x + y + z \le 47$) – (Number of solution of $x + y + z \le 16$); $x, y, z \in W$

(Whole number set)

$= [{}^{49}C_2 + {}^{48}C_2 + {}^{47}C_2 + ... + {}^2C_2] - [{}^{18}C_2 + {}^{17}C_2 + {}^{16}C_2 + ... + {}^2C_2] = [{}^{50}C_3 - {}^{19}C_3]$

51. (b) Let x, y, z be the number of questions attempted from section A, B and C respectively.

Since at least one question is to be attempted from each section $1 \le x, y, z \le 3$ and $x + y + z = 5$

$\Rightarrow$ $(x - 1) + (y - 1) + (z - 1) = 2$; $x_1 - 1 \ge 0$ etc.

$\Rightarrow$ $x' + y' + z' = 2$; $2 \ge x' \ge 0$ etc.

Number of ways = ${}^4C_2 = 6$, which are (1, 1, 3); (1, 3, 1); (3, 1, 1); (2, 2, 1); (2, 1, 2); (1, 2, 2)

$\therefore$ Required number of ways = $3[{}^4C_1 \times {}^4C_1 \times {}^4C_3 + {}^4C_2 \times {}^4C_2 \times {}^4C_1] = 624$

52. (a) Out of six married couples, one couple can be selected in 6 ways. The other two persons are two be selected from remaining 5 married couple, so that *a* couple is not selected

$\therefore$ Number of ways = $6[{}^{10}C_2 - 5] = 240$

53. (c) For exactly 18 correct forecasts out of 21, 3 must be incorrect and can occur in ${}^{21}C_3$ ways. Now each of the 3 incorrect forecasts has two ways of incorrectness.

Hence total number of ways = ${}^{21}C_3 \times 2 \times 2 \times 2 = 8({}^{21}C_3)$

54. (a) Every group of 4 points on the circumference of circle would provide an interior point of intersection as shown below

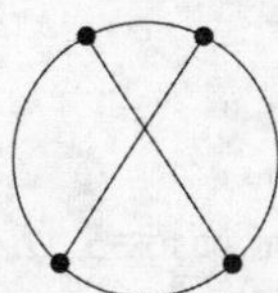

Maximum number of interior points of intersection =

${}^9C_4 = \dfrac{9\times8\times7\times6}{4\times3\times2\times1} = 126$

55. (a) Number of ways – ${}^5C_3 \times {}^8C_7 + {}^5C_4 \times {}^8C_6 + {}^5C_5 \times {}^8C_5 =$ 10 × 8 + 5 × 28 + 1 × 56 = 80 + 140 + 56 = 276

56. (d) Required number of ways = Coefficient of x^8 in $(1 + x + x^2 + ... + x^{10})^4$

= Coefficient of x^8 in $\left[\dfrac{1-x^{11}}{1-x}\right]^4$

= Coefficient of x^8 in $(1 - x^{11})^4\,(1 - x)^{-4}$

= Coefficient of x^8 in $[{}^4C_0 - {}^4C_1\,x^{11} + ...]$

$\left[1+4x+\dfrac{4(5)x^2}{2!}+\dfrac{4(5)(6)x^3}{3!}+....+\dfrac{(4)(5)(6)....(11)}{8!}x^8+...\right]$

$= \dfrac{4(5)(6)....(11)}{8!} = \dfrac{9\times10\times11}{3\times2\times1} = {}^{11}C_3$

57. (b) Required number of ways = Coefficient x^{12} in $(x + x^2 + x^3)^6$

= Coefficient of x^{12} in $x^6(1 + x + x^2)^6$

= Coefficient of x^6 in $(1 + x + x^2)^6$

= Coefficient of x^6 in $\left[\dfrac{1-x^3}{1-x}\right]^6$

= Coefficient of x^6 in $(1 - x^3)^6\,(1 - x)^6$

= Coefficient of x^6 in $[{}^6C_0 - {}^6C_1x^3 + {}^6C_2x^6] \times [1 + {}^{6+3-1}C_3x^3 + {}^{6+6-1}C_6x^6]$

$= {}^{11}C_6 - {}^6C_1.{}^8C_3 + {}^6C_2 = 141$

58. (b) We have 4 groups of different nations, they can be arranged on *a* circle in 3! Ways Further the people inside the groups can be arranged among themselves in 2!, 3! And 4! Ways respectively.

$\therefore$ Total number of ways = $2(3!)^3.4!$

59. (c) Required number of ways = (Total number of ways of arranging 7 persons) – (Number of ways where two American are together + Number of ways when two Britishian are together – Number of ways when both American and both Britishian are together)

= 6! – [2 × 5! + 2 × 5! – 4! × 2! × 2!)] = 720 – [480 – 96] = 240 + 96 = 336

60. (d) 4 boys can be arranged around a circular table in 3! ways Now after arranging 4 boys, 4 places are created in between the boys, in which 4 girls can be arranged in 4! ways.

$\therefore$ Number of ways when boys and girls are separated = 3! × 4! = 144

Now out of these ways we are to exclude those ways in which *a* particular boy and *a* particular girl are together say B_1 and G_1

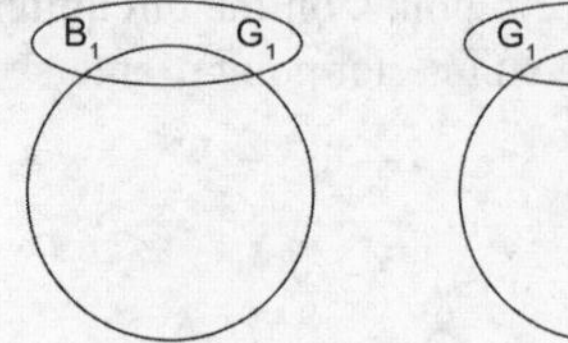
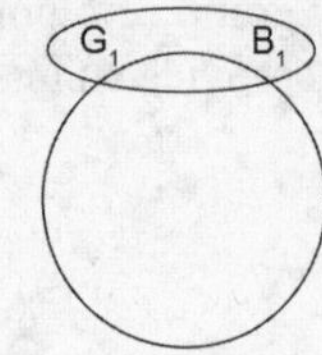

Now each of two cases B_2, B_3, B_4 can be arranged in 3! ways.

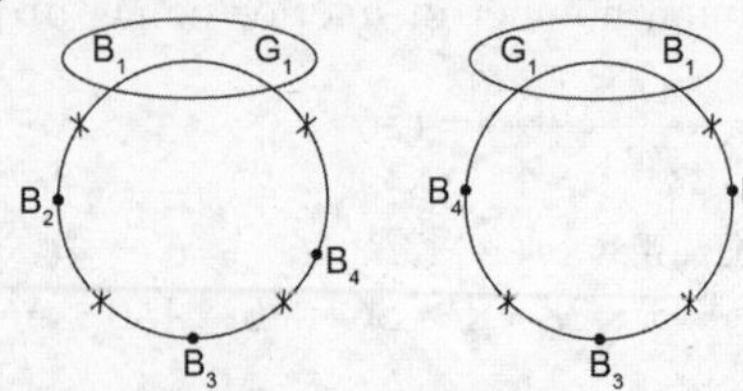

Now G_2, G_3 and G_4 can be arranged in position marked (X) in 3! ways

∴ Total number of ways when B_1 and G_1 are together = 2 × 3! × 3! = 72

∴ Number of ways when girls and boys are separated and *a* particular boy and *a* particular girl are not together = 144 – 72 = 72

61. (a) 4 different Prizes can be given to *a* particular student in ${}^9C_4$ ways

Rest 5 different prizes are to be given to rest 4 students. Each of rest 5 different prizes has 4 options.

∴ Total number of ways = ${}^9C_4 \times 4 \times (4) \times 4 \times 4 \times 4 = {}^9C_4 (4)^5 = {}^9C_4 (2)^{10}$.

62. (c) Two balls which are to be put in the boxes of same colour can be selected in ${}^5C_2$ ways i.e., 10 ways

Now, the remaining 3 balls are to be put in three boxes such that no ball goes to the box of its own colour, which can be done in $3!\left[1-\frac{1}{1!}+\frac{1}{2!}-\frac{1}{3!}\right]$ ways i.e., in 2 ways

∴ Total number of required ways = 10 × 2 = 20

63. (a) Number of ways of distributing *p* identical white balls in n different bags

= Number of solutions of equation $x_1 + x_2 + x_3 + \ldots. + x_n = p;\ x_i \geq 0$

$= {}^{p+n-1}C_{n-1} = {}^{p+n-1}C_p$ ways

Similarly for *q* identical balls = ${}^{q+n-1}C_q$ ways and for *r* identical balls = ${}^{r+n-1}C_r$ ways

∴ Total number of distribution = ${}^{p+n-1}C_p \cdot {}^{q+n-1}C_q \cdot {}^{r+n-1}C_r$ ways

64. (c) For the time being, let three A's are different i.e., A_1, A_2, A_3

Let *x* be the actual number of circular permutations

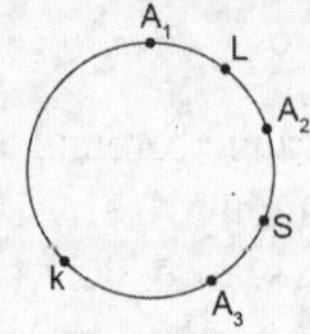

Then, $x.3! = (6-1)! \Rightarrow \frac{5!}{3!} = 20$

65. (d) 10 identical boxes can contain 12 balls such that each box contains at least one ball in the following cases:

Case (i): 8 boxes single ball each + 2 boxes single balls each

Single ball boxes	Boxes with double balls
$2W, 6B$;	$(WW)(WW)$
$3W, 5B$;	$(WW)(WB)$
$4W, 4B$;	$(WW)(BB)$;$(WB)(WB)$
$5W, 3B$;	$(WB)(BB)$
$6W, 2B$;	$(BB)(BB)$

Case (ii): 9 boxes single ball each + 1 box containing 3 balls

Single ball boxes	Triple ball boxes
$3W + 6B$;	(WWW)
$4W + 5B$;	(WWB)
$5W + 4B$;	(WBB)
$6W + 3B$;	(BBB)

∴ Total 10 ways are there

66. (c) $L = {}^{p+q}C_p = {}^{p+q}C_q$

$M = ({}^{p+q}C_p + {}^{p+q}C_q) = 2L$

$N = {}^{p+q}C_p = L$

∴ $2L = M = 2N$

67. (a) There are two possible ways of distribution as given below:

Case (i): 2 books, 2books, 4 books

Number of ways of selection of 2, 2 and 4 books = ${}^8C_2 \times {}^6C_2 \times {}^4C_4$ = 28 × 15 = 420

Case (ii): 3 books, 3 books, 2 books,

Number of ways of selection of 3, 3 and 2 books = ${}^8C_3 \times {}^5C_3 \times {}^2C_2$ = 56 × 10 = 560

∴ Total number of ways of selection of (2, 2, 4) or (3, 3, 2) books = 420 + 560 = 980

Now, 2 student getting same numbers of books (i.e., (2, 2) or (3, 3)) and 3rd student getting (3 or 4) books can be selected in 3 ways.

(1, 2) → (2 or 3 each); 3 → (4 or 2)

(2, 3) → (2 or 3 each); 1 → (4 or 2)

(1, 3) → (2 or 3 each); 2 → (4 or 2)

∴ Total number of ways of distribution = 980 × 3 = 2940

68. (b) Required number of ways = Number of solutions of equation $(x_1 + x_2 + x_3 + x_4 = 8;\ x_i \geq 0)$ – (Number of ways when any one gets 5 or more angles

$$= {}^{11}C_3 - \left[\overbrace{{}^4C_1 \times {}^5C_2}^{(5\text{ oranges})} + \overbrace{{}^4C_1 \times {}^4C_2}^{(6\text{ oranges})} + \overbrace{{}^4C_1 \times {}^3C_2}^{(7\text{ oranges})} + \overbrace{{}^4C_1 \times 1}^{(8\text{ oranges})} + \left(\overbrace{{}^4C_1 \times {}^6C_2}^{(4\text{ oranges})} - \overbrace{{}^4C_2}^{(4\text{ oranges two persons})}\right)\right]$$

= 165 – [40 + 24 + 12 + 4 + 54] = 31

69. (b) Number of ways of forming groups of 2, 3 and 4 people = ${}^9C_2 \times {}^7C_3 \times {}^4C_4$

Now, three floors out of 10 floors (except for ground floor) can be permutated in ${}^{10}P_3$ ways

∴ Total number of ways in which 9 people can leave the lift in the groups of 2, 3 and 4

$= {}^9C_2 \times {}^7C_3 \times {}^4C_4 \times {}^{10}P_3$

$= \frac{9!}{2!7!} \times \frac{7!}{3!4!} \times 1 \times \frac{10!}{7!} = \frac{9 \times 8 \times 10!}{2 \times 6 \times 24} = \frac{10!}{4}$

70. (a)

8 Teachers	8 Boys	4 Girls	Number of ways of forming group
4	3	3	${}^8C_4 \times {}^8C_3 \times {}^4C_3$
4	4	2	${}^8C_4 \times {}^8C_4 \times {}^4C_2$
4	2	4	${}^8C_4 \times {}^8C_2 \times {}^4C_4$
5	3	2	${}^8C_5 \times {}^8C_3 \times {}^4C_2$
5	2	3	${}^8C_5 \times {}^8C_2 \times {}^4C_3$
6	2	2	${}^8C_6 \times {}^8C_2 \times {}^4C_2$

∴ Total number of ways = 15680 + 29400 + 1960 + 18816 + 6272 + 4704 = 76832

71. (b) Let T_1 denotes the days when two train departs *a* day for three days. T_2 denotes the days when one train departs *a* day for two days and T_3 denotes the days when three trains depart *a* day for two days.

∴ Required number of ways of compiling time tables = Number of permutations of $T_1T_1T_1T_2T_2T_3T_3$

$= \frac{7!}{3!2!2!} = 7 \times 5 \times 3 \times 2 = 210$ ways

72. (a) Any number between 1 to 999 is of the form abc when $0 \le a, b, c, \le 9$. Let us first count the numbers in which 3 occurs exactly once. Since 3 can occur at one place in, $1 \times {}^3C_1 \times 9 \times 9 = 234$ ways. Next 3 can occur in exactly two places in, ${}^3C_2 \times 9 = 27$

Lastly, 3 can occur in all three digits in only one way. Hence the number of times 3 occur is = 1 × 243 + 27 × 2 + 1 × 3 = 243 + 54 + 3 = 300

Alter: Since 3 do not occurs in 1000

∴ We have to count number from 1 to 999.

Any number between 1 and 999 is form xyz; $0 \le x, y, z \le 9$

Case I: 3 occur exactly once.

∴ 3 can occur at any place out of 3 in ${}^3C_1$ ways remaining place can be filled in 9 × 9 ways.

∴ Numbers = 3 × 9 × 9 = 243.

Case II: 3 occurs twice: ${}^3C_2 \times 9 = 27$

27 number are that 3 occurs twice

3 occurs twice (2 × 27) times = 54 times.

Case III: 3 occurs thrice: Only 1 numbers

3 occurs 3 times is = 1 × 234 + 27 × 2 + 1 × 3 + 243 + 54 + 3 = 300.

73. (c) $x + y + 3z = 33$; $x, y, z \ge 0 \Rightarrow x + y = 33 - 3z$

$\Rightarrow$ Number of solutions $= \sum_{t=0}^{11} {}^{33-3t+1}C_1$

$= {}^{34}C_1 + {}^{31}C_1 + {}^{28}C_1 + {}^{25}C_1 + \ldots + {}^1C_1$

$= 1 + 4 + 7 + \ldots + 31 + 34 = \frac{12}{2}[1 + 34] = 210$

74. (b) Required number of ways = Coefficient of x^{50} in $(1 + x + x^2 + \ldots + x^{25})^2 (1 + x + x^2 + \ldots + x^{100})$

$= \text{Coefficient of } x^{50} \text{ in } \left(\frac{1-x^{26}}{1-x}\right)^2 (1 + x + x^2 + \ldots + x^{50})$

$= \text{Coefficient of } x^{50} \text{ in } (1 - x^{26})^2 (1 - x)^{-2} (1 - x^{51}) (1 - x)^{-1}$

$= \text{Coefficient of } x^{50} \text{ in } (1 - x^{26})^2 (1 - x^{51}) (1 - x)^{-3}$

$= \text{Coefficient of } x^{50} \text{ in } (1 - 2x^{26}) (1) (1 - x)^{-3}$

$= \text{Coefficient } x^{50} \text{ in } (1 - 2x^{26}) ({}^{3+50-1}C_{50}x^{50} + {}^{3+24-1}C_{24}x^{24})$

$= {}^{52}C_{50} - 2({}^{26}C_{24}) = {}^{52}C_2 - 2({}^{26}C_2) = 676$

75. (b) Required ways = ${}^8C_5$ – Number of ways when any one of three rows remains empty

$= \frac{8 \times 7 \times 6}{3 \times 2 \times 1} - \left[\underbrace{{}^6C_5}_{\text{Row 1 empty}} + \underbrace{{}^6C_5}_{\text{Row 2 empty}}\right] = 56 - 2 \times 6 = 44$

76. (c) If we want to fill AAABBB, so that none of R_1, R_2, R_3, R_4, R_5 remains empty, then we are to use R_2 and R_4 and from R_1, R_3 and R_5 use any two boxes of one of the three rows and one box of reaming two rows.

∴ Number of ways of selection =

$\underset{R_2}{1} \times \underset{R_4}{1} \times \left(\underbrace{3({}^3C_2)}_{R_1 \text{ or } R_3 \text{ or } R_5 \text{ uses 2 boxes}} \times \underbrace{{}^3C_1}_{\text{Single box}} \times \underbrace{{}^3C_1}_{\text{Single box}}\right)$

$= 3 \times (3) \times 3 \times 3 = 81$

∴ Required ways of permutations of AAABBB in these 81 ways of selection

$= \frac{81 \times 3!}{3! \times 3!} = \frac{81 \times 720}{6 \times 6} = 1620$

77. (b) Required ways = ${}^8C_5$ – (Number of ways when R_2 or R_3 are unused)

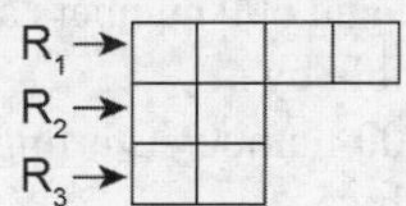

$= {}^8C_5 - ({}^6C_5 + {}^6C_5) = {}^8C_5 - (12) = 56 - 12 = 44$

78. (c) Number of diagonals of n sided polygon are given by = ${}^nC_2 - n = 104$ (given)

$\Rightarrow \frac{n(n-1)}{2} - n = 104 \quad \Rightarrow \frac{n}{2}[n - 1 - 2] = 104$

$\Rightarrow n(n - 3) = 208 \quad \Rightarrow n^2 - 3n - 208 = 0$

$\Rightarrow n = 16$

79. (a) Case 1: If there is only one line: Number of sub parts = 2

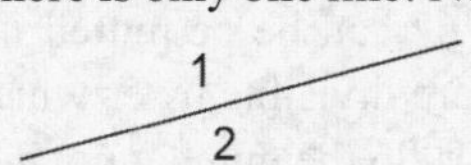

Case 2: If two lines are there: Number of sub parts = 2 + 2 = 4

Case 3: If three lines are there: Number of sub parts = 2 + 2 + 3 = 7

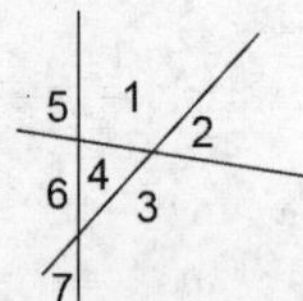

Case 4: If four line are there: Number of sub parts = 2 + 2 + 3 + 4 = 11

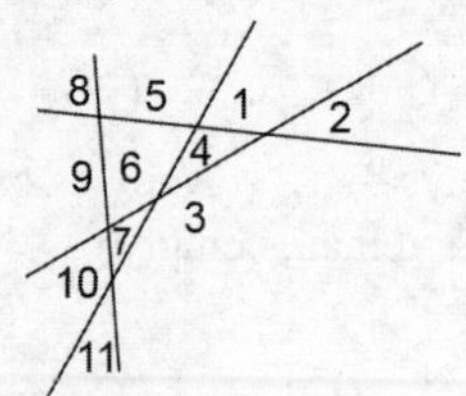

Case 5: If five line are there: Number of sub parts = 2 + 2 + 3 + 4 + 5 = 16

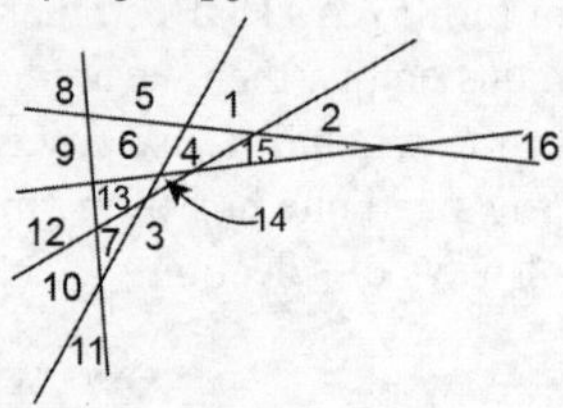

And in generally, if there are n-lines, Number of sub parts = $1 + 1 + 2 + 3 + 4 + \ldots + n$

$= 1+\frac{n(n+1)}{2} = \frac{n^2+n+2}{2}$

80. (a) The number of numbers starting with 1 and not divisible by 5 = (6! – 5!) = 600

$\left(\because 1, \underbrace{2,3,4,5,6,7}_{6!}; 1, \underbrace{2,3,4,6,7}_{5!},5\right)$

Similarly 600 numbers are there starting with 2 and not divisible by 5 and 600 numbers are there starting with 2 and not divisible by 5.

∴ There are 1800 numbers starting with 1, or 2 or 3 and not divisible by 5

Next, fix 41 in first two places 41, $\underbrace{2,3,5,6,7}_{5!\text{ ways}}$; 41 $\underbrace{2,3,6,7}_{4!\text{ ways}}$

∴ Number of numbers not divisible by 5 = (5! – 4!) = 96

Similarly number of numbers starting with 42 and not divisible by 5 = 96

∴ Total 1800 + 96 + 96 = 1992 numbers are there upto the numbers starting with 42 and not divisible by 5.

∴ Number will be 1992 number will be 42, 76, 531

∴ Number will be 1993 number will be 43, 12, 567

Number 5, 67 can be permuted in 3! = 6 ways out of which two are divisible by 5, which are 675 and 765.

∴ 1992 + 4 = 1996 the number not divisible by 5 is 43, 12, 756

Clearly 1997 in number will be starting with 4315, and ends the smallest permutation of 2, 7 and 6

Now 276 can be permuted in 6 ways (1996 + 6); 2002 number will be 43,15, $\underbrace{762}_{\text{greatest permutation}}$

⇒ 2001 number will be 43, 15, 726

81. (b) 6 left gloves can be distributed to 6 persons in 6! ways. Now distribute 6 right gloves so that at least 3 persons get *a* complete pair.

Number of ways corresponding to each of 6! distribution of left gloves, when right gloves distributed

So that exactly 3 or 4 or all for *a* complete pair.

$= {}^6C_3\left[3!\left(1-\frac{1}{1!}+\frac{1}{2!}+\frac{1}{3!}\right)\right]+{}^6C_4\left[2!\left(1-\frac{1}{1!}+\frac{1}{2!}\right)\right]+1=$

20 [2] + 15 (1) + 1 = 56

∴ Total number of ways when atleast three persons get *a* complete pair = 6! × 56 = 6! × 7 × 8 = 8!

82. (a) c.d. = 2; (1, 3, 5); (2, 4, 6); (3, 5, 7); …. (21, 23, 25)

∴ Total groups = 21

c.d. = 4; (1, 5, 9); (2, 6, 10); ….. ;(17, 21, 25)

∴ Total groups = 17

c.d. = 6; (1, 7, 13); (2, 8, 14); …., (13, 19, 25)

∴ Total group = 13

c.d. = 12; (1, 13, 25)

∴ Total group = 1

∴ Total number of groups of three numbers in A.P. with even common difference

$= 1 + 5 + 9 + \ldots.. + 21 = \frac{6}{2}(1+21) = 66$

83. (c) Unit place has 3 choices i.e., 0, 2 or 4. Each of these digits occur in 5 × 6 × 6 = 180 times.

∴ Sum contributed by unit place digits = 180 (0 + 2 + 4) = 1080

Now thousand place digit has 5 choices i.e., 1, 2, 3, 4 or 5 Each of there digits occur in 6 × 6 × 3 = 108 times

∴ Sum contributed by thousand place digit = 10^3 × 108 (1 + 2 + 3 + 4 + 5) = 1620 × 10^3

Similarly contribution to sum by hundred and ten's place digits each of 0, 1, 2, 3, 4, 5, occurring

5 × 6 × 3 = 90 times = 10^2 × 90(0 + 1 + 2 + 3 + 4 + 5) = 1350 × 10^2

And 10 × 90 (0 + 1 + 2 + 3 + 4 + 5) = 1350 × 10

∴ Sum of al even numbers = 1620 × 10^3 + 1350 (10^2 + 10) + 1080 = 1769580

84. (a) There are 7 types of notes of denominations 5 Rs, 10Rs, 20Rs, 50Rs, 100Rs, 500Rs and 100Rs.

Now in a set order containing 10 Currency notes can be displayed in $\underbrace{7\times7\times7\times\ldots..\times7}_{(10\ times)} = (7)^{10}$ ways

(∵ Currency notes may be repeated)

After selecting one note of each denomination, we are to select 3 more notes

Following cases are possible:

Case (i): All 3 are of same denomination i.e., 7 ways.

Number of ways of forming set order = $\frac{10!}{4!}\times 7$

Case (ii): 2 of same denomination and 1 of different i.e., ${}^7C_2\times 2$

Number of ways of forming set order = $\frac{10!}{3!2!}\times {}^7C_2\times 2$

Case (iii): All 3 are of different denominations i.e., ${}^7C_3$ ways

Number of ways of forming set order = $\frac{10!}{2!2!2!} \times {}^7C_3$

∴ Total number of ways

$= \frac{10!}{4!} \times 7 + {}^7C_2 \times 2 \times \frac{10!}{3!2!} + \frac{10!}{2!2!} \times {}^7C_3$

$= 10!(7)\left[\frac{1}{4!} + \frac{6}{2!} \times 2 \times \frac{1}{3!2!} + \frac{6\times5}{2!2!2!3!}\right]$

$= 10!(7)\left[\frac{1}{4!} + \frac{2}{4} + \frac{5}{8}\right] = 10!(7)\left[\frac{1+12+15}{24}\right]$

$= 10!(7)\left(\frac{28}{24}\right) = 10!\left(\frac{49}{6}\right)$

85. **(a)** Following cases are possible

Case (i): All some digits 9 numbers of this type (11111, 22222, …., 99999)

Case (ii): Exactly 2 different digits number of ways of selecting 2 different digits ${}^{10}C_2 = 45$.

Sub case (a): When one of two different digits is 0 and other is non-zero e,g., 50000, 50500; 55500 etc

Corresponding to each of such 9 selections, first place has exactly one choice i.e., non-zero digit each of next 4 places has two choices 0 and non-zero digits.

∴ Number of such numbers formed = $9(1 \times 2 \times 2 \times 2 \times 2 - 1)$ = 135 (one way is subtracted when each digit is same)

Sub case (b): When both different digits are non-zeros. e.g., 57757

Number of ways of selection = ${}^9C_2 = 36$

Now each of such 36 elections, each place has 2 choices

∴ Number of such numbers formed = $36(2 \times 2 \times 2 \times 2 \times 2 - 2) = 1080$

Two ways are subtracted when all digits are same in two ways)

= 9 + 135 + 1080 = 1224

86. **(c)** Let the fixed seats of master and mistress be as shown below:

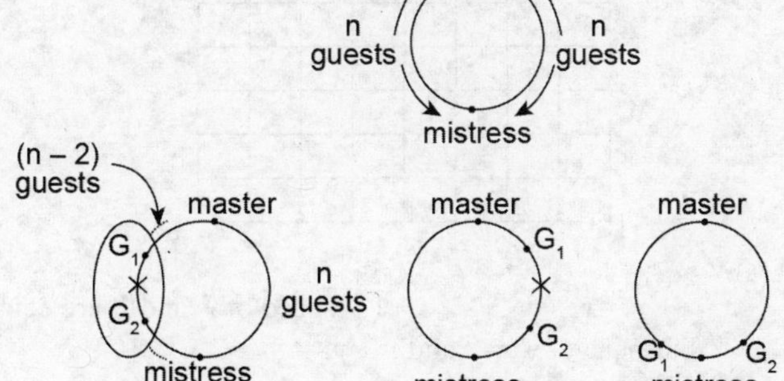

Case (i): When G_1G_2 are on left half or right half of circular table.

Number of ways of selection and arrange

$= 2\left[{}^{2n-2}C_n . n!\{n! - (n-1)! \times 2\}\right]$

$= 2\left[\frac{(2n-2)!}{n!(n-2)!} . n!\{(n-1)!(n-2)!\}\right]$

$= 2[(2n-2)!\ ((n-1)(n-2))] = (2n-2)!\ (2n^2 - 6n + 4)$

Case (ii): When G_1 and G_2 are on left and right side misters.

Number of ways of selection and argument = $2[{}^{2n-2}C_{n-1}$. n! . n!] = $2\left(\frac{(2n-2)!}{(n-1)!(n-1)!} \times n! \times n!\right) = 2(2n-2)!\ .\ n^2$

∴ Total number of ways of argument = $(2n-2)!\ [2n^2 - 6n + 4 + 2n^2] = (2n-2)!\ [4n^2 - 6n + 4]$

87. **(a)** **Case (i):** When difference is 1, pair of numbers can be (1, 2); (2, 3), …., (99, 100) i.e., 99

Case (ii): When difference is 2, pair of numbers can be (1, 3); (2, 4), …., (98, 100) i.e., 98

Case (iii): When difference is 3, pair of numbers can be (1, 4); (2, 5), …., (97, 100) i.e., 97 and so on

Finally when difference 10, pair of numbers can be (1, 11); (2, 12); (3, 13), ….. ,(90, 100) i.e., 90

∴ All possible pairs with difference atmost 10 = 90 + 91 + 92 + …. + 99

$= \frac{(99)(100)}{2} - \frac{(89)(90)}{2} = 945$

SECTION–IV

1. **(a), (b)** Given n distincts objects $a_1, a_2, ….. a_n$ (each in abundance)

Number of ways of choosing r ($r > n$) taking each of these at least once

= Number of ways of distributing $(r - n)$ identical objects to n types

$= \underbrace{0000...0}_{r-n \text{ balls}}\ \underbrace{1111....}_{n-1 \text{ seperate}} = \frac{(r-n+n-1)!}{(r-n)!(n-1)!} = {}^{r-1}C_{r-n}$ or ${}^{r-1}C_{n-1}$

2. **(b), (c)** $P = n(n^2 - 1^2)\ (n^2 - 2^2)\ (n^2 - 3^2)…..\ (n^2 - r^2)$; n > r

⇒ $P = n(n+1)\ (n-1)\ (n+2)\ (n-2)\ (n+3)\ (n-3)\ ….\ (n+r)\ (n-r)$

⇒ $P = (n-r)\ (n-(r-1)\ ….\ (n-3)\ (n-2)\ (n-1) \times n(n+1)\ (n+2)\ (n+3)\ …..\ (n+r)$

⇒ P is the product of $(2r+1)!$, consecutive integer

⇒ P is divisible by $(2r+1)!$, also $(2r+1)! = (2r+1)\ (2r)\ (2r-1)!$

⇒ P is also divisible by $(2r-1)!$

3. **(a), (d)** $x + y + z + w = 19$

Number of positive integer solution = number of whole number solution of the equation $x_1 + y_1 + z_1 + w_1 = 15$

= Number of ways of distributing 15 identical objects to 4 persons

= Number of arrays of $\underbrace{00000.0}_{15 \text{ identical balls}}\ \underbrace{111}_{3 \text{ seperate}} = {}^{18}C_3$

= Coefficient of x^{19} in $(x + x^2 + x^3 + … + x^{19})^4$

4. **(b), (c), (d)** Total number of ways = $\frac{(200)!}{(100)!(2!)^{100}}$, we divided by (100)! since the groups are unnamed. ⇒ (c)

$= \frac{100!.(101)(102)(103)....(200)}{(100)!(2!)^{100}}$

$= \left(\frac{101}{2}\right)\left(\frac{102}{2}\right)\left(\frac{103}{2}\right)...\left(\frac{200}{2}\right) \Rightarrow$ (b)

Also $\dfrac{(200)!}{(100)!(2)^{100}} = \dfrac{(1.3.5...199)(2.4.6...198.200)}{(100)!(2)^{100}}$

$= \dfrac{(1.3.5...199)(2)^{100}(1.2.3...99.100)}{(100)!(2)^{100}} = (1.\ 3.\ 5.\ \ldots\ 199)$

$\Rightarrow$ (d)

5. (a), (b), (c), (d)

Let number of a's be k and number of b's be $2n - k$

$\Rightarrow$ Number of arrangements $= \dfrac{2n!}{k!(2n-k)!}$ to be maximum; $k = 2n - k$

$\Rightarrow k = n = \dfrac{2n(2n-1)(2n-2)....4.3.2.1}{n!.n!} = {}^{2n}C_n$

$\Rightarrow$ (a) $= \dfrac{1.3.5.7...(2n-1).2^n(1.2.3....n)}{n!}$

$= \dfrac{2.6.10.14.......(4n-2)}{n!} \Rightarrow$ (b)

Also $\dfrac{2n(2n-1)(2n-2).....(n+3)(n+2)(n+1)}{n!} \Rightarrow$ (c)

Also ${}^{2n}C_n = \dfrac{2^n n![1.3...(2n-1)]}{(n!)^2} = \dfrac{2^n[1.3...(2n-1)]}{n!} \Rightarrow$ (d)

6. (a), (b), (c)

Total number of ways = Number of ways when R and W together = 8! – 7! 2! $\Rightarrow$ (a)

= 7! (8 – 2) = 6 (7!) $\Rightarrow$ (b)

Now, Arrange 6 balls excluding R in 6! ways and in 7 gaps 2 balls R and W can be arranged in ${}^7p_2$ ways.

$\Rightarrow$ Total number of ways = ${}^7p_2 \times 6!$ ways = 2.6! .${}^7C_2$

$\Rightarrow$ (c)

7. (a), (b), (c), (d)

Let the friends be $F_1, F_2, F_3, F_4, \ldots\ldots, F_8, F_9, F_{10}, F_{11}$

Thus required ways = Total number of ways – Number of ways when two particular friends F_1 and F_2 (say) are invited

$= {}^{11}C_5 - n(F_1 F_2 \ldots..) = {}^{11}C_5 - {}^9C_3$ ways

$\Rightarrow$ (a)

Also, $n(F_1\overline{F_2}...)\times{}^9C_4 + n(F_2\overline{F_1}...)\times{}^9C_4 + n(\overline{F_1}\,\overline{F_2}...)\times{}^9C_5$

$\Rightarrow {}^9C_5 + 2\,({}^9C_4) = {}^9C_4 + 2({}^9C_4) = 3\,({}^9C_4)$ ways $= 3\times(126) =$ 378 ways

8. (a), (b), (c)

Let x, y, z, u be the number of vertices left between any two chosen vertices

$\Rightarrow x, y, z, u \geq 1$ and $x + y + z + u = 16$ (i)

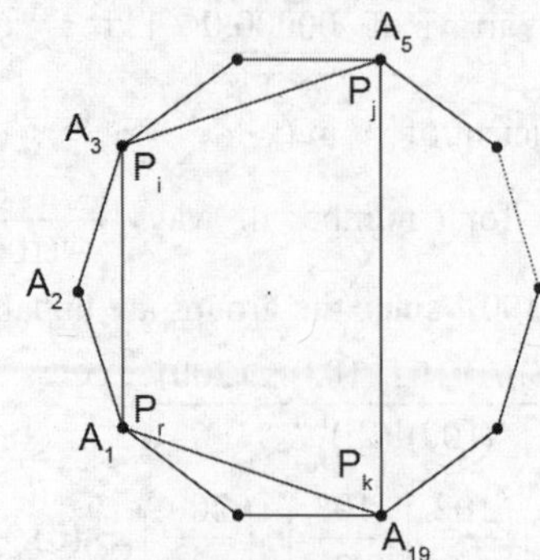

Equivalently, $x + y + z + u = 12$; $x, y, z, u \geq 0$

Required ways $= \dfrac{20\times{}^{15}C_3}{4} = \dfrac{5\times15\times14\times13}{3\times2} = 2275$

Also on choosing one of the vertices (say A)

9. (a), (d) Case (i): When two points from non-collinear points and two points from collinear points are taken to form *a* quadrilateral.

Number of possible quadrilaterals = ${}^7C_2\times{}^5C_2$.

Case (ii): When three points from non-collinear points and one point from collinear points are taken to form *a* quadrilateral.

Number of possible quadrilaterals = ${}^7C_3 \times {}^5C_1$.

Case (iii): All the four points are taken from non-collinear points to form *a* quadrilateral

Number of possible quadrilaterals = ${}^7C_4$

$\therefore$ Total possible quadrilaterals = ${}^7C_2 \times {}^5C_2 + {}^7C_3 \times {}^5C_1 + {}^7C_4 = 21 \times 10 + 35 \times 5 + 35 = 420 = 7 \times 6 \times 5 \times 2 = 2\left(\dfrac{7!}{4!}\right) = 2.{}^7P_3$

10. (c), (d) Number of non-negative integer solutions of $x + y + z + w = 10 = {}^{13}C_3 = {}^{13}C_{10}$

Number of ways of distributing 10 identical objects in four different boxes.

$\Rightarrow$ (a) is correct option

Also it is the same as number of selections of 10 objects from *a* lot containing 4 varieties of objects

$\Rightarrow$ (b) is correct option

Clearly (c) and (d) are incorrect.

11. (a), (b), (c), (d) Let x the number of horizontal steps taken by I_1 and x' that by I_2 and let y be the number of vertical steps taken by I_1 and y' by I_2.

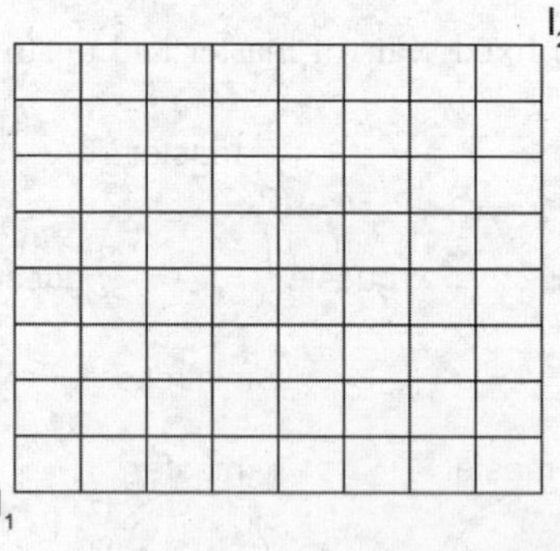

$\therefore\ x + y = x' + y'$ ($\because$ speed of I_1 and I_2 are equal)

Further $x + x' = 8$ and $y + y' = 8$

$\Rightarrow x' = 8 - x;\ y' = 8 - y$

$\therefore\ x + (y) = (8 - x) + (8 - y)$

$\Rightarrow 2(x + y) = 16 \qquad \Rightarrow x + y = 8$

$\Rightarrow y = 8 - x$

$\therefore$ To meet at any point

	Horizontal	Vertical
I_1	x	$8 - x$
I_2	$8 - x$	x

Number of ways in which I_1 can take x horizontal steps and $(8 - x)$ vertical steps

$= \frac{[x+(8-x)]!}{x!(8-x)!} = \frac{8!}{x!(8-x)!} = {}^8C_x$

Similarly I_2 can take $(8 - x)$ horizontal steps and x vertical in ${}^8C_x$ ways.

∴ The two can meet corresponding to *a* particular value of x in ${}^8C_x \times {}^8C_x = ({}^8C_x)^2$ ways

But $x \in \{0, 1, 2, 3, 4, 5, 6, 7, 8\}$

∴ Total number of ways in which two insects can meet during their joining

$= \sum_{x=0}^{8} ({}^8C_x)^2 = ({}^8C_0)^2 + ({}^8C_2)^2 + ... + ({}^8C_8)^2$

$= {}^8C_0 . {}^8C_8 + {}^8C_1 . {}^8C_7 + {}^8C_2 . {}^8C_6 + ... + {}^8C_8 . {}^8C_0 = {}^{16}C_8$

⇒ (d) is correct option.

Further ${}^{16}C_8 = \frac{16\times15\times14\times13\times12\times11\times10\times9}{1\times2\times3\times4\times5\times6\times7\times8}$

⇒ (a) is correct.

$= \frac{(2)^4\times2\times(2)^2(15\times7\times13\times3\times11\times5\times9)}{1\times2\times3\times4\times5\times6\times7\times8}$

$= (2)^8\left(\frac{1}{1}\right)\left(\frac{3}{2}\right)\left(\frac{5}{3}\right)\left(\frac{7}{4}\right)\left(\frac{9}{5}\right)\left(\frac{11}{6}\right)\times\left(\frac{13}{7}\right)\times\left(\frac{15}{5}\right)$

⇒ (b) is correct.

$= \left(\frac{2}{1}\right)\left(\frac{6}{2}\right)\left(\frac{10}{3}\right)\left(\frac{14}{4}\right)\left(\frac{18}{5}\right)\left(\frac{22}{6}\right)\times\left(\frac{26}{7}\right)\times\left(\frac{30}{8}\right)$

⇒ (c) is correct.

12. (b), (c), (d) Let the occupied seat is represented by G and vacant by R, thus we are booking for permutation of $4G$ and $6R$ such that no two G are together.

$\underbrace{(1)R(2)R(3)R(4)R(5)R(6)R(7)}$

Clearly it is equal to number of ways of choosing 4 places out 7 vacant place $= {}^7C_4$

⇒ Number of ways of arranging 4 people in 7 is required ways $= {}^7C_4 \times 4! = {}^7C_3 \times 4! = 840$

13. (a), (b) Case 1: Let n = 2*m* + 1 (odd)

c.d. = 1; (1, 2, 3); (2, 3, 4) ….. $(n - 2, n - 1, n)$

c.d. = 2; (1, 3, 8); (2, 4, 6) ….. $(n - 4, n - 2, n)$

c.d. = 3; (1, 4, 7); (2, 5, 8) ….. $(n - 5, n - 3, n)$

c.d. = *m*; $(1, 1 + m, 2m + 1)$

∴ Number of 3 numbers in AP = 1 + 3 + 5 + …. + $(n - 2)$

$= \frac{m}{2}[1+(n-2)] = \frac{m}{2}(n-1) = \left(\frac{n-1}{4}\right)(n-1) = \frac{(n-1)^2}{4}$

⇒ (a) is correct.

Case (ii): If n is even; n = 2*m*

c.d. = 1; (1, 2, 3); (2, 3, 4) ….. $(2m - 2, 2m - 1, 2m)$

c.d. = 2; (1, 3, 5); (2, 4, 6) ….. $(2m - 4, m - 2, 2m)$

c.d. = 3; (1, 4, 7); (2, 5, 8) ….. $(2m - 6, 2m - 3, 2m)$

c.d. = 4; (1, 5, 9); (2, 6, 10) ….. $(2m - 8, 2m - 4, 2m)$

c.d. = $(m - 2)$; $(1, m - 1, 2m - 3)$; $(2, m, 2m - 2)$ ….. $(3, m + 1, 2m - 1)$; $(4, m + 2, 2m)$

c.d. = $(m - 1)$; (1, m, 2*m*–1); $(2, m + 1, 2m)$

c.d. = m; $(1, 1 + m, 2m + 1)$; (impossible)

∴ Number of 3 terms in AP = 2 + 4 + 6 + …. + $(2m - 2)$

$= \frac{(m-1)}{2}[2+2m-2)] = m(m-1)$

$= \frac{n}{2}\left(\frac{n}{2}-1\right) = \frac{n(n-2)}{4}$

⇒ (b) is correct option.

14. (a), (b) $a \le b < c$; $a, b, c \in \{1, 2, 3, n\}$

Case (i): $a < b < c$ select any 3 out of n; and arrange them in ascending order and naming *a, b, c*

Number of ways = ${}^nC_3$.

Case (ii): a = $b < c$ select any 2 out of n; and arrange in ascending order first are becomes *a* and *b* and the second one becomes *c*.

Number of ways = ${}^nC_2$.

∴ Total ways = ${}^nC_3 + {}^nC_2$

⇒ (a) is correct option.

$= {}^{n+1}C_3$ (by Pascal's rule)

⇒ (b) is correct option.

15. (a), (b), (c)

←—•——•——•——•——•——•—→
–2 –1 0 1 2 3

He will stop after 5 steps or after reaching 3 or –2

(a) Number of ways of reaching (–2) are

0 → (–1) → (–2)
(0) → (–1) → (0) → (–1) → (–2)
(0) → (1) → (0) → (–1) → (–2)
⇒ 3 ways ⇒ (a)

(b) Ways of reaching (3) are

(0) → (1) → (2) → (3)
(0) → (1) → (–1) → (–2) → (3)
(0) → (1) → (2) → (1) → (2) → (3)
(0) → (–1) → (0) → (1) → (2) → (3)
⇒ 4 ways ⇒ (b)

(c) Total ways in which he stops after five steps are

(0) → (1) → (0) → (1) → (0) → (1)
(0) → (1) → (2) → (1) → (0) → (1)
(0) → (1) → (2) → (1) → (2) → (1)
(0) → (1) → (2) → (1) → (2) → (3)
(0) → (–1) → (0) → (–1) → (0) → (–1)
(0) → (–1) → (0) → (1) → (2) → (3)
(0) → (–1) → (0) → (1) → (0) → (–1)
(0) → (1) → (0) → (–1) → (0) → (1)
(0) → (1) → (2) → (1) → (0) → (–1)
(0) → (1) → (0) → (–1) → (0) → (–1)
(0) → (–1) → (0) → (–1) → (0) → (1)
(0) → (1) → (0) → (1) → (2) → (3)

Which are = 12 ⇒ (c)

(d) Total ways of completing the experiment = 16

⇒ (d) (incorrect)

16. (a), (b) Number of times the teacher visits the zoological garden = ${}^{25}C_5$.

Number of time each child visits the zoo = ${}^{24}C_4$.

∴ Number of times the teacher visit the zoo exceed the number of times each child visit = ${}^{25}C_5 - {}^{24}C_4$.
∴ By Pascal's rule ${}^{24}C_4 + {}^{24}C_5 = {}^{25}C_5$
⇒ ${}^{25}C_5 - {}^{24}C_4 = {}^{24}C_5$
⇒ (a) and (b) are correct option.

SECTION–V: (ASSERTION REASONS)

1. (b) Maximum number of points of intersection of 8 circles $= 2.{}^8C_2 = 56$ ⇒ Assertion is correct.
Further 4 circles and 4 straight lines can intersect at maximum $= 2.{}^4C_2 + {}^4C_2 + (4 \times 2) \times 4 = 12 + 6 + 32 = 50$
⇒ Reason is also correct, but being no link between assertion and reason.

2. (a) $\frac{n!}{(n-3)!} = n(n-1)(n-2)$ = Product of 3 consecutive integers must be divisible by 3!.
⇒ Assertion is correct. Also reason is correct explanation of assertion.

3. (a) Clearly reason is true
∵ $L_1, L_3, L_5 \rightarrow E_1, E_3, E_5$
So that number letter goes to correct envelope.
Corresponding number of ways $= 3!\left(1 - \frac{1}{1!} + \frac{1}{2!} - \frac{1}{3!}\right) = 2$
Similarly $L_2, L_4, L_6 \rightarrow E_2, E4_5, E_6$
So that no letter goes to correct envelope.
Corresponding number of ways = 2
∴ Total ways = 2 × 2 = 4
⇒ Assertion is true and reason correctly explanation of the assertion.

4. (d) Clearly the reason is correct
To find exponent of 50 in 100!
Exponent of 2 in 100 =

$$\left[\frac{100}{2}\right] + \left[\frac{100}{2^2}\right] + \left[\frac{100}{2^3}\right] + \left[\frac{100}{2^4}\right] + \left[\frac{100}{2^5}\right] + \left[\frac{100}{2^6}\right] = 50 +$$

25 + 12 + 6 + 3 + 1 = 97
Exponent of 5 in 100! $= \left[\frac{100}{5}\right] + \left[\frac{100}{5^2}\right] = 20 + 4 = 24$
∴ $100! = (2)^{97} (5)^{24} (3)^k (7)^l \ldots..$
$= (2)^{97} (25)^{12} (3)^k (7)^l \ldots.$
$= (2 \times 25)^{12} (2)^{85} (3)^k (7)^l \ldots..$
$= (50)^{12} (2)^{85} (3)^k (7)^l \ldots\ldots$
⇒ Exponent of 50 in 100! = 12
⇒ $k = 12$ ⇒ Assertion is incorrect

5. (d) Clearly reason is correct
Sum of all given digits = 0 + 1 + 2 + 3 + 4 + 5 = 15
To get *a* group of 5 digits having their sum divisible by 3, we are to exclude *a* digit divisible by 3
i.e., 0 or 3
∴ Number of five digit numbers divisible by 3 = 5! + (5! – 4!) = 216, but then are the number without repetition. Obviously, it repetition is allowed, then three will be more such numbers including there 216 numbers
∴ Assertion is incorrect.

6. (a) Clearly the reason is correct standard result for number of de-arrangements.
It f: $\{a, b, c, d, e\} \rightarrow \{a, b, c, d, e\}$ is onto and $f(x) \neq x$
⇒ All the elements of sets $\{a, b, c, d, e\}$ are to be mapped to elements of itself and no element is image of itself.
⇒ Number of ways $= 5!\left(1 - \frac{1}{1!} + \frac{1}{2!} - \frac{1}{3!} + \frac{1}{4!} - \frac{1}{5!}\right) = 44$
⇒ Assertion is correct

7. (a) It can be verified that 1! + 2! + 3! + …. + 9! = 409113
Also for $n!$; $n \geq 20$
$n! = 5 \times 10 \times 20k$; where $k = (4! \times 6 \times 7 \times 5 \times 9 \times 11 \times 12 \times \ldots.. \times 19) \times m$; $m \in \mathbb{Z}$
⇒ $n!$ is divisible by 1000
⇒ Reason is correct option.
Now, 1! + 2! + 3! + …. + 4! + 20! + 21! + … + 49!
$= 409113 + \left(\overline{a_1a_2a_3 \ldots a_k000} + \overline{b_1b_2b_3 \ldots b_l000} + \ldots + \overline{n_1n_2n_3 \ldots n_p000}\right)$
$= \overline{t_1t_2t_3 \ldots t_l113}$; having its one place digit, ten's place digit 1 and hundred's place digit 1.
⇒ Assertion is true and correctly explained by reason.

8. (a) Total permutation = 9!, when 4 maths lecture are together $M_1\ M_2\ M_3\ M_4\ B_1\ B_2\ B_3\ B_4\ B_5$
∴ No of permutation = 4! × 6!
∴ Required permutation = 9! – 6! × 4! = 6!. [9.8.7 – 24] = 6! × 24[21 – 1] = 6! × 24 × 20 = 6.5!. 24. 20 = 5! × 5! × 4 = 4 (5!)^2
⇒ Both assertion and reason are correct and also reason is the correct explanation of assertion.

9. (d) Clearly reason is correct as it is the standard result of obtaining sum of positive integer divisors.
Now, $720 = (2)^4 \times (3)^2 \times (5)^1$
⇒ Sum of positive odd divisors of 720 = $(1 + 3 + 3^2)$ (1 + 5) = 78
Now, perfect square odd divisors of 720 are 1 and 9 only
∴ Sum of positive odd divisors of 720, which are not perfect square = 78 – (1 + 9) = 68
⇒ Assertion is incorrect

10. (d) Reason is standard result and hence correct.
Since by using all digits 1, 2, 3, 4, 0, every number starts with *a* non-zero digit
∴ Sum of all such number will be $= (1 + 2 + 3 + 4)\ 4!\ (10^4) + (1 + 2 + 3 + 4)\ (4! - 3!)\ (10^3 + 10^2 + 10 + 1)$
$= 240\ (10^4) + 180(10^3 + 10^2 + 10 + 1)$
$= 240 \times 10^4 + 180(1111)$
$= 240 \times 10^4 + 240\ (1111) - 60(1111)$
$= 240 \times (11111) - 60(1111)$
⇒ Assertion is incorrect

11. (c) Out of 4 collinear and 4 non-collinear points *a* quadrilateral can be formed if we take

(i) Two non-collinear points and 2 collinear points.
Number of such quadrilaterals formed = ${}^4C_2 \times {}^4C_2$ = 36

(ii) 3 non-collinear points and 1 collinear point.
Number of such quadrilateral formed = ${}^4C_3 \times {}^4C_1$ = 16

(iii) 4 points from non-collinear points,
Number of quadrilaterals formed = ${}^4C_4 = 1$

$\therefore$ Total number of quadrilateral formed = 36 + 16 + 1 = 53

$\therefore$ Obviously reason is incorrect.

SECTION–VI: (PASSAGE)

Passage A:

1. (d) $x_1 + x_2 + x_3 + x_4 + x_5 = 25; x_i \geq 1$
$\Rightarrow a + b + c + d + e = 20$
$\therefore$ Required number of ways = ${}^{20+5-1}C_{5-1} = {}^{24}C_4$

2. (a) Let $x_i = 2A_i + 1$
$\therefore$ Required ways = Number of integral solutions of $A_1 + A_2 + A_3 + A_4 + A_5 = 10$
$\therefore$ Required ways = ${}^{10+5-1}C_4 = {}^{14}C_4$

3. (c) Required number of ways = coefficient of x^{25} in $(x + x^2 + x^3 + ... + x^{11})^5$
= coefficient of x^{20} in $(1 + x + ...+ x^{10})^5$
= coefficient of x^{20} in $(1 - x^{11})^5 (1 - x)^{-5}$
= coefficient of x^{20} in $(1 - {}^5C_1 x^{11} ....)(1 - x)^{-5}$
= coefficient of x^{20} in $(1 - x)^{-5} - 5 \times$ coefficient of x^9 in $(1 - x)^{-5}$
$= {}^{5+20-1}C_{20} - 5 \times {}^{5+9-1}C_9 = {}^{24}C_{20} - 5 \times {}^{13}C_9 = {}^{24}C_4 - 5 \times {}^{13}C_4$

Passage B:

4. (b) Number of ways of selection = ${}^4C_2$

5. (d) $B_1\, B_2\, B_3\, B_4\, B_5\, B_6\, B_7\, B_8$
Total ways = 3^8
Number of ways when 1 boy receive no ball = 3×2^8 (ways for selection of 1 boy)
Number of ways when 2 boys receive no ball = ${}^3C_2\,(1)^8$
$\therefore$ Required number of ways = $3^8 - 3.2^8 + {}^3C_2 \,.\, (1)^8$
Aliter: Number of ways of distributing 'n' different things into 'r' different group when no box should remains empty is $r^n - {}^rC_1\,(r-1)^n + {}^rC_2\,(r-2)^n + ... + (-1)^{r-1}\,.{}^rC_{r-1}$
Here $n = 8$ and $r = 3$
$\therefore$ Required number of ways = $3^8 - {}^3C_1 .\, 2^8 + {}^3C_2 .1^8$

6. (a) Since each letters can be posted in 3 ways
$\therefore$ Required number of ways = 3^5

Passage C:

7. (a) 8 Batsman, 6 Bowlers, 4 All rounder, 2 Wicket keepers
Required number of ways:
(a) No All rounder, No Wicket keepers
(b) No All rounder, 1 Wicket keeper
(c) 1 All rounder, No Wicket keeper
(d) 1 All rounder, 1 wicket keeper
$\therefore$ ${}^{14}C_{11} + {}^2C_1 \times {}^{14}C_{10} + {}^4C_1 \times {}^{14}C_{10} + {}^4C_1 . {}^2C_1 . {}^{14}C_9$

8. (a) **Case I:** When particular Bowler players:
Number of ways of selection = selection of 10 persons from 6 batsman, 5 bowlers, 4 all rounder, 2 wicket keepers. = ${}^{17}C_{10}$
Case II: When that particular bowler does not play!
Numbers of ways = ${}^{19}C_{11}$
$\therefore$ Total number of ways = ${}^{17}C_{10} + {}^{19}C_{11}$

9. (b) **Case I:** Batsman plays: Number of ways = ${}^{18}C_{10}$
Case II: Batsman does not play: Number of ways = ${}^{19}C_{11}$
$\therefore$ Total number of ways ${}^{18}C_{10} + {}^{19}C_{11}$

Passage D:

10. (b) MM, AA, TT, HE, C, S, I

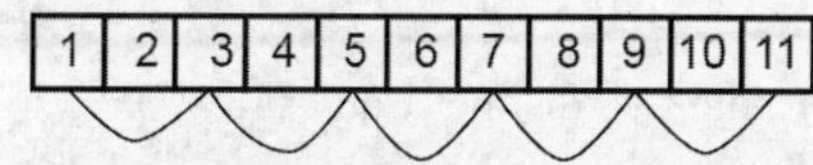

Required number of ways = Total Number of ways – Number of ways when no repeating letter is at odd place = $\frac{11!}{\lfloor 2 \lfloor 2 \lfloor 2}$

[Repeating letters are 6,
Number of even places 5
$\therefore$ Atleast one letter occupies odd place
$\therefore$ Numbers of ways = 0]

11. (a) Both M's and both A' S are together
$\boxed{MM}, \boxed{AA}$, TT, HE, C, S, I
$\therefore$ Number of ways = $\frac{9!}{2!}$
$\Rightarrow$ Number of ways when both M' S, A's and T' S are together
$\boxed{MM}, \boxed{AA}, \boxed{TT}$, HE, C, S, I = 8!
$\therefore$ Required number of ways = $\frac{9!}{2!} - 8! = {}^8C_2 .7!$

12. (a) Firstly arrange consonants and then vowels at empty space (CROSS MARK METHOD)
$\times M \times M \times T \times T \times H \times C \times S \times$
$\therefore$ Required number of ways
$= \frac{7!}{2!2!} \times \underbrace{{}^8C_4}_{\text{Selection of 4 spaces}} \cdot \underbrace{\frac{4!}{2!}}_{\text{Arrangement of 4 vowels(AAEI)}}$

13. (b) Number of ways = ${}^8C_3 \times {}^4C_2 = 56 \times 6 = 336$

14. (a) Number of ways = (2 non-official and 3-official) + (3 non-official × 2 official) + (4 non-official × 1 official)
$= ({}^4C_2 \times {}^8C_3) + ({}^4C_3 \times {}^8C_2) + ({}^4C_4 \times {}^8C_1) = (336) + (112) + (8) = 456$
Aliter: Number of ways = Total ways – [Number of ways when 1 non-official is selected + when no non-official is selected] $= {}^{12}C_5 - [({}^8C_4 \times {}^4C_1) + {}^8C_5]$
$= \frac{12.11.10.9.8}{120} - \left[\frac{8.7.6.5.4}{24} + \frac{8.7.6.5.4}{120}\right] = 792 - [280 + 56] = 792 - 336 = 456$

15. (d) Required number of ways = ${}^{11}C_5$

$$= \frac{11.10.9.8.7}{120} = 11 \times 42 = 462$$

SECTION–VIII: (MATRIX MATCH TYPE)

1. (i)→(c); (ii)→(d); (iii)→(a); (iv)→(b)

(i) Case (i): Using single distinct digit x(say); $x \neq 0$

| x | x | x | x | x | x | ; 9 numbers formed

Case (ii): (a) Using two distinct digit x, y both non-zeros

| x | x | x | y | y | y | *or* | x | x | y | y | y | y |

$$= {}^9C_2 \times \left[\left(\frac{6!}{3!3!}\right)+2\left(\frac{6!}{2!4!}\right)\right] = 1800$$

(b) Using two distinct x and y: $x = 0, y \neq 0$

$$\text{Number of ways} = {}^9C_1\left[\frac{5!}{4!}+\frac{5!}{3!2!}+\frac{5!}{3!2!}\right] = 225$$

Case (iii) (a): Using three different digits, $x, x, y, y, z, z, x, y, z \neq 0$

$$\text{Number of ways} = {}^9C_3\left[\frac{6!}{2!2!2!}\right] = 7560$$

(b) $x = 0, y \neq 0, z \neq 0$

$$\text{Number of ways} = {}^9C_2\left[\frac{5!}{2!2!}+\frac{5!}{2!2!}\right] = 2160$$

∴ Total number of ways = 9 + 1800 + 225 + 7560 + 2160 = 11754

(ii) (3, 1, 1); (2, 2, 1)

$$\text{Now of ways} = {}^5C_3 + \frac{{}^5C_2 \times {}^3C_2}{2!} = 25$$

(iii) $\underbrace{(6)}_{\text{ways of selection of 5P's}} \; \underbrace{(7)}_{\text{ways of selection of 6Q's}} - \underbrace{1}_{\text{when non of pad Q are selected}} = 41$

∴

(iv) First letter can be used in 26 ways and second letter can also be used in 26 ways for different first two initials

∴ 26 × 26 = 676 students can have two different initials.

∴ There should be atleast (676 + 1) = 677 students in the school to guarantee.

2. (i)→(c); (ii)→(b); (iii)→(d); (iv)→(a)

(i) 20 = 1 × 2 × 2 × 5 × 1 = 1 × 4 × 5 × 1 × 1

∴ Required number of numbers

$$= \frac{5!}{2!\times 2!} + \frac{5!}{3!} = 30 + 20 = 50$$

(ii) Required number of ways = 5! – (Number of ways when exactly 1 play was put in its positio*n* + *N*umber of play was put in its position)

$$= 5! - \left[{}^5C_1.4!\left(1-\frac{1}{1!}+\frac{1}{2!}-\frac{1}{3!}+\frac{1}{4!}\right)+5!\left(1-\frac{1}{1!}+\frac{1}{2!}-\frac{1}{3!}+\frac{1}{4!}-\frac{1}{5!}\right)\right]$$

$$= 5! - [5(12-4+1)+60-20+5-1] = 120 - [45 + 44] = 31$$

(iii) Form 1 to 1000; for atleast two consecutive same integers the number must be either of two digits or 3 digits.

For two digits numbers, number of ways = 9

For three digit number,

Number of ways

$$= \underbrace{9}_{\text{ten's \& hundred place digit same}} \times \underbrace{9}_{\text{unit place digit (different)}} + \underbrace{9}_{\text{type(500)}} + \underbrace{8\times 9}_{\text{numbers of type 788}} + \underbrace{9}_{\text{numbers of type 777}} + \underbrace{1}_{(1000)} = 172$$

∴ Total numbers = 9 + 172 = 181

(iv) $\frac{1}{15}\sum\sum_{1\le i\le j\le 9} i.j$

$$= \frac{1}{15}\left[\frac{(1+2+3+\ldots+9)^2+(1^2+2^2+3^2+\ldots+9^2)}{2}\right]$$

$$= \frac{1}{15}\left[\frac{(45)^2+15\times19}{2}\right] = \frac{1}{15}\left[\frac{15(135+19)}{2}\right] = 77$$

3. (i)→(c); (ii)→(a); (iii)→(c); (iv)→(c)

(i) Required number of arrangement = Coefficients of x^4 in

$$4!\left(1+\frac{x}{1!}+\frac{x^2}{2!}\right)^2(1+x)^4$$

$$= 4!\left[{}^4C_4 + {}^4C_2 + \frac{1}{4} + 2.{}^4C_3 + ({}^4C_1) + ({}^4C_2)\right] = 606$$

(ii) Required number of ways = Coefficients of x^4 in

$$4!\left(1+x+\frac{x^2}{2!}\right)^3(1+x)^5$$

= Coefficient of x^4 in

$$4!\left[{}^3C_0\left(x+\frac{x^2}{2!}\right)^0 + {}^3C_1\left(x+\frac{x^2}{2}\right) + {}^3C_2\left(x+\frac{x^2}{2}\right)^2 + {}^3C_3\left(x+\frac{x^2}{2}\right)^3\right]$$

$$\times [{}^5C_0 + {}^5C_1x + {}^5C_2x + {}^5C_2x^2 + {}^5C_3x^3 + {}^5C_4x^4 + {}^5C_5x^5]$$

= Coefficient of x^4 in

$$= 4!\left[1+3x+\frac{3x^2}{2}+3\left(x^2+\frac{x^4}{4}+x^3\right)+x^3+\frac{x^6}{8}+\frac{3x^4}{4}+\frac{3x^5}{4}\right]$$

$$\times (1 + x + 10x^2 + 10x^3 + 5x^4 + x^5)$$

$$= 4!\left[5+30+15+30+\frac{3}{4}+15+5+\frac{3}{2}\right] = 24\left(100+\frac{3}{4}+\frac{3}{2}\right)$$

$$= \frac{409}{4}\times 24 = 2454$$

(iii) Number of selection of 4 letters from the word ASSASSINATION

= Coefficient of x^4 in $(1 + x + x^2 + x^3 + x^4)(1 + x + x^2 + x^3)(1 + x + x^2)^2 \times (1 + x)^2$

= Coefficient of x^4 in $(1 + 2x + 3x^2 + 4x^3 + 4x^4)(1 + x^2 + x^4 + 2x + 2x^3 + 2x^2)(1 + x^2 + 2x)$

= Coefficient of x^4 in $(1 + 2x + 3x^2 + 4x^3 + 4x^4)(1 + 4x + 8x^2 + 10x^3 + 8x^4)$

= 8 + 20 + 24 + 16 + 4 = 72

(iv) We can choose *a* student from section I in 9 ways and from section II in 8 ways.

Total number of ways = 9 × 8 = 72 ways

4. (i) → (a); (ii) → (a), (b), (c); (iii) → (a), (b), (c), (d); (iv) → (a)

(i) Total number of ways of selection = (4 × 5 × 3) – 1 – 59 > 50

(ii) Number of triangle formed = ${}^{12}C_3 - {}^7C_3 = 1857 > 100 > 50$

(iii) Coefficient of x^{10} in $(1 + x + x^2 + x^3 + ...)^4$

$= \text{Coefficient of } x^{10} \text{ in } \left[\frac{1}{1-x}\right]^4$

$= \text{Coefficient of } x^{10} \text{ in } (1 - x)^{-4} = {}^{4+10-1}C_{10} = {}^{13}C_3 = 286$

$> 200 > 150 > 100 > 50$

(iv) $38808 = 2 \times 2 \times 2 \times 3 \times 3 \times 3 \times 7 \times 7 \times 11 = (2)^3 \times (3)^2 \times (7)^2 \times 11$

∴ Number of proper positive integer devisors $= (4 \times 3 \times 3 \times 2) - (2) = 70 > 50$

5. (i) → (a); (ii) → (d); (iii) → (b); (iv) → (b)

(i) (ENDEA), N, O, E, L

Number of permutations = 5!

(ii) $E,\underbrace{(N,D,E,A,N,O,L)}_{7!/2!},E$

Number of permutations $= \frac{7!}{2} = 7 \times 3(5!) = 21(5!)$

(iii) First four positions are reserved for D, L, N, N

∴ D, L, N, N can be arranged in first four positions in $= \frac{4!}{2!} = 12$ ways

The remaining 5 letters can be arranged in $\frac{5!}{3!}$

∴ Total number of required ways $= 12 \times \frac{5!}{3!} = 2 \times 5!$

(iv) A, E, O occurs only in odd positions i.e., in 1st, 3rd, 5th, 7th, and 9th positions i.e., A, E, E, E, O occur with any order in 1st, 3rd, 5th, 7th and 9th positions in $\frac{5!}{3!}$ ways.

The other 4 letters D, L, N, N can be arranged in remaining 4 places in $\frac{4!}{2!}$ ways.

∴ Total number of ways $= \frac{5!}{3!} \times \frac{4!}{2!} = 2 \times 5!$

6. (i) → (a); (ii) → (b); (iii) → (b); (iv) → (c); (v) → (d)

(i) Required number of numbers $= {}^6P_3 = 6 \times 5 \times 4 = 120$

(ii) For numbers less than 400 hundred's place has 2 choices i.e., 2 and 3

∴ Ten's place and unit place has respectively 5 and 4 choices.

∴ Numbers less than $400 = 2 \times 5 \times 4 = 40$

(iii) Numbers which are even, have number of choices for unit place = 2

For ten's and hundred place number of choices = 5 and 4

∴ Required number of numbers $= 5 \times 4 \times 2 = 40$

(iv) Number of odd numbers $= 120 - 40 = 80$

(v) For *a* number to be *a* multiple of 5; unit place has only one choice, and ten's place and hundred place has 5 and 4 choices

∴ Total number of such numbers $= 5 \times 4 \times 1 = 20$

SECTION–VIII: (INTEGER-TYPE QUESTION)

1. Sum of there digit numbers formed $= (1 + 2 + 3 + 4) \times 25 \times 10^2 + (0 + 1 + 2 + 3 + 4)(4 \times 5) \times 10 + (0 + 1 + 2 + 3 + 4)(4 \times 5) \times 1$

Sum of 4 digit numbers (< 4000) formed $= (1 + 2 + 3)(125) \times 10^3 + (0 + 1 + 2 + 3 + 4)(3 \times 5 \times 5) \times 10^2 + (0 + 1 + 2 + 3 + 4)(3 \times 5 \times 5) \times 10 + (0 + 1 + 2 + 3 + 4)(3 \times 5 \times 5) \times 1$

∴ Sum of 3 and 4 digit numbers formed from 100 on to 4000

$= 10(2500 + 200 + 20) + 750{,}000 + 75000 + 7500 + 750 + 4000$

$= 27{,}000 + 7{,}50{,}000 + 75{,}000 + 82{,}550 + 8{,}250 + 4000$

$= 947000$

2. ${}^nC_2 - n = 35 \Rightarrow n(n-1) - 2n = 70$

$\Rightarrow n^2 - 3n - 70 = 0 \Rightarrow (n - 10)(n + 7) = 0$

$\Rightarrow n = 10$

3. Coefficient of x^6 in $(1 + x)^3 (1 + x + x^2)^2 (1 + x + x^2 + x^3)$

$= \text{Coefficient of } x^6 \text{ in } [1 + 3x + 3x^2 + x^3]\left[\frac{1-x^3}{1-x}\right]^2\left[\frac{1-x^4}{1-x}\right]$

$= \text{Coefficient of } x^6 \text{ in } (1 + 3x + 3x^2 + x^3)(1 + x^6 - 2x^3)(1 - x^4) \times (1 - x)^{-3}$

$= \text{Coefficient of } x^6 \text{ in } (1 + 3x + 3x^2 + x^3)[1 - x^4 + x^6 - 2x^3] \times (1 - x)^{-3}$

$= \text{Coefficient of } x^6 \text{ in } (1 + 3x + 3x^2 - (2)x^3 + x^3 - x^4 - 6x^4 - 9x^5 + x^6 - 3x^6 - 2x^6)(1 - x)^{-3}$

$= \text{Coefficient of } x^6 \text{ in } (1 + 3x + 3x^2 - x^3 - 7x^4 - 9x^5 - 4x^6)(1 - x)^{-3}$

$= \text{Coefficient of } x^6 \text{ in } (1 + 3x + 3x^2 - x^3 - 7x^4 - 9x^5 - 4x^6)(1 + 3x + 6x^2 + 10x^3 + 15x^4 + 21x^5 + 28x^8)$

$= 28 + 63 + 45 - 10 - 42 - 27 - 4 = 53$

4. $x \in \mathbb{N}$; and ${}^{x-1}C_4 - {}^{x-1}C_3 - \frac{5}{4} \cdot {}^{x-2}P_2 < 0$

$\Rightarrow \frac{(x-1)!}{4!(x-5)!} - \frac{(x-1)!}{3!(x-4)!} - \frac{5\,(x-2)!}{4\,(x-4)!} < 0$

$\Rightarrow \frac{(x-2)!}{(x-5)!}\left[\frac{(x-1)}{4!} - \frac{(x-1)}{3!(x-4)} - \frac{5}{4} \times \frac{1}{(x-4)}\right] < 0$

$\Rightarrow \frac{x-1}{24} - \frac{(x-1)}{6(x-4)} - \frac{5}{4(x-4)} < 0$

$\Rightarrow \frac{(x-1)(x-4) - 4(x-1) - 30}{12} < 0$

$\Rightarrow x^2 - 9x - 22 < 0$

$\Rightarrow (x - 11)(x + 2) < 0$

$\Rightarrow -2 < x < 11$

$\Rightarrow x \in \{1, 2, 3, ...10\}$

∴ 10 is then greatest possible value of x.

5. A can won the match if he makes the sum even at 1st and 3rd turn of match or at 1st and 5th turn of match or at 3rd and 5th turn of match, initially sum = 0

1st	2nd	3rd	4th	5th	6th
A	B	A	B	A	B

A makes sum even at 1st and 3rd then

Even	Odd	Odd	–	–	–
(1)	(0)	(2)	–	–	–
Even	Even	Even	–	–	–
(1)	(1)	(2)	–	–	–

A makes sum even at 1st and 5th then

Even	Even	Odd	Even	Odd
(1)	(1)	(1)	(1)	(2)
Even	Odd	Even	Even	Odd
(1)	(0)	(1)	(0)	(2)
Even	Odd	Even	Odd	Even
(1)	(0)	(1)	(1)	(2)

A makes sum even at 3rd and 5th turn

A	B	A	B	A
Odd	Even	Odd	Even	Even
(0)	(0)	(1)	(1)	(2)

∴ Total number of ways in which A can won the match
$= (3 \times 3 \times 2 + 3 \times 2 \times 1) + (3 \times 2 \times 3 \times 1 \times 2 + 3 \times 3 \times 2 \times 1 \times 2) + (3 \times 3 \times 2 \times 2 \times 1)$
$= 24 + 4 \times 36 = 168$ ways

6. $2x + y + z = 20;\ x, y, z \geq 0$
$y + z = 20 - 2x;\ 0 \leq x \leq 10$
∴ Number of solutions $= \sum_{x=0}^{10} {}^{20-2x+1}C_1 = 21 + 19 + 17 + \ldots + 1 = 121$

7. $3x + y + z \leq 30$
Let there be a stack variable t, $0 \leq t \leq 30$
∴ $3x + y + z + t = 30$
⇒ $y + z + t = 30 - 3x;\ 0 \leq x \leq 10$
∴ Number of solution $= \sum_{x=0}^{10} {}^{30-3x+2}C_2$
$= {}^{32}C_2 + {}^{29}C_2 + {}^{26}C_2 + \ldots + {}^{2}C_2$
$= \frac{32\times31}{2} + \frac{29\times28}{2} + \frac{26\times25}{2} + \ldots + \frac{2\times1}{2}$
$= \frac{1}{2}[1.2 + 4.5 + \ldots + 25.26 + 28.29 + 31.32]$
$= -\sum^{11}[1+(n-1)(3)][2+(n-1)(3)]$
$= \frac{1}{2}\sum_{n=1}^{11}[3n-2][3n-1] = -\sum^{11}(9n\ -9n+2)$
$= \frac{9}{2}\sum_{n=1}^{11} n\ - \frac{9}{2}\sum_{n=1}^{11} n + \sum_{n=1}^{11}$
$= \frac{9}{2}\left(\frac{11(12)(23)}{6}\right) - \frac{9}{2}\frac{(11)(12)}{2} + 11$
$= 2277 - 297 + 11 = 1991$

8. $x_1 + x_2 + x_3 = 5;\ x_k \geq 0$ has number of solutions $= {}^7C_2 = 21$
Now $x_1 + x_2 + x_3 + x_4 + x_5 = 20$
⇒ $5 + x_4 + x_5 = 20$ ⇒ $x_4 + x_5 = 15$
Having number of solutions $= {}^{16}C_1 = 16$
∴ Total number of solutions $= 21 \times 16 = 336$

9. (a) For divisibility by 25, last two digits must by $\overline{25}$ or $\overline{75}$ i.e., the number must be of the type $= \overline{a\,b\,25}$ or $\overline{a\,b\,75}$
∴ Number of possible 4 digits numbers formed by using the digits 1, 2, 3, 4, 5, 6, 7 which are divisible by 25 $= 5 \times 4 \times 2 = 40$

(b) For divisibility by 4; 2(ten's place digit) + unit plane digit must be divisible by 4 i.e., of the form, $\overline{a\,b\,c\,d}$; $(2c + d)$ must be divisible by 4
$c = 1;\ d = 2;\ d = 6;$
$c = 2;\ d = 4;$
$c = 3;\ d = 2;\ d = 6$
$c = 4;\ d =$ impossible
$c = 5;\ d = 2;\ d = 6$
$c = 6;\ d = 4;$
$c = 7;\ d = 2;\ d = 6$
∴ Number of numbers divisible by 4
$= 5 \times 4 \times 2 + 5 \times 4 + 5 \times 4 \times 2 + 5 \times 4 \times 2 + 5 \times 4 + 5 \times 4 \times 2 = 200$

10. If exactly 6 of his matching are correct, then the remaining 4 statements from column I must be incorrectly matched with 4 statements from column II
∴ Number of ways $= {}^{10}C_6 \cdot 4!\left[1 - \frac{1}{1!} + \frac{1}{2!} - \frac{1}{3!} + \frac{1}{4!}\right]$
$= \frac{10!}{6!4!} \cdot 4!\left[\frac{1}{2} - \frac{1}{6} + \frac{1}{24}\right]$
$= (10\times9\times8\times7)\left[\frac{12-4+1}{24}\right] = 1890$

11. Required number of ways = Total number of ways – Number of ways when number one goes to wrong envelope
$= (5! - 1) = 120 - 1 = 119$

12. One-one onto functions
$f: A \to A;\ A = \{1, 2, 3, 4, 5\}$ for which $f(k) \neq k$
$= 5!\left[1 - \frac{1}{1!} + \frac{1}{2!} - \frac{1}{3!} + \frac{1}{4!} - \frac{1}{5!}\right] = 44 = 11p$ (gives)
⇒ $p = 4$

13. $S = \{1, 2, 3, 4\}$
Let P and Q be two subsets of S such that $P \cap Q = \phi$ and for unordered pairs $(P, Q) = (Q, P)$

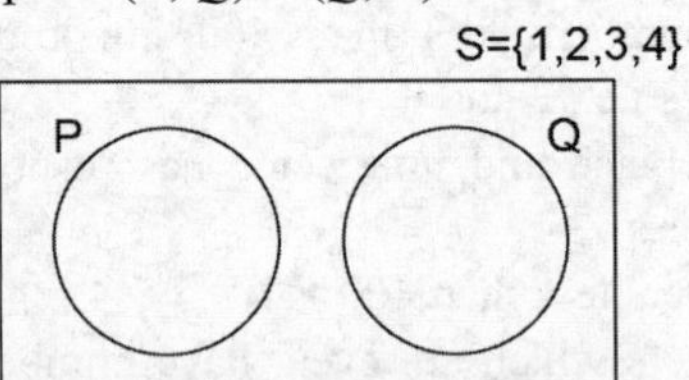

Now each element of S has 3 choices i.e., P or Q or $(P \cup Q)'$
∴ Number of ordered pair of disjoint sets formed $= 3 \times 3 \times 3 \times 3 = 81$
Out of which one pair is (ϕ, ϕ)
∴ Remaining 80 are ordered pair such that at least one element of each pair is non-empty.
But in above collection we have pair of the type (P, Q) and (Q, P) both.
∴ Number of unordered pairs of disjoint sets $= \frac{80}{2} = 40$
Also (ϕ, ϕ) is one of the unordered pair.
∴ Total $40 + 1 = 41$ unordered pair of disjoint sets are there

Binomial Theorem

CHAPTER 7

INTRODUCTION

Binomial [Bi (two) + Nomial (terms)] is an expression containing sum of two different terms

e.g., $a + x$, $b + cx$, $p + qx^2$, $x + y$, $x^2 + 1/y^2$ etc.

Any power of binomial expression $\{(a + x)^2\}$ can be expanded in the form of a series which is obtained by process of continuous multiplication as below: $(a + x)^2 = (a + x)(a + x) = a^2 + ax + xa + x^2 = a^2 + 2ax + x^2$ which can be explained as the terms of expansion are obtained when any one of two terms a or x are selected from each factor and finally they are multiplied together. When number a is chosen from each factor, a^2 is obtained. When only one x is selected from two factors, (which is done in ${}^2C_1$ ways) the term $2ax$ is obtained and when all x are selected, then x^2 is formed.

So $(a + x)^2 = {}^2C_0\, a^2 x^0 + {}^2C_1\, a^1x^1 + {}^2C_2\, a^0 x^2$

$= {}^2C_0\, a^2 + {}^2C_1\, ax + {}^2C_2\, x^2$

Similarly, expansion of $(a + x)^3 = {}^3C_0\, a^3 + {}^3C_1\, a^2x + {}^3C_2\, a^1x^2 + {}^3C_3x^3$

Binomial Theorem

After finding above expressions, mathematician observed that all of them follow a definite pattern. Observing these patterns, the expression for $(a + x)^n$ has been obtained, where n is a positive integer which is given by

$$(a + x)^n = {}^nC_0\, a^n x^0 + {}^nC_1\, a^{n-1} x^1 + {}^nC_2\, a^{n-2} x^2 + {}^nC_3\, a^{n-3} x^3 + ... + {}^nC_{n-1}\, ax^{n-1} + {}^nC_n\, a^0 x^n$$

(n is a positive integer known as index of binomial and ${}^nC_r$ is binomial co-efficient)

$$(a - x)^n = {}^nC_0\, a^n x^0 - {}^nC_1\, a^{n-1} x^1 + {}^nC_2\, a^{n-2} x^2 - {}^nC_3\, a^{n-3} x^3 + ... + {}^nC_{n-1}\, ax^{n-1} + (-1)^n\, {}^nC_n\, a^0 x^n$$

Explanation: The expansion of $(a + x)^n$ (i.e., multiplication of $(a + x)(a + x) ....(a + x)$, n times) will contain ${}^nC_0$ number of $a^n x^0$ (when number a is chosen from each and no x from n-factors factor i.e., ${}^nC_0$ ways).

${}^nC_1$ number $a^{n-1} x$ (when one x is chosen from any one of n binomial factors and remaining $(n - 1)$ a's in ${}^nC_1$ ways). Similarly, the other terms can be obtained.

ILLUSTRATION 1: Obtain the expansion of $(a - x)^n$.

SOLUTION: We know that $(a + x)^n = {}^nC_0a^n + {}^nC_1\, a^{n-1}\, x + {}^nC_2\, a^{n-2}\, x^2 + ... + {}^nC_nx^n$ (i)

Replacing $-x$ by x in (i), we get

$(a - x)^n = [a + (-x)]^n = {}^nC_0a^n + {}^nC_1\, a^{n-1}\, (-x) + {}^nC_2\, a^{n-2}\, (-x)^2 + ... + {}^nC_n(-x)^n$

$= {}^nC_0a^n - {}^nC_1\, a^{n-1}\, x + {}^nC_2\, a^{n-2}\, x^2 - .... + (-1)^n\, {}^nC_n\, x^n$

ILLUSTRATION 2: Find the value of $(x+\sqrt{x^2-1})^7 + (x-\sqrt{x^2-1})^7$.

SOLUTION: Here, we have to find the sum of two expansions whose terms are numerically the same, but in the second expansion the even terms are negative, and therefore cancel the corresponding terms of the first expansion. Hence, the given expression

$= 2\ \{x^7 + 21x^5\, (x^2 - 1) + 35x^3\, (x^2 - 1)^2 + 7x\, (x^2 - 1)^3\ \} = 2x\, (64x^6 - 112\, x^4 + 56\, x^2 - 7)$

Properties of binomial expansion

1. ${}^nC_0, {}^nC_1, {}^nC_2, \ldots\ldots {}^nC_n$ are known as **binomial co-efficients.**
2. n is called as **index** of binomial.
3. $a + x$ is known as **base** of binomial.
4. The binomial expansion is homogenous in a and x. i.e., **sum of powers of a and x in each term remains constant** and this constant is equal to index of binomial.
5. Number of **distinct terms** in the expansion is equal to $(n + 1)$
6. **General term** is known as representative term of binomial and it is $(r + 1)^{\text{th}}$ term of the expansion and is given by $T_{r+1} = {}^nC_r\, a^{n-r} x^r$.
7. The equidistant binomial co-efficients from beginning and end are equal.

Proof: Writing the expansion of $(a + x)^n$ and $(x + a)^n$

$$(a + x)^n = {}^nC_0 a^n x^0 + {}^nC_1 a^{n-1} x^1 + {}^nC_2 a^{n-2} x^2 + {}^nC_3 a^{n-3} x^3 + \ldots + {}^nC_{n-1} a\, x^{n-1} + {}^nC_n a^0 x^n \quad \text{(i)}$$

$$(x + a)^n = {}^nC_0 x^n a^0 + {}^nC_1 x^{n-1} a^1 + {}^nC_2 x^{n-2} a^2 + {}^nC_3 x^{n-3} a^3 + \ldots {}^nC_{n-1} x\, a^{n-1} + {}^nC_n x^0 a^n \quad \text{(ii)}$$

and comparing the co-efficients of different power terms of x, we can say

$${}^nC_0 = {}^nC_n, {}^nC_1 = {}^nC_{n-1}, {}^nC_2 = {}^nC_{n-2}, {}^nC_3 = {}^nC_{n-3}, \ldots\ldots\ldots, {}^nC_r = {}^nC_{n-r}$$

Adding the expansions of $(a + x)^n$ and $(a - x)^n$ we get

$$(a + x)^n + (a - x)^n = 2\{a^n + {}^nC_2 a^{n-2} x^2 + {}^nC_4 a^{n-4} x^4 + \ldots\} = 2 \text{ \{sum of terms at odd places\}}$$

The last term is ${}^nC_n x^n$ or ${}^nC_{n-1} a\, x^{n-1}$ according as n is even or odd respectively.

NOTES

1. *The number of terms in the above expansion will be $\frac{n}{2} + 1$, when n is even and $\frac{n+1}{2}$ when n is odd. Subtracting*
   $(a + x)^n - (a - x)^n = 2\{{}^nC_1 a^{n-1} x^1 + {}^nC_3 a^{n-3} x^3 + \ldots\} = 2$ *{sum of terms at even places}*
   The last term is ${}^nC_{n-1} a x^{n-1}$ or ${}^nC_n x^n$ according as n is even or odd respectively.
2. *The number of terms in the above expansion will be $\frac{n}{2}$, when n is even and $\frac{n+1}{2}$ when n is odd*

ILLUSTRATION 3: Find the total number of terms in the expansion of $(x + a)^{100} - (x - a)^{100}$ after simplification.

SOLUTION: Since n is even, therefore number of terms $= \frac{100}{2} = 50$

ILLUSTRATION 4: Find the number of terms in the expansion of $(x + \sqrt{x^2 + 1})^{101} - (x - \sqrt{x^2 - 1})^{101}$.

SOLUTION: Since n is odd, therefore number of terms $= \frac{101+1}{2} = 51$

General term $(r + 1)^{\text{th}}$ term from beginning

The term ${}^nC_r\, x^{n-r} y^r$ is the $(r + 1)$ th term from beginning in the expansion of $(x + y)^n$. It is usually called the general term and it is denoted by T_{r+1}. i.e., $T_{r+1} = {}^nC_r\, x^{n-r} y^r$

ILLUSTRATION 5: Find the 7th term in the expansion of $\left(4a - \frac{1}{2\sqrt{a}}\right)^{13}$.

SOLUTION: Seventh term $T_7 = T_{6+1} = {}^{13}C_6 (4a)^{13-6} \left(-\frac{1}{2\sqrt{a}}\right)^6 = {}^{13}C_6\, 4^7 a^7 \frac{1}{2^6 a^3} = {}^{13}C_6\, 2^8 a^4$

NOTE

k

k^{th} term from end

k^{th} term from end in the expansion of $(x + y)^n = (n - k + 2)^{th}$ term from beginning in $(x + y)^n$ or k^{th} term from beginning in $(y + x)^n$

ILLUSTRATION 6: Find the 4th term from the end in the expansion of $(a^3/2 - 2/a^2)^7$.

SOLUTION: 4th term from end $= (7 - 4 + 2)^{th}$ term from beginning in the given expansion

$$= T_5 = T_{4+1} = {}^7C_4\,(a^3/2)^{7-4}\,(-2/a^2)^4 = {}^7C_3\,(a^3/2)^3\,(-2/a^2)^4 = \frac{7.6.5}{1.2.3}.\frac{a^9}{8}.\frac{16}{a^8} = 70a$$

NOTES

General term is used to find the following in binomial expansion:

(i) *A particular term e.g., Term independent of x*

(ii) *Rational term, real term etc.*

(iii) *Middle term, greatest term*

(iv) *Term containing greatest co-efficient of x*

ILLUSTRATION 7: Find the number of irrational terms in the expansion of $(7^{1/8} + 3^{1/6})^{100}$.

SOLUTION: $T_{r+1} = {}^{100}C_r\,(7^{1/8})^{100-r}.\,(3^{1/6})^r$

As 3 and 7 are coprime, T_{r+1} will be rational if $100 - r$ is a multiple of 8 and r is a multiple of 6. Also $0 \le r \le 100$ and $0 \le 100 - r \le 100$.

$\therefore\ r \in \{0, 6, 12, ..., 96\}$

$\therefore\ 100 - r \in \{4, 10, 16, ...88, 94, 100\}$ (i)

But $100 - r$ is to be a multiple of 8

$\Rightarrow\ 100 - r \in \{0, 8, 16, 24, .., 96\}$ (ii)

The common terms in (i) and (ii) are 16, 40, 64, 88

$\therefore\ r \in \{88, 64, 40, 16\}$ give rational terms

$\therefore$ the number of irrational terms $= 101 - 4 = 97$

TEXTUAL EXERCISE–1 (SUBJECTIVE)

1. (a) Expand and find the number of terms in the following binomial expansion:

(i) $((2x - y)^5)^3$

(ii) $(2x + 5y)^{15}$

(iii) $(1 + x + x^2)^3$

(b) Evaluate the following binomial expansion:

(i) $\left(\sqrt{3}+1\right)^6 - \left(\sqrt{3}-1\right)^6$

(ii) $\left(1+\sqrt{2}\right)^5 + \left(1-\sqrt{2}\right)^5$

(c) Use binomial theorem to evaluate the approximate value of the following:
(i) $(1003)^6$ (ii) $(9999)^{10}$
(iii) $(1.01)^{10}$

(d) Find the number of terms in the expansion of L.H.S. of equation $(x+\sqrt{x^2+1})^5+(x-\sqrt{x^2+1})^5=0$ and also find the value of x^2.

(e) Find the 3rd term from the end in the expansion of $\left(x^{-2/3}-\frac{3}{x^2}\right)^8$.

(f) Find the degree of the expression $[x+(x^3-1)^{1/2}]^5+[x-(x^3-1)^{1/2}]^5$.

2. If the fourth term in the expansion of $(ax+1/x)^n$ is (5/2) for any value of x, find the value of n and a.

3. Find the value of x in the expansion of $(x+x^{\log_{10}x})^5$ if third term = 1000000.

4. If the 3rd, 4th, 5th and 6th term in the expansion of $(x+\alpha)^n$ be a, b, c, d respectively, prove that $\frac{b^2-ac}{c^2-bd}=\frac{5a}{3c}$.

5. Find the co-efficient of:

(i) x^7 in $\left(ax^2+\frac{1}{bx}\right)^{11}$

(ii) x^5 in $(1+x^2)^5(1+x)^4$

(iii) x^{11} in $(2x^2+x-3)^6$

(iv) x^{20} in $(1+x^2)^{40}.(x^2+2+1/x^2)^{-5}$

(v) x^4 in $(1+x+x^2+x^3)^{11}$ and $(2-x-3x^2)^6$

(vi) x^{13} in $(1-x)^5(1+x+x^2+x^3)^4$.

(vii) x^3 in $(1+x+x^2)^n$

(viii) x^p in the expansion of $(x^2+1/x)^{2n}$ (when it exists)

6. Find the term independent of x in the expansion of

(i) $\left[\sqrt{\frac{x}{3}}+\frac{3}{2x^2}\right]^{10}$

(ii) $(1+x+2x^3)\left(\frac{3}{2}x^2-\frac{1}{3x}\right)^9$

7. If n and r are integers, such that $r>1$ and $n>2$, and the co-efficient of $(3r)$ and $(r+2)$th powers of x in the expansion of $(1+x)^{2n}$ are equal, show that $n=2r+1$.

8. Find the number of terms in the following expansions:

(a) $(1+x+x^2)^{50}$

(b) $(1+x+x^2+x^3)^{20}$

(c) $(1+x^2+x^4+x^6)^{50}$

(d) $(1+x+x^2+x^3+x^4+x^5)^n$

(e) $(1-x+x^2-x^3+x^4\,........\infty)^{-n}$ where $|x|<1$, $n\in\mathbb{N}$

9. (a) Find the number of real negative, real positive and imaginary terms in the binomial expansion of $(1+ix)^{4n-2}$; $n\in\mathbb{N}$; $x>0$.

(b) Find the number of terms in expansion of $(x^2+1+1/x^2)^n$, $n\in\mathbb{N}$.

(c) Find the number of terms in the expansion of $(x+y+z)^n$, $n\in\mathbb{N}$

(d) Find the number of rational, irrational term and nature of middle term in the expansion of $\left(\sqrt[3]{4}+\frac{1}{\sqrt[4]{6}}\right)^{20}$.

(e) Show that there will be no term containing x^{2r} in the expansion of $(x+x^{-2})^{n-3}$, if $n-2r$ is positive but not a multiple of 3.

10. (a) Find the sum of numerical co-efficients in the expansion of $(1+x/3+2y/3)^{12}$.

(b) Find the sum of last 10 co-efficients in the expansion of $(1+x)^{19}$, when expanded in ascending powers of x.

11. In the expansion of $(1+x)^{20}$

(i) Sum of I^{st} 10 co-efficients

(ii) Sum of I^{st} 11 co-efficients

Answer Keys

1. (a) (i) $\sum_{r=0}^{15}(-1)^r 2^{15-r}.\,{}^{15}C_r.x^{15-r}.\,y^r$; Number of terms = 16

(ii) $\sum_{r=0}^{15}2^{15-r}.5^r.\,{}^{15}C_r.\,x^{15-r}.\,y^r$; Number of terms = 16

(iii) $x^6+3x^5+6x^4+7x^3+6x^2+3x+1$; Number of terms = 7

(b) (i) $240\sqrt{3}$ (ii) 82

(c) (i) 1.018×10^{18} (ii) 0.999×10^{40} (iii) 1.1

(d) 3 terms, $\frac{-5 \pm \sqrt{5}}{8}$ (e) $20412.\ x^{-40/3}$ (f) 7

2. $a = 1/2$, $n = 6$ **3.** $10^{-5/2}$, 10

5. (i) $\frac{^{11}C_5 a^6}{b^5}$ (ii) 60 (iii) 192 (iv) $^{30}C_{25}$

(v) 990, 780 (vi) 4 (vii) $\frac{n(n-1)(n+4)}{6}$ (viii) $\frac{(2n)!}{\left(\frac{4n-p}{3}\right)!\left(\frac{2n+p}{3}\right)!}$

6. (i) 5/4 (ii) 17/54

8. (a) 101 (b) 61 (c) 151 (d) $5n + 1$ (e) $n + 1$

9. (a) $n, n, 2n - 1$ (b) $2n + 1$ (c) $\frac{(n+1)(n+2)}{2}$

(d) rational = 2; irrational = 19; middle term is irrational

10. (a) 2^{12} (b) 2^{18}

11. (i) $\frac{2^{20} - {}^{20}C_{10}}{2}$ (ii) $\frac{2^{20} + {}^{20}C_{10}}{2}$

TEXTUAL EXERCISE–1 (OBJECTIVE)

1. r^{th} term in the expansion of $(a + 2x)^n$ is

(a) $\frac{n(n+1)....(n-r+1)}{r!}a^{n-r+1}(2x)^r$

(b) $\frac{n(n-1)....(n-r+2)}{(r-1)!}a^{n-r+1}(2x)^{r-1}$

(c) $\frac{n(n+1)....(n-r)}{(r+1)!}a^{n-r}(x)^r$

(d) None of these

2. If the $(r+1)^{th}$ term in the expansion of $\left(\sqrt[3]{\frac{a}{\sqrt{b}}} + \sqrt{\frac{b}{\sqrt[3]{a}}}\right)^{21}$ has the same power of a and b, then the value of r is

(a) 9 (b) 10
(c) 8 (d) 6

3. The expression $(x + \sqrt{x^3 - 1})^6 + (x - \sqrt{x^3 - 1})^6$ is a polynomial of degree

(a) 6 (b) 7
(c) 8 (d) 9

4. The total number of terms in the expansion of $(x + a)^{100} + (x - a)^{100}$ after simplification will be

(a) 202 (b) 51
(c) 50 (d) None of these

5. $(\sqrt{2}+1)^6 - (\sqrt{2}-1)^6 =$

(a) 101 (b) $70\sqrt{2}$
(c) $140\sqrt{2}$ (d) $120\sqrt{2}$

6. If $T_0, T_1, T_2, ...T_n$ represent the terms in the expansion of $(x + a)^n$, then $(T_0 - T_2 + T_4 - ....)^2 + (T_1 - T_3 + T_5 - ...)^2 =$

(a) $(x^2 + a^2)$ (b) $(x^2 + a^2)^n$
(c) $(x^2 + a^2)^{1/n}$ (d) $(x^2 + a^2)^{-1/n}$

7. If the sum of the co-efficients in the expansion of $(\alpha^2x^2 - 2\alpha x + 1)^{51}$ vanishes, then the value of α is

(a) 2 (b) –1
(c) 1 (d) –2

8. In the expansion of $(5^{1/2} + 7^{1/8})^{1024}$, the number of integral terms is

(a) 128 (b) 129
(c) 130 (d) 131

9. If the ratio of the magnitudes of co-efficient of third and fourth terms in the expansion of $\left(x - \frac{1}{2x}\right)^n$ is 1:2, then the value of n will be

(a) 18 (b) 16
(c) 12 (d) 14

10. In $\left(\sqrt[3]{2} + \frac{1}{\sqrt[3]{3}}\right)^n$ if the ratio of 7th term from the beginning to the 7th term from the end is 1/6, then $n =$

(a) 7 (b) 8
(c) 9 (d) None of these

11. If the co-efficient of x^7 in the expansion of $\left(ax^2 + \frac{1}{bx}\right)^{11}$ and the co-efficient of x^{-7} in the expansion of $\left(ax - \frac{1}{bx^2}\right)^{11}$ are equal, then

(a) $ab = 1$ (b) $ab = 11$
(c) $ab = 7$ (d) $ab = 6$

12. If $x + y = 1$, then value of $\sum_{r=0}^{n}(r)({}^nC_r)x^{n-r}y^r$ is

(a) 1 (b) 0
(c) nx (d) ny

Answer Keys

1. (b) **2.** (a) **3.** (d) **4.** (b) **5.** (c) **6.** (b) **7.** (c) **8.** (b) **9.** (d) **10.** (c)
11. (a) **12.** (d)

Middle term

The middle term depends upon the value of n.

Case I

If n is even: Then total number of terms in the expansion of $(x + y)^n$ is $n + 1$ (odd). So there is only one middle term i.e., $[(n/2 + 1)]$th term is the middle term.

i.e., $T_{(n/2)+1} = {}^nC_{n/2}\, x^{n/2}\, y^{n/2}$

Case II

If n is odd: Then total number of terms in the expansion of $(x + y)^n$ is $n + 1$ (even). So there are two middle terms i.e., $\left(\frac{n+1}{2}\right)$th and $\left(\frac{n+3}{2}\right)$th are two middle terms.

They are given by ${}^nC_{\frac{n-1}{2}}x^{\frac{n+1}{2}}y^{\frac{n-1}{2}}$ and ${}^nC_{\frac{n+1}{2}}x^{\frac{n-1}{2}}y^{\frac{n+1}{2}}$.

ILLUSTRATION 8: Find the middle term in the expansion of $(a/x + bx)^{12}$.

SOLUTION: The number of terms in the expansion of $(a/x + bx)^{12}$ is 13 (odd), its middle term is $[(12/2) + 1)]^{\text{th}}$ term.

$\therefore$ Required term $= T_7 = T_{6+1} = {}^{12}C_6\,(a/x)^{12-6}\,(bx)^6 = {}^{12}C_6(a^6/x^6)\,b^6x^6 = {}^{12}C_6\,a^6\,b^6$

ILLUSTRATION 9: Prove that middle term in the expansion of $(x + 1/x)^{2n}$ is $\frac{1.3.5.....(2n-1)}{n!}.2^n$

SOLUTION: Since $2n$ is even, Therefore $[(2n/2) + 1)]^{\text{th}}$ i.e., $(n + 1)$th term will be the middle term.

Now $(n + 1)$th term i.e., middle term in $(x + 1/x)^{2n}$ is given by

$$T_{n+1} = {}^{2n}C_n\,x^{2n-n}\,(1/x)^n = {}^{2n}C_n\,x^n\,\frac{1}{x^n} = {}^{2n}C_n$$

$$= \frac{(2n)!}{n!n!} = \frac{2n(2n-1)(2n-2)(2n-3).....4.3.2.1}{n!n!} = \frac{[1.3.5....(2n-1)].2^n[(n-1)(n-2)(n-3).......2.1]}{n!n!}$$

$$= \frac{1.3.5....(2n-1)2^n n!}{n!n!} = \frac{1.3.5....(2n-1)2^n}{n!}$$

Term free from radicals in $(a^{1/p} + b^{1/q})^n$

First find the general term of $(a^{1/p} + b^{1/q})^n$

i.e., $T_{r+1} = {}^nC_r\,(a^{1/p})^{n-r}\,(b^{1/q})^r \quad \Rightarrow T_{r+1} = {}^nC_r\,a^{(n-r)/p}\,b^{r/q}$

By putting the values of $0 \le r \le n$, when indices of a and b are integers i.e., $(n - r)$ is a multiple of p and r is a multiple of q.

NOTE

Number of irrational terms = Total terms - number of rational terms.

ILLUSTRATION 10: Find the sum of the rational terms in the expansion of $(3^{1/5} + 2^{1/3})^{15}$.

SOLUTION: The general term of given expansion is $T_{r+1} = {}^{15}C_r\,(3^{1/5})^{15-r}\,(2^{1/3})^r$

$\Rightarrow T_{r+1} = {}^{15}C_r\,3^{3-(r/5)}.\,2^{r/3}$

For rational terms $r = 0, 15$ then $T_{0+1} = {}^{15}C_0\,.\,3^3\,2^0 = 27$

$T_{15+1} = {}^{15}C_{15}\,3^0\,2^5 = 32$

$\therefore$ sum of rational terms $= T_1 + T_{16} = 27 + 32 = 59$

Problems regarding consecutive terms or co-efficients

(i) If consecutive co-efficients are given:

In this case, divide consecutive co-efficients pair wise. We get equations and then solve them.

(ii) If consecutive terms are given:

In this case, divide consecutive terms pair wise i.e., if four consecutive terms be $T_r, T_{r+1}, T_{r+2}, T_{r+3}$.

Then find $\frac{T_r}{T_{r+1}}, \frac{T_{r+1}}{T_{r+2}}, \frac{T_{r+2}}{T_{r+3}}$

$\Rightarrow \lambda_1, \lambda_2, \lambda_3$ (say), then divide λ_1 by λ_2 and λ_2 by λ_3 and solve.

ILLUSTRATION 11: If x, y, z and w be any four consecutive co-efficients in the expansion of $(1 + a)^n$, prove that $\frac{x}{x+y} + \frac{z}{z+w} = \frac{2y}{y+z}$.

SOLUTION: Let x, y, z and w be the co-efficients of the rth, $(r + 1)^{th}$ $(r + 2)^{th}$ and the $(r + 3)^{th}$ terms respectively in the expansion of $(1 + a)^n$,

then $T_r = T_{(r-1)+1} = {}^nC_{r-1}\,a^{r-1}$ $\quad\therefore\ x = {}^nC_{r-1}$ (i)

$\Rightarrow T_{r+1} = {}^nC_r\,a^r$ $\quad\Rightarrow y = {}^nC_r$ (ii)

$\Rightarrow T_{r+2} = {}^nC_{r+1}\,a^{r+1}$ $\quad\Rightarrow z = {}^nC_{r+1}$ (iii)

$\Rightarrow T_{r+3} = {}^nC_{r+2}\,a^{r+2}$ $\quad\Rightarrow w = {}^nC_{r+2}$ (iv)

Dividing (ii) by (i), we get $\frac{y}{x} = \frac{{}^nC_r}{{}^nC_{r-1}} = \frac{n-r+1}{r}$ (v)

Dividing (iii) by (ii), we get $\frac{z}{y} = \frac{{}^nC_{r+1}}{{}^nC_r} = \frac{n-r}{r+1}$ (vi)

Dividing (iv) by (iii), we get $\frac{w}{z} = \frac{{}^nC_{r+2}}{{}^nC_{r+1}} = \frac{n-r-1}{r+2}$ (vii)

$$\therefore\ \text{L.H.S} = \frac{x}{x+y} + \frac{z}{z+w} = \frac{1}{1+(y/x)} + \frac{1}{1+(w/z)}$$

$$= \frac{1}{1+\left(\frac{n-r+1}{r}\right)} + \frac{1}{1+\left(\frac{n-r-1}{r+2}\right)} = \frac{r}{n+1} + \frac{r+2}{n+1} = 2\left(\frac{r+1}{n+1}\right)$$

$$\Rightarrow \frac{2}{\left(\frac{n+1}{r+1}\right)} = \frac{2}{1+\frac{n+1}{r+1}-1} = \frac{2}{1+\frac{n-r}{r+1}}$$

$$\Rightarrow \frac{2}{1+z/y} = \frac{2y}{y+z} = \text{R.H.S}$$

Concept of divisibility

To show that an expression is divisible by an integer

(i) If x, y, n, r are positive integers, then $x^{yn+r} = x^{yn}.x^r = (x^y)^n.x^r$

(ii) If the given expression is divisible by c, then write as $x^y = \{1 + (x^y - 1)\}$, if some power of $(x^y - 1)$ has c as a factor or $x^y = \{2 + (x^y - 2)\}$, if some power of $(x^y - 2)$ has c as a factor or $x^y = \{3 + (x^y - 3)\}$,
....
if some power of $(x^y - 3)$ has c as a factor or $x^y = \{k + (x^y - k)\}$, if some power of $(x^y - k)$ has c as a factor.

(iii) $(1 + x)^n - 1 = {}^nC_1\, x + {}^nC_2\, x^2 + ... + {}^nC_n\, x^n$ is divisible by x.
$(1 + x)^n - nx - 1$ is always divisible by x^2
$(1 + x)^n - 1 - nx - \dfrac{n(n-1)}{2}x^2 = {}^nC_3\, x^3 + {}^nC_4\, x^4 + ... + {}^nC_n\, x^n = M(x^3)$

ILLUSTRATION 12: If 7^{103} is divided by 25, then find the remainder.

SOLUTION: Since $7^{103} = 7(49)^{51} = 7(50 - 1)^{51} = 7(50^{51} - {}^{51}C_1\, 50^{50} + {}^{51}C_2\, 50^{49} - ..... - 1)$
$= 7(50^{51} - {}^{51}C_1\, 50^{50} + {}^{51}C_2\, 50^{49} - .....) - 7 + 18 - 18$
$= 7(50^{51} - {}^{51}C_1\, 50^{50} + {}^{51}C_2\, 50^{49} - .....) - 25 + 18 = k + 18$

k is divisible by 25, hence remainder is 18.

ILLUSTRATION 13: Show that

(a) $2^{4n} - 2^n(7n + 1)$ is divisible by 14^2 $\quad \forall\, n \geq 2$

(b) $a^n - b^n$ is divisible by $(a - b)$ $\quad \forall\, n$

SOLUTION: (a) $2^{4n} - 2^n(7n + 1) = 2^n(2^{3n} - 7n - 1) = 2^n\,[(1 + 7)^n - 7n - 1]$
$= 2^n\,(7^2k)$ where $k \in \mathbb{Z}$

[from (iii) point of concept of divisibility, see above]

when $n \geq 2$, clearly, the expression is divisible by 14^2

(b) $a^n - b^n = [(a - b) + b\,]^n - b^n$

Expanding binomially, we get

$[(a - b)^n + (a - b)^{n-1}\, b + (a - b)^{n-2}\, b^2 + ... + (a - b)\, b^{n-1} + (a - b)^0\, b^n] - b^n$
$= (a - b)\,[\,(a - b)^{n-1} + (a - b)^{n-2}b + (a - b)^{n-3}\, b^2 ......(a - b)^0 b^{n-1}]$
$= (a - b).\,k$ (where k is an integer) Hence proved.

Useful results and remarks

Pascal's triangle

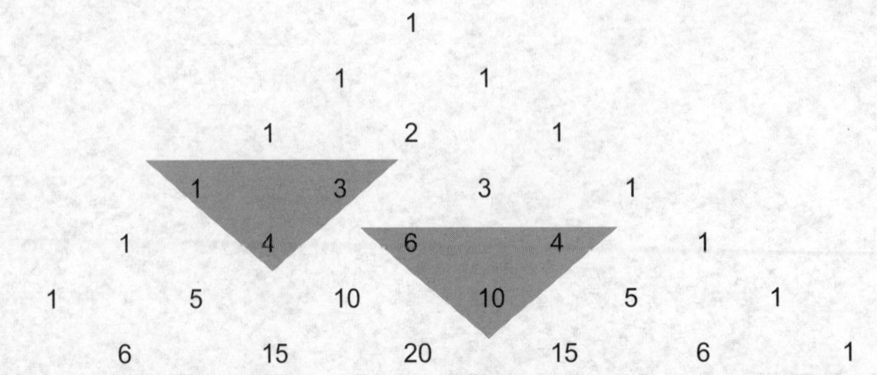

NOTES

In Pascal's triangle, successive entries can be obtained by adding the nearest entries in the row above it (as illustrated in the shaded region). So from the above property, we can complete the binomial expansion for any natural number n.

- *Pascal's triangle gives the binomial co-efficients directly.*
- *Binomial co-efficients of $(x + y)^n$ is given by $(n + 1)^{th}$ row of pascal.*

How to construct a pascal's triangle

Binomial co-efficient in the expansion of $(x + y)^3$ are

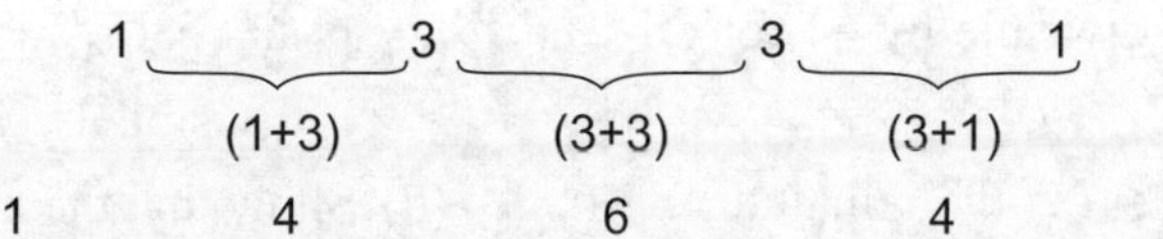

the binomial co-efficients in the expansion of $(x + a)^4$

ILLUSTRATION 14: Expand following using Pascal's triangle.

(a) $(x + y)^4$ (b) $(a + b)^5$

SOLUTION: (a) Since the co-efficient in the 5th row of triangle are 1, 4, 6, 4, 1.

Therefore, $(x + y)^4 = 1.x^4 + 4.x^3y + 6x^2 .y^2 + 4.x.y^3 + y^4$

$= x^4 + 4x^3 y + 6x^2y^2 + 4xy^3 + y^4$

(b) Similarly, $(a + b)^5 = a^5 + 5a^4 b + 10 a^3 b^2 + 10 a^2 b^3 + 5 ab^4 + b^5$

TEXTUAL EXERCISE–2 (SUBJECTIVE)

1. (a) Show that the middle term in the expansion of $(1 + x)^{2n}$ is $\dfrac{1.3.5...(2n-1)}{n!}.2^n.x^n$.

(b) Show that the co-efficient of the middle term in the expansion of $(1 + x)^{2n}$ is the sum of the co-efficient of the two middle terms in the expansion of $(1 + x)^{2n-1}$.

2. Find the middle term in the expansion of $\left(\dfrac{a}{x}+bx\right)^{12}$ and show that it is of the form $3.7.11.2^2.(ab)^6$.

3. Find the middle term of expansion $\left(x-\dfrac{1}{x}\right)^{2n}$ and show that it is equal to $\dfrac{(2n)!}{(n!)(n!)}(-1)^n$.

4. (a) If the co-efficients of the 5th, 6th and 7th terms in the expansion of $(1 + x)^n$ are in *A.P.* then determine the value of n and also find n if the above co-efficients are in G.P.

(b) If a_1, a_2, a_3 and a_4 are any four consecutive co-efficients in the expansion of $(1 + x)^n$, then show that $\dfrac{a_1}{a_1+a_2}+\dfrac{a_3}{a_3+a_4}=\dfrac{2a_2}{a_2+a_3}$.

(c) If the co-efficient of second, third and fourth terms in the expansion of $(1 + x)^{2n}$ are in *A.P.*, show that $2n^2 - 9n + 7 = 0$

(d) The co-efficient of $(r - 1)^{th}$, r^{th} and $(r + 1)^{th}$ terms in the expansion of $(x + 1)^n$ are in the ratio 1:3:5, then find the value of r and n.

(e) The co-efficients of three consecutive terms in the expansion of $(1 + a)^n$ are in the ratio 1: 7: 42, find n.

(f) If the 2nd, 3rd and 4th terms in the expansion of $(x + y)^n$ are 240, 720 and 1080 respectively. Find x, y and n.

5. Find the sum of the rational terms in the expansion of $(3^{1/5} + 2^{1/3})^{15}$.

6. If P be the sum of odd terms and Q that of even terms in the expansion of $(x + y)^n$, then prove the following results:

(a) $(x^2 - y^2)^n = P^2 - Q^2$

(b) $(x + y)^{2n} - (x - y)^{2n} = 4PQ$

(c) $(x + y)^{2n} + (x - y)^{2n} = 2(P^2 + Q^2)$

7. Show that $(1 + x)^n - nx - 1$ is always divisible by x^2(non-zero number) $\forall\, n \in \mathbb{N}$ and hence or otherwise,

(a) Show that $9^{n+1} - 8n - 9$ is divisible by 64 for all positive integers n.

(b) Show that $6^n - 5n$ always leaves the remainder 1 when divided by 25.

8. (a) Show that $2^{4n} - 2^n(7n + 1)$ is some multiple of the square of 14 where n is a positive integer.

(b) If a and b are distinct integers, show that $a^n - b^n$ is divisible by $a - b$ for each positive integer n.

(c) If n be an odd natural number greater than 1, then find the number of zeros at the end of sum $99^n + 1$.

9. (a) Find the remainder

(i) when 2^{60} is divided by 7.

(ii) when 7^{103} is divided by 25.

(b) Find the last three digits of 17^{256}.

(c) Prove that $1992^{1998} - 1955^{1998} - 1938^{1998} + 1901^{1998}$ is divisible by 1998.

(d) Show that the number $101^{100} - 1$ is divisible by 10^4 but not by 10^5.

Answer Keys

2. $924a^6b^6$ **3.** $\dfrac{2n!}{n!n!}(-1)^n$ **4.** (a) $n = 7$ or 14; $n = -1$ which is not possible (d) $n = 7, r = 3$ (e) $n = 55, r = 7$ (f) $x = 2, y = 3, n = 5$ **5.** 59 **8.** (c) 2 **9.** (a) (i) 1 (ii) 18 (b) 681

TEXTUAL EXERCISE–2 (OBJECTIVE)

1. The co-efficient of middle term in the expansion of $(1 + x)^{10}$ is

(a) $\dfrac{10!}{5!6!}$ (b) $\dfrac{10!}{(5!)^2}$

(c) $\dfrac{10!}{5!7!}$ (d) None of these

2. The middle term in the expansion of $\left(x+\dfrac{1}{x}\right)^{10}$ is

(a) ${}^{10}C_4\dfrac{1}{x}$ (b) ${}^{10}C_5$

(c) ${}^{10}C_5x$ (d) ${}^{10}C_7x^4$

3. If the middle term in the expansion of $\left(x^2+\dfrac{1}{x}\right)^n$ is $924x^6$, then $n =$

(a) 10 (b) 12

(c) 14 (d) None of these

4. The last digit in 7^{300} is

(a) 7 (b) 9

(c) 1 (d) 3

5. The remainder when 2^{2003} is divided by 17 is

(a) 1 (b) 2

(c) 8 (d) None of these

Answer Keys

1. (b) **2.** (b) **3.** (b) **4.** (c) **5.** (c)

■ PROPERTIES OF BINOMIAL CO-EFFICIENT

The binomial co-efficient for general term of the expansion $(a + x)^n$ is given as ${}^nC_r$ which states the number of ways the term $a^{n-r}x^r$ occurs in the expansion.

Properties of ${}^nC_r$

${}^nC_r$ is defined as number of selections of r objects out of n different objects and is given by, ${}^nC_r = \dfrac{n!}{r!(n-r)!}$, when $n \geq r$, ($= 0$ if $n < r$). ${}^nC_r$ is always an integer. Product of r consecutive integers is always divisible by $r!$.

$\therefore \quad {}^nC_r = \dfrac{n(n-1)(n-2)(n-3).....(n-r+1)}{r!} \in I$

Clearly, the numerator being the product of r consecutive integer is completely divisible by r!

^nC_r has following properties

1. $^nC_r = {}^nC_{n-r}$
2. $^nC_x = {}^nC_y \Rightarrow x = y$ or $x + y = n$
3. $^nC_r + {}^nC_{r-1} = {}^{n+1}C_r$
4. $^nC_r = \dfrac{n}{r}\left({}^{n-1}C_{r-1}\right) = \dfrac{n}{r}\left(\dfrac{n-1}{r-1}\right){}^{n-2}C_{r-2} = ...$
5. $^nC_r = {}^{n+1}C_{r+1}\cdot\left(\dfrac{r+1}{n+1}\right) = \dfrac{(r+1)(r+2)}{(n+1)(n+2)}\ {}^{n+2}C_{r+2}$
6. $r.{}^nC_r = n\ {}^{n-1}C_{r-1}$ and $\dfrac{{}^nC_r}{r+1} = \left(\dfrac{{}^{n+1}C_{r+1}}{n+1}\right)$

NOTES

By virtue of definition of ^nC_r, the following results follow automatically:

(a) $0! = 1$.

(b) $k! = -\infty$, *when* $k < 0$.

(c) $^nC_k = 0$, *when* $k < 0$. ***(Think why?)***

Properties of co-efficients

Most of the properties of the binomial co-efficients are derived from the basic expansion:

$$(1 + x)^n = \sum_{r=0}^{n} {}^nC_r x^r = {}^nC_0 + {}^nC_1 x + {}^nC_2 x^2 + ... + {}^nC_r x^r + ... + {}^nC_n x^n \quad \text{(i)}$$

$$(1-x)^n = \sum_{r=0}^{n} (-1)^r\ {}^nC_r x^r = {}^nC_0 - {}^nC_1 x + {}^nC_2 x^2 - .... + (-1)^n\ {}^nC_n x^n \quad \text{(ii)}$$

Property 1: Show that sum of binomial co-efficients of $(1 + x)^n$ will be equal to 2^n.

$$\sum_{r=0}^{n} {}^nC_r x^r = {}^nC_0 + {}^nC_1 + {}^nC_2 + ...+ {}^nC_n = 2^n$$

Proof: Put $x = 1$ in expansion (i)

$$2^n = {}^nC_0 + {}^nC_1 + {}^nC_2 + ... + {}^nC_n = \sum_{r=0}^{n} {}^nC_r$$

Property 2:

$$\sum_{r=0}^{n} (-1)^r\ {}^nC_r = {}^nC_0 - {}^nC_1 + {}^nC_2 - .....+(-1)^n\ {}^nC_n = 0$$

Proof: It is obtained by substituting $x = -1$ in expansion (i)

Property 3: The sum of the binomial co-efficients of the odd terms in the expansion of $(1 + x)^n$ is equal to the sum of the binomial co-efficients of the even terms and each is equal to 2^{n-1}.

$$C_0 + C_2 + C_4 + ... = C_1 + C_3 + C_5 + ... = 2^{n-1}.$$

Proof: Automatically follows from **(Property 2)**.

Alternatively adding the series (i) and (ii), we get

$(1 + x)^n + (1-x)^n = 2({}^nC_0 + {}^nC_2 x^2 + ...)$,

putting $x = 1$ in it, we get $^nC_0 + {}^nC_2 + {}^nC_4 + ...$

$$= \frac{2^n}{2} = 2^{n-1}$$

Similarly, the sum of the binomial co-efficients of odd terms can be obtained from the expansion of $(1 + x)^n - (1 - x)^n = 2\ ({}^nC_1 x + {}^nC_3 x^3 + ...)$, now put $x = 1$, we get $2^n = 2\ [{}^nC_1 + {}^nC_3 + {}^nC_5 ....] \Rightarrow 2^{n-1} = {}^nC_1 + {}^nC_3 + ...$

Property 4:

$$\sum_{r=0}^{n} r\ {}^nC_r = 1C_1 + 2C_2 + 3C_3 + ... + nC_n = n\ 2^{n-1}$$

Proof: Since $r\ [{}^nC_r] = r.(n/r)\ {}^{n-1}C_{r-1} = n\ {}^{n-1}C_{r-1}$ for $r \geq 1$

Now, $\displaystyle\sum_{r=0}^{n} r.{}^nC_r = \sum_{r=1}^{n} n\ {}^{n-1}C_{r-1} = n\sum_{r=1}^{n} {}^{n-1}C_{r-1} =$

$= n\ ({}^{n-1}C_0 + {}^{n-1}C_1 + ... + {}^{n-1}C_{n-1}) = n(2^{n-1})$

Property 5:

$$\sum_{r=0}^{n} r^2\ {}^nC_r = 1^2 C_1 + 2^2 C_2 + 3^2 C_3 + ... + n^2 C_n = n(n+1)(2)^{n-2}$$

Proof $r^2.\ {}^nC_r = (r^2 - r)\ {}^nC_r + r.\ {}^nC_r = r(r-1){}^nC_r + r\ {}^nC_r$

$= r\,(r-1)\left(\dfrac{n}{r}\right)\left(\dfrac{n-1}{r-1}\right){}^{n-2}C_{r-2} + r\left(\dfrac{n}{r}\right).\ {}^{n-1}C_{r-1}$

$= n(n-1).\ {}^{n-2}C_{r-2} + n.\ {}^{n-1}C_{r-1}$

So $\displaystyle\sum_{r=1}^{n} r^2\ {}^nC_r = n(n-1)\sum_{r=2}^{n} {}^{n-2}C_{r-2} + n\sum_{r=1}^{n} {}^{n-1}C_{r-1}$

$= n(n-1).\ 2^{n-2} + n.2^{n-1} = n(n+1).\ 2^{n-2}$

NOTE

In any problem of summation carrying binomial coefficient on replacing 'r' by 'n–r' never changes the value of summation.

Property 6:

$$\sum_{r=0}^{n}\frac{C_r}{r+1}=\frac{C_0}{1}+\frac{C_1}{2}+\frac{C_2}{3}+\ldots\ldots\ldots\ldots\ldots\ldots+\frac{C_n}{n+1}.$$

Proof: $\frac{^nC_r}{r+1}=\frac{1}{n+1}\left(\frac{(n+1)}{r+1}.{}^nC_r\right)=\frac{1}{n+1}\left({}^{n+1}C_{r+1}\right)$

Therefore, $\sum_{r=0}^{n}\frac{^nC_r}{r+1}=\frac{1}{n+1}\sum_{r=0}^{n}{}^{n+1}C_{r+1}$

$$=\frac{1}{n+1}\left[{}^{n+1}C_1+{}^{n+1}C_2+{}^{n+1}C_3+\ldots\ldots\ldots\ldots+{}^{n+1}C_{n+1}\right]$$

$$=\left(\frac{2^{n+1}-1}{n+1}\right)$$

Property 7: $\sum_{r=1}^{n}r.\frac{^nC_r}{^nC_{r-1}}=\sum_{k=0}^{n}k=\frac{n(n+1)}{2}$

Proof: $\sum_{r=1}^{n}r.\left(\frac{n-r+1}{r}\right)$

$$=\sum_{r=1}^{n}(n+1)-\sum_{r=1}^{n}r=n(n+1)-\frac{n(n+1)}{2}=\frac{n(n+1)}{2}$$

Use of complex numbers

If certain number (k) of binomial co-efficients are missing from the binomial series alternatively, then we substitute $(k+1)^{th}$ root of unity in place of x in the expansion on $(1+x)^n$.

ILLUSTRATION 15: Evaluate $C_0 + C_3 + C_6 + C_9$.......

SOLUTION: Putting $x = 1, \omega, \omega^2$ in the expansion of

$(1+x)^n = {}^nC_0x^0 + {}^nC_1x + {}^nC_2x^2 + {}^nC_3x^3 + \ldots\ldots + {}^nC_{n-1}x^{n-1} + {}^nC_nx^n$ and then adding we get,

$$\Rightarrow C_0+C_3+C_6+C_9+\ldots\ldots\ldots=\frac{\left(2^n+(1+\omega)^n+(1+\omega^2)^n\right)}{3}$$

$$\Rightarrow C_0+C_3+C_6+\ldots\ldots\ldots=\frac{2^n+(-1)^n\omega^{2n}+(-1)^n\omega^n}{3}$$

$$=\frac{2^n+(-1)^n(\omega^n+\overline{\omega}^n)}{3}$$

$$=\frac{2^n+(-1)^n2\cos\frac{2n\pi}{3}}{3}$$

Use of differentiation

This method is applied when the power (numeral) of terms occurs as the product to the binomial co-efficients.

(i) If last term of the series leaving the plus or minus sign be m, then divide m by n, where q is the quotient and r is the remainder. i.e., $m = nq + r$ then replace x by x^q in the given series and multiplying both sides of the expression by x^r.

(ii) After process (i), differentiate both sides with respect to x and put $x = 1$ or -1 or $-i$ etc., according to the given series.

(iii) If there be product of two numericals (or square of numericals) or three numericals (or cube of numericals), then differentiate twice or thrice, as required.

ILLUSTRATION 16: If $(1 + x)^n = C_0 + C_1x + C_2x^2 + ... + C_nx^n$, then prove that

(a) $C_1 + 2C_2 + 3C_3 + ...+ nC_n = n2^{n-1}$

(b) $2.1C_2 + 3.2C_3 + 4.3C_4 + ...(n-1).nC_n = n(n-1)2^{n-2}$

(c) $1^2.C_1 + 2^2.C_2 + 3^2.C_3 + ... + n^2.C_n = n(n+1).2^{n-2}$

SOLUTION: (a) Differentiating both sides of given expansion

$$n(1+x)^{n-1} = \sum_{r=0}^{n} {}^nC_r \frac{d}{dx}x^r = \sum_{r=0}^{n} r\,{}^nC_r x^{r-1}$$

$$= {}^nC_1 + {}^nC_2(2x) + {}^nC_3(3x^2) + ... + {}^nC_n\, n.x^{n-1} \quad \text{(i)}$$

(If we apply any mathematical operation to both sides of an identity, the resulting expression remains identity).

put $x = 1$ in (i), $n.2^{n-1} = {}^nC_1 + 2.{}^nC_2 + 3.{}^nC_3 + ...+ n.{}^nC_n$

ALITER: $S = {}^0C_0 + 1C_1 + 2C_2 + 3C_3 + 4C_4 + ... (n-2)\,C_{n-2} + (n-1)C_{n-1} + nC_n$

Reverse: $S = nC_n + n-1C_{n-1} + n-2C_{n-2} + ... + 2C_2 + 1C_1 + 0C_0$

Adding $2S = ({}^nC_0 + {}^nC_1 + {}^nC_2 + ... + {}^nC_{n-2} + {}^nC_{n-1} + {}^nC_n).n$

$= n(C_0 + C_1 + C_2 + ... + C_n) = n2^n \Rightarrow S = n.2^{n-1}$

(b) $(1+x)^n = \sum_{r=0}^{n} {}^nC_r x^r$

Differentiating both sides with respect to x,

$$n(1+x)^{n-1} = \sum_{r=0}^{n} {}^nC_r \times r \times x^{r-1}$$

Again differentiating with respect to x,

$$n(n-1)(1+x)^{n-2} = \sum_{r=0}^{n} {}^nC_r\, r(r-1)x^{r-2}$$

Put $x = 1$ in above identity, $n(n-1)\,2^{n-2} = \sum_{r=0}^{n} r(r-1)\,{}^nC_r$

(c) $(1+x)^n = C_0 + C_1x + C_2x^2 + ... + C_nx^n$

Differentiating both sides with respect to x, we get

$$n(1+x)^{n-1} = C_1 + 2C_2x + ... + n\,C_nx^{n-1} \quad \text{(i)}$$

Multiplying both sides of (i) by x, we get $nx(1+x)^{n-1} = C_1x + 2C_2x^2 + ... + n\,C_nx^n$

Again differentiating both sides with respect to x, we get

$n\{x.(n-1)(1+x)^{n-2} + (1+x)^{n-1}.1\} = C_1.1 + 2^2C_2x + 3^2C_3x^2 + ...+ n^2C_nx^{n-1}$

putting $x = 1$, $n\{1.(n-1)\,2^{n-2} + 2^{n-1}\} = C_1.1 + 2^2C_2 + 3^2C_3 + ...+ n^2C_n$

or $1^2C_1 + 2^2C_2 + 3^2C_3 + ... + n^2C_n = n(n+1).2^{n-2}$

Use of integration

This method is applied only when power (numeral) of term occurs in the denominator of the binomial co-efficient.

If $(1 + x)^n = C_0 + C_1x + C_2x^2 + C_3x^3 + ... + C_nx^n$, then integrate both sides between the suitable limits which gives the required series.

(i) If the sum contains $C_0, C_1, C_2, ..., C_n$ are all positive signs, then integrate between limits 0 to 1.

(ii) If the sum contains alternate signs (i.e., + , –) then integrate between limits – 1 to 0

(iii) If the sum contains odd co-efficients (i.e., C_0, C_2, C_4, ...), then integrate between – 1 to 1

(iv) If the sum contains even co-efficients (i.e., C_1, C_3, C_5..), then subtracting (ii) from (i) and then divide by 2.

(v) If denominator of binomial co-efficient contains product of two numericals, then integrate two times, first time take limits between 0 to x and second time take suitable limits.

ILLUSTRATION 17: Prove that $C_0 - \frac{C_1}{2} + \frac{C_2}{3} - ..... + (-1)^n \frac{C_n}{n+1} = \frac{1}{n+1}$

SOLUTION: $(1 + x)^n = C_0 + C_1x + C_2x^2 + ... + C_nx^n$ (i)

Integrate both sides of (i) within limits –1 to 0

$$\int_{-1}^{0}(1+x)^n dx = \int_{-1}^{0}(C_0 + C_1x + C_2x^2 + ... + C_nx^n)dx$$

$$\Rightarrow \left[\frac{(1+x)^{n+1}}{n+1}\right]_{-1}^{0} = \left[C_0x + \frac{C_1x^2}{2} + \frac{C_2x^3}{3} + ... + \frac{C_nx^{n+1}}{n+1}\right]_{-1}^{0}$$

$$\Rightarrow \frac{1+0}{n+1} - 0 = -\left(-C_0 + \frac{C_1}{2} - \frac{C_2}{3} + ... + (-1)^{n+1}\frac{C_n}{n+1}\right)$$

$$\Rightarrow \frac{1}{n+1} = C_0 - \frac{C_1}{2} + \frac{C_2}{3} - ..... + (-1)^n \frac{C_n}{n+1}. \text{ Hence } C_0 - \frac{C_1}{2} + \frac{C_2}{3} - ... + (-1)^n \frac{C_n}{n+1} = \frac{1}{n+1}$$

Binomial series containing multiplication of binomial co-efficient

$$\sum_{r=0}^{n} C_r^2 = C_0^2 + C_1^2 + C_2^2 + ... + C_n^2$$

$$\sum_{r=0}^{n-1} C_rC_{r+1} = C_0C_1 + C_1C_2 + C_2C_3 + ... + C_{n-1}C_n$$

$$\sum_{r=0}^{n-2} C_rC_{r+2} = C_0C_2 + C_1C_3 + C_2C_4 + ... + C_{n-2}C_n$$

....

$$\sum_{r=0}^{n-k} C_rC_{r+k} = C_0C_k + C_1C_{k-1} + C_2C_{k+2} + ... + C_{n-k}C_n$$

Case I: When each term of series is positive

$(1 + x)^n = C_0 + C_1x + C_2x^2 + ... + C_nx^n$ (i)

$(x + 1)^n = C_0x^n + C_1x^{n-1} + C_2x^{n-2} .... + C_nx^0$ (ii)

Multiplying (i) and (ii), we get

$(1 + x)^{2n} = x^n(C_0^2 + C_1^2 + C_2^2 + ... + C_n^2)$
$+ x^{n-1}[C_0C_1 + C_1C_2 + C_2C_3 + ...C_{n-1}C_n)$
$+ x^{n-2}[C_0C_2 + C_1C_3 + C_2C_4 + ... + C_{n-2}C_n] + ...$
$+ x^{n-k}[C_0C_k + C_1C_{k+1} + C_2C_{k+2} + ... + C_{n-k}C_n]$

But $(1 + x)^{2n} = {}^{2n}C_0x^0 + {}^{2n}C_1x^1 + {}^{2n}C_2x^2 + ...{}^{2n}C_{n-3}x^{n-3} + {}^{2n}C_{n-2}x^{n-2} + {}^{2n}C_{n-1}x^{n-1} + {}^{2n}C_nx^n$

- $C_0^2 + C_1^2 + C_2^2 + ... + C_n^2 = {}^{2n}C_n$,
- $C_0C_1 + C_1C_2 + C_2C_3 + ... + C_{n-1}C_n = {}^{2n}C_{n-1}$,
- $C_0C_2 + C_1C_3 + C_2C_4 + ... + C_{n-2}C_n = {}^{2n}C_{n-2}$,
- $C_0C_k + C_1C_{k+1} + ... + C_{n-k}C_n = {}^{2n}C_{n-k}$

Case II: If the terms of the series are alternatively positive and negative.

$(1 - x)^n = C_0 - C_1x + C_2x^2 - .... + (-1)^nC_nx^n$ (i)

$(x + 1)^n = C_0x^n + C_1x^{n-1} + C_2x^{n-2} + ... + C_n$ (ii)

Ist Method: Multiply (i) and (ii) and get the co-efficient for the suitable power of x on both sides.

IInd method: Replacing x by $1/x$ in (i), we get

$(1 - 1/x)^n = C_0 - \frac{C_1}{x} + \frac{C_2}{x^2} - ..... + \frac{(-1)^nC_n}{x^n}$ (iii)

multiply (i) and (iii) to equate the co-efficient.

TEXTUAL EXERCISE–3 (SUBJECTIVE)

1. If $(1 + x)^n = C_0 + C_1x + C_2x^2 + \ldots\ldots + C_nx^n$ Then evaluate the sum of following series:

(a) $\sum_{r=0}^{n}(-1)^{r+2}\,C_{2r}$

(b) $\sum_{r=0}^{n}(-1)^r\,{}^nC_r\left(\frac{1}{2}\right)^r$

(c) ${}^nC_0 + 2.\,{}^nC_1 + 4.\,{}^nC_2 + 8.\,{}^nC_3 + \ldots n+1.$ terms

(d) ${}^nC_0 + \frac{{}^nC_1}{2} + \frac{{}^nC_2}{4} + \frac{{}^nC_3}{8} + \ldots n+1$ terms

(e) ${}^nC_0 - \frac{1}{3}{}^nC_1 + \frac{1}{9}{}^nC_2 - \frac{1}{27}{}^nC_3 + \ldots n+1$ terms

(f) $\sum_{r=1}^{n} r(C_r)$

(g) $\sum_{r=3}^{n} r(r-1)(r-2)C_r$

(h) $\sum_{r=1}^{n} r^2\ {}^nC_r$

(i) $\sum_{r=0}^{n}\frac{C_r}{r+1}$

(j) $\sum_{r=0}^{n}\frac{C_r}{(r+1)(r+2)}$

2. If $(1 + x)^n = C_0 + C_1x + C_2x^2 + \ldots\ldots + C_nx^n$ then evaluate the sum of following series:

(a) $\sum_{r=0}^{n} C_r^2 = C_0^2 + C_1^2 + \ldots\ldots + C_n^2$

(b) $\sum_{r=1}^{n} r\left(\frac{{}^nC_r}{{}^nC_{r\text{-}1}}\right) = \frac{{}^nC_1}{{}^nC_0} + 2\frac{{}^nC_2}{{}^nC_1} + \ldots . n\frac{{}^nC_n}{{}^nC_{n\text{-}1}}$

(c) $\sum_{r=1}^{n} r^2\left(\frac{{}^nC_r}{{}^nC_{r-1}}\right) = \frac{{}^nC_1}{{}^nC_0} + 2^2\frac{{}^nC_2}{{}^nC_1} + \ldots . n^2\frac{{}^nC_n}{{}^nC_{n-1}}$

(d) $\sum_{r=1}^{n} r^3\left(\frac{{}^nC_r}{{}^nC_{r-1}}\right) = \frac{{}^nC_1}{{}^nC_0} + 2^3\frac{{}^nC_2}{{}^nC_1} + \ldots . n^3\frac{{}^nC_n}{{}^nC_{n-1}}$

(e) $\sum_{r=1}^{n} r^2\left(\frac{{}^nC_r}{{}^nC_{r-1}}\right)^2 = 1^2\left(\frac{{}^nC_1}{{}^nC_0}\right)^2 +$ $2^2\left(\frac{{}^nC_2}{{}^nC_1}\right)^2 + \ldots . n^2\left(\frac{{}^nC_n}{{}^nC_{n-1}}\right)^2$

(f) $\sum_{r=2}^{n} r(r-1)\frac{{}^nC_r}{{}^nC_{r-2}} = 2.1\frac{{}^nC_2}{{}^nC_0} +$ $3.2\frac{{}^nC_3}{{}^nC_1} + 4.3\frac{{}^nC_4}{{}^nC_2} + \ldots .$

3. Find the co-efficient of x^6 in $(1 + x)^{15} + (1 + x)^{16} + \ldots\ldots\ldots\ldots + (1 + x)^{30}$.

4. Prove that

(a) ${}^nC_m + {}^{n-1}C_m + \ldots\ldots\ldots\ldots + {}^mC_m = {}^{n+1}C_{m+1}$

(b) ${}^nC_m + 2\,{}^{n-1}C_m + 3\,{}^{n-2}C_m + \ldots\ldots + (n - m + 1)\,{}^mC_m = {}^{n+2}C_{m+2}$

5. Prove that ${}^nC_n + {}^{n+1}C_n + {}^{n+2}C_n + \ldots\ldots\ldots + {}^{n+k}C_n = {}^{n+k+1}C_{n+1}$

6. Show that $101^{50} > 99^{50} + 100^{50}$.

7. Find the sum of series:

$$\sum_{r=0}^{n}(-1)^r C_r\left[\frac{1^r}{2^r} + \frac{3^r}{2^{2r}} + \frac{7^r}{2^{3r}} + \ldots\ldots m \text{ terms}\right].$$

8. If $C_0, C_1, C_2, C_3, \ldots . C_n$ denote the co-efficients in the expansion of $(1 + x)^n$, prove that

$$2C_0 + \frac{2^2C_1}{2} + \frac{2^3C_2}{3} + \frac{2^4C_3}{4} + \ldots\ldots + \frac{2^{n+1}C_n}{n+1} = \frac{3^{n+1}-1}{n+1}.$$

9. Find the summation of following series:

(a) $C_0 - C_2 + C_4 - C_6 + \ldots\ldots\ldots$

(b) $C_0 + C_3 + C_6 + \ldots\ldots$

(c) $C_3 + C_7 + C_{11} + \ldots\ldots\ldots$

(d) $C_0 + C_4 + C_8 + \ldots .$

(e) $C_1 + C_4 + C_7 + \ldots\ldots$

(f) $C_2 + C_6 + C_{10} + C_{14} + \ldots .$

(g) $C_2 + C_5 + C_8 + C_{11} + C_{14} \ldots .$ (where C_r denotes ${}^nC_r$)

10. Evaluate the sum of following binomial series:

(a) $\frac{C_0}{1} + \frac{C_2}{3} + \frac{C_4}{5} + \ldots .$

(b) $\frac{C_1}{2} + \frac{C_3}{4} + \frac{C_5}{6} + \ldots .$

(c) $\frac{C_0}{1.2} - \frac{C_1}{2.3} + \frac{C_2}{3.4} - \frac{C_3}{4.5} + \ldots$ to $(n+1)$ terms

(d) $C_0 - 3C_1 + 5C_2 - \ldots\ldots + (-1)^n(2n + 1)C_n$

(e) $C_1^2 - 2C_2^2 + 3C_3^2 - \ldots\ldots - 2n\,C_{2n}^2;\ C_r = {}^{2n}C_r$

Answer Keys

1. (a) $\frac{(1+i)^n+(1-i)^n}{2}$ (b) $(1/2)^n$ (c) 3^n (d) $\left(\frac{3}{2}\right)^n$

(e) $\left(\frac{2}{3}\right)^n$ (f) $n.2^{n-1}$ (g) $n(n-1)(n-2)\,2^{n-3}$ (h) $n(n+1)2^{n-2}$

(i) $\frac{2^{n+1}-1}{n+1}$ (j) $\frac{2^{n+2}-n-3}{(n+1)(n+2)}$

2. (a) ${}^{2n}C_n$ (b) $\frac{n(n+1)}{2}$ (c) $\frac{n(n+1)(n+2)}{6}$ (d) $\frac{n(n+1)^2}{12}(n+2)$

(e) $\frac{n(n+1)(2n+1)}{6}=\sum_{k=1}^{n}k^2$ (f) $\frac{n(n^2-1)}{3}$ **3.** ${}^{31}C_7-{}^{15}C_7$ **7.** $\frac{2^{mn}-1}{2^{mn}(2^n-1)}$

9. (a) $2^{n/2}.\cos\frac{n\pi}{4}$ (b) $\frac{2^n+(-1)^n\left(2\cos\frac{2n\pi}{3}\right)}{3}$ (c) $\frac{1}{2}\left\{2^{n-1}-2^{n/2}\sin\frac{n\pi}{4}\right\}$

(d) $\frac{1}{2}\left\{2^{n-1}+2^{n/2}\cos\frac{n\pi}{4}\right\}$ (e) $\frac{(2)^n-2\cos(n+1)\frac{\pi}{3}}{3}$ (f) $\frac{1}{2}\left\{(2)^{n-1}-(2)^{n/2}\cos\frac{n\pi}{4}\right\}$ (g) $\frac{(2)^n-2\cos(n-1)\frac{\pi}{3}}{3}$

10. (a) $\frac{2^n}{n+1}$ (b) $\frac{2^n-1}{n+1}$ (c) $\frac{1}{n+2}$ (d) 0 (e) $(-1)^{n+1}(2n).\,{}^{2n-1}C_{n-1}$

TEXTUAL EXERCISE–3 (OBJECTIVE)

1. $C_0C_r+C_1C_{r+1}+C_2C_{r+2}+\ldots+C_{n-r}C_n=$

(a) $\frac{(2n)!}{(n-r)!(n+r)!}$ (b) $\frac{n!}{(-r)!(n+r)!}$

(c) $\frac{n!}{(n-r)!}$ (d) None of these

2. ${}^nC_0-\frac{1}{2}{}^nC_1+\frac{1}{3}{}^nC_2-\ldots\ldots+(-1)^n\frac{{}^nC_n}{n+1}$

(a) n (b) $1/n$

(c) $\frac{1}{n+1}$ (d) $\frac{1}{n-1}$

3. If $(1+x)^n=C_0+C_1x+C_2x^2+\ldots.+C_nx^n$, then $\frac{C_1}{C_0}+\frac{2C_2}{C_1}+\frac{3C_3}{C_2}+\ldots.+\frac{nC_n}{C_{n-1}}=$

(a) $\frac{n(n-1)}{2}$ (b) $\frac{n(n+2)}{2}$

(c) $\frac{n(n+1)}{2}$ (d) $\frac{(n-1)(n-2)}{2}$

4. $\frac{C_0}{1}+\frac{C_2}{3}+\frac{C_4}{5}+\frac{C_6}{7}+\ldots.=$

(a) $\frac{2^{n+1}}{n+1}$ (b) $\frac{2^{n+1}-1}{n+1}$

(c) $\frac{2^n}{n+1}$ (d) None of these

5. $\frac{1}{1!(n-1)!}+\frac{1}{3!(n-3)!}+\frac{1}{5!(n-5)!}+\ldots=$

(a) $\frac{2^n}{n!}$: for all even values of n

(b) $\frac{2^{n-1}}{n!}$: for all values of n i.e., all even, odd values

(c) 0

(d) None of these

6. The sum to $(n+1)$ terms of the following series: $\frac{C_0}{2}-\frac{C_1}{3}+\frac{C_2}{4}-\frac{C_3}{5}+\ldots..$ is

(a) $\frac{1}{n+1}$ (b) $\frac{1}{n+2}$

(c) $\frac{1}{n(n+1)}$ (d) None of these

7. If a and d are two complex numbers, then the sum to $(n + 1)$ terms of the following series $aC_0 - (a + d)C_1 + (a + 2d)C_2 - \ldots$ is

(a) $\frac{a}{2^n}$ (b) na

(c) 0 (d) None of these

8. If n is an integer greater than 1, then $a - {}^nC_1(a - 1) + {}^nC_2(a - 2) + \ldots + (-1)^n(a - n) =$

(a) a (b) 0

(c) a^2 (d) 2^n

9. If $C_0, C_1, C_2, \ldots C_n$ are the binomial co-efficients, then $2C_1 + 2^3.C_3 + 2^5.C_5 + \ldots$equals

(a) $\frac{3^n + (-1)^n}{2}$ (b) $\frac{3^n - (-1)^n}{2}$

(c) $\frac{3^n + 1}{2}$ (d) $\frac{3^n - 1}{2}$

10. The expression $C_0 + 2C_1 + 3C_2 + \ldots + (n + 1)C_n$ is equal to

(a) 2^{n-1} (b) $n(2^{n-1})$

(c) $n(2^{n-1}) + 2^n$ (d) $(n + 1)2^n$

11. If $n > 1$, then value of the expression $C_0 - 2C_1 + 3C_2 - 4C_3 + \ldots + (-1)^n (n + 1)C_n$ is

(a) –1 (b) 0

(c) 1 (d) None of these

12. Value of the expression $C_0^2 - 2C_1^2 + \ldots + (n + 1)C_n^2$ is

(a) $(2n + 1)({}^{2n}C_n)$

(b) $(-1)^{n/2}\left(\frac{n}{2}+1\right).{}^nC_{n/2}$, if n is even

(c) $(-1)^{n/2}.(n+2).{}^{n-1}C_{n/2}$, if n is even

(d) $(-1)^{\frac{n+1}{2}}.n.{}^{n-1}C_{\frac{n-1}{2}}$, if n is even

13. If A and B are co-efficients of x^n in the expansions of $(1 + x)^{2n}$ and $(1 + x)^{2n-1}$ respectively, then A/B is equal to

(a) 1 (b) 2

(c) 1/2 (d) $1/n$

14. The co-efficient of x^k in the expansion of $(0 \le k \le n)$ $E = 1 + (1 + x) + (1 + x)^2 + \ldots + (1 + x)^n$ is

(a) ${}^nC_k$ (b) ${}^{n+1}C_k$

(c) ${}^{n+1}C_{k+1}$ (d) None of these

15. Sum of the last 30 co-efficients in the expansion of $(1 + x)^{59}$, when expanded in ascending powers of x, is

(a) 2^{29} (b) 2^{28}

(c) ${}^{60}C_{30} - 2^{19}$ (d) 2^{58}

16. The value of $2C_0 + \frac{2^2}{2}C_1 + \frac{2^3}{3}C_2 + \ldots + \frac{2^{11}}{11}C_{10}$, is

(a) $\frac{1}{11}(2^{11} - 1)$ (b) $\frac{1}{11}(3^{11} - 1)$

(c) $\frac{1}{11}(11^3 - 1)$ (d) $\frac{1}{11}(11^2 - 1)$

17. If $C_r = {}^nC_r$, then value of $2\left(\frac{C_1}{C_0} + 2\frac{C_2}{C_1} + 3\frac{C_3}{C_2} + \ldots n\frac{C_n}{C_{n-1}}\right)$ is

(a) $n(n - 1)$ (b) $n(n + 1)$

(c) $n^2 - 1$ (d) $n^2 + 1$

18. Sum of the series $\sum_{r=0}^{10}(-1)^r\left({}^{10}C_r\right)\left[\frac{1}{3^r} + \frac{8^r}{3^{2r}}\right]$ is

(a) $\frac{6^{10} + 1}{3^{20}}$ (b) $\frac{2^{10} - 1}{3^{20}}$

(c) $\frac{2^{20} - 1}{2^{20}}$ (d) None of these

19. If m and n are positive integers, then value of ${}^mC_0\,{}^nC_k + {}^mC_1\,{}^nC_{k-1} + \ldots + {}^mC_k\,{}^nC_0$

(a) ${}^{m+n}C_k$ (b) ${}^{m+n}C_{m+k}$

(c) ${}^{m+n}C_{n+k}$ (d) None of these

20. If ${}^{2n+1}C_1 + {}^{2n+1}C_2 + \ldots + {}^{2n+1}C_n = 4095$ then value of n is

(a) 6 (b) 7

(c) 5/2 (d) 7/2

21. Let P_n denote the product of all the binomial co-efficients of $(1 + x)^n$, then $\frac{P_{n+2}}{P_n}$ is equal to

(a) $\frac{(n+2)!}{(n+1)^{n+1}}$ (b) $\left(1+\frac{1}{n+1}\right)^{-n+1}$

(c) $\left(1+\frac{1}{n+2}\right)^n$ (d) None of these

22. Value of $C_0 + 7C_1 + 13C_2 + \ldots + (6n + 1)C_n$ is equal to

(a) $(2n + 1)2^{2n}$ (b) $(3n + 1)2^n$

(c) $n.\ 2^n$ (d) $(3n - 1)^{2n}$

Answer Keys

1. (a)	**2.** (c)	**3.** (c)	**4.** (c)	**5.** (b)	**6.** (d)	**7.** (c)	**8.** (b)	**9.** (b)	**10.** (c)
11. (b)	**12.** (b,c,d)	**13.** (b)	**14.** (c)	**15.** (d)	**16.** (b)	**17.** (b)	**18.** (a)	**19.** (a)	**20.** (a)
21. (d)	**22.** (b)								

NUMERICALLY GREATEST TERM OF THE BINOMIAL EXPANSION

Let T_{r+1} be the numerically greatest term in $(a + x)^n$.

$\Rightarrow |T_r| \le |T_{r+1}| \ge |T_{r+2}|$, where $T_{r+1} = {}^nC_r\, a^{n-r} x^r$

$\Rightarrow \dfrac{|T_{r+1}|}{|T_r|} \ge 1;\ 1 \le r \le n$ (1)

Case I: $\dfrac{|T_{r+1}|}{|T_r|} \ge 1 \Rightarrow \left|\dfrac{{}^nC_r a^{n-r} x^r}{{}^nC_{r-1} a^{n-r+1} x^{r-1}}\right| \ge 1$

$\Rightarrow \left|\dfrac{n-r+1}{r}\dfrac{x}{a}\right| \ge 1 \Rightarrow \left|\dfrac{n-r+1}{r}\right|\left|\dfrac{x}{a}\right| \ge 1$ (ii)

$\Rightarrow \left(\dfrac{n+1}{r}-1\right) \ge \left|\dfrac{a}{x}\right| \Rightarrow \dfrac{n+1}{r} \ge \left|\dfrac{a}{x}\right| + 1$

$\Rightarrow r \le \dfrac{n+1}{1+\left|\dfrac{a}{x}\right|}$ as $\dfrac{n+1}{r} > 1$

Case II: $\left|\dfrac{T_{r+2}}{T_{r+1}}\right| \le 1 \Rightarrow \left|\dfrac{{}^nC_{r+1} a^{n-r-1} x^{r+1}}{{}^nC_r a^{n-r} x^r}\right| \le 1$

$\Rightarrow \left|\dfrac{n-r}{r+1}\right|\left|\dfrac{x}{a}\right| \le 1 \Rightarrow \left|\dfrac{n-r+1-1}{r+1}\right| \le \left|\dfrac{a}{x}\right|$

$\Rightarrow \dfrac{n+1}{r+1} - 1 \le \left|\dfrac{a}{x}\right| \Rightarrow \dfrac{n+1}{r+1} \le \left|\dfrac{a}{x}\right| + 1 \Rightarrow r+1 \ge \dfrac{n+1}{1+\left|\dfrac{a}{x}\right|}$

$\Rightarrow r \ge \dfrac{n+1}{1+\left|\dfrac{a}{x}\right|} - 1 \Rightarrow \alpha - 1 \le r \le \alpha$, where $\alpha = \dfrac{n+1}{1+\left|\dfrac{a}{x}\right|}$

Conclusion:

- If α is not an integer. Then $r = [\alpha]$
  $\Rightarrow$ So there is only one numerically greatest term given by $T_{[\alpha]+1} = {}^nC_{[\alpha]}\, a^{n-[\alpha]} x^{[\alpha]}$
- In case α is an integer, then r has 2 possible values,
  $\Rightarrow r = [\alpha]$ and $r = [\alpha] - 1$

$\therefore$ 2 numerically largest terms.

$T_{\alpha+1} = {}^nC_\alpha\, a^{n-\alpha} x^\alpha$ and $T_\alpha = {}^nC_{\alpha-1}\, a^{n-\alpha+1} x^{\alpha-1}$.

NOTE

To find the greatest term in the expansion of $(x + y)^n$.
Since $(x + y)^n = x^n(1 + y/x)^n$ and then find the greatest term in $(1 + y/x)^n$.

ILLUSTRATION 18: If $x = 1/3$, find the greatest term in the expansion of $(1 + 4x)^8$.

SOLUTION: We have $T_r = {}^8C_{r-1}\,(4/3)^{r-1}$ and $T_{r+1} = {}^8C_r\,(4/3)^r$

Now $\dfrac{T_{r+1}}{T_r} = \dfrac{{}^8C_r(4/3)^r}{{}^8C_{r-1}(4/3)^{r-1}} = \dfrac{9-r}{r}.\dfrac{4}{3} \Rightarrow T_{r+1} = \dfrac{9-r}{r}.\dfrac{(4)T_r}{3}$ (A)

Therefore, $T_{r+1} > T_r$ if $\dfrac{9-r}{r} \times \dfrac{4}{3} > 1 \Rightarrow 36 > 7r$ (B)

The greatest value of 'r' satisfying (B) is 5. Therefore $r = 5$ and thus sixth term of the expansion is the greatest term.

ILLUSTRATION 19: Find the greatest term in the expansion of $(3 + 2x)^{15}$ when $x = 5/2$.

SOLUTION: $(3 + 2x)^{15} = 3^{15}\,(1 + 2x/3)^{15}$

It is enough to find the greatest term in the expansion of $(1 + 2x/3)^{15}$ at $x = 5/2$

Proceeding as in earlier example, we get $T_{r+1} = \left(\dfrac{16-r}{r}\right).\dfrac{5}{3}T_r$ (A)

Hence $T_{r+1} > T_r$ if $\left(\dfrac{16-r}{r}\right).\dfrac{5}{3} > 1 \Rightarrow 80 > 8r \Rightarrow r > 10$ (B)

Hence for all values of r up to 9, we have $T_{r+1} > T_r$ but if $r = 10$ if we have $T_{r+1} = T_r$ and these are the greatest terms. Thus the 10th and 11th terms are numerically equal and greater than any other term. The required answer is $T_{10} = T_{11} = 3^{15}\,{}^{15}C_{10}\,(5/3)^{10}$

GREATEST CO-EFFICIENT

To determine the greatest co-efficient in the binomial expansion of $(1 + x)^n$, consider the following:

$$\left(\frac{T_{r+1}}{T_r}\right) = \frac{C_r}{C_{r-1}} = \frac{n-r+1}{r} = \frac{n+1}{r} - 1$$

Now the $(r + 1)$th binomial co-efficient will be greater than the rth binomial co-efficient when,

$$\Rightarrow \quad \frac{n+1}{r} - 1 > 1 \Rightarrow \frac{n+1}{2} > r \qquad \text{(i)}$$

But r must be an integer, and therefore when n is even, the greatest binomial co-efficient is given by the greatest value of r, consistent with (i) i.e., $r = n/2$ and hence the greatest binomial co-efficient is ${}^nC_{n/2}$.

NOTES

(a) If n is even, then greatest co-efficient = ${}^nC_{n/2}$

(b) If n is odd, then greatest co-efficients are ${}^nC_{(n-1)/2}$ *and* ${}^nC_{(n+1)/2}$

ILLUSTRATION 20: If in the expansion of $(1 + x)^{43}$, the co-efficient of $(2r + 1)^{\text{th}}$ term is equal to the co-efficient of $(r + 2)$th term, find r.

SOLUTION: Given in the expansion of $(1 + x)^{43}$

co-efficient of $(2r + 1)$th term = co-efficient of $(r + 2)$th term

$\therefore \quad {}^{43}C_{2r} = {}^{43}C_{r+1} \qquad \Rightarrow 2r + r + 1 = 43 \qquad \Rightarrow \qquad r = 14$

ILLUSTRATION 21: Show that if the greatest term in the expansion of $(1 + x)^{2n}$ has also the greatest co-efficient, then x lies between $\frac{n}{n+1}$ and $\frac{n+1}{n}$.

SOLUTION: In the expansion of $(1 + x)^{2n}$, the middle term is $\left(\frac{2n}{2}+1\right)$th i.e., $(n + 1)$th term, we know that from binomial expansion, middle term has greatest co-efficient.

$(\because$ Terms $T_1, T_2, T_3, \ldots, T_n, T_{n+1}, T_{n+2}, \ldots) \qquad \therefore \quad T_n < T_{n+1} > T_{n+2}$

If $\;T_n < T_{n+1} \qquad \Rightarrow T_{n+1} > T_n$

$$\Rightarrow \quad \frac{T_{n+1}}{T_n} > 1 \quad \left(\because \frac{T_{r+1}}{T_r} = \frac{n-r+1}{r}x, \text{ here } n = 2n\right)$$

$$\Rightarrow \quad \frac{2n-n+1}{n}x > 1 \qquad \Rightarrow x > \frac{n}{n+1} \qquad \text{(i)}$$

and if $T_{n+1} > T_{n+2} \qquad \Rightarrow \frac{T_{n+2}}{T_{n+1}} < 1$

$$\Rightarrow \quad \frac{2n-(n+1)+1}{n+1}x < 1 \qquad \therefore \quad x < \frac{n+1}{n} \qquad \text{(ii)}$$

From (i) and (ii), we get, $\frac{n}{n+1} < x < \frac{n+1}{n}$

■ MULTINOMIAL THEOREM

Multinomial theorem for a positive integral index.

The idea of binomial theorem carries over from binomials to sums of more than two elements

As an example, consider the expression $(x + y + z + w)^{16}$; this by definition, is a product of sixteen identical factors $x + y + z + w$; i.e., $(x + y + z + w)(x + y + z + w)....(x + y + z + w)$ (16 times)

The expansion of this has a term, for example, of the form $x^3y^5z^6w^2$ because the sum of the exponents is $3 + 5 + 6 + 2 = 16$. This particular term occurs in the expansion as often as x can be chosen from three of the sixteen factors, y from five of the remaining thirteen factors, z from six of the remaining eight factors, and w, then taken automatically from the other two factors. Paralleling the argument made in the case of the binomial expansion, we see that this is simply

$$^{16}C_3 \cdot {}^{13}C_5 \cdot {}^{8}C_6\, 1 = \frac{16!}{13!3!} \cdot \frac{13!}{8!5!} \cdot \frac{8!}{6!2!}$$

The expansion of $(x + y + z + w)^{16}$ has been shown to contain the term $\frac{16!}{3!5!6!2!} x^3 y^5 z^6 w^2$.

The co-effcient is equivalent to calculating the number of ways of ordering the following sixteen letters.

$x\,x\,x\,y\,y\,y\,y\,y\,z\,z\,z\,z\,z\,z\,w\,w$

More generally, we can say that the expansion of $(x + y + z + w)^{16}$ is the sum of all terms of the form

$$\frac{16!}{a!b!c!d!} x^a y^b z^c w^d$$

Where a, b, c, d range over all possible sets of non-negative intergers satisfying $a + b + c + d = 16$.As a simple case, we note the solution $a = 16, b = 0, c = 0, d = 0$, belonging to term

$$\frac{16!}{16!0!0!0!} x^{16} y^0 z^0 w^0$$

or more simply x^{16} in the expansion. Other solutions of $a + b + c + d = 16$ are for example, $a = 4, b = 5, c = 5, d = 2$ and $a = 3, b = 5, c = 2, d = 6$ and belong to the terms

$$\frac{16!}{4!5!5!2!} x^4 y^5 z^5 w^2 \text{ and } \frac{16!}{3!5!2!6!} x^3 y^5 z^2 w^6 \text{ respectively}$$

Further generalizations apparent. For any positive integer, (in place of the special number 16) we see that expansion of $(x + y + z + w)^n$ is the sum of all terms of the form

$$\frac{n!}{a!b!c!d!} x^a y^b z^c w^d$$

Where a, b, c, d range over all solutions of $a + b + c + d = n$ in non-negative integers

There is no reason to restrict attention to a sum of four elements x, y, z, w.

For any positive integer n, the multinomial expansion of $(x + y + z + w + ...)^n$ is the sum of all terms of the form

$$\frac{n!}{a!b!c!d!....} \left(x^a y^b z^c w^d ....\right),$$

Where a, b, c, d...... range over all solutions of $a + b + c + d + ...+ = n$ in non-negative integers

The number of terms in the expansion of $(x_1 + x_2 + ... + x_r)^n$

= Number of whole number solutions of

$a_1 + a_2 + ... + a_r = n$

$= {}^{n+r-1}C_n$ or ${}^{n+r-1}C_{r-1}$

EXAMPLES

(i) *The binomial expansion can also be written as* $(x + y)^n = \sum_{\alpha+\beta=n} \frac{n!}{\alpha!\beta!} x^\alpha y^\beta$

Here the summation runs over all those non-negative integers whose sum is n

e.g., $\alpha = 0, \beta = n; \alpha = 1. \beta = n - 1$ *and so on*

(ii) $(x + y + z)^n = \sum_{\alpha+\beta+\gamma=n} \frac{n!}{\alpha!\beta!\gamma!} x^\alpha y^\beta z^\gamma$

(iii) *In the expansion of* $(a - b - c + d)^6$, *the co-efficient of* a^3b^2c *is* $(-1)^3 \frac{6!}{3!2!1!0!} = -60$

ILLUSTRATION 22: Find the co-efficient of x^8 in the expansion of $(1 + x^2 - x^3)^9$

SOLUTION: We have

$$(1 + x^2 - x^3)^9 = \sum_{\alpha+\beta+\gamma=9} \frac{9!}{\alpha!\beta!\gamma!} 1^{\alpha} (x^2)^{\beta}(-x^3)^{\gamma} = \sum_{\alpha+\beta+\gamma=9} \frac{9!}{\alpha!\beta!\gamma!}(-1)^{\gamma} \times x^{2\beta+3\gamma}$$

Now we must have $2\beta + 3\gamma = 8$ also $\alpha + \beta + \gamma = 9$. It is easy to see that there are only two triplets of values of α, β, γ which can satisfy both equations, namely,

(6, 1, 2) and (5, 4, 0). Thus the co-efficient of x^8 is $\frac{9!}{6!1!2!}(-1)^2 + \frac{9!}{5!4!0!}(-1)^0 = 378$

ALTERNATIVE: $(1 + x^2 - x^3)^9 = (1 + x^2)^9 + {}^9C_1 (1 + x^2)^8 (-x^3) + {}^9C_2 (1 + x^2)^7 (-x^3)^2 + {}^9C_3 (1 + x^2)^6 (-x^3)^3 + \ldots$

Now, there is no need to consider fourth term and terms after that, since the smallest power of x in these will be 12. There will not be a term containing x^8.

Therefore co-efficient of x^8 in $(1 + x^2)^9 - {}^9C_1$ (Co-efficient of x^5 in $(1 + x^2)^8\}$ + ${}^9C_2$ (coefficient of x^2 in $(1 + x^2)^7) = {}^9C_4 - {}^9C_1.(0) + {}^9C_2.{}^7C_1 = 378$

ILLUSTRATION 23: Find sum of rational terms in $(\sqrt{2} + \sqrt[3]{3} + \sqrt[6]{5})^{10}$

SOLUTION: The general term of the given expression $= \frac{10!}{\alpha!\beta!\gamma!} 2^{\alpha/2}.3^{\beta/3}.(5)^{\gamma/6}$

where α, β, γ satisfy the following properties:

$0 \le \alpha, \beta, \gamma \le 10$; $\alpha + \beta + \gamma = 10$

$\therefore$ $\alpha = 0, 2, 4, 6, 8, 10$; $\beta = 0, 3, 6$; $\gamma = 0, 6$

Hence possible pairs of (α, β, γ) are (4, 6, 0); (4, 0, 6); (10, 0, 0)

$\therefore$ There exists three rational terms

So, sum of rational terms $= \frac{10!}{4!6!}.2^2.3^2 + \frac{10!}{4!.6!}.2^2.5 + \frac{10!}{10!}.2^5 = 11792$

ILLUSTRATION 24: Find the co-efficient of $a^2b^3c^4\,d$ in the expansion of $(a - b - c + d)^{10}$.

SOLUTION: $(a - b - c + d)^{10} = \sum_{r_1+r_2+r_3+r_4=10} \frac{(10)!}{r_1!r_2!r_3!r_4!} (a)^{r_1} (-b)^{r_2} (-c)^{r_3} (d)^{r_4}$

Since we want to get $a^2\,b^3\,c^4\,d$ this implies that, $r_1 = 2, r_2 = 3, r_3 = 4, r_4 = 1$

$\therefore$ Co-efficient of $a^2\,b^3\,c^4\,d = \frac{-10!}{2!3!4!1!}$

ILLUSTRATION 25: Find the co-efficients of x^7 in the expansion of $(1 + 3x - 2x^3)^{10}$

SOLUTION: Co-efficient of x^7 in the expansion of

$(1 + 3x - 2x^3)^{10}$ is $\sum_{n_1+n_2+n_3=10} \frac{10!}{n!n!n_3!} (1)^{n_1} (3x)^{n_2} (-2x^3)^{n_3}$

where $n_1 + n_2 + n_3 = 10$ and $n_2 + 3n_3 = 7$, the possible values of n_1, n_2 and n_3 are shown here

n_1	n_2	n_3
3	7	0
5	4	1
7	1	2

$\therefore$ The co-effcient of $x^7 = \frac{10!}{3!7!0!}(1)^3 (3)^7 (-2)^0 + \frac{10!}{5!4!1!}(1)^5 (3)^4 (-2)^1 + \frac{10!}{7!1!2!}(1)^7 (3)^1 (-2)^2$

$= 262440 - 204120 + 4320 = 62640$

NOTE

The greatest co-effcient in the expansion of

$(a_1+a_2+a_3+\ldots\ldots\ldots+a_m)^n$ *is* $\dfrac{n!}{(q!)^{m-r}\left((q+1)!\right)^r}$

Where q is the quotient and r is the remainder when n is divided by m.

ILLUSTRATION 26: Find the greatest co-efficient in the expansion of $(a+b+c+d)^{15}$.

SOLUTION: Here $n = 15$ and $m = 4$

($\because$ *a, b, c, d* are four terms)

$15 = 4 \times 3 + 3 \therefore q = 3$ and $r = 3$. Hence the greatest co-efficient $= \dfrac{15!}{(3!)^1(4!)^3}$

ILLUSTRATION 27: Find the numerically greatest term in the expansion of $(4 - 3x)^7$ when $x = \dfrac{2}{3}$, also find its co-efficient.

SOLUTION: $\left|\dfrac{T_{r+1}}{T_r}\right| = \left|\dfrac{{}^7C_r(4)^{7-r}(-3x)^r}{{}^7C_{r-1}(4)^{8-r}(-3x)^{r-1}}\right| = \left|\dfrac{{}^7C_r}{{}^7C_{r-1}}\dfrac{1}{(4)}(-3x)\right| = \left|\dfrac{7!}{r!(7-r)!}\times\dfrac{(r-1)!(8-r)!}{7!}\dfrac{(-3x)}{4}\right|$

$= \left|\dfrac{8-r}{r}\left(\dfrac{-3x}{4}\right)\right| = \dfrac{8-r}{r}\left(\dfrac{3}{4}\right)|x|$

$\therefore\ |T_{r+1}| \ge |T_r|$

$\Rightarrow\ \dfrac{(8-r)}{r}.\dfrac{3}{4}|x| \ge 1$

when $x = 2/3$

$\dfrac{8-r}{r}\dfrac{3}{4}\left|\dfrac{2}{3}\right| \ge 1$, we get —— $\ge 1 \Rightarrow 8 - r \ge 2r$

$\Rightarrow\ 3r \le 8$ $\qquad\qquad \Rightarrow\ r \le 8/3$

$\Rightarrow\ r \le 2$ for $|T_{r+1}| > |T_r|$ $\qquad\qquad \therefore\ |T_1| < |T_2| < |T_3|$

and $|T_{r+1}| \le |T_r| \Rightarrow \dfrac{8-r}{2r} \le 1 \Rightarrow 8 \le 3r$

$\Rightarrow\ r \ge \dfrac{8}{3}$ $\qquad\qquad \Rightarrow\ |T_{r+1}| < |T_r|$ for $r \ge 3$

$|T_3| > |T_4| > |T_5| > |T_6| > |T_7| > |T_8| > |T_9|$

$\therefore\ |T_1| < |T_2| < |T_3| > |T_4| > |T_5| \ldots\ldots|T_9|$

$\therefore$ The numerically greatest term is T_3, having numerical value ${}^7C_2(4)^5(3x)^2$

$= {}^7C_2(4)^5(9)x^2 = \dfrac{7\times 6}{2\times 1}\times(4)^5\,9\times\dfrac{4}{9} = 86016.$

ALITER:

We know that T_{r+1} has greatest numerical value where $r = \left[\frac{(n+1)|x|}{|x|+|a|}\right]$; [.] = gint

function $\Rightarrow r = \left[\frac{(7+1)|-3x|}{|-3x|+|4|}\right] = \left[\frac{8\left(3.\frac{2}{3}\right)}{3\left(\frac{2}{3}\right)+4}\right] = \left[\frac{16}{6}\right] = 2$

$\therefore$ T_3 will be the term with greatest numerical value and $T_3 = {}^7C_2\,(4)^5\,(3x)^2 = 86016$ for $x = 2/3$.

ILLUSTRATION 28: Find all rational terms in the expansion of $\left(\sqrt{x}+\frac{1}{2\sqrt[4]{x}}\right)^n$ if the first 3 co-efficients form an arithmetic progression, where x is a prime number.

SOLUTION: Given that first 3 co-efficients

${}^nC_0, {}^nC_1\left(\frac{1}{2}\right), {}^nC_2\left(\frac{1}{2}\right)^2$ are in A.P $\quad \Rightarrow 1, \frac{n}{2}, \frac{n(n-1)}{8}$ are in A.P

$\Rightarrow n = 1 + \frac{n(n-1)}{8}$ $\quad \Rightarrow 8n = n^2 - n + 8$

$\Rightarrow n^2 - 9n + 8 = 0$ $\quad \Rightarrow (n-1)(n-8) = 0$

$\Rightarrow n = 1$ or $n = 8$

But $n = 1$ is impossible, otherwise other expansion would not contain three terms, i.e., $n = 1$ is an extraneous root.

$\therefore$ $n = 8$

$\therefore$ n = 8, thus $T_{r+1} = {}^nC_r(\sqrt{x})^{n-r}\left(\frac{1}{2\sqrt[4]{x}}\right)^r = {}^8C_r.\frac{1}{(2)^r}(x)^{\left(4-\frac{3r}{4}\right)} = {}^8C_r\,\frac{1}{(2)^r}(x)^{\frac{16-3r}{4}}$

$\therefore$ For rational terms; $16 - 3r$ must be divisible by 4 and $0 \le r \le 8$

$\Rightarrow r = 0, r = 4, r = 8 \;\Rightarrow T_1, T_5$ and T_9 are rational terms

TEXTUAL EXERCISE–4 (SUBJECTIVE)

1. (a) If $T_{k+1} > T_k$ and $T_{k+1} > T_{k+2}$ in the expansion of $(1+\sqrt{3})^{100}$, then find the value of k.

   (b) Find the greatest term in the expansion of $\sqrt{3}\left(1+\frac{1}{\sqrt{3}}\right)^{20}$.

2. (a) Find the greatest term in the expansion of $(2 + 3x)^9$ if $x = 3/2$.

   (b) Find the greatest term in the expansion of $(1 + 4x)^8$ if $x = 1/3$.

3 (i) Find the co-efficient of following term in the expansion of $(x + y + z)^{12}$.

   (a) $x^3y^4z^5$ (b) $x^4y^6z^2$

   (c) x^5yz^6 (d) $x^3y^2z^5$

   (e) x^2y^7z

   (ii) Find the co-efficient of

   (a) $a^{10}\,b^7\,c^3$ in the expansion of $(bc + ca + ab)^{10}$.

   (b) $(a^3.b^6\,c^8.d^9.e^4.f)$ in the expansion of $(a + b + c - d - e - f)^{31}$

   (c) $(a^3.b^6\,c^8.d^9.e.f)$ in the expansion of $(a + b + c - d - e - f)^{20}$

4. Find the co-efficient of $a^3b^3c^2d$ in the expansion of $(a - b + c - d)^9$.

5. (a) Find the greatest co-efficient in $(x_1 + x_2 + ... + x_m)^n$

   (b) Find the greatest co-efficient in the expansion of $(a + b + c + d)^{15}$.

6 Find the co-efficient of x^{50} in the polynomials after parenthesis have been removed and like terms have been collected in the expansions.

   (a) $(1 + x)^{1000} + x(1 + x)^{999} + x^2(1 + x)^{998} + ... + x^{1000}$

   (b) $(1 + x) + 2(1 + x)^2 + 3(1 + x)^3 + ... + 1000(1 + x)^{1000}$

7. Find the value of

$$\frac{18^3+7^3+3.18.7.25}{3^6+6.243.2+15.81.4+20.27.8+15.9.16+6.3.32.+64}.$$

8. Find the total number of terms in the expansion of $(x+y+z+w)^n$, $n \in \mathbb{N}$.

9. Find the number of terms in the expansion of $(\sqrt[4]{9}+\sqrt[6]{8})^{500}$ which are integers.

Answer Keys

1. (a) $k = 64$ (b) 8th term $= \frac{^{20}C_7}{27}$ **2.** (a) 7 th term $= {}^9C_3\,(81/2)^3$ (b) 6th term $= {}^8C_3\,(4/3)^5$

3. (i) (a) $\frac{12!}{3!4!5!}$ (b) $\frac{12!}{2!4!6!}$ (c) $\frac{12!}{5!6!}$ (d) zero (e) zero

(ii) (a) 120 (b) $\frac{(31)!}{3!6!8!9!4!}$ (c) 0 **4.** $\frac{9!}{3!3!2!}$

5 (a) $\frac{n!}{(q!)^{m-r}((q+1)!)^r}$ (b) $\frac{15!}{(3!)^1(4!)^3}$ **6.** (a) $\frac{1001!}{50!951!}$ (b) $\frac{(51050)\,1001!}{52!950!}$

7. 1 **8.** $\frac{(n+3)(n+2)(n+1)}{6}$ **9.** 251

TEXTUAL EXERCISE–4 (OBJECTIVE)

1. The greatest co-efficient in the expansion of $(1+x)^{2n+2}$ is

(a) $\frac{(2n)!}{(n!)^2}$ (b) $\frac{(2n+2)!}{\{(n+1)!\}^2}$

(c) $\frac{(2n+2)!}{n!(n+1)!}$ (d) $\frac{(2n)!}{n!(n+1)!}$

2. If n is even positive integer, then the condition that the greatest term in the expansion of $(1+x)^n$ may have the greatest co-efficient also is

(a) $\frac{n}{n+2}<|x|<\frac{n+2}{n}$ (b) $\frac{n+1}{n}<|x|<\frac{n}{n+1}$

(c) $\frac{n}{n+4}<|x|<\frac{n+4}{4}$ (d) None of these

3. The interval in which x must lie so that the greatest term in the expansion of $(1+x)^{2n}$ has the greatest co-efficient, is

(a) $\left(\frac{n-1}{n},\frac{n}{n-1}\right)$ (b) $\left(\frac{n}{n+1},\frac{n+1}{n}\right)$

(c) $\left(\frac{n}{n+2},\frac{n+2}{n}\right)$ (d) None of these

4. The greatest co-efficient in the expansion of $(1+x)^{2n+1}$ is

(a) $\frac{(2n+1)!}{n!(n+1)!}$ (b) $\frac{(2n+2)!}{n!(n+1)!}$

(c) $\frac{(2n+1)!}{[(n+1)!]^2}$ (d) $\frac{(2n)!}{(n!)^2}$

5. Given that the 4th term in the expansion of $\left(2+\frac{3x}{8}\right)^{10}$ has the maximum numerical value; then x lies in the interval

(a) $\left(2,\frac{64}{21}\right)$ (b) $\left(-\frac{60}{23},-2\right)$

(c) $\left(-\frac{64}{21},-2\right)$ (d) $\left(2,-\frac{60}{23}\right)$

Answer Keys

1. (b) **2.** (a) **3.** (b) **4.** (a) **5.** (a, c)

AN IMPORTANT APPLICATION OF BINOMIAL THEOREM

To analyse the problems related to integrated fraction, roots of number the application of binomial theorem can be understood by the following illustration.

ILLUSTRATION 29: If $R = (5 + 2\sqrt{6})^{2n+1}$ and $f = R\text{-}[R]$, where $[R]$ denotes the greatest integer less than or equal to x. Prove that $R(1 - f) = 1$.

SOLUTION: Clearly, $[R] = I$ (say) and f are respectively the integral and fractional parts of $(5 + 2\sqrt{6})^n$.

Let $G = (5 - 2\sqrt{6})^n$. Since $0 < (5 - 2\sqrt{6}) < 1$, therefore $0 < G < 1$

Now, $I + f + G = (5 + 2\sqrt{6})^n + (5 - 2\sqrt{6})^n$

$= 2\ [{}^nC_0\, 5^n + {}^nC_2\, 5^{n-2}\, (2\sqrt{6})^2 + {}^nC_4\, 5^{n-4}\, (2\sqrt{6})^4 + ...1$

$=$ an even integer λ (say)

$$\Rightarrow f + G = \lambda - I \Rightarrow f + G \text{ is an integer } \begin{bmatrix} \because & \lambda \in \mathbb{Z}, I \in \mathbb{Z} \\ \Rightarrow & \lambda - I \in \mathbb{Z} \end{bmatrix} \Rightarrow f + G = 1$$

$[\because\ 0 < f < 1, 0 < G < 1 \Rightarrow 0 < f + G < 2 \Rightarrow f + G$ is an integer between 0 and $2 \Rightarrow f + G = 1]$

$\Rightarrow\ G = 1 - f$. Now, $(I + f)\,(1 - f) = R.G = R(1 - f) = (5 + 2\sqrt{6})^n\,(5 - 2\sqrt{6})^n = 1^n = 1$

Algorithm to solve the problems of this kind

Step1: Write the given expression equal to $\boldsymbol{I + F}$, where I is its integral part and F is the fractional part.

Step2: Define $\boldsymbol{G}$ by replacing '+' sign in the given expression by '–' . Note that G always lies between 0 and 1.

Step3: Either add $\boldsymbol{G}$ to the expression in Step 1 or subtract G from the expression in step 1 so that RHS is an integer.

Step 4: If $\boldsymbol{G}$ is added to the expression in Step 1, then $\boldsymbol{G + F}$ will always come out to be equal to 1 i.e., $\boldsymbol{G = 1 - F}$. If G is subtracted from the expression in Step 1, then G will always come out to be equal to $\boldsymbol{F}$.

Step 5: Obtain the value of the desired expression after getting F in terms of G.

ILLUSTRATION 30: Show that integral part of $(3+\sqrt{7})^n$ is always odd.

SOLUTION: Note that $0 < 3-\sqrt{7} < 1$ and therefore $0 < (3-\sqrt{7})^n < 1$ for all n.

Let $(3+\sqrt{7})^n = I + \beta$

where I is the integral part and β be the fractional part i.e., $0 < \beta < 1$.

We have $(3+\sqrt{7})^n + (3-\sqrt{7})^n = 2\left[3^n + {}^nC_2 3^{n-2}(\sqrt{7})^2 + ...\right] = E$(say) (even number)

The bracketed quantity on RHS is an integer since $(\sqrt{7})^2, (\sqrt{7})^4 ....$ are integers.

Now we can write $I + \beta + \beta' = E$; where $0 < \beta < 1$ and $\beta' = (3-\sqrt{7})^n \in (0,1)$

$\Rightarrow\ \beta + \beta'$ must be an integer

$\Rightarrow\ \beta + \beta' = 1$ essentially, since both β and β' lie between 0 and 1

$\Rightarrow\ I + 1 = E \Rightarrow I = E - 1\ \therefore$ I is odd.

ILLUSTRATION 31: If $(6\sqrt{6}+14)^{2n+1} = N$ and $F = N-[N]$. Show that $NF = 20^{2n+1}$; where $[N]$ denotes greatest integer $\le N$.

SOLUTION: It is clear that F is the fractional part of the irrational number N.

Consider $(6\sqrt{6}+14)^{2n+1} - (6\sqrt{6}-14)^{2n+1}$

$= 2\left[{}^{2n+1}C_1(6\sqrt{6})^{2n}(14) + {}^{2n+1}C_3(6\sqrt{6})^{2n-2}(14)^3 + ...\right]$ which is an integer.

Now since $0 < 6\sqrt{6}-14 < 1, 0 < (6\sqrt{6}-14)^{2n+1} < 1$ for all n,

$\therefore\ [N]+F-(6\sqrt{6}-14)^{2n+1} \in \mathbb{Z} \qquad \Rightarrow F-(6\sqrt{6}-14)^{2n+1} \in \mathbb{Z}$

Also $-1 < F-(6\sqrt{6}-14)^{2n+1} < 1 \qquad \Rightarrow F = (6\sqrt{6}-14)^{2n+1}$

$\therefore\ NF = (6\sqrt{6}+14)^{2n+1}(6\sqrt{6}-14)^{2n+1} = [(6\sqrt{6})^2-(14)^2]^{2n+1} = 20^{2n+1}$

Series involving product of binomial co-efficients

Such series are obtained by multiplying two expansions, one involving the first factors as co-efficients and the other involving the second factors as co-efficients and finally equating the co-efficients of a suitable power of x on both sides.

Illustrations related to such type are categorised in following discussed cases.

Case (i): If difference of the lower suffices of binomial co-efficients in each term is the same

ILLUSTRATION 32: Evaluate the sum ${}^nC_0{}^nC_2 + {}^nC_1{}^nC_3 + {}^nC_2{}^nC_4 + {}^nC_3{}^nC_5 + ... + {}^nC_{n-2}{}^nC_n$

SOLUTION: Here 2 – 0 = 3 – 1 = 4 – 2 = 5 – 3 = ... = n – (n – 2) = 2

Since each term of series is positive consider

$(1 + x)^n = C_0 + C_1x + C_2x^2 + ... + C_nx^n$ (1)

Interchanging 1 and x, we have $(x + 1)^n = C_0x^n + C_1x^{n-1} + C_2x^{n-2} + ... + C_n$ (2)

Multiplying (1) and (2), we have

$(1 + x)^n(x + 1)^n = (C_0 + C_1x + C_2x^2 + ... + C_nx^n) \times (C_0x^n + C_1x^{n-1} + C_2x^{n-2} + ... + C_n)$

Equating the co-efficient of x^{n-2} on both sides, we get $C_0C_2 + C_1C_3 + C_2C_4 + ... + C_{n-2}C_n$

Thus the required sum is equal to co-efficient of x^{n-2} in $(1 + x)^{2n}$ which is equal to ${}^{2n}C_{n-2}$

Study Tip

(i) ${}^nC_0{}^nC_r + {}^nC_1{}^nC_{r+1} + ... + {}^nC_{n-r}{}^nC_n$ = co-effcient of x^{n-r} in $(1 + x)^{2n} = {}^{2n}C_{n-r}$

(ii) $({}^nC_0)^2 + ({}^nC_1)^2 + ({}^nC_2)^2 + ... + ({}^nC_r)^2 + ... + ({}^nC_n)^2 = {}^{2n}C_n$

ILLUSTRATION 33: Prove that $({}^{2n}C_0)^2 - ({}^{2n}C_1)^2 + ({}^{2n}C_2)^2 - ... + (-1)^{2n}({}^{2n}C_{2n})^2 = (-1)^n\,{}^{2n}C_n$.

SOLUTION: Since the terms of the series are alternately positive and negative, we consider one of the expansions with alternate sings.

$(1 - x)^{2n} = {}^{2n}C_0 - {}^{2n}C_1x + {}^{2n}C_2x^2 - .... + (-1)^{2n}.\ {}^{2n}C_{2n}x^{2n}$, (1)

and $(x + 1)^{2n} = {}^{2n}C_0x^{2n} + {}^{2n}C_1x^{2n-1} + {}^{2n}C_2x^{2n-2} + ... + {}^{2n}C_{2n}$ (2)

Multiplying (1) and (2), we get

$(x^2-1)^{2n} = ({}^{2n}C_0 - {}^{2n}C_1x + {}^{2n}C_2x^2 - ... + (-1)^{2n}\,.{}^{2n}C_{2n}x^{2n}).({}^{2n}C_0\,x^{2n} + {}^{2n}C_1x^{2n-1} + ... + {}^{2n}C_{2n})$ (3)

Now, co-efficient of x^{2n}in **R. H. S.**

$= ({}^{2n}C_0)^2 - ({}^{2n}C_1)^2 + ({}^{2n}C_2)^2 - .... + (-1)^{2n}\,({}^{2n}C_{2n})^2,$

$\because$ General term in **L.H.S.,** $T_{r+1} = {}^{2n}C_r(x^2)^{2n-r}(-1)^r$

Putting $2\,(2n-r) = 2n$ $\quad\therefore\;$ $r = n,\ T_{n+1} = {}^{2n}C_nx^{2n}(-1)^n$

Hence co-efficient of x^{2n} **L.H.S.** $= (-1)^n\cdot{}^{2n}C_n$ But (3) is an identity, therefore co-efficient of x^{2n} in **R.H. S.** = Cofficient of x^{2n} in **L.H.S**

$\Rightarrow ({}^{2n}C_0)^2 - ({}^{2n}C_1)^2 + ({}^{2n}C_2)^2 - ... + (-1)^{2n}\,({}^{2n}C_{2n})^2 = (-1)^n.\,{}^{2n}C_n$

Case II : If sum of the lower suffices of binomial coefficients in each term is the same

ILLUSTRATION 34: Evaluate the sum

$$C_0C_n + C_1C_{n-1} + C_2C_{n-2} + ... + C_nC_0$$

SOLUTION: Here $0 + n = 1 + (n-1) = 2 + (n-2) = ... = n + 0 = n.$

Since each term of series is positive, consider

$(1+x)^n = C_0 + C_1x + C_2x^2 + ... + C_nx^n,$ (1)

and $(x+1)^n = C_0x^n + C_1x^{n-1} + ... + C_n$ (2)

Multiplying (1) and (2), we get

$(1+x)^{2n} = (C_0 + C_1x + C_2x^2 + ... + C_nx^n) \times (C_0x^n + C_1x^{n-1} + C_2x^{n-2} + ... + C_n)$

and equating the co-efficients of x^n on both sides, we get ${}^{2n}C_n = C_0C_0 + C_1C_1 + C_2C_2 + ... + C_nC_n$

$= C_0C_n + C_1C_{n-1} + C_2C_{n-2} + ... + C_nC_0$

ILLUSTRATION 35: Prove that $C_0C_n - C_1C_{n-1} + C_2C_{n-2} - ... + (-1)^nC_n = 0$ or $(-1)^{n/2}\dfrac{n!}{(n/2)!(n/2)!}$ according as n is odd or even.

SOLUTION: Since the terms of the series are alternately positive and negative, we consider one of the expansions with alternate signs.

$(1+x)^n = C_0 + C_1x + C_2x^2 + ... + C_{n-2}x^{n-2} + C_{n-1}x^{n-1} + C_nx^n$ (1)

$(1-x)^n = C_0 - C_1x + C_2x^2 + ... + (-1)^n\,C_nx^n$ (2)

Multiplying (1) and (2), we get,

$(1-x^2)^n = (C_0 + C_1x + ...C_{n-2}x^{n-2} + C_{n-1}x^{n-1} + C_nx^n).(C_0 - C_1x + C_2x^2 - ... + (-1)^n\,C_nx^n)$ (3)

Now, co-efficient of x^n in R.H.S $= C_0C_n - C_1C_{n-1} + C_2C_{n-2} - ... + (-1)^nC_nC_0$

Now general term in L.H.S. $= T_{r+1} = {}^nC_r(-x^2)^r = (-1)^r.{}^nC_rx^{2r}$; put $2r = n$

$\Rightarrow r = n/2,\ T_{n/2+1} = (-1)^{n/2}.{}^nC_{n/2}x^n$

$\therefore$ The co-ffcient of x^n in L.H.S. $= (-1)^{n/2}.{}^nC_{n/2} = (-1)^{n/2}\dfrac{n!}{(n/2)!(n/2)!}$

$$= \begin{cases} 0 & \text{if } n \text{ is odd} \\ (-1)^{n/2} \dfrac{n!}{(n/2)!(n/2)!} & \text{if } n \text{ is even} \end{cases}$$

But (3) is an identity, therefore the co-efficient of x^n in R.H.S = co-efficient of x^n in L.H.S.

$\Rightarrow C_0C_n - C_1C_{n-1} + C_2C_{n-2} - .... + (-1)^n C_nC_0$

$$= \begin{cases} 0 & \text{if } n \text{ is odd} \\ (-1)^{n/2} \dfrac{n!}{(n/2)!(n/2)!} & \text{if } n \text{ is even} \end{cases}$$

ILLUSTRATION 36: If $(1 + x)^n = C_0 + C_1x + C_2x^2 + ... + C_nx^n$, then show that the sum of the products of the C_i's taken two at a time represented by $\sum\sum_{0\le i<j\le n} C_iC_j$ is equal to $2^{n-1} - \dfrac{2n!}{2.n!n!}$.

SOLUTION: Since $(C_0 + C_1 + C_2 + ... + C_{n-1} + C_n)^2$

$= (C_0^2 + C_1^2 + C_2^2 + ... + C_{n-1}^2 + C_n^2) + 2\,(C_0C_1 + C_0C_2 + C_0C_3 + ... + C_0C_n + C_1C_2 + ...+ C_{n-1}C_n$

$= {}^{2n}C_n + 2\sum\sum_{0\le i<j\le n} C_iC_j$

Hence $\sum\sum_{0\le i<j\le n} C_iC_j = 2^{n-1} - \dfrac{2n!}{2.n!n!}$

ILLUSTRATION 37: Prove that $\sum\sum_{0\le i<j\le n} (i+j)C_iC_j = n\left(2^{2n-1} - \frac{1}{2}\,{}^{2n}C_n\right)$

SOLUTION: Let $P = \sum\sum_{0\le i<j\le n} (i+j)C_iC_j$

Replacing i by $n - i$ and j by $n - j$, we get,

$P = \sum\sum_{0\le i<j\le n} (n-i+n-j)C_{n-i}C_{n-j} = \sum\sum_{0\le i<j\le n} \{2n-(i+j)\}C_iC_j$

$= 2n\left(2^{2n-1} - \dfrac{{}^{2n}C_n}{2}\right) - P \Rightarrow 2P = n.2^{2n} - n.\,{}^{2n}C_n$

$\therefore\ P = n\left(2^{2n-1} - \frac{1}{2}\,{}^{2n}C_n\right)$

Hence $\sum\sum_{0\le i<j\le n} (i+j)C_iC_j = n\left(2^{2n-1} - \frac{1}{2}\,{}^{2n}C_n\right)$

Series involving products of binomial co-efficients with variable upper indices

ILLUSTRATION 38: Show that (i) $C_0\,{}^{2n}C_n - C_1\,.\,{}^{2n-1}C_n + C_2\,.\,{}^{2n-2}C_n - C_3\,.\,{}^{2n-3}C_n + ... + (-1)^n C_n\,.\,{}^nC_n = 1$

(ii) $C_0\,{}^{2n}C_n - C_1\,.\,{}^{2n-2}C_n + C_2\,.\,{}^{2n-4}C_n - .... = 2^n$

SOLUTION: (i) Here, all co-efficients have the same lower suffix

${}^{2n}C_n$ = co-effcient of x^n in$(1 + x)^{2n}$

${}^{2n-1}C_n$ = co-efficient of x^n in $(1 + x)^{2n-1}$

${}^{2n-2}C_n$ = co-efficient of x^n in $(1 + x)^{2n-2}$

${}^{2n-3}C_n$ = co-efficient of x^n in $(1 + x)^{2n-3}$

....

^nC_n = co-efficient of x^n in $(1 + x)^n$

L.H.S $= C_0\,{}^{2n}C_n - C_1\,.\,{}^{2n-1}C_n + C_2.\,{}^{2n-2}C_n - C_3.\,{}^{2n-3}C_n + \ldots + (-1)^n C_n\,.{}^nC_n$

= Coefficient of x^n in $[C_0(1+x)^{2n} - C_1(1+x)^{2n-1}$
$+ C_2(1+x)^{2n-2} - C_3(1+x)^{2n-3} + \ldots. + (-1)^n C_n(1+x)^n]$

= co-efficient of x^n in $(1+x)^n[C_0(1+x)^n - C_1(1+x)^{n-1}$
$+ C_2(1+x)^{n-2} - C_3(1+x)^{n-3} + \ldots. + (-1)^n C_n$.

= co-efficient of x^n in $(1+x)^n[(1+x)-1]^n$ = co-efficient of x^n in $(1+x)^n x^n = 1$ = R.H.S

(ii) L.H.S $= C_0\,{}^{2n}C_n - C_1\,.{}^{2n-2}C_n + C_2.{}^{2n-4}C_n - \ldots\ldots\ldots.$

= Co-efficient of x^n in $[C_0(1+x)^{2n} - C_1(1+x)^{2n-2} + C_2(1+x)^{2n-4} - \ldots.]$

= Co-efficient of x^n in $[(1+x)^2 - 1]^n$

= Co-efficient of x^n in $(2x + x^2)^n$ = Co-efficient of x^0 in $(2+x)^n = 2^n$ = R.H.S.

ILLUSTRATION 39: If C_r stands for ^nC_r, then simplify $^nC_0.{}^{2n}C_r - {}^nC_1\,.\,{}^{2n-2}C_r + \ldots$

SOLUTION: $^nC_0\,.\,{}^{2n}C_r - {}^nC_1\,.{}^{2n-2}C_r + \ldots$

= Co-efficient of x^r in $[C_0(1+x)^{2n} - C_1(1+x)^{2n-2} + C_2$
$(1+x)^{2n-4} \ldots\ldots + (-1)^n C_n(1+x)^0]$

= Co-efficient of x^r in $[(1+x)^2 - 1]^n$ = Co-efficient of x^r in $x^n(2+x)^n$

= Co-efficient of x^{r-n} in $(2+x)^n = \begin{cases} {}^nC_{r-n}2^{2n-r} & \text{if } r > n \\ 0 & \text{if } r < n \end{cases}$

ILLUSTRATION 40: Find the sum of the series

$^nC_0\,.\,{}^{n+1}C_n + {}^nC_1\,.{}^nC_{n-1} + {}^nC_2\,.\,{}^{n-1}C_{n-2} + {}^nC_3.{}^{n-2}C_{n-3} + \ldots\ldots.. + {}^nC_n.{}^1C_0$

SOLUTION: Let $S = {}^nC_0.{}^{n+1}C_n + {}^nC_1\,.\,{}^nC_{n-1} + {}^nC_2\,{}^{n-1}C_{n-2} + {}^nC_3\,.\,{}^{n-2}C_{n-3} + \ldots.. + {}^nC_n.{}^1C_0$

Also $S = {}^nC_0.{}^1C_0 + {}^nC_{n-1}\,{}^2C_1 + {}^nC_{n-2}.{}^3C_1 + \ldots\ldots.. + {}^nC_0.{}^{n+1}C_1$

Adding the two series

$2S = {}^nC_0({}^{n+1}C_1 + {}^1C_0) + {}^nC_1({}^nC_1 + {}^2C_1) + \ldots + {}^nC_n.({}^{n+1}C_1 + {}^1C_1)$

$= (n+2)\,[{}^nC_0 + {}^nC_1 + {}^nC_2 + \ldots. + {}^nC_n]$

$S = (n+2)2^{n-1}$

TEXTUAL EXERCISE–5 (SUBJECTIVE)

1. (a) If $(5+2\sqrt{6})^n = I + f$, where $I \in \mathbb{N}$, $n \in \mathbb{N}$ and $0 \le f < 1$, then prove that $I = \dfrac{1}{1-f} - f$.

(b) Show that $(\sqrt{2}+1)^6 + (\sqrt{2}-1)^6 = 198$. Hence find the integral part of $(\sqrt{2}+1)^6$.

(c) Show that $[(\sqrt{3}+1)^{2n}] + 1$ is divisible by 2^{n+1} for all $n \in \mathbb{N}$. (where [ ] denotes the G.I.F)

(d) Let $R = (5\sqrt{5}+11)^{2n+1}$ and $f = R - [R]$, then prove that $Rf = 4^{2n+1}$. (where [ ] denotes the G.I.F)

2. If $(1 + x)^n = C_0 + C_1x + C_2x^2 + \ldots.. + C_nx^n$, then evaluate the sum of following series:

(a) $\sum_{r=0}^{n-1} C_r C_{r+1} = C_0C_1 + C_1C_2 + \ldots. + C_{n-1}C_n$

(b) $\sum_{r=0}^{n-2} C_r C_{r+2} = C_0C_2 + C_1C_3 + \ldots. + C_{n-2}C_n$

(c) $\sum_{r=0}^{n-3} C_r C_{r+3} = C_0C_3 + C_1C_4 + \ldots. + C_{n-3}C_n$

3. Evaluate the sum of the following binomial series:

(a) $(C_0 + C_1)(C_1 + C_2)(C_2 + C_3) \ldots\ldots (C_{n-1} + C_n)$

(b) $\sum\sum_{0 \le i < j \le n} C_iC_j$

4. Prove that $({}^3C_3 + {}^4C_3 + {}^5C_3 + ... + {}^nC_3)\,({}^nC_3 + {}^nC_4 + {}^nC_5 + ... + {}^nC_n) = \left[\dfrac{(n+1)!}{4!(n-3)!}\right]\left[2^n - \dfrac{n(n-1)}{2} - n - 1\right]$

5. If $(1 + x)^n = C_0 + C_1x + C_2x^2 + ...C_nx^n$ then evaluate the following binomial series:

(a) $\sum\sum_{0 \le i < j \le n} (C_i + C_j)^2$

(b) $\sum\sum_{0 \le i < j \le n} (C_i + C_j)$

(c) $\sum\sum_{0 \le i < j \le n} (i + j)(C_i + C_j)$

(d) $\sum\sum_{0 \le i < j \le n} (C_i - C_j)^2$

(e) $\sum\sum_{0 \le i < j \le n} (i + j)C_iC_j$

6. If $(1 + x)^n = \sum_{r=0}^{n} {}^nC_r.x^r$ & $\sum_{r=0}^{n} \dfrac{1}{{}^nC_r} = a,$ then evaluate $\sum\sum_{0 \le i < j \le n} \left(\dfrac{i}{{}^nC_i} + \dfrac{j}{{}^nC_j}\right)$ in term of a and n.

7. Evaluate $\sum_{r=1}^{n} \dfrac{P_r}{r}.{}^nC_r$; where P_r denotes the sum of the first r natural numbers.

Answer Keys

1. (b) 197

2. (a) ${}^{2n}C_{n-1}$ (b) ${}^{2n}C_{n-2}$ (c) ${}^{2n}C_{n-3}$

3. (a) $\dfrac{(n+1)^n}{n!}.C_1.C_2....C_n$ (b) $\dfrac{2^{2n} - {}^{2n}C_n}{2}$

5. (a) $(n - 1).{}^{2n}C_n + 2^{2n}$ (b) $n(2^n)$ (c) $n^2(2^n)$

(d) $(n + 1){}^{2n}C_n - 2^{2n}$ (e) $n\left(2^{2n-1} - \dfrac{1}{2}\,{}^{2n}C_n\right)$

6. $\left(\dfrac{n^2}{2}\right)a$

7. $(n+2)2^{n-2} - \dfrac{1}{2}$

TEXTUAL EXERCISE–5 (OBJECTIVE)

1. The integer next above $(\sqrt{3}+1)^{2m}$ contains

(a) 2^{m+1} as a factor (b) 2^{m+2} as a factor
(c) 2^{m+3} as a factor (d) 2^m as a factor

2. If n is positive integer and $(3\sqrt{3} + 5)^{2n+1} = \alpha + \beta,$ where α is an integer and $0 < \beta < 1$, then

(a) α is an even integer

(b) $(\alpha + \beta)^2$ is divisible by 2^{2n+1}

(c) The integer just below $(3\sqrt{3} + 5)^{2n+1}$ divisible by 3

(d) α is divisible by 10

3. If $(8 + 3\sqrt{7})^n = P + F$, where P is an integer and F is a proper fraction, then

(a) P is an odd integer (b) P is an even integer
(c) $F.(F + P) = 1$ (d) $(1- F)(P + F) = 1$

4. Integral part of $(6\sqrt{6}+14)^{2n+1}$ is

(a) an even integer (b) an odd integer
(c) a prime integer (d) None of these

5. If $[x]$ denotes greatest integer $\le x$, then $[(2+\sqrt{3})^P] - 2^{P+1} + 1$, where P is prime number greater than 2 is

(a) is not divisible by P

(b) is divisible by P

(c) cannot say anything

(d) None of these

6. If $x = (2 + \sqrt{3})^n$, $n \in \mathbb{N}$ and $f = x - [x]$ then $\dfrac{f^2}{1-f}$ is

(a) an irrational number

(b) a non-integer rational number

(c) an odd number

(d) an even number

Answer Keys

1. (a) **2.** (a, c, d) **3.** (a, d) **4.** (a) **5.** (b) **6.** (d)

MULTIPLE-CHOICE QUESTIONS

SECTION–I

OBJECTIVE-TYPE SOLVED EXAMPLES

1. Co-efficient of x^5 in the expansion of $(1 + x^2)^5.(1 + x)^4$ is

(a) 30 (b) 40
(c) 20 (d) 60

Solution: (d) Co-efficient of x^5 in $(1 + x^2)^5.(1 + x)^4$

i.e., in $(1 + {}^5C_1x^2 + {}^5C_2x^4 + {}^5C_3x^6 + \dots\dots) \times (1 + x)^4$

i.e., in $(1 + 5x^2 + 10x^4 + \dots\dots) \times (1 + x)^4$

$= 5.{}^4C_3 + 10.{}^4C_1 = 60$

2. Co-efficient of x^4 in the expansion of $(1 + x + x^2 + x^3)^{11}$ is

(a) 920 (b) 850
(c) 890 (d) 990

Solution: (d) $(1 + x + x^2 + x^3)^{11}$

$= ((1 + x) + x^2(1 + x))^{11}$

$= (1 + x)^{11}(1 + x^2)^{11}$

$= (1 + {}^{11}C_1x + {}^{11}C_2x^2 + {}^{11}C_3x^3 + {}^{11}C_4x^4 + \dots..) \times$

$(1 + {}^{11}C_1x^2 + {}^{11}C_2x^4 + \dots) \Rightarrow$ Cofficient of x^4

$= (1.{}^{11}C_2 + {}^{11}C_2.{}^{11}C_1 + {}^{11}C_4.1)$

$= ({}^{11}C_2 + {}^{11}C_4 + {}^{11}C_2\,{}^{11}C_1) = 55 + 330 + 605 = 990$

3. Co-efficient of x^4 in the expansion of $(2 - x + 3x^2)^6$ is

(a) 3600 (b) 3660
(c) 3590 (d) None of these

Solution: (b) The general term of $(2 - x + 3x^2)^6$

is given by $\sum_{r_1+r_2+r_3=6} \frac{6!}{r_1!r_2!r_3!}(2)^{r_1}(-x)^{r_2}(3x^2)^{r_3}$

$= \sum_{r_1+r_2+r_3=6} \frac{6!}{r_1!r_2!r_3!}(2)^{r_1}(-1)^{r_2}(3)^{r_3}x^{r_2+2r_3}$

$\Rightarrow$ For terms containing x^4

$r_2 + 2r_3 = 4 \Rightarrow r_2 = 4 - 2r_3$ and

$r_1 + r_2 + r_3 = 6 \Rightarrow r_1 = 2 + r_3$

r_1	r_2	r_3
$2 + r_3$	$4 - 2r_3$	r_3
2	4	0
3	2	1
4	0	2

so the co-efficient of x^4 is

$= \frac{6!}{2!4!0!}(2)^2(-1)^4 + \frac{6!}{3!2!1!}(2)^3(-1)^2(3)^1 + \frac{6!}{4!0!2!}(2)^4(-1)^0(3)^2$

$= 6!\left[\frac{2\times2}{2\times4\times3\times2} + \frac{2\times2\times2\times3}{3\times2\times2} + \frac{2\times2\times4\times9}{4\times3\times4}\right]$

$= 6!\left[\frac{1}{12} + 2 + 3\right] = 3660.$

4. Numerically greatest term in the expansion of $(2 + 3x)^9$, when $x = \frac{3}{2}$ is

(a) T_4 (b) T_5
(c) T_7 (d) None of these

Solution: (c) $r = \left[\frac{n+1}{1+\left|\frac{a}{x}\right|}\right] = \left[\frac{9+1}{1+\left|\frac{2}{3x}\right|}\right]$

$= \left[\frac{10}{1+\left|\frac{2}{3.3}.2\right|}\right] = \left[\frac{90}{13}\right] = 6$

Thus there will be a single numerically greatest term and is $T_{r+1} = T_{6+1} = T_7$

5. Which one is/are numerically greatest term in $(3 - 5x)^{15}$; $x = \frac{1}{5}$?

(a) T_2 (b) T_3
(c) T_4 (d) T_5

Solution: (c, d)

$r = \left[\frac{n+1}{1+\left|\frac{a}{x}\right|}\right] = \left[\frac{15+1}{1+\left|\frac{3}{5x}\right|}\right] = \left[\frac{16}{1+\left(\frac{3}{5}.\frac{5}{1}\right)}\right] = [4]$

$\Rightarrow r = [4]$ or $r = [4] - 1$ i.e., $r = 4$ or 3

Thus there will be two numerically greatest terms T_4 and T_5.

6. The index n of the binomial $\left(\frac{x}{5}+\frac{2}{5}\right)^n$ if the 9th term of the expansion has numerically the greatest coefficient ($n \in \mathbb{N}$) is

(a) 4 (b) 6
(c) 8 (d) 12

Solution: (d) $8 < \frac{n+1}{1+\left|\frac{a}{x}\right|} < 9 \quad \left(\because r = 8 = \left[\frac{n+1}{1+\left|\frac{a}{x}\right|}\right]\right)$

$\Rightarrow \; 8 < \frac{n+1}{1+\left|\frac{x}{2}\right|} < 9$; $x = 1$ for greatest coefficient.

$\Rightarrow \; 8 < \frac{n+1}{1+\frac{1}{2}} < 9 \qquad \Rightarrow \; 11 < n < 12.5 = n = 12$

7. For which positive value of x, the fourth term in the expansion of $(5 + 3x)^{10}$ is greatest?

(a) $\left(0, \frac{20}{21}\right)$ (b) $\left(\frac{5}{8}, \frac{20}{21}\right)$
(c) $\left(\frac{5}{4}, \frac{20}{21}\right)$ (d) None of these

Solution: (b) $3 < \frac{10+1}{1+\left|\frac{5}{3x}\right|} < 4 \quad \left(\because r = 3 = \left[\frac{n+1}{1+\left|\frac{a}{x}\right|}\right]\right)$

$\Rightarrow \; 3 < \frac{11}{1+\left|\frac{5}{3x}\right|} < 4$

$\Rightarrow \; \frac{5}{8} < |x| < \frac{20}{21}$

$\Rightarrow \; x \in \left(-\frac{20}{21}, -\frac{5}{8}\right) \cup \left(\frac{5}{8}, \frac{20}{21}\right)$; but $x \in \mathbb{R}^+$

$\Rightarrow \; x \in \left(\frac{5}{8}, \frac{20}{21}\right)$.

8. The number of positive integer divisors of the number $N = {}^{2000}C_1 + 2.\,{}^{2000}C_2 + 3.{}^{2000}C_3 + \ldots\ldots + 2000.\,{}^{2000}C_{2000}$ are

(a) 8016 (b) 8000
(c) 4000 (d) None of these

Solution: (a) $N = {}^{2000}C_1 + 2.\,{}^{2000}C_2 + 3.{}^{2000}C_3 + \ldots\ldots + 2000.\,{}^{2000}C_{2000}$.

Let $(1 + x)^{2000} = {}^{2000}C_0 + {}^{2000}C_1x^1 + \ldots + {}^{2000}C_{2000}x^{2000}$

Diff. w.r.t. x, we get $2000\,(1 + x)^{1999} = {}^{2000}C_1 + 2\,{}^{2000}C_2x + 3\,{}^{2000}C_3x^2 + \ldots\ldots + 2000\;{}^{2000}C_{2000}x^{1999}$

Putting $x = 1$, we have $2000.2^{1999} = {}^{2000}C_1 + 2\,{}^{2000}C_2 + \ldots\ldots + 2000\;{}^{2000}C_{2000} = N$

$\Rightarrow \; N = 2000\,.\,2^{1999}$

$= 2.10^3.\,2^{1999} = 2^{2000}.\,(2.5)^3 = 2^{2003}.\,5^3$

$\Rightarrow$ Number of positive integer divisors = (2003 + 1) (3 + 1) = 2004 × 4 = 8016

9. The number of terms in the expansion of $(ax^2 + bx + c)^9$ containing x^6 are

(a) 3 (b) 4
(c) 5 (d) 6

Solution: (b) The general term

$= \sum_{r_1+r_2+r_3=9} \frac{9!}{r_1!r_2!r_3!} a^{r_1} b^{r_2} c^{r_3} x^{2r_1+r_2}$

For x^6, $2r_1 + r_2 = 6$, $r_1 + r_2 + r_3 = 9$

r_1	r_2	r_3
r_1	$6 - 2r_1$	$3 + r_1$
0	6	3
1	4	4
2	2	5
3	0	6

∴ There will be 4 terms containing x^6.

10. The co-efficient of $x^2y^3z^4$ in the expansion of $(ax - by + cz)^9$ is

(a) 1220 (b) −1260
(c) 1300 (d) None of these

Solution: (b) The general term of $(ax - by + cz)^9$

$= \sum_{r_1+r_2+r_3=9} \frac{9!}{r_1!r_2!r_3!} (a)^{r_1} (-b)^{r_2} (c)^{r_3} x^{r_1} y^{r_2} z^{r_3}$

For $x^2y^3z^4$, $r_1 = 2$, $r_2 = 3$ and $r_3 = 4$

$\Rightarrow$ Coefficient of $x^2y^3z^4 = \frac{9!}{2!3!4!}(a)^2(-b)^3(c)^4$

$= -1260\,a^2b^3c^4$ **Ans**

11. The co-efficient of $a^2b^3c^4d$ in the expansion of $(a - b - c + d)^{10}$ is

(a) −12600 (b) 12000
(c) 10000 (d) None of these

Solution: (a) The general term of $(a - b - c + d)^{10}$

$\Rightarrow \; \sum_{r_1+r_2+r_3+r_4=10} \frac{10!}{r_1!r_2!r_3!r_4!}(a)^{r_1}(-b)^{r_2}(-c)^{r_3}(d)^{r_4}$

For $a^2 b^3 c^4 d$, $r_1 = 2, r_2 = 3, r_3 = 4, r_4 = 1$

$\Rightarrow$ Coefficient of $a^2b^3c^4d$

$$= \sum_{r_1+r_2+r_3+r_4=10} \frac{10!}{2!3!4!1!}(1)^2(-1)^3(-1)^4(1)^1 = -12600$$

12. Let $a = (4^{1/401} - 1)$ and for each $n \ge 2$, let $b_n = {}^nC_1 + {}^nC_2 \cdot a + {}^nC_3 \cdot a^2 + ... + {}^nC_n \cdot a^{n-1}$, then the value of $(b_{2006} - b_{2005})$ is

(a) $(4)^{2004/401}$ (b) $(4)^{2005/400}$
(c) $(4)^5$ (d) None of these

Solution: (c) $b_n = {}^nC_1 + {}^nC_2\, a + {}^nC_3\, a^2 + ... + {}^nC_n a^{n-1}$

$$\Rightarrow b_n = \frac{1}{a}\,[a\,{}^nC_1 + {}^nC_2 a^2 + {}^nC_3 a^3 + ... + {}^nC_n a^n]$$

$$\Rightarrow b_n = \frac{1}{a}[{}^nC_0 + {}^nC_1 a + {}^nC_2 a^2 + {}^nC_2 a^3 + ... + {}^nC_n a^n - 1]$$

$$\Rightarrow b_n = \frac{1}{a}((1+a)^n - 1)$$

$$\Rightarrow b_{2006} - b_{2005} = \frac{1}{a}[(1+a)^{2006} - 1] - \frac{1}{a}[(1+a)^{2005} - 1]$$

$$= \frac{1}{a}(1+a)^{2005}(1+a-1) = (1+a)^{2005}$$

$$= \left(1 + 4^{\frac{1}{401}} - 1\right)^{2005} = 4^{\frac{2005}{401}} = (4)^5$$

13. The remainder when $x = 5^{5^{5^{\cdot^{\cdot^{5}}}}}$ (24 times 5) is divided by 24 is

(a) 1 (b) 3
(c) 5 (d) 23

Solution: (c) Note that $x = 5^{5^{5^{\cdot^{\cdot^{5}}}}}$ (23 times 5) is an odd natural number, Therefore let it be $(2m + 1)$

$\Rightarrow x = 5^{2m+1} = (25^m)5$

where m is a natural number. Thus,

$x = (24 + 1)^m \cdot 5 = 5$ + a multiple of 24

Hence, the desired remainder is 5.

14. The co-efficient of t^{50} in $(1+t^2)^{25}\,(1+t^{25})\,(1+t^{40})\,(1+t^{45})\,(1+t^{47})$ …(1) is

(a) $1 + {}^{25}C_5$ (b) $1 + {}^{25}C_5 + {}^{25}C_7$
(c) $1 + {}^{25}C_7$ (d) None of these

Solution: (a) As we are interested in co-efficient of t^{50}, we shall ignore all the terms with exponents more than 50. Thus, we can write (1) as $(1 + {}^{25}C_1 t^2 + \dots {}^{25}C_{25} t^{50}) \times (1 + t^{25} + t^{40} + t^{45} + t^{47})$

As all the terms in the first expression have even exponents, we can ignore t^{25}, t^{45}, t^{47} too. Thus, co-efficient of $t^{50} = {}^{25}C_{25} + {}^{25}C_5 = 1 + {}^{25}C_5$

15. If $\sum_{r=0}^{2n} a_r (x-100)^r = \sum_{r=0}^{2n} b_r (x-101)^r$ and $a_k = \frac{2^k}{{}^kC_n}$ $\forall k \ge n$, then b_n equals

(a) $2^n(2^{n+1} - 1)$ (b) $2^n(2^n + 1)$
(c) $2^n(2^n - 1)$ (d) $2^{n+1}(2^n - 1)$

Solution: (a) Put $x - 101 = t$, so that

$$\sum_{r=0}^{2n} b_r t^r = \sum_{r=0}^{2n} a_r (t+1)^r \qquad (1)$$

$\therefore$ b_n = Co-efficient t^n on the R.H.S of (1)

$$= {}^nC_n a_n + {}^{n+1}C_n a_{n+1} + ... + {}^{2n}C_n . a_{2n}$$

$$= \sum_{k=n}^{2n} {}^kC_n a_k = \sum_{k=n}^{2n} 2^k \left(\because a_k = \frac{2^k}{{}^kC_n}\right)$$

$$= 2^n \sum_{k=n}^{2n} 2^{k-n} = 2^n\left(2^{n+1} - 1\right)$$

16. If $x \in \mathbb{R}$ and

$$S = 1 - C_1\frac{1+x}{1+nx} + C_2\frac{1+2x}{(1+nx)^2} - C_3\frac{1+3x}{(1+nx)^3} + \dots\text{upto}$$

$(n + 1)$ terms, then S

(a) equals x^2 (b) equals 1
(c) equals 0 (d) is independent of x

Solution: (c, d) Putting $\frac{1}{1+nx} = y$, we can write

$$S = \left[C_0 - C_1 y + C_2 y^2 - ... + (-1)^n C_n y^n\right]$$

$$-xy\left[C_1 - 2C_2 y + 3C_3 y^2 - ... + (-1)^{n-1} nC_n y^{n-1}\right]$$

$$= (1-y)^n + xy\frac{d}{dy}\left\{(1-y)^n\right\}$$

$$= (1-y)^n - nxy(1-y)^{n-1}$$

$$= (1-y)\quad\left[1 - (1+nx)y\right] = 0$$

17. Value of $\sum_{k=0}^{n} {}^nC_k \sin(kx)\cos(n-k)x$ is

(a) $2^{n-1}\sin(nx)$ (b) $2^n\sin(nx)$
(c) $2^n\cos(nx)$ (d) none of these

Solution: (a) $S = \sum_{k=0}^{n} {}^nC_k \sin(kx)\cos(n-k)x \qquad$ (i)

Writing the terms in the reverse order, we have

$$S = \sum_{k=0}^{n} {}^nC_{n-k} \sin(n-k)x\cos(kx)$$

$$= \sum_{k=0}^{n} {}^nC_k \sin(n-k)x\cos(kx) \qquad \text{(ii)}$$

Adding (i) and (ii), we get

$$2S = \sum_{k=0}^{n} {}^nC_k \ \{\sin(kx)\cos(n-k)x + \sin(n-k)x\cos(kx)\}$$

$$\Rightarrow \ 2S = \sum_{k=0}^{n} ({}^nC_k) \ \sin(nx) = 2^n \sin(nx)$$

$$\Rightarrow \ S = 2^{n-1} \sin(nx)$$

18. Value of $S = \sum_{k=1}^{\infty} \sum_{r=0}^{k} \frac{1}{3^k} ({}^kC_r)$ is

(a) 2 (b) 2/3

(c) 1/3 (d) None of these

Solution:(a) $\sum_{r=0}^{k} \frac{1}{3^k}({}^kC_r) = \frac{1}{3^k}\sum_{r=0}^{k} {}^kC_r = \frac{2^k}{3^k}$

Thus, $S = \frac{2/3}{1-2/3} = 2$

19. Sum of the series

$$S = \sum_{r=0}^{n} \frac{3^{r+4}({}^nC_r)}{{}^{r+4}C_4} + \sum_{r=0}^{3} \frac{{}^{n+4}C_r 3^r}{{}^{n+4}C_4} \text{ is}$$

(a) 4^{n+4} (b) $n^{n+4}({}^{2n}C_4)$

(c) $\frac{4^{n+4}}{{}^{n+4}C_4}$ (d) $\frac{3^{n+4}+2^{n+4}}{{}^{n+4}C_4}$

Solution: (c) $\frac{{}^nC_r}{{}^{r+4}C_4} = \frac{n!}{r!(n-r)!} \frac{4!r!}{(r+4)!}$

$$= \frac{4!}{(n+1)(n+2)(n+3)(n+4)}({}^{n+4}C_{r+4}) = \frac{{}^{n+4}C_{r+4}}{{}^{n+4}C_4}$$

Thus,

$$S = \frac{1}{{}^{n+4}C_4}\left[\sum_{r=0}^{n} 3^{r+4}({}^{n+4}C_{r+4}) + \sum_{r=0}^{3} {}^{n+4}C_r 3^r\right]$$

$$= \frac{1}{{}^{n+4}C_4}\sum_{k=0}^{n+4} {}^{n+4}C_k 3^k = \frac{4^{n+4}}{{}^{n+4}C_4}$$

20. The number of seven digit positive integers, with sum of the digits equal to 10 and formed by using the digits 1, 2 and 3 only, is

(a) 55 (b) 66

(c) 77 (d) 88

Solution: (c) Number of numbers of required type

= Co-efficient of x^{10} in $(x + x^2 + x^3)^7$

= Co-efficient of x^3 in $(1 + x + x^2)^7$

= Co-efficient of x^3 in $(1 - x^3)^7 (1 - x)^{-7}$

$= {}^{7+3-1}C_3 - 7 = {}^9C_3 - 7 = \frac{9 \times 8 \times 7}{6} - 7 = 77.$

Alternate:

The digits are 1, 1, 1, 1, 1, 2, 3

or 1, 1, 1, 1, 2, 2, 2

Hence number of seven digit numbers formed

$= \frac{7!}{5!} + \frac{7!}{4!3!} = 77.$

21. For $r \in \{0, 1, \ldots, 10\}$; let A_r, B_r and C_r denotes, respectively the co-efficient of x^r in the expansion of $(1 + x)^{10}$, $(1 + x)^{20}$ and $(1 + x)^{30}$. Then $\sum A_r(B_{10}B_r - C_{10}A_r)$ is equal to

(a) $B_{10} - C_{10}$ (b) $A_{10}(B_{10}^2 - C_{10}A_{10})$

(c) 0 (d) $C_{10} - B_{10}$

Solution: (d)

Let $y = \sum_{r=1}^{10} A_r(B_{10}B_r - C_{10}A_r)$

$\sum_{r=1}^{10} A_rB_r$ = co-efficient of x^{20} in $((1 + x)^{10} (x + 1)^{20}) - 1$

$= {}^{30}C_{20} - 1 = {}^{30}C_{10} - 1 = C_{10} - 1$ and $\sum_{r=1}^{10}(A_r)^2$ = co-efficient of x^{10} in $((1 + x)^{10} (x + 1)^{10}) - 1$

$= {}^{20}C_{10} - 1 \ B_{10} - 1$

$\Rightarrow y = B_{10}(C_{10} - 1) - C_{10}(B_{10} - 1) = C_{10} - B_{10}$

22. The value of

$$\binom{30}{0}\binom{30}{10} - \binom{30}{1}\binom{30}{11} + \binom{30}{2}\binom{30}{12} - \ldots + \binom{30}{20}\binom{30}{30}$$

is, where $\binom{n}{r} = {}^nC_r$.

(a) $\binom{30}{10}$ (b) $\binom{30}{15}$

(c) $\binom{60}{30}$ (d) $\binom{31}{10}$

Solution: (a) Let

$$\binom{30}{0}\binom{30}{10} - \binom{30}{1}\binom{30}{11} + \binom{30}{2}\binom{30}{12} - \ldots.. + \binom{30}{20}\binom{30}{30}$$

$\therefore \ A = {}^{30}C_0 . {}^{30}C_{10} - {}^{30}C_1 . {}^{30}C_{11} + {}^{30}C_2 . {}^{30}C_{12} - \ldots.. + {}^{30}C_{20} . {}^{30}C_{30}$

= co-efficient of x^{20} in $(1 + x)^{30} (1 - x)^{30}$

= co-efficient of x^{20} in $(1 - x^2)^{30}$

= co-efficient of x^{20} in $\sum_{r=0}^{30}(-1)^r . {}^{30}C_r . (x^2)^r$

$= (-1)^{10} \ {}^{30}C_{10}$ (for co-efficient of x^{20}, put $r = 10$)

$= {}^{30}C_{10}$

Aliter: The given expression is the co-efficient of x^{20} in the product $(1 + x)^{30} (1 - x)^{30} = (1 - x^2)^{30}$

$\Rightarrow$ the given expression $= {}^{30}C_{10}$

23. If the second, third and fourth terms in the expansion of $(x + y)^n$ are 135, 30 and 10/3 respectively, then

(a) $n = 7$ (b) $n = 5$
(c) $n = 6$ (d) None of these

Solution: (b)

We have:

$T_2 = 135 \Rightarrow {}^nC_1\, x^{n-1} y^1 = 135$

$T_3 = 30 \Rightarrow {}^nC_2\, x^{n-2} y^2 = 30$

$T_4 = \frac{10}{3} \Rightarrow {}^nC_3 x^{n-3} y^3 = \frac{10}{3}$

Now, $\frac{T_2 \times T_4}{T_3^2} = \frac{135 \times \frac{10}{3}}{(30)^2}$

$$\Rightarrow \frac{({}^nC_1 x^{n-1} y^1) \times ({}^nC_3 x^{n-3} y^3)}{({}^nC_2 x^{n-2} y^2)^2} = \frac{135 \times \frac{10}{3}}{(30)^2}$$

$$\Rightarrow \frac{{}^nC_1 \times {}^nC_3}{({}^nC_2)^2} = \frac{135 \times 10}{2700} \Rightarrow n = 5$$

24. The co-efficient of the term independent of x in the expansion of $(1 + x + 2x^3)\left(\frac{3}{2}x^2 - \frac{1}{3x}\right)^9$ is

(a) $\frac{1}{3}$ (b) $\frac{19}{54}$
(c) $\frac{17}{54}$ (d) $\frac{1}{4}$

Solution: (c)

$$(1+x+2x^3)\left(\frac{3}{2}x^2 - \frac{1}{3x}\right)^9$$

$$= (1+x+2x^3)\left[\sum_{r=0}^{9} {}^9C_r \left(\frac{3}{2}x^2\right)^{9-r}\left(-\frac{1}{3x}\right)^r\right]$$

$$= (1+x+2x^3)\left[\sum_{r=0}^{9} {}^9C_r \left(\frac{3}{2}\right)^{9-r}\left(-\frac{1}{3}\right)^r x^{18-3r}\right]$$

$$= \left(\sum_{r=0}^{9} {}^9C_r \left(\frac{3}{2}\right)^{9-r}\left(-\frac{1}{3}\right)^r x^{18-3r}\right) +$$

$$\left(\sum_{r=0}^{9} {}^9C_r \left(\frac{3}{2}\right)^{9-r}\left(-\frac{1}{3}\right)^r x^{19-3r}\right) +$$

$$2\left(\sum_{r=0}^{9} {}^9C_r \left(\frac{3}{2}\right)^{9-r}\left(-\frac{1}{3}\right)^r x^{21-3r}\right)$$

Clearly, first and third expansions contain terms independent of x and are obtained by equation $18 - 3r = 0$ and $21 - 3r = 0$ respectively.

So, co-efficient of the term independent of x

$$= {}^9C_6 \left(\frac{3}{2}\right)^{9-6}\left(-\frac{1}{3}\right)^6 + 2\left({}^9C_7 \left(\frac{3}{2}\right)^{9-7}\left(\frac{-1}{3}\right)^7\right)$$

$$= \frac{7}{18} - \frac{2}{27} = \frac{17}{54}$$

25. The number of non-negative integral solutions of the equation $x + y + 3z = 33$ is

(a) 120 (b) 135
(c) 210 (d) 520

Solution: (c)

$x + y + 3z = 33 \Rightarrow x + y = 33 - 3z$

Let $z = k$. Then, $x + y = 33 - 3k$.

The number of non-negative integral solution of $x + y = 33 - 3z$ is ${}^{33-3k+2-1}C_{2-1} = {}^{34-3k}C_1 = (34 - 3k)$

But $0 \le 33 - 3k \le 33 \Rightarrow 0 \le k \le 11$

Hence, total number of solution $= \sum_{k=0}^{11}(34 - 3k) = 210$

26. The co-efficient of x^r $\{0 \le r \le (n-1)\}$ in the expansion of $(x + 3)^{n-1} + (x + 3)^{n-2} + (x + 3)^{n-3} (x + 2)^2 + \ldots.. + (x + 2)^{n-1}$ is

(a) ${}^nC_r\,(3^r - 2^n)$ (b) ${}^nC_r\,(3^{n-r} - 2^{n-r})$
(c) ${}^nC_r\,(3^r + 2^{n-r})$ (d) None of these

Solution: (b)

We have,

$(x + 3)^{n-1} + (x + 3)^{n-2} (x + 2) + \ldots.. + (x + 2)^{n-1}$

$$= \frac{(x+3)^n - (x+2)^n}{(x+3)-(x+2)} = (x+3)^n - (x+2)^n$$

∴ Co-efficient of x^r in the given expression

$=$ co-efficient of x^r in $[(x + 3)^n - (x + 2)^n]$

$= {}^nC_r \,.\, 3^{n-r} - {}^nC_r\, 2^{n-r} = {}^nC_r\,(3^{n-r} - 2^{n-r})$.

27. If $n \in \mathbb{N}$ such that $(7+4\sqrt{3})^n = I + F$, where $I \in \mathbb{N}$ and $0 < F < 1$, then the value of $(I + F)(I - F)$ is

(a) 0 (b) 1
(c) 7^{2n} (d) 2^{2n}

Solution: (b)

Let $G = (7-4\sqrt{3})^n$, then $0 < G < 1$ as $7 - 4\sqrt{3} \in (0,1)$.

Now $I + F + G = (7+4\sqrt{3})^n + (7-4\sqrt{3})^n$

$= 2({}^nC_0 7^n + {}^nC_2 7^{n-2}(4\sqrt{3})^2 + \ldots)$, which is an integer

$\Rightarrow F + G = 1$ as $F + G \in (0, 2) \Rightarrow G = 1 - F$

$\Rightarrow (I + F)(1 - F) = (I + F)G$

$= (7+4\sqrt{3})^n (7-4\sqrt{3})^n = 1.$

28. The remainder, when 5^{99} is divided by 13 is

(a) 6 (b) 8
(c) 9 (d) 10

Solution: (b)
We have, $5^{99} = 5^3.5^{96} = (13 \times 9 + 8)(1 + 13 \times 48)^{24}$
$= (13 \times 9 + 8)\,[1 + {}^{24}C_1\,(13 \times 48) + ... + {}^{24}C_{24}\,(13 \times 48)^{24}]$
$= 8 + 13$ (an integer) $\Rightarrow$ remainder $= 8$.

29. The value of $\frac{1}{81^n} - \frac{10}{81^n}\,{}^{2n}C_1 + \frac{10^2}{81^n}\,{}^{2n}C_2 + ... + \frac{10^{2n}}{81^n}$ is

(a) 2 (b) 0
(c) $\frac{1}{2}$ (d) 1

Solution: (d)
We have,

$$\frac{1}{81^n} - \frac{10}{81^n}\,{}^{2n}C_1 + \frac{10^2}{81^n}\,{}^{2n}C_2 - \frac{10^3}{81^n}\,{}^{2n}C_3 + ... + \frac{10^{2n}}{81^n}$$
$$= \frac{1}{81^n}\,[{}^{2n}C_0 - {}^{2n}C_1\,10^1 + {}^{2n}C_2\,10^2 - {}^{2n}C_3\,10^3 + ... + {}^{2n}C_{2n}\,10^{2n}] = \frac{1}{81^n}[1-10]^{2n} = \frac{(-9)^{2n}}{81^n} = \frac{81^n}{81^n} = 1$$

30. The approximate value of $(7.995)^{\frac{1}{3}}$ correct to four decimal places is

(a) 1.9995 (b) 1.9996
(c) 1.9990 (d) 1.9991

Solution: (b)

$$(7.995)^{\frac{1}{3}} = (8 - 0.005)^{\frac{1}{3}} = 8^{\frac{1}{3}}\left[1 - \frac{0.005}{8}\right]^{\frac{1}{3}}$$
$$= 2\left[1 - \frac{1}{3} \times \frac{0.005}{8} + \frac{1}{3}\frac{\left(\frac{1}{3}-1\right)}{2!}\left(\frac{0.005}{8}\right)^2 + ...\right]$$
$$= 2[1 - 0.000208] = 1.999584 = 1.9996$$

31. The greatest term in the expansion of $\sqrt{3}\left(1 + \frac{1}{\sqrt{3}}\right)^{20}$ is

(a) $\frac{25840}{9}$ (b) $\frac{24840}{9}$
(c) $\frac{26840}{9}$ (d) None of these

Solution: (a)
Let $(r + 1)$th term be the greatest term. Then
$T_{r+1} = \sqrt{3}\,.\,{}^{20}C_r\left(\frac{1}{\sqrt{3}}\right)^r$ and $T_r = \sqrt{3}\;{}^{20}C_{r-1}\left(\frac{1}{\sqrt{3}}\right)^{r-1}$

Now $\frac{T_{r+1}}{T_r} = \frac{20 - r + 1}{r}\left(\frac{1}{\sqrt{3}}\right) \Rightarrow r \le \frac{21}{\sqrt{3}+1}$

$\therefore\ T_{r+1} \ge T_r \Rightarrow r(\sqrt{3}+1) \Rightarrow r \le 7.686 \Rightarrow r = 7.$
Hence, the greatest term is

$$T_8 = \sqrt{3}\;{}^{20}C_7\left(\frac{1}{\sqrt{3}}\right)^7 = \frac{25840}{9}$$

32. The largest co-efficient in the expansion of $(1 + x)^n$, given that the sum of co-efficients of the terms in its expansion is 4096 is

(a) ${}^{18}C_9$ (b) ${}^{14}C_9$
(c) ${}^{12}C_6$ (d) ${}^{20}C_{10}$

Solution: (c) Largest co-efficient in $(1 + x)^n = {}^nC_{n/2}$
$C_0 + C_1 + C_2 + ... + C_n = 4096$ (given)
$\Rightarrow 2^n = 4096$
$\Rightarrow 2^n = 2^{12} \Rightarrow$ Largest co-efficient $= {}^nC_{\frac{n}{2}} = {}^{12}C_6$

33. In the binomial expansion of $(a - b)^n$, $n \ge 5$, the sum of the 5th and 6th terms is zero, then $\frac{a}{b}$ equals

(a) $\frac{n-5}{6}$ (b) $\frac{n-4}{5}$
(c) $\frac{5}{n-4}$ (d) $\frac{6}{n-5}$

Solution: (b) Given, $T_5 + T_6 = 0$
$\Rightarrow {}^nC_4a^{n-4}b^4 - {}^nC_5a^{n-5}b^5 = 0 \Rightarrow {}^nC_4a^{n-4}b^4 = {}^nC_5a^{n-5}b^5$
$\Rightarrow \frac{a}{b} = \frac{{}^nC_5}{{}^nC_4} = \frac{n-4}{5}$

SECTION–II

SUBJECTIVE-TYPE SOLVED EXAMPLE

1. If the sum of the co-efficient in the expansion of $(\alpha x^2 - 2x + 1)^{35}$ is equal to the sum of the co-efficients in the expansion of $(x - \alpha y)^{35}$, then find the value of α.

Solution: $(\alpha x^2 - 2x + 1)^{35} = (x - \alpha y)^{35}$; $x = y = 1$(given)
$\Rightarrow (\alpha - 1)^{35} = (1 - \alpha)^{35}$
$\Rightarrow (\alpha - 1)^{35} = -(\alpha - 1)^{35} \Rightarrow 2(\alpha - 1)^{35} = 0 \Rightarrow \alpha = 1$

2. In the expansion of $(3^{-x/4} + 3^{5x/4})^n$, the sum of the binomial co-efficients is 64 and the term with the greatest binomial co-efficient exceeds the third by $(n - 1)$, then find the value of x.

Solution: $(3^{-x/4} + 3^{5x/4})^n = 64$ for $3^{-x/4} = 3^{5x/4} = 1$(given)

$\therefore$ $(1 + 1)^n = 64 \Rightarrow 2^n = 64 \Rightarrow n = 6$

We know that the middle term has the greatest binomial co-efficient,

Here $n = 6$

$\therefore$ middle term $= [(6/2) + 1]^{th}$ term = 4th term $= T_4$

and given $T_4 = (n - 1) + T_3 \Rightarrow T_{3+1} = (n - 1) + T_{2+1}$

$\Rightarrow {}^6C_3 (3^{-x/4})^3 (3^{5x/4})^3 = (6 - 1) + {}^6C_2 (3^{-x/4})^4 (3^{5x/4})^2$

$\Rightarrow \dfrac{6.5.4}{1.2.3} 3^{-3x/4} .3^{15x/4} = 5 + \dfrac{6.5}{1.2} 3^{-x} .3^{5x/2}$

$\Rightarrow 20.3^{3x} = 5 + 15.3^{3x/2}$

Let $3^{3x/2} = t$...(i) $(t > 0)$

$\therefore$ $20t^2 - 15t - 5 = 0 \Rightarrow 4t^2 - 3t - 1 = 0$

$\Rightarrow (4t + 1)(t - 1) = 0 \Rightarrow t \neq -1/4$

$\Rightarrow$ t = 1 from (i), $3^{3x/2} = 1 \Rightarrow x = 0$

3. The sum of the co-efficients in the first three terms of the expansion of $(x^2 - 2/x)^m$ is 97. Show that the co-efficient of x^4 is 1120.

Solution: We have $(x^2 - 2/x)^m = (x^2)^m + {}^mC_1(x^2)^{m-1} (-2/x) + {}^mC_2 (x^2)^{m-2} (-2/x)^2 + ...$

Now, sum of the co-efficients in the first three terms:

$= 1 - {}^mC_1 . 2 + {}^mC_2 . 4 = 97$ (given)

$\Rightarrow m^2 - 2m - 48 = 0 \Rightarrow m = 8, -6$

The value -6 is inadmissible since m must be a positive integer. Thus the given binomial is $(x^2 - 2/x)^8$ in which the general term

$T_{r+1} = {}^8C_r (x^2)^{8-r} (-2/x)^r = {}^8C_r(-2)^r x^{16-3r}$

The value of r corresponding to the term containing x^4 is given by $16 - 3r = 4$

$\Rightarrow r = 4$. Thus the co-eff. of x^4 is ${}^8C_4(-2)^4$

$= 70 \times 16 = 1120$.

4. Show that $2^{4n} - 15n - 1$ is divisible by 225.

Solution: $2^{4n} = (2^4)^n = 16^n$

$\therefore$ $(2^4)^n = (1 + 15)^n$

or $2^{4n} = 1 + {}^nC_1 . 15 + {}^nC_2 . 15^2 + {}^nC_3 . 15^3 + ...$

$\therefore$ $2^{4n} - 1 - 15n = 15^2 [{}^nC_2 + 15({}^nC_3) + ...]$

$\therefore$ $2^{4n} - 1 - 15n = 225m$ (where $m = {}^nC_2 + 15 . {}^nC_3 +$ ....and m is also an integer)

Hence, $2^{4n} - 1 - 15n$ is divisible by 225.

6. Find out which is larger $99^{50} + 100^{50}$ or 101^{50}.

Solution: $101^{50} - 99^{50} = (100 + 1)^{50} - (100 - 1)^{50}$

$= (C_0 100^{50} + C_1 100^{49} + C_2 .100^{48} + ...)$
$-(C_0 100^{50} - C_1 100^{49} + C_2 .100^{48} - .....) = 2 [C_1 100^{49} + C_3 .100^{47} + ...]$

$= 2 [50. 100^{49} + C_3 .100^{47} + ...] = 100^{50} + 2 [C_3 .100^{47} + ...] > 100^{50} \Rightarrow 101^{50} > 99^{50} + 100^{50}$

5. Show that the co-efficient of x^{24} in the expansion of $(1 + 3x + 6x^2 + 10x^3 + ...\infty)^{2/3}$ is 25.

Solution: Let $S = 1 + 3x + 6x^2 + 10x^3 + ...\infty$

and $xS = 0 + x + 3x^2 + 6x^3 + ...\infty$

Subtracting, we get $S(1 - x) = 1 + 2x + 3x^2 + 4x^3 + ...\infty = \dfrac{1}{(1-x)^2}$ or $S = \dfrac{1}{(1-x)^3} = (1-x)^{-3}$

$\therefore$ $(1 + 3x + 6x^2 + 10x^3 + ...\infty)^{2/3}$

$= [(1 - x)^{-3}]^{2/3} = (1 - x)^{-2}$

$= 1 + 2x + 3x^2 + ... (r + 1)x^r + ... \infty$

$\therefore$ Co-efficient of x^{24} (Taking $r = 24$) $= 24 + 1 = 25$

6. If $(a + x)^n = t_0 + t_1 + t_2 + ... + t_n$, prove that $(a^2 + x^2)^n = (t_0 - t_2 + t_4 - ....)^2 + (t_1 - t_3 + t_5 - ....)^2$

Solution: $(a + x)^n = a^n + {}^nC_1a^{n-1}x + {}^nC_2a^{n-2}x^2 + ...$

$\Rightarrow t_0 = a^n, t_1 = {}^nC_1a^{n-1}x$, etc

Now, $(a + ix)^n = a^n + {}^nC_1a^{n-1}(ix) + {}^nC_2a^{n-2}(ix)^2 + {}^nC_3a^{n-3}(ix)^3 + {}^nC_4a^{n-4}(ix)^4 + {}^nC_5a^{n-5}(ix)^5 + ...$

On collecting the real and imaginary parts, we get

$(a + ix)^n = (t_0 - t_2 + t_4 + ...) + i (t_1 - t_3 + t_5 - ....)$ (i)

On taking the conjugate of (i), we get,

$(a - ix)^n = (t_0 - t_2 + t_4 + ...) - i (t_1 - t_3 + t_5 - ....)$ (ii)

Multiplying (i) and (ii), we get

$(a^2 + x^2)^n = (t_0 - t_2 + t_4 + ...)^2 + (t_1 - t_3 + t_5 - ....)^2$

7. Find the co-efficient of x^{50} in the expansion of $(1 + x)^{1000} + 2x (1 + x)^{999} + 3x^2 (1 + x)^{998} + ... + 1001x^{1000}$.

Solution: Let $S = (1 + x)^{1000} + 2x (1 + x)^{999} + 3x^2 (1 + x)^{998} + ... + 1001x^{1000}$ (i)

Let $r = \dfrac{x}{x+1}$ and $d = 1$

$\dfrac{x}{x+1} S = x (1 + x)^{999} + 2x^2 (1 + x)^{998} + ... + 1000x^{1000} + \dfrac{1001^{1001}}{}$ (ii)

Subtracting (ii) from (i), we get

$\left(1 - \dfrac{x}{1+x}\right) S = (1 + x)^{1000} + x(1 + x)^{999} + ... + x^{1000} - \dfrac{1001x^{1001}}{1+x}$

or $S = (1 + x)^{1001} + x(1 + x)^{1000} + x^2(1 + x)^{999} + ... + x^{1000}(1 + x) - 1001x^{1001}$

This is G.P. and sum is $S = (1 + x)^{1002} - x^{1002} - 1002\,x^{1001}$

So the co-efficient of x^{50} is ${}^{1002}C_{50}$

8. If K be a quantity, so small that K^3 may be neglected in comparison with m^3, show that $\sqrt{\dfrac{m}{m+K}}+\sqrt{\dfrac{m}{m-K}}$ is very nearly equal to $2+\dfrac{3K^2}{4m^2}$.

Solution: We have

$$\sqrt{\frac{m}{m+K}}+\sqrt{\frac{m}{m-K}}=\left[\frac{m+K}{m}\right]^{-1/2}+\left[\frac{m-K}{m}\right]^{-1/2}$$

$$=\left(1+\frac{K}{m}\right)^{-1/2}+\left(1-\frac{K}{m}\right)^{-1/2}$$

$$=\left[1+(-1/2)\frac{K}{m}+\frac{(-1/2)(-1/2-1)}{1.2}\cdot\frac{K^2}{m^2}+......\right]$$

$$+\left[1+(-1/2)\left(-\frac{K}{m}\right)+\frac{(-1/2)(-1/2-1)}{1.2}\cdot\left(-\frac{K}{m}\right)^2+..\right] \quad \text{(i)}$$

{*Higher terms are neglected*}

$$=\left(1-\frac{K}{2m}+\frac{3}{8}\cdot\frac{K^2}{m^2}\right)+\left(1+\frac{K}{2m}+\frac{3}{8}\cdot\frac{K^2}{m^2}\right)=2+\frac{3}{4}\cdot\frac{K^2}{m^2}$$

9. Show that $\sum_{k=0}^{n}{}^nC_k(\sin kx)\cos(n-k)x=2^{n-1}\sin(nx)$.

Solution: $\sum_{k=0}^{n}{}^nC_k(\sin kx)\cos(n-k)x$

$$=\frac{1}{2}\sum_{k=0}^{n}{}^nC_k[\sin(kx+nx-kx)+\sin(kx-nx+kx)]$$

$$=\frac{1}{2}\sum_{k=0}^{n}{}^nC_k\sin nx+\frac{1}{2}\sum_{k=0}^{n}{}^nC_k\sin(2kx-nx)$$

$$=\frac{1}{2}\sin nx\sum_{k=0}^{n}{}^nC_k+\frac{1}{2}[{}^nC_0\sin(-nx)+{}^nC_1\sin(2-n)x$$

$$+......+{}^nC_{n-1}\sin(n-2)x+{}^nC_n\sin nx]$$

$= 2^{n-1}\sin nx + 0$ (Hence it is proved)

10. Prove that $13^{99} - 19^{93}$ is divisible by 162.

Solution: Hence $13^{99} - 19^{93} = (1 + 3.4)^{99} - (1 + 9.2)^{93}$

$= \{{}^{99}C_0 + {}^{99}C_1.\,3.4 + {}^{99}C_2.(3.4)^2 + ... + {}^{99}C_{99}\,(3.4)^{99}\}$

$\quad - \{{}^{93}C_0 + {}^{93}C_1.\,9.2 + {}^{93}C_2.\,(9.2)^2 + ... + {}^{93}C_{93}(9.2)^{93}\}$

$= (99 \times 12 - 93 \times 18) + \{{}^{99}C_2\,12^2 + {}^{99}C_3\,12^3\} + 3^4 \times$ integer

$= 1188 - 1674 + 144\,\{{}^{99}C_2 + {}^{99}C_3 \times 12\} + 81 \times$ integer

$= -486 + 144\,\{99\,.\,49 + 99.\,98.\,97\,.\,2\} + 81 \times$ integer

$= -81.6 + 16.81\,\{11.49 + 11.98.97\,.\,2\} + 81 \times$ integer

$= 81\,\{-6 + 16\,(11.49 + 11.98.97.2) +$ integer$\}$

$= 81 \times$ integer

$\therefore$ $13^{99} - 19^{93}$ is divisible by 81

But $13^{99} - 19^{93}$

= odd number – odd number = even number

$\therefore$ $13^{99} - 19^{93}$ is divisible by 2

But 2 and 81 are co-prime

$\therefore$ $13^{99} - 19^{93}$ is divisible by 81×2, i.e., 162

11. If $(15+6\sqrt{6})^{2n+1} = P$, then prove that $P(1 - F) = 9^{2n+1}$ (where F is the fractional part of P).

Solution: $P = (15+6\sqrt{6})^{2n+1} = \mathrm{I} + F$.

Let $F' = (15-6\sqrt{6})^{2n+1}$

Now $I + F = C_0(15)^{2n+1} + C_1\,(15)^{2n}\,6\sqrt{6} + C_2\,(15)^{2n-1}\,(6\sqrt{6})^2 + ...$

$F' = C_0(15)^{2n+1} - C_1\,(15)^{2n}\,6\sqrt{6} + C_2\,(15)^{2n-1}\,(6\sqrt{6})^2 + ...$

$\Rightarrow I + F + F' = 2[C_0(15)^{2n+1} + C_2\,(15)^{2n-1}\,(6\sqrt{6})^2 + ...]$

$\Rightarrow I + F + F' =$ Even integer $\Rightarrow F + F' =$ Integer

But, $0 < F < 1$ and (F is fractional part)

$0 < F' < 1 \Rightarrow 0 < F + F' < 2$

Hence $F + F' = 1 \Rightarrow F' = (1 - F)$

$\therefore$ $P(1 - F) = (15+6\sqrt{6})^{2n+1}(15-6\sqrt{6})^{2n+1} = 9^{2n+1}$

12. If n is a positive integer and if $(1 + x + x^2)^n = \sum_{r=0}^{2n} a_r x^r$, then prove that

(a) $a_r = a_{2n-r}$ for $0 \le r \le 2n$

(b) $a_0 + a_1 + ... + a_{n-1} = \frac{1}{2}(3^n - a_n)$

(c) $(r+1)\,a_{r+1} = (n-r)a_r + (2n-r+1)\,a_{r-1}$ $(0 < r < 2n)$

Solution: (a) We have $(1 + x + x^2)^n = \sum_{r=0}^{2n} a_r x^r$ (i)

$$\sum_{r=0}^{2n} a_r\left(\frac{1}{x}\right)^r = \left(1+\frac{1}{x}+\frac{1}{x^2}\right)^n = \frac{1}{x^{2n}}(x^2+x+1)^n$$

$$\Rightarrow \sum_{r=0}^{2n} a_r x^{2n-r} = (x^2+x+1)^n = \sum_{r=0}^{2n} a_r x^r = \sum_{r=0}^{2n} a_{2n-r}x^{2n-r} \quad \text{(ii)}$$

Equating the co-efficients of x^{2n-r} on both sides, we get, $a_r = a_{2n-r}$ for $0 \le r \le 2$

(b) Putting $x = 1$ in (i), we get $a_0 + a_1 + ...+ a_n + a_{n+1} +...+ a_{2n} = (3)^n$

But $a_r = a^{2n-r}$ for $0 \le r \le n-1$

$\Rightarrow 2(a_0 + a_1 + ... + a_{n-1}) + a_n = 3^n$

$\Rightarrow a_0 + a_1 + ... + a_{n-1} = \frac{1}{2}(3_n - a_n)$

(c) Differentiating (i) with respect to x, we get

$$n(1 + 2x)(1 + x + x^2)^{n-1} = \sum_{r=0}^{2n} ra_r x^{r-1}$$

$$\Rightarrow n(1 + 2x)(1 + x + x^2)^n = (1 + x + x^2)\sum_{r=0}^{2n} ra_r x^{r-1}$$

$$\Rightarrow n(1 + 2x)\sum_{r=0}^{2n} a_r x^r = (1 + x + x^2)\sum_{r=0}^{2n} ra_r x^{r-1}$$

Equating the co-efficients of x_r, $(0 < r < 2n)$, we get

$na_r + 2na_{r-1} = (r + 1)a_{r+1} + ra_r + (r - 1)a_{r-1}$

$\Rightarrow (r + 1)a_{r+1} = (n - r)a_r + (2n - r + 1)a_{r-1}$

13. Prove that $\sum_{r=1}^{k}(-3)^{r-1}\,{}^{3n}C_{2r-1} = 0$ when $k = \frac{3n}{2}$ and n is an even positive integer.

Solution: Since n is even integer, let $n = 2m$,

$\therefore\ k = \frac{3n}{2} = \frac{6m}{2} = 3m$ and

$$S = \sum_{r=1}^{k}(-3)^{r-1}\,{}^{3n}C_{2r-1} = \sum_{r=1}^{3m}(-3)^{r-1}\,{}^{6m}C_{2r-1}$$

Now, $(1 + x)^{6m} = {}^{6m}C_0 + {}^{6m}C_1 x + {}^{6m}C_2 x^2 + ...$
$+ {}^{6m}C_{6m-1} x^{6m-1} + {}^{6m}C_{6m} x^{6m}$ (i)

$(1 - x)^{6m} = {}^{6m}C_0 + {}^{6m}C_1(-x) + {}^{6m}C_2(-x)^2 + ...$
$+ {}^{6m}C_{6m-1}(-x)^{6m-1} + {}^{6m}C_{6m}(-x)^{6m}$ (ii)

$\Rightarrow (1 + x)^{6m} - (1 - x)^{6m} = 2[{}^{6m}C_1 x + {}^{6m}C_3 x^3 + ... + {}^{6m}C_{6m-1} x^{6m-1}]$

$$\Rightarrow \frac{(1+x)^{6m} - (1-x)^{6m}}{2x}$$

$= [{}^{6m}C_1 + {}^{6m}C_3 x^2 + ... + {}^{6m}C_{6m-1} x^{6m-2}]$

Let $x^2 = y \Rightarrow \frac{(1+\sqrt{y})^{6m} - (1-\sqrt{y})^{6m}}{2\sqrt{y}}$

$= {}^{6m}C_1 + {}^{6m}C_3 y + ... {}^{6m}C_{6m-1} y^{3m-1}$

Put $y = -3$, R.H.S. becomes S

$$\text{L.H.S.} = \frac{(1+i\sqrt{3})^{6m} - (1-i\sqrt{3})^{6m}}{(2\sqrt{3})i},$$

Let $z = 1 + (\sqrt{3})i = 2e^{i\pi/3}$

$\bar{z} = 1 - (\sqrt{3})i = 2e^{-i\pi/3}$

$$\therefore\ S = \frac{(z)^{6m} - (\bar{z})^{6m}}{2i\sqrt{3}} = \frac{2i\sin(6m\frac{\pi}{3})}{2i\sqrt{3}} = 0$$

14. For what value of x, the sixth term in the expansion of $[7^{\log_{10}(10-3^x)^{1/2}} + \{7^{(x-2)\log_{10}3}\}^{1/5}]^n$ is equal to 21, if it is given that co-efficient of 2nd, 3rd and 4th terms in the expansion represent respectively the first, third and fifth terms of an *A.P.*?

Solution: Co-efficient of 2nd, 3rd and 4th terms will be ${}^nC_1$, ${}^nC_2$ and ${}^nC_3$.

Since they are the first, third and fifth terms of an *A.P.*, we may write

$${}^nC_3 - {}^nC_2 = {}^nC_2 - {}^nC_1 \quad \Rightarrow n = 7, 2$$

But $n \neq 2$ because then there will be only three terms in the expansion. So we take $n = 7$ and in this case 6th term will be 21 if

$${}^7C_5\left[7^{\log_{10}(10-3^x)1/2}\right]^{(7-5)}\left[7^{(x-2)\log_{10}3}\right]^{5/5} = 21$$

$$\Rightarrow \frac{7.6}{1.2}.7^{\log_{10}(10-3^x)}.7^{(x-2)\log_{10}3} = 21$$

$$\Rightarrow 21.7^{\log_{10}(10-3^x) + \log_{10}3^{(x-2)}} = 21$$

Hence, $7^{\left[\log_{10}(10-3^x).3^{x-2}\right]} = 7^0$

$\Rightarrow \log_{10}[(10 - 3^x)(3^{x-2})] = 0 = \log_{10}1$

$\Rightarrow (10 - 3^x)(3^{x-2}) = 1$

$\Rightarrow 3^{2x-2} - 10.3^{x-2} + 1 = 0$ or $3^{2x}.\frac{1}{9} - 10.3^x.\frac{1}{9} + 1 = 0$

$\Rightarrow 3^{2x} - 10.3^x + 9 = 0$ or $(3^x - 1)(3^x - 9) = 0$

$\therefore\ 3^x - 1 = 0$ which gives $x = 0$

and $3^x - 9 = 0$ which gives $x = 2$. Hence $x = 0$ or 2.

15. Prove that $C_1^2 - 2C_2^2 + 3C_3^2 - ..... - 2nC_{2n}^2 = (-1)^{n-1} nC_n$; where $C_r = {}^{2n}C_r$

Solution: $(1 + x)^{2n} = {}^{2n}C_0 + {}^{2n}C_1 x + {}^{2n}C_2 x^2 + ... + {}^{2n}C_{2n} x^{2n}$ (i)

Differentiating w.r.t.x, we get

$2n(1 + x)^{2n-1} = C_1 + 2C_2 x + 3C_3 x^2 + ... + 2nC_{2n} x^{2n-1}$ (ii)

Also $\left(1 - \frac{1}{x}\right)^{2n} = C_0 - C_1\frac{1}{x} + C_2\frac{1}{x^2} + ... + C_{2n}\frac{1}{x^{2n}}$ (iii)

where $C_r = {}^{2n}C_r$

Multiplying (ii) and (iii), we get $2n(1 + x)^{2n-1}(1 - 1/x)^{2n}$

$= (C_1 + 2C_2 x + 3C_3 x^2 + ... + 2nC_{2n} x^{2n-1})$

$(C_0 - C_1\frac{1}{x} + C_2\frac{1}{x^2} - ...... + C_{2n}\frac{1}{x^{2n}})$

The co-efficient of $1/x$ in RHS is $-(C_1^2 - 2C_2^2 + 3C_3^2 - ..... + 2nC_{2n}^2)$ (v)

Also the co-efficient of $1/x$ in $2n\,(1+x)^{2n-1}\,(1-1/x)^{2n}$

$= $ co-efficient of $1/x$ in $2n\,.\,\dfrac{(1+x)^{2n-1}(x-1)^{2n}}{x^{2n}}$

$= $ co-efficient of $1/x$ in $\dfrac{2n}{x^{2n}}.\,(1-x^2)^{2n-1}(1-x)$

$= $ co-efficient of x^{2n-1} in $2n(1-x^2)^{2n-1}\,(1-x)$

$= $ co-efficient of x^{2n-2} in $2n\,(1-x^2)^{2n-1}$ × co-efficient of x in $(1-x)$

$$= 2n\,(-1)^{n-1}\,{}^{2n-1}C_{n-1}\,(-1) = (-1)^n\,2n\,\frac{(2n-1)!}{(n-1)!n!}$$

$$= (-1)^n\,\frac{(2n)!}{n(n-1)!n!}n = (-1)^n\,\frac{(2n)!}{n!n!}n = -(-1)^{n-1}\,nC_n \qquad \text{(vi)}$$

From (v) and (vi), we get

$C_1^{\,2} - 2C_2^{\,2} + 3C_3^{\,2} - \dots + 2nC_{2n}^{\,2} = (-1)^{n-1}\,nC_n;\ C_r = {}^{2n}C_r$

16. Show that

$$(C_0+C_1)(C_1+C_2)\ldots\ldots\ldots(C_{n-1}+C_n) = \frac{(n+1)^n}{n!}C_1\,C_2\,C_3\ldots\ldots\ldots C_n.$$

Solution: $C_0 + C_1 = 1 + n;\ C_1 + C_2 = n + \dfrac{n(n-1)}{2}$

$$= (n+1)\frac{n}{2} = \frac{(n+1)}{2}.C_1$$

$$C_2 + C_3 = \frac{n(n-1)}{1.2} + \frac{n(n-1)(n-2)}{1.2.3}$$

$$= \frac{n(n-1)}{1.2}\left(1+\frac{(n-2)}{3}\right) = \frac{(n+1)}{3}.C_2$$

Similarly,

$$C_3 + C_4 = \frac{(n+1)}{4}.C_3,\ C_4 + C_5$$

$$= \frac{(n+1)}{5}C_4,\ldots,C_{n-1}+C_n = \frac{(n+1)}{n}C_{n-1}$$

$\therefore\ (C_0+C_1)\,(C_1+C_2)\,(C_2+C_3)\ldots\ldots.(C_{n-1}+C_n)$

$$= \frac{(n+1)^n}{1.2.3..n}C_1\;C_2\;C_3\ldots..C_{n-1}$$

$$= \frac{(n+1)^n}{n!}C_1\;C_2\;C_3\;\ldots..C_{n-1}.C_n$$

17. Show that for $m \le n$

${}^mC_1\,{}^nC_m - {}^mC_2\,{}^{2n}C_m + {}^mC_3\,{}^{3n}C_m - \ldots\ldots + (-1)^{m-1}.\,{}^mC_m.\,{}^{mn}C_m = (-1)^{m-1}\,.\,n^m$

Solution: We have ${}^mC_1\,{}^nC_m - {}^mC_2\,{}^{2n}C_m + {}^mC_3\,{}^{3n}C_m - \ldots\ldots + (-1)^{m-1}\,.\,{}^mC_m.\,{}^{mn}C_m$

$= $ co-efficient of x^m in

${}^mC_1(1+x)^n - {}^mC_2(1+x)^{2n} + {}^mC_3\,(1+x)^{3n} - \ldots + (-1)^{m-1}.\,{}^mC_m\,.\,(1+x)^{mn} = $ co-efficient of x^m in

${}^mC_0 - [{}^mC_0 - {}^mC_1(1+x)^n + {}^mC_2\,(1+x)^{2n}$
$- {}^mC_3(1+x)^{3n} + \ldots\ldots + (-1)^m.\,{}^mC_m.\,(1+x)^{mn}]$

$= $ co-efficient of x^m in $[1 - \{1 - (1+x)^n\}^m]$

$= $ co-efficient of x^m in $[1 - \{-nx - {}^nC_2x^2 - {}^nC_3x^3 - \ldots. - {}^nC_n\,x^n\}^m]$ i.e., in $(1+x)$

$= -(-n)^m = -(-1)^m\,n^m = (-1)^{m-1}n^m$

18. If k and n are two positive integers and $S_k = 1^k + 2^k + \ldots. + n^k$, then show that ${}^{m+1}C_1S_1 + {}^{m+1}C_2S_2 + \ldots. + {}^{m+1}C_mS_m = (1+n)^{m+1} - (1+n)$

Solution: We have $(1+p)^{m+1} = {}^{m+1}C_0 + {}^{m+1}C_1\,p + {}^{m+1}C_2\,p^2 + \ldots.+ {}^{m+1}C_{m+1}p^{m+1}$. Putting $p = 1, 2, 3, \ldots\ldots, n$, we have $2^{m+1} - 1 = {}^{m+1}C_0 + {}^{m+1}C_1\,(1) + {}^{m+1}C_2\,(1)^2 + \ldots\ldots + {}^{m+1}C_m\,(1)^m$;

$3^{m+1} - 2^{m+1} = {}^{m+1}C_0 + {}^{m+1}C_1\,(2) + {}^{m+1}C_2\,(2)^2 + \ldots\ldots + {}^{m+1}C_m\,(2)^m$;

$4^{m+1} - 3^{m+1} = {}^{m+1}C_0 + {}^{m+1}C_1\,(3) + {}^{m+1}C_2\,(3)^2 + \ldots\ldots + {}^{m+1}C_m\,(3)^m$;

....

$(1+n)^{m+1} - n^{m+1} = {}^{m+1}C_0 + {}^{m+1}C_1\,(n) + {}^{m+1}C_2\,(n)^2 + \ldots\ldots + {}^{m+1}C_m(n)^m$

Adding all these terms, we get

$(1+n)^{m+1} - 1 = {}^{m+1}C_0\,(n) + {}^{m+1}C_1\,\Sigma(n) + {}^{m+1}C_2\,\Sigma(n)^2 + \ldots\ldots + {}^{m+1}C_m\Sigma(n)^m$

$(1+n)^{m+1} - 1 = {}^{m+1}C_0\,(n) + {}^{m+1}C_1S_1 + {}^{m+1}C_2\,S_2 + \ldots\ldots + {}^{m+1}C_mS_m$

$\Rightarrow {}^{m+1}C_1S_1 + {}^{m+1}C_2S_2 + \ldots. + {}^{m+1}C_mS_m = (1+n)^{m+1} - (1+n)$ (Hence proved).

19. Show that

(a) $\dfrac{C_0}{1} - \dfrac{C_1}{4} + \dfrac{C_2}{7} - \dfrac{C_3}{10} + \ldots + \dfrac{(-1)^nC_n}{3n+1} = \displaystyle\int_0^1 (1-x^3)^n\,dx$

(b) $C_1^2 - 2C_2^2 + 3C_3^2 - \ldots\ldots - 2n.C_{2n}^2 = (-1)^{n-1}.n\,{}^{2n}C_n$

(c) $\displaystyle\sum_{i=1}^{n} i^2.C_i = n(n+1)\;2^{n-2}$

Solution: (a) Consider $(1-x^3)^n = C_0 - C_1x^3 + C_2x^6 - C_3x^9 + \ldots\ldots. + (-1)^n\,C_nx^{3n}$

Integrating between the limits 0 to 1, we get

$$\int_0^1 (1-x^3)^n\,dx = \int_0^1 \left[\begin{matrix} C_0 - C_1x^3 + C_2x^6 - \ldots\ldots \\ + (-1)^n C_n x^{3n} \end{matrix}\right] dx$$

$$= \left| C_0 x - C_1 . \frac{x^4}{4} + C_2 . \frac{x^7}{7} + \ldots.. + (-1)^n C_n . \frac{x^{3n+1}}{3n+1} \right|_0^1$$

$$= C_0 - \frac{C_1}{4} + \frac{C_2}{7} - \frac{C_3}{10} + \ldots + (-1)^n \frac{C_n}{3n+1}$$

(b) We know

$(1 + x)^{2n} = C_0x^{2n} + C_1x^{2n-1} + C_2x^{2n-2} + \ldots. + C_{2n}$ (i)

and $(1 - x)^{2n} = C_0 - C_1x + C_2x^2 - C_3x^3 + \ldots\ldots. + C_{2n}x^{2n}$ (ii)

Differentiating (ii), w.r.t .x, we have

$-2n(1 - x)^{2n-1} = - C_1 + 2C_2x - 3C_3x^2 + \ldots\ldots\ldots + 2nC_{2n}x^{2n-1}$ or

$2nx(1 - x)^{2n-1} = C_1x - 2C_2x^2 + 3C_3x^3 - \ldots\ldots\ldots - 2n C_{2n}x^{2n}$ (iii)

Multiplying (i) by (iii) and comparing co-efficient of x^{2n} on both sides, we have

$\therefore\ C_1^2 - 2\,C_2^2 + 3\,C_3^2 + \ldots\ldots. - 2n\,C_{2n}^2$

= The co-efficient of x^{2n} in $(x + 1)^{2n}. [2nx(1 - x)^{2n-1}]$

= The co-efficient of x^{2n} in $2nx(1 + x)(1 - x^2)^{2n-1}$

= The co-efficient of x^{2n-1} in $2n(1 + x)(1 - x^2)^{2n-1}$

= The co-efficient of x^{2n-2} in $2n(1 - x^2)^{2n-1}$

$$= 2n.\ {}^{2n-1}C_{n-1}(-1)^{n-1} = 2n.\frac{(2n-1)!}{(n-1)!\,n!}(-1)^{n-1}$$

$$= \frac{2n!}{(n-1)!\,n!}(-1)^{n-1} = \frac{2n!}{n!n!}n(-1)^{n-1} = n.\ {}^{2n}C_n(-1)^{n-1}$$

(c) We know that

$(1 + x)^n = C_0 + C_1x + C_2x^2 + C_3x^3 + \ldots\ldots\ldots + C_nx^n$

Differentiating w. r. t. x, we have $n(1 + x)^{n-1} = C_1 + 2C_2x + 3C_3x^2 + \ldots\ldots\ldots + nC_nx^{n-1}$ (1)

Multiplying (1) by x, we get $nx(1 + x)^{n-1} = C_1x + 2C_2x^2 + 3C_3x^3 + \ldots\ldots\ldots + n.C_nx^n$

Again differentiating w. r. t. x, we get

$n[(n - 1)x. (1 + x)^{n-2} + 1. (1 + x)^{n-1}] = C_1 + 2^2C_2x + 3^2C_3x^2 + \ldots\ldots. + n^2. C_nx^{n-1}$

Putting, $x = 1$, we have

$n[(n-1)\,2^{n-2} + 2^{n-1}] = 1^2\,C_1 + 2^2C_2 + 3^2C_3 + \ldots\ldots\ldots + n^2C_n$

or $1^2\,C_1 + 2^2C_2 + 3^2C_3 + \ldots\ldots\ldots + n^2C_n = n.2^{n-2}(n - 1 + 2)$

$$\therefore\ \sum_{i=1}^{n} i^2.C_i = n(n+1)\ 2^{n-2}$$

20. If $(1 + x)^n = C_0 + C_1x + C_2x^2 + \ldots\ldots + C_nx^n$ $(n \in \mathbb{N})$, then show that $\sum_{k=1}^{n} k^3\left[\frac{C_k}{C_{k-1}}\right] = \frac{1}{12}(n)(n+1)^2(n+2)$.

Solution: $\because\ \frac{C_r}{C_{r-1}} = \frac{n-r+1}{r}$ for $r \geq 1$

$$\Rightarrow\ r^3\frac{C_r}{C_{r-1}} = \left(\frac{n+1-r}{r}\right)r^3 = (n+1)r^2 - r^3$$

$$\Rightarrow\ \sum_{r=1}^{n} r^3\frac{C_r}{C_{r-1}} = (n+1)\sum_{r=1}^{n} r^2 - \sum_{r=1}^{n} r^3$$

$$= \frac{(n+1)n(n+1)(2n+1)}{6} - \frac{n^2(n+1)^2}{4}$$

$$= \frac{n(n+1)}{12}[4n^2 + 6n + 2 - 3n^2 - 3n]$$

$$= \frac{n(n+1)(n^2+3n+2)}{12}$$

$$= \frac{n(n+1)(n+1)(n+2)}{12} = \frac{n(n+1)^2(n+2)}{12}$$

21. If $(1 + x)^n = C_0 + C_1x + C_2x^2 + \ldots. + C_nx^n$, then show that

(i) $\sum\sum_{0 \leq i < j \leq n} C_iC_j = 2^{2n-1} - \frac{2n!}{2(n!)^2}$

(ii) $\sum_{0 \leq i < j \leq n} (C_i + C_j)^2 = (n-1)\ {}^{2n}C_n + 2^{2n}$

(iii) $\sum\sum_{0 \leq i < j \leq n} (i+j)C_iC_j = n\left(2^{2n-1} - \frac{1}{2}\,{}^{2n}C_n\right)$

Solution: (i) We have

$(C_0 + C_1 + C_2 + \ldots + C_n)^2 =$

$C_0^{\,2} + C_1^{\,2} + \ldots + C_n^{\,2} + 2\sum\sum_{0 \leq i < j \leq n} C_iC_j$

we get, $(2^n)^2 = {}^{2n}C_n + 2\sum\sum_{0 \leq i < j \leq n} C_iC_j$

therefore $\sum\sum_{0 \leq i < j \leq n} C_i\,C_j = 2^{2n-1} - \frac{2n!}{2(n!)^2}$

(ii) $\sum\sum_{0 \leq i < j \leq n} (C_i + C_j)^2 = n\ (C_0^{\,2} + C_1^{\,2} + C_2^{\,2} + \ldots + C_n^{\,2}) + 2\sum\sum_{0 \leq i < j \leq n} C_iC_j$

$$= n\ {}^{2n}C_n + 2\left\{2^{2n-1} - \frac{(2n)!}{2(n!)^2}\right\} \ldots..\text{(using part (i))}$$

$= n\ {}^{2n}C_n + 2^{2n} - {}^{2n}C_n = (n - 1)\ {}^{2n}C_n + 2^{2n}$

(iii) Let $\sum\limits_{0\le i<j\le n}\sum (i+j)C_iC_j$

replacing i by $(n-i)$ and j by $(n-j)$, we have

$$P=\sum_{0\le i<j\le n}\sum (2n-i-j)C_{n-i}C_{n-j}$$

$$=\sum_{0\le i<j\le n}\sum (2n-(i+j))C_iC_j \qquad [\because {}^nC_r={}^nC_{n-r}]$$

$$=2n\sum_{0\le i<j\le n}\sum C_iC_j-P$$

$$\therefore\quad \sum_{0\le i<j\le n}\sum (i+j)C_iC_j=n\left(2^{2n-1}-\frac{1}{2}{}^{2n}C_n\right)$$

22. Show that $\sum\limits_{r=0}^{n} r(n-r)C_r^2=n^2({}^{2n-2}C_n)$.

Solution: We have $(1+x)^n=C_0+C_1x+C_2x^2+\ldots.+C_nx^n$ (i)

$(x+1)^n=C_0x^n+C_1x^{n-1}+C_2x^{n-2}+\ldots.+C_{n-1}x+C_n$ (ii)

Differentiating both sides of (i) with respect to x, we get,

$n(1+x)^{n-1}=C_1+2C_2x+3C_3x^2+\ldots.+nC_nx^{n-1}$ (iii)

Differentiating both sides of (ii) with respect to x, we get

$n(x+1)^{n-1}=nC_0x^{n-1}+(n-1)C_1x^{n-2}+(n-2)C_2x^{n-3}+\ldots.+C_{n-1}$ (iv)

Multiplying (iii) and (iv), we have

$n^2(1+x)^{n-1}(x+1)^{n-1}=n^2(1+x)^{2n-2}$

$=[C_1+2C_2x+3C_3x^2+\ldots.+nC_nx^{n-1}]$

$\times[nC_0x^{n-1}+(n-1)C_1x^{n-2}+(n-2)C_2x^{n-3}+\ldots.+C_{n-1}]$ (v)

The co-efficient of x^{n-2} on the LHS of (v) is $n^2\,{}^{2n-2}C_{n-2}$ $=n^2\,{}^{2n-2}C_n$

The co-efficient of x^{n-2} of the RHS is $1.(n-1)C_1^{\,2}+2(n-2)C_2^{\,2}+\ldots.(n-1)\,1C_{n-1}^2$

$$=\sum_{r=0}^{n-1} r(n-r)\,C_r^2=\sum_{r=0}^{n} r(n-r)\,C_r^2.$$

Hence $\sum\limits_{r=0}^{n} r(n-r)\,C_r^2=n^2({}^{2n-2}C_n)$

23. Show that

$$\frac{C_0}{n}-\frac{C_1}{n+1}+\frac{C_2}{n+2}-\ldots\ldots+(-1)^n\frac{C_n}{2n}=\frac{n!(n-1)!}{(2n)!}$$

Solution: We have $(1-x)^n=C_0-C_1x+C_2x^2-\ldots.+(-1)^nC_nx^n$

$$\Rightarrow \int_0^1 x^{n-1}(1-x)^n\,dx=$$

$$\int_0^1 (C_0x^{n-1}-C_1x^n+C_2x^{n+1}-\ldots..+(-1)^n C_nx^{2n-1})dx$$

$$=\left(\frac{C_0}{n}x^n-\frac{C_1}{n+1}x^{n+1}+\frac{C_2}{n+2}x^{n+2}-\ldots\ldots+(-1)^n\frac{C_n}{2n}x^{2n}\right)\Bigg|_0^1$$

$$=\frac{C_0}{n}-\frac{C_1}{n+1}+\frac{C_2}{n+2}-\ldots\ldots+(-1)^n\frac{C_n}{2n}$$

Let us now evaluate $\int_0^1 x^{n-1}(1-x)^n\,dx$. Consider the integral $\int_0^1 [tx+(1-x)]^{2n-1}dx$

We have $\int_0^1 [tx+(1-x)]^{2n-1}dx=\int_0^1 [1-(1-t)x]^{2n-1}dx$

$$=\frac{1}{2n(t-1)}[1+(t-1)x]^{2n}\Big|_0^1=\frac{1}{2n}\left(\frac{t^{2n}-1}{t-1}\right)$$

$$=\frac{1}{2n}(t^{2n-1}+t^{2n-2}+\ldots\ldots+t+1)$$

also $\int_0^1 [tx+(1-x)]^{2n-1}dx=$

$$\int_0^1\left[\sum_{k=0}^{2n-1}{}^{2n-1}C_k(tx)^{2n-1-k}(1-x)^k\right]dx$$

$$=\sum_{k=0}^{2n-1}\left[{}^{2n-1}C_k t^{2n-1-k}\int_0^1 x^{2n-1-k}(1-x)^k\,dx\right]$$

Thus $\sum\limits_{k=0}^{2n-1}\left[{}^{2n-1}C_k t^{2n-1-k}\int_0^1 x^{2n-1-k}(1-x)^k\,dx\right]=$

$$\frac{1}{2n}(t^{2n-1}+t^{2n-2}+\ldots\ldots+t+1)$$

Equating the co-efficient of t^{n-1} on both sides, we get,

$${}^{2n-1}C_n\int_0^1 x^{n-1}(1-x)^n\,dx=\frac{1}{2n}$$

$$\Rightarrow \int_0^1 x^{n-1}(1-x)^n\,dx=\frac{n!(n-1)!}{2n(2n-1)!}=\frac{n!(n-1)!}{(2n)!}$$

Hence $\dfrac{C_0}{n}-\dfrac{C_1}{n+1}+\dfrac{C_2}{n+2}-\ldots\ldots+(-1)^n\dfrac{C_n}{2n}=\dfrac{n!(n-1)!}{(2n)!}$

24. Show that

(a) $(1+x)^n-nx-1$ is divisible by x^2 where $n\in\mathbb{N}$

(b) $2^{3n}-7n-1$ is divisible by 49. Hence show that $2^{3n+3}-7n-8$ is divisible by 49, $n\in\mathbb{N}$

Solution: (a) Since $(1+x)^n=1+{}^nC_1x+{}^nC_2x^2+\ldots.+x^n=1+nx+\dfrac{n(n-1)}{2}x^2+{}^nC_3\,x^3+\ldots+x^n$

$\therefore\quad (1+x)^n-(nx+1)=x^2\left[\dfrac{n(n-1)}{2}+{}^nC_3\,x+\ldots.+x^{n-2}\right]$

i.e.,$(1+x)^n-nx-1$ is divisible by x^2 as $n(n-1)$ is even

(b) Put $x=7$ in the above result as we want $2^{3n}=8^n$

$\therefore\quad (1+7)^n-n(7)-1$ is divisible by 7^2

$\therefore\quad 8^n-7n-1$ is divisible by 49

$\therefore\quad 2^{3n}-7n-1$ is divisible by 49

$\therefore\ 2^{3n} = 49k + 7n + 1, k \in \mathbb{N}$

$\therefore\ 2^{3n+3} - 7n - 8 = 2^{3n} \times 2^3 - 7n - 8$

$= 8\,(49k + 7n + 1) - 7n - 8$

$= 8 \times 49\,k + 56n - 7n = 8 \times 49\,k + 49\,n$

$= 49(8k + n)$

$\therefore\ 2^{3n+3} - 7n - 8$ is divisible by 49.

25. Prove that HCF of ${}^{2n}C_1, {}^{2n}C_3, {}^{2n}C_5, \ldots, {}^{2n}C_{2n-1}$ is 2^{m+1} where $n = 2^m.\,q$; q being an odd integer.

Solution: We have ${}^{2n}C_1 + {}^{2n}C_3 + {}^{2n}C_5 + \ldots + {}^{2n}C_{2n-1} = (2)^{2n-1}$

HCF of numbers divides each number and so it divides their sum also. So the $HCF = 2^k$; where $0 \le k \le 2n - 1$

Now, every number n can be expressed as $2^m.q$; q being an odd integer and m is an integer ≥ 0.

$\therefore\ 2n = {}^{2n}C_1 = 2.2^m.q = 2^{m+1}.\,q$, where q is odd

Now ${}^{2n}C_p = p/p.\ {}^{2n}C_p = \frac{1}{p}.2n.\ {}^{2n-1}C_{p-1}$

$[\because (r.\,{}^nC_r = n.\,{}^{n-1}C_{r-1})]$

$= 2n.\,(\frac{1}{p}.\,{}^{2n-1}C_{p-1}) = 2^{2m+1}.\,q\,(\frac{1}{p}\,{}^{2n-1}C_{p-1})$

$= 2^{m+1}\,\dfrac{q.\,{}^{2n-1}C_{p-1}}{p}$

For $p = 1, 3, 5, \ldots, 2n - 1$; ${}^{2n}C_p$ is an integer.

So $q.\,{}^{2n-1}C_{p-1}$ is divisible by the integer p.

Let $\dfrac{q.\,{}^{2n-1}C_{p-1}}{p} = Q_p$ integer. $\Rightarrow {}^{2n}C_p = 2^{m+1}.Q_p$

$\therefore\ {}^{2n}C_p = 2^{m+1}.\,2^r.\,M_p$; where $Q_p = 2^r\,M_p$ and M_p is an odd integer as well as $r \ge 0$.

$\therefore$ required $HCF = HCF$ of $\{2^{m+1}.\,q,\ 2^{m+1},\ 2^r.\,M_p\}$ $= 2^{m+1}$, where $n = 2^m.\,q$

Matrix Match Type Question

26. For $n \ge 2$, let $C_r = \binom{n}{r}$ and $a_n = \sum_{r=0}^{n} \frac{1}{C_r}$

(i) $\sum_{r=0}^{n} \frac{r}{C_r}$	(a) na_n
(ii) $\sum_{r=0}^{n} \frac{n-r}{C_r}$	(b) $\frac{1}{n}a_{n-1}$
(iii) $\sum_{r=1}^{n} \frac{1}{rC_r}$	(c) $\frac{1}{2}na_n$
(iv) $\sum_{r=0}^{n-1} \frac{1}{(n-r)C_r}$	(d) $\frac{1}{2n}a_{n-1}$

Answer: (i)→(c); (ii)→(c); (iii)→(b); (iv)→(b)

Solution: Using $C_r = C_{n-r}$, we get

$$\sum_{r=0}^{n} \frac{r}{C_r} = \sum_{r=0}^{n} \frac{r}{C_{n-r}} = \sum_{r=0}^{n} \frac{n-r}{C_r}$$

$$\Rightarrow 2\sum_{r=0}^{n} \frac{r}{C_r} = na_n \Rightarrow \sum_{r=0}^{n} \frac{r}{C_r} = \frac{1}{2}na_n$$

Similarly, $\sum_{r=0}^{n} \frac{n-r}{C_r} = \frac{1}{2}na_n$

Using $r.C_r = n.\,{}^{n-1}C_{r-1}$, we get

$$\sum_{r=1}^{n} \frac{1}{r.C_r} = \frac{1}{n}\sum_{r=1}^{n} \frac{1}{{}^{n-1}C_{r-1}} = \frac{1}{n}a_{n-1}$$

$$\sum_{r=0}^{n-1} \frac{1}{(n-r)C_r} = \sum_{r=0}^{n-1} \frac{1}{(n-r)C_{n-r}} = \sum_{k=1}^{n} \frac{1}{kC_k} = \frac{1}{n}a_{n-1}$$

Assertion and Reason Type

27. A: $\sum_{r=0}^{n}(r+1).{}^nC_r = (n+2)^{n-1}$

R: $\sum_{r=0}^{n} {}^nC_r(r+1)x^r = (1+x)^n + nx(1+x)^{n-1}$

Solution: We know that

$$\sum_{r=0}^{n} {}^nC_r x^r = (1+x)^n$$

Multiplying both sides by x, we get

$$\sum_{r=0}^{n} {}^nC_r x^{r+1} = (1+x)^n x$$

Differentiating both sides w.r.t x, we get

$$\sum_{r=0}^{n} {}^nC_r(r+1)x^r = (1+x)^n + nx(1+x)^{n-1}$$

Putting $x = 1$, we have

$$\sum_{r=0}^{n} {}^nC_r(r+1) = (2)^n + n(2)^{n-1}$$

$= (2)^{n-1}\,(2 + n) = (n + 2)\,(2)^{n-1}$

$\therefore$ Assertion is incorrect, but the reason is correct.

$\therefore$ **Ans.** (d)

28. A: If 'n' is an odd prime, then the integral part of $(\sqrt{5} + 2)^n - 2^{n+1}$ is divisible by $20n$

R: $(a + b)^n - (a - b)^n = 2\,[{}^nC_1\,a^{n-1}\,b + {}^nC_3\,a^{n-3}\,b^3 + \ldots + {}^nC_n\,b^n]$

Solution: Let $(\sqrt{5} + 2)^n = [x] + f$

where $f \in (0, 1)$

and let $(\sqrt{5} - 2)^n = f' \in (0, 1)$

$\therefore\ (\sqrt{5} + 2)^n - (\sqrt{5} - 2)^n = [x] + (f - f')$

Now $f - f' \in (-1, 1)$

$\therefore\ 2[{}^nC_1(\sqrt{5})^{n-1}(2)^1 + {}^nC_3(\sqrt{5})^{n-3}(2)^3 + {}^nC_5(\sqrt{5})^{n-5}(2)^5 + \ldots + {}^nC_n(\sqrt{5})^0(2)^n]$

$= [x] + (f - f')$ (i)

As n is prime, ${}^nC_1, {}^nC_3, {}^nC_5, \ldots, {}^nC_{n-2}$ are divisible by n as 1, 3, 5,....,$(n-2) < n$ and n being prime, no one of 1, 3, 5, ...,$(n-2)$ can cancel n.

$\therefore$ L.H.S of (1) – $(2)^{n+1}$ is divisible by 20 n

i.e., $(\sqrt{5}+2)^n - (\sqrt{5}-2)^n - (2)^{n+1}$ divisible by 20 n

$\Rightarrow f - f' = 0 \Rightarrow f = f'$

$\therefore$ $[x] + f - f' - (2)^{n+1}$ is divisible by 20 n

$\Rightarrow$ $[x] - (2)^{n+1}$ is divisible by 20 n [$\because f - f' = 0$]

$\Rightarrow$ Assertion as well as the reason both are correct and reason correctly explain the assertion.

Ans. (a)

29. A: The co-efficient of x^n in the binomial expansion of $(1-x)^{-2}$ is $(n+1)$

R: The co-efficient of x^r in $(1-x)^{-n}$, where $n \in \mathbb{N}$ is ${}^{n+r-1}C_r$

Solution: The co-efficient of x^r in the expansion of $(1-x)^{-n}$ is ${}^{n+r-1}C_r$

$\therefore$ The co-efficient of x^n in the expansion of $(1-x)^{-2}$ is ${}^{2+n-1}C_n = {}^{n+1}C_n = {}^{n+1}C_1 = (n+1)$

$\therefore$ Assertion and reason both are true and reason is correct explanation of assertion.

$\therefore$ **Ans.** (a)

30. A: The term independent of x in the expansion of $\left(x+\dfrac{1}{x}+2\right)^m$ is $\dfrac{(4m)!}{(2m)!}$

R: The co-efficient of x^k in the expansion of $(1+x)^n$ is ${}^nC_k$

Solution: $\left(x+\dfrac{1}{x}+2\right)^m = \left(\dfrac{x^2+2x+1}{x}\right)^m = \dfrac{(1+x)^{2m}}{x^m}$

Term independent of x will be co-efficient of x^m in the expansion of $(1+x)^{2m}$

$= {}^{2m}C_m = \dfrac{(2m)!}{((m)!)^2}$

$\Rightarrow$ incorrect but reason is correct.

$\therefore$ **Ans.** (d)

Comprehension Type

A: Consider the product $\prod_{i=1}^{n}(x+\alpha_i) = (x+\alpha_1)$ $(x+\alpha_2)(x+\alpha_3)\ldots\ldots\ldots(x+\alpha_n)$

$= x^n + (\alpha_1+\alpha_2+\alpha_3+\ldots\ldots+\alpha_n)x^{n-1} +$
$(\alpha_1\alpha_2+\alpha_1\alpha_3+\ldots.+\alpha_{n-1}\alpha_n)x^{n-2}+\ldots.+$
$(\alpha_1.\alpha_2.\alpha_3\ldots..\alpha_n)$ (i)

Let us denote $\alpha_1+\alpha_2+\alpha_3+\ldots.+\alpha_n = \sum_{i=1}^{n}\alpha_i$ by S_1

$\alpha_1\alpha_2+\alpha_1\alpha_3+\ldots..+\alpha_{n-1}\alpha_n = \sum\sum_{0\le i<j\le n}\alpha_i\alpha_j$ by S_2

and $\alpha_1\alpha_2\alpha_3+\alpha_1\alpha_2\alpha_4+\ldots.+\alpha_{n-2}\alpha_{n-1}\alpha_n$

$= \sum\sum\sum_{0\le i<j<k\le n}\alpha_i\alpha_j\alpha_k$ by S_3

....

and $\alpha_1\alpha_2\alpha_3\ldots\ldots\ldots\ldots\alpha_n$ by S_n

$\therefore$ (i) becomes $(x+\alpha_1)(x+\alpha_2)(x+\alpha_3)\ldots(x+\alpha_n)$
$= x^n + S_1x^{n-1} + S_2x^{n-2} + \ldots + S_n$

On the basis of the above information, answer the following questions:

31. Co-efficient of x^{n-1} in the expression $(x+C_0)(x+C_1)(x+C_2)\ldots\ldots(x+C_n)$ is; [Here $C_r = {}^nC_r$]

(a) $2^{2n} - \dfrac{(2n)!}{2(n!)^2}$ (b) $2^{2n-1} - \dfrac{(2n)!}{2(n!)^2}$

(c) $2^{2n+1} - \left(\dfrac{(2n)!}{2(n!)^2}\right)$ (d) $2^{2n-2} - \dfrac{(2n)!}{2(n!)^2}$

32. The value of $\sum\sum_{0\le i<j\le n}(i+j)C_iC_j$ is

(a) $n\sum\sum_{0\le i<j\le n}C_iC_j$ (b) $(n+1)\sum\sum_{0\le i<j\le n}C_iC_j$

(c) $(n-1)\sum\sum_{0\le i<j\le n}C_iC_j$ (d) $2\sum\sum_{0\le i<j<n}C_iC_j$

33. The value of $\sum\sum_{0\le i<j\le n}(i+j)(C_i+C_j+C_iC_j)$ is;

where $k = \sum\sum_{0\le i<j\le n}C_iC_j$

(a) $n(2^n+k)$ (b) $n^2.2^n+k$

(c) $n(n.2^n+k)$ (d) None of these

34. If $\sum_{r=0}^{n}\dfrac{1}{{}^nC_r} = \lambda$; then the value of $\sum\sum_{0\le i<j\le n}\left(\dfrac{i}{C_i}+\dfrac{j}{C_j}\right)$ will be

(a) $\dfrac{n\lambda}{2}$ (b) $\dfrac{n^2\lambda}{2}$

(c) $\dfrac{n\lambda^2}{2}$ (d) $\dfrac{n^2\lambda^2}{2}$

38. The value of $(k_1 - k_2)$; where k_1 is coeffcient of x^6 and k_2 is co-efficient of x^7 in the expansion of $(2+x)^3(3+x)^2(5+x)^3$ is

(a) 339 (b) 312

(c) 285 (d) None of these

Solution: 31. $(x+C_0)(x+C_1)(x+C_2)\ldots.(x+C_n)$

$= x^{n+1} + \sum_{i=0}^{n}C_i\,x^n + \sum\sum_{0\le i<j\le n}C_iC_j\,x^{n-1} + \ldots. + (C_0C_1C_2\ldots.C_n)$

$\therefore$ Co-efficient of x^{n-1} is $\sum\sum_{0\le i<j\le n} C_iC_j$

$=\frac{1}{2}\{(C_0 + C_1 + C_2 + ...C_n)^2 - (C_1^2 + C_2^2 + C_3^2 + ... + C_n^2)\}$

$= \frac{1}{2}\left[\left(2^n\right)^2 - \left[{}^{2n}C_n\right]\right] = \frac{1}{2}\left[2^{2n} - \frac{(2n)!}{(n!)^2}\right]$

$= 2^{2n-1} - \frac{(2n)!}{2(n!)^2} \Rightarrow$ Ans (b)

32. $P = \sum\sum_{0\le i<j\le n}(i+j)C_iC_j = \sum\sum_{0\le i<j\le n}(i+j)\,{}^nC_i\,{}^nC_j$ (i)

Replacing i by $(n - i)$ and j by $(n - j)$, we get,

$= \sum\sum_{0\le 1<j\ \le i}(n-i+n-j)\,{}^nC_{n-i}\,{}^nC_{n-j}$

$= \sum_{0\le i<j\le n}\left[2n-(i+j)\right]{}^nC_i.{}^nC_j$ (ii)

Adding (i) and (ii), we get

$2P = 2n\sum\sum_{0\le i<j\le n}{}^nC_i.{}^nC_j \Rightarrow P = n\sum\sum_{0\le i<j\le n}C_iC_j$

33. Let $P = \sum_{0\le i<j\le n}\sum(i+j)\left(C_i + C_j + C_iC_j\right)$ (i)

Replacing i by $(n - i)$ and j by $(n - j)$, we get

$P = \sum\sum_{0\le i\le j\le n}(n-i+n-j)\left(C_{n-i} + C_{n-j} + C_{n-i}C_{n-j}\right)$

$P = \sum\sum_{0\le i<j\le n}\{2n-(i+j)\}\left(C_i + C_j + C_iC_j\right)$ (ii)

Adding (i) and (ii), gives

$2P = \sum\sum_{0\le i<j\le n}2n\left(C_i + C_j + C_iC_j\right)$

$= 2n\sum\sum_{0\le i<j\le n}\left(C_i + C_j\right) + 2n\sum\sum_{0\le i<j\le n}C_iC_j$

$= 2n(n(2)^n) + 2nk = 2n^2(2)^n + 2nk$

$2P = 2n(n.2^n + k)$

$\Rightarrow P = n(n.2^n + k) \Rightarrow$ **Ans.** (c)

34. Let $P = \sum\sum_{0\le i<j\le n}\left(\frac{i}{{}^nC_i} + \frac{j}{{}^nC_j}\right)$ (i)

Replacing i by $(n-i)$ and j by $(n - j)$, we get

$P = \sum\sum_{0\le i<j\le n}\left(\frac{n-i}{{}^nC_{n-i}} + \frac{n-j}{{}^nC_{n-j}}\right)$ (ii)

Adding (i) and (ii), we get

$2P = \sum\sum_{0\le i<j\le n}n\left[\frac{1}{{}^nC_i} + \frac{1}{{}^nC_j}\right]$

$\Rightarrow 2P = n\sum_{i=0}^{n}n\left(\frac{1}{{}^nC_i}\right) = n^2\sum_{i=0}^{n}\frac{1}{{}^nC_i} = n^2\lambda$

$\Rightarrow P = \frac{n^2\lambda}{2} \Rightarrow$ **Ans.** (b)

35. $(2 + x)^3(3 + x)^2(5 + x)^3 = (2 + x)(2 + x)(2 + x)(3 + x)(3 + x)(5 + x)(5 + x)(5 + x) = x^8 + (2 + 2 + 2 + 3 + 3 + 5 + 5 + 5)x^7 +$

$(2.2 + 2.2 + 2.3 + ...5.5)x^6 +$ ....

→ {Product of (2, 2, 2, 3, 3, 5, 5, 5) taking 2 at a time}

$\therefore k_2$ = Co-efficient of $x^7 = (2 + 2 + 2 + 3 + 3 + 5 + 5 + 5) = 27$

and k_1 = co-efficient $x^6 = \frac{1}{2}[(2 + 2 + 2 + 3 + 3 + 5 + 5 + 5)^2 - (2^2 + 2^2 + 2^2 + 3^2 + 3^2 + 5^2 + 5^2 + 5^2)]$

$= \frac{1}{2}[(27)^2 - (105)] = 312$

$\therefore k_1 - k_2 = 312 - 27 = (285)$

$\therefore$ **Ans.** (c)

36. The greatest term of $\sqrt{3}\left[1+\frac{1}{\sqrt{3}}\right]^{20}$ is T_λ, then λ = ?

Solution: We know that the term with greatest magnitude in $(1 + x)^n$ is given by T_{r+1}; where

$r = \left[\frac{(n+1)|x|}{|x|+1}\right]$; where [.] stands for gint function

$\therefore r = \left[\frac{(21).\frac{1}{\sqrt{3}}}{\left|\frac{1}{\sqrt{3}}\right|+1}\right] = \left[\frac{21}{1+\sqrt{3}}\right] = \left[(10.5)\left(\sqrt{3}-1\right)\right]$

$= [(10.5)(0.732)] = [7.6860] = 7$

$\therefore T_{r+1} = T_8$ will be the greatest term

$\therefore \lambda = 8$

37. For what value of (m), the sum $\sum_{i=0}^{20}{}^{20}C_i\,{}^{40}C_{m-i}$ has maximum value $(m \ge 20)$?

Solution: The given sum $= ({}^{20}C_0.{}^{40}C_m + {}^{20}C_1.{}^{40}C_{m-1} + ..{}^{20}C_{20}.{}^{40}C_{m-20})$ = co-efficient of x^m in the expression

$({}^{20}C_0 + {}^{20}C_1x + {}^{20}C_2x^2 + ... + {}^{20}C_mx^m + ... {}^{20}C_{20}x^{20})$

$\times ({}^{40}C_{30}x^{30} + ... + {}^{40}C_mx^m + {}^{40}C_{m-1}x^{m-1} + {}^{40}C_{m-2}x^{m-2} + ... + {}^{40}C_{m-2}x^{m-20} + ...+{}^{40}C_1x^1 + {}^{40}C_0$

Co-efficient of x^m in the expansion of $(1 + x)^{20}(1 + x)^{40} = (1 + x)^{60} = {}^{60}C_m$

which will be maximum and is equal to ${}^{60}C_{30}$ for $m = 30$

$\therefore$ **Ans.** 30

38. If $\sum_{r=0}^{n}(r^2+r+1)r! = (2000)(2000)!$, then evaluate the co-efficient of x^{n+1} in the expansion of $\left(x+\frac{1}{x}\right)^{2000}$.

Solution: $\sum_{r=0}^{n}\{r^2(r)! + (r+1)!\}$

$$= \sum_{r=0}^{n}(r^2-1+1)r! + \sum_{r=0}^{n}(r+1)!$$

$$= \sum_{r=0}^{n}(r+1)(r-1)(r!) + \sum_{r=0}^{n}r! + \sum_{r=0}^{n}(r+1)!$$

$$= \sum_{r=0}^{n}(r+1)!(r-1) + \sum_{r=0}^{n}r! + \sum_{r=0}^{n}(r+1)!$$

$$= \sum_{r=0}^{n}((r+2)-3)(r+1)! + \sum_{r=0}^{n}r! + \sum_{r=0}^{n}(r+1)!$$

$$= \sum_{r=0}^{n}(r+2)! + \sum_{r=0}^{n}r! - 2\sum_{r=0}^{n}(r+1)!$$

$$= \sum_{r=0}^{n}\{(r+2)! - (r+1)!\} - \sum_{r=0}^{n}\{(r+1)! - r!\}$$

$$= \sum_{r=0}^{n}(r+1)(r+1)! - \sum_{r=0}^{n}r(r!)$$

$$1.(1!) - 0.(0!)$$
$$+2.(2!) - 1.(1!)$$
$$+3.(3!) - 2.(2!)$$
$$+4.(4!) - 3.(3!)$$
$$= + \quad \vdots \quad \vdots \quad \vdots \quad \vdots \quad \vdots$$
$$(n+1)\,(n+1)! - n\,(n!)$$

$= (n+1)(n+1)!$

$\Rightarrow n = 1999$

Now $(x + 1/x)^{2000} = x^{-2000}(x^2+1)^{2000}$

$\therefore$ Co-efficient of x^{n+1} is co-efficient of x^{2000} in the expansion of $x^{-2000}(1+x^2)^{2000}$

= Co-efficient of x^{4000} in the expansion of $(1+x^2)^{2000}$

$= {}^{2000}C_{2000} = 1$

$\therefore$ **Ans.** 1

39. If the co-efficients of the $(2r+4)^{th}$, $(r-2)^{th}$ terms in the expansion of $(1+x)^{18}$ are equal, find r.

Solution: For $(1+x)^{18}$,

$T_{2r+4} = {}^{18}C_{2r+3}\,(1)^{18-2r-3}\,(x)^{2r+3}$ and

$T_{r-2} = {}^{18}C_{r-3}\,(1)^{18-r+3}\,x^{r-3}$

Given that coefficients are equal, ${}^{18}C_{2r+3} = {}^{18}C_{r-3}$

$\Rightarrow 2r+3+r-3 = 18$ or $2r+3 = r-3$

$\Rightarrow r = 6$ or $r = -6 \quad \Rightarrow r = 6$ as $r \geq 2$ and $r \in W$.

40. If the co-efficients of the rth, $(r+1)^{th}$, $(r-2)^{th}$ terms in the expansion of $(1+x)^{14}$ are in A.P., then find $\sqrt{s+2}$ (where s = sum of all possible values of r).

Solution: Here $T_r = {}^{14}C_{r-1}.(x)^{r-1}$;

$T_{r+1} = {}^{14}C_r\,.\,(x)^r$;

and $T_{r+2} = {}^{14}C_{r+1}.(x)^{r+1}$

$\because\ {}^{14}C_{r-1}, {}^{14}C_r, {}^{14}C_{r+1}$ are in A.P. (Given)

$2.\,{}^{14}C_r = {}^{14}C_{r-1} + {}^{14}C_{r+1}$

$$\Rightarrow \frac{2.14!}{(14-r)!r!} = \frac{14!}{(14-r+1)!(r-1)!} + \frac{14!}{(14-r-1)!\,(r+1)!}$$

$$\Rightarrow \frac{2}{(14-r)(13-r)!r(r-1)!} = \frac{1}{(15-r)(14-r)(13-r)!(r-1)!} + \frac{1}{(13-r)!\,(r+1)r(r-1)!}$$

$$\Rightarrow \frac{2}{(14-r)r} = \frac{1}{(15-r)\,(14-r)} + \frac{1}{r(r+1)}$$

$$\Rightarrow \frac{2}{(14-r)r} - \frac{1}{r(r+1)} = \frac{1}{(15-r)\,(14-r)}$$

$$\Rightarrow \frac{3r-12}{r(r+1)} = \frac{1}{(15-r)}$$

$\Rightarrow r = 5$ or $9 \Rightarrow s = 5+9 = 14$

$\Rightarrow \sqrt{s+2} = \sqrt{14+2} = 4$

41. Find the value of x for which the fourth term in the expansion of $\left(5^{\frac{2}{5}\log_5\sqrt{4^x+44}} + \frac{1}{5^{\log_5\sqrt[3]{2^{x-1}+7}}}\right)^8$ is 336.

Solution: $\left(5^{\frac{2}{5}\log_5\sqrt{4^x+44}} + \frac{1}{5^{\log_5\sqrt[3]{2^{x-1}+7}}}\right)^8$

$$= \left(\left(\sqrt{4^x+44}\right)^{2/5} + \left(\frac{1}{\sqrt[3]{2^{x-1}+7}}\right)\right)^8$$

$$\left[\because a^{\log_a f(x)} = f(x)\right]$$

$$= \left((4^x+44)^{1/5} + \frac{1}{(2^{x-1}+7)^{1/3}} \right)^8$$

Fourth term (T_4)

$$= T_{3+1} = {}^8C_3\,(4^x+44)^{1/5})^{8-3} \times \frac{1}{((2^{x-1}+7)^{1/3})^3}$$

$$336 = {}^8C_3\left(\frac{4^x+44}{2^{x-1}+7}\right)$$

$$\Rightarrow 336 = {}^8C_3\left(\frac{2^{2x}+44}{2^x.2^{-1}+7}\right)$$

$$336 = {}^8C_3\left(\frac{y^2+44}{(y/2)+7}\right)$$

$$\Rightarrow\ 336 = \frac{8\times7\times6}{3\times2\times1}.\left(\frac{2(y^2+44)}{y+14}\right),$$

where $2^x = y$

$\Rightarrow\ 3y + 42 = y^2 + 44$

$\Rightarrow\ 2^x = 0$ or $2^x = 2$

$\Rightarrow\ x = 1$

$(\because\ 2^x > 0\forall x \in \mathbb{R})$

42. In the expansion of $\left(1+x+\frac{7}{x}\right)^{11}$, find the number of terms not containing x.

Solution: The general term of $\left(1+x+\frac{7}{x}\right)^{11}$ is

$$\sum_{r_1+r_2+r_3=11} \frac{11!}{r_1!r_2!r_3!}(1)^{r_1}(x)^{r_2}\left(\frac{7}{x}\right)^{r_3}$$

i.e., $$\sum_{r_1+r_2+r_3=11} \frac{11!}{r_1!r_2!r_3!}x^{r_2-r_3}\,7^{r_3}$$

For terms independent of x, $r_2 - r_3 = 0$

$\Rightarrow\ r_2 = r_3$

$\therefore\ r_1 + r_2 + r_3 = 11$

$\Rightarrow\ r_1 = 11 - 2r_2$

r_1	r_2	r_3
$11–2r_2$	r_2	r_2
11	0	0
9	1	1
7	2	2
5	3	3
3	4	4
1	5	5

So, $(r_1,r_2,r_3) \in \{(11, 0, 0); (9, 1, 1)\ (7, 2, 2); (5, 3, 3); (3, 4, 4); (1, 5, 5)\}$ for terms independent of x.

Thus there will be total 6 such terms.

43. If $(7+4\sqrt{3})^n = p+\beta$; where n and p are positive integers and β is a proper fraction then evaluate $(1-\beta)(p+\beta)$.

Solution: $(p+\beta) = (7+4\sqrt{3})^n$; $G = (7-4\sqrt{3})^n \in (0, 1)$; $p + \beta + G \in \mathbb{Z}$

$\Rightarrow\ \beta + G = 1$ as $\beta + G \in (0, 2)$

$\Rightarrow (1-\beta)(p+\beta) = G(p+\beta) = (7-4\sqrt{3})^n(7+4\sqrt{3})^n$

$= (49 - 48)^n = 1$

44. Let $a = 3^{\frac{1}{223}}+1$ and for all $n \geq 3$, let $f(n) = {}^nC_0.a^{n-1} - {}^nC_1.\,a^{n-2} + {}^nC_2.a^{n-3} - .... + (-1)^{n-1}.{}^nC_{n-1}\,.\,a^0$. If the value of $f(2007) + f(2008) = (3)^k$; where $k \in \mathbb{N}$, then find k.

Solution: $f(n) = {}^nC_0a^{n-1} - {}^nC_1\,a^{n-2} + {}^nC_2a^{n-3} + ... + (-1)^{n-1}\,{}^nC_{n-1}a^0$

$$= \frac{1}{a}({}^nC_0\ a^n - {}^nC_1\ a^{n-1} + {}^nC_2\ a^{n-2} + ... + (-1)^{n-1}C_{n-1}\,a)$$

$$= \frac{1}{a}((a-1)^n - (-1)^n\,{}^nC_n) = \frac{1}{a}\left(((3)^{n/223} - (-1)^n)\right)$$

$$\Rightarrow\ f(n) = \frac{3^{\frac{n}{223}} - (-1)^n}{\left(3^{\frac{1}{223}}+1\right)};\ f(2007) = \frac{3^{\frac{2007}{223}}+1}{3^{\frac{1}{223}}+1};$$

$$f(2008) = \frac{3^{\frac{2008}{223}}-1}{3^{\frac{1}{223}}+1};$$

$$f(2007)+f(2008) = \frac{3^{\frac{2007}{223}}+3^{\frac{2008}{223}}}{3^{\frac{1}{223}}+1}$$

$$= \frac{3^9+3^{9+\frac{1}{223}}}{3^{\frac{1}{223}}+1}$$

$$= 3^9\frac{\left(1+3^{\frac{1}{223}}\right)}{\left(1+3^{\frac{1}{223}}\right)} = 3^9 = 3^k \Rightarrow k = 9$$

SECTION–III

OBJECTIVE-TYPE (ONLY ONE CORRECT ANSWER)

1. If the $(r+1)^{th}$ term in the expansion of $\left(\sqrt[3]{\frac{a}{\sqrt{b}}}+\sqrt{\frac{b}{\sqrt[3]{a}}}\right)^{21}$ has the same power of a and b, then the value of r is

(a) 9 (b) 10
(c) 8 (d) 6

2. If the sum of the coeffecients in the expansion of $(a+b)^n$ is 2048, then the greatest co-efficient in the expansion is

(a) ${}^{12}C_5$ (b) ${}^{11}C_5$
(c) ${}^{12}C_7$ (d) ${}^{11}C_7$

3. If the co-efficient of 2nd, 3rd and 4th term in the expansion of $(1+x)^n$, $n \in N$ are in $A.P.$ then n is

(a) 7 (b) 14
(c) 2 (d) None of these

4. If, in the expansion of $(1+x)^m(1-x)^n$, the co-efficient of x and x^2 are respectively 3 and – 6, then value of m is

(a) 6 (b) 9
(c) 12 (d) 24

5. If x^m occurs in the expansion of $[x+(1/(x)^2)]^{2n}$, then the co-efficient of the x^m is

(a) $\dfrac{(2n)!}{m!(2n-m)!}$

(b) $\dfrac{(2n)!\,3!\,3!}{(2n-m)!}$

(c) $\dfrac{(2n)!}{[(2n-m)/3]!\,[(4n+m)/3]!}$

(d) None of these

6. The positive value of a so that the co-efficent of x^5 and x^{15} are equal in the expansion of $\left(x^2+\frac{a}{x^3}\right)^{10}$.

(a) $\dfrac{1}{2\sqrt{3}}$ (b) $\dfrac{1}{\sqrt{3}}$
(c) 1 (d) None of these

7. The co-efficient of x in the expansion of $(1-2x^2+3x^5)[1+(1/x)]^8$ is

(a) 56 (b) 65
(c) 194 (d) 62

8. The co-efficient of x^7 in the expansion of $(1-x^4)(1+x)^9$ is

(a) ${}^9C_7$ (b) ${}^9C_3$
(c) ${}^9C_7-{}^9C_3$ (d) None of these

9. The co-efficient of x^{17} in the expansion of $[(x-1)(x-2)(x-3)\ldots.(x-18)]$ is

(a) 342 (b) $\dfrac{171}{2}$
(c) –171 (d) 684

10. The co-efficient of x^6 in $(1+x)^6+(1+x)^7+\ldots.+(1+x)^{15}$ is

(a) ${}^{16}C_9$ (b) ${}^{16}C_5-{}^6C_5$
(c) ${}^{16}C_6-1$ (d) None of these

11. If 6th term in the expansion of $\left[\frac{1}{x^{8/3}}+x^2\log_{10}x\right]^8$ is 5600, then x is equal to

(a) 5 (b) 4
(c) 8 (d) 10

12. If $(1+x-2x^2)^8 = a_0+a_1x+a_2x^2+\ldots+a_{16}x^{16}$, then the sum $a_0+a_2+a_4+\ldots+a_{16}$ is

(a) -2^7 (b) 2^7
(c) 2^8 (d) None of these

13. If $n \in \mathbb{N}$, then $C_1-2C_2x+3C_3x^2-4C_4x^3+$ *up to* n terms is equal to

(a) $n(1-x)^{n-1}$ (b) $n(1+x)^{n-1}$
(c) $(-1)^n.n(1+x)^{n-1}$ (d) $(-1)^r.n(1+x)^{n-1}$

14. The largest term in the expansion of $(3+2x)^{50}$ where $x = 1/5$ is

(a) 5th (b) 51st
(c) 7th (d) 61th

15. The co-efficient of $a^8b^6c^4$ in the expansion of $(a+b+c)^{18}$ is

(a) ${}^{18}C_{14}.\,{}^{14}C_8$ (b) ${}^{18}C_{12}.\,{}^{10}C_6$
(c) ${}^{18}C_{16}.\,{}^{12}C_8$ (d) ${}^{18}C_{14}.\,{}^{14}C_6$

16. The sum of $\frac{1}{2}\,{}^{10}C_0-{}^{10}C_1+2.\,{}^{10}C_2-2^2.\,{}^{10}C_3+\ldots\ldots.\,2^9.\,{}^{10}C_{10}$ is equal to.

(a) 1/2 (b) 0
(c) $1/2.\,3^{10}$ (d) None of these

17. The remainder when 2^{2003} is divided by 17 is
(a) 1 (b) 2
(c) 8 (d) None of these

18. In the expansion of $\left[\sqrt[3]{4}+\frac{1}{\sqrt[4]{6}}\right]^{20}$
(a) the number of rational terms = 4
(b) the number of irrational terms = 18
(c) the middle term is irrational
(d) the number of irrational terms = 7

19. The number of irrational terms in the expansion of $(5^{1/6} + 2^{1/8})^{100}$ is
(a) 96 (b) 97
(c) 98 (d) 99

20. The co-efficient of x^{13} in the expansion of $(1 - x)^5 (1 + x + x^2 + x^3)^4$ is
(a) 4 (b) – 4
(c) 0 (d) None of these

21. Co-efficient of x^5 in the expansion of $(1 + x^2)^5 (1 + x)^4$ is
(a) 40 (b) 50
(c) 30 (d) 60

22. In the binomial expansion of $(a - b)^n$, $n \geq 5$ the sum of the 5th and 6th terms is zero. Then a/b equals
(a) $\frac{n-5}{6}$ (b) $\frac{n-4}{5}$
(c) $\frac{5}{n-4}$ (d) $\frac{6}{n-5}$

23. Co-efficient of x^n in the expansion of $\left(\frac{1-x}{1+x}\right)^2$ is
(a) $(-1)^n 4n$ (b) $4n$
(c) $(-1)^n (n + 4)$ (d) None of these

24. If $(1 + x)^n = C_0 + C_1x + C_2x^2 + ... + C_nx^n$, then $\frac{C_1}{C_0}+\frac{2C_2}{C_1}+\frac{3C_3}{C_2}+....+\frac{nC_n}{C_{n-1}}$ is equal to
(a) $\frac{n(n-1)}{2}$ (b) $\frac{n(n+2)}{2}$
(c) $\frac{n(n+1)}{2}$ (d) $\frac{(n-1)(n-2)}{2}$

25. The expression ${}^{n+1}C_2 + 2\,({}^2C_2 + {}^3C_2 + {}^4C_2 .. + {}^nC_2)$ reduces to
(a) $\frac{n(n+1)(n+2)}{6}$ (b) $\frac{n(n-1)(n-2)}{3}$
(c) $\frac{n(n+1)(2n+1)}{6}$ (d) None of these

26. If m and n are any two odd positive integers with $n < m$, then the largest positive integer which divides all numbers of the form $(m^2–n^2)$ is
(a) 4 (b) 6
(c) 8 (d) 9

27. The co-efficient of $x^n y^n$ in the expansion of $[(1 + x)(1 + y)(x + y)]^n$ is
(a) $2n$ (b) $\sum_{r=0}^{n} C_r^3 32^{32^{32}}$
(c) $\sum_{r=0}^{n} C_r^3$ (d) None of these

28. If $a_n = \sum_{r=0}^{n}\frac{1}{{}^nC_r}$ then $\sum_{r=0}^{n}\frac{r}{{}^nC_r}$ equals (where n is even + ve integer)
(a) $(n - 1)a_n$ (b) $(n - 2)a_n$
(c) $(n/2)a_n$ (d) None of these

29. If $A = (300)^{600}$, $B = (600)!$, $C = (200)^{600}$, then
(a) $A < B < C$ (b) $A > B > C$
(c) $A > C$ and $C = B$ (d) $A = B$ and $B > C$

30. In the expansion of $\left(3-\sqrt{\frac{17}{4}+3\sqrt{2}}\right)^{15}$, the 11th term is a
(a) positive integer
(b) positive irrational number
(c) negative integer
(d) negative irrational number

31. Co-efficient of x^6 in the expansion of $\frac{1}{(1-x+x^2)^3}$, $|x| < 1$ is
(a) 9 (b) –3
(c) 6 (d) None of these

32. Let n be an odd integer, If $\sin n\theta = \sum_{r=0}^{n} b_r \sin^r\theta$ for every value of θ, then
(a) $b_0 = 1, b_1 = 3$ (b) $b_0 = 0, b_1 = n$
(c) $b_0 = -1, b_1 = n$ (d) $b_0 = 0, b_1 = n^2 - 3n + 3$

33. The co-efficient of x^4 in the expansion of $(1 + x + x^2 + x^3)^n$ is
(a) ${}^nC_4$ (b) ${}^nC_4 + {}^nC_2$
(c) ${}^nC_4 + {}^nC_2 + {}^nC_4 . {}^nC_2$ (d) ${}^nC_2 + {}^{n+1}C_3 + {}^{n+2}C_4$

34. If $n \in N$ and $0 < x < 1$, then $C_1x(1 - x)^{n-1} + 2C_2x^2(1 - x)^{n-2} + 3C_3x^3(1 - x)^{n-3} + ... + n.{}^nC_nx^n$ is equal to
(a) nx (b) $n(n - 1)x^2$
(c) $nx(1 - x)^n$ (d) $n(n + 1)x^2$

35. The positive integer just greater than $(1 + 0.0001)^{10000}$ is

(a) 4 (b) 5
(c) 2 (d) 3

36. The last digit in 7^{300} is

(a) 7 (b) 9
(c) 1 (d) 3

37. The sum to $(n + 1)$ terms of the following series

$\frac{C_0}{2} - \frac{C_1}{3} + \frac{C_2}{4} - \frac{C_3}{5} + ...$ is

(a) $\frac{1}{n+1}$ (b) $\frac{1}{n+2}$
(c) $\frac{1}{n(n+1)}$ (d) None of these

38. The value of x for which the 6th term in the expansion of $\left\{ \log\sqrt{(9 \quad 7)} \quad \frac{}{(1/5)\log(3 \quad 1)} \right\}$ is 84 is

(a) 4 (b) 3
(c) 2 (d) 10

39. Let $f(n) = 10^n + 3.4^{n+2} + 5$, $n \in N$. The greatest value of the integer which divides $f(n)$ for all n is

(a) 27 (b) 9
(c) 3 (d) None of these

40. If $n > 3$ and $a, b \in \mathbb{R}$, then the value of $ab - n(a-1)(b-1) + \frac{n(n-1)}{1.2}(a-2)(b-2)$ ..... $+ (-1)^n(a-n)(b-n)$

(a) $a^n + b^n$ (b) $\frac{a^n - b^n}{a-b}$
(c) $(a\ b)^n$ (d) None of these

41. When $32^{32^{32}}$ is divided by 7, then the remiander is

(a) 2 (b) 3
(c) 4 (d) 5

42. The last two digits of the number 17^{256} are

(a) 61 (b) 81
(c) 68 (d) 01

43. $\sum_{r=0}^{n} (-1)^r\ {}^nC_r \frac{1 + r\log_e 10}{(1 + \log_e 10^n)^r}$ equals

(a) 1 (b) –1
(c) n (d) None of these

44. Integral part of $(6\sqrt{6} + 14)^{2n+1}$ is

(a) an even integer (b) an odd integer
(c) a prime integer (d) None of these

45. If $[x]$ denotes greatest integer $\le x$, then $[(2+\sqrt{3})^P] - 2^{P+1} + 1$, where P is prime number greater than 2 is

(a) is not divisible by P
(b) is divisible by P
(c) cannot say anything
(d) None of these

46. Given positive integers $r > 1$, $n > 2$ and that the coefficient of $(3r)^{\text{th}}$ and $(r + 2)^{\text{th}}$ terms in the binomial expansion of $(1 - x)^{2n}$ are equal. Then

(a) $n = 2r$ (b) $n = 2r + 1$
(c) $n = 3r$ (d) None of these

47. The expression $\left(x + (x^3 - 1)^{\frac{1}{2}}\right)^6 + \left(x - (x^3 - 1)^{\frac{1}{2}}\right)^6$ is a polynomial of degeree

(a) 5 (b) 6
(c) 9 (d) 8

48. The sum $\sum_{i=0}^{m} \binom{10}{i}\binom{20}{m-i}$, (where $\binom{p}{q} = 0$ if $p < q$) is maximum when m is

(a) 5 (b) 10
(c) 15 (d) 20

49. Co-efficient of t^{24} in $(1 + t^2)^{12}(1 + t^{12})(1 + t^{24})$ is

(a) ${}^{12}C_6 + 3$ (b) ${}^{12}C_6 + 1$
(c) ${}^{12}C_6$ (d) ${}^{12}C_6 + 2$

50. If ${}^{n-1}C_r = (k^2 - 3)\ {}^nC_{r+1}$, then $k \in$

(a) $(-\infty, -2]$ (b) $[2, \infty)$
(c) $[-\sqrt{3}, \sqrt{3}]$ (d) $(-\sqrt{3}, 2]$

51. If C_r stands for ${}^nC_r$, then the sum of the series

$\frac{2\left(\frac{n}{2}\right)!\left(\frac{n}{2}\right)!}{n!}[C_0^2 - 2C_1^2 + 3C_2^2 - ......+(-1)^n(n+1)C_n^2]$,

where n is an even positive integer, is equal to

(a) 0 (b) $(-1)^{n/2}(n + 1)$
(c) $(-1)^{n/2}(n + 2)$ (d) None of these

SECTION–IV

OBJECTIVE-TYPE (MORE THAN ONE CORRECT ANSWER)

1. If P_n denotes the product of all the co-efficients in the expansion of$(1 + x)^n$, then $\frac{P_{n+1}}{P_n}$

(a) $\frac{(n+1)^n}{n!}$ (b) $\frac{(n+1)^{n+1}}{(n+1)!}$

(c) $\frac{(n+1)^{n+1}}{n!}$ (d) $\frac{(n+1)^n}{(n+1)!}$

2. The co-efficient of x^{33} in the expansion of $\sum_{r=0}^{50} {}^{50}C_r (x-4)^{50-r} 3^r$ is

(a) ${}^{50}C_{33}$ (b) $-{}^{50}C_{33}$

(c) $-{}^{50}C_{17}$ (d) ${}^{50}C_{17}$

3. The co-efficient of $a^8\, b^6\, c^4$ in the expansion of $(a + b + c)^{18}$ is

(a) ${}^{18}C_{14}\ {}^{14}C_8$ (b) ${}^{18}C_{10}.\ {}^{10}C_6$

(c) ${}^{18}C_6.\ {}^{12}C_8$ (d) ${}^{18}C_4.\ {}^{14}C_6$

4. In the expansion of $\left(\sqrt[3]{4}+\frac{1}{\sqrt[4]{6}}\right)^{20}$,

(a) the number of rational terms = 2

(b) the number of irrational terms = 20

(c) the middle term is irrational

(d) the number of irrational terms = 17

5. In the expansion of $(x + y + z)^{25}$

(a) every term is of the form ${}^{25}C_r.\ {}^rC_k.x^{25-r}.y^{r-k}.z^k$

(b) the co-efficient of $x^8\, y^9\, z^9$ is 0

(c) the number of terms is 325

(d) None of these

6. The value of $C_0^2 + 3C_1^2 + 5C_2^2 + \ldots$ to$(n + 1)$ terms is (given that $C_r \equiv {}^nC_r$)

(a) ${}^{2n-1}C_{n-1}$ (b) $(2n + 1).\ {}^{2n-1}C_n$

(c) $2(n + 1).\ {}^{2n-1}C_n$ (d) ${}^{2n-1}C_n + (2n + 1).{}^{2n-1}C_{n-1}$

7. The number of distinct terms in the expansion of $(x + 2y - 3z + 5w - 7u)^n$ is

(a) $n + 1$

(b) ${}^{n+4}C_4$

(c) ${}^{n+4}C_n$

(d) $\frac{(n+1)(n+2)(n+3)(n+4)}{24}$

8. If n is positive integer and $(3\sqrt{3} + 5)^{2n+1} = \alpha + \beta$ where α is an integer and $0 < \beta < 1$, then

(a) α is an even integer

(b) $(\alpha + \beta)^2$ is divisible by 2^{2n+1}

(c) The integer just below $(3\sqrt{3} + 5)^{2n+1}$ divisible by 3

(d) α is divisible by 10

9. If $(8 + 3\sqrt{7})^n = P + F$, where P is an integer and F is a proper fraction, then

(a) P is an odd integer (b) P is an even integer

(c) $F.(F + P) = 1$ (d) $(1- F)(P + F) = 1$

10. Let $a_n = (1 + 1/n)^n$, then for each $n \in \mathbb{N}$.

(a) $a_n \geq 2$ (b) $a_n < 3$

(c) $a_n < 4$ (d) $a_n < 2$

11. The number $101^{100} - 1$ is divisible by

(a) 100 (b) 1000

(c) 10000 (d) 100000

12. The sum of the series $\sum_{r=0}^{n} (-1)^r.{}^nC_r\ [\sin r\,\theta - i\cos r\,\theta]$ is

(a) 0 if $\theta = 2\pi$

(b) 0 if $\theta = 0$

(c) $-2^{2m+1}\, i$ if $n = 2m + 1$ and $\theta = \pi$

(d) None of these

SECTION–V

ASSERTION AND REASON TYPE

The questions given below consist of an assersion (A) and the reason (R). Use the following key to choose the appropriate answer.

(a) If both assertion and reason are correct and reason is the correct explanation of the assertion.

(b) If both assertion and reason are correct but reason is not correct explanation of the assertion.

(c) If assertion is correct, but reason is incorrect

(d) If assertion is incorrect, but reason is correct

Now consider the following statements:

1. **A:** The term independent of x in the expansion of $\left(x+\dfrac{1}{x}+2\right)^m$ is $\dfrac{(2m!)}{(m!)^2}$

   R: The co-efficient of x^b in the expansion of $(1+x)^n$ is ${}^nC_b$.

2. **A:** If $S_n = {}^nC_1 - \dfrac{{}^nC_2}{2} + \dfrac{{}^nC_3}{3} - \ldots\ldots + \dfrac{(-1)^{n-1}\,{}^nC_n}{n}$ and $T_n = 1+\dfrac{1}{2}+\dfrac{1}{3}+\ldots.+\dfrac{1}{n}$, then $S_n = T_n$ for all n

   R: $S_{n+1} - S_n = T_{n+1} - T_n$

3. **A:** If $A = \sum_{r=0}^{n} \dfrac{1}{C_r}$ and $S = \sum\sum_{0\le i<j\le n}\left(\dfrac{i}{C_i}+\dfrac{j}{C_j}\right)$ then $S = \dfrac{n^2 A}{2}$

   R: If $T = \sum\sum_{0\le i<j\le n}\left(\dfrac{1}{C_i}+\dfrac{1}{C_j}\right)$ then $T = nA$

4. **A:** $\dfrac{1}{m!}C_0 + \dfrac{n}{(m+1)!}C_1 + \dfrac{n(n-1)}{(m+2)!}C_2 + \ldots\ldots. + \dfrac{n(n-1)\ldots\ldots2.1}{(m+n)!}C_n = \dfrac{(m+n+1)(m+n+2)\ldots(m+2n)}{(m+n)!}$

   R: For $r \ge 0$, $\binom{m}{r}C_o + \binom{m}{r-1}C_1 + \binom{m}{r-2}C_2 + \ldots. + \binom{m}{0}C_r = \binom{m+n}{r}$

5. **A:** $\sum_{r=1}^{n}(r)C_r^2 = n\binom{2n-1}{n-1}$

   R: $\sum_{r=0}^{n}C_r^2 = \binom{2n}{n}$

6. **A:** For non-negative integers m, n, r and k, $\sum_{m=0}^{k}(n-m)\dfrac{(r+m)!}{m!} = \dfrac{(r+k+1)!}{k!}\left[\dfrac{n}{r+1}-\dfrac{k}{r+2}\right]$

   R: $\sum_{m=0}^{k}\binom{r+m}{m} = \binom{r+k+1}{k}$.

7. **A:** In the expansion of $(3-5x)^{15}$, for $x = 1/5$, 4th terms is numerically greatest.

   R: In the expansion of $(a+x)^n$, if $r = \dfrac{(n+1)|x|}{|a|+|x|}$ is an integer for some given value of x say x_0, for $x = x_0$ then $(r+1)$th term is numerically greatest term in the expansion.

8. **A:** Co-efficient of $a^2b^3c^4$ in the expansion of $(a+b+c)^8$ is zero.

   R: Co-efficient of $a^\alpha b^\beta c^\gamma$ where $\alpha+\beta+\gamma = n$, in the expansion of $(\alpha+\beta+\gamma) = n$ is the expansion of $(a+b+c)^n$ is $\dfrac{n!}{\alpha!\beta!\gamma!}$.

9. **A:** The greatest value of ${}^{40}C_0 . {}^{60}C_r + {}^{40}C_1\,{}^{60}C_{r-1}$ ...... ${}^{40}C_{40} . {}^{60}C_{r-40}$ is ${}^{100}C_{50}$

   R: The greatest value of ${}^{2n}C_r$ occurs at $r = n$.

10. **A:** Co-efficient of x^4 in the expansion of $\left(x^2+\dfrac{1}{x}\right)^{11}$ is $\dfrac{11!}{6!5!}$.

    R: Co-efficient of x^p in the expansion of $\left(x^2+\dfrac{1}{x}\right)^n$, where p, n∈N and $2n-p$ is positive and divisible by 3, is $\dfrac{(n)!}{\left(\dfrac{2n-p}{3}\right)!\left(\dfrac{n+p}{3}\right)!}$.

SECTION–VI

LINKED COMPREHENSION TYPE

Passage 1:

Let T_r and T_{r+1} be r[th] and $(r+1)$[th] terms respectively in the expansion of binomial $(x+a)^n$. Then

$$T_r = {}^nC_{r-1}\,x^{n-r+1}a^{r-1} \text{ and } T_{r+1} = {}^nC_r\,x^{n-r}a^r$$

$$\therefore \quad \frac{T_{r+1}}{T_r} = \frac{n-r+1}{r}\frac{a}{x}$$

Now, $T_{r+1} >,=,< T_r$ According as $\left(\dfrac{n-r+1}{r}\right)\dfrac{a}{x} >,=,< 1$, i.e., according as $\dfrac{n+1}{r}-1 >,=,< \dfrac{x}{a}$, i.e., according as $<,=,> \dfrac{\dfrac{n+1}{\dfrac{x}{a}+1}}{}$. So, if $\dfrac{n+1}{\dfrac{x}{a}+1}$ is an integer, say p, then $T_{r+1} > T_r$ if $r < p$ otherwise $T_{r+1} \le T_r$.

So, $T_p = T_{p+1}$ (numerically) and these are greater than any other term in the expansion.

Next, if $\frac{n+1}{\frac{x}{a}+1}$ is a non-integer, suppose m be its integral part then $T_{r+1} < T_r$ if $r \le m$ and $T_{r+1} < T_r$ if $r > m$.

So, T_{m+1} is the numerically greatest term among the terms of the expansion.

Again, we can also write that k^{th} term is numerically greatest if $T_k > T_{k+1}$ and $T_k > T_{k-1}$.

1. The numerical value of numerically greatest term in the expansion of $(1 - 2x)^8$, when $x = 2$ is
   (a) ${}^8C_6\,4^6$ (b) ${}^8C_4\,4^4$
   (c) 2^{17} (d) None of these
2. Magnitude wise the greatest term in the expansion of $(3 - 2x)^9$ when $x = 1$ is
   (a) ${}^9C_2\,3^7\,2^2$ (b) ${}^9C_3\,3^6\,2^3$
   (c) ${}^9C_4\,3^5\,2^4$ (d) both (b) and (c)
3. If $x > 0$ and the 4th term in the expansion of $\left(2+\frac{3}{8}x\right)^{10}$ has maximum value, then the posibilities are
   (a) $2 < x < 3$ (b) $3 < x < \frac{10}{3}$
   (c) $4 < x < 5$ (d) None of these
4. If n is even positive integer, then the condition that the numerically greatest term in the expansion of $(1 + x)^n$ may have the greatest co-efficient also is
   (a) $\frac{n}{n+2} < |x| < \frac{n+2}{n}$ (b) $\frac{n}{n+1} < |x| < \frac{n}{n+1}$
   (c) $\frac{n}{n+4} < |x| < \frac{n+4}{n}$ (d) None of these
5. The interval to which x must belong so that the numerically greatest term in the expansion of $(1 - x)^{21}$ has the greatest co-efficient is $(x > 0)$.
   (a) $\left[\frac{5}{6}, \frac{6}{5}\right]$ (b) $\left[\frac{5}{6}, \frac{6}{5}\right)$
   (c) $\left(\frac{4}{5}, \frac{5}{4}\right)$ (d) $\left[\frac{4}{5}, \frac{5}{4}\right]$

Passage 2:

We know that if ${}^nC_0$, ${}^nC_1$, ${}^nC_2$, ..., ${}^nC_n$ are binomial co-efficients, then

Various relations among binomial co-efficients can be derived by putting $x = \pm 1, \pm i, \omega, \omega^2$; where $i = \sqrt{-1}, \omega = \frac{-1+i\sqrt{3}}{2}$. Some other identities can be derived by adding and subtracting two such identities. The expression $(a + ib)^n$ can be evaluated by using Demoivre's theorem by putting a $= r\cos\theta$, $b = r\sin\theta$. Now answer the following questions:

6. The value of the expression $({}^nC_0 - {}^nC_2 + {}^nC_4 - {}^nC_6 + \ldots)^2 + ({}^nC_1 - {}^nC_3 + {}^nC_5 \ldots)^2$ must be
   (a) 2^{2n} (b) 2^n
   (c) 2^{n2} (d) None of these
7. The value of ${}^nC_0 + {}^nC_4 + {}^nC_8 + \ldots$ must be
   (a) $2^{n/2}\cos\frac{n\pi}{8}$ (b) $2^{n/2}\sin\frac{n\pi}{8}$
   (c) $2^n + 2^{n/2}\cos\frac{n\pi}{4}$ (d) $2^{n-2} + 2^{\frac{n-2}{2}}\cos\frac{n\pi}{4}$
8. The value of $\sum_{r=1}^{k}(-3)^{r-1}\,{}^{3n}C_{2r-1}$ where, n is an even positive integer and $k = \frac{3n}{2}$, must be
   (a) 3^n (b) 3^{n-1}
   (c) 6^n (d) 0

Passage 3:

For any real x, let us define $(x)_r = x(x-1)(x-2)\ldots\ldots(x-r+1)$ with $(x)_0 = 1$. We can observe that, if x is a positive integer n, then $(x)_r = {}^nC_r$.

Let us also define $\binom{x}{r}$ as $\binom{x}{r} = \frac{(x)_r}{r!}$ for every real x and for every non-negative integer r.

Now answer the following questions:

9. $\binom{-1}{r}$ must be equal to
   (a) $(-1)^r$ (b) $(-1)^{r+1}$
   (c) 0 (d) None of these
10. $\binom{-2}{r}$ must be equal to
   (a) $(-1)^r\, r$ (b) $(-1)^r(r + 1)$
   (c) $(-1)^{r+1}(r + 1)$ (d) None of these
11. The number of ways of distributing n identical balls in r distinct boxes must be equal to
   (a) $(-1)^r\binom{-r}{n}$ (b) $\binom{-n}{r}$
   (c) $\binom{n}{r}$ (d) $\binom{r}{n}$

Passage 4:

Observing $(x + y + z)^n$ intuitively we observe that each term of expansion must be of the form $x^\alpha y^\beta z^\gamma$ where α, β, γ are non-negative integers satisfying $\alpha + \beta + \gamma = n$. Again the term $x^\alpha y^\beta z^\gamma$ can be obtained in $\frac{n!}{\alpha!\beta!\gamma!}$ multiplication so that we can write $(x+y+z)^n = \sum \frac{n!}{\alpha!\beta!\gamma!}x^\alpha y^\beta z^\gamma$

The above theorem is called multinomial theorem. Now answer the following questions:

12. The value of the sum $\sum_{x+y+z=10} \frac{10!}{x!y!z!}$ must be equal to

(a) 3^{10} (b) 10^3
(c) 45 (d) None of these

13. The co-efficient of $a^3b^4c^5$ in expansion of $(ab + bc + ca)^6$ must be

(a) $\frac{12!}{3!4!5!}$ (b) 60
(c) 18 (d) 120

14. The number of terms in the expansion of $(x + 2y + 3z)^{20}$ must be

(a) 190 (b) 231
(c) 200 (d) None of these

15. The co-efficient of x^4 in the expansion of $(1 + x - 2x^2)^7$ must be

(a) –81 (b) –91
(c) 81 (d) + 91

16. The co-efficient of x^6 in the expansion of $\left(x^2 + \frac{4}{x^2} + 4\right)^5$ must be

(a) 90 (b) 180
(c) 100 (d) 120.

Passage 5:

If $C_r = {}^nC_r$ then to evalutate the expression $P = \sum\sum_{0\le r<s\le n} C_rC_s$ we make use of $C_0^2 + C_1^2 + C_2^2 + \ldots\ldots\ldots\ldots + C_n^2 = {}^{2n}C_n$ and expansion of $(C_0 + C_1 + \ldots\ldots C_n)^2$. Now answer the following questions:

17. Value of $P = \sum\sum_{0\le r<s\le n} C_rC_s$ is

(a) $2^{2n} - \frac{1}{2}({}^{2n}C_n)$ (b) $2^{2n-1} - \frac{1}{2}({}^{2n}C_n)$
(c) $2^{2n} - {}^{2n}C_n$ (d) None of these

18. Value of $Q = \sum\sum_{0\le r<s\le n} (C_r - C_s)^2$ is

(a) $(n + 1)({}^{2n}C_n) - 2^n$ (b) $(n + 1)({}^{2n}C_n) - 2^{2n}$
(c) $(n + 1)^n - 2^{2n}$ (d) None of these

19. Value of the expression $R = \sum\sum_{0\le r<s\le n} (r+s)C_rC_s$ is

(a) $n(2^{2n-1})$
(b) $n(2^{2n-1}) + {}^{2n}C_n$
(c) $n(2^{2n-1}) - \frac{1}{2}({}^{2n}C_n)$
(d) None of these

20. If $S = \sum\sum_{0\le r<s\le n} (r+s)(C_r - C_s)^2$, then S equals

(a) 0
(b) ${}^{2n}C_n - (n + 1)\,2^{2n}$
(c) $n[(n + 1)]({}^{2n}C_n) - 2^{2n}]$
(d) $n[(n+1)2^{2n} - \frac{1}{2}({}^{2n}C_n)]$

21. If $T = \sum\sum_{0\le r<s\le n} (C_r + C_S)^2$ then T equals

(a) $(n - 1)({}^{2n}C_n) + 2^{2n}$ (b) ${}^{2n}C_n + 2^{2n}$
(c) ${}^{2n}C_n - (n + 1)(2^{2n})$ (d) None of these

SECTION–VII

MATRIX MATCH TYPE

1. If $R = (5\sqrt{5}+11)^{2n+1}$ (n is a positive integer) and if $f = R - [R]$ (i.e., fractional part of R), then match the following:

Column-I

(i) f
(ii) Rf
(iii) $[R]$

Column - II

(a) $(5\sqrt{5}-11)^{2n+1}$
(b) $(5\sqrt{5}+11)^{2n+1} - (5\sqrt{5}-11)^{2n+1}$
(c) 4^{2n+1}

2. **Column-I**

(i) Number of distinct terms in the expansion $(x + y - z)^{16}$
(ii) Number of terms in the expansion of $(x+\sqrt{x^2-1})^6 + (x-\sqrt{x^2-1})^6$
(iii) The number of irrational terms in $(\sqrt[8]{5}+\sqrt[6]{2})^{100}$
(iv) The sum of numerical co-efficients in the expansion of $\left(1+\frac{x}{3}+\frac{2y}{3}\right)^{12}$

Column-II

(a) 2^{12}
(b) 97
(c) 4

(d) 153

(e) 1

3. Column-I

(i) If the co-efficient of x^2 and x^3 in $(3 + \alpha x)^9$ are equal, then value of α is

(ii) If a denotes the co-efficient of x^n in $(1 + x)^{2n}$ and b denotes the co-efficient of x^{n-1} in $(1 + x)^{2n-1}$, then $\left(\frac{a-b}{a+b}\right)^3$ equals

(iii) If $\{x\}$ denote the fractional part of x, then $\left\{\frac{3^{2008}}{7}\right\}$ is

(iv) The term independent of x in the expansion of $(1+x+2x^2)\left(\frac{3x^2}{2}+\frac{1}{3x}\right)^7$

Column-II

(a) 4/7

(b) 9/7

(c) 1/27

(d) 7/36

4. For $n \geq 2$, let $C_r = \binom{n}{r}$ and $a_n = \sum_{r=0}^{n} \frac{1}{C_r}$

Column-I	Column-II
(i) $\sum_{r=0}^{n} \frac{r}{C_r}$	(a) na_n
(ii) $\sum_{r=0}^{n} \frac{n-r}{C_r}$	(b) $\frac{1}{n}a_{n-1}$
(iii) $\sum_{r=1}^{n} \frac{1}{r.C_r}$	(c) $\frac{1}{2}na_n$
(iv) $\sum_{r=0}^{n-1} \frac{1}{(n-r)C_r}$	(d) $\frac{1}{2n}a_{n-1}$

5. Match the expressions on the left with their properties on the right.

Column-I

(i) $E = \frac{C_1}{C_0} + 2\frac{C_2}{C_1} + ... + n\frac{C_n}{C_{n-1}}$ and $S = 2^n E$

(ii) $E = \frac{C_1^2}{C_0} + 2\frac{C_2^2}{C_1} + ... + n\frac{C_n^2}{C_{n-1}}$ and $S = (n + 1) + E$

(iii) $S = C_0 + 3C_1 + ... + (2n + 1)C_n$

(iv) A is a set containing $(2n + 1)$ elements and S = the number of subsets of A containing at most n elements.

Column-II

(a) $2^{n-1} | S$

(b) $2^n | S$

(c) $n|S$

(d) $(n + 1) |S$

6. Column-I

(i) If $(r + 1)^{\text{th}}$ term is the first negative term in the expansion of $(1 + x)^{7/2}$, then the value of r(where $|x| < 1$) is

(ii) The co-effcient of y in the expansion of $(y^2 + 1)^5$ is

(iii) If the second term in the expansion $\left(a^{\frac{1}{13}} + \frac{a}{\sqrt{a^{-1}}}\right)^n$ is $14a^{5/2}$, then the value of n is

(iv) The co-efficient of x^4 in the expression $(1 + 2x + 3x^2 + 4x^3 + ...\text{up to } \infty)^{1/2}$ is c, $(c \in N)$, then $c + 1$ (where $|x| < 1$) is

Column-II

(a) divisible by 2

(b) divisible by 5

(c) divisible by 10

(d) a prime number

SECTION–VIII

INTEGER-TYPE QUESTIONS

1. If $(1 + x + 2x^2)^{10} = a_0 + a_1x + a_2x^2 + ... + a_{20}x^{20}$, then evaluate $a_0 + a_2 + a_4 + ...a_{18}$

2. If the value of ${}^{15}C_0 + {}^{15}C_1 + {}^{15}C_2 + ... + {}^{15}C_7$ is $(m)^2$, then find the value of m.

3. $10! + \frac{11!}{1!} + \frac{12!}{2!} + \frac{13!}{3!} +$ upto 12 terms $= \frac{(2k)!}{k(k!)}$ then find k

4. Find the remainder when 2^{1990} is divided by 1990.

5. If the co-efficient of x^{40} in the expression $(1 + x)^{1000} + 2x(1 + x)^{999} + 3x^2(1 + x)^{998} + ... + 1001\,x^{1000}$ is ${}^nC_{4k}$; $k \in \mathbb{Z}^+$; then evaluate $(n + k)$

6. The sum of the cofefficients of the expression $(1 + x - 3x^2)^{2163}$ is k ; then evaluate |k|.

7. If $(1 + ax)^n = 1 + 8x + 24x^2 + ...$ then evaluate $a + n$.

8. The sum of the rational terms in the expansion of $(\sqrt{2}+3^{1/5})^{10}$ is λ; then evaluate $\frac{(\lambda+1)}{14}$

9. Let $R=(5\sqrt{5}+11)^{2n+1}$ and $f = R - [R]$, where [ ] dentoes the greatest integer function, then $Rf = (k)^{2n+1}$, then evaluate k.

10. If the greatest integer less than or equal to $(\sqrt{2}+1)^6$ is λ, then evaluate $\sqrt{\sqrt{\lambda-1}+2}$.

11. If the integer just greater than $(\sqrt{3}+1)^{18}$ contains 2^{m+1} as a factor, then evaluate m; (where m is the maximum possible power).

12. If the co-efficient of x^{49} in the polynomial

$$\left(x-\frac{C_1}{C_0}\right)\left(x-2^2.\frac{C_2}{C_1}\right)\left(x-3^2.\frac{C_3}{C_2}\right)\cdots\left(x-50^2.\frac{C_{50}}{C_{49}}\right);$$

where $C_r = {}^{50}C_r$ is 1, then evaluate $\sqrt{22149+\lambda}$.

Answers Keys

SECTION–II

1. (a)	**2.** (b)	**3.** (a)	**4.** (c)	**5.** (c)	**6.** (a)	**7.** (c)	**8.** (c)	**9.** (c)	**10.** (a)
11. (d)	**12.** (b)	**13.** (a)	**14.** (c)	**15.** (a)	**16.** (a)	**17.** (c)	**18.** (c)	**19.** (b)	**20.** (a)
21. (d)	**22.** (b)	**23.** (a)	**24.** (c)	**25.** (c)	**26.** (c)	**27.** (c)	**28.** (d)	**29.** (b)	**30.** (b)
31. (d)	**32.** (b)	**33.** (d)	**34.** (a)	**35.** (d)	**36.** (c)	**37.** (d)	**38.** (c)	**39.** (b)	**40.** (d)
41. (c)	**42.** (b)	**43.** (d)	**44.** (a)	**45.** (b)	**46.** (a)	**47.** (c)	**48.** (c)	**49.** (d)	**50.** (d)
51. (c)									

SECTION–III

1. (a, b)	**2.** (b, c)	**3.** (a, b, c, d)	**4.** (b, c)	**5.** (a, b)
6. (c, d)	**7.** (b, c, d)	**8.** (a, b, d)	**9.** (a, d)	**10.** (a, b, c)
11. (a, b, c)	**12.** (a, b, c)			

SECTION–IV

1. (a)	**2.** (a)	**3.** (a)	**4.** (a)	**5.** (b)	**6.** (a)	**7.** (d)	**8.** (b)	**9.** (a)	**10.** (a)

SECTION–V

1. (c)	**2.** (d)	**3.** (a)	**4.** (a)	**5.** (a, b)	**6.** (b)	**7.** (d)	**8.** (d)	**9.** (a)	**10.** (b)
11. (a)	**12.** (a)	**13.** (b)	**14.** (b)	**15.** (b)	**16.** (b)	**17.** (b)	**18.** (b)	**19.** (d)	**20.** (c)
21. (a)									

SECTION–VI

1. (i) → (a),	(ii) → (c),	(iii) → (b)	
2. (i) → (d),	(ii) → (c),	(iii) → (b),	(iv) → (a)
3. (i) → (b),	(ii) → (c),	(iii) → (a),	(iv) → (d)
4. (i) → (c),	(ii) → (c),	(iii) → (b),	(iv) → (b)
5. (i) → (a, b, c, d),	(ii) → (a),	(iii) → (a, b, d),	(iv) → (a), (b)
6. (i) → (b, d),	(ii) → (a, b, c)	(iii) → (a)	(iv) → (a, d)

SECTION–VII

1. 523776	**2.** 128	**3.** 11	**4.** 1682	**5.** 1012	**6.** 1	**7.** 6	**8.** 3	**9.** 4	**10.** 4
11. 10	**12.** 7								

HINTS AND SOLUTIONS

TEXTUAL EXERCISE: 1(SUBJECTIVE)

1. (a) (i) $\because\ (a+b)^n = \sum_{r=0}^{n} {}^nC_r(a)^{n-r}.(b)^r$

$\therefore\ ((2x-y)^5)^3 = (2x-y)^{15}$

$= \sum_{r=0}^{15} {}^{15}C_r(2x)^{15-r}(-y)^r = \sum_{r=0}^{15}(-1)^r.{}^{15}C_r(2)^{15-r}x^{15-r}(y)^r$;

Number of terms = 16 ($\because r \in \{0,1,2,\ldots 15\}$)

(ii) $(2x+5y)^{15} = \sum_{r=0}^{15} {}^{15}C_r(2x)^{15-r}.(5y)^r$

$= \sum_{r=0}^{15} {}^{15}C_r(2)^{15-r}.(5)^r.x^{15-r}.y^r$; Number of terms = 16

($\because r \in \{0, 1, 2, \ldots 15\}$)

(iii) $(1+x+x^2)^3 = \sum_{r=0}^{3} {}^3C_r(1)^{3-r}(x+x^2)^r = \sum_{r=0}^{3} {}^3C_r.x^r(1+x)^r$

$= {}^3C_0 + {}^3C_1\, x(1+x) + {}^3C_2x^2(1+x)^2 + {}^3C_3x^3(1+x)^3$

$= 1 + 3x + 3x^2 + 3x^2 + 3x^4 + 6x^3 + x^3(1 + x^3 + 3x + 3x^2)$

$= x^6 + 3x^5 + 6x^4 + 7x^3 + 6x^2 + 3x + 1$

Number of terms = 7 (By observation)

(Also, no of terms in $(1 + x + x^2 + \ldots + x^r)^n = nr + 1$)

(b) (i) $\left(\sqrt{3}+1\right)^6 - \left(\sqrt{3}-1\right)^6$

$= 2\left[{}^6C_1\left(\sqrt{3}\right)^5 + {}^6C_3\left(\sqrt{3}\right)^3 + {}^6C_5\left(\sqrt{3}\right)^1\right]$

$= 2\left[6\left(9\sqrt{3}\right) + 20\left(3\sqrt{3}\right) + 6\sqrt{3}\right] = 240\sqrt{3}$

(ii) $\left(1+\sqrt{2}\right)^5 + \left(1-\sqrt{2}\right)^5$

$= 2\left[{}^5C_0 + \left(\sqrt{2}\right)^0 + {}^5C_2\left(\sqrt{2}\right)^2 + {}^5C_4\left(\sqrt{2}\right)^4\right]$

$= 2[1 + 20 + 20] = 82$

(c) (i) $(1003)^6 = (1000 + 3)^6$

$= {}^6C_0\,(10^3)^6\,(3)^0 + {}^6C_1\,(10^3)^5(3)^1 + {}^6C_2\,(10^3)^4\,(3)^2 + {}^6C_3\,(10^3)^3(3)^3 + {}^6C_4(10^3)^2(3)^4 + {}^6C_5\,(10^3)^1(3)^5 + {}^6C_6(10^3)^0\,(3)^6$

$= 10^{18} + 18(10)^{15} + 135(10)^{12} + 54(10)^{10} + 1215\,(10)^6 + 1458(10)^3 + 729$

= Taking first two terms and neglecting the other terms for approximation $\simeq 10^{18} + 0.18 \times 10^{15} = (1.018) \times 10^{18}$

(ii) $(9999)^{10} = (10{,}000 - 1)^{10} = {}^{10}C_0(10^4)^{10} - {}^{10}C_1(10^4)^9 + \ldots$

$\simeq (10)^{40} - 10(10)^{36} = (10)^{40} - 0.0010 \times 10^{40} = 0.999 \times 10^{40}$

(iii) $(1.01)^{10} = (1 + 0.01)^{10} = {}^{10}C_0\,(1)^{10}\,(0.01)^0 + {}^{10}C_1(1)^9(0.01)^1 + \ldots$

Negatively other terms $\simeq 1 + 10(0.01) = 1.1$

(d) $\left(x+\sqrt{x^2+1}\right)^5 + \left(x-\sqrt{x^2+1}\right)^5 = 0$ (i)

Number of terms in the expansion of L.H.S. of equation (i) $= \dfrac{n+1}{2} = \dfrac{5+1}{2} = 3$

($\because$ Numbers of terms in $(a+b)^n \pm (a-b)^n) = \dfrac{n+1}{2}$ for n = odd positive integer)

On expanding the expansion, equation (i) becomes

$2\left[{}^5C_0(x)^5\left(\sqrt{x^2+1}\right)^0 + {}^5C_2(x)^3\left(\sqrt{x^2+1}\right)^2 + {}^5C_4(x)^1\left(\sqrt{x^2+1}\right)^4 = 0\right]$

$\Rightarrow x^5 + 10x^3\,(x^2+1) + 5x\,(x^2+1)^2 = 0$

$\Rightarrow x^4 + 10x^4 + 10x^2 + 5x^4 + 5 + 10x^2 = 0$

$\Rightarrow 16x^4 + 20x^2 + 5 = 0$

$\Rightarrow x^2 = \dfrac{-20 \pm \sqrt{400-320}}{32}$

$\Rightarrow x^2 = \dfrac{-20 \pm 4\sqrt{5}}{32}$

$\Rightarrow x^2 = \dfrac{-5 \pm \sqrt{5}}{8}$; but $x^2 \geq 0$

$\Rightarrow x^2 = \dfrac{-5-\sqrt{5}}{8}; \dfrac{-5+\sqrt{5}}{8}$

Clearly both values $\in (-1, 0)$ i.e., x will be imaginary.

Also for the validity of equation (i); $x^2 + 1 \geq 0$

$\Rightarrow x^2 \geq -1$

$\Rightarrow x^2 \in [-1, \infty)$, which holds for the given value of x^2

(e) To find 3rd term from the end in the expansion of $\left(x^{-2/3} - \dfrac{3}{x^2}\right)^8$

Rth term from end in the expansion of $(a+b)^n = (n-r+2)^{th}$ term from beginning in $(a+b)^n$

$\therefore$ 3rd term from end = (8 – 3 + 2) i.e., 7th term of $\left(x^{-2/3} - \dfrac{3}{x^2}\right)^8$

$= T_{6+1} = {}^8C_6(x^{-2/3})^2\left(\dfrac{-3}{x^2}\right)^6 = 28\,(3)^6 \times \dfrac{1}{x^{12+4/3}} = 20412.\,x^{-40/3}$

(f) To find degree expression

$[x + (x^3-1)^{1/2}]^5 + [x - (x^3-1)^{1/2}]^5$

$= 2[{}^5C_0x^5\,(x^3-1)^0 + {}^5C_2\,x^3(x^3-1)^1 + {}^5C_4\,x(x^3-1)^2]$

$= 2[x^5 + 10x^6 - 10x^3 + 5x(x^6 + 1 - 2x^3)]$

$= 2[5x^7 + 10x^6 + x^5 - 10x^4 - 10x^3 + 5x]$

$\Rightarrow$ degree = 7

2. T_4 of $(ax + 1/x)n = 5/2$ (given)

$\Rightarrow {}^nC_3(ax)^{n-3}\left(\dfrac{1}{x}\right)^3 = \dfrac{5}{2}$

$\Rightarrow \dfrac{n(n-1)(n-2)}{6}.\,a^{n-3}.x^{n-6} = \dfrac{5}{2}$ (Constant term)

$\Rightarrow n = 6$ (Power of $x = 0$)

$\Rightarrow 20.\,a^{n-3} = 5/2 \quad \Rightarrow a^{n-3} = 1/8$

$\Rightarrow a^3 = 1/8$

$\Rightarrow a = 1/2$

$\therefore\ n = 6;\ a = 1/2$

3. $T_3 = 106$ for the expansion of $(x + x\log 10x)^5$

$\Rightarrow {}^5C_2(x)^3 (x^{\log_{10} x})^2 = 10^6$

$\Rightarrow x^3.((x)^{\log_{10} x})^2 = 10^5$ (i)

Let $\log_{10}x = y$

$\Rightarrow x = 10y$ (ii)

$\therefore$ From (i) and (ii), we have, $(10y)^3 [x^y]^2 = 10^5$

$\Rightarrow (10)^{3y}.[10^y]^{2y} = 10^5 \Rightarrow (10)^{2y^2+3y} = (10)^5$

$\Rightarrow 2y^2 + 3y = 5$

$\Rightarrow y = -\frac{5}{2}$ or $y = 1 \Rightarrow x = 10^{-5/2}$ or 10

4. T_3, T_4, T_5, T_6 of $(x + a)^n$ are a, b, c, d

$\Rightarrow {}^nC_2\, x^{n-2}\alpha^2 = a$ (i)

${}^nC_3 x^{n-3}\alpha^3 = b$ (ii)

${}^nC_4 x^{n-4}\alpha^4 = c$ (iii)

and ${}^nC_5 x^{n-5}\alpha^5 = d$ (iv)

Now,

$$\text{L.H.S.} = \frac{b^2 - ac}{c^2 - bd} = \frac{({}^nC_3)^2 x^{2n-6}\alpha^6 - {}^nC_2.{}^nC_4 x^{2n-6}.\alpha^6}{({}^nC_4)^2 x^{2n-8}\alpha^8 - {}^nC_3.{}^nC_5 x^{2n-8}.\alpha^8}$$

$$= \frac{\left[({}^nC_3)^2 - {}^nC_2.{}^nC_4\right].x^2}{\left[({}^nC_4)^2 - {}^nC_3.{}^nC_5\right]\alpha^2} \quad \text{(v)}$$

$$\text{R.H.S.} = \frac{5a}{3c} = \frac{5.{}^nC_2 x^{n-2}\alpha^2}{3.{}^nC_4 x^{n-4}\alpha^4} = \frac{5.{}^nC_2}{3.{}^nC_4}\cdot\frac{x^2}{\alpha^2} \quad \text{(vi)}$$

$$\therefore \text{We require to prove, } \frac{({}^nC_3)^2 - {}^nC_2.{}^nC_4}{({}^nC_4)^2 - {}^nC_3.{}^nC_5} = \frac{5}{3}\left(\frac{{}^nC_2}{{}^nC_4}\right) \quad \text{(vii)}$$

$$\text{R.H.S. of 7} = \frac{5}{3}\cdot\frac{n(n-1)\times 12}{n(n-1)(n-2)(n-3)} = \frac{20}{(n-2)(n-3)}$$

$$\text{And L.H.S of 7} = \frac{({}^nC_3)^2 - {}^nC_2.{}^nC_4}{({}^nC_4)^2 - {}^nC_3.{}^nC_5} = \frac{1 - \dfrac{{}^nC_2.{}^nC_4}{({}^nC_3)^2}}{\left(\dfrac{{}^nC_4}{{}^nC_3}\right)^2 - \left(\dfrac{{}^nC_5}{{}^nC_3}\right)}$$

$$= \frac{1 - \left(\dfrac{{}^nC_2}{{}^nC_3}\right)\cdot\left(\dfrac{{}^nC_4}{{}^nC_3}\right)}{\left(\dfrac{{}^nC_4}{{}^nC_3}\right)^2 - \left(\dfrac{{}^nC_5}{{}^nC_4}\times\dfrac{{}^nC_4}{{}^nC_3}\right)} = \frac{1 - \left(\dfrac{3}{n-2}\right)\left(\dfrac{n-3}{4}\right)}{\left(\dfrac{n-3}{4}\right)^2 \left(\dfrac{n-4}{5}\times\dfrac{n-3}{4}\right)}$$

$\left(\because \dfrac{{}^nC_r}{{}^nC_{r-1}} = \dfrac{n-r+1}{r}\right)$; on solving, we get $\dfrac{20}{(n-2)(n-3)}$

$\therefore$ L.H.S. = R.H.S.

5. (i) Co-efficient of x^7 in $\left(ax^2 + \frac{1}{bx}\right)^{11}$

General term $= T_{r+1} = {}^{11}C_r\,(ax^2)^{11-r}\left(\frac{1}{bx}\right)^r$

$= {}^{11}C_r \frac{a^{11-r}}{b^r}.(x)^{22-3r}$ for coefficient of x^7; $22 - 3r = 7$

$\Rightarrow 3r = 15 \qquad \Rightarrow r = 5$

$\therefore$ Coefficient of $x^7 = \dfrac{{}^{11}C_5.a^6}{b^5}$

(ii) Coefficient of x^5 in $(1 + x^2)^5 (1 + x)^4$ = Coefficient of x^5 in $[{}^5C_0 + {}^5C_1x^2 + {}^5C_2x^4] \times [{}^4C_0 + {}^4C_1\,x + {}^4C_2x^2 + {}^4C_3x^3 + {}^4C_4x^4] = {}^5C_1.{}^4C_3 + {}^5C_2.{}^4C_1 = 20 + 40 = 60$

(iii) Coefficient of x^{11} in $(2x^2 + x - 3)^6$

= Coefficient of x^{11} in $(2x + 3)^6 (x - 1)^6$

= Coefficient of x^{11} in $\sum_{r=0}^{6} {}^6C_r(2x)^{6-r}(3)^r.\sum_{k=0}^{6} {}^6C_k(x)^{6-k}(-1)^k$

For coefficient of x^{11}; $6 - r + 6 - k = 11$

$\Rightarrow r + k = 1$

$\therefore$ Coefficient of $x^{11} = {}^6C_0(2)^6(3)^0.{}^6C_1(-1)^1 + {}^6C_1(2)^5(3)^1.{}^6C_0(-1)^0 = -384 + 576 = 192$

(iv) Coefficient of x^{20} in $(1 + x^2)^{40}.(x^2 + 2 + 1/x^2)^{-5}$

= Coefficient of x^{20} in $(1 + x^2)^{40}.\left(x + \frac{1}{x}\right)^{-10}$

= Coefficient of x^{20} in $(1 + x^2)^{40}.x^{10}(1 + x^2)^{-10}$

= Coefficient of x^{20} in $x^{10}(1 + x^2)^{30}$

= Coefficient of x^{10} in $(1 + x^2)^{30}$

$= {}^{30}C_5 = {}^{30}C_{25}$

(v) Co-efficient of x^4 in $(1 + x + x^2 + x^3)^{11}$ and $(2 - x - 3x^2)^6$

Here $(1 + x + x^2 + x^3)^{11} = \left(\frac{1-x^4}{1-x}\right)^{11}$

$= (1 - x^4)^{11}.(1 - x)^{-11}$

$= \sum_{r=0}^{11}(-1)^r.{}^{11}C_r(x)^{4r}.\sum_{k=0}^{\infty} {}^{11+k-1}C_k\,x^k$

$\therefore$ For coefficient of x^4; $4r + k = 4$

$\Rightarrow r = 1, k = 0$ and $r = 0, k = 4$

$\therefore$ Coefficient of $x^4 = -{}^{11}C_1.{}^{10}C_0 + {}^{11}C_0.{}^{14}C_4 = -11 + 1001 = 990$

Now, $(2 - x - 3x^2)^6 = (3x^2 + x - 2)^6 = (3x - 2)^6 (x + 1)^6$

$= \sum_{r=0}^{6} {}^6C_r(3r)^{6-r}(-2)^r.\sum_{k=0}^{6} {}^6C_k(x)^{6-k}$

$\therefore$ For coefficient of x^4; $6 - r + 6 - k = 4$

$\Rightarrow r + k = 8$

$\therefore$ Coefficient of $x^4 = {}^6C_2(3)^{6-2}.(-2)^2.{}^6C_6 + {}^6C_3(3)^3(-2)^3.{}^6C_5 + {}^6C_4(3)^2(-2)^4.{}^6C_4 + {}^6C_5(3)^1(-2)^5.{}^6C_3 + {}^6C_6(3)^0(-2)^6.{}^6C_2$

$= (15)(81)(4) - (20)(27)(8)(6) + (135)(16).(15) + 6(3)(-32)(20) + 64 \times 15$

$= 4860 - 960 \times 27 + (135)(240) - 360(32) + 960 = 780$

(vi) Coefficient of x^{13} in $(1 - x)^{15}(1 + x + x^2 + x^3)^4$

= Coefficient of x^{13} in $(1 - x)^5\left[\frac{1-x^4}{1-x}\right]^4$

= Coefficient of x^{13} in $(1 - x)^5(1 - x^4)^4(1 - x)^{-4}$

= Coefficient of x^{13} in $(1 - x)(1 - x^4)^4$

= Coefficient of x^{13} in $(1-x)\sum_{r=0}^{4}(-1)^r.{}^4C_r\,x^{4r}$

$= -(-1)^3.{}^4C_3 = 4$

(vii) Coefficient of x^3 in $(1 + x + x^2)^n$

= Coefficient of x^3 in $\left(\frac{1-x^3}{1-x}\right)^n$

$= \text{Coefficient of } x^3 \text{ in } (1-x^3)^n (1-x)^{-n}$

$= \text{Coefficient of } x^3 \text{ in } \sum_{r=0}^{n} (-1)^r . {}^nC_r x^{3r} . \sum_{k=0}^{\infty} {}^{n+k-1}C_k x^k$; for x^3; $3r + k = 3$

$\Rightarrow r = 0; k = 3; r = 1; k = 0$

$\therefore$ Coefficient of $x^3 = (-1)^0 . {}^nC_0 . {}^{n+2}C_3 + (-1)^1 . {}^nC_1 . {}^{n-1}C_0$

$= {}^{n+2}C_3 - n = \frac{(n+2)(n+1)(n) - 6n}{6} = \frac{n(n-1)(n+4)}{6}$

(viii) Coefficient of x^p in $\left(x^2 + \frac{1}{x}\right)^{2n}$ if exists

$\left(x^2 + \frac{1}{x}\right)^{2n} = \frac{(1+x^3)^{2n}}{x^{2n}}$

$\therefore$ Coefficient of x^p in $\frac{(1+x^3)^{2n}}{x^{2n}}$

$=$ Coefficient of $x^{(p+2n)}$ in $(1+x^3)^{2n}$

$=$ Coefficient $x^{(p+2n)}$ in $\sum_{r=0}^{2n} {}^{2n}C_r x^{3r}$

$\Rightarrow 3r = p + 2n \qquad \Rightarrow r = \frac{2n+p}{3}$

$\therefore$ Coefficient of $x^{(p+2n)} = {}^{2n}C_{\frac{2n+p}{3}} = \frac{(2n)!}{\left(\frac{4n-p}{3}\right)! \left(\frac{2n+p}{3}\right)!}$

6. (i) $\left[\sqrt{\frac{x}{3}} + \frac{3}{2x^2}\right]^{10} = \sum_{r=0}^{10} {}^{10}C_r \left(\frac{x}{3}\right)^{\frac{10-r}{2}} . \left(\frac{3}{2x^2}\right)^r$

For term independent of x; $\frac{10-r}{2} - 2r = 0$, $r = 2$

$\therefore$ Term independent of x has value ${}^{10}C_2 \left(\frac{1}{3}\right)^4 \left(\frac{3}{2}\right)^2 = \frac{5}{4}$

(ii) $(1 + x + 2x^3)\left(\frac{3}{2}x^2 - \frac{1}{3x}\right)^9$

$= (1 + x + 2x^3) \sum_{r=0}^{9} {}^9C_r \left(\frac{3}{2}x^2\right)^{9-r} \left(-\frac{1}{3x}\right)^r$

$= (1 + x + 2x^3) \sum_{r=0}^{9} (-1)^r \, {}^9C_r \frac{(3)^{9-2r}}{(2)^{9-r}} . x^{(18-3r)}$

For term independent of x, $18 - 3r = 0$

$\Rightarrow r = 6$ and $21 - 3r = 0 \Rightarrow r = 7$

$\therefore$ Term independent of x is

$= 1.(-1)^6 . {}^9C_6 \frac{(3)^{-3}}{(2)^3} + 2.(-1)^7 . {}^9C_7 \frac{(3)^{-5}}{(2)^2}$

$= \frac{7}{18} - \frac{2}{27} = \frac{21-4}{54} = \frac{17}{54}$

7. Given $r > 1$ and $n > 2$, and Coefficient of $3r$ = Coefficient of $xr + 2$ in the expansion of $(1 + x)^{2n}$

$\Rightarrow {}^{2n}C_{3r} = {}^{2n}C_{r+2}$

$\Rightarrow$ Either $3r = r + 2$ or $3r + r + 2 = 2n$

$(\because {}^nC_k = {}^nC_p \qquad \Rightarrow k = p \text{ or } k + p = n)$

$\Rightarrow$ Either $r = 1$ or $n = 2r + 1$, but $r > 1$ (given)

$\Rightarrow n = 2r + 1$

8. (a) Number of terms in $(1 + x + x^2)^{50} = 2(50) + 1 = 101$

(b) Number of terms in $(1 + x + x^2 + x^3)^{20} = 3\,(20) + 1 = 61$

(c) Number of terms in $(1 + x^2 + x^4 + x^6)^{50} = \frac{6(50)}{2} + 1 = 151$

(d) Number of terms in $(1 + x + x^2 + x^4 + x^5)^n = (5n + 1)$

(e) Number of terms in $(1 - x + x^2 - x^3 + x^4 + \ldots\infty)^{-n}$; $|x| < 1$; $n \in \mathbb{N}$ i.e., $\left(\frac{1}{1+x}\right)^{-n} = (1+x)^n$

$\Rightarrow$ Number of terms $= (n + 1)$

9. (a) $(1 + ix)^{4n-2}$; $n \in \mathbb{N}$; $x > 0$

$= \sum_{r=0}^{4n-2} {}^{4n-2}C_r (ix)^r$

For real negative terms: $r = 4k + 2$; $k \in W$

$r \in \{2, 6, 10, \ldots, 4n - 2\}$

$\Rightarrow$ Number of terms (k) given by $2 + (k - 1)(4) = 4n - 2$

$\Rightarrow k = n$

For real positive terms: $r = 4k$; $k \in W$

$\Rightarrow r \in \{0, 4, 8, \ldots, 4(n - 1)\}$

$\Rightarrow$ Number of terms $= n$

For imaginary terms: $r = 4k + 1$ or $4k + 3$; $k \in W$

$\Rightarrow r \in \{1, 3, 5, 7, 9, 11, \ldots, 4n - 3\}$ or directly (Total terms) – (Real terms) $= (4n - 1) - (2n) = 2n - 1$

(b) $\left(x^2 + 1 + \frac{1}{x^2}\right)^n$; $n \in \mathbb{N} = \left(x + \frac{1}{x}\right)^{2n} = \frac{(x^2+1)^{2n}}{x^{2n}}$

$\therefore$ Number of terms in $(x^2 + 1 + 1/x^2)^n$

$=$ Number of terms in $(1 + x^2)^{2n} = \frac{4n}{2} + 1 = 2n + 1$

(c) $(x + y + z)^n$; $n \in \mathbb{N}$

$= {}^nC_0 (x + y)^n + {}^nC_1 (x + y)^{n-1}.z + {}^nC_2 (x + y)^{n-2}. z^2 + \ldots +$ ${}^nC_n (x + y)^0.z^n$

$\therefore$ Number of terms $= (n + 1) + (n) + (n - 1) + \ldots + (1)$ terms

$= \frac{(n+1)(n+2)}{2} = {}^{n+2}C_2$

(d) $\left(\sqrt[3]{4} + \frac{1}{\sqrt[4]{6}}\right)^{20} = \sum_{r=0}^{20} {}^{20}C_r \left(\sqrt[3]{4}\right)^{20-r} . \left(\frac{1}{\sqrt[4]{6}}\right)^r$

$= \sum_{r=0}^{20} {}^{20}C_r (4)^{\frac{20-r}{3}} . \frac{1}{(6)^{r/4}}$

For rational terms, $(20 - r) = 3k$ and $r = 4m$; $k, m \in W$

$\therefore$ $r = 8$; $k = 4$ and $r = 20$; $k = 0$

$\therefore$ Terms corresponding to $r = 8$ and $r = 20$ i.e., 9th and 21st terms will be rational

$\therefore$ Remaining $21 - 2 = 19$ terms will be irrational

Middle term $= T_{\frac{20+2}{2}} = T_{11} =$ irrational as T_9 and T_{21} are the only rational terms.

(e) $(x + x^{-2})^{n-3} = \sum_{k=0}^{n-3} {}^{n-3}C_k (x)^{n-3-k} (x^{-2})^k$

$= \sum_{k=0}^{n-3} {}^{n-3}C_k (x)^{n-3-3k}$

For term containing x^{2r}; $n - 3 - 3k = 2r$

$\Rightarrow n - 2r = 3 + 3k \qquad \because k \geq 0 \Rightarrow n - 2r > 0$

$\because$ R.H.S. is a multiple of 3

$\Rightarrow$ L.H.S. must also be a multiple of 3

$\therefore$ Three will be no terms containing x^{2r} if $n - 2r > 0$ but $(n - 2r)$ not a multiple of 3

10. (a) Sum of numerical coefficients can be obtained by substituting $x = y = 1$ i.e., $\left(1+\frac{1}{3}+\frac{2}{3}\right)^{12} = (2)^{12}$

(b) $(1 + x)^{19} = {}^{19}C_0 + {}^{19}C_1x + {}^{19}C_2x^2 + \ldots + {}^{19}C_{19}\,x^{19}$

Sum of last 10 coefficients $= {}^{19}C_{19} + {}^{19}C_{18} + \ldots.. + {}^{19}C_{10}$

$=\frac{1}{2}\left[\left({}^{19}C_{19}+{}^{19}C_0\right)+\left({}^{19}C_{18}+{}^{19}C_1\right)+\ldots+\left({}^{19}C_{11}+{}^{19}C_8\right)+\left({}^{19}C_{10}+{}^{19}C_9\right)\right]$

$= \frac{1}{2}(2)^{19} = (2)^{18}$

11. (i) Sum of first 10 coefficient in the expansion of $(1 + x)^{20}$

$= {}^{20}C_0 + {}^{20}C_1 + {}^{20}C_2 + \ldots + {}^{20}C_9$

$=\frac{1}{2}\left[{}^{20}C_0+{}^{20}C_1+{}^{20}C_2+\ldots.+{}^{20}C_9+{}^{20}C_{11}+{}^{20}C_{12}+\ldots+{}^{20}C_{18}+{}^{20}C_{18}+{}^{20}C_{19}\right]$

$= \frac{1}{2}\left[(2)^{20} - {}^{20}C_{10}\right]$

(ii) Sum of first 11 coefficients ${}^{20}C_0 + {}^{20}C_1 + {}^{20}C_2 + \ldots + {}^{20}C_{10}$

$=\frac{1}{2}\left[{}^{20}C_0+{}^{20}C_1+{}^{20}C_2+\ldots+{}^{20}C_9+{}^{20}C_{10}+{}^{20}C_{11}+{}^{20}C_{12}+\ldots+{}^{20}C_{19}+{}^{20}C_{20}\right]$

$= \frac{1}{2}\left[(2)^{20} + {}^{20}C_{10}\right]$

TEXTUAL EXERCISE–1: (OBJECTIVE)

1. (b) rth term of $(a + 2x)^n = {}^nC_r - 1(a)^n - r + 1(2x)r - 1$

$= \frac{n(n-1)(n-2)\ldots.(n-(r-2))}{(r-1)!}.a^{n-r+1}.(2x)^{r-1}$

2. (a) $T_{r+1} = {}^{21}C_r\left(\frac{a^{1/3}}{b^{1/6}}\right)^{21-r}\cdot\left(\frac{b^{1/2}}{a^{1/6}}\right)^r$

$= {}^{21}C_r\,(a)^{\frac{(21-r)}{3}-\frac{r}{6}}\cdot(b)^{\frac{r}{2}-\frac{(21-r)}{6}}$

According to question; $\frac{(21-r)}{2}-\frac{r}{6}=\frac{r}{2}-\frac{(21-r)}{6}$

$\Rightarrow \frac{(21-r)}{2}=\frac{2r}{3}$ $\Rightarrow r = 9$

3. (d) $\left(x+\sqrt{x^3-1}\right)^6+\left(x-\sqrt{x^3-1}\right)^6 = 2[{}^6C_0(x)^6 + {}^6C_2\,x^4$ $(x^3 - 1) + {}^6C_4\,x^2\,(x^3 - 1)^2 + {}^6C_6\,x^0(x^3 - 1)^3]$

Which is clearly of degree 9.

4. (b) $(x + a)100 + (x - a)100$ has $\frac{100}{2}+1=51$ terms

5. (c) $2\left[{}^6C_1\left(\sqrt{2}\right)^5+{}^6C_3\left(\sqrt{2}\right)^3+{}^6C_5\left(\sqrt{2}\right)^1\right]$

$= 2\left[6\left(4\sqrt{2}\right)+20\left(2\sqrt{2}\right)+6\sqrt{2}\right] = 140\sqrt{2}$

6. (b) $(x + a)^n = T_0 + T_1 + T_2 + T_3 + \ldots\ldots + T_n$

$= {}^nC_0x^n + {}^nC_1x^{n-1}.a + {}^nC_2x^{n-2}.a^2 + {}^nC_3x^{n-3}.a^3 + \ldots + {}^nC_n.a^n$

$\equiv T_0 + T_1 + T_2 + T_n$

Replacing a by a_i, we get

$(x+ai)^n = {}^nC_0x^n + {}^nC_1x^{n-1}ai - {}^nC_2\,x^{n-2}a^2 - i\,{}^nC_3\,x^{n-3}a^3 + ..+ {}^nC_n(i)^n a^n$

$= (T_0 - T_2 + T_4 \ldots\ldots.) + i(T_1 - T_3 + T_5 + \ldots.)$ (i)

Further (replacing a by $-a_i$)

$(x - ai)^n = (T_0 - T_2 + T_4 \ldots) - i\,(T_1 - T_3 + T_5 \ldots)$ (ii)

Equation (i) × (ii), gives $(x + ai)^n .(x - ai)^n = (T_0 - T_2 + T_4 \ldots)^2 - \text{i}\,(T_1 - T_3 + T_5 \ldots)^2$

$\Rightarrow (x^2 + a^2)^n$

7. (c) Sum of coefficients in $(\alpha^2 x^2 - 2\alpha x + 1)^{51}$

$= \alpha^2 - 2\alpha + 1 = 0 \quad \Rightarrow \quad (\alpha - 1)^2 = 0$

$\Rightarrow \alpha = 1$

8. (b) $(5^{1/2} + 7^{1/8})^{1024} = \sum_{r=0}^{1024} {}^{1024}C_r(5)^{\frac{1024-r}{2}} \times (7)^{r/8}$

$\therefore$ For integral terms $1024 - r = 2k$; $k \in W$ and $r = 8m$; $m \in W$ and r must be a multiple of 8.

$\Rightarrow r \in \left\{0,8,16,\ldots.,\left[\frac{1024}{8}\right]\times 8\right\}$ i.e., $\in \{0, 8, 16 \ldots.,1024\}$

$\Rightarrow$ There will 129

9. (d) $\frac{T_3}{T_4} = \frac{{}^nC_2(x)^{n-2}\left(-\frac{1}{2x}\right)^2}{{}^nC_3(x)^{n-3}\left(-\frac{1}{2x}\right)^3}$ $\frac{\left|{}^nC_2\left(\frac{1}{4}\right)\right|}{\left|{}^nC_3\left(-\frac{1}{8}\right)\right|} = \frac{1}{2}$

$\Rightarrow \frac{3}{(n-3+1)}(2) = \frac{1}{2}$

$\Rightarrow n - 2 = 12 \qquad \Rightarrow n = 14$

10. (c) $\frac{T_7}{(n-7+2)} = \frac{1}{6}$

$\Rightarrow \frac{{}^nC_6\left(\sqrt[3]{2}\right)^{n-6}\left(\frac{1}{\sqrt[3]{3}}\right)^6}{{}^nC_{n-6}\left(\sqrt[3]{2}\right)^6\left(\frac{1}{\sqrt[3]{3}}\right)^{n-6}} = \frac{1}{6}$

$\Rightarrow \left(\sqrt[3]{2}\right)^{n-12}\left(\sqrt[3]{3}\right)^{n-12} = \frac{1}{6}$

$\Rightarrow (6)^{\frac{n-12}{3}} = (6)^{-1} \qquad \Rightarrow n = 9$

11. (a) $\left(ax^2+\frac{1}{bx}\right)^{11} = \sum_{r=0}^{11} {}^{11}C_r(ax^2)^{11-r}\left(\frac{1}{bx}\right)^r$

$= \sum_{r=0}^{11} {}^{11}C_r(a)^{11-r}(b)^{-r}.(x)^{22-3r}$

$\therefore$ For term containing x^7; $r = 5$

$\therefore$ Coefficient of $x^7 = {}^{11}C_5\,(a)^6(b)^{-5}$ and

$\left(ax-\frac{1}{bx^2}\right)^{11} = \sum {}^{11}C_r(a)^{11-r}(-b)^{-r}(x)^{11-3r}$

$\therefore$ For term containing x^{-7}; $r = 6$

$\therefore$ Coefficient of $x^{-7} = {}^{11}C_6\,(a)^5\,(-b)^{-6}$

According to question ${}^{11}C_5\,a^6\,b^{-5} = {}^{11}C_6\,a^5\,(-b)^{-1}$

$\Rightarrow a = (b)^{-1} \qquad \Rightarrow ab = 1$

12. (d) $\sum_{r=0}^{n}(r)({}^nC_r)x^{n-r}.y^r = \sum_{r=1}^{n} r\,{}^nC_r\,x^{n-r}.y^r$

$= \sum_{r=1}^{n} r.\frac{n}{r}({}^{n-1}C_{r-1})x^{n-r}.y^r = n\sum_{r=1}^{n}({}^{n-1}C_{r-1})x^{n-r}.y^{r-1}.y$

$= ny(x+y)^{n-1} = ny(1)$ $(\because x + y = 1 \text{ given})$

$= ny$

TEXTUAL EXERCISE: 2(SUBJECTIVE)

1. (a) $(1+x)^{2n}$ has $\left(\frac{2n+2}{2}\right)$th term as its middle term

$\therefore$ $T_{(n+1)}$ = middle term

$\therefore$ $T_{n+1} = {}^{2n}C_n\,x^n = \frac{(2n)!}{n!(n!)}.x^n$

$= \frac{1.2.3.4.5.6......(2n-2)(2n-1)(2n)}{n!\,.\,n!}$

$= \frac{[1.3.5.7.....(2n-1)].[2.4.6...(2n-2)(2n)].x^n}{n!\,.n!}$

$= \frac{[1.3.5.7.....(2n-1)].(2)^n[1.2.3...(n-1)(n)].x^n}{n!\;n!}$

$= \frac{(1.3.5.7....(2n-1)}{n!}(2)^n.(x)^n$

(b) As in part (a); the coefficient of middle term of $(1+x)^{2n}$ $= {}^{2n}C_n$

Further, the sum of coefficients of two middle terms of $(1+x)^{2n-1}$ = Sum of coefficients of T_n and $T_{(n+1)}$ terms $= {}^{2n-1}C_{n-1} + {}^{2n-1}C_n = {}^{2n}C_n$ (By pascal's rule)

2. Middle term of $\left(\frac{a}{x}+bx\right)^{12} = T_{\frac{12+2}{2}} = T_7 = {}^{12}C_6\left(\frac{a}{x}\right)^6\left(\frac{b}{x}\right)^6 =$

${}^{12}C_6\,a^6.\,b^6 = 924\,a^6\,b^6$

$= 12 \times 11 \times 7\,(ab)^6 = (2)^2 \times (3)^1 \times (7) \times (11)\,.(ab)^6$

3. Middle term of $\left(x-\frac{1}{x}\right)^{2n} = T_{\frac{2n+2}{2}} = T_{n+1} = {}^{2n}C_n(x)^n\left(-\frac{1}{x}\right)^n =$

${}^{2n}C_n(-1)^n = \frac{2n!}{n!n!}(-1)^n$

4. (a) Coefficient of T_5, T_6, T_7 of $(1+x)^n$ are ${}^nC_4$, ${}^nC_5$ and ${}^nC_6$ respectively. There are given to be in AP

$\Rightarrow 2({}^nC_5) = {}^nC_4 + {}^nC_6 \quad \Rightarrow 2 = \frac{{}^nC_4}{{}^nC_5} + \frac{{}^nC_6}{{}^nC_5}$

$\Rightarrow 2 = \frac{5}{n-5+1} + \frac{n-6+1}{6}$

$\Rightarrow 2 = \frac{5}{n-4} + \frac{n-5}{6} \quad \Rightarrow n = 14 \text{ or } n = 7$

Further if these coefficients are in G.P., then $({}^nC_5)^2 = {}^nC_4.{}^nC_6$

$\Rightarrow 1 = \frac{{}^nC_4}{{}^nC_5}.\frac{{}^nC_6}{{}^nC_5} \quad \Rightarrow 1 = \left(\frac{5}{n-5+1}\right)\times\left(\frac{n-6+1}{6}\right)$

$\Rightarrow 1 = \frac{5}{6}.\frac{(n-5)}{(n-4)}$

$\Rightarrow n = -1$; but $n \in \mathbb{N}$

$\therefore$ The three terms can't be in G.P.

(b) Let a_1, a_2, a_3, a_4 be the coefficients of T_r, T_{r+1}, T_{r+2} and T_{r+3} th term; $(r \in \mathbb{N})$ of $(1+x)^n$

$\Rightarrow a_1 = {}^nC_{r-1};\ a_2 = {}^nC_r;\ a_3 = {}^nC_{r+1};\ a_4 = {}^nC_{r+2}$

Now, L.H.S. $= \frac{a_1}{a_1+a_2} + \frac{a_3}{a_3+a_4}$

$= \frac{{}^nC_{r-1}}{{}^nC_{r-1}+{}^nC_r} + \frac{{}^nC_{r+1}}{{}^nC_{r+1}+{}^nC_{r+2}}$

$= \frac{1}{1+\left(\frac{{}^nC_r}{{}^nC_{r-1}}\right)} + \frac{1}{1+\left(\frac{{}^nC_{r+2}}{{}^nC_{r+1}}\right)}$

$= \frac{1}{1+\left(\frac{n-r+1}{r}\right)} + \frac{1}{1+\left(\frac{n-(r+2)+1}{r+2}\right)}$

$= \frac{r}{n+1} + \frac{r+2}{(n+1)} = \frac{2(r+1)}{(n+1)}$ and

R.H.S $= \frac{2a_2}{a_2+a_3} = \frac{2\,{}^nC_r}{{}^nC_r+{}^nC_{r+1}}$

$= \frac{2}{1+\left(\frac{{}^nC_{r+1}}{{}^nC_r}\right)} = \frac{2}{1+\left(\frac{n-(r+1)+1}{(r+1)}\right)} = \frac{2(r+1)}{(n+1)}$

$\therefore$ L.H.S. = R.H.S.

(c) Given that coefficient of 2nd, 3rd and 4th terms of $(1+x)^{2n}$ are in A.P.

$\Rightarrow {}^{2n}C_1;\ {}^{2n}C_2;\ {}^{2n}C_3$ are in A.P.

$\Rightarrow 2[{}^{2n}C_2] = {}^{2n}C_1 + {}^{2n}C_3$

$\Rightarrow 2 = \frac{{}^{2n}C_1}{{}^{2n}C_2} + \frac{{}^{2n}C_3}{{}^{2n}C_2}$

$\Rightarrow 2 = \left(\frac{2}{2n-2+1}\right) + \left(\frac{2n-3+1}{3}\right)$

$\Rightarrow 2 = \frac{2}{2n-1} + \frac{2n-2}{3}$

$\Rightarrow 6(2n-1) = 6 + (4n^2 - 6n + 2)$

$\Rightarrow 4n^2 - 18n + 14 = 0$

$\Rightarrow 2n^2 - 9n + 7 = 0$

(d) (Given) ${}^nC_{r-2};\ {}^nC_{r-1};\ {}^nC_r = 1 : 3 : 5$

$\Rightarrow {}^nC_{r-2} : {}^nC_{r-1} = 1 : 3$ and ${}^nC_{r-1} : {}^nC_r = 3:5$

$\Rightarrow \frac{{}^nC_{r-1}}{{}^nC_{r-2}} = \frac{3}{1}$ and $\frac{{}^nC_r}{{}^nC_{r-1}} = \frac{5}{3}$

$\Rightarrow \frac{n-(r+1)+1}{(r-1)} = 3;\ \frac{n-r+1}{r} = \frac{5}{3}$

$\Rightarrow (n+1) = 4(r-1);\ 3(n+1) = 8r$

$\Rightarrow 3 = 2\left(\frac{r}{r-1}\right) \Rightarrow r = 3 \Rightarrow n = 7$

(e) Let the consecutive coefficient be ${}^nC_{r-1};\ {}^nC_r;\ {}^nC_{r+1}$

$\therefore$ According to question; ${}^nC_{r-1};\ {}^nC_r;\ {}^nC_{r+1} = 1 : 7 : 42$

$\Rightarrow \dfrac{{}^nC_r}{{}^nC_{r-1}} = \dfrac{7}{1}$ and $\dfrac{{}^nC_{r+1}}{{}^nC_r} = \dfrac{42}{7}$

$\Rightarrow \dfrac{n-r+1}{r} = 7$ and $\dfrac{n-(r+1)+1}{(r+1)} = 6$

$\Rightarrow (n+1) = 8r$ and $(n+1) = 7(r+1)$

$\Rightarrow r = 7 \qquad \Rightarrow n = 55$

(f) $T_2 = 240$; $T_3 = 720$; $T_4 = 1080$

$\Rightarrow \dfrac{T_3}{T_2} = 3;\ \dfrac{T_4}{T_3} = \dfrac{3}{2}$

$\Rightarrow \dfrac{{}^nC_2 x^{n-2}.y^2}{{}^nC_1 x^{n-1}.y^1} = 3;\ \dfrac{{}^nC_3 x^{n-3}.y^3}{{}^nC_2 x^{n-2}.y^2} = \dfrac{3}{2}$

$\Rightarrow \dfrac{n-2+1}{2}.\dfrac{y}{x} = 3;\ \dfrac{n-3+1}{3}.\dfrac{y}{x} = \dfrac{3}{2}$

$\Rightarrow \dfrac{3(n-1)}{2(n-2)} = 2 \qquad 3n - 3 = 4n - 8$

$\Rightarrow n = 5$

$\Rightarrow \dfrac{y}{x} = \dfrac{3}{2} \qquad \Rightarrow 2y = 3x \qquad$ (i)

Also $T_2 = 240 \qquad \Rightarrow {}^nC_1 x^{n-1}.y = 240$

$\Rightarrow {}^5C_1 x^4.y = 240 \qquad \Rightarrow 5x^4(3/2x) = 240$

$\Rightarrow x^5 = \dfrac{240 \times 2}{15} = 32 \qquad \Rightarrow x = 2$

$\Rightarrow y = 3$

5. $(31/5 + 21/3)15 = \sum_{r=0}^{15} {}^{15}C_r (3)^{\frac{15-r}{5}}.(2)^{\frac{r}{3}}$. Now for integer terms, $(15 - r)$ must be a multiple of 5

$\Rightarrow r$ must be a multiple of 5; Also r must be multiple of 3

$\Rightarrow r = 15k;\ k \in W$

$\Rightarrow r \in \{0, 15\}$

$\therefore$ Sum of integer terms $= {}^{15}C_0(3)^3(2)^0 + {}^{15}C_{15}(3)^0(2)^5 = 27 + 32 = 59$

6. (a) $P = {}^nC_0 + {}^nC_2 x^n - 2y^2 + {}^nC_4 x^{n-4} y^4 + ...$

$Q = {}^nC_1 x^{n-1} y + {}^nC_3 x^{n-3} y^3 + {}^nC_5 x^{n-5}.y^5 + ...$

$\therefore (x+y)^n = P + Q$

Also $(x-y)^n = P - Q$

$\Rightarrow (x+y)^n (x-y)^n = P^2 - Q^2$

$\Rightarrow (x^2 - y^2)^n = P^2 - Q^2$

(b) $(x+y)^{2n} - (x-y)^{2n} = [(x+y)^n]^2 - [(x-y)^n]^2 = (P+Q)^2 - (P-Q)^2 = 4.PQ$

(c) $(x+y)^{2n} + (x-y)^{2n} = (P+Q)^2 + (P-Q)^2 = 2(P^2 + Q^2)$

7. $(1+x)^{2n} - nx - 1 \qquad$ (i)

$= ({}^nC_0 + {}^nC_1 x + {}^nC_2 x^2 + {}^nC_3 x^3 + ... + {}^nC_n x^n - nx - 1)$

$= {}^nC_2 x^2 + {}^nC_3 x^3 + ... + {}^nC_n x^n$

$= x^2({}^nC_2 + {}^nC_3 x + ... + {}^nC_n x^{n-2})$

Which is divisible by $x^2\ \forall\ x \geq 2$. Also for $n = 1$; $(1+x)^n - nx - 1 = 0$

Which is divisible $x^2\ (\neq 0)$

(a) Now $(9)^{n+1} - 8n - 9$

$= (1+8)^{n+1} - 8(n+1) - 1 \qquad$ (ii)

Comparing (ii) with (1), we have $x = 8$

$\therefore$ Given expression is divisible x^2 i.e., 64

(b) $6^n - 5n = [(1+5)^n - 5n - 1] + 1 \qquad$ (iii)

Comparing (3) with (1); $[(1+5)^n - 5n - 1]$ is divisible by x^2 i.e., 25

$\therefore 6^n - 5n = 25k + 1;\ k \in \mathbb{Z}$

i.e., $6^n - 5n$ always leave remainder 1 when divided by 25.

8. (a) $2^{4n} - 2^n(7n+1) = 2^n.2^{3n} - 2^n(7n+1) = 2^n[(8)^n - 7n - 1] = 2^n[(1+7)^n - 7n - 1]$

We know that $(1+x)^n - nx - 1$ is divisible by $x^2\ \forall\ n \in \mathbb{N}$

$\therefore 2^n[(1+7)^n - 7x - 1] = 2^n(7)^2 k = 2^{n-2}.(2 \times 7)^2.k = (14)^2.k'$ for $n \geq 2$

For $n = 1$; $(2)^4 - 2^1(7+1) = 0$, which is also divisible by $(14)^2$

$\therefore (2)^{4n} - 2^n(7n+1)$ is divisible by some multiple of $(14)^2$

(b) $a, b \in \mathbb{Z}$ and $a \neq b$

Consider $a^n = (a - b + b)^n$

$= {}^nC_0(a-b)^n + {}^nC_1(a-b)^{n-1}.b + {}^nC_2(a-b)^{n-2}.b^2 + {}^nC_3(a-b)^{n-3}.b^3 + ... + {}^nC_{n-1}(a-b)^1.b^{n-1} + {}^nC_n.b^n$

$\Rightarrow a^n - b^n = {}^nC_0(a-b)^n + {}^nC_1(a-b)^{n-1}.b + ... + {}^nC_{n-1}(a-b).b^{n-1}$

$\Rightarrow a^n - b^n$ is divisible by $(a-b)\ \forall\ n \in \mathbb{N}$

(c) Let $n = 2m + 1$; $m \in \mathbb{N}$

$\Rightarrow n \geq 3$ and $n \in \mathbb{N}$

$\therefore (99)^n + 1 = (10^2 - 1)^n + 1$

$= {}^nC_0 10^{2n} - {}^nC_1(10)^{2n-2} + {}^nC_2(10)^{2n-4} + ... + {}^nC_{n-1}(10^2) - {}^nC_n + 1$

$= {}^nC_0(10)^{2n} - {}^nC_1(10)^{2n-2} + {}^nC_2(10)^{2n-4} ...... + {}^nC_{n-1}(10)^2$

$= (10)^2[{}^nC_0(10)^{2n-2} - {}^nC_1(10)^{2n-4} + {}^nC_2(10)^{2n-6} - .... - {}^nC_{n-2}(10)^2 + n]$

Since all terms upto second last are even, their sum or difference will be even and when it is added to odd (n), the sum inside the bracket becomes odd i.e., ends with 1, 3, 5, 7 and 9

$\therefore$ When it is multiplied by $(10)^2$, there will be exactly 2 zeroes at the end.

9. (a) (i) $(2)^{60} = (23)^{20} = (1+7)^{20}$

$= {}^{20}C_0 + {}^{20}C_1(7) + {}^{20}C_2(7)^2 + {}^{20}C_3(7)^3 + ... + {}^{20}C_{20}(7)^{20}$

$= 1 + 7k;\ k \in \mathbb{Z}$

$\Rightarrow$ Remainder will be 1, when divided by 7

(ii) $(7)^{103} = (7)(7)^{102} = 7(7^2)^{51}$

$= 7(50-1)^{51} = -7[(1-50)^{51}]$

$= -7[{}^{51}C_0 - {}^{51}C_1(50) + {}^{51}C_2(50)^2 - {}^{51}C_3(50)^3 + ... + {}^{51}C_{50}(50)^{50} - {}^{51}C_{51}(50)^{51}]$

$= -7 + 25k = 25k + (18 - 25)$

$= 25(k-1) + 18 = 25k' + 18$

$\Rightarrow$ Remainder will be 18, when divided by 25

(b) If $(17)^{256} = 10^3.q + r$; then r will be a remainder of 3 digits giving last 3 digits of the number $(17)^{256}$

Now, $(17)^{256} = (17^2)^{128}$

$= (289)^{128} = (290 - 1)^{128}$

$= (1 - 290)^{128}$

$= {}^{128}C_0 - {}^{128}C_1(290) + {}^{128}C_2(290)^2 - {}^{128}C_3(290)^3 + ... + {}^{128}C_{127}(290)^{127} + {}^{128}C_{128}(290)^{128}$

$= 1 - 128(290) + \frac{128 \times 127}{2}(290)^2 + 1000k_1 = 103k_1 + r$

$\Rightarrow r = 1 - (128)(290) + (64)(127)(290)^2$

$\Rightarrow r = 1 + 64 \times 290 [(127)(290) - 2]$

$\Rightarrow r = 1 + 128 \times 290 [127 \times 145 - 1]$

$\Rightarrow r = 1 + [100 + 28][200 + 90][127 \times 45 - 1]$

$\Rightarrow r = 1 + [2 \times 10^4 + 9 \times 10^3 + 56 \times 10^2 + 252 \times 10][127 \times 45 - 1]$

$\Rightarrow r = 1 + [56 \times 10^2 + 252 \times 10][127 \times 45 - 1]$

$\Rightarrow r = 1 + [5 \times 10^3 + 6 \times 10^2 + 2 \times 10^3 + 520] \times [127 \times 45 - 1]$

$\Rightarrow r = 1 + [1120][127 \times 45 - 1]$

$\Rightarrow r = 1 + (1120)(4 \times 10^3 + 10^3 + 715 - 1)$

$\Rightarrow r = 1 + (10^3 + 120)(4 \times 10^3 + 10^3 + 714)$

$\Rightarrow r = 1 + (10^2 + 20)(7 \times 10^2 + 10 + 4)$

$\Rightarrow r = 1 + (400 + 200 + 80) = 681$

(c) $1992^{1998} - 1955^{1998} - 1938^{1998} + 1901^{1998}$

$= [(1992)^{1998} - (1955)^{1998}] - [(1938)^{1998} - (1901)^{1998}]$

We know by binomial theorem that $a^n - b^n$ is divisively $(a - b)$

$\therefore$ $(1992)^{1998} - (1955)^{1998}$ is divisible by $1992 - 1955 = 37$

Similarly $(1938)^{1998} - (1901)^{1998}$ is divisible by $1938 - 1901 = 37$

$\therefore$ Given expression is divisible by 37

Also given expression is $[(1992)^{1998} - (1938)^{1998}] - [(1955)^{1998} - (1901)^{1998}]$ is divisible by $(1992 - 1938) = 54$ or $(1955 - 1901) = 54$

Also g.c.d (37, 54) = 1

$\therefore$ The given expression is divisible by $37 \times 54 = 1998$

(d) $(101)^{100} - 1 = (100 + 1)^{100} - 1 = (1 + 10^2)^{100} - 1$

$= {}^{100}C_0 + {}^{100}C_1(10^2) + {}^{100}C_2(10^2)^2 + {}^{100}C_3(10^2)^3 + \ldots + {}^{100}C_{100}(10^2)^{100} - 1$

$= {}^{100}C_1(10)^2 + {}^{100}C_2(10)^4 + {}^{100}C_3(10)^6 + \ldots + (10)^{200}$

$= (10)^4 + {}^{100}C_2(10)^4 + {}^{100}C_3(10)^6 + \ldots + (10)^{200}$

$= (10)^4 + (1 + (50 \times 99) + {}^{100}C_3(10)^2 + \ldots + (10)^{96}]$

The sum inside the bracket is an odd number with 1 as its unit place.

Thus the given no is divisible by 104 and not by 10^5

TEXTUAL EXERCISE–2: (OBJECTIVE)

1. (b) Middle term of $(1 + x)^{10}$ $T_{\frac{10+2}{2}} = T_6 = {}^{10}C_5 x^5$ having coefficient $= {}^{10}C_5 = \frac{10!}{(5!)^2}$

2. (b) Middle term of $\left(x + \frac{1}{x}\right)^{10} \Rightarrow T_{\frac{10+2}{2}}$ i.e.,

$T_6 = {}^{10}C_5 x^5 . \frac{1}{x^5} = {}^{10}C_5$

3. (b) $\left(x^2 + \frac{1}{x}\right)^n$ has only one middle term

$\Rightarrow$ n must be even and the middle term $= T_{\frac{n+2}{2}} = T_{\frac{n}{2}+1}$

$= {}^nC_{n/2}(x^2)^{n - \frac{n}{2}}\left(\frac{1}{x}\right)^{n/2} = {}^nC_{n/2}\, x^{n/2} = 924x^6$ (given)

$\Rightarrow n = 12$

4. (c) $(7)^{300} = q.(10)^3 + r$; we need to find r.

Now $(7^2)^{150} = (49)^{150} = (50 - 1)^{150} = (1 - 50)^{150}$

$= 1 - {}^{150}C_1(50) + {}^{150}C_2(50)^2 - {}^{150}C_3(50)^3 + \ldots +$

$= 1 - 7500 + \frac{150 \times 149}{2}(2500) + 10^3q_1$

$= 1 - 7500 + (70 + 5) \times (150 - 1)\, 2500 + 10^3q_1$

$= 1 - 500 + (-5)(2500) + 10^3q_2$

$= 1 - 500 - 12500 + 10^3q_2$

$= 1 - 13000 + 10^3q_2 = 1 + 10^3(q_2 - 13)$

$= 1 + 10^3q_3$ $\Rightarrow$ last digit = 1,

$(\because q_2 - 13 > 0$ as $(7)^{300} > 0)$

5. (c) $2^{2003} = 8(24)^{500}$

$= 8(1 - 17)^{500} = 8({}^{500}C_0 - {}^{500}C_1\, 17 + {}^{500}C_2(17)^2 + \ldots + {}^{500}C_{500}(17)^{500}) = 8 + 17k;\ k \in \mathbb{Z}$

$\Rightarrow$ On dividing by 17, 8 will be the remainder

TEXTUAL EXERCISE–3: (SUBJECTIVE)

1. (a) $\sum_{r=0}^{n}(-1)^{r+2}C_{2r} = \sum_{r=0}^{n}(-1)^r.C_{2r} = C_0 - C_2 + C_4 - C_6 + \ldots + (-1)^n C_{2n}$

Sign's are alternatively +ve and –ve and one terms is missing from the three consecutive terms.

$\therefore$ Put $x = (-1)^{1/2}$ in the expansion of $(1 + x)^n = C_0 + C_1x + C_2x^2 + C_3x^3 + \ldots$

$\Rightarrow (1 + i)^n = C_0 + C_1i - C_2 - C_3i + C_4 + C_5i - C_6 + \ldots$ and

$(1 - i)^n = C_0 - C_1i - C_2 - C_3i + C_4 - C_5i - C_6 + \ldots$

Adding, $\frac{(1+i)^n + (1-i)^n}{2} = C_0 - C_2 + C_4 - C_6 + \ldots$

$\therefore \frac{(1+i)^n + (1-i)^n}{2}$

(b) $\sum_{r=0}^{n}(-1)^r.{}^nC_r\left(\frac{1}{2}\right)^r = \left(1 - \frac{1}{2}\right)^n = \left(\frac{1}{2}\right)^n$

(c) ${}^nC_0 + 2\,{}^nC_1 + 4.{}^nC_2 + 8.{}^nC_3 + \ldots + (n + 1)$terms

$= \sum_{r=0}^{n} {}^nC_r(2)^r = (1+2)^n = (3)^n$

(d) ${}^nC_0 + \frac{{}^nC_1}{2} + \frac{{}^nC_2}{4} + \frac{{}^nC_3}{8} + \ldots + (n+1)$ terms

$= \sum_{r=0}^{n} {}^nC_r.\left(\frac{1}{2}\right)^r = \left(1 + \frac{1}{2}\right)^n = \left(\frac{3}{2}\right)^n$

(e) ${}^nC_0 - \frac{1}{3}.{}^nC_1 + \frac{1}{9}{}^nC_2 - \frac{1}{27}.{}^nC_3 + \ldots + (n+1)$ terms

$= \sum_{r=0}^{n} {}^nC_r\left(-\frac{1}{3}\right)^r = \left(1 - \frac{1}{3}\right)^n = \left(\frac{2}{3}\right)^n$

(f) $\sum_{r=1}^{n} r.C_r = \sum_{r=1}^{n} r.\frac{n}{r}.{}^{n-1}C_{r-1} = n\sum_{r=1}^{n} {}^{n-1}C_{r-1} = n(2)^{n-1}$

(g) $\sum_{r=3}^{n} r(r-1)(r-2)C_r$

$= \sum_{r=3}^{n} r(r-1)(r-2).\frac{n}{r}.\frac{(n-1)}{(r-1)}.\frac{(n-2)}{(r-2)}.{}^{n-3}C_{r-3}$

$= n(n-1)(n-2)\sum_{r=3}^{n} {}^{n-3}C_{r-3} = n(n-1)(n-2)(2)^{n-3}$

(h) $\sum_{r=1}^{n} r^2.{}^{n}C_r = \sum_{r=1}^{n} r^2.\frac{n}{r}{}^{n-1}C_{r-1}$

$= n\sum_{r=1}^{n} r.{}^{n-1}C_{r-1} = n\sum_{r=1}^{n}(r-1+1).{}^{n-1}C_{r-1}$

$= n\sum_{r=1}^{n}(r-1).{}^{n-1}C_{r-1} + n\sum_{r=1}^{n}{}^{n-1}C_{r-1}$

$= n(n-1)\sum_{r=2}^{n}{}^{n-2}C_{r-2} + n(2)^{n-1}$

$= n(n-1)(2)^{n-2} + n(2)^{n-1} = n(2)^{n-2}[n-1+2] = n(n+1)(2)^{n-2}$

(i) $\sum_{r=0}^{n}\frac{C_r}{(r+1)} = \sum_{r=0}^{n}\frac{1}{(r+1)}\times\frac{(r+1)}{(n+1)}{}^{n+1}C_{r+1}$

$= \frac{1}{(n+1)}\sum_{r=0}^{n}{}^{n+1}C_{r+1} = \frac{1}{n+1}\left(\sum_{r=0}^{(n+1)}{}^{n+1}C_r - {}^{n+1}C_0\right)$

$= \frac{1}{(n+1)}\left[(2)^{n+1}-1\right]$

(j) $\sum_{r=0}^{n}\frac{C_r}{(r+1)(r+2)}$

$= \sum_{r=0}^{n}\frac{1}{(r+1)(r+2)}\times\frac{r+1}{(n+1)}\times\frac{r+2}{n+2}\times{}^{n+2}C_{r+2}$

$= \frac{1}{(n+1)(n+2)}\sum_{r=0}^{n}{}^{n+2}C_{r+2}$

$= \frac{1}{(n+1)(n+2)}\left(\sum_{r=0}^{n+2}{}^{n+2}C_r - {}^{n+2}C_0 - {}^{n+2}C_1\right)$

$= \frac{1}{(n+1)(n+2)}((2)^{n+2}-1-n-2) = \frac{(2)^{n+2}-n-3}{(n+1)(n+2)}$

2. (a) $\sum_{r=0}^{n}C_r^2 = \sum_{r=0}^{n}C_r.C_r = \sum_{r=0}^{n}{}^{n}C_r.{}^{n}C_{n-r} = {}^{2n}C_n$

(b) $\sum_{r=1}^{n} r\left(\frac{{}^{n}C_r}{{}^{n}C_{r-1}}\right) = \sum_{r=1}^{n} r\left(\frac{n-r+1}{r}\right)$

$= \sum_{r=1}^{n}(n-r+1) = n(n+1) - \frac{n(n+1)}{2} = \frac{n(n+1)}{2} = {}^{n+1}C_2$

(c) $\sum_{r=1}^{n} r^2\left(\frac{{}^{n}C_r}{{}^{n}C_{r-1}}\right) = \sum_{r=1}^{n} r^2\left(\frac{n-r+1}{r}\right)$

$= \sum_{r=1}^{n} r(n-r+1) = \frac{n^2(n+1)}{2} - \frac{n(n+1)(2n+1)}{6} + \frac{n(n+1)}{2}$

$= \frac{n(n+1)}{2}\left[n - \frac{(2n+1)}{3} + 1\right]$

$= \frac{n(n+1)}{2}\left[\frac{n+2}{3}\right] = \frac{n(n+1)(n+2)}{6}$

(d) $\sum_{r=1}^{n} r^3\left(\frac{{}^{n}C_r}{{}^{n}C_{r-1}}\right) = \sum_{r=1}^{n} r^2(n-r+1)$

$= \frac{n^2(n+1)(2n+1)}{6} - \left[\frac{n(n+1)}{2}\right]^2 + \frac{n(n+1)(2n+1)}{6}$

$= \frac{n(n+1)}{2}\left[\frac{n(2n+1)}{3} - \frac{n(n+1)}{2} + \frac{(2n+1)}{3}\right]$

$= \frac{n(n+1)}{2}\left[\frac{(n+1)(n+2)}{6}\right] = \frac{n(n+1)^2}{12}(n+2)$

(e) $\sum_{r=1}^{n} r^2\left(\frac{{}^{n}C_r}{{}^{n}C_{r-1}}\right)^2 = \sum_{r=1}^{n} r^2\left(\frac{n-r+1}{r}\right)^2 = \sum_{r=1}^{n}(n-r+1)^2$

$= \sum_{r=1}^{n}\{(n+1)^2 + r^2 - 2(n+1)r\}$

$= n(n+1)^2 + \frac{n(n+1)(2n+1)}{6} - \frac{2(n+1)^2 n}{2}$

$= n(n+1)\left[(n+1) + \frac{(2n+1)}{6} - (n+1)\right]$

$= \frac{n(n+1)(2n+1)}{6} = \sum_{k=1}^{n} k^2$

(f) $\sum_{r=2}^{n} r(r-1).\frac{{}^{n}C_r}{{}^{n}C_{r-2}} = \sum_{r=2}^{n} r(r-1).\frac{{}^{n}C_r}{{}^{n}C_{r-1}}\times\frac{{}^{n}C_{r-1}}{{}^{n}C_{r-2}}$

$= \sum_{r=2}^{n} r(r-1)\left(\frac{n-r+1}{r}\right)\left(\frac{n-r+1+1}{r-1}\right)$

$= \sum_{r=2}^{n}(n-r+1)(n-r+2)$

$= 1.2 + 2.3 + 3.4 + \ldots + (n-1)(n)$

$= \sum_{r=1}^{n-1} r(r+1) = \sum_{r=1}^{n-1}(r^2+r)$

$= \frac{(n-1)(n)(2n-1)}{6} + \frac{(n-1)(n)}{2}$

$= \frac{n(n-1)}{2}\left[\frac{2n-1}{3}+1\right] = \frac{n(n^2-1)}{3}$

3. Coefficient $x^6 = {}^{15}C_6 + {}^{16}C_6 + \ldots + {}^{30}C_6 = ({}^{15}C_7 + {}^{15}C_6 + {}^{16}C_6 + \ldots + {}^{30}C_6 - {}^{15}C_7) = {}^{16}C_7 + {}^{16}C_6 + \ldots + {}^{30}C_6 - {}^{15}C_7$.

(Using pascal's rule repeatedly)

$= {}^{30}C_7 + {}^{30}C_6 - {}^{15}C_7 = {}^{31}C_7 - {}^{15}C_7$

4. (a) ${}^{n}C_m + {}^{n-1}C_m + \ldots + {}^{m}C_m = {}^{n+1}C_{m+1}$

L.H.S. $= {}^{m}C_m + {}^{m+1}C_m + {}^{m+2}C_m + \ldots + {}^{n-1}C_m + {}^{n}C_m$

$= {}^{m+1}C_{m+1} + {}^{m+1}C_m + {}^{m+2}C_m + \ldots + {}^{n-1}C_m + {}^{n}C_m$

$= {}^{m+2}C_{m+1} + {}^{m+2}C_m + \ldots + {}^{n}C_m$ (using pascal's rule repeatedly)

$= {}^{n}C_{m+1} + {}^{n}C_m = {}^{n+1}C_{m+1}$ = R.H.S.

(b) $^nC_m + 2.^{n-1}C_m + 3.^{n-2}C_m + \ldots + (n-(m-1)).^mC_m = {}^{n+2}C_{m+2}$

L.H.S. = $(^nC_m + {}^{n-1}C_m + {}^{n-2}C_m + \ldots + {}^mC_m) + (^{n-1}C_m + {}^{n-2}C_m + \ldots + {}^mC_m) + (^{n-2}C_m + \ldots + {}^mC_m) + \ldots + (^{m+1}C_m + {}^mC_m) + (^mC_m)$

(using (a))

$= {}^{n+1}C_{m+1} + {}^nC_{m+1} + {}^{n-1}C_{m+1} + \ldots + {}^{m+2}C_{m+1} + {}^{m+1}C_{m+1}$

$= {}^{m+1}C_{m+1} + {}^{m+2}C_{m+1} + {}^{m+3}C_{m+1} + \ldots + {}^{n-1}C_{m+1} + {}^nC_{m+1} + {}^{n+1}C_{m+1}$

$= {}^{m+2}C_{m+2} + {}^{m+2}C_{m+1} + {}^{m+3}C_{m+1} + \ldots + {}^{n+1}C_{m+1}$

$= {}^{m+3}C_{m+2} + {}^{m+3}C_{m+1} + \ldots + {}^{n+1}C_{m+1}$

$= {}^{n+1}C_{m+2} + {}^{n+1}C_{m+1} = {}^{n+2}C_{m+2}$ = R.H.S.

5. L.H.S. = $^nC_n + {}^{n+1}C_n + {}^{n+2}C_n + \ldots + {}^{n+k}C_n$

$= {}^{n+k}C_{n+1} + {}^{n+1}C_n + {}^{n+2}C_n + \ldots + {}^{n+k}C_n$

$= {}^{n+2}C_{n+1} + {}^{n+1}C_n + \ldots + {}^{n+k}C_n$

$= {}^{n+k}C_{n+1} + {}^{n+k}C_n = {}^{n+k+1}C_{n+1}$ = R.H.S.

6. Consider $101^{50} - 99^{50} = (100+1)^{50} - (100-1)^{50} = (1+100)^{50} - (1-100)^{50}$

$= 2[^{50}C_1(10^2) + {}^{50}C_3(10^2)^3 + {}^{50}C_5(10^2)^5 + \ldots + {}^{50}C_{49}(10^2)^{49}]$

Each of $^{50}C_r \geq 50$ and $^{50}C_3 = \dfrac{50\times 49\times 48}{6} = 50 \times 49 \times 8 > 51$

$\therefore$ $(101)^{50} - (99)^{50} > 2[50(10)^2 + 51(10^6) + 50(10^{10}) + \ldots + 50(10^{98})]$

$= 100[(10)^2 + (10)^6 + (10)^{10} + \ldots + (10)^{98}] + 2 \times 10^6$

$= 100(10^2)\left[\dfrac{(10^4)^{25}-1}{(10^4)-1}\right] + 2\times 10^6$

$= \left(\dfrac{10^4}{10^4-1}\right)\left[(100)^{50}-1\right] + 2\times 10^6 > (100)^{50} - 1 + (2 \times 10^6) > (100)^{50}$

$\Rightarrow$ $(101)^{50} > (99)^{50} + (100)^{50}$

$\Rightarrow$ $(101)^{50} > (99)^{50} + (100)^{50}$

7. $\sum_{r=0}^{n}(-1)^r.C_r\left[\dfrac{1^r}{2^r} + \dfrac{3^r}{2^{2r}} + \dfrac{7^r}{2^{3r}} + \ldots + m \text{ terms}\right]$

$= \sum_{r=0}^{n}(-1)^r.C_r\left[\left(\dfrac{1}{2}\right)^r + \left(\dfrac{3}{4}\right)^r + \left(\dfrac{7}{8}\right)^r + \ldots + m \text{ terms}\right]$

$= \left(1-\dfrac{1}{2}\right)^n + \left(1-\dfrac{3}{4}\right)^n + \left(1-\dfrac{7}{8}\right)^n + \ldots$upto m terms

$= \left(\dfrac{1}{2}\right)^n + \left(\dfrac{1}{4}\right)^n + \left(\dfrac{1}{8}\right)^n + \ldots$upto n terms

$= \left(\dfrac{1}{2}\right)^n + \left(\dfrac{1}{2}\right)^{2n} + \left(\dfrac{1}{2}\right)^{3n} + \ldots$upto n terms

$= \left(\dfrac{1}{2}\right)^n \dfrac{\left[\left[\left(\dfrac{1}{2}\right)^n\right]^m - 1\right]}{\left(\dfrac{1}{2}\right)^n - 1} = \left[\dfrac{1-(2)^{mn}}{1-(2)^n}\right]\dfrac{1}{2}\times\dfrac{1}{2^{mn}}\times\dfrac{2^n}{1}$

$= \dfrac{(2^{mn}-1)}{2^{mn}(2^n-1)}$

8. L.H.S. $= 2C_0 + \dfrac{2^2C_1}{2} + \dfrac{2^3C_2}{3} + \dfrac{2^4.C_3}{4} + \ldots + \dfrac{2^{n+1}.C_n}{(n+1)}$

$= \sum_{r=0}^{n}\dfrac{^nC_r.(2)^{r+1}}{(r+1)} = \sum_{r=0}^{n}\dfrac{r+1}{n+1}.\dfrac{1}{(r+1)}.{}^{n+1}C_{r+1}(2)^{r+1}$

$= \sum_{r=0}^{n}\dfrac{1}{(n+1)}.{}^{n+1}C_{r+1}(2)^{r+1} = \dfrac{1}{(n+1)}\sum_{r=1}^{n+1}{}^{n+1}C_r(2)^r$

$= \dfrac{1}{(n+1)}\left(\sum_{r=0}^{n+1}{}^{n+1}C_r(2)^r - 1\right)$

$= \dfrac{1}{(n+1)}\left[(1+2)^{n+1}-1\right] = \dfrac{(3)^{n+1}-1}{(n+1)}$ = R.H.S.

9. (a) $(1+x)^n = C_0 + C_1x + C_2x^2 + \ldots + C_nx^n$

Put $x = (-1)^{1/2} = i$ and $-i$

$\Rightarrow$ $(1+i)^n = C_0 + C_1i - C_2 - C_3i + C_4 + \ldots$ and $(1-i)^n = C_0 - C_1i - C_2 + C_3i + C_4 + \ldots$

Adding; $\dfrac{(1+i)^n + (1-i)^n}{2} = C_0 - C_2 + C_4\ldots$

$\therefore$ Required sum

$= \dfrac{1}{2}\left\{\left[\sqrt{2}\left(\cos\dfrac{\pi}{4} + i\sin\dfrac{\pi}{4}\right)\right]^n + \left[\sqrt{2}\left(\cos\dfrac{\pi}{4} - i\sin\dfrac{\pi}{4}\right)\right]^n\right\}$

$= \dfrac{1}{2}\left\{\left(\sqrt{2}\right)^n\left[2\cos\dfrac{n\pi}{4}\right]\right\} = (2)^{n/2}\cos\dfrac{n\pi}{4}$

(b) $(1+x)^n = C_0 + C_1x + C_2x^2 + \ldots + C_nx^n$

Put $x = (1)^{1/3}$ i.e., 1, ω and ω²

$\Rightarrow$ $(2)^n = C_0 + C_1 + C_2 + C_3 + \ldots + C_n$

$\Rightarrow$ $(1+\omega)^n = C_0 + C_1\omega + C_2\omega^2 + C_3\omega^3 + \ldots + C_n\omega^{2n}$

$\Rightarrow$ $(1+\omega^2)^n = C_0 + C_1\omega^2 + C_3\omega^4 + C_3\omega^6 + \ldots C_n\omega^2n$

Adding, $\dfrac{(2)^n + (1+\omega)^n + (1+\omega^2)^n}{3} = C_0 + C_3 + C_6 + \ldots$

$\Rightarrow$ Required Sum $= \dfrac{(2)^n + (-\omega^2)^n + (-\omega)^n}{3}$

$= \dfrac{(2)^n + (-1)^n\left[\omega^{2n} + \omega^n\right]}{3} = \dfrac{(2)^n + (-1)^n[\omega^n + (\omega^2)^n]}{3}$

$\Rightarrow \dfrac{(2)^n + (-1)^n\left[\left(-\dfrac{1}{2} + \dfrac{\sqrt{3}}{2}i\right)^n + \left(-\dfrac{1}{2} - \dfrac{\sqrt{3}}{2}i\right)^n\right]}{3}$

$= \dfrac{(2)^n + (-1)^n\left[\left[cis\left(\dfrac{2\pi}{3}\right)\right]^n + \left[cis\left(-\dfrac{2\pi}{3}\right)\right]^n\right]}{3}$

$= \dfrac{(2)^n + (-1)^n 2\cos\left(\dfrac{2n\pi}{3}\right)}{3}$

(c) $(1+x)^n = C_0 + C_1x + C_2x^2 + C_3x^3 + \ldots + C_nx^n$ (i)

Here 3 terms are missing and all terms are positive.

$\therefore$ We are to substitutes x = 4th roots of unity i.e., 1, –1, i, –i, but before that we are to make C_3 the coefficient of x^4 (∵ 4rth root)

$\therefore$ Multiplying (i) by x both sides, we get $(1+x)^n.\,x = C_0x + C_1x^2 + C_2x^3 + C_3x^4 + C_4x^5 + C_5x^6 + C_6x^7 + C_7x^8$ ...(ii)

Put $x = 1, -1, i, -i$ in (ii), we get $(2)^n = C_0 + C_1 + C_2 + C_3 + C_4 + C_5 + C_6 + C_7 + \ldots$ $0 = -C_0 + C_1 - C_2 + C_3 - C_4 + C_5 - C_6 + C_7 + \ldots$ $(1+i)^n.i = C_0i - C_1 - C_2i + C_3 + C_4i - C_5 - C_6i + C_7 + \ldots$ $(1+i)^n.(-i) = -C_0i - C_1 + C_2i + C_3 - C_4i - C_5 + C_6i + C_7 + \ldots$

Adding above equation, we get $\dfrac{(2)^n+(1+i)^n.i-(1-i)^n.i}{4} = C_3 + C_7 + \ldots$

$$\text{Required Sum} = \frac{(2)^n + i[(1+i)^n-(1-i)^n]}{4}$$

$$= \frac{(2)^n + i\left[(\sqrt{2})^n\left(cis\dfrac{\pi}{4}\right)^n - (\sqrt{2})^n\left(cis-\dfrac{\pi}{4}\right)^n\right]}{4}$$

$$= \frac{(2)^n + i(2)^{n/2}\left[2\sin\dfrac{n\pi}{4}\right]}{4}$$

$$= \frac{1}{2}\left\{(2)^{n-1} - (2)^{n/2}\sin\frac{n\pi}{4}\right\}$$

(d) Put $x = (1)^{1/4} = 1, -1, i, -i$ in binomial expansion, we get

$(2)^n = C_0 + C_1 + C_2 + C_3 + C_4 + \ldots$

$0 = C_0 - C_1 + C_2 - C_3 + C_4 + \ldots$

$(1+i)^n = C_0 + C_1i - C_2 - C_3i + C_4 + \ldots$

$(1-i)^n = C_0 - C_1i - C_2 + C_3i + C_4 + \ldots$

Adding, we get $\dfrac{(2)^n+(1+i)^n+(1-i)^n}{4} = C_0 + C_4 + C_8 + \ldots$

$$\Rightarrow \text{Required sum} = \frac{(2)^n + (\sqrt{2})^n\left[2\cos\dfrac{n\pi}{4}\right]}{4}$$

$$= \frac{1}{2}\left\{(2)^{n-1} + (2)^{n/2}\cos\frac{n\pi}{4}\right\}$$

(e) Two terms are missing, thus substituting $x = 1, \omega, \omega^2$, after C_1 coefficient of x^3, we have

$(1+x)^n.\,x^2 = C_0x^2 + C_1x^3 + C_2x^4 + C_3x^5 + C_4x^6 + \ldots$

$\Rightarrow (2)^n = C_0 + C_1 + C_2 + C_3 + C_4 + \ldots$

$\Rightarrow \omega^2(1+\omega)^n = C_0\omega^2 + C_1\omega^3 + C_2\omega^4 + C_3\omega^5 + C_4\omega^6 + \ldots$

$\Rightarrow \omega^4(1+\omega^2)^n = C_0\omega^4 + C_1\omega^6 + C_2\omega^8 + C_3\omega^{10} + C_4\omega^{12}$

Adding above equation, we get

$$\frac{(2)^n + \omega^2(1+\omega)^n + \omega^4(1+\omega^2)^n}{3} = C_1 + C_4 + C_7 + \ldots$$

$$\therefore \text{Required sum} = \frac{2^n + \omega^2(-1)^n.\omega^{2n} + \omega(-1)^n\omega^n}{3}$$

$$= \frac{2^n + (-1)^n[\omega^{2n+2} + \omega^{n+1}]}{3}$$

$$= \frac{2^n + (-1)^n\left[cis(2n+2)\dfrac{2\pi}{3} + cis(n+1)\dfrac{2\pi}{3}\right]}{3}$$

$$= \frac{(2)^n + (-1)^n.2(-1)^{n+1}\cos(n+1)\dfrac{\pi}{3}}{3}$$

$$= \frac{(2)^n + 2(-1)^{2n+1}\cos(n+1)\dfrac{\pi}{3}}{3}$$

$$= \frac{(2)^n - 2\cos(n+1)\dfrac{\pi}{3}}{3}$$

(f) 3 terms are missing between any two consecutive terms.

$\therefore$ Put $x = 4^{\text{th}}$ roots of unity in the expansion of $(1+x)^n.x^2 = C_0x^2 + C_1x^3 + C_2x^4 + C_3x^5 + C_4x^6 + C_5x^7 + C_6x^8 + \ldots$

$\Rightarrow (2)^n = C_0 + C_1 + C_2 + C_3 + C_4 + C_5 + C_6 + \ldots$

$\Rightarrow 0 = C_0 - C_1 + C_2 - C_3 + C_4 - C_5 + C_6 + \ldots$

$\Rightarrow (1+i)^n.\,1^2 = -C_0 - C_1i + C_2 + C_3i - C_4 - C_5i + C_6 + \ldots$

$\Rightarrow (1-i)^n.1^2 = -C_0 + C_1i + C_2 - C_3i - C_4 + C_5i + C_6 + \ldots$

Adding, above equations we get

$$\frac{(2)^n - (1+i)^n - (1-i)^n}{4} = C_2 + C_6 + \ldots$$

$$\Rightarrow S = \frac{(2)^n - (\sqrt{2})^n\left[cis\dfrac{n\pi}{4} + cis\left(-\dfrac{n\pi}{4}\right)\right]}{4}$$

$$\Rightarrow S = \frac{(2)^n - (2)^{n/2}.2\cos\dfrac{n\pi}{4}}{4}$$

$$\Rightarrow S = \frac{1}{2}\left\{(2)^{n-1} - (2)^{n/2}\cos\frac{n\pi}{4}\right\}$$

(g) $(1+x)^n.\,x = C_0x + C_1x^2 + C_2x^3 + C_3x^4 + C_4x^5 + C_5x^6 + C_6x^7 + C_7x^8 + C_8x^9 + \ldots$

Put $x = 1, \omega, \omega^2$

$\Rightarrow (2)^n = C_0 + C_1 + C_2 + C_3 + C_4 + C_5 + \ldots$

$\Rightarrow (1+\omega)^n.\,\omega = C_0\,\omega + C_1\,\omega^2 + C_2\,\omega^3 + C_2\,\omega^3 + C_3\,\omega^4 + C_4\,\omega^5 + C^5\,\omega^6 + \ldots$

$\Rightarrow (1+\omega^2)^n.\,\omega^2 = C_0\,\omega^2 + C_1\,\omega^4 + C_2\,\omega^6 + C_3\,\omega^8 + C_4\,\omega^{10} + C_5\,\omega^{12} + \ldots$

Adding, above equations, we get

$$\frac{(2)^n + (1+\omega)^n.\omega + (1+\omega^2)^n.\omega^2}{3} = C_2 + C_5 + \ldots$$

$$\therefore S = \frac{(2)^n + \omega(-1)^n\omega^{2n} + (-1)^n.\omega^n.\omega^2}{3}$$

$$\Rightarrow S = \frac{(2)^n + (-1)^n.n[\omega^{2n+1} + \omega^{n+2}]}{3}$$

$$\Rightarrow S = \frac{(2)^n + (-1)^n\left[cis(2n+1)\dfrac{2\pi}{3} + cis(n+2)\dfrac{2\pi}{3}\right]}{3}$$

$$\Rightarrow S = \frac{(2)^n + (-1)^n\left[2(-1)^{n+1} + \cos(n-1)\dfrac{\pi}{3}\right]}{3}$$

$$\Rightarrow S = \frac{(2)^n + 2(-1)^{2n+1}\cos(n-1)\dfrac{\pi}{3}}{3}$$

$$S = \frac{(2)^n - 2\cos(n-1)\dfrac{\pi}{3}}{3}$$

10. (a) $\frac{C_0}{1}+\frac{C_2}{3}+\frac{C_4}{5}+.....$

Consider $(1+x)^n = C_0 + C_1x + C_2x^2 + C_3x^3 + ...$

$(1-x)^n = C_0 - C_1x + C_2x^2 - C_3x^3 + ...$

Adding, we get $(1+x)^n + (1-x)^n = 2[C_0 + C_2x^2 + C_4x^4 + ...]$

Integrating both sides w.r.t. with in the limits $x=0$ to $x=1$, we get

$$\left[\frac{(1+x)^{n+1}}{(n+1)}+\frac{(1-x)^{n+1}}{(-1)(n+1)}\right]_0^1 = 2\left[\cos x+\frac{C_2x^3}{3}+\frac{C_4x^5}{5}+....\right]_0^1$$

$$\Rightarrow \frac{(2)^{n+1}}{n+1}-\left(\frac{1}{n+1}-\frac{1}{n+1}\right)=2\left[C_0+\frac{C_2}{3}+\frac{C_4}{5}+...\right]$$

$$\Rightarrow \frac{C_0}{1}+\frac{C_2}{3}+\frac{C_4}{5}+....=\frac{(2)^n}{(n+1)}=\frac{2^n}{(n+1)}$$

(b) As in part (a), $(1+x)^n - (1-x)^n = 2[C_1x + C_3x^3 + ...]$

Integrating both sides with in the limit $x = 0$ to $x = 1$

$$\Rightarrow \left[\frac{(1+x)^{n+1}}{(n+1)}+\frac{(1-x)^{n+1}}{(n+1)}\right]_0^1=2\left[\frac{C_1}{2}+\frac{C_3}{4}+\frac{C_5}{6}+....\right]$$

$$\Rightarrow \frac{(2)^{n+1}}{n+1}-2\left(\frac{1}{n+1}\right)=2\left[\frac{C_1}{2}+\frac{C_3}{4}+....\right]$$

$$\Rightarrow \frac{C_1}{2}+\frac{C_3}{4}+.....=\frac{(2)^n-1}{(n+1)}$$

(c) $(1-x)^n = C_0 - C_1x + C^2x^2 - C_3x^3 + ...$

Integrating w.r.t. x with the limit $x = 0$ to $x = x$

$$\Rightarrow \left[\frac{(1-x)^{n+1}}{-(n+1)}\right]_0^x=\left(C_0x-\frac{C_1x^2}{2}+\frac{C_2x^3}{3}-\frac{C_3x^4}{4}+...\right)$$

$$\Rightarrow \frac{-(1-x)^{n+1}}{(n+1)}+\frac{1}{n+1}=C_0x-\frac{C_1}{2}x^2+\frac{C_2}{3}x^3-\frac{C_3}{4}x^4+...$$

Now integrating w.r.t. with in the limit $x = 0$ to $x = 1$, we get

$$\left[\frac{(1-x)^{n+2}}{(n+1)(n+2)}+\frac{x}{n+1}\right]_0^1=\left[\frac{C_0x^2}{1.2}-\frac{C_1x^3}{2.3}+\frac{C_2x^4}{3.4}-\frac{C_3x^5}{4.5}+...\right]_0^1$$

$$\Rightarrow \frac{1}{(n+1)}-\frac{1}{(n+1)(n+2)}=\frac{C_0}{1.2}-\frac{C_1}{2.3}+\frac{C_2}{3.4}-\frac{C_3}{4.5}+...$$

$$\Rightarrow \frac{C_0}{1.2}-\frac{C_1}{2.3}+\frac{C_2}{3.4}+...=\frac{1}{(n+2)}$$

(d) $C_0 - 3C_1 + 5C_2 + ...+ (-1)^n(2n+1)C_n$

$$= \sum_{r=0}^{n}(-1)^r(2r+1).\,^nC_r$$

$$= 2\sum_{r=0}^{n}(-1)^r.r.\,^nC_r+\sum_{r=0}^{n}(-1)^r.\,^nC_r$$

$$= 2\sum_{r=1}^{n}(-1)^r\,r.\frac{n}{r}.\,^{n-1}C_{r-1}+(0)$$

$$= 2n\sum_{r=1}^{n}(-1)^r.\,^{n-1}C_{r-1}$$

$$= -2n\sum_{r=1}^{n}(-1)^{r-1}.\,^{n-1}C_{r-1} = (-2n)\,(0) = 0$$

(e) $S = C_1^2 - 2C_2^2 + 3C_3^2 + ... - 2nC_{2n}^2$

$$= \sum_{r=1}^{2n}(-1)^{r+1}.(^{2n}C_r)^2(r)$$

$$= \sum_{r=1}^{2n}(-1)^{r+1}.r.(^{2n}C_r.\,^{2n}C_r)$$

$$= (-1)(2n)\sum_{r=1}^{2n}(-1)^r\,^{2n-1}C_{r-1}.\,^{2n}C_r$$

Let $2n = m$(even)

$$= (-m)\sum_{r=1}^{m}(-1)^r\,^{m-1}C_{r-1}.\,^mC_r \qquad \text{(i)}$$

Now consider, $(1+x)^{m-1}(1-x)^m$

$= [^{m-1}C_0 + {}^{m-1}C_1x + {}^{m-1}C_2x^2 + ...+ {}^{m-1}C_{m-1}x^{m-1}] \times [^mC_0 - {}^mC_1x + {}^mC_2x^2 - {}^mC_3x^3 + ...+ (-1)^m.{}^mC_mx^m]$

Now coefficient of x^{m-1} in R.H.S.

$= (-1)^{m-1}.\,^mC_{m-1}.\,^{m-1}C_0 + (-1)^{m-2}.\,^mC_{m-2}.\,^{m-1}C_1 + (-1)^{m-3}.\,^mC_{m-3}.\,^{m-1}C_2 + ...+(-1)^0.\,^{m-1}C_{m-1}x^{m-1}.\,^mC_0$

$(\because m = 2n \Rightarrow (-1)^m = 1$ and $^mC_r = {}^mC_{m-r})$

$= -^mC_1.\,^{m-1}C_0 + {}^mC_2.\,^{m-1}C_1 - {}^mC_3.\,^{m-1}C_2 + ...+ {}^{m-1}C_{m-1}.\,^mC_m$

$$= \sum_{r=1}^{m}(-1)^r\,^mC_r.\,^{m-1}C_{r-1} \qquad \text{(ii)}$$

$\therefore$ From (i) and (ii) we note that required sum = $(-m)$ coefficient of x^{m-1} in $(1+x)^{m-1}(1-x)^m$

= $(-m)$ coefficient of x^{m-1} in $(1-x)[1-x^2]^{m-1}$

=(m) coefficient of x^{m-2} in $(1-x^2)^{m-1}$

=(m) coefficient of x^{m-2} in $\sum_{r=1}^{m-1}(-1)^r.\,^{m-1}C_r.\,x^{2r}$

$$= (m)\left[(-1)^{\frac{m}{2}-1}.\,^{m-1}C_{\frac{m}{2}-1}\right]=-m(-1)^{\frac{m}{2}}.\,^{m-1}C_{\frac{m}{2}-1}$$

$= -(2n)(-1)^n.\,^{2n-1}C_{n-1} = (-1)^{n+1}(2n).\,^{2n-1}C_{n-1}$

TEXTUAL EXERCISE–3: (OBJECTIVE)

1. (a) $\sum_{k=0}^{n-r}\,^nC_k.\,^nC_{r+k}\ ;\ 0\le r\le n = \sum_{k=0}^{n-r}\,^nC_{n-k}.\,^nC_{r+k} = {}^{2n}C_{n+r}$

$$= \frac{(2n)!}{(n+r)!(n-r)!}$$

2. (c) $\sum_{r=0}^{n}\frac{(-1)^r.\,^nC_r}{r+1}=\sum_{r=0}^{n}\frac{(-1)^r}{(r+1)}.\frac{(r+1)}{(n+1)}.\,^{n+1}C_{r+1}$

$$= \frac{1}{(n+1)}\sum_{r=0}^{n}(-1)^r.\,^{n+1}C_{r+1}=\frac{-1}{(n+1)}\left[\sum_{r=0}^{n}(-1)^{r+1}.\,^{n+1}C_{r+1}\right]$$

$$= \frac{-1}{n+1}\left[\sum_{r=0}^{n+1}(-1)^r.\,^{n+1}C_r-1\right]=\frac{-1}{(n+1)}(0-1)=\frac{1}{(n+1)}$$

3. (c) $\sum_{r=0}^{n-1}\frac{(r+1)C_{r+1}}{C_r}=\sum_{r=0}^{(n-1)}(r+1).\frac{n-(r+1)+1}{(r+1)}$

$$= \sum_{r=0}^{(n-1)}(n-r)=\sum_{r=0}^{n-1}n-\sum_{r=0}^{(n-1)}r = n^2-\frac{(n-1)(n)}{2}$$

$$= \frac{2n^2-n^2+n}{2}=\frac{n(n+1)}{2}$$

4. (c) $\sum_{r=0}^{m} \frac{{}^nC_{2r}}{(2r+1)}; m = \begin{cases} \frac{n}{2} \text{ if } n \text{ is even} \\ \frac{n-1}{2} \text{ if } n \text{ is odd} \end{cases}$

$= \sum_{r=0}^{m} \frac{2r+1}{n+1} \cdot {}^{n+1}C_{2r+1} \times \frac{1}{(2r+1)} = \frac{1}{(n+1)} \sum_{r=0}^{m} {}^{n+1}C_{2r+1}$

$= \frac{1}{(n+1)}\left((2)^{n+1-1}\right) = \frac{(2)^n}{(n+1)}$

5. (b) $\sum_{r=0}^{m} \frac{1}{(2r+1)!} \cdot \frac{1}{(n-2r-1)!}; m = \begin{cases} n \text{ if } n \text{ is odd} \\ (n-1) \text{ if } n \text{ is even} \end{cases}$

$= \frac{1}{n!} \sum_{r=0}^{m} \frac{n!}{(2r+1)!\,[n-(2r+1)]!} = \frac{1}{n!} \sum_{r=0}^{m} {}^nC_{2r+1}$

$= \frac{1}{n!}\left((2)^{n-1}\right) = \frac{(2)^{n-1}}{n!}$

6. (d) $\sum_{r=0}^{n} \frac{(-1)^r \cdot {}^nC_r}{(r+2)} = \sum_{r=0}^{n} (-1)^r \cdot \frac{r+1}{(n+1)} \cdot \frac{r+2}{(n+2)} \cdot {}^{n+2}C_{r+2} \cdot \frac{1}{(r+2)}$

$= \frac{1}{(n+1)(n+2)} \sum_{r=0}^{n} (-1)^r \cdot (r+1) \cdot {}^{n+2}C_{r+2}$

$= \frac{1}{(n+1)(n+2)} \sum_{r=0}^{n} (-1)^r \cdot (r+2-1) \cdot {}^{n+2}C_{r+2}$

$= \frac{1}{(n+1)(n+2)} \left[\sum_{r=0}^{n} (-1)^r (r+2) \cdot {}^{n+2}C_{r+2} - \sum_{r=0}^{n} (-1)^r \cdot {}^{n+2}C_{r+2} \right]$

$= \frac{1}{(n+1)(n+2)} \left[\sum_{r=0}^{n} (-1)^r (r+2) \frac{(n+2)}{(r+2)} \cdot {}^{n+1}C_{r+1} - \sum_{r=0}^{n} (-1)^{r+2} \cdot {}^{n+2}C_{r+2} \right]$

$= \frac{1}{(n+1)(r+2)} \left[(n+2) \sum_{r=0}^{n} (-1)^r \cdot {}^{n+1}C_{r+1} - \left(\sum_{k=0}^{n+2} (-1)^k \, {}^{n+2}C_k \right) + 1 \right]$

$= \frac{1}{(n+1)(n+2)} [(n+2)(0) - 0 + 1] = \frac{1}{(n+1)(n+2)}$

7. (c) $\sum_{r=0}^{n} (-1)^r (a+rd)\, {}^nC_r = \sum_{r=0}^{n} (-1)^r . a . {}^nC_r + \sum_{r=0}^{n} (-1)^r . rd . {}^nC_r$

$= a \sum_{r=0}^{n} (-1)^r . {}^nC_r + d \sum_{r=1}^{n} (-1)^r . r . \frac{n}{r}$

$= (a)(0) + d.n \sum_{r=1}^{n} (-1)^r . {}^{n-1}C_{r-1}$

$= a(0) - dn(0) = 0$

8. (b) $\sum_{r=0}^{n} (-1)^r . {}^nC_r (a-r)$

$= a \sum_{r=0}^{n} (-1)^r . {}^nC_r - \sum_{r=1}^{n} r . (-1)^r . \frac{n}{r} . {}^{n-1}C_{r-1}$

$= a(0) + n \sum_{r=1}^{n} (-1)^{r-1} . {}^{n-1}C_{r-1} = 0 + n(0) = 0$

9. (b) $\sum_{r=0}^{k} (2)^{2r+1} . {}^nC_{2r+1}; \ (2k+1) = \begin{cases} n \text{ if } n \text{ odd} \\ (n-1) \text{ if } n \text{ is even} \end{cases}$

$= \frac{1}{2}\left[(1+2)^n - (1-2)^n\right] = \frac{1}{2}\left[(3)^n - (-1)^n\right]$

10. (c) $\sum_{r=0}^{n} (r+1) . {}^nC_r = \sum_{r=1}^{n} r . {}^nC_r + \sum_{r=0}^{n} {}^nC_r = n \sum_{r=1}^{n} {}^{n-1}C_{r-1} + (2)^n$

$= n(2)n - 1 + (2)n = (2)n - 1\ (n + 2)$

11. (b) $\sum_{r=0}^{n} (-1)^r (r+1)\, {}^nC_r$

$= \sum_{r=1}^{n} (-1)^r . r . \frac{n}{r} . {}^{n-1}C_{r-1} + \sum_{r=0}^{n} (-1)^r . {}^nC_r$

$= -n \sum_{r=1}^{n} (-1)^{r-1} . {}^{n-1}C_{r-1} + (0) = -n(0) + 0 = 0$

12. (b), (c), (d) $\sum_{r=0}^{n} (-1)^r . ({}^nC_r)^2 (r+1)$

$= \sum_{r=0}^{n} (-1)^r ({}^nC_r . {}^nC_r)(r) + \sum_{r=0}^{n} (-1)^r ({}^nC_r)^2$

$= \sum_{r=0}^{n} (-1)^r . \frac{n}{r} . {}^{n-1}C_{r-1} . {}^nC_r . r + \sum_{r=0}^{n} (-1)^r . n . {}^nC_r$

$= n \sum_{r=0}^{n} (-1)^r . {}^{n-1}C_{n-r} . {}^nC_r + \sum_{r=0}^{n} (-1)^r . {}^nC_{n-r} . {}^nC_r$ (i)

Consider, $(1+x)^{n-1}(1-x)^n = (1-x)(1-x^2)^{n-1}$

$\Rightarrow \sum_{r=0}^{n-1} {}^{n-1}C_r x^r . \sum_{k=0}^{n} (-1)^k . {}^nC_k x^k = (1-x) \sum_{r=0}^{n-1} (-1)^r . {}^{n-1}C_r x^{2r}$

Equating the coefficient of x^n on both sides, we get

$\sum_{r=0}^{n} {}^{n-1}C_{n-r} (-1)^r . {}^nC_r = \begin{cases} (-1)^{\frac{n}{2}} . {}^{n-1}C_{\frac{n}{2}} \text{ if } n \text{ is even} \\ (-1)^{\frac{n+1}{2}} . {}^{n-1}C_{\frac{n-1}{2}} \text{ if } n \text{ is odd} \end{cases}$

Again consider, $(1+x)^n (1-x)^n = (1-x^2)^n$

$\Rightarrow \sum_{k=0}^{n} {}^nC_k . x^k . \sum_{r=0}^{n} (-1)^r . {}^nC_r x^r = \sum_{r=0}^{n} (-1)^r . {}^nC_r x^{2r}$

Equating the coefficient of x^n, we get

$\sum_{r=0}^{n} (-1)^r . {}^nC_r . {}^nC_{n-r} = \begin{cases} (-1)^{\frac{n}{2}} . {}^nC_{\frac{n}{2}} \text{ if } n \text{ is even} \\ 0 \text{ if } n \text{ is odd} \end{cases}$ (iii)

Using (ii) and (iii) in (i), we get

$S = n\left[(-1)^{\frac{n}{2}} . {}^{n-1}C_{\frac{n}{2}}\right] + (-1)^{\frac{n}{2}} . {}^nC_{\frac{n}{2}}$ if n is even

And $S = n\left[(-1)^{\frac{n+1}{2}} . {}^{n-1}C_{\frac{n-1}{2}}\right]$ if n is odd

$\Rightarrow S = (-1)^{\frac{n}{2}} \left\{ n . {}^{n-1}C_{\frac{n}{2}} + {}^nC_{\frac{n}{2}} \right\}$

If n is even and $S = (-1)^{\frac{n+1}{2}} n . {}^{n-1}C_{\frac{n-1}{2}}$ if n is odd

After further solving

$\Rightarrow\ S=(-1)^{\frac{n}{2}}.(n+2).^{n-1}C_{\frac{n}{2}}$; if n is even

And $S=(-1)^{\frac{n+1}{2}}.n.^{n-1}C_{\frac{n-1}{2}}$; if n is odd

$\Rightarrow$ (c) and (d) are correct

Also for n = even, $S=(-1)^{n/2}(n+1)^{n-1}C_{n/2}$

$$=(-1)^{\frac{n}{2}}(n+2).\frac{(n-1)!}{\frac{n}{2}!\left(\frac{n}{2}-1\right)!}=\frac{(-1)^{\frac{n}{2}}\left(\frac{n+2}{n}\right)n!}{\frac{n}{2}!\frac{n}{2}!\frac{n}{2}!}$$

$$=(-1)^{n/2}\left(\frac{n}{2}+1\right).^nC_{n/2}\quad\therefore\ \text{(b) is also correct}$$

13. (b) $(1+x)^{2n}=\sum_{r=0}^{2n}{}^{2n}C_r\,x^r$

$\Rightarrow$ Coefficient of $x^n=A={}^{2n}C_n$ and $(1+x)^{2n-1}=\sum^{2n-1}{}^{2n-1}C\,.x^r$

$\Rightarrow$ Coefficient of $x^n=B={}^{2n-1}C_n$

$$\therefore\ \frac{A}{B}=\frac{{}^{2n}C_n}{{}^{2n-1}C_n}=\frac{\frac{2n}{n}\,{}^{2n-1}C_{n-1}}{{}^{2n-1}C_n}=2\left[\frac{n}{2n-1-n+1}\right]=2$$

14. (c) $E=1\left[\frac{(1+x)^{n+1}-1}{(1+x)-1}\right]=\left[\frac{(1+x)^{n+1}-1}{x}\right]$

$$=\frac{\left(\sum_{r=0}^{n+1}{}^{n+1}C_r.x^r-1\right)}{x}=\frac{\sum_{r=1}^{n+1}{}^{n+1}C_r.x^r}{x}=\sum_{r=1}^{n+1}{}^{n+1}C_r(x)^{r-1}$$

$\Rightarrow$ Coefficient of $x^k={}^{n+1}C_{k+1}$

15. (d) $(1+x)^{59}=\sum_{r=0}^{59}{}^{59}C_r\,x^r$

Sum of last 30 coefficient = Sum of first 30 coefficient

$$=\sum_{r=0}^{29}{}^{59}C_r=\frac{1}{2}\sum_{r=0}^{59}{}^{59}C_r=\frac{1}{2}(2)^{59}=(2)^{58}$$

16. (b) $\sum_{r=0}^{10}\frac{(2)^{r+1}.{}^{10}C_r}{(r+1)}=\sum_{r=0}^{10}\frac{(2)^{r+1}}{(r+1)}.\frac{(r+1)^{11}}{11}.{}^{11}C_{r+1}$

$$=\frac{1}{11}\sum_{r=0}^{10}(2)^{r+1}.{}^{11}C_{r+1}=\frac{1}{11}\sum_{k=1}^{11}(2)^k.{}^{11}C_k=\frac{1}{11}\left((1+2)^{11}-1\right)$$

$$=\frac{1}{11}\left((3)^{11}-1\right)$$

17. (b) $2\sum_{r=0}^{n-1}\frac{(r+1)\,{}^nC_{r+1}}{{}^nC_r}=2\sum_{r=0}^{n-1}\frac{(r+1)[n-(r+1)+1]}{(r+1)}$

$$=2\sum_{r=0}^{n-1}[n-r]=2\sum_{r=0}^{n-1}n-2\sum_{r=1}^{n-1}r=2n^2-2\left[\frac{(n-1)n}{2}\right]$$

$= 2n^2 - (n^2 - n) = n^2 + n = n\,(n + 1)$

18. (a) $\sum_{r=0}^{10}(-1)^r.({}^{10}C_r)\left[\frac{1}{3^r}+\frac{8^r}{3^{2r}}\right]$

$$=\sum_{r=0}^{10}(-1)^r.{}^{10}C_r\left(\frac{1}{3}\right)^r+\sum_{r=0}^{10}(-1)^r.{}^{10}C_r\left(\frac{8}{9}\right)^r$$

$$=\left(1-\frac{1}{3}\right)^{10}+\left(1-\frac{8}{9}\right)^{10}=\left(\frac{2}{3}\right)^{10}+\left(\frac{1}{9}\right)^{10}$$

$$=\frac{(2)^{10}}{(3)^{10}}+\frac{1}{(3)^{20}}=\frac{(6)^{10}+1}{(3)^{20}}$$

19. (a) $\sum_{r=0}^{k}{}^mC_r.{}^nC_{k-r}={}^{m+n}C_k$

20. (a) $\sum_{r=1}^{n}{}^{2n+1}C_r=4095\quad\Rightarrow\quad\frac{1}{2}\left(\sum_{r=1}^{2n}{}^{2n+1}C_r\right)=4095$

$\Rightarrow\ \frac{1}{2}\left((2)^{2n+1}-2\right)=4095$

$\Rightarrow\ (2)^{2n}-1=4095\quad\Rightarrow\ (2)^{2n}=4096=(2)^{12}$

$n = 6$

21. (d) $P_n=C_0.\,C_1.C_2.C_3\ldots\ldots C_n;\ C_r={}^nC_r$

$$\Rightarrow\ \frac{P_{n+2}}{P_n}=\frac{{}^{n+2}C_0.\,{}^{n+2}C_1.\,{}^{n+2}C_2.\,{}^{n+2}C_3\ldots{}^{n+2}C_{n+2}}{{}^nC_0.\,{}^nC_1.\,{}^nC_2.\,{}^nC_3\ldots{}^nC_n}$$

$$=\frac{\frac{(n+2)^{n+2}}{(n+2)!}\left[{}^{n+1}C_0.\,{}^{n+1}C_1.\,{}^{n+1}C_2\ldots{}^{n+1}C_{n+1}\right]}{\left(\frac{(n+1)!}{(n+1)^n}\right)\left[{}^{n+1}C_2.\,{}^{n+1}C_3.\,{}^{n+1}C_4\ldots{}^{n+1}C_{n+1}\right]}$$

$$=\frac{(n+2)^{n+2}}{(n+2)!}\times\frac{(n+1)^n}{(n+1)!}\times(n+1)=\frac{(n+2)^{n+2}(n+1)^{n+1}}{(n+2)!(n+1)!}$$

$$=\frac{(n+2)^{n+1}(n+1)^n}{(n+1)!\,n!}=\frac{(n+2)^{n+1}(n+1)^{n-1}}{(n!)^2}$$

22. (b) $\sum_{r=0}^{n}(6r+1).\,{}^nC_r=6\sum_{r=0}^{n}r.\,{}^nC_r+\sum_{r=0}^{n}{}^nC_r$

$$=6\sum_{r=1}^{n}r.\frac{n}{r}.{}^{n-1}C_{r-1}+(2)^n=6n\sum_{r=1}^{n}{}^{n-1}C_{r-1}+(2)^n=6n\ (2)$$

$n–1 + (2)n = (2)n\ (3n + 1)$

TEXTUAL EXERCISE–4: (SUBJECTIVE)

1. (a) In the expansion of $\left(1+\sqrt{3}\right)^{100}$, $T_{k+1}>T_k$ and $T_{k+1}>T_{k+2}$

$\Rightarrow\ T_k<T_{k+1}>T_{k+2}$

$\Rightarrow\ T_{k+1}$ is the greatest term,

$$\Rightarrow\ k=\left[\frac{100+1}{\frac{1}{\sqrt{3}}+1}\right]\quad\Rightarrow\ k=\left[\frac{(101)\sqrt{3}}{1+\sqrt{3}}\right]$$

$$\Rightarrow\ k=\left[\frac{101\times1.732}{2.732}\right]\quad\Rightarrow\ k=\left[\frac{174.932}{2.732}\right]=64$$

(b) $\sqrt{3}\left(1+\frac{1}{\sqrt{3}}\right)^{20}$; greatest term = √3

(greatest term of $\left(\left(1+\frac{1}{\sqrt{3}}\right)20\right)$

$= \sqrt{3}\,(T_{r+1})$; where $r = \left[\dfrac{20+1}{\left|\dfrac{1}{\frac{1}{\sqrt{3}}}\right|+1}\right] = \left[\dfrac{21}{\sqrt{3}+1}\right]$

$= \left[\dfrac{21}{2.732}\right] = [7.6] = 7$

∴ Greatest term = √3 $\left(T_8 \text{ of } \left(1+\frac{1}{\sqrt{3}}\right)^{20}\right)$

$= \sqrt{3}\left[{}^{20}C_7\left(\frac{1}{\sqrt{3}}\right)^7\right] = \dfrac{{}^{20}C_7}{(\sqrt{3})^6}$

∴ 8th term will be the greatest term and $= \dfrac{{}^{20}C_7}{27}$

2. (a) $r = \left[\dfrac{9+1}{\left|\dfrac{2}{3x}\right|+1}\right] = \left[\dfrac{10}{\frac{4}{9}+1}\right] = \left[\dfrac{90}{13}\right] = 6$

∴ 7th term will be the greatest term $= {}^9C_6(2)^3(3x)^6$; $x = 3/2$
$= {}^9C_3\,(8)\,(9/2)^6 = {}^9C_3\,(81/2)^3$

(b) $r = \left[\dfrac{8+1}{\left|\dfrac{1}{4x}\right|+1}\right] = \left[\dfrac{9}{\frac{3}{4}+1}\right] = \left[\dfrac{36}{7}\right]$

∴ T_6 will be greatest term $= {}^8C_5(4x)^5 = {}^8C_5\,(4/3)^5 = {}^8C_3\,(4/3)^5$

3. (i) (a) Coefficient of $x^3y^4z^5$ in $(x+y+z)^{1/2} = \dfrac{12!}{3!4!5!}$

(b) Coefficient of $x^4y^6z^2 = \dfrac{12!}{4!6!2!}$

(c) Coefficient of $x^5y\,z^6 = \dfrac{12!}{5!1!6!}$

(d) Coefficient of $x^3y^2z^5 = 0$

(∵ Every term must be of degree 12)

(e) Coefficient of $x^2y^7z = 0$ (By same reason as for (d))

(ii) (a) Coefficient of $a^{10}\,b^7\,c^3$ in $(bc+ca+ab)^{10}$

Every term of expansion will contain the terms of the form

$\dfrac{10!}{\ell!m!n!}\cdot(bc)^\ell\cdot(ca)^m\cdot(ab)^n$ i.e., $\dfrac{10!}{\ell!m!n!}a^{m+n}.b^{n+\ell}.c^{n+\ell}$

∴ For coefficient of $a^{10}\,b^7\,c^3$; $m+n=10$; $n+\ell=7$; $m+\ell=3$

⇒ $m=3, =0, n=7$

∴ Required coefficient $= \dfrac{10!}{3!7!} = \dfrac{10\times9\times8}{3\times2\times1} = 120$

(b) Coefficient of $(a^3.b^6.c^8.d^9.e^4.f)$ in $(a+b+c-d-e-f)^{31}$
$= \dfrac{(-1)^{9+4+1}.(31)!}{3!\,6!\,8!\,9!\,4!} = \dfrac{(31)!}{3!6!8!9!4!}$

(c) Coefficient of $(a^3.\,b^6.\,c^8.\,d^9.\,e.\,f)$ in $(a+b+c-d-e-f)^{20} = 0$ as each term must be of degree 20

4. Coefficient of $a^3b^3c^2d$ in the expansion of $(a-b+c-d)^9$

$= \dfrac{(-1)^4\,(9!)}{3!3!2!} = \dfrac{9!}{3!3!2!}$

5. (a) Greatest coefficient in $(x^1+x^2+x^3+\ldots+x^m)^n$ is given by $\dfrac{n!}{(q!)^{m-r}\,((q+1)!)^r}$; where $n = mq+r$

(b) Greatest coefficient in the expansion of $(a+b+c+d)^{15}$

$= \dfrac{15!}{(3!)^{4-3}(4!)^3} = \dfrac{15!}{3!(4!)}$

6. (a) $S = (1+x)^{1000}\left[\dfrac{\left(\frac{x}{1+x}\right)^{1001}-1}{\left(\frac{x}{1+x}\right)-1}\right]$

$= (1+x)^{1000}\left[\dfrac{(x)^{1001}-(1+x)^{1001}}{(1+x)^{1001}\left[\frac{-1}{1+x}\right]}\right] = [(1+x)^{1001} - x^{1001}]$

∴ Coefficient of $x^{50} = {}^{1001}C_{50}$

(b) $S = (1+x) + 2(1+x)^2 + 3(1+x)^3 + \ldots + 1000(1+x)^{1000}$

⇒ $(1+x)S = (1+x)^2 + 2\,(1+x)^3 + \ldots + 999\,(1+x)^{1000} + 1000\,(1+x)^{1001}$

⇒ $(1-1-x)S = (1+x) + (1+x)^2 + (1+x)^3 + \ldots + (1+x)^{1000} - 1000(1+x)^{1001}$

⇒ $-xS = (1+x)\left[\dfrac{(1+x)^{1000}-1}{(1-x)-1}\right] - 1000\,(1+x)^{1001}$

⇒ $S = \dfrac{1000(1+x)^{1001}}{x} - \dfrac{(1+x)[(1+x)^{1000}-1]}{x}$

⇒ $S = \dfrac{1000}{x}(1+x)^{1001} - \dfrac{(1+x)^{1001}}{x^2} + \dfrac{(1+x)}{x^2}$

∴ Coefficient of $x^{50} = (1000)[{}^{1001}C_{51}] - {}^{1001}C_{52}$

$= \dfrac{(1000)(1001)!}{51!\,950!} - \dfrac{(1001)!}{52!\,949!}$

$= \dfrac{(1001)!}{52!950!}[1000\times52 - 950] = \dfrac{(51050)(1001)!}{52!\ 950!}$

7. $E = \dfrac{18^3+7^3+3.18.7.25}{3^6+6.243.2+15.81.4+20.27.8+15.9.16+6.3.32+64}$

$= \dfrac{(18+7)^3}{(3+2)^6} = \dfrac{(25)^3}{(5)^6} = 1$

8. Total number of terms in $(x + y + z + w)^n$ = Number of non-negative solutions of equation $a + b + c + d = n$

i.e., $= {}^{n+3}C_3 = \dfrac{(n+3)(n+2)(n+1)}{6}$

9. $\left(\sqrt[4]{9}+\sqrt[6]{8}\right)^{500}$

$$= \sum_{r=0}^{500} {}^{500}C_r(9)^{\frac{500-r}{4}}(8)^{\frac{r}{6}} = \sum_{r=0}^{500} {}^{500}C_r(3)^{\frac{500-r}{2}}(2)^{\frac{r}{2}}$$

∴ For integer terms $2/(500 - r)$ and $2/r$

⇒ r must be an even integer

⇒ $r \in \{0, 2, 4, 6,\ldots\ldots,500\}$ i.e., 251 terms

$$\Rightarrow 3=\left[\frac{10+1}{\left|\frac{2\times 8}{3x}\right|+1}\right] \quad \Rightarrow 3\le\frac{11}{\left|\frac{16}{3x}\right|+1}<4$$

$$\Rightarrow \left|\frac{16}{3x}\right|+1\le\frac{11}{3} \text{ and } \left|\frac{16}{3x}\right|+1>\frac{1}{4}$$

$$\Rightarrow \frac{16}{3}\cdot\frac{1}{|x|}\le\frac{8}{3} \text{ and } \frac{16}{3|x|}>\frac{7}{4}$$

⇒ $|x| \ge 2$ and $|x| < 64/21$

⇒ $2 \le |x| < 64/21$

$$\Rightarrow x\in\left(-\frac{64}{21},-2\right]\cup\left[2,\frac{64}{21}\right)$$

TEXTUAL EXERCISE–4: (OBJECTIVE)

1. (b) Greatest coefficient of $(1 + x)^{2n} + 2 = 2n + {}^2C_n + 1$

$$= \frac{(2n+2)!}{(n+1)!(n+1)!}$$

2. (a) n = even positive integer (given)

⇒ Greatest coefficient of $(1 + x)^n = {}^nC_{n/2}$

Let T_{r+1} be the greatest term of $(1 + x)^n$; $r = n/2$ and

$$\frac{n+1}{\left|\frac{1}{x}\right|+1}-1<r<\frac{n+r}{\left|\frac{1}{x}\right|+1}$$

$$\Rightarrow \frac{(n+1)|x|}{1+|x|}-1<r<\frac{|x|(n+1)}{1+|x|}$$

$$\Rightarrow \frac{n|x|+|x|-1-|x|}{1+|x|}<r<\frac{|x|(n+1)}{1+|x|}$$

$$\Rightarrow \frac{n|x|-1}{1+|x|}<r<\frac{|x|(n+1)}{1+|x|}$$

⇒ $n|x| -1 < r (1 + |x|) < |x| (n + 1)$

⇒ $n|x| -1 < n/2 (1 + |x|) < |x|(n + 1)$

⇒ $2n|x| - 2 < n + n|x|$ and $n + n|x| < 2n|x| + 2|x|$

⇒ $n|x| < n + 2$ and $n|x| + 2|x| > n$

$$\Rightarrow |x|<\frac{n+2}{n} \text{ and } |x|>\frac{n}{n+2}$$

3. (b) From (2.)

The condition must be $\dfrac{2n}{2n+2}<|x|<\dfrac{2n+2}{2n}$

$$\Rightarrow \frac{n}{n+1}<|x|<\frac{n+1}{n}$$

$$\Rightarrow x\in\left(-\frac{n+1}{n},\frac{-n}{n+1}\right)\cup\left(\frac{n}{n+1},\frac{n+1}{n}\right)$$

4. (a) The greatest coefficient in the expansion of $(1 + x)^{2n+1}$

$= {}^{2n+1}C_{\frac{2n+1-1}{2}}$ or ${}^{2n+1}C_{\frac{2n+1+1}{2}}$ i.e., ${}^{2n+1}C_n$

5. (a), (c) 4th term in the expansion of $\left(2+\dfrac{3x}{8}\right)^{10}$ has the maximum numerical value

TEXTUAL EXERCISE–5: (SUBJECTIVE)

1. (a) Given $\left(5+2\sqrt{6}\right)^n = I + f$; $I, n \in N$ and $0 \le f < 1$. Let

$(5 - 2\sqrt{6}) = \dfrac{}{5\ \ 2\sqrt{6}} \in (0,1)$

⇒ $(5 - 2\sqrt{6})^n \in (0, 1)$

So let $(5 - 2\sqrt{6})^n = f' \in (0, 1)$

Now, $(5 + 2\sqrt{6})^n + (5 - 2\sqrt{6})^n = I + f + f'$

⇒ $2[{}^nC_0(5)^n + {}^nC_2(5)^{n-2}(2\sqrt{6})^2 + \ldots.] = I + f + f'$

⇒ $2[(5)^n + {}^nC_2(5)^{n-2}(24) + \ldots] = I + f + f'$

Left side is an integer

⇒ $f + f' \in \mathbb{Z}$

But $0 < f + f' < 2$ ⇒ $f + f' = 1$

$f' = 1 - f$

∴ $(5 - 2\sqrt{6})^n = 1 - f$ ⇒ $\dfrac{1}{\left(5+2\sqrt{6}\right)^n}=1-f$

⇒ $I + f = 1 - f$

⇒ $I+f=\dfrac{1}{1-f}$ ⇒ $I=\dfrac{1}{1-f}-f$

(b) Let $\left(\sqrt{2}+1\right)^6 = I + f$ (i)

Now $\left(\sqrt{2}-1\right)^6=\dfrac{1}{\left(\sqrt{2}+1\right)^6}=\dfrac{1}{I+f}\in(0,1)$

Let $\left(\sqrt{2}-1\right)^6 = f' \in (0,1)$

Now $\left(\sqrt{2}+1\right)^6+\left(\sqrt{2}-1\right)^6 = I + f + f'$

$$\Rightarrow 2\left[{}^6C_0\left(\sqrt{2}\right)^6+{}^6C_2\left(\sqrt{2}\right)^4+{}^6C_4\left(\sqrt{2}\right)^2+{}^6C_6\right]=I+f+f'$$

⇒ $f + f' \in \mathbb{Z}$, But $0 < f + f' < 2$

⇒ $f + f' = 1$ ⇒ $f' = 1 - f$

∴ $\left(\sqrt{2}+1\right)^6+\left(\sqrt{2}-1\right)^6 = I + 1 = 198$

⇒ $I = 197$

(c) $\left(\sqrt{3}+1\right)^{2n}=\left[(\sqrt{3}+1)^2\right]^n=(2)^n(2+\sqrt{3})^n$ (i)

Let $(2)^n(2+\sqrt{3})^n = I + f; 0 < f < 1$

Now $\left(\sqrt{3}-1\right)\in(0,1) \Rightarrow \left(\sqrt{3}-1\right)^{2n}=f'\in(0,1)$

$\therefore\ f' = (2)^n\left(2-\sqrt{3}\right)^n$

$\therefore\ I + f + f' = (2)^n\left[(2+\sqrt{3})^n + (2-\sqrt{3})^n\right] = (2)^n.2[{}^nC_0(2)^n$
$(\sqrt{3})^0 + {}^nC_2(2)^{n-2}(\sqrt{3})^2 + \ldots] = (2)^{n+1}.(k);\ k \in \mathbb{Z}$

Now $f + f'$ must be equal to 1 as $f + f' \in (0, 2)$

$\Rightarrow\ I + 1 = (2)^{n+1}.k$

$\Rightarrow\ [(\sqrt{3}+1)^{2n}] + 1$ divisible by $2^{n+1}\ \forall\ n \in \mathbb{N}$

(d) $R = \left(5\sqrt{5}+11\right)^{2n+1};\ f = R - [R]$

$\Rightarrow\ R = \left(5\sqrt{5}+11\right)^{2n+1} = [R] + f;\ f \in [0,1)$

$\Rightarrow\ \dfrac{1}{R} = \dfrac{1}{(5\sqrt{5}+11)^{2n+1}} = \dfrac{(5\sqrt{5}-11)^{2n+1}}{(4)^{2n+1}} = \dfrac{f'}{(4)^{2n+1}};\ f' \in (0,1)$

Now, $\left(5\sqrt{5}+11\right)^{2n+1} - (5\sqrt{5}-11)^{2n+1} = [R] + f - f'$

$\Rightarrow\ 2\left[{}^{2n+1}C_1\left(5\sqrt{5}\right)^{2n}(11) + {}^{2n+1}C_3\left(5\sqrt{5}\right)^{2n-2}(11)^3 + \ldots\right] = [R] + f - f'$

$\Rightarrow\ f - f' \in \mathbb{Z}$, but $-1 < f - f' < 1$

$\Rightarrow\ f - f' = 0 \qquad \Rightarrow\ f' = f$

$\therefore\ \dfrac{1}{R} = \dfrac{f'}{(4)^{2n+1}} = \dfrac{f}{(4)^{2n+1}} \Rightarrow\ Rf = (4)^{2n+1}$

2. (a) $\sum_{r=0}^{n-1} C_rC_{r+1} = C_0.C_1 + C_1.C_2 + \ldots + C_{n-1}.C_n$

$= \sum_{r=0}^{n-1} {}^nC_{n-r}.{}^nC_{r+1} = {}^{2n}C_{n+1}$

(b) $\sum_{r=0}^{n-2} C_r.C_{r+2} = \sum_{r=0}^{n-2} {}^nC_{n-r}.{}^nC_{r+2} = {}^{2n}C_{n+2} = {}^{2n}C_{n-2}$

(c) $\sum_{r=0}^{n-3} C_r.C_{r+3} = \sum_{r=0}^{n-3} {}^nC_{n-r}.{}^nC_{r+3} = {}^{2n}C_{n+3} = {}^{2n}C_{n-3}$

3. (a) $(C_0 + C_1)(C_1 + C_2)(C_2 + C_3) \ldots (C_{n-1} + C_n)$

$= (C_0.C_1.C_2.C_3\ldots C_{n-1})\left(1+\dfrac{C_1}{C_0}\right)\left(1+\dfrac{C_2}{C_1}\right)$

$\ldots\ldots\left(1+\dfrac{C_1}{C_2}\right)\ldots\left(1+\dfrac{C_n}{C_{n-1}}\right)$

$= C_1.C_2.C_3\ldots\ldots C_{n-1}.\prod_{r=1}^{n}\left(1+\dfrac{C_r}{C_{r-1}}\right)$

$= C_1.C_2.C_3\ldots\ldots C_{n-1}\prod_{r=1}^{n}.\left[1+\dfrac{n-r+1}{r}\right]$

$= C_1.C_2.C_3\ldots\ldots C_{n-1}\prod_{r=1}^{n}\left[\dfrac{n+1}{r}\right]$

$= C_1.C_2.C_3\ldots.C_{n-1}(n+1)^n.\dfrac{1}{n!}$

$= \dfrac{(n+1)^n}{n!}.C_1.C_2.C_3\ldots.C_{n-1}$

$= \dfrac{(n+1)^n}{n!}.C_1.C_2.C_3\ldots\ldots C_{n-1}.C_n \qquad (\because\ C_n = 1)$

(b) $\sum\sum_{0\le i<j\le n} C_iC_j = \dfrac{(C_0 + C_1 + C_2 + \ldots + C_n)^2 - \sum_{k=0}^{n} C_k^2}{2}$

$= \dfrac{(2)^{2n} - 2\left({}^{2n}C_n\right)}{2}$

4. L.H.S. $= \left({}^3C_3 + {}^4C_3 + {}^5C_3 + .. + {}^nC_3\right)\times\left({}^nC_3 + {}^nC_4 + {}^nC_5 + \ldots + {}^nC_n\right)$

$= \left({}^4C_4 + {}^4C_3 + {}^5C_3 + .. {}^nC_3\right)\times\left((2)^n - \left(1+n+\dfrac{n(n-1)}{2}\right)\right)$

$= \left[{}^{n+1}C_4\right]\left(\dfrac{(2)^{n+1} - 2 - 2n - n^2 - 2}{2}\right)$

$= ({}^{n+1}C_4)\left(\dfrac{(2)^{n+1} - n^2 - n - 2}{2}\right)$ or

$\dfrac{(n+1)!}{4!(n-3)!}\left[2^n - \dfrac{n(n-1)}{2} - n - 1\right]$

5. (a) $\sum\sum_{0\le i<j\le n}(C_i + C_j)^2 = \sum\sum_{0\le i<j\le n}(C_i^2 + Cj^2 + 2C_iC_j)$

$= \sum\sum_{0\le i<j\le n}\left(C_i^2 + Cj^2\right) + 2\sum\sum_{0\le i<j\le n}C_i.C_j$

$= n(C_0^2 + C_1^2 + \ldots + C_n^2) +$
$[(C_0 + C_1 + C_2 + \ldots + C_n)^2 - (C_0^2 + C_1^2 + \ldots + C_n^2)]$

$= n\left[{}^{2n}C_n\right] + \left[2^{2n} - {}^{2n}C_n\right] = (n-1)^{2n}C_n + (2)^{2n}$

(b) $\sum\sum_{0\le i<j\le n}(C_i + Cj) = n(C_0 + C_1 + C_2 + \ldots + C_n) = n(2)^n$

(c) $\sum\sum_{0\le j<i\le n}(n - i + n - j)(C_{n-i} + C_{n-j})$

$= \sum\sum_{0\le j<i\le n}[2n - (i+j)](C_i + C_j)$

$= 2n\sum\sum_{0\le j<i\le n}(C_i + C_j) - \sum\sum_{0\le j<i\le n}(i+j)\times(C_i + C_j)$

$= 2n\ (n(2)^n) - S$

$\Rightarrow\ 2S = 2n^2(2)^n \qquad \Rightarrow\ S = n^2(2)^n$

(d) $\sum\sum_{0\le i<j\le n}(C_i - C_j)^2 = \sum\sum_{0\le i<j\le n}(C_i^2 + Cj^2 - 2C_iC_j)$

$= n\left(C_0^2 + C_1^2 + C_2^2 + \ldots + C_n^2\right)$
$-[(C_0 + C_1 + C_2 + \ldots\ldots + C_n)^2 - (C_0^2 + C_1^2 + \ldots + C_n^2)]$

$= n({}^{2n}C_n) - \left[2^{2n} - {}^{2n}C_n\right] = (n+1)^{2n}C_n - (2)^{2n}$

(e) $\sum\sum_{0\le i<j\le n}(i+j)C_iC_j = S(say)$

$= \sum\sum_{0\le j<i\le n}(n - i + n - j)C_{n-i}.C_{n-j}$

$= \sum\sum_{0\le j<i\le n}2n - (i+j)C_{n-i}.C_{n-j}$

$= 2n\sum\sum_{0\le j<i\le n}C_{n-i}C_{n-j} - \sum\sum_{0\le j<i\le n}(i+j)C_{n-i}.C_{n-j}$

$$= 2n\sum_{0\le i<j\le n}\sum C_iC_j - \sum_{0\le i<j\le n}(i+j)C_iC_j$$

$$= \left[\left(\sum_{i=0}^{n}C_i\right)^2 - \sum_{i=0}^{n}C_i^2\right] - S$$

$$\Rightarrow 2S = n[(2)^{2n} - {}^{2n}C_n]$$

$$\Rightarrow S = n(2)^{2n-1} - n/2({}^{2n}C_n) = n\left[(2)^{2n-1} - \frac{1}{2}.{}^{2n}C_n\right]$$

6. $$S = \sum_{0<i<j<n}\sum\left(\frac{i}{{}^nC_i} + \frac{1}{{}^nC_j}\right) = \sum_{0<i<j<n}\sum\left(\frac{n-i}{{}^nC_{n-i}} + \frac{n-j}{{}^nC_{n-j}}\right)$$

$$= \sum_{0\le i<j\le n}\sum\left(\frac{n-i}{{}^nC_i} + \frac{n-i}{{}^nC_j}\right)$$

$$= n\sum_{0\le i<j\le n}\sum\left(\frac{1}{{}^nC_i} + \frac{1}{{}^nC_j}\right) - \sum_{0\le i<j\le n}\sum\left(\frac{i}{{}^nC_i} + \frac{j}{{}^nC_j}\right)$$

$$= n\left[\sum_{i=0}^{n-1}\frac{n-i}{{}^nC_i} + \sum_{j=1}^{n}\frac{j}{{}^nC_i}\right] - S$$

$$= n\left[\sum_{i=0}^{n-1}\frac{1}{{}^nC_i} - \sum_{i=0}^{n-1}\frac{i}{{}^nC_i} + \sum_{j=1}^{n}\frac{j}{{}^nC_j}\right] - S$$

$$= n\left[n\sum_{i=0}^{n-1}\frac{1}{{}^nC_i} - \sum_{i=1}^{n-1}\frac{i}{{}^nC_i} + \sum_{j=1}^{n}\frac{j}{{}^nC_j}\right] - S$$

$$= n\left[\underbrace{\sum_{i=0}^{n}\frac{1}{{}^nC_i}}_{\text{added } n} - \underbrace{\sum_{i=1}^{n}\frac{i}{{}^nC_i}}_{\text{subtracted } n} + \sum_{j=1}^{n}\frac{j}{{}^nC_j}\right] - S$$

$\therefore\ S = n[n(a)] - S \qquad \Rightarrow\ 2S = n^2a$

$$\Rightarrow\ S = \frac{n^2}{2}(a)$$

7. $$\sum_{r=1}^{n}\frac{P_r}{r}.{}^nC_r = \sum_{r=1}^{n}\frac{1}{r}\left(\frac{r(r+1)}{2}\right).{}^nC_r = \sum_{r=1}^{n}\frac{(r+1)}{2}.{}^nC_r$$

$$= \frac{1}{2}\sum_{r=1}^{n}r.{}^nC_r + \frac{1}{2}\sum_{r=1}^{n}.{}^nC_r = \frac{1}{2}\sum_{r=1}^{n}n^{n-1}C_{r-1} + \frac{1}{2}((2)^n - 1)$$

$$= \frac{n}{2}\left[(2)^{n-1}\right] + \frac{1}{2}\left[(2)^n - 1\right]$$

$$= n(2)^{n-2} + (2)^{n-1} - \frac{1}{2} = (n+2)^2 2 - \frac{1}{2}$$

TEXTUAL EXERCISE–5: (OBJECTIVE)

1. (a) $\left(\sqrt{3}+1\right)^{2m} = \left(4+2\sqrt{3}\right)^m = (2)^m\left(2+\sqrt{m}\right)^m$ (i)

Let $\left(2+\sqrt{3}\right)^m = p + f$ .... (ii), $p \in \mathbb{Z}, f \in (0, 1)$ and

$\left(2-\sqrt{3}\right)^m = f'\in(0,1)$

Next, $\left(2+\sqrt{3}\right)^m + \left(2-\sqrt{3}\right)^m = p + f + f'$

$$\Rightarrow\ 2\left[{}^mC_0(2)^m + {}^mC_2(2)^{m-2}\left(\sqrt{3}\right)^2 + {}^mC_4(2)^{m-4}\left(\sqrt{3}\right)^4 + ...+\right]$$

$= p + f + f'$

$\therefore$ L.H.S. is an even integer and $f + f' \in (0, 2)$

$\Rightarrow\ f + f' = 1$

$$\Rightarrow\ p+1 = 2\left[{}^mC_0(2)^m + {}^mC_2(2)^{m-2}\left(\sqrt{3}\right)^2 + {}^mC_4(2)^{m-4}\left(\sqrt{3}\right)^4 + ...\right]$$

$= k$ (say)

$$\left(\sqrt{3}+1\right)^{2m} = (2)^m[p+f] = (2)^m[p+1-f']$$

$$= (2)^m\left[(p+1) - \left(2-\sqrt{3}\right)^m\right] = (2)^m(p+1) - (2)^m\left(2-\sqrt{3}\right)$$

$$= (2)^m[k] - \left(\frac{2}{2+\sqrt{3}}\right)^m = (2)^m(k) - 1 + \left[1 - \left(\frac{2}{2+\sqrt{3}}\right)^m\right]$$

$$\Rightarrow\ \left[\left(\sqrt{3}+1\right)^{2m}\right] + 1 = 2^m.\ k = 2^{m+1}$$

$$\left[{}^mC_0 2^m + {}^mC_2 2^{m-2}\left(\sqrt{3}\right)^2 + ...+\right]$$

$\Rightarrow$ divisible by $(2)^{m+1}$

2. (a), (c), (d) $n \in N$,

$\left(3\sqrt{3}+5\right)^{2n+1} = \alpha + \beta;\ \alpha \in \mathbb{Z};\ \beta \in (0, 1)$

Let $\left(3\sqrt{3}-5\right)^{2n+1} = \beta' \in (0, 1)$

Now $\left(3\sqrt{3}+5\right)^{2n+1} - \left(3\sqrt{3}-5\right)^{2n+1} = \alpha + \beta - \beta'$

$$\Rightarrow\ 2\left[{}^{2n+1}C_1\left(3\sqrt{3}\right)^{2n}(5)^1 + {}^{2n+1}C_3\left(3\sqrt{3}\right)^{2n-2}(5)^3 + {}^{2n+1}C_5\left(3\sqrt{3}\right)^{2n-4}(5)^5 + ...\right]$$

$= \alpha + (\beta - \beta')$

L.H.S. is an even integer and $\beta - \beta' \in (-1, 1)$

$\Rightarrow\ \beta = \beta'$

$$\Rightarrow\ \alpha = 2\left[\begin{array}{l}{}^{2n+1}C_1(5)(3)^{3n} + {}^{2n+1}C_3(3)^{3(n-1)}.(5)^3 + \\ {}^{2n+1}C_5(3)^{3(n-2)}.(5)^5 + ... + {}^{2n+1}C_{2n+1}(3)^0(5)^{2n+1}\end{array}\right]$$

$\Rightarrow\ \alpha$ is an even integer $\Rightarrow$ option (a) is correct

Here $\beta = \beta' = \left(3\sqrt{3}-5\right)^{2n+1}$ and $(\alpha + \beta)^2$

$$= \left[\left(3\sqrt{3}+5\right)^2\right]^{(2n+1)}$$

$$= \left[27 + 25 + 30\sqrt{3}\right]^{(2n+1)} = \left[52 + 30\sqrt{3}\right]^{(2n+1)}$$

$$= (2)^{2n+1}\left[26 + 15\sqrt{3}\right]^{(2n+1)}$$

Which is not divisible by $(2)^{(2n+1)}$ as the other factor is not an integer $\Rightarrow$ option (b) is incorrect

$\alpha - 1 = 2\left[3k_1 + (5)^{2n+1}\right] - 1;\ k_1 \in \mathbb{Z}$

$= 6k_1 + 2(5)^{2n+1} - 1;\ k_1 \in \mathbb{Z}$

$= 6k_1 + 2[(5)^{2n+1} + 1] - 3$

$= 6k_1 + 2(5 + 1)k_2 - 3;\ k_2 \in \mathbb{Z}$

$= 6k_1 + 12k_2 - 3$, which is divisible by 3

$\Rightarrow$ option (c) is correct

Clearly, $\alpha = 2\left[{}^{2n+1}C_1(5)(3)^{3n} + ... + {}^{2n+1}C_{2n+1}(5)^{2n+1}\right]$; which is divisible by 10

$\Rightarrow$ option (d) is correct

3. (a), (d) $\left(8+3\sqrt{7}\right)^n = P + F$ (i)

Let $\left(8-3\sqrt{7}\right)^n = F$ (ii)

Now $8-3\sqrt{7} = \dfrac{\left(8+3\sqrt{7}\right)\left(8-3\sqrt{7}\right)}{\left(8+3\sqrt{7}\right)} = \dfrac{1}{8+3\sqrt{7}} \in (0, 1)$

$\Rightarrow \left(8-3\sqrt{7}\right)^n = F' \in (0, 1)$.

Now, $\left(8+3\sqrt{7}\right)^n + \left(8-3\sqrt{7}\right)^n = P + (F + F')$

$\Rightarrow 2\left[{}^nC_0(8)^n + {}^nC_0(8)^{n-2}\left(3\sqrt{7}\right)^2 + {}^nC_4(8)^{n-4}\left(3\sqrt{7}\right)^4 + ...\right]$

$= P + (F + F')$

Clearly L.H.S. is an even integer,

$\Rightarrow$ $P + (F + F')$ must be an even integer, but $F + F' \in (0, 2)$ and hence $F + F' = 1$

$\Rightarrow$ P must be an integer $\Rightarrow$ Option (a) is correct

Further $F' = (1 - F)$

$\Rightarrow (P + F).F' = (P + F)(1 - F) = \left(8+3\sqrt{7}\right)^n\left(8-3\sqrt{7}\right)^n$

$= (1)^n = 1$

$\Rightarrow$ Option (d) is correct

If (c) holds, then $F = 1 - F$

$\Rightarrow F = \dfrac{1}{2} \Rightarrow F' = \dfrac{1}{2}$ and $F + P = 2$

$\Rightarrow \left(8+3\sqrt{7}\right)^n = 2$; which is an absurd, thus Option (c) is incorrect

4. (a) $\left(6\sqrt{6}+14\right)^{2n+1} = (2)^{2n+1}\left[3\sqrt{6}+7\right]^{(2n+1)}$

Let $\left[3\sqrt{6}+7\right]^{(2n+1)} = P + f$ (i)

And $\left[3\sqrt{6}-7\right]^{(2n+1)} = f \in (0, 1)$

And $\left[3\sqrt{6}+7\right]^{(2n+1)} - \left(3\sqrt{6}-7\right)^{2n+1} = p + f - f'$

$$\Rightarrow 2\begin{bmatrix} {}^{2n+1}C_1\left(3\sqrt{6}\right)^{2n}(7)^1 + {}^{2n+1}C_3\left(3\sqrt{6}\right)^{2n-2}(7)^3 + ... \\ + {}^{2n+1}C_{2n-1}\left(3\sqrt{6}\right)^2(7)^{2n-1} + (7)^{2n+1} \end{bmatrix}$$

$= p + (f - f')$

$\therefore$ L.H.S is an even integer, and $f - f \in (-1, 1)$

$\Rightarrow f - f' = 0$

$\Rightarrow$ p is an even integer, but p has two prime factors 2 and 7, hence P is not a prime integer.

5. (b) Let $\left(2+\sqrt{3}\right)^p = n + f$; $n \in \mathbb{Z}$ and $f \in (0, 1)$ (i)

And $\left(2-\sqrt{3}\right)^p = f \in (0, 1)$ (ii)

Now, $\left(2+\sqrt{3}\right)^p + \left(2-\sqrt{3}\right)^p = n + f + f$

$$\Rightarrow 2\begin{bmatrix} {}^pC_0(2)^p\left(\sqrt{3}\right)^0 + {}^pC_2(2)^{p-2}\left(\sqrt{3}\right)^2 + \\ {}^pC_4(2)^{p-4}\left(\sqrt{3}\right)^4 + ... + {}^pC_{p-1}(2)^1\left(\sqrt{3}\right)^{p-1} \end{bmatrix} = n + f + f'$$

Now L.H.S. is an even integer as P is an odd prime and $f + f \in (0, 2)$, hence $(f + f') = 1$

$\Rightarrow$ n is an odd integer given by

$\left[\left(2+\sqrt{3}\right)^p\right] = 2$

$$\begin{bmatrix} {}^pC_0(2)^p + {}^pC_2(2)^{p-2}\left(\sqrt{3}\right)^2 + {}^pC_4(2)^{p-4}\left(\sqrt{3}\right)^4 + ... \\ + {}^pC_{p-1}(2)\left(\sqrt{3}\right)^{p-1} \end{bmatrix} - 1$$

$\Rightarrow \left[\left(2+\sqrt{3}\right)^p\right] - 2^{p+1} + 1$

$= {}^pC_2(2)^{p-2}\left(\sqrt{3}\right)^2 + {}^pC_4(2)^{p-4}\left(\sqrt{3}\right)^4 + ... + {}^pC_{p-1}(2)\left(\sqrt{3}\right)^{p-1}$

$= p.\ k$ where $k \in \mathbb{Z}$, as, ${}^pC_r = \dfrac{p(p-1)(p-2)...(p-r+1)}{1.2.3....r}$ and $r \le (p - 1)$

$\Rightarrow$ Each of 1, 2, 3,…,$r < p$ and p is prime

$\Rightarrow$ None of 1, 2, 3,….,r can divide p

$\Rightarrow$ ${}^pC_r$ is divisible by p for each r

6. (d) $x = \left(2+\sqrt{3}\right)^n$; $n \in N$

Let $\left(2+\sqrt{3}\right)^n = p + f$ (i)

And $\left(2-\sqrt{3}\right)^n = f' \in (0, 1)$

As solved in above question, $f + f' = 1$

$\Rightarrow f' = 1 - f$ (ii)

Next, $\left(2+\sqrt{3}\right)^n\left(2-\sqrt{3}\right)^n = (p + f)(f')$

$\Rightarrow 1 = (p + f)(1 - f)$

$\Rightarrow 1 = p - pf + f - f^2$

$\Rightarrow f^2 = p - pf + f - 1$

$\Rightarrow f^2 = p(1 - f) - 1(1 - f)$

$\Rightarrow \dfrac{f^2}{1-f} = p - 1 = [x] - 1$

$\Rightarrow \dfrac{f^2}{1-f}$ is $(p - 1)$ an even integer.

SECTION–III: (SINGLE CORRECT)

1. (a) $T_{r+1} = {}^{21}C_r\left[\left(\dfrac{a}{b^{1/2}}\right)^{1/3}\right]^{21-r}.\left[\left(\dfrac{b}{a^{1/3}}\right)^{r/2}\right]$

$= {}^{21}C_r(a)^{7-\frac{r}{3}-\frac{r}{6}}.(b)^{\frac{r}{2}-\frac{21}{6}+\frac{r}{6}} = {}^{21}C_r(a)^{\frac{42-3r}{6}}.(b)^{\frac{4r-21}{6}}$

$\Rightarrow 42 - 3r = 4r - 21$

$\Rightarrow 7r = 63$

$\Rightarrow r = 9$

2. (b) Sum of coefficient of $(a+b)^n = 2048$

$\Rightarrow (2)^n = 2048 \quad \Rightarrow n = 11$

$\therefore$ Greatest coefficient $= {}^{11}C_{\frac{11+1}{2}}$ or ${}^{11}C_{\frac{11-1}{2}}$ i.e., ${}^{11}C_5$ or ${}^{11}C_6$

3. (a) ${}^nC_1, {}^nC_2$ and ${}^nC_3$ are in A.P.

$= 2({}^nC_2) = {}^nC_1 + {}^nC_3$

$\Rightarrow 2 = \frac{{}^nC_1}{{}^nC_2} + \frac{{}^nC_3}{{}^nC_2} \quad \Rightarrow 2 = \left[\frac{2}{n-2+1}\right] + \left[\frac{n-3+1}{3}\right]$

$\Rightarrow 2 = \left[\frac{2}{n-1}\right] + \left[\frac{n-2}{3}\right] \quad 2 = \frac{6+(n-2(n-1)}{3(n-1)}$

$\Rightarrow 6n - 6 = n^2 - 3n + 8 \Rightarrow n^2 - 9n + 14 = 0$

$\Rightarrow n = 7$ or $n = 2$, but for n = 2, fourth terms are impossible

$\Rightarrow n = 7$

4. (c) $(1+x)^m(1-x)^n = \sum_{r=0}^{m} {}^mC_r.x^r.\sum_{k=0}^{n} {}^nC_k(-1)^k.x^k$

Now, for coefficient of x; $r + k = 1$

$\Rightarrow r = 0, k = 1$ and $r = 1, k = 0$

$\therefore$ Sum of coefficient $x^1 = {}^mC_0.{}^nC_1(-1)^1 + {}^mC_1(-1)^0.{}^nC_0$

$= -n + m = (m-n) = 3$ (i)

And for coefficient x^2; $r + k = 2$

$\Rightarrow r = 0, k = 2; r = 1, k = 1, r = 2, k = 0$

$\therefore$ Sum of coefficient of $x^2 = {}^mC_0.{}^nC_2(-1)^2 + {}^mC_1.{}^nC_1(-1)^1 + {}^mC_2.{}^nC_0(-1)^0$

$\Rightarrow {}^nC_2 - mn + \frac{m(m-1)}{2} = -6$

$\Rightarrow n(n-1) - 2mn + m(m-1) = -12$

$\Rightarrow n^2 + m^2 - m - n - 2mn = -12$

$\Rightarrow (m-n)^2 - (m+n) = -12$

$\Rightarrow (m+n) = 9 + 12 = 21$ (ii)

$\therefore$ From (i) and (ii), we get $m = 12$; $n = 9$

5. (c) $\left[x + \frac{1}{x^2}\right] = \sum_{r=0}^{2n} {}^{2n}C_r.x^{2n-r}.x^{-2r}$

Coefficient of $x^m = {}^{2n}C_r$; where $m = 2n - 3r$ i.e., $r = \frac{2n-m}{3}$

i.e., ${}^{2n}C_{\left(\frac{2n-m}{3}\right)} = \frac{2n!}{\left[\frac{(2n-m)}{3}\right]!.\left[\frac{4n+m}{3}\right]!}$

6. (a) $\left(x^2 + \frac{a}{x^3}\right)^{10} = \sum_{r=0}^{10} {}^{10}C_r\left(x^2\right)^{10-r}.\left(\frac{a}{x^3}\right)^r$

$= \sum_{r=0}^{10} {}^{10}C_r.a^r.x^{20-2r-3r} = \sum_{r=0}^{10} {}^{10}C_r.a^r.x^{20-5r}$

$\Rightarrow$ Coefficient of $x^5 = {}^{10}C_3a^3$ and Coefficient of $x^{15} = {}^{10}C_1a^1$

A.T.Q.; $= {}^{10}C_3a^3 = {}^{10}C_1$a

$\Rightarrow \frac{10\times9\times8}{10\times6}a^2 = 1 \quad \Rightarrow a = \frac{1}{2\sqrt{3}}$

7. (c) $(1-2x^2+3x^5)(1+1/x)^8 = (1-2x^2+3x^5).\sum_{r=0}^{8} {}^8C_r.\frac{1}{x^r} =$

$(1-2x^2+3x^5).\sum_{r=0}^{8} {}^8C_r.x^{-r}$

$\therefore$ Coefficient of $x = -2\left({}^8C_1\right) + 3\left({}^8C_4\right) = -16 + 210 = 194.$

8. (c) $(1-x^4)(1+x)^9 = \sum_{r=0}^{9} {}^9C_rx^r - \sum_{k=0}^{9} {}^9C_k.x^{k+4}$

$\therefore$ Coefficient of $x^7 = {}^9C_7 - {}^9C_3$

9. (c) Coefficient of $x^{17} = -1-2-3-\ldots-18 = -\frac{(18)(19)}{2} = -171$

10. (a) The coefficient of x^6 in $(1+x)^6 + (1+x)^7 + \ldots + (1+x)^{15}$

$= \underline{{}^6C_6 + {}^7C_6} + {}^8C_6 + \ldots\ldots + {}^{15}C_6$

$= \underline{{}^7C_7 + {}^7C_6} + {}^8C_6 + \ldots\ldots + {}^{15}C_6$

$= {}^8C_7 + {}^8C_6 + \ldots\ldots + {}^{15}C_6$

$= {}^{15}C_7 + {}^{15}C_6 = {}^{16}C_7 = {}^{16}C_9$

11. (d) $\left[\frac{1}{x^{8/3}} + x^2\log_{10}x\right]^8 = \sum_{r=0}^{8} {}^8C_r\left(\frac{1}{x^{8/3}}\right)^{8-r}.\left(x^2\log_{10}x\right)^r$

$= T_6 = {}^8C_5\left(\frac{1}{x^{8/3}}\right)^3(x^2\log_{10}x)^5 = 5600$ (given)

$\Rightarrow \frac{56\times6}{3!}(\log_{10}x)^5.x^2 = 5600$

$\Rightarrow x^2(\log_{10}x)^5 = 100$

Put $\log_{10}x = t \quad \Rightarrow x = 10^t$

$\Rightarrow 10^{2t}(t)^5 = 100 \quad \Rightarrow t^5 = 10^{2-2t}$

$\Rightarrow (\log_{10}x)^5 = 10^{2-2t} \quad \Rightarrow 5\log_{10}(\log_{10}x) = 2 - 2t$

$\Rightarrow t = 1 \quad \Rightarrow \log_{10}x = 1$

$\Rightarrow x = 10$

12. (b) $(1+x-2x^2) = a_0 + a_1x + a_2x^2 + \ldots + a_{16}x^{16}$, $a_0 + a_2 + a_4 + \ldots + a_{16} = ?$

Put $n = 1$

$\Rightarrow 0 = a_0 + a_1 + a_2 + \ldots + a_{16}$ (i)

Put $x = -1$

$\Rightarrow (2)^8 = a_0 - a_1 + a_2 + \ldots + a_{16}$ (ii)

Adding, we get $(2)^8 = 2[a_0 + a_2 + \ldots + a_{16}]$

$\Rightarrow a_0 + a_2 + \ldots + a_{16} = (2)^7$

13. (a) Given series is $\sum_{r=1}^{n} r.C_rx^{r-1}(-1)^{r-1}$

$= \sum_{r=1}^{n} r.\frac{n}{r}.{}^{n-1}C_{r-1}.x^{r-1}.(-1)^{r-1}$

$= n\sum_{r=1}^{n} {}^{n-1}C_{r-1}.x^{r-1}(-1)^{r-1} = n(1-x)^{n-1}$

14. (c) Let T_{r+1} be the largest term of $(3+2x)^{50}$.

$\Rightarrow r = \left[\frac{(50+1)}{\left|\frac{3}{2x}\right|+1}\right] = \left[\frac{51}{\frac{3}{2}\cdot\frac{1}{|x|}+1}\right]$

$\Rightarrow r = \left[\frac{51}{\frac{3}{2}(5)+1}\right] = \left[\frac{102}{17}\right] = 6$

$\therefore$ T_7 is the largest terms

15. (a) Coefficient of $a^8b^6c^4$ in $(a+b+c) = \frac{18!}{8!6!4!} = {}^{18}C_4 . {}^{14}C_6$

$= {}^{18}C_{14}.{}^{14}C_8$

16. (a) Given sum = $\sum_{r=0}^{10}(-1)^r.(2)^{r-1}.{}^{10}C_r = \frac{1}{2}\sum_{r=0}^{10}(-1)^r.(2)^r.{}^{10}C_r$

$= \frac{1}{2}(1-2)^{10} = \frac{1}{2}(-1)^{10} = \frac{1}{2}$

17. (c) $(2)^{2003} = 8[2^4]^{500} = 8[1-17]^{500}$
$= 8[{}^{500}C_0 - {}^{500}C_1(17) + {}^{500}C_2(17)^2 - {}^{500}C_3(17)^3 + ... + (-1)^{500}.{}^{500}C_{500}(17)^{500}]$
$= 8[1 + 17k] = 14k_1 + 8$, which leave remainder 8 when divided by 8

18. (c) $\left[\sqrt[3]{4} + \frac{1}{\sqrt[4]{6}}\right]^{20} = \sum_{r=0}^{20}{}^{20}C_r[(2)^{2/3}]^{20-r}(2\times 3)^{-r/4}$

$= \sum_{r=0}^{20}{}^{20}C_r(2)^{\frac{40-2r}{3}-\frac{r}{4}}.(3)^{-r/4} = \sum_{r=0}^{20}{}^{20}C_r(2)^{\left[\frac{160-8r-3r}{12}\right]}.(3)^{-\frac{r}{4}}$

$\therefore$ For rational terms, $\frac{12}{160-11r}$ and $\frac{4}{r}$

$\Rightarrow r = 4k;\ k \in W$

$\Rightarrow \frac{12}{160-44k}$ $\quad \frac{3}{40-11k}$

$\Rightarrow k = 2$ $\quad \Rightarrow r = 8$

There is only one rational term and 20 irrational terms, middle term is $\frac{T_{n+2}}{2} = T_{11}$ which will be irrational.

19. (b) $(5^{1/6} + 2^{1/8})^{100} = \sum_{r=0}^{100}{}^{100}C_r(5^{1/6})^{100-r}.(2^{1/8})^r$

$= \sum_{r=0}^{100}{}^{100}C_r(15)^{\frac{100-r}{6}}.(2)^{\frac{r}{8}}$

$\therefore$ For rational terms, $6/(100-r)$ and $8/r$

$\Rightarrow r = 8k;\ k \in W$

$\Rightarrow \frac{6}{100-8k}$ $\quad \frac{3}{(50-4k)}$

$\Rightarrow k \in \{2, 5, 8, 11\}$ $\quad \Rightarrow r \in \{16, 40, 64, 88\}$

$\Rightarrow$ There will be 97 irrational terms.

20. (a) $(1-x)^5(1+x+x^2+x^3)^4 = (1-x)^5[(1+x)(1+x^2)]^4$
$= (1-x)(1-x^4) = (1-x^4)^4 - x(1-x^4)^4$

$= \sum_{r=0}^{4}{}^4C_r(-x^4)^r - \sum_{r=0}^{4}{}^4C_r(-1)^r.x^{4r+1}$

$\therefore$ Coefficient of $x^{13} = -(-1)^3.{}^4C_3 = 4$

21. (d) Coefficient of x5 in $(1+x^2)^5(1+x)^4$ i.e., coefficient of x^5 in $\sum_{r=0}^{5}{}^5C_rx^{2r}.\sum_{k=0}^{4}{}^4C_kx^k$

For coefficient x^5; $r = 1, k = 3$; $r = 2, k = 1$

$\therefore$ Coefficient of $x^5 = {}^5C_1.{}^4C_3 + {}^5C_2.{}^4C_1 = 20 + 40 = 60$

22. (b) $(a-b)^n = \sum_{r=0}^{n}{}^nC_r(a)^{n-r}.(-b)^r$

$\therefore$ $T_5 + T_6 = {}^nC_4(a)^{n-4}(-b)^4 + {}^nC_5(a)^{n-5}(-b)^5$

$\Rightarrow {}^nC_4a^{n-4}b^4 - {}^nC_5a^{n-5}b^5 = 0$

$\Rightarrow ({}^nC_4a - {}^nC_5b) = 0$

$\Rightarrow \frac{a}{b} = \frac{{}^nC_5}{{}^nC_4} = \frac{n-5+1}{5} = \frac{n-4}{5}$

23. (a) $\left(\frac{1-x}{1+x}\right)^2 = (1-x)^2(1+x)^{-2}$

$= (1+x^2-2x)\sum_{r=0}^{\infty}{}^{2+r-1}C_rx^r(-1)^r$

$= (1+x^2-2x)\sum_{r=0}^{\infty}{}^{r+1}C_r.x^r.(-1)^r$

$= (1+x^2-2x)\sum_{r=0}^{\infty}(r+1).x^r.(-1)^r$

$\therefore$ Coefficient of $x^n = (-1)^n(n+1) + (n-1)(-1)^{n-2} - 2(n)(-1)^{n-1}$
$= (-1)^n[n + 1 + n - 1 + 2n] = (-1)^n(4n)$

24. (c) $\sum_{r=1}^{n}\frac{r(C_r)}{C_{r-1}} = \sum_{r=1}^{n}r.\left[\frac{n-r+1}{r}\right] = \sum_{r=1}^{n}r(n-r+1)$

$= n(n+1) - \frac{n(n+1)}{2} = \frac{n(n+1)}{2}$

25. (c) ${}^{n+1}C_2 + 2({}^2C_2 + {}^3C_2 + ... + {}^nC_2)$
$= {}^{n+1}C_2 + 2[{}^3C_3 + {}^3C_2 + {}^4C_2 + ... + {}^nC_2]$
$= {}^{n+1}C_2 + 2[{}^nC_3 + {}^nC_2]$ (using pascla's rule repeated)
$= {}^{n+1}C_2 + 2({}^{n+1}C_3) = {}^{n+1}C_2 + {}^{n+1}C_3 + {}^{n+1}C_3 = {}^{n+2}C_3 + {}^{n+1}C_3$
$= \frac{(n+2)(n+1)(n) + (n+1)(n)(n-1)}{6}$

$= (n+1)(n)\left[\frac{n+2+n-1}{6}\right] = \frac{n(n+1)(2n+1)}{6}$

26. (c) $m^2 - n^2$; Let $m = 2k_1 + 1$; $n = 2k_2 + 1$; $k_1, k_2 \in W$; $k_1 > k_2$ $(\because m > n)$
Now, $m^2 - n^2 = (2k_1+1)^2 - (2k_2+1)^2 = (4k_1^2 - 4k_2^2) + (4k_1 - 4k_2) = 4(k_1-k_2)[k_1+k_2+1]$
$\because$ $k_1 - k_2$ and $k_1 + k_2$ have same parity i.e., either both odd or both even
If $k_1 - k_2$ = even, then $k_1 + k_2$ = even.
$\Rightarrow$ $(k_1 - k_2)$ = even, $k_1 + k_2 + 1$ = odd
$\therefore$ $(m^2 - n^2) = 8k$, for some $k \in \mathbb{N}$
Similarly if $k_1 - k_2$ = odd
$\Rightarrow$ $k_1 + k_2$ = odd $\quad \Rightarrow k_1 + k_2 + 1$ = even
$\Rightarrow$ $(m^2 - n^2) = 8k'$, for some $k' \in \mathbb{N}$
$\therefore$ 8 is the largest positive integer of the form $m^2 - n^2$; where m and n are any two positive odd integer.

27. (c) $[(1+x)(1+y)(x+y)]^n =$

$\sum_{r=0}^{n}{}^nC_r.x^r.\sum_{k=0}^{n}{}^nC_k.y^k.\sum_{p=0}^{n}{}^nC_p.x^{n-p}.y^p$

$\therefore$ For coefficient of $x^n.y^n$; $r + n - p = n$; $k + p = n$
$\Rightarrow r - p = 0;\ k + p = n$
$\Rightarrow p = r;\ k = n - r$
$\therefore$ $r = 0, 1, 2, ..., n$
$\Rightarrow k = n, n-1, n-2, ..., 10$

$\therefore$ Coefficient of $x^n.y^n = {}^nC_0 . {}^nC_n . {}^nC_0 + {}^nC_1 . {}^nC_{n-1} . {}^nC_1 + {}^nC_2 . {}^nC_{n-2} . {}^nC_2 + ... + {}^nC_n . {}^nC_0 . {}^nC_n$

$= \sum_{r=0}^{n} {}^nC_r . {}^nC_{n-r} . {}^nC_r = \sum_{r=0}^{n} ({}^nC_r)^3$

28. (d) $a_n = \sum_{r=0}^{n} \frac{1}{{}^nC_r}$; $\sum_{r=0}^{n} \frac{r}{{}^nC_r} = \sum_{r=0}^{n} \frac{(r+1-1)}{{}^nC_r}$

$= (n+1)\sum_{r=0}^{n} \frac{1}{\frac{(n+1)}{(r+1)}.{}^nC_r} - \sum_{r=0}^{n} \frac{1}{{}^nC_r}$

$= (n+1)\sum_{r=0}^{n} \frac{1}{{}^{n+1}C_{r+1}} - a_n = (n+1)[a_{n+1} - 1] - a_n$

29. (b) $A = (300)^{600}$; $B = (600)!$; $C = (200)^{600}$

By inequality $\left(\frac{n}{2}\right)^n > n! > \left(\frac{n}{3}\right)^n$

$\Rightarrow \left(\frac{600}{2}\right)^{600} > 600! > \left(\frac{600}{3}\right)^{600}$

$\Rightarrow (300)^{600} > 600! > (200)^{600}$

$\Rightarrow A > B > C$

30. (b) $\left(3 - \sqrt{\frac{17}{45}} + 3\sqrt{2}\right)^{15}$; $T_{11} = {}^{15}C_{10}(3)^{15-10}\left(-\sqrt{\frac{17}{4}} + 3\sqrt{2}\right)^{10}$

$\Rightarrow T_{11} = {}^{15}C_{10}(3)^5\left(\frac{17}{4} + 3\sqrt{2}\right)^5$; which is irrational but positive.

31. (d) $\frac{1}{(1-x+x^2)^3} = (1-(x-x^2))^{-3} = \sum_{r=0}^{\infty} {}^{3+r-1}C_r(x-x^2)^r$

$= \sum_{r=0}^{\infty} {}^{2+r}C_r\, x^r(1-x)^r = \sum_{r=0}^{\infty} {}^{2+r}C_r x^r \left(\sum_{k=0}^{r} {}^rC_k(-1)^k.x^k\right)$

$\therefore$ Coefficient of x^n; $k = n - r$, for each r.

$\therefore$ Coefficient of $x^n = \sum_{r=0}^{n} {}^{2+r}C_r . {}^rC_{n-r}(-1)^{n-r}$

$\therefore$ Coefficient of $x^6 = ({}^5C_3 . {}^3C_3 (-1)^3 + {}^6C_4 . {}^4C_2 (-1)^{6-4} + {}^7C_5 . {}^5C_1 (-1)^1 + {}^8C_6 . {}^6C_0(-1)^0)$

$= -10 + 15 \times 6 - (21)(5) + 28 = 3$

32. (b) $(\cos\theta + i\sin\theta)^n = \sum_{r=0}^{n} {}^nC_r(\cos\theta)^{n-r}(i\sin\theta)^r$

$= i\sin n\theta = \sum_{r=0}^{k} {}^nC_{2r+1}(\cos\theta)^{n-(2r+1)}(i\sin\theta)^{2r+1}$; where $n = 2k + 1$

$= i\sin n\theta = \sum_{r=0}^{k} {}^{2k+1}C_{2r+1}(\cos\theta)^{2(k-r)}(i\sin\theta)^{2r+1}$

$= \sum_{r=0}^{k} {}^{2k+1}C_{2r+1}(1-\cos^2\theta)^{k-r}.(i\sin\theta)^{2r+1}$

$= \sum_{r=0}^{k} {}^{2k+1}C_{2r+1}(i\sin\theta)^{2r+1}.\sum_{t=0}^{k-r} {}^{k-r}C_t(-1)^t \sin\theta^2 t$

$= \sum_{r=0}^{k} {}^{2k+1}C_{2r+1}(i)^{2r+1}.(\sin\theta)^{2r+1}.\sum_{t=0}^{k-r} {}^{k-r}C_t(-1)^t \sin^2\theta t$

$\therefore$ For $b_0(\sin\theta)^0$; $2r + 1 + 2t = 0$; which is impossible as $r, t \geq 0$

For $b_1(\sin\theta)^1$; $2r + 1 + 2t = 1$

$\Rightarrow r = t = 0$

$\therefore b_1\, i \sin\theta = {}^{2k+1}C_1(i)^1 \sin\theta . {}^kC_0 (-1)^0 (\sin\theta)^0$

$\Rightarrow b_1 = (2k + 1) = \text{n}$

33. (d) Coefficient of x^4 in $(1 + x + x^2 + x^3)^n$

$=$ Coefficient of x^4 in $\left[\frac{1-x^4}{1-x}\right]^n$

$=$ Coefficient of x^4 in $(1 - x^4)^n (1 - x)^{-n}$

$=$ Coefficient of x^4 in $\sum_{r=0}^{n} {}^nC_r.(-1)^r.(x^{4r}) \times \sum_{k=0}^{\infty} {}^{n+k-1}C_k x^k$

$\therefore$ For coefficient x^4; $4r + k = 4$

$\Rightarrow r = 0, k = 4; r = 1, k = 0$

$\therefore$ Coefficient of $x^4 = {}^nC_0 (-1)^0 . {}^{n+3}C_4 + {}^nC_1(-1)^1 . {}^{n-1}C_0 = {}^{n+3}C_4 - {}^nC_1$ $\quad (\because {}^nC_1 + {}^nC_2 = {}^{n+1}C_2)$

$\Rightarrow {}^{n+1}C_2 + {}^{n+1}C_3 = {}^{n+2}C_3$

$\Rightarrow {}^{n+2}C_3 + {}^{n+2}C_4 = {}^{n+3}C_4$

$\therefore {}^{n+3}C_4 = {}^nC_1 + {}^nC_2 + {}^{n+1}C_3 + {}^{n+2}C_4$

$\Rightarrow {}^{n+3}C_4 - {}^nC_1 = {}^nC_2 + {}^{n+1}C_3 + {}^{n+2}C_4$

34. (a) $x \in \mathbb{N}$; $0 < x < 1$; we have $\sum_{r=1}^{n} r.{}^nC_r x^r (1-x)^{n-r}$

$= \sum_{r=1}^{n} r.\frac{n}{r}.{}^{n-1}C_{r-1} x^r (1-x)^{n-r}$

$= n\sum_{r=1}^{n} {}^{n-1}C_{r-1} x.x^{r-1}(1-\text{x})^{[(x-1)-(r-1)]}$

$= nx\sum_{k=0}^{n-1} {}^{n-1}C_k x^k (1-\text{x})^{[(\text{n}-1-\text{k})]} = nx[x + (1 - x)]^{n-1} = nx$

35. (d) $(1 + 10^{-4})^{10000} = 1 + {}^{10000}C_1(10^{-4})^1 + {}^{10000}C_2 (10^{-4})^2 + ... \approx 1 + (10^4)(10^{-4}) + \frac{(10000)(9999)(10^{-8})}{2}$

$= 1 + \frac{1}{10} + \frac{(0.9999)}{2} = 1 + 1 + 0.4999 = 2.5999$

$\therefore$ The positive integer just greater is 3.

36. (c) $(7)^{300} = (7^2)^{1500} = (1 - 50)^{150}$

$= {}^{150}C_0 - {}^{150}C_1 (50) + {}^{150}C_2 (50)^2 - {}^{150}C_3 (50)^3 + ...$

$= 1 - (150)(50) + \frac{(150)(149)(50)^2}{2} + 10^3 k_1$

$= 1 - 7500 + 75 \times 149 \times 2500 + 10^3 k_1$

$= 1 - 7000 - 500 + (70 + 5)(150 - 1) \times 2500 + 10^3 k_1$

$= 1 - 500 - 5(2500) + 10^3 k_2$

$\Rightarrow 1 + 10^3 k_3 \quad \Rightarrow$ last digit = 1

37. (d) Given sum is $\sum_{r=0}^{n} \frac{C_r}{r+2}(-1)^r$

$= (1 - x)^n = C_0 - C_1x + C_2x^2 - C_3x^3 + ...$

$= (1 - x)^n . x = C_0x - C_1x^2 + C_2x^3 - C_3x^4 + ...$

Integrating both sides with respect to x and with in the limits from $x = 0$ to $x = 1$

$\int_0^1 (1-x)^n dx = \left[C_0x - \frac{C_1x^3}{3} + \frac{C_2x^4}{4} - \frac{C_3x^5}{5} + ...\right]_0^1$

In L.H.S.; put $(1 - x) = t$

$\Rightarrow$ $-dx = dt$

$$\int_1^0 t^n(1-t)(-dt) = C_0 - \frac{C_1}{3} + \frac{C_2}{4} - \frac{C_3}{5} + ...$$

$$\Rightarrow \int_1^0 (t^n - t^{n+1})dt = C_0 - \frac{C_1}{3} + \frac{C_2}{4} - \frac{C_3}{5} + ...$$

$\therefore$ Given sum

$$= \left[\frac{t^{n+1}}{n+1} - \frac{t^{n+2}}{n+2}\right]_0^1 = \frac{1}{(n+1)} - \frac{1}{(n+2)} = \frac{1}{(n+1)(n+2)}$$

38. (c) $T_6 = {}^7C_5\left(\sqrt{9^{x-1}+7}\right)^2\left(3^{x-1}+1\right)^{-\frac{1}{5}\times 5}$

$$= {}^7C_2(9^{x-1}+7)(3^{x-1}+1)^{-1} = 84$$

$$\Rightarrow \frac{9^{x-1}+7}{3^{x-1}+1} = 4 \quad \Rightarrow \quad \frac{y^2}{9} + 7 = 4\left(\frac{y}{3}+1\right); y = 3^x$$

$\Rightarrow$ $(y^2 + 6^3) = 12(y + 3)$ $\Rightarrow$ $y^2 - 12y + 27 = 0$

$\Rightarrow$ $(y - 9)(y - 3) = 0$ $\Rightarrow$ $x = 1$ or 2

39. (b) $f(x) = 10^n + 3.4^{n+2} + 5; n \in \mathbb{N}$

$\Rightarrow$ $f(x) = 10^n + 48(4)^n + 5; n \in \mathbb{N}$

$\Rightarrow$ $10^n = (1 + 9)^n = 1 + {}^nC_1(9) + {}^nC_1(9)^2 + ... + {}^nC_n(9)^n$.

Which is $1 + 9k_1$ (say)

Again $48(4)^n = 48[1 + 3]^n$

$= 48(1 + {}^nC_1(3) + {}^nC_2(3)^2 + {}^nC_3(3)^3 + ... + {}^nC_n(3)^9]$

$\therefore$ $48 + 144k_2$

$\therefore$ $f(x) = 1 + 9k_1 + 48 + 144k_2 + 5$

$= 9k_1 + 144k_2 + 54 = 9(k_1 + 16k_2 + 6)$

$\Rightarrow$ 9 is the greatest integer which divides $f(x)$ $\forall$ $n \in \mathbb{N}$

40. (d) Given sum $= \sum_{r=0}^{n} {}^nC_r(a-r)(b-r)(-1)^r$

$$= \sum_{r=0}^{n} {}^nC_r ab(-1)^r + \sum_{r=0}^{n} (-1)^{r+1}.{}^nC_r(a+b)r + \sum_{r=0}^{n} {}^nC_r r^2.(-1)^r$$

$$= ab\sum_{r=0}^{n}(-1)^r.{}^nC_r - (a+b)\sum_{r=0}^{n}(-1)^r.r.{}^nC_r + \sum_{r=0}^{n}{}^nC_r(r^2)(-1)^r$$

$$= ab(0) - (a+b)\sum_{r=1}^{n}(-1)^r.n.{}^{n-1}C_{r-1} + \sum_{r=0}^{n} nr.{}^{n-1}C_{r-1}.(-1)^r$$

$$= n(a+b)\sum_{r=1}^{n}(-1)^{r-1}.{}^{n-1}C_{r-1} + n\sum_{r=1}^{n}(r-1+1){}^{n-1}C_{r-1}(-1)^r$$

$$= n(a+b)(0) + n\sum_{r=1}^{n}(r-1).{}^{n-1}C_{r-1}(-1)^r + n\sum_{r=1}^{n}{}^{n-1}C_{r-1}(-1)^r$$

$$= n\sum_{r=2}^{n}(r-1).\frac{n-1}{r-1}.{}^{n-2}C_{r-2}(-1)^{r-2}(-1)^2 + n\sum_{r=1}^{n}{}^{n-1}C_{r-1}(-1)^{r-1}(-1)$$

$$= n(n-1).\sum_{r=2}^{n}{}^{n-2}C_{r-2}(-1)^{r-2} - n\sum_{r=1}^{n}{}^{n-1}C_{r-1}(-1)^{r-1}(-1)$$

$- 0 - 0 = 0$

41. (c) $\because$ $32^{32} = (33 - 1)^{32} = 33m + 1$ where $m \in \mathbb{Z}$

Now $32^{32^{32}} = 32^{3m+1} = 32(2^5)^{3m} = 32(2^3)^{5m} = 32(1 + 7)^{5m}$

$= 32(7k + 1)$ where $k \in \mathbb{Z}$

$= 7q + 4 =$ clearly remainder is 4.

42. (b) $(17)^{256} = (17)^{2\times128} = (289)^{128} = (1 - 290)^{128}$

$= 1 - {}^{128}C_1(290) + {}^{128}C_2(290)^2 ......$

$= 1 - (128)(290) + 100k_1$

$= 1 - (100 + 28)(200 + 90) + 100k_1$

$= 1 - 28(90) + 100k_2$

$= 1 - (20 + 8)(90) + 100k_2$

$= 1 - 8(90) + 100k_3$

$= 1 - 720 + 100k_3$

$= 1 - 20 + 100k_4$

$= - 19 + 100k_4$

$= 81 - 100 + 100k_4$

$= 81 + 100k_5$

$\Rightarrow$ The last two digits will be 81

43. (d) $\sum_{r=0}^{n}(-1)^r.{}^nC_r.\frac{1+r\log_e 10}{(1+\log_e 10^n)^r}$

$$= \sum_{r=0}^{n}(-1)^r.{}^nC_r.\frac{1}{(1+\log_e 10^n)^r} + \log_e 10$$

$$\sum_{r=1}^{n}(-1)^r.{}^nC_r.r.\frac{1}{(1+\log_e 10^n)^r}$$

$$= \left[1 - \frac{1}{(1+\log_e 10^n)}\right]^n +$$

$$\log_e 10\sum_{r=1}^{n}(-1)^r.n.{}^{n-1}C_{r-1}\frac{1}{(1+\log_e 10^n)^r}$$

$$= \left[\frac{\log_e 10^n}{1+\log_e 10^n}\right]^n - \frac{\log_e 10.n}{(1+\log_e 10^n)}\sum_{r=1}^{n}{}^{n-1}C_{r-1}(-1)^{r-1}\frac{1}{(1+\log_e 10^n)^{r-1}}$$

$$= \left[\frac{\log_e 10^n}{1+\log_e 10^n}\right]^n - \frac{n\log_e 10}{(1+\log_e 10^n)}\left[1 - \frac{1}{1+\log_e 10^n}\right]$$

$$= \left(\frac{\log_e 10^n}{1+\log_e 10^n}\right)^n - \left(\frac{\log_e 10^n}{1+\log_e 10^n}\right)^n = 0$$

44. (a) $(6\sqrt{6} + 14)^{2n+1} = I + f$ where $0 < f < 1$ (i)

$$(6\sqrt{6} - 14) = \frac{(6\sqrt{6})^2 - (14)^2}{(6\sqrt{6}+14)} = \frac{20}{6\sqrt{6}+14} \in (0,1)$$

$\Rightarrow$ $(6\sqrt{6} - 14)^{2n+1} \in (0, 1)$

Let it be f' $\Rightarrow$ $f' \in (0, 1)$

Now $(6\sqrt{6} + 14)^{2n+1} - (6\sqrt{6} - 14)^{2n+1} = 2[{}^{2n+1}C_1(6\sqrt{6})^{2n}(14)^1 + {}^{2n+1}C_3(6\sqrt{6})^{2n-2}(14)^3 + ...] \in \mathbb{Z}$ (set of integer)

$\Rightarrow$ $I + f - f' \in \mathbb{Z}$ but $-1 < f < f' < 1$

$\therefore$ $2[{}^{2n+1}C_1(6\sqrt{6})^{2n}(14) + {}^{2n+1}C_3(6\sqrt{6})^{2n-2}.(14)^3 + ...] = I$

$\Rightarrow$ Integer part is an even integration

45. (b) $(2 + \sqrt{3})^p = I + f; 0 < f < 1$

$(2 - \sqrt{3})^p = f' \in (0, 1)$

$\therefore$ $I + f + f' = (2 + \sqrt{3})^p + (2 - \sqrt{3})^p$

$= 2[{}^pC_0(2)^p(\sqrt{3})^0 + {}^pC_2(2)^{p-2}(\sqrt{3})^2 + {}^pC_4(2)^{p-4}(\sqrt{3})^4 + ... + {}^pC_{p-1}(2)^1(\sqrt{3})^{p-1}]$

$= 2^{p+1} + 2[{}^pC_2(2)^{p-2}(3) + {}^pC_4(2)^{p-4}(3)^2 + ... + {}^pC_{p-1}(2)(\sqrt{3})^{p-1}]$

$\therefore$ $I + f + f' \in \mathbb{Z}$ $\Rightarrow$ $f + f' = 1$

$\therefore$ $I + 1 - 2^{p+1} = 2[{}^pC_2\,(2)^{p-2}\,(3) + {}^pC_4\,(2)^{p-4}\,(3)^2 + \ldots + {}^pC_{p-1}(2)\,(\sqrt{3})^{p-1}]$

Now 2, 3, 4, ..., $p - 1 < p$ and p is a prime and no natural number less than prime p can divide p

$\Rightarrow$ ${}^pC_2, {}^pC_4, \ldots, {}^pC_{p-1}$ will contain the factor p and each is an integer

$\Rightarrow$ $I + 1 - 2^{p+1}$ is divisible by p.

46. (a) $(1-x)^{2n} = \sum_{r=0}^{2n} {}^{2n}C_r(-1)^r x^r$

$\therefore$ Coefficient of $(3r)^{\text{th}}$ term $= {}^{2n}C_{3r-1}\,(-1)^{3r-1}$ and coefficient of $(r + 2)^{\text{th}}$ term $= {}^{2n}C_{r+1}\,(-1)^{r+1}$

A.T.Q.; ${}^{2n}C_{3r-1}\,(-1)^{3r-1} = {}^{2n}C_{r+1}\,(-1)^{r+1}$

$\Rightarrow$ ${}^{2n}C_{3r-1}\,(-1)^{2r-2} = {}^{2n}C_{r+1}$

$\Rightarrow$ ${}^{2n}C_{3r-1} = {}^{2n}C_{r+1}$

$\Rightarrow$ $3^{r-1} = r + 1$ or $3r - 1 + r + 1 = 2n$

$\Rightarrow$ $2r = 2$ or $4r = 2n$

$\Rightarrow$ $r = 1$ or $n = 2r$, but $r > 1$ (given)

$\Rightarrow$ $n = 2r$

47. (c) $(x + (x^3 - 1)^{1/2})^6 + (x - (x^3 - 1)^{1/2})^6$

$= 2[{}^6C_0 x^6\,(x^3 - 1)^0 + {}^6C_2\,x^4(x^3 - 1) + {}^6C_4 x^2\,(x^3 - 1)^2 + {}^6C_6\,x^0\,(x^3 - 1)^3]$

Which is a polynomial of degrees 9.

48. (c) $\sum_{i=0}^{m}\binom{10}{i}\binom{20}{m-i} = \sum_{i=0}^{m} {}^{10}C_i.{}^{20}C_{m-i} = {}^{30}C_m$

Which is maximum for $\frac{30}{2}$ i.e., 15

49. (d) $(1 + t^2)^{12}\,(1 + t^{12})\,(1 + t^{24})$

$=$ Coefficient of t^{24} in $\sum_{r=0}^{12} {}^{12}C_r t^{2r}.\left(1+t^{12}+t^{24}+t^{36}\right)$

$=$ Coefficient of t^{24} in $\left(1+t^{12}+t^{24}+t^{36}\right).\sum_{r=0}^{12} {}^{12}C_r t^{2r}$

$=$ Coefficient of t^{24} in $\sum_{r=0}^{12} {}^{12}C_r t^{2r}$ + Coefficient of t^{12} in $\sum_{r=0}^{12} {}^{12}C_r t^{2r}$ + Coefficient of t^0 in $\sum_{r=0}^{12} {}^{12}C_r t^{2r}$

$= {}^{12}C_{12} + {}^{12}C_6 + {}^{12}C_0 = {}^{12}C_6 + 2$

50. (d) ${}^{n-1}C_r = (k^2 - 3).{}^nC_{r+1}$ $\quad {}^{n-1}C_r = (k^2-3).\frac{n}{(r+1)}.{}^{n-1}C_r$

$\Rightarrow$ $(k^2-3) = \frac{r+1}{n}$

$\Rightarrow$ $k^2 = 3 + \frac{r+1}{n}$ (i)

$\Rightarrow$ $0 \le r \le n-1$ $\quad\Rightarrow$ $1 \le r+1 \le n$

$\Rightarrow$ $\frac{1}{n} \le \frac{r+1}{r} \le 1$ $\quad\Rightarrow$ $3+\frac{1}{n} \le 3+\frac{r+1}{n} \le 4$

$\Rightarrow$ $3+\frac{1}{n} \le k^2 \le 4$ as $n \to \infty$; $3 + 1/n \to 3$

$\therefore$ $k^2 \in (3, 4]$ $\quad\Rightarrow$ $k \in [-2, -\sqrt{3}) \cup (\sqrt{3}, 2]$

$\therefore$ $k \in (-\sqrt{3}, 2]$ $\quad$ ($\because$ If $x \in A \subseteq B \Rightarrow x \in B$)

51. (c) $\frac{2\left(\frac{n}{2}\right)!\left(\frac{n}{2}\right)!}{n!}$ $[C_0^2 - 2C_1^2 + 3C_2^2 - \ldots + (-1)^n\,(n + 1)\,C_n^2]$; n is an even positive integer.

Given expression $= \frac{2}{{}^nC_{n/2}}\left[\sum_{r=0}^{n}(-1)^r.(r+1)({}^nC_r)^2\right]$

$= \frac{2}{{}^nC_{n/2}}\left[\sum_{r=0}^{n}(-1)^r.r.{}^nC_r.{}^nC_r + \sum_{r=0}^{n}(-1)^r.({}^nC_r)^2\right]$

$- \frac{2}{{}^nC_{n/2}}\left[\sum_{r=1}^{n}(-1)^r.n.{}^{n-1}C_{r-1}.{}^nC_r + \sum_{r=0}^{n}(-1)^r.{}^nC_r.{}^nC_r\right]$

$= \frac{2}{{}^nC_{n/2}}\left[n\sum_{r=1}^{n}(-1)^r.{}^{n-1}C_{r-1}.{}^nC_r + \sum_{r=0}^{n}(-1)^r.{}^nC_r.{}^nC_{n-r}\right]$ (i)

Now $(1+x)^{n-1}(1-x)^n = \sum_{k=0}^{n-1} {}^{n-1}C_k.x^k.\sum_{r=0}^{n}(-1)^r.{}^nC_r.x^r$

$\therefore$ Coefficient of x^n from R.H.S. $= \sum_{r=1}^{n} {}^{n-1}C_{n-r}(-1)^r.{}^nC_r.x^r$

and coefficient of x^n from L.H.S. i.e., $(1 - x)(1 - x^2)^{n-1}$

i.e., coefficient of x^n in $\sum_{r=0}^{n-1} {}^{n-1}C_r.(-1)^r.x^{2r}$ – Coefficient of x^{n-1} in $\sum_{r=0}^{n-1} {}^{n-1}C_r(-1)^r x^{2r}$

$\because$ n = even; $n - 1$ = odd

$\Rightarrow$ Coefficient of x^n from L.H.S. $= {}^{n-1}C_{n/2}\,(-1)^{n/2}$

$= \sum_{r=1}^{n}(-1)^r.{}^{n-1}C_{n-r}.{}^nC_r = (-1)^{n/2}.{}^{n-1}C_{n/2}$ (ii)

Also $\sum_{r=0}^{n}(-1)^r.{}^nC_r.{}^nC_{n-r}$ is the coefficient of x^n in $(1-x)^n.(1 + x)^n$

$\Rightarrow$ $\sum_{r=0}^{n}(-1)^r.{}^nC_r.{}^nC_{n-r}$ = coefficient of x^n in $(1 - x^2)^n$

$= (-1)^{n/2}\,.\,{}^nC_{n/2}$ (iii)

Using (ii) and (iii) in (i), we get

$\frac{2}{{}^nC_{n/2}}\left[n.(-1)^{n/2}.{}^{n-1}C_{n/2} + (-1)^{n/2}.{}^nC_{n/2}\right]$

$= \frac{2}{{}^nC_{n/2}}(-1)^{n/2}\left[n.{}^{n-1}C_{n/2} + {}^nC_{n/2}\right]$

$= 2(-1)^{n/2}\left[\frac{n({}^{n-1}C_{n/2})}{{}^nC_{n/2}} + 1\right]$

$= 2(-1)^{n/2}\left[\frac{n!}{\frac{n}{2}!\left(\frac{n}{2}-1\right)!} \times \frac{\frac{n}{2}!\,\frac{n}{2}!}{n!} + 1\right]$

$= 2(-1)^{n/2}\left[\frac{n}{2}+1\right] = (-1)^{n/2}(n+2)$

SECTION–IV (MORE THAN ONE CORRECT)

1. (a), (b) $\dfrac{P_{n+1}}{P_n} = \dfrac{{}^{n+1}C_0.{}^{n+1}C_1.{}^{n+1}C_2......{}^{n+1}C_n.{}^{n+1}C_{n+1}}{{}^{n}C_0.{}^{n}C_1.{}^{n}C_2.......{}^{n}C_{n-1}.{}^{n}C_n}$

$$= \frac{{}^{n+1}C_0.{}^{n+1}C_n.{}^{n+1}C_2....{}^{n+1}C_n.{}^{n+1}C_{n+1}}{\left(\frac{1.2.3....n+1}{(n+1)^{n+1}}\right)\left({}^{n+1}C_1.{}^{n+1}C_2.{}^{n+1}C_3....{}^{n+1}C_n.{}^{n+1}C_{n+1}\right)}$$

$$= \left[\frac{\frac{1}{n!}}{(n+1)^n}\right] = \frac{(n+1)^n}{n!} = \frac{(n+1)^{n+1}}{(n+1)!}$$

2. (b), (c) $\sum\limits_{r=0}^{50} {}^{50}C_r(x-4)^{50-r}.3^r = (x-4+3)^{50} = (x-1)^{50}$

$= (1-x)^{50} = \sum\limits_{r=0}^{50} {}^{50}C_r(-1)^r.x^r$

∴ Coefficient of $x^{33} = (-1)^{33}.{}^{50}C_{33} = -{}^{50}C_{33} = -{}^{50}C_{17}$

⇒ (b) and (c) are correct option.

3. (a), (b), (c), (d)

$(a+b+c)^{18} = \sum\limits_{l+m+n=18} a^l.b^m.c^n.\dfrac{18!}{l!.m!.n!}$

∴ Coefficient of $a^8b^6c^4 = \dfrac{18!}{8!6!64!} = {}^{18}C_4.{}^{14}C_6 = {}^{18}C_{14}.{}^{14}C_6$

$= {}^{18}C_{14}.{}^{14}C_8$

Also $\dfrac{18!}{8!6!4!} = {}^{18}C_{10}.{}^{10}C_6$ and $\dfrac{18!}{8!6!4!} = {}^{18}C_6.{}^{12}C_8$

4. (b), (c) $\left(\sqrt[3]{4}+\dfrac{1}{\sqrt[4]{6}}\right)^{20} = \sum\limits_{r=0}^{20} {}^{20}C_r(4^{1/3})^{20-r}\left((6)^{-\frac{1}{4}}\right)^r$

$= \sum\limits_{r=0}^{20} {}^{20}C_r(2)^{\frac{40-2r}{3}}.(2)^{-r/4}.(3)^{-r/4}$

$= \sum\limits_{r=0}^{20} {}^{20}C_r(2)^{\frac{160-11r}{12}}.(3)^{-r/4}$

∴ For rational terms, $4/r$

⇒ $r = 4k$; $k \in W$ (say)

Now, $\dfrac{12}{160-44k}$; $k \in W$.

⇒ $k \in \{2\}$ ⇒ $r = 8$

∴ 9th terms is the only rational term

⇒ 20 terms are irrational; middle term is $\dfrac{T_{20+2}}{2} = T_{11}$ which will be irrational

5. (a), (b) $(x+y+z)^{25} = \sum\limits_{a+b+c=25} \dfrac{25!}{a!b!c!}x^a.y^b.z^c$

Let $c = k$ ⇒ $a + b + k = 25$

⇒ $a + b = 25 - k = (25 - r) + (r - k)$ say

Let $a = 25 - r$, $b = r - k$

⇒ $\dfrac{25}{a!b!c!} = \dfrac{25!}{(25-r)!(r-k)!k!} = {}^{25}C_r.{}^{r}C_k$

∴ It contains terms of the form ${}^{25}C_r.{}^{r}C_k.x^{25-r}y^{r-k}.z^k$

∴ Coefficient of $x^8y^9z^9$ is 0

∵ degree of terms is 26 > 25

6. (c), (d) Given sum is $\sum\limits_{r=0}^{n}(2r+1)\left({}^nC_r\right)^2$

$= \sum\limits_{r=0}^{n} 2.r.{}^nC_r.{}^nC_r + \sum\limits_{r=0}^{n}({}^nC_r)^2 = 2\sum\limits_{r=1}^{n} {}^{n.n-1}C_{r-1}.{}^nC_r + ({}^{2n}C_n)$

$= 2n\sum\limits_{r=1}^{n} {}^{n-1}C_{r-1}.{}^nC_r + {}^{2n}C_n = 2n\sum\limits_{r=1}^{n} {}^{n-1}C_{r-1}.{}^nC_{n-r}.{}^nC_r + {}^{2n}C_n$

$= 2n$ (Coefficient of x^n in $(1+x)^{n-1}.(1+x)^n$) $+ {}^{2n}C_n = 2n$ $[{}^{2n-1}C_n] + {}^{2n}C_n$.

$= \dfrac{2n!}{n!(n-1)!} + {}^{2n}C_n = \dfrac{(2n)(2n-1)!}{n!(n-1)!} + \dfrac{2n(2n-1)!}{n!n!}$

$= 2n\left({}^{2n-1}C_n\right) + 2\left[\dfrac{2n-1}{n!(n-1)!}\right]$ ⇒ (c) is correct option.

Also $= 2n({}^{2n-1}C_n) + {}^{2n+1}C_n + {}^{2n-1}C_n = (2n)({}^{2n-1}C_{n-1}) + {}^{2n-1}C_{n-1} + {}^{2n-1}C_n = (2n+1).{}^{2n-1}C_{n-1} + {}^{2n-1}C_n$

7. (b), (c), (d)

Number of terms in $(x + 2y - 3z + 5w - 7u)^n$

= Number of ways of distribution of n identical things to 5 people

$= {}^{n+4}C_4 = {}^{n+4}C_n = \dfrac{(n+4)(n+36)(n+2)(n+1)}{24}$

8. (a), (b), (d) $(3\sqrt{3}+5)^{2n+1} = \alpha + \beta$; where α = integral part and β = fractional part

Now $(3\sqrt{3}-5)^{2n+1} \in (0, 1)$; $= \beta'$(say)

∴ $\alpha + \beta - \beta' = (3\sqrt{3}+5)^{2n+1} - (3\sqrt{3}-5)^{2n+1}$

$= 2[{}^{2n+1}C_1(3\sqrt{3})^{2n}(5) + {}^{2n+1}C_3(3\sqrt{3})^{2n-2}(5)^3 + ... + {}^{2n+1}C_{2n+1}(3\sqrt{3})^0(5)^{2n+1}] \in \mathbb{Z}$

Now $-1 < \beta - \beta' < 1$ ⇒ $\beta - \beta' = 0$

⇒ $\alpha = 2k$; $k \in \mathbb{Z}$ ⇒ α is an even integer

⇒ (a) is correct option

Now $\alpha = 2[{}^{2n+1}C_1(3\sqrt{3})^{2n}(5)] + {}^{2n+1}C_3(3\sqrt{3})^{2n-2}(5)^3 + ... + {}^{2n+1}C_{2n+1}(5)^{2n+1}]$

⇒ $\alpha = 2(5)[{}^{2n+1}C_1(3\sqrt{3})^{2n} + {}^{2n+1}C_3(3\sqrt{3})^{2n-2}(5)^2 + ... + {}^{2n+1}C_{2n+1}(5)^{2n}]$

⇒ α is divisible by 10 ⇒ (d) is correct option.

Further $(\alpha+\beta)^2 = [(3\sqrt{3}+5)^2]^{2n+1} = [52+30\sqrt{3}]^{2n+1}$.

$= (2)^{2n+1}.[26+15\sqrt{3}]^{2n+1}$ which is divisible by $(2)^{2n+1}$

⇒ (b) is correct.

Clearly last term of α does not contain 3 i.e., α is not divisible by 3.

9. (a), (d) $(8+3\sqrt{7})^n = P + F$; $F \in (0, 1)$ and $(8-3\sqrt{7})^n = F'$; $F' \in (0, 1)$

Now $P + F + F' = 2[{}^nC_0(8)^{n-2}(3\sqrt{7})^0 + {}^nC_2(8)^{n-2}(3\sqrt{7})^2 + {}^nC_4(3\sqrt{7})^4 + ...] \in \mathbb{Z}$

⇒ $F + F' = 1$ as $0 < F < F' < 2$

∴ $P + 1 = 2k$; $k \in \mathbb{Z}$

⇒ P is an odd integer

Now $F'.(P+F) = (8-3\sqrt{7})^n(8+3\sqrt{7})^n = (64-63)^n = 1$

⇒ $F'.(P+F) = 1$

⇒ $(1-F).(P+F) = 1$ $(\because F' = 1-F)$

10. (a), (b), (c) $a_n = \left(1+\frac{1}{n}\right)^n$

⇒ $a_1 = 2$, as the function a_n is increasing function

⇒ $a_n > a_1 = 2\ \forall\ n \in \mathbb{N}$

⇒ $\lim\limits_{x\to\infty} a_n = \lim\limits_{x\to\infty}\left(1+\frac{1}{n}\right)^n = e < 3$

⇒ $2 \le a_n < 3$

∴ Clearly (a), (b), (c) option are correct

11. (a), (b), (c) $(101)^{100} - 1 = (1+10^2)^{100} - 1$

$= ({}^{100}C_0 + {}^{100}C_1(10^2) + {}^{100}C_2(10^2)^2 + {}^{100}C_3(10^2)^3 + ... + {}^{100}C_{100}(10^2)^{100}) - 1$

$= \left(10^4 + \frac{100\times 99}{2}(10^4) + {}^{10}C_3 10^6 + ... + (10)^{200}\right)$

$= 10^4(1 + 50\times 99 + {}^{10}C_3\,10^2 + ... + 10^{196})$

Which is divisible by 10^4 and hence by 100, 1000, but not by 10^5.

12. (a), (b), (c) $\sum\limits_{r=0}^{n}(-1)^r.{}^nC_r[\sin r\theta - i\cos r\theta]$

$= \sum\limits_{r=0}^{n}(-1)^r.{}^nC_r(-i)[\cos r\theta + i\sin r\theta]$

$= \sum\limits_{r=0}^{n}(-1)^r.{}^nC_r(-i)e^{ir\theta} = -i\sum\limits_{r=0}^{n}{}^nC_r(-e^{i\theta})^r = -i[(1-e^{i\theta})^n]$

⇒ Sum = 0, if $\theta = 2\pi$, $\theta = 0$

$= -i[1-(-1)]^{2m+1} = -(-2)^{2m+1}.i$, if $n = 2m+1$ and $\theta = \pi$.

SECTION-V: (ASSERTION-REASON TYPE)

1. (a) $\left(x+\frac{1}{x}+2\right)^m = \left[\frac{x^2+2x+1}{x}\right]^m = \frac{(x+1)^{2m}}{x^m} = \frac{(1+x)^{2m}}{x^m}$

∴ The term independent of x

= Coefficient of x^m in $(1+x)^{2m} = {}^{2m}C_m = \frac{(2m)!}{(m!)^2}$

Both assertion and reason are correct and reason is correct explanation of assertion.

2. (a) ${}^nC_1 - \frac{{}^nC_2}{2} + \frac{{}^nC_3}{3} + ... + \frac{(-1)^{n-1}.{}^nC_n}{n}$

⇒ $S_n = \sum\limits_{r=1}^{n}\frac{{}^nC_r(-1)^{r-1}}{r}$ ⇒ $S_{n+1} = \sum\limits_{r=1}^{n+1}\frac{{}^{n+1}C_r(-1)^{r-1}}{r}$

∴ $S_{n+1} - S_n = \sum\frac{\left({}^{n+1}C_r - {}^nC_r\right)(-1)^{r-1}}{r} + \frac{(\ 1)}{(n\ \ 1)}\quad C_{n+1}$

$= \sum\limits_{r=1}^{n}\frac{{}^nC_{r-1}(-1)^{r-1}}{r} + \frac{(-1)^n}{(n+1)}$

$= \sum\limits_{r=1}^{n}\frac{r}{n+1}.\frac{1}{r}.{}^{n+1}C_r(-1)^{r-1} + \frac{(-1)^n}{(n+1)}$

$= \sum\limits_{r=1}^{n}\frac{1}{(n+1)}.{}^{n+1}C_r(-1)^{r-1} + \frac{(-1)^n}{(n+1)}$

$= \frac{-1}{n+1}\left(\sum\limits_{r=0}^{n+1}(-1)^r.{}^{n+1}C_r - 1 - (-1)^{n+1}.{}^{n+1}C_{n+1}\right) + \frac{(-1)^n}{n+1}$

$= -\frac{1}{(n+1)}[0 - 1 - (-1)^{n+1}] + \frac{(-1)^n}{n+1}$

$= \frac{1}{n+1} + \frac{(-1)^{n+1}}{n+1} + \frac{(-1)^n}{n+1} = \frac{1}{n+1}\ \forall\ n \in \mathbb{N} = T_{n+1} - T_n$

∴ $S_{n+1} - S_n = T_{n+1} - T_n\ \forall\ n \in N$ (i)

Also $T_1 = S_1 = 1$

Let $T_k = T_k$ for some positive integer k.

∴ $S_{k+1} - S_k = T_{k+1} - T_k$

⇒ $S_{k+1} = T_{k+1}$

∴ By P.M.I.; $T_n = S_n\ \forall\ n \in N$

∴ Assertion on well as reason both are correct and reason is the correct explanation of assertion.

3. (a) $S = \sum\limits_{0\le i<j\le n}\sum\left(\frac{i}{C_i}+\frac{j}{C_j}\right) = \sum\limits_{0\le i<j\le n}\sum\left(\frac{n-i}{C_{n-i}}+\frac{n-j}{C_{n-j}}\right)$

$= \sum\limits_{0\le i<j\le n}\sum n\left(\frac{1}{C_i}+\frac{1}{C_j}\right) - \sum\limits_{0\le i<j\le n}\sum\left(\frac{i}{C_i}+\frac{j}{C_j}\right)$

⇒ $2S = \sum\limits_{0\le i<j\le n}\sum n\left(\frac{1}{C_i}+\frac{1}{C_j}\right)$ (i)

Now $\sum\limits_{0\le i<j\le n}\sum\left(\frac{1}{C_i}+\frac{1}{C_j}\right)$

$= \sum\limits_{i=0}^{n-1}\frac{n-i}{C_i} + \sum\limits_{j=1}^{n}\frac{j}{C_j} = \sum\limits_{i=0}^{n}\frac{n-i}{C_i} + \sum\limits_{j=0}^{n}\frac{j}{C_j}$

$= n\sum\limits_{i=0}^{n}\frac{i}{C_i} - \sum\limits_{i=0}^{n}\frac{i}{C_i} + \sum\limits_{j=0}^{n}\frac{j}{C_j}$

$= n\sum\limits_{i=0}^{n}\frac{1}{C_i} = nA$ $\left(\because A = \sum\limits_{r=0}^{n}\frac{1}{C_r}\right)$ (ii)

∴ From (i) and (ii), we get $2S = n.(nA)$

⇒ $S = \frac{n^2A}{2}$

∴ Assertion as well as reason both are true and reason, correctly explanation the assertion

4. (a) Clearly ${}^mC_r.{}^nC_0 + {}^mC_{r-1}.{}^nC_1 + {}^mC_{r-2}.{}^nC_2 + ... + {}^mC_0.{}^nC_r = {}^{m+n}C_r$.

⇒ Reason is correct.

Now given series is $\sum\limits_{r=0}^{n}\frac{n!}{(n-r)!(m+r)!}C_r$

$= \frac{n!}{(m+n)!}\sum\limits_{r=0}^{n}\frac{(m+n)!}{(n-r)!(m+r)!}.C_r$

$= \frac{n!}{(m+n)!}\sum\limits_{r=0}^{n}{}^{m+n}C_{m+r}.{}^nC_r$

$= \frac{n!}{(m+n)!}.\sum\limits_{r=0}^{n}{}^{m+n}C_{m+r}.{}^nC_{n-r} = \frac{n!}{(m+n)!}\left({}^{m+2n}C_{m+n}\right)$ (By reason)

$$= \frac{n!}{(m+n)!}\left[\frac{(m+2n)!}{(m+n)!n!}\right] = \frac{(m+2n)!}{(m+n)!(m+n)!}$$

$$= \frac{(m+n)!(m+n+1)(m+n+2)...(m+2n)}{(m+n)!(m+n)!}$$

$$= \frac{(m+n+1)(m+n+2)...(m+2n)}{(m+n)!}$$

⇒ Assertion is also true and reason correctly explains the assertion.

5. (b) $\sum_{r=0}^{n} C_r^2 = {}^{2n}C_n$ is standard result, implies reason is correct

Now $\sum_{r=1}^{n} r.C_r^2 = \sum_{r=1}^{n} r.{}^nC_r.{}^nC_r = \sum_{r=1}^{n} r.\frac{n}{r}.{}^{n-1}C_{r-1}.{}^nC_r$

$$= n\sum_{r=1}^{n} {}^{n-1}C_{r-1}.{}^nC_r \quad n\sum_{r=1}^{n} {}^{n-1}C_{r-1}.{}^nC_{n-r} = n({}^{2n-1}C_{n-1})$$

⇒ Assertion is also correct but reason does not explain the assertion

6. (a) m, n, r, k are non-negative integers.

$$\sum_{m=0}^{k} {}^{r+m}C_m = {}^rC_0 + {}^{r+1}C_1 + {}^{r+2}C_2 + ... + {}^{r+k}C_k$$

$$= \underbrace{{}^{r+1}C_0 + {}^{r+1}C_1} + {}^{r+2}C_2 + ... + {}^{r+k}C_k = {}^{r+2}C_1 + {}^{r+2}C_2 + ...$$

$+ {}^{r+k}C_k$ (Applying Pascal's rule repeatedly)

$$= {}^{r+k}C_{k-1} + {}^{r+k}C_k = {}^{r+k+1}C_k$$

⇒ Reason is correct.

Now $\sum_{m=0}^{k} (n-m)\frac{(r+m)!}{m!} = n\sum_{m=0}^{k}\frac{(r+m)!}{m!} - \sum_{m=1}^{k}\frac{m.(r+m)!}{m!}$

$$= (r!).n\sum_{m=0}^{k} {}^{r+m}C_m - \sum_{m=1}^{k}\frac{(r+m)!}{(m-1)!}$$

$$= r!n\left[{}^{r+k+1}C_k\right] - (r+1)!\sum_{m=1}^{k}\frac{(r+m)!}{(r+1)!(m-1)!}$$

$$= r!(n)\left[{}^{r+k+1}C_k\right] - (r+1)!\left[\sum_{m=1}^{k} {}^{r+m}C_{m-1}\right]$$

$$= r!(n)({}^{r+k+1}C_k) - (r+1)!\left[\sum_{m=1}^{k} {}^{(r+1)+m-1}C_{m-1}\right]$$

$$= r!(n)({}^{r+k+1}C_k) - (r+1)!\sum_{t=0}^{k-1} {}^{r+1+t}C_t$$

$$= r!(n)({}^{r+k+1}C_k) - (r+1).{}^{r+1+k}C_{k-1}$$

$$= r!n\left(\frac{(r+k+1)!}{k!(r+1)!}\right) - (r+1).\frac{(r+k+1)!}{(k-1)!(r+2)!}$$

$$= \frac{n(r+k+1)!}{k!(r+1)!} - \frac{k(r+k+1)!}{k(k-1)!(r+2)!}$$

$$= \frac{(r+k+1)!}{k!}\left[\frac{n}{r+1} - \frac{k}{r+2}\right]$$

⇒ Assertion is correct and reason correctly explain the assertion.

7. (d) Clearly, the reason is correct

Now $r = \left[\frac{15+1}{\left|\frac{3}{-5x}\right|+1}\right]_{x=1/5} = \left[\frac{16}{\left|\frac{3}{5}\times 5\right|+1}\right] = \left[\frac{16}{4}\right] = 4$

∴ $= T_5$ is the numerically greatest term.

⇒ Assertion is incorrect

8. (b) Clearly coefficient of $a^2b^3c^4$ in the explanation of $(a + b + c)^8$ is zero as $a^2b^3c^4$ is of 9th degree.

⇒ Assertion is correct.

Clearly reason being standard result is also true. If would explain the assertion if along with the given information, it is also given that coefficient is zero for terms of degree not equal to n.

9. (a) ${}^{40}C_0 . {}^{60}C_r + {}^{40}C_1 . {}^{60}C_{r-1} + ... + {}^{40}C_{40} . {}^{60}C_{r-40} = {}^{100}C_r$

Its greatest value $= {}^{100}C_{50}$

⇒ Assertion is correct and correctly explained by reason.

10. (a) $\left(x^2 + \frac{1}{x}\right)^{11} = \sum_{r=0}^{11} {}^{11}C_r (x^2)^{11-r}\left(\frac{1}{x}\right)^r = \sum_{r=0}^{11} {}^{11}C_r (x)^{22-3r}$

For coefficient of x^4; $22 - 3r = 4$

⇒ $x = 6$

∴ Coefficient of $x^4 = {}^{11}C_6 = \frac{11!}{6!.5!}$

⇒ Assertion is correct

Also coefficient of x^p in $\left(x^2 + \frac{1}{x}\right)^n = {}^nC_r$; where $p = 2n - 3r$

$= {}^{11}C_{\left(\frac{2n-p}{3}\right)} = \frac{11!}{\left(\frac{2n-p}{3}\right)!\left(\frac{n+p}{3}\right)!}$; when $(2n - p)$ is positive and divisible by 3

⇒ Reason is also correct and correctly explain the assertion

SECTION–IV: (COMPREHENSION TYPE)

Passage: 1

1. (c) $r = \left[\frac{8+1}{\left|\frac{1}{-2x}\right|+1}\right]_{x=2}$ ⇒ $r = \left[\frac{9\times 4}{5}\right] = 7$

∴ Numerical value of numerically greatest term $= |T_8| = |{}^8C_7 (-2\times 2)| = |-{}^8C_1 (4)^7| = |-2^{17}| = 2^{17}$

2. (d) $r = \left[\frac{10}{\left|\frac{3}{-2x}\right|+1}\right]_{x=1} = [4] = 4$

∴ Magnitude of greatest magnitude term $= |{}^9C_4 (3)^5 (-2(1))^4| = {}^9C_4 (3)^5 (2)^4$

⇒ (c) is correct option

$= \dfrac{9\times8\times7\times6}{4\times3\times2\times1}\times(3)^5(2)^4$

$= {}^9C_3\left(\dfrac{6}{4}\right)(3)^5(2)^4 = {}^9C_3(3)^6(2)^3$ i.e., $T_3 = T_4$ = greatest numerical value term.

$\Rightarrow$ (b) is correct option

3. (a) $3 = \left[\dfrac{10+1}{\left|\dfrac{2}{3x}\times 8\right|+1}\right] \Rightarrow 3 = \left[\dfrac{11}{\left|\dfrac{16}{3x}\right|+1}\right]$

$3 \le \dfrac{11}{\dfrac{16}{3|x|}+1} < 4 \quad \Rightarrow \quad 3 \le \dfrac{11\times3|x|}{16+3|x|} < 4$

$\Rightarrow$ $48 + 9|x| \le 33|x| < 64 + 12|x|$

$\Rightarrow$ $24\,|x| \ge 48;\ 21\,|x| < 64$

$\Rightarrow$ $|x| \ge 2;\ |x| < 64/21 \quad \Rightarrow \quad 2 \le x < 3\dfrac{1}{21}$

4. (a) Let T_{r+1} be the term with greatest numerical value of coefficients

$\therefore \quad r = \left[\dfrac{n+1}{\dfrac{1}{|x|}+1}\right] \qquad r \le \dfrac{(n+1)(|x|)}{1+|x|} < (r+1)$

$\Rightarrow$ $r + r|x| \le n|x| + |x| < (r + 1)(1 + |x|)$

But for greatest coefficient $r = n/2$ $\qquad (\because n = \text{even})$

$\Rightarrow$ $\dfrac{n}{2}+\dfrac{n}{2}|x| \le x|x|+|x| < \left(\dfrac{n}{2}+1\right)(1+|x|)$

$\Rightarrow$ $\dfrac{n}{2}(1+|x|) \le (n+1)|x| < \left(\dfrac{n+2}{2}\right)(1+|x|)$

$\Rightarrow$ $n + n|x| \le 2x|x| + 2|x|$ and $2x|x| + 2|x| < (x + 2) + (n + 2)|x|$

$\Rightarrow$ $n \le (n + 2)\,|x|$ and $n|x| < (x + 2)$

$\Rightarrow$ $\dfrac{n}{n+2} \le |x| < \dfrac{x+2}{n}$

5. (a), (b) $(1-x)^{21} = \sum_{r=0}^{21}(-1)^r.{}^{21}C_r x^r$

Numerical value of coefficients = ${}^{21}C_r$ greatest of numerical values of coefficients = ${}^{21}C_{10}$ or ${}^{21}C_{11}$

$\Rightarrow r = 10 \qquad \Rightarrow 10 = \left[\dfrac{21+1}{\left|\dfrac{1}{-x}\right|+1}\right]$

$\Rightarrow 10 = \left[\dfrac{22}{\left|\dfrac{1}{|x|}\right|+1}\right]$

$\Rightarrow 10 \le \dfrac{22}{\dfrac{1}{|x|}+1} < 11 \qquad \Rightarrow \dfrac{10}{|x|}+10 \le 22 < \dfrac{11}{|x|}+11$

$\Rightarrow \dfrac{10}{|x|} \le 12$ and $\dfrac{11}{|x|} > 11$

$\Rightarrow |x| \ge \dfrac{5}{6}$ and $|x| < 1 \qquad \dfrac{5}{6} \le |x| < 1$

$\because x > 0 \qquad \Rightarrow x \in \left[\dfrac{5}{6}, 1\right) \le \left[\dfrac{5}{6}, \dfrac{6}{5}\right)$

Passage: 2

6. (b) $(C_0 - C_2 + C_4 - C_6 + \ldots\ldots)^2 + (C_1 - C_3 + C_5 \ldots\ldots\ldots)^2$
$= A^2 + B^2$ (say)

Now, $A = C_0 - C_2 + C_4 - C_6 + \ldots\ldots\ldots$

$(1 + x)^n = C_0 + C_1x + C_2x^2 + C_3x^3 + C_4x^4 \ldots\ldots\ldots\ldots$

Put $x = (-1)^{1/2} = i, -i$

$\therefore$ $(1 + i)^n = C_0 + C_1i - C_2 - iC_3 + C_4 + \ldots\ldots\ldots\ldots$

$(1 - i)^n = C_0 - C_1i - C_2 + iC_3 + C_4 + \ldots\ldots\ldots\ldots$

$\Rightarrow$ $(1 + i)^n + (1 - i)^n = 2[C_0 - C_2 + C_4 + \ldots\ldots\ldots]$

$\Rightarrow$ $A = \dfrac{(1+i)^n + (1-i)^n}{2}$

$= \dfrac{(\sqrt{2})^n}{2}\left[\left(cis\dfrac{\pi}{4}\right)^n + \left(cis\left(\dfrac{-\pi}{4}\right)\right)^n\right]$

$= \dfrac{(\sqrt{2})^n}{2}\left[2\cos\dfrac{x\pi}{4}\right] = (2)^{n/2}\cos\dfrac{n\pi}{4}$

Again, $(1 + x)^n.x = C_0x + C_1x^2 + C_2x^3 + C_3x^4 + C_4x^5 + \ldots\ldots$

Put $x = (-1)^{1/2} = i, -i$

$\Rightarrow$ $(1 + i)^n\, i = C_0i + C_1(-1) + C_2(-i) + C_3 + C_4i + \ldots\ldots\ldots\ldots$

And $(1 - i)^n\,(-i)\ C_0(-i) + C_1(-1) + C_2(i) + C_3 - C_4i + \ldots\ldots\ldots\ldots\ldots$

$\Rightarrow$ $i((1 + i)^n - (1 - i)^n) = -2[C_1 - C_3 + \ldots\ldots\ldots]$

$\Rightarrow$ $\dfrac{i\left[(\sqrt{2})^n\left(cis\dfrac{n\pi}{4} - cis\left(-\dfrac{n\pi}{4}\right)\right)\right]}{-2} = B$

$\Rightarrow$ $B = \dfrac{i}{-2}\left[(2)^{n/2}\left(2i\sin\dfrac{n\pi}{4}\right)\right] = (2)^{n/2}\sin\dfrac{n\pi}{4}$

$\therefore$ $A^2 + B^2 = (2)^n\left[\cos^2\dfrac{n\pi}{4} + \sin^2\dfrac{n\pi}{4}\right] = (2)^n$

7. (d) ${}^nC_0 + {}^nC_4 + {}^nC_8 + \ldots\ldots$

Put $x = (1)^{1/4} = 1, -1, i, -i$ in $(1 + x)^n = C_0 + C_1x + C_2x^2 + C_3x^3 + C_4x^4 + \ldots\ldots$

$(2)^n = C_0 + C_1 + C_2 + C_3 + C_4 + \ldots\ldots$

$0 = C_0 - C_1 + C_2 - C_3 + C_4 - \ldots\ldots\ldots\ldots$

$(1 + i)^n = C_0 + C_1i - C_2 - iC_3 + C_4 + \ldots\ldots$

$(1 - i)^n = C_0 - C_1i - C_2 + iC_3 + C_4 + \ldots\ldots$

Adding, $\dfrac{(2)^n + (1+i)^n + (1-i)^n}{4} = [C_0 + C_4 + \ldots..]$

$\therefore$ Sum $= \dfrac{(2)^n + (\sqrt{2})^n\left[2\cos\dfrac{n\pi}{4}\right]}{4} = (2)^{n-2} + (2)^{\frac{n-2}{2}}\cos\dfrac{n\pi}{4}$

8. (d) $\sum_{r=1}^{k}(-3)^{r-1}.{}^{3n}C_{2r-1} = {}^{3n}C_1 - 3^1.{}^{3n}C_3 + 3^2.{}^{3n}C_6 - \ldots..$

In the expression $(1 + x)^{3n}.x = {}^{3n}C_0x + {}^{3n}C_1x^2 + {}^{3n}C_2x^3 + {}^{3n}C_3x^4 + {}^{3n}C_4x^5 + \ldots.$

Put $x = (-3)^{1/2} = \sqrt{3}i, -\sqrt{3}i$

Gives $\dfrac{\sqrt{3}i\left[\left(1-\sqrt{3}i\right)^{3n}-\left(1+\sqrt{3}i\right)^{3n}\right]}{3} = {}^{3n}C_1 - 3.{}^{3n}C_3 + 3^2.{}^{3n}C_5 + \ldots$

i.e., $\sum_{r=1}^{k}(-3)^{r-1}.{}^{3n}C_{2r-1};\left(k=\dfrac{3n}{2}\right)$

$= \dfrac{-i}{\sqrt{3}}\left[(1+\sqrt{3}i)^{3n}-(1-\sqrt{3}i)^{3n}\right]$

$= \dfrac{-i}{\sqrt{3}}\left[(2)^{3n}\left\{\left(\dfrac{1}{2}+\dfrac{\sqrt{3}}{2}i\right)^{3n}-\left(\dfrac{1}{2}-\dfrac{\sqrt{3}}{2}i\right)^{3n}\right\}\right]$

$= \dfrac{-i}{\sqrt{3}}(2)^{3n}\left[cis3n.\dfrac{\pi}{3}-cis\left(3n.\dfrac{\pi}{3}\right)\right] = \dfrac{-i}{\sqrt{3}}(2)^{3n}\left[2i\sin n\pi\right]=0$

Passage: 3

9. (a) $\dbinom{-1}{r} = \dfrac{-(1)r}{r!} = \dfrac{(-1)(-2)(-3)\ldots(-1-(r-1))}{r!} = (-1)^r.r!/r! = (-1)^r$

10. (b) $\dbinom{-2}{r} = \dfrac{(-2)r}{r!} = \dfrac{(-2)(-3)(-4)\ldots[-2-(r-1)]}{r!}$

$= \dfrac{(-1)^r(2.3.4\ldots(r+1))}{r!} = \dfrac{(-1)^r(r+1)!}{r!} = (-1)^r(r+1)$

11. (a) Number of ways of distributing n identical balls in r – distinct boxes $= {}^{n+r-1}C_{r-1} = \dfrac{(n+r-1)}{(r-1)!.n!}$

$= \dfrac{(n+r-1)(n+r-2)\ldots(n+1)(n!)}{(r-1)!n!}$

$= \dfrac{(n+1)(n+2)(n+3)\ldots(n+r-1)}{(r-1)!}$

$= \dfrac{(n+1)(n+2)(n+3)\ldots(n+r-1).n!}{n!(r-1)!}$

$= \dfrac{1.2.3\ldots n.(n+1)(n+2)\ldots(n+r-1)}{n!(r-1)!}$

$= \dfrac{1.2.3\ldots(r-1).r.(r+1)\ldots(r+n-1)}{n!(r-1)!}$

$= \dfrac{r(r+1)(r+2)\ldots(r+n-1)}{n!}$

$= (-1)^n\dfrac{[(-r)(-r-1)(-r-2)\ldots(-r-n+1)]}{n!}$

$= (-1)^n\dbinom{-r}{n}$

Passage: 4

12. (a) $\sum_{x+y+z=10}\dfrac{10!}{x!y!z!}$ = Sum of coefficients of $(x+y+z)^{10} = (1+1+1)^{10} = 3^{10}$

13. (b) The coefficient of $a^3b^4c^5$ in $(ab+bc+ca)^6 = \dfrac{6!}{\alpha!\beta!\gamma!}$

Where $(ab)^\alpha (bc)^\beta (ca)^\gamma = a^3b^4c^5$ i.e., $a^{\alpha+\gamma}.b^{\alpha+\beta}.c^{\beta+\gamma} = a^3b^4c^5$

$\Rightarrow \alpha+\gamma=3;\ \alpha+\beta=4;\ \beta+\gamma=5 \Rightarrow \alpha=1;\ \beta=3;\ \gamma=2$

$\therefore$ Required coefficient $= \dfrac{6!}{1!3!2!} = 60$

14. (b) Number of terms in $(x+2y+3z)^{20}$

Number of ways of distributing 20 identical balls to 3 persons

$= {}^{20+2}C_2 = {}^{22}C_2 = \dfrac{22\times 21}{2} = 231$

15. (b) $(1+x-2x^2)^7 = [(1-x)(1+2x)]^7 = (1-x)^7(1+2x)^7$

$= \sum_{r=0}^{7}{}^7C_r(-1)^r.x^r.\sum_{p=0}^{7}{}^7C_p2^p.x^p$

$\therefore$ For coefficient of x^4; $r+p=4$

$\Rightarrow r=0;\ p=4;\ r=1;\ p=3;\ r=2,\ p=2;\ r=3,\ p=1;\ r=4;\ p=0$

$= {}^7C_0.{}^7C_4(2)^4 - {}^7C_1.{}^7C_3(2)^3 + {}^7C_2.{}^7C_2(2)^2 - {}^7C_3.{}^7C_1(2)^1 + {}^7C_4.{}^7C_0(2)^0$

$= 560 - 1960 + 1764 - 490 + 35 = -91$

16. (b) $\left(x^2+\dfrac{4}{x^2}+4\right)^5 = \left(\dfrac{x^4+4x^2+4}{x^2}\right)^5 = \left(\dfrac{(x^2+2)^2}{x^2}\right)^5 = \dfrac{(x^2+2)^{10}}{x^{10}}$

$\therefore$ Coefficient of x^6 in $\dfrac{(x^2+2)^{10}}{x^{10}}$

= Coefficient of x^{16} in $(x^2+2)^{10}$

= Coefficient of x^{16} in $\sum_{r=0}^{10}{}^{10}C_r(2)^{10-r}(x^2)^r$

= Coefficient of $x^{16} = {}^{10}C_r(2)^{10-r}$; where $2r = 16$

$= {}^{10}C_8(2)^2 = {}^{10}C_2(4) = 180$

Passage: 5

17. (b) $P = \sum\sum_{0\le r<s\le n} C_rC_s$

$= \dfrac{(C_0+C_1+C_2+\ldots+C_n)^2-(C_0^2+C_1^2+C_2^2+\ldots+C_n^2)}{2}$

$= \dfrac{2^{2n}-({}^{2n}C_n)}{2} = (2)^{n-1} - \dfrac{1}{2}({}^{2n}C_n)$

18. (b) $Q = \sum\sum_{0\le r<s\le n}(C_r-C_s)^2 = \sum\sum_{0\le r<s\le n}(C_r^2+C_s^2-2C_r.C_s)$

$= \sum\sum_{0\le r<s\le n}(C_r^2+C_s^2) - 2\sum\sum_{0\le r<s\le n}C_r.C_s$

$= \sum_{r=0}^{n-1}(n-r)C_r^2 + \sum_{s=1}^{n}s.C_s^2 - [(C_0+C_1+C_2+\ldots+C_n)^2 - (C_0^2+C_1^2+\ldots+C_n^2)]$

$= \sum_{r=0}^{n}(n-r)C_r^2 + \sum_{S=0}^{n}s.C_s^2 - \left[2^{2n}-{}^{2n}C_n\right]$

$= n\sum_{r=0}^{n}C_r^2 - \left[2^{2n}-{}^{2n}C_n\right]$

$= n({}^{2n}C_n) - 2^{m} + {}^{2n}C_n = (n+1)({}^{2n}C_n) - 2^{2n}$.

19. **(d)** $R=\sum\sum_{0\le r<s\le n}(r+s)C_r.C_s=\sum\sum_{0\le r<s\le n}(n-r+n-s)C_{n-r}.C_{n-s}$

$=\sum\sum_{0\le r<s\le n}(2n-(r+s))C_r.C_s$

$=2n\sum\sum_{0\le r<s\le n}C_r.C_s-R=2R=n\left[\left(\sum_{r=0}^{n}C_r\right)^2-\left(\sum_{k=0}^{n}C_k^2\right)\right]$

$=R=\frac{n}{2}[2^{2n}-{}^{2n}C_n]=n.(2)^{2n-1}-\frac{n}{2}\left({}^{2n}C_n\right)$

20. **(c)** $S=\sum\sum_{0\le r<s\le n}(r+s)(C_r-C_s)^2$

$=\sum\sum_{0\le r<s\le n}(n-r+n-s)[C_{n-r}-C_{n-s}]^2$

$=\sum\sum_{0\le r<s\le n}(2n-(r+s))(C_r-C_s)^2$

$=2n\sum\sum_{0\le r<s\le n}(C_r-C_s)^2-S=2S=2n\sum\sum_{0\le r<s\le n}(C_r-C_s)$

$\Rightarrow$ $2S=2nQ$ (From Q. no. 18)

$\Rightarrow$ $S=nQ=n[(n+1)({}^{2n}C_n)-2^{2n}]$

21. **(a)** $T=\sum\sum_{0\le r<s\le n}(C_r+C_s)^2=\sum\sum_{0\le r<s\le n}(C_r^2+C_s^2+2C_rC_s)$

$=\sum\sum_{0\le r<s\le n}(C_r^2+C_s^2)+2\sum\sum_{0\le r<s\le n}C_rC_s$

$=\sum_{r=0}^{n-1}Cr^2(n-r)+\sum_{s=1}^{n}s.C_s^2+(2^{2n}-{}^{2n}C_n)$

$=\sum_{r=0}^{n}Cr^2(n-r)+\sum_{s=0}^{n}s.Cs^2+(2^{2n}-{}^{2n}C_n)$

$=n\sum_{r=0}^{n}Cr^2+(2^{2n}-{}^{2n}C_n)=(n-1)\,{}^{2n}C_n+2^{2n}$

SECTION–VII: (COLUMN MATCHING)

1. **(i) → (a); (ii) → (c); (iii) → (b)**

$R=\left(5\sqrt{5}+11\right)^{2n+1}=[R]+f;0<f<1$

Now $\left(5\sqrt{5}-11\right)^{2n+1}=f'\in(0,1)$

Now, $\left(5\sqrt{5}+11\right)^{2n+1}-\left(5\sqrt{5}-11\right)^{2n+1}$

$=2\begin{bmatrix}{}^{2n+1}C_1(5\sqrt{5})^{2n}(11)^1+{}^{2n+1}C_3(5\sqrt{5})^{2n-2}(11)^3+\ldots\\+{}^{2n-1}C_{2n+1}(11)^{2n+1}\end{bmatrix}\in\mathbb{Z}$

$\Rightarrow$ $[R]+f-f'=2k;\ k\in\mathbb{Z}$

$\Rightarrow$ $f-f'\in\mathbb{Z}$; but $-1<f-f'<1$

$\Rightarrow$ $f-f'=0$ $\Rightarrow$ $f=f'=(5\sqrt{5}-11)^{2n+1}$

$\therefore$ **(i) → (a)**

Now $RF=\left(5\sqrt{5}+11\right)^{2n+1}.\left(5\sqrt{5}-11\right)^{2n+1}$

$=(125-121)^{2n+1}=(4)^{2n+1}$ $\therefore$ **(ii) → (c)**

Further $[R]=\left(5\sqrt{5}+11\right)^{2n+1}-\left(5\sqrt{5}-11\right)^{2n+1}$

$\therefore$ **(iii) → (b)**

2. **(i) → (d) ; (ii) → (c) ; (iii) → (b) ; (iv) → (a)**

(i) Number of distinct term in the expansion of $(x+y-z)^{16}$

$={}^{16+2}C_2={}^{18}C_2=\frac{18\times17}{2}=153$

$\therefore$ **(i) → (d)**

(ii) $\left(x+\sqrt{x^2-1}\right)^6+(x-\sqrt{x^2-1}))^6$ has terms $=\frac{6}{2}+1=4$

$\left(\frac{n}{2}+1\text{ if } n \text{ is even}\right)$

$\therefore$ **(ii) → (c)**

(iii) $\left(\sqrt[8]{5}+\sqrt[6]{2}\right)^{100}=\sum_{r=0}^{100}{}^{100}C_r(5)^{100}$

$\therefore$ For rational terms, $6/r$ and $8/(100-r)$

Let $r=6k$; $k\in W$

$\therefore$ $8/(100-6k)$

$\Rightarrow$ $4/(50-3k)$

$\Rightarrow$ $k\in\{2,6,10,14\}$

$\Rightarrow$ $r\in\{12,36,60,84\}$

$\therefore$ These are 4 rational terms

$\Rightarrow$ No of irrational terms = 101 – 4 = 97

$\therefore$ **(iii) → (b)**

(iv) Sum of numerical coefficients in $\left(1+\frac{x}{3}+\frac{2y}{3}\right)^{12}=$

$\left(1+\frac{1}{3}+\frac{2}{3}\right)^{12}=(2)^{12}$ $\therefore$ **(iv) → (b)**

3. **(i) → (b), (ii) → (c) , (iii) →a; (iv) → (d)**

(i) $(3+\alpha x)^9=\sum_{r=0}^{9}{}^9C_r(3)^{9-r}(\alpha x)^r$

$\therefore$ Coefficient of $x^2={}^9C_2(3)^7\alpha^2$ and coefficient of $x^3={}^9C_3(3)^6\alpha^3$

$\therefore$ A.T.Q, ${}^9C_2(3)^7.\alpha^2={}^9C_3(3)^6.\alpha^3$

$\Rightarrow$ $3=\frac{{}^9C_3}{{}^9C_2}.\alpha$ $\Rightarrow$ $3=\left(\frac{9-3+1}{3}\right)\alpha$

$\Rightarrow$ $a=9/7$ $\Rightarrow$ **(i) → (b)**

(ii) a = coefficient of x^n in $(1+x)^{2n}$ and b = coefficient of x^{n-1} in $(1+x)^{2n-1}$

$\Rightarrow$ $a={}^{2n}C_n$; $b={}^{2n-1}C_{n-1}$

$\therefore$ $\left(\frac{a-b}{a+b}\right)^3=\left(\frac{{}^{2n}C_n-{}^{2n-1}C_{n-1}}{{}^{2n}C_n+{}^{2n-1}C_{n-1}}\right)^3$

$=\left[\frac{\frac{2n}{n}.{}^{2n-1}C_{n-1}-{}^{2n-1}C_{n-1}}{\frac{2n}{n}.{}^{2n-1}C_{n-1}+{}^{2n-1}C_{n-1}}\right]^3=\left(\frac{2-1}{2+1}\right)^3=\frac{1}{27}$

(iii) If $\{x\}$ = fractional part of x

$3^{2008}=3.3^{2007}=3\,(3^3)^{669}$

$=3[27]^{669}=3[28-1]^{669}$

$=-3(1-28)^{669}$

$=-3[{}^{669}C_0-{}^{669}C_1(28)+{}^{669}C_2(28)^2\ldots]$

$=-3+28k$

$=25+(28k-28)=25+25k';\ k'\in Z$

Now, $\left\{\frac{3^{2008}}{7}\right\}=\left\{\frac{25+28k'}{7}\right\}=\left\{\frac{25}{7}\right\}\left\{3+\frac{4}{7}\right\}=\frac{4}{7}$

$\therefore$ **(iii) → (a)**

(iv) $(1+x+2x^2)\left(\frac{3x^2}{2}+\frac{1}{3x}\right)^7$

$= (1+x+2x^2)\left[\sum_{r=0}^{7}{}^7C_r\left(\frac{3x^2}{2}\right)^{7-r}\cdot\left(\frac{1}{3r}\right)^r\right]$

$= \left(1+x+2x^2\right)\left[\sum_{r=0}^{7}{}^7C_r.\frac{(3)^{7-2r}}{(2)^{7-r}}.(x)^{14-3r}\right]$

$\therefore$ Term independent of $x = {}^7C_5\frac{(3)^{-3}}{(2)^2}={}^7C_2.\frac{1}{(27)(4)}$

$=\frac{21}{27\times4}=\frac{7}{36}$

$\therefore$ **(iv) → (d)**

4. (i) → c; (ii) → (c); (iii) → (b); (iv) → b

(i) $\sum_{r=0}^{n}\frac{r}{C_r}=\sum_{r=0}^{n}\frac{n-r}{C_{n-r}}=\sum_{r=0}^{n}\frac{n-r}{C_r}=2\sum_{r=0}^{n}\frac{r}{C_r}=n\sum_{r=0}^{n}\frac{1}{C_r}$

$=\sum_{r=0}^{n}\frac{r}{C_r}=\frac{n}{2}$ $\therefore$ **(i) → (c)**

(ii) $\sum_{r=0}^{n}\frac{n-r}{C_r}=n\sum_{r=0}^{n}\frac{1}{C_r}-\sum_{r=0}^{n}\frac{r}{C_r}=n.a_n-\frac{n}{2}a_n=\frac{n}{2}a_n$

$\therefore$ **(ii) → (c)**

(iii) $\sum_{r=1}^{n}\frac{1}{{}^7C_r}=\sum_{r=1}^{n}\frac{1}{r.\frac{n}{r}.{}^{n-1}C_{r-1}}=\frac{1}{n}\sum_{r=1}^{n}\frac{1}{{}^{n-1}C_{r-1}}=\frac{1}{n}.a_{n-1}$

$\therefore$ **(iii) → (b)**

(iv) $\sum_{r=0}^{n-1}\frac{1}{(n-r)C_r}=\sum_{r=0}^{n-1}\frac{1}{(n-r){}^nC_{n-r}}=\sum_{r=1}^{n}\frac{1}{r.C_r}=\frac{1}{n}a_{n-1}$

$\therefore$ **(iv) → (b)**

5. (i) → (a), (b), (c), (d); (ii) → (a); (iii) → (a), (b), (d); (iv) → (a), (b)

Sol. (i) $E=\sum_{r=1}^{n}\frac{r.C_r}{C_{r-1}}=\sum_{r=1}^{n}r.\left(\frac{n-r+1}{r}\right)$

$=\sum_{r=1}^{n}(n-r+1)=n(n+1)-\frac{n(n+1)}{2}=\frac{n(n+1)}{2}={}^{n+1}C_2$

$\therefore$ $S = 2^nE = (2)^{n-1}.n(n+1)$

$\Rightarrow$ $2^{n-1}/S$

$\therefore$ **option (a)**

Also n(n + 1) being even $\Rightarrow$ $S = 2^n.k;\ k \in \mathbb{Z}$

$\Rightarrow$ $2^n/s$ $\therefore$ **option (b)**

Also $S = (2)^{n-1}.\ n(n+1) \Rightarrow\ n/s$

$\therefore$ **option (c)**

And $S = (2)^{n-1}.\ n(n+1) \Rightarrow\ (n+1)/S$

$\therefore$ **option (d)**

$\therefore$ **(i) → (a), (b), (c), (d)**

(ii) $E=\sum_{r=1}^{n}r.\frac{Cr^2}{C_{r-1}}=\sum_{r=1}^{n}r.C_r.\frac{C_r}{C_{r-1}}=\sum_{r=1}^{n}r.C_r\left(\frac{n-r+1}{r}\right)$

$=\sum_{r=1}^{n}(n-r+1)C_r=(n+1)\sum_{r=1}^{n}C_r-\sum_{r=1}^{n}r.C_r$

$=(n+1)(2^n-1)-\sum_{r=1}^{n}r.\frac{n}{r}.{}^{n-1}C_{r-1}=(n+1)(2^n-1)-n$

$\sum_{r=1}^{n}{}^{n-1}C_{r-1}=(n+1)(2^n-1)-n\,(2)^{n-1}$

Now $S = (n+1) + E$

$\Rightarrow$ $S = (n+1) + (n+1)(2^n-1) - n(2)^{n-1}$

$\Rightarrow$ $S = (n+1)(2^n) - n(2)^{n-1} = (2)^{n-1}(2n+2-n) = (n+2)(2)^{n-1}$

$\Rightarrow$ $2^{n-1}/S$ $\therefore$ **(ii) → (a)**

(iii) $S=\sum_{r=0}^{n}(2r+1)C_r=2\sum_{r=1}^{n}rC_r+\sum_{r=0}^{n}C_r$

$=2\sum_{r=1}^{n}r.\frac{n}{r}.{}^{n-1}C_{r-1}+(2)^n$

$= 2n\,(2)^{n-1} + (2)^n = n(2)^n + (2)^n = (n+1)(2)^n$

$\Rightarrow$ $2^{n-1}\left|s;(2)^n\right|S;(n+1)\,|\,S$ $\therefore$ **(iii) → (a), (b), (d)**

(iv) $n(A) = (2n+1)$

S = Number of subsets of A containing at most n-elements

$={}^{2n+1}C_0+{}^{2n+1}C_1+{}^{2n+1}C_2+\ldots..+{}^{2n+1}C_n$

$=\frac{1}{2}[{}^{2n+1}C_0+{}^{2n+1}C_1+{}^{2n+1}C_2+..+{}^{2n+1}C_n]$

$=\frac{1}{2}(2)^{2n+1}=(2)^{2n}$ $\Rightarrow$ $(2)^n\,|\,S;(2)^{n-1}\,|\,s$

$\therefore$ **(iv) → (a), (b)**

6. (i) → (b),(d); (ii) → (a), (b), (c); (iii) → (a); (iv) → (a), (d)

(i) $T_r > 0$ $\Rightarrow$ $T_{(r-1+1)} > 0$

$\Rightarrow$ $\frac{\left(\frac{7}{2}\right)\left(\frac{7}{2}-1\right)\ldots..\left(\frac{7}{2}-(r-1)+1\right)}{(r-1)!}x^{r-1}>0$

$\Rightarrow$ $\frac{\left(\frac{7}{2}\right)\left(\frac{5}{2}\right)\left(\frac{3}{2}\right)\left(\frac{1}{2}\right)}{(r-1)!}(x)^{r-1}>0$

$\Rightarrow$ $\frac{7}{2}-r+2=\frac{1}{2}$ $\Rightarrow$ $r = 5$

Which is divisible by 5 and is a prime number

$\therefore$ **(i) → (b), (d)**

(ii) $(y^2+1)^5=(1+y^2)^5=\sum_{r=0}^{5}{}^5C_r(y^2)^r=\sum_{r=0}^{5}{}^5C_r\,y^{2r}$

$\Rightarrow$ Coefficient of $y = 0$; which is divisile by 2, 5 and 10

$\therefore$ **(ii) → (a), (b), (c)**

(iii) $\sum_{r=0}^{n} {}^nC_r(a^{1/13})^{n-r}.(a.a^{1/2})^r$

$\Rightarrow\ T_2 = {}^nC_1\left(a^{\frac{1}{13}}\right)^{n-1}\left(a^{3/2}\right)^1 = 14a^{5/2}$

$\Rightarrow\ n(a)^{\frac{n-1}{13}+\frac{3}{2}} = 14(a)^{5/2}$

$\Rightarrow\ n(a)^{\frac{2n-2+39}{26}} = 14(a)^{5/2}$

$\Rightarrow\ n(a)^{\frac{2n+37}{26}} = 14(a)^{5/2}$

$\Rightarrow$ $n = 14$ which is divisible by 2

$\therefore$ **(iii) → (a)**

(iv) $(1 + 2x + 3x^2 + 4x^3 + \ldots \infty)^{1/2}$

$= [(1-x)^{-2}]^{1/2} = (1-x)^{-1}; (\because |x|<1|)$

$= 1 + x + x^2 + x^3 + \ldots.$

$\therefore$ Coefficient $x^4 = 1 = C$;

$\Rightarrow$ $C + 1 = 2$

which is divisible by 2 as well as a prime numbers.

$\therefore$ **(iv) → (a), (d)**

SECTION–VIII: INTEGER-TYPE QUESTIONS

1. $(1 + x + 2x^2)10 = a_0 + a_1x + a_2x^2 + \ldots a_{20}x^{20}$

Put $x = 1; -1$

$\Rightarrow$ $(4)^{10} = a_0 + a_1 + a_2 + \ldots a_{20}$ and $(2)^{10} = a_0 - a_1 + a_2 + \ldots. a_{20}$

$\Rightarrow$ $(4)^{10} + (2)^{10} = 2\,[a_0 + a_2 + \ldots a_{20}]$

Clearly $(2x^2)^{10}$ would give $a_{20}\,x^{20}$

$\Rightarrow$ $a_{20} = (2)^{10}$

$\therefore$ $\frac{(4)^{10}\quad(2)^{10}}{} = a_0 + a_2 + \ldots. + a_{18} + (2)^{10}$

$\Rightarrow\ a_0 + a_2 + \ldots + a_{18} = \frac{(4)^{10}+(2)^{10}}{2} - (2)^{10} = \frac{(4)^{10}-(2)^{10}}{2}$

$= (2)^{10}\frac{(2^{10}-1)}{2} = (2^9)(1023) = (512)\,(1023) = 523776$

2. ${}^{15}C_0 + {}^{15}C_1 + {}^{15}C_0 + \ldots. + {}^{15}C_7 = m^2$

$\Rightarrow\ \frac{1}{2}\left[{}^{15}C_0 + {}^{15}C_1 + {}^{15}C_2 + \ldots + {}^{15}C_7 + {}^{15}C_8 + {}^{15}C_9 + .. + {}^{15}C_{15}\right] = m^2$

$\Rightarrow\ \frac{1}{2}\left((2)^{15}\right) = m^2$ $\qquad\Rightarrow\ (2)^{14} = m^2$

$\Rightarrow\ (2^7)^2 = m^2$ $\qquad\Rightarrow\ m = (2)^7 = 128$

3. $\frac{10!}{0!} + \frac{11!}{1!} + \frac{12!}{2!} + \frac{13!}{3!} + \ldots$ upto 12 terms

$= 10!\left(\frac{10!}{0!10!} + \frac{11!}{10!1!} + \frac{12!}{10!2!} + \frac{13!}{10!\,3!} + \ldots + \frac{21!}{10!11!}\right)$

$= 10!({}^{10}C_0 + {}^{11}C_1 + {}^{12}C_2 + \ldots + {}^{21}C_{11})$

$= 10!({}^{11}C_0 + {}^{11}C_1 + {}^{12}C_2 + \ldots + {}^{21}C_{11})$

$= 10!\left[{}^{12}C_1 + {}^{12}C_2 + \ldots + {}^{21}C_{11}\right]$

$= 10!\left[{}^{21}C_{10} + {}^{21}C_{11}\right]$ (By using pascal's rule repeatedly)

$= 10![{}^{22}C_{11}]$

$= 10!\left(\frac{22!}{11!11!}\right) = \frac{22!}{11(11)!} = \frac{(2k)!}{k(k)!}$

$\Rightarrow\ k = 11$

4. $2^{1990} = 2^{10}.2.^{1980} = 2^{10}\,[2^{11}]^{180} = (2)^{10}\,[2048]^{180} = (2)^{10}[58 + 1990]^{180} = (2)^{10}\,[{}^{180}C_0(58) + 1990k] = (2)^{10}(58) + 1990\,k_1 = (1024)\,(58) + 1990k_1 = (995 + 29)\,(50 + 8) + 1990k_1 = (199 \times 5 + 29)\,(50 + 8) + 1990\,k_1$
$= 199 \times 5 \times 8 + 29 \times 50 + 29 \times 8 + 1990\,.k_2 + 29 \times 58 + 1990k_3 = 1682$

5. $S = (1 + x)^{1000} + 2x\,(1 + x)^{999} + 3x^2\,(1 + x)^{998} + \ldots + 1001\,x^{1000}$

$\frac{x}{(1+x)}S = x(1+x)^{999} + 2x^2(1+x)^{998} + \ldots 1000x^{1000} + \frac{1001x^{1001}}{(1+x)}$

Subtract, we get $\left(1-\frac{x}{1+x}\right)S = (1+x)^{1000} + x(1+x)^{999} +$

$x^2(1+x)^{998} + \ldots + x^{1000} - \frac{1001}{(1+x)}x^{1001}$

$\Rightarrow\ \frac{1}{1+x}.S = (1+x)^{1000}\left[\frac{\left(\frac{x}{1+x}\right)^{1001} - 1}{\left(\frac{x}{1+x}\right) - 1}\right] - \frac{1001}{1+x}x^{1001}$

$\Rightarrow\ \frac{S}{1+x} = (1+x)^{1000}\left[\frac{x^{1001} - (1+x)^{1001}}{(1+x)^{1000}(-1)}\right] - \frac{1001}{1+x}.x^{1001}$

$\Rightarrow\ \frac{S}{1+x} = [(1+x)^{1001} - x^{1001}] - \frac{1001}{1+x}.\,x^{1001}$

$\Rightarrow\ S = (1+x)^{1002} - x^{1001}(1+x) - 1001.\,x^{1001}$

$\Rightarrow$ Coefficient of $x^{40} = {}^{1002}C_{40} = {}^nC_{4k}$

$\Rightarrow$ $n = 1002;\ k = 10$

$\therefore$ $n + k = 1012$

6. Sum of coefficient in $(1 + x - 3x^2)^{2163}$

$= (1 + 1 - 3)^{2163} = (-1)^{2163} = -1 = k$

$\Rightarrow$ $|k| = 1$

7. $(1 + ax)^n = 1 + 8x + 24x^2 + \ldots.$

$\Rightarrow\ 1 + nax + \frac{n(n-1)a^2x^2}{2!} + \ldots = 1 + 8x + 24x^2 + \ldots.$

$\Rightarrow\ na = 8;\ \frac{n(n-1)a^2}{2} = 24$

$\Rightarrow$ $n^2a^2 = 64;\ n(n-1)\,a^2$

$\Rightarrow\ \frac{n}{(n-1)} = \frac{4}{3}$ $\qquad\Rightarrow\ n = 4\,;\ a = 2$

$\Rightarrow$ $a + n = 6$

8. $\left(\sqrt{2} + 3^{1/5}\right)^{10} \sum_{r=0}^{10} {}^{10}C_r\left(\sqrt{2}\right)^{10-r}(3^{r/5}) = \sum_{r=0}^{10} {}^{10}C_r(2)^{\frac{10-r}{2}}(3)^{r/5}$

$\therefore$ For rational terms, $2/10 - r$ and $5/r$

$\therefore$ $2/10 - 5k$

$\Rightarrow$ $k \in \{0, 2\}$

$\therefore$ Sum of rational terms = ${}^{10}C_0(2)^5 + {}^{10}C_{10}(3)^2 = 32 + 9 = 41 = \lambda$

$\therefore$ $\left(\frac{\lambda+1}{4}\right) = \frac{42}{14} = 3$

9. $R = (5\sqrt{5}+11)^{2n+1} = [R] + f; 0 < f < 1$ and

$[5\sqrt{5}-11]^{2n+1} = f' \in (0,1)$

Now $[R] + f - f' = (5\sqrt{5}+11)^{2n+1} - (5\sqrt{5}-11)^{2n+1}$

$= 2\left[{}^{2n+1}C_1(5\sqrt{5})^{2n}(11)^1 + {}^{2n+1}C_3(5\sqrt{5})^{2n-2}(11)^3 + ...\right]$

$= 2k; k \in \mathbb{Z}$

But $-1 < f - f' < 1 \Rightarrow f - f' = 0$

$\Rightarrow$ $f = f'$

$\therefore$ $[R] = 2k$

$\therefore$ $f = (5\sqrt{5} - 11)^{2n+1}$

$\therefore$ $Rf = (5\sqrt{5}+11)^{2n+1}.(5\sqrt{5}-11)^{2n+1} = (125 - 121)^{2n+1} = (4)^{2n+1} = (k)^{2n+1}$

$\Rightarrow$ $k = 4$

10. Let $(\sqrt{2}+1)^6 = R + f$; where $R = [\sqrt{2}+1]^6$ and

$f = \left\{(\sqrt{2}+1)^6\right\}$

$\therefore$ $f \in (0, 1)$

Now let $f'(\sqrt{2}-1)^6 \in (0, 1)$

$\therefore$ $R + f + f' = (\sqrt{2}+1)^6 + (\sqrt{2}-1)^6 = 2[{}^6C_0(\sqrt{2})^6 + {}^6C_2(\sqrt{2})^4 + {}^6C_4(\sqrt{2})^2) + {}^6C_6(\sqrt{2})^0] = 2k$ (say); $k \in \mathbb{Z}$

$\Rightarrow$ $f + f' \in \mathbb{Z}$ but $f + f' \in (0, 2)$

$\Rightarrow$ $f + f' = 1$

$\therefore$ $R + 1 = 2[8 + 60 + 30 + 1]$

$\Rightarrow$ $R = 197 = \lambda$ (given)

$\therefore$ $\sqrt{\sqrt{\lambda-1}+2} = \sqrt{\sqrt{196}+2} = 4$

11. $(\sqrt{3}+1)^{18} = \left[(\sqrt{3}+1)^9\right]^2$

Let $(\sqrt{3}+1)^9 = R + f; 0 < f < 1$ and let

$(\sqrt{3}-1)^9 = f'; 0 < f' < 1$

Now $R + f - f' = (\sqrt{3}+1)^9 - (\sqrt{3}-1)^9$

$= 2\left[{}^9C_1(\sqrt{3})^8 + {}^9C_3(\sqrt{3})^6 + {}^9C_5(\sqrt{3})^4 + {}^9C_7(\sqrt{3})^2 + {}^9C_9\right]$

$= 2[9(3)^4 + 84(27) + 126(9) + 36(3) + 1]$

$= 2[729 + 2268 + 1134 + 109] = 8480$, but $f - f' = 0$ as $-1 < f - f' < 1$

$\therefore$ $R = 8480$

Now $(\sqrt{3}+1)^{18}$ $(R + f)^2 = R^2 + 2Rf + f^2$ (i)

Now, $(\sqrt{3}+1)^9 = R + f$

$\Rightarrow$ $(\sqrt{3}+1)^9 . f = Rf + f^2$

$\Rightarrow$ $(\sqrt{3}+1)^9 . f' = Rf + f^2$

$\Rightarrow$ $(\sqrt{3}+1)^9 . (\sqrt{3}-1)^9 = Rf + f^2$

$\Rightarrow$ $(3 - 1)^9 = Rf + f^2$

$\Rightarrow$ $(2)^9 = Rf + f^2$

$\Rightarrow$ $(2)^{10} = 2Rf + 2f^2$

$\Rightarrow$ $2Rf + f^2 = (2)^{10} - f^2$

$\therefore$ $(\sqrt{3}+1)^{18} = R^2 + 2Rf + f^2 = (8480)^2 + (2)^{10} - f^2 = (8480)^2 + (2)^{10} - (f')^2 = (8480)^2 + (2)^{10} - (\sqrt{3}-1)^{18}$

$\therefore$ $\left[(\sqrt{3}+1)^{18}\right] = (8480)^2 + (2)^{10} - 1$

$\therefore$ $\left[(\sqrt{3}+1)^{18}\right] + 1 = (8480)^2 + (2)^{10} = (2^5 \times 265)^2 + (2)^{10} = (2)^{10}[(265)^2 + 1]$

$\Rightarrow$ $m = (2)^{10}(70226) = (2)^{11}(35113) = (2)^{m+1}(35113)$

$\Rightarrow$ $m = 10$

12. Coefficient $x^{49} = \frac{-C_1}{C_0} - 2^2.\frac{C_2}{C_1} - 3^2.\frac{C_3}{C_2} - .... - 50^2\frac{C_{50}}{C_{49}}$

$= -\sum_{r=1}^{50} \frac{r^2 C_r}{C_{r-1}} = -\sum_{r=1}^{50} r^2.\left(\frac{50-r+1}{r}\right)$

$= -\sum_{r=1}^{50} r(51-r) = -51\sum_{r=1}^{50} r + \sum_{r=1}^{50} r^2$

$= -51\left(\frac{50 \times 51}{2}\right) + \frac{(50)(51)(101)}{6}$

$= -(51)^2 \times 25 + (25)(17)(101) = -22100 = \lambda$ (given)

$\therefore$ $\sqrt{22149+\lambda} = \sqrt{22149-22100} = \sqrt{49} = 7$

8 CHAPTER

Infinite Series

INTRODUCTION

In this chapter, we study the expansions which have infinite number of terms particularly binomial theorem for any index, exponential and logarithmic series.

These expansions have great use in different branches of Mathematics and Engineering Calculus. In algebra, the understanding of multinomial theorem too depends much over these concepts and expansions.

Using any of these expansions as identity and applying different mathematical operations over them to create new identities and subsequently deriving different useful and interesting results which will be always of a great fun to science loving students.

BINOMIAL THEOREM FOR ANY INDEX

It is more general form of binomial theorem in which the index (exponent) need not be always a natural number. The statement of theorem is given below: For any rational value of n,

$$(1+x)^n = 1+\frac{n}{1!}x+\frac{n(n-1)}{2!}x^2+\frac{n(n-1)(n-2)}{3!}x^3+....$$
$$....+\frac{n(n-1)(n-2)...(n-r+1)}{r!}x^r+...\text{to}\infty;$$

where $|x| < 1$ i.e., $-1 < x < 1$.

Expansion of $(x + a)^n$ for any rational index

Case I: When $|x| > |a|$ i.e., $|a/x| < 1$

In this case, $(x + a)^n = \{x(1 + a/x)\}^n = x^n (1 + a/x)^n$

$$= x^n\left\{1+n\frac{a}{x}+\frac{n(n-1)}{2!}(a/x)^2+\frac{n(n-1)(n-2)}{3!}(a/x)^3+.....\right\}$$

Case II: When $|x| < |a|$ i.e., $|x/a| < 1$

In this case, $(x + a)^n = \{a(1 + x/a)\}^n = a^n (1 + x/a)^n$

$$= a^n\left\{1+n\frac{x}{a}+\frac{n(n-1)}{2!}\left(\frac{x}{a}\right)^2+\frac{n(n-1)(n-2)}{3!}\left(\frac{x}{a}\right)^3+...\right\}$$

General term of $(1+x)^n$

The $(r + 1)^{th}$ term is called the general term and is denoted by T_{r+1} and $(r + 1)^{th}$ term in the expansion of $(1 + x)^n$ is given by $T_{r+1}=\frac{n(n-1)(n-2)...(n-r+1)}{r!}x^r$

ILLUSTRATION 1: If x is positive, then which is the second negative term in the expansion of $(1 + x)^{27/5}$?

SOLUTION: $T_{r+1}<0 \Rightarrow \frac{\left(\frac{27}{5}\right)\left(\frac{27}{5}-1\right).....\left(\frac{27}{5}-r+1\right)(x)^r}{r!}<0$

$$\Rightarrow \left(\frac{27}{5}\right)\left(\frac{22}{5}\right)\left(\frac{17}{5}\right)...\left(\frac{32-5r}{5}\right)\frac{(x)^r}{r!}<0$$

$$\frac{32-5r}{5}<0 \Rightarrow r>\frac{32}{5}\Rightarrow r\geq 7\ [\because r \text{ is a positive integer})$$

$\therefore$ 8th term is first negative term

$\Rightarrow$ 9th term will be + *ve*

$\Rightarrow$ 10th term will be – *ve*

$\therefore$ 10th term will be second – *ve* term

ILLUSTRATION 2: If x is so small that its square and higher power may be neglected, find the value of $(1-7x)^{1/3}(1-2x)^{-3/4}$.

SOLUTION:
$$(1-7x)^{1/3}(1-2x)^{-3/4} = \left[1-\frac{1}{3}(7x)+\left(\frac{1}{3}\right)\left(\frac{1}{3}-1\right)\left(-\frac{7x}{2!}\right)^2+\ldots\right]$$
$$\times\left[1+\left(\frac{-3}{4}\right)(-2x)+\left(\frac{-3}{4}\right)\left(\frac{-3}{4}-1\right)\left(-\frac{2x}{2!}\right)^2+\ldots.\right]$$
$$= 1+\frac{3}{2}x-\frac{7}{3}x \text{ (neglecting terms containing } x^2 \text{ and higher powers of } x) = 1-\frac{5x}{6}$$

ILLUSTRATION 3: Find the 8th term of $\dfrac{1}{\sqrt{1-3x}}$.

SOLUTION: $T_8 = (1-3x)^{-1/2}$
$$=\left(\frac{-1}{2}\right)\left(\frac{-1}{2}-1\right)\left(\frac{-1}{2}-2\right)\ldots.\left(\frac{-1}{2}-r+1\right)\left(-\frac{3x}{r!}\right)^r \text{; where } r=7$$
$$=\left(\frac{-1}{2}\right)\left(\frac{-3}{2}\right)\left(\frac{-5}{2}\right)\ldots.\left[-\left(\frac{1}{2}+r-1\right)\right](-3)^r\frac{x^r}{r!}\text{; } r=7$$
$$=\frac{(-1)^{2r}(1.3.5\ldots\ldots(2r-1))}{(2)^r}\frac{(3)^r.x^r}{r!}=\frac{(1.3.5\ldots..13)(3)^7x^7}{(2)^7\quad 7!}=\frac{(\pm\pm\pm\pm\pm\pm\pm\quad)}{7!}\left(\frac{3x}{2}\right)^7$$

ILLUSTRATION 4: Find the coefficient of x^5 in the expansion of $(1-2x)^{-5/2}$

SOLUTION:
$$T_{r+1}=\frac{\left(\frac{-5}{2}\right)\left(\frac{-5}{2}-1\right)\left(\frac{-5}{2}-2\right)\ldots\left(\frac{-5}{2}-r+1\right)(-2x)^r}{r!}$$

for coefficient of x^5; $r = 5$
$$\therefore\ T_6=\frac{(-5)(-7)(-9)(-11)(-13)}{5!}(-2)^5x^5=\frac{5\times7\times9\times11\times13\times32}{5\times4\times3\times2\times1}x^5=12012x^5$$

$\therefore$ Coefficient of $x^5 = 12012$

REMARKS

- *In the expansion of (1 + x)n for n $\in \mathbb{Q}$*
- *${}^nC_r$ can't be used because it is defined only for natural number.*
- *The expansion contains an infinite number of terms.*
- *If n is not a positive integer, we should write $(x+a)^n$ as $[x^n[1+a/x]^n]$, if $|x|>|a|$ and $(a+x)^n$ as $a^n[1+x/a]^n$, if $|x|<|a|$.*
- *If x be so small that its square and higher powers may be neglected, then approximate value of $(1+x)^n = 1+nx$.*

GREATEST TERM

To find the numerically greatest term in the expansion of $(1 + x)^n$. If T_{r+1} is the greatest term, then $|T_{r+1}| \geq |T_r|$

$\therefore \left|\frac{T_{r+1}}{T_r}\right| \geq 1$ or $\left|\frac{n-r+1}{r}x\right| \geq 1$. After simplification,

$$r \leq m; \text{ where } r = \left|\frac{|x|(n+1)}{|x|+1}\right|$$

Procedure: To find the greatest term in the expansion of $(1 + x)^n$; $|x| < 1$; $n \in \mathbb{Q}$

(a) Calculate $m = \left|\frac{|x|(n+1)}{|x|+1}\right|$

(b) If m is integer, then T_m and T_{m+1} are equal and both are greatest terms.

(c) If m is not integer, then $T_{[m]+1}$ is the greatest term where [.] denotes the greatest integer function.

Some important deductions

1. Replacing n by $-n$ in the expansion for $(1 + x)^n$, we get

$$(1+x)^{-n} = 1 - nx + \frac{n(n+1)}{2!}x^2 - \frac{n(n+1)(n+2)}{3!}x^3 + ... + (-1)^r\frac{n(n+1)(n+2)...(n+r-1)}{r!}x^r + ...$$

The general term in this expansion is $T_{r+1} = (-1)^r \frac{n(n+1)(n+2)...(n+r-1)}{r!}x^r$

2. Replacing x by $-x$ and n by $-n$ in the expansion of $(1 + x)^{-n}$, we get $(1 - x)^{-n} = 1 + nx + \frac{n(n+1)}{2!}x^2 - \frac{n(n+1)(n+2)}{3!}x^3 + ... + (-1)^r\frac{n(n+1)(n+2)...(n+r-1)}{r!}x^r + ...$

The general term in this expansion is

$$T_{r+1} = \frac{n(n+1)(n+2)...(n+r-1)}{r!}x^r$$

Putting $n = 1, 2, 3$ in the expansion of $(1 + x)^{-n}$, we get

$(1 + x)^{-1} = 1 - x + x^2 - x^3 + x^4 + ... + (-1)^r x^r + ...,$

$(1 + x)^{-2} = 1 - 2x + 3x^2 - 4x^3 + 5x^4 + ... + (-1)^r(r + 1)x^r + ...,$

$(1 + x)^{-3} = 1 - 3x + 6x^2 - 10x^3 + .. + (-1)^r\frac{(r+1)(r+2)}{2}x^r + ...$

Replacing x by $-x$ in the above expansions, we get

$(1 - x)^{-1} = 1 + x + x^2 + x^3 + ... + x^r + ...$

$(1 - x)^{-2} = 1 + 2x + 3x^2 + ... + (r + 1)x^r + ...$ and

$(1 - x)^{-3} = 1 + 3x + 6x^2 + ... + \frac{(r+1)(r+2)}{2}x^r + ...$

ILLUSTRATION 5: Show that $(53)^{53} - (33)^{33}$ is divisible by 10.

SOLUTION: $(53)^{53} = (50 + 3)^{53} = {}^{53}C_0(50)^{53}(3)^0 + {}^{53}C_1(50)^{52}(3)^1 + ... + {}^{53}C_{52}(50)^1(3)^{52} + {}^{53}C_{53}(50)^0(3)^{53}$

$= 10k_1 + (3)^{53}$; where $10k_1$ = sum of first 53 terms; $k_1 \in \mathbb{Z}^+$

We know that periodicity of 3 is 4

$\therefore (3)^{53} = (3)^{4(13)+1}$

$\Rightarrow$ Last digit of $(3)^{53}$ is 3

$\therefore$ Last digit of $(53)^{53}$ is 3

Also: $(33)^{33} = (30 + 3)^{33}$

$= {}^{33}C_0(30)^{33}(3)^0 + {}^{33}C_1(30)^{32}(3)^1 + ... + {}^{33}C_{32}(30)^0(3)^{32} + {}^{33}C_{33}(30)^0(3)^{33} = 10k_2 + (3)^{33}$

Again last digit at $(3)^{33}$ is 3

$\therefore$ Last digit of $(33)^{33}$ is 3

$\therefore$ Last digit of $(53)^{33} - (33)^{33}$ will be 0

$\Rightarrow (53)^{33} - (33)^{33}$ is divisible by 10

ILLUSTRATION 6: If x is so small that its square and higher powers may be neglected, find the value of $\frac{(8+3x)^{2/3}}{(2+3x)\sqrt{4-5x}}$.

SOLUTION: We have $\dfrac{(8+3x)^{2/3}}{(2+3x)\sqrt{4-5x}} = \dfrac{8^{2/3}(1+3x/8)^{2/3}}{(2)^2(1+3x/2)\sqrt{1-5x/4)}}$

$= \dfrac{2^2(1+3x/8)^{2/3}}{2^2(1+3x/2)(1-5x/8)}$ $[\because (1+x)^n = 1 + nx] = \dfrac{[(1+(2/3)\times(3x/8)]}{(1-5x/8+3x/2)} = \dfrac{[1+x/4]}{[1+7x/8]}$

$= (1+x/4)(1+7x/8)^{-1} = (1+x/4)(1-7x/8) = 1-7x/8+x/4 = 1-5x/8$

ILLUSTRATION 7: Find the coefficient of x^4 in the expansion of $\dfrac{1+x}{1-x}$ if $|x| < 1$.

SOLUTION: $\dfrac{1+x}{1-x} = (1+x)(1-x)^{-1}$

$= (1+x)\left[1+\dfrac{(-1)}{1!}(-x)+\dfrac{(-1)(-1-1)}{2!}(-x)^2+\dfrac{(-1)(-1-1)(-1-2)}{3!}(-x)^3+....\text{to}\,\infty\right]$

$= (1+x)(1+x+x^2+x^3+x^4+ \ldots \text{ to } \infty)$

$= 1+2x+2x^2+2x^3+2x^4+2x^5 \ldots \text{ to } \infty$

Hence the coefficient of $x^4 = 2$

ILLUSTRATION 8: Find a, b so that the coefficient of x^n in the expansion of $\dfrac{a+bx}{(1-x)^2}$ may be $2n+1$ and hence find the sum of the series $1+3(1/2)+5(1/2)^2+\ldots$

SOLUTION: $\dfrac{a+bx}{(1-x)^2} = (a+bx)(1-x)^{-2}$

or $\dfrac{a+bx}{(1-x)^2} = (a+bx)[1+2x+3x^2+\ldots+nx^{n-1}+(n+1)x^n+\ldots]$ (i)

$\therefore$ coefficient of $x^n = nb+(n+1)a = (a+b)n+a$

Given $(a+b)n+a = 2n+1$

Equating the coefficient of n and constant term, we get, $a+b=2$ (ii)

and $a = 1$ (iii)

Putting $a = 1$ in (ii), we get $b = 1$

Putting the values of a and b in (i), we get $\dfrac{1+x}{(1-x)^2} = (1+x)(1+2x+3x^2+\ldots)$

$= 1+3x+5x^2+7x^3+\ldots$

Putting $x = 1/2$, we get, $1+3(1/2)+5(1/2)^2+\ldots\ldots = \dfrac{1+1/2}{(1-1/2)^2} = 6$

TEXTUAL EXERCISE–1 (SUBJECTIVE)

1. Write down the first five terms in the expansion of $(1+x)^{-2}$, when $|x| < 1$.

2. Find the coefficient of x^n in the expansion of $(1-2x+3x^2-4x^3+\ldots\ldots..\infty)^3$ $|x| < 1$.

3. Write first four terms in the expansion of $\dfrac{\quad}{(4\quad 5\ ^2)^{1/2}}$.

   For what value of x is this expansion valid? Also find the general term.

4. Prove that the coefficient of x^r in the expansion of $(1-4x)^{-1/2}$ is $\dfrac{(2r)!}{(r!)^2}$.

5. Prove that the coefficient of x^n in the expansion of $\left(\dfrac{1+x}{1-x}\right)^2$ is $4n$ when $|x| < 1$. is it true, when $n = 0$? Find the coefficient when $n = 0$.

6. Find the coefficient of x^3 in the expansion of $\dfrac{3-2x}{1+3x^3}$ assuming that the expansion is possible.

7. If x be so small that its squares and higher powers are neglected, prove that

(a) $\dfrac{(1-3x)^{1/2}+(1-x)^{5/3}}{(4-x)^{1/2}}=1-\dfrac{35}{24}x$

(b) $\dfrac{\sqrt{1-x}+(1+x)^{2/3}}{1-x+\sqrt{(1-x)^{5/3}}}=1+x$

(c) $\left(1+\dfrac{3x}{4}\right)^{-4}(4-3x)^{1/2}=2-\dfrac{27}{4}x$

8. If x is nearly equal to 1, prove that

(a) $\dfrac{mx^m-nx^n}{m-n}=x^{m+n}$ (b) $\dfrac{mx^n-nx^m}{x^n-x^m}=\dfrac{1}{1-x}$

9. Compute

(a) $\sqrt{30}$ to 4 places of decimal

(b) Evaluate $\sqrt[3]{126}$ correct to 5 decimal places.

10. If $|x| < 1$, show that

(a) $(1+x)^{-2} = 1 - 2x + 3x^2 - 4x^3 + ...\infty$

(b) $(1-x)^{-3} = 1 + 3x + 6x^2 + 10x^3 + ...\infty$

11. Verify each of the following series as an expansion of a powers of a binomial and find its sum.

(a) $1+\dfrac{1}{6}+\dfrac{1.4}{6.12}+\dfrac{1.4.7}{6.12.18}+.........\text{to } \infty$

(b) $1+\dfrac{3}{4}+\dfrac{3.5}{4.8}+\dfrac{3.5.7}{4.8.12}+.........\text{to } \infty$

12. Find the coefficient of x^{24} in the multinomial expansion of $(1 + 3x + 6x^2 + 10x^3 + ...\text{to } \infty)^{2/3}$

13. If c be a quantity so small that c^3 may be neglected in comparison with l^3, show that $\sqrt{\left(\dfrac{l}{l+c}\right)}+\sqrt{\left(\dfrac{l}{l-c}\right)}$ is very nearly equal to $2+\dfrac{3c^2}{4l^2}$.

Answer Keys

1. $(1 - 2x + 3x^2 - 4x^3 + 5x^4)$

2. ${}^{n+5}C_5(-1)^n$

3. condition: $\dfrac{-2}{\sqrt{5}}<x<\dfrac{2}{\sqrt{5}};1+\dfrac{5}{16}x^2+\dfrac{75}{256}x^4+...$, coefficient of x^{2r}: ${}^{2r}C_r\left(\dfrac{5}{2^4}\right)^r X^{2r}$ first three terms values of x^2 and higher powers neglected.

5. 1

6. –9

9. (a) 5.4775 (b) 5.01329

11. (a) $3\sqrt{2}$ (b) $2\sqrt{2}$

12. 25

TEXTUAL EXERCISE–1 (OBJECTIVE)

1. The fourth term in the expansion of $(1 - 2x)^{3/2}$ will be

(a) $-\dfrac{3}{4}x^4$ (b) $\dfrac{x^3}{2}$

(c) $-\dfrac{x^3}{2}$ (d) $\dfrac{3}{4}x^4$

2. The expansion of $\dfrac{1}{(4-3x)^{1/2}}$ binomial theorem will be valid, if

(a) $x < 1$ (b) $|x| < 1$

(c) $-\dfrac{2}{\sqrt{3}}<x<\dfrac{2}{\sqrt{3}}$ (d) None of these

3. If $(a + bx)^{-2} = \dfrac{1}{4} - 3x + ...$, then $(a, b) =$

(a) (2, 12) (b) (–2, 12)

(c) (2, – 12) (d) None of these

4. $\dfrac{1}{\sqrt[3]{6-3x}}=$

(a) $6^{1/3}\left[1+\dfrac{x}{6}+\dfrac{2x^2}{6^2}+....\right]$

(b) $6^{-1/3}\left[1+\dfrac{x}{6}+\dfrac{2x^2}{6^2}+....\right]$

(c) $6^{1/3}\left[1-\dfrac{x}{6}+\dfrac{2x^2}{6^2}-....\right]$

(d) $6^{-1/3}\left[1-\dfrac{x}{6}+\dfrac{2x^2}{6^2}-....\right]$

5. $\left(\frac{a}{a+x}\right)^{\frac{1}{2}}+\left(\frac{a}{a-x}\right)^{\frac{1}{2}}=$

(a) $2+\frac{3x^2}{4a^2}+.....$ (b) $1+\frac{3x^2}{8a^2}+.....$

(c) $2+\frac{x}{a}+\frac{3x^2}{4a^2}+.....$ (d) $2-\frac{x}{a}+\frac{3x^2}{4a^2}+.....$

6. $(r+1)^{th}$ term in the expansion of $(1-x)^{-4}$ will be

(a) $\frac{x^r}{r!}$ (b) $\frac{(r+1)(r+2)(r+3)}{6}x^r$

(c) $\frac{(r+2)(r+3)}{2}x^r$ (d) None of these

7. In the expansion of $\left(\frac{1+x}{1-x}\right)^2$, the coefficient of x^n will be

(a) $4n$ (b) $4n-3$

(c) $4n+1$ (d) None of these

8. $\frac{1}{\left(x^2+\frac{1}{x}\right)^{\frac{4}{3}}}$ can be expanded by binomial theorem, if

(a) $x<1$ (b) $|x|<1$

(c) $x>1$ (d) $|x|>1$

9. If $|x|<1$ then the coefficient of x^n in the expansion of $(1+x+x^2+...)^2$ will be

(a) 1 (b) n

(c) $n+1$ (d) None of these

10. If $|x|<1$, then in the expansion of $(1+2x+3x^2+4x^3+....)^{1/2}$, the coefficient of x^n is

(a) n (b) $n+1$

(c) 1 (d) -1

11. The sum of $1+n\left(1-\frac{1}{x}\right)+\frac{n(n+1)}{2!}\left(1-\frac{1}{x}\right)^2+......\infty$, will be

(a) x^n (b) x^{-n}

(c) $\left(1-\frac{1}{x}\right)^n$ (d) None of these

12. If $(r+1)^{th}$ term is the first negative term in the expansion of $(1+x)^{7/2}$, then the value of r is

(a) 5 (b) 6

(c) 4 (d) 7

13. If x is so small that x^3 and higher powers of x may be neglected, then $\frac{(1+x)^{\frac{3}{2}}-\left(1+\frac{1}{2}x\right)^3}{(1-x)^{\frac{1}{2}}}$ may be approximated as

(a) $-\frac{3}{8}x^2$ (b) $\frac{x}{2}-\frac{3}{8}x^2$

(c) $1-\frac{3}{8}x^2$ (d) $3x+\frac{3}{8}x^2$

Answer Keys

1. (b) **2.** (d) **3.** (a) **4.** (b) **5.** (a) **6.** (b) **7.** (a) **8.** (d) **9.** (c) **10.** (c)
11. (a) **12.** (a) **13.** (a)

■ MACLAURIN'S EXPANSION

Any function f(x) can be written as a polynomial with infinite degree in variable x as:

$$f(x)=f(0)+f'(0)\frac{x}{1!}+f''(0)\frac{x^2}{2!}+f'''(0)\frac{x^3}{3!}+...\infty;$$

provided $f(0), f'(0), f''(0), f'''(0)$, ... exist finitely.

Proof: Let $f(x)=a_0+a_1x+a_2x^2+a_3x^3+....\infty$ (i)

$\Rightarrow f(0)=a_0$ (ii)

$\because f'(x)=a_1+2a_2x+3a_3x^2+....$

$\Rightarrow f'(0)=a_1$ (iii)

$\Rightarrow f''(x)=2a_2+3.2\,a_3x+4.3a_4x^2+...$

$\Rightarrow \frac{f''(0)}{2!}=a_2$ (iv)

Proceeding similarly and substituting in (i), we get the result i.e., $f(x)=f(0)+f'(0)\frac{x}{1!}+f''(0)\frac{x^2}{2!}+...\infty$

■ TAYLOR'S EXPANSION

Any function f(x) can be written as a polynomial with infinite degree in variable $(x-a)$ as:

$$f(x)=f(a)+\frac{(x-a)}{1!}f'(a)+\frac{(x-a)^2}{2!}f''(a)+....\infty$$

Proof: Let $f(x) = a_0 + a_1(x - a) + a_2(x - a)^2 + a_3(x - a)^3 + \ldots\ldots \infty$ (i)

$\Rightarrow f'(x) = a_1 + 2a_2(x - a) + 3a_3(x - a)^2 + \ldots \infty$ (i)

$\Rightarrow f''(x) = 2a_2 + 3.2a_3(x - a) + \ldots\ldots \infty$ (iii)

Substituting $x = a$, we get

$f(a) = a_0 = a_0$

$f'(a) = a_1 = 1!(a_1)$

$f''(a) = 2a_2 = 2!(a_2)$ and so on.

Substituting all these values in (i), we get

$$f(x) = f(a) + \frac{f'(a)}{1!}(x-a) + \frac{f''(a)}{2!}(x-a)^2 + \frac{f'''(a)}{3!} + (x-a)^3 + \ldots\ldots\infty$$

ILLUSTRATION 9: Using Mac Lauren's series, find the expansion of following functions.

(a) e^x (b) $\sin x$

SOLUTION: (a) Let $f(x) = e^x \Rightarrow f'(x) = e^x \Rightarrow f''(x) = e^x \ldots\ldots$

$$\Rightarrow f(0) = 1 \text{ and } f'(0) = 1 \text{ and } f''(0) = 1 \Rightarrow e^x = 1 + \frac{x}{1!} + \frac{x^2}{2!} + \ldots.$$

(b) Let $f(x) = \sin x \Rightarrow f'(x) = \cos x \Rightarrow f''(x) = -\sin x \Rightarrow f'''(x) = -\cos x\ldots.$

$\Rightarrow f(0) = 0$ and $f'(0) = 1$ and $f'' = (0)$ and $f''(0) = -1$ and so on

$$\Rightarrow \sin x = x - \frac{x^3}{3!} + \frac{x^5}{5!} - \frac{x^7}{7!} + \ldots.$$

ILLUSTRATION 10: By expanding using Mac Lauren's theorem, prove the following:

(i) $\ln(1+x) = x - \frac{x^2}{2} + \frac{x^3}{3} - \frac{x^4}{4} + \ldots.[-1 < x \le 1]$

(ii) $\cos x = 1 - \frac{x^2}{2!} + \frac{x^4}{4!} - \frac{x^6}{6!} + \ldots.$

(iii) $\tan x = x + \frac{x^3}{3} + \frac{2x^5}{15} + \frac{17}{315}.x^7 + \ldots.$

(iv) $\tan^{-1} x = x - \frac{x^3}{3} + \frac{x^5}{5} - \frac{x^7}{7} + \ldots.$

SOLUTION: (i) $f(x) = \ln(1 + x) \ldots.; -1 < x \le 1$

$$\Rightarrow f'(x) = \frac{1}{1+x} \quad \Rightarrow f''(x) = \frac{-1}{(1+x)^2} \quad \Rightarrow f'''(x) = \frac{2}{(1+x)^3}$$

$$\Rightarrow f''''(x) = \frac{-6}{(1+x)^4} \text{ and so on}$$

$\Rightarrow f(0) = \ln 1 = 0 \quad \Rightarrow f'(0) = 1$

$\Rightarrow f''(0) = -1 \quad \Rightarrow f''(0) = 2$

$\Rightarrow f'''(0) = -6$ ($\therefore$ By Mac Lauren's theorem)

$$\Rightarrow f(x) = 0 + x + \frac{(-1)x^2}{2!} + \frac{(2)x^3}{3!} + \frac{(-6)x^4}{4!} + \ldots. \text{ or } \ln x = x - \frac{x^2}{2} + \frac{x^3}{3} - \frac{x^4}{4} + \ldots.$$

(ii) $f(x) = \cos x$

$\Rightarrow f'(x) = -\sin x$

$\Rightarrow f''(x) = -\cos x$

$\Rightarrow f'''(x) = \sin x$

$\Rightarrow f''''(x) = \cos x$ and so on.

$\Rightarrow f(0) = 1, f'(0) = 0; f''(0) = -1; f'''(0) = 0; f'''' (0) = 1,$

$\therefore$ By Mac Lauren's theorem; $f(x) = 1 + 0x + \frac{(-1)x^2}{2!} + \frac{(0)x^3}{3!} + \frac{(1)x^4}{4!} + ...$

$\Rightarrow \cos x = 1 - \frac{x^2}{2!} + \frac{x^4}{4!} + ...$

(iii) $f(x) = \tan x$

$\Rightarrow f'(x) = \sec^2 x$

$\Rightarrow f''(x) = 2\sec^2 x \tan x$

$\Rightarrow f'''(x) = 2\sec^4 x + 2\tan x\,(2\sec^2 x \tan x)$

$= 2\sec^4 x + 4\sec^2 x \tan^2 x$

$\Rightarrow f''''(x) = 2(4) \sec^3 x \sec x \tan x$

$+ 4\sec^2 x\,(2 \tan x.\sec^2 x)$

$+ 4 \tan^2 x\,(2\sec^2 x \tan x) = 16\sec^4 x \tan x + 8\sec^2 x \tan^3 x$

$\Rightarrow f(0) = 0; f'(0) = 1; f''(0) = 0$

$f'''(0) = 2; f''''(0) = 0$ and $f'''''(x)$ $(16 \sec^6 x)$ + terms containing $\tan x$

$\Rightarrow f'''''(0) = 16$

$\therefore$ By Mac Lauren's theorem,

$$f(x) = 0 + \frac{(1)x}{1!} + \frac{(0)x^2}{2!} + \frac{(2)x^3}{3!} + \frac{(0)(x^4)}{4!} + \frac{(16)x^5}{5!} + ... \Rightarrow \tan x = x + \frac{x^3}{3} + \frac{2}{15}x^5 + ...$$

(iv) $f(x) = \tan^{-1} x \quad \Rightarrow \quad f'(x) = \frac{1}{1+x^2} = (1+x^2)^{-1}$

$\Rightarrow f''(x) = (-1)\,(1 + x^2)^{-2}\,(2x) = -2x(1 + x^2)^{-2}$

$\Rightarrow f'''(x) = -2(1 + x^2)^{-2} - 2x\,(-2)\,(1 + x^2)^{-3}\,(2x)$

$\Rightarrow f''''(x) = (-2)\,(-2)\,(1 + x^2)^{-3}\,(2x) + 8x^2\,(-3)\,(1 + x^2)^{-4}\,(2x) + 8\,(1 + x^2)^{-3}\,(2x)$ and so on

$\Rightarrow f(0) = 0; f'(0) = 1; f''(0) = 0; f'''(0) = -2$ and so on

$\therefore$ By Mac Lauren's theorem, $f(x) = 0 + \frac{(1)x}{1!} + \frac{(0)x^2}{2!} + \frac{(-2)x^3}{3!} + ...$

$\Rightarrow f(x) = x - \frac{x^3}{3} + \frac{x^5}{5} - \frac{x^7}{7} + ...\infty$

EXPONENTIAL SERIES

The concept of 'e' was introduced by a great Swiss Mathematician Leonhard Euler, in his text of calculus in 1748. That is why, e is known as Euler Number.

Definition: (The number *e*)

The summation of the infinite series $1 + \frac{1}{1!} + \frac{1}{2!} + \frac{1}{3!} + \frac{1}{4!} + ...\infty$ is denoted by e which is equal to the limiting value of $(1 + 1/n)^n$ as n tends to infinity.

Proof: Let n be a natural number greater than 1, then $1/n < 1$. Using binomial theorem, we have $(1 + 1/n)^n$

$$= 1.n\frac{1}{n} + \frac{n(n-1)}{2!}(1/n)^2 + \frac{n(n-1)(n-2)}{3!}(1/n)^3 + ...$$

$\Rightarrow (1 + 1/n)^n = 1 + 1 + \frac{1}{2!}(1 - 1/n) + \frac{1}{3!}(1 - 1/n)\,(1 - 2/n) + ...$

This is an identity and it is true for all values of n, however large. If n is indefinitely large i.e., $n \to \infty$, then $1/n$, $2/n$, $3/n$ etc. will approach to zero.

$\therefore \quad \lim_{n\to\infty}(1+1/n)^n = 1+1+\frac{1}{2!}+\frac{1}{3!}+\frac{1}{4!}+...$

$\Rightarrow \quad \lim_{n\to\infty}(1+1/n)^n = 1+1+\frac{1}{2!}+\frac{1}{3!}+\frac{1}{4!}+... = e$

$\Rightarrow$ Thus $e = \lim_{n\to\infty}\left(1+\frac{1}{n}\right)^n = 1+\frac{1}{1!}+\frac{1}{2!}+\frac{1}{3!}+\frac{1}{4!}+...\infty$

Properties of *e*

(a) e lies between 2 and 3 i.e., $2 < e < 3$

$\left(\text{since } \frac{1}{n!} \le \frac{1}{2^{n-1}} \text{ for } n \ge 2\right)$

(b) The value of e, correct to 10 places of decimals, is 2.7182818284.

(c) e is an irrational (incommensurable) number.

(d) e is the base of natural logarithm (Napier logarithm). i.e., $\ln x = \log_e x$

The value of factorial of zero and $\frac{1}{(n-m)!}$ when $n < m$, i.e., $(n - m)$ is negative

(i) $0! = 1$

(ii) $\frac{1}{(n-m)!} = 0$

■ EXPANSION OF e^x IN TERMS OF X

For $x \in \mathbb{R}$, $e^x = 1+\frac{x}{1!}+\frac{x^2}{2!}+\frac{x^3}{3!}+...+\frac{x^r}{r!}+...\infty$

or $\quad e^x = \sum_{n=0}^{\infty}\frac{x^n}{n!}$

The above series is known as exponential series and e^x is called exponential function. Exponential function is also denoted by exp. x i.e., $\exp A = e^A \therefore \exp x = e^x$

Some standard results

1. e lies between 2 and 3.

Proof: We have, $e = 1+\frac{1}{1!}+\frac{1}{2!}+\frac{1}{3!}+\frac{1}{4!}+...\infty$

$\Rightarrow e = 2+\frac{1}{2!}+\frac{1}{3!}+\frac{1}{4!}+...\infty$

$\Rightarrow e-2 = \frac{1}{2!}+\frac{1}{3!}+\frac{1}{4!}+...\infty$

$\Rightarrow e - 2 =$ a positive number $\Rightarrow e > 2$ (i)

We know that $n! > 2^{n-1}$ for all $n > 2$

$\therefore \quad \frac{1}{n!} < \frac{1}{2^{n-1}}$ for all $n > 2$

$\Rightarrow \frac{1}{3!} < \frac{1}{2^2}, \frac{1}{4!} < \frac{1}{2^3}, \frac{1}{5!} < \frac{1}{2^4}...$

$\Rightarrow \frac{1}{3!}+\frac{1}{4!}+\frac{1}{5!}+....... < \frac{1}{2^2}+\frac{1}{2^3}+\frac{1}{2^4}+...$

$\Rightarrow 1+\frac{1}{1!}+\frac{1}{2!}+\frac{1}{3!}+\frac{1}{4!}+\frac{1}{5!}.......$

$< 1+\frac{1}{1!}+\frac{1}{2!}+\frac{1}{2^2}+\frac{1}{2^3}+\frac{1}{2^4}+...$

$\Rightarrow 1+\frac{1}{1!}+\frac{1}{2!}+\frac{1}{3!}+\frac{1}{4!}+....$

$< 1+1+\frac{1}{2}+\frac{1}{2^2}+\frac{1}{2^3}+\frac{1}{2^4}+...$

$\Rightarrow e < 1+\frac{1}{(1-1/2)} \left[\because 1+\frac{1}{2}+\frac{1}{2^2}+..... = \frac{1}{(1-1/2)} = 2\right]$

$\Rightarrow e < 1+2 = 3$ (ii)

From (i) and (ii), we get $2 < e < 3$.

2. e is an irrational number:

Proof: In fact, e is an irrational number and its value, to 10 places of decimal is 2.7182818284. Let us now prove that e is an irrational number.

If possible, let $e = p/q$, where p and q are positive integers. Then

$\frac{p}{q} = \left(1+\frac{1}{1!}+\frac{1}{2!}+...+\frac{1}{q!}\right)+$

$\left(\frac{1}{(q+1)!}+\frac{1}{(q+2)!}+...\infty\right)$

Multiplying both sides of (ii) by $q!$, we get,

$p(q-1)! = \left(1+\frac{1}{1!}+\frac{1}{2!}+...+\frac{1}{q!}\right)(q!)+$ (iii)

$\left(\frac{1}{(q+1)}+\frac{1}{(q+1)(q+2)}+....\right)$

Note that $p(q - 1)!$ and $\left(1+\frac{1}{1!}+\frac{1}{2!}+...+\frac{1}{q!}\right)(q!)$ are positive integer, therefore, from (iii), we get

$m = \frac{1}{q+1}+\frac{1}{(q+1)(q+2)}+\frac{1}{(q+1)(q+2)(q+3)+...}$

must be a positive integer.

But $\frac{1}{q+1}+\frac{1}{(q+1)(q+2)}+\frac{1}{(q+1)(q+2)(q+3)}+... <$

$$\frac{1}{q+1}+\frac{1}{(q+1)^2}+\frac{1}{(q+1)^3}+\ldots\left[\because \frac{1}{q+r}<\frac{1}{q+1}\ \forall r\geq 2\right]$$

$$=\frac{\frac{1}{q+1}}{1-\frac{1}{q+1}}=\frac{1}{q+1}\cdot\frac{q+1}{q}=\frac{1}{q}$$

Thus $m < 1/q$. But q is a positive integer. Therefore, $1/q \leq 1$ or $m < 1$. But this is not possible, as m is a positive integer.

Therefore, e cannot be a rational number.

3. If $a > 0$, then a^x is

$$a^x = 1+\frac{x}{1!}(\ln a)+\frac{x^2}{2!}(\ln a)^2+\frac{x^3}{3!}(\ln a)^3+\ldots..\infty \text{ for all}$$

real values of x.

Proof: We have, $e^x = 1 + x + \frac{x^2}{2!}+\frac{x^3}{3!}+\ldots$

Replacing x by cx in this series, we get

$$e^{cx} = \left(1+cx+\frac{(cx)^2}{2!}+\frac{(cx)^3}{3!}+\ldots.\infty\right)$$

$$\Rightarrow e^{cx} = 1+cx+\frac{c^2}{2!}x^2+\frac{c^3}{3!}x^3+\ldots.\infty$$

Let $e^c = a$. Then $c = \ln a$ and $e^{cx} = (e^c)^x = a^x$

Putting these values in (i), we get

$$a^x = 1+x(\ln a)+\frac{x^2}{2!}(\ln a)^2+\frac{x^3}{3!}(\ln a)^3+\ldots..\infty$$

Important deductions from exponential series

$$e^x = 1+\frac{x}{1!}+\frac{x^2}{2!}+\ldots+\frac{x^r}{r!}+\ldots\infty=\sum_{r=0}^{\infty}\frac{x^r}{r!} \quad (1)$$

$$e^{-x} = 1-\frac{x}{1!}+\frac{x^2}{2!}-\ldots+\frac{x^r(-1)^r}{r!}+\ldots\infty=\sum_{r=0}^{\infty}\frac{x^r(-1)^r}{r!} \quad (2)$$

$$\Rightarrow \frac{e^x+e^{-x}}{2}=1+\frac{x^2}{2!}+\frac{x^4}{4!}+\frac{x^6}{6!}+\ldots+\frac{x^{2r}}{2r\,!}+\ldots \quad (3)$$

$$\Rightarrow \frac{e^x+e^{-x}}{2}=\sum_{r=0}^{\infty}\frac{x^{2r}}{(2r)!}$$

and $$\frac{e^x-e^{-x}}{2}=\frac{x}{1!}+\frac{x^3}{3!}+\frac{x^5}{5!}+\ldots+\frac{x^{2r+1}}{(2r+1)!}+\ldots \quad (4)$$

or $$\frac{e^x-e^{-x}}{2}=\sum_{r=0}^{\infty}\frac{x^{2r+1}}{(2r+1)!}$$

Putting $x = 1$ in (1), (2), (3) and (4), we obtain

$$e=1+\frac{1}{1!}+\frac{1}{2!}+\frac{1}{3!}+\ldots\infty \text{ or } e=\sum_{r=0}^{\infty}\frac{1}{r!} \quad (5)$$

$$e^{-1}=1-\frac{1}{1!}+\frac{1}{2!}-\frac{1}{3!}+\ldots\infty \text{ or } e^{-1}=\sum_{r=0}^{\infty}\frac{(-1)^r}{r!} \quad (6)$$

$$\frac{e+e^{-1}}{2}=1+\frac{1}{2!}+\frac{1}{4!}+\frac{1}{6!}+\ldots\infty \text{ or } \frac{e+e^{-1}}{2}=\sum_{r=0}^{\infty}\frac{1}{2r!} \quad (7)$$

and $$\frac{e-e^{-1}}{2}=\frac{1}{1!}+\frac{1}{3!}+\frac{1}{5!}+\ldots\infty \text{ or}$$

$$\frac{e-e^{-1}}{2}=\sum_{r=0}^{\infty}\frac{1}{(2r+1)!} \quad (8)$$

ILLUSTRATION 11: Find the sum of the infinite series:

(a) $\frac{2}{3!}+\frac{4}{5!}+\frac{6}{7!}+\frac{8}{9!}+\ldots\infty$ (b) $\frac{2}{1!}+\frac{4}{3!}+\frac{6}{5!}+\frac{8}{7!}+\ldots\infty$

SOLUTION: (a) Given series is $S=\frac{2}{3!}+\frac{4}{5!}+\frac{6}{7!}+\frac{8}{9!}+\ldots\infty$

$$=\left(\frac{3-1}{3!}\right)+\left(\frac{5-1}{5!}\right)+\left(\frac{7-1}{7!}\right)+\ldots\infty=\left(\frac{1}{2!}-\frac{1}{3!}\right)+\left(\frac{1}{4!}-\frac{1}{5!}\right)+\left(\frac{1}{6!}-\frac{1}{7!}\right)+\ldots\infty$$

$$=1-\frac{1}{1!}+\frac{1}{2!}-\frac{1}{3!}+\frac{1}{4!}-\frac{1}{5!}+\frac{1}{6!}-\frac{1}{7!}+\ldots.\infty=e^{-1}$$

(b) $$S=\frac{2}{1!}+\frac{4}{3!}+\frac{6}{5!}+\frac{8}{7!}+\ldots\infty=\left(\frac{1+1}{1!}\right)+\left(\frac{3+1}{3!}\right)+\left(\frac{5+1}{5!}\right)+\left(\frac{7+1}{7!}\right)+\ldots\infty$$

$$=1+\frac{1}{1!}+\frac{1}{2!}+\frac{1}{3!}+\frac{1}{4!}+\frac{1}{5!}+\frac{1}{6!}+\frac{1}{7!}+\ldots.\infty=e$$

ILLUSTRATION 12: Show that $\frac{4}{1!}+\frac{11}{2!}+\frac{22}{3!}+\frac{37}{4!}+\frac{56}{5!}+\ldots$ to $=6e-1$

SOLUTION: If U_n be the nth term of the given series. Then

$$U_n=\frac{n\text{th term of the series } 4,11,22,\ldots\ldots\ldots}{n!}$$

Let T_n be the nth term of the series 4,11,22,......... and S_n be the sum of n terms. Then

$S_n=4+11+22+37+\ldots\ldots\ldots+T_{n-1}+T_n$

Also $S_n=4+11+22+\ldots\ldots\ldots+T_{n-1}+T_n$

Subtracting, we get

$0=4+[7+11+15+19+\ldots\ldots\text{ to } (n-1) \text{ terms}]-T_n$

$\therefore\ T_n=4+\left(\frac{n-1}{2}\right)\left[2(7)+(n-2)4\right]$ (Summing up the A.P. series)

$=4+(n-1)\,[7+2n-4]\ =4+(n-1)\,(2n+3)\ =\ 2n^2+n+1$

$$\therefore\ U_n=\frac{2n^2+n+1}{n!}=\frac{2n(n-1)+3n+1}{n!}=\frac{2}{(n-2)!}+\frac{3}{(n-1)!}+\frac{1}{n!}$$

$$\Rightarrow\ S_n=2\sum_{n=1}^{\infty}\frac{1}{(n-2)!}+3\sum_{n=1}^{\infty}\frac{1}{(n-1)!}+\sum_{n=1}^{\infty}\frac{1}{n!}=2e+3e+(e-1)=6e-1$$

TEXTUAL EXERCISE–2 (SUBJECTIVE)

1. Prove that

(i) $\frac{5}{1!}+\frac{9}{2!}+\frac{13}{3!}+\frac{17}{4!}+\ldots\ldots\infty=5e-1$

(ii) $\frac{1}{3!}+\frac{1}{4!}+\frac{1}{5!}+\ldots\ldots=e-\frac{5}{2}$

(iii) $\frac{3e}{2}-\frac{1}{2e}-3=\frac{5}{3!}+\frac{7}{5!}+\frac{9}{7!}+\ldots\ldots\infty$

2. Find the sum of the series $1+\frac{1+2}{2!}+\frac{1+2+2^2}{3!}+\frac{1+2+2^2+2^3}{4!}+\ldots\infty$.

3. If $y=x-\frac{x^2}{2}+\frac{x^3}{3}-\frac{x^4}{4}+\ldots$ show that

$x=y+\frac{y^2}{2!}+\frac{y^3}{3!}+\ldots=(e^y-1)$

4. If $y=x-x^2+x^3-x^4+\ldots\infty$ then show that $x=y+y^2+y^3+\ldots\infty$.

5. Prove that the coefficient of x^n in the expansion of e^{e^x} is $\frac{1}{n!}\sum_{k=1}^{\infty}\frac{k^n}{k!}$

6. Find the coefficient of x^{10} in the expansion of e^{2+3x}. Also find the coefficient of x^n.

7. Find the coefficient of x^n in the expansion of $\frac{e^{5x}+e^x}{3e^{3x}}$.

8. Prove that...... $\frac{e^2-1}{2e}=\frac{1}{1!}+\frac{1}{3!}+\frac{1}{5!}\ldots\ldots$to ∞.

9. Sum the series up to infinite terms, whose n^{th} term is......

(a) $\frac{1}{(2n+3)!}$ (b) $\frac{1}{(n-2)!}$

10. If $a=\sum_{n=1}^{\infty}\frac{1}{(2n-1)!}$, $b=\sum_{n=0}^{\infty}\frac{1}{(2n)!}$. then find the quadratic equation whose roots are a and b.

11. Prove that $\frac{1.4}{0!}+\frac{2.5}{1!}+\frac{3.6}{2!}+\frac{4.7}{3!}+\ldots\ldots=11e$

12. Prove that

$$\left(1+\frac{1}{2!}+\frac{1}{4!}+\frac{1}{6!}+\ldots\right)^2-\left(1+\frac{1}{3!}+\frac{1}{5!}+\frac{1}{7!}+\ldots\right)^2=1$$

13. Prove that

$$\frac{e-1}{e+1}=\left(\frac{1}{2!}+\frac{1}{4!}+\frac{1}{6!}+....\right)\div\left(\frac{1}{1!}+\frac{1}{3!}+\frac{1}{5!}+....\right)$$

14. Prove that

$$\frac{e^2-1}{e^2+1}=\left(\frac{1}{1!}+\frac{1}{3!}+\frac{1}{5!}+....\right)\div\left(1+\frac{1}{2!}+\frac{1}{4!}+\frac{1}{6!}+....\right)$$

Answer Keys

2. $e^2 - e$

6. $\frac{e^2.3^n}{n!}, \frac{e^2 3^{10}}{\underline{|10}}$

7. $\begin{cases} 0 & \text{if } n \text{ is odd} \\ \frac{2^{n+1}}{3n!} & \text{if } n \text{ is odd} \end{cases}$

9. (a) $\frac{e-e^{-1}}{2}-1$ (b) e

10. $a=\frac{e-e^{-1}}{2}, b=\frac{e+e^{-1}}{2}; x^2-e.x+\frac{1}{4}\left(e^2-e^{-2}\right)=0$

TEXTUAL EXERCISE–2 (OBJECTIVE)

1. The coefficient of x^{10} in the series of e^2x is

(a) $\frac{2}{14175}$ (b) $\frac{4}{14175}$

(c) $\frac{1}{14175}$ (d) None of these

2. The coefficient of x^n in the expansion of e^{a+bx} in powers of x is

(a) $\frac{e^a b}{n!}$ (b) $\frac{e^{na}b^n}{n!}$

(c) $e^a\left(\frac{b^n}{n!}\right)$ (d) None of these

3. The coefficient of x^n in the expansion of $\frac{a+bx+cx^2}{e^x}$ is

(a) $\frac{(-1)^n}{n!}[a-bn+cn(n-1)]x^n$

(b) $\frac{1}{n!}\left[a-bn+\left(n(n-1)\right]\right.$

(c) $\frac{(-1)^n}{n!}\left[a+bn+\left(n(n-1)\right]\right.$

(d) None of these

4. Sum of the series $\sum_{n=1}^{\infty}\frac{1}{(n+1)!}$ is

(a) $e+1$ (b) $e-1$

(c) $e-2$ (d) None of these

5. Sum of the series $\sum_{n=1}^{\infty}\frac{1}{(2n+1)!}$ is

(a) $\frac{e+e^{-1}}{2}$ (b) $\frac{e-e^{-1}}{2}$

(c) $e-e^{-1}$ (d) None of these

6. Sum of the series $\sum_{n=1}^{\infty}\frac{x^n}{(n-2)!}$ is

(a) xe^x (b) x^3e^x

(c) x^2e^{-x} (d) x^2e^x

7. The value of $\frac{\left\{1+\frac{1}{2!}+\frac{1}{4!}+\frac{1}{6!}+....\infty\right\}}{\left\{1+\frac{1}{3!}+\frac{1}{5!}+\frac{1}{7!}+......\infty\right\}}$ is

(a) $\frac{e^2+1}{e^2-1}$ (b) $\frac{e^2-1}{e^2+1}$

(c) $\frac{e-1}{e+1}$ (d) $\frac{e^3-1}{e^3+1}$

8. The sum of infinite series $x+\frac{2^2}{2!}x^2+\frac{3^2}{3!}x^3+.....+\infty$

(a) x^2e^x (b) $(x+x^2)e^x$

(c) $(1+x)e^x$ (d) None of these

9. The sum of infinite series $\frac{2}{1!}+\frac{4}{3!}+\frac{6}{5!}+\frac{8}{7!}+......\infty$ is

(a) e^{-1} (b) e^2

(c) e^3 (d) e

10. The value of $\frac{1}{3!}+\frac{1}{5!}+\frac{1}{7!}+...$ is

(a) $\frac{e-e^{-1}-2}{2}$ (b) $\frac{e-e^{-1}}{2}$

(c) $\frac{e+e^{-1}}{2}$ (d) $\frac{e+e^{-1}-2}{2}$

Answer Keys

1. (b) **2.** (c) **3.** (a) **4.** (c) **5.** (d) **6.** (d) **7.** (a) **8.** (b) **9.** (d) **10.** (a)

LOGARITHMIC SERIES

We know that logarithm of any number N to the given base a is the exponent or index of the power to which the base must be raised to obtain the number N. Thus if $a^x = N$, x is called the Logarithm of N to the base a. It is also called designated as $\log_a N$.

$\therefore \quad \log_a N = x;\ a^x = N,\ a > 0,\ a \neq 1$ and $N > 0$

In Logarithmic series, we are taking number e as the base of the logarithm. Logarithms of numbers calculated to the base e are called *Naperian Logarithms* or *Natural logarithms* and the logarithms to the base 10 are known as *Common Logarithms*. Now, we will obtain an expansion for $\log_e(1 + x)$ as a series in powers of x which is valid only when $|x| < 1$.

If $-1 < x \leq 1$, then

$$\log_e (1 + x) = x - \frac{x^2}{2} + \frac{x^3}{3} - \frac{x^4}{4} + \ldots \infty \text{ or}$$

$$\log_e (1 + x) = \sum_{r=1}^{\infty} (-1)^{r-1} \frac{x^r}{r}.$$

Proof: $\dfrac{1}{1+x} = 1 - x + x^2 - x^3 + x^4 - x^5 + \ldots..$

$$\int_0^x \frac{1}{1+x}dx = x - \frac{x^2}{2} + \frac{x^3}{3} - \frac{x^4}{4} + \frac{x^5}{5} \ldots..\{(1+x)^{-1}\} \text{ using}$$

$$\Rightarrow \quad \ln[1+x] = x - \frac{x^2}{2} + \frac{x^3}{3} - \frac{x^4}{4} + \frac{x^5}{5} - \ldots.$$

Important deductions from logarithmic series

Since, $\log_e (1 + x) = x - \dfrac{x^2}{2} + \dfrac{x^3}{3} - \dfrac{x^4}{4} + \ldots,\ (-1 < x \leq 1)$ (1)

Replacing x by $-x$ in (1), we get

$$\log_e (1 - x) = -x - \frac{x^2}{2} - \frac{x^3}{3} - \frac{x^4}{4} - \ldots,\ (-1 \leq x < 1) \quad (2)$$

Adding (1) and (2), we get

$$\log_e [(1 + x)(1 - x)] = -2\left(\frac{x^2}{2} + \frac{x^4}{4} + \frac{x^6}{6} + \ldots\right),$$

$(-1 < x < 1)$ (3)

Subtracting (2) from (1), then

$$\log_e \left(\frac{1+x}{1-x}\right) = 2\left(x + \frac{x^3}{3} + \frac{x^5}{5} + \ldots \infty\right),\ (-1 < x < 1) \quad (4)$$

ILLUSTRATION 13: Show that the coefficient of x^n in the expansion of $\log(1+ x+ x^2)$ is -2/n or 1/n according as n is a multiple of 3 or not a multiple of 3.

SOLUTION: $\log(1+ x+ x^2) = \log\dfrac{(1+x+x^2)(1-x)}{1-x}$

$$= \log\left(\frac{1+x^3}{1-x}\right) = \log(1+x^3) - \log(1-x)$$

$$= \left[-x^3 - \frac{(x^3)^2}{2} - \frac{(x^3)^3}{3} - \ldots\right] - \left[-x - \frac{x^2}{2} - \frac{x^3}{3} - \ldots\right]$$

If n is a multiple of 3, the coefficient of

$$x^n = -\frac{1}{n/3} + \frac{1}{n} = -\frac{3}{n} + \frac{1}{n} = -\frac{2}{n}$$

If n is not a multiple of 3, the coefficient of $x^n = 1/n$

TEXTUAL EXERCISE–3 (SUBJECTIVE)

1. If α, β be the roots of the equation $ax^2 + bx + c = 0$, show that $\log(a - bx + cx^2) = \log a + (\alpha + \beta)x - \dfrac{(\alpha^2+\beta^2)}{2}x^2 + \ldots\ldots\ldots\infty$.

2. Prove that $2\log x - \log(x+1) - \log(x-1) = \dfrac{1}{x^2} + \dfrac{1}{2x^4} + \dfrac{1}{3x^6} + \ldots$

3. Prove that
$$\log[(1+x)^{1+x}(1-x)^{1-x}] = 2\left[\frac{x^2}{1.2} + \frac{x^4}{3.4} + \frac{x^6}{5.6} + \ldots\infty\right]$$

4. Evaluate the sum of the series $\dfrac{1}{1.2} - \dfrac{1}{2.3} + \dfrac{1}{3.4} - \dfrac{1}{4.5} + \ldots\ldots\ldots$ to ∞.

5. Evaluate the sum of the series
$$1 + \left(\frac{1}{2} + \frac{1}{3}\right)\frac{1}{4} + \left(\frac{1}{4} + \frac{1}{5}\right)\frac{1}{4^2} + \left(\frac{1}{6} + \frac{1}{7}\right)\frac{1}{4^3} + \ldots\ldots\ldots$$

6. Show that $\dfrac{2}{1}.\dfrac{1}{3} + \dfrac{3}{2}.\dfrac{1}{9} + \dfrac{4}{3}.\dfrac{1}{27} + \dfrac{5}{4}.\dfrac{1}{81} + \ldots\ldots = \dfrac{1}{2} + \log_e 3 - \log_e 2$

7. Prove that $\dfrac{(\log_e 2)^2}{2!} + \dfrac{(\log_e 2)^4}{4!} + \ldots\ldots\ldots\infty = \dfrac{1}{4}$.

8. Prove that $\log_e(x+a) - \log_e(x-a) = 2\left(\dfrac{a}{x} + \dfrac{a^3}{3x^3} + \dfrac{a^5}{5x^5} + \ldots\ldots\ldots\ldots\infty\right)$

9. Prove that

(a) $\log_e\left(\dfrac{x+1}{x}\right) = 2\left[\dfrac{1}{2x+1} + \dfrac{1}{3(2x+1)^3} + \dfrac{1}{5(2x+1)^5} + \ldots\ldots\ldots\infty\right]$

(b) $\log_e(x+2h) = 2\log_e(x+h) - \log_e x - \left[\left(\dfrac{h}{x+h}\right)^2 + \dfrac{1}{2}\left(\dfrac{h}{x+h}\right)^4 + \dfrac{1}{3}\left(\dfrac{h}{x+h}\right)^6 + \ldots\ldots\ldots\infty\right]$

10. Prove that ....

(a) $1 + \dfrac{1}{3.2^2} + \dfrac{1}{5.2^4} + \dfrac{1}{7.2^6} \ldots\ldots\ldots\infty = \log_e 3$

(b) $\dfrac{1}{1.3} + \dfrac{1}{2.5} + \dfrac{1}{3.7} + \ldots\ldots\ldots\infty = 2 - \log_e 2$

11. Prove that $\dfrac{1}{2.3} + \dfrac{1}{4.5} + \dfrac{1}{6.7} + \ldots\infty = 1 - \log_e 2$

12. Prove that
$$\frac{1}{2}\left(\frac{1}{2} + \frac{1}{3}\right) - \frac{1}{4}\left(\frac{1}{2^2} + \frac{1}{3^2}\right) + \frac{1}{6}\left(\frac{1}{2^3} + \frac{1}{3^3}\right) - \ldots\ldots = \ln\sqrt{2}$$

Answer Keys

4. $\log(4/e)$ 5. $\dfrac{1}{2}\log 12$

TEXTUAL EXERCISE–3 (OBJECTIVE)

1. The value of $\left(\dfrac{a-b}{a}\right) + \dfrac{1}{2}\left(\dfrac{a-b}{2}\right)^2 + \dfrac{1}{3}\left(\dfrac{a-b}{a}\right)^3 \ldots\ldots\ldots\ldots\ldots\infty$ is

(a) $\ell n\left(\dfrac{a}{b}\right)$ (b) $-\ell n\left(\dfrac{2b}{a}\right)$

(c) $\ell n(a+b)$ (d) $\ell n(a-b)$

2. The value of $\ell n\left(\dfrac{1+3x}{1-2x}\right)$ is

(a) $x - \dfrac{x^2}{2} + \dfrac{x^3}{3} - \dfrac{x^4}{4} + \ldots\infty$

(b) $5x - \dfrac{5}{2}x^2 + \dfrac{35}{3}x^3 - \dfrac{65}{4}x^4 \ldots\ldots\ldots\infty$

(c) $3x - \dfrac{9}{2}x^2 + \dfrac{27}{8}x^3 - \dfrac{64}{16}x^4 + \ldots\infty$

(d) None of these

3. The value of $\ell n\left(\dfrac{x+a}{x-a}\right)$ is

(a) $\left(\dfrac{a}{x} + \dfrac{a^3}{3x^3} + \dfrac{a^5}{5x^5} + \ldots\ldots\infty\right)$

(b) $\left(1 + \dfrac{a^2}{2x^2} + \dfrac{a^4}{4x^4} + \ldots\infty\right)$

(c) $2\left(\dfrac{a}{x} + \dfrac{a^3}{3x^3} + \dfrac{a^5}{5x^5} + \ldots\right)$

(d) $2\left(1 + \dfrac{a^2}{2x^2} + \dfrac{a^4}{4x^4} + \ldots\infty\right)$

4. The coefficient x^n in the expansion of $ln\,(1 + 3x + 2x^2)$ is

(a) $\frac{1}{n}\left(1+3^n\right)$ (b) $\frac{(-1)^{n-1}}{n}\left(1+2^n\right)$

(c) $\frac{(-1)^{n-1}}{n}\left(1+3^n\right)$ (d) None of these

5. The sum of infinite series $\frac{5}{1.2.3}+\frac{7}{3.4.5}+\frac{9}{5.6.7}+\ldots\infty$ is

(a) $\ell n\,2-1$ (b) $3\ell n\,2-1$

(c) $\ell n\left(\frac{8}{e}\right)$ (d) None of these

6. The sum of infinite series $\left(\frac{1}{1.2.3}+\frac{1}{3.4.5}+\frac{1}{5.67}+\ldots\infty\right)$

(a) $\ell n\,2-1$ (b) $\ell n\,2-\frac{1}{2}$

(c) $\frac{\ell n3}{\ell n2}$ (d) None of these

7. The sum of $\frac{1}{2}-\frac{1}{2.2^2}+\frac{1}{3.2^3}-\frac{1}{4.2^4}+\ldots$is

(a) $\ell n\left(\frac{2}{3}\right)$ (b) $\ell n\left(\frac{3}{2}\right)$

(c) $\frac{\ell n^3}{\ell 2}$ (d) None of these

8. The sum of $\frac{1}{5}+\frac{1}{2.5^2}+\frac{1}{3.5^3}+\frac{1}{4.5^4}+\ldots$ is

(a) $\ell n(4/5)$ (b) $\ell n(5/4)$

(c) $\frac{\ell n5}{\ell n4}$ (d) None of these

9. The sum of $1+\frac{1}{3}.\frac{1}{2^2}+\frac{1}{5}.\frac{1}{2^4}+\frac{1}{7}.\frac{1}{2^6}+\ldots$ is

(a) $ln3$ (b) $ln2$

(c) $ln4$ (d) $7n$

Answer Keys

1. (a) **2.** (b) **3.** (c) **4.** (b) **5.** (b) **6.** (b) **7.** (b) **8.** (b) **9.** (a)

MULTIPLE-CHOICE QUESTIONS

SECTION–I

OBJECTIVE-TYPE SOLVED EXAMPLES

1. The coefficient of x^n in the expansion of $\left(\frac{1+x}{1-x}\right)^2$ is

(a) $2n$ (b) $3n$
(c) $4n$ (d) $-3n$

Solution: (c) $\left(\frac{1+x}{1-x}\right)^2 = (1+x)^2(1-x)^{-2}$

$= (1+2x+x^2)[1+2x+3x^2+4x^3+...+ (n-1)x^{n-2}+nx^{n-1}+(n+1)x^n+...]$

$\therefore$ Coefficient of x^n in $\left(\frac{1+x}{1-x}\right)^2 = 1 \times (n+1) + 2 \times (n) + 1 \times (n-1) = n + 1 + 2n + n - 1 = 4n$

2. The coefficient of x^4 in the expansion of $(1 + 2x + 3x^2 + 4x^3 + ...)^{1/2}$ is

(a) 2 (b) 1
(c) 4 (d) 3

Solution: (b) We have, $(1 + 2x + 3x^2 + 4x^3 + ...)^{1/2}$
$= [(1-x)^{-2}]^{1/2} = (1-x)^{-1} = 1 + x + x^2 + ... + x^n + ..$
Hence, coefficient of $x^4 = 1$.

3. If x is nearly equal to 1, $\frac{ax^b - bx^a}{x^b - x^a}$ is nearly equal to

(a) $\frac{a}{x-1}$ (b) $\frac{a}{2x+1}$
(c) $\frac{a}{1+x}$ (d) $\frac{1}{1-x}$

Solution: (d) Let $x = 1 + h$, where h is so small that its square and higher powers can be neglected.

$$\therefore \frac{ax^b - bx^a}{x^b - x^a} = \frac{a(1+h)^b - b(1+h)^a}{(1+h)^b - (1+h)^a} = \frac{a(1+bh) - b(1+ah)}{(1+bh)-(1+ah)}$$

[Neglecting h^2 and higher powers of h]

$$= \frac{a-b}{(b-a)h} = -\frac{1}{h} = \frac{1}{1-x} \quad [\because x = 1+h]$$

4. The value of $(0.98)^{-3}$ upto 2 decimal places is

(a) 1 (b) 1.06
(c) 1.24 (d) 1.08

Solution: (b) $(0.98)^{-3} = (1 - 0.02)^{-3}$

$$= \left[1+(-3)(-0.02)+\frac{(-3)(-3-1)}{2!}(-0.02)^2 + \frac{(-3)(-3-1)(-3-2)}{3!}\times(-0.02)^3+...\right]$$

$= 1 + 0.0600 + 0.0024$

[Neglecting other terms as they contain 3 or more zeros just after decimal]
$= 1.0624 = 1.06$ upto two places of decimal

5. The coefficient of x^n in the expansion of e^{a+bx} in powers of x is

(a) $-e^a\left(\frac{b^n}{n!}\right)$ (b) $e^a\left(\frac{b^n}{2n!}\right)$
(c) $e^a\left(\frac{b^n}{n!}\right)$ (d) None of these

Solution: (c) We have $e^a.e^{bx} = e^a\left(\sum_{n=0}^{\infty}\frac{(bx)^n}{n!}\right)$

or $e^{a+bx} = e^a\left(1+\frac{(bx)}{1!}+\frac{(bx)^2}{2!}+\frac{(bx)^3}{3!}+...+\frac{(bx)^n}{n!}+...\right)$

$\therefore$ Coefficient of x^n in $e^{a+bx} = e^a\left(\frac{b^n}{n!}\right)$

6. The coefficient of x^2 in the expansion of e^{2x+3} as a series in powers of x is

(a) $-2e^4$ (b) $2e^3$
(c) -2 e (d) $-2e^6$

Solution: (b) We have $e^{2x+3} = e^{2x}.\ e^3 = e^3\left(\sum_{n=0}^{\infty}\frac{(2x)}{n!}\right)^n$

$\Rightarrow e^{2x+3} = e^3.\left(1+\frac{(2x)}{1!}+\frac{(2x)^2}{2!}+...+\frac{(2x)^n}{n!}+...\right)$

$\Rightarrow$ Coefficient of x^2 in $e^{2x+3} = e^3\left(\frac{2^2}{2!}\right) = 2e^3$.

7. If $S=\sum_{n=2}^{\infty} {}^nC_2 \frac{3^{n-2}}{n!}$, then $2S$ is

(a) e (b) e^2

(c) -2 e (d) e^3

Solution: (d) $T_n = {}^nC_2 \cdot \left(\frac{3^{n-2}}{n!}\right); n \in \{2,3,...\infty\}$

Then,

$$T_n = \frac{n!}{(n-2)!2!} \cdot \frac{3^{n-2}}{n!} = \frac{1}{2!}\frac{3^{n-2}}{(n-2)!} = \frac{1}{2}\left(\frac{3^{n-2}}{(n-2)!}\right)$$

$$\therefore \quad S = \sum_{n=2}^{\infty} T_n = \frac{1}{2}\sum_{n=2}^{\infty}\frac{3^{n-2}}{(n-2)!}$$

$$= \frac{1}{2}\left[\frac{3^0}{0!}+\frac{3^1}{1!}+\frac{3^2}{2!}+\frac{3^3}{3!}+...\infty\right] = \frac{1}{2}e^3$$

$\Rightarrow 2S = e^3$.

8. If $\frac{e^x}{1-x} = B_0 + B_1x + B_2x^2 + ... + B_nx^n$, then the value of $(B_n - B_{n-1})$ is

(a) 1 (b) $\frac{1}{n!}$

(c) $\frac{1}{2n!}$ (d) None of these

Solution: (b) We have,

$$\frac{e^x}{1-x} = B_0 + B_1x + B_2x^2 + ... + B_nx^n + ...\infty$$

$$\Rightarrow \quad e^x(1-x)^{-1} = B_0 + B_1x + B_2x^2 + ... + B_nx^n + ...\infty$$

$$\Rightarrow \quad \left(1+\frac{x}{1!}+\frac{x^2}{2!}+..+\frac{x^{n-1}}{(n-1)!}+\frac{x^n}{n!}+...\right)$$

$$(1+x+x^2+x^3+...+x^{n-1}+x^n+...\infty)$$

$$= B_0 + B_1x + B_2x^2 + .. + B_nx^n + ... \infty$$

On equating the coefficients of x^n and x^{n-1} on both sides, we get

$$\Rightarrow \quad \frac{1}{n!}+\frac{1}{(n-1)!}+...+\frac{1}{2!}+\frac{1}{1!}+1 = B_n$$

and $\frac{1}{(n-1)!}+\frac{1}{(n-2)!}+...+\frac{1}{2!}+\frac{1}{1!}+1 = B_{n-1}$.

$$\therefore \quad B_n - B_{n-1} = \frac{1}{n!}$$

9: The results of

$\left[\left(\frac{a-b}{a}\right)+\frac{1}{2}\left(\frac{a-b}{a}\right)^2+\frac{1}{3}\left(\frac{a-b}{a}\right)^3+...\infty\right]$ is equal to

(a) $2\log_e b + 2\log_e$ (b) $\log_e a + \log_e b$

(c) $\log_e b - \log_e a$ (d) None of these

Solution: (c) Let $x = \frac{a-b}{a}$.

Then the given series is $\left(x+\frac{x^2}{2}+\frac{x^3}{3}+...\infty\right)$

$$= -\left(-x-\frac{x^2}{2}-\frac{x^3}{3}-....\infty\right) = -\log_e(l-x)$$

$$= -\log_e\left(1-\frac{a-b}{a}\right) = -\log_e\left(\frac{b}{a}\right) = \log_e a - \log_e b$$

10. $\log(1 + 3x + 2x^2) = ...$

(a) $3x-\frac{5}{2}x^2+\frac{9}{3}x^3-\frac{17}{4}x^4+...$

(b) $x-\frac{3}{4}x^4+\frac{2}{3}x^3+\frac{10}{2}x^2+...$

(c) $2x-\frac{2}{3}x^3+\frac{7}{2}x^2+\frac{11}{4}x^4+...$

(d) None of these

Solution: (a) $\log(1 + 3x + 2x^2) = \log\{(1 + x)(1 + 2x)\} = \log(1 + x) + \log(1 + 2x)$

$$= \left(x-\frac{x^2}{2}+\frac{x^3}{3}-\frac{x^4}{4}+....\infty\right) + \left(2x-\frac{(2x)^2}{2}+\frac{(2x)^3}{3}-\frac{(2x)^4}{4}+...\infty\right)$$

$$= 3x - x^2\left(\frac{1}{2}+\frac{2^2}{2}\right)+x^3\left(\frac{1}{3}+\frac{2^3}{3}\right)-x^4\left(\frac{1}{4}+\frac{2^4}{4}\right)+....$$

$$= 3x-\frac{5}{2}x^2+\frac{9}{3}x^3-\frac{17}{4}x^4+..$$

11. $\dfrac{(a-1)-\frac{1}{2}(a-1)^2+\frac{1}{3}(a-1)^3-.....\infty}{(b-1)-\frac{1}{2}(b-1)^2+\frac{1}{3}(b-1)^3-....\infty}$ is equal to

(a) $\log_b a$ (b) $\log a$

(c) $-\log_a b$ (d) $\log_a b$

Solution: (a) Let $x = a - 1$ and $y = b - 1$. Then,

$$\frac{(a-1)-\frac{1}{2}(a-1)^2+\frac{1}{3}(a-1)^3-.....}{(b-1)-\frac{1}{2}(b-1)^2+\frac{1}{3}(b-1)^3-....} = \frac{x-\frac{x^2}{2}+\frac{x^3}{3}-...}{y-\frac{y^2}{2}+\frac{y^3}{3}-...}$$

$$= \frac{\log_e(1+x)}{\log_e(1+y)} = \frac{\log_e(1+a-1)}{\log_e(1+b-1)} = \frac{\log_e a}{\log_e b} = \log_b a.$$

12. The coefficient of x^n in the expansion of $\log_e(1 + 3x + 2x^2)$ is

(a) $\frac{(1)^{n-1}}{n}(1-2^n)$ (b) $\frac{(-1)^n}{n}(1-2^n)$

(c) $\frac{(-1)^{n-1}}{n}(1+2^n)$ (d) None of these

Solution: (c) We have,

$\log_e(1+3x+2x^2) = \log_e\{(1+x)(1+2x)\}$

$= \log_e(1+x) + \log_e(1+2x)$

$= \left(x - \frac{x^2}{2} + \frac{x^3}{3} - ... + (-1)^{n-1}\frac{(x)^n}{n} + ...\right)$

$+ \left(2x - \frac{(2x)^2}{2} + \frac{(2x)^3}{3} - ... + (-1)^{n-1}\frac{(2x)^n}{n} + ...\right)$

$\therefore$ Coefficient of x^n in $\log_e(1+3x+2x^2)$

$= \frac{(-1)^{n-1}}{n} + (-1)^{n-1}\frac{2^n}{n} = \frac{(-1)^{n-1}}{n}(1+2^n)$

13. $\left(\frac{1}{3} + \frac{1}{3.3^3} + \frac{1}{5.3^5} + \frac{1}{7.3^7} + ...\infty\right)$ is equal to

(a) 1/2 $\log_e 3$ (b) $\log_e 2$

(c) $\log_e 3$ (d) (1/2) $\log_e 2$

Solution: (d) We have:

$\left(\frac{1}{3} + \frac{1}{3.3^3} + \frac{1}{5.3^5} + \frac{1}{7.3^7} + ...\infty\right) =$

$\left(x + \frac{x^3}{3} + \frac{x^5}{5} + \frac{x^7}{7} + ...\infty\right)$, where $x = \frac{1}{3}$

$= \frac{1}{2}\log_e\left(\frac{1+x}{1-x}\right) = \frac{1}{2}\log_e\left(\frac{1+\frac{1}{3}}{1-\frac{1}{3}}\right) = \frac{1}{2}\log_e 2$

SECTION–II

SUBJECTIVE-TYPE SOLVED EXAMPLES

1: If the series $1 + \frac{x^3}{3!} + \frac{x^6}{6!} + ...; x + \frac{x^4}{4!} + \frac{x^7}{7!} + ...$ $\frac{x^2}{2!} + \frac{x^5}{5!} + \frac{x^8}{8!} + ...$ be denoted by S_1, S_2 and S_3, then show that $S_1^3 + S_2^3 + S_3^3 - 3S_1 S_2 S_3 = 1$

Solution: If ω is an imaginary cube root of unity

$S_1^3 + S_2^3 + S_3^3 - 3S_1 S_2 S_3 =$

$(S_1+S_2+S_3)(S_1+S_2\omega+S_3\omega)(S_1+S_2\omega^2+S_3\omega)$

Now $S_1 + S_2 + S_3 = 1 + x + \frac{x^2}{2!} + \frac{x^3}{3!} + \frac{x^4}{4!} + \frac{x^5}{5!} + ... = e^x$

and $S_1 + S_2\omega + S_3\omega^2 = \left(1 + \frac{x^3}{3!} + \frac{x^6}{6!} + ...\right) +$

$\omega\left(x + \frac{x^4}{4!} + \frac{x^7}{7!} + ...\right) + \omega^2\left(\frac{x^2}{2!} + \frac{x^5}{5!} + \frac{x^8}{8!} + ...\right)$

$= 1 + \omega x + \frac{\omega^2 x^2}{2!} + \frac{\omega^3 x^3}{3!} + \frac{\omega^4 x^4}{4!} + \frac{\omega^5 x^5}{5!} + ... = e^{\omega x}$

Similarly, $S_1 + \omega^2 S_2 + \omega S_3 = e^{\omega^2 x}$.

$\therefore\ S_1^3 + S_2^3 + S_3^3 - 3S_1 S_2 S_3 = e^x . e^{wx} . e^{w^2 x}$

$= e^{0.x} = e^0 = 1$ [$\because$ $(1+\omega+\omega^2) = 0$]

2. Prove that the coefficient of x^n in the expansion of e^{e^x} is $\frac{1}{n!}\sum_{i=1}^{n}\frac{i^n}{1!}$.

Solution:

$\because\ e^{kx} = 1 + kx + \frac{k^2x^2}{2!} + ... + \frac{k^n x^n}{n!} + ...$

$\therefore$ Coefficient of x^n in $e^{kx} = \frac{k^n}{n!}$

Now, $e^{e^x} = 1 + e^x + \frac{(e^x)^2}{2!} + \frac{(e^x)^3}{3!} + ...$

$= 1 + e^x + \frac{e^{2x}}{2!} + \frac{e^{3x}}{3!} + ... + \frac{e^{nx}}{n!} + ...$

$\therefore$ Coefficient of x^n in the expansion of e^{e^x}

$= \frac{1^n}{n!} + \frac{2^n}{2!n!} + \frac{3^n}{3!n!} + ... + \frac{n^n}{n!n!} = \frac{1}{n!}\sum_{i=1}^{n}\frac{i^n}{1!}$

3. Show that the coefficient of x^{24} in the expansion of $(1+3x+6x^2+10x^3+.......to\ \infty)^{2/3}$ is 25.

Solution: Let $S = 1+3x+6x^2+10x^3+$...........to ∞

and $xS = 0+x+3x^2+6x^3+$...........to ∞

Subtracting, we get

$S(1-x) = 1+2x+3x^2+4x^3+$.......to $\infty = \frac{1}{(1-x)^2}$

or $S = \frac{1}{(1-x)^3} = (1-x)^{-3}$

$\therefore\ (1+3x+6x^2+10x^3+........to\ \infty)^{2/3}$

$= [(1-x)^{-3}]^{2/3} = (1-x)^{-2}$

$= 1+2x+3x^2+......(r+1)x^r+$.......to ∞

$\therefore$ Coefficient of x^{24} (Taking $r = 24$) = 24 + 1 = 25

4. Prove that $1+\left(\frac{1}{2}+\frac{1}{3}\right)\frac{1}{4}+\left(\frac{1}{4}+\frac{1}{5}\right)\frac{1}{4^2}+\left(\frac{1}{6}+\frac{1}{7}\right)$

$$\frac{1}{4^3}+\ldots=\frac{1}{2}\ln 12$$

Solution: L. H. S.

$$=1+\left(\frac{1}{2}+\frac{1}{3}\right)\frac{1}{4}+\left(\frac{1}{4}+\frac{1}{5}\right)\frac{1}{4^2}+\left(\frac{1}{6}+\frac{1}{7}\right)\frac{1}{4^3}+\ldots\ldots\ldots\ldots$$

$$=\left(1+\frac{1}{3}\cdot\frac{1}{4}+\frac{1}{5}\cdot\frac{1}{4^2}+\frac{1}{7}\cdot\frac{1}{4^3}+\ldots\ldots\right)+$$

$$\left(\frac{1}{2}\cdot\frac{1}{4}+\frac{1}{4}\cdot\frac{1}{4^2}+\frac{1}{6}\cdot\frac{1}{4^3}+\ldots\ldots\right)$$

$$=\left(1+\frac{1}{3}\cdot\frac{1}{2^2}+\frac{1}{5}\cdot\frac{1}{2^4}+\frac{1}{7}\cdot\frac{1}{2^6}+\ldots\ldots\right)+$$

$$\left(\frac{1}{2}\cdot\frac{1}{2^2}+\frac{1}{4}\cdot\frac{1}{2^4}+\frac{1}{6}\cdot\frac{1}{2^6}+\ldots\ldots\right)$$

$$=2\left[\frac{1}{2}+\frac{1}{3}\left(\frac{1}{2}\right)^3+\frac{1}{5}\left(\frac{1}{2}\right)^5+\frac{1}{7}\left(\frac{1}{2}\right)^7+\ldots\ldots\right]+$$

$$\left[\frac{1}{2}\left(\frac{1}{2}\right)^2+\frac{1}{4}\left(\frac{1}{2}\right)^4+\frac{1}{6}\left(\frac{1}{2}\right)^6+\ldots\ldots\right]$$

$$=2\left[x+\frac{x^3}{3}+\frac{x^5}{5}+\frac{x^7}{7}+\ldots\ldots\right]+\left[\frac{x^2}{2}+\frac{x^4}{4}+\frac{x^6}{6}+\ldots\right]$$

$$\left(\text{where } x=\frac{1}{2}\right)$$

$$=2\left[\frac{1}{2}\ln\frac{1+x}{1-x}\right]+\left[-\frac{1}{2}\ln\{(1+x)(1-x)\}\right]$$

$$=\ln\frac{1+x}{1-x}-\frac{1}{2}\ln(1+x)(1-x);x=\frac{1}{2}$$

$$=\ln\frac{1+1/2}{1-1/2}-\frac{1}{2}\ln\left(1+\frac{1}{2}\right)\left(1-\frac{1}{2}\right)$$

$$=\ln 3-\frac{1}{2}\ln\frac{3}{4}=\ln 3-\frac{1}{2}\ln 3+\frac{1}{2}\ln 4$$

$$=\frac{1}{2}(\ln 3+\ln 4)=\frac{1}{2}\ln 3.4=\frac{1}{2}\ln 12=\text{R.H.S.}$$

5. Prove that $\log\left(1+\frac{1}{y}\right)^y=1-\frac{1}{1.2(y+1)}-$

$$\frac{1}{2.3(y+1)^2}-\frac{1}{3.4(y+1)^3}-\ldots\ldots$$

Solution: Put $\frac{1}{y+1}=x$, then

$$\text{R. H. S.}=1-\frac{x}{1.2}-\frac{x^2}{2.3}-\frac{x^3}{3.4}-\ldots\ldots$$

$$=1-\left(1-\frac{1}{2}\right)x-\left(\frac{1}{2}-\frac{1}{3}\right)x^2-\left(\frac{1}{3}-\frac{1}{4}\right)x^3-\ldots\ldots\ldots\ldots$$

$$=\left(1+\frac{1}{2}x+\frac{1}{3}x^2+\frac{1}{4}x^3+\ldots\right)-\left(x+\frac{1}{2}x^2+\frac{1}{3}x^3+\ldots\right)$$

$$=\frac{1}{x}\left(x+\frac{1}{2}x^2+\frac{1}{3}x^3+\ldots\ldots\right)-\left(x+\frac{1}{2}x^2+\frac{1}{3}x^3+\ldots\ldots\right)$$

$$=-\frac{1}{x}\ln(1-x)+\ln(1-x)=\left(1-\frac{1}{x}\right)\ln(1-x)$$

$$=\left[1-\frac{1}{\{1/(y+1)\}}\right]\ln\left[1-\frac{1}{(y+1)}\right]\left(\because\ x=\frac{1}{y+1}\right)$$

$$=-y\ln\left(\frac{y}{y+1}\right)=\ln\left(\frac{y+1}{y}\right)^y=\text{L.H.S.}$$

6. If m is nearly equal to n, then the value of the expression $\frac{(n+2m)}{(m+2n)}$ is nearly equal to $(m/n)^{1/3}$.

Solution: Since m is nearly equal to n

$\therefore$ $m = (1 + \lambda)n$ $\Rightarrow$ or $m/n = 1 + \lambda$ (i)

Where λ is so small that λ^2 and higher powers of λ may be neglected

$$\therefore\ \frac{(n+2m)}{(m+2n)}=\frac{1+2(m/n)}{(m/n)+2}$$

$$=\frac{1+2(1+\lambda)}{1+\lambda+2}=\frac{3+2\lambda}{3+\lambda}=\frac{1+2\lambda/3}{1+\lambda/3}$$

$$=\left(1+\frac{2\lambda}{3}\right)\left(1+\frac{\lambda}{3}\right)^{-1}=\left(1+\frac{2\lambda}{3}\right)\left(1-\frac{\lambda}{3}\right)$$

$$=1-\frac{\lambda}{3}+\frac{2\lambda}{3}=1+\frac{\lambda}{3}$$

$= (1 + \lambda)^{1/3} = (m/n)^{1/3}$ (from (i))

7. Find the sum of first n terms of the harmonic series $\frac{1}{(a+b)}+\frac{1}{(a+2b)}+\frac{1}{(a+3b)}+\ldots$; where b is so small in comparison with a, such that b_2, b_3, ...etc., can be neglected.

Solution: Let,

$$S=\frac{1}{(a+b)}+\frac{1}{(a+2b)}+\frac{1}{(a+3b)}+\ldots\text{upto } n \text{ terms}$$

$$=\frac{1}{a(1+b/a)}+\frac{1}{a(1+2b/a)}+\frac{1}{a(1+3b/a)}+\ldots+t_n$$

$$= \frac{1}{a}\left[\frac{1}{(1+b/a)} + \frac{1}{(1+2b/a)} + \frac{1}{(1+3b/a)} + ... + t'_n\right]$$

$$= \frac{1}{a}\left[\left(1+\frac{b}{a}\right)^{-1} + \left(1+\frac{2b}{a}\right)^{-1} + \left(1+\frac{3b}{a}\right)^{-1} + ... + t'_n\right]$$

$$= \frac{1}{a}\left[\left(1-\frac{b}{a}\right) + \left(1-\frac{2b}{a}\right) + \left(1-\frac{3b}{a}\right) + ... + t'_n\right]$$

[∵ b is so small , ∴ (b/a) is very small, ∴ $(b/a)^2$, $(b/a)^3$, ...can be neglected]

$$= \frac{1}{a}\left[(1+1+1+...n \text{ terms}) - \frac{b}{a}(1+2+3+....n \text{ terms})\right]$$

$$= \frac{1}{a}\left[n - \frac{b}{a}.\frac{n(n+1)}{2}\right] = \frac{n}{a}\left[1 - \frac{b(n+1)}{2a}\right]$$

8. Show that the coefficient of x^n in the expansion of $\frac{x}{(x-a)(x-b)}$ in ascending powers of x is $\frac{a^n - b^n}{a-b}.\frac{1}{a^n b^n}$ and that coefficient of x^{2n} in the expansion of $\frac{(1+x^2)^n}{(1-x)^3}$ is $2^{n-1}(n^2+4n+2)$.

Solution: Since $\frac{x}{(x-a)(x-b)} = \frac{A}{x-a} + \frac{B}{x-b}$

∴ $A = \frac{a}{a-b}$ and $B = -\frac{b}{a-b}$

$$∴ \frac{x}{(x-a)(x-b)} = \frac{a}{a-b}\frac{1}{x-a} - \frac{b}{a-b}\frac{1}{x-b}$$

$$= \frac{a}{(a-b)(-a)(1-x/a)} - \frac{b}{(a-b)(-b)(1-x/b)}$$

$$= -\frac{1}{a-b}\left(1-\frac{x}{a}\right)^{-1} + \frac{1}{(a-b)}\left(1-\frac{x}{b}\right)^{-1}$$

$$= \frac{-1}{a-b}\left[1+\frac{x}{a}+\frac{x^2}{a^2}+....+\frac{x^n}{a^n}+....\right] + \frac{1}{(a-b)}\left[1+\frac{x}{b}+\frac{x^2}{b^2}+....+\frac{x^n}{b^n}+....\right]$$

Hence coefficient of x^n in $\frac{x}{(x-a)(x-b)}$ is

$$\frac{1}{(a-b)a^n} + \frac{1}{(a-b)b^n} = \frac{a^n - b^n}{a-b}.\frac{1}{a^n b^n}$$

Now $\frac{(1+x^2)^n}{(1-x)^3} = (1+x^2)^n(1-x)^{-3}$

$= (1 + {}^nC_1\, x^2 + {}^nC_2\, x^4 + ... + {}^nC_{n-2}\, x^{2n-4} + {}^nC_{n-1}\, x^{2n-2} + {}^nC_n\, x^{2n}) \times (1 + {}^3C_1\, x + {}^4C_2\, x^2 + ... + {}^{2n+2}C_{2n}\, x^{2n} + ...)$

∴ coefficient of x^{2n} in $\frac{(1+x^2)^n}{(1-x)^3}$

$= {}^nC_0 + 6\,{}^nC_1 + 15\,{}^nC_2 + 28\,{}^nC_3 + ...+ (n+1)(2n+1)\,{}^nC_n$

$$= \sum_{r=0}^{n}(r+1)(2r+1)^n C_r$$

$$= 2\sum_{r=0}^{n} r^2\ {}^nC_r + 3\sum_{r=0}^{n} r\ {}^nC_r + \sum_{r=0}^{n} {}^nC_r \qquad \text{(i)}$$

Now $(1+x)^n = {}^nC_0 + {}^nC_1\, x + {}^nC_2\, x^2 + ... + {}^nC_n\, x^n$

Differentiating both sides w.r.to x, we get

$n(1+x)^{n-1} = {}^nC_1 + 2\,{}^nC_2\, x + 3\,{}^nC_3\, x^2 + ... + n\,{}^nC_n\, x^{n-1}$

Multiplying both sides by x

$nx(1+x)^{n-1} = {}^nC_1\, x + 2\,{}^nC_2\, x^2 + 3\,{}^nC_3\, x^3 + ... + n\,{}^nC_n\, x^n$

again differentiating both sides w.r.to x we get

$n[x(n-1)(1+x)^{n-2} + (1+x)^{n-1}.1] = {}^nC_1 + 2^2\,{}^nC_2\, x + 3^2\,{}^nC_3\, x^2 + ... + n^2\,{}^nC_n\, x^{n-1}$

Putting $x = 1$ in (ii), (iii) and (iv), we get

$$2^n = \sum_{r=0}^{n} {}^nC_r\ ,\ n.2^{n-1}\sum_{r=0}^{n} r.{}^nC_r, n(n+1)2^{n-2} = \sum_{r=0}^{n} r^2.{}^nC_r$$

Putting these values in (i), then coefficient of x^{2n} in $\frac{(1+x^2)^n}{(1-x)^3}$

$= 2n(n+1)\,2^{n-2} + 3n\,2^{n-1} + 2^n = n(n+1)2^{n-1} + 3n2^{n-1} + 2^n$

$= 2^{n-1}[n^2 + n + 3n + 2] = 2^{n-1}(n^2 + 4n + 2)$

9. If s_n denotes the sum of the first n natural numbers, prove that

(i) $(1-x)^{-3} = s_1 + s_2 x + s_3 x^2 + ... + s_n x^{n-1} + ...$

(ii) $2(s_1 s_{2n} + s_2 s_{2n-1} + s_n s_{n+1}) = \frac{(2n+4)!}{5!(2n-1)!}$

Solution: Given $s_n = \Sigma n = \frac{n(n+1)}{2}$

Coefficient of x^n in $(1-x)^{-3}$

$$= \frac{(-3)(-4)(-5)...(-3-n+1)}{n!}(-1)^n$$

$$= (-1)^n\frac{[3.4.5...(n+2)]}{n!}(-1)^n$$

$$= (-1)^{2n}\frac{[1.2.3.4.5...n(n+1)(n+2)]}{1.2.n!}$$

$$= \frac{(n+1)(n+2)}{2} = s_{n+1} = {}^{n+2}C_2$$

(i) $(1-x)^{-3} = 1 + 3x + 6x^2 + 10x^3 + ...$

$= 1 + {}^3C_1\, x + {}^4C_2\, x^2 + {}^5C_3\, x^3 + ... + {}^{n+1}C_{n-1}\, x^{n-1} + ...$

$= 1 + {}^3C_2\, x + {}^4C_2\, x^2 + {}^5C_2\, x^3 + ... + {}^{n+1}C_2\, x^{n-1} + ...$

$= {}^2C_2\, x + {}^3C_2\, x^2 + {}^4C_2 x^3 + ... + {}^{n+1}C_2\, x^{n-1} + ...$

$= s_1 + s_2 x + s_3\, x^2 + ... + s_n\, x^{n-1} + ...$

(ii) Since $s_1 + s_2 x + s_3\, x^2 + ... + s_n\, x^{n-1} + ...+ s_{2n-1}\, x^{2n-2} + s_{2n} x^{2n-1} + ... = (1-x)^{-3}$

squaring both sides, we get

$(s_1 + s_2 x + s_3\, x^2 + ... + s_n\, x^{n-1} + ... + s_{2n-1}\, x^{2n-2} + s_{2n} x^{2n-1} + ...)^2 = (1-x)^{-6}$

Now coefficient of x^{2n-1} in L.H.S

$= 2(s_1\, s_{2n} + s_2\, s_{2n-1} + ... + s_n\, s_{n+1})$

and coefficient of x^{2n-1} in R.H.S

$$= \frac{(-6)(-7)(-8)....[-6-(2n-1)+1]}{(2n-1)!}(-1)^{2n-1}$$

$$= (-1)^{2n-1}\frac{6.7.8....(2n+4)}{(2n-1)!}(-1)^{2n-1}$$

$$= (-1)^{4n-2}\frac{5!\,6.7.8....(2n+4)}{5!\,(2n-1)!}(-1)^{2n-1}$$

$$= 1.\frac{(2n+4)!}{5!\,(2n-1)!} = \frac{(2n+4)!}{5!\,(2n-1)!}$$

10. If p is nearly equal to q and $n > 1$, show that $\dfrac{(n+1)p+(n-1)q}{(n-1)p+(n+1)q} = \left(\dfrac{p}{q}\right)^{1/n}$. Hence, find the approximate value of $\left(\dfrac{99}{101}\right)^{1/6}$.

Solution: Let $p = q + h$ (say), where h is so small that its square and higher powers may be neglected. Then

$$\frac{(n+1)p+(n-1)q}{(n-1)p+(n+1)q} = \frac{(n+1)(q+h)+(n-1)q}{(n-1)(q+h)+(n+1)q}$$

$(\because p = q + h)$

$$= \frac{2nq+(n+1)h}{2nq+(n-1)h} = \frac{\left[1+\left(\dfrac{n+1}{2nq}\right)h\right]}{\left[1+\left(\dfrac{n-1}{2nq}\right)h\right]}$$

$$= \left[1+\left(\frac{n+1}{2nq}\right)h\right]\left[1+\left(\frac{n-1}{2nq}\right)h\right]^{-1}$$

$$= \left[1+\left(\frac{n+1}{2nq}\right)h\right]\left[1-\left(\frac{n-1}{2nq}\right)h\right]$$

$$= 1-\frac{nh}{2nq}+\frac{h}{2nq}+\frac{nh}{2nq}+\frac{h}{2nq} = 1+\frac{2h}{2nq}$$

$$= 1+\frac{h}{nq} = \left(1+\frac{h}{q}\right)^{1/n} = \left(\frac{q+h}{q}\right)^{1/n} = \left(\frac{p}{q}\right)^{1/n}$$

$(\because q + h = p)$

Deduction: Since $\dfrac{(n+1)p+(n-1)q}{(n-1)p+(n+1)q} = \left(\dfrac{p}{q}\right)^{1/n}$

Putting $p = 99$, $q = 101$ and $n = 6$

then, $$\frac{(6+1)\times 99+(6-1)\times 101}{(6-1)\times 99+(6+1)\times 101} = \left(\frac{99}{101}\right)^{1/6}$$

$$\Rightarrow \frac{1198}{1202} = \left(\frac{99}{101}\right)^{1/6} \quad \Rightarrow \frac{599}{601} = \left(\frac{99}{101}\right)^{1/6}$$

Hence approximate value of $\left(\dfrac{99}{101}\right)^{1/6}$ is $\dfrac{599}{601}$.

11. Find the first negative term in the expansion of $(1 + x)^{7/2}$ and $0 < x < 1$.

Solution: $$T_{r+1} \frac{\dfrac{7}{2}\left(\dfrac{7}{2}-1\right)\left(\dfrac{7}{2}-2\right)...\left(\dfrac{7}{2}-r+1\right)}{r!}x^r$$

This will be the first negative term when $\dfrac{7}{2}-r+1$ is negative.

That is when $\dfrac{9}{2}-r<0$ or $r>\dfrac{9}{2}$ i.e, what $r>4\dfrac{1}{2}$

Hence when $r = 5$, we get the first negative term and this is

$$\frac{\dfrac{7}{2}\left(\dfrac{7}{2}-1\right)\left(\dfrac{7}{2}-2\right)\left(\dfrac{7}{2}-3\right)\left(\dfrac{7}{2}-4\right)}{5!}x^5 = -\frac{7}{256}x^5$$

12. Find the coefficient of x^7 in the expansion of $(x - 2x^2)^{-3}$; $|x| < 1/2$.

Solution: Let x^7 occurs in T_{r+1}

Now, $$T_{r+1} = x^{-3}\frac{(-3)(-3-1)...(-3-r+1)}{r!}\left(\frac{2x^2}{x}\right)^r$$

$$= \frac{3.4.5.............(r+2)}{r!}2^r.x^{r-3}$$

Hence $r - 3 = 7 \quad \Rightarrow r = 10$

$\therefore$ Coefficient of x^7

$$= \frac{3.4.5...(10+2)}{10!}2^{10} = 66\times 2^{10} = 67584$$

13. If $y = 3x + 6x^2 + 10x^3 + ...$,

Prove that $x = \dfrac{y}{3}-\dfrac{1.4}{3^2 2!}y^2+\dfrac{1.4.7}{3^3.3!}y^3 - ....$

Solution: $y = 3x + 6x^2 + 10x^3 + ...$

$\Rightarrow 1 + y = 1 + 3x + 6x^2 + 10x^3 + ... = (1-x)^{-3}$;

$\therefore (1-x) = (1+y)^{-1/3}$

$$= 1+\left(-\frac{1}{3}\right)y+\frac{\left(-\frac{1}{3}\right)\left(-\frac{1}{3}-1\right)}{2!}y^2+$$

$$\frac{\left(-\frac{1}{3}\right)\left(-\frac{1}{3}-1\right)\left(-\frac{1}{3}-2\right)}{3!}y^3+.......$$

$$\therefore \quad x=\frac{y}{3}-\frac{1.4}{3^2 2!}y^2+\frac{1.4.7}{3^3 3!}y^3+......$$

14. Find the numericaly greatest term in $(1 + x)^{15/2}$; where $x = 2/3$.

Solution: Here

$$\frac{T_{r+1}}{T_r}=\frac{n-r+1}{r}.x=\frac{\frac{15}{2}-r+1}{r}.\frac{2}{3}=\frac{17-2r}{3r}$$

$\therefore$ $T_{r+1} \geq T_r$, according as $17 - 2r \geq 3r$

i.e., according as $r \leq 3\frac{2}{5} \Rightarrow r \leq 3$

Hence 4th term is the greatest term.

15. Find the coefficient of x^n in the expansion $\frac{(1+x)^2}{(1-x)^3}$ and write down the coefficient of x^5 and x^7.

Solution: $\frac{(1+x)^2}{(1-x)^3} = (1 + 2x + x^2)(1-x)^{-3}$

$= (1 + 2x + x^2)$

$.[1 + 3x + 6x^2+...+ \frac{1}{2}(n+1)(n+2)x^n+...]$

$\therefore$ Coefficient of

$$x^n=\frac{1}{2}(n+1)(n+2)+2.\frac{1}{2}n(n+1)+\frac{1}{2}(n-1)n$$

$$=\frac{1}{2}\left(n^2+3n+2+2n^2+2n+n^2-n\right)$$

$$=\frac{1}{2}\left(4n^2+4n+2\right)=2n^2+2n+1$$

$\therefore$ Coefficient of $x^5 = 2.5^2 + 2.5 + 1 = 61$

and coefficient of $x^7 = 2.7^2 + 2.7 + 1 = 113$

Remember

(1) If $|x| < 1$, and $n \in \mathbb{N}$

$(1 - x)^{-n} = 1 + {}^nC_1 x + {}^{(n+1)}C_2 x^2 + {}^{(n+2)}C_3 x^3 +...+ {}^{(n+r-1)}C_r x^r +...$

(i) General Term $T_{r+1} = {}^{(n+r-1)}C_r x^r$

(ii) Coeff. of x^r = coeff of $T_{r+1} = {}^{(n+r-1)}C_r$

(2) If $|x| < 1$, and $n \in \mathbb{N}$

$(1 + x)^{-n} = 1\ {}^nC_1 x + {}^{(n+1)}C_2 x^2 - {}^{(n+2)}C_3 x^3 +..+ (-1)^r\,{}^{(n+r-1)}C_r x^r +...$

(i) General term $T_{r+1} = (-1)^r\,{}^{(n+r-1)}C_r x^r$

(ii) Coeff. of x^r = coeff. of $T_{r+1} = (-1)^r\,{}^{(n+r-1)}C_r$

16. If $\ln\frac{1}{1+x+x^2+x^3}$ be expanded in ascending power of x, show that the coefficients of x^n is $-1/n$ if n is odd or of the form $4m + 2$ and $3/n$ if n is of the form $4m$.

Solution: $\ln\frac{1}{1+x+x^2+x^3}=\ln\frac{1}{(1+x)(1+x^2)}$

$$=\ln\left[(1+x)(1+x)^2\right]^{-1}$$

$$=-\ln(1+x)-\ln(1+x^2)$$

$$=-\left\{x-\frac{1}{2}x^2+\frac{1}{3}x^3-.....\right\}-\left\{x^2-\frac{1}{2}x^4+\frac{1}{3}x^6-...\right\}$$

Let n be odd. Then there is no term containing x^n in the second series.

$\therefore$ Coefficient of $x^n=-\frac{1}{n}$

Let $n = 4m + 2$

Then coeffcient of x^n = coefficient of x^{4m+2}

$$=\frac{1}{4m+2}-\frac{1}{2m+1}=-\frac{1}{4m+2}=-\frac{1}{n}$$

Let, $n = 4m$

Then coefficient of x^n = coefficient of

$$x^{4m}=\frac{1}{4m}+\frac{1}{2m}=3.\frac{1}{4m}=\frac{3}{n}$$

17. If x is small and if the expansion of $\frac{1}{(1-x)^2}+\frac{1}{(a+bx)^2}$ is equal to $2 + 3x +... \infty$, then find (a, b) and also the coefficient of x^n.

Solution: Given expression $=(1-x)^{-2}+\frac{1}{a^2}\left(1+\frac{bx}{a}\right)^{-2}$

$$=\left\{1+{}^2C_1x+{}^3C_2x^2+{}^4C_3x^3+....\right\}+$$

$$\frac{1}{a^2}\left\{1-{}^2C_1\left(\frac{bx}{a}\right)+{}^3C_2\left(\frac{bx}{a}\right)^2-...\right\}$$

Equating constant terms

$$\Rightarrow 1+\frac{1}{a^2}=2\Rightarrow a=\pm 1$$

Equating coefficient of x

$$\Rightarrow 2-\frac{1}{a^2}\left(\frac{2b}{a}\right)=3\Rightarrow b=\frac{-1}{2}a^3$$

Thus, $(a,b)=\left(1,\frac{-1}{2}\right),\left(-1,\frac{1}{2}\right)$

$$\Rightarrow \text{Coefficient of } x^n=(n+1)+\frac{(-1)^n}{a^2}(n+1)\left(\frac{b}{a}\right)^n$$

$$=(n+1)\left(1+\frac{1}{2^n}\right)$$

18. Find the coefficient of x^2 in $(1+x+x^2)^{10}$.

Solution: $(1+x+x^2)^{10} = \left[\frac{(1-x^3)}{1-x}\right]^{10}$

$$= \frac{(1-x^3)^{10}}{(1-x)^{10}}$$

$$= (1-x^3)^{10}(1-x)^{-10}$$

∴ Coefficient of x^2 in $(1+x+x^2)^{10}$

= Coefficient of x^2 in $(1-x^3)^{10}(1-x)^{-10}$

= Coefficient of x^2 in $(1-x)^{-10} = {}^{11}C_2 = 55$

19. If x is so small that x^3 and higher powers can be neglected, then $\frac{(1+2x)^{5/2}-\left(1-\frac{1}{3}x\right)^2}{(1+3x)^{1/2}} \simeq a + bx + cx^2$, then evaluate a, b and c.

Solution: $\frac{(1+2x)^{5/2}-\left(1-\frac{1}{3}x\right)^2}{(1+3x)^{1/2}}$

$$= \frac{\left[1+\frac{5}{2}(2x)+\frac{\left(\frac{5}{2}\right)\left(\frac{3}{2}\right)(2x)^2}{2!}\right]}{(1+3x)^{1/2}} - \frac{\left[1+2\left(\frac{-1}{3}x\right)+\frac{(2)(1)\left(\frac{-1}{3}x\right)^2}{2!}\right]}{(1+3x)^{1/2}}$$

$$= \frac{\left[1+5x+\frac{15x^2}{2}\right]-\left[1-\frac{2}{3}x+\frac{1}{9}x^2\right]}{(1+3x)^{1/2}}$$

$$= \left[\left(5+\frac{2}{3}\right)x+\left(\frac{15}{2}-\frac{1}{9}\right)x^2\right](1+3x)^{-1/2}$$

$$= \left[\frac{17}{3}x+\left(\frac{135-2}{18}\right)x^2\right](1+3x)^{-1/2}$$

$$= \left[\frac{17}{3}x+\frac{133}{18}x^2\right]\left(1-\frac{3}{2}x\right)$$

[neglecting terms giving x^3 and higher powers of x]

$$= \frac{17}{3}x+\frac{133}{18}x^2-\frac{17}{2}x^2 = \frac{17}{3}x-\frac{20}{18}x^2 = \frac{17}{3}x-\frac{10}{9}x^2$$

$$\Rightarrow a=0; b=\frac{17}{3}; c=\frac{-10}{9}$$

SECTION–III

OBJECTIVE-TYPE (ONLY ONE CORRECT ANSWER)

1. If $|x| < 1$, then the coefficient of x^n in the expansion of $(1+x+x^2+x^3......)^2$ is

(a) n (b) $n-1$
(c) $n+2$ (d) $n+1$

2. The coefficient of x^4 in the expansion of $(1+x+x^2+x^3)^{11}$ is

(a) 900 (b) 909
(c) 990 (d) 999

3. The sum of the series $1+\frac{3}{1!}+\frac{5}{2!}+\frac{7}{3!}+....$ is

(a) $2e$ (b) $e-1$
(c) $3e$ (d) $5e-7$

4. If $|x| < 1$, the coefficient of x^3 in the expansion of $\frac{1}{e^x.(1+x)}$ is

(a) $\frac{17}{6}$ (b) $-\frac{17}{6}$
(c) $-\frac{11}{6}$ (d) None of these

5. The constant term in the expansion of $\frac{x+\log_e(1-x)}{x^3}$.

(a) –1/3 (b) 0
(c) –1/2 (d) 1/3

6. $\frac{1}{0!}+\frac{2}{1!}+\frac{3}{2!}+\frac{4}{3!}+....$ to ∞ is equal to

(a) $4e$ (b) $3e$
(c) $2e$ (d) None of these

7. The general term in the expansion of $(1-2x)^{3/4}$ is

(a) $-\frac{3^r}{2^r r!}x^r$ (b) $-\frac{3}{2^r r!}x^r$

(c) $-\frac{3^r}{2^r(2r)!}x^r$ (d) None of these

8. If $|x|<1$, then the value of $1+n\left(\frac{2x}{1+x}\right)+\frac{n(n+1)}{2!}\left(\frac{2x}{1+x}\right)^2+\ldots$to ∞

(a) $\left(\frac{1-x}{1+x}\right)^n$ (b) $\left(\frac{2x}{1+x}\right)^n$

(c) $\left(\frac{1+x}{1-x}\right)^n$ (d) $\left(\frac{2x}{1+x}\right)^{n-1}$

9. If x be very small compared with unity such that $\frac{\sqrt{(1+x)}+\sqrt[3]{(1+x)^2}}{\sqrt{(1+x)}+(1+x)}=a+bx$, then the value of a and b are

(a) $a=1, b=\frac{1}{6}$ (b) $a=1, b=-\frac{1}{6}$

(c) $a=1, b=\frac{1}{3}$ (d) $a=1, b=-\frac{1}{3}$

10. The coefficient of x^n in the expansion of $(1-9x+20x^2)^{-1}$ is

(a) $4^{n+1}-3^{n+1}$ (b) $5^{n+1}-4^{n+1}$

(c) 4^n+3^n (d) 5^n+4^n

11. If $(2+3x)^{-5}$ expanded in ascending powers of x, then $x\in$

(a) $[-1, 1]$ (b) $\left(-\frac{1}{3},1\right)$

(c) $\left(-\frac{1}{3},\frac{2}{3}\right)$ (d) $\left(-\frac{2}{3},\frac{2}{3}\right)$

12. The sum of the series $\frac{2}{3!}+\frac{4}{5!}+\frac{6}{7!}+\ldots$ is equal to

(a) $2e^{-2}$ (b) e^{-2}

(c) e^{-1} (d) $2e^{-1}$

13. $2\left[\frac{m-n}{m+n}+\frac{1}{3}\left(\frac{m-n}{m+n}\right)^3+\frac{1}{5}\left(\frac{m-n}{m+n}\right)^5+\ldots\right]$ is equal to

(a) $\log_e\left(\frac{m}{n}\right)$ (b) $\log_e\left(\frac{n}{m}\right)$

(c) $\log_e mn$ (d) $2\log_e mn$

14. If $y+\frac{y^3}{3}+\frac{y^5}{5}+\ldots\infty=2\left[x+\frac{x^3}{3}+\frac{x^5}{5}+\ldots\infty\right]$ then relation between x and y is

(a) $xy^2=2x-y$ (b) $xy^2=x-2y$

(c) $x^2y=2x-y$ (d) $xy^2=x-2y$

15. $\sum_{n=1}^{\infty}\frac{n^2}{n!}=$

(a) $e/2$ (b) e

(c) $2e$ (d) $4e$

6. The coefficient of x^4 in the expansion of $(1+2x+3x^2+\ldots)^{1/2}$ is

(a) 0 (b) 1

(c) 2 (d) 3

17. The coefficient of x^n in the expansion of $\frac{1}{(1-x)(3-x)}$ is

(a) $\frac{3^{n+1}-1}{2.3^{n+1}}$ (b) $\frac{3^{n+1}-1}{3^{n+1}}$

(c) $2\left(\frac{3^{n+1}-1}{3^{n+1}}\right)$ (d) None of these

18. If $x-\frac{x^2}{2}+\frac{x^3}{3}-\frac{x^4}{4}+\ldots$.to $\infty=y$ then $y+\frac{y^2}{2!}+\frac{y^3}{3!}+\ldots$.to ∞ is equal to

(a) $-x$ (b) x

(c) $x+1$ (d) None of these

19. If $\frac{e^x}{1-x}=B_0+B_1x+B_2x^2+\ldots.+B_nx^n+\ldots..$, then B_n-B_{n-1} equals

(a) $\frac{1}{n!}$ (b) $\frac{1}{(n-1)!}$

(c) $\frac{1}{n!}-\frac{1}{(n-1)!}$ (d) 1

20. The coefficient of x^n in the expansion of $\log_a(1+x)$ is

(a) $\frac{(-1)^{n-1}}{n}$ (b) $\frac{(-1)^{n-1}}{n}\log_a e$

(c) $\frac{(-1)^{n-1}}{n}\log_e a$ (d) $\frac{(-1)^n}{n}\log_a e$

21. The coefficient of x^4 in the expansion of $\frac{1}{(1-x)(3-x)}$ is

(a) $\frac{121}{243}$ (b) $\frac{242}{243}$

(c) $\frac{484}{243}$ (d) None of these

22. The coefficient of x^4 in the expansion of $\frac{(1+x)^2}{(1-x)^3}$ is

(a) n^2+2n+1 (b) $2n^2+n+1$

(c) $2n^2+2n+1$ (d) n^2+2n+1

23. If $y = x - x^2 + x^3 - x^4 + ...$ to ∞, then the value of x is

(a) $y/(1 - y)$ (b) $y/(1 + y)$

(c) $y - (1/y)$ (d) $y + (1/y)$

24. The approximate value of $(7.995)^{1/3}$ correct to four decimal places is

(a) 1.9995 (b) 1.9996

(c) 1.9990 (d) 1.9991

25. The sum of the series $1-\frac{1}{2}\left(\frac{1}{2}\right)+\frac{1.3}{2.4}\left(\frac{1}{2}\right)^2-\frac{1.3.5}{2.4.6}\left(\frac{1}{2}\right)^3+\frac{1.3.5.7}{2.4.6.8}\left(\frac{1}{2}\right)^4$ ......is

(a) $\sqrt{\frac{3}{2}}$ (b) $\sqrt{\frac{2}{3}}$

(c) $\sqrt{\frac{1}{3}}$ (d) $\left(\frac{1}{3}\right)^{1/3}$

26. If x is so small that its two and higher powers can be neglected and if $(1 - 2x)^{-1/2} (1 - 4x)^{-5/2} = 1 + kx$, then k is equal to

(a) 1 (b) –2

(c) 10 (d) 11

27. $y = -x^3 + \frac{x^6}{2} - \frac{x^9}{3} + ...$ to ∞ then the value of x^3 is

(a) $1 + e^y$ (b) $1 - e^y$

(c) e^y (d) $e^y - 1$

28. If $e^x = y + \sqrt{(1+y^2)}$, then the value of y is

(a) $e^x - e^{-x}$ (b) $1/2\ (e^x - e^{-x})$

(c) $e^x + e^{-x}$ (b) $1/2(e^x + e^{-x})$

29. If $S = \frac{1}{1.2} - \frac{1}{2.3} + \frac{1}{3.4} - \frac{1}{4.5} + ... + \infty$, then e^s equals

(a) $\log_e (4/3)$ (b) $4/e$

(c) $\log_e (e/4)$ (d) $e/4$

30. If $a=\sum_{n=1}^{\infty}\frac{2n}{(2n-1)!}$, $b=\sum_{n=1}^{\infty}\frac{2n}{(2n+1)!}$, then ab equals

(a) 1 (b) e^2

(c) $\frac{e-1}{e+1}$ (d) $\frac{e+1}{e-1}$

31. $1+\frac{1}{3}x+\frac{1.4}{3.6}x^2+\frac{1.4.7}{3.6.9}x^3+...$ is

(a) x (b) $(1 + x)^{1/3}$

(c) $(1 - x)^{1/3}$ (d) $(1 - x)^{-1/3}$

32. The sum of the series

$$1+\frac{1+a}{2!}+\frac{1+a+a^2}{3!}+\frac{1+a+a^2+a^3}{4!}+....\text{ is}$$

(a) $\frac{e^a-e}{a-1}$ (b) $\frac{e^a}{a-1}$

(c) $\frac{e^a-a}{a-1}$ (d) $\frac{e^a+e^{-a}}{a-1}$

33. The sum of the series $\frac{1.4}{0!}+\frac{2.5}{1!}+\frac{3.6}{2!}+\frac{4.7}{3!}+\frac{5.8}{4!}+....$ is

(a) 11 e (b) 10 e

(c) 9 e (d) 8 e

34. The sum of the series $\frac{1}{2}-\frac{1}{2.2^2}+\frac{1}{3.2^3}-\frac{1}{4.2^4}+...$ is

(a) log 2 (b) log (1/2)

(c) log (3/2) (d) None of these

35. If $S=\frac{y-1-\frac{1}{2}(y-1)^2+\frac{1}{3}(y-1)^3-....}{a-1-\frac{1}{2}(a-1)^2+\frac{1}{3}(a-1)^3-....}$, then S is equal to

(a) $\log_e y$ (b) $\log_a y$

(c) $\log_e a$ (d) $\log_y a$

36. If x is very large, the value of $\sqrt{(x^2+16)}-\sqrt{(x^2+9)}$ is

(a) $25/(2x)$ (b) $7/(2x)$

(c) $5/(2x)$ (d) $3/(2x)$

37. If $y = \frac{2}{6}+\frac{2.5}{6.12}+\frac{2.5.8}{6.12.18}+...\infty$, then the value of $(y + 1)$ is

(a) $2^{1/3}$ (b) $3^{1/3}$

(c) $4^{1/3}$ (d) $5^{1/3}$

38. The value of $(a + b)(a - b) + \frac{1}{2!}(a + b)(a - b)(a^2 + b^2) + \frac{1}{3!}(a + b)(a - b)(a^4 + a^2b^2 + b^4) + ...$ is

(a) $e^{a^2}-e^{b^2}$ (b) $e^{a^2}+e^{b^2}$

(c) $e^{a^2-b^2}$ (d) None of these

39. $\sum_{n=0}^{\infty}\frac{(\ln x)^n}{n!}$ is equal to

(a) $\ln x$ (b) x

(c) $1/\ln x$ (d) $1/x$

40. The coefficient of n^{-1} in the expansion of $\log_{10}\left(\frac{n}{n-1}\right)$ is

(a) $\frac{1}{n\log_e 10}$ (b) $-\frac{1}{n\log_e 10}$

(c) $-\frac{1}{n!\log_e 10}$ (d) $\frac{1}{n!\log_e 10}$

41. If x is small and $\frac{\left(1+\frac{3}{4}x\right)^{-4}\sqrt{(16-3x)}}{(8+x)^{2/3}} = P + Qx$, then (P, Q) is

(a) $\left(2,-\frac{307}{196}\right)$ (b) $\left(1,-\frac{305}{96}\right)$

(c) $\left(2,\frac{-305}{196}\right)$ (d) $\left(1,-\frac{307}{96}\right)$

42. In the expansion of $(1 + x)^{-3}$

(a) the third term is ${}^4C_2\,x^2$, if $|x| < 1$

(b) the third term is ${}^4C_2\left(\frac{1}{x}\right)^2$, if $x > 1$

(c) the value of the third term is – 3/2, when $x = 1/2$

(d) the value of the third term is – 2/81, when $x = -3$

43. $2\left[\frac{1}{2n+1}+\frac{1}{3(2n+1)^3}+\frac{1}{5(2n+1)^5}+...\right] = \log\left(\frac{n+1}{n}\right)$ is valid for

(a) all $n \neq 0, -1$ (b) $-1 < n < 0$

(c) $n < -1$ or $n > 0$ (d) no value of n

44. The sum of the series $\log_4 2 - \log_8 2 + \log_{16} 2 - ...$ is

(a) e^2 (b) $\log_e 2 - 1$

(c) $\log_e 3 - 2$ (d) $1 - \log_e 2$

45. Let $S = \frac{1}{n+1}+\frac{1}{2(n+1)^2}+\frac{1}{3(n+1)^3}+...$ and

$T = \frac{1}{n}-\frac{1}{2n^2}+\frac{1}{3n^3}-...$ then

(a) $S = 2T$ (b) $2S = T$

(c) $S = T$ (d) $S = 3T$

SECTION-IV

OBJECTIVE-TYPE (MORE THEN ONE CORRECT ANSWER)

1. If $x-\frac{x^2}{2}+\frac{x^3}{3}-\frac{x^4}{4}+...to\ \infty = y$ then $y+\frac{y^2}{2!}+\frac{y^3}{3!}+...$to ∞ is equal to

(a) $-x$ (b) x

(c) $x + 1$ (d) $e^y - 1$

2. The value of $\frac{1}{2}-\frac{1}{8}+\frac{1}{24}-\frac{1}{64}+...\infty$ is

(a) $\ln\frac{3}{2}$ (b) $\ln\frac{2}{3}$

(c) $\ln\left(\log_2 2\sqrt{2}\right)$ (d) None of these

3. The sum of infinite series $\frac{4}{1.3}-\frac{6}{2.4}+\frac{12}{5.7}-\frac{14}{6.8}+...\infty$ is

(a) $ln3$ (b) $ln2$

(c) $ln(\log_3 9)$ (d) None of these

4. The value of $\sum_{k=1}^{\infty}\sum_{r=0}^{k}\frac{1}{5k}\cdot{}^kC_r$ is

(a) $\frac{2}{3}$ (b) $\sum_{r=1}^{\infty}\left(\frac{2}{5}\right)^r$

(c) $\frac{2}{5}$ (d) None of these

SECTION-V

ASSERTION AND REASON TYPE

The questions given below consist of an assertion (A) and the reason (R). Use the following key to choose the appropriate answer.

(a) If both assertion and reason are correct and reason is the correct explanation of the assertion.

(b) If both assertion and reason are correct but reason is not correct explanation of the assertion.

(c) If assertion is correct, but reason is incorrect

(d) If assertion is incorrect, but reason is correct

Now consider the following statements:

1. A: $\sum_{n=1}^{\infty} \frac{{}^nC_0 + {}^nC_1 + {}^nC_2 + \dots\dots\dots + {}^nC_n}{{}^nP_n} = e^2$

R: $\sum_{r=0}^{\infty} \frac{x^r}{r!} = e^x$

2. A: Co-efficient of x^5 in $(1-x)^{-8}$ is ${}^{13}C_5$

R: Co-efficient of x^m in $(1-x)^{-n}$ is ${}^{n+1}C_m$.

3. A: $\left(\tan\theta + \frac{\tan^3\theta}{3} + \frac{\tan^5\theta}{5} + \dots\infty\right)$ where $|\tan\theta| < 1$ equals $\ln\sqrt{\tan\left(\frac{\pi}{4}+\theta\right)}$

R: $\ln(1+x) = x - \frac{x^2}{2} + \frac{x^3}{3} - \frac{x^4}{4} + ..$ and

$\ln(1-x) = -x - \frac{x^2}{2} - \frac{x^3}{3} - \frac{x^4}{4} - \dots for\ |x| < 1.$

4. A: Binomial expansion for $\left(1 - \frac{2}{\sqrt{3}}\sin\theta\right)^{-7/3}$ is valid for $\theta \in \left(-\infty, \frac{-\pi}{3}\right) \cup \left(\frac{\pi}{3}, \infty\right)$.

R: Binomial expansion for $(1+x)^n$; where n is -ve or fractional index is valid for $|x| < 1$.

SECTION–VI

LINKED COMPREHENSION TYPE

A: When 'n' is a negative integer or negative or positive fraction and $|x| < 1$ then

$(1+x)^n = 1 + nx + \frac{n(n-1)}{2!} + \frac{n(n-1)(n-2)}{3!} + \dots\dots$

In this case, we cannot expand $(1+x)^n$ as $C_0 + C_1x + C_2x^2 + \dots\dots$

$\because$ C_0, C_1C_2 are not defined then. Using above theorem, we have the following useful expansion.

$(1+x)^{-n} = 1 - nx + \frac{n(n+1)}{2}x^2 - \frac{n(n+1)(n+2)}{3!}x^3 + \dots\dots\dots\infty$ and

$(1-x)^{-n} = 1 + nx + \frac{n(n+1)}{2!}x^2 + \frac{n(n+1)(n+2)}{3!}x^3 \dots\dots\dots\dots\dots\infty$

Where $|x| < 1$.

If $n \in N$ then above two expansions can be written as

$(1+x)^{-n} = 1 - {}^nC_1x + {}^{n+1}C_2x^2 - {}^{n+2}C_3x^3 + \dots\dots\dots\dots\infty$

$= \sum_{r=0}^{\infty} {}^{n+r-1}C_r(-1)^r x^r$ and $(1-x)^{-n} = 1 - {}^nC_1x + {}^{n+1}C_2x^2 + {}^{n+2}C_3x^3 + \dots\dots\dots\dots\infty$

$= \sum_{r=0}^{\infty} {}^{n+r-1}C_r\, x^r$

Using the above results, we can find co-efficients of various powers of x in the expansion of $(1+x)^{-n}$ or $(1-x)^{-n}$.

1. Co-efficient of x^n in the expansion of $[1 + 3x + 6x^2 + 10x^3 + \dots\dots\dots\dots]^{-n}$ is, $n \in \mathbb{N}$.

(a) ${}^{3n}C_n$ (b) ${}^{3n}C_n(-1)^n$

(c) $-{}^{3n}C_n$ (d) None of these

2. Co-efficient of x^n in the expansion of $\frac{1+x^2-x^4}{(1+x)^3}$ is

(a) $\frac{x^2+5n-8}{2}$ (b) $(-1)^n({}^{n+2}C_2 - {}^{n-2}C_2)$

(c) $(-1)^n\left(\frac{n^2+7n-4}{2}\right)$ (d) None of these

3. Co-efficient of x^5 in the expansion of $(1-x)^{-3}$ is

(a) ${}^7C_2$ (b) ${}^7C_3$

(c) ${}^7C_4$ (d) ${}^7C_5$

B: Consider the following types of infinite series:

(i) $e^x = 1 + x + \frac{x^2}{2!} + \frac{x^3}{3!} + \dots\infty;\ x \in \mathbb{R}$

(ii) $\ln(1+x) = x - \frac{x^2}{2} + \frac{x^3}{3} - \frac{x^4}{4} + \dots$to ∞; $|x| < 1$

(iii) $\frac{1}{2}\ln\left(\frac{1+x}{1-x}\right) = x + \frac{x^3}{3} + \frac{x^5}{5} + \dots$to ∞; $|x| < 1$

(iv) $(1+x)^n = 1 + nx + \frac{n(n-1)x^2}{2!} + \frac{n(n-1)(n-2)x^3}{3!} + \dots + \frac{n(n-1)(n-2)\dots(n-r+1)x^r}{r!} + \dots$

for $|x| < 1$

n any –ve or fractional index.

(v) $a + ar + ar^2 + ar^3 + \dots = \frac{a}{1-r};\ |r| < 1;\ r \neq 0$

On the basis of above expansions and their corresponding domains, answer the following questions.

4. The value of $1-\frac{x}{1.2}-\frac{x^2}{2.3}-\frac{x^3}{3.4}-.....$ is

(a) $\ln(1-x)^{\left(\frac{x}{x-1}\right)}$ (b) $\ln(1-x)^{\left(\frac{x-1}{x}\right)}$

(c) $\ln(x)^{\left(\frac{x}{x-1}\right)}$ (d) None of these

5. The value of

$1+n\left(1-\frac{1}{x}\right)+n\left(\frac{n+1}{2!}\right)\left(1-\frac{1}{x}\right)^2+.....$ to ∞ will be

(a) x^{-n} (b) x^n

(c) $\left(1-\frac{1}{x}\right)^n$ (d) None of these

6. The sum of the series

$\cos\theta+\frac{\cos\theta}{\sin^2\theta}+\frac{\cos\theta}{\sin^4\theta}+\frac{\cos\theta}{\sin^6\theta}+..$ exist when

(a) $0<\theta<\frac{\pi}{2}$ (b) $\theta=\frac{\pi}{2}$

(c) $\frac{\pi}{2}<\theta<\pi$ (d) None of these

C: A function which exists at $x = 0$ and whose first derivative $\{f'(x)\}$, second derivative $\{f''(x)\}$ and so on exist at $x = 0$, can be expanded using $f(x) = f(0) +$ $f'(0)x+f''(0)\frac{x^2}{2!}+f'''(0)\frac{x^3}{3!}+......\infty$, and is called Mclaurin's expansion. Using this, we can expand functions like e^x, $In(1 + x)$ $\sin x$, $\tan x$, $\cos x$ etc.

For example: $e^x=e^0+e^0.x+e^0.\frac{x^2}{2!}+e^0.\frac{x^3}{3!}+..........\infty$

$\Rightarrow e^x=1+x+\frac{x^2}{2!}+\frac{x^3}{3!}+.........\infty=\sum_{n=0}^{\infty}\frac{x^n}{n!}$

Replacing x by $-x$;

$e^{-x}=1-x+\frac{x^2}{2!}-\frac{x^3}{3!}.........\infty=\sum_{n=0}^{\infty}(-1)^n\frac{x^n}{n!}$

Also we can expand $ln\,(1 + x)$

$ln(1+x)=x-\frac{x^2}{2}+\frac{x^3}{3}............\infty$

$=\sum_{n=0}^{\infty}(-1)^{n-1}\frac{x^n}{n}$, expansion is valid for $|x| < 1$ and $x = 1$

$ln\,(1-x)=-x-\frac{x^2}{2}-\frac{x^3}{3}............\infty$

$=-\sum_{n=0}^{\infty}\frac{x^n}{n}$. using above facts, answer the following questions:

7. Co-efficient of x^n in the expansion of $1-\left(\frac{x+1}{1!}\right)+\frac{(x+1)^2}{2!}-\frac{(x+1)^3}{3!}+...........\infty$

(a) $\frac{1}{e}$ (b) $\frac{1}{ne}$

(c) $\frac{(-1)^n}{n!e}$ (d) None of these

8. Co-efficient of x^4 in the expansion of $\frac{1-3x+x^2}{e^x}$ is

(a) $\frac{5}{24}$ (b) $\frac{4}{25}$

(c) $\frac{25}{24}$ (d) $\frac{24}{25}$

9. $1+\frac{1}{4.2!}+\frac{1}{16.4!}+\frac{1}{64.6!}+........\infty$ is

(a) $\frac{e+1}{\sqrt{e}}$ (b) $\frac{e-1}{\sqrt{e}}$

(c) $\frac{e+1}{2\sqrt{e}}$ (d) $\frac{e-1}{2\sqrt{e}}$

10. Co-efficient of x^6 in the expansion of $\log\,[(1 + x)^{1+x}.\,(1 - x)^{1-x}]$ is

(a) $\frac{1}{45}$ (b) $\frac{1}{30}$

(c) $\frac{1}{10}$ (d) $\frac{1}{15}$

SECTION–VII

MATRIX MATCH TYPE

1. Column-1

(i) $\frac{1^2}{1!}+\frac{2^2}{2!}+\frac{3^2}{3!}+......\infty$

(ii) $\sum_{n=0}^{\infty}\frac{n^2-n+1}{n!}$

(iii) $1.3+\frac{2.4}{1.2}+\frac{3.5}{1.2.3}+\frac{4.6}{1.2.3.4}+....\infty$

(iv) $\frac{12}{2!}+\frac{28}{3!}+\frac{50}{4!}+\frac{78}{5!}+....\infty$

Column-2

(a) $4e$

(b) $5e$

(c) $2e$

(d) $1+\frac{2^3}{2!}+\frac{3^3}{3!}+\frac{4^3}{4!}+....\infty$

2. Column-1

(i) If $(r + 1)$th term is the first negative term in the expansion of $(1 + x)^{7/2}$ then value of r (where $|x| < 1$) is

(ii) Co-efficient of x^4 in the expansion of $(1 + 2x + 3x^2 + 4x^3 + ...\infty)^{1/2}$ is c, $c \in \mathbb{N}$ then $c + 1$ where $|x| < 1$

(iii) Co-efficient of x^{401} in the expansion of $(1 + x + x^2 + ...x^9)^{-1}$ where $|x| < 1$ is

(iv) Number of values of r satisfying $^{69}C_{3r-1} - {}^{69}C_{r^2} = {}^{69}C_{r^2-1} - {}^{69}C_{3r}$

Column-2

(a) Divisible by 5

(b) A prime Number

(c) Divisible by 2

(d) < 0

3. Column-1

(i) $1+\frac{1}{3.2^2}+\frac{1}{5.2^4}+\frac{1}{7.2^6}+..........\infty$

(ii) $\frac{1}{1.2}-\frac{1}{2.3}+\frac{1}{3.4}-\frac{1}{4.5}...........\infty$

(iii) $1+\left(\frac{1}{2}+\frac{1}{3}\right)\frac{1}{4}+\left(\frac{1}{4}+\frac{1}{5}\right)\frac{1}{4^2}+...............\infty$

(iv) $\frac{1}{2}\left(\frac{1}{5}\right)^2+\frac{2}{3}\left(\frac{1}{5}\right)^3+\frac{3}{4}\left(\frac{1}{5}\right)^4+...........\infty$

Column-2

(a) $\frac{1}{4}+\log\frac{4}{5}$

(b) $\log_e 3$

(c) $\log\frac{4}{e}$

(d) $\log_e \sqrt{12}$

SECTION–VIII

INTEGER-TYPE QUESTIONS

1. If $|x| < 1$, then the co-efficient of x^{35} in the expansion of $(1 + x + x^2 + x^3 + ...)^2$ is λ, then evaluate $\sqrt{\lambda}$.

2. If x is so small such that its square and higher powers many be neglected, then the value of $\frac{(1-3x)^{1/2}+(1-x)^{5/3}}{(4-x)^{1/2}} \simeq 1-\frac{\lambda}{\mu}x$; where $\frac{\lambda}{\mu}$ is in lowest fraction, then evaluate $(2\mu - \lambda)$.

3. The co-efficient of x^{100} in $\frac{3-5x}{(1-x)^2}$ is k, then evaluate $\sqrt{\sqrt{|k|-1}+2}$.

4. If the value of $\left(1+\frac{1+2}{2!}+\frac{1+2+3}{3!}+\frac{1+2+3+4}{4!}+....\infty\right)$ is $\left(\frac{k}{\lambda}\right)e$; where gcd(k,l) = 1 then evaluate $(k + l)$.

5. If $\left(\frac{1}{1.3}+\frac{1}{1.2.3.5}+\frac{1}{1.2.3.4.5.7}+.....\infty\right)=e^k$ then evaluate $|k|$.

6. $1+\frac{2^3}{2!}+\frac{3^3}{3!}+\frac{4^3}{4!}+..... = \lambda e$ then evaluate λ.

7. If $1+\frac{1}{3.2^2}+\frac{1}{5.2^4}+\frac{1}{7.2^6}+....\infty = \log_e \lambda$, then evaluate λ.

8. If $\frac{1}{1.2}+\frac{1}{3.4}+\frac{1}{5.6}+.... = \frac{1}{2}+\frac{1}{1.2.3}+\frac{1}{3.4.5}+\frac{1}{5.6.7}+ ....$ ln $\sqrt{k}$, then find k.

9. If $\frac{1}{2}-\frac{1}{2.2^2}+\frac{1}{3.2^3}-\frac{1}{4.2^4}+..... = \log\left(\frac{m}{n}\right)$, where gcd (m, n) = 1 then evaluate $(m^2 - n^2)$

10. If the sum of the series $\frac{3}{1!}+\frac{5}{2!}+\frac{9}{3!}+\frac{15}{4!}+\frac{23}{5!}+....\infty = (ke-l)$; then evaluate $\sqrt{k^2+l^2}$.

11. In the expansion of $(1 + x)^{-2}$; $|x| < 1$; the 5th term is kx^4; then find the value of k

12. If the value of $1+\frac{1}{3}.\frac{1}{4}+\frac{1}{5}.\frac{1}{4^2}+\frac{1}{7}.\frac{1}{4^3}+... = \ln k$, then evaluate k.

Answers Keys

SECTION–III

1. (d)	**2.** (c)	**3.** (c)	**4.** (b)	**5.** (a)	**6.** (c)	**7.** (d)	**8.** (c)	**9.** (b)	**10.** (b)
11. (d)	**12.** (c)	**13.** (a)	**14.** (c)	**15.** (c)	**16.** (b)	**17.** (a)	**18.** (b)	**19.** (a)	**20.** (b)
21. (a)	**22.** (c)	**23.** (a)	**24.** (b)	**25.** (b)	**26.** (d)	**27.** (d)	**28.** (b)	**29.** (a)	**30.** (a)
31. (d)	**32.** (a)	**33.** (a)	**34.** (c)	**35.** (b)	**36.** (b)	**37.** (c)	**38.** (a)	**39.** (b)	**40.** (a)
41. (b)	**42.** (a)	**43.** (c)	**44.** (d)	**45.** (c)					

SECTION–IV

1. (b,d) **2.** (a,c) **3.** (b,c) **4.** (a,b)

SECTION–V

1. (d) **2.** (d) **3.** (d) **4.** (d)

SECTION–VI

1. (b) **2.** (c) **3.** (a) **4.** (b) **5.** (b) **6.** (d) **7.** (c) **8.** (c) **9.** (d) **10.** (d)

SECTION–VII

1. (i) → (c)	(ii) → (c)	(iii) → (a)	(iv) → (b, d)
2. (i) → (a, b)	(ii) → (b, c)	(iii) → (d)	(iv) → (b, c)
3. (i) → (b)	(ii) → (c)	(iii) → (d)	(iv) → (a)

SECTION–VIII

1. 6	**2.** 13	**3.** 4	**4.** 5	**5.** 1	**6.** 5	**7.** 3	**8.** 2	**9.** 5	**10.** 5
11. 5	**12.** 3								

HINTS AND SOLUTIONS

TEXTUAL EXERCISE–1: (SUBJECTIVE)

1. $(1 + x)^{-2}$

$(1+x)^{-n} = 1 - nx + \frac{n(n+1)}{2!}.x^2 - \frac{n(n+1)(n+2)}{3!}.x^3 + \frac{n(n+1)(n+2)(n+3)}{4!}.x^4$ ..... [upto 5 terms]

So, putting $n = 2$

$\Rightarrow (1+x)^{-2} = 1 - 2x + \frac{2(3)}{2!}x^2 - \frac{2(3)(4)}{3!}x^3 + \frac{2(3)(4)(5)}{4!}x^4 + ...$

$= 1 - 2x + 3x^2 - 4x^3 + 5x^4 + ...$

2. $(1 - 2x + 3x^2 - 4x^3 + ... \infty)^3$

$\Rightarrow (1+x)^{-2} = 1 - 2x + 3x^2 - 4x^3 + ...\infty$ (as shown in previous examples)

$\Rightarrow [(1+x)^{-2}]^3 \qquad \Rightarrow (1+x)^{-6}$

$\Rightarrow 1 - 6x + \frac{6(6+1)x^2}{2!} - \frac{(6)(7)(8)}{3!}x^3 + ... + \frac{(-1)^r(6)(6+1)(6+2).....(6+r-1)x^r}{r!} + ...$

The general term $T_{n+1} = \frac{(-1)^n \times (6)(6+1)(6+2)...(6n+1)x^n}{n!}$

So, the coefficient of x^n is $\frac{(-1)^n(6)(7)(8)...(5+n)}{n!} = (-1)^n\frac{(1\times2\times3\times4\times5)(6)(7)(8).....(5+n)}{n!\times(5\times4\times3\times2\times1)} = (-1)^n\frac{(5+n)!}{n!(5!)} =$

$(-1)^n\ {}^{(5+n)}C_5$

3. $\frac{1}{(4-5x^2)^{1/2}}$; taking 4 common out of the denominator

$\Rightarrow \frac{1}{2\left(1-\frac{5x^2}{4}\right)^{1/2}} \qquad \Rightarrow \frac{1}{2}\times\left(1-\frac{5x^2}{4}\right)^{1/2}$

Now for the expansion of $(1-x)^{-n}$ to be valid on this expression $-1 < \frac{5x^2}{4} < 1$

$\Rightarrow -4 < 5x^2 < 4 \qquad \Rightarrow -4 < 5x^2 < 4$

$\Rightarrow \frac{-4}{5} < x^2 < \frac{4}{5} \qquad \Rightarrow 0 < x^2 < 4/5$

$\Rightarrow -\frac{2}{\sqrt{5}} < x < \frac{2}{\sqrt{5}} \qquad \Rightarrow \frac{1}{2}\left(1-\frac{5x^2}{4}\right)^{1/2}$

$\Rightarrow \frac{1}{2}\left[1 + \frac{1}{2}\times\left(\frac{5x^2}{4}\right) + \frac{(1/2)(1/2+1)}{2!}\left(\frac{5x^2}{4}\right)^2\right]$

$+ ..... + \frac{(-1)^r\frac{1}{2}\left(\frac{1}{2}+1\right)...\left(\frac{1}{2}+r-1\right)}{r!}\times x^r$

$\Rightarrow \frac{1}{2} + \frac{5x^2}{16} + \frac{75}{256}x^4 + ...$

The general term is

$(-1)^r\frac{\frac{1}{2}\left(\frac{1}{2}+1\right)\left(\frac{1}{2}+2\right) + ... + \left(\frac{1}{2}+r-1\right)}{r!}\times\left(\frac{5x^2}{4}\right)^r$

$\Rightarrow (-1)^2\frac{\frac{1}{2}\frac{(1+2)}{2}\frac{(1+4)}{2} + ... + \frac{(1+2r-2)}{2}}{r!}\times\left(\frac{5x^2}{2^2}\right)^r$

$\Rightarrow (-1)^r\times\frac{1.3.5.7...(2r-1)}{2^r\times r!}\times\left(\frac{5}{2^2}\right)^r\times x^{2r}$

$\Rightarrow (-1)^r\times\frac{1.3.5.7...(2r-1)\times2.4.6.8...2r}{2^r\times r!\times2\times4\times6\times.....\times2r}\times\left(\frac{5}{2^2}\right)^r\times x^{2r}$

$\Rightarrow (-1)^r\times\frac{(2r)!}{2^r\times r!\times2^r(1\times2\times3\times....\times r)}\times\left(\frac{5}{2^2}\right)^r\times x^{2r}$

$\Rightarrow (-1)^r\times\frac{(2r)!}{2^{2r}\times r!\times r!}\times\left(\frac{5}{2^2}\right)^r\times x^{2r}$

$\Rightarrow (-1)^r\times\frac{(2r)!}{(r!)^2}\times\left(\frac{5}{2^4}\right)^r\times x^{2r}$

4. $(1-4x)^{-1/2}$

The general terms in the expression is $(1-x)^n$

$\Rightarrow T_r = (-1)^r\times\frac{(n)(n+1)(n+2)....(n+r-1)}{r!}\times(x)^r$ in the above term, we have to replace $n = 1/2$, $x = -4x$

$\Rightarrow (-1)^r\times\frac{\left(\frac{1}{2}\right)\left(\frac{1}{2}+1\right)\left(\frac{1}{2}+2\right) + ... + \left(\frac{1}{2}+r-1\right)\times(-4x)^r}{r!}$

$\Rightarrow (-1)^r\times\frac{(-4)^r\times\left(\frac{1}{2}\right)\left(\frac{1}{2}+1\right)\left(\frac{1}{2}+2\right) + ... + \left(\frac{1}{2}+r-1\right)\times(x)^r}{r!}$

$\Rightarrow (4)^r\times\frac{1\times3\times5\times7....(2r-1)}{2^r\times r!}\times x^r$

$\Rightarrow \frac{(2^2)^r}{2^r}\times\frac{1\times2\times3\times4....2r}{2^r(1\times2\times3...r)\times r!}\times x^r$

$\Rightarrow \frac{(2^2)^r}{(2^{2r})}\times\frac{2r!}{(r!)^2}\times x^r$

$\Rightarrow \frac{(2r)!}{(r!)^2}$ is the coefficient of x^n

5. $\left(\frac{1+x}{1-x}\right)^2 \quad (1+x)^2(1-x)^{-2}$

$\Rightarrow (1 + x^2 + 2x)\,[1 + 2x + 3x^2 + ... + (x+4)x^n]$

$\Rightarrow$ The coefficient of x^4 are $(1)(n+1) + (n-1)(1) + n \times 2 = n + 1 + n - 1 + 2n = 4n$

If $n = 0$ (it is not true for n = 0)

$\Rightarrow (1+x)^2[1-x^o] \qquad \Rightarrow [1 + x^o + x^2 + 2x]\,[1.x]^o$

$\Rightarrow 1.x^o \qquad \Rightarrow$ The coefficient of x^o is 1.

6. $\frac{3-2}{1+3x^3}$ $\Rightarrow$ $(3-2x)(1+3x^3)^{-1}$

$\Rightarrow$ $(3-2x)[1-(3x^3)+\ldots]$

The coefficient of x^3 is -9

7. (a) $\frac{(1-3x)^{1/2}+(1-x)^{5/3}}{(4-x)^{1/2}}=1-\frac{35}{24}x$

$\Rightarrow$ $\frac{\left[1-(3x)\times\frac{1}{2}\right]+\left[1-(x)\frac{5}{3}\right]}{2\left[1-\frac{x}{4}\right]^{1/2}}$ [Square and above room neglected]

$\Rightarrow$ $\frac{1-\frac{3x}{2}+1-\frac{5x}{3}}{2\left[1-\frac{1}{2}\times\left(\frac{x}{4}\right)\right]}$ $\frac{2-\frac{19x}{6}}{2-\frac{x}{4}}$

$\frac{12-19x}{3}\times\frac{4}{8-x}$ $\frac{24-38x}{24-3x}$

$\Rightarrow$ $1-\frac{35x}{(24-3x)}$ $1-\frac{35x}{24}\times\left(1-\frac{x}{8}\right)^{-1}$

$\Rightarrow$ $1-\frac{35x}{24}\times\left[1+\frac{x}{8}\right]\Rightarrow 1-\frac{35x}{24}$ [Square and above terms neglected

(b) $\frac{\sqrt{1-x}+(1+x)^{2/3}}{1-x+\sqrt{(1-x)^{5/3}}}=1+x=\frac{(1-x)^{1/2}+(1+x)^{2/3}}{1-x+(1-x)^{5/6}}=$

$\frac{1-\frac{1}{2}x+1+\frac{2}{3}x}{1-x+1--x}$ [square of higher terms neglected]

$=\frac{2+\frac{1}{6}}{2-\frac{11}{6}x}=\frac{12+x}{12-11x}=\frac{(12+x)}{12}\left(1-\frac{11x}{12}\right)^{-1}$

$=\frac{(12+x)}{12}\left[1+\frac{11x}{12}\right]=\frac{(12+x)}{12}\times\frac{(12+11x)}{12}$

$=\frac{144+12x+132x+11x^2}{144}$ [x^2 again neglected]

$=\frac{144+144x}{144}=1+x$

(c) $\left(1+\frac{3x}{4}\right)^{-4}$ $(4-3x)^{1/2}=2-\frac{27}{4}x$

$=2\left[1-4\times\frac{3x}{4}\right]\left[1-\frac{3x}{4}\times\frac{1}{2}\right]$ [square and above term neglected]

$=2[1-3x]\left[1-\frac{3x}{8}\right]=\frac{2}{8}[1-3x][8-3x]$

$=1/4[8-24x-3x+9x^2]$ [square term neglected]

$=\frac{1}{4}[8-27x]=2-\frac{27x}{4}$

8. (a) $\frac{mx^n-nx^n}{m-n}=x^{m+n}$

Let $x=1+h$ where h is small that square and above terms are neglected

$=\frac{m(1+h)^m-n(1+h)^n}{m-n}=\frac{m[1+mh]-n[1+nh]}{m-n}$

$=\frac{(m-n)+(m^2-n^2)h}{m-n}=1+(m+n)h$

$=(1+h)^{m+n}$ (approximately) $=x^{m+n}$

(b) $\frac{mx^n-nx^m}{x^n-x^m}=\frac{1}{1-x}$

Let $x=1+h$, where h is every small, and square and higher terms can neglected

$=\frac{m(1+h)^n-n(1+h)^m}{(1+h)^n-(1+h)^m}=\frac{m(1+nh)-n(1+mh)}{1+nh-1-mh}$

$=\frac{m+mhh-n-mnh}{(n-m)h}=\frac{-1}{h}=\frac{1}{1-x}$

9. (a) $(5+25)^{1/2}=5\left(1+\frac{1}{5}\right)^{1/2}$

$=5\left[1+\frac{1}{2}+\frac{1}{5}+\frac{\left(\frac{1}{2}\right)\left(\frac{1}{2}-1\right)}{2!}\times\frac{1}{(5)^2}+\frac{\left(\frac{1}{2}\right)\left(\frac{1}{2}-1\right)\left(\frac{1}{2}-1\right)}{3!}\times\frac{1}{(5)^3}\right]$

$=5\left[1+\frac{1}{10}-\frac{1}{8}\times\frac{1}{25}+\frac{1}{16}+\frac{1}{125}\right]$

$=5\left[1+0.1-\frac{1}{200}+\frac{1}{16\times125}\right]$

$=5[1+0.1-0.005+0.0005]=5.4775$

(b) $(125+1)^{1/3}=5\left(1+\frac{1}{125}\right)^{1/3}$

$=5\left[1+\frac{1}{3}\times\frac{1}{125}+\frac{\left(\frac{1}{3}\right)\left(\frac{1}{3}+1\right)}{2!}\times\frac{1}{(125)^2}+\frac{\left(\frac{1}{3}\right)\left(\frac{1}{3}+1\right)\left(\frac{1}{3}+2\right)}{3!}\times\right.$

$\left.\frac{1}{(125)^3}+\frac{\left(\frac{1}{3}\right)\left(\frac{1}{3}+1\right)\left(\frac{1}{3}+3\right)}{4!}\times\frac{1}{(125)^4}\right]$

$=5\times[1+0.00266+0.000014]$

$=5\times1.00267=5.01335$

10. (a) $(1+x)^{-2}=1-2x+3x^2-4x^3+\ldots..\infty$

Since $|x|<1$

$\Rightarrow$ $(1+x)^n=1+nx+\frac{(n)(n-1)}{2!}\times x^2+\ldots$ [general expansion]

Replacing n with $-n$

$\Rightarrow$ $(1+x)^{-n}=1-nx+\frac{(-n)(-n-1)\times x^2}{2!}+\ldots$

$=1-nx+\frac{n(n+1)}{2}\times x^2+\ldots+$

$\frac{(-1)^r n(n+1)(n+2)\ldots(n+r-1)x^r}{r!}+\ldots$

$\Rightarrow\ (1+x)^{-2} = 1-2x+\frac{2(2+1)}{2!}\times x^2+\ldots+$

$\frac{(-1)^r 2(2+1)(2+2)\ldots(2+r-1)}{r!}\times x^r$

$= 1 - 2x + 3x^2 - 4x^3 + \ldots (-1)^r (r+1)x^r + \ldots$

(b) $(1-x)^{-3} = 1 + 3x + 6x^2 + 10x^3 + \ldots \infty$

Since $|x| < 1$

$\Rightarrow\ (1+x)^{-n} = 1-nx+\frac{n(n-1)}{2!}\times x^2-\frac{n(n+1)(n+2)}{3!}\times x^3$

$+\ldots+(-1)^r\frac{n(n-1)(n-2)\ldots(n+r-1)x^r}{r!}$

Replacing x with $-x$

$\Rightarrow\ (1-x)^{-n} = 1-n(-x)+\frac{n(n+1)(-x^2)}{2!}+\ldots$

$+\frac{(-1)^r n(n+1)(n+2)\ldots(n+r-1)\times(-x)^r}{r!}$

$\Rightarrow\ (1-x)^{-n} = 1 + nx + \frac{n(n+1)}{2!}x^2+\ldots+$

$\frac{n(n+1)\ldots(n+r-1)}{r!}+\ldots$

Putting $n = 3$

Multiplying and dividing every term by 2

$\Rightarrow\ 1+\frac{2\times 3x}{2}+\frac{2\times 3\times 4\times x^2}{2!\times 2}+\ldots+\frac{2\times(3)(4)\ldots(r+2)}{r!\times 2}\times x^r+\ldots$

$\Rightarrow\ 1 + 3x + 6x^2 + 10x^3 + \ldots + \frac{(r+2)(r+1)}{2}\times x^r + \ldots$

11. (a) $1+\frac{1}{6}+\frac{1.4}{6.12}+\frac{1.4.7}{6.12.18}+\ldots\text{to}\infty$

Comparing it with the expansion of $(1+x)^n$

$= 1+nx+\frac{n(n-1)}{2!}x^2+\ldots+\frac{(n)(m-1)(n-r+1)}{r!}\times x^r$

$= nx = \frac{1}{6},\ \frac{n(n-1)}{2}x^2 = \frac{1}{6}.\frac{4}{12}$

$= (n\times x)\times\frac{(n-1)x}{2} = \frac{1}{6}.\frac{4}{12}$

$= \frac{(n-1)x}{2} = \frac{1}{3} = (n-1)x = 2/3 = nx - x = 2/3$

$= 1/6 - x = 2/3 = \frac{1}{6}-\frac{2}{3} = x = -1/2 = x$

$\Rightarrow\ nx = 1/6 \qquad \Rightarrow\ nx-\frac{1}{2}=\frac{1}{6}\Rightarrow n=-\frac{1}{3}$

The expression is equivalent to $= \left(1-\frac{1}{2}\right)^{-1/3} = \left(\frac{1}{2}\right)^{-1/3}$

$= (2)^{1/3} = \sqrt[3]{2}$

(b) $1+\frac{3}{4}+\frac{3}{4}.\frac{5}{8}+\frac{3.5.7}{4.8.12}+\ldots\text{to}\infty$

Comparing it with the expansion of $(1+x)^n$

$nx = 3/4$ (i)

$\Rightarrow\ \frac{n(n-1)}{2!}\times x^2 = \frac{3}{4}.\frac{5}{8}$ (ii)

$\Rightarrow\ nx\times\frac{(n-1)x}{2} = \frac{3}{4}.\frac{5}{8} \qquad \Rightarrow\ \frac{1}{4}\frac{(n-1)x}{2} = \frac{5}{8}.\frac{3}{4}$

$\Rightarrow\ nx - x = 5/4 \qquad \Rightarrow\ \frac{3}{4}-x=\frac{5}{4}$

$\Rightarrow\ \frac{-1}{2} = x \qquad \Rightarrow\ nx = \frac{3}{4}$

$\Rightarrow\ -\frac{1}{2}\times n = \frac{3}{4} = n = -\frac{3}{2}$

The series is equivalent to $\left(1-\frac{1}{2}\right)^{-3/2} = \left(\frac{1}{2}\right)^{-3/2}$

$= (2)^{3/2} - (8)^{1/2} = 2\sqrt{2}$

12. $(1 + 3x + 6x^2 + 10x^3 + \ldots \text{ to } \infty)^{2/3}$ (i)

$\Rightarrow\ 1 + 3x + 6x^2 + 10x^3 \ldots \text{ to } \infty$

The above expression is the expansion for $(1-x)^{-3}$

$\therefore$ The equation (i) reduced to $((1-k)^{-3})^{2/3}$

$\Rightarrow\ (1-x)^{-\frac{2}{3}\times 3} \qquad (1-x)^{-2}$

$\Rightarrow\ 1 + 2x + 3x^2 + 4x^3 + \ldots + (r+1)x^r$

$\Rightarrow$ Coefficient of x^{24} is $= 24 + 1 = 25$

13. $\sqrt{\frac{\ell}{\ell+1}}+\sqrt{\frac{\ell}{\ell-c}} \qquad \Rightarrow\ \sqrt{\ell}\left[(\ell+c)^{-1/2}+(\ell-c)^{-1/2}\right]$

$\Rightarrow\ \left[\left(1+\frac{c}{\ell}\right)^{-1/2}+\left(1-\frac{c}{\ell}\right)^{-1/2}\right]$

Expending the expression

$1-\frac{1}{2}\times\frac{c}{\ell}+\frac{\left(\frac{1}{2}\right)\left(\frac{1}{2}+1\right)}{2}\times\left(\frac{c}{\ell}\right)^2+$

$1+\frac{1}{2}.\frac{c}{\ell}+\frac{3}{8}.\frac{c^2}{\ell^2}+\frac{\left(\frac{1}{2}\right)\left(\frac{1}{2}+1\right)}{2}\left(\frac{c}{\ell}\right)^2$

$\Rightarrow\ 2+2.\frac{3}{8}\left(\frac{c}{\ell}\right)^2 \qquad 2+\frac{3}{4}\left(\frac{c}{\ell}\right)^2$

TEXTUAL EXERCISE–1: (OBJECTIVE)

1. (b) $(1-2x)^{3/2}$

On expanding the above term the fourth terms,

$T_4 = \frac{\left(\frac{3}{2}\right)\left(\frac{3}{2}-1\right)\left(\frac{3}{2}-2\right)}{3!}\times(-2x)^3$

$\Rightarrow\ \frac{3\times 1\times -1}{2\times 2\times 2\times 3\times 2}\times(2)^3\times(-1)^3\times x^3 = \frac{x^3}{2}$

2. (d) $\frac{1}{(4-3x)^{1/2}}$

Taking 4 common out of $(4-3x)^{1/2}$ term gives us

$\frac{1}{2\left(1-\frac{3x}{4}\right)^{1/2}}$

Now, for expansion to be valid $-1<\frac{3x}{4}<1$

$\Rightarrow\ -4<3\ <4 \qquad -\frac{4}{3}<x<\frac{4}{3}$

3. (a) $(a+bx)^{-2}=\frac{1}{4}-3x+..$

L.H.S. $\Rightarrow\ a^{-2}\left[1+\frac{bx}{a}\right]^{-2}$

$a^{-2}\left[1-\frac{2bx}{a}+.....\right] \Rightarrow \frac{1}{a^2}-\frac{2bx}{a^3}+.....$

Comparing this with the R.H.S. gives us

$\frac{1}{a^2}=\frac{1}{4}$ (i)

& $\frac{-2b}{a^3}=-3$ (ii)

Equation (i) gives us $a^2 = 2$

$\Rightarrow\ a\pm 2$

Solving equation (ii) $-\frac{2b}{a^3}=-3$

$\frac{2b}{a^3}=3 \qquad \frac{2b}{3}=a^3$

If $a=-2 \qquad \Rightarrow \frac{2b}{3}=-3$

$b=-12$

If $a=2 \qquad \Rightarrow \frac{2b}{3}=8$

$b=2$

so $(a, b) = (-2, -12)$ or $(2, 12)$

4. (b) $\frac{1}{\sqrt[3]{6-3x}}=\frac{1}{(6-3x)^{1/3}}=\frac{1}{(6)^{1/3}\left(1-\frac{x}{2}\right)^{1/3}}$

$=\frac{1}{(6)^{1/3}}\left[1-\frac{x}{2}\right]^{1/3}=\frac{1}{(6)^{1/3}}\left[1+\frac{x}{6}+\frac{\left(\frac{1}{3}\right)\left(\frac{1}{3}+1\right)}{2!}\left(\frac{x}{2}\right)^2+..\right]$

$=\frac{1}{(6)^{1/3}}\left[1+\frac{x}{6}+\frac{2x^2}{6^2}+..\right]$

5. (a) $\left(\frac{a}{a+x}\right)^{1/2}+\left(\frac{a}{a-x}\right)^{1/2} \Rightarrow \left(\frac{1}{1+\frac{x}{a}}\right)^{1/2}+\left(\frac{1}{1-\frac{x}{a}}\right)^{1/2}$

$\Rightarrow\ \left(1+\frac{x}{a}\right)^{-1/2}+\left(1-\frac{x}{a}\right)^{-1/2}$

$\Rightarrow\ \left[1-\frac{1}{2}\frac{x}{a}+\frac{\left(\frac{1}{2}\right)\left(\frac{1}{2}+1\right)}{2!}\times\left(\frac{x}{a}\right)^2+..\right]+$

$\left[1+\frac{x}{2a}+\frac{\left(\frac{1}{2}\right)\left(\frac{1}{2}+1\right)}{2!}\left(\frac{x}{a}\right)^2+...\right]$

$\Rightarrow\ 2\left[1+\frac{3}{8}\left(\frac{x}{a}\right)^2+..\right]$

$\Rightarrow\ 2+\frac{3}{4}\frac{x^2}{a^2}+...$

6. (b) $(1-x)^{-4}$

$T_{r+1}=\frac{(n)(n+1)(n+2)....(n+r-1)}{r!}.x^r$

Putting $n = 4$, we get $\frac{(4)(5)(6)....(r+2)}{r!}(r+3).x^r$

Multiplying and dividing by 3!

$\Rightarrow\ \frac{1\times2\times3\times4\times5\times....(r+3)}{3!\times r!}\times x^r$

$\Rightarrow\ \frac{(r+3)!}{r!\times 6}\times x^r$

$\Rightarrow\ \frac{(r+1)(r+2)(r+3)}{6}\times x^r$

7. (a) $\frac{(1+x)^2}{(1-x)^2}=(1+x)^2\,[1-x]^{-2}=(1+x^2+2x)\,[1+2x+3x$ $+.....]$

Term of x^n in the above expansion $= (n+1)x^n + (n-1)$ $x^n + 2nx^n = 4n\,x^n$

8. (d) $\frac{1}{\left(x^2+\frac{1}{x}\right)^{4/3}} \qquad \frac{1}{(x)^{8/3}\left(1+\frac{1}{x^3}\right)^{4/3}}$

$-1<\frac{1}{x^3}<1 \qquad x^3<-1$ and $1<x^3$

$\Rightarrow\ x\in(-\infty,-1)\cup(1,\infty)$

$\Rightarrow\ |x|>1$

9. (c) $(1+x+x^2+...)^2$

$\because\ (1+x+x^2+....)=(1-x)^{-1}$

$((1-x)^{-1})^2$

$\Rightarrow\ (1-x)^{-2} \qquad \Rightarrow\ 1+2x+3x^2+....(n+1)x^n$

10. (c) $(1+2x+3x^2+4x^3+...)^{1/2}$

$(1+2x+3x^2\ ...=(1-x)^{-2})$

$[(1-x)^{-2}]^{1/2}$

$\Rightarrow\ (1-x)^{-1}$

$1+x+x^2+x^3+..$

$\Rightarrow$ Coefficient of $x^n = 1$

11. (a) $1+n\left(1-\frac{1}{x}\right)+\frac{n(n+1)}{2!}\left(1-\frac{1}{x}\right)^2+....$

$\Rightarrow\ \left(1-\left(1-\frac{1}{x}\right)\right)^{-n} \qquad \Rightarrow\ \left(1-1+\frac{1}{x}\right)^{-n}$

$\Rightarrow\ \left(\frac{1}{x}\right)^{-n} \qquad \Rightarrow\ x^n$

12. (a) $(1+x)^{7/2}$

$$T_{r+1}=\frac{(n)(n-1)(n-2)....(n-r+1)}{r!}\times x^r<0$$

For me first negative term $n-r+1<0$

$$\frac{7}{2}-r+1<0 \quad \Rightarrow \quad \frac{9}{2}-r<0$$

$$\frac{9}{2}<r$$

For $r=5$, the first negative term

13. (a) $\dfrac{(1+x)^{3/2}-\left(1+\frac{1}{2}x\right)^3}{(1-x)^{1/2}}$

$$\left[\left[1+\frac{3}{2}x+\frac{3}{8}x^2\right]-\left[1+\frac{3}{2}x+\frac{3}{4}x^2\right]\right](1-x)^{-1/2}$$

$$\Rightarrow \left[-\frac{3}{8}\right]x^2\left[1+\frac{1}{2}x+....\right] \quad \frac{-3}{8}x^2-\frac{3}{16}x^3+...$$

$\Rightarrow \dfrac{-3}{8}x^2$ (x^3 and higher terms neglected)

TEXTUAL EXERCISE–2: (SUBJECTIVE)

1. (i) $\dfrac{5}{1!}+\dfrac{9}{2!}+\dfrac{13}{3!}+\dfrac{17}{4!}+...\infty=5e-1$

$$\frac{4\times1+1}{1!}+\frac{4\times2+1}{2!}+\frac{2\times4\times1}{3!}+..$$

$$\Rightarrow 4\left[1+\frac{1}{1!}+\frac{1}{2!}+\frac{1}{3!}+....\right]+\frac{1}{1!}+\frac{1}{2!}$$

$$\Rightarrow 4e+1+\frac{1}{1!}+\frac{1}{2!}+...1$$

$$\Rightarrow 4e+e-1 \quad \Rightarrow 5e-1$$

(ii) $\dfrac{1}{3!}+\dfrac{1}{4!}+\dfrac{1}{5!}+...=e-\dfrac{5}{2} \quad \Rightarrow \dfrac{1}{3!}+\dfrac{1}{4!}+\dfrac{1}{5!}+...$

$$\Rightarrow 1+\frac{1}{1!}+\frac{1}{2!}+\frac{1}{3!}+...-1-\frac{1}{1!}-\frac{1}{2!}$$

$$\Rightarrow e-1-1-1/2 \quad \Rightarrow e-2-\frac{1}{2}$$

(iii) $\dfrac{3e}{2}-\dfrac{1}{2e}-3=\dfrac{5}{3!}+\dfrac{7}{5!}+\dfrac{9}{7!}+..$

$$\Rightarrow \frac{5}{3!}+\frac{7}{5!}+\frac{9}{7!}+...\infty \quad \Rightarrow \frac{3+2}{3!}+\frac{5+2}{5!}+\frac{7+2}{7!}+....\infty$$

$$\Rightarrow \frac{1}{2!}+\frac{2}{3!}+\frac{1}{4!}+\frac{2}{5!}+\frac{1}{6!}+\frac{2}{7!}+...$$

$$\Rightarrow \left[\frac{1}{2!}+\frac{1}{4!}+\frac{1}{6!}+...\right]+2\left[\frac{1}{3!}+\frac{1}{5!}+\frac{1}{7!}+..\right]$$

$$\Rightarrow \left[\left(1+\frac{1}{2!}+\frac{1}{4!}+...\infty\right)-1\right]+2\left[\left(1+\frac{1}{3!}+\frac{1}{5!}+...\infty\right)-1\right]$$

$$\Rightarrow \left[\frac{e+e^{-1}}{2}-1\right]+2\left[\frac{e^{-}+e^{-1}}{2}-1\right] \quad \frac{3}{2}e-\frac{e^{-1}}{2}-3$$

2. $1+\dfrac{1+2}{2!}+\dfrac{1+2+2^2}{3!}+...\infty$

$$\Rightarrow T_r=\frac{1+2+2^2+...2^{r-1}}{r}$$

$$\Rightarrow \frac{1\frac{(1-2^r)}{1-2}}{2} \quad \Rightarrow \frac{2^r-1}{r!}$$

$\Rightarrow$ Sum of series $=\Sigma T_r$

$$\Rightarrow \sum\frac{2^r-1}{r!} \quad \Rightarrow \sum\frac{2^r}{r!}-\sum\frac{1}{r!}$$

$$\Rightarrow \left[1+\frac{2}{1!}+\frac{2^?}{2!}+\frac{2^3}{3!}\right]-e \Rightarrow e^2-e$$

3. $y=x-\dfrac{x^2}{2}+\dfrac{x^3}{3}-\dfrac{x^4}{4}+....$

$$\Rightarrow y=n(1+x) \quad \Rightarrow e^y=1+x$$

$$\Rightarrow e^y-1=x$$

$$\Rightarrow \left(1+\frac{y}{1!}+\frac{y^2}{2!}+\frac{y^3}{3!}+...\right)-1=x$$

$$\Rightarrow \frac{y}{1!}+\frac{y^2}{2!}+\frac{y^3}{3!}+..=x \quad \Rightarrow x=y+\frac{y^2}{2!}+\frac{y^3}{3!}+..$$

4. $y=x-x^2+x^3-x^4+...+\infty$

$(1+x)^{-1}=1-x+x^2-x^3+..$

$(1+x)^{-1}-1=-x+x^2+x^3+x^4+...$

$1-(1+x)^{-1}=x-x^2+x^3-x^4+...$

$$\Rightarrow y=1-(y+x)^{-1} \quad \Rightarrow (1+x)^{-1}=1-y$$

$$\Rightarrow \frac{1}{1-y}=1+x \quad \Rightarrow \frac{1}{1-y}-1=x$$

$$\Rightarrow \frac{y}{1-y}=x \quad \Rightarrow x=y(1-y)^{-1}$$

$$\Rightarrow x=y[1+y+y^2+y^3+...]$$

$$\Rightarrow x=y+y^2+y^3+y^4......\infty$$

5. e^{e^x}

$1+\dfrac{e^x}{1!}+\dfrac{e^{2x}}{2!}+\dfrac{e^{3x}}{3!}$..... ; Each of the term in the above expression contains x^n and sum of term will give us the coefficient of x^n in e^{e^x}

Term	Coefficient
$\dfrac{e^x}{1!}$	$\dfrac{1}{n!}$
$\dfrac{e^{2x}}{2!}$	$\dfrac{1}{2!}\times\dfrac{2^n}{n!}$
.	.
.	.
$\dfrac{e^{nx}}{n!}$	$\dfrac{1}{n!}\times\dfrac{n^n}{n!}$

Sum of coefficient $=\dfrac{1}{n!}\times\dfrac{1}{2!\left(\frac{n}{2}\right)}+\dfrac{1}{3!\left(\frac{n}{3}\right)!}$

$$T_r \frac{1}{r!\left(\frac{n}{r}\right)!} = \frac{1}{1!n!} + \frac{1}{2!} \times \frac{2^n}{n!} + \frac{3^n}{3!n!} \cdots \frac{1}{n!} \times \frac{n^n}{n!} + ..$$

$$\text{General term} = \frac{r^n}{n! \times r!}$$

$$\text{Sum} = \sum_1^{\infty} \frac{r^n}{n!r!} = \frac{1}{n!}\sum_1^{\infty} \frac{r^n}{r!}$$

6. e^{2+3x}

$$T_{10} = e^2.e^{3x}$$

$$T_{11} = e^2.\left[\frac{(3x)^{10}}{10!}\right] = \frac{e^2.3^{10}}{10!} \times x^{10}$$

$$\text{Coefficient of } x^n = e^2\left[\frac{(3x)^n}{n!}\right]$$

$$\Rightarrow \frac{e^2.3^n}{n!} \times x^n$$

7. $$\frac{e^{5x}+e^x}{3e^{3x}} = \frac{(e^{5x}+e^x)}{3}(e^{-3x}) = \frac{e^{2x}+e^{-2x}}{3}$$

$$= \frac{2}{3}\left[1 + \frac{(2x)^2}{2!} + \frac{(2x)^4}{4!} + ...\right]$$

The coefficient of x^n is 0 if n is odd and $\frac{1}{3} \times \frac{2^{n+1}}{n!}$ if n is even

8. $$\frac{e^2-1}{2e} = \frac{1}{1!} + \frac{1}{3!} + \frac{1}{5!} + ... + \infty \quad \Rightarrow \left(\frac{c^2-1}{2e}\right)$$

$$\Rightarrow \frac{(e^2-1)e^{-1}}{2}$$

$$\Rightarrow \frac{\left[1 + \frac{1}{1!} + \frac{1}{2!} + ... - \left(1 - \frac{1}{1!} + \frac{1}{2!} + \frac{1}{3!}\right)\right]}{2}$$

$$\Rightarrow \frac{2\left(\frac{1}{1!} + \frac{1}{3!} + \frac{1}{5!} + ...\right)}{2} \quad \Rightarrow \frac{1}{1!} + \frac{1}{3!} + \frac{1}{5!} + \frac{1}{7!} + ..$$

9. **(a)** $$\frac{1}{(2n+3)!} \qquad T_n = \frac{1}{(2n+3)!}$$

$$T_0 = \frac{1}{3!}, T_1 = \frac{1}{5!}, T_2 = \frac{1}{7!} + ...$$

$$\text{Adding then} \Rightarrow S = \frac{1}{3!} + \frac{1}{5!} + \frac{1}{7!} + ...$$

$$\Rightarrow S = 1 - 1 + \frac{1}{3!} + \frac{1}{5!} + \frac{1}{7!} + ...$$

$$\Rightarrow \frac{e-e^{-1}}{2} - 1$$

(b) $$\frac{1}{(n-2)!}$$

$$T_n = \frac{1}{(n-2)!}$$

$$S = \sum \frac{1}{(n-2)!} \qquad S = 1 + \frac{1}{1!} + \frac{1}{2!} + ..$$

$$S = e$$

10. $$a = \sum_{n=1}^{\infty} \frac{1}{(2n-1)!}, b = \sum_{n=0}^{\infty} \frac{1}{(2n)!}$$

$$a = \sum_{n=1}^{\infty} \frac{1}{(2n-1)!} = \frac{1}{1!} + \frac{1}{3!} + \frac{1}{5!} + .. = \frac{e-e^{-1}}{2}$$

$$b = \sum_{n=0}^{\infty} \frac{1}{(2n)!} = 1 + \frac{1}{2!} + \frac{1}{4!} + .. = \frac{e+e^{-1}}{2}$$

The quadratic equation having a and b as roots is $x^2 - (a + b)\, x + ab = 0$

$$\Rightarrow x^2 - \left(\frac{e+e^{-1}}{2} + \frac{e-e^{-1}}{2}\right)x + \left(\frac{e+e^{-1}}{2}\right)\left(\frac{e-e^{-1}}{2}\right) = 0$$

$$\Rightarrow x^2 - e.x + \frac{e^2-e^{-2}}{4} = 0$$

11. $$\frac{1.4}{0!} + \frac{2.5}{1!} + \frac{3.6}{2!} + \frac{4.7}{3!} + ...$$

$$T_{n+1} = \frac{(n+1)(n+4)}{n!} = \frac{n^2+5n+4}{n!} = \frac{n(n-1)+6n+4}{n!}$$

$$\text{Sum} = \sum_0^4 T_{n+1} = \sum_0^4 \frac{n(n-1)+6n+4}{n!}$$

$$= \left[\frac{1}{0!} + \frac{1}{1!} + \frac{1}{2!} + ..\right] + 6\left[\frac{1}{0!} + \frac{1}{1!} + \frac{1}{2!} + ...\right] + 4\left[\frac{1}{0!} + \frac{1}{1!} + \frac{1}{2!} + ...\right]$$

$$= 0e + 6e + 4e = 11e$$

12. $$\left(1 + \frac{1}{2!} + \frac{1}{4!} + \frac{1}{6!} + ...\right)^2 - \left(1 + \frac{1}{3!} + \frac{1}{5!} + ...\right) = 1$$

$$= \left(\frac{e+e^{-1}}{2}\right)^2 - \left(\frac{e-e^{-1}}{2}\right)^2 = \frac{e^2+e^{-2}+2}{4} - \frac{(e^2-e^{-2}-2)}{4}$$

$$= \frac{4}{4} = 1$$

13. $$\left(\frac{e-1}{e+1}\right) = \left(\frac{1}{2!} + \frac{1}{4!} + \frac{1}{6!} + ...\right) \div \left(\frac{1}{1!} + \frac{1}{3!} + \frac{1}{5!} + ...\right)$$

$$= \frac{\left(\frac{1}{2!} + \frac{1}{4!} + \frac{1}{6!} + ...\right)}{\left(\frac{1}{1!} + \frac{1}{3!} + \frac{1}{5!} + ...\right)} = \frac{\left(\frac{e+e^{-1}}{2} - 1\right)}{\left(\frac{e-e^{-1}}{2}\right)} = \frac{e+e^{-1}-2}{e-e^{-1}}$$

$$= \frac{e^2-2e+1}{e^2-1} = \frac{(e-1)}{(e+1)}$$

14. $$\frac{e^2-1}{e^2+1} = \left(\frac{1}{1!} + \frac{1}{3!} + \frac{1}{5!} + ...\right) \div \left(1 + \frac{1}{2!} + \frac{1}{4!} + ..\right)$$

$$= \frac{\left(\frac{1}{1!} + \frac{1}{3!} + \frac{1}{5!} + ...\right)}{\left(1 + \frac{1}{2!} + \frac{1}{4!} + ..\right)} = \frac{\left(\frac{e-e^{-1}}{2}\right)}{\left(\frac{e+e^{-1}}{2}\right)} = \frac{e-e^{-1}}{e+e^{-1}} = \frac{e^2-1}{e^2+1}$$

TEXTUAL EXERCISE–2: (OBJECTIVE)

1. **(b)** e^{2x} $$\Rightarrow \frac{1}{(10)!} \times (2x)^{10}$$

$$\Rightarrow \frac{1024}{(10)!} \times x^{10} \qquad \Rightarrow \frac{4}{14175} \times x^{10}$$

2. (c) $e^{a+bx} = e^a . e^{bx} = e^a.\left[1+\frac{bx}{1!}+\frac{(bx)^2}{2!}+...\right]$

Term with $x^n = e^a \times \frac{(bx)^n}{n!} = e^a \times \frac{b^n x^n}{n!}$

3. (a) $\frac{a+bx+cx^2}{e^x} = (a + bx + cx^2)(e^{-x})$

$= (a + bx + cx^2)\left(1-\frac{x}{1!}+\frac{x^2}{2!}-\frac{x^3}{3!}+...\right)$ terms with x^{10}

$= (-1)\frac{ax^n}{n!}+\frac{b(-1)^{n-1}x^n}{(n-1)!}+\frac{c(-1)^{n-2}}{(n-2)!}x^n$

$\Rightarrow \frac{(-1)^n}{n!}[a-bn+cn(n-1)]x^n$

4. (c) $\sum_{n=1}^{\infty}\frac{1}{(n+1)!} = \frac{1}{2!}+\frac{1}{3!}+\frac{1}{4!}+.. = -2+1+\frac{1}{1!}+\frac{1}{2!}+\frac{1}{3!}+...$

$= -2 + e$

5. (d) $\sum_{n=1}^{\infty}\frac{1}{(2n+1)!} = \frac{1}{3!}+\frac{1}{5!}+\frac{1}{7!}+... = -1+\frac{1}{1!}+\frac{1}{3!}+\frac{1}{5!}+.....$

$= -1+\frac{e-e^{-1}}{2}$

6. (d) $\sum_{n=1}^{\infty}\frac{x^n}{(n-2)!} = 0+\frac{x^2}{0!}+\frac{x^3}{1!}+\frac{x^4}{2!}+...$

$= x^2\left[1+\frac{x}{1!}+\frac{x^2}{2!}+...\right] = 1/2 = x^2 e^x$

7. (a) $\frac{\left\{1+\frac{1}{2!}+\frac{1}{4!}+\frac{1}{6!}+...\infty\right\}}{\left\{1+\frac{1}{3!}+\frac{1}{5!}+\frac{1}{7!}+...\infty\right\}} = \frac{\frac{e+e^{-1}}{2}}{\frac{e-e^{-1}}{2}} = \frac{e+e^{-1}}{e-e^{-1}} = \frac{e^2+1}{e^2-1}$

8. (b) $x+\frac{2^2}{2!}x^2+\frac{3^2}{3!}x^3+...\infty$

$T_n = \frac{n^2}{n!}\times x^n = \frac{n(n-1)+n}{n!}\times x^n$

$S = \sum\frac{n(n-1)+n}{n!}\times x^n = \sum\frac{x^n}{(n-2)!}+\sum\frac{x^n}{(n-1)!}$

$= x^2 + e^x + x. e^x = (x^2 + x)e^x$

9. (d) $\frac{2}{1!}+\frac{4}{3!}+\frac{6}{5!}+\frac{8}{7!}+......\infty$

$T_n = \frac{2n}{(2n-1)!}$

$T_n = \frac{(2n-1)}{(2n-1)!}+\frac{1}{(2n-1)!} = \frac{1}{(2n-2)!}+\frac{1}{(2n-1)!}$

Sum $= \Sigma T_n = \sum\frac{1}{(2n-2)!}+\sum\frac{1}{(2n-1)!}$

$= \frac{e+e^{-1}}{2}+\frac{e-e^{-1}}{2} = e$

10. (a) $\frac{1}{3!}+\frac{1}{5!}+\frac{1}{7!}+... = -1+1+\frac{1}{3!}+\frac{1}{5!}+\frac{1}{7!}+...$

$= -1+\frac{e-e^{-1}}{2} = \frac{e-e^{-1}-2}{2}$

TEXTUAL EXERCISE–3: (SUBJECTIVE)

1. $ax^2 + bx + c = 0$

Since α and β are the roots

$\alpha+\beta = -\frac{b}{a}$; $\alpha\beta = \frac{c}{a}$

Now, $\log (a - bx + cx^2)$

$\Rightarrow \log a\left(1-\frac{b}{a}x-1+\frac{c}{a}x^2\right)$

$\Rightarrow \log a+\log\left(\frac{c}{a}x^2-\frac{b}{a}x+1\right)$

$\Rightarrow \log a + \log(\alpha\beta x^2 + (\alpha + \beta) x + 1)$

$\Rightarrow \log a + \log (\alpha\beta x^2 + \alpha x + \beta x + 1)$

$\Rightarrow \log a + \log (\alpha x + 1) (\beta x + 1)$

$\Rightarrow \log a + \log (1 + \alpha x) (1 + \beta x)$

$\Rightarrow \log a + \log(1+ \alpha x) + \log (1 + \beta x)$

$\Rightarrow \log a+\alpha x-\frac{(\alpha x)^2}{2}+\frac{(\alpha x)^3}{3}+.....+\beta x-\frac{(\beta x)^2}{2}+\frac{(\beta x)^3}{3}...$

$\Rightarrow \log a + (\alpha + \beta)x - \frac{(\alpha^2+\beta^2)}{2}x^2+\frac{(\alpha^2+\beta^3)}{3}x^3.........$

2. $2\log x - \log (x + 1) - \log(x - 1)$

$\Rightarrow -2\log x - \log(x^2 - 1)$

$\Rightarrow 2\log x^2 - \log(x^2 - 1)$

$\Rightarrow -\log\left(\frac{x^2-1}{x^2}\right)$

$\Rightarrow -\log\left(1-\frac{1}{x^2}\right)$

$\Rightarrow \left[-\left(\frac{1}{x^2}\right)-\frac{1}{2(x^2)^2}-\frac{1}{3}\times\frac{1}{(x^2)^3}+..\right]$

$\Rightarrow \frac{1}{x^2}+\frac{1}{2x^4}+\frac{1}{3x^6}+..$

3. $\log[(1 + x)^{1+x} (1 - x)^{1-x}]$

$\Rightarrow \log(1 + x)^{1+x} + \log (1 - x)^{1-x}$

$\Rightarrow (1 + x) \log(1 + x) + (1 - x) \log (1 - x)$

$\Rightarrow (1+x)\left[x-\frac{x^2}{2}+\frac{x^3}{3}+....\right]+(1-x)\left[-x-\frac{x^2}{2}-\frac{x^3}{3}+...\right]$

$\Rightarrow \left[x-\frac{x^2}{2}+\frac{x^3}{3}+...\right]+\left[x^2-\frac{x^3}{2}+\frac{x^4}{3}..\right]$

$\left[-x-\frac{x^2}{2}-\frac{x^3}{3}...\right]+\left[x^2+\frac{x^3}{2}+\frac{x^4}{3}+...\right]$

$\Rightarrow 2\left[x^2+\frac{x^4}{3}+\frac{x^6}{5}+..\right]+2\left[-\frac{x^2}{2}-\frac{x^4}{4}-..\right]$

$\Rightarrow 2\left[x^2-\frac{x^2}{2}+\frac{x^4}{3}-\frac{x^4}{4}+\frac{x^6}{5}-\frac{x^6}{6}+...\right]$

$\Rightarrow 2\left[\frac{x^2}{1.2}+\frac{x^4}{3.4}+\frac{x^6}{5.6}+..\right]$

4. $\frac{1}{1.2}-\frac{1}{2.3}+\frac{1}{3.9}-\frac{1}{4.5}+\ldots\text{to}\infty$

$\Rightarrow \left[1-\frac{1}{2}-\frac{1}{2}+\frac{1}{3}+\frac{1}{3}-\frac{1}{4}+\ldots\right]$

$\Rightarrow \left[1-2\left[\frac{1}{2}\right]+2\left[\frac{1}{3}\right]-2\left[\frac{1}{4}\right]+\ldots\right]$

$\Rightarrow 2\left[1-\frac{1}{2}+\frac{1}{3}-\frac{1}{4}\ldots\ldots\right]-1$

$\Rightarrow$ 2log(1 + 1) – 1 $\Rightarrow$ 2 log 2 – 1

$\Rightarrow$ log 4 – log *e* $\Rightarrow$ log(4/*e*)

5. $1+\left(\frac{1}{2}+\frac{1}{3}\right)\frac{1}{4}+\left(\frac{1}{4}+\frac{1}{5}\right)\frac{1}{4^2}+\left(\frac{1}{6}+\frac{1}{7}\right)\frac{1}{4^3}+\ldots$

$\Rightarrow \frac{1}{2}\times\frac{1}{4}+\frac{1}{4}\times\frac{1}{4^2}+\ldots$

$\Rightarrow 1+\frac{1}{3}\times\frac{1}{4}+\frac{1}{5}\times\frac{1}{4^2}+\frac{1}{7}\times\frac{1}{4^3}+\ldots$

$\Rightarrow -\frac{1}{2}\times\log_e\left(1+\frac{1}{2}\right)\left(1-\frac{1}{2}\right)$

$+2\left[\frac{1}{2}+\frac{1}{3}\times\frac{1}{2^3}+\frac{1}{5}\times\frac{1}{2^5}+\frac{1}{7}\times\frac{1}{2^7}+..\right]$

$= -\frac{1}{2}\log_e\left(1+\frac{1}{2}\right)\left(1-\frac{1}{2}\right)+\log_e\frac{(1+1/2)}{(1-1/2)}$

$= \frac{-1}{2}\log_e\left(\frac{3}{2}\right)\left(\frac{1}{2}\right)+\log_e\frac{3}{2}\times 2$

$= \frac{1}{2}\log_e\frac{3}{4}+\log_e 3 = \log_e\frac{2}{\sqrt{3}}+\log_e 3 = \log_e 2\sqrt{3}$

$= \frac{1}{2}\log_e 12$

6. $\frac{2}{1}\cdot\frac{1}{3}+\frac{3}{2}\cdot\frac{1}{9}+\frac{4}{3}\cdot\frac{1}{27}+\frac{5}{4}\cdot\frac{1}{81}+\ldots = \frac{1}{2}+\log_e 3-\log_e 2$

General term $= \frac{(n+1)n}{n}\times\frac{1}{3^n}$

Sum $= \sum_1^n\frac{(n+1)}{n}\times\frac{1}{3^n} = \sum_1^n\left(\frac{1}{n}\times\frac{1}{3^n}\right)+\sum_1^n\frac{1}{3^n}$

$= \frac{1}{3}+\frac{1}{2.3^2}+\frac{1}{3.3^3}+\ldots+\frac{1}{3}+\frac{1}{3^2}+\frac{1}{3^3}+\ldots$

$= -\left[\log_e\left(1-\frac{1}{3}\right)\right]+\frac{1}{3}\left[1+\frac{1}{3}+\frac{1}{3^2}+..\right]$

$= -\log_e 2/3 + \frac{1}{3}\times\frac{1}{1-\frac{1}{3}}$

$= \log_e\frac{3}{2}+\frac{1}{3}\times\frac{1}{2/3} = \log_e 3-\log_e 2+\frac{1}{2}$

7. $\frac{(\log_e 2)^2}{2!}+\frac{(\log_e 2)^4}{4!}+\ldots\infty = \frac{1}{4}$

Simply let $\log_e 2 = x$

We can write the entire series as $\frac{x^2}{2!}+\frac{x^4}{4!}+\frac{x^6}{6!}+\ldots\infty$

Which can be written as $\frac{e^x+e^{-x}}{2}-1 = \frac{e^{\log_e 2}+e^{-\log_e 2}}{2}-1$

$= \frac{2+\frac{1}{2}}{2}-1 = \frac{1}{4}$

$\Rightarrow \frac{(\log_e 2)^2}{2!}+\frac{(\log_e 2)^4}{4!}+\ldots\infty = \frac{1}{4}$

8. $\log_e(x+a)-\log_e(x-a)$

$\Rightarrow \log_e\left(\frac{x+a}{x-a}\right)$

$\Rightarrow \log_e\left(\frac{1+a/x}{1-a/x}\right)$

$\left\{\left(\text{using}\log_e\frac{(1+x)}{(1-x)} = 2\left[x+\frac{x^3}{3}+\frac{x^6}{5}+\ldots\right]\right)\right\}$

$\Rightarrow 2\left[\frac{a}{x}+\frac{1}{3}\left(\frac{a}{x}\right)^3\times\frac{1}{5}\left(\frac{a}{x}\right)^5+\ldots\infty\right]$

9. (a) $\log_e\frac{(x+1)}{x} = \left[\frac{1}{2x+1}+\frac{1}{3(2x+1)^3}+\ldots\right]$

$\Rightarrow \log_e\left(\frac{2x+1+1}{2x+1-1}\right)$

$\Rightarrow \log_e\frac{(1+(2x+1))}{((2x+1)-1)} \Rightarrow \log_e\frac{\left(1+\left(\frac{1}{2x+1}\right)\right)}{\left(1-\left(\frac{1}{2x+1}\right)\right)}$

$\Rightarrow 2\left[\frac{1}{2x+1}+\frac{1}{3(2x+1)^3}+\frac{1}{5(2x+1)^5}+\ldots\infty\right]$

(b) R.H.S. $= 2\log_e(x+h)-\log_e x-$

$\left[\left(\frac{h}{x+h}\right)^2+\frac{1}{2}\left(\frac{h}{x+h}\right)^4+\frac{1}{3}\left(\frac{h}{x+h}\right)^6+\ldots\infty\right]$

$=2\log_e(x+h)-\log_e x-2\left[\frac{1}{2}\left(\frac{h}{x+h}\right)^2+\frac{1}{4}\left(\frac{h}{x+h}\right)^4+\ldots\infty\right]$

$= 2\log_e(x+h)-\log_e x+\log_e\left(1+\frac{h}{x+h}\right)\left(1-\frac{h}{x+h}\right)$

$= \log_e(x+h)^2-\log_e x+\log_e\left(1-\frac{h^2}{(x+h)^2}\right)$

$= \log_e(x+h)^2+\log_e\left(\frac{(x+h)^2-h^2}{(x+h)^2}\right)-\log_e x$

$= \log_e\left((x+h)^2\times\frac{((x+h)^2-h^2)}{(x+h)^2}\right)-\log_e x$

$= \log_e[x^2+2xh]-\log_e x-\log_e x$

$= \log e\frac{[x^2+2xh]}{x} = \log_e(x+2h) =$ L.H.S.

10. (a) $1+\frac{1}{3.2^2}+\frac{1}{5.2^4}+\frac{1}{7.2^6}+...=\log_e 3$

$\Rightarrow\ 2\left[\frac{1}{2}+\frac{1}{3.2^3}+\frac{1}{5.2^5}+\frac{1}{7.2^7}+....\right]$

$\Rightarrow\ \log_e\frac{\left(1+\frac{1}{2}\right)}{\left(1-\frac{1}{2}\right)}\quad\Rightarrow\ \log_e\frac{3/2}{1/2}$

$\Rightarrow\ \log_e 3$

(b) $\frac{1}{1.3}+\frac{1}{2.5}+\frac{1}{3.7}+...\infty=2\ \log_e 2$

General term $=\frac{1}{n(2n+1)}=\frac{1}{n}-\frac{2}{2n+1}$

Sum $=\sum_1^n\frac{1}{n}-\frac{2}{2n+1}$

$=\left[1+\frac{1}{2}+\frac{1}{3}+\frac{1}{4}+...\right]-2\left[\frac{1}{3}+\frac{1}{5}+\frac{1}{7}+....\right]$

$=\left[1+\frac{1}{2}+\frac{1}{3}+\frac{1}{4}+...\right]-\left[\frac{1}{2}+\frac{1}{3}-\frac{1}{4}+\frac{1}{5}+...\right]$

$-\left[\frac{1}{2}+\frac{1}{3}+\frac{1}{4}+\frac{1}{5}+..\right]$

$=\left[1+\frac{1}{2}+\frac{1}{3}+\frac{1}{4}+...\right]-\left[1+\frac{1}{2}+\frac{1}{3}+\frac{1}{4}...\right]$

$+1-\left[-\frac{1}{2}+\frac{1}{3}-\frac{1}{4}....\right]$

$=1-\left[1-\frac{1}{2}+\frac{1}{3}-\frac{1}{4}+..\right]+1=2-\log_e 2$

11. $\frac{1}{2.3}+\frac{1}{4.5}+\frac{1}{6.7}...\infty=1-\log_e 2$

$\Rightarrow\ \frac{1}{2}-\frac{1}{3}+\frac{1}{4}-\frac{1}{5}+\frac{1}{6}-\frac{1}{7}+...\infty$

$\Rightarrow\ 1-1+\frac{1}{2}-\frac{1}{3}+\frac{1}{4}-\frac{1}{5}+\frac{1}{6}-\frac{1}{7}+..\infty$

$\Rightarrow\ 1-\left[1-\frac{1}{2}+\frac{1}{3}-\frac{1}{4}+\frac{1}{5}....\infty\right]$

$\Rightarrow\ 1-\log_e(2)$

12. $\frac{1}{2}\left(\frac{1}{2}+\frac{1}{3}\right)-\frac{1}{4}\left(\frac{1}{2^2}+\frac{1}{3^2}\right)+\frac{1}{6}\left(\frac{1}{2^3}+\frac{1}{3^3}\right)+...=\ell n\sqrt{2}$

$\Rightarrow\ \frac{1}{2}\left[\frac{1}{2}+\frac{1}{3}-\frac{1}{2}\left(\frac{1}{2^2}\right)-\frac{1}{2}\frac{1}{3^2}+\frac{1}{3}\left(\frac{1}{2^3}+\frac{1}{3^3}\right)-....\infty\right]$

$\Rightarrow\ \frac{1}{2}\left[\ell n\left(1+\frac{1}{2}\right)+\ell n\left(1+\frac{1}{3}\right)\right]$

$\Rightarrow\ \frac{1}{2}\left[\ell n\frac{3}{2}+\ell n\frac{4}{3}\right]\quad\Rightarrow\ \frac{1}{2}\ell n^2$

$\Rightarrow\ \ell n\sqrt{2}$

TEXTUAL EXERCISE–3: (OBJECTIVE)

1. (a) $\left(\frac{a-b}{a}\right)+\frac{1}{2}\left(\frac{a-b}{a}\right)^2+\frac{1}{3}\left(\frac{a-b}{a}\right)^3+.....$

$\Rightarrow\ \left[-\frac{(a-b)}{a}-\frac{1}{2}\left(\frac{(a-b)}{a}\right)^2-\frac{1}{3}\left(\frac{a-b}{a}\right)^3...\infty\right]$

$\rightarrow\ \left[-\ell n\left[1\ \frac{(a-b)}{a}\right]\right]$

$\Rightarrow\ -\left[\ell n\frac{[b]}{a}\right]\quad\Rightarrow\ \ell n\left(\frac{a}{b}\right)$

2. (b) $\ell n\left(\frac{1+3x}{1-2x}\right)\quad\Rightarrow\ \ell n(1+3x)-\ell n(1-2x)$

$\Rightarrow\ 3x-\frac{(3x)^2}{2}+\frac{(3x)^3}{3}+....+\left[2x+\frac{(2x)^2}{2}+\frac{(2x)}{3}+...\right]$

$\Rightarrow\ 5x-\left[\frac{9x^2-4x^2}{2}\right]+\left[\frac{27x^3+8x^3}{3}\right]+...$

$\Rightarrow\ 5x-\frac{5x^2}{5}+\frac{35x^3}{3}+..$

3. (c) $\ell n\frac{(x+a)}{(x-a)}\Rightarrow\ \ell n\left(\frac{1+\frac{a}{x}}{1-\frac{a}{x}}\right)$

$\Rightarrow\ 2\left[\frac{a}{x}+\frac{1}{3}\left(\frac{9}{x}\right)^3+\frac{1}{5}\left(\frac{9}{x}\right)^5+...\infty\right]$

4. (b) ln $(1+3x+2x^2)\quad\Rightarrow\ \ell n\left(2x^2+2x+x+1\right)$

$\Rightarrow\ \ell n(2x+1)(x+1)\quad\Rightarrow\ \ell n(2x+1)+\ell n(x+1)$

$\Rightarrow\ \left[2x-\frac{(2x)^2}{2}+\frac{(2x)^3}{3}-....\infty\right]+\left[x-\frac{x^2}{2}+\frac{x^3}{3}....\infty\right]$

$\Rightarrow$ Coefficient of $x^n\quad\Rightarrow\ (-1)^{n+1}\frac{2^n}{n}+(-1)^{n+1}\frac{1}{n}$

$\Rightarrow\ \frac{(-1)^{n+1}}{n}\left[2^n+1\right]$

5. (b) $\frac{5}{1.2.3}+\frac{7}{3.4.5}+\frac{9}{5.6.7}+...\infty$

General Term $=\frac{2n+3}{(2n-1)(2n)(2n+1)}$

$=\frac{2}{2n-1}-\frac{3}{2n}+\frac{1}{2n+1}$

$=2\left[1+\frac{1}{3}+\frac{1}{5}+...\right]-3\left[\frac{1}{2}+\frac{1}{4}+\frac{1}{6}+\frac{1}{8}+...\right]+\left[\frac{1}{3}+\frac{1}{5}+\frac{1}{7}+\frac{1}{9}...\right]$

$=3\left[1+\frac{1}{3}+\frac{1}{5}+\frac{1}{7}+...\right]-3\left[\frac{1}{2}+\frac{1}{4}+\frac{1}{6}+....\right]-1$

$=3\left[1-\frac{1}{2}+\frac{1}{3}-\frac{1}{5}+...\right]-1=3\log_e 2-1$

6. (b) $\frac{1}{1.2.3}+\frac{1}{3.4.5}+\frac{1}{5.6.7}+..\infty$

General term $=\frac{1}{(2n-1)(2n)(2n+1)}$

$=\frac{1}{2(2n-1)}-\frac{1}{2n}+\frac{1}{2(2n+1)}$

Sum $=\sum\frac{1}{2(2n-1)}-\frac{1}{2n}+\frac{1}{2(2n+1)}$

$=\frac{1}{2}\left[1+\frac{1}{3}+\frac{1}{5}+...\right]\left[\frac{1}{2}+\frac{1}{4}+\frac{1}{6}+..\right]+\frac{1}{2}\left[\frac{1}{3}+\frac{1}{5}+\frac{1}{7}+..\right]$

$=\left[\frac{1}{2}+\frac{1}{3}+\frac{1}{8}+...\right]-\left[\frac{1}{2}+\frac{1}{4}+\frac{1}{6}+..\right]-\frac{1}{2}$

$=\log_e 2-1/2$

7. (b) $\frac{1}{2}-\frac{1}{2.2^2}+\frac{1}{3.2^3}-\frac{1}{4.2^4}+...=\ell n(1+1/2)=\ell n(3/2)$

8. (b) $\frac{1}{5}+\frac{1}{2.5^2}+\frac{1}{3.5^3}+\frac{1}{4.5^4}+...$

$\Rightarrow -\left[-\frac{1}{5}-\frac{1}{2.5^2}-\frac{1}{3.5^3}-\frac{1}{4.5^4}+..\right]$

$\Rightarrow -\left[\ell n\left(1-\frac{1}{5}\right)\right] \quad \Rightarrow n(4/5)$

$\Rightarrow \ell n\, 5/4$

9. (a) $1+\frac{1}{3}\cdot\frac{1}{2^2}+\frac{1}{5.2^4}+\frac{1}{7.2^6}+..=\ell n\frac{\left[1+\frac{1}{2}\right]}{\left[1-\frac{1}{2}\right]}=\ell n\frac{\left(\frac{3}{2}\right)}{\left(\frac{1}{2}\right)}=\ell n\, 3$

SECTION-III: (SINGLE CORRECT)

1. (d) $(1+x+x^2+x^3+...)^2=((1-x)^{-1})^2=(1-x)^{-2}$
$=(1+2x+3x^2+4x^3+...)=(n+1)$

2. (c) $(1+x+x^2+x^3.....)^{11}=(1+x+x^2(1+x))^{11}$
$=((1+x)(1+x^2))^{11}=(1+x)^{11}(1+x^2)^{11}$

$=\left[1+11x+\frac{(11)(10)}{2!}\times x^2+\frac{(11)(10)(9)}{3!}\times x^3+\frac{(11)(10)(9)(8)}{4!}\times x^4....\right]$

$=\left[1+11x^2+\frac{(11)(10)}{2!}\times x^4+..\right]$

Coefficient of $x^4=\frac{11\times10}{2}+\frac{11^2\times10}{2}+\frac{11\times10\times9\times8}{4\times3\times2}=55+605+330=990$

3. (c) $1+\frac{1}{3!}+\frac{5}{2!}+\frac{7}{3!}+...$

General term $=\frac{2n-1}{(n-1)!}=\frac{2(n-1)+1}{(n-1)!}$

Sum $=\sum_{10}^{\infty}\frac{2(n-1)+1}{(n-1)!}=\sum_{1}^{\infty}\frac{2}{(n-2)!}+\frac{1}{(n-1)!}$

$=2\left[0+1+\frac{1}{1!}+\frac{1}{2!}+...\right]+\left[1+\frac{1}{1!}+\frac{1}{2!}+..\right]$

$=2e+e=3e$

4. (b) $\frac{1}{e^x.(1+x)}=e^{-x}(1+x)^{-1}$

$=\left[1-\frac{x}{1!}+\frac{x^2}{2!}-\frac{x^3}{3!}+...\right]+\left[1-x+x^2-x^3+..\right]$

Coefficient of $x^3=-1-1-\frac{1}{2}-\frac{1}{6}=-\frac{17}{6}$

5. (a) $\frac{x+\log_e(1-x)}{x^3}=\frac{1}{x^2}+\frac{1}{x^3}\left[-x-\frac{x^2}{2}-\frac{x^3}{3}-\frac{x^4}{4}.....\right]$

Constant term is $\frac{1}{x^3}\times-\frac{x^3}{3}=-\frac{1}{3}$

6. (c) $\frac{1}{0!}+\frac{2}{1!}+\frac{3}{2!}+\frac{4}{3!}+..$

General term $=\frac{n}{(n-1)!}=\frac{(n-1)+1}{(n-1)!}$

Sum $=\sum_{1}^{\infty}\frac{1}{(n-2)!}+\frac{1}{(n-1)!}$

$=\left[0+\frac{1}{1!}+\frac{1}{1!}+\frac{1}{2!}+...\right]+\left[\frac{1}{0!}+\frac{1}{1!}+\frac{1}{2!}+..\right]=e+e$

$=2e$

7. (d) $(1-2x)^{3/4}=1-\frac{3}{4}\times(2x)+\frac{\left(\frac{3}{4}\right)-\left(\frac{3}{4}-1\right)}{2!}\times(2x)^2+...$

The general term is

$=(-1)^{r+1}\times\frac{\left(\frac{3}{4}\right)\left(\frac{3}{4}-1\right)\left(\frac{3}{4}-2\right)-\left(\frac{3}{4}-r+1\right)}{r!}\times(2x)^r$

$=(-1)^{r+1}\times\frac{(3)(-1)(-5)(-9)...(7-4r)\times x^r\times2^r}{4^r\times r!}\times x^r\times2^r$

$=\frac{(-1)^{r+1}\times(3)(-1)(-5)(-9)}{2^r\times r!}(7-4r)\times x^r$

8. (c) $1+n\left(\frac{2x}{1+x}\right)+\frac{n(n+1)}{2!}\times\left(\frac{2x}{1+x}\right)^2+...\infty$

$=\left(1-\frac{2x}{1+x}\right)^{-n}=\left(\frac{1+x-2x}{1+x}\right)^{-n}=\left(\frac{1-x}{1+x}\right)^{-n}=\left(\frac{1+x}{1-x}\right)^{n}$

9. (b) $\frac{\sqrt{1+x}+\sqrt[3]{(1+x)^2}}{\sqrt{1+x}+(1+x)}=a+bx \quad = \frac{(1+x)^{1/2}+(1+x)^{2/3}}{(1+x)^{1/2}+(1+x)}=$

$\frac{1+\frac{1}{2}x+1+\frac{2}{3}x}{1+\frac{1}{2}x+1+x}$ [square & higher terms neglected]

$=\frac{2+\frac{7}{6}x}{2+\frac{3}{2}x}=\frac{1+\frac{7}{12}x}{1+\frac{3}{4}x}=\left(1+\frac{7}{12}\right)x\left(1+\frac{3}{4}x\right)^{-1}$

$=\left(1+\frac{7}{12}x\right)\left(1-\frac{3}{4}x\right)=1+\frac{7}{12}x-\frac{3}{4}x-\frac{21}{24}x^2$ [x^2 again rejected]

$=1-\frac{2}{12}x=1-\frac{x}{6}=a=1,\ b=-1/6$

10. (b) $(1-9x+20x^2)^{-1} = (20x^2-5x-4x+1)^{-1} = (5x(4x-1)$ $-1(4x-1))^{-1} = [(5x-1)(4x-1)]^{-1} = [(1-5x)(1-4x)]^{-1}$

$=(1-5x)^{-1}(1-4x)^{-1} = \sum_{r=0}^{\infty}(5x)^r.\sum_{k=0}^{\infty}(4x)^k = \sum_{r=0}^{\infty}\sum_{k=0}^{\infty}(5)^r(4)^k.x^{r+k}$

Coefficient of $x^n = [4^n + 5.4^{n-1} + 5^2.4^{n-2} + \ldots + 5^{n-1}.4 + 5^n]$

$$= \frac{(4)^n[(4)^{n+1}-(5)^{n+1}]4}{(4)^{n+1}(-1)} = (5)^{n+1}-(4)^{n+1}$$

11. (d) $(2+3x)^{-5} = \frac{1}{32}\left[1+\frac{3}{2}x\right]^{-5} = -1 < \frac{3x}{2} < 1 = -2 < 3x < 2 =$ $-2/3 < x < 2/3$

$\Rightarrow x \in (-2/3, 2/3)$

12. (c) $\frac{2}{3!}+\frac{4}{5!}+\frac{4}{7!}+\ldots$

General term $= \frac{2n}{(2n+1)!} = \frac{(2n+1)-1}{(2n+1)!} = \frac{1}{2n!} - \frac{1}{(2n+1)!}$

Sum $= \sum\frac{1}{2n!} - \sum\frac{1}{(2n+1)!}$

$$= \left[\frac{1}{2!}+\frac{1}{4!}+\frac{1}{6!}+\ldots\right] - \left[\frac{1}{3!}+\frac{1}{5!}+\frac{1}{7!}+\ldots\right]$$

$$= 1-1+\frac{1}{2!}-\frac{1}{3!}+\frac{1}{4!}-\frac{1}{5!}+\ldots = e^{-1}$$

13. (a) $2\left[\frac{m-n}{m+n}+\frac{1}{3}\left(\frac{m-n}{m+n}\right)^3+\frac{1}{5}\left(\frac{m-n}{m+n}\right)^3+\ldots\right]$

$$= \log\left(\frac{1+\left(\frac{m-n}{m+n}\right)}{1-\left(\frac{m-n}{m+n}\right)}\right) = \log\left(\frac{m+n+m-n}{m+n-m+n}\right) = \log\left(\frac{2m}{2n}\right)$$

$$= \log\left(\frac{m}{n}\right)$$

14. (c) $y+\frac{y^3}{3}+\frac{y^5}{5}+\ldots\infty = 2\left[x+\frac{x^3}{3}+\frac{x^5}{5}+\ldots\infty\right]$

$\Rightarrow \frac{1}{2}\log\left(\frac{1+y}{1-y}\right) = \log\left(\frac{1+x}{1-x}\right) \Rightarrow \frac{1+y}{1-y} = \left(\frac{1+x}{1-x}\right)^2$

$\Rightarrow (1+y)(1+x^2-2x) = (1-y)(1+x^2+2x)$

$\Rightarrow 2y + 2x^2y = 4x$

$\Rightarrow x^2y = 2x - y$

15. (c) $\sum_{n=1}^{\infty}\frac{n^2}{n!} = 1 = \sum_{n=1}^{\infty}\frac{n}{(n-1)!}$

$$= \sum_{n=1}^{\infty}\frac{(n-1)}{(n-1)!}+\frac{1}{(n-1)!} = \sum_{n=1}^{\infty}\frac{1}{(n-2)!}+\frac{1}{(n-1)!}$$

$$= \left[0+1+\frac{1}{2!}+\frac{1}{3!}+\ldots\right]+\left[1+\frac{1}{2!}+\frac{1}{3!}+\ldots\right] = e + e = 2e$$

16. (b) $(1+2x+3x^2+\ldots)^{1/2} = ((1-x)^{-2})^{1/2} = (1-x)^{-1}$

$= 1+x+x^2+x^3+x^4+\ldots\ldots\infty$

Coefficient of $x^4 = 1$

17. (a) $\frac{1}{(x+1)(3-x)} = (1-x)^{-1}(3-x)^{-1}$

$$= \frac{1}{3}(1-x)^{-1}(1-x/3)^{-1}$$

$$= \frac{1}{3}[1+x+x^2+x^3+\ldots]\left[1+\frac{x}{3}+\left(\frac{x}{3}\right)^2+\ldots\right]$$

Coefficient of $x^4 =$

$$\frac{1}{3}\left[\left(\frac{x}{3}\right)^n.x^0+\left(\frac{x}{3}\right)^{n-1}.x^1+\left(\frac{x}{3}\right)^{n-2}.x^2+\ldots+\left(\frac{x}{3}\right)^0.x^n\right]$$

$$= \frac{1}{3}\left[\left(\frac{1}{3}\right)^n+\left(\frac{1}{3}\right)^{n-1}+\ldots+\left(\frac{1}{3}\right)^0\right]$$

$$\frac{a(\quad r\quad)}{(\quad)}$$

S = Sum of GP

A = initial term of GP

R = common product $\left(1-\left(\frac{1}{3}\right)^{n+1}\right) = \frac{1}{3}\left[\frac{1}{1-\frac{1}{3}}\right]$

$$= \frac{1}{3}\left[\frac{3^{n+1}-1}{3^{n+1}}\right]\times\frac{3}{2} = \frac{1}{2}\left[\frac{3^{n+1}-1}{3^{n+1}}\right]$$

18. (b) $x-\frac{x^2}{2}+\frac{x^3}{3}-\frac{x^4}{4}+\ldots\infty = y$

$\Rightarrow \log(1+x) = y$

$\Rightarrow 1+x = e^y \qquad \Rightarrow x = e^y - 1$

Now, $y+\frac{y^2}{2!}+\frac{y^3}{3!}+\ldots\infty$

$\Rightarrow \left[1+y+\frac{y^2}{2!}+\frac{y^3}{3!}+\ldots\infty\right]-1$

$\Rightarrow e^y - 1 = x$

19. (a) $\frac{e^x}{1-x} = B_0+B_1x+B_2x^2+\ldots+B_nx^4 = (e^x)(1-x)^{-1}$

$$= \left[1+x+\frac{x^2}{2!}+\frac{x^3}{3!}+\ldots\infty\right][1+x+x^2+x^3+\ldots\ldots\infty]$$

Coefficient of $x^4 = \left[1+1+\frac{1}{2!}+\frac{1}{3!}+\ldots+\frac{1}{n!}\right]$

Coefficient of $x^{n-1} = \left[1+1+\frac{1}{2!}+\frac{1}{3!}+\ldots+\frac{1}{(n-1)!}\right] = \frac{1}{n!}$

20. (b) $\log_a(1+x) = \frac{1}{\log_e a}[\log_e(1+x)]$

$$= \frac{1}{\log_e a}\left[x-\frac{x^2}{2}+\frac{x^3}{3}-\frac{x^4}{4}+\ldots\infty\right]$$

Coefficient of $x^4 = \frac{1}{\log_e a}\left[(-1)^{n-1}.\frac{1}{n}\right] = \frac{(-1)^{n-1}}{n}\log_a e$

21. (a) $\dfrac{1}{(1-x)(3-x)} = \dfrac{1}{3}(1-x)^{-1}\left(1-\dfrac{x}{3}\right)^{-1}$

$= \dfrac{1}{3}\left[1+x+x^2+x^3+x^4+...\infty\right].$

$\left[1+\dfrac{x}{3}+\left(\dfrac{x}{3}\right)^2+\left(\dfrac{x}{3}\right)^3+\left(\dfrac{x}{3}\right)^4....\right]$

$= \dfrac{1}{3}\left[\left(\dfrac{1}{3}\right)^4+\left(\dfrac{1}{3}\right)^3+\left(\dfrac{1}{3}\right)^2+\dfrac{1}{3}+1\right]$

$= \dfrac{1}{3}\left[\dfrac{1\left(1-\left(\dfrac{1}{3}\right)^{n+1}\right)}{\left(1-\dfrac{1}{3}\right)}\right]$; where $n = 4$

$= \dfrac{1}{3}\left[\dfrac{1\left(1-\left(\dfrac{1}{3}\right)^5\right)}{\dfrac{2}{3}}\right] = \dfrac{1}{3}\times\dfrac{242}{243}\times\dfrac{3}{2} = \dfrac{121}{243}$

22. (c) $\dfrac{(1+x)^2}{(1-x)^3} = (1+x)^2(1-x)^{-3}$

$= (1+x^2+2x)$

$\left(1+3x+\dfrac{3.4(x^2)}{2}+\dfrac{3\times4\times5}{3\times2}\times x^3+\dfrac{3\times4\times5\times6}{4\times3\times2}\times x^4+....\infty\right)$

Coefficient of x^n =

$\dfrac{3\times4\times5\times..(n+2)}{n!}+\dfrac{3\times4\times5\times...(n)}{(n-2)!}+2\times\left(\dfrac{3\times4\times5....\times(n+1)}{(n-1)!}\right)$

$= \dfrac{(n+1)(n+2)}{2}+\dfrac{(n)(n-1)}{2}+(n-1)(n)$

$= \dfrac{n^2+n+2n+2+n^2-n+2n^2+2n}{2} = \dfrac{4n^2+4n+2}{2}$

$= 2n^2+2n+1$

23. (a) $y = x - x^2 + x^3 - x^4 + ... \infty$

$\Rightarrow y = [-1 + x - x^2 + x^3 - x^4 + ... + \infty] + 1$

$\Rightarrow y = -1[1 - x + x^2 - x^3 + x^4 + ... \infty] + 1$

$\Rightarrow y = -(1+x)^{-1} + 1 \quad \Rightarrow y - 1 = (1+x)^{-1}$

$\Rightarrow \dfrac{1}{y-1} = 1+x \quad \Rightarrow \dfrac{1}{y-1}+1 = x$

$\Rightarrow \dfrac{1+y-1}{y-1} = x \quad \Rightarrow \dfrac{y}{y-1} = x$

24. (b) $(7.995)^{1/3} = (8-0.005)^{1/3} = 2\left[1-\dfrac{0.005}{8}\right]^{1/3}$

$= 2[1-0.000625]^{1/3}$

$= 2\left[1-\dfrac{1}{3}\times0.000625+\dfrac{\left(\dfrac{1}{3}\right)\left(\dfrac{1}{3}-1\right)}{4}\times(0.00625)^2+...\infty\right]$

$= 2[1 - 0.0002083]$ [square & above terms neglected]

$= 2[0.99979] = 1.99958 = 1.9996$

25. (b) $1-\dfrac{1}{2}\left(\dfrac{1}{2}\right)+\dfrac{1}{2}.\dfrac{3}{4}\times\left(\dfrac{1}{2}\right)^2-\dfrac{1.3.5}{2.4.6}\times\left(\dfrac{1}{2}\right)^3+....$

$= 1-\dfrac{\left(\dfrac{1}{2}\right)}{1!}\left(\dfrac{1}{2}\right)+\dfrac{\left(\dfrac{1}{2}\right)\left(\dfrac{1}{2}+1\right)}{2!}\left(\dfrac{1}{2}\right)^2-\dfrac{\left(\dfrac{1}{2}\right)\left(\dfrac{1}{2}+1\right)\left(\dfrac{1}{2}+2\right)}{3!}\times\left(\dfrac{1}{2}\right)^2+...\infty$

$= \left(1+\dfrac{1}{2}\right)^{-1/2} = \left(\dfrac{3}{2}\right)^{-1/2} = \left(\dfrac{3}{2}\right) = \sqrt{\dfrac{2}{3}}$

26. (d) $(1-2x)^{-1/2}(1-4x)^{-5/2} = 1 + kx$

$= \left[1-2\times\dfrac{-1}{2}\times x\right]\left[1-4x\times-\dfrac{5}{2}\right] = [1+x][1+10x]$

$= 1 + x + 10x + 10x^2$ (x^2 neglected) $= 1 + 11k$

27. (d) $y = -x^3+\dfrac{x^6}{2}-\dfrac{x^9}{3}+....\text{to}\,\infty$

$\Rightarrow y = -\left[x^3-\dfrac{(x^3)^2}{2}+\dfrac{(x^3)^3}{3}+.....\infty\right]$

$\Rightarrow y = -[\log(1+x^3)] \quad \Rightarrow -y = \log(1+x^3)$

$\Rightarrow e^{-y} = 1 + x^3 \quad \Rightarrow e^{-y} - 1 = x^3$

28. (b) $e^x = y+\sqrt{1+y^2} \quad \Rightarrow e^x = y+(1+y^2)^{1/2}$

$\Rightarrow e^x - y(1+y^2)^{1/2} \quad \Rightarrow e^{2x} + y^2 - 2e^x.y = 1 + y^2$

$\Rightarrow e^{2x} - 1 = 2e^x.y \quad \Rightarrow y = \dfrac{e^{2x}-1}{2e^x}$

$\Rightarrow y = \dfrac{(e^x-e^{-x})}{2}$

29. (a) $S = \dfrac{1}{1.2}-\dfrac{1}{2.3}+\dfrac{1}{3.4}-\dfrac{1}{4.5}+....+\infty$

General term $= (-1)^{n-1}\dfrac{1}{(n)(n+1)} = (-1)^{n-1}\times\dfrac{1}{(n)(n-1)}$

Sum $= \sum(-1)^{n-1}\dfrac{1}{(n)(n-1)}$

$= \sum(-1)^{n-1}.\dfrac{1}{n}-\sum(-1)^{n-1}\times\dfrac{1}{n+1}$

$= \left[1-\dfrac{1}{2}+\dfrac{1}{3}-\dfrac{1}{4}+...\infty\right]-\left[\dfrac{1}{2}-\dfrac{1}{3}+\dfrac{1}{4}-....\infty\right]$

$= \log 2 + \left[1-\dfrac{1}{2}+\dfrac{1}{3}-\dfrac{1}{4}+....\infty-1\right]$

$= \log2 + \log2 - 1$

$= \log4 - \log e = \log(4/e)$

30. (a) $a = \sum_{n=1}^{\infty}\dfrac{2n}{(2n-1)!},\ b = \sum_{1}^{\infty}\dfrac{2n}{(2n+1)!}$

$\Rightarrow a = \sum_{n=1}^{\infty}\dfrac{1}{(2n-2)!}+\dfrac{1}{(2n-1)!}$

$\Rightarrow b = \sum_{1}^{\infty}\dfrac{1}{(2n)!}-\dfrac{1}{(2n+1)!}$

$\Rightarrow a = \left[1+\dfrac{1}{2!}+\dfrac{1}{4!}+....\right]+\left[1+\dfrac{1}{3!}+\dfrac{1}{5!}+...\right]$

$\Rightarrow\ b=\left[\frac{1}{2!}+\frac{1}{4!}+\frac{1}{6!}+\ldots\infty\right]-\left[\frac{1}{3!}+\frac{1}{5!}+\frac{1}{6!}+\ldots\infty\right]$

$\Rightarrow\ a=e \qquad \Rightarrow\ b=e^{-1}$

$\Rightarrow\ ab=e\times e^{-1}=1$

31. (d) $1+\frac{1}{3}x+\frac{1}{3}\cdot\frac{4}{6}x^2+\frac{1}{3}\times\frac{4}{6}\times\frac{7}{9}\times x^3+\ldots\infty$

$\Rightarrow\ 1+\frac{1}{3}x+\frac{\frac{1}{3}\times\left(\frac{1}{3}+1\right)}{2!}x^2+\frac{\frac{1}{3}\left(\frac{1}{3}+1\right)\left(\frac{1}{3}+2\right)}{3!}\times x^3+\ldots\infty$

$\Rightarrow\ (1-x)^{-1/3}$

32. (a) $1+\frac{1+a}{2!}+\frac{1+a+a^2}{3!}+\frac{1+a+a^2+a^3}{4!}+..$

General term $=\frac{1+a+a^2+a^3+\ldots+a^{n-1}}{(n)!}=\frac{1\times(1-a^n)}{(1-a)n!}$

$=\frac{1}{(a-1)}\left[\frac{a^n-1}{n!}\right]$

Sum $=\frac{1}{(a-1)}\left[(a-1)+\frac{(a^2-1)}{2!}+\frac{(a^3-1)}{3!}+\ldots\right]$

$=\frac{1}{(a-1)!}\left[a+\frac{a^2}{2!}+\frac{a^3}{3!}+\ldots\infty-1\left[1+\frac{1}{2!}+\frac{1}{3!}+\ldots\infty\right]\right]$

$=\frac{1}{a-1}\left[e^a-1-e+1\right]=\frac{e^a-e}{a-1}$

33. (a) $\frac{1.4}{0!}+\frac{2.5}{1!}+\frac{3.6}{2!}+\frac{4.7}{3!}+\ldots$

General term $=\frac{(n)(n+3)}{(n-1)!}$

Sum $=\sum_0^\infty\frac{(n)(n+3)}{(n-1)!}=\sum_0^\infty\frac{(n^2-2n+1+5n-5+4)}{(n-1)!}$

$=\sum_0^\infty\frac{(n-1)^2}{(n-1)!}+\frac{5(n-1)}{(n-1)!}+\frac{4}{(n-1)!}$

$=\sum_0^\infty\frac{(n-1)}{(n-2)!}+\frac{5}{(n-2)!}+\frac{4}{(n-1)!}$

$=\sum_0^\infty\frac{1}{(n-3)!}+\frac{6}{(n-2)!}+\frac{4}{(n-1)!}$

$=\left[0+\frac{1}{1!}+\frac{1}{2!}+\frac{1}{3!}+\ldots\right]+6\left[0+\frac{1}{1!}+\frac{1}{2!}+\frac{1}{3!}+..\infty\right]$

$+\ 4\left[0+\frac{1}{1!}+\frac{1}{2!}+\ldots\infty\right]=e+6e+4e=11e$

34. (c) $\frac{1}{2}-\frac{1}{2.2^2}+\frac{1}{3.2^3}-\frac{1}{4.2^4}$

$=\left(\frac{1}{2}\right)-\left(\frac{1}{2}\right)\times\left(\frac{1}{2}\right)^2+\frac{1}{3}\left(\frac{1}{2}\right)^3-\frac{1}{4}\left(\frac{1}{2}\right)^4+\ldots\infty$

$=\log\left(1+\frac{1}{2}\right)=\log\left(\frac{3}{2}\right)$

35. (b) $S=\frac{y-1-\frac{1}{2}(y-1)^2+\frac{1}{3}(y-1)^3\ldots\infty}{a-1-\frac{1}{2}(a-1)^2+\frac{1}{3}(a-1)^3\ldots\infty}$

$\Rightarrow\ S=\frac{\log(1+y-1)}{\log(1+a-1)}=\frac{\log y}{\log a}=\log_a y$

36. (b) $\sqrt{x^2+16}-\sqrt{x^2+9}=x\sqrt{1+\frac{16}{x^2}}-x\sqrt{1+\frac{9}{x^2}}$

$=x\left(1+\frac{16}{x^2}\right)^{1/2}-x\left(1+\frac{9}{x^2}\right)^{1/2}=x\left[1+\frac{1}{2}+\frac{16}{x^2}\right]-x\left[1+\frac{9}{2x^2}\right]$

$=x\frac{\left[x^2+8\right]}{x^2}-x\frac{\left[2x^2+9\right]}{2x^2}$ [Neglected x^2 & higher terms]

$=\frac{8}{x}-\frac{9}{2x}=\frac{7}{2x}$

37. (c) $y=\frac{2}{6}+\frac{2.5}{6.12}+\frac{2.5.8}{6.12.18}+\ldots\infty$

$\Rightarrow\ (1+y)=1+\frac{2}{6}+\frac{2}{6}\cdot\frac{5}{12}+\frac{2}{6}\cdot\frac{5}{12}\cdot\frac{8}{18}+\ldots\infty$

$=(1+x)^n$ (say)

$\Rightarrow\ nx=\frac{2}{6};\frac{n(n-1)x^2}{2!}=\frac{2}{6}\cdot\frac{5}{12};\frac{n(n-1)(n-2)x^3}{3!}=\frac{2}{6}\times\frac{5}{12}\times\frac{8}{18},\ldots$

$\Rightarrow\ \frac{(n-1)}{2}x=\frac{5}{12}\Rightarrow\frac{1}{3}-x=\frac{5}{6}\Rightarrow x=\frac{1}{3}-\frac{5}{6}=\frac{-1}{2}$

$\Rightarrow\ n=\frac{-2}{3}\Rightarrow\ (1+y)=(1+x)^n=\left(1-\frac{1}{2}\right)^{-\frac{2}{3}}=\left(2^{-1}\right)^{-\frac{2}{3}}=(4)^{\frac{1}{3}}$

38. (a) $(a+b)(a-b)+1/2!\,(a+b)(a-b)(a^2-b^2)+1/3!\,(a+b)$ $(a-b)(a^4+a^2b^2+b^4)+\ldots$

$(a^2-b^2)+1/2!\,(a^2-b^2)(a^2+b^2)+1/3!\,(a^2-b^2)(a^4+a^2b^2+a^4)+\ldots\infty$

$\Rightarrow\ (a^2-b^2)+\frac{1}{2!}(a^4-b^4)+\frac{1}{3!}(a^6-b^6)+\ldots$

$=a^2+\frac{a^4}{2!}+\frac{a^6}{3!}+\ldots\infty-\left[b^2+\frac{b^4}{2!}+\frac{b^6}{3!}+\ldots\right]=e^{a^2}\ \ e^{b^2}$

39. (b) $\sum_0^\infty\frac{(\ell nx)^n}{n!}=1+\frac{(\ell nx)}{1!}+\frac{(\ell nx)^2}{2!}+\frac{(\ell nx)^3}{3!}+\ldots\infty=e^{\ln x}=x$

40. (a) $\log_{10}\left(\frac{n}{n-1}\right)=\frac{-1}{\log_e 10}\times\log_e\left(\frac{n-1}{n}\right)$

$=-\frac{1}{log_e 10}\times\log_e\left(1-\frac{1}{n}\right)=\frac{-1}{\log_e 10}\left[-\frac{1}{n}-\frac{1}{2}\times\left(\frac{1}{n}\right)^2-\ldots\infty\right]$

Coefficient of n^{-1} is $\frac{1}{n\log_e 10}$

41. (b) $\frac{\left(1+\frac{3}{4}x\right)^{-4}\sqrt{16-3x}}{(8+x)^{2/3}}=\frac{\left(1+(-4)\times\frac{3}{4}x\right)4\left(1-\frac{3x}{16}\right)^{1/2}}{4\left(1+\frac{x}{8}\right)^{2/3}}$

$$=\frac{(1-3\ )\left(1-\frac{1}{2}\cdot\frac{3}{16}\right)}{\overline{24}}=\left[1-3x-\frac{3x}{32}+\frac{9x^2}{32}\right]\left[1+\frac{x}{12}\right]^{-1}$$

$$=\left[1-\frac{99x}{32}\right]\left[x-\frac{x}{12}\right]=\ -\frac{x}{32}-\frac{99x}{32}-\frac{99x}{33\times 12}$$

$$=1-\frac{(8x+297x)}{96}=1-\frac{305x}{96}$$

$$\Rightarrow (P, Q)\equiv\left(1,-\frac{305}{96}\right)$$

42. **(a)** $(1+x)^{-3}$; If $|x|<1$

$$=1-3x+\frac{3\times4}{2!}\times x^2-\frac{3\times4\times5}{3!}\times x^3+....\infty$$

$$\text{Third term}=\frac{3\times4x^2}{2!}=\frac{2\times3\times4x^2}{2\times2}={}^4C_2x^2$$

43. **(c)** $2\left[\frac{1}{(2n+1)}+\frac{1}{3(2n+1)^3}+\frac{1}{5(2n+1)^5}+....\right]=\ell n\left(\frac{n+1}{n}\right)$

$$\because\ \ln\left(\frac{1+x}{1-x}\right)=2\left[x+\frac{x^3}{3}+\frac{x^5}{5}+....\right]=-1<x<1$$

$$\Rightarrow \ell n\left(\frac{1+\frac{1}{2n+1}}{1-\frac{1}{2n+1}}\right)=\ell n\left(\frac{n+1}{n}\right);\ \text{which is valid}$$

$$\text{For } -1<\frac{1}{2n+1}<1$$

$$\Rightarrow \frac{1}{2n+1}+1>0 \text{ and } \frac{1}{2n+1}-1<0$$

$$\Rightarrow \frac{2n+2}{2n+1}>0 \text{ and } \frac{-2n}{2n+1}<0$$

$$\Rightarrow (n+1)(2n+1)>0 \text{ and } (2n)(2n+1)>0$$

$$\Rightarrow n<-1 \text{ or } n>\frac{-1}{2} \text{ and } n<\frac{-1}{2} \text{ or } n>0$$

$$\Rightarrow n<-1 \text{ or } n>0$$

44. **(d)** $\log_4 2-\log_8 2+\log_{16} 2+.......$

$$=\frac{\log2}{2\log2}-\frac{\log2}{3\log2}+\frac{\log2}{4\log2}+...=\frac{1}{2}-\frac{1}{3}+\frac{1}{4}+.....$$

$$=1-\left[1-\frac{1}{2}+\frac{1}{3}-\frac{1}{4}+...\right]=1-\log_e 2$$

45. **(c)** $S=\frac{1}{n+1}+\frac{1}{2(n+1)^2}+\frac{1}{3(n+1)^3}+.....\infty$

$$T=\frac{1}{n}-\frac{1}{2n^2}+\frac{1}{3n^3}.....\infty$$

$$S=-\log\left(1-\frac{1}{n+1}\right)\quad S=-\log\left(\frac{n}{n+1}\right)$$

$$T=\log\left(1+\frac{1}{n}\right)\quad T=\log\left(\frac{n+1}{n}\right)$$

$$S=T$$

SECTION–IV (MORE THAN ONE CORRECT)

1. **(b), (d)** $x-\frac{x^2}{2}+\frac{x^3}{3}-\frac{x^4}{4}+......\text{to}\infty=4$

$$\Rightarrow \log(1+x)=y \qquad \Rightarrow 1+x=e^y$$

$$\Rightarrow x=e^y-1\ y+\frac{y^2}{2!}+\frac{y^3}{3!}+.....\text{to }\infty$$

$$\Rightarrow y+\frac{y^2}{2!}+\frac{y^3}{3!}+..\infty \qquad e^y-1$$

$$\Rightarrow x$$

2. **(a), (c)** $\frac{1}{2}-\frac{1}{8}+\frac{1}{24}-\frac{1}{64}+...\infty$

$$=\frac{1}{2}-\frac{1}{2.2^2}+\frac{1}{3.2^3}-\frac{1}{4.2^4}+...\infty=\log\left(1+\frac{1}{2}\right)=\log(3/2)$$

$$=\log 3/2\ \log_2 2 \qquad \Rightarrow \log\log_2(2)^{3/2}$$

$$\Rightarrow \ell n\,(\log_2 2\sqrt{2})$$

3. **(b), (c)** $\frac{4}{1.3}-\frac{6}{2.4}+\frac{12}{5.7}-\frac{14}{6.8}+...\infty$

$$=\frac{1+3}{1.3}-\frac{(2+4)}{2.4}+\frac{5+7}{5.7}-\frac{6+8}{6.8}+...\infty$$

$$=\left[\frac{1}{3}+1\right]-\left[\frac{1}{4}+\frac{1}{2}\right]+\left[\frac{1}{7}+\frac{1}{5}\right]-\left[\frac{1}{8}+\frac{1}{6}\right]+...\infty$$

$$=1-\frac{1}{2}+\frac{1}{3}-\frac{1}{4}+\frac{1}{5}-\frac{1}{6}+\frac{1}{7}-\frac{1}{8}+....\infty$$

$$=\log(1+1)=\log 2=\log 2\log_3 3=\log\log_3 9$$

4. **(a), (b)** $\sum_{k=1}^{\infty}\sum_{r=1}^{k}\frac{1}{5^k}.{}^kC_r$

$$=\sum_{k=1}^{\infty}\frac{1}{5^k}\ ({}^kC_0+{}^kC_1+{}^kC_2+....+{}^kC_k)$$

$$=\sum_{k=1}^{\infty}\frac{1}{5^k}((2)^k)=\sum_{k=1}^{\infty}\frac{2^k}{5^k}$$

$$=\left(\sum_{r=1}^{\infty}\left(\frac{2}{5}\right)^r\right)=\frac{\frac{2}{5}}{1-\frac{2}{5}}=\frac{\frac{2}{5}}{\frac{3}{5}}=\frac{2}{3}\qquad\left(\because S_\infty=\frac{a}{1-r}\text{ for } G.P.\right)$$

SECTION–V: (ASSERTION–REASON TYPE)

1. **(d)** $\sum_{n=1}^{\infty}\frac{{}^nC_0+{}^nC_1+{}^nC_2+...+{}^nC_n}{{}^nP_n}=e^2$

$$\text{General term}=\frac{{}^nC_0+{}^nC_1+{}^nC_2+...+{}^nC_n}{{}^nP_n}$$

$$=\frac{(1+1)^n}{\left(\frac{n!}{(n-n)!}\right)}=\frac{(2)^n}{\left(\frac{n!}{1}\right)}=\frac{2^n}{n!}$$

$$\text{Sum} = \sum_{1}^{\infty}\frac{2^n}{n!} = 2+\frac{2^2}{2!}+\frac{2^3}{3!}+\frac{2^4}{4!}+....\infty$$

$$= \left[1+2+\frac{2^2}{2!}+\frac{2^3}{3!}+\frac{2^4}{4!}+..\infty\right]-1 = e^2-1$$

Assertion is wrong, reason is correct

2. (d) $(1-x)^{-n} = 1 + {}^nC_1x + {}^{n+1}C_2x^2 + {}^{n+2}C_3x^3 + ...$

∴ The coefficient of x^m will be ${}^{n+1}C_m$

∴ In $(1-x)^{-8}$ coefficient of $x^5 = {}^9C_5$

∴ Assertion is wrong

∴ Reason is correct

3. (d) $\left(\tan\theta+\frac{\tan^3\theta}{3}+\frac{\tan^5\theta}{5}+....\infty\right)$; where $|\tan\theta|<1$

$$= \frac{1}{2}\ell n\left(\frac{1+\tan\theta}{1-\tan\theta}\right) = \frac{1}{2}\ell n\left(\tan\left(\frac{\pi}{4}+\theta\right)\right)$$

$$= \sqrt{\ell n\tan\left(\frac{\pi}{4}+\theta\right)}$$

⇒ Assertion is incorrect, but obviously reason is correct.

4. (d) Clearly, reason is correct,

For the validity of assertion, $\left|\frac{2}{\sqrt{3}}\sin\theta\right|<1$

$$\Rightarrow |\sin\theta|<\frac{\sqrt{3}}{2} \quad \Rightarrow \frac{-\sqrt{3}}{2}<\sin\theta<\frac{\sqrt{3}}{2}$$

$$\Rightarrow \theta\in\left(2n\pi-\frac{\pi}{3},(2n+1)\pi+\frac{\pi}{3}\right);x\in\mathbb{Z}$$

⇒ Assertion is in correct

SECTION–IV: (COMPREHENSION TYPE)

1. (b) $[1 + 3x + 6x^2 + 10x^3 + ...]^{-n} = [(1-x)^{-3}]^{-n} = (1-x)^{3n}$

$$= 1-3nx+\frac{(3n-1)(3n)}{2!}x^2+....$$

$= (n+1)^{th}$ term $= {}^{3n}C_n(-1)^n$

2. (c) $\frac{1+x^2-x^4}{(1+x)^3} = (1+x^2-x^4)(1+x)^{-3}$

$$= (1+x^2-x^4)\left(1-3x+\frac{3\times4}{2!}x^2-\frac{3\times4\times5}{3!}x^3+...\right)$$

Coefficient of

$$x^n = (-1)^n\left[\frac{(n+2)!}{(n)!(2)!}+\frac{(n)!}{(n-2)!(2)!}-\frac{(n-2)!}{(n-4)!2!}\right]$$

$$= (-1)^n\left[\frac{(n+2)(n+1)}{2}+\frac{(n)(n-1)}{2}-\frac{(n-2)(n-3)}{2}\right]$$

$$= (-1)^n\left[\frac{n^2+3n+2+n^2-n-n^2+5n-6}{2}\right]$$

$$= (-1)^n\left[\frac{n^2+7n-4}{2}\right]$$

3. (a) $(1-x)^3$

$$= 1+3x+\frac{3\times4}{2!}\times x^2+\frac{3\times4\times5}{3!}\times x^3+...$$

$$\text{Coefficient of } x^5 = \frac{3\times4\times5\times6\times7}{5!} = \frac{7!}{5!2!} = {}^7C_2$$

4. (b) $1-\frac{x}{1.2}-\frac{x^2}{2.3}-\frac{x^3}{3.4}-...$

$$\text{General term} = \frac{-1}{(n)(n+1)}\times x^n = -\left[\frac{1}{n-1}-\frac{1}{n}\right]x^{n-1}$$

$$= 1-\sum_{2}^{\infty}\left(\frac{1}{n-1}-\frac{1}{n}\right)x^{n-1} - \left[x+\frac{x^2}{2}+\frac{x^3}{3}+\frac{x^4}{4}+...\right] - \left(1+\frac{x}{2}+\frac{x^2}{3}+\frac{x^3}{4}+...\right)$$

$= \log(1-x) - 1/x\log(1-x)$

$= \log(1-x) - \log(1-x)^{1/x} = \log(1.x)^{x-1/x}$

5. (b) $1+n\left(1-\frac{1}{x}\right)+n\frac{(n+1)}{2!}\left(1-\frac{1}{x}\right)^2+.. = \left(1-\left(1-\frac{1}{x}\right)\right)^{-n}$

$$= \left(\frac{1}{x}\right)^{-n} = x^n$$

6. (d) $\cos\theta+\frac{\cos\theta}{\sin^2\theta}+\frac{\cos\theta}{\sin^4\theta}+\frac{\cos\theta}{\sin^6\theta}+....$

$$= \cos\theta\left[1+\frac{1}{\sin^2\theta}+\frac{1}{\sin^4\theta}+\frac{1}{\sin^6\theta}+...\infty\right]$$

$$= \cos\theta\left[1-\frac{1}{\sin\theta}\right]^{-1}$$

The above expansion holds true only and only if $-1<\frac{1}{\sin^2\theta}<1$, but this is never possible since $\sin^2\theta>1$

So the sum of series does not exit.

7. (c) $1-\frac{(x+1)}{1!}+\frac{(x+1)^2}{2!}-\frac{(x+1)^3}{2!}+...\infty = e^{-(x+1)} = \frac{1}{e}\left[e^{-x}\right]$

$$= \frac{1}{e}\left[1-x+\frac{x^2}{2!}+\frac{x^3}{3!}+...\infty\right]$$

$$\text{Coefficient of } x^n = \frac{1}{e}\times\frac{(-1)^n}{(n)!}$$

8. (c) $(1+3x+x^2)(e^{-x})$

$$= (1-3x+x^2)\left[1-x+\frac{x^2}{2!}+\frac{x^3}{3!}+...\infty\right]$$

$$\text{Coefficient of } x^4 = \frac{1}{4!}+3\times\frac{1}{3!}+\frac{1}{2!} = \frac{1}{24}+\frac{1}{62}+\frac{1}{2}$$

$$= \frac{1+12+12}{24} = \frac{25}{24}$$

9. (d) $1+\frac{1}{4.2!}+\frac{1}{16.4!}+\frac{1}{64.6!}+....\infty$

$$= 1+\frac{1}{2^2 2!}+\frac{1}{2^4 4!}+\frac{1}{2^6 6!}+...\infty$$

$$= \frac{(e)^{1/2}-e^{-1/2}}{2} = \frac{e-1}{2(e)^{1/2}}$$

10. (d) $\log\left[(1+x)^{1+x}(1-x)^{1-x}\right]$

$= (1+x)\log[1+x]+(1-x)\log[1-x]$

$=(1+x)\left[x-\frac{x^2}{2}+\frac{x^3}{3}-\frac{x^4}{4}+...\infty\right]-[1-x]\left[x+\frac{x^2}{2}+\frac{x^3}{3}+...\infty\right]$

$=$ Coefficient of $x^6 = \frac{1}{5}-\frac{1}{6}-\left[\frac{1}{5}+\frac{1}{6}\right]$

$\Rightarrow \frac{1}{5}-\frac{1}{6}+\frac{1}{5}-\frac{1}{6} \qquad \Rightarrow \frac{2}{5}-\frac{2}{6}$

$\Rightarrow 2\left[\frac{1}{30}\right] \Rightarrow \frac{1}{15}$

SECTION–VII: (COLUMN MATCHING)

1. (i)→(c); (ii)→(c); (iii)→(a); (iv)→(b, d)

(i) $\frac{1^2}{1!}+\frac{2^2}{2!}+\frac{3^2}{3!}+....\infty$

Which is equivalent to $\sum_{n=1}^{\infty}\frac{n^2}{n!}$

Which can be written as $\sum_{n=1}^{\infty}\frac{n}{(n-1)!}=1+\frac{2}{1!}+\frac{3}{2!}+\frac{4}{3!}+...$

Which can be further simplified as $1+\frac{1+1}{1!}+\frac{2+1}{2!}+\frac{3+1}{3!}+....=1+\frac{1}{1!}+\frac{1}{1!}+\frac{2}{2!}+\frac{1}{2!}+\frac{1}{3!}+\frac{1}{3!}+...$

Since $1+\frac{1}{1!}+\frac{1}{2!}+\frac{1}{3!}+\frac{1}{4!}+..=e$

The above expression can be reduced as $2\left(1+\frac{1}{1!}+\frac{1}{2!}+\frac{1}{3!}+...\right)=2e$

∴ (i)→(c)

(ii) $\sum_{n=0}^{\infty}\frac{n^2-n+1}{n!}$

Which is equivalent to writing $\sum_{n=0}^{\infty}\frac{n^2}{n!}-\sum_{n=0}^{\infty}\frac{n}{n!}+\sum_{n=0}^{\infty}\frac{1}{n!}$

Using the result from previous question = $2e - e + e = 2e$

∴ (ii)→(c)

(iii) $1.3+\frac{2.4}{1.2}+\frac{3.5}{1.2.3}+\frac{4.6}{1.2.3.4}+..$

This infinite expansion can be reduced as $1.3+\frac{4}{1}+\frac{5}{1.2}+\frac{6}{1.2.3}+..$

$1.3+\frac{4}{1}+\frac{5}{2!}+\frac{6}{3!}$, which is equivalent to $\sum\frac{n(n+2)}{n!}=$

$\sum\frac{n^2}{n!}+2\sum\frac{n}{n!} = 2e + 2e = 4e$

∴ (iii)→(a)

(iv) $\frac{12}{2!}+\frac{28}{3!}+\frac{50}{4!}+\frac{78}{5!}+...$

$U_n = \frac{n^{th}\text{term of...}}{n!}$

$S_n = 12 + 28 + 50 + ... + T_{n-1} + T_n = 12 + 28 + ...+ T_n$

$\Rightarrow 0 = 12 + 16 + 22 + 28 +....T_n$

$\Rightarrow T_n = 12 + 16 + 22 + 28 ....$

$= \frac{12+(n-1)(16+(n-2)3)}{n!} = \frac{3n^2+7n-2}{n!}$

Putting n = 2, 3, 4....

$= e + 3e + e = 5e$

The series $1+\frac{2^3}{2!}+\frac{3^3}{3!}+\frac{4^3}{4!}+$

Which summation of $\sum_{n=1}^{\infty}\frac{n^3}{n!} = \sum_{n=1}^{\infty}\frac{n^2}{(n-1)!}$

$= \frac{1}{0!}+\frac{2^2}{1!}+\frac{3^2}{2!}+\frac{4^2}{3!}+...$

$\sum_{n=1}^{\infty}\frac{n(n-1)+n}{(n-1)!} = \sum_{n=1}^{\infty}\frac{n}{(n-2)!}+\sum_{n=1}^{\infty}\frac{n}{(n-1)!}$

$= \sum_{n=1}^{\infty}\frac{n-2+2}{(n-2)!}+\sum_{n=1}^{\infty}\frac{n}{(n-1)}$

$= \sum_{n=1}^{\infty}\frac{1}{(n-3)!}+2\sum_{n=1}^{\infty}\frac{1}{(n-2)!}+\sum_{n=1}^{\infty}\frac{n}{(n+1)!}$

$= e + 2e + 2e = 5e$

∴ (iv)→(b), (d)

2. (i)→(a, b); (ii)→(b, c); (iii)→(d); (iv)→(b, c)

(i) Expansion of $(1 + x)^{7/2}$ for the first negative term $\left(\frac{7}{5}-r+1\right)<0$

$\Rightarrow \left(\frac{12}{5}-r\right)<0 \qquad \Rightarrow r > 12/5$

$\Rightarrow r > 2.4$

⇒ First negative term = 5th

∴ (i) (a, b)

(ii) $(1 + 2x + 3x^2 + 4x^3 + ... \infty)^{1/2}$

$= ((1 - x)^{-2})^{1/2} = (1 - x)^{-1}$

$= \frac{1}{1-x} = 1 + x + x^2 + ...$

Coefficient of $x^4 = 1$

$c + 1 = 2$

∴ (ii)→(b, c)

(iii) $\left(\frac{1-x^{10}}{1-x}\right)^{-1} = (1 - x^{10})^{-1}(1 - x) = (1 - x)(1 - x^{10})^{-1}$

$= (1-x)\sum_{r=0}^{\infty}\frac{(-1)(-2)(-3)...(-1-r+1)(-x^{10})^r}{r!}$

$= (1-x)\sum_{r=0}^{\infty}\frac{(-1)(-2)(-3)...(-r)(-x^{10})^r}{r!}$

∴ Coefficient of x^{401}, $10r = 400$

$\Rightarrow$ $r = 40$

$\therefore$ Coefficient of $x^{401} = -1 < 0$

$\therefore$ (iii)→(d)

(iv) ${}^{69}C_{3r-1} - {}^{69}C_{r^2} = {}^{69}C_{r^2-1} - {}^{69}C_{3r}$

Which can be written as ${}^{69}C_{3r} + {}^{69}C_{3r-1} = {}^{69}C_{r^2} + {}^{69}C_{r^2-1}$

$= {}^{70}C_{3r} = {}^{70}C_{r^2}$

$\Rightarrow$ $3r = r^2$ or $r^2 + 3r = 70$

$\Rightarrow$ $r^2 - 3r = 0$ or $r^2 + 3r - 70 = 0$

$\Rightarrow$ $r(r-3) = 0$ or $r^2 + 10r - 7r - 70 - 0$

$\Rightarrow$ $r = 0$ or $r = 3$ or $r(r+10) - 7(r+10) = 0$

$\Rightarrow$ $r = 0, r = 3$ or $(r+10)(r-7) = 0$

$\Rightarrow$ $r = 0, 3, -10, 7$ $\quad\Rightarrow$ r is not clearly $-10, 0$

$\Rightarrow$ $r = 3, 7$

$\Rightarrow$ 2 numbers, which is a prime number

$\therefore$ (iv)→(b, c)

3. (i)→(b); (ii)→(c); (iii)→(d); (iv)→(a)

(i) $1+\frac{1}{3.2^2}+\frac{1}{5.2^4}+\frac{1}{7.2^6}+....\infty = 2\left(\frac{1}{2}+\frac{1}{3.2^3}+\frac{1}{5.2^5}+...\right)$

Which can be compared with $2\left(x+\frac{x^3}{3}+\frac{x^5}{5}+...\right)$

$x = 1/2$

$= \log_e\left(\frac{1+x}{1-x}\right) - \log\left[\frac{1+1/2}{1-1/2}\right] = \log_2 3$

$\therefore$ (i)→(b)

(ii) $\frac{1}{1.2}-\frac{1}{2.3}+\frac{1}{3.4}-\frac{1}{4.5}.+....\infty$

$T_n = (-1)^{n-1}\frac{1}{n(n+1)} = (-1)^{n-1}\left[\frac{1}{n}-\frac{1}{n+1}\right]$

$T_1 = 1-\frac{1}{2}$; $T_2 = -\frac{1}{2}+\frac{1}{3}$; $T_3 = \frac{1}{3}-\frac{1}{4}$; $T_4 = \frac{-1}{4}+\frac{1}{5}$

Adding, we get $1+2\left(-\frac{1}{2}+\frac{1}{3}-\frac{1}{4}+\frac{1}{5}-...\right) = 1 + 2\log(2)$

$-2 = \log 4/e$

$\therefore$ (ii)→(c)

(iii) $1+\left(\frac{1}{2}+\frac{1}{3}\right)+\frac{1}{4}\left[\frac{1}{4}+\frac{1}{5}\right]\frac{1}{4^2}+.....$

$\Rightarrow$ $\frac{1}{2}\times\frac{1}{4}+\frac{1}{4}\times\frac{1}{4^2}+.....$

$\Rightarrow$ $1+\frac{1}{3}\times\frac{4}{4}+\frac{1}{5}\times\frac{1}{4^2}+\frac{1}{7}+\frac{1}{4^3} = -\frac{1}{2}\log_e\left(1+\frac{1}{2}\right)\left(1-\frac{1}{2}\right)$

$= 2\left[\frac{1}{2}+\frac{1}{3}\times\frac{1}{2^3}+\frac{1}{5}\times\frac{1}{2^5}+....\right] = -\frac{1}{2}\log_e\left(1+\frac{1}{2}\right)\left(1-\frac{1}{2}\right)$

$\Rightarrow$ $-\frac{1}{2}\log_e\left(\frac{3}{2}\right)\left(\frac{1}{2}\right)+\log_e 3$

$\Rightarrow$ $\log_e\frac{2}{\sqrt{3}}+\log_e 3$ $\quad\Rightarrow$ $\log_e\sqrt{12}$ \

$\therefore$ (iii)→(d)

(iv) $\frac{1}{2}\left(\frac{1}{5}\right)^2+\frac{2}{3}\left(\frac{1}{5}\right)^3+\frac{3}{4}\left(\frac{1}{5}\right)^4+....$

$= \left(1-\frac{1}{2}\right)x^2+\left(1-\frac{1}{3}\right)x^3+\left(1-\frac{1}{4}\right)x^4+....; x=\frac{1}{5}$

$= (x^2+x^3+x^4+...)-\left(\frac{1}{2}x^2+\frac{1}{3}x^3+\frac{1}{4}x^4+...\right)$

$= (x+x^2+x^3+x^4+...)-\left(x+\frac{x^2}{2}+\frac{x^3}{3}+.....\right)$

$= \frac{x}{1-x}-\ln(1-x) = \frac{\frac{1}{5}}{1-\frac{1}{5}}-\ln\left(1-\frac{1}{5}\right) = \frac{\frac{1}{5}}{\frac{4}{5}}-\ln\left(\frac{4}{5}\right)$

$= \frac{1}{4}+\ln\left(\frac{4}{5}\right)$

$\therefore$ (iv)→(a)

SECTION–VIII: (INTEGER-TYPE QUESTIONS)

1. Consider $S = 1 + x + x^2 + x^3 + ...\infty$

This is the infinite G.P. with common ratio $= r = x$

$\Rightarrow$ $S = \frac{1}{1-x} = (1-x)^{-1}$

$\Rightarrow$ $(5)^2 = (1-x)^{-2} = 1 + 2x + 3x^2 + ...+ (r+1)x^r +....$

$\Rightarrow$ Coefficient of x^r is $r + 1$

$\Rightarrow$ Coefficient of $x^{35} = 36$

$\Rightarrow$ $\sqrt{\lambda} = 6$

2. $\frac{(1-3x)^{\frac{1}{2}}+(1-x)^{\frac{5}{3}}}{(4-x)^{\frac{1}{2}}} = \frac{\left[1+\frac{1}{2}(-3x)\right]+\left[1+\frac{5}{3}(-x)\right]}{\left(\left[4\left(1-\frac{x}{4}\right)\right]\right)^{\frac{1}{2}}}$ (sin ax^2 and higher power can be neglected)

$= \frac{1}{2}\left(2-\frac{19}{6}x\right)\left(1-\frac{x}{4}\right)^{-\frac{1}{2}} = \left(1-\frac{19}{12}x\right)\left[1-\frac{1}{2}\left(-\frac{x}{4}\right)\right]$

$= 1+\frac{x}{8}-\frac{19}{12}x = 1-\frac{35}{24}x$

In simplest form $\lambda = 35$; $\mu = 24$

$\therefore$ $2\mu - \lambda = 48 - 35 = 13$

3. Let us consider the expression $(3 - 5x)(1 - x)^{-2} = -5\left(x-\frac{3}{5}\right)(1 + 2x + 3x^2 + ...)$

Coefficient of $x^{100} = -5\left(100-\frac{303}{5}\right) = -197$

$= \sqrt{\sqrt{197-1}+2} = \sqrt{14+2} = \sqrt{16} = 4$

4. We can write $T_n = \frac{1+2+3+.....+n}{n!} = \frac{\frac{n(n+1)}{2}}{n!} = \frac{n(n+1)}{2(n!)}$

$$= \frac{n-1}{2(n-1)!} + \frac{1}{(n-1)!} = \frac{n-1}{2(n-1)(n-2)!} + \frac{1}{(n-1)!}$$

$$= \frac{1}{2(n-2)!} + \frac{1}{(n-1)!}$$

$$\sum_{n=1}^{\infty} T_n = \frac{1}{2}\left(1+\frac{1}{1!}+\frac{1}{2!}+....\right)+\left(1+\frac{1}{1!}+\frac{1}{2!}+....\right) = \frac{1}{2}e + e = \frac{3}{2}+e$$

$\therefore\ k = 3; \lambda = 2$

$\Rightarrow\ k + \lambda = 5$

5. $S_\infty = \frac{1}{1.3} + \frac{1}{1.2.3.5} + \frac{1}{1.2.3.4.5.7} + ...\infty$

$$= \frac{2}{1.2.3} + \frac{4}{1.2.3.4.5} + \frac{6}{1.2.3.4.5.6.7} + ...$$

$$= \frac{3-1}{1.2.3} + \frac{5-1}{1.2.3.4.5} + \frac{7-1}{1.2.3.4.5.6.7.} + ...$$

$$= \frac{3}{1.2.3} - \frac{1}{1.2.3} + \frac{5}{1.2.3.4.5} + \frac{-1}{1.2.3.4.5} + \frac{7}{1.2.3...7} - \frac{1}{1.2.3.4.5.6.7}$$

$$= 1 - \frac{1}{1!} + \frac{1}{2!} - \frac{1}{3!} + \frac{1}{4!} - \frac{1}{5!} + ... = e^{-1}$$

By the question $e^{-1} = e^k$

$\Rightarrow\ |k| = 1$

6. $T_n = \frac{n^3}{n!} = \frac{n^2}{(n-1)!} = \frac{n^2-1+1}{(n-1)!} = \frac{(n-1)(n+1)+1}{(n-1)!}$

$$= \frac{(n-2)+3}{(n-2)!} + \frac{1}{(n-1)!} = \frac{1}{(n-3)!} + \frac{3}{(n-2)!} + \frac{1}{(n-1)!}$$

$$= \frac{1}{(n-1)!} + \frac{3}{(n-2)!} + \frac{1}{(n-3)!}$$

The sum of the given series

$$\sum_{n-1}^{\infty} \frac{1}{(n-1)!} + 3\sum_{n=2}^{\infty} \frac{1}{(n-2)!} + \sum_{n=3}^{\infty} \frac{1}{(n-3)!}$$

$$= \left(1+1!+\frac{1}{2!}+\frac{1}{3!}+....\right)+3\left(1+\frac{1}{1!}+...\right)+\left(1+\frac{1}{1!}+\frac{1}{2!}+\frac{1}{3!}+...\right)$$

$= e + 3e + e = 5e \quad \Rightarrow k = 5$

7. $S = 1 + \frac{1}{3.2^2} + \frac{1}{5.2^4} + \frac{1}{7.2^6} + ...\infty$

$$= 2\left(\frac{1}{2} + \frac{1}{3.2^3} + \frac{1}{5.2^5} + \frac{1}{7.2^7} + ...\infty\right)$$

$$= 2\left(x + \frac{x^3}{3} + \frac{x^5}{5} + \frac{x^7}{7} + ...\infty\right) \text{ where } x = 1/2$$

$$= \log_e \left[\frac{1+\frac{1}{2}}{1-\frac{1}{2}}\right] = \log_e 3 = \log_e \lambda$$

$\Rightarrow\ \lambda = 3$

8. $S_\infty = \frac{1}{1.2} + \frac{1}{3.4} + \frac{1}{5.6} + ...\infty$

We can written the same as $\frac{2-1}{1.2} + \frac{4-3}{3.4} + \frac{6-5}{5.6} + ...$

$= 1 - \frac{1}{2} + \frac{1}{3} - \frac{1}{4} + \frac{1}{5} + ... = \log_e (1 + 1) = \ln 2$

$\Rightarrow\ k = 2$

9. L.H.S $= \frac{1}{2} - \frac{1}{2.2^2} + \frac{1}{3.2^3} - \frac{1}{4.2^4} + ...$

$$= x - \frac{x^2}{2} + \frac{x^3}{3} - \frac{x^4}{4} + ... \text{ where } x = 1/2$$

$$= \log(1+x) = \log\left(1+\frac{1}{2}\right) = \log\left(\frac{3}{2}\right) = \text{R.H.S}$$

$\therefore\ m = 3; n = 2$

$\Rightarrow\ m^2 - n^2 = 9 - 4 = 5$

10. $S_\infty = \frac{3}{1!} + \frac{5}{2!} + \frac{9}{3!} + \frac{15}{4!} + \frac{23}{5!} + ...\infty$

$$T_n = \frac{n(n-1)+3}{n!} = \frac{1}{(n-2)!} + \frac{3}{n!}$$

$$\therefore\ \sum \frac{1}{n!} = e - 1$$

Putting values

$$\Rightarrow \left(\frac{2}{2!} + \frac{6}{3!} + \frac{12}{4!} + ...\right) + 3\left(1 + \frac{1}{2!} + \frac{1}{3!} + ...\right)$$

$$\Rightarrow \left(1 + \frac{1}{1!} + \frac{1}{2!} + \frac{1}{3!} ....\right) + 3\left(1 + \frac{1}{2!} + \frac{1}{3!} + ...\right)$$

$\Rightarrow\ 4e - 3$

$\Rightarrow\ k = 4;\ \ell = 3$

Required number $= \sqrt{k^2 + \ell^2} = 5$

11. Consider the expansion of $(1 + x)^{-2}$

$$\therefore\ T_{r+1} = \frac{n(n-1)(n-2)......(n-r+1)}{r_1}.x^r$$

We are interested in $T_5 = T_{4+1}$

Which is given by $T_{4+1} = \frac{n(n-1)(n-2)(n-3)}{4!}.x^4$

$n = -2$ (exponent of the binomial term)

$$\Rightarrow\ T_{4+1} = \frac{5.4!.x^4}{4!} = 5x^4$$

$\Rightarrow\ k = 5$

12. $S_\infty = 1 + \frac{1}{3.4} + \frac{1}{5.4^2} + \frac{1}{7.4^3} + ... = \ell nk.$

We can replace $4 = 2^2$

$$\Rightarrow S_\infty = 1 + \frac{1}{3.2^2} + \frac{1}{5.2^4} + \frac{1}{7.2^6} + ...$$

$$= 2\left(\frac{1}{2} + \frac{1}{3.2^3} + \frac{1}{5.2^5} + \frac{1}{7.2^7} + ...\right) = \left(\log_e \left(\frac{1+\frac{1}{2}}{1-\frac{1}{2}}\right)\right)$$

$= \log_e 3$

$\Rightarrow\ k = 3$